CW00418805

WHO'S WHO OF CRICKETERS

WHO'S WHO OF CRICKETERS

a complete who's who of all cricketers who have played first-class cricket in England, with full career records

PHILIP BAILEY PHILIP THORN
PETER WYNNE-THOMAS

Published by NEWNES BOOKS in association with
THE ASSOCIATION OF CRICKET STATISTICIANS

Published by Newnes Books
a Division of the Hamlyn Publishing Group Limited
84–88, The Centre, Feltham, Middlesex, England
and distributed for them by
The Hamlyn Publishing Group Limited
Rushden, Northants, England

First published 1984

ISBN 0 600 34692 7

Phototypeset by Input Typesetting Limited, London
Printed in Great Britain

Acknowledgements

The authors acknowledge their debt to the many previously published works that have given biographical details of cricketers. Apart from the work of Arthur Haygarth and F. S. Ashley-Cooper, noted in the Introduction, a major source has been all the cricket annuals, ranging from the *Wisden Cricketers' Almanack* and *Playfair Annual* of the present day to the many Annuals, both national and local, which have appeared only briefly, and all the County Yearbooks, as well as the biographies of players. The number of books consulted runs into four figures; the principal ones are listed on another page.

As stated in the Introduction the present research began with the Association of Cricket Statisticians' 'County' booklets in 1973, and the names of those who researched for these booklets are included below. We particularly wish however to acknowledge our thanks to Maurice Alexander for his very extensive researches during the last two years, to Peter Arnold for his guidance throughout the project and to Leigh Scaife for her assistance.

The help of the following was also much appreciated:

C. D. Adams
R. L. Arrowsmith
N. S. Asgarali
D. St. E. Atkinson
Sir John Aubrey-Fletcher
G. L. B. August
S/Ldr A. Bacon
J. A. Baiss
I. Balfour
P. Banham
C. J. Bartlett
A. Beecroft
K. E. Bridger
R. W. Brooke
D. Brookes
R. B. Bruce-Lockhart
J. Burrell
G. Byrne
J. H. Cameron
D. S. Carmichael
E. Cawston
P. B. Clift
R. H. Cobbold
J. R. Cole
F. Collins
H. R. Cox
B. A. C. Croudy
R. L. B. Cunliffe
J. H. Doggart
A. Dossa
M. Down
W. M. Eadon
R. M. Edwards
S. Emsley
J. A. Evetts
J. Featherstone
M. Featherstone
L. C. Fielding
T. E. J. Fitton
C. B. Fordham
R. A. C. Forrester
T. W. Fraser
R. E. G. Fulljames
P. F. Garthwaite
P. W. Gooden
J. Goulstone
E. W. Greenhalgh
J. N. Grover
R. J. L. Hammond
L. W. Hancock
M. N. Harbottle
S. T. Harper-Scott
R. Harragan
T. M. Hart
S. B. Hassan
L. Hatton
D. Heesom
I. C. Henry
G. E. Hewan
Gen Sir R. Hewetson
A. Hignell
B. J. W. Hill
M. Hill
J. W. Holder
R. A. A. Holt
R. H. Horsley
R. E. H. Hudson
B. Hunt
V. Isaacs
R. Isherwood
D. H. James
N. Jenkinson
H. H. H. Johnson
W. R. H. Joynson
W. G. Kalaugher
M. A. C. P. Kaye
D. King
F. King
L. King
N. S. Knight
C. H. Knott
H. J. H. Lamb
D. A. Lambert
P. D. Lashley
J. H. Lee
J. E. Liddle
W. S. P. Lithgow
R. A. Lord
C. W. S. Lubbock
R. E. Luyt
S. Lynch
A. E. Mallalieu
D. A. Marriott
R. W. S. Miller
J. M. Mills
H. Milton
M. J. H. Morton
A. H. Musson
C. J. Myburgh
P. G. E. Nash
L. Newell
L. Newnham
Capt D. Oakley
P. C. Oldfield
H. Osborne
D. G. Oswald
R. K. Page
Roger Page
F. G. Peach
S. S. Perera
S. Pether
R. H. Priestley
S. Proffitt
T. B. Raikes
O. L. Roberts
H. B. O. Robinson
B. W. Rought-Rought
J. V. D. Rowley
G. W. Russ
R. Sargent
G. G. A. Saulez
H. E. Scott
P. Sichel
R. G. Simons
F. W. Simpson
R. W. Skene
D. Smith
E. E. Snow
R. G. Stainton
J. Stockwell
D. W. Stokes
P. M. Studd
G. C. Tovey
K. Trushell
K. C. Turner
A. W. Tyler
A. H. Wagg
P. Wakefield
R. Warburton
K. Warsop
A. Wharton
R. C. C. Whittaker
A. Wiggett
K. Williams
D. Wilshin
D. C. Wilson
M. Wong
A. Woodhouse
A. J. Wreford-Brown
J. E. L. Wright
D. E. Young

Bibliography

Of the many books and journals consulted, the authors found the following particularly useful, and thank the authors, contributors and publishers.

Adamson, J. A. *Denstone Cricket 1874–1952* (Wilde, Shrewsbury, 1952)

Aitchison, Rev James *Kilmarnock C. C. Hundred Not Out* (Kilmarnock, 1952)

All England Cricket and Football Journal 1877–79 (Hurst, Sheffield, 1877–79)

American Cricket Annual 1890–1901 (various publishers, New York)

Anthony, Edwyn *Herefordshire Cricket* (the author, Hereford, 1903)

Ashley-Cooper, F. S. *New Zealand Cricket Guide* 1927, 1931 (Richards, Nottingham)

Ashley-Cooper, F. S. *West Indies Cricket Guide* 1928 (Richards, Nottingham)

Ashley-Cooper, F. S. manuscript biographical notes

Athletic News Cricket Annual 1888–1939 (London and Manchester)

Ayres' Cricket Companion 1902–1932 (Ayres, London)

Betham, J. D. *Oxford and Cambridge, Scores and Biographies* (Simpkin, Marshall, London, 1905)

Bettesworth, W. A. *Chats on the Cricket Field* (Merritt and Hatcher, London, 1910)

British Sports and Sportsmen (London, 1917)

Canynge Caple, S. *The Cricketers' Who's Who* (Williams, London, 1934)

Canynge Caple, S. *The Cricketer's Who Who A-E* (C.B.S., Hunstanton, 1947)

Burke's Peerage (London, various years)

Burke's Landed Gentry (London, various years)

Cambridge University Calendar

Clarke, James *History of Cricket in Kendal* (Thompson, Kendal, 1906)

Coldham, J. D. *Northamptonshire Cricket* (Heinemann, London, 1959)

Cochrane, A. *Records of the Harlequin Cricket Club* (Eyre and Spottiswoode, London, 1930)

Cricket: A Weekly Record of the Game 1882 to 1914 (London, various years)

Cricket Field 1892–94 (London, various years)

Cricket Quarterly 1963–70 (Bowen, Eastbourne and Mullion, various years)

Cricket Society Journal 1961 to date (Cricket Society)

Cricket Spotlight 1957 to 1970 (Barker, Northampton, various years)

The Cricketer 1921 to date (London)

The Cricketer Quarterly 1973 to date (Tunbridge Wells)

Crockford's Clerical Directory

Daily News Cricket Annual 1913 to 1930 (*Daily News*, London)

De Lugo, A. B. *Surrey at the Wicket* (the author, Madrid, 1888)

Derbyshire County Year Book 1957 to date (Derby, various years)

Dorey, H. V. *Cricket Who's Who 1909 to 1913* (London)

Duffus Louis *South African Cricket, Vol 3* (Johannesburg, 1948)

Essex County Cricket Club Year Book (London and Chelmsford, various years)

Flagstaff Cricket Annual 1953 to 1969 (Flagstaff, London, various years)

Glamorgan County Cricket Club Year Books 1933 to date (Cardiff)

Gloucestershire County Cricket Club Year Books 1923 to date (Bristol)

Gordon, Home *Cricket Form at a Glance* (Constable, London, 1902)

Goulstone, John *Sports Quarterly* (the author, Bexleyheath, various years)

Hampshire County Cricket Club Guides 1892 to 1939 (Southampton)

Harris, Lord *The History of Kent Cricket* (Eyre and Spottiswoode, London, 1907)

Haygarth, A. *Lillywhite's Scores & Biographies, Vols 1–4* (London, 1862)

Haygarth, A. *MCC Scores & Biographies, Vols 5–15* (Longmans, London, various years)

Indian Cricket Almanacks 1946 to date (Kasturi and Sons, Madras, various years)

Indian Cricket Field Annual 1957 to 1964 (Rutnagur, Bombay, various years)

Kent County Cricket Club Year Book (Blue Book) 1877–1945

James Lillywhite's Cricketer's Annual 1872–1900 (London, various years)

John Lillywhite's Cricketers' Companion 1865–85 (London, various years)

Luckin, M. W. *South African Cricket, Vols 1 and 2* (Hortor, Johannesburg, 1915)

Lyon, W. R. *The Elevens of Three Great Schools* (Spottiswoode, Eton, 1930)

Morning Leader Cricket Annual 1907–12

Martin-Jenkins, C. D. A. *Who's Who of Test Cricketers* (Orbis, London, 1983)

News Chronicle Cricket Annual 1932–62 (London, various years)

Norman, Philip *Scores and Annals of the West Kent C. C.* (Eyre and Spottiswoode, London, 1897)

Pentelow, J. N. *Guide to Cricketers* (Simpkin, Marshall, Kent, 1911)

Playfair Cricket Annual 1948 to date (London, various years)

Playfair Cricket Monthly 1960 to 1973 (London, various years)

Pullin, A. W. *Talks with Old English Cricketers* (Blackwood, Edinburgh, 1900)

Pullin, A. W. *Talks with Old Yorkshire Cricketers* (*Yorkshire Post*, Leeds, 1898)

Reese, T. W. *New Zealand Cricket, Vols 1 and 2* (Whitcombe & Toombs, Auckland, 1936)

Richards, C. H. *Notts Cricket Scores & Biographies* (Richards, Nottingham, 1901)

Snow, E. E. *A History of Leicestershire Cricket, Vols 1 and 2* (Backus, Leicester, 1949)

South African Cricket Annual 1951 to date (Durban, various years)

Standing, P. C. *The Cricketers' Birthday Book* (Dent, London, 1898)

Surrey County Cricket Club Yearbooks 1884 to date (London, various years)

Thomas, P. *Yorkshire Cricketers 1839–1939* (Hodgson, Cheshire 1973)

Trinidad Cricket Council Yearbook (Port of Spain, various years)

Washbrook, C. *Cricket Annual 1949* (Sportsguide, London, 1949)

West Indies Cricket Annual 1970 to date

Who's Who/Who was Who (A. and C. Black, London, various years)

Wisden Cricketers' Almanack 1864 to date

Wisden Cricket Monthly 1979 to date (London)

Wynne-Thomas, P. *Notts Cricketers, Vols 1 and 2* (Nottingham, 1971, 1981)

Wynne-Thomas, P. *England on Tour* (Hamlyn, London, 1982)

Yorkshire County Cricket Club Yearbooks 1893 to date

INTRODUCTION

The concept of a volume containing the biographies of every notable English cricketer is not a new one. Arthur Haygarth, whilst at Harrow School in the 1840s, began a search for famous players of the past, a search which was to last a lifetime. Haygarth died in 1903 and his work was continued by F. S. Ashley-Cooper, who edited the fifteenth and final volume of Haygarth's monumental *Scores and Biographies*. The task of researching and collating biographical material on English cricketers, other than contemporary players, more or less died with Ashley-Cooper, except for certain specialist areas, such as specific clubs or families.

When the Association of Cricket Statisticians was formed in 1973, it was found that a number of members had an interest in reviving the type of biographical research formerly undertaken by Haygarth and Ashley-Cooper, and had in fact been quietly ferreting out details of the cricketers who had eluded their predecessors. The Association was anxious to continue this research and to try to direct the footsteps of the researchers in order to avoid duplication of effort. It was decided to publish brief biographical details of English first-class cricketers on a County by County basis. Before much progress could be made, however, it was necessary to solve a problem that had confounded cricket historians and statisticians for fifty years, the compilation of a precise list of English first-class matches, for without such a list, it was impossible to compose a list of English first-class cricketers.

Although the modern concept of first-class cricket evolved during the 1860s, it was not until 1947 that a 'first-class' match was officially defined. For about eighty years therefore, the decision as to which matches to include in the season's 'First-class Averages' was largely in the hands of the sporting press, though since 1890 the MCC had decided which Counties could boast first-class status.

The Association of Cricket Statisticians gathered in the views of all known interested parties, held meetings, published preliminary lists, conducted fresh research into contemporary newspapers and periodicals, held further meetings, and the result of three years intensive study was *A Guide to First Class Cricket Matches Played in the British Isles*, published in 1976. This work found general acceptance among statisticians, because it gave historical reasons for the inclusion, or exclusion, of the matches on the borderline of first-class status. The guide commences with the 1864 season when the modern concept of 'first-class' cricket was being evolved. Further research led to the publication of *A Guide to Important Cricket Matches Played in the British Isles 1709–1863*, published in 1981. This publication gives a list of important matches from 1801–1863 and a list of 18th century matches which includes most matches that are known to have been played. The career records in this book start from 1801.

Now, at last, the biographical researchers could produce a list of 'first-class' cricketers and the task of detection, with its blind alleys, false trails, and, in most cases, eventual success, could begin in earnest. The story of the tracing of these hundreds of 'lost' cricketers is a saga on its own. We can only thank all those members of the Association who have helped on our 'County' booklets, and indeed the many first-class cricketers, their friends or relatives, who have provided the clues without which many of the facts contained in this volume could not have been discovered. There are still a few 'lost' cricketers; we will of course continue to search for them, but we would be most grateful for any clues that might help that research and any addenda or errata will be published and acknowledged in the next edition of this book.

May we close this introduction by dedicating this work to all the cricketers contained herein, for the pleasure they have given to cricket followers throughout the British Isles.

Philip J. Bailey
Haughton Mill, Retford — Philip R. Thorn
April 1984 — Peter Wynne-Thomas

The Association of Cricket Statisticians

Enquiries about the publications, or membership of, the Association of Cricket Statisticians should be addressed to the Secretary at The Bungalow, Haughton Mill, Retford, Notts.

EXPLANATION OF THE ENTRIES

Scope
This book contains every cricketer who played in a first-class match in the British Isles from 1864 to 1983. Some of the most prominent players before this date are also included. A list of first-class teams appears on a separate page in this book.

The Order
Players are listed in alphabetical order; those of the same surname are listed in order of their initials, not their first forenames. Those who in the course of their lives changed their names, are shown under the names they used when playing cricket, except for the handful who played under aliases. Cricketers who changed their name during the course of their cricket career are cross-referenced.

Names
For players born in the British Isles the forenames given are those on their birth certificates. If a player adopted an additional name, for example Robert George (Dylan) Willis, the adopted name is given in brackets. Nicknames are not shown. Relatives are shown only where the exact relationship is known.

Decorations are not given unless they are awarded for services to cricket. Services ranks, because of the complexity of the subject, especially in the 19th century, are not shown except for ranks of General and the Navy and RAF equivalents.

Status
The players are described as professional or amateur if their career began before 1962. Those whose career began after 1962 are shown as 'cricketer', since the distinction, in first-class cricket, was abolished that year. The convention of describing overseas tourists as 'amateur' is followed in most cases.

Dates and places of birth and death
For players born or dying in England and Wales, dates and places have been checked against the records of the General Register Office, London, where possible, and thus many details given will differ from previously published information.

The cause of death is stated if it is unusual, or, when known, in the case of a player who died young. There are players who may be presumed dead because of their birth date but for whom no definite information about date of death exists.

Type of Player
A player's style may vary at different stages of his career, for example a fast bowler may become medium pace, or in the 19th century, an under-arm bowler change to round-arm, or a lower order batsman in County cricket may be an opening batsman in local club cricket. The description given here is of the player during his first-class career only, unless stated to the contrary. The description is in the order of batting, bowling and fielding characteristics, whatever the player's principal activity.

School
A player's school is given only if the school is one of those whose records are usually found in cricketing periodicals.

Teams
The first-class County(ies) for which the player appeared are given with dates indicating the extent of his career and number of first-class matches. Dates are also given for appearances for London County, Scotland, Ireland, Oxford U, Cambridge U and Dublin U. If a player did not represent a first-class County then the principal first-class team is given with appropriate dates. The overseas equivalents of English first-class Counties are given as appropriate with dates, but the number of matches are only included for the Australian States. In the case of players of Oxford and Cambridge Universities, the year(s) in which blues were obtained are stated.

If a player made his first-class debut, or his final first-class appearance, for a side not mentioned under 'teams', the details are given separately.

Tours
All tours involving first-class matches are shown as appropriate, plus those tours which the authors feel are of significance to the biography.

Test Matches
The countries for which the player appeared in an official Test match are given with seasons of first and last appearance and number of matches.

Career Records
The first-class career record for each player is given, except for 18th century players. Details of the matches included can be found in the various 'Guides' published by the Association of Cricket Statisticians. The Career records are complete to the end of the 1983 English season. The line of batting figures is composed as follows:

matches–innings–not outs–runs–highest score–average–100s–catches–stumpings

The line of bowling figures are:

runs conceded–wickets–average–five wickets in an innings–ten wickets in a match–best bowling in an innings

In cases where a bowler took wickets but no bowling analyses are extant then these wickets are shown thus (+21) between the wickets figure and the average.
A bowler who did not take a wicket is given an abbreviated record, for example: 27–0.

Where no bowling figures are given, it is to be assumed that the player did not bowl in first-class cricket. Test career records are set out in similar fashion.

Abbreviations
The abbreviations used in the entries are:
b born *d* died *Sch* School *ct* caught *st* stumped *not out

Seasons
Seasons overseas, where the cricket season takes place in the English winter, are indicated in the style: 1981/2. Career spans are shown thus: 1975–79, except where an overseas season is concerned, when the style is: 1975 to 1978/9.

First Class Teams 1864 to 1983

The following is the list of teams considered to have played first-class cricket matches in the British Isles.

All England Eleven (1864–78)
L. E. G. Ames XI (1957)
Army (1912–39)
Australians (1878 to date)
Australian Imperial Forces (AIF) (1919)
Australian Services (1945)
J. Bamford's XI (1907–09)
Barbados (1969)
R. G. Barlow's XI (1883)
Sir Julien Cahn's XI (1932–38)
F. S. G. Calthorpe's XI (1926)
Cambridgeshire (1864–71)
Cambridgeshire and Yorkshire (1864)
Cambridge University (1864 to date)
Cambridge University Past and Present (1882–90)
Canada (1954)
Capped (1923)
Civil Service (1927)
D. B. Close's XI (1982–83)
S. H. Cochrane's XI (1909)
Commonwealth (1950–61)
Lord Cowdray's XI (1923–24)
R. Daft's XI (1870–80)
Demobilised Officers (1919)
Derbyshire (1871 to date)
Dominions (1945)
Dublin University (1895–1926)
East (1892–1948)
East Africa (1975)
T. Emmett's XI (1881–83)
England (1864 to date)
Essex (1894 to date)
Essex and Middlesex (1947)
H. K. Foster's XI (1912–19)
Free Foresters (1912–68)
C. B. Fry's XI (1912)
Gentlemen (1864–1962)
Gentlemen of Kent (1864–80)
Gentlemen of Middlesex (1865)
Gentlemen of the North (1867–80)
Gentlemen of the South (1864–1920)
A. E. R. Gilligan's XI (1925–66)
Glamorgan (1921 to date)
Gloucestershire (1870 to date)
Gloucestershire and Yorkshire (1877)
W. G. Grace's XI (1871–1907)
L. Hall's XI (1885–91)
Hambledon XII (1908)
Hampshire (1864 to date)
Harlequins (1924–28)
Lord Hawke's XI (1885–1930)
H. T. Hewett's XI (1892)
Home Counties (1899)
Hurst Park (1890)
Indians (1911 to date)
International Cavaliers (1969)
International XI (1975)
Ireland (1902 to date)
I Zingari (1866–1904)
Jamaica (1970)
D. R. Jardine's XI (1955–58)
G. L. Jessop's XI (1911)
V. W. C. Jupp's XI (1926)
Kent (1864 to date)
Kent and Gloucestershire (1874–76)
Kent and Nottinghamshire (1864)
Kent and Surrey (1947)
Kent and Sussex (1902)
Kent and Yorkshire (1913)
Lancashire (1865 to date)
Lancashire and Yorkshire (1883–1909)
W. H. Laverton's XI (1890)
Left-handed (1870)
Leicestershire (1894 to date)
H. D. G. Leveson-Gower's XI (1902–50)
M. Leyland's XI (1947)
Liverpool and District XI (1882–94)
Lord Londesborough's XI (1886–1913)
London County (1900–04)
Lyric Club (1890)
Lord March's XI (1886)
Married (1871–92)
MCC (1864 to date)
MCC Australian XI (1904–73)
MCC President's XI (1964–66)
MCC South African XI (1910–48)
MCC West Indian XI (1935)
J. R. Mason's XI (1913)
Middlesex (1864 to date)
Midland Counties (1896–99)
Minor Counties (1912 to date)
Navy (1912–29)
Navy and Army (1910–19)
New Zealanders (1927 to date)
New Zealand Services (1945)
Non-Smokers (1884)
North (1864–1961)
Northamptonshire (1905 to date)
Nottinghamshire (1864 to date)
Nottinghamshire and Lancashire (1883)
Nottinghamshire and Yorkshire (1872–83)
Old Oxford University (1881)
Orleans Club (1878–83)
Oxford University (1864 to date)
Oxford and Cambridge Universities (1910–81)
Oxford University Past and Present (1888–99)
Oxford and Cambridge Universities, Past and Present (1874–93)
Over 30s (1879–1949)
Over 32s (1950)
Over 33s (1945)
Pakistanis (1954 to date)
Pakistan Eaglets (1963)
Sir L. Parkinson's XI (1933–35)
T. N. Pearce's XI (1951–78)
Philadelphians (1897–1908)
H. Philipson's XI (1891)
R. Pilling's XI (1889)
Players (1864–1962)
Players of the North (1873–87)
Players of the South (1864–1920)
Rest of England (1901–74)
Rest of the World (1965–70)
A. W. Ridley's XI (1879)
Right-handed (1870)
L. Robinson's XI (1912–21)
RAF (1927–46)
RAF (Ex-Service) (1922)
Scotland (1905 to date)
Second Class Counties (1893)
Services (1920–64)
J. Sharp's XI (1923)
A. Shaw's XI (1881–85)
Lord Sheffield's XI (1881–96)
M. Sherwin's XI (1889–91)
A. Shrewsbury's XI (1888–93)
Single (1871–92)
Smokers (1884)
Somerset (1882 to date)
South (1864–1961)
South Africans (1901–65)
South African Fezelas (1961)
South African Universities
South Americans (1932)
Southgate (1864–68)
South Wales (1912)
Sri Lankans (1975 to date)
L. C. Steven's XI (1960–61)
A. E. Stoddart's XI (1895–98)
Surrey (1864 to date)
Surrey and Middlesex (1868–1912)
Surrey and Sussex (1867–1900)
Surrey Club (1865–73)
Sussex (1864 to date)
Hon. L. H. Tennyson's XI (1923–26)
TCCB XI (1981)
C. I. Thornton's XI (1882–1929)
C. E. de Trafford's XI (1896)
Uncapped (1923)
Under 25s (1968–71)
Under 30s (1879–1949)
Under 32s (1950)
Under 33s (1945)
United Eleven (1882)
United All England Eleven (1864–69)
United North of England Eleven (1870–76)
United South of England Eleven (1870–80)
Wales (1923–30)
R. D. Walker's XI (1866)
P. F. Warner's XI (1903–47)
Earl de la Warr's XI (1896)
Warwickshire (1894 to date)
G. J. V. Weigall's XI (1904–14)
A. J. Webbe's XI (1885–1901)
Wembley Park (1896)
West (1892–1948)
West Indians (1906 to date)
Woodbrook Club and Ground (1912)
Worcestershire (1899 to date)
G. N. Wyatt's XI (1886)
Sir F. M. M. Worrell's West Indian XI (1964)
Yorkshire (1864 to date)
Young England (1973–78)

WHO'S WHO OF CRICKETERS

Aamer Hameed
Cricketer. *b:* 18.10.1954, Lahore. Lower order right-hand batsman, right-arm medium fast bowler. Punjab University. *Teams* Universities (1972/3 to 1973/4); Lahore (1974/5 to 1976/7); Punjab (1974/5 to 1977/8); Servis Industries (1975/6 to 1977/8); National Bank (1976/7); United Bank (1977/8); Oxford U (1979, blue). *Tour* Pakistan to England 1978.
Career batting
53–69–10–872–103–14.77–2–*ct* 15
Bowling 4123–110–37.48–5–1–7/36
Although awarded his blue in 1979, Aamer Hameed's bowling record for the University was a very modest 7 wickets (av 74.57).

Abberley, Robert Neal
Cricketer. *b:* 22.4.1944, Birmingham. Opening or middle order right-hand batsman, occasional right-arm medium pace bowler. *Team* Warwickshire (1964–79, 258 matches). *Tour* MCC Under 25 Team to Pakistan 1966/7.
Career batting
261–439–27–10082–117*–24.47–3–*ct* 171
Bowling 294–5–58.80–0–0–2/19
He had his best season in 1966 with 1,315 runs (av 28.58) and exceeded 1,000 runs on two other occasions, but never lived up to his early promise.

Abbey, David Robert
Cricketer. *b:* 11.12.1941, Edmonton, North London. Right-hand batsman, slow left-arm bowler. *Team* Middlesex (1967, 2 matches).
Career batting
2–2–0–14–12–7.00–0–*ct* 0
Bowling 23–0

Abbott, Alan Wesley
Professional. *b:* 15.11.1926, Sutton-in-the-Elms, Leics. Right-hand batsman. *Team* Leicestershire (1946, 1 match).
Career batting
1–2–0–5–5–2.50–0–*ct* 0
Bowling 8–0

Abbott, Herbert Edward Stacey
Amateur. *b:* 6.4.1855, Calcutta, India. *d:* 13.6.1939, Richmond, Surrey. *Sch* Elizabeth College, Guernsey. *Team* MCC (1902, 1 match).
Career batting
1–2–0–19–18–9.50–0–*ct* 0

Abbott, J. D.
Amateur. Middle order batsman. *Team* Worcestershire (1919–20, 3 matches).
Career batting
3–5–0–63–42–12.60–0–*ct* 0

Abbott, William
Amateur. *b:* 28.10.1856, Walton-on-Thames, Surrey. *d:* 22.12.1935, East Woking, Surrey. Son of C. J. (Surrey, 1844). Middle order batsman, wicket-keeper. *Sch* Winchester. *Team* Surrey (1877, 3 matches).
Career batting
3–5–0–9–5–1.80–0–*ct* 7–*st* 2

Abdul Hafeez *(see under* Kardar, A. H.)

Abdul Qadir Khan
Cricketer. *b*: 15.9.1955, Lahore, Pakistan. Lower order right-hand batsman, leg break and googly bowler. *Teams* Punjab (1975/6); Lahore (1975/6); Habib Bank (1975/6 to 1982/3). *Tours* Pakistan to England 1978, 1982; to India 1979/80. *Tests* Pakistan (1977/8 to 1982/3, 19 matches).

Career batting
113–134–28–2102–112–19.83–1–*ct* 51
Bowling 11301–573–19.72–46–11–9/49
Test batting
19–22–4–255–38–14.16–0–*ct* 6
Bowling 2197–65–33.80–2–1–7/142

He achieved very little on the 1978 tour to England and did not appear in the Tests. In 1982, however, he was the leading wicket taker in first-class matches with 57, av 20.82, and played in all three Tests. In 1982/3 he took 103 wickets during the Pakistan season, the first bowler to take 100 wickets in a season in Pakistan.

Abdy, Brig-Gen Anthony John
Amateur. *b:* 26.4.1856. *d:* 4.7.1924, La Tour-de-Peilz, Switzerland. Useful opening batsman. *Sch* Charterhouse. *Team* Hampshire (1881, 1 match).
Career batting
1–2–0–30–23–15.00–0–*ct* 0

Notable Army cricketer with Royal Artillery, Southern Division, etc.

Abdy, Robert Burlton
Amateur. *b:* 1857, Worksop, Notts. *d:* 21.5.1899, Great Yarmouth. Middle order batsman. *Team* MCC (1888, 2 matches).
Career batting
2–4–0–8–6–2.00–0–*ct* 1

a'Beckett, Edward Lambert
Amateur. *b:* 11.8.1907, East St Kilda, Victoria, Australia. Father of E.C. (Victoria, 1966/7). Attractive right-hand batsman, right-arm fast medium bowler, good field anywhere. Melbourne University. *Team* Victoria (1927/8 to 1931/2, 25 matches). *Tours* Australia to England 1930. *Tests* Australia (1928/9 to 1931/2, 4 matches).
Career batting
47–64–8–1636–152–29.21–2–*ct* 35
Bowling 3062–105–29.16–3–0–6/119
Test batting
4–7–0–143–41–20.42–0–*ct* 4
Bowling 317–3–105.66–0–0–1/41

Illness on his tour to England in 1930 deprived him of the opportunity of acclimatising himself and he therefore had a moderate tour. His only real moment was the brilliant catch he took in the third Test (acting as sub) to dismiss Hobbs. He left first-class cricket while still young, to concentrate on his career as a barrister.

Abel, Robert
Professional. *b:* 30.11.1857, Rotherhithe, Surrey. *d:* 10.12.1936, Stockwell, London. Father of T. E. (Surrey and Glamorgan) and W. J. (Surrey). Very sound opening right-hand batsman, who could hit if required. Right-hand slow round arm bowler. *Team* Surrey (1881–1904, 514 matches). *Tours* Vernon to Australia 1887/8; Warton to S.Africa 1888/9; Sheffield to Australia 1891/2. *Tests* England (1888–96, 13 matches).
Career batting
627–1007–73–33124–357*–35.46–74–*ct* 586
Bowling 6314–263–24.00–3–0–6/15
Test batting
13–22–2–744–132*–37.20–2–*ct* 13

'The Guv'nor', as he was affectionately termed, did not make his first-class debut until he was 23 and then made little impact on the cricketing world for the next six years. It was an innings of 144 in 1886 against the Australians which really made his name and in the same summer he reached 1,000 runs for the first of 14 times. An eye infection seemed likely to close prematurely his career in 1893, but happily he recovered and the next decade saw his run tally vastly increase. For eight successive seasons (1895–02) he exceeded 2,000 runs, and in one glorious summer acquired no less than 3,309 to create a new first-class record. That was in 1901, but two years earlier he had hit 357 not out for Surrey v Somerset at the Oval, an innings which remains the second highest ever in Championship cricket.

After 1902 he again suffered from eye trouble and, although wearing glasses helped a little, his first-class days were brought to a rather abrupt end in 1904.

As an opening batsman he shared in many large partnerships, usually for the first wicket with W. Brockwell, but his record-breaking effort was for the fourth wicket with T. W. Hayward, the pair adding 447 for Surrey against Yorkshire at the Oval in 1899 – a world record for nearly fifty years and still the English record.

Abel was on the short side for a batsman and somewhat ungainly, but his perseverance during his early years at the Oval, when the authorities retained him as much for his fielding as batting, paid dividends in the long term, both for himself and for Surrey.

Abel, Thomas Ernest
Professional. *b:* 10.9.1890, Kennington, London. *d:* 23.1.1937, Lambeth, London. Son of Robert (Surrey and England), brother of W. J. (Surrey). Hard hitting opening right-hand batsman, slow right-arm bowler. *Team* Surrey (1919–20, 12 matches); Glamorgan (1922–25, 32 matches)
Career batting
44–68–2–1045–107–15.83–1–*ct* 19
Bowling 976–31–31.48–0–0–3/30

Abel, William John
Professional. *b:* 29.8.1887, South Bermondsey, Surrey. *d:* 23.3.1934, Stockwell, London. Son of

Robert (Surrey and England), brother of T. E. (Surrey and Glamorgan). Hard hitting right-hand batsman, right-arm fast medium, later leg break and googly bowler, good slip field. *Team* Surrey (1909–26, 170 matches).
Career batting
171–246–29–4988–117–22.98–1–*ct* 143
Bowling 5753–187–30.76–3–0–5/28

His health was seriously affected while serving in the First World War, and this led to his death at the early age of 46.

Abell, Sir George Edmond Brackenbury
Amateur. *b:* 22.6.1904, Worcester. Father of J. N. (Oxford) and T. G. (Free Foresters). Hard-hitting right-hand batsman, wicket-keeper. *Sch* Marlborough. *Teams* Oxford U (1924–27, blue 1924, 1926 and 1927); Worcestershire (1923–39, 34 matches); Europeans (1928/9 to 1929/30); Northern India (1934/5 to 1941/2).
Career batting
75–124–16–2666–210–24.68–4–*ct* 97–*st* 33
Bowling 4–0

His most famous innings was on his debut in the Ranji Trophy when he hit 210 for Northern India v Army at Lahore 1934/5. From 1946 to 1967 he was the First Civil Service Commissioner.

Abell, John Norman
Amateur. *b:* 18.9.1931, Chelsfield, Kent. Son of G. E. B. (Worcs), brother of T. G. (Free Foresters). Forcing right-hand batsman, wicket-keeper. *Sch* Marlborough. *Team* Oxford U (1952–53).
Career batting
3–5–0–56–25–11.20–0–*ct* 2–*st* 5

Abell, Roy Beverley
Cricketer. *b:* 21.1.1931, Birmingham. Tail end right-hand batsman, leg break bowler. *Team* Warwickshire (1967, 1 match).
Career batting
1 match, did not bat–*ct* 1
Bowling 112–4–28.00–0–0–3/64

Abell, Timothy George
Amateur. *b:* 29.4.1930, Lahore, India. Son of G. E. B. (Worcs), brother of J. N. (Oxford U). Lower order right-hand batsman, off break bowler. *Team* Free Foresters (1954).
Career Batting
1–2–1–4–4*–4.00–0–*ct* 0
Bowling 1–0

Abercrombie, Cecil Halliday
Amateur. *b:* 12.4.1886, Mozufferpore, India. *d:* 31.5.1916. Killed in the naval action off Jutland (HMS *Defence*). Dashing middle order right-hand batsman. *Sch* Berkhamsted. *Team* Hampshire (1913, 13 matches).
Career batting
16–31–3–1126–165–40.21–4–*ct* 11
Bowling 329–8–41.12–0–0–3/27

His first-class debut was for Army and Navy in 1910. He scored a century for Navy v Army at Lord's in 1912 and was drafted into the Hampshire side in 1913, hitting 126 on his debut v Oxford U at Southampton. Owing to Service commitments he could not appear for Hampshire in 1914. He represented Scotland at Rugby Football.

Aberdare, Lord (*see under* Bruce, Hon C. N.)

Abidali Sardarali, Syed
Cricketer. *b:* 9.9.1941, Hyderabad. Lower order right-hand batsman, right-arm medium fast bowler. *Team* Hyderabad (1959/60 to 1978/9). *Tours* India to England 1971, 1974, to Australia and New Zealand 1967/8, to West Indies 1970/1; State Bank India to Ceylon 1968/9; Rest of World to Pakistan 1970/1. *Tests* India (1967/8 to 1974/5, 29 matches).
Career batting
212–333–35–8732–173*–29.30–13–*ct* 190–*st* 5
Bowling 11336–397–28.55–14–0–6/23
Test batting
29–53–3–1018–81–20.36–0–*ct* 32
Bowling 1980–47–42.12–1–0–6/55

He was for several years the best seam bowler in India, but his returns in Test cricket were very modest, and though he could show the lowest average in first-class matches during the 1974 tour to England, his 32 wickets cost 30.15 runs apiece.

Ablack, Robert Kenneth
Amateur. *b:* 5.1.1919, Port of Spain, Trinidad. Slow left-arm bowler. *Team* Northants (1946–49, 3 matches).
Career batting
3–4–2–24–16–12.00–0–*ct* 0
Bowling 220–6–36.66–0–0–3/32

He became well-known as a cricket commentator on radio.

Abraham, Thomas Smyth
Amateur. *b:* 1838, Exeter, Devon. *d:* 14.12.1873, Algiers. *Team* Gentlemen of England (1870).
Career batting
1–2–0–9–9–4.50–0–*ct* 0
Bowling 45–0

He played non-first-class County cricket for Cornwall, Devon, Wiltshire and Somerset.

Abrahams, John
Cricketer. *b*: 21.7.1952, Salt River, Cape Town,

South Africa. Middle order right-hand batsman, off break bowler, cover field. *Team* Lancashire (1973–83, 167 matches).
Career batting
168–255–34–6077–178–27.49–6–*ct* 108
Bowling 2225–43–51.74–0–0–3/27
He hit 1,000 runs in a season twice (best 1,261, av 39.40, in 1983).

Absolom, Charles Alfred
Amateur. *b:* 7.6.1846, Blackheath, Kent. *d:* 30.7.1889, Port-of-Spain, Trinidad – he was employed as purser on a ship which was loading sugar cane when a crane collapsed, crushing him. He lingered on in great agony for three days before dying. Right hand bat, being a lively but eccentric hitter, useful medium pace right-arm bowler, good field. Privately educated. *Teams* Cambridge U (1866–69, blue each year); Kent (1868–79, 57 matches). *Tour* England to Australia 1878/9. *Test* England (1878/9, 1 match).
Career batting
99–178–11–2515–94–15.05–0–*ct* 127
Bowling 5471–281+1–19.11–19–3–7/45
Test batting
1–2–0–58–52–29.00–0–*ct* 0
He was an all round athlete, representing Cambridge at putting the shot and the long jump, and a noted footballer. The last ten years of his life were spent roving America, spending much time with the Red Indians. As a cricketer he always played for his side and never for himself, a philosophy which he carried into other walks of life. He also appeared in non-first-class cricket for Essex.

Aburrow, Edward
Professional. *b:* 1747, Hambledon, Hants. *d:* 6.10.1835, Hambledon, Hants. Safe and steady right-hand batsman, right-hand under-arm bowler, good long-field. *Team* Hampshire.
He played before 1801, so career records are inapplicable.

Acfield, David Laurence
Cricketer. *b*: 24.7.1947, Chelmsford, Essex. Lower order right-hand batsman, off break bowler. *School* Brentwood. *Teams* Essex (1966–83, 310 matches); Cambridge U (1966–68, blue 1967 and 1968). *Tours* MCC to East Africa 1973/4.
Career batting
352–355–182–1504–42–8.69–0–*ct* 116
Bowling 22846–830–27.52–30–4–8/55
His best season was 1981 with 76 wickets, av 22.61. A noted fencer he represented Cambridge and Great Britain in the Olympic Games and was British sabre champion.

Acheson, Lord Archibald Brabazon-Sparrow (4th Earl of Gosford)
Amateur. *b:* 19.8.1841, Worlingham Hall, Beccles, Suffolk. *d:* 11.4.1922, Paddington, London. Brother of the Hon. E. A. B. (MCC). Fair right-hand batsman, right medium pace round-arm bowler. *Sch* Harrow. *Team* MCC (1864).
Career batting
1–2–1–6–4*–6.00–0–*ct* 1
Bowling 7–1–7.00–0–0–1/7
He succeeded to the Earldom in 1864. He was Vice-Chamberlain to Queen Alexandra.

Acheson, Hon Edward Archibald Brabazon
Amateur. *b:* 22.5.1844, Worlingham Hall, Beccles, Suffolk. *d:* 3.7.1921, London. Brother of A. B. S., Earl of Gosford (MCC). Fair right-hand batsman, round-arm bowler, excellent field. *Sch* Harrow. *Team* MCC (1866).
Career batting
1–1–0–0–0–0.00–0–*ct* 1

Achong, Ellis Edgar
Amateur. *b:* 16.2.1904, Belmont, Port of Spain, Trinidad. Left-hand batsman, slow left-arm bowler. *Team* Trinidad (1929/30 to 1934/5). *Tour* West Indies to England 1933. *Tests* West Indies (1929/30 to 1934/5, 6 matches).
Career batting
38–55–20–503–45*–14.37–0–*ct* 20
Bowling 3326–110–30.23–3–1–7/73
Test batting
6–11–1–81–22–8.10–0–*ct* 6
Bowling 378–8–47.25–0–0–2/64
Of Chinese descent – the first such to play in a Test match – Achong was the leading slow bowler of the 1933 touring side, but achieved little due to the unresponsive wickets that year. It is sometimes said that the term 'Chinaman', for a left-hander's googly, was inspired by him, but this appears to have no basis in fact.

Ackerman, Hylton Michael
Cricketer. *b*: 28.4.1947, Springs, South Africa. Sound opening or middle order left-hand batsman, right-arm medium pace bowler. *Teams* Border (1963/4 to 1965/6); North East Transvaal (1966/7 to 1967/8); Northants (1967–71, 98 matches); Natal (1968/9 to 1969/70); Western Province (1970/1 to 1981/2). *Tour* Rest of World to Australia 1971/2.
Career batting
234–409–33–12219–208–32.75–20–*ct* 199
Bowling 1400–32–43.75–0–0–4/61
He hit 1,000 runs in a season three times (best

1,565, av 33.29, in 1970). His only double century in England was 208 for Northants v Leicestershire at Leicester in 1970.

Ackroyd, Alfred
Amateur. *b:* 29.8.1858, Birkenshaw, Leeds, Yorkshire. *d:* 3.10.1927, Eccles, Lancashire. Fair right-hand batsman, right-arm fast bowler. *Sch* Uppingham. *Team* Yorkshire (1879, 1 match).
Career batting
2–3–2–15–13*–15.00–0–*ct* 0
Bowling 32–3–10.66–0.0–3/25
He made his first-class debut for the England XI in 1878.

Ackroyd, Archibald
Professional. *b:* 18.5.1897, Heanor, Derbyshire. *d:* 25.6.1968, Dudley, Worcs. Lower order right-hand batsman, right-arm medium fast bowler. *Teams* Derbyshire (1924–25, 11 matches); Scotland (1937).
Career batting
12–20–1–79–15–4.15–0–*ct* 5
Bowling 707–20–35.35–0–0–4/63

A'Court, Dennis George
Professional. *b:* 27.7.1937, Bedwelty, Monmouth. Tail end right-hand batsman, right-arm fast medium bowler. *Team* Gloucestershire (1960–63, 49 matches).
Career batting
49–68–31–420–47*–11.35–0–*ct* 10
Bowling 3890–145–26.82–5.0.–6/25
He was on the Gloucestershire staff for ten years, but rarely commanded a regular place in the Eleven.

Acton, James
Amateur. *Team* Hampshire (1880–82, 2 matches).
Career batting
2–3–0–41–31–13.66–0–*ct* 0
Bowling 12–0

Adair, John Frederick
Amateur. *b:* 1851, Dublin. *d:* 1.4.1913, Ballsbridge, Co. Dublin. Wicket-keeper. *Team* An England Eleven (1875).
Career batting
2–2–1–31–17–31.00–0–*ct* 2

Adair, Robert Emile
Amateur. *b:* 1876, Ireland. *d:* 18.3.1951, Westcliff-on-Sea, Essex. Middle order right-hand batsman, right-arm fast medium pace bowler. *Team* Ireland (1902).
Career batting
4–7–1–86–32–14.33–0–*ct* 3
Bowling 37–1–37.00–0–0–1/29

Adams, Alfred
Professional. *b:* 14.11.1814, Saffron Walden Essex. *d:* 1.10.1868, Saffron Walden, Essex. Brother of James (Essex). Fine hitter.
His chief claim to fame is an innings of 279 which he hit in a minor match in 1837 – at the time the highest recorded score.

Adams, Cyril Douglas
Amateur. *b:* 18.9.1897, Parkstone, Dorset. Useful middle order right-hand batsman, right-arm fast bowler. *Team* RAF (1928–32).
Career batting
5–10–1–173–46*–19.22–0–*ct* 4
Bowling 373–11–33.90–0–0–3/62
He also appeared for Dorset.

Adams, Donald
Professional. *b:* 8.6.1880, Ockley, Surrey. *d:* 8.1.1976, Walton-on-Thames, Surrey. Moderate batsman, opening bowler. *Team* Surrey (1902, 1 match)
Career batting
1–2–0–26–14–13.00–0–*ct* 2
Bowling 83–1–83.00–0–0–1/28
His only first-class wicket was that of W. G. Grace, the match being Surrey v London County at Crystal Palace, 1902.

Adams, Douglas Howe
Amateur. Middle order batsman. *Sch* Haverford College. *Teams* Philadelphia (1898–1908). *Tour* Philadelphians to England 1908.
Career batting
3–6–0–27–19–4.50–0–*ct* 2
Bowling 46–0

Adams, E.J.
Amateur. Middle order batsman. *Team* Somerset (1935, 1 match).
Career batting
1–1–0–5–5–5.00–0–*ct* 0

Adams, Geoffrey Coker Arding
Amateur. *b:* 24.5.1909, London. Hard-hitting right-hand batsman, excellent cover-point, fair change bowler. *Sch* Radley. *Team* Hampshire (1928–30, 18 matches).
Career batting
18–33–2–421–42–13.58–0–*ct* 3
Bowling 162–4–40.50–0–0–1/0
He played in various trial matches at Cambridge with little success, and for Hampshire in the vacation.

Adams, Henry James
Professional. *b:* 25.4.1852, Croydon, Surrey. *d:* 21.2.1922, Edmonton, Middlesex. Tail end right-

hand batsman, wicket-keeper, right-arm medium pace bowler. *Team* Surrey (1887–89, 4 matches).
Career batting
5–9–4–25–9–5.00–0–*ct* 4–*st* 2

Adams, Keith
Amateur. *b:* 3.8.1932, Pudsey, Yorkshire. Stylish right-hand batsman. *Sch* St Peter's, York. *Team* Cambridge U (1954).
Career batting
1–2–0–34–34–17.00–0–*ct* 1

Adams, Lestock Handley
Amateur. *b:* 10.9.1887, Ormskirk, Lancashire. *d:* 22.4.1918. He was killed in action at Placaut Wood, France. Tail end batsman, useful bowler. *Sch* St Lawrence College, Ramsgate. *Team* Cambridge U (1908–10).
Career batting
6–10–5–61–21*–12.20–0–*ct* 1
Bowling 531–17–31.23–1–0–6/86

Adams, Percy William
Amateur. *b:* 5.9.1900, Northampton. *d:* 28.9.1962, Westminster, London. Lower order right-hand batsman, wicket-keeper. *Sch* Cheltenham. *Team* Sussex (1922, 1 match).
Career batting
1–2–1–2–1*–2.00–0–*ct* 0–*st* 1

Adams, Sidney Clarke
Amateur. *b:* 1904, Northampton. *d:* 24.3.1945, Berlin. Middle order right-hand batsman, useful leg break bowler. *Team* Northants (1926–32, 10 matches).
Career batting
11–16–1–158–87–10.53–0–*ct* 5
Bowling 250–13–19.23–1–0–6/32

On his first-class debut for Northants v Dublin Univ (Northampton), Adams hit 87 and took two wickets with the first two balls he delivered, ending with 6/32.

Adams, Thomas Miles
Professional. *b:* 2.5.1813, Gravesend, Kent. *d:* 20.1.1894, Gravesend, Kent. Fine, punishing right-hand batsman, medium round-arm bowler. *Teams* Kent (1836–58, 99 matches); Hampshire (1848, 1 match); Lancashire (1851, 1 match).
Career batting
157–290–11–3435–78–12.31–0–*ct* 144
Bowling 449–33+117–13.60–5–1–7/?

He played County cricket for about 20 years, and unusually for round-arm bowlers bowled over the wicket. On 18 July 1849 in the match between I Zingari and Royal Artillery, he had a hand in dismissing all ten of his opponents in both innings.

Adams, William
Amateur. *b:* 17.4.1885. *d:* 6.4.1957, Ashton, Northants. Defensive opening left-hand batsman. *Team* Northants (1920–29, 37 matches).
Career batting
38–67–5–1125–154*–18.14–2–*ct* 5
Bowling 67–0

Adamson, Charles Lodge
Amateur. *b:* 18.5.1906, Durham. *d:* 18.11.1979, Durham. Middle order right-hand batsman. *Sch* Durham School. *Team* Minor Counties (1934).
Career batting
1–2–0–15–15–7.50–0–*ct* 0

He played for Durham.

Adcock, Neil Amwin Treharne
Amateur. *b:* 8.3.1931, Cape Town, S. Africa. Tail end right-hand batsman, hostile right-arm fast bowler. *Teams* Transvaal (1952/3 to 1959/60); Natal (1960/1 to 1962/3). *Tours* South Africa to England 1955, 1960; Commonwealth to New Zealand 1961/2. *Tests* South Africa (1953/4 to 1961/2, 26 matches).
Career batting
99–117–35–451–41–5.50–0–*ct* 23
Bowling 6989–405–17.25–19–4–8/39
Test batting
26–39–12–146–24–5.40–0–*ct* 4
Bowling 2195–104–21.10–5–0–6/43

Adcock appeared in Test cricket after only 9 first-class matches, but initially his career was plagued by injuries and it was not until the 1960 tour to England that he was physically capable of playing continuous first-class cricket. In this tour he was South Africa's principal bowler, equalling the record for the most wickets by a South African in a Test Series (26) and taking more wickets in an English season (108 at 14.02) than any previous South African visitor.

Adcock, Robert Alfred
Professional. *b:* 3.11.1916, Ibstock, Leicestershire. Middle order right-hand batsman, right-arm medium bowler. *Team* Leicestershire (1938, 5 matches).
Career batting
5–9–0–89–27–9.88–0–*ct* 2
Bowling 29–1–29.00–0–0–1/29

He also appeared for Lincolnshire.

Adderley, Charles Henry
Amateur. *b:* 16.9.1912, Kings Heath, Birmingham. Lower order right-hand batsman, right-arm medium pace opening bowler. *Team* Warwickshire (1946, 5 matches).

Career batting
5–8–2–27–12–4.50–0–*ct* 1
Bowling 255–4–63.75–0–0–1/19

Addis, Charles Frederick
Amateur. *b:* 2.2.1902, Finedon, Northants. Lower order left-hand batsman, left-arm medium pace bowler. *Team* Northants (1924–26, 2 matches).
Career batting
2–1–0–38–38–38.00–0–*ct* 1
Bowling 155–5–31.00–0–0–3/78

Addison, James Paul
Cricketer. *b*: 14.11.1965, Leek, Staffordshire. Middle order right-hand batsman, slow left-arm bowler. *Team* Leicestershire (1983, 1 match).
Career batting
1–2–0–67–51–33.50–0–*ct* 0

Adhikari, Hemchandra Ramachandra
Amateur. *b:* 31.7.1919, Poona, Baroda, India. Middle order right-hand batsman, occasional leg break bowler, brilliant cover point. *Teams* Gujarat (1936/7); Baroda (1937/8 to 1949/50); Services (1950/51 to 1959/60); Hindus (1941/2 to 1944/5). *Tours* India to Australia 1947/8; to England 1952. *Tests* India (1947/8 to 1958/9, 21 matches).
Career batting
152–236–28–8683–230*–41.74–17–*ct* 97
Bowling 1859–49–37.93–0–0–3/2
Test batting
21–36–8–872–114*–31.14–1–*ct* 8
Bowling 82–3–27.33–0–0–3/68

Although he began his first-class career as an attractive stroke playing batsman, the weakness of the Indian batting in the 1950s changed him into a dour defensive player. In the field he was regarded as second only to R. N. Harvey at cover. His highest score was 230* Services v Rajasthan in 1951/2.

Adshead, Frank Hand
Amateur, *b:* 9.2.1894, Dudley, Worcestershire. *d:* 22.11.1977, Twyford Abbey, Ealing. Middle order right-hand batsman. *Team* Worcestershire (1927, 2 matches).
Career batting
2–3–0–26–14–8.66–0–*ct* 2

Adshead, Dr William Ewart
(later known as Barnie-Adshead)
Amateur. *b:* 10.4.1901, Dudley, Worcs. *d:* 26.1.1951, Birmingham. Middle order right-hand batsman. *Team* Worcestershire (1922–28, 12 matches).
Career batting
12–22–1–244–51–11.61–0–*ct* 15

A noted soccer player, he appeared for Aston Villa.

Aers, David Roland
Cricketer. *b:* 3.10.1946, Lahore, India. Right-hand batsman, slow left-arm bowler. *Sch* Tonbridge. *Team* Cambridge U (1966–68, blue 1967).
Career batting
15–26–2–288–48–12.00–0–*ct* 3
Bowling 882–18–49.00–1–0–5/116

Afaq Hussain
Cricketer. *b:* 31.12.1939, Lucknow, India. Right-hand batsman, right-arm off break bowler, good field. *Teams* Karachi (1957/8 to 1963/4); Karachi University (1959/60 to 1960/61); Universities (1959/60); PIA (1964/5 to 1973/4); PWD (1967/8). *Tours* Pakistan to England 1962, to Australia 1964/5; Pakistan Eaglets to England 1963. *Tests* Pakistan (1961/2 to 1964/5, 2 matches).
Career batting
67–83–24–1448–122*–24.54–1–*ct* 52
Bowling 4156–214–19.42–14–5–8/108
Test batting
2–4–4–66–35*–no av–0–*ct* 2
Bowling 106–1–106.00–0–0–1/40

Aftab Baloch
Cricketer. *b*: 1.4.1953, Karachi, Pakistan. Sound middle order right-hand batsman, off break bowler. *Teams* PWD (1969/70); PIA (1970/1 to 1982/3); Karachi (1971/2 to 1973/4); Sind (1972/3 to 1975/6); National Bank (1975/6 to 1976/7). *Tours* Pakistan Under-25 to Sri Lanka 1973/4; Pakistan to England 1974; PIA to Zimbabwe 1981/2. *Tests* Pakistan (1969/70 to 1974/5, 2 matches).
Career batting
150–231–36–8289–428–42.50–20–*ct* 125–*st* 3
Bowling 5916–188–31.46–10–2–8/171
Test batting
2–3–1–97–60*–48.50–0–*ct* 0
Bowling 17–0

On his 1974 tour to England he hit 101 runs, av 25.25, and did not appear in the Tests. He hit 428 for Sind v Baluchistan at Karachi in 1973/4.

Aftab Gul
Cricketer. *b:* 31.3.1946, Gujar Khan, India. Opening right-hand batsman, slow right-arm bowler. *Teams* Punjab University (1964/5 to 1969/70); Lahore (1964/5 to 1975/6); Punjab (1972/3 to 1977/8); Servis Industries (1976/7). *Tours* Pakistan to England 1971, 1974. *Tests* Pakistan (1968/9 to 1971, 6 matches).

Career batting
100–173–7–6131–140–36.93–11–*ct* 46
Bowling 465–14–33.21–0–0–2/20
Test batting
6–8–0–182–33–22.75–0–*ct* 3
Bowling 4–0

He was most successful on his 1971 visit to England, hitting 1,154 runs (av 46.16) and appearing in all 3 Tests, but on his return in 1974 failed to strike form and did not play against England. He played in a Test for Pakistan whilst on bail.

Agar, Charles
Professional. *b:* 1877, Birstall, Leics. *d:* 10.11.1921, Birstall, Leics. Lower order right-hand batsman, useful right-arm medium pace bowler. *Team* Leicestershire (1898–1900, 23 matches).
Career batting
23–40–6–381–48–11.20–0–*ct* 14
Bowling 1711–38–45.02–0–0–4/80

Agnew, Jonathan Philip
Cricketer. *b*: 4.4.1960, Macclesfield, Cheshire. Lower order right-hand batsman, right-arm fast bowler. *Sch* Uppingham. *Team* Leicestershire (1978–83, 57 matches). *Tour* Leicestershire to Zimbabwe 1980/1.
Career batting
58–56–7–444–56–9.06–0–*ct* 19
Bowling 4033–125–32.26–2–0–6/70

Agnew, Vice-Adm Sir William Gladstone
Amateur. *b:* 2.12.1898, London. *d:* 12.7.1960, Alverstoke, Hants. *Team* Royal Navy (1920).
Career batting
1–2–0–68–48–24.00–0–*ct* 0

Ahl, Frank Douglas
Professional. *b:* 24.11.1908, Potchefstroom, South Africa. *d:* 3.5.1967, Ashford, Middx. Punishing right-hand batsman, wicket-keeper, change bowler. *Team* Worcestershire (1931–33, 35 matches).
Career batting
35–53–3–592–43–11.84–0–*ct* 24–*st* 2
Bowling 384–13–29.54–0–0–4/44

Ahsan ul Hak
Amateur. *b:* 16.7.1878, Jullundur City, Punjab, India. *d: circa* 1943, Punjab. Good right-hand batsman with excellent drive, useful right-arm medium pace change bowler. Aligarh College. *Team* Middlesex (1902, 3 matches).
Career batting
4–6–0–64–25–10.66–0–*ct* 3
Bowling 90–0

He made his first-class debut for MCC in 1901. Coming to England to study the law, Ahsan ul Hak scored many runs for Hampstead in club cricket, but when he had just gained his place in the Middlesex side, he was called to the bar and returned to India.

Aikman, Andrew Miller
Amateur. *b:* 9.4.1885, Galashiels, Selkirkshire, Scotland. *d:* 14.4.1959, Galashiels. Lower order right-hand batsman, wicket-keeper. *Team* Scotland (1921).
Career batting
1–1–0–1–1–1.00–0–*ct* 0

Ainley, Joe
Professional. *b:* 28.10.1878, Huddersfield, Yorks. *d:* 18.11.1907, Sparkbrook, Birmingham. Tail end right-hand batsman, good wicket-keeper. *Team* Worcestershire (1905–06, 19 matches).
Career batting
19–25–16–64–13–7.11–0–*ct* 25–*st* 5

Ainley died of consumption when only 29 – his obituary in Wisden is mistakenly given under Hinley.

Ainscough, Thomas
Amateur. *b:* 23.2.1865, Lancaster House, Parbold, Lancs. *d:* 20.11.1927, Lancaster House, Parbold, Lancs. Useful left-hand batsman. *Sch* Ampleforth. *Team* Lancashire (1894–1906, 2 matches).
Career batting
5–9–1–194–61*–24.25–0–*ct* 3

He played first-class cricket for Liverpool and District, for whom he made his first-class debut in 1891, and was a prolific batsman in club cricket in the Liverpool area.

Ainsworth, Cyrus Gerald
Amateur. *b:* 1888, Bury, Lancashire. *d:* 20.2.1940, Elton, Lancashire. Hard hitting batsman. *Team* Royal Navy (1919).
Career batting
1–2–0–77–71–38.50–0–*ct* 0

Ainsworth, George William Bromilow
Amateur. *b:* 21.3.1876, Formby, Lancashire. *d:* 1941, Watford, Hertfordshire. Brother of J. L. (Lancs). Middle order batsman. *Sch* Marlborough. *Team* Leveson-Gower's XI (1902).
Career batting
1–1–1–10–10*–no av–0–*ct* 0

Ainsworth, Jerry Lionel
Amateur. *b:* 11.9.1877, Formby, Lancashire. *d:* 30.12.1923, Falmouth, Cornwall. Brother of G. W. B. (Leveson-Gower's XI). Good left-arm

slow bowler. *Sch* Marlborough. *Teams* Lancashire (1899, 4 matches), Europeans (1904/5). *Tour* Warner's Team to America 1898.
Career batting
11–16–5–44–11–4.00–0–*ct* 7
Bowling 791–50–15.82–5–2–7/61

He had great success in America taking 75 wickets (av 6.33) including 11 for 67 against the Philadelphians. This success led to his four matches with Lancashire, when he took 18 wickets. He would probably have obtained a regular place in the County side if he had cared to play cricket. He was a well-known racehorse owner.

Ainsworth, Michael Lionel Yeoward
Amateur. *b:* 13.5.1922, Hooton, Cheshire. *d:* 28.8.1978, Hillingdon, Middlesex. Excellent right-hand batsman with good off-drive. *Sch* Shrewsbury. *Team* Worcestershire (1948–50, 17 matches).
Career batting
49–86–2–2034–137–24.22–3–*ct* 26
Bowling 126–2–63.00–0–0–1/4

Service duties prevented him from appearing regularly in County cricket, but he captained the Combined Services in 1950 and did not make his final first-class appearance until 1964, playing for the Free Foresters. His first-class debut was for Combined Services in 1946.

Aird, Ronald
Amateur. *b:* 4.5.1902, London. Middle order stylish right-hand batsman, right-arm medium pace bowler, brilliant cover-point. *Sch* Eton. *Teams* Hampshire (1920–38, 108 matches), Cambridge U (1923, blue).
Career batting
136–223–19–4482–159–21.97–4–*ct* 52
Bowling 413–7–59.00–0–0–2/35

His best year was 1924 when he hit 1,072 runs (av 24.36). He is best remembered as Secretary to MCC (1953–62) and President of the premier club in 1968–69.

Airey, Robert Berkeley
Amateur. *b:* 21.9.1874, Southminster, Essex. *d:* 23.6.1933, Westminster, London. Middle order right-hand batsman. *Sch* Tonbridge. *Team* Hampshire (1911, 3 matches).
Career batting
3–5–0–52–30–10.40–0–*ct* 2

Aislabie, Benjamin
Amateur. *b:* 14.1.1774, London. *d:* 2.6.1842, Regents Park, London. Right-hand batsman. *Sch* Eton. *Teams* MCC (1818–41); Surrey (1808–17); Hampshire (1819); Kent (1823); Sussex (1827).
Career batting
55–99–29–224–15*–3.20–0–*ct* 7

Though he played his last match of importance in 1841 – MCC v Cambridge U – at the age of 67 and had therefore appeared for the MCC in all grades of cricket for about 40 seasons, he was never more than a moderate cricketer. His fame rests with the fact that he was Secretary of MCC for many years and as such organised many matches:

'He doats on the game, has played many a year, Weighs at least seventeen stones, on his pins rather queer, But he still takes the bat, and there's no better fun, Than to see him when batting attempting a run.'

Aitchison, Rev James
Amateur. *b:* 26.5.1920, Kilmarnock, Ayrshire, Scotland. Opening right-hand batsman, right-arm medium pace bowler. *Team* Scotland (1946–63).
Career batting
50–87–2–2786–190*–32.78–5–*ct* 22
Bowling 3–0

Aitchison, John Edward
Professional. *b:* 27.12.1928, Gillingham, Kent. Lower order right-hand batsman, off break bowler. *Team* Kent (1949–50, 3 matches).
Career batting
3–3–0–6–4–2.00–0–*ct* 0
Bowling 88–3–29.33–0–0–3/33

Aizazuddin, Fakir Syed
Amateur. *b:* 17.8.1935, Lahore, India. Middle order right-hand batsman, leg break bowler. *Teams* Cambridge U (1957); Khairpur (1959/60 to 1968/9); Karachi (1965/6 to 1971/2). *Tours* Pakistan Eaglets to England 1963; Pakistan to Ceylon 1964/5, to England 1967.
Career batting
43–79–4–1872–187–24.95–3–*ct* 12
Bowling 762–19–40.10–0–0–4/36

He was known as S. A. U. Fakir whilst at Cambridge U.

Akers-Douglas, Ian Stanley
Amateur. *b:* 16.11.1909, Kensington, London. *d:* 16.12.1952, Frant, Tunbridge Wells, Kent, as the result of a shot-gun accident. Stylish right-hand batsman with excellent cover-drive. *Sch* Eton. *Teams* Oxford U (1929–30); Kent (1929–38, 48 matches).
Career batting
60–86–3–1965–123–23.66–2–*ct* 12
Bowling 100–4–25.00–0–0–2/20

He hit 158 for Eton v Harrow in 1928 and scored centuries in both the Freshmen's Match of

1929 and the Seniors' Match of 1930, but did not get a blue. In 1933 he won the Open Rackets Championship of the British Isles.

Akroyd, Bayly Nash
Amateur. *b:* 27.4.1850, Streatham, Surrey. *d:* 24.11.1926, Marylebone, London. Brother of S. H. (Surrey). Steady right-hand batsman, occasional slow round-arm bowler, good field at point. *Sch* Radley. *Team* Surrey (1872–73, 6 matches).
Career batting
8–15–0–129–30–8.60–0–*ct* 9
Bowling 14–0
His final first-class match was for MCC in 1879.

Akroyd, Swainson Howden
Amateur. *b:* 13.11.1848, Streatham, Surrey. *d:* 5.12.1925, Marylebone, London. Brother of B. N. (Surrey). Useful opening right-hand batsman, good field. *Sch* Radley. *Team* Surrey (1869–78, 23 matches).
Career batting
33–55–1–930–87–17.22–0–*ct* 7

Alabaster, John Chaloner
Amateur. *b:* 11.7.1930, Invercargill, New Zealand. Brother of G. D. (Otago, Canterbury, Northern Districts). Lower order right-hand batsman, right-arm leg break and googly bowler. *Team* Otago (1956/7 to 1971/2). *Tours* New Zealand to England 1958, to India and Pakistan 1955/6, to South Africa 1961/2, to West Indies 1971/2, to Australia 1967/8. *Tests* New Zealand (1955/6 to 1971/2, 21 matches).
Career batting
143–212–30–2427–82–13.33–0–*ct* 94
Bowling 12688–500–25.37–25–4–7/41
Test batting
21–34–6–272–34–9.71–0–*ct* 7
Bowling 1863–49–38.02–0–0–4/46
The unusual aspect of Alabaster's career was that he had not appeared at all in first-class cricket when he visited India and Pakistan as part of the 1955/6 New Zealand side. His only visit to England was not very successful, though he appeared in two of the Tests.

Alderman, Albert Edward
Professional. *b:* 30.10.1907, Alvaston, Derbyshire. Sound right-hand opening batsman, smart field, occasional wicket-keeper. *Team* Derbyshire (1928–48, 318 matches).
Career batting
318–529–52–12376–175–25.14–12–*ct* 202–*st* 2
Bowling 171–4–42.75–0–0–3/37
He completed 1,000 runs each season from 1934 to 1939 (best 1,509, av 32.53, in 1937). He was a first class umpire. He also played for Berkshire. He played professional football for Burnley and Derby County.

Alderman, Terence Michael
Cricketer. *b*: 12.6.1956, Subiaco, Western Australia. Lower order right-hand batsman, right-arm fast medium bowler. *Team* Western Australia (1974/5 to 1982/3, 51 matches). *Tours* Australia to England 1981, to New Zealand 1981/2, to Pakistan 1982/3. *Tests* Australia (1981 to 1982/3, 16 matches).
Career batting
77–77–37–248–26*–6.20–0–*ct* 52
Bowling 6869–293–23.44–15–3–7/28
Test batting
16–21–11–51–12*–5.10–0–*ct* 16
Bowling 1890–66–28.63–4–0–6/135
He was most successful on the 1981 tour to England, heading both Test and first-class bowling averages with 42 wickets, av 21.26, and 51 wickets, av 20.86 respectively.

Alderson, Ralph
Professional. *b:* 7.6.1920, Newton-le-Willows, Lancashire. Sound right-hand batsman. *Team* Lancashire (1948–49, 2 matches).
Career batting
2–2–0–55–55–27.50–0–*ct* 0
He scored 55 for Lancs v Kent (Old Trafford) in his only Championship match, adding 120 for the 4th wicket with G. A. Edrich.

Alderwick, Ernest Ewart Gladstone
Amateur. *b:* 14.4.1886, Bristol, Gloucs. *d:* 26.8.1917, Peronne, France. He was killed in action. Right-hand batsman. *Team* Gloucestershire (1908, 2 matches).
Career batting
2–3–0–7–5–2.33–0–*ct* 0
He also appeared for Suffolk.

Aldridge, Keith John
Professional. *b:* 13.3.1935, Evesham, Worcs. Tail end right-hand batsman, right-arm fast medium bowler. *Teams* Worcestershire (1956–60, 73 matches); Tasmania (1961/2 to 1963/4, 6 matches).
Career batting
79–112–35–511–24*–6.63–0–*ct* 33
Bowling 6033–256–23.56–7–0–6/26
In July 1959 he was no-balled for throwing by J. S. Buller; and no-balled again in 1960 for the same reason.

Alexander, Charles Dallas
Amateur. *b:* 25.12.1839, Calcutta, India. *d:* 22.1.1917, Tankerton, Kent. *Sch* Cheltenham and Harrow. *Team* Kent (1864, 1 match).
Career batting
1–2–0–11–8–5.50–0–*ct* 0

Alexander, Charles Robert
Amateur. *b:* 8.11.1847, Kensington, London. *d:* 17.2.1902, Westminster, London. Steady right-hand batsman, good field – longstop. *Sch* Eton. *Teams* Kent (1867–69, 4 matches); Cambridge U (1870–71).
Career batting
6–9–0–88–41–9.77–0–*ct* 2

In 1867 he is reported to have scored 1,016 runs for Eton, being the captain that year. He was also a noted sprinter.

Alexander, Franz Copeland Murray
Amateur. *b:* 2.11.1928, Kingston, Jamaica. Aggressive right-hand batsman, skilful wicket-keeper. *Sch* Wolmer's (Jamaica). *Teams* Cambridge U (1952–53, blue both years); Jamaica (1956/7 to 1959/60). *Tours* West Indies to England 1957, to India and Pakistan 1958/9, to Australia 1960/1; played for Governor-General's XI v MCC in New Zealand 1960/61. *Tests* West Indies (1957 to 1960/1, 25 matches).
Career batting
92–141–30–3238–108–29.17–1–*ct* 217–*st* 39
Bowling 7–0
Test batting
25–38–6–961–108–30.03–1–*ct* 85–*st* 5

Known as 'Gerry', Alexander's last Test series was undoubtedly the highlight of his career, for he not only hit his single Test hundred (at Sydney in the 3rd match), but also ended the series at the top of the West Indies batting averages (484 runs, av 60.50). Usually coming in at no. 7 or 8, he hit at least one fifty in each of the five Tests. He also played for Cambridgeshire.

Alexander, Frederick Russell
Professional. *b:* 4.6.1924, Acton Green, London. Forcing right-hand batsman, right-arm medium, or off break, bowler. *Team* Middlesex (1951, 2 matches).
Career batting
2–3–0–15–8–5.00–0–*ct* 0

He 'appeared' for England in the fill-up game played when the Lord's Test of 1951 finished early.

Alexander, George
Amateur. *b:* 22.4.1851, Fitzroy, Victoria, Australia. *d:* 6.11.1930, Melbourne, Australia. Dashing right-hand batsman, fast right round-arm bowler, excellent field. *Team* Victoria (1875/6 to 1879/80, 6 matches). *Tours* Australia to England 1880 and 1884. *Tests* Australia (1880 to 1884/5, 2 matches).
Career batting
24–35–5–466–75–15.53–0–*ct* 16
Bowling 607–33–18.39–1–0–5/57
Test batting
2–4–0–52–33–13.00–0–*ct* 2
Bowling 93–2–46.50–0–0–2/69

Alexander acted as manager to both the 1880 and 1884 Australian teams in England.

Alexander, George Caledon
Amateur. *baptised:* 8.11.1842, Epsom, Surrey. *d:* 8.4.1913, St James, London. Batsman. *Team* Surrey (1869, 1 match).
Career batting
3–4–0–14–10–3.50–0–*ct* 0

Apart from his match with Surrey his only other first-class appearances were with Gentlemen of South in 1866 and Gentlemen of England in 1876.

Alexander, Gilbert William Arbuthnot
Amateur. *b:* 7.9.1895. *d;* 10.4.1957, Finchley, Middlesex. Middle order right-hand batsman, right-arm medium place bowler. *Sch* Glenalmond. *Team* Scotland (1922–32).
Career batting
13–22–0–617–136–28.04–1–*ct* 12
Bowling 113–3–37.66–0–0–2/30

Alexander, Robert
Amateur. *b:* 24.9.1910, Belfast. *d:* 19.7.1943, Sicily. Right-hand batsman, right-arm fast medium bowler. *Sch* Royal Belfast Academical Institution. *Team* Ireland (1932).
Career batting
1–2–0–29–22–14.50–0–*ct* 0
Bowling 55–0

He was also an Irish Rugby International.

Ali, Inshan
Cricketer. *b:* 25.9.1949, Preysel Village, Trinidad. Lower order left-hand batsman, slow left-arm bowler. *Team* Trinidad (1965/6 to 1979/80). *Tours* West Indies to England 1973, to Australia 1975/6. *Tests* West Indies (1970/1 to 1976/7, 12 matches).
Career batting
91–118–21–1341–63–13.82–0–*ct* 44
Bowling 9491–328–28.93–17–4–8/58
Test batting
12–18–2–172–25–10.75–0–*ct* 7
Bowling 1621–34–47.67–1–0–5/59

On his visit to England in 1973, Inshan Ali bowled well, taking 38 wickets (av 26.84) and was unfortunate not to play in more than one Test.

Alim-ud-Din
Amateur. *b:* 15.12.1930, Ajmer, India. Brother of Azim-ud-Din (Rajputana). Opening or middle order right-hand batsman, occasional leg break bowler. *Teams* Rajputana (1942/3); Gujarat (1944/5 to 1947/8); Muslims (1945/6); Sind (1948/9); Bahawalpur (1953/4); Karachi (1954/5 to 1965/6); PWD (1967/8). *Tours* Pakistan to Ceylon 1948/9, to England 1954, 1962, to West Indies 1957/8, to India 1960/1. *Tests* Pakistan (1954–62, 25 matches).
Career batting
140–238–16–7276–142–32.77–14–*ct* 65
Bowling 959–40–23.97–0–0–4/33
Test batting
25–45–2–1091–109–25.37–2–*ct* 8
Bowling 75–1–75.00–0–0–1/17
He was the youngest cricketer in first-class matches when he appeared for Rajputana v Baroda at Rajkot in 1942/3, aged 12 years and 45 days. He hit 1,083 runs, av 30.94, in 1954.

Alison, Charles Hugh
Amateur. *b:* May 1883, Preston, Lancashire. *d:* 20.10.1952, Rondesbosch, Cape Province, South Africa. Useful all-rounder. *Sch* Malvern. *Team* Somerset (1902–05, 4 matches).
Career batting
4–5–2–36–20–12.00–0–*ct* 3
Bowling 23–0
He played in the Oxford Freshmen's match of 1902. He also played for Buckinghamshire.

Allan, David Walter
Cricketer. *b:* 5.11.1937, Hastings, Barbados. Lower order right-hand batsman, wicket-keeper. *Team* Barbados (1955/6 to 1965/6). *Tours* West Indies to England 1963 and 1966. *Tests* West Indies (1961/2 to 1966, 5 matches).
Career batting
54–64–12–764–56–14.69–0–*ct* 117–*st* 24
Test batting
5–7–1–75–40*–12.50–*ct* 15–*st* 3
Allan came to England as the wicket-keeper on the 1963 tour, and was regarded as the principal keeper on the 1966 visit, but lost his Test place following a poor performance in the Second Test.

Allan, Francis Erskine
Amateur. *b:* 2.12.1849, Allansford, Victoria, Australia. *d:* 9.2.1917, Melbourne, Australia. Tail-end left-hand batsman, excellent fast-medium left round-arm bowler, slip field. *Team* Victoria (1867/8 to 1882/3, 14 matches). *Tour* Australia to England and USA 1878. *Test* Australia (1878/9, 1 match).
Career batting
31–50–16–371–35*–10.91–0–*ct* 14
Bowling 1638–124–13.20–11–2–8/20
Test batting
1–1–0–5–5–5.00–0–*ct* 0
Bowling 80–4–20.00–0–0–2/30
He was one of the first Australian bowlers to develop the art of swerving the ball in the air and deceived many batsmen, especially on his visit to England in 1878.

Allan, John
Amateur. *b:* 20.1.1911, Hamilton, Scotland. Right-hand batsman, right-arm medium pace bowler. *Team* Scotland (1951).
Career batting
1–2–0–2–2–1.00–0–*ct* 1
Bowling 78–3–26.00–0–0–3/78

Allan, James Moffat
Amateur. *b:* 2.4.1932, Leeds, Yorkshire. Determined right-hand batsman, who went in at no. 11 for Oxford in 1953 but by 1955 opened for Kent, accurate slow left arm spinner. *Sch* Edinburgh Academy. *Teams* Oxford U (1953–56, blue all four years); Kent (1954–57, 40 matches); Warwickshire (1966–68, 48 matches); Scotland (1954–72).
Career batting
179–268–45–4988–153–22.36–5–*ct* 124
Bowling 11179–435–25.69–18–2–7/54
He had an amazing start to his first-class career, bowling ten successive maidens and taking three wickets before conceding a run. In 1955 he was just 5 wickets short of achieving the 'double'. He hit 1,000 runs in a season twice (best 1,369, av 27.93, in 1955).

Allan, Walter Ramsay
Amateur. *b:* 26.10.1927, Riccarton, Ayrshire. Right-hand batsman. *Sch* Edinburgh Academy. *Team* Scotland (1950).
Career batting
3–6–0–73–30–12.16–0–*ct* 3

Allbrook, Mark Edward
Cricketer. *b:* 15.11.1954, Frimley, Surrey. Tail end right-hand batsman, right-arm off break bowler. *Sch* Tonbridge. *Teams* Cambridge U (1975–78, blue all four years); Nottinghamshire (1976–80, 12 matches).
Career batting
47–56–19–320–39–8.64–0–*ct* 15
Bowling 3504–76–46.10–2–0–7/79

Allchurch, Thomas
Amateur. *b:* 1883, Stourbridge, Worcs. *d:* 23.10.1934, Halesowen, Worcs. Middle order

right-hand batsman, slow right-arm bowler. *Team* Worcestershire (1919–20, 3 matches).
Career batting
3–6–0–74–51–12.33–0–*ct* 2
Bowling 280–10–28.00–1–0–5/70

Allcock, Charles Howard
Amateur. *b:* 16.4.1855, Harborne, Staffs. *d:* 30.9.1947, Aberdovey. Brother of Rev. A. E. (Warwickshire, non-first-class). Fair right-hand batsman, slow round-arm bowler, slip field. *Teams* Cambridge U (1878); MCC (1883).
Career batting
5–8–0–29–14–3.62–0–*ct* 4
Bowling 250–14–17.85–0–0–4/51

He appeared for Staffordshire and later Buckinghamshire, being a master at Eton College. His final first-class match was for Cambridge U (Past and Present) in 1884.

Allcott, Cyril Francis Walter
Amateur. *b:* 7.10.1896, Lower Moutere, New Zealand. *d:* 21.11.1973, Auckland, New Zealand. Attacking left-hand batsman, slow left-arm bowler. *Teams* Hawke's Bay (1920/1); Auckland (1921/2 to 1931/2); Otago (1945/6). *Tours* New Zealand to Australia 1925/6, 1927/8, to England 1927, 1931. *Tests* New Zealand (1929/30 to 1931/32, 6 matches).
Career batting
82–116–26–2514–131–27.93–5–*ct* 62
Bowling 5892–220–26.78–13–2–7/75
Test batting
6–7–2–113–33–22.60–0–*ct* 3
Bowling 541–6–90.16–0–0–2/102

Originally Allcott made his mark as a bowler, but by 1927 had developed into an all-rounder. On the 1931 tour to England he acted as assistant manager and treasurer.

Alldis, James Stephen
Cricketer. *b:* 27.12.1949, Paddington, London. Left-hand batsman, slow left-arm bowler. *Team* Middlesex (1970, 2 matches).
Career batting
2–4–1–7–4*–2.33–0–*ct* 0
Bowling 37–1–37.00–0–0–1/33

Allen, Antony William
Amateur. *b:* 22.12.1912, Evenley Hall, Brackley, Northants. Brilliant right-hand opening batsman. *Sch* Eton. *Teams* Cambridge U (1932–34, blue in 1933 and 1934); Northants (1932–36, 8 matches).
Career batting
35–64–1–1928–144–30.60–4–*ct* 13

Allen hit a century (112) before lunch for Eton v Harrow at Lord's in 1931, helping in a record opening stand of 208. It was Northants' misfortune that he gave up serious cricket after leaving Cambridge. His final first-class match was for Free Foresters in 1947.

Allen, Basil Oliver
Amateur. *b:* 13.10.1911, Clifton, Gloucs. *d:* 1.5.1981, Chewton Mendip, Somerset. Solid middle order left-hand batsman, who could hit if required, fine close leg-side field. *Sch* Clifton. *Teams* Cambridge U (1932–33, blue 1933); Gloucestershire (1932–51, 285 matches).
Career batting
308–512–20–14195–220–28.85–14–*ct* 310
Bowling 429–3–143.00–0–0–2/80

He captained Gloucestershire 1937–38, 1947–50. His highest score was 220 v Hants (Bournemouth) 1947. He scored 1,000 runs in a season 7 times between 1934 and 1949 (best 1,785, av 34.32, in 1938).

Allen, Charles
Amateur. *b:* 1878. *d:* 22.5.1958, Cirencester, Gloucestershire. Hard hitting batsman. *Sch* Cranleigh. *Team* Gloucestershire (1909, 2 matches).
Career batting
2–3–0–51–35–17.00–0–*ct* 2

Allen, David Arthur
Professional. *b:* 29.10.1935, Bristol. Dependable right-hand lower order batsman, consistent off spin bowler with subtle variations of flight, fine outfield with accurate throw. *Team* Gloucestershire (1953–72, 349 matches). *Tours* MCC to West Indies 1959/60, New Zealand 1960/1, Ceylon, India and Pakistan 1961/2, Australia 1962/3, South Africa 1964/5, Australia and New Zealand 1965/6; Commonwealth to Pakistan 1967/8. *Tests* England (1959/60 to 1966, 39 matches).
Career batting
456–641–147–9291–121*–18.80–1–*ct* 252
Bowling 28586–1209–23.64–56–8–8/34
Test batting
39–51–15–918–88–25.50–0–*ct* 10
Bowling 3779–122–30.97–4–0–5/30

Though making his debut in 1953, Allen did not come to the fore until 1959, when he gained a regular place in the Gloucestershire side and was chosen for the winter tour to West Indies. As a useful all-rounder he then remained on the Test scene for six years. His best season was 1961, when he performed the double. He hit 1,000 runs twice (best 1,165, av 24.78, in 1964) and took 100 wickets once (124, av 19.43, in 1961).

Allen, Ernest George
Amateur. *b:* 24.6.1880, Worksop, Notts. *d:* 28.5.1943, Harrogate, Yorkshire. Right-hand

middle order batsman. *Sch* Lancing. *Team* Nottinghamshire (1903, 2 matches).
Career batting
2–3–0–48–19–16.00–0–*ct* 0

Allen, George Oswald Browning, CBE
Amateur. *b:* 31.7.1902, Bellevue Hill, Sydney, New South Wales, Australia. Nephew of R. C. (N.S.W. and Australia). Forceful right-hand batsman, fast right-arm bowler. *Sch* Eton. *Teams* Cambridge U (1922–23, blue both years); Middlesex (1921–50, 146 matches). *Tours* MCC to South America 1926–7, to Australia and New Zealand 1932–3 and 1936–7, to West Indies 1947–8 (captain on last two). *Tests* England (1930 to 1947–8, 25 matches).
Career batting
265–376–54–9232–180–28.67–11–*ct* 131
Bowling 17518–788–22.23–48–9–10/40
Test batting
25–33–2–750–122–24.19–1–*ct* 20
Bowling 2379–81–29.37–5–1–7/80

Although he was never really a regular County player, due to business commitments, Allen nevertheless remained for most of the period between the First and Second World Wars one of the leading fast bowlers in the game. He first appeared for Middlesex in the year that he was regarded as the best Public School bowler, and his performances for the County won immediate praise. His success continued during two years at Cambridge, but not a great deal was seen of him in the following seasons, and his selection for the MCC team to Australia in 1932–33 was the subject of some controversy, which was subsequently silenced by his all-round performances on that 'Bodyline' tour – it was notable that he himself did not use leg-theory bowling. His best bowling was 10/40 for Middlesex v Lancashire at Lord's in 1929.

He led England on the next visit to Australia and had the mortification to find his side winning the first two Tests but still losing the series.

After the Second World War he was persuaded to lead England on the ill-fated tour of West Indies, when not a single match was won. He played his last first-class match for Free Foresters in 1954.

After his first-class career Allen became one of the most influential figures behind the scenes at Lord's. He was chairman of the Test selectors from 1955 to 1961; treasurer of MCC from 1964 to 1976 and held the office of President in 1963–64.

Allen, James Stephen
Professional. *b:* 4.11.1881, Croydon, Surrey. *d:* 1958, Raunds, Northants. Left-hand batsman, slow left-arm bowler. *Team* Northants (1905, 2 matches).
Career batting
2–3–1–0–0*–0.00–0–*ct* 0
Bowling 154–1–154.00–0–0–1/58

Allen, John Wallace
Amateur. *b:* 17.2.1921, Cullion, Co Londonderry. Right-hand batsman. *Team* Ireland (1948).
Career batting
1–1–0–0–0–0.00–0–*ct* 0

Allen, Michael Henry John
Cricketer. *b:* 7.1.1933, Bedford. Tail end right-hand batsman, accurate slow left-arm bowler, good close field. *Sch* Bedford School. *Teams* Northants (1956–63, 155 matches); Derbyshire (1964–66, 31 matches).
Career batting
193–231–56–1723–59–9.84–0–*ct* 171
Bowling 11219–500–22.43–25–3–8/48

He took 8–88 in the first first-class innings in which he bowled (it was his second first-class match).

Allen, Spencer
Amateur. *b:* 20.12.1893, Halifax, Yorkshire. *d:* 9.10.1978, Bradford. Lower order left-hand batsman, slow left-arm bowler. *Team* Yorkshire (1924, 1 match).
Career batting
1–2–0–8–6–4.00–0–*ct* 0
Bowling 116–2–58.00–0–0–2/116

Allen played for Yorkshire when four of the first eleven were appearing in a 'Test Trial'.

Allen, Wentworth
Amateur. *b:* 30.1.1894, Dublin. *d:* 22.2.1943, Shankhill, Co Dublin. Lower order right-hand batsman, right-arm medium pace bowler. *Teams* Ireland (1920–25); Dublin University (1926).
Career batting
7–10–5–23–10*–4.60–0–*ct* 3
Bowling 435–15–29.00–0–0–2/20

Allen, William Reginald
Professional. *b:* 14.4.1893, Featherstone, Yorkshire. *d:* 14.10.1950, Normanton, Yorkshire. Useful right-hand batsman, wicket-keeper. *Team* Yorkshire (1921–25, 30 matches).
Career batting
30–32–10–475–95–21.59–0–*ct* 45–*st* 21

In his later years, when playing for Castleford in the Yorkshire Council, he weighed about 20 stones.

Allenby, Marmaduke Cecil
Amateur. *b:* 30.8.1873, York. *d:* 16.4.1932, Plymouth. *Team* Hampshire (1900, 1 match).
Career batting
1–1–0–0–0–0.00–0–*ct* 0
He also appeared for Devon.

Allerton, Jeremy William Orde
Cricketer. *b:* 2.2.1944, Windsor, Berkshire. Middle order left-hand batsman, right-arm medium pace bowler. *Sch* Stowe. *Team* Oxford U (1967–69, blue 1969).
Career batting
15–26–1–605–67–24.20–0–*ct* 2
Bowling 7–0

Alletson, Edwin Boaler
Professional. *b:* 6.3.1884, Welbeck Estate, Notts. *d:* 5.7.1963, Worksop, Notts. Hard hitting middle order right-hand batsman, occasional right-arm medium leg break bowler. *Team* Nottinghamshire (1906–14, 118 matches).
Career batting
119–179–6–3217–189–18.59–1–*ct* 74
Bowling 628–33–19.03–1–0–6/74
Alletson created a sensation in the match between Notts and Sussex at Hove in 1911, when he hit 189 in 90 minutes, the last 142 coming in 40 minutes, including 34 off one over from Killick. He was never able to reproduce this form, though earlier in his career he hit several fast fifties.

Alley, William Edward
Professional. *b:* 2.3.1919, Hornsby, Sydney, New South Wales, Australia. Aggressive left-hand batsman, right-arm fast-medium or medium pace bowler. *Teams* New South Wales (1945/6 to 1947/8, 12 matches); Somerset (1957–68, 350 matches). *Tours* Commonwealth to India, Pakistan and Ceylon 1949/50, to Rhodesia 1962/3, to Pakistan 1963/4; Cavaliers to South Africa 1962/3.
Career batting
400–682–67–19612–221*–31.88–31–*ct* 293
Bowling 17421–768–22.68–30–1–8/65
After a moderate cricket career in Australia and nine years in League cricket in Lancashire, Alley joined Somerset at the age of 38 and began a most successful all-round career in County cricket. The highlight of this was his aggregate of 3,019 runs (av 56.96) in 1961, and in all he reached 1,000 runs on 10 occasions. His highest innings was 221* v Warwicks (Nuneaton) 1961. He performed the 'double' in 1962, taking 112 wickets, av 20.74. He became a first-class umpire.
Alley is a colourful character and a great inspiration to lesser players – nothing daunts him. In his early years he was a noted boxer, winning all his 28 professional fights at welterweight.

Alleyne, Hartley Leroy
Cricketer. *b:* 28.2.1957, Bridgetown, Barbados. Lower order right-hand batsman, right-arm fast bowler. *Teams* Barbados (1978/9 to 1982/3); Worcestershire (1980–82, 38 matches). *Tour* Young West Indies to Zimbabwe 1981/2.
Career batting
49–54–11–538–72–12.51–0–*ct* 10
Bowling 4099–157–26.10–6–2–8/43
He also played for Lincolnshire in 1979.

Allin, Anthony William
Cricketer. *b:* 20.4.1954, Bideford, Devon. Moderate right-hand batsman, excellent left-arm slow bowler. *Sch* Belmont College, Barnstaple. *Team* Glamorgan (1976, 13 matches).
Career batting
13–16–8–108–32–13.50–0–*ct* 3
Bowling 1011–44–22.97–4–1–8/63
He headed the Glamorgan bowling averages in 1976 with 44 wickets (av 22.97), his best bowling being 8/63 v Sussex (Cardiff). He declined an offer of a two-year contract with Glamorgan, preferring to return to farming and Minor County cricket with Devon.

Allison, David Farquhar
Cricketer. *b:* 26.6.1948, London. Right-hand batsman, wicket-keeper. *Sch* Greenmore College. *Team* Oxford U (1970, blue).
Career batting
6–9–2–48–21–6.85–0–*ct* 4

Alliston, Cyril George Prat
Amateur. *b:* 1.11.1891, Fulham. *d:* 21.7.1973, Southport, Lancashire. Right-hand batsman, right-arm medium pace bowler. *Sch* Repton. *Team* Kent (1922, 1 match).
Career batting
1–1–0–0–0–0.00–0–*ct* 0

Allom, Anthony Thomas Carrick
Amateur. *b:* 21.10.1938, Bletchingly, Surrey. Son of M. J. C. (Surrey). Hard-hitting right-hand batsman, accurate right-arm medium fast bowler, fine slip field. *Sch* Charterhouse. *Team* Surrey (1960, 1 match).
Career batting
5–8–3–94–34*–18.80–0–*ct* 1
Bowling 439–15–29.26–1–0–5/79
His debut was for the Free Foresters in 1959 and final match for the same team in 1961.

Allom, Maurice James Carrick
Amateur. *b:* 23.3.1906, Northwood, Middlesex. Father of A. T. C. (Surrey). Useful lower order right-hand batsman, effective right-arm medium fast bowler. *Sch* Wellington. *Teams* Cambridge U (1926–28, blue 1927–28); Surrey (1927–37, 100 matches). *Tours* MCC to Australia and New Zealand 1929/30, to South Africa 1930/1; Tennyson to Jamaica 1927/8. *Tests* England (1929/30 to 1930/1, 5 matches).
Career batting
179–203–51–1953–64–12.84–0–*ct* 83
Bowling 14291–605–23.62–30–3–9/55
Test batting
5–3–2–14–8*–14.00–0–*ct* 0
Bowling 265–14–18.92–1–0–5/38

Allom's most noteworthy feat was the dismissal of four men in five balls (including the hat-trick) on his Test debut for England v New Zealand at Christchurch in 1929/30. His best English season was 1930 when he took 108 wickets (av 23.33). His best bowling was for 9 for 55 for Cambridge U v. Army at Cambridge in 1927. His final first-class match was for Free Foresters in 1938.

Allott, Paul John Walter
Cricketer. *b*: 14.9.1956, Altrincham, Cheshire. Lower order right-hand batsman, right-arm fast medium bowler, good deep field. *Team* Lancashire (1978–83, 78 matches). *Tours* England to India and Sri Lanka 1981/2; International XI to Jamaica 1982/3. *Tests* England (1981–82, 5 matches).
Career batting
93–86–25–809–52*–13.26–0–*ct* 26
Bowling 6522–224–29.11–9–0–8/48
Test batting
5–6–2–119–52*–29.75–0–*ct* 2
Bowling 414–6–69.00–0–0–2/17

Allsop, Richard
Professional. *b:* 10.6.1849, Wirksworth, Derbyshire. *d:* 20.3.1908, Burton-on-Trent, Staffordshire. Fair right-hand batsman, slip field. *Team* Derbyshire (1872–74, 3 matches).
Career batting
3–5–0–42–33–8.40–0–*ct* 3

Allsopp, Hon Frederic Ernest
Amateur. *b:* 21.9.1857, Hindlip Hall, Worcs. *d:* 20.12.1928, Droitwich, Worcs. Brother of Hon H. T. (Cambridge U). Sound right-hand batsman, slow round-arm bowler. *Sch* Cheltenham. *Team* MCC (1884).
Career batting
2–3–0–46–34–15.33–0–*ct* 1
Bowling 23–2–11.50–0–0–1/8

He appeared for Worcestershire in the County's non-first-class period.

Allsopp, Hon Herbert Tongue
Amateur. *b:* 5.12.1855, Foremark Hall, Derbyshire. *d:* 31.1.1920, Walton Bury, Staffordshire. Brother of Hon F. E. (MCC). Useful right-hand batsman, fast round-arm bowler, good field at third man. *Sch* Cheltenham. *Team* Cambridge U (1876, blue).
Career batting
5–8–1–80–22–11.42–0–*ct* 4
Bowling 58–6–9.66–0–0–3/15

He appeared for Worcestershire in the County's non-first-class period.

Allsopp, Thomas C.
Professional. *b:* 18.12.1880, Leicester. *d:* 7.3.1919, Norwich. Lower order left-hand batsman, good slow left-arm spin bowler. *Team* Leicestershire (1903–05, 36 matches).
Career batting
37–55–17–347–32–9.13–0–*ct* 10
Bowling 2490–88–28.29–4–1–6/85

He made quite an impression as a bowler in 1904, but was dropped from the Leicestershire side the following year and later appeared with success for Norfolk. A well-known soccer player, he appeared for Leicester Fosse.

Alpass, Herbert John Hampden
Amateur. *b:* 7.8.1906, Berkeley, Gloucs. Fair right-hand batsman, slow left-arm bowler, who could spin or swing the ball. *Sch* Clifton. *Team* Gloucestershire (1926–28, 7 matches).
Career batting
7–9–2–36–18*–5.14–0–*ct* 3
Bowling 114–4–28.50–0–0–2/42

He was a brilliant schoolboy bowler, who might well have developed into a good County cricketer.

Alston, Hallam Newton Egerton
Amateur. *b:* 10.6.1908, Cheltenham, Gloucs. Right-hand middle order batsman, right-arm medium pace bowler. *Sch* Cheltenham. *Team* Somerset (1933, 1 match).
Career batting
1–2–0–6–4–3.00–0–*ct* 0
Bowling 6–1–6.00–0–0–1/6

Altham, Harry Surtees
Amateur. *b:* 30.11.1888, Camberley, Surrey. *d:* 11.3.1965, Sheffield. Father of R. J. L. (Oxford U). Useful right-hand batsman, occasional right-

arm medium pace bowler. *Sch* Repton. *Teams* Oxford U (1909–12, blue 1911–12); Surrey (1908–12, 10 matches); Hampshire (1919–23, 24 matches).
Career batting
55–87–9–1537–141–19.70–1–*ct* 26
Bowling 47–0

He was better known 'behind the scenes' rather than on the field; cricket coach at Winchester for 30 years; member of MCC Committee for 25 years; Test Selector in 1954; author with E. W. Swanton of 'The History of Cricket', which was the standard work on the game. His final first-class match was for Gentlemen of England v New Zealand in 1931.

Altham, Richard James Livingstone
Amateur. *b:* 21.1.1924, Winchester, Hants. Son of H. S. (Hants and Surrey). Middle order right-hand batsman, right-arm medium pace bowler. *Sch* Marlborough. *Team* Oxford U (1947).
Career batting
2–3–0–14–14–4.66–0–*ct* 2

His County cricket was for Hertfordshire. He made his final first-class appearance for Free Foresters in 1948.

Alwyn, Nicholas
Amateur. *b:* 13.6.1938, Finchley, London. Right-hand batsman. *Team* Cambridge U (1961).
Career batting
5–10–0–141–41–14.10–0–*ct* 0

Amarnath, Mohinder Bhardwaj
Cricketer. *b*: 24.9.1950, Patiala, India. Son of L. Amarnath (India), brother of Surinder (India) and Rajinder (Punjab and Delhi). Middle order right-hand batsman, right-arm medium pace bowler. *Teams* Punjab (1966/67 to 1973/4); Delhi (1974/5 to 1981/2). *Tours* Indian Universities to Sri Lanka 1970/1; India to West Indies 1975/6, 1982/3, to New Zealand 1975/6, to Australia 1977/8, to Pakistan 1978/9, 1982/3, to England 1979. *Tests* India (1969/70 to 1982/3, 37 matches).
Career batting
178–280–47–9946–207–42.68–21–*ct* 125
Bowling 8169–257–31.78–8–1–7/27
Test batting
37–64–5–2648–120–44.88–7–*ct* 32
Bowling 1476–26–56.76–0–0–4/63

On the 1979 tour to England he hit 592 runs, av 45.53, and appeared in two Tests. He hit over 2,000 runs in the 1982/3 season, whilst playing in India, Pakistan and West Indies.

Amarnath, Nanik Bhardwaj
(known as Lala Amarnath)
Amateur. *b:* 11.9.1911, Lahore, India. Father of M.B. (India), Surinder (India) and Rajinder (Delhi and Punjab). Middle order right-hand batsman, excellent right-arm medium pace bowler. Aligarh University. *Teams* Hindus (1929/30 to 1939/40); S. Punjab (1933/4 to 1951/2); Gujerat (1952/3); Patiala (1953/4 to 1957/8); Uttar Pradesh (1956/7); Railways (1958/9 to 1960/61). *Tours* India to England 1936, 1946, to Ceylon 1944/5, to Australia 1947/8, to Pakistan 1954/5; Indian Starlets to Pakistan 1959/60; also appeared in Ceylon 1933/4. *Tests* India (1933/4 to 1952/3, 24 matches).
Career batting
184–282–33–10323–262–41.45–31–*ct* 9–*st* 2
Bowling 10488–457–22.94–19–3–7/27
Test batting
24–40–4–878–118–24.38–1–*ct* 13
Bowling 1481–45–32.91–2–0–5/96

At Aligarh University, Amarnath was principally a wicket-keeper, but by the time of the 1933/4 MCC tour to India, he had developed into an attacking batsman and hit a century on his Test debut. It was whilst in the nets prior to this Test that Amarnath's bowling potential was discovered, and within a short while he became one of the best all-rounders in India. He was expected to play a leading part in the 1936 tour to England, but was sent home for disciplinary reasons on the eve of the first Test. On the 1946 Tour he headed the Test bowling averages – the peculiarity of his bowling was that he bowled off the wrong foot, using a three pace run-up. His first class debut was for Hindus in the Lahore Tournament in 1929/30. His highest score was 262 for Indians in England v. Rest at Calcutta in 1946/7. His final first class match was for Maharashtra Governor's XI in 1963/4.

Amar Singh, Ladhabhai Nakum
Amateur. *b:* 4.12.1910, Rajkot, India. *d:* 21.5.1940, Jamnagar, India. Brother of L. Ramji (Hindus, Western India, India), uncle of Vajehsingh Nakum (Nawanagar and Saurashtra). Punishing right-hand batsman, right-arm fast medium bowler. *Teams* Patiala (1931/2 to 1932/3); Western India (1933/4 to 1935/6); Nawanagar (1936/7 to 1939/40); Hindus (1934/5 to 1939/40). *Tours* India to England 1932 and 1936; also appeared in England in 1935

and 1938, and in Ceylon in 1933/4. *Tests* India (1932–36, 7 matches).
Career batting
91–149–12–3338–140*–24.36–5–*ct* 76
Bowling 9199–498–18.47–41–14–8/23
Test batting
7–14–1–292–51–22.46–0–*ct* 3
Bowling 858–28–30.64–2–0–7/86

The best Indian fast bowler of his generation, he died tragically of pneumonia at the early age of 29. He was the first man to take 100 wickets in Ranji Trophy matches and he was a brilliant hitter – in a match at Rajkot he hit a century in 22 minutes. He took 111 wickets, av. 20.78, in 1932. His first class debut was for Rest of India in 1930/1.

Ambler, Joe
Professional. *b:* 12.2.1860, Lascelles Hall, Yorkshire. *d:* 1899, Huddersfield, Yorkshire. Middle order batsman, right-arm fast medium bowler. *Teams* Somerset (1883, 4 matches); Yorkshire (1886, 4 matches).
Career batting
8–14–0–197–76–14.07–0–*ct* 5–*st* 2
Bowling 222–7–31.71–0–0–4/54

According to MCC 'Scores and Biographies', vol XIV, p lxxxvi, the cricketer who appeared for Yorkshire was John Ambler of Lascelles Hall, b 1845, but this is incorrect.

Ames, Leslie Ethelbert George, CBE
Professional. *b:* 3.12.1905, Elham, Kent. Forcing right-hand batsman, usually at no 3, brilliant wicket-keeper. *Team* Kent (1926–51, 430 matches). *Tours* MCC to Australia 1928/9, 1932/3, 1936/7, to South Africa 1938/39, to West Indies 1929/30, 1934/5, to New Zealand 1932/3; Commonwealth to Ceylon and India 1950/1. *Tests* England (1929 to 1938/9, 47 matches).
Career batting
593–951–95–37248–295–43.51–102–*ct* 703–*st* 418
Bowling 801–24–33.37–0–0–3/23
Test batting
47–72–12–2434–149–40.56–8–*ct* 74–*st* 23

The outstanding wicket-keeper-batsman of the 1930s, Ames joined the Kent staff in 1923 as a batsman, but soon took up wicket-keeping. He obtained a regular place in the County side for the first time in 1927, scoring over 1,000 runs in the season, a feat he was to accomplish 17 times, his highest being in 1933 when 3,058 runs, av. 58.80, flowed from his bat. In 1927 he also hit the first of 102 centuries – completing his century of centuries in 1950. His highest innings was 295 for Kent v Gloucs at Folkestone in 1933 and he hit eight other double centuries.

In 1928 he created a new seasonal first-class record by picking up 122 dismissals behind the stumps, but the following year he again broke the record with a total of 128, which remains the English record. In 1932 he achieved 100 dismissals for the third time (104), but this time included 64 stumpings in his bag, another record which still stands. In his career he achieved 418 stumpings, another first-class record. Most of his triumphs behind the wicket were accomplished in harness with A. P. Freeman, the prolific leg spinner.

Ames played regularly for England as a wicket-keeper-batsman through the 1930s, but when first-class cricket resumed after the Second World War, he forsook his position behind the wicket (giving way to T. G. Evans) and remained in the County side purely as a batsman. In 1950 he was the first professional to be appointed as a Test Selector and served for eight seasons, then from 1960 to 1974 he took the post as secretary/manager to Kent. On three occasions, including the riot-torn Pakistan tour of 1968/9, he managed MCC teams abroad.

In one capacity or another his career in first-class cricket has spanned over 50 years. He also played soccer for Clapton Orient and Gillingham.

Ames, Neville Laurenson
Amateur. *b:* 31.7.1891, Fulham, London *d:* 21.3.1956, St Johns Wood, London. Hard hitting right-hand batsman, right-arm fast medium bowler, good field. *Sch* Radley. *Team* Leveson-Gower's XI (1912).
Career batting
1–2–0–0–0–0.00–0–*ct* 0
Bowling 11–0

Amherst, Hon Joceline George Herbert
Amateur. *b:* 7.6.1846, Grosvenor St, London. *d:* 1.2.1900, Darlinghurst, West Australia. Steady right-hand batsman, slow round-arm bowler. *Sch* Harrow. *Teams* MCC (1866); Gentlemen of Kent (1864).
Career batting
2–4–0–15–7–3.75–0–*ct* 0
Bowling 36–3–12.00–0–0–2/26

It is very difficult to separate the performances of this player and his brother (Hon Jeffrey Charles Amherst, 1845–1877), but it is believed that the two appearances in first-class matches were both by J. G. H. Amherst. He held various high political offices.

Amherst, Rev Hon Percy Arthur
Amateur. *b:* 30.11.1839, Sevenoaks, Kent. *d:* 30.1.1910, Ossington, Notts. *Sch* Eton. *Team* MCC (1871).

Amir Elahi

Career batting
1–2–0–2–2–1.00–0–*ct* 0
He played non-first-class cricket for Northants.

Amir Elahi
Amateur. *b:* 1.9.1908, Lahore, India. *d:* 28.12.1980, Multan, Pakistan. Lower order right-hand batsman, right-arm bowler, originally medium, but later leg-break and googly. *Teams* Muslims (1935/6 to 1944/5); Northern India (1934/5 to 1943/4); S. Punjab (1937/8 to 1949/50); Baroda (1944/5 to 1949/50); Bahawalpur (1953/4). *Tours* India to England 1936, to Australia 1947/8; Pakistan to India 1952/3. *Tests* India (1947/8, 1 match); Pakistan (1952/3, 5 matches).
Career batting
123–168–20–2462–96–16.63–0–*ct* 65
Bowling 13005–505–25.75–30–6–8/94
Test batting
6–9–1–82–47–10.25–0–*ct* 0
Bowling 248–7–35.42–0–0–4/134

Neither on the tour to England in 1936, nor the visit to Australia in 1947/8 did Amir Elahi attain much distinction, but he was comparatively successful in his later years for Pakistan when he not only became one of the few cricketers to represent two countries, but also one of the oldest (44) of Test players. He took 5 wickets in 5 balls in the Surat Tournament, 1944/5.

Amiss, Dennis Leslie
Professional. *b*: 7.4.1943, Harborne, Birmingham. Sound opening right-hand batsman, slow left-arm bowler, good close field. *Team* Warwickshire (1960–83, 444 matches). *Tours* MCC to Pakistan 1966/7, to India, Pakistan and Sri Lanka 1972/3, to West Indies 1973/4, to Australia and New Zealand 1974/5, to India, Sri Lanka and Australia 1976/7; International XI to India, Ceylon and Pakistan 1967/8; Rest of World to Pakistan 1970/1; SAB to South Africa 1981/2. *Tests* England (1966–77, 50 matches).
Career batting
555–954–102–36879–262*–43.28–85–*ct* 358
Bowling 718–18–39.88–0–0–3/21
Test batting
50–88–10–3612–262*–46.30–11–*ct* 24

He hit 1,000 runs in a season in England 19 times, going on to 2,000 twice (best 2,110, av 65.93, in 1976). Of his three double centuries two were for England and one for Warwickshire, the highest being 262* for England v West Indies at Kingston in 1973/4. His career in Test cricket ended when he signed for Packer's World Series Cricket.

Amor, Stanley Long
Amateur. *b:* 22.7.1887, Bath, Somerset. *d:* 7.8.1965, Bath, Somerset. Right-hand batsman, wicket-keeper. *Team* Somerset (1908–30, 26 matches).
Career batting
29–51–20–220–21–7.09–0–*ct* 29–*st* 22
He also represented Somerset at hockey.

Amory, J. H. (*see under* Heathcoat-Amory, J.)

Amory, L. H. (*see under* Heathcoat-Amory, L.)

Anderson, Albert Edwin
Amateur. *b:* 13.4.1889, Comber, Co Down. *d:* 21.9.1944, Comber, Co Down. Middle order right-hand batsman. *Team* Ireland (1926).
Career batting
1–2–0–18–18–9.00–0–*ct* 1

Anderson, Charles Stewart
Amateur. *b: circa* 1881. *d:* 1.3.1943, Portrush, Co Antrim. Lower order right-hand batsman, right-arm medium pace off break bowler. *Team* Ireland (1926).
Career batting
1–1–0–0–0–0.00–0 *ct* 0
Bowling 25–0

Anderson, Ewan William
Amateur. *b:* 28.3.1938, Bromley, Kent. Right-hand batsman, right-arm fast medium bowler. *Sch* Dulwich. *Team* Oxford U (1961–62).
Career batting
12–15–5–38–13*–3.80–0–*ct* 1
Bowling 727–18–40.38–0–0–3/69

Anderson, George
Professional. *b:* 20.1.1826, Aiskew, Bedale, Yorkshire. *d:* 27.11.1902, Bedale, Yorkshire. Hard-hitting right-hand batsman, excellent mid-wicket or long-leg field. *Team* Yorkshire (1850–69, 35 matches). *Tour* Parr to Australia 1863/4.
Career batting
99–171–16–2535–99*–16.35–0–*ct* 74

One of the most prominent professionals of his day, Anderson appeared for the All England Eleven for about 20 years. Late in his career he was offered the captaincy of Yorkshire but refused because it would mean playing against Surrey, there being a dispute between the leading Northern professionals and the authorities at the Oval. Anderson's refusal resulted in him missing a number of County matches – the argument continuing for several years (1862–66).

Anderson, Ivan John
Cricketer. *b:* 13.8.1944, Armagh, Ireland. Right-hand batsman, off break bowler. *Team* Ireland (1966–82).
Career batting
19–33–8–947–147–37.88–3–*ct* 9
Bowling 249–17–14.64–1–0–5/21

Anderson, Ian Mair
Amateur. *b:* 11.5.1931, Calcutta, India. Middle order right-hand batsman, right-arm fast medium pace bowler. *Sch* Dollar. *Team* Scotland (1951–53).
Career batting
5–8–0–114–40–14.25–0–*ct* 2

Anderson, Iain Stuart
Cricketer. *b:* 24.4.1960, Derby. Opening or middle order right-hand batsman, off break bowler. *Team* Derbyshire (1978–83, 73 matches).
Career batting
73–112–20–2425–112–26.35–2–*ct* 62
Bowling 836–15–55–73–0–0–4/35
He hit 1,233 runs, av 37.36, in 1983.

Anderson, Joseph
Amateur. *b:* 31.1.1878, Perth, Scotland. *d:* 10.6.1961, Perth, Scotland. Right-hand batsman. *Team* Scotland (1906–12).
Career batting
5–9–0–139–31–15.44–0–*ct* 3

Anderson, James Duncan
Amateur. *b:* 17.12.1931, Melbourne, Australia. Right-hand batsman, right-arm medium pace off break bowler. *Sch* Melbourne G.S. *Team* Oxford U (1955).
Career batting
2–3–2–4–4*–4.00–0–*ct* 3
Bowling 118–4–29.50–0–0–4/68
He won a half-blue for athletics and represented Australia at Australian Rules Football.

Anderson, John Theodore
Amateur. *b:* 10.8.1878, Warrnambool, Victoria, Australia. *d:* 20.8.1926, Geelong, Victoria, Australia. *Teams* Scotland (1905–06); W. Australia (1908/9 to 1909/10, 4 matches).
Career batting
6–11–2–68–17*–7.55–0–*ct* 4
Bowling 351–16–21.93–0–0–4/51

Anderson, Michael Herbert
Amateur, *b:* 10.12.1916, Devonport, Devon. *d:* 10.5.1940. He was killed in action (with 600 Squadron, based at Manston, Kent). Opening right-hand batsman, wicket-keeper. *Sch* Clifton. *Team* Cambridge U (1937–38).
Career batting
4–7–2–92–60–18.40–0–*ct* 3–*st* 3
He also played for Hertfordshire.

Anderson, Reginald Mervyn Bulford
Amateur. *b:* 25.4.1914, Swansea, Glamorgan. *d:* 12.8.1972, Swansea, Glamorgan. Tail end right-hand batsman, right-arm fast medium bowler. *Team* Glamorgan (1946, 1 match).
Career batting
1–1–0–0–0–0.00–0–*ct* 0
Bowling 60–0

Anderson, Robert Wickham
Cricketer. *b*: 2.10.1948, Christchurch, New Zealand. Son of W. McD. (New Zealand). Attacking opening right-hand batsman, good deep field. *Teams* Canterbury (1967/8); Northern Districts (1969/70); Otago (1971/2 to 1976/7); Central Districts (1977/8 to 1981/2). *Tours* New Zealand to England 1973, 1978 to Pakistan 1976/7. *Tests* New Zealand (1976 to 1978/9, 9 matches).
Career batting
111–197–14–5609–155–30.65–8–*ct* 79
Bowling 154–5–30.80–0–0–4/49
Test batting
9–18–0–423–92–23.50–0–0–*ct* 1
He played in all three Test matches on the 1978 tour, scoring 739 runs, av 35.19, in first-class matches.

Anderson, William Alexander
Amateur. *b:* 28.7.1909, Eastry, Kent. *d:* 21.4.1975, Harlow, Essex. Middle order left-hand batsman. *Sch* Charterhouse. *Team* Free Foresters (1946).
Career batting
1–1–0–14–14–14.00–0–*ct* 0

Anderson, William Burn
Amateur. *b:* 12.11.1871, London. *d:* 31.1.1948, Bury St Edmunds, Suffolk. Right-hand batsman, right-arm medium fast bowler, good field. *Sch* Harrow. *Team* Middlesex (1891, 1 match).
Career batting
1–2–0–2–2–1.00–0–*ct* 1

Anderson, William Williamson
Amateur. *b:* 27.11.1894, Dunfermline, Scotland. *d:* 16.6.1973, Dunfermline, Scotland. Lower order right-hand batsman, right-arm fast bowler. *Team* Scotland (1922–36).
Career batting
16–26–3–241–27–10.47–0–*ct* 14
Bowling 1147–54–21.24–3–0–6/51

Anderton, Frederic Michael
Amateur. *b:* 8.12.1931, Agra, India. Sound right-hand batsman, off break bowler. *Sch* Sherborne. *Team* Cambridge U (1953).
Career batting
3–5–1–64–38–16.00–0–*ct* 2
Bowling 11–0

Andreae, Charles Montagu
Amateur. *b:* 16.12.1906, Marylebone, London. *d:* 22.6.1970, Sunningdale, Berkshire. Attacking right-hand batsman, slow right-arm bowler. *Sch* Harrow. *Team* Cambridge U (1929).
Career batting
2–3–0–44–18–14.66–0–*ct* 1
Bowling 118–2–59.00–0–0–2/60

Andrew, Frederick James
Professional. *b:* 29.5.1937, Southmead, Bristol. Tail end right-hand batsman, right-arm fast medium opening bowler. *Team* Gloucestershire (1959–63, 21 matches).
Career batting
21–26–7–53–6–2.78–0–*ct* 13
Bowling 1366–57–23.96–2–1–5/8

His only performance of note was for Gloucestershire v Kent (Dartford) 1962, when he took 5 for 8 and 5 for 83 in the two innings.

Andrew, Keith Vincent
Professional. *b:* 15.12.1929, Oldham, Lancs. Lower order right-hand batsman, brilliant wicket-keeper. *Team* Northants (1953–66, 351 matches). *Tours* MCC to Australia and New Zealand 1954/5, to West Indies 1959/60; Commonwealth to Pakistan 1963/4, to India 1964/5. *Tests* England (1954/5 to 1963, 2 matches).
Career batting
390–476–160–4230–76–13.38–0–*ct* 723–*st* 181
Bowling 31–2–15.50–0–0–2/9
Test batting
2–4–1–29–15–9.66–0–*ct* 1

By some he was regarded as the most talented wicket-keeper of his generation, but his lack of batting ability meant few Test calls. He captained Northants from 1962 to 1966. His debut was for Combined Services in 1952. He became the NCA Director of Coaching.

Andrew, Walter
(known as William Andrew)
Amateur. *b:* 22.3.1869, Bournemouth. *d:* 30.3.1911, Sligo, Ireland. Middle order right-hand batsman, right-arm medium pace bowler. *Team* Hampshire (1897–98, 12 matches).
Career batting
12–22–1–312–106–14.85–1–*ct* 3
Bowling 626–23–27.21–1–0–5/157

His fame rests with an innings of 106 for Hants v Warwickshire at Southampton in 1897, when he shared a partnership of 222 with A. J. L. Hill and saved the match. He was tried in several matches the following season, but could not repeat his success. He also appeared for Dorset.

Andrews, Arthur John
Amateur. *b:* August 1856, Southampton. *d:* 26.2.1943, Aldershot. Defensive right-hand batsman, wicket-keeper. *Team* Hampshire (1880–85, 7 matches).
Career batting
7–12–1–236–62*–21.45–0–*ct* 6–*st* 2
Bowling 2–0

He also appeared for Wiltshire.

Andrews, Clifford Jack
Amateur. *b:* 6.8.1912, Swindon, Wilts. *d:* 11.12.1973, Eastleigh, Hants. Brother of W. H. R. (Somerset). Lower order right-hand batsman, wicket-keeper. *Team* Hampshire (1938–48, 7 matches).
Career batting
7–10–1–127–29–14.11–0–*ct* 6–*st* 1

Andrews, Norman Palmer
Amateur. *b:* 1.5.1899, Bromley, Kent. *d:* 5.11.1971, Westminster School, London. Opening or middle order right-hand batsman. *Sch* Westminster. *Team* Northants (1922–23, 6 matches).
Career batting
6–12–1–122–45*–11.09–0–*ct* 1

Andrews, Oscar
Amateur. *b:* 24.7.1876, Liverpool. *d:* 30.10.1956, Belfast. Right-hand batsman, right-arm medium pace bowler. *Sch* Rossall. *Team* Ireland (1902).
Career batting
4–7–2–82–29*–16.40–0–*ct* 5
Bowling 36–2–18.00–0–0–2/8

Andrews, Thomas James Edwin
Amateur. *b:* 26.8.1890, Newtown, New South Wales, Australia. *d:* 28.1.1970, Sydney, New South Wales, Australia. Attractive right-hand batsman, leg break and googly bowler. *Teams* New South Wales (1912/3 to 1928/9, 74 matches). *Tours* Australia to England 1921, 1926, to South Africa 1921/2; New South Wales to New Zealand 1923/4. *Tests* Australia (1921–26, 16 matches).
Career batting
151–222–17–8095–247*–39.48–14–*ct* 85
Bowling 3050–95–32.10–3–0–6/109
Test batting
16–23–1–592–94–26.90–0–*ct* 12
Bowling 116–1–116.00–0–0–1/23

Andrews toured England twice and on both

occasions appeared in the Tests. He never made his mark in International cricket, though he was a successful member of the New South Wales side for many years. His play was characterised by the straightness of his bat. He hit 1,000 runs in a season twice (best 1,234, av. 38.56, in 1926). His highest score was 247* for New South Wales v Victoria at Sydney, 1919/20.

Andrews, Walter Hermann
Amateur. *b:* 17.4.1865, Dulwich, Surrey. *d:* 26.11.1908, Stanger, Natal, South Africa. Son of H. W. (Kent). Hard-hitting left-hand batsman, fast left-arm bowler, good field. *Sch* Radley. *Team* Sussex (1888–92, 37 matches).
Career batting
37–69–4–864–67–13.29–0–*ct* 27
Bowling 1–0

Andrews, William Harry Russell
Professional. *b:* 14.4.1908, Swindon, Wilts. Brother of C. J. (Hampshire). Aggressive right-hand batsman, right-arm fast medium bowler. *Team* Somerset (1930–47, 226 matches).
Career batting
231–371–54–5000–80–15.77–0–*ct* 96
Bowling 18033–768–23.48–40–6–8/12

Andrews was unfortunate to be released by Somerset at the end of the 1932 season due to economy measures, but returning to the staff in 1935 he looked a much improved player and in 1937 and 1938 achieved the 'double'. He hit 1,000 runs in a season twice (best 1,141, av 20.74, in 1937) and took 100 wickets four times (best 143, av 20.53, in 1937). His bowling, with a deceptive swing and accurate length, was little short of the highest standard. He was released by the County a second time in 1947, but returned later as coach. He also played for Devon.

Angell, Frederick Leslie
Amateur turned professional in 1949. *b:* 29.6.1922, Norton St Philip, Somerset. Steady right-hand batsman, good slip field. *Team* Somerset (1947–56, 132 matches).
Career batting
132–251–11–4596–114–19.15–1–*ct* 52
Bowling 31–0

He exceeded 1,000 runs once : 1125 (av 22.95) in 1954.

Angus, Alexander William
Amateur. *b:* 11.11.1889, Sydney, Australia. *d:* 23.3.1947, Edinburgh. Right-hand batsman. *Sch* George Watson's College. *Team* Scotland (1921–22).
Career batting
4–7–0–108–29–15.42–0–*ct* 2

Angus, Thomas
Professional. *b:* 23.11.1934, Gateshead, Co Durham. Tail end left-hand batsman, useful right-arm fast medium bowler. *Team* Middlesex (1956–57, 7 matches).
Career batting
7–11–5–49–18*–8.16–0–*ct* 4
Bowling 353–23–15.34–0–0–4/81

In 1958 it was announced that he would be having a trial with Somerset, but in fact he did not appear in that side.

Anscombe, John Parker
Professional. *b:* 4.1.1838, Brighton, Sussex. *d:* 1881, Hurstpierpoint, Sussex. Fair right-hand batsman, wicket-keeper. *Sch* Hurstpierpoint. *Team* Sussex (1862–66, 3 matches).
Career batting
3–5–1–7–2–1.75–0–*ct* 1–*st* 3

Anson, Claude Esmond
Amateur. *b:* 14.10.1889, Bradford, Yorkshire. *d:* 26.3.1969, Cawood, Selby, Yorkshire. Right-hand batsman. *Sch* Pocklington. *Team* Yorkshire (1924, 1 match).
Career batting
1–2–0–27–14–13.50–0–*ct* 1

Anson, Geoffrey Frank
Amateur. *b:* 8.10.1922, Sevenoaks, Kent. *d:* 4.12.1977, Birchington, Kent. Attacking right-hand batsman. *Sch* Harrow. *Teams* Cambridge U (1947); Kent (1947, 7 matches).
Career batting
10–18–0–460–106–25.55–*ct* 6

Anson was originally at Cambridge in 1942, but returned in 1947 and looked certain to get his blue when he abruptly took up an appointment in the Colonial Service and left the University.

Anson, Hon Rupert
Amateur. *b:* 7.11.1889, Marylebone, London. *d:* 20.12.1966, Blandford St Mary, Dorset. Useful right-hand batsman, slow right-arm bowler. *Sch* Harrow. *Team* Middlesex (1910–14, 30 matches).
Career batting
33–49–4–1030–97–22.88–0–*ct* 16
Bowling 233–10–23.30–1–0–5/39

His final first-class match was for Leveson-Gower's XI in 1919.

Anstead, Walter Henry
Professional, but Amateur in 1872. *b:* 26.2.1845, Twickenham, Middlesex. *d:* 14.5.1933, Bournemouth, Hants. Middle order right-hand batsman, excellent right-arm fast bowler. *Team* Surrey (1870–72, 7 matches).

Career batting
7–12–2–61–17–6.10–0–*ct* 2
Bowling 542–48–11.29–5–1–6/27

He performed brilliantly for Surrey in the school holidays of 1870 – his occupation being that of a schoolmaster in Weybridge – but in 1871 he was appointed Assistant-Inspector of Schools and this virtually ended his important cricket. He also played for Bedfordshire.

Anstruther, Alexander William
(he changed his name to Anstruther-Duncan in 1897)
Amateur. *b:* 3.10.1846, Rajahmundry, Madras, India. *d:* 18.10.1902, Dundee. Useful right-hand batsman, excellent field at long-stop or short-leg. *Team* Sussex (1875–78, 7 matches).
Career batting
14–27–3–281–43–11.70–0–*ct* 4
Bowling 12–0

His most notable innings was 120 for Gentlemen of England v Gentlemen of Kent in 1877 – the match was XIII-a-side and not first-class. His first-class debut was for MCC in 1873, and his final match for the same team in 1887.

Anthony, Alfred Feargus O'Connor
Professional. *b:* 22.5.1841, Arnold, Notts. *d:* 10.6.1900, Sheffield, Yorkshire. Uncle of G. (Notts) and H. (Notts). Lower order right-hand batsman, wicket-keeper, occasional under-arm or round-arm bowler. *Team* Nottinghamshire (1875–76, 3 matches).
Career batting
3–6–0–14–11–2.33–0–*ct* 2–*st* 2

Anthony, George
Professional. *b:* 25.6.1875, Arnold, Notts. *d:* 13.5.1907, Arnold, Notts. Nephew of A. F. O'C.(Notts). Middle order right-hand batsman, right-arm fast medium bowler. *Team* Nottinghamshire (1900–05, 85 matches).
Career batting
85–126–13–1721–89–15.23–0–*ct* 33
Bowling 2619–82–31.93–3–0–6/72

He died of consumption aged 31, which cut short a promising career.

Anthony, Henry
Professional. *b:* 16.5.1873, Old Basford, Notts. Nephew of A. F. O'C. (Notts). Right-hand batsman, medium pace right-arm bowler. *Team* Nottinghamshire (1898–02, 4 matches).
Career batting
4–7–1–52–13*–8.66–0–*ct* 3
Bowling 81–2–40.50–0–0–1/15

He also appeared for Cheshire.

Antliff, William Norris
Amateur. *b:* 23.8.1848, Bottesford, Leics. *d:* 29.4.1909, Draycott, Derbyshire. Fair right-hand batsman. *Sch* Shireland Hall, Birmingham. *Team* Derbyshire (1880, 2 matches).
Career batting
2–4–0–17–5–4.25–0–*ct* 0

Anton, John Hamish Hugh
Amateur. *b:* 19.9.1926, Kidderminster, Worcs. Attractive hard-hitting right-hand batsman. *Sch* Rugby. *Teams* Cambridge U (1949–50); Worcestershire (1950, 4 matches).
Career batting
14–24–1–361–45–15.69–0–*ct* 2

Antrobus, Edward Philip
Cricketer. *b:* 28.9.1938, Cradock, Cape Province, South Africa. Right-hand batsman, leg break bowler. *Team* Cambridge U (1963).
Career batting
2–4–0–53–31–13.25–0–*ct* 1
Bowling 20–0

Antrobus, Geoffrey John
Amateur. *b:* 26.5.1904, South Africa. Tail end batsman, right-arm medium pace bowler. *Team* Cambridge U (1925).
Career batting
2–4–0–2–1–0.50–0–*ct* 1
Bowling 194–3–64.66–0–0–3/121

Antrobus, Robert Crawfurd
Amateur. *b:* 21.3.1830. *d:* 12.2.1911, Westminster, London. *Sch* Eton. *Teams* Gentlemen of England (1850); I Zingari (1866).
Career batting
2–4–1–17–12*–5.66–0–*ct* 0
Bowling 10–1+1–10.00–0–0–1/10

Appleby, Arthur
Amateur. *b:* 22.7.1843, Enfield, near Clayton le Moors, Lancs. *d:* 24.10.1902, Enfield, near Clayton le Moors, Lancs. Free hitting left-hand batsman, left fast medium bowler with a round-arm action. *Sch* Grange School, Yorks. *Team* Lancashire (1866–87, 58 matches). *Tour* Fitz-Gerald to North America 1872.
Career batting
81–131–22–1249–99–11.45–0–*ct* 54–*st* 1
Bowling 5269–336–15.68–24–3–9/25

His best bowling was 9/25 for Lancs v Sussex (Hove) 1877. He was twice invited to tour Australia (1873/4 and 1878/9) but had to decline for business reasons. During the 1870s he was perhaps the best amateur fast bowler in England.

Appleton, Charles
Amateur. *b:* 15.5.1844, Hull. *d:* 26.2.1925, Bradley Hall, Standish, Wigan, Lancs. Useful right-hand batsman, wicket-keeper. *Sch* Rossall. *Team* Yorkshire (1865, 3 matches).
Career batting
3–6–1–56–18–11.20–0–*ct* 0
An all-round athlete he excelled at running, pole-jumping and putting 'the stone'. He left Yorkshire shortly after playing for the County and appeared regularly in London Club cricket.

Appleyard, Francis
Amateur. *b:* 26.9.1905, Clifton, Yorkshire. *d:* 11.10.1971, Stevenage, Herts. Lower order right-hand batsman, steady right-arm fast medium bowler. *Team* Essex (1946–47, 14 matches).
Career batting
18–25–14–74–15*–6.72–0–*ct* 10
Bowling 1210–30–40.33–2–0–5/14
A leading bowler with Herts in the 1930s and with the British Empire XI during the 1939–45 war. His first-class debut was for Minor Counties in 1939 and his final match for MCC in 1950.

Appleyard, Robert
Professional. *b:* 27.6.1924, Wibsey, Bradford. Tail end right-hand batsman, versatile right-arm bowler – medium pace or off-breaks. *Team* Yorkshire (1950–58, 133 matches). *Tour* MCC to Australia and New Zealand 1954/5. *Tests* England (1954–56, 9 matches).
Career batting
152–145–54–776–63–8.52–*ct* 80
Bowling 10965–708–15.44–57–17–8/76
Test batting
9–9–6–51–19*–17.00–0–*ct* 4
Bowling 554–31–17.87–1–0–5/51
Appleyard took the cricket world by storm, when in 1951, virtually as an unknown, he took 200 wickets (av 14.14) and headed the first-class averages. The secret of his success lay in the way he concealed his variation of pace. A prolonged illness prevented him from playing except on one occasion in 1952 and he was not seen at all in 1953, but quite astonishingly he came back in 1954 to come second in the averages with 154 wickets (av 14.42) and win his Test cap, also a place in the MCC side to Australia the following winter. Appleyard was dropped from the Yorkshire side during 1958 and then left County cricket.

Apte, Arvindrao Laxmanrao
Amateur. *b:* 24.10.1934, Bombay, India. Brother of M. L. (Bombay and India). Opening right-hand batsman, right-arm medium pace bowler. *Teams* Bombay (1957/8 to 1964/65); Rajasthan (1968/9 to 1970/71). *Tour* India to England 1959. *Test* India (1959, 1 match).
Career batting
58–91–8–2782–165–33.51–6–*ct* 13–*st* 1
Bowling 76–2–38.00–0–0–1/21
Test batting
1–2–0–15–8–7.50–0–*ct* 0
His debut was for Indian Universities in 1955/6.

Arber, Ralph Herbert
Professional. *b:* 1846, Cambridge. Tail end batsman, useful bowler. *Team* Cambridgeshire (1871, 1 match).
Career batting
1–2–0–6–6–3.00–0–*ct* 0
Bowling 51–2–25.50–0–0–2/29

Arbuthnot, Reginald James Hugh
Amateur. *b:* 2.6.1853, Brighton. *d:* 19.9.1917, Brighton. Uncle of W. H. Spottiswoode (Kent). Useful right-hand batsman, good field. *Sch* Rugby. *Team* Kent (1881–90, 2 matches).
Career batting
2–4–0–8–5–2.00–0–*ct* 0
The reason for the nine years gap between his appearances for Kent was that he was resident in India in the interim.

Archdale, Arthur Somerville
Amateur. *b:* 8.9.1882, Baldock, Herts. *d:* 30.3.1948, Camberley, Surrey. *Sch* Repton. *Teams* Army (1920–21), Services (1920–21).
Career batting
5–8–3–91–38*–18.20–0–*ct* 5
Bowling 447–19–23.52–0–0–4/102

Archdale, J.
Amateur. *Team* MCC (1876).
Career batting
1–2–0–7–7–3.50–0–*ct* 0

Archer, Alfred German
Amateur. *b:* 6.12.1871, Richmond, Surrey. *d:* 15.7.1935, Seaford, Sussex. Lower order right-hand batsman, good wicket-keeper. *Sch* Haileybury. *Team* Worcestershire (1900–01, 4 matches). *Tour* Hawke to South Africa 1898/9. *Test* England (1898/9, 1 match).
Career batting
12–24–3–231–43–11.00–0–*ct* 10–*st* 2
Test batting
1–2–1–31–24*–31.00–0–*ct* 0
The unusual aspect of Archer's career was that not only did he appear in a Test for England before playing in first-class County cricket, but he was not even in the XI at Haileybury. He did not keep wicket in his only Test, but played in emergency, owing to the absence through injury

of Bromley-Davenport. He also played for Shropshire and his final first-class match was for MCC in 1903.

Archer, Kenneth Alan
Amateur. *b:* 17.1.1928, Yeerongpilly, Queensland, Australia. Brother of R. G. (Queensland and Australia). Right-hand batsman, off break bowler. *Teams* Queensland (1946/7 to 1956/7, 58 matches); Commonwealth XI at Hastings (1954). *Tour* Australians to South Africa 1949/50. *Tests* Australia (1950/1 to 1951/2, 5 matches)
Career batting
82–139–13–3774–134–29.95–3–*ct* 56–*st* 1
Bowling 698–13–53.69–0–0–2/16
Test batting
5–9–0–234–48–26.00–0–*ct* 0
His one appearance in England was made when he was professional for Accrington in the Lancashire League in 1954, when he hit a record 1,116 runs (av 93.00) for the club.

Archer, Ronald Graham
Amateur. *b:* 25.10.1933, Brisbane, Australia. Brother of K. A. (Queensland and Australia). Hard-hitting right-hand batsman, excellent right-arm fast bowler. *Team* Queensland (1951/2 to 1958/9, 35 matches). *Tours* Australia to England 1953, 1956, to West Indies 1954/5, to Pakistan 1956/7. *Tests* Australia (1952/3 to 1956/7, 19 matches).
Career batting
98–137–19–3768–148–31.93–4–*ct* 105
Bowling 5958–255–23.36–9–1–7/56
Test batting
19–30–1–713–128–24.58–1–*ct* 20
Bowling 1318–48–27.45–1–0–5/53
The peak of his brief career was the 1956 Test series in England, when his bowling was most effective and he was hailed as Lindwall's successor.

Ardagh, Osmond Charles
Amateur. *b:* 1.11.1900, Hambledon, Hants. *d:* 1.2.1954. He drowned in River Thames, near Wallingford, Berkshire. Useful middle order left-hand batsman. *Sch* Epsom. *Team* Oxford U (1922).
Career batting
1–1–0–2–2–2.00–0–*ct* 0

Arden-Davis, Rev Richard
Amateur. *b:* 31.1.1855, Malins Lee, Shropshire. *d:* 29.6.1917, Branksome Park, Dorset. *Team* Middlesex (1881, 1 match).
Career batting
1–2–0–14–14–7.00–0–*ct* 1
He also played for Suffolk.

Ardington, Anthony John
Cricketer. *b:* 26.3.1940, New Zealand. Middle order right-hand batsman. *Team* Oxford U (1965).
Career batting
3–5–0–29–11–5.80–0–*ct* 1.

Arenhold, John Adolf
Amateur. *b:* 9.5.1931, Cape Town, S. Africa. Forcing right-hand batsman, right-arm fast medium bowler, slip field. *Sch* Diocesan College, S. Africa. *Teams* Oxford U (1953–55, blue 1954); Ceylon (1956/7); Orange Free State (1959/60).
Career batting
33–47–7–403–45–10.07–0–*ct* 14
Bowling 2226–82–27.14–4–1–7/97
He also represented Ceylon at rugby football.

Argent, E.
Professional. *b:* 6.2.1902. Lower order right-hand batsman, right-arm off break bowler. *Team* Worcestershire (1928, 2 matches).
Career batting
2–4–1–22–19–7.33–0–*ct* 0
Bowling 63–0

Arif Butt
Cricketer. *b:* 17.5.1944, Lahore, India. Right-hand batsman, right-arm fast medium bowler. *Teams* Lahore (1960/1 to 1961/2); Railways (1962/3 to 1977/8). *Tours* Pakistan to Australia and New Zealand 1964/5, to England 1967. *Tests* Pakistan (1964/5, 3 matches).
Career batting
97–154–16–4017–180–29.10–4–*ct* 44
Bowling 5386–201–26.79–10–2–8/45
Test batting
3–5–0–59–20–11.80–0–*ct* 0
Bowling 288–14–20.57–1–0–6/89

Arkell, Henry John Denham
Amateur. *b:* 26.6.1898, London. *d:* 12.3.1982, Oxford. Father of R. H. M. (Oxford U). Middle order right-hand batsman. *Team* Northants (1921, 2 matches).
Career batting
2–2–0–11–6–5.50–0–*ct* 0

Arkell, Richard Henry Myles
Amateur. *b:* 26.6.1932, Northampton. Son of H. J. D. (Northants). Lower order right-hand batsman, slow left-arm bowler. *Sch* Aldenham. *Team* Cambridge U (1953–55).
Career batting
3–5–1–18–10–4.50–0–*ct* 1
Bowling 125–6–20.83–0–0–3/39

Arkwright, Francis Godfrey Bertram
Amateur. *b:* 30.1.1905, Bramdean, Hants. *d:* 1.7.1942, Knightsbridge, near Acroma, Libya. Hard hitting right-hand batsman, rather weak in defence. *Sch* Eton. *Team* Hampshire (1923, 3 matches).
Career batting
4–7–0–67–23–9.57–0–*ct* 2

His best innings was 175 for Eton v Winchester in 1923, on the strength of which he appeared later in the year for Hampshire. He also represented the Army, for whom he played his last first-class match in 1925.

Arkwright, Henry
Amateur. *b:* 16.12.1837, Hampton Court, Leominster, Herefordshire. *d:* 13.10.1866. He was killed by avalanche whilst ascending Mont Blanc, France. Free hitting right-hand batsman, fast underhand bowler, but changed to slow round-arm in 1853. *Sch* Harrow. *Teams* Cambridge U (1858, blue).
Career batting
17–32–3–144–26–4.96–0–*ct* 16
Bowling 976–86+11–11.34–10–2–9/43

For Gentlemen of MCC v Gentlemen of Kent at Canterbury in 1861 he took 18 of the 22 wickets to fall (12-a-side match), including 9/43, being his best innings bowling analysis. He was Aide-de-camp to Lord Lieutenant of Ireland at his death. He also played for Herefordshire and his final first-class match was for Gentlemen of MCC in 1866.

Arkwright, Harold Arthur
Amateur. *b:* 10.11.1872, Oswestry, Shropshire. *d:* 10.12.1942, Virginia Water, Surrey. Fair right-hand batsman, useful right-arm medium pace bowler. *Sch* Eton. *Teams* Oxford U (1893–95, blue 1895); Essex (1894–95, 3 matches). *Tour* Mitchell to North America, 1895.
Career batting
23–40–4–436–38–12.11–0–*ct* 15
Bowling 1659–71–23.36–5–1–8/40

His final first-class match was for MCC in 1903.

Arlington, George Harwood Ashley
Amateur. *b:* 28.5.1872, Dover, Kent. *d: circa* 1940, Australia. Free hard-hitting right-hand batsman, good wicket-keeper. *Sch* Brighton G.S. *Team* Sussex (1894–98, 29 matches).
Career batting
29–50–0–614–73–12.28–0–*ct* 13
Bowling 36–1–36.00–0–0–1/13

In club cricket in Sussex it is believed that he scored over 100 centuries, his highest being 309 for Sheffield Park v Nutley, 1897.

Armitage, Alan Kenneth
Amateur. *b:* 25.1.1930, Nottingham. Middle order right-hand batsman, wicket-keeper. *Sch* Nottingham H.S. *Teams* Nottinghamshire (1950–51, 5 matches); Oxford U (1951).
Career batting
7–12–2–348–115–34.80–1–*ct* 3

Armitage, Charles Ingram
Amateur. *b:* 28.4.1849, Birkby Grange, Huddersfield, Yorkshire. *d:* 24.4.1917, Honley, Yorkshire. Middle order right-hand batsman, good left-arm fast bowler. *Team* Yorkshire (1873–78, 3 matches).
Career batting
3–5–0–26–12–5.20–0–*ct* 0
Bowling 29–0

Armitage, Edward Leathley
Amateur. *b:* 26.4.1891, Omagh, Ireland. *d:* 24.11.1957, St Leonards, Sussex. Middle order right-hand batsman. *Sch* Cheltenham. *Teams* Hampshire (1919–25, 8 matches); Europeans (1929/30).
Career batting
20–35–2–576–105–17.45–1–*ct* 11
Bowling 476–26–18.30–1–0–5/67

His final first-class match was in India for Viceroy's XI in 1931/2.

Armitage, Thomas
Professional. *b:* 25.4.1848, Walkley, Sheffield, Yorkshire. *d:* 21.9.1922, Pullman, Chicago, USA. Excellent right-hand batsman, both in attack and defence, right-arm medium pace bowler or underhand lobs, all-round fieldsman. *Team* Yorkshire (1872–79, 51 matches). *Tour* Lillywhite to Australia and New Zealand 1876/7. *Tests* England (1876/7, 2 matches).
Career batting
56–92–8–1122–95–13.55–0–*ct* 23
Bowling 1699–119–14.27–12–3–7/26
Test batting
2–3–0–33–21–11.00–0–*ct* 0
Bowling 15–0

Although principally a batsman, Armitage had some startling successes as a lob bowler and in 1876 returned figures of 13 for 46 for Yorks v Surrey at Bramall Lane.

Armitage, Vernon Kirk
Amateur. *b:* 20.10.1842, Pendleton, Manchester. *d:* 8.5.1911, Birkdale, Lancashire. Fair right-hand batsman, good cover point. *Sch* Harrow. *Teams* Cambridge U (1864).
Career batting
1–1–0–6–6–6.00–0–*ct* 0

Armitstead, Rev Sydney Henry
Amateur. *b:* 13.6.1837, Holmes Chapel, Cheshire. *d:* 29.1.1912, Glyngarth, Anglesey. Brother of W. G. (Oxford U). Useful middle order batsman, medium pace round-arm bowler, wicket-keeper. *Sch* Charterhouse. *Teams* Gentlemen of North (1862); MCC (1864).
Career batting
2–2–0–0–0–0.00–0–*ct* 1
He was one of the founder-members of the Free Foresters. He also played for Cheshire, Herefordshire and Shropshire.

Armitstead, Rev William George
Amateur. *b:* 22.3.1833, Holmes Chapel, Cheshire. *d:* 12.3.1907, Goostrey, Cheshire. Brother of S. H. (MCC). Hard hitting right-hand batsman, excellent long-stop. *Sch* Westminster. *Team* Oxford U (1853–57, blue 1853,1854,1856 and 1857).
Career batting
14–25–1–293–38–12.20–0–*ct* 6
Bowling 2 wickets (no analysis available)
His first-class debut was for Manchester in 1852 and his last match for MCC in 1864. He also played for Cheshire, Shropshire and Oxfordshire.

Armstrong, Gregory de Lisle
Cricketer. *b:* 11.5.1950, Bank Hall, Barbados. Tail end right-hand batsman, right-arm fast bowler. *Teams* Barbados (1973/4 to 1977/8); Glamorgan (1974–76, 30 matches).
Career batting
40–54–12–642–93–15.28–0–*ct* 13
Bowling 3199–91–35.15–2–0–6/91
He signed on a three-year contract after glowing reports on his prospects, but never realised his promise in County cricket.

Armstrong, H. H.
Amateur. Fair right-hand batsman, useful right-arm medium pace bowler. *Team* Hampshire (1882–85, 23 matches).
Career batting
23–42–7–502–68–14.34–0–*ct* 10
Bowling 1376–68–20.23–2–0–7/33

Armstrong, Norman Foster
Amateur, but turned professional in 1926. *b:* 22.12.1892, Loughborough, Leics. Sound defensive middle order right-hand batsman, right-arm medium pace change bowler. *Team* Leicestershire (1919–39, 386 matches).
Career batting
386–637–61–19002–186–32.98–36–*ct* 223
Bowling 4459–110–40.53–0–0–4/21
Though he did not take up regular County cricket until well into his thirties, Armstrong developed into the mainstay of the batting – so often did he rescue the side from collapse that he was known as the 'Valiant Armstrong'. In 1933 he became the first man to hit 2,000 runs in a season for the County, totalling 2,113, av 43.12, for the summer. He reached 1,000 runs in a season 13 times between 1927 and 1939.

Armstrong, Philip Alexander Nikolas
Cricketer. *b:* 23.1.1962, Lambeth, London. Middle order right-hand batsman. *Sch* Eastbourne. *Team* Oxford U (1982).
Career batting
1–2–0–34–34–17.00–0–*ct* 0

Armstrong, Robert Lloyd George
Amateur. *b:* 22.5.1914, Donaghcloney, Co Armagh, Ireland. *d:* 9.4.1959, Downpatrick, Co Down, Ireland. Right-hand batsman, right-arm medium pace bowler. *Team* Ireland (1948–53).
Career batting
5–10–1–121–29*–13.44–0–*ct* 1
Bowling 129–6–21.50–0–0–4/16

Armstrong, Thomas
Professional. *b:* 16.3.1872, Keyworth, Notts. *d:* 5.7.1938, Keyworth, Notts. Fair right-hand middle order batsman, right-arm medium pace bowler, useful outfield. *Teams* Nottinghamshire (1892–96, 6 matches).
Career batting
6–11–2–67–20*–7.44–0–*ct* 1

Armstrong, Thomas Hugh
Amateur. *b:* 1849, Wingate, Co Durham. *d:* 27.1.1929, East Grinstead, Sussex. *Sch* Rossall. *Team* Oxford U (1869).
Career batting
1–2–0–6–6–3.00–0–*ct* 0
Bowling 43–1–43.00–0–0–1/43
He also played for Shropshire.

Armstrong, Thomas Riley
Professional. *b:* 13.10.1909, Clay Cross, Derbyshire. Tail end left-hand batsman, useful left-arm spin bowler. *Team* Derbyshire (1929–50, 58 matches).
Career batting
58–83–33–314–28*–6.28–0–*ct* 18
Bowling 3239–133–24.35–7–0–7/36
His career was, for a professional, most unusual, spanning 22 years, but he never commanded a regular place in the County side. He played for the most part in place of regular bowlers, injured or otherwise absent.

Armstrong, Warwick Windridge
Amateur. *b:* 22.5.1879, Kyneton, Victoria, Australia. *d:* 13.7.1947, Darling Point, New South Wales, Australia. Excellent right-hand batsman, originally fast medium right-arm, but by 1905 leg-break, bowler. *Team* Victoria (1898/9 to 1921/2, 83 matches). *Tours* Australians to England 1902, 1905, 1909, 1921, to South Africa 1902/3, to New Zealand 1904/5, 1909/10, 1913/4. *Tests* Australia (1901/2 to 1921, 50 matches).
Career batting
269–406–61–16158–303*–46.83–45–*ct* 274
Bowling 16406–832–19.71–50–5–8/47
Test batting
50–84–10–2863–159*–38.68–6–*ct* 44
Bowling 2923–87–33.59–3–0–6/35

Of all the cricketers to visit England, Armstrong has the most remarkable all-round record – on three of his four tours, 1905, '09 and '21 he achieved the 'double', and indeed in 1905 narrowly missed 2,000 runs. His best season in England was 1905 with 1,902 runs, av 50.05; and 122 wickets, av 1820.

Considering also that he captained Australia to eight successive Test victories over England, the stature of Armstrong is apparent – his physical stature in fact matched his performances, for he was over 1.83m (6 feet) in height and on his last tour to England weighed over 127kg (20 stone). He was known as 'The Big Ship'.

In his later career, he was accused, as many successful men have been, of arrogance, and no-one can deny that he was a man who liked his own way, but he had certainly earned that right! It was however unfortunate that in his retirement he should put his name to press articles which were almost designed to cause bitterness and ill-feeling.

Armstrong was a splendid stroke-player, but his real worth was to be found on difficult wickets. He survived long after his so-called equals were back in the pavilion. As a bowler he used accuracy of length and variation of flight rather than an ability to turn the ball, and he could bottle up one end with no difficulty. His highest score was 303* v Somerset at Bath on the 1905 tour, but a better innings was his 248* against the Gentlemen at Lord's on the same visit.

Arnall, Harry Thompson
(he assumed the name of Arnall-Thompson in 1885)
Amateur. *b:* 7.4.1864, Belgrave, Leicester. *d:* 28.12.1916, Anstey Frith, Leics. Brother of W. E. (Leics, non-first-class). Fair right-hand batsman, capital slow left-arm bowler (fast until 1878), slip field. *Sch* Rugby. *Team* Oxford U (1886, blue).
Career batting
6–9–3–56–25–9.33–0–*ct* 5
Bowling 352–16–22.00–1–0–7/82

He appeared for Leicestershire (non-first-class) in 1883–90, captain 1888. Batting for Leics v MCC in 1889, the ball flew off his bat on to his eyebrow from whence it rebounded to the bowler. After being stunned and stemming the flow of blood Arnall-Thompson prepared to continue batting only to be informed he was out 'caught'.

His first-class debut was for Gentlemen of England in 1885 and his final match for MCC in 1887.

Arnold, Alban Charles Phidias
Amateur. *b:* 19.11.1892, Fareham, Hants. *d:* 7.7.1916. He was killed in action at Ovilliers La Boiselle, France. Good middle order right-hand batsman, wicket-keeper. *Sch* Malvern. *Teams* Cambridge U (1912–14, blue 1914); Hampshire (1912–14, 16 matches).
Career batting
22–35–2–836–89–25.33–0–*ct* 13–*st* 2
Bowling 0–0

Arnold, Arnold Peter
Professional. *b:* 16.10.1926, Wellington, New Zealand. Attacking right-hand opening batsman, occasional right-arm medium pace bowler. *Teams* Northants (1951–60, 167 matches); Canterbury (1953–4).
Career batting
174–306–15–8013–122–27.53–7–*ct* 79
Bowling 85–3–28.33–0–0–1/5

He played as a middle order batsman for the first three years with Northants, but had only limited success. Being promoted to open in 1954 made all the difference. Hit 1,000 runs in a season three times (best 1,699, av 30.89, in 1955).

Arnold, Charles
Professional. *b:* 10.2.1822, Cambridge. *d:* 1.2.1873, Cambridge. Brother of Mark (Cambridge Town Club). A 'tremendous-paced round-armed bowler delivering many shooting balls, which have proved very fatal and destructive' (Scores and Biographies, vol IV p514). *Team* Cambridge Town Club (1843–56); Cambridgeshire (1857, 1 match).
Career batting
22–35–5–203–29–6.76–0–*ct* 23
Bowling 258–27+106–9.55–13–5–8/?

For a few years about 1850, Arnold was one of the most notable bowlers in England, and in 1853 was engaged by the All England Eleven. He played non-first-class cricket for Suffolk, Hereford, Essex, Warwickshire, Huntingdonshire and Worcestershire.

Arnold, Edward George
Professional. *b:* 7.11.1876, Exmouth, Devon. *d:* 25.10.1942, Worcester. Useful right-hand batsman, medium to fast medium right-arm bowler. safe close field. *Teams* Worcestershire (1899–1913, 301 matches); London County (1900). *Tour* MCC to Australia 1903–04. *Tests* England (1903/4 to 1907, 10 matches).
Career batting
343–592–62–15853–215–29.91–24–*ct* 187
Bowling 24763–1069–23.16–63–13–9/64
Test batting
10–15–3–160–40–13.33–0–*ct* 8
Bowling 788–31–25.41–1–0–5/37

Arnold was the best all-round cricketer in the Worcestershire side of 187, but ill-health more or less stopped his cricket in 1898. When Worcestershire were promoted to the Championship in 1899, he did nothing spectacular, but in 1902 he achieved the 'double' for the first of four times. The following year he won a place in the MCC team to Australia and performed well in both Tests and other matches. He had the knack of making the ball lift off a good length, even on docile wickets, and bowled with a beautiful action. Ill-health (he was never very strong physically) brought his career to a close in 1913. He hit 1,000 runs in a season ten times (best 1,767, av 50.48, in 1906) and took 100 wickets four times (best 143, av 17.44, in 1903). His highest score was 215 for Worcestershire v Oxford U at Oxford in 1910, and his best bowling 9/64 against the same team in 1905. He also played for Devon.

Arnold, Frederick George
Amateur. *b:* 18.11.189, Dover, Kent. *d:* 16.12.1980, Broughton, Hants. Tail end right-hand batsman, right-arm fast medium bowler. *Teams* Army (1926–30); Europeans (1935/6).
Career batting
6–6–4–33–15–16.50–0–*ct* 2
Bowling 493–18–27.38–1–0–6/41

Arnold, Geoffrey Graham
Cricketer. *b*: 3.9.1944, Earlsfield, Surry. Lower order right-hand batsman, right-arm fast medium bowler. *Teams* Surrey (1963–77, 218 matches); Sussex (1978–82, 77 matches); Orange Free State (1976/7). *Tours* MCC to Pakistan 1966/7, to Ceylon 1969/70, to India, Pakistan and Sri Lanka 1972/3, to West Indies 1973/4, to Australia and New Zealand 1974/5; International XI to India and Pakistan 1967/8. *Tests* England (1967–75, 34 matches).
Career batting
365–379–90–3952–73–13.67–0–*ct* 122
Bowling 24761–1130–21.91–46–3–8/41
Test batting
34–46–11–421–59–12.02–0–*ct* 9
Bowling 3254–115–28.29–6–0–6/45

He took 109 wickets, av 18.22, in 1967. About 1970 he was one of the most effective bowlers in England and his Test place would have been more secure if he had been as deadly overseas as he was on damp English wickets. He also suffered more than his fair share of injuries.

Arnold, John
Professional. *b:* 30.11.1907, Cowley, Oxford. *d:* 3.4.1984, Southampton, Hants. Attractive opening right-hand batsman, particularly effective against spin bowling, right-arm slow bowler, excellent deep field with strong throw. *Team* Hampshire (1929–50, 396 matches). *Test* England (1931, 1 match).
Career batting
402–710–45–21831–227–32.82–37–*ct* 184
Bowling 1182–17–69.52–0–0–3/34
Test batting
1–2–0–34–34–17.00–0–*ct* 0

He scored 1,000 runs in season 14 times (best 2,261, av 48.10, in 1934); his highest score being 227 Hants v Glamorgan (Cardiff) 1932. He also played for Oxfordshire. He became a first-class umpire. He played soccer as outside left for Southampton and Fulham and played for England v Scotland 1932–33, thus becoming a double international.

Arnold, James Frederick
Amateur. *b:* 1869, Chorlton, Lancashire. *d:* 1944, Worthing, Sussex. Good middle order right-hand batsman. *Team* Lancashire (1896, 3 matches).
Career batting
3–5–0–94–37–18.80–0–*ct* 2

Arnott, Trevor
Amateur. *b:* 16.2.1902, Radyr, Glamorgan. *d:* 2.2.1975, Wilton, Ross-on-Wye, Herefordshire. Hard-hitting right-hand batsman, right-arm fast medium pace swing bowler. *Sch* Wycliffe. *Teams* Glamorgan (1921–30, 188 matches); Wales (1924–30). *Tours* Tennyson to Jamaica 1927/8; Cahn to South America 1929/30.
Career batting
216–370–30–5791–153–17.03–3–*ct* 104
Bowling 13511–408–33.11–10–0–7/40

He captained Glamorgan in 1928 and also played for Monmouthshire. His final first-class match was MCC in 1931.

Arrowsmith, Robert
Cricketer. *b:* 21.5.1952, Denton, Lancashire. Lower order right-hand batsman, left-arm spin

bowler. *Team* Lancashire (1976–79, 43 matches).
Career batting
43–40–12–286–39–10.21–0–*ct* 13
Bowling 2796–99–28.24–4–0–6/29
He has played for Northumberland since 1983.

Arshad Pervez
Cricketer. *b:* 1.10.1952, Sargodha, Pakistan. Middle order batsman, useful bowler. *Teams* Sargodha (1969/70 to 1975/6); Lahore (1971/2); Universities (1972/3 to 1974/5); Punjab University (1973/4); Servis Industries (1975/6); Habib Bank (1975/6 to 1982/3), Punjab (1976/7). *Tour* Pakistan to England 1978.
Career batting
127–212–18–7666–251*–39.51–20–*ct* 87
Bowling 650–17–38.23–0–0–3/37
He played in only three first-class matches on the 1978 tour.

Asgarali, Nyron Sultan
Amateur. *b:* 28.12.1920, St James, near Port of Spain, Trinidad. Right-hand opening batsman, right-arm medium pace bowler. *Teams* Trinidad (1940/1 to 1961/2); Commonwealth XI (1956). *Tour* West Indies to England 1957. *Tests* West Indies (1957, 2 matches).
Career batting
50–89–5–2761–141*–32.86–7–*ct* 29
Bowling 966–23–42.00–0–0–4/72
Test batting
2–4–0–62–29–15.50–0–*ct* 0
He hit 1,011 runs, av 29.73, in 1957.

Ash, David Leslie
Cricketer. *b:* 18.2.1944, Bingley, Yorkshire. Right-hand batsman, slow left-arm bowler. *Team* Yorkshire (1965, 3 matches).
Career batting
3–3–0–22–12–7.33–0–*ct* 0
Bowling 22–0
He began playing for Cumberland in 1968.

Ash, Edward Philip
Amateur. *b:* 25.12.1842, Brisley, Norfolk. *d:* 25.5.1909, Petersfield, Hants. Good right-hand batsman. *Sch* Rugby. *Team* Cambridge U (1865, blue).
Career batting
5–10–0–126–47–12.60–0–*ct* 3
He also played for Norfolk, hitting 130 for that County v I Zingari in 1866, and for Warwickshire (non-first-class), Suffolk and Herts.

Ashby, David (Alexander)
Professional. *b:* 11.6.1852, Beddington, Surrey. *d:* 2.6.1934, Christchurch, New Zealand. Right-hand batsman, right-arm medium to fast bowler. *Teams* Surrey Club (1873); Surrey (1874, 1 match); Canterbury (1875/6 to 1889/90).
Career batting
17–31–4–468–59–17.33–0–*ct* 12
Bowling 586–53–11.05–4–1–6/27

Ashby, William
Professional. *b:* 12.1.1786, Linton, Maidstone, Kent. *d:* 10.4.1847, London. Poor batsman, excellent slow round-arm bowler. *Teams* Kent (1815–29); Sussex (1823); Hants (1825–26); Surrey (1830).
Career batting
45–78–24–242–18–4.48–0–*ct* 26
Bowling 164 wickets (no analyses available)
After John Willes he was, perhaps, the first bowler of note to bowl 'round-arm'. His first important match was for England in 1808.

Ashcroft, Edward Maynard
Amateur. *b:* 27.9.1875, Chorlton, Manchester. *d:* 26.2.1955, Upton-by-Chester, Cheshire. Free scoring right-hand batsman, occasional off break bowler. *Sch* Owens College. *Team* Derbyshire (1897–1906, 100 matches).
Career batting
101–170–13–4581–162–29.17–8–*ct* 33
Bowling 1186–24–49.41–1–0–5/18
His highest score was 162 v Leics (Leicester) 1902. He was joint captain of Derbyshire 1904–05. He also played for Herefordshire.

Ashdown, William Henry
Professional. *b:* 27.12.1898, Bromley, Kent. *d:* 15.9.1979, Rugby, Warwickshire. Opening right-hand batsman, noted for the square drive and cut, right-arm medium fast bowler, good field. *Team* Kent (1920–37, 482 matches).
Career batting
487–812–77–22589–332–30.73–39–*ct* 400–*st* 1
Bowling 19551–602–32.47–13–0–6/23
Ashdown actually made his first-class debut aged 15 for G. J. V. Weigall's Team v Oxford in 1914 and his final first-class match was for M. Leyland's XI at Harrogate in 1947. Thus he is the only cricketer to appear in first-class matches both before the First World War and after the Second.
He is among the very few batsmen to hit two triple centuries in County cricket: 332 v Essex (Brentwood) 1934 and 305* v Derbyshire (Dover) 1935. He reached 1,000 runs in a season 11 times between 1926 and 1937, his best being 2,247 (av 43.21) in 1928.

Ashenden, Martin
Professional. *b:* 4.8.1937, Bexhill-on-Sea, Sussex. Lower order right-hand batsman, right-arm fast

medium bowler. *Teams* Northants (1959–61, 19 matches); Gloucestershire (1962–65, 15 matches).
Career batting
34–41–12–70–15–2.41–0–*ct* 9
Bowling 2095–64–32.73–0–0–4/50

He created a sensation by taking all 10 wickets (for 15) for Bedfordshire v Shropshire in 1958 and then signed as a professional for Northants and subsequently Gloucestershire, but he never gained a regular place in first-class cricket.

Asher, Sir Augustus Gordon Grant
(also known as Grant-Asher)
Amateur. *b:* 18.12.1861, Poona, India. *d:* 15.7.1930, Kingussie, Scotland. Middle order right-hand batsman, right-arm fast-medium bowler, good deep field. *Sch* Loretto. *Team* Oxford U (1883–84, blue 1883).
Career batting
10–17–0–346–182–20.35–1–*ct* 2
Bowling 88–3–29.33–0–0–3/62

He was a noted rugby footballer, playing at half-back against Cambridge University in 1881 and the next three years. He also represented Scotland seven times. He won a third blue for Athletics, being the Oxford champion long-jumper and later champion pole-vaulter for Scotland.

Ashley, Richard
Amateur. *b:* 27.10.1902, Axbridge, Somerset. *d:* 8.8.1974, Bognor Regis, Sussex. Useful right-hand batsman, good opening bowler. *Teams* Somerset (1932, 2 matches); Mysore (1937/8); Europeans (1939/40).
Career batting
4–6–0–61–17–10.16–0–*ct* 1
Bowling 180–8–22.50–0–0–3/26

Ashman, John Robert
Professional. *b:* 20.5.1926, Rotherham, Yorkshire. Tail end left-hand batsman, useful slow left-arm bowler. *Teams* Yorkshire (1951, 1 match); Worcestershire (1953–54, 33 matches).
Career batting
34–41–15–149–24–5.73–0–*ct* 25
Bowling 2546–61–41.73–3–0–7/111

Ashman had an extended trial in the Worcestershire side of 1953 due to Jenkins' injury, but did not realise his promise.

Ashmore, William Scott
Professional. *b:* 29.10.1929, St John's Wood, London. Moderate left-hand batsman, useful left-arm medium fast bowler. *Team* Middlesex (1946–47, 2 matches).
Career batting
3–5–3–24–15*–12.00–0–*ct* 1
Bowling 129–3–43.00–0–0–2/37

Both his matches for Middlesex were against Cambridge U at Fenner's – in 1948 he made a single appearance for Combined Services.

Ashton, Claude Thesiger
Amateur. *b:* 19.2.1901, Calcutta, India. *d:* 31.10.1942. He was killed on active service with the RAF at Carmarthen. Brother of Gilbert (Cambridge U and Worcestershire), Hubert (Cambridge U and Essex) and Percy (Essex). Attacking right-hand batsman, right-arm medium pace bowler. *Sch* Winchester. *Teams* Cambridge U (1921–23, blue all three years); Essex (1921–38, 89 matches).
Career batting
127–204–15–4723–118–24.98–4–*ct* 113
Bowling 4299–139–30.92–5–1–7/51

An all-round sportsman, he played soccer for England and obtained his blue for soccer and hockey as well as cricket. Three of the brothers captained Cambridge at cricket in successive seasons. Whilst flying his plane he collided with the plane of R. de W. K. Winlaw, both men being killed.

Ashton, Gilbert
Amateur. *b:* 27.9.1896, Bromley, Kent. *d:* 6.2.1981, Abberley, Worcs. Brother of C. T. (Cambridge U and Essex); Hubert (Cambridge U and Essex) and Percy (Essex). Fine right-hand batsman, excellent cover-point, occasional slow left-arm bowler. *Sch* Winchester. *Teams* Cambridge U (1919–21, blue all three years); Worcestershire (1922–36, 27 matches).
Career batting
62–100–3–2329–125–24.01–2–*ct* 24
Bowling 521–14–35.78–0–0–3/49

He captained Cambridge U in 1921 and played in the match v Australians at Eastbourne that year. He lost a thumb in action in the First World War, but this did not seem to impede his cricket. The headmaster of a private school in Worcestershire after leaving University, his appearances for the County were confined to the school holidays.

Ashton, Sir Hubert
Amateur. *b:* 13.2.1898, Calcutta, India. *d:* 17.6.1979, South Weald, Essex. Brother of C. T. (Cambridge U and Essex); Gilbert (Cambridge U and Worcs) and Percy (Essex). Attractive and sound right-hand batsman, fine outfield. *Sch* Winchester. *Teams* Cambridge U (1920–22, blue all three years); Essex (1921–39, 21 matches); Europeans (1926/7); Burma (1926/7).

Career batting
71–115–11–4025–236*–38.70–8–*ct* 72
Bowling 14–0

His highest score was 236* Cambridge U v Free Foresters (Fenner's) 1920, but his most famous innings was 75 for an England XI v Australians at Eastbourne in 1921, when with G. A. Faulkner he added 154 runs for the 5th wicket, a partnership which enabled his side to defeat the tourists. He hit 1,000 runs in a season twice (best 1,294, av 39.21, in 1921).

He played football for Clapton Orient and Bristol Rovers. He was MP for Chelmsford, 1950–64 and President of MCC, 1960.

Ashton, Nicholas Charles Ellis
Amateur. *b:* 8.10.1904, Scaftworth, Notts. Sound right-hand batsman, wicket-keeper. *Sch* Repton. *Team* Oxford U (1924).
Career batting
1–1–0–0–0–0.00–0–*ct* 1–*st* 2

Ashton, Percy
Amateur. *b:* 27.2.1895, Calcutta, India. *d:* 18.9.1934, Bigbury-on-Sea, Devon. Brother of C. T. (Cambridge U and Essex), Gilbert (Cambridge U and Worcs) and Hubert (Cambridge U and Essex). Right-arm fast medium bowler. *Sch* Winchester. *Team* Essex (1924, 1 match).
Career batting
1–2–0–52–31–26.00–0–*ct* 0
Bowling 55–1–55.00–0–0–1/55

Ashwell, Arthur Harry
Professional. *b:* 2.8.1908, Charing, Kent. Lower order right-hand batsman, right-arm medium pace bowler. *Team* Kent (1933–34, 4 matches).
Career batting
4–5–2–42–21*–14.00–0–*ct* 1
Bowling 139–0

Ashwell, Arthur Thomas
Amateur. *b:* 8.2.1853, Nottingham. *d:* 30.9.1925, Canterbury. Brother of C. T. (Gentlemen of North). Middle order right-hand batsman. *Sch* Rugby. *Team* Nottinghamshire (1876, 2 matches).
Career batting
2–2–0–0–0–0.00–0–*ct* 0

He represented Notts County at the inaugural meeting of the Football League in 1888.

Ashwell, Charles Tebbutt
Amateur. *b:* 31.1.1851, Nottingham. *d:* 18.4.1928, Nottingham. Brother of A. T. (Notts). *Team* Gentlemen of North (1870).
Career batting
1–2–1–21–19–21.00–0–*ct* 0

Ashwell, Thomas Geoffrey Lyon
Amateur. *b:* 18.7.1897, Nottingham. *d:* 21.12.1969, Chelsea, London. Lower order right-hand batsman, leg break bowler. *Sch* Rugby. *Team* Oxford U (1919).
Career batting
1–2–1–3–2–3.00–0–*ct* 2
Bowling 19–0

Ashworth, David Anthony
Cricketer. *b:* 18.7.1944, Rani, India. Middle order right-hand batsman, off break bowler. *Sch* Uppingham. *Team* Oxford U (1966–67).
Career batting
7–13–0–173–67–13.30–0–*ct* 3

Ashworth, John Thomas
Amateur. *b:* 1850, Haslingden, Lancashire. *d:* 20.10.1901, Oldham, Lancashire. Middle order batsman. *Team* Lancashire (1871–73, 2 matches).
Career batting
2–3–0–28–19–9.33–0–*ct* 0

Asif Ahmed
Cricketer. *b:* 1.4.1942, Karachi, India. Right-hand batsman, wicket-keeper. *Teams* Oxford U (1963–64); Karachi University (1959/60 to 1960/1); Universities (1959/60); Karachi (1961/2 to 1970/1); PWD (1971/2). *Tour* Pakistan to England 1962.
Career batting
60–94–13–2140–148–26.41–4–*ct* 27
Bowling 97–0

Asif Din, Mohamed
Cricketer. *b*: 21.9.1960, Kampala, Uganda. Middle order right-hand batsman, leg break bowler. *Team* Warwickshire (1981–83, 59 matches).
Career batting
59–92–9–2144–102–25.83–1–*ct* 36
Bowling 1790–28–63.92–1–0–5/100

Asif Iqbal Razvi
Professional. *b*: 6.6.1943, Hyderabad, India. Nephew of Ghulam Ahmed (India). Attacking middle order right-hand batsman, right-arm medium pace bowler, good cover field. *Teams* Hyderabad (1959/60 to 1960/1); Karachi (1961/2 to 1968/9); PIA (1964/5 to 1979/80); National Bank (1976/7); Kent (1968–82, 243 matches).
Tours Pakistan to Australia and New Zealand 1964/5, 1972/3, 1978/9; to England 1967, 1971, 1974, to Australia and West Indies 1976/7, to India 1979/80, to Ceylon 1964/5, 1972/3; Pakistan Eaglets to England 1963; PIA to East Africa 1964/5. *Tests* Pakistan (1964/5 to 1979/80, 58 matches).

Asif Masood

Career batting
441–703–76–23375–196–37.28–45–*ct* 304
Bowling 8776–291–30.15–5–0–6/45
Test batting
58–99–7–3575–175–38.85–11–*ct* 36
Bowling 1502–53–28.33–2–0–5/48

After playing in India, he emigrated to Pakistan in 1961. He appeared in all three Tests on the 1967 tour to England, his most successful match being the third Test when he hit 146. In 1971 he again appeared in all three Tests and hit a century in the first. On his final English tour in 1974, he made little impression in the Tests, though he played in all three. He was vice-captain on both the 1971 and 1974 tours and he led Pakistan in six Tests, all against India. He also captained Kent in 1977 and in 1981–82. He hit 1,000 runs in England seven times (best 1,379, av 39.40, in 1970).

Asif Masood
Cricketer. *b:* 23.1.1946, Lahore, India. Right-hand batsman, right-arm fast medium bowler. *Teams* Lahore (1963/4 to 1968/9); Punjab U (1965/6 to 1968/9); PIA (1969/70 to 1976/7). *Tours* Pakistan to England 1971, 1974, to Sri Lanka, New Zealand and Australia 1972/3, to West Indies and Australia 1976/7, to Sri Lanka 1975/6; Rest of World to Australia 1971/2; PIA to England (non-first-class) 1969. *Tests* Pakistan (1968/9 to 1976/7, 16 matches).
Career batting
121–119–46–635–34–8.69–0–*ct* 38
Bowling 8854–305–29.02–9–0–8/97
Test batting
16–19–10–93–30*–10.33–0–*ct* 5
Bowling 1568–38–41.26–1–0–5/111

In 1971 on his first Test tour to England he took 13 wickets (av 26.46) in the three Tests, but in 1974 was not so successful. He also played for Northumberland.

Askew, John Garbutt
Amateur. *b:* 2.9.1908, Gateshead. *d:* 31.8.1942, Stannington, Northumberland. Right-hand batsman. *Sch* Durham. *Team* Cambridge U (1931).
Career batting
2–4–0–30–11–7.50–0–*ct* 1

His County cricket was for Durham. A noted rugby footballer, he appeared both for Cambridge U and England.

Askham, Sydney Thomas
Amateur. *b:* 9.9.1896, Wellingborough, Northants. *d:* 21.8.1916. He was killed in action at Maillet Wood, Sheepal, France. Lower order right-hand batsman, right-arm fast medium bowler. *Sch* Wellingborough. *Team* Northants (1914, 5 matches).
Career batting
5–9–3–83–28*–13.83–0–*ct* 0
Bowling 86–2–43.00–0–0–2/68

He appeared for Northants with still a full year left at school and in 1915 was regarded as one of the best Public School players in England – it was tragic that he should die at the age of 19.

Aslett, Derek George
Cricketer. *b:* 12.2.1958, Dover, Kent. Middle order right-hand batsman, leg break bowler. *Team* Kent (1981–83, 38 matches).
Career batting
38–68–8–2419–168–40.31–4–*ct* 32
Bowling 561–10–56.10–0–0–4/119

He hit 1,437 runs, av 43.54, in 1983. On his first-class debut in 1981 he made 146* for Kent v Hampshire at Bournemouth.

Aspinall, F.
Amateur. *Team* Liverpool and District (1892).
Career batting
1–2–1–27–16–27.00–0–*ct* 0

He also played for Cheshire.

Aspinall, Ronald
Professional. *b:* 26.10.1918, Almondbury, Yorkshire. Hard hitting right-hand batsman, right-arm fast medium bowler, good field. *Team* Yorkshire (1946–50, 36 matches).
Career batting
36–48–8–763–75*–19.07–0–*ct* 18
Bowling 2670–131–20.37–8–2–8/47

His bowling in 1947 and 1948 was such that he was regarded as an England prospect, but a strained Achilles tendon ended his first-class career in 1950. He then appeared for Durham for seven seasons. He became a first-class umpire.

Aspinall, Walter
Professional. *b:* 24.3.1858, Elland, Yorkshire. Moderate right-hand batsman, wicket-keeper, occasional fast bowler. *Team* Yorkshire (1880, 2 matches).
Career batting
3–4–0–19–14–4.75–0–*ct* 5

His final first-class match was for Under 30s in 1882.

Asquith, John Patrick Kenyon
Amateur. *b:* 1.2.1932, Carshalton, Surrey. Right-hand batsman, wicket-keeper. *Sch* Purley G.S. *Team* Cambridge U (1953–54).
Career batting
5–8–1–46–12–6.57–0–*ct* 4–*st* 1

He won a rugby blue 1953–54.

Asquith, Thomas Frederick
Professional. *b:* 5.2.1870, Halifax, Yorkshire. *d:* 11.1.1916, Hull, Yorkshire. Wicket-keeper. *Team* Yorkshire (1903, 1 match).
Career batting
1–1–0–0–0–0.00–0–*ct* 2

Astill, William Ewart
Professional. *b:* 1.3.1888, Ratby, Leicestershire. *d:* 10.2.1948, Leicester Hospital, after a long illness. Originally a tail end right-hand batsman, he developed into a good middle order player, right-arm slow to medium bowler, turning the ball either way, excellent slip field. *Team* Leicestershire (1906–39, 628 matches). *Tours* MCC to West Indies 1925/6, 1929/30, to South Africa 1927/8, to India and Ceylon 1926/7; Cahn to Jamaica 1928/9; Joel to South Africa 1924/5; Tennyson to West Indies 1930/1. *Tests* England (1927/8 to 1929/30, 9 matches).
Career batting
733–1153–145–22731–164*–22.55–15–*ct* 464
Bowling 57783–2431–23.76–140–22–9/41
Test batting
9–15–0–190–40–12.67–0–*ct* 7
Bowling 856–25–34.24–0–0–4/58

After making his first-class debut with a single appearance for Leicestershire during 1906, Astill then appeared in every match for the County during the next four seasons. He headed the County's bowling averages in both 1907 and 1908 and an international career was confidently forecast for him. Curiously, however, he seemed to lose his bowling and by 1911 was dropped from the Leicestershire team for several matches.

He appeared to be re-born after demobilisation and in 1921 completed his first of nine 'doubles'. For year after year he was near the top of both Leicester's batting and bowling and in his 40th year – in 1927–28 – finally made his England debut. If he had represented a more fashionable County, no doubt his tally of 9 Tests would have been much higher.

His best season with the bat was 1925 with 1,601 runs (av 32.03), having 1,000 runs in a season 11 times, and with the ball, 1921 with 153 wickets (av 20.99), having 100 wickets in a season 9 times and the 'double' 9 times. His best bowling was 9/41 v Warwickshire at Birmingham in 1923. He was an accomplished billiards player, winning several titles, whilst he was also a noted vocalist, singing to his own piano accompaniment. In his final years he did much coaching, showing himself to be an expert in this field.

Aston, John Gordon
Amateur. *b:* 20.11.1882, Dublin. *d:* 9.1.1951, Selly Oak, Birmingham. Right-hand batsman, right-arm medium pace bowler. *Team* Ireland (1925).
Career batting
2–4–1–68–53*–22.66–0–*ct* 1
Bowling 82–8–10.25–1–0–5/58

Atfield, Alfred John
Professional. *b:* 3.3.1868, Ightham, Kent. *d:* 1.1.1949, Caterham, Surrey. Useful hard-hitting right-hand batsman, right-arm medium pace bowler, good field. *Teams* Gloucestershire (1893, 3 matches); Natal (1897/8); London County (1900); Transvaal (1906/7).
Career batting
8–13–2–137–45–12.45–0–*ct* 5
Bowling 102–3–34.00–0–0–3/102

He is principally known as a coach in South Africa and a first-class umpire, both in South Africa and England. He also played for Wiltshire.

Athey, Charles William Jeffrey
Cricketer. *b*: 27.9.1957, Middlesbrough, Yorkshire. Middle order right-hand batsman, off break bowler, slip field. *Team* Yorkshire (1976–83, 151 matches). *Tours* Robins to New Zealand 1979/80; England to West Indies 1980/1. *Tests* England (1980 to 1980/1, 3 matches).
Career batting
163–268–21–6803–134–27.54–11–*ct* 150–*st* 2
Bowling 1060–21–50.47–0–0–3/38
Test batting
3–6–0–17–9–2.83–0–*ct* 2

He hit 1,000 runs in a season twice (best 1,339 av 43.19, in 1982).

Atkins, Frederick Mark
Amateur. *b:* 28.3.1864, Boxley, Kent. *d.* 13.1.1941, Rochester, Kent. Good left-hand batsman, useful wicket-keeper. *Team* Kent (1882–97, 27 matches).
Career batting
25–46–2–425–52–9.65–0–*ct* 21–*st* 1

He scored very heavily in club cricket in Kent, including 364 for Mote Park v Shorncliffe Camp in 1887.

Atkins, Gerald
Amateur. *b:* 14.5.1938, Great Missenden, Buckinghamshire. Left-hand batsman, leg break bowler. *Sch* Challenors, Amersham. *Teams* Combined Services (1958–59); Cambridge U (1960–61, blue 1960).
Career batting
20–36–3–394–49–11.93–0–*ct* 8
Bowling 96–2–48.00–0–0–2/25

He also appeared for Buckinghamshire.

Atkinson, Bernard Gerard Wensley

Amateur. *b:* 11.9.1900, Crediton, Devon. *d:* 4.9.1966, London. Brother of N. S. M. (Middx). Hard-hitting right-hand batsman, useful right-arm fast medium bowler. *Sch* St Paul's. *Teams* Northants (1922–25, 13 matches); Middlesex (1933–34, 9 matches).

Career batting
22–37–2–554–94–15.82–0–*ct* 17
Bowling 867–25–34.68–0–0–4/97

He went to Cambridge University where he captained his college at cricket and had trials for the University at both cricket and rugby, but failed to obtain a blue at either. A master at Edinburgh Academy, he appeared in four non-first-class matches for Scotland (1935–48).

Atkinson, Colin Ronald Michael

Cricketer. *b:* 23.7.1931, Thornaby, Yorkshire. Right-hand middle order batsman, leg spin bowler, but altered to right-arm medium in 1965 due to arthritis in the hand. *Team* Somerset (1960–67, 163 matches).

Career batting
164–240–41–3796–97–19.07–0–*ct* 75
Bowling 5982–192–31.15–7–0–7/54

He originally appeared for Northumberland and then Durham. He retired in 1963 from County cricket, but was released by Millfield School, where he was a master, to captain Somerset 1965–67. His first-class debut was for Minor Counties in 1959. He hit 1,120 runs, av 26.04, in 1966.

Atkinson, Denis St Eval

Amateur. *b:* 9.8.1926, Christchurch, Barbados. Brother of E. St. E. (Barbados and West Indies). Good middle order right-hand batsman, right-arm medium pace off-break bowler. *Teams* Trinidad (1947/8 to 1949/50); Barbados (1946/7 to 1960/1). *Tours* West Indies to India, Pakistan and Ceylon 1948/9, to Australia 1951/2, to New Zealand 1951/2, 1955/6, to England 1957. *Tests* West Indies (1948/9 to 1957/8, 22 matches).

Career batting
78–115–16–2812–219–28.40–5–*ct* 39
Bowling 5291–200–26.45–6–2–8/58
Test batting
22–35–6–922–219–31.79–1–*ct* 11
Bowling 1647–47–35.04–3–0–7/53

Atkinson captained West Indies in 7 Tests, including the fourth Test v Australia at Bridgetown, when he hit his only first-class double-century (219) and in the process created a new 7th wicket Test partnership record of 348 with C. C. Depeiza. He was by far the best West Indian bowler in this series, heading the averages and taking most wickets. On his only visit to England he suffered from injury and was rarely seen on the top of his form.

Atkinson, Graham

Professional. *b:* 29.3.1938, Lofthouse, Wakefield, Yorkshire. Sound right-hand opening batsman, occasional off break bowler, good outfield. *Teams* Somerset (1954–66, 271 matches); Lancashire (1967–69, 62 matches).

Career batting
347–608–41–17654–190–31.13–27–*ct* 189
Bowling 260–5–52.00–0–0–4/63

He made his first-class debut for Somerset at the age of 16; reached 1,000 runs in a season 9 times: best 2,078 (av 37.10) in 1961. His highest score was 190 for Somerset v Glamorgan (Bath) 1960.

Atkinson, Geoffrey Bean

Amateur. *b:* 29.1.1896, Lambeth, London. *d:* 1951, Worthing, Sussex. Right-hand batsman, right-arm fast-medium bowler. *Sch* Forest. *Team* Middlesex (1930, 2 matches).

Career batting
3–6–2–25–14–6.25–0–*ct* 2
Bowling 57–2–28.50–0–0–2/27

His final appearance in first-class cricket was for Leveson-Gower's Team in 1933.

Atkinson, George (Robert)

Professional. *b:* 21.9.1830, Ripon, Yorkshire. *d:* 3.5.1906, Bradford, Yorkshire. Stylish right-hand batsman, right medium-fast round-arm bowler, good slip field. *Team* Yorkshire (1858–70, 32 matches).

Career batting
62–95–21–935–66–12.60–0–*ct* 32
Bowling 2782–161+3–17.27–8–2–6/18

Atkinson was 29 before he took part in the major matches of the day, but through the 1860s was one of the leading Yorkshire all-rounders. The great facet of his bowling was its accuracy at a time when the faster round-arm bowlers tended to be wayward in direction. His final first-class match was for United North in 1871. He also played for Wiltshire.

Atkinson, Harry

Professional. *b:* 1.2.1881, Bramley, Yorkshire. *d:* 22.12.1959. *Team* Yorkshire (1907, 1 match).

Career batting
1–2–0–0–0–0.00–0–*ct* 0
Bowling 17–0

He was drafted into the Yorkshire side when three of the regulars were appearing for England, but had no success.

Atkinson, John
Professional. *b:* 7.6.1878, Nether Green, Notts. *d:* 1951, Bentley, Doncaster, Yorkshire. Lower order left-hand batsman, useful left-arm slow bowler. *Team* Nottinghamshire (1899–1901, 7 matches).
Career batting
7–12–4–40–19–5.00–0–*ct* 1
Bowling 236–10–23.60–0–0–4/22
He was dismissed in five consecutive innings for 0 (1899–1900).

Atkinson, Nigel Samuel Mitford
Amateur. *b:* 26.7.1899, Hong Kong. *d:* 24.10.1966, St John's Wood, London. Brother of B. G. W. (Middlesex and Northants). Right-hand batsman, useful slow/medium left-arm bowler. *Sch* St. Paul's. *Team* Middlesex (1923, 2 matches).
Career batting
2–2–0–41–39–20.50–0–*ct* 2
Bowling 147–12–12.25–1–0–5/16
He was a leading figure with Hampstead CC for many years.

Atkinson, Thomas
Professional. *b:* 27.9.1930, Millom, Cumberland. Useful middle order right-hand batsman, right-arm fast medium bowler. *Team* Nottinghamshire (1957–60, 64 matches).
Career batting
64–104–19–1127–48–13.25–0–*ct* 30
Bowling 5157–116–44.46–2–1–6/61
He also played for Cumberland.

Atkinson-Clark, John Cecil
Amateur. *b:* 9.7.1912, Kensington, London. *d:* 2.10.1969, Alderwasley, Derbyshire. Useful right-hand batsman. *Sch* Eton. *Team* Middlesex (1930–32, 8 matches).
Career batting
8–12–0–116–66–9.66–0–*ct* 2
Bowling 13–1–13.00–0–0–1/13
He hit 135 for Eton v Harrow at Lord's in 1930 and made his first-class debut for Middlesex with still a full school year ahead of him.

Attenborough, Thomas
Professional. *b:* July 1833, Ilkeston, Derbyshire. *d:* 21.1.1907, Ilkeston, Derbyshire. Useful right-hand batsman, good slow left-arm bowler. *Team* Derbyshire (1871–74, 6 matches).
Career batting
6–9–0–72–27–8.00–0–*ct* 2
Bowling 29–2–14.50–0–0–1/9
A good all-rounder, his best days were prior to Derbyshire being first-class. He also played for Lincolnshire.

Attewell, Thomas
Professional. *b:* 7.11.1869, Keyworth, Notts. *d:* 6.7.1937, Nottingham. Brother of William (Notts and England); cousin of Walter (Notts). Lower order right-hand batsman, right-arm medium pace bowler. *Team* Nottinghamshire (1891–94, 7 matches).
Career batting
7–10–3–53–23*–7.57–0–*ct* 2
Bowling 12–0
He was on the MCC staff at Lord's 1893 to 1925.

Attewell, Walter
Professional. *b:* 29.1.1865, Keyworth, Notts. *d:* 3.2.1919, Keyworth, Notts. Cousin of Thomas (Notts) and William (Notts and England). Fair right-hand batsman, excellent field. *Team* Nottinghamshire (1891, 1 match).
Career batting
1–2–0–0–0–0.00–0–*ct* 0
Bowling 10–0
He was the cricket coach at Shrewsbury School from 1906 to 1912 and is immortalised in the writing of Neville Cardus.

Attewell, William
Professional. *b:* 12.6.1861, Keyworth, Notts. *d:* 11.6.1927, Long Eaton, Derbyshire. Brother of Thomas (Notts), cousin of Walter (Notts). Useful right-hand lower order batsman, accurate medium pace right-arm bowler, excellent mid-field. *Team* Nottinghamshire (1881–1900, 283 matches). *Tours* Lillywhite, Shaw and Shrewsbury to Australia 1884/5; Vernon to Australia 1887/8; Sheffield to Australia 1891/2. *Tests* England (1884/5 to 1891/2, 10 matches).
Career batting
429–644–68–8083–102–14.03–1–*ct* 363
Bowling 29896–1950–15.33–134–27–9/23
Test batting
10–15–6–150–43*–16.66–0–*ct* 9
Bowling 626–27–23.18–0–0–4/42
Accuracy of length and direction was the prime facet of Attewell's bowling, and throughout the 1880s and 1890s he returned a continuous string of very economical bowling analyses. Three examples for Notts are: 10–9–2–3 v MCC (Lord's) 1881; 52.2–42–19–4 v Kent (Trent Bridge) 1887; 14–12–6–4 v Sussex (Trent Bridge) 1891.
He first took 100 wickets in a season in 1884 and in all performed the feat on ten occasions (best 153 wickets, av 13.93, in 1891). His best bowling was 9/23 for Notts v Sussex at Trent Bridge in 1886.
All but one of his ten Test appearances were in Australia and on the last two of his three tours there he was the most successful bowler.

His first-class batting is remarkable for the fact that his first and only century came in 1897 – sixteen seasons after his debut.

He was a man who never got on anyone's nerves and whose good nature was proverbial.

Aubrey-Fletcher, Sir John Henry Lancelot
Amateur. *b:* 22.8.1912, London. Middle order right-hand batsman, right-arm medium pace bowler. *Sch* Eton. *Teams* Oxford U (1933); Minor Counties (1933).
Career batting
2–3–3–66–48*–no av–0–*ct* 2
Bowling 133–5–26.60–0–0–2/46
He appeared for Buckinghamshire.

Audland, John Heslop
Amateur. *b:* 5.10.1852, Tintern, Monmouth. *d:* 4.10.1931, Ackenthwaite, Westmorland. Wicket-keeper. *Team* Oxford U (1875).
Career batting
1–1–0–2–2–2.00–0–*ct* 1–*st* 1
He played for Wiltshire.

August, George Lawrence Bagley
Amateur. *b:* 16.9.1917, Mymensingh, India. Middle order right-hand batsman. *Sch* Bedford. *Team* Minor Counties (1950–53).
Career batting
2–4–0–41–27–10.25–0–*ct* 0
He represented Bedfordshire, and is secretary of the County Club.

Austen-Leigh, S. (*See under* Leigh, S. A.)

Austin, Edward James
Amateur. *b:* 1847, Weymouth, Dorset. *d:* 13.4.1891, Pimlico, London. Right-hand batsman, medium pace round-arm bowler. *Sch* Sherborne. *Team* Oxford U (1869).
Career batting
1–2–1–10–10–10.00–0–*ct* 1
Bowling 58–2–29.00–0–0–2/58
He played for Dorset.

Austin, Geoffrey Lewis
Amateur. *b:* 11.9.1837, Canterbury, Kent. *d:* 29.5.1902, Chelsea, London. *Team* Kent (1861–68, 2 matches).
Career batting
3–6–0–64–23–10.66–0–*ct* 1

Austin, Harry
Professional. *b:* 17.4.1892, Moseley, Birmingham. *d:* 29.8.1968, Canterbury, Kent. Lower order left-hand batsman, slow left-arm bowler. *Teams* Warwickshire (1919, 4 matches); Worcestershire (1928, 2 matches).
Career batting
6–10–2–67–13–8.37–0–*ct* 3
Bowling 290–3–96.66–0–0–1/41

Austin, Sir Harold Bruce Gardiner
Amateur. *b:* 15.7.1877, Bridgetown, Barbados. *d:* 27.7.1943, Collymore Rock, Barbados. Brother of A. P. G. (British Guiana), M. B. G. (British Guiana) and H. F. (Barbados). Middle order right-hand batsman. *Sch* Harrison College, Barbados. *Teams* Barbados (1894/5 to 1927/8); MCC (1909–26). *Tours* West Indies to England 1906, 1923.
Career batting
67–104–7–2667–129–27.49–1–*ct* 51–*st* 3
Bowling 304–15–20.26–0–0–3/7
Austin was the captain of both the first and second first-class West Indies tours to England. Knighted in 1935, he was Speaker of the House of Assembly, Barbados.

Austin, Harold McPherson
Amateur. *b:* 8.3.1903, Skipton, Victoria, Australia. *d:* 31.7.1981, Timboon, Victoria, Australia. Middle order right-hand batsman, leg break bowler. *Sch* Melbourne, Australia. *Teams* Cambridge U (1924, blue); Victoria (1924/5, 6 matches – all on tour of New Zealand). *Tour* Victoria to New Zealand 1924/5.
Career batting
17–25–2–599–87–26.04–0–*ct* 11
Bowling 1047–41–25.53–3–0–6/79

Austin, Mervyn Neville
Amateur. *b:* 1.8.1913, Melbourne, Australia. Tail end right-hand batsman, leg break and googly bowler. *Sch* Melbourne G.S. *Team* Oxford U (1938).
Career batting
4–5–4–14–6–14.00–0–*ct* 2
Bowling 234–7–33.42–0–0–4/36

Austin, Robert Gordon Lefroy
Amateur. *b:* 28.12.1871, Cheltenham, Gloucestershire. *d:* 26.5.1958, Stellenbosch, Cape Province, South Africa. Hard-hitting right-hand batsman, but liable to throw away his wicket, good field. *Sch* Cheltenham. *Team* Oxford U (1894).
Career batting
1–2–0–7–7–3.50–0–*ct* 0
Bowling 4–0

Avery, Alfred Victor
Professional. *b:* 19.12.1914, New Beckton, Essex. Sound right-hand opening batsman, slow left-arm bowler, close field. *Team* Essex (1935–54, 268 matches).

Career batting
269–455–35–14137–224–33.65–25–*ct* 119
Bowling 627–9–69.66–0–0–1/11

His highest score was 224 for Essex v Northants (Northampton) 1952. He scored 1,000 runs in a season 7 times between 1939 and 1953 (best: 1,890 av 46.09, in 1948).

Avory, Henry Kemp
Amateur. *b:* 4.10.1848, Clapham, Surrey. *d:* 16.4.1918, Weybridge, Surrey. Hard-hitting opening right-hand batsman, useful outfield. *Team* Surrey (1876, 2 matches).
Career batting
2–4–0–82–42–20.50–0–*ct* 0

A solicitor, he was for many years Clerk to the Central Criminal Court.

Awdry, Charles Edwin
Amateur. *b:* 29.4.1906, Paddington, London. *d:* 16.11.1965, Lacock, Wilts. Nephew of R. W. (Oxford U). Middle order batsman, right-arm fast-medium bowler, good extra cover. *Sch* Winchester. *Teams* West of England (1927); Minor Counties (1937).
Career batting
2–3–0–16–8–5.33–0–*ct* 1
Bowling 80–3–26.66–0–0–2/56

He was the leading all-rounder in the Wiltshire side for many years.

Awdry, Robert William
Amateur. *b:* 20.5.1881, London. *d:* 3.2.1949, Devizes, Wilts. Uncle of C. E. (Minor Counties). Good opening right-hand batsman. *Sch* Winchester. *Team* Oxford U (1902–04, blue 1904).
Career batting
9–16–0–383–72–23.93–0–*ct* 5

He was a mainstay of Wiltshire cricket for many years, first as player then as hon. secretary and treasurer. He was a Chairman of Wilts County Council.

Aworth, Christopher John
Cricketer. *b:* 19.2.1953, Wimbledon, London. Good middle order left-hand batsman, occasional left-arm slow bowler. *Sch* Tiffin School. *Teams* Cambridge U (1973–75, blue all three years); Surrey (1974–76, 26 matches).
Career batting
56–104–6–2552–135–26.04–3–*ct* 22
Bowling 476–7–68.00–0–0–2/23

His best season was 1975 when he hit 1,057 runs (av 31.08).

Axford, William Ian
Amateur. *b:* 2.1.1933, New Zealand. Right-hand middle order batsman, right-arm medium pace bowler. *Team* Cambridge U (1960).
Career batting
2–2–0–13–7–6.50–0–*ct* 1

Ayling, Cyril Edgar
Amateur. *b:* 26.10.1910, Buenos Aires, Argentina. Brother of D. E. (Argentine), Cecil (Argentine) and Eric (Argentine). Lower order right-hand batsman, right-arm fast medium bowler. *Team* Argentine (1937/8). *Tour* South America to England 1932.
Career batting
9–15–2–200–50–15.38–0–*ct* 8
Bowling 674–24–28.08–1–0–5/48

Ayling, Dennet Ernest
Amateur. *b:* 8.6.1906, Buenos Aires, Argentina. Brother of Cecil (Argentine), Cyril (Argentine) and Eric (Argentine). Middle order right-hand batsman, off spin bowler. *Team* Argentine (1926/7 to 1937/8). *Tour* South America to England 1932.
Career batting
16–29–2–653–88–24.18–0–*ct* 6
Bowling 1297–79–16.41–7–2–6/10

Ayling, William
Professional. *b: circa* 1766, Cocking, Chichester, Sussex. *d:* 1826, Bromley, Kent. Hard-hitting batsman, fine outfield. *Teams* Kent (1806); England (1801–10).
Career batting
21–38–5–271–45–8.21–0–*ct* 7

In his early days he was a bit of a poacher and on this account moved from Sussex. When batting he stood square to the bowler and held the bat in his right hand only, grasping it with his left immediately before receiving the ball.

Aylmer, Edward Arthur
Amateur. *b:* 20.3.1892, Falmouth, Cornwall. *d:* 30.10.1974, Askerswell, Dorset. *Team* Royal Navy (1920).
Career batting
1–2–1–20–10*–20.00–0–*ct* 1
Bowling 38–1–38.00–0–0–1/19

Aylward, James
Professional. *b:* 1741, Warnford, Droxford, Hants. *d:* 27.12.1827, Marylebone, Middlesex. Brother of John and Thomas (both noted players in their day). Excellent left-hand batsman. *Team* Hampshire.

He played almost entirely before 1801, so career records are inapplicable. He hit 167 for

Hampshire v England at Sevenoaks in 1777 – at the time the highest score ever made in an important match. He continued to play cricket until 1802, when his age was 61, his career thus being one of the longest on record, but many of his early scores are lost. In his later years he became well-known as a captain.

Ayres, George White
Professional. *b:* 5.7.1871, Thames Ditton, Surrey. *d:* 28.8.1934, Felpham, Sussex. Steady right-hand batsman, brilliant fieldsman and change bowler. *Teams* Surrey (1892–96, 25 matches); Essex (1899, 12 matches). *Tour* Read to South Africa 1891/2 (he did not play in a first-class match).
Career batting
38–52–2–672–83–13.44–0–*ct* 22
Bowling 166–5–33.20–0–0–1/2

Azad, Kirti Vardhan Bhagwat Jha
Cricketer. *b*: 2.1.1959, Purnea, India. Middle order, right-hand batsman, off break bowler, good outfield. *Teams* Delhi (1977/8 to 1982/3); D. B. Close's XI (1983). *Tour* India to Australia and New Zealand 1980/1. *Tests* India (1980/1 to 1981/2, 4 matches)
Career batting
49–66–5–2327–186–38.14–6–*ct* 33
Bowling 2264–89–25.43–3–0–7/63
Test batting
4–6–0–107–24–17.83–0–*ct* 2
Bowling 158–1–158.00–0–0–1/35
His first-class debut was for India Under 22s in 1976/7.

Azmat Rana
Cricketer. *b*: 3.11.1951, Lahore, Pakistan. Brother of Shafqat Rana (PIA). Opening or middle order left-hand batsman. *Teams* Bahawalpur (1969/70); PIA (1969/70 to 1974/5); Punjab (1976/7 to 1977/8); Muslim Commercial Bank (1976/7 to 1982/3). *Tours* Pakistan to England 1971, to New Zealand 1972/3. *Test* Pakistan (1979/80, 1 match).
Career batting
88–131–17–5529–206*–48.50–15–*ct* 72
Bowling 84–0
Test batting
1–1–0–49–49–49.00–0–*ct* 0
He hit 192 runs, av 21.33, on the 1971 tour to England and did not appear in the Tests.

BACCHUS, SHEIK FAOUD AHUMUL FASIEL
Cricketer. *b*: 31.1.1954, Georgetown, British Guiana. Opening or middle order right-hand batsman, right-arm medium pace bowler, good outfield. *Team* Guyana (1973/4 to 1982/3). *Tours* West Indies to India and Sri Lanka 1978/9, to England 1980, to Pakistan 1980/1, to Australia 1981/2; Young West Indies to Zimbabwe 1981/2. *Tests* West Indies (1977/8 to 1982/3, 19 matches).
Career batting
88–140–12–4694–250–36.67–7–*ct* 70
Bowling 27–0
Test batting
19–30–0–782–250–26.06–1–*ct* 17
Bowling 3–0
His first-class debut was for Demerera in 1971/2. In first-class matches on the 1980 tour he hit 710 runs, av 33.80, and played in all five Tests, but with little success.

Bache, Harold Godfrey
Amateur. *b:* 20.8.1889, Churchill, Worcs. *d:* 15.2.1916, Comines Canal Bank, Ypres, Belgium. Useful left-hand batsman, slow bowler. *Sch* K.E.S., Birmingham. *Teams* Worcestershire (1907–10, 17 matches); Cambridge U (1910).
Career batting
20–31–1–270–36–9.00–0–*ct* 5
Bowling 39–3–13.00–0–0–2/4
He was better known as a soccer player, appearing for Cambridge U, West Bromwich and the Corinthians. He also represented Cambridge at lawn tennis.

Bacher, Dr Aron
Amateur. *b:* 24.5.1942, Roodepoort, South Africa. Middle order right-hand batsman, brilliant field. Witswatersrand University. *Team* Transvaal (1959/60 to 1973/4). *Tour* South Africa to England 1965. *Tests* South Africa (1965 to 1969/70, 12 matches).
Career batting
120–212–10–7894–235–39.07–18–*ct* 110 *st* 1
Bowling 87–2–43.50–0–0–1/8
Test batting 12–22–1–679–73–32.33–0 *ct* 10
On his only visit to England Bacher hit 1,008 runs (av 40.32) and was one of the successes of the tour. In 1969/70 he captained South Africa to a great victory over the Australians, winning all four of the Tests.

Backhouse, Edgar Norman
Professional. *b:* 13.5.1901, Malton, Yorkshire. *d:* 1.11.1936. He was killed in a motor accident at

High Wycombe, Bucks. Fair right-hand batsman, medium pace left-arm bowler. *Teams* Yorkshire (1931, 1 match); MCC (1932).
Career batting
2–3–0–3–2–1.00–0–*ct* 0
Bowling 134–3–44.66–0–0–3/130

Oldroyd was taken ill when Yorkshire arrived in London to play as Champion County v The Rest and as they brought only 11 men, Backhouse, on the staff at Lord's, was brought into the County side at the last moment. It proved to be one of two appearances in first-class cricket, though he appeared for Staffordshire for some years.

Bacmeister, Lucas Henry
Amateur. *b:* 22.11.1869, Islington, Middlesex. *d:* 23.5.1962, Wollage Green, Barham, Kent. Lower order right-hand batsman, useful right-arm fast-medium bowler. *Team* Middlesex (1889–90, 9 matches).
Career batting
11–17–4–59–15–4.53–0–*ct* 9
Bowling 688–31–22.19–1–0–5/22

Bacmeister made his first-class debut for Gentlemen of England v Oxford U in May 1889 and took 5/22 in the second innings. He was immediately drafted into the Middlesex side, but discarded after a handful of games, though his record was most promising. After an interval of 14 years he reappeared in first-class cricket in one match in 1904 – Weigall's XI v Cambridge U.

Bacon, Francis Hugh
Originally professional, but turned amateur in 1903. *b:* 24.6.1869, Colombo, Ceylon. *d:* 31.10.1915. He was drowned off the coast of Belgium, the ship, *Yacht Aries*, in which he was serving being sunk by a mine. Good right-hand batsman, slow right-arm bowler. *Sch* St Augustine's, Canterbury. *Team* Hampshire (1895–1911, 75 matches).
Career batting
75–132–11–1909–110–15.77–1–*ct* 34
Bowling 190–6–31.66–0–0–2/23

Bacon hit 114 in 130 minutes on his debut for Hampshire v Warwickshire in 1894 (this match is not ranked as first-class). He was appointed Secretary of Hampshire in 1903 and remained in that post until his death.

Bacon, John
Professional. *b:* 1872, Cosby, Leicestershire. *d:* 16.10.1942, Broughton-Astley. Leics. Right-hand batsman, useful right-arm medium pace bowler. *Team* Leicestershire (1895, 4 matches).
Career batting
4–8–1–42–14–6.00–0–*ct* 0
Bowling 21–1–21.00–0–0–1/18

He also played for Cambridgeshire.

Badat, Yunus
Cricketer. *b:* 1943, Northern Rhodesia, Middle order right-hand batsman. *Team* East Africa (1975). *Tour* East Africans to England 1975.
Career batting
1–2–0–3–3–1.50–0–*ct* 0

Badcock, Clayvel Lindsay
Amateur. *b:* 10.4.1914, Exton, Tasmania. *d:* 13.12.1982, Exton, Tasmania. Punishing opening or middle order right-hand batsman. *Teams* Tasmania (1929/30 to 1933/4, 19 matches); South Australia (1934/5 to 1940/1, 40 matches). *Tour* Australia to England 1938. *Tests* Australia (1936/7 to 1938, 7 matches).
Career batting
97–159–16–7371–325–51.54–26–*ct* 41
Bowling 44–0
Test batting
7–12–1–160–118–14.54–1–*ct* 3

His only success in Test matches came at Melbourne in 1936/7 when, in the fifth Test, he hit 118 in 205 minutes. On his visit to England in 1938, he batted well in the ordinary matches, returning an aggregate of 1,604 runs (av 45.82) but totally failed in the Tests – in 8 innings his best score was 9. His highest score was 325 for South Australia v Victoria at Adelaide in 1935/6.

Badcock, Frederick Theodore
Professional. *b:* 9.8.1897, Abbottabad, India. *d:* 19.9.1982, South Perth, Australia. Attacking opening or middle order right-hand batsman, right-arm fast-medium bowler. *Sch* Wellington (UK). *Teams* Wellington (1924/5 to 1929/30); Otago (1930/1 to 1936/7). *Tour* New Zealand Services to England 1945. *Tests* New Zealand (1929/30 to 1932/33, 7 matches).
Career batting
53–96–3–2383–155–25.62–4–*ct* 38
Bowling 5211–221–23.57–14–5–7/50
Test batting
7–9–2–137–64–19.57–0–*ct* 1
Bowling 610–16–38.12–0–0–4/80

Badcock went out to New Zealand as coach to Wellington in 1924/5 and after six years moved on to Otago. He played for New Zealand only in home Tests and his two appearances in English first-class cricket occurred in 1945 playing for the New Zealand Forces team, and for L. Parkinson's XI in 1935.

Badcock, John
Professional. *b:* 4.10.1883, Christchurch, Hants. *d:* 24.8.1940, Marylebone, London. Useful tail end right-hand batsman, right-arm fast bowler. *Team* Hampshire (1906–08, 63 matches).
Career batting
63–102–19–1199–74–14.44–0–*ct* 30
Bowling 5414–212–25.53–12–3–8/44
Badcock had a most successful debut season with 96 wickets (av 24.81), but his first-class career lasted only three years.

Bader, Sir Douglas Robert Steuart
Amateur. *b:* 21.2.1910, Marylebone, London. *d:* 5.9.1982, Chiswick, London. Hard hitting right-hand batsman, fast bowler. *Sch* St Edward's, Oxford. *Team* RAF (1931).
Career batting
1–2–0–66–65–33.00–0–*ct* 0
Also a noted rugby footballer for the RAF and Combined Services, Bader lost both legs in a flying accident in 1931. The way in which he overcame this disability and returned to the RAF to become a hero of the Second World War was the subject of books and a film. He set out to encourage other disabled people to conquer their difficulties and lead an ordinary life.

Badger, Henry Dixon
Amateur. *b:* 7.3.1900, York. *d:* 10.8.75, Barnard Castle, Co. Durham. Lower order right-hand batsman, fast right-arm bowler. *Sch* Shrewsbury. *Teams* Yorkshire (1921–22, 2 matches); Oxford U (1921).
Career batting
5–7–4–33–17*–11.00–0–*ct* 2
Bowling 325–15–21.66–0–0–4/53

Badham, Peter Henry Christopher
Amateur. *b:* 11.2.1911, Bagworth, Leics. *d:* 10.4.83, Upton, Dorset. Lower order right-hand batsman, right-arm medium pace bowler. *Sch* Winchester. *Teams* Leicestershire (1933, 1 match); Oxford U (1934).
Career batting
4–6–0–67–38–11.16–0–*ct* 4
Bowling 311–10–31.10–0–0–4/70
He played for Leics v Oxford University only, appearing in the same year for Buckinghamshire in the Minor Counties Championship. He also played for Dorset.

Baggallay, Mervyn Eric Claude
Amateur. *b:* 7.12.1887, Kensington, London. *d:* 19.3.1961, Kensington, London. Brother of R.R.C. (Derbyshire), cousin of T.W. (Surrey). Hard hitting lower order right-hand batsman, wicket-keeper. *Sch* Eton. *Team* Cambridge U (1911, blue).
Career batting
8–14–3–119–22–10.81–0–*ct* 6–*st* 4
Though at Cambridge in 1908, he did not play in a first-class match for the University until 1911.

Baggallay, Richard Romer Claude
Amateur. *b:* 4.5.1884, Kensington, London. *d:* 12.12.1975, Kensington, London. Brother of M.E.C. (Cambridge U), cousin of T.W. (Surrey). Right-hand bat, wicket-keeper. *Sch* Marlborough. *Team* Derbyshire (1912–19, 31 matches).
Career batting
31–59–1–688–88–11.86–0–*ct* 25
Captained Derbyshire 1913–1919 (jointly with J. Chapman in 1919).

Baggallay, Thomas Weeding
(he changed his name to Weeding in 1868)
Amateur. *b:* 11.6.1847, St Pancras, Middlesex. *d:* 19.12.1929, Addlestone, Surrey. Cousin of R.R.C. (Derbyshire) and M.E.C. (Cambridge U). Opening or middle order right-hand batsman, slow round-arm bowler, wicket-keeper. *Sch* Marlborough. *Team* Surrey (1865–74, 8 matches).
Career batting
9–15–0–181–82–12.06–0–*ct* 4
A keen yachtsman, he took up sailing to the detriment of his cricket.

Bagguley, Robert
Professional. *b:* 10.7.1873, Ruddington, Notts. *d:* 8.10.1946, Bradmore, Notts. Brother of William (Derbyshire). Middle order right-hand batsman, useful left-arm medium pace bowler. *Team* Nottinghamshire (1891–96, 45 matches).
Career batting
48–76–12–766–110–11.96–*ct* 25
Bowling 930–38–24.47–3–0–6/74
On the staff at Lord's from 1893 to 1902, Bagguley made his final appearance in first-class cricket for MCC in 1900.

Bagguley, William
Professional. *b:* 9.9.1866, Ruddington, Notts. *d:* 18.4.1936, Nottingham. Brother of Robert (Notts). Useful middle order batsman. *Team* Derbyshire (1905, 1 match).
Career batting
1–1–0–5–5–5.00–0–*ct* 0

Bagnall, Hamer Fraser
Amateur. *b:* 18.2.1904, Field Burcote, Northants. *d:* 2.9.1974, London. Middle order right-hand batsman with splendid off-drive, leg break bowler. *Sch* Harrow. *Teams* Northants (1921–28, 64 matches); Cambridge U (1923–25, blue 1923).

Tour Tennyson to Jamaica 1931/2 (but played no first-class matches).
Career batting
85–158–3–2956–128*–19.71–3–*ct* 40
Bowling 59–0

He made his debut for Northants with still a full year to go at school. He scored well on fast wickets and against fast bowlers, but failed too often against the slower bowlers. His final first-class match was for MCC in 1929.

Bagshaw, Henry
Professional. *b:* 1.9.1859, Foolow, Tideswell, Derbyshire. *d:* 31.1.1927, Crowden, Cheshire. Free hitting left-hand batsman, useful right-arm medium pace bowler. *Team* Derbyshire (1887–1902, 123 matches).
Career batting
125–218–9–5456–127*–26.10–7–*ct* 36
Bowling 2119–73–29.03–2–0–5/18

He was buried in his umpire's coat and with a cricket ball in his hand. He hit 1,055 runs, 29.30, in 1900.

Baig, Abbasali Humayunali
Amateur. *b:* 19.3.1939, Hyderabad, India. Brother of M.H. (Oxford U) and Mazhar Ali (Hyderabad). Attractive middle order right-hand batsman, leg break bowler. Osmania University. *Teams* Hyderabad (1954/5 to 1975/6); Oxford U (1959–62, blue all four years); Somerset (1960–62, 23 matches). *Tours* India to England 1959, 1971; Hyderabad Blues to Ceylon 1966/7; Swanton to West Indies 1960/1. *Tests* India (1959 to 1966/7, 10 matches).
Career batting
235–391–29–12367–224*–34.16–21–*ct* 154
Bowling 432–9–48.00–0–0–2/26
Test batting
10–18–0–428–112–23.77–1–*ct* 6
Bowling 15–0

Baig's only Test hundred was made on his debut for India v England at Old Trafford in 1959 – he made 112 – when he was co-opted into the touring side after being at Oxford. His first first-class century was scored in his second first-class match: 105 for Hyderabad v Mysore in 1954/5.

He hit over 1,000 runs in each of his 3 full seasons in England (best 1821, av 39.58, in 1959). His highest score was 224* for South Zone v North Zone at Delhi in 1966/7.

Baig, Murtazaali Humayunali
Amateur. *b:* 8.11.1941, Hyderabad, India. Brother of A.H. (Oxford U, Somerset and India) and Mazhar Ali (Hyderabad). Middle order right-hand batsman, off break bowler. Osmania University. *Teams* Oxford U (1961–64, blue 1962–64); Hyderabad (1958/9 to 1970/1).
Career batting
47–81–12–1898–103–27.50–1–*ct* 13
Bowling 299–6–49.83–0–0–4/44

In 1962 both M.A.Baig and his brother appeared for Oxford at Lord's – the first time two brothers had done this since 1928.

Bailey, Albert E.
Professional. *b:* 14.3.1872, Norwood, Surrey. Lower order right-hand batsman, good slow left-arm bowler. *Teams* Somerset (1900–11, 40 matches); Scotland (1908–09).
Career batting
43–70–27–322–25*–7.48–0–*ct* 15
Bowling 3541–133–26.62–7–2–8/46

He also played for Surrey in non-first-class matches in 1892.

Bailey, David
Cricketer. *b:* 9.9.1944, West Hartlepool, Durham. Middle order right-hand batsman, off break bowler, excellent cover point. *Sch* Malvern. *Team* Lancashire (1968–69, 27 matches).
Career batting
32–46–2–1265–136–28.68–1–*ct* 13
Bowling 139–3–46.33–0–0–3/67

His cricket has been mainly in the Minor Counties Championship, with Durham 1961–68 and Cheshire 1973–81. He has appeared regularly in representative Minor Counties sides. His final first-class match was for Minor Counties in 1981.

Bailey, Sir Derrick Thomas Louis
Amateur. *b:* 15.8.1918, London. Son of Sir Abe Bailey (Transvaal). Middle order right-hand batsman, right-arm medium pace change bowler. *Sch* Winchester. *Team* Gloucestershire (1949–52, 60 matches).
Career batting
60–95–12–2029–111–24.44–2–*ct* 36
Bowling 398–12–33.16–0–0–2/19

He captained Gloucestershire, 1951–52. He hit 1,003, av 30.39, in 1951. He also played for Oxfordshire and Herefordshire.

Bailey, Frederick Raymond
Amateur. *b:* 2.11.1919, Newcastle, Staffs. Opening left-hand batsman. *Team* Minor Counties (1950–60).
Career batting
3–5–1–118–79–29.50–0–*ct* 0

He played for Staffordshire.

Bailey, George Herbert
Amateur. *b:* 29.10.1853, Colombo, Ceylon. *d:* 10.10.1926, Hobart, Tasmania. Hard hitting

lower order right-hand batsman, right-hand fast round-arm bowler, deep field. *Sch* Elizabeth College, Guernsey, C.I. *Team* Tasmania (1872/3 to 1892/3, 2 matches). *Tour* Australia to England and North America 1878.
Career batting
15–27–5–367–57*–16.68–0–*ct* 9
Bowling 102–4–25.50–0–0–1/5

He was also invited to tour England with the 1880 Australians, but had to decline.

Bailey, Harry John
Cricketer. *b:* 23.4.1940, West Hartlepool, Co Durham. Middle order right-hand batsman, left-arm medium pace bowler. *Team* Minor Counties (1967–69).
Career batting
3–4–0–50–25–12.50–0–*ct* 1
Bowling 68–3–22.66–0–0–2/20

He played for Durham.

Bailey, James
Professional. *b:* 6.4.1908, Shawford, Winchester, Hants. Solid left-hand opening batsman, good left-arm slow bowler, gully. *Team* Hampshire (1927–52, 242 matches).
Career batting
248–418–37–9500–133–24.93–5–*ct* 64
Bowling 12886–473–27.23–25–5–7/7

Hitting 1,000 runs in a season four times (best 1,410, av 30.00, in 1946), he did not play regularly for the County through the 1930s, being engaged in League cricket. His outstanding year was 1948 when he performed the 'double' with 1,399 runs (av 31.79) and 121 wickets (av 18.13).

Bailey, Jack Arthur
Amateur. *b:* 22.6.1930, Brixton, London. Lower order right-hand batsman, right-arm fast medium bowler. *Sch* Christ's Hospital. *Teams* Essex (1953–58, 71 matches); Oxford U (1956–58, blue all three years).
Career batting
112–148–38–641–29*–5.82–0–*ct* 67
Bowling 7504–347–21.62–20–2–8/24

J.A. Bailey has been Secretary of MCC since June 1974. During the 1960s he appeared frequently in MCC matches. He took 7/32 in the second innings of his first-class debut match: Essex v Notts (Southend) 1953.

His final first-class match was for Free Foresters in 1968.

Bailey, Michael John
Cricketer. *b*: 1.8.1954, Cheltenham, Gloucs. Lower order left-hand batsman, off break bowler. *Team* Hampshire (1979–82, 20 matches).
Career batting
20–29–9–228–24–11.40–0–*ct* 8
Bowling 996–18–55.33–1–0–5/89

Bailey, Ronald Anthony
Amateur. *b:* 30.7.1923, Camberwell, London. Tail end batsman, right-arm medium pace bowler. *Team* Kent (1948, 3 matches).
Career batting
3–5–1–0–0*–0.00–0–*ct* 0
Bowling 250–2–125.00–0–0–1/76

Bailey, Robert John
Cricketer. *b*: 28.10.1963, Biddulph, Staffs. Middle order right-hand batsman, off break bowler. *Team* Northamptonshire (1982–83, 5 matches).
Career batting
5–8–1–110–37*–15.71–0–*ct* 6
Bowling 35–3–11.66–0–0–3/33

He also played for Staffordshire.

Bailey, Raymond Reginald
Cricketer. *b:* 16.5.1944, Bedford. Lower order right-hand batsman, right-arm fast medium bowler. *Team* Northants (1964–73, 48 matches).
Career batting
49–48–21–253–25–9.37–0–*ct* 27
Bowling 2906–108–26.90–5–0–5/25

He also appeared for Bedfordshire in 1963 and for Buckinghamshire since 1975. He played soccer for Bedford Town, Gillingham and Northampton Town (centre half).

Bailey, Trevor Edward
Amateur. *b:* 3.12.1923, Westcliff-on-Sea, Essex. Tenacious middle order right-hand bat, right-arm fast-medium bowler, brilliant close field. *Sch* Dulwich. *Teams* Essex (1946–67, 482 matches); Prime Minister's XI in India (1963/64); Cambridge U (1947–48, blue both years). *Tours* MCC to Australia and New Zealand 1950/1, 1954/5, to Australia 1958/9, to South Africa 1956/7, to West Indies 1953/4; Cavaliers to West Indies 1963/4, 1964/5. *Tests* England (1949 to 1958/9, 61 matches).
Career batting
682–1072–215–28641–205–33.42–28–*ct* 428
Bowling 48170–2082–23.13–110–13–10/90
Test batting
61–91–14–2290–134*–29.74–1–*ct* 32
Bowling 3856–132–29.21–5–1–7/34

The best English all-round cricketer of the 1950s, Bailey became famous for his defensive batting against the Australians, particularly in the 1953 and 1954/5 series when he time and again saved England from collapse. His great innings at Lord's v Australia in 1953 went a long way towards bringing back the Ashes to England for the first time since the war. In the record books his two most dogged innings were: 68 in 458 minutes v Australia at Brisbane in 1958/9 and 8 in 120 minutes v South Africa at Headingley in 1955. He opened the England bowling for several series with A.V.Bedser and on the latter's retirement from Tests, Bailey continued as the main back-up bowler to Statham and Tyson. He hit 1,000 runs 17 times, going on to 2,000 once (2,011, av 46.76, in 1959) and took 100 wickets 9 times (best 133, av 21.01, in 1961).

In County cricket he was Essex's leading bowler and his batting was much more attractive than in the Test arena. Achieving the 'double' on eight occasions, he performed the feat of 2,000 runs and 100 wkts in 1959, the only post-war cricketer to attain this milestone. His highest innings was 205 for Essex v Sussex (Eastbourne) 1947 and his best bowling 10/90 for Essex v Lancashire (Clacton) 1949. From 1961 to 1966 he captained the County and from 1954 to 1967 was the County Secretary. His first-class debut was for Under-33s in 1945.

A talented soccer player, Bailey won his blue at Cambridge and went on to obtain an FA Amateur Cup medal with Walthamstow in 1951/2. He is the author of several books and other publications on cricket and is well-known as a sports commentator.

Bailey, William Henry
Professional. *b:* 2.10.1869, Melton Mowbray, Leics. *d:* 19.10.1930, Melton Mowbray, Leics. Hard hitting right-hand batsman. *Team* Leicestershire (1896, 2 matches).
Career batting
2–4–0–49–15–12.25–0–*ct* 1

Bailey, W. P.
Amateur. Opening batsman. *Team* Hampshire (1864, 1 match).
Career batting
1–2–0–14–10–7.00–0–*ct* 0

Baillie, William Hunter
Amateur. *b:* 1838, Cheltenham, Gloucs. *d:* 17.3.1895, Paddington, London. Middle order batsman. *Sch* Eton. *Team* Gloucestershire (1870, 1 match).
Career batting
1–1–0–7–7–7.00–0–*ct* 1

Baily, Cyril Alexander Highett
Amateur. *b:* 17.7.1880, Glastonbury, Somerset. *d:* 21.9.1924, Burnham-on-Sea, Somerset. Right-hand batsman. *Team* Somerset (1902, 1 match).
Career batting
1–2–1–8–4*–8.00–0–*ct* 2

Baily, Edward Peter
Amateur. *b:* 18.1.1852, London. *d:* 21.1.1941, Tupsley, Hereford. Father of R.E.H. (Surrey). Middle order right-hand batsman, wicket-keeper. *Sch* Harrow. *Teams* Cambridge U (1872–74, blue 1872 and 1874); Middlesex (1872, 1 match).
Career batting
10–17–3–172–26–12.28–0–*ct* 15–*st* 2

He also played non-first-class cricket for Somerset in 1880.

Baily, Henry Paul
Amateur. *b:* 3.9.1868, Philadelphia. Lower order right-hand batsman, right-arm off break bowler. *Sch* Haverford College. *Team* Philadelphia (1891–1903). *Tour* Philadelphia to England 1897.
Career batting
25–41–6–327–40–9.34–0–*ct* 16
Bowling 1825–78–23.39–3–1–7/65

He also visited England with the non-first-class side in 1889 and was most successful on that visit. He appeared 3 times for United States v Canada 1890, 1892 and 1894.

He was always cheerful and nothing could change his tranquil manner.

Baily, Robert Edward Hartwell
Amateur. *b:* 6.6.1885, Godstone, Surrey. *d:* 19.9.1973, Hereford. Son of E.P. (Cambridge U and Middlesex). Opening or middle order right-hand batsman, wicket-keeper. *Sch* Harrow. *Teams* Surrey (1904–06, 5 matches); Cambridge U (1905–08, blue 1908).
Career batting
28–51–2–825–61–16.83–0–*ct* 37–*st* 12

Bainbridge, Alfred Brian
Cricketer. *b:* 15.10.1932, Middlesbrough, Yorkshire. Lower order right-hand batsman, useful off break bowler. *Team* Yorkshire (1961–63, 5 matches).
Career batting
5–10–0–93–24–9.30–0–*ct* 3
Bowling 358–20–17.90–2–1–6/53

In his second match for Yorkshire (v Essex at Harrogate, 1961) he took 12 for 111. He also played for Durham.

Bainbridge, Herbert William
Amateur. *b:* 29.10.1862, Gowhatti, Assam, India. *d:* 3.3.1940, Leamington, Warwickshire. Opening right-hand batsman, slow round-arm, later changed to fast, good field. *Sch* Eton. *Teams* Surrey (1883–85, 11 matches); Cambridge U (1884–86, blue all three years); Warwickshire (1894–1902, 118 matches). *Tour* Sanders to North America 1886.

Career batting
177–288–21–6878–162–25.76–7–*ct* 101
Bowling 988–31–31.87–0–0–3/21

He first appeared for Warwickshire (non-first-class) in 1886, but was unqualified and an objection by Leicestershire was upheld by MCC. From 1888 to 1902 he captained Warwickshire and in 1903 he was appointed Hon. Secretary of the County Club. He scored 1,000 runs in a season twice (best 1,162, av 34.17, in 1895).

Bainbridge, Rear-Admiral John Hugh
Amateur. *b:* 31.5.1845, Co. Cork. *d:* 10.8.1901, Frankfield, Co. Cork. *Team* MCC (1882)
Career batting
1–2–0–0–0–0.00–0 *ct* 0

Bainbridge, Philip
Cricketer. *b*: 16.4.1958, Sneyd Green, Stoke-on-Trent, Staffs. Middle order right-hand batsman, right-arm medium pace bowler, good field. *Team* Gloucestershire (1977–83, 100 matches).
Career batting
100–171–27–4320–146–30.00–5–*ct* 51
Bowling 3926–104–37.75–2–0–6/59

He hit 1,000 runs in a season three times (best 1,217, av 29.68, in 1983).

Baines, Francis Edmund
Amateur. *b:* 18.6.1864, Sheffield. *d:* 17.11.1948, Worksop, Notts. *Team* Yorkshire (1888, 1 match).
Career batting
1–1–0–0–0–0.00–0–*ct* 0

Baines, Michael Fitzroy Talbot
Amateur. *b:* 3.9.1898, Kasauli, India. Tail end batsman, right-arm medium-fast bowler. *Sch* Cheltenham. *Team* Army (1926).
Career batting
1–2–1–0–0*–0.00–0–*ct* 0
Bowling 39–0

Baines, Matthew Talbot
Amateur *b:* 19.9.1863, East Molesey, Surrey. *d:* 6.5.1925, Beckley, Sussex. Middle order right-hand batsman, fast bowler, brilliant field at point. *Sch* Harrow. *Team* Cambridge U (1883).
Career batting
8–14–1–109–29–8.38–0–*ct* 1

Baines played two of the best innings ever seen in a Freshmen's match – 104 and 48* – in 1883, both innings made without a chance, but he did little in other matches for Cambridge and was not awarded his blue. His final first-class match was for MCC in 1890.

Baines, Threlfall Werge Talbot
Amateur. *b:* 20.6.1908, Johannesburg, South Africa. Opening right-hand batsman, leg break bowler. *Teams* Cambridge U (1930); Eastern Province (1925/6 to 1926/7); Transvaal (1931/2 to 1936/7).
Career batting
20–36–1–1045–96–29.85–0–*ct* 18
Bowling 453–2–226.50–0–0–1/8

Bairamian, Robert
Amateur. *b:* 18.3.1935, Nicosia, Cyprus. Middle order right-hand batsman, off break bowler. *Sch* Dover College. *Team* Cambridge U (1957).
Career batting
2–3–1–45–24–22.50–0–*ct* 1
Bowling 6–1–6.00–0–0–1/6

Baird, Henry Hulme Chisholm
Amateur. *b:* 13.4.1878, Haverfordwest, Pembrokeshire. *d:* 22.2.1950, Sandwich, Kent. Hard hitting middle order right-hand batsman. *Sch* Cheltenham. *Teams* MCC (1910); Army (1912–13). *Tour* MCC to South America 1911/12.
Career batting
9–16–0–308–81–19.25–0–*ct* 10
Bowling 451–31–14.54–2–0–5/43

He hit 111* in 130 minutes for the Army v Navy at Lord's in 1910 (non-first-class).

Bairstow, Arthur
Professional. *b:* 14.8.1868, Bradford, Yorkshire. *d:* 7.12.1945, Bucklow, Cheshire. Tail end right-hand batsman, wicket-keeper. *Team* Yorkshire (1896–1900, 23 matches).
Career batting
25–26–12–79–12–5.64–0–*ct* 41–*st* 18

His final first-class match was for an England XI v Australians in 1902.

Bairstow, David Leslie
Cricketer. *b*: 1.9.1951, Bradford, Yorkshire. Hard hitting middle or lower order right-hand batsman, wicket-keeper, right-arm medium pace bowler. *Teams* Yorkshire (1970–83, 308 matches); Griqualand West (1976/7 to 1977/8). *Tours* England to Australia 1978/9 (no first-class matches), 1979/80, to West Indies 1980/1. *Tests* England (1979 to 1980/1, 4 matches).
Career batting
334–482–92–9498–145–24.35–4–*ct* 731–*st* 109
Bowling 208–6–34.66–0–0–3/82
Test batting
4–7–1–125–59–20.83–0–*ct* 12–*st* 1

In the match between Yorkshire and Derbyshire at Scarborough in 1981 he caught out 11 batsmen, equalling the world first-class record. He hit 1,000 runs in a season twice (best 1,102, av 38.00, in 1983).

Baiss, James Archibald
Amateur. *b:* 27.5.1909, London. Sound opening right-hand batsman, leg break bowler. *Sch* Tonbridge. *Team* Oxford U (1929).
Career batting
3–5–0–59–19–11.80–0–*ct* 4
His final first-class match was for Free Foresters in 1937.

Baiss, Reginald Sydney Habershon
Amateur. *b:* 6.3.1873, Belvedere, Kent. *d:* 2.5.1955, Tunbridge Wells, Kent. Useful right-hand batsman with strong defence, wicket-keeper. *Sch* Tonbridge. *Teams* Oxford U (1895); Kent (1895–1901, 7 matches).
Career batting
10–19–4–379–52*–25.26–0–*ct* 7

Baitup, Frederick Henry
Professional. *b:* 19.6.1896, Tunbridge Wells, Kent. Middle order batsman, change bowler. *Team* Somerset (1924, 1 match).
Career batting
1–1–0–11–11–11.00–0–*ct* 1
Bowling 8–0

Bajana, Manek Pallon
Amateur. *b:* 14.9.1886, India. *d:* 28.4.1927, Bethnal Green, London. Right-hand opening batsman, change bowler. *Team* Somerset (1912–20, 51 matches). *Tour* India to England 1911.
Career batting
55–96–1–1975–115–20.78–3–*ct* 36
Bowling 132–4–33.00–0–0–2/14
He never appeared in first-class cricket in India.

Baker, Albert
Professional. *b:* 28.11.1872, Hale, Farnham, Surrey. *d:* 17.4.1948, Farnham, Surrey. Sound defensive middle order right-hand batsman. *Teams* Surrey (1900–07, 104 matches); Ireland (1912).
Career batting
108–168–18–3863–155*–25.75–5–*ct* 40
Bowling 116–2–58.00–0–0–1/3
Easily his best season was 1905 when he hit 1,257 runs (av 31.42). After his County career, Baker was engaged in Ireland by S.H.Cochrane at Bray.

Baker, Air Marshal Sir Brian Edmund
Amateur. *b:* 31.8.1896, Hertford. *d:* 8.10.1979, Nocton Hall, Lincs. Middle order right-hand batsman. *Sch* Haileybury. *Team* RAF (1927–32).
Career batting
8–13–1–303–66–25.25–0–*ct* 5

Baker, Cyril
Amateur. *d:* 8.10.1949. Lower order right-hand batsman, right arm medium pace bowler. *Team* Northants (1906–22, 4 matches).
Career batting
4–8–1–17–7–2.42–0–*ct* 2
Bowling 198–11–18.00–0–0–3/38
Baker's career in first-class County cricket was unusual in that he played in three matches at the beginning of the 1906 season for Northants and headed the season's bowling averages, then reappeared once only – in 1922.

Baker, Charles Shaw
Professional. *b:* 5.1.1883, Moss Side, Manchester. *d:* 16.12.1976, Lelant, Cornwall. Sound middle order left-hand batsman, right-arm leg break bowler. *Team* Warwickshire (1905–20, 214 matches).
Career batting
214–355–42–9244–155*–29.53–10–*ct* 98
Bowling 1017–22–46.23–0–0–4/59
Baker hit 1,000 runs in a season on 3 occasions (best 1,242, av 33.56, in 1913). After leaving Warwickshire he appeared for Cornwall as an amateur with considerable success. He also became a well-known cartoonist and worked for some time on the *Daily Express.* He played football for Aston Villa.

Baker, Clare Valentine
Amateur. *b:* 23.11.1885, London. *d:* 7.12.1947, Betchworth, Surrey. Middle order right-hand batsman. *Sch* Harrow. *Team* Middlesex (1906–12, 31 matches).
Career batting
38–58–5–726–53–13.69–0–*ct* 19

Baker, David William
Cricketer. *b:* 26.7.1935, Hull, Yorkshire. Lower order right-hand batsman, leg break and googly bowler. *Teams* Kent (1961–63, 27 matches); Nottinghamshire (1964–65, 7 matches).
Career batting
34–37–13–101–15–4.20–0–*ct* 11
Bowling 2856–78–36.61–3–0–5/47

Baker, Edward
Professional. *b:* 9.2.1846, Plaxtol, Kent. *d:* 30.6.1913, Maidenhead, Berkshire. Tail end batsman, right-arm medium pace bowler. *Team* Kent (1875, 1 match).

Career batting
1–2–0–0–0–0.00–0–*ct* 0
Bowling 19–1–19.00–0–0–1/19

Baker, Edward Conrad
Amateur. *b:* 7.1.1892, Carmarthen. *d:* 2.4.1969, Maidenhead. Lower order right-hand batsman, right-arm fast medium bowler. *Sch* Brighton. *Teams* Cambridge U (1912–14, blue 1912 and 1914); Sussex (1912–19, 8 matches); Somerset (1921, 1 match).
Career batting
25–43–14–334–63*–11.51–0–*ct* 5
Bowling 1815–69–26.30–2–0–5/18

Baker, Edward Stanley
Amateur. *b:* 9.11.1910, Moseley, Birmingham. Tail end right-hand batsman, wicket-keeper. *Sch* K.E.S. Birmingham. *Team* Worcestershire (1933–34, 32 matches).
Career batting
32–44–19–160–21*–6.40–0–*ct* 35–*st* 5

Baker, Francis
Amateur. *b:* 5.12.1847, Cirencester, Gloucs. *d:* 15.4.1901. Fine free left-hand batsman, occasional right-arm medium pace bowler (or left-arm slow bowler in another report). *Sch* Cheltenham. *Team* Gloucestershire (1875, 1 match).
Career batting
8–15–2–199–53–15.30–0–*ct* 4
He made his first-class debut for Gentlemen of the South in 1866 when he still had a further year at Cheltenham.

Baker, Frank Adam Conyers
Amateur. *b:* 6.12.1889. *d:* 17.3.1961, Witley, Surrey. Middle order batsman. *Team* Royal Navy (1920).
Career batting
1–2–0–34–28–17.00–0–*ct* 0

Baker, George Dashwood
Amateur. *b:* 4.3.1849, Compton-Martin, Somerset. *d:* 1879, Brighton, Sussex. Middle order right-hand batsman, occasional right-arm fast bowler. *Sch* Rugby. *Team* Middlesex (1872, 1 match).
Career batting
1–2–0–5–5–2.50–0–*ct* 2
He also played for Hertfordshire.

Baker, George Robert
Professional. *b:* 18.4.1862, Malton, Yorkshire. *d:* 6.2.1938, Wing, Bucks. Sound right-hand batsman, useful right-arm medium pace bowler, good field. *Teams* Yorkshire (1884, 7 matches); Lancashire (1887–99, 228 matches).
Career batting
249–382–30–7563–186–21.48–4–*ct* 153
Bowling 3616–145–24.93–6–0–6/18
His best season was 1897 when he hit 1,444 runs (av 32.81). In all he hit 1,000 runs in three seasons, but his form was very variable and he went through long periods when he was unable to build a good innings. He was coach at Harrow for 12 years after leaving County cricket.

Baker, Harold Frank
Amateur. *b:* 4.5.1884, Walsall, Staffs. *d:* 4.5.1954, Hagley, Worcs. Lower order right-hand batsman, slow left-arm bowler. *Team* Worcestershire (1911, 2 matches).
Career batting
2–4–1–21–8*–7.00–0–*ct* 0
Bowling 66–0

Baker, Hugh Thomas
Amateur. *b:* 19.7.1906, Midleton, Co Cork. Right-hand batsman. *Team* Dublin University (1926).
Career batting
1–2–1–2–2–2.00–0–*ct* 0

Baker, Herbert Zouch
Amateur. *b:* 7.2.1880, Beckenham, Kent. *d:* 26.8.1958, Orpington, Kent. Middle order right-hand batsman. *Sch* Wellington. *Team* Kent (1903(USA)–04, 11 matches). *Tour* Kent to USA 1903.
Career batting
12–18–0–211–82–11.72–0–*ct* 6
Bowling 108–5–21.60–0–0–2/68
His final first-class match was for J.R.Mason's XI in 1913.

Baker, John
Amateur. *b:* 18.5.1933, Weston-super-Mare, Somerset. Middle order right-hand batsman, right-arm medium pace bowler. *Sch* Taunton. *Teams* Somerset (1952–54, 9 matches); Oxford U (1955).
Career batting
15–24–6–338–91*–18.77–0–*ct* 4
Bowling 424–9–47.11–0–0–2/26
His last appearance in first-class cricket was for Combined Services in 1956. He also played for Dorset.

Baker, Leslie George
Amateur. *b:* 19.5.1904, High Wycombe, Bucks. *d:* 9.8.1976, High Wycombe, Bucks. Opening right-hand batsman. *Sch* Bedford. *Team* Minor Counties (1939).

Career batting
1–1–0–6–6–6.00–0–*ct* 1
He played for Buckinghamshire.

Baker, Nigel Ernest Westby
Amateur. *b:* 9.1.1914, London. *d:* 10.3.1968, Cuckfield, Sussex. Tail end right-hand batsman, fast bowler. *Sch* Eton. *Team* Cambridge U (1934–35).
Career batting
3–3–2–19–10*–19.00–0–*ct* 3
Bowling 190–11–17.27–0–0–4/22
His County cricket was for Berkshire.

Baker, Percy Charles
Amateur. *b:* 2.5.1874, Bromley, Kent. *d:* 30.12.1939, Northwood, Middlesex. Fast scoring right-hand batsman. *Sch* Uppingham. *Team* Kent (1900–02, 41 matches).
Career batting
41–67–2–1600–130–24.61–2–*ct* 14
Though Baker failed to get into the Eleven at either Uppingham or Oxford, he batted so well for Beckenham that he obtained a place in the Kent side of 1900. His highest innings was 130 v Notts at Trent Bridge in 1900, but in the same year he also hit an excellent 89 v Yorkshire at Headingley.

Baker, Robert
Amateur. *b:* 3.7.1849, Hunmanby, Yorkshire. *d:* 21.6.1896, Scarborough, Yorkshire. Useful right-hand batsman, right-arm fast-medium bowler, slip field. *Team* Yorkshire (1874–75, 3 matches).
Career batting
3–5–1–45–22–11.25–0–*ct* 3
Bowling 43–0
He was for about 25 years the leading light in Scarborough cricket and organised the annual Festival. In a minor match, but involving good class batsmen, he once took 5 wickets with 5 balls for Scarborough.

Baker, Richard Kenneth
Cricketer. *b:* 28.4.1952, Gidea Park, Essex. Middle order right-hand batsman, wicket-keeper. *Sch* Brentwood. *Teams* Essex (1972, 1 match); Cambridge U (1973–74, blue both years).
Career batting
20–34–3–505–59*–16.29–0–*ct* 25–*st* 1

Baker, Raymond Paul
Cricketer. *b:* 9.4.1954, Carshalton, Surrey. Lower order right-hand batsman, right-arm medium pace bowler. *Team* Surrey (1973–78, 54 matches).
Career batting
54–56–30–563–91–21.65–0–*ct* 24
Bowling 2942–104–28.28–1–0–6/29
In 1977 he headed the season's batting averages – but with only three completed innings.

Baker, W.
Amateur. Lower order batsman, change bowler. *Team* Worcestershire (1920, 2 matches).
Career batting
2–4–0–24–7–6.00–0–*ct* 1
Bowling 38–1–38.00–0–0–1/38

Baker, William Beresford
Amateur. *b:* 31.10.1849. *d:* 20.2.1933, Dover, Kent. Right-hand batsman. *Team* MCC (1895).
Career batting
1–2–0–33–30–16.50–0–*ct* 0
His County cricket was for Hertfordshire.

Bakewell, Alfred Harry
Professional. *b:* 2.11.1908, Walsall, Staffs. *d:* 23.1.1983, Westbourne, Dorset. Opening right-hand batsman, useful change bowler, brilliant short-leg. *Team* Northants (1928–36, 227 matches). *Tour* MCC to India and Ceylon 1933/4. *Tests* England (1931–35, 6 matches).
Career batting
250–453–24–14570–257–33.96–31–*ct* 225
Bowling 1271–22–57.77–0–0–2/17
Test batting
6–9–0–409–107–45.44–1–*ct* 3
Bowling 8–0
Coming into the Northants team midway through the 1928 season, Bakewell was an immediate success, and from 1929 to 1936 exceeded 1,000 runs each season: 2,149 (av 46.71) in 1933 being his best. He also scored two double centuries in 1933, including 257 v Glamorgan at Swansea, the highest innings till then ever made for Northants. His career was brought to a sudden end due to a motor accident at the end of the 1936 season – his right arm being badly injured.

Balaskas, Xenophon Constantine
Amateur. *b:* 15.10.1910, Kimberley, South Africa. Useful middle order right-hand batsman, leg break and googly bowler. *Teams* Western Province (1934/5 to 1935/6); Transvaal (1936/7 to 1946/7); Griqualand West (1926/7 to 1932/3); NE Transvaal (1938/9); Border (1933/4). *Tours* South Africa to Australia and New Zealand 1931/2, to England 1935. *Tests* South Africa (1930/1 to 1938/9, 9 matches).

Career batting
75–107–13–2696–206–28.68–6–*ct* 47
Bowling 6656–276–24.11–20–9–8/60
Test batting
9–13–1–174–122*–14.50–1–*ct* 5
Bowling 806–22–36.63–1–0–5/49

Owing to an elbow injury, Balaskas missed many matches on his single visit to England, but when fit he was most effective.

Balderstone, John Christopher
Professional. *b:* 16.11.1940; Longwood, Huddersfield, Yorkshire. Opening or middle order right-hand batsman, slow left-arm bowler, gully field. *Teams* Yorkshire (1961–69, 68 matches); Leicestershire (1971–83, 260 matches). *Tour* Leicestershire to Zimbabwe 1980/1. *Tests* England (1976, 2 matches).
Career batting
331–520–53–16093–178*–34.46–26–*ct* 183
Bowling 7880–305–25.86–5–0–6/25
Test batting
2–4–0–39–35–9.75–0–*ct* 1
Bowling 80–1–80.00–0–0–1/80

He hit 1,000 runs in a season nine times (best 1,482, av 39.00, in 1982). A good soccer player, he appeared for Huddersfield Town, Carlisle United, Doncaster Rovers and Queen of the South.

Baldock, William Frederick
Amateur. *b:* 1.8.1900, Wellington, Somerset. *d:* 30.12.1941, Jabor Valley, Trengganu, Malaya. Son of W.S. (Hants). Middle order right-hand batsman. *Sch* Winchester. *Team* Somerset (1920–36, 10 matches).
Career batting
10–16–2–238–63*–17.00–0–*ct* 2

Baldock, William Stanford
Amateur. *b:* 20.1.1847, Chilworth, Hants. *d:* 30.8.1923, Wellington, Somerset. Father of W.F. (Somerset). Middle order batsman, change bowler. *Team* Hampshire (1877–82, 7 matches).
Career batting
7–13–1–155–40–12.91–0– *ct* 4
Bowling 48–2–24.00–0–0–1/10

He played in 1878 as W. Stanford.

Baldry, Dennis Oliver
Professional. *b:* 26.12.1931, Acton, Middlesex. Middle order right-hand batsman, useful off-break bowler. *Teams* Middlesex (1953–58, 49 matches); Hampshire (1959–62, 85 matches).
Career batting
139–242–19–4661–151–20.90–3–*ct* 63
Bowling 3076–83–37.06–1–0–7/76

After six seasons with Middlesex without achieving a great deal, Baldry hit 151 for Hampshire on his debut (v Glamorgan, Portsmouth, 1959) and later in the same season took 7/76 v Lancs at Old Trafford. This initial success with his adopted county however did not develop into an extended first-class career and he dropped out of first-class county cricket in 1962. His best season was in 1959 with 1,715 runs, av 29.06

Baldwin, Charles
Professional. *b:* 29.12.1864, Bury St Edmunds, Suffolk. *d:* 2.5.1947, Tylers Green, Penn, Bucks. Son of Thomas (pro for Suffolk in 1860s). Sound middle order right-hand batsman, occasional medium pace bowler, good field at point. *Team* Surrey (1892–98, 80 matches).
Career batting
80–126–12–2757–234–24.17–3–*ct* 55
Bowling 87–0

His best year was 1897 when he scored 1,211 runs (av 30.27) including an innings of 234 for Surrey v Kent at the Oval – easily the highest score of his career. After leaving Surrey he appeared in the ranks of his native county.

Baldwin, George Frederick
Professional. *b:* 3.4.1878, Northampton. *d:* 1970, Burton-on-Trent. Lower order batsman, useful bowler. *Team* Northants (1906, 1 match).
Career batting
1–1–0–6–6–6.00–0–*ct* 0
Bowling 18–0

Baldwin, Henry
Professional. *b:* 27.11.1860, Wokingham, Berkshire. *d:* 12.1.1935, Aldershot, Hants. Father of H.G. (Surrey). Hard-hitting right-hand batsman, right-arm off-break bowler. *Team* Hampshire (1877–1905, 150 matches).
Career batting
151–241–66–1873–55*–10.70–0–*ct* 54
Bowling 14383–580–24.79–41–6–8/74

Unfortunately the best ten years of his career occurred whilst Hampshire were not ranked as first-class. His best first-class season was 1895 when he took 114 wickets (av 15.80). He was the first Hampshire professional to be granted a benefit.

Baldwin, Herbert George
Professional. *b:* 16.3.1893, Hartley Wintney, Hampshire *d:* 7.3.1969, Hartley Wintney. Son of Henry (Hampshire). Middle order right-hand batsman, leg break bowler, brilliant field at cover-point. *Team* Surrey (1922–30, 32 matches).

Career batting
32–46–8–509–63*–13.39–0–*ct* 10
Bowling 321–3–107.00–0–0–2/83

After his playing career, Baldwin became a noted umpire, standing in nine Tests. He caused a sensation in 1938, when, in the opening match of the Australian tour, he no-balled McCormick 19 times in three overs.

Bale, Ernest William
Professional. *b:* 18.9.1878, Mitcham, Surrey. *d:* 6.7.1952, Carshalton, Surrey. Lower order right-hand batsman, wicket-keeper. *Teams* Surrey (1904, 1 match); Worcestershire (1908–20, 138 matches); London County (1904).
Career batting
148–233–86–1222–43–8.31–*ct* 252–*st* 90
Bowling 230–9–25.55–0–0–3/46

Bale, Frank
Professional. *b:* 7.1.1891, Leicester. *d:* 16.1.1969, Leicester. Moderate left-hand batsman, slow medium left-arm bowler, slip field. *Team* Leicestershire (1920–28, 134 matches).
Career batting
134–202–53–1426–52–9.57–0–*ct* 62
Bowling 6431–231–27.83–3–0–5/62

A most promising all-rounder, Bale never really realised his full potential.

Balfour, Leslie Melville
(from 1893, Balfour-Melville)
Amateur. *b:* 9.3.1854, Bonnington, Edinburgh. *d:* 16.7.1937, North Berwick, Scotland. Father of J.E. (Scotland). Excellent right-hand batsman, wicket-keeper. *Sch* Edinburgh Academy. *Teams* I Zingari (1888); MCC (1892); Scotland (1909–10).
Career batting
4–7–0–121–91–17.28–0–*ct* 6–*st* 1

Known as 'The W.G.Grace of Scotland', no Scottish representative eleven was complete without him for about 40 years (1874–1914). He captained Scotland in their first 'official' match with Ireland in 1909. Aside from cricket he excelled at golf, winning the Amateur Championship in 1905; he won the Scottish Lawn Tennis Championship, also the billiards title, and represented Scotland at rugby.

Balfour, Robert Drummond
Amateur. *b:* 1.3.1844, Putney, Surrey. *d:* 7.5.1915, Welwyn, Herts. Brother of Edward (Oxford U 1852–54). Steady right-hand batsman, wicket-keeper. *Sch* Westminster, Bradfield. *Team* Cambridge U (1863–66, blue all four years).
Career batting
32–59–4–685–82–12.45–0–*ct* 22–*st* 11

He played for I Zingari and MCC, playing his final first-class match for MCC in 1873.

Balfour-Melville, James Elliot
Amateur. *b:* 9.7.1882, Edinburgh. *d:* 25.9.1915, Loos, France. Son of L.M. (Scotland). Right-hand batsman, wicket-keeper. *Sch* Malvern. *Team* Scotland (1913).
Career battting
2–4–0–46–32–11.50–0–*ct* 1

He was at Oxford, but did not play in any first-class matches whilst there.

Ball, Edgar Cedric
Amateur. *b:* 11.1.1892, Richmond, Surrey. *d:* 15.5.1969, Vancouver, British Columbia, Canada. Son of E.W. (Gloucs). Middle order left-hand batsman, occasional left-arm bowler. *Sch* Clifton. *Team* Somerset (1914, 3 matches).
Career batting
3–6–0–35–20–5.83–0–*ct* 0

He also played for Devon.

Ball, Edward William
Amateur. *b:* 10.2.1859, Clifton, Gloucs. *d:* 31.7.1917, Tonbridge, Kent. Father of E.C. (Somerset). Lower order batsman. *Sch* Clifton. *Team* Gloucestershire (1880–81, 3 matches).
Career batting
3–3–0–0–0–0.00–0–*ct* 3

Ball, George Armstrong
Amateur. *b:* 27.2.1914, Barwell, Leics. Middle order right-hand batsman. *Team* Leicestershire (1933–36, 11 matches).
Career batting
11–17–2–206–44*–13.73–0–*ct* 7

Ball, Kenneth John
Professional. *b:* 16.5.1889, Northampton. *d:* 16.1.1958, Northampton. Middle order right-hand batsman, change bowler. *Team* Northants (1921, 12 matches).
Career batting
12–22–1–178–49–8.47–0–*ct* 7
Bowling 384–13–29.53–0–0–4/52

Ball, Wilfred Joseph
Professional. *b:* 1895, Thrapston, Northants. *d:* 23.7.1965, Hollowell, Northants. Tail end right-hand batsman, wicket-keeper. *Team* Northants (1924–31, 4 matches).
Career batting
4–6–2–10–8–2.50–0–*ct* 2

Ballance, Tristan George Lance
Amateur. *b:* 21.4.1916, Norwich. *d:* 4.12.1943. He was killed in action near Naples, Italy. Lower order right-hand batsman, slow left-arm bowler. *Sch* Uppingham. *Team* Oxford U (1935–37, blue 1935 and 1937).
Career batting
23–32–12–190–63–9.50–0–*ct* 18
Bowling 1875–51–36.76–2–0–5/30

He appeared for Norfolk from 1932 to 1939 with great success.

Ballantyne, David
Amateur. *b:* 31.10.1914, Peebles, Scotland. Right-hand batsman. *Sch* Merchiston. *Team* Scotland (1937).
Career batting
1–2–0–11–10–5.50–0–*ct* 0

Baloo, Babaji Palvankar
Amateur. *b:* 19.3.1876, Bombay, India. *d:* 4.7.1955, Bombay, India. Father of Y.B. Palvankar (Bombay), brother of P. Shivram, P. Ganpat and P. Vithal (Hindus). Useful lower order batsman, slow left-arm bowler. *Team* Hindus (1905/6 to 1920/1). *Tour* Indians to England 1911.
Career batting
33–58–3–753–75–13.69–0–*ct* 12
Bowling 2724–179–15.21–17–4–7/57

He was easily the best bowler of the 1911 Indians in England and in all matches on the tour took 114 wickets, av 18.86. In India he performed well for the Hindus for over ten years.

Bamber, Martin John
Cricketer. *b*: 7.1.1961, Cheam, Surrey. Middle order right-hand batsman, right-arm medium pace bowler. *Sch* Millfield. *Team* Northamptonshire (1982–83, 8 matches).
Career batting
8–16–1–418–77–27.86–0–*ct* 5

Bancroft, Claud Keith
Amateur. *b:* 30.10.1885, Bridgetown, Barbados. *d:* 12.1.1919, Toronto, Canada. Fair middle order right-hand batsman, wicket-keeper. *Team* Barbados (1904/5). *Tour* West Indians to England 1906.
Career batting
14–27–7–293–53–14.65–0–*ct* 14–*st* 6

He appeared in some trials for Cambridge but not in any first-class matches for the University.

Bancroft, John
Professional. *b:* 1879, Swansea, Glamorgan. *d:* 7.1.1942, Swansea, Glamorgan. Tail end right-hand batsman, wicket-keeper. *Team* Glamorgan (1922, 9 matches).
Career batting
9–18–3–36–5*–2.40–0–*ct* 4–*st* 3

Bancroft, William James
Professional. *b:* 2.3.1871, Swansea, Glamorgan. *d:* 3.3.1959, Swansea, Glamorgan. Opening right-hand batsman. *Teams* South Wales (1912); West of England (1910).
Career batting
2–4–0–38–16–9.50–0–*ct* 3

He played for Glamorgan from 1897 to 1914 and was perhaps the county's leading batsman of the non-first-class days. He was more famous on the rugby field, representing Wales on 33 successive occasions as full back – his local club was Swansea.

Banerjee, Sarbindu Surendrakumar
(known as Shute Nath Banerjee)
Amateur. *b:* 3.10.1913, Calcutta, India. *d:* 14.10.1980, Calcutta, India. Lower order right-hand batsman, right-arm fast-medium bowler. *Teams* Hindus (1935/6 to 1945/6); Bengal (1935/6 to 1936/7); Nawanagar (1937/8 to 1941/2); Bihar (1942/3 to 1957/8); Madhya Pradesh (1959/60). *Tours* India to England 1936, 1946, to Ceylon 1944/5; Indian Univ Occasionals to Ceylon 1935/6. Also Combined XI v Commonwealth in Ceylon 1950/1. *Test* India (1948/9, 1 match).
Career batting
138–209–29–3715–138–20.63–5–*ct* 74
Bowling 10274–385–26.68–15–2–8/25
Test batting
1–2–0–13–8–6.50–0–*ct* 0
Bowling 127–5–25.40–0–0–4/54

Although he performed well in Indian domestic cricket, Banerjee was not very successful on his two tours to England and is remembered chiefly for his 10th wicket partnership with Sarwate v Surrey at the Oval in 1946, when 249 runs were added – Banerjee hit 121. His first-class debut was for Patiala's XII in 1931/2.

Banes-Walker, Frederick Cecil
Amateur. *b:* 19.6.1888, Bridgwater, Somerset. *d:* 9.5.1915. He was killed in action near Ypres, Belgium. Aggressive right-hand batsman. *Sch* Tonbridge. *Team* Somerset (1914, 5 matches).
Career batting
5–10–1–172–40–19.11–0–*ct* 3

He played hockey for Gloucestershire.

Banfield, Arthur Ernest
Amateur. *b:* 28.1.1897, Hackney, London. *d:* 3.1.1972, Raynes Park, Surrey. Lower order

batsman, useful bowler. *Team* Essex (1921, 1 match).
Career batting
1–2–1–0–0*–0.00–0–*ct* 0
Bowling 62–2–31.00–0–0–2/62

Banham, Stanley Tattersall
Professional. *b:* 21.9.1913, Bacup, Lancs. Tail end right-hand batsman, wicket-keeper. *Team* Lancashire (1939, 1 match).
Career batting
1 match, did not bat–*ct* 1

Banister, Stephen Michael Alvin
Amateur. *b:* 7.10.1918, Llandegai, Caernarvon. Tail end right-hand batsman, right-arm off break bowler. *Sch* Eton. *Team* Cambridge U (1938–39).
Career batting
6–5–2–8–4*–2.66–0–*ct* 2
Bowling 350–5–70.00–0–0–2/73

Banks, David Andrew
Cricketer. *b:* 11.1.1961, Pensnett, Staffs. Middle order right-hand batsman, right-arm medium pace bowler. *Team* Worcestershire (1983, 7 matches).
Career batting
7–13–1–363–100–30.25–1–*ct* 3
He hit 100 and 53 on his first-class debut for Worcestershire v Oxford U at Oxford in 1983.

Banks, Percy d'Aguilar
Amateur. *b:* 9.5.1885, Bath, Somerset. *d:* 28.4.1915. He was killed in action near Ypres, Belgium. Attractive right-hand batsman. *Sch* Cheltenham. *Team* Somerset (1903–08, 7 matches).
Career batting
7–14–1–161–30–12.23–0–*ct* 1
He hit 103 for Cheltenham v Haileybury at Lord's in 1902 – an innings regarded as the best ever made by a schoolboy at Lord's. He also played with success in India and was well-known as a polo player.

Banner, George
Professional. *b:* 21.1.1864, Sutton-in-Ashfield, Notts. *d:* 20.3.1890, Sutton-in-Ashfield, Notts. Right-hand batsman, fast right-arm bowler. *Team* Nottinghamshire (1885, 1 match).
Career batting
1–1–0–5–5–5.00–0–*ct* 0
Bowling 33–2–16.50–0–0–2/33

Bannerman, Alexander Chalmers
Began as amateur, but professional for most of his first-class career. *b:* 21.3.1854, Paddington, New South Wales, Australia. *d:* 19.9.1924, Paddington, New South Wales, Australia. Brother of Charles (New South Wales and Australia). Defensive right-hand opening batsman, right-hand medium pace round-arm bowler, excellent field. *Team* New South Wales (1876/7 to 1893/4, 46 matches). *Tours* Australia to England, 1878, 1880, 1882, 1884, 1888, 1893, to North America 1878, 1893. *Tests* Australia (1878/9 to 1893, 28 matches).
Career batting
219–381–28–7816–134–22.14–5–*ct* 154
Bowling 656–22–29.81–0–0–3/12
Test batting
28–50–2–1108–94–23.08–0–*ct* 21
Bowling 163–4–40.75–0–0–3/111
He was described as the most famous of all Australian stonewall batsmen, his patience being inexhaustible. His most notable innings was of 91 for Australia v England at Sydney in 1891/2 when he was at the crease seven and a half hours and won the match for his side. He took his cricket very seriously indeed. He hit 1,000 runs twice (best 1,144, av 22.88, in 1882).

Bannerman, Charles
Professional. *b:* 23.7.1851, Woolwich, Kent. *d:* 20.8. 1930, Surry Hills, New South Wales, Australia. Brother of A.C. (New South Wales and Australia). Excellent opening right-hand batsman, fine outfield, occasional bowler. *Team* New South Wales (1870/1 to 1887/8, 23 matches). *Tour* Australia to England and North America 1878. *Tests* Australia (1876/7 to 1878/9, 3 matches).
Career batting
44–84–6–1687–165*–21.62–1–*ct* 20
Bowling 44–0
Test batting
3–6–2–239–165*–59.75–1–*ct* 0
His most noteworthy innings and his only first-class century was the first ever Test hundred; he hit 165 retired hurt v England at Melbourne in 1876/7. On his only visit to England he headed the tourists' batting averages.

Bannister, Arthur Frederick
Professional. *b:* 15.6.1874, Birmingham. *d:* 1933, Kidderminster, Worcs. Tail-end batsman, slow right-arm bowler with plenty of spin, or left-arm slow bowler in another account. *Team* Worcestershire (1900–02, 38 matches).
Career batting
38–62–16–354–44–7.69–*ct* 18
Bowling 2175–92–23.64–5–1–7/29
In his debut season of 1900, Bannister had the encouraging return of 65 wickets at a cost of 20.47, but he fell away badly in 1901 and lost his place in the County side.

Bannister, Charles Stuart
Cricketer. *b:* 22.5.1956, Redhill, Surrey. Right-hand batsman, right-arm medium pace bowler. *Sch* Caterham. *Team* Cambridge U (1975–77, blue 1976).
Career batting
17–30–2–383–50–13.67–0–*ct* 2
Bowling 813–19–42.78–1–0–5/50
He has played for Hertfordshire since 1982.

Bannister, Herbert Milburn
Amateur. *b:* 3.6.1889, Lutterworth, Leics. *d:* 18.6.1959, Hammersmith, London. Sound right-hand batsman, right-arm medium pace bowler. *Sch* Tonbridge. *Team* Leicestershire (1912–21, 11 matches).
Career batting
11–20–3–227–64–13.35–0–*ct* 4
Bowling 793–26–30.50–1–0–5/90
Business prevented him from appearing regularly in first-class cricket, but he was a stalwart of the Bank of England team for many years.

Bannister, John David
Professional. *b:* 23.8.1930, Wolverhampton, Staffs. Lower order right-hand batsman, right-arm fast medium bowler. *Team* Warwickshire (1950–68, 368 matches).
Career batting
374–456–123–3140–71–9.42–0–*ct* 168
Bowling 26258–1198–21.91–53–6–10/41
He took 100 wickets in a season on four occasions (best 137, av 20.83, in 1961). His best bowling performance was 10 for 41 for Warwickshire v Combined Services in 1959 and in 1955 he took 9 for 35 v Yorkshire at Bramall Lane.

Bannon, Bernard Douglas
Amateur. *b:* 7.12.1874, Goudhurst, Kent. *d:* 18.12.1938, Virginia Water, Surrey. Stylish right-hand opening batsman. *Sch* Tonbridge. *Teams* Oxford U (1897–98, blue 1898); Kent (1895–1900, 25 matches).
Career batting
36–60–4–1078–78–19.25–0–*ct* 10
Played for Oxford in the University Hockey match of 1897 and threw the hammer in the University Sports of 1898. Owing to his profession, the Law, he was unable to devote much time to County cricket.

Baptiste, Eldine Ashworth Elderfield
Cricketer. *b*: 12.3.1960, Liberta, Antigua. Middle order right-hand batsman, right-arm fast medium bowler, deep field. *Teams* Kent (1981–83, 41 matches); Leeward Islands (1981/2 to 1982/3).
Career batting
51–78–13–1759–136*–27.06–2–*ct* 33
Bowling 3620–128–28.28–4–0–5/37

Baqa Khan Jilani, Mohammad
Amateur. *b:* 20.7.1911, Jullundur, India. *d:* 2.7.1941, Jullundur, India. Lower order right-hand batsman, right-arm medium-fast bowler. *Teams* Northern India (1934/5 to 1938/9); Muslims (1934/5). *Tour* India to England 1936. *Test* India (1936, 1 match).
Career batting
29–53–4–896–113–18.28–1–*ct* 12
Bowling 1585–81–19.56–3–1–7/37
Test batting
1–2–1–16–12–16.00–0–*ct* 0
Bowling 55–0

Barber, Arthur Norman
Professional. *b:* 23.11.1898, West Ham, Essex. Lower order batsman, opening bowler. Team Essex (1925, 2 matches).
Career batting
2–4–0–46–31–11.50–0–*ct* 2
Bowling 76–1–76.00–0–0–1/42

Barber, Alan Theodore
Amateur. *b:* 17.6.1905, Eccleshall, Sheffield. Fine right-hand middle order or opening batsman. *Sch* Shrewsbury. *Teams* Oxford U (1927–29, blue all three years); Yorkshire (1929–30, 42 matches.)
Career batting
70–100–3–2261–119–23.30–2–*ct* 52
Bowling 0–0
Brought in to captain Yorkshire in 1930, with virtually no County cricket experience, he proved to be the best leader Yorkshire had had for some years. Unfortunately owing to his profession he had to retire from first-class cricket at the end of 1930. An all-round sportsman, he also won a blue for soccer.

Barber, Eric George
Professional. *b:* 22.7.1915, Coventry, Warwickshire. Middle order right-hand batsman. *Team* Warwickshire (1936, 2 matches).
Career batting
2–3–0–31–13–10.33–0–*ct* 2

Barber, Frederick Arthur
Professional. *b:* 13.5.1887, Ilkeston, Derbyshire. *d:* 4.6.1943, Mickleover, Derbyshire. Tail-end batsman, useful change bowler. *Team* Derbyshire (1907–20, 5 matches).
Career batting
5–10–1–30–10–3.33–0–*ct* 3
Bowling 267–9–29.66–0–0–2/19
He also played for Cumberland.

Barber, Henry William
Amateur. *b:* 5.11.1841, Bloomsbury, London. *d:* 10.7.1924, Draycott, Cheddar, Somerset. Hard hitting right-hand batsman, fast right-hand round-arm bowler. *Sch* King's School, Canterbury. *Team* Kent (1861–64, 9 matches).
Career batting
13–26–5–218–45–10.38–0–*ct* 4
Bowling 18–0
He did not appear in first-class matches whilst at Oxford U.

Barber, Horatio William
Amateur. *b:* 1843, Salford, Lancashire. *d:* 1869, Hastings, Sussex. Left-hand batsman, right-arm bowler. *Sch* Rossall. *Team* Lancashire (1866–67, 3 matches).
Career batting
5–10–0–69–20–6.90–0–*ct* 6

Barber, John Benjamin
Amateur. *b:* 1849, Chorlton, Lancashire. *d:* 1908, Camberwell, London. Middle order batsman. *Team* Lancashire (1874–76, 3 matches).
Career batting
3–6–3–39–12*–13.00–0–*ct* 2

Barber, Robert William
Amateur. *b:* 26.9.1935, Manchester. Attractive left-hand opening batsman, leg break and googly bowler. *Sch* Ruthin. *Teams* Cambridge U (1955–57, blue 1956–57); Lancashire (1954–62, 155 matches); Warwickshire (1963–69, 124 matches). *Tours* MCC to New Zealand 1960/1, to Ceylon, India and Pakistan 1961/2, to South Africa 1964/5, to Australia 1965/6; Swanton to West Indies 1960/1; Rest v Barbados 1966/7. *Tests* England (1960–68, 28 matches).
Career batting
386–651–52–17631–185–29.43–17–*ct* 210
Bowling 16176–549–29.46–12–0–7/35
Test batting
28–45–3–1495–185–35.59–1–*ct* 21
Bowling 1806–42–43.00–0–0–4/132
An outstanding schoolboy cricketer – he achieved the 'double' at Ruthin in 1953 – his initial County career with Lancashire was one surrounded in controversy and it was not until he moved to Warwickshire that his full potential was realised. The highest and best innings of his career was 185 for England v Australia at Sydney in 1965/6. He hit 1,000 runs in a season seven times, his best being 1,573 (av 31.46) in 1964. He also played for Cheshire.

Barber, Thomas David
Amateur. *b:* 18.11.1937, Carlton-in-Lindrick, Notts. Great-nephew of W.D. (Notts). Right-hand batsman, off break bowler. *Sch* Eton. *Team* Nottinghamshire (1960, 1 match).
Career batting
2–3–1–5–3–2.50–0–*ct* 2
He did not play in a first-class match for the University, whilst at Cambridge.

Barber, Wilfred
Professional. *b:* 18.4.1901, Cleckheaton, Yorkshire. *d:* 10.9.1968, Bradford, Yorkshire. Defensive middle order or opening right-hand batsman, right-arm fast medium bowler, brilliant outfield. *Team* Yorkshire (1926–47, 354 matches). *Tour* MCC to New Zealand and Australia 1935/6. *Tests* England (1935, 2 matches).
Career batting
373–526–49–16402–255–34.38–29–*ct* 183
Bowling 419–16–26.18–0–0–2/1
Test batting
2–4–0–83–44–20.75–0–*ct* 1
Bowling 0–1–0.00–0–0–1/0
He did not obtain a regular place in the Yorkshire team until 1932, after which he was a model of consistency. He hit 1,000 runs in a season on eight occasions (best 2,147, av 42.09, in 1935) – his highest innings of 255 for Yorks v Surrey at Bramall Lane came in the same year.

Barber, William
Amateur. *b:* 25.10.1920, Dalston, London. Lower order batsman, wicket-keeper. *Team* Combined Services (1946, 1 match).
Career batting
1–2–1–4–4–4.00–0–*ct* 3
He also appeared for the Army at Lord's in 1946.

Barber, William Douglas
Amateur. *b:* 17.10.1881, Lambclose, Eastwood, Notts. *d:* 26.4.1971, Ranby, Notts. Great-uncle of T.D. (Notts). Right-hand batsman, wicket-keeper. *Sch* Eton. *Team* Nottinghamshire (1904, 1 match).
Career batting
2–3–0–13–7–4.33–0–*ct* 2–*st* 1
For many years he appeared in Army matches and in 1924 made his second and final appearance in first-class cricket for the Army v Oxford U at Oxford.

Barber, William Henry
Professional. *b:* 23.7.1906, Nuneaton, Warwickshire. *d:* 14.1.1981, Coventry. Lower order right-hand batsman, right-arm fast-medium bowler. *Team* Warwickshire (1927–33, 5 matches).

Career batting
5–6–1–71–23–14.20–0–*ct* 0
Bowling 253–7–36.14–0–0–3/81

He also played for Cheshire.

Barbery, Alfred Edward
Professional. *b:* 13.10.1884, Marylebone, London. *d:* 23.5.1973, Solihull, Warwickshire. Tail end right-hand batsman, right-arm fast-medium bowler. *Team* Warwickshire (1906–07, 2 matches).
Career batting
2–3–0–13–6–4.33–0–*ct* 0
Bowling 245–3–81.66–0–0–2/64

Barbour, Robert Roy Pitty
Amateur. *b:* 29.3.1899, Ashfield, New South Wales, Australia. Brother of E.P. (New South Wales). Opening right-hand batsman. *Teams* Queensland (1919/20, 2 matches); Oxford U (1922–23).
Career batting
6–11–0–172–41–15.63–0–*ct* 2

Barchard, Harry George
Amateur. *b:* June 1860, Eccles, Manchester. *d:* 1935, Axminster, Devon. Middle order batsman. *Sch* Uppingham. *Team* Lancashire (1888, 1 match).
Career batting
1–2–0–45–40–22.50–0–*ct* 1

Barclay, John Robert Troutbeck
Cricketer. *b*: 22.1.1954, Bonn, West Germany. Opening or middle order right-hand batsman, off break bowler, good slip field. *Sch* Eton. *Teams* Sussex (1970–83, 215 matches); Orange Free State (1978/9). *Tours* MCC to West Africa 1975/6, to Bangladesh 1976/7 (not first-class).
Career batting
224–379–35–8623–119–25.06–9–*ct* 182
Bowling 7935–257–30.87–7–1–6/61

He hit 1,000 in a season four times (best 1,093, av 32.14, in 1979). He was appointed captain of Sussex in 1981.

Barcroft, Peter
Professional. *b:* 14.8.1929, Bacup, Lancashire. *d:* 26.8.1977, Bacup, Lancashire. Middle order right-hand batsman, leg break bowler. *Team* Lancashire (1956, 3 matches).
Career batting
3–3–0–40–29–13.33–0–*ct* 1

Bardsley, Robert Vickers
Amateur. *b:* 28.6.1890, Manchester. *d:* 26.7.1952, Coldwaltham, Pulborough, Sussex. Useful middle order right-hand batsman, leg break bowler. *Sch* Shrewsbury. *Teams* Oxford U (1910–13, blue 1911, 1912, 1913); Lancashire (1910–20, 7 matches).
Career batting
31–52–0–964–72–18.53–0–*ct* 18
Bowling 344–12–28.66–0–0–3/15

He represented Oxford at billiards and golf. He was Governor of the Blue Nile Province, Sudan, 1928–32. His final first-class match was for Free Foresters in 1922.

Bardsley, Warren
Amateur. *b:* 7.12.1882, Nevertire, Warren, New South Wales, Australia. *d:* 20.1.1954, Collaroy, New South Wales, Australia. Brother of Raymond (New South Wales). Stylish left-hand opening batsman. *Team* New South Wales (1903/4 to 1925/6, 83 matches). *Tours* Australia to England 1909, 1912, 1921, 1926, to South Africa 1921/2, to New Zealand 1909/10, to North America 1913; New South Wales to New Zealand 1923/4. *Tests* Australia (1909 to 1926, 41 matches).
Career batting
250–376–35–17025–264–49.92–53–*ct* 112
Bowling 41–0
Test batting
41–66–5–2469–193*–40.47–6–*ct 12*

Regarded as one of the most correct of batsmen, he was exceedingly successful on all his visits to England, hitting over 2,000 runs on three of the four trips (best 2,365, av 51.41, in 1912). His highest score was 264 for Australian XI v Rest at Melbourne in 1908/9. He hit six other double centuries. He was the first batsman to score a hundred in each innings of a Test, a feat he accomplished at the Oval in 1909. In 1926 he hit 193 in the Lord's Test – the highest score made up to that date in a Lord's Test. His final first-class match was for Australian XI in 1926/7.

Bardswell, Gerald Roscoe
Amateur. *b:* 7.12.1873, Woolton, Liverpool. *d:* 29.12.1906, New Orleans, USA. Useful middle order right-hand batsman, right-arm medium pace bowler, brilliant slip field. *Sch* Uppingham. *Teams* Oxford U (1894–97, blue 1894, 1896, 1897); Lancashire (1894–1902, 21 matches). *Tours* Lord Hawke to North America 1894, to West Indies 1896/7.
Career batting
59–92–13–1585–97–20.06–0–*ct* 104
Bowling 1618–63–25.68–4–0–6/36

He died unexpectedly at the age of 33 following an operation. He was on both the Lancashire and MCC Committees. Owing to business, Bardswell was unable to play regularly in County cricket.

Barford, Michael Thomas
Cricketer. *b:* 7.6.1950, Eastbourne, Sussex. Opening right-hand batsman, right-arm slow bowler. *Sch* Eastbourne. *Team* Cambridge U (1970–71, blue both years).
Career batting
15–27–4–606–95–26.34–0–*ct* 7

Baring, Amyas Evelyn Giles
Amateur. *b:* 21.1.1910, Roehampton, London. Tail end right-hand batsman, fast right-arm bowler. *Sch* Gresham's Holt. *Teams* Cambridge U (1930–31); Hampshire (1930–39, 62 matches).
Career batting
70–103–27–664–46–8.73–0–*ct* 29
Bowling 5607–197–28.46–10–2–9/26

Making a promising debut, Baring was unfortunate to dislocate both knees in a motor accident in 1931, which prevented him appearing at all in 1932, though he was able to play occasionally in later seasons. He was easily the fastest Hampshire bowler of his time. His final first-class match was for MCC in 1946. His best bowling was 9/26 for Hampshire v Essex at Colchester in 1931.

Barkass-Williamson, J. G.
(*see under* Williamson, J. G. B.)

Barker, Andrew Hunter
Cricketer. *b:* 7.8.1945, Salisbury, Wilts. Middle order left-hand batsman, left-arm spin bowler. *Sch* Charterhouse. *Team* Oxford U (1964–67, blue 1964, 1965 and 1967).
Career batting
44–67–8–864–94–14.64–0–*ct* 24
Bowling 2906–70–41.51–2–0–5/42

His County cricket was for Wiltshire.

Barker, Antony Royston Paul
Cricketer. *b:* 30.5.1947, May Bank, Newcastle-under-Lyme, Staffs. Middle order right-hand batsman, good close field. *Team* Worcestershire (1967–69, 27 matches).
Career batting
27–43–3–544–67–13.60–0–*ct* 12

He also played for Staffordshire.

Barker, Gordon
Professional. *b:* 6.7.1931, Bramley, Leeds, Yorkshire. Opening right-hand batsman, occasional right-arm medium pace bowler, fine field. *Team* Essex (1954–71, 444 matches).
Career batting
451–809–46–22288–181*–29.21–30–*ct* 236
Bowling 200–5–40.00–0–0–2/34

He scored a century on his first-class debut (Essex v Canadians 1954) and hit 1,000 runs in 15 seasons (best 1,741, av 36.27, in 1960). He played soccer for Southend United.

Barker, J.
Professional. *Team* North (1880).
Career batting
1–2–1–19–16–19.00–0–*ct* 0

Barker, Kenneth Edgar Mylne
Amateur. *b:* 27.10.1877, Godstone, Surrey. *d:* 6.8.1938, Blakeney, Norfolk. Sound middle order right-hand batsman, right-arm fast medium bowler. *Sch* Uppingham. *Teams* Cambridge U (1899); Surrey (1899–03, 6 matches).
Career batting
10–14–0–203–52–14.50–0–*ct* 2
Bowling 31–0

Barker made his first-class debut for MCC in 1898.

Barker, Montague Merton
Amateur. *b:* 1867. *d:* 12.1.1954, Epsom Downs, Surrey. Attacking middle order right-hand batsman, occasional bowler, excellent cover field. *Sch* Radley. *Team* MCC (1895–96). *Tour* Lucas to West Indies 1894/5.
Career batting
10–15–1–106–30–7.57–0–*ct* 11
Bowling 7–0

A brilliant hockey player, he captained England in 1898.

Barker, Maurice Percy
Amateur. *b:* 4.2.1917, Leamington Spa, Warwickshire. Lower order right-hand batsman, right-arm fast medium bowler. *Team* Warwickshire (1946, 5 matches).
Career batting
5–9–2–55–17–7.85–0–*ct* 1
Bowling 378–16–23.62–1–0–7/68

His one day of triumph in County cricket was at the expense of Yorkshire, when at Edgbaston in 1946 he took 7 for 68.

Barker, Philip David
Cricketer. *b:* 22.9.1951, Edmonton, Middlesex. Right-hand batsman, left-arm medium or slow bowler. *Sch* Latymer G.S. *Team* Oxford U (1974).
Career batting
1–2–0–15–14–7.50–0–*ct* 0

He won a blue for hockey 1972/3 and 1973/4. He played both hockey and cricket for Suffolk.

Barker, Thomas
Professional. *b:* 15.11.1798, Carlton, Notts. *d:* 2.3.1877, Nottingham. Good right-hand

batsman, fast under-arm, then fast round-arm bowler. *Teams* Nottinghamshire (1826–45); Yorkshire (1836).
Career batting
72–132–12–1269–58–10.57–0–*ct* 36
Bowling 266–18+191–14.77–15–3–7/?
In 1843, whilst travelling with the Notts team to Southampton to play Hampshire, he was involved in an accident, being thrown out of a horse-drawn cab in London and breaking a leg. This virtually ended his career.

Barker, W.
Amateur. Tail end right-hand batsman, left-arm fast bowler. *Team* Surrey (1882, 1 match).
Career batting
1–2–0–1–1–1.00–0–*ct* 0
Bowling 40–0

Barkham, Frederick
Amateur. *b:* 26.10.1905, Scarborough, Yorkshire. Right-hand batsman, right arm medium pace bowler. *Team* Scotland (1948–49).
Career batting
2–4–1–7–3*–2.33–0–*ct* 0

Barley, Jack Charles
Amateur. *b:* 4.12.1887, Eton, Bucks. *d: circa* 1960, Surfers Paradise, Queensland, Australia. Fair batsman, wicket-keeper. *Sch* Tonbridge. *Teams* Sussex (1908, 1 match); Oxford U (1909); Worcestershire (1909, 1 match).
Career batting
4–7–2–12–8–2.40–0–*ct* 4–*st* 1

Barling, Henry Thomas
(known as Thomas Henry)
Professional. *b:* 1.9.1906, Kensington, London. Forcing middle order right-hand batsman. *Team* Surrey (1927–48, 389 matches).
Career batting
391–609–54–19209–269–34.61–34–*ct* 171
Bowling 550–7–78.57–0–0–3/46
His best season was 1946 when he hit 2,014 runs (av 43.78). In all he exceeded 1,000 runs in a season nine times. His two double centuries were both for Surrey: 269 v Hants (Southampton) 1933 and 233* v Notts (Oval) 1946. A good soccer player, he represented Surrey.

Barlow, Alfred
Professional. *b:* 31.8.1915, Little Lever, Lancs. *d:* 9.5.1983, Middleton, Lancs. Useful right-hand batsman, wicket-keeper. *Team* Lancashire (1947–51, 74 matches). *Tour* Commonwealth to Ceylon and India 1950/1.
Career batting
85–100–25–863–44–11.50–0–*ct* 116–*st* 52
Bowling 0–0

Barlow, Charles Sydney
Amateur. *b:* 10.5.1905, Durban, South Africa. *d:* 1.6.1979, Sotto Grande, Spain. Forcing right-hand batsman, steady right-arm medium fast bowler, brilliant field. *Sch* Clifton. *Team* Somerset (1925–26, 2 matches).
Career batting
2–4–0–24–23–6.00–0–*ct* 1
Bowling 120–2–60.00–0–0–2/98

Barlow, Edwin Alan
Amateur. *b:* 24.2.1912, Ashton-under-Lyne, Lancs. *d:* 27.6.1980, Gretton, Gloucs. Useful lower order right-hand batsman, slow-medium off break bowler. *Sch* Shrewsbury. *Teams* Oxford U (1932–34, blue all three years); Lancashire (1932, 7 matches).
Career batting
36–53–11–582–46–13.85–0–*ct* 21
Bowling 2793–102–27.38–4–0–6/44
He also played for Denbighshire.

Barlow, Edgar John
Professional. *b:* 12.8.1940, Pretoria, South Africa. Sound opening right-hand batsman, right-arm medium pace bowler, excellent slip field. *Teams* Transvaal (1959/60 to 1961/2); Eastern Province (1964/5 to 1965/6); Western Province (1968/9 to 1980/1); Derbyshire (1976–78, 60 matches); Boland (1981/2 to 1982/3). *Tours* South Africa to Australia and New Zealand 1963/4, to England 1965; Rest of the World to England 1970. *Tests* South Africa (1961/2 to 1969/70, 30 matches).
Career batting
283–493–28–18212–217–39.16–43–*ct* 335
Bowling 13785–571–24.14–16–2–7/24
Test batting
30–57–2–2516–201–45.74–6–*ct* 35
Bowling 1362–40–34.05–1–0–5/85
On the 1965 tour to England he hit 971 runs, av 38.84, and played in all three Tests. In England he hit 1,000 runs in a season twice (best 1,162, av 29.05, in 1976). His highest score in England was 217 for Derbyshire v Surrey at Ilkeston on 1976. He captained Derbyshire from midway through 1976 to the close of the 1978 season. For the Rest of the World v England at Headingley in 1970 he took 4 wickets in 5 balls.

Barlow, Graham Derek
Cricketer. *b*: 26.3.1950, Folkestone, Kent. Determined opening or middle order left-hand batsman, right-arm medium pace bowler, excel-

lent cover field. *Team* Middlesex (1969–83, 195 matches). *Tour* MCC to India, Sri Lanka and Australia 1976/7. *Tests* England (1976/7 to 1977, 3 matches).
Career batting
207–330–52–9947–177–35.78–19–*ct* 119
Bowling 54–3–18.00–0–0–1/6
Test batting
3–5–1–17–7*–4.25–0–*ct* 0

He hit 1,000 runs in a season six times (best 1,545, av 48.28, in 1983).

Barlow, Keith
Amateur. *b:* 27.8.1890, Kensington, London. *d:* 5.4.1930, Kensington, London. Middle order right-hand batsman. *Team* Kent (1910, 2 matches).
Career batting
2–3–0–11–6–3.66–0–*ct* 1

Barlow, Micah Yates
Amateur. *b:* 6.2.1873, Bury, Lancs. *d:* 13.1.1936, Grange-over-Sands, Lancashire. Middle order batsman, good field at cover. *Sch* Harrow. *Team* Oxford U (1894).
Career batting
1–2–0–9–6–4.50–0–*ct* 0

Barlow, Richard Gorton
Professional. *b:* 28.5.1851, Barrow Bridge, Bolton, Lancs. *d:* 31.7.1919, Blackpool, Lancs. Defensive opening right-hand batsman, left-arm medium pace bowler, excellent field. *Team* Lancashire (1871–91, 249 matches). *Tours* Shaw and Shrewsbury to Australia 1881/2, 1886/7; Bligh to Australia 1882/3. *Tests* England (1881/2 to 1886/7, 17 matches).
Career batting
351–608–64–11217–117–20.61–4–*ct* 266
Bowling 13797–951–14.50–66–14–9/39
Test batting
17–30–4–591–62–22.73–0–*ct* 14
Bowling 767–34–22.55–3–0–7/40

Runs were always at a premium when Barlow was playing – the epitome of the 'stonewaller', the accurate bowler and brilliant field, he served Lancashire well for over 20 years.

As a batsman he concentrated on defending his wicket; it was reckoned that his opening partner, Hornby, made a 100 runs for every 10 that Barlow scored. On two occasions, Lancs v Sussex at Old Trafford in 1876, and v Notts at Trent Bridge in 1882, he batted two and a half hours for 5 runs and in the latter innings spent 80 minutes without scoring. In first-class matches he carried his bat through a completed innings 11 times and in all on 51 occasions. Although he never scored a Test century, his batting materially assisted in the winning of two Tests – at Lord's in 1884 and at Old Trafford in 1886. He hit 1,000 runs in a season once (1,138, av 27.09, in 1882) and took 100 wickets three times (best 130, av 13.18, in 1884). His best bowling was 9/39 for Lancashire v Sussex at Old Trafford in 1886.

The best performance of his career was for the North against the Australians in 1884 at Trent Bridge: he hit a century on a wicket on which Spofforth claimed the entire side would not make 60, and Barlow also took ten wickets for 48 in the match.

His bowling was rarely off a length and in the Lancashire v Sussex match at Old Trafford in 1885 he bowled for an hour conceding just a single.

Physically he kept himself very fit and played football for 12 years, keeping goal for Lancashire. In addition he won numerous awards as a sprint runner.

In contrast to his dour cricket, Barlow was the most amiable of men. He claimed that no one could possibly have enjoyed a career in first-class cricket as much as he had done.

Barmby, Francis James
Amateur. *b:* 21.12.1863, Durham. *d:* 30.9.1936, Oxford. Stylish middle order right-hand batsman, useful right-arm medium pace bowler, good slip field. *Sch* Charterhouse. *Team* Oxford U (1885).
Career batting
1–2–0–6–6–3.00–0–*ct* 1

He was awarded his soccer blue in 1886. His County cricket was for Berkshire.

Barnard, Francis Herbert
Amateur. *b:* 6.5.1902, St. Lucia, West Indies. Hard hitting right-hand batsman, right-arm medium pace bowler. *Sch* Charterhouse. *Team* Oxford U (1922–24, blue 1922 and 1924).
Career batting
23–37–1–571–61–15.86–0–*ct* 19
Bowling 766–28–27.14–0–0–3/17

Barnard, Henry Michael
Professional. *b:* 18.7.1933, Portsmouth, Hampshire. Middle order right-hand batsman, occasional right-arm medium pace bowler. *Sch* Portsmouth G.S. *Team* Hampshire (1952–66, 276 matches).
Career batting
276–463–41–9314–128*–22.07–6–*ct* 313
Bowling 563–16–35.18–0–0–3/35

His best year was 1962 when he reached 1,000 runs for the only time in his career (1,114, av 27.17). He played soccer for Portsmouth.

Barnardo, Freeman Frederick Thomas
Amateur. *b:* 16.5.1918, Bombay, India. *d:* 25.10.1942, ten miles west of El Alamein, Egypt. Middle order right-hand batsman. *Sch* Eton. *Teams* Middlesex (1939, 1 match); Cambridge U (1939).
Career batting
2–3–0–75–75–25.00–0–*ct* 0

Barnato, Joel Woolf
Amateur. *b:* 27.9.1895, Westminster, London. *d:* 27.7.1948, Marylebone, London. Tail end right-hand batsman, wicket-keeper. *Sch* Charterhouse. *Team* Surrey (1928–30, 6 matches).
Career batting
6–8–1–23–7–3.28–0–*ct* 19–*st* 1

He was best known as a long distance motor racing driver and was the son of the diamond merchant, Barney Barnato.

Barnby, Arthur Charles
Amateur. *b:* 10.9.1881, London. *d:* 30.10.1937, Rochester Airport, Kent. Lower order right-hand batsman, wicket-keeper. *Sch* Westminster. *Team* Royal Navy (1913).
Career batting
1–2–1–1–1*–1.00–0–*ct* 0

Barne, Rev George Dunsford
Amateur. *b:* 6.5.1879. *d:* 18.6.1954, Hammersmith, London. *Sch* Clifton. *Team* Somerset (1904, 1 match).
Career batting
1–2–1–10–9*–10.00–0–*ct* 0

Barnes, Alan Sedgwick
Amateur. *b:* 9.10.1850, West Derby, Liverpool. *d:* 17.5.1915, Twyford Abbey, Willesden, Middlesex. Right-hand batsman. *Team* Derbyshire (1878, 3 matches).
Career batting
13–20–2–107–16–5.93–0–*ct* 4

He was at Cambridge, but not in the Eleven. His first-class debut was for MCC in 1877 and his final first-class match was for MCC in 1879.

Barnes, Frederic Barrie
Amateur. *b:* 4.5.1923, South Africa. Lower order left-hand batsman, wicket-keeper. *Team* Cambridge U (1948).
Career batting
2–2–0–61–39–30.50–0–*ct* 3

Barnes, George Corbett
Amateur. *b:* 9.3.1847, Umballa, India. *Sch* Brighton. *Team* Gentlemen of Kent (1866).
Career batting
1–1–0–3–3–3.00–0–*ct* 1

Barnes, Henry Marshall
Amateur. *b:* 27.6.1869, Newbridge, Co. Kildare, Ireland. *d:* 8.6.1946, Ipswich Suffolk. Middle order batsman. *Sch* Marlborough. *Team* MCC (1907).
Career batting
1–1–1–3–3*–no av–0–*ct* 0

Barnes, John Hamilton
Amateur. *b:* 14.11.1916, Armagh, Ireland. *d:* 22.4.1943, Kneesall, Notts. Brother of R.J. Right-hand batsman, right-arm fast bowler. *Team* Ireland (1937).
Career batting
1–2–0–0–0–0.00–0–*ct* 0
Bowling 7–0

Barnes, John Reginald
Amateur. *b:* 18.5.1897, Ormskirk, Lancs. *d:* 22.7.1945, Grange-over-Sands, Lancs. Stylish right-hand batsman, occasional leg break bowler, good field. *Sch* Marlborough. *Team* Lancashire (1919–30, 89 matches).
Career batting
94–145–23–3643–133–29.86–4–*ct* 40
Bowling 53–0

Barnes scored heavily in Lancashire club cricket, but business (he was a Liverpool cotton merchant) limited his first-class appearances. His final first-class match was for MCC in 1931.

Barnes, James William
Professional. *b:* 14.8.1886, Sutton-in-Ashfield, Notts. *d:* 9.9.1963, Mansfield, Notts. Son of William (Notts and England), nephew of Thomas (Notts). Lower order batsman, right-arm medium pace bowler. *Team* Nottinghamshire (1908–10, 3 matches).
Career batting
3–5–0–19–12–3.80–0–*ct* 0
Bowling 105–2–52.50–0–0–1/30

Barnes, Hon Ronald Gorell
(succeeded as 2nd Baron Gorell in 1917)
Amateur. *b:* 16.4.1884, Kensington, London. *d:* 2.5.1963, Burpham, Sussex. Lower order right-hand batsman, left-arm medium pace bowler. *Sch* Winchester and Harrow. *Team* Oxford U (1906–07, blue both years).
Career batting
19–33–2–431–77–13.90–0–*ct* 17
Bowling 1127–43–26.20–1–0–5/48

His final first-class match was for MCC in 1920, and his County cricket for Suffolk.

Barnes, Rev Robert James
Amateur. *b:* 25.3.1911, Armagh, Ireland. Brother of J.H. Left-hand batsman, slow left-arm bowler. *Team* Ireland (1930–47).
Career batting
8–15–1–199–48–14.21–0–*ct* 7
Bowling 99–9–11.00–0–0–4/18
He was an Irish rugby international.

Barnes, Sydney Francis
Professional. *b:* 19.4.1873, Smethwick, Staffordshire. *d:* 26.12.1967, Chadsmoor, Staffordshire. Useful right-hand batsman, right-arm fast-medium to slow-medium bowler. *Teams* Warwickshire (1894–96, 4 matches); Lancashire (1899–1903, 46 matches); Wales (1927–30). *Tours* MacLaren to Australia 1901/2; MCC to Australia 1907/8, 1911/2, to South Africa 1913/4. *Tests* England (1901/02 to 1913/4, 27 matches).
Career batting
133–173–50–1573–93–12.78–0–*ct* 72
Bowling 12289–719–17.09–68–18–9/103
Test batting
27–39–9–242–38*–8.06–0–*ct* 12
Bowling 3106–189–16.43–24–7–9/103
Regarded by his contemporary players as the greatest of bowlers, Barnes was not only a master of length and of deception in flight, but also had the knack of making the ball turn either to the off or the leg. He could alter his bowling to suit all types of wicket and few if any batsmen were happy against him.
A rather gaunt, cold character, he remained aloof from the humdrum world of first-class county cricket. Twice he tried it – with Warwickshire, then Lancashire – but soon rejected it as too irksome. Those in authority at Lord's were very wary of him and though his career spanned over 40 years and for most of that time he was taking wickets at minimal cost – he captured all ten wickets in an innings seven times – his name is to be found in only ten Test Matches played in England.
MacLaren really introduced him to the public at large when the Lancashire amateur picked him for the 1901/2 tour to Australia. His visit was only a partial success due to injury, and it was not until the tours of 1911/2 to Australia and 1913/4 to South Africa that he demonstrated his art to its full. On the latter tour, with only four Tests, he took 49 wickets, whilst on the former he took 34. He took 100 wickets in a season once: 131 av 17.85, in 1903 and his best bowling was 9/103 for England v South Africa at Johannesburg in 1913/14.
After the First World War Barnes confined himself mainly to League cricket and Minor Counties Championship matches with Staffordshire – at the age of 55 he took 76 wickets (av 8.21) for his native County. According to his biography he took 6,229 wickets (av 8.33) in competitive matches during his career.

Barnes, Sidney George
Amateur. *b:* 5.6.1916, Charters Towers, Queensland, Australia. *d:* 16.12.1973, Collaroy, New South Wales, Australia. Excellent right-hand opening batsman, leg break bowler. *Team* New South Wales (1936/7 to 1952/3, 56 matches). *Tours* Australia to England 1938, 1948, to New Zealand 1945/6. *Tests* Australia (1938 to 1948, 13 matches).
Career batting
110–164–10–8333–234–54.11–26–*ct* 80–*st* 4
Bowling 1836–57–32.21–0–0–3/0
Test batting
13–19–2–1072–234–63.05–3–*ct* 14
Bowling 218–4–54.50–0–0–2/25
He was unfortunate to fracture a wrist on his 1938 visit to England and thereby miss the first half of the tour; in 1948 on his second visit, however, he was a great success, averaging 82.25 in the Tests and hitting a century in the Lord's Test. In the 1946/7 series in Australia he made 234 at Sydney, creating a record 405 fifth wicket stand with Bradman. He hit 1,354 runs, av 56.81, in 1948. After 1948 he was increasingly at loggerheads with the Australian authorities and wrote many caustic criticisms in the press, which ended his first-class career. In 1973 he took his own life.

Barnes, Thomas
Professional. *b:* 11.5.1849, Sutton-in-Ashfield, Notts. *d:* 22.9.1873, Sutton-in-Ashfield, Notts. Brother of William (Notts and England), uncle of J. W. (Notts). Right-hand batsman, right-arm medium pace bowler. *Team* Nottinghamshire (1872, 5 matches).
Career batting
6–8–0–70–33–8.75–0–*ct* 2
Bowling 23–2–11.50–0–0–2/23
His first-class debut was in 1870 for R. Daft's XI v U.N.E.E. He died of typhoid aged 24.

Barnes, Terry Peter
Professional. *b:* 13.11.1933, Coventry, Warwickshire. Lower order right-hand batsman, wicket-keeper. *Team* Warwickshire (1956, 1 match).
Career batting
1–1–0–7–7–7.00–0–*ct* 1
He played soccer for Coventry.

Barnes, William
Professional. *b:* 27.5.1852, Sutton-in-Ashfield, Notts. *d:* 24.3.1899, Mansfield Woodhouse, Notts. Brother of Thomas (Notts); father of J.W. (Notts). Middle order right-hand batsman, right-arm fast medium bowler. *Team* Nottinghamshire (1875–94, 257 matches). *Tours* Daft to North America 1879 (not first-class); Bligh to Australia 1882/3; Shaw and Shrewsbury to Australia 1884/5 and 1886/7. *Tests* England (1880–90, 21 matches.).
Career batting
459–725–60–15425–160–23.19–21–*ct* 342–*st* 3
Bowling 15448–903–17.10–45–10–8/64
Test batting
21–33–2–725–134–23.38–1–*ct* 19
Bowling 793–51–15.54–3–0–6/28

A regular member of the England team during the 1880s, Barnes was the leading professional all-rounder of his day. His greatest triumphs occurred on the second of his three visits to Australia, when he finished the tour at the head of both batting and bowling tables – his batting on that tour included a brilliant 134 in the first Test on a tricky wicket at Adelaide. In the second Test he took 6 for 31 in Australia's second innings to enable England to win by ten wickets. The third Test was the scene of his refusal to bowl when asked to do so by the England captain and in fact his rather rumbustious character caused him more trouble on his third visit to Australia for he got involved in a fracas with one of the Australian players and so injured his hand that he missed many of the matches.

In England he exceeded 1,000 runs in a season five times, his best being 1,308, av 27.82, in 1883, but the nearest he got to 100 wickets was 97 in both 1885 and 1888. He was at loggerheads with the Notts Committee on several occasions and due to this was omitted from the County side two or three years earlier than might otherwise have been the case.

Barnett, Benjamin Arthur, AM
Amateur. *b:* 23.3.1908, Auburn, Victoria, Australia. *d:* 29.6.1979, Newcastle, New South Wales, Australia. Middle order left-hand batsman, occasional slow bowler, wicket-keeper. *Team* Victoria (1929/30 to 1946/7, 73 matches). *Tours* Australia to England 1934, 1938, to South Africa 1935/6; Commonwealth to India 1953/4. *Tests* Australia (1938, 4 matches).
Career batting
173–243–42–5531–131–27.51–4–*ct* 216–*st* 142
Bowling 20–1–20.00–0–0–1/3
Test batting
4–8–1–195–57–27.85–0–*ct* 3–*st* 2

After a relatively successful career in first-class and Test cricket, Barnett moved to London in 1949 and appeared for Buckinghamshire from 1951 to 1964. During this time he took part in a number of first-class matches, usually end of season festival games, and his last first-class game was in 1961 for Commonwealth XI in England. He was an excellent Australian Rules footballer and represented Victoria.

Barnett, Charles John
Amateur on debut but turned professional in 1929. *b:* 3.7.1910, Cheltenham, Gloucs. Son of C.S. (Gloucs), nephew of E.P. (Gloucs) and P.P. (Gloucs). Excellent opening or middle order right-hand batsman, good right-arm medium pace bowler, fine outfield. *Sch* Wycliffe. *Teams* Gloucestershire (1927–48, 424 matches). *Tours* MCC to Ceylon and India 1933/4, to Australia and New Zealand 1936/7; Commonwealth to India 1953/4. *Tests* England (1933–48, 20 matches).
Career batting
498–821–45–25389–259–32.71–48–*ct* 319
Bowling 12207–394–30.98–12–2–6/17
Test batting
20–35–4–1098–129–35.41–2–*ct* 14
Bowling 93–0

For the first few years of his career Barnett was a hard-hitting middle order batsman, but in 1932 he began opening the innings for Gloucestershire and became much more consistent. He reached 1,000 runs in a season twelve times, including over 2,000 on four occasions, his best being 2,489 (av 40.14) in 1937. He also hit four double centuries – highest 259 for MCC v Queensland (Brisbane) 1936/7. His benefit realised £4,164 in 1947, a Gloucestershire record at that time. His last first-class match in England was for the Commonwealth XI in 1952.

Barnett, Charles Sherborne
Amateur. *b:* 24.2.1884, Cheltenham, Gloucs. *d:* 20.11.1962, Gloucester. Brother of E.P. (Gloucs) and P.P. (Gloucs), father of C.J. (Gloucs and England). Right-hand opening batsman. *Sch* Wycliffe. *Team* Gloucestershire (1904–26, 107 matches).
Career batting
107–191–18–3690–157–21.32–2–*ct* 50
Bowling 66–0

His best season was 1921 when he hit two centuries, but was unable to play regularly for the County.

Barnett, E.E.
Amateur. Middle order batsman. *Team* MCC (1908).
Career batting
1–2–0–71–70–35.50–0–*ct* 1

Barnett, Edgar Playle
Amateur. *b:* 22.3.1885, Cheltenham, Gloucs. *d:* 20.1.1922, Cheltenham. Brother of C.S. (Gloucs) and P.P. (Gloucs), uncle of C.J. (Gloucs and England). Good right-hand batsman. *Sch* Wycliffe. *Team* Gloucestershire (1903–21, 64 matches).
Career batting
64–119–8–1925–95–17.34–0–*ct* 58

Barnett, Kim John
Cricketer. *b:* 17.7.1960, Stoke-on-Trent, Staffs. Middle order right-hand batsman, leg break bowler, cover field. *Teams* Derbyshire (1979–83, 98 matches); Boland (1982/3). *Tour* Robins to New Zealand 1979/80.
Career batting
106–158–19–4154–121–29.88–5–*ct* 59
Bowling 1365–18–75.83–0–0–4/76
He hit 1,423 runs, av 38.45, in 1983. He captained Derbyshire in 1983.

Barnett, Percival Playle
Amateur. *b:* 1889, Cheltenham. *d:* 1966, Westmorland. Brother of C.S. (Gloucs) and E.P. (Gloucs), uncle of C.J. (Gloucs and England). Middle order batsman. *Sch* Wycliffe. *Team* Gloucestershire (1908–09, 4 matches).
Career batting
4–7–0–36–16–5.14–0–*ct* 2

Barnfather, James David
Professional. *b:* 22.7.1896, Leicester. *d:* 21.8.1957, Grays, Thurrock, Essex. Lower order right-hand batsman, right-arm fast medium bowler. *Team* Essex (1924, 5 matches).
Career batting
5–5–3–50–28*–25.00–0–*ct* 1
Bowling 355–13–27.30–1–0–6/32

Barnie-Adshead, W.E.
(*see under* Adshead, W.E.)

Barnsdale, John Davison
Amateur. *b:* 24.5.1878, Mapperley Park, Nottingham. *d:* 5.8.1960, Frensham, Surrey. Lower order right-hand batsman, wicket-keeper. *Sch* Nottingham High School and Sedbergh. *Team* Nottinghamshire (1905, 1 match).
Career batting
1–2–0–10–10–5.00–0–*ct* 0–*st* 1
He played soccer for Nottm. Forest 1904/5.

Barnwell, Charles John Patrick
Amateur. *b:* 23.6.1914, Stoke-on-Trent, Staffs. Uncle of L.M.L. (Somerset). Middle order right-hand batsman. *Sch* Repton. *Team* Somerset (1935–48, 69 matches).
Career batting
69–111–6–1592–83–15.16–0–*ct* 18
Bowling 40–0

Barnwell, Lionel Michael Lowry
Cricketer. *b:* 12.8.1943, Crewkerne, Somerset. Nephew of C.J.P. (Somerset). Opening right-hand batsman, right-arm medium pace bowler. *Sch* Repton. *Teams* Cambridge U (1965–66); Somerset (1967–68, 6 matches); Eastern Province (1969/70 to 1970/1).
Career batting
19–33–2–612–74–19.74–0–*ct* 10
Bowling 194–3–64.66–0–0–1/11
He was awarded a blue for soccer at Cambridge.

Baroda, The Gaekwad of, HH Maharajkumar Shiyajirao
Amateur. *b:* 31.8.1890, India. *d:* 24.11.1919, India. Second son of the Maharajah of Baroda, father of Udaysingh (Cambridge U), uncle of F.P., R.P. and S.P. Gaekwad (all Baroda). Stylish opening or middle order right-hand batsman. *Teams* Oxford U (1911–12); Hindus (1909/10). *Tour* Indians to England 1911.
Career batting
14–27–1–406–62–15.62–0–*ct* 4–*st* 1
An accident in 1912 which resulted in concussion of the brain cut short his cricket at Oxford when he would probably have gained a blue. His last first-class match in England was for Gentlemen in 1913 and his final first-class match for Hindus and Muslims in 1916/7.

Barr, Douglas
Amateur. *b:* 1.2.1935, Edinburgh. Right-hand batsman, right-arm fast medium bowler. *Team* Scotland (1954–70).
Career batting
41–70–9–1199–86–19.65–0–*ct* 34
Bowling 2747–88–31.21–2–0–6/89

Barraclough, Eric Scott
Professional. *b:* 30.3.1923, Bradford, Yorkshire. Lower order right-hand batsman, fast medium bowler. *Team* Yorkshire (1949–50, 2 matches).
Career batting
2–4–2–43–24*–21.50–0–*ct* 2
Bowling 136–4–34.00–0–0–2/39

Barratt, Edward (D'Oyley)
Professional. *b:* 21.4.1844, Stockton-on-Tees, Durham. *d:* 27.2.1891, Kennington, Surrey. Hard-hitting left-hand batsman, excellent slow left-arm bowler, good field. *Team* Surrey (1876–85, 130 matches).

Career batting
153–245–57–1595–67–8.48–0–*ct* 75
Bowling 13862–790–17.54–69–17–10/43

He created a sensation in 1872, when, as an unknown, he took 8/60 on his first-class debut in the second innings of North v South at Prince's. He then joined the Oval staff and qualified by residence for Surrey. He took 100 wickets in a season three times, his best being 148, av 17.25, in 1883. The best performance of his career was for Players v Australians at the Oval in 1878 when he took all ten wickets in an innings (for 43). He also played for Durham. His final first-class match was for C.I. Thornton's XI in 1886.

Barratt, Fred
Professional. *b:* 12.4.1894, Annesley, Notts. *d:* 29.1.1947, Nottingham. Powerful lower order right-hand batsman, right-arm fast bowler. *Team* Nottinghamshire (1914–31, 353 matches). *Tour* MCC to New Zealand and Australia 1929/30. *Tests* England (1929 to 1929/30, 5 matches).
Career batting
371–467–52–6445–139*–15.99–2–*ct* 174
Bowling 27811–1224–22.72–69–11–8/26
Test batting
5–4–1–28–17–9.33–0–*ct* 2
Bowling 235–5–47.00–0–0–1/8

Barratt took 100 wickets in his debut season of 1914 and in all obtained 100 wickets in five seasons (best 129, av 21.24, in 1929). His great year was 1928 when he also hit 1,000 runs and achieved the 'double' for the only time, scoring 1,167 runs, av 29.17, that year. He was noted for hitting sixes and twice hit three in succession. His highest score of 139 v Warwickshire at Coventry in 1928 took 84 minutes. He played soccer for Aston Villa and Sheffield Wednesday.

Barratt, Roy James
Professional. *b:* 3.4.1942, Leicester. Lower order left-hand batsman, slow left-arm bowler. *Team* Leicestershire (1961–70, 70 matches).
Career batting
70–88–16–604–39–8.38–0–*ct* 50
Bowling 4007–141–28.41–7–1–7/35

Barratt left the Leicestershire staff after 1962 and did not play at all in 1963, 1966 or 1967.

Barrell, Ben
Professional. *b:* 14.5.1885, Orford, Suffolk. *d:* 1969, Bootle, Lancs. Middle order batsman, useful change bowler. *Team* Lancashire (1911–23, 3 matches).
Career batting
3–3–1–45–25–22.50–0–*ct* 1
Bowling 135–9–15.00–0–0–3/10

Barrett, Alexander Gould
Amateur. *b:* 17.11.1866, Taunton, Somerset. *d:* 12.3.1954, Taunton, Somerset. Middle order batsman. *Sch* Eton. *Team* Somerset (1896, 1 match).
Career batting
1–2–0–6–6–3.00–0–*ct* 0

Barrett, Arthur George
Cricketer. *b:* 4.4.1944, Kingston, Jamaica. Lower order right-hand batsman, leg break and googly bowler. *Team* Jamaica (1966/7 to 1980/1). *Tours* Jamaica to England 1970; West Indies to India and Pakistan 1974/5. *Tests* West Indies (1970/1 to 1974/5, 6 matches).
Career batting
57–75–13–1086–102*–17.51–1–*ct* 54
Bowling 5276–169–31.21–9–2–7/90
Test batting
6–7–1–40–19–6.66–0–*ct* 0
Bowling 603–13–46.38–0–0–3/43

His appearances in English first-class cricket were limited to four, on the Jamaican tour of 1970.

Barrett, Edward
Amateur. *b:* 11.6.1846. *d:* 23.12.1923. Father of E.I.M. (Hants). Lower order batsman, useful bowler. *Sch* Cheltenham. *Team* Hampshire (1885, 2 matches).
Career batting
2–4–2–22–13*–11.00–0–*ct* 1
Bowling 48–0

Barrett, Edward Ivo Medhurst
Amateur. *b:* 22.6.1879, Pitt, Winchester. *d:* 10.7.1950, Boscombe, Hants, following an accident. Son of Edward (Hants). Fine hard-hitting middle order right-hand batsman. *Sch* Cheltenham. *Team* Hampshire (1896–1925, 80 matches).
Career batting
86–133–15–3804–215–32.23–6–*ct* 36
Bowling 40–0

Service abroad prevented him from appearing regularly for the County, but in 1912 he hit 1,381 runs (av 40.61) and also exceeded 1,000 runs in 1920. His highest score was 215 for Hampshire v Gloucs at Southampton in 1920. When Commissioner for Police in Shanghai, he appeared often in the matches between Shanghai and Hong Kong and in 1921 hit a record 165 in this match series. An excellent rugby footballer, he represented England in 1903.

Barrett, Dr John Edward
Amateur. *b:* 15.10.1866, South Melbourne, Australia. *d:* 6.2.1916, Peak Hill, West Australia.

Defensive left-hand opening or middle order batsman, right-arm medium pace bowler. *Team* Victoria (1884/5 to 1892/3, 15 matches). *Tour* Australia to England 1890. *Tests* Australia (1890, 2 matches).
Career batting
50–91–12–2039–97–25.81–0–*ct* 16
Bowling 336–21–16.00–3–1–6/49
Test batting
2–4–1–80–67*–26.66–0–*ct* 1

His batting was regarded as the success of the 1890 Australian tour to England and his great innings came at Lord's in the Test when he carried out his bat, having gone in first, for 67*. His profession considerably reduced his opportunities in first-class cricket. He hit 1,226 runs, av 20.03, in 1890.

Barrett, Peter
Cricketer. *b:* 3.6.1955, Winchester, Hants. *d:* 28.10.1983, Everton, Hants. He was killed in a moped accident. Opening left-hand batsman. *Team* Hampshire (1975–76, 6 matches).
Career batting
6–11–0–138–26–12.54–0–*ct* 0
Bowling 4–0

Barrick, Desmond William
Professional. *b:* 28.4.1926, Fitzwilliam, Yorkshire. Attractive middle order right-hand batsman, useful leg-break and googly bowler, good outfield. *Team* Northants (1949–60, 267 matches). *Tours* Commonwealth to India 1953/4; Norfolk to Jamaica 1956/7.
Career batting
301–490–62–13970–211–32.64–20–*ct* 116
Bowling 3575–79–45.25–2–0–5/71

He scored 1,000 runs in a season seven times (best 1,570, av 37.38, in 1952). His highest score was 211 for Northants v Essex at Northampton in 1952.

Barrington, George Bainbridge
(at birth G. Bainbridge)
Amateur. *b:* 20.4.1857, Pimlico, London. *d:* 29.3.1942, Kirk Langley, Derbyshire. Good right-hand batsman, slow round-arm bowler. *Sch* Repton. *Team* Derbyshire (1880–87, 24 matches).
Career batting
25–48–1–455–50–9.68–0–*ct* 7
Bowling 27–1–27.00–0–0–1/27

Barrington, Kenneth Frank
Professional. *b:* 24.11.1930, Reading, Berkshire. *d:* 14.3.1981, Needham's Point, Bridgetown, Barbados. Very sound middle order right-hand batsman, leg break bowler, fine field. *Team* Surrey (1953–68, 362 matches). *Tours* MCC to Pakistan 1955/6, to West Indies 1959/60, to Ceylon, India and Pakistan 1961/2, to Australia and New Zealand 1962/3, to India 1963/4; to South Africa 1964/5; to Australia 1965/6, to West Indies 1967/8; Surrey to Rhodesia 1959/60; Cavaliers to South Africa 1960. *Tests* England 1955 to 1968 (82 matches).
Career batting
533–831–136–31714–256–45.63–76–*ct* 515
Bowling 8907–273–32.62–8–0–7/40
Test batting
82–131–15–6806–256–58.67–20–*ct* 58
Bowling 1300–29–44.82–0–0–3/4

The key to Barrington's success in County and Test cricket was determination. He was no infant prodigy, for although he joined the Oval staff in 1948, it was not until 1953 that he made his first-class debut for the County and it took another six years to establish himself in the Test side. The England selectors gave him a chance in 1955, but he failed and this made him practise until he had eliminated every risky stroke from his repertoire. By 1959, when he became an integral part of the England Eleven, he was technically the soundest bat in the team.

The highlight of his career was the 1962/3 MCC tour to Australia – his Test average that winter was 72.75 and his average in all first-class matches 80.13. No-one else approached either figure and without him the series would undoubtedly have been lost. He was at times criticised for slow play and sometimes justifiably – against the weak New Zealanders of 1965 he took seven and a quarter hours to make 137. The selectors disciplined him by omitting him from the side for the next match. It is true that he was a match saver rather than a winner and perhaps Surrey suffered because of this.

Barrington hit 2,000 runs in a season three times (best 2,499, av 54.32, in 1959) and reached 1,000 runs on nine other occasions in England. His highest score came in the 1964 Test at Old Trafford v Australia – he made 256. He also compiled one 200 for Surrey and one for MCC in Australia.

A heart attack in 1968 brought his first-class career to a premature end, but he continued to play an active role as manager/coach until he suffered a second fatal heart attack in the West Indies, whilst assistant manager to the English touring party.

Barrington, William Edward James
Cricketer. *b*: 4.1.1960, Carshalton, Surrey. Middle order right-hand batsman. *Sch* Lancing. *Team* Cambridge U (1982, blue).
Career batting
4–6–1–174–59–34.80–0–*ct* 1

Barrington-Chance, G.H.
(*see under* Chance, G.H.B.)

Barron, William
Professional. *b:* 26.10.1917, Herrington, Co. Durham. Forcing left-hand batsman, slip field or occasional wicket-keeper. *Teams* Lancashire (1945, 1 match); Northants (1946–51, 118 matches).
Career batting
120–200–13–4772–161*–25.51–6–*ct* 98–*st* 2
Bowling 200–5–40.00–0–0–1/1
He hit 1,000 runs in a season twice (best 1,123, av 26.11, in 1946). He also appeared for Durham. He played soccer at full-back for Northampton Town, Charlton and Wolverhampton Wanderers.

Barrow, Arthur William
Professional. *b:* 1897, Cheltenham, Gloucs. *d:* 19.7.1943, Stoke Bishop, Bristol. Fair lower order batsman, useful change bowler. *Team* Gloucestershire (1919, 6 matches).
Career batting
6–11–1–162–37–16.20–0–*ct* 2
Bowling 196–3–65.33–0–0–2/51

Barrow, Charles Deans
Amateur. *b:* 4.4.1875, Tunbridge Wells, Kent. *d:* 20.9.1944, Farmington, Gloucs. Middle order right-hand batsman. *Sch* Eton. *Team* MCC (1903).
Career batting
2–2–0–25–25–12.50–0–*ct* 0

Barrow, Ivan
Amateur. *b:* 6.1.1911, Kingston, Jamaica. *d:* 2.4.1979, Kingston, Jamaica. Opening right-hand batsman, wicket-keeper. *Team* Jamaica (1928/9 to 1945/6). *Tours* West Indies to England 1933, 1939, to Australia 1930/1. *Tests* West Indies (1929/30 to 1939, 11 matches).
Career batting
67–113–6–2551–169–23.84–3–*ct* 71–*st* 27
Bowling 34–0
Test batting
11–19–2–276–105–16.23–1–*ct* 17–*st* 5
His most illustrious innings was at Old Trafford in the second Test v England, 1933. He hit 109, becoming the first West Indian to make a Test hundred in England. In the course of his innings he added 200 for the second wicket with G.A. Headley. He hit 1,046 runs, av 23.77, in 1933.

Barrow, Patrick Lindsay
Amateur. *b:* 22.1.1893, Bromley, Kent. *d:* 7.5.1974, Adstock, Bucks. Useful middle order left-hand batsman. *Sch* Wellington. *Team* Essex (1922, 1 match).
Career batting
1–1–0–0–0–0.00–0–*ct* 0
Bowling 43–1–43.00–0–0–1/21
He also appeared for Dorset. He was a composer of some repute.

Barrs, Frank Arthur
Amateur. *b:* 24.4.1871, Repton, Derbyshire. *d:* 16.12.1963, Vancouver, Canada. Middle order left-hand batsman, left-arm fast bowler. Team Derbyshire (1900–01, 3 matches).
Career batting
3–5–0–68–58–13.60–0–*ct* 0
Bowling 29–1–29.00–0–0–1/17

Barry, Edward Albert
Amateur. *b:* 8.6.1898, Hong Kong. *d:* 24.11.1965, Liphook, Hants. Left-hand batsman, left arm medium pace bowler. *Team* Ireland (1926).
Career batting
2–3–1–20–15–10.00–0–*ct* 1
Bowling 70–1–70.00–0–0–1/44

Barry, Gerald
Amateur. *b:* 18.12.1896, London. *d:* 21.2.1977, Great Witchingham, Norfolk. Tail end batsman, opening bowler. *Sch* Eton. *Team* Combined Services (1922).
Career batting
1–2–0–2–2–1.00–0–*ct* 1
Bowling 68–0

Bartels, Clarence Wilfred
Professional. *b:* 24.6.1922, Colombo, Ceylon. Right-hand batsman, right-arm medium pace bowler. *Teams* Commonwealth XI (1957–58); Ceylon (1952/3 to 1953/4). *Tour* Ceylon to India (1952/3).
Career batting
5–8–1–215–88–30.71–0–*ct* 8
Bowling 317–14–22.54–0–0–3/24
He was engaged by Ashton in the Central Lancashire League when he appeared for the Commonwealth XI.

Bartholomew, Amos
Professional. *b:* 26.5.1825, Sevenoaks, Kent. *d:* 4.11.1907, Sevenoaks, Kent. Right-hand batsman. *Team* Kent (1858–64, 2 matches).
Career batting
4–7–0–17–6–2.42–0–*ct* 2
Bowling 11–2–5.50–0–0–2/11
His first important match was for Combined Kent and Sussex in 1853.

Bartholomew, Arthur Churchill
Amateur. *b:* 21.2.1846, Lympstone, Devon. *d:* 29.3.1940, Reading, Berkshire. Brother of Robert (MCC). Steady middle order right-hand batsman, good field in the covers. *Sch* Marlborough. *Team* Oxford U (1866–68, blue 1868).
Career batting
8–13–3–158–54–15.80–0–*ct* 5
His County cricket was for Devonshire.

Bartholomew, Robert
Amateur. b: 27.1.1841, Lympstone, Devon. *d:* March 1918, Marylebone, London. Brother of A. C. (Oxford U). Middle order batsman. *Sch* Uppingham. *Team* MCC (1872).
Career batting
1–1–0–0–0–0.00–0–*ct* 1
His County cricket was for Devon.

Bartlett, Edward Lawson
Amateur. *b:* 18.3.1906, Barbados. *d:* 21.12.1976, Henrys, nr Bridgetown, Barbados. Quick scoring middle order right-hand batsman. *Team* Barbados (1923/4 to 1938/9). *Tours* West Indies to England 1928, to Australia 1930/1. *Tests* West Indies (1928 to 1930/1, 5 matches).
Career batting
42–72–4–1581–109–23.25–1–*ct* 8
Test batting
5–8–1–131–84–18.71–0–*ct* 2
A broken finger on the West Indies tour to England in 1928 forced him to miss some matches in mid-tour and later he could not recover his confidence.

Bartlett, Ezra William
Amateur. *b:* 1861, Doncaster, Yorkshire. *d:* 16.3.1942, Taunton, Somerset. Lower order batsman, wicket-keeper. *Team* Somerset (1894–95, 6 matches).
Career batting
6–12–1–126–40–11.45–0–*ct* 2
Bowling 16–0

Bartlett, Hugh Tryon
Amateur. *b:* 7.10.1914, Balaghat, India. Fine hard-hitting left-hand batsman. *Sch* Dulwich. *Teams* Surrey (1933–35, 3 matches); Cambridge U (1934–36, blue all three years); Sussex (1937–49, 152 matches). *Tours* MCC to South Africa 1938/9; also selected for MCC to India 1939/40 (tour cancelled).
Career batting
217–350–34–10098–183–31.95–16–*ct* 70
Bowling 269–10–26.90–0–0–1/0
His greatest season was his first full year with Sussex, 1938. He hit 175 for the Gentlemen v Players at Lord's and also the fastest hundred of the year – for Sussex v Australians at Hove in 57 minutes. His record for 1938 was 1,548 runs, av 57.33 – he also hit 1,000 runs in 1939, 1947 and 1948. He was captain of Sussex from 1947 to 1949, but then resigned after a disagreement with the County Committee. His final first-class appearance was for Free Foresters in 1951.

Bartlett, John Norton
Amateur. *b:* 16.6.1928, Mickleover, Derbyshire. Lower order right-hand batsman, left-arm slow bowler. *Teams* Oxford U (1946–51, blue 1946, 1951); Sussex (1946–50, 7 matches). *Tour* MCC to Canada 1951.
Career batting
49–70–32–351–28–9.23–0–*ct* 34
Bowling 3443–107–32.17–2–0–5/77
An unusual feature of Bartlett's career is that he was awarded his blue in 1946 and then not again until 1951 – he was on National Service in 1947 and 1948. His final first-class match was for Free Foresters in 1953.

Bartley, Edward Leslie Dayrell
Amateur. *b:* 2.3.1896, Clifton, Bristol. *d:* 7.10.1969, Stonehouse, Plymouth. Middle order left-hand batsman, wicket-keeper. *Team* Hampshire (1931, 3 matches). *Tour* Tennyson to South Africa 1924/5.
Career batting
27–44–12–649–84–20.28–0–*ct* 43–*st* 19
He was for many years a leading figure in Naval cricket and made his first-class debut for the Royal Navy in 1914.

Barton, Arthur
Professional. *b:* 30.9.1874, Shipley, Ilkeston, Derbyshire. *d:* 19.1.1949, Ealing, Middlesex. Middle order right-hand batsman, change bowler. *Team* Derbyshire (1901, 3 matches).
Career batting
3–6–0–24–7–4.00–0–*ct* 0
Bowling 61–0

Barton, Charles Gerard
Amateur. *b:* 26.4.1860, Romsey, Hants. *d:* 3.11.1919, Hatfield-Peverel, Essex. Fair right-hand batsman, good slow left-arm bowler. *Sch* Sherborne and Tonbridge. *Teams* Hampshire (1895–96, 4 matches); Europeans (1893/4).
Career batting
6–8–2–29–22–4.83–0–*ct* 0
Bowling 206–9–22.88–1–0–6/27
His best County cricket was played whilst Hampshire were not considered first-class and in 1891 he took 42 wickets (av 9.79) for the County.

Barton, Harold George Mitford
Amateur. *b:* 10.10.1882, Christchurch, Hants. *d:* 3.7.1970, Bassett, Southampton. Middle order right-hand batsman. *Sch* Sherborne. *Team* Hampshire (1910–12, 8 matches).
Career batting
8–15–2–146–31–11.23–0–*ct* 2
He also appeared for Buckinghamshire.

Barton, Joseph
Professional. *b:* 1859, Meriden, Warwickshire. *d:* 31.1.1945, Selly Oak, Birmingham. Tail end right-hand batsman, right-arm fast bowler. *Team* Warwickshire (1895–96, 3 matches).
Career batting
3–4–0–38–16–9.50–0–*ct* 0
Bowling 165–7–23.57–1–0–5/73
He took 5 for 73 in the first County Championship match ever played by Warwickshire (v Essex, Edgbaston, 1895). He also played for Staffordshire.

Barton, Michael Richard
Amateur. *b:* 14.10.1914, Dereham, Norfolk. Sound middle order right-hand batsman, good slip field. *Sch* Winchester. *Teams* Oxford U (1935–37, blue 1936–37); Surrey (1948–54, 110 matches).
Career batting
147–247–16–5965–192–25.82–7–*ct* 117
Barton played for Norfolk from 1935 to 1947, but joined Surrey in 1948 and captained that County from 1949 to 1951. His final first-class appearance was for Free Foresters in 1955. He hit 1,000 runs in a season three times (best 1,187, av 22.82, in 1948).

Barton, Victor Alexander
Professional. *b:* 6.10.1867, Netley, Hants. *d:* 23.3.1906, Southampton, Hants. Attractive hard-hitting right-hand batsman, useful right-arm medium pace bowler. *Teams* Kent (1889–90, 11 matches); Hampshire (1895–1902, 143 matches). *Tour* Read to South Africa 1891/2. *Test* England (1891/2, 1 match).
Career batting
157–282–15–6413–205–24.01–6–*ct* 101
Bowling 4036–141–28.62–3–0–6/28
Test batting
1–1–0–23–23–23.00–0–*ct* 0
Barton first came to notice when playing for the Royal Artillery v MCC at Lord's in 1889 – he hit 91 and 102 and took 6 for 53. He then appeared for Kent as 'Bombardier Barton', but in 1891 purchased his discharge from the Army and began his career with Hampshire. His highest score was 205 for Hants v Sussex at Hove in 1900. His on-drives were noted for their power and fieldsmen at mid-on had a 'wholesome dread of him'. He hit 1,000 runs in a season twice (best 1,060, av 27.17, in 1900).

Barwell, Terence Ian
Cricketer. *b:* 29.4.1937, Transvaal, South Africa. Middle order right-hand batsman, wicket-keeper. *Team* Somerset (1959–68, 43 matches).
Career batting
44–77–8–1344–84*–19.47–0–*ct* 39–*st* 1
His final first-class match was in 1973 for Minor Counties – he played for Wiltshire from 1971 to 1976.

Barwick, Stephen Royston
Cricketer. *b:* 6.9.1960, Neath, Glamorgan. Low order right-hand batsman, right-arm medium pace bowler. *Team* Glamorgan (1981–83, 27 matches).
Career batting
27–29–14–177–24–11.80–0–*ct* 8
Bowling 1646–50–32.82–2–0–8/42

Bashford, Rev Alfred Myddleton
Amateur. *b:* 23.7.1881, Wickhampton, Norfolk. *d:* 31.7.1949, Colham Green, Hillingdon, Middlesex. Middle order right-hand batsman. *Sch* Merchant Taylors'. *Team* Middlesex (1906, 2 matches).
Career batting
2–4–0–27–14–6.75–0–*ct* 1
Bowling 29–1–29.00–0–0–1/12
He played in the Seniors' Match at Cambridge in 1903, but never in a first-class game for the University.

Baskervyle-Glegg, John
Amateur. *b:* 10.11.1940, Windsor, Berkshire. Opening right-hand batsman, wicket-keeper. *Sch* Eton. *Team* Combined Services (1962).
Career batting
1–2–0–43–35–21.50–0–*ct* 0

Bass, Hamar Alfred
Amateur. *b:* 30.7.1842, Burton on Trent. *d:* 8.4.1898, Needwood, Staffs. Middle order batsman. *Sch* Cheltenham and Harrow. *Team* MCC (1865).
Career batting
1–2–0–6–3–3.00–0–*ct* 0
His County cricket was for Staffordshire and Derbyshire (non-first-class). From 1878 to 1885 he was MP for Tamworth, then for West Staffs until his death.

Bass, Henry John
Professional. *b:* 14.10.1852, Canterbury, Kent. *d:*

24.1.1904, Canterbury, Kent. *Team* Kent (1871–75, 3 matches).
Career batting
3–5–0–11–8–2.20–0–*ct* 1

He was employed as groundsman at Canterbury from 1879 until his death.

Bass, John George
Amateur. *b:* 9.8.1903, Northampton. Right-hand batsman, change bowler. *Team* Northants (1935, 2 matches).
Career batting
2–4–0–43–16–10.75–0–*ct* 0
Bowling 31–0

Bassett, Hubert
Amateur. *b:* 5.10.1868, Stanton St John, Oxford. *d:* 13.6.1943, Oxford. Middle order left-hand batsman, left-arm medium pace bowler. *Team* Oxford U (1888–91, blue last three years).
Career batting
21–39–6–292–54*–8.84–0–*ct* 15
Bowling 1722–78–22.07–4–0–6/50

He also represented Oxfordshire and Suffolk.

Bastard, Edward William
Amateur. *b:* 28.2.1862, Wilton, Somerset. *d:* 2.4.1901, Taunton, Somerset. Fair left-hand batsman, excellent left-arm slow bowler, slip field. *Sch* Sherborne. *Teams* Oxford U (1882–85, blue last three years); Somerset (1883–85, 15 matches).
Career batting
37–60–19–278–47–6.78–0–*ct* 15
Bowling 2887–137–21.07–8–2–8/54

He continued to appear for Somerset in non-first-class matches until 1889. He also played for Dorset.

Bastow, John
Professional. *b:* 30.10.1850, Bromley-by-Bow, Middlesex. *d:* 1.6.1927, Haverstock Hill, Middlesex. Fair right-hand batsman, wicket-keeper. *Team* Middlesex (1874–77, 5 matches).
Career batting
5–10–2–118–35–14.75–0–*ct* 3–*st* 5

He also appeared for Essex in the county's non-first-class days, commencing 1886.

Batchelor, Rev William Jesse
Amateur. *b:* 14.11.1846, Hayes, Kent. *d:* 19.11.1917, Epsom, Surrey. Good middle order right-hand batsman, fine field. *Sch* Perse. *Team* Cambridgeshire (1868, 2 matches).
Career batting
2–4–0–14–7–3.50–0–*ct* 1
Bowling 42–0

He was educated at Cambridge and was asked to play for the University but declined, as he was the senior mathematical scholar of his college. He appeared for Warwickshire (non-first-class) in 1876. His scores in minor matches were quite extraordinary.

Bateman, Arthur Cyril
Amateur. *b:* 31.10.1890, Bailieborough, Co Cavan, Ireland. *d:* 28.3.1918, nr Arras, France. Right-hand batsman. *Sch* Portora Royal School. *Team* Ireland (1913–14).
Career batting
2–4–0–149–52–37.25–0–*ct* 2

Bateman, Edward Louis
Amateur. *b:* 15.9.1834, Mickleover, Derbyshire. *d:* 25.1.1909, Rowditch Lodge, Derbyshire. Brother of Augustus (Cambridge U and Notts). Right-hand batsman, excellent field. *Sch* Marlborough. *Teams* Oxford U (1854–55, blue both years); Nottinghamshire (1855, 1 match).
Career batting
8–15–1–269–68*–19.21–0–*ct* 4

His last first-class match was for the Gentlemen of England v Gentlemen of Middlesex at Islington in 1865. He was on the MCC Committee for many years and was Auditor to the Club from 1904 to his death. He also played non-first-class cricket for Leicestershire.

Bateman, Richard
Amateur. *b:* 1849, Farnham, Surrey. *d:* 5.11.1913, Ash Vale, Surrey. Middle order batsman. *Team* Hampshire (1883, 1 match).
Career batting
1–2–1–18–14*–18.00–0–*ct* 0

Bateman-Champain, Claude Edward
Amateur. *b:* 30.3.1875, Richmond, Surrey. *d:* 13.10.1956, Budleigh Salterton, Devon. Brother of F.H. (Gloucs), H.F. (Gloucs) and J.N. (Gloucs). Middle order right-hand batsman, slow right-arm bowler. *Sch* Cheltenham. *Team* Gloucestershire (1898–1907, 16 matches).
Career batting
18–28–4–226–29–9.42–0–*ct* 8
Bowling 14–0

Bateman-Champain, Francis Henry
Amateur. *b:* 17.6.1877, Richmond, Surrey. *d:* 29.12.1942, Tiverton, Devon. Brother of C.E. (Gloucs), H.F. (Gloucs) and J.N. (Gloucs). Stylish opening/middle order right-hand batsman, slow right-arm bowler, good field. *Sch* Cheltenham. *Teams* Gloucestershire (1895–1914, 83 matches); Oxford U (1897–1900, blue all four years).

Career batting
114–198–8–4677–149–24.61–5–*ct* 103
Bowling 418–17–24.59–1–0–6/62

Bateman-Champain, Brig-Gen Hugh Frederick
Amateur. *b:* 6.4.1869, Ashford, Middlesex. *d:* 7.10.1933, London. Brother of C.E. (Gloucs), F.H. (Gloucs) and J.N. (Gloucs). Middle order right-hand batsman. *Sch* Cheltenham. *Team* Gloucestershire (1888–1902, 11 matches).
Career batting
12–18–1–142–35–8.35–0–*ct* 8

Owing to his military duties he was unable to play much County cricket, but he appeared in Army and other matches in India.

Bateman-Champain, Rt Rev John Norman
Amateur. *b:* 14.3.1880, Richmond, Surrey. *d:* 22.10.1950, Westbury-on-Trym, Gloucs. Brother of C.E. (Gloucs), F.H. (Gloucs) and H.F. (Gloucs). Middle order right-hand batsman. *Sch* Cheltenham. *Team* Gloucestershire (1899, 2 matches).
Career batting
5–9–2–36–17–5.14–0–*ct* 2
Bowling 7–0

His final first-class match was for Free Foresters in 1920. Whilst at Cambridge he played in both the Freshmen's and Seniors' Trials, but never in a first-class match. He also played for Shropshire.

Bates, Arthur John
Professional. *b:* 18.6.1852, New Radford, Notts. *d:* 13.2.1925, Lenton, Notts. Right-hand batsman, slow right-arm bowler. *Team* Nottinghamshire (1878, 2 matches).
Career batting
2–4–0–5–5–1.25–0–*ct* 0

He played soccer at right wing for Nottingham Forest in 1879.

Bates, Donald Lawson
Professional. *b:* 10.5.1933, Hove. Lower order right-hand batsman, right-arm fast medium bowler, good field. *Team* Sussex (1950–71, 315 matches).
Career batting
315–358–157–1525–37*–7.58–0–*ct* 118
Bowling 22776–880–25.88–34–2–8/51

Bates took 100 wickets in a season three times (best 113, av 22.65, in 1961). His benefit in 1968 realised £8,000. A talented soccer player, he appeared at right-half for Lewes and Brighton and Hove Albion.

Bates, F.H.
Amateur. *b:* 1875, Philadelphia. Right-hand middle order batsman, right-arm medium pace bowler. *Team* Philadelphia (1897–1903). *Tours* Philadelphia to England, 1897 and 1903.
Career batting
16–30–1–224–24–7.72–*ct* 8
Bowling 355–7–50.71–0–0–2/17

He scored prolifically in club cricket in the United States, but failed completely on both his visits to England. He appeared for United States v Canada in 1898 and 1899.

Bates, Frederick Stanley
Amateur. *b:* 25.2.1899, Lambourn, Berkshire. *d:* 13.8.1969, Hammersmith, London. Middle order batsman. *Sch* Marlborough. *Team* Hampshire (1920, 2 matches).
Career batting
2–3–0–18–9–6.00–0–*ct* 0

Bates, Henry Alfred
Professional. *b:* 3.12.1880, Brentford, Middlesex. *d:* 1942, Reading, Berkshire. Middle order right-hand batsman, right-arm medium pace bowler. *Team* Middlesex (1909, 2 matches).
Career batting
2–3–0–18–10–6.00–0–*ct* 0

Bates, James
Professional. *b:* 10.1.1856, Paddington, Middlesex. *d:* 7.12.1915, London. Middle order right-hand batsman, right-arm medium pace bowler. *Team* Middlesex (1880, 1 match).
Career batting
1–2–0–9–8–4.50–0–*ct* 2

Bates, Leonard Thomas Ashton
Professional. *b:* 20.3.1895, in the groundsman's house at Edgbaston. *d:* 11.3.1971, Coldwaltham, Sussex. Brother of S.H. (Warwickshire). Sound middle order right-hand batsman, right-arm medium pace bowler. *Team* Warwickshire (1913–35, 441 matches).
Career batting
444–749–53–19380–211–27.84–21–*ct* 160
Bowling 471–9–52.33–0–0–2/16

He exceeded 1,000 runs in a season twelve times (best 1,518, av 33.73, in 1926). His highest score was 211 for Warwickshire v Gloucs at Gloucester, 1932.

Bates, Samuel Harold
Professional. *b:* 16.6.1890, Edgbaston Cricket Ground. *d:* 28.8.1916. He was killed in action near Hardecourt, France. Brother of L.T.A. (Warwickshire). Lower order right-hand batsman, slow left-arm bowler. *Team* Warwickshire (1910–12, 5 matches).

Career batting
5–9–1–24–13–3.00–0–*ct* 0
Bowling 182–6–30.33–0–0–3/56

Bates, Willie
Professional. *b:* 19.11.1855, Lascelles Hall, Huddersfield, Yorkshire. *d:* 8.1.1900, Lepton, Yorkshire. Father of W. E. (Yorkshire and Glamorgan). Very hard-hitting middle order right-hand batsman, right-arm slow off break bowler. *Team* Yorkshire (1877–87, 202 matches). *Tours* Daft to North America 1879 (not first-class); Shaw and Shrewsbury to Australia 1881/2, 1884/5 and 1886/7; Bligh to Australia 1882/3; Vernon to Australia 1887/8. *Tests* England (1881/2 to 1886/7, 15 matches).
Career batting
299–495–20–10249–144*–21.57–10–*ct* 238
Bowling 14980–874–17.13–52–10–8/21
Test batting
15–26–2–656–64–27.33–0–*ct* 9
Bowling 821–50–16.42–4–1–7/28

An excellent all-rounder, though his fielding tended to let him down, Bates took 121 wickets av 16.28, in 1881 and scored 1,000 runs five times (best 1,161, av 25.23, in 1885). His most famous feat was the hat-trick he performed against Australia in 1882/3 when his victims were McDonnell, Giffen and Bonnor. During net practice on the 1887/8 tour to Australia, Bates was hit in the eye and nearly lost his sight – the accident ended his first-class career.

Bates, William Ederick
Professional. *b:* 5.3.1884, Kirkheaton, Yorkshire. *d:* 17.1.1957, Belfast, N. Ireland. Son of Willie (Yorkshire and England). Opening or middle order right-hand batsman, slow left-arm bowler, brilliant field. *Teams* Yorkshire (1907–13, 113 matches); Glamorgan (1921–31, 283 matches); Wales (1923-30).
Career batting
406–684–30–15964–200*–24.40–13–*ct* 248
Bowling 8671–230–37.70–4–0

After being unable to obtain a regular place in the Yorkshire side, Bates became one of the mainstays of Glamorgan. He reached 1,000 runs in seven seasons (best 1,692, av 43.48, in 1927). His highest score was 200* for Glamorgan v Worcs (Kidderminster) 1927. He also played for Cheshire. He played soccer for Leeds United and Bolton Wanderers.

Bather, Rev William Henry
Amateur. *b:* 12.12.1861, Meole Brace, Shropshire. *d:* 3.1.1939, Bournemouth, Hants. Hard hitting right-hand batsman. *Sch* Rossall. *Teams* Cambridge U (1882–83); MCC (1883).
Career batting
6–10–1–119–33–13.22–0–*ct* 6

He also appeared for Hertfordshire and Shropshire.

Bathurst, F. H. H
(see under Hervey-Bathurst, F. H)

Bathurst, F. T. A. H
(see under Hervey-Bathurst, F. T. A)

Bathurst, Lawrence Charles Villebois
Amateur. *b:* 4.6.1871, Gressenhall, Dereham, Norfolk. *d:* 22.2.1939, Bonchurch, Isle of Wight. Steady right-hand batsman, useful left-arm medium pace bowler, good field. *Sch* Radley. *Teams* Oxford U (1893–94, blue both years); Middlesex (1894–95, 8 matches). *Tour* Lord Hawke to North America 1894.
Career batting
33–56–11–671–45*–14.91–0–*ct* 19
Bowling 1908–96–19.87–6–1–8/44

His final first-class appearance was for MCC in 1899. He also appeared for Norfolk.

Batson, Richard Erstine
Amateur. *b:* 11.6.1891, Bridgetown, Barbados. *d:* 25.1.1971, Islington, London. Right-hand batsman. *Teams* Scotland (1920–23); Barbados (1909/10 to 1911/12).
Career batting
6–10–0–260–111–26.00–1–*ct* 2

Batson, W.
Amateur. Middle order right-hand batsman. *Team* Northants (1920–21, 2 matches).
Career batting
2–4–0–45–34–11.25–0–*ct* 0

Battcock, Oliver Gordon
Amateur. *b:* 16.9.1903, Slough, Buckinghamshire. *d:* 26.9.1970, Guy's Hospital, London. Left-hand batsman, left-arm medium pace bowler. *Sch* Harrow. *Team* MCC (1938–39).
Career batting
2–2–1–30–27–30.00–0–*ct* 0
Bowling 102–2–51.00–0–0–1/10

He appeared for Bucks from 1923 to 1952 and was reputed to have captured about 6,000 wickets in local cricket. He appeared on the stage as 'Oliver Gordon'.

Battersby, Terence Esmond Maxwell
Amateur. *b:* 29.10.1893, Meerut, Bengal, India. *d:* 10.1.1972, Goring Heath, Berkshire. Opening left-hand batsman, change bowler. *Sch* Marlborough. *Teams* Army (1926); Europeans (1923/4).

Career batting
3–6–0–110–41–18.33–0–*ct* 1
Bowling 126–2–63.00–0–0–2/60
He also played for Suffolk and Devon.

Battersea, Howard
Tail end batsman, bowler. *Team* H.K. Foster's XI (1919).
Career batting
1–1–0–1–1–1.00–0–*ct* 0
Bowling 163–0

Baucher, Frederick William
Amateur. *b:* 6.11.1878, Wigan, Lancashire. *d:* 7.6.1947, Blundellsands, Lancashire. Right-hand batsman, wicket-keeper. *Team* Lancashire (1903, 1 match).
Career batting
1–2–0–12–8–6.00–0–*ct* 0

Bawtree, John Francis
Amateur. *b:* 26.11.1873, Witham, Essex. *d:* 25.3.1938, Great Totham, Essex. Useful batsman, slow left-arm bowler. *Sch* Haileybury. *Team* Essex (1895–96, 5 matches).
Career batting
5–9–1–96–47–12.00–0–*ct* 5
Bowling 66–2–33.00–0–0–1/16

Baxter, Arthur Douglas
Amateur. *b:* 20.1.1910, Edinburgh, Scotland. Right-hand batsman, right-arm fast medium bowler. *Sch* Loretto. *Teams* Scotland (1929–37); Lancashire (1933–34, 3 matches); Middlesex (1938, 2 matches). *Tour* MCC to Australia and New Zealand 1935/6.
Career batting
42–56–18–273–26*–7.18–0–*ct* 10
Bowling 4109–189–21.74–16–4–7/33
His final first-class match was for Free Foresters in 1939. He also appeared for Devon.

Baxter, Austin Godfrey
Amateur. *b:* 21.9.1931, West Bridgford, Notts. Stylish right-hand batsman, occasional right-arm medium pace bowler. *Team* Nottinghamshire (1952–53, 13 matches).
Career batting
13–22–1–314–98–14.95–0–*ct* 4
Bowling 8–0
He was a most promising batsman, but unable to play regularly in County cricket owing to business commitments.

Baxter, Herbert Wood
Amateur. *b:* 1883, Stockport, Cheshire. *d:* 25.4.1962, Stockport, Cheshire. Hard-hitting batsman. *Team* Glamorgan (1921, 1 match).
Career batting
1–2–0–11–10–5.50–0–*ct* 0

Bayes, George William
Professional. *b:* 27.2.1884, Flamborough, Yorkshire. *d:* 6.12.1960, Flamborough, Yorkshire. Tail end right-hand batsman, right-arm fast bowler. *Team* Yorkshire (1910–21, 18 matches).
Career batting
18–24–11–165–36–12.69–0–*ct* 7
Bowling 1534–48–31.95–1–0–5/83

Bayford, Robert Augustus
Amateur. *b:* 13.3.1838, Albury, Surrey. *d:* 24.8.1922, Netley, Hants. Hard-hitting right-hand batsman, slow round-arm bowler. *Teams* Cambridge U (1857–59, blue all three years); Surrey (1860–61, 4 matches); Middlesex (1861–64, 5 matches); Cambridgeshire (1858, 1 match).
Career batting
30–51–1–822–92–16.44–0–*ct* 7–*st* 4
Bowling 128–7+5–18.28–0–0–4/42
His final first-class appearance was for Southgate in 1867.

Bayley, Henry Peter
Amateur. *b:* 9.4.1916. Sound middle order right-hand batsman, good field. *Team* British Guiana (1935/6 to 1950/1). *Tour* West Indies to England 1939.
Career batting
28–50–4–1577–268–34.28–3–*ct* 11
Bowling 10–0
Coming to England with a reputation built on his record breaking innings of 268 for British Guiana v Barbados at Bridgetown in 1937/8, Bayley failed to find any sort of form and was not selected for the Tests.

Bayley, John
Professional. *b:* 17.5.1794, Mitcham, Surrey. *d:* 7.11.1874, Mitcham, Surrey. Uncle of Morton (Surrey). Fair hard-hitting right-hand batsman, good slow round-arm bowler. *Teams* Middlesex (1830); Surrey (1839–47, 5 matches); Hampshire (1843).
Career batting
83–144–17–936–54–7.37–0–*ct* 52–*st* 5
Bowling 259–12+338–21.58–31–9–7/?
His first important match was for the Bs v England in 1822 and from 1823 to 1854 he was on the staff at Lord's. His bowling was at its best in the late 1830s when he was well over 40 years of age. His final first-class match was for MCC in 1850.

Bayley, Morton
Professional. *b:* 7.5.1843, Mitcham, Surrey. *d:* 6.3.1926, Mitcham, Surrey. Nephew of John

(Surrey). Fair right-hand batsman, right-arm medium pace bowler. *Team* Surrey (1866, 1 match).
Career batting
1–1–1–8–8*–no av–0–*ct* 1
Bowling 19–0

Bayley, Martin George
Cricketer. *b:* 10.7.1952, Leamington Spa, Warwickshire. Lower order right-hand batsman, slow left-arm bowler. *Team* Warwickshire (1969, 2 matches).
Career batting
2–2–1–2–1*–2.00–0–*ct* 2
Bowling 125–3–41.66–0–0–2/54

Baylis, Keith Rodney
Cricketer. *b:* 5.11.1947, Redditch, Worcs. Lower order right-hand batsman, leg break bowler, good close field. *Sch* Ellesmere. *Team* Worcestershire (1966–67, 6 matches).
Career batting
6–7–1–89–26–14.83–0–*ct* 2
Bowling 495–14–35.35–0–0–4/112

Bayliss, Edward George
Amateur. *b:* 5.1.1918, Worcester. Right-hand batsman. *Team* Worcestershire (1939, 1 match).
Career batting
1–2–0–0–0–0.00–*ct* 0

Baynton, Robert Geoffrey
Amateur. *b:* 5.3.1900, Moseley, Birmingham. *d:* 26.9.1924. He died after a motor accident, King's Heath, Birmingham. Lower order right-hand batsman, left-arm medium pace bowler. *Team* Warwickshire (1921–23, 13 matches).
Career batting
13–19–1–212–36–11.77–0–*ct* 3
Bowling 479–14–34.21–0–0–4/56

Beadle, Sydney Wilford
Amateur. *b:* 9.11.1885, Wadhwan, India. *d:* 24.7.1937, Reading Street, Tenterden, Kent. Middle order right-hand batsman, slow right-arm bowler. *Sch* Rossall. *Team* Hampshire (1911, 1 match).
Career batting
3–6–0–88–28–14.66–0–*ct* 2
Bowling 53–0

He also represented the Navy v Army at Lord's in 1911 and 1912.

Beadsmoore, Walter Arthur
Amateur. *b:* 15.10.1891, Basford, Notts. *d:* 1964, Watford, Herts. Lower order left-hand batsman, slow left-arm bowler. *Team* Minor Counties (1924).
Career batting
1–2–1–10–7–10.00–0–*ct* 0
Bowling 55–5–11.00–0–0–4/53

His county cricket was for Norfolk, commencing 1921.

Beagley, Thomas
Professional. *b:* 5.10.1789, Farringdon, Alton, Hants. *d:* 21.2.1858, London. Brother of Henry (Hants) and John (Hants). Fine batsman, splendid long-stop. *Team* Hampshire (1816–28).
Career batting
70–127–15–1916–113*–17.10–1–*ct* 32
Bowling 7 wickets, no analyses

His most celebrated innings was 113* – the first century ever scored in the Gentlemen v Players series of matches – hit at Lord's in 1821. He appeared in important matches from 1816 to 1839.

Beal, Charles William
Amateur. *b:* 24.6.1855, Sydney, New South Wales, Australia. *d:* 5.2.1921, Randwick, New South Wales, Australia. Nephew of J.C. (New South Wales). *Tour* Manager of the 1882 and 1888 Australians to England.
Career batting
1–1–0–5–5–5.00–0–*ct* 0

He appeared in first-class cricket in England in 1882, playing in emergency for the Australian tourists. He was Secretary to the New South Wales Cricket Association.

Bean, George
Professional. *b:* 7.3.1864, Sutton-in-Ashfield, Notts. *d:* 16.3.1923, Warsop, Notts. Brother of Joseph (Sussex). Hard-hitting middle order, or opening right-hand batsman, right-arm medium pace bowler, good cover-point. *Teams* Nottinghamshire (1885, 5 matches); Sussex (1886–98, 202 matches). *Tours* Sheffield to Australia 1891/2. *Tests* England (1891/2, 3 matches).
Career batting
247–438–21–8634–186–20.70–9–*ct* 145
Bowling 7087–260–27.25–9–2–8/29
Test batting
3–5–0–92–50–18.40–0–*ct* 4

He reached 1,000 runs in a season twice (best 1,277, av 28.38, in 1893).

Bean, Joseph
Professional. *b:* 16.2.1876, Sutton-in-Ashfield, Notts. *d:* 12.1.1922, Sutton-in-Ashfield, Notts. Brother of George (Notts and Sussex). Middle order batsman, change bowler. *Team* Sussex (1895–1903, 40 matches).
Career batting
40–57–4–453–46–8.54–0–*ct* 27
Bowling 841–35–24.02–1–0–5/34

Bean, John Reginald
Amateur. *b:* 16.1.1913, Bangalore, India. Middle order right-hand batsman, leg break bowler. *Sch* Ampleforth. *Team* Army (1936).
Career batting
1–2–0–20–19–10.00–0–*ct* 0

Bean, Leslie Hugh
Amateur. *b:* 2.2.1906, Burnham-on-Sea, Somerset. Middle order right-hand batsman, right-arm medium pace bowler. *Sch* Sherborne. *Team* Somerset (1929, 3 matches).
Career batting
3–6–0–35–17–5.83–0–*ct* 1
Bowling 24–1–24.00–0–0–1/4
He also appeared for Dorest with some success.

Bear, Michael John
Professional. *b:* 23.2.1934, Brentwood, Essex. Opening left-hand batsman, occasional leg break bowler, excellent outfield. *Team* Essex (1954–68, 322 matches). *Tour* MCC to New Zealand 1960/1 (played in emergency in non-first-class match).
Career batting
322–562–44–12564–137–24.25–9–*ct* 113
Bowling 53–0
He hit 1,000 runs in a season four times (best 1,833, av 32.15, in 1966). He played soccer for Romford.

Beard, Bertram Ferryman
Amateur. *b:* 1874, Lewes, Sussex. *d:* 1959, Westminster, London. Middle order right-hand batsman, right-arm medium pace bowler. *Sch* Wellington. *Team* Sussex (1899, 2 matches).
Career batting
2–2–0–4–4–2.00–0–*ct* 1
Bowling 9–0

Beard, Graeme Robert
Cricketer. *b:* 19.8.1950, Auburn, New South Wales, Australia. Lower order right-hand batsman, right-arm medium off break bowler. *Team* New South Wales (1975/6 to 1981/2, 39 matches). *Tours* Australia to Pakistan 1979/80, to Sri Lanka 1980/81, to England 1981. *Tests* Australia (1979/80, 3 matches).
Career batting
54–71–16–1441–75–23.62–0–*ct* 22
Bowling 3524–125–28.19–7–1–5/33
Test batting
3–5–0–114–49–22.80–0–*ct* 0
Bowling 109–1–109.00–0–0–1/26
He was given few opportunities on the 1981 tour to England and did not appear in the Tests.

Beardmore, William Joseph Montague
Amateur. *b:* 18.7.1894, Renfrew, Scotland. *d:* 29.12.1978, Haywards Heath, Sussex. Right-hand batsman. *Sch* Loretto. *Team* Scotland (1924).
Career batting
1–2–0–5–3–2.50–0–*ct* 0

Beart, Frederick Robert
Amateur. *b:* 6.7.1850, Godmanchester, Hunts. *d:* 4.3.1895, Godmanchester, Hunts. Hard hitting middle order batsman, moderate field. *Sch* Marlborough. *Team* Oxford U (1871).
Career batting
1–1–0–0–0–0.00–0–*ct* 1
His County cricket was for Huntingdonshire.

Beasley, Joseph Noble
Amateur. *b:* 1882, Northampton. *d:* 23.1.1960, Stony Stratford. Brother of R.N. (Northants). Hard-hitting tail end right-end batsman, right-arm fast medium bowler. *Team* Northants (1911–19, 16 matches).
Career batting
16–22–6–100–21–6.25–0–*ct* 9
Bowling 261–5–52.20–0–0–1/6
From 1911 to 1914 he lived in Australia. He was a good rugby footballer, appearing for Northampton.

Beasley, Rev Robert Noble
Amateur. *b:* 17.12.1882, Northampton. *d:* 21.1.1966, Stony Stratford, Bucks. Brother of J.N. (Northants). Useful batsman. *Team* Northants (1907–11, 10 matches).
Career batting
10–15–0–109–28–7.26–0–*ct* 4
He was an excellent rugby footballer, appearing for Northants.

Beattie, Fred Demetrius
Amateur. *b:* 18.8.1909, Manchester. Middle order right-hand batsman, right-arm medium pace bowler. *Sch* Rossall. *Team* Lancashire (1932, 5 matches).
Career batting
7–12–2–172–36–17.20–0–*ct* 0
He also played for the Minor Counties in first-class matches in 1930 and 1933.

Beauclerk, Rev Lord Frederick
Amateur. *b:* 8.5.1773. *d:* 22.4.1850, London. Father of C.W. (Oxford U, 1836). Brilliant right-hand batsman, slow under-arm bowler, slip field. *Teams* Hampshire (1805–07); Kent (1806).
Career batting
99–181–14–4555–129*–27.27–4–*ct* 81–*st* 1
Bowling 251 wickets, no analyses
He followed William Beldham as the best batsman in England and for some years was regarded as the finest amateur single-wicket crick-

eter in the country. Like Beldham's, his career was a very long one, extending over 35 years, and in his retirement he was a frequenter of Lord's, being regarded as the autocrat of the game. His uncontrollable temper made him a man with whom few cared to cross swords. His final important match was in 1825.

Beaumont, David John
Cricketer. *b:* 17.9.1944, West Bridgford, Nottingham. Middle order right-hand batsman, right-arm off break bowler. *Team* Cambridge U (1977–78, blue 1978).
Career batting
11–16–1–258–44–17.20–0–*ct* 4

Beaumont, Harold
Professional. *b:* 14.10.1916, Huddersfield, Yorkshire. Hard hitting middle order right-hand batsman, useful bowler. *Team* Yorkshire (1946–47, 28 matches).
Career batting
28–46–6–716–60–17.90–0–*ct* 11
Bowling 236–9–26.22–0–0–4/31

Beaumont, John
Professional. *b:* 16.9.1854, Armitage Bridge, Yorkshire. *d:* 1.5.1920, Lambeth, London. Lower order right-hand batsman, fast right-arm bowler. *Teams* Yorkshire (1877–78, 4 matches); Surrey (1885–90, 91 matches). *Tour* Vernon to Australia 1887/8.
Career batting
112–158–52–878–60–8.28–0–*ct* 37
Bowling 7808–467–16.71–31–7–8/40

Easily his best season was his first with Surrey, when he captured 129 wickets, av 16.57, the only time in his career he passed 100.

Beaumont, Rolland
Amateur. *b:* 4.2.1884, Newcastle, Natal, South Africa. *d:* 25.5.1958, Durban, South Africa. Hard hitting middle order right-hand batsman, fine field. *Team* Transvaal (1911/2 to 1913/4). *Tour* South Africans to England 1912. *Tests* South Africa (1912 to 1913/4, 5 matches).
Career batting
31–47–4–1086–121–25.25–1–*ct* 11
Bowling 2–0
Test batting
5–9–0–70–31–7.77–0–*ct* 2
Bowling 0–0

His first-class debut was for Wanderers CC in South Africa in 1908/9.

Becher, Adrian William Bay
Amateur. *b:* 12.5.1897, Stow-in-the-Wold, Gloucs. *d:* 29.3.1957, Swindon Village, Cheltenham. Middle order right-hand batsman. *Sch* Repton. *Teams* Gloucestershire (1925–29, 9 matches); Europeans (1924/5 to 1925/6).
Career batting
12–21–0–327–64–15.57–0–*ct* 18
Bowling 209–0

Becher, Arthur William Reddie
Amateur. *b:* 6.12.1842, Allahabad, India. *d:* 25.3.1926, Maida Vale, London. Middle order batsman. *Team* MCC (1872).
Career batting
1–2–0–13–8–6.50–0–*ct* 1

Becher, Sir William Fane Wrixon
Amateur. *b:* 7.9.1915, Co.Cork, Ireland. Middle order right-hand batsman. *Sch* Harrow. *Team* Sussex (1939, 3 matches).
Career batting
3–5–0–48–20–9.60–0–*ct* 0

He also played for Wiltshire.

Beck, Geoffrey Edward
Amateur. *b:* 16.6.1918, Wisbech, Cambridgeshire. Opening or middle order right-hand batsman, off break bowler. *Sch* Whitgift. *Team* Oxford U (1946).
Career batting
3–6–0–72–50–12.00–0–*ct* 0

He played for Oxford v Cambridge in 1945 (not first-class).

Beckett, Samuel Barclay
Amateur. *b:* 13.4.1906, Dublin. Left-hand batsman, left-arm medium pace bowler. *Sch* Portora Royal School. *Team* Dublin University (1925–26).
Career batting
2–4–0–35–18–8.75–0–*ct* 2
Bowling 64–0

A well-known author whose works include 'Waiting for Godot', 'Murphy' and 'Molloy', he was awarded the Nobel Prize for Literature in 1969.

Beddow, Alan Michael
Cricketer. *b:* 12.10.1941, St Helens, Lancashire. Attacking middle-order right-hand batsman, right-arm medium pace bowler. *Team* Lancashire (1962–66, 33 matches).
Career batting
33–54–3–775–112*–15.19–1–*ct* 14
Bowling 473–15–31.53–0–0–3/10

He was a well-known Rugby League footballer with St Helens.

Bedford, Edward Henry Rilands
Amateur. *b:* 7.6.1903, Aston, Birmingham. *d:*

9.10.1976, Chelmsford, Essex. Grandson of Rev W.K.R. Bedford (co-founder of Free Foresters). Middle order right-hand batsman. *Sch* Winchester. *Team* Derbyshire (1924, 1 match).
Career batting
1–2–0–3–3–1.50–0–*ct* 0

Bedford, H.
Amateur. Lower order batsman, useful bowler. *Team* Hampshire (1882, 1 match).
Career batting
1–1–0–3–3–3.00–0–*ct* 0
Bowling 5–1–5.00–0–0–1/5

Bedford, Harry
Professional. *b:* 17.7.1907, Morley, Leeds, Yorkshire. *d:* 5.7.1968, Croydon, Surrey. Lower order right-hand batsman, slow left-arm bowler. *Team* Yorkshire (1928, 5 matches).
Career batting
5–5–1–57–24–14.25–0–*ct* 0
Bowling 179–8–22.37–1–0–6/91

Bedford, Philip Ian
Amateur. *b:* 11.2.1930, Friern Barnet, Middlesex. *d:* 18.9.1966, on way to Wanstead Hospital. Lower order right-hand batsman, leg break bowler. *Team* Middlesex (1947–62, 65 matches). *Tours* MCC to South America 1958/9, 1963/4, to North America 1959 (not first-class).
Career batting
77–84–24–979–75*–16.31–0–*ct* 46
Bowling 4208–128–32.87–5–0–6/52

As a 17-year-old he created a most favourable impression in 1947, when he came second in the Middlesex bowling averages with 25 wickets, av 19.36, but he failed to maintain this form and soon left County cricket. He was recalled by Middlesex in 1961 as captain, and led the side for two seasons. He collapsed whilst batting in a club match at Buckhurst Hill in 1966 and died on the way to hospital; he had played his last first-class match – for MCC – only a fortnight before his death.

Bedford, Walter
Professional. *b:* 24.2.1879, Barnsley, Yorkshire. *d:* July 1939, Doncaster, Yorkshire. Hard hitting lower order right-hand batsman, right-arm fast-medium bowler. *Team* Yorkshire (1903, 2 matches).
Career batting
2–2–1–38–30*–38.00–0–*ct* 1
Bowling 117–2–58.50–0–0–2/38

Bedi, Bishansingh Giansingh
Cricketer. *b*: 25.9.1946, Amritsar, India. Hard-hitting tail end right-hand batsman, slow left-arm bowler. *Teams* Northern Punjab (1961/2 to 1966/7); Delhi (1968/9 to 1980/1); Northants (1972–77, 110 matches). *Tours* India to England 1967, 1971, 1974, 1979, to Australia and New Zealand 1967/8, to Australia 1977/8, to East Africa 1967/8, to West Indies 1970/1, 1975/6, to New Zealand 1975/6, to Pakistan 1978/9; State Bank of India to Ceylon 1968/9; International XI to Pakistan 1981/2. *Tests* India (1966/7 to 1979, 67 matches).
Career batting
370–426–111–3584–61–11.37–0–*ct* 172
Bowling 33843–1560–21.69–106–20–7/5
Test batting
67–101–28–656–50*–8.98–0–*ct* 26
Bowling 7637–266–28.71–14–1–7/98

He played in all but one of the Tests during his four tours to England, but was not very successful, his best Test series being 1971 with 11 wickets, av 29.54. In 1971 and 1974 he took 58 wickets and 53 wickets respectively. He proved, however, most effective for Northants and twice reached 100 wickets in a season (best 112, av 24.64, in 1974). He captained India in 22 Tests, but none in England.

Bedser, Alec Victor, OBE
Professional. *b:* 4.7.1918, Reading, Berkshire. Twin brother of E.A. (Surrey). Lower order right-hand batsman, outstanding right-arm medium-fast bowler. *Team* Surrey (1939–60, 371 matches). *Tours* MCC to Australia and New Zealand 1946/7, 1950/1, to Australia 1954/5, to South Africa 1948/9; Howard to India 1956/7; Surrey to Rhodesia 1959/60. *Tests* England (1946 to 1955, 51 matches).
Career batting
485–576–181–5735–126–14.51–1–*ct* 289
Bowling 39279–1924–20.41–96–16–8/18
Test batting
51–71–15–714–79–12.75–0–*ct* 26
Bowling 5876–236–24.89–15–5–7/34

Although he played for Surrey in 1939, Bedser's first-class career really began in 1946, when he was quickly recognised as the principal seam bowler in England. His Test debut – the first post-war Test – provided him with figures of 11 for 145, and in the second Test he captured another 11 wickets (for 93). From that moment until 1954 he was the major force in the England attack. His total of 236 Test wickets created a new world record and if he had not declined invitations to go on several winter tours he would probably have topped the 300 mark.

Bedser's name is inseparably linked with the first four post-war series against Australia – in the 1950/1 matches he took 30 wickets (av 16.06) and in the 1953 matches 39 wickets (av 17.48). The latter included 14 for 99 at Trent Bridge – the outstanding performance of his career. His most effective delivery was the one which went from leg to off, but unlike many bowlers of his pace, he employed a number of subtle variations which were undoubtedly the essence of his success. The way in which he uncovered a flaw in Bradman's technique and dismissed the master batsman on several occasions was a credit to Bedser's endeavour.

He took 100 wickets in a season on eleven occasions with 162 (av 16.67) in 1953 his best, and he constituted a major force in Surrey's famous run of seven consecutive Championships.

In 1962 he was appointed as an England selector and from 1969 to 1981 was Chairman of the Selection Committee. He managed the tours to Australia of 1974/5 and 1979/80, after being assistant manager on the 1962/3 visit. He was awarded an OBE for his services to cricket.

Bedser, Eric Arthur
Professional. *b:* 4.7.1918, Reading, Berkshire. Twin brother of A.V. (Surrey and England). Middle order right-hand batsman, right-arm off break bowler. *Team* Surrey (1939–61, 443 matches). *Tours* MCC to Australia 1950/1 (1 match); Surrey to Rhodesia 1959/60.
Career batting
457–692–79–14716–163–24.00–10–*ct* 236
Bowling 20784–833–24.95–24–4–7/33

He hit 1,000 runs in a season six times (best 1,740, av 34.11, in 1949). His final first-class match was for MCC in 1962.

Beeching, Thomas Hugh Pitt
Amateur. *b:* 10.3.1900, Maidstone, Kent. *d:* 31.12.1971, Aldershot, Hants. Hard hitting middle order right-hand batsman. *Sch* Charterhouse. *Team* Kent (1920–21, 10 matches).
Career batting
10–13–0–217–38–16.69–0–*ct* 1

Beers, Hector George
Amateur. *b:* 1876, Potterspury, Northants. *d:* 11.2.1954, Northampton. Middle order batsman, slow right-arm bowler. *Sch* Wellingborough. *Team* Northants (1914–21, 17 matches).
Career batting
17–30–1–175–31–6.03–0–*ct* 9
Bowling 232–4–58.00–0–0–1/8

Beet, George
Professional. *b:* 24.4.1886, Somercotes, Derbyshire. *d:* 13.12.1946, Somercotes, Derbyshire. Father of G.H.C. (Derbyshire), grandfather of G.A. (Derbyshire). Middle order right-hand batsman, wicket-keeper. *Team* Derbyshire (1910–25, 47 matches).
Career batting
48–88–10–1277–92*–16.37–0–*ct* 59–*st* 11
Bowling 27–0

He was a noted umpire after retiring from County cricket.

Beet, Gordon Albert
Professional. *b:* 5.5.1939, Heanor, Derbyshire. Son of G.H.C. (Derbyshire), grandson of George (Derbyshire). Lower order right-hand batsman, right-arm off break bowler. *Team* Derbyshire (1956–61, 6 matches).
Career batting
6–7–2–36–17–7.20–0–*ct* 3
Bowling 100–2–50.00–0–0–1/42

Beet, George Hector Cook
Professional. *b:* 30.5.1904, Somercotes, Derbyshire. *d:* 22.8.1949, Somercotes, Derbyshire. Father of G.A. (Derbyshire), son of George (Derbyshire). Middle order right-hand batsman, wicket-keeper. *Team* Derbyshire (1928–32, 5 matches).
Career batting
11–19–2–277–61–16.29–0–*ct* 14–*st* 2

His last appearance in first-class cricket was for MCC in 1938.

Beevor, John Grosvenor
Amateur. *b:* 1.1.1845, Barnby Moor, Notts. *d:* 5.5.1903, Barnby Moor, Notts. Hard-hitting middle order right-hand batsman, slow right-hand round-arm bowler. *Sch* Uppingham. *Team* Nottinghamshire (1868–70, 5 matches).
Career batting
7–13–1–322–88–26.83–0–*ct* 2

His final first-class match was for Gentlemen of North in 1871.

Begbie, Denis Warburton
Amateur. *b:* 12.12.1914, Middleburg, Transvaal, South Africa. Middle order right-hand batsman, off break bowler. *Team* Transvaal (1933/4 to 1949/50). *Tour* South Africans to England 1947. *Tests* South Africa (1948/9 to 1949/50, 5 matches).
Career batting
58–85–9–2727–207*–35.88–6–*ct* 27
Bowling 2085–88–23.69–5–2–7/96
Test batting
5–7–0–138–48–19.71–0–*ct* 2
Bowling 130–1–130.00–0–0–1/38

He had only limited success on his tour to England and did not appear in any of the Tests. His best innings against English bowling was for

Transvaal v MCC in 1948/9, when he hit 154. His highest score was 207* for Transvaal v OFS at Johannesburg in 1937/8.

Beisiegel, William Karl
Amateur. *b:* 13.7.1907, Uppingham, Rutland. *d:* 8.1.1973, Halton, Bucks. Middle order right-hand batsman, excellent cover field. *Sch* Uppingham. *Team* Leicestershire (1934, 10 matches).
Career batting
15–25–3–357–54–16.22–0–*ct* 9
His debut in first-class matches was for the RAF in 1928.

Belcher, Charles (Frank)
Amateur. *b:* 1872, Thornbury, Gloucs. *d:* 1.4.1938, Caernarvon, North Wales. Sound right-hand middle order batsman, right-arm medium pace bowler. *Team* Gloucestershire (1890–92, 7 matches).
Career batting
7–12–2–157–60*–15.70–0–*ct* 2
Bowling 55–1–55.00–0–0–1/13

Belcher, Gordon
Amateur. *b:* 26.9.1885, Brighton College. *d:* 16.5.1915. He was killed in action nr Richebourg L'Avoue, Belgium. Son of T.H. (Oxford U). Right-hand batsman, right-arm medium pace bowler. *Sch* Brighton. *Team* Hampshire (1905, 1 match).
Career batting
1–2–0–0–0–0.00–0 *ct* 0
Bowling 3–0
He appeared in the Freshmen's match of 1905 at Cambridge, but did not play in any first-class games for the University. He also played for Berkshire.

Belcher, Rev Thomas Hayes
Amateur. *b:* 12.9.1847, Faringdon, Berkshire. *d:* 26.11.1919, Bramley, Hants. Father of Gordon (Hants). Lower order right-hand batsman, right-arm fast round-arm bowler. *Sch* Magdalen College School. *Team* Oxford U (1869–70, blue 1870).
Career batting
7–13–8–58–23–11.60–*ct* 4
Bowling 391–19+1–20.57–0–0–4/22
He played for Herefordshire and Worcestershire (non-first-class).

Beldam, Cyril Asplan
Amateur. *b:* 15.10.1869, North Aylesford, Kent. *d:* 7.9.1940, Marylebone, London. Brother of E.A. (Middlesex) and cousin of G.W. (Middlesex). Lower order right-hand batsman. *Sch* King's College School, London. *Team* Middlesex (1896, 2 matches). *Tour* Priestley to West Indies 1896/7.
Career batting
12–20–4–185–24*–11.56–0–*ct* 5
Bowling 272–7–38.85–1–0–5/97
His final first-class match was for A. J. Webbe's XI in 1899.

Beldam, Ernest Asplan
Amateur. *b:* 30.6.1879, Brentford, Middlesex. *d:* 28.11.1958, Horsell, Surrey. Brother of C.A. (Middlesex) and cousin of G.W. (Middlesex). Middle order right-hand batsman. *Team* Middlesex (1903–07, 37 matches).
Career batting
39–63–5–1225–105–21.12–1–*ct* 19
His only first-class hundred was made for Middlesex v Somerset at Lord's in 1904, when he and his cousin, G.W., both reached three figures and featured in a partnership of 201 for the fifth wicket.

Beldam, George William
Amateur. *b:* 1.5.1868, New Cross, Kent. *d:* 23.11.1937, Lower Bourne, Surrey. Cousin of C.A. (Middlesex) and E.A. (Middlesex). Sound middle order right-hand batsman, right-arm medium slow bowler. *Teams* Middlesex (1900–07, 102 matches); London County (1900–03).
Career batting
141–233–16–6562–155*–30.23–9–*ct* 83
Bowling 3278–107–30.63–4–0–5/28
He hit 1,000 runs in a session three times (best 1,158, av 38.60, in 1901). A pioneer in action photography, he produced the plates for 'Great Batsmen, Their Methods at a Glance' published in 1907 and a remarkable book for its time. Beldam also wrote books on golf and tennis.

Beldham, William
Professional. *b:* 21.3.1766, Wrecclesham, Farnham, Surrey. *d:* 26.2.1862, Tilford, Surrey. Excellent right-hand batsman, medium pace under-arm bowler. *Teams* Surrey (1801–17); Hampshire (1805–07); Kent (1806).
Career batting
72–131–8–2374–82–19.30–0–*ct* 111–*st* 42
Bowling 48 wickets, no analyses
He was regarded as the best batsman of his time, his career in great matches lasting 35 seasons. He was the last survivor of the famous cricketers of the Hambledon era and details of many of his early performances are unfortunately lost. His final important match was for Godalming in 1821.

Bell, Alexander John
Amateur. *b:* 15.4.1906, East London, South Africa. Tail end right-hand batsman, right-arm

fast-medium bowler. *Teams* Western Province (1925/6 to 1930/1); Rhodesia (1938/9). *Tours* South Africans to England 1929, 1935, to Australia and New Zealand 1931/2. *Tests* South Africa (1929–35, 16 matches).
Career batting
63–79–45–311–32*–9.14–0–*ct* 27
Bowling 5312–228–23.29–10–1–8/34
Test batting
16–23–12–69–26*–6.27–0–*ct* 6
Bowling 1567–48–32.64–4–0–6/99

On his first visit to England, Bell's best performance was his 6/99 in the Lord's Test. His second visit was unfortunately marred by injury.

Bell, Alexander Patrick
Amateur. *b:* 23.2.1915, Rosario, Argentina. *d:* 12.4.1956, Oxford. Middle order right-hand batsman. *Sch* Warwick. *Team* Northants (1934, 3 matches).
Career batting 3–6–0–37–24–6.16–0–*ct* 2

He also played for Hertfordshire.

Bell, David Lauder
Cricketer. *b:* 28.4.1949, Edinburgh, Scotland. Middle order right-hand batsman. *Sch* Rugby. Teams Oxford U (1971); Scotland (1979–81).
Career batting
7–13–3–234–60–23.40–0–*ct* 3

Bell, Frederick William
Professional. *b:* 2.1.1830, St Neots, Hunts. *d:* 18.9.1871, Cambridge. Lower order right-hand batsman, round-arm medium pace bowler, brilliant outfield. *Team* Cambridgeshire (1857–64, 17 matches).
Career batting
58–100–18–921–50*–11.23–0–*ct* 23
Bowling 1090–69+10–15.79–4–1–6/25

His first-class debut was for the Cambridge Town Club in 1846. He also played for Herefordshire, Worcestershire (non-first-class) and Dorset.

Bell, Geoffrey Foxall
Amateur. *b:* 16.4.1896, Stapenhill, Staffs. *d*: 17.1. 1984, Haslemere, Surrey. Cousin of the brothers Evershed (Derbyshire). Middle order right-hand batsman. *Sch* Repton. *Teams* Derbyshire (1914–20, 5 matches); Oxford U (1919, blue).
Career batting
12–21–0–336–64–16.00–0–*ct* 6

Bell, John Thomson
Professional. *b:* 16.6.1895, Batley, Yorkshire. *d:* 14.8.1974, Guiseley, Leeds, Yorkshire. Stylish opening right-hand batsman. *Teams* Yorkshire (1921–23, 7 matches); Glamorgan (1924–31, 166 matches); Wales (1924–30).
Career batting
184–307–20–8390–225–29.23–12–*ct* 63
Bowling 205–2–102.50–0–0–1/2

He hit 1,000 runs in a season four times (best 1,701, av 31.50, in 1929). He hit two double centuries, the higher being 225 for Glamorgan v Worcs at Dudley in 1926.

Bell, Percy Harrison
Amateur. *b:* 1892, Headington, Oxon. *d:* 4.2.1956, Durban, South Africa. Middle order batsman. *Teams* Gloucestershire (1911–12, 8 matches); Orange Free State (1912/3, 2 matches).
Career batting
10–18–1–293–64–17.23–0–*ct* 9

This cricketer has two obituary notices in Wisden, one for 1956 and the other for 1971. It is believed, but is by no means certain, that 1956 is correct.

Bell, Roland
Amateur. *b:* 16.5.1857, Bishops Stortford, Herts. *d:* 29.1.1935, Leamington Spa, Warwickshire. Middle order right-hand batsman, slow round arm bowler. *Team* Surrey (1876, 1 match).
Career batting
1–2–0–4–3–2.00–0–*ct* 0

Bell, Richard Moor
Amateur. *b:* 1.1.1874, Wigton, Cumberland. *d:* 10.6.1953, Elm Grove, Brighton, Sussex. Lower order right-hand batsman, slow off-break bowler. *Sch* The Leys. *Team* London County (1902–04). *Tour* Brackley to Egypt 1909 (not first-class).
Career batting
15–26–6–225–31*–11.25–0–*ct* 10
Bowling 889–31–28.67–2–0–6/88

He was a noted cricketer in London Club cricket, appearing for Sutton CC (Surrey) for about 40 years.

Bell, Ronald Victor
Professional. *b:* 7.1.1931, Chelsea, London. Tail end left-hand batsman, slow left-arm bowler. *Teams* Middlesex (1952–54, 5 matches); Sussex (1957–64, 183 matches).
Career batting
189–233–54–1558–53*–8.70–0–*ct* 150
Bowling 11111–392–28.34–19–1–8/54

He also played for Norfolk. He played soccer for Chelsea.

Bellamy, Benjamin Walter
Professional. *b:* 22.4.1891, Wollaston, Northants. Middle order right-hand batsman, wicket-keeper. *Team* Northants (1920–37, 353 matches).

Career batting
354–625–66–9247–168–16.54–4–*ct* 529–*st* 125
Bowling 57–0

His best season with the bat was 1928 when he hit 1,116 runs, av 22.77 – this was the only time he reached 1,000 runs for the season. He played soccer for Northampton Town.

Belle, Brian Henry
Amateur. *b:* 7.4.1914, Woodford Green, Essex. Middle order right-hand batsman, right-arm medium bowler. *Sch* Forest. *Teams* Essex (1935–37, 26 matches); Oxford U (1935–36, blue 1936). *Tour* Oxford and Cambridge to Jamaica 1938/9.
Career batting
43–72–5–1235–70–18.43–0–*ct* 29
Bowling 33–1–33.00–0–0–1/10

He also played for Suffolk and appeared in first-class matches for the Minor Counties in 1949 and 1950. His first-class debut was for MCC in 1934.

Beloe, Gerald Harry
Amateur. *b:* 21.11.1877, Clifton, Gloucs. *d:* 1.10.1944, Clifton, Gloucs. Middle order left-hand batsman, slow left-arm bowler. *Sch* Marlborough. *Team* Gloucestershire (1898–99, 6 matches).
Career batting
6–11–2–153–52*–17.00–0–*ct* 4

Bembridge, Henry
Professional. *b:* 27.6.1852, Bulwell, Notts. Lower order right-hand batsman, right-arm fast bowler. *Team* Nottinghamshire (1878, 1 match).
Career batting
1–2–1–17–15*–17.00–0–*ct* 0
Bowling 34–0

Benaud, Richard, OBE
Amateur. *b:* 6.10.1930, Penrith, New South Wales, Australia. Brother of John (New South Wales and Australia). Forcing middle-order right-hand batsman, excellent leg break and googly bowler. *Team* New South Wales (1948/9 to 1963/4, 86 matches). *Tours* Australia to England 1953, 1956, 1961, to South Africa 1957/8, to West Indies 1954/5, to New Zealand 1956/7, to Pakistan and India 1956/7, 1959/60; Cavaliers to South Africa 1960/1, to India, Pakistan and New Zealand 1961/2, to India and South Africa 1962/3; Swanton to India 1963/4; Commonwealth to Pakistan 1967/8. *Tests* Australia (1951/2 to 1963/4, 63 matches).
Career batting
259–365–44–11719–187–36.50–23–*ct* 254
Bowling 23370–945–24.73–56–9–7/18
Test batting
63–97–7–2201–122–24.45–3–*ct* 65
Bowling 6704–248–27.03–16–1–7/72

Although originally selected for New South Wales as a batsman, Benaud developed into the best Australian all-rounder of his generation, and indeed his bowling latterly became even more effective than his batting. It was the tour to South Africa in 1957/8, when he took 106 wickets in addition to making 817 runs, that really established him. The following year he was chosen to lead Australia against England and his shrewd captaincy plus brilliant bowling won the Ashes by four Tests to nil. He captained Australia in England in 1961 and again won the series, though injury curtailed his bowling ability. He is a noted journalist and broadcaster.

Benbow, Herbert Clifton
Amateur. *b:* 4.10.1861, Uxbridge, Middlesex. *d:* 2.2.1941, Brampton, Cumberland. Useful middle order right-hand batsman, wicket-keeper. *Sch* Westminster. *Team* Cambridge U (1881).
Career batting
2–4–1–28–12–9.33–0–*ct* 2–*st* 3

Bencraft, Sir Henry William Russell
(also known as Russell-Bencraft)
Amateur. *b:* 4.3.1858, Southampton, Hants. *d:* 25.12.1943, Compton, Winchester, Hants. Right-hand batsman, fast right-arm bowler. *Sch* St Edward's, Oxford. *Team* Hampshire (1876–96, 44 matches).
Career batting
46–78–18–932–62*–15.53–0–*ct* 32
Bowling 197–5–39.40–0–0–2/15

For many years he was Hampshire cricket, being Secretary to the County Club from 1882 to 1904, captain from 1893 to 1895 and on the Committee of the Club for many years, finally being the President in 1936. He was also a noted rugby player.

Bendall, Frederick George
Professional. *b:* 18.12.1865, Cheltenham, Gloucs. *d:* 27.4.1941, Cheltenham, Gloucs. Lower order right-hand batsman, right-arm medium pace bowler. *Team* Gloucestershire (1887, 1 match).
Career batting
1–2–0–3–3–1.50–0–*ct* 0
Bowling 42–1–42.00–0–0–1/42

Bengough, Clement Stuart
Amateur. *b:* 14.1.1861, Frampton-Cotterell, Bristol. *d:* 19.11.1934, Laramie, Wyoming, USA.

Lower order hard-hitting right-hand batsman, wicket-keeper. *Sch* Marlborough. *Team* Gloucestershire (1880, 2 matches).
Career batting
2–3–0–8–8–2.66–0–*ct* 3

Benham, Charles Edward
Professional. *b:* 24.6.1881, East Ham, Essex. *d:* 13.12.1961, Bangour Hospital, West Lothian. Father of F.C. (Scotland). Lower order right-hand batsman, right-arm fast bowler. *Teams* Essex (1904–09, 57 matches); Scotland (1912).
Career batting
59–84–11–1047–65*–14.34–0–*ct* 33
Bowling 2338–70–33.40–4–0–7/60

Benham, Frederick Charles
Professional. *b:* 18.12.1905, Bexley, Kent. Son of C.E. (Essex). Right-hand batsman. *Team* Scotland (1949).
Career batting
1–2–1–9–9–9.00–0–*ct* 0

Benjamin, Harold Lewis
Amateur. *b:* 1892, Birmingham. *d:* 7.8.1942, Tettenhall, Staffs. Lower order right-hand batsman, right-arm fast medium bowler. *Teams* Warwickshire (1919, 2 matches); Northants (1928, 1 match).
Career batting
3–4–0–37–23–9.25–0–*ct* 1
Bowling 182–6–30.33–0–0–3/38

Benka, Herbert Frank
Amateur. *b:* 27.10.1909, Regent's Park, London. *d:* 22.4.1970, Westminster, London. Middle order right-hand batsman, slow left-arm bowler. *Team* Middlesex (1933–36, 11 matches).
Career batting
13–23–1–359–59–16.31–0–*ct* 12
Bowling 331–12–27.58–0–0–4/78
His last first-class match was for MCC in 1939.

Benke, Andrew Frederick
Amateur. *b:* 3.9.1938, Southampton, Hants. Lower order right-hand batsman, right-arm off break bowler. *Sch* Cheltenham. *Team* Cambridge U (1962, blue).
Career batting
19–29–4–240–26–9.60–0–*ct* 4
Bowling 1964–50–39.28–2–0–5/75
He did not make his first-class debut for the University until his third year and then proceeded to win his blue and capture 50 wickets in the University season.

Benn, Anthony
Amateur. *b:* 7.10.1912, London. Middle order right-hand batsman, right-arm medium pace bowler. *Sch* Harrow. *Team* Oxford U (1934–35, blue 1935).
Career batting
12–20–0–378–90–18.90–0–*ct* 6
Bowling 135–0

Bennet, Ferdinando Wallis
Amateur. *b:* 13.12.1850, Newlyn, Cornwall. *d:* 17.10.1929, Northam, Devon. Middle order right-hand batsman, good field. *Sch* Sherborne. *Team* Kent (1874, 1 match).
Career batting
4–6–1–119–47–23.80–0–*ct* 2
Bowling 40–1–40.00–0–0–1/22
He was a prolific batsman in military cricket. His final first-class match was for MCC in 1878.

Bennett, Albert
Professional. *b:* 21.5.1910, St Helens, Lancs. Lower order right-hand batsman, leg break and googly bowler. *Teams* New South Wales (1930/1, 1 match); Lancashire (1932–33, 16 matches).
Career batting
17–16–1–254–51–16.93–0–*ct* 12
Bowling 906–24–37.75–0–0–4/49

Bennett, Alfred Charles Leopold
Amateur. *b:* 31.12.1914, West Norwood, London. *d:* 24.9.1971, Surrey. Middle order right-hand batsman. *Sch* Dulwich. *Team* Northants (1947–49, 16 matches).
Career batting
16–29–0–586–68–20.20–0–*ct* 8
A noted batsman in London Club cricket and one time captain of the Club Cricket Conference, his work with the BBC prevented him from playing regular County cricket.

Bennett, Arthur Robert
Amateur. *b:* 16.11.1868, Mapperley, Notts. *d:* 7.5.1899, Marylebone, London. Tail-end right-hand batsman, right-arm fast-medium bowler. *Team* Nottinghamshire (1893–96, 7 matches).
Career batting
7–11–1–40–17–4.00–0–*ct* 2
Bowling 498–17–29.29–1–0–5/81

Bennett, Barry William Prosser
Cricketer. *b:* 6.2.1955, RAF Abyad, Ismailia, Egypt. Middle order right-hand batsman. *Sch* Welbeck. *Team* Cambridge U (1979, blue).
Career batting
2–2–0–4–4–2.00–0–*ct* 0

Bennett, Charles Oatley
Amateur. *b:* 15.8.1872, Ticehurst, Sussex. *d:* May 1921, Bath, Somerset. Middle order right-hand

batsman, leg break bowler. *Sch* Haileybury. *Team* Somerset (1902, 2 matches).
Career batting
2–4–2–10–6–5.00–0–*ct* 1

Bennett, Cecil Tristram
Amateur. *b:* 10.8.1902, Lambeth, London. *d:* 3.2.1978, Islington, London. Opening or middle order right-hand batsman, good slip field. *Sch* Harrow. *Teams* Cambridge U (1923–25, blue 1923 and 1925); Surrey (1922, 4 matches); Middlesex (1926–27, 3 matches). *Tour* MCC to West Indies 1925/6.
Career batting
50–85–9–1335–88–17.56–0–*ct* 43
Bowling 4–0

He was regarded as one of the most promising cricketers at Harrow, but never made his mark in County cricket. His last first-class match was for MCC in 1928.

Bennett, Donald
Professional. *b:* 18.12.1933, Wakefield, Yorkshire. Middle order right-hand batsman, right-arm fast-medium bowler. *Team* Middlesex (1950–68, 392 matches).
Career batting
404–612–125–10656–117*–21.88–4–*ct* 158
Bowling 20598–784–26.27–24–1–7/47

He scored 1,000 runs in a season twice (1,144, av 22.00, best). A noted soccer player, he appeared for Arsenal and Coventry City.

Bennett, Enoch Harvey
Amateur. *b:* 21.12.1894, Dudley, Worcs. Hard hitting middle order batsman. *Team* Worcestershire (1925, 3 matches).
Career batting
4–8–0–157–73–19.62–0–*ct* 1

In 1927 he played for the Civil Service against the New Zealanders and scored 73 and 60 – easily the best batting for his side. This match is regarded as first-class. He also played for Staffordshire.

Bennett, George
Professional. *b:* 12.2.1829, Shorne Ridgway, Gravesend, Kent. *d:* 16.8.1886, Shorne Ridgway. Very defensive right-hand batsman, slow right-hand round arm bowler, good outfield. *Team* Kent (1853–73, 126 matches). *Tour* Stephenson to Australia 1861/2.
Career batting
169–307–22–4199–100–14.73–1–*ct* 122
Bowling 10173–601+12–16.92–41–12–9/113

He was one of the best all-rounders of his day. His most notable innings was 100 for South v North in 1865. His bowling was very slow, flighted high in the air and most deceptive. His best bowling was 9/113 for Kent v Sussex at Hove in 1871.

Bennett, George Guy Marsland
Amateur. *b:* 22.4.1883, Charlton, Kent. *d:* 6.2.1966, Sunningdale, Berkshire. Middle order right-hand batsman. *Sch* Harrow. *Team* Oxford U (1903–05).
Career batting
8–16–0–380–131–23.75–1–*ct* 6
Bowling 49–2–24.50–0–0–1/20

He played for Berkshire for some 20 years.

Bennett, Geoffrey Michael
Amateur. *b:* 17.12.1909, Bruton, Somerset. *d:* 26.7.1982, Toronto, Canada. Middle order right-hand batsman, right-arm medium pace bowler. *Sch* King's Bruton. *Team* Somerset (1928–39, 109 matches).
Career batting
109–173–21–2330–73–15.32–0–*ct* 52
Bowling 448–14–32.00–0–0–4/39

Bennett, Howard Alfred
Amateur. *b:* 20.8.1892, Alcester, Warwickshire. *d:* 13.1.1973, Southbourne, Hants. Lower order right-hand batsman, leg break bowler. *Sch* Wellingborough. *Team* Northants (1920, 1 match).
Career batting
1–2–0–1–1–0.50–0–*ct* 1
Bowling 51–0

Bennett, Rev Hugh Frederic
Amateur. *b:* 10.11.1862, Pershore, Worcs. *d:* 26.7.1943, Malvern, Worcs. Middle order right-hand batsman, slow right-hand bowler. *Sch* Bradfield. *Team* Worcestershire (1901, 2 matches).
Career batting
2–3–1–63–31*–31.50–0–*ct* 0

He also played for Shropshire.

Bennett, Henry Simpson
Professional. *b:* 1869, Pilsley, Bakewell, Derbyshire. *d*: 1921, Chapel-en-le-Frith, Derbyshire. Tail end batsman, wicket-keeper. *Team* Lancashire (1894, 1 match).
Career batting
1–2–0–16–11–8.00–0–*ct* 4

Bennett, John
Professional. *b:* 1777, Kingsley, Hants. *d:* July 1857, Kingsley, Hants. Cousin of James (Hants, 1803). Free hitting left-hand batsman, fast bowler, wicket-keeper. *Team* Hampshire (1803–18).

Career batting
51–93–7–1200–72–13.95–0–*ct* 41–*st* 1
Bowling 55 wickets, no analyses
His career in great matches lasted about 20 years, during which he was one of the leading Hampshire cricketers.

Bennett, John William
(registered at death as William)
Professional. *b:* 22.2.1864, Lower Whitfield, Glossop, Derbyshire. *d:* 10.11.1928, Stockport, Cheshire. Lower order right-hand batsman, left-arm medium or slow bowler. *Team* Derbyshire (1895–96, 16 matches).
Career batting
16–25–2–257–43–11.17–0–*ct* 7
Bowling 701–35–20.02–3–0–5/8
He played for Cheshire before representing his native County.

Bennett, M.
Middle order batsman. *Team* Worcestershire (1946, 1 match).
Career batting
1–2–0–10–8–5.00–0–*ct* 1

Bennett, Montague Valentine
Amateur. *b:* 1912, Glentham, Lincs. *d:* 17.12.1940, at sea off coast of Norway, serving in HMS *Acheron*. Lower order batsman, opening bowler. *Team* Minor Counties (1935).
Career batting
1–2–1–22–16*–22.00–0–*ct* 2
Bowling 54–2–27.00–0–0–2/27
He represented Lincolnshire.

Bennett, Nigel Harvie
Amateur. *b:* 23.9.1912, Walton-on-Thames, Surrey. Lower order right-hand batsman. *Sch* Stowe. *Team* Surrey (1946, 31 matches).
Career batting
31–45–2–688–79–16.00–0–*ct* 6
Bowling 25–1–25.00–0–0–1/1
He was captain of Surrey in 1946.

Bennett, Robert
Professional. *b:* 1831, Tunbridge Wells, Kent. *d:* 5.10.1875, Chichester, Sussex. Lower order batsman, wicket-keeper. *Teams* Sussex (1860, 1 match); Kent (1863–64, 6 matches).
Career batting
7–14–0–35–12–2.50–0–*ct* 9–*st* 2

Bennett, Robert
Cricketer. *b:* 16.6.1940, Bacup, Lancs. Opening right-hand batsman. *Sch* Rossall. *Team* Lancashire (1962–66, 49 matches).
Career batting
49–82–3–1814–112–22.96–2–*ct* 14
Bowling 0–0

Bennett, Richard Alexander
Amateur. *b:* 12.12.1872, Bournemouth, Hants. *d:* 16.7.1953, Thornbury, Gloucs. Steady right-hand batsman, wicket-keeper. *Sch* Eton. *Team* Hampshire (1896–99, 23 matches). *Tours* Warner to USA 1897; His own side to West Indies 1901/02.
Career batting
37–60–6–683–47–12.64–0–*ct* 44–*st* 29
His final first-class match was for Gentlemen in 1903.

Bennett, Sydney John
Professional. *b:* 7.2.1905, Hackleton, Northants. *d:* 1969, Worthing, Sussex. Lower order right-hand batsman, slow right-arm bowler. *Team* Northants (1933–34, 3 matches).
Career batting
3–6–1–37–19*–7.40–0–*ct* 0
Bowling 107–2–53.50–0–0–1/40

Benskin, William Ewart
Professional. *b:* 8.4.1880, Leicester. *d:* 1.6.1956, Leicester. Lower order right-hand batsman, right-arm fast bowler. *Teams* Leicestershire (1906–24, 100 matches); Scotland (1912–13).
Career batting
105–162–48–954–79*–8.36–0–*ct* 30
Bowling 8408–325–25.87–17–5–8/86
After appearing briefly for Leicestershire, Benskin took an engagement in Scotland, playing in five first-class matches for that country, and did not return to County cricket until 1919. Injury ended his first-class cricket in 1924. A noted soccer player he was a half-back with Leicester Fosse.

Benson, Edward Turk
Amateur. *b:* 20.11.1907, Cardiff. *d:* 11.9.1967, Cape Town, South Africa. Tail end right-hand batsman, wicket-keeper. *Sch* Blundell's. *Teams* Oxford U (1928–29, blue both years); Gloucestershire (1929–31, 5 matches). *Tour* MCC to Australia and New Zealand 1929/30.
Career batting
38–55–14–520–42–12.68–0–*ct* 50–*st* 11
Bowling 0–0
Whilst he was in New Zealand in 1929/30, he was adjudged out 'handled ball', though there was some doubt as to whether he actually touched it.

Benson, Gwynfor Leonard
Professional. *b:* 7.1.1941, Birmingham. Middle order right-hand batsman, right-arm off break

bowler. *Team* Warwickshire (1959–61, 3 matches).
Career batting
3–5–2–102–46–34.00–0–*ct* 1
Bowling 32–2–16.00–0–0–2/25

Benson, Mark Richard
Cricketer. *b:* 6.7.1958, Shoreham, Sussex. Middle order left-hand batsman, off break bowler. *Sch* Sutton Valence. *Team* Kent (1980–83, 69 matches).
Career batting
69–116–13–3926–152*–38.11–9–*ct* 33
Bowling 72–0
He hit 1,000 runs in a season three times (best 1,515, av 44.55, in 1983).

Benstead, Charles Richard
Amateur. *b:* 21.4.1896, Cambridge. *d:* 3.7.1980, Solihull, Warwickshire. Lower order right-hand batsman, right-arm medium pace bowler. *Teams* Cambridge U (1920–21); Royal Navy (1923).
Career batting
3–4–1–28–16–9.33–0–*ct* 2
Bowling 259–11–23.54–1–0–5/32
His County cricket was for Cambridgeshire.

Benthall, William Henry
Amateur. *b:* 3.7.1837, Westminster, London. *d:* 4.1.1909, St Leonard's, Sussex. Middle order right-hand batsman, good field at point, occasional slow bowler. *Sch* Marlborough. *Teams* Cambridge U (1858–60, blue all three years); Middlesex (1862–68, 6 matches).
Career batting
37–70–8–1030–103–16.61–1–*ct* 33
Bowling 74–4+1–18.50–0–0–3/24
He also represented Cambridge at rackets and played cricket for Devon and Buckinghamshire. Owing to his duties at the India Office, his appearances in first-class cricket were very limited, though he appeared seven times for the Gentlemen v Players.

Bentinck, Bernhard Walter
Amateur. *b:* 16.7.1877, Hartley-Wintney, Hants. *d:* 27.6.1931, Petersfield, Hants. Hard-hitting right-hand batsman. *Sch* Winchester. *Team* Hampshire (1900–02, 2 matches).
Career batting
2–4–0–26–15–6.50–0–*ct* 1

Bentley, Michael
Professional. *b:* 14.2.1934, Rotherham, Yorkshire. Opening left-hand batsman. *Team* Derbyshire (1957, 1 match).
Career batting
1–2–0–12–10–6.00–0–*ct* 0

Benton, Charles Henry
Amateur. *b:* 8.1.1868, Glossop, Derbyshire. *d:* 19.5.1918. He died by his own hand at Knutsford, Cheshire. Middle order right-hand batsman, occasional left-arm medium pace bowler. *Sch* Harrow. *Team* Lancashire (1892–1901, 29 matches).
Career batting
29–50–6–663–68–15.06–0–*ct* 15
He also played for Cheshire and was on the MCC Committee.

Benton, Rev William (Manstead)
Amateur. *b:* July 1873, Chelsea, London. *d:* 17.8.1916. He was killed in action on the Somme, Belgium. *Sch* Framlingham. *Team* Middlesex (1913, 2 matches).
Career batting
2–3–1–25–19*–12.50–0–*ct* 0

Beresford, Richard Augustus Agincourt
Amateur. *b:* 12.8.1869, Castor, nr Peterborough. *d:* 12.7.1941, Derby. Hard-hitting middle order right-hand batsman, useful change bowler. *Sch* Oundle. *Team* Cambridge U (1889–91).
Career batting
7–14–1–177–40–13.61–0–*ct* 2
Bowling 6–0
He put the weight for Cambridge in 1891 and 1892. His County cricket was played for Northants (non-first-class) and later Norfolk.

Beresford, Hon Seton Robert de la Poer Horsley
Amateur. *b:* 25.7.1868, Ireland. *d:* 28.5.1928, Cap d'Ail, France. Middle order batsman. *Sch* Eton. *Team* Middlesex (1909, 2 matches).
Career batting
8–13–0–161–45–12.38–0–*ct* 9
His final first-class match was for MCC in 1910.

Bergin, Bernard Francis
Amateur. *b:* 20.9.1913, Dublin, Ireland. Brother of S.F. (Ireland). Right-hand batsman. *Team* Ireland (1937).
Career batting
1–2–0–16–12–8.00–0–*ct* 0

Bergin, Stanley Francis
Amateur. *b:* 18.12.1926, Dublin, Ireland. *d:* 4.8.1969, Dublin, Ireland. Brother of B.F. (Ireland). Left-hand batsman. *Team* Ireland (1949–65).
Career batting
27–52–5–1610–137–34.25–2–*ct* 6

Berkeley, George Fitz-Hardinge
Amateur. *b:* 29.1.1870, Dublin, Ireland. *d:* 14.11.1955, Hanwell Castle, Banbury. Lower order right-hand batsman, good left-arm medium pace bowler. *Sch* Wellington. *Team* Oxford U (1890–93, blue all four years).
Career batting
32–60–28–324–38–10.12–0–*ct* 17
Bowling 2719–131–20.75–9–1–8/70
He appeared occasionally for Oxfordshire, commencing 1904. His final first-class match was for Leveson-Gower's XI in 1906.

Berkeley, Robert George Wilmot
Amateur. *b:* 23.4.1898, Romford, Essex. *d:* 28.8.1969, Bristol. Middle order right-hand batsman. *Sch* Downside. *Team* Worcestershire (1919–22, 4 matches).
Career batting
4–7–0–37–16–5.28–0–*ct* 0
In 1933 he was High Sheriff of Worcestershire.

Berkley, Rev Maurice
Amateur. *b:* 6.9.1872, Navestock, Essex. *d:* 9.8.1947, Bangor, Caernarvonshire. Lower order right-hand batsman, right-arm slow bowler. *Sch* Fettes. *Team* Essex (1894, 2 matches).
Career batting
2–3–1–6–5–3.00–0–*ct* 2
Bowling 103–7–14.71–1–0–6/50
He appeared in a number of trials whilst at Oxford (1892–94), but never in first-class games for the University.

Bernard, Charles Albert
Amateur. *b:* 16.2.1876, Bristol. *d:* 26.9.1953, Bristol. Opening right-hand batsman, moderate field. *Sch* Eton. *Team* Somerset (1896–1901, 33 matches).
Career batting
33–62–6–1705–122–30.43–2–*ct* 21
Bowling 30–0

Bernard, John Richard
Amateur. *b:* 7.12.1938, Clifton, Bristol. Right-hand opening batsman, right-arm medium pace bowler. *Sch* Clifton. *Teams* Gloucestershire (1956–61, 11 matches); Cambridge U (1958–60, blue all three years).
Career batting
56–100–17–1891–119*–22.78–1–*ct* 28
Bowling 1705–35–48.71–0–0–4/44
His final first-class match was for MCC in 1964.

Bernau, Ernest Henry Lovell
Amateur. *b:* 6.4.1896, Napier, New Zealand. *d:* 7.1.1966, Wanganui, New Zealand. Hard hitting left-hand batsman, left-arm medium pace bowler, moderate field. *Teams* Hawke's Bay (1914/5); Wellington (1922/3 to 1927/8). *Tours* New Zealand to England 1927.
Career batting
28–39–2–651–117–17.59–1–*ct* 10
Bowling 1672–58–28.82–1–0–6/35

Berners, John Anstruther
Amateur. *b:* 23.9.1869, London. *d:* 2.3.1934, Woolverstone, Suffolk. Middle order batsman. *Sch* Eton. *Team* Middlesex (1904, 1 match).
Career batting
2–4–0–59–50–14.75–0–*ct* 0
He also played for Suffolk.

Bernstein, Rodney Elliott
Amateur. *b:* 15.12.1937, Dublin, Ireland. Right-hand batsman, right-arm fast medium bowler. *Team* Ireland (1960–62).
Career batting
6–10–0–89–18–8.90–0–*ct* 1
Bowling 406–16–25.37–0–0–4/23

Berridge, Edward Henry Stuart
Amateur. *b:* 1873, Islington, Middlesex. *d:* 30.1.1927, Charing Cross, London. Middle order batsman. *Team* London County (1900).
Career batting
1–1–0–0–0–0.00–0–*ct* 0

Berridge, William
Professional. *b:* 7.9.1892, Leicester. *d:* 1.4.1968, Leicester. Middle order right-hand batsman, right-arm medium pace bowler. *Team* Leicestershire (1923–24, 13 matches).
Career batting
13–21–0–146–33–6.95–0–*ct* 5
Bowling 27–0

Berridge, Dr William Claude Morpott
Amateur. *b:* 2.12.1894, Enderby, Leics. *d:* 25.2.1973, Oxshott, Surrey. Useful right-hand batsman, right-arm slow-medium bowler. *Sch* Malvern. *Team* Leicestershire (1914–22, 22 matches).
Career batting
23–40–5–411–61–11.74–0–*ct* 6
Bowling 839–30–27.96–1–0–5/58

Berrington, Edwin Henry
Professional. *b:* 1850, Lambeth, Surrey. *d:* 1880, Uxbridge, Middlesex. Lower order batsman, right-arm medium pace bowler. *Team* Surrey (1872, 1 match).
Career batting
1–2–0–16–8–8.00–0–*ct* 0
Bowling 4–0

Berry, Fred
Professional. *b:* 13.2.1910, Kirkheaton, Yorkshire. Useful lower order right-hand batsman, right-arm medium fast bowler. *Team* Surrey (1934–39, 46 matches).
Career batting
47–66–11–1053–104*–19.14–1–*ct* 28
Bowling 2376–83–28.62–2–0–6/81
He also played for Berkshire.

Berry, George Leslie
(known as Leslie George)
Professional. *b:* 28.4.1906, Dorking, Surrey. Attractive opening right-hand batsman, good field. *Team* Leicestershire (1924–51, 605 matches).
Career batting
609–1056–57–30225–232–30.25–45–*ct* 181
Bowling 606–10–60.60–0–0–1/1
For many years the mainstay of Leicestershire's batting, Berry hit 1,000 runs in a season 18 times between 1925 and 1950. His best year, and the only time he exceeded 2,000 runs, was 1937 with 2,446, av 52.04. His highest score was 232 for Leics v Sussex at Leicester, 1930. He hit one other double century for the County. He captained Leics from 1946 to 1948. A good soccer player, he appeared for Sheffield Wednesday, Bristol Rovers and Swindon Town.

Berry, John
Professional. *b:* 10.1.1824, Dalton, Yorkshire. *d:* February 1895, Huddersfield, Yorkshire. Nephew of George (Yorkshire 1845–51). Sound right-hand batsman, round-arm medium pace bowler. *Team* Yorkshire (1849–67, 24 matches).
Career batting
47–83–7–1069–78–14.06–0–*ct* 34
Bowling 247–17+23–14.52–3–0–6/31
He also played non-first-class cricket for Northamptonshire.

Berry, Joseph
Professional. *b:* 29.11.1829, Dalton, Yorkshire. *d:* 20.4.1894, Fartown, Huddersfield, Yorkshire. Opening right-hand batsman, right-arm medium pace bowler. *Team* Yorkshire (1861–74, 5 matches).
Career batting
5–8–0–82–30–10.25–0–*ct* 2

Berry, Robert
Professional. *b:* 29.1.1926, Manchester. Tail-end left-hand batsman, slow left-arm bowler, good outfield. *Teams* Lancashire (1948–54, 93 matches); Worcestershire (1955–58, 94 matches); Derbyshire (1959–62, 54 matches). *Tours* MCC to Australia 1950/51; Commonwealth to India 1953/4. *Tests* England (1950, 2 matches).
Career batting
273–305–112–1463–40–7.58–0–*ct* 138
Bowling 17389–703–24.73–34–5–10/102
Test batting
2–4–2–6–4*–3.00–0–*ct* 2
Bowling 228–9–25.33–1–0–5/63
Most promising spin bowler, he failed miserably on his only tour to Australia in 1950/1 and despite gaining County Caps with both Worcestershire and Derbyshire (in addition to his Lancashire one) he never really fulfilled early promise. His best year was 1953 (98 wickets, av 18.97) and in the same year he took all 10 wickets (for 102) for Lancashire v Worcestershire at Blackpool.

Berry, Wilfred Ernest
Amateur. *b:* 12.10.1897, Hertford. *d:* 1951. Lower order batsman, useful bowler. *Team* Somerset (1926, 1 match).
Career batting
1–1–1–1–1*–no av–0 *ct* 0
Bowling 34–0

Berwick, John Albert
Professional. *b:* 30.7.1867, Northampton. *d:* 31.7.1946, Glossop. Lower order left-hand batsman, left-arm fast-medium bowler. *Team* Derbyshire (1895–1901, 16 matches).
Career batting
16–29–6–138–27–6.00–0–*ct* 7
Bowling 892–24–37.16–2–0–5/61
He also played non-first-class cricket for Northamptonshire.

Beslee, George Prior
Professional. *b:* 27.3.1904, Cliffe, Kent. *d:* 3.11.1975, Tonbridge, Kent. Lower order right-hand batsman, right-arm fast medium bowler. *Team* Kent (1925–30, 63 matches).
Career batting
63–86–25–439–24–7.19–0–*ct* 30
Bowling 4199–133–31.57–0–0–4/27

Bessant, John (George) William Thomas
Professional. *b:* 11.11.1892, Bedminster, Somerset. *d:* 17.1.1982, Frenchay, Bristol. Lower order right-hand batsman, right-arm medium pace bowler. *Team* Gloucestershire (1921–28, 113 matches).
Career batting
113–170–53–1200–50–10.25–0–*ct* 81
Bowling 4615–130–35.50–5–0–5/29

Best, William Finlay
Amateur. *b:* 30.5.1865, Smarden, Staplehurst, Kent. *d:* 3.8.1942, Preston, Lancashire. Right-

hand batsman, slow right-arm bowler. *Team* Kent (1890–92, 5 matches).
Career batting
5–8–0–103–26–12.87–0–*ct* 2
Bowling 69–5–13.80–0–0–3/29

For Kent v Somerset at Taunton in 1891, Best performed the hat-trick. His first-class cricket however was very limited and his most noted performances were for Preston in Lancashire.

Bestwick, Robert Saxton
Professional. *b:* 29.9.1899, Heanor, Derbyshire. *d:* 3.7.1980, St Ouen, Jersey. Son of William (Derbyshire). Tail end right-hand batsman, right-arm fast medium bowler. *Team* Derbyshire (1920–22, 5 matches).
Career batting
5–9–1–29–10–3.62–0–*ct* 2
Bowling 151–2–75.50–0–0–2/47

Bestwick, William
Professional. *b:* 24.2.1875, Heanor, Derbyshire. *d:* 2.5.1938, Nottingham. Father of R.S. (Derbyshire). Right-hand tail end batsman, excellent right-arm fast medium bowler. *Team* Derbyshire (1898–1925, 321 matches).
Career batting
323–524–183–1607–39–4.71–0–*ct* 89
Bowling 30998–1457–21.27–104–27–10/40

Employing a short run up, he was able to bowl for long spells without tiring. He took 100 wickets in a season four times (best 147, av 16.72 in 1921). In 1921 he also took 10 wickets in an innings (for 40) v Glamorgan at Cardiff. Owing to his intemperance, the Derbyshire Committee dispensed with his services in 1909 and he moved to South Wales where he qualified by residence for Glamorgan and appeared for that County (non-first-class) in 1914. He resumed his first-class career with Derbyshire in 1919.

Betham, Sir Geoffrey Lawrence
Amateur. *b:* 8.4.1889, Belgaum, India. *d:* 6.11.1963, Chelsea, London. Opening right-hand batsman, change bowler. *Sch* Dulwich. *Teams* Free Foresters (1922); Europeans (1917/8 to 1926/7); Rajputana (1937/8).
Career batting
7–13–3–129–30–12.90–0–*ct* 3
Bowling 139–4–34.75–0–0–2/27

His first class debut was for Europeans and Parsis XI in 1916/7.

Bethell, John Arthur L.
Cricketer. *b:* 18.12.1940, St Thomas, Barbados. Sound middle order left-hand batsman, left-arm bowler. *Team* Barbados (1963/4 to 1969/70). *Tour* Barbados to England 1969.
Career batting
16–25–6–496–84*–26.10–0–*ct* 7
Bowling 391–10–39.10–0–0–2/16

Bethune, Henry Beauclerk
Amateur. *b:* 16.11.1844, Horsham, Sussex. *d:* 16.4.1912, Horsham, Sussex. Right-hand batsman, slow bowler – latterly under-arm. *Team* Hampshire (1885–97, 2 matches).
Career batting
2–4–1–26–9–8.66–0–*ct* 1
Bowling 27–1–27.00–0–0–1/27

He made many large scores in club cricket, notably in the army and for Gentlemen of Hampshire.

Beton, Sydney Lionel
Professional. *b:* 22.11.1895, Paddington, London. *d:* 30.11.1972, London. Middle order right-hand batsman. *Team* Middlesex (1923–28, 32 matches).
Career batting
32–46–10–688–49–19.11–0–*ct* 7

Bettesworth, Walter Ambrose
Amateur. *b:* 24.11.1856, Horndean, Hants. *d:* 23.2.1929, Hampstead, London. Middle order right-hand batsman, slow round-arm bowler, good cover field. *Sch* Ardingly. *Team* Sussex (1878–83, 21 matches).
Career batting
22–43–3–716–77–17.90–0–*ct* 12
Bowling 986–38–25.47–1–0–5/66

A noted author and journalist, he was cricket editor of 'The Field' from 1906 to 1928 and wrote several books on the game.

Bettington, Brindley Cecil John
Amateur. *b:* 2.9.1898, Merriwa, New South Wales, Australia. *d:* 26.8.1931, Merriwa, New South Wales, Australia. Brother of R.H.B. (Middlesex, Oxford U and New South Wales). Middle order right-hand batsman, leg break and googly bowler. *Teams* Oxford U (1920–22); New South Wales (1927/8, 1 match).
Career batting
4–7–2–153–69–30.60–*ct* 1
Bowling 229–8–28.62–0–0–3/35

Bettington, Dr Reginald Henshall Brindley
Amateur. *b:* 24.2.1900, Merriwa, New South Wales, Australia. *d:* 24.6.1969. He was killed in a motor accident, Gisborne, New Zealand. Brother of B.C.J. (Oxford U and New South Wales). Hard hitting middle order right-hand batsman, slow leg-break and googly bowler. *Teams* Oxford U (1920–23, blue all four years); Middlesex (1928, 15 matches); New South Wales (1928/9 to 1931/2, 5 matches).

Career batting
86–142–21–3314–127–27.38–4–*ct* 60
Bowling 8496–357–23.79–21–5–8/66

A fine all-round sportsman, he also obtained his blue for rugby and golf. He qualified for Middlesex whilst studying medicine at St Bartholomew's. His final first-class match was for Free Foresters in 1938.

Betts, George
Professional. *b:* 19.9.1841, Sheffield, Yorkshire. *d:* October 1902, Sheffield, Yorkshire. Hard-hitting right-hand batsman. *Team* Yorkshire (1873–74, 2 matches).
Career batting
2–4–1–56–44*–18.66–0–*ct* 0

Betts, Gilbert Frederick
Amateur. *b:* 21.12.1916, Witney, Oxfordshire. *d:* 5.1.1982, Abingdon, Berkshire. Lower order batsman, right-arm fast medium bowler. *Team* Minor Counties (1951).
Career batting
1–2–0–1–1–0.50–0–*ct* 1
Bowling 95–5–19.00–1–0–5/95

He played for Oxfordshire.

Betts, Morton Peto
Amateur. *b:* 30.8.1847, St Pancras, Middlesex. *d:* 19.4.1914, Mentone, France. Middle order batsman. *Sch* Harrow. *Teams* Middlesex (1872, 1 match); Kent (1872–81, 2 matches).
Career batting
3–5–2–83–39*–27.66–0–*ct* 0

From 1887 to 1890 he was Secretary to Essex CCC. He was well-known on the soccer field, playing for Wanderers in the first FA Cup final of 1872, when he played under a pseudonym, A.H.Chequer (he had played for Harrow Chequers in an earlier round), and scored the only goal. He also played for England in 1877.

Betts, William Hammond
Amateur. b: 25.8.1846. *d:* 14.6.1884, Diss, Norfolk. Middle order batsman. *Sch* Harrow. *Team* MCC (1866).
Career batting
1–2–0–1–1–0.50–0–*ct* 0

Bevan, David George
Cricketer. *b:* 11.6.1943, Gloucester. Middle order right-hand batsman, right-arm medium pace bowler. *Teams* Gloucestershire (1964–70, 33 matches); Eastern Province (1973/4).
Career batting
36–57–4–706–80–13.32–0–*ct* 13
Bowling 30–3–10.00–0–0–3/30

He left the Gloucestershire staff after the 1967 season to become a lecturer at Cape Town University, but returned to Gloucestershire for 1970.

Bevan, Thomas
Amateur. *b:* 14.2.1900, Crayford, Kent. *d:* 12.6.1942, Libya. Middle order right-hand batsman. *Sch* Eton. *Team* Army (1928).
Career batting
1–2–0–7–6–3.50–0–*ct* 0

His County cricket was for Suffolk.

Beveridge, Robert
Professional. *b:* 16.9.1909, Paddington, London. Lower order right-hand batsman, slow left-arm bowler. *Team* Middlesex (1930–34, 41 matches).
Career batting
41–57–19–352–49–9.26–0–*ct* 21
Bowling 1350–41–32.92–2–0–6/66

He emigrated to New Zealand.

Beves, Gordon
Amateur. *b:* 15.3.1862, Brighton, Sussex. *d:* 22.3.1927, Johannesburg, South Africa. Useful right-hand batsman, change bowler. *Sch* The Leys. *Teams* Nottinghamshire (1888–91, 9 matches); Transvaal (1894/5 to 1898/9).
Career batting
18–31–1–370–60–12.33–0–*ct* 11
Bowling 201–8–25.12–0–0–2/13

A noted rugby footballer he represented Sussex. He was Chairman of the South African Cricket Association.

Bevington, John Currey
Amateur. *b:* 6.4.1872, Sydenham, Kent. *d:* 4.4.1933, Chelmsford, Essex. Brother of T.A.D. (Middlesex). Middle order right-hand batsman. *Sch* Harrow. *Team* Middlesex (1900, 1 match).
Career batting
1–2–0–8–6–4.00–0–*ct* 1

He did not appear in a first-class match whilst at Cambridge. He played for Essex in a few non-first-class matches commencing 1891.

Bevington, Timothy Arthur Dent
Amateur. *b:* 22.8.1881, Ware, Herts. *d:* 4.5.1966, Vancouver, Canada. Brother of J.C. (Middlesex). Middle order left-hand batsman. *Sch* Harrow. *Team* Middlesex (1900–04, 6 matches).
Career batting
14–22–2–359–91–17.95–0–*ct* 4
Bowling 77–3–25.66–0–0–3/21

Bevington emigrated to Winnipeg, Canada, and played a large part in cricket in Canada in the years immediately prior to the First World War.

He represented Canada v United States in 1911. His last first-class match was for USA and Canada v Australia in 1913.

Bewick, Alfred William George
Professional. *b:* 25.1.1876, Hempstead, Gloucs. *d:* 15.10.1949, Cheltenham, Gloucs. Tail end left-hand batsman, left-arm fast bowler. *Team* Gloucestershire (1903, 1 match).
Career batting
1–2–0–5–5–2.50–0–*ct* 0
Bowling 51–1–51.00–0–0–1/31

Bezer, Arthur Herbert
Professional. *b:* 20.10.1875, Bath, Somerset. *d:* 11.7.1944, Bath, Somerset. Lower order batsman, left-arm bowler. *Team* Somerset (1914, 1 match).
Career batting
1–2–0–1–1–0.50–0 *ct* 1
Bowling 12–0

Bhatia, Anand Narain
Cricketer. *b:* 22.1.1947, Lucknow, India. Lower order right-hand batsman, right-arm off break bowler. *Teams* Delhi (1966/7); Cambridge U (1969, blue).
Career batting
13–21–2–277–43–14.57–0–*ct* 7
Bowling 866–30–28.66–0–0–4/36

Bick, Donald (Albert)
Professional. *b:* 22.2.1936, Hampstead, London. Useful right-hand batsman, right-arm off spin bowler. *Team* Middlesex (1954–67, 145 matches).
Career batting
147–190–31–2221–85–13.96–0–*ct* 35
Bowling 6482–234–27.70–5–0–5/22
He also played for Hertfordshire.

Bickley, John
Professional. *b:* 16.1.1819, Keyworth, Notts. *d:* 15.11.1866, Nottingham. Lower order right-hand batsman, fast right-hand round-arm bowler, good slip. *Teams* Nottinghamshire (1847–60, 15 matches); Surrey (1852, 1 match as given man); Kent (1854, 1 match as given man).
Career batting
38–60–8–228–27–4.38–0–*ct* 37
Bowling 1639–140+1–11.70–9–4–8/7
For England against Kent and Sussex at Lord's in 1856 he took 8 wickets for 7 runs.

Bickmore, Arthur Frederic
Amateur. *b:* 19.5.1899, Tonbridge, Kent. *d:* 18.3.1979, Tonbridge, Kent. Good right-hand opening batsman, brilliant outfield. *Sch* Clifton. *Teams* Kent (1919–29, 48 matches); Oxford U (1920–21, blue both years).
Career batting
64–104–7–2254–120–23.23–2–*ct* 41
Bowling 120–0
In both his University matches he hit the highest score for his side and in 1921 also made the highest score for Kent in the match v Australians. Owing to his scholastic duties his first-class appearances were very limited.

Biddle, Lynford A.
Amateur. *b:* 1876, Chestnut Hill, Philadelphia. *d:* 24.1.1941, Philadelphia. Sound opening left-hand batsman. *Team* Philadelphia (1896–97). *Tour* Philadelphians to England 1897.
Career batting
9–16–3–155–30*–11.92–0–*ct* 10
Bowling 7–0
He represented the United States v Canada in 1893,1894,1896 and 1903.

Biddulph, George Henry
Amateur. *b:* 28.3.1858, Manchester. *d:* 21.4.1937, Melbourne, Australia. Middle order right-hand batsman, right-arm medium pace bowler. *Team* Lancashire (1885, 1 match).
Career batting
1–2–0–19–18–9.50–0–*ct* 1
Bowling 13–0

Biddulph, Kenneth David
Professional. *b:* 29.5.1932, Chingford, Essex. Tail end right-hand batsman, right-arm fast medium bowler. *Team* Somerset (1955–61, 91 matches).
Career batting
91–119–50–468–41–6.78–0–*ct* 37
Bowling 7457–270–27.59–10–0–6/30
He also played for Durham.

Biddulph, Samuel
Professional. *b:* 23.12.1840, Hyson Green, Notts. *d:* 7.3.1876, Nottingham. Tail end right-hand batsman, wicket-keeper, occasional right-hand round-arm medium pace bowler. *Team* Nottinghamshire (1862–75, 76 matches).
Career batting
176–291–51–2287–60–9.52–0–*ct* 164–*st* 123
Bowling 117–5+2–23.40–0–0–3/31
From 1863 to his death he was on the staff at Lord's and played in many MCC matches.

Bielby, Stephen Richard
Cricketer. *b:* 9.3.1947, Windsor, Berkshire. Middle order right-hand batsman, right-arm off break bowler. *Sch* Radley. *Team* Nottinghamshire (1967–71, 43 matches).

Bigg

Career batting
43–58–12–837–62–18.19–0–*ct* 16
Bowling 161–3–53.66–0–0–1/14
He also played for Buckinghamshire.

Bigg, George Ashburner
Amateur. *b:* 1861, Ulverston, Lancashire. *d:* 27.10.1931, Barrow-in-Furness. *Team* Lancashire (1887, 1 match).
Career batting
1–1–0–16–16–16.00–0–*ct* 1
Bowling 13–1–13.00–0–0–1/13

Bigge, George Orde
Amateur. *b:* 13.1.1869, Ferezepore, India. *d:* 26.3.1935, Stone-in-Oxney, Kent. Middle order right-hand batsman, right-arm medium pace bowler. *Sch* Mill Hill. *Team* MCC (1898).
Career batting
1–2–0–12–11–6.00–0–*ct* 0

Biggs, Anthony Llewellyn
Amateur. *b:* 26.4.1946, Graaff-Reinet, South Africa. Opening right-hand batsman, right-arm off break bowler. *Team* Eastern Province (1964/5 to 1980/1). *Tour* SA Universities to England 1967.
Career batting
62–112–8–3409–156–32.77–8–*ct* 35
Bowling 2811–82–34.28–4–1–7/62

Bignall, Thomas
Professional. *b:* 8.1.1842, Chilwell, Notts. *d:* 19.9.1898, Hyson Green, Notts. Powerful opening rght-hand batsman, occasional fast round-arm bowler. *Team* Nottinghamshire (1863–78, 60 matches).
Career batting
90–155–10–2656–116*–18.31–1–*ct* 19
Bowling 104–1+1–104.00–0–0–1/12
He also played for Devon.

Bignell, Guy Newcombe
Amateur. *b:* 3.12.1886, Mozufferpore, India. *d:* 10.6.1965, Lausanne, Switzerland. Brother of H.G. (Hants). Middle order right-hand batsman, right-arm medium pace bowler. *Sch* Haileybury. *Teams* Hampshire (1904–25, 55 matches); Europeans (1923/4).
Career batting
58–86–5–1670–109–20.61–1–*ct* 27
Bowling 759–17–44.64–0–0–3/67
In 1908 for Hambledon XII he appeared under the assumed name of G.N. Deer and in 1919 for Hampshire under the assumed name G. Newcombe.

Bignell, Hugh Glennie
Amateur. *b:* 4.10.1882, Mozufferpore, India. *d:* 6.5.1907, of enteric fever, Rawalpindi, India. Brother of G.N. (Hants). Middle order right-hand batsman, right-arm fast bowler. *Sch* Haileybury. *Teams* Hampshire (1901–02, 5 matches); Europeans (1901/2).
Career batting
6–11–2–140–49*–15.55–0–*ct* 2
Bowling 29–0

Bigwood, Alfred
Professional. *b:* 3.8.1857, Mortlake, Surrey. *d:* 12.9.1940, Wandsworth, London. Lower order right-hand batsman, slow round-arm bowler. *Team* Surrey (1878, 1 match).
Career batting
1–2–1–5–4–5.00–0–*ct* 2

Bilbie, Anthony Robin
Professional. *b:* 29.4.1942, Nottingham. Middle order right-hand batsman. *Team* Nottinghamshire (1960–63, 14 matches).
Career batting
14–27–1–291–39–11.19–0–*ct* 12

Billham, Frank Denis
Amateur. *b:* 27.9.1896, Georgetown, British Guiana. *d:* 16.11.1980, Sudbury, Suffolk. Lower order right-hand batsman, slow left-arm bowler. *Sch* Framlingham. *Team* Essex (1924, 2 matches).
Career batting
2–3–1–12–12*–6.00–0–*ct* 0
Bowling 72–0
For many years he was on the Council of the Club Cricket Conference.

Billingsley, Charles William
Amateur. *b:* 1.1.1910, Belfast, N Ireland. *d:* 4.11.1951, Belfast, N Ireland. Right-hand batsman, right-arm fast medium bowler. *Team* Ireland (1936–38).
Career batting
5–10–5–19–6*–3.80–0–*ct* 1
Bowling 265–18–14.72–0–0–4/19

Billyeald, James
Amateur. *b:* 20.1.1835, Hyson Green, Nottingham. *d:* 8.7.1890, Nottingham. Middle order right-hand batsman, round-arm medium pace bowler. *Team* Derbyshire (1871, 1 match).
Career batting
1–2–1–15–11*–15.00–0–*ct* 0

Bilton, Edmund John
Professional. *b:* 1839, Cambridge. *d:* 24.8.1916, Cambridge. Middle order batsman. *Team* Cambridgeshire (1866, 1 match).

Career batting
3–5–0–25–10–5.00–0–*ct* 3
His debut was for Cambridge Town Club in 1859.

Bingham, Dr Frank Miller
Amateur. *b:* 17.9.1874, Alfreton, Derbyshire. *d:* 22.5.1915. He was killed in action, Sanctuary Wood, Ypres, Belgium. Lower order batsman, right-arm medium pace bowler. *Sch* St Peter's, York. *Team* Derbyshire (1896, 1 match).
Career batting
1–2–0–17–11–8.50–0–*ct* 0
He also played rugby for Blackheath.

Binks, James Graham
Professional. *b:* 5.10.1935, Hull, Yorkshire. Lower order right-hand batsman, leg break bowler, wicket-keeper. *Team* Yorkshire (1955–69, 491 matches). *Tours* MCC to Ceylon, India and Pakistan 1961/2, to India 1963/4. *Tests* England (1963/4, 2 matches).
Career batting
502–598–129–6910–95–14.73–*ct* 895–*st* 176
Bowling 82–0
Test batting
2–4–0–91–55–22.75–0–*ct* 8
Binks appeared in 412 consecutive County Championship matches for Yorkshire between 1955 and 1969. In 1960 he dismissed 107 batsmen (96 ct, 11 st). He also played for Lincolnshire.

Binns, John
Professional. *b:* 1872, Upper Wortley, Leeds, Yorkshire. *d:* 8.12.1934, Leeds, Yorkshire. Lower order batsman, wicket-keeper. *Team* Yorkshire (1898, 1 match).
Career batting
1–1–0–4–4–4.00–0–*ct* 0–*st* 3

Birch, Albert Edgar
Professional. *b:* 11.8.1868, Bethnal Green, Middlesex. *d:* 6.11.1936. Lower order batsman, fast-medium right-arm bowler. *Team* Kent (1894, 1 match).
Career batting
1–2–0–3–3–1.50–0–*ct* 0

Birch, John Dennis
Cricketer. *b*: 18.6.1955, Nottingham. Hard hitting middle order right-hand batsman, right-arm medium pace bowler, gully field. *Team* Nottinghamshire (1973–83, 146 matches).
Career batting
146–219–33–4951–125–26.61–4–*ct* 109
Bowling 1836–38–48.31–1–0–6/64
He hit 1,000 runs in a season twice (best 1,086, av 30.16, in 1983).

Birch, William
Professional. *b:* 1863, Brentford, Middlesex. *d:* 1940, Brentford, Middlesex. Lower order batsman, useful bowler. *Team* Middlesex (1887, 2 matches).
Career batting
2–4–1–6–4–2.00–0–*ct* 0
Bowling 95–2–47.50–0–0–2/28

Bird, Albert
Professional. *b:* 17.8.1867, Moseley, Warwickshire. *d:* 17.6.1927, Worcester. Lower order right-hand batsman, slow right-hand off break bowler, good field. *Team* Worcestershire (1899–1909, 143 matches).
Career batting
143–225–63–1951–64*–12.04–0–*ct* 55
Bowling 7403–292–25.35–20–3–7/41
Bird played for Warwickshire (non-first-class) from 1887 to 1890 and began his career with Worcestershire in 1892 (not first-class until 1899).

Bird, Austin Carlos
Amateur. *b:* 26.1.1884, Toxteth Park, Liverpool. *d:* 4.1.1938, Buxted, Sussex. Son of George (Middlesex and Lancashire), brother of M.C. (Lancashire and Surrey). Middle order batsman. *Sch* Malvern. *Teams* MCC (1914); Army in India (1934/5).
Career batting
2–4–0–25–21–6.25–0–*ct* 1
He spent most of his career with the Army in India.

Bird, Rev Frederick Nash
Amateur. *b:* 13.12.1875, Framlingham, Suffolk. *d:* 3.3.1965, Chichester, Sussex. Middle order right-hand batsman, right-arm medium pace bowler. *Teams* Gloucestershire (1899–1900, 6 matches); Northants (1908–09, 10 matches).
Career batting
16–28–4–398–61*–16.58–0–*ct* 11
He also played for Buckinghamshire, Devon and Suffolk.

Bird, George
Amateur. *b:* 30.7.1849, Crouch Hill, Middlesex. *d:* 28.10.1930, Esher, Surrey. Father of M.C. (Lancashire and Surrey) and A.C. (MCC). Elegant middle order right-hand batsman. *Sch* Highgate. *Teams* Middlesex (1872–77, 13 matches); Lancashire (1880, 1 match).
Career batting
21–36–3–477–75–14.45–0–*ct* 6–*st* 5
Bowling 0–0
He was a member of the MCC for 60 years.

His best innings was 112 for Fifteen of the MCC v Anglo-American Team of 1872 at Lord's in 1873 (non-first-class).

Bird, Harold Denis
Professional. *b:* 19.4.1933, Barnsley, Yorkshire. Opening right-hand batsman, right-arm medium pace bowler. *Teams* Yorkshire (1956–59, 14 matches); Leicestershire (1960–64, 79 matches).
Career batting
93–170–10–3314–181*–20.71–2–*ct* 28
Bowling 22–0

He hit 1,028 runs, av 21.41, in 1960.

Appointed as a first-class umpire in 1970, he stood in a Test match for the first time in 1973, since when he has been regularly on the panel of Test match umpires.

Bird, Morice Carlos
Amateur. *b:* 25.3.1888, Toxteth Park, Liverpool. *d:* 9.12.1933, Broadstone, Dorset. Son of George (Middlesex and Lancashire), brother of A.C. (MCC). Fine forcing right-hand batsman, right-arm medium pace bowler. *Sch* Harrow. *Teams* Lancashire (1907, 5 matches); Surrey (1909–21, 127 matches); Cooch-Behar's XI (1917/8); Bird's XI (1918/19). *Tours* MCC to South Africa 1909/10, 1913/4, to the Argentine 1911/2. *Tests* England (1909/10 to 1913/4, 10 matches).
Career batting
192–306–14–6938–200–23.76–7–*ct* 112
Bowling 3828–149–25.69–2–1–5/48
Test batting
10–16–1–280–61–18.66–0–*ct* 5
Bowling 120–8–15.00–0–0–3/11

The outstanding schoolboy cricketer of 1907, Bird hit a century in each innings (100 and 131) for Harrow v Eton at Lord's, the only boy ever to perform such a feat in that fixture. In County cricket he hit 1,000 runs in a season three times (best 1,404, av 30.52, in 1919). He captained Surrey from 1911 to 1913. His highest score, 200, was made for MCC v Orange Free State in 1913/4, but his record on his two tours to South Africa was a modest one.

Bird, Percy John
Amateur. *b:* 27.5.1877, West Cowes, Isle of Wight. *d:* 11.11.1942, Freshwater, Isle of Wight. Middle order left-hand batsman, slow left-arm bowler. *Sch* Cheltenham. *Team* Hampshire (1900, 1 match).
Career batting
1–2–0–37–28–18.50–0–*ct* 0

Bird, Ronald Ernest
Amateur. *b:* 4.4.1915, Quarry Bank, Staffs. Forcing middle order right-hand batsman, occasional right-arm fast medium bowler. *Team* Worcestershire (1946–54, 190 matches).
Career batting
195–327–32–7700–158*–26.10–7–*ct* 156
Bowling 1121–23–48.73–0–0–3/26

He hit 1,000 runs in a season three times (best 1,591, av 37.00, in 1952). He captained Worcs 1952–54. His last first-class match was for MCC in 1958.

Bird, Walter
Amateur. *b:* 22.7.1845, Hackney, Middlesex. *d:* 27.7.1921, Eastbourne. Middle order batsman. *Sch* Highgate. *Team* MCC (1880).
Career batting
1–2–0–13–13–6.50–0–*ct* 2

Bird, Wilfred Stanley
Amateur. *b:* 28.9.1883, Yiewsley, Middlesex. *d:* 9.5.1915, Richebourg, France. Lower order right-hand batsman, wicket-keeper. *Sch* Malvern. *Teams* Oxford U (1904–06, blue all three years); Middlesex (1905–08, 11 matches).
Career batting
55–92–16–969–57–12.75–0–*ct* 92–*st* 17

His final first-class appearance was for MCC in 1913.

Birkenshaw, Jack
Professional. *b:* 13.11.1940, Rothwell, Yorkshire. Middle/lower order left-hand batsman, right-arm off break bowler, good slip field. *Teams* Yorkshire (1958–60, 30 matches); Leicestershire (1961–80, 420 matches); Worcestershire (1981, 10 matches). *Tours* MCC to Pakistan, India and Sri Lanka 1972/3, to West Indies 1973/4. *Tests* England (1972/3 to 1973/4, 5 matches).
Career batting
490–665–123–12780–131–23.76–4–*ct* 318
Bowling 29276–1073–27.28–44–4–8/94
Test batting
5–7–0–148–64–21.14–0–*ct* 3
Bowling 469–13–36.07–1–0–5/57

He took 100 wickets in a season twice (best 111, av 21.41, in 1967).

He was appointed to the first-class umpires' list in 1982.

Birkett, William
(also known as Burkitt)
Professional. *b:* 27.2.1874, Coal Aston, Derbyshire. *d:* 2.5.1934, Norton, Sheffield, Yorkshire. *Team* Derbyshire (1898–1901, 4 matches).
Career batting
4–7–0–20–10–2.85–0–*ct* 0
Bowling 115–3–38.33–0–0–2/28

Birks, Douglas Thomas Montague
Amateur. *b:* 4.7.1919, St Austell, Cornwall. Middle order right-hand batsman, right-arm fast medium bowler. *Sch* Radley. *Team* Free Foresters (1949).
Career batting
1–1–0–3–3–3.00–0–*ct* 0
His County cricket was for Suffolk.

Birley, Francis Hornby
Amateur. *b:* 14.3.1850, Manchester. *d:* 1.8.1910, Dormansland, Surrey. Moderate right-hand batsman, useful slow right-arm bowler, excellent field. *Sch* Winchester. *Teams* Lancashire (1870–72, 4 matches); Surrey (1879, 1 match).
Career batting
5–8–1–65–18–9.28–0–*ct* 1
Bowling 120–4–30.00–0–0–3/76
He also appeared for Cheshire. He played in the Freshmen's Match of 1869 but not in any first-class matches for Oxford U. A well-known soccer player, he was a member of the Oxford side which won the FA Cup in 1874 and of the Wanderers who won the Cup in 1876 and 1877. He appeared in two internationals for England.

Biron, Rev Henry Brydges
Amateur. *b:* 13.6.1835, Hythe, Kent. *d:* 7.4.1915, Derringstone, Canterbury, Kent. Middle order right-hand batsman. *Sch* King's School, Canterbury. *Teams* Cambridge U (1857); Kent (1857–64, 15 matches).
Career batting
20–33–3–314–53–10.46–0–*ct* 9
Bowling 64–2–32.00–0–0–1/29
He scored many runs in club cricket, including an innings of 214 for the Quidnuncs at Brighton in 1864.

Birrell, Henry Berson
Amateur. *b:* 12.12.1927, Pietermaritzburg, South Africa. Middle order right-hand batsman, right-arm medium or slow bowler, brilliant cover field. *Sch* St Andrews, South Africa. *Teams* Eastern Province (1947/8 to 1956/7); Rhodesia (1957/8 to 1959/60); Oxford U (1953–54, blue both years).
Career batting
54–95–3–2446–134–26.58–3–*ct* 18
Bowling 1939–55–35.25–2–0–5/20
He was also awarded his rugby blue 1953/4.

Birtle, Thomas William
Professional. *b:* 28.3.1926, Stockton-on-Tees, Durham. Lower order right-arm batsman, right-arm fast-medium bowler. *Team* Nottinghamshire (1952, 7 matches).
Career batting
7–7–2–12–4*–2.40–0 *ct* 4
Bowling 593–8–74.12–0–0–2/68
He also played for Durham.

Birtles, Thomas James (Denton)
Professional. *b:* 26.10.1886, Barnsley, Yorkshire. *d:* 13.1.1971, Attenborough, Notts. Middle order right-hand batsman. *Team* Yorkshire (1913–24, 37 matches).
Career batting
37–57–11–876–104–19.52–1–*ct* 19
Bowling 20–0
He played football for Barnsley and Northampton.

Birtwell, Alexander Joseph
Amateur. *b:* 17.12.1908, Burnley, Lancashire. *d:* 20.11.1974, Nelson, Lancashire. Tail end right-hand batsman, leg break bowler. *Team* Lancashire (1937–39, 14 matches).
Career batting
14–16–6–103–31–10.30–0–*ct* 12
Bowling 999–25–39.96–0–0–4/78
Prior to playing for Lancashire he had appeared for Buckinghamshire, but his best cricket was for Nelson in the Lancashire League.

Bisgood, Bertram Lewis
Amateur. *b:* 11.3.1881, Glastonbury, Somerset. *d:* 19.7.1968, Canford Cliffs, Hants. Brother of E.D. (Somerset). Middle order right-hand batsman, wicket-keeper. *Sch* Prior Park College. *Team* Somerset (1907–21, 67 matches).
Career batting
67–126–12–2143–116*–18.79–2–*ct* 23–*st* 1
Bisgood made a remarkable first-class debut; playing for Somerset v Worcs at Worcester in 1907 he hit 82 and 116*.

Bisgood, Eustace Denis
Amateur. *b:* 1878, Glastonbury, Somerset. *d:* 4.3.1958, Sidmouth, Devon. Brother of B.L. (Somerset). *Team* Somerset (1909, 1 match).
Career batting
1–2–0–6–6–3.00–0–*ct* 1

Bishop, Arthur Theodore
Amateur. b: 2.9.1863, West Ham, Essex. *d:* 8.9.1931, St John's Wood, London. Brother of F.A. (Essex). Lower order right-hand batsman, useful bowler. *Team* Middlesex (1883, 1 match).
Career batting
1–2–2–0–0*–no av–0–*ct* 0
Bowling 76–2–38.00–0–0–2/72
From 1885 he appeared for Essex (non-first-class).

Bishop, Charles Frederick
Amateur. *b:* 1879, Stroud, Gloucs. *d:* 1943, Plymouth, Devon. Middle order batsman. *Team* Somerset (1920–21, 2 matches).
Career batting
2–4–1–9–3*–3.00–0–*ct* 0

Bishop, Francis Augustus
Amateur. *b:* 11.6.1862, Wanstead, Essex. *d:* 1942, Hendon, Middlesex. Brother of A.T. (Middlesex). Tail end right-hand batsman, useful fast right-arm bowler. *Team* Gentlemen (1889).
Career batting
1–2–0–1–1–0.50–0–*ct* 1
Bowling 108–1–108.00–0–0–1/74

He was one of the principal bowlers of the Essex team in 1889 when he was chosen to represent the Gentlemen – the selection was criticised on account of his doubtful bowling action.

Bishop, John Fillingham
Amateur. *b:* 21.11.1891, Radcliffe-on-Trent, Notts. *d:* 14.12.1963, Brighton, Sussex. Right-hand opening batsman, slip field. *Sch* Uppingham. *Team* Nottinghamshire (1923–25, 3 matches).
Career batting
3–4–2–21–15*–10.50–0–*ct* 4

Bishop, Michael Mark
Cricketer. *b:* 20.10.1952, Marlborough, Wiltshire. Tail end right-hand batsman, right-arm medium pace bowler. *Team* Cambridge U (1976–78).
Career batting
3–4–1–4–3–1.33–0–*ct* 1
Bowling 165–2–82.50–0–0–1/13

Bishop, S.
Amateur. Lower order batsman, change bowler. *Team* H.K. Foster's XI (1919).
Career batting
1–2–0–30–20–15.00–0–*ct* 0
Bowling 54–1–54.00–0–0–1/54

Bisseker, Robert Godlonton
Amateur. *b:* 19.11.1878, Port Elizabeth, South Africa. *d:* 9.3.1965, Hindhead, Surrey. Lower order batsman, change bowler. *Sch* King Edward VI, Birmingham. *Team* Cambridge U (1904).
Career batting
1–1–1–9–9*–no av–0–*ct* 1
Bowling 44–2–22.00–0–0–1/16

Bisset, Arthur Vintcent Crossley
Amateur. *b:* 15.1.1879, Cape Town, South Africa. *d:* 8.3.1955, South Africa. Brother of Murray (Western Province). Middle order right-hand batsman. *Team* Western Province (1902/3 to 1921/2). *Tour* South Africans to England 1901.
Career batting
25–47–2–697–94–15.48–0–*ct* 13
Bowling 265–7–37.85–0–0–2/33

Bisset, Sir Murray
Amateur. *b:* 14.4.1876, Port Elizabeth, South Africa. *d:* 24.10.1931, Salisbury, Rhodesia. Brother of A.V.C. (Western Province). Good middle order right-hand batsman, occasional left-arm bowler, wicket-keeper. *Team* Western Province (1894/5 to 1909/10). *Tour* South Africans to England 1901. *Tests* South Africa (1898/9 to 1909/10, 3 matches).
Career batting
40–70–9–1436–184–23.54–2–*ct* 51–*st* 13
Bowling 122–5–24.40–0–0–2/20
Test batting
3–6–2–103–35–25.75–0–*ct* 2–*st* 1

He captained the tourists on the 1901 visit to England and also led South Africa in two Tests in 1898/9. At the time of his death he was acting-Governor of Rhodesia.

Bissett, George Finlay
Amateur. *b:* 5.11.1905, Kimberley, South Africa. *d:* 14.11.1965, Bothas Hill, near Durban, South Africa. Tail end right-hand batsman, fast right-arm bowler. *Teams* Griqualand West (1922/3 to 1927/8); Transvaal (1929/30). *Tour* South Africans to England 1924. *Tests* South Africa (1927/8, 4 matches).
Career batting
21–31–12–294–33–15.47–0–*ct* 8
Bowling 1816–67–27.10–5–0–7/29
Test batting
4–4–2–38–23–19.00–0–*ct* 0
Bowling 469–25–18.76–2–0–7/29

Injury considerably reduced his cricket in England in 1924, but he was very effective in the 1927/8 series in South Africa, and the press deplored the fact that he did not come to England with the 1929 tourists.

Bissex, Michael
Cricketer. *b:* 25.9.1944, Bath, Somerset. Middle order right-hand batsman, slow left-arm bowler. *Team* Gloucestershire (1961–72, 204 matches). *Tour* MCC Under-25 to Pakistan 1966/7.
Career batting
212–354–35–6492–104*–20.35–2–*ct* 133
Bowling 6783–237–28.62–11–2–7/50

He hit 1,316 runs, av 37.60, in 1970. He also played for Cheshire.

Blaber, Archibald
Professional. *b:* 15.12.1867, Horsted Keynes,

Sussex. *d:* 15.5.1905, Cuckfield, Sussex. Lower order batsman, change bowler. *Team* Sussex (1890–94, 2 matches).
Career batting
2–3–1–29–28*–14.50–0–*ct* 0
Bowling 68–1–68.00–0–0–1/32

Black, Christopher James Robert
Cricketer. *b:* 15.12.1947, Johannesburg, South Africa. Lower order right-hand batsman, right-arm medium pace bowler. *Sch* Stowe. *Team* Middlesex (1970–73, 17 matches).
Career batting
17–26–1–400–71–16.00–0–*ct* 8
Bowling 649–13–49.92–0–0–3/51
He was also a noted hockey player.

Black, George Gordon
Amateur. *b:* 19.1.1885, Darling Point, New South Wales, Australia. *d:* 6.12.1954, Orange, New South Wales, Australia. Middle order right-hand batsman, right-arm medium pace bowler. *Teams* London County (1903); New South Wales (1903/4, 1 match).
Career batting
2–3–0–104–72–34.66–0–*ct* 1
Bowling 143–2–71.50–0–0–2/41

Black, Lennox Graham
Amateur. *b:* 1880. *d:* c. 1950, Quebec, Canada. Lower order right-hand batsman, right-arm fast bowler. *Team* Hampshire (1903–1919, 4 matches).
Career batting
4–5–0–36–21–7.20–0–*ct* 3
Bowling 229–1–229.00–0–0–1/27
His first-class career for Hampshire was confined to 1903 and 1919. He appeared for Canada v USA in 1907.

Black, Thomas MacMillan
Cricketer. *b:* 7.2.1956, Greenock, Scotland. Right-hand batsman, right-arm medium pace bowler. *Team* Scotland (1979).
Career batting
1–2–0–88–57–44.00–0–*ct* 2

Blackburn, Benjamin Fielding
Amateur. *b:* 10.9.1855, Nottingham. *d:* 6.5.1907, Bournemouth. Middle order right-hand batsman. *Team* Nottinghamshire (1879, 2 matches).
Career batting
2–3–1–6–4*–3.00–0–*ct* 2

Blackburn, John Derek Hepburn
Amateur. *b:* 27.10.1924, Leeds, Yorkshire. Middle order right-hand batsman. *Team* Yorkshire (1956, 1 match).
Career batting
1–2–0–18–15–9.00–0–*ct* 0

Blackburn, Joseph Scott
Professional. *b:* 24.9.1852, Holbeck, Yorkshire. *d:* 1922, Bramley, Yorkshire. Useful lower-order right-hand batsman, right-arm fast bowler. *Team* Yorkshire (1876–77, 6 matches).
Career batting
7–13–1–122–28–10.16–0–*ct* 4
Bowling 218–8–27.25–0–0–2/19

Blackburn, Paul Hamer
Amateur. *b:* 29.3.1934, Stockport, Cheshire. Tail end right-hand batsman, right-arm medium pace bowler. *Sch* Cheltenham. *Team* Cambridge U (1954).
Career batting
1–2–0–7–5–3.50–0–*ct* 0
Bowling 30–0

Blackburn, William Edward
Amateur. *b:* 24.11.1888, Clitheroe, Lancashire. *d:* 3.6.1941, Heaton, Bolton, Lancashire. Tail end right-hand batsman, right-arm fast-medium bowler. *Team* Yorkshire (1919–20, 10 matches).
Career batting
10–13–6–26–6*–3.71–0–*ct* 9
Bowling 1113–45–24.73–4–0–5/17

Blacker, William
Amateur. *b:* 29.9.1853, Dublin, Ireland. *d:* 21.11.1907, Weston Straffan, Co Kildare, Ireland, as the result of a hunting accident. Opening/middle order right-hand batsman. *Sch* Harrow. *Team* Cambridge U (1873–76, blue all four years).
Career batting
32–55–2–856–86–16.15–0–*ct* 10
Bowling 34–1–34.00–0–0–1/24

Blackham, John McCarthy
Amateur. *b:* 11.5.1854, North Fitzroy, Victoria, Australia. *d:* 28.12.1932, Melbourne, Australia. Stubborn defensive right-hand batsman, brilliant wicket-keeper. *Team* Victoria (1874/5 to 1894/5, 45 matches). *Tours* Australians to England 1878, 1880, 1882, 1884, 1886, 1888, 1890, 1893, to North America 1878, 1893. *Tests* Australia (1876/7 to 1894/5, 35 matches).
Career batting
275–442–61–6395–109–16.78–1–*ct* 273–*st* 180
Bowling
138–2–69.00–0–0–1/8
Test batting
35–62–11–800–74–15.68–0–*ct* 36–*st* 24
He went on every one of the first eight tours made by the Australians to England.Though at

the start of his career he had a rival in W.L. Murdoch, he was soon regarded as the 'Prince' of Australian wicket-keepers. Generally standing up very close to the stumps he was able to gather the ball and whip off the bails in a single movement. Unlike some keepers of his day he never played to the gallery.

Blackledge, Joseph Frederick
Amateur. *b:* 15.4.1928, Chorley, Lancashire. Lower order right-hand batsman. *Sch* Repton. *Team* Lancashire (1962, 26 matches).
Career batting
26–41–4–569–68–15.37–0–*ct* 9
Bowling 10–0
A useful club cricketer, Blackledge was appointed captain of Lancashire for 1962 without ever having appeared in first-class cricket. This experiment by the County Committee was not successful.

Blacklidge, Henry George
Professional. *b:* 14.7.1884, Stoughton, Surrey. *d:* 23.5.1917, Amara, Mesopotamia. Lower order left-hand batsman, left-arm fast-medium bowler or slow left-arm in another account. *Team* Surrey (1908–13, 7 matches).
Career batting
7–9–2–100–45–14.28–0–*ct* 8
Bowling 334–10–33.40–0–0–4/26
He moved to Hampshire in 1914 in order to qualify for that County.

Blackman, Arthur
Amateur. *b:* 13.10.1853, Dartford, Kent. *d:* 6.4.1908, Preston, Sussex. Half-brother of F. Martin (Kent). Lower order right-hand batsman, right-hand medium pace round-arm bowler, good deep field. *Teams* Surrey (1878, 1 match); Kent (1879–80, 3 matches); Sussex (1881–87, 15 matches).
Career batting
20–35–1–399–73–11.73–0–*ct* 9
Bowling 263–7–37.57–0–0–2/20

Blackman, William
Amateur. *b:* 27.11.1862, Arundel, Sussex. *d:* 2.6.1885, Fitzroy, Melbourne, Australia. Hard hitting middle-order right-hand batsman, right-arm fast bowler, good outfield. *Sch* Ardingly. *Team* Sussex (1881–84, 34 matches).
Career batting
34–65–7–1070–89–18.44–0–*ct* 21
Bowling 1883–87–21.64–3–0–7/86
His bowling was objected to in 1882 as unfair. He went to Australia for the benefit of his health, but died within a few months of consumption.

Blackmore, David
Amateur. *b:* 1910, Swansea. Middle order batsman. *Team* Glamorgan (1934, 1 match).
Career batting
1–1–0–34–34–34.00–0–*ct* 1

Blackmore, Ernest George
Amateur. *b:* 21.5.1895, Bedminster, Gloucs. *d:* October 1955, Pretoria, South Africa. Tail end right-hand batsman, right-arm fast-medium bowler. *Team* Gloucestershire (1925, 3 matches).
Career batting
3–5–0–11–5–2.20–0–*ct* 0
Bowling 140–2–70.00–0–0–1/38

Blackmore, George Patrick Maxwell
Amateur. *b:* 8.10.1908, Gillingham, Kent. *d:* 29.1.1984, Isleworth, Middlesex. Tail end right-hand batsman, right-arm fast medium bowler. *Sch* Blundell's. *Teams* Europeans (India) 1944/5; Kent (1948, 2 matches).
Career batting
3–3–0–12–8–4.00–0–*ct* 1
Bowling 127–2–63.50–0–0–1/14

Blackstock, Richard
Amateur. *b:* 13.7.1838, Oxton, Cheshire. *d:* 3.2.1893, Oxton, Cheshire. Middle order right-hand batsman. *Team* Lancashire (1865, 1 match).
Career batting
4–8–1–154–47–22.00–0–*ct* 3–*st* 1
Bowling 11–1–11.00–0–0–1/11
His first-class debut was for Gentlemen of North in 1858.

Blackwell, Henry
Amateur. *b:* 16.12.1876, Wirksworth, Derbyshire. *d:* 24.1.1900, Wirksworth, Derbyshire. Middle order right-hand batsman, right-arm medium pace bowler. *Team* Derbyshire (1895–98, 4 matches).
Career batting
4–6–2–41–15–10.25–0–*ct* 1
Bowling 105–4–26.25–0–0–2/23
He also played for Cornwall.

Blades, Colin Francis
Cricketer. *b:* 13.8.1944, Barbados. Middle order right-hand batsman. *Team* Barbados (1963/4 to 1969/70). *Tour* Barbados in England 1969.
Career batting
12–22–0–406–75–18.45–0–*ct* 11
Bowling 21–0
He represented Bermuda in the World Cup.

Blagg, Edward Arthur
Professional. *b:* 9.2.1918, Shireoaks, Notts. *d:* 28.10.1976, Shireoaks, Notts. Lower order right-

hand batsman, right-arm fast-medium bowler. *Team* Nottinghamshire (1948, 1 match).
Career batting
1 match, did not bat–*ct* 0
Bowling 20–0
He was a noted League footballer with Nottingham Forest and Southport.

Blagg, Peter Henry
Amateur. *b:* 11.9.1918, Basford, Notts. *d:* 18.3.1943. He was presumed killed in action in Burma. Tail end right-hand batsman, wicket-keeper. *Sch* Shrewsbury. *Team* Oxford U (1939).
Career batting
10–13–5–67–28*–8.37–0–*ct* 17–*st* 12

Blagrave, Herbert Henry Gratwicke
Amateur. *b:* 3.3.1899, Cheltenham, Gloucs. *d:* 4.7.1981, Beckhampton, Wiltshire. Lower order batsman, slow bowler. *Sch* Cheltenham. *Team* Gloucestershire (1922, 1 match).
Career batting
1–2–0–12–12–6.00–0–*ct* 0
He was a well-known racehorse trainer.

Blaikie, Kenneth Guy
Amateur. *b:* 8.5.1897, Johannesburg, South Africa. *d:* 8.6.1968, Lennoxville, Quebec, Canada. Hard-hitting middle order left-hand batsman, left-arm medium or slow bowler. *Teams* Oxford U (1921–24, blue 1924); Somerset (1921–23, 9 matches).
Career batting
27–48–1–1080–120–22.97–2–*ct* 20
Bowling 1196–46–26.00–0–0–4/14
Blaikie produced perhaps the best all-round performance seen in an Oxford Freshmen's match, scoring a century and taking 13 wickets for 58, but he could not obtain a regular place in the Oxford team until 1924, when he hit two brilliant hundreds and topped the Oxford batting averages.

Blair, Major-Gen Everard McLeod
Amateur. *b:* 26.7.1866, Bangalore, India. *d:* 16.5.1939, Northampton. Hard hitting middle order right-hand batsman, slow leg break bowler. *Sch* Cheltenham. *Team* Kent (1893–1900, 7 matches).
Career batting
7–10–0–190–61–19.00–0–*ct* 2
He was also a noted rackets player.

Blair, Philbert Duncan
Cricketer. *b:* 30.10.1943, Georgetown, British Guiana. Tail end batsman, right-arm fast bowler. *Team* Guyana. *Tour* West Indians to England 1969.
Career batting
31–34–10–142–30–5.91–0–*ct* 5
Bowling 2630–77–34.15–3–0–5/60
He made little impact on his only visit to England and did not appear in any of the Tests.

Blair, Robert William
Amateur. *b:* 23.6.1932, Petone, New Zealand. Aggressive tail-end right-hand batsman, right-arm fast-medium bowler. *Teams* Wellington (1951/2 to 1964/5); Central Districts (1955/6). *Tours* New Zealanders to England 1958, to South Africa and Australia 1953/4. *Tests* New Zealand (1952/3 to 1963/4, 19 matches).
Career batting
119–172–36–1672–79–12.29–0–*ct* 46
Bowling 9961–537–18.54–41–12–9/72
Test batting
19–34–6–189–64*–6.75–0–*ct* 5
Bowling 1515–43–35.23–0–0–4/85
On his single visit to England he did very little in the Tests, and in first-class matches took 51 wickets (av 23.58). He was the leading wicket-taker in New Zealand first-class cricket, until overtaken by H.J. Howarth. His best bowling was 9/72 for Wellington v Auckland at Wellington in 1956/7.

Blair-White, Arthur
Amateur. *b:* 3.7.1891, Monkstown, Co Dublin, Ireland. *d:* 19.4.1975, Lifford, Co Donegal, Ireland. Right-hand batsman, wicket-keeper. *Sch* Rugby. *Team* Ireland (1913).
Career batting
1–2–0–30–25–15.00–0–*ct* 0

Blake, David Eustace
Amateur. *b:* 27.4.1925, Havant, Hants. Brother of J.P. (Hants). Attractive middle order left-hand batsman, wicket-keeper. *Sch* Aldenham. *Team* Hampshire (1949–58, 50 matches). *Tours* Swanton to West Indies 1955/6; Norfolk to Jamaica 1956/7.
Career batting
73–129–9–2909–100–24.24–2–*ct* 91–*st* 30
His County cricket was restricted due to his profession. His final first-class match was for Free Foresters in 1961.

Blake, John Philip
Amateur. *b:* 17.11.1917, Portsmouth, Hants. *d:* 3.6.1944, Vis Island, Yugoslavia. Brother of D.E. (Hants). Free scoring opening/middle order right-hand batsman. *Sch* Aldenham. *Teams* Hampshire (1937–39, 14 matches); Cambridge U (1938–39, blue 1939).
Career batting
29–51–3–1095–88–22.81–0–*ct* 18

Blake, Peter Douglas Stuart
Amateur. *b:* 23.5.1927, Calcutta, India. Stylish middle order right-hand batsman, fine field. *Sch* Eton. *Teams* Sussex (1946–51, 23 matches); Oxford U (1950–52, blue all three years).
Career batting
58–99–6–2067–130–22.22–3–*ct* 26
Bowling 52–0
His final first-class match was for Free Foresters in 1953.

Blake, Wilfred
Professional. *b:* 29.11.1854, Embsay, Skipton, Yorkshire. Middle order right-hand batsman, right-hand medium pace round-arm bowler, good deep field. *Teams* Lancashire (1877, 1 match); Yorkshire (1880, 2 matches).
Career batting
3–4–0–70–26–17.50–0–*ct* 0
Bowling 17–1–17.00–0–0–1/17

Blaker, Richard Norman Rowsell
Amateur. *b:* 24.10.1879, Bayswater, London. *d:* 11.9.1950, Eltham, Kent. His twin daughters both played cricket for England. Grandson of R.N. (Cambridge U 1842–3). Hard-hitting middle order right-hand batsman, right-arm fast bowler, brilliant field. *Sch* Westminster. *Teams* Kent (1898–1908, 119 matches); Cambridge U (1899–1902, blue 1900–02). *Tour* Bennett to West Indies 1901/2.
Career batting
161–262–25–5359–122–22.61–2–*ct* 142
Bowling 226–9–25.11–0–0–2/1
He also obtained a soccer blue, playing as centre-forward.

Blake-Kelly, G. N. (*see under* Kelly, G. N. B.)

Blake-Kelly, G. W. F.
(*see under* Kelly, G. W. F. B.)

Blakey, George Matthew
Professional. *b:* 1907, Fylde, Lancashire. *d:* 1968, Stoke-on-Trent, Staffordshire. Middle order batsman, change bowler. *Team* Worcestershire (1939, 3 matches).
Career batting
3–4–1–46–42–15.33–0–*ct* 1
Bowling 87–0
He also played for Shropshire.

Blamires, Emmanuel
Professional. *b:* 31.7.1850, Bradford, Yorkshire. *d:* 22.3.1886, Bradford, Yorkshire. Lower order left-hand batsman, left-hand fast round-arm bowler. *Teams* Yorkshire (1877, 1 match); Surrey (1878–81, 32 matches).
Career batting
36–61–15–440–31–9.56–0–*ct* 28
Bowling 2743–137–20.02–9–2–8/77
He was a noted player of the game called knur and spell.

Blanckenberg, James Manuel
Amateur. *b:* 31.12.1893, Newlands, Cape Town, South Africa. Middle order right-hand batsman, right-arm medium pace bowler. *Teams* Western Province (1912/3 to 1922/3); Natal (1923/4). *Tours* South Africans to England 1924. *Tests* South Africa (1913/4 to 1924, 18 matches).
Career batting
74–116–16–2232–171–22.32–1–*ct* 53
Bowling 6230–293–21.26–21–3–9/78
Test batting
18–30–7–455–59–19.78–0–*ct* 9
Bowling 1817–60–30.28–4–0–6/76
Although he took 119 wickets (av 22.40) on his single tour to England, Blanckenberg was ineffective against the major English batsmen and admitted that he could not bowl well on turf wickets. His most successful series was the 1913/14 Tests in South Africa. His style of bowling was similar to T. G. Wass, in that he delivered a fast leg break. His best bowling was 9/78 for Western Provinces v Transvaal at Johannesburg in 1920/1.

Bland, Cyril Harold George
Professional. *b:* 23.5.1872, Leake, Boston, Lincs. *d:* 1.7.1950. He was found dead in the canal at Cowbridge, Boston. Very moderate right-hand batsman, right-arm fast bowler. *Team* Sussex (1897–1904, 145 matches).
Career batting
147–190–35–998–59–6.43–0–*ct* 80
Bowling 13524–557–24.28–44–11–10/48
Bland's career was short but brilliant. He took 129 wickets (av 21.69) in his debut season of 1897, 82 wickets in 1898, 108 in 1899 and 112 in 1900 and then faded completely away. This sudden failure was perhaps due to his being warned that his bowling action was suspect. In 1899 he took all ten wickets in the innings (for 48) for Sussex v Kent at Tonbridge. He also played for Lincolnshire.

Bland, Kenneth Colin
Amateur. *b:* 5.4.1938, Bulawayo, Rhodesia Middle order right-hand batsman, right-arm medium pace bowler, brilliant outfield. *Teams* Rhodesia (1956/7 to 1968/9); Orange Free State (1972/3 to 1973/4); Eastern Province (1969/70 to 1970/1). *Tours* South Africans to Australia and New Zealand 1963/4, to England 1965; International XI to Pakistan 1961/2; SA Fezela to

England 1961; Rest of World to England 1966, 1967. *Tests* South Africa (1961/2 to 1966/7, 21 matches).
Career batting
131–219–28–7249–197–37.95–13–*ct* 51
Bowling 1512–43–35.16–0–0–4/40
Test batting
21–39–5–1669–144*–49.08–3–*ct* 10
Bowling 125–2–62.50–0–0–2/16

On his only Test playing visit to England, Bland was most successful, batting well in two of the three internationals, hitting 906 runs (av 37.75) in first-class matches and bringing delight to the crowds with his outstanding fielding, his pick-ups and returns to the wicket being rarely equalled for speed. He hit 1,048 runs, av 69.86, in South Africa in 1964/5.

Bland, Robert Dennis Fraser
Amateur. *b:* 16.5.1911, West Bridgford, Notts. Lower order right-hand batsman, left-arm medium pace bowler. *Sch* Shrewsbury. *Team* Nottinghamshire (1929–34, 33 matches).
Career batting
33–39–14–240–20*–9.60–0–*ct* 13
Bowling 2697–73–36.95–1–0–5/61

Blaney, Frederick Andrews
Amateur. *b:* 17.3.1918, Lisburn, Ireland. Right-hand batsman. *Sch* Royal Belfast Academical Institution. *Team* Ireland (1939).
Career batting
1–2–0–14–13–7.00–0–*ct* 0

Blatcher, Richard Brian
Amateur. *b:* 2.4.1934, Barnes, Surrey. Lower order right-hand batsman, right-arm medium-fast bowler. *Sch* Kingston Grammar School. *Team* Cambridge U (1955).
Career batting
2–3–1–16–15–8.00–0–*ct* 1
Bowling 120–4–30.00–0–0–2/42

Blaxland, Rev Lionel Bruce
Amateur. *b:* 25.3.1898, Lilleshall, Shropshire. *d:* 29.4.1976, Temple Ewell, Kent. Middle order right-hand batsman, right-arm fast-medium bowler, good field. *Sch* Shrewsbury. *Team* Derbyshire (1925–47, 19 matches).
Career batting
19–31–1–483–64–16.10–0–*ct* 7
Bowling 18–0

Whilst at Oxford he was awarded his blue for soccer and played in some cricket trials, but not in first-class matches for the University.

Bleackley, Edward Overall
Amateur. *b:* 10.3.1898, Salford, Lancashire. *d:* 17.2.1976, London. Middle order batsman. *Sch* Harrow. *Team* Lancashire (1919, 2 matches).
Career batting
3–5–0–31–21–6.20–0–*ct* 0

Blenkiron, William
Professional. *b:* 21.7.1942, Newfield, Co Durham. Lower order right-hand batsman, right-arm fast-medium bowler. *Team* Warwickshire (1964–74, 117 matches). *Tour* MCC to Ceylon 1969/70 (not first-class).
Career batting
118–139–30–1467–62–13.45–0–*ct* 55
Bowling 8149–287–28.39–7–0–5/37

He also played for Durham.

Blewitt, Charles Percy
Amateur. *b:* 1877, Dudley, Worcs. *d:* 15.12.1937, Danesford, Shropshire. Right-hand batsman. *Team* Worcestershire (1912, 1 match).
Career batting
1–2–0–7–4–3.50–0–*ct* 0

Bligh, Algernon Stuart
Amateur. *b:* 6.10.1888, Marylebone, London. *d:* 27.12.1952, Minehead, Somerset. Son of L.E. (Kent). Middle order right-hand batsman, wicket-keeper. *Sch* Eton. *Team* Somerset (1922–26, 14 matches).
Career batting
14–27–1–455–73*–17.50–0–*ct* 13
Bowling 14–0

Bligh, General The Hon Edward
Amateur. *b:* 19.9.1769. *d:* 2.11.1840, Thames Ditton, Surrey. Brother of the 4th Earl of Darnley. One of the best amateur batsmen of his day. *Sch* Eton. *Teams* Kent (1806); Hampshire (1806).
Career batting
25–46–10–382–42*–10.61–0–*ct* 14

His final match was for Bligh's XI in 1813.

Bligh, Hon and Rev Edward Vesey
Amateur. *b:* 28.2.1829, Grosvenor Place, London. *d:* 22.4.1908, West Malling, Kent. Brother of 6th Earl of Darnley, father of L.E. (Kent). Hard-hitting lower order right-hand batsman, slow round-arm bowler. *Sch* Eton. *Teams* Oxford U (1850, blue); Kent (1849–64, 23 matches); Middlesex (1862, 1 match).
Career batting
40–73–10–786–53–12.47–0–*ct* 21–*st* 2
Bowling 178–9+14–19.77–1–0–6/?

From 1850 to 1855 his cricket was limited as he was successively Attache at Hanover, Florence and Berlin. He later left the Diplomatic Service and entered the Church. His first important match was for Gentlemen of Kent in 1848. He also appeared for Oxfordshire.

Bligh, Hon Ivo Francis (Walter)
(became 8th Earl of Darnley in 1900)
Amateur. *b:* 13.3.1859, Bruton St, London. *d:* 10.4.1927, Puckle Hill, Cobham, Kent. Brother of Lord Clifton (Kent). Opening right-hand batsman, good deep field. *Sch* Eton. *Teams* Kent (1877–83, 47 matches); Cambridge U (1878–81, blue all four years). *Tour* Bligh to Australia 1882/3. *Tests* England (1882/3, 4 matches).
Career batting
84–143–11–2734–113*–20.71–2–*ct* 81
Test batting
4–7–1–62–19–10.33–0–*ct* 7

He hit 1,013 runs, av 30.69, in 1880.

Owing to ill-health his career in first-class cricket was relatively brief and he is remembered for his team which went to Australia in the winter of 1882/3 and recaptured 'The Ashes' for England. Apart from cricket he represented Cambridge at tennis, both singles and doubles.

Bligh, Lodovick Edward
Amateur. *b:* 24.11.1854, Dover, Kent. *d:* 16.5.1924, Minehead, Somerset. Son of Hon and Rev E.V. (Kent), father of A.S. (Somerset). Sound middle order right-hand batsman, right-arm fast bowler. *Sch* Eton. *Team* Kent (1878–84, 10 matches).
Career batting
10–18–4–107–20–7.64–0–*ct* 6
Bowling 157–5–31.40–0–0–2/36

He was not in the Eleven whilst at Eton or Cambridge.

Block, Spencer Allen
Amateur. *b:* 15.7.1908, Esher, Surrey. *d:* 7.10.1979, Meadle, Bucks. Attacking opening or middle order right-hand batsman, brilliant deep field. *Sch* Marlborough. *Teams* Cambridge U (1928–29, blue 1929); Surrey (1928–33, 30 matches). *Tour* Martineau to Egypt 1929 (not first-class).
Career batting
58–93–4–2488–117–27.95–2–*ct* 33
Bowling 40–2–20.00–0–0–1/0

His final first-class match was for Free Foresters in 1948. He also excelled at rugby football and hockey.

Blofeld, Henry Calthorpe
Amateur. *b:* 23.9.1939, Hoveton, Norfolk. Right-hand opening batsman, wicket-keeper. *Sch* Eton. *Team* Cambridge U (1958–59, blue 1959).
Career batting
17–32–1–758–138–24.45–1–*ct* 11
Bowling 15–0

He played County cricket for Norfolk. He is a well-known cricket journalist and broadcaster. His final first-class match was for Free Foresters in 1960.

Blomley, Benjamin
Professional. *b:* November 1879, Oldham, Lancashire. *d:* 12.3.1949, Chadderton, Lancashire. Tail end right-hand batsman, wicket-keeper. *Team* Lancashire (1903–22, 69 matches).
Career batting
69–87–32–316–41–5.74–0–*ct* 109–*st* 33

Bloodworth, Bernard Sydney
Professional. *b:* December 1893, Cheltenham, Gloucs. *d:* 19.2.1967, Bristol. Impetuous middle order left-hand batsman, slow left-arm bowler, wicket-keeper. *Team* Gloucestershire (1919–32, 142 matches).
Career batting
142–237–9–3714–115–16.28–1–*ct* 74–*st* 27
Bowling 47–0

He was also a good rugby footballer, playing for Cheltenham. After he finished as a first-class cricketer he remained with the County Club as scorer and groundsman at Bristol until 1965.

Bloom, George Raymond
Cricketer. *b:* 13.9.1941, Aston, Sheffield. Middle order left-hand batsman. *Team* Yorkshire (1964, 1 match).
Career batting
1–1–0–2–2–2.00–0–*ct* 2

Bloomfield, Horace Orlando
Amateur. *b:* 15.7.1891, Brixton, Surrey. *d:* 31.5.1973, Hillhead, near Fareham, Hants. Son-in-law of F.C. Holland (Surrey). Middle order right-hand batsman. *Team* Surrey (1921–22, 4 matches).
Career batting
4–7–2–180–107*–36.00–1–*ct* 2

He scored a century (107*) on his first-class debut – Surrey v Northants at Northampton in 1921. He was a noted figure in London Club cricket and appeared in representative matches for the Club Cricket Conference.

Bloor, James Henry
Amateur. *b:* 1857, Clifton, Gloucs. *d:* 9.3.1935, Brynmawr, Breconshire. Middle order batsman, change bowler. *Team* Gloucestershire (1887, 3 matches).

Career batting
3–5–0–44–22–8.80–0–*ct* 2
Bowling 14–0

Blore, Rev Edward William
Amateur. *b:* 24.1.1828, London. *d:* 24.6.1885, Cambridge. Lower order right-hand batsman, slow round-arm bowler. *Sch* Eton. *Teams* Cambridge U (1848–54, blue 1848–51).
Career batting
18–34–6–230–22–8.21–0–*ct* 5
Bowling 41–0+104–no av–7–2–8/?
He was the greatest schoolboy bowler of his day, taking no less than 68 wickets for Eton against Harrow and Winchester in three seasons. He was also successful at Cambridge and captained the University in his fourth year. He also played for Buckinghamshire. His final first-class match was for MCC in 1855.

Blount, Albert
Professional. *b:* 8.8.1889, Morton, Derbyshire. *d:* 10.11.1961, New Rossington, Yorkshire. Tail end right-hand batsman, slow left-arm bowler. *Team* Derbyshire (1912–26, 7 matches).
Career batting
7–11–2–52–17–5.77–0–*ct* 3
Bowling 215–7–30.71–0–0–4/53

Blount, Air Vice Marshal Charles Hubert Boulby
Amateur. *b:* 26.10.1893, Kampti, India. *d:* 23.10.1940. He was killed in an air crash at Hendon, Middlesex. Hard hitting middle order right-hand batsman, slow right-arm bowler. *Sch* Harrow. *Teams* Services (1920–24); RAF (1927–30).
Career batting
10–17–0–575–110–33.82–1–*ct* 9
Bowling 303–12–25.37–0–0–3/16
His County cricket was for Suffolk.

Bloy, Nigel Clement Francis
Amateur. *b:* 2.1.1923, Plymouth. Middle order left-hand batsman, leg break bowler. *Sch* Dover. *Team* Oxford U (1946–48, blue 1946–47).
Career batting
31–53–9–964–77–21.90–0–*ct* 15
Bowling 613–8–76.62–0–0–3/80
He appeared occasionally for Gloucestershire 2nd XI, but more frequently for Devon in the 1950s. His final first-class match was for MCC in 1958.

Bluett, John Douglas Jeremy
Amateur. *b:* 29.5.1930, Kensington, London. Stylish middle-order right-hand batsman, off break bowler. *Sch* Cranbrook. *Team* Kent (1950, 2 matches).
Career batting
2–2–0–16–10–8.00–0–*ct* 1

Blundell, Dermot Howard (Blundell Hollinshead)
Amateur. *b:* 27.2.1874, London. *d:* 26.10.1910, Kensington, London. Middle order right-hand batsman. *Sch* Wellington. *Team* MCC (1902).
Career batting
1–1–0–45–45–45.00–0–*ct* 0
His County cricket was for Berkshire.

Blundell, Sir Edward Denis
Amateur. *b:* 29.5.1907, Wellington, New Zealand. Tail end left-hand batsman, right-arm fast-medium bowler. *Teams* Cambridge U (1928–29, blue both years); Wellington (1930/1 to 1937/8). *Tour* New Zealanders to England 1927 (one match).
Career batting
48–68–22–400–27*–8.69–*ct* 16
Bowling 4924–195–25.25–11–1–6/25
He was Governor-General of New Zealand from 1972 to 1977.

Blundell, Frederick (John)
Amateur. *b:* 1850, South Stoneham, Hants. *d:* 26.4.1929, Botley, Southampton. Lower order right-hand batsman, slow right-arm bowler. *Team* Hampshire (1880, 1 match).
Career batting
1–1–0–2–2–2.00–0–*ct* 1
Bowling 22–2–11.00–0–0–2/22

Blundell, Joseph Wagstaff
Amateur. *b:* 1845, Droitwich, Worcs. *d:* 11.1.1933, Hove, Sussex. Middle order batsman. *Team* MCC (1882).
Career batting
1–2–0–3–2–1.50–0–*ct* 0

Blunden, Arthur
Professional. *b:* 5.9.1906, East Malling, Kent. Tail end right-hand batsman, right-arm fast-medium bowler. *Team* Kent (1931–33, 11 matches).
Career batting
11–12–4–33–9*–4.12–0–*ct* 3
Bowling 586–18–32.55–0–0–4/31
He also played for Durham.

Blunt, Leonard
Professional. *b:* 29.3.1921, Worcester. Tail end right-hand batsman, right-arm fast medium bowler. *Team* Worcestershire (1946–48, 14 matches).

Career batting
14–19–5–109–18–7.78–0–*ct* 4
Bowling 885–33–26.84–1–0–5/60
He also played for Cheshire.

Blunt, Roger Charles, MBE
Amateur. *b:* 3.11.1900, Durham. *d:* 22.6.1966, London. Middle order right-hand batsman, leg break bowler. *Teams* Canterbury (1917/8 to 1924/5); Otago (1926/7 to 1931/2); MCC (1934). *Tours* New Zealand to Australia 1925/6, 1927/8, to England 1927 and 1931. *Tests* New Zealand (1929/30 to 1931/2, 9 matches).
Career batting
123–209–15–7953–338*–40.99–15–*ct* 88
Bowling 6638–214–31.01–5–1–8/99
Test batting
9–13–1–330–96–27.50–0–*ct* 5
Bowling 472–12–39.33–0–0–3/17
His highest innings of 338* was scored for Otago v Canterbury at Christchurch in 1931/2. He was originally purely a leg-break bowler, but developed into a fine bat. His two visits to England were most successful. In 1927 he hit 1,540 runs (av 44.00) and in 1931, 1,592 (av 43.02). His highest innings in England was 225 v Gentlemen at Eastbourne in 1931. His final first-class match was for Sir J. Cahn's XI in 1935.

Blythe, Colin
Professional. *b:* 30.5.1879, Deptford, Kent. *d:* 8.11.1917. He was killed in action near Passchendaele, Belgium. Tail end right-hand batsman, slow left-arm bowler. *Team* Kent (1899–1914, 381 matches). *Tours* MacLaren to Australia 1901/2; MCC to Australia 1907/8, to South Africa 1905/6, 1909/10; Kent to USA 1903. *Tests* England (1901/2 to 1909/10, 19 matches).
Career batting
439–587–137–4443–82*–9.87–0–*ct* 206
Bowling 42099–2503–16.81–218–71–10/30
Test batting
19–31–12–183–27–9.63–0–*ct* 6
Bowling 1863–100–18.63–9–4–8/59
Blythe and Rhodes were the two principal left-arm spin bowlers of the Edwardian era. Contemporaries were in two minds as to which was the greater. Ranjitsinhji chose Blythe, but others equally qualified picked theYorkshireman.

Blythe's great quality was his deceptive flight, but he was also a master of the sticky or crumbling wicket, and the fact that he could deliver a faster ball coming through with his arm without any noticeable change of action proved the downfall of many batsmen.

He appeared in first-class cricket for 15 full seasons (1900–14) and in 14 of them captured over 100 wickets – in 1901 ill-health hampered him, but he still had 93 victims to his name. His best year was 1909 when his total reached 215 (av 14.54). His best bowling was 10/30 for Kent v Northants at Northampton in 1907.

Blythe first played for England during MacLaren's 1901/02 tour to Australia and on both that visit and his return in 1907/8 he came second in the bowling table to the redoubtable Barnes. Both his visits to South Africa were also most successful.

His best Test performances in England occurred in the 1909 series against Australia, when in the Edgbaston Test he took 11 for 102, which brought England victory by 10 wickets. His international career was marred to some extent by the fact that he suffered from epilepsy and for this reason he was omitted from the England team on several occasions.

Blythe's death in the First World War was a major loss to cricket since, in normal circumstances, his career would have lasted about another ten seasons and in 1914 he was still at the top of his profession.

Boak, John
Professional. *b:* 27.6.1837, Edinburgh. *d:* 29.10.1876, Bermondsey, Surrey. He was killed by a train whilst crossing the line. Tail end right-hand batsman, right-arm fast bowler. *Sch* Royal High School, Edinburgh. *Team* Middlesex (1873, 1 match).
Career batting
1–2–0–19–11–9.50–0–*ct* 2
Bowling 37–1–37.00–0–0–1/20
He emigrated to Australia in 1858 and was employed as a professional cricketer there, but returned to England about 1868. He played for New South Wales and Queensland, but not in first-class matches.

Board, John Henry
Professional. *b:* 23.2.1867, Clifton, Gloucs. *d:* 15.4.1924, on board *SS Kenilworth Castle* en route from South Africa from heart failure. Sound middle order right-hand batsman, wicket-keeper. *Teams* Gloucestershire (1891–1914, 430 matches); London County (1900–04); Hawke's Bay (1910/11 to 1914/5). *Tours* Stoddart to Australia 1897/8; Hawke to South Africa 1898/9; MCC to South Africa 1905/6. *Tests* England (1898/9 to 1905/6, 6 matches).
Career batting
525–906–97–15674–214–19.37–9–*ct* 852–*st* 355
Bowling 46–0
Test Batting
6–12–2–108–29–10.80–0–*ct* 8–*st* 3
He hit 1,000 runs in a season six times (best 1,132, av 24.08, in 1900). He went abroad most

winters coaching, either in South Africa or New Zealand. His highest score was 214 for Gloucs v Somerset at Bristol in 1900.

Boardman, Alfred Joseph
Professional. *b:* 11.5.1859, Islington, Middlesex. *d:* 1928, Epsom, Surrey. Middle order right-hand batsman, right-arm medium pace bowler. *Team* Surrey (1878–80, 9 matches).
Career batting
10–19–2–162–33–9.52–0–*ct* 1
Bowling 37–0

Bocking, Henry
Professional. *b:* 10.12.1835, Sheffield. *d:* February 1907, Sheffield. *Team* Yorkshire (1865, 2 matches).
Career batting
2–2–0–14–11–7.00–0–*ct* 0
He appeared for Yorkshire in two matches in 1865, when the leading five County players were in dispute with the Committee.

Boddam-Whetham, John Whetham
Amateur. *b:* May, 1843, Southwell, Notts. *d:* 23.3.1918, Folkestone, Kent. Middle order batsman. *Team* Gentlemen of North (1870, 1 match).
Career batting
1–2–0–12–7–6.00–0–*ct* 0
Bowling 13–0

Boddington, Myles Alan
Amateur. *b:* 30.11.1924, Hale, Cheshire. Son of R.A. (Lancs). Tail end left-hand batsman, opening bowler. *Sch* Rugby. *Team* RAF (1946).
Career batting
1–2–0–23–23–11.50–0–*ct* 1
Bowling 13–0

Boddington, Robert Alan
Amateur. *b:* 30.6.1892, Manchester. *d:* 5.8.1977, Fifield, Oxford. Father of M.A. (RAF). Middle order right-hand batsman, wicket-keeper. *Sch* Rugby. *Teams* Lancashire (1913–24, 52 matches); Oxford U (1914).
Career batting
56–83–19–801–69–12.35–0–*ct* 76–*st* 21

Bodell, Ernest Herbert
Amateur. *b:* 17.8.1928, Dublin, Ireland. Right-hand batsman, right-arm fast medium pace bowler. *Team* Ireland (1954–59).
Career batting
5–8–4–25–11*–6.25–0–*ct* 1
Bowling 464–11–42.18–0–0–4/27

Boden, Rev Cecil Arthur
Amateur. *b:* 18.12.1890, Countesthorpe, Leics. *d:* 31.5.1981, Hampstead Marshall, Newbury, Berks. Opening right-hand batsman, occasional right-arm medium pace bowler. *Sch* Christ's Hospital. *Team* Leicestershire (1911–13, 11 matches).
Career batting
11–19–0–196–40–10.31–0–*ct* 5

Boden, John George
Amateur. *b:* 27.12.1848, Birstall, Leeds, Yorkshire. *d:* 3.1.1928, Ilkley, Yorkshire. Lower order right-hand batsman, wicket-keeper. *Team* Yorkshire (1878, 1 match).
Career batting
1–1–0–6–6–6.00–0–*ct* 1

Boden, R.
Professional. Middle order batsman. *Team* Lancashire (1907, 1 match).
Career batting
1–2–0–8–5–4.00–0–*ct* 0

Boden, Timothy Walter
Amateur. *b:* 19.5.1901, Sherborne, Dorset. *d:* 5.9.1969, Churchill, Axminster, Devon. Great nephew of Walter (Derbyshire). Middle order batsman. *Sch* Eton. *Team* Derbyshire (1920, 1 match).
Career batting
1–2–0–14–9–7.00–0–*ct* 0

Boden, Walter
Amateur. *b:* 6.8.1837, Derby. *d:* 16.9.1905, Mickleover, Derbyshire. Great uncle of T.W. (Derbyshire). Right-hand batsman. *Sch* Rugby. *Team* Derbyshire (1874, 1 match).
Career batting
2–4–2–18–11–9.00–0–*ct* 0
His only other first-class match was for Gentlemen of the North at the Oval in 1859. Boden was one of the prime movers in the creation of Derbyshire CCC in 1870. He was hon secretary to the County Club from 1870 to 1881.

Bodington, Cecil Herbert
Amateur. *b:* 20.1.1880, Suffield, Norfolk. *d:* 11.4.1917. He was killed in action near Arras, France. Middle order right-hand batsman, change bowler. *Sch* Charterhouse/King's, Canterbury. *Team* Hampshire (1901–02, 10 matches).
Career batting
10–18–4–154–36–11.00–0–*ct* 4
Bowling 287–9–31.88–0–0–3/19
He appeared in the Seniors' Match at Cambridge in 1901 and 1902, but not in any first-class matches at the University.

Bodkin, Peter Ernest
Amateur. *b:* 15.9.1924, Barnet, Herts. Middle order left-hand batsman, left-arm medium pace bowler. *Sch* Bradfield. *Team* Cambridge U (1946, blue).
Career batting
9–17–0–328–52–19.29–0–*ct* 9
Bowling 330–8–41.25–0–0–2/27
He captained Cambridge in 1946, having appeared in the non-first-class war time matches v Oxford, and led Cambridge in the 1945 game. His County cricket was for Hertfordshire.

Boger, Alnod John
Amateur. *b:* 31.8.1871, Plymouth, Devon. *d:* 3.6.1940, Oxford. Middle order right-hand batsman, right-arm slow bowler, slip field. *Sch* Winchester. *Team* Oxford U (1891–92, blue 1891).
Career batting
6–12–1–143–41*–13.00–0–*ct* 1
Bowling 225–9–25.00–1–0–6/63
His County cricket was played for Hertfordshire, 1889–97. In 1925 he was appointed Sheriff of Cornwall.

Bohlen, Francis Hermann
Amateur. *b:* 31.7.1868, Philadelphia, USA. *d:* 9.12.1942, USA. Forcing middle order right-hand batsman, occasional right-arm fast-medium bowler. *Teams* Philadelphians (1891–1908); MCC (1894–1904); London County (1904). *Tours* Philadelphians to England 1897, 1903 and 1908.
Career batting
58–104–4–2266–118–22.66–2–*ct* 18
Bowling 6–0
In Philadelphia he played for the Germantown Club. He appeared regularly in the USA v Canada match, but his most famous innings was 118 for the Gentlemen of Philadelphia v Australians in 1893. He was a brilliant batsman on hard fast wickets, but never really flourished on English pitches.

Boissier, Arthur Paul
Amateur. *b:* 25.1.1881, Bloxham, Oxfordshire. *d:* 2.10.1953, Tarves, Aberdeenshire. Middle order batsman, change bowler. *Sch* St John's, Leatherhead. *Team* Derbyshire (1901–06, 2 matches).
Career batting
2–4–0–13–6–3.25–0–*ct* 0
Bowling 32–2–16.00–0–0–2/32
He batted well in the Oxford Freshmen's Match of 1901, but did not appear in first-class cricket for the University. He was awarded his blue for soccer in 1904.

Bokhari, Iftikhar Ali
Amateur. *b:* 6.7.1935, Lahore, India. Opening right-hand batsman, right-arm medium pace bowler. *Teams* Cambridge U (1957); Sargodha (1964/5); Lahore (1958/9 to 1965/6); Punjab (1957/8).
Career batting
18–30–6–938–203*–39.08–3–*ct* 4
Bowling 25–0
His highest score was 203 for Lahore v Punjab U at Lahore in 1960/1. He also played for Cambridgeshire.

Bolitho, William Edward Thomas
Amateur. *b:* 2.7.1862, Penzance, Cornwall. *d:* 21.2.1919, Bath, Somerset. Middle order right-hand batsman, excellent cover field. *Sch* Harrow. *Teams* Oxford U (1883 and 1885, blue both years; injury prevented him playing in 1884). *Tour* Sanders to North America 1885.
Career batting
10–19–1–339–45*–18.83–0–*ct* 1
He played for and captained Cornwall, being one of the mainstays of cricket in the West Country for many years.

Bollon, Stanley
Amateur. *b:* 1890, Islington, London. Lower order batsman, opening bowler. *Team* Demobilised Officers (1919).
Career batting
1–1–0–9–9–9.00–0–*ct* 2
Bowling 81–6–13.50–1–0–5/59

Bolton, Alan
Professional. *b:* 1.7.1939, Darwen, Lancashire. Opening or middle order right-hand batsman, right-arm off break bowler. *Team* Lancashire (1957–61, 40 matches).
Career batting
40–71–6–1223–96–18.81–0–*ct* 15
Bowling 80–2–40.00–0–0–1/17

Bolton, Benjamin Charles
Amateur. *b:* 23.9.1862, Cottingham, Yorkshire. *d:* 18.11.1910. He died from injuries sustained falling from an express train en route to Hull. Tail end right-hand batsman, right-arm fast-medium bowler. *Team* Yorkshire (1890–91, 4 matches).
Career batting
4–6–0–25–11–4.16–0–*ct* 2
Bowling 252–13–19.30–1–0–5/40
He took 8 for 26 on his Yorkshire debut v Warwickshire in 1890 – not first-class.

Bolton, Robert Henry Dundas
Amateur. *b:* 13.1.1893, Koppa Kadur, Mysore, India. *d:* 30.10.1964, St Pancras, London. Middle

order right-hand batsman. *Sch* Rossall. *Team* Hampshire (1913–22, 7 matches).
Career batting
7–12–0–121–24–10.08–0–*ct* 2
He played for Dorset whilst still at school and later, when Chief Constable of Northants, he was on the Committee of that County Club.

Bolus, Frank
Professional. *b:* 2.11.1864, Wolverhampton, Staffs. *d:* 1939, Coventry, Warwickshire. Middle order right-hand batsman. *Team* Somerset (1893–94, 10 matches).
Career batting
10–18–3–111–23–7.40–0–*ct* 5
Bowling 7–0

Bolus, John Brian
Cricketer. *b:* 31.1.1934, Whitkirk, Leeds, Yorkshire. Opening right-hand batsman, occasional left-arm medium pace bowler. *Teams* Yorkshire (1956–62, 107 matches); Nottinghamshire (1963–72, 269 matches); Derbyshire (1973–75, 64 matches). *Tour* MCC to India 1963/4. *Tests* England (1963 to 1963/4, 7 matches).
Career batting
469–833–81–25598–202*–34.03–39–*ct* 201
Bowling 886–24–36.91–0–0–4/40
Test batting
7–12–0–496–88–41.33–0–*ct* 2
Bowling 16–0
He hit 1,000 runs in a season on 14 occasions, including two seasons over 2,000 (best 2,190, av 41.32, in 1963). His only double century was 202* for Notts v Glamorgan in 1963. He captained Notts in 1972 and Derbyshire in 1973–75. He was awarded his County Cap for all three of his first-class Counties.

Bomford, Sir Hugh
Amateur. *b:* 12.8.1882, Calcutta, India. *d:* 19.1.1939, Meerut, India. Lower order right-hand batsman, wicket-keeper. *Sch* Marlborough. *Team* Oxford U (1901–03).
Career batting
9–11–4–52–16*–7.42–0–*ct* 19–*st* 9

Bompas, Hugh Steele
Amateur. *b:* 9.12.1881, Hampstead. *d:* 19.7.1944, Chelsea, London. Opening right-hand batsman, wicket-keeper. *Sch* Westminster. *Teams* Cambridge U (1901–03); London County (1901).
Career batting
7–11–2–35–15–3.88–0–*ct* 5–*st* 4
He was most successful with the bat in his final year (1900) at school and then hit 109 and 59 in the Cambridge Freshmen's Match of 1901, but totally failed to make runs in first-class cricket.

Bond, John David
Cricketer. *b:* 6.5.1932, Kearsley, Lancashire. Middle order right-hand batsman, occasional leg break bowler. *Teams* Lancashire (1955–72, 344 matches); Nottinghamshire (1974, 17 matches).
Career batting
362–548–80–12125–157–25.90–14–*ct* 222
Bowling 69–0
He hit over 1,000 runs in a season twice (best 2,125, av 36.01, in 1962). He was appointed captain of Lancashire in 1968 when the County was at a low ebb and took the team to the top with three Gillette Cup Championships and two John Player League successes. After retiring in 1972, having led Lancashire for five seasons, he was appointed captain and manager of Notts in 1974, but had little success. In 1982 he held the post of manager of Lancashire.

Bond, Raymond Ernest
Cricketer. *b:* 7.9.1944, Slough, Bucks. Tail end left-hand batsman, right-arm medium-fast bowler. *Team* Minor Counties (1973).
Career batting
1 match, did not bat–*ct* 0
Bowling 107–2–53.50–0–0–1/33
His County cricket was for Buckinghamshire 1965–1979.

Bonham-Carter, Lothian George
Amateur. *b:* 29.9.1858, Petersfield, Hants. *d:* 13.1.1927, Buriton, Hants. Father of S.S. (Royal Navy). Free hitting opening right-hand batsman, useful slow round-arm bowler. *Sch* Clifton. *Team* Hampshire (1880–85, 8 matches).
Career batting
8–15–0–260–67–17.33–0–*ct* 5
Bowling 63–2–31.50–0–0–2/22

Bonham-Carter, Sir Maurice
Amateur. *b:* 11.10.1880, Paddington, London. *d:* 7.6.1960, Bayswater, London. Middle order right-hand batsman, slow bowler, wicket-keeper. *Sch* Winchester. *Teams* Oxford U (1901–02, blue 1902); Kent (1902, 1 match).
Career batting
14–23–3–391–86–19.55–0–*ct* 8–*st* 1
Bowling 430–9–47.77–0–0–2/5
From 1910 to 1916 he was Private Secretary to the Prime Minister, Mr Asquith.

Bonham-Carter, Philip Herman
Amateur. *b:* 12.11.1891, Karachi, India. *d:*

7.1.1934, Hampstead, London. Middle order batsman. *Team* Royal Navy (1919–29).
Career batting
3–6–0–35–16–5.83–0–*ct* 0

Bonham-Carter, Sir Stuart Sumner
Amateur. *b:* 9.7.1889, Portsmouth, Hants. *d:* 5.9.1972, Petersfield, Hants. Son of L.G. (Hants). Middle order batsman. *Sch* Clifton. *Team* Royal Navy (1925–26).
Career batting
2–4–0–47–18–11.75–0–*ct* 0

Bonner, John Wardell
Amateur. *b:* 3.4.1869, Mile End, Middlesex. *d:* 26.11.1936, Bournemouth, Hants. Middle order right-hand batsman. *Sch* Forest. *Team* Essex (1896–98, 16 matches).
Career batting
16–27–1–339–59–13.03–0–*ct* 5

Bonnor, George John
Amateur. *b:* 25.2.1855, Bathurst, New South Wales, Australia. *d:* 27.6.1912, East Orange, New South Wales, Australia. Very hard-hitting middle order right-hand batsman. *Teams* Victoria (1881/2 to 1884/5, 10 matches); New South Wales (1884/5 to 1890/1, 5 matches). *Tours* Australians to England 1880, 1882, 1884, 1886, 1888. *Tests* Australia (1880–88, 17 matches).
Career batting
148–244–17–4820–128–21.23–5–*ct* 127–*st* 1
Bowling 470–12–39.16–0–0–3/34
Test batting
17–30–0–512–128–17.06–1–*ct* 16
Bowling 84–2–42.00–0–0–1/5

Known as 'The Colonial Hercules', Bonnor was the most powerful hitter of his day – he stood about 6ft 6ins and weighed 16st. His best innings in England, though not his highest, was 119 for Australians v Gentlemen at Lord's in 1888, whilst his outstanding innings in Test cricket came at Sydney in 1884/5, when he hit the fastest Test hundred (in 100 mins) up to that date. From 1886 to 1889 he lived in England. He hit 1,000 runs in a season twice (best 1,155, av 20.26, in 1886).

Boobbyer, Brian
Amateur. *b:* 25.2.1928, Ealing, Middlesex. Opening right-hand batsman, right-arm medium pace bowler, brilliant field. *Sch* Uppingham. *Team* Oxford U (1949–52, blue all four years).
Career batting
40–75–2–1970–126–26.95–2–*ct* 35
Bowling 19–0

In addition to his cricket he was a brilliant rugby footballer, obtaining his blue at Oxford and also being capped for England at centre.

Boock, Stephen Lewis
Cricketer. *b*: 20.9.1951, Dunedin, New Zealand. Lower order right-hand batsman, slow left-arm bowler. *Teams* Otago (1973/4 to 1982/3); Canterbury (1975/6 to 1977/8). *Tours* New Zealand to England 1978, to Australia 1980/1. *Tests* New Zealand (1977/8 to 1979/80, 12 matches).
Career batting
92–115–43–592–35*–8.20–0–*ct* 48
Bowling 7583–363–20.88–24–3–8/59
Test batting
12–19–6–37–8–2.84–0–*ct* 8
Bowling 706–19–37.15–1–0–5/67

He came second in the first-class bowling averages for the 1978 tour to England with 39 wickets, av 22.17, and played in all three Tests.

Booden, Christopher Derek
Cricketer. *b:* 22.6.1961, Newport Pagnell, Bucks. Lower order right-hand batsman, right-arm medium pace bowler. *Team* Northants (1980–81, 4 matches).
Career batting
4–3–2–10–6*–10.00–0–*ct* 2
Bowling 258–3–86.00–0–0–2/30

He also played for Buckinghamshire.

Bookman, Louis
(originally Buckhalter)
Amateur. *b:* 1890, Dolphins Barn, Dublin, Ireland. *d:* 10.6.1943, Dublin, Ireland. Right-hand batsman, right-arm medium pace bowler. *Team* Ireland (1920–29).
Career batting
9–17–0–342–53–20.11–0–*ct* 5
Bowling 189–3–63.00–0–0–2/32

He played soccer for Bradford City, West Bromwich Albion and Luton Town, and was an international for Northern Ireland, 1914–22.

Boon, Ronald Winston
Amateur. *b:* 11.6.1909, Barry, Glamorgan. Middle order right-hand batsman, right-arm medium pace bowler. *Team* Glamorgan (1931–32, 11 matches).
Career batting
11–19–2–229–33–13.47–0–*ct* 4
Bowling 40–0

Boon was much better known on the rugby field, being a Welsh cap.

Boon, Timothy James
Cricketer. *b*: 1.11.1961, Doncaster, Yorkshire. Middle order right-hand batsman, right-arm medium pace bowler. *Team* Leicestershire (1980–83, 38 matches). *Tour* Leicestershire to Zimbabwe 1980/1.

Career batting
38–63–6–1150–90–20.17–0–*ct* 10
Bowling 57–0

Boot, Jesse
Professional. *b:* 18.3.1860, South Normanton, Derbyshire. *d:* 1.3.1940, Chesterfield. Lower order right-hand batsman, wicket-keeper. *Team* Derbyshire (1895, 1 match).
Career batting
1–2–0–4–4–2.00–0–*ct* 2

Booth, Arthur
Professional. *b:* 3.11.1902, Featherstone, Yorkshire. *d:* 17.8.1974, Rochdale, Lancashire. Tail end right-hand batsman, left-arm slow bowler. *Team* Yorkshire (1931–47, 36 matches).
Career batting
38–40–16–137–29–5.70–0–*ct* 12
Bowling 1931–131–14.74–7–1–6/21

His career was altogether a remarkable one. Given a brief trial in County cricket in 1931, Booth was not again seen in Yorkshire matches until 1945 when he played twice. In 1946 however he carried all before him and ended the season at the head of the first-class bowling averages with 111 wickets (av 11.61). The following year he appeared in just four matches and then retired back into League cricket. He also played for Northumberland.

Booth, Arthur
Professional. *b:* 8.1.1926, Droylsden, Lancashire. Middle order right-hand batsman. *Team* Lancashire (1950–51, 4 matches).
Career batting
4–5–0–81–49–16.20–0–*ct* 1

His most notable performance was an innings of 253 for Lancs 2nd XI v Lincs in 1950.

Booth, Brian Charles
Amateur. *b:* 19.10.1933, Perthville, Bathurst, New South Wales, Australia. Elegant middle order right-hand batsman, right-arm medium pace or off-break bowler, good field. *Team* New South Wales (1954/5 to 1968/9, 93 matches). *Tours* Australians to England 1961, 1964, to West Indies 1964/5, to India and Pakistan 1964/5, to New Zealand 1959/60, 1966/7. *Tests* Australia (1961 to 1965/6, 29 matches.)
Career batting
183–283–35–11265–214*–45.42–26–*ct* 119
Bowling 956–16–59.75–0–0–2/29
Test batting
29–48–6–1773–169–42.21–5–*ct* 17
Bowling 146–3–48.66–0–0–2/33

On his first tour to England he forced his way into the Australian Test side and proved a most useful acquisition. In first-class matches he hit 1,279 runs (av 44.10). Returning in 1964 as Australia's vice-captain he hit 1,551 runs (av 55.39) but had only one good Test innings. His only first-class double century (214*) was made v Central Districts at Palmerston North on his 1966/7 tour to New Zealand.

Booth, Brian Joseph
Professional. *b:* 3.10.1935, Blackburn, Lancashire. Opening right-hand batsman, leg break and googly bowler. *Teams* Lancashire (1956–63, 117 matches); Leicestershire (1964–73, 232 matches).
Career batting
350–600–52–15298–183*–27.91–18–*ct* 135
Bowling 4677–146–32.03–1–0–7/143

He hit over 1,000 runs in a season eight times (best 1,752, av 31.85, in 1961).

Booth, Rev Cecil
Amateur. *b:* 21.2.1896, Aylesbury, Bucks. Middle/lower order right-hand batsman, leg break bowler. *Sch* Alleyn's. *Team* Cambridge U (1923).
Career batting
7–10–1–94–24*–10.44–0–*ct* 1
Bowling 382–7–54.57–0–0–2/16

Booth, Clement
Amateur. *b:* 11.5.1842, Friskney, Boston, Lincs. *d:* 14.7.1926, Hundleby, Spilsby, Lincs. Opening/middle order right-hand batsman, excellent deep field. *Sch* Rugby. *Teams* Cambridge U (1862–65, blue all four years); Hampshire (1875–80, 20 matches).
Career batting
75–135–6–1922–78–15.37–0–*ct* 34
Bowling 186–5–37.20–0–0–1/4

He also represented Cambridge at Athletics. He appeared for Lincolnshire, being hon secretary of the County Club 1867–71. In 1874 he was appointed hon secretary to Hampshire, resigning in 1879 and latterly represented Huntingdonshire. His final first-class match was for MCC in 1886.

Booth, Frank Stanley
Professional. *b:* 12.2.1907, Cheetham Hill, Lancashire. *d:* 21.1.1980, Shoreham-by-Sea, Sussex. Tail end right-hand batsman, right-arm fast-medium bowler. *Team* Lancashire (1927–37, 140 matches).
Career batting
140–157–25–1330–54–10.07–0–*ct* 56
Bowling 11180–457–24.46–24–3–7/59

He joined the Lancashire staff in 1924, but after a few years with limited opportunity in County cricket left to play in the Leagues. Returning in 1932 to Old Trafford he quickly gained a regular place in the County Eleven and remained for six seasons before retiring due to injury. His best year was 1934 when he took 101 wickets (av 23.46). He also played for Durham.

Booth, Lionel Edward Blakeney
Amateur. *b:* 21.12.1850, Marylebone, Middlesex. *d:* 9.7.1912, Newport, Isle of Wight. Middle order batsman. *Team* MCC (1885).
Career batting
1–1–0–8–8–8.00–0–*ct* 1

Booth, Major William
Professional. *b:* 10.12.1886, Pudsey, Yorkshire. *d:* 1.7.1916. He was killed in action near La Cigny, France. Middle/lower order right-hand batsman, right-arm medium-fast bowler. *Team* Yorkshire (1908–14, 144 matches). *Tour* MCC to South Africa 1913/4. *Tests* England (1913/4, 2 matches).
Career batting
162–243–39–4753–210–23.29–2–*ct* 121
Bowling 11953–603–19.82–43–9–8/47
Test batting
2–2–0–46–32–23.00–0–*ct* 0
Bowling 130–7–18.57–0–0–4/49

Major was his Christian name, not rank. His career was tragically cut short, for he did not obtain a regular place in the Yorkshire team until 1910 and was at the top of his profession when the war broke out. He scored 1,000 runs in a season twice (best 1,239, av 25.81, in 1911) and took 100 wickets in a season three times (best 181, av 18.46, in 1913) – in 1913 he performed the 'double'. His only double century was 210 for Yorks v Worcs at Worcester in 1911.

Booth, Peter
Cricketer. *b:* 2.11.1952, Shipley, Yorkshire. Lower order right-hand batsman, right-arm fast-medium bowler. *Team* Leicestershire (1972–81, 90 matches). *Tour* Leicestershire to Zimbabwe 1980/1.
Career batting
90–80–21–767–58*–13.00–0–*ct* 27
Bowling 4549–162–28.08–1–0–6/93

Booth, Paul Antony
Cricketer. *b*: 5.9.1965, Huddersfield, Yorkshire. Lower order left-hand batsman, slow left-arm bowler. *Team* Yorkshire (1982–83, 2 matches).
Career batting
2–3–1–0–0*–0.00–0–*ct* 0
Bowling 72–0

Booth, Roy
Professional. *b:* 1.10.1926, Marsden, Yorkshire. Lower order right-hand batsman, occasional right-arm medium pace bowler, wicket-keeper. *Teams* Yorkshire (1951–55, 65 matches); Worcestershire (1956–70, 402 matches). *Tours* Worcestershire on World Tour 1964/5; to Jamaica 1965/6.
Career batting
468–671–135–10139–113*–18.91–2–*ct* 949–*st* 177
Bowling 3–0

In 1959 he exceeded 1,000 runs in a season for the only time (1,042, av 27.42). In 1960 he had 101 victims behind the wicket and in 1964 100.

Booth, Stephen Charles
Cricketer. *b*: 30.10.1963, Leeds, Yorkshire. Lower order right-hand batsman, slow left-arm bowler. *Team* Somerset (1983, 10 matches).
Career batting
10–12–5–24–9–3.42–0–*ct* 7
Bowling 849–21–40.42–0–0–4/26

Booth-Jones, Timothy Douglas
Cricketer. *b:* 6.8.1952, Dover, Kent. Middle order right-hand batsman. *Team* Sussex (1980–81, 26 matches).
Career batting
26–44–1–1034–95–24.04–0–*ct* 8

Booton, Walter Thomas
Amateur. *b:* 13.1.1941, Kidderminster, Worcs. Right-hand batsman, right-arm fast medium pace bowler. *Team* Ireland (1970).
Career batting
1–1–0–12–12–12.00–0–*ct* 0
Bowling 72–2–36.00–0–0–2/72

Borde, Chandrakant Gulabrao
Amateur. *b:* 21.7.1934, Poona, India. Father of R.G. (Maharashta). Middle order right-hand batsman, leg break bowler. *Teams* Baroda (1952/3 to 1953/4); Maharashtra (1953/4 to 1972/3). *Tours* Indians to England 1959, 1967, to West Indies 1961/2, to Australia and New Zealand 1967/8, to Pakistan 1954/5; Commonwealth to South Africa 1962/3. *Tests* India (1958/9 to 1969/70, 55 matches).
Career batting
251–370–57–12805–207*–40.91–30–*ct* 159
Bowling 9044–331–27.32–14–3–8/52
Test batting
55–97–11–3061–177*–35.59–5–*ct* 37
Bowling 2417–52–46.48–1–0–5/88

He was the great success of the 1959 Indian tour to England, hitting 1,060 runs and taking 72 wickets, but returning in 1967 he had given up bowling and did very little in the Tests. His highest score was 207* for Maharashtra v Bengal at Poona in 1972/3. Borde's greatest achievement was early in his career when he scored 109 and 96 for India v West Indies at Delhi against the formidable attack of Hall and Gilchrist. He also played for Northumberland. His last first-class match was for Birhan Maharashtra Sugar Syndicate XI (1973/4).

Border, Allan Robert
Cricketer. *b*: 27.7.1955, Cremorne, New South Wales, Australia. Middle order left-hand batsman, slow left-arm bowler, slip field. *Teams* New South Wales (1976/7 to 1979/80, 25 matches); Gloucestershire (1977, 1 match); Queensland (1980/1 to 1982/3, 17 matches). *Tours* Australia to India 1979/80, to England 1980, 1981, to Sri Lanka 1980/1, 1982/3, to Pakistan 1979/80, 1982/3, to New Zealand 1981/2. *Tests* Australia (1978/9 to 1982/3, 51 matches).
Career batting
116–198–30–8067–200–48.01–19–*ct* 111
Bowling 1662–47–35.36–0–0–4/61
Test batting
51–91–16–3539–162–47.18–9–*ct* 58
Bowling 513–15–34.20–0–0–3/20
On the 1981 tour to England he proved to be the best batsman with 533 runs, av 59.22, in the six Tests and 807 runs, av 50.43, in all first-class matches; he scored most runs in both categories.

Bore, Michael Kenneth
Cricketer. *b*: 2.6.1947, Hull, Yorkshire. Lower order right-hand batsman, left-arm medium pace bowler, deep field. *Teams* Yorkshire (1969–78, 74 matches); Nottinghamshire (1979–83, 74 matches).
Career batting
148–149–51–828–37*–8.44–0–*ct* 49
Bowling 10445–346–30.18–8–0–8/89

Borgnis, Richard Peter
(later Hammond-Chambers-Borgnis)
Amateur. *b:* 25.8.1910, Newbury, Berkshire. Middle order right-hand batsman, right-arm medium pace bowler. *Team* Combined Services (1937).
Career batting
1–2–0–124–101–62.00–1–*ct* 1
Bowling 57–3–19.00–0–0–3/38
He hit 101 for Combined Services v New Zealanders at Portsmouth in 1937 in his only first-class match. He played for Berkshire.

Boroughs, William Frederick
Professional. *b:* 1865, Cheltenham, Gloucs. *d:* 16.1.1943, Birmingham. Tail end batsman, wicket-keeper. *Team* Gloucestershire (1899–1901, 5 matches).
Career batting
5–7–3–45–25–11.25–0–*ct* 3–*st* 4

Borradaile, Oswell Robert
Amateur. *b:* 9.5.1859, Westminster, London. *d:* 11.5.1935, Bexhill, Essex. Opening or middle order right-hand batsman, right-arm medium pace bowler, good field at point. *Sch* Westminster. *Team* Essex (1894, 1 match).
Career batting
1–2–0–7–5–3.50–0–*ct* 1
He was Secretary to Essex CCC from 1890 to 1921 and had much to do with the promotion of Essex to first-class status. He captained Stoics CC for 10 years and was a major force in London Club cricket.

Borrett, Norman Francis
Amateur. *b:* 1.10.1917, Wanstead, Essex. Middle order right-hand batsman, slow left-arm bowler. *Sch* Framlingham. *Team* Essex (1937–46, 3 matches).
Career batting
3–4–2–33–15*–16.50–0–*ct* 2
Bowling 43–0
At Cambridge he performed the hat-trick in the Seniors' Match of 1939, but did not appear in a first-class match whilst there. He played for Devon fairly often in the 1950s.

Borrill, Peter David
Cricketer. *b:* 4.7.1951, Leeds, Yorkshire. Tail end right-hand batsman, right-arm fast-medium bowler. *Team* Yorkshire (1971, 2 matches).
Career batting
2 matches, did not bat–*ct* 0
Bowling 61–5–21.20–0–0–2/6

Borrington, Anthony John
Cricketer. *b:* 8.12.1948, Derbyshire. Middle order right-hand batsman, leg-break bowler. *Team* Derbyshire (1971–80, 122 matches).
Career batting
122–203–24–4230–137–23.63–3–*ct* 57
Bowling 19–0

Borrowes, Sir Kildare Dixon, 10th Bart
Amateur. *b:* 21.9.1852, Exeter, Devon. *d:* 19.10.1924, Wateringbury, Kent. Free hitting middle order right-hand batsman, wicket-keeper. *Sch* Cheltenham. *Team* Middlesex (1882, 5 matches).
Career batting
6–9–0–40–20–4.44–0–*ct* 8–*st* 7
He appeared in the Essex side in 1878, when his regiment was stationed at Colchester, and was prominent in military cricket in Natal when stationed in South Africa in the 1890s.

Borwick, Peter Malise
Amateur. *b:* 21.11.1913, York. *d:* 23.12.1983,

Haslebeach, Northants. Lower order right-hand batsman, slow left-arm bowler. *Sch* Harrow. *Team* Northants (1932, 3 matches).
Career batting
3–6–0–25–11–4.16–0–*ct* 0
Bowling 98–3–32.66–0–0–1/25

Bosanquet, Bernard James Tindal
Amateur. *b:* 13.10.1877, Enfield, Middlesex. *d:* 12.10.1936, Ewhurst, Surrey. Hard-hitting middle order right-hand batsman, right-arm fast bowler until 1900, later leg-break and googly. *Sch* Eton. *Teams* Oxford U (1898–1900, blue all three years); Middlesex (1898–1919, 123 matches). *Tours* Warner to North America 1898; Ranjitsinhji to North America 1899; Bosanquet to North America 1901; Bennett to West Indies 1901/2; Hawke to New Zealand and Australia 1902/3; MCC to Australia 1903/4. *Tests* England (1903/4 to 1905, 7 matches).
Career batting
235–382–32–11696–214–33.41–21–*ct* 191
Bowling 14974–629–23.80–45–10–9/31
Test batting
7–14–3–147–27–13.36–0–*ct* 9
Bowling 604–25–24.16–2–0–8/107

One of the most remarkable of all English cricketers, Bosanquet holds a place in the history of the game by virtue of perfecting the googly – an off-break bowled with a leg-break action. Despite the fact that his length when delivering this ball tended to be wayward, for several seasons he baffled the best batsmen even on good wickets.

His outstanding summer with the ball was 1904 when he took 132 wickets (av 21.62). In the previous winter he had taken 6 for 51 for England in the fourth Test v Australia to bring victory to his side. In 1905 he performed the feat of taking 11 wickets and hitting a century in each innings of the same match – Middlesex v Sussex at Lord's.

His bowling declined after 1905, but as a batsman he grew in stature until his astonishing success in 1908, when he headed the first-class averages with 1,081 runs (av 54.05) and hit his most famous innings of 214 in 195 minutes for the Rest of England v Champion County at the Oval. In all he topped 1,000 runs in a season six times (best 1,405, av 36.02, in 1904) – in 1904 he achieved the 'double' for the only time in his career. His best bowling was 9/31 for Oxford U v Sussex at Oxford in 1900.

After 1908 Bosanquet played very infrequently in first-class matches but it was not until 1919 that he made his final appearance for Middlesex.

Apart from cricket he achieved a considerable reputation at other sports, representing Oxford at throwing the hammer and at billiards, whilst also being an accomplished ice-hockey player. He was the father of television news-reader and personality Reginald Bosanquet.

Bose, Gopal
Cricketer. *b:* 20.5.1947, Calcutta, India. Opening right-hand batsman, off break bowler. *Team* Bengal (1968/9 to 1978/9). *Tours* India to England 1974, to Sri Lanka 1973/4.
Career batting
77–126–5–3741–170–30.91–8–*ct* 37
Bowling 1905–71–26.85–1–0–5/67

He failed to make any impression on his single tour of England, hitting 328 runs, av 18.22, and was not selected for the Tests.

Boshier, Brian Stanley
Professional. *b:* 6.3.1932, Leicester. Tail end right-hand batsman, right-arm medium pace bowler. *Team* Leicestershire (1953–64, 169 matches).
Career batting
170–226–92–579–30–4.32–0–*ct* 56
Bowling 11742–510–23.02–23–2–8/45

He took 100 wickets in a season twice – each time 108 (in 1958, av 18.77; in 1961, av 17.87). In 1955 he began the season with nine successive scoreless innings.

Bosomworth, William Edward
Professional. *b:* 8.3.1847, Carlton-Husthwaite, Thirsk, Yorkshire. *d:* 7.6.1891, Malton, Yorkshire. Lower order right-hand batsman, right-arm fast round-arm bowler. *Team* Yorkshire (1872–80, 4 matches).
Career batting
4–7–1–20–7–3.33–0–*ct* 2
Bowling 140–9–14.44–0–0–2/5

In 1874 Bosomworth joined the short-lived Yorkshire United team, and thus his opportunities to appear in bona fide Yorkshire matches were limited.

Bostock, Herbert
Professional. *b:* 4.5.1869, Ilkeston, Derbyshire. *d:* 20.2.1954, Ilkeston, Derbyshire. Middle order right-hand batsman. *Team* Derbyshire (1897, 4 matches).
Career batting
4–6–2–75–36–18.75–0–*ct* 1

Bostock, Lionel Carrington
Amateur. *b:* 13.2.1888, Colombo, Ceylon. *d:* 30.1.1962, Ifield, Sussex. Lower order right-hand batsman, right-arm medium pace bowler. *Sch* Marlborough. *Team* Army (1925).
Career batting
1–2–1–5–3–5.00–0–*ct* 1
Bowling 58–2–29.00–0–0–2/58

Bostock-Hill, A. J. (*see under* Hill, A. J. B.)

Boston, Granger Farwell
Amateur. *b:* 24.5.1921, Liverpool, Lancashire. *d:* 4.2.1958, Marylebone, London. Middle order right-hand batsman. *Sch* Wellington. *Team* Cambridge U (1946).
Career batting
3–6–0–38–19–6.33–0–*ct* 0

Boswell, Cecil Stanley Reginald
Professional. *b:* 19.1.1910, Edmonton, London. Tail end right-hand batsman, right-arm leg break and googly bowler. *Team* Essex (1932–36, 30 matches).
Career batting
30–46–8–406–69–10.68–0–*ct* 12
Bowling 1345–36–37.36–0–0–4/22

After leaving Essex he appeared with some success for Norfolk.

Boswell, William Gerald Knox
Amateur. *b:* 24.6.1892, Chelsea, London. *d:* 28.7.1916. He died of wounds, Thiepval, France. Middle order right-hand batsman, change bowler. *Sch* Eton. *Team* Oxford U (1912–14, blue 1913–14).
Career batting
14–26–1–756–101*–30.24–1–*ct* 2
Bowling 343–14–24.50–0–0–4/22

Bosworth-Smith, B. N.
(*see under* Smith, B. N. B.)

Botham, Ian Terence
Cricketer. *b*: 24.11.1955, Heswall, Cheshire. Attacking middle order right-hand batsman, right-arm fast medium bowler, good close field. *Teams* Somerset (1974–83, 136 matches). *Tours* England to Pakistan and New Zealand 1977/8, to Australia 1978/9, to Australia and India 1979/80, to West Indies 1980/1, to India and Sri Lanka 1981/2, to Australia and New Zealand 1982/3. *Tests* England (1977–83, 63 matches).
Career batting
226–351–25–10701–228–32.82–23–*ct* 214
Bowling 19430–777–25.00–44–7–8/34
Test batting
63–100–3–3548–208–36.57–12–*ct* 72
Bowling 6876–277–24.82–20–4–8/34

Since his Test debut in 1977 he has been England's leading all-round cricketer. Of his many outstanding performances the greatest was perhaps achieved in Bombay in 1979/80 for England v India when he hit 114 in his single innings and took 13 for 106 (6–58 and 7–48) – this was the first time that the all-round feat of scoring a century and taking ten wickets had been accomplished in a Test match. He reached the Test career double of 1,000 runs and 100 wickets in 21 matches; his tally of 100 wickets was reached after 2 years and 9 days, both these feats being new records, the latter since beaten by Kapil Dev. He was also the youngest cricketer to take 200 wickets in a Test career and he went on to perform the second career double of 2,000 runs and 200 wickets in record time, both by age and number of Tests (42).

Because of his frequent absences from County cricket, due to his selection for England in both Tests and one-day internationals, he has only hit 1,000 runs in a season three times (best 1,241, av 44.32, in 1982). He took 100 wickets, av 16.40, in 1978. His highest innings is 208 for England v India at the Oval in 1982, and his best bowling 8 for 34 for England v Pakistan at Lord's in 1978.

He captained England in 12 Tests and on the tour to West Indies in 1980/1, but the cares of leadership affected his performances on the field and he resigned as captain in 1981.

He is also a useful soccer player with Scunthorpe United.

Although his second Christian name has been spelt in a variety of different ways, a copy of his birth certificate confirms this to be Terence.

Botten, James Thomas
Amateur. *b:* 21.6.1938, Pretoria, South Africa. Lower order right-hand batsman, right-arm fast-medium bowler. *Team* N.E. Transvaal (1957/8 to 1971/2). *Tours* South Africans to England 1965; SA Fezela to England 1961. *Tests* South Africa (1965, 3 matches).
Career batting
98–143–31–1775–90–15.84–0–*ct* 52
Bowling 8125–399–20.36–24–5–9/23
Test batting
3–6–0–65–33–10.83–0–*ct* 1
Bowling 337–8–42.12–0–0–2/56

He had a very rapid rise to fame, when in 1958/9 he took 55 wickets in the Currie Cup, creating a new record in what was his first full season in the competition. With the Fezelas in England in 1961, he was the most successful bowler with 70 wickets in all matches. In 1965, on his only Test tour to England, he bowled well without being outstanding. His best bowling was 9/23 for NE Transvaal v Griqualand West at Pretoria in 1958/9.

Botting, Stephen Hovey
Professional. *b:* 5.11.1845, Higham, Kent. *d:* 23.1.1927, Shorne, Gravesend, Kent. Right-hand

batsman, right-arm medium pace bowler. *Team* Kent (1867–75, 2 matches).
Career batting
2–4–0–27–20–6.75–0–6–*ct* 0

Bottom, Daniel
Professional originally, but amateur in 1901. *b:* 2.10.1864, Whitwell, Derbyshire. *d:* 16.2.1937, Bulwell, Nottingham. Lower order right-hand batsman, right-arm medium pace bowler. *Teams* Derbyshire (1894–1901, 3 matches); Nottinghamshire (1899, 3 matches).
Career batting
6–10–0–42–9–4.20–0–*ct* 2
Bowling 250–9–27.77–1–0–5/34

Bottom had a rather unusual if brief first-class career, playing three times for Derbyshire – once each in 1894, 1898 and 1901 – and three times for Notts in 1899, for whom he was qualified by residence.

Bottomley, Isaac Henry
Amateur. *b:* 9.4.1855, Shelf, Halifax, Yorkshire. *d:* 23.4.1922, Heysham, Lancashire. Middle order right-hand batsman, right-arm fast round-arm bowler. *Team* Yorkshire (1878–80, 9 matches).
Career batting
9–12–0–166–32–13.83–0–*ct* 1
Bowling 75–1–75.00–0–0–1/17

Bottomley, Thomas
Professional. *b:* 26.12.1910, Rawmarsh, Yorkshire. *d:* 19.2.1977, Rotherham, Yorkshire. Middle order right-hand batsman, right-arm medium pace bowler. *Team* Yorkshire (1934–35, 6 matches).
Career batting
6–7–0–142–51–20.28–0–*ct* 5
Bowling 188–1–188.00–0–0–1/46

Botton, Norman Denis
Cricketer. *b:* 21.1.1954. Hammersmith, London. Lower order left-hand batsman, left-arm medium pace bowler. *Team* Oxford U (1974–75, blue 1974).
Career batting
15–30–6–286–38*–11.91–0–*ct* 10
Bowling 714–11–64.90–0–0–2/53

Bouch, Herbert Edward
Amateur. *b:* 15.4.1868, Bickley, Kent. *d:* 28.7.1929, Keston, Kent. Lower order right-hand batsman, right-arm bowler. *Sch* Eastbourne. *Team* Kent (1892, 1 match).
Career batting
1–2–0–7–7–3.50–0–*ct* 1
Bowling 52–1–52.00–0–0–1/52

Boucher, James Chrysostom
Amateur. *b:* 22.12.1910, Dublin, Ireland. Right-hand batsman, off break bowler. *Team* Ireland (1930–54).
Career batting
28–51–5–625–85–13.58–0–*ct* 23
Bowling 2359–168–14.04–18–5–7/13

He was for many years the outstanding Irish cricketer, and after retiring from first-class cricket was Hon Secretary to the Irish Cricket Union from 1954 to 1973.

Boucher, Sidney
Amateur. *b:* 17.9.1899, Rochester, Kent. *d:* 4.8.1963, Wadhurst, Sussex. Lower order left-hand batsman, left-arm seam bowler. *Teams* Kent (1922, 1 match); Royal Navy (1923–29).
Career batting
9–15–0–147–43–9.80–0–*ct* 4
Bowling 613–14–43.78–0–0–2/15

Boughton, Hubert James
Amateur. *b:* 11.10.1858, Westbury-on-Severn, Gloucs. *d:* 26.3.1902, Gloucester. Brother of W.A. (Gloucs). Middle order right-hand batsman. *Team* Gloucestershire (1884–88, 7 matches).
Career batting
7–12–2–114–41–11.40–0–*ct* 3

Boughton, William Albert
Amateur. *b:* 23.12.1854, Westbury-on-Severn, Gloucs. *d:* 26.11.1936, Canton, Cardiff. Brother of H.J. (Gloucs). Middle order right-hand batsman, right-arm medium pace bowler. *Team* Gloucestershire (1879–83, 3 matches).
Career batting
3–3–0–3–3–1.00–0–*ct* 1

Boult, Farrington Holker
Amateur. *b:* 12.6.1852, Bath, Somerset. *d:* 21.5.1882, Marylebone, Middlesex. Steady middle order right-hand batsman, fast round-arm bowler, good point field. *Sch* Epsom. *Team* Surrey (1872–73, 22 matches). *Tour* Grace to Australia 1873/4 (not first-class).
Career batting
25–46–0–570–65–12.39–0–*ct* 15
Bowling 1161–55–21.10–1–0–5/32

Boultbee, St John
Amateur. *b:* 30.4.1843, Bedford. *d:* 4.9.1898, Minster, Kent. Lower order right-hand batsman, slow round-arm bowler. *Team* Surrey (1867, 2 matches).

Career batting
3–6–2–57–35–14.25–0–*ct* 5
Bowling 94–3–31.33–0–0–2/54
He also played for Bedfordshire.

Boumphrey, Colin
Amateur. *b:* 7.1.1897, Birkenhead, Cheshire. *d:* 1.2.1945, Liverpool. Brother of Donald (Wales). Middle order right-hand batsman. *Sch* Shrewsbury. *Team* RAF (1932).
Career batting
1–2–0–31–31–15.50–0–*ct* 0
His County cricket was for Cheshire.

Boumphrey, Donald
Amateur. *b:* 4.10.1892, Birkenhead, Cheshire. *d:* 12.9.1971, Holt Green, Aughton, Lancashire. Brother of Colin (RAF). Opening batsman. *Sch* Shrewsbury. *Team* Wales (1928).
Career batting
1–2–0–10–6–5.00–0–*ct* 0
His County cricket was played for Cheshire.

Boundy, Gerald Oscar
Amateur. *b:* 1895, Little Torrington, Devon. *d:* 8.2.1964, Hammersmith, London. Middle order right-hand batsman. *Team* Somerset (1926–30, 2 matches).
Career batting
2–4–1–22–10*–7.33–0–*ct* 1

Bourchier, Rev Wilfred La Rive
Amateur. *b:* 22.3.1884, Cahir, Co Tipperary, Ireland. *d:* 7.9.1973, Cork, Ireland. Right-hand batsman. *Team* Ireland (1908–09).
Career batting
3–6–0–47–19–7.83–0–*ct* 0

Bourdillon, Thomas Edmund
Amateur. *b:* 31.5.1890, Bloemfontein, South Africa. *d:* 28.5.1961, Salisbury, Rhodesia. Brother of V. E. (Sussex). Middle order batsman. *Sch* Tonbridge. *Teams* Sussex (1919, 1 match); Rhodesia (1909/10 to 1924/5).
Career batting
7–13–0–176–60–13.53–0–*ct* 4
Bowling 173–3–57.66–0–0–2/51

Bourdillon, Victor Edmund
Amateur. *b:* 18.6.1897, Bloemfontein, South Africa. Brother of T. E. (Sussex). Middle order right-hand batsman. *Team* Sussex (1919, 3 matches).
Career batting
3–6–0–15–7–2.50–0–*ct* 0

Bourne, Alfred Allinson
Amateur. *b:* 16.4.1848, Atherstone, Warwickshire. *d:* 17.7.1931, Cheltenham, Gloucs. Lower order right-hand batsman, slow left-arm bowler, good close field. *Sch* Rugby. *Team* Cambridge U (1870, blue).
Career batting
4–6–2–6–3*–1.50–0–*ct* 1
Bowling 494–28–17.64–3–1–7/65
He also played for Warwickshire in 1876.

Bourne, Edmund Horace
Amateur. *b:* 14.2.1885, Stoke-on-Trent. *d:* 1962, Reigate, Surrey. Middle order batsman, change bowler. *Team* Minor Counties (1912).
Career batting
1–1–0–16–16–16.00–0–*ct* 0
His County cricket was for Staffordshire.

Bourne, John James
Professional. *b:* 2.11.1872, Church Gresley, Derbyshire. *d:* 23.12.1952, Burton-on-Trent, Staffs. Tail end batsman, left-arm medium pace bowler. *Team* Derbyshire (1898, 1 match).
Career batting
1–1–0–6–6–6.00–0–*ct* 0
Bowling 103–3–34.33–0–0–2/63

Bourne, William Anderson
Cricketer. *b:* 15.11.1952, Clapham, Barbados. Lower order right-hand batsman, right-arm fast-medium bowler. *Teams* Barbados (1970/1); Warwickshire (1973–77, 59 matches).
Career batting
60–78–15–1325–107–21.03–1–*ct* 39
Bowling 4164–128–32.53–2–0–6/47

Bousfield, Donald Greenhill
Amateur. *b:* 9.4.1914, Broxbourne, Herts. Middle order right-hand batsman, leg break bowler. *Sch* Winchester. *Team* Cambridge U (1935).
Career batting
2–4–0–38–37–9.50–0–*ct* 0
He also played for Hertfordshire and Buckinghamshire.

Bousfield, Edwin James
Amateur. *b:* 21.5.1838, Manchester. *d:* 8.1.1895, Torquay, Devon. Middle order right-hand batsman, splendid deep field, wicket-keeper. *Team* Lancashire (1865–78, 12 matches).
Career batting
16–27–2–321–32–12.84–0–*ct* 23–*st* 5
His first-class debut was for Gentlemen of North in 1860.

Bovill, Walter Denman
Amateur. *b:* 12.8.1857, London. *d:* 5.1.1940, Westminster, London. Middle order right-hand

batsman, medium pace round-arm bowler. *Sch* Clifton. *Team* MCC (1874).
Career batting
1–2–1–30–19–30.00–0–*ct* 1

In a minor match in 1886 he took all ten wickets in an innings and hit 28 not out and 115, going in first and being last man out. He was only 16 years old at the time of his only first-class match – as he seems to have been successful in minor matches, it is not known why he was not seen again in first-class cricket.

Bowden, Ernest
Amateur. *b:* 13.6.1892, Lancaster. *d:* 14.10.1972, Slyne, Lancashire. Tail end batsman, bowler. *Team* Lancashire (1914, 4 matches).
Career batting
4–6–0–27–10–4.50–0–*ct* 5
Bowling 453–12–37.75–1–0–6/78

Bowden, Jack
Amateur. *b:* 17.10.1916, Lisburn, Ireland. Right-hand batsman, slow left-arm bowler. *Team* Ireland (1946–55).
Career batting
6–9–0–52–34–5.77–0–*ct* 6
Bowling 369–19–19.42–2–0–6/23

Bowden, Joseph
Professional. *b:* 8.10.1884, Glossop, Derbyshire. *d:* 1.3.1958, Glossop, Derbyshire. Sound opening right-hand batsman, right-arm medium pace bowler. *Team* Derbyshire (1909–30, 231 matches).
Career batting
231–395–25–7613–120–20.57–4–*ct* 75
Bowling 54–1–54.00–0–0–1/0

He hit 1,000 runs in a season twice (best 1,221, av 30.52, in 1926).

Bowden, Montague Parker
Amateur. *b:* 1.11.1865, Stockwell, Surrey. *d:* 19.2.1892, Umtali, Mashonaland. Middle order right-hand batsman, wicket-keeper. *Sch* Dulwich. *Teams* Surrey (1883–88, 72 matches); Transvaal (1889/90). *Tours* Vernon to Australia 1887/8; Warton to South Africa 1888/9. *Tests* England (1888/9, 2 matches).
Career batting
86–132–17–2316–189*–20.13–3–*ct* 73–*st* 14
Bowling 33–2–16.50–0–0–2/5
Test batting
2–2–0–25–25–12.50–0–*ct* 1

He captained the England team in the second Test of 1888/9 v South Africa, owing to the absence of C.A. Smith. After the 1888/9 tour, Bowden remained in Southern Africa.

Bowell, Horace Alexander William
Professional. *b:* 27.4.1880, Oxford. *d:* 28.8.1957, Oxford. Father of N.H. (Hants). Sound right-hand opening batsman, latterly middle order, right-arm medium fast bowler, brilliant cover-point. *Team* Hampshire (1902–27, 473 matches).
Career batting
475–810–43–18509–204–24.13–25–*ct* 255–*st* 2
Bowling 1766–34–51.94–0–0–4/20

He hit 1,000 runs in a season 8 times (best 1,627, av 31.28, in 1913). His only double century was 204 for Hants v Lancs at Bournemouth in 1914.

Bowell, Norman Henry
Professional. *b:* 2.2.1904, Oxford. *d:* 5.3.1943, at sea. Son of H.A.W. (Hants). Middle order right-hand batsman, slow right-arm bowler. *Teams* Hampshire (1924, 2 matches); Northants (1925, 1 match).
Career batting
3–3–0–56–48–18.66–0–*ct* 0
Bowling 72–0

His only appearance for Northants was v Dublin University, when the County fielded a very weak side. He also played for Oxfordshire.

Bowen, Elfyn
Professional. *b:* 1907, Llanelly, Glamorgan. *d:* 24.8.1965, Pontardulais, Glamorgan. Middle order left-hand batsman, slow left-arm bowler. *Team* Glamorgan (1928–33, 3 matches).
Career batting
3–5–1–40–22–10.00–0–*ct* 0
Bowling 14–0

Bowen, Edward Ernest
Amateur. *b:* 30.3.1836, Glenmore, Co Wicklow, Ireland. *d:* 8.4.1901, at Moux, in France, whilst on a cycling tour. Middle order right-hand batsman, occasional wicket-keeper. *Sch* Kings College, London. *Team* Hampshire (1864, 1 match).
Career batting
1–2–0–0–0–0.00–0 *ct* 0

He was educated at Cambridge, but was not in the Eleven. He played soccer for England in the first unofficial match with Scotland in 1870, and also appeared for Wanderers on the winning side in the first two FA Cup finals, 1872 and 1873.

Bower, Philip Salkeld Syndercombe
Amateur. *b:* 24.9.1898, York. *d:* 12.10.1978, Magaliesberg, Transvaal, South Africa. Grandfather of C.E.B. Rice (Transvaal and Notts). Middle order right-hand batsman. *Sch* Repton. *Team* Oxford U (1919).

Career batting
5–7–0–105–78–15.00–0–*ct* 7
Bowling 467–11–42.45–0–0–3/103

Bower, Wallace
Professional. *b:* 2.1.1895, Eastwood, Notts. *d:* July, 1971, Welbeck Colliery Village, Notts. Lower order right-hand batsman, right-arm fast-medium bowler. *Team* Nottinghamshire (1914, 1 match).
Career batting
1–1–0–0–0–0.00–*ct* 0
Bowling 51–1–51.00–0–0–1/31

Bower, William Henry
Professional. *b:* 17.10.1857, Bradford, Yorkshire. *d:* 1943, Nelson, Lancashire. Middle order right-hand batsman, good field. *Teams* Yorkshire (1883, 1 match); Lancashire (1885–86, 4 matches).
Career batting
5–8–0–55–23–6.87–0–*ct* 1

Bower
Professional. Tail end batsman, opening bowler. *Team* Hampshire (1897–98, 3 matches).
Career batting
3–4–1–14–8–4.66–0–*ct* 0
Bowling 166–8–20.75–0–0–4/43

Bowerman, Alfred James
Amateur. *b:* 1873, Bridgwater, Somerset. *d:* 1959, Brisbane, Australia. Middle order batsman. *Team* Somerset (1900–05, 2 matches).
Career batting
2–4–0–8–3–2.00–0–*ct* 1

Bowers, Robert Bruce
Amateur. *b:* 1.3.1897, Lambeg, Co Antrim, Ireland. *d:* 25.11.1956, Belfast, Ireland. Right-hand batsman, right-arm medium pace bowler. *Team* Ireland (1926).
Career batting
1–2–0–10–5–5.00–0–*ct* 2
Bowling 52–0

Bowes, John Barton
Professional. *b:* 2.1.1918, Stretford, Manchester. *d:* 1969, Manchester. Lower order batsman, right-arm medium pace bowler. *Team* Lancashire (1938–48, 10 matches).
Career batting
10–13–1–106–39–8.83–0–*ct* 6
Bowling 602–21–28.66–0–0–4/103

Bowes, William Eric
Professional. *b:* 25.7.1908, Elland, Yorkshire. Tail end right-hand batsman, fast medium/medium right-arm bowler. *Team* Yorkshire (1929–47, 301 matches). *Tours* MCC to Australia and New Zealand 1932/3; Yorkshire to Jamaica 1935/6. *Tests* England (1932–46, 15 matches).
Career batting
372–326–148–1530–43*–8.59–0–*ct* 138
Bowling 27470–1639–16.76–116–27–9/121
Test batting
15–11–5–28–10*–4.66–0–*ct* 2
Bowling 1519–68–22.33–6–0–6/33

It would not be an injustice to other County cricketers to state that Bowes was the most intelligent bowler of his era, and because of that he was one of the very few performers who never had an 'off' season, right from his first games with MCC to his retirement at the close of the 1947 season.

Perhaps due to his poor batting and rather moderate showing as a fieldsman, he appeared in only 15 Tests for England, but his true worth can be demonstrated by the standing of Yorkshire in the County Championship between 1929 and 1939, when the County attack was built around Bowes and Verity.

Bowes studied the weaknesses of each batsman and exploited them through his controlled use of both the out and in-swinger. He could also make the ball come very sharply off the wicket, though he was never one to over-use the bouncer or to employ leg theory. He took 100 wickets in a season nine times with 193, av 15.44, in 1935 as his best return. His best bowling was 9/121 for Yorkshire v Essex at Scarborough in 1932.

During the Second World War he was taken prisoner and physically never really recovered from the time spent in enemy hands, but in 1946 he still proved an effective bowler, even if his pace was slowed to a brisk medium. Since retiring from first-class cricket he has built himself a considerable reputation as a cricket writer. His first-class debut was for MCC in 1928.

Bowes-Lyon, Hon John Herbert
Amateur. *b:* 1.4.1886, Glamis, Scotland. *d:* 7.2.1930, Glamis, Scotland. Lower order batsman, opening bowler. *Sch* Eton. *Team* Oxford U (1906–07).
Career batting
3–5–2–50–28–16.66–0–*ct* 2
Bowling 165–2–82.50–0–0–2/17

Bowie, Thomas Alexander
Amateur. *b:* 21.2.1877, Alloa, Scotland. *d:* 23.1.1974, Stirling, Scotland. Right-hand batsman, right-arm medium pace bowler. *Team* Scotland (1906–13).

Career batting
8–15–1–252–66–18.00–0–*ct* 4
Bowling 156–4–39.00–0–0–3/35

Bowles, John Jesse
Professional. *b:* 3.4.1890, Lower Slaughter, Gloucs. *d:* 27.11.1971, Salisbury, Wilts. Lower order right-hand batsman, left-arm medium or slow bowler. *Teams* Gloucestershire (1911–20, 18 matches); Worcestershire (1926–28, 62 matches).
Career batting
80–136–15–1392–73–11.50–0–*ct* 46–*st* 1
Bowling 3457–83–41.65–1–0–5/56

Bowles, Roger Andrew
Amateur. *b:* 11.2.1936, Carshalton, Surrey. Opening right-hand batsman, leg break bowler. *Team* Oxford U (1957).
Career batting
3–6–0–92–43–15.33–0–*ct* 0

Bowley, Edward Henry
Professional. *b:* 6.6.1890, Leatherhead, Surrey. *d:* 9.7.1974, Winchester. Sound right-hand opening batsman, slow right-arm leg break bowler. *Teams* Sussex (1912–34, 458 matches); Auckland (1926/7 to 1928/9). *Tours* Joel to South Africa 1924/5; MCC to New Zealand and Australia 1929/30; Tennyson to Jamaica 1931/2. *Tests* England (1929 to 1929/30, 5 matches).
Career batting
510–859–47–28378–283–34.94–52–*ct* 372
Bowling 19257–741–25.98–28–2–9/114
Test batting
5–7–0–252–109–36.00–1–*ct* 2
Bowling 116–0

He reached 1,000 runs in a season fifteen times and on four of those exceeded 2,000 (best 2,360, av 43.70, in 1929). He hit four double centuries, all for Sussex, his highest of 283 being against Middlesex at Hove in 1933. During this innings he was involved in a record Sussex 1st wicket stand of 490 with J.G. Langridge. His best bowling was 9/114 for Sussex v Derbyshire at Hove in 1919.

Bowley, Frederick James
Professional. *b:* 20.2.1909, Ratby, Leics. Brother of H.B. (Leics). Tail end right-hand batsman, slow left-arm bowler. *Team* Leicestershire (1930–31, 13 matches).
Career batting
13–17–7–33–6–3.30–0–*ct* 4
Bowling 770–23–33.47–0–0–4/46

Bowley, Frederick Lloyd
Professional. *b:* 9.11.1873, Brecon. *d:* 31.5.1943, Worcester. Sound opening right-hand batsman, excellent deep field. *Team* Worcestershire (1899–1923, 396 matches).
Career batting
405–738–25–21122–276–29.62–38–*ct* 148
Bowling 101–4–25.25–0–0–1/6

He exceeded 1,000 runs in a season 14 times (best 1,629, av 39.73, in 1906). He scored three double centuries, all for Worcs, the highest being 276 v Hants (Dudley) 1914.

Bowley, Herrick Browett
Professional. *b:* 10.1.1911, Kirby-Muxloe, Leics. Brother of F.J. (Leics). Middle order right-hand batsman, leg break bowler. *Team* Leicestershire (1933–37, 13 matches).
Career batting
13–18–1–113–25–6.65–0–*ct* 3
Bowling 919–17–54.06–0–0–4/17

Bowley, Thomas
Professional. *b:* 28.2.1857, Old Basford, Notts. *d:* 8.11.1939, Sherborne, Dorset. Lower order right-hand batsman, right-arm fast bowler. *Team* Surrey (1885–91, 76 matches).
Career batting
83–111–26–730–46–8.58–0–*ct* 42
Bowling 4441–264–16.82–9–1–7/64

He appeared for Northants (non-first-class) before joining the Oval staff, and from 1896 for Dorset.

Bowling, Kenneth
Professional. *b:* 10.11.1931, Leyland, Lancashire. Stylish middle order right-hand batsman, good deep field. *Team* Lancashire (1954, 1 match).
Career batting
1–2–1–7–4*–7.00–0–*ct* 0

Bowman, Richard
Amateur. *b:* 26.1.1934, Cleveleys, Lancashire. Lower order right-hand batsman, right-arm fast bowler. *Sch* Fettes. *Teams* Oxford U (1955–57, blue 1957); Lancashire (1957–59, 9 matches).
Career batting
26–37–9–454–75–16.21–0–*ct* 15
Bowling 1902–51–37.29–2–0–7/60

His final first-class match was for MCC in 1964. He also played for Cumberland.

Bowmer, Herbert Edgar
Amateur. *b:* 4.7.1891, Wirksworth, Derbyshire. *d:* 1.6.1966, Derby. Middle order right-hand batsman, right-arm fast-medium bowler. *Sch* Wellingborough. *Team* Derbyshire (1909–11, 3 matches).
Career batting
3–6–0–6–3–1.00–0–*ct* 1

Bowring, Charles James
Professional. *b:* 1888, Weymouth, Dorset. *d:* 16.1.1959, Yeovil, Somerset. Middle order batsman. *Team* Somerset (1913, 4 matches).
Career batting
4–7–0–42–15–6.00–0–*ct* 0
Bowling 26–3–8.66–0–0–3/24

Bowring, Trevor
Amateur. *b:* 8.11.1887, Long Ditton, Surrey. *d:* 7.8.1908, Ditton Hill, Surrey. Cousin of W. B. Stoddart (Lancs). Opening right-hand batsman, slow bowler. *Sch* Rugby. *Team* Oxford U (1907–08, blue both years).
Career batting
17–32–2–722–228–24.06–1–*ct* 5
Bowling 535–20–26.75–0–0–3/10
In 1908 he hit 228 in 210 minutes, adding 338 for the lst wicket with H. Teesdale for Oxford v Gentlemen, but within two months of this great innings he died from blood poisoning aged only 20.

Bowstead, John
Amateur. *b:* 14.5.1872, Edenhall, Penrith, Cumberland. *d:* 17.1.1939, Ealing, Middlesex. Middle order right-hand batsman, slow round-arm bowler. *Sch* Repton. *Team* Middlesex (1909, 1 match).
Career batting
1–2–0–21–16–10.50–0–*ct* 0

Box, Joseph William
Professional. *b:* 1842, Bermondsey, Surrey. *d:* 2.10.1873, Bow Common. Lower order batsman, wicket-keeper. *Team* Middlesex (1866–68, 4 matches).
Career batting
4–7–1–33–17–5.50–0–*ct* 3–*st* 1

Box, Thomas
Professional. *b:* 7.2.1808, Ardingly, Sussex. *d:* 12.7.1876, Prince's Cricket Ground, London. Middle order right-hand batsman, wicket-keeper. *Teams* Sussex (1826–56, 108 matches); Surrey (1849, 2 matches as given man); Hampshire (1844–45).
Career batting
247–456–43–4936–79–11.95–0–*ct* 235–*st* 162
Bowling 66–5+3–13.20–1–0–5/45
He was regarded in his day as the best wicket-keeper in England. After retiring he kept the Brunswick Cricket Ground in Brighton and latterly was ground-keeper at Prince's, where he fell down dead during the Middlesex v Notts match of 1876 – the match was abandoned as soon as his death was known.

Boxall, Thomas
Professional. Excellent bowler. *Teams* Kent (pre-1801); England (1801–03).
Career batting
5–9–2–42–17*–6.00–0–*ct* 3
Bowling 10 wickets, no analyses
For about fifteen seasons commencing 1790 he was regarded as one of the best bowlers in England, but nowhere is his type of bowling recorded. It is believed that he was born in Ripley in Surrey and played for Kent by reason of residing at Barming.

Boxill, Darnley Da Costa
Cricketer. *b:* 2.10.1944, Christ Church, Barbados. Lower order right-hand batsman, wicket-keeper. *Team* Barbados (1964/5 to 1971/2). *Tour* Barbados to England 1969.
Career batting
15–19–1–149–38–8.27–0–*ct* 29–*st* 12

Boyce, Keith David
Cricketer. *b:* 11.10.1943, near Ashton Hall, Barbados. Hard hitting middle order right-hand batsman, right-arm fast-medium bowler, excellent field. *Teams* Barbados (1964/5 to 1974/5); Essex (1966–77, 211 matches). *Tours* West Indies to England 1973, India, Sri Lanka and Pakistan 1974/5, Australia 1975/6; Commonwealth to Pakistan 1967/8; Rest of World to Pakistan 1973/4. *Tests* West Indies (1970/1 to 1975/6, 21 matches).
Career batting
285–420–27–8800–147*–22.39–4–*ct* 215
Bowling 21324–852–25.02–35–7–9/61
Test batting
21–30–3–657–95*–24.33–0–*ct* 5
Bowling 1801–60–30.01–2–1–6/77
The high point of his career was the 1973 Test series between West Indies and England, when he took 19 wickets (av 15.47) in the three matches and averaged 25.80 with the bat, being the major factor in winning the rubber for his country. He has been outstandingly successful in limited overs matches for Essex and was the first player ever to reach 1,000 runs and 100 wickets in the John Player League. In first-class matches he hit 1,000 runs in 1972 (1,023, av 30.08). His best bowling was 9/61 for Essex v Cambridge U at Brentwood in 1966, on his County debut. A serious knee injury prematurely ended his career in 1977.

Boycott, Geoffrey, OBE
Professional. *b*: 21.10.1940, Fitzwilliam, Yorkshire. Very sound and determined opening right-hand batsman, right-arm medium pace bowler. *Teams* Yorkshire (1962–83, 361 matches); Northern Transvaal (1971/2). *Tours* MCC to

South Africa 1964/5, to Australia and New Zealand 1965/6, 1970/1, to West Indies 1967/8, 1973/4, to Ceylon 1969/70; England to Pakistan and New Zealand 1977/8, to Australia 1978/9, to Australia and India 1979/80, to West Indies 1980/1, to India and Sri Lanka 1981/2; SAB to South Africa 1981/2. *Tests* England (1964 to 1981/2, 108 matches).
Career batting
555–925–139–44210–261*–56.24–139–*ct* 227
Bowling 1405–45–31.22–0–0–4/14
Test batting
108–193–23–8114–246*–47.72–22–*ct* 33
Bowling 382–7–54.57–0–0–3/47

The most prolific and controversial batsman of the present day, he is the only cricketer to average more than 100 in an English first-class season twice. His two great years were 1979 with 1,538 runs, av 102.53, and 1971 with 2,503, av 100.12. 1971 was his own record aggregate season, but he has exceeded 1,000 runs in England 21 times and gone on to 2,000 three times. Of his ten double centuries, seven were for Yorkshire, two for MCC (including his highest which was 261* v President's XI in Bridgetown in 1973/4) and one for England – 246* v India at Headingley in 1967. He performed the feat of scoring his 100th 100 in first-class cricket on the same ground in the 1977 Test v Australia.

His aggregate of 8,114 runs set a world record for Test cricket (he passed Sobers' total in 1981) and would be larger had it not been for two factors, first that he indicated that he was not available for selection for England in 1975 and 1976 and for several overseas tours, and secondly that he was banned from Test cricket for three years following his 1981/2 tour to South Africa.

He captained England in four Tests in 1977/8 and led Yorkshire from 1971 to 1978. At the close of the 1983 season his contract with Yorkshire was not renewed and this action caused a resumption of the discontent within the Yorkshire Club which had flared up when he was dropped as County captain.

Boyd, James Lawrence
Amateur. *b:* 18.8.1891, Amoy, China. *d:* 15.6.1930, Arosa, Switzerland. Lower order batsman, bowler. *Team* Royal Navy (1913–19).
Career batting
2–4–1–25–10*–8.33–0–*ct* 1
Bowling 56–1–56.00–0–0–1/30

He played rugby for Scotland.

Boyd-Moss, Robin James
Cricketer. *b*: 16.12.1959, Hatton, Ceylon. Middle order right-hand batsman, slow left-arm bowler. *Sch* Bedford. *Teams* Cambridge U (1980–83, blue all four years); Northamptonshire (1980–83, 43 matches).
Career batting
79–139–11–3987–139–31.14–8–*ct* 34
Bowling 1231–32–38.46–1–0–5/27

He hit 1,602 runs, av 44.50 in 1982, and 1,437, av 35.04, in 1983. He scored 139 and 124 for Cambridge v Oxford in the 1983 match at Lord's, the first time two hundreds had been hit by one batsman in this fixture. A good rugby footballer, he appeared in the University matches of 1980/1 and 1981/2.

Boyers, Michael John Herbert
Cricketer. *b:* 16.4.1948, Plaistow, Essex. Lower order right-hand batsman, right-hand fast-medium bowler. *Team* Essex (1969, 1 match).
Career batting
1–2–0–2–2–1.00–0–*ct* 0

Boyes, George Stuart
Amateur in 1921 but turned professional in 1922. *b:* 31.3.1899, Southampton, Hants. *d:* 11.2.1973, Southampton. Began as tail-end, but later lower order, right-hand batsman, slow left-arm bowler, splendid field at short-leg. *Team* Hampshire (1921–39, 474 matches). *Tour* MCC to India, Burma and Ceylon, 1926/7.
Career batting
504–709–169–8078–104–14.95–2–*ct* 498
Bowling 34610–1472–23.81–74–11–9/57

He took 100 wickets in a season three times (best 111, av 26.75, in 1933). His best bowling was 9/57 for Hampshire v Somerset at Yeovil in 1938.

Boyle, Sir Courtenay Edmund
Amateur. *b:* 21.10.1845, Kingston, Jamaica. *d:* 19.5.1901, Granville Place, London. Cousin of C.W. (Oxford U). Steady middle order right-hand batsman, change bowler, wicket-keeper. *Sch* Charterhouse. *Team* Oxford U (1865–67, blue all three years).
Career batting
24–41–0–575–55–14.02–0–*ct* 22–*st* 5

In 1866 and 1867 he was champion tennis player at Oxford and in both years defeated the Cambridge champion. At the time of his death he was Permanent Secretary to the Board of Trade. His final first-class match was for MCC in 1872, and his County cricket was for Northants (non-first-class) and Buckinghamshire.

Boyle, Cecil William
Amateur. *b:* 16.3.1853, London. *d:* 5.4.1900. He was killed in action at Boshof, Orange Free State, South Africa. Cousin of C.E. (Oxford U). Lower order right-hand batsman, right-arm fast bowler,

slip field. *Team* Oxford U (1873–74, blue 1873).
Career batting
6–8–3–52–16–10.40–0–*ct* 3
Bowling 309–30–10.30–2–1–7/33

He excelled on the rugby field and represented England. By some he was regarded as one of the three fastest bowlers of his day.

Boyle, Henry Frederick
Amateur. *b:* 10.12.1847, Sydney, Australia. *d:* 21.11.1907, Bendigo, Victoria, Australia. Lower order right-hand batsman, right-hand medium pace round-arm bowler, good field. *Team* Victoria (1871/2 to 1887/8, 28 matches). *Tours* Australians to England 1878, 1880, 1882, 1884, 1888 and as player/manager in 1890, to North America 1878. *Tests* Australia (1878/9 to 1884/5, 12 matches).
Career batting
140–215–48–1711–108–10.24–1–*ct* 125
Bowling 5692–370–15.38–26–6–7/32
Test batting
12–16–4–153–36*–12.75–0–*ct* 10
Bowling 641–32–20.03–1–0–6/42

Boyle was an invaluable bowler for keeping down the runs; he kept an immaculate length and proved an excellent foil to Spofforth, especially in the 1882 Tests in England. He took 125 wickets, av 12.18, in 1882.

Boyns, Cedric Nigel
Cricketer. *b:* 14.8.1954, Harrogate, Yorkshire. Middle order right-hand batsman, right-arm medium pace bowler. *Teams* Cambridge U (1976); Worcestershire (1976–79, 33 matches).
Career batting
37–54–7–871–95–18.53–0–*ct* 37
Bowling 1668–36–46.33–0–0–3/24

He also played for Shropshire.

Boys, Frank Cecil
Amateur. *b:* 21.6.1918, London. Middle order right-hand batsman, right-arm medium pace bowler. *Team* Combined Services (1947–51).
Career batting
7–13–0–273–84–21.00–0–*ct* 4

Boys, John James
Professional. *b:* 17.8.1856, Titchfield, Hants. *d:* 1.8.1883, Woolwich, Kent. Right-hand opening batsman, right-arm fast round-arm bowler, good field. *Team* Kent (1875–81, 3 matches).
Career batting
3–5–0–34–21–6.80–0–*ct* 4–*st* 2

A musician in the band of the Royal Artillery stationed at Woolwich, he could only occasionally obtain leave to play County cricket. His end was a melancholy one, for he died, aged 26, on the day on which he was to be married, having been busy preparing on the previous day.

Boys, Richard
Professional. *b:* 17.6.1849, Burnley, Lancashire. *d:* 4.1.1896, Burnley, Lancashire. Lower order right-hand batsman, wicket-keeper. *Team* Lancashire (1877, 1 match).
Career batting
1–2–1–13–10–13.00–0–*ct* 2

He did not keep wicket in his only first-class match. He was killed when an industrial chimney collapsed on him.

Bracewell, B. P. (*see entry at end of book*)

Bracewell, J. G. (*see entry at end of book*)

Bracey, Frederick Cecil
Professional. *b:* 20.7.1887, Derby. *d:* 28.3.1960, Derby. Lower order left-hand batsman, slow left-arm bowler. *Team* Derbyshire (1906–14, 77 matches).
Career batting
77–132–54–562–28–7.20–0–*ct* 20
Bowling 3122–132–23.65–5–1–6/36

A noted soccer player, he appeared for Leicester Fosse.

Bracher, Frederick Charles
Amateur. *b:* 25.10.1868, Bedminster, Gloucs. *d:* 23.12.1947, Portishead, Somerset. Middle order batsman. *Team* Gloucestershire (1895–97, 13 matches).
Career batting
13–23–1–163–21–7.40–0–*ct* 9

Brackin, Thomas
Professional. *b:* 5.1.1859, Thornes, Wakefield, Yorkshire. *d:* 1924, Barnsley, Yorkshire. Opening right-hand batsman, right-arm slow bowler, good field. *Team* Yorkshire (1882, 3 matches).
Career batting
3–6–0–12–9–2.00–0–*ct* 0

Brackley, Lord John Francis Granville Scrope Egerton
(Succeeded as 4th Earl of Ellesmere in 1914)
Amateur. *b:* 14.11.1872, Westminster, London. *d:* 24.8.1944, Mertoun, Berwickshire. Middle order right-hand batsman. *Sch* Eton. *Team* MCC (1898–1905). *Tours* Brackley's Team to West Indies 1904/5; MCC to Egypt 1909 (not first-class).
Career batting
12–18–3–210–34–14.00–0–*ct* 6–*st* 1

Brackpool, Alfred
Professional. *b* 11.10.1857, Crawley Down, Sussex. *d:* 24.10.1927, East Grinstead, Sussex.

Middle order right-hand batsman, right arm medium pace bowler. *Team* Sussex (1880, 1 match).
Career batting
1–2–0–2–2–1.00–0–*ct* 0
Bowling 62–1–62.00–0–0–1/62

Bradbury, Leslie
Cricketer. *b:* 19.4.1938, Matlock, Derbyshire. Lower order right-hand batsman, right-arm fast-medium bowler. *Team* Derbyshire (1971, 1 match).
Career batting
1 match, did not bat –*ct* 1
Bowling 53–1–53.00–0–0–1/53

Bradbury, Thomas F.
Amateur. *b:* 1856. *d:* 1934, Barton-on-Irwell, Lancashire. *Team* Lancashire (1881, 1 match).
Career batting
1–2–1–6–6*–6.00–0–*ct* 1

Bradby, Edwin Hugh Falkwin
Amateur. *b:* 8.11.1867, Harrow, Middlesex. *d:* 7.11.1947, Kensington, London. Brother of H. C. (Oxford U). Middle order right-hand batsman, change bowler. *Sch* Rugby. *Team* Oxford U (1886).
Career batting
1–2–0–4–4–2.00–0–*ct* 0
He represented Oxford in the inter-university sports.

Bradby, Henry Christopher
Amateur. *b:* 28.12.1868, Haileybury, Herts. *d:* 28.6.1947, Berkhamsted, Herts. Brother of E.H.F. (Oxford U). Middle order right-hand batsman. *Sch* Rugby. *Team* Oxford U (1890, blue).
Career batting
6–11–2–178–40*–19.77–0–*ct* 5
He played County cricket for Hertfordshire.

Braddell, Robert Lyttleton Lee
Amateur. *b:* 14.12.1888, Malacca, Malaya. *d:* 17.3.1965, Sintra, Portugal. Middle order right-hand batsman, right-arm medium pace bowler. *Sch* Charterhouse. *Team* Oxford U (1908–11, blue 1910–11).
Career batting
20–37–2–648–96–18.51–0–*ct* 11
Bowling 247–11–24.45–0–0–2/1
His County cricket was for Suffolk. His final first-class match was for Leveson-Gower's XI in 1926.

Braddock, J.
Professional. Opening batsman. *Team* Lancashire (1873, 1 match).
Career batting
1–2–0–13–11–6.50–0–*ct* 0

Bradfield, Arthur
Professional. *b:* 5.1.1892, Box, Wiltshire. *d:* 25.12.1978, Mochdre, Colwyn Bay, North Wales. Tail end right-hand batsman, wicket-keeper. *Team* Essex (1922, 5 matches).
Career batting
5–7–3–7–4*–1.75–0–*ct* 2–*st* 3

Bradfield, Geoffrey W.
Cricketer. *b:* 1950, South Africa. Middle order batsman. *Team* Northants (1970, 1 match).
Career batting
1–1–0–50–50–50.00–0–*ct* 0

Bradford, Sir Evelyn Ridley, 2nd Bart
Amateur. *b:* 16.4.1869, Goonah, India. *d:* 14.9.1914. He was killed in action at Soissons, France. Grandson of E. Knight (Hants and Kent). Opening right-hand batsman, right-arm fast bowler. *Sch* Eton. *Team* Hampshire (1895–1905, 8 matches).
Career batting
8–14–2–311–102–25.91–1–*ct* 5
Bowling 328–20–16.40–2–1–6/28
In 1899 his name was on the list of bowlers with 'doubtful' deliveries.

Bradley, George
Professional. *b:* 29.4.1850, Derby. *d:* 24.4.1887, Derby. Lower order right-hand batsman, change bowler. *Team* Derbyshire (1875, 1 match).
Career batting
1–2–0–1–1–0.50–0–*ct* 0
Bowling 17–0

Bradley, James
Professional. *b:* 3.10.1913, Pleasley Hill, Notts. Tail end batsman, slow left-arm bowler. *Team* Nottinghamshire (1937–39, 9 matches).
Career batting
9–8–3–30–13–6.00–0–*ct* 4
Bowling 781–19–41.10–0–0–4/116

Bradley, Michael Ewart
Amateur. *b:* 29.3.1934, Halesowen, Worcs. Tail end right-hand batsman, slow left-arm bowler. *Team* Worcestershire (1951–52, 9 matches).
Career batting
9–9–7–9–6*–4.50–0–*ct* 0
Bowling 867–23–37.69–1–0–6/162

Bradley, Peter
Cricketer. *b:* 3.3.1937, Gee Cross, Hyde, Cheshire. Lower order left-hand batsman, right-

arm medium pace bowler. *Team* Minor Counties (1973–74).
Career batting
2–3–2–11–9*–11.00–0–*ct* 3
Bowling 249–9–27.66–0–0–4/57
He represented Shropshire from 1957 to 1976.

Bradley, Walter Morris
Amateur. *b:* 2.1.1875, Sydenham, Kent. *d:* 19.6.1944, Wandsworth Common. Very moderate tail-end right-hand batsman, right-arm fast bowler. *Sch* Alleyn's. *Teams* Kent (1895–1903, 123 matches); London County (1903). *Tour* Kent to USA 1903. *Tests* England (1899, 2 matches).
Career batting
Bowling 14341–633–22.65–44–10–9/87
Test batting
2–2–1–23–23*–23.00–0–*ct* 0
Bowling 233–6–38.83–1–0–5/67
His two great seasons were 1899 (156 wickets, av 19.10) and 1901 (128, av 23.39) – these were the only years in which he took 100 wickets. His best bowling was 9/87 for Kent v Hampshire at Tonbridge in 1901. He regarded himself as one of the poorest batsmen of all time, but once or twice rose above this modest description. His final first-class match was for Weigall's XI in 1904.

Bradman, Sir Donald George
Amateur. *b:* 27.8.1908, Cootamundra, New South Wales, Australia. Outstanding middle order right-hand batsman, occasional leg break bowler. *Teams* New South Wales (1927/8 to 1933/4, 41 matches); South Australia (1935/6 to 1948/9, 44 matches). *Tours* Australia to England 1930, 1934, 1938, 1948. *Tests* Australia (1928/9 to 1948, 52 matches).
Career batting
234–338–43–28067–452*–95.14–117–*ct* 131–*st* 1
Bowling 1367–36–37.97–0–0–3/35
Test batting
52–80–10–6996–334–99.94–29–*ct* 32
Bowling 72–2–36.00–0–0–1/8
The most effective batsman the game has yet produced, Bradman was as successful in England as he was in his native Australia. By the time of his first English tour in 1930 he had established himself as Australia's leading batsman and he followed one triumph after another as the season progressed. His return in 1934 was no less triumphant and though his first tour as captain, in 1938, resulted only in a drawn series of Tests, his final visit in 1948 was totally successful, both from the team's results and his own, save perhaps for his failure in the fifth Test at the Oval on his farewell appearance against England.
His record during his four English tours is so remarkable that it deserves being chronicled in full:

	M	I	NO	R	HS	Avge	100s
1930	27	36	6	2960	334	98.66	10
1934	22	27	3	2020	304	84.16	7
1938	20	26	5	2429	278	115.66	13
1948	23	31	4	2428	187	89.92	11

Both the triple hundreds noted above were hit in the Leeds Test matches – in 1930 he actually hit 309* by the close of the first day's play. His 334 was a new Test record. The previous winter in Australia he scored 452* for NSW v Queensland at Sydney which was the world record for first-class cricket; a record which stood for almost thirty years, and remains unbeaten in Australia.
No other cricketer has remotely challenged his career average either in Tests or in all first-class matches. Bradman's achievements remain without parallel.

Bradshaw, James Cecil
Amateur, but changed to professional in 1926. *b:* 25.1.1902, Romford, Essex. Brother of W. H. (Leics), cousin of J. W. M. (Leics). Stylish middle order right-hand batsman, brilliant field. *Sch* Stamford. *Team* Leicestershire (1923–33, 181 matches)
Career batting
181–286–20–5051–140–18.98–3–*ct* 68
Bowling 80–0
He hit 1,000 runs in a season once – 1,119, av 25.43, in 1929. An excellent hockey player, he represented Leicestershire for six seasons.

Bradshaw, James (William) Montgomery
Amateur. *b:* 23.11.1906, Oakham, Rutland. *d:* 5.12.1938, Oakham, Rutland. Cousin of J. C. (Leics) and W. H. (Leics). Middle order left-hand batsman, right-arm bowler. *Sch* Oakham. *Team* Leicestershire (1935–38, 3 matches).
Career batting
3–3–0–95–82–31.66–0–*ct* 3
Bowling 103–1–103.00–0–0–1/25

Bradshaw, Stanley William
Amateur. *b:* 16.1.1898, Leicester, *d:* 9.1.1980, Oadby, Leics. Middle-order right-hand batsman. *Team* Leicestershire (1923, 3 matches).
Career batting
3–6–0–9–5–1.50–0–*ct* 2

Bradshaw, Walter Harry
Professional. *b:* 2.8.1906, Teddington, Middlesex. Brother of J. C. (Leics); cousin of J. W. M. (Leics). Middle order right-hand batsman.

Sch Stamford. *Team* Leicestershire (1929, 3 matches).
Career batting
3–5–0–38–20–7.60–0–*ct* 0

Bradshaw, Walter Hulatt
Amateur. *b:* 22.1.1909, Adelaide, Australia. Lower order right-hand batsman, right-arm fast medium bowler. *Sch* Malvern. *Team* Oxford U (1929–31, blue 1930–31); Rajputana (1935/6 to 1938/9); Europeans (1936/7 to 1937/8).
Career batting
25–37–7–330–81–11.00–0–*ct* 12
Bowling 2001–76–26.32–3–1–8/68
His County cricket was for Buckinghamshire.

Brailsford, Frank Colliss
Professional. *b:* 26.8.1933, Chesterfield, Derbyshire. Opening right-hand batsman, right-arm medium pace in-swing bowler. *Team* Derbyshire (1958, 3 matches).
Career batting
3–5–0–41–14–8.20–0–*ct* 1
Bowling 2–1–2.00–0–0–1/2

Brain, Brian Maurice
Professional. *b:* 13.9.1940, Worcester. Lower order right-hand batsman, right-arm fast-medium bowler. *Sch* Kings, Worcester. *Teams* Worcestershire (1959–75, 149 matches); Gloucestershire (1976–81, 110 matches). *Tours* Worcestershire World Tour 1964/5, to Jamaica 1965/66.
Career batting
259–271–68–1704–57–8.39–0–*ct* 50
Bowling 20194–824–24.50–33–6–8/55
Whilst at Worcestershire he left the staff twice (in 1960 and 1971), but rejoined after a break of a season or two.

Brain, Joseph Hugh
Amateur. *b:* 11.9.1863, Kingswood, Bristol, Gloucs. *d:* 26.6.1914, Bonvilston, Cardiff, Glamorgan. Brother of W. H. (Oxford U and Gloucs), uncle of J. H. P. (Glamorgan) and M. B. (Glamorgan). Opening or middle order right-hand batsman, right-arm medium pace bowler, occasional wicket-keeper. *Sch* Clifton. *Teams* Oxford U (1884–87, blue all four years), Gloucestershire (1883–89, 68 matches).
Career batting
101–180–6–3393–143–19.50–3–*ct* 83–*st* 4
Bowling 306–8–38.25–0–0–4/54
The most promising schoolboy batsman of his year, although he did reasonably well in County cricket, he never realised his promise. In 1890 he began playing for Glamorgan and was one of the mainstays of the Welsh County in its pre first-class days. His final first-class match was for MCC in 1901.

Brain, John Henry Patrick
Amateur. *b:* 17.3.1896, Cardiff. *d:* 11.12.1945, Dinas Powis, Glamorgan. Son of W. H. (Gloucs), brother of M. B. (Glamorgan), nephew of J. H. (Gloucs). Lower order right-hand batsman, wicket-keeper. *Sch* Winchester. *Team* Glamorgan (1921–28, 6 matches).
Career batting
7–13–3–86–19*–8.60–0–*ct* 4–*st* 1

Brain, Michael Benjamin
Amateur. *b:* 13.4.1910, Cardiff. *d:* 24.8.1971, Trelleck, Monmouth. Son of W. H. (Gloucs), brother of J. H. P. (Glamorgan), nephew of J. H. (Gloucs). Middle order right-hand batsman, wicket-keeper. *Sch* Repton. *Team* Glamorgan (1930, 1 match).
Career batting
1–2–0–9–9–4.50–0–*ct* 0

Brain, William Henry
Amateur. *b:* 21.7.1870, Clifton, Bristol, Gloucs. *d:* 20.11.1934, Dinas Powis, Glamorgan. Brother of J. H. (Oxford U and Gloucs), father of J. H. P. (Glamorgan) and M. B. (Glamorgan). Lower order right-hand batsman, wicket-keeper. *Sch* Clifton. *Teams* Oxford U (1891–93, blue all three years); Gloucestershire (1893, 7 matches).
Career batting
30–55–15–458–65*–11.45–0–*ct* 39–*st* 22
In 1894 he began to play for Glamorgan under residential qualification. Whilst at Oxford he was awarded his soccer blue, being a goalkeeper. His great feat as wicket-keeper came for Gloucs v Somerset in 1893 when he achieved a hat-trick of stumpings, the bowler being C. L. Townsend.

Brampton, Charles
Professional. *b:* 5.2.1828, Hyson Green, Nottingham. *d:* 12.6.1895, Marlborough, Wilts. Right-hand opening batsman, right-arm medium pace round-arm bowler. *Team* Nottinghamshire (1854–67, 36 matches).
Career batting
73–133–12–1973–89–16.30–0–*ct* 36
Bowling 758–40+16–18.95–2–1–6/16
He also played for Herefordshire, Wiltshire and Devon.

Bramwell, Thomas Young
Amateur. *b:* 15.10.1850, North Shields, Northumberland. *d:* 23.4.1924, Wetherall, Cumberland. Middle order batsman. *Sch* Cheltenham. *Team* MCC (1875).

Career batting
1–2–0–44–44–22.00–0–*ct* 0
His County cricket was for Northumberland.

Brancker, Rawle Clive
Cricketer. *b:* 19.11.1937, Barbados. Middle order left-hand batsman, slow left-arm bowler. *Team* Barbados (1955/6 to 1969/70). *Tours* West Indies to England 1966; Barbados to England 1969.
Career batting
47–68–7–1666–135*–27.31–5–*ct* 21
Bowling 2895–106–27.31–4–0–7/77
He had only very modest success during his 1966 tour of England.

Brand, Hon David Francis
(succeeded to the title 5th Viscount Hampden in 1965)
Amateur. *b:* 14.6.1902, Welwyn, Herts. *d:* 4.9.1975, Glynde, Sussex. Grandson of H. R. (Sussex). Attractive middle order right-hand batsman, right-arm medium pace bowler. *Sch* Eton. *Team* Cambridge U (1922). *Tours* MCC to New Zealand and Australia 1922/3.
Career batting
14–18–2–246–60–15.37–0–*ct* 5
Bowling 757–27–28.03–0–0–4/31
He was regarded as a most promising all-rounder, but gave up first-class cricket after his tour to Australia and New Zealand. His County cricket was for Hertfordshire.

Brand, Rt Hon Henry Robert
(succeeded to the title 2nd Viscount Hampden in 1892)
Amateur. *b:* 2.5.1841, Devonport, Devon. *d:* 22.11.1906, Westminster, London. Grandfather of D. F. (Cambridge U). Middle order right-hand batsman, good field. *Sch* Rugby. *Team* Sussex (1860–67, 2 matches).
Career batting
2–4–0–16–9–4.00–0–*ct* 2
His County cricket was for Hertfordshire.

Brand, James Samson
Amateur. *b:* 5.3.1913, Arbroath, Scotland. Right-hand batsman, wicket-keeper. *Team* Scotland (1939).
Career batting
1–2–0–12–12–6.00–0–*ct* 1–*st* 1

Brander, Edward Richard Spieker
Amateur. *b:* 21.7.1845, Dartford, Kent. *d:* 2.5.1883, Southbourne-on-Sea, Hants. *Sch* Cheltenham. *Team* Orleans Club (1878).
Career batting
1–1–0–2–2–2.00–0–*ct* 0

Brandt, Druce Robert
Amateur. *b:* 20.10.1887, Streatham, Surrey. *d:* 6.7.1915, Boesinghe, Belgium. Middle order right-hand batsman, wicket-keeper. *Sch* Harrow. *Team* Oxford U (1907–08, blue 1907).
Career batting
8–15–3–105–23–8.75–0–*ct* 6–*st* 3
At Harrow he was a noted light-weight boxer, winning the Public School Championship.

Brann, George
Amateur. *b:* 23.4.1865, near Eastbourne, Sussex. *d;* 14.6.1954, Surbiton Hill, Surrey. Originally a hard-hitting but latterly, stubborn defensive, right-hand batsman, right-arm fast bowler, good deep field. *Sch* Ardingly. *Team* Sussex (1883–1905, 271 matches). *Tours* Shrewsbury to Australia 1887/8; Read to South Africa 1891/2 (no first-class matches); Ranjitsinhji to North America 1899.
Career batting
291–479–43–11205–161–25.69–25–*ct* 146–*st* 2
Bowling 3058–69–44.31–1–0–5/73
He reached 1,000 runs in a season twice (best 1,626, av 36.42, in 1897). An excellent soccer player, he was capped for England in 1886 and 1891.

Branston, George Trevor
Amateur. *b:* 3.9.1884, Newark, Notts. *d:* 12.8.1969, London. Attacking middle order right-hand batsman, right-arm medium pace bowler. *Sch* Charterhouse. *Teams* Nottinghamshire (1903–13, 44 matches); Oxford U (1904–06, blue all three years). *Tours* MCC to New Zealand 1906/7, to North America 1907, to Egypt 1909 (not first-class).
Career batting
89–144–16–3301–194*–25.78–3–*ct* 96
Bowling 4303–153–28.12–6–0–6/66

Branston, John Richard Martin
Amateur. *b:* 20.4.1932, Nuneaton, Warwickshire. Lower order right-hand batsman, right-arm medium pace bowler. *Team* Oxford U (1956).
Career batting
5–6–2–32–19–8.00–0–*ct* 2
Bowling 235–9–26.11–0–0–3/50
His first-class debut was for Free Foresters in 1955.

Brassington, Andrew James
Cricketer. *b*: 9.8.1954, Bagnall, Staffs. Lower order right-hand batsman, wicket-keeper. *Team* Gloucestershire (1974–82, 122 matches).
Career batting
122–150–43–856–35–8.00–0–*ct* 207–*st* 47
Bowling 10–0

Braund, Leonard Charles
Professional. *b:* 18.10.1875, Clewer, Berkshire. *d:* 23.12.1955, Putney, London. Middle order right-hand batsman, leg break bowler, excellent slip field. *Teams* Surrey (1896–98, 21 matches); Somerset (1899–1920, 281 matches); London County (1900–04). *Tours* MacLaren to Australia 1901/2; MCC to Australia 1903/4, 1907/8. *Tests* England (1901/2 to 1907/8, 23 matches).
Career batting
432–752–57–17801–257*–25.61–25–*ct* 545–*st* 1
Bowling 30388–1114–27.27–80–16–9/41
Test batting
23–41–3–987–104–25.97–3–*ct* 39
Bowling 1810–47–38.51–3–0–8/81

As a young man Braund played County cricket for Surrey but with little success. In 1899 he switched his allegiance to Somerset, only to discover that he was not qualified, and he thus spent a year appearing in non-Championship cricket for London County. Re-appearing for Somerset in 1901 he took the critics by surprise, completing the 'double' and being rewarded by selection for the England team to Australia in 1901/2. His success continued through 1902; he again completed the 'double' and represented England in all five Tests. A third and last 'double' was completed in 1903, and though he went with MCC on two further visits to Australia and appeared for Somerset until 1920, his career showed a gradual decline from those three great summers of 1901, 1902 and 1903. His highest score was 257* for Somerset v Worcs at Worcester in 1913 and best bowling 9/41 for Somerset v Yorkshire at Sheffield in 1902.

In all he hit 1,000 runs in a season 6 times (best 1,587, av 36.06, in 1901) and took 100 wickets 4 times (best 172, av 19.80, in 1902). His great asset which does not show in the averages was his slip fielding and several catches he took during his Test career were quite exceptional. He was a player who could rise to the big occasion and he never appeared to suffer from nerves. After leaving County cricket he was a first-class umpire for about 15 seasons.

Bray, Charlie
Amateur. *b:* 6.4.1898, Brighton, Sussex. Defensive middle order right-hand batsman. *Team* Essex (1927–37, 95 matches).
Career batting
95–154–14–3474–129–24.81–5–*ct* 54
Bowling 104–2–52.00–0–0–1/1

He was a noted sporting journalist with the *Daily Herald.*

Bray, Sir Edward
Amateur. *b:* 19.8.1849, Shere, Surrey. *d:* 19.6.1926, Kensington, London. Father of E. H. (Cambridge U and Middlesex). Lower order right-hand batsman, right-arm slow bowler. *Sch* Westminster. *Teams* Surrey (1870–78, 14 matches); Cambridge U (1871–72, blue both years).
Career batting
30–52–10–399–38–9.50–0–*ct* 18
Bowling 1757–108–16.26–8–2–7/32

His final first-class match was for MCC in 1879. At the time of his death he was County Court Judge for Bloomsbury and Brentford.

Bray, Sir Edward Hugh
Amateur. *b:* 15.4.1874, London. *d:* 27.11.1950, Playden, Rye, Sussex. Son of Edward (Cambridge U and Surrey). Middle/lower order right-hand batsman, wicket-keeper. *Sch* Charterhouse. *Teams* Cambridge U (1896–97, blue both years); Middlesex (1895–1906, 21 matches). *Tours* Warner to North America 1898.
Career batting
42–60–9–684–49–13.41–0–*ct* 71–*st* 12

He was in business in Bengal for many years.

Bray, James
Professional. *b:* 18.1.1853, Limehouse, Middlesex. *d:* 30.8.1898, St Pancras, London. Tail end right-hand batsman, right-arm medium pace bowler. *Team* Kent (1879–82, 22 matches).
Career batting
22–37–10–74–9–2.74–0–*ct* 16
Bowling 1464–87–16.82–6–1–8/103

From 1887 he appeared for Essex.

Bray, Leslie Lingwood
Amateur. *b:* 14.1.1895, West Ham, Essex. *d:* 29.11.1957, Ampthill, Bedfordshire. *Team* RAF (1927).
Career batting
1–1–1–10–10*–no av–0–*ct* 1

Braybrooke, Henry Mellor
Amateur. *b:* 11.2.1869, Kandy, Ceylon. *d:* 28.10.1935, Hawkhurst, Kent. Opening/middle order right-hand batsman, right-arm medium pace bowler. *Sch* Wellington. *Teams* Kent (1891–99, 21 matches); Cambridge U (1891).
Career batting
28–51–3–690–53–14.37–0–*ct* 15
Bowling 21–0

He represented Cambridge against Oxford at golf in 1890 and 1891 and was also a noted runner and tobogganer.

Brayshay, Peter Beldon
Amateur. *b:* 14.10.1916, Leeds, Yorkshire. Tail end right-hand batsman, right-arm fast bowler.

Teams Yorkshire (1952, 2 matches); Europeans (1945/6).
Career batting
3–5–1–23–13–5.75–0–*ct* 0
Bowling 223–4–55.75–0–0–2/48

Brazier, Alan Frederick
Professional. *b:* 7.12.1924, Paddington, London. Middle order right-hand batsman, right-arm medium pace bowler. *Teams* Surrey (1948–54, 36 matches); Kent (1955–56, 20 matches).
Career batting
58–94–14–1366–92–17.07–0–*ct* 20
Bowling 158–4–39.50–0–0–2/45

In 1949 he created a new aggregate run record for Minor County cricket, hitting 1,212 runs (av 80.80) for Surrey 2nd XI.

Breakwell, Dennis
Cricketer. *b:* 2.7.1948, Brierley Hill, Staffs. Middle order left-hand batsman, slow left-arm bowler. *Teams* Northants (1969–72, 64 matches); Somerset (1973–83, 165 matches).
Career batting
231–306–64–4792–100*–19.80–1–*ct* 80
Bowling 13008–422–30.82–12–1–8/39

Brearley, Horace
Amateur. *b:* 26.6.1913, Heckmondwike, Yorkshire. Father of J. M. (Cambridge U, Middlesex and England). Middle order right-hand batsman. *Teams* Yorkshire (1937, 1 match); Middlesex (1949, 2 matches).
Career batting
5–10–0–134–37–13.40–0–*ct* 3

Brearley, John Michael, OBE
Amateur. *b*: 28.4.1942, Harrow, Middlesex. Son of Horace (Yorkshire and Middlesex). Sound opening right-hand batsman, right-arm medium pace bowler, occasional wicket-keeper. *Sch* City of London. *Teams* Cambridge U (1961–64, blue all four years); Middlesex (1961–83, 291 matches). *Tours* MCC to South Africa 1964/5, to Pakistan 1966/7, to East Africa 1973/4, to India, Sri Lanka and Australia 1976/7; England to Pakistan and New Zealand 1977/8, to Australia 1978/9, to Australia and India 1979/80; Kent to West Indies 1972/3 (not first-class); International XI to Pakistan 1973/4; Middlesex to Zimbabwe 1980/1; Overseas XI to India 1980/1. *Tests* England (1976–81, 39 matches).
Career batting
455–768–102–25185–312*–37.81–45–*ct* 418–*st* 12
Bowling 192–3–64.00–0–0–1/6
Test batting
39–66–3–1442–91–22.88–0–*ct* 52

He hit 1,000 runs in a season eleven times, going on to 2,000 once: 2,178, av 44.44, in 1964. His highest innings was 312* for MCC v North Zone at Peshawar in 1966/7, and both his double centuries were also for MCC overseas. He captained Middlesex with great success from 1971 to 1982 and England in 31 Tests, including the overseas tours of 1966/7, 1977/8, 1978/9 and 1979/80. He is generally regarded as England's best captain in recent years and in fact commanded a place in the Test team rather for his flair as leader than for his batting.

Brearley, Walter
Amateur. *b:* 11.3.1876, Bolton, Lancashire. *d:* 13.1.1937, Middlesex Hospital, London. Tail end right-hand batsman, right-arm fast bowler. *Teams* Lancashire (1902–11, 106 matches); London County (1904). *Tests* England (1905–12, 4 matches).
Career batting
134–185–31–907–38–5.88–0–*ct* 52
Bowling 16305–844–19.31–93–27–9/47
Test batting
4–5–2–21–11*–7.00–0–*ct* 0
Bowling 359–17–21.11–1–0–5/110

His first-class career was marred by continual quarrels with the Lancashire Committee. He refused to play for the County for most of 1906 and all of 1907 and the final break came at the end of the 1911 season, so that in 1912 he played Test cricket for England whilst appearing for Cheshire. He was the epitome of the explosive fast bowler. In three seasons he took over 100 wickets (best 181, av 19.25, in 1905). His final first-class match was for an England XI v Australians in 1921. His best bowling was 9/47 for Lancashire v Somerset at Old Trafford in 1905.

Breeden, Carl Louis
Amateur. *b:* 10.2.1891, Moseley, Warwickshire. *d:* 2.11.1951, Claverdon, Warwickshire. Middle order right-hand batsman, right-arm medium pace bowler. *Sch* KES, Birmingham. *Team* Warwickshire (1910, 5 matches).
Career batting
5–8–1–80–27–11.42–0–*ct* 4
Bowling 29–0

Brelsford, James
(also known as Bralsford)
Professional. *b:* 19.12.1855, Brimington, Derbyshire. *d:* 24.12.1924, Hale, Cheshire. Lower order right-hand batsman, right-arm medium pace bowler. *Team* Derbyshire (1883–86, 8 matches).
Career batting
8–14–1–56–16–4.30–0–*ct* 4
Bowling 482–24–20.08–1–0–5/31

He also played for Cheshire under residential qualification.

Bremner, Colin David
Amateur. *b:* 29.1.1920, Hawthorn, Victoria, Australia. Lower order right-hand batsman, wicket-keeper. *Teams* Dominions (1945); Australian Services (1945/6). *Tour* Australian Services to India 1945/6.
Career batting
7–9–6–8–4*–2.66–0–*ct* 4–*st* 6
He was a member of the RAAF team stationed in England in 1945.

Brennan, Donald (Vincent)
Amateur. *b:* 10.2.1920, Eccleshill, Yorkshire. Lower order right-hand batsman, wicket-keeper. *Sch* Downside. *Team* Yorkshire (1947–53, 204 matches). *Tour* MCC to India, Pakistan and Ceylon 1951/2. *Tests* England (1951, 2 matches).
Career batting
232–258–74–1937–67*–10.52–0–*ct* 318–*st* 122
Test batting
2–2–0–16–16–8.00–0–*ct* 0–*st* 1

Bretherton, James
Amateur. *b:* 5.1.1862, Whiston, Lancashire. *d:* 1926, Wirral, Cheshire. Tail end right-hand batsman, right-arm fast-medium bowler, slip field. *Team* Liverpool and District (1890–94).
Career batting
6–11–1–165–50–16.50–0–*ct* 2
Bowling 396–24–16.50–1–0–5/30
His County cricket was for Cheshire.

Brett, Patrick John
Amateur. *b:* 18.4.1910, Johannesburg, South Africa. *d:* 9.12.1982, Hook Heath, Surrey. Middle order right-hand batsman, right-arm medium-fast bowler. *Sch* Winchester. *Team* Oxford U (1929, blue).
Career batting
8–13–1–490–106–40.83–1–*ct* 2
Bowling 242–4–60.50–0–0–2/32

Brett, Thomas
Professional. *b:* 1747, Catherington, Hants. *d:* 31.12.1809, Kingston, Portsmouth, Hants. Hard hitting lower order batsman, very fast under-arm bowler. *Team* Hampshire.
First-class career figures are inappropriate as he played before 1801. In the 1770s he was regarded as the fastest and straightest of the Hambledon Club bowlers, but about 1778 he left the Club and seems to have retired from the game.

Brettell, David Norman
Cricketer. *b:* 10.3.1956, Woking, Surrey. Lower order left-hand batsman, slow left-arm bowler. *Sch* Cheltenham. *Team* Oxford U (1975–78, blue 1977).
Career batting
13–19–4–175–39–11.66–0–*ct* 4
Bowling 549–18–30.50–0–0–3/22

Brewer, Thomas Tanner
Amateur. *b:* 1868, Bridgewater, Somerset. Middle order batsman. *Team* London County (1903).
Career batting
5–8–1–88–59–12.57–0–*ct* 5
His final first-class match was for Gentlemen of England in 1905. His County cricket was for Cheshire.

Brewster, Vincent Crescedo
Cricketer. *b:* 2.1.1940, Bridgetown, Barbados. Lower order left-hand batsman, slow left-arm bowler. *Team* Warwickshire (1965, 2 matches).
Career batting
2–4–1–58–35*–19.33–0–*ct* 1
Bowling 175–10–17.50–1–0–7/58

Brice, Edward Archibald
(changed his name to Bruce in 1875)
Amateur. *b:* 1.9.1849, Secunderabad, India. *d:* 14.11.1918, Steyning, Sussex. Middle/lower order right-hand batsman, right-arm fast bowler. *Sch* Cheltenham. *Team* Gloucestershire (1872–73, 4 matches).
Career batting
6–9–0–22–13–2.44–0–*ct* 3
Bowling 264–20–13.20–2–1–6/34
In 1874 he was stationed in India and therefore lost to County cricket. After retiring from the Army he was Hon Sec and Chairman of Sussex CCC. He played for Somerset in non-first-class matches.

Brice, Gordon Harry Joseph
Professional. *b:* 4.5.1924, Bedford. Lower order right-hand batsman, right-arm fast medium bowler. *Sch* Bedford Modern. *Team* Northants (1949–52, 25 matches).
Career batting
25–35–5–412–82*–13.73–0–*ct* 14
Bowling 2426–72–33.69–4–1–8/124
He also played for Bedfordshire. He was an excellent soccer player, appearing at centre half for Reading, Luton, Fulham and Wolves.

Bridge, Derek James Wilson
Amateur. *b:* 30.11.1921, Manchester. Lower order right-hand batsman, off break bowler. *Teams* Northants (1947, 3 matches); Oxford U (1947).
Career batting
4–7–1–55–25*–9.16–0–*ct* 1
Bowling 261–5–52.20–0–0–2/14

An excellent rugby player he was awarded his blue at Oxford. He also played for Dorset.

Bridge, Walter Basil
Professional. *b:* 29.5.1938, Selly Oak, Birmingham. Lower order right-hand batsman, right-arm off break bowler. *Team* Warwickshire (1955–68, 98 matches).
Career batting
99–133–33–1058–56*–10.58–0–*ct* 59
Bowling 7438–283–26.28–13–2–9/56
He took more than 100 wickets in a season once – 123, av 22.99, in 1961.

Bridgeman, Charles George Orlando
Amateur. *b:* 13.7.1852, Wells, Somerset. *d:* 19.12.1933, St John's Wood, London. Stylish lower order right-hand batsman, right-hand slow round-arm bowler, excellent deep field. *Sch* Harrow. *Team* Cambridge U (1872).
Career batting
3–6–1–87–27–17.40–0–*ct* 1
Bowling 20–0
His County cricket was for Staffordshire. His last first-class match was for an England XI in 1874.

Bridgeman, William Clive
(created 1st Viscount Bridgeman in 1929)
Amateur. *b:* 31.12.1864, London. *d:* 14.8.1935, Leigh, Salop. Middle order right-hand batsman, good field at point. *Sch* Eton. *Team* Cambridge U (1887–88, blue 1887).
Career batting
13–20–3–361–162*–21.23–1–*ct* 5
His County cricket was for Shropshire and Staffordshire. His final first-class match was for MCC in 1894. A well-known MP, he was Home Secretary in 1922 and First Lord of the Admiralty in 1924. He represented Oswestry from 1906 to 1929.

Bridger, Rev John Richard
Amateur. *b:* 8.4.1920, Dulwich, Surrey. Stylish opening right-hand batsman, leg break bowler. *Sch* Rugby. *Team* Hampshire (1946–54, 38 matches).
Career batting
40–69–4–1883–142–28.96–2–*ct* 30
Bowling 56–0
He appeared for Cambridge U against Oxford in 1941 and 1943. His first-class debut was for Under 33s in 1945. Being in the scholastic profession his County cricket was limited mainly to August.

Bridges, John Henry
Amateur. *b:* 26.3.1852, Horsham, Sussex. *d:* 12.2.1925, Eastbourne, Sussex. Free scoring middle order right-hand batsman, good deep field. *Sch* Winchester. *Team* Surrey (1876, 2 matches).
Career batting
2–2–0–9–8–4.50–0–*ct* 0
He did not appear in any first-class matches whilst at Oxford, but won his blue for soccer. He was Champion Archer of Scotland in 1905 and from 1919 to 1920 High Sheriff of Surrey.

Bridges, James (John)
Professional to 1914, amateur from 1919. *b:* 28.6.1887, Timsbury, Somerset. *d:* 26.9.1966, Hackney, London. Tail end right-hand batsman. Right-arm fast-medium bowler. *Team* Somerset (1911–29, 214 matches).
Career batting
216–348–108–2418–99*–10.07–0–*ct* 128
Bowling 17613–685–25.71–44–4–7/41

Bridges, Leslie Walter
Amateur. *b:* 14.2.1890, Christchurch, New Zealand. *d:* 6.8.1959, Antwerp, Belgium. Middle order batsman, change bowler. *Team* Cambridge U (1911).
Career batting
1–2–0–34–25–17.00–0–*ct* 0
Bowling 39–0
He performed well in the Seniors' Match at Cambridge in 1911, taking 13 wickets and hitting 74, but did little in his other Trials at the University.

Brierley, Thomas Leslie
Professional. *b:* 15.6.1910, Southampton. Middle order right-hand batsman, wicket-keeper. *Teams* Glamorgan (1931–39, 181 matches); Lancashire (1946–48, 46 matches); Canada (1951–54). *Tour* Canadians to England 1954.
Career batting
232–362–33–6244–116*–18.97–4–*ct* 215–*st* 91
Bowling 45–0
He hit 1,183 runs, av 23.66, in 1938. He emigrated to Canada after leaving Lancashire and appeared for Canada against the MCC touring team in 1951. He later returned to the UK.

Briers, Norman
Cricketer. *b:* 10.2.1947, Leicester. Cousin of N. E. (Leics). Lower order right-hand batsman, right-arm fast medium bowler. *Team* Leicestershire (1967, 1 match).
Career batting
1–1–0–1–1–1.00–0–*ct* 0
Bowling 31–0

Briers, Nigel Edwin
Cricketer. *b:* 15.1.1955, Leicester. Cousin of Norman Briers (Leicestershire). Middle order right-hand batsman; right-arm medium pace bowler, cover field. *Team* Leicestershire (1971–83, 143 matches). *Tour* Leicestershire to Zimbabwe 1980/1.
Career batting
143–228–23–6056–201*–29.54–9–*ct* 59
Bowling 343–10–34.30–0–0–2/11
He hit 1,000 runs in a season three times (best 1,289, av 40.28, in 1983). His highest innings is 201* for Leicestershire v Warwickshire at Edgbaston in 1983.

Briggs, Rev Charles Edward
Amateur. *b:* 17.9.1873, Ashbourne, Derbyshire. *d:* 16.12.1949, Sherborne, Dorset. Middle order batsman. *Sch* Winchester. *Team* Hampshire (1900, 6 matches).
Career batting
6–10–0–158–58–15.80–0–*ct* 4
He also played for Buckinghamshire.

Briggs, John
Professional. *b:* 3.10.1862, Sutton-in-Ashfield, Notts. *d:* 11.1.1902, Cheadle, Cheshire. Brother of J. B. (Notts). Hard-hitting middle/lower order right-hand batsman, slow left-arm bowler, brilliant cover field. *Team* Lancashire (1879–1900, 391 matches). *Tours* Lillywhite, Shaw and Shrewsbury to Australia 1884/5, 1886/7, 1887/8; Warton to South Africa 1888/9; Sheffield to Australia 1891/2; Stoddart to Australia 1894/5, 1897/8. *Tests* England (1884/5 to 1899, 33 matches).
Career batting
535–826–55–14092–186–18.27–10–*ct* 259
Bowling 35432–2221–15.95–200–52–10/55
Test batting
33–50–5–815–121–18.11–1–*ct* 12
Bowling 2094–118–17.74–9–4–8/11
'Boy' Briggs – he was only 5ft 5in tall and made his first-class debut at the age of 16 – was one of the most popular professionals of his generation. He is remembered now chiefly for his slow bowling, but in 1879 he won his place in the Lancashire team as a fieldsman and retained it for six years as a batsman. It was not until 1885 that his skill with the ball was of paramount importance – in 1884 he had only 9 first-class wickets to his credit. The first of his many good performances for England came in the Lord's Test of 1886, when he took 11 for 74 to win the match for England. He exceeded 100 wickets in a season 12 times, but it is difficult to pinpoint his best year, so consistent was his success. In 1893 he took most wickets in his career with 166 (av 15.89), but he had effectively headed the bowling table in 1890 with 158 wickets (av 12.34) and in 1888 his 160 wickets were obtained at the low cost of 10.49 runs each. His best bowling was 10/55 for Lancashire v Worcestershire at Old Trafford in 1900.
He visited Australia with no less than six English Test-playing sides and was a success on all but the last trip.
From about 1889 he suffered from a form of epilepsy which became increasingly serious. He had a particularly bad seizure during the Leeds Test of 1899 and it seemed as if his career were at an end, but he recovered and bowled with all his old skill in 1900. That, however, was the farewell season, for he had another more serious attack and was confined to Cheadle Asylum where he died in the winter of 1901/2 at the early age of 39.

Briggs, John
Professional. *b:* 8.4.1916, Haslingden, Lancashire. Tail end batsman, slow left-arm bowler. *Team* Lancashire (1939, 4 matches).
Career batting
4–2–2–0–0*–no av–0–*ct* 2
Bowling 391–10–39.10–0–0–4/48
He also played for Cheshire.

Briggs, Joseph (Banner)
Professional. *b:* 4.6.1860, Sutton-in-Ashfield, Notts. *d:* 30.11.1902, Bramley, Leeds, Yorkshire. Brother of John (Lancs and England). Lower order right-hand batsman, slow left-arm bowler. *Team* Nottinghamshire (1888, 6 matches).
Career batting
7–11–0–26–9–2.36–0–*ct* 2
Bowling 168–14–12.00–1–0–5/34
His first-class debut was in 1885 for L. Hall's XI v A. Shaw's XI.

Briggs, Kenneth Robert
Amateur. *b:* 17.7.1933, Woking, Surrey. Middle order right-hand batsman, off break bowler. *Sch* KCS, Wimbledon. *Team* Combined Services (1961).
Career batting
1–2–1–29–17*–29.00–0–*ct* 2
Bowling 44–1–44.00–0–0–1/32

Briggs, Patrick David
Cricketer. *b:* 24.8.1940, Timperley, Cheshire. Middle order right-hand batsman. *Sch* Pocklington. *Team* Cambridge U (1963–64).
Career batting
21–35–2–533–91–16.15–0–*ct* 17
Bowling 7–0

His County cricket was for Cheshire and Bedfordshire.

Briggs, Canon Rawdon
Amateur. *b:* 30.12.1854, Warkworth, Northumberland. *d:* 21.8.1936, Bedford. Middle order right-hand batsman, right-hand fast round-arm bowler. *Sch* Winchester. *Team* Oxford U (1875–76, blue both years).
Career batting
10–17–1–342–71–21.37–0–*ct* 8
Residing in Yorkshire in the 1870s, he was a notable player with the Gentlemen of that County and also appeared for the breakaway Yorkshire United side.

Bright, Raymond James
Cricketer. *b*: 13.7.1954, Footscray, Victoria, Australia. Lower order right-hand batsman, slow left-arm bowler. *Team* Victoria (1972/3 to 1982/3). *Tours* Australia to New Zealand 1973/4, 1976/7, 1981/2, to England 1977, 1980 and 1981, to Pakistan 1979/80, 1982/3, to Sri Lanka 1980/1. *Tests* Australia (1977 to 1982/3, 16 matches).
Career batting
125–173–37–2769–108–20.36–1–*ct* 83
Bowling 9891–332–29.79–17–2–7/87
Test batting
16–27–5–303–33–13.77–0–*ct* 8
Bowling 1343–37–36.29–3–1–7/87
He headed the first-class bowling averages on the 1977 tour to England with 39 wickets, av 20.35, and played in three Tests. He appeared in the Centenary Test of 1980 and in five Tests on the 1981 tour, but made little impression.

Brindle, Reginald Gordon
Professional. *b:* 3.10.1925, Warrington, Cheshire. Middle order right-hand batsman. *Team* Warwickshire (1949, 1 match).
Career batting
1–2–0–74–42–37.00–0–*ct* 0

Brindley, Thomas
Amateur. *b:* 3.6.1841, Chester. *d:* 1.3.1911, Bournemouth. Hard hitting right-hand batsman, slow underarm bowler. *Team* MCC (1867).
Career batting
2–4–1–31–13*–10.33–0–*ct* 0
He appeared for Gloucestershire and Warwickshire before these Counties were first-class.

Brindley, William Thomas
Amateur. *b:* 4.12.1896, High Wycombe, Buckinghamshire. *d:* 13.8.1958, Virginia Water, Surrey. Opening right-hand batsman, change bowler. *Teams* Ceylon (1925/6 to 1933/4); Minor Counties (1930–35).
Career batting
9–15–2–221–59*–17.00–0–*ct* 4
Bowling 389–14–27.78–1–0–5/40
He played for Buckinghamshire, but joined the Ceylon Police Force and his English cricket was thereby very restricted.

Brinton, Percival Robert
Amateur. *b:* 5.2.1873, Kidderminster, Worcs. *d:* 14.5.1958, Oxford. Brother of R. S. (Worcs). Middle order batsman. *Sch* Winchester. *Team* Worcestershire (1904, 1 match).
Career batting
1–1–0–1–1–1.00–0–*ct* 0

Brinton, Ronald Lewis
Amateur. *b:* 26.2.1903, Kidderminster, Worcs. *d:* 19.4.1980, Malvern, Worcs. Lower order right-hand batsman, change bowler. *Sch* Shrewsbury. *Team* Worcestershire (1924, 2 matches).
Career batting
2–4–0–22–10–5.50–0–*ct* 0
Bowling 22–0

Brinton, Reginald Seymour
Amateur. *b:* 15.12.1869, Lower Mitton, Worcs. *d:* 23.2.1942, Kidderminster, Worcs. Brother of P. R. (Worcs). Steady middle order right-hand batsman, right-arm fast-medium bowler. *Sch* Winchester. *Team* Worcestershire (1903–09, 13 matches).
Career batting
13–24–7–332–72*–19.53–0–*ct* 3
Bowling 13–0

Briscoe, Henry
Professional. *b:* 20.5.1861, Bonehill, Staffs. *d:* 7.3.1911, Fenton, Staffs. Lower order right-hand batsman, right-arm fast-medium bowler. *Team* An England XI (1888).
Career batting
1–2–1–4–4*–4.00–0–*ct* 0
Bowling 28–0
His County cricket was for Staffordshire.

Bristow, John
Professional. *b:* 13.4.1840, Esher, Surrey. *d:* 25.1.1912, Brookwood, Surrey. Lower order right-hand batsman, left-arm medium pace bowler, occasional wicket-keeper. *Team* Surrey (1867–73, 32 matches).
Career batting
32–58–8–514–79–10.28–0–*ct* 17–*st* 1
Bowling 1503–73–20.58–5–0–7/45

Bristowe, Orme Chesshyre
Amateur. *b:* 12.4.1895, Great Baddow, Essex. *d:* 27.12.1938, of heart failure whilst out shooting at Freiston Shore, Lincs. Hard hitting lower order right-hand batsman, leg break and googly bowler, good field. *Sch* Eton. *Teams* Essex (1913–14, 11 matches); Oxford U (1914, blue).
Career batting
21–33–2–567–81–18.29–0–*ct* 6
Bowling 1751–74–23.66–4–0–6/81
He also played for Cheshire.

Britton, George
Professional. *b:* 17.4.1843 Hunslet, Leeds. *d:* 3.1.1910, Leeds. Opening right-hand batsman. *Team* Yorkshire (1867, 1 match).
Career batting
1–2–0–3–3–1.50–0–*ct* 0
In 1870 he performed the unusual feat of carrying his bat through the completed innings of a team of Twenty-Two of Hull v All England.

Broad, Brian Christopher
Cricketer. *b*: 29.9.1957, Bristol. Opening left-hand batsman, right-arm medium pace bowler. *Team* Gloucestershire (1979–83, 89 matches).
Career batting
89–159–9–4804–145–32.02–8–*ct* 35
Bowling 656–11–59.63–0–0–2/14
He hit 1,000 runs in a season three times (best 1,153, av 28.12, in 1982).

Broadbent, Arthur
Professional. *b:* 7.6.1879, Armley, Yorkshire. *d:* 19.7.1958, Aberdeen, Scotland. Middle order right-hand batsman, right-arm fast medium bowler. *Teams* Scotland (1907–12); Yorkshire (1909–10, 3 matches).
Career batting
6–11–1–141–32–14.10–0–*ct* 1
Bowling 545–16–34.06–0–0–4/61
He was a most successful player for Yorkshire 2nd XI, taking 100 wickets in 1910 (av 13.20), but did little in first-class matches.

Broadbent, Robert Gillespie
Amateur for first season, professional afterwards. *b:* 21.6.1924, Beckenham, Kent. Aggressive middle order right-hand batsman, occasional right-arm fast-medium bowler, good field. *Sch* Caterham. *Team* Worcestershire (1950–63, 307 matches).
Career batting
307–520–56–12800–155–27.58–13–*ct* 297
Bowling 382–4–95.50–0–0–1/16
He hit 1,000 runs in a season 7 times (best 1556, av 33.10, in 1952). He also played for Hertfordshire.

Broadbridge, James
Professional. *b:* 1796, Duncton, Sussex. *d:* 12.2.1843, Duncton. Brother of William (Sussex). Hard hitting opening left-hand or right-hand batsman, right-arm medium pace round-arm bowler. *Teams* Sussex (1815–40); Godalming (1822–24); Kent (1828); Surrey (1829).
Career batting
102–184–23–2671–135–16.59–1–*ct* 51
Bowling 243–13+310–18.69–8–1–6/?
He was considered for some seasons the best all round cricketer in England and was partly responsible for the introduction of round-arm bowling in 1827. When batting he stood at the wicket 'with his bat over his shoulder'. In 1825 in important matches he hit 552 runs, av 46.00. His first important match was for Osbaldeston's XI in 1814.

Broadbridge, William
Professional. *b:* 1.10.1790, Duncton, Sussex. *d:* 19.4.1860, Duncton, Sussex. Brother of James (Sussex). Hard-hitting right-hand batsman, wicket-keeper. *Team* Sussex (1817–30).
Career batting
25–45–2–609–61–14.16–0–*ct* 14–*st* 22
Bowling 3 wickets, no analyses
He was one of the mainstays of the old Sussex team for many years, commencing 1817, but details of his early performances appear to have been lost.

Broadhead, William Bedford
Professional. *b:* 31.5.1903, East Ardsley, Yorkshire. Right-hand opening batsman, leg-break bowler. *Team* Yorkshire (1929, 1 match).
Career batting
1–2–0–5–3–2.50–0–*ct* 1

Broberg, Ralph Francis
Amateur. *b:* 21.7.1899, Birmingham. *d:* 3.9.1938, Hall Green, Birmingham. Lower order batsman, left-arm slow bowler. *Team* Warwickshire (1920, 1 match).
Career batting
1–1–0–4–4–4.00–0–*ct* 0
Bowling 16–0

Brockbank, John
Amateur. *b:* 22.8.1848, Whitehaven, Cumberland. *d:* 29.1.1904, Bowness-on-Windermere. Middle order right-hand batsman. *Sch* Shrewsbury. *Team* MCC (1874).
Career batting
1–2–0–5–4–2.50–0–*ct* 0
He appeared at various times for Shropshire, Cumberland, Cambridgeshire, Brecon, Herefordshire and Staffordshire; he was not however in

the Eleven whilst at Cambridge University, being better known as a soccer player. He was awarded his soccer blue and went on to play for England in 1873. By profession he was an actor.

Brocklebank, Sir John Montague, Bart
Amateur. *b:* 3.9.1915, Wirral, Cheshire. *d:* 13.9.1974, Palazz Zejtun, Malta. Brother of T. A. L. (Cambridge U), nephew of F.S. Jackson (Yorkshire and England). Tail end right-hand batsman, medium pace, leg break bowler. *Sch* Eton. *Teams* Cambridge U (1936, blue); Lancashire (1939, 4 matches); Bengal (1947/8). *Tours* MCC to Canada 1937 (not first-class); MCC to India 1939/40 (team selected but owing to war the tour was cancelled).
Career batting
21–26–14–112–23–9.33–0–*ct* 7
Bowling 1998–68–29.38–4–2–6/92

His final first-class match was for Free Foresters in 1949. He also played for Cheshire. Chairman of the Cunard shipping line, he placed the order for the QE2.

Brocklebank, Sir Thomas Aubrey Lawies
Amateur. *b:* 23.10.1899, Chelsea, London. *d:* 15.9.1953, Ruthin, North Wales. Brother of J. M. (Lancs), nephew of F. S. Jackson (Yorks). Middle order batsman. *Sch* Eton. *Team* Cambridge U (1919).
Career batting
2–4–2–42–37*–21.00–0–*ct* 2

His County cricket was for Cheshire.

Brocklehurst, Benjamin Gilbert
Amateur. *b:* 18.2.1922, Knapton, Norfolk. Hard-hitting middle order right-hand batsman. *Sch* Bradfield. *Team* Somerset (1952–54, 64 matches).
Career batting
64–116–9–1671–89–15.61–0–*ct* 26
Bowling 36–1–36.00–0–0–1/9

He was Captain of Somerset 1953–54. He also played for Berkshire. He is Managing Director and Proprietor of 'The Cricketer' Magazine.

Brockwell, George
Professional. *b:* 14.8.1811, Kingston-on-Thames, Surrey. *d:* 12.12.1876, Hackney, London. Uncle of William (Surrey). Very hard-hitting lower-order left-hand batsman, left-hand slow round-arm bowler. *Team* Surrey (1844–57, 34 matches).
Career batting
44–77–7–790–57–11.28–0–*ct* 17
Bowling 208–9+77–23.11–2–1–7/?

When bowling he had a very curious delivery, striking himself on the chest just before the ball left his hand. In wet weather this left a large round mark in the centre of his shirt. He was employed at the Oval from the opening of the ground in 1845 to 1862, when he was retired on half-pay.

Brockwell, William
Professional. *b:* 21.1.1865, Kingston-on-Thames, Surrey. *d:* 30.6.1935, Richmond, Surrey. Nephew of George (Surrey). Stylish opening right-hand batsman, right-arm fast-medium bowler, good slip field. *Teams* Surrey (1886–1903, 314 matches); Kimberley (1889/90); London County (1901–03). *Tours* Read to South Africa 1891/2 (no first-class matches); Stoddart to Australia 1894/5. *Tests* England (1893–99, 7 matches).
Career batting
357–539–47–13285–225–27.00–21–*ct* 250–*st* 1
Bowling 13680–553–24.73–24–1–8/22
Test batting
7–12–0–202–49–16.83–0–*ct* 6
Bowling 309–5–61.80–0–0–3/33

He exceeded 1,000 runs in a season 6 times, his highest aggregate being 1,686, av 38.31, in 1898, but his best being 1,491, av 38.23, in 1894, when he headed the first-class averages, that season being a very difficult one for batsmen. His highest score was 225 for Surrey v Hampshire at the Oval in 1897. His single visit to Australia was not very successful. In 1899 he took 105 wickets, av 25.26, his best season with the ball, and he completed the double that year. He fell on hard times after leaving first-class cricket and died in abject poverty.

Broderick, Vincent
Professional. *b:* 17.8.1920, Bacup, Lancashire. Opening/middle order left-hand batsman, slow left-arm bowler. *Team* Northants (1939–57, 245 matches).
Career batting
253–384–44–7530–190–22.14–6–*ct* 65
Bowling 15007–548–27.38–23–4–9/35

He performed the 'double' in 1948 (1,066 runs, av 26.65, and 100 wickets, av 22.77); he also exceeded 1,000 runs in one other season. His best bowling was 9/35 for Northants v Sussex at Horsham in 1948.

Brodhurst, Arthur Hugh
Amateur. *b:* 21.7.1916, Buenos Aires, Argentina. Middle order right-hand batsman, off-break bowler, excellent field. *Sch* Malvern. *Teams* Cambridge U (1937–39, blue 1939); Gloucestershire (1939–46, 6 matches). *Tours* Oxford and Cambridge Universities to Jamaica 1938/39; MCC to Canada 1951.
Career batting
20–33–2–658–111–21.22–2–*ct* 8
Bowling 321–6–53.50–0–0–4/83

Brodhurst, Bernard Maynard Lucas
Amateur. *b:* 6.8.1873, Benares, India. *d:* 27.4.1915. He was killed in action near Ypres, Belgium. Lower order right-hand batsman, right-arm fast medium bowler. *Sch* Clifton. *Team* Hampshire (1897, 1 match).
Career batting
1–1–0–9–9–9.00–0–*ct* 1
Bowling 23–0

Brodie, James Bruce
Amateur. *b:* 19.3.1937, Graaff-Reinet, South Africa. Lower order right-hand batsman, right-arm fast-medium bowler. *Teams* Cambridge U (1959–60, blue 1960); Commonwealth (1960); Eastern Province (1961/2 to 1963/4).
Career batting
22–36–11–305–37–12.20–0–*ct* 7
Bowling 1743–48–36.31–2–0–5/47
He appeared for Berkshire with considerable success in 1960.

Brodie, James Lothian
Amateur. *b:* 17.10.1893, Glasgow. *d:* 2.7.1939, Glasgow. Right-hand batsman. *Team* Scotland (1924–25).
Career batting
3–5–0–57–20–11.40–0–*ct* 0

Brodrick, Peter Dawson
Amateur. *b:* 11.5.1937, North Shields, Northumberland. Lower order right-hand batsman, slow left-arm bowler. *Sch* Newcastle GS. *Team* Cambridge U (1959–61, blue 1961).
Career batting
22–34–11–321–49–13.95–0–*ct* 7
Bowling 1927–44–43.79–0–0–4/74
He played County cricket for Northumberland.

Bromfield, Harry Dudley
Amateur. *b:* 26.6.1932, Mossel Bay, South Africa. Lower order right-hand batsman, right-arm off break bowler. *Team* Western Province (1956/7 to 1968/9). *Tour* South Africa to England 1965. *Tests* South Africa (1961/2 to 1965, 9 matches).
Career batting
62–91–32–374–44–6.33–0–*ct* 68
Bowling 5256–205–25.63–13–1–7/60
Test batting
9–12–7–59–21–11.80–0–*ct* 13
Bowling 599–17–35.23–1–0–5/88
On his single visit to England he failed to do himself justice and appeared in only one Test, with little success.

Bromley, Ernest Harvey
Amateur. *b:* 2.9.1912, Fremantle, West Australia. *d:* 1.2.1967, Clayton, Victoria, Australia. Middle order left-hand batsman, slow left-arm bowler, brilliant field. *Teams* Western Australia (1929/30 to 1931/2, 6 matches); Victoria (1932/3 to 1938/9, 22 matches): Europeans (1936/7). *Tour* Australia to England 1934. *Tests* Australia (1932/3 to 1934, 2 matches).
Career batting
52–78–6–2055–161–28.54–3–*ct* 43
Bowling 1651–39–42.33–0–0–4/50
Test batting
2–4–0–38–26–9.50–0–*ct* 2
Bowling 19–0
Although he appeared in one of the Tests on his single tour to England, he had few days of success during the visit, save that his fielding was always a great asset to the team.

Bromley, Philip Harry
Amateur. *b:* 30.7.1930, Stratford-on-Avon, Warwickshire. Middle order right-hand batsman, right-arm off break bowler. *Sch* Warwick. *Team* Warwickshire (1947–56, 49 matches).
Career batting
49–66–11–1183–121*–21.50–1–*ct* 37
Bowling 1264–35–36.11–1–0–5/61
He also played for Shropshire.

Bromley, Richard Charles
Cricketer. *b:* 23.6.1946, Oxted, Surrey. Middle order left-hand batsman, wicket-keeper. *Team* Cambridge U (1970, blue).
Career batting
5–9–0–78–18–8.66–0–*ct* 6

Bromley-Davenport, Hugh Richard
Amateur. *b:* 18.8.1870, Capesthorne, Cheshire. *d:* 23.5.1954, South Kensington, London. Lower order right-hand batsman, fast left-arm bowler, slip field. *Sch* Eton. *Teams* Cambridge U (1892–93, blue both years); Middlesex (1896–98, 28 matches). *Tours* Lucas to West Indies 1894/5; Hawke to West Indies 1896/7; Hawke to South Africa 1895/6, 1898/9. *Tests* England (1895/6 to 1898/9, 4 matches).
Career batting
76–119–21–1801–91–18.37–0–*ct* 48
Bowling 3352–187–17.92–12–1–7/17
Test batting
4–6–0–128–84–21.33–0–*ct* 1
Bowling 98–4–24.50–0–0–2/46
He was one of the few players of his era to play cricket wearing glasses. His most successful cricket was on his two visits to the West Indies, when he headed the bowling averages each time. From 1886 to 1895 he appeared for Cheshire. His final first-class match was in 1899. His brother William played soccer for England.

Bromley-Martin, Eliot George
Amateur. *b:* 2.10.1866, St Cloud, Worcester. *d:* 23.1.1946, Walton, Radnorshire. Brother of G. E. (Worcs). Lower order right-hand batsman, right-arm slow bowler. *Sch* Eton. *Team* Worcestershire (1899–1900, 10 matches).
Career batting
12–17–1–257–42–16.06–0–*ct* 2
Bowling 274–10–27.40–0–0–4/33
Whilst at Oxford he appeared in various trials, but no first-class matches. He did, however, win his soccer blue in 1888. Most of his County cricket for Worcs was played before that side was in the County Championship. He acted as Hon. Sec. to the County Club in the 1890s.

Bromley-Martin, Granville Edward
Amateur. *b:* 18.10.1875, Callow End, Worcs. *d:* 31.5.1941, Hassocks, Sussex. Brother of E. G. (Worcs). Middle order right-hand batsman, slow right-arm bowler. *Sch* Eton. *Teams* Oxford U (1897–98, blue both years); Worcestershire (1899–1904, 32 matches).
Career batting
48–83–1–1779–137–21.69–2–*ct* 21
Bowling 93–1–93.00–0–0–1/11
He was also an excellent fives player.

Brook, Arthur John
Amateur. *b:* 1844, Battle, Sussex. *d:* 19.12.1917, Bexhill, Sussex. Middle order batsman. *Team* Sussex (1873, 1 match).
Career batting
1–1–0–10–10–10.00–0–*ct* 0

Brook, George Wilfred
Professional. *b:* 30.8.1888, Mirfield, Yorkshire. *d:* 24.7.1966, Bournemouth, Hants. Lower order right-hand batsman, slow left-arm bowler. *Team* Worcestershire (1930–35, 150 matches).
Career batting
150–218–17–1877–56–9.33–0–*ct* 77
Bowling 12841–461–27.85–23–4–7/50
He enjoyed great success in his initial County Championship season of 1930 taking 132 wickets (av 21.88) at the age of 41.

Brook, James William
Professional. *b:* 1.2.1897, Ossett, Yorkshire. Middle order right-hand batsman, right-arm medium pace bowler. *Team* Yorkshire (1923, 1 match).
Career batting
1–1–0–0–0–0.00–0–*ct* 0

Brooke, Bernard
Professional. *b:* 3.3.1930, Huddersfield, Yorkshire. Tail end right-hand batsman, right-arm, medium fast bowler. *Team* Yorkshire (1950, 2 matches).
Career batting
2–4–0–16–14–4.00–0–*ct* 0
Bowling 191–2–95.50–0–0–1/64

Brooke, Vice Admiral Basil Charles Barrington
Amateur. *b:* 6.4.1895, Boddington, Northants. *d:* 20.1.1983, Saffron Walden, Essex. Middle order batsman, bowler. *Sch* Malvern. *Team* Royal Navy (1919–26)
Career batting
2–4–0–61–28–15.25–0–*ct* 3
Bowling 59–3–19.66–0–0–2/48

Brooke, Francis Ralph Russell
Amateur. *b:* 2.10.1884, Bowdon, Cheshire. *d:* 20.6.1960, Basingstoke, Hants. Middle/lower order hard-hitting right-hand batsman, wicket-keeper. *Sch* Harrow. *Teams* Lancashire (1912–13, 29 matches); Europeans (1910/11 to 1926/7); Ceylon (1925/6 to 1926/7).
Career batting
62–92–6–2197–115–25.54–2–*ct* 85–*st* 21
Bowling 9–1–9.00–0–0–1/9
Owing to his military career he played little County cricket, but was one of the mainstays of the Army team, his final first-class match being for the Army in 1929.

Brooke, Rev Richard Hubert John
Amateur. *b:* 6.6.1909, Eton, Buckinghamshire. *d:* 3.5.1973, Great Canfield, Essex. Opening right-hand batsman, right-arm medium pace bowler. *Sch* St Edward's, Oxford. *Teams* Oxford U (1931–32, blue 1931); Gloucestershire (1931, 1 match). *Tour* Martineau to Egypt 1933 (not first-class).
Career batting
18–29–3–1043–140–40.11–5–*ct* 14
Bowling 331–14–23.64–0–0–3/7
He played with success for Buckinghamshire and his final first-class match was for Minor Counties in 1935.

Brooke-Short, Cecil
Amateur. *b:* 1894, Daventry, Northants. *d:* 28.6.1937, Wei-Hai-Wei, China. *Team* Royal Navy (1925).
Career batting
1–2–1–4–3*–4.00–0–*ct* 0

Brooke-Taylor, David Charles
Amateur. *b:* 15.6.1920, Bakewell, Derbyshire. Son of G. P. (Derbyshire and Cambridge U). Middle order right-hand batsman. *Sch* Cheltenham. *Team* Derbyshire (1947–49, 15 matches).

Career batting
15–26–1–375–61*–15.00–0–*ct* 6

Brooke-Taylor, Geoffrey Parker
Amateur. *b:* 25.10.1895, Bakewell, Derbyshire. *d:* 13.1.1968, Hurlingham, Buenos Aires, Argentina. Father of D. C. (Derbyshire). Middle order left-hand batsman, wicket-keeper. *Sch* Cheltenham. *Teams* Cambridge U (1919–20, blue both years); Derbyshire (1920, 1 match); Argentine (1926/7 to 1929/30).
Career batting
25–40–1–778–84–19.94–0–*ct* 13–*st* 3
He played in the North v South match in Argentina.

Brooker, Mervyn Edward William
Cricketer. *b:* 24.3.1954, Burton-on-Trent, Staffs. Lower order right-hand batsman, medium-fast bowler. *Team* Cambridge U (1974–76, blue 1976).
Career batting
15–28–15–43–9–3.30–0–*ct* 3
Bowling 1149–25–45.96–0–0–4/58

Brookes, Dennis
Professional. *b:* 29.10.1915, Kippax, Leeds, Yorkshire. Sound stylish opening right-hand batsman, right-arm medium pace bowler. *Team* Northants (1934–59, 492 matches). *Tour* MCC to West Indies 1947/8. *Test* England (1947/8, 1 match).
Career batting
525–925–70–30874–257–3610–71–*ct* 205
Bowling 127–3–42.33–0–0–1/7
Test batting
1–2–0–17–10–8.50–0–*ct* 1
He hit 1,000 runs in a season 17 times, exceeding 2,000 on six occasions (best 2229, av 47.42, in 1952). His highest score was 257 for Northants v Gloucs at Bristol in 1949 and he made five other double centuries, all for Northants. On his only MCC tour overseas he was unlucky to be injured and return home early. He captained Northants 1954 to 1957.

Brooks, Alfred James
Professional. *b:* 24.3.1848, Sutton-in-Ashfield, Notts. *d:* 20.11.1911, Sutton-in-Ashfield, Notts. Lower order right-hand batsman, right-arm fast-medium bowler, cover field. *Team* Nottinghamshire (1877, 2 matches).
Career batting
2–4–1–10–6–3.33–0–*ct* 0
Bowling 85–5–17.00–0–0–2/10
He also appeared for Somerset in 4 non-first-class matches in 1880, and for Dorset.

Brooks, Abraham (W.)
Professional. *b:* 1853. *d:* 1925, Bolton, Lancashire. Tail end batsman, wicket-keeper. *Team* Lancashire (1877, 1 match).
Career batting
1–1–0–6–6–6.00–0–*ct* 2

Brooks, Edward William John
Professional. *b:* 6.7.1898, Camberwell, Surrey. *d:* 10.2.1960, Rustington, Sussex. Lower order right-hand batsman, wicket-keeper. *Team* Surrey (1925–39, 354 matches).
Career batting
359–442–98–4497–70–13.07–0–*ct* 725–*st* 96
Bowling 6–0

Brooks, Joseph
Professional. *b:* 10.9.1870, South Normanton, Derbyshire. *d:* 15.5.1937, Shuttlewood, Derbyshire. Tail end batsman, left-arm fast-medium bowler. *Team* Derbyshire (1895–96, 5 matches).
Career batting
5–7–4–8–6–2.66–0–*ct* 1
Bowling 190–2–95.00–0–0–1/22

Brooks, J.
Professional. Tail end batsman, medium pace bowler. *Team* Gloucestershire (1892, 1 match).
Career batting
1–2–0–0–0–0.00–0–*ct* 1
Bowling 31–1–31.00–0–0–1/31

Brooks, Kevin Graham
Cricketer. *b:* 15.10.1959, Reading, Berkshire. Right-hand batsman, right-arm medium pace bowler. *Team* Derbyshire (1980, 1 match).
Career batting
1–2–0–11–8–5.50–0–*ct* 2
He played for Lincolnshire in 1983.

Brooks, Paul Wilson
Professional. *b:* 1921, Marylebone, London., *d:* 27.1.1946, St Mary's Hospital, London, as a result of wounds received whilst on active service in Italy. Middle order left-hand batsman, left-arm fast-medium bowler. *Team* Middlesex (1939, 1 match).
Career batting
1–1–1–44–44*–no av–0–*ct* 0

Brooks, Richard
(generally known as R. B. Brooks, but he has only one Christian name)
Amateur. *b:* 29.7.1863, Sutton-on-Sea, Lincolnshire. *d:* 9.4.1927, Kensington, London. Lower order right-hand batsman, wicket-keeper. *Sch* Cranleigh. *Teams* Surrey (1889, 1 match); London County (1900–03).

Career batting
7–8–1–56–18*–8.00–0–*ct* 8–*st* 12

He was regarded as one of the best wicket-keepers of his day, but owing to his profession could not afford the time for County cricket. He appeared mainly in London Club matches for the Wanderers CC.

Brooks, Richard Alan
Cricketer. *b:* 14.6.1943, Edgware, Middlesex. Lower order right-hand batsman, wicket-keeper. *Teams* Oxford U (1967, blue); Somerset (1968, 26 matches).
Career batting
35–45–16–317–44–10.93–0–*ct* 53–*st* 7

After one full season with Somerset, Brooks took up a teaching post at Bradfield College, which ended his first-class career.

Brooks, Gen Sir Reginald Alexander Dallas
(also known as Dallas-Brooks)
Amateur. *b:* 2.8.1896, Cambridge. *d:* 22.3.1966, Frankston, Victoria, Australia. Middle order right-hand batsman, right-arm medium pace bowler. *Sch* Dover. *Team* Hampshire (1919–21, 9 matches).
Career batting
29–53–1–1070–143–20.57–2–*ct* 15
Bowling 1092–38–28.73–1–0–8/90

His final first-class match was for Combined Services in 1931. A prominent sportsman, he captained the Royal Navy at golf and at hockey, also representing England in the latter. From 1949 to 1963 he was Governor of Victoria.

Brooks, Ronald Clifton
Amateur. *b:* 3.3.1899, Kingston, Surrey. *d:* 14.8.1980, Chelsea, London. Lower order right-hand batsman, wicket-keeper. *Sch* Haileybury. *Team* Cambridge U (1919).
Career batting
5–6–2–99–27–24.75–0–*ct* 1–*st* 2

His final first-class match was for Free Foresters in 1929.

Brooks, Victor Charles George
Cricketer. *b:* 29.6.1948, East Ham, London. Middle order left-hand batsman. *Team* Essex (1970–71, 3 matches).
Career batting
3–5–0–53–22–10.60–0–*ct* 1

Brooks, Walter Tyrrell
Amateur. *b:* 23.2.1884, Kensington, London. *d:* 3.6.1965, Tunbridge Wells, Kent. Lower order batsman, bowler. *Sch* Marlborough. *Team* Leveson-Gower's XI (1906).
Career batting
1–2–1–14–13*–14.00–0–*ct* 0
Bowling 47–2–23.50–0–0–1/9

He played for Oxfordshire.

Brophy, James Noel
Amateur. *b:* 8.1.1912, Cork, Ireland. Right-hand batsman, wicket-keeper. *Team* Ireland (1938).
Career batting
1–2–0–13–9–6.50–0–*ct* 0

Brotherhood, Rowland
Amateur. *b:* 18.11.1841, Brinkworth, Wiltshire. *d:* 4.3.1883, Redland, Bristol, Gloucs. Lower order left-hand batsman, left-hand fast under-arm bowler, good deep field. *Sch* King's College, Wimbledon. *Team* Gloucestershire (1875, 3 matches).
Career batting
3–6–2–3–2–0.75–0–*ct* 1
Bowling 67–2–33.50–0–0–2/49

From 1869 to 1874 he was residing in South America. He belonged to a family of eleven brothers and on several occasions the eleven played as a team.

Brougham, Henry
Amateur. *b:* 8.7.1888, Wellington College, Somerset. *d:* 18.2.1923, La Croix, Var, France. Opening/middle order right-hand batsman, brilliant field. *Sch* Wellington. *Team* Oxford U (1911, blue).
Career batting
5–9–0–214–84–23.77–0–*ct* 1

His County cricket was for Berkshire. A noted rugby footballer, he appeared for Harlequins and England. He represented Oxford at rackets in 1908 and 1909. Invalided out of the Army in 1917, he died in 1923 after five years illness.His final first-class match was for Minor Counties in 1912.

Broughton, Ernest Alfred
Amateur. *b:* 22.4.1905, Wigston, Leics. *d:* 19.2.1982, Wigston, Leics. Middle order right-hand batsman, off break bowler. *Team* Leicestershire (1928–33, 25 matches).
Career batting
25–38–1–482–61–13.02–0–*ct* 12
Bowling 18–0

Broughton, John Jarvis
Professional. *b:* 8.9.1873, Grantham, Lincolnshire. *d:* 3.4.1952, Billinge, Lancashire. Middle order right-hand batsman. *Team* Lancashire (1901–02, 6 matches).
Career batting
6–7–0–153–99–21.85–0–*ct* 3
Bowling 69–2–34.50–0–0–2/28

He had the unusual distinction of scoring 99 on his first-class debut – Lancs v Essex 1901. He also represented Lincolnshire.

Broughton, Peter Norman
Professional. *b:* 22.10.1935, Castleford, Yorkshire. Tail end right-hand batsman, right-arm fast medium bowler. *Teams* Yorkshire (1956, 6 matches); Leicestershire (1960–62, 24 matches).
Career batting
30–33–17–162–17*–10.12–0–*ct* 12
Bowling 2430–85–28.59–5–0–6/38
He also played for Cumberland.

Broughton, Robert John Porcher
Amateur. *b:* 11.7.1816, Farnham, Surrey. *d:* 15.6.1911, Chipperfield, Herts. Hard-hitting middle order batsman, round-arm slow bowler, excellent cover field. *Sch* Harrow. *Team* Cambridge U (1836–39, blue 1836, 1838 and 1839).
Career batting
24–46–5–477–40–11.63–0–*ct* 4
Bowling 2 wickets, no analyses
His final first-class match was for MCC in 1864.

Brown, Alan
Professional. *b:* 17.10.1935, Rainworth, Notts. Lower order right-hand batsman, right-arm fast medium bowler. *Team* Kent (1957/70, 237 matches). *Tour* MCC to India, Pakistan and Ceylon 1961/2. *Tests* England (1961/2, 2 matches).
Career batting
251–312–87–2189–81–9.72–0–*ct* 104
Bowling 18326–743–24.66–26–4–8/47
Test batting
2–1–1–3–3*–no av–0–*ct* 1
Bowling 150–3–50.00–0–0–3/27
He took 100 wickets in a season once – 116, av 19.04, in 1965. Also a useful soccer player, he appeared for Gravesend at centre forward.

Brown, Alan
Cricketer. *b:* 23.12.1957, Darwen, Lancashire. Lower order right-hand batsman, wicket-keeper. *Team* Worcestershire (1979, 1 match).
Career batting
1 match, did not bat–*ct* 2

Brown, Albert
Amateur. *b:* 10.7.1911, Birmingham. Lower order right-hand batsman, right-arm fast medium bowler. *Team* Warwickshire (1932, 1 match).
Career batting
1–1–1–1–1*–no av–0–*ct* 1
Bowling 96–2–48.00–0–0–2/96
He was a well-known snooker and billiards player.

Brown, Alexander
Cricketer. *b:* 7.10.1950, Coatbridge, Scotland. Right-hand batsman, right-arm medium pace bowler. *Team* Scotland (1977–82).
Career batting
5–7–0–64–25–9.14–0–*ct* 7

Brown, Alfred
Professional. *b:* 10.6.1854, Malton, Yorkshire. *d:* 2.11.1900, Malton, Yorkshire. Opening right-hand batsman, right-hand fast round-arm bowler, good field. *Team* Yorkshire (1872, 2 matches).
Career batting
2–3–0–9–5–3.00–0–*ct* 4
Bowling 47–3–15.66–0–0–2/17

Brown, Andrew John Trevor
Amateur. *b:* 27.6.1935, Edinburgh, Scotland. Middle order left-hand batsman, off break bowler. *Team* Combined Services (1960).
Career batting
2–4–1–41–40*–13.66–0–*ct* 1

Brown, Anthony Stephen
Professional. *b:* 24.6.1936, Bristol, Gloucs. Middle/lower order right-hand batsman, right-arm medium fast bowler, excellent close field. *Team* Gloucestershire (1953–76, 489 matches). *Tours* Robins to South Africa 1972/3; International XI to South Africa 1974/5.
Career batting
496–808–99–12851–116–18.12–3–*ct* 493
Bowling 31546–1230–25.64–54–8–8/80
He exceeded 1,000 runs in a season once (1,149, av 20.15, in 1964) and 100 wickets twice (best 110, av 23.08, in 1959).
In the match between Gloucs and Notts at Trent Bridge in 1966, he held 7 catches in one innings, equalling the world first-class record. In 1977 he was appointed secretary-manager to Gloucs CCC, but moved to Somerset in 1983.

Brown, Charles
Professional. *b:* 22.1.1815, Nottingham. *d:* 28.9.1875, Nottingham. Middle order right-hand batsman, occasional round-arm bowler, wicket-keeper. *Team* Nottinghamshire (1842–61, 25 matches).
Career batting
33–59–10–435–43*–8.87–0–*ct* 32–*st* 26
Bowling 92–7+3–13.14–0–0–4/27
He was regarded as one of the leading wicket-keepers of his day and played for the England team v Kent in 1844, 1848 and 1849. He could bowl 'behind his back' i.e. putting his right-arm

behind his back and delivering from his left side and in minor matches was quite successful with this strange delivery.

Brown, Charles Atherton
Amateur. *b:* 8.6.1854, Sydney, New South Wales, Australia. *d:* 8.7.1917, Grendon, Warwickshire. Tail end right-hand batsman, left-hand first round arm bowler. *Sch* Highgate. *Team* Sussex (1876–78, 11 matches).
Career batting
11–20–5–137–26–9.13–0–*ct* 10
Bowling 576–25–23.04–2–0–7/58

Brown, Colin Edwin
Amateur. *b:* 1878. *d:* 25.6.1936, Whitby, Yorkshire. Middle order batsman, change bowler. *Team* Somerset (1902–05, 8 matches).
Career batting
8–15–3–151–53–12.62–0–*ct* 6
Bowling 15–0

Brown, Air Vice-Marshal Cecil Leonard Morley
Amateur. *b:* 16.7.1895, Melton Mowbray, Leics. *d:* 6.12.1955, Crowthorne, Berks. Middle order right-hand batsman, right-arm medium pace bowler. *Sch* Worksop. *Team* Leicestershire (1920–21, 7 matches).
Career batting
7–11–0–74–33–6.72–0–*ct* 1

Brown, David
Amateur. *b:* 29.7.1900, Dunfermline, Scotland. *d:* 30.1.1951, Dunfermline, Scotland. Right-hand batsman, right-arm medium pace bowler. *Team* Scotland (1927–30).
Career batting
2–3–0–21–13–7.00–0–*ct* 1
Bowling 43–1–43.00–0–0–1/10

Brown, David Basil Stuart
Cricketer. *b:* 14.6.1941, Insch, Aberdeenshire. Left-hand batsman. *Team* Scotland (1973–76).
Career batting
3–6–0–115–58–19.16–0–*ct* 2

Brown, David John
Professional, *b*: 30.1.1942, Walsall, Staffs. Lower order right-hand batsman, right-arm fast medium bowler. *Team* Warwickshire (1961–82, 326 matches). *Tours* MCC to South Africa 1964/5, to Australia and New Zealand 1965/6, to Pakistan 1966/7, to West Indies 1967/8, to Ceylon and Pakistan 1968/9; Rest of World to Pakistan 1970/1; Robins to South Africa 1972/3. *Tests* England (1965–69, 26 matches).
Career batting
390–446–111–4110–79–12.26–0–*ct* 157
Bowling 28961–1165–24.85–46–5–8/60
Test batting
26–34–5–342–44*–11.79–0–*ct* 7
Bowling 2237–79–28.31–2–0–5/42
He captained Warwickshire from 1975–77 and was appointed manager of the County in 1981.

Brown, David Wyndham James
Cricketer. *b:* 26.2.1942, Cheltenham, Gloucs. Middle order right-hand batsman, right-arm off break bowler. *Team* Gloucestershire (1964–67, 88 matches).
Career batting
89–153–11–2863–142–20.16–1–*ct* 37
Bowling 84–3–28.00–0–0–3/84

Brown, Edward
Professional. *b:* 27.11.1911, Newcastle-on-Tyne. Lower order right-hand batsman, right-arm medium-fast bowler. *Team* Warwickshire (1932–34, 28 matches).
Career batting
28–29–9–134–19*–6.70–0–*ct* 10
Bowling 1877–56–31.37–3–0–8/35
He also played for Durham.

Brown, Frederick Richard, MBE
Amateur. *b:* 16.12.1910, Lima, Peru. Hard hitting middle order right-hand batsman, right-arm medium or leg-break and googly bowler. *Sch* The Leys. *Teams* Cambridge U (1930–31, blue both years); Surrey (1931–48, 106 matches); Northants (1949–53, 102 matches). *Tours* MCC to Australia and New Zealand 1932/3, 1950/1; Martineau to Egypt 1934, 1936, 1939 (not first-class); MCC to South Africa 1956/7 (manager); MCC to East Africa 1957/8 (not first-class); Brown to East Africa 1961/2 (not first-class). *Tests* England (1931–53, 22 matches).
Career batting
Bowling 32007–1221–26.21–62–11–8/34
Test batting
22–30–1–734–79–25.31–0–*ct* 22
Bowling 1398–45–31.06–1–0–5/49
After a short but brilliant career at Cambridge, where he headed the batting averages as a Freshman, then in his only other season headed the bowling table, Brown made a tremendous impact in his first full season of County cricket by performing the 'double' and being selected to tour Australia with Jardine's 1932/33 team. His talents were scarcely required on this venture and afterwards his County cricket career seemed to be destined to follow the pattern of so many other amateurs – just appearing in a handful of first-class games each season. During the Second

World War he was a POW for three years and afterwards very little was seen of him – in three seasons he made one solitary appearance in a Championship match for Surrey.

In 1949 however came his appointment as captain of Northants and overnight he was transformed back into the brilliant all-rounder of the early 1930s – he performed the 'double' for the second time in his career and was soon recalled to the England team, this time as captain. His leadership revitalised England on the 1950/51 tour to Australia, just as it had revitalised Northants. This second career lasted until 1953, when he retired from the Northants captaincy, but he went on appearing in occasional first-class matches until 1961 – his farewell match being for Free Foresters.

He hit 1,000 runs in a season 4 times (best 1,135, av 32.42, in 1932), and took 100 wickets three times (best 120, av 20.46 in 1932), achieving the 'double' twice. His only double century was 212 for Surrey v Middlesex in 1932.

He was a Test Selector from 1951 to 1953, being Chairman in the last year and Chairman of the Cricket Council 1974–79. He was awarded the MBE for services to cricket.

Brown, George
Professional. *b:* 27.4.1783, Stoughton, Sussex. *d:* 25.6.1857, Sompting, Sussex. Father of G. G. (Sussex). Hard hitting right-hand batsman, very fast under-arm bowler. *Teams* Hampshire (1819–23); Sussex (1825–38).
Career batting
51–96–4–1053–70–11.44–0–*ct* 50
Bowling 68–6+83–11.33–5–1–6/?

He was rated as the fastest of bowlers, placing nearly all his fieldsmen behind the wicket and his wicket-keeper, Dench, had a sack stuffed with straw fastened to his chest for protection. He was the father of no less than seventeen children.

Brown, George
Professional. *b:* 6.10.1887, Cowley, Oxon. *d:* 3.12.1964, Winchester, Hants. Opening/middle order left-hand batsman, right-arm medium pace bowler, wicket-keeper/brilliant close field. *Team* Hampshire (1908–33, 539 matches). *Tours* MCC to West Indies 1910/11, to South Africa 1922/23, to India, Burma and Ceylon 1926/27; Tennyson to Jamaica 1931/2. *Tests* England (1921 to 1922/3, 7 matches).
Career batting
612–1012–52–25649–232*–26.71–37–*ct* 568–*st* 78
Bowling 18666–626–29.81–23–2–8/55
Test batting
7–12–2–299–84–29.90–0–*ct* 9–*st* 3

In his day one of the most brilliant all-round cricketers ever seen, Brown's batting tended to be inconsistent as well as moving unpredictably from attack to dour defence. He could be given the wicket-keeper's job at a moment's notice and perform to Test match standard. He made 1,000 runs in a season 11 times, exceeding 2,000 once – 2,040 runs, av 40.00, in 1926. The highest of his three double-centuries was 232* for Hants v Yorks (Leeds) 1920.

Brown, George Grainger
Professional. *b:* 16.6.1821, Brighton, Sussex. *d:* 21.3.1875, Battersea, London. Son of George (Sussex). Steady middle order right-hand batsman, slow under-arm bowler, long-stop. *Team* Sussex (1851–58, 37 matches).
Career batting
46–78–10–898–86–13.20–0–*ct* 18
Bowling 508–35–14.51–3–0–5/25

Brown, George Rainy Reynolds
Amateur. *b:* 8.12.1905, Maldon, Essex. Lower order right-hand batsman, slow left-arm bowler. *Sch* Felsted. *Teams* Essex (1924–32, 23 matches); Cambridge U (1925); Europeans (1936/7 to 1945/6).
Career batting
29–46–12–396–38*–11.64–0–*ct* 15
Bowling 1358–46–29.52–1–0–5/55

Brown, H. W.
Amateur. Middle order batsman, useful bowler. *Team* Gloucestershire (1890–94, 16 matches).
Career batting
16–31–5–210–41–8.08–0–*ct* 4
Bowling 1023–36–28.41–1–0–6/155

Brown, James
Amateur. *b:* 7.2.1864, Gainford, Co Durham. *d:* December, 1916, Copenhagen. Middle order left-hand batsman, left-arm medium-fast bowler, slip field. *Team* Sussex (1890, 2 matches).
Career batting
3–4–0–31–19–7.75–0–*ct* 0
Bowling 26–0

He also appeared in the Durham County side. His final first-class match was for the South in 1896.

Brown, James
Amateur. *b:* 24.9.1931, Perth, Scotland. Right-hand batsman, wicket-keeper. *Team* Scotland (1953–73).
Career batting
59–85–18–1306–90–19.49–0–*ct* 83–*st* 23

Brown, John
Professional. *b:* 1862, Bingham, Notts. Brother of Thomas (Notts). Middle order left-hand

batsman, left-arm medium pace bowler. *Team* Nottinghamshire (1888, 3 matches).
Career batting
3–6–2–33–24–8.25–0–*ct* 1
Bowling 15–0
He also played for Staffordshire.

Brown, John Dowell
Professional. *b:* 25.8.1890, Coventry, Warwickshire. *d:* 18.3.1968, Leamington, Warwickshire. Lower order batsman, slow left-arm bowler. *Team* Warwickshire (1913–14, 9 matches)
Career batting
9–12–5–12–7–1.71–0–*ct* 4
Bowling 264–9–27.11–0–0–4/18

Brown, Joseph Henry
Professional. *b:* 26.1.1872, Earl Shilton, Leicestershire. *d:* May 1915, Earl Shilton, Leicestershire. Brother of Lewis (Leics). Middle order right-hand batsman, right-arm off break bowler. *Team* Leicestershire (1898–05, 15 matches).
Career batting
15–28–3–305–53*–12.20–0–*ct* 16
Bowling 325–7–46.42–0–0–2/6

Brown, John Thomas
Professional. *b:* 20.8.1869, Driffield, Yorkshire. *d:* 4.11.1904, Westminster, London. Opening right-hand batsman, slow right-arm bowler, excellent field. *Team* Yorkshire (1889–1904, 346 matches). *Tour* Stoddart to Australia 1894/5. *Tests* England (1894/5 to 1899, 8 matches).
Career batting
383–634–47–17920–311–30.52–29–*ct* 221
Bowling 5627–190–29.61–4–0–6/52
Test batting
8–16–3–470–140–36.15–1–*ct* 7
Bowling 22–0
One of the greatest of Yorkshire's batsmen, Brown was the only one to hit two triple centuries for the County – 311 v Sussex at Bramall Lane in 1897 and 300 v Derbyshire at Chesterfield in 1898. During the latter innings he and Tunnicliffe created a new first-class record first wicket partnership of 554. His only other score over 200 was 203 v Middlesex at Lord's in 1896, in which match he and Tunnicliffe added 139 in the first innings and 147 without being parted in the second.

He scored over 1,000 runs in a season in 10 successive years (1894 to 1903) with 1873, av 35.33, in 1896 best. He went to Australia in 1894/5 and hit his only Test hundred whilst there. His career was marred by ill-health. Though he made his first-class debut in 1889, it was not until 1893 that he did anything exceptional and then after a decade of run getting he was obliged to drop out of first-class cricket in May 1904 due to heart trouble, which initially was not regarded as serious, but he in fact never recovered, and died in November of the same year, aged only 35. His love of tobacco unfortunately did little to help his health, for apart from his heart condition he suffered with asthma.

Brown, John Thomas
Professional. *b:* 24.11.1874, Darfield, Yorkshire. *d:* 12.4.1950, Duckmanton, Derbyshire. Brother of William (Yorkshire). Tail end right-hand batsman, right-arm fast bowler. *Team* Yorkshire (1897–1903, 30 matches).
Career batting
30–32–3–333–37*–11.48–0–*ct* 18
Bowling 2071–97–21.35–8–2–8/40
Regarded as one of the fastest bowlers of his time, his career ended suddenly when he dislocated his shoulder.

Brown, Lewis
Professional. *b:* 12.3.1874, Earl Shilton, Leics. *d:* 14.10.1951, Earl Shilton, Leics. Brother of J. H. (Leics). Opening right-hand batsman, right-arm medium pace bowler. *Team* Leicestershire (1896–1903, 62 matches).
Career batting
62–110–7–1660–110–16.11–1–*ct* 23
Bowling 385–7–55.00–0–0–3/39

Brown, Lionel George
Amateur. *b:* 23.4.1872, Ancaster, Lincolnshire. *d:* 16.12.1938, Chorlton, Staffs. Middle/lower order right-hand batsman, wicket-keeper. *Sch* Bedford Modern. *Team* Oxford U (1892).
Career batting
1–2–0–22–14–11.00–0–*ct* 1
His County cricket was for Berkshire and Bedfordshire.

Brown, Reynolds Driver
Amateur. *b:* 6.5.1869, Newcastle, Delaware, USA. *d:* 6.4.1956, Charleston, South Carolina. Son of H. W. (USA) and brother of H. I. (USA). Defensive middle order right-hand batsman, right-arm fast bowler. *Sch* Harvard. *Team* Philadelphia (1891–1903). *Tours* Philadelphians to England 1889 (not first-class) and 1903.
Career batting
18–34–2–532–103–16.62–1–*ct* 6
Bowling 35–0
He achieved very little on his 1903 visit to England, but hit two hundreds in minor matches on the 1889 trip. His best innings was probably 103 for Philadelphia v Bosanquet's Team of 1901. He appeared in three matches for USA v Canada.

Brown, Robin David
Cricketer. *b*: 11.3.1951, Gatooma, Rhodesia. Middle order right-hand batsman, wicket-keeper. *Team* Rhodesia/Zimbabwe (1976/7 to 1982/3). *Tour* Zimbabwe to England 1982.
Career batting
30–57–3–1422–200*–26.33–3–*ct* 37–*st* 9

Brown, Samuel
Professional. *b:* 26.2.1857, Kimberley, Notts. *d:* 5.9.1938, Edgeley, Cheshire. Lower order right-hand batsman, right-arm fast medium bowler. *Team* Nottinghamshire (1896–97, 14 matches).
Career batting
17–23–3–288–43–14.40–0–*ct* 7
Bowling 1159–49–23.65–3–0–6/55

His first-class debut was for North v South at Lord's in 1884. Notts first asked him to play for the County in 1883, but his club, Stockport, refused to release him and later in the same year he made his debut for Cheshire, but his appearance was objected to as he was not qualified.

Brown, Sidney J.
Professional. Middle order batsman. *Team* MCC (1930–33).
Career batting
2–3–0–26–21–8.66–0–*ct* 1

His County cricket was for Hertfordshire.

Brown, Sydney Maurice
Professional. *b:* 8.12.1917, Eltham, Kent. Forcing right-hand opening batsman, good deep field, occasional wicket-keeper. *Team* Middlesex (1937–55, 313 matches).
Career batting
329–580–40–15756–232*–29.17–22–*ct* 152–*st* 2
Bowling 80–3–26.66–0–0–2/19

He hit 1,000 runs in a season nine times, exceeding 2,000 once – 2,078, av 37.78, in 1947. He scored two double centuries, both for Middlesex, his higher being 232* v Somerset (Lord's) 1951.

Brown, Stevens William
Professional. *b:* 15.4.1875, Cliffe, Kent. *d:* 21.10.1957, Watford, Herts. Lower order batsman, bowler. *Team* Kent (1899, 3 matches).
Career batting
3–6–1–3–1*–0.60–0–*ct* 1
Bowling 217–5–43.40–0–0–2/36

Brown, Thomas
Professional. *b:* 9.8.1845, Rusper, Sussex. Lower order right-hand batsman, right-hand medium pace round-arm bowler. *Team* Surrey (1868–74, 9 matches).
Career batting
9–15–2–58–10–4.46–0–*ct* 6
Bowling 123–7–17.57–0–0–4/16

Brown, Thomas
Professional. *b:* 14.6.1848, Bingham, Notts. Brother of John (Notts). Middle order right-hand batsman, right-arm medium pace bowler. *Team* Nottinghamshire (1881, 4 matches).
Career batting
4–7–0–118–74–16.85–0–*ct* 0
Bowling 42–0

Brown, Thomas Austin
Professional. *b:* 11.4.1863, Wollaston, Northants. *d:* 12.3.1930, Dunstable, Bedfordshire. Lower order right-hand batsman, right-arm fast bowler. *Team* MCC (1894–1901).
Career batting
12–22–3–333–64*–17.52–0–*ct* 9
Bowling 342–12–28.50–1–0–6/82

His County cricket was for Northants and Bedfordshire, but he was mainly involved in cricket at Lord's, being on the MCC staff, until forced to retire through ill-health. He also played for Hertfordshire.

Brown, Thomas Charles
Professional. *b:* 25.3.1854, Ampthill, Bedfordshire. *d:* 26.4.1936, Isleworth, Middlesex. Lower order right-hand batsman, right-hand fast-medium round-arm bowler. *Team* Sussex (1890, 6 matches).
Career batting
6–12–1–142–38–12.91–0–*ct* 3
Bowling 161–1–161.00–0–0–1/38

In 1877 and 1878 he resided in Surrey to qualify for the County, but never in fact was included in the County side. He also played for Bedfordshire and Northants (non-first-class).

Brown, William
Professional. *b:* 1892. Lower order batsman, opening bowler. *Team* Lancashire (1919–22, 10 matches).
Career batting
10–17–2–239–39–15.66–0–*ct* 10
Bowling 474–22–21.54–0–0–4/22

Brown, William
Professional. *b:* 13.6.1866, Brierley Hill, Staffs. Middle order right-hand batsman, left-arm medium pace bowler. *Team* Lancashire (1894, 2 matches).
Career batting
2–3–0–17–7–5.66–0–*ct* 1
Bowling 12–0

He also played for Staffordshire.

Brown, William
Professional. *b:* 19.11.1876, Darfield, Yorkshire. *d:* 27.7.1945, Barnsley, Yorkshire. Brother of J. T. (Darfield) (Yorkshire). Tail end right-hand batsman, right-arm fast bowler. *Team* Yorkshire (1902–08, 2 matches).
Career batting
2–2–1–2–2–2.00–0–*ct* 0
Bowling 84–4–21.00–0–0–3/61

Brown, William
Professional. *b:* 11.4.1888, Old Woodhouse, Leics. *d:* 3.9.1964, Heywood, Lancs. Lower order left-hand batsman, left-arm slow medium bowler. *Team* Leicestershire (1910–1919, 46 matches).
Career batting
46–72–23–347–35–7.08–0–*ct* 22
Bowling 3161–114–27.72–4–1–7/51

Brown, William Alfred
Amateur. *b:* 31.7.1912, Toowoomba, Queensland, Australia. Excellent opening right-hand batsman, brilliant field. *Team* New South Wales (1932/3 to 1934/5, 22 matches); Queensland (1936/7 to 1949/50, 50 matches). *Tours* Australia to England 1934, 1938, 1948, to South Africa 1935/6, to New Zealand 1945/6, 1949/50. *Tests* Australia (1934–48, 22 matches).
Career batting
189–284–15–13838–265*–51.44–39–*ct* 110–*st* 1
Bowling 110–6–18.33–0–0–4/16
Test batting
22–35–1–1592–206*–46.82–4–*ct* 14

On each of his three visits to England he hit over 1,000 runs, having an almost identical average on the last two tours – 1,448 runs (av 57.92) in 1934 and 1,854 (av 57.93) in 1938. His two great innings in England were both at Lord's. In 1934 he hit 105, the only score of substance for Australia in that match, and in 1938 he made 206*. Despite his high scoring in 1948, he was not required in three of the Tests. At times Brown could be a most stubborn batsman, but usually he was an elegant quick-scoring player. His highest score was 265* for Australians v Derbyshire at Chesterfield in 1938.

Brown, William Cecil
Amateur. *b:* 13.11.1900, Wellingborough, Northants. Middle order right-hand batsman. *Sch* Charterhouse. *Team* Northants (1925–37, 127 matches).
Career batting
127–214–29–2601–103*–14.06–1–*ct* 57
Bowling 1–0

He captained Northants 1932–35 and was later Honorary Secretary.

Brown, Walter Medlicott Rodney
Amateur. *b:* 31.7.1868, Benares, India. *d:* 13.8.1954, Cheltenham, Gloucs. Middle order right-hand batsman. *Sch* Cheltenham. *Team* Gloucestershire (1895, 1 match).
Career batting
1–2–0–19–11–9.50–0–*ct* 0

Brown, William Stanley Alston
Amateur. *b:* 23.5.1877, Clifton, Bristol, Gloucs. *d:* 12.9.1952, Bristol, Gloucs. Attractive middle-order right-hand batsman, medium/slow left-arm bowler, excellent field. *Sch* Leys School. *Team* Gloucestershire (1896–1919, 161 matches); London County (1900).
Career batting
164–277–23–4820–155–18.97–2–*ct* 140
Bowling 6510–195–33.38–3–0–6/56

One of the leading all-round sportsmen of his County, Brown represented Gloucestershire at soccer, hockey, lacrosse, golf and bowls, as well as playing rugby for Bristol.

Browne, Cyril Ross
Amateur. *b:* 7.2.1893, King's Norton, Warwickshire. *d:* 30.4.1948, Eastbourne, Sussex. Middle order right-hand batsman, right-arm medium pace bowler. *Teams* Cambridge U (1913–14); Sussex (1913–19, 3 matches).
Career batting
10–18–0–146–23–8.11–0–*ct* 2
Bowling 329–11–29.90–0–0–4/8

Browne, Cyril Rutherford
Amateur. *b:* 8.10.1890, Bridgetown, Barbados. *d:* 12.1.1964, Georgetown, British Guiana. Brother of C. A. (Barbados). Hard-hitting middle/lower order right-hand batsman, right-arm medium pace bowler. *Teams* Barbados (1908/9 to 1910/11); British Guiana (1921/2 to 1938/9). *Tours* West Indies to England 1923, 1928. *Tests* West Indies (1928 to 1929/30, 4 matches).
Career batting
74–115–11–2077–103–19.97–3–*ct* 59
Bowling 6228–278–22.40–17–6–8/58
Test batting
4–8–1–176–70*–25.14–0–*ct* 1
Bowling 288–6–48.00–0–0–2/72

On both tours to England he produced some useful all-round performances, without doing anything outstanding. Before the First World War he was seen in London Club cricket, being in England to study law.

Browne, Rev Elliott Kenworthy
Amateur. *b:* 10.10.1847. Goldington, Bedfordshire. *d:* 10.3.1915, Bournemouth, Hants. Brother of G. E. K. (Gloucs). Middle order right-

hand batsman, right-arm fast bowler, useful deep field. *Sch* Rugby. *Team* Gloucestershire (1872, 4 matches).
Career batting
4–6–1–136–52–27.20–0–*ct* 1
Bowling 19–1–19.00–0–0–1/7
He was not in the Eleven whilst at Oxford. In 1868 he appeared for the Gentlemen of Hampshire, but never for that County in first-class matches.

Browne, Canon Francis Bernard Ross
Amateur. *b:* 28.7.1899, Eastbourne. *d:* 11.3.1970, Pewsey, Wiltshire. Lower order right-hand batsman, right-arm fast-medium bowler. *Sch* Eastbourne. *Teams* Sussex (1919–32, 49 matches); Cambridge U (1921–22, blue 1922).
Career batting
75–89–31–333–26*–5.74–0–*ct* 34
Bowling 5223–252–20.72–15–1–8/39
He had a very strange delivery, bowling off the wrong foot, which earned him the soubriquet 'Tishy', after a cross-legged racehorse of the time.

Browne, Franklin Doughty
Amateur. *b:* 4.3.1873, Tufnell Park, London. *d:* 12.8.1946, Cobham, Kent. Middle order right-hand batsman. *Sch* Dulwich. *Team* Kent (1899–1903, 10 matches).
Career batting
10–17–3–262–53*–18.71–0–*ct* 8
Whilst at Oxford he captained Trinity College, but did not appear in any first-class matches.

Browne, Gerald Elliott Kenworthy
(later Kenworthy-Browne)
Amateur. *b:* 14.5.1850, Goldington, Bedfordshire. *d:* 6.7.1910, Glencormac, Co Wicklow, Ireland. Brother of E. K. (Gloucs). Middle order right-hand batsman. *Sch* Rugby. *Team* Gloucestershire (1874, 2 matches).
Career batting
2–3–0–20–12–6.66–0–*ct* 0
He also played non-first-class cricket for Somerset.

Browne, George Fairbrother
Amateur. *b:* 1835. *d:* 28.5.1919, Lowestoft, Suffolk. Middle order batsman. *Team* Sussex (1864, 1 match); Middlesex (1864, 1 match).
Career batting
2–3–0–19–11–6.33–0–*ct* 0
Since he played for Sussex against Middlesex, it is probable that he was a native of the former County, but resided in the latter in 1864 – both his first-class appearances took place on the Middlesex home ground at Islington.

Browne, Horace James
Amateur. *b:* 1.12.1842, Cambridge. *d:* 19.3.1896, Byfleet, Surrey. Middle order batsman. *Sch* Bury St Edmunds. *Team* Cambridgeshire (1865–69, 7 matches).
Career batting
7–13–2–111–28–10.09–0–*ct* 0

Brownell, Eric Lindsay Douglas
Amateur. *b:* 7.11.1876, Hobart, Tasmania. *d:* 22.10.1945, Windsor, New South Wales, Australia. Middle order batsman. *Team* Worcestershire (1908, 1 match).
Career batting
1–2–0–28–21–14.00–0–*ct* 1
He also played in Ceylon but not in first-class matches.

Brownfield, Douglas Harold
Amateur. *b:* 30.3.1856, Hanley, Staffs. *d:* 5.8.1917, Llandudno, Wales. Middle order right-hand batsman. *Sch* Rugby. *Team* An England XI (1888).
Career batting
1–2–0–4–4–2.00–0–*ct* 0
He played for Staffordshire.

Brownhill, Thomas
Professional. *b:* 10.10.1838, Sheffield, Yorkshire. *d:* 6.1.1915, Wortley, Yorkshire. Middle order right-hand batsman, excellent deep field. *Team* Yorkshire (1862–71, 12 matches).
Career batting
14–26–4–202–25–9.18–0–*ct* 12

Browning, Francis Henry
Amateur. *b:* 23.6.1868, Dublin. *d:* 26.4.1916, Dublin. Right-hand batsman, wicket-keeper. *Sch* Marlborough. *Team* Ireland (1902–09).
Career batting
9–18–1–356–56–20.94–0–*ct* 7–*st* 3
He was 'killed by the Irish rebels'.

Browning, Frederick Henry
Amateur. *b:* 1.8.1870, Thingoe, Suffolk. *d:* 13.10.1929, Flaxley, Gloucs. Sound middle order right-hand batsman, wicket-keeper. *Sch* Wellington. *Team* MCC (1907). *Tour* MCC to North America 1907.
Career batting
3–5–1–38–27–9.50–0–*ct* 0
He did not appear in any first-class matches whilst at Oxford, but represented his University at rackets in 1893 and 1895.

Brownlee, Leigh Dunlop
Amateur. *b:* 17.12.1882, Redland, Bristol, Gloucs. *d:* 22.9.1955, Clifton, Bristol. Brother of

W. M. (Gloucs). Middle order right-hand batsman, slow right-arm bowler, good deep field. *Sch* Clifton. *Teams* Gloucestershire (1901–09, 65 matches); Oxford U (1902–04, blue 1904); Somerset (1902, 1 match).
Career batting
82–138–5–1946–103–14.63–1–*ct* 62
Bowling 407–15–27.13–0–0–3/40

Brownlee, Wilfred Methven
Amateur. *b:* 18.4.1890, Cotham, Bristol, Gloucs. *d:* 12.10.1914, Wyke Regis, Dorset. Brother of L. D. (Gloucs and Oxford U). Free scoring middle order right-hand batsman, right-arm fast-medium bowler, brilliant field. *Sch* Clifton. *Team* Gloucestershire (1909–14, 32 matches).
Career batting
33–53–4–773–68–15.77–0–*ct* 26
Bowling 1251–46–27.19–3–0–6/61

Brownrigg, George Neville
Professional. *b:* 16.7.1896, Queen's County, Ireland. *d:* 1981, Westminster, London. Lower order batsman, left-arm bowler. *Sch* Rossall. *Team* Sussex (1921–22, 3 matches).
Career batting
3–5–2–26–11–8.66–0–*ct* 2
Bowling 103–4–25.75–0–0–4/31

Bruce, Hon Clarence Napier
(succeeded to the title 3rd Baron Aberdare in 1929)
Amateur. *b:* 2.8.1885, London. *d:* 4.10.1957. Motoring near Kotor, Yugoslavia, he was drowned when the car in which he was travelling went over a precipice into a river. Hard-hitting middle order right-hand batsman. *Sch* Winchester. *Teams* Oxford U (1905–08, blue 1907–08); Middlesex (1908–29, 62 matches); Wales (1925–29).
Career batting
96–159–10–4326–149–29.03–6–*ct* 34
Bowling 13–0

A brilliant rackets player he was the Amateur Champion in 1922 and 1931 and ten times Doubles Champion. He represented Oxford at both rackets and golf and for 20 years was on the International Olympic Executive.

Bruce, William
Amateur. *b:* 22.5.1864, South Yarra, Victoria, Australia. *d:* 3.8.1925. He was found drowned at St Kilda, Victoria. Aggressive middle order left-hand batsman, left-arm medium pace bowler. *Team* Victoria (1882/3 to 1903/4, 61 matches). *Tours* Australia to England 1886, 1893, to North America 1893. *Tests* Australia (1884/5 to 1894/5, 14 matches).
Career batting
145–250–11–5731–191–23.97–4–*ct* 103
Bowling 4244–143–29.67–5–0–7/72
Test batting
14–26–2–702–80–29.25–0–*ct* 12
Bowling 440–12–36.66–0–0–3/88

He was an excellent hitter, but had little defence. His first visit to England in 1886 was not successful, but in 1893 he scored 1227 runs (av 25.01) and his best innings was 191 v Combined Universities, made in 220 minutes. His best year in Test cricket was 1891/2 in Australia.

Bruce-Lockhart, John Harold
Amateur. *b:* 4.3.1889, Beith, Ayrshire, Scotland. *d:* 4.6.1956, Marylebone, London. Father of R. B. (Cambridge U). Lower order right-hand batsman, leg break and googly bowler. *Sch* Sedbergh. *Teams* Cambridge U (1909–11, blue 1909–10); Scotland (1910–11, 2 matches).
Career batting
24–38–3–306–42–8.74–0–*ct* 12
Bowling 2418–121–19.90–10–3–8/45

Cambridge were greatly criticised for omitting him from the 1911 University match. His County cricket was for Berkshire. An excellent rugby footballer, he represented Cambridge and Scotland at fly half.

Bruce-Lockhart, Rab Brougham
Amateur. *b:* 1.12.1916, Rugby, Warwickshire. Son of J. H. (Cambridge U and Scotland). Middle/lower order right-hand batsman, leg break bowler. *Sch* Edinburgh Academy. *Team* Cambridge U (1937–38).
Career batting
3–5–1–32–17–8.00–0–*ct* 3
Bowling 146–1–146.00–0–0–1/76

Brumfitt, Jack
Amateur. *b:* 18.2.1917, Guiseley, Yorkshire. Middle order right-hand batsman. *Team* Yorkshire (1938, 1 match).
Career batting
1–1–0–9–9–9.00–0–*ct* 0

Brune, Charles Julius
Amateur. *b:* 16.4.1843, Cuba. *d:* 13.1.1877, Boulogne, France. Stubborn defensive lower order right-hand batsman, right-hand medium fast pace round-arm bowler, good deep field. *Team* Cambridge U (1866–69, blue 1867–69); Middlesex (1866–75, 19 matches).
Career batting
56–91–20–738–41–10.39–0–*ct* 21
Bowling 1872–107–17.49–6–1–8/31

He was the first Treasurer of the Incogniti (commencing 1861). He also played for Hertfordshire and Staffordshire.

Brunskill, John Handfield
Amateur. *b:* 17.4.1875, Dublin. *d:* 21.7.1940, Lincoln. Left-hand batsman, right-arm medium pace bowler. *Team* Dublin University (1895).
Career batting
4–8–0–134–58–16.75–0–*ct* 0
Bowling 50–0

Brunton, Rev John du Vallon
Amateur. *b:* 23.7.1869, Benares, India. *d:* 12.11.1962, Knutsford, Cheshire. Middle order right-hand batsman. *Sch* Lancaster GS. *Team* Cambridge U (1894, blue).
Career batting
6–11–0–258–66–23.45–0–*ct* 4
He was also a rugby blue, playing three times against Oxford.

Brunwin, Herbert Jack
Amateur. *b:* 28.4.1912, Layer-de-la-Haye, Essex. Tail end right-hand batsman, right-arm medium-fast bowler. *Team* Essex (1937, 1 match).
Career batting
1–1–1–2–2*–no av–0–*ct* 0
Bowling 5–1–5.00–0–0–1/5

Bruton, Charles Lamb
Amateur. *b:* 6.4.1890, Gloucester. *d:* 26.3.1969, Lower Shiplake, Oxon. Middle order right-hand batsman. *Sch* Radley. *Team* Gloucestershire (1922, 3 matches).
Career batting
3–6–1–60–24–12.00–0–*ct* 0
He was Resident Commissioner in Swaziland 1937–42 and Commissioner of the East African Refugee Association 1942–47.

Brutton, Charles Phipps
Amateur. *b:* 20.1.1899, Southsea, Hampshire. *d:* 11.5.1964, Dorchester. Son of Septimus (Hants), nephew of E. B. (Liverpool). Middle order right-hand batsman. *Sch* Winchester. *Team* Hampshire (1921–30, 81 matches).
Career batting
82–129–12–2055–119*–17.56–1–*ct* 35
Bowling 125–0
He also appeared for Denbighshire, Dorset and Cheshire.

Brutton, Rev Ernest Bartholomew
Amateur. *b:* 29.7.1864, Newcastle-on-Tyne. *d:* 19.4.1922, Aylesbeare, Devon. Brother of Septimus (Hants) and uncle of C. P. (Hants). Hard-hitting right-hand batsman, right-arm fast bowler. *Sch* Durham. *Teams* C. I. Thornton's XI (1885); Liverpool and District (1892).
Career batting
2–4–1–33–18*–11.00–0–*ct* 1
Bowling 37–0
He represented Northumberland and Devon. An excellent rugby footballer, he gained a blue at Cambridge and went on to represent England.

Brutton, Septimus
Amateur. *b:* 1869, Newcastle-on-Tyne. *d:* 29.9.1933, Marylebone, London. Brother of E. B. (Cambridge U, Northumberland), father of C. P. (Hants). Middle order batsman. *Sch* Leatherhead. *Team* Hampshire (1904, 1 match).
Career batting
1–2–0–22–15–11.00–0–*ct* 1
Before playing for Hampshire he appeared for Northumberland.

Bruyns, André
Cricketer. *b:* 19.9.1946, Pietermaritzburg, South Africa. Excellent middle order right-hand batsman, wicket-keeper. *Teams* Western Province (1965/6 to 1976/7); Natal (1972/3). *Tour* South African Universities to England 1967.
Career batting
90–160–9–5050–197–33.44–11–*ct* 106
Bowling 25–1–25.00–0–0–1/1
He is also a notable rugby footballer.

Bryan, Frank
Amateur. *b:* 1853, Amersham, Buckinghamshire. *d:* 11.6.1923, Quainton, Buckinghamshire. Lower order batsman, wicket-keeper. *Team* Middlesex (1891, 1 match).
Career batting
1–2–0–0–0–0.00–0–*ct* 0

Bryan, Godfrey James
Amateur. *b:* 29.12.1902, Beckenham, Kent. Brother of J. L. (Cambridge U and Kent) and R. T. (Kent). Excellent opening/middle order left-hand batsman, slow bowler. *Sch* Wellington. *Team* Kent (1920–33, 51 matches).
Career batting
70–114–8–3192–229–30.11–6–*ct* 46
Bowling 1753–35–50.08–1–0–5/148
Bryan was an exceptional schoolboy batsman, hitting 699 runs (av 116.50) in his last year at Wellington. On his first-class debut in August of the same year (Kent v Notts, Trent Bridge, 1920) he hit 124. Joining the Army and being stationed abroad meant that his County cricket was very limited. His final first-class match was for the Army in 1935. His highest score was 229 for Combined Services v South Africans at Portsmouth in 1924.

Bryan, John
Amateur. *b:* 17.10.1841, Lower Slaughter, Gloucs. *d:* 24.6.1909, Minchinhampton, Gloucs. Middle order right-hand batsman, excellent long-stop. *Sch* Gloucester College. *Team* Gloucestershire (1873, 2 matches).
Career batting
2–3–1–34–24–17.00–0–*ct* 4

Bryan, John Lindsay
Amateur. *b:* 26.5.1896, Beckenham, Kent. Brother of G. J. (Kent) and R. T. (Kent). Opening/middle order left-hand batsman, excellent cover field. *Sch* Rugby. *Teams* Kent (1919–32, 119 matches); Cambridge U (1921, blue). *Tour* MCC to Australia 1924/5.
Career batting
165–260–20–8702–236–36.25–17–*ct* 89
Bowling 675–15–45.00–0–0–2/18

Bryan had a most unusual career at Cambridge; in 1919 and 1920 he was not even afforded a trial, but in 1921 hit a century in the Seniors' Match and ended the season top of the batting table, being so successful that he was chosen as a Wisden 'Cricketer of the Year'. In 1921 he hit 1,858 runs, av 50.21. Thereafter he could only play County cricket in August owing to his scholastic duties, but in most seasons produced a few brilliant innings. He hit two double centuries, the highest being 236 for Kent v Hants at Canterbury in 1923. His final first-class match was for Leveson-Gower's XI in 1933.

Bryan, Ronald Thurston
Amateur. *b:* 30.7.1898, Beckenham. *d:* 27.7.1970, Pevensey Bay, Sussex. Brother of G. J. (Kent) and J. L. (Cambridge U and Kent). Middle order left-hand batsman, leg break and googly bowler. *Sch* Rugby. *Team* Kent (1920–37, 40 matches).
Career batting
40–60–9–1154–89*–22.62–0–*ct* 30
Bowling 22–1–22.00–0–0–1/9

Like his brothers his profession prevented his regular participation in County cricket, though in 1937 he obtained three months' leave of absence to captain Kent.

Bryan, William
Professional. *b:* 22.9.1856, Kimberley, Notts. *d:* 22.5.1933, Cambridge. Lower order right-hand batsman, right-arm medium pace bowler. *Team* South v North (1886).
Career batting
1–2–0–11–7–5.50–0–*ct* 0
Bowling 14–0

His County cricket was for Cambridgeshire, commencing 1891.

Bryan
Professional. *b:* West Indies. Middle order batsman, change bowler. *Team* MCC (1902).
Career batting
1–2–0–10–5–5.00–0–*ct* 0
Bowling 15–0

Bryans, F. A.
Amateur. Bowler. *Teams* Leveson-Gower's XI (1933); Argentina (1926/7 to 1929/30).
Career batting
9–17–2–240–65–16.00–0–*ct* 3
Bowling 420–18–23.33–1–0–5/67

Bryant, David John
Cricketer. *b:* 29.10.1950, London. Tail end right-hand batsman, right-arm fast medium bowler. *Team* Oxford U (1970–71).
Career batting
6–10–7–19–6*–6.33–0–*ct* 1
Bowling 423–8–52.87–0–0–3/40

Bryant, Edwin Harvey
Amateur. *b:* 12.9.1886, Bromsgrove, Worcs. *d:* 24.10.1948, Barnt Green, Worcs. Middle order batsman. *Team* Worcestershire (1923–25, 16 matches).
Career batting
16–30–0–329–63–10.96–0–*ct* 5

Bryant, Herbert William
Amateur. *b:* 30.6.1867, Uxbridge, Middlesex. *d:* 23.2.1910, St Mary, Azores. Punishing lower order right-hand batsman, excellent wicket-keeper. *Team* Middlesex (1888–89, 8 matches).
Career batting
8–12–3–71–38–7.88–0–*ct* 13–*st* 12

The demands of business took him abroad in 1890 and he was therefore lost to County cricket.

Bryant, James Mark
Professional. *baptised:* 24.10.1826, Caterham, Surrey. *d:* 10.12.1881, Sale, Victoria, Australia. Right-hand batsman, right-arm medium pace bowler. *Teams* Surrey (1852, 2 matches); Victoria (1856/7 to 1861/2, 8 matches).
Career batting
11–19–2–182–32–10.70–0–*ct* 9
Bowling 238–22–10.81–0–0–3/11

He emigrated to Australia shortly after appearing for Surrey and was for some years the curator of the Melbourne Cricket Ground.

Bryant, Leonard Eric
Professional. *b:* 2.6.1936, Weston-super-Mare, Somerset. Tail end left-hand batsman, slow left-arm bowler. *Team* Somerset (1958–60, 22 matches).

Career batting
22–29–14–133–17–8.86–0–*ct* 10
Bowling 943–34–27.97–1–0–5/64

Bryant, Michael
Cricketer. *b*: 5.4.1959, Beacon, Camborne, Cornwall. Middle order right-hand batsman, right-arm fast medium bowler. *Team* Somerset (1982, 2 matches).
Career batting
2–2–0–6–6–3.00–0–*ct* 1
Bowling 158–2–79.00–0–0–1/29
He played for Cornwall 1978 to 1981.

Buchanan, David
Amateur. *b:* 16.1.1830, Edinburgh, Scotland. *d:* 30.5.1900, Northfield, Rugby. Lower order left-hand batsman, originally fast left round-arm bowler, but changed to slow-medium spin bowling about 1864. *Sch* Rugby. *Teams* Cambridge U (1850–51, blue 1850).
Career batting
62–106–39–257–27–3.83–0–*ct* 17
Bowling 5718–366+42–15.62–40–11–9/82
He appeared for Warwickshire (non-first-class) from 1862 to 1885. He was about 40 years old before he made much of a mark in first-class cricket and declined an invitation to tour Australia with the 1878/9 team. Regarded by many as the best amateur slow bowler in the 1870s, he wrote a much valued essay on the subject, which was published in 1894. He also played for Lincolnshire. His final first-class match was for Gentlemen in 1881. His best bowling was 9/82 for Gentlemen v Players at the Oval in 1868.

Buchanan, John Nevile
Amateur. *b:* 30.5.1887, Grahamstown, South Africa. *d:* 31.10.1969, St John's Wood, London. Opening/middle order right-hand batsman, right-arm medium fast bowler, brilliant field. *Sch* Charterhouse. *Team* Cambridge U (1906–09, blue all four years).
Career batting
34–60–2–1536–118–26.48–4–*ct* 45
Bowling 1094–26–42.07–0–0–4/56
His County cricket was for Buckinghamshire. His final first-class match was for Free Foresters in 1922.

Buck, William Dalton
Cricketer. *b:* 30.9.1946, Southampton. Lower order right-hand batsman, right-arm medium pace bowler. *Teams* Somerset (1969, 1 match); Hampshire (1969, 1 match).
Career batting
2–2–0–11–6–5.50–0–*ct* 0
Bowling 135–2–67.50–0–0–2/54

Buck's career in first-class cricket is a curiosity – he played for Somerset and for Hampshire in the same season, but neither game was in the County Championship, the Somerset match being against New Zealanders and the Hampshire one against West Indians.

Buckenham, Claude Percival
Professional. *b:* 16.1.1876, Herne Hill, Surrey. *d:* 23.2.1937, Dundee, Scotland. Middle/lower order right-hand batsman, right-arm fast bowler. *Sch* Alleyn's. *Team* Essex (1899–1914, 258 matches). *Tour* MCC to South Africa 1909/10. *Tests* England (1909/10, 4 matches).
Career batting
307–468–79–5641–124–14.50–2–*ct* 172
Bowling 29110–1150–25.31–85–17–8/33
Test batting
4–7–0–43–17–6.14–0–*ct* 2
Bowling 593–21–28.23–1–0–5/115
He took 100 wickets in a season 6 times (best 135, av 24.13, in 1906). Regarded as one of the deadliest fast bowlers of his time, he would have had a much better record had it not been for catches missed in the slips.

Buckingham, Amyand David
Amateur. *b:* 28.1.1930, Sydney, Australia. Opening/middle order right-hand batsman, right-arm off break bowler. *Team* Cambridge U (1955).
Career batting
10–20–1–349–61–18.36–0–*ct* 3
Bowling 43–0
His final first-class match was for Free Foresters in 1960.

Buckingham, John
Professional. *b:* 21.1.1903, Grimethorpe, Yorkshire. Forcing middle/lower order right-hand batsman, wicket-keeper. *Team* Warwickshire (1933–39, 93 matches).
Career batting
93–142–23–2840–137*–23.87–3–*ct* 132–*st* 92
He hit 1,054 runs, av 31.00, in 1938.

Bucklan, Joseph Edwin
Professional. *b:* 24.9.1916, Surrey. Lower order batsman, left-arm fast-medium bowler. *Team* Somerset (1948, 1 match).
Career batting
1–2–2–17–17*–no av–0–*ct* 2
Bowling 55–3–18.33–0–0–2/35

Buckland, Edward Hastings
Amateur. *b:* 20.6.1864, Laleham-on-Thames, Middlesex. *d:* 10.2.1906, Winchester, Hants. Brother of F. M. (Oxford U and Middlesex). Middle order right-hand batsman, originally fast

under-arm, afterwards slow off break bowler. *Sch* Marlborough. *Teams* Oxford U (1884–87, blue all four years); Middlesex (1885–88, 9 matches); Hampshire (1895, 4 matches). *Tour* Sanders to North America 1886.
Career batting
48–82–4–1414–148–18.12–1–*ct* 54
Bowling 2159–110–19.62–8–1–7/17
He also represented Oxford U at rackets and played both soccer and golf to a high standard. He also played for Wiltshire.

Buckland, Francis Matthew
Amateur. *b:* 27.8.1854, Laleham-on-Thames, Middlesex. *d:* 7.3.1913, Bexhill-on-Sea, Sussex. Brother of E. H. (Oxford U and Middlesex). Middle order right-hand batsman, right-hand medium pace round-arm bowler, close field. *Sch* Eton. *Teams* Oxford U (1874–77, blue 1875–77); Middlesex (1877–78, 5 matches).
Career batting
24–40–5–829–117*–23.68–2–*ct* 21
Bowling 1199–71–16.88–4–2–6/48
Whilst at Eton he bowled leg-breaks, but in first-class cricket relied entirely on accuracy of length and direction. His final first-class appearance was for MCC in 1891.

Buckland, Tom George
Professional. *b:* 20.11.1860, Sutton-in-Ashfield, Notts. *d:* 18.7.1915, Sutton-in-Ashfield, Notts. Lower order right-hand batsman, right-arm fast-medium bowler. *Team* Nottinghamshire (1888, 2 matches).
Career batting
2–3–1–23–12–11.50–0–*ct* 0
Bowling 68–4–17.00–0–0–2/13

Buckle, Frederick
Professional. *b:* 25.9.1849, Thames Ditton, Surrey. *d:* 1884, Kingston-on-Thames, Surrey. Lower order right-hand batsman, wicket-keeper, change bowler. *Team* Surrey (1867–72, 15 matches).
Career batting
15–25–4–156–31–7.42–0–*ct* 4
Bowling 165–6–27.50–0–0–2/40

Buckley, Cyril Francis Stewart
Amateur. *b:* 21.2.1905, Chelsea, London. *d:* 11.6.1974, London. Middle order batsman. *Sch* Eton. *Team* Leveson-Gower's XI (1934–36).
Career batting
3–5–0–53–50–10.60–0–*ct* 5
He also played for Berkshire.

Buckley, George Arthur
Amateur. *b:* 3.2.1889, Skegby, Notts. *d:* 1.12.1935, Norton Lees, Yorkshire. Middle order right-hand batsman, right-arm fast medium bowler. *Team* Derbyshire (1921, 1 match).
Career batting
1–2–0–10–8–5.00–0–*ct* 1
Bowling 48–0
Buckley was selected to play for Notts in 1913 v Leics, but forced to withdraw due to injury. He also played for Cheshire. A useful soccer player he appeared for Sheffield United.

Bucknell, John
Professional. *b:* 1872, Taunton, Somerset. *d:* 5.3.1925, Middleton-on-Row, Co Durham. Lower order batsman, right-arm medium pace bowler. *Team* Somerset (1895–1905, 10 matches).
Career batting
10–19–7–144–33–12.00–0–*ct* 3
Bowling 617–10–61.70–0–0–3/93
He also played for Durham.

Buckston, George Moreton
Amateur. *b:* 12.3.1881, Hope, Derbyshire. *d:* 24.11.1942, Sutton-on-the-Hill, Derbyshire. Father of R. H. R. (Derbyshire). Lower order right-hand batsman, wicket-keeper. *Sch* Eton. *Teams* Cambridge U (1903); Derbyshire (1905–21, 33 matches).
Career batting
39–75–3–852–96–11.83–0–*ct* 8–*st* 1
Most of his first-class cricket was confined to 1921, when he was appointed captain of Derbyshire and served the County well at a time of great difficulty.

Buckston, Robin Henry Rowland
Amateur. *b:* 10.10.1908, Kensington, London. *d:* 16.5.1967, Burton-on-Trent, Staffs. Son of G. M. (Cambridge U and Derbyshire). Lower order right-hand batsman, wicket-keeper. *Sch* Eton. *Team* Derbyshire (1928–39, 72 matches).
Career batting
74–104–24–944–60*–11.80–0–*ct* 18–*st* 2
Bowling 10–0
He captained Derbyshire from 1937 to 1939.

Budd, Edward Hayward
Amateur. *b:* 23.2.1785, Great Missenden, Bucks. *d:* 29.3.1875, Wroughton, Wilts. Hard-htting middle order right-hand batsman, medium pace under-arm bowler, but with his hand extended from his side, wicket-keeper. *Teams* Middlesex (1808); Norfolk (1820); Hampshire (1823).
Career batting
73–125–9–2728–105–23.51–1–*ct* 51–*st* 27
Bowling 173 wickets, no analyses
He first played at Lord's in 1802 and for about 30 years was one of the best all-rounder cricketers

in England, his complete career extending over 50 years. His first important match was for H. C. Woolridge's XI in 1803 and his final one for England in 1831.

Budd, William Lloyd
Professional. *b:* 25.10.1913, Hawkley, Hants. Lower order right-hand batsman, right-arm fast medium bowler. *Team* Hampshire (1934–46, 60 matches).
Career batting
60–98–16–941–77*–11.47–0–*ct* 24
Bowling 2506–64–39.15–0–0–4/22
He became a Test match umpire.

Budden, Charles
Professional. *b:* 18.7.1879, Fareham, Hants. *d:* 26.11.1969, Winchester. Lower order batsman, bowler. *Team* Hampshire (1900, 2 matches).
Career batting
2–3–1–35–32*–17.50–0–*ct* 0
Bowling 102–2–51.00–0–0–1/30

Budden, James Thomas W. F.
Amateur. *b:* 1882, Southampton. *d:* 1965, Southampton. Useful bowler. *Team* Hampshire (1912, 1 match).
Career batting
1 match, did not bat–*ct* 0
Bowling 46–0

Budgen, Harry
Amateur. *b:* 1.4.1879, Reigate, Surrey. *d:* 13.3.1944, Redhill, Surrey. Lower order right-hand batsman, slow left-arm bowler. *Team* Surrey (1904–09, 3 matches).
Career batting
3–4–0–58–30–14.50–0–*ct* 1
Bowling 213–3–71.00–0–0–3/112

Budgen, Henry Richard
Professional. *b:* 1865, Brighton, Sussex. *d:* 1929, Romford, Essex. Right-hand batsman. *Team* Sussex (1886–92, 10 matches).
Career batting
10–20–4–120–32–7.50–0–*ct* 6
Bowling 19–0

Buggé, David Anthony Bowdell
Cricketer. *b:* 12.12.1956, Aden. Tail end right-hand batsman, right-arm medium fast bowler. *Sch* Cranleigh. *Team* Oxford U (1977).
Career batting
1 match, did not bat –*ct* 0
Bowling 22–0

Bulcock, Leslie
Professional. *b:* 5.1.1913, Colne, Lancashire. Right-hand batsman, off break bowler. *Team* Lancashire (1946, 1 match).
Career batting
1–1–0–1–1–1.00–0–*ct* 0
Bowling 90–2–45.00–0–0–2/41

Bull, Arthur Herbert
Amateur. *b:* 23.1.1892, Wellingborough, Northants. *d:* 18.12.1965, Ingoldisthorpe, Norfolk. Lower order right-hand batsman. *Sch* Wellingborough, Mill Hill. *Team* Northants (1913–24, 36 matches).
Career batting
36–57–4–538–44–10.15–0–*ct* 12
He captained Northants in 1923 and 1924. Much better known as a bowls player, he represented England 45 times and captained the national side in 1939.

Bull, Charles Harry
Professional. *b:* 29.3.1909, Lewisham, Kent. *d:* 28.5.1939. He was killed in a road accident at Margaretting, Chelmsford. Opening/middle order right-hand batsman. *Teams* Kent (1929–30, 4 matches); Worcestershire (1931–39, 171 matches).
Career batting
175–308–20–6801–161–23.61–5–*ct* 63
Bowling 120–0
He hit 1,000 runs in a season 4 times with 1,619, av 28.40, in 1937 his best.

Bull, Eric Alister
Amateur. *b:* 28.9.1886, Bourke, New South Wales, Australia. *d:* 14.5.1954, Mt Kuring-Gai, New South Wales, Australia. Middle order right-hand batsman, right-arm medium/leg break bowler. *Team* New South Wales (1913/4 to 1914/5, 3 matches). *Tours* AIF to England and South Africa 1919; AIF in Australia 1919/20.
Career batting
23–33–2–595–42–19.19–0–*ct* 8
Bowling 100–4–25.00–0–0–2/8
He had a very modest record in English first-class cricket in 1919.

Bull, Frederick George
Amateur, but changed to professional in 1905. *b:* 2.4.1875, Hackney, Essex. *d:* 16.9.1910. He was found drowned at St Annes-on-Sea, Lancashire. Tail end right-hand batsman, right-arm slow off break bowler. *Teams* Essex (1895–1900, 88 matches); Scotland (1905). *Tour* Warner to United States 1897.
Career batting
95–138–35–1274–51–12.36–0–*ct* 46
Bowling 9042–416–21.74–34–7–9/93

He took 100 wickets in a season twice (best 120, av 21.95, in 1897). His best bowling was 9/93 for Essex v Surrey at the Oval in 1897.

Bull, G.
Professional. Lower order batsman, bowler. *Team* Hampshire (1900, 2 matches).
Career batting
2–3–1–12–10–6.00–0–*ct* 0
Bowling 25–0

Bull, Henry Edward
Amateur. *b:* 8.3.1843, Lothbury Rectory, Newport Pagnell, Bucks. *d:* 31.5.1905, Maids Moreton, near Buckingham. Opening right-hand batsman, excellent deep field. *Sch* Westminster. *Team* Oxford U (1863, blue).
Career batting
21–36–1–494–46–14.11–0–*ct* 9
Bowling 20–0
His County cricket was for Oxfordshire 1863–64 and Buckinghamshire 1864–68, being the first Hon. Sec. of the latter County. He also played for Northants (non-first-class), Herts and Bedfordshire. His final first-class match was for MCC in 1876.

Bull
Professional. Lower order batsman, change bowler. *Team* Kent (1871, 1 match).
Career batting
1–2–1–10–8*–10.00–0–*ct* 0
Bowling 22–0

Bullen, Christopher Keith
Cricketer. *b*: 5.11.1962, Clapham, London. Middle order right-hand batsman. *Team* Surrey (1982, 1 match).
Career batting
1 match, did not bat – *ct* 0
Bowling 29–0

Buller, Charles Edward
Professional. *b:* 23.8.1892, Wellingborough, Northants. *d:* 16.12.1969, Northampton. Tail end right-hand batsman, bowler. *Team* Northants (1931, 1 match).
Career batting
1–2–1–2–1*–2.00–0–*ct* 0
Bowling 35–0

Buller, Charles Francis
Amateur. *b:* 26.5.1846, Colombo, Ceylon. *d:* 22.11.1906, Lyme Regis, Dorset. Son of Arthur (Gentlemen 1836). Very stylish right-hand middle order batsman, right-hand slow round-arm bowler, excellent deep field. *Sch* Harrow. *Team* Middlesex (1865–77, 24 matches).
Career batting
90–158–14–3140–106–21.80–2–*ct* 46
Bowling 220–7+5–31.42–1–0–5/?
His debut in first-class matches was for England v XIII of Kent in 1864. He also played for Devon. An excellent athlete he was a noted long jumper.

Buller, Eric Tremayne
(later Buller-Leybourne-Popham)
Amateur. *b:* 3.1.1894, Highworth, Wilts. *d:* 8.8.1973, Bath, Somerset. Lower order batsman, useful bowler. *Sch* Harrow. *Team* Army (1919).
Career batting
1–2–1–58–46–58.00–0–*ct* 0
Bowling 71–0
His County cricket was for Devon.

Buller, John Sydney, MBE
Professional. *b:* 23.8.1909, Bramley, Yorkshire. *d:* 7.8.1970, Edgbaston, Birmingham. Lower order right-hand batsman, wicket-keeper. *Teams* Yorkshire (1930, 1 match); Worcestershire (1935–46, 110 matches).
Career batting
112–171–44–1746–64–13.74–0–*ct* 178–*st* 71
He was better known as an umpire than a player and was the leading figure in the elimination of 'throwing' in the early 1960s, notably in the case of the South African bowler, Griffin. Buller became a first-class umpire in 1951 and died at Edgbaston whilst officiating in the match between Warwickshire and Notts. He stood regularly as an umpire in Test matches and was awarded the MBE for his services to cricket.

Bullock, Burnett (Wedlake)
Professional. *b:* 5.10.1896, Redhill, Surrey. *d:* 22.12.1954, Balham, South London. Middle order right-hand batsman. *Team* Surrey (1922–24, 5 matches).
Career batting
6–8–1–121–40–17.28–0–*ct* 0

Bullock, Mark
Professional. *b:* 1872, Dudley, Worcs. *d:* 1925, Leicester. Middle order batsman. *Team* Worcestershire (1900, 4 matches).
Career batting
4–6–0–59–27–9.83–0–*ct* 1

Bullock, Percy George
Professional. *b:* 28.8.1893, Birmingham. Middle/lower order right-hand batsman, slow left-arm bowler. *Team* Worcestershire (1921, 3 matches).
Career batting
3–5–0–11–9–2.20–0–*ct* 3

Bullough, John
Professional. *b:* 1893, Bolton, Lancashire. *d:* 3.6.1967, Westhoughton, Lancashire. Tail end right-hand batsman, slow right-arm bowler. *Team* Lancashire (1914–19, 8 matches).
Career batting
8–8–3–24–17–4.80–0–*ct* 2
Bowling 573–13–44.07–1–0–5/123

Bulmer, John Robert L.
Professional. *b:* 28.12.1867, Guisborough, Yorkshire. *d:* 1917, Oldham, Lancashire. Tail end batsman, right-arm fast medium bowler. *Team* Yorkshire (1891, 1 match).
Career batting
1–2–0–0–0–0.00–0–*ct* 0
Bowling 79–1–79.00–0–0–1/51

Bulpett, Charles William Lloyd
Amateur. *b:* 18.8.1852, Chertsey, Surrey. *d:* 11.7.1939, Nairobi, Kenya. Lower order right-hand batsman, right-arm fast bowler. *Sch* Rugby. *Team* Middlesex (1880, 1 match).
Career batting
5–9–2–76–23*–10.85–0–*ct* 2
Bowling 163–5–32.60–0–0–4/21

His first appearance in first-class cricket was for MCC in 1877. He was at Oxford, but not in the Eleven. His final first-class match was for Gentlemen in 1882. He appeared in some matches under the name 'C. W. Lloyd'. In 1887 he backed himself for £200 to walk a mile, run a mile and ride a mile in 18 minutes and won the bet. In 1888 for a bet of £1,000 to £400 he set himself 16 minutes 30 seconds to achieve the same feat and again won.

Bulsara, Maneksha Dadabhai
Amateur. *b:* 2.9.1877, Daman, Portugese India. Lower order right-hand batsman, right-arm medium fast bowler. *Team* Parsis (1899/1900 to 1921/2). *Tour* India to England 1911.
Career batting
30–47–14–228–24*–6.90–0–*ct* 14
Bowling 1885–119–15.84–7–2–8/31

Bunce, William Newman
Amateur. *b:* 17.4.1911, Pill, Bristol. *d:* 29.5.1981, Pill, Bristol. Lower order left-hand batsman, right-arm medium fast bowler. *Team* Somerset (1936–37, 14 matches).
Career batting
14–21–3–227–46–12.61–0–*ct* 4
Bowling 186–4–46.50–0–0–3/81

Bunting, Dr Edward Lancelot
Amateur. *b:* 10.12.1883, Tillington, Staffs. *d:* 26.2.1962, Barnwood, Gloucs. Middle order right-hand batsman, right-arm medium pace bowler. *Sch* Blundell's. *Team* Worcestershire (1922, 1 match).
Career batting
1–2–0–1–1–0.50–0–*ct* 0
Bowling 38–0

Bunting, Walter Henry
Amateur. *b:* 18.6.1854, Cambridge. *d:* 28.10.1922, Burnham, Somerset. Lower order right-hand batsman, right-arm fast bowler. *Team* Middlesex (1877, 3 matches).
Career batting
3–6–1–6–2*–1.20–0–*ct* 3
Bowling 107–0

He played under the assumed name of Walter Gray.

Bunyard, Graham Stuart
Amateur. *b:* 17.10.1939, Eastern Province, South Africa. Lower order right-hand batsman, right-arm fast bowler. *Teams* Transvaal (1959/60 to 1960/1); Rhodesia (1962/3). *Tour* SA Fezela to England 1961.
Career batting
14–17–3–192–35–13.71–0–*ct* 7
Bowling 1082–48–22.54–1–0–5/35

Burbidge, Arthur
Amateur. *b:* 1836, Camberwell, Surrey. *d:* 18.12.1890, Swanage, Dorset. Brother of Frederick (Surrey). Middle order batsman. *Team* Surrey (1857, 2 matches).
Career batting
4–8–1–54–13–7.71–0–*ct* 0

His last first-class match was for Gentlemen of South in 1862.

Burbidge, Frederick
Amateur. *b:* 23.11.1832, Champion Hill, London. *d:* 12.12.1892, Micklefield, Rickmansworth, Herts. Brother of Arthur (Surrey). Sound middle order right-hand batsman, good field. *Team* Surrey (1854–66, 41 matches).
Career batting
64–110–11–1475–101–14.89–1–*ct* 58

His last first-class match was for Gentlemen of South in 1868. Owing to his profession he was unable to appear regularly for Surrey. He also played for Bedfordshire.

Burch, Geoffrey Worth
Professional. *b:* 12.4.1937, Leicester. Useful lower order right-hand batsman, wicket-keeper. *Team* Leicestershire (1958–64, 46 matches).
Career batting
46–79–10–1067–64*–15.46–0–*ct* 55
Bowling 3–0

Burchell, Thomas James
Professional in 1905, but amateur in 1919. *b:* 26.4.1875, Steyning, Sussex. *d:* 16.2.1951, Brighton, Sussex. Tail end batsman, wicket-keeper. *Team* Sussex (1905–19, 2 matches).
Career batting
2–4–2–13–6*–6.50–0–*ct* 8–*st* 1

Burchnall, Richard Langley
Cricketer. *b:* 8.8.1948, Oxford. Opening right-hand batsman. *Sch* Winchester. *Team* Oxford U (1968–71, blue 1970–71).
Career batting
32–57–2–874–85–15.89–0–*ct* 14

Burden, Mervyn Derek
Professional. *b:* 4.10.1930, Southampton. Lower order right-hand batsman, right-arm off-break bowler. *Team* Hampshire (1953–63, 174 matches).
Career batting
174–191–59–901–51–6.82–0–*ct* 76
Bowling 12559–481–26.11–23–4–8/38

Burdett, John Willder
Amateur. *b:* 16.8.1888, Leicester. *d:* 16.4.1974, Melton Mowbray, Leics. Son of Thomas (Hon. Sec., Leics CCC 1883–1907). Middle order right-hand batsman. *Sch* Oundle. *Team* Leicestershire (1919, 1 match).
Career batting
1–2–0–1–1–0.50–0–*ct* 0

Burge, Gerard Rodon
Amateur. *b:* 9.8.1857, Dinapore, India. *d:* 15.2.1933, London. Lower order right-hand batsman, right-arm fast bowler. *Sch* Marlborough. *Team* Middlesex (1885, 1 match).
Career batting
2–4–1–1–1–0.33–0–*ct* 1
Bowling 103–5–20.60–1–0–5/46

His last first-class appearance was for Gentlemen at Scarborough in 1886. He also played for Bedfordshire and Hertfordshire.

Burge, Peter John Parnell
Amateur. *b:* 17.5.1932, Buranda, Queensland, Australia. Sound middle order right-hand batsman. *Team* Queensland (1952/3 to 1967/8, 91 matches). *Tours* Australia to England 1956, 1961, 1964, to West Indies 1954/5, to New Zealand 1956/7, 1966/7, to South Africa 1957/8, to India 1956/7, 1959/60, 1964/5. to Pakistan 1959/60, 1964/5. *Tests* Australia (1954/5 to 1965/6, 42 matches).
Career batting
233–354–46–14640–283–47.53–38–*ct* 166–*st* 4
Bowling 129–1–129.00–0–0–1/0
Test batting
42–68–8–2290–181–38.16–4–*ct* 23

He hit 1,000 runs in a season twice on his tours to England (best 1,376, av 55.04, in 1961). His two great innings in England were 181 in the Oval Test of 1961 and 160 in the Leeds Test of 1964. His highest score was 283 for Queensland v NSW at Brisbane in 1963/4.

Burger, Christopher George de Villiers
Amateur. *b:* 12.7.1935, Randfontein, Transvaal, South Africa. Middle order right-hand batsman, fine field. *Teams* Free Foresters (1955); Natal (1955/6 to 1965/6). *Tour* SA Fezela to England 1961. *Tests* South Africa (1957/8, 2 matches).
Career batting
48–74–5–2073–131–30.04–2–*ct* 47
Bowling 17–1–17.00–0–0–1/8
Test batting
2–4–1–62–37*–20.66–0–*ct* 1

Burgess, Arthur Austen
Amateur. *b:* 2.1.1906, Peterborough. Lower order right-hand batsman, leg break bowler. *Sch* Wellingborough. *Team* Northants (1929, 1 match).
Career batting
1–2–0–14–13–7.00–0–*ct* 1
Bowling 13–0

Burgess, Alan Thomas
Amateur. *b:* 1.5.1920, Christchurch, New Zealand. Lower order right-hand batsman, left-arm bowler. *Team* Canterbury (1940/1 to 1951/2). *Tour* New Zealand Services in England 1945.
Career batting
14–23–2–466–61*–22.19–0–*ct* 12
Bowling 491–16–30.68–1–0–6/52

Burgess, Charles Thomas
Amateur. *b:* 30.6.1886, Hastings. *d:* 14.1.1978, Crediton, Devon. Middle order right-hand batsman, slow right-arm bowler. *Team* Sussex (1919, 1 match).
Career batting
1–2–0–2–1–1.00–0–*ct* 1
Bowling 39–3–13.00–0–0–3/39

Burgess, Graham Iefvion
Cricketer. *b:* 5.5.1943, Glastonbury, Somerset. Middle/lower order right-hand batsman, right-arm medium pace bowler. *Sch* Millfield. *Team* Somerset (1966–79, 252 matches).

Career batting
252–414–37–7129–129–18.90–2–*ct* 120
Bowling 13543–474–28.57–18–2–7/43
He also played for Wiltshire.

Burgess, Henry
Amateur. *b:* 1879, Carlton-Curlieu, Leics. *d:* 16.4.1964, Middleton, Northants. Brother of John (Leics). Lower order right-hand batsman, right-arm fast bowler. *Sch* Wellingborough. *Teams* Leicestershire (1900–02, 8 matches); Northants (1905, 1 match).
Career batting
9–13–1–63–20–5.25–0–*ct* 4
Bowling 556–11–50.54–0–0–3/106

Burgess, John
Amateur. *b:* 22.11.1880, Carlton-Curlieu, Leics. *d:* 2.11.1953, East Carlton, Northants. Brother of Henry (Leics and Northants). Hard-hitting middle order right-hand batsman, wicket-keeper. *Sch* Oakham. *Team* Leicestershire (1902–13, 12 matches).
Career batting
12–18–0–230–39–12.77–0–*ct* 7–*st* 2

Burgess, Mark Gordon
Cricketer. *b:* 17.7.1944, Auckland, New Zealand. Son of G. C. (Auckland). Middle order right-hand batsman, right-arm off break bowler. *Team* Auckland (1966/7 to 1979/80). *Tours* New Zealand to England 1969, 1973, 1978, to Australia 1967/8, 1969/70, 1970/1, 1980/1, to West Indies 1971/2, to India and Pakistan 1969/70, 1976/7. *Tests* New Zealand (1967/8 to 1980/1, 50 matches).
Career batting
192–322–35–10281–146–35.82–20–*ct* 151
Bowling 1148–30–38.26–0–0–3/23
Test batting
50–92–6–2684–119*–31.20–5–*ct* 34
Bowling 212–6–35.33–0–0–3/23
His first-class debut was for New Zealand Under 23 in 1963/4. The most successful of his three tours to England was in 1973 when he hit 836 runs, av 49.17, including a Test hundred. He captained the 1978 touring side.

Burgess, Thomas
Professional. *b:* 1861. *d:* 22.2.1922, Harrogate, Yorkshire. Useful middle order batsman. *Team* Yorkshire (1895, 1 match).
Career batting
1–2–1–0–0*–0.00–0–*ct* 2
The professional with the Harrogate Club, he played in emergency for Yorkshire in one match at Harrogate, when one of the County team failed to arrive.

Burgess, William Arthur
Amateur. *b:* 31.1.1888, Williton, Somerset. *d:* 20.6.1970, Minehead, Somerset. Middle order right-hand batsman, left-arm bowler. *Team* Somerset (1921–22, 7 matches).
Career batting
7–12–0–211–79–17.58–0–*ct* 7
Bowling 246–6–41.00–0–0–2/39

Burghes, Arthur
Professional. *b:* 8.9.1848, London. *d:* 1916, Poplar, East London. Middle or lower order right-hand batsman, right-hand medium pace round-arm bowler. *Team* Middlesex (1876–77, 7 matches).
Career batting
7–11–1–245–104–24.50–1–*ct* 4
Bowling 82–0
He also played non-first-class cricket for Essex.

Burgin, Eric
Professional. *b:* 4.1.1924, Sheffield, Yorkshire. Lower order right-hand batsman, right-arm medium pace bowler. *Team* Yorkshire (1952–53, 12 matches).
Career batting
12–10–3–92–32–13.14–0–*ct* 0
Bowling 795–31–25.64–2–0–6/43
A noted soccer player, he appeared for York City and Sheffield United.

Burke, Cecil
Amateur. *b:* 22.3.1914, Auckland, New Zealand. Defensive lower order right-hand batsman, leg-break and googly bowler, good close field. *Team* Auckland (1937/8 to 1953/4). *Tour* New Zealand to England 1949. *Tests* New Zealand (1945/6, 1 match).
Career batting
58–70–17–935–51–17.64–0–*ct* 29
Bowling 5047–194–26.01–7–1–6/23
Test batting
1–2–0–4–3–2.00–0–*ct* 0
Bowling 30–2–15.00–0–0–2/30
On his single tour to England he was not selected for any of the Tests, but in all first-class matches took 54 wickets, av 29.83.

Burke, Charles Carrington
Amateur. *b:* 8.7.1853, Paddington, London. *d:* 22.5.1904, Godalming, Surrey. *Sch* Harrow. *Team* MCC (1882).
Career batting
1–2–0–7–7–3.50–0–*ct* 0

Burke, George Humphrey
Professional. *b:* 18.8.1848, Greenwich, Kent. *d:* 21.7.1920, Peckham, South London. Lower order right-hand batsman, right-arm fast bowler. *Team* Kent (1877, 1 match).
Career batting
1–1–0–9–9–9.00–0–*ct* 2
Bowling 51–4–12.75–0–0–3/16

Burke, Joseph Patrick
Amateur. *b:* 31.1.1923, Dublin. Right-hand batsman, right-arm fast medium bowler. *Team* Ireland (1953–58).
Career batting
3–4–1–36–19*–12.00–0–*ct* 2
Bowling 105–3–35.00–0–0–2/32

Burke, James Wallace
Amateur. *b:* 12.6.1930, Mosman, New South Wales, Australia. *d:* 2.2.1979, Manly, New South Wales, Australia. He died by his own hand. Defensive opening right-hand batsman, right-arm off break bowler. *Team* New South Wales (1948/9 to 1958/9, 67 matches). *Tours* Australia to England, Pakistan and India 1956, to South Africa 1957/8, to New Zealand 1949/50. *Tests* Australia (1950/1 to 1958/9, 24 matches).
Career batting
130–204–36–7563–220–45.01–21–*ct* 59
Bowling 2941–101–29.11–3–0–6/40
Test batting
24–44–7–1280–189–34.59–3–*ct* 18
Bowling 230–8–28.75–0–0–4/37

He was one of the few successful players of the 1956 Australian tour of England, heading the Test batting averages and in all first-class matches hitting 1339 runs, av 47.82. His highest score was 220 for NSW v South Australia at Adelaide in 1956/7. An injury on his 1957/8 tour to South Africa put an end to his career, undermining his confidence. As a bowler he was more than useful, but a suspect action curtailed his career in this direction. After retiring he was a well-known sports commentator.

Burki, Javed
Amateur. *b:* 8.5.1938, Meerut, India. Middle order right-hand batsman, right-arm medium pace bowler. Cousin of Imran Khan Niazi (Pakistan) and Majid Jahangir Khan (Pakistan). *Team* Oxford U (1958–60, blue all three years); Punjab (1955/6 to 1956/7); Lahore (1961/2 to 1970/1); Karachi (1963/4 to 1967/8); Rawalpindi (1967/8 to 1972/3); NWFP (1974/5). *Tours* Pakistan to England 1962, 1967, to India 1960/1, to Australia and New Zealand 1964/5, to Ceylon 1964/5. *Tests* Pakistan (1960/1 to 1969/70, 25 matches).
Career batting
177–290–31–9421–227–36.37–22–*ct* 100
Bowling 1554–35–44.40–0–0–4/13
Test batting
25–48–4–1341–140–30.47–3–*ct* 7
Bowling 23–0

Although he had an excellent cricket career at Oxford, neither of his visits to England with the Pakistani team was very successful. He captained the 1962 side and hit 1,257 runs av 33.07, including a century in the Lord's Test, but his leadership came in for considerable criticism. In 1967, he was promoted to opening batsman, an experiment which failed.

Burkitt, H. W. *(see under* Birkett, W.)

Burls, Charles William
Amateur. *b:* 8.3.1847, Peckham Rye, Surrey. *d:* 17.12.1923, Datchet, Bucks. Middle order right-hand batsman, change bowler. *Team* Surrey (1873–80, 10 matches).
Career batting
17–29–0–304–37–10.48–0–*ct* 8
Bowling 23–0

His final first-class match was for Gentlemen in 1887.

Burlton, Arthur Temple
Amateur. *b:* 10.3.1900, Coimbatore, India. *d:* 10.2.1980, Ballochneck, Thornhill, Stirling, Scotland. Middle order right-hand batsman, off break bowler. *Sch* Repton. *Team* Worcestershire (1922, 5 matches).
Career batting
5–10–1–114–35*–12.66–0–*ct* 3
Bowling 38–1–38.00–0–0–1/22

He also appeared for Devon. He wrote a book on 'cricketing manners.'

Burman, John
Professional. *b: circa* 1838. *d:* 1900, Hunslet, Yorkshire. *Team* Yorkshire (1867, 1 match).
Career batting
1–2–1–1–1*–1.00–0–*ct* 0

Burn, Edmund Holcroft Miller
Amateur. *b:* 1922, Glanford Brigg, Lincs. *d:* 22.10.1969. He was killed in a road accident at Grimsby Beach, Ontario, Canada. Middle order right-hand batsman, change bowler. *Team* Canada (1954). *Tour* Canada to England 1954.
Career batting
2–4–0–31–12–7.75–0–*ct* 1

He appeared for Canada v MCC (non-first-class) in 1951 and was one of the mainstays of cricket in Ontario. He produced, edited and published '*The Canadian Cricketer*' from 1952 to 1965.

Burn, Edwin James Kenneth
Amateur. *b:* 17.9.1862, Richmond, Tasmania. *d:* 20.7.1956, Hobart, Tasmania. Opening/middle order right-hand batsman. *Team* Tasmania (1883/4 to 1909/10, 25 matches). *Tours* Australians to England 1890; Tasmania to New Zealand 1883/4. *Tests* Australia (1890, 2 matches).
Career batting
48–90–8–1750–119–21.34–2–*ct* 31
Bowling 320–14–22.85–0–0–3/15
Test batting
2–4–0–41–19–10.25–0–*ct* 0

Burn was chosen as reserve wicket-keeper on the 1890 tour to England owing to a dispute among the selectors, but on the voyage to England it was then discovered that he had never kept wicket! He was a prolific batsman in Tasmania, but never came to terms with conditions in England.

Burn, Sir Roland Clive Wallace
Amateur. *b:* 29.10.1882, Streatham, Surrey. *d:* 8.5.1955, London. Lower order batsman, left-arm slow bowler. *Sch* Winchester/Merchant Taylors. *Team* Oxford U (1902–05, blue all four years). *Tours* Brackley to West Indies 1904/5; MCC to North America 1905.
Career batting
45–71–23–420–59–8.75–0–*ct* 30
Bowling 3284–123–26.69–4–0–5/88

His final first-class match was for Leveson-Gower's XI in 1919.

Burnand, Lewis Whitmore
Amateur. *b:* 5.5.1839, Bloomsbury, London. *d:* 31.1.1923, Worthing, Sussex. Lower order batsman, bowler. *Sch* Harrow. *Team* MCC (1863–64).
Career batting
2–3–0–4–4–1.33–0–*ct* 1
Bowling 11–0

He played for Hertfordshire.

Burnell, Henry Blomfield
Amateur. *b:* 14.11.1853, Upper Clapton, Middlesex. *d:* 19.10.1910, St John's Wood, London. *Sch* Harrow. *Team* MCC (1879).
Career batting
1–1–0–1–1–1.00–0–*ct* 0

Burnell, Philip John
Cricketer. *b:* 12.6.1945, Woodford Green, Essex. Lower order right-hand batsman, wicket-keeper. *Sch* Chigwell. *Team* Oxford U (1967).
Career batting
6–10–3–71–28–10.14–0–*ct* 3–*st* 1

Burnet, John Ronald
Amateur. *b:* 11.10.1918, Saltaire, Shipley, Yorkshire. Middle order right-hand batsman. *Team* Yorkshire (1958–59, 54 matches).
Career batting
55–77–6–897–54–12.63–0–*ct* 7
Bowling 26–1–26.00–0–0–1/8

Appointed captain of Yorkshire in 1958, without previously having appeared in first-class cricket, he led the County for two seasons (1958–59).

Burnett, Anthony Compton
(later known as Compton-Burnett)
Amateur. *b:* 26.10.1923, Chipstead, Surrey. Father of R. J. Compton-Burnett (Cambridge U). Middle order right-hand batsman, good close field, occasional wicket-keeper. *Sch* Lancing. *Teams* Cambridge U (1949–50, blue 1949); Glamorgan (1958, 8 matches).
Career batting
27–40–6–790–79*–23.23–0–*ct* 20
Bowling 16–0

Burnett, Ernest Wildman
Amateur. *b:* 22.9.1844, Brighton, Sussex. *d:* 22.12.1931, Oxford. Cousin of J. D. (Surrey). Hard-hitting lower order right-hand batsman, slow round-arm bowler. *Sch* Harrow. *Teams* Gentlemen of South (1867); Southgate (1868).
Career batting
5–7–0–45–26–6.42–0–*ct* 1
Bowling 60–2–30.00–0–0–2/39

He also played for Staffordshire. His first-class debut was for South in 1862.

Burnett, John David
Amateur. *b:* 25.2.1840, Vauxhall, Surrey. *d:* 18.6.1878, Pietermaritzburg, South Africa. Cousin of E. W. (Gentlemen of South 1867). Middle order right-hand batsman, brilliant cover field. *Sch* Harrow. *Team* Surrey (1862, 1 match).
Career batting
5–7–0–68–39–9.71–0–*ct* 4

He appeared in several trials whilst at Oxford, but not against Cambridge. His first-class debut was for Gentlemen of South in 1861 and his final first-class match for the same side in 1863.

Burnham, George Joseph
Professional. *b:* 5.11.1878, Nottingham. *d:* 7.3.1971, Nottingham. Middle order right-hand batsman. *Team* Derbyshire (1912, 5 matches).
Career batting
5–6–1–30–15–6.00–0–*ct* 3

Burnham, Gordon Le Roy
Amateur. *b:* 18.12.1886. *d:* 1.9.1964, Gessenay, Berne, Switzerland. Middle order batsman, useful change bowler. *Teams* Europeans (1910/11); Sussex (1914, 1 match).
Career batting
3–4–0–42–18–10.50–0–*ct* 2
Bowling 60–3–20.00–0–0–2/48

Burnham, John William
Professional. *b:* 6.6.1839, Nottingham. *d:* 20.4.1914, Derby. Opening/middle order right-hand batsman. *Team* Derbyshire (1871–76, 6 matches).
Career batting
6–11–0–55–31–5.00–0–*ct* 2
He also played for Suffolk.

Burns, James (Henry)
Professional. *b:* 20.6.1865, Liverpool. *d:* 11.9.1957, Hampstead, London. Brother of Rt Hon John Burns. Opening right-hand batsman, slow left-arm bowler. *Team* Essex (1894–96, 26 matches).
Career batting
41–70–4–1134–114–17.18–1–*ct* 15
Bowling 460–15–30.66–1–0–6/41
He appeared in non-first-class matches for Lancashire from 1884 to 1886 and commenced his connection with Essex in 1887. His first-class debut was for MCC in 1890 and his final first-class match for the same club in 1901. An excellent soccer player, he appeared for West Bromwich Albion and Notts County.

Burns, William Beaumont
Amateur. *b:* 29.8.1883, Rugeley, Staffs. *d:* 7.7.1916, Contalmaison, France. Hard-hitting middle order right-hand batsman, right-arm fast bowler, brilliant field. *Sch* King's School, Ely. *Team* Worcestershire (1903–13, 196 matches). *Tour* MCC to New Zealand 1906/7.
Career batting
217–374–23–9479–196–27.00–12–*ct* 147
Bowling 6334–214–29.59–8–1–6/41
He hit 1,000 runs in a season 5 times (best 1438, av 31.95, in 1911). His bowling was very fast, but the fairness of his delivery was often in question. He also played for Staffordshire. At the close of the 1913 season he emigrated to Canada.

Burnup, Cuthbert James
Amateur. *b:* 21.11.1875, Blackheath, Kent. *d:* 5.4.1960, Golders Green, London. Sound right-hand opening batsman, slow right-arm bowler, splendid outfield. *Sch* Malvern. *Teams* Cambridge U (1895–98, blue 1896–98); Kent (1896–1907, 157 matches); London County (1901). *Tours* Warner to North America 1898; Hawke to New Zealand and Australia 1902/03; Kent to USA 1903.
Career batting
228–395–25–13614–200–36.79–26–*ct* 107
Bowling 3178–98–32.42–4–0–6/36
He hit 1,000 runs in a season 8 times (best 2,048, av 39.38, in 1902). His only double century was 200 for Kent v Lancs at Old Trafford in 1900. He captained Kent in 1903. An excellent soccer player he was awarded his blue at Cambridge and went on to gain an England cap in 1896.

Burr, Frederick Bonham
Amateur. *b:* 2.8.1887, Hastings, Sussex. *d:* 12.3.1915, Kemmel, Belgium. Middle order batsman. *Sch* Denstone. *Team* Worcestershire (1911, 1 match).
Career batting
1–2–1–46–39–46.00–0–*ct* 1

Burrell, Rev Herbert John Edwin
Amateur. *b:* 15.11.1866, Kirtling, Cambs. *d:* 22.5.1949, Cambridge. Brother of R. J. (Essex). Middle order right-hand batsman, right-arm medium pace bowler. *Sch* Charterhouse. *Teams* Essex (1895, 2 matches); Oxford U (1889).
Career batting
3–5–0–15–10–3.00–0–*ct* 0
Bowling 78–2–39.00–0–0–1/37
He also represented Hertfordshire and Norfolk.

Burrell, Reginald John
Amateur. *b:* 26.8.1870, Kirtling, Cambs. *d:* 16.3.1948, Risby, Suffolk. Brother of H. J. E. (Essex). Middle order batsman. *Sch* Charterhouse. *Team* Essex (1894–95, 6 matches).
Career batting
10–17–1–200–40–12.50–0–*ct* 2
His final first-class match was for MCC in 1897. He also played for Suffolk.

Burridge, Alan James
Cricketer. *b:* 8.10.1936, Sunderland, Co Durham. Middle order left-hand batsman, right-arm slow bowler. *Team* Minor Counties (1973).
Career batting
1–2–0–42–37–21.00–0–*ct* 0
He played for Durham 1961 to 1972, Lincolnshire 1973 and 1974 and Hertfordshire commencing 1975.

Burrington, George
Amateur. *b:* 1864, Tiverton, Devon. *d:* 22.1.1942, Newhaven, Sussex. Middle order batsman. *Team* Somerset (1901–02, 3 matches).
Career batting
3–5–0–40–15–8.00–0–*ct* 1

Burrington, Humphrey Sandford
Amateur. *b:* 5.4.1882, Bridgwater, Somerset. *d:* 15.4.1957, Barnstaple, Devon. Middle order batsman. *Sch* Haileybury. *Team* Somerset (1903–05, 5 matches).
Career batting
5–7–1–65–20–10.83–0–*ct* 3
Bowling 10–0

Burrough, George Baker
Amateur. *b:* 1907, Wells, Somerset. *d:* 9.5.1965 Butleigh, Somerset. Lower order batsman, useful spin bowler. *Team* Somerset (1936, 1 match).
Career batting
1–1–0–27–27–27.00–0–*ct* 2
Bowling 38–1–38.00–0–0–1/23

Burrough, Herbert Dickinson
Amateur. *b:* 6.2.1909, Wedmore, Somerset. Son of W. G. (Somerset); nephew of John (Cambridge U). Sound middle order right-hand batsman. *Sch* King's Bruton. *Team* Somerset (1927–47, 171 matches).
Career batting
171–272–18–5316–135–20.92–4–*ct* 82
Bowling 14–0

He appeared in the Seniors' Match whilst at Cambridge, but not in first-class matches. His best season was 1933 when he reached 1007 runs, av 25.17 – the only year he exceeded 1,000 runs.

Burrough, Rev John
Amateur. *b:* 5.9.1873, Clun, Shropshire. *d:* 26.12.1922, St Leonards-on-Sea, Sussex. Brother of W. G. (Somerset), uncle of H. D. (Somerset) and J. W. (Oxford U and Gloucs). Middle order right-hand batsman, right-arm medium pace bowler. *Sch* King's School, Bruton and Shrewsbury. *Team* Cambridge U (1893–96, blue 1895).
Career batting
24–39–5–780–127–22.94–1–*ct* 15
Bowling 1929–65–29.64–4–2–6/29

His County cricket was for Herefordshire. His final first-class match was for Free Foresters in 1914. An excellent athlete he put the shot.

Burrough, Rev John Wilson
Amateur. *b:* 17.6.1904, Headington, Oxfordshire. *d:* 11.9.1969. He was killed in a road accident at Seale, Surrey. Nephew of John (Cambridge U) and W. G. (Somerset). Middle order right-hand batsman, right-arm fast-medium bowler. *Sch* Lancing. *Teams* Oxford U (1924–26); Gloucestershire (1924–37, 7 matches).
Career batting
10–16–4–146–46–12.16–0–*ct* 6
Bowling 349–6–58.16–0–0–2/26

Burrough, William George
Amateur. *b:* 22.7.1875, Clun, Shropshire. *d:* 30.12.1939, Wedmore, Somerset. Brother of John (Cambridge U), father of H. D. (Somerset); uncle of J. W. (Oxford U and Gloucs). Lower order batsman, opening bowler. *Sch* Bruton. *Team* Somerset (1906, 4 matches).
Career batting
4–7–0–40–11–5.71–0–*ct* 2
Bowling 344–7–49.14–0–0–2/102

Burrowes, Dr James Taylor
Amateur. *b:* 28.2.1914, Jamaica. Batsman. *Team* Oxford U (1934).
Career batting
1–1–0–3–3–3.00–0–*ct* 0
Bowling 37–0

Burrows, Arthur Dixon
Professional. *b:* 2.7.1865, Awsworth, Notts. *d:* 6.2.1890, Eastwood, Notts. Middle order right-hand batsman, right-arm fast-medium bowler. *Team* Nottinghamshire (1887, 1 match).
Career batting
1–2–0–2–1–1.00–0–*ct* 1
Bowling 19–0

Burrows, Matthew
Professional. *b:* 18.8.1855, Chesterfield, Derbyshire. *d:* 29.5.1893, Beeston, Leeds, Yorkshire. Middle order right-hand batsman, occasional right-hand fast round-arm bowler. *Team* Yorkshire (1880, 6 matches); Derbyshire (1884, 1 match).
Career batting
7–12–0–95–23–7.91–0–*ct* 2
Bowling 10–0

Burrows, Lieut-General Montagu Brocas
Amateur. *b:* 31.10.1894, Reigate, Surrey. *d:* 17.1.1967, Marylebone, London. Middle order right-hand batsman, right-arm fast-medium bowler. *Sch* Eton. *Teams* Oxford U (1914–21); Surrey (1921, 1 match). *Tour* Incogniti to North America 1920 (not first-class).
Career batting
28–45–5–1283–112–32.07–1–*ct* 29
Bowling 1998–85–23.51–2–0–6/27

He appeared in many Army matches and his last first-class game was for the Army in 1932. He also played for Oxfordshire.

Burrows, Robert Dixon
Professional. *b:* 6.6.1871, Eastwood, Notts. *d:* 12.2.1943, Hill Top, near Eastwood, Notts. Hard-hitting lower order right-hand batsman, right-arm fast bowler. *Team* Worcestershire (1899–1919, 277 matches).

Career batting
277–436–65–5223–112–14.07–2–*ct* 138
Bowling 23604–894–26.40–57–9–8/48

He twice took exactly 100 wickets in a season – 1910 (av 23.46) and 1913 (av 21.41). After retiring from first-class cricket he became a noted County umpire.

Burrows, William
Professional. *b:* 31.12.1844, Preston, Lancashire. Lower order batsman, right-hand medium pace round-arm bowler, good long-stop. *Team* Lancashire (1867–73, 14 matches).
Career batting
14–26–1–255–39–10.20–0–*ct* 2
Bowling 6–0

Burt, George Peter
Amateur. *b:* 11.11.1886, Glasgow, Scotland. *d:* 20.1.1935, Murtle, Aberdeenshire, Scotland. Right-hand batsman. *Team* Scotland (1924–25).
Career batting
2–3–0–35–26–11.66–0–*ct* 1

Burton, Clifford
Amateur. *b:* 15.6.1931, Moston, Manchester. Tail end right-hand batsman, right-arm fast-medium bowler. *Team* Lancashire (1956, 2 matches).
Career batting
2–1–0–0–0–0.00–0–*ct* 2
Bowling 80–0

Burton, David Cecil Fowler
Amateur. *b:* 13.9.1887, Bridlington, Yorkshire. *d:* 24.9.1971, Surrey. Brother of R. C. (Yorkshire), cousin of D. S. G. (MCC in West Indies). Middle order right-hand batsman, excellent field at cover. *Sch* Rugby. *Team* Cambridge U (1907–08); Yorkshire (1907–21, 104 matches). *Tours* MCC to West Indies 1910/11, 1912/13.
Career batting
130–171–20–3057–142*–20.24–2–*ct* 54

He captained Yorkshire 1919–21. His final first-class match was for MCC in 1922. At Cambridge he was awarded his blue for rugby football and was also a noted sprinter.

Burton, Frederick Alfred
Professional. *b:* 28.12.1885, Islington, Middlesex. *d:* 7.1.1978, Weston-super-Mare, Somerset. Son of George (Middlesex). Lower order right-hand batsman, right-arm medium fast bowler. *Teams* MCC (1921–25); Minor Counties (1924).
Career batting
7–13–5–99–35*–12.37–0–*ct* 0
Bowling 564–11–51.27–0–0–4/101

During the 1920s he was the prinicipal Hertfordshire bowler. His final first-class match was for East of England in 1927.

Burton, George
Professional. *b:* 1.5.1851, Hampstead, Middlesex. *d:* 7.5.1930, Westminster, London. Father of F. A. (MCC). Lower order right-hand batsman, right-hand slow round-arm bowler. *Team* Middlesex (1881–93, 111 matches).
Career batting
128–205–62–1150–34–8.04–0–*ct* 98
Bowling 10446–608–17.18–47–12–10/59

For Middlesex v Surrey at the Oval in 1888 he took all ten wickets (for 59) in the first innings.

Burton, Geoffrey Cecil
Amateur. *b:* 14.12.1909, Hackney, North London. Middle order right-hand batsman. *Sch* Cheltenham. *Team* Middlesex (1930, 1 match).
Career batting
1–2–0–1–1–0.50–0–*ct* 0

Burton, Henry (Herbert)
Amateur. *b:* 1874, Lambeth, London. *d:* 4.2.1964, Streatham, Surrey. Middle order right-hand batsman. *Teams* Surrey (1904, 3 matches); London County (1904).
Career batting
6–12–1–261–59–23.72–0–*ct* 0

His final first-class match was for Gentlemen in 1905.

Burton, John Chambers
Professional. *b:* 7.5.1837, Oare, Faversham, Kent. *d:* 19.2.1887, Sittingbourne, Kent. Stylish middle order right-hand batsman, good field. *Team* Kent (1862–64, 12 matches).
Career batting
12–24–2–162–40–7.36–0–*ct* 3

Burton, Joseph Parkin
Professional. *b:* 10.12.1873, Somercotes, Derbyshire. *d:* 25.1.1940, Somercotes, Derbyshire. Middle order right-hand batsman. *Team* Derbyshire (1901, 7 matches).
Career batting
7–12–1–200–51*–18.18–0–*ct* 4

Burton, Michael St John Whitehead
Cricketer. *b:* 14.2.1944, Bulawayo, Rhodesia. Middle order right-hand batsman, right-arm off break bowler. *Teams* Eastern Province (1964/5 to 1967/8); Oxford U (1969–71, blue all three years).
Career batting
37–59–5–821–84–15.20–0–*ct* 15
Bowling 3317–77–43.07–2–0–5/96

Burton, Oswald
Professional. *b:* 21.8.1874, Gorton, Lancashire. *d:* 4.7.1944, Bristol. Lower order right-hand batsman, right-arm medium-fast bowler. *Team* Derbyshire (1901–05, 3 matches).
Career batting
3–4–4–21–9*–no av–0–*ct* 2
Bowling 156–5–31.20–0–0–2/44

Burton, Robert Claude
Amateur. *b:* 11.4.1891, Bridlington, Yorkshire. *d:* 30.4.1971, Pevensey, Sussex. Brother of D. C. F. (Cambridge U and Yorkshire), cousin of D. S. G. (MCC in West Indies). Hard-hitting lower order right-hand batsman, right-arm medium-fast bowler. *Sch* Malvern. *Teams* Oxford U (1911–13); Yorkshire (1914, 2 matches).
Career batting
12–16–2–312–71–22.28–0–*ct* 8
Bowling 886–33–26.24–0–0–4/95

He played much cricket with the Harlequins and Free Foresters. His final first-class match was for Harlequins in 1928.

Burton, Reginald Henry Markham
Amateur. *b:* 23.3.1900, Leamington, Warwickshire. *d:* 19.10.1980, Rugby, Warwickshire. Middle order right-hand batsman. *Team* Warwickshire (1919, 1 match).
Career batting
1–1–0–47–47–47.00–0–*ct* 0

Burton, W. J.
Professional. *b:* 31.1.1878, Barbados. Hard-hitting lower order batsman, bowler. *Team* British Guiana (1901/2 to 1904/5). *Tours* West Indians to England 1900 (non-first-class), 1906.
Career batting
10–18–4–161–38*–11.50–0–*ct* 14
Bowling 857–57–15.03–5–3–7/54

Burton was regarded as the best bowler in the West Indies at the turn of the century and performed well on the 1900 tour with 78 wickets (av 21.55) and the remarkable figures of 10.4–7–9–8 v Norfolk, but in 1906 he played in few games and had no success.

Burtt, Leonard Lionel
Amateur. *b:* 1886, Fulham, Middlesex. *d:* 8.11.1942, Hampstead, North London. Middle order right-hand batsman, change bowler. *Team* Middlesex (1921, 2 matches).
Career batting
2–4–1–78–50–26.00–0–*ct* 1
Bowling 9–1–9.00–0–0–1/8

Burtt, Thomas Browning
Amateur. *b:* 22.1.1915, Christchurch, New Zealand. Brother of N. V. (Canterbury). Lower order right-hand batsman, slow left-arm bowler. *Team* Canterbury (1943/4 to 1954/5). *Tour* New Zealand to England 1949. *Tests* New Zealand (1946/7 to 1952/3, 10 matches).
Career batting
84–124–29–1644–68*–12.17–0–*ct* 53
Bowling 9054–408–22.19–29–4–8/35
Test batting
10–15–3–252–42–21.00–0–*ct* 2
Bowling 1170–33–35.45–3–0–6/162

On his single tour to England, Burtt was easily the most successful New Zealand bowler, both in terms of wickets taken and average: 128 wickets, av 22.88

Bury, Lindsay
Amateur. *b:* 9.7.1857, Withington, Manchester. *d:* 30.10.1935, Stanford Wood, Reading, Berkshire. Lower order right-hand batsman, right-hand fast round-arm bowler. *Sch* Eton. *Teams* Cambridge U (1877–78, blue 1877); Hampshire (1877, 1 match).
Career batting
9–15–3–115–21–9.58–0–*ct* 6
Bowling 249–18–13.83–0–0–4/26

A well-known soccer player, he was awarded his blue at Cambridge and went on to be capped by England. He also threw the hammer for Cambridge in the University sports and was a noted sprinter.

Bury, Thomas Edward Oswell
Cricketer. *b:* 14.5.1958, Chelmsford, Essex. Right-hand batsman, wicket-keeper. *Sch* Charterhouse. *Team* Oxford U (1979–80, blue 1980).
Career batting
4–4–1–32–22–10.66–0–*ct* 2

Bury, Rev William
Amateur. *b:* 14.10.1839, Radcliffe-on-Trent, Notts. *d:* 21.5.1927, Borough Green, Sevenoaks, Kent. Brother of T. W. (Cambridge U, 1855). Hard-hitting right-hand batsman, brilliant deep field. *Teams* Cambridge U (1860–62, blue 1861–62); Nottinghamshire (1861–62, 3 matches).
Career batting
9–13–0–245–121–18.84–1–*ct* 9
Bowling 4–0

He played non-first-class for Northants from 1867 to 1870. In 1920 he had the odd experience of reading his own obituary notice twice within a few months.

Buse, Herbert Francis Thomas
Professional. *b:* 5.8.1910, Bristol. Steady middle/lower order right-hand batsman, right-

arm medium pace bowler. *Team* Somerset (1929–53, 304 matches).
Career batting
304–523–55–10623–132–22.69–7–*ct* 151
Bowling 18908–657–28.77–20–0–8/41

He hit 1,000 runs in a season 5 times (best 1279, av 26.10, in 1948).

Bush, Frederick William
Amateur. *b:* 27.2.1852, East Dulwich, Surrey. *d:* 8.1.1937, Bournemouth, Hants. Brother of H. S. (Surrey). Right-hand batsman, slow round-arm bowler. *Sch* Dulwich. *Team* Surrey (1879–85, 7 matches). *Tours* Lucas to West Indies 1894/5; Priestley to West Indies 1896/7.
Career batting
22–35–1–481–101–14.14–1–*ct* 10
Bowling 1071–65–16.47–5–2–7/25

His last appearance in first-class cricket was in the West Indies in 1896/7. He also played for Shropshire and Suffolk.

Bush, Harry Stebbing
Amateur. *b:* 7.10.1871, Dulwich, Surrey. *d:* 18.3.1942, South Farnborough, Hants. Brother of F. W. (Surrey). Stylish middle order right-hand batsman, right-arm medium pace bowler. *Sch* Dover. *Team* Surrey (1901–12, 70 matches).
Career batting
72–113–7–2607–135–24.59–4–*ct* 40
Bowling 204–2–102.00–0–0–1/12

His final first-class match was for the Army in 1914 – he was most successful in County cricket, but his military duties prevented him from appearing at all frequently.

Bush, James Arthur
Amateur. *b:* 28.7.1850, Cawnpore, India. *d:* 21.9.1924, Clevedon, Somerset. Brother of R. E. (Gloucs). Lower order left-hand batsman, wicket-keeper. *Sch* Clifton. *Team* Gloucestershire (1870–90, 136 matches). *Tour* Grace to Australia 1873/4.
Career batting
148–224–67–1263–57–8.04–0–*ct* 206–*st* 93
Bowling 65–0

He also excelled as a rugby footballer and gained five international caps.

Bush, John Edgar
Amateur. *b:* 28.8.1928, Oxford. Opening right-hand batsman. *Sch* Magdalen School, Oxford. *Team* Oxford U (1950–52, blue 1952).
Career batting
8–15–1–417–67–29.78–0–*ct* 6

His County cricket was for Oxfordshire, and in 1949 he assisted in an opening partnership of 264 for the County v Buckinghamshire.

Bush, Robert Edwin
Amateur. *b:* 11.10.1855, Redland, Bristol, Gloucs. *d:* 29.12.1939, Stoke Bishop, Bristol. Brother of J. A. (Gloucs). Middle order right-hand batsman, wicket-keeper. *Sch* Clifton. *Team* Gloucestershire (1874–77, 16 matches).
Career batting
17–24–1–221–42–9.60–0–*ct* 6

He emigrated to Australia in the 1880s, remaining there as a sheep-farmer for about 30 years.

Bush, Robert (Thompson)
Professional. *b:* 14.1.1839, Kennington, Surrey. *d:* 24.12.1874, Kennington, Surrey. Steady middle order right-hand batsman, fine field. *Team* Surrey (1864–68, 2 matches).
Career batting
2–4–1–21–8*–7.00–0–*ct* 0

Bushby, Edward
Professional. *b:* 3.4.1817, Sompting, Sussex. *d:* 29.2.1856, Henfield, Sussex. Fine free hitting right-hand batsman. *Team* Sussex (1843–54, 50 matches).
Career batting
64–114–12–1485–86–14.55–0–*ct* 27
Bowling 25–0

He was regarded as one of the best bats of his day, but latterly suffered from ill-health and died aged only 38.

Bushby, Michael Howard
Amateur. *b:* 29.7.1931, Macclesfield, Cheshire. Sound opening right-hand batsman, right-arm medium pace bowler. *Sch* Dulwich. *Team* Cambridge U (1952–54, blue all three years).
Career batting
46–78–1–1919–113–24.92–3–*ct* 12
Bowling 11–1–11.00–0–0–1/7

His final first class match was for MCC in 1966. An excellent rugby footballer he toured Japan with Cambridge U in 1953.

Bushe, Edwin Alexander
Cricketer. *b:* 11.4.1951, Lurgan, Co Armagh, Ireland. Right-hand batsman, wicket-keeper. *Team* Ireland (1979–80).
Career batting
2–2–1–14–14–14.00–0–*ct* 7 *st* 1

Busher, Harold Aston
Amateur. *b:* 2.8.1876, Sparkhill, Birmingham. *d:* October 1954, Australia. Brother of S. E. (Surrey and Worcestershire). Middle order right-hand batsman. *Team* Warwickshire (1908, 1 match).

Career batting
1–2–1–15–15–15.00–0–*ct* 0
He also played for Suffolk.

Busher, Sydney Edmund
Amateur. *b:* 19.12.1882, Solihull, Warwickshire. *d:* June 1953, Turramurra, New South Wales, Australia. Brother of H. A. (Warwickshire). Lower order right-hand batsman, right-arm fast-medium bowler. *Teams* Surrey (1908, 1 match); Worcestershire (1908–10, 4 matches).
Career batting
5–8–1–84–52–12.00–0–*ct* 2
Bowling 380–26–14.61–3–0–6/63
He lived in Australia for many years.

Busk, Richard Dawson
Amateur. *b:* 21.6.1895, Marylebone. *d:* 24.12.1961, Rampisham, Dorset. Middle/lower order right-hand batsman, right-arm fast bowler. *Sch* Marlborough. *Team* Hampshire (1919, 2 matches).
Career batting
5–6–2–50–43–12.50–0–*ct* 1
Bowling 365–11–33.18–0–0–4/60
His last first-class appearance was for West of England in 1927. He played regularly for Dorset during the 1920s and 1930s.

Buss, Antony
Professional. *b:* 1.9.1939, Brightling, Sussex. Brother of M. A. (Sussex). Lower order right-hand batsman, right-arm fast-medium bowler. *Team* Sussex (1958–74, 304 matches).
Career batting
310–412–76–4415–83–13.13–0–*ct* 131
Bowling 23989–958–25.04–44–3–8/23
He took 100 wickets in a season three times (best 120, av 20.30, in 1965 and 120, av 22.55, in 1966).

Buss, Clarence Harold Henry
Amateur. *b:* 19.2.1913, Weybridge, Surrey. *d:* 6.12.1974, Addlestone, Surrey. Lower order left-hand batsman, slow left-arm bowler. *Team* Surrey (1934, 1 match).
Career batting
1–2–0–47–42–23.50–0–*ct* 0
Bowling 143–2–71.50–0–0–2/90

Buss, Michael Alan
Professional. *b:* 24.1.1944, Brightling, Sussex. Brother of Antony (Sussex). Middle order, then from 1966 opening left-hand batsman, slow left arm, later medium pace bowler. *Teams* Sussex (1961–78, 297 matches); Orange Free State (1972/3 to 1977/8). *Tour* MCC Under 25 to Pakistan 1966/7.
Career batting
316–547–47–11996–159–23.99–11–*ct* 230
Bowling 15349–547–28.06–18–0–7/58
He hit 1,000 runs in a season 4 times (best 1,379, av 37.27, in 1970).

Buswell, John Edgar
Professional. *b:* 3.7.1909, Barnwell, Northants. Tail end right-hand batsman, right-arm medium pace bowler. *Team* Northants (1936–39, 61 matches).
Career batting
61–99–29–525–30–7.50–0–*ct* 19
Bowling 5653–172–32.86–5–1–7/61

Buswell, Walter Alfred
Professional. *b:* 12.1.1875, Welford, Northants. *d:* 24.4.1950, Swinford, Leics. Son of Alfred (Leics 1879–83). Lower order hard-hitting right-hand batsman, wicket-keeper. *Team* Northants (1906–21, 205 matches).
Career batting
205–327–76–2670–101*–10.63–1–*ct* 288–*st* 115

Butchaart, Iain Peter
Cricketer. *b*: 9.5.1960, Bulawayo, Rhodesia. Sound middle order right-hand batsman, right-arm medium pace bowler. *Team* Zimbabwe (1980/1 to 1982/3). *Tour* Zimbabwe to England 1982.
Career batting
9–14–1–200–54–15.38–0–*ct* 7
Bowling 209–4–52.25–0–0–2/22

Butcher, Arthur
Amateur. *b:* 8.11.1863, Tring, Hertfordshire. *d:* 17.9.1955, Kensington, London. Middle order right-hand batsman, right-arm slow bowler. *Sch* Mill Hill. *Team* MCC (1902–05).
Career batting
2–4–1–35–24*–11.66–0–*ct* 0
His County cricket was for Hertfordshire.

Butcher, Alan Raymond
Cricketer. *b:* 7.1.1954, Croydon, Surrey. Brother of I. P. (Leics) and M. S. (Surrey). Attractive opening left-hand batsman, left-arm medium or slow bowler, good close field. *Team* Surrey (1972–83, 217 matches). *Tours* Overseas XI to India 1980/1; International XI to Jamaica 1982/3. *Test* England (1979, 1 match).
Career batting
224–378–36–11278–216*–32.97–22–*ct* 103
Bowling 3920–99–39.59–1–0–6/48
Test batting
1–2–0–34–20–17.00–0–*ct* 0
Bowling 9–0
He hit 1,000 runs in a season five times (best

1,713, av 46.29, in 1980). His only double century is 216* for Surrey v Cambridge U at Fenner's in 1980.

Butcher, Basil Fitzherbert
Professional. *b:* 3.9.1933, Sugar Estate near Port Mourant, Berbice. Excellent middle order right-hand batsman, right-arm leg break bowler, fine field. *Team* British Guiana (1954/5 to 1970/1). *Tours* West Indies to England 1963, 1966, 1969, to Australia and New Zealand 1968/9, to India and Pakistan 1958/9; to India and Ceylon 1966/7; Rest of World to England 1968; Commonwealth to Pakistan 1963/4. *Tests* West Indies (1958/9 to 1969, 44 matches).
Career batting
169–262–29–11628–209*–49.90–31–*ct* 67
Bowling 1217–40–30.42–1–0–5/34
Test batting
44–78–6–3104–209*–43.11–7–*ct* 15
Bowling 90–5–18.00–1–0–5/34

He was very successful on all of his three tours to England, hitting 1,294 runs (av 44.62) in 1963, 1,105 (av 48.04) in 1966 and 984 (av 61.50) in 1969. His best innings in England was his 133 in the Lord's Test of 1963, but he also hit a splendid 209* in the Trent Bridge Test of 1966, saving his side. His final first-class match was for Berbice in 1971/2.

Butcher, Cecil Frank
Professional. *b:* 31.10.1872, Steyning, Sussex. *d:* 22.3.1929, Hove, Sussex. Tail end right-hand batsman, right-arm fast medium bowler. *Team* Sussex (1894–96, 6 matches).
Career batting
6–12–0–36–13–3.00–*ct* 1
Bowling 355–9–39.44–0–0–3/107

Butcher, Douglas Harry
Amateur. *b:* 15.5.1876, Mitcham, Surrey. *d:* 4.7.1945, Wallington, Surrey. Middle order right-hand batsman. *Team* Surrey (1900–13, 7 matches).
Career batting
7–11–1–187–71–18.70–0–*ct* 1

Butcher, Ian Paul
Cricketer. *b*: 1.7.1962, Farnborough, Kent. Brother of A. R. (Surrey) and M. S. (Surrey). Middle order right-hand batsman. *Team* Leicestershire (1980–83, 25 matches).
Career batting
25–41–4–1211–139–32.32–3–*ct* 22
Bowling 2–1–2.00–0–0–1/2

His best season was 1983 with 973 runs, av 33.55.

Butcher, Martin Simon
Cricketer. *b*: 17.5.1958, Thornton Heath, Surrey. Brother of A. R. (Surrey) and I. P. (Leics). Middle order right-hand batsman. *Team* Surrey (1982, 1 match).
Career batting
1 match, did not bat– *ct* 1
Bowling 2–0

Butcher, Roland Orlando
Cricketer. *b*: 14.10.1953, East Point, St Philip, Barbados. Hard-hitting middle order right-hand batsman, right-arm medium pace bowler, good close field. *Teams* Barbados (1974/5); Middlesex (1974–83, 125 matches); Tasmania (1982/3, 2 matches). *Tours* Middlesex to Zimbabwe 1980/1; England to West Indies 1980/1; International XI to Pakistan 1981/2, to Jamaica 1982/3. *Tests* England (1980/1, 3 matches).
Career batting
153–238–18–6491–197–29.50–10–*ct* 188–*st* 1
Bowling 76–0
Test batting
3–5–0–71–32–14.20–0–*ct* 3

In 1982 he hit 1,058 runs, av 42.32.

Butler, Hon Brian Danvers
Amateur. *b:* 18.4.1876, Belturbet, Co Cavan, Ireland. *d:* 18.8.1916, Longueval, France. Middle order batsman. *Sch* Eton. *Team* MCC (1913–14).
Career batting
2–4–0–42–29–10.50–*ct* 0

Butler, Edward Henry
Amateur. *b:* 15.3.1851, Hobart, Tasmania. *d:* 5.1.1928, Lower Sandy Bay, Tasmania. Middle order right-hand batsman, fast right-arm bowler. *Teams* Tasmania (1870/1 to 1883/4, 5 matches); Victoria (1872/3, 1 match); MCC (1877). *Tour* Tasmania to New Zealand 1883/4.
Career batting
10–17–3–98–26–7.00–0–*ct* 7
Bowling 148–7–21.14–1–0–6/62

Butler, Edward Montagu
Amateur. *b:* 3.12.1866, Harrow, Middlesex. *d:* 11.2.1948, Rogate, Sussex. Middle order right-hand batsman. *Sch* Harrow. *Teams* Middlesex (1885, 2 matches); Cambridge U (1888–89, blue both years).
Career batting
13–22–2–362–47–18.10–0–*ct* 4
Bowling 11–0

He was an all-round athlete, representing Cambridge at both tennis and rackets and winning the 100 yards at the University sports in 1885. He also played for Cambridgeshire.

Butler, Frederick
Professional. *b:* 29.12.1857, Radcliffe-on-Trent, Notts. *d:* 26.2.1923, Sailors' Snug Harbor, Staten Island, USA. Brother of Robert (Notts), nephew of George Parr (Notts). Opening/middle order right-hand batsman. *Team* Nottinghamshire (1881–90, 45 matches).
Career batting
48–76–7–1042–171–15.10–1–*ct* 26
Bowling 11–0
He did not play for Notts in 1885–86, being in America and went to live there permanently about 1900. He also played for Durham and Northumberland.

Butler, F. L.
Amateur. *Team* South (1877).
Career batting
1–2–2–3–3*–no av–0–*ct* 0

Butler, George Stephen
Amateur. *b:* 16.12.1900, Marlborough, Wilts. *d:* 21.9.1969, Kingswear, Devon. Attractive right-hand opening batsman. *Sch* Marlborough. *Team* Somerset (1920, 1 match).
Career batting
8–14–0–411–121–29.35–1–*ct* 7
Bowling 22–0
He appeared regularly for Wiltshire from 1920 to 1939 and made several appearances in first-class cricket for the Minor Counties, the final one being in 1939. He also played for Devon.

Butler, Harold James
Professional. *b:* 12.3.1913, Clifton, Nottingham. Hard-hitting lower order right-hand batsman, right-arm fast-medium bowler. *Teams* Nottinghamshire (1933–54, 306 matches); Services in India (1943/4 to 1944/5). *Tour* MCC to West Indies 1947/8. *Tests* England (1947 to 1947/8, 2 matches).
Career batting
319–381–100–2962–62–10.54–0–*ct* 111
Bowling 23276–952–24.44–46–6–8/15
Test batting
2–2–1–15–15*–15.00–0–*ct* 1
Bowling 215–12–17.91–0–0–4/34
He took 100 wickets in a season twice (best 106, av 22.55 in 1947).

Butler, John
Professional. *b:* 29.8.1863, Clifton, Nottingham. *d:* 1945, Belper, Derbyshire. Nephew of George Wootton (Notts). Middle order right-hand batsman. *Team* Nottinghamshire (1889, 6 matches).
Career batting
6–8–1–111–56–15.85–0–*ct* 1

Butler, Robert
Generally amateur but played as professional in a few matches. *b:* 8.3.1852, Radcliffe-on-Trent, Notts. *d:* 18.12.1916, Sutton-cum-Granby, Notts. Brother of Frederick (Notts), nephew of George Parr (Notts). Middle order right-hand batsman. *Team* Nottinghamshire (1870–77, 7 matches).
Career batting
10–16–0–163–60–10.18–0–*ct* 8–*st* 1

Butler, Samuel Evan
Amateur. *b:* 15.4.1850, Colombo, Ceylon. *d:* 30.4.1903, Bath, Somerset. Lower order right-hand batsman, right-hand fast round-arm bowler, good field. *Sch* Eton. *Team* Oxford U (1870–73, blue all four years).
Career batting
21–34–6–256–31–9.14–0–*ct* 17
Bowling 1419–99+7–14.33–10–3–10/38
His fame rests with the feat of taking all ten wickets (for 38) in the first innings of Cambridge during the University match at Lord's in 1871. He also played for Devon and Somerset.

Butt, Henry Rigden
Professional. *b:* 27.12.1865, Sands End, Fulham, Middlesex. *d:* 21.12.1928, Hastings, Sussex. Hard-hitting tail end right-hand batsman, wicket-keeper. *Team* Sussex (1890–1912, 517 matches). *Tour* Hawke to South Africa 1895/6. *Tests* England (1895/6, 3 matches).
Career batting
550–801–225–7391–96–12.83–0–*ct* 953–*st* 275
Bowling 33–0
Test batting
3–4–1–22–13–7.33–0–*ct* 1–*st* 1

Butt, John Alec Steuart
Amateur. *b:* 7.5.1892, Sutton, Surrey. *d:* 30.10.1966, Kensington, London. Middle order left-hand batsman. *Sch* Marlborough. *Team* Sussex (1923, 1 match).
Career batting
1–2–0–10–8–5.00–0–*ct* 0

Butterfield, Edward Banks
Amateur. *b:* 1849, Keighley, Yorkshire. *d:* 1899, Keighley. Opening batsman. *Team* Yorkshire (1870, 1 match).
Career batting
1–2–0–8–8–4.00–0–*ct* 0

Butterfield, Walter
Professional. *b:* 6.8.1870, Dewsbury, Yorkshire. *d:* 19.7.1954, West Bridgford, Nottingham. Useful right-hand batsman, right-arm medium pace bowler. *Team* Derbyshire (1896, 2 matches).

Career batting
2–4–0–11–7–2.75–0–*ct* 0
Bowling 20–1–20.00–0–0–1/10

Butterworth, Hugh Montagu
Amateur. *b:* 1.11.1885, Saffron Walden, Essex. *d:* 25.9.1915. He was killed in action, Hooge, Belgium. Opening batsman. *Sch* Marlborough. *Team* Oxford U (1906).
Career batting
3–6–0–78–31–13.00–0–*ct* 2
He represented Oxford at rackets in 1905 and 1906. After leaving the University he emigrated to Wanganui, New Zealand, and his name can be found in matches there – in the 1914/15 season he hit consecutive innings of 296 and 311. He also played for Wiltshire.

Butterworth, Henry Rhodes Whittle
Amateur. *b:* 4.2.1909, Rochdale, Lancashire. *d:* 9.10.1958, Hollingworth Lake, near Littleborough, Lancashire. Middle/lower order right-hand batsman, leg break bowler. *Sch* Rydal. *Teams* Cambridge U (1929–30, blue 1929); Lancashire (1931–36, 25 matches).
Career batting
47–68–11–1014–107–17.78–1–*ct* 23
Bowling 2909–80–36.26–3–1–6/50
His final first-class match was for Minor Counties in 1937. He also played for Denbighshire.

Butterworth, John Compton
Amateur. *b:* 17.8.1905, Samarang, Java. *d:* 18.3.1941, Greenwich, Kent. Brother of R. E. C. (Oxford U and Middlesex). Middle order right-hand batsman. *Sch* Harrow. *Teams* Middlesex (1925, 1 match); Oxford U (1926).
Career batting
3–6–1–49–16*–9.80–0–*ct* 1

Butterworth, Reginald Edmund Compton
Amateur. *b:* 16.8.1906, Samarang, Java. *d:* 30.5.1940. He was killed in action. Brother of J. C. (Middlesex and Oxford U). Opening right-hand batsman, right-arm fast medium bowler. *Sch* Harrow. *Teams* Oxford U (1926–27, blue 1927); Middlesex (1935–37, 14 matches). *Tours* Cahn to Ceylon 1936/7.
Career batting
38–63–2–1189–110–19.49–2–*ct* 15
Bowling 2078–50–41.56–0–0–3/11
His final first-class match was for MCC in 1939.

Butterworth, Wilfred Selkirk
Amateur. *b:* 11.10.1855, Rochdale, Lancashire. *d:* 9.4.1908, Rochdale, Lancashire. Middle order right-hand batsman, wicket-keeper. *Sch* Lancing. *Team* Lancashire (1876–82, 9 matches).
Career batting
9–14–1–73–22–5.61–0–*ct* 4

Buttery, John
Professional. *b:* 21.12.1815, Nottingham. *d:* 5.12.1873, Nottingham. Lower order batsman, excellent bowler. *Teams* Nottinghamshire (1843–45, 4 matches); Lancashire (1849, 1 match); Manchester (1852).
Career batting
9–16–1–148–36–9.86–0–*ct* 6
Bowling 47–3+19–15.66–1–0–8/?

Buttle, Cecil Frederick Douglas
Professional. *b:* 11.2.1906, Norton Fitzwarren, Somerset. Lower order right-hand batsman, right-arm fast medium bowler. *Team* Somerset (1926–28, 2 matches).
Career batting
2–4–1–8–4*–2.66–0–*ct* 0
Bowling 54–0

Buttress, William
Professional. *b:* 25.11.1827, Cambridge. *d:* 25.8.1866, Cambridge. Lower order batsman, right-arm medium pace spin bowler. *Team* Cambridge Town Club (1849–61); Cambridgeshire (1857–61, 3 matches).
Career batting
17–27–10–65–9*–3.82–0–*ct* 11
Bowling 558–37+46–15.08–9–2–7/35
He was regarded as one of the best bowlers of his day, but, for some reason unknown, was rarely selected for important matches. He also played for Norfolk, Leicestershire, Devon, Cheshire and Durham.

Buxton, Cyril Digby
Amateur. *b:* 25.6.1865, Woodford, Essex. *d:* 10.5.1892, Woodford, by his own hand. Opening right-hand batsman, right-arm medium pace bowler, brilliant field. *Sch* Harrow. *Team* Cambridge U (1885–88, blue all four years).
Career batting
40–68–4–1213–108*–18.95–1–*ct* 30
Bowling 1522–60–25.36–2–1–5/16
His County cricket was for Essex (non-first-class) 1883–1891. His final first-class match was for MCC in 1891. He also excelled at tennis and rackets.

Buxton, Ian Ray
Professional. *b:* 17.4.1938, Cromford, Derbyshire. Middle order right-hand batsman, right-arm medium pace bowler. *Team* Derbyshire (1959–73, 350 matches).
Career batting
350–579–86–11803–118*–23.94–5–*ct* 199
Bowling 12742–483–26.38–12–2–7/33
He hit 1,000 runs in a season 5 times (best 1,219, av 28.34, in 1964). He was captain of Derbyshire 1970–72. He was also a good soccer player, appearing for Derby County, Luton Town, Notts County and Port Vale.

Buxton, Joseph Herbert
Professional. *b:* 20.12.1912, Kirkby-in-Ashfield, Notts. Lower order right-hand batsman, right-arm fast-medium bowler. *Team* Nottinghamshire (1937, 1 match).
Career batting
1–1–0–6–6–6.00–0–*ct* 2
Bowling 90–1–90.00–0–0–1/54

Buxton, Noah
Professional. *b:* 6.11.1876, Codnor, Derbyshire. *d:* 26.5.1967, Pontefract, Yorkshire. Uncle of J. H. (Notts). Lower order right-hand batsman, right-arm fast medium bowler. *Team* Derbyshire (1902–11, 7 matches).
Career batting
7–14–2–40–7–3.33–0–*ct* 1
Bowling 171–5–34.20–0–0–2/14
He also played for Staffordshire and Cheshire.

Buxton, Robert Vere
Amateur. *b:* 29.4.1883, London. *d:* 1.10.1953, Itchen-Abbas, Hants. Opening/middle order right-hand batsman. *Sch* Eton. *Teams* Oxford U (1906, blue); Middlesex (1906–09, 10 matches).
Career batting
17–31–1–664–76–22.13–*ct* 10
Bowling 15–0
He also played for Hertfordshire.

Byass, John Edmund
Amateur. *b:* 8.5.1854, Upper Clapton, Middlesex. *d:* 6.6.1936, Shepparton, Victoria, Australia. Middle order right-hand batsman, right-arm fast bowler, slip field. *Sch* Christ College, Finchley. *Team* Kent (1874–76, 3 matches).
Career batting
4–8–0–34–17–4.25–0–*ct* 2
He emigrated to Australia as a young man and was therefore lost to County cricket.

Byng, Arthur Maitland
Amateur. *b:* 26.9.1872, Ireland. *d:* 14.9.1914. He was killed in action at Vailly, France. Sound right-hand middle order batsman. *Teams* Hampshire (1905, 3 matches); Jamaica (1896/7).
Career batting
8–15–0–252–70–16.80–0–*ct* 8
Bowling 168–7–24.00–0–0–3/53
He was one of the best batsmen in Army cricket during the ten years prior to the First World War.

Bynoe, Michael Robin
Cricketer. *b:* 23.2.1941, Christchurch, Barbados. Opening right-hand batsman, slow left-arm bowler. *Team* Barbados (1957/8 to 1971/2). *Tours* West Indies to India and Pakistan 1958/9, to India and Ceylon 1966/7; Barbados to England 1969. *Tests* West Indies (1958/9 to 1966/7, 4 matches).
Career batting
56–97–10–3572–190–41.05–6–*ct* 44
Bowling 246–9–27.33–0–0–2/7
Test batting
4–6–0–111–48–18.50–0–*ct* 4
Bowling 5–1–5.00–0–0–1/5

Byrne, George Robert
Amateur. *b:* 28.5.1892, Northfield, Birmingham. *d:* 23.6.1973, Torteval, Guernsey. Middle order right-hand batsman, right-arm medium pace bowler. *Team* Warwickshire (1912, 8 matches); Worcestershire (1914–21, 4 matches).
Career batting
12–20–0–64–18–3.20–0–*ct* 1
Bowling 239–7–34.14–0–0–3/9
He took 3 wickets in 4 balls during his first-class debut match for Warwickshire in 1912.

Byrne, James Frederick
Amateur. *b:* 19.6.1871, Birmingham. *d:* 10.5.1954, Edgbaston, Birmingham. Middle order right-hand batsman, right-arm fast-medium bowler. *Sch* Downside. *Team* Warwickshire (1897–1912, 138 matches).
Career batting
140–219–10–4766–222–22.75–4–*ct* 81
Bowling 2248–74–30.37–1–0–5/37
His highest score was 222 for Warwickshire v Lancashire at Edgbaston in 1905. He captained Warwickshire 1903–06. A brilliant rugby footballer, he played for Moseley and England at full-back, leading England in the 1897/8 season.

Byrom, John Lewis
Amateur. *b:* 20.7.1851, Saddleworth, Yorkshire. *d:* 24.8.1931, Delph, Oldham, Lancashire. Middle order right-hand batsman, right-arm

medium pace bowler, good field. *Team* Yorkshire (1874, 2 matches).
Career batting
3–5–0–20–11–4.00–0–*ct* 1
His final first-class match was for Gentlemen of North in 1877.

Bythell, William John
Amateur. *b:* 9.9.1862, Poona, India. *d:* 30.6.1920, Elm Grove, Southsea, Hants. Useful batsman. *Team* MCC (1903).
Career batting
1–2–0–8–6–4.00–0–*ct* 0

CADELL, ALEXANDER RICHARD
Amateur. *b:* 19.8.1900, Ferozepore, India. *d:* 14.5.1928, Petersfield Cottage Hospital, Hampshire, as the result of a motor accident. Middle/lower order right-hand batsman, right-arm medium fast bowler. *Teams* Royal Navy (1922–25); Hampshire (1923–27, 2 matches).
Career batting
12–19–2–226–48–13.29–0–*ct* 6
Bowling 854–21–40.66–0–0–3/37

Cadman, Samuel William (Anthony)
Professional. *b:* 29.1.1877, Denton, Lancashire. *d:* 6.5.1952, Glossop, Derbyshire. Steady opening/middle order right-hand batsman, right-arm medium pace bowler. *Team* Derbyshire (1900–26, 375 matches).
Career batting
377–690–34–14077–126–21.45–8–*ct* 277
Bowling 20370–807–25.24–30–2–8/70
He hit 1,000 runs in a season twice (best 1,036, av 29.60, in 1911). After leaving first-class cricket he played for Glossop and continued with that club until the age of 70.

Cadogan, Edward Henry
Amateur. *b:* 11.9.1908, Kasauli, India. Lower order right-hand batsman, right-arm fast bowler. *Sch* Winchester. *Teams* Europeans (1929/30); Army (1933–36); Hampshire (1933–35, 5 matches).
Career batting
9–15–5–148–36*–14.80–0–*ct* 4
Bowling 652–29–22.48–1–0–5/52

Caesar, Julius
Professional. *b:* 25.3.1830, Godalming, Surrey. *d:* 6.3.1878, Godalming, Surrey. Brother of F. B. (Surrey 1859–62). Opening/middle order right-hand batsman, occasional right-hand fast round-arm bowler, excellent field. *Team* Surrey (1849–67, 121 matches); Lancashire (1851, 1 match). *Tours* Parr to North America 1859 (not first-class), to Australia 1863/4.
Career batting
194–333–24–4879–132*–15.78–3–*ct* 181
Bowling 134–6+8–22.33–0–0–3/?

He was one of the best batsmen of his day and excelled at the on-drive. Unfortunately he was also very temperamental, getting most dejected when he made a small score. Out with a shooting party, his gun went off accidentally and killed one of the gamekeepers; Caesar never really recovered from the shock.

Caesar, William Cecil
Amateur. *b:* 25.11.1899, Clapham, Surrey. Lower order right-hand batsman, right-arm medium-fast bowler. *Teams* Surrey (1922, 1 match); Somerset (1946, 3 matches).
Career batting
4–4–1–14–7–4.66–0–*ct* 3
Bowling 252–10–25.20–0–0–4/59
A noted soccer player he represented England in amateur internationals and appeared for Dulwich Hamlet, Darlington, Fulham, Walsall and Brentford.

Caffarey, James
Professional. *b:* 1861, Mitcham, Surrey. *d:* December, 1913, Wandsworth, South London. Middle order batsman, change bowler. *Team* Surrey (1881–82, 3 matches).
Career batting
3–5–0–18–6–3.60–0–*ct* 2
Bowling 44–0

Caffyn, William
Professional. *b:* 2.2.1828, Reigate, Surrey. *d:* 28.8.1919, Reigate, Surrey. Nephew of W. W. (Surrey 1844). Stylish middle order right-hand batsman, right-hand medium pace round-arm bowler. *Teams* Surrey (1849–73, 89 matches); Kent (1858, 2 matches as given man); Lancashire (1851, 1 match); New South Wales (1865/6 to 1870/1, 5 matches). *Tours* Parr to North America 1859 (not first-class), to Australia 1863/4; Stephenson to Australia 1861/2.
Career batting
200–350–23–5885–103–17.99–2–*ct* 149
Bowling 7773–577+24–13.47–49–11–9/29
Regarded as one of the leading batsmen of his time, Caffyn stayed behind in Australia after the 1863/4 tour and his coaching had much to do with

raising the standard of cricket in Australia. He returned to England in 1871. His best bowling was 9/29 for Surrey and Sussex v England at the Oval in 1857.

Cahn, Sir Julien
Amateur. *b:* 21.10.1882, Cardiff. *d:* 26.9.1944, Stanford Hall, Notts. Right-hand batsman, right-arm slow bowler. *Team* Cahn's XI (1928/9 to 1935). *Tours* Cahn to Jamaica 1928/9, to Argentine 1929/30, to North America 1933 (not first-class), to Ceylon 1936/7 (no first-class matches), to New Zealand 1938/9 (no first-class matches).
Career batting
6–9–2–70–17–10.00–0–*ct* 0
Bowling 149–2–74.50–0–0–1/1

The major patron of English cricket between the two World Wars, Cahn ran his own cricket team with its home ground at Loughborough Road, West Bridgeford, Notts.

Cairns, Bernard Lance
Cricketer. *b*: 10.10.1949, Picton, New Zealand. Hard hitting lower order right-hand batsman, right-arm medium pace bowler. *Teams* Central Districts (1972/3 to 1975/6); Otago (1976/7 to 1979/80); Northern Districts (1981/2 to 1982/3). *Tours* New Zealand to Australia 1973/4, 1980/1, to Pakistan and India 1976/7, to England 1978, 1983. *Tests* New Zealand (1973/4 to 1983, 32 matches).
Career batting
119–185–22–3389–110–20.79–1–*ct* 73
Bowling 10224–394–25.94–23–5–8/46
Test batting
32–51–7–739–52*–16.79–0–*ct* 24
Bowling 3096–97–31.91–5–1–7/74

He took 35 wickets, av 25.20, on the 1978 tour to England and played in two Tests, but with little success. In 1983 he played in all four Tests and after Hadlee was the leading bowler with 16 wickets, av 28.81. His first-class debut was for New Zealand Under 23s in 1971/2.

Cairns, John David
Amateur. *b:* 10.2.1925, Gibraltar. Opening right-hand batsman. *Sch* Highgate. *Team* Oxford U (1946).
Career batting
7–14–0–179–36–12.78–0–*ct* 2

His final first-class match was for Free Foresters in 1949.

Calder, Henry
Amateur. *b:* 14.4.1858, South Stoneham, Hants. *d:* 19.5.1938, Southampton, Hants. Middle order batsman, useful change bowler. *Teams* Hampshire (1882–85, 5 matches); Eastern Province (1896/7); Western Province (1892/3 to 1894/5).
Career batting
10–19–2–288–44–16.94–0–*ct* 5
Bowling 222–10–22.00–0–0–3/24

Caldwell, Rev William Somerville
Amateur. *b:* 26.2.1878, Altrincham, Cheshire. *d:* 14.1.1964, Littlemore, Oxon. Patient middle order right-hand batsman. *Team* Worcestershire (1901–04, 20 matches).
Career batting
20–33–1–673–133–21.03–2–*ct* 6
Bowling 40–2–20.00–0–0–2/23

He also played for Cheshire and Oxfordshire.

Callington, A. (*see under* Lord, A.)

Calnan, Clement Noel
Amateur. *b:* 25.12.1888, Mile End, London, *d:* 30.1.1974, Southend, Essex. Middle order batsman, change bowler. *Team.* Essex (1919–29, 4 matches).
Career batting
4–8–0–49–24–6.12–0–*ct* 1
Bowling 25–0

Calthorpe, Hon Frederick Somerset (Gough)
Amateur. *b:* 27.5.1892, Kensington, London. *d:* 19.11.1935, Worplesdon, Surrey. Middle order right-hand batsman, right-arm medium pace bowler. *Sch* Repton. *Teams* Cambridge U (1912–14, 1919, blue all four years); Sussex (1911–12, 2 matches); Warwickshire (1919–30, 231 matches). *Tours* MCC to Australia and New Zealand 1922/3, to West Indies 1925/6, 1929/30. *Tests* England (1929/30, 4 matches).
Career batting
369–576–52–12596–209–24.03–13–*ct* 216
Bowling 23390–782–29.91–18–0–6/53
Test batting
4–7–0–129–49–18.42–0–*ct* 3
Bowling 91–1–91.00–0–0–1/38

He captained England in the four Tests in which he appeared and also captained Warwickshire from 1920 to 1929. He hit 1,000 runs in a season five times (best 1,546 av 30.92, in 1925). His only double century was 209 for Warwickshire v Hampshire at Edgbaston in 1921. He took 100 wickets, av 24.26, in 1920, performing the 'double' in the same season. His final first-class match was for MCC in 1935.

Calvert, Charles
Amateur. *b:* 21.3.1833, Kneller Hall, Middlesex. *d:* 7.4.1905, Ecclefechan, Dumfries-shire. Middle order right-hand batsman, right-hand fast round-arm bowler. *Sch* Rugby. *Teams* Middlesex

(1865–66, 9 matches); Surrey (1868, 13 matches).
Career batting
27–43–4–541–67*–13.87–0–*ct* 14
Bowling 102–2–51.00–0–0–1/9

Camacho, George Stephen
Cricketer. *b:* 15.10.1945, Georgetown, British Guiana. Opening right-hand batsman, leg break and googly bowler. Grandson of G. C. Learmond (Barbados and Trinidad). *Team* Guyana (1964/5 to 1978/9). *Tours* West Indies to England 1969, 1973, to Australia and New Zealand 1968/9. *Tests* West Indies (1967/8 to 1970/1, 11 matches).
Career batting
76–125–8–4079–166–34.86–7–*ct* 47
Bowling 216–8–27.00–0–0–3/10
Test batting
11–22–0–640–87–29.09–0–*ct* 4
Bowling 12–0

He was most successful on his 1969 tour of England, heading the Test batting averages, but in 1973 he had the misfortune to suffer a severe injury and played in only two first-class matches. He is Secretary of the West Indies Board of Control.

Came, Kenneth Charles
Amateur. *b:* 29.10.1925, Reading, Berkshire. Lower order left-hand batsman, right-arm medium pace bowler. *Team* Free Foresters (1957).
Career batting
1–2–0–12–6–6.00–0–*ct* 1
Bowling 46–0

Cameron, Francis James
Amateur. *b:* 22.6.1923, Kingston, Jamaica. Son of J. J. (Jamaica) and brother of J. H. (Somerset, West Indies). Middle order right-hand batsman, off-break bowler. *Teams* Jamaica (1945/6 to 1958/9); Canada (1954). *Tours* West Indies to India, Pakistan and Ceylon 1948/9; Canada to England 1954. *Tests* West Indies (1948/9, 5 matches).
Career batting
21–27–5–551–75*–25.04–0–*ct* 9
Bowling 1411–29–48.65–0–0–4/52
Test batting
5–7–1–151–75*–25.16–0–*ct* 0
Bowling 278–3–92.66–0–0–2/74

Cameron, Francis James
Amateur. *b:* 1.6.1932, Dunedin, New Zealand. Tail end right-hand batsman, right-hand medium-fast bowler. *Team* Otago (1952/3 to 1966/7). *Tours* New Zealand to South Africa and Australia 1961/2, to India and Pakistan 1964/5, to England 1965. *Tests* New Zealand (1961/2 to 1965, 19 matches).
Career batting
119–176–92–993–43–11.82–0–*ct* 26
Bowling 9658–447–21.60–21–0–7/27
Test batting
19–30–20–116–27*–11.60–0–*ct* 2
Bowling 1849–62–29.82–3–0–5/34

Although he ended the 1965 tour to England with 47 wickets av 24.42, he was ineffective in the two Tests in which he played. By dint of having 12 not out innings he headed the first-class batting averages for the tour.

Cameron, Horace Brakendridge
Amateur. *b:* 5.7.1905, Port Elizabeth, South Africa. *d:* 2.11.1935, Johannesburg, South Africa, of enteric fever. Excellent middle order right-hand batsman, wicket-keeper. *Teams* Transvaal (1924/5 to 1934/5); Eastern Province (1929/30); Western Province (1930/1). *Tours* South Africa to England 1929, 1935, to Australia and New Zealand 1931/2. *Tests* South Africa (1927/8 to 1935, 26 matches).
Career batting
107–161–17–5396–182–37.47–11–*ct* 155–*st* 69
Bowling 13–0
Test batting
26–45–4–1239–90–30.21–0–*ct* 39–*st* 12

In 1935 he was regarded as a wicket-keeper the equal of the Australian, Oldfield, and his batting was of great value to South Africa – in first-class matches he hit 1,458 runs, av 41.65. He captained the South Africans in Australia in 1931/2, and was vice-captain in 1935. He died after only a few days' illness, having just returned to South Africa from England.

Cameron, John Hemsley
Amateur. *b:* 8.4.1914, Kingston, Jamaica. Son of J. J. (Jamaica), brother of F. J. (Jamaica and Canada). Middle order right-hand batsman, off break, leg break and googly bowler. *Sch* Taunton. *Teams* Cambridge U (1934–37, blue 1935–37); Somerset (1932–47, 48 matches); Jamaica (1945/6). *Tours* West Indies to England 1939; Oxford and Cambridge to Jamaica 1938/9. *Tests* West Indies (1939, 2 matches).
Career batting
105–164–12–2772–113–18.23–4–*ct* 63
Bowling 5662–184–30.77–7–0–7/73
Test batting
2–3–0–6–5–2.00–0–*ct* 0
Bowling 88–3–29.33–0–0–3/66

His greatest triumph was in The Rest v Public Schools match at Lord's in 1931, when in one innings his return read: 19.1–3–49–10

Cameron, Dr John Joseph
Amateur. *b:* 18.5.1882, Kingston, Jamaica. *d:* 12.12.1954, Kingston, Jamaica. Father of J. H.

(Somerset and West Indies) and F. J. (Jamaica and Canada). Right-hand batsman, right-arm slow bowler. *Teams* Jamaica (1908/9 to 1927/8); Gentlemen of England (1908). *Tour* West Indies to England 1906.
Career batting
13–21–2–272–52–14.31–0–*ct* 7
Bowling 213–10–21.30–1–0–5/83

Cammish, James W.
Professional. *b:* 21.5.1921, Scarborough, Yorkshire. *d: circa* 1975, New Zealand. Lower order right-hand batsman, leg break and googly bowler. *Teams* Auckland (1950/1); Yorkshire (1954, 2 matches).
Career batting
7–10–3–31–7*–4.42–0–*ct* 8
Bowling 781–25–31.24–2–0–6/93

Campbell, Alistair Keyon
Amateur. *b:* 29.5.1890, South Stoneham, Hants. *d:* 16.6.1943, Cosham, Hants. Right-hand batsman. *Team* Hampshire (1908–09, 7 matches).
Career batting
7–10–0–91–21–9.10–0–*ct* 1
He played soccer for Southampton.

Campbell, Andrew Neville
Cricketer. *b:* 17.6.1949, Amersham, Buckinghamshire. Middle order left-hand batsman. *Sch* Berkhamsted. *Team* Oxford U (1968–70, blue 1970).
Career batting
15–27–1–530–73–20.38–0–*ct* 5
His County cricket was for Buckinghamshire.

Campbell, Anthony U.
Cricketer. *b:* 25.9.1950, Jamaica. Opening/middle order batsman, wicket-keeper. *Team* Jamaica (1969/70 to 1979/80). *Tour* Jamaica to England 1970.
Career batting
22–35–3–509–48*–15.90–0–*ct* 49–*st* 9

Campbell, Donald
Amateur. *b:* 18.9.1851, Loddon Plains, Victoria, Australia. *d:* 14.9.1887, South Yarra, Victoria, Australia. Opening right-hand batsman. *Teams* Oxford U (1873-76, blue 1874–76); Victoria (1868/9 to 1880/1, 8 matches).
Career batting
25–44–3–643–55–15.68–0–*ct* 13
Bowling 61–2–30.50–0–0–1/0
His County cricket was for Cheshire.

Campbell, Frederick
Amateur. *b:* 15.6.1843, Edinburgh, Scotland. *d:* 13.9.1926, Sydenham Hill, South London. Father of J. M. (Middlesex). Middle order batsman, bowler. *Team* MCC (1867–69).
Career batting
4–6–0–52–34–8.66–0–*ct* 4
Bowling 116–13–8.92–1–0–6/37
He was a well-known club cricketer for many years, appearing for I Zingari, Gentlemen of Hampshire and in military matches.

Campbell, G.
Amateur. Middle order batsman, change bowler. *Team* W.G.Grace's XI (1871).
Career batting
1–1–0–0–0–0.00–0–*ct* 1
Bowling 73–1–73.00–0–0–1/73

Campbell, George Augustus
Amateur. *b:* July 1847, Tonbridge, Kent. *d:* 12.9.1930, Brackley, Northants. Batsman. *Sch* Wellington. *Team* Lancashire (1866, 1 match).
Career batting
1–2–0–18–10–9.00–0–*ct* 0

Campbell, George Gordon
Amateur. *b:* 12.9.1893, Durban, South Africa. *d:* 5.5.1977, Durban, South Africa. Batsman. *Team* Scotland (1921).
Career batting
1–2–0–9–6–4.50–0–*ct* 0

Campbell, Gerald Victor
Amateur. *b:* 29.4.1884, Kensington, London. *d:* 26.3.1950, Lymington, Hants. Lower order right-hand batsman, right-arm medium pace bowler. *Sch* Eton. *Teams* Surrey (1912, 1 match); Europeans (1905/6).
Career batting
2–3–0–16–14–5.33–0–*ct* 0
Bowling 86–0
He was for many years a stalwart of the Sussex Martlets, taking over 1,000 wickets for the Club. He also played for Norfolk.

Campbell, Sir Harold George
Amateur. *b:* 6.4.1888, London. *d:* 9.6.1969, Rolvenden, Kent. Lower order right-hand batsman, right-arm medium pace bowler. *Team* Royal Navy (1912–14).
Career batting
2–4–1–76–38–25.33–0–*ct* 2
Bowling 65–2–32.50–0–0–2/45

Campbell, Ian Parry
Amateur, *b:* 5.2.1928, Purley, Surrey. Hard-hitting middle/lower order right-hand batsman, wicket-keeper. *Sch* Canford. *Teams* Kent (1946, 1 match); Oxford U (1949–51, blue 1949–50). *Tour* MCC to Canada 1951.

Career batting
22–36–4–482–60*–15.06–0–*ct* 24–*st* 17

His fame as a cricketer rests with his quite remarkable achievement at Canford School. In 1945 he hit 1,027 runs (av 79.00) and in 1946 1,277 runs (av 116.00) including three double centuries. In first-class cricket his performances were quite modest, but he was also a noted rugby footballer for Kent and London Counties and was awarded a blue for hockey at Oxford. His final first-class match was for MCC in 1954.

Campbell, Ian Percy Fitzgerald
Amateur. *b:* 25.11.1890, Palampur, Kanga Valley, Punjab, India. *d:* 25.12.1963, Redgorton, Perthshire, Scotland. Middle order right-hand batsman, change bowler. *Sch* Repton. *Teams* Surrey (1910–27, 25 matches); Oxford U (1911–13, blue all three years); Europeans (1925/6 to 1926/7).
Career batting
59–102–3–2413–120–24.37–3–*ct* 28
Bowling 205–5–41.00–0–0–3/12

He also was awarded his blue for soccer and was an excellent fives player. His final first-class match was for Indian XI v MCC in 1933/4.

Campbell, John Maxwell
(known as Ian Maxwell Campbell)
Amateur. *b:* 3.10.1870, London. *d:* 6.3.1954, Amersham, Bucks. Son of Frederick (MCC). Middle order right-hand batsman, right-arm medium pace bowler. *Sch* Dulwich. *Teams* Middlesex (1900, 1 match); London County (1900–02).
Career batting
4–6–0–65–37–10.83–0–*ct* 2
Bowling 57–1–57.00–0–0–1/57

Campbell, Percival
Amateur. *b:* 26.12.1887, West Ham, Essex. *d:* 18.3.1960, Woodford, Essex. Middle order batsman, change bowler. *Sch* Eastbourne. *Team* Essex (1911–19, 13 matches).
Career batting
13–21–2–270–35–14.21–0–*ct* 6
Bowling 26–0

Campbell, Thomas
Amateur. *b:* 9.2.1882, Edinburgh, Scotland. *d:* 5.10.1924, Milndale, Natal, South Africa, in a railway accident. Middle/lower order right-hand batsman, wicket-keeper. *Team* Transvaal (1906/7 to 1908/9). *Tours* South Africa to England 1912; to Australia 1910/11. *Tests* South Africa (1909/10 to 1912, 5 matches).
Career batting
29–42–12–365–48–12.16–0–*ct* 40–*st* 12
Test batting
5–9–3–90–48–15.00–0–*ct* 7–*st* 1

On his single visit to England he was deputy wicket-keeper to Sherwell and had little to do. In view of the nature of his death it should be recorded that he fell out of a train in 1916 and suffered severe head injuries, from which it was thought he would not recover.

Candler, David Cecil
Amateur. *b:* 18.10.1924, Bulawayo, Southern Rhodesia. Middle order right-hand batsman, leg break bowler. *Team* Oxford U (1950–51).
Career batting
5–7–0–115–54–16.42–0–*ct* 2
Bowling 4–0

Candler, Dr John Pycock
Amateur. *b:* 7.10.1873, Alresford, Hants. *d:* 4.12.1942, Finsbury, London. Tail end batsman, bowler. *Sch* Merchant Taylors. *Team* Cambridge U (1894–95).
Career batting
7–10–5–8–8*–1.60–0–*ct* 5
Bowling 662–18–36.77–0–0–3/91

He failed to score in nine consecutive first-class innings.

Candlett, William
Professional. *b: circa* 1847. *d:* 20.6.1904, Salford, Lancashire. Tail end right-hand batsman, right-arm medium bowler. *Team* Kent (1880, 1 match).
Career batting
1–2–1–3–3–3.00–0–*ct* 0
Bowling 29–0

Cangley, Barron George Merriman
Amateur. *b:* 12.9.1922, Blakesley, Towcester, Northants. Middle order right-hand batsman. *Sch* Felsted, *Team* Cambridge U (1947).
Career batting
8–14–1–295–76–22.69–0–*ct* 3

His County cricket was for Cambridgeshire.

Canning, Ernest George
Professional. *b:* 1902, Marylebone, London. Middle order right-hand batsman. *Team* Middlesex (1929–31, 36 matches).
Career batting
37–62–7–829–85–15.07–0–*ct* 11
Bowling 12–0

He also played for Hertfordshire.

Cannings, Victor Henry Douglas
Professional. *b:* 3.4.1919, Bighton, Hants. Lower order right-hand batsman, right-arm medium

pace bowler. *Teams* Warwickshire (1947–49, 53 matches); Hampshire (1950–59, 230 matches).
Career batting
285–373–128–2660–61–10.85–0–*ct* 103
Bowling 21077–927–22.73–42–4–7/52
He took 100 wickets in a season 4 times (best 112, av 21.56, in 1952). He also played for Buckinghamshire.

Cantelupe, Viscount
(*see under* De La Warr, Earl)

Cantlay, Charles Peter Thrale
Cricketer. *b:* 4.2.1954, Victoria, London. Lower order right-hand batsman, right-arm medium fast bowler. *Sch* Radley. *Team* Oxford U (1975).
Career batting
6–9–5–19–9–4.75–0–*ct* 0
Bowling 419–19–38.09–0–0–4/85

Cantrell, Arthur Stanley
Amateur. *b:* 8.5.1883. *d:* 22.5.1954, Black-Notley, Essex. Lower order right-hand batsman, right-arm medium fast bowler. *Sch* Bedford. *Team* Royal Navy (1913–29).
Career batting
15–27–14–308–32*–23.69–0–*ct* 6
Bowling 1256–49–25.63–3–0–6/58

Cantwell, Noel Euchuria Cornelious
Amateur. *b:* 28.12.1932, Cork, Ireland. Left-hand batsman, right-arm medium pace bowler. *Team* Ireland (1956).
Career batting
1–2–1–48–31–48.00–0–*ct* 0
Bowling 13–0
He played football for West Ham and Manchester United, and was an international for the Republic of Ireland.

Capel, David John
Cricketer. *b*: 6.2.1963, Northampton. Middle order right-hand batsman, right-arm medium pace bowler. *Team* Northamptonshire (1981–83, 32 matches).
Career batting
32–48–10–1031–109*–27.13–1–*ct* 20
Bowling 664–9–73.77–0–0–2/14

Capel-Cure, George Nigel
Amateur. *b:* 28.9.1908, London. Nephew of Arthur and Francis (both Essex, pre first-class). Opening left-hand batsman, leg break bowler. *Sch* Eton. *Team* Essex (1929, 1 match).
Career batting
1–2–0–6–6–3.00–0–*ct* 0
Bowling 58–2–29.00–0–0–2/58
He played in Cambridge Freshmen's Match of 1928 and the Seniors' of 1930, but in no first-class matches at the University.

Capes, Charles John
Amateur. *b:* 5.1.1898, Forest Hill. *d:* 16.2.1933, Ospedaletti, Italy. Hard-hitting lower order right-hand batsman, medium pace left-arm bowler. *Sch* Malvern. *Team* Kent (1923–28, 33 matches).
Career batting
33–41–8–534–65*–16.18–0–*ct* 16
Bowling 1381–55–25.10–2–0–7/20
He was better known as an English International hockey player.

Caplan, Jeremy John Notley
Amateur. *b:* 9.10.1941, Champion Reef, India. Lower order right-hand batsman, off break bowler. *Sch* Cheltenham. *Team* Cambridge U (1962).
Career batting
2–3–0–38–26–12.66–0–*ct* 0
Bowling 97–3–32.33–0–0–1/25

Caple, Robert Graham
Professional. *b:* 8.12.1939, Chiswick, Middlesex. Middle order left-hand batsman, right-arm medium pace bowler. *Teams* Middlesex (1959, 2 matches); Hampshire (1961–67, 65 matches).
Career batting
68–103–17–1581–64*–18.38–0–*ct* 32
Bowling 1235–34–36.62–1–0–5/54
His first-class debut was for MCC in 1958.

Caplen, Tom
Amateur. *b:* 23.11.1879, Rusthall, Tunbridge Wells, Kent. *d:* 17.4.1945, Hove, Sussex. Lower order batsman, bowler. *Team* Kent (1897, 1 match).
Career batting
1–2–1–6–5*–6.00–0–*ct* 0
Bowling 74–2–37.00–0–0–2/74
He appeared for Cornwall in 1898, but later moved to India, and his name can be found in a number of important matches there.

Capon, Stephen
Amateur. *b:* 25.4.1927, Snodland, Kent. Lower order right-hand batsman, right-arm fast medium bowler. *Team* Kent (1950, 1 match).
Career batting
1–1–0–4–4–4.00–0–*ct* 0
Bowling 98–0

Caprani, Joseph Desmond
Amateur. *b:* 27.5.1920, Clontarf, Co Dublin, Ireland. Right-hand batsman. *Team* Ireland (1948–60).

Career batting
5–10–0–95–44–9.50–0–*ct* 5

Capron, Frederick William
Amateur. *b:* 1.10.1860, London. *d:* 18.1.1942, Kensington, London. Middle order right-hand batsman. *Sch* Tonbridge/Rugby. *Team* MCC (1881–82).
Career batting
2–3–0–13–11–4.33–0–*ct* 0

Carbutt, Noel John Obelin
Amateur. *b:* 25.12.1895, Gingindhlovu, Zululand. *d:* 31.10.1964, Durban, South Africa. Lower order right-hand batsman, leg break and googly bowler. *Sch* Pietermaritzburg College, South Africa. *Teams* Essex (1923, 2 matches); Madras (1926/7).
Career batting
15–19–5–135–45–9.64–0–*ct* 7
Bowling 1386–36–38.50–2–0–5/20

He was a noted figure in Army cricket for many years. His first-class debut was for Combined Services in 1920 and last match for the Army in 1928.

Card, Anthony John
Professional. *b:* 13.9.1929, Doncaster, Yorkshire. Lower order batsman, slow left-arm bowler. *Team* MCC (1955–58).
Career batting
2–4–2–51–19*–25.50–0–*ct* 2
Bowling 87–7–12.42–0–0–4/26

Carew, Michael Conrad
Amateur. *b:* 15.9.1937, Woodbrook, Port of Spain, Trinidad. Opening left-hand batsman, right-arm medium, or off break, bowler. *Team* Trinidad (1955/6 to 1972/3). *Tours* West Indies to England 1963, 1966, 1969, to Australia and New Zealand 1968/9. *Tests* West Indies (1963 to 1971/2, 19 matches).
Career batting
129–221–18–7810–182–38.47–13–*ct* 83
Bowling 3215–108–29.76–5–0–5/28
Test batting
19–36–3–1127–109–34.15–1–*ct* 13
Bowling 437–8–54.62–0–0–1/11

Of his three tours to England his best was in 1969, when he hit 677 runs, av 45.13; in 1963 he made 1,060 runs, av 30.28. His final first-class match was for North Trinidad 1973/4.

Carey, P.A.D. (*see under* Dobree-Carey, P.A.)

Carey, Thomas Falkland
Amateur. *b:* 12.2.1903, California, USA. *d:* December 1966, Acle, Norfolk. Right-hand batsman, right-arm medium pace bowler. *Team* Dublin University (1924).
Career batting
1–2–0–21–15–10.50–0–*ct* 0
Bowling 41–2–20.50–0–0–2/41

Carkeek, William (Barlow)
Amateur. *b:* 17.10.1878, Walhalla, Victoria, Australia. *d:* 20.2.1937, Prahran, Victoria, Australia. Lower order left-hand batsman, wicket-keeper. *Team* Victoria (1903/4 to 1914/5, 53 matches). *Tours* Australia to England 1909, 1912, to North America 1912. *Tests* Australia (1912, 6 matches).
Career batting
95–146–32–1388–68–12.17–0–*ct* 114–*st* 45
Test batting
6–5–2–16–6*–5.33–0–*ct* 6

Although he was the principal wicket-keeper on the 1912 tour, he did not approach the standard of his contemporary, H. Carter.

Carless, Ernest Francis
Professional in 1934, amateur in 1946. *b:* 9.9.1912, Barry, Glamorgan. Lower order right-hand batsman, wicket-keeper. *Team* Glamorgan (1934–46, 3 matches).
Career batting
3–3–0–35–25–11.66–0–*ct* 1

He also played for Devon. A noted soccer player he appeared for Cardiff City and Plymouth Argyle.

Carlin, John
Professional. *b:* 3.11.1861, New Eastwood, Notts. *d:* 28.11.1944, Eastwood, Notts. Originally a left-hand batsman, he changed to right-hand when being tried for Notts, wicket-keeper. *Team* Nottinghamshire (1887–1901, 58 matches).
Career batting
76–113–20–1578–85–16.96–0–*ct* 101–*st* 39
Bowling 121–5–24.20–0–0–3/25

From 1888 to 1912 he was on the staff at Lord's.

Carlin, Robert McKenzie
Professional. *b:* 24.2.1871, Eastwood, Notts. *d:* 10.3.1950, Conisbrough, Yorkshire. Middle order right-hand batsman, right-arm medium pace bowler. *Team* Derbyshire (1905–08, 15 matches).
Career batting
15–28–1–306–37–11.33–0–*ct* 5
Bowling 208–5–41.60–0–0–2/53

Carling, Philip George
Cricketer. *b:* 25.11.1946, Carshalton, Surrey. Sound opening left-hand batsman, wicket-keeper.

Sch Kingston GS. *Team* Cambridge U (1967–70, blue 1968 and 1970).
Career batting
30–55–3–1160–104–22.30–1–*ct* 13
Bowling 25–0
Chief Executive of Notts CCC 1979–82; of Glamorgan CCC since 1983.

Carlisle, Frederick
Amateur. *b:* 4.11.1849, Liverpool, Lancashire. *d:* 22.10.1920, Eastbourne, Sussex. Middle order batsman. *Sch* Harrow. *Team* Lancashire (1869, 2 matches).
Career batting
2–4–0–37–18–9.25–0–*ct* 0
He also played for Cheshire.

Carlisle, Kenneth Methven
Amateur. *b:* 7.8.1882, Lymm, Cheshire. *d:* 15.5.1967, Bardwell, Suffolk. Father of K. R. M. (Sussex), brother of M. M. (MCC). Middle order right-hand batsman, slow right-arm bowler. *Sch* Harrow. *Team* Oxford U (1903–05, blue all three years).
Career batting
30–55–4–1211–114*–23.70–2–*ct* 19
Bowling 279–6–46.50–0–0–2/39
In 1908 he represented South v North Argentine.

Carlisle, Kenneth Ralph Malcolm
Amateur. *b:* 28.3.1908, Buenos Aires, Argentina. *d:* 23.7.1983, London. Son of K. M. (Oxford U), nephew of M.M. (MCC). Middle/lower order right-hand batsman, right-arm medium pace bowler. *Sch* Harrow. *Teams* Sussex (1927–28, 3 matches); Oxford U (1929).
Career batting
5–7–0–101–34–14.42–0–*ct* 2

Carlisle, Malcolm Methven
Amateur. *b:* 5.7.1884, Lymm, Cheshire. *d:* 24.5.1906, Lucknow, India. Brother of K. M. (Oxford U), uncle of K.R.M. (Sussex). Middle order right-hand batsman. *Sch* Harrow. *Team* MCC (1904).
Career batting
1–2–0–12–12–6.00–0–*ct* 0
Bowling 26–0

Carlstein, Peter Rudolph
Amateur. *b:* 28.10.1938, Klerksdorp, South Africa. Middle order right-hand batsman, fine field, occasional wicket-keeper. *Teams* Orange Free State (1954/5 to 1957/8); Transvaal (1958/9 to 1971/2); Natal (1964/5 to 1966/7); Rhodesia (1967/8 to 1979/80). *Tours* South Africa to England 1960, to Australia 1963/4. *Tests* South Africa (1957/8 to 1963/4, 8 matches).
Career batting
148–255–16–7554–229–31.60–9–*ct* 82
Bowling 480–9–53.33–0–0–3/37
Test batting
8–14–1–190–42–14.61–0–*ct* 3
He appeared in all five Tests on his 1960 tour to England, but only averaged 13.22; in all first-class matches he just missed reaching 1,000 runs. His highest score was 229 for Transvaal v Cavaliers at Johannesburg in 1962/3.

Carmichael, Duncan Smart
Amateur. *b:* 8.11.1915, Matelli, Jailpaiguri, India. Lower order right-hand batsman, right-arm medium pace bowler. *Sch* Fettes. *Team* Cambridge U (1936–37).
Career batting
9–11–4–13–5–1.85–0–*ct* 1
Bowling 658–20–32.90–1–0–6/103

Carmichael (of Carmichael), Evelyn George Massey
Amateur. *b:* 3.4.1871, Worcester. *d:* 14.7.1959, Berrington, Shrewsbury. Middle order right-hand batsman, right-arm medium pace bowler. *Sch* Harrow. *Team* Worcestershire (1903, 1 match).
Career batting
1–2–0–6–5–3.00–0–*ct* 1
He did not appear in first-class cricket whilst at Oxford U.

Carmichael, John
Amateur. *b:* 4.7.1858, Howden, Yorkshire. *d:* 24.8.1914, USA, as the result of a motor accident. Middle order right-hand batsman, wicket-keeper. *Team* Surrey (1876–81, 14 matches).
Career batting
14–24–1–243–47–10.56–0–*ct* 11–*st* 3
Bowling 9–0

Carmody, Douglas Keith
Amateur. *b:* 16.2.1919, Mosman, New South Wales, Australia. *d:* 21.10.1977, Concord, New South Wales, Australia. Opening/middle order right-hand batsman, right-arm medium pace bowler. *Teams* New South Wales (1939/40 to 1946/7, 13 matches); Western Australia (1947/8 to 1955/6, 35 matches). *Tour* Australian Services to England and India 1945.
Career batting
65–123–2–3496–198–28.89–2–*ct* 39–*st* 3
Bowling 187–3–62.33–0–0–1/0
He was captain of the RAAF team in England in 1945, after being a prisoner-of-war. In 1947/8

he captained West Australia to its Sheffield Shield Championship and his close-to-the-wicket field placings earned the name 'Carmody Umbrella'.

Carnegie-Brown, Dr George
Amateur. *b:* 28.1.1906, Jerusalem. *d:* 26.3.1964, Lincoln. Attractive middle order left-hand batsman, good field. *Sch* Leys. *Team* Cambridge U (1926).
Career batting
4–7–0–78–32–11.14–0–*ct* 2

His County cricket was played for Cambridgeshire, Dorset and Lincolnshire. His final first-class match was for the Minor Counties in 1937.

Carnie, William
Amateur. *b:* 27.1.1907, Caputh, Perthshire. Right-hand batsman, right-arm fast medium bowler. *Team* Scotland (1925).
Career batting
1–2–1–6–6*–6.00–0–*ct* 1
Bowling 21–0

Carnill, Denys John
Amateur. *b:* 11.3.1926, Hampstead, North London. Lower order left-hand batsman, leg break bowler. *Sch* Hitchin GS. *Team* Oxford U (1950).
Career batting
1–1–0–8–8–8.00–0–*ct* 0
Bowling 33–1–33.00–0–0–1/33

He also played for Hertfordshire. An excellent hockey player, he represented Oxford and England.

Carpenter, Charles Wilson
Amateur. *b:* 1837, Brighton, Sussex. *d:* 5.3.1876, Nagpore, India as the result of a fall from his horse whilst steeplechasing. Middle order right-hand batsman. *Sch* Brighton. *Team* Sussex (1868, 2 matches).
Career batting
3–6–0–47–15–7.83–0–*ct* 2
Bowling 45–3–15.00–0–0–3/32

His debut in first-class matches was for Gentlemen of Kent and Sussex in 1857.

Carpenter, David
Professional. *b:* 12.9.1935, Rodborough, Stroud, Gloucestershire. Opening right-hand batsman, off break bowler. *Team* Gloucestershire (1954–63, 117 matches).
Career batting
117–210–6–3741–95–18.33–0–*ct* 72
Bowling 36–0

He reached 1,000 runs in a season once : 1,353, av 23.32, 1961.

Carpenter, Herbert Arthur
Professional. *b;* 12.7.1869, Cambridge. *d:* 12.12.1933, Whipps Cross, Essex. Son of R. P. (Cambs), uncle of J. O'Connor (Essex), nephew of George (CTC). Opening right-hand batsman, off break bowler. *Team* Essex (1894–1920, 262 matches).
Career batting
310–551–26–14939–199–28.45–25–*ct* 257
Bowling 2246–50–44.92–0–0–4/57

He scored 1,000 runs in a season 7 times (best 1852, av 37.04, in 1901). His career with Essex commenced in 1888. Latterly he was handicapped by ill-health and left first-class cricket to appear for Cambridgeshire, but made a final appearance for Essex in 1920. His debut in first-class matches was for MCC in 1893.

Carpenter, Robert Pearson
Professional. *b:* 18.11.1830, Mill Road, Cambridge. *d:* 14.7.1901, Cambridge. Father of H. A. (Essex), brother of George (Cambridge Town Club). Fine middle-order right-hand batsman, brilliant point field. *Team* Cambridgeshire (1861–71, 32 matches). *Tours* Parr to North America 1859 (not first-class), to Australia 1863/4.
Career batting
143–233–19–5220–134–24.39–4–*ct* 190–*st* 1
Bowling 290–18+1–16.11–0–0–4/29

About 1860 he was regarded as the finest batsman in England but for various reasons he did not play in important matches at Lord's as often as he deserved. He was associated mainly with the United All England Eleven. His debut in first-class matches was for Cambridge Town Club in 1855 and his final match for the North in 1876.

Carr, Austin Michael
Amateur. *b:* 29.9.1898, Chester. *d:* 20.12.1946, Great Witley, Worcs. Middle order right-hand batsman, *Sch* Eton. *Team* Worcestershire (1921–25, 6 matches).
Career batting
6–10–0–150–82–15.00–0–*ct* 2
Bowling 10–0

Carr, Arthur William
Amateur. *b:* 21.5.1893, Mickleham, Surrey. *d:* 7.2.1963, West Witton, Yorkshire. Hard-hitting middle order right-hand batsman, right-arm medium pace bowler. *Sch* Sherborne and Eton. *Team* Nottinghamshire (1910–34, 416 matches). *Tour* MCC to South Africa 1922/3. *Tests* England (1922/3 to 1929, 11 matches).

Career batting
468–709–42–21051–206–31.56–45–*ct* 393–*st* 1
Bowling 1150–31–37.09–0–0–3/14
Test batting
11–13–1–237–63–19.75–0–*ct* 3

An inspiring but controversial captain, Carr led Notts from 1919 to 1934 and England in the first four Tests v Australia in 1926 and in two Tests v South Africa in 1929. He was dismissed from the England captaincy in 1926 and the Notts captaincy in 1934, in each case in circumstances that resulted in much ill-feeling.

An attacking batsman, he hit 1,000 runs in a season 11 times, exceeding 2,000 runs once (2338, av 51.95, in 1925). He hit two double centuries, his highest being 206 for Notts v Leics at Leicester in 1925. Also in 1925 he hit no less than 48 sixes, which is believed to have created a new record.

The close of his first-class career was brought about by the arguments concerning 'bodyline' bowling. He was dismissed by the Notts Committee in December 1934, but forced an Extra-ordinary General Meeting of the County Club which demanded the sacking of the Committee and reinstatement of Carr. Subtle manoeuvring however managed to reverse the decision of the Extra-ordinary Meeting at the club's AGM and Carr was not seen again in County cricket, though he appeared in a final first-class match for Sir Lindsay Parkinson's XI in 1935.

Carr, Donald Bryce
Amateur. *b:* 28.12.1926, Wiesbaden, Germany. Son of J. L. (Army), father of J.D. (Middlesex). Attractive middle-order right-hand batsman, slow left-arm bowler, excellent close field. *Sch* Repton. *Teams* Derbyshire (1946–63, 336 matches); Oxford U (1949–51, blue all three years). *Tours* MCC to India, Pakistan and Ceylon 1951/2, to Pakistan 1955/6, to South America 1958/9 (not first-class). *Tests* England (1951/2, 2 matches).
Career batting
446–745–72–19257–170–28.61–24–*ct* 499
Bowling 11396–328–34.74–5–0–7/53
Test batting
2–4–0–135–76–33.75–0–*ct* 0
Bowling 140–2–70.00–0–0–2/84

His first-class debut was for England v Australian Services in the Victory 'Test' of 1945 at Lord's. He reached 1,000 runs 11 times (best 2,292, av 44.07, in 1959). On his 1951/2 MCC tour, he captained England in the Madras Test v India. County Captain of Derbyshire 1955 to 1962 and Secretary of the County from 1959 to 1961; Secretary of TCCB since 1973 and Secretary of the Cricket Council since 1974. He managed three MCC Test tours: to South Africa 1964/5, to India/Pakistan 1972/3, to West Indies 1973/4. His final first-class match was for Free Foresters in 1968. He also gained a soccer blue and appeared in the Amateur FA Cup Final for Pegasus in 1950/1 and 1952/3.

Carr, Douglas Ward
Amateur. *b:* 17.3.1872, Cranbrook, Kent. *d:* 23.3.1950, Sidmouth, Devon. Lower order right-hand batsman, right-arm medium bowler, changed to googly bowler about 1906. *Sch* Sutton Valence. *Team* Kent (1909–14, 49 matches). *Test* England (1909, 1 match).
Career batting
58–68–18–447–48–8.94–0–*ct* 19
Bowling 5585–334–16.72–31–8–8/36
Test batting
1–1–0–0–0–0.00–0–*ct* 0
Bowling 282–7–40.28–1–0–5/146

At Oxford he played in the Freshmen's Match of 1891, but a football injury prevented him appearing in any major matches. After years in good class club cricket, he suddenly developed an aptitude for bowling 'googlies' and achieved almost instant fame in 1909, when soon after being introduced into the Kent team he was selected for the Gentlemen and then for England.

Carr, Harry Lascelles
Amateur. *b:* 8.10.1907, Lambeth, London. *d:* 18.8.1943, Marylebone, London. Lower order right-hand batsman, wicket-keeper. *Sch* Clifton. *Team* Glamorgan (1934, 1 match).
Career batting
3–5–0–54–33–10.80–0–*ct* 4–*st* 2

His debut in first-class matches was for Leveson-Gower's XI in 1931.

Carr, John Donald
Cricketer. *b*: 15.6.1963, St John's Wood, London. Son of D. B. (Derbyshire), grandson of J. L. (Army). Lower order right-hand batsman, off break bowler. *Sch* Repton. *Teams* Oxford U (1983, blue); Middlesex (1983, 3 matches).
Career batting
9–10–4–67–18–11.16–0–*ct* 5
Bowling 476–9–52.88–0–0–2/59

He also played for Hertfordshire.

Carr, John Lillington
Amateur. *b:* 16.5.1892, Palambottah, India. *d:* 3.2.1963, Derby. Father of D. B. (Derbyshire), grandfather of J. D. (Middlesex). Middle order right-hand batsman. *Sch* Repton and St Lawrence, Ramsgate. *Teams* MCC (1913); Army (1926).
Career batting
4–7–0–114–46–16.28–0–*ct* 3

He played for Berkshire.

Carr, Michael Lewis
(originally Kerner-Cohen)
Amateur. *b:* 24.6.1933, Alexandria, Egypt. Lower order right-hand batsman, wicket-keeper. *Sch* Malvern. *Team* Cambridge U (1953).
Career batting
1–2–1–1–1*–1.00–0–*ct* 2

Carr, Ronald Bernard
Professional. *b:* 12.1.1938, Johannesburg, South Africa. Lower order right-hand batsman, leg break and googly bowler. *Teams* Essex (1960, 1 match); Transvaal (1964/5).
Career batting
2–3–2–35–28*–35.00–0–*ct* 2
Bowling 107–0

Carrick, Phillip
Cricketer. *b*: 16.7.1952, Armley, Leeds, Yorkshire. Middle or lower order right-hand batsman, slow left-arm bowler. *Teams* Yorkshire (1970–83, 222 matches); Eastern Province (1976/7); Northern Transvaal (1982/3). *Tours* Robins to South Africa 1975/6, to Sri Lanka 1977/8.
Career batting
241–305–59–5426–131*–22.05–3–*ct* 119
Bowling 17701–611–28.97–30–3–8/33

Carrick, James Stewart
Amateur. b: 6.9.1855, Glasgow, Scotland. *d:* 2.1.1923, Seattle, USA. Hard-hitting middle order left-hand batsman, slow bowler, good field. *Sch* Glasgow Academy. *Team* MCC (1882).
Career batting
1–2–0–13–10–6.50–0–*ct* 0

In 1885 he hit 419* for West of Scotland v Priory Park at Chichester, batting 11¼ hours. For many years the best bat in Scotland he regularly appeared for his Country. Also an excellent rugby player he represented Scotland v England. In addition he was a noted golfer.

Carrington, Elijah
Professional. *b:* 25.3.1914, Blackwell, Derbyshire. Middle order right-hand batsman. *Team* Derbyshire (1934–37, 50 matches).
Career batting
50–77–4–1470–80–20.13–0–*ct* 18
Bowling 32–0

Carris, Bertram Dudley
Amateur. *b:* 23.10.1917, Flixton, Lancashire. Brother of H. E. (Middlesex). Opening right-hand batsman. slow left-arm bowler. *Sch* Harrow. *Teams* Cambridge U (1937–39, blue 1938-39); Middlesex (1937–39, 12 matches).
Career batting
32–55–2–1214–87–22.90–0–*ct* 14
Bowling 955–26–36.73–0–0–4/59

Carris, Harold Edward
Amateur. *b:* 7.7.1909, Flixton, Lancashire. *d:* 29.7.1959, Cheadle Hulme, Cheshire. Brother of B. D. (Middlesex). Middle order left-hand batsman, right-arm bowler. *Sch* Mill Hill. *Teams* Middlesex (1928–33, 36 matches); Cambridge U (1930, blue).
Career batting
44–71–3–1418–98–20.85–0–*ct* 11
Bowling 65–2–32.50–0–0–1/5

He was awarded his rugby blue in 1929.

Carroll, James
Professional. *b:* 18.3.1843, Gravesend, Kent. *d:* 1.4.1926, Gravesend, Kent. Opening/middle order right-hand batsman, bowler, good outfield. *Team* Kent (1865–69, 33 matches).
Career batting
33–56–6–610–48–12.20–0–*ct* 12
Bowling 257–8–32.12–0–0–2/21

Carroll, Peter Robert
Cricketer. *b:* 7.11.1941, New South Wales, Australia. Middle order right-hand batsman, right-arm medium pace bowler. *Team* Oxford U (1969–71, blue 1971).
Career batting
14–27–2–403–60*–16.12.–0–*ct* 11
Bowling 64–0

Carse, James Alexander
Cricketer. *b*: 13.12.1958, Salisbury, Rhodesia. Lower order right-hand batsman, right-arm fast medium bowler. *Teams* Rhodesia (1977/8 to 1979/80); Eastern Province (1981/2 to 1982/3); Northants (1983, 11 matches); Western Province (1980/1).
Career batting
39–49–20–367–44–12.65–0–*ct* 10
Bowling 2904–87–33.37–3–0–6/50

A good all-round sportsman, he has represented Rhodesia at rugby football and athletics.

Carson, William Nicol
Amateur. 16.7.1916, Gisborne, New Zealand. *d:* 8.10.1944, He died at sea of wounds received in Italy. Middle order left-hand batsman, left-arm bowler. *Team* Auckland (1936/7 to 1939/40). *Tours* New Zealand to England 1937, to Australia 1937/8.
Career batting
31–51–7–1535–290–34.88–4–*ct* 27
Bowling 752–35–21.48–0–0–4/20

Coming to England with a big reputation, Carson had a very modest tour and was not selected for the Tests. He shared the world record 3rd wicket stand of 445 with P. E. Whitelaw, Auckland v Otago at Dunedin in 1936/7, making his highest score of 290. He was perhaps better known as a rugby player, and played for New Zealand.

Carter, Rev Arthur
Amateur. *b:* 1847, Slingsby, Yorkshire. *d:* 9.4.1923, Thrussington, Leics. Lower order right-hand batsman, right-hand fast round-arm bowler. *Team* MCC (1885).
Career batting
1–1–0–8–8–8.00–0–*ct* 1
He was at Cambridge but not in the Eleven and appeared later for Hertfordshire.

Carter, Arthur Gervase
(known as Jarvis Carter)
Professional. *b:* 1868, Ruddington, Notts. *d:* 19.7.1933, General Hospital, Nottingham. Middle order right-hand batsman, right-arm medium pace bowler. *Team* Nottinghamshire (1895, 2 matches).
Career batting
2–3–1–16–13–8.00–0–*ct* 1

Carter, Charles Edward Peers
Cricketer. *b:* 7.8.1947, Richmond, Surrey. Tail end right-hand batsman, wicket-keeper. *Sch* Radley. *Team* Somerset (1968–69, 26 matches).
Career batting
26–35–10–73–16–2.92–0–*ct* 47–*st* 6

Carter, Claude Paget
Amateur, but professional for Cornwall. *b:* 23.4.1881, Durban, South Africa. *d:* 8.11.1952, Durban. Lower order right-hand batsman, slow left-arm bowler. *Teams* Natal (1897/8 to 1923/4); Transvaal (1910/11). *Tours* South Africa to England 1912, 1924. *Tests* South Africa (1912–24, 10 matches).
Career batting
107–142–28–1333–80*–11.69–0–*ct* 64
Bowling 6796–366–18.56–23–2–7/37
Test batting
10–15–5–181–45–18.10–0–*ct* 2
Bowling 694–28–24.78–2–0–6/50
During the 1924 tour to England, he headed the tourists' bowling averages with 65 wickets, av 19.86. His real skill however was on the South African matting pitches. He came back to England after the 1924 visit to play for Cornwall, returning to South Africa in 1939.

Carter, Rev Edmund Sardinson
Amateur. *b:* 3.2.1845, Malton, Yorkshire. *d:* 23.5.1923, Scarborough, Yorkshire. Middle order right-hand batsman, right-hand fast round-arm and lob bowler, good slip field. *Sch* Durham. *Teams* Oxford U (1865–68, blue 1866 and 1867); Victoria (1868/9, 1 match); Yorkshire (1876–81, 14 matches).
Career batting
29–44–7–503–63–13.59–0–*ct* 17
Bowling 601–36+3–16.69–0–0–4/58
He played for Victoria whilst on holiday recovering from pleurisy. He is one of the few cricket blues who also won a rowing blue at Oxford. His last first-class match was for I Zingari in 1882.

Carter, Frederic Asgill
Amateur. *b:* 13.6.1853, Newnham, Gloucestershire. *d:* 1.8.1924, London. Lower/middle order right-hand batsman, right-hand fast round-arm bowler. *Sch* Cheltenham. *Team* Gloucestershire (1871–73, 10 matches).
Career batting
10–13–3–75–13*–7.50–0–*ct* 6
Bowling 88–2–44.00–0–0–1/15

Carter, George
Amateur. *b:* 4.8.1846, Warblington, Hants. Opening right-hand batsman, right-hand fast round-arm bowler, good field. *Team* Hampshire (1869–78, 12 matches).
Career batting
12–23–0–274–34–11.91–0–*ct* 4
Bowling 12–1–12.00–0–0–1/11
He played for Herefordshire.

Carter, George
Amateur. *b:* 10.5.1901, Stoke Newington, London. Middle order right-hand batsman, right-arm medium pace bowler. *Team* Essex (1921–23, 7 matches).
Career batting
7–11–1–163–44*–16.30–0–*ct* 3
Bowling 18–0
He later played in Canada, and now lives in Florida, USA.

Carter, Hanson
Amateur. *b:* 15.3.1878, Halifax, Yorkshire. *d:* 8.6.1948, Bellevue Hill, New South Wales, Australia. Lower order right-hand batsman, wicket-keeper. *Team* New South Wales (1897/8 to 1924/5, 44 matches). *Tours* Australia to England 1902, 1909, 1921, to South Africa 1902/3, 1921/2. *Tests* Australia (1907/8 to 1921/2, 28 matches).

Career batting
128–175–31–2897–149–20.11–2–*ct* 182–*st* 89
Test batting
28–47–9–873–72–22.97–0–*ct* 44–*st* 21

After being reserve on the 1902 tour, he was principal wicket-keeper in 1909 and 1921 and was regarded as the best Australia had had since Blackham. He was in addition a more than useful lower order batsman.

Carter, Horatio Stratton
Professional. *b:* 21.12.1913, Hendon, Sunderland. Lower order right-hand batsman, right-arm medium pace bowler. *Team* Derbyshire (1946, 3 matches).
Career batting
3–4–0–8–7–2.00–0–*ct* 1
Bowling 46–2–23.00–0–0–2/39

He also played for Durham. One of the great soccer players, he appeared as inside-forward for Sunderland, Derby County and Hull City winning FA Cup winners' medals with Sunderland in 1937 and Derby County in 1946, a League Championship medal in 1935/6, and an Irish Cup Winners' medal in 1953 with Cork Athletic. He was capped 13 times by England between 1934 and 1947.

Carter, John William
Professional. *b:* 23.6.1935, Oxford. Middle order right-hand batsman. *Sch* Magdalen College School. *Team* Leicestershire (1959, 7 matches).
Career batting
7–14–0–209–41–14.92–0–*ct* 0

He also played for Oxfordshire.

Carter, Reginald
Professional. b: 7.11.1933, Whitwell, Derbyshire. Lower order right-hand batsman. slow left-arm bowler. *Team* Derbyshire (1953–55, 17 matches).
Career batting
17–22–4–130–25–7.22–0–*ct* 6
Bowling 752–30–25.06–1–0–7/46

A useful soccer player he was left half for Worksop.

Carter, Richard Dring
Amateur. *b:* 19.7.1891, Boston, Lincolnshire. *d:* 24.8.1969, Wiggenhall, St. Mary Magdalen, Norfolk. Middle order right-hand batsman. *Team* East (v New Zealanders 1927).
Career batting
1–2–0–1–1–0.50–0–*ct* 0

His County cricket was for Norfolk.

Carter, Raymond George
Professional. *b:* 14.4.1933, Billesley, Birmingham. Lower order right-hand batsman, right-arm fast-medium or off break bowler. *Team* Warwickshire (1951–61, 88 matches).
Career batting
89–109–20–635–37–7.13–0–*ct* 43
Bowling 6759–243–27.81–7–1–8/82

Carter, Robert George Mallaby
Professional. *b:* 11.7.1937, Horden, Co Durham. Lower order left-hand batsman, right-arm fast-medium bowler. *Team* Worcestershire (1961–72, 177 matches).
Career batting
178–165–95–324–23–4.62–0–*ct* 56
Bowling 13714–523–26.22–17–2–7/61

His final first-class match was for MCC in 1973.

Carter, Robert Michael
Cricketer. *b*: 25.5.1960, Kings Lynn, Norfolk. Lower order right-hand batsman, right-arm medium pace bowler. *Teams* Northamptonshire (1978–82, 51 matches); Canterbury (1982/3).
Career batting
58–81–16–1042–79–16.03–0–*ct* 33
Bowling 1566–39–40.15–0–0–4/27

He played soccer for Norwich City.

Carter, Wilfred
Professional. *b:* 19.6.1896, Annesley, Notts. *d:* 1.11.1975, Watford, Herts. Middle order right-hand batsman, slow right-arm donkey-drop bowler. *Teams* Derbyshire (1920–26, 65 matches).
Career batting
65–112–10–1812–145–17.76–2–*ct* 26
Bowling 707–16–44.18–0–0–3/12

He played soccer at left-half for Watford.

Carter, William John
Professional. *b:* 21.1.1841, Kennington, Surrey. *d:* 18.11.1888, Kingston-on-Thames, Surrey. Lower order right-hand batsman, right-arm fast bowler. *Team* Surrey (1871–74, 7 matches).
Career batting
8–14–3–91–21*–8.27–0–*ct* 2
Bowling 41–4–10.25–0–0–2/15

At the time of his death he was in the service of the Jockey Club as a kind of private detective.

Carter-Shaw, Robert
Amateur. *b:* 21.11.1941, Berkhamsted, Herts. Tail end right-hand batsman, slow left-arm bowler. *Sch* Radley. *Team* Cambridge U (1962).
Career batting
1–1–0–2–2–2.00–0–*ct* 0
Bowling 78–1–78.00–0–0–1/33

Cartledge, J. (or W.)
Professional. *b: circa* 1857. *Team* Derbyshire (1878, 1 match).
Career batting
1–2–0–1–1–0.50–0–*ct* 0

It is not clear from the match report whether the player involved is John Cartledge of Burton Joyce, Notts, who died at Stoke Bardolph, Notts on 8 July 1907 aged 50, or W. Cartledge of Woodsetts, Derbyshire.

Cartman, William Henry
Professional. *b:* 20.6.1861, Skipton, Yorkshire. *d:* 16.1.1935, Skipton, Yorkshire. Middle order right-hand batsman. *Team* Yorkshire (1891, 4 matches).
Career batting
5–9–0–129–49–14.33–0–*ct* 1

Cartridge, Donald Colin
Professional. *b:* 31.12.1933, Southampton, Hants. Middle order right-hand batsman, off break bowler. *Team* Hampshire (1953, 3 matches).
Career batting
3–6–0–6–4–1.00–0–*ct* 2

Cartwright, George Hamilton Grahame Montagu
Amateur. *b:* 23.4.1889, Westminster, London. *d:* 4.8.1976, Westminster, London. Middle order right-hand batsman, right-arm fast-medium bowler. *Sch* Eton. *Team* Oxford U (1909–10).
Career batting
17–28–5–523–65*–22.73–0–*ct* 2
Bowling 1143–32–35.71–0–0–4/79

He was Secretary of the Eton Ramblers 1919–1955 and then President until his death. His final first-class match was for MCC in 1928.

Cartwright, Harold
Cricketer. *b:* 12.5.1951, Half Way Houses, Derbyshire. Middle order right-hand batsman. *Team* Derbyshire (1973–79, 82 matches).
Career batting
82–128–16–2384–141*–21.28–1–*ct* 31
Bowling 11–0

Cartwright, Philip
Amateur. *b:* 26.9.1880, Gibraltar. *d:* 21.11.1955, Virginia Water, Surrey. Defensive middle order left-hand batsman, left-arm medium bowler. *Team* Sussex (1905–22, 84 matches).
Career batting
84–134–7–2463–101–19.39–1–*ct* 36
Bowling 547–16–34.18–0–0–3/29

Cartwright, Thomas William
Professional. *b:* 22.7.1935, Coventry, Warwickshire. Middle order right-hand batsman, right-arm medium pace bowler. *Teams* Warwickshire (1952–69, 353 matches); Somerset (1970–76, 101 matches); Glamorgan (1977, 7 matches). *Tours* MCC to South Africa 1964/5, to East Africa 1963/4, 1973/4; Warwickshire to East Africa 1967/8 (not first-class). *Tests* England (1964–65, 5 matches).
Career batting
479–737–94–13710–210–21.32–7–*ct* 332
Bowling 29357–1536–19.11–94–18–8/39
Test batting
5–7–2–26–9–5.20–0–*ct* 2
Bowling 544–15–36.26–1–0–6/94

He hit 1,000 runs in a season three times (best 1,668, av 30.88, in 1961) and took 100 wickets in a season 8 times (best 147, av 15.52 in 1967). He accomplished the 'double' in 1962. His highest innings and only double century was 210 for Warwickshire v Middlesex at Nuneaton in 1962. It was his withdrawal from the England touring party to South Africa in 1968/9 and his replacement by d'Oliveira that led to the cancellation of the tour, the 'd'Oliveira Affair' and the cessation of Test matches with South Africa. He was cricket manager to Glamorgan.

Cartwright, Vincent Henry
Amateur. *b:* 10.9.1882, Nottingham. *d:* 25.11.1965, Loughborough, Leics. Opening right-hand batsman, good slip field. *Sch* Rugby. *Team* Nottingham (1901–04, 7 matches).
Career batting
7–8–0–60–22–7.50–0–*ct* 4

Whilst at Oxford he appeared in various Trials, but no first-class matches. He was a famous rugby footballer, gaining his blue at Oxford and going on to play for England, being captain in 1905 and 1906. He was later an England selector and President of the Rugby Union.

Carty, Richard Arthur
Professional. *b:* 28.7.1922, Southampton. Lower order right-hand batsman, right-arm fast-medium bowler. *Team* Hampshire (1949–54, 55 matches).
Career batting
55–79–25–798–53–14.77–0–*ct* 24
Bowling 4164–138–30.17–8–1–7/29

Carver, George James
Professional. *b:* 4.5.1879, Long Ditton, Surrey. *d:* 1.10.1912, Bootle, Lancashire. He was killed in an accident at the docks. Lower order batsman, opening bowler. *Team* Surrey (1907, 1 match).
Career batting
1–2–0–36–36–18.00–0–*ct* 0
Bowling 42–1–42.00–0–0–1/42

Caryer, Reginald George
Professional. *b:* 1895, Dover, Kent. *d:* 7.6.1957, Reading, Berkshire. Right-hand batsman, right-arm medium fast bowler. *Team* Sussex (1922, 1 match).
Career batting
1–2–0–12–7–6.00–0–*ct* 0
Bowling 13–0
He also played for Berkshire.

Case, Cecil Charles Coles
Amateur. *b:* 7.9.1895, Frome, Somerset. *d:* 11.11.1969, Keyford, Somerset. Defensive middle order right-hand batsman. *Sch* King's, Bruton. *Team* Somerset (1925–35, 255 matches).
Career batting
257–424–36–8574–155–22.09–9–*ct* 47
Bowling 128–0
He reached 1,000 runs in a season four times (best 1,146, av 26.65, in 1933). He also played for Dorset.

Case, George Henry
Amateur. *b:* 4.4.1839, Fareham, Hants. *d:* 21.4.1911, Fareham, Hants. Middle order right-hand batsman. *Sch* University College, London. *Team* Hampshire (1864, 2 matches).
Career batting
2–3–0–85–48–28.33–0–*ct* 0
Bowling 21–0

Case, Thomas
Amateur. *b:* 14.7.1844, Liverpool. *d:* 31.10.1925, Falmouth, Cornwall. Father of T. B. (Oxford U) and W. S. (MCC). Middle order right-hand batsman, good long-stop. *Sch* Rugby. *Teams* Oxford U (1864–67, blue 1864, 1865 and 1867); Middlesex (1864–68, 12 matches).
Career batting
35–56–4–982–116–18.88–1–*ct* 12
His final first-class match was for MCC in 1869.

Case, Thomas Bennett
Amateur. *b:* 19.2.1871, Upton, Berkshire. *d:* 10.11.1941, Donnybrook, Co Dublin, Ireland. Son of Thomas (Oxford U and Middlesex), brother of W. S. (MCC). Opening right-hand batsman. *Sch* Winchester. *Team* Oxford U (1891–92, blue both years).
Career batting
15–28–2–330–55–12.69–0–*ct* 5
He appeared for and captained Oxfordshire for several years. In 1891 he gained his blue only because Thesiger was injured whilst fielding on the first day and Case took his place with the consent of the opposing captain. His debut in first-class cricket was for Gentlemen of England in 1890.

Case, William Sterndale
Amateur. *b:* 24.8.1873, Oxford. *d:* 18.3.1922, St. Giles, Oxford. Son of Thomas (Oxford U and Middlesex), brother of T. B. (Oxford U). Defensive opening left-hand batsman, slow left-arm bowler. *Sch* Winchester. *Teams* Gentlemen of England (1895); MCC (1896).
Career batting
2–4–0–26–11–6.50–0–*ct* 0
He did not appear in any first-class matches whilst at Oxford U. His County cricket was for Oxfordshire.

Cass, George Rodney
Cricketer. *b:* 23.4.1940, Overton, Yorkshire. Middle/lower order left-hand batsman, wicket-keeper. *Teams* Essex (1964–67, 45 matches); Worcestershire (1969–75, 104 matches); Tasmania (1970/1 to 1972/3, 6 matches).
Career batting
155–231–34–4304–172*–21.84–2–*ct* 213–*st* 28
He has played for Shropshire since 1976.

Cassels, Field Marshal Sir Archibald James Halkett
Amateur. *b:* 28.2.1907, Quetta, India. Middle/lower order right-hand batsman, right-arm medium fast, or off break, bowler. *Sch* Rugby. *Teams* Europeans (1927/8); Army (1932–35).
Career batting
5–6–1–197–72–39.40–0–*ct* 5
Bowling 415–20–20.75–2–0–6/51

Cassidy, John Joseph
Cricketer. *b:* 31.1.1963, Leeds, Yorkshire. Lower order right-hand batsman, right-arm medium pace bowler. *Team* Oxford U (1982).
Career batting
1–1–0–0–0–0.00–0–*ct* 0
Bowling 12–0

Casswell, Arthur Henry Seymour
Amateur. *b: circa* 1894. *d:* 29.10.1940, Tardebigg, Bromsgrove, Worcestershire. Lower order batsman, opening bowler. *Team* Royal Navy (1927).
Career batting
1–2–1–7–7*–7.00–0–*ct* 1
Bowling 44–0

Castell, Alan Terry
Professional, *b:* 6.8.1943, Oxford. Lower order right-hand batsman, leg break and googly bowler, changing in 1966 to right-arm medium. *Team*

Hampshire (1961–71, 110 matches). *Tour* Cavaliers to Jamaica 1963/4.
Career batting
112–141–39–1622–76–15.90–0–*ct* 89
Bowling 7094–229–30.97–8–1–6/22
He also played for Berkshire.

Castle, Frederick
Amateur. *b:* 8.4.1909, Elham, Kent. Fast-scoring middle order right-hand batsman, leg-break bowler, good field. *Team* Somerset (1946–49, 23 matches).
Career batting
23–36–3–686–60*–20.78–0–*ct* 6
Bowling 43–1–43.00–0–0–1/16
Being in the scholastic profession he was only able to appear during the school holidays.

Castle, Sidney
Amateur. *b:* 21.1.1864, Westminster. *d:* 5.12.1937, Plymstock, Devon. Stylish middle order right-hand batsman. *Sch* Rugby. *Team* Kent (1890–93, 5 matches).
Career batting
5–6–0–25–6–4.16–0–*ct* 6

Castledine, Stafford William Thomas
Professional. *b:* 10.4.1912, Bingham, Notts. Middle order right-hand batsman, slow left-arm bowler. *Team* Nottinghamshire (1933–34, 5 matches).
Career batting
5–7–0–22–15–3.14–0–*ct* 6
Bowling 25–0

Castor, Brian Kenneth
Amateur. *b:* 21.10.1889, Mahaica, British Guiana. *d:* 2.10.1979, Maida Hill, London. Middle order right-hand batsman. *Team* Essex (1932, 1 match).
Career batting
1–1–0–13–13–13.00–0–*ct* 0
He was Secretary of Essex CCC 1930–46 and of Surrey CCC 1947–57.

Cater, Charles Alexander
Amateur. *b:* 24.1.1844, Liverpool. *d:* 3.2.1892, Harrow, Middlesex. Opening/middle order right-hand batsman. *Sch* Harrow. *Team* Middlesex (1866–67, 3 matches).
Career batting
3–4–0–22–20–5.50–0–*ct* 2

Catling, William
Professional. *b:* 9.9.1836, Highgate, Middlesex. *d:* 1899, London. Lower order right-hand batsman, right-hand medium pace round-arm bowler. *Team* Middlesex (1864–65, 8 matches).
Career batting
8–12–7–53–24*–10.60–0–*ct* 5
Bowling 150–18–8.33–1–0–5/29

Catlow, Charles Stanley
Amateur. *b:* 21.2.1908, Darwen, Lancashire. Middle order right-hand batsman. *Sch* Haileybury. *Team* Northants (1929, 2 matches).
Career batting
2–3–1–18–10*–9.00–0–*ct* 0

Catt, Anthony William
Professional. *b:* 2.10.1933, Edenbridge, Kent. Lower order right-hand batsman, wicket-keeper. *Teams* Kent (1954–64, 126 matches); Western Province (1965/6 to 1967/8).
Career batting
138–218–37–3123–162–17.25–1–*ct* 284–*st* 37
Bowling 2–0
After the 1964 English season, he emigrated to South Africa. Playing for Kent v Leics at Maidstone in 1962 he was put in to bat as nightwatchman and proceeded to hit 162, including making 121 before lunch on the second morning.

Catterall, Robert Hector
Amateur. *b:* 10.7.1900, Port Elizabeth, South Africa. *d:* 2.1.1961, Johannesburg, South Africa. Middle order, later opening, right-hand batsman, right-arm medium pace bowler, excellent deep field. *Teams* Natal (1925/6 to 1927/8); Rhodesia (1924/5); Orange Free State (1928/9); Transvaal (1920/1 to 1933/4). *Tours* South Africa to England 1924, 1929. *Tests* South Africa (1922/3 to 1930/1, 24 matches).
Career batting
124–203–8–5849–147–29.99–9–*ct* 52
Bowling 1629–53–30.73–0–0–4/22
Test batting
24–43–2–1555–120–37.92–3–*ct* 12
Bowling 162–7–23.14–0–0–3/15
He did very well on his two visits to England – on the first, as a free scoring middle order batsman, he hit 1,329 runs, av 28.48, and on the second 1,411, av 28.79, as a defensive opener.

Cattley, Arthur Cyril
Amateur. *b:* 27.11.1861, Croydon, Surrey. *d:* 21.9.1895, Dorking, Surrey. Brother of S. W. (Surrey). Middle order right-hand batsman, right-arm fast or medium bowler. *Sch* Eton. *Team* Surrey (1882, 1 match).
Career batting
1–2–0–45–45–22.50–0–*ct* 1

Cattley, Stephen William
Amateur. *b:* 28.10.1860, Croydon, Surrey. *d:*

11.4.1925, Sparsholt, Winchester, Hants. Brother of A. C. (Surrey). Middle/lower order right-hand batsman, occasional wicket-keeper. *Sch* Eton. *Team* Surrey (1879–83, 23 matches).
Career batting
23–41–1–562–89–14.05–0–*ct* 9
Bowling 13–0

Causton, Edward Postle Gwyn
Amateur. *b:* 1877, Fulham, Middlesex. *d:* 18.4.1957, Torquay, Devon. Middle order batsman. *Team* Hampshire (1919, 1 match).
Career batting
1–1–0–21–21–21.00–0–*ct* 0
Bowling 4–0

Cave, Sir Basil Shillito
Amateur. *b:* 14.11.1865, Mill Hill, Middlesex. *d:* 9.10.1931, Tunbridge Wells, Kent. Lower order right-hand batsman, wicket-keeper. *Sch* Merchant Taylors. *Team* MCC (1902).
Career batting
1–1–0–13–13–13.00–0–*ct* 1
He was Consul-General at Algiers.

Cave, Henry Butler
Amateur. *b:* 10.10.1922, Wanganui, New Zealand. Lower order right-hand batsman, right-arm medium pace bowler. *Teams* Wellington (1945/6 to 1949/50); Central Districts (1950/1 to 1958/9). *Tours* New Zealand to England 1949, 1958, to India and Pakistan 1955/6. *Tests* New Zealand (1949–1958, 19 matches).
Career batting
117–175–39–2187–118–16.08–2–*ct* 69
Bowling 8664–362–23.93–13–1–7/31
Test batting
19–31–5–229–22*–8.80–0–*ct* 8
Bowling 1467–34–43.14–0–0–4/21
His bowling on the two tours he made to England was steady and reliable, but he did very little in the Tests. He captained the 1955/6 New Zealand team to India and Pakistan.

Cave, Walter Frederick
Amateur. *b:* 17.9.1863, Clifton, Gloucs. *d:* 7.1.1939, London. Sound middle order right-hand batsman. *Sch* Eton. *Team* Gloucestershire (1883, 3 matches).
Career batting
4–8–0–74–42–9.25–0–*ct* 0

Cave-Rogers, R.A. (*see under* Rogers, R.A.C.)

Cawston, Edward
Amateur. *b:* 16.1.1911, Wantage, Berkshire. Opening/middle order right-hand batsman, right-arm medium-fast bowler. *Sch* Lancing. *Teams* Sussex (1928–31, 6 matches); Cambridge U (1932–33, blue 1932). *Tours* Martineau to Egypt 1934, 1936 (not first-class).
Career batting
25–43–3–668–93–16.70–0–*ct* 16
Bowling 1305–39–33.46–2–0–7/53
An outstanding schoolboy cricketer, he appeared for Sussex with still another year to complete at Lancing. He also represented Berkshire.

Cawthray, George
Professional. *b:* 28.9.1913, Brayton, Selby, Yorkshire. Middle/lower order left-hand batsman, right-arm medium pace bowler. *Team* Yorkshire (1939–52, 4 matches).
Career batting
4–6–0–114–30–19.00–0–*ct* 1
Bowling 304–4–76.00–0–0–2/64

Cazalet, Peter Victor Ferdinand
Amateur. *b:* 15.1.1907, Westminster, London. *d:* 29.5.1973, Plaxtol, Kent. Opening right-hand batsman. *Sch* Eton. *Teams* Oxford U (1927–28, blue 1927); Kent (1927–32, 4 matches).
Career batting
22–36–2–744–150–21.88–1–*ct* 6
He also represented Oxford at rackets, lawn tennis and squash. Later he was a steeplechase jockey until a bad fall ended his career in 1938. For 25 years he was in charge of the horses of Queen Elizabeth the Queen Mother. In 1960 he was High Sheriff of Kent.

Cecil, Aubrey Bruce Cooper
Amateur. *b:* 10.3.1847, Toddington, Bedfordshire. *d:* 26.8.1918, South Brisbane, Australia. Brother of E. D. C. (Hants). *Sch* Chatham House, Ramsgate. *Team* Hampshire (1876, 1 match).
Career batting
1–2–0–6–4–3.00–0–*ct* 0

Cecil, Egerton Dodge Cooper
Amateur. *b:* 1853, Worthing Sussex. *d:* 25.9.1928, Mortlake, Surrey. Brother of A. B. C. (Hants). *Team* Hampshire (1875, 1 match).
Career batting
1–1–0–4–4–4.00–0–*ct* 0
Bowling 8–0

Chadd, John Etheridge
Professional. *b:* 27.10.1933, Whitestone, Hereford. Lower order right-hand batsman, off break bowler. *Team* Worcestershire (1955–56, 2 matches).

Career batting
2–1–0–4–4–4.00–0–*ct* 1
Bowling 98–2–49.00–0–0–2/84

Chadwick, Edmund Leach
Amateur. *b:* 31.8.1847, Rochdale, Lancashire. *d:* 6.8.1918, Parkstone, Dorset. Middle order right-hand batsman, good long-stop. *Sch* Marlborough. *Team* Lancashire (1875–81, 13 matches).
Career batting
13–24–3–254–42–12.09–0–*ct* 2

Chadwick, John Peter Granville
Professional. *b:* 8.11.1934, Pateley Bridge, Yorkshire. Middle order right-hand batsman, right-arm medium pace bowler, slip field. *Team* Yorkshire (1960–65, 6 matches).
Career batting
6–9–3–106–59–17.66–0–*ct* 7
Bowling 67–2–33.50–0–0–2/58

Chadwick, Mark Robert
Cricketer. *b*: 9.2.1963, Rochdale, Lancashire. Middle order right-hand batsman, right-arm medium pace bowler. *Team* Lancashire (1983, 1 match).
Career batting
1–2–0–2–1–1.00–0–*ct* 1

Chakorsab, Prince (*see under* Rajkot, T. S.)

Chalk, Frederick Gerald Hudson
(registered at birth as Gerald Frederick Hudson) Amateur. *b:* 7.9.1910, Sydenham, Kent. *d:* 17.2.1943. He was reported missing, presumed killed in action, over English Channel. Nephew of H. E. W. Prest (Cambridge U and Kent). Forcing middle order right-hand batsman, bowler. *Sch* Uppingham. *Teams* Oxford U (1931–34, blue all four years); Kent (1933–39, 101 matches).
Career batting
156–259–20–6732–198–28.16–11–*ct* 62
Bowling 409–7–58.42–0–0–2/22

He hit 1,000 runs in a season 4 times (best 1,306, av 29.02, in 1939). For several seasons his cricket was limited due to his profession, but in 1938 and 1939 he captained Kent. At Oxford he also obtained a hockey blue and was a noted rugby footballer and fives player.

Challen, John Bonamy
Amateur. *b:* 26.3.1863, Ruthin, Denbighshire. *d:* 5.6.1937, Eastbourne, Sussex. Hard-hitting middle order right-hand batsman, right-arm fast-medium bowler, excellent cover-point. *Sch* Marlborough. *Team* Somerset (1884–99, 52 matches).
Career batting
52–90–6–1656–108–19.71–1–*ct* 32
Bowling 572–16–35.75–0–0–4/43

Being in the scholastic profession, his appearances in County cricket were limited. An excellent soccer player, he was chosen to represent Wales in five matches.

Challenor, Brig-Gen Edward Lacy
Amateur. *b:* 10.3.1873, Speightstown, Barbados. *d:* 15.9.1935, Hampstead, London. Brother of George (West Indies), V. and R. L. (Barbados). Middle order right-hand batsman. *Teams* Natal (1897/8); Western Province (1895/6 to 1896/7); Barbados (1894/5 to 1895/6); Leicestershire (1906–14, 10 matches).
Career batting
29–52–1–1106–111–21.68–1–*ct* 23
Bowling 15–0

His final first-class match was for MCC in 1914. He also played in important matches in India.

Challenor, George
Amateur. *b:* 28.6.1888, Waterloo, Barbados. *d:* 30.7.1947, Collymore Rock, St Michael, Barbados. Brother of E. L. (Leics), V. and R. L. (Barbados). Fine opening right-hand batsman, right-arm medium pace bowler. *Team* Barbados (1905/6 to 1929/30). *Tours* West Indies to England 1906, 1923, 1928. *Tests* West Indies (1928, 3 matches).
Career batting
95–160–9–5822–237*–38.55–15–*ct* 25
Bowling 1290–54–23.88–0–0–4/16
Test batting
3–6–0–101–46–16.83–0–*ct* 0

He reached 1,000 runs in 1923 and 1928, the former year being his great season with 1556 runs (av 51.86). His highest score was 237* for Barbados v Jamaica at Bridgetown in 1924/5.

Chalmers, George Keay
Amateur. *b:* 13.6.1881, Dundee, Scotland. *d:* 5.1.1946, Carnoustie, Angus. Right-hand batsman, wicket-keeper. *Team* Scotland (1908–20).
Career batting
7–11–4–118–40*–16.85–0–*ct* 7–*st* 7

Chamberlain, William Richard Frank
Amateur. *b:* 13.4.1925, Elton, Huntingdonshire. Middle order right-hand batsman, leg break bowler. *Sch* Uppingham. *Team* Northants (1946, 6 matches).
Career batting
6–9–0–67–14–7.44–0–*ct* 3

He also played for Bedfordshire.

Chambers, Charles Graham
Amateur. *b:* 12.7.1870, Wantage, Berkshire. *d:* 30.1.1921, Reading, Berkshire. Hard-hitting middle order right-hand batsman, good cover point. *Sch* Marlborough. *Team* Liverpool and District (1894).
Career batting
1–2–0–21–16–10.50–0–*ct* 0
Bowling 13–0
He played for Cheshire and Dorset.

Chambers, George Henry
Professional. *b:* 6.10.1875, Nottingham. Lower order batsman, left-arm fast bowler. *Team* Nottinghamshire (1896–99, 3 matches).
Career batting
3–4–2–25–26–12.50–0–*ct* 2
Bowling 235–6–39.16–0–0–3/44

Chambers, George Henry
Professional. *b:* 24.3.1884, Kimberley, Notts. *d:* 13.9.1947, Bentley, Doncaster, Yorkshire. Lower order right-hand batsman, slow left-arm bowler. *Team* Nottinghamshire (1903–05, 4 matches).
Career batting
4–6–1–58–30–11.60–0–*ct* 1
Bowling 54–0

Chambers, Meshack
Professional. *b:* 23.12.1867, Awsworth, Notts. *d:* 23.6.1920, Newcastle-on-Tyne. Lower order batsman, medium pace bowler. *Team* Nottinghamshire (1894, 1 match).
Career batting
1–2–0–6–4–3.00–0–*ct* 0
Bowling 22–1–22.00–0–0–1/22
He also played for Northumberland.

Chambers, Robert Edwin Jeffery
Cricketer. *b:* 19.11.1943, Battle, Sussex. Opening right-hand batsman. *Sch* Forest. *Team* Cambridge U (1966, blue).
Career batting
12–22–0–386–58–17.54–0–*ct* 9
Bowling 4–0
His County cricket was for Hertfordshire and Staffordshire.

Champain, C. E. B.
(*see under* Bateman-Champain, C. E.)

Champain, F. H. B.
(*see under* Bateman-Champain, F. H.)

Champain, H. F. B.
(*see under* Bateman-Champain, H. F.)

Champain, J. N. B.
(*see under* Bateman-Champain, J. N.)

Champion, Albert
Professional. *b:* 27.12.1851, Hollins End, Handsworth, Yorkshire. *d:* 30.6.1909, Sheffield, Yorkshire. Middle order left-hand batsman, right-arm medium pace bowler. *Teams* Yorkshire (1876–79, 14 matches); Lancashire (1886, 1 match).
Career batting
18–31–4–219–29–8.11–0–*ct* 9
Bowling 17–1–17.00–0–0–1/10
His final first-class match was for Liverpool and District in 1890.

Champion, George Ernest
Amateur. *b:* 15.7.1867, Stockbury, Kent. *d:* 30.9.1933, Linton, Kent. Middle order right-hand batsman, right-arm medium pace bowler. *Team* Kent (1892, 1 match).
Career batting
1–2–0–0–0–0.00–0–*ct* 0

Chance, Geoffrey Henry Barrington
(also known as Barrington-Chance)
Amateur. *b:* 16.12.1893, Burghfield, Berkshire. Hard-hitting lower order left-hand batsman, right-arm medium pace bowler. *Sch* Eton. *Team* Hampshire (1913, 1 match).
Career batting
2–2–1–0–0*–0.00–0–*ct* 0
Bowling 47–0
His final first-class match was for MCC in 1922. He also played for Berkshire.

Chandler, Allen
Amateur. *b:* 5.12.1849, Kensington, London. *d:* 25.12.1926, Haslemere, Surrey. Middle order right-hand batsman, good field. *Sch* Cheltenham. *Team* Surrey (1873–77, 27 matches).
Career batting
29–50–1–716–74–14.61–0–*ct* 17
He captained Surrey in 1876.

Chandler, G.
Professional. Lower order batsman, wicket-keeper. *Team* Hampshire (1865, 1 match).
Career batting
1–2–0–16–16–8.00–0–*ct* 1–*st* 2

Chandler, Gordon Mountford
Amateur. *b:* 23.10.1909, Purley, Surrey. Lower order right-hand batsman, right-arm medium pace bowler. *Sch* Uppingham. *Team* Cambridge U (1929).
Career batting
2–1–0–11–11–11.00–0–*ct* 3
Bowling 173–2–86.50–0–0–1/39

Chandless, John
Amateur. *b:* 21.8.1884, Cardiff, Wales. *d:*

1.6.1968, Whitchurch, Glamorgan. Lower order right-hand batsman, right-arm medium pace bowler. *Teams* Wales (1926); Glamorgan (1927, 1 match).
Career batting
2–1–0–2–2–2.00–0–*ct* 0
Bowling 95–6–15.83–0–0–3/13

Chandrasekhar, Bhagwat Subramanya
Cricketer. *b:* 18.5.1945, Bangalore, India. Tail end right-hand batsman, right-arm medium pace leg break bowler. *Teams* Mysore/Karnataka (1963/4 to 1979/80). *Tours* India to England 1967, 1971, 1974, 1979, to Australia 1967/8, 1977/8, to West Indies 1975/6, to New Zealand 1975/6, to Pakistan 1978/9, to East Africa 1967. *Tests* India (1963/4 to 1979, 58 matches).
Career batting
246–244–114–600–25–4.61–0–*ct* 107
Bowling 25547–1063–24.03–75–19–9/72
Test batting
58–80–39–167–22–4.07–0–*ct* 25
Bowling 7199–242–29.74–16–2–8/79
He was successful on his first two visits to England, taking 57 wickets, av 22.21, in 1967 and 50, av 24.86, in 1971, but his 1974 and 1979 tours were not so fruitful. His best bowling was 9/72 for Mysore v Kerala at Bijapur in 1969/70.

Chanmugam, Dennis Ravindran
Cricketer. *b:* 13.8.1948, Colombo, Ceylon. Right-hand batsman, right-arm fast medium bowler. *Team* Sri Lanka (1973/4 to 1975/6). *Tours* Sri Lanka to England 1975, to India 1974/5, 1975/6, to Pakistan 1973/74.
Career batting
14–18–2–180–35–11.25–0–*ct* 8
Bowling 780–19–41.05–0–0–4/60
His first-class debut was for R. Senanayaka's XI in Sri Lanka in 1972/3.

Chapel, David
Amateur. *b:* 23.6.1882, St Vigeans, Angus Scotland. *d:* 4.5.1912, Arbroath, Scotland. Right-hand batsman, left-arm fast medium bowler. *Team* Scotland (1909–11).
Career batting
4–6–1–68–36–13.60–0–*ct* 2
Bowling 325–18–18.05–2–0–5/34

Chaplin, Herbert Percy
Amateur. *b:* 1.3.1883, London. *d:* 6.3.1970, Deal, Kent. Middle order right-hand batsman, right-arm medium pace bowler. *Sch* Harrow. *Teams* Sussex (1905–14, 169 matches); Europeans (1904/5 to 1906/7).
Career batting
176–292–26–6497–213*–24.42–7–*ct* 59
Bowling 370–8–46.25–0–0–3/47

His single double century was 213* for Sussex v Notts at Hove in 1914 and in the same season he hit 1,158 runs, av 33.08, his best year – in all he reached 1,000 runs in 4 seasons.

Chapman, Allinson George
Amateur. *b:* 7.3.1892, Langton, Kent. *d:* 21.10.1982, Tunbridge Wells, Kent. Lower order right-hand batsman, right-arm fast opening bowler. *Team* Civil Service (v New Zealanders 1927).
Career batting
1–2–0–22–22–11.00–0–*ct* 0
Bowling 73–3–24.33–0–0–3/73

Chapman, Arthur Percy Frank
Amateur. *b:* 3.9.1900, Reading, Berkshire. *d:* 16.9.1961, Alton Hospital, Hants. Attacking middle order left-hand batsman, brilliant close field, slow left-arm, later medium pace, bowler. *Sch* Oakham and Uppingham. *Teams* Cambridge U (1920–22, blue all three years); Kent (1924–38, 194 matches). *Tours* MCC to Australia and New Zealand 1922/3, to Australia 1924/5, 1928/9, to South Africa 1930/1; Tennyson to Jamaica 1931/2; Martineau to Egypt 1938 (not first-class). *Tests* England (1924 to 1930/1, 26 matches).
Career batting
394–554–44–16309–260–31.97–27–*ct* 356
Bowling 921–22–41.86–1–0–5/40
Test batting
26–36–4–925–121–28.90–1–*ct* 32
Bowling 20–0
In the 1920s and early 1930s, Chapman was regarded as the epitome of the English amateur cricketer. A brilliant career at school – in 1917 he hit 668 runs at an average of 111.33 – was crowned by a century on his first-class debut for Oxford U v Essex in 1920 and later a century in the University match of 1922. His carefree batting won him an England cap in 1924 in spite of the fact that his County cricket had been only for Berkshire. In that season however began his connection with Kent. He was in splendid form in 1926, when he was selected to captain England at the Oval and won back the Ashes – winning this Test, after the first four of the series had all been drawn. He captained England on the 1928/9 tour to Australia and returned home victorious by 4 matches to 1. His leadership of England was ended temporarily for the final Test of 1930, when on the grounds that his batting was too unpredictable, Wyatt was selected, but Chapman led England to South Africa the following winter. This, however, proved to be the close of his Test career – at the early age of 30. He captained Kent from 1931 to 1936, though not regularly. His final first-class match was for MCC in 1939.

Considering his ability it is surprising that he reached 1,000 runs in only three seasons (best 1,387, av 66.04, in 1927) and hit only one double century – 260 for Kent v Lancashire at Maidstone in 1927, but his qualities as a leader and fieldsman must be added to his batting to give a complete picture of Chapman as a cricketer.

Chapman, Charles Edward
Amateur. *b:* 26.8.1860, Swinstead, Lincolnshire. *d:* 23.8.1901, Scrivelsby, Lincolnshire. Lower order right-hand batsman, right-arm fast bowler. *Sch* Trent. *Team* Cambridge U (1882–83).
Career batting
5–8–2–59–33*–9.83–0–*ct* 1
Bowling 190–7–27.14–0–0–3/19

His County cricket was for Lincolnshire and Berkshire. A noted rugby footballer, he represented Cambridge and England.

Chapman, David Macklin Braby
Amateur. *b:* 12.9.1855, St Paul's, Ruperts Land, Red River, Canada. *d:* 24.3.1934, Hailsham, Sussex. Lower order batsman, bowler. *Sch* Trent College. *Team* Cambridge U (1876–77).
Career batting
2–4–0–7–5–1.75–0–*ct* 0
Bowling 128–4–32.00–0–0–3/56

Chapman, Ivan
Amateur. *b:* 21.10.1906, Pudsey, Yorkshire. *d:* February 1976, Hamilton, New Zealand. Middle order right-hand batsman, right-arm fast-medium bowler. *Team* Essex (1929, 1 match).
Career batting
1–1–0–9–9–9.00–0–*ct* 0
Bowling 18–0

Chapman, John
Professional and amateur at various times. *b:* 28.11.1814, Nottingham. *d:* 14.4.1896, Gainsborough, Lincs. Stepson of William Clarke (Notts 1826–55). Middle order right-hand batsman, right-arm fast bowler. *Team* Nottinghamshire (1842–48, 8 matches).
Career batting
13–22–4–179–41–9.94–0–*ct* 3
Bowling 167–8+2–20.87–0–0–2/6

He succeeded William Clarke as manager of Trent Bridge Cricket Ground and ran the ground for about four seasons. He also played for Durham.

Chapman, John
Amateur. *b:* 11.3.1877, Frocester, Gloucestershire. *d:* 12.8.1956, Dunford Bridge, Yorkshire. Attractive middle order right-hand batsman, excellent cover field. *Sch* Uppingham. *Team* Derbyshire (1909–20, 113 matches).
Career batting
113–210–15–3624–198–18.58–2–*ct* 35
Bowling 241–1–241.00–0–0–1/42

He was Derbyshire captain, 1910 to 1912, and joint-captain, 1919 and 1920. With A. Warren he created a world record 9th wicket partnership of 283 for Derbyshire v Warwickshire at Blackwell in 1910.

Chapman, Mat
Professional. *b:* 13.4.1865, Arnesby, Leics. *d:* 1909, Fleckney, Leics. Middle order right-hand batsman, right-arm medium pace bowler, wicket-keeper. *Team* Leicestershire (1894-95, 27 matches).
Career batting
28–54–6–633–56–13.18–0–*ct* 21–*st* 2
Bowling 30–0

His first-class debut was for Liverpool and District in 1893.

Chapman, Thomas Alan
Professional. *b:* 14.5.1919, Barwell, Leics. *d:* 19.2.1979, Marandellas, Rhodesia. Middle order right-hand batsman, fine field. *Teams* Leicestershire (1946–50, 53 matches); Rhodesia (1952/3).
Career batting
58–95–5–1413–124*–15.70–1–*ct* 20–*st* 1
Bowling 23–0

He emigrated to Rhodesia at the end of the 1950 season.

Chappell, Gregory Stephen
Cricketer. *b*: 7.8.1948, Unley, South Australia. Brother of I. M. and T. M. (Australia), grandson of V.Y. Richardson (Australia). Stylish middle order right-hand batsman, right-arm medium pace bowler, brilliant slip field. *Teams* South Australia (1966/7 to 1972/3, 57 matches); Somerset (1968–69, 52 matches); Queensland (1973/4 to 1982/3, 51 matches). *Tours* Australia to New Zealand 1969/70, 1973/4, 1976/7, 1981/2, to England 1972, 1975, 1977, 1980, to West Indies 1972/3, to Pakistan 1979/80, to Sri Lanka 1982/3; International Wanderers to South Africa 1975/6. *Tests* Australia (1970/1 to 1982/3, 82 matches).
Career batting
306–520–68–23581–247*–52.71–71–*ct* 357
Bowling 8255–286–28.85–5–0–7/40
Test batting
82–145–18–6746–247*–53.11–22–*ct* 114
Bowling 1758–47–37.40–1–0–5/61

He hit 1,260 runs, av 70.00, in first-class matches on his first tour to England in 1972 and 437 runs, av 48.55, in the Tests. In 1975 he was not very successful, but in 1977, when he captained the tourists, he hit 1,182 runs, av 59.10, in first-class matches and 371, av 41.22 in the Tests, being the leading batsman of the tour. He hit 1,000 runs during both his seasons with Somerset. He was one of the leading players to join Packer's World Series Cricket and announced his retirement from Test cricket at that time, but resumed as Australia's captain in 1979; however he declined to come to England on the 1981 tour.

Chappell, Ian Michael
Cricketer. *b:* 26.9.1943, Unley, South Australia. Grandson of V. Y. Richardson (Australia), brother of G. S. (Australia) and T. M. (Australia). Brilliant middle order right-hand batsman, leg break and googly bowler, excellent slip field. *Teams* South Australia (1961/2 to 1979/80, 109 matches); Lancashire (1963, 1 match). *Tours* Australia to England 1968, 1972, 1975, to South Africa 1966/7, 1969/70, to West Indies 1972/3, to India and Sri Lanka 1969/70; International XI to South Africa 1974/5, 1975/6. *Tests* Australia (1964/5 to 1979/80, 75 matches).
Career batting
262–448–41–19680–209–48.35–59–*ct* 312–*st* 1
Bowling 6614–176–37.57–2–0–5/29
Test batting
75–136–10–5345–196–42.42–14–*ct* 105
Bowling 1316–20–65.80–0–0–2/21

He reached 1,000 runs on all 3 tours to England (best 1,261, av 48.50, in 1968) and also hit 1,000 runs six times in Australia. He was the captain of both the 1972 and 1975 tours. Of his three double centuries, the highest is 209 for Australians v Barbados at Bridgetown in 1972/3. He came out of retirement to play for Packer's World Series Cricket, and resumed his first class career.

Chappell, Trevor Martin
Cricketer. *b*: 21.10.1952, Glenelg, South Australia. Brother of I. M. (Australia) and G. S. (Australia), grandson of V. Y. Richardson (Australia). Middle order right-hand batsman, right-arm medium pace bowler. *Teams* South Australia (1972/3 to 1975/6, 17 matches); Western Australia (1976/7, 4 matches); New South Wales (1979/80 to 1982/3, 43 matches). *Tours* Australia to England 1981; Robins to South Africa 1975/6. *Tests* Australia (1981, 3 matches).
Career batting
80–137–13–3834–150–30.91–5–*ct* 45
Bowling 1082–52–20.80–0–0–4/12
Test batting
3–6–1–79–27–15.80–0–*ct* 2

Although he played in three Tests on the 1981 tour of England he achieved very little.

Chard, Herbert William
Amateur. *b:* 1869, Clifton, Gloucestershire. *d:* 9.1.1932, Cotham, Gloucestershire. Middle/lower order right-hand batsman, right-arm medium pace bowler. *Team* Gloucestershire (1889, 2 matches).
Career batting
2–4–0–35–32–8.75–0–*ct* 3
Bowling 136–3–45.33–0–0–2/27

Charles, Stephen Flockton
Amateur. *b:* 17.8.1858, Romford, Essex. *d:* 24.6.1950, Wroxham, Norfolk. Lower order right-hand batsman, wicket-keeper. *Sch* Harrow. *Teams* MCC (1895–1905); Gentlemen (1897–98)
Career batting
8–12–5–143–30–20.42–0–*ct* 5–*st* 5

He played for Norfolk.

Charlesworth, Alfred
Amateur. *b:* 9.5.1865, Simmondley, Glossop, Derbyshire. *d:* 4.12.1928, St Annes-on-Sea, Lancashire. Lower order batsman, change bowler. *Team* Derbyshire (1898, 7 matches).
Career batting
7–10–1–92–23–10.22–0–*ct* 2
Bowling 47–0

Charlesworth, Albert Percy
Professional. *b:* 19.2.1865, Sheepscar, Leeds, Yorkshire. *d:* May 1926, Hull, Yorkshire. Free-hitting middle order right-hand batsman. *Team* Yorkshire (1894–95, 7 matches).
Career batting
7–12–1–241–63–21.90–0–*ct* 2

Charlesworth, Crowther
Professional. *b:* 12.2.1875, Swinton, Lancashire. *d:* 15.6.1953, Halifax, Yorkshire. Middle order right-hand batsman, right-arm fast medium bowler. *Team* Warwickshire (1898–1921, 372 matches).
Career batting
372–632–27–14289–216–23.61–15–*ct* 195
Bowling 8878–294–30.20–7–1–6/45

He reached 1,000 runs in a season 5 times (best 1,376, av 38.22, in 1911). He hit two double centuries, the highest being 216 for Warwickshire v Derbyshire at Blackwell in 1910.

Charlton, Percie Chater
Amateur. *b:* 9.4.1867, Surry Hills, New South Wales, Australia. *d:* 30.9.1954, Pymble, New South Wales, Australia. Tail end right-hand batsman, right-arm fast-medium bowler. *Team* New South Wales (1888/9 to 1897/8, 14 matches). *Tour* Australia to England 1890. *Tests* Australia (1890, 2 matches).

Career batting
40–65–13–648–50–12.46–0–*ct* 38
Bowling 1937–97–19.96–6–1–7/44
Test batting
2–4–0–29–11–7.25–0–*ct* 0
Bowling 24–3–8.00–0–0–3/18

He had only modest success during his tour to England, not being able to adapt his bowling to English conditions.

Charlwood, Alexander Evelyn
Professional. *b:* 25.11.1888, Eastbourne, Sussex. *d:* 23.6.1974, Hove, Sussex. Middle/lower order right-hand batsman. *Team* Sussex (1911–14, 12 matches).
Career batting
12–17–2–165–34–11.00–0–*ct* 1

Charlwood, Charles Robert
Professional. *b:* 22.11.1842, Horsham, Sussex. *d:* 16.5.1880, Horsham, Sussex. Brother of H. R. J. (Sussex). Opening right-hand batsman, right-arm medium pace bowler. *Team* Sussex (1869, 3 matches).
Career batting
3–5–0–40–15–8.00–0–*ct* 6

Charlwood, Henry Rupert James
Professional. *b:* 19.12.1846, Horsham, Sussex. *d:* 6.6.1888, Scarborough, Yorkshire. Brother of C. R. (Sussex). Fine middle order right-hand batsman, lob bowler, excellent cover point. *Team* Sussex (1865–82, 127 matches). *Tours* Willsher to North America 1868 (not first-class); Lillywhite to Australia 1876/7. *Tests* England (1876/7, 2 matches).
Career batting
197–350–19–7017–155–21.19–5–*ct* 89
Bowling 89–4–22.25–0–0–2/12
Test batting
2–4–0–63–36–15.75–0–*ct* 0

He was regarded as one of the best batsmen in England and was referred to as the 'Hope of Sussex'. About 1872 he moved to Chesterfield and then to Scarborough and for this reason ceased to play for Sussex earlier than would otherwise have been the case.

Charlwood, John Armstrong
Professional. *b:* 1871, East Grinstead, Sussex. *d:* 1923, Westminster, London. Middle order batsman, fine field. *Team* Sussex (1890, 3 matches).
Career batting
3–6–1–44–23*–8.80–0–*ct* 3

Charman, William
Amateur. *b:* 23.9.1850, Epsom, Surrey. *d:* 14.2.1913, Horsham, Sussex. Opening right-hand batsman, occasional right-arm fast-medium bowler. *Team* Surrey (1875, 1 match).
Career batting
1–2–0–11–7–5.50–0–*ct* 0
Bowling 24–0

Charteris, Hon Hugo Francis (Wemyss) (Lord Elcho)
Amateur. *b:* 28.12.1884, Wilbury, Wiltshire. *d:* 23.4.1916. He was killed in action, Katia, Egypt. Lower order right-hand batsman, change bowler. *Sch* Eton. *Team* Gloucestershire (1910, 1 match).
Career batting
1–1–0–1–1–1.00–0–*ct* 0

He was at Oxford, but did not appear in first-class cricket whilst there.

Charters, Frank Henry
Professional. *b:* 1884, Plymouth, Devon. *d:* 1953, Bournemouth. Middle order right-hand batsman. *Team* Hampshire (1913, 1 match).
Career batting
1–2–0–14–9–7.00–0–*ct* 0

Chater, Leathley
Amateur. *b:* 23.12.1858, London. *d:* 5.5.1931, Littlehampton, Sussex. Middle order right-hand batsman, good field at long stop. *Sch* Harrow. *Team* MCC (1881).
Career batting
1–1–1–6–6*–no av–0–*ct* 0

Chatfield, Ewen John
Cricketer. *b*: 3.7.1950, Dannevirke, New Zealand. Lower order right-hand batsman, right-arm medium fast bowler. *Team* Wellington (1973/4 to 1982/3). *Tours* New Zealand to Australia 1980/1, 1982/3, to England 1983. *Tests* New Zealand (1974/5 to 1983, 10 matches).
Career batting
81–75–34–377–24*–9.19–0–*ct* 29
Bowling 7242–365–19.84–20–7–8/24
Test batting
10–14–7–60–13*–8.57–0–*ct* 0
Bowling 1073–29–37.00–1–0–5/95

On the 1983 tour to England he took 28 wickets, av 29.21, and played in three Tests.

He was knocked unconscious whilst batting for New Zealand v England at Auckland in 1974/5, when a ball from P. Lever hit him on the temple. He did not regain consciousness until he had been taken to hospital, but happily fully recovered from his injury.

Chatham, Charles Henry
Amateur. *b:* 18.6.1910, Tewkesbury, Worcestershire. Middle order right-hand batsman, right-

arm medium pace bowler. *Sch* Wycliffe. *Team* Worcestershire (1934, 1 match).
Career batting
1–2–0–12–8–6.00–0–*ct* 0
Bowling 65–1–65.00–0–0–1/49

Chatterton, James
Professional. *b:* 1.4.1836, Newark, Notts. *d:* 13.2.1891, Newark, Notts. Hard-hitting opening right-hand batsman, right-hand slow round-arm bowler. *Team* Nottinghamshire (1856-65, 6 matches).
Career batting
21–39–4–414–47*–11.82–0–*ct* 6
Bowling 44–5+1–8.80–0–0–2/14
His final first-class match was for MCC in 1867.

Chatterton, Joseph (Deeley)
Professional. *b:* 14.2.1867, Thornsett, Derbyshire. *d:* 7.11.1886, Derby, of typhoid fever aged 19. Brother of William (Derbyshire). Middle order right-hand batsman, slow right-arm bowler. *Team* Derbyshire (1884–86, 11 matches).
Career batting
11–22–2–108–21–5.40–0–*ct* 3
Bowling 119–5–23.80–0–0–1/9

Chatterton, William
Professional. *b:* 27.12.1861, Thornsett, Derbyshire. *d:* 19.3.1913, Flowery Field, Hyde, Cheshire. Brother of Joseph (Derbyshire). Middle order right-hand batsman, right-arm slow bowler, excellent field. *Team* Derbyshire (1882–1902, 196 matches). *Tour* Read to South Africa 1891/2. *Test* England (1891/2, 1 match).
Career batting
289–510–39–10914–169–23.17–8–*ct* 239–*st* 4
Bowling 4465–208–21.46–4–1–6/42
Test batting
1–1–0–48–48–48.00–0–*ct* 0
He reached 1,000 runs in a season three times (best 1,193, av 38.49, in 1896). He captained Derbyshire jointly in 1887 and solely in 1888 and 1889. In the period when Derbyshire were not first class (1888-93), he appeared regularly in first-class matches for MCC, being on the Lord's staff. He played soccer for Derby County.

Chauhan, Chetandra Pratapsingh Navaratansingh
Cricketer. *b*: 21.7.1947, Bareilly, India. Sound opening right-hand batsman, off break bowler. *Teams* Maharashtra (1967/8 to 1974/5); Delhi (1978/6 to 1982/3). *Tours* India to Australia 1977/8, to Pakistan 1978/9, to England 1979, to Australia and New Zealand 1980/1. *Tests* India (1969/70 to 1980/1, 40 matches).
Career batting
170–283–20–10514–207–39.97–20–*ct* 181
Bowling 1660–50–33.20–1–0–6/26
Test batting
40–68–2–2084–97–31.57–0–*ct* 38
Bowling 106–2–53.00–0–0–1/4
He hit 561 runs, av 28.05, on the 1979 tour to England and appeared in all four Tests.

Chaytor, Joshua David Gerald
Amateur. 13.5.1903, Dunshaughlin, Co Meath. *d:* 4.3.1937, Meerut, India as the result of a polo accident. Hard-hitting middle/lower order right-hand batsman, right-arm fast-medium bowler. *Sch* Wellington. *Team* Free Foresters (1924).
Career batting
1–1–1–9–9*–no av–0–*ct* 0
Whilst at Cambridge he played in the Freshmen's match and Seniors' Match but not in first-class matches.

Cheatle, Robert Giles Lenthall
Cricketer. *b*: 31.7.1953, Paddington, London. Lower order left-hand batsman, slow left-arm bowler, good field. *Sch* Stowe. *Teams* Sussex (1974–79, 42 matches); Surrey (1980–83, 18 matches).
Career batting
60–44–18–338–49–13.00–0–*ct* 54
Bowling 3303–104–31.75–6–0–6/32

Checksfield, Martin Frederic James
Amateur. *b:* 29.4.1939, London. Middle order right-hand batsman. *Sch* Bryanston. *Teams* Free Foresters (1960); Oxford U (1961).
Career batting
2–4–0–59–42–14.75–0–*ct* 0

Cheetham, Albert George
Amateur. *b:* 7.12.1915, Ryde, New South Wales, Australia. Middle order right-hand batsman, right-arm fast medium bowler. *Team* New South Wales (1936/7 to 1939/40, 20 matches). *Tour* Australian Services to England 1945.
Career batting
24–46–3–899–85–20.90–0–*ct* 7
Bowling 1517–42–36.11–0–0–4/75
His final first-class match was for Australian Services in Australia 1945/6.

Cheetham, John Erskine
Amateur. *b:* 26.5.1920, Cape Town, South Africa. *d:* 21.8.1980, Johannesburg, South Africa. Father of J. R. (Transvaal) and R. S. (Transvaal). Defensive middle order right-hand batsman, excellent field. *Team* Western Province (1939/40 to 1954/5). *Tours* South Africa to England 1951,

1955, to Australia and New Zealand 1952/3. *Tests* South Africa (1948/9 to 1955, 24 matches).
Career batting
108–170–35–5697–271*–42.20–8–*ct* 67
Bowling 376–8–47.00–0–0–2/38
Test batting
24–43–6–883–89–23.86–0–*ct* 13
Bowling 2–0

On his 1951 visit to England he hit 1,196 runs, av 42.71, and appeared in all five Tests, but in 1955, when he captained the team, he missed two Tests through injury and did not complete 1,000 runs. Good though his batting was, his reputation rests mainly on his splendid captaincy, especially during the 1952/3 tour to Australia, when his unsung side drew the rubber two-all and confounded all the critics. His highest score was 271* for Western Province v OFS at Johannesburg in 1950/1.

Cheetham, John Leslie
Amateur. *b:* 17.3.1918, Hull. Lower order right-hand batsman, wicket-keeper. *Team* Gentlemen (v Players 1947).
Career batting
1–2–0–9–6–4.50–0–*ct* 1

Chenery, Charles John
Amateur. *b:* 1.1.1850, Lambourn, Berkshire. Middle order right-hand batsman, right-arm fast bowler, excellent field. *Team* Surrey (1872–73, 12 matches).
Career batting
13–24–2–309–40*–14.04–0–*ct* 4
Bowling 48–1–48.00–0–0–1/11

He also played non-first-class cricket for Northants. One of the best soccer players of his day, he appeared for England in three matches in 1873 and 1874.

Cherrington, Peter Ralph
Professional. *b:* 24.11.1917, Newark, Notts. *d:* 23.1.1945, Momywa, Burma. Middle/lower order right-hand batsman, leg break and googly bowler. *Sch* Wellingborough. *Team* Leicestershire (1938, 10 matches).
Career batting
10–14–0–85–33–6.07–0–*ct* 3
Bowling 127–0

Chessher, John Robert
Cricketer. *b*: 21.8.1962, Banstead, Surrey. Middle order right-hand batsman, right-arm medium pace bowler. *Sch* Ipswich. *Team* Oxford U (1982–83).
Career batting
4–6–1–78–47–15.60–0–*ct* 0

Chester, Arthur
Professional. *b:* 18.12.1851, Kingston-on-Thames, Surrey. *d:* 13.5.1915, Lambeth, South London. Son of James (Surrey 1846-58). Middle order right-hand batsman, change bowler. *Team* Surrey (1872-83, 17 matches).
Career batting
17–27–2–272–54*–10.88–0–*ct* 5

He was a mainstay of Kingston-on-Thames CC for many years and captained the Club for nine seasons.

Chester, Charles
Professional. *b:* 7.2.1869, Eastwood, Notts. *d:* 9.2.1940, Forest Town, Mansfield, Notts. Lower order right-hand batsman, right-arm medium pace bowler. *Team* Derbyshire (1899, 1 match).
Career batting
1–2–0–0–0–0.00–0–*ct* 1
Bowling 9–1–9.00–0–0–1/9

Chester, Frank
Professional. *b:* 20.1.1895, Bushey, Hertfordshire. *d:* 8.4.1957, Bushey, Hertfordshire. Middle order left-hand batsman, slow left-arm bowler. *Team* Worcestershire (1912–14, 54 matches).
Career batting
55–92–18–1773–178*–23.95–4–*ct* 25
Bowling 2561–81–31.61–2–0–6/43

Having lost an arm in the First World War, he became a first-class umpire and stood in many Tests, retiring in 1955, by which time he had become the most respected member of his profession.

Chester, James
Professional. *b:* 30.5.1823, Kingston-on-Thames, Surrey. *d:* 23.6.1888, Wimbledon, Surrey. Father of Arthur (Surrey). Hard-hitting middle order right-hand batsman, right-hand medium pace round-arm bowler. *Team* Surrey (1846–58, 26 matches).
Career batting
45–79–5–853–64–11.52–0–*ct* 15
Bowling 7–0+46–no av–3–1–9/?

He was regarded as one of the best all-round cricketers of his day, but he did not play regularly in important matches. His final first-class match was for MCC in 1859. His best bowling was for MCC v Cambridge U at Cambridge in 1850.

Chester-Master, Algernon William
(registered as A. W. C. Master at death)
Amateur. *b:* 27.9.1851, Almondsbury, Gloucestershire. *d:* 1.9.1897, Northampton. Father of

Edgar (Gloucs). *Sch* Marlborough. *Team* Gloucestershire (1870, 2 matches).
Career batting
2–2–1–5–5–5.00–0–*ct* 4

Chester-Master, Edgar
(registered as E. C. Master at birth)
Amateur. *b:* 6.5.1888, London. *d:* 17.9.1979, Durban, South Africa. Son of A. W. (Gloucs). *Sch* Repton. *Team* Gloucestershire (1911, 1 match).
Career batting
1–2–1–4–4–4.00–0–*ct* 0
Bowling 25–1–25.00–0–0–1/9

Chesterton, George Herbert
Amateur. *b:* 15.7.1922, Chirbury, Salop. Lower order right-hand batsman, right-arm medium pace bowler. *Sch* Malvern. *Teams* Oxford U (1949, blue); Worcestershire (1950–57, 47 matches). *Tour* MCC to Canada 1951 (no first-class matches).
Career batting
72–102–34–598–43–8.79–0–*ct* 37
Bowling 5993–263–22.78–18–1–7/14
His first-class debut was for Free Foresters in 1948 and his final first-class appearance for MCC in 1966. He also played for Cornwall.

Chichester-Constable, Brig Raleigh Charles Joseph
(born R. C. J. Chichester, his name changed in 1895).
Amateur. *b:* 21.12.1890, Wycombe, Buckinghamshire. *d:* 26.5.1963, Burton-Constable, Yorkshire. Lower order right-hand batsman, right-arm fast bowler. *Sch* Stonyhurst. *Team* Yorkshire (1919, 1 match). *Tour* MCC to India, Burma and Ceylon 1926/7.
Career batting
24–19–2–152–47*–8.94–0–*ct* 6
Bowling 243–4–60.75–0–0–2/42
He captained Yorkshire 2nd XI 1926–38. His final first-class match was for Minor Counties in 1935.

Chidgey, Graham James
Amateur. *b:* 5.1.1937, London. Middle order right-hand batsman, off break bowler. *Sch* City of London. *Team* Free Foresters (1962–64).
Career batting
3–6–0–164–113–27.33–1–*ct* 6

Chidgey, Harry
Professional. *b:* 25.7.1879, Flax Bourton, Somerset. *d:* 16.11.1941, Flax Bourton, Somerset. Tail end right-hand batsman, wicket-keeper. *Team* Somerset (1900–21, 98 matches).
Career batting
99–169–64–717–45–6.82–0–*ct* 135–*st* 55

Chignell, Thomas Alexander
Amateur. *b:* 31.10.1880, Havant, Hants. *d:* 25.8.1965, Portsmouth, Hants. Lower order left-hand batsman, right-arm medium slow bowler. *Team* Hampshire (1901–04, 18 matches).
Career batting
18–28–10–181–29*–10.05–0–*ct* 11
Bowling 1108–33–33.57–1–0–5/68

Childs, John Henry
Cricketer. *b:* 15.8.1951, Plymouth, Devon. Lower order left-hand batsman, slow left-arm bowler, deep field. *Team* Gloucestershire (1975–83, 158 matches).
Career batting
158–145–70–523–34*–6.97–0–*ct* 61
Bowling 12728–406–31.34–21–2–9/56
His best bowling in an innings was 9 for 56 for Gloucestershire v Somerset at Bristol in 1981, when he took 75 wickets, av 26.16.

Childs-Clarke, Arthur William
Amateur. *b:* 13.5.1905, Exeter, Devon. *d:* 19.2.1980, Mevagissey, Cornwall. Middle/lower order right-hand batsman, change bowler. *Sch* Christ's Hospital. *Teams* Middlesex (1923–34, 10 matches); Northants (1947–48, 53 matches). *Tours* Martineau to Egypt 1936, 1937, 1938, 1939 (not first class).
Career batting
66–107–9–1674–68–17.08–0–*ct* 31
Bowling 1098–25–43.92–0–0–3/72
He captained Northants in 1947 and 1948.

Chinnery, Esmé Fairfax
Amateur. *b:* 28.3.1886, Hatchford, Cobham, Surrey. *d:* 18.1.1915. He was killed in a plane crash at Issy, France. Half-brother of H. B. (Middlesex and Surrey). Middle order right-hand batsman. *Sch* Eton. *Team* Surrey (1906, 1 match).
Career batting
1–1–0–47–47–47.00–0–*ct* 0

Chinnery, Harry Brodrick
Amateur. *b:* 6.2.1876, Teddington, Middlesex. *d:* 28.5.1916. He was killed in action at Monchy-le-Preux, France. Half-brother of E. F. (Surrey). Stylish opening right-hand batsman, slow left-arm bowler. *Sch* Eton. *Teams* Surrey (1897–1904, 30 matches); Middlesex (1899–02, 9 matches). *Tours* Warner to North America 1897; Oxford U Authentics to India 1902/3.
Career batting
66–108–6–2536–165–24.85–4–*ct* 25
Bowling 554–12–46.16–0–0–4/51

Although he retired from first-class County cricket relatively young, he was a noted player for MCC, Eton Ramblers and I Zingari until 1914. His final first-class match was for Gentlemen of England in 1910.

Chipperfield, Arthur Gordon
Amateur. *b:* 17.11.1905, Ashfield, New South Wales, Australia. Middle order right-hand batsman, leg break bowler, excellent slip field. *Team* New South Wales (1933/4 to 1939/40, 30 matches). *Tours* Australia to England 1934, 1938, to South Africa 1935/6. *Tests* Australia (1934–38, 14 matches).
Career batting
96–129–17–4295–175–38.34–9–*ct* 92
Bowling 2582–65–39.72–1–1–8/66
Test batting
14–20–3–552–109–32.47–1–*ct* 15
Bowling 437–5–87.40–0–0–3/91
Although failing to reach 1,000 runs on either of his visits to England, he appeared in all 5 Tests on the 1934 tour, hitting 99 on his Test debut at Trent Bridge. On his visit in 1938 he was struck down with appendicitis and appeared in only one Test.

Chisholm, Jack Richardson
Professional. *b:* 9.10.1924, Enfield, Middlesex. *d:* September 1977, Waltham Forest, Essex. Lower order right-hand batsman, right-arm fast bowler. *Team* Middlesex (1947, 1 match).
Career batting
1–2–0–14–12–7.00–0–*ct* 0
Bowling 33–1–33.00–0–0–1/15
He also played for Bedfordshire and Devon. He was better known as a soccer player with Brentford, Spurs, Sheffield United and Plymouth Argyle.

Chisholm, Ronald Harry Eddie
Amateur. *b:* 22.5.1927, Aberdeen, Scotland. Right-hand batsman, leg break googly bowler. *Team* Scotland (1948–71).
Career batting
61–106–6–2354–105–23.54–1–*ct* 18
Bowling 839–26–32.26–0–0–4/9

Chitty, Arthur John
Amateur. *b:* 27.5.1859, London. *d:* 6.1.1908, South Kensington, London. Son of J. W. (Oxford U 1848–49). Lower order right-hand batsman, wicket-keeper. *Sch* Eton. *Team* Oxford U (1879).
Career batting
2–3–1–23–10*–11.50–0–*ct* 2

Chowdhury, Nirode Ranjan
Amateur. *b:* 20.1.1926, Jamshedpur, India. *d:* 14.12.1979, Durgapur, Pakistan. Tail end right-hand batsman, right-arm medium pace off break bowler. *Teams* Bengal (1944/5 to 1954/5); Bihar (1941/2 to 1957/8). *Tour* India to England 1952. *Tests* India (1948/9 to 1951/2, 2 matches).
Career batting
58–85–27–419–30*–7.22–0–*ct* 22
Bowling 5029–200–25.14–10–2–7/79
Test batting
2–2–1–3–3*–3.00–0–*ct* 0
Bowling 205–1–205.00–0–0–1/130
He was given very few opportunities on his 1952 tour to England and did not appear in a Test. His final first-class match was for Bihar Governor's XI 1958/9.

Christen, Brian
Amateur. *b:* 1927, North Bierley, Yorkshire. Lower order batsman, left-arm fast-medium bowler. *Team* Canada (1951–54). *Tour* Canada to England 1954.
Career batting
5–7–3–29–9*–4.83–0–*ct* 2
Bowling 384–17–22.58–1–0–7/80
He was the leading opening bowler in Canada for several seasons.

Christian Victor of Schleswig-Holstein, HRH Prince Albert Ludwig Ernest Anton
Amateur. *b:* 14.4.1867, Windsor Castle, Buckinghamshire. *d:* 29.10.1900, Pretoria, South Africa, of enteric fever whilst serving in the Boer War. Grandson of Queen Victoria. Middle order right-hand batsman, wicket-keeper. *Sch* Wellington. *Team* I Zingari (1887).
Career batting
1–2–0–35–35–17.50–0–*ct* 1
Most of his cricket was played in India in the 1890s. He was at Oxford but did not appear in any first-class matches there.

Christiani, Cyril Marcel
Amateur. *b:* 28.10.1913, Georgetown, British Guiana. *d:* 4.4.1938, Georgetown, British Guiana. Brother of E. S. (British Guiana) and R. J. (British Guiana). Lower order right-hand batsman, wicket-keeper. *Team* British Guiana (1931/2 to 1937/8). *Tour* West Indies to England 1933. *Tests* West Indies (1934/5, 4 matches).
Career batting
28–44–4–658–79–16.45–0–*ct* 44–*st* 20
Bowling 6–0
Test batting
4–7–2–98–32*–19.60–0–*ct* 6–*st* 1
As reserve wicket-keeper on his only tour of England, his opportunites were very limited. He

was a good batsman in club cricket and with his brother E. S. Christiani added 296 for the 1st wicket in a match in British Guiana.

Christiani, Robert Julian
Amateur. *b:* 19.7.1920, Georgetown, British Guiana. Brother of C. M. (British Guiana) and E. S. (British Guiana). Middle order right-hand batsman, leg break bowler, wicket-keeper. *Team* British Guiana (1938/9 to 1953/4). *Tours* West Indies to India, Ceylon and Pakistan 1948/9, to England 1950, to Australia and New Zealand 1951/2. *Tests* West Indies (1947/8 to 1953/4, 22 matches).
Career batting
88–142–16–5103–181–40.50–12–*ct* 96–*st* 12
Bowling 1088–18–60.44–0–0–3/11
Test batting
22–37–3–896–107–26.35–1–*ct* 19–*st* 2
Bowling 108–3–36.00–0–0–3/52

On his tour to England he hit 1,094 runs, av 45.58, and played in all four Tests.

Christie, John Cubie
Amateur. *b:* 12.7.1903, Edinburgh, Scotland. *d:* 27.5.1978, Wroxham, Norfolk. Right-hand batsman. *Team* Scotland (1923).
Career batting ·
2–3–2–13–11*–13.00–0–*ct* 3
Bowling 132–6–22.00–0–0–3/31

Christie, Robert Douglas
Cricketer. *b:* 7.3.1942, New Delhi, India. Lower order right-hand batsman, right-arm medium pace bowler. *Sch* Eton. *Team* Oxford U (1964).
Career batting
4–6–2–47–21–11.75–0–*ct* 0
Bowling 315–8–39.37–0–0–4/44

Christopherson, John Clifford
Amateur. *b:* 1.6.1909, Blackheath, Kent. Middle order right-hand batsman, right-arm medium pace bowler. *Sch* Uppingham. *Teams* Cambridge U (1931, blue); Kent (1931–35, 3 matches).
Career batting
16–29–2–486–75–18.00–0–*ct* 5
Bowling 32–1–32.00–0–0–1/8

His final first-class match was for Leveson Gower's XI in 1936.

Christopherson, Percy
Amateur. *b:* 31.3.1866, Blackheath, Kent. *d:* 4.5.1921, Folkestone, Kent. Brother of Stanley (Kent). Middle order right-hand batsman, right-arm medium pace bowler, good field. *Sch* Bedford Grammar. *Teams* Kent (1887, 1 match); Oxford U (1889).
Career batting
2–3–0–27–27–9.00–0–*ct* 0

He also played for Berkshire. An excellent rugby footballer, he represented Oxford and England.

Christopherson, Stanley
Amateur. *b:* 11.11.1861, Blackheath, Kent. *d:* 6.4.1949, London. Brother of Percy (Kent). Lower order right-hand batsman, very fast right-arm bowler, fine field. *Sch* Uppingham. *Team* Kent (1883–90, 50 matches). *Tests* England (1884, 1 match).
Career batting
66–109–12–923–47–9.51–0–*ct* 41
Bowling 5332–241–22.12–13–3–8/41
Test batting
1–1–0–17–17–17.00–0–*ct* 0
Bowling 69–1–69.00–0–0–1/52

He played little serious cricket after 1886, when an injury to his arm affected his bowling. From 1939 to 1946 he was President of MCC. He was one of ten brothers, and the family, with his father, fielded a fairly strong Eleven in a few matches in the 1880s.

Christy, James Alexander Joseph
Amateur. *b:* 12.12.1904, Pretoria, South Africa. *d:* 1.2.1971, Durban, South Africa. Stylish opening/middle order right-hand batsman, right-arm medium pace bowler. *Teams* Transvaal (1925/6 to 1929/30); Queensland (1934/5 to 1935/6, 13 matches). *Tours* South Africa to England 1929, to Australia and New Zealand 1931/2. *Tests* South Africa (1929 to 1931/2, 10 matches).
Career batting
65–108–9–3670–175–37.07–11–*ct* 33
Bowling 894–32–27.93–0–0–4/19
Test batting
10–18–0–618–103–34.33–1–*ct* 3
Bowling 92–2–46.00–0–0–1/15

Owing to a finger injury, his opportunities were limited during his single visit to England.

Chubb, Geoffrey Walter Ashton
Amateur. *b:* 12.4.1911, East London, South Africa. *d:* 28.8.1982, East London, South Africa. Originally opening, later lower order right-hand batsman, right-arm medium-fast bowler. *Teams* Border (1931/2); Transvaal (1936/7 to 1950/1). *Tour* South Africa to England 1951. *Tests* South Africa (1951, 5 matches).

Career batting
49–61–15–835–71*–18.15–0–*ct* 12
Bowling 3826–160–23.91–7–0–7/54
Tests batting
5–9–3–63–15*–10.50–0–*ct* 0
Bowling 577–21–27.47–2–0–6/51

Chosen for his first tour to England at the age of 40, Chubb completely justified his selection and appeared in all five Tests. He bowled most overs on the tour and took most wickets: 76, av 26.38.

Church, L.
Amateur. Middle order batsman, bowler. *Team* D. R. Jardine's XI (v Oxford U 1957).
Career batting
1–2–0–1–1–0.50–0–*ct* 0
Bowling 16–0

Churchill, Smith Wild
Amateur. *b:* 17.5.1838, Shepshed, Leicestershire. *d:* 13.2.1902, Mapperley, Derbyshire. *Sch* Christ's Hospital. *Team* MCC (1865).
Career batting
1–2–2–1–1*–no av–0–*ct* 0

Churchill, William
Amateur. *b:* 6.10.1840, Winterborne-Stickland, Dorset, *d:* 20.10.1907, Woking, Surrey. Opening/middle order batsman. *Sch* Brighton. *Team* MCC (1870–72).
Career batting
2–3–0–16–12–5.33–0–*ct* 0

He played for Dorset.

Churchill, Rev William Henry
Amateur. *b:* 9.4.1855, Satara, India. *d:* 8.9.1936, Kensington, London. Middle order right-hand batsman, change bowler. *Sch* Marlborough. *Team* An England XI (1877).
Career batting
1–2–0–13–13–6.50–0–*ct* 2

A noted athlete, he represented Cambridge at soccer and also in the quarter mile in 1877 and 1878, but did not appear in any first-class matches whilst at University.

Clapp, Albert Edward
Amateur until 1890, then professional. *b:* 3.5.1867, Chelsea, Middlesex. *d:* 1936, Bristol. Middle order right-hand batsman, right-arm medium pace bowler. *Team* Somerset (1885–95, 10 matches).
Career batting
10–17–3–152–60*–10.85–0–*ct* 1
Bowling 12–0

He also played for Shropshire commencing 1886 – appearing for both that County and Somerset in the same year.

Clapp, Robert John
Cricketer. *b:* 12.12.1948, Weston-super-Mare, Somerset. Lower order right-hand batsman, right-arm medium pace bowler. *Team* Somerset (1972–77, 15 matches).
Career batting
15–16–5–49–32–4.45–0–*ct* 1
Bowling 734–25–29.36–0–0–3/15

A schoolmaster his first-class cricket was very limited, but in Limited Overs County matches in 1974 he took 51 wickets (av 15.90).

Clapperton, Dr Thomas James Milner
Amateur. *b:* 3.9.1875, Bourn, Cambridge. *d:* 26.5.1939, Corby, Northants. Lower order batsman, change bowler. *Sch* Epsom. *Team* Northants (1909, 1 match).
Career batting
1–1–0–0–0–0.00–0–*ct* 0
Bowling 29–0

Clare, Thomas
Amateur. *b:* 1883, Stourbridge, Worcs. *d:* 6.5.1940, Hagley, Worcs. Middle order right-hand batsman. *Team* Worcestershire (1920–25, 2 matches).
Career batting
2–4–0–63–34–25.75–0–*ct* 3

Clark, Augustus Gilbert Finnis
Professional. *b:* 1862, Dover, Kent. *d:* 7.5.1928, Hastings, Sussex. Lower order left-hand batsman, left-arm medium pace bowler. *Team* Sussex (1886, 1 match).
Career batting
1–2–0–1–1–0.50–0–*ct* 0
Bowling 19–0

He was for many years associated with cricket in Hastings.

Clark, Arthur Henry Seymour
Professional. *b:* 26.3.1902, Weston-super-Mare, Somerset. Tail end right-hand batsman, wicket-keeper. *Team* Somerset (1930, 5 matches).
Career batting
5–9–2–0–0*–0.00–0–*ct* 8

He had a most unfortunate batting record in first-class matches, failing to score a run in any of 9 innings.

Clark, Antony Roy
Cricketer. *b*: 7.11.1956, Grahamstown, South

Africa. Middle order right-hand batsman. *Team* Cambridge U (1981).
Career batting
1–2–0–13–12–6.50–0–*ct* 0

Clark, Charles Manning Hope
Amateur. *b:* 3.3.1915, Burwood, New South Wales, Australia. Middle order right-hand batsman, wicket-keeper. *Sch* Melbourne GS, Australia. *Team* Oxford U (1939).
Career batting
3–6–0–87–22–14.50–0–*ct* 1–*st* 1

Clark, David Graham
Amateur. *b:* 27.1.1919, Barming, Kent. Stubborn opening/middle order right-hand batsman, good close field. *Sch* Rugby. *Team* Kent (1946–51, 75 matches).
Career batting
75–133–9–1959–78–15.79–0–*ct* 46
Bowling 44–1–44.00–0–0–1/19

He was captain of Kent 1949–51 and President of MCC 1977/78. He was Chairman of a sub-committee set up in 1966 to examine the future of County cricket.

Clark, Edward Austen
Professional. *b:* 15.4.1937, Balham, South London. Middle order right-hand batsman, left-arm medium pace bowler. *Team* Middlesex (1959–76, 196 matches). *Tours* MCC to East Africa 1973/4; he also captained MCC on three minor tours : West Africa 1975/6, Bangladesh 1976/7 and 1978/9.
Career batting
200–339–39–8733–149–29.11–6–*ct* 106
Bowling 1883–58–32.46–2–0–5/61

He reached 1,000 runs in a season 5 times (best 1,454, av 32.31 in 1964). He ceased to appear regularly in County cricket after 1966.

Clark, Edward Winchester
Professional. *b:* 9.8.1902, Elton, Hunts. *d:* 28.4.1982, near King's Lynn, Norfolk. Tail end left-hand batsman, left-arm fast bowler. *Team* Northants (1922–47, 307 matches). *Tours* Tennyson to Jamaica 1927/8; MCC to India and Ceylon 1933/4. *Tests* England (1929–34, 8 matches).
Career batting
338–510–195–1971–30–6.25–0–*ct* 104
Bowling 25967–1208–21.49–63–15–8/59
Test batting 8–9–5–36–10–9.00–0–*ct* 0
Bowling 899–32–28.09–1–0–5/98

He took 100 wickets in a season twice (best 149, av 19.10, in 1929). Although his County career extended from 1922 to 1947, it contained two breaks – in 1927 and in 1938 – when he left Northants to play in League cricket. He also played for Cambridgeshire and Huntingdonshire.

Clark, Horace George
Amateur. *b:* 23.1.1889, West Ham, Essex. *d:* 28.2.1967, Epping, Essex. Middle order batsman. *Team* Essex (1923, 2 matches).
Career batting
2–3–0–13–11–4.33–0–*ct* 0

Clark, H. L.
Amateur. *b:* 1866, Germantown, Philadelphia, USA. *d:* February 1940. Brother of P. H. (Philadelphia). Middle order right-hand batsman, good field. *Team* Philadelphia (1897). *Tour* Philadelphia to England 1897.
Career batting
6–9–0–91–22–10.11–0–*ct* 2

He was completely unable to find his form on his visit to England.

Clark, John
Cricketer. *b:* 9.12.1943, Greenock, Scotland. Right-hand batsman, right-arm fast medium bowler. *Team* Scotland (1969–82).
Career batting
13–16–3–104–29–8.00–0–*ct* 13
Bowling 800–43–18.60–0–0–4/10

Clark, Leonard Stanley
Amateur. *b:* 6.3.1914, Manor Park, Essex. Opening right-hand batsman, right-arm medium pace bowler. *Team* Essex (1946–47, 24 matches).
Career batting
24–44–3–745–64–18.17–0–*ct* 11
Bowling 15–0

Clark, Percy Hamilton
Amateur. *b:* 7.8.1873, Germantown, Philadelphia, USA. *d:* 12.8.1965, Villanova, Pennsylvania, USA. Brother of H. L. (Philadelphia). Lower order right-hand batsman, right-arm fast-medium bowler. *Team* Philadelphia (1896–1913). *Tours* Philadelphia to England 1897 and 1903.
Career batting
50–85–17–852–67–12.52–0–*ct* 31
Bowling 4346–197–22.06–11–4–8/91

On his second visit to England in 1903 he was most successful, taking 85 wickets (av 20.50) in all matches. He appeared regularly for USA v Canada and was regarded as one of the best bowlers in North American cricket.

Clark, Ronald Disston
Amateur. *b:* 22.2.1895, Romford, Essex. *d:* 1983, Chichester, Sussex. Lower order right-hand

batsman, wicket-keeper. *Sch* Christ's Hospital. *Team* Essex (1912–19, 7 matches).
Career batting
7–11–1–61–14–6.10–0–*ct* 10–*st* 1

Clark, Robert Selbie
Amateur. *b:* 11.9.1882, Aberdeen, Scotland. *d:* 29.9.1950, Aberdeen, Scotland. Right-hand batsman. *Team* Scotland (1912–24).
Career batting
2–4–0–19–10–4.75–0–*ct* 2

Clark, Thomas Henry
Professional. *b:* 5.10.1924, Luton, Beds. *d:* 14.6.1981, Luton, Beds. Sound opening/middle order right-hand batsman, right-arm off break bowler. *Team* Surrey (1947 to 1959/60, 260 matches). *Tour* Surrey to Rhodesia 1959/60.
Career batting
263–426–35–11490–191–29.38–12–*ct* 104
Bowling 2314–75–30.85–1–0–5/23

He reached 1,000 runs in a season 6 times (best 1,570, av 32.70, in 1957). He also played for Bedfordshire. He played soccer for Walsall and Aston Villa.

Clark, William
Amateur. *b:* 8.9.1905, Crieff, Perthshire, Scotland. Right-hand batsman, wicket-keeper. *Team* Scotland (1946).
Career batting
1–2–0–13–9–6.50–0–*ct* 1–*st* 1

Clarke, Alfred
Professional. *b:* 16.2.1831, Nottingham. *d:* 23.10.1878, Ruddington, Notts. Son of William Clarke (Notts 1835–55). Middle order right-hand batsman, good deep field. *Team* Nottinghamshire (1851–63, 25 matches). *Tour* Parr to Australia and New Zealand 1863/4.
Career batting
55–95–10–936–57–11.01–0–*ct* 30

Clarke, A.
Professional. Lower order batsman, fast bowler. *Team* Leicestershire (1902, 1 match).
Career batting
1 match, did not bat–*ct* 0
Bowling 70–2–35.00–0–0–2/70

Clarke, Alfred Ferrier
Amateur. *b:* 12.8.1865, Farnworth, Lancashire. *d:* 1935, Hastings, Sussex. Lower order right-hand batsman, wicket-keeper. *Sch* University College School, London. *Team* Surrey (1890–92, 8 matches).
Career batting
8–8–2–61–30–10.16–0–*ct* 8–*st* 6

Clarke, Basil Frederick
Amateur. *b:* 26.9.1885, Madras, India. *d:* 4.5.1940, Hove, Sussex. Middle order right-hand batsman. *Sch* Marlborough. *Teams* Gloucestershire (1914–20, 12 matches); Leicestershire (1922, 5 matches).
Career batting
20–32–3–349–108*–12.03–1–*ct* 10
Bowling 24–0

Clarke, Charles
Professional. *b:* 11.4.1878, Partick, Scotland. Son of William (Notts and Middlesex). Lower order batsman, left-arm medium pace bowler. *Team* Sussex (1902, 3 matches).
Career batting
3–4–2–17–10–8.50–0–*ct* 2
Bowling 122–1–122.00–0–0–1/56

Clarke, Dr Carlos Bertram
Amateur. *b:* 7.4.1918, Bridgetown, Barbados. Lower order right-hand batsman, leg break and googly bowler. *Teams* Barbados (1937/8 to 1938/9); Northants (1946–49, 49 matches); Essex (1959–60, 18 matches). *Tour* West Indies to England 1939. *Tests* West Indies (1939, 3 matches).
Career batting
97–145–40–1292–86–12.30–0–*ct* 42
Bowling 8782–333–26.37–20–1–7/75
Test batting
3–4–1–3–2–1.00–0–*ct* 0
Bowling 261–6–43.50–0–0–3/59

He captained the British Empire XI in England during the Second World War and in post-war years played club cricket in the Home Counties. His final first-class match was for MCC in 1961.

Clarke, Charles Cyril
Amateur. *b:* 22.12.1910, Burton-on-Trent, Staffs. Middle order right-hand batsman. *Sch* Repton. *Teams* Derbyshire (1929–33, 25 matches); Sussex (1947, 3 matches).
Career batting
28–43–3–472–35*–11.80–0–*ct* 8

He also played for Staffordshire.

Clarke, Charles Frederick Carlos
Amateur. *b;* 26.4.1853, Welton, Northants. *d:* 29.1.1931, Virginia Water, Surrey. Brother of M. C. (Surrey). Middle order right-hand batsman, right-arm slow bowler. *Team* Surrey (1873–82, 10 matches).
Career batting
24–40–3–437–65–11.81–0–*ct* 19–*st* 1
Bowling 154–4–38.50–0–0–2/50

His final first-class match was for I Zingari in 1890.

Clarke, Donald Hugh
Amateur. *b:* 15.5.1926, Bromborough, Cheshire. Opening right-hand batsman. *Sch* Oundle. *Team* Cambridge U (1946).
Career batting
2–4–0–32–24–8.00–0–*ct* 0

Clarke, Frank
Professional. *b:* 8.10.1936, Cardiff. Lower order right-hand batsman, right-arm fast-medium bowler. *Team* Glamorgan (1956–60, 31 matches).
Career batting
31–41–14–98–31–3.62–0–*ct* 10
Bowling 1868–50–37.36–1–0–5/66

Clarke, George William
Amateur. *b:* 1869, Northampton. *d:* 26.8.1955, Northampton. Lower order batsman, bowler. *Team* Northants (1908, 1 match).
Career batting
1–2–0–0–0–0.00–0–*ct* 1
Bowling 58–2–29.00–0–0–2/58

Clarke, J.
Professional. Lower order batsman, bowler. *Team* Lancashire (1905, 1 match).
Career batting
1–1–0–0–0–0.00–0–*ct* 0
Bowling 35–0

Clarke, John Michael
Cricketer. *b:* 25.12.1948, Barcombe, Sussex. Middle order left-hand batsman. *Team* Sussex (1969, 1 match).
Career batting
1–2–0–0–0–0.00–0–*ct* 1

Clarke, Morice Carlos
Amateur. *b:* 1852, Welton, Northants. *d:* 14.7.1887, Virginia Water, Surrey. Brother of C. F. C. (Surrey). Middle order right-hand batsman. *Team* Surrey (1875–80, 9 matches).
Career batting
9–17–1–115–26–7.18–0–*ct* 6
He also appeared for Northants (non-first-class).

Clarke, Peter
Professional. *b:* 1882, Middlesex. *d:* December, 1915, Dublin, Ireland. Tail end right-hand batsman, leg break and googly bowler. *Teams* Ireland (1912); Middlesex (1913–14, 11 matches).
Career batting
19–28–12–125–28–7.81–0–*ct* 7
Bowling 1376–47–29.27–2–0–5/62
He bowled with great success for Woodbrook Club and Ground in Ireland and as a result was given a place in the Test Trial of 1912, without ever having appeared in English County cricket.

Clarke, Robert Wakefield
Professional. *b:* 22.4.1924, Finedon, Northants. *d:* 3.8.1981, Sherborne, Dorset. Hard-hitting tail end left-hand batsman, left-arm fast bowler, fine close field. *Team* Northants (1947–57, 208 matches).
Career batting
212–263–84–2745–56–15.33–0–*ct* 150
Bowling 16749–484–34.60–16–1–8/26
He also played for Devon.

Clarke, Simon John Scott
Amateur. *b:* 2.4.1938, Westcliff, Essex. Middle order right-hand batsman. *Sch* Wellington. *Teams* Combined Services (1958); Cambridge U (1961–62).
Career batting
8–14–0–99–19–7.07–0–*ct* 5
An excellent rugby footballer, he represented Cambridge U and England.

Clarke, Sylvester Theophilus
Cricketer. *b*: 11.12.1954, Lead Vale, Christchurch, Barbados. Attacking lower order right-hand batsman, right-arm fast bowler, gully field. *Teams* Barbados (1977/8 to 1981/2); Surrey (1979–83, 98 matches). *Tours* West Indies to India and Sri Lanka 1978/9, to Pakistan 1980/1, to Australia 1981/2; West Indies XI to South Africa 1982/3. *Tests* West Indies (1977/8 to 1981/2, 11 matches).
Career batting
133–146–24–1858–100*–15.22–1–*ct* 68
Bowling 10654–507–21.01–29–4–7/34
Test batting
11–16–5–172–35*–15.63–0–*ct* 2
Bowling 1171–42–27.88–1–0–5/126
His best season in England was 1982 with 85 wickets, av 19.95.

Clarke (or Clark), William
Professional. *b:* 24.12.1798, Nottingham. *d:* 25.8.1856, Wandsworth, Surrey. Father of Alfred (Notts), step-father of John Chapman (Notts). Right-hand batsman, slow right-hand under-arm bowler. *Teams* Nottinghamshire (1826–55); Surrey (1852, 1 match as given man); Sussex (1854, 1 match as given man); Kent (1854, 1 match as given man).
Career batting
143–243–37–2133–75–10.35–0–*ct* 55
Bowling 4144–409+386–10.13–82–25–9/29
He did not become prominent as a player, outside his native County, until he was about 45 years old, and then for some ten seasons his

bowling was most successful – he practised the art of under-arm deliveries, an art which had more or less died with the coming of round-arm bowling.

In 1838 he laid out Trent Bridge cricket ground and in 1846 created the All England Eleven – the first professional wandering cricket team, which proved to be immensely popular. His best bowling was 9/29 for Notts v Kent at Trent Bridge in 1845.

Clarke, William
Professional. *b:* 17.3.1849, Kirkby-in-Ashfield, Notts. *d:* 29.5.1935, Mapperley, Notts. Lower order left-hand batsman, right-arm fast bowler. *Team* Nottinghamshire (1876–77, 6 matches).
Career batting
6–10–0–82–17–8.20–0–*ct* 1
Bowling 126–4–31.50–0–0–2/60

Clarke, William (Benjamin)
Professional. *b:* 5.11.1846, Old Basford, Nottingham. *d:* 18.8.1902, Hyson Green, Nottingham. Father of Charles (Sussex). Lower order right-hand batsman, right-hand medium pace round-arm bowler. *Teams* Nottinghamshire (1874–76, 13 matches); Middlesex (1880–84, 21 matches).
Career batting
39–64–13–409–40–8.01–0–*ct* 38
Bowling 1741–101–17.23–10–0–7/51

Clarkson, Anthony
Cricketer. *b:* 5.9.1939, Killinghall, Harrogate, Yorkshire. Opening right-hand batsman, off break bowler. *Teams* Yorkshire (1963, 6 matches); Somerset (1966–71, 104 matches).
Career batting
110–189–12–4458–131–25.18–2–*ct* 52
Bowling 367–13–28.23–0–0–3/51

He reached 1,000 runs in a season twice (best 1,346, av 27.68, in 1970). He also played for Devonshire.

Clarkson, William
Professional. *b:* Lancashire. Lower order left-hand batsman, left-arm medium pace bowler. *Team* Warwickshire (1922–23, 2 matches).
Career batting
2–4–0–59–41–14.75–0–*ct* 0
Bowling 52–2–26.00–0–0–2/24

Claughton, Hugh Marsden
Professional. *b:* 24.12.1891, Wharfedale, Yorkshire. *d:* 18.10.1980, Staincliffe, Yorkshire. Middle/lower order right-hand batsman, right-arm medium fast bowler. *Team* Yorkshire (1914–19, 4 matches).
Careeer batting
4–6–0–39–15–6.50–0–*ct* 1
Bowling 176–3–58.66–0–0–1/27

Claughton, John Alan
Cricketer. *b:* 17.9.1956, Leeds, Yorkshire. Opening right-hand batsman, slow left-arm bowler, brilliant field. *Sch* KES Birmingham. *Teams* Oxford U (1976–79, blue all four years); Warwickshire (1979–80, 18 matches).
Career batting
55–96–7–1910–130–21.46–4–*ct* 21
Bowling 4–0

He scored 51 and 112 for Oxford U v Gloucestershire at Oxford in 1976 on his first-class debut. He played for Berkshire commencing 1982.

Clay, John Charles
Amateur. *b:* 18.3.1898, Bonvilston, Glamorgan. *d:* 12.8.1973, St Hilary, near Cowbridge, Glamorgan. Lower order right-hand batsman, originally fast-medium bowler, slow-medium from about 1926. *Sch* Winchester. *Teams* Glamorgan (1921–49, 358 matches); Wales (1923–26). *Test* England (1935, 1 match).
Career batting
373–555–90–7186–115*–15.45–2–*ct* 177
Bowling 26028–1317–19.76–105–28–9/54
Test batting
1 match, did not bat –*ct* 1
Bowling 75–0

He took 100 wickets in a season three times (best 176, av 17.34, in 1937). Captain of Glamorgan 1924–27, jointly in 1929 and 1946. Test Selector 1947–48. His best bowling was 9/54 for Glamorgan v Northants, Llanelly, 1935.

Clay, John Desmond
Professional. *b:* 25.10.1924, West Bridgford, Notts. Opening right-hand batsman, good slip field. *Team* Nottinghamshire (1948–61, 236 matches).
Career batting
236–400–17–9991–192–26.08–11–*ct* 164
Bowling 133–0

He hit 1,000 runs 6 times (best 1,497, av 25.81, in 1961). In 1961 he captained Notts.

Clayton, Frederick George Hugh
Amateur. *b:* 5.5.1873, Wylam, Northumberland. *d:* 20.3.1946, Warkworth, Northumberland. Middle order right-hand batsman, right-arm medium pace bowler. *Sch* Harrow. *Team* Oxford U (1893–96). *Tour* Oxford U Authentics to India 1902/3.
Career batting
9–16–0–332–68–20.75–0–*ct* 5
Bowling 525–18–29.16–1–0–7/70

Appearing in the Oxford Freshmen's Match of 1893 he hit 230 and 70* – a remarkable feat – but failed to obtain his blue. He was for many years a member of the Northumberland team.

Clayton, Geoffrey
Professional. *b:* 3.2.1938, Mossley, Lancashire. Lower order right-hand batsman, wicket-keeper. *Teams* Lancashire (1959–64, 183 matches); Somerset (1965–67, 89 matches).
Career batting
274–415–66–6154–106–17.63–1–*ct* 601–*st* 65
His first-class debut was for Combined Services in 1957.

Clayton, John Morton
Amateur. *b:* 17.11.1857, Chesterfield, Derbyshire. *d:* 1.4.1938, West Southbourne, Hants. Lower order right-hand batsman, right-arm fast medium bowler. *Team* Derbyshire (1881–83, 2 matches).
Career batting
2–3–0–3–2–1.00–0–*ct* 1
Bowling 11–0

Clayton, Robert Owen
Professional. *b:* 1.1.1844, Otley, Yorkshire. *d:* 26.11.1901, Gainsborough, Lincs. Hard-hitting lower order right-hand batsman, right-arm fast bowler. *Team* Yorkshire (1870–79, 70 matches).
Career batting
121–201–34–1709–62–10.23–0–*ct* 48
Bowling 4255–254–16.75–18–2–8/66
He joined the MCC ground staff in 1872 and remained there until his death. He also played for Northumberland and Lincolnshire. His final first-class match was for MCC in 1881.

Clayton, William Clayton
(changed name from W. C. Walters in 1849).
Amateur. *b:* 23.4.1839, Stella Hall, Newcastle-on-Tyne. *d:* 26.12.1876, Delhi, India, as the result of a polo accident. Lower order right-hand batsman, wicket-keeper. *Sch* Harrow. *Teams* Gentlemen of England (1858–59); MCC (1861–67).
Career batting
6–8–0–90–26–11.25–0–*ct* 0–*st* 4
In a minor match in Sheffield, he was responsible as wicket-keeper for the dismissal of 4 batsmen in 4 balls, stumping one, catching two and running out the last. At the time of his death he was aide-de-camp to the Viceroy of India.

Cleaton, Howard
Cricketer. *b:* 15.11.1949, Merthyr-Tydfil, Glamorgan. Lower order right-hand batsman, off break bowler. *Team* Gloucestershire (1971, 1 match).
Career batting
1–1–0–1–1–1.00–0–*ct* 1
Bowling 23–0

Clegg, Henry
Professional. *b:* 8.12.1850, Dewsbury, Yorkshire. *d:* 1920, Dewsbury, Yorkshire. Middle order right-hand batsman, fine field. *Team* Yorkshire (1881, 6 matches).
Career batting
8–11–2–96–27–10.66–0–*ct* 2
His final first-class match was for Emmett's XI in 1883.

Clegg, William Gavin
Amateur. *b:* 29.6.1869, Altrincham, Cheshire. *d:* 18.5.1949, Barrow, Cheshire. Hard-hitting lower order right-hand batsman, right-arm medium pace bowler. *Sch* Winchester. *Team* Oxford U (1891).
Career batting
2–4–0–35–35–8.75–0–*ct* 1
Bowling 62–5–12.40–0–0–3/35

Clements, Simon Mark
Cricketer. *b:* 29.4.1956, Felixstowe, Suffolk. Middle order left-hand batsman, right-arm medium pace bowler. *Sch* Ipswich. *Team* Oxford U (1976–79, blue 1976 and 1979).
Career batting
29–47–5–860–91–20.47–0–*ct* 18
Bowling 205–3–68.33–0–0–1/29
Since 1974 he has played for Suffolk.

Cleveley, Alan Barnard
Professional. *b:* 5.1.1932, Chaddesden, Derbyshire. Lower order right-hand batsman, right-arm fast medium bowler. *Team* Nottinghamshire (1955, 1 match).
Career batting
1–2–1–4–4*–4.00–0–*ct* 0
Bowling 107–3–35.66–0–0–3/63

Cliff, Alfred Talbot
Amateur. *b:* 27.10.1878, Glanford Brigg, Lincs. *d:* 25.1.1966, Oxford. Middle order right-hand batsman, slow left-arm bowler. *Team* Worcestershire (1912–20, 39 matches).
Career batting
39–74–2–986–81*–13.69–0–*ct* 12
Bowling 410–8–51.25–0–0–1/4

Clifford, Christopher Craven
Cricketer. *b:* 5.7.1942, Hovingham, Yorkshire. Lower order right-hand batsman, off break

bowler. *Teams* Yorkshire (1972, 11 matches); Warwickshire (1978–80, 36 matches).
Career batting
47–45–16–210–26–7.24–0–*ct* 16
Bowling 4740–126–37.61–6–0–6/89
He appeared for Yorks 2nd XI in 1963, but lived in South Africa 1969–72.

Clifford, Frank Leonard
Professional. *b:* 29.8.1891, London. *d:* 13.6.1982, Enfield, Middlesex. Lower order batsman. *Team* Middlesex (1921, 1 match).
Career batting
1–2–2–0–0*–no av–0–*ct* 0
Bowling 7–0

Clifford, George
Professional. *b:* 19.4.1852, Barnes, Surrey. *d:* 1941, Surrey. Middle/lower order right-hand batsman, change bowler. *Team* Surrey (1871–78, 15 matches).
Career batting
16–30–1–282–45–9.72–0–*ct* 7
Bowling 355–13–27.30–0–0–3/15
His final first-class match was for the South in 1879.

Clift, Patrick Bernard
Cricketer. *b*: 14.7.1953, Salisbury, Rhodesia. Middle order right-hand batsman, right-arm medium pace bowler, slip field. *Teams* Rhodesia (1971/2 to 1979/80); Leicestershire (1975–83, 146 matches); Natal (1980/1 to 1981/2).
Career batting
228–327–73–6075–100*–23.90–1–*ct* 120
Bowling 15230–627–24.29–20–1–8/17

Clift, Phil Brittain
Professional. *b:* 3.9.1918, Usk, Monmouth. Opening right-hand batsman, off break bowler, brilliant field at short leg. *Team* Glamorgan (1937–55, 183 matches).
Career batting
183–306–21–6055–125*–21.24–7–*ct* 169
Bowling 675–11–61.36–0–0–3/6
He hit 1,000 runs in a season three times (best 1,226, av 26.08, in 1949). He was Secretary of Glamorgan, retiring in 1982.

Clifton, Charles
Professional. *b:* 13.1.1846, Ruddington, Notts. Son-in-law to James Grundy (Notts). Middle order right-hand batsman, right-hand fast round-arm bowler, good field. *Team* Nottinghamshire (1873–76, 9 matches).
Career batting
10–18–2–168–45–10.50–0–*ct* 9

Clifton, Cecil Cooper
Professional. *b:* 8.12.1885, Eastwood, Notts. *d:* 12.3.1930, Liverpool. Lower order right-hand batsman, right-arm fast medium bowler. *Team* Nottinghamshire (1908–10, 24 matches).
Career batting
24–36–10–154–22–5.92–0–*ct* 10
Bowling 1334–50–26.68–0–0–4/25
He also played for Northumberland and Cheshire.

Clifton, Ernest George
Cricketer. *b:* 15.6.1939, Lambeth, South London. Lower order right-hand batsman, wicket-keeper. *Team* Middlesex (1962–66, 25 matches).
Career batting
25–29–16–128–25–9.84–0–*ct* 43–*st* 7

Clifton, Lord Edward Henry Stuart
(succeeded as 7th Earl of Darnley in 1896)
Amateur. *b:* 21.8.1851, Cobham Hall, Gravesend, Kent. *d:* 30.10.1900, Cobham, Kent. Elder brother of Hon Ivo Bligh (Kent and England). Hard-hitting middle order right-hand batsman, right-hand fast round-arm bowler. *Sch* Eton. *Team* Kent (1871–79, 6 matches).
Career batting
11–21–2–200–52–10.52–0–*ct* 2
Bowling 22–0
His final first-class match was for MCC in 1880.

Clinton, Grahame Selvey
Cricketer. *b*: 5.5.1953, Sidcup, Kent. Opening left-hand batsman, right-arm medium pace bowler. *Teams* Kent (1974–78, 32 matches), Surrey (1979–83, 95 matches); Zimbabwe-Rhodesia (1979/80).
Career batting
131–224–23–5854–172*–29.12–9–*ct* 39
Bowling 97–4–24.25–0–0–2/8
He scored 1,000 runs in a season three times (best 1,240, av 37.57, in 1980).

Clode, Harry Pile
Professional. *b:* 7.9.1877, Kensington, London. *d:* 1964, Sunderland, Co Durham. Lower order right-hand batsman, slow right-arm bowler. *Team* Surrey (1899–1903, 40 matches).
Career batting
40–56–6–596–50*–11.92–0–*ct* 20
Bowling 2884–111–25.98–6–1–6/31
He also played for Durham.

Close, Dennis Brian
Professional. *b*: 24.2.1931, Rawdon, Leeds, Yorkshire. Versatile left-hand batsman, right-arm medium pace or off break bowler. *Teams* Yorkshire (1949–70, 536 matches); Somerset (1971–77, 142 matches). *Tours* MCC to Australia and New

Zealand 1950/1, to Pakistan 1955/6; Robins to South Africa 1973/4, 1974/5; Commonwealth to South Africa 1959/60; International XI to South Africa 1972/3, 1973/4; Yorkshire to North America 1964 (not first-class). *Tests* England (1949–76, 22 matches).
Career batting
783–1220–170–34911–198–33.24–52–*ct* 811–*st* 1
Bowling 30841–1168–26.40–43–3–8/41
Test batting
22–37–2–887–70–25.34–0–*ct* 24
Bowling 532–18–29.55–0–0–4/35

Close achieved so much in his first year in first-class cricket that any subsequent success was almost bound to be an anti-climax – at the age of 18 in 1949 he became the youngest player to attain the 'double', the youngest to gain a Yorkshire cap and the youngest to represent England in Test cricket. Looking back on his County career, which spanned 29 seasons to 1977, it is apparent, however, that he might well have remained as successful as he was in 1949 had not he become a magnet for controversy. Several times he won himself the praise of all connected with the game, only then to be entangled in discord. In 1963 he was made captain of Yorkshire and took to the responsibility with such success that he was recalled to the England side and held the country's batting together. In 1966 he was given the English captaincy and looked to be set for a long reign when suddenly he was at loggerheads with the authorities and his international career abruptly ended.

He captained Yorkshire from 1963 to 1970, Somerset from 1971 to 1977 and England in seven Tests. In all he reached 1,000 runs in a season 20 times (best 1,985, av 35.44, in 1961) and took 100 wickets in a season twice (best 114, av 24.08, in 1952). In 1949 and 1952 he achieved the 'double'. His final first-class match was for D. B. Close's XI in 1983.

Apart from his cricketing ability, he was a good soccer player, appearing for Leeds United, Arsenal and Bradford City.

Close, Peter Alwen
Cricketer. *b:* 1.6.1943, Murree, India. Middle order right-hand batsman, off break bowler. *Sch* Haileybury. *Team* Cambridge U (1964–65, blue 1965).
Career batting
15–27–2–344–54–13.76–0–*ct* 15
Bowling 44–1–44.00–0–0–1/6

He also played for Dorset.

Clowes, Henry
Amateur. *b:* 1.7.1863, Cheadle, Cheshire. *d:* 6.4.1899, Bloomsbury, London. Middle order right-hand batsman, occasional wicket-keeper. *Sch* Cheltenham. *Team* Gloucestershire (1884, 4 matches).
Career batting
4–8–0–82–22–10.25–0–*ct* 1

Clube, Stace Victor Murray
Amateur. *b:* 22.10.1934, Merton, Surrey. Lower order right-hand batsman, slow right-arm bowler. *Sch* St John's, Leatherhead. *Team* Oxford U (1956–57, blue 1956).
Career batting
17–25–3–132–25–6.00–0–*ct* 11
Bowling 1514–47–32.20–1–0–5/49

His final first-class match was for Free Foresters in 1959.

Clugston, David Lindsey
Amateur. *b:* 5.2.1908, Belfast, Northern Ireland. Lower order batsman, slow left-arm bowler. *Team* Warwickshire (1928–46, 6 matches).
Career batting
6–9–0–64–17–7.11–0–*ct* 3
Bowling 475–4–118.75–0–0–2/75

Coates, Arthur Edward
Amateur. *b:* 2.8.1848, Wigan, Lancashire. *d:* 19.8.1898, Los Angeles, USA. Middle order right-hand batsman, useful change bowler. *Sch* Shrewsbury. *Team* Gloucestershire (1873, 1 match).
Career batting
1–1–0–2–2–2.00–0–*ct* 0

Coates, Crawford
Amateur. *b:* 24.5.1866, Cape Town, South Africa. *d:* 9.10.1944, Manhattan Beach, California, USA. Middle order right-hand batsman, good outfield. *Team* Philadelphia (1891–97). *Tour* Philadelphia to England 1897.
Career batting
18–28–0–511–84–18.25–0–*ct* 16
Bowling 42–0

Although he did well for Belmont in Philadelphian Club cricket, he achieved little either on his 1897 visit to England or his five appearances for USA v Canada.

Coates, Joseph
Amateur. *b:* 13.11.1844, Huddersfield, Yorkshire. *d:* 9.9.1896, Sydney, Australia. Lower order left-hand batsman, left-arm medium pace bowler. *Teams* New South Wales (1867/8 to 1879/80, 13 matches); North (1877).
Career batting
15–26–6–158–36*–7.90–0–*ct* 3
Bowling 885–76–11.64–5–1–7/39

In 'Scores and Biographies' it is incorrectly stated that he played for Surrey.

Cobb, Arthur Rhodes
Amateur. *b:* 12.3.1864, Adderbury, Banbury, Oxon. *d:* 6.11.1886, Cotefield, Banbury, of typhoid fever. Brother of C. E. (A. J. Webbe's XI). Middle order right-hand batsman, wicket-keeper. *Sch* Winchester. *Team* Oxford U (1884–86, blue 1886). *Tours* Sanders to America 1885 and 1886.
Career batting
17–30–2–323–51–11.53–0–*ct* 15–*st* 4
He appeared for Warwickshire in 1885 and 1886. He had only just returned from America at the time of his death.

Cobb, Charles Edward
Amateur. *b:* 26.3.1863, Adderbury, Banbury, Oxon. *d:* 6.7.1922, Marylebone, London. Brother of A. R. (Oxford U). Lower order right-hand batsman, wicket-keeper. *Sch* Rugby. *Team* A. J. Webbe's XI v Oxford U 1900.
Career batting
1–2–0–36–19–18.00–0–*ct* 1
He also played for Buckinghamshire.

Cobb, Humphry Henry
Amateur. *b:* 12.7.1873, Kensington, London. *d:* 13.12.1949, Camber, Sussex. Middle order right-hand batsman. *Sch* Sedbergh. *Team* Middlesex (1898–1901, 10 matches).
Career batting
11–16–4–160–55*–13.33–0–*ct* 10
His first-class debut was for MCC in 1896. He captained Rosslyn Park FC for three seasons and was at one time President of the Bear Skating Club. He also played for Hertfordshire.

Cobb, Russell Alan
Cricketer. *b*: 18.5.1961, Leicester. Opening right-hand batsman, left-arm medium pace bowler. *Sch* Trent College. *Team* Leicestershire (1980–83, 41 matches). *Tours* Robins to New Zealand 1979/80 (no first-class matches); Leicestershire to Zimbabwe 1980/1.
Career batting
41–63–1–1193–63–19.24–0–*ct* 24
Bowling 5–0

Cobbett, James
Professional. *b:* 12.1.1804, Frimley, Surrey. *d:* 31.3.1842, Marylebone, London. Middle order right-hand batsman, right-hand slow round-arm bowler. *Teams* Middlesex (1826); Surrey (1839, 1 match); Yorkshire (1835).
Career batting
100–172–17–1573–60–10.01–0–*ct* 71–*st* 5
Bowling 111–9+525–12.33–41–14–8/?
He was on the staff at Lord's for 16 seasons and was regarded as one of the best all-round cricketers of his day. His final first-class match was for MCC in 1841.

Cobbold, Philip Wyndham
Amateur. *b:* 5.1.1875, Ipswich, Suffolk. *d:* 28.12.1945, Tattingstone, Ipswich. Lower order right-hand batsman, slow leg break bowler, fine slip field. *Sch* Eton. *Team* Cambridge U (1896, blue).
Career batting
18–31–5–249–49*–9.57–0–*ct* 13
Bowling 1601–67–23.89–3–0–6/56
He played for Suffolk from 1902, captaining the County for several seasons. His final first-class match was for Free Foresters in 1922. He represented Cambridge at both tennis and rackets.

Cobbold, Ralph Hamilton
Amateur. *b:* 22.5.1906, Calne, Wiltshire. Middle order right-hand batsman, off break bowler. *Sch* Eton. *Team* Cambridge U (1926–27, blue 1927).
Career batting
14–18–1–456–100*–26.82–1–*ct* 6
Bowling 558–9–62.00–0–0–4/81
His final first-class match was for Free Foresters in 1928.

Cobden, Frank Carroll
Amateur. *b:* 14.10.1849, Lambley, Notts. *d:* 7.12.1932, Capel Curig, Caernarvonshire. Brother of H. S. (Gloucestershire). Hard-hitting lower order right-hand batsman, right-arm fast bowler. *Sch* Highgate, Brighton and Harrow. *Team* Cambridge U (1870–72, blue all three years).
Career batting
22–37–4–471–73*–14.27–0–*ct* 9
Bowling 1119–65–17.21–4–1–6/36
His most famous feat on the cricket field occurred in the 1870 University Match. Oxford required only 4 to win with three wickets in hand when Cobden bowled the last over. A single was hit off the first delivery, then Cobden performed the 'hat-trick' to win the game for Cambridge by 2 runs. For many years he ran Radnor CCC. He played for Shropshire and Herefordshire.

Cobden, Halsted Sayer
Amateur. *b:* 20.11.1845, London. *d:* 5.1.1909, Wincanton, Somerset. Brother of F. C. (Cambridge U). Lower order right-hand batsman, right-hand fast round-arm bowler. *Sch* Repton and Brighton. *Team* Gloucestershire (1872, 4 matches).
Career batting
4–5–2–11–5*–3.66–0–*ct* 0
Bowling 21–1–21.00–0–0–1/21

Cobham, 8th Viscount *(see under* Lyttelton, Hon C.G.)

Cobham, 9th Viscount, formerly Lyttelton, Hon John Cavendish
(succeeded to title in 1922)
Amateur. *b:* 23.10.1881, Hagley Hall, Worcs. *d:* 31.7.1949, Bromsgrove, Worcs. Son of C. G. Lyttelton (Cambridge U), father of C. J. Lyttelton (Cambridge U, Worcs). Lower order right-hand batsman, change bowler. *Sch* Eton. *Team* Worcestershire (1924–25, 3 matches).
Career batting
3–6–1–63–30–12.60–0–*ct* 0
He was Conservative MP for Droitwich, 1910–16; Parliamentary Secretary of State for War, 1939–40. At the time of his death Treasurer of MCC and President of Worcs CCC.

Cobham, 10th Viscount
(see under Lyttelton, Hon C.J.)

Cobham, Michael David
Amateur. *b:* 11.5.1930, Boynton, Yorkshire. Middle order right-hand batsman, right-arm medium fast bowler. *Sch* Stowe. *Team* Free Foresters (1953).
Career batting
1–2–0–0–0–0.00–0–*ct* 0
Bowling 54–2–27.00–0–0–2/21
He also played for Berkshire.

Cobley, Arthur
Professional. *b:* 5.10.1874, Barwell, Leics. *d:* 21.4.1960, Barwell, Leics. Lower order right-hand batsman, right-arm medium pace bowler. *Team* Leicestershire (1897–1904, 9 matches).
Career batting
9–18–0–139–22–7.72–0–*ct* 4
Bowling 142–1–142.00–0–0–1/9

Cochrane, Alfred Henry John
Amateur. *b:* 26.1.1865, Mauritius. *d:* 14.12.1948, Elmhurst, Batheaston, Somerset. Lower order right-hand batsman, left-arm medium pace off-break bowler. *Sch* Repton. *Teams* Derbyshire (1884–86, 4 matches); Oxford U (1885–88, blue 1885, 1886 and 1888)
Career batting
28–48–15–347–61*–10.51–0–*ct* 16
Bowling 1956–103–18.99–4–0–7/66
Injury prevented him from appearing in the University match of 1887. He played for Northumberland from 1891 to 1897. He was a noted writer and apart from books on cricket, contributed many articles to cricket magazines.

Cochrane, Roy Dundonald
Amateur. *b:* 13.2.1892, Kensington, London. *d:* 5.12.1968, Kensington, London. Middle order batsman. *Sch* Marlborough. *Team* Sussex (1913, 1 match).
Career batting
1–1–0–6–6–6.00–0–*ct* 0
Bowling 37–2–18.50–0–0–2/37
Whilst at Cambridge he appeared in the Seniors' Match, but no first-class games.

Cochrane, Sir Stanley Herbert
Amateur. *b:* 19.9.1877, Ireland. *d:* 23.10.1949, Bray, Co Dublin, Ireland. Lower order batsman, wicket-keeper. *Team* Woodbrook C and G v South Africans 1912.
Career batting
1–1–0–5–5–5.00–0–*ct* 1
He was the originator of Woodbrook CC which played on his private ground at Bray.

Cock, David Frederick
Amateur. *b:* 22.10.1914, Great Dunmow, Essex. Middle order right-hand batsman. *Sch* Bishops Stortford. *Team* Essex (1939–46, 14 matches).
Career batting
14–20–2–355–98–19.72–0–*ct* 5
He also appeared for Cambridgeshire and Hertfordshire.

Cockbain, Ian
Cricketer. *b*: 19.4.1958, Bootle, Lancashire. Opening or middle order right-hand batsman, slow left-arm bowler. *Team* Lancashire (1979–83, 46 matches).
Career batting
46–78–9–1456–98–21.10–0–*ct* 22
Bowling 14–0

Cockburn, Sir William Robert Marshall
Amateur. *b:* 26.4.1891, Paisley, Scotland. *d:* 1.9.1957, Winchester. Useful all rounder. *Team* Scotland (1921).
Career batting
1–2–0–11–11–5.50–0–*ct* 0
Bowling 20–1–20.00–0–0–1/20

Cockburn-Hood, Rev J.S.E.
(see under Hood, J.S.E.)

Cockerell, Rev Louis Arthur
Amateur. *b:* 20.11.1836, North Weald, Essex. *d:* 4.3.1929, Oxford. Lower order batsman, useful bowler. *Sch* Rugby and Radley. *Team* Gentlemen of Kent (1865).
Career batting
1–1–0–8–8–8.00–0–*ct* 0
Bowling 10–0

He appeared for Essex and at the time of his death was the oldest member of the Harlequins.

Cockett, John Ashley
Amateur. *b:* 23.12.1927, Broadstairs, Kent. Middle order right-hand batsman. *Sch* Aldenham. *Teams* Cambridge U (1951, blue).
Career batting
8–15–2–311–121–23.92–1–*ct* 3
Bowling 6–0
His County cricket was for Buckinghamshire. His final first-class match was for Minor Counties in 1953.

Cocks, Arthur Denis Bradford
Amateur. *b:* 29.7.1904, Dharmsala, India. *d:* 6.6.1944, Normandy, France. Lower order right-hand batsman, useful bowler. *Sch* Bedford. *Team* Army (1927).
Career batting
2–3–1–30–26*–15.00–0–*ct* 3
Bowling 113–0

Coe, Geoffrey
Cricketer. *b:* 29.3.1943, Earl Shilton, Leics. Lower order left-hand batsman, left-arm medium pace bowler. *Team* Leicestershire (1963, 1 match).
Career batting
1 match, did not bat –*ct* 0
Bowling 77–2–38.50–0–0–1/26

Coe, Samuel
Professional. *b:* 3.6.1873, Earl Shilton, Leics. *d:* 4.11.1955, Earl Shilton, Leics. Middle order left-hand batsman, left-arm slow-medium bowler. *Teams* Leicestershire (1896–1923, 448 matches); London County (1900–04).
Career batting
452–775–69–17438–252*–24.69–19–*ct* 176
Bowling 10789–335–32.20–3–0–6/38
He reached 1,000 runs in a season 7 times (best 1,258, av 37.00, in 1914). His only double century was 252* for Leics v Northants at Leicester in 1914, which was the highest score for the County. From 1931 he was the Leics County scorer.

Cogger, Gerald Lyndley
Professional. *b:* 7.9.1933, Uckfield, Sussex. Tail end right-hand batsman, right-arm medium-fast bowler. *Team* Sussex (1954–57, 8 matches).
Career batting
8–8–1–12–5–1.71–0–*ct* 5
Bowling 286–7–40.85–0–0–3/20

Coghlan, Timothy Boyle Lake
Amateur. *b:* 29.3.1939, Chelsea, London. Lower order right-hand batsman, right-arm fast bowler. *Sch* Rugby. *Team* Cambridge U (1958–60, blue 1960).
Career batting
20–33–8–257–24–10.28–0–*ct* 12
Bowling 1622–30–54.06–0–0–3/70
His final first-class match was for L. C. Steven's XI in 1961.

Cohen, Aaron Neville
Amateur. *b:* 11.9.1913, Calcutta, India. Middle order right-hand batsman, leg break bowler. *Sch* Cheltenham. *Team* Oxford U (1934).
Career batting
3–3–2–27–15*–27.00–0–*ct* 2
Bowling 269–4–67.25–0–0–2/79

Cohen, Mark Francis
Cricketer. *b:* 27.3.1961, Cork, Ireland. Right-hand batsman. *Team* Ireland (1980).
Career batting
1–1–0–0–0–0.00–0–*ct* 1
He was on the Middlesex staff in 1981.

Cohen, Rudolph A.
Cricketer. *b:* 23.5.1943, Kingston, Jamaica. Lower order right-hand batsman, right-arm fast-medium bowler. *Team* Jamaica (1963/4 to 1966/7). *Tour* West Indies to England 1966.
Career batting
37–42–20–160–32*–7.27–0–*ct* 15
Bowling 2576–81+1–31.80–1–0–6/71
Visiting England in 1966 in the place of the injured Lester King, Cohen, though not obtaining a place in the Tests, proved fairly effective with 40 wickets, av 24.22.

Cokayne-Frith, Colin
Amateur. *b:* 27.3.1900, Canterbury, Kent. *d:* 18.5.1940, Near Escaut River, Belgium. He was killed in action. Middle order batsman. *Sch* Eton. *Team* Army (1939).
Career batting
1–1–0–54–54–54.00–0–*ct* 1

Colah, Sorabji Hormasji Munchersha
Amateur. *b:* 22.9.1902, Bombay, India. *d:* 11.9.1950, Ahmedabad, India. Brother of N. H. (Parsis). Middle order right-hand batsman, right-arm medium pace bowler, fine close field. *Sch* St Xavier's College, Bombay. *Teams* Parsis (1922/3 to 1939/40); Bombay (1926/7 to 1933/4); Western India (1934/5 to 1935/6); Nawanagar (1936/7 to 1941/2). *Tour* India to England 1932. *Tests* India (1932 to 1933/4, 2 matches).

Career batting
74–130–9–3435–185*–28.38–5–*ct* 50
Bowling 279–5–55.80–0–0–2/14
Test batting
2–4–0–69–31–17.25–0–*ct* 2

He had a moderate tour to England in 1932 – his fielding being perhaps his major asset.

Colbeck, Leonard George
Amateur. *b:* 1.1.1884, Hendon, Middlesex. *d:* 3.1.1918. He died at sea in HMS *Ormonde*. Middle order right-hand batsman. *Sch* Marlborough. *Teams* Cambridge U (1905–06, blue both years); Middlesex (1906–08, 10 matches); Europeans (1913/14).
Career batting
32–60–5–1368–175*–24.87–3–*ct* 16

His great innings was for Cambridge in the University match of 1905 when he hit 107 and added 143 for the 7th wicket after 6 batsmen had gone for 77. His last first-class match in England was for MCC in 1911.

Coldham, John Maurice
Amateur. *b:* 17.1.1901, Cheadle, Cheshire. Middle order right-hand batsman. *Sch* Repton. *Team* Oxford U (1925).
Career batting
2–4–0–73–40–18.25–0–*ct* 0

His first-class debut was for the Minor Counties XI in 1924 and he represented Norfolk for many years.

Coldwell, Leonard John
Professional. *b:* 10.1.1933, Newton Abbot, Devon. Tail end right-hand batsman, right-arm fast-medium bowler. *Team* Worcestershire (1955–69, 296 matches). *Tours* MCC to Australia and New Zealand 1962/3; Worcestershire World Tour 1964/5, to Jamaica 1965/6. *Tests* England (1962–64, 7 matches).
Career batting
310–347–100–1474–37–5.96–0–*ct* 89
Bowling 22791–1076–21.18–60–7–8/38
Test batting
7–7–5–9–6*–4.50–0–*ct* 1
Bowling 610–22–27.72–1–0–6/85

He took 100 wickets in a season twice (best 152, av 17.90, in 1962). He appeared for Devon, 1953–54.

Coldwell, William Rodney
Professional. *b:* 4.6.1932, Petersfield, Hampshire. Middle order batsman. *Team* MCC (1954–55).
Career batting
2–4–0–15–8–3.75–0–*ct* 0

Cole, A.
Professional. Middle/lower order batsman, bowler. *Team* Middlesex (1879, 2 matches).
Career batting
3–6–0–45–21–7.50–0–*ct* 0
Bowling 51–3–17.00–0–0–3/29

He also played non-first-class cricket for Essex.

Cole, Colin Gibson
Professional. *b:* 7.7.1916, Sittingbourne, Kent. Lower order right-hand batsman, right-arm fast-medium bowler. *Team* Kent (1935–38, 27 matches).
Career batting
27–43–14–228–23*–7.86–0–*ct* 15
Bowling 2110–61–34.55–2–0–6/62

Cole, Derek Henry
Amateur. *b:* 9.3.1925, Dawlish, Devon. Opening right-hand batsman, right-arm fast medium and off-break bowler. *Team* Minor Counties (1959–67).
Career batting
3–4–0–86–36–21.50–0–*ct* 1
Bowling 82–2–41.00–0–0–1/11

His County cricket was played for Devon. He made his first-class debut for South v North in 1956.

Cole, Major-General Eric Stuart
Amateur. *b:* 10.2.1906, Malta. Middle/lower order right-hand batsman, right-arm medium pace bowler. *Teams* Army (1933–38); Kent (1938, 3 matches).
Career batting
10–15–0–147–36–9.80–0–*ct* 13
Bowling 912–25–36.48–0–0–4/78

His first-class debut was for Free Foresters in 1931.

Cole, Frederick Livsey
Amateur. *b:* 4.10.1852, Patricroft, Lancashire. *d:* 1.7.1941, Sheffield, Yorkshire. Middle order right-hand batsman, right-arm medium pace bowler. *Team* Gloucestershire (1879–90, 15 matches).
Career batting
15–25–2–188–36–8.17–0–*ct* 8–*st* 1
Bowling 41–0

He also assisted Somerset (non-first-class).

Cole, Canon George Lamont
Amateur. *b:* 5.9.1885, Hastings, Sussex. *d:* 14.10.1964, Faversham, Kent. Middle order right-hand batsman. *Sch* Sherborne. *Teams* Cambridge U (1908); Hampshire (1909–11, 6 matches).
Career batting
7–12–1–122–33–11.09–0–*ct* 4

Cole, George Thomas
(known as Thomas George Cole)
Amateur. *b:* 16.2.1846, Poplar, Middlesex. *d:* 1900, Islington, London. Middle order right-hand batsman, right-hand fast round-arm bowler. *Team* Surrey Club (1873).
Career batting
2–4–0–55–21–13.75–0–*ct* 0

Cole, John Richard
Amateur. *b:* 15.2.1907, London. Opening right-hand batsman. *Sch* Emanuel. *Team* Army (1930–32).
Career batting
4–8–0–112–63–14.00–0–*ct* 5

Cole, Terence George Owen
Amateur. *b:* 14.11.1877, Llanrhaiadr, Denbighshire. *d:* 15.12.1944, Stoke Court, near Taunton, Somerset. Opening/middle order right-hand batsman, slow left-arm bowler. *Sch* Harrow. *Teams* Cambridge U (1898); Lancashire (1904, 1 match); Derbyshire (1913, 6 matches); Somerset (1922, 1 match). *Tour* Brackley to West Indies 1904/5.
Career batting
20–35–3–499–68–15.59–0–*ct* 9
Bowling 17–0
In addition to the three first-class counties, Cole also appeared for Denbighshire in 1905.

Colebrooke, Rev Edward Lotherington
Amateur. *b:* 29.10.1858, Southborough, Kent. *d:* 10.8.1939, Canterbury, Kent. Opening/middle order right-hand batsman. *Sch* Charterhouse. *Teams* Oxford U (1880, blue); Gentlemen of Kent (1880).
Career batting
7–14–2–161–34*–13.41–0–*ct* 6
He made his first-class debut for Gentlemen of England in 1879.

Colegrave, Henry Manby
Amateur. *b:* 1872, Kensington, London. *d:* 21.4.1955, Brighton, Sussex. Middle order right-hand batsman, right-arm fast bowler. *Sch* Oscott College. *Team* London County (1901).
Career batting
2–2–1–36–36*–36.00–0–*ct* 2

Coleman, Charles Alfred Richard
Professional. *b:* 7.7.1906, Gumley, Leics. *d:* 14.6.1978, Market Harborough, Leics. Hard-hitting lower order batsman, right-arm fast-medium bowler. *Team* Leicestershire (1926–35, 114 matches).
Career batting
114–170–10–2403–114–15.01–1–*ct* 60
Bowling 3576–100–35.76–1–0–5/30
A first-class umpire, he officiated in Test matches.

Coleman, Edward Charles
Amateur. *b:* 5.9.1891, Southend, Essex. *d:* 2.4.1917, Salonica, Greece. He was killed in action. Lower order left-hand batsman, wicket-keeper. *Sch* Dulwich. *Team* Essex (1912, 2 matches).
Career batting
3–5–1–14–6–3.50–0–*ct* 2–*st* 1
He did not appear in a first-class match whilst at Cambridge. His first-class debut was for Combined Oxford and Cambridge Universities in 1911.

Coleman, William Ezra
Professional. *b:* 1879, Hitchin, Herts. *d:* 17.1.1960, Napsbury, St Albans, Hertfordshire. Middle/lower order right-hand batsman, right-arm fast medium bowler. *Team* MCC (1902–09).
Career batting
10–18–2–180–37–11.25–0–*ct* 4
Bowling 483–23–21.00–1–0–6/30
He appeared for Hertfordshire 1896–1914.

Coles, George Edward
Amateur. *b:* 11.2.1851, Bombay, India. *d:* 21.6.1903, Naini Tal, India. Middle order right-hand batsman, right-hand fast round-arm bowler. *Team* Kent (1873, 2 matches).
Career batting
2–4–0–39–19–9.75–0–*ct* 0
Bowling 98–11–8.90–1–1–6/23

Coles, Percival
Amateur. *b:* 2.5.1865, Eastbourne, Sussex. *d:* 24.2.1920, St Leonard's-on-Sea, Sussex. Opening right-hand batsman, occasional right-arm fast-medium bowler, good field. *Sch* Rugby. *Teams* Sussex (1885, 4 matches); Oxford U (1885–86).
Career batting
10–20–2–174–45–9.66–0–*ct* 3
He played in the Oxford Rugby XV for three years, being captain in 1886.

Coles, Walter Neill
Amateur. *b:* 11.2.1928, Northwood, Middlesex. Middle order right-hand batsman. *Sch* Eton. *Team* Cambridge U (1949).
Career batting
2–3–0–26–14–8.66–0–*ct* 1

Colhoun, Osmund David
Amateur. *b:* 6.6.1939, Sion Mills, Co Tyrone,

Ireland. Right-hand batsman, wicket-keeper. *Team* Ireland (1959–79).
Career batting
28–35–19–74–9*–4.62–0–*ct* 44–*st* 2

Colledge, Fred
Amateur. *b:* 7.5.1915, Renfrew, Scotland. Right-hand batsman, right-arm fast medium bowler. *Team* Scotland (1949–52).
Career batting
4–4–2–21–12*–10.50–0–*ct* 2
Bowling 267–6–44.50–0–0–2/50

Collett, Gilbert Faraday
Amateur. *b:* 18.7.1879, Gloucester. *d:* 25.2.1945, Barnwood, near Gloucester. Middle order right-hand batsman, change bowler, good slip field. *Sch* Cheltenham. *Team* Gloucestershire (1900–14, 9 matches).
Career batting
9–16–0–155–41–9.68–0–*ct* 8
Bowling 144–4–36.00–0–0–2/37

Collett, William Eustace
Professional. *b:* 23.9.1839, Lambeth, Surrey. *d:* 1.5.1904, Kennington, Surrey. Middle order right-hand batsman, right-hand fast round-arm bowler. *Team* Surrey (1869–74, 4 matches).
Career batting
4–8–0–44–19–5.50–0–*ct* 1

Colley, David John
Cricketer. *b:* 15.3.1947, Mosman, New South Wales, Australia. Lower order right-hand batsman, right-arm fast-medium bowler. *Team* New South Wales (1969/70 to 1977/8, 71 matches). *Tour* Australia to England 1972. *Tests* Australia (1972, 3 matches).
Career batting
87–123–23–2374–101–23.74–1–*ct* 44
Bowling 7459–236–31.60–8–0–6/30
Test batting
3–4–0–84–54–21.00–0–*ct* 1
Bowling 312–6–52.00–0–0–3/83

Although he had a place in three of the five Tests on the 1972 tour to England, his performance on the visit was a modest one, his 33 first-class wickets costing 28.66 runs each.

Collier, Christopher George Arthur
Professional. *b:* 23.8.1886, Banff, Scotland. *d:* 25.8.1916, near Mametz, France. He was killed in action. Middle order right-hand batsman, change bowler. *Team* Worcestershire (1910–14, 52 matches).
Career batting
53–87–8–1021–72–12.92–0–*ct* 13
Bowling 369–10–36.90–0–0–3/28

Collier, Robert
(Succeded as 2nd Baron Monkswell in 1886)
Amateur. *b:* 26.3.1845, London. *d:* 22.12.1909, Chelsea, London. Middle order batsman. *Sch* Eton. *Team* Cambridgeshire (1866–67, 3 matches).
Career batting
3–6–0–33–14–5.50–0–*ct* 0
Bowling 15–0

He was Under Secretary for War in 1895.

Collin, Spencer Compton
Amateur. *b:* 1.8.1852, Saffron Walden, Essex. *d:* 25.11.1923, Brighton, Sussex. Middle order batsman, excellent cover field. *Sch* Winchester. *Team* An All England Eleven (1873, 1 match).
Career batting
1–2–0–4–4–2.00–0–*ct* 0

Whilst at Cambridge he did not appear in any first-class matches. He played non-first-class cricket for Essex.

Collin, Thomas
Professional, amateur after 1937. *b:* 7.4.1911, South Moor, Co Durham. Middle order left-hand batsman, slow left-arm bowler. *Team* Warwickshire (1933–36, 52 matches).
Career batting
52–75–7–1399–105*–20.57–1–*ct* 35
Bowling 1302–26–50.07–0–0–3/45

He also appeared for Durham.

Collinge, John Gregory
Cricketer. *b:* 10.5.1939, New Zealand. Middle order right-hand batsman, off break bowler. *Team* Oxford U (1964).
Career batting
2–3–0–18–9–6.00–0–*ct* 1

Collinge, Rex Alan
Amateur. *b:* 23.1.1935, Nottingham. Lower order right-hand batsman, right-arm fast medium bowler. *Sch* Bedford. *Team* Combined Services (1962).
Career batting
2–4–0–101–41–25.25–0–*ct* 2
Bowling 186–11–16.90–1–0–6/52

His County cricket was for Suffolk.

Collinge, Richard Owen
Cricketer. *b:* 2.4.1946, Wellington, New Zealand. Lower order right-hand batsman, left-arm medium fast bowler. *Teams* Central Districts (1963/4 to 1969/70); Wellington (1967/8 to 1974/5); Northern Districts (1975/6 to 1977/8). *Tours* New Zealand to England 1965, 1969, 1973, 1978, to Australia 1967/8, 1969/70, 1970/1, to

India and Pakistan 1964/5, 1976/7. *Tests* New Zealand (1964/5 to 1978, 35 matches).
Career batting
163–178–50–1848–68*–14.43–0–*ct* 57
Bowling 12793–524–24.41–22–4–8/64
Test batting
35–50–13–533–68*–14.40–0–*ct* 10
Bowling 3393–116–29.25–3–0–6/63

Of his four tours to England, his 1973 visit was easily the most successful, in that he headed both first-class and Test bowling averages with 51 wickets, av 21.92, and 12 wickets, av 24.08, respectively.

Collings, Algernon William
Amateur. *b:* 4.9.1853, Guernsey. *d:* 14.5.1945, Burghfield Common, Berkshire. Middle order batsman, good field. *Sch* Winchester. *Team* Gloucestershire (1874, 1 match).
Career batting
1–1–0–1–1–1.00–0–*ct* 0

Collings, Edward Peter
Amateur. 30.1.1892, Lichfield, Staffs. *d:* 14.9.1968, Combe Down, Somerset. Lower order right-hand batsman, right-arm bowler. *Sch* King's, Canterbury. *Team* Somerset (1921–25, 4 matches).
Career batting
4–8–1–42–16–6.00–0–*ct* 2
Bowling 156–2–78.00–0–0–2/125

Collingwood, Boris Esmond
Amateur. *b:* 8.1.1920, Lewisham, Kent. *d:* 18.11.1968, Storrington, Sussex. Middle order right-hand batsman, good outfield. *Sch* Dulwich. *Teams* Cambridge U (1948); Somerset (1953, 1 match).
Career batting
2–3–0–21–15–7.00–0–*ct* 2

Collins, Arthur
Amateur. *b:* 1872, East Grinstead, Sussex. *d:* 22.7.1945, Hadlow Down, Sussex. Middle/lower order right-hand batsman, slow left-arm bowler. *Team* Sussex (1895–1902, 53 matches).
Career batting
53–89–18–1812–102–25.52–1–*ct* 29
Bowling 1656–36–46.00–1–0–5/61

Collins, Bernard Abdy
Amateur. *b:* 17.2.1880, Saxmundham, Suffolk. *d:* 22.10.1951, Bedford. Lower order right-hand batsman, wicket-keeper. *Sch* Malvern. *Team* Oxford U (1901).
Career batting
1–2–1–83–83*–83.00–0–*ct* 1

He also played for Suffolk. He was Director-General of Commerce and Industry in Hyderabad State.

Collins, Brian George
Cricketer. *b:* 11.8.1941, Enfield, Middlesex. Lower order right-hand batsman, right-arm fast medium bowler. *Team* Minor Counties (1979). *Tour* Minor Counties to Kenya 1978 (not first-class).
Career batting
1 match, did not bat–*ct* 0
Bowling 110–3–36.66–0–0–3/83

His County cricket was for Hertfordshire, commencing 1965.

Collins, Christopher
Professional. *b:* 14.10.1859, Cobham, Kent. *d:* 11.8.1919, Gravesend, Kent. Brother of George (Kent), father of G. C. (Kent). Lower order right-hand batsman, right-arm fast-medium bowler. *Team* Kent (1881–85, 8 matches).
Career batting
8–13–2–97–41–8.81–0–*ct* 5
Bowling 305–16–19.06–0–0–4/9

Owing to his bowling action being suspect, his County career was of short duration.

Collins, Dr David Charles
Amateur. *b:* 1.10.1887, Wellington, New Zealand. *d:* 2.1.1967, Tauranga, New Zealand. Son of W. E. (Wellington). Opening right-hand batsman, right-arm medium pace bowler. *Sch* Wellington College, New Zealand. *Teams* Cambridge U (1908–11, blue 1910–11); Wellington (1905/6 to 1926/7).
Career batting
53–96–8–2604–172–29.59–6–*ct* 33–*st* 1
Bowling 870–32–27.18–0–0–4/10

He returned to New Zealand after coming down from Cambridge. His final first-class match in England was for Free Foresters in 1912.

Collins, Frank
Professional. *b:* 3.2.1903, Eastbourne, Sussex. Tail end right-hand batsman, right-arm medium pace bowler. *Team* Sussex (1923, 1 match).
Career batting
1–2–0–27–27–13.50–0–*ct* 0
Bowling 33–0

Collins, George
Professional. *b:* 29.10.1851, Cobham, Kent. *d:* 11.3.1905, Tunbridge Wells, Kent. Brother of Christopher (Kent), uncle of G. C. (Kent). Lower order right-hand batsman, right-hand fast round-arm bowler. *Team* Kent (1874–82, 13 matches).

Career batting
14–22–4–183–36–10.16–0–*ct* 5
Bowling 68–3–22.66–0–0–2/15

His first-class debut was for W.G. Grace's XI in 1873.

Collins, Geoffrey A.
Professional. *b:* 1918, Brighton. Opening right-hand batsman. *Team* Sussex (1939, 1 match).
Career batting
1–2–0–19–17–9.50–0–*ct* 1

Collins, Geoffrey Albert Kirwan
Amateur. *b;* 16.5.1909, Steyning, Sussex. *d:* 7.8.1968, Hove, Sussex. Opening right-hand batsman. *Sch* Lancing. *Team* Sussex (1928–34, 49 matches).
Career batting
50–72–12–1140–90–19.00–0–*ct* 17

He was a useful soccer player, appearing for The Casuals. Demands of business restricted his County cricket.

Collins, George Christopher
Professional. *b:* 21.9.1889, Gravesend, Kent. *d:* 23.1.1949, Rochester, Kent. Son of Christopher (Kent), nephew of George (Kent). Middle/lower order left-hand batsman, right-arm fast-medium bowler. *Team* Kent (1911–28, 212 matches). *Tour* MCC to West Indies 1925/6.
Career batting
218–321–37–6280–110–22.11–4–*ct* 81–*st* 1
Bowling 9065–379–23.91–24–3–10/65

In 1923 he hit 1036 runs, av 22.04. His best bowling was 10/65 for Kent v Notts at Dover in 1922.

Collins, Gordon Thomas
Professional. *b:* 26.12.1914, Sunbury-on-Thames, Middlesex. Opening right-hand batsman, wicket-keeper. *Team* Northants (1938, 3 matches).
Career batting
3–5–0–44–17–8.80–0–*ct* 0

He also played for Cambridgeshire.

Collins, Herbert Leslie
Amateur. *b:* 21.1.1889, Darlinghurst, New South Wales, Australia. *d:* 28.5.1959, Sydney, New South Wales, Australia. Brother of R. S. (Civil Service 1927). Sound opening right-hand batsman, slow left-arm bowler. *Team* New South Wales (1909/10 to 1925/6, 52 matches). *Tours* Australia to England 1921, 1926, to South Africa 1921/2, to New Zealand 1913/4, to North America 1913; AIF to England and South Africa 1919. *Tests* Australia (1920/1 to 1926, 19 matches).
Career batting
168–258–10–9924–282–40.01–32–*ct* 115
Bowling 3871–181–21.38–8–2–8/31
Test batting
19–31–1–1352–203–45.06–4–*ct* 13
Bowling 252–4–63.00–0–0–2/47

Captaining the AIF in England in 1919, he was most successful, performing the 'double' with 1,615 runs, av 38.45, and 106 wickets, av 16.55. On his two official tours, however, he was beset by injury and neither time reached 1,000 runs in first-class matches, whilst his bowling was of little account. He captained Australia on the 1926 tour. Of his three double centuries, two were made in South Africa, including 203 in the Johannesburg Test of 1921/2, and the last for New South Wales. His highest score was 282 for NSW v Tasmania at Hobart in 1912/3.

Collins, Ian Glen
Amateur. *b:* 23.4.1903, Glasgow, Scotland. *d:* 20.3.1975, Bearsden, Dunbartonshire, Scotland. Opening/middle order right-hand batsman, change bowler. *Sch* Harrow. *Teams* Oxford U (1925); Scotland (1927).
Career batting
2–4–0–69–34–17.25–0–*ct* 1

A broken leg prevented him from playing cricket in his first year at Oxford. He gained half-blues for golf and tennis and represented Great Britain in the Davis Cup.

Collins, Lionel Peter
Amateur. *b:* 27.11.1878, Reading, Berkshire. *d:* 28.9.1957, Fleet, Hants. Middle order right-hand batsman. *Sch* Marlborough. *Team* Oxford U (1899, blue). *Tour* MCC to North America 1907.
Career batting
19–35–3–858–102*–26.81–1–*ct* 5

His County cricket was for Berkshire. For several years commencing 1901 he was stationed in India. His final first-class match was for Free Foresters in 1913.

Collins, Roy
Professional. *b:* 10.3.1934, Clayton, Manchester. Brother-in-law of J. Cumbes (Lancs). Middle/lower order right-hand batsman, off break bowler, good slip field. *Team* Lancashire (1954–62, 139 matches).
Career batting
120–183–18–3436–107*–20.79–2–*ct* 80
Bowling 4831–159–30.38–4–0–6/63

He also played for Cheshire.

Collins, Ross Phillip
Cricketer. *b*: 9.12.1945, Paddington, New South Wales, Australia. Middle order right-hand

batsman, right-arm medium pace bowler. *Teams* New South Wales (1967/8 to 1975/6, 22 matches); International Cavaliers (1969).
Career batting
23–43–3–1061–88*–26.52–0–*ct* 20
Bowling 910–31–29.35–1–0–5/54

Collins, R. S.
Amateur. *b:* 1890, Darlinghurst, New South Wales, Australia. Brother of H. L. (New South Wales). Lower order batsman, bowler. *Team* Civil Service (1927).
Career batting
1–2–0–11–11–5.50–0–*ct* 1
Bowling 47–2–23.50–0–0–2/47

Collins, Thomas Hugh
Professional. *b:* 4.3.1895, Nottingham. *d:* 19.5.1964, Edwalton, Notts. Lower order left-hand batsman, left-arm slow-medium bowler. *Teams* Nottinghamshire (1921, 2 matches); Hampshire (1935, 2 matches).
Career batting
4–6–0–32–13–5.33–0–*ct* 2
Bowling 80–4–20.00–0–0–1/17

Collins, William Edmund Wood
Amateur. *b:* 16.6.1848, Cheriton, Glamorgan. *d:* 7.1.1932, Heacham, Norfolk. Hard-hitting lower order right-hand batsman, left-arm fast bowler. *Sch* Radley. *Teams* Gentlemen (1884).
Career batting
7–10–2–157–56*–19.62–0–*ct* 3
Bowling 448–19–23.57–3–0–6/35

Although considered one of the best amateur cricketers of his day, he rarely appeared in first-class matches, confining himself mainly to Free Foresters and Country House games, though he played occasionally for Shropshire. His final first-class match was for H. Philipson's XI in 1891. He was a noted author, his subjects including cricket.

Collins, William Ronald
Amateur. *b:* 29.1.1868, Hackney, Middlesex. *d:* 10.12.1942, Clapton, Thrapston, Northants. Middle order right-hand batsman, right-arm fast bowler. *Sch* Wellington, *Team* Middlesex (1892, 1 match).
Career batting
1–2–0–0–0–0.00–0–*ct* 0

Collinson, John
Amateur. *b:* 2.10.1911, Sotterley, Suffolk. *d:* 29.8.1979, Hove, Sussex. Middle order right-hand batsman, off break bowler. *Sch* St John's, Leatherhead. *Teams* Middlesex (1939, 2 matches); Worcestershire (1946, 1 match).
Career batting
3–6–0–109–34–18.16–0–*ct* 1

Collinson, Robert Whiteley
Amateur. *b:* 6.11.1875, Halifax, Yorkshire. *d:* 26.12.1963, Norwich. Middle order batsman. *Team* Yorkshire (1897, 2 matches).
Career batting
2–3–0–58–34–19.33–0–*ct* 0

He also played for Norfolk.

Collishaw, William Frederick
Professional. *b:* 2.10.1860, Hickling, Notts. *d:* 31.1.1936, Saltley, Birmingham. Middle order right-hand batsman, right-arm medium pace bowler. *Team* An England XI (1886).
Career batting
1–1–0–0–0–0.00–0–*ct* 0

He played non-first-class cricket for Warwickshire, 1885 to 1892.

Collyer, Francis Edward
Cricketer. *b:* 4.2.1947, Brentford, Middlesex. Lower order right-hand batsman, wicket-keeper. *Teams* Cambridge U (1967–69); Minor Counties (1973–79).
Career batting
5–8–1–96–46–13.71–0–*ct* 11–*st* 1

He represented Hertfordshire commencing 1965.

Collyer, William James
Amateur. *b:* 1.6.1841, Chobham, Surrey. *d:* 1.9.1908, Bruges, Belgium. Opening/middle order right-hand batsman, good long-stop. *Sch* Windlesham House School. *Team* Surrey (1866–69, 18 matches).
Career batting
18–34–3–386–69–12.45–0–*ct* 6

He did not appear in any first-class matches whilst at Oxford U.

Collyer, William Robert
Amateur. *b:* 11.1.1842, London. *d:* 27.10.1928, Hackford-by-Reepham, Norfolk. Middle order right-hand batsman. *Sch* Rugby. *Team* Cambridge U (1864).
Career batting
1–2–0–2–2–1.00–0–*ct* 2

His County cricket was played for Norfolk. From 1903 until 1906 he was Attorney-General of the Straits Settlements.

Colman, Geoffrey Russell Rees
Amateur. *b:* 14.3.1892, Norwich. *d:* 18.3.1935, Framlingham, Norwich. Cousin of Stanley (Surrey). Attractive opening right-hand batsman, occasional slow bowler, brilliant cover point. *Sch*

Eton. *Team* Oxford U (1912–14, blue 1913–14). *Tour* Incogniti to North America 1913 (not first-class).
Career batting
23–41–2–958–127–24.56–1–*ct* 17
Bowling 14–1–14.00–0–0–1/14
He played for Norfolk until 1930, when he was obliged to retire due to ill-health. His final first-class match was for Minor Counties in 1924.

Colman, Stanley
Amateur. *b:* 6.1.1862, Clapham, Surrey. *d:* 27.2.1942, Walton-on-the-Hill, Surrey. Cousin of G. R. R. (Oxford U). Opening/middle order right-hand batsman. *Team* Surrey (1882, 6 matches).
Career batting
6–10–0–81–63–8.10–0–*ct* 2
Captain of the South London club, Wanderers CC, for over 50 years, he was regarded as the 'W. G. Grace' of club cricket.

Colquhoun, James Clifton
Amateur. *b:* 1.12.1893, Scotland. *d:* 9.2.1977, London. Opening right-hand batsman. *Sch* Glenalmond. *Team* G. J. V. Weigall's XI v Oxford U 1914.
Career batting
1–2–0–30–15–15.00–0–*ct* 0
He appeared for Kent 2nd XI and later occasionally for Cornwall.

Comber, George
Professional. *b:* 12.10.1856, Redhill, Surrey. *d:* 18.10.1929, Redhill, Surrey. Middle/lower order right-hand batsman, wicket-keeper. *Team* Surrey (1880–85, 6 matches).
Career batting
6–11–2–44–19–4.88–0–*ct* 2–*st* 1

Comber, John Howard
Professional. *b:* 8.1.1861, Brighton, Sussex. Middle/lower order batsman, change bowler. *Team* Sussex (1885, 3 matches).
Career batting
3–6–1–28–8–5.60–0–*ct* 0
Bowling 20–0
He emigrated to Philadelphia in 1886.

Comber, Joseph Thomas Henry
Amateur. *b:* 26.2.1911. *d:* 3.5.1976, Chelsea, London. Lower order right-hand batsman, wicket-keeper. *Sch* Marlborough. *Team* Cambridge U (1931–33, blue all three years).
Career batting
57–78–18–833–62–13.88–*ct* 84–*st* 42
He also played for Cambridgeshire. His final first-class match was for MCC in 1948.

Commaille, John McIllwain Moore
Amateur. *b:* 21.2.1883, Cape Town, South Africa. *d:* 27.7.1956, Cape Town, South Africa. Opening right-hand batsman. *Teams* Western Province (1904/5 to 1923/4); Natal (1919/20); Orange Free State (1924/5 to 1928/9); Griqualand West (1929/30 to 1930/1). *Tours* South Africa to England 1924, to Australia 1910/11. *Tests* South Africa (1909/10 to 1927/8, 12 matches).
Career batting
96–169–13–5026–186–32.21–9–*ct* 32
Bowling 33–1–33.00–0–0–1/15
Test batting
12–22–1–355–47–16.90–0–*ct* 1
Over 40 when he came to England as vice-captain of the 1924 team, he hit 1,170 runs, av 26.00, and whilst doing nothing extraordinary achieved as much as was expected of him.

Compton, Denis Charles Scott, CBE
Professional, changed to amateur after 1957 season. *b:* 23.5.1918, Hendon, Middlesex. Brother of L. H. (Middlesex). Brilliant middle order right-hand batsman, slow left-arm bowler. *Teams* Middlesex (1936–58, 296 matches); Holkar (1944/5); Europeans (1945/6). *Tours* MCC to Australia and New Zealand 1946/7, 1950/1, 1954/5, to South Africa 1948/9, 1956/7, to West Indies 1953/4; Commonwealth to South Africa 1959/60; Cavaliers to Jamaica 1963/4. *Tests* England (1937 to 1956/7, 78 matches).
Career batting
515–839–88–38942–300–51.85–123–*ct* 415
Bowling 20074–622–32.27–19–3–7/36
Test batting
78–131–15–5807–278–50.06–17–*ct* 49
Bowling 1410–25–56.40–1–0–5/70
Of his many achievements on the cricket field all are dwarfed by Compton's incredible success in 1947. Scoring 3,816 runs at an average of 90.85 with 18 centuries, he created new records both for the most runs in first-class cricket in a season and most centuries. The South African tourists, who visited England that summer, suffered greatly from his appetite, conceding 6 centuries to him and in the Tests 753 runs at an average of 94.12. His success continued, though slightly reduced, through 1948 and the tour to South Africa in 1948/9, when he hit his highest innings of 300 for MCC v North-East Transvaal – this innings, which took 181 minutes, was the fastest triple hundred ever made in a first-class match. In both 1948 and 1949, Compton reached 2,000 runs in a season, as he had done in 1939 and 1946, but his run glut was halted by an old soccer injury, which meant that despite several operations he was never as fluent after 1949 as he had been previously. In all he exceeded 1,000 runs in

a season 14 times in England and three more times overseas.

He scored nine double hundreds, his highest in England being 278 for England v Pakistan at Trent Bridge in 1954. Owing to his football commitments he did not tour overseas with MCC until 1946/7, but he made many runs whilst serving in India during the Second World War. He played outside left for Arsenal, gaining an FA Cup winner's medal in 1950, and, in wartime internationals, for England.

He captained Middlesex jointly with W. J. Edrich in 1951 and 1952 and was vice-captain of MCC on the 1950/1 tour to Australia. His final first-class match was for MCC in 1964.

Compton, Edward Denison
Amateur. *b:* 11.4.1872, Frome, Somerset. *d:* 11.10.1940, Rye, Sussex. Lower order right-hand batsman, wicket-keeper. *Sch* Lancing. *Teams* Somerset (1894–1907, 4 matches); Oxford U (1896).
Career batting
6–11–4–51–22*–7.28–0–*ct* 4–*st* 1
He also played for Oxfordshire.

Compton, Leslie Harry
Professional. *b:* 12.9.1912, Woodford, Essex. Brother of D. C. S. (Middlesex). Lower order right-hand batsman, wicket-keeper, right-arm medium pace bowler. *Team* Middlesex (1938–56, 272 matches).
Career batting
274–393–46–5814–107–16.75–1–*ct* 468–*st* 131
Bowling 569–12–47.41–0–0–2/21
A noted soccer player, he was centre-half for Arsenal, winning an FA Cup winners medal in 1950, and in 1950/1 gained two caps for England.

Compton-Burnett, A.
(*see under* Burnett, A. C.)

Compton-Burnett, Richard James
Cricketer. *b*: 1.7.1961, Windsor, Berkshire. Son of A. C. Burnett (Glamorgan). Middle order right-hand batsman. *Sch* Eton. *Team* Cambridge U (1981).
Career batting
1–2–0–23–18–11.50–0–*ct* 0

Comyn, Andrew Daniel
Amateur. *b:* 23.9.1872, Kilconnell, Co Galway, Ireland. *d:* 21.5.1949, Dublin, Ireland. Right-hand batsman, leg break bowler. *Teams* Ireland (1902); Dublin University (1895).
Career batting
8–16–0–290–54–18.12–0–*ct* 1
Bowling 102–0

Conan Doyle, Sir Arthur Ignatius
Amateur. *b:* 22.5.1859, Edinburgh, Scotland. *d:* 7.7.1930, Crowborough, Sussex. Lower order right-hand batsman, slow bowler. *Sch* Stonyhurst. *Team* MCC (1900–07).
Career batting
10–18–6–231–43–19.25–0–*ct* 1
Bowling 50–1–50.00–0–0–1/4
He was a well-known author, the creator of Sherlock Holmes.

Conde-Williams, Maurice Marcel Frederic
Amateur. *b:* 16.1.1885. *d:* 16.11.1967, Chelsea, London. Opening batsman. *Sch* Brighton. *Team* Royal Navy (1913–23).
Career batting
2–4–0–54–30–13.50–0–*ct* 2
Bowling 10–0

Coney, Jeremy Vernon
Cricketer. *b*: 21.6.1952, Wellington, New Zealand. Sound middle order right-hand batsman, right-arm medium pace bowler. *Team* Wellington (1971/2 to 1982/3). *Tours* New Zealand to Australia 1973/4, 1980/1, 1982/3, to England 1983. *Tests* New Zealand (1973/4 to 1983, 24 matches).
Career batting
104–180–30–4632–120*–30.88–4–*ct* 125
Bowling 2332–80–29.15–1–0–6/17
Test batting
24–42–6–1146–84–31.83–0–*ct* 28
Bowling 486–15–32.40–0–0–3/28
He proved a useful all-rounder on the 1983 tour to England and played in all four Tests. His first-class debut was for New Zealand Under 23s in 1970/1.

Congdon, Bevan Ernest
Amateur. *b:* 11.2.1938, Motueka, New Zealand. Opening/middle order right-hand batsman, right-arm medium pace bowler. *Teams* Central Districts (1960/1 to 1970/1); Wellington (1971/2); Otago (1972/3 to 1973/4); Canterbury (1974/5 to 1977/8). *Tours* New Zealand to England 1965, 1969, 1973, 1978, to Australia 1967/8, 1969/70, 1970/1, 1972/3, 1973/4, to West Indies 1971/2, to India and Pakistan 1964/5, 1969/70. *Tests* New Zealand (1964/5 to 1978, 61 matches).
Career batting
241–416–40–13101–202*–34.84–23–*ct* 201
Bowling 6125–204–30.02–4–0–6/42
Test batting
61–114–7–3448–176–32.22–7–*ct* 44
Bowling 2154–59–36.50–1–0–5/65
Although touring England four times and playing in all three Tests on each visit, he was only really successful in 1973, when he hit 1,081

runs, av 60.05, and averaged 72.40 in the Tests. His highest score was 202* for Central District v Otago at Nelson in 1968/9.

Congdon, Charles Hector
Amateur. *b:* 29.8.1891. *d:* 11.1.1958, Boughton, Kent. Opening right-hand batsman. *Team* Royal Navy (1921–29).
Career batting
9–17–0–652–128–38.35–2–*ct* 4
Bowling 75–3–25.00–0–0–2/11

Conibere, William John
Amateur. *b:* 11.8.1923, Wellington, Somerset. *d:* 19.8.1982, Torbay, Devon. Lower order right-hand batsman, left-arm medium-fast bowler. *Team* Somerset (1950, 4 matches).
Career batting
4–5–0–16–8–3.20–0–*ct* 4
Bowling 220–7–31.42–0–0–4/66
A noted rugby footballer, he appeared for Somerset.

Coningham, Arthur
Amateur. *b:* 14.7.1863, South Melbourne, Victoria, Australia. *d:* 13.6.1939, Gladesville, New South Wales, Australia. Middle/lower order left-hand batsman, left-arm fast-medium bowler, brilliant field. *Teams* New South Wales (1892/3 to 1898/9, 13 matches); Queensland (1893/4 to 1895/6, 4 matches). *Tour* Australia to England and North America 1893. *Test* Australia (1894/5, 1 match).
Career batting
35–59–2–896–151–15.71–1–*ct* 27
Bowling 2603–112–23.24–7–0–6/38
Test batting
1–2–0–13–10–6.50–0–*ct* 0
Bowling 76–2–38.00–0–0–2/17
For some unexplained reason he was given very few opportunities to bowl on his only visit to England, but did well when called upon. He was a noted athlete, holding records for the quarter-mile hurdles, half-mile flat, one-mile flat and five mile flat races.

Connaughton, Joseph Maurice Francis
Amateur. *b:* 1918, Paddington, London. *d:* 12.2.1945, Burma. Lower order right-hand batsman, leg break bowler. *Sch* Oratory. *Teams* Oxford U (1939); Middlesex (1939, 1 match).
Career batting
2–3–1–22–16*–11.00–0–*ct* 1
Bowling 85–3–28.33–0–0–3/19

Connell, Francis Gerard
Amateur. *b:* 13.1.1902, Dublin, Ireland. *d:* 16.3.1983, Dublin. Right-hand batsman. *Team* Ireland (1934–38).
Career batting
5–10–0–262–87–26.20–0–*ct* 2

Connolly, Alan Norman
Amateur. *b:* 29.6.1939, Skipton, Victoria, Australia. Lower order right-hand batsman, right-arm fast-medium bowler. *Team* Victoria (1959/60 to 1970/1, 83 matches); Middlesex (1969–70, 44 matches). *Tours* Australia to England 1964, 1968, to South Africa 1969/70, to India 1964/5, 1969/70, to New Zealand 1966/7. *Tests* Australia (1964/5 to 1970/1, 29 matches).
Career batting
201–215–93–1073–40–8.79–0–*ct* 77
Bowling 17974–676–26.58–25–4–9/67
Test batting
29–45–20–260–37–10.40–0–*ct* 17
Bowling 2981–102–29.22–4–0–6/47
Minor injuries affected his 1964 tour to England and he did not appear in any Tests, but in 1968 he headed both Test and first-class bowling averages. He continued in 1969 to bowl well for Middlesex taking 74 wickets, av 23.24, but retired from first-class cricket in 1970/1 due to back trouble. His best bowling was 9/67 for Victoria v Queensland at Brisbane in 1964/5.

Connor, Edward James
Professional. *b:* 1872, Hackney, Middlesex. *d:* 11.1.1947, Enfield, Middlesex. Lower order batsman, right-arm medium pace bowler. *Team* Essex (1905, 2 matches).
Career batting
2–4–0–43–26–10.75–0–*ct* 0
Bowling 131–2–65.50–0–0–2/21

Conradi, Eric Ralph
Amateur. *b:* 25.7.1920, London. *d:* 22.8.1972, Droitwich, Worcestershire. Middle order left-hand batsman, excellent field. *Sch* Oundle. *Team* Cambridge U (1946, blue).
Career batting
7–13–3–164–50*–16.40–0–*ct* 8
He was very successful for Cambridge U in the wartime matches of 1940.

Considine, Stanley George Ulick
Amateur. *b:* 11.8.1901, Bilaspur, India. *d:* 31.8.1950, Bath, Somerset. Middle order right-hand batsman. *Sch* Blundell's. *Team* Somerset (1919–35, 89 matches).
Career batting
89–155–16–2965–130*–21.33–1–*ct* 43
Bowling 0–0
An excellent rugby footballer, he represented Bath, Somerset and England.

Constable, Bernard
Professional. *b:* 19.2.1921, East Molesey, Surrey. Brother of Dennis (Northants). Middle order right-hand batsman, leg-break bowler, excellent cover-point. *Team* Surrey (1939–64, 434 matches). *Tour* Surrey to Rhodesia 1959/60.
Career batting
446–701–82–18849–205*–30.45–27–*ct* 181
Bowling 3017–64–47.14–1–0–5/131

He reached 1,000 runs in a season 12 times (best 1,799, av 39.97, in 1961). His only double century was 205* for Surrey v Somerset at the Oval in 1952.

Constable, Dennis
Professional. *b:* 14.8.1925, East Molesey, Surrey. Brother of Bernard (Surrey). Lower order right-hand batsman, wicket-keeper. *Team* Northants (1949, 2 matches).
Career batting
2–2–0–20–12–10.00–0–*ct* 5–*st* 1

Constable, William Thomas
Professional. *b:* 21.3.1851, Poplar, Middlesex. *d:* 31.1.1894, Rochester, Kent. Middle order right-hand batsman, right-hand fast round-arm bowler. *Team* Kent (1876, 1 match).
Career batting
1–2–0–1–1–0.50–0–*ct* 0

Constant, David John
Professional. *b:* 9.11.1941, Bradford-on-Avon, Wilts. Middle order left-hand batsman, slow left-arm bowler. *Teams* Kent (1961–63, 8 matches); Leicestershire (1965–68, 53 matches).
Career batting
61–93–14–1517–80–19.20–0–*ct* 33
Bowling 36–1–36.00–0–0–1/28

He was appointed a first-class umpire in 1969 and Test umpire in 1971.

Constantine, Lord Learie Nicholas, MBE
Amateur. *b:* 21.9.1901, Petit Valley, Diego Martin, Trinidad. *d:* 1.7.1971, Hampstead, London. Son of L. S. (Trinidad). Hard-hitting middle order right-hand batsman, right-arm fast bowler, later also medium, brilliant fielder. *Teams* Trinidad (1921/2 to 1934/5); Freelooters (India) (1934/5); Barbados (1938/9). *Tours* West Indies to England 1923, 1928, 1933, 1939, to Australia 1930/1. *Tests* West Indies (1928–39, 18 matches).
Career batting
119–197–11–4475–133–24.05–5–*ct* 133
Bowling 8991–439–20.25–25–4–8/38
Test batting
18–33–0–635–90–19.24–0–*ct* 28
Bowling 1746–58–30.10–2–0–5/75

The best West Indian all-rounder of his generation, he first toured England in 1923, when fielding was his most notable asset; in 1928 he performed the 'double' and was the outstanding figure of the visit, but in 1933 he was playing for Rochdale and only assisted the tourists in five matches. In 1939 he was easily the best bowler, again taking 100 wickets. His best season's batting was in 1928 with 1381 runs, av 34.52; he took 107 wickets that season, but at 22.95 each compared with 103, at 17.77, in 1939. His final first-class match was for Dominions in 1945. He was High Commissioner for Trinidad and Tobago from 1962 to 1964 and was created a life peer in 1969.

Constantine, Lebrun Samuel
Amateur. *b:* 25.5.1874, Maraval, Trinidad. *d:* 5.1.1942, Tunapuna, Trinidad. Father of L. N. (Trinidad). Opening/middle order right-hand batsman. *Team* Trinidad (1893/4 to 1922/3). *Tours* West Indies to England 1900 (not first-class), 1906.
Career batting
56–100–4–2433–116–25.34–1–*ct* 95–*st* 18
Bowling 632–46–13.73–1–0–6/17

He was one of the best West Indian batsmen on both of his visits to England, but the tourists were of modest strength on each occasion.

Contractor, Nariman Jamshedji
Amateur. *b:* 7.3.1934, Godra, Gujerat, India. Father of H. N. (Bombay). Opening left-hand batsman, right-arm medium pace bowler. *Teams* Gujerat (1952/3 to 1970/1); Railways (1958/9 to 1959/60). *Tours* India to England 1959, to West Indies 1961/2, to Ceylon 1956/7. *Tests* India (1955/6 to 1961/2, 31 matches).
Career batting
138–234–18–8611–176–39.86–22–*ct* 72
Bowling 1040–26–40.00–0–0–4/85
Test batting
31–52–1–1611–108–31.58–1–*ct* 18
Bowling 80–1–80.00–0–0–1/9

He scored a century in each innings on his first-class debut: 152 and 102 for Gujerat v Baroda at Baroda in 1952/3. When visiting England in 1959 he hit 1,183 runs, av 31.13. He captained India in 12 Tests, including 1961/2 series v England, which India won 2-0. His skull was fractured by a ball from C. C. Griffith in the match between Indians and Barbados in 1961/2 and this ended his Test career.

Conway, Arthur Joseph
Professional. *b:* 1.4.1885, Stirchley, Worcs. *d:* 29.10.1954, Blackpool, Lancashire. Lower order right-hand batsman, right-arm fast bowler. *Team* Worcestershire (1910–19, 29 matches).

Career batting
31–52–14–165–20*–4.34–0–*ct* 6
Bowling 2039–57–35.77–2–1–9/38
He played soccer for Wolverhampton Wanderers. His best bowling was 9/38 for Worcs v Gloucs at Moreton-in-Marsh in 1914.

Coode, Arthur Trevenen
Amateur. *b:* 5.2.1876, St Helier, Jersey. *d:* 28.12.1940, Hazlemere, Bucks. Opening right-hand batsman. *Sch* Beccles. *Teams* Cambridge U (1898, blue); Middlesex (1898, 1 match).
Career batting
11–19–2–280–38–16.47–0–*ct* 3
Bowling 3–0
His last first-class match was for MCC in 1901. A noted soccer player, he obtained his blue for Cambridge and also appeared for Middlesex.

Cook, Cecil
Professional. *b:* 23.8.1921, Tetbury, Gloucs. Tail end right-hand batsman, slow left-arm bowler. *Team* Gloucestershire (1946–64, 498 matches). *Test* England (1947, 1 match).
Career batting
506–612–248–1965–35*–5.39–0–*ct* 153
Bowling 36578–1782–20.52–99–15–9/42
Test batting
1–2–0–4–4–2.00–0–*ct* 0
Bowling 127–0
He took 100 wickets in a season 9 times (best 149, av 14.16, in 1956). He is now a first-class umpire. His best bowling was 9/42 for Gloucs v Yorks at Bristol in 1947.

Cook, Charles John
Cricketer. *b:* 5.6.1946, Retford, Notts. Lower order right-hand batsman, off break bowler. *Team* Nottinghamshire (1974–75, 2 matches).
Career batting
2–2–1–1–1–1.00–0–*ct* 1
Bowling 105–1–105.00–0–0–1/50

Cook, Colin Roy
Cricketer. *b:* 11.1.1960, Edgware, Middlesex. Middle order right-hand batsman. *Sch* Merchant Taylors. *Team* Middlesex (1981–82, 9 matches).
Career batting
9–15–2–287–79–22.07–0–*ct* 7

Cook, David Roland
Cricketer. *b:* 2.9.1936, Birmingham. Brother of M. S. (Warwickshire). Lower order right-hand batsman, left-arm fast medium bowler. *Sch* Warwick School. *Team* Warwickshire (1962–68, 9 matches).
Career batting
9–13–5–108–28*–13.50–0–*ct* 7
Bowling 534–23–23.21–0–0–4/66
He played once for Warwickshire in 1962, but did not re-appear until 1967. A noted rugby footballer, he represented Coventry and Warwickshire.

Cook, Enoch
Professional. *b:* 23.4.1845, Sandiacre, Derbyshire. *d:* 14.4.1927, Long Eaton, Derbyshire. Middle order right-hand batsman. *Teams* Derbyshire (1878–79, 8 matches).
Career batting
8–15–2–92–23*–7.07–0–*ct* 3

Cook, Geoffrey
Cricketer. *b:* 9.10.1951, Middlesbrough, Yorkshire. Sound opening right-hand batsman, slow left-arm bowler, good close field. *Teams* Northamptonshire (1971–83, 275 matches); Eastern Province (1978/9 to 1980/1). *Tours* England to India and Sri Lanka 1981/2, to Australia and New Zealand 1982/3 (New Zealand not first-class). *Tests* England (1981/2 to 1982/3, 7 matches).
Career batting
320–563–39–16079–172–30.68–24–*ct* 333–*st* 3
Bowling 570–14–40.71–0–0–3/47
Test batting
7–13–0–203–66–15.61–0–*ct* 9
Bowling 27–0
He hit 1,000 runs in a season eight times (best 1,759, av 43.97, in 1981). He was appointed Northants captain in 1981.

Cook, Geoffrey William
Amateur. *b:* 9.2.1936, Beckenham, Kent. Middle order right-hand batsman, off break bowler. *Sch* Dulwich. *Teams* Cambridge (1956–58, blue 1957–58); Kent (1957, 4 matches). *Tour* MCC to East Africa 1957/8 (not first-class).
Career batting
47–77–11–1858–140–28.15–3–*ct* 26
Bowling 2309–64–36.07–0–0–4/45
He also played for Berkshire. His final first-class match was for Free Foresters in 1961.

Cook, Jeremy
Cricketer. *b:* 20.7.1941, Leicester. Lower order batsman, bowler. *Team* MCC (1961–63).
Career batting
2–4–0–52–35–13.00–0–*ct* 3
Bowling 103–7–14.71–1–0–5/48

Cook, John Gilbert
Amateur. *b:* 16.5.1911, Houghton Regis, Bedfordshire. *d:* 10.9.1979, Overstrand, Norfolk.

Right-hand batsman. *Sch* Bedford. *Team* Ireland (1936).
Career batting
1–2–0–27–21–13.50–0–*ct* 0
Bowling 31–1–31.00–0–0–1/15
He also played for Bedfordshire. He was a rugby international for England.

Cook, Lawrence Whalley
Professional. *b:* 28.3.1885, Preston, Lancashire. *d:* 2.12.1933, Wigan, Lancashire. Brother of William (Lancashire). Lower order right-hand batsman, right-arm medium pace bowler. *Team* Lancashire (1907–23, 203 matches).
Career batting
206–263–93–2126–54*–12.50–0–*ct* 138
Bowling 17791–839–21.19–46–8–8/39
He took 100 wickets in a season three times (best 156, av 14.88, in 1920).

Cook, Michael Stephen
Amateur. *b:* 19.2.1939, Birmingham. Brother of D. R. (Warwickshire). Opening left-hand batsman, wicket-keeper. *Sch* Warwick School. *Team* Warwickshire (1961–62, 2 matches).
Career batting
2–4–0–110–52–27.50–0–*ct* 0

Cook, Nicholas Grant Billson
Cricketer. *b:* 17.6.1956, Broughton-Astley, Leics. Lower order right-hand batsman, slow left-arm bowler. *Team* Leicestershire (1978–83, 115 matches). *Tours* Robins to New Zealand 1979/80; Leicestershire to Zimbabwe 1980/1. *Tests* England (1983, 2 matches).
Career batting
121–118–36–993–75–12.10–0–*ct* 71
Bowling 9207–354–26.00–14–1–7/63
Test batting
2–4–0–51–26–12.75–0–*ct* 3
Bowling 275–17–16.17–2–0–5/35
His best season was 1982 with 90 wickets, av 23.25.

Cook, Thomas Edwin Reed
Professional. *b:* 5.2.1901, Cuckfield, Sussex. *d:* 15.1.1950, Brighton, Sussex. Middle order right-hand batsman, right-arm medium pace bowler. *Team* Sussex (1922–37, 459 matches).
Career batting
460–730–65–20198–278–30.22–32–*ct* 169–*st* 1
Bowling 2880–80–36.00–1–0–5/24
He reached 1,000 runs in a season ten times including once over 2,000: 2,132, av 54.66, in 1934. He hit three double centuries, all for Sussex, the highest being 278 v Hants at Hove in 1930. In 1937 he left County cricket for a coaching position in South Africa. A noted soccer player with Brighton and Hove Albion and Bristol Rovers, he appeared as centre-forward for England in 1925.

Cook, William
Professional. *b:* 16.1.1882, Preston, Lancashire. *d:* 18.12.1947, Burnley, Lancashire. Brother of L. W. (Lancashire). Lower order batsman, right-arm fast medium bowler. *Team* Lancashire (1905–07, 11 matches).
Career batting
11–17–3–307–46–21.92–0–*ct* 4
Bowling 946–51–18.54–3–1–7/64
He played soccer for Preston and Oldham Athletic.

Cook, William Thomas
Amateur. *b:* 6.12.1891, Brixton, Surrey. *d:* 22.9.1969. Shirley, Surrey. Middle order left-hand batsman. *Team* Surrey (1921–33, 32 matches).
Career batting
39–66–4–1441–92–23.24–0–*ct* 12
Bowling 111–2–55.50–0–0–1/1
He was for many years captain of Surrey 2nd XI and appeared for the Minor Counties in several matches.

Cooke, Sir Cyril Bertram
Amateur. *b:* 28.6.1895, Dorking, Surrey. *d:* 27.9.1972, Rustington, Sussex. Lower order batsman, right-arm fast bowler. *Team* RAF (1927–30).
Career batting
6–8–2–51–20–8.50–0–*ct* 4
Bowling 490–23–21.30–2–0–7/76

Cooke, Geoffrey Charles Sidney Bancroft
Amateur. *b:* 8.1.1897, Farnborough, Hants. *d:* 4.12.1980, Sunningdale, Berkshire. Lower order right-hand batsman, bowler. *Sch* Charterhouse. *Team* Army (1925–26).
Career batting
2–3–1–25–13–12.50–0–*ct* 3
Bowling 120–6–20.00–0–0–4/39

Cooke, John
Professional. *b:* 7.3.1851, Wirksworth, Derbyshire. *d:* 22.11.1908, Wirksworth, Derbyshire. Lower order right-hand batsman, wicket-keeper. *Team* Derbyshire (1874, 1 match).
Career batting
1–2–0–6–6–3.00–0–*ct* 0

Cooke, Noel H.
Professional. *b:* 5.1.1935, West Derby. Liverpool. Middle order right-hand batsman, off break

bowler. *Sch* Liverpool College. *Team* Lancashire (1958–59, 12 matches).
Career batting
12–16–0–242–33–15.12–0–*ct* 2
Bowling 93–3–31.00–0–0–2/10
He also played for Cheshire.

Cooke, Robert
Professional. *b:* 25.5.1900, Selly Oak, Birmingham. *d:* 14.1.1957, Selly Oak, Birmingham. Tail end right-hand batsman, right-arm fast medium bowler. *Team* Warwickshire (1925–26, 15 matches).
Career batting
15–21–4–66–14–3.88–0–*ct* 6
Bowling 507–16–31.68–1–0–5/22

Cooke, Robert Michael Oliver
Cricketer. *b:* 3.9.1943, Adlington, Cheshire. Middle order left-hand batsman, leg break and googly bowler. *Sch* Rossall. *Team* Essex (1973–75, 40 matches).
Career batting
42–70–5–1450–139–22.30–2–*ct* 25
Bowling 184–4–46.00–0–0–2/55
He played for Cheshire in 1969 and returned to that County after leaving Essex. His first-class debut was for Minor Counties in 1972 and his final match for the same side in 1976.

Cooke, W.
Amateur. *Team* Hurst Park Club v Australians 1890.
Career batting
1–2–0–1–1–0.50–0–*ct* 0

Cookson, William Whicher
Amateur. *b:* 29.8.1862, Mufsoorie, India. *d:* 23.12.1922, Winscombe, Somerset. Batsman. *Sch* Clifton. *Team* Somerset (1882, 1 match).
Career batting
1–1–0–8–8–8.00–0–*ct* 0

Cooley, Bertram Clifford
Amateur. *b:* 1874, Durban, South Africa. *d:* 17.8.1935, Durban, South Africa. Middle order right-hand batsman, bowler. *Team* Natal (1893/4 to 1906/7). *Tour* South Africa to England 1901.
Career batting
19–32–4–564–126*–20.14–2–*ct* 11
Bowling 361–15–24.06–0–0–4/34
He returned very modest results on his only visit to England.

Coomaraswamy, Indrajit
Cricketer. *b:* 3.4.1950, Colombo, Ceylon. Middle order right-hand batsman, slow left-arm bowler. *Sch* Harrow. *Team* Cambridge U (1971–72).
Career batting
2–4–0–7–4–1.75–0–*ct* 0

Coomb, Arthur Grenfell
Amateur. *b:* 3.3.1929, Bedford. Lower order right-hand batsman, right-arm medium-fast bowler. *Sch* Bedford Modern. *Team* Combined Services (1948–49).
Career batting
5–10–4–55–16–9.16–0–*ct* 1
Bowling 321–8–40.12–0–0–3/61
His County cricket was for Bedfordshire and Norfolk and his last first-class match for Minor Counties in 1953.

Coope, Miles
Professional. *b:* 28.11.1917, Gildersome, Yorkshire. *d:* 5.7.1974, Gildersome, Yorkshire. Hard-hitting middle order right-hand batsman. *Team* Somerset (1947–49, 70 matches).
Career batting
71–136–4–2789–113–21.12–2–*ct* 20
Bowling 479–8–59.87–0–0–3/29
He hit 1,172 runs, av 22.11, in 1948.

Cooper, Archibald Henry Hedges
Professional. *b:* 14.8.1878, Cowley, Oxon. *d:* 13.1.1922, Chesterfield, Derbyshire. Lower order batsman, bowler. *Team* Derbyshire (1902, 1 match).
Career batting
1–1–0–0–0–0.00–0–*ct* 1
Bowling 12–0

Cooper, Albert Vincent
Amateur. *b:* 3.12.1893, Stoke Newington, Middlesex. *d:* 3.5.1977, Stoke Newington, Middlesex. Middle order right-hand batsman, right-arm slow bowler. *Sch* Bancroft's. *Team* Essex (1923, 1 match).
Career batting
1–2–0–14–12–7.00–0–*ct* 0

Cooper, Alfred William Madison
Amateur. *b*: 12.6.1932, Dublin. Right-hand batsman, right-arm fast medium bowler. *Team* Ireland (1954).
Career batting
1–2–0–50–31–25.00–0–*ct* 0
Bowling 38–2–19.00–0–0–2/35

Cooper, Bransby Beauchamp
Amateur. *b:* 15.3.1844, Dacca, India. *d:* 7.8.1914, Geelong, Victoria, Australia. Middle order right-hand batsman, wicket-keeper. *Sch* Rugby. *Teams* Middlesex (1863–67, 8 matches); Kent (1868–69,

9 matches); Victoria (1870/1 to 1877/8, 11 matches). *Test* Australia (1876/7, 1 match).
Career batting
50–83–5–1600–101–20.51–1–*ct* 41–*st* 20
Test batting
1–2–0–18–15–9.00–0–*ct* 2
In 1870 he moved to the USA and his name is found in some matches there, then he settled permanently in Australia.

Cooper, Charles Osborn
Amateur. *b:* 5.8.1868, Plaistow, Essex. *d:* 23.11.1943, Southborough, Kent. Steady right-hand batsman, right-arm medium pace bowler. good slip. *Sch* Dulwich. *Team* Kent (1894–96, 10 matches).
Career batting
10–19–1–237–44–13.16–0–*ct* 7

Cooper, Edgar
Amateur. *b:* November 1891, Briton-Ferry, Glamorgan. *d:* 15.3.1959, Kettering, Northants. Lower order batsman, right-arm fast medium bowler. *Team* Glamorgan (1921, 4 matches).
Career batting
4–8–0–46–14–5.75–0–*ct* 3
Bowling 406–10–40.60–0–0–4/61

Cooper, Edwin
Professional. *b:* 30.11.1915, Bacup, Lancashire. *d:* 29.10.1968, Birmingham. Brother of Frederick (Lancashire and Worcs). Sound opening right-hand batsman, fine deep field. *Team* Worcestershire (1936–51, 249 matches).
Career batting
250–444–28–13304–216*–31.98–18–*ct* 99
Bowling 44–0
He reached 1,000 runs nine times (best 1916, av 43.54, in 1949). His only double century was 216* for Worcs v Warwickshire at Dudley in 1938. He also played for Devon.

Cooper, Frederick
Professional. *b:* 18.4.1921, Bacup, Lancashire. Brother of Edwin (Worcs). Opening right-hand batsman, leg break bowler. *Teams* Lancashire (1946, 4 matches); Worcestershire (1947–50, 39 matches).
Career batting
44–84–13–1369–113*–19.28–1–*ct* 17
Bowling 30–0

Cooper, Frederick Joseph
Amateur. *b:* 1888, Wetherby, Yorkshire. *d:* 27.6.1958, York. Lower order batsman, right-arm medium pace bowler. *Team* Essex (1921–23, 10 matches).
Career batting
10–18–1–170–52–10.00–0–*ct* 3
Bowling 385–8–48.12–1–0–5/71
He also appeared for Shropshire. A useful soccer player he represented Bradford. In 1921 it is believed that he played in two matches under the assumed name of A. Brown, but this is by no means certain and A. Brown may perhaps be another cricketer altogether.

Cooper, Graham Charles
Professional. *b:* 2.9.1936, East Grinstead, Sussex. Middle/lower order right-hand batsman, off break bowler. *Team* Sussex (1955–69, 252 matches).
Career batting
252–407–56–8134–142–23.17–2–*ct* 149
Bowling 3677–100–36.77–5–0–5/13
He reached 1,000 runs in three seasons (best 1095, av 28.81, in 1961). He played soccer for Hastings United.

Cooper, Herbert
Professional. *b:* 25.12.1883, Dukinfield, Cheshire. *d:* 6.12.1963, Oldham, Lancashire. Middle order right-hand batsman. *Team* Derbyshire (1905–10, 15 matches).
Career batting
15–28–4–216–23–9.00–0–*ct* 7

Cooper, Howard Pennett
Cricketer. *b*: 17.4.1949, Great Horton, Bradford, Yorkshire. Lower order left-hand batsman, right-arm medium pace bowler. *Teams* Yorkshire (1971–80, 98 matches); Northern Transvaal (1973/4).
Career batting
101–113–30–1191–56–14.34–0–*ct* 62
Bowling 6529–233–28.02–4–1–8/62

Cooper, John Frederick
Amateur. *b:* 14.2.1855, Henley-on-Thames, Oxon. *d:* 30.1.1928, Henley-on-Thames, Oxon. Middle order right-hand batsman. *Sch* Marlborough. *Team* MCC (1881).
Career batting
1–1–0–0–0–0.00–0–*ct* 0
He appeared occasionally for Shropshire and Wiltshire.

Cooper, Kevin Edwin
Cricketer. *b*: 27.12.1957, Sutton-in-Ashfield, Notts. Lower order left-hand batsman, right-arm fast medium bowler, deep field. *Team* Nottinghamshire (1976–83, 134 matches).
Career batting
135–138–30–996–38*–9.22–0–*ct* 44
Bowling 8937–320–27.82–11–0–7/33

Cooper, Norman Charles
Amateur. *b:* 12.7.1870, Long Ditton, Surrey. *d:* 30.7.1920, Hampden Park, Eastbourne. Opening/middle order right-hand batsman, right-arm medium pace bowler. *Sch* Brighton. *Team* Cambridge U (1891–92).
Career batting
13–24–1–275–45–11.95–0–*ct* 10
Bowling 15–0
His first-class debut was for Oxford and Cambridge, Past and Present v Australians 1890. His final first-class match was for C. I. Thornton's XI in 1893. He also played for Surrey, but not in a first-class match. An excellent soccer player, he represented both Cambridge U and England at wing half.

Cooper, Nicholas Henry Charles
Cricketer. *b:* 14.10.1953, Bristol, Gloucs. Opening left-hand batsman. *Teams* Gloucestershire (1975–78, 17 matches); Cambridge U (1979, blue).
Career batting
24–39–2–825–106–22.29–1–*ct* 10
Bowling 277–7–39.57–0–0–2/11
After being on the Gloucs staff, he went on a one-year post-graduate course at Cambridge.

Cooper, Philip Edward
(later Whiteoak-Cooper)
Amateur. *b:* 19.2.1885, Rotherham, Yorkshire. *d:* 21.5.1950, Wroxham, Norfolk. Middle order right-hand batsman. *Sch* Queen's College, Taunton. *Team* Yorkshire (1910, 1 match).
Career batting
1–2–0–0–0–0.00–0–*ct* 0

Cooper, Richard Claude
Cricketer. *b:* 9.12.1945, Malmesbury, Wiltshire. Middle order right-hand batsman, right-arm medium pace bowler. *Team* Somerset (1972, 1 match).
Career batting
1–2–0–4–4–2.00–0–*ct* 0
Originally he played for Wiltshire, commencing 1967, and returned to that County in 1975, being on the Somerset staff 1972–74.

Cooper, Rustom Sorabji
Amateur. *b:* 15.12.1922, Bombay, India. Attractive right-hand batsman. *Teams* Parsis (1941/2 to 1944/5); Middlesex (1949–51, 8 matches).
Career batting
22–29–6–1205–127*–52.39–3–*ct* 7
Bowling 61–0

Cooper, Sydney Hyde
Amateur. *b:* 5.2.1913, Carshalton, Surrey. *d:* 20.1.1982, Wallington, Surrey. Lower order right-hand batsman, wicket-keeper. *Team* Surrey (1936, 2 matches).
Career batting
2–2–1–11–11*–11.00–0–*ct* 2–*st* 3

Cooper, Walter
Professional. Middle order left-hand batsman, slow left-arm bowler. *Team* Essex (1905–10, 3 matches).
Career batting
3–6–0–32–18–5.33–0–*ct* 1
Bowling 69–0

Cooper, William Henry
Amateur. *b:* 11.9.1849, Maidstone, Kent. *d:* 5.4.1939, Malvern, Victoria, Australia. Great grandfather of A. P. Sheahan (Australia). Lower order right-hand batsman, slow right-arm leg (1878/9 to 1882/3, 15 matches). *Tour* Australia to England 1884. *Tests* Australia (1881/2 to 1884/5, 2 matches).
Career batting
26–39–15–247–46–10.29–0–*ct* 16
Bowling 1739–71–24.49–5–0–7/37
Test batting
2–3–1–13–7–6.50–0–*ct* 1
Bowling 226–9–25.11–1–0–6/120
His only visit to England was a complete failure: in all matches he took just 7 wickets, av 46.43, and he did not appear in any of the Tests. His final first-class match was for Non-Smokers in 1886/7.

Cooper-Key, Charles Aston Whinfield
Amateur. *b:* 13.11.1856, Stretton Sugwas, Hereford. *d:* 13.7.1936, Paddington, London. Middle order right-hand batsman, right-arm fast bowler. *Sch* Rugby. *Team* Oxford U (1877).
Career batting
1–2–1–2–1*–2.00–0–*ct* 1
Bowling 11–3–3.66–0–0–3/8

Coote, Cyril Ernest
Amateur. *b:* 13.4.1909, Cambridge. Opening left-hand batsman, left-arm medium pace bowler. *Team* Minor Counties XI (1935).
Career batting
4–6–0–120–49–20.00–*ct* 1
His County cricket was for Cambridgeshire commencing 1932. He was for many years the Head Groundsman at Fenner's.

Coote, Charles Purdon
Amateur. *b:* 8.8.1847, Weymouth, Dorset. *d:* 20.9.1893, Co Cork, Ireland. Middle order right-hand batsman, change bowler. *Sch* Harrow. *Team* MCC (1869–74).

Career batting
13–21–0–192–35–9.14–0–*ct* 5

Coote, David Edward
Cricketer. *b:* 8.4.1955, Winkburn, Notts. Middle order left-hand batsman. *Team* Nottinghamshire (1977, 1 match).
Career batting
1–1–0–20–20–20.00–0–*ct* 0

Cope, Geoffrey Alan
Cricketer. *b:* 23.2.1947, Leeds, Yorkshire. Lower order right-hand batsman, off break bowler. *Team* Yorkshire (1966–80, 230 matches). *Tours* Robins to South Africa 1975/6; MCC to India and Sri Lanka 1976/7; England to Pakistan and New Zealand 1977/8. *Tests* England (1977/8, 3 matches).
Career batting
246–261–93–2383–78–14.18–*ct* 70
Bowling 16948–686–24.70–35–6–8/73
Test batting
3–3–0–40–22–13.33–0–*ct* 1
Bowling 277–8–34.62–0–0–3/102
His first-class career was marred by doubts concerning his bowling action and he was twice suspended by the TCCB (1972 and 1978). He appeared for Lincolnshire commencing 1981.

Cope, John James
Amateur. *b:* 1.8.1908, Ellesmere Port, Cheshire. Middle order right-hand batsman. *Team* Glamorgan (1935, 3 matches).
Career batting
3–5–1–27–14*–6.75–0–*ct* 1
He also played for Monmouthshire.

Cope, Sidney Alfred
Professional. *b:* 12.8.1904, Hastings, Sussex. Lower order left-hand batsman, left-arm fast bowler. *Team* Kent (1924, 1 match).
Career batting
1–1–0–0–0–0.00–0–*ct* 1
Bowling 27–1–27.00–0–0–1/27

Copeland, William
Professional. *b:* 1856, Stockton-on-Tees, Co Durham. *d:* 28.1.1917, South Shields, Co Durham. Lower order batsman, left-arm medium pace bowler. *Team* Lancashire (1885, 1 match).
Career batting
1–2–1–21–21*–21.00–0–*ct* 0
Bowling 23–1–23.00–0–0–1/23
He appeared for Durham between 1886 and 1894, being for about 30 years, professional with South Shields.

Copland-Crawford, Robert Erskine Wade
(added Copland to his name in 1872)
Amateur. *b:* 5.9.1852. *d:* 23.5.1894, Hendon, Middlesex. Stylish middle order right-hand batsman, lob bowler. *Sch* Harrow. *Team* MCC (1872–73).
Career batting
3–6–0–20–9–3.33–0–*ct* 0

Copley, Sydney Herbert
Professional. *b:* 1.11.1905, Hucknall Torkard, Notts. Middle order right-hand batsman, slow left-arm bowler, brilliant field. *Team* Nottinghamshire (1930, 1 match).
Career batting
1–2–0–7–4–3.50–0–*ct* 0
Bowling 28–0
Whilst fielding as substitute in the England v Australia Test at Trent Bridge in 1930, he took a magnificent catch which changed the course of the game. A useful soccer player, he played for Rotherham United.

Coppinger, Charles
Amateur. *b:* 10.4.1851, Bexleyheath, Kent. *d:* 1.8.1877, New Cross, Kent. Brother of E. T. (Kent) and William (Kent), nephew of Septimus (Sussex). *Team* Kent (1870, 1 match).
Career batting
1–2–1–13–11*–13.00–0–*ct* 0

Coppinger, Edward Thomas
Professional. *b:* 25.11.1846, Bexley, Kent. *d:* 26.2.1927, Surbiton, Surrey. Brother of Charles (Kent) and William (Kent), nephew of Septimus (Sussex). Middle order right-hand batsman, wicket-keeper. *Team* Kent (1873, 2 matches).
Career batting
2–4–0–17–10–4.25–0–*ct* 1
Bowling 29–5–5.80–1–0–5/29
In 1890/1 he was Mayor of Kingston-on-Thames.

Coppinger, Septimus
Professional. *b:* 15.9.1828, Northiam, Sussex. *d:* 8.4.1870, Epsom, Surrey. Uncle of Charles (Kent), E. T. (Kent) and William (Kent). Middle order right-hand batsman. *Team* Sussex (1857–61, 8 matches).
Career batting
9–16–1–126–43–8.40–0–*ct* 2
One of eight brothers – the family occasionally put an eleven into the field – his youngest brother, Octavius, was a noted local cricketer, but never appeared in first-class matches. His final first-class match was for the New All England Eleven in 1862.

Coppinger, William
Professional. *b:* 3.6.1849, Bexley, Kent. Brother of Charles (Kent), E. T. (Kent), nephew of Septimus (Sussex). Middle order right-hand batsman, slow under-hand bowler, good field. *Team* Kent (1868–73, 7 matches).
Career batting
7–14–3–52–16–4.72–0–*ct* 1
Bowling 98–2–49.00–0–0–2/49

Copson, William Henry
Professional. *b:* 27.4.1908, Stonebroom, Derbyshire. *d:* 13.9.1971, Clay Cross, Derbyshire. Lower order right-hand batsman, right-arm fast-medium bowler with short run. *Team* Derbyshire (1932–50, 261 matches). *Tour* MCC to Australia and New Zealand 1936/7. *Tests* England (1939–47, 3 matches).
Career batting
279–359–108–1711–43–6.81–0–*ct* 103
Bowling 20752–1094–18.96–66–6–8/11
Test batting
3–1–0–6–6–6.00–0–*ct* 1
Bowling 297–15–19.80–1–0–5/85
He took 100 wickets in a season three times (best 160, av 13.34, in 1936). For Derbyshire v Warwickshire at Derby in 1937 he obtained four wickets in four balls. He became a first-class umpire.

Corbett, Alexander Merlin
Amateur. *b:* 25.11.1854, Aston, Rotherham, Yorkshire. *d:* 7.10.1934, Sheffield, Yorkshire. Middle order batsman. *Team* Yorkshire (1881, 1 match).
Career batting
1–2–0–0–0–0.00–0–*ct* 1

Corbett, Bertie Oswald
Amateur. *b:* 15.5.1875, Thame, Oxon. *d:* 30.11.1967, Portesham, Dorset. Brother of C. J. (Derbyshire). Middle order right-hand batsman. *Team* Derbyshire (1910, 1 match).
Career batting
1–2–0–1–1–0.50–0–*ct* 0
He also appeared for Buckinghamshire. A noted soccer player, he represented England as an outside-left and played for the Corinthians.

Corbett, Cornelius John
(known as John Cornelius Corbett)
Amateur. *b:* 8.3.1883, Thame, Oxon. *d:* 10.4.1944, Chandlers Ford, Hants. Brother of B. O. (Derbyshire). Middle order right-hand batsman, change bowler. *Sch* Eastbourne. *Team* Derbyshire (1911–24, 27 matches).
Career batting
27–48–4–633–61–14.38–0–*ct* 7
Bowling 54–0

Corbett, Leonard James
Amateur. *b:* 12.5.1897, Bristol, Gloucs. *d:* 26.1.1983, Taunton, Somerset. Middle order right-hand batsman. *Team* Gloucestershire (1920–25, 9 matches).
Career batting
9–18–0–373–55–20.72–0–*ct* 9
Bowling 19–0
He played rugby as a three-quarter for England.

Corbett, Percival Thomas
Professional. *b:* 1900, Droitwich, Worcs. *d:* 26.6.1944, West Malvern, Worcs. Middle/lower order right-hand batsman, change bowler. *Team* Worcestershire (1922-23, 7 matches).
Career batting
7–13–3–57–20–5.70–0–*ct* 2
Bowling 77–0

Cordaroy, Terence Michael
Cricketer. *b:* 26.5.1944, Hampstead, London. Middle order right-hand batsman. *Team* Middlesex (1968, 2 matches). *Tour* MCC to West Africa 1975/6 (not first-class).
Career batting
2–3–0–104–81–34.66–0–*ct* 1
He also played for Buckinghamshire.

Corden, Charles Frederic
Professional. *b:* 30.12.1874, Croydon, Surrey. *d:* 26.2.1924, Croydon, Surrey. Middle order batsman. *Team* Worcestershire (1900–03, 17 matches).
Career batting
17–33–4–479–64–16.51–0–*ct* 6
He played for Surrey 2nd XI in the 1890s.

Cording, George Ernest
Amateur. *b:* 1.1.1878, Tredegar, Monmouthshire. *d:* 2.2.1946, St Mellons, Monmouthshire. Middle order right-hand batsman, occasional wicket-keeper, fine slip field. *Team* Glamorgan (1921–23, 19 matches).
Career batting
19–34–4–498–101–16.60–1–*ct* 16–*st* 2
He first appeared for Glamorgan in 1900.

Cordingley, Albert
Professional. *b:* 13.5.1871, Eccleshill, Bradford, Yorkshire. *d:* 30.4.1945, Horsham, Sussex. Lower order batsman, slow left-arm bowler. *Team* Sussex (1901–05, 15 matches).
Career batting
15–14–5–47–24*–5.22–0–*ct* 9
Bowling 546–16–34.12–1–0–5/22
He appeared once for Yorkshire, in 1898 v Worcestershire (a non-first-class match).

Cordle, Anthony Elton
Cricketer. *b*: 21.9.1940, Bridgetown, Barbados. Lower order right-hand batsman, right-arm fast medium bowler, deep field. *Team* Glamorgan (1963–80, 312 matches). *Tour* Glamorgan to West Indies 1969/70.
Career batting
312–433–76–5239–81–14.67–0–*ct* 141
Bowling 19281–701–27.50–19–2–9/49
His best innings analysis was 9/49 for Glamorgan v Leicestershire at Colwyn Bay in 1969.

Cordner, Arthur Douglas
Amateur. *b:* 30.8.1887. *d:* 3.7.1946, Dublin, Ireland. Right-hand batsman, wicket-keeper. *Team* Ireland (1926).
Career batting
1–2–1–3–3*–3.00–0–*ct* 0
He played for Canada v USA in 1909.

Cordner, John Pruen
Amateur. *b:* 20.3.1929, Diamond Creek, Victoria, Australia. Second cousin of L. O. (Victoria). Lower order right-hand batsman, left-arm fast-medium bowler. *Teams* Victoria (1951/2, 3 matches); Warwickshire (1952, 1 match).
Career batting
4–4–2–13–8*–6.50–0–*ct* 3
Bowling 236–3–78.66–0–0–2/37

Corke, Martin Dewe
Amateur. *b:* 8.6.1923, Murree, India. Opening/middle order right-hand batsman. *Sch* Radley. *Team* Free Foresters (1953–58).
Career batting
5–10–0–116–53–11.60–0–*ct* 0
His County cricket was for Suffolk.

Corlett, Samuel
Professional. *b:* 8.5.1852, Withington, Lancashire. *d:* 1921, Chorlton, Lancashire. Lower order right-hand batsman, right-arm medium-fast bowler. *Team* Lancashire (1871–75, 2 matches).
Career batting
2–3–0–6–4–2.00–0–*ct* 0

Corlett, Simon Charles
Cricketer. *b*: 18.1.1950, Blantyre, Nyasaland. Lower order right-hand batsman, right-arm fast medium bowler. *Sch* Worksop. *Teams* Oxford U (1970–72, blue 1971, 1972); Ireland (1974–83).
Career batting
29–41–7–520–60–15.29–0–*ct* 24
Bowling 2028–65–31.20–4–0–7/82

Corley, Harry Hegarty
Amateur. *b: circa* 1879, Dublin, Ireland. *d:* February 1936, Dublin, Ireland. Right-hand batsman. *Team* Ireland (1907–09).
Career batting
4–8–1–50–27–7.14–0–*ct* 4
He was a rugby international for Ireland.

Corling, Grahame Edward
Cricketer. *b:* 13.7.1941, Newcastle, New South Wales, Australia. Lower order right-hand batsman, right-arm fast-medium bowler. *Team* New South Wales (1963/4 to 1968/9, 46 matches). *Tour* Australia to England 1964. *Tests* Australia (1964, 5 matches).
Career batting
65–78–32–484–42*–10.52–0–*ct* 11
Bowling 5546–173–32.05–6–0–5/44
Test batting
5–4–1–5–3–1.66–0–*ct* 0
Bowling 447–12–37.25–0–0–4/60
The youngest member of the 1964 tourists to England, he appeared in all five Tests and in first-class matches took 44 wickets, av 31.38.

Cornelius, Bernard William
Amateur. *b:* 16.3.1919, Northampton. Middle order right-hand batsman, leg break bowler. *Team* Northants (1947, 1 match).
Career batting
1–2–1–9–9*–9.00–0–*ct* 1

Cornelius, Norman Stanley
Amateur. *b:* 5.6.1886, Blundellsands, Lancashire. *d:* 21.10.1963, West Felton, Shropshire. Middle order right-hand batsman, brilliant outfield. *Sch* Malvern. *Team* Gloucestershire (1910–11, 6 matches).
Career batting
6–9–1–99–40–12.37–0–*ct* 0
He appeared in the Freshmen's and Seniors' matches at Cambridge, but not in first-class cricket.

Cornell, Henry
Professional. *b:* 19.12.1822, Cambridge. *d:* October, 1869, Cambridge. Brother of Edward (Cambridge Town Club). Hard-hitting right-hand batsman, good long-stop. *Team* Cambridge Town Club (1844–49).
Career batting
11–18–1–266–61–15.64–0–*ct* 5
The leading batsman of the Cambridge Town Club in the 1840s, he appeared for England v Kent in 1846.

Cornell, William
(also known as William Cornwell)
Professional. *b: circa* 1838, Lode, Cambridgeshire. *d.:* 21.4.1915, Lode, Cambridgeshire.

Lower order batsman. *Team* Cambridgeshire (1864–68, 5 matches).
Career batting
5–8–3–22–12–4.40–0–*ct* 3–*st* 1

Cornford, James Henry
Professional. *b:* 9.12.1911, Crowborough, Sussex. Tail end right-hand batsman, right-arm fast-medium bowler. *Team* Sussex (1931–52, 330 matches).
Career batting
332–399–145–1357–34–5.34–0–*ct* 116
Bowling 26999–1019–26.49–39–6–9/53

He several times took 90 wickets in a season, but never reached 100 (best 97, av 25.52, in 1949). His best bowling was 9/53 for Sussex v Northants at Rushden in 1949.

Cornford, Walter Latter
Professional. *b:* 25.12.1900, Hurst Green, Sussex. *d:* 6.2.1964, Brighton, Sussex. Lower order right-hand batsman, wicket-keeper. *Team* Sussex (1921–47, 484 matches). *Tour* MCC to Australia and New Zealand 1929/30. *Tests* England (1929/30, 4 matches).
Career batting
496–649–211–6554–82–14.96–0–*ct* 675–*st* 342
Bowling 65–0
Test batting
4–4–0–36–18–9.00–0–*ct* 5–*st* 3

He retired from first-class cricket in 1939, but appeared once in 1947 in emergency.

Cornish, Harry Hemming
Amateur. *b:* 1871, Westminster, London. *d:* 1918, Philadelphia, USA. Lower order batsman, bowler. *Team* Middlesex (1893, 1 match).
Career batting
1–2–0–7–6–3.50–0–*ct* 0
Bowling 27–0

He emigrated to the USA and was Editor of the *American Cricketer* commencing 1906. He appeared in Philadelphian Club cricket for Belmont and in 1909, in emergency, made a single appearance for USA v Canada. He died in the influenza epidemic that swept the USA in 1918.

Cornock, Walter Berkeley
Professional. *b:* 1.1.1921, Bondi, New South Wales, Australia. Middle order right-hand batsman, left-arm medium pace bowler. *Team* Leicestershire (1948, 26 matches).
Career batting
26–43–2–801–60–19.53–0–*ct* 24
Bowling 1007–15–67.13–0–0–3/46

He played soccer for Rochdale.

Cornu, Geoffrey
Amateur. *b:* 29.6.1913, Sheffield, Yorkshire. Lower order right-hand batsman, leg break and googly bowler. *Sch* Malvern. *Team* Free Foresters (1934–37).
Career batting
5–5–3–60–21*–30.00–0–*ct* 4
Bowling 513–13–39.46–0–0–3/92

Cornwall, Alan Edward Cripps
Amateur. *b:* 12.8.1898, Monmouth. *d:* 26.2.1984, Lustleigh, Devon. Middle order right-hand batsman. *Sch* Marlborough. *Team* Gloucestershire (1920, 1 match).
Career batting
1–2–0–5–3–2.50–0–*ct* 2

Cornwall, Anthony Ewart Frank
Amateur. *b:* 19.8.1929. Lower order batsman, opening bowler. *Sch* Radley. *Team* Free Foresters (1949).
Career batting
1–2–0–0–0–0.00–0–*ct* 4
Bowling 60–3–20.00–0–0–3/60

Cornwallis, Hon Oswald Wykeham
Amateur. *b:* 16.3.1894, Linton, Kent. *d:* 28.1.1974, Froxfield, Hants. Brother of W. S. (Kent). Opening right-hand batsman. *Teams* Royal Navy (1920–26); Hampshire (1921, 1 match).
Career batting
4–6–0–91–31–15.16–0–*ct* 0

Cornwallis (2nd Baron), Wykeham Stanley
Amateur. *b:* 14.3.1892, Linton, Kent. *d:* 4.1.1982, Ashurst, Kent. Brother of O. W. (Hampshire). Lower order right-hand batsman, right-arm fast-medium bowler. *Team* Kent (1919–26, 105 matches).
Career batting
106–129–47–964–91–11.75–0–*ct* 35
Bowling 3830–118–32.45–5–0–6/37

He was captain of Kent, 1924 to 1926.

Corrall, Percy
Professional. *b:* 16.7.1906, Aylestone Park, Leicester. Lower order right-hand batsman, wicket-keeper. *Teams* Leicestershire (1930–51, 285 matches); Europeans (1944/5); Services (1944/5).
Career batting
288–422–126–2846–64–9.61–0–*ct* 381–*st* 187

In 1933 he received a serious injury, being struck on the head by an opponent's bat whilst keeping wicket – it was feared that the accident would end his career, but happily he fully recovered.

Corran, Andrew John
Amateur. *b:* 25.11.1936, Norwich. Lower order right-hand batsman, right-arm medium pace bowler. *Sch* Gresham's. *Teams* Oxford U (1958–60, blue all three years); Nottinghamshire (1961–65, 101 matches).
Career batting
132–207–55–2476–75–16.28–0–*ct* 78
Bowling 10556–410–25.73–21–1–7/45
He captained Notts in 1962. He also played for Norfolk, 1958–60. An excellent hockey player he was awarded his blue at Oxford. He took 111 wickets, av 20.31, in 1965.

Corry, Charles Victor
Amateur. *b:* 26.11.1940, Belfast, Ireland. Right-hand batsman. *Team* Ireland (1959–66).
Career batting
4–7–1–40–17–6.66–0–*ct* 2

Cosh, Nicholas John
Cricketer. *b:* 6.8.1946, Denmark Hill, South London. Middle order right-hand batsman, off break bowler. *Sch* Dulwich. *Teams* Cambridge U (1966–68, blue all three years); Surrey (1969, 6 matches).
Career batting
36–64–6–1731–138–29.84–2–*ct* 25
Bowling 34–1–34.00–0–0–1/8
A noted rugby footballer, he was awarded his blue and played for Blackheath.

Cosh, Stephen Hunter
Amateur. *b:* 31.1.1920, Ayr, Scotland. Right-hand batsman, wicket-keeper. *Sch* Edinburgh Academy, *Team* Scotland (1950–59).
Career batting
36–57–3–873–99–16.16–0–*ct* 36–*st* 7
Bowling 7–0

Cosier, Gary John
Cricketer. *b:* 25.4.1953, Richmond, Victoria, Australia. Middle order right-hand batsman, right-arm medium pace bowler. *Teams* Victoria (1971/2 to 1980/1, 4 matches); South Australia (1974/5 to 1976/7, 24 matches); Queensland (1977/8 to 1979/80, 26 matches). *Tours* Australia to England 1977, to New Zealand 1976/7, to West Indies 1977/8. *Tests* Australia (1975/6 to 1978/9, 18 matches).
Career batting
91–161–9–5005–168–32.92–7–*ct* 75
Bowling 2301–75–30.68–0–0–3/20
Test batting
18–32–1–897–168–28.93–2–*ct* 14
Bowling 341–5–68.20–0–0–2/26
He achieved only modest results on his 1977 tour of England and was not selected for the Tests.

Coskerry, Joseph Whiteside
Amateur. *b:* 22.7.1895, Ballynahinch, Co Down, Ireland. *d:* 24.9.1965, Bangor, Co Down, Ireland. Left-hand batsman. *Team* Ireland (1924).
Career batting
1–2–1–7–4*–7.00–0–*ct* 0

Cottam, Francis
Amateur. *b:* 6.6.1900, Redhill, Surrey. Lower order right-hand batsman, slow left-arm bowler. *Team* Essex (1922, 1 match).
Career batting
1 match, did not bat –*ct* 0
Bowling 25–0

Cottam, Robert Michael Henry
Cricketer. *b:* 16.10.1944, Cleethorpes, Lincs. Lower order right-hand batsman, right-arm fast-medium bowler. *Team* Hampshire (1963–71, 188 matches); Northants (1972–76, 76 matches). *Tours* MCC to Ceylon and Pakistan 1968/9, to India, Pakistan and Sri Lanka 1972/3; Robins to West Indies 1974/5 (not first-class); Commonwealth to Pakistan 1970/1. *Tests* England (1968/9 to 1972/3, 4 matches).
Career batting
289–280–97–1278–62*–6.98–0–*ct* 153
Bowling 21125–1010–20.91–58–6–9/25
Test batting
4–5–1–27–13–6.75–0–*ct* 2
Bowling 327–14–23.35–0–0–4/50
He took 100 wickets in a season three times (best 130, av 17.56, in 1968). His best bowling was 9/25 for Hampshire v Lancashire at Old Trafford in 1965. He appeared for Devon 1977–78.

Cotter, Albert
Amateur. *b:* 3.12.1884, Sydney, Australia. *d:* 31.10.1917, Beersheba, Palestine. He was killed in action. Lower order right-hand batsman, right-arm fast bowler. *Team* New South Wales (1901/2 to 1913/4, 38 matches). *Tours* Australia to England 1905, 1909, to New Zealand 1904/5. *Tests* Australia (1903/4 to 1911/2, 21 matches).
Career batting
113–157–10–2484–82–16.89–0–*ct* 63
Bowling 10730–442–24.27–31–4–7/15
Test batting
21–37–2–457–45–13.05–0–*ct* 8
Bowling 2549–89–28.64–7–0–7/148
He was the fastest bowler on both his visits to England and though prone to inaccuracy, his sheer pace proved too much for many batsmen. He took 119 wickets, av 20.41 in 1905, but did not exceed 100 in 1909.

Cotterell, Thomas Archbold
Cricketer. *b*: 12.5.1963, Marylebone, London. Lower order right-hand batsman, slow left-arm bowler. *Sch* Downside. *Team* Cambridge U (1983, blue).
Career batting
10–12–3–81–22–9.00–0–*ct* 2
Bowling 758–17–44.58–1–0–5/89
He has also represented Cambridge at real tennis.

Cotterill, Rev George Edward
Amateur. *b:* 28.7.1839, Madras, India. *d:* 2.6.1913, Cambridge. Brother of J. M. (Sussex), father of G. H. (Sussex). Hard-hitting middle order right-hand batsman, right-arm medium-fast, or slow underhand, bowler, good deep field. *Sch* Brighton. *Teams* Cambridge U (1858–60, blue all three years); Sussex (1869–74, 8 matches); Cambridgeshire (1858, 1 match).
Career batting
18–32–1–447–55–14.41–0–*ct* 5–*st* 2
Bowling 182–14–13.00–1–0–5/23
He also appeared for Norfolk in 1866 and 1867.

Cotterill, George Huth
Amateur. *b:* 4.4.1868, Brighton, Sussex. *d:* 1.10.1950, Llandaff, Glamorgan. Son of G. E. (Sussex), nephew of J. M. (Sussex). Middle order right-hand batsman, slow right-arm bowler. *Sch* Brighton. *Teams* Cambridge U (1888–89); Sussex (1886–90, 8 matches).
Career batting
17–31–1–305–27–10.16–0–*ct* 9
Bowling 115–3–38.33–0–0–2/59
An excellent soccer player, he was awarded his blue at Cambridge and appeared for the Corinthians and for England as centre-forward in four matches 1891–94. He also played rugby for Richmond and Surrey, was an excellent long-jumper and rowed with Weybridge RC.

Cotterill, Sir Joseph Montague
Amateur. *b:* 23.11.1851, Brighton, Sussex. *d:* 30.12.1933, Edinburgh, Scotland. Brother of G. E. (Sussex) and uncle of G. H. (Sussex). Sound middle order right-hand batsman, right-arm medium pace bowler, good deep field. *Sch* Brighton. *Team* Sussex (1870–88, 27 matches).
Career batting
37–65–2–1708–191–27.11–1–*ct* 16
Bowling 214–6–35.66–0–0–2/44
He moved to Edinburgh in 1871 and this greatly restricted his appearances in first-class cricket. He was famous for throwing the cricket ball – his own authenticated record being 121 yards in 1875. He was one of the best-known surgeons of his day.

Cotton, John
Professional. *b:* 7.11.1940, Newstead, Notts. Hard-hitting lower order right-hand batsman, right-arm fast-medium bowler. *Teams* Nottinghamshire (1958–64, 138 matches); Leicestershire (1965–69, 94 matches).
Career batting
239–298–107–1631–58–8.53–0–*ct* 74
Bowling 16674–652–25.57–21–1–9/29
His best bowling was 9/29 for Leics v Indians at Leicester in 1967.

Cotton, Robert Henry
Amateur. *b:* 5.11.1909, Birmingham. *d:* 17.1.1979, Warley, Staffs. Lower order right-hand batsman, right-arm fast bowler. *Team* Warwickshire (1947, 2 matches).
Career batting
2–3–1–0–0*–0.00–0–*ct* 0
Bowling 128–2–64.00–0–0–2/42

Cottrell, Clement Edward
Amateur. *b:* 28.5.1854, London. *d:* 21.1.1897, Brighton, Sussex. Middle/lower order right-hand batsman, right-arm fast-medium bowler. *Sch* Harrow. *Team* Middlesex (1876–85, 14 matches). *Tour* Sanders to USA 1886.
Career batting
26–43–6–464–46–12.54–0–*ct* 14
Bowling 1407–59–23.84–4–0–5/55
He was a noted club cricketer in the London area, appearing mainly for Esher.

Cottrell, Graham Allan
Cricketer. *b:* 23.3.1945, Datchet, Slough, Bucks. Middle order right-hand batsman, right-arm medium pace bowler. *Sch* Kingston GS. *Team* Cambridge U (1966–68, blue all three years).
Career batting
39–70–4–1108–81–16.78–0–*ct* 17
Bowling 2121–60–35.35–0–0–4/31
His County cricket was for Cambridgeshire.

Cottrell, Peter Richard
Cricketer *b:* 22.5.1957, Welling, Kent. Lower order right-hand batsman, wicket-keeper. *Team* Cambridge U (1979, blue).
Career batting
10–9–1–119–34–14.87–0–*ct 17–st* 4

Coulson, Sydney Samuel
Professional. *b:* 17.10.1898, South Wigston, Leics. *d:* 3.10.1981, Gainsborough, Lincolnshire. Steady opening right-hand batsman. *Team* Leicestershire (1923–27, 53 matches).
Career batting
53–94–6–1094–80–12.43–0–*ct* 11
He also played for Lincolnshire.

Coulthurst, Josiah
Amateur. *b:* 24.12.1893, Blackburn, Lancashire. *d:* 6.1.1970, Lytham, Lancashire. Lower order batsman, left-arm fast medium bowler. *Team* Lancashire (1919), 1 match).
Career batting
1 match did not bat –*ct* 0
He was one of the best amateur bowlers ever to appear in the Lancashire League, and in 1919 created a record for the East Lancashire Club by taking 101 wickets, av 9.78.

Coup, Edwin
(known as Coupe)
Professional. *b:* 9.6.1861, Ripley, Derbyshire. *d:* 2.7.1892, Mickleover, Derbyshire. Middle order left-hand batsman, excellent field at point. *Team* Derbyshire (1885–87, 13 matches).
Career batting
13–26–3–195–33–8.47–0–*ct* 2

Court, Richard Charles Lucy
(later Lucy-Court)
Professional. *b:* 23.10.1916, Ambala, India. *d:* 10.4.1974, Southampton. Lower order right-hand batsman, right-arm fast bowler. *Team* Hampshire (1937–39, 18 matches).
Career batting
18–27–5–224–35–10.18–0–*ct* 8
Bowling 1228–33–37.21–0–0–4/53

Court, William Thomas
Amateur. *b:* 1842, Sydney, New South Wales, Australia. *d:* 31.5.1910, Red Hill, Wateringbury, Kent. Middle order right-hand batsman, wicket-keeper. *Team* Kent (1867, 1 match).
Career batting
1–2–0–11–11–5.50–0–*ct* 0

Courtenay, Geofrey William List
Amateur. *b:* 16.12.1921, Castle Cary, Somerset. *d:* 17.10.1980, Edinburgh, Scotland. Middle order right-hand batsman. *Sch* Sherborne. *Teams* Somerset (1947, 4 matches); Scotland (1955–57).
Career batting
8–14–0–168–69–12.00–0–*ct* 1
He appeared for Dorset, commencing 1953.

Courtenay, Peter Jeofry Searle
Amateur. *b:* 11.3.1914, Weymouth, Dorset. *d:* 7.4.1959, Broadstone, Dorset. Attractive middle order right-hand batsman. *Sch* Marlborough. *Team* Somerset (1934, 2 matches).
Career batting
2–4–0–15–9–3.75–0–*ct* 2
He went up to Cambridge in 1933, but did not appear in any first-class matches whilst there.

Cousens, Peter
Professional. *b:* 15.5.1932, Durban, South Africa. Lower order right-hand batsman, slow left-arm bowler. *Team* Essex (1950–55, 39 matches).
Career batting
39–50–26–72–13–3.00–0–*ct* 3
Bowling 1707–40–38.79–0–0–4/63

Coutts, Ian Douglas Freeman
Amateur. *b:* 27.4.1928, Herne Hill, South London. Lower order right-hand batsman, right-arm medium-fast bowler. *Sch* Dulwich, *Team* Oxford U (1951–52, blue 1952).
Career batting
15–25–5–108–16*–5.40–0–*ct* 4
Bowling 1180–33–35.75–1–0–5/64
A noted rugby footballer, he was awarded his blue at Oxford and won a cap for Scotland.

Coventry, Hon Henry Thomas
Amateur. *b:* 3.5.1868, Cumberland Place, London. *d:* 2.8.1934, Westminster, London. Brother of Hon C. J. (England in South Africa), uncle of Hon J. B. (Worcs). Middle order right-hand batsman, slow right-arm bowler, good field. *Sch* Eton. *Team* MCC (1888).
Career batting
2–4–0–28–15–7.00–0–*ct* 0
Bowling 12–1–12.00–0–0–1/12
His County cricket was played for Worcestershire. He did not appear in first-class matches at Oxford U.

Coventry, Hon John Bonynge
Amateur. *b:* 9.1.1903, London. *d:* 4.7.1969, Pirton, Worcs. Nephew of Hon C. J. (England in South Africa) and Hon H. T. (MCC). Lower order right-hand batsman, slow left-arm bowler. *Sch* Eton. *Team* Worcestershire (1919–35, 75 matches).
Career batting
75–133–13–1774–86–14.78–0–*ct* 28
Bowling 733–16–45.81–0–0–2/18
He did not appear in any first-class matches whilst at Oxford U. He captained Worcs, 1929–30.

Coverdale, Stephen Peter
Cricketer. *b*: 20.11.1954, York. Opening right-hand batsman, wicket-keeper. *Sch* St Peter's, York. *Teams* Yorkshire (1973–80, 6 matches); Cambridge U (1974–77, blue all four years).
Career batting
45–75–6–1245–85–18.04–0–*ct* 41–*st* 10
Bowling 0–1–0.00–0–0–1/0

Coverdale, William
Amateur. *b:* 8.7.1862, Pickering, Yorkshire. *d:* 23.9.1934, Bridlington, Yorkshire. Middle order

batsman, wicket-keeper. *Team* Yorkshire (1888, 2 matches).
Career batting
2–2–0–2–1–1.00–0–*ct* 2

Coverdale, Walter William
Professional. *b:* 30.5.1912. *d:* 6.10.1972, Gateshead, Co Durham. Middle order right-hand batsman, right-arm medium pace bowler. *Team* Northants (1931–32, 31 matches).
Career batting
31–53–4–512–35*–10.44–0–*ct* 4
Bowling 62–1–62.00–0–0–1/25
He appeared for Durham, commencing 1946.

Covill, Reginald John
Professional. *b:* 10.8.1905, Cambridge. Middle order right-hand batsman, right-arm fast bowler. *Team* MCC (1930–35).
Career batting
12–19–3–322–48–20.12–0–*ct* 4
Bowling 589–23–25.60–1–0–5/31
He represented Norfolk and later Cambridgeshire. His first-class debut was for East in 1927.

Covington, Frederick Ernest
Amateur. *b:* 29.10.1912, Kingston, Surrey. Steady middle order left-hand batsman, slow left-arm bowler. *Sch* Harrow. *Teams* Cambridge U (1935); Middlesex (1936, 6 matches). *Tour* Brinckman to South America 1937/8.
Career batting
12–21–4–301–83–17.70–0–*ct* 4
Bowling 25–0

Cowan, Charles Frederic Roy
Amateur. *b:* 17.9.1883, Glangrwyney, Brecon. *d:* 22.3.1958, Leamington Spa, Warwickshire. Middle order right-hand batsman. *Team* Warwickshire (1909–21, 27 matches).
Career batting
29–53–3–846–78–16.92–0–*ct* 10
Bowling 9–0
He captained Warwickshire 2nd XI in the 1930s and was later Treasurer to the County Club.

Cowan, James Ferguson
Amateur. *b:* 17.5.1929, Milton Bridge, Midlothian, Scotland. Left-hand batsman. *Team* Scotland (1960–62).
Career batting
3–5–0–52–18–10.40–0–*ct* 1

Cowan, Michael Joseph
Professional. *b:* 10.6.1933, Leeds, Yorkshire. Lower order left-hand batsman, left-arm fast-medium bowler. *Team* Yorkshire (1953–62, 91 matches). *Tour* MCC to Pakistan 1955/6.
Career batting
99–94–52–233–22–5.54–0–*ct* 40
Bowling 6783–276–24.57–13–2–9/43
His first-class career was marred by injury. On the tour to Pakistan in 1955/6 he went home early due to back strain and missed most of the 1956 English season in consequence. He also missed the 1959 and most of 1961 seasons due to injury and illness. His best bowling was 9/43 for Yorkshire v Warwickshire at Edgbaston in 1960.

Cowan, Ralph Stewart
Cricketer. *b:* 30.3.1960, Hamlin, West Germany. Middle order right-hand batsman, right-arm medium pace bowler. *Teams* Oxford U (1980–82, blue all three years); Sussex (1982–83, 6 matches).
Career batting
28–52–5–1406–143*–29.91–3–*ct* 17–*st* 1
Bowling 798–9–88.66–0–0–2/75

Cowans, Norman George
Cricketer. *b:* 17.4.1961, Enfield, St Mary, Jamaica. Lower order right-hand batsman, right-arm fast bowler, deep field. *Team* Middlesex (1980–83, 27 matches). *Tours* Middlesex to Zimbabwe 1980/1; England to Australia and New Zealand 1982/3 (New Zealand not first-class). *Tests* England (1982/3 to 1983, 8 matches).
Career batting
39–41–7–201–36–5.91–0–*ct* 17
Bowling 2619–99–26.45–5–0–6/77
Test batting
8–14–2–90–36–7.50–0–*ct* 3
Bowling 843–23–36.65–1–0–6/77

Coward, Cornelius
Professional. *b:* 27.1.1838, Preston, Lancashire. *d:* 15.7.1903, Preston, Lancashire. Brother of Frederick (Lancashire). Middle order right-hand batsman, right-arm medium pace bowler, fine deep field. *Team* Lancashire (1865–76, 36 matches).
Career batting
49–86–5–1210–85–14.93–0–*ct* 15
Bowling 44–0

Coward, Frederick
Professional. *b:* 11.2.1842, Preston, Lancashire. *d:* 15.12.1905, Preston, Lancashire. Brother of Cornelius (Lancashire). Middle order right-hand batsman, good field. *Team* Lancashire (1867–68, 7 matches).
Career batting
8–14–1–38–9–2.92–0–*ct* 5

Cowderoy, John
Professional. *b:* 19.4.1851, Battersea, Surrey. *d:*

1934, Fulham, London. Lower order right-hand batsman, left-hand fast round-arm bowler. *Team* Surrey (1876, 1 match).
Career batting
1–2–0–4–2–2.00–0–*ct* 0
Bowling 11–0

Cowdrey, Christopher Stuart
Cricketer. *b:* 20.10.1957, Farnborough, Kent. Son of M. C. (Kent), grandson of E. A. (Europeans). Middle order right-hand batsman, right-arm medium pace bowler, good field. *Sch* Tonbridge. *Team* Kent (1977–83, 134 matches). *Tours* Robins to Sri Lanka 1977/8, to New Zealand 1979/80.
Career batting
138–197–34–5124–123–31.43–6–*ct* 123
Bowling 1943–45–43.17–0–0–3/17

He hit 1,364 runs, av 56.83, in 1983.

Cowdrey, Michael Colin, CBE
Amateur. *b:* 24.12.1932, Pulumala, Ootacamund, India. Father of C. S. (Kent), son of E. A. (Europeans). Brilliant middle order right-hand batsman, leg break bowler, slip field. *Sch* Tonbridge. *Teams* Kent (1950–76, 402 matches); Oxford U (1952–54, blue all three years). *Tours* MCC to Australia and New Zealand 1954/5, 1958/9, 1962/3, 1965/6, 1970/1, 1974/5, to South Africa 1956/7, to West Indies 1959/60, 1967/8, to India 1963/4, to Ceylon and Pakistan 1968/9; Swanton to West Indies 1955/6; International XI to India and Pakistan 1961/2; Commonwealth to India 1964/5; Norfolk to West Indies 1969/70; Kent to West Indies 1972/3 (non first-class); MCC to West Africa 1975/6 (non first-class). *Tests* England (1954/5 to 1974/5, 114 matches).
Career batting
692–1130–134–42719–307–42.89–107–*ct* 638
Bowling 3329–65–51.21–0–0–4/22
Test batting
114–188–15–7624–182–44.06–22–*ct* 120
Bowling 104–0

Beginning his public career as the youngest cricketer to appear in an important match at Lord's – aged 13 for Tonbridge School – Cowdrey developed into the most accomplished batsman in England. He broke many batting records, but lacking the ruthlessness of some he made comparatively few high scores – only three innings over 200 in a total of 107 centuries. Most cricketers with 100 hundreds had at least 10 double centuries.

In the opinion of many his best innings came on the first of his six tours to Australia – a brilliant 102, when England were all out for 191 in the third Test at Melbourne, 1954/5. The highest innings of his first-class career was 307 for MCC v South Australia at Adelaide in 1962/3. He exceeded 1,000 runs in a season 21 times, but only in 1959 and 1965 did he reach 2,000: 2,093, av 63.42, in the latter season being his best. He also exceeded 1,000 runs in an overseas season on six occasions.

He created a new record of 114 for appearances in Test cricket and his partnership of 411 for the 4th wicket with P. B. H. May for England v West Indies at Edgbaston in 1957 was also a new record stand for England.

From 1957 to 1971 he captained Kent, and between 1959 and 1968/9 he led England in 27 Tests. On four of his Australian tours he was the vice-captain, but he was never chosen as captain for this major overseas trip, the selectors apparently under the impression that he was not quite rigorous enough for the task.

Cowell, Edward
Professional. *b:* 22.3.1848, Cambridge. *d:* 17.11.1885, Cambridge. Lower order right-hand batsman, right-arm fast bowler. *Team* Cambridgeshire (1867, 3 matches).
Career batting
3–5–0–37–13–7.40–0–*ct* 1
Bowling 61–4–15.25–0–0–3/11

Cowie, Alexander Gordon
Amateur. *b:* 27.2.1889, Lymington, Hants. *d:* 7.4.1916, Amara, Mesopotamia. He died of wounds. Lower order right-hand batsman, right-arm fast bowler. *Sch* Charterhouse. *Teams* Cambridge U (1910–11, blue 1910); Hampshire (1910, 2 matches); Army (1913).
Career batting
14–20–6–98–28–7.00–0–*ct* 6
Bowling 1395–58–24.05–5–0–6/87

He created a sensation in the University match of 1910, bowling 2 wides and taking 2 wickets in his opening over – he was a very fast bowler, but erratic.

Cowie, John
Amateur. *b:* 30.3.1912, Auckland, New Zealand. Right-hand lower order batsman, right-arm fast-medium bowler. *Team* Auckland (1932/3 to 1949/50). *Tours* New Zealand to England 1937, 1949, to Australia 1937/8. *Tests* New Zealand (1937–49, 9 matches).
Career batting
86–104–29–762–54–10.16–0–*ct* 35
Bowling 8001–359–22.28–20–1–6/3
Test batting
9–13–4–90–45–10.00–0–*ct* 3
Bowling 969–45–21.53–4–1–6/40

The outstanding player of the 1937 tourists, he took 114 wickets, av 19.95, in first-class matches and 19 wickets, av 20.78, in the Tests, heading both bowling tables. In 1949 he was at the veteran stage as a fast bowler and, suffering from various strains, was not as effective, but he played in all four Tests and came second in the Test bowling figures with 14 wickets, av 32.21.

Cowley, John Norman
Amateur. *b:* 7.2.1885, London. *d:* 5.8.1957, Bovingdon, Herts. *Sch* Harrow. *Team* Free Foresters (1914).
Career batting
1–2–0–0–0–0.00–*ct* 0
He played for Hertfordshire.

Cowley, Nigel Geoffrey
Cricketer. *b*: 1.3.1953, Shaftesbury, Dorset. Middle order right-hand batsman, off break bowler. *Team* Hampshire (1974–83, 182 matches).
Career batting
182–264–38–4725–109*–20.90–2–*ct* 72
Bowling 9313–271–34.36–4–0–6/48

Cownley, John Michael
Amateur. *b:* 24.2.1929, Wales, near Sheffield, Yorkshire. Middle order left-hand batsman, leg break and googly bowler. *Team* Yorkshire (1952, 2 matches); Lancashire (1962, 2 matches).
Career batting
4–6–1–64–25–12.80–0–*ct* 1
Bowling 155–3–51.66–0–0–2/36
He appeared for Cheshire in 1961. A noted amateur boxer at light-heavyweight, he represented Sheffield University.

Cowper, Robert Maskew
Amateur. *b:* 5.10.1940, Kew, Victoria, Australia. Brother of D. R. (Victoria). Middle order left-hand batsman, off break bowler. *Teams* Victoria (1959/60 to 1969/70, 66 matches); MCC (1966); Western Australia (1968/9, 3 matches). *Tours* Australia to England 1964, 1968, to South Africa 1966/7, to West Indies 1964/5, to India and Pakistan 1964/5. *Tests* Australia (1964–68, 27 matches).
Career batting
147–228–31–10595–307–53.78–26–*ct* 151
Bowling 5709–183–31.19–1–0–7/42
Test batting
27–46–2–2061–307–46.84–5–*ct* 21
Bowling 1139–36–31.63–0–0–4/48
Despite hitting 1,286 runs, av 51.44, he appeared in only one Test on his first visit to England in 1964. On his return in 1968, he played in four Tests, being omitted from the last only due to injury, but was nothing like as successful – 744 runs, av 37.20. His most famous innings was 307 for Australia v England at Melbourne in the 1965/6 series, but it was a feat of endurance rather than entertainment.

Cox, Arthur Leonard
Professional. *b:* 22.7.1907, Northampton. Son of Mark (Northants), brother of M. H. D. (Northants). Middle order right-hand batsman, medium-slow leg break bowler. *Team* Northants (1926–47, 229 matches).
Career batting
230–410–31–6631–104–17.49–1–*ct* 121
Bowling 7926–199–39.07–4–0–7/91

Cox, Alexander Robb
Amateur. *b:* 6.8.1865, Liverpool. *d:* 21.11.1950, Newmarket, Suffolk. Lower order batsman, wicket-keeper. *Sch* Harrow. *Team* Cambridge U (1887).
Career batting
2–3–0–6–4–2.00–0–*ct* 4
He was a well-known racehorse owner.

Cox, Dennis Frank
Professional. *b:* 21.12.1925, Bermondsey, South London. Lower order right-hand batsman, right-arm fast-medium bowler. *Team* Surrey (1949–57, 42 matches).
Career batting
42–52–17–660–57–18.85–0–*ct* 38
Bowling 2316–68–34.05–2–1–7/22
He also played for Cheshire.

Cox, David William
Cricketer. *b:* 19.5.1946, Oakhill, Somerset. Lower order right-hand batsman, right-arm fast medium bowler. *Team* Somerset (1969, 1 match).
Career batting
1–2–0–8–8–4.00–0–*ct* 2
Bowling 77–1–77.00–0–0–1/50

Cox, E.
Amateur. *Team* London County (1900).
Career batting
1–2–0–9–7–4.50–0–*ct* 1

Cox, George (jun)
Professional. *b:* 23.8.1911, Horsham, Sussex. Son of G. R. (Sussex). Aggressive middle order right-hand batsman, left-arm medium pace bowler, excellent cover field. *Team* Sussex (1931–60, 448 matches).
Career batting
455–754–57–22949–234*–32.92–50–*ct* 139
Bowling 5935–192–30.91–3–0–6/125
He reached 1,000 runs in a season 13 times, twice going on to 2,000 (best 2,369, av 49.35, in 1950). All four of his double centuries were for

Sussex, the highest being 234* v Indians at Hove in 1946. His final first-class match was for L. C. Steven's XI in 1961. A noted soccer player he appeared as centre-forward for Arsenal, Fulham and Luton.

Cox, Gilbert Clifford
Amateur. *b:* 5.7.1908, Stroud, Gloucestershire. *d:* 31.3.1974, Alcester, Warwickshire. Middle order batsman. *Sch* Worcester RGS. *Team* Worcestershire (1935, 2 matches).
Career batting
2–4–0–28–19–7.00–0–*ct* 0

Cox, George Robert
Amateur. *b:* November 1859, Brentford, Middlesex. *d:* 24.2.1936, Hoylake, Cheshire. Middle order right-hand batsman. *Sch* Uppingham. *Team* Liverpool and District XI (1884).
Career batting
1–2–0–0–0–0.00–0–*ct* 0

Cox, George Rubens (sen)
Professional. *b:* 29.11.1873, Warnham, Sussex. *d:* 23.3.1949, Dorking, Surrey. Father of George jun (Sussex). Sound middle order right-hand batsman, medium pace left-arm bowler, later slow, good field. *Team* Sussex (1895–1928, 618 matches).
Career batting
634–978–198–14643–167*–18.77–2–*ct* 551
Bowling 42136–1843–22.86–111–13–9/50
He reached 1,000 runs once – 1,158, av 25.73, in 1906 and 100 wickets five times (best 170, av 21.87, in 1905). During four winters he went out coaching in South Africa and once to India at Cooch Behar. His best bowling was 9/50 for Sussex v Warwickshire at Horsham in 1926.

Cox, Henry Ramsay
Amateur. *b:* 19.5.1911, Radcliffe-on-Trent, Notts. Middle/lower order right-hand batsman, right-arm medium pace bowler. *Sch* Uppingham. *Teams* Nottinghamshire (1930–54, 23 matches); Cambridge U (1934).
Career batting
30–42–9–419–64–12.69–0–*ct* 12
Bowling 1556–47–33.10–2–0–6/30
He was also a useful soccer player.

Cox, Joseph Lovell
Amateur. *b:* 28.6.1886, Pietermaritzburg, South Africa. *d:* 4.7.1971, South Africa. Lower order right-hand batsman, right-arm medium-fast bowler, good slip field. *Sch* St Charles's College, Pietermaritzburg. *Team* Natal (1910/11 to 1921/2). *Tours* South Africa to England 1912. *Tests* South Africa (1913/4, 3 matches).
Career batting
42–55–12–357–51–8.30–0–*ct* 14
Bowling 2704–120–22.53–4–1–8/20
Test batting
3–6–1–17–12*–3.40–0–*ct* 1
Bowling 245–4–61.25–0–0–2/74
He was not given enough bowling to do on his only visit to England, and his results were therefore moderate.

Cox, Mark (sen)
Professional. *b:* 10.5.1879, Northampton. *d:* December 1968, Northampton. Father of A. L. (Northants) and M. H. D. (Northants). Originally tail end left-hand batsman, developing into a defensive opener, right-arm medium pace bowler. *Team* Northants (1905–19, 75 matches).
Career batting
75–134–10–1808–78–14.58–0–*ct* 22
Bowling 984–25–39.36–0–0–3/22
His career with Northants commenced in the pre-first-class days in 1897. He retired in 1909, but returned briefly in 1919.

Cox, Mark Henry D.
Professional. *b:* 1906, Northampton. *d:* 1979, Pontypridd, Glamorgan. Son of Mark senior (Northants), brother of A. L. (Northants). Middle order right-hand batsman, slow right-arm bowler. *Team* Northants (1932, 3 matches).
Career batting
3–4–0–8–5–2.00–0–*ct* 1
Bowling 62–2–31.00–0–0–2/11

Cox, Roger
Cricketer. *b:* 27.4.1947, Luton, Bedfordshire. Middle order right-hand batsman. *Team* Minor Counties XI (1971).
Career batting
1–2–1–24–24–24.00–0–*ct* 0
His County cricket was for Bedfordshire.

Cox, Sydney
Professional. *b:* 23.5.1905, Northampton. *d:* 5.3.1969, Northampton. Middle order right-hand batsman, right-arm medium pace bowler. *Team* Northants (1932, 6 matches).
Career batting
6–11–1–89–25–8.90–0–*ct* 2
Bowling 45–1–45.00–0–0–1/10

Coxhead, Maurice Edward
Amateur. *b:* 24.5.1889, London. *d:* 3.5.1917. He was killed in action near Douai, France. Middle/lower order right-hand batsman, right-arm fast bowler. *Sch* Eastbourne. *Teams* Oxford U (1909–10); Middlesex (1911, 1 match).

Career batting
6–8–0–29–9–3.62–0–*ct* 4
Bowling 300–13–23.07–1–0–5/33

Coxon, Alexander
Professional. *b:* 18.1.1916, Huddersfield, Yorkshire. Lower order right-hand batsman, right-arm medium fast bowler. *Team* Yorkshire (1945–50, 142 matches). *Test* England (1948, 1 match).
Career batting
146–188–33–2814–83–18.15–0–*ct* 126
Bowling 9893–473–20.91–24–2–8/31
Test batting
1–2–0–19–19–9.50–0–*ct* 0
Bowling 172–3–57.33–0–0–2/90
He took 100 wickets in a season twice (best 131, av 18.60, in 1950). He left County cricket after the 1950 season to go into the Leagues. He also played for Durham.

Coxon, Alan John
Amateur. *b:* 18.3.1930, London. Aggressive lower order left-hand batsman, left-arm fast-medium bowler. *Team* Oxford U (1951–54, blue 1952).
Career batting
18–26–14–144–43*–12.00–0–*ct* 4
Bowling 1350–28–48.21–0–0–3/55
His final first-class match was for MCC in 1958.

Coxon, Ernest James De Veuille
Amateur. *b:* 1858, Taunton, Somerset. *d:* 8.4.1924, Nevilly-sur-Seine, France. Lower order left-hand batsman, left-arm medium pace bowler. *Team* Gentlemen of England v Oxford U (1890).
Career batting
1–2–0–31–21–15.50–0–*ct* 2
Bowling 5–0
He was no-balled for throwing in his only first-class match and was therefore taken off after three overs.

Coyle, Frederick Thomas
Professional. *b:* 1869, Taunton, Somerset. *d:* 12.9.1925, Halifax, Yorkshire. Middle/lower order right-hand batsman, right-arm fast-medium bowler. *Team* Somerset (1903–05, 2 matches).
Career batting
2–3–2–14–10–14.00–0–*ct* 4
Bowling 54–0
He also played for Northumberland.

Crabtree, Frederick
Professional. *b:* 10.3.1867, Baildon, Shipley, Yorkshire. *d:* 28.11.1893, Nelson, Lancashire, of ulceration of the stomach caused by a cricket ball. Lower order batsman, wicket-keeper. *Team* Lancashire (1890, 1 match).
Career batting
1–1–0–1–1–1.00–0–*ct* 1
He appeared for Yorkshire in a few matches in 1893, but only in non-first-class matches.

Crabtree, Frederick Lane
Amateur. *b:* 13.9.1872, Darlington, Co Durham. *d:* 19.8.1951, Canterbury, Kent. Middle order right-hand batsman, left-arm medium pace bowler. *Sch* Eton. *Team* Cambridge U (1894).
Career batting
3–6–1–66–27*–13.20–0–*ct* 2
Commencing 1898 he played for Hertfordshire.

Crabtree, Herbert
Professional. *b:* 1880, Colne, Lancashire. *d:* March 1951, Colne, Lancashire. Middle order right-hand batsman, medium pace bowler, brilliant slip field. *Team* Lancashire (1902–08, 5 matches).
Career batting
5–8–0–116–49–14.50–0–*ct* 1
Bowling 34–0

Crabtree, Harry Pollard
Amateur. *b:* 30.4.1906, Barnoldswick, Yorkshire. *d:* 28.5.1982, Brentwood, Essex. Opening right-hand batsman, right-arm medium pace bowler. *Sch* St Peters, York. *Team* Essex (1931–47, 24 matches).
Career batting
24–41–1–1281–146–32.03–4–*ct* 12
Bowling 63–0
Owing to his scholastic duties he was unable to appear regularly for Essex.

Craddy, Wilfred Hartland
Amateur. *b:* 1.9.1905, Bristol, Gloucs. *d:* 4.1.1979, Westbury-on-Trym, Bristol. Middle order left-hand batsman. *Team* Gloucestershire (1928, 3 matches).
Career batting
3–5–0–47–29–9.40–0–*ct* 0

Cragg, James Richard Allen
Cricketer. *b:* 28.10.1946, Stockport, Cheshire. Middle order right-hand batsman. *Team* Cambridge U (1970).
Career batting
7–13–0–149–55–11.46–0–*ct* 2
He also played for Cheshire.

Cragg, James Stanley
Amateur. *b:* 18.10.1886, Stockport, Cheshire. *d:* 27.7.1979, Manchester. Middle order batsman. *Team* Lancashire (1908, 1 match).

Career batting
1–2–0–10–9–5.00–0–*ct* 0
He was President of Lancashire CCC in 1966.

Craib, James Derek Graham
Amateur. *b:* 27.11.1917, Kandy, Ceylon. Lower order right-hand batsman, right-arm fast-medium bowler. *Sch* Eastbourne. *Team* Cambridge U (1937).
Career batting
2–3–0–100–62–33.33–0–*ct* 0
Bowling 109–4–27.25–0–0–2/34

Craig, Edward John
Amateur. *b:* 26.3.1942, Formby, Lancashire. Opening right-hand batsman. *Sch* Charterhouse. *Teams* Cambridge U (1961–63, blue all three years); Lancashire (1961–62, 6 matches).
Career batting
50–93–7–3103–208*–36.08–7–*ct* 43
Bowling 16–0
He reached 1,000 runs in a season twice (best 1,528, av 42.44 in 1961). He was one of the few Cambridge cricket blues to be placed in the First Class in three Triposes. His highest score was 208* for Cambridge U v L. C. Steven's XI at Eastbourne in 1961.

Craig, Hartley Samuel
Amateur. *b:* 19.9.1917, Prospect, Adelaide, Australia. Left-hand opening batsman. *Team* Dominions (1945).
Career batting
1–2–0–88–56–44.00–0–*ct* 0

Craig, Ian David
Amateur. *b:* 12.6.1935, Yass, New South Wales, Australia. Middle order right-hand batsman, excellent deep field. *Teams* New South Wales (1951/2 to 1961/2, 55 matches); Free Foresters (1957). *Tours* Australia to England 1953, 1956, to South Africa 1957/8, to India and Pakistan 1956/7, to New Zealand 1956/7, 1959/60; Commonwealth to South Africa 1959/60, to New Zealand and India 1961/2. *Tests* Australia (1952/3 to 1957/8, 11 matches).
Career batting
144–208–15–7328–213*–37.96–15–*ct* 70
Bowling 127–1–127.00–0–0–1/3
Test batting
11–18–0–358–53–19.88–0–*ct* 2
Only 17 years of age when he toured England in 1953, he had a very modest tour and did not appear in the Tests; his second visit was an improvement, but he failed to reach 1,000 runs and did little in either of the Tests for which he was chosen. He captained Australia in five Tests. His highest score was 213* for NSW v South Africa at Sydney in 1952/3.

Craig, Ian Thornton
Amateur. *b:* 26.1.1931, Maidstone, Kent. Lower order right-hand batsman, right-arm medium fast bowler. *Sch* Leys. *Team* Minor Counties (1959).
Career batting
1–1–0–1–1–1.00–0–*ct* 0
Bowling 85–2–42.50–0–0–2/46
His County cricket was for Cambridgeshire.

Craig, Dr Leslie
Amateur. *b:* 14.10.1904, Edinburgh, Scotland. Wicket-keeper. *Team* Scotland (1928–29).
Career batting
2–3–0–30–17–10.00–0–*ct* 4–*st* 1

Craig, Victor Alexander
Amateur. *b:* 27.7.1917, Strabane, Co Tyrone, Ireland. Left-hand batsman, wicket-keeper. *Team* Ireland (1948).
Career batting
1–1–0–12–12–12.00–0–*ct* 2

Craig, Walter Reid
Amateur. *b:* 1847, Bury, Lancashire. *d:* 6.7.1923, Hangleton, Sussex. Opening batsman. *Sch* Shrewsbury. *Team* Lancashire (1874, 1 match).
Career batting
1–2–0–8–7–4.00–0–*ct* 0

Craigie, Edmund Warren
Amateur. *b:* 8.5.1842, Goruckpore, India. *d:* 8.6.1907, Putney, London. *Sch* Harrow. *Team* MCC (1870).
Career batting
1–2–0–0–0–0.00–0–*ct* 0

Crake, Eric Hamilton
Amateur. *b:* 25.1.1886, Madras, India. *d:* 3.2.1948, Nakuru, Kenya. Brother of R. H. (MCC). Middle order batsman. *Sch* Harrow. *Team* MCC (1912).
Career batting
1–1–0–1–1–1.00–0–*ct* 0
He emigrated to Kenya about 1912.

Crake, Ralph Hamilton
Amateur. *b*: 13.4.1882, Madras, India. *d*: 26.1.1952, Edinburgh, Scotland. Brother of E. H. (MCC). Lower order batsman, wicket-keeper. *Sch* Harrow. *Team* MCC (1901); Europeans (1920/1).
Career batting
2–4–0–47–37–11.75–0–*ct* 1

Cranfield, Beaumont
Professional. *b:* 28.8.1874, Bath, Somerset. *d:* 20.1.1909, Montpelier, Bristol, of pneumonia contracted whilst watching a soccer match. Tail end batsman, left-arm slow bowler. *Teams* Somerset (1897–1908, 125 matches); London County (1902–03).
Career batting
137–228–95–1307–42–9.82–0–*ct* 64
Bowling 14896–621–23.98–47–12–8/39

He took 100 wickets in a season three times (best 141, av 18.56, in 1902).

Cranfield, Lionel Lord
Professional. *b:* 11.10.1883, Brixton, Surrey. *d:* 17.5.1968, Sale, Cheshire. Father of L. M. (Gloucs). Lower order right-hand batsman, slow left-arm bowler. *Teams* Gloucestershire (1903–22, 25 matches); Somerset (1906, 4 matches).
Career batting
29–51–5–612–51*–13.30–0–*ct* 15
Bowling 1760–59–29.83–2–0–6/67

Cranfield, Lionel Montague
Professional. *b:* 29.8.1909, Bristol. Son of L. L. (Gloucs and Somerset). Lower order right-hand batsman, off break bowler. *Team* Gloucestershire (1934–51, 162 matches).
Career batting
162–228–55–2466–90–14.25–0–*ct* 38
Bowling 7670–233–32.91–8–2–8/45

He was on the Old Trafford staff in 1933.

Crankshaw, Sir Eric Norman Spencer
Amateur. *b:* 1.7.1885, Over Peover, Cheshire. *d:* 24.6.1966, Reading, Berkshire. Opening/middle order right-hand batsman. *Sch* Eton. *Team* Gloucestershire (1909, 1 match).
Career batting
1–2–0–2–1–1.00–0–*ct* 0

Cranmer, Peter
Amateur. *b:* 10.9.1914, Acocks Green, Birmingham. Middle order right-hand batsman, right-arm medium-fast bowler, good field. *Sch* St Edward's School, Oxford. *Teams* Warwickshire (1934–54, 166 matches); Europeans (1944/5); Services (1944/5).
Career batting
175–284–13–5833–113–21.59–4–*ct* 126
Bowling 1208–29–41.65–1–0–7/52

He played in the Freshmen's Match at Oxford, but no first-class matches. He reached 1,000 runs in a season three times (best 1,192, av 22.49, in 1947). He captained Warwickshire 1938–47. His final first-class match was for MCC in 1959. A noted rugby footballer, he played at centre three-quarter for Oxford and England. He later became a well-known sporting journalist and commentator.

Cranston, James
Amateur. *b:* 9.1.1859, Birmingham. *d:* 10.12.1904, Bristol. Middle order left-hand batsman, left-arm bowler, fine outfield. *Sch* Taunton College. *Team* Gloucestershire (1876–99, 103 matches). *Test* England (1890, 1 match).
Career batting
118–195–20–3450–152–19.71–5–*ct* 49
Bowling 19–0
Test batting
1–2–0–31–16–15.50–0–*ct* 1

He appeared occasionally for Warwickshire in 1886 and 1887, having moved away from Bristol, but returned to Gloucestershire in 1889. During a match for the latter County in 1891 he was seized with a fit and this ended his first-class career, apart from a brief re-appearance in 1899. He also played for Worcestershire.

Cranston, Kenneth
Amateur. *b:* 20.10.1917, Aigburgh, Liverpool, Lancashire. Middle order right-hand batsman, right-arm medium pace bowler. *Team* Lancashire (1947–48, 50 matches). *Tour* MCC to West Indies 1947/8. *Tests* England (1947–48, 8 matches).
Career batting
78–104–15–3099–156*–34.82–3–*ct* 46
Bowling 4985–178–28.00–10–1–7/43
Test batting
8–14–0–209–45–14.92–0–*ct* 3
Bowling 461–18–25.61–0–0–4/12

He captained Lancashire in 1948 and England in one match v West Indies 1947/8. He hit 1,000 runs in a season twice (best 1,228, av 33.18, in 1947). A dentist by profession, he retired from first-class cricket after the 1948 season. His final first-class match was for Leveson-Gower's XI in 1950.

Cranston, Robert S.
Amateur. Right-hand batsman, wicket-keeper. *Team* Scotland (1922–23).
Career batting
3–5–3–35–31–17.50–0–*ct* 4–*st* 2

Crapp, John Frederick
Professional. *b:* 14.10.1912, St Columb, Cornwall. *d:* 15.2.1981, Bristol. Sound left-hand batsman, excellent slip field. *Team* Gloucestershire (1936–56, 422 matches). *Tours* MCC to South Africa 1948/9; Commonwealth to India 1953/4. *Tests* England (1948 to 1948/9, 7 matches).

Career batting
452–754–80–23615–175–35.03–38–*ct* 386
Bowling 306–6–51.00–0–0–3/24
Test batting
7–13–2–319–56–29.00–0–*ct* 7

He reached 1,000 runs in a season 14 times, but 2,000 runs only once – 2,014, av 45.77, in 1949. He captained Gloucestershire in 1953 and 1954. After retiring from first-class cricket, he became a noted umpire, officiating in a number of Tests.

Crawford, Alexander Basil
Amateur. *b:* 24.5.1891, Coleshill, Warwickshire. *d:* 10.5.1916. He was killed in action near Richebourg, France. Hard-hitting middle order right-hand batsman, right-arm fast medium bowler. *Sch* Oundle. *Teams* Warwickshire (1911, 7 matches); Nottinghamshire (1912, 11 matches).
Career batting
18–27–4–381–51–16.56–0–*ct* 5
Bowling 607–21–28.90–1–0–6/36

Crawford, Frank Fairbairn
Amateur. *b:* 17.6.1850, Hastings, Sussex. *d:* 16.1.1900, at the military base hospital, Pietermaritzburg, South Africa. Brother of J. C. (Kent), uncle of V. F. S. (Surrey), J. N. (Surrey and South Australia) and R. T. (Leics). Middle order right-hand batsman, splendid outfield. *Sch* Maidstone. *Teams* Kent (1870–79, 15 matches); Natal (1889/90).
Career batting
25–48–6–579–38–13.78–0–*ct* 13
Bowling 17–0

He went to India with his Regiment in 1874/5 and then to South Africa, his appearances in County cricket being therefore very limited. His last first-class match in England was for MCC in 1884.

Crawford, George Henry
Professional. *b:* 15.12.1890, Hull. *d:* 28.6.1975, Hull. Lower order right-hand batsman, right-arm fast bowler. *Team* Yorkshire (1914–26, 9 matches).
Career batting
9–8–0–46–21–5.75–0–*ct* 3
Bowling 541–21–25.76–1–0–5/59

After playing for Yorkshire in 1914, he was not seen again in the County side until 1925.

Crawford, Ian Cunningham
Cricketer. *b:* 13.9.1954, Bristol. Middle order right-hand batsman, off break bowler. *Team* Gloucestershire (1975–78, 5 matches).
Career batting
5–7–0–104–73–14.85–0–*ct* 5
Bowling 174–3–58.00–0–0–1/18

He did not play in first-class cricket in either 1976 or 1977.

Crawford, Rev John Charles
Amateur. *b:* 29.5.1849, Hastings, Sussex. *d:* 21.2.1935, Wimbledon, Surrey. Brother of F. F. (Kent and Natal), father of R. T. (Leics), J. N. (Surrey and South Australia), V. F. S. (Surrey and Leics). Middle order batsman, being right-hand usually, but left-hand when hitting out; also right-hand fast bowler and left-hand slow bowler, brilliant deep field. *Sch* Maidstone. *Team* Kent (1872–77, 10 matches).
Career batting
11–22–1–202–35–9.61–0–*ct* 0
Bowling 174–6–29.00–0–0–3/5

He did not play in any first-class matches whilst at Oxford. In 1878 he was a curate in Leicester and appeared for that County. At one time he was reputed to be the fastest bowler in England. He also played for Hereford. His debut in first-class matches was for W. G. Grace's XI 1871.

Crawford, John Neville
Amateur. *b:* 1.12.1886, Cane Hill, Surrey. *d:* 2.5.1963, Epsom, Surrey. Son of J. C. (Kent), brother of R. T. (Leics) and V. F. S. (Surrey and Leics), nephew of F. F. (Kent). Middle order right-hand batsman, right-arm medium pace off-break bowler. *Sch* Repton. *Teams* Surrey (1904–21, 120 matches); South Australia (1909/10 to 1913/4, 22 matches); Wellington (1917/8); Otago (1914/5). *Tours* MCC to South Africa 1905/6, to Australia 1907/8; Australia to New Zealand 1913/4, to North America 1913/4. *Tests* England (1905/6 to 1907/8, 12 matches).
Career batting
210–325–34–9488–232–32.60–15–*ct* 162
Bowling 16842–815–20.66–57–12–8/24
Test batting
12–23–2–469–74–22.33–0–*ct* 13
Bowling 1150–39–29.48–3–0–5/48

As a schoolboy with still a year ahead of him at Repton, Crawford made his first-class debut for Surrey in August 1904. By the season's close he had taken 44 wickets at a cost of 16.93 each, only two occasional bowlers standing ahead of him in the first-class averages. Shortly after leaving school in 1905 he was on his way to South Africa with the MCC team and made his Test debut in the first match of the 1905/6 series. Back in England for the 1906 season he accomplished the 'double', repeated the feat in 1907 and missed it by two wickets in 1908. A quarrel in the middle of the 1909 summer abruptly ended his career with Surrey. He quit England and began a new life in Australia, playing for South Australia. Only the outbreak of war in 1914 brought him back to England and after it was over, his quarrel forgotten, he reappeared for Surrey and demonstrated how much his County had missed by coming third in the first-class batting table with an average of 61.00. That was more or less the swansong of one of England's most remarkable players, though his final first-class match was not until 1921.

In all he reached 1,000 runs in three seasons (best 1,371, av 37.05, in 1908) and 100 wickets twice (best 124, av 16.95, in 1907). His single 200 was 232 for Surrey v Somerset at the Oval in 1908, but mention should be made of his 354 in 330 minutes for an Australian XI v XV of South Canterbury in 1914, he and Trumper adding 298 in 69 minutes!

Crawford, Michael Grove
Amateur. *b:* 30.7.1920, Leeds, Yorkshire. Father of N. C. (Cambridge U). Middle order right-hand batsman, good cover point. *Sch* Shrewsbury. *Team* Yorkshire (1951, 1 match).
Career batting
1–2–0–22–13–11.00–0–*ct* 1

He later became Chairman of Yorkshire CCC.

Crawford, Neil Cameron
Cricketer. *b:* 26.11.1958, Leeds, Yorkshire. Son of M. G. (Yorkshire). Lower order right-hand batsman, right-arm medium pace bowler. *Sch* Shrewsbury. *Team* Cambridge U (1978–80, blue 1979–80).
Career batting
22–22–2–262–46–13.10–0–*ct* 5
Bowling 1030–32–32.18–1–0–6/80

Crawford, R. E. W.
(*see under* Copland-Crawford, R. E. W.)

Crawford, Robert Ogilvy
Amateur. *b:* 1.10.1869, Bedford. *d:* 27.2.1917, Weston-Super-Mare, Somerset. Middle order right-hand batsman. *Sch* Monkton Combe and Highgate. *Team* Cambridge U (1891).
Career batting
1–2–0–8–4–4.00–0–*ct* 0

Crawford, Reginald Trevor
Amateur. *b:* 11.6.1882, Leicester. *d:* 15.11.1945, Swiss Cottage, London, after a long illness. Son of J. C. (Kent); brother of J. N. (Surrey and South Australia) and V. F. S. (Surrey and Leics), nephew of F. F. (Kent). Middle order right-hand batsman, right-arm fast-medium bowler. *Team* Leicestershire (1901–11, 96 matches).
Career batting
112–187–13–3190–99*–18.33–0–*ct* 100
Bowling 5686–221–25.72–15–5–7/71

A well known singer, his concert engagements limited his appearances in first-class cricket.

Crawford, Thomas Alan
Amateur. *b:* 18.2.1910, Hoo, Kent. *d:* 5.12.1979, Westminster, London. Attacking middle order right-hand batsman, occasional off break bowler, good close field. *Sch* Tonbridge. *Team* Kent (1930–51, 13 matches).
Career batting
13–16–1–150–32–10.00–0–*ct* 2
Bowling 13–0

He appeared in the Cambridge Freshmen's match of 1931, but not in first-class matches whilst at University. Most of his cricket was for Kent Second XI.

Crawford, Vivian Frank Shergold
Amateur. *b:* 11.4.1879, Leicester. *d:* 21.8.1922, Merton, Surrey. Son of J. C. (Kent), brother of J. N. (Surrey and South Australia) and R. T. (Leics), nephew of F. F. (Kent). Hard-hitting middle order right-hand batsman, right-arm fast bowler. *Sch* Whitgift. *Teams* Surrey (1896–1902, 110 matches); Leicestershire (1903–10, 165 matches). *Tour* Bosanquet to North America 1901.
Career batting
293–479–32–11909–172*–26.64–16–*ct* 262
Bowling 875–17–51.47–0–0–3/14

He reached 1,000 runs in a season five times (best 1,511, av 32.14, in 1901). In 1903 he was appointed Secretary to Leics CCC and therefore, being qualified by birth, removed from Surrey to his native County. He was one of the greatest of schoolboy batsmen, hitting 1,340 runs for his school in 1897. After leaving Leics he emigrated to Ceylon, becoming a tea-planter, but returned to serve in the First World War.

Crawford, Sir Walter Ferguson
Amateur. *b:* 11.4.1894, Melbourne, Australia. *d:* 28.3.1978, Churt, Surrey. Middle/lower order batsman, bowler. *Team* Oxford U (1919).
Career batting
3–5–0–23–11–4.60–0–*ct* 3
Bowling 136–3–45.33–0–0–2/43

Crawford, William Patrick Anthony
Amateur. *b:* 3.8.1933, Sydney, Australia. Lower order right-hand batsman, right-arm fast bowler. *Team* New South Wales (1954/5 to 1957/8, 14 matches). *Tours* Australia to England 1956, to India 1956/7. *Tests* Australia (1956 to 1956/7, 4 matches).
Career batting
37–42–20–424–86–19.27–0–*ct* 18
Bowling 2313–110–21.02–5–1–6/55
Test batting
4–5–2–53–34–17.66–0–*ct* 1
Bowling 107–7–15.28–0–0–3/28

On his only tour of England in 1956, he achieved a modest return and appeared in a single Test, in which his bowling was scarcely required.

Crawfurd, John William Frederick Arthur
Amateur. *b:* 15.11.1878, Dulwich, Surrey. *d:* 22.6.1939, Dublin. Lower order left-hand batsman, left-arm fast medium bowler. *Sch* Merchant Taylors. *Teams* Oxford U (1900–01, blue both years); Ireland (1907–23).
Career batting
19–31–3–644–72–23.00–0–*ct* 15
Bowling 403–13–31.00–0–0–3/30
He appeared for Surrey in a non-first-class match. His last first-class match was for Harlequins in 1927. A noted rugby player he gained his blue in 1900.

Crawley, Aidan Merivale
Amateur. *b:* 10.4.1908, Beneden, Kent. Son of A. S. (MCC), brother of C. S. (Hants and Middlesex), nephew of Eustace (Cambridge U) and H. E. (Cambridge U). Attacking opening right-hand batsman, right-arm medium pace off break bowler. *Sch* Harrow. *Teams* Oxford U (1927–30, blue all four years); Kent (1927–47, 33 matches).
Career batting
87–141–6–5061–204–37.48–11–*ct* 44
Bowling 565–15–37.66–0–0–2/40
He also played for Buckinghamshire. He hit 1,316 runs, av 48.74, in 1928 and his highest score was 204 for Oxford U v Northants at Wellingborough in 1929. His final first-class match was for Free Foresters in 1949. He was Labour MP for Buckingham 1945–51 and Conservative MP for West Derbyshire 1962–67. A noted journalist and author, he was at one time Editor-in-Chief of Independent Television News.

Crawley, Canon Arthur Stafford
Amateur. *b:* 18.9.1876, Sutherland. *d:* 8.10.1948, Clewer, Berkshire. Brother of Eustace (Cambridge U) and H. E. (Cambridge U), father of A. M. (Kent) and C. S. (Hants and Middlesex). Middle order right-hand batsman, good cover point. *Sch* Harrow. *Team* MCC (1897–98).
Career batting
3–4–0–19–12–4.75–0–*ct* 4
He appeared in the Freshmen's and Seniors' Matches at Oxford, but no first-class games. He played a little for Hertfordshire.

Crawley, Charles Lambart
Amateur. *b:* 1.5.1908, Brandon, Suffolk. *d:* 24.7.1935, Sunderland, Co Durham. Brother of L. G. (Essex and Worcestershire). Middle order batsman. *Sch* Harrow. *Team* Essex (1929, 1 match).
Career batting
1–2–0–3–3–1.50–0–*ct* 1

Crawley, Cosmo Stafford
Amateur. *b:* 27.5.1904, Chelsea, London. Son of A. S. (MCC), brother of A. M. (Kent), nephew of Eustace (Cambridge U) and H. E. (Cambridge U). Middle order right-hand batsman, right-arm medium pace bowler. *Sch* Harrow. *Teams* Hampshire (1923, 1 match); Oxford U (1924–25); Middlesex (1929, 1 match).
Career batting
6–11–0–243–81–22.09–0–*ct* 1

Crawley, Eustace
Amateur. *b:* 19.4.1868, Highgate, Middlesex. *d:* 2.11.1914, Hollebeke, Belgium. He was killed in action. Brother of H. E. (Cambridge U) and A. S. (MCC), uncle of A. M. (Kent) and C. S. (Hants and Middlesex). Opening right-hand batsman, good field. *Sch* Harrow. *Team* Cambridge U (1887–89, blue all three years).
Career batting
17–28–2–424–103*–16.30–1–*ct* 8
He played occasional County cricket for Hertfordshire and Worcestershire. An excellent tennis player he represented Cambridge.

Crawley, Henry Ernest
Amateur. *b:* 19.8.1865, Highgate, Middlesex. *d:* 18.6.1931, Walton-on-the-Hill, Surrey. Brother of Eustace (Cambridge U) and A. S. (MCC), uncle of A. M. (Kent) and C. S. (Hants and Middlesex). Middle order right-hand batsman, good field. *Sch* Harrow. *Team* Cambridge U (1886).
Career batting
4–8–0–132–54–16.50–0–*ct* 3
His debut in first-class matches was for C. I. Thornton's XI 1885 and his final match for MCC in 1887. His County cricket was for Hertfordshire. He was amateur tennis champion in 1892 to 1894 and represented Cambridge. He was also a noted chess champion.

Crawley, Leonard George
Amateur. *b:* 26.7.1903, Nacton, Suffolk. *d:* 9.7.1981, Worlington, Suffolk. Brother of C. L. (Essex). Opening/middle order right-hand batsman, right-arm fast-medium bowler. *Sch* Harrow. *Teams* Cambridge U (1923–25, blue all three years); Essex (1926–36, 56 matches); Worcestershire (1922–23, 6 matches). *Tour* MCC to West Indies 1925/6.
Career batting
109–177–9–5227–222–31.11–8–*ct* 42
Bowling 57–0
Regarded as one of the most talented crticketers of his generation, he unfortunately was unable to play regularly in County cricket. His single 200

was 222 for Essex v Glamorgan at Swansea in 1928. His final first-class match was for MCC in 1939. He was a talented golfer, appearing four times in the Walker Cup, and also a good rackets player, representing Cambridge.

Crawley, William Parry
Amateur. *b:* 24.8.1842, Bryngwyn, Monmouthshire. *d:* 9.5.1907, Walberton, Sussex. Middle order batsman. *Sch* Marlborough. *Team* MCC (1867).
Career batting
1–1–0–0–0–0.00–0–*ct* 0
Had several Trials whilst at Cambridge, but did not appear for the University. He played non-first-class cricket for Somerset.

Cray, Stanley J.
Professional. *b:* 29.5.1921, Stratford, Essex. Opening right-hand batsman. *Teams* Essex (1938–50, 99 matches); Europeans (1943/4 to 1944/5).
Career batting
102–177–6–4218–163–24.66–7–*ct* 23
Bowling 40–1–40.00–0–0–1/0
He hit 1,000 runs twice (best 1,339, av 26.78, in 1947).

Creber, Arthur Brynley
Professional. *b:* 11.10.1909, Sketty, Glamorgan. *d:* 10.8.1966, Colwyn Bay. Son of Harry (Glamorgan). Middle order right-hand batsman, right-arm medium pace bowler. *Teams* Glamorgan (1929, 1 match); Scotland (1937).
Career batting
2–4–0–45–23–11.25–0–*ct* 1
Bowling 80–1–80.00–0–0–1/80

Creber, Harry
Professional. *b:* 30.4.1872, Birkenhead, Cheshire. *d:* 27.3.1939, Uplands, Swansea. Father of A. B. (Glamorgan). Lower order right-hand batsman, left-arm medium pace bowler. *Team* Glamorgan (1921–22, 33 matches).
Career batting
34–60–29–157–13*–5.06–0–*ct* 6
Bowling 2671–98–27.25–5–1–7/47
He was a leading figure in South Wales cricket prior to the First World War and for 40 years professional and groundsman at St Helens, Swansea. His first-class debut was for South Wales in 1912.

Creese, William Leonard Charles
Professional. *b:* 28.12.1907, Park Town, Transvaal, South Africa. *d:* 9.3.1974, Dover, Kent. Son of W. H. (Transvaal). Hard-hitting middle order left-hand batsman, left-arm medium pace bowler. *Team* Hampshire (1928–39, 278 matches).
Career batting
281–455–42–9938–241–24.06–6–*ct* 205
Bowling 11246–410–27.42–15–1–8/37
He reached 1,000 runs in a season five times (best 1,421, av 28.42, in 1938) and missed the 'double' by only five wickets in 1936. His highest score was 241 for Hampshire v Northants at Northampton in 1939. His last first-class match was for Combined Services in 1946. He also played for Dorset.

Cregar, Edward Mathews
Amateur. *b:* 28.12.1868, Philadelphia, USA. *d:* 6.5.1916, Philadelphia, USA. Hard-hitting middle/lower order right-hand batsman, right-arm fast-medium, later slow, bowler. *Team* Philadelphia (1895–1908). *Tours* Philadelphia to England 1897, 1903, 1908.
Career batting
37–65–6–713–57–12.08–0–*ct* 12
Bowling 1757–70–25.10–3–0–8/35
He achieved a fairly good bowling record on his first two visits to England, but was clearly too old for the 1908 tour. Appearing in ten matches for USA v Canada, he took 25 wickets, av 14.12, and also performed usefully with the bat.

Creighton, Ernest
Professional. *b:* 9.7.1859, Hemsworth, Yorkshire. *d:* 17.2.1931, Leeds. Lower order batsman, left-arm fast bowler (or slow in another account). *Team* Yorkshire (1888, 4 matches)
Career batting
4–8–2–33–10–5.50–0–*ct* 0
Bowling 181–10–18.10–0–0–4/22

Crerar, George Graham
Amateur. *b:* 1.10.1914, Glasgow, Scotland. Right-hand batsman, slow left-arm bowler. *Sch* Glasgow Academy. *Team* Scotland (1947–48).
Career batting
2–4–0–76–36–19.00–0–*ct* 1

Cresswell, George Fenwick
Amateur. *b:* 22.3.1915, Wanganui, New Zealand. *d:* 10.1.1966, Blenheim, New Zealand. He was found dead with a shot gun by his side. Brother of A. E. (Wellington). Tail end left-hand batsman, slow-medium right-arm bowler. *Teams* Wellington (1949/50, 3 matches); Central Districts (1950/1 to 1954/5, 7 matches). *Tour* New Zealand to England 1949. *Tests* New Zealand (1949 to 1950/51, 3 matches).

Career batting
33–36–19–89–12*–5.23–0–*ct* 11
Bowling 2794–124–22.53–8–0–8/100
Test batting
3–5–3–14–12*–7.00–0–*ct* 0
Bowling 292–13–22.46–1–0–6/168

He had only appeared in one first-class match when he was selected to tour England in 1949, but proved successful with 62 wickets, av 26.09. He played only in the final Test however, when he took 6 for 168 in the single innings. His first-class debut was for Rest of New Zealand in 1948/9.

Cresswell, Joseph
Professional. *b:* 22.12.1865, Denby, Derbyshire. *d:* 7.8.1932, Marehay, Derbyshire. Uncle of J. A. (Derbyshire). Lower order right-hand batsman, right-arm medium-fast bowler, good close field. *Team* Warwickshire (1895–99, 15 matches).
Career batting
15–22–9–137–16–10.54–0–*ct* 12
Bowling 1144–42–27.23–1–0–6/69

He first appeared for Warwickshire in 1889 and his best years occurred before the County was raised to first-class status.

Cresswell, James Arthur
Professional. b: 16.3.1903, Marehay, Derbyshire. Nephew of Joseph (Warwickshire). Lower order right-hand batsman, left-arm fast-medium bowler. *Team* Derbyshire (1923–27, 21 matches).
Career batting
21–34–13–160–28–7.61–0–*ct* 17
Bowling 1022-25–40.88–0–0–4/65

Cressy-Hall, John Walter
Amateur. *b:* 4.8.1843. *d:* 7.4.1894, Kimberley, South Africa. Middle order batsman, change bowler. *Sch* Merchant Taylors and Brighton. *Team* MCC (1873–80).
Career batting
3–5–0–27–12–5.40–0–*ct* 4
Bowling 48–2–24.00–0–0–2/48

Crichton, Henry Thompson
Amateur. *b:* 18.5.1884, Edgbaston, Birminghm. *d:* 1.7.1968, Branksome Park, Poole, Dorset. Middle/lower order right-hand batsman, right-arm medium pace bowler. *Team* Warwickshire (1908, 2 matches).
Career batting
2–3–0–26–26–8.66–0–*ct* 0
Bowling 30–2–15.00–0–0–2/21

He also played for Berkshire.

Crichton, Ian Gordon
Cricketer. *b:* 7.1.1943, St Annes-on-Sea, Lancashire. Tail end left-hand batsman, medium-fast bowler. *Team* Oxford U (1963).
Career batting
1–1–0–4–4–4.00–0–*ct* 0
Bowling 61–0

Crick, Harry
Professional. *b:* 29.1.1910, Sheffield. *d:* 10.2.1960, Near Wyke, Bradford, in a road accident. Lower order right-hand batsman, wicket-keeper. *Teams* Yorkshire (1937–47, 8 matches); Combined Services (1949).
Career batting
11–15–2–124–22–9.53–0–*ct* 20–*st* 8

Crisp, James George
Amateur. *b:* 15.11.1927, Newtown, Montgomeryshire. Lower order right-hand batsman, right-arm fast medium bowler. *Sch* Alleyns. *Team* Oxford U (1951).
Career batting
1–2–1–12–12–12.00–0–*ct* 0
Bowling 26–0

He also played for Suffolk.

Crisp, Robert James
Amateur. *b:* 28.5.1911, Calcutta, India. Lower order right-hand batsman, right-arm fast bowler. *Teams* Rhodesia (1929/30 to 1930/1); Western Province (1931/2 to 1935/6); Worcestershire (1938, 8 matches). *Tours* South Africa to England 1935; Cahn to Ceylon 1936/7. *Tests* South Africa (1935 to 1935/6, 9 matches).
Career batting
62–82–14–888–45–13.05–0–*ct* 27
Bowling 5487–276–19.88–21–4–9/64
Test batting
9–13–1–123–35–10.25–0–*ct* 3
Bowling 747–20–37.35–1–0–5/99

His single tour to England proved most successful: 107 wickets, av 19.58. He moved to England in 1936 and during that summer and the following one played for Sir Julien Cahn's XI, taking 105 wickets in 1936 and 165 in 1937. In 1938 he appeared for Worcs, but an injury limited his County matches. His best bowling was 9/64 for Western Province v Natal at Durban in 1933/4.

Cristofani, Desmond Robert
Amateur. *b:* 14.11.1920, Waverley, New South Wales, Australia. Middle/lower order right-hand batsman, right-arm medium leg break bowler. *Team* New South Wales (1941/2 to 1946/7, 3 matches). *Tour* Australian Services to England, India and Ceylon 1945.

Career batting
18–30–2–749–110*–26.75–1–*ct* 13
Bowling 1581–48–32.93–2–0–5/49

Critchley-Salmonson, Humphrey Seymour Ramsay
Amateur. *b:* 19.1.1894, Chalbury, Dorset. *d:* 24.4.1956, St Mary Church, Devon. Lower order right-hand batsman, right-arm fast-medium bowler. *Sch* Winchester. *Team* Somerset (1910–28, 14 matches). *Tour* Cahn to the Argentine 1929/30.
Career batting
16–23–0–205–66–8.91–0–*ct* 16
Bowling 773–25–30.92–1–0–5/23

He was regarded as the best Public School bowler of his day, bowling at the speed of S. F. Barnes and having the knack of making the ball swerve in late.

Crocker, Jonathan Alfred
Amateur. *b:* 8.10.1874, London. *d:* 21.7.1944, Westminster, London. Middle order batsman, change bowler. *Sch* Eton. *Team* Cambridge U (1894).
Career batting
4–7–1–65–29–10.83–0–*ct* 2
Bowling 132–5–26.40–0–0–2/27

He also played for Hertfordshire.

Crockford, Eric Bertram
Amateur. *b:* 13.10.1888, Wylde Green, Warwickshire. *d:* 17.1.1958, Four Oaks, Sutton Coldfield, Warwickshire. Middle order right-hand batsman. *Sch* Eastbourne. *Team* Warwickshire (1911–22, 21 matches).
Career batting
21–35–0–394–55–11.25–0–*ct* 6
Bowling 199–2–99.50–0–0–1/7

Croft, Colin Everton Hunte
Cricketer. *b*: 15.3.1953, Lancaster Village, Demerara, British Guiana. Lower order right-hand batsman, right-arm fast bowler, deep field. *Teams* Guyana (1971/2 to 1981/2); Lancashire 1977–82, 49 matches). *Tours* West Indies to Australia and New Zealand 1979/80, to England 1980, to Pakistan 1980/1, to Australia 1981/2; West Indies XI to South Africa 1982/3 (no first-class matches). *Tests* West Indies (1976/7 to 1981/2, 27 matches).
Career batting
118–131–50–853–46*–10.53–0–*ct* 25
Bowling 10277–419–24.52–17–1–8/29
Test batting
27–37–22–158–33–10.53–0–*ct* 8
Bowling 2913–125–23.30–3–0–8/29

He played in three Tests on the 1980 tour to England, but took only 9 wickets, av 34.00, and was scarcely more successful in the other first-class matches.

Croft, Peter Downton
Amateur. *b:* 7.7.1933, Purley, Surrey. Middle order right-hand batsman, off break bowler. *Sch* Gresham's Holt. *Team* Cambridge U (1955–57, blue 1955).
Career batting
18–29–2–402–47*–14.88–0–*ct* 8
Bowling 29–0

Croft, Sydney James
Amateur. *b*: 14.1.1883, Gravesend, Kent. *d*: 16.7.1965, Dartford, Kent. Middle order right-hand batsman. *Team* Kent (1902, 2 matches).
Career batting
2–4–0–18–13–4.50–0–*ct* 0

Crofton, Edward Hugh
Amateur. *b:* 7.9.1854, Plymouth. *d:* 15.5.1882, Kilmainham, Dublin. Middle order batsman, bowler. *Team* Hampshire (1881, 3 matches).
Career batting
3–5–0–32–23–6.40–0–*ct* 0
Bowling 42–1–42.00–0–0–1/21

Crofts, Edmund Sclater
Amateur. *b:* 23.1.1859, Winchester, Hampshire. *d:* 23.12.1939, Carlton, Bedford. Middle order batsman. *Sch* Winchester. *Team* Hampshire (1885, 1 match).
Career batting
1–2–0–5–3–2.50–0–*ct* 0

Crole, Gerard Bruce
Amateur. *b:* 7.6.1894, Edinburgh, Scotland. *d:* 31.3.1965, Aberdeen, Scotland. Middle order batsman. *Sch* Edinburgh Academy. *Teams* Oxford U (1920); Scotland (1920).
Career batting
2–3–0–90–47–30.00–0–*ct* 1
Bowling 16–3–5.33–0–0–3/16

Cromack, Bernard
Professional. *b:* 5.6.1937, Rothwell, Leeds, Yorkshire. Lower order right-hand batsman, slow left-arm bowler. *Team* Leicestershire (1959–68, 34 matches).
Career batting
34–55–2–626–55–11.81–0–*ct* 13
Bowling 1006–38–26.47–1–0–6/48

He left the Leics staff at the end of the 1961 season, but re-appeared for the County in one match in 1968.

Cromb, Ian Burns
Amateur. *b:* 25.6.1905, Christchurch, New Zealand. *d:* 6.3.1984, Christchurch, New Zealand. Hard-hitting lower/middle order right-hand batsman, right-arm fast-medium bowler. *Team* Canterbury (1929/30 to 1946/7). *Tour* New Zealand to England 1931. *Tests* New Zealand (1931 to 1931/2, 5 matches).
Career batting
88–148–12–3950–171–29.04–3–*ct* 102
Bowling 6152–222–27.71–10–2–8/70
Test batting
5–8–2–123–51*–20.50–0–*ct* 1
Bowling 442–8–55.25–0–0–3/113
He bowled usefully on his 1931 visit to England and was expected to develop into a very effective bowler, but his later career was confined mainly to Provincial cricket in which he was a leading all-rounder.

Crommelin-Brown, John Louis
Amateur. *b:* 20.10.1888, Delhi, India. *d:* 11.9.1953, Minehead, Somerset. Opening/middle order right-hand batsman. *Sch* Winchester. *Team* Derbyshire (1922–26, 16 matches).
Career batting
16–28–2–659–74–25.34–0–*ct* 9
Bowling 70–1–70.00–0–0–1/29
At Cambridge he appeared in the Freshmen's Match, but no first-class matches. He played soccer for the Corinthians and was a fine billiard player.

Crooke, Frederick James
Amateur. *b:* 21.4.1844, Liverpool. *d:* 6.8.1923, Southsea, Hants. Middle order right-hand batsman, right-hand fast round-arm bowler. *Sch* Winchester. *Teams* Lancashire (1865, 1 match); Gloucestershire (1874–75, 8 matches).
Career batting
21–35–1–573–56*–16.85–0–*ct* 10
Bowling 12–0
From 1866 to 1886 he lived in India and was for many years captain of Calcutta CC. His appearances for Gloucestershire were made whilst home on leave.

Crookes, Dennis Victor
Amateur. *b:* 18.6.1931, Durban, South Africa. Middle/lower order right-hand batsman, leg break bowler. *Sch* Michaelhouse. *Team* Cambridge U (1953–54, blue 1953).
Career batting
11–16–3–227–33–17.46–0–*ct* 4
Bowling 125–3–41.66–0–0–1/0

Crookes, John Edward
Amateur. *b:* 7.3.1890, Horncastle, Lincolnshire. *d:* 8.9.1948, Cuddington, Surrey. Middle order batsman. *Team* Hampshire (1920, 3 matches).
Career batting
3–5–1–50–36*–12.50–0–*ct* 3
Bowling 6–0
He also played for Lincolnshire. He was a sergeant-major in the army.

Crookes, Norman Samuel
Cricketer. *b:* 15.11.1935, Renishaw, Natal, South Africa. Lower order right-hand batsman, off break bowler. *Team* Natal (1962/3 to 1969/70). *Tour* South Africa to England 1965.
Career batting
50–64–5–1123–68–19.03–0–*ct* 51
Bowling 4489–153–29.33–6–1–8/47
Although he was not selected for any of the Tests on his visit to England, he returned the satisfactory figures of 47 wickets, av 19.44.

Crookes, Ralph
Professional. *b:* 9.10.1846, Sheffield, Yorkshire. *d:* 15.2.1897, Sheffield, Yorkshire. Lower order batsman, bowler. *Team* Yorkshire (1879, 1 match).
Career batting
1–2–1–2–2*–2.00–0–*ct* 0
Bowling 14–0

Croom, Alfred John William
Professional. *b:* 23.5.1896, Reading, Berkshire. *d:* 16.8.1947, Oldbury, Worcs. Father of L. C. B. (Warwickshire). Opening/middle order right-hand batsman, right-arm spin bowler. *Team* Warwickshire (1922–39, 394 matches).
Career batting
398–628–65–17692–211–31.42–24–*ct* 296
Bowling 6072–138–44.00–2–0–6/65
He reached 1,000 runs in a season 12 times (best 1,584, av. 38.63, in 1931). His only double century was 211 for Warwickshire v Worcs at Edgbaston in 1934. He appeared for Berkshire as an amateur before joining Warwickshire.

Croom, Leslie Charles Brine
Professional. *b:* 20.4.1920, Reading, Berkshire. Son of A. J. W. (Warwickshire). Opening right-hand batsman. *Team* Warwickshire (1949, 4 matches).
Career batting
4–8–0–73–26–9.12–0–*ct* 0

Croome, Arthur Capel Molyneux
Amateur. *b:* 21.2.1866, Stroud, Gloucestershire. *d:* 11.9.1930, Taplow, Berkshire. Father of Victor (RAF). Middle order right-hand batsman, slow

right-arm bowler. *Sch* Wellington. *Teams* Gloucestershire (1885–92, 30 matches); Oxford U (1887–89, blue 1888–89).
Career batting
51–86–13–978–81–13.39–0–*ct* 38
Bowling 1539–53–29.03–1–1–6/73

He suffered a terrible accident whilst playing for Gloucestershire at Old Trafford in 1887 – in attempting to stop a ball travelling over the boundary he impaled himself in the spike of the railings, the spike entering his neck, and it was at first thought that the injury would prove fatal. Happily he recovered completely. His final first-class appearance was for Gentlemen of England in 1908. He also played for Berkshire. A noted athlete, he took part in the University Sports of 1886 to 1889, winning the hurdles in 1886.

Croome, Victor
Amateur. *b:* 30.11.1899, London. *d:* 1.9.1973, Thaxted, Essex. Son of A. C. M. (Gloucs). Lower order right-hand batsman, wicket-keeper. *Sch* Westminster. *Team* RAF (1928–30).
Career batting
5–8–1–124–36–17.71–0–*ct* 6–*st* 4

Cropper, William
Professional. *b:* 27.12.1862, Brimington, Derbyshire. *d:* 13.1.1889, Grimsby, Lincolnshire, as the result of an accident on the football field. Middle order right-hand batsman, left-arm medium pace bowler. *Team* Derbyshire (1882–87, 56 matches).
Career batting
60–113–4–1636–93–15.00–0–*ct* 26
Bowling 2930–171–17.13–8–0–7/25

His final first-class match was for an England XI 1888.

Crosdale, Gordon
Amateur. *b:* 14.7.1880. *d:* 12.9.1954, Cold Ash, Newbury, Berkshire. Lower order right-hand batsman, wicket-keeper. *Sch* Charterhouse. *Team* Middlesex (1905, 3 matches).
Career batting
3–4–2–30–17*–15.00–0–*ct* 1

Crosfield, Sydney Morland
Amateur. *b:* 12.11.1861, Warrington, Lancashire. *d:* 30.1.1908, Las Palmas, Canary Islands. Hard hitting middle order right-hand batsman, right-arm fast, but after 1882, slow bowler, good cover field. *Sch* Wimbledon School. *Team* Lancashire (1883–99, 90 matches).
Career batting
96–150–14–2027–82*–14.90–0–*ct* 49
Bowling 151–3–50.33–0–0–1/1

He also appeared for Cheshire. A fine shot, he won the Grand Prix de Casino at Monte Carlo in two successive years.

Cross, Anthony John
Cricketer. *b:* 5.8.1945, Fulmer, Buckinghamshire. Middle order right-hand batsman. *Teams* Cambridge U (1966–67); Warwickshire (1969, 1 match).
Career batting
6–10–1–151–39*–16.77–0–*ct* 2
Bowling 19–0

Cross, Eric Percival
Amateur. *b:* 25.6.1896, Handsworth, Birmingham. Lower order right-hand batsman, wicket-keeper. *Sch* Denstone. *Team* Warwickshire (1921–23, 7 matches).
Career batting
7–12–4–61–12*–7.62–0–*ct* 9–*st* 1

He also played for Staffordshire.

Cross, Graham Frederick
Professional. *b:* 15.11.1943, Leicester. Middle/lower order right-hand batsman, right-arm medium pace bowler. *Team* Leicestershire (1961–76, 83 matches).
Career batting
83–128–15–2079–78–18.39–0–*ct* 61
Bowling 2756–92–29.95–0–0–4/28

He was a noted soccer player, appearing for Leicester City, Brighton and Hove Albion, Chesterfield, Preston North End and Lincoln City, and in English Under-23 Internationals.

Cross, James
Professional. *b:* 6.2.1862, Leyland, Lancashire. *d:* 22.3.1927, Great Harwood, Lancashire. Lower order batsman, bowler. *Team* Derbyshire (1897, 9 matches).
Career batting
9–15–4–82–29*–7.45–0–*ct* 4
Bowling 634–22–28.81–0–0–4/68

Cross, Joseph John
Amateur. *b:* February 1849, Merriott, Somerset. *d:* 2.11.1918, Bath, Somerset. Middle order right-hand batsman. *Sch* Uppingham. *Team* Gloucestershire (1870, 2 matches).
Career batting
2–2–0–5–5–2.50–0–*ct* 0

Crosse, Charles William
Amateur. *b:* 13.6.1854, Bushey, Middlesex. *d:* 28.5.1905, Paris, France. Middle order right-hand batsman, good field. *Sch* Rugby. *Team* Oxford U (1875).
Career batting
1–2–0–13–8–6.50–0–*ct* 1

He also played for Devon. He was an excellent rugby footballer, representing England.

Crosse, Edmund Mitchell
Amateur. *b:* 11.12.1882, London. *d:* 28.6.1963, Wandsworth, London. Opening/middle order right-hand batsman. *Sch* Cheltenham. *Team* Northants (1905–10, 48 matches).
Career batting
48–90–4–1168–65–13.58–0–*ct* 16
He captained Northants in 1907.

Crosskey, Thomas Roland
Professional. *b:* 4.7.1905, Hastings, Sussex. *d:* 1971, Newton Abbot, Devon. Right-hand batsman, right-arm fast medium bowler. *Team* Scotland (1949–50).
Career batting
4–8–0–236–81–29.50–0–*ct* 2
Bowling 26–0
He played soccer for Crystal Palace, Hearts and Albion Rovers.

Crossland, Andrew
Professional. *b:* 30.11.1817, Dalton, Huddersfield, Yorkshire. *d:* 17.11.1902, Hull, Yorkshire. Brother of Joseph (Yorkshire 1850), father of S. M. (Yorkshire). Middle order right-hand batsman, right-hand medium pace round-arm bowler. *Team* Yorkshire (1844–55).
Career batting
8–16–1–138–28–9.20–0–*ct* 3–*st* 2
Bowling 146–11+1–13.27–0–0–4/11
He was regarded as the best Yorkshire bowler of his day. His final first-class match was for AEE in 1857.

Crossland, John
Professional. *b:* 2.4.1853, Sutton-in-Ashfield, Notts. *d:* 26.9.1903, Blackburn, Lancashire. Hard-hitting lower order batsman, very fast right-arm bowler, excellent deep field. *Team* Lancashire (1878–85, 71 matches).
Career batting
84–132–25–1172–51–10.95–0–*ct* 32
Bowling 4019–322–12.48–25–6–8/57
His bowling was regarded a 'pure throw' by many experts and several counties refused to play Lancashire so long as Crossland and Nash were in the County Eleven. He was finally forced out of County cricket on the grounds that he was not qualified for Lancashire – his *bona fide* residence being in the County of his birth. His final first-class match was for C. I. Thornton's XI in 1887. He took 112 wickets, av 10.06, in 1882.

Crossland, Samuel Moorhouse
Professional. *b:* 16.8.1851, Leeds, Yorkshire. *d:* 11.4.1906, Wakefield, Yorkshire. Son of Andrew (Yorkshire), nephew of Joseph (Yorkshire 1850). Middle/lower order right-hand batsman, wicket-keeper. *Team* Yorkshire (1883–86, 4 matches).
Career batting
4–6–2–32–20–8.00–0–*ct* 3–*st* 5

Crossman, George Lytton
Amateur. *b:* 18.2.1877, Hambrook, Bristol. *d:* 17.1.1947, Colchester, Essex. Middle order right-hand batsman, leg break bowler. *Sch* Radley. *Team* Gloucestershire (1896, 2 matches).
Career batting
2–4–0–11–5–2.75–0–*ct* 0

Crothers, George Marcus
Amateur. *b:* 30.1.1909, Belfast, Ireland. Right-hand batsman, wicket-keeper. *Sch* Royal Belfast Academical Institution. *Team* Ireland (1931–47).
Career batting
10–19–1–174–41–9.66–0–*ct* 6–*st* 3

Crothers, John Graham
Cricketer. *b:* 8.4.1949, Belfast, Ireland. Right-hand batsman. *Team* Ireland (1972).
Career batting
1–2–0–10–10–5.00–0–*ct* 1

Crouch, Henry Russell
Amateur. *b:* 10.12.1914, Calcutta, India. Middle order right-hand batsman, right-arm medium pace bowler. *Sch* Tonbridge. *Team* Surrey (1946, 1 match). *Tour* Martineau to Egypt 1939 (not first-class).
Career batting
3–3–0–11–7–3.66–0–*ct* 1
Bowling 101–2–50.50–0–0–1/34
His debut in first-class matches was for Minor Counties XI in 1935 – he was a mainstay of Surrey 2nd XI for many years.

Crouch, Maurice Alfred
Amateur. *b:* 9.8.1917, Wisbech, Cambridgeshire. Opening right-hand batsman. *Sch* Oundle. *Teams* MCC (1950); Minor Counties (1952).
Career batting
4–7–0–205–81–29.28–0–*ct* 7
His County cricket was for Cambridgeshire.

Crowder, Alfred James
Amateur. *b:* 1878, Market Harborough, Leics. *d:* 12.10.1961, Isleworth, Middlesex. Opening or middle order batsman. *Team* Somerset (1908, 3 matches).
Career batting
3–6–0–44–24–7.33–0–*ct* 1

Crowder, Frederick
Amateur. *b:* 8.10.1845. *d:* 27.3.1938, Oxford. Opening batsman. *Sch* Rugby. *Team* MCC (1874).
Career batting
3–6–1–25–14–5.00–0–*ct* 1
His first-class debut was for Gentlemen of England in 1873 and his County cricket for Berkshire.

Crowdy, Rev James Gordon
Amateur. *b:* 2.7.1847, Faringdon, Berkshire. *d:* 16.12.1918, Sarum, Winchester, Hants. Middle order right-hand batsman. *Sch* Rugby. *Team* Hampshire (1875–84, 6 matches).
Career batting
7–12–0–112–21–9.33–0–*ct* 0
Bowling 31–1–31.00–0–0–1/31
He did not appear in any first-class matches whilst at Oxford. His first-class debut was for MCC in 1872, playing against Oxford U. He also played for Berkshire, Worcestershire (non-first-class) and Devon.

Crowe, George Lawson
Amateur. *b:* 8.1.1885, Worcester. *d:* 23.6.1976, Bromley, Kent. Middle order right-hand batsman. *Sch* Westminster and Tonbridge. *Team* Worcestershire (1906–13, 23 matches).
Career batting
23–38–2–584–78–16.22–0–*ct* 5
Bowling 35–2–17.50–0–0–1/6

Crowe, Jeffrey John
Cricketer. *b*: 14.9.1958, Auckland, New Zealand. Son of D. W. (Wellington), brother of M. D. (New Zealand). Middle order right-hand batsman. *Teams* South Australia (1977/8 to 1981/2, 34 matches); Auckland (1982/3). *Tours* New Zealand to Australia 1982/3, to England 1983. *Tests* New Zealand (1982/3 to 1983, 4 matches).
Career batting
49–90–10–2554–157–31.92–5–*ct* 52
Bowling 19–1–19.00–0–0–1/10
Test batting
4–7–0–81–36–11.57–0–*ct* 3
He appeared in two Tests on the 1983 tour of England.

Crowe, Martin David
Cricketer. *b*: 22.9.1962, Auckland, New Zealand. Son of D. W. (Wellington), brother of J. J. (New Zealand). Middle order right-hand batsman. *Team* Auckland (1979/80 to 1982/3). *Tours* New Zealand to Australia 1982/3, to England 1983. *Tests* New Zealand (1981/2 to 1983, 7 matches).
Career batting
46–77–12–2731–150–42.01–8–*ct* 49
Bowling 728–28–26.00–1–0–5/69
Test batting
7–12–0–183–46–15.25–0–*ct* 8
Bowling 72–2–36.00–0–0–2/35
He headed the first-class batting averages on the 1983 tour to England with 819 runs, av 58.50, and played in all four Tests. His first-class debut in England was for D. B. Close's XI in 1982.

Crowe, Dr Philip John
Cricketer. *b*: 27.10.1955, Westminster, London. Lower order left-hand batsman, left-arm medium pace bowler. *Team* Oxford U (1982).
Career batting
1–2–0–11–11–5.50–0–*ct* 0
Bowling 121–1–121.00–0–0–1/105
A good rugby footballer, he gained his blue at Oxford and was capped six times for Australia.

Crowhurst, William
Amateur. *b:* 24.10.1849, Chislehurst, Kent. *d:* 4.7.1915, St Mary Cray, Kent. Tail end batsman, right-arm fast bowler. *Team* Kent (1877, 1 match).
Career batting
1–2–0–1–1–0.50–0–*ct* 0
Bowling 46–1–46.00–0–0–1/26

Crowther, Arthur
Professional. *b:* 1.8.1878, Leeds, Yorkshire. *d:* 4.6.1946, Bradford, Yorkshire. Lower order batsman. *Team* Yorkshire (1905, 1 match).
Career batting
1–2–0–0–0–0.00–0–*ct* 1

Crowther, Fred
Amateur. *b:* 22.1.1857, Birstall, Leeds, Yorkshire. *d:* 1899, North Bierley, Yorkshire. Opening right-hand batsman. *Team* L. Hall's XI (1891).
Career batting
1–2–1–60–43*–60.00–0–*ct* 0
He appeared for Yorkshire in 1890 in a non-first-class match.

Crowther, Peter Gwynne
Cricketer. *b:* 26.4.1952, Neath, Glamorgan. Middle order right-hand batsman, off break bowler. *Team* Glamorgan (1977–78, 9 matches).
Career batting
9–14–0–185–99–13.21–0–*ct* 3
Bowling 22–1–22.00–0–0–1/22
He his 99 for Glamorgan v Cambridge U at Fenner's on his first-class debut.

Croxford, Henry
Professional. *b:* 14.6.1845, Hadlow, Kent. *d:* 15.12.1892, Faversham, Kent. Hard-hitting lower order right-hand batsman, right-hand fast round-arm bowler. *Team* Kent (1869–77, 27 matches).
Career batting
27–51–11–472–53–11.80–0–*ct* 9
Bowling 677–31–22.83–2–0–6/45

Crozier, William Magee
Amateur. *b:* 5.12.1873, Dublin, Ireland. *d:* 1.7.1916, Thiepval, France. Right hand batsman. *Sch* Repton. *Team* Dublin University (1895).
Career batting
1–2–0–7–4–3.50–0–*ct* 0
Bowling 42–0

Crump, Brian Stanley
Professional. *b:* 25.4.1938, Stoke-on-Trent, Staffs. Cousin of D. S. Steele (Northants and Derbyshire). Middle order right-hand batsman, right-arm medium off break bowler. *Team* Northants (1960–72, 317 matches).
Career batting
321–479–111–8789–133*–23.88–5–*ct* 144
Bowling 20163–814–24.77–30–5–7/29

He reached 1,000 runs in a season twice (best 1,396, av 29.08, in 1961) and 100 wickets in a season also twice (best 112, av 18.88, in 1965).

Crump, Rev Thomas
Amateur. *b:* 1845, Bristol. *d:* 8.1.1907, East Pennard, Somerset. Middle order right-hand batsman, lob bowler. *Team* Somerset (1885, 1 match).
Career batting
1–1–0–8–8–8.00–0–*ct* 0

He also played for Herefordshire.

Crush, Edmund
Amateur. *b:* 25.4.1917, Dover, Kent. Lower order right-hand batsman, right-arm medium pace off break bowler. *Team* Kent (1946–49, 45 matches).
Career batting
45–72–5–1078–51–16.08–0–*ct* 23
Bowling 3163–83–38.10–2–0–6/50

Crutchley, Edward
Amateur. *b:* 2.4.1922, Paddington, London. *d:* 18.10.1982, Guildford, Surrey. Son of G. E. V. (Middlesex). Middle order right-hand batsman. *Sch* Harrow. *Team* Middlesex (1947, 2 matches).
Career batting
2–4–0–28–14–7.00–0–*ct* 1

Crutchley, Gerald Edward Victor
Amateur. *b:* 19.11.1890, London. *d:* 17.8.1969, St John's Wood, London. Father of Edward (Middlesex). Opening/middle order batsman, right-arm medium pace leg break bowler. *Sch* Harrow. *Teams* Oxford U (1910–12, blue 1912); Middlesex (1910–30, 54 matches).
Career batting
123–200–17–4112–181–22.46–5–*ct* 53
Bowling 2191–67–32.70–0–0–4/52

In the 1912 University match he was 99 not out at the close on the first day, then taken ill with measles overnight and compelled to retire from the match. His last first-class match was for Leveson-Gower's XI in 1932. During the First World War he was a prisoner in Germany for almost four years.

Crutchley, Percy Edward
Amateur. *b:* 24.7.1855, Parsontown, King's County, Ireland. *d:* 16.10.1940, Sunninghill, Berkshire. Hard-hitting middle order right-hand batsman, right-hand slow round-arm bowler, excellent long-stop. *Sch* Harrow. *Team* MCC (1876).
Career batting
3–5–1–128–84–32.00–0–*ct* 0
Bowling 68–2–34.00–0–0–2/68

Whilst at Cambridge he did not appear in any first-class matches. His final first-class match was for Gentlemen in 1878.

Cruwys, Rev Robert Geoffrey
Amateur. *b:* 10.3.1884, Cruwys-Morchard, Devon. *d:* 25.8.1951, Cruwys-Morchard, Devon. Middle order batsman, useful bowler. *Sch* Blundell's. *Team* Oxford U (1907).
Career batting
1–2–0–29–19–14.50–0–*ct* 0

He played for Devon commencing 1903.

Crwys-Williams, Gareth
Amateur. *b:* 27.12.1907, Crickhowell, Breconshire. *d:* 8.3.1970, Llangollen, Denbighshire. Lower order batsman, left-arm medium fast bowler. *Sch* Bancrofts. *Team* MCC (1934).
Career batting
1–1–1–0–0*–no av–0–*ct* 0
Bowling 18–0

He also played for Monmouthshire and Lincolnshire.

Cudworth, Henry
Amateur. *b:* 1873, Burnley, Lancashire. *d:* 5.4.1914, Burnley, Lancashire. Middle order batsman. *Team* Lancashire (1900, 1 match).
Career batting
1–1–0–4–4–4.00–0–*ct* 0

He hit a fine century for Lancs v West Indies in 1900 – the West Indies tour that year however was not first class.

Cuffe, Charles Richard
Amateur. *b:* 5.8.1914, Dublin, Ireland. *d:* 10.11.1972, Dublin, Ireland. Left-hand batsman, wicket-keeper. *Sch* Stonyhurst. *Team* Ireland (1936–39).
Career batting
3–6–2–61–18–15.25–0–*ct* 2–*st* 4

Cuffe, John Alexander
Professional. *b:* 26.6.1880, Toowoomba, Queensland, Australia. *d:* 16.5.1931. He was found drowned at Burton-on-Trent, Staffs. Middle order right-hand batsman, slow left-arm bowler. *Teams* New South Wales (1902/3, 1 match); Worcestershire (1903–14, 215 matches).
Career batting
221–368–32–7476–145–22.25–4–*ct* 126
Bowling 18803–738–25.47–33–7–9/38

He reached 1,000 runs in a season three times (best 1,112, av 31.77, in 1906) and 100 wickets twice (best 110, av 23.56, in 1911). In 1911 he performed the 'double'. His best bowling was 9/38 for Worcestershire v Yorkshire at Bradford in 1907. He played soccer for Glossop. At the time of his death he had just taken up an appointment as coach at Repton School.

Cull, George
Professional. *b:* 1856, Lymington, Hants. *d:* 9.5.1898, Sandown, Isle of Wight. Lower order batsman, wicket-keeper. *Team* Hampshire (1877, 2 matches).
Career batting
2–4–0–14–7–3.50–0–*ct* 1

Cullen, Alexander Coney
Amateur. *b:* 17.1.1889, Uddingston, Lanarkshire, Scotland. *d:* 25.2.1922, Glasgow, Scotland. Left-hand batsman, leg break bowler. *Team* Scotland (1912–21).
Career batting
4–7–2–34–11–6.80–0–*ct* 2
Bowling 42–0

Cullen, Leonard
Professional. *b:* 23.11.1914, Johannesburg, South Africa. Lower order right-hand batsman, right-arm medium pace bowler. *Sch* St Andrew's College, Bloemfontein, South Africa. *Team* Northants (1934–35, 18 matches).
Career batting
18–31–1–253–40–8.43–0–*ct* 4
Bowling 650–11–59.09–0–0–3/73

Whilst playing for Northants v Glamorgan at Llanelly in 1935, he had the frightening experience of falling out of his bedroom window whilst sleep-walking and was badly bruised.

Cullimore, Martin Henry
Amateur. *b:* 4.12.1908, Stroud, Gloucs. Middle order right-hand batsman. *Sch* Wycliffe. *Team* Gloucestershire (1929, 3 matches).
Career batting
3–3–0–19–15–6.33–0–*ct* 0

Cullinan, Mark Ronald
Cricketer. *b:* 3.4.1957, Johannesburg, South Africa. Lower order right-hand batsman, wicket-keeper. *Team*: Oxford U (1983, blue).
Career batting
9–9–2–60–27–8.57–0–*ct* 16

His first-class debut was for South African Universities in 1979/80.

Cumberbatch, C. P.
Professional. *b:* 22.11.1882, Barbados. *d:* 15.2.1922, Port of Spain, Trinidad. Lower order batsman, fast bowler. *Team* Trinidad (1904/5 to 1921/2). *Tour* West Indies to England 1906.
Career batting
30–50–10–804–127*–20.10–1–*ct* 31
Bowling 1636–92–17.78–6–2–8/27

He performed moderately on his single tour to England.

Cumberlege, Barry Stephenson
Amateur. *b:* 5.6.1891, Newcastle-on-Tyne. *d:* 22.9.1970, Folkestone, Kent. Son of C. F. (Surrey). Opening right-hand batsman. *Sch* Durham. *Teams* Cambridge U (1913, blue); Kent (1923–24, 6 matches).
Career batting
14–23–3–763–172–38.15–1–*ct* 5
Bowling 13–0

He also played for Durham and Northumberland. A noted rugby footballer, he played for Cambridge against Oxford four times as scrum-half and for Blackheath and England in the 1920s.

Cumberlege, Charles Farrington
Amateur. *b:* 29.7.1851, Kurreebee, India. *d:* 12.2.1929, Ealing, Middlesex. Father of B. S. (Kent). Middle order right-hand batsman. *Sch* Rossall. *Team* Surrey (1872, 2 matches).
Career batting
2–4–0–30–26–7.50–0–*ct* 1

He also appeared for Northumberland and Wiltshire.

Cumbes, James
Cricketer. *b*: 4.5.1944, East Didsbury, Manchester, Lancashire. Brother-in-law of R.

Collins (Lancashire). Lower order right-hand batsman, right-arm fast medium bowler. *Teams* Lancashire (1963–71, 9 matches); Surrey (1968–69, 29 matches); Worcestershire (1972–81, 109 matches); Warwickshire (1982, 14 matches).
Career batting
161–133–67–499–43–7.56–0–*ct* 38
Bowling 11447–379–30.20–13–0–6/24
A good soccer player, he kept goal for Tranmere Rovers, West Bromwich Albion, Aston Villa and Worcester City.

Cuming, Thomas
Amateur. *b:* 21.4.1893, Woolwich, Kent. *d:* 18.8.1960, Bexhill, Sussex. Stylish middle order batsman, change bowler. *Sch* Malvern. *Teams* Middlesex (1913, 1 match); Ceylon (1925/6 to 1930/1).
Career batting
5–8–0–112–36–14.00–0–*ct* 1
Bowling 22–1–22.00–0–0–1/12

Cumming, Bruce Leonard
Amateur. *b:* 11.7.1916, Germiston, Transvaal, South Africa. *d:* 5.5.1968, Johannesburg, South Africa. Hard-hitting middle order right-hand batsman, right-arm medium pace bowler. *Teams* Oxford U (1936–37); Sussex (1936–38, 17 matches).
Career batting
24–36–1–684–60–19.54–0–*ct* 10
Bowling 52–2–26.00–0–0–2/19

Cunis, Robert Smith
Cricketer. *b:* 5.1.1941, Whangarei, New Zealand. Middle/lower order right-hand batsman, right-arm fast medium bowler. *Teams* Auckland (1960/1 to 1973/4); Northern Districts (1975/6 to 1976/7). *Tours* New Zealand to England 1969, to India and Pakistan 1969/70, to Australia 1969/70, 1970/1, to West Indies 1971/2; Rest of World to Australia 1971/2. *Tests* New Zealand (1965/6 to 1971/2, 20 matches).
Career batting
132–157–45–1849–111–16.50–1–*ct* 30
Bowling 10287–386–26.65–18–2–7/29
Test batting
20–31–8–295–51–12.82–0–*ct* 1
Bowling 1887–51–37.00–1–0–6/76
On his 1969 visit to England he was unable to find his form until late in the tour. His 38 first-class wickets cost 27.76.

Cunliffe, Charles Morley
Amateur. *b:* 2.9.1858, Leyton, Essex. *d:* 15.10.1884, Davos-Platz, Switzerland, of consumption aged 26. Middle order right-hand batsman, right-hand medium pace round-arm bowler. *Sch* Rugby. *Team* Kent (1877–80, 23 matches).
Career batting
25–44–4–378–47–9.45–0–*ct* 18
Bowling 1395–93–15.00–11–3–7/25

Cunliffe, Sir Foster Hugh Egerton
Amateur. *b:* 17.8.1875, Acton Park, Wrexham, Denbighshire. *d:* 10.7.1916, of wounds at Ovilliers La Boiselle, France. Lower order left-hand batsman, left-arm medium pace bowler. *Sch* Eton. *Teams* Oxford U (1895–98, blue all four years); Middlesex (1897–03, 18 matches).
Career batting
56–85–16–1053–70–15.26–0–*ct* 25
Bowling 5120–235–21.78–15–5–8/26
He also played for Shropshire. His final first-class match was for I Zingari in 1904. He was a distinguished military historian.

Cunliffe, Robert Lionel Brooke
Amateur. *b:* 15.3.1895, Woolwich, Kent. Lower order right-hand batsman, leg break and googly bowler. *Team* Royal Navy (1914–29).
Career batting
10–18–2–335–87–23.92–0–*ct* 2
Bowling 582–16–36.37–1–0–5/78

Cunningham, Alec George Gordon
Amateur. *b:* 15.7.1905, Knowle, Somerset. *d:* 21.7.1981, Keynsham, Bristol. Tail end right-hand batsman, wicket-keeper. *Team* Somerset (1930, 2 matches).
Career batting
2–3–2–10–6*–10.00–0–*ct* 3–*st* 1

Cunningham, Edward James
Cricketer. *b*: 16.5.1962, Oxford. Middle order left-hand batsman; off break bowler. *Sch* Marlborough. *Team* Gloucestershire (1982–83, 8 matches).
Career batting
8–12–3–109–29*–12.11–0–*ct* 4
Bowling 194–4–48.50–0–0–2/55

Cunningham, William Henry Ranger
Amateur. *b:* 23.1.1900, Christchurch, New Zealand. Lower order right-hand batsman, right-arm medium-fast bowler. *Team* Canterbury (1922/3 to 1930/1). *Tours* New Zealand to Australia 1925/6, to England 1927.
Career batting
32–50–16–396–33*–11.64–0–*ct* 8
Bowling 3122–91–34.30–4–0–6/33
Although he proved the best bowler on his tour to Australia, his form in England in 1927 was a complete disappointment.

Cupitt, Joseph
Professional. *b:* 25.9.1867, Barrow Hill, Derbyshire. *d:* 6.5.1932, South Kirkby, Yorkshire. Lower order batsman, left-arm medium pace off break bowler. *Team* Derbyshire (1905, 2 matches).
Career batting
2–4–2–19–13–9.50–0–*ct* 0
Bowling 145–3–48.33–0–0–2/24

Curgenven, Gilbert
Amateur. *b:* 1.12.1882, Derby. *d:* 26.5.1934, Birmingham. Brother of H. G. (Derbyshire), son of W. G. (Derbyshire). Middle order right-hand batsman, slow bowler. *Sch* Repton. *Team* Derbyshire (1901–22, 95 matches).
Career batting
95–169–5–3440–124–20.97–3–*ct* 40
Bowling 1163–25–46.52–0–0–3/32

Curgenven, Henry Grafton
Amateur. *b:* 22.12.1875, Derby. *d:* 14.2.1959, Bridgend, Glamorgan. Brother of Gilbert (Derbyshire) and son of W. G. (Derbyshire). middle order right-hand batsman, right-arm fast-medium bowler. *Sch* Repton. *Teams* Derbyshire (1896–97, 9 matches); Cambridge U (1897).
Career batting
11–14–1–125–26–9.61–0–*ct* 6
Bowling 223–7–31.85–0–0–2/9
He was later engaged as a club professional.

Curgenven, Dr William Grafton
Amateur. *b:* 30.11.1841, Plymouth, Devon. *d:* 18.3.1910, Fareham, Hants. Father of Gilbert (Derbyshire) and H. G. (Derbyshire). Middle order right-hand batsman. *Sch* Wellingborough and Aldenham. *Team* Derbyshire (1872–78, 17 matches).
Career batting
17–30–0–376–71–12.53–0–*ct* 5

Curle, Arthur Charles
Amateur. *b:* 27.7.1895, Leamington Spa, Warwickshire. *d:* 1966, Aylesbury, Bucks. Brother of Gerald (Warwickshire). Middle order left-hand batsman, left-arm bowler. *Teams* Warwickshire (1920, 3 matches); Rhodesia (1922/3).
Career batting
4–6–1–102–40–20.40–0–*ct* 0
Bowling 14–0

Curle, Gerald
Amateur. *b:* 7.6.1893, Leamington Spa, Warwickshire. *d:* 4.3.1977, Budleigh Salterton, Devon. Brother of A. C. (Warwickshire). Middle order right-hand batsman, off break bowler. *Sch* King Edward's, Birmingham. *Team* Warwickshire (1913, 5 matches).
Career batting
5–9–0–54–34–6.00–0–*ct* 2
Bowling 3–1–3.00–0–0–1/3

Curley, Simon Andrew
Amateur. *b:* 21.7.1917, Dublin, Ireland. Left-hand batsman. *Team* Ireland (1948–51).
Career batting
5–10–1–175–43–19.44–0–*ct* 6

Curran, Kevin Malcolm
Cricketer. *b*: 7.9.1959, Rusape, Rhodesia. Middle order right-hand batsman, right-arm fast medium bowler. *Team* Zimbabwe (1980/1 to 1982/3). *Tour* Zimbabwe to England 1982.
Career batting
12–17–4–323–96–24.86–0–*ct* 3
Bowling 627–25–25.08–0–0–4/24

Currie, Cecil Edmund
Amateur. *b:* 4.4.1861, Bright Waltham, Berkshire. *d:* 2.1.1937, Staines, Middlesex. Lower order right-hand batsman, right-arm slow bowler, splendid field. *Sch* Marlborough. *Teams* Hampshire (1881–85, 16 matches); Cambridge U (1883).
Career batting
20–35–10–300–32–12.00–0–*ct* 9
Bowling 1426–64–22.28–2–1–8/57
His last first-class appearance was for Oxford and Cambridge, Past and Present in 1890.

Currie, Frederick Alexander
Amateur. *b:* 23.9.1851, India. *d:* 13.6.1902, Aldeburgh, Suffolk. Middle order right-hand batsman. *Sch* Harrow. *Team* MCC (1894).
Career batting
1–2–0–10–7–5.00–0–*ct* 1

Currie, John David
Amateur. *b:* 3.5.1932, Clifton, Bristol. Attacking middle order right-hand batsman. *Sch* Bristol GS. *Teams* Somerset (1953, 1 match); Oxford U (1956–57).
Career batting
10–20–1–283–38–14.89–0–*ct* 4
An excellent rugby footballer he played for Gloucester, Oxford U and England.

Cursham, Arthur William
Amateur. *b:* 14.3.1853, Wilford, Notts. *d:* 24.12.1884, Florida, USA, of yellow fever. Brother of H. A. (Notts). Middle order right-hand batsman, slow round-arm bowler, brilliant cover field. *Sch* Oakham School. *Teams*

Nottinghamshire (1876–78, 12 matches); Derbyshire (1879–80, 9 matches).
Career batting
21–35–0–314–67–8.97–0–*ct* 10
Bowling 49–1–49.00–0–0–1/39

A noted soccer player with Notts County and Nottingham Forest, he represented England six times at outside right 1876–83, on two occasions with his brother H. A. in the side. He emigrated to Florida, but died within a year of reaching there.

Cursham, Henry Alfred
Amateur. *b:* 27.11.1859, Wilford, Notts. *d:* 6.8.1941, Holme Pierrepont, Notts. Brother of A. W. (Notts and Derbyshire). Lower order right-hand batsman, wicket-keeper. *Sch* Repton. *Team* Nottinghamshire (1880–1904, 2 matches).
Career batting
2–3–1–41–25*–20.50–0–*ct* 1
Bowling 43–0

His two appearances in first-class cricket were separated by 24 years. A noted soccer player for Notts County and Corinthians, he appeared in eight internationals for England, 1880-84, on two occasions with his brother A. W. in the side.

Curteis, Edward Witherden
Amateur. *b:* 17.4.1853, Warminster, Wiltshire. *d:* 25.2.1902, Mottram, Macclesfield, Cheshire. Middle order right-hand batsman. *Sch* Tonbridge. *Team* Kent (1877, 1 match).
Career batting
2–3–0–17–8–5.66–0–*ct* 0

His final first-class match was for MCC in 1887.

Curteis, Francis Algernon
Amateur. *b:* 26.6.1856, Bideford, Devon. *d:* 1.5.1928, Tenby, Pembrokeshire. Lower order batsman, fast bowler. *Sch* Malvern. *Team* Gloucestershire (1884, 6 matches).
Career batting
6–10–1–72–27*–8.00–0–*ct* 3
Bowling 127–0

He also played for Devon.

Curteis, Herbert
Amateur. *b:* 14.4.1849, Windmill Hill, Hailsham, Sussex. *d:* 28.10.1919, Windmill Hill, Hailsham, Sussex. Son of H. M. (Sussex), brother of R. M. (Sussex). Lower order right-hand batsman, right-hand medium round-arm bowler. *Sch* Westminster. *Team* Sussex (1873, 1 match).
Career batting
4–6–1–48–25–9.60–0–*ct* 0

His last first-class match was for MCC in 1880. He did not appear in any first-class matches whilst at Oxford U.

Curteis, Herbert Mascall
Amateur. *b:* 8.1.1823, Florence, Italy. *d:* 16.6.1895, Windmill Hill, Hailsham, Sussex. Father of Herbert (Sussex) and R. M. (Sussex). Middle order right-hand batsman, slow round-arm bowler, good deep field. *Sch* Westminster. *Teams* Oxford U (1841–42, blue both years); Sussex (1846–60, 43 matches).
Career batting
57–102–20–560–29–6.82–0–*ct* 11
Bowling 27–1+10–27.00–0–0–3/?

He was for many years a liberal supporter of Sussex cricket. He was MP for Rye.

Curteis, Robert Mascall
Amateur. *b:* 12.10.1851, Windmill Hill, Hailsham, Sussex. *d:* 21.1.1927, Uckfield, Sussex. Son of H. M. (Sussex), brother of Herbert (Sussex). Middle order right-hand batsman, good field. *Sch* Westminster. *Team* Sussex (1873–78, 9 matches).
Career batting
11–18–1–117–41–6.93–0–*ct* 6

He did not appear in any first-class matches whilst at Oxford U. His last first-class match was for MCC in 1881.

Curteis, Rev Thomas Spencer
Amateur. *b:* 10.3.1843, Shelton, Norfolk. *d:* 5.6.1914, Brampton, Suffolk. Lower order batsman, left-hand fast round-arm bowler. *Sch* Bury St Edmunds School. *Team* Cambridge U (1864-65, blue both years).
Career batting
7–13–4–65–16–7.22–0–*ct* 6
Bowling 447–23+1–19.43–0–0–4/23

He played for Norfolk, Suffolk and Cheshire at various times.

Curtis, Andrew David
Cricketer. *b:* 12.1.1943, Bedford. Opening right-hand batsman. *Team* Oxford U (1966).
Career batting
1–1–0–15–15–15.00–0–*ct* 0

His County cricket was for Bedfordshire.

Curtis, Ian James
Cricketer. *b*: 13.5.1959, Purley, Surrey. Lower order left-hand batsman, slow left-arm bowler. *Sch* Whitgift. *Teams* Oxford U (1980–82, blue 1980 and 1982); Surrey (1983, 13 matches).
Career batting
30–29–13–76–20*–4.75–0–*ct* 7
Bowling 2073–50–41.46–2–0–6/28

He also represented Oxford at rugby fives.

Curtis, John Stafford
Professional. *b:* 21.12.1887, Barrow-upon-Soar, Leics. *d:* 8.3.1972, Leicester. Lower order right-hand batsman, off break bowler. *Team* Leicestershire (1906–21, 36 matches).
Career batting
36–57–4–868–66–16.37–0–*ct* 14
Bowling 2334–71–32.87–4–0–7/75

Curtis, Timothy Herbert William
(registered at birth as Roderick Herbert William Curtis)
Amateur. *b:* 3.8.1882, Elham, Kent. *d:* 11.6.1966, Little Waltham, Essex. Middle order batsman. *Sch* Harrow. *Team* Sussex (1912, 1 match).
Career batting
1–2–0–3–2–1.50–0–*ct* 0

Curtis, Timothy Stephen
Cricketer. *b*: 15.1.1960, Chislehurst, Kent. Middle order right-hand batsman, leg break bowler. *Sch* RGS Worcester. *Teams* Worcestershire (1979–83, 27 matches); Cambridge U (1983, blue).
Career batting
38–68–11–1404–92–24.63–0–*ct* 19
Bowling 172–4–43.00–0–0–2/53

Curtis, William Frederick
Amateur. *b:* 29.5.1881, Leicester. *d:* 23.12.1962, Leicester. Middle order right-hand batsman. *Team* Leicestershire (1911–20, 5 matches).
Career batting
5–8–0–69–38–8.62–0–*ct* 0
Being in the legal profession he was unable to appear regularly in County cricket, but was a stalwart of the Leicester Ivanhoe Club.

Curwen, Wilfred John Hutton
Amateur. *b:* 14.4.1883, Beckenham, Kent. *d:* 9.5.1915, near Poperinghe, Belgium. He was killed in action. Middle/lower order right-hand batsman, right-arm fast-medium bowler. *Sch* Charterhouse. *Teams* Oxford U (1906, blue); Surrey (1909, 4 matches). *Tours* MCC to New Zealand 1906/7, to Australia 1911/2 (minor matches only).
Career batting
25–44–5–511–76–13.10–0–*ct* 12
Bowling 851–26–32.73–1–0–5/81
His final first-class match was for MCC in 1910, after which he went to Australia, and thus played in emergency for MCC in 1911/12. An excellent soccer player he was awarded his blue at Oxford.

Curzon, Christopher Colin
Cricketer. *b:* 22.12.1958, Lenton, Notts. Brother of J. T. (Notts). Lower order right-hand batsman, wicket-keeper. Nottinghamshire (1978–80, 17 matches); Hampshire (1981, 1 match).
Career batting
18–23–5–307–45–17.05–0–*ct* 32–*st* 3

Curzon, John Timothy
Cricketer. *b:* 4.6.1954, Lenton, Notts. Brother of C. C. (Notts and Hants). Lower order right-hand batsman, right-arm medium pace bowler. *Team* Nottinghamshire (1978, 1 match).
Career batting
1–1–0–1–1–1.00–0–*ct* 1
Bowling 22–0

Cushing, Vincent Gordon Burke
Cricketer. *b:* 17.1.1950, Chichester, Sussex. Middle order right-hand batsman. *Sch* KCS, Wimbledon. *Team* Oxford U (1971–73, blue 1973).
Career batting
14–25–5–565–77*–28.25–0–*ct* 7

Cuthbertson, Arthur
Professional. *b:* 25.8.1901, Belford, Northumberland. *d:* 13.2.1979, Reading, Berkshire. Lower order right-hand batsman, right-arm medium pace bowler. *Team* MCC (1924)
Career batting
1–2–0–7–6–3.50–0–*ct* 0
Bowling 33–1–33.00–0–0–1/23
His County cricket was for Hertfordshire.

Cuthbertson, Edward Hedley
Amateur. *b:* 15.12.1887, Hackney, Middlesex. *d:* 24.7.1917, Amara, Mesopotamia. He was killed in action. Brother of G. B. (Sussex and Middlesex). Sound defensive left-hand batsman, wicket-keeper. *Sch* Malvern. *Team* Cambridge U (1908–10).
Career batting
3–6–1–32–18–6.40–0–*ct* 4–*st* 3
His County cricket was for Hertfordshire. His final first-class match was for MCC in 1914. He obtained his blue for soccer.

Cuthbertson, Geoffrey Bourke
Amateur. *b:* 23.3.1901, Hampstead, London. Brother of E. H. (Cambridge U). Hard-hitting opening right-hand batsman. *Sch* Malvern. *Teams* Cambridge U (1920–22); Sussex (1920, 1 match); Middlesex (1921–27, 17 matches); Northants (1935–38, 43 matches).
Career batting
79–140–9–1991–96–15.19–0–*ct* 32
He captained Northants in 1936 and 1937. He also played for Hertfordshire.

Cuthbertson, John Layton
Amateur. *b:* 24.2.1942, Bombay, India. Middle order right-hand batsman, right-arm medium pace bowler. *Sch* Rugby. *Teams* Oxford U (1962–63, blue both years); Surrey (1963, 7 matches).
Career batting
28–51–7–1294–94–29.40–0–*ct* 21
Bowling 1646–34–48.41–1–0–5/32
He was awarded his hockey blue whilst at Oxford.

Cutler, Roy William
Cricketer. *b:* 28.3.1945, West Hartlepool, Co Durham. Lower order batsman, right-arm medium-fast bowler. *Team* Cambridge U (1965–66).
Career batting
6–12–1–79–18–7.18–0–*ct* 1
Bowling 341–9–37.88–1–0–5/39

Cutmore, James Albert
Professional. *b:* 28.12.1898, Walthamstow, Essex. Opening right-hand batsman, right-arm medium pace bowler. *Team* Essex (1924–36, 342 matches).
Career batting
342–593–36–15937–238*–28.61–15–*ct* 121
Bowling 687–11–62.45–0–0–2/31
He reached 1,000 runs in 11 seasons (best 1876, av 40.78, in 1934). His single double century was 238* for Essex v Gloucs at Bristol in 1927.

Cuttell, William
Professional. *b:* 28.1.1835, Sheffield, Yorkshire. *d:* 10.6.1896, Sheffield, Yorkshire. Father of W. R. (Lancashire). Middle order right-hand batsman, 'excellent' bowler. *Team* Yorkshire (1862–71, 15 matches).
Career batting
15–29–7–272–56–12.36–0–*ct* 4
Bowling 596–36+2–16.55–2–0–6/48

Cuttell, Willis Robert
Professional. *b:* 13.9.1864, Sheffield, Yorkshire. *d:* 9.12.1929, Nelson, Lancashire. Son of William (Yorkshire). Middle/lower order right-hand batsman, right-arm slow-medium leg break bowler. *Team* Lancashire (1896–1906, 213 matches). *Tours* Hawke to South Africa 1898/9. *Tests* England (1898/9, 2 matches).
Career batting
227–315–31–5938–137–20.90–5–*ct* 140
Bowling 15519–792–19.59–49–8–8/105
Test batting
2–4–0–65–21–16.25–0–*ct* 2
Bowling 73–6–12.16–0–0–3/17
He appeared in two non-first-class matches for Yorkshire in 1890. He scored 1,000 runs in a season twice (best 1054, av 26.35, in 1899) and took 100 wickets in a season four times (best 120, av 16.45, in 1897). In 1898 he performed the 'double'.

Cuyler, Sir Charles
Amateur. *b:* 15.8.1867, Oakleaze, Gloucestershire. *d:* 1.10.1919, Shotover, Oxon. Left-hand batsman. *Sch* Clifton. *Team* MCC (1895).
Career batting
1–2–0–0–0–0.00–0–*ct* 0

DA COSTA, OSCAR C.
Amateur. *b:* 11.9.1907, Jamaica, *d:* 1.10.1936, Jamaica. Middle order right-hand batsman, right-arm medium pace bowler. *Team* Jamaica (1928/9 to 1934/5). *Tour* West Indies to England 1933. *Tests* West Indies (1929/30 to 1934/5, 5 matches).
Career batting
39–64–11–1563–105*–29.49–1–*ct* 30
Bowling 1766–44–40.13–0–0–4/16
Test batting
5–9–1–153–39–19.12–0–*ct* 5
Bowling 175–3–58.33–0–0–1/14
In 1933 in England he hit 1,046 runs, av 26.82.

Dacre, Charles Christian Ralph
Amateur, but changed to professional in 1930. *b:* 15.5.1899, Devenport, New Zealand. *d:* 2.11.1975, Devenport, New Zealand. Middle order right-hand batsman, slow left-arm bowler, good field. *Teams* Auckland (1914/5 to 1932/3); Gloucestershire (1928–36, 191 matches). *Tours* New Zealand to England 1927, to Australia 1925/6, 1927/8; Tennyson to Jamaica 1931/2.
Career batting
268–439–20–12230–223–29.19–24–*ct* 166–*st* 6
Bowling 1219–39–31.25–1–0–5/35
An outstanding schoolboy cricketer, he hit 1,817 runs and took 149 wickets in all cricket 1912/3, and made his first-class debut in 1914/15. He hit 1,000 runs in a season seven times (best 1,413, av 33.64, in 1930). His only double century was 223 for Gloucs v Worcs at Worcester in 1930.

Daer, Arthur George
Amateur. *b:* 22.11.1906, Bishopsgate, London. *d:* 16.7.1980, Torquay, Devon. Brother of H.B. (Essex). Lower order right-hand batsman, right-arm fast-medium bowler. *Teams* Essex (1925–35, 100 matches).
Career batting
100–141–42–1469–59–14.83–0–*ct* 48
Bowling 6182–195–31.70–3–0–6/38

Daer, Harry Bruce
Professional, *b:* 10.12.1918, Hammersmith, London, *d:* 19.12.1980, Plymouth, Devon. Brother of A.G. (Essex). Tail end right-hand batsman, right-arm medium pace bowler. *Team* Essex (1938–39, 9 matches).
Career batting
9–12–3–60–17–6.66–0–*ct* 4
Bowling 387–11–35.18–0–0–3/21

D'Aeth, Edward Knatchbull Hughes
Amateur, *b:* 11.9.1866, Wingham, Kent. *d:* 19.9.1923, New York, USA. Brother of L. N. H. (MCC). Hard hitting middle order right-hand batsman, right-arm fast medium bowler. *Sch* Haileybury. *Team* Oxford U (1885).
Career batting
3–5–0–44–22–8.80–*ct* 1

D'Aeth, Lewis Narbrough Hughes
Amateur. *b:* 13.3.1858, Wingham, Kent. *d:* 21.10.1920, Mark Cross, Sussex. Brother of E.K.H. (Oxford U). Useful middle order batsman. *Sch* Harrow. *Team* MCC (1894).
Career batting
1–2–0–0–0–0.00–0–*ct* 0

Daffen, Arthur
Amateur, *b:* 30.12.1861, East Retford, Notts. *d:* 9.7.1938, Victoria Park, Perth, Australia. Sound middle order right hand batsman, right-arm fast bowler, good deep field. *Team* Kent (1890–91, 16 matches).
Career batting
16–27–3–399–72*–16.62–0–*ct* 8
Bowling 144–7–20.57–0–0–4/5
He also appeared for Berkshire.

Daft, Charles Frederick
Professional. *b:* 8.6.1830, Nottingham. *d:* 9.3.1915, Nottingham. Brother of Richard (Notts), uncle of H.B. (Notts) and R.P. (Notts). Middle order right-hand batsman, right-hand medium pace round arm bowler. *Team* Nottinghamshire (1862–64, 14 matches).
Career batting
17–29–1–392–46–14.00–0–*ct* 6

Daft, Harry Butler
Amateur until 1890, professional from 1891. *b:* 5.4.1866, Radcliffe on Trent, Notts. *d:* 12.1.1945, High Cross, Herts. Son of Richard (Notts), brother of R.P. (Notts), nephew of C.F. (Notts). Defensive middle order right-hand batsman, occasional slow bowler. *Sch* Trent College. *Team* Nottinghamshire (1885–99, 190 matches).
Career batting
200–309–34–4370–92*–15.89–0–*ct* 81
Bowling 2239–86–26.03–1–0–5/79
An excellent soccer player he was outside left for Notts County, Nottingham Forest, and England; he also played in the lacrosse England trials.

Daft, Richard
Amateur to 1858, professional 1859 to 1880, amateur 1881 to retirement. *b:* 2.11.1835, Nottingham. *d:* 18.7.1900, Radcliffe on Trent, Notts. Brother of C.F. (Notts), father of H.B. (Notts) and R.P. (Notts). Brilliant middle order right-hand batsman, occasional slow bowler, good field. *Team* Nottinghamshire (1858–91, 157

matches). *Tour* Daft to North America 1879 (not first-class).
Career batting
254–431–36–9788–161–25.42–7–*ct* 155
Bowling 1070–51–20.98–2–0–6/59

About 1870 he was regarded as the best professional batsman in England. He captained Notts 1871–80. He headed the first-class batting averages in 1867 (377 runs, av 53.85) and was second to W. G. Grace in 1869, 1870, 1871 and 1873.

Daft, Richard Parr
Amateur. *b:* 25.10.1863, Radcliffe on Trent, Notts. *d:* 27.3.1934, Radcliffe on Trent, Notts. Son of Richard (Notts), brother of H.B. (Notts), nephew of C.F. (Notts). Middle order right-hand batsman, right-arm medium pace bowler. *Sch* Trent College. *Team* Nottinghamshire (1886, 1 match).
Career batting
1–1–0–5–5–5.00–0–*ct* 0

He also played for Berkshire.

Daily, Charles Edwin
Professional. *b:* 28.4.1900, Ockley, Surrey. *d:* 30.6.1974, Ockley, Surrey. Middle order right hand batsman. *Team* Surrey (1923–29, 45 matches).
Career batting
45–60–4–998–91–17.82–0–*ct* 15
Bowling 11–1–11.00–0–0–1/11

Dainty, Harold William
Amateur. *b:* 2.6.1892, Rushton, Northants. *d:* 17.4.1961, Kettering, Northants. Lower order right-hand batsman, right-arm fast bowler. *Team* Northants (1922, 3 matches).
Career batting
3–5–2–20–8–6.66–0–*ct* 0
Bowling 47–0

He played soccer for New Brighton and Leicester City.

Dakin, Samuel
Professional. *b:* 12.4.1808, Sileby, Leics. *d:* 27.12.1876, Cambridge. Middle order right-hand batsman, medium pace round arm bowler. *Teams* Nottinghamshire (1845, 1 match); Cambridge Town Club (1853).
Career batting
45–80–10–834–64–11.91–0–*ct* 21
Bowling 9–8+27–1.12–0–0–4/3

He appeared in first-class matches from 1840 to 1855.

Dale, Jack Hillen
Amateur. *b:* 29.10.1901, Northampton. *d:* 28.4.1965, Battle, Sussex. Son of P.W. (Northants Secretary). Middle order right-hand batsman, slow right-arm bowler. *Teams* Northants (1922, 7 matches); Royal Navy (1922–28).
Career batting
9–17–1–323–76–20.18–0–*ct* 2
Bowling 119–2–59.50–0–0–1/19

His career in the Royal Navy curtailed his appearances in County cricket.

Dale, John Ronald
Professional. *b:* 24.10.1930, Cleethorpes, Lincs. Lower order right hand batsman, slow left-arm bowler. *Team* Kent (1958, 1 match),
Career batting
1–1–0–0–0–0.00–0–*ct* 0
Bowling 31–1–31.00–0–0–1/31

He appeared for Lincolnshire from 1949 to 1979.

Dale, John William
Amateur. *b:* 21.6.1848, Lincoln. *d:* 26.6.1895, Westminster. Opening/middle order right-hand batsman, right-hand fast round arm bowler. *Sch* Tonbridge. *Teams* Cambridge U (1868–70, blue all three years); Middlesex (1874–78, 7 matches).
Career batting
56–98–2–1625–132–16.93–1–*ct* 39
Bowling 174–6–29.00–0–0–2/16

His final first-class match was for MCC in 1882. He also played for Lincolnshire.

Dales, Hartley Horace
Amateur. *b:* 12.5.1909, North Transvaal, South Africa. Middle/lower order right-hand batsman, wicket keeper. *Team* Cambridge U (1929–31).
Career batting
4–6–2–6–3–1.50–0–*ct* 9–*st* 1

Dales, Hugh Lloyd
Amateur. *b:* 18.5.1888, Lanchester, Co Durham. *d:* 4.5.1964, Whitley Bay, Northumberland. Opening left-hand batsman, slow left-arm bowler. *Team* Middlesex (1920–30, 108 matches). *Tour* MCC to West Indies 1925/6.
Career batting
118–190–15–4643–143–26.53–8–*ct* 32
Bowling 206–4–51.50–0–0–2/28

He played for Durham 1911–13. He hit 1,000 runs in a season twice (best 1,138, av 29.17, in 1923).

Daley, John Valiant
Professional. *b:* 1.2.1906, Beccles, Suffolk. Tail end right-hand batsman, slow left-arm bowler. *Team* Surrey (1936–38, 28 matches).
Career batting
28–34–24–75–26*–7.50–0–*ct* 13
Bowling 1942–67–28.98–3–1–6/47

He was nine years in the Army before starting

his County cricket career. He also played for Norfolk and Suffolk.

A well-known soccer player he appeared for Kingstonian in the FA Amateur Cup Final.

Dalkeith, Earl of
(Walter Henry Montagu-Douglas-Scott, known as Lord Eskdaill until 1884)
Amateur. *b:* 17.1.1861, London. *d:* 18.9.1886, Achnacarry Forest, Loch Arkaig, Fort William. Brother of G.W. Montagu-Douglas-Scott (MCC). Opening/middle order batsman. *Sch* Eton. *Team* MCC (1881–85).
Career batting
3–4–0–9–7–2.25–0–*ct* 0

He accidentally shot himself whilst deer-stalking.

Dallas-Brooks, R. A.
(*see under* Brooks, R. A. D.)

Dalmeny, Lord Albert Edward Harry Mayer Archibald Primrose
(succeeded as 6th Earl of Rosebery in 1929)
Amateur. *b:* 8.1.1882, Westminster, London. *d:* 30.5.1974, Mentmore House, Bucks. Father of Lord Dalmeny (Middlesex). Middle order right-hand batsman, right-arm fast bowler. *Sch* Eton. *Teams* Middlesex (1902, 2 matches); Surrey (1903–08, 94 matches); Scotland (1905).
Career batting
102–164–6–3551–138–22.47–2–*ct* 50
Bowling 100–3–33.33–0–0–2/16

He captained Surrey 1905–07.

In 1901 he appeared for Buckinghamshire. His final first-class match was for MCC in 1920. He hit 1,000 runs in a season twice (best 1,150, av 25.55, in 1907).

He left £9,650,986 net.

Dalmeny, Lord Archibald Ronald Primrose
Amateur. *b:* 1.8.1910, London. *d:* 11.11.1931, Oxford, of blood poisoning. Son of Lord Dalmeny (Middlesex and Surrey). Middle order right-hand batsman, right-arm fast medium bowler. *Sch* Eton. *Teams* Middlesex (1929–31, 2 matches); Oxford U (1930).
Career batting
3–3–0–29–29–9.66–0–*ct* 6
Bowling 62–2–31.00–0–0–1/15

Dalrymple, John James Hamilton
Cricketer. *b:* 14.10.1957, St John's Wood, London. Tail end right-hand batsman, right-arm fast medium bowler. *Team* Oxford U (1978).
Career batting
3–4–2–27–15–13.50–0–*ct* 1
Bowling 260–7–37.14–0–0–3/34

Dalton, Andrew John
Cricketer. *b:* 14.3.1947, Horsforth, Yorkshire. Middle order right-hand batsman. *Team* Yorkshire (1969–72, 21 matches).
Career batting
21–31–2–710–128–24.48–3–*ct* 6

Dalton, Eric Londesbrough
Amateur. *b:* 2.12.1906, Durban, South Africa. *d:* 3.6.1981, Durban, South Africa. Son of G.L. (Transvaal). Middle order right-hand batsman, leg break bowler. *Team* Natal (1924/5 to 1946/7). *Tours* South Africa to England 1929, 1935, to Australia, and New Zealand 1931/2. *Tests* South Africa (1929 to 1938/9, 15 matches).
Career batting
121–180–19–5333–157–33.12–13–*ct* 72
Bowling 3588–139–25.81–5–0–6/42
Test batting
15–24–2–698–117–31.72–2–*ct* 5
Bowling 490–12–40.83–0–0–4/59

He hit 1446 runs, av 37.07, in 1935.

After retiring from first-class cricket he became a noted golfer and won the South African Amateur Championship.

Daly, Arthur Raine
Amateur. *b:* 1831. *d:* 1.2.1898, London. Lower order left-hand batsman, left-hand medium round arm bowler. *Teams* Middlesex (1866, 1 match).
Career batting
1–1–0–0–0–0.00–*ct* 1
Bowling 26–1–26.00–0–0–1/26

Daly, Guy Nolan
Amateur. *b:* 4.9.1908, Bramley, Hampshire. Lower order right-hand batsman, right-arm medium pace bowler. *Team* Glamorgan (1938, 1 match)
Career batting
1–1–0–9–9–9.00–0–*ct* 0
Bowling 17–0

Daniel, Adrian Richard Huw
Cricketer. *b:* 17.1.1955, Ealing, Middlesex. Middle order right-hand batsman, right-arm medium pace bowler. *Team* Cambridge U (1976–77).
Career batting
4–5–0–96–75–19.20–0–*ct* 0

Daniel, Arthur William Trollope
Amateur. *b:* 3.1.1841, London. *d:* 26.1.1873, Clapham, Surrey, of consumption. Middle order right-hand batsman, brilliant field. *Sch* Harrow. *Teams* Cambridge U (1861–64, blue all four years); Middlesex (1861–69, 16 matches).

Career batting
37–64–2–1102–87–17.77–0–*ct* 23–*st* 6
Bowling 74–4–18.50–0–0–2/8

In 1861 he was rackets champion at Cambridge and in 1864 won the 120 yards hurdles in the inter-University athletics meeting.

Daniel, Wayne Wendell
Cricketer. *b*: 16.1.1956, St Philip, Barbados. Tail end right-hand batsman, right-arm fast bowler, deep field. *Teams* Barbados (1975/6 to 1982/3); Middlesex (1977–83, 137 matches); Western Australia (1981/2, 2 matches). *Tours* West Indies to England 1976; Young West Indies to Zimbabwe 1981/2. *Tests* West Indies (1975/6 to 1976, 5 matches)
Career batting
176–156–67–1137–53*–12.78–0–*ct* 41
Bowling 12088–592–20.41–26–7–9/61
Test batting
5–5–2–29–11–9.66–0–*ct* 2
Bowling 381–15–25.40–0–0–4/53

On the 1976 tour to England he appeared in four of the five Tests and took 13 wickets, av 24.38, his record in first-class matches being 52, av 21.26. His best season for Middlesex was 1978 with 76 wickets, av 14.65, and his best innings analysis is 9 for 61 for Middlesex v Glamorgan at Swansea in 1982.

Daniell, John
Amateur. *b:* 12.12.1878, Bath, Somerset. *d:* 24.1.1963, Holway, Somerset. Hard hitting middle order right-hand batsman, right-arm fast bowler, brilliant close field. *Sch* Clifton. *Teams* Somerset (1898–1927, 287 matches); Cambridge U (1899–1901, blue all three years).
Career batting
304–531–54–10468–174*–21.94–*ct* 228
Bowling 171–7–24.42–0–0–1/0

Despite scoring over 10,000 runs in his first-class career, he never hit 1,000 in a season. He captained Somerset 1908–12 and 1919–26.

An excellent rugby footballer, he was awarded his blue and went on to captain England. He was later President of the Rugby Football Union.

Daniels, David Michael
Cricketer. *b:* 29.3.1942, Bexleyheath, Kent. Opening right-hand batsman. *Team* Cambridge U (1964–65, blue both years).
Career batting
18–32–0–562–82–17.56–0–*ct* 7
Bowling 7–0

His County cricket was for Dorset, commencing 1969, and later Bedfordshire.

Daniels, John Giles Upton
Cricketer. *b:* 25.1.1942, Edgbaston, Birmingham. Middle order right-hand batsman. *Sch* Cheltenham. *Team* Gloucestershire (1964, 1 match).
Career batting
2–4–0–51–22–12.75–0–*ct* 1

Apart from his appearance for Gloucs, his only other first-class match was for Combined Services, also in 1964.

Daniels, Rupert Chandos
Cricketer. *b:* 28.6.1945, Birmingham. Middle order right-hand batsman, off break bowler. *Sch* Eton. *Team* Oxford U (1965–66).
Career batting
7–14–1–97–26–7.46–0–*ct* 1
Bowling 148–1–148.00–0–0–1/29

Daniels, Simon Antony Brewis
Cricketer. *b*: 23.8.1958, Darlington, Co Durham. Lower order right-hand batsman, right-arm fast medium bowler. *Sch* Sedbergh. *Team* Glamorgan (1981–82, 16 matches).
Career batting
16–23–10–227–73–17.46–0–*ct* 7
Bowling 1162–28–41.50–0–0–3/33

He also played for Durham.

Darby, James Herbert
Amateur. *b:* 26.10 1865, Fareham, Hants. *d:* 7.11.1943, Fareham, Hants. Middle order batsman. *Team* Hampshire (1884–97, 4 matches).
Career batting
4–7–1–78–35–13.00–0–*ct* 1
Bowling 24–0

Darbyshire, Rev Benjamin Stewart
Amateur. *b:* 1845. *d:* 18.1.1907, Birkdale, Lancashire. Middle/lower order batsman, bowler. *Team* Oxford U (1864–66).
Career batting
2–2–0–4–4–2.00–0–*ct* 0
Bowling 9–3+5–3.00–1–0–5/?

D'Arcy, John William
Amateur. *b:* 23.4.1936, Christchurch, New Zealand. Opening right-hand batsman. *Teams* Canterbury (1955/6 to 1958/9); Wellington (1959/60); Otage (1960/1 to 1961/2). *Tour* New Zealand to England 1958. *Tests* New Zealand (1958, 5 matches).
Career batting
53–90–3–2009–89–23.09–0–*ct* 26
Bowling 12–1–12.00–0–0–1/0
Test batting
5–10–0–136–33–13.60–0–*ct* 0

Despite hitting only 522 runs, av 16.31, on the 1958 tour to England, he appeared in all five Tests as as an opening bat.

Dare, Reginald
Professional. *b:* 26.11.1921, Blandford, Dorset. Middle order right-hand batsman, slow left-arm bowler. *Team* Hampshire (1949–54, 109 matches).
Career batting
109–169–32–1679–109*–12.25–1–*ct* 70
Bowling 6479–185–35.02–5–0–6/28
He also played for Buckinghamshire. He played soccer for Southampton and Exeter.

Dargan, Michael James
Amateur. *b:* 9.10.1928, Dublin, Ireland. Right-hand batsman. *Team* Ireland (1954).
Career batting
1–2–0–10–7–5.00–0–*ct* 3
He was an Irish rugby international.

Darke, Robert Henry
Amateur. *b:* 25.1.1876. *d:* 19.7.1961, Balham, South London. *Sch* Dulwich. *Team* Gentlemen of England (1905, 1 match).
Career batting
1 match, did not bat–*ct* 0

Darks, Geoffrey Chalton
Professional. *b:* 28.6.1926, Bewdley, Worcs. Lower order right-hand batsman, right-arm medium pace bowler. *Team* Worcestershire (1946–50, 7 matches).
Career batting
7–8–3–89–39–17.80–0–*ct* 6
Bowling 452–13–34.76–1–0–5/49

Darling, Joseph
Amateur. *b:* 21.11.1870, Glen Osmond, Adelaide, Australia. *d:* 2.1.1946, Hobart, Tasmania. Opening/middle order left-hand batsman, slow bowler, good field. *Team* South Australia (1893/4 to 1907/08, 42 matches). *Tours* Australia to England 1896, 1899, 1902, 1905, to South Africa 1902/3, to North America 1896. *Tests* Australia (1894/5 to 1905, 34 matches).
Career batting
202–333–25–10635–210–34.52–19–*ct* 148
Bowling 55–1–55.00–0–0–1/5
Test batting
34–60–2–1657–178–28.56–3–*ct* 27
He captained the Australian teams to England in 1899, 1902 and 1905, also to South Africa 1902/3. He hit 1,000 runs on all four of his tours to England (best 1,941, av 41.29, in 1899).
His only double century was 210 for South Australia v Queensland at Brisbane in 1898/9.

Darling, Leonard Stuart
Amateur. *b:* 14.8.1909, South Yarra, Victoria, Australia. Middle order left-hand batsman, right-arm medium pace bowler. *Team* Victoria (1926/7 to 1936/7, 47 matches). *Tours* Australia to England 1934, to South Africa 1935/6. *Tests* Australia (1932/3 to 1936/7, 12 matches).
Career batting
100–143–7–5780–188–42.50–16–*ct* 59
Bowling 1504–32–47.00–0–0–3/57
Test batting
12–18–1–474–85–27.88–0–*ct* 8
Bowling 65–0
On his 1934 tour to England he hit 1,022 runs, av 34.06. He appeared in four out of five Tests on that tour, but had little success.

Darling, Robert Stormonth
Amateur. *b:* 6.6.1880, Scotland. *d:* 20.5.1956, Kelso, Roxburghshire, Scotland. Middle order right-hand batsman, right-arm medium bowler. *Sch* Winchester. *Team* Oxford U (1902–03).
Career batting
10–16–0–188–54–11.75–0–*ct* 3
Bowling 84–3–28.00–0–0–2/35

Darnton, Thomas
Professional. *b:* 12.2.1836, Stockton on Tees, Durham. *d:* 25.20.1874, Stockton on Tees, of consumption. Opening right-hand batsman, right-hand medium pace round arm bowler. *Team* Yorkshire (1858–68, 15 matches).
Career batting
20–35–2–402–81*–12.18–0–*ct* 4
Bowling 492–18–27.33–0–0–3/57
He also played for Durham.

Darvell, Bruce Stanley
Professional. *b:* 29.4.1931, Chipperfield, Hertfordshire. Right-hand batsman, off break bowler. *Team* Kent (1952, 1 match).
Career batting
1–1–0–5–5–5.00–0–*ct* 1
Bowling 2–0
He also played for Hertfordshire.

Darwall-Smith, John Anderton
Amateur. *b:* 12.4.1912, London. *d:* 22.6.1976, Hemel Hempstead, Herts. Brother of R.F.H. (Sussex). Lower order right-hand batsman, right-arm fast medium bowler. *Sch* Winchester. *Team* Oxford U (1933–34).
Career batting
5–9–1–98–36–12.25–0–*ct* 2
Bowling 393–13–30.23–0–0–4/106

His final first-class match was for Free Foresters in 1937.

He was awarded his soccer blue and also played for Corinthians.

Darwall-Smith, Randle Frederick Hines
Amateur. *b:* 11.7.1914, London. Brother of J.A. (Oxford U). Lower order right-hand batsman, right-arm fast medium bowler. *Sch* Charterhouse. *Teams* Oxford U (1935–38, blue all four years); Sussex (1946, 5 matches).
Career batting
46–69–16–649–54–12.24–0–*ct* 16
Bowling 4153–151–27.50–6–1–7/44

Dashwood, Thomas Henry Knyvett
Amateur. *b:* 3.1.1876, Hitchin, Herts. *d:* 24.1.1929, London. Middle order right-hand batsman, good field. *Sch* Wellington. *Teams* Hampshire (1904, 2 matches); Oxford U (1899). *Tour* Bennett to West Indies 1901/2.
Career batting
18–29–1–334–70–11.92–0–*ct* 14

He also appeared for Hertfordshire and Cornwall.

Datta, Punya Brata
Amateur. *b:* 21.6.1924, India. Lower order right-hand batsman, slow left-arm bowler. *Teams* Cambridge U (1947, blue); Bengal (1944/5 to 1955/6).
Career batting
34–52–3–1459–143–29.77–4–*ct* 12
Bowling 1520–41–37.07–1–0–5/52

Dauglish, Maurice John
Amateur. *b:* 2.10.1867, Gordon Square, London, WC. *d:* 30.4.1922, Hunton Bridge, Herts. Middle order right-hand batsman, lob bowler, wicket-keeper. *Sch* Harrow. *Teams* Middlesex (1886–90, 9 matches); Oxford U (1889–90, blue both years).
Career batting
14–24–3–165–46*–7.85–0–*ct* 11–*st* 5
Bowling 13–0

He also appeared for Berkshire.

Dauncey, John Gilbert
Professional. *b:* 9.4.1936, Ystalyfera, Glamorgan. Middle order right-hand batsman. *Team* Glamorgan (1957, 2 matches).
Career batting
2–4–0–54–34–13.50–0–*ct* 1

Davenport, Rev Edward
Amateur. *b:* 26.3.1844, Oxford. *d:* 5.3.1915, Stoke Talmage, Oxon. Steady middle order right-hand batsman, excellent long stop. *Sch* Rugby. *Team* Oxford University (1864–66, blue 1866).
Career batting
7–10–0–318–107–31.80–1–*ct* 2–*st* 1

He appeared for Oxfordshire 1863–64, and also played non-first-class cricket for Northants.

Davenport, George
Professional. *b:* 5.5.1860, Nantwich, Cheshire. *d:* 4.10.1902, Nantwich, Cheshire. Middle order right-hand batsman, wicket-keeper, right-arm medium pace bowler. *Team* MCC (1884–96).
Career batting
27–46–8–625–101*–16.44–1–*ct* 22–*st* 12

He appeared with great success for Cheshire, commencing 1883.

Davenport, Horace John
Amateur. *b:* 11.1.1875, London. *d:* 20.8.1946. Right-hand batsman. *Sch* Repton. *Team* MCC (1898).
Career batting
1–2–0–2–2–1.00–0–*ct* 1

Davenport, H. R. B.
(*see under* Bromley-Davenport, H. R.)

Davey, Clive Frederick
Amateur. *b:* 2.6.1932, Petherton, Somerset. Middle order right-hand batsman, leg break bowler. *Team* Somerset (1953–55, 13 matches).
Career batting
13–25–4–261–46–12.42–0–*ct* 4

Davey, Jack
Cricketer. *b:* 4.9.1944, Tavistock, Devon. Tail end left-hand batsman, left-arm fast medium bowler. *Team* Gloucestershire (1966–78, 175 matches).
Career batting
175–208–90–918–53*–7.77–0–*ct* 32
Bowling 11720–411–28.51–9–0–6/95

He also played for Devon, 1964–65.

Davey, John George
Professional. *b:* 21.6.1847, Brighton, Sussex. *d:* 4.5.1878, Brighton, Sussex. Lower order right-hand batsman, right-hand medium pace round arm bowler, wicket-keeper. *Team* Sussex (1869–73, 4 matches).
Career batting
7–13–3–80–32–8.00–0–*ct* 8

His final first-class match was for MCC in 1876.

Davey, Philip John
Amateur. *b:* 10.8.1913, Taunton, Somerset. Tail end right-hand batsman, right-arm medium bowler. *Sch* Taunton. *Team* Somerset (1934–37, 16 matches).

Career batting
16–26–3–235–30–10.21–0–*ct* 10
Bowling 621–22–28.22–1–0–6/9

David, Rodney Felix Armine
Amateur. *b:* 19.6.1907, Cardiff. *d:* 2.7.1969, Warbleton, Sussex. Middle order right-hand batsman. *Sch* Wellington. *Team* Glamorgan (1925–29, 3 matches).
Career batting
3–5–0–20–17–4.00–0–*ct* 0

Davidge, Guy Mortimer Coleridge
Amateur. *b:* 2.3.1878, Woolwich. *d:* 17.2.1956, Hove. Middle order batsman. *Sch* Newton College. *Team* Worcestershire (1911, 1 match).
Career batting
1–1–0–0–0–0.00–0–*ct* 1

Davidson, Alan Keith
Amateur. *b:* 14.6.1929, Lisarow, Gosford, New South Wales, Australia. Middle order left-hand batsman, left-arm fast-medium bowler. *Team* New South Wales (1949/50 to 1962/3, 72 matches). *Tours* Australia to England 1953, 1956, 1961, to South Africa 1957/8, to West Indies 1954/5, to India and Pakistan 1956/7, 1959/60, to New Zealand 1949/50. *Tests* Australia (1953 to 1962/3, 44 matches).
Career batting
193–246–39–6804–129–32.86–9–*ct* 168
Bowling 14048–672–20.90–33–2–7/31
Test batting
44–61–7–1328–80–24.59–0–*ct* 42
Bowling 3819–186–20.53–14–2–7/93

Although he did not reach 1,000 runs or take 100 wickets in a season on any of his three visits to England (in 1956 he missed many matches due to injury), he was one of the best all-rounders of his day and his bowling was especially effective in England in 1961, when he topped the Test averages with 23 wkts, av 24.86.

Davidson, Frank
Professional. *b:* 1.10.1872, Brimington, Derbyshire. *d:* 7.6.1951, Chesterfield, Derbyshire. Son of Joseph (Derbyshire), brother of G.A. (Derbyshire). Lower order right-hand batsman, right-arm medium pace bowler. *Team* Derbyshire (1897–99, 14 matches).
Career batting
14–23–4–129–43–6.78–0–*ct* 11
Bowling 1094–43–25.44–2–0–6/36

Davidson, George Arthur
Professional. *b:* 29.6.1866, Brimington, Derbyshire. *d:* 8.2.1899, Tividale, Staffs, of pneumonia. Son of Joseph (Derbyshire), brother of Frank (Derbyshire). Stylish middle order right-hand batsman, right-arm fast-medium bowler, good field. *Team* Derbyshire (1886–98, 95 matches).
Career batting
158–260–27–5546–274–23.80–3–*ct* 135
Bowling 11341–621–18.26–43–10–9/39

The best all-rounder in the Derbyshire side, his appearances in first-class matches were restricted, first because of the demotion of Derbyshire and then because of his sudden death at the early age of 32. He hit 1,000 runs in a season three times (best 1,296, av 28.18, in 1895); in the same year he took over 100 wickets, for the only time – 138, av. 16.79 – thus completing the 'double'. His only double century, 274 for Derbyshire v Lancs at Old Trafford in 1896, remains the highest individual innings for the County. His best bowling was 9/39 for Derbyshire v Warwickshire at Derby in 1895.

Davidson, Joseph
Professional. *b:* 9.8.1846, Brimington, Derbyshire. *d:* 3.12.1901, Brimington, Derbyshire. Father of Frank (Derbyshire) and G.A. (Derbyshire). Tail end right-hand batsman, right-arm medium off break bowler. *Team* Derbyshire (1871–74, 4 matches).
Career batting
4–6–3–14–8–4.66–0–*ct* 2
Bowling 96–6–16.00–0–0–3/33

Davidson, John Ewen
Amateur. *b:* 2.3.1841, London. *d:* 2.9.1923, Oxford. Middle order batsman. *Sch* Harrow. *Team* MCC (1864, 1 match).
Career batting
1–2–0–13–13–6.50–0–*ct* 0

He played for Hertfordshire.

Davidson, James Norman Grieve
Amateur. *b:* 28.1.1931, Hawick, Scotland. Right-hand batsman. *Team* Scotland (1951).
Career batting
4–7–1–86–40–14.33–0–*ct* 1

He was a Scottish rugby international.

Davidson, Kenneth Richard
Amateur in 1933, then professional from 1934. *b:* 24.12.1905, Calverley, Yorkshire. *d:* 25.12.1954, Prestwick Aerodrome, Scotland, in a plane crash. Middle order right-hand batsman. *Teams* Yorkshire (1933–35, 30 matches); Scotland (1938).
Career batting
31–48–5–1355–128–31.51–2–*ct* 18
Bowling 4–0

He hit 1,241 runs, av 34.47, in 1934.

He emigrated to USA in 1935 and became a noted badminton player. It was during a badminton world tour with a United States team that he was killed.

Davidson, William Leslie
Amateur. *b:* 31.1.1850. Inchmarlo, Kincardineshire. *d:* 3.8.1915, Rouen, France. Middle order batsman. *Team* MCC (1877, 1 match).
Career batting
1–1–0–0–0–0.00–0–*ct* 0
He also played for Northants. He was killed in action at the age of 65 and is thought to be the oldest first-class cricketer to be killed in the First World War.

Davidson, Rev William Watkins
Amateur. *b:* 20.3.1920, Poplar, London. Lower order right-hand batsman, wicket-keeper. *Sch* Brighton. *Teams* Oxford U (1947–48, blue both years); Sussex (1948–51, 5 matches).
Career batting
22–23–6–118–31–6.94–0–*ct* 34–*st* 6
His final first-class match was for MCC in 1956.

Davies, Andrew George
Cricketer. *b*: 15.5.1962, Altrincham, Cheshire. Tail end right-hand batsman, wicket-keeper. *Sch* Birkenhead. *Team* Cambridge U (1982–83).
Career batting
5–4–0–17–13–4.25–0–0–*ct* 5

Davies, Conrad Stephen
Amateur. *b:* 27.6.1907, Edgbaston, Birmingham. Lower order right-hand batsman, slow left-arm bowler. *Sch* Chatham House, Ramsgate. *Team* Warwickshire (1930–36, 8 matches).
Career batting
8–11–0–112–63–10.18–0–*ct* 3
Bowling 672–14–48.00–0–0–3/26

Davies, David
(known as Dai)
Professional. *b:* 26.8.1896, Llanelly, Carmarthen. *d:* 16.7.1976, Llanelly, Carmarthen. Middle order right-hand batsman, right-arm medium pace off break bowler. *Teams* Glamorgan (1923–39, 411 matches); Wales (1923–30).
Career batting
421–696–62–15390–216–24.27–16–*ct* 195
Bowling 9633–275–35.02–4–0–6/50
He hit 1,000 runs in a season seven times (best 1539, av 34.97, in 1930). His only double century was 216 for Glamorgan v Somerset at Newport in 1939.
Commencing in 1946 he was a noted first-class umpire, standing in 23 Tests.

Davies, David Aubrey
Professional. *b:* 11.7.1915, Swansea. Lower order right-hand batsman, leg break and googly bowler. *Team* Glamorgan (1934–38, 46 matches).
Career batting
46–64–16–600–55–12.50–0–*ct* 28
Bowling 760–14–54.28–0–0–3/63
He also played for Devon.

Davies, David Emrys
Professional. *b:* 27.6.1904, Sandy, Llanelly, Carmarthen. *d:* 10.11.1975, Llanelly, Carmarthen. Brother of Gwyn (Glamorgan). Opening left-hand batsman, left-arm slow bowler, sound deep field. *Teams* Glamorgan (1924–54, 612 matches); Wales (1926–29). *Tour* Selected to tour India with MCC 1939/40 (tour cancelled).
Career batting
621–1033–80–26566–287*–27.87–32–*ct* 217
Bowling 26458–903–29.26–32–2–6/24
He hit 1,000 runs in a season 16 times, exceeding 2,000 once – 2,012, av 40.24, in 1937. He took 100 wickets in a season twice (best 103, av 23.03, in 1937). In 1935 and 1937 he performed the 'double', in the latter year achieving the feat of 2,000 runs and 100 wickets in the same year.
He hit two double centuries, his highest being 287* for Glamorgan v Gloucs at Newport in 1939.
He was a first-class umpire for some seasons and stood in two Tests.

Davies, David Roy
Professional. *b:* 12.8.1928, Llanelly, Carmarthen. Brother of H.G. (Glamorgan). Right-hand batsman. *Team* Glamorgan (1950, 1 match),
Career batting
1–1–0–7–7–7.00–0–*ct* 0

Davies, Gwyn
Professional. *b:* 12.8.1908, Sandy, Llanelly, Carmarthen. *d:* 10.3.1972, Llanelly, Carmarthen. Brother of D.E. (Glamorgan). Middle/lower order right-hand batsman, right-arm medium bowler. *Team* Glamorgan (1932, 7 matches).
Career batting
7–9–1–77–44–9.62–0–*ct* 2
Bowling 134–3–44.66–0–0–2/18

Davies, Gwyn
Professional. *b:* 10.6.1919, Cardiff. Right-hand batsman, right-arm medium bowler. *Team* Glamorgan (1947–48, 2 matches).
Career batting
2–2–0–9–7–4.50–0–*ct* 0

Davies, Geoffrey Boisselier
Amateur. *b:* 26.10.1892, Poplar, London. *d:* 26.9.1915, Hulluch, France. He was killed in

action. Opening/middle order right-hand batsman, right-arm slow-medium bowler. *Sch* Rossall. *Teams* Essex (1912–14, 32 matches); Cambridge U (1913–14, blue both years).
Career batting
54–90–9–1487–118–18.35–2–*ct* 43
Bowling 2935–141–20.81–4–1–8/67

Davies, Harry Donald
Amateur. *b:* 13.3.1892, Pendleton, Manchester. *d:* 6.2.1958, Riem Airport, near Munich, Germany, He was killed in air crash involving the Manchester United football team. Middle order right-hand batsman. *Team* Lancashire (1924–25, 11 matches).
Career batting
11–15–0–260–46–17.33–0–*ct* 4
He played soccer for Bolton Wanderers and obtained an Amateur International cap with England. Latterly he was a well-known journalist, reporting soccer for *The Guardian* under the title 'An Old International'.

Davies, Hugh Daniel
Professional. *b:* 23.7.1932, Pembrey, Llanelly, Carmarthen. Tail end right-hand batsman, right-arm medium fast bowler. *Team* Glamorgan (1955–60, 52 matches).
Career batting
52–70–26–247–28–5.61–0–*ct* 17
Bowling 3659–115–31.81–4–0–6/85

Davies, Haydn George
Professional. *b:* 23.4 1912, Llanelly, Carmarthen. Brother of D.R. (Glamorgan). Lower order right-hand batsman, wicket-keeper. *Team* Glamorgan (1935–58, 423 matches).
Career batting
427–601–96–6613–80–13.09–0–*ct* 585–*st* 203
Bowling 20–1–20.00–0–0–1/20
He was also a noted squash player.

Davies, Henry Gwyn Saunders
(later Davies-Scourfield. He was also known as Saunders-Davies)
Amateur. *b:* 2.2.1865, Pembroke. *d:* 4.12.1934, Patching, Sussex. Middle order right-hand batsman. *Sch* Winchester. *Team* Hampshire (1883, 1 match).
Career batting
1–2–0–45–42–22.50–0–*ct* 0
A noted rider, he headed the Gentlemen Riders Steeplechasing for four years 1891–94.

Davies, John Anthony
Amateur. *b:* 3.2.1926, Pontypridd, Glamorgan. Hard hitting middle order right-hand batsman, leg break and googly bowler. *Team* Glamorgan (1952, 1 match).
Career batting
1–2–0–11–11–5.50–0–*ct* 0

Davies, Jack Gale Wilmot
Amateur. *b:* 10.9.1911, Broadclyst, Devon. Stylish middle order right-hand batsman, right-arm off break bowler. *Sch* Tonbridge. *Teams* Cambridge U (1931–34, blue 1933–34); Kent (1934–51, 99 matches).
Career batting
153–262–12–5982–168–23.92–4–*ct* 87
Bowling 7847–258–30.41–6–1–7/20
He scored 1246 runs, av 32.78, in 1946. His final first-class match was for MCC in 1961.
A noted rugby footballer, he appeared for Blackheath and Kent.

Davies, John Trevor
Amateur. *b:* 26.12.1932, Shrewsbury. Middle order right-hand batsman. *Team* Cambridge U (1956–58).
Career batting
8–15–0–94–29–6.26–0–*ct* 4

Davies, Llewellyn John
Amateur. *b:* 1894, Northampton. *d:* 28.10.1965, Selly Oak, Birmingham. Lower order right-hand batsman, bowler. *Team* Northants (1919–21, 6 matches).
Career batting
6–9–1–43–20–5.37–0–*ct* 2
Bowling 96–2–48.00–0–0–1/9
He played soccer for Northampton Town.

Davies, Morean Kimsley
Cricketer. *b:* 13.10.1954, Clydach, Glamorgan. Lower order left-hand batsman, wicket-keeper. *Team* Glamorgan (1975–76, 2 matches).
Career batting
2–2–1–14–12–14.00–0–*ct* 2–*st* 2
He also played rugby for Aberavon.

Davies, Mark Nicholas
Cricketer. *b*: 28.12.1959, Maesteg, Glamorgan. Middle order left-hand batsman. *Team* Glamorgan (1982, 2 matches).
Career batting
2–1–0–0–0–0.00–0–*ct* 1

Davies, Philip Havelock
Amateur. *b:* 30.8.1893, Brighton. *d:* 30.1.1930, Catholic Military Hospital, Catterick, Yorkshire. Lower order right-hand batsman, right-arm slow bowler. *Sch* Brighton. *Teams* Oxford U (1913–14, blue both years); Sussex (1914, 1 match).

Career batting
27–41–8–286–55–8.66–0–*ct* 23
Bowling 2370–98–24.18–3–0–6/59

His final first-class match was for the Army in 1927.

Davies, Richard John
Cricketer. *b:* 11.2.1954, Selly Oak, Birmingham. Opening right-hand batsman, right-arm medium pace bowler. *Team* Warwickshire (1976, 1 match).
Career batting
1–2–0–18–18–9.00–0–*ct* 1

Davies, Terry
Cricketer. *b:* 25.10.1960, St Albans, Herts. Lower order right-hand batsman, wicket-keeper. *Team* Glamorgan (1979–83, 23 matches).
Career batting
23–33–8–558–69*–22.32–0–*ct* 46–*st* 4

Davies, Thomas Clive
Cricketer. *b:* 7.11.1951, Pontrhydyfen, Glamorgan. Lower order right-hand batsman, slow left-arm bowler. *Team* Glamorgan (1971–72, 7 matches).
Career batting
7–6–4–9–5–4.50–0–*ct* 0
Bowling 625–18–34.72–0–0–3/22

Davies, Trefor E.
Professional. *b:* 14.3.1938, Stourbridge, Worcs. Middle order right-hand batsman, leg break bowler. *Team* Worcestershire (1955–61, 20 matches).
Career batting
20–30–5–481–76–19.24–0–*ct* 8
Bowling 169–6–28.16–0–0–2/22

Davies, William David E.
Professional. *b:* 28.6.1906, Briton-Ferry, Glamorgan. *d:* 1.10.1971, Briton-Ferry, Glamorgan. Middle order right-hand batsman, leg break and googly bowler. *Team* Glamorgan (1932–35, 7 matches).
Career batting
7–12–1–122–32–11.09–0–*ct* 2
Bowling 60–0

Davies, William George
Professional. *b:* 3.7.1936, Barry, Glamorgan. Opening right-hand batsman, right-arm medium fast bowler. *Team* Glamorgan (1954–60, 32 matches).
Career batting
32–58–0–674–64–11.62–0–*ct* 14
Bowling 646–16–40.37–0–0–2/23

Davies, William Henry
Amateur. *b:* 7.8.1901, Briton Ferry, Glamorgan. Lower order right-hand batsman, right-arm medium pace bowler. *Team* Glamorgan (1922–27, 5 matches).
Career batting
5–10–2–33–8*–4.12–0–*ct* 0
Bowling 130–3–43.33–0–0–2/35

Davis, Arthur Edward
Amateur, *b:* 4.8.1882, Leicester. *d:* 4.11.1916, near Albert, France. He was killed in action. Middle order right-hand batsman, wicket-keeper. *Sch* Mill Hill. *Team* Leicestershire (1901–08, 21 matches).
Career batting
21–31–4–334–55–12.37–0–*ct* 37–*st* 10

Davis, Anthony Tilton
Cricketer. *b:* 14.8.1931, Reading, Berkshire. *d:* 20.11.1978, Reading, Berkshire. Middle order right-hand batsman, slow left-arm bowler. *Teams* Minor Counties (1967); MCC (1967).
Career batting
2–3–0–57–47–19.00–0–*ct* 0

He was a mainstay of Berkshire, captaining the side 1960–70.

Davis, Bryan Allan
Cricketer. *b:* 2.5.1940, Belmont, Port of Spain, Trinidad. Brother of C.A. (Trinidad). Middle order right-hand batsman, right-arm off break bowler. *Teams* Trinidad (1959–60 to 1970–1); Glamorgan (1968–70, 60 matches). *Tours* West Indies to India and Ceylon 1966/7; Glamorgan to West Indies 1969/70. *Tests* West Indies (1964/5, 4 matches).
Career batting
112–193–14–6231–188*–34.81–5–*ct* 127
Bowling 434–9–48.22–0–0–4/79
Test batting
4–8–0–245–68–30.62–0–*ct* 1

He hit 1,000 runs in a season twice (best 1,532, av 31.26, in 1970).

Davis, Charles Allan
Cricketer. *b:* 1.1.1944, Belmont, Port of Spain, Trinidad. Brother of B.A. (Trinidad and Glamorgan). Middle order right-hand batsman, right-arm medium pace bowler. *Team* Trinidad (1960/1 to 1974/5). *Tours* West Indies to Australia and New Zealand 1968/9, to England 1969. *Tests* West Indies (1968/9 to 1972/3, 15 matches).

Career batting
90–152–18–5538–41.32–14–*ct* 44
Bowling 2480–63–39.36–3–0–7/106
Test batting
15–29–5–1301–183–54.20–4–*ct* 4
Bowling 330–2–165.00–0–0–1/27

He was successful on his tour of England, scoring 848 runs, av 42.40, and was the only tourist to hit a century in the Tests. His final first-class match was for North Trinidad in 1975/6.

Davis, Charles Percy
(known as Percy Charles)
Professional. *b:* 24.5.1915, Brackley, Northants. Brother of Edward (Northants). Sound opening right-hand batsman, right-arm medium pace bowler, wicket-keeper. *Team* Northants (1935–52, 169 matches).
Career batting
169–303–22–6363–237–22.64–10–*ct* 72–*st* 10
Bowling 492–6–82.00–0–0–2/13

He hit 1,000 runs in a season three times (best 1435, av 32.61, in 1946). His only double century was 237 for Northants v Somerset at Northampton 1947.

Davis, Edward
Professional. *b:* 8.3.1922, Brackley, Northants. Brother of C. P. (Northants). Middle order right-hand batsman. *Team* Northants (1947–56, 104 matches).
Career batting
104–159–14–4126–171–28.45–3–*ct* 27
Bowling 8–1–8.00–0–0–1/0

He also played for Cambridgeshire.

Davis, Francis John
Amateur. *b:* 23.3.1939, Cardiff. Brother of R.C. (Glamorgan). Lower order right-hand batsman, slow left-arm bowler. *Sch* Blundell's. *Teams* Glamorgan (1959–67, 14 matches); Oxford U (1963, blue).
Career batting
28–47–13–552–63–16.23–0–*ct* 17
Bowling 1694–52–32.57–2–0–5/67

He was at Oxford on a one-year course only.

Davis, Ian Charles
Cricketer. *b*: 25.6.1953, North Sydney, New South Wales, Australia. Stylish opening or middle order right-hand batsman. *Teams* New South Wales (1973/4 to 1982/3); Queensland (1975/6, 9 matches). *Tours* Australia to New Zealand 1973/4, 1976/7, to England 1977. *Tests* Australia (1973/4 to 1977, 15 matches).
Career batting
88–147–9–4609–156–33.39–7–*ct* 48
Bowling 7–0
Test batting
15–27–1–692–105–26.61–1–*ct* 9

On the 1977 tour to England he hit 608 runs, av 30.40, and played in three Tests, but with little success.

Davis, John Percy
Amateur. *b:* 26.1.1884, Lye, Worcs. *d:* 16.2.1951, Stourbridge, Worcs. Brother of Major (Worcs). Middle order right-hand batsman. *Team* Worcestershire (1922, 4 matches).
Career batting
4–8–1–48–38*–6.85–0–*ct* 0
Bowling 45–0

Davis, John William
Professional. *b:* 10.4.1882, Ironville, Derbyshire. *d:* 29.10.1963, Ripley, Derbyshire. Middle order right-hand batsman. *Team* Derbyshire (1920, 1 match).
Career batting
1–2–0–9–8–4.50–0–*ct* 2

He played soccer for Grimsby Town and Derby County.

Davis, Major
Amateur. *b:* 1882, Lye, Worcs. *d:* 27.4.1959, Kidderminster, Worcs. Brother of J.P. (Worcs). Middle order right-hand batsman, wicket-keeper. *Team* Worcestershire (1911, 1 match).
Career batting
1–2–0–35–29–17.50–0–*ct* 1

Davis, Michael John
Professional. *b:* 18.8.1943, Bolton, Lancashire. Lower order right-hand batsman, right-arm fast medium bowler. *Sch* King's School, Macclesfield. *Team* Northants (1963, 1 match).
Career batting
1 match, did not bat–*ct* 1
Bowling 58–2–29.00–0–0–1/21

He played for Cheshire in 1961.

Davis, Mark Richard
Cricketer. *b*: 26.2.1962, Kilve, Somerset. Tail end left-hand batsman, left-arm fast medium bowler. *Team* Somerset (1982–83, 23 matches).
Career batting
23–29–7–190–21*–8.63–0–*ct* 9
Bowling 1354–37–36.59–0–0–4/34

Davis, Percy Vere
Professional. *b:* 4.4.1922, Forest Hill. Middle order right-hand batsman. *Team* Kent (1946, 6 matches).

Career batting
10–17–0–276–136–16.23–1–*ct* 4

Davis, Roger Clive
Cricketer. *b:* 1.1.1946, Cardiff. Brother of F.J. (Glamorgan, Oxford U). Opening right-hand batsman, right-arm off break bowler. *Sch* Blundell's. *Team* Glamorgan (1964–76, 213 matches). *Tour* Glamorgan to West Indies 1969/70.
Career batting
214–371–30–7367–134–21.60–5–*ct* 208
Bowling 7793–241–32.33–6–0–6/82
He hit 1,000 runs in a season once; 1,243, av 31.07, in 1975.

Davis, Thomas
Professional. *b:* 27.11.1827, Nottingham. *d:* 29.5.1898, Nottingham. Middle order right-hand batsman, right-arm medium pace bowler. *Team* Nottinghamshire (1854–65, 12 matches).
Career batting
18–31–2–326–72–11.24–0–*ct* 16

Davis, W.
Professional. Middle/lower order batsman, change bowler. *Team* Essex (1920, 4 matches).
Career batting
4–6–0–26–13–4.33–0–*ct* 2
Bowling 69–1–69.00–0–0–1/67

Davis, William Ernest
Professional. *b:* 26.11.1880, Wimbledon, Surrey. *d:* 27.1.1959, Balham, South London. Middle order right-hand batsman, leg break bowler. *Teams* Surrey (1903–11, 111 matches); London County (1904).
Career batting
113–178–12–3504–112–21.10–3–*ct* 76
Bowling 919–17–54.05–0–0–4/51

Davis, Winston Walter
Cricketer. *b*: 18.9.1958, Kingstown, St Vincent, West Indies. Lower order right-hand batsman, right-arm fast medium bowler. *Teams* Windward Islands (1979/80 to 1982/3); Glamorgan (1982–83, 28 matches). *Tour* Young West Indies to Zimbabwe 1981/2. *Test* West Indies (1982/3, 1 match).
Career batting
49–61–25–432–60–12.00–0–*ct* 15
Bowling 4906–183–26.80–9–1–7/70
Test batting
1–1–0–14–14–14.00–0–*ct* 1
Bowling 175–4–43.75–0–0–2/54

Davison, Brian Fettes
Cricketer. *b*: 21.12.1946, Bulawayo, Rhodesia. Attacking middle order right-hand batsman, right-arm medium pace bowler, good field. *Teams* Rhodesia (1967/8 to 1978/9); Leicestershire (1970–83, 303 matches); Tasmania (1979/80 to 1981/2, 21 matches).
Career batting
415–680–64–24608–189–39.94–48–*ct* 312
Bowling 2635–82–32.13–1–0–5/52
He hit 1,000 runs in a season 13 times (best 1,818, av 56.81, in 1976). In 1980 he captained Leicestershire. A good hockey player, he represented Rhodesia.

Davison, Ian Joseph
Professional. *b:* 4.10.1937, Hemel Hempstead, Herts. Lower order right-hand batsman, right-arm medium fast bowler. *Team* Nottinghamshire (1959–66, 177 matches).
Career batting
178–246–65–1641–60*–9.06–0–*ct* 91
Bowling 15588–541–28.81–22–2–7/28
He took 111 wickets, av 21.92, in 1963.
He played for Bedfordshire 1955–58, and 1967–69.

Davy, Charles Vinicombe Butler
Amateur. *b:* 24.10.1869, Mercara, India. *d:* 10.9.1931, Vancouver, British Columbia. Middle/lower order left-hand batsman, slow left-arm bowler. *Sch* Cheltenham. *Team* Kent (1892, 1 match); Europeans (1902/3).
Career batting
3–6–1–58–32–11.60–0–*ct* 3
Bowling 41–1–41.00–0–0–1/6

Dawes, Albert George
Professional. *b:* 23.4.1907, Aldershot, Hants. *d:* 23.6.1973, Goring-by-Sea, Sussex. Middle order batsman. *Team* Northants (1933, 1 match).
Career batting
1–2–0–16–16–8.00–0–*ct* 1
He was a noted soccer player with Northampton, Crystal Palace and Luton Town.

Dawes, Joseph
Professional. *b:* 14.2.1836, Hallam, Sheffield. Lower order right-hand batsman, right-hand fast round arm bowler. *Team* Yorkshire (1865, 5 matches).
Career batting
6–11–2–104–28*–11.55–0–*ct* 3
Bowling 236–6–39.33–0–0–2/24
His last first-class match was for the North in 1866.

Dawkes, George Owen
Professional. *b:* 19.7.1920, Leicester. Lower order right-hand batsman, wicket-keeper. *Teams* Leicestershire (1937–39, 63 matches); Derbyshire

(1947–61, 392 matches). *Tour* Commonwealth to India and Pakistan 1949/50.
Career batting
482–736–105–11411–143–18.08–1–*ct* 895–*st* 148
Bowling 20–0

A good soccer player he appeared as goalkeeper for Leicester City.

Dawson, Edwin
Professional. *b:* 1.5.1835, Dalton, Huddersfield, Yorkshire. *d:* 1.12.1888, Bradford, Yorkshire, whilst watching a football match. Middle order right-hand batsman, right-hand medium pace round arm bowler. *Team* Yorkshire (1862–74, 16 matches).
Career batting
16–27–1–256–30–9.84–0–*ct* 5

Dawson, Edward William
Amateur. *b:* 13.2.1904, London. *d:* 4.6.1979, Idmiston, Wilts. Opening right-hand batsman. *Sch* Eton. *Teams* Leicestershire (1922–34, 174 matches); Cambridge U (1924–27, blue all four years). *Tours* MCC to South Africa 1927/8, to Australia and New Zealand 1929/30; Cahn to Jamaica 1928/9; Martineau to Egypt 1932, 1933 (not first-class). *Tests* England (1927/8 to 1929/30, 5 matches).
Career batting
282–482–177–12598–146–27.09–14–*ct* 110
Bowling 68–0
Test batting
5–9–0–175–55–19.44–0–*ct* 0

He hit 1,000 runs in a season six times (best 1,909, av 31.29, in 1929).

He captained Leicestershire 1928, 1929, 1931 and 1933.

Dawson, G.A.
Amateur. Lower order batsman, wicket-keeper. *Team* MCC (1871).
Career batting
2–4–0–24–18–6.00–0–*ct* 3

He played County cricket for Brecon. His first-class debut was for Gentlemen of South in 1860.

Dawson, Gilbert Wilkinson
Professional. *b:* 9.12.1916, Bradford, Yorkshire. *d:* 24.5.1969, Glasgow. He was found dead in his crashed car. Opening right hand batsman. *Team* Hampshire (1947–49, 60 matches).
Career batting
60–107–7–2643–158*–26.43–4–*ct* 36
Bowling 7–0

He hit 1,000 runs in a season twice (best 1,229, av 23.63, in 1948).

Dawson, Harold
Professional. *b:* 10.8.1914, Todmorden, Yorkshire. Middle order right-hand batsman, right-arm medium pace bowler. *Team* Hampshire (1947–48, 10 matches).
Career batting
10–19–1–236–37–13.11–0–*ct* 6
Bowling 8–0

He also played for Devon.

Dawson, Oswald Charles
Amateur. *b:* 1.9.1919, Rossburgh, Durban, South Africa. Middle order right-hand batsman, right-arm medium pace bowler, good slip field. *Teams* Natal (1938/9 to 1949/50); Border (1951/2 to 1961/2). *Tour* South Africa to England 1947. *Tests* South Africa (1947 to 1948/9, 9 matches).
Career batting
75–119–9–3804–182–34.58–6–*ct* 76
Bowling 3429–123–27.87–3–0–5/42
Test batting
9–15–1–293–55–20.92–0–*ct* 10
Bowling 578–10–57.80–0–0–2/57

In England in 1947 he hit 1,002 runs, av 32.32.

Dawson, William Arthur
Amateur. *b:* 3.12.1850, Bradford, Yorkshire. *d:* 6.3.1916, Ilkley, Yorkshire. Lower order right-hand batsman, right-arm medium pace bowler. *Sch* Marlborough. *Team* Yorkshire (1870, 1 match).
Career batting
1–2–0–0–0–0.00–0–*ct* 1

He did not appear in first-class matches whilst at Cambridge, but represented the University in the 100 yards, being Champion of England at that distance.

He also represented Yorkshire at rugby football.

Day, Albert George
Amateur. *b:* 20.9.1865, Dewsbury, Yorkshire. *d:* 16.10.1908, Dewsbury, Yorkshire. Middle order batsman. *Sch* Mill Hill. *Team* Yorkshire (1885–88, 6 matches).
Career batting
6–10–0–78–25–7.80–0–*ct* 3

Day, Arthur Percival
Amateur. *b:* 10.4.1885, Blackheath, Kent. *d:* 22.1.1969, Budleigh Salterton, Devon. Brother of S.E. (Kent) and S.H. (Kent). Middle order right-hand batsman, right-arm fast and leg break bowler. *Sch* Malvern. *Team* Kent (1905–25, 143 matches).
Career batting
157–243–25–7174–184*–32.90–13–*ct* 92
Bowling 3480–132–26.36–4–0–8/49

He scored 1,000 runs in a season twice (best 1,149, av 32.82, in 1905). For Kent v Hampshire at Southampton in 1911 he hit 100* in 55 minutes.

Day, Alan Richard
Cricketer. *b:* 12.11.1938, Edmonton, Middlesex. Middle order right-hand batsman. *Team* MCC (1968).
Career batting
1–1–0–5–5–5.00–0–*ct* 0
He appeared for Hertfordshire, commencing 1962, and later Berkshire.

Day, Anthony Samuel
Amateur. *b:* 20.6.1930, Ascot, Berks. Middle order right-hand batsman. *Sch* Harrow. *Team* Cambridge U (1953).
Career batting
1–2–0–3–2–1.50–0–*ct* 1

Day, Daniel
Professional. *b:* 14.6.1807, Streatham, Surrey. *d:* 22.11.1887, Southampton. Lower order right-hand batsman, right-hand fast medium round arm bowler, good close field. *Teams* Hampshire (1843–50, 13 matches); Surrey (1846–52, 23 matches).
Career batting
50–86–15–395–70–5.57–0–*ct* 36
Bowling 1120–95+157–11.78–22–8–8/?
He also played for Dorset. His first-class debut was for England in 1842.

Day, Frederick Gordon Kenneth
Amateur. *b:* 25.6.1919, Yatton, Somerset. Lower order right-hand batsman, wicket-keeper. *Team* Somerset (1950–56, 7 matches).
Career batting
7–13–2–201–56*–18.27–0–*ct* 7–*st* 8

Day, Harold Lindsay Vernon
Amateur. *b:* 12.8.1898, Darjeeling, India. *d:* 15.6.1972, Hadley Wood, Herts. Middle order right-hand batsman. *Sch* Bedford Modern. *Team* Hampshire (1922–31, 78 matches).
Career batting
80–129–5–3142–142–25.33–4–*ct* 26
Bowling 46–0
He appeared for Bedfordshire before joining Hampshire. A well-known rugby player, he represented Leicestershire and England as wing three quarter.

Day, James John
Amateur. *b:* 1850, London. *d:* 19.2.1895, Wandsworth, London. Middle order batsman. *Team* Gentlemen of South (1870); W.G. Grace's XI (1871–73).
Career batting
3–3–0–1–1–0.33–0–*ct* 2

Day, John William
Professional. *b:* 16.9.1882, Sutton on Trent, Notts. *d:* 9.11.1949, Saxilby, Lincs. Middle order right-hand batsman, medium pace bowler. *Team* Nottinghamshire (1903–07, 61 matches).
Career batting
61–96–8–1233–88–14.01–0–*ct* 34
Bowling 950–27–35.18–1–0–5/50
He also played for Lincolnshire. He played soccer for Gainsborough Trinity.

Day, Kenneth Brian
Professional. *b:* 19.5.1935, Hendon, Middlesex. *d:* 19.1.1971, Fulham, London. Lower order right-hand batsman, wicket-keeper. *Team* Middlesex (1959, 1 match).
Career batting
3 matches, did not bat–*ct* 4–*st* 4
He made his first-class debut in 1958 for MCC.

Day, Leonard Morrison
Amateur. *b:* 24.12.1859, York. *d:* 25.4.1943, Hornsey, Middlesex. Middle/lower order right-hand batsman, lob bowler, wicket-keeper. *Team* Gloucestershire (1880–82, 15 matches).
Career batting
16–23–8–164–34*–10.93–0–*ct* 7–*st* 3

Day, Sydney Ernest
Amateur. *b:* 9.2.1884, Blackheath, Kent. *d:* 7.7.1970, West Malling, Kent. Brother of A.P. (Kent) and S.H. (Kent). Middle order right-hand batsman. *Sch* Malvern. *Team* Kent (1922–25, 11 matches).
Career batting
11–17–4–245–45*–18.84–0–*ct* 4
An excellent soccer player, he appeared for Corinthians.

Day, Samuel Hulme
Amateur. *b:* 29.12.1878, Peckham Rye, Surrey. *d:* 21.2.1950, Chobham, Surrey. Brother of A.P. (Kent) and S.E. (Kent). Middle order right-hand batsman, right-arm fast bowler. *Sch* Malvern. *Teams* Kent (1897–1919, 128 matches); Cambridge U (1899–02, blue all four years).
Career batting
171–285–25–7722–152*–29.70–7–*ct* 58
Bowling 317–8–39.62–0–0–3/46
He twice hit 1,000 runs in a season (best 1,167, av 34.32, in 1901).
A noted soccer player, he appeared for Corinthians and three times for England.

Days, John Edward
Professional. *b:* 1872, Pershore, Worcs. *d:* 1947, Walsall, Staffs. Lower order batsman, bowler. *Team* Worcestershire (1900–07, 2 matches).
Career batting
2–3–0–8–5–2.66–0–*ct* 0
Bowling 42–2–21.00–0–0–2/42
He also played for Staffordshire.

Deakin, Michael John
Cricketer. *b:* 5.5.1957, Bury, Lancashire. Lower order right-hand batsman, wicket-keeper. *Team* Derbyshire (1981, 4 matches).
Career batting
4–6–0–45–15–7.50–0–*ct* 9

Dean, David
Professional. *b:* 27.7.1847, Duncton, Sussex. *d:* 1919, Midhurst, Sussex. Brother of James, jun (Sussex), nephew of James, sen (Sussex). Middle order batsman. *Team* Sussex (1871, 2 matches).
Career batting
2–3–0–8–6–2.66–0–*ct* 1

Dean, Harry
Professional. *b:* 13.8.1884, Burnley, Lancashire. *d:* 12.3.1957, Garstang, Lancashire. Lower order left-hand batsman, left-arm fast medium bowler. *Team* Lancashire (1906–21, 256 matches). *Tests* England (1912, 3 matches).
Career batting
267–370–122–2559–49*–10.31–0–*ct* 120
Bowling 23606–1301–18.14–97–24–9/31
Test batting
3–4–2–10–8–5.00–0–*ct* 2
Bowling 153–11–13.90–0–0–4/19
He took 100 wickets in a season eight times (best 183, av 17.43, in 1911). His best bowling was 9/31 for Lancashire v Somerset at Old Trafford in 1909.
He also played for Cheshire.

Dean, James
Professional. *b:* 4.1.1816, Duncton, Sussex. *d:* 25.12. 1881, Duncton, Sussex. Uncle of David (Sussex) and James, jun (Sussex). Lower order right-hand batsman, right-hand fast round arm bowler, wicket-keeper. *Team* Sussex (1835–60, 112 matches).
Career batting
305–548–63–5115–99–10.54–0–*ct* 205
Bowling 6805–491+649–13.85–86–18–9/34
He often bowled from one end and then remained there to keep wicket for the following over. His best bowling was 9/34 for MCC v Notts at Trent Bridge in 1843. He took 100 wickets in 1845.
His final first-class match was for MCC in 1861.

Dean, James
Professional. *b:* 7.4.1842, Petworth, Sussex. *d:* 6.3.1869, Duncton, Sussex. Brother of David (Sussex) nephew of James, sen (Sussex). Hard hitting middle order right-hand batsman. *Team* Sussex (1862–66, 12 matches).
Career batting
12–22–4–220–39*–12.22–0–*ct* 5
Bowling 23–1–23.00–0–0–1/13

Dean, Philip James
Cricketer. *b:* 4.6.1955, Skipton, Yorkshire. Middle order left-hand batsman. *Sch* Mill Hill. *Team* Oxford U (1978).
Career batting
2–4–0–75–39–18.75–0–*ct* 1

Dean, T.
Professional. Middle order batsman. *Team* Gloucestershire (1908, 1 match).
Career batting
1–2–0–15–11–7.50–0–*ct* 0

Dean, Thomas Arthur
Professional. *b:* 21.11.1920, Gosport, Hants. Middle/lower order right-hand batsman, leg break bowler. *Teams* Hampshire (1939–49, 28 matches); Eastern Province (1956/7).
Career batting
29–46–13–285–26–8.63–0–*ct* 31
Bowling 1706–54–31.59–4–1–7/51
He was brought up in South Africa and returned there as a cricket coach after leaving Hampshire.
He also played for Devon.

Dean, William H.
Professional. *b:* 3.11.1928, Leeds, Yorkshire. Lower order right-hand batsman, right-arm fast medium bowler. *Team* Somerset (1952, 1 match).
Career batting
1–2–1–21–21–21.00–0–*ct* 0
Bowling 17–0

Dean
Professional. *b:* Australia. *Team* Hampshire (1907, 1 match).
Career batting
1–1–1–3–3*–no av–0–*ct* 2
Bowling 52–2–26.00–0–0–2/52

Deane, Charles Gerard
Amateur. *b:* 1885, Oakhill, Somerset. *d:* 14.12.1914, Multan, India, of fever. Middle order right-hand batsman, right-arm medium pace bowler. *Sch* Taunton. *Team* Somerset (1907–13, 36 matches).

Career batting
36–69–6–753–78–11.95–0–*ct* 25
Bowling 206–8–25.75–0–0–2/36

Deane, Hubert Gouvaine
Amateur. *b:* 21.7.1895, Eshowe, Zululand. *d:* 21.10.1939, Johannesburg, South Africa. Son of H.P. (Natal). Middle order right-hand batsman, brilliant close field. *Teams* Natal (1919/20 to 1922/3); Transvaal (1923/4 to 1929/30). *Tours* South Africa to England 1924, 1929. *Tests* South Africa (1924 to 1930/1, 17 matches).
Career batting
100–138–12–3795–165–30.11–6–*ct* 63
Bowling 99–3–33.00–0–0–3/23
Test batting
17–27–2–628–93–25.12–0–*ct* 8

He hit 1,239, av 34.41, runs on his 1929 tour of England. He captained the South Africans in England in 1929 and in all led his country in 12 Tests. His final first-class match was in South Africa in 1930/1.

Deane, Marmaduke William
Professional. *b:* 23.5.1857, Petersham, Surrey. *d:* 1936, Surrey. Lower order right-hand batsman, wicket-keeper. *Teams* Surrey (1880, 1 match); Hampshire (1895, 4 matches).
Career batting
5–9–2–16–8–2.28–0–*ct* 5–*st* 4

Dearden, John
Amateur. *b:* 26.12 1891, St Helens, Lancashire. *d:* 4.5.1972, Belfast, Ireland. Right-hand batsman, wicket-keeper. *Team* Ireland (1922–26).
Career batting
2–3–0–84–84–28.00–0–*ct* 1–*st* 1

Dearlove, Alfred John
Amateur. *b:* 1869, Clifton, Gloucs. *d:* 17.3.1955, Bristol. Middle order right-hand batsman, change bowler. *Team* Gloucestershire (1895–1900, 6 matches).
Career batting
6–10–1–129–34*–14.33–0–*ct* 1
Bowling 141–5–28.20–0–0–3/56

Dearlove, John Allan
Amateur. *b:* 30.4.1931, London. Lower order right-hand batsman, right-arm medium pace bowler. *Sch* Downside. *Team* Cambridge U (1954).
Career batting
1–1–0–6–6–6.00–0–*ct* 1
Bowling 74–0

Dearnaley, Irvine
Professional in 1900, but amateur 1905–07. *b:* 18.2.1877, Glossop, Derbyshire. *d:* 14.3.1965, Ashton-under-Lyne, Lancashire, following a road accident. Middle order right-hand batsman. *Team* Derbyshire (1905–07, 4 matches).
Career batting
4–8–0–51–34–6.37–0–*ct* 3

He played for Derbyshire v West Indies (pre-first-class) in 1900.

Deas, Kenneth Robin
Amateur. *b:* 10.7.1927, Papatoetoe, New Zealand. Right-hand batsman, slow left-arm bowler. *Teams* Scotland (1955–56); Auckland (1947/8 to 1960/1).
Career batting
18–34–4–522–73–17.40–0–*ct* 7
Bowling 313–9–34.77–0–0–4/81

Debnam, Alexander Frederick Henry
Amateur in 1948, professional from 1949. *b:* 12.10.1922, Belvedere, Kent. Middle/lower order right-hand batsman, leg break bowler. *Teams* Kent (1948–49, 11 matches); Hampshire (1950–51, 10 matches).
Career batting
21–33–6–327–64–12.11–0–*ct* 12
Bowling 862–20–43.10–1–0–5/87

De Burgh, Hubert Henry
Amateur. *b:* 16.2.1879, Old Town, Naas, Co Kildare, Ireland. *d:* 6.10.1960, Old Town, Naas, Co Kildare, Ireland. Right-hand batsman. *Team* Ireland (1926); Europeans (1905–06).
Career batting
2–3–0–39–28–13.00–0–*ct* 0

De Courcy, James Harry
Amateur. *b:* 18.4.1927, Newcastle, New South Wales, Australia. Middle order right-hand batsman. *Team* New South Wales (1947/8 to 1957/8, 50 matches). *Tour* Australia to England 1953. *Tests* Australia (1953, 3 matches).
Career batting
79–113–11–3778–204–37.03–6–*ct* 51
Bowling 67–0
Test batting
3–6–1–81–41–16.20–0–*ct* 3

In 1953 in England he hit 1,214 runs, av 41.86. His only double century was made during that tour v Combined Services at Kingston.

Deed, John Arthur
Amateur. *b:* 12.9.1901, Sevenoaks, Kent. *d:* 19.10.1980, Ide Hill, Kent. Opening or middle order left-hand batsman. *Sch* Malvern. *Team* Kent (1924–30, 62 matches).
Career batting
62–99–17–1863–133–22.71–2–*ct* 16

He appeared in the Seniors' match whilst at Cambridge, but no first-class games.

De Grey, Rev Hon Arnald
Amateur. *b:* 11.9.1856, London. *d:* 15.11.1889, Hyeres, France. Half-brother of Hon Thomas (Cambridge U). Middle order right-hand batsman. *Sch* Eton. *Team* I Zingari (1880).
Career batting
1–1–0–1–1–1.00–0–*ct* 1
Bowling 32–0

De Grey, Hon Thomas
(succeeded as 6th Baron Walsingham in 1870)
Amateur. *b:* 29.7.1843, Mayfair, London. *d:* 3.12.1919, Hampstead, London. Half-brother of Rev Hon Arnald (I Zingari). Opening/middle order right-hand batsman, excellent cover point. *Sch* Eton. *Team* Cambridge U (1862–64, blue 1862–63).
Career batting
15–27–1–380–62–14.62–0–*ct* 9

His final first-class match was for MCC in 1866. He would have played in the University match of 1864 but for rheumatism.

He was at one time the best shot in England and had a record of 1,070 grouse in one day.

He was MP for West Norfolk, 1865–1870.

Deighton, John Harold Greenway
Amateur. *b:* 5.4.1920, Prestwich, Lancashire. Hard hitting middle/lower order right-hand batsman, right-arm fast medium bowler. *Sch* Denstone. *Teams* Lancashire (1948–50, 7 matches); Combined Services (1947–62).
Career batting
35–63–13–994–79–19.88–0–*ct* 17
Bowling 3081–127–24.25–6–1–6/50

He also played for Northumberland.

Delacombe, William Barclay
Amateur. *b:* 20.7.1860, Georgetown, Ascension Island. *d:* 14.10.1911, Nottingham. Lower order batsman, change bowler, good field. *Sch* King's, Bruton. *Team* Derbyshire (1894–1900, 10 matches).
Career batting
10–13–3–95–23*–9.50–0–*ct* 2
Bowling 44–0

He was Hon Secretary to Derbyshire CCC from 1889 to 1907 and, as a good club cricketer, appeared for the County if required.

De La Warr, Earl, Gilbert George Reginald Sackville
(Viscount Cantelupe, becoming 3rd Earl in 1895)
Amateur. *b:* 22.3.1869, London. *d:* 16.12 1915, Messina, Sicily. Batsman. *Sch* Charterhouse. *Teams* Lord Sheffield's XI (1891); Earl De La Warr's XI (1896)
Career batting
2–2–0–2–1–1.00–0–*ct* 2

Delisle, Gustave Peter Saprine
Amateur. *b:* 25.12.1934, Basseterre, St Kitts, West Indies. Middle order right-hand batsman, off break bowler. *Sch* Stonyhurst. *Teams* Oxford U (1954–56, blue 1955–56); Middlesex (1954–57, 55 matches). *Tour* Surridge to Bermuda 1961 (not first-class).
Career batting
91–163–16–3283–130–22.03–3–*ct* 40

His last first-class match was for Combined Services in 1958. He hit 1,185 runs, av 22.78, in 1955.

De Lisle, John Adrian Frederick March Phillipps
Amateur. *b:* 27.9.1891, London. *d:* 4.11.1961, Leicester. Middle/lower order right-hand batsman. *Sch* Downside and Beaumont. *Team* Leicestershire (1921–30, 33 matches).
Career batting
33–50–4–530–88–11.52–0–*ct* 13

He captained Leicestershire in 1930, his only season playing regularly in County cricket.

De Little, Ernest Robert
Amateur. *b:* 19.6.1868, Melbourne, Australia. *d:* 1.10.1926, Caramut, Victoria, Australia. Lower order right-hand batsman, right-arm fast bowler, good field. *Team* Cambridge U (1888–89, blue 1889). *Tour* Vernon to India 1889/90 (not first-class).
Career batting
9–16–7–104–22–11.55–0–*ct* 4
Bowling 548–27–20.29–2–1–7/27

Deller, Reginald Patrick
Professional. *b:* 27.3.1933, Paddington, London. Lower order right-hand batsman, right-arm fast medium bowler. *Team* Middlesex (1951–53, 3 matches).
Career batting
3–3–3–4–3*–no av–0–*ct* 0
Bowling 127–2–63.50–0–0–1/35

Delmé-Radcliffe, Arthur Henry
Amateur. *b:* 23.11.1870, South Tidworth, Hants. *d:* 30.6.1950, Branksome Park, near Bournemouth, Hants. Middle order right-hand batsman, slow bowler. *Sch* Sherborne. *Team* Hampshire (1896–1900, 7 matches).
Career batting
7–13–0–190–43–14.61–0–*ct* 3

Whilst at Oxford he played in the Freshmen's Match, but no first-class games. His County cricket began with Hampshire in 1889, during a period when Hampshire were not considered first-class, and later he played for Berkshire.

De Mel, Asantha Lakdasa Francis
Cricketer. *b:* 9.5.1959, Colombo, Ceylon. Middle order right-hand batsman, right-arm fast medium bowler. *Team* Sri Lanka (1980/1 to 1982/3). *Tours* Sri Lanka to India 1980/1, 1982/3, to England 1981, to Pakistan 1981/2, to Australia and New Zealand 1982/3, to Zimbabwe 1982/3. *Tests* Sri Lanka (1981/2 to 1982/3, 6 matches).
Career batting
22–32–6–613–100*–23.57–1–*ct* 14
Bowling 2102–48–43.79–1–0–5/68
Test batting
6–12–2–154–34–15.40–0–*ct* 5
Bowling 905–25–36.20–1–0–5/68

De Montezuma, Leonidas De Toledo Marcondes
Amateur. *b:* 16.4.1869, Crowborough, Sussex. *d:* 18.3.1937, Dartford, Kent. Middle order right-hand batsman, useful change bowler. *Teams* Sussex (1898, 7 matches); London County (1904).
Career batting
9–15–4–285–80*–25.90–0–*ct* 2
Bowling 83–4–20.75–0–0–4/71

De Montmorency, Reymond Hervey
Amateur. *b:* 6.10.1871, Gondah, India. *d:* 19.12.1938, Sunningdale, Berkshire. Middle order right-hand batsman, right-arm slow medium bowler. *Sch* Cheltenham and St Paul's. *Team* Oxford U (1899, blue).
Career batting
4–7–0–230–62–32.85–0–*ct* 1
Bowling 123–5–24.60–0–0–3/16
His first-class debut was for Oxford U, Past and Present in 1897. His County cricket was for Hertfordshire and Buckinghamshire. A useful all round sportsman, he represented Oxford at golf and rackets.

Dempsey, General Sir Miles Christopher
Amateur. *b:* 15.12.1896, Wallasey, Cheshire. *d:* 5.6.1969, Newbury, Berkshire. Middle order right-hand batsman, slow left-arm bowler. *Sch* Shrewsbury. *Team* Sussex (1919, 2 matches).
Career batting
2–3–0–5–4–1.66–0–*ct* 1
He also played for Berkshire.
He commanded the Second Army in the 1944 invasion of Normandy.

Dempster, Charles Stewart
Amateur. *b:* 15.11.1903, Wellington, New Zealand. *d:* 14.2.1974, Wellington, New Zealand. Opening/middle order right-hand batsman, right-arm slow bowler. *Teams* Wellington (1921/2 to 1947/8); Scotland (1934); Leicestershire (1935–39, 69 matches); Warwickshire (1946, 3 matches). *Tours* New Zealand to England 1927, 1931, to Australia 1927/8; Cahn to Ceylon 1936/7, to New Zealand 1938/9. *Tests* New Zealand (1929/30 to 1932/3, 10 matches).
Career batting
184–306–36–12145–212–44.98–35–*ct* 94–*st* 2
Bowling 300–8–37.50–0–0–2/4
Test batting
10–15–4–723–136–65.72–2–*ct* 2
Bowling 10–0
One of the greatest of all New Zealand batsmen, he began in County cricket after two successful tours to England with the New Zealand team. He hit 1,000 runs in a season five times (best 1,778, av 59.26, in 1931). The highest of his two double centuries was 212 for New Zealanders v Essex at Leyton in 1931. He captained Leicestershire 1936–38.

Dench, Charles Edward
Professional. *b:* 6.9.1873, East Stoke, Notts. *d:* 28.6.1958, Sherwood, Nottingham. Middle/lower order right-hand batsman, right-arm medium pace bowler. *Team* Nottinghamshire (1897–1902, 91 matches).
Career batting
91–136–17–2660–88–22.35–0–*ct* 60
Bowling 2191–78–28.09–4–0–7/28
He took 7 for 28 on his first-class debut, Notts v MCC at Lord's in 1897.

Denham, Harold Alfred
Amateur. *b:* 13.10.1872, Howrah, India. *d:* 25.2.1946, Eastbourne, Sussex. Middle order batsman. *Team* Hampshire (1896, 1 match).
Career batting
1–2–0–8–7–4.00–0–*ct* 0

Denman, Henry Wynne
Amateur. *b:* 5.7.1929, Liverpool. Lower order right-hand batsman, wicket-keeper. *Sch* Oundle. *Team* Cambridge U (1950–52).
Career batting
7–5–4–4–3–4.00–0–*ct* 5–*st* 2

Denman, John
Cricketer. *b:* 13.6.1947, Crawley, Sussex. Lower order right-hand batsman, right-arm medium pace bowler. *Team* Sussex (1970–73, 49 matches).

Career batting
49–65–20–713–50*–15.84–0–*ct* 26
Bowling 3065–70–43.78–1–0–5/45

Denness, Michael Henry
Cricketer. *b:* 1.12.1940, Bellshill, Lanarkshire, Scotland. Opening/middle order right-hand batsman, right-arm medium pace off break bowler. *Sch* Ayr Academy. *Teams* Scotland (1959–67); Kent (1962–76, 333 matches); Essex (1977–80, 83 matches). *Tours* International XI to East Africa, India, Pakistan and Ceylon 1967/8; Norfolk to West Indies 1969/70; MCC to India, Pakistan and Sri Lanka 1972/3, to West Indies 1973/4, to Australia and New Zealand 1974/5; International Wanderers to South Africa 1975/6; Robins to Sri Lanka 1977/8. *Tests* England (1969–75, 28 matches).
Career batting
501–838–65–25886–195–33.48–33–*ct* 411
Bowling 62–2–31.00–0–0–1/7
Test batting
28–45–3–1667–188–39.69–4–*ct* 28

He reached 1,000 runs in a season 14 times (best 1,606, av 31.49, in 1966). He captained Kent from 1972 to 1976 and England in 19 Tests between 1973/4 and 1975, including the Test tours of 1973/4 and 1974/5. He dropped himself from the fourth Test in Australia in 1974/5, but resumed his place later.

Dennett, Edward George
Professional. *b:* 27.4.1879, Upway, Dorset. *d:* 15.9.1937, Cheltenham, Gloucs. Lower order left-hand batsman, slow left-arm bowler. *Teams* Gloucestershire (1903–26, 387 matches); Bengal Governor's XI (1917/18).
Career batting
401–651–254–4102–71–14.33–0–*ct* 297
Bowling 42640–2151–19.82–211–57–10/40

He took 100 wickets in a season 12 times, exceeding 200 once – 201, av 16.05, in 1907.

He performed the feat of taking all ten wickets in an innings (for 40 runs) for Gloucs v Essex at Bristol in 1906.

An all-round sportsman, he also excelled at soccer, fives, billiards and shooting.

Denning, Peter William
Cricketer. *b*: 16.12.1949, Chewton Mendip, Somerset. Middle order left-hand batsman, off break bowler, deep field. *Sch* Millfield. *Team* Somerset (1969–83, 264 matches).
Career batting
264–439–41–11221–184–28.19–8–*ct* 130
Bowling 96–1–96.00–0–0–1/4

He hit 1,000 runs in a season six times (best 1,222, av 42.13, in 1979).

Dennis, Frank
Professional. *b:* 11.6.1907, Leeds, Yorkshire. Uncle of S. J. (Yorkshire), brother in law of L. Hutton (Yorkshire). Lower order left-hand batsman, right-arm fast bowler. *Team* Yorkshire (1928–33, 90 matches).
Career batting
93–105–29–1500–95–19.73–0–*ct* 59
Bowling 4770–163–29.26–5–0–6/42

He appeared for Cheshire 1935–39 and his final first-class match was for Minor Counties in 1939.

After the Second World War he lived in New Zealand and was an official of the Canterbury Club.

Dennis, Joseph
Professional. *b:* 1779, Nottingham. *d:* 16.11.1831, Nottingham. Wicket-keeper. *Team* Nottingham (1803–29).
Career batting
7–13–0–48–14–3.69–0–*ct* 4–*st* 4

He was regarded as one of the greatest wicket-keepers of his era.

Dennis, John Newman
Amateur. *b:* 4.1.1913, Leytonstone, Essex. Middle order right-hand batsman. *Sch* Forest. *Team* Essex (1934–39, 22 matches).
Career batting
22–33–3–530–53–17.66–0–*ct* 13

Dennis, Simon John
Cricketer. *b*: 18.10.1960, Scarborough, Yorkshire. Nephew of L. Hutton (Yorkshire) and F. Dennis (Yorkshire). Tail end right-hand batsman, left-arm fast medium bowler. *Teams* Yorkshire (1980–83, 33 matches); Orange Free State (1982/3).
Career batting
38–42–16–209–37*–8.03–0–*ct* 11
Bowling 3199–111–28.81–3–0–5/35

Dennison, David George
Cricketer. *b*: 22.12.1961, Banbridge, Co Down, Ireland. Opening right-hand batsman. *Team* Ireland (1983).
Career batting
1–2–0–17–16–8.50–0–*ct* 1

Denny, Ernest Wriothesley
Amateur. *b:* 5.2.1872, London. *d:* 20.10.1949, Garboldisham, Norfolk. Lower order right-hand batsman, right-arm fast medium bowler. *Sch* Wellington. *Team* Oxford U (1891).
Career batting
1–2–2–1–1*–no av–0–*ct* 0
Bowling 14–0

Dent, Henry James
Amateur. *b:* 1875, Weobley, Herefordshire. *d:* 27.8.1929, Stoke Edith, Herefordshire. Lower order batsman, useful bowler. *Team* H.K. Foster's XI (1919).
Career batting
1–1–0–1–1–1.00–0–*ct* 0
Bowling 38–0
He also played for Herefordshire.

Denton, Arthur Donald
Amateur. *b:* 21.10.1896, Rushden, Northants. *d:* 23.1.1961, Higham Ferrers, Northants. Brother of J.S. (Northants) and W.H. (Northants). Middle order right-hand batsman, lob bowler. *Sch* Wellingborough. *Team* Northants (1914–20, 7 matches).
Career batting
7–13–2–176–51*–25.09–0–*ct* 3
Bowling 5–0
He lost part of a leg in the First World War, but continued to play cricket with the aid of a runner.

Denton, David
Professional. *b:* 4.7.1874, Thornes, Wakefield, Yorkshire. *d;* 16.2.1950, Wakefield, Yorkshire. Brother of Joe (Yorkshire). Middle order right-hand batsman, right-arm medium fast bowler, brilliant outfield. *Team* Yorkshire (1894–1920, 676 matches). *Tours* MCC to South Africa 1905/6, 1909/10. *Tests* England (1905 to 1909/10, 11 matches).
Career batting
741–1161–70–36440–221–33.40–69–*ct* 396–*st* 1
Bowling 983–34–28.91–1–0–5/42
Test batting
11–22–1–424–104–20.19–1–*ct* 8
He hit 1,000 runs in a season 21 times, exceeding 2,000 on five occasions (best 2,405, av 42.19, in 1905). His three double centuries were all for Yorkshire, the highest being 221 v Kent at Tunbridge Wells in 1912.

Denton, Joe
Professional. *b:* 3.2.1865, Thornes, Wakefield. *d:* 19.7.1946, Pontefract, Yorkshire. Brother of David (Yorkshire). Middle order right-hand batsman. *Team* Yorkshire (1887–88, 15 matches).
Career batting
15–24–1–222–57–9.65–0–*ct* 6

Denton, John Sidney
Amateur. *b:* 2.11.1890, Rushden, Northants. *d:* 9.4.1971, Rushden, Northants. Twin brother of W.H. (Northants) and brother of A.D. (Northants). Opening right-hand batsman, leg break and googly bowler. *Sch* Wellingborough. *Team* Northants (1909–19, 104 matches).
Career batting
104–178–26–3298–124–21.69–2–*ct* 53
Bowling 1883–67–28.10–2–0–5/39
He hit 1,007 runs, av 17.97, in 1913.

Denton, William Herbert
Amateur. *b:* 2.11.1890, Rushden, Northants. *d:* 23.4.1979, Bedford. Twin brother of J.S. (Northants) and brother of A.D. (Northants). Opening right-hand batsman, good field. *Sch* Wellingborough. *Team* Northants (1909–24, 119 matches).
Career batting
119–205–19–4449–230*–23.94–4–*ct* 54
Bowling 42–0
In 1913 he hit 1,055 runs, av 34.03. He also scored his only double century in the same year: 230* for Northants v Essex at Leyton.

De Paravicini, Harry Farquhar
Amateur. *b:* 20.10.1859, London. *d:* 28.10.1942, Hove. Brother of P.J. (Middlesex). Middle order right-hand batsman. *Sch* Harrow. *Team* MCC (1882–85).
Career batting
6–9–3–64–28*–10.66–0–*ct* 1
He was not in the eleven at Cambridge, but excelled at rackets. His final first-class match was for I Zingari in 1888.

De Paravicini, Percy John
Amateur. *b:* 15.7.1862, London. *d:* 11.10.1921, Pangbourne, Berkshire. Brother of H.F. (MCC). Middle order right-hand batsman, right-hand slow round arm bowler, excellent deep field. *Sch* Eton. *Teams* Middlesex (1881–92, 62 matches); Cambridge U (1882–85, blue all four years).
Career batting
122–200–26–2699–77–15.51–0–*ct* 70
Bowling 1048–32–32.75–0–0–4/26
In a minor match he went to the wicket with time nearly up and fifteen runs required – he hit the first ball for eight and the second for seven! He also played for Buckinghamshire. He played soccer for Cambridge University and England, and played in two FA Cup finals for Old Etonians, on the winning side against Blackburn Rovers in 1882.

Dermont, Roger Wayne Archie
Cricketer. *b:* 1.4.1945, Hitchin, Herts. Lower order batsman, bowler. *Team* MCC (1967).
Career batting
1–1–0–0–0–0.00–0–*ct* 0
Bowling 31–2–15.50–0–0–2/23

Derrick, John
Cricketer. *b:* 15.1.1963, Cwmaman, Glamorgan. Right-hand batsman, right-arm medium pace bowler. *Team* Glamorgan (1983, 5 matches).
Career batting
5–5–3–52–24*–26.00–0–*ct* 3
Bowling 31–0

Desai, Avinash Harkant
Professional. *b:* 7.8.1932, Surat, India. Son of Harkant Desai (Baroda and Gujerat). Lower order right-hand batsman, leg break and googly bowler. *Teams* Commonwealth XI (1957); Rajputana (1947/8); Bombay (1952/3 to 1957/8); Railways (1958/9 to 1963/4).
Career batting
41–51–12–1700–147*–43.58–5–*ct* 18
Bowling 1378–54–25.51–4–1–6/108

Desai, Ramakant Bhikaji
Amateur. *b:* 20.6.1939, Bombay, India. Lower order right-hand batsman, right-arm fast medium bowler. *Team* Bombay (1958/9 to 1968/9). *Tours* India to England 1959, to West Indies 1961/2, to Australia and New Zealand 1967/8; Wadekar to Sri Lanka 1975/6. *Tests* India (1958/9 to 1967/8, 28 matches).
Career batting
150–179–48–2384–107–18.19–1–*ct* 49
Bowling 11282–468–24.10–22–2–7/46
Test batting
28–44–13–418–85–13.48–0–*ct* 9
Bowling 2761–74–37.31–2–0–6/56
He took 45 wickets, av 41.42, on the 1959 tour to England and played in all five Tests. His final first-class match in India was for A.C.C. in 1971/2.

De Saram, Frederick Cecil
Amateur. *b:* 5.9.1912, Colombo, Ceylon. *d:* 11.4.1983, Colombo, Sri Lanka. Middle order right-hand batsman. Nephew of D. L. and F. R. (Ceylon). *Teams* Oxford U (1934–35, blue both years); Ceylon (1930/1 to 1953/4). *Tour* Ceylon to India 1940/1.
Career batting
40–74–4–2789–208–39.84–6–*ct* 17
Bowling 81–0
In 1934 he hit 1,119 runs, av 50.86, and scored his only double century, 208 for Oxford U v Leveson-Gower's XI at Reigate.
He also played for Hertfordshire.

Deshon, David Peter Tower
Amateur. *b:* 19.6.1923, London. Middle order right-hand batsman. *Sch* Sherborne. *Team* Somerset (1947–53, 4 matches).
Career batting
4–8–1–82–21–11.71–0–*ct* 1

De Silva, Deva Lokesh Stanley
Cricketer. *b:* 17.11.1956, Ambalangoda, Ceylon. *d:*12.4.1980, Sri Lanka, in a motor cycle accident. Tail end right-hand batsman, right-arm fast medium bowler. *Team* Sri Lanka (1979). *Tour* Sri Lanka to England 1979.
Career batting
4–3–1–11–7–5.50–0–*ct* 2
Bowling 199–6–33.16–0–0–2/28
He was the principal seam bowler on the 1979 tour to England.

De Silva, Dandeniyage Somachandra
Cricketer. *b:* 11.6.1944, Galle, Ceylon. Middle order right-hand batsman, leg break and googly bowler. *Teams* Sri Lanka (1966/7 to 1982/3). *Tours* Sri Lanka to India 1972/3, 1975/6, 1982/3, to Pakistan 1973/4, 1981/2, to England 1975, 1979, 1981, to Australia and New Zealand 1982/3; to Zimbabwe 1982/3. *Tests* Sri Lanka (1981/2 to 1982/3, 8 matches).
Career batting
56–85–14–1638–97–23.07–0–*ct* 30
Bowling 5889–217–27.13–14–5–8/46
Test batting
8–16–2–364–61–26.00–0–*ct* 3
Bowling 969–27–35.88–1–0–5/59
He also played for Lincolnshire. He captained Sri Lanka in two Tests in 1982/3.

De Silva, Ginigalgodage Ramba Ajit
Cricketer. *b:* 12.12.1952, Ambalagoda, Ceylon. Lower order left-hand batsman, slow left-arm bowler. *Team* Sri Lanka (1973/4 to 1982/3). *Tours* Sri Lanka to Pakistan 1973/4, 1981/2, to India 1974/5, 1975/6, 1976/7, 1982/3, to England 1975, 1979, 1981; Sri Lanka XI to South Africa 1982/3. *Tests* Sri Lanka (1981/2 to 1982/3, 4 matches).
Career batting
53–68–27–317–75–7.73–0–*ct* 21
Bowling 4418–161–27.44–4–0–6/30
Test batting
4–7–2–41–14–8.20–0–*ct* 0
Bowling 385–7–55.00–0–0–2/38

De Silva, John Albert
Amateur. *b:* 19.1.1901, Colombo, Ceylon. *d:* 30.11.1981, Colombo, Sri Lanka. Middle order left-hand batsman, right-arm medium pace bowler. *Teams* Oxford U (1924–27); Ceylon (1929/30 to 1930/1).
Career batting
8–14–3–214–65–19.45–0–*ct* 4
Bowling 187–4–46.75–0–0–1/5

De Soysa, Gahmini Ryle Johannes
Amateur. *b:* 21.6.1917, Colombo, Ceylon.

Middle order left-hand batsman, leg break and googly bowler. *Sch* Newton College. *Teams* Oxford U (1938); Ceylon (1944/5). *Tour* Universities to Jamaica 1938/9.
Career batting
8–16–1–314–67–20.93–0–*ct* 0
Bowling 15–2–7.50–0–0–2/15

De Trafford, Charles Edmund
Amateur. *b:* 21.5.1864, Trafford Park, Manchester. *d:* 11.11.1951, Rothley Temple, Leics. Brother-in-law to Sir T.C. O'Brien (Middlesex). Hard hitting middle order right-hand batsman. *Sch* Beaumont. *Teams* Lancashire (1884, 1 match); Leicestershire (1894–1920, 231 matches); London County (1904). *Tours* Hawke to USA 1894; MCC to New Zealand 1906/7, to South America 1911/2.
Career batting
292–526–13–9581–137–18.67–6–*ct* 98
Bowling 95–2–47.50–0–0–2/47

He played for Leicestershire from 1888 and led the County from 1890 to 1906.

De Uphaugh, Richard George Duppa
Amateur. *b:* 12.3.1895, London. *d:* 25.10.1972, Hollingbourne, Kent. Middle order batsman. *Sch* Harrow. *Team* Oxford U (1919).
Career batting
1–2–1–47–43*–47.00–0–*ct* 0

Devapriya, Hettiwatte Hemantha
Cricketer. *b*: 12.4.1958, Galle, Ceylon. Middle order right-hand batsman, wicket-keeper. *Team* Sri Lanka (1980/1 to 1982/3). *Tours* Sri Lanka to India 1980/1, to England 1981; Sri Lanka XI to South Africa 1982/3.
Career batting
10–20–0–522–95–26.10–0–*ct* 13–*st* 5

Deverell, Sir Colville Montgomery
Amateur. *b:* 27.2.1906, Clonskea, Dublin, Ireland. Right-hand batsman. *Sch* Portora Royal School, Enniskillen. *Team* Dublin University (1926).
Career batting
1–2–0–3–2–1.50–0–*ct* 0

Devereux, Louis Norman
Professional. *b:* 20.10.1931, Heavitree, Exeter, Devon. Middle order right-hand batsman, right-arm off break bowler, fine field. *Teams* Middlesex (1949, 2 matches); Worcestershire (1950–55, 79 matches); Glamorgan (1956–60, 106 matches).
Career batting
192–327–47–5560–108*–19.85–1–*ct* 107
Bowling 6286–178–35.31–2–0–6/29

He hit 1,039 runs, av 22.58, in 1957. He represented England at table tennis in 1949.

Devereux, Richard Jaynes
Cricketer. *b:* 24.12.1938, Castle Bromwich, Warwickshire. Hard hitting lower order right-hand batsman, left-arm medium pace bowler. *Sch* Malvern. *Team* Worcestershire (1963, 11 matches).
Career batting
11–16–3–216–55*–16.61–0–*ct* 13
Bowling 581–13–44.69–0–0–3/44

Devey, John Henry George
Professional. *b:* 26.12.1866, Birmingham. *d:* 11.10.1940, Moseley, Birmingham. Opening/middle order right-hand batsman, right-arm medium pace bowler. *Team* Warwickshire (1894–1907, 153 matches).
Career batting
154–253–20–6550–246–28.11–8–*ct* 70
Bowling 655–16–40.93–0–0–3/65

His best season was 1906 when he hit 1,237 runs, av 41.23. His only double century was 246 for Warwickshire v Derbyshire at Birmingham in 1900.

A noted soccer player he represented West Bromwich Albion, Aston Villa and England as a forward, and won three FA Cup winners medals, one with West Brom and two with Villa.

De Ville, Roger Thomas
Cricketer. *b:* 21.1.1935, Uttoxeter, Staffs. Middle/lower order right-hand batsman, leg break bowler. *Sch* Denstone. *Team* Derbyshire (1963–64, 3 matches)
Career batting
3–5–2–26–17–8.66–0–*ct* 0
Bowling 146–2–73.00–0–0–2/47

He appeared for Staffordshire commencing 1959.

De Villiers, John Oliver
Amateur. *b:* 28.2.1930, Cape Town, South Africa. Middle order right-hand batsman. *Teams* Oxford U (1951–52); Orange Free State (1953/4).
Career batting
11–20–4–347–81–21.68–0–*ct* 3
Bowling 38–0

Dew, David Gerveys du Breul
Amateur. *b:* 16.9.1935, London. Lower order right-hand batsman, wicket-keeper. *Sch* Stowe. *Team* Cambridge U (1959).
Career batting
2–2–0–4–4–2.00–0–*ct* 1

Dew, Dr John Alexander
Amateur. *b:* 12.5.1920, Horsham, Sussex. Middle order right-hand batsman, wicket-keeper. *Sch* Tonbridge. *Team* Sussex (1947, 2 matches).
Career batting
3–5–0–60–29–12.00–0–*ct* 5–*st* 1
His final first-class match was for L.C. Steven's XI in 1961.

Dewar, Arthur
Amateur. *b:* 15.3.1934, Perth, Scotland. Right-hand batsman, right-arm fast medium bowler. *Team* Scotland (1960–62).
Career batting
5–7–4–15–4*–5.00–0–*ct* 1
Bowling 366–11–33.27–1–0–7/71

Dewdney, David Thomas
Amateur. *b:* 23.10.1933, Kingston, Jamaica. Lower order right-hand batsman, right-arm fast bowler. *Teams* Jamaica (1954/5 to 1957/8); Commonwealth (1961). *Tours* West Indies to England 1957, to New Zealand 1955/6, to Australia 1960/1. *Tests* West Indies (1954/5 to 1957/8, 9 matches).
Career batting
40–49–19–171–37*–5.70–0–*ct* 6
Bowling 2828–92–30.73–4–0–7/55
Test batting
9–12–5–17–5*–2.42–0–*ct* 0
Bowling 807–21–38.42–1–0–5/21
He only performed modestly on his tour of England.

Dewé, Charles Douglas Eyre
Amateur. *b:* 2.5.1879, Kingsdown, Kent. *d:* 24.5.1955, Fleet, Hants. Lower order batsman, fast medium bowler. *Sch* Marlborough. *Team* Cambridge U (1901).
Career batting
2–4–1–33–16–11.00–0–*ct* 0
Bowling 130–2–65.00–0–0–2/66

Dewes, Anthony Roy
Cricketer. *b:* 2.6.1957, Rugby. Son of J.G. (Middlesex). Middle order right-hand batsman, leg break bowler. *Sch* Dulwich. *Team* Cambridge U (1978–79, blue 1978).
Career batting
14–21–1–368–84–18.40–0–*ct* 3
Bowling 146–1–146.00–0–0–1/52

Dewes, John Gordon
Amateur. *b:* 11.10.1926, North Latchford, Cheshire. Father of A.R. (Cambridge U). Opening left-hand batsman, right-arm medium pace bowler, excellent outfield. *Sch* Aldenham. *Teams* Cambridge U (1948–50, blue all 3 years); Middlesex (1948–56, 62 matches). *Tour* MCC to Australia and New Zealand 1950/1. *Tests* England (1948 to 1950/1, 5 matches).
Career batting
137–229–24–8564–212–41.77–18–*ct* 46
Bowling 71–2–35.50–0–0–1/0
Test batting
5–10–0–121–67–12.10–0–*ct* 0
He made his first-class debut for England v Australia at Lord's in 1945 and his final first-class appearance for L.E.G. Ames XI in 1957. His batting at Cambridge was quite exceptional, but his appearances in County cricket after 1950 were very restricted due to his profession.
He hit 1,000 runs in a season three times (best 2,432, av 59.31, in 1950). The highest of his two double centuries (both for Cambridge) was 212 v Sussex at Hove in 1950.
A good hockey player he gained his blue in 1949 and 1950.

Dewfall, Ernest George
Amateur. *b:* 12.8.1911, Long Ashton, Bristol. *d:* 11.11.1982, Cleeve, Somerset. Lower order right-hand batsman, right-arm fast bowler. *Team* Gloucestershire (1938, 2 matches).
Career batting
2–2–0–0–0–0.00–0–*ct* 1
Bowling 148–4–37.00–0–0–3/82

Dewhurst, George Alric R.
Amateur. *d:* 1954, Trinidad. Lower order right-hand batsman, wicket-keeper. *Team* Trinidad (1919/20 to 1929/30). *Tour* West Indies to England 1923.
Career batting
31–51–10–665–58–16.21–0–*ct* 47–*st* 13

Dewhurst, Robert
Amateur. *b:* 11.5.1851, Clitheroe, Lancashire. *d:* 15.3.1929, Bispham, Lancashire. Middle order right-hand batsman, right-arm medium round or under arm bowler, good field. *Team* Lancashire (1872–75, 13 matches).
Career batting
13–22–1–266–59–12.66–0–*ct* 8
He also played for Cheshire.

De Winton, George Seton
Amateur. *b:* 5.9.1869, Clifton, Gloucs. *d:* 28.6.1930, Froxfield, Wilts. Middle order left-hand batsman. *Team* Gloucestershire (1890–1901, 28 matches).
Career batting
28–51–9–669–80–15.93–0–*ct* 13
Bowling 3–0

Dews, George
Professional. *b:* 5.6.1921, Ossett, Yorkshire. Forcing middle order right-hand batsman, brilliant outfield. *Team* Worcestershire (1946–61, 374 matches).
Career batting
376–642–53–16803–145–28.52–20–*ct* 351
Bowling 202–2–101.00–0–0–1/31

He hit 1,000 runs in a season 11 times (best 1,752, av 41.71, in 1959).

A well-known soccer player he appeared at inside left for Plymouth Argyle, Walsall and Middlesbrough.

Dewse, Harry
Professional. *b:* 23.2.1836, York. *d:* 8.7.1910, York. Lower order batsman, lob bowler, wicket-keeper. *Team* Yorkshire (1873, 1 match).
Career batting
1–2–0–14–12–7.00–0–*ct* 1
Bowling 15–0

He also played for Northumberland.

Dexter, Edward Ralph
Amateur. *b:* 15.5.1935, Milan, Italy. Brilliant middle order right-hand batsman, right-arm medium pace bowler. *Sch* Radley. *Teams* Cambridge U (1956–58, blue all three years); Sussex (1957–68, 137 matches). *Tours* MCC to Australia and New Zealand 1958/9, 1962/3, to West Indies 1959/60, to India, Pakistan and Ceylon 1961/2, to South Africa 1964/5; Cavaliers to Jamaica 1963/4, 1969/70, to South Africa 1962/3. *Tests* England (1958–68, 62 matches).
Career batting
327–567–48–21150–205–40.75–51–*ct* 234
Bowling 12539–419–29.92–9–2–7/24
Test batting
62–102–8–4502–205–47.89–9–*ct* 30
Bowling 2306–66–34.93–0–0–4/10

Regarded, when he was in his first year at Cambridge, as one of the greatest of modern batsmen, Dexter's career was unfortunately barely ten years in length, first because he chose to retire from regular first-class cricket after 1965, and secondly because he suffered a number of injuries which reduced his opportunites, even in this period. Captain of Sussex from 1960 to 1965 and captain of England in 30 Tests from 1961/2 in India to the series in 1964 against Australia. After this he decided to stand, unsuccessfully as it happened, for Parliament and lost the leadership in the meanwhile. His best summer was 1962 when he hit 2,148 runs and took 76 wickets. In all he hit over 1,000 runs in a season eight times, going on to 2,000 on three occasions, with 2,217 (av 43.47) in 1960 his highest.

Of his two double centuries, the higher was 205 for England v Pakistan at Karachi in 1961/2 and the other 203 for Sussex v Kent at Hastings in 1968, when he made a brief re-appearance in first-class cricket.

He was at his best attacking the bowling, but often found himself forced to play a defensive game. As a bowler he was under-rated and he might easily have achieved the 'double' had his ambitions been in that direction.

After retiring from cricket he became a noted golfer.

Dexter, Hermon Walter
Professional. *b:* 3.5.1877, Nottingham. *d:* 1961, Nottingham. Middle/lower order batsman, right-arm fast medium bowler. *Team* Nottinghamshire (1902–03, 10 matches).
Career batting
10–17–6–223–38*–20.27–0–*ct* 3
Bowling 33–0

Dexter, Roy Evatt
Cricketer. *b:* 13.4.1955, Nottingham. Middle order right-hand batsman. *Sch* Nottingham HS. *Team* Nottinghamshire (1975–81, 22 matches).
Career batting
22–36–6–464–57–15.46–0–*ct* 23

Deyes, George
Professional. *b:* 11.2.1878, Sculcoates, Hull. *d:* January 1963, Scotland. Lower order right-hand batsman, right-arm fast bowler. *Team* Yorkshire (1905–07, 17 matches).
Career batting
17–24–4–44–12–2.20–0–*ct* 6
Bowling 944–41–23.02–3–0–6/62

In 1907 he had 14 successive innings and scored just three singles.

He also played for Staffordshire.

De Zoete, Herman Walter
Amateur. *b:* 13.2.1877, Bromley, Kent. *d:* 26.3.1957, Ipswich, Suffolk. Lower order right-hand batsman, left-arm medium pace/spin bowler. *Sch* Eton. *Teams* Cambridge U (1897–98, blue both years); Essex (1897, 2 matches).
Career batting
18–26–4–151–29–6.86–0–*ct* 7
Bowling 1033–55–18.78–3–0–6/53

An excellent golfer he represented Cambridge in 1896, 1897 and 1898.

Dias, Roy Luke
Cricketer. *b*: 18.10.1952, Colombo, Ceylon. Middle order right-hand batsman, excellent cover field. *Team* Sri Lanka (1974/5 to 1982/3). *Tours* Sri Lanka to India 1974/5, 1975/6, 1976/7, 1982/3, to England 1979, 1981, to Pakistan

1981/2, to Zimbabwe 1982/3, to Australia and New Zealand 1982/3. *Tests* Sri Lanka (1981/2 to 1982/3, 6 matches).
Career batting
52–89–11–2620–127–33.58–2–*ct* 19
Bowling 6–0
Test batting
6–12–0–543–109–45.25–1–*ct* 2

On the 1981 tour to England he hit 607 runs, av 40.46, and scored the only first-class century of the tour.

Dible, William Guy
(known as William Charles)
Professional. *b:* 5.11.1861, Sholing Common, Southampton, Hants. *d:* 15.8.1894, Fareham, Hants. Middle/lower order right-hand batsman, right-arm fast bowler. *Teams* Surrey (1882, 1 match); Hampshire (1883–85, 25 matches).
Career batting
26–47–8–503–68–12.89–0–*ct* 18
Bowling 1996–90–22.17–5–1–7/60

Dick, Arthur Edward
Cricketer. *b:* 10.10.1936, Middlemarch, Otago, New Zealand. Middle order right-hand batsman, wicket-keeper. *Teams* Otago (1956/7 to 1960/1); Wellington (1962/3 to 1968/9). *Tours* New Zealand to Australia and South Africa 1961/2 to Pakistan 1964/5, to England 1965. *Tests* New Zealand (1961/2 to 1965, 17 matches).
Career batting
78–126–12–2315–127–20.30–1–*ct* 148–*st* 21
Bowling 20–0
Test batting
17–30–4–370–50*–14.23–0–*ct* 47–*st* 4

On his tour of England in 1965, he appeared in two of the three Tests.

Dick, Robert Douglas
Amateur. *b:* 16.4.1889, Middlesbrough. Tail end right-hand batsman, right-arm fast bowler. *Team* Yorkshire (1911, 1 match).
Career batting
1–1–0–2–2–2.00–0–*ct* 1
Bowling 37–2–18.50–0–0–1/3

Dickens, Alfred
Amateur. *b:* 1884, Brixworth, Northants. *d:* 1937, Bedford. Lower order batsman, bowler. *Team* Northants (1907, 1 match).
Career batting
1–2–0–3–3–1.50–0–*ct* 0
Bowling 4–1–4.00–0–0–1/4

Dickens, Frederick
Professional. *b:* 23.4.1873, Stratford on Avon, Warwickshire. *d:* 20.2.1935, Warwick. Lower order batsman, left-arm medium pace bowler. *Team* Warwickshire (1898–1903, 29 matches).
Career batting
29–32–6–172–35–6.61–0–*ct* 7
Bowling 1782–75–23.77–3–1–6/23

Dickins, George Caldwell
Amateur. *b:* 17.11.1821, Elmham, Norfolk. *d:* 5.12.1903, Coldstream, Berwickshire, Scotland. Middle order left-hand batsman, right-arm lob bowler. *Sch* Harrow. *Team* Kent (1849–64, 2 matches).
Career batting
7–13–2–158–44–14.36–0–*ct* 1

His debut in first-class matches was for Gentlemen of Kent in 1848.

Dickinson, David Christopher
Amateur. *b:* 11.12.1929, Blackheath, Kent. Lower order right-hand batsman, right-arm medium pace bowler. *Sch* Clifton. *Team* Cambridge U (1953, blue).
Career batting
13–18–7–111–36*–10.90–0–*ct* 4
Bowling 653–24–26.36–0–0–4/22

His final first-class match was for Free Foresters in 1957.

Dickinson, Harold J.
Professional. *b:* 1912, Barry, Glamorgan. Lower order batsman, right-arm fast medium bowler. *Team* Glamorgan (1934–35, 7 matches).
Career batting
7–13–6–37–14*–5.28–0–*ct* 3
Bowling 335–6–55.83–0–0–3/91

Dickinson, John Edward
Amateur. *b:* 20.5.1914, Ashby-de-la-Zouch, Leics. Forcing middle order left-hand batsman, slow left-arm bowler. *Team* Leicestershire (1933–35, 2 matches).
Career batting
2–4–0–27–16–6.75–0–*ct* 1
Bowling 63–0

He also played for Devon.

Dickinson, Patrick John
Amateur. *b:* 28.8.1919, Upper Barian, India. *d:* 28.5.1984, St Pancras, London. Middle/lower order right-hand batsman, right-arm medium slow bowler. *Sch* KCS Wimbledon. *Teams* Cambridge U (1939, blue); Surrey (1939, 10 matches); Bombay (1947/8 to 1948/9); Madras (1950/1 to 1952/3).
Career batting
27–39–1–782–122–20.57–2–*ct* 16
Bowling 1052–28–37.57–1–0–5/95

Dickinson, Stanley Patrick
Amateur. *b:* 7.3.1890, Norton, Derbyshire. *d:* 25.6.1972, Wern, North Wales. Middle/lower order right-hand batsman, right-arm fast medium bowler. *Sch* Haileybury. *Team* Derbyshire (1909, 2 matches).
Career batting
2–3–1–13–10*–6.50–0–*ct* 0
Bowling 45–1–45.00–0–0–1/38

Dickinson, Thomas Eastwood
Amateur. *b:* 11.1.1931, Parramatta, Australia. Lower order left-hand batsman, right-arm fast medium bowler. *Team* Lancashire (1950–51, 4 matches); Somerset (1957, 5 matches).
Career batting
9–12–6–21–9–3.50–0–*ct* 5
Bowling 419–20–20.95–1–0–5/36

Dickinson, William Vicris Digby
Amateur. *b:* 2.11.1889, Swansea. *d:* 24.11.1948, Nairobi, Kenya. Middle order right-hand batsman, left-arm fast medium bowler. *Sch* Cheltenham. *Team* Army (1919–23).
Career batting
14–23–4–614–150–32.31–1–*ct* 8
Bowling 1286–57–21.79–5–1–7/111

He opened the batting whilst at Cheltenham, but in post-war Services matches usually went in at 7 or 8.

Dickson, A.W. *(see under* Dixon, A.W.)

Dickson, Maurice Rhynd
Amateur. *b:* 2.1.1882, Panbride, Angus, Scotland. *d:* 10.1.1940, Arbroath, Scotland. Right-hand batsman, right-arm medium pace bowler. *Sch* Marlborough. *Team* Scotland (1905–14).
Career batting
13–26–1–723–98–28.92–0–*ct* 6
Bowling 16–1–16.00–0–0–1/9

He was a Scottish rugby international.

Digby, Reginald
Amateur. *b:* 30.4.1847, Tittleshall, Norfolk. *d:* 29.9.1927, Colehill, Wimborne, Dorset. Brother of Sir K.E. (Oxford U 1856–59). Middle order right-hand batsman, good cover point. *Sch* Harrow. *Team* Oxford U (1867–69, blue all 3 years).
Career batting
14–25–2–429–88–18.65–0–*ct* 3

He also appeared for Norfolk.

Dilawar Hussain, Dr
Amateur. *b:* 19.3.1907, Lahore, India. *d:* 26.8.1967, Lahore, Pakistan. Father of Waqar Ahmed (Lahore). Very steady opening right-hand batsman, wicket-keeper. *Teams* Muslims (1924/5 to 1939/40); Northern India (1926/7 to 1934/5); Madras (1933/4); Central India (1934/5 to 1938/9); Uttar Pradesh (1940/1). *Tours* India to England 1936; Vizianagram's XI to India and Ceylon 1930/1. *Tests* India (1933/4 to 1936, 3 matches).
Career batting
57–94–9–2394–122–28.16–4–*ct* 70–*st* 32
Bowling 40–0
Test batting
3–6–0–254–59–42.33–0–*ct* 6–*st* 1

In residence at Cambridge, he was co-opted into the 1936 touring team and was most successful, coming second in the batting table (620 runs, av 44.28) and appearing in one Test. He did not appear in any first-class matches for Cambridge, missing the 1935 summer through illness.

A notable figure in Pakistan cricket he was a member of the Board of Control and a Test selector.

Dilley, Graham Roy
Cricketer. *b*: 18.5.1959, Dartford, Kent. Lower order left-hand batsman, right-arm fast bowler, deep field. *Team* Kent (1977–83, 78 matches). *Tours* England to Australia and India 1979/80, to West Indies 1980/1, to India and Sri Lanka 1981/2. *Tests* England (1979/80 to 1983, 17 matches).
Career batting
110–115–40–1158–81–15.44–0–*ct* 52
Bowling 7431–259–28.69–9–1–6/66
Test batting
17–27–7–328–56–16.40–0–*ct* 5
Bowling 1453–45–32.28–0–0–4/24

Dilley, Michael Reginald
Professional. *b:* 28.3.1939, Rushden, Northants. Lower order right-hand batsman, right-arm fast medium bowler. *Sch* Wellingborough. *Team* Northants (1957–63, 33 matches).
Career batting
33–38–16–232–31*–10.54–0–*ct* 13
Bowling 2471–80–30.88–2–0–6/74

Dillon, Edward Wentworth
Amateur. *b:* 15.2.1881, Penge, Kent. *d:* 20.4.1941, Totteridge, Herts. Hard hitting left-hand opening batsman, slow left-arm bowler. *Sch* Rugby. *Teams* Kent (1900–23, 223 matches); Oxford U (1901–02, blue both years); London County (1900). *Tours* Bennett to West Indies 1901/2; Kent to USA 1903.

Career batting
260–414–25–11006–143–28.29–15–*ct* 213
Bowling 2426–74–32.78–0–0–4/11

A noted rugby footballer, he played three-quarter for Blackheath and England.

Diment, Robert Anthony
Amateur. *b:* 9.2.1927, Tortworth, Gloucs. Middle order right-hand batsman, right-arm medium pace bowler. *Teams* Gloucestershire (1952, 1 match); Leicestershire (1955–58, 59 matches).
Career batting
60–102–5–1595–71–16.44–0–*ct* 35
Bowling 4–0

Secretary of Leics CCC, 1957–60.

Dindar, Andrew
Cricketer. *b:* 26.6.1942, Johannesburg, South Africa. Lower order right-hand batsman, right-arm medium pace bowler. *Team* Gloucestershire (1962–63, 7 matches).
Career batting
7–10–2–100–55–12.50–0–*ct* 2
Bowling 70–3–23.33–0–0–3/32

He has played for Berkshire since 1981.

Dineen, Patrick Joseph
Amateur. *b:* 13.5.1937, Cork, Ireland. Left-handed batsman. *Team* Ireland (1962–71).
Career batting
7–12–2–179–84–17.90–0–*ct* 3

Dines, William James
Professional. *b:* 14.9.1916, Colchester, Essex. Lower order right-hand batsman, right-arm medium pace off break bowler. *Team* Essex (1947–49, 20 matches).
Career batting
20–30–7–431–69*–18.73–0–*ct* 7
Bowling 980–15–65.33–0–0–3/35

Dinsdale, Stephen Charles
Cricketer. *b:* 30.12.1948, Buckhurst Hill, Essex. Opening middle order left-hand batsman, left-arm medium pace bowler. *Teams* Rhodesia (1969/70); Essex (1970, 5 matches); Transvaal (1974/5 to 1975/6).
Career batting
15–26–2–581–88–24.20–0–*ct* 8
Bowling 160–8–20.00–0–0–4/24

Dinwiddy, Hugh Pochin
Amateur. *b:* 16.10.1912, Kensington, London. Opening/middle order right-hand batsman, leg break and googly bowler, excellent cover field. *Sch* Radley. *Teams* Kent (1933–34, 10 matches); Cambridge U (1934–35).
Career batting
15–24–3–258–45–12.28–0–*ct* 9
Bowling 35–0

Dipper, Alfred Ernest
Professional. *b:* 9.11.1885, Apperley, Gloucs. *d:* 7.11.1945, St Thomas's Hospital, London. Solid opening right-hand batsman, right-arm medium pace bowler, moderate field. *Team* Gloucestershire (1908–32, 478 matches). *Test* England (1921, 1 match).
Career batting
481–865–69–28075–252*–35.27–53–*ct* 210
Bowling 4903–161–30.45–5–1–7/46
Test batting
1–2–0–51–40–25.50–0–*ct* 0

He hit 1,000 runs in a season 15 times, going on to complete 2,000 five times (best 2,365, av 55.00, in 1928). He scored three double centuries, all for Gloucs, the highest being 252* v Glamorgan at Cheltenham in 1923. For some years he was on the first-class umpires' list.

He was also a noted bowls player.

Dippie, William Russell Hennessy
Amateur. *b:* 9.6.1907, Edinburgh, Scotland. Right-hand batsman, right-arm fast medium bowler. *Team* Scotland (1939).
Career batting
1–2–1–7–7*–7.00–0–*ct* 1
Bowling 71–3–23.66–0–0–3/41

Disbury, Brian Elvin
Professional. *b:* 30.9.1929, Bedford. Opening right-hand batsman, right-arm medium pace bowler. *Sch* Bedford School. *Team* Kent (1954–57, 14 matches).
Career batting
14–21–3–288–74*–16.00–0–*ct* 11
Bowling 204–5–40.80–0–0–2/76

Disney, Charles Ronald
Amateur. *b:* 21.11.1894, Stourbridge, Worcs. *d:* 11.4.1963, Linthorpe, Yorkshire. Middle order right-hand batsman, right-arm fast medium bowler. *Sch* Clifton and Rossall. *Team* Gloucestershire (1923, 1 match).
Career batting
1–2–0–2–2–1.00–0–*ct* 0

Disney, James Joseph
Professional. *b:* 20.11.1859, Butterley, Derbyshire. *d:* 24.6.1934, Ripley, Derbyshire. Lower order right-hand batsman, wicket-keeper. *Team* Derbyshire (1881–87, 53 matches).
Career batting
57–101–30–377–27*–5.30–0–*ct* 97–*st* 12

His final first-class match was for Liverpool and District in 1894.

He also played for Cheshire.

Disney-Roebuck, Claude Delaval
Amateur. *b:* 1.3.1876, East Stonehouse, Devon. *d:* 10.5.1947, Hindhead, Surrey. Middle order batsman. *Sch* Weymouth. *Team* MCC (1906–07).
Career batting
2–4–1–20–8*–6.66–0–*ct* 1

Disney-Roebuck, Francis Henry Algernon
Amateur. *b:* 7.10.1846, Trinidad. *d:* 9.1.1919, Kensington, London. Middle order batsman. *Sch* Wimbledon. *Team* MCC (1878–82).
Career batting
4–6–0–33–10–5.50–0–*ct* 1

His County cricket was for Devon.

Divecha, Ramesh Vithaldas
Amateur. *b:* 18.10.1927, Bombay, India. Brother of A.V. (Maharashtra). Middle order right-hand batsman, right-arm fast medium/slow off break bowler. Bombay University. *Teams* Oxford U (1948–51, blue 1950–51): Northants (1948, 1 match); Madhya Pradesh (1954/5); Bombay (1951/2); Saurashtra (1962/3). *Tour* India to England 1952. *Tests* India (1951/2 to 1952/3, 5 matches).
Career batting
61–88–18–1423–92–20.32–0–*ct* 35
Bowling 5401–217–24.88–9–0–8/74
Test batting
5–5–0–60–26–12.00–0–*ct* 5
Bowling 361–11–32.81–0–0–3/102

Diver, Alfred John Day
Professional. *b:* 6.7.1824, Cambridge. *d:* 25.3.1876, Rugby, Warwickshire. Uncle of E.J. (Surrey and Warwickshire). Middle order right-hand batsman, right-hand fast medium round arm and lobs. *Teams* Middlesex (1850, 1 match); Cambridgeshire (1857–66, 15 matches); Nottinghamshire (1858, 1 match). *Tour* Parr to North America 1859 (not first-class).
Career batting
75–136–12–1579–65–12.73–0–*ct* 39–*st* 3
Bowling 256–13+72–19.69–6–1–7/?

He also played for Suffolk and Huntingdonshire.

Diver, Edwin James
Amateur to 1885 then professional. *b:* 20.3.1861, Cambridge. *d:* 27.12.1924, Pontardawe, Glamorgan. Nephew of A.J.D. (Middlesex and Notts). Opening/middle order right-hand batsman, right-arm medium pace bowler. wicket-keepr. *Sch* Perse School. *Teams* Surrey (1883–86, 75 matches); Warwickshire (1894–1901, 118 matches).
Career batting
205–329–14–7245–184–23.00–5–*ct* 116–*st* 4
Bowling 311–6–51.83–1–0–6/58

He hit 1,096 runs, av 29.62, in 1899). He also appeared for Cambridgeshire, being joint secretary and treasurer of that County Club in 1889, and later he played for Monmouthshire. He played soccer for Aston Villa.

Dixie-Smith, J.W. *(see under* Smith, J.W.)

Dixon, Alan Leonard
Professional. *b:* 27.11.1933, Dartford, Kent. Middle order right-hand batsman, right-arm medium pace off break bowler, excellent cover field. *Team* Kent (1950–70, 378 matches). *Tour* MCC to East Africa (1973/4).
Career batting
381–580–71–9589–125*–18.83–3–*ct* 155
Bowling 24060–935–25.73–46–10–8/61

He hit 1,000 runs in a season three times (best 1,170, av 24.37, in 1961).

He created a Gillette Cup record in taking 7 for 15 for Kent v Surrey at the Oval in 1967. He took 100 wickets three times (best 122, av 23.89, in 1964).

Dixon, Anthony Sumner
Cricketer. *b:* 17.11.1948, Bristol. Middle order right-hand batsman. *Sch* Clifton. *Team* Cambridge U (1971).
Career batting
1–2–0–12–12–6.00–0–*ct* 0

Dixon, Alexander Willoughby
(also known as Dickson)
Professional. *b:* 1876, Liverpool. *d:* 1.3.1953, Leicester. Lower order left-hand batsman, slow left-arm bowler. *Team* Leicestershire (1900, 5 matches).
Career batting
5–9–1–36–18–4.50–0–*ct* 2
Bowling 266–5–53.20–0–0–2/79

Dixon, Cecil Donovan
Amateur. *b:* 12.2.1891, Potchefstroom, Transvaal, South Africa. *d:* 9.9.1969, Johannesburg, South Africa. Lower order right-hand batsman, right-arm medium pace bowler. *Team* Transvaal (1912/3 to 1924/5) *Tour* South Africa to England 1924. *Test* South Africa (1913/14, 1 match).

Career batting
33–39–8–184–27–5.93–0–*ct* 19
Bowling 2556–106–24.11–6–1–7/16
Test batting
1–2–0–0–0–0.00–0–*ct* 1
Bowling 118–3–39.33–0–0–2/62

He only returned very modest figures on his visit to England and did not appear in the Tests.

Dixon, Cecil Egerton
Amateur. *b:* 21.7.1903, Scotland. *d:* 3.3.1973, Battle, Sussex. Middle order batsman, change bowler. *Sch* Wellington. *Team* Hampshire (1929, 2 matches).
Career batting
2–4–0–10–5–2.50–0–*ct* 0

Dixon, Eric John Hopkins
Amateur. *b:* 22.9.1915, Horbury, Yorkshire. *d:* 20.4.1941, presumed killed on active service. Solid right-hand opening batsman. *Sch* St Edward's School, Oxford. *Teams* Oxford U (1937–39, blue all three years); Northants (1939, 8 matches). *Tour* Combined Oxford and Cambridge to Jamaica 1938/9.
Career batting
49–86–4–2356–123–28.73–2–*ct* 19
Bowling 29–0

Dixon, Dr Francis
Amateur. *b:* 31.7.1855, Derby. *d:* 20.8.1943, Eastwood, Notts. Middle order right-hand batsman, off break bowler. *Team* Derbyshire (1885, 1 match).
Career batting
2–4–0–23–15–5.75–0–*ct* 1
Bowling 7–0

His last first-class match was for A. Shrewsbury's Notts XI in 1891.

Dixon, J.
Amateur. *Team* Lancashire (1878, 1 match).
Career batting
1–2–0–2–2–1.00–0–*ct* 0

Dixon, John Auger
Amateur. *b:* 27.5.1861, Grantham, Lincs. *d:* 8.6.1931, Nottingham. Opening/middle order right-hand batsman, right-arm medium pace bowler. *Sch* Nottingham HS. *Team* Nottinghamshire (1882–1905, 235 matches).
Career batting
253–419–25–9527–268*–24.18–13–*ct* 180
Bowling 5080–184–27.42–2–0–5/28

He hit 1,100 runs, av 44.00, in 1897. His only double century was 268* for Notts v Sussex in 1897. He captained Notts 1889–99.

A noted soccer player, he appeared for Notts County and England as a forward.

Dixon, Joseph Gilbert
Amateur. *b:* 3.9.1895, Chelmsford, Essex. *d:* 19.11.1954, Great Baddow, Essex. Middle order right-hand batsman, right-arm fast-medium bowler. *Sch* Felsted. *Team* Essex (1914–22, 93 matches).
Career batting
93–148–12–2214–173–16.27–3–*ct* 48
Bowling 6484–206–31.47–9–2–7/61

Dixon, John Henry
Cricketer. *b:* 3.3.1954, Bournemouth, Hants. Tail end right-hand batsman, right-arm medium fast bowler. *Sch* Monkton Combe. *Team* Gloucestershire (1973–81, 16 matches).
Career batting
16–20–8–77–13*–6.41–0–*ct* 6
Bowling 1136–21–54.09–2–0–5/44

Whilst at Oxford, he appeared for the University in the Benson and Hedges Cup, but not in first-class matches.

Dixon, J.T.
Amateur. Lower order batsman, bowler. *Team* Middlesex (1908, 1 match).
Career batting
1–2–0–7–7–3.50–0–*ct* 2
Bowling 22–0

Dixon, Patrick O'Madigan
Amateur. *b:* 9.10.1907, Rohtak, India. Brother of T.H. (Ireland). Right-hand batsman, right-arm medium pace or leg break and googly bowler. *Teams* Dublin University (1926); Ireland (1932).
Career batting
3–6–0–69–47–11.50–*ct* 1
Bowling 30–0

Dixon, Thomas Hartigan
Amateur. *b:* 22.1.1906, Dhaipai, India. (Brother of P.O'M. (Ireland). Right-hand batsman, right-arm fast medium bowler. *Teams* Dublin University (1926); Ireland (1927–32); Delhi (1934/5 to 1936/7).
Career batting
14–27–5–312–45*–14.16–0–*ct* 4
Bowling 1043–50–20.86–3–1–7/51

Dobell, Percy
Amateur. *b:* 29.4.1864, Huyton, Liverpool. *d:* 5.1.1903, Liverpool. Middle order right-hand batsman, *Sch* Birkenhead. *Team* Lancashire (1886–87, 7 matches).
Career batting
10–17–2–142–28–9.46–0–*ct* 4

His final first-class match was for Liverpool and District in 1888.

Dobree-Carey, Paul Alexander Huntly
(also known as P.A.D. Carey)
Professional. *b:* 21.5.1920, Horsham, Sussex. Lower order left-hand batsman, right-arm fast bowler. *Teams* Baroda (1942/3); Services (1943/4); Bengal (1944/5); Europeans (1944/5 to 1945/6); Sussex (1946–48, 42 matches).
Career batting
52–81–16–869–96–13.36–0–*ct* 24
Bowling 4448–136–32.70–7–0–6/80
He also represented Dorset and Durham.

Dobson, Arthur
Professional. *b:* 22.2.1854, Ilkley, Yorkshire. *d:* 17.9.1932, Horsforth, Yorkshire. Lower order right-hand batsman, right-arm medium pace bowler, fine cover point. *Team* Yorkshire (1879, 2 matches).
Career batting
2–3–0–1–1–0.33–0–*ct* 1

Dobson, Alban Tabor Austin
Amateur. *b:* 29.6.1885, Ealing Middlesex. *d:* 19.5.1962, Walsham-le-Willows, Suffolk. Middle order batsman. *Sch* Clifton. *Team* Gentlemen (1905).
Career batting
1–2–0–1–1–0.50–0–*ct* 0

Dobson, Frederick
Amateur. *b:* 12.10.1898, Olton, Warwickshire. *d:* 15.10.1980, Burley, Hants. Lower order right-hand batsman, slow left-arm bowler. *Team* Warwickshire (1928, 3 matches).
Career batting
3–3–0–9–7–3.00–0–*ct* 0
Bowling 138–7–19.71–0–0–3/51

Dobson, Kenneth William Cecil
Amateur. *b:* 28.8.1900, Barrow-on-Trent, Derbyshire. *d:* 6.3.1960, Torquay, Devon. Lower order right-hand batsman, right-arm medium pace bowler. *Sch* Repton. *Teams* Derbyshire (1920, 3 matches); Warwickshire (1925, 2 matches).
Career batting
5–10–3–33–12*–4.71–0–*ct* 0
Bowling 123–1–123.00–0–0–1/25
He also played for Staffordshire.

Dobson, Thomas Kell
Amateur. *b:* 1901, South Shields. *d:* 3.10.1940, Whitburn, Sunderland. Middle order left-hand batsman, bowler. *Team* Minor Counties (1929–34).
Career batting
8–12–2–305–126–30.50–1–*ct* 6
Bowling 377–6–62.83–0–0–4/70
His County cricket was for Durham.

Docker, Cyril Talbot
Amateur. *b:* 3.3.1884, Ryde, North South Wales, Australia. *d:* 26.3.1975, Double Bay, New South Wales, Australia. Brother of K.B. (NSW) and P.W. (NSW), nephew of E.B. (NSW) and A.R.M. (NSW). Lower order right-hand batsman, right-arm fast medium bowler. *Team* New South Wales (1909/10, 1 match). *Tours* AIF to England 1919, to South Africa 1919/20.
Career batting
24–32–10–371–52*–16.86–0–*ct* 17
Bowling 1091–58–18.81–5–0–5/20

Docker, Frank Dudley
Amateur. *b:* 26.8.1862, Smethwick, Staffs. *d:* 8.7.1944, Colteshill, Amersham, Bucks. Brother of L.C. (Derbyshire and Warwickshire and Ralph (Derbyshire). Middle order batsman. *Sch* KES, Birmingham. *Team* Derbyshire (1881–82, 2 matches).
Career batting
2–3–0–33–25–11.00–0–*ct* 3

Docker, George Arthur Murray
Amateur. *b:* 18.11.1876, New South Wales, Australia. *d:* 17.11.1914, near Le Touquet, Belgium. Son of A.R.M. (NSW). Hard hitting middle order right-hand batsman, right-arm fast bowler. *Sch* Highgate. *Team* MCC (1911–14). *Tour* MCC to West Indies 1912/3.
Career batting
11–18–2–185–34*–11.56–0–*ct* 3
Bowling 169–5–33.80–0–0–2/66

Docker, Ludford (Charles)
Amateur. *b:* 26.11.1860, Smethwick, Staffs. *d:* 1.8.1940, Alveston, Warwickshire. Brother of F.D. (Derbyshire) and Ralph (Derbyshire). Opening/middle order right-hand batsman, right-arm fast, later medium-fast bowler. *Sch* KES Birmingham. *Teams* Derbyshire (1881–86, 48 matches); Warwickshire (1894–95, 11 matches). *Tour* Shrewsbury to Australia 1887/8.
Career batting
77–136–8–2665–107–20.82–1–*ct* 41
Bowling 280–9–31.11–0–0–3/38
He captained Derbyshire in 1884, but in 1887 moved to Warwickshire. He also occasionally appeared for Worcestershire.

Docker, Ralph
Amateur. *b:* 31.8.1855, Harborne, Staffs. *d:* 7.7.1910, Tunbridge Wells, Kent. Brother of F.D.

(Derbyshire) and L.C. (Derbyshire and Warwickshire). Middle order batsman. *Team* Derbyshire (1879, 2 matches).
Career batting
2–4–0–9–6–2.25–0–*ct* 2
He also played non-first-class cricket for Worcestershire, Staffordshire and Warwickshire.

Docwra, Edward David
Cricketer. *b:* 24.4.1953, Paddington, London. *Sch* Canford. Opening right-hand batsman, leg break bowler. *Team* Oxford U (1974).
Career batting
1–2–0–26–20–13.00–0–*ct* 0

Dodd, William Thomas Francis
Amateur. *b:* 8.3.1908, Steep, Hants. Lower order left-hand batsman, slow left-arm bowler. *Team* Hampshire (1931–35, 10 matches).
Career batting
10–16–2–95–31–6.78–0–*ct* 3
Bowling 321–10–32.10–1–0–5/63

Dodds, Thomas Carter
Amateur in 1946, professional from 1947. *b:* 19.5.1919, Bedford. Opening right-hand batsman, right-arm medium pace or leg break bowler. *Sch* Wellingborough and Warwick. *Teams* Essex (1946–59, 380 matches); Services (in India) (1943/4).
Career batting
396–693–18–19407–157–28.75–17–*ct* 187
Bowling 1126–36–31.27–0–0–4/34
He hit 1,000 runs in a season 13 times, exceeding 2,000 once – 2,147, av 38.33, in 1947.
His final first-class match was for MCC in 1961.

Dods, Harold William
Amateur. *b:* 25.3.1909, Gosberton, Lincolnshire. *d:* 18.6.1944, London. Middle order left-hand batsman, *Sch* Tonbridge. *Team* Minor Counties (1936–38). *Tour* Brinckman to South America 1937/8.
Career batting
3–5–0–172–104–34.40–1–*ct* 0
His County cricket was for Lincolnshire, and he was that side's leading batsman for many years.

Dodsworth, George Edward
Amateur. *b:* 2.12.1841, York. *d:* 14.6.1876, Morar Gualior, India. Middle order left-hand batsman. *Sch* Repton. *Team* MCC (1868, 1 match).
Career batting
1–2–1–5–3–5.00–0–*ct* 0

Doggart, Alexander Graham
Amateur. *b:* 2.6.1897, Bishop Auckland, Co. Durham. *d:* 7.6.1963, London, whilst chairing the AGM of the Football Association. Father of A.P. (Sussex) and G.H.G. (Sussex), brother of J.H. (Cambridge U), grandfather of S.J.G. (Cambridge U). Middle order right-hand batsman, right-arm medium pace bowler. *Sch* Bishop's Stortford. *Teams* Cambridge U (1919–22, blue 1921–22); Middlesex (1925, 4 matches).
Career batting
46–69–9–1716–116–28.60–2–*ct* 53
Bowling 2582–85–30.37–2–0–5/58
He also played for Durham.
His final first-class match was for Free Foresters in 1930. A noted soccer player he appeared for Cambridge U, Darlington, Corinthians and England as inside left.

Doggart, Arthur Peter
Amateur. *b:* 3.12.1927, London. *d:* 17.3.1965, Epsom, Surrey. Son of A.G. (Middlesex); brother of G.H.G. (Sussex). Middle order right-hand batsman, right-arm medium pace bowler. *Sch* Winchester. *Team* Sussex (1947–51, 9 matches).
Career batting
9–16–3–228–43–17.53–0–*ct* 2
Bowling 41–2–20.50–0–0–2/8
He was on the staff of *The Cricketer* magazine until his death.

Doggart, George Hubert Graham
Amateur. *b:* 18.7.1925, Earls Court, London. Son of A.G. (Middlesex), brother of A.P. (Sussex), father of S.J.G. (Cambridge U). Middle order right-hand batsman, off break bowler, brilliant close field. *Sch* Winchester. *Teams* Cambridge U (1948–50, blue all 3 years); Sussex (1948–61, 155 matches). *Tours* Swanton to West Indies 1955/6; MCC to East Africa 1957/8, to South America 1958/9 (neither first-class). *Tests* England (1950, 2 matches).
Career batting
210–347–28–10054–219*–31.51–20–*ct* 199
Bowling 2057–60–34.28–0–0–4/50
Test batting
2–4–0–76–29–19.00–0–*ct* 3
He hit 1,000 runs in a season four times (best 2,063, av. 45.84, in 1949).
Both his double centuries were for Cambridge U, the highest being 219* v Essex at Cambridge in 1949, when he and J.G. Dewes put on 429* for the 2nd wicket, constituting a new record in English first-class cricket. He captained Sussex in 1954.

A brilliant all round sportsman, he was awarded his blue for soccer and also represented Cambridge at squash, rackets and rugby fives.

Doggart, James Hamilton
Amateur. *b:* 22.1.1900, Bishop Auckland, Co. Durham. Brother of A.G. (Middlesex). Middle order right-hand batsman, right-arm fast bowler. *Sch* Bishops Stortford. *Team* Cambridge U (1919).
Career batting
1–1–0–0–0–0.00–0–*ct* 1
Bowling 69–1–69.00–0–0–1/50
He also played for Durham.

Doggart, Simon Jonathon Graham
Cricketer. *b*: 8.2.1961, Winchester. Son of G. H. G. (Sussex), grandson of A. G. (Cambridge U). Middle order left-hand batsman, off break bowler. *Sch* Winchester. *Team* Cambridge U (1980–83, blue all four years).
Career batting
35–50–11–878–70–22.51–0–*ct* 14
Bowling 2223–34–65.38–0–0–3/3

Dolbey, Hugh Owen
Amateur. *b:* 27.11.1879, Sutton, Surrey. *d:* 14.7.1936, Glemsford, Suffolk. Lower order right-hand batsman, right-arm fast bowler. *Sch* Dulwich/Cranleigh. *Team* Surrey (1899–1902, 3 matches).
Career batting
3–6–2–21–18*–5.25–0–*ct* 1
Bowling 235–7–33.57–0–0–4/96
His career in County cricket was very brief since he worked in East Africa, where he was a District Judge.
He also played for Shropshire.

Dolding, Desmond Leonard
Professional. *b:* 13.12.1922, Oordegem, Belgium. *d:* 23.11.1954, Wembley, Middlesex, as the result of a motor accident. Lower order right-hand batsman, right-arm leg break bowler, brilliant field. *Team* Middlesex (1951, 1 match).
Career batting
3–3–1–11–8–5.50–0–*ct* 0
Bowling 103–3–34.33–0–0–3/43
He made his first-class debut in 1950 for MCC.
A noted soccer player he appeared for QPR, Chelsea and Norwich City as wing forward.

D'Oliveira, Basil Lewis, OBE
Cricketer. *b:* 4.10.1931, Signal Hill, Cape Town, South Africa. Brother of Ivan (Leics), father of D.B. (Worcs). Middle order right-hand batsman, right-arm medium pace or off break bowler. *Team* Worcestershire (1964–80, 274 matches). *Tours* Commonwealth to Rhodesia 1961/2, 1962/3, to Pakistan 1963/4; Worcs World Tour 1964/5, to Jamaica 1965/6; Rest of World to West Indies 1966/7; MCC to West Indies 1967/8, to Ceylon and Pakistan 1968/9, to Australia and New Zealand 1970/1; International XI to South Africa 1972/3. *Tests* England (1966–72, 44 matches).
Career batting
362–566–88–18919–227–39.57–43–*ct* 211
Bowling 15021–548–27.41–17–2–6/29
Test batting
44–70–8–2484–158–40.06–5–*ct* 29
Bowling 1859–47–39.55–0–0–3/46
After attaining great success in local club cricket in South Africa, d'Oliveira, a Cape Coloured, was forced to emigrate to England in order to achieve an opportunity of playing cricket at the highest standard. He began in 1960 with Middleton in the Central Lancashire League and then in 1965 qualified to play for Worcestershire. The following summer he won a place in the England team. When he was chosen as a member of the MCC team to tour South Africa, his acceptance caused the cancellation of the tour and brought the problems of apartheid more forcibly before the British public.
His first-class debut had been made in Rhodesia in 1961/2 and he appeared in a handful of first-class matches before his regular County cricket commenced in 1965. He hit over 1,000 runs in a season nine times with 1,691, av 43.35, in 1965 as his best. His only double century was 227 for Worcestershire v Yorkshire at Hull in 1974. He was made an OBE in the 1969 Birthday Honours list. Receipts from his benefit in 1975 amounted to £27,000.
On retiring from first-class cricket he was appointed coach to Worcestershire.

D'Oliveira, Damian Basil
Cricketer. *b*: 19.10.1960, Cape Town, South Africa. Son of B. L. (Worcs), nephew of Ivan (Leics). Middle order right-hand batsman, right-arm medium or off break bowler. *Team* Worcestershire (1982–83, 26 matches).
Career batting
26–46–3–1037–102–24.71–1–*ct* 15
Bowling 262–4–65.50–0–0–1/12

D'Oliveira, Ivan
Cricketer. *b:* 19.3.1941, Cape Town, South Africa. Brother of B.L. (Worcs), uncle of D.B. (Worcs). Middle order right-hand batsman, right-arm medium pace bowler. *Team* Leicestershire (1967, 1 match).
Career batting
1–1–0–0–0–0.00–0–*ct* 0

Doll, Christian Charles Tyler
Amateur. *b:* 22.3.1880, London. *d:* 5.4.1955, Meldreth, Cambs. Brother of M.H.C. (Middlesex). Middle order right-hand batsman, excellent field. *Sch* Charterhouse. *Teams* MCC (1900–04); Cambridge U (1901).
Career batting
27–45–9–774–224*–21.50–2–*ct* 17
Bowling 15–0

He also played for Hertfordshire. His highest score was for MCC v London County at Crystal Palace in 1901.

Doll, Mordaunt Henry Caspers
Amateur. *b:* 5.4.1888, London, *d:* 30.6.1966, Devizes, Wilts. Brother of C.C.T. (Cambridge U). Hard hitting middle order right-hand batsman. *Sch* Charterhouse. *Teams* Cambridge U (1908); Middlesex (1912–1919, 24 matches). *Tour* MCC to West Indies 1912/3.
Career batting
43–63–4–1097–102*–18.59–1–*ct* 32
Bowling 655–15–43.66–1–0–5/52

He also appeared for Hertfordshire.

Dollery, Horace Edgar
Amateur to 1933, professional from 1934. *b:* 14.10.1914, Reading, Berkshire. Excellent middle order right-hand batsman, fine slip field. occasional wicket-keeper. *Sch* Reading. *Teams* Warwickshire (1934–55, 413 matches); Wellington (1950/1). *Tour* Selected for MCC to India 1939/40 (tour cancelled). *Tests* England (1947–50, 4 matches).
Career batting
436–717–66–24413–212–37.50–50–*ct* 291–*st* 13
Bowling 32–0
Test batting
4–7–0–72–37–10.28–0–*ct* 1

He played for Berkshire 1931–33 and made his first-class debut for Minor Counties in 1933. He exceeded 1,000 runs in a season 15 times and completed 2,000 twice (best 2,084, av 47.36, in 1949). Both his double centuries were for Warwickshire, the highest being 212 v Leics at Birmingham in 1952.

He captained Warwickshire jointly in 1948 and alone 1949–55.

A useful soccer player he appeared for Reading.

Dollery, Keith Robert
Professional. *b:* 9.12.1924, Cooroy, Queensland. Lower order right-hand batsman, right-arm fast medium bowler. *Teams* Queensland (1947/8, 2 matches); Auckland (1949/50); Tasmania (1950/51, 3 matches); Warwickshire (1951–56, 73 matches).
Career batting
80–107–27–958–41–11.97–0–*ct* 24
Bowling 6018–227–26.51–9–2–8/42

Dolman, Charles Eric
Amateur. *b:* 17.7.1903, Abertillery. *d:* 6.6.1969, Bristol. Lower order right-hand batsman, bowler. *Sch* Allhallows, Honiton. *Team* Wales (1926–28).
Career batting
2–2–0–46–35–23.00–0–*ct* 0
Bowling 85–2–42.50–0–0–1/22

He appeared for Monmouthshire 1922–26.

He was Lord Mayor of Cardiff.

Dolphin, Arthur
Professional. *b:* 24.12.1885, Wilsden, Yorkshire. *d:* 23.10.1942, Heaton, Bradford, Yorkshire. Lower order right-hand batsman, wicket-keeper. *Teams* Yorkshire (1905–27, 428 matches); Patiala (1926/7). *Tours* MCC to Australia 1920/1, to India 1926/7 (in emergency). *Test* England (1920/1, 1 match).
Career batting
449–465–164–3402–66–11.30–0–*ct* 608–*st* 273
Bowling 28–1–28.00–0–0–1/18
Test batting
1–2–0–1–1–0.50–0–*ct* 1

He umpired in first-class matches after retiring from County cricket.

Donald, Peter Colligan Graham
Cricketer. *b:* 8.8.1957, Bristol. Middle order left-hand batsman, right-arm medium pace or off break bowler. *Sch* Sherborne. *Team* Oxford U (1978).
Career batting
1–1–0–1–1–1.00–0–*ct* 0

Donald, William Alexander
Cricketer. *b*: 29.7.1953, Huntly, Aberdeenshire, Scotland. Right-hand batsman, right-hand medium pace bowler. *Team* Scotland (1978–83).
Career batting
5–8–1–126–45–18.00–0–*ct* 1
Bowling 64–1–64.00–0–0–1/46

Donaldson, Thomas Hubert
Amateur. *b:* 6.8.1882. *d: circa* 1960, South Africa. Lower order batsman, bowler. *Team* Oxford U (1906).
Career batting
1–2–1–38–26*–38.00–0–*ct* 0
Bowling 26–0

Donaldson, William Patrick
Amateur. *b:* 4.3.1871, Scotland. *d:* 27.3.1923, Dollar, Scotland. Lower order batsman, left-arm fast medium bowler, good close field. *Sch* Loretto. *Team* Oxford U (1894).

Career batting
1–2–1–1–1*–1.00–0–*ct* 1
He was a Scottish rugby international.

Donnan, Henry
Amateur. *b:* 12.11.1864, Liverpool, New South Wales, Australia. *d:* 13.8.1956, Bexley, New South Wales, Australia. Brother in law of S.E. Gregory (New South Wales and Australia). Defensive opening right-hand batsman, right-arm medium pace bowler. *Team* New South Wales (1887/8 to 1900/1, 58 matches). *Tour* Australia to England and North America 1896. *Tests* Australia (1891/2 to 1896, 5 matches).
Career batting
94–160–14–4262–167–29.19–6–*ct* 37
Bowling 1191–29–41.06–0–0–3/14
Test batting
5–10–1–75–15–8.33–0–*ct* 1
Bowling 22–0
He began his career mainly as a bowler and did not become noted as a batsman until the 1890s. He hit 1,009 runs, av 23.46, in 1896.

Donnellan, Rory Owen
Cricketer. *b:* 20.6.1941, South Africa. Opening right-hand batsman. *Team* Oxford U (1963).
Career batting
5–10–0–173–47–17.30–0–*ct* 3

Donnelly, J.A.
Amateur. *Team* Ireland (1914).
Career batting
1–2–0–65–59–32.50–0–*ct* 1

Donnelly, Martin Paterson
Amateur. *b:* 17.10.1917, Ngaruawahia, New Zealand. Forcing middle order left-hand batsman, slow left-arm bowler, brilliant field. *Teams* Wellington (1936/7 to 1940/1); Canterbury (1938/9 to 1939/40); Middlesex (1946, 1 match); Oxford U (1946–47, blue both years); Warwickshire (1948–50, 20 matches). *Tours* New Zealand to England 1937, 1949, to Australia 1937/8. *Tests* New Zealand (1937–49, 7 matches).
Career batting
131–221–26–9250–208*–47.43–23–*ct* 74
Bowling 1683–43–39.13–0–0–4/32
Test batting
7–12–1–582–206–52.90–1–*ct* 7
Bowling 20–0
He scored 1,000 runs in a season five times, exceeding 2,000 once (2,287, av 61.81, in 1949).
His highest innings was 208* for MCC v Yorkshire at Scarborough in 1948; his other double century was 206 for New Zealand v England at Lord's in 1949. He met with great success as a batsman in England, but in 1950 he took up a business appointment in Australia.
His final first-class match was for Governor-General's XI in 1960/1.
An excellent rugby player he appeared for Oxford U and England.

Donovan, E.J.
Amateur. *Team* Ireland (1907).
Career batting
1–2–1–5–3*–5.00–0–*ct* 0
Bowling 36–1–36.00–0–0–1/36

Donovan, Robert Leo
Amateur. *b:* 1899, Dublin, Ireland. *d:* 26.2.1932, Dublin, Ireland. Left-hand batsman, left-arm medium pace bowler. *Team* Ireland (1921).
Career batting
1–1–0–3–3–3.00–0–*ct* 0

Dooland, Bruce
Professional. *b:* 1.11.1923, Adelaide, Australia. *d:* 8.9.1980, Adelaide, Australia. Middle/lower order right-hand batsman, leg break and googly bowler, good field. *Teams* South Australia (1945/6 to 1957/8, 29 matches); Nottinghamshire (1953–57, 140 matches). *Tours* Australia to New Zealand 1945/6; Commonwealth to India and Ceylon 1950/1; Howard to India 1956/7. *Tests* Australia (1946/7 to 1947/8, 3 matches).
Career batting
214–326–33–7141–115*–24.37–4–*ct* 186
Bowling 22332–1016–21.98–84–23–8/20
Test batting
3–5–1–76–29–19.00–0–*ct* 3
Bowling 419–9–46.55–0–0–4/69
He took 100 wickets in a season five times (best 196, av 15.48, in 1954) and hit 1,000 runs twice (best 1,604, av 28.64 in 1957). He performed the 'double' in 1954 and 1957.

Dorey, Lewis Hugh John
Amateur. *b:* 23.10.1901, St Albans, Herts. Middle/lower order batsman. *Sch* Harrow. *Team* Hampshire (1925, 1 match).
Career batting
1–2–0–0–0–0.00–0–*ct* 1

Dorman, Rev Arthur William
Amateur. *b:* 24.10.1862, Sydenham, Kent. *d:* 7.1.1914, Hinton Charterhouse, Bath, Somerset. Lower order batsman, left arm slow bowler. *Sch* Dulwich. *Team* Cambridge U (1886, blue).
Career batting
8–12–5–31–15–4.42–0–*ct* 6
Bowling 655–25–26.20–1–0–5/55

Dorrell, Philip George
Amateur. *b:* 6.12.1914, Worcester. Middle order right-hand batsman. *Sch* Bromsgrove. *Team* Worcestershire (1946, 1 match).
Career batting
1–1–0–1–1–1.00–0–*ct* 0

Dorrinton, William
Professional. *b:* 29.4.1809, Town Malling, Kent. *d:* 8.11.1848, Town Malling. Brother of Alban (Kent, 1836). Lower order right-hand batsman, wicket-keeper. *Team* Kent (1836–48, 55 matches); Hampshire (1845, 2 matches).
Career batting
95–175–13–1440–65–8.88–0–*ct* 89–*st* 25
Bowling 2 wickets, no analyses
He was an excellent wicket-keeper and earlier excelled as a long stop.

Dorset, 3rd Duke of, John Frederick
(succeeded to title in 1769)
Amateur. *b:* 24.3.1745. *d:* 19.7.1799, Knowle, Sevenoaks, Kent. Middle order batsman, bowler. *Sch* Harrow. *Team* Kent (1773–83).
As he played before 1801, career figures are inappropriate.
He was one of the greatest supporters of the game and employed several of the most famous cricketers on his estate.
He more or less gave up playing in 1784 when he was appointed ambassador to France. He was partially responsible for the proposed cricket tour to Paris in 1789 – the tour was abandoned due to the Revolution.

Doshi, Dilip Rasiklal
Cricketer. *b*: 22.12.1947, Rajkot, India. Tail end left-hand batsman, slow left-arm bowler. *Teams* Bengal (1968/9 to 1982/3); Nottinghamshire (1973–78, 44 matches); Warwickshire (1980–81, 43 matches). *Tours* Indian Universities to Ceylon 1970/1; India to Australia and New Zealand 1980/1, to England 1982, to Pakistan 1982/3. *Tests* India (1979/80 to 1982/3, 32 matches).
Career batting
221–234–67–1335–44–7.99–0–*ct* 57
Bowling 21955–836–26.26–39–5–7/29
Test batting
32–37–10–129–20–4.77–0–*ct* 10
Bowling 3450–113–30.53–6–0–6/102
For Warwickshire in 1980 he took 101 wickets, av 26.73. On the 1982 tour to England he played in all three Tests and headed the Test bowling averages with 13 wickets, av 35.00.
He has also played for Northumberland and Hertfordshire.

Doughty, David George
Professional. *b:* 9.11.1937, Chiswick, Middlesex. Lower order left-hand batsman, slow left-arm bowler. *Team* Somerset (1963–64, 17 matches).
Career batting
17–20–5–104–22–6.93–0–*ct* 6
Bowling 710–35–20.28–2–1–6/58

Doughty, Richard James
Cricketer. *b*: 17.11.1960, Bridlington, Yorkshire. Lower order right-hand batsman, right-arm medium pace bowler. *Team* Gloucestershire (1981–83, 13 matches).
Career batting
13–18–7–210–32*–19.09–0–*ct* 2
Bowling 939–23–40.82–1–0–6/43

Doughty, Stephen
Professional. *b:* 16.10.1855, Staveley, Derbyshire. *d:* 11.11.1929, Halton East, Skipton, Yorkshire. Lower order right-hand batsman, right-arm medium pace off break bowler. *Team* Derbyshire (1880–86, 4 matches).
Career batting
4–7–1–40–13*–6.66–0–*ct* 1
Bowling 79–4–19.75–0–0–3/28

Douglas, Arthur Coates
Amateur. *b:* 16.8.1902, Belfast, Ireland. *d:* 27.6.1937, Stranmillis, Belfast, Ireland. Right-hand batsman, right-arm fast medium bowler. *Sch* Royal Belfast Academical Institution. *Team* Ireland (1925–33).
Career batting
7–14–0–262–63–18.71–0–*ct* 4
Bowling 341–12–28.41–0–0–4/35
He was an Irish rugby international.

Douglas, Archibald Philip
Amateur. *b:* 7.6.1867, Norwood Green, Middlesex. *d:* 24.1.1953, Taunton, Somerset. Brother of James (Middlesex), R.N. (Middlesex and Surrey) and Sholto (Middlesex). Middle order right-hand batsman, good cover field. *Sch* Dulwich. *Teams* Surrey (1887, 1 match); Europeans (1898/9 to 1911/2); Middlesex (1902, 2 matches).
Career batting
9–14–1–328–91–25.23–0–*ct* 9
Bowling 48–8–6.00–1–0–6/34
Being stationed for many years in India, his County cricket was very restricted.

Douglas, Cecil Herbert
Amateur. *b:* 28.6.1886, Clapton. *d:* 30.9.1954, Frinton, Essex. Brother of J.W.H.T. (Essex). Middle order right-hand batsman, right-arm slow

bowler. *Sch* Felsted. *Team* Essex (1912–19, 21 matches).
Career batting
21–27–0–326–78–12.07–0–*ct* 4
Bowling 350–6–58.33–0–0–3/46

Douglas, James
Amateur. *b:* 8.1.1870, Norwood Green, Middlesex. *d:* 8.2.1958, Cheltenham, Gloucs. Brother of A.P. (Surrey and Middlesex), R.N. (Surrey and Middlesex) and Sholto (Middlesex), right-hand opening batsman, slow left-arm bowler, excellent field. *Sch* Dulwich. *Teams* Cambridge U (1892–94, blue all 3 years); Middlesex (1893–13, 164 matches).
Career batting
197–336–22–9099–204–28.97–15–*ct* 179
Bowling 1732–58–29.86–2–0–5/45

His only double century was 204 for Middlesex v Gloucs in 1903. Being in the scholastic profession his County cricket was restricted mainly to the holidays.

Douglas, Joseph Stanley
Professional. *b:* 4.4.1903, Bradford, Yorkshire. *d:* 27.12.1971, Torbay, Devon. Lower order left-hand batsman, left-arm medium fast bowler. *Team* Yorkshire (1925–34, 23 matches).
Career batting
23–26–8–125–19–6.94–0–*ct* 14
Bowling 1310–49–26.73–2–0–6/59

Douglas, John William Henry Tyler
Amateur. *b:* 3.9.1882, Clapton, Middlesex. *d:* 19.12.1930. He was drowned in a shipping accident off the island of Laeso, Denmark. Brother of C.H. (Essex). Originally hard hitting, but later stolid, middle order right-hand batsman, right-arm fast medium bowler. *Sch* Felsted. *Teams* Essex (1901–28, 459 matches); London County (1903–04). *Tours* MCC to New Zealand 1906/7, to USA 1907, to Australia 1911/2, 1920/1, 1924/5, to South Africa 1913/4. *Tests* England (1911/2 to 1924/5, 23 matches).
Career batting
651–1035–156–24531–210*–27.90–26–*ct* 364
Bowling 44159–1893–23.32–113–23–9/47
Test batting
23–35–2–962–119–29.15–1–*ct* 9
Bowling 1486–45–33.02–1–0–5/46

An all-round sportsman, Douglas excelled at boxing, winning the Olympic middleweight title in 1908, at soccer, obtaining an England amateur international cap, and at cricket. He captained Essex from 1911 to 1928 and led England on two tours to Australia – in 1911/2, when he had the captaincy thrust upon him by Warner's illness, and in 1920/1. He also captained the MCC to South Africa in 1913/4. In all he led England in 18 Tests.

His batting was of the stubborn variety and he was the ideal man to save a match. He hit 1,000 runs in a season 10 times with 1,547 (av 37.73) in 1921 his best. Five times he completed the 'double' and seven times he completed 100 wickets in a season, his best being 147 (av 21.38) in 1920. His highest score and only double hundred was 210* for Essex v Derbyshire at Leyton in 1921. His best bowling was 9/47 for Essex v Derbyshire at Leyton in 1921.

His final first-class match was for MCC in 1930.

He died whilst attempting to save his father when the ship in which they were travelling, SS *Oberon*, was in collision with another in dense fog.

Douglas, Rev Robert Noel
Amateur. *b:* 9.11.1868, Norwood Green, Middlesex. *d:* 27.2.1957, Colyton, Devon. Brother of A.P. (Middlesex and Surrey); James (Middlesex) and Sholto (Middlesex). Middle order right-hand batsman. *Sch* Dulwich. *Teams* Cambridge U (1890–92, blue all three years); Surrey (1890–91, 4 matches); Middlesex (1898–1905, 45 matches).
Career batting
75–122–7–2669–131–23.20–1–*ct* 48–*st* 3

Being in the scholastic profession, his first-class appearances were limited.

A noted soccer player he was awarded his blue in 1891.

Douglas, Sholto
Amateur. *b:* 8.9.1873, Norwood Green, Middlesex. *d:* 28.1.1916, Cambrin, Arras, France. He was killed in action. Brother of A.P. (Middlesex and Surrey), James (Middlesex), and R.N. (Surrey and Middlesex). Middle order right-hand batsman. *Sch* Dulwich. *Team* Middlesex (1906, 1 match).
Career batting
1–2–0–30–16–15.00–0–*ct* 1

Douglas-Home, Sir Alec
(*see under* Dunglass, Lord)

Douglas-Home, Andrew
Cricketer. *b:* 14.5.1950, Galashiels, Scotland. Tail end left-hand batsman, right-arm fast medium bowler. *Sch* Eton. *Team* Oxford U (1970).
Career batting
4–6–1–33–23–6.60–0–*ct* 1
Bowling 273–9–30.33–0–0–3/71

Douglas-Jones, Stanley Douglas
Amateur. *b:* 19.11.1885, Hendon, Middlesex. *d:* 12.10.1969, Glyndyfrdwy, Merionethshire. Middle order batsman. *Team* MCC (1913–14).
Career batting
2–4–1–30–12–10.00–0–*ct* 0–*st* 1

Douglas-Pennant, Sir Cyril Eustace
Amateur. *b:* 7.4.1894, London. *d:* 3.4.1961, Westminster, London. Middle order batsman. *Team* Royal Navy (1924–25).
Career batting
2–3–0–29–15–9.66–0–*ct* 0

Douglas-Pennant, Simon
Amateur. *b:* 28.6.1938, Glasgow, Scotland. Tail end right-hand batsman, left-arm fast medium bowler. *Sch* Eton. *Team* Cambridge U (1959–61, blue 1959).
Career batting
35–53–31–101–14*–4.59–0–*ct* 6
Bowling 3031–83–36.57–3–1–7/56

Douthwaite, Harold
Amateur. *b:* 12.8.1900, Lancaster. *d:* 9.7.1972, Lancaster. Middle order right-hand batsman. *Sch* Lancaster GS. *Team* Lancashire (1920–21, 3 matches).
Career batting
3–5–0–85–29–17.00–0–*ct* 1
A prolific scorer in school cricket, he made over 1,000 runs for Lancaster GS in 1919 at an average of 112.

Dovey, Raymond Randall
Professional. *b:* 18.7.1920, Chislehurst, Kent. *d:* 27.12.1974, Tunbridge Wells, Kent. Lower order right-hand batsman, right-arm slow off break bowler. *Sch* Eltham College. *Team* Kent (1938–54, 249 matches). *Tour* Commonwealth to India and Ceylon 1950/1.
Career batting
263–404–74–3841–65*–11.63–0–*ct* 79
Bowling 21391–777–27.53–25–2–8/23
He took 102 wkts, av 25.48, in 1950.
After leaving Kent he appeared for Dorset.

Dow, William David Fraser
Professional. *b:* 27.11.1933, Glasgow, Scotland. Lower order right-hand batsman, right-arm fast medium bowler. *Teams* Scotland (1956–67, 11 matches); Essex (1958–59, 2 matches).
Career batting
13–16–4–107–18–8.91–0–*ct* 2
Bowling 1015–38–26.71–2–1–6/56
He also appeared for Cumberland.

Dowding, Alan Lorimer
Amateur. *b:* 4.4.1929, Adelaide, Australia. Forcing middle order right-hand batsman, good field. *Team* Oxford U (1951–53, blue 1952–53).
Career batting
43–73–5–1950–105–28.67–2–*ct* 27
Bowling 116–1–116.00–0–0–1/4
His final first-class match was for MCC in 1956.
He was awarded his soccer blue at Oxford.

Dowell, Alistair McQueen
Amateur. *b:* 17.5.1920, Kinross, Scotland. Right-hand batsman, right-arm fast medium bowler. *Team* Scotland (1951–55).
Career batting
3–4–1–6–5–2.00–0–*ct* 0
Bowling 136–2–68.00–0–0–2/51

Dowen, Neville Thomas
Amateur. *b:* 18.8.1901, Bulwell, Notts. *d:* 25.10.1964, Evington, Leics. Middle order left-hand batsman, right-arm fast medium bowler. *Team* Leicestershire (1925–38, 7 matches).
Career batting
7–12–0–187–44–15.58–0–*ct* 3
Bowling 25–0

Dowling, Geoffrey Charles Walter
Amateur. *b:* 12.8.1891. *d:* 30.7.1915, Hooge, Belgium. He was killed in action. Middle order batsman. *Sch* Charterhouse. *Team* Sussex (1911–13, 4 matches).
Career batting
4–8–0–123–48–15.37–0–*ct* 4
Bowling 19–1–19.00–0–0–1/19
Whilst at Cambridge he appeared in various trials, but no first-class matches for the University.

Dowling, Graham Thorne
Cricketer. *b:* 4.3.1937, Christchurch, New Zealand. Opening right-hand batsman. *Teams* Canterbury (1958/9 to 1971/2); Prime Minister's XI (in India) (1967/8). *Tours* New Zealand to England 1965, 1969, to South Africa 1961/2, to India and Pakistan 1964/5, 1969/70, to West Indies 1971/2, to Australia 1961/2, 1970/1. *Tests* New Zealand (1962/3 to 1971/2, 39 matches).
Career batting
158–282–13–9399–239–34.94–16–*ct* 111
Bowling 378–9–42.00–0–0–3/100
Test batting
39–77–3–2306–239–31.16–3–*ct* 23
Bowling 19–1–19.00–0–0–1/19
He played in all the Tests on his two tours to England, being captain in 1969, and was reasonably successful.

In first-class matches he hit two double centuries, the highest being 239 for New Zealand v India at Christchurch in 1967/8.

Down, J. H.
Professional. Lower order left-hand batsman, slow left-arm bowler. *Team* Hampshire (1914, 2 matches).
Career batting
2–3–1–32–31*–16.00–0–*ct* 0
Bowling 53–1–53.00–0–0–1/33

Downend, Richard Hugh
Cricketer. *b:* 19.1.1945, Manchester. Lower order right-hand batsman, right-arm medium pace bowler. *Team* Minor Counties (1972).
Career batting
1–2–0–6–5–3.00–0–*ct* 0
Bowling 71–1–71.00–0–0–1/71
His County cricket was for Staffordshire.

Downer, Harry Rodney
Amateur. *b:* 19.10.1915, Southampton. Middle order right-hand batsman, *Team* Hampshire (1946, 2 matches).
Career batting
2–4–0–8–4–2.00–0–*ct* 0

Downes, Keith Drummond
Amateur. *b:* 12.6.1917, Liverpool. Middle/lower order right-hand batsman, wicket-keeper. *Sch* Rydal. *Team* Cambridge U (1939, blue).
Career batting
8–13–2–102–27–9.27–0–*ct* 6–*st* 1
He played for Denbighshire.

Downs, Alexander
Amateur. *b:* 28.5.1876, Uddingston, Lanarkshire, Scotland. *d:* 17.7.1924, Uddingston, Lanarkshire, Scotland. Lower order batsman, wicket-keeper. *Team* Scotland (1907).
Career batting
1–2–0–1–1–0.50–0–*ct* 0

Downton, George Charles
Professional. *b:* 1.11.1928, Bexley, Kent. Father of P.R. (Kent and Middlesex). Lower order right-hand batsman, wicket-keeper. *Team* Kent (1948, 8 matches).
Career batting
10–15–5–88–20–8.80–0–*ct* 26–*st* 1
His final first-class match was for MCC in 1959.

Downton, Paul Rupert
Cricketer. *b:* 4.4.1957, Farnborough, Kent. Son of G. C. (Kent). Right-hand batsman, wicket-keeper. *Sch* Sevenoaks. *Teams* Kent (1977–79, 45 matches); Middlesex (1980–83, 80 matches). *Tours* England to Pakistan and New Zealand 1977/8, to West Indies 1980/1; Middlesex to Zimbabwe 1980/1. *Tests* England (1980/1 to 1981, 4 matches).
Career batting
142–160–28–2437–90*–18.46–0–*ct* 305–*st* 42
Test batting
4–7–1–59–26*–9.83–0–*ct* 8

Dowson, Edward
Amateur. *b:* 17.2.1838, Camberwell, Surrey. *d:* 29.4.1922, Surbiton, Surrey. Father of E.M. (Surrey). Middle order right-hand batsman, good deep field. *Sch* Shrewsbury. *Team* Surrey (1860–70, 54 matches).
Career batting
74–120–6–1927–94–16.90–0–*ct* 41
Bowling 13–0
His first-class debut was for Gentlemen of Surrey and Sussex in 1856.
He also played for Bedfordshire, Buckinghamshire and Lincolnshire.

Dowson, Edward Maurice
Amateur. *b:* 21.6.1880, Weybridge, Surrey. *d:* 22.7.1933, Hele, Ashburton, Devon. Son of Edward (Surrey). Middle order right-hand batsman, slow left-arm bowler. *Sch* Harrow. *Teams* Cambridge U (1900–03, blue all four years); Surrey (1900–03, 44 matches). *Tours* Hawke to Australia and New Zealand 1902/3; Bosanquet to North America 1901; Bennett to West Indies 1901/2.
Career batting
113–187–14–5047–135–29.17–8–*ct* 61
Bowling 8544–357–23.93–23–3–8/21
He hit 1,000 runs in a season three times (best 1,343, av 34.43, in 1903).
His last first-class match was for MCC in 1913, but he appeared in very few important matches after 1903.

Draffan, Nigel Gordon Helm
Cricketer. *b:* 1.9.1950, Kenya. Opening/middle order right-hand batsman. *Team* Cambridge U (1971–72).
Career batting
4–7–1–35–29–5.83–0–*ct* 1

Drake, Alonzo
Professional. *b:* 16.4.1884, Parkgate, Rotherham, Yorkshire. *d:* 14.2.1919, Honley, Huddersfield, Yorkshire. Middle order left-hand batsman, left-arm slow medium bowler. *Team* Yorkshire (1909–14, 156 matches).

Career batting
157–246–24–4816–147*–21.69–3–*ct* 94
Bowling 8656–480–18.03–29–1–10/35

He took 100 wickets in a season twice (best 158, av 15.30, in 1914).

His career was dogged by ill-health. His best bowling was 10/35 for Yorkshire v Somerset at Weston in 1914. He hit 1,000 runs in a season twice (best 1,487, av 30.97, in 1911) and completed the 'double' in 1913.

He played soccer for Sheffield United.

Drake, Cyril Henry
Professional. *b:* 9.1.1922, Leicester. Lower order right-hand batsman, right-arm fast bowler. *Team* Leicestershire (1939, 8 matches).
Career batting
8–11–3–43–13–5.37–0–*ct* 3
Bowling 605–19–31.84–1–0–5/21

Drake, Edward Joseph
Professional. *b:* 16.8.1912, Southampton. Middle order right-hand batsman. *Team* Hampshire (1931–36, 16 matches).
Career batting
16–27–0–219–45–8.11–0–*ct* 10
Bowling 171–4–42.75–0–0–2/37

One of the best known centre forwards of his day, Drake played soccer for Southampton, Arsenal and England, gaining five international caps.

Drake, Rev Edward Tyrwhitt
Amateur. *b:* 15.5.1832, Bucknall, Bicester, Oxon. *d:* 20.6.1904, Amersham, Bucks. Hard hitting right-hand batsman, right-hand lob bowler. *Sch* Westminster. *Team* Cambridge U (1852–54, blue all three years).
Career batting
55–102–8–1412–88–15.02–0–*ct* 41
Bowling 2003–154+43–13.00–20–8–8/61

His last first-class match was for MCC in 1871. He was regarded as one of the best lob bowlers, though at times very expensive. He entered the church in 1860 and rarely appeared in first-class matches after that – it was thought that the clergy should not take part in matches which involved betting.

He also played for Buckinghamshire and Hertfordshire.

Drake, John
Professional. *b:* 1.9.1893, Tong Park, Baildon, Yorkshire. *d:* 22.5.1967, Meanwood, Yorkshire. Lower order left-hand batsman, left-arm fast medium bowler. *Team* Yorkshire (1923–24, 3 matches).
Career batting
3–4–1–21–10–7.00–0–*ct* 2
Bowling 117–1–117.00–0–0–1/44

Drakes, Thomas Edwin
Amateur. *b:* 7.3.1908, Bardney, Lincs. *d:* 10.5.1974, Hainault, Essex. Middle/lower order right-hand batsman, right-arm fast medium bowler. *Sch* Stamford. *Team* Cambridge U (1929).
Career batting
8–11–1–140–39*–14.00–0–*ct* 6
Bowling 648–20–32.40–1–0–5/70

His County cricket was for Lincolnshire.

Draper, Robert William
Amateur. *b:* 20.1.1903, Calcutta, India. Lower order right-hand batsman, left-arm medium pace bowler. *Team* Somerset (1925–29, 3 matches).
Career batting
3–5–0–20–11–4.00–0–*ct* 2
Bowling 221–6–36.83–0–0–3/73

Draper, William
Professional. *b:* 12.11.1849, Penshurst, Kent. *d:* 13.3.1919, Tonbridge, Kent. Brother of Henry (noted umpire). Lower order left-hand batsman, right-arm medium pace bowler. *Team* Kent (1874–80, 9 matches).
Career batting
9–17–2–108–28–7.71–0–*ct* 3
Bowling 290–20–14.50–1–0–5/51

Dredge, Colin Herbert
Cricketer. *b*: 4.8.1954, Frome, Somerset. Lower order left-hand batsman, right-arm medium pace bowler, deep field. *Team* Somerset (1976–83, 138 matches).
Career batting
138–158–50–1535–56*–14.21–0–*ct* 58
Bowling 9499–327–29.04–11–0–6/37

Drew, Thomas Michael
Amateur. *b:* 9.11.1875, Australia. *d:* 9.1.1928, Toowoomba, Queensland, Australia. Lower order batsman, bowler. *Teams* South Australia (1897/8, 3 matches); London County (1903).
Career batting
4–7–2–65–33*–13.00–0–*ct* 4
Bowling 33–0

Driffield, Lancelot Townshend
Amateur. *b:* 10.8.1880, Old, Northants. *d:* 9.10.1917, Leatherhead, Surrey. Lower order left-hand batsman, left-arm slow bowler. *Sch* St John's, Leatherhead. *Teams* Cambridge U (1900–02, blue 1902); Northants (1905–08, 40 matches).

Career batting
61–98–19–851–56–10.77–0–*ct* 32
Bowling 4102–137–29.94–6–1–7/7
A noted soccer player, he obtained his blue at Cambridge.

Dring, Clive Frederick
Professional. *b:* 30.6.1934, Shooters Hill, Kent. Middle order right-hand batsman, right-arm medium pace bowler. *Team* Kent (1955, 1 match).
Career batting
1–2–0–8–8–4.00–0–*ct* 0

Drinnan, William Murdoch Ross
Amateur. *b:* 28.5.1883, St. Quivox, Ayrshire, Scotland. *d:* 10.3.1948, Ayr, Scotland. Left-hand batsman, slow left-arm bowler. *Team* Scotland (1928).
Career batting
1–2–2–24–24*–no av–0–*ct* 0
Bowling 102–3–34.00–0–0–2/43

Driver, Jeremiah
Professional. *b:* 16.5.1861, Keighley, Yorkshire. *d:* 10.12.1946, Bradford, Yorkshire. Lower order batsman, wicket-keeper. *Team* Yorkshire (1889, 2 matches).
Career batting
2–4–1–24–8–8.00–0–*ct* 2

Druce, Eliot Albert Cross
Amateur. *b:* 20.6.1876, Weybridge, Surrey. *d:* 24.10.1934, Westminster, London. Cousin of W.G. (Cambridge U) and N.F. (Cambridge U and Surrey). Middle order right-hand batsman, right-arm medium pace bowler. *Sch* Marlborough. *Teams* Cambridge U (1897–98); Kent (1898–1900, 3 matches).
Career batting
10–14–2–185–43–15.41–0–*ct* 6
Bowling 213–13–16.38–0–0–4/28
His final first-class match was for Free Foresters in 1913.
He played hockey for Cambridge U in 1897/8.

Druce, Norman Frank
Amateur. *b:* 1.1.1875, Denmark Hill, Surrey. *d:* 27.10.1954, Milford on Sea, Hants. Brother of W.G. (Cambridge U), cousin of E.A.C. (Kent). Middle order right-hand batsman. *Sch* Marlborough. *Teams* Cambridge U (1894–97, blue all four years); Surrey (1895–97, 12 matches). *Tours* Mitchell to North America 1895; Stoddart to Australia 1897/8. *Tests* England (1897/8, 5 matches).
Career batting
66–105–8–3416–227*–35.21–9–*ct* 66
Bowling 268–8–33.50–0–0–1/8
Test batting
5–9–0–252–64–28.00–0–*ct* 5
His double century was for Cambridge U v C.I. Thornton's XI in 1897.
After leaving Cambridge he appeared in very few first-class matches, but his final game was not until 1913, for Free Foresters.

Druce, Walter George
Amateur. *b:* 16.9.1872, Denmark Hill, Surrey. *d:* 8.1.1963, Sherborne, Dorset. Brother of N.F. (Surrey) and cousin of E.A.C. (Kent). Middle order right-hand batsman, good cover point. *Sch* Marlborough. *Team* Cambridge U (1894–95, blue both years).
Career batting
39–67–11–1568–129–28.00–3–*ct* 47–*st* 5
Bowling 18–0
His final first-class match was for MCC in 1913.

Drummond, Alexander Victor
Amateur. *b:* 20.10.1888, London. *d:* 29.4.1937, Tunbridge Wells, Kent. Brother of G.H. (Northants). Middle order batsman. *Sch* Harrow. *Team* MCC (1911–21). *Tour* MCC to Egypt 1909 (not first-class).
Career batting
8–15–1–182–30–13.00–0–*ct* 2
Bowling 157–3–52.33–0–0–2/44
He also played for Buckinghamshire.

Drummond, Duncan Weir
Amateur. *b:* 12.5.1923, Greenock, Scotland. Right-hand batsman, right-arm medium pace bowler. *Sch* Merchiston. *Team* Scotland (1951–61).
Career batting
17–22–1–263–33–12.52–0–*ct* 3
Bowling 771–20–38.55–0–0–4/73

Drummond, George Henry
Amateur. *b:* 3.3.1883. London. *d:* 12.10.1963, Braddan, Isle of Man. Brother of A.V. (MCC). Middle order right-hand batsman. *Sch* Harrow. *Team* Northants (1920–22, 4 matches). *Tours* MCC to Australia 1903/4 (he played in emergency); Brackley to West Indies 1904/5.
Career batting
15–27–1–186–34–7.15–0–*ct* 5
Bowling 21–0
Whilst at Cambridge he did not appear in first-class games. He made his first-class debut in England for MCC in 1906.
He was High Sheriff of Northants.

Drury, John Joseph
Professional. *b:* 28.5.1874, Kimberley, Notts. *d:* 16.10.1919, Dobcross, Yorkshire. Lower order right-hand batsman, right-arm fast bowler. *Team* Nottinghamshire (1899–1902, 4 matches).
Career batting
4–3–0–21–19–7.00–0–*ct* 0
Bowling 71–4–17.75–0–0–1/1

Drybrough, Colin David
Amateur. *b:* 31.8.1938, Melbourne, Australia. Lower order right-hand batsman, slow left-arm bowler, good close field. *Sch* Highgate. *Teams* Middlesex (1958–64, 92 matches); Oxford U (1960–62, blue all 3 years).
Career batting
133–161–41–1848–88–15.40–0–*ct* 99
Bowling 9270–319–29.05–10–1–7/35

He captained Middlesex 1963–64.

His final first-class match was for MCC in 1967.

D'Souza, Antao
Cricketer. *b:* 17.1.1939, Goa, India. Tail end right-hand batsman, right-arm medium pace off break bowler. *Teams* Karachi (1956/7 to 1962/3); Peshawar (1959/60); PIA (1960/1 to 1966/7). *Tours* Pakistan to England 1962; Pakistan Eaglets to England 1963; PIA to East Africa 1964. *Tests* Pakistan (1958/9 to 1962, 6 matches).
Career batting
61–72–29–815–45–18.95–0–*ct* 20
Bowling 4946–190–26.03–12–1–7/33
Test batting
6–10–8–76–23*–38.00–0–*ct* 3
Bowling 745–17–43.82–1–0–5/112

On his only Test tour to England he took 58 wickets, av 34.79.

Du Boulay, Arthur Houssemayne
Amateur. *b:* 18.6.1880, Chatham, Kent. *d:* 25.10.1918, Fillieres, France, of influenza. Opening/middle order right-hand batsman, right-arm medium pace bowler. *Sch* Cheltenham. *Teams* Kent (1899, 5 matches); Gloucestershire (1908, 3 matches).
Career batting
9–14–3–303–58–27.54–0–*ct* 2
Bowling 177–3–59.00–0–0–1/4

His final first-class match was for MCC in 1910.

He was a prolific scorer in military cricket, his most famous innings being 402* for School of Military Engineering v Royal Navy and Marines at Chatham in 1907.

Ducat, Andrew
Professional. *b:* 16.2.1886, Brixton, Surrey. *d:* 23.7.1942, Lord's Cricket Ground. He died of heart failure whilst batting. Sound right-hand batsman, slow right-arm bowler. *Team* Surrey (1906–31, 422 matches). *Tour* MCC to Australia 1929/30 (in emergency). *Test* England (1921, 1 match).
Career batting
428–669–59–23373–306*–38.63–52–*ct* 205
Bowling 903–21–43.00–0–0–3/12
Test batting
1–2–0–5–3–2.50–0–*ct* 1

He hit 1,000 runs in a season 14 times, exceeding 2,000 once : 2,067, av 49.21, in 1930. He scored eight double centuries, all for Surrey, including one 300 – 306* v Oxford U at the Oval 1919. A noted soccer player he appeared for Aston Villa, Southend, Woolwich Arsenal and Fulham and was capped six times for England. He captained Aston Villa to win the FA Cup in 1920.

Duckfield, Richard George
Amateur in 1930, professional from 1931. *b:* 2.7.1907, Maesteg, Glamorgan. *d:* 30.12.1959, Bridgend, Glamorgan. Right-hand middle order batsman, right-arm medium pace bowler. *Team* Glamorgan (1930–38, 191 matches).
Career batting
192–302–39–7000–280*–26.61–10–*ct* 27
Bowling 255–0

He hit 1,000 runs in a season three times (best 1,343, av 37.30 in 1933). His only double century was 280* for Glamorgan v Surrey at the Oval in 1936.

A useful rugby footballer, he appeared for Maesteg.

Duckworth, Christopher Anthony Russell
Amateur. *b:* 22.3.1933, Que Que, Southern Rhodesia. Opening right-hand batsman, wicket-keeper. *Teams* Natal (1952/3 to 1953/4); Rhodesia (1954/5 to 1962/3). *Tours* South Africa to England 1955, 1960. *Tests* South Africa (1956/7, 2 matches).
Career batting
77–124–12–2572–158–22.96–3–*ct* 91–*st* 13
Test batting
2–4–0–28–13–7.00–0–*ct* 3

Selected as reserve wicket-keeper on his two visits to England, his opportunities were very limited.

Duckworth, George
Professional. *b:* 9.5.1901, Warrington, Lancashire. *d:* 5.1.1966, Warrington, Lancashire. Lower order right-hand batsman, wicket-keeper. *Teams* Lancashire (1923–38, 424 matches). *Tours* MCC to Australia 1928/9, to South Africa 1930/1,

to Australia and New Zealand 1932/3, 1936/7. *Tests* England (1924–36, 24 matches).
Career batting
504–545–206–4945–75–14.58–0–*ct* 754–*st* 341
Bowling 73–0
Test batting
24–28–12–234–39*–14.62–0–*ct* 45–*st* 15

He managed three Commonwealth teams to the Indian subcontinent: 1949/50, 1950/1 and 1953/4.

One of the outstanding wicketkeepers of his day, he was small of stature but loud of voice.

His final first-class match was for North v South in 1947.

He also played for Cheshire.

Dudhia, Maqbul Hussein Ebrahim Mahomed
Cricketer. *b*: 24.8.1954, Lusaka, Zambia. Lower order right-hand batsman, right-arm medium pace bowler. *Team* Zimbabwe (1980/1 to 1982). *Tour* Zimbabwe to England 1982.
Career batting
2–1–0–0–0–0.00–0–*ct* 0
Bowling 71–5–14.20–0–0–2/13

Dudleston, Barry
Cricketer. *b*: 16.7.1945, Bebington, Cheshire. Sound opening or middle order right-hand batsman, slow left-arm bowler, occasional wicket-keeper. *Teams* Leicestershire (1966–80, 262 matches); Gloucestershire (1981–83, 9 matches); Rhodesia (1976/7 to 1979/80). *Tour* Robins to West Indies 1974/5 (not first-class).
Career batting
295–501–47–14747–202–32.48–32–*ct* 234–*st* 7
Bowling 1365–47–29.04–0–0–4/6

He hit 1,000 runs in a season eight times (best 1,374, av 31.22, in 1970). His only double century was 202 for Leicestershire v Derbyshire at Leicester in 1979. He was appointed coach to Gloucestershire in 1981.

Dudley-Jones, Robert David Louis
Cricketer. *b:* 26.5.1952, Bridgend, Glamorgan. Lower order right-hand batsman, right-arm medium pace bowler. *Sch* Millfield. *Team* Glamorgan (1972–73, 5 matches).
Career batting
5–7–2–15–5–3.00–0–*ct* 1
Bowling 351–13–27.00–0–0–4/31

Dudman, Leonard Charles
Amateur. *b:* 4.8.1933, Dundee, Scotland. Right-hand batsman. *Team* Scotland (1955–68).
Career batting
35–61–3–1286–161–22.17–1–*ct* 20

Dudney, William Hudson
Amateur. *b:* 8.1.1860, Portslade, Sussex. *d:* 16.6.1922, Hove, Sussex. Middle order right-hand batsman, wicket-keeper. *Sch* Cranleigh. *Teams* Canterbury (1883/4); Sussex (1887–93, 29 matches).
Career batting
36–67–4–912–97–14.47–0–*ct* 38–*st* 6

Duff, Alan Robert
Amateur. *b:* 12.1.1938, Kinver, Staffs. Lower order right-hand batsman, leg break and googly bowler. *Sch* Radley. *Teams* Oxford U (1959–61, blue 1960–61); Worcestershire (1960–61, 6 matches). *Tours* MCC to South America 1964/5, to Bangladesh 1976/7, 1978/9 (none of these first-class).
Career batting
36–57–16–676–55*–16.48–0–*ct* 33
Bowling 1396–54–25.85–0–0–4/24

His final first-class match was for MCC in 1968.

Duff, Reginald Alexander
Amateur. *b:* 17.8.1878, Sydney, New South Wales, Australia. *d:* 13.12.1911, North Sydney, New South Wales, Australia. Brother of W.S. (NSW). Opening right-hand batsman, right-arm medium pace bowler. *Team* New South Wales (1898/9 to 1907/8, 38 matches). *Tours* Australia to England 1902, 1905, to South Africa 1902/3, to New Zealand 1904/5. *Tests* Australia (1901/2 to 1905, 22 matches).
Career batting
121–197–9–6589–271–35.04–10–*ct* 73
Bowling 478–14–34.14–0–0–2/17
Test batting
22–40–3–1317–146–35.59–2–*ct* 14
Bowling 85–4–21.25–0–0–2/43

He hit 1,000 runs on both his tours to England (best 1,403, av 22.50, in 1902).

His only double century was 271 for NSW v South Australia at Sydney in 1903/4.

Duffield, John
Profesional. *b:* 12.8.1915, Worthing, Sussex. *d:* 7.9.1956, Worthing, Sussex. Lower order right-hand batsman, right-arm fast medium bowler. *Team* Sussex (1938–47, 16 matches).
Career batting
16–23–6–263–60*–15.35–0–*ct* 3
Bowling 1043–29–35.96–1–0–5/38

A noted soccer player he appeared for Portsmouth.

Duffy, Gerald Andrew Anthony
Amateur. *b:* 4.11.1930, Dublin, Ireland. Right-hand batsman, leg break bowler. *Team* Ireland (1953–73).

Career batting
16–27–6–317–55*–15.09–0–*ct* 12
Bowling 426–15–28.40–0–0–3/8

He appeared in all three Tests on the 1965 tour to England and in all first-class matches hit 429 runs, av 22.57, and took 31 wickets, av 21.70.

Duleepsinhji, Kumar Shri
(known in India as Jawansinhji Jadeja Duleepsinhji)
Amateur. *b:* 13.6.1905, Sarodar, India. *d:* 5.12.1959, Bombay, India. Nephew of K.S. Ranjitsinhji. Middle order right-hand batsman, good slip field, leg break bowler. *Sch* Cheltenham. *Teams* Cambridge U (1925–28, blue 1925–26 and 1928); Sussex (1924–32, 119 matches); Hindus (1928/9). *Tour* MCC to Australia and New Zealand 1929/30. *Tests* England (1929–31, 12 matches).
Career batting
205–333–23–15485–333–49.95–50–*ct* 256
Bowling 1345–28–48.03–0–0–4/49
Test batting
12–19–2–995–173–58.52–3–*ct* 10
Bowling 7–0

He hit 1,000 runs in a season 7 times, going on to 2,000 three times (best 2,684, av 54.77, in 1931). His highest innings was 333 for Sussex v Northants at Hove in 1930 and he made three other scores over 200. He captained Sussex in 1931–32.

Ill-health forced him to retire from first-class cricket in 1932. In the 1950s he was Indian High Commissioner in Australia and New Zealand.

Dumbleton, Horatio Norris
Amateur. *b:* 23.10.1858, Ferozepore, India. *d:* 18.12.1935, Winchester, Hants. Middle order right-hand batsman, slow round-arm bowler. *Sch* Wimbledon. *Team* Hampshire (1884, 1 match).
Career batting
1–2–0–16–9–8.00–0–*ct* 0
Bowling 14–0

A noted cricketer in military matches he hit 325 for the Royal Engineers v Royal Marines at Portsmouth in 1884.

Dumbrill, Richard
Cricketer. *b:* 19.11.1938, London. Middle/lower order right-hand batsman, right-arm medium pace bowler. *Team* Natal (1960/1 to 1967/8). *Tour* South Africa to England 1965. *Tests* South Africa (1965 to 1966/7, 5 matches).
Career batting
51–82–7–1761–94–23.48–0–*ct* 35
Bowling 2909–132–22.03–5–1–5/34
Test batting
5–10–0–153–36–15.30–0–*ct* 3
Bowling 336–9–37.33–0–0–4/30

Duminy, Dr Jacobus Petrus
Amateur. *b:* 16.12.1897, Bellville, Cape Province, South Africa. *d:* 31.1.1980, Cape Town, South Africa. Middle order left-hand batsman, slow right-arm bowler. *Teams* Western Province (1919/20); Oxford U (1921); Transvaal (1927/8 to 1928/9). *Tour* South Africa to England 1929. *Tests* South Africa (1927/8 to 1929, 3 matches).
Career batting
13–23–4–557–168*–29.31–1–*ct* 11
Bowling 368–12–30.66–1–0–6/40
Test batting
3–6–0–30–12–5.00–0–*ct* 2
Bowling 39–1–39.00–0–0–1/17

He was on holiday in Switzerland when, due to injuries, he was co-opted into the 1929 South Africa team in England.

Dummer, William
Professional. *b:* 8.10.1847, Petworth, Sussex. *d:* 1909, Southampton. Middle order right-hand batsman, right-hand fast round arm bowler. *Team* Sussex (1869, 3 matches).
Career batting
3–6–2–60–35*–15.00–0–*ct* 3
Bowling 43–0

Duncan, Anthony Arthur
Amateur. *b:* 10.12.1914, Cardiff. Opening/middle order right-hand batsman. *Sch* Rugby. *Teams* Glamorgan (1934, 2 matches); Oxford U (1935).
Career batting
3–5–1–18–15*–4.50–0–*ct* 0

He was a well-known golfer.

Duncan, Arthur James
Amateur. *b:* 1856, Southampton. *d:* 1936, Wandsworth, London. Brother of D.W.J. (Hants). Middle order batsman. *Team* Hampshire (1878–83, 2 matches).
Career batting
2–4–0–28–26–7.00–0–*ct* 0

Duncan, Adam Seymour Dickson
Amateur. *b:* 1852. *d:* 1940, Hatfield, Herts. Middle order batsman. *Sch* Eton. *Team* Cambridge U (1873).
Career batting
14–25–2–313–42–13.60–0–*ct* 5

His final first-class match was for MCC in 1879.

Duncan, Alexander William
Amateur. *b:* 19.6.1881, Crichton, Midlothian, Scotland. *d:* 18.11.1934, Angmering-on-Sea, Sussex. Right-hand batsman, right-arm fast bowler. *Sch* Merchiston. *Team* Scotland (1909).
Career batting
1–1–0–31–31–31.00–0–*ct* 0
Bowling 22–0
He was a Scottish rugby international.

Duncan, Dunbar Wilson Johnston
Amateur. *b:* 8.7.1852, Southampton. *d:* 12.12.1919, Regent's Park, London. Brother of A.J. (Hants). Middle order right-hand batsman. *Team* Hampshire (1875–85, 17 matches).
Career batting
17–29–3–581–87*–22.34–0–*ct* 4
Bowling 18–3–6.00–0–0–1/1

Dunglass, Lord Alexander Frederick
(later Sir Alexander Douglas-Home, then Lord Home of the Hirsel)
Amateur. *b:* 2.7.1903, London. Lower order right-hand bat, right-arm fast-medium, bowler. *Sch* Eton. *Teams* Middlesex (1924–25, 2 matches); Oxford U (1926). *Tours* MCC to South America 1926/7.
Career batting
10–15–6–147–37*–16.33–0–*ct* 9
Bowling 363–12–30.25–0–0–3/43
His final first-class match was for Harlequins in 1927.
He was Unionist MP for South Lanark 1931–45; Conservative MP for Lanark 1950–51; Secretary of State for Commonwealth Relations 1955–60; Lord President of the Council and Leader of the House of Lord's 1957–60; Secretary of State for Foreign Affairs 1960–63; Prime Minister 1963–64; Leader of the Opposition 1964–65; Secretary of State for Foreign and Commonwealth Affairs 1970–74. He disclaimed his peerage in 1963 and returned to the House of Commons as Conservative MP for Kinross and West Perthshire until 1974, when he was made a Life Peer.

Dunham, Norman Leonard
Professional. *b:* 9.12.1925, Quorn, Leics. Lower order right-hand batsman, right-arm medium pace bowler. *Team* Leicestershire (1949, 1 match).
Career batting
1–2–1–15–12*–15.00–0–*ct* 1
Bowling 60–0

Dunkels, Paul Renton
Cricketer. *b:* 26.11.1947, Marylebone, London. Lower order left-hand batsman, right-arm medium bowler. *Teams* Warwickshire (1971, 1 match); Sussex (1972, 1 match).
Career batting
3–2–1–3–3*–3.00–0–*ct* 0
Bowling 253–3–84.33–0–0–2/60
He also played for Devon.

Dunkley, Frederick John
Professional. *b:* 9.9.1862, Chelsea, London. *d:* 1901, Marylebone, London. Lower order left-hand batsman, left-arm fast bowler. *Team* Middlesex (1886–88, 15 matches).
Career batting
15–21–4–58–11–3.41–0–*ct* 13
Bowling 1170–49–23.87–4–0–6/42

Dunkley, Maurice Edward Frank
Professional. *b:* 19.2.1914, Kettering, Northants. Middle order right-hand batsman. *Team* Northants (1937–39, 36 matches).
Career batting
36–64–4–904–70–15.06–0–*ct* 17
Bowling 12–0
He was a noted soccer player with Northampton Town and Manchester City.

Dunlop, Charles Edward
Amateur. *b:* 25.6.1870, Edinburgh, Scotland. *d:* 21.8.1911, London. Middle order right-hand batsman, good field. *Sch* Merchiston. *Team* Somerset (1892–1905, 43 matches).
Career batting
43–77–6–1172–65–16.50–0–*ct* 20
Bowling 41–2–20.50–0–0–2/29
He played in several trials at Oxford, but no first-class matches.

Dunlop, George Colquhoun Hamilton
Amateur. *b:* 28.7.1846, Edinburgh, Scotland. *d:* 7.6.1929, Dumfries, Scotland. Opening right-hand batsman. *Sch* Edinburgh Academy. *Team* Lancashire (1868, 1 match).
Career batting
1–2–0–17–16–8.50–0–*ct* 0

Dunlop, Sir Thomas Charles
Amateur. *b:* 4.2.1878, Ayr, Scotland. *d:* 13.8.1960, Ayr, Scotland. Right-hand batsman, wicket-keeper. *Sch* Eton. *Team* Scotland (1911).
Career batting
1–1–0–0–0–0.00–0–*ct* 0–*st* 2

Dunn, John
Amateur. *b:* 8.6.1862, Hobart, Tasmania. *d:* 10.10.1892, Sand Is, Pescadores, Formosa. He was drowned in a shipwreck on board SS *Bokhara*. Hard hitting middle order right-hand batsman, good field. *Sch* Harrow. *Team* Surrey

(1881, 4 matches). *Tour* Gentlemen of Ireland to North America 1888 (not first-class).
Career batting
7–12–1–95–38*–8.63–0–*ct* 1

He was drowned with the rest of the Hong Kong Cricket Team, which was returning from their annual match with Shanghai, when the shipwreck occurred.

His final first-class match was for Gentlemen of England in 1889.

Dunning, John Angus
Amateur. *b:* 6.2.1903, Omaha, Rodney, Auckland, New Zealand. *d:* 24.6.1971, Adelaide, Australia. Lower order right-hand batsman, right-arm medium pace off break bowler. *Teams* Oxford U (1928); Otago (1923/4 to 1937/8); Auckland (1928/9). *Tour* New Zealand to England 1937. *Tests* New Zealand (1932/3 to 1937, 4 matches).
Career batting
60–95–14–1057–45–13.04–0–*ct* 34
Bowling 6290–228–27.58–15–2–6/42
Test Batting
4–6–1–38–19–7.60–0–*ct* 2
Bowling 493–5–98.60–0–0–2/35

On the 1937 tour he took 83 wickets, av 30.10, but failed in the Tests.

Dunning, Michael Lindsay
Cricketer. *b:* 11.3.1941, Windsor, Berkshire. Middle order batsman, bowler. *Sch* Eton. *Team* Combined Services (1962–64).
Career batting
2–4–0–134–85–33.50–0–*ct* 0
Bowling 22–0

Dunstan, Malcolm Stephen Thomas
Cricketer. *b:* 14.10.1950, Redruth, Cornwall. Middle order right-hand batsman, right-arm medium pace bowler. *Team* Gloucestershire (1971–74, 12 matches).
Career batting
12–20–3–283–52–16.64–0–*ct* 4

He played for Cornwall commencing 1969 and returned to that County after appearing for Gloucestershire.

Durack, John Philip
Cricketer. *b:* 18.5.1956, Perth, Australia. Opening right-hand batsman, leg break bowler. *Team* Oxford U (1980).
Career batting
7–13–0–136–45–10.46–0–*ct* 3
Bowling 32–0

Durandu, Arthur
Amateur. *b:* 25.12.1860, Liverpool. *d:* 4.2.1903, Crosby, Liverpool. Middle order batsman. *Team* Lancashire (1887, 1 match).
Career batting
2–3–0–5–5–1.66–0–*ct* 2

Durden-Smith, Neil
Cricketer. *b:* 18.8.1933, Richmond, Surrey. Middle order right-hand batsman, off break bowler. *Sch* Aldenham. *Team* Combined Services (1961).
Career batting
4–6–1–111–50–22.20–0–*ct* 0

His last first-class match was for MCC in 1967.

He is married to TV personality Judith Chalmers.

Durlacher, Patrick Neville
Amateur. *b:* 17.3.1903, Paddington, London. *d:* 26.2.1971, Ireland. Opening right-hand batsman. *Sch* Wellington. *Team* Middlesex (1921–23, 5 matches).
Career batting
5–4–0–43–27–10.75–0–*ct* 3

He also played for Buckinghamshire.

Durley, Anthony William
Professional. *b:* 30.9.1933, Ilford, Essex. Lower order right-hand batsman, wicket-keeper. *Team* Essex (1957, 5 matches).
Career batting
5–8–0–38–16–4.75–0–*ct* 3

He also represented Bedfordshire.

Durnell, Thomas Wilfred
Amateur. *b:* 17.6.1901, Cannon Hill, Birmingham. Lower order left-hand batsman, right-arm fast bowler. *Team* Warwickshire (1921–30, 14 matches).
Career batting
14–13–3–21–5*–2.10–0–*ct* 7
Bowling 1190–42–28.33–3–1–7/29

Durose, Antony Jack
Cricketer. *b:* 10.10.1944, Dukinfield, Cheshire. Lower order right-hand batsman, right-arm fast medium bowler. *Team* Northants (1964–69, 70 matches).
Career batting
70–71–23–447–30–9.31–0–*ct* 24
Bowling 4035–150–26.90–2–1–7/23

He played for Cheshire in 1964.

Durston, Frederick John
Professional. *b:* 11.7.1893, Clophill, Beds. *d:* 8.4.1965, Norwood Green, Southall, Middlesex. Hard hitting lower order right-hand batsman, right-arm fast bowler, latterly medium pace. *Team* Middlesex (1919–33, 349 matches). *Tours*

Cahn to Jamaica 1928/9; Brinckman to South America 1937/8 (no first-class matches). *Test* England (1921, 1 match).
Career batting
386–473–144–3918–92*–11.90–0–*ct* 257
Bowling 29279–1329–22.03–72–11–8/27
Test batting
1–2–1–8–6*–8.00–0–*ct* 0
Bowling 136–5–27.20–0–0–4/102

He took 100 wickets in a season six times (best 136, av 19.50, in 1921).

He kept goal for Brentford.

Dury, Guy Alexander Ingram
Amateur. *b:* 4.12.1895, Hendon, Middlesex. *d:* 10.8.1976, Eastbourne, Sussex. Son of T.S. (Yorkshire). Middle order batsman, bowler. *Sch* Harrow. *Teams* Leveson-Gower's XI (1919); Army (1922); Free Foresters (1926).
Career batting
3–5–0–70–51–14.00–0–*ct* 0
Bowling 131–3–43.66–0–0–2/51

Dury, Theodore Seton
Amateur. *b:* 12.6.1854, Ripley, Yorkshire. *d:* 20.3.1932, London. Father of G.A.I. (Leveson-Gower's XI). Middle order right-hand batsman, right-hand medium pace round arm bowler. *Sch* Harrow. *Teams* Oxford U (1875–76, blue 1876); Yorkshire (1878–81, 13 matches).
Career batting
24–42–1–565–46–13.78–0–*ct* 8
Bowling 158–3–52.66–0–0–2/38

He also represented Oxford U at rackets, both singles and doubles.

Duthie, Arthur Murray
Amateur. *b:* 12.6.1881, Saharanpur, India. *d:* 3.6.1973, Chideock, Dorset. Lower order batsman, opening bowler. *Sch* Marlborough. *Team* Hampshire (1911, 1 match).
Career batting
1–2–0–6–5–3.00–0–*ct* 1
Bowling 141–5–28.20–0–0–3/85

He also played for Madras in Ceylon.

Dutnall, Frank
Professional. *b:* 30.3.1896, Canterbury, Kent. *d:* 24.10.1971, Burnley, Lancashire. Brother of William (Kent). Middle order right-hand batsman, right-hand medium bowler. *Team* Kent (1919–20, 4 matches).
Career batting
4–5–0–26–16–5.20–0–*ct* 1
Bowling 9–0

Dutnall, William
Amateur. *b:* 29.8.1888, Canterbury, Kent. *d:* 18.3.1960, Canterbury, Kent. Brother of Frank (Kent). Middle order right-hand batsman, right-hand slow medium bowler. *Team* Kent (1923, 1 match).
Career batting
2–4–0–33–30–8.25–0–*ct* 0
Bowling 69–0

His first-class debut was for the Army in 1919.

He and his brother frequently opened the batting for Kent Second Eleven – William playing as an amateur and his brother, a professional.

Dutton, Henry John
Amateur. *b:* 17.1.1847, Kensington, London. *d:* 1.1.1935, Southampton. Lower order batsman, change bowler. *Sch* Eton. *Team* Hampshire (1875, 1 match).
Career batting
1–2–2–7–7*–no av–0–*ct* 0
Bowling 8–0

Dutton, Ronald Moore
Amateur. *b:* 24.11.1902, Chester. Middle order left-hand batsman, left-arm bowler. *Sch* Oakham. *Team* Minor Counties (1936–37).
Career batting
2–4–0–160–56–40.00–0–*ct* 1
Bowling 37–0

He played for Cheshire.

Dutton, Richard Stuart
Cricketer. *b*: 24.11.1959, Liverpool, Lancashire. Lower order right-hand batsman, right-arm medium pace bowler. *Sch* Wrekin. *Team* Cambridge U (1981–82).
Career batting
6–6–4–7–7*–3.50–0–*ct* 2
Bowling 261–1–261.00–0–0–1/45

Dwyer, John Elicius Benedict Bernard Placid Quirk Carrington
Professional. *b:* 3.5.1876, Sydney, New South Wales, Australia. *d:* 19.10.1912, Crewe, Cheshire. Hard hitting lower order right-hand batsman, right-arm fast-medium bowler. *Team* Sussex (1904–09, 60 matches).
Career batting
60–92–9–986–63*–11.87–0–*ct* 21
Bowling 5002–179–27.95–10–2–9/35

His best bowling was 9/35 for Sussex v Derbyshire at Hove in 1906. He was the great-grandson of Michael Dwyer, who was transported to Australia after the Irish insurrection of 1798.

Dyas, William George
Amateur. *b:* 1872, Madeley, Salop. *d:* 14.1.1940, Madeley, Salop. Middle order batsman, bowler. *Team* London County (1901–02).

Career batting
4–6–0–136–83–22.66–0–*ct* 0
Bowling 68–2–34.00–0–0–1/16
He played for Shropshire.

Dye, John Cooper James
Cricketer. *b:* 24.7.1942, Gillingham, Kent. Tail end right-hand batsman, left-arm fast medium bowler. *Teams* Kent (1962–71, 149 matches); Northants (1972–77, 112 matches); Eastern Province (1972/3).
Career batting
266–247–125–778–29*–6.37–0–*ct* 53
Bowling 17272–725–23.82–22–2–7/45
He also played for Bedfordshire.

Dyer, Alan Willoughby
Cricketer. *b:* 8.7.1945, Winchester. Middle order right-hand batsman, wicket-keeper. *Sch* Mill Hill. *Team* Oxford U (1965–66, blue both years).
Career batting
25–41–9–765–67–23.90–0 *ct* 34–*st* 2

Dyer, David Dennis
Cricketer. *b:* 3.12.1946, Durban, South Africa. Son of D. V. (Natal) and brother of G. D. (Western Province). Middle order right-hand batsman, wicket-keeper. *Teams* Natal (1967/8 to 1974/5); Transvaal (1975/6 to 1981/2). *Tour* South African Universities to England 1967.
Career batting
109–191–18–5651–196*–32.66–8–*ct* 149–*st* 8
Bowling 46–0
He made his first-class debut for South African Universities in 1965/6.

Dyer, Dennis Victor
Amateur. *b:* 2.5.1914, Durban, South Africa. Father of D.D. (Natal and Transvaal) and G.D. (Western Province). Opening right-hand batsman. *Team* Natal (1939/40 to 1948/9). *Tour* South Africa to England 1947. *Tests* South Africa (1947, 3 matches).
Career batting
34–53–7–1725–185–37.50–3–*ct* 20
Bowling 16–0
Test batting
3–6–0–96–62–16.00–0–*ct* 0
He had a modest tour in 1947, being hampered by ill-health.

Dyer, Robin Ian Henry Benbow
Cricketer. *b*: 22.12.1958, Hereford. Middle order right-hand batsman, right-arm medium pace bowler. *Team* Warwickshire (1981–83, 16 matches).
Career batting
16–24–4–323–93–16.15–0–*ct* 8
Bowling 2–0

Dyke, Rev Canon Edwin Francis
Amateur. *b:* 27.9.1842, London. *d:* 26.8.1919, Maidstone, Kent. Lower order right-hand batsman, left-arm medium pace bowler, goodfield *Sch* Eton. *Team* Cambridge U (1864–65, blue 1865).
Career batting
6–11–2–132–46–14.66–0–*ct* 6
Bowling 248–19–13.05–1–1–6/14
His final first-class match was for MCC in 1866.

Dymock, Geoffrey
Cricketer. *b*: 21.7.1945, Maryborough, Queensland, Australia. Lower order left-hand batsman, left-arm fast medium bowler. *Team* Queensland (1971/2 to 1981/2, 87 matches). *Tours* Australia to New Zealand 1973/4, to England 1977, 1980, to Pakistan and India 1979/80. *Tests* Australia (1973/4 to 1979/80, 21 matches).
Career batting
126–159–54–1518–101*–14.45–1–*ct* 41
Bowling 11438–425–26.91–13–1–7/67
Test batting
21–32–7–236–31*–9.44–0–*ct* 1
Bowling 2116–78–27.12–5–1–7/67
He took only 15 wickets, av 31.20, on the 1977 tour to England and did not appear in the Tests. On the brief visit in 1980 he achieved little.

Dynes, Ernest (Desmond)
Amateur. *b:* 30.3.1903, Bedford. *d:* 21.6.1968, Ipswich, Suffolk. Middle order right-hand batsman, right-arm leg break bowler. *Sch* Bedford Modern. *Teams* Minor Counties (1928–30); Army (1929–31).
Career batting
9–17–2–410–127–27.33–1–*ct* 7
Bowling 511–34–15.02–2–0–5/31
He played for Bedfordshire.

Dyson, Arnold Herbert
Professional. *b:* 10.7.1905, Halifax, Yorkshire. *d:* 7.6.1978, Goldsborough, Yorkshire. Sound opening right-hand batsman, excellent field. *Team* Glamorgan (1926–48, 412 matches). *Tour* Cahn to New Zealand 1938/9.
Career batting
413–697–37–17922–208–27.15–24–*ct* 243–*st* 1
Bowling 160–1–160.00–0–0–1/9
He hit 1,000 runs in a season ten times (best 1,884, av 40.95, in 1938). His only double century was 208 for Glamorgan v Surrey at The Oval in 1932.

Dyson, Edward Martin
Amateur. *b:* 21.10.1935, Wakefield, Yorkshire. Opening right-hand batsman. *Team* Oxford U (1958–60, blue 1958).
Career batting
27–48–3–819–68*–18.20–0–*ct* 16
Bowling 8–0
His final first-class match was for MCC in 1968.

Dyson, Jack
Professional. *b:* 8.7.1934, Oldham, Lancashire. Opening right-hand batsman, right-arm off break bowler. *Team* Lancashire (1954–64, 150 matches).
Career batting
150–242–35–4433–118*–21.41–1–*ct* 54
Bowling 4447–161–27.62–8–1–7/83
He hit 1,087 runs in 1956, av 27.17.
A noted soccer player he was inside left for Manchester City, scoring in their 1956 FA Cup final victory.

Dyson, John
Cricketer. *b*: 11.6.1954, Randwick, New South Wales, Australia. Steady opening right-hand batsman. *Team* New South Wales (1975/6 to 1982/3, 57 matches). *Tours* Australia to England 1980, 1981, to Sri Lanka 1980/1, to New Zealand 1981/2, to Pakistan 1982/3. *Tests* Australia (1977/8 to 1982/3, 27 matches).
Career batting
100–178–19–6025–197–37.89–11–*ct* 51
Bowling 20–1–20.00–0–0–1/18
Test batting
27–52–7–1282–127*–28.48–2–*ct* 10
On the 1981 tour to England he hit 582 runs, av 30.63, and appeared in five of the six Tests.

Dyson, John Humphrey
Amateur. *b:* 28.9.1913, Honley, Yorkshire. Lower order right-hand batsman, slow left-arm bowler. *Sch* Charterhouse. *Team* Oxford U (1933–36, blue 1936).
Career batting
26–40–12–211–35–7.53–0–*ct* 8
Bowling 2144–68–31.51–3–0–6/47
His last first-class match was for Free Foresters in 1938.

Dyson, William Lord
Professional. *b:* 11.12.1857, Halifax, Yorkshire. *d:* 1.5.1936, Brighouse, Yorkshire. Middle order batsman. *Team* Yorkshire (1887, 2 matches).
Career batting
2–4–0–8–6–2.00–0–*ct* 2

EADIE, JOHN
(known as John Thom Clarke Eadie)
Amateur. *b:* 25.9.1861, Burton-on-Trent, Staffs. *d:* 19.8.1923, Aldershawe, Staffs. Brother of W.S. (Derbyshire). Lower order batsman, bowler. *Team* Derbyshire (1882, 1 match).
Career batting
1–2–1–8–8*–8.00–0–*ct* 0
Bowling 6–1–6.00–0–0–1/6

Eadie, William Stewart
Amateur. *b:* 27.11.1864, Burton-on-Trent, Staffs. *d:* 20.9.1914, Barrow-upon-Trent, Derbyshire. Brother of J.T.C. (Derbyshire). Middle order right-hand batsman. *Sch* Dollar and Edinburgh Institution (later Melville College). *Team* Derbyshire (1885–89, 23 matches).
Career batting
23–41–3–399–62–10.50–0–*ct* 7
Bowling 13–0
Owing to business commitments, his appearances were limited.

Eadon, Wilfred Myles
Amateur. *b:* 19.6.1915, Milstead, Kent. Middle/lower order right-hand batsman, leg break and googly bowler. *Sch* Canford. *Team* Oxford U (1934).
Career batting
1–2–0–17–14–8.50–0–*ct* 0
Bowling 88–3–29.33–0–0–2/61

Eady, Charles John
Amateur. *b:* 29.10.1870, Hobart, Tasmania. *d:* 20.12.1945, Hobart, Tasmania. Middle order right-hand batsman, right-arm fast bowler. *Team* Tasmania (1889/90 to 1907/8, 19 matches). *Tour* Australia to England and North America 1896. *Tests* Australia (1896 to 1901/2, 2 matches).
Career batting
42–71–6–1490–116–22.92–3–*ct* 45
Bowling 3146–136–23.13–12–5–8/34
Test batting
2–4–1–20–10*–6.66–0–*ct* 2
Bowling 112–7–16.00–0–0–3/30
He achieved little on his tour of England. His most famous feat was an innings of 566 for Break o' Day v Wellington in March 1902.

Eagar, Edward Desmond Russell
Amateur. *b:* 8.12.1917, Cheltenham, Gloucs. *d:* 13.9.1977, Kingsbridge, Devon. Middle order right-hand batsman, slow left-arm bowler, excellent close field. *Sch* Cheltenham. *Teams* Gloucestershire (1935–39, 21 matches); Hampshire (1946–57, 311 matches); Oxford U (1938–39, blue 1939). *Tour* Norfolk to Jamaica 1956/57.
Career batting
363–599–42–12178–158*–21.86–10–*ct* 369
Bowling 1481–31–47.77–1–0–6/66
He hit 1,000 runs in a season 6 times (best 1,200, av 26.66, in 1949). He captained Hampshire 1946–57 and was Secretary to the County from 1946 to his death.
He obtained his blue for hockey at Oxford.
He was an authority on the history of cricket. His son, Patrick, is a well-known cricket photographer.

Eagar, Michael Anthony
Amateur. *b:* 20.3.1934, Kensington, London. Middle order right-hand batsman. *Sch* Rugby. *Teams* Oxford U (1956–59, blue all four years); Gloucestershire (1957–61, 6 matches).
Career batting
58–105–8–2465–125–25.41–1–*ct* 45
Bowling 4–0
A noted hockey player, he was awarded his blue and was capped for Ireland at right-wing.

Eaglestone, James Thomas
Professional. *b:* 24.7.1923, London. Hard hitting middle order left-hand batsman. *Teams* Middlesex (1947, 9 matches); Glamorgan (1948–49, 50 matches).
Career batting
60–97–7–1420–77–15.77–0–*ct* 23

Ealham, Alan George Ernest
Cricketer. *b*: 30.8.1944, Willesborough, Kent. Middle order right-hand batsman, off break bowler, good outfield. *Team* Kent (1966–82, 305 matches).
Career batting
305–466–68–10996–153–27.62–7–*ct* 175
Bowling 189–3–63.00–0–0–1/1
He hit 1,000 runs in a season three times (best 1,363, av 34.94, in 1971). From 1978 to 1980 he captained Kent.

Eames, David George Roniel
Professional. *b:* 15.4.1937, London Colney, Herts. Middle order batsman, bowler. *Team* MCC (1958).
Career batting
1–2–0–21–14–10.50–0–*ct* 0
Bowling 9–0

Earl, George Burrill
(also known as Earle)
Professional. *b:* 7.8.1859, Melbourne, Derbyshire. *d:* 20.4.1933, Melbourne, Derbyshire. Middle order right-hand batsman, right-arm fast medium bowler. *Team* Derbyshire (1883, 1 match).

Career batting
1–1–0–4–4–4.00–0–*ct* 1

Earl, Kenneth John
Amateur. *b:* 10.11.1925, Gateshead, Co. Durham. Lower order right-hand batsman, right-arm fast medium bowler. *Team* Minor Counties (1950).
Career batting
2–4–0–4–4–1.00–0–*ct* 2
Bowling 162–9–18.00–1–0–5/75
His County cricket was for Northumberland.

Earle, Guy Fife
Amateur. *b:* 24.8.1891, Newcastle-on-Tyne. *d:* 30.12.1966, Wincanton, Somerset. Hard hitting middle order right-hand batsman, right-arm fast bowler. *Sch* Harrow. *Teams* Surrey (1911–21, 4 matches); Somerset (1922–31, 152 matches). *Tours* MCC to India, Burma and Ceylon 1926/7, to New Zealand and Australia 1929/30; Martineau to Egypt 1932, 1933 and 1934 (not first-class).
Career batting
188–295–7–5810–130–20.17–2–*ct* 112
Bowling 3107–104–29.87–1–0–5/137
He captained Harrow in the famous 1910 Fowler's Match. For Somerset v Gloucs at Taunton in 1929 he hit 59 in 15 minutes, and for MCC v Taranaki in 1929/30 his 98 came in 40 minutes.
He was badly injured in a motor cycle accident in Egypt in 1932 and retired from first-class cricket.

Earls-Davis, Michael Richard Gratwicke
Amateur. *b:* 21.2.1921, Hampstead, London. Lower order left-hand batsman, right-arm fast medium bowler. *Sch* Sherborne. *Teams* Somerset (1950, 1 match); Cambridge U (1947).
Career batting
6–7–1–14–4–2.33–0–*ct* 2
Bowling 361–12–30.08–0–0–4/87
He appeared for Cambridge U in 1940 in non first-class wartime matches, then returned to the University in 1947.

Earnshaw, George Russell Bell
Amateur. *b:* 5.5.1857, Clapham, Surrey. *d:* 29.12.1894, Meran, Austria. Son of Alfred (Surrey, 1847). Middle order right-hand batsman, good close field. *Sch* King's College. *Team* Surrey (1880, 2 matches).
Career batting
2–4–1–31–13*–10.33–0–*ct* 1
Bowling 4–0

Earnshaw, Richard Oliver
Amateur. *b:* 8.1.1939, Huddersfield, Yorkshire. Lower order batsman, fast medium bowler. *Team* Combined Services (1960–61).
Career batting
2–3–1–11–9–5.50–0–*ct* 0
Bowling 211–0

Earnshaw, Wilson
Professional. *b:* 20.9.1867, Morley, Leeds, Yorkshire. *d:* 24.11.1941, Bradford, Yorkshire. Lower order right-hand batsman, wicket-keeper. *Team* Yorkshire (1893–96, 6 matches).
Career batting
6–7–3–44–23–11.00–0–*ct* 6–*st* 2

Easby, J.
Professional. Middle order batsman. *Team* Players of the North (1878).
Career batting
1–1–0–13–13–13.00–0–*ct* 2

Easby, Joseph William
Professional. *b:* 12.8.1867, Appleton-Wiske, Yorkshire. *d:* 7.2.1915, Dover, Kent. Sound right-hand batsman, right-arm medium pace bower, wicket-keeper. *Team* Kent (1894–99, 62 matches).
Career batting
62–110–9–1851–73–18.32–0–*ct* 26–*st* 3
Bowling 424–13–32.61–0–0–2/8
A regular soldier, he showed so much promise in military matches that he was persuaded to resign and take the post of groundsman at St Lawrence, Canterbury in order to qualify for Kent. Though scoring brilliantly in club matches, he did little in first-class cricket, however.
He also played for Hampshire in non first-class matches.

East, David Edward
Cricketer. *b*: 27.7.1959, Clapton, London. Lower order right-hand batsman, wicket-keeper. *Team* Essex (1981–83, 63 matches).
Career batting
63–81–15–1304–91–19.75–0–*ct* 149–*st* 19

East, Raymond Eric
Cricketer. *b*: 20.6.1947, Manningtree, Essex. Lower order and right-hand batsman, slow left-arm bowler, close field. *Team* Essex (1965–83, 401 matches). *Tours* Robins to South Africa 1973/4; Overseas XI to India 1980/1.
Career batting
406–515–112–7148–113–17.73–1–*ct* 254
Bowling 25886–1008–25.68–49–10–8/30

East, William
Professional. *b:* 29.8.1872, Northampton. *d:* 19.12.1926, Northampton. Middle/lower order

right-hand batsman, right-arm medium pace bowler. *Team* Northants (1905–14, 157 matches).
Career batting
163–270–38–4012–86*–17.29–0–*ct* 77
Bowling 10431–499–20.90–28–4–7/71

He first appeared for Northants in 1894 and was a major force in gaining that County first-class status.

His first-class debut was for MCC in 1902.

Easter, John Nicholas Cave
Cricketer. *b:* 17.12.1945, Shawford, Hants. Tail end right-hand batsman, right-arm medium pace bowler. *Sch* St Edwards, Oxford. *Team* Oxford U (1966–68, blue 1967–68).
Career batting
28–36–13–90–14–3.91–0–*ct* 8
Bowling 1940–58–33.44–1–0–5/62

He was a well-known squash player.

Eastman, George Frederick
Professional. *b:* 7.4.1903, Leyton, Essex. Brother of L.C. (Essex). Tail end right-hand batsman, wicket-keeper. *Team* Essex (1926–29, 48 matches).
Career batting
48–66–28–265–35*–6.97–0–*ct* 29–*st* 21

A useful soccer player, he appeared for Clapton Orient.

Eastman, Lawrence Charles
Amateur, but turned professional in 1927. *b:* 3.6.1897, Enfield Wash, Middlesex. *d:* 17.4.1941, Harefield, Middlesex, in hospital after an operation. Brother of G.F. (Essex). Middle/opening right-hand batsman, originally right-arm medium, later leg break bowler. *Team* Essex (1920–39, 442 matches); Otago (1927/8 to 1928/9). *Tour* Brinckman to South America 1937/8.
Career batting
451–693–50–13385–161–20.81–7–*ct* 259
Bowling 26940–1006–26.77–30–3–7/28

He hit 1,000 runs in a season 5 times (best 1,338, av 32.63, in 1933). His best bowling season was 1935 when he took 99 wickets, av 19.58.

Eastwood, David
Professional. *b:* 30.3.1848, Lascelles Hall, Yorkshire. *d:* 17.5.1903, Huddersfield, Yorkshire. Middle order right-hand batsman, right-hand fast round arm bowler. *Team* Yorkshire (1870–77, 29 matches).
Career batting
36–63–2–807–68–13.22–0–*ct* 20
Bowling 714–36–19.83–1–0–6/69

His final first-class match was for London United in 1879.

He also represented Durham and Northumberland.

Eato, Alwyn
Professional. *b:* 15.2.1929, Duckmanton, Derbyshire. Tail end right-hand batsman, right-arm fast medium bowler. *Team* Derbyshire (1950–55, 25 matches).
Career batting
25–28–5–220–44–9.56–0–*ct* 7
Bowling 1429–50–28.58–1–0–5/14

Eaton, Hubert Francis Joseph
Amateur. *b:* 19.1.1864, London. *d:* 25.3.1910, Ketton, Rutland. Opening/middle order right-hand batsman. *Sch* Oratory. *Team* Cambridge U (1885).
Career batting
8–14–2–173–64*–14.41–0–*ct* 4

His first-class debut was for C.I. Thornton's XI in 1884, and his last first-class match was for MCC in 1894.

His County cricket was for Rutland and Lincolnshire.

Eaton, Vivian John
Professional. *b:* 19.6.1902, Steyning, Sussex. *d:* 31.12.1972, Worthing, Sussex. Lower order right-hand batsman, wicket-keeper. *Team* Sussex (1926–46, 36 matches).
Career batting
36–52–8–465–44–10.56–0–*ct* 52–*st* 29
Bowling 5–0

Ebden, Charles Hotson Murray
Amateur. *b:* 29.6.1880, London. *d:* 24.5.1949, Newton House, near Elvanfoot, Lanarkshire. Opening right-hand batsman. *Sch* Eton. *Teams* Cambridge U (1902–03, blue both years); Sussex (1904, 3 matches); Middlesex (1905, 2 matches); Scotland (1906). *Tour* Brackley to West Indies 1904/05.
Career batting
40–74–3–1465–137–20.63–1–*ct* 24
Bowling 89–2–44.50–0–0–1/15

His last first-class match was for MCC in 1909.

A noted hockey player, he represented both Cambridge and England.

Ebdon, Edward William
Amateur. *b:* 22.4.1870, Wellington, Somerset. *d:* 6.12.1950, Yatton, Somerset. Brother of J.F. and P.J. (Somerset). Tail end right-hand batsman, wicket-keeper. *Team* Somerset (1891–98, 2 matches).
Career batting
2–4–1–9–5–3.00–0–*ct* 1–*st* 2

Ebdon, John Francis
Amateur. *b:* 1876, Wellington, Somerset. *d:* 1.11.1952, Burley-in-Wharfedale, Yorkshire. Brother of E.W. and P.J. (Somerset). Tail end right-hand batsman, slow right-arm bowler. *Team* Somerset (1898, 1 match).
Career batting
1–2–0–2–1–1.00–0–*ct* 2
Bowling 73–0

Ebdon, Percy John
Amateur. *b:* 16.3.1874, Wellington, Somerset. *d:* 16.2.1943, Wellington, Somerset. Brother of E.W. and J.F. (Somerset). Opening/middle order batsman. *Team* Somerset (1894, 2 matches).
Career batting
2–4–0–13–7–3.25–0–*ct* 1
He played rugby for England.

Ebeling, Hans Irvine
Amateur. *b:* 1.1.1905, Avoca, Victoria, Australia. *d:* 12.1.1980, East Bentleigh, Victoria, Australia. Lower order right-hand batsman, right-arm fast medium bowler. *Team* Victoria (1923/4 to 1937/8, 44 matches). *Tours* Australia to England 1934; Victoria to New Zealand 1924/5. *Test* Australia (1934, 1 match).
Career batting
73–83–12–1005–76–14.15–0–*ct* 38
Bowling 5768–217–26.58–7–2–7/33
Test batting
1–2–0–43–41–21.50–0–*ct* 0
Bowling 89–3–29.66–0–0–3/74
He performed usefully on his tour to England, but was always in the shadow of Grimmett and O'Reilly.
He was the prime mover in the staging of the Centenary Test Match at Melbourne in 1977.

Eccles, Alexander
Amateur. *b:* 16.3.1876, Ashton-on-Ribble, Lancashire. *d:* 17.3.1919, Bilsborough Hall, Preston, Lancashire. Middle order right-hand batsman, good field. *Sch* Repton. *Teams* Oxford U (1896–99, blue last three years); Lancashire (1898–1907, 123 matches).
Career batting
152–244–23–5129–139–23.20–6–*ct* 96
Bowling 88–1–88.00–0–0–1/17
He hit 1,070 runs, av 26.09, in 1899.

Eccles, Charles Vernon
Amateur. *b:* 20.8.1843, Davenham, Cheshire. *d:* 21.2.1890, Bareilly, India. Brother of W.H. (MCC). Middle order right-hand batsman, slow lob bowler. *Sch* Cheltenham. *Team* Hampshire (1870–75, 2 matches).
Career batting
3–5–0–42–23–8.40–0–*ct* 0
Bowling 44–0
He also played for Devon.

Eccles, Henry
Amateur. *b:* March 1863, Roby, Lancashire. *d:* 10.2.1931, Roby, Lancashire. Middle order right-hand batsman, right-arm fast bowler. *Sch* Uppingham. *Team* Lancashire (1885–86, 5 matches).
Career batting
6–9–1–40–14–5.00–0–*ct* 1
Bowling 5–0
His final first-class match was for Liverpool and District in 1889.

Eccles, Joseph
Amateur. *b:* 13.4.1863, Accrington, Lancashire. *d:* 2.9.1933, Barton, Preston, Lancashire. Middle order right-hand batsman. *Team* Lancashire (1886–89, 47 matches).
Career batting
49–79–6–1802–184–24.68–2–*ct* 17
Bowling 38–0

Eccles, William Hall
Amateur. *b:* 24.3.1838, Davenham, Cheshire. *d:* 18.4.1900, Folkestone, Kent. Brother of C.V. (Hants). Middle order right-hand batsman, good field. *Sch* Eton. *Team* MCC (1866–67)
Career batting
2–4–2–30–17–15.00–0–*ct* 0
He was Hon Sec of Hampshire CCC 1867–69, but never appeared in first-class matches for that County.

Eckersley, Peter Thorp
Amateur. *b:* 2.7.1904, Newton-le-Willows, Lancashire. *d:* 13.8.1940. He was killed whilst serving in the RNVR in a flying accident from Eastleigh, Hants. Middle order right-hand batsman, good field. *Sch* Rugby. *Team* Lancashire (1923–35, 256 matches). *Tours* MCC to India, Burma and Ceylon 1926/7; Tennyson to Jamaica 1927/8; Cahn to Argentina 1929/30.
Career batting
292–339–51–5629–102*–19.54–1–*ct* 121
Bowling 348–7–49.71–0–0–2/21
He captained Lancashire 1929–35. In 1928 he gave up a political career for cricket, then in 1935 gave up cricket for politics, being Conservative MP for Manchester Exchange at his death.
Whilst at Cambridge University he did not appear in first-class matches. His final first-class match was for an England XI in 1938.

Eckersley, Ronald
Amateur. *b:* 4.9.1925, Bingley, Yorkshire. Tail end batsman, left-arm medium fast bowler. *Team* Yorkshire (1945, 1 match).
Career batting
1–1–1–9–9*–no av–0–*ct* 0
Bowling 62–0
He appeared in wartime matches for Cambridge U.

Edbrooke, Roger Michael
Cricketer. *b:* 30.12.1960, Bristol. Middle order right-hand batsman. *Team* Oxford U (1982–83).
Career batting
3–4–1–171–84–57.00–0–*ct* 1

Eddie, William
Amateur. *b:* 19.12.1891, Brechin, Scotland. *d:* 3.9.1979, Brechin, Scotland. Right-hand batsman, right-arm medium pace bowler. *Team* Scotland (1913).
Career batting
1–2–1–6–4–6.00–0–*ct* 1
Bowling 90–0

Eddington, Roderick Ian
Cricketer. *b:* 2.1.1950, Perth, Australia. Lower order left-hand batsman, slow left-arm bowler. *Team* Oxford U (1975–76).
Career batting
8–14–4–130–24–13.00–0–*ct* 4
Bowling 329–8–41.12–0–0–3/48

Eddis, Sir Basil Eden Garth
Amateur. *b:* 17.9.1881, Calcutta, India. *d:* 5.11.1971, Aldeburgh, Suffolk. Brother of B.L. (Army and Navy). Sound middle order right-hand batsman, useful change bowler. *Sch* Charterhouse. *Team* MCC (1908, 1 match).
Career batting
1–2–0–62–40–31.00–0–*ct* 0

Eddis, Bruce Lindsay
Amateur. *b:* 17.8.1883, Calcutta, India. *d:* 12.5.1966, Beaconsfield, Bucks. Brother of B.E.G. (MCC). Middle order batsman. *Sch* Rugby. *Team* Army and Navy (1919, 1 match).
Career batting
1–2–1–21–21*–21.00–0–*ct* 1

Ede, Edward Lee
Amateur. *b:* 22.2.1834, Southampton. *d:* 7.7.1908, Southampton. Twin brother of G.M. (Hants), father of E.M.C. (Hants). Middle/lower order right-hand batsman, lob bowler. *Sch* Eton. *Team* Hampshire (1861–70, 17 matches).
Career batting
17–32–4–265–49–9.46–0–*ct* 6
Bowling 400–15–26.66–0–0–4/79

Ede, Edward Murray Charles
Amateur. *b:* 24.4.1881, Southampton. Son of E.L. (Hants), nephew of G.M. (Hants). Lower order left-hand batsman, slow left-arm bowler. *Sch* Eton. *Teams* Hampshire (1902–06, 14 matches).
Career batting
16–28–8–245–43–12.25–0–*ct* 11
Bowling 1247–40–31.17–2–1–7/72
His last first-class match was for Hambledon in 1908.

Ede, George Matthew
Amateur. *b:* 22.2.1834, Southampton. *d:* 13.3.1870, Aintree, Liverpool. Twin brother of E.L. (Hants), uncle of E.M.C. (Hants). Middle order right-hand batsman. *Sch* Eton. *Team* Hampshire (1864–69, 15 matches).
Career batting
15–29–2–257–52–9.51–0–*ct* 0
Bowling 22–1–22.00–0–0–1/22
A well-known amateur jockey he was killed whilst riding in the Grand National.

Eden, E.
Professional. Middle order batsman. *Teams* Gloucestershire (1921, 1 match); Worcestershire (1923, 1 match).
Career batting
2–4–1–30–18*–10.00–0–*ct* 0
He played football for Walsall.

Edgar, Bruce Adrian
Cricketer. *b:* 23.11.1956, Wellington, New Zealand. Stylish opening left-hand batsman, occasional wicket-keeper. *Team* Wellington (1975/6 to 1982/3). *Tours* New Zealand to England 1978, 1983, to Australia 1980/1. *Tests* New Zealand (1978–83, 24 matches).
Career batting
94–171–13–6128–161–38.78–11–*ct* 68–*st* 1
Bowling 26–1–26.00–0–0–1/17
Test batting
24–43–2–1481–161–36.12–3–*ct* 13
He came second in the first-class batting averages of the 1978 tour to England with 823 runs, av 37.40, and was again successful in 1983 with 742 runs, av 39.05. He appeared in all Tests on both visits.

Edgar, Samuel James
Amateur. *b:* 23.9.1913, Lisburn, Northern Ireland. *d:* 31.1.1937, Lisburn, Northern Ireland.

Right-hand batsman, right-arm medium pace bowler. *Team* Ireland (1934).
Career batting
1–2–0–32–32–16.00–0–*ct* 0

Edge, Cyril Arthur
Professional. *b:* 17.12.1916, Ashton-under-Lyne, Lancashire. Tail end right-hand batsman, right-arm fast medium bowler. *Team* Lancashire (1936–38, 8 matches).
Career batting
9–6–3–17–15*–5.66–0–*ct* 2
Bowling 873–29–30.10–0–0–4/71
His last first-class match was for Minor Counties in 1939.

Edge, Geoffrey D.
Amateur. *b:* 12.8.1936, Eccles, Lancashire. Middle order right-hand batsman, off break bowler. *Sch* Manchester G.S. *Team* Cambridge U (1957).
Career batting
2–4–0–55–33–13.75–0–*ct* 0
Bowling 2–0

Edge, Harold Emerton
Professional. *b:* 1892, Market Drayton, Shropshire. *d:* 24.1.1944, Middlewich, Cheshire. Tail end batsman, useful medium pace bowler. *Teams* Lancashire (1913, 1 match); Wales (1927–29).
Career batting
3–5–1–27–19*–6.75–0–*ct* 5
Bowling 276–4–69.00–0–0–4/115
He also played for Denbighshire.

Edgson, Charles Leslie
Amateur. *b:* 22.8.1915, Morcott, Rutland. *d:* 28.6.1983, Brentwood, Essex. Middle order right-hand batsman. *Sch* Stamford. *Team* Leicestershire (1933–39, 14 matches).
Career batting
14–24–0–321–49–13.37–0–*ct* 4
He played in the Freshmen's Match at Oxford in 1936, but no first-class matches.
He was also a noted rugby and hockey player.

Edlmann, Herbert Gottlieb
Amateur. *b:* July 1840, Peckham, Kent. *d:* 2.3.1912, Wokingham, Berkshire. Middle order batsman, change bowler. *Team* Gentleman of Kent (1864, 1 match).
Career batting
1–2–1–17–13*–17.00–0–*ct* 0
Bowling 8–0

Edmeades, Brian Ernest Arthur
Professional. *b:* 17.9.1941, Matlock, Derbyshire. Opening right-hand batsman, right-arm medium pace bowler. *Team* Essex (1961–76, 335 matches).
Career batting
335–555–69–12593–163–25.91–14–*ct* 105
Bowling 9688–374–25.90–10–1–7/37
He hit 1,000 runs in a sesaon 5 times (best 1,620, av 35.21, in 1970) and took 100 wickets in a season once – 106, av 18.59, in 1966.

Edmeades, James Frederick
Amateur. *b:* 8.7.1843, Nursteed, Kent. *d:* 6.2.1917, Northfleet, Kent. Middle order batsman, change bowler. *Sch* Harrow. *Team* Gentlemen of Kent (1866, 1 match).
Career batting
1–2–0–26–24–13.00–0–*ct* 1
Bowling 17–0

Edmonds, James William
Cricketer. *b:* 4.6.1951, Smethwick, Staffs. Tail end right-hand batsman, left-arm fast medium bowler. *Team* Lancashire (1975, 1 match).
Career batting
1 match, did not bat–*ct* 0
Bowling 82–3–27.33–0–0–3/52

Edmonds, Philippe-Henri
Cricketer. *b*: 8.3.1951, Lusaka, Northern Rhodesia. Aggressive middle order right-hand batsman, slow left-arm bowler, good field. *Sch* Cranbrook. *Teams* Cambridge U (1971–73, blue all three years); Middlesex (1971–83, 193 matches); Eastern Province (1975/6). *Tours* England to Pakistan and New Zealand 1977/8, to Australia 1978/9; International Wanderers to South Africa 1975/6. *Tests* England (1975–83, 23 matches).
Career batting
282–368–64–5966–141*–19.62–2–*ct* 266
Bowling 23152–944–24.52–43–8–8/80
Test batting
23–28–6–430–64–19.54–0–*ct* 23
Bowling 1733–59–29.37–2–0–7/66
His best season was 1983 with 92 wickets, av 21.45.

Edmonds, Roger Bertram
Professional. *b:* 2.3.1941, Birmingham. Middle order right-hand batsman, right-arm medium off break bowler. *Team* Warwickshire (1962–67, 78 matches). *Tour* Warwickshire to East Africa 1967/8 (not first-class).
Career batting
78–100–31–1006–102*–14.57–1–*ct* 35
Bowling 3994–146–27.36–2–0–5/40

Edrich, Brian Robert
Professional. *b:* 18.8.1922, Cantley, Norfolk. Brother of W.J. (Middlesex), E.H. (Lancs) and G.A. (Lancs), cousin of J.H. (Surrey). Forcing middle order left-hand batsman, right-arm off break bowler, close field. *Teams* Kent (1947–53, 128 matches); Glamorgan (1954–56, 52 matches).
Career batting
181–302–25–5529–193*–19.96–4–*ct* 130
Bowling 4546–137–33.18–4–0–7/41

His last first-class match was for Minor Counties in 1967. He hit 1,267 runs, av 26.39, in 1951.

He also played for Oxfordshire.

Edrich, Eric Harry
Amateur but turned professional in 1946. *b:* 27.3.1914, Lingwood, Norfolk. Brother of W.J. (Middlesex), G.A. (Lancs) and B.R. (Kent and Glamorgan), cousin of J.H. (Surrey). Middle order right-hand batsman, wicket-keeper. *Team* Lancashire (1946–48, 33 matches).
Career batting
36–46–5–949–121–23.14–2–*ct* 38–*st* 15

He played for Norfolk, commencing 1935.

His first-class debut was for Minor Counties XI in 1938.

Edrich, Geoffrey Arthur
Professional. *b:* 13.7.1918, Lingwood, Norfolk. Brother of B.R. (Kent and Glamorgan); E.H. (Lancs) and W.J. (Middlesex), cousin of J.H. (Surrey). Middle order right-hand batsman, fine leg-slip. *Team* Lancashire (1946–58, 322 matches). *Tour* Commonwealth to India 1953/4.
Career batting
339–508–60–15600–167*–34.82–26–*ct* 333
Bowling 399–5–79.80–0–0–1/8

He hit 1,000 runs in a season eight times, exceeding 2,000 once : 2,067, av. 41.34, in 1952.

He also played for Norfolk and Cumberland.

Edrich, John Hugh, MBE
Professional. *b:* 21.6.1937, Blofield, Norfolk. Cousin of B.R. (Kent and Glamorgan), E.H. (Lancashire), G.A. (Lancashire) and W.J. (Middlesex). Opening left-hand batsman, right-arm medium pace bowler. *Team* Surrey (1958–78, 410 matches). *Tours* Surrey to Rhodesia 1959/60; MCC to India 1963/4, to Australia and New Zealand 1965/6, 1970/1, 1974/5, to West Indies 1967/8, to Ceylon and Pakistan 1968/9; Cavaliers to South Africa 1962/3; Robins to South Africa 1972/3, 1973/4. *Tests* England (1963–76, 77 matches).
Career batting
564–979–104–39790–310*–45.47–103–*ct* 311
Bowling 53–0
Test batting
77–127–9–5138–310*–43.54–12–*ct* 43
Bowling 23–0

Commencing his County career with Norfolk in 1954, Edrich made his first-class debut for Combined Services in 1956 and his Surrey debut in 1958. The following season he began his long career as Surrey's opening batsman, and despite two injuries easily completed 1,000 runs – a feat he was to achieve 19 times plus twice more in overseas seasons. In six summers he went on to 2,000 runs; 1962, with 2,482, av. 51.70, being his most prolific. His highest innings came in 1965 when he made 310* for England v New Zealand at Headingley; the three other scores he made over 200 were all for Surrey.

For some 12 years he was in the England side and proved one of the most dependable of post-war Test openers. His runs were made generally by concentration and application and he kept his wicket by being rarely tempted into indiscretion – not for him the dazzling footwork and fluent strokes to which many batsman aspire.

He captained Surrey from 1973 to 1977 and led England in one Test – at Sydney in 1974/5; he was vice-captain of the MCC touring party that winter. After leaving first-class cricket he returned to play for his native Norfolk.

He was awarded the MBE in the 1977 Birthday Honours.

Edrich, William John
Professional, but turned amateur 1947. *b:* 26.3.1916, Lingwood, Norfolk. Brother of E.H. (Lancs), G.A. (Lancs) and B.R. (Kent and Glamorgan), cousin of J.H. (Surrey). Aggressive middle order right-hand batsman, right-arm fast medium bowler, also off breaks from about 1952. *Team* Middlesex (1937–58, 389 matches). *Tours* Tennyson to India 1937/8; MCC to South Africa 1938/9, to Australia and New Zealand 1946/7, 1954/5; Howard to India 1956/7. *Tests* England (1938 to 1954/5, 39 matches).
Career batting
571–964–92–36965–267*–42.39–86–*ct* 529–*st* 1
Bowling 15956–479–33.31–11–3–7/48
Test batting
39–63–2–2440–219–40.00–6–*ct* 39
Bowling 1693–41–41.29–0–0–4/68

After five successful seasons with his native Norfolk, Edrich qualified for Middlesex in 1937 – he had made his first-class debut for Minor Counties in 1934 – and the following summer won his England cap. In each of his three pre-war seasons he hit over 2,000 runs, but his greatest year came in 1947, when his total reached 3,539, av 80.43, with 12 centuries, and he and Compton broke many records. In all he exceeded 1,000 runs in a season 15 times, going on to 2,000 nine times. Of his nine double centuries, eight were for Middlesex, with the highest 267* v Northants at Northampton in 1947. His other 200 was for England – 219 v South Africa at Durban in 1938/9. In 1938 he performed the great feat of reaching 1,000 runs before the end of May.

A most determined and courageous cricketer, his batting was none too elegant, relying mainly on pulls and hooks. His bowling was of the slinging variety and very fast for a few overs. In the field he excelled at slip. A somewhat controversial figure, he was several times dropped from the England side, only to be recalled when the Test team needed some gumption in the middle order, or even at the start.

He captained Middlesex from 1951 to 1957, the first two years being in harness with D.C.S. Compton. After retiring from Middlesex he returned to the Norfolk side for several more years of cricket.

He played football for Tottenham Hotspur. During the war he was awarded the DFC.

Edward, William Alfred
Amateur. *b:* 19.6.1916, Glasgow, Scotland. Right-hand batsman, right-arm medium pace bowler. *Team* Scotland (1947–55).
Career batting
28–43–5–898–99–23.63–0–*ct* 10
Bowling 1475–38–39.13–0–0–4/51

Edwards, Aubrey M.
Amateur. *b:* 1918, Pontypridd, Glamorgan. Lower order right-hand batsman, right-arm medium pace bowler. *Team* Glamorgan (1947, 1 match).
Career batting
1–1–0–0–0–0.00–0–*ct* 0
Bowling 71–3–23.66–0–0–2/34

Edwards, Charles William
Amateur. *b:* 18.10.1884, Burton-on-Trent. *d:* 22.5.1938, Earls Court, London. Middle order batsman. *Sch* Cheltenham. *Team* Gloucestershire (1911–12, 7 matches).
Career batting
7–14–0–184–42–13.14–0–*ct* 7
Bowling 28–0

Edwards, Frank
Professional. *b:* 23.5.1885, Merstham, Surrey. *d:* 10.7.1970, Winscombe, Somerset. Lower order left-hand batsman, originally medium then slow left-arm bowler. *Team* Surrey (1909, 1 match).
Career batting
6–8–0–31–10–3.87–0–*ct* 1
Bowling 399–19–21.00–1–1–8/98

He joined Buckinghamshire in 1914 and from then until the Second World War was one of the leading Minor County bowlers. In all he took over 1,000 wickets for his adopted County. His final first-class match was for the Minor Counties in 1933.

Edwards, Sir Fleetwood Isham
Amateur. *b:* 21.4.1842, Kingston on Thames, Surrey. *d:* 14.8.1910, Lindfield, Sussex. Middle order right-hand batsman. *Sch* Harrow and Uppingham. *Team* I Zingari (1866, 1 match).
Career batting
1–2–1–39–27*–39.00–0–*ct* 0
Bowling 8–1–8.00–0–0–1/8

Edwards, Gordon
Cricketer. *b:* 17.9.1947, Glapthorn, Northants. Lower order left-hand batsman, off break bowler. *Team* Nottinghamshire (1973, 9 matches).
Career batting
9–16–4–191–46*–15.91–0–*ct* 5
Bowling 224–12–18.66–1–0–5/44

Edwards, Guy Janion
Amateur. *b:* 11.5.1881, Kensington. *d:* 30.9.1962, Upper Slaughter, Gloucs. Middle order right-hand batsman. *Sch* Eton. *Team* Essex (1907, 2 matches).
Career batting
2–3–0–45–21–15.00–0–*ct* 2

Edwards, Graham Neil
Cricketer. *b*: 27.5.1955, Nelson, New Zealand. Attacking middle order right-hand batsman, wicket-keeper. *Team* Central Districts (1973/4 to 1981/2). *Tour* New Zealand to England 1978. *Tests* New Zealand (1976/7 to 1980/1, 8 matches).
Career batting
91–163–8–4585–177*–29.58–5–*ct* 126–*st* 16
Bowling 32–0
Test batting
8–15–0–377–55–25.13–0–*ct* 7

The main wicket-keeper on the 1978 tour to England, he played in the first two Tests, but was then dropped due to lack of form.

Edwards, Herbert Charles
Amateur. *b:* 3.12.1913, Colley Gate, Staffs. Middle order right-hand batsman, leg break bowler. *Team* Worcestershire (1946, 1 match).
Career batting
1–2–0–11–10–5.50–0–*ct* 1

Edwards, Herbert Ivor Powell
(also known as Powell-Edwards)
Amateur. *b:* 12.3.1884, London. *d:* 24.9.1946, Cowes, Isle of Wight. Middle order right-hand batsman. *Sch* Winchester. *Team* Sussex (1908, 1 match).
Career batting
1–2–0–22–15–11.00–0–*ct* 0

Edwards, H. R.
Amateur. Middle order batsman. *Team* Sussex (1885, 1 match).
Career batting
1–2–0–0–0–0.00–0–*ct* 0

Edwards, John Dunlop
Amateur. *b:* 12.6.1862, Prahan, Victoria, Australia. *d:* 31.7.1911, Hawksburn, Victoria, Australia. Steady middle order right-hand batsman, leg break bowler. *Team* Victoria (1880/1 to 1889/90, 9 matches). *Tour* Australia to England 1888. *Tests* Australia (1888, 3 matches).
Career batting
50–84–14–961–65–13.72–0–*ct* 19
Bowling 194–7–27.71–0–0–2/6
Test batting
3–6–1–48–26–9.60–0–*ct* 1

He achieved very little on his single visit to England.

Edwards, Michael John
Professional. *b:* 1.3.1940, Balham, South London. Opening right-hand batsman, off break bowler, excellent close field. *Sch* Alleyns. *Teams* Cambridge U (1960–62); Surrey (1961–74, 236 matches). *Tours* Commonwealth to Pakistan 1967/8; Norfolk to West Indies 1969/70.
Career batting
256–452–26–11378–137–26.70–12–*ct* 273
Bowling 179–2–89.50–0–0–2/53

He hit 1,000 runs in a season five times (best 1,428, av. 36.61, in 1969).

Edwards, Philip George
Professional. *b:* 6.12.1906, Hoxton, London. Lower order right-hand batsman, slow left-arm bowler. *Team* Middlesex (1930–33, 4 matches).
Career batting
4–5–2–12–10–4.00–0–*ct* 1
Bowling 140–1–140.00–0–0–1/35

Edwards, Ross
Cricketer. *b:* 1.12.1942, Cottesloe, West Australia. Middle order right-hand batsman. Son of E. K. (Western Australia). *Teams* Western Australia (1964/5 to 1974/5, 71 matches); New South Wales (1979/80, 5 matches). *Tours* Australia to England 1972, 1975, to West Indies 1972/3. *Tests* Australia (1972–75, 20 matches).
Career batting
126–212–25–7345–170*–39.27–14–*ct* 111–*st* 11
Bowling 75–1–75.00–0–0–1/24
Test batting
20–32–3–1171–170*–40.37–2–*ct* 7
Bowling 20–0

Edwards, Richard Martin
Cricketer. *b:* 3.6.1940, Garden Gap, Worthing, Barbados, West Indies. Lower order right-hand batsman, right-arm fast bowler. *Team* Barbados (1961/2 to 1969/70). *Tours* Barbados to England 1969; West Indies to Australia and New Zealand 1968/9. *Tests* West Indies (1968/9, 5 matches).
Career batting
35–43–10–389–34–11.78–0–*ct* 15
Bowling 2831–78–36.29–3–0–6/45
Test batting
5–8–1–65–22–9.28–0–*ct* 0
Bowling 626–18–34.77–1–0–5/84

Edwards, Reginald Owen
Amateur. *b:* 17.10.1881, Yarmouth, Norfolk. *d:* 15.11.1925, Bishop's Stortford, Herts. Middle order right-hand batsman. *Sch* Christs Hospital. *Team* Rest of England (1922).
Career batting
1–2–1–1–1–1.00–0–*ct* 0

He appeared occasionally for Norfolk and Cambridgeshire and went on minor tours abroad with Incognti and MCC.

During an expedition to Southern Russia just after the First World War, he lost all his baggage save for his set of Wisdens which always travelled with him.

Edwards, Timothy David Warneford
Cricketer. *b*: 6.12.1958, Merton, Surrey. Middle order left-hand batsman. *Sch* Sherborne. *Team* Cambridge U (1979–81, blue 1981).
Career batting
12–21–2–393–57–20.68–0–*ct* 5
Bowling 58–1–58.00–0–0–1/17

Edwards, William
Amateur. *b:* 27.6.1859, Bloomsbury, London. *d:* 21.8.1947, St Pancras, London. Middle order right-hand batsman, right-arm slow bowler. *Sch* Hurstpierpoint. *Team* Kent (1884, 2 matches).
Career batting
2–4–1–44–25–14.66–0–*ct* 0
Bowling 27–3–9.00–0–0–3/16

He broke his leg playing football in 1885 and this injury handicapped his cricket.

Eele, Peter James
Professional. *b:* 27.1.1935, Taunton, Somerset. Lower order left-hand batsman, wicket-keeper.

Sch Taunton. *Team* Somerset (1958–65, 54 matches).
Career batting
54–70–20–612–103*–12.24–1–*ct* 87–*st* 19

In 1981 he was appointed to the first-class Umpires' List. He also played for Devon.

Eggar, John Drennan
Amateur. *b:* 1.12.1916, Nowshera, India. *d:* 3.5.1983, Hinton St George, Somerset, while playing tennis. Sound middle order right-hand batsman, right-arm bowler. *Sch* Winchester. *Teams* Oxford U (1938, blue); Hampshire (1938, 2 matches); Derbyshire (1946–54, 31 matches).
Career batting
41–64–6–1847–219–31.84–4–*ct* 20
Bowling 193–1–193.00–0–0–1/2

His only double century was 219 for Derbyshire v Yorkshire at Bradford in 1949.

His County cricket was restricted due to his scholastic duties.

Eglington, Richard
Amateur. *b:* 1.4.1908, Esher, Surrey. *d:* 20.3.1979, Winchester. Middle order right-hand batsman. *Sch* Sherborne. *Team* Surrey (1938, 2 matches).
Career batting
3–4–0–82–34–20.50–0–*ct* 1

He captained Surrey 2nd XI in the Minor Counties Competition in 1938–39 and his last first-class match was for the Minor Counties XI in 1939.

Ehtesham-ud-din
Cricketer. *b*: 4.9.1950, Lahore, Pakistan. Lower order right-hand batsman, right-arm medium pace bowler. *Teams* Punjab Univ (1969/70); Lahore (1970/1 to 1974/5); Punjab (1973/4); PIA (1972/3); National Bank (1974/5 to 1981/2); United Bank (1982/3). *Tours* Pakistan Under 25 to Sri Lanka 1973/4; Pakistan to India 1979/80, to England 1982. *Tests* Pakistan (1979/80 to 1982, 5 matches).
Career batting
120–134–45–1030–83–11.56–0–*ct* 32
Bowling 9251–442–20.92–34–7–8/45
Test batting
5–3–1–2–2–1.00–0–*ct* 2
Bowling 375–16–23.94–1–0–5/47

He was co-opted into the 1982 touring team and appeared in two matches, one of which was the third Test.

Elam, Frederick William
Amateur. *b:* 13.9.1871, Hunslet, Yorkshire. *d:* 19.3.1943, Headingley, Leeds, Yorkshire. Opening right-hand batsman, right-arm fast bowler. *Team* Yorkshire (1900–02, 2 matches).
Career batting
2–3–1–48–28–24.00–0–*ct* 0

Elder, John Watson George
Cricketer. *b:* 16.8.1949, Bangor, Co Down, Northern Ireland. Right-hand batsman, right-arm fast medium bowler. *Team* Ireland (1973–80).
Career batting
8–8–2–25–7–4.16–0–*ct* 6
Bowling 310–12–25.83–0–0–3/56

Elderkin, Thomas
Amateur. *b:* 1909, Peterborough. *d:* 9.12.1961, Peterborough. Middle order right-hand batsman. *Team* Northants (1934, 1 match).
Career batting
1–2–0–13–13–6.50–0–*ct* 0

Elderton, Merrick Beaufoy
Amateur. *b:* 21.2.1884, Brentford, Middlesex. *d:* 11.12.1939, Sherborne, Dorset. Middle order right-hand batsman, wicket-keeper. *Sch* Merchant Taylors. *Team* Cambridge U (1907).
Career batting
5–6–0–74–24–12.33–0–*ct* 4–*st* 5

His County cricket was for Dorset and his final first-class match for the Minor Counties in 1931.

Elers, Charles George Carew
Amateur. *b:* 2.1.1867, Lyme Regis, Dorset. *d:* 11.12.1927, Antony, Torpoint, Cornwall. Attractive middle order batsman, wicket-keeper. *Team* West of England (1910).
Career batting
1–1–0–4–4–4.00–0–*ct* 5–*st* 1

His County cricket was for Devon and Glamorgan.

Elgie, Michael Kelsey
Amateur. *b:* 6.3.1933, Durban, South Africa. Middle order right-hand batsman, slow left-arm bowler. *Team* Natal (1957/8 to 1961/2). *Tour* SA Fezela to England 1961. *Tests* South Africa (1961/2, 3 matches).
Career batting
32–55–5–1834–162*–36.68–3–*ct* 25
Bowling 405–10–40.50–0–0–3/16
Test batting
3–6–0–75–56–12.50–0–*ct* 4
Bowling 46–0

An excellent rugby footballer, he represented Middlesex and Scotland.

Elgood, Bernard Cyril
Amateur. *b:* 10.3.1922, Hampstead, London.

Eliot

Middle order right-hand batsman, *Sch* Bradfield. *Teams* Cambridge U (1948, blue).
Career batting
14–21–2–631–127*–33.21–2–*ct* 5
He played for Berkshire.

Eliot, Robert Francis
Amateur. *b:* 7.3.1942, Gloucester. Lower order left-hand batsman, left-arm medium pace bowler. *Sch* Radley. *Team* Oxford U (1961).
Career batting
2–4–2–55–30–27.50–0–*ct* 0
Bowling 140–1–140.00–0–0–1/70

Ellcock, Ricardo McDonald
Cricketer. *b*: 17.6.1965, Bridgetown, Barbados. Lower order right-hand batsman, right-arm fast medium bowler. *Sch* Malvern. *Team* Worcestershire (1982–83, 13 matches).
Career batting
13–20–5–167–36–11.13–0–*ct* 2
Bowling 1021–28–36.46–0–0–4/70

Elliot, Edgar William
Amateur. *b:* 9.7.1878, Roker, Sunderland, Co Durham. *d:* 23.3.1931, Vancouver, Canada. Attractive middle order right-hand batsman, right-arm medium fast bowler. *Sch* Wellington. *Team* Gentlemen of England (1907).
Career batting
2–4–2–30–15–15.00–0–*ct* 1
His County cricket was for Durham, 1897–1907. His most famous innings came for Borderers v Newcastle Garrison in 1905 when he hit 332 in 225 minutes.
An excellent rugby player, he appeared for Durham and England as a three quarter.

Elliott, Charles Standish
Professional. *b:* 24.4.1912, Bolsover, Derbyshire. Nephew of Harry (Derbyshire). Opening right-hand batsman, off break bowler, good slip field. *Team* Derbyshire (1932–53, 275 matches).
Career batting
275–468–29–11965–215–27.25–9–*ct* 210–*st* 1
Bowling 526–11–47.81–0–0–2/25
His only double century was 215 for Derbyshire v Notts at Trent Bridge in 1947. He hit 1,000 runs in a season 6 times (best 1,599, av 34.76, in 1952). He was later a first-class and Test umpire.
He played football for Coventry City.

Elliott, George Frederick
Professional. *b:* 1.5.1850, Farnham, Surrey. *d:* 23.4.1913, Farnham, Surrey. Sound middle order right-hand batsman, right-arm fast bowler. *Teams* Kent (1874, 2 matches); Surrey (1875–80, 44 matches).
Career batting
51–93–8–1163–53–13.68–0–*ct* 9
Bowling 485–8–60.62–0–0–1/2

Elliott, Harold
Professional. *b:* 15.6.1904, Hindley, Wigan, Lancashire. *d:* 15.4.1969, Hindley, Wigan, Lancashire. Tail end right-hand batsman, wicket-keeper. *Team* Lancashire (1930, 1 match).
Career batting
1–1–0–4–4–4.00–0–*ct* 2–*st* 1

Elliott, Harry
Professional. *b:* 2.11.1891, Scarcliffe, Derbyshire. *d:* 2.2.1976, Derby. Uncle of C.S. (Derbyshire). Lower order right-hand batsman, wicket-keeper. *Team* Derbyshire (1920–47, 520 matches). *Tours* MCC to South Africa 1927/28, to India 1933/34. *Tests* England (1927/8 to 1933/4, 4 matches).
Career batting
532–764–220–7580–94–13.93–0–*ct* 904–*st* 302
Bowling 5–0
Test batting
4–5–1–61–37*–15.25–0–*ct* 8–*st* 3
He was a noted first-class umpire.

Elliott, Herbert Denis Edleston
Amateur. *b:* 30.3.1887, Newport, Salop. *d:* 26.4.1973, Bognor Regis, Sussex. Tail end batsman, bowler. *Team* Essex (1913, 2 matches).
Career batting
2–4–0–3–3–0.75–0–*ct* 1
Bowling 107–1–107.00–0–0–1/67

Elliott, John William
Cricketer. *b:* 12.2.1942, Worcester. Lower order left-hand batsman, wicket-keeper. *Sch* Worcester RGS. *Team* Worcestershire (1959–65, 10 matches).
Career batting
10–11–3–66–18*–8.25–0–*ct* 18–*st* 8

Elliott, William
Professional. *b:* 15.11.1842, Bulwell, Notts. Lower order right-hand batsman, right-arm fast bowler. *Team* Nottinghamshire (1871, 2 matches).
Career batting
3–4–0–12–5–3.00–0–*ct* 0
Bowling 73–2–36.50–0–0–1/18
His first-class debut was for R. Daft's XI in 1870.
He also played for Durham.

Ellis, Charles Howard
Professional. *b:* 9.8.1830, Ditchling, Sussex. *d:*

17.1.1880, Brighton, Sussex. Hard hitting middle order right-hand batsman, wicket-keeper, lob bowler. *Team* Sussex (1856–68, 65 matches).
Career batting
80–136–10–1811–83–14.37–*ct* 97–*st* 36
Bowling 2108–100–21.08–5–1–8/96

Ellis, Frank Edgar
Professional. *b:* 1893, Bristol. *d:* 29.4.1961, Keynsham, Somerset. Lower order batsman, bowler. *Team* Gloucestershire (1914–21, 26 matches).
Career batting
26–44–19–241–24*–9.64–0–*ct* 6
Bowling 2185–70–31.21–4–0–6/90

Ellis, Geoffrey Phillip
Cricketer. *b:* 24.5.1950, Llandudno. Opening or middle order right-hand batsman, right-arm medium pace bowler. *Team* Glamorgan (1970–76, 75 matches).
Career batting
75–139–10–2673–116–20.72–1–*ct* 24
Bowling 1418–24–59.08–0–0–2/20

Ellis, Harold
Professional. *b:* 13.3.1883, Burnley, Lancashire. *d:* 31.12.1962, Stockport, Cheshire. Tail end right-hand batsman, wicket-keeper. *Team* Northants (1908–10, 18 matches).
Career batting
18–27–10–72–18–4.23–0–*ct* 27–*st* 7

Ellis, Henry Willson
Amateur. *b:* 1840, Cambridge. *d:* 13.5.1902, Cambridge. Middle order batsman. *Team* Cambridgeshire (1864, 1 match).
Career batting
1–2–0–12–10–6.00–0–*ct* 1

Ellis, Jeremy
Professional. *b:* 1866, Summerseat, Lancashire. *d:* 14.8.1943, Billington, Lancashire. Father of Stanley (Lancs) and Walker (Lancs). Lower order batsman, left-arm bowler. *Team* Lancashire (1892–98, 6 matches).
Career batting
6–9–1–56–26*–7.00–0–*ct* 8–*st* 3
Bowling 240–21–11.42–1–1–8/21

Ellis, John Ernest
Professional. *b:* 10.11.1864, Sheffield, Yorkshire. *d:* 1.12.1927, Sheffield, Yorkshire. Tail end right-hand batsman, wicket-keeper. *Team* Yorkshire (1888–92, 11 matches).
Career batting
11–15–6–14–4*–1.55–0–*ct* 11–*st* 10

Ellis, John Leslie
Amateur. *b:* 9.5.1890, Malvern, Victoria, Australia. *d:* 26.7.1974, Glen Iris, Victoria, Australia. Lower order right-hand batsman, wicket-keeper. *Team* Victoria (1918/9 to 1929/30, 72 matches). *Tours* Australia to England 1926, to India 1935/6; Victoria to New Zealand 1924/5.
Career batting
101–141–30–2351–119–21.18–2–*ct* 187–*st* 107

As the reserve wicket-keeper, he was not required for any of the Tests on his tour to England.

Ellis, Peter Michael
Professional. *b:* 15.9.1932, Orpington, Kent. Father of R.G.P. (Oxford U and Middlesex). Lower order right-hand batsman, right-arm medium fast bowler. *Team* MCC (1953).
Career batting
1 match, did not bat–*ct* 0
Bowling 120–0

Ellis, Robert
Cricketer. *b:* 19.5.1940, Kilmarnock, Scotland. Left-hand batsman, right-arm medium pace bowler. *Team* Scotland (1963–74).
Career batting
10–13–3–133–35–13.33–0–*ct* 6
Bowling 379–6–63.16–0–0–1/3

Ellis, Richard Gary Peter
Cricketer. *b*: 20.12.1960, Paddington, London. Son of P. M. (MCC). Middle order right-hand batsman, off break bowler. *Sch* Haileybury. *Tours* Oxford U (1981–83, blue all three years); Middlesex (1982–83, 9 matches).
Career batting
37–68–3–1943–105*–29.89–2–*ct* 19
Bowling 264–4–66.00–0–0–2/40

Ellis, Reginald Sidney
Amateur. *b:* 26.11.1917, Angaston, South Australia. Tail end left-hand batsman, slow left-arm bowler. *Team* South Australia (1945/6, 1 match). *Tours* Australian Services to England 1945, to Ceylon and India 1945/6.
Career batting
21–28–12–47–10*–2.93–0–*ct* 6
Bowling 2070–78–26.53–6–1–6/144

Ellis, Robert Thomas
Amateur. *b:* 16.9.1853, Burgess Hill, Sussex. *d:* 23.9.1937, Stone, Kent. Steady opening right-hand batsman, right-hand fast round arm bowler. *Sch* Brighton. *Teams* Sussex (1877–86, 65 matches).

Career batting
70–133–7–2356–103–18.69–2–*ct* 28
Bowling 70–0

In 1880 he was captain and manager of Sussex. Owing to ill-health he was obliged to retire early from first-class matches.

Ellis, Samuel
Amateur. *b:* 23.11.1851, Dewsbury, Yorkshire. *d:* 28.10.1930, Sandal, Wakefield, Yorkshire. Middle order right-hand batsman. *Team* Yorkshire (1880, 2 matches).
Career batting
3–5–0–16–9–3.20–0–*ct* 2

His debut in first-class matches was for An England Eleven at Dewsbury in 1878.

Ellis, Stanley
Professional. *b:* 1896, Summerseat, Lancashire. Brother of Walker (Lancs), son of Jeremy (Lancs). Lower order batsman, right-arm medium pace bowler. *Team* Lancashire (1923–24, 8 matches).
Career batting
8–7–1–57–25–9.50–0–*ct* 0
Bowling 252–14–18.00–1–0–5/21

He also played for Durham.

Ellis, S.E.
Amateur. Middle order batsman. *Team* Somerset (1902, 1 match).
Career batting
1–2–0–5–5–2.50–0–*ct* 0

Ellis, Walker
Professional. *b:* 27.1.1895, Summerseat, Lancashire. *d:* 25.11.1974, Eccleston, Lancashire. Brother of Stanley (Lancs), son of Jeremy (Lancs). Opening right-hand batsman. *Team* Lancashire (1920–23, 36 matches).
Career batting
36–55–4–846–138*–16.58–1–*ct* 14

Ellis, William
Professional. *b:* 28.8.1876, Whitwell, Derbyshire. *d:* 22.1.1931, Huddersfield, Yorkshire. Middle order batsman, change bowler. *Team* Derbyshire (1898–1906, 18 matches).
Career batting
18–32–2–361–58–12.03–0–*ct* 7
Bowling 120–0

Ellis, William
Professional. *b:* 15.8.1919, Rolleston, Notts. Lower order right-hand batsman, right-arm fast medium bowler. *Team* Nottinghamshire (1948, 2 matches).
Career batting
2–1–0–29–29–29.00–0–*ct* 0
Bowling 77–1–77.00–0–0–1/49

Ellis, William Arnot
Amateur. *b:* 16.9.1923, Carriden, West Lothian, Scotland. Right-hand batsman. *Team* Scotland (1954).
Career batting
1–1–0–6–6–6.00–0–*ct* 1

Ellison, Charles Christopher
Cricketer. *b*: 11.2.1962, Pembury, Kent. Brother of R. M. (Kent). Lower order right-hand batsman, right-arm medium pace bowler. *Sch* Tonbridge. *Team* Cambridge U (1982–83, blue both years).
Career batting
11–13–6–105–21–15.00–0–*ct* 5
Bowling 467–12–38.91–0–0–4/36

Ellison, Rev Henry Richard Nevile
Amateur. *b:* 16.7.1868, Blyth, Notts. *d:* 7.10.1948, Elstead, Surrey. Son of C.C. (Cambridge U, 1830s). Middle order batsman, change bowler. *Sch* Rugby. *Team* Nottinghamshire (1897, 1 match).
Career batting
1–2–0–5–3–2.50–0–*ct* 0
Bowling 5–0

He also appeared for Lincolnshire and later Wiltshire. Commencing 1930, he was Hon Sec of Derbyshire CCC.

Ellison, Michael Joseph
Amateur. *b:* 1.6.1817, Worksop, Notts. *d:* 12.7.1898, Sheffield, Yorkshire. Middle order right-hand batsman. *Teams* Yorkshire (1849–55, 4 matches); Nottinghamshire (1852, 1 match).
Career batting
16–28–0–195–6.96–0–*ct* 1
Bowling 15–0+1–no av–0–0–1/?

He was the prime mover in the establishment of the County cricket ground at Bramall Lane, Sheffield, and was President of Yorkshire CCC from 1864 to his death, and Treasurer 1863–1893.

His first important match was for Sheffield in 1846.

Ellison, Richard Mark
Cricketer. *b*: 21.9.1959, Ashford, Kent. Brother of C. C. (Cambridge U). Middle order left-hand batsman, right-arm medium pace bowler. *Sch* Tonbridge. *Team* Kent (1981–83, 36 matches).
Career batting
36–43–16–759–63–28.11–0–*ct* 20
Bowling 2068–71–29.12–1–0–5/73

Elms, John Emmanuel
Professional. *b:* 24.12.1874, Sheffield, Yorkshire. *d:* 7.11.1951, Sheffield, Yorkshire. Lower order batsman, right-arm medium or slow bowler. *Team* Yorkshire (1905, 1 match).
Career batting
1–2–0–20–20–10.00–0–*ct* 1
Bowling 28–1–28.00–0–0–1/20

Elms, Richard Burtenshaw
Cricketer. *b:* 5.4.1949, Sutton, Surrey. Tail end right-hand batsman, off break bowler. *Teams* Kent (1970–76, 55 matches); Hampshire (1977–78, 17 matches).
Career batting
72–73–23–558–48–11.16–0–*ct* 17
Bowling 4606–116–39.70–4–0–5/38

Elsby, George
Professional. *b:* 1902, Sandiford, Staffs. Middle order right-hand batsman, right-arm medium pace bowler. *Team* Wales (1927).
Career batting
1–2–0–36–22–18.00–0–*ct* 0
Bowling 36–0
His County cricket was for Caernarvonshire.

Elsdon, Harold
Professional. *b:* 19.2.1921, Lemington, Northumberland. Lower order right-hand batsman, right-arm fast bowler. *Team* Minor Counties (1949, 1 match).
Career batting
1–2–1–12–12*–12.00–0–*ct* 1
Bowling 100–3–33.33–0–0–3/51
His County cricket was for Northumberland.

Else, Robert
Professional. *b:* 17.11.1876, Leawood, Matlock, Derbyshire. *d:* 16.9.1955, Sheffield, Yorkshire. Middle order left-hand batsman. *Team* Derbyshire (1901–03, 5 matches).
Career batting
5–10–2–59–28–7.37–0–*ct* 3
Bowling 61–1–61.00–0–0–1/56

Elson, Geoffrey
Amateur. *b:* 19.3.1913, Coventry. Tail end left-hand batsman, slow left-arm bowler. *Sch* Rydal. *Team* Warwickshire (1947, 1 match).
Career batting
1–2–1–7–4–7.00–0–*ct* 0
Bowling 116–1–116.00–0–0–1/99

Elstob, Eric Bramley
Amateur. *b:* 2.8.1885, Brentford, Middlesex. *d:* 15.5.1949, Hawkhurst, Kent. Middle order batsman. *Sch* Marlborough. *Team* Royal Navy (1913–23).
Career batting
2–4–1–23–14–7.66–0–*ct* 0
Bowling 46–2–23.00–0–0–1/5

Elviss, Richard William
Cricketer. *b:* 19.7.1945, Sheffield, Yorkshire. Lower order right-hand batsman, off break bowler. *Sch* Leeds Grammar School. *Team* Oxford U (1966–67, blue both years).
Career batting
19–26–9–114–16–6.70–0–*ct* 4
Bowling 1718–65–26.43–4–0–5/83

Emburey, John Ernest
Cricketer. *b*: 20.8.1952, Peckham, London. Stubborn lower order right-hand batsman, off break bowler, excellent gully field. *Teams* Middlesex (1973–83, 152 matches); Western Province 1982/3). *Tours* England to Australia 1978/9, to Australia and India 1979/80, to West Indies 1980/1, to India and Sri Lanka 1981/2; Robins to Sri Lanka 1977/8; Middlesex to Zimbabwe 1980/1; SAB to South Africa 1981/2. *Tests* England (1978 to 1981/2, 22 matches).
Career batting
213–253–61–3986–133–20.76–2–*ct* 196
Bowling 16956–745–22.80–42–8–7/36
Test batting
22–33–6–326–57–12.07–0–*ct* 17
Bowling 1696–56–30.28–2–0–6/33
His best season was 1983 with 103 wickets, av 17.88.

Emery, Kevin St John Dennis
Cricketer. *b*: 28.2.1960, Swindon, Wiltshire. Lower order right-hand batsman, right-arm fast medium bowler. *Team* Hampshire (1982–83, 30 matches).
Career batting
30–27–15–45–18–3.75–0–*ct* 3
Bowling 2231–88–25.35–3–1–6/51
He took 83 wickets, av 23.72, in 1982, his debut season.

Emery, Sidney Hand
Amateur. *b:* 16.10.1885, Sydney, Australia. *d:* 7.1.1967, Petersham, New South Wales, Australia. Lower order right-hand batsman, leg break and googly bowler. *Team* New South Wales (1908/9 to 1912/3, 20 matches). *Tours* Australia to England and North America 1912, to New Zealand 1909/10, to North America 1913. *Tests* Australia (1912, 4 matches).

Career batting
58–80–15–1192–80*–18.33–0–*ct* 30
Bowling 4355–183–23.79–11–3–7/28
Test batting
4–2–0–6–5–3.00–0–*ct* 2
Bowling 249–5–49.80–0–0–2/46

Although he bowled fairly well in the county matches, he proved ineffective in the Tests on his visit to England.

Emery, William
Professional. *b:* 1897, Merthyr-Tydfil, Glamorgan. *d:* 1962, Gowerton, Glamorgan. Lower order right-hand batsman, right-arm fast medium bowler. *Team* Glamorgan (1922, 2 matches); Wales (1925).
Career batting
3–5–0–16–11–3.20–0–*ct* 0
Bowling 246–6–41.00–0–0–2/25

Emmett, Arthur
Professional. *b:* 1872, Linthorpe, Yorkshire. *d:* 1935, Leicester. Son of Thomas (Yorkshire). Lower order right-hand batsman, right-arm medium pace bowler. *Team* Leicestershire (1902, 3 matches).
Career batting
3–4–0–12–10–3.00–0–*ct* 0
Bowling 240–5–48.00–0–0–3/48

In a minor match in 1905 for Leicester v Oakham he bowled the first four batsmen with his first four deliveries.

Emmett, George Malcolm
Professional. *b:* 2.12.1912, Agra, India. *d:* 18.12.1976, Bristol. Opening right-hand batsman, right-arm medium pace bowler, good field. *Team* Gloucestershire (1936–59, 454 matches). *Tours* Commonwealth to India and Ceylon 1950/1, to India 1953/4. *Test* England (1948, 1 match).
Career batting
509–865–50–25602–188–31.41–37–*ct* 296
Bowling 2641–60–44.01–2–0–6/137
Test batting
1–2–0–10–10–5.00–0–*ct* 0

He hit 1,000 runs in a season 13 times plus once overseas and went on to 2,000 runs three times (best 2,115, av 35.25, in 1953). He captained Gloucestershire 1955–58.

He also appeared for Devon 1932–35.

Emmett, Thomas
Professional. *b:* 3.9.1841, Halifax, Yorkshire. *d:* 30.6.1904, Leicester. Father of Arthur (Leics). Middle order left-hand batsman, right-hand fast round arm bowler. *Team* Yorkshire (1866–88, 298 matches). *Tours* Lillywhite to Australia 1876/7; Harris to Australia 1878/9; Daft to North America 1879 (not first-class); Lillywhite, Shaw and Shrewsbury to Australia 1881/2. *Tests* England (1876/7 to 1881/2, 7 matches).
Career batting
426–700–90–9053–104–14.84–1–*ct* 274
Bowling 21334–1572–13.57–121–29–9/23
Test batting
7–13–1–160–48–13.33–0–*ct* 9
Bowling 284–9–31.55–1–0–7/68

He took 100 wickets in a season on four occasions, (best 124, av 12.83, in 1886). His best bowling was 9/23 for Yorkshire v Cambridgeshire at Hunslet in 1869.

Emmitt, Herbert William
(known as Emmett)
Professional. *b:* 6.8.1857, Nottingham. *d:* 23.4.1901, Nottingham. Middle order batsman. *Team* Nottinghamshire (1888, 2 matches).
Career batting
3–5–1–6–4*–1.50–0–*ct* 2

He was a noted soccer player, appearing for both Notts County and Nottingham Forest.

His first-class debut was for North v South in 1884.

Endean, William Russell
Amateur. *b:* 31.5.1924, Johannesburg, South Africa. Middle order right-hand batsman, wicket-keeper, brilliant close field. *Team* Transvaal (1945/6 to 1960/1). *Tours* South Africa to England 1951, 1955, to Australia and New Zealand 1952/3. *Tests* South Africa (1951 to 1957/8, 28 matches).
Career batting
134–230–25–7757–247–37.83–15–*ct* 158–*st* 13
Bowling 73–2–36.50–0–0–1/1
Test batting
28–52–4–1630–162*–33.95–3–*ct* 41

He came to England in 1951 as the principal wicket-keeper, but found himself deposed by Waite, and had only a moderate season with the bat. In 1955 he hit 1,242 runs, av 34.50, and appeared in all five Tests as a batsman. He hit three double hundreds for Transvaal and against Orange Free State in 1954/5 hit a record 197* runs before lunch, going on to 235.

His final first-class match was for MCC in 1964.

Enfield, Henry
Amateur. *b:* 12.9.1849, Hampstead, Middlesex. *d:* 19.9.1923, Nottingham. Middle order right-hand batsman, brilliant close field. *Sch* Brighton. *Team* Nottinghamshire (1869–72, 2 matches).
Career batting
2–4–0–6–4–1.50–0–*ct* 3

Engineer, Farokh Maneksha
Professional. *b:* 25.2.1938. Bombay, India.

Brother of D.M. (Mysore). Opening/middle order right-hand batsman, wicket-keeper, leg break bowler. *Teams* Bombay (1959/60 to 1974/5); Lancashire (1968–76, 175 matches). *Tours* Indian Starlets to Pakistan 1959/60; India to West Indies 1961/2, to England 1967, 1974, to Australia and New Zealand 1967/8, to East Africa 1967; Rest of World to Pakistan 1970/1, to Australia 1971/2. *Tests* India (1961/2 to 1974/5, 46 matches).
Career batting
335–510–55–13436–192–29.52–13–*ct* 703–*st* 121
Bowling 117–1–117.00–0–0–1/40
Test Batting
46–87–3–2611–121–31.08–2–*ct* 66–*st* 16

His first-class debut was for Combined Indian Universities 1958/9. He did not exceed 1,000 runs in a season in England, but made 1,050, av 47.72, in India in 1964/5.

England, Richard Michael
Amateur. *b:* 23.8.1918, Midgham, Berkshire. Lower order right-hand batsman, wicket-keeper. *Sch* Eton. *Team* Oxford U (1938–39).
Career batting
2–3–1–59–43*–29.50–0–*ct* 4

He played for Berkshire.

English, Edward Apsey
Amateur. *b:* 1.1.1864, Dorking, Surrey. *d:* 8.9.1966, Tiverton, Devon. Middle order right-hand batsman. *Team* Hampshire (1898–1901, 18 matches).
Career batting
18–32–2–565–98–18.83–0–*ct* 5
Bowling 101–1–101.00–0–0–1/11

As far as is known he was the oldest first-class cricketer, living to the age of 102.

English, Ernest Robert Maling
Amateur. *b:* 2.12.1874, Cheltenham. *d:* 18.8.1941, South Kensington. Middle order right-hand batsman. *Sch* Wellington. *Team* Gloucestershire (1909, 1 match).
Career batting
1–2–0–2–2–1.00–0–*ct* 0

He also played for Shropshire.

English, Winston
Cricketer. *b: circa* 1945, British Guiana. Lower order left-hand batsman, left-arm fast bowler. *Teams* Guyana (1966/7 to 1969/70); D.H. Robins' XI (1969).
Career batting
12–16–5–479–112–43.54–1–*ct* 8
Bowling 916–27–33.92–0–0–4/111

Ennis, James Tench
Amateur. *b:* 27.2.1900, Naul, Co Dublin, Ireland. *d:* 15.10.1976, Dublin, Republic of Ireland. Right-hand batsman.
Team Dublin University (1926).
Career batting
1–2–0–0–0–0.00–0–*ct* 0

Ensor, Ernest
Amateur. *b:* 1871, Cheltenham, Gloucs. *d:* 13.8.1929, Cork, Ireland. Right-hand batsman, right-arm fast medium bowler. *Team* Dublin University (1895).
Career batting
4–7–0–65–18–9.28–0–*ct* 1
Bowling 468–23–20.35–2–0–5/74

Enthoven, Henry John
Amateur. *b:* 4.6.1903, Cartagena, Spain. *d:* 29.6.1975, London. Middle order right-hand batsman, right-arm medium pace bowler. *Sch* Harrow. *Teams* Middlesex (1925–36, 123 matches); Cambridge U (1923–26, blue all four years). *Tour* MCC to Canada 1937 (not first-class).
Career batting
194–301–30–7362–139–27.16–9–*ct* 78
Bowling 8099–252–32.13–5–1–6/64

He captained Middlesex jointly with N.E. Haig in 1933–34. He hit 1,129 runs, av 31.36, in 1926.

His final first-class match was for MCC in 1948.

Entwistle, Robert
Cricketer. *b:* 20.10.1941, Burnley, Lancashire. Middle order right-hand batsman, good outfield. *Team* Lancashire (1962–66, 48 matches).
Career batting
49–81–4–1612–85–20.93–0–*ct* 16

He hit 1,030 runs, av 28.61, in 1964.

Commencing 1967 he appeared for Cumberland, and his final first-class match was for Minor Counties in 1976.

Eskdaill, Lord (*see under* Earl of Dalkeith)

Estcourt, Noël Sidney Dudley
Amateur. *b:* 7.1.1929, Ralolia, Southern Rhodesia. Middle order right-hand batsman, off break bowler. *Team* Cambridge U (1953–54, blue 1954).
Career batting
21–34–7–513–56*–19.00–0–*ct* 6
Bowling 1262–23–54.86–0–0–4/79

An excellent rugby footballer, he represented Cambridge and England.

Estridge, Edward
Amateur. *b:* 28.4.1843, Hounslow, Middlesex. *d:* 30.8.1919, Abingdon, Berkshire. Middle order batsman. *Sch* Tonbridge. *Team* Derbyshire (1874, 1 match).
Career batting
1–1–0–4–4–4.00–0–*ct* 0

Estridge, George Tyler
Amateur. *b:* 11.8.1835, Carshalton, Surrey. *d:* 26.6.1862, Belgaum, India. Brother of H.W. (Gentlemen of South). Sound middle order right-hand batsman, good field at point. *Team* Surrey (1859–60, 5 matches).
Career batting
8–13–2–168–47–15.27–0–*ct* 3
Bowling 105–7–15.00–1–0–6/44

His career in County cricket was brief as he joined the army in India in 1861.

Estridge, Henry Whatley
Amateur. *b:* 1837, Carshalton, Surrey. *d:* 15.1.1902, Hailey, Oxon. Brother of G.T. (Surrey). Middle order right-hand batsman, slow round arm bowler. *Team* Gentlemen of South (1868).
Career batting
1–2–0–14–14–7.00–0–*ct* 0

Etheridge, Charles Robert
Professional. *b:* 1870, Horsham, Sussex. *d:* 14.2.1948, Horsham, Sussex. Lower order batsman, slow left-arm bowler. *Team* Sussex (1896–1901, 3 matches).
Career batting
3–5–2–22–17*–7.33–0–*ct* 1
Bowling 251–3–83.66–0–0–3/105

Etheridge, Robert James
Professional. *b:* 25.3.1934, Gloucester. Lower order right-hand batsman, wicket-keeper. *Team* Gloucestershire (1955–56, 39 matches).
Bowling 39–64–14–796–48–15.92–0–*ct* 33–*st* 8

He played soccer for Bristol City.

Etheridge, Sydney Graver
Amateur. *b:* 3.11.1882, New Barnet, Herts. *d:* 3.9.1945, Barnet, Herts. Middle order right-hand batsman. *Sch* Aldenham. *Team* Middlesex (1908–10, 8 matches).
Career batting
8–12–2–81–22–8.10–0–*ct* 6

He also played for Hertfordshire.

Etherington, Maurice William
Professional. *b:* 24.8.1916, North Hammersmith, London. Lower order right-hand batsman, right-arm fast bowler. *Teams* Middlesex (1946, 2 matches); Leicestershire (1948, 3 matches).
Career batting
5–9–2–64–27–9.14–0–*ct* 1
Bowling 292–8–36.50–0–0–3/23

Evan-Thomas, Charles Marmaduke
Amateur. *b:* 5.11.1897, Builth, Brecon. *d:* 28.3.1953, Llanwrtyd Wells, Brecon. Middle/lower order batsman, opening bowler. *Teams* Royal Navy (1919–20); MCC (1929).
Career batting
3–6–0–45–19–7.50–0–*ct* 1
Bowling 59–1–59.00–0–0–1/16

Evans, Sir Alfred Englefield
Amateur. *b:* 30.1.1884, South Africa. *d:* 29.12.1944, Cranbourne, Dorset. Brother of D.M. (Hants) and W.H.B. (Hants and Worcs). Lower order right-hand batsman, right-arm medium pace bowler. *Teams* Royal Navy (1914–25); Hampshire (1919–20, 5 matches).
Career batting
13–22–0–310–77–14.09–0–*ct* 8
Bowling 841–23–36.56–0–0–4/74

Evans, Alfred Henry
Amateur. *b:* 14.6.1858, Madras, India. *d:* 26.3.1934, Saunton, Devon. Father of A.J. (Hants and Kent) and R. du B. (Hants). Middle order right-hand batsman, right-arm fast medium bowler. *Sch* Rossall and Clifton. *Teams* Oxford U (1878–81, blue all four years); Somerset (1882–84, 6 matches); Hampshire (1885, 3 matches).
Career batting
44–74–8–908–59*–13.75–0–*ct* 45
Bowling 3234–201+3–16.08–20–6–9/59

He was awarded his rugby blue at Oxford and was also a noted athlete. His best bowling was 9/59 for England XI v Daft's XI at Lord's in 1880.

Evans, Alfred John
Amateur. *b:* 1.5.1889, Newtown, Hampshire. *d:* 18.9.1960, Marylebone, London. Son of A.H. (Hants and Somerset), brother of R. du B. (Hants). Middle order right-hand batsman, right-arm medium fast bowler. *Sch* Winchester. *Teams* Hampshire (1908–20, 7 matches); Oxford Univ (1909–12, blue all four years); Kent (1921–28, 36 matches). *Test* England (1921, 1 match).
Career batting
90–148–6–3499–143–24.64–6–*ct* 94
Bowling 3062–110–27.83–4–1–7/50
Test batting
1–2–0–18–14–9.00–0–*ct* 0

He represented Oxford at rackets in 1910 and golf in 1909–10.

During the First World War he won fame for his escapes from German prisoner-of-war camps.

Evans, Bertram Sutton
Amateur. *b:* 17.12.1872, Guildford, Surrey. *d:* 2.3.1919, Paris, France. Middle order batsman. *Team* Hampshire (1900–09, 5 matches).
Career batting
5–8–2–67–18*–11.16–0–*ct* 2

His County cricket was very limited due to his naval career.

Evans, Charles
Professional. *b:* 19.2.1866, Whittington Moor, Derbyshire. *d:* 14.1.1956, Chesterfield, Derbyshire. Lower order right-hand batsman, right-arm fast medium bowler. *Team* Derbyshire (1894–95, 9 matches).
Career batting
9–14–2–157–31–13.08–0–*ct* 7
Bowling 526–19–27.68–0–0–4/46

Evans, Charles William Henry
Amateur. *b:* 19.8.1851, Guernsey. *d:* 2.11.1909, Bognor, Sussex. Middle order right-hand batsman. *Sch* Haileybury. *Teams* Cambridge U (1871); Gentlemen of England (1879).
Career batting
3–6–1–33–8*–6.60–0–*ct* 2–*st* 2

Evans, David Gwilliam Lloyd
Professional. *b:* 27.7.1933, Lambeth, London. Lower order right-hand batsman, wicket-keeper. *Team* Glamorgan (1956–69, 270 matches).
Career batting
270–364–91–2875–46*–10.53–0–*ct* 503–*st* 55
Bowling 12–0

He was awarded a Winston Churchill Scholarship in 1967–68 to travel around the world studying cricket coaching. He is a first-class umpire and has stood in Tests.

Evans, David Linzee
Amateur. *b:* 13.4.1869, West Town, Somerset. *d:* 11.11.1907, West Town, Somerset. Aggressive middle order right-hand batsman, right-arm fast medium bowler. *Sch* Loretto. *Teams* Gloucestershire (1889–91, 7 matches); Somerset (1894–1902, 15 matches).
Career batting
22–42–3–382–60–9.79–0–*ct* 8
Bowling 51–1–51.00–0–0–1/7

He played for Gloucestershire whilst still at school.

Evans, Dudley MacNeil
Amateur. *b:* 11.12.1886, South Africa. *d:* 18.12.1972, Petersfield, Hants. Brother of A.E. (Hants) and W.H.B. (Hants and Worcs). Middle order right-hand batsman, right-arm fast medium bowler. *Sch* Winchester. *Team* Hampshire (1904–11, 15 matches).
Career batting
16–29–3–382–64–14.69–0–*ct* 17
Bowling 1449–55–26.34–4–0–6/81

Evans, Edwin
Amateur. *b:* 6.3.1849, Emu Plains, New South Wales, Australia. *d:* 2.7.1921, Walgett, New South Wales, Australia. Lower order right-hand batsman, right-arm fast medium bowler. *Team* New South Wales (1874/5 to 1887/8, 27 matches). *Tour* Australia to England 1886. *Tests* Australia (1881/2 to 1886, 6 matches).
Career batting
65–105–23–1006–74*–12.26–0–*ct* 63
Bowling 3356–201–16.69–18–4–7/16
Test batting
6–10–2–82–33–10.25–0–*ct* 5
Bowling 332–7–47.42–0–0–3/64

He achieved very little on his single visit to England.

Evans, Ernest Dering
Amateur. *b:* 21.8.1861, Clifton, Bristol. *d:* 4.11.1948, Clifton, Bristol. *Sch* Clifton. *Team* Somerset (1891, 1 match).
Career batting
1–1–0–0–0–0.00–0–*ct* 1

Evans, Edward Noel
Amateur. *b:* 7.12.1911, Edmonton, London. *d:* 12.2.1964, Kensington, London. Middle order left-hand batsman, leg break and googly bowler. *Sch* Haileybury. *Team* Oxford U (1931–33, blue 1932).
Career batting
22–37–3–617–91–18.14–0–*ct* 5
Bowling 224–5–44.80–0–0–2/56

His final first-class match was for MCC in 1934.

Evans, Canon Frederic Rawlins
Amateur. *b:* 1.6.1842, Griff, Warwickshire. *d:* 4.3.1927, Bedworth, Warwickshire. Middle order right-hand batsman, right-hand fast round arm bowler. *Sch* Cheltenham and Rugby. *Team* Oxford U (1863–65, blue all three years).
Career batting
12–17–1–302–43–18.87–0–*ct* 6
Bowling 177–12+1–14.75–1–0–5/32

After leaving Oxford he appeared for Warwickshire and Worcestershire and was a leading member of the Free Foresters. In 1863 he was no-balled for having his hand above his shoulder and for this reason his bowling was not used as much as his ability warranted.

He was a nephew of the author George Eliot (Mary Ann Evans).

Evans, Gwynn
Amateur. *b:* 13.8.1915, Bala, Merioneth. Middle order right-hand batsman, right-arm medium fast bowler. *Teams* Oxford U (1938–39, blue 1939); Glamorgan (1939, 7 matches); Leicestershire (1949, 10 matches).
Career batting
33–56–6–824–65*–16.48–0–*ct* 19
Bowling 2458–72–34.13–2–0–6/80

Evans, George Herbert David
Amateur. *b:* 22.8.1928, Bristol. Middle order right-hand batsman, right-arm medium pace bowler. *Team* Somerset (1953, 8 matches).
Career batting
8–14–0–180–42–12.85–0–*ct* 5
Bowling 22–0

Evans, Henry
Amateur. *b:* 8.7.1857, Stoneyford, Codnor, Derbyshire. *d:* 30.7.1920, Spondon, Derbyshire. Brother of Thomas (Derbyshire). Lower/middle order right-hand batsman, right-arm fast medium bowler. *Team* Derbyshire (1878–82, 5 matches).
Career batting
5–10–0–41–10–4.10–0–*ct* 4
Bowling 252–19–13.26–2–0–7/47

Evans, Harold Ernest
Amateur. *b:* 20.10.1891. Hampstead. *d:* 24.9.1980, Crowthorne, Berkshire. Middle order batsman. *Team* Royal Navy (1920).
Career batting
1–2–0–5–3–2.50–0–*ct* 1

Evans, Herbert Price
Amateur. *b:* 30.8.1894, Llandaff, Cardiff. *d:* 19.11.1982, Llandough, Penarth, Glamorgan. Middle order right-hand batsman. *Team* Glamorgan (1922, 1 match).
Career batting
1–2–0–9–9–4.50–0–*ct* 0

Evans, James
Professional. *b:* 14.7.1891. *d:* 26.8.1973, Upham, Hants. Middle order right-hand batsman, slow right-arm bowler. *Team* Hampshire (1913–21, 15 matches).
Career batting
15–26–7–196–41–10.31–0–*ct* 10–*st* 1
Bowling 81–1–81.00–0–0–1/34

Evans, John Brian
Professional. *b:* 9.11.1936, Clydach, Glamorgan. Lower order right-hand batsman, right-arm fast medium bowler. *Team* Glamorgan (1958–63, 87 matches).
Career batting
88–131–19–1535–62*–13.70–0–*ct* 46
Bowling 6789–251–27.04–10–0–8/42

After leaving Glamorgan he appeared for Lincolnshire and his last first-class match was for Minor Counties in 1969.

Evans, Michael
Amateur. *b:* 3.5.1908, Leicester. *d:* 14.11.1974, Leicester. Tail end right-hand batsman, right-arm fast medium bowler. *Team* Leicestershire (1946, 2 matches).
Career batting
2–4–1–26–14*–8.66–0–*ct* 0
Bowling 130–6–21.66–0–0–3/30

Evans, Martin James
Amateur. *b:* 16.10.1904, Kingsclere, Hants. Tail end batsman, opening bowler. *Team* Royal Navy (1925, 1 match).
Career batting
1–2–1–8–7*–8.00–0–*ct* 0
Bowling 42–0

Evans, Nicholas John
Cricketer. *b:* 9.9.1954, Weston super Mare, Somerset. Lower order right-hand batsman, right-arm medium pace bowler. *Team* Somerset (1976, 1 match).
Career batting
1–1–0–0–0–0.00–0–*ct* 0
Bowling 62–0

Evans, P.S.
Amateur. Tail end batsman, slow left-arm bowler. *Team* Worcestershire (1928, 5 matches).
Career batting
5–9–3–15–5–2.50–0–*ct* 3
Bowling 199–3–66.33–0–0–3/84

Evans, Ralph Du Boulay
Amateur. *b:* 1.10.1891, Newtown, Newbury, Berkshire. *d:* 27.7.1929, Wheelers Ridge, Los Angeles, USA. He was killed in a road accident. Brother of A.J. (Kent and Hants), son of A.H. (Hants and Somerset). Tail end right-hand batsman, right-arm medium pace bowler. *Sch* Winchester. *Team* Hampshire (1912, 1 match); Cambridge U (1913).

Career batting
5–7–4–102–70–34.00–0–*ct* 1
Bowling 227–5–45.40–0–0–3/37

His last first-class match was for Free Foresters in 1914.

Evans, Ronald Ernest
Amateur. *b:* 22.7.1922, East Ham, Essex. Sound middle order right-hand batsman. *Team* Essex (1950–57, 17 matches).
Career batting
17–29–0–482–79–16.62–0–*ct* 8

Evans, Robert Gordon
Amateur. *b:* 20.8.1899, Great Barton, Suffolk. *d:* 2.8.1981, Sidlesham, Sussex. Lower order left-hand batsman, right-arm fast medium bowler. *Team* Cambridge U (1920–21, blue 1921).
Career batting
14–20–9–248–46*–22.54–0–*ct* 5
Bowling 1191–50–23.82–3–0–6/45

His last first-class match was for Free Foresters in 1923.

He played occasional County cricket for Berkshire.

Evans, Talfryn
Professional. *b:* 10.6.1914, Sandy, Llanelly, Glamorgan. *d:* March, 1944, Llanelly. Lower order left-hand batsman, slow left-arm bowler. *Team* Glamorgan (1934, 1 match).
Career batting
1–2–1–0–0*–0.00–0–*ct* 0
Bowling 25–0

Evans, Thomas
Amateur. *b:* 3.6.1852, Stoneyford, Codnor, Derbyshire. *d:* 2.12.1916, Heaton Moor, Lancashire. Brother of Henry (Derbyshire). Lower order right-hand batsman, right-arm slow medium bowler. *Team* Derbyshire (1883, 2 matches).
Career batting
4–7–0–91–35–13.00–0–*ct* 2
Bowling 150–6–25.00–0–0–2/27

He appeared in first-class matches for Liverpool and District in 1886 and 1889.

Evans, Thomas Godfrey
Professional. *b:* 18.8.1920, Finchley, Middlesex. Hard hitting lower order right-hand batsman, brilliant wicket-keeper. *Team* Kent (1939–67, 258 matches). *Tours* MCC to Australia and New Zealand 1946/7, 1950/1, 1954/5, 1958/9, to West Indies 1947/8, 1953/4, to South Africa 1948/9, 1956/7; Commonwealth to South Africa 1959/60; Cavaliers to Jamaica 1963/4, to West Indies 1964/5; Prime Minister's XI in India 1963/4. *Tests* England (1946–59, 91 matches).
Career batting
465–753–52–14882–144–21.22–7–*ct* 816–*st* 250
Bowling 245–2–122.50–0–0–2/50
Test batting
91–133–14–2439–104–20.49–2–*ct* 173–*st* 46

Though he appeared in a handful of Kent matches in 1939, Evans' regular County cricket began in 1946, and within twelve months he was recognised as the leading wicket-keeper in England. In contrast to most of his contemporaries behind the stumps, he was a very extrovert cricketer, relishing the acrobatics and flourishes that can be introduced into wicket-keeping, not that this showmanship detracted from his performances – he was the automatic choice for England both at home and overseas.

He hit 1,000 runs in a season four times with 1,613, av 28.80, in 1952 as his best, but ever keen to play to the gallery, he rarely treated the bowling seriously. To prove however that he could bat, he saved England from collapse on several occasions, including the famous 1946/7 Adelaide Test, when he was at the crease 95 minutes before scoring.

He retired from full-time first-class cricket in 1959, soon after being dropped as the England stumper, but he played his last first-class match for Cavaliers in 1969 and made fleeting re-appearances in Charity matches much later.

Evans, Victor James
Professional. *b:* 4.3.1912, Woodford, Essex. *d:* 28.3.1975, Barking, Essex. Lower order right-hand batsman, right-arm medium pace off break bowler. *Team* Essex (1932–37, 62 matches).
Career batting
62–96–37–469–23*–7.94–0–*ct* 12
Bowling 3843–129–29.79–5–1–6/47

Evans, William Henry Brereton
Amateur. *b:* 29.1.1883, South Africa. *d:* 7.8.1913, Farnborough, Hants. Brother of A.E. (Hants) and D.M. (Hants). Middle order right-hand batsman, right-arm fast bowler. *Sch* Malvern. *Teams* Worcestershire (1901, 6 matches); Oxford U (1902–05, blue all four years); Hampshire (1902–10, 20 matches).
Career batting
66–114–5–3175–142–29.12–5–*ct* 61
Bowling 4550–175–26.00–12–2–7/41

Being in the Egyptian Civil Service, his County cricket was very limited, but it was thought that he would have represented England, had he been able to play regular first-class cricket. He was awarded his soccer blue 1902–05 and was also a noted racquets player. He was killed in a flying accident with the well known aviator Colonel Cody.

Evans, William Lewis
Amateur. *b:* 1898, Wandsworth, Surrey. *d:* 25.4.1966, Epsom, Surrey. Middle order batsman, useful bowler. *Team* Civil Service (1927)
Career batting
1–2–1–23–15*–23.00–0–*ct* 1
Bowling 52–0

Eve, Stanley Charles
Amateur. *b:* 18.12.1925, Stepney, London. Middle order right-hand batsman, right-arm medium pace bowler. *Team* Essex (1950–57, 32 matches).
Career batting
32–51–4–1041–120–22.14–1–*ct* 17
He did not appear for Essex in the years 1952–56 inclusive.

Evelyn, Francis Lyndon
Amateur. *b:* 24.5.1859, Presteigne, Radnorshire. *d:* 8.12.1910, Kinsham, Herefordshire. Middle order right-hand batsman, good deep field. *Sch* Rugby. *Team* Oxford U (1880–81, blue 1880).
Career batting
5–10–0–33–10–3.30–0–*ct* 1
He appeared for Radnorshire and for Herefordshire 1879–91.

Everard, Sir William Lindsay
Amateur. *b:* 13.3.1891, Knighton, Leicester. *d:* 11.3.1949, Torquay, Devon. Opening right-hand batsman. *Sch* Harrow. *Team* Leicestershire (1924, 1 match).
Career batting
1–2–0–3–3–1.50–0–*ct* 0
A pioneer of private flying, he had his own aerodrome near Ratcliffe Hall, Leicestershire.
He was Unionist MP for Melton 1924–35.

Everett, Harold
Amateur. *b:* 13.11.1891. *d:* 27.4.1979, East Preston, Sussex. Middle order right-hand batsman, right-arm slow medium bowler. *Team* Civil Service (1927).
Career batting
1–2–0–2–2–1.00–0–*ct* 0
Bowling 34–0

Everett, Samuel Charles
Amateur. *b:* 17.6.1901, Sydney, Australia. *d:* 10.10.1970, Sydney, Australia. Tail end left-hand batsman, right-arm fast bowler. *Team* New South Wales (1921/2 to 1929/30, 28 matches). *Tours* Australia to England 1926; New South Wales to New Zealand 1923/4.
Career batting
45–51–9–617–77–14.69–0–*ct* 26
Bowling 3634–134–27.11–8–0–6/23
He accomplished very little on his tour to England.

Everitt, Russell Stanley
Amateur. *b:* 8.9.1881, Kings Heath, Birmingham. *d:* 11.5.1973, Kew Gardens, Surrey. Middle order right-hand batsman, wicket-keeper. *Sch* Malvern. *Teams* Worcestershire (1901, 1 match); Warwickshire (1909, 3 matches).
Career batting
4–7–1–63–38–10.50–0–*ct* 3

Evers, Ralph Denis Mark
Amateur. *b:* 11.8.1913, Stourbridge, Worcs. Middle order right-hand batsman. *Sch* Haileybury. *Team* Worcestershire (1936–38, 15 matches).
Career batting
15–26–1–383–60*–15.32–0–*ct* 7

Evershed, Edward
Amateur. *b:* 3.11.1867, Stapenhill, Burton-on-Trent, Staffs. *d:* 18.2.1957, Handsworth Wood, Birmingham. Brother of S.H. and Wallis (Derbyshire). Middle order right-hand batsman. *Team* Derbyshire (1898, 1 match).
Career batting
1–1–0–1–1–1.00–0–*ct* 2
A noted rugby footballer, he appeared for Rosslyn Park.

Evershed, Sir Sydney Herbert
Amateur. *b:* 13.1.1861, Burton-on-Trent, Staffs. *d:* 7.3.1937, Burton-on-Trent, Staffs. Brother of Edward (Derbyshire) and Wallis (Derbyshire). Opening right-hand batsman, right-arm medium pace bowler. *Sch* Clifton. *Team* Derbyshire (1880–1901, 75 matches).
Career batting
76–129–2–3137–153–24.70–4–*ct* 35
Bowling 122–5–24.40–1–0–5/19
An excellent rugby footballer, he played for Midland Counties as half-back and was reserve for England. He captained Derbyshire 1891–98.

Evershed, Wallis
(entered at Clifton as Wallis Emerond Evershed) Amateur. *b:* 10.5.1863, Stapenhill, Burton-on-Trent, Staffs. *d:* 8.5.1911, Kendal, Westmorland. Brother of E. and S.H. (Derbyshire). Middle order right-hand batsman, right-arm medium pace bowler. *Sch* Clifton. *Team* Derbyshire (1882–84, 13 matches).

Career batting
13–24–0–357–92–14.87–0–*ct* 6
Bowling 8–3–2.66–0–0–3/8

Every, Trevor
Professional. *b:* 19.12.1909, Llanelly, Glamorgan. Lower order right-hand batsman, wicket-keeper. *Team* Glamorgan (1929–34, 128 matches).
Career batting
128–198–44–2518–116–16.35–1–*ct* 109–*st* 70
Bowling 49–0
Failing eyesight, which eventually led to total blindness, caused his retirement in 1934.

Evetts, Julian Arthur
Amateur. *b:* 24.11.1911, Tackley Park, Oxon. Opening right-hand batsman. *Sch* Westminster. *Team* Oxford U (1933).
Career batting
1–1–0–0–0–0.00–*ct* 0
He played for Oxfordshire.

Evetts, William
Amateur. *b:* 30.6.1847, Tackley Park, Thame, Oxon. *d:* 7.4.1936, Tackley Park, Thame, Oxon. Hard hitting middle order right-hand batsman, brilliant deep field. *Sch* Harrow. *Teams* Oxford U (1868–69, blue both years); MCC (1875–82).
Career batting
22–36–2–531–102–15.61–1–*ct* 4
He also appeared for Buckinghamshire.

Ewbank, Rev Christopher Cooper
Amateur. *b:* 10.3.1845, Cambridge. *d:* 9.7.1933, Langford, Bedfordshire. Middle order right-hand batsman, wicket-keeper. *Sch* Cheam School. *Team* Sussex (1867–79, 3 matches).
Career batting
4–8–0–95–31–11.87–0–*ct* 2
He was not in the Eleven whilst at Cambridge U. His first-class debut was for MCC in 1866. He also played for Bedfordshire.

Ewens, Percival Charles
Amateur. *b:* 23.11.1882, Yeovil, Somerset. *d:* 21.7.1961, Taunton, Somerset. Middle order right-hand batsman. *Team* Somerset (1923–26, 7 matches).
Career batting
7–11–4–114–27–16.28–0–*ct* 3

Exham, Percy George
Amateur. *b:* 26.6.1859, Cork, Ireland. *d:* 7.10.1922, Repton, Derbyshire. Middle order right-hand batsman, good cover field. *Sch* Repton. *Teams* Cambridge U (1880–81); Derbyshire (1883, 1 match).
Career batting
6–10–0–88–43–8.80–0–*ct* 3
He appeared for Dorset in 1884.

Exton, Rodney Noel
Amateur. *b:* 28.12.1927, Bournemouth. Middle/lower order right-hand batsman, right-arm slow off break bowler. *Sch* Clifton. *Team* Hampshire (1946, 4 matches).
Career batting
4–5–1–39–24*–9.75–0–*ct* 1
Bowling 40–0

Eyre, Charles Howard
Amateur. *b:* 26.3.1883, Liverpool. *d:* 25.9.1915, Loos, France. He was killed in action. Middle order right-hand batsman. *Sch* Harrow. *Team* Cambridge U (1903–06, blue 1904–06). *Tour* MCC to North America 1905.
Career batting
30–53–2–1092–153–21.41–1–*ct* 40
Bowling 50–2–25.00–0–0–1/9

Eyre, John
Amateur. *b:* 29.10.1859, Shaw, Berkshire. *d:* 24.11.1941, Bayswater, London. Middle order right-hand batsman. *Sch* Winchester. *Team* MCC (1887, 1 match).
Career batting
1–1–0–9–9–9.00–0–*ct* 0
He was at Oxford U, but did not appear in first-class matches whilst there.

Eyre, John Arthur
Professional. *b:* 25.7.1885, North Wingfield, Derbyshire. *d:* 12.6.1964, Bolton-on-Dearne, Yorkshire. Middle order right-hand batsman. *Team* Derbyshire (1908, 1 match).
Career batting
1–2–1–2–1*–1.00–0–*ct* 0

Eyre, John Richard
Cricketer. *b:* 13.6.1944, Glossop, Derbyshire. Middle order right-hand batsman, right-arm medium pace bowler. *Team* Derbyshire (1963–67, 48 matches).
Career batting
48–84–4–1194–106–14.92–1–*ct* 17
Bowling 248–1–248.00–0–0–1/6

Eyre, Thomas John Peter
Professional. *b:* 17.10.1939, Brough, Derbyshire. Lower order left-hand batsman, right-arm fast medium bowler. *Team* Derbyshire (1959–72, 197 matches).

Career batting
197–264–49–3436–102–15.98–1–*ct* 83
Bowling 10305–359–28.70–8–0–8/65
In 1965 he was reported to MCC as having a suspect bowling action.

Ezekowitz, Raymond Alan Bryan
Cricketer. *b:* 19.1.1954, Durban, South Africa. Opening right-hand batsman. *Team* Oxford U (1980–81, blue both years).
Career batting
18–32–1–635–93–20.48–0–*ct* 13

FABER, MARK JAMES JULIAN
Cricketer. *b:* 15.8.1950, Horsted Keynes, Sussex. Middle order right-hand batsman, right-arm medium pace bowler. *Sch* Eton. *Teams* Oxford U (1970–72, blue 1972); Sussex (1973–76, 57 matches). *Tours* Oxford and Cambridge to Malaysia 1972/3 (not first-class).
Career batting
78–144–8–3009–176–22.12–3–*ct* 42
Bowling 66–1–66.00–0–0–1/11
He hit 1,060 runs, av 30.28, in 1975. He is a grandson of the former Prime Minister Harold Macmillan.

Fabian, Aubrey Howard
Amateur. *b:* 20.3.1909, East Finchley, Middlesex. Lower order right-hand batsman, right-arm medium pace bowler. *Sch* Highgate. *Team* Cambridge U (1929–31, blue all three years). *Tour* Oxford and Cambridge to Jamaica 1938/9.
Career batting
35–51–22–763–76–26.31–0–*ct* 22
Bowling 2280–61–37.37–2–0–8/69
He played soccer for Derby County.

Fabling, Arthur Hugh
Amateur. *b:* 6.9.1888, Grandborough, Warwickshire. *d:* 11.10.1972, Grandborough. Middle order right-hand batsman, wicket-keeper. *Sch* Wellingborough. *Team* Warwickshire (1921, 1 match).
Career batting
1–2–0–8–7–4.00–0–*ct* 0
A noted soccer player, he represented Northampton.

Fagg, Arthur Edward
Professional. *b:* 18.6.1915, Chartham, Kent. *d:* 13.9.1977, Tunbridge Wells, Kent. Opening right-hand batsman, right-arm medium pace bowler, occasional wicket-keeper. *Team* Kent (1932–57, 414 matches). *Tour* MCC to Australia 1936/7. *Tests* England (1936–39, 5 matches).
Career batting
435–803–46–27291–269*–36.05–58–*ct* 425–*st* 7
Bowling 47–0
Test batting
5–8–0–150–39–18.75–0–*ct* 5
Ill health reduced his opportunities in Test cricket, but he was very successful for Kent. He completed 1,000 runs 13 times, going on to 2,000 five times, his best being 2,456 (av 52.25) in 1938. In the same season he performed the unique feat of hitting a double century in both innings of the same match : 244 and 202* for Kent v Essex at Colchester. Of his six double centuries, the highest was 269* for Kent v Notts at Trent Bridge in 1953.
He was a county umpire from 1959 to his death and stood in Test Matches from 1967 to 1976.

Fairbairn, Alan
Amateur. *b:* 25.1.1923, Winchmore Hill, London. Opening left-hand batsman. *Sch* Haileybury. *Team* Middlesex (1947–51, 20 matches).
Career batting
21–34–4–776–110*–25.86–2–*ct* 10
Bowling 2–0
He hit 108 on his first-class debut for Middlesex v Somerset, Taunton, 1947.

Fairbairn, Gordon Armytage
Amateur. *b:* 26.6.1892, Logan Downs, Queensland, Australia. *d:* 5.11.1973, Ocean Grove, Victoria, Australia. Middle order left-hand batsman, leg break bowler. *Sch* Geelong GS, Australia. *Teams* Cambridge U (1912–14, 1919, blue 1913, 1914 and 1919); Middlesex (1919, 4 matches).
Career batting
32–52–9–971–112–22.58–1–*ct* 29
Bowling 2396–80–29.95–6–1–5/55
His final first-class match was for Free Foresters in 1924.

Fairbairn, Sir Robert Duncan
Amateur. *b:* 25.9.1910, Perth, Scotland. Right-hand batsman. *Teams* Scotland (1938); Europeans (1944/5).

Career batting
2–4–0–19–13–4.75–0–*ct* 1

Fairbanks, Walter
Amateur. *b:* 13.4.1852, Luton, Chatham, Kent. *d:* 25.8.1924, Guildford, Surrey. Middle order right-hand batsman, good point field. *Sch* Clifton. *Teams* Cambridge U (1875); Gloucestershire (1877–84, 24 matches).
Career batting
27–38–7–316–46–10.19–0–*ct* 21
He was awarded his rugby blue whilst at Cambridge.

Fairbanks-Smith, Cuthbert
Amateur. *b:* 18.3.1885, Lewisham, Kent. *d:* 25.5.1948, Middleton, Sussex. *Sch* Bradfield. *Team* Somerset (1921, 2 matches).
Career batting
2–3–1–6–6–3.00–0–*ct* 1

Fairbrother, Neil Harvey
Cricketer. *b*: 9.9.1963, Warrington, Lancashire. Middle order left-hand batsman, left-arm medium pace bowler. *Team* Lancashire (1982–83, 17 matches).
Career batting
17–26–5–759–94*–36.14–0–*ct* 8
Bowling 1–0

Fairclough, Peter Moss
Professional. *b:* 25.9.1887, Bickershaw, Lancashire. *d:* 16.11.1952, Blackpool, Lancashire. Lower order right-hand batsman, slow left-arm bowler. *Team* Lancashire (1911–23, 20 matches).
Career batting
20–27–14–140–19–10.76–0–*ct* 9
Bowling 1158–52–22.26–2–0–7/27

Fairfax, Alan Geoffrey
Amateur. *b:* 16.6.1906, Summer Hill, New South Wales, Australia. *d:* 17.5.1955, Kensington, London. Middle order right-hand batsman, right-arm fast medium bowler. *Team* New South Wales (1928/9 to 1931/2, 21 matches). *Tour* Australia to England 1930. *Tests* Australia (1928/9 to 1930/1, 10 matches).
Career batting
55–76–10–1910–104–28.93–1–*ct* 41
Bowling 3735–134–27.87–2–0–6/54
Test batting
10–12–4–410–65–51.25–0–*ct* 15
Bowling 645–21–30.71–0–0–4/31
He emigrated to England in 1932, running a cricket school, and his final first-class match was for Gentlemen v Players in 1934.

Fairservice, Colin
Professional. *b:* 6.8.1909, Hadlow, Kent. Son of W.J. (Kent). Middle order right-hand batsman, right-arm off break bowler. *Teams* Kent (1929–33, 59 matches); Middlesex (1936, 6 matches).
Career batting
74–107–13–1650–110–17.57–1–*ct* 44
Bowling 694–18–38.55–0–0–3/49

Fairservice, William John
Professional. *b:* 16.5.1881, Nunhead, London. *d:* 26.6.1971, Canterbury, Kent. Father of Colin (Kent and Middlesex). Tail end right-hand batsman, right-arm medium pace off break bowler. *Team* Kent (1902–21, 301 matches).
Career batting
302–419–96–4939–61*–15.29–0–*ct* 164
Bowling 19419–859–22.60–39–7–7/44
He completed 100 wickets in a season once, in 1920 : 113, av 17.46. He also appeared for Northumberland.

Fairweather, James Henry Whitton
Cricketer. *b:* 16.7.1946, Edinburgh, Scotland. Right-hand batsman. *Team* Scotland (1971).
Career batting
2–4–0–23–9–5.75–0–*ct* 2

Fakir S. A. U. (*see under* Aizazuddin, F. S.)

Falck, Ernest Dyson
Amateur. *b:* 21.10.1907, Huddersfield, Yorkshire. *d:* 19.2.1982, Bridport, Dorset. Middle order right-hand batsman. *Team* Somerset (1935–36, 4 matches).
Career batting
4–8–1–74–28–10.57–0–*ct* 2

Falcon, Joseph Henry
Amateur. *b:* 9.4.1892, Norwich. *d:* 11.2.1950, Lowestoft, Suffolk. Brother of Michael (Cambridge U). Lower order right-hand batsman, right-arm fast medium, bowler. *Sch* Harrow. *Team* Cambridge U (1914).
Career batting
2–1–1–3–3*–no av–0–*ct* 0
Bowling 165–5–33.00–0–0–3/72
He appeared for Norfolk.

Falcon, Michael
Amateur. *b:* 21.7.1888, Norwich. *d:* 27.2.1976, Norwich. Brother of J.H. (Cambridge U). Middle order right-hand batsman, right-arm fast medium bowler, fine field. *Sch* Harrow. *Team* Cambridge U (1908–11, blue all four years). *Tour* Incogniti to USA 1913 (not first-class).

Career batting
89–155–25–3282–134–25.24–4–*ct* 44
Bowling 5727–231–24.79–20–1–7/70

He played for Norfolk from 1906 to 1946, being captain from 1912 to 1946. One of the greatest of regular Minor Counties cricketers, he might have played for England if he had appeared more often in first-class cricket.

His final first-class match was for Free Foresters in 1936.

He was MP for East Norfolk.

Falconer, Roderick
Professional. *b:* 1886, Hoxne, Suffolk. *d:* 8.3.1966, Malvern, Worcs. Lower order right-hand batsman, right-arm medium pace bowler. *Team* Northants (1907–10, 7 matches).
Career batting
7–12–4–29–12*–3.62–0–*ct* 1
Bowling 228–9–25.33–0–0–2/13

He also played for Norfolk

Falding, Sydney Wheatley
Professional *b:* 1891, Leeds, Yorkshire. *d:* 7.11.1959, Leeds, Yorkshire. Lower order left-hand batsman, left-arm opening bowler. *Team* Northants (1921, 1 match).
Career batting
2–3–0–8–8–2.66–0–*ct* 0
Bowling 168–3–56.00–0–0–2/49

He appeared for Devon, commencing 1925, and for Lincolnshire.

His final first-class match was for West of England in 1927.

Fallows, John Armstrong
Amateur. *b:* 25.7.1907, Woodley, Cheshire. *d:* 20.1.1974, Macclesfield, Cheshire. Lower order right-hand batsman. *Sch* Worksop. *Team* Lancashire (1946, 25 matches).
Career batting
25–22–1–171–35–8.14–0–*ct* 10

He also appeared for Cheshire. Appointed as Lancashire's captain in 1946, he played first-class County cricket for just that summer, but later served on the Lancashire Committee.

Fane, Frederick Luther
Amateur. *b:* 27.4.1875, Curragh Camp, Ireland. *d:* 27.11.1960, Brentwood, Essex. Opening right-hand batsman. *Sch* Charterhouse. *Teams* Essex (1895–1922, 292 matches); Oxford U (1896–98, blue 1897 and 1898); London County (1901). *Tours* Bennett to West Indies 1901/2; Hawke to New Zealand and Australia 1902/3; MCC to South Africa 1905/6, 1909/10, to Australia 1907/8; Leveson-Gower's XI to Rhodesia 1909/10. *Tests* England (1905/6 to 1909/10, 14 matches).
Career batting
417–721–44–18548–217–27.39–25–*ct* 194
Bowling 49–2–24.50–0–0–2/17
Test batting
14–27–1–682–143–26.23–1–*ct* 6

He captained Essex 1904–06 and England in five Tests – three in Australia in 1907/8 and two in South Africa in 1909/10; on both occasions he was the vice-captain of the MCC touring party.

He hit 1,000 runs in a season five times (best 1,572, av 34.93, in 1906).

His two double centuries were for Essex, the highest being 217 v Surrey at the Oval in 1911.

His final first-class match was for Leveson-Gower's XI in 1924.

Fantham, William Edward
Professional. *b:* 14.5.1918, Birmingham. Middle order right-hand batsman, off break bowler. *Team* Warwickshire (1935–48, 63 matches).
Career batting
63–103–12–1168–51–12.83–0–*ct* 33
Bowling 2907–64–45.42–2–0–5/55

Faragher, Harold Alker
Amateur. *b:* 20.7.1917, Reddish, Lancashire. Middle order right-hand batsman, right-arm medium or leg break bowler. *Team* Essex (1949–50, 6 matches).
Career batting
6–9–2–274–85*–39.14–0–*ct* 4

Farebrother, Michael Humphrey
Amateur. *b:* 28.2.1920, Chelsea, London. Lower order right-hand batsman, left-arm fast medium bowler. *Sch* Eton. *Team* Oxford U (1939)
Career batting
1–2–0–1–1–0.50–0–*ct* 2
Bowling 128–4–32.00–0–0–2/49

Fargus, Rev Archibald Hugh Conway
Amateur. *b:* 15.12.1878, Clifton, Bristol. *d:* 1963, Bristol. Lower order right-hand batsman, right-arm fast bowler. *Sch* Clifton and Haileybury. *Teams* Cambridge U (1900–01, blue both years); Gloucestershire (1900–01, 15 matches).
Career batting
28–51–9–507–61–12.07–0–*ct* 19
Bowling 2048–60–34.13–2–1–7/55

He also appeared for Devonshire.

He was the son of a well-known Victorian novelist.

Farmer, Charles George Edgar
Amateur. *b:* 28.11.1885, Chelsea, London. *d:* 18.8.1916, Longueval, France. He was killed in

action. Middle order batsman. *Sch* Eton. *Team* MCC (1905–06).
Career batting
2–3–0–78–55–26.00–0–*ct* 1
He appeared in the Freshmen's and Seniors' Matches at Oxford, but no first-class games.

Farmer, John James Stewart
Amateur. *b:* 5.8.1934, Surrey. Middle order right-hand batsman. *Sch* Eton. *Team* Oxford U (1958).
Career batting
2–4–0–10–6–2.50–0–*ct* 0

Farnes, Kenneth
Amateur. *b:* 8.7.1911, Leytonstone, Essex. *d:* 20.10.1941, Chipping-Warden, Northants. He was killed while flying on active service. Tail end right-hand batsman, right-arm fast bowler. *Teams* Essex (1930–39, 79 matches); Cambridge U (1931–33, blue all three years). *Tours* MCC to West Indies 1934/5, to Australia and New Zealand 1936/7, to South Africa 1938/9. *Tests* England (1934 to 1938/9, 15 matches).
Career batting
168–201–59–1182–97*–8.32–0–*ct* 84
Bowling 14804–690–21.45–44–8–8/38
Test batting
15–17–5–58–20–4.83–0–*ct* 1
Bowling 1719–60–28.65–3–1–6/96
Although the best amateur fast bowler of the 1930s, Farnes' County cricket was very restricted – after leaving Cambridge in 1933 he was a master at Worksop College. He twice took 100 wickets in a season (best 113, av 18.38, in 1933). He tragically died shortly after qualifying as a pilot in the RAF.

Farnfield, Geoffrey George
Amateur. *b:* 13.7.1897, West Ham, Essex. *d:* 22.3.1974, Leamington Spa, Warwickshire. Middle order right-hand batsman. *Team* Essex (1921, 12 matches).
Career batting
12–20–1–252–41–13.26–0–*ct* 5

Farnfield, Percy Hamilton
Amateur, *b:* 16.6.1881, Guildford, Surrey. *d:* 19.8.1962, Solihull, Warwickshire. Middle order right-hand batsman. *Team* Worcestershire (1925, 1 match).
Career batting
1–1–0–0–0–0.00–0–*ct* 0

Farnsworth, Andrew William
Professional. *b:* 1887, Sydney, Australia. *d:* 30.10.1966, Sydney, Australia. Middle order right-hand batsman. *Team* Lancashire (1919, 1 match); New South Wales (1908/9, 1 match).
Career batting
2–4–0–78–69–19.50–0–*ct* 0

Farooq Hamid
Cricketer. *b:* 3.3.1945, Lahore, India. Tail end right-hand batsman, right-arm fast medium bowler. *Teams* Lahore (1961/2 to 1968/9); PIA (1962/3 to 1969/70). *Tours* Pakistan Eaglets to England 1963; Pakistan to Australia and New Zealand 1964/5, to Ceylon 1964/5; PIA to East Africa 1964/5. *Test* Pakistan (1964/5, 1 match).
Career batting
43–54–12–546–38–13.00–0–*ct* 27
Bowling 2799–111–25.21–3–1–7/16
Test batting
1–2–0–3–3–1.50–0–*ct* 0
Bowling 107–1–107.00–0–0–1/82

Farquhar, John Stewart
Amateur, *b:* 8.4.1904, Cargill, Perthshire, Scotland. Lower order right-hand batsman, right-arm fast medium bowler. *Team* Scotland (1930–39).
Career batting
6–9–7–20–6*–10.00–0–*ct* 1
Bowling 422–22–19.18–0–0–4/13

Farr, Bryan Henry
Amateur. *b:* 16.3.1924, Nottingham. Middle or lower order right-hand batsman, right-arm medium pace bowler. *Sch* Harrow. *Team* Nottinghamshire (1949–51, 6 matches).
Career batting
7–12–2–143–37–14.30–0–*ct* 2
Bowling 538–10–53.80–1–0–5/96
He appeared for Cambridge U against Oxford in 1943.
His final first-class match was for Free Foresters in 1952.

Farrands, Frank Henry
(registered as Farrand at death)
Professional. *b:* 28.3.1835, Sutton-in-Ashfield, Notts. *d:* 22.9.1916, Sutton-in-Ashfield, Notts. Lower order right-hand batsman, right-hand fast round arm bowler. *Team* Nottinghamshire (1871, 2 matches).
Career batting
30–49–15–212–41–6.23–0–*ct* 13
Bowling 1925–127+1–15.15–12–4–6/23
His first-class debut was for MCC in 1868 and his final first-class match was for the same club in 1880.
He was a noted umpire and stood in County and Test matches.

Farrant, Percy Robert
Amateur. *b:* 25.4.1868, Llandudno, Caernarvonshire. *d:* 4.9.1921, at sea on board ss *Ortesa*.

Middle order right-hand batsman, right-arm fast bowler. *Sch* Repton. *Team* Oxford U (1890).
Career batting
2–4–1–12–5*–4.00–0–*ct* 1
Bowling 30–1–30.00–0–0–1/20

His County cricket was for Worcestershire (not first-class).

Farrar, Albert
Professional. *b:* 29.4.1883, Brighouse, Yorkshire. *d:* 25.12.1953, Brighouse, Yorkshire. Middle order batsman. *Team* Yorkshire (1906, 1 match).
Career batting
1–1–0–2–2–2.00–0–*ct* 1

A rugby league footballer, he appeared for Rochdale Hornets.

Farrar, Harry
Amateur. *b:* 14.3.1931, Radcliffe, Lancashire. Lower order left-hand batsman, left-arm fast medium bowler. *Team* Lancashire (1955, 1 match).
Career batting
1 match, did not bat–*ct* 0
Bowling 25–0

Farrar, Hubert Lister
Amateur. *b:* 2.4.1881, Broughton Park, Manchester. *d:* 4.7.1939, Bowden, Cheshire. Middle order right-hand batsman. *Sch* Repton. *Team* Lancashire (1904, 1 match).
Career batting
1–2–0–28–25–14.00–0–*ct* 0

Farren, George Clement
Amateur. *b:* 1873, Rugby, Warwickshire. *d:* 2.11.1956, Coventry, Warwickshire. Middle order right-hand batsman. *Team* Warwickshire (1912, 1 match).
Career batting
1–1–0–0–0–0.00–0–*ct* 0

Farrimond, William
Professional. *b:* 23.5.1903, Daisy Hill, Lancashire. *d:* 14.11.1979, Westhoughton, Bolton, Lancashire. Middle order right-hand batsman, wicket-keeper. *Team* Lancashire (1924–45, 134 matches). *Tours* MCC to South Africa 1930/1, to West Indies 1934/5. *Tests* England (1930/1 to 1935, 4 matches).
Career batting
153–168–45–2908–174–23.64–1–*ct* 255–*st* 177
Bowling 16–0
Test batting
4–7–0–116–35–16.57–0–*ct* 5–*st* 2

Although selected to play for England in four matches, Farrimond did not at that time command a regular place in his County team, being deputy to Duckworth. His only full seasons in County cricket were 1938 and 1939.

Fasih-ud-din
Cricketer. *b:* 28.12.1939, Quetta, India. Middle order right-hand batsman, wicket-keeper. *Teams* Karachi (1957/8 to 1961/2); Quetta (1962/3 to 1974/5); Baluchistan (1972/3 to 1973/4). *Tour* Pakistan to England 1967.
Career batting
51–83–5–2286–237–29.30–6–*ct* 81–*st* 35

As reserve wicket-keeper to Wasim Bari on the 1967 Tour to England, he was only required for six matches. His only double century was for Quetta v East Pakistan at Karachi in 1962/3.

Fasken, David Kenneth
Amateur. *b:* 23.3.1932, Batu Gajah, Ipoh, Federated Malay States. Lower order right-hand batsman, right-arm medium fast bowler. *Sch* Wellington *Team* Oxford U (1953–55, blue all three years).
Career batting
36–53–8–559–61–12.42–0–*ct* 21
Bowling 2862–73–39.20–1–0–5/108

His final first-class match was for Free Foresters in 1962.

Faulkner, George Aubrey
Amateur. *b:* 17.12.1881, Port Elizabeth, South Africa. *d:* 10.9.1930, Walham Green, London, of gas poisoning. Brilliant middle order right-hand batsman, googly bowler. *Teams* Transvaal 1902/03 to 1909/10); MCC (1912–20). *Tours* South Africa to England 1907, 1912, 1924 (1 match); to Australia 1910/11. *Tests* South Africa (1905/6 to 1924, 25 matches).
Career batting
118–197–23–6366–204–36.58–13–*ct* 94
Bowling 7826–449–17.42–33–8–7/26
Test batting
25–47–4–1754–204–40.79–4–*ct* 20
Bowling 2180–82–26.58–4–0–7/84

He was very successful on his two full tours to England, scoring over 1,000 runs on each (best 1,206, av 29.82, in 1907) and in 1912 taking 163 wickets, av 15.42. He also performed brilliantly in 1909/10 in the Tests against England in South Africa and in the following season in Australia. In 1913 he moved to England and after serving with distinction in the First World War opened an indoor cricket school in London, which became world famous. His last first-class match in South Africa was in 1910/11. His highest score was 204 for South Africa v Australia at Melbourne in 1910/11.

Faulkner, William George
Amateur. *b:* 5.5.1923, Poplar, London. Lower order right-hand batsman, right-arm fast medium bowler. *Team* RAF (1946).
Career batting
1–2–0–23–18–11.50–1–*ct* 1
Bowling 56–0

Faviell, William Frederick Oliver
Amateur. *b:* 5.6.1882, Loughton, Essex. *d:* 14.2.1950, Nairobi, Kenya. Middle order right-hand batsman, right-arm medium pace bowler. *Sch* Forest. *Teams* Essex (1908, 7 matches); Europeans (1903/04 to 1909/10).
Career batting
14–24–5–241–66*–12.68–0–*ct* 11
Bowling 261–10–26.10–0–0–3/40

Fawcett, Arthur Henry
Amateur. *b:* 16.9.1880, Sculcoates, Hull. *d:* 1957, Northumberland. Lower order batsman, wicket-keeper. *Teams* Europeans (1916/17 to 1918/19); Gentlemen (1922).
Career batting
6–8–3–29–9–5.80–0–*ct* 6–*st* 1

Fawcett, Edward Boyd
Amateur. *b:* 10.10.1839, Poona, India. *d:* 26.9.1884, Teignmouth, Devon. Middle order right-hand batsman, right-hand fast medium round arm bowler. *Sch* Brighton. *Teams* Cambridge U (1859–60, blue both years); Sussex (1860–63, 10 matches).
Career batting
21–37–0–326–53–8.81–0–*ct* 17
Bowling 534–28+29–19.07–4–1–6/57
He also played for Devonshire and Brecon.

Fawcett, George Walter
Amateur. *b:* 6.8.1929, Ardglass, Co Down, Ireland. Lower order right-hand batsman, wicket-keeper. *Team* Ireland (1956–59).
Career batting
6–9–2–56–21–8.00–0–*ct* 8–*st* 4

Fawcus, Charles Leslie Dinsdale
Amateur. *b:* 8.12.1898, Bromley, Kent. *d:* 8.12.1967, West Chiltington, Sussex. Opening left-hand batsman, left-arm medium pace bowler. *Sch* Bradfield. *Teams* Kent (1924, 1 match); Oxford U (1925–26); Worcestershire (1925, 1 match).
Career batting
7–13–0–202–70–15.53–0–*ct* 2
Bowling 21–0
He also appeared for Dorset.

Fawcus, Ernest Augustus
Amateur. *b:* 10.11.1895, Newcastle-on-Tyne. *d:* 30.6.1966, Halton, Wendover, Bucks. Middle order right-hand batsman, right-arm bowler. *Team* RAF (1927–29).
Career batting
5–8–1–291–115–41.57–1–*ct* 4
Bowling 206–8–25.75–0–0–4/51
His County cricket was for Buckinghamshire.

Fawcus, Lieut Gen Sir Harold Ben
Amateur. *b:* 20.7.1876, South Charlton, Northumberland. *d:* 24.10.1947, Hillingdon, Middlesex. Middle/lower order right-hand batsman, useful bowler. *Sch* Durham. *Teams* Orange Free State (1910/11); Army (1913–14).
Career batting
9–15–0–276–56–18.40–0–*ct* 6
Bowling 619–45–13.75–3–2–7/19
He appeared for Durham.

Fawkes, John
Amateur. *b:* 9.10.1933, Chesterfield, Derbyshire. Middle order left-hand batsman, wicket-keeper. *Team* Combined Services (1959–60).
Career batting
4–6–0–117–41–19.50–0–*ct* 5–*st* 2

Fazal Mahmood
Amateur. *b:* 18.2.1927, Lahore, India. Lower order right-hand batsman, right-arm fast medium bowler. *Teams* Northern India (1943/44 to 1946/47); Punjab (1951/2 to 1956/7); Lahore (1958/59). *Tours* Pakistan to England 1954, 1962, to West Indies 1957/8, to India 1952/3, 1960/1, to Ceylon 1948/9. *Tests* Pakistan (1952/3 to 1962, 34 matches).
Career batting
111–146–33–2602–100*–23.02–1–*ct* 38
Bowling 8792–460–19.11–38–8–9/43
Test batting
34–50–6–620–60–14.09–0–*ct* 11
Bowling 3434–139–24.70–13–4–7/42
Vice-captain of the first Pakistan Test team to tour England, Fazal proved to be the outstanding bowler of the visit, and mainly through his efforts Pakistan gained their first Test victory at The Oval. During the tour he took 77 wickets, av 17.53. However he was not very successful on his second tour in 1962. He played for MCC in England in 1962 and his last first-class match was for President's XI in Pakistan in 1963/4. His best bowling was 9/43 for Punjab v Services at Lahore in 1956/7.

Fear, Harold Percival
Amateur. *b:* 1908, Barnet, Herts. *d:* 13.5.1943, Bishop's Hull, Somerset. Middle order right-hand

batsman. *Sch* Taunton. *Team* Somerset (1934, 2 matches).
Career batting
2–3–0–28–23–9.33–0–*ct* 0
Bowling 29–0

Fearnley, Charles Duncan
Professional. *b:* 12.4.1940, Pudsey, Yorkshire. Brother of M. C. (Yorkshire). Middle order left-hand batsman, off break bowler, close field. *Team* Worcestershire (1962–68, 97 matches).
Career batting
97–174–14–3294–112–20.58–1–*ct* 28
Bowling 37–1–37.00–0–0–1/37
He also played for Lincolnshire.
He runs a well-known firm of cricket outfitters.

Fearnley, Michael Carruthers
Cricketer. *b:* 21.8.1936, Horsforth, Leeds, Yorkshire. *d:* 7.7.1979, East Bierley, Yorkshire, whilst playing cricket. Brother of C.D. (Worcs). Lower order right-hand batsman, right-arm medium pace bowler. *Team* Yorkshire (1962–64, 3 matches).
Career batting
3–4–2–19–11*–9.50–0–*ct* 0
Bowling 133–6–22.16–0–0–3/56

Featherby, William Dixon
Professional. *b:* 18.8.1888, Goodmanham, Yorkshire. *d:* 23.11.1958, Goodmanham, Yorkshire. Lower order batsman, bowler. *Team* Yorkshire (1920, 2 matches).
Career batting
2 matches, did not bat–*ct* 0
Bowling 12–0

Featherstone, Norman George
Cricketer. *b*: 20.8.1949, Que Que, Rhodesia. Middle order right-hand batsman, off break bowler, slip field. *Teams* Transvaal (1967/8 to 1977/8); Middlesex (1968–79, 216 matches); Glamorgan (1980–81, 45 matches); Northern Transvaal (1981/2).
Career batting
329–528–54–13922–147–29.37–12–*ct* 277
Bowling 4986–181–27.54–4–0–5/32
He hit 1,000 runs in a season four times (best 1,156, av 35.03, in 1975).

Fee, Francis
Amateur. *b:* 14.5.1934, Belfast, Ireland. Lower order right-hand batsman, right-arm medium pace off break bowler. *Team* Ireland (1956–59).
Career batting
5–9–2–57–15*–8.14–0–*ct* 4
Bowling 356–37–9.62–3–2–9/26
On his first-class debut he took 14/100 for Ireland v MCC at Dublin in 1956. His best bowling was 9/26 for Ireland v Scotland at Dublin in 1957.

Felix, Nicholas
(real name Wanostrocht)
Amateur. *b:* 5.10.1804, Camberwell, Surrey. *d:* 3.9.1876, Wimborne Minster, Dorset. Excellent middle order left-hand batsman, left-arm underhand slow bowler, point field. *Teams* Kent (1834–52, 55 matches); Surrey (1846–52, 23 matches).
Career batting
148–264–13–4556–113–18.15–2–*ct* 112
Bowling 14–0+9–no av–0–0–3/?
One of the greatest players of his day, he did not become well known until the 1830s, and then appeared in most of the important matches until about 1852. He invented the 'Catapulta' bowling machine and also tubular india rubber batting gloves. In his later years he was an artist and painted the likenesses of a number of cricketers.
He expressed the wish that his biography should appear under his alias, when consulted by Arthur Haygarth.
His debut in important matches was for MCC in 1830.

Fell, Desmond Robert
Amateur. *b:* 16.12.1912, Pietermaritzburg, South Africa. Opening left-hand batsman, off break bowler. *Team* Natal (1931/32 to 1949/50); Dominions (1945).
Career batting
39–64–2–1958–161–31.58–5–*ct* 14
Bowling 1–0
His single appearance in first-class matches in England was for the Dominion side in 1945; he played some matches for Sussex (not first-class) in the same season.

Fell, Mark Andrew
Cricketer. *b:* 17.11.1960, Newark, Notts. Middle order right-hand batsman, slow left-arm bowler. *Team* Nottinghamshire (1982–83, 15 matches).
Career batting
15–27–0–408–108–15.11–1–*ct* 13
Bowling 157–1–157.00–0–0–1/20

Fellowes, Rev Edward Lyon
Amateur. *b:* 23.4.1845, Lingwood, Norfolk. *d:* 23.7.1896, Papworth, Cambs. Lower order right-hand batsman, right-hand fast round-arm bowler, Slip field. *Sch* Marlborough. *Teams* Oxford U (1865–68, blue 1865, 1866, and 1868).
Career batting
17–25–5–376–56–18.80–0–*ct* 17
Bowling 1009–71+14–14.21–6–1–7/46

In 1889 he was elected President of the resuscitated Cambridgeshire CCC.

His final first-class match was for Gentlemen of England 1869.

Fellowes, James
Amateur. *b:* 25.8.1841, Cape of Good Hope, South Africa. *d:* 3.5.1916, Dedham, Essex. Father-in-law of W. C. Hedley (Somerset). Hard hitting lower order right-hand batsman, right-hand fast round-arm bowler. *Teams* Kent (1873–81, 9 matches); Hampshire (1883–85, 11 matches).
Career batting
23–41–6–431–32–12.31–0–*ct* 23
Bowling 1139–60–18.98–4–1–7/24

He made his first-class debut for MCC in 1870. Most of his cricket was for the Royal Engineers, but latterly he appeared for Devon, being founder of the Devon Dumplings as well as the Hampshire Hogs.

Fellows, Harvey Winson
Amateur. *b:* 11.4.1826, Rickmansworth, Herts. *d:* 13.1.1907, Rickmansworth, Herts. Brother of Walter (Oxford U 1854–57). Middle order right-hand batsman, right-hand round-arm fast bowler, good cover point. *Sch* Eton. *Team* MCC (1847–69).
Career batting
67–115–15–1019–61*–10.19–0–*ct* 32–*st* 8
Bowling 441–54+115–8.16–16–7–8/?

In 1848 and 1849 he was regarded as one of the fastest bowlers ever to appear, but after 1849 his pace was much reduced. His County cricket was for Hertfordshire.

Fellows, John Pulteney
Amateur. *b:* 28.3.1881, Beeston, Notts. *d:* 3.2.1942, Hove, Sussex. Middle order batsman, change bowler. *Sch* Repton. *Team* Nottinghamshire (1904–05, 2 matches)
Career batting
2–3–1–23–18*–11.50–0–*ct* 1
Bowling 36–1–36.00–0–0–1/3

Fellows-Smith, Jonathan Payn
Amateur. *b:* 3.2.1932, Durban, South Africa. Aggressive middle order right-hand batsman, right-arm medium pace bowler. *Teams* Oxford U (1953–55, blue all three years); Northants (1957, 13 matches); Transvaal (1958/9 to 1959/60). *Tour* South Africa to England 1960. *Tests* South Africa (1960, 4 matches).
Career batting
94–157–21–3999–109*–29.40–5–*ct* 69
Bowling 4414–149–29.62–6–1–7/26
Test batting
4–8–2–166–35–27.66–0–*ct* 2
Bowling 61–0

He also gained his rugby blue at Oxford.

His final first-class match was for an International XI (in South Africa) in 1960/1.

Feltham, Mark Andrew
Cricketer. *b*: 26.6.1963, Wandsworth, London. Right-hand batsman, right-arm medium fast bowler. *Team* Surrey (1983, 1 match).
Career batting
1 match, did not bat– *ct* 0
Bowling 44–2–22.00–0–0–1/19

Feltham, Walter George
Professional. *b:* 1864, Ringwood, Hants. *d:* 23.9.1904, Ringwood, Hants. Tail end left-hand batsman, left-arm fast bowler. *Team* Hampshire (1884, 3 matches).
Career batting
3–5–1–1–1–0.25–0–*ct* 1
Bowling 254–12–21.16–0–0–4/54

Felton, Nigel Alfred
Cricketer. *b*: 24.10.1960, Guildford, Surrey. Middle order left-hand batsman. *Sch* Millfield. *Team* Somerset (1982–83, 15 matches).
Career batting
15–24–1–722–173*–31.39–1–*ct* 6

Felton, Robert
Amateur. *b:* 27.12.1909, Streatham, South London. *d:* 4.10.1982, Ealing, Middlesex. Middle order right-hand batsman, right-arm fast medium bowler. *Sch* St Paul's. *Team* Middlesex (1935–48, 11 matches).
Career batting
13–22–0–558–171–25.36–1–*ct* 5
Bowling 152–2–76.00–0–0–1/4

Fender, Percy George Herbert
Amateur. *b:* 22.8.1892, Balham, South London. Nephew of P. Herbert (Gentlemen of South). Hard hitting middle order right-hand batsman, right-arm medium pace leg break bowler, brilliant slip field. *Sch* St Paul's. *Teams* Sussex (1910–13, 52 matches); Surrey (1914–35, 413 matches). *Tours* MCC to Australia 1920/1, to South Africa 1922/3; Tennyson to Jamaica 1926/7. *Tests* England (1920/1 to 1929, 13 matches).

Career batting
556–783–69–19034–185–26.65–21–*ct* 600
Bowling 47440–1894–25.04–100–16–8/24
Test batting
13–21–1–380–60–19.00–0–*ct* 14
Bowling 1185–29–40.86–2–0–5/90

His name is remembered for his famous century in 35 minutes made in the match between Surrey and Northants at Northampton in 1920 – he scored 113* in 42 minutes. He was, however, probably a greater bowler than batsman, though such was his all round ability that few cricketers can equal him, when his fielding and captaincy is added to his batting and bowling.

He initially played for Sussex and did not make much of a mark until he joined Surrey in 1914. In all he took 100 wickets in a season seven times (best 178, av 19.98, in 1923) and hit 1,000 runs nine times (best 1,625, av 33.16, in 1929). He completed the 'double' six times.

He captained Surrey from 1921 to 1931, but was never invited to lead England, and in fact only appeared in five Tests in England, never commanding a regular place in the side. A noted writer on the game, he published books on four series between England and Australia.

Fenley, Stanley
Amateur to 1924, but professional from 1925. *b:* 4.1.1896, Kingston-on-Thames, Surrey. *d:* 2.9.1972, Bournemouth, Hants. Tail end right-hand batsman, leg break bowler. *Teams* Surrey (1924–29, 116 matches); Hampshire (1935, 3 matches).
Career batting
119–117–45–421–26–5.84–0–*ct* 52
Bowling 10084–346–29.14–19–4–8/69

Fenner, Derek Alfred
Amateur. *b:* 17.9.1933, Walthamstow, Essex. Lower order right-hand batsman, slow left-arm bowler. *Sch* Epsom. *Team* Cambridge U (1954).
Career batting
1–1–0–21–21–21.00–0–*ct* 0
Bowling 63–2–31.50–0–0–2/33

Fenner, Francis Phillips
Professional. *b*: 1.3.1811, Cambridge. *d.* 22.5.1896, Bath, Somerset. Stylish middle order right-hand batsman, right-hand fast round-arm bowler, slip field. *Teams* Cambridge Town Club (1829–56); Hampshire (1843).
Career batting
55–97–8–1232–87*–14.06–0–*ct* 27–*st* 1
Bowling 19–1+182–19.00–14–4–9/?

A noted player for Cambridge Town his lasting memorial is the cricket ground at Cambridge, which he laid out in 1846. It was described soon after its opening as 'perhaps the smoothest ground in England – being in fact too easy, causing too much run getting.' He took 17 wickets in a match for Cambridge Town Club v Cambridge U in 1844.

Fenner, George David
Professional. *b:* 15.11.1896, Linton, Kent. *d:* 14.9.1971, Linton, Kent. Father of M.D.(Kent). Right-hand batsman. *Team* Kent (1925–27, 2 matches).
Career batting
7–11–1–163–63–16.30–0–*ct* 2
Bowling 52–1–52.00–0–0–1/12

His final first-class match was for MCC in 1929.

He was a noted coach and groundsman.

Fenner, Maurice David
Amateur. *b:* 16.2.1929, Linton, Kent. Son of G.D.(Kent). Middle order left-hand batsman, wicket-keeper. *Sch* Maidstone GS. *Teams* Combined Services (1949–64); Kent (1951–54, 14 matches).
Career batting
33–54–6–708–77–14.75–0–*ct* 47–*st* 13
Bowling 1–1–1.00–0–0–1/1

He was one of the leading cricketers in the RAF for some seasons.

In 1977 he was appointed Secretary to Kent CCC.

Fennex, William
Professional. *b*: *circa* 1764, Gerrards Cross, Buckinghamshire. *d*: *circa* 1839, London. Elegant middle order right-hand batsman, right-hand fast under-arm bowler, good field. *Teams* Middlesex (1816); England (1802–06).
Career batting
9–18–3–90–44–6.00–0–*ct* 7
Bowling 16 wickets, no analyses

He was best known as a single-wicket player, but was regularly picked for England in the 1780s and 1790s.

Fereday, John Benjamin
Professional. *b:* 24.11.1873, Burnt Tree, Dudley, Worcs. *d:* 1.1.1958, Holy Cross, Worcs. Opening right-hand batsman, off break bowler. *Team* Worcestershire (1899–1901, 10 matches).
Career batting
10–19–0–211–37–11.10–0–*ct* 5
Bowling 103–2–51.50–0–0–1/27

He also played for Staffordshire.

Ferguson, George William
Amateur. *b:* 17.9.1912, Buenos Aires, Argentina. Middle order right-hand batsman. *Team* Argen-

tine (1929/30 to 1937/38). *Tour* South America to England 1932.
Career batting
12–23–0–445–85–19.34–0–*ct* 9
Bowling 1–0

Ferguson, William Henry Noel
Amateur. *b:* 6.12.1927, Downpatrick, Co Down, Ireland. Left-hand batsman, right-arm medium pace bowler. *Team* Ireland (1951–64).
Career batting
5–9–1–122–37–15.25–0–*ct* 3
Bowling 375–19–19.73–1–0–6/37

Fergusson, John Alexander
Amateur. *b:* 24.6.1882. *d:* 28.4.1947, Perth, Scotland. Right-hand batsman, right-arm medium pace bowler. *Team* Scotland (1911–23).
Career batting
8–15–1–283–103*–20.21–1–*ct* 7
Bowling 226–9–25.11–1–0–5/36

Fernandes, Maurius Pacheco
Amateur. *b:* 12.8.1897, British Guiana. *d:* 8.5.1981, Georgetown, Guyana. Father of Leslie (British Guiana). Middle order right-hand batsman. *Team* British Guiana (1922/3 to 1931/2). *Tours* West Indies to England 1923, 1928. *Tests* West Indies (1928 to 1929/30, 2 matches).
Career batting
46–79–5–2087–141–28.20–4–*ct* 30
Bowling 183–5–36.60–0–0–2/29
Test batting
2–4–0–49–22–12.25–0–*ct* 0

He batted well on his first visit to England in 1923, being second in the averages (523 runs, av 34.86), but in 1928 quite failed to live up to his reputation.

Fernando, Edward Ranjit
Cricketer. *b:* 22.2.1944, Colombo, Ceylon. Middle order right-hand batsman, wicket-keeper. *Team* Sri Lanka (1964/5 to 1978/9). *Tours* Sri Lanka to India 1964/5, 1966/7, 1968/9, 1970/1, 1975/6, to Pakistan 1973/4, to England 1975.
Career batting
38–65–4–1349–81–22.11–0–*ct* 51–*st* 15

Fernando, Lantra Jayantha
Cricketer. *b*: 20.8.1956, Colombo, Ceylon. Right-hand batsman, right-arm medium-fast bowler. *Team* Sri Lanka (1980/1 to 1982/3). *Tours* Sri Lanka to India 1980/1, to England 1981; Sri Lanka XI to South Africa 1982/3.
Career batting
8–7–1–65–21–10.83–0–*ct* 4
Bowling 430–5–86.00–0–0–2/61

He played in only four first-class matches on the 1981 tour.

Fernie, Arthur Ernest
Amateur. *b:* 9.4.1877, Stone, Staffs. *d:* 24.7.1959, Bideford, Devon. Lower order right-hand batsman, slow left-arm bowler. *Sch* Wellingborough. *Team* Cambridge U (1897–1900, blue 1897, 1900).
Career batting
22–32–16–121–24–7.56–0–*ct* 11
Bowling 1558–61–25.54–1–0–6/104

His County cricket was for Staffordshire and Berkshire. His final first-class match was for MCC in 1901.

Ferreira, Anthonie Michal
Cricketer. *b*: 13.4.1955, Pretoria, South Africa. Lower order right-hand batsman, right-arm medium pace bowler, good field. *Teams* Northern Transvaal (1974/5 to 1982/3); Warwickshire (1979–83, 75 matches).
Career batting
119–180–29–4109–112*–27.21–2–*ct* 58
Bowling 9636–308–31.25–11–1–8/38

Ferris, George John Fitzgerald
Cricketer. *b*: 18.10.1964, Urlings Village, Antigua. Lower order right-hand batsman, right-arm fast bowler, deep field. *Teams* Leeward Islands (1982/3); Leicestershire (1983, 13 matches).
Career batting
15–16–6–67–26–6.70–0–*ct* 2
Bowling 1315–56–23.48–3–1–7/42

Ferris, John James
Amateur. *b:* 21.5.1867, Sydney, New South Wales, Australia. *d:* 21.11.1900, Durban, South Africa, of enteric fever whilst fighting in the Boer War. Tail end left-hand batsman, slow or medium left-arm bowler. *Teams* New South Wales (1886/7 to 1897/8, 19 matches); Gloucestershire (1892–95, 63 matches); South Australia (1895/6, 1 match). *Tours* Australia to England 1888, 1890; Read to South Africa 1891/2. *Tests* Australia (1886/7 to 1890, 8 matches); England (1891/2, 1 match).
Career batting
198–328–56–4264–106–15.67–1–*ct* 90
Bowling 14260–813–17.53–63–11–8/41
Test batting
For Aus: 8–16–4–98–20*–8.16–0–*ct* 4
For Eng: 1–1–0–16–16–16.00–0–*ct* 0
Bowling For Aus: 684–48–14.25–4–0–5/26
For Eng: 91–13–7.00–2–1–7/37

He was outstandingly successful on his Australian tours to England, taking 199 wickets, av 14.74, in 1888 and 186, av 14.28, in 1890, but his skill deserted him as the 1890s progressed, so that he had dropped out of first-class cricket soon after he was 30. He hit 1,056 runs, av 22.46, in 1893.

Ferris, Stuart Wesley
Amateur. *b:* 2.5.1927, Lurgan, Co Armagh, Ireland. Right-hand batsman, right-arm medium pace bowler. *Team* Ireland (1956).
Career batting
2–3–2–10–4*–10.00–0–*ct* 0
Bowling 144–4–36.00–0–0–4/106

Fetherstonhaugh, Charles Bateman Robert
Amateur. *b:* 17.11.1932, Tavistock, Devon. Middle/lower order right-hand batsman, wicket-keeper. *Sch* Millfield. *Teams* MCC (1956); Free Foresters (1962–64). *Tour* Surridge to Bermuda 1961 (not first-class).
Career batting
4–8–2–59–20*–9.83–0–*ct* 4–*st* 1
His County cricket was for Devon.

Few, Harry Gleaves
Professional. *b:* 8.9.1848, Willingham, Cambs. *d:* 9.4.1931, Cambridge. Lower order right-hand batsman, left-hand medium pace round arm bowler. *Team* Cambridgeshire (1866, 2 matches).
Career batting
2–4–0–4–4–1.00–0–*ct* 1
Bowling 170–8–21.25–1–0–5/72
He also played for Huntingdonshire.

Fewings, James
Amateur. *b:* 1849, Bristol. *d:* 20.8.1920, Southampton. Lower order right-hand batsman, wicket-keeper. *Team* Gloucestershire (1872, 2 matches).
Career batting
2–4–1–4–3*–1.33–0–*ct* 0

Fewkes, Alfred
Amateur. *b:* 31.8.1837, Basford, Notts. *d:* 1.4.1912, Bulwell, Notts. Lower order batsman, wicket-keeper. *Team* Nottinghamshire (1864, 1 match).
Career batting
1–2–0–11–9–5.50–0–*ct* 2–*st* 2

Fiddian-Green, Charles Anderson Fiddian
Amateur. *b:* 22.12.1898, Handsworth, Birmingham. *d:* 5.9.1976, Malvern, Worcs. Middle order right-hand batsman, right-arm medium pace bowler. *Sch* The Leys. *Teams* Warwickshire (1920–28, 64 matches); Cambridge U (1921–22, blue both years); Worcestershire (1931–34, 24 matches).
Career batting
107–169–29–4350–120–31.07–4–*ct* 71–*st* 1
Bowling 372–6–62.00–0–0–1/6
He hit 1,000 runs in a season twice (best 1,079, av 31.73, in 1921). An excellent hockey player he represented both Cambridge and England; he also played golf for Cambridge.

Fiddling, Kenneth
Professional. *b:* 13.10.1917, Hebden Bridge, Yorkshire. Lower order right-hand batsman, wicket-keeper. *Teams* Yorkshire (1938–46, 18 matches); Northants (1947–53, 142 matches).
Career batting
160–191–73–1380–68–11.69–0–*ct* 226–*st* 76

Field, Edwin
Amateur. *b:* 18.12.1871, Hampstead, Middlesex. *d:* 9.1.1947, South Bromley, Kent. Opening/middle order right-hand batsman, right-arm medium pace bowler, good field. *Sch* Clifton. *Teams* Cambridge U (1893–94, blue 1894); Middlesex (1904–06, 6 matches).
Career batting
17–31–2–618–107*–21.31–1–*ct* 13
Bowling 48–0
He also played for Berkshire.
A noted rugby footballer, he was awarded his blue at Cambridge and went on to represent England in 1893.

Field, Ernest Frank
(known as Frank Ernest)
Professional. *b:* 23.9.1874, Weethley, Warwickshire. *d:* 25.8.1934, Droitwich, Worcs. Lower order right-hand batsman, right-arm fast bowler. *Teams* Warwickshire (1897–1920, 256 matches); London County (1900).
Career batting
264–352–104–1900–39–7.66–0–*ct* 108
Bowling 24091–1026–23.48–80–17–9/104
He took 100 wickets in a season three times (best 146, av 20.37, in 1911). He performed a most remarkable piece of bowling for Warwickshire v Worcs at Dudley in 1914. Going on with the total 85 for 4, he returned figures of 8.4–7–2–6, there being only one scoring stroke off him despite five no-balls. His best bowling was 9/104 for Warwickshire v Leics at Leicester in 1899.

Field, Frank
Professional. *b:* 29.2.1908, Langley, Worcs. *d:* 25.4.1981, Stourbridge, Worcs. Tail end right-hand batsman, right-arm fast medium bowler. *Team* Worcestershire (1928–31, 2 matches).

Career batting
3–6–2–26–12–6.50–0–*ct* 0
Bowling 194–4–48.50–0–0–4/60

His final first-class match was for MCC in 1932.

Field, George
Amateur. *b:* 30.9.1871, Dudley, Worcs. *d:* 9.6.1942, Portseath, Cornwall. Lower order right-hand batsman, wicket-keeper. *Sch* Uppingham. *Team* Oxford U (1893).
Career batting
1–2–0–4–4–2.00–0–*ct* 0–*st* 1

Field, Maxwell Nicholas
Cricketer. *b:* 23.3.1950, Coventry, Warwickshire. Lower order right-hand batsman, right-arm medium pace bowler. *Teams* Cambridge U (1974, blue); Warwickshire (1974–75, 3 matches).
Career batting
11–15–5–122–39*–12.20–0–*ct* 1
Bowling 896–24–37.33–0–0–4/76

Fielder, Arthur
Professional. *b:* 19.7.1877, Plaxtol, Tonbridge, Kent. *d:* 30.8.1949, Lambeth, London. Lower order right-hand batsman, right-arm fast bowler. *Team* Kent (1900–14, 253 matches). *Tour* MCC to Australia 1903/4, 1907/8. *Tests* England (1903/4 to 1907/8, 6 matches).
Career batting
287–380–175–2320–112*–11.31–1–*ct* 119
Bowling 26852–1277–21.02–97–28–10/90
Test batting
6–12–5–78–20–11.14–0–*ct* 4
Bowling 711–26–27.34–1–0–6/82

He took 100 wickets in a season five times (best 186, av 20.19, in 1906). His most famous feat was performed in the Players v Gentlemen match of 1906, when he took all 10 wickets in an innings at Lord's (for 90 runs).

Though not much of a batsman, he achieved the unusual distinction of hitting a century when coming in at no.11 – for Kent v Worcs at Stourbridge in 1909. He and Woolley added 235 for the last wicket, a record in English County cricket.

Fielder, Albert Edward
Professional. *b:* 3.4.1889, Sarisbury Green, Hants. *d:* 29.4.1947, Fareham, Hants. Lowei order right-hand batsman, right-arm fast medium bowler. *Team* Hampshire (1911–13, 3 matches).
Career batting
3–4–1–38–35–12.66–0–*ct* 4
Bowling 225–6–37.50–1–0–5/128

Fielder, Walter George
Professional. *b:* 6.3.1899, Fareham, Hants. *d:* 7.1.1968, Sarisbury Green, Hants. Lower order batsman, bowler. *Team* Hampshire (1923, 1 match).
Career batting
1–1–1–2–2*–no av–0–*ct* 0
Bowling 26–0

Fielding, Felix
Amateur. *b:* 24.2.1858, Lewisham, Kent. *d:* 4.2.1910, Surbiton, Surrey. Lower / middle order right-hand batsman, wicket-keeper. *Sch* Malvern. *Team* Surrey (1889, 2 matches).
Career batting
4–6–1–100–75–20.00–0–*ct* 4–*st* 3

His last first-class match was for the South in 1890.

Fieldwick, Edward
Amateur. *b:* 1868, Prescot, Lancashire. *d:* 1910, Prescot, Lancashire. Middle order batsman. *Team* Liverpool and District (1894).
Career batting
1–2–0–0–0–0.00–0–*ct* 2
Bowling 39–0

Figg, George
Professional. *b:* 13.6.1824, Horsham, Sussex. *d:* 20.7.1888, Horsham. Lower order right-hand batsman, right-hand medium pace round-arm bowler. *Teams* Middlesex (1850, 1 match); Sussex (1865–66, 10 matches).
Career batting
11–19–7–77–26*–6.41–0–*ct* 7
Bowling 702–38–18.47–3–0–6/42

For about 10 years he managed a cricket ground in Norwich, commencing in or about 1851.

He also played for Suffolk and Norfolk.

Filgas, Frank Miroslav
Amateur. *b:* 3.11.1926, Carlow, Co Carlow, Ireland. Right-hand batsman, wicket-keeper. *Team* Ireland (1948).
Career batting
1–2–0–3–3–1.50–0–*ct* 1

Filgate, Charles Roden
Amateur. *b:* 16.10.1849, Ardee, Co Louth, Ireland. *d:* 1.9.1930, Pinner, Middlesex. Middle order right-hand batsman, fine deep field. *Sch* Cheltenham. *Team* Gloucestershire (1870–77, 15 matches).
Career batting
25–41–5–563–93–15.63–0–*ct* 18

His first-class debut was for MCC in 1869. He played much cricket in Ireland, notably for County Louth.

Fillary, Edward William Joseph
Cricketer. *b:* 14.4.1944, Heathfield, Sussex. Opening right-hand batsman, leg break and googly bowler. *Sch* St Lawrence College, Ramsgate. *Teams* Oxford U (1963–65, blue all three years); Kent (1963–66, 13 matches).
Career batting
45–83–11–1371–75–19.04–0–*ct* 24
Bowling 2163–82–26.37–5–0–6/77

Fillery, Richard
Professional. *b:* 4.2.1842, Henfield, Sussex. *d:* 22.11.1881, Henfield, Sussex. Middle order right-hand batsman, right-hand medium pace round-arm bowler. *Team* Sussex (1862–79, 102 matches).
Career batting
123–210–28–2676–105–14.70–1–*ct* 87
Bowling 6104–318–19.19–28–4–7/24

Fillingham, George Henry
Amateur. *b:* 24.8.1841, Syerston Hall, Newark, Notts. *d:* 17.1.1895, Syerston Hall, Newark, following a shooting accident. Middle order batsman, change bowler. *Sch* Harrow. *Team* Gentlemen of South (1870).
Career batting
1–1–0–0–0–0.00–0–*ct* 0

In his only first-class match he appeared for the Gentlemen of South in emergency, being in fact a prominent member of the Gentlemen of Notts CC.

Finan, Nicholas Hugh
Cricketer. *b:* 3.7.1954, Knowle, Bristol. Lower order right-hand batsman, right-arm medium pace bowler. *Team* Gloucestershire (1975–79, 8 matches).
Career batting
8–4–2–26–18–13.00–0–*ct* 1
Bowling 313–4–78.25–0–0–2/57

Finch, Henry Randolph
Amateur. *b:* 18.10.1842, Kensington, London. *d:* 6.12.1935, Oakham, Rutland. Middle order batsman. *Sch* Harrow. *Team* MCC (1864).
Career batting
2–3–1–34–19–17.00–0–*ct* 0

He did not appear in first-class matches whilst at Oxford U, but was later a notable member of the Harlequins and Free Foresters. He played non-first-class cricket for Northants. His final first-class match was for Southgate in 1866.

Fincham, Anthony Leonard Rupert
Cricketer. *b:* 19.3.1955, Lambeth, London. Lower order right-hand batsman, right-arm medium pace bowler. *Sch* Tonbridge. *Team* Oxford U (1976).
Career batting
1–1–1–3–3*–no av–0–*ct* 0
Bowling 64–5–12.80–0–0–4/42

Findlay, Francis
Amateur. *b:* 4.2.1920, Aberdeen, Scotland. *d:* 16.6.1963, Kilmarnock, Scotland. Right-hand batsman. *Team* Scotland (1948).
Career batting
2–3–0–9–6–3.00–0–*ct* 1

Findlay, Thomas Alexander
Amateur. *b:* 22.3.1918, Aberdeen, Scotland. Right-hand batsman. *Team* Scotland (1947).
Career batting
1–2–0–19–19–9.50–0–*ct* 1

Findlay, Thaddeus Michael
Cricketer. *b:* 19.10.1943, Troumaca, St Vincent. Lower order right-hand batsman, wicket-keeper. *Team* Windward Is (1964/5 to 1977/8). *Tours* West Indies to England 1969, 1976, to Australia and New Zealand 1968/9. *Tests* West Indies (1969 to 1972/3, 10 matches).
Career batting
110–170–25–2927–90–20.18–0–*ct* 209–*st* 43
Test batting
10–16–3–212–44*–16.30–0–*ct* 19–*st* 2

He appeared in two Tests on his 1969 tour of England, but in 1976 was reserve wicket-keeper to D.L.Murray and did not take part in any Tests.

Findlay, William
Amateur. *b:* 22.6.1880, Liverpool. *d:* 19.6.1953, Tenterden, Kent. Steady middle order right-hand batsman, wicket-keeper. *Sch* Eton. *Teams* Oxford U (1901–03, blue all three years); Lancashire (1902–06, 58 matches). *Tour* MCC to Argentine 1911/2.
Career batting
87–131–29–1984–81–19.45–0–*ct* 140–*st* 27
Bowling 15–0

In 1907 he was appointed Secretary to Surrey CCC; in 1919 he became Assistant Secretary to MCC and then Secretary from 1926 to 1936. In 1937 he headed the 'Findlay Commission' into the problems of County Cricket Clubs.

Findlay, William Schreiner
Amateur. *b:* 2.1.1908, South Africa. Lower order batsman, bowler. *Team* Cambridge U (1930).
Career batting
1–1–1–30–30*–no av–0–*ct* 0
Bowling 102–4–25.50–0–0–3/53

Fingleton, John Henry Webb
Amateur. *b:* 28.4.1908, Waverley, New South Wales, Australia. *d:* 22.11.1981, Killara, New

South Wales, Australia. Right-hand opening batsman, excellent close field. *Team* New South Wales (1928/9 to 1939/40, 49 matches). *Tours* Australia to South Africa 1935/6, to England 1938. *Tests* Australia (1931/2 to 1938, 18 matches).
Career batting
108–166–13–6816–167–44.54–22–*ct* 81–*st* 4
Bowling 54–2–27.00–0–0–1/6
Test batting
18–29–1–1189–136–42.46–5–*ct* 13
He only had a moderate return on his 1938 tour of England with 1,141 runs, av 38.03, and appearing in four of the five Tests he could muster only 123 runs, av 20.50.
A noted author and journalist, he wrote several major cricket books.

Finlay, Aubrey James
Amateur. *b:* 2.3.1938, Sion Mills, Co Tyrone, Ireland. Right-hand batsman. *Team* Ireland (1957–65).
Career batting
9–16–1–170–30–11.33–0–*ct* 12

Finlay, Frank Dazell
Amateur. *b:* 1868, Belfast, Ireland. *d:* 21.1.1947, Biarritz, France. Opening right-hand batsman. *Sch* UCS. *Team* MCC (1902).
Career batting
1–1–0–19–19–19.00–0–*ct* 0
He played for Northumberland

Finlay, Ian William
Cricketer. *b:* 14.5.1946, Woking, Surrey. Opening / middle order left-hand batsman, left-arm medium pace bowler, good field. *Teams* Surrey (1965–67, 23 matches); Northern Transvaal (1968/9 to 1975/6); Transvaal B (1967/8).
Career batting
43–69–5–1640–150–25.62–2–*ct* 29
Bowling 691–18–38.38–0–0–3/17

Finney, Roger John
Cricketer. *b*: 2.8.1960, Darley Dale, Derbyshire. Middle order right-hand batsman, left-arm medium pace bowler. *Team* Derbyshire (1982–83, 21 matches).
Career batting
21–36–2–617–71–18.14–0–*ct* 5
Bowling 1010–31–32.58–1–0–5/58

Finney, William
Professional. *b:* 13.8.1866, Newtown, Montgomery. *d:* 8.5.1927, Stamford, Lincs. Sound middle/lower order right-hand batsman, right-arm medium fast, later slow, bowler. *Team* Leicestershire (1894, 3 matches).
Career batting
3–5–1–29–14*–7.25–0–*ct* 0
Bowling 123–3–41.00–0–0–1/7
His County career with Leicestershire began in 1890 (pre-first-class).

Firbeck, Godfrey Christopher
Amateur. *b:* 19.6.1895, Wrington, Somerset. *d:* 8.7.1947, Kings Somborne, Hants. Lower order batsman, slow left-arm bowler. *Sch* Cheltenham. *Teams* Services (1922); Army (1927).
Career batting
2–4–2–0–0*–0.00–0–*ct* 0
Bowling 177–5–35.40–0–0–3/67

Firth, Alfred
Amateur. *b:* 1847, Dewsbury, Yorkshire. *d:* 16.1.1927, Wyke, Bradford, Yorkshire. Middle order batsman. *Team* Yorkshire (1869, 1 match).
Career batting
1–1–0–4–4–4.00–0–*ct* 0

Firth, Rev Edgar Beckwith
Amateur. *b:* 11.4.1863, Malton, Yorkshire. *d:* 25.7.1905, Matjesfontein, Cape Province, South Africa. Middle order batsman. *Team* Yorkshire (1894, 1 match).
Career batting
1–1–0–1–1–1.00–0–*ct* 0

Firth, Edward Loxley
(also known as Loxley-Firth)
Amateur. *b:* 7.3.1886, Hope, Derbyshire. *d:* 8.1.1949, Syracuse, New York, USA. Middle order batsman. *Sch* Charterhouse. *Team* Yorkshire (1912, 2 matches).
Career batting
2–4–0–43–37–10.75–0–*ct* 1

Firth, Jack
Professional. *b:* 27.6.1918, Cottingley, Yorkshire. *d:* 7.9.1981, Cottingley, Yorkshire. Lower order right-hand batsman, wicket-keeper. *Teams* Yorkshire (1949–50, 8 matches); Leicestershire (1951–58, 223 matches).
Career batting
235–340–94–3588–90*–14.58–0–*ct* 373–*st* 95
He played football for York City.

Firth, Canon John D'Ewes Evelyn
Amateur. *b:* 21.2.1900, Nottingham. *d:* 21.9.1957, Winchester. Lower order right-hand batsman, leg break bowler. *Sch* Winchester. *Teams* Oxford U (1919–20); Nottinghamshire (1919, 2 matches).
Career batting
4–4–1–22–19*–7.33–0–*ct* 2
Bowling 248–8–31.00–0–0–2/22

Fisher, Charles Dennis
Amateur. *b:* 19.6.1877, Blatchington Court, Sussex. *d:* 31.5.1916, aboard HMS *Invincible* at Jutland. Steady middle order right-hand batsman, right-arm medium pace off break bowler. *Sch* Westminster. *Teams* Oxford U (1899–1900, blue 1900); Sussex (1898–1903, 15 matches).
Career batting
21–33–1–429–80–13.40–0–*ct* 7
Bowling 242–8–30.25–0–0–2/8

Fisher, Horace
Professional. *b:* 3.8.1903, Pontefract, Yorkshire. *d:* 16.4.1974, Overton, Wakefield, Yorkshire. Lower order left-hand batsman, slow left-arm bowler. *Team* Yorkshire (1928–36, 52 matches). *Tour* Yorkshire to Jamaica 1935/6.
Career batting
52–58–14–681–76*–15.47–0–*ct* 22
Bowling 2621–93–28.18–2–0–6/11

For Yorkshire v Somerset at Bramall Lane in 1932 he performed the hat trick by dismissing all three batsmen lbw.

Fisher, John
Professional. *b:* 4.8.1897, Hodthorpe, Derbyshire. *d:* 22.6.1954, Castleford, Yorkshire. Middle/lower order left-hand batsman, right-arm medium pace bowler. *Team* Derbyshire (1921–22, 3 matches).
Career batting
3–6–1–52–39*–10.40–0–*ct* 0
Bowling 15–0

He was a noted soccer player with Chesterfield, Burnley, Lincoln City and Mansfield.

Fisher, Paul Bernard
Cricketer. *b:* 19.12.1954, Edmonton, Middlesex. Lower order right-hand batsman, wicket-keeper. *Teams* Oxford U (1974–78, blue 1975–78); Middlesex (1979, 2 matches); Worcestershire (1980–81, 14 matches).
Career batting
57–85–14–654–42–9.21–0–*ct* 92–*st* 11

Fisher, Reginald Wordsworth Cecil
Amateur. *b:* 17.4.1872, Grantham, Lincs. *d:* 31.12.1939, Hemel Hempstead, Herts. Middle order right-hand batsman, change bowler, good point. *Sch* Haileybury. *Team* Hampshire (1898, 1 match).
Career batting
1–1–0–3–3–3.00–0–*ct* 0

Fishlock, Laurence Barnard
Professional. *b:* 2.1.1907, Battersea, South London. Opening left-hand batsman, slow left-arm bowler. *Team* Surrey (1931–52, 347 matches). *Tours* MCC to Australia and New Zealand 1936/7, 1946/7; Commonwealth to India, and Ceylon 1950/1. *Tests* England (1936 to 1946/7, 4 matches).
Career batting
417–699–54–25376–253–39.34–56–*ct* 216
Bowling 504–11–45.81–0–0–4/62
Test batting
4–5–1–47–19*–11.75–0–*ct* 1

He hit 1,000 runs in a season 12 times plus once overseas and went on to exceed 2,000 runs in six seasons (best 2426, av 45.77, in 1949). Both his double centuries were for Surrey, the higher being 253 v Leics at Leicester in 1948.

A noted soccer player he appeared for Crystal Palace, Millwall, Aldershot, Southampton and Gillingham as a forward, and he also obtained an amateur international cap for England.

Fishwick, Tom Silvester
Amateur. *b:* 24.7.1876, Stone, Staffs. *d:* 21.2.1950, Sandown, IOW. Middle order right-hand batsman, brilliant slip field. *Sch* Wellingborough. *Teams* Warwickshire (1896–1909, 206 matches); London County (1901).
Career batting
210–349–13–8833–140*–26.28–13–*ct* 231–*st* 2
Bowling 35–0

He hit 1,000 runs in a season twice (best 1440, av 32.00, in 1905). He appeared for Staffordshire 1892 to 1894.

Fisk, Eric
Amateur. *b:* 27.3.1931, East Ardsley, Yorkshire. Lower order left-hand batsman, slow left-arm bowler. *Team* Combined Services (1950–51).
Career batting
3–5–0–37–16–7.40–0–*ct* 1
Bowling 123–2–61.50–0–0–1/19

He appeared for Yorks 2nd XI.

Fitton, Thomas Edmond John
Amateur. *b:* 16.8.1911, Killarney, Co Kerry, Ireland. Lower order right-hand batsman, right-arm medium fast bowler. *Sch* Trent. *Team* Oxford U (1932).
Career batting
1–2–2–7–4*–no av–0–*ct* 0
Bowling 76–2–38.00–0–0–2/76

Fitzgerald, Alfred William
Amateur. *b:* 1849, Shalstone, Bucks. *d:* 30.7.1871, Shalstone, Bucks. Brother of R.A.(Middlesex) and M.N.R.P.(Sussex). Middle order batsman. *Sch* Eton. *Team* MCC (1868).
Career batting
1–2–0–3–3–1.50–0–*ct* 0

His County cricket was for Buckinghamshire.

Fitzgerald, Francis John
Amateur. *b:* 4.7.1864, Australia. *d:* 24.2.1939, Chelsea, London. Brother of P.D. (MCC). Lower order batsman, useful bowler. *Sch* Oscott College. *Team* MCC (1890).
Career batting
1–2–0–3–3–1.50–0–ct0
Bowling 15–0

Fitzgerald, James Francis
Cricketer. *b:* 28.11.1946, Sutton Coldfield, Warwickshire. Tail end right-hand batsman, slow left-arm bowler. *Team* Cambridge U (1966–68, blue 1968).
Career batting
15–24–11–147–27*–11.30–0–*ct* 4
Bowling 894–29–30.82–1–0–6/70

Fitzgerald, Maurice Noel Ryder Purcell
Amateur. *b:* 22.12.1835, Torquay, Devon. *d:* 17.12.1877, Boulge Hall, Woodbridge, Suffolk. Brother of A.W. (MCC) and R.A. (Middlesex). Steady opening right-hand batsman. *Sch* Brighton. *Team* Sussex (1864, 1 match).
Career batting
2–2–0–8–8–4.00–0–*ct* 1
His final first-class match was for MCC in 1866.
He also played for Suffolk.

Fitzgerald, Brig Gen Percy Desmond
Amateur. *b:* 18.4.1875, Australia. *d:* 17.8.1933, Marylebone, London. Brother of F. J. (MCC). Middle order batsman. *Sch* Oscott College. *Team* MCC (1897).
Career batting
1–2–0–5–4–2.50–0–*ct* 0

Fitzgerald, Robert Allan
Amateur. *b:* 1.10.1834, Purley, Berkshire. *d:* 28.10.1881, Chorley Wood, Herts. Brother of A.W. (MCC) and M.N.R.P. (Sussex). Middle order right-hand batsman, right-hand fast round-arm bowler. *Sch* Harrow. *Teams* Cambridge U (1854–56, blue 1854 and 1856); Middlesex (1864, 1 match). *Tour* Fitzgerald to North America 1872 (not first-class).
Career batting
46–79–7–1123–91*–15.59–0–*ct* 34
Bowling 112–4+3–28.00–0–0–3/23
He was Honorary Secretary of MCC 1863–76.
His final first-class match was for MCC in 1874. He also played for Berkshire, Buckinghamshire and Hertfordshire.

Fitzherbert, Edward Herbert
Amateur. *b:* 3.12.1885, Poona, India. *d:* 1.8.1979, Wandsworth, London. Middle order batsman. *Sch* Rossall. *Team* Army (1923).
Career batting
1–2–0–3–3–1.50–0–*ct* 0

Fitzmaurice, Desmond Michael John
Amateur. *b:* 16.10.1917, Carlton, Victoria, Australia. *d:* 19.1.1981, Prahan, Victoria, Australia. Brother of D.J.A.(Victoria). Lower order right-hand batsman, right-arm fast medium bowler. *Team* Victoria (1947/8, 2 matches). *Tour* Commonwealth to India Pakistan and Ceylon 1949/50.
Career batting
17–18–2–272–45–17.00–0–*ct* 3
Bowling 798–28–28.50–0–0–3/29
His final first-class match, and only one in England, was for a Commonwealth XI in 1950.

Fitzroy, Hon John Maurice
(later Fitzroy-Newdegate)
Amateur. *b:* 20.3.1897, Chelsea, London. *d:* 7.5.1976, Nuneaton. Hard hitting middle order right-hand batsman, slip field. *Sch* Eton. *Team* Northants (1925–27, 56 matches).
Career batting
56–101–6–1373–50–14.45–0–*ct* 47
Bowling 82–6–13.66–0–0–4/14
He captained Northants 1925 to 1927 – an injury in the latter season ending his first-class cricket.

Flaherty, Kevin Frederick
Cricketer. *b:* 17.9.1939, Birmingham. Tail end right-hand batsman, off break bowler. *Team* Warwickshire (1969, 1 match).
Career batting
1 match, did not bat–*ct* 0
Bowling 107–4–26.75–0–0–3/38

Flamson, William Henry
Professional. *b:* 12.8.1904, Heather, Leicestershire. *d:* 9.1.1945, Heather, Leicestershire. Tail end right-hand batsman, right-arm medium fast bowler. *Team* Leicestershire (1934–39, 49 matches).
Career batting
49–67–20–351–50*–7.46–0–*ct* 24
Bowling 4971–151–32.92–7–0–7/46

Flanagan, John Patrick Douglas
Cricketer. *b:* 20.9.1947, Johannesburg, South Africa. Middle/lower order right-hand batsman, right-arm medium pace bowler. *Team* Transvaal (1965/6 to 1977/8). *Tour* SA Universities to England 1967.

Career batting
57–91–15–1835–98–24.14–0–*ct* 48
Bowling 3191–116–27.50–3–1–8/113

Flanagan, Michael
Professional. *b:* 15.3.1842, Glen Colombkill, Co Clare, Ireland. *d:* 14.1.1890, London. Tail end right-hand batsman, right-hand fast round arm bowler, slip field. *Team* Middlesex (1873–78, 15 matches).
Career batting
18–32–9–100–14–4.34–0–*ct* 7
Bowling 1094–68–16.08–3–1–9/78

His best bowling was 9/78 for MCC v Surrey at Lord's in 1876.

Flavell, John Alfred
Professional. *b:* 15.5.1929, Wall Heath, Staffs. Tail end left-hand batsman, right-arm fast medium bowler. *Team* Worcestershire (1949–67, 392 matches). *Tours* Worcs World Tour 1964/5, to Jamaica 1965/6. *Tests* England (1961–64, 4 matches).
Career batting
401–453–141–2032–54–6.51–0–*ct* 128
Bowling 32847–1529–21.48–86–15–9/30
Test batting
4–6–2–31–14–7.75–0–*ct* 0
Bowling 367–7–52.42–0–0–2/65

He took 100 wickets in a season eight times (best 171, av 17.79, in 1961). His best bowling was 9/30 for Worcs. v Kent at Dover in 1955. In 1963 he had the unusual distinction of dismissing three batsmen lbw with successive deliveries – Worcs v Lancs at Old Trafford. He played football for Walsall.

Flaxington, Samuel
Professional. *b:* 14.10.1860, Otley, Yorkshire. *d:* 10.3.1895, Otley, Yorkshire. Middle order right-hand batsman, good field. *Team* Yorkshire (1882, 4 matches).
Career batting
4–8–0–121–57–15.12–0–*ct* 1

Fleetwood-Smith, Leslie O'Brien
Amateur. *b:* 30.3.1910, Stawell, Victoria, Australia. *d:* 16.3.1971, Fitzroy, Victoria, Australia. Lower order right-hand batsman, slow left-arm bowler with chinamen. *Team* Victoria (1931/2 to 1939/40, 51 matches). *Tours* Australia to England 1934, 1938, to South Africa 1935/6. *Tests* Australia (1935/6 to 1938, 10 matches).
Career batting
112–117–33–617–63–7.34–0–*ct* 42
Bowling 13519–597–22.64–57–18–9/36
Test batting
10–11–5–54–16*–9.00–0–*ct* 0
Bowling 1570–42–37.38–2–1–6/110

Due to his very moderate batting and fielding, Fleetwood-Smith did not appear in any of the Tests on his 1934 visit to England, but his bowling was most successful – 106 wkts, av 19.20 – and he was second to O'Reilly in the averages. He returned similar figures in 1938, but appeared in four Tests, when unfortunately his uncertain length and direction counter-balanced his well concealed spin. His best bowling was 9/36 for Victoria v Tasmania at Melbourne in 1932/3.

Fleming, Charles Barnett
Amateur. *b:* 28.2.1887, Derby. *d:* 22.9.1918, Grevillers, France. Middle order right-hand batsman. *Team* Derbyshire (1907, 1 match).
Career batting
1–2–0–5–3–2.50–0–*ct* 0

Fleming, F.E.
Amateur. *Team* London County (1901).
Career batting
1–2–0–10–5–5.00–0–*ct* 0

Fleming, Ian Douglas Keith
Amateur. *b:* 21.8.1908, Georgetown, British Guiana. Middle order right-hand batsman, right-arm medium pace bowler. *Sch* Winchester. *Team* Kent (1934, 3 matches).
Career batting
5–8–2–183–66–30.50–0–*ct* 5

His last first-class match was for Leveson-Gower's XI in 1935.

Fleming, James Millar
Amateur. *b:* 5.9.1901, Philpstoun, West Lothian, Scotland. *d:* 4.9.1962, Murrayfield, Edinburgh, Scotland. Right-hand batsman, wicket-keeper. *Team* Scotland (1926).
Career batting
1–1–1–51–51*–no av–0–*ct* 4–*st* 1

Fleming, Robert Christopher John
Cricketer. *b:* 20.7.1953, Woking, Surrey. Lower order right-hand batsman, off break bowler. *Team* Cambridge U (1974).
Career batting
9–15–7–60–13*–7.50–0–*ct* 5
Bowling 522–7–74.57–0–0–3/91

Fletcher, Barry Elyston
Professional. *b:* 7.3.1935, Birmingham. Middle order left-hand batsman, right-arm medium pace bowler, fine field. *Team* Warwickshire (1956–61, 49 matches).
Career batting
49–79–13–1511–102*–22.89–1–*ct* 39
Bowling 13–0

He was a Welsh badminton International

Fletcher, Christopher David Bryan
Cricketer. *b:* 10.12.1957, Harrogate, Yorkshire. Lower order left-hand batsman, right-arm fast medium bowler. *Team* Sussex (1979, 1 match).
Career batting
1 match, did not bat–*ct* 0
Bowling 51–1–51.00–0–0–1/35

Fletcher, Duncan Andrew Gwynne
Cricketer. *b:* 27.9.1948, Salisbury, Rhodesia. Brother of A. W. R. (Rhodesia) Middle order left-hand batsman, right-arm fast-medium bowler. *Team* Rhodesia/Zimbabwe (1969/70 to 1982/3). *Tour* Zimbabwe to England 1982.
Career batting
102–181–21–3745–89–23.40–0–*ct* 70
Bowling 5793–211–27.45–5–1–6/31
He captained the Zimbabwe team in the 1982 tour and the 1983 World Cup. In 1977 he appeared for Cambridgeshire.

Fletcher, David George William
Professional. *b:* 6.7.1924, Sutton, Surrey. Stylish opening right-hand batsman, right-arm fast bowler. *Team* Surrey (1946–61, 300 matches). *Tours* Commonwealth to India 1953/4; Surrey to Rhodesia 1959/60.
Career batting
316–519–41–14461–194–30.25–22–*ct* 178
Bowling 0–0
He hit 1,000 runs in a season four times (best 1,960, av 37.69 in 1952). Illness and injury reduced his chances of further honours in the game.

Fletcher, Geoffrey Everingham
Amateur. *b:* 20.7.1919, Godalming, Surrey. *d:* 27.3.1943, near El Hamma, Tunisia. Middle order right-hand batsman. *Sch* Marlborough. *Teams* Oxford U (1939); Somerset (1939, 1 match).
Career batting
5–10–1–165–65–18.33–0–*ct* 4
Bowling 15–0

Fletcher, Henry
Professional. *b:* 25.7.1882, Clay Cross, Derbyshire. *d:* 27.10.1937, Chaddesden, Derby. Middle order batsman. *Team* Derbyshire (1907–08, 5 matches).
Career batting
5–10–2–17–4–2.12–0–*ct* 2

Fletcher, Keith William Robert
Professional. *b:* 20.5.1944, Worcester. Sound middle order right-hand batsman, leg break bowler, good slip field. *Team* Essex (1962–83, 470 matches). *Tours* MCC to Pakistan 1966/7, to Ceylon and Pakistan 1968/9, to Ceylon 1969/70, to Australia and New Zealand 1970/1, to India, Pakistan and Sri Lanka 1972/3, to West Indies 1973/4, to Australia and New Zealand 1974/5, to India, Sri Lanka and Australia 1976/7, to India and Sri Lanka 1981/2; Cavaliers to West Indies 1964/5; International XI to India, Pakistan and Ceylon 1967/8. *Tests* England (1968 to 1981/2, 59 matches).
Career batting
626–1025–146–33957–228*–38.63–59–*ct* 564
Bowling 2224–50–44.48–1–0–5/41
Test batting
59–96–14–3272–216–39.90–7–*ct* 54
Bowling 193–2–96.50–0–0–1/6
He hit 1,000 runs in a season 19 times (best 1,890, av 41.08, in 1968). He scored two double centuries, 228* for Essex v Sussex at Hastings in 1968 and 216 for England v New Zealand at Auckland 1974/5. He captained Essex from 1974 to 1983 and England in seven Tests including the tour to India and Sri Lanka in 1981/2.

Fletcher, Stuart David
Cricketer. *b:* 8.6.1964, Keighley, Yorkshire. Lower order right-hand batsman, right-arm medium pace bowler. *Team* Yorkshire (1983, 3 matches).
Career batting
3–4–2–14–12–7.00–0–*ct* 0
Bowling 186–8–23.25–0–0–4/71

Fletcher, Thomas
Amateur. *b:* 15.6.1881, Heanor, Derbyshire. *d:* 29.9.1954, Derby. Middle order right-hand batsman, right-arm medium pace bowler. *Team* Derbyshire (1906, 1 match).
Career batting
1–1–0–28–28–28.00–0–*ct* 0
Bowling 3–0
A noted amateur soccer player, he appeared for Derby County and Leicester Fosse.

Fletcher, William
Professional. *b:* 16.2.1866, Leeds, Yorkshire. *d:* 1.6.1935, Knaresborough, Yorkshire. Middle or lower order right-hand batsman, right-arm fast bowler. *Teams* Yorkshire (1891–92, 6 matches).
Career batting
6–10–2–100–31*–12.50–0–*ct* 7
Bowling 222–9–24.66–0–0–4/45

Flick, Barry John
Cricketer. *b:* 5.3.1952, Coventry, Warwickshire. Tail end right-hand batsman, wicket-keeper. *Team* Warwickshire (1969–73, 16 matches).
Career batting
16–14–8–46–18–7.66–0–*ct* 17–*st* 4

Flint, Benjamin
Professional. *b:* 12.1.1893, Underwood, Notts. *d:* 20.7.1959, Nottingham. Brother of W.A. (Notts), father of Derrick (Warwickshire). Lower order right-hand batsman, right-arm fast bowler. *Team* Nottinghamshire (1919–20, 13 matches).
Career batting
13–13–4–81–36–9.00–0–*ct* 5
Bowling 564–19–29.68–0–0–3/28

Flint, Derrick
Professional. *b:* 14.6.1924, Creswell, Derbyshire. Son of Benjamin (Notts), nephew of W.A. (Notts), husband of Rachael Heyhoe Flint (England Women). Tail end right-hand batsman, leg break and googly bowler. *Team* Warwickshire (1948–49, 10 matches).
Career batting
10–10–3–33–11–4.71–0–*ct* 5
Bowling 465–12–38.75–0–0–4/67

Flint, Joseph
Professional. *b:* 23.4.1840, Wirksworth, Derbyshire. *d:* 2.11.1912, Wirksworth, Derbyshire. Lower order right-hand batsman, right-hand slow round arm bowler, good slip. *Team* Derbyshire (1872–79, 14 matches).
Career batting
14–24–3–143–24–6.80–0–*ct* 11
Bowling 601–44–13.65–2–0–6/28

His most famous bowling feat was to take 6 wickets for 7, when Derbyshire dismissed Notts for 14 (not first-class).

Flint, Louis Edward
Amateur. *b:* 10.1.1895, Ripley, Derbyshire. *d:* 3.4.1958, Sutton-in-Ashfield, Notts. Lower order left-hand batsman, right-arm fast medium bowler. *Team* Derbyshire (1919–20, 7 matches).
Career batting
7–11–0–100–35–9.09–0–*ct* 1
Bowling 291–8–36.37–0–0–3/30

Flint, William Arthur
Professional. *b:* 21.3.1890, Underwood, Notts. *d:* 5.2.1955, West Bridgford, Nottingham. Brother of Benjamin (Notts), uncle of Derrick (Warwickshire) Middle order right-hand batsman, right-arm medium pace bowler. *Team* Nottinghamshire (1919–29, 145 matches).
Career batting
145–195–22–3345–103–19.33–1–*ct* 77
Bowling 6665–236–29.51–6–1–6/23

A well-known soccer player, he appeared for Notts County as a half-back from 1908 to 1926.

Flockton, Raymond George
Amateur. *b:* 14.3.1930, Paddington, New South Wales, Australia. Middle order right-hand batsman, right-arm medium pace bowler. *Team* New South Wales (1951/2 to 1962/3, 34 matches).
Career batting
35–50–9–1695–264*–41.34–2–*ct* 11
Bowling 1027–27–38.03–0–0–4/33

His only first-class match in England was for a Commonwealth XI in 1956. His highest score was 264* for NSW v South Australia at Sydney in 1959/60.

Flood, Dr John Wellesley
Amateur. *b:* 22.4.1884, Australia. *d:* 1934, Rabaul, New Guinea, Australasia. Right-hand batsman, right-arm fast medium bowler. *Sch* Rossall. *Team* Ireland (1909).
Career batting
1–2–0–25–16–12.50–0–*ct* 0
Bowling 27–0

Flood, Raymond David
Professional. *b:* 20.11.1935, Southampton. Middle order right-hand batsman, off break bowler. *Team* Hampshire (1956–60, 24 matches).
Career batting
24–43–5–885–138*–23.28–1–*ct* 10
Bowling 9–0

Flower, Russell William
Cricketer. *b:* 6.11.1942, Stone, Staffs. Tail end left-hand batsman, slow left-arm bowler. *Team* Warwickshire (1978, 9 matches).
Career batting
9–8–4–23–10*–5.75–0–*ct* 0
Bowling 554–10–55.40–0–0–3/45

He appeared for Staffordshire commencing 1964.

Flowers, John
Amateur. *b:* 1882, Steyning, Sussex. *d:* 8.5.1968, Brighton, Sussex. Lower order batsman, bowler. *Team* Sussex (1905, 2 matches).
Career batting
2–3–0–9–5–3.00–0–*ct* 0
Bowling 59–0

Flowers, Thomas
Professional. *b:* 25.10.1868, Daybrook, Notts. *d:* 26.3.1939, Daybrook, Notts. Cousin of Wilfred (Notts). Lower order right-hand batsman, right-arm slow medium bowler. *Team* Nottinghamshire (1894, 1 match).
Career batting
1–2–0–16–11–8.00–0–*ct* 0
Bowling 10–0

Flowers, Wilfred
Professional. *b:* 7.12.1856, Calverton, Notts. *d:* 1.11.1926, Carlton, Nottingham. Cousin of Thomas (Notts). Middle order right-hand

batsman, right-arm off break bowler, good deep field. *Team* Nottinghamshire (1877–96, 281 matches). *Tours* Lillywhite, Shaw and Shrewsbury to Australia 1884/5, 1886/7. *Tests* England (1884/5 to 1893, 8 matches).
Career batting
442–696–54–12891–173–20.07–9–*ct* 223
Bowling 18887–1188–15.89–73–17–8/22
Test batting
8–14–0–254–56–18.14–0–*ct* 3
Bowling 296–14–21.14–1–0–5/46

He hit 1,000 runs in a season twice and took 100 wickets in a season twice, his best year with both bat and ball being 1883 when he achieved the 'double': 1,144 runs (av 24.86) and 113 wickets (av 15.03).

He stood as an umpire in first-class matches after retiring from County cricket.

Flynn, Vincent Anthony
Cricketer. *b:* 3.10.1955, Aylesbury, Bucks. Lower order right-hand batsman, wicket-keeper. *Team* Northants (1976–78, 3 matches).
Career batting
3–2–1–21–15–21.00–0–*ct* 4

He also played for Buckinghamshire.

Foat, James Clive
Cricketer. *b:* 21.11.1952, Salford Priors, Warwickshire. Middle order right-hand batsman, right-arm medium pace bowler, brilliant field. *Sch* Millfield *Team* Gloucestershire (1972–79, 91 matches).
Career batting
91–150–15–2512–126–18.60–5–*ct* 39
Bowling 40–0

Foley, Cyril Pelham
Amateur. *b:* 1.11.1868, London. *d:* 9.3.1936, Witchampton, Dorset. Defensive opening right-hand batsman, slow right-arm bowler, deep field. *Sch* Eton. *Teams* Cambridge U (1889–91, blue all three years); Middlesex (1893–1906, 57 matches). *Tour* Brackley to West Indies 1904/5.
Career batting
123–207–16–3175–117–16.62–2–*ct* 43
Bowling 26–1–26.00–0–0–1/14

He took part in the Jameson Raid of 1895 and later fought in both the Boer War and First World War.

His debut in first-class matches was for MCC in 1888, in which year he also appeared in non-first-class cricket for Worcestershire.

Foley, Charles Windham
Amateur. *b:* 26.8.1856, Wadhurst, Sussex. *d:* 20.11.1933, Kensington, London. Lower order bat – originally left hand, but 'foolishly' changed to right. Wicket-keeper. *Sch* Eton. *Team* Cambridge U (1880, blue).
Career batting
7–11–0–51–12–4.63–0–*ct* 7–*st* 12

He was awarded his soccer blue, playing against Oxford in 1880. His last first-class match was for MCC in 1891.

Foley, Edward Francis Walwyn
Amateur. *b:* 6.10.1851, Derby. *d:* 21.10.1923, Kensington, London. Right-hand batsman. *Sch* Repton. *Team* Derbyshire (1871, 1 match).
Career batting
1–2–0–0–0–0.00–0–*ct* 1

He did not appear in first-class matches whilst at Oxford U.

Foley, Henry Thomas Hamilton
Amateur. *b:* 25.4.1905, Hereford. *d:* 13.12.1959, Stoke Edith, Hereford. Middle order left-hand batsman. *Sch* Eton. *Team* Worcestershire (1925, 1 match).
Career batting
1–2–1–6–6–6.00–0–*ct* 0

He also played for Monmouthshire.

Foley, Dr James Henry
Amateur. *b:* 1.11.1898, Macroom, Co Cork, Ireland. *d:* 30.3.1969, Cork, Ireland. Right-hand batsman. *Team* Ireland (1926).
Career batting
1–2–0–26–16–13.00–0–*ct* 0
Bowling 54–0

Foley, Paul Henry
Amateur. *b:* 19.3.1857, London. *d:* 21.1.1928, Westminster, London. Middle order left-hand batsman, right-hand slow underarm bowler. *Sch* Eton. *Team* MCC (1891).
Career batting
1–2–0–21–13–10.50–0–*ct* 0

He played for Worcestershire (pre-first-class) commencing 1878 and was Honorary Secretary to the County Club until 1908.

Foljambe, Edward Walter Savile
Amateur. *b:* 19.9.1890, Southwell, Notts. *d:* 22.8.1960, Sheffield, Yorkshire. Son of G. S. (Notts). Opening/middle order batsman. *Sch* Eton. *Team* Oxford U (1912).
Career batting
3–6–1–91–38–18.20–0–*ct* 1

Foljambe, Godfrey Acheson Thornhagh
Amateur. *b:* 21.10.1869, London. *d:* 16.3.1942, The Lizard, Cornwall. Lower order batsman, left-arm medium pace bowler. *Sch* Eton. *Team* MCC (1892–93). *Tour* Hawke to India 1892/3.

Career batting
5–8–0–97–34–12.12–0–*ct* 2
Bowling 145–9–16.11–0–0–4/32

He appeared in the Cambridge Seniors' Match of 1892, but no first-class matches for the University.

He also played for Cambridgeshire.

Foljambe, George Savile
Amateur. *b:* 10.10.1856, Osberton, Notts. *d:* 13.9.1920, Kensington, London. Father of E.W.S. (Oxford U). Middle order right-hand batsman, left-arm medium pace bowler. *Sch* Eton. *Team* Nottinghamshire (1879–81, 7 matches).
Career batting
24–38–2–297–99–8.25–0–*ct* 12

He did not appear in first-class cricket whilst at Oxford U. His last first-class match was for MCC in 1882.

Folkes, Castell
Cricketer. *b:* 29.7.1944, Jamaica. Tail end right-hand batsman, right-arm fast-medium bowler. *Team* Jamaica (1967/8 to 1970/1). *Tour* Jamaica to England 1970.
Career batting
13–9–1–36–9–4.50–0–*ct* 1
Bowling 745–25–29.80–2–0–5/22

He bowled well on his single tour to England.

Follett, Edward Charles
Amateur. *b:* 16.2.1842. *d:* 6.6.1869, Birmingham. Middle order right-hand batsman, slow round-arm bowler. *Sch* Eton. *Team* MCC (1868).
Career batting
1–2–0–3–3–1.50–0–*ct* 0

He was at Oxford U, but not in the eleven.

He played for Berkshire.

Folley, Ian
Cricketer. *b*: 9.1.1963, Burnley, Lancashire. Lower order right-hand batsman, left-arm medium pace bowler. *Team* Lancashire (1982–83, 29 matches).
Career batting
29–24–8–256–36–16.00–0–*ct* 6
Bowling 1280–34–37.64–0–0–4/40

Foord, Charles William
Professional. *b:* 11.6.1924, Scarborough, Yorkshire. Lower order right-hand batsman, right-arm fast medium bowler. *Team* Yorkshire (1947–53, 51 matches).
Career batting
52–36–16–125–35–6.25–0–*ct* 19
Bowling 3469–128–27.10–5–0–6/63

Foord, E.
Amateur. *Team* W.G. Grace's XI (1871).
Career batting
1–1–0–0–0–0.00–0–*ct* 0

Foord played in emergency for Grace's XI against his own county, Kent.

Foord-Kelcey, John
(changed name from Foord in May 1872)
Amateur. *b:* 1860, Smeeth, Ashford, Kent. *d:* 10.1.1931, Gloucester. Brother of William (Kent). Middle order right-hand batsman, useful bowler. *Sch* Chatham House, Ramsgate. *Team* Oxford U (1883).
Career batting
2–3–0–36–23–12.00–0–*ct* 0
Bowling 125–11–11.36–1–0–6/58

Foord-Kelcey, William
(changed name from Foord in May 1872)
Amateur. *b:* 21.4.1854, Smeeth, Ashford, Kent. *d:* 3.1.1922, Woolwich, Kent. Brother of John (Oxford U). Middle order right-hand batsman, right-hand fast round-arm bowler, good field. *Sch* Chatham House, Ramsgate. *Team* Oxford U (1874–75, blue both years); Kent (1874–83, 64 matches).
Career batting
78–135–9–1790–105–14.20–1–*ct* 66
Bowling 4828–274–17.62–19–7–8/49

Forbes, Carlton
Professional. *b:* 9.8.1936, Cross Roads, Kingston, Jamaica. Lower order left-hand batsman, left-arm medium pace bowler. *Team* Nottinghamshire (1959–73, 244 matches).
Career batting
245–319–69–3597–86–14.38–0–*ct* 145
Bowling 17993–707–25.44–23–2–7/19

He hit 1,000 runs in a season once : 1,020 (av 20.40) in 1961 and took 100 wickets in a season three times (best 117, av 19.64, in 1965).

Forbes, Dudley Henry
Amateur. *b:* 13.1.1873, Callander, Perthshire, Scotland. *d:* 21.4.1901, Kronstad, South Africa, of enteric fever. Lower order right-hand batsman, right-arm fast bowler. *Sch* Eton. *Team* Oxford U (1894–95, blue 1894).
Career batting
12–21–3–83–25*–5.18–0–*ct* 9
Bowling 1121–44–25.47–3–0–6/86

His last first-class match was for Oxford U, Past and Present, in 1899.

Forbes, George Thomson
Amateur. *b:* 25.11.1906, Aberdeen, Scotland.

Right-hand batsman, right-arm fast medium bowler. *Team* Scotland (1936–38).
Career batting
4–8–0–122–29–15.25–0–*ct* 3
Bowling 173–11–15.72–0–0–3/25

Forbes, Walter Francis
Amateur. *b:* 20.1.1858, Malvern Link, Worcs. *d:* 29.3.1933, Marylebone, London. Middle order right-hand batsman, right-hand fast round-arm bowler, good deep field. *Sch* Eton. *Teams* I Zingari (1878); Gentlemen (1877–84).
Career batting
11–18–0–382–80–21.22–0–*ct* 6
Bowling 679–31–21.90–2–0–6/32
He did not appear in first-class County cricket, most of his matches being for Yorkshire Gentlemen and I Zingari. In 1876 he threw the cricket ball 132 yards, though only 18 years old.

Forbes-Adam, Eric Graham
Amateur. *b:* 3.10.1888, Bombay, India. *d:* 7.7.1925, Constantinople, Turkey. Middle order batsman. *Sch* Eton. *Team* Cambridge U (1911).
Career batting
1–2–0–27–17–13.50–0–*ct* 1
He was First Secretary at the British Embassy in Constantinople at the time of his death.

Ford, Alexander Clark
Amateur. *b:* 8.11.1900, Uddingston, Lanarkshire, Scotland. Father of J. M. C. (Scotland). Right-hand batsman, right-arm medium pace bowler. *Team* Scotland (1924–25).
Career batting
2–3–0–18–17–6.00–0–*ct* 0
Bowling 78–1–78.00–0–0–1.64

Ford, Augustus Frank Justice
Amateur. *b:* 12.9.1858, Sussex Square, London. *d:* 20.5.1931, Marylebone, London. Brother of F. G. J. (Middlesex) and W. J. (Middlesex), uncle of N. M. (Derbyshire, Oxford U and Middlesex). Lower order right-hand batsman, right-hand medium pace round-arm bowler, good field. *Sch* Repton. *Teams* Cambridge U (1878–81, blue all four years); Middlesex (1879–82, 18 matches).
Career batting
51–77–8–984–102–14.49–1–*ct* 58
Bowling 2484–153–16.23–9–2–7/32
His final first-class match was for Cambridge U, Past and Present, in 1886. He was a noted billiards player, and represented Cambridge.

Ford, Charles Richard
Professional. *b:* 8.8.1838, Bungay, Suffolk. Middle/lower order right-hand batsman, right-hand medium pace round-arm bowler, slip field. *Team* England (1874).
Career batting
1–2–0–7–5–3.50–0–*ct* 0
He appeared for Staffordshire.
A noted coach and umpire, he was engaged at Cambridge U for at least 15 years, commencing 1865.

Ford, Cecil W.
Amateur. *b:* 1913, Watford, Herts. Middle order right-hand batsman, right-arm medium fast bowler. *Team* Minor Counties (1936).
Career batting
1–2–0–5–3–2.50–0–*ct* 1
Bowling 31–0
His County cricket was for Hertfordshire and Devonshire.

Ford, Ernest Claudius Bramhall
Amateur. *b:* 23.7.1855, Cheltenham, Gloucs. *d:* 19.6.1900, Southend, Essex. Middle/lower order right-hand batsman, wicket-keeper. *Sch* Clifton. *Team* Gloucestershire (1874–75, 6 matches).
Career batting
6–9–2–75–32*–10.71–0–*ct* 3–*st* 1

Ford, Edgar Samuel
Amateur. *b:* 1876, Bradford-on-Avon, Wilts. *d:* 1943, Isle of Wight. Lower order batsman, wicket-keeper. *Team* London County (1902, 1 match).
Career batting
1–1–1–0–0*–no av–0–*ct* 0–*st* 1
His County cricket was for Wiltshire.

Ford, Francis Gilbertson Justice
Amateur. *b:* 14.12.1866, Paddington, London. *d:* 7.2.1940, Burwash, Sussex. Brother of A. F. J. (Middlesex) and W. J. (Middlesex), uncle of N. M. (Derbyshire, Oxford U and Middlesex). Attractive middle order left-hand batsman, slow left-arm bowler, slip field. *Sch* Repton. *Teams* Middlesex (1886–99, 102 matches); Cambridge U (1887–90, blue all four years). *Tour* Stoddart to Australia 1894/5. *Tests* England (1894/5, 5 matches).
Career batting
168–289–17–7359–191–27.05–14–*ct* 131
Bowling 4757–200–23.78–8–1–7/65
Test batting
5–9–0–168–48–18.66–0–*ct* 5
Bowling 129–1–129.00–0–0–1/47
His final first-class match was for an England XII in 1908. He hit 1,000 runs in a season twice (best 1,195, av 28.45, in 1899). A noted goal-keeper, he was awarded his blue at Cambridge.

Ford, John Kenneth
Professional. *b:* 5.3.1934, Redland, Bristol. Tail end right-hand batsman, right-arm fast bowler. *Team* Gloucestershire (1951, 1 match).
Career batting
1–1–0–0–0–0.00–0–*ct* 0
Bowling 44–1–44.00–0–0–1/44

Ford, James Malcolm Clark
Amateur. *b:* 29.12.1936, Edinburgh, Scotland. Son of A. C. (Scotland). Left-hand batsman. *Team* Scotland (1960–66).
Career batting
10–17–4–235–50–18.07–0–*ct* 7

Ford, Neville Montague
Amateur. *b:* 18.11.1906, Repton, Debyshire. Nephew of A. F. J. (Middlesex), F. G. J. (Middlesex) and W. J. (Middlesex). Middle order right-hand batsman. *Sch* Harrow. *Teams* Derbyshire (1926–34, 31 matches); Oxford U (1928–30, blue all three years); Middlesex (1932, 1 match). *Tour* MCC to Canada 1937 (not first-class).
Career batting
75–121–9–2925–183–26.11–5–*ct* 15
Bowling 117–1–117.00–0–0–1/19

He hit 1,096 runs, av 37.79, in 1930. His last first-class match was for Free Foresters in 1935. He also played for Devon.

Ford, Percy Hadley
Amateur. *b:* 5.7.1877, Wheatenhurst, Gloucs. *d:* 2.12.1920, Gloucester, of septic pneumonia. Lower order right-hand batsman, right-arm fast bowler. *Sch* Wycliffe. *Team* Gloucestershire (1906–08, 29 matches).
Career batting
29–51–9–419–36–9.97–0–*ct* 10
Bowling 2148–87–24.69–7–2–6/24

Business restricted his appearances in County cricket.

Ford, Reggie Gilbert
Professional. *b:* 5.3.1907, Bristol. *d:* Oct 1981, Bristol. Middle order right-hand batsman, right-arm medium pace bowler. *Team* Gloucestershire (1929–36, 51 matches).
Career batting
51–70–23–496–37*–10.55–0–*ct* 23
Bowling 493–10–49.30–0–0–2/11

Ford, William Justice
Amateur. *b:* 7.11.1853, Paddington, London. *d:* 3.4.1904, Kensington, London. Brother of A. F. J. (Middlesex) and F. G. J. (Middlesex), uncle of N. M. (Derbyshire, Oxford U and Middlesex). Very hard hitting middle order right-hand batsman, right-hand slow round-arm bowler, good point. *Sch* Repton. *Teams* Cambridge U (1873–74, blue 1873); Middlesex (1879–94, 7 matches); Nelson (1886/7 to 1888/9).
Career batting
25–42–2–711–75–17.77–0–*ct* 19–*st* 2
Bowling 213–13–16.38–1–0–6/56

He was regarded second only to C. I. Thornton as a hitter. A noted writer on cricket, his works included Histories of Cambridge University CC and Middlesex CCC.

His final first-class match was for MCC in 1896.

He also played for Wiltshire.

Ford, Walter Ronald
Amateur. *b:* 19.10.1913, Teddington, Middlesex. Lower order left-hand batsman, wicket-keeper. *Team* Combined Services (1946–49).
Career batting
4–7–0–69–36–9.85–0–*ct* 7

Fordham, Cyril Bernard
Amateur. *b:* 22.9.1906, Puckeridge, Herts. Middle order right-hand batsman, off break bowler. *Sch* Bishop Stortford. *Team* Minor Counties (1931–37).
Career batting
5–10–2–414–140–51.75–2–*ct* 2
Bowling 91–2–45.50–0–0–2/34

His County cricket was for Hertfordshire.

Fordham, James
Professional. *b:* 19.3.1839, Cambridge. *d:* 2.4.1901, Cambridge. Middle order right-hand batsman. *Team* Cambridgeshire (1865–69, 5 matches).
Career batting
5–9–1–27–10–3.37–0–*ct* 5
Bowling 11–1–11.00–0–0–1/11

Foreman, Dennis Joseph
Professional. *b:* 1.2.1933, Cape Town, South Africa. Middle/lower order right-hand batsman, off break bowler, slip field. *Teams* Western Province (1951/2); Sussex (1952–67, 125 matches).
Career batting
130–203–23–3277–104–18.20–1–*ct* 124
Bowling 273–9–30.33–0–0–4/64

He played soccer for Brighton and Hove Albion at outside left.

Forman, Rev Arthur Francis Emilius
Amateur. *b:* 26.7.1850, Gibraltar. *d:* 13.2.1905, Repton, Derbyshire. Father of Humphrey (Somerset). Middle order right-hand batsman, right-hand fast round-arm bowler, deep field. *Sch* Sherborne. *Team* Derbyshire (1877–82, 5 matches).

Career batting
5–7–0–90–36–12.85–0–*ct* 0
Bowling 3–0

He did not play in first-class matches whilst at Oxford U. His cricketing fame rests with his coaching when a master at Repton. He also played for Dorset and Somerset (non-first-class).

Forman, Frederick Gerald
Amateur. *b:* 30.8.1884, Chellaston, Derbyshire. *d:* 8.12.1960, Penzance, Cornwall. Middle/lower order batsman, change bowler. *Team* Derbyshire (1911, 1 match).
Career batting
1–2–0–3–3–1.50–0–*ct* 1

A well-known hockey player, he represented Derbyshire.

Forman, Humphrey
Amateur. *b:* 26.4.1888, Repton, Derbyshire. *d:* 21.5.1923, Bangkok, Siam. Son of A. F. E. (Derbyshire). Middle order batsman, left-arm medium pace bowler. *Sch* Shrewsbury. *Teams* Cambridge U (1910); Somerset (1910, 1 match).
Career batting
2–4–0–13–8–3.25–0–*ct* 0
Bowling 159–5–31.80–0–0–4/62

Forman, Peter Ralph
Amateur. *b:* 9.3.1934, West Bridgford, Nottingham. Lower order right-hand batsman, slow left-arm bowler. *Sch* Oakham. *Team* Nottinghamshire (1959–62, 16 matches).
Career batting
16–25–8–180–26–10.58–0–*ct* 14
Bowling 1291–40–32.27–1–0–5/73

Formby, Miles Robert
Amateur. *b:* 14.2.1906, Ormskirk, Lancashire. Lower order right-hand batsman, right-arm medium fast bowler. *Sch* Cheltenham. *Team* Cambridge U (1925).
Career batting
2–4–2–18–11–9.00–0–*ct* 0
Bowling 106–2–53.00–0–0–2/27

Forrester, Alexander Roxburgh
Amateur. *b:* 26.10.1899, Glasgow, Scotland. *d:* 11.12.1976, Glasgow, Scotland. Lower order right-hand batsman, leg break and googly bowler. *Sch* Glasgow Academy. *Team* Scotland (1925–27).
Career batting
3–4–2–43–25*–21.50–0–*ct* 1
Bowling 290–17–17.05–1–0–5/66

Forrester, George Douglas
Amateur. *b:* 22.5.1890, Colinton, Edinburgh, Scotland. *d:* 6.5.1959, Barwon Heads, Victoria, Australia. Middle order right-hand batsman. *Sch* Rugby. *Team* Oxford U (1912–13).
Career batting
6–11–0–235–82–21.36–0–*ct* 4
Bowling 17–0

Forrester, Thomas
(known as Forester)
Amateur. *b:* 21.9.1873, Clay Cross, Derbyshire. *d:* 27.12.1927, Nottingham. Lower order left-hand batsman, right-arm medium pace bowler. *Sch* Saltley College. *Teams* Warwickshire (1896–99, 26 matches); Derbyshire (1902–20, 105 matches).
Career batting
131–212–33–2829–87–15.80–0–*ct* 62
Bowling 8920–347–25.70–17–3–7/18

His bowling action was unusual in that he appeared to bowl off the wrong foot.

Forster, Grant
Cricketer. *b*: 27.5.1961, Seaham, Co Durham. Lower order left-hand batsman, off break bowler. *Teams* Northamptonshire (1980, 1 match); Leicestershire (1980/1 to 1982, 4 matches). *Tour* Leicestershire to Zimbabwe 1980/1.
Career batting
5–4–2–45–22*–22.50–0–*ct* 3
Bowling 275–4–68.75–0–0–2/30

Forster, Harold Thomas
Amateur. *b:* 14.11.1878, Winchester. *d:* 29.5.1918, near Ventalay, France. He was killed in action. Lower order left-hand batsman, left-arm medium slow bowler. *Team* Hampshire (1911, 5 matches).
Career batting
5–8–3–33–13–6.60–0–*ct* 3
Bowling 212–10–21.20–1–0–5/38

A Colour Sergeant in the Royal Berkshire Regiment, Forster created a great impression on his debut for Hants, taking 9–92 in the match, but did very little in his other first-class games.

Forster, Henry William
(created Lord Forster of Lepe in 1919)
Amateur. *b:* 31.1.1866, South End, Catford, Kent. *d:* 15.1.1936, Marylebone, London. Middle order right-hand batsman, slow left-arm bowler, splendid field. *Sch* Eton. *Teams* Hampshire (1885–95, 5 matches); Oxford U (1886–89, blue 1887–89).
Career batting
43–75–6–807–60*–11.69–0–*ct* 43
Bowling 2923–135–21.65–7–2–8/119

He was MP for Sevenoaks 1892–1919; Governor-General of Australia commencing 1919.

Forster, Ralph
Amateur. *b:* 21.7.1835, Springhill, Co Durham. *d:* 17.2.1879, Rome, Italy. Right-hand batsman, excellent long stop. *Sch* Harrow. *Team* Cambridge U (1859).
Career batting
16–27–7–110–40*–5.50–0–*ct* 5
His final first-class match was for MCC in 1870 and his County cricket was for Buckinghamshire.

Forsyth, Harry Hollingsworth
Amateur. *b:* 18.12.1903, Dublin, Ireland. Left-hand batsman, wicket-keeper. *Team* Dublin University (1926).
Career batting
1–2–0–49–43–24.50–0–*ct* 2–*st* 1

Fortescue, Rev Arthur Trosse
Amateur. *b:* 7.4.1848, Fallapit, Totnes, Devon. *d:* 21.11.1899, Marylebone, London. Opening right-hand batsman, deep field. *Sch* Marlborough. *Team* Oxford U (1868–70, blue all three years). *Tour* Sanders to North America 1886.
Career batting
19–32–0–480–68–15.00–0–*ct* 12
Bowling 291–16–18.18–0–0–4/28
His final first-class match in England was for the Gentlemen in 1872. He played county cricket for Devon, Warwickshire (not first-class), Essex (not first-class) and Lincolnshire.

Fortin, Richard Chalmers Gordon
Cricketer. *b:* 12.4.1940, Singapore. Opening right-hand batsman, wicket-keeper. *Sch* Wellington. *Team* Oxford U (1963).
Career batting
2–4–0–52–25–13.00–0–*ct* 0
He played for Berkshire.

Fosh, Matthew Kailey
Cricketer. *b:* 26.9.1957, Epping, Essex. Middle order left-hand batsman, right-arm medium pace bowler. *Sch* Harrow. *Teams* Essex (1976–78, 14 matches); Cambridge U (1977–78, blue both years).
Career batting
30–48–2–1069–109–23.23–1–*ct* 9
He was awarded his rugby blue whilst at Cambridge. In 1975 he hit 161* for Harrow v Eton at Lord's, the third highest innings recorded to that date in this fixture.

Foster, Arthur Webster
Amateur. *b:* 12.8.1894, Deritend, Birmingham. *d:* 9.1.1954, Acocks Green, Birmingham. Brother of F.R. (Warwickshire). Lower order right-hand batsman, wicket-keeper. *Sch* Repton. *Team* Warwickshire (1914, 1 match).
Career batting
1–2–1–1–1*–1.00–0–*ct* 2

Foster, Basil Samuel
Amateur. *b:* 12.2.1882, Malvern, Worcs. *d:* 28.9.1959, Hillingdon, Middlesex. Brother of H. K., M. K., N. J. A., R. E., G. N. and W. L. (all Worcs), uncle of C. K. (Worcs) and P. G. (Kent). Middle order right-hand batsman. *Sch* Malvern. *Teams* Worcestershire (1902–11, 7 matches); Middlesex (1912, 12 matches).
Career batting
34–52–1–753–86–14.76–0–*ct* 32
Bowling 50–0
He was a well-known actor on the London stage.

Foster, Christopher Knollys
Amateur. *b:* 27.9.1904, Ledbury, Worcs. *d:* 4.12.1971, Kingsthorne, Hereford. Son of H. K. (Worcs), nephew of B. S., M. K., N. J. A., R. E., G. N. and W. L. (all Worcs), cousin of P. G. (Kent). Middle order right-hand batsman. *Sch* Malvern. *Team* Worcestershire (1927, 3 matches).
Career batting
3–5–2–34–16*–11.33–0–*ct* 0

Foster, David Charles Geoffrey
Cricketer. *b:* 19.9.1959, Holbeach, Lincs. Middle order left-hand batsman, slow left-arm bowler. *Sch* Sutton Valence. *Team* Oxford U (1980).
Career batting
4–6–1–124–67–24.80–0–*ct* 0

Foster, Derek George
Amateur. *b:* 19.3.1907, Sutton Coldfield, Warwickshire. *d:* 13.10.1980, Chipping Campden, Gloucs. Lower order right-hand batsman, right-arm fast medium bowler. *Sch* Shrewsbury. *Team* Warwickshire (1928–34, 52 matches).
Career batting
58–79–7–757–70–10.51–0–*ct* 51
Bowling 4120–150–27.48–8–1–742

Foster, Ernest
Amateur. *b:* 23.11.1873, Bramley, Yorkshire. *d:* 16.4.1956, Leeds, Yorkshire. Lower order batsman, bowler. *Team* Yorkshire (1901, 1 match).
Career batting
1–1–0–2–2–2.00–0–*ct* 0
Bowling 27–0

Foster, Francis George
Amateur. *b:* 6.11.1848, Havant, Hants. Middle order right-hand batsman. *Team* Hampshire (1876, 1 match).

Career batting
1–2–0–12–10–6.00–0–*ct* 1

Foster, Frank Rowbotham
Amateur. *b:* 31.1.1889, Deritend, Birmingham. *d:* 3.5.1958, Northampton. Brother of A. W. (Warwickshire). Middle order right-hand batsman, left-arm fast medium bowler. *Sch* Solihull. Team Warwickshire (1908–14, 127 matches). *Tour* MCC to Australia 1911/12. *Tests* England (1911/12 to 1912, 11 matches).
Career batting
159–263–17–6548–305*–26.61–7–*ct* 121
Bowling 14879–718–20.72–53–8–9/118
Test batting
11–15–1–330–71–23.57–0–*ct* 11
Bowling 926–45–20.57–4–0–6/91

He hit 1,000 runs in a season twice (best 1,614, av 42.47, in 1911) and took 100 wickets in a season four times (best 141, av 20.31, in 1911). In 1911 and 1914 he performed the 'double'.

His highest score of 305* was for Warwickshire v Worcs at Dudley in 1914 and his only other double century was also for Warwickshire. His best bowling was 9/118 for Warwickshire v Yorkshire at Edgbaston in 1911.

He captained his County from 1911 to 1914. A motor cycle accident during the First World War ended any chance he had of resuming his first-class career in 1919.

He was one of the first bowlers to employ 'leg-theory'.

Foster, Geoffrey Norman
Amateur. *b:* 16.10.1884, Malvern, Worcs. *d:* 11.8.1971, Westminster, London. Brother of B. S., H. K., M. K., N. J. A., R. E. and W. L. (all Worcs), father of P. G. (Kent), uncle of C. K. (Worcs), father-in-law of F. G. H. Chalk (Kent). Middle order right-hand batsman, excellent field. *Sch* Malvern. *Teams* Worcestershire (1903–14, 81 matches); Oxford U (1905–08, blue all four years); Kent (1921–22, 10 matches); Europeans (1909/10).
Career batting
141–249–16–6600–175–28.32–11–*ct* 160–*st* 1
Bowling 284–8–35.50–0–0–2/21

He hit 1,000 runs in a season three times (best 1,182, av 40.75, in 1907). His final first-class match was for MCC in 1931. He gained his soccer blue at Oxford and went on to win an amateur international cap for England.

Foster, Henry Knollys
Amateur. *b:* 30.10.1873, Malvern, Worcs. *d:* 23.6.1950, Kingsthorne, Herefordshire. Brother of B. S., G. N., M. K., N. J. A., R. E., and W. L., father of C. K. (all Worcs), uncle of P. G. (Kent). Opening/middle order right-hand batsman, right-arm fast medium bowler. *Sch* Malvern. *Teams* Oxford U (1894–96, blue all three years); Worcestershire (1899–1925, 246 matches).
Career batting
289–524–21–17154–216–34.10–29–*ct* 206
Bowling 444–15–29.60–0–0–3/63

He hit 1,000 runs in a season eight times (best 1,635, av 43.02, in 1904). Both his double centuries were for Worcs, the highest being 216 v Somerset at Worcester in 1903.

He captained Worcestershire 1901–10, 1913.

A noted rackets player, he was the English Amateur Champion.

Foster, James Bryan
(also known as Hone-Foster and Hone)
Amateur. *b:* 9.3.1854, Ramsgate, Kent. *d:* 22.11.1914, Stirchley, Warwickshire. Middle/lower order right-hand batsman, right-arm medium pace bowler. *Team* Kent (1880–81, 2 matches).
Career batting
2–3–0–10–6–3.33–0–*ct* 2

Foster, Jack Heygate Nedham
Amateur. *b:* 8.9.1905, Chatham, Kent. *d:* 16.11.1976, Bough Beach, Kent. Middle order right-hand batsman. *Sch* Harrow. *Team* Kent (1930, 2 matches).
Career batting
2–2–0–1–1–0.50–0–*ct* 0

Foster, Maurice Kirshaw
Amateur. *b:* 1.1.1889, Malvern, Worcs. *d:* 3.12.1940, Lichfield, Staffs. Brother of B. S., G. N., H. K., N. J. A., R. E., and W. L. (all Worcs), uncle of C. K. (Worcs) and P. G. (Kent). Middle order right-hand batsman, right-arm medium pace bowler. *Sch* Malvern. *Teams* Worcestershire (1908–34, 157 matches); Bengal Governor's XI (1917/8).
Career batting
170–301–12–8295–158–28.70–12–*ct* 139–*st* 4
Bowling 282–3–94.00–0–0–2/17

He hit 1,000 runs in five seasons (best 1,615, av 32.95, in 1926). He captained Worcestershire 1923 to 1925.

His final first-class match was for MCC in 1936.

Foster, Maurice Linton Churchill
Cricketer. *b:* 9.5.1943, St Mary, Jamaica. Middle order right-hand batsman, right-arm off break bowler. *Team* Jamaica (1963/4 to 1977/8). *Tours* West Indies to England 1969, 1973; Jamaica to

England 1970. *Tests* West Indies (1969 to 1977/8, 14 matches).
Career batting
112–175–26–6731–234–45.17–17–*ct* 37
Bowling 4056–132–30.72–2–0–5/65
Test batting
14–24–5–580–125–30.52–1–*ct* 3
Bowling 600–9–66.66–0–0–2/41

In both 1969 and 1973 he appeared in only one Test, but in the latter year his batting in first-class matches was very successful – 828 runs, av 63.69. His highest score was 234 for Jamaica v Trinidad at Montego Bay in 1976/7. There was some criticism of his non-selection for all the 1973 Tests.

Foster, Neil Alan
Cricketer. *b*: 6.5.1962, Colchester, Essex. Lower order right-hand batsman, right-arm fast medium bowler, deep field. *Team* Essex (1980–83, 19 matches). *Test* England (1983, 1 match).
Career batting
20–22–7–306–40*–20.40–0–*ct* 6
Bowling 1811–68–26.63–1–0–6/46
Test batting
1–2–0–13–10–6.50–0–*ct* 1
Bowling 75–1–75.00–0–0–1/35

Foster, Neville John Acland
Amateur. *b:* 28.9.1890, Malvern, Worcs. *d:* 8.1.1978, Malvern, Worcs. Brother of B. S., G. N., H. K., M. K., R. E., and W. L. (all Worcs), uncle of C. K. (Worcs) and P. G. (Kent). Middle order right-hand batsman. *Sch* Malvern. *Team* Worcestershire (1914–23, 8 matches).
Career batting
8–14–4–219–40*–21.90–0–*ct* 5

He spent most of his life in Malaya and captained the Federated Malay States side.

Foster, Peter Geoffrey
Amateur. *b:* 19.10.1916, Beckenham, Kent. Son of G. N. (Worcs and Kent), nephew of B. S., H. K., M. K., N. J. A., R. E., W. L. (all Worcs), cousin of C. K. (Worcs). Middle order right-hand batsman, left-arm bowler, excellent deep field. *Sch* Winchester. *Teams* Kent (1939–46, 25 matches); Oxford U (1936–38).
Career batting
30–50–2–882–107–18.37–1–*ct* 16
Bowling 7–0

Foster, Reginald Erskine
Amateur. *b:* 16.4.1878, Malvern, Worcs. *d:* 13.5.1914, Kensington, London, of diabetes. Brother of B. S., G. N., H. K., M. K., N. J. A., and W. L. (all Worcs), uncle of C. K. (Worcs) and P. G. (Kent). Brilliant middle order right-hand batsman, right-arm fast bowler. *Sch* Malvern. *Teams* Oxford U (1897–1900, blue all four years); Worcestershire (1899–1912, 80 matches). *Tours* MCC to Australia 1903/4. *Tests* England (1903/4 to 1907, 8 matches).
Career batting
139–234–17–9076–287–41.82–22–*ct* 179
Bowling 1153–25–46.12–0–0–3/54
Test batting
8–14–1–602–287–46.30–1–*ct* 13

He could not afford the time for regular County cricket and in fact only had one full English season – 1901 – when he hit 2,128 runs, av 50.66. He also exceeded 1,000 runs in 1899 and 1900. His most famous innings was 287 for England v Australia in the Sydney Test of 1903/4, which was a record for the series for many years. He captained England v South Africa in 1907 and Oxford and Worcs in 1900. A noted soccer player, he won his blue and went on to play for Corinthians and England.

Foster, Thomas
Professional. *b:* 15.12.1848, Mill Town, Glossop, Derbyshire. *d:* 22.3.1929, East Glossop, Derbyshire. Middle order right-hand batsman, right-hand fast round arm bowler, excellent field. *Team* Derbyshire (1873–84, 85 matches).
Career batting
90–167–6–2594–101–16.11–1–*ct* 64
Bowling 233–9–25.88–0–0–2/18

Foster, Thomas William
Professional. *b:* 12.11.1871, Birkdale, Lancashire. *d:* 31.1.1947, Dewsbury, Yorkshire. Lower order right-hand batsman, right-arm medium pace bowler. *Team* Yorkshire (1894–95, 14 matches).
Career batting
14–20–5–138–25–9.20–0–*ct* 6
Bowling 952–58–16.41–5–3–9/59

His best bowling was 9/59 for Yorkshire v MCC at Lord's in 1894.

Foster, William
Professional. *b:* 8.6.1859, Beeston, Notts. *d:* 1.11.1944, Arnold, Notts. Middle order batsman. *Team* Nottinghamshire (1889, 1 match).
Career batting
1–2–0–0–0–0.00–0–*ct* 0

Foster, William John
Cricketer. *b:* 3.2.1934, Milton, Hants. Opening right-hand batsman. *Sch* Harrow. *Team* Combined Services (1964).
Career batting
2–4–0–79–36–19.75–0–*ct* 1
Bowling 13–0

Foster, Wilfrid Lionel
Amateur. *b:* 2.12.1874, Malvern, Worcs. *d:* 22.3.1958, Ryton Grove near Shifnal, Salop. Brother of B. S., G. N., H. K., M. K., N. J. A., and R. E. (all Worcs), uncle of C. K. (Worcs) and P. G. (Kent). Opening right-hand batsman. *Sch* Malvern. *Team* Worcestershire (1899–1911, 29 matches).
Career batting
38–67–2–1993–172*–30.66–3–*ct* 18
Bowling 13–0
Owing to his military duties his only season of regular first-class cricket was 1899. He hit 1,041 runs, av 34.70, that year.
He was an excellent soccer player with Corinthians and a noted rackets player.

Fothergill, Arnold James
Amateur, then professional from 1877. *b:* 26.8.1854, Newcastle on Tyne. *d:* 1.8.1932, Newcastle on Tyne. Lower order left-hand batsman, left-arm medium fast bowler. *Team* Somerset (1882–84, 16 matches). *Tour* Warton to South Africa 1888/9. *Tests* England (1888/9, 2 matches).
Career batting
39–69–9–843–74–14.05–0–*ct* 15
Bowling 2164–119–18.18–6–1–6/43
Test batting
2–2–0–33–32–16.50–0–*ct* 0
Bowling 90–8–11.25–0–0–4/19
He was on the staff at Lord's commencing 1882 and much of his first-class cricket was for MCC.
His final first-class match in England was for South of England in 1887.
He also appeared for Northumberland.

Foulds, Frederick George
Professional. *b:* 23.4.1935, Leicester. Forcing middle order right-hand batsman. *Team* Leicestershire (1952–56, 2 matches).
Career batting
2–4–0–1–1–0.25–0–*ct* 0
He was on National Service in 1953 and 1954.

Foulke, William Henry
(registered at birth as Foulk and death as Foulkes)
Professional. *b:* 12.4.1874, Dawley, Salop. *d:* 1.5.1916, Sheffield, Yorkshire. Middle order batsman. *Team* Derbyshire (1900, 4 matches).
Career batting
4–7–1–65–53–10.83–0–*ct* 2
Bowling 92–2–46.00–0–0–2/15
Famous as a goalkeeper, he represented Sheffield United, Chelsea Bradford City and England. In 1901 he weighed 21 stone, but was still very active. He died from pneumonia, caught on Blackpool Sands, where he made a living inviting the public to score goals against him.

Fowke, Gustavus Henry Spencer
Amateur. *b:* 14.10.1880, Brighton, Sussex. *d:* 24.6.1946, Wansford, Northants. Opening, later middle order, right-hand batsman, right-arm fast medium bowler, good slip. *Sch* Uppingham. *Team* Leicestershire (1899–1927, 159 matches).
Career batting
160–261–27–4438–113–18.96–2–*ct* 89
Bowling 738–13–56.76–0–0–2/13
After making his County debut in 1899, Fowke went to fight in the Boer War and then was stationed in India. His County cricket was very restricted until he was appointed County captain in 1922, a post he held until 1927.
He had the unusual misfortune to be a Prisoner of War both in the Boer War and the First World War.

Fowler, Archibald John Burgess
Professional. *b:* 1.4.1891, Marylebone, London. *d:* 7.5.1977, London. Lower order right-hand batsman, slow left-arm bowler. *Team* Middlesex (1921–30, 26 matches).
Career batting
30–39–15–167–21–6.95–0–*ct* 16
Bowling 1293–43–30.06–1–0–5/29
He was head coach at Lord's in the 1930s

Fowler, Gerald
Amateur. *b:* 27.7.1866, Leytonstone, Essex. *d:* 24.5.1916, Trull, Somerset, after an operation for appendicitis. Brother of W. H. (Somerset) and Howard (Oxford U). Lower order right-hand batsman, right-arm fast medium bowler. *Sch* Clifton. *Teams* Oxford U (1888–89, blue 1888); Somerset (1891–1903, 119 matches).
Career batting
132–231–19–3571–118–16.84–1–*ct* 66
Bowling 2858–92–31.07–4–0–6/50
He appeared for Essex 1884–89. From 1896 to his death he was Hon Treasurer of Somerset CCC.

Fowler, Graeme
Cricketer. *b*: 20.4.1957, Accrington, Lancashire. Hard-hitting opening left-hand batsman, occasional wicket-keeper, good cover field. *Team* Lancashire (1979–83, 71 matches). *Tours* England to Australia and New Zealand 1982/3 (New Zealand not first-class); International XI to Jamaica 1982/3. *Tests* England (1982–83, 6 matches).

Career batting
75–123–9–4636–156*–40.66–14–*ct* 41–*st* 5
Bowling 32–0
Test batting
6–12–0–436–105–36.33–1–*ct* 2
He hit 1,000 runs in a season three times (best 1,560, av 39.00, in 1981).

Fowler, Howard
Amateur. *b:* 20.10.1857, Tottenham, Middlesex. *d:* 6.5.1934, Burnham-on-Sea, Somerset. Brother of Gerald and W. H. (both Somerset). Hard hitting middle order right-hand batsman, wicket-keeper. *Sch* Clifton. *Team* Oxford U (1877–80, blue 1877, 1879 and 1880).
Career batting
17–30–1–471–63–16.24–0–*ct* 13–*st* 7
He appeared for Somerset and later Essex.
A noted rugby footballer, he represented both Oxford and England.
His final first-class match was for MCC in 1884.

Fowler, Rev Richard Harold
Amateur. *b:* 5.3.1887, Islington, Middlesex. *d:* 27.10.1970, Clent, Worcs. Lower order right-hand batsman, right-arm fast medium bowler. *Team* Worcestershire (1921, 4 matches).
Career batting
4–7–1–72–35–12.00–0–*ct* 3
Bowling 105–7–15.00–1–0–5/33
Due to a doubtful bowling action, his County career was very short.

Fowler, Robert Henry
Amateur. *b:* 28.6.1857, Mellifont, Co Louth, Ireland. *d:* 11.5.1957, Rahinstown, Enfield, Co Meath, Ireland. Father of R. St L. (Hampshire). Middle order right-hand batsman. *Sch* Cheltenham *Team* Cambridge U (1876).
Career batting
1–2–0–4–3–2.00–0–*ct* 0

Fowler, Robert St Leger
Amateur. *b:* 7.4.1891, Enfield, Co Meath, Ireland. *d:* 13.6.1925, Enfield, Co Meath, Ireland. Son of R. H. (Cambridge U). Middle/lower order right-hand batsman, off break bowler. *Sch* Eton. *Team* Hampshire (1924, 3 matches). *Tours* Appointed captain of the MCC Team to West Indies 1924/25, but the tour was postponed until the following winter and Fowler died in June 1925.
Career batting
24–38–4–957–92*–28.14–0–*ct* 21
Bowling 1462–59–24.77–2–0–7/22
His most famous match was Eton v Harrow in 1910. Captain of Eton, he hit 64 to save an innings defeat and then with Harrow needing only 55 to win, Fowler took 8 wickets to achieve victory by 5 runs. The game is always referred to as 'Fowler's Match'. His military career prevented him from appearing in all but a handful of first-class matches, his first-class debut being in 1913 for MCC.

Fowler, Thomas Frederick
Amateur. *b:* 12.3.1841, Kennington Park, London. *d:* 7.1.1915, Woolston, Hants. Middle/lower order right-hand batsman, right-hand fast round arm bowler, cover point. *Sch* Uppingham. *Team* Cambridge U (1863–64, blue 1864).
Career batting
10–16–5–208–38*–18.90–0–*ct* 6
Bowling 98–9–10.88–1–0–5/37
His final first-class match was for MCC in 1867.
He appeared for Huntingdonshire 1862 to 1879, being Honorary Secretary and captain of that County club 1862 to 1868.
He also played for Northants.

Fowler, Theodore Humphrey
Amateur. *b:* 25.9.1879, Cirencester, Gloucs. *d:* 17.8.1915, London County Hospital, Epsom, Surrey. Opening/middle order batsman, wicket-keeper. *Sch* Lancing. *Team* Gloucestershire (1901–14, 46 matches).
Career batting
46–78–4–1057–114–14.28–1–*ct* 35–*st* 1
Bowling 36–0
He was an excellent long distance runner. He twice declined a commission in the HAC whilst serving in the First World War. He also played for Dorset.

Fowler, William Herbert
Amateur. *b:* 28.5.1856, Tottenham, Middlesex. *d:* 13.4.1941, Chelsea, London. Brother of Gerald (Somerset) and Howard (Oxford U). Hard hitting middle order right-hand batsman, right-arm fast bowler. *Team* Somerset (1882–84, 15 matches).
Career batting
26–49–0–905–139–18.47–1–*ct* 6
Bowling 521–23–22.65–0–0–4/8
He appeared for Essex in 1877. His debut in first-class matches in 1880 and his final first-class match in 1885 were both for MCC.

Fowler, William Peter
Cricketer. *b*: 13.3.1959, St Helens, Lancashire. Middle order right-hand batsman, slow left-arm bowler. *Teams* Northern Districts (1979/80 to 1980/81); Auckland (1981/2); Derbyshire (1983, 17 matches).

Career batting
27–44–5–875–91–22.43–0–*ct* 17
Bowling 661–9–73.44–0–0–2/44
He played for Derbyshire in John Player League matches in 1982.

Fox, Charles John Macdonald
Amateur. *b:* 5.12.1858, Dum Dum, India. *d:* 1.4.1901, Albury, New South Wales, Australia. Opening/middle order right-hand batsman, right-arm medium pace bowler, fine field. *Sch* Westminster. *Teams* Surrey (1876, 1 match); Kent (1888–93, 74 matches).
Career batting
80–135–10–2147–103–17.31–1–*ct* 40
Bowling 818–46–17.78–3–0–5/21
About 1890 he was a very prolific scorer in London Club cricket, mainly for the Crystal Palace club.

Fox, Frederick Isaac
Amateur. *b:* 7.11.1863, Nottingham. *d:* 21.8.1935, Beltinge, Kent. Middle order right-hand batsman, deep field. *Sch* Nottingham HS. *Team* Nottinghamshire (1890, 2 matches).
Career batting
2–4–2–34–23–17.00–0–*ct* 0

Fox, Henry
Amateur. *b:* 30.9.1856, Wellington, Somerset. *d:* on or after 30.8.1888, Georgia, Russia. *Team* Somerset (1882, 3 matches).
Career batting
3–6–0–16–6–2.66–0–*ct* 0
He was lost in the Caucasus Mountains.

Fox, Herbert Francis
Amateur. *b:* 1.8.1858, Brislington, Somerset. *d:* 20.1.1926, London. Sound middle order right-hand batsman, left-arm bowler. *Sch* Clifton. *Team* Somerset (1882–91, 10 matches).
Career batting
10–18–1–133–31–7.82–0–*ct* 5
He appeared in the Oxford Freshmen's match of 1878 and later for both Oxfordshire and Suffolk.

Fox, John
Professional. *b:* 7.9.1904, Northfield, Birmingham. *d:* 15.11.1961, Birmingham. He collapsed and died on a bus whilst on his way home from work. Lower order right-hand batsman, slow left-arm bowler. *Teams* Warwickshire (1922–28, 46 matches); Worcestershire (1929–33, 94 matches).
Career batting
140–209–35–2907–73–16.70–0–*ct* 30
Bowling 2193–46–47.67–0–0–4/27

Fox, John Charles Ker
Amateur. *b:* 10.3.1851, Castle Dillon, County Armagh, Ireland. *d:* 10.8.1929, Brislington, Somerset. Middle order right-hand batsman. *Sch* Clifton. *Team* Gloucestershire (1872, 2 matches).
Career batting
2–3–1–13–11*–6.50–0–*ct* 1

Fox, John George
Professional. *b:* 22.7.1929, Norton-on-Tees, Co Durham. Lower order right-hand batsman, wicket-keeper. *Team* Warwickshire (1959–61, 43 matches).
Career batting
43–54–6–515–52–10.72–0–*ct* 91–*st* 14
Bowling 0–0
He appeared for Durham from 1950 to 1964.

Fox, Ronald Henry
Amateur. *b:* 23.1.1880, Caversham, New Zealand. *d:* 27.8.1952, Bloxham, Oxon. Tail end right-hand batsman, wicket-keeper. *Sch* Haileybury. *Team* MCC (1906–10). *Tours* MCC to New Zealand 1906/7; New Zealand to England 1927 (1 first-class match).
Career batting
19–32–6–407–54–15.65–0–*ct* 26–*st* 8
Bowling 51–2–25.50–0–0–1/17
His debut was for Gentlemen of England in 1904.

Fox, Raymond Wodehouse
Amateur. *b:* 11.7.1873, Frampton-Cotterell, Gloucs. *d:* 21.8.1948, Ticehurst, Sussex. Tail end right-hand batsman, wicket-keeper. *Sch* Wellington. *Teams* Oxford U (1896–98, blue 1897–98); Sussex (1896–1900, 7 matches).
Career batting
27–38–18–106–20–5.30–0–*ct* 39–*st* 13
His final first-class match was for H. D. G. Leveson-Gower's XI in 1909.

Fox, Dr Thomas Calcott
Amateur. *b:* 1849, Broughton, Hants. *d:* 11.4.1916, London. Lower order batsman, bowler. *Sch* U.C.S. *Team* Hampshire (1875, 2 matches).
Career batting
2–4–0–10–7–2.50–0–*ct* 1
Bowling 26–0

Fox, Thomas Seely
Amateur. *b:* 23.8.1878, Upton, Essex. *d:* 3.4.1931, Bournemouth, Hants. Lower order batsman, wicket-keeper. *Team* Middlesex (1905, 1 match).
Career batting
1 match, did not bat–*ct* 0

Fox, William Victor
Professional. *b:* 8.1.1898, Middlesbrough, Yorkshire. *d:* 17.2.1949, Withington, Manchester, Lancashire. Middle order right-hand batsman. *Team* Worcestershire (1923–32, 163 matches).
Career batting
163–281–31–6654–198–26.61–11–*ct* 87
Bowling 137–2–68.50–0–0–1/13
He hit 1,000 runs in a season three times (best 1,457, av 31.00, in 1929). He began his cricket with Worcestershire in 1923, but it was found that he was not qualified and he had to wait for two years before being permitted to make any further appearances in the Championship.
He played football for Middlesborough, Wolves and Newport.

Foy, Frederick George
Professional. *b:* 11.4.1915, Maidstone, Kent. Middle order right-hand batsman, slow left-arm bowler. *Team* Kent (1937–38, 11 matches).
Career batting
11–17–1–153–25–9.56–0–*ct* 5
Bowling 18–0

Foy, Philip Arnold
Amateur. *b:* 16.10.1891, Axbridge, Somerset. *d:* 12.2.1957, Buenos Aires, Argentine. Middle/lower order right-hand batsman, right-arm fast medium bowler. *Sch* Bedford GS. *Teams* Somerset (1919–30, 21 matches); Argentine (1911/2 to 1929/30).
Career batting
25–40–4–504–72–14.00–0–*ct* 20
Bowling 1524–78–19.53–7–1–7/84
He was for some years one of the leading bowlers in Argentine cricket.

Francis, Arthur Stopford
Amateur. *b:* 14.6.1854, Upminster, Essex. *d:* Jan 1908. Brother of C.K. (Middlesex). Middle order right-hand batsman, right-hand medium pace round arm bowler. *Sch* Rugby. *Team* Middlesex (1880, 2 matches).
Career batting
3–6–0–98–26–16.33–0–*ct* 1
His final first-class match was for South of England in 1887.

Francis, Bruce Colin
Cricketer. *b:* 18.2.1948, Sydney, New South Wales, Australia. Opening right-hand batsman, right-arm medium pace bowler. *Teams* New South Wales (1968/9 to 1972/3, 32 matches); Essex (1971–73, 47 matches). *Tours* Australia to England 1972; International Wanderers to Rhodesia 1972/3; D.H.Robins to South Africa 1973/4, 1974/5. *Tests* Australia (1972, 3 matches).
Career batting
109–192–10–6183–210–33.97–13–*ct* 42
Bowling 15–1–15.00–0–0–1/10
Test batting
3–5–0–52–27–10.40–0–*ct* 1
He hit 1,000 runs in both his seasons with Essex (1971 and 1973), the best being 1,578, av 38.48, in 1971, but achieved little in 1972 with the Australian Touring Team, except his highest innings of 210 v Combined Universities at Oxford.

Francis, Conway James
Amateur. *b:* 1870, Clifton, Gloucs. *d:* 15.4.1924, Staple Hill, Bristol. Brother of H.H. (Gloucs). Middle order right-hand batsman, right-arm fast bowler. *Sch* Blundell's. *Team* Gloucestershire (1895, 1 match).
Career batting
1–1–0–8–8–8.00–0–*ct* 0
Bowling 11–0

Francis, Charles King
Amateur. *b:* 3.2.1851, Upminster, Essex. *d:* 28.10.1925, Crichel, Dorset. Brother of A.S. (Middlesex). Lower order right-hand batsman, right-hand fast round arm bowler. *Sch* Rugby. *Teams* Oxford U (1870–73, blue all four years); Middlesex (1875–77, 9 matches). *Tour* Fitzgerald to North America 1872 (not first-class).
Career batting
47–75–10–717–45–11.03–0–*ct* 38
Bowling 2797–136+6–20.56–5–1–7/12
He gained a tremendous reputation in school cricket as a fast bowler, but after his first year at Oxford, proved a very moderate success.
His final first-class match was for MCC in 1879.

Francis, David Arthur
Cricketer. *b*: 29.11.1953, Clydach, Glamorgan. Middle order right-hand batsman, off break bowler, mid-wicket. *Team* Glamorgan (1973–83, 136 matches).
Career batting
136–234–36–4911–142*–24.80–3–*ct* 60
Bowling 31–0
His best season was 1982 with 1,076 runs, av 38.42.

Francis, Francis Philip
Amateur. *b:* 15.9.1852, Upminster, Essex. *d:* 18.1.1926, Claygate, Surrey. Lower order batsman, wicket-keeper. *Team* Middlesex (1881, 1 match).
Career batting
1–1–0–0–0–0.00–0–*ct* 0

Francis, Guy
Amateur. *b:* 16.8.1860, Maugersbury, Gloucs. *d:* 18.5.1948, Wynne's Parc, Denbigh. Middle order right-hand batsman, right-arm fast bowler. *Sch* Cheltenham. *Team* Gloucestershire (1884–88, 31 matches).
Career batting
32–57–7–670–89–13.40–0–*ct* 9
Bowling 23–1–23.00–0–0–1/16

Francis, George Nathaniel
Professional. *b:* 7.12.1897, Bridgetown, Barbados. *d:* 12.1.1942, Barbados. Lower order right-hand batsman, right-arm fast bowler. *Team* Barbados (1924/5 to 1929/30). *Tours* West Indies to England 1923, 1928, 1933, to Australia 1930/1. *Tests* West Indies (1928–33, 10 matches).
Career batting
62–91–23–874–61–12.85–0–*ct* 42
Bowling 5159–223–23.13–8–2–7/50
Test batting
10–18–4–81–19*–5.78–0–*ct* 7
Bowling 763–23–33.17–0–0–4/40

He was the outstanding success of the 1923 West Indian tour with 82 wickets, av 15.58, but in 1928 achieved only a modest return. In 1933 he was a professional with the Radcliffe Club and appeared for the West Indies only in the Lord's Test.

His final first-class match in the West Indies was for C. A. Merry's XI in 1932/3.

Francis, Howard Henry
Amateur. *b:* 26.5.1868, Clifton, Bristol. *d:* 7.1.1936, Cape Town, South Africa. Brother of C. J. (Gloucs). Middle order batsman. *Teams* Gloucestershire (1890–94, 18 matches); Western Province (1895/6 to 1902/03). *Tests* South Africa (1898/9, 2 matches).
Career batting
25–44–3–529–55–12.90–0–*ct* 13–*st* 1
Test batting
2–4–0–39–29–9.75–0–*ct* 1

Francis, Percy Thomas
Amateur. *b:* 1875, Suffolk. *d:* 8.9.1964, Branksome, Poole, Dorset. Opening batsman. *Team* Worcestershire (1901–02, 3 matches).
Career batting
3–5–1–95–66–23.75–0–*ct* 0

He also appeared for Suffolk.

Francis, Thomas Egerton Seymour
Amateur. *b:* 21.11.1902, South Africa. *d:* 24.2.1969, Bulawayo, Rhodesia. Opening right-hand batsman. *Sch* Tonbridge. *Teams* Somerset (1921–25, 16 matches); Cambridge U (1923–25, blue 1925); Eastern Province (1927/8).
Career batting
34–56–4–804–79–15.46–0–*ct* 14
Bowling 202–3–64.00–0–0–2/100

A noted rugby player, he gained a blue at Cambridge as stand-off half and was capped for England in 1925/6.

Francis, Dr William
Amateur. *b:* 21.3.1856, Little Waltham, Chelmsford, Essex. *d:* 28.4.1917, Forest Gate, Essex. Hard hitting middle order right-hand batsman, good deep field. *Team* Sussex (1877–79, 7 matches).
Career batting
7–13–1–83–17–6.91–0–*ct* 5

He also appeared in non-first-class matches for Essex.

Frank, Joseph
Amateur. *b:* 27.12.1857, Helmsley, Yorkshire. *d:* 22.10.1940, Ryedale, Yorkshire. Lower order left-hand batsman, very fast right-arm bowler. *Team* Yorkshire (1881, 1 match).
Career batting
7–13–1–198–46–16.33–0–*ct* 9
Bowling 258–9–28.66–0–0–3/70

His bowling action was very suspect, which probably limited his appearances in first-class cricket.

His final first-class appearance was for A. J. Webbe's XI in 1887.

Frank, Robert Wilson
Amateur. *b:* 29.5.1864, Pickering, Yorkshire. *d:* 9.9.1950, Hungate, near Pickering, Yorkshire. Opening/middle order right-hand batsman, slow right-arm bowler, excellent deep field. *Team* Yorkshire (1889–1903, 19 matches).
Career batting
20–31–4–430–92–15.92–0–*ct* 9
Bowling 9–0

He captained Yorkshire 2nd XI from 1900 to 1914.

Franklin, Henry William Fernehough
Amateur. *b:* 30.6.1901, Ford End, Essex. Brother of R. C. (Essex). Middle/lower order right-hand batsman, leg break bowler. *Sch* Christ's Hospital. *Teams* Oxford U (1921–24, blue 1924); Surrey (1921, 1 match); Essex (1921–31, 73 matches). *Tour* Martineau to Egypt 1931 (not first-class).
Career batting
92–134–19–2212–106–19.23–2–*ct* 41
Bowling 2002–46–43.52–0–0–4/40

Franklin, Reginald Carey
Amateur. *b:* 30.4.1880, Coventry, Warwickshire. *d:* 25.6.1957, Brighton, Sussex. Middle order

right-hand batsman, leg break bowler. *Sch* Repton. *Team* Warwickshire (1900, 1 match).
Career batting
1–1–0–0–0–0.00–0–*ct* 1

Franklin, Ronald Christian
Amateur. *b:* 9.9.1904, Ford End, Essex. *d:* 28.9.1982, Prestwood, Bucks. Brother of H. W. F. (Essex). Lower order right-hand batsman, right-arm medium pace bowler. *Sch* Christ's Hospital. *Team* Essex (1924, 1 match).
Career batting
1–2–0–1–1–0.50–0–*ct* 1
Bowling 41–1–41.00–0–0–1/20

Franklin, Trevor John
Cricketer. *b*: 15.3.1962, Auckland, New Zealand. Opening right-hand batsman, right-arm medium pace bowler. *Team* Auckland (1980/1 to 1982/3). *Tour* New Zealand to England 1983. *Test* New Zealand (1983, 1 match).
Career batting
35–65–5–1863–136–31.05–3–*ct* 18
Bowling 10–0
Test batting
1–2–0–9–7–4.50–0–*ct* 0
On the 1983 tour he hit 539 runs, av 35.93, and played in one Test.

Franklin, Walter Bell
Amateur. *b:* 16.8.1891, Croydon, Surrey. *d:* 5.3.1968, Knoddishall, Suffolk. Lower order right-hand batsman, wicket-keeper. *Sch* Repton. *Team* Cambridge U (1911–13, blue 1912).
Career batting
60–91–19–1362–77–18.91–0–*ct* 61–*st* 54
He played for Buckinghamshire 1911 to 1946, captaining the County from 1919 to 1946.
His final first-class match was for Minor Counties in 1937.

Franks, Jonathan Guy
Cricketer. *b*: 23.9.1962, Stamford, Lincolnshire. Middle order right-hand batsman, wicket-keeper. *Sch* Stamford. *Team* Oxford U (1983).
Career batting
5–7–0–98–29–14.00–0–*ct* 2
His County cricket has been for Lincolnshire since 1980.

Frasat Ali
Cricketer. *b:* 1950, Kenya. Right-hand batsman, right-arm medium pace bowler. *Tour* East Africa to England 1975.
Career batting
1–2–0–42–30–21.00–0–*ct* 0
Bowling 82–2–41.00–0–0–2/37

Fraser, Alan
Amateur. *b:* 13.7.1892, Perth, Scotland. *d:* 28.8.1962, Dundee, Scotland. Brother of W. L. (Scotland). Right-hand batsman. *Sch* Merchiston. *Team* Scotland (1921).
Career batting
1–1–0–9–9–9.00–0–*ct* 1
Bowling 28–0

Fraser, David Dempster
Cricketer. *b:* 9.4.1943, Edinburgh, Scotland. Lower order right-hand batsman, right-arm fast medium bowler. *Sch* Royal High School, Edinburgh. *Team* Scotland (1967–69).
Career batting
4–2–2–0–0*–no av–0–*ct* 1
Bowling 363–8–45.37–0–0–3/29

Fraser, John Neville
Amateur. *b:* 6.8.1890, Toorak, Victoria, Australia. *d:* 23.1.1962, Lindfield, New South Wales, Australia. Lower order right-hand batsman, leg break and googly bowler. *Team* Oxford U (1912–14, blue 1912–13).
Career batting
17–28–11–195–33–11.47–0–*ct* 13
Bowling 1391–59–23.57–4–0–6/35

Fraser, Patrick Shaw
Amateur. *b:* 15.6.1892, India. *d:* 1962, Liverpool. Opening/middle order left-hand batsman, leg break bowler. *Sch* Rugby. *Teams* Scotland (1911–13); MCC (1925–27).
Career batting
9–17–0–289–79–17.00–0–*ct* 4
Bowling 54–1–54.00–0–0–1/14
He also played for Buckinghamshire.

Fraser, Thomas William
Amateur. *b:* 26.6.1912, South Africa. Lower order right-hand batsman, slow left-arm bowler. *Teams* Cambridge U (1936–37, blue 1937); Orange Free State (1937/8 to 1946/7).
Career batting
22–37–11–249–61*–9.57–0–*ct* 11
Bowling 1834–58–31.62–3–0–8/71
His final first-class match was for Free Foresters in 1948.

Fraser, William Lovat
Amateur. *b:* 7.11.1884, Perth, Scotland. *d:* 21.11.1968, Scone, Perthshire, Scotland. Brother of Alan (Scotland). Right-hand batsman, right-arm medium pace bowler. *Sch* Merchiston. *Team* Scotland (1909–13).
Career batting
3–5–1–53–44–13.25–0–*ct* 3
Bowling 278–15–18.53–1–0–5/50

Frazer, Charles Ewan
Amateur. *b:* 23.9.1905. *d:* 30.4.1971, Tenterden, Kent. Brother of J. E. (Sussex). Opening/middle order right-hand batsman, slow right-arm bowler, good field. *Sch* Winchester. *Team* Oxford U (1927–28).
Career batting
4–8–0–101–43–12.62–0–*ct* 2

Frazer, John Ewan
Amateur. *b:* 2.4.1901, Lydney, Gloucs. *d:* 2.1.1927, Davos Platz, Switzerland, as the result of a ski-ing accident. Brother of C. E. (Oxford U). Middle order left-hand batsman, left-arm medium fast bowler, fine field. *Sch* Winchester. *Teams* Somerset (1921, 1 match); Sussex (1921–24, 23 matches); Oxford U (1924, blue).
Career batting
37–65–0–887–81–13.64–0–*ct* 13

He also gained his blue for soccer. In 1921 he appeared for both Somerset and Sussex, but for the former only against Oxford.

His last first-class match was for Free Foresters in 1925.

Frearson, Raymond Eric
Amateur. *b:* 14.1.1904, Lincoln. Middle order right-hand batsman, leg break bowler. *Sch* Eastbourne. *Teams* Minor Counties (1929–31).
Career batting
3–3–0–19–13–6.33–0–*ct* 1

His first-class debut was for East of England in 1927.

His County cricket was for Lincolnshire.

Frederick, Sir Edward Boscawen
Amateur. *b:* 29.6.1880, Wem, Salop. *d:* 26.10.1956, Marylebone, London. Lower order right-hand batsman, slow right-arm bowler. *Sch* Eton. *Teams* Hampshire (1903–04, 5 matches); Europeans (1907/8).
Career batting
6–11–4–36–11–5.14–0–*ct* 12
Bowling 362–10–36.20–0–0–3/41

Frederick, John St John
Amateur. *b:* 6.1.1846, London. *d:* 10.9.1907, Camberley, Surrey. Hard hitting middle order right-hand batsman, very fast right-hand round-arm bowler, excellent deep field. *Sch* Eton. *Teams* Oxford U (1864–67, blue 1864 and 1867); Hampshire (1864–69, 5 matches); Middlesex (1864, 1 match).
Career batting
25–43–0–635–44–14.76–0–*ct* 15
Bowling 106–4–26.50–0–0–4/45

Though bowling very fast, his direction was rather erratic. A severe accident prevented him playing for Oxford in 1865. He was on the MCC Committee for several years.

Frederick, Michael Campbell
Amateur. *b:* 6.5.1927, St Peter, Barbados. Middle order right-hand batsman, excellent field. *Teams* Jamaica (1953/4); Barbados (1944/5); Derbyshire (1949, 2 matches). *Test* West Indies (1953/4, 1 match).
Career batting
6–10–0–294–84–29.40–0–*ct* 3
Test batting
1–2–0–30–30–15.00–0–*ct* 0

Fredericks, Roy Clifton
Cricketer. *b:* 11.11.1942, Blairmont, Berbice, British Guiana. Opening left-hand batsman, slow left-arm bowler. *Teams* British Guiana/Guyana (1963/4 to 1982/3); Glamorgan (1971–73, 45 matches). *Tours* West Indies to Australia and New Zealand 1968/9, to England 1969, 1973, 1976, to India, Pakistan and Ceylon 1974/5, to Australia 1975/6. *Tests* West Indies (1968/9 to 1976/7, 59 matches).
Career batting
223–391–34–16384–250–45.89–40–*ct* 177
Bowling 2846–75–37.94–0–0–4/36
Test batting
59–109–7–4334–169–42.49–8–*ct* 62
Bowling 548–7–78.28–0–0–1/12

He was most successful on his three tours to England, scoring over 1,000 runs on each visit; he also made 1,000 runs for Glamorgan in 1971. His best English season was 1973 with 1,506 runs, av 43.02, but he completed 1,000 runs in 1968/9 and 1971/2. Of the four double centuries he scored the highest was 250 for Guyana v Barbados in 1974/5 and the only one in England was 228* for Glamorgan v Northants at Swansea in 1972. He was a leading member of the World Series Cricket in Australia. He re-appeared after three years in 1982/3 and scored 217 and 103 in his only two innings. He is Minister of Sport in the Guyana Government.

Freeland, Sir Ian Henry
Amateur. *b:* 14.9.1912, Milton, Hant. *d:* 2.7.1979, Foxley, Norfolk. Middle order right-hand batsman. *Teams* Army (1937); Europeans (1937/8).
Career batting
3–5–0–44–26–8.80–0–*ct* 1
Bowling 47–1–47.00–0–0–1/8

Freeman, Albert
Professional. *b:* 3.6.1844, Croydon, Surrey. *d:* 27.3.1920, Holloway, North London. Lower order right-hand batsman, right-arm medium

pace bowler, good point field. *Team* Surrey (1871–75, 29 matches).
Career batting
30–56–5–419–32–8.21–0–*ct* 18
Bowling 478–11–43.45–0–0–3/20
He also played non-first-class cricket for Essex.

Freeman, Arthur Ernest B.
Amateur. *b:* 1871, Chipping Sodbury, Gloucs. *d:* 30.11.1948, Bath, Somerset. Lower order batsman, fast bowler. *Team* Somerset (1905, 1 match).
Career batting
1–1–0–3–3–3.00–0–*ct* 0

Freeman, Albert James
Professional. *b:* 19.7.1887, Kennington, Surrey. *d:* 1945, Greenwich, Kent. Tail end right-hand batsman, right-arm medium fast bowler. *Team* Surrey (1919, 1 match).
Career batting
1–1–1–0–0*–no av–0–*ct* 0
Bowling 67–0

Freeman, Alfred James
Professional. *b:* 2.4.1892, Edmonton, London. *d:* 28.4.1972, Chelmsford, Essex. Tail end batsman, left-arm medium pace bowler. *Team* Essex (1920, 1 match).
Career batting
1–2–1–1–1–1.00–0–*ct* 0
Bowling 95–0

Freeman, Alfred Percy
Professional. *b:* 17.5.1888, Lewisham, Kent. *d:* 28.1.1965, Bearsted, Kent. Brother of J. R. (Essex), nephew of E. C. (Essex), cousin of E. J. (Essex). Lower order right-hand batsman, leg break and googly bowler. *Team* Kent (1914–36, 506 matches). *Tours* MCC to Australia and New Zealand 1922/3, to Australia 1924/5, 1928/9, to South Africa 1927/8. *Tests* England (1924/5 to 1929, 12 matches).
Career batting
592–716–194–4961–66–9.50–0–*ct* 238–*st* 1
Bowling 69577–3776–18.42–386–140–10/53
Test Batting
12–16–5–154–50*–14.00–0–*ct* 4
Bowling 1707–66–25.86–5–3–7/71
The most consistent of all bowlers in County Championship cricket, Freeman is the only cricketer to capture over 300 wickets in a single summer: 304, av 18.05, in 1928. In the seven seasons following that record-breaking feat, he took over 200 wickets, thus acquiring a total of 2,090 wickets in eight English seasons. In all he took at least 100 wickets in a season 17 times.
Despite this prodigious success, Freeman proved only a moderate player in Test matches, appearing in little more than one tenth of the English Tests played during his career and, more surprisingly, during his really great County years from 1930 to 1935, he played no Test cricket at all. His bowling relied on a perfect length, which no doubt soon forced the ordinary County cricketer into indiscretion, but in Test cricket the more experienced batsmen just bided their time. His best bowling was 10/53 for Kent v Essex at Southend in 1930.

Freeman, Charles Redfern
Professional. *b:* 22.8.1887, Overseal, Derbyshire. *d:* 16.3.1956, Fulham, London. Middle order right-hand batsman. *Team* Derbyshire (1911, 1 match).
Career batting
1–2–0–7–4–3.50–0–*ct* 1
He played football for Chelsea.

Freeman, Douglas Percy
Professional. *b:* 21.7.1914, Sherborne, Dorset. Son of E. J. (Essex), grandson of E. C. (Essex). Middle order left-hand batsman. *Team* Kent (1937, 1 match).
Career batting
1–2–0–10–6–5.00–0–*ct* 0
He also played for Dorset.

Freeman, Edward
Professional. *b:* 1887, Northampton. *d:* 7.12.1945, Northampton. Lower order right-hand batsman, right-arm medium pace bowler. *Team* Northants (1908–20, 16 matches).
Career batting
16–26–5–133–30–6.33–0–*ct* 4
Bowling 416–6–69.33–0–0–3/62
He was a noted soccer player with Northampton Town.

Freeman, Edward Charles
Professional. *b:* 7.12.1860, Lewisham, Kent. *d:* 16.10.1939, Westbury, near Sherborne, Dorset. Father of E. J. (Essex), grandfather of D. P. (Kent), uncle of A. P. (Kent) and J. R. (Essex). Middle order right-hand batsman. *Team* Essex (1894–96, 5 matches).
Career batting
5–9–0–95–35–10.55–0–*ct* 1
Bowling 40–0
Most of his cricket with Essex was played prior to that County being first class. He was for many years head groundsman at Leyton.

Freeman, Edward John
Professional. *b:* 16.10.1880, Ladywell, Lewisham, Kent. *d:* 22.2.1964, Sherborne,

Dorset. Son of E. C. (Essex), father of D. P. (Kent), cousin of J. R. (Essex) and A. P. (Kent). Middle order batsman. *Team* Essex (1904–12, 55 matches).
Career batting
55–91–3–1280–84–14.54–0–*ct* 14
Bowling 50–1–50.00–0–0–1/6
He also appeared for Dorset.
A noted soccer player, he represented Essex.

Freeman, Eric Walter
Cricketer. *b:* 13.7.1944, Largs Bay, South Australia. Middle/lower order right-hand batsman, right-arm fast medium bowler, excellent field. *Team* South Australia (1964/5 to 1973/4, 44 matches). *Tours* Australia to England 1968, to South Africa 1969/70, to India 1969/70, to New Zealand 1966/67. *Tests* Australia (1967/8 to 1969/70, 11 matches).
Career batting
83–123–6–2244–116–19.17–1–*ct* 60
Bowling 6690–241–27.75–7–2–8/47
Test batting
11–18–0–345–76–19.16–0–*ct* 5
Bowling 1128–34–33.17–0–0–4/52
He appeared in two Tests on his 1968 tour to England, but did not do as well as expected.

Freeman, George
Professional until 1872, then amateur. *b:* 28.7.1843, Boroughbridge, Yorkshire. *d:* 18.11.1895, Sowerby, near Thirsk, Yorkshire of Bright's disease. Hard hitting middle order right-hand batsman, right-hand very fast round-arm bowler, good slip. *Team* Yorkshire (1865–80, 32 matches). *Tour* Willsher to North America 1868 (not first-class).
Career batting
44–70–3–918–53–13.70–0–*ct* 20
Bowling 2797–284+4–9.84–32–10–8/11
Regarded as the greatest fast bowler of his time – succeeding Jackson and Tarrant – Freeman's career was very short, for after five seasons, 1867–1871, he virtually retired from first-class cricket to devote his time to business.
He also played for Northumberland.

Freeman, John Robert
Professional. *b:* 3.9.1883, Ladywell, Lewisham, Kent. *d:* 8.8.1958, Napsbury, Herts. Brother of A. P. (Kent), nephew of E. C. (Essex), cousin of E. J. (Essex). Middle order right-hand batsman, right-arm medium pace bowler, wicket-keeper. *Team* Essex (1905–28, 336 matches).
Career batting
337–579–56–14602–286–27.91–26–*ct* 231–*st* 46
Bowling 365–10–36.50–0–0–3/31
He hit 1,000 runs in a season seven times (best 1,958, av 41.65, in 1926). His only double century was 286 for Essex v Northants at Northampton in 1921.

Freeman, Sidney Thomas
Amateur. *b:* 21.8.1888, Gloucester. *d:* 6.6.1971, Whitbourne, Hereford. Middle order batsman. *Team* Gloucestershire (1920–21, 3 matches).
Career batting
6–9–2–163–58–23.28–0–*ct* 4
Bowling 183–10–18.30–0–0–4/31
His first-class debut was for H. K. Foster's XI in 1919.

Freeman, Terence
Amateur. *b:* 21.10.1931, Wellingborough, Northants. Tail end right-hand batsman, right-arm fast medium bowler. *Team* Northants (1954, 1 match).
Career batting
1–1–0–4–4–4.00–0–*ct* 0
Bowling 90–1–90.00–0–0–1/43

Freeman-Thomas, F. (*see under* Thomas, F. F.)

Freemantle, Frederick William
Professional. *b:* 1871, Whitchurch, Hants. *d:* 12.9.1943, Stockbridge, Hants. Lower order batsman, opening bowler. *Team* Hampshire (1900, 2 matches).
Career batting
2–4–1–28–26–9.33–0–*ct* 0
Bowling 53–0

Freethy, Albert Edwin
Amateur. *b:* 27.4.1885, Swansea. *d:* 1966, Cimla, Neath. Opening batsman. *Team* Glamorgan (1921, 3 matches).
Career batting
3–4–1–79–31–26.33–0–*ct* 1
He was a well-known rugby referee.

French, Bruce Nicholas
Cricketer. *b*: 13.8.1959, Warsop, Notts. Lower order right-hand batsman, wicket-keeper. *Team* Nottinghamshire (1976–83, 143 matches).
Career batting
144–189–38–2606–91–17.25–0–*ct* 302–*st* 30

French, Hon Edward Gerald Fleming
Amateur. *b:* 11.12.1883, Woburn, Bucks. *d:* 17.9.1970, Hove, Sussex. Middle order left-hand batsman. *Sch* Wellington. *Team* MCC (1922–36).
Career batting
2–2–0–10–5–5.00–0–*ct* 0
Bowling 32–0
He appeared for Devon 1924 to 1927 and was a noted member of I Zingari for over 60 years.

French, Edward Lee
Amateur. *b:* 22.7.1857, Thrandeston, Suffolk. *d:* 17.5.1916, Bath, Somerset. Son of T. L. (Cambridge U 1841-44). Lower order batsman, wicket-keeper. *Sch* Marlborough. *Teams* London County (1902); Gentlemen of India (1892/3).
Career batting
3–5–2–17–8*–5.66–0–*ct* 4–*st* 2
He played for Suffolk.

French, John
Professional. *b:* 1834, Histon, Cambridgeshire. Middle order batsman. *Team* Cambridgeshire (1864, 1 match).
Career batting
1–2–0–1–1–0.50–0–*ct* 0

Frere, Henry Tobias
Amateur. *b:* 27.9.1830, Odiham, Hants. *d:* 15.8.1881, Westbourne, Hants. Middle order right-hand batsman, right-hand fast round-arm bowler, slip field. *Teams* Hampshire (1850–66, 7 matches); Sussex (1868, 1 match).
Career batting
13–24–6–177–26–9.83–0–*ct* 5–*st* 2
Bowling 647–24–26.95–1–0–5/20
He also played for Wiltshire.
He was also noted as a crack shot.

Frere, Lionel Robert Temple
Amateur. *b:* 10.12.1870, London. *d:* 15.3.1936, Kensington, London. Middle order right-hand batsman, wicket-keeper. *Sch* Haileybury. *Team* Cambridge U (1892).
Career batting
1–2–0–3–2–1.50–0–*ct* 2
He also appeared for Norfolk.

Friend, Major General Hon Lovick Bransby
Amateur. *b:* 25.4.1856, Penhill, Halfway Street, Kent. *d:* 19.11.1944, West Kensington, London. Middle order right-hand batsman, wicket-keeper. *Sch* Cheltenham. *Team* Kent (1886–87, 3 matches).
Career batting
6–12–1–189–72–17.18–0–*ct* 2
He also appeared for Northumberland occasionally, but was best known in military cricket, mainly for the Royal Engineers.
His final first-class match was for MCC in 1891.

Frisby, Joseph Brankin
Amateur. *b:* 26.2.1908, Carlton-Curlieu, Leics. *d:* 2.11.1977, Leicester. Lower order right-hand batsman, wicket-keeper. *Sch* Harrow. *Team* Leicestershire (1938, 1 match).
Career batting
1–1–0–4–4–4.00–0–*ct* 3
He was Hon Secretary to Leicestershire CCC 1937–39.

Frith, William Frederick Lowndes
(also known as Lowndes-Frith and as Lowndes)
Amateur. *b:* 1.7.1871, Wandsworth, London. *d:* 6.10.1956, West Wittering, Sussex. Father of W. G. L. F. Lowndes (Hants). Lower order batsman, useful bowler. *Team* London County (1901–02).
Career batting
2–1–0–4–4–4.00–*ct* 0
Bowling 23–1–23.00–0–0–1/23

Frost, George
Professional. *b:* 16.10.1848, Wirksworth, Derbyshire. *d:* 12.2.1913, Wirksworth, Derbyshire. Brother of J. H. (Derbyshire). Opening/middle order right-hand batsman. *Team* Derbyshire (1872–80, 36 matches).
Career batting
37–67–4–771–52–12.23–0–*ct* 10

Frost, Graham
Cricketer. *b:* 15.1.1947, Old Basford, Notts. Opening right-hand batsman, right-arm medium pace bowler. *Team* Nottinghamshire (1967–73, 102 matches).
Career batting
104–169–17–3439–107–22.62–2–*ct* 83
Bowling 680–15–45.33–0–0–3/33

Frost, John Henry
Professional. *b:* 30.1.1847, Wirksworth, Derbyshire. *d:* 1.11.1916, Ashover, Derbyshire. Brother of George (Derbyshire). Middle order batsman. *Team* Derbyshire (1874, 1 match).
Career batting
1–2–0–19–18–9.50–0–*ct* 2

Frost, Patrick David
Amateur. *b:* 3.10.1940, Antigua, West Indies. Middle order right-hand batsman. *Team* Oxford U (1961).
Career batting
1 match, did not bat–*ct* 1

Fry, Charles Anthony
Amateur. *b:* 14.1.1940, Henley-in-Arden, Warwickshire. Son of Stephen (Hants), grandson of C. B. (Hants and Sussex). Middle order right-hand batsman, wicket-keeper. *Sch* Repton. *Teams* Oxford U (1959–61, blue all three years); Hampshire (1960, 5 matches); Northants (1962, 2 matches). *Tours* MCC to Bangladesh 1978/9 (not first-class).

Career batting
50–85–7–1952–103*–25.02–2–*ct* 38
Bowling 13–0

His last first-class match was for Free Foresters in 1968.

Fry, Charles Burgess
Amateur. *b:* 25.4.1872, West Croydon, Surrey. *d:* 7.9.1956, Hampstead, London. Father of Stephen (Hants), grandfather of C. A. (Hants and Northants), cousin of K. R. B. (Sussex). Brilliant opening or middle order right-hand batsman, right-arm fast medium bowler, good field. *Sch* Repton. *Teams* Oxford U (1892–95, blue all four years); Sussex (1894–1908, 236 matches); London County (1900–02); Hampshire (1909–21, 44 matches); Europeans (1921/2). *Tour* Hawke to South Africa 1895/6. *Tests* England (1895/6 to 1912, 26 matches).
Career batting
394–658–43–30886–258*–50.22–94–*ct* 240
Bowling 4872–166–29.34–9–2–6/78
Test batting
26–41–3–1223–144–32.18–2–*ct* 17
Bowling 3–0

Perhaps the most talented of all English athletes, C. B. Fry was a triple blue at Oxford – cricket, soccer and athletics – and would have been awarded his rugby blue, but for injury just before the University match. He played soccer for England (v Ireland in 1901) and for Southampton in the 1902 FA Cup Final, and held the world long jump record in addition to his career in English Test cricket. Although he made his Test debut in 1895/6, he did not really come to the forefront of English batsmen until 1898, when he averaged 54.18 with the bat. The following year he completed 2,000 runs for the first of six times and in 1901 reached 3,147 (av 78.67). In this season he hit six centuries in successive innings and had a total of 13 hundreds to his name. In all he completed 1,000 runs in a season 12 times.

His appearances in Test cricket were restricted by the fact that he never toured Australia, although invited to do so at least twice.

He captained England during the 1912 Triangular Series and did not lose a match; he also led Sussex from 1904 to 1908 (jointly in 1906 with C. L. A. Smith). Of his 16 double centuries, 13 were for Sussex, two for Hampshire and one for the Gentlemen v Players at Lord's. His highest first-class innings was 258* for Hampshire v Gloucester at Southampton in 1911.

He stood for Parliament several times but failed to be elected and after the war acted as India's representative at the League of Nations. He was offered the Kingship of Albania, but declined.

A noted writer on cricket and other games he published his own magazine for some years as well as his autobiography in 1939.

Fry, Kenneth Robert Burgess
Amateur. *b:* 15.3.1883, Surat, India. *d:* 21.6.1949, Chelsea, London. Cousin of C. B. (Sussex, Hants). Middle order right-hand batsman, wicket-keeper. *Sch* Cheltenham. *Teams* Sussex (1901–02, 4 matches); Cambridge U (1902–04, blue 1904).
Career batting
26–46–0–1036–129–22.52–2–*ct* 15–*st* 2

Fry, Stephen
Amateur. *b:* 23.5.1899, Portsmouth. *d:* 18.5.1979, London. Son of C. B. (Sussex and Hants), father of C. A. (Hants and Northants). Lower order right-hand batsman, wicket-keeper. *Team* Hampshire (1922–31, 29 matches).
Career batting
29–50–2–508–78–10.58–0–*ct* 16–*st* 1

Fryer, Frederick Eustace Reade
Amateur. *b:* 7.1.1849, Holbrook, Suffolk. *d:* 1.10.1917, Poplar, London. Middle order right-hand batsman, right-arm medium pace bowler. *Sch* Harrow. *Team* Cambridge U (1870–73, blue all four years).
Career batting
58–103–5–2149–91–21.92–0–*ct* 31
Bowling 1131–39–29.00–2–0–5/49

His County cricket was for Suffolk.

His first-class debut was for Gentlemen of the South in 1869 and his final match for Orleans Club in 1883.

In his later years he was a noted golfer.

Fryer, Philip Algernon
Amateur. *b:* 26.6.1870, Wymondham, Norfolk. *d:* 4.11.1950, Wilby, Northants. Opening right-hand batsman, lob bowler. *Sch* Wellingborough. *Team* Northants (1908, 2 matches).
Career batting
2–4–0–83–38–20.75–0–*ct* 1
Bowling 66–3–22.00–0–0–3/35

He did not appear for Cambridge whilst at the university, but missed his soccer blue only through injury.

From 1890 to 1906 he appeared for Norfolk.

Fryer, William Henry
Professional. *b:* 29.3.1829, Greenwich, Kent. *d:* 19.1.1919, Loose, Maidstone, Kent. Opening right-hand batsman, right-hand medium fast round-arm bowler, wicket-keeper. *Team* Kent (1852–72, 75 matches).

Career batting
88–161–9–1666–67–10.96–0–*ct* 73–*st* 25
Bowling 950–49–19.38–1–0–8/40

In September 1862 he was thrown out of a trap and lost the sight of one eye as a result of the accident, but continued to appear in County cricket, though he gave up keeping wicket.

Fulcher, Arthur William
Amateur. *b:* 7.5.1855, Pau, France. *d:* 17.5.1932, Bayswater, London. Father of E. J. (Kent). Middle order right-hand batsman, right-hand slow round arm bowler, good deep field. *Sch* Westminster. *Team* Kent (1878–87, 7 matches).
Career batting
7–12–1–156–44*–14.18–0–*ct* 2

Fulcher, Eric Jesser
Amateur. *b:* 12.3.1890, Bearsted, Kent. *d:* 14.2.1923, Llandogo, Monmouth, as the result of a gun accident. Son of A. W. (Kent). Hard hitting middle order right-hand batsman, splendid field. *Sch* Radley. *Team* Kent (1919, 4 matches). *Tour* MCC to Argentine 1911/2.
Career batting
10–18–1–329–64–19.35–0–*ct* 9
Bowling 228–4–57.00–0–0–2/35

He appeared with success for Norfolk; his first-class debut in England was for L. Robinson's Team in 1913 and his final first-class match for MCC in 1921.

Fuller, Edward Russell Henry
Amateur. *b:* 2.8.1931, Worcester, Cape Province, South Africa. Hard hitting lower order right-hand batsman, right-arm fast medium bowler, fine field. *Team* Western Province (1950/1 to 1959/60). *Tours* South Africa to England 1955, to Australia and New Zealand 1952/3. *Tests* South Africa (1952/3 to 1957/8, 7 matches).
Career batting
59–86–16–1062–69–15.10–0–*ct* 29
Bowling 5026–190–26.45–11–3–7/40
Test batting
7–9–1–64–17–8.00–0–*ct* 3
Bowling 668–22–30.36–1–0–5/66

Although he only appeared in two Tests during his one tour to England – he was competing with Heine and Adcock – he had a successful visit, taking 49 wickets (av 19.51).

His final first-class match in England was for the Commonwealth XI in 1958.

Fullerton, George Murray
Amateur. *b:* 8.12.1922, Johannesburg, South Africa. Middle order right-hand batsman, wicket-keeper. *Team* Transvaal (1945/6 to 1950/1). *Tours* South Africa to England 1947, 1951. *Tests* South Africa (1947–51, 7 matches).
Career batting
63–97–8–2768–167–31.10–3–*ct* 64–*st* 18
Bowling 107–3–35.66–0–0–2/41
Test batting
7–13–0–325–88–25.00–0–*ct* 10–*st* 2

In 1947 he came into the last two Tests as wicket-keeper, but in 1951 appeared in the first three Tests as a batsman. On the latter tour he hit 1,129 runs, av 31.36.

His first-class debut was for the Rest of South Africa in 1942/3.

Fullerton, Ian R.
Amateur. *b:* 24.9.1935, Johannesburg, South Africa. Opening right-hand batsman. *Team* Transvaal (1958/9 to 1965/66). *Tour* South African Fezela to England 1961.
Career batting
31–56–2–1853–145–34.31–5–*ct* 11
Bowling 8–0

He also played hockey for Transvaal.

Fulljames, Reginald Edgar Gilbert
Amateur. *b:* 13.11.1896, Southsea, Hants. Lower order left-hand batsman, slow left-arm bowler. *Sch* St Paul's. *Team* RAF (1927–32).
Career batting
8–14–2–173–47–14.41–0–*ct* 7
Bowling 795–38–20.92–5–1–7/25

Fullwood, Walter
Professional. *b:* 8.2.1907, Holmewood, Derbyshire. Tail end right-hand batsman, wicket-keeper. *Team* Derbyshire (1946, 6 matches).
Career batting
6–10–1–41–13–4.55–0–*ct* 5–*st* 1

Fulton, Herbert Angus
Amateur. *b:* 3.10.1872, Bangalore, India. *d:* 23.12.1951, Minehead, Somerset. Lower order batsman, wicket-keeper. *Team* Worcestershire (1914, 1 match).
Career batting
1–1–1–2–2*–no av–0–*ct* 0

He also played for Bedfordshire.

Furley, John
Amateur. *b:* 24.3.1847, Oakham, Rutland. *d:* 30.6.1909, Oakham, Rutland. Middle order right-hand batsman, right-hand fast round arm bowler, slip field. *Sch* Oakham. *Teams* North (1875); England (1877).
Career batting
2–4–0–13–5–3.25–0–*ct* 0

He appeared in several matches under the alias 'A. Yorker'. His county cricket was for

Northants (non-first-class), Rutland and Lincolnshire.

Furniss, John Brian
Professional. *b:* 16.11.1934, Baslow, Derbyshire. Lower order right-hand batsman, right-arm fast medium bowler. *Team* Derbyshire (1955–56, 4 matches).
Career batting
4–5–1–9–6–2.25–0–*ct* 2
Bowling 259–7–37.00–0–0–3/52

Fursdon, Edward David
Cricketer. *b:* 20.12.1952, Sevenoaks, Kent. Middle/lower right-hand batsman, right-arm medium fast bowler. *Sch* Sherborne. *Teams* Oxford U (1973–75, blue 1974–75).
Career batting
17–29–6–484–112*–21.04–1–*ct* 2
Bowling 1428–43–33.20–1–0–6/60
His County cricket was for Devon.

Fussell, Philip Hillier
Amateur. *b:* 12.2.1931, Rode, Bath. Lower order right-hand batsman, right-arm medium pace bowler, close field. *Sch* Monkton Combe. *Team* Somerset (1953–56, 2 matches).
Career batting
2–4–0–10–5–2.50–0–*ct* 1
Bowling 71–1–71.00–0–0–1/26

Fyfe, Douglas Munro
Amateur. *b:* 1824. *d:* 1871, Westminster, London. Middle order batsman. *Teams* Gentlemen of South (1866); MCC (1868–69).
Career batting
5–8–0–60–31–7.50–0–*ct* 2
He played for Devon, Hampshire (non-first-class), Wiltshire and Monmouthshire.

Fyffe, Alan Herbert
Amateur. *b:* 30.4.1884, Kensington, London. *d:* 5.3.1939, Minchinhampton, Gloucs. Lower order right-hand batsman, right-arm fast medium bowler. *Sch* Winchester. *Team* Oxford U (1906).
Career batting
13–24–4–130–39–6.50–0–*ct* 7
Bowling 1149–40–28.72–0–0–4/62
His final first-class match was for Harlequins in 1925.
He played County cricket for Denbighshire and Cheshire.

Fynn, Charles Garnet
Amateur. *b:* 24.4.1897, Marylebone, London. *d:* 26.8.1976, Bournemouth, Hants. Lower order right-hand batsman, right-arm slow bowler. *Team* Hampshire (1930–31, 9 matches).
Career batting
9–12–5–45–21–6.42–0–*ct* 2
Bowling 446–11–40.54–0–0–3/92

GABE-JONES, A. R.
(*see under* Jones, A. R. G.)

Gaddum, Frederick Ducange
Amateur. *b:* 28.6.1860, Didsbury, Manchester. *d:* 14.10.1900, Stockport, Cheshire, as the result of a bicycling accident. Tail end left-hand batsman, slow left-arm bowler, moderate field. *Sch* Uppingham and Rugby. *Teams* Cambridge U (1880–82, blue 1882); Lancashire (1884, 1 match).
Career batting
11–20–7–87–16–6.69–0–*ct* 9
Bowling 406–21–19.33–0–0–4/34

Gaekwad, A. D. *(see entry at back of book)*

Gaekwad, Dattajirao Krishnarao
Amateur. *b:* 27.10.1928, Baroda, India. Father of A. D. (India). Opening/middle order right hand batsman, right-arm medium pace or leg break bowler. *Team* Baroda (1947/8 to 1963/4). *Tours* India to England 1952, 1959, to West Indies 1952/3. *Tests* India (1952 to 1960/1, 11 matches).
Career batting
110–172–13–5788–249*–36.40–17–*ct* 50
Bowling 1016–25–40.64–0–0–4/117
Test batting
11–20–1–350–52–18.42–0–*ct* 5
Bowling 12–0

In 1952 he batted adequately in first-class matches, but was required for only one Test; in 1959 he hit 1,174 runs, av 34.52, and appeared in four Tests, but made little impact against England. He hit three double centuries, all for Baroda, his highest being 249* v Maharashtra at Poona in 1959/60.

His first-class debut was for D. B. Deodhar's XI in 1943/44.

Gaekwad, Hiralal Ghasulal
Amateur. *b:* 29.8.1923, Nagpur, India. Lower order left-hand batsman, left-arm medium pace or slow spin bowler. *Teams* C. P. and Berar (1941/2); Holkar (1943/4 to 1954/5); Madhya Bharat (1955/6 to 1956/7); Madhya Pradesh (1957/8 to 1963/4). *Tours* India to England 1952; Holkar to Ceylon 1947/8. *Test* India (1952/3, 1 match).
Career batting
101–147–19–2487–164–19.42–2–*ct* 43
Bowling 8859–375–23.62–21–5–7/67
Test batting
1–2–0–22–14–11.00–0–*ct* 0
Bowling 47–0

Gaekwar, HH Prince Udayasinhrao Shivajirao
(later Maharajah of Baroda)
Amateur. *b:* 11.6.1918, Baroda, India. Lower order right-hand batsman, right-arm fast medium bowler. *Team* Cambridge U (1939).
Career batting
4–5–3–16–13*–8.00–0–*ct* 0
Bowling 188–2–94.00–0–0–1/12

Gale, Henry
Amateur. *b:* 11.7.1836, Winchester. *d:* 3.3.1898, Bournemouth, Hants. Middle order right-hand batsman. *Sch* Marlborough. *Teams* Hampshire (1865–66, 5 matches).
Career batting
6–9–0–144–44–16.00–0–*ct* 2

He also appeared for Norfolk.

Gale, Leslie Edward
Amateur. *b.* 11.11.1904, Solihull, Warwickshire. *d:* 22.1.1982, Dudley, West Midlands. Middle order right-hand batsman. slow right-arm bowler. *Team* Worcestershire (1923–28, 14 matches).
Career batting
14–26–6–155–19–7.75–0–*ct* 6
Bowling 394–10–39.40–1–0–5/49

He also played for Staffordshire.

Gale, Percival George
Amateur. *b:* 22.5.1865, Kensington, London. *d:* 7.9.1940, Croydon, Surrey. Middle order right-hand batsman. *Team* London County (1901–04).
Career batting
11–17–1–140–40–8.75–0–*ct* 5
Bowling 37–0

He was mainly associated with the Wanderers CC of London. His final first-class match was for W. G. Grace's XI in 1906.

Gale, Robert Alec
Professional. *b:* 10.12.1933, Old Warden, Bedfordshire. Opening left-hand batsman, right-arm medium pace, or leg break bowler. *Sch* Bedford Modern. *Team* Middlesex (1956–65, 219 matches). *Tours* Swanton to West Indies 1960/1; Brown to East Africa 1961/2 (not first-class); MCC to South America 1964/5 (not first-class).
Career batting
242–439–13–12505–200–29.35–15–*ct* 124
Bowling 1748–47–37.19–0–0–4/57

He hit 1,000 runs in a season six times (best 2,211, av 38.78, in 1962). His only double century was 200 for Middlesex v Glamorgan at Newport in 1962.

His first-class debut was for Combined Services in 1955 and his final first-class match for Free Foresters in 1968.

Gallacher, Thomas Nesbitt
Cricketer. *b:* 3.4.1936, Kilmarnock, Scotland. Right-hand batsman. *Team* Scotland (1965–66).
Career batting
4–5–0–126–73–25.20–0–*ct* 0

Gallaugher, Robert George
Amateur. *b:* 8.1.1923, Auckland, New Zealand. Lower order left-hand batsman, slow left-arm bowler: *Tour* New Zealand Services to England 1945.
Career batting
1–1–0–2–2–2.00–0–*ct* 0
Bowling 27–0

Galley, James
Cricketer. *b:* 4.10.1945, Brislington, Somerset. Middle order right-hand batsman. *Team* Somerset (1969, 3 matches).
Career batting
3–6–1–27–17–5.40–0–*ct* 1
A noted rugby player, he appeared for Bath at scrum-half.

Gallichan, Norman
Amateur. *b:* 3.6.1906, Palmerston North, New Zealand. *d:* 25.3.1969, Taupo, New Zealand. Middle/lower order right-hand batsman, slow left-arm bowler. *Team* Wellington (1928/9 to 1938/9). *Tour* New Zealand to England 1937. *Test* New Zealand (1937, 1 match).
Career batting
31–43–8–636–62–18.17–0–*ct* 22
Bowling 2244–86–26.09–4–1–6/46
Test batting
1–2–0–32–30–16.00–0–*ct* 0
Bowling 113–3–37.66–0–0–3/99
Although only a last minute selection for the 1937 tour of England he bowled better than anticipated, taking 59 wickets, av 23.92, and earning a place in one Test.
His first-class debut was for The Rest v New Zealand 1927/8.

Gallop, Henry George
Amateur. *b:* 21.8.1857, Redland, Bristol. *d:* 21.8.1940, Bitton, Gloucs. Lower order right-hand batsman, right-arm medium pace bowler. *Team* Gloucestershire (1877–83, 6 matches).
Career batting
6–10–2–43–16–5.37–0–*ct* 4
Bowling 104–5–20.80–0–0–3/47

Galpin, John George
Professional. *b:* 13.1.1843, Gosport, Hants. *d:* 1917, Luton, Bedfordshire. Lower order right-hand batsman, right-hand fast round arm bowler. *Team* Hampshire (1875–80, 7 matches).
Career batting
7–14–5–100–27–11.11–0–*ct* 4
Bowling 462–28–16.50–2–0–6/68
He also played for Buckinghamshire and Northants (not first-class).

Gamble, Frederick Charles
Professional. *b:* 29.5.1905, Charing Cross, London. *d:* 15.5.1965, Lambeth, London. Lower order right-hand batsman, right-arm medium pace bowler. *Team* Surrey (1933–35, 19 matches).
Career batting
19–25–10–132–29–8.80–0–*ct* 10
Bowling 1555–40–38.87–0–0–4/82
He also played for Devon. A well-known soccer player, he was a centre forward for West Ham, Aldershot and Reading.

Gamble, George (F.)
Professional. *b:* 24.10.1877, Leicester. *d:* 1949, Leicester. Tail end right-hand batsman, left-arm bowler. *Teams* London County (1900–03); Surrey (1906, 8 matches).
Career batting
11–13–7–54–21*–9.00–0–*ct* 5
Bowling 691–26–26.57–1–0–5/78

Gamble, Neil Walton
Cricketer. *b:* 17.1.1943, Macclesfield, Cheshire. Lower order right-hand batsman, right-arm medium pace bowler. *Sch* Stockport GS. *Team* Oxford U (1967, blue).
Career batting
13–17–5–87–24–7.25–0–*ct* 8
Bowling 786–19–41.36–0–0–4/57
His County cricket was for Cheshire.

Game, William Henry
Amateur. *b:* 2.10.1853, Stoke Newington, Middlesex. *d:* 11.8.1932, Brancaster, Norfolk. Hard hitting middle order right-hand batsman, right-arm slow bowler, brilliant outfield. *Sch* Sherborne. *Teams* Surrey (1871–83, 39 matches); Oxford U (1873–76, blue all four years).
Career batting
59–104–5–1862–141–18.80–2–*ct* 33
Bowling 308–5–61.60–0–0–1/5
He also played for Dorset. He won his blue for rugby football.

Gamlin, Herbert Temlett
Professional. *b:* 12.2.1878, Wellington, Somerset. *d:* 12.7.1937, North Cheam, Surrey. Tail end right-hand batsman, off-break bowler. *Team* Somerset (1895–96, 3 matches).
Career batting
3–6–0–7–5–1.16–0–*ct* 4
Bowling 207–2–103.50–0–0–2/100
A noted rugby footballer, he appeared for England at full-back.

Gamsy, Dennis
Amateur. *b:* 17.2.1940, Durban, South Africa. Opening right-hand batsman, wicket-keeper.

Team Natal (1958/9 to 1972/3). *Tour* South Africa to England 1965. *Tests* South Africa (1969/70, 2 matches).
Career batting
93–145–14–3106–137–23.70–2–*ct* 277–*st* 33
Bowling 13–0
Test batting
2–3–1–39–30*–19.50–0–*ct* 5
He was reserve wicket-keeper on the 1965 tour to England and did not appear in any Tests.

Gandon, Nicholas John Charles
Cricketer. *b:* 7.7.1956, Leicester. Right-hand batsman, off break bowler. *Sch* Haileybury. *Team* Oxford U (1979).
Career batting
8–13–1–170–38–14.16–0–*ct* 6
He appeared for Hertfordshire commencing 1975.

Gandy, Christopher Henry
Professional. *b:* 1867, Bethnal Green, Middlesex. *d:* 18.6.1907, Billericay, Essex. Lower order batsman, opening left-arm bowler. *Team* Hampshire (1900, 2 matches).
Career batting
2–4–1–6–6*–2.00–0–*ct* 1
Bowling 117–3–39.00–0–0–2/84

Gange, Thomas Henry
Professional. *b:* 15.4.1891, Pietermaritzburg, South Africa. *d:* 11.7.1947, Swansea, Glamorgan. Lower order right-hand batsman, right-arm fast bowler. *Team* Gloucestershire (1913–20, 37 matches).
Career batting
37–64–7–571–39–10.01–0–*ct* 12
Bowling 3265–103–31.69–6–0–7/91
In Wisden's Almanack for 1950, Gange is given an obituary stating he died in March 1949, but this is incorrect.
He also played for Wiltshire.

Ganly, James Blandford
Amateur. *b:* 7.3.1904, Dublin, Ireland. *d:* 22.7.1976, Oughterand, Co Galway, Ireland. Right-hand batsman, right-arm fast medium bowler. *Teams* Ireland (1921–37); Dublin University (1924).
Career batting
15–29–1–486–62*–17.36–0–*ct* 5
Bowling 177–7–25.28–0–0–2/22
He played rugby for Ireland.

Gannon, Jack Rose Compton
Amateur. *b:* 1.11.1882. *d:* 25.4.1980, near Eastshaw, Midhurst, Sussex. Lower order batsman, wicket-keeper. *Sch* Sutton Valence. *Teams* MCC (1908–10); Europeans (1917/8).
Career batting
8–15–3–158–48–13.16–0–*ct* 10–*st* 3

Ganteaume, Andrew Gordon
Amateur. *b:* 22.1.1921, Belmont, Port of Spain, Trinidad. Opening right-hand batsman, bowler, wicket-keeper. *Team* Trinidad (1940/1 to 1962/3). *Tour* West Indies to England 1957. *Test* West Indies (1947/8, 1 match).
Career batting
50–85–5–2785–159–34.81–5–*ct* 34–*st* 3
Bowling 51–0
Test batting
1–1–0–112–112–112.00–1–*ct* 0
He was brought into the West Indies Test side as deputy for the injured Stollmeyer and hit a century on his Test debut. This proved to be his only Test. In 1957 he only had a modest tour of England with the bat.

Gard, Trevor
Cricketer. *b:* 2.6.1957, West Lambrook, Somerset. Lower order right-hand batsman, wicket-keeper. *Team* Somerset (1976–83, 43 matches).
Career batting
43–49–10–618–51*–15.84–0–*ct* 67–*st* 16
Bowling 8–0

Gardiner, Peter Leitham
Amateur. *b:* 22.7.1896, Perth, Scotland. *d:* 15.6.1975, Perth, Scotland. Right-hand batsman, right-arm medium pace bowler. *Team* Scotland (1925–31).
Career batting
2–4–0–67–42–16.75–0–*ct* 1
Bowling 136–3–45.33–0–0–2/7

Gardiner, Robert P.
Amateur. Right-hand batsman, wicket-keeper. *Team* Scotland (1909–14).
Career batting
3–5–0–130–72–26.00–0–*ct* 6

Gardiner, Stuart James
Cricketer. *b:* 19.3.1947, Bloemfontein, South Africa. Lower order left-hand batsman, left-arm medium pace bowler. *Teams* Cambridge U (1978, blue); Orange Free State (1967/8 to 1973/4).
Career batting
34–49–16–556–40*–16.84–0–*ct* 13
Bowling 2772–111–24.97–5–0–6/49

Gardiner-Hill, Peter Farquhar
Amateur. *b:* 22.10.1926, London. Middle order

right-hand batsman. *Sch* Eton. *Team* Oxford U (1949).
Career batting
2–2–0–78–50–39.00–0–*ct* 0

Gardner, Fred Charles
Amateur in 1947, professional from 1948. *b:* 4.6.1922, Bell Green, Coventry, Warwickshire. *d:* 12.1.1979, Coventry. Right-hand opening batsman, fine slip field. *Team* Warwickshire (1947–61, 338 matches).
Career batting
340–597–66–17905–215*–33.71–29–*ct* 198
Bowling 99–0

He hit 1,000 runs in a season 10 times (best 1,911, av 45.50, in 1950). His only double century was 215* for Warwickshire v Somerset at Taunton in 1950.

He played soccer for Coventry City and Newport County.

Gardner, Harry
Amateur. *b:* 12.6.1890, London. *d:* 12.2.1939, East Grinstead, Sussex. Middle order batsman. *Sch* King's, Canterbury. *Team* Army (1914).
Career batting
2–4–0–42–17–10.50–0–*ct* 1

Gardner, Herbert Wilson
Amateur. *b:* 19.1.1852, Rugeley, Staffs. *d:* 5.12.1924, Armitage, Staffs. Middle order right-hand batsman, good cover point. *Sch* Rugby. *Team* MCC (1882).
Career batting
1–2–0–2–1–1.00–0–*ct* 0

His County cricket was for Staffordshire.

Gardner, Leslie Robin
Professional. *b:* 23.2.1934, Ledbury, Herefordshire. Middle order right-hand batsman, right-arm medium pace bowler. good slip field. *Team* Leicestershire (1954–62, 126 matches).
Career batting
126–227–19–4119–102*–19.80–2–*ct* 63
Bowling 199–5–39.80–0–0–3/54

He his 1,000 runs, av 27.77, in 1959. He also played for Hertfordshire.

A useful soccer player, he appeared as inside right for Hereford.

Gardom, Barrie Keith
Cricketer. *b:* 31.12.1952, Birmingham. Middle order right-hand batsman, leg break and googly bowler. *Team* Warwickshire (1973–74, 17 matches).
Career batting
17–25–2–427–79*–18.56–0–*ct* 6
Bowling 700–17–41.17–1–0–6/39

Garforth, William Henry
Amateur. *b:* 14.1.1856, Otherington, Yorkshire. *d:* 15.6.1931, Malton, Yorkshire. Lower order batsman, bowler. *Sch* Uppingham. *Team* I Zingari (1887).
Career batting
1–2–0–0–0–0.00–0–*ct* 1
Bowling 3–0

Garland-Wells, Herbert Montandon
Amateur. *b:* 14.11.1907, Brockley, Surrey. Hard hitting middle order right-hand batsman, right-arm medium pace bowler. *Sch* St Paul's. *Teams* Oxford U (1927–30, blue 1928–30); Surrey (1928–39, 130 matches).
Career batting
190–283–23–6068–128–23.34–4–*ct* 141
Bowling 7617–185–41.17–2–0–5/25

He captained Surrey in 1939. He hit 1,270 runs, av 43.79, in 1928.

A good soccer player, he played for Clapton Orient and England in an Amateur International as goalkeeper.

Garlick, Richard Gordon
Professional. *b:* 11.4.1917, Kirkby Lonsdale, Westmorland. Lower order right-hand batsman, right-arm medium pace off break bowler, good field. *Teams* Lancashire (1938–47, 44 matches); Northants (1948–50, 77 matches).
Career batting
121–152–32–1664–62*–13.86–0–*ct* 39
Bowling 8670–332–26.11–10–1–6/27

Garlies, Lord Alan Plantagenet Stewart
(succeeded as 10th Earl of Galloway in 1873)
Amateur. *b:* 21.10.1835, London. *d:* 7.2.1901, Cumloden, Newton Stewart, Kirkcudbrightshire. Steady opening right-hand batsman, good deep field. *Sch* Harrow. *Team* MCC (1858–64).
Career batting
5–9–2–96–24–13.71–0–*ct* 1–*st* 2

He was President of MCC in 1858.

He also played for Rutland.

He was MP for Wigtownshire 1868–73.

Garne, William Henry
Amateur. *b:* 9.5.1861, Middle Aston, Oxon. *d:* 24.5.1895, Wellingborough, Northants. Middle order right-hand batsman, right-arm medium pace bowler. *Sch* Framlingham. *Team* Gloucestershire (1884, 1 match).
Career batting
1–2–0–2–2–1.00–0–*ct* 0

Garner, Joel
Cricketer. *b*: 16.12.1952, Christchurch, Barbados. Hard hitting lower order right-hand

batsman, right-arm fast bowler, gully field. *Teams* Barbados (1975/6 to 1982/3); Somerset (1977–83, 60 matches); South Australia (1982/3, 8 matches). *Tours* West Indies to Australia and New Zealand 1979/80, to England 1980, to Pakistan 1980/1, to Australia 1981/2. *Tests* West Indies (1976/7 to 1982/3, 32 matches).
Career batting
134–151–36–2049–104–17.81–1–*ct* 91
Bowling 10653–595–17.90–36–7–8/31
Test batting
32–40–6–424–60–12.47–0–*ct* 26
Bowling 2861–131–21.83–2–0–6/56

On the 1980 tour to England he headed both Test and first-class bowling tables with 26 wickets, av 14.26, and 49 wickets, av 13.93, respectively. His best season with Somerset was 1981 with 88 wickets, av 15.32.

Garnett, Harold Gwyer
Amateur. *b:* 19.11.1879, Aigburgh, Liverpool. *d:* 3.12.1917, Marcoing, Cambrai, France. He was killed in action. Dashing opening left-hand batsman, slow left-arm bowler, wicket-keeper. *Sch* Clifton. *Teams* Lancashire (1899–1914, 144 matches); Argentine (1911/12). *Tours* MacLaren to Australia 1901/2.
Career batting
152–245–22–5798–139–26.00–5–*ct* 185–*st* 18
Bowling 224–8–28.00–0–0–2/18

He his 1,000 runs in a season twice (best 1758, av 35.87, in 1901).

He was absent from England for several years, being in business in Argentina, but returned home in 1912.

Garnett, Rev Lionel
Amateur. *b:* 25.12.1843, Lancaster. *d:* 1.5.1912, Belfast, Northern Ireland. Middle order batsman, bowler. *Sch* Eton. *Team* Southgate (1864).
Career batting
1–1–1–3–3*–no av–0–*ct* 0

He played for Cheshire.

Garnett, Thomas Ronald
Amateur. *b:* 1.1.1915, Stockport, Cheshire. Opening/middle order right-hand batsman, off break bowler. *Sch* Charterhouse. *Team* Somerset (1935–39, 5 matches).
Career batting
5–8–0–161–75–20.12–0–*ct* 6

He appeared in the Freshmen's Match and Seniors' Match at Cambridge, but no first-class games. He also played for Wiltshire.

Garnham, Michael Anthony
Cricketer. *b*: 20.8.1960, Johannesburg, South Africa. Lower order right-hand batsman, wicket-keeper. *Teams* Gloucestershire (1979, 3 matches); Leicestershire (1980–82, 31 matches).
Career batting
34–49–8–875–74–21.34–0–*ct* 62–*st* 13

Garnier, Rev Edward Southwell
Amateur. *b:* 5.4.1850, Paddington, London. *d:* 8.8.1938, Shropham, Norfolk. Brother of T. P. (Hants). Opening right-hand batsman, right-hand medium pace round arm bowler. *Sch* Marlborough. *Team* Oxford U (1871–73, blue 1873).
Career batting
10–18–2–187–66*–11.68–0–*ct* 3
Bowling 60–0

He played for Shropshire and Bedfordshire. He was an excellent athlete, both as a hurdler and at throwing the hammer.

Garnier, Rev Thomas Parry
Amateur. *b:* 22.2.1841, Longford, Derbyshire. *d:* 18.3.1898, St Moritz, Switzerland. Brother of E. S. (Oxford U). Opening/ middle order right-hand batsman, good deep field. *Sch* Winchester. *Teams* Oxford U (1861–63, blue all three years); Hampshire (1864, 1 match).
Career batting
13–24–3–287–35–13.66–0–*ct* 4

He also played for Lincolnshire and Norfolk.

Garofall, Alan Robert
Cricketer. *b:* 1.6.1946, Kingston, Surrey. Tail end right-hand batsman, right-arm medium pace bowler. *Sch* Latymer Upper. *Team* Oxford U (1966–68, blue 1967–68).
Career batting
27–47–0–874–99–18.59–0–*ct* 19
Bowling 8–0

He appeared for Hertfordshire commencing 1970.

Garratt, Humphry Stone
Amateur. *b:* 12.1.1898, Kingston-on-Thames, Surrey. *d:* 1.9.1974, Worplesden Hill, Surrey. Lower order batsman, wicket-keeper. *Sch* Haileybury. *Team* Worcestershire (1925–28, 5 matches).
Career batting
5–9–0–111–39–12.33–0–*ct* 3

Garrett, Charles Richard
Amateur. *b:* 3.3.1901, Puri, India. *d:* 15.2.1968. Lower order batsman, useful bowler. *Team* Royal Navy (1926–29).
Career batting
4–7–1–70–23–11.66–0–*ct* 5
Bowling 240–7–34.28–0–0–3/124

Garrett, Hubert Frederic
Amateur. *b:* 13.11.1885, Melbourne, Australia.

d: 4.6.1915, near Achi Baba, Gallipoli, Turkey. He was killed in action. Son of T. W. (New South Wales). Lower order right-hand batsman, leg break bowler. *Team* Somerset (1913, 8 matches).
Career batting
11–21–3–220–37*–12.22–0–*ct* 4
Bowling 755–34–22.20–2–1–6/60

He did not appear for Cambridge whilst at the University. His final first-class match was for MCC in 1914.

Garrett, Thomas William
Amateur. *b:* 26.7.1858, Wollongong, New South Wales, Australia. *d:* 6.8.1943, Warrawee, Sydney, Australia. Father of H. F. (Somerset). Lower order right-hand batsman, right-arm fast medium bowler. *Team* New South Wales (1876/7 to 1897/8, 56 matches). *Tours* Australia to England 1878, 1882, 1886, to North America 1878. *Tests* Australia (1876/7 to 1887/8, 19 matches).
Career batting
160–256–29–3673–163–16.18–2–*ct* 80
Bowling 8353–445–18.77–29–4–7/38
Test batting
19–33–6–339–51*–12.55–0–*ct* 7
Bowling 970–36–26.94–2–0–6/78

Of his three tours to England, his most successful was 1882 when he took 118 wickets, av 14.35, in first-class matches.

He was also a noted sprinter.

Garrett, William Thomas
Amateur. *b:* 9.1.1876, Camberwell, Surrey. *d:* 16.2.1953, Buckhurst Hill, Essex. Middle order right-hand batsman, change bowler. *Team* Essex (1900–03, 15 matches).
Career batting
15–25–1–516–92–21.50–0–*ct* 4
Bowling 142–1–142.00–0–0–1/72

Garthwaite, Clive Charlton
Amateur. *b:* 22.10.1909, Guisborough, Yorkshire. *d:* 20.1.1979, Wendover, Bucks. Twin brother of P. F. (Oxford U). Sound right-hand middle order batsman, right-arm medium pace bowler. *Sch* Wellington. *Team* Army (1930).
Career batting
1–2–0–7–7–3.50–0–*ct* 0
Bowling 22–0

Garthwaite, Peter Fawcitt
Amateur. *b:* 22.10.1909, Guisborough, Yorkshire. Twin brother of C. C. (Army). Lower order right-hand batsman, leg break bowler. *Sch* Wellington. *Team* Oxford U (1929–30, blue 1929).
Career batting
11–15–5–99–31–9.90–0–*ct* 7
Bowling 917–23–39.86–1–0–5/74

Gatacre, Admiral Galfry George Ormond
Amateur. *b:* 11.6.1907, Wooroolin, Queensland, Australia. Lower order batsman, bowler. *Team* Royal Navy (1928).
Career batting
1–2–0–19–12–9.50–0–*ct* 0
Bowling 34–1–34.00–0–0–1/24

Gatehouse, Peter Warlow
Professional. *b:* 3.5.1936, Caerphilly, Glamorgan. Lower order right-hand batsman, left-arm fast medium bowler. *Team* Glamorgan (1957–62, 19 matches).
Career batting
19–23–8–85–20–5.66–0–*ct* 3
Bowling 1551–53–29.26–3–1–7/94

A well known rugby footballer, he played for Caerphilly.

Gatting, Michael William
Cricketer. *b*: 6.6.1957, Kingsbury, Middlesex. Aggressive middle order right-hand batsman, right-arm medium pace bowler, good close field. *Team* Middlesex (1975–83, 153 matches). *Tours* England to Pakistan and New Zealand 1977/8, to West Indies 1980/1, to India and Sri Lanka 1981/2; Middlesex to Zimbabwe 1980/1. *Tests* England (1977/8 to 1983, 24 matches).
Career batting
192–291–44–10219–216–41.37–22–*ct* 175
Bowling 2355–92–25.59–2–0–5/34
Test batting
24–42–3–918–81–23.53–0–*ct* 21
Bowling 52–0

He hit 1,000 runs in a season five times (best 1,651, av 58.96, in 1982). His highest innings was 216 for Middlesex v New Zealand at Lord's in 1983. He was appointed Middlesex captain 1983.

Gaukrodger, George Warrington
Professional. *b:* 1877, Belfast, Ireland. *d:* 13.12.1937, Low Moor, Bradford, Yorkshire. Middle/lower order right-hand batsman, wicket-keeper. *Team* Worcestershire (1900–10, 114 matches).
Career batting
115–179–46–2241–91–16.84–0–*ct* 169–*st* 62

Gauld, Dr George Ogg
Amateur. *b:* 21.6.1873, Aberdeen, Scotland. *d:* 16.6.1950, Nottingham. Lower order right-hand batsman, right-arm fast bowler. *Team* Nottinghamshire (1913–19, 14 matches).

Career batting
14–19–0–350–90–18.42–0–*ct* 9
Bowling 250–5–50.00–0–0–1/11

He captained Notts in 1913 and 1914 in the absence through illness of A. O. Jones.

Gaunt, Rev Canon Howard Charles Adie
Amateur. *b:* 13.11.1902, Edgbaston, Warwickshire. *d:* 1.2.1983, Winchester, Hants. Middle order right-hand batsman. *Sch* Tonbridge. *Team* Warwickshire (1919–22, 11 matches).
Career batting
11–20–1–147–32–7.73–0–*ct* 6

Gaunt, Ronald Arthur
Amateur. *b:* 26.2.1934, Yarlu, Western Australia. Lower order left-hand batsman, right-arm fast bowler. *Teams* Western Australia (1955/6 to 1959/60, 29 matches); Victoria (1960/1 to 1963/4, 18 matches). *Tours* Australia to South Africa 1957/8, to New Zealand 1956/7, 1959/60, to England 1961. *Tests* Australia (1957/8 to 1963/4, 3 matches).
Career batting
85–92–33–616–32*–10.44–0–*ct* 31
Bowling 7143–266–26.85–10–0–7/104
Test batting
3–4–2–6–3–3.00–0–*ct* 1
Bowling 310–7–44.28–0–0–3/53

Though he headed the tourists' first-class bowling averages in 1961 with 40 wickets, av 21.12, he appeared in only one Test.

Gauntlett, Gilbert Bernard
Amateur. *b:* 19.9.1936, Dolgelley, Merioneth. Lower order right-hand batsman, wicket-keeper. *Team* Oxford U (1957).
Career batting
1 match, did not bat–*ct* 3

Gavaskar, Sunil Manohar
Cricketer. *b:* 10.7.1949, Bombay, India. Excellent opening right-hand batsman, right-arm medium pace bowler, slip field. Nephew of M. K. Mantri (India), brother-in-law of G. R. Visnawath India). *Teams* Bombay (1967/8 to 1981/2); Somerset (1980, 15 matches). *Tours* Indian Universities to Ceylon 1970/1; India to West Indies 1970/1, to England 1971, 1974, 1979, 1982, to Ceylon 1973/4, to New Zealand and West Indies 1975/6, to Australia 1977/8, 1980/1, to Pakistan 1978/9, 1982/3, to New Zealand 1980/1, to West Indies 1982/3; Rest of World to Australia 1971/2. *Tests* India (1970/1 to 1982/3, 90 matches).
Career batting
287–471–49–21543–340–51.04–68–*ct* 251
Bowling 1137–21–54.14–0–0–3/43
Test batting
90–158–12–7625–221–52.22–27–*ct* 80
Bowling 173–1–173.00–0–0–1/34

On his first tour to England in 1971 he hit 1,141 runs, av 43.88, and played in all three Tests. In 1974 his record was 993 runs, av 41.37, and he again appeared in all three Tests, hitting the only century for the Indians in the series at Old Trafford. His performances in 1979 improved even on his previous visits, with 1,062 runs, av 55.89, and an innings of 221 in the Test at the Oval. He captained India on the 1982 tour but was not very successful as a batsman.

His first-class debut was for Vazir Sultan Colts XI in 1966/7.

Gavin, Norman Leslie
Amateur. *b:* 5.9.1922, London. Tail end left-hand batsman, slow left-arm bowler. *Team* RAF (1946).
Career batting
1–2–1–52–29–52.00–0–*ct* 1
Bowling 102–3–34.00–0–0–3/76

Gay, David William Maurice
Amateur. *b:* 2.4.1920, London. Lower order right-hand batsman, right-arm medium pace bowler. *Sch* Shrewsbury. *Team* Sussex (1949, 2 matches).
Career batting
4–6–1–16–11–3.20–0–*ct* 1
Bowling 288–9–32.00–0–0–4/57

Gay, Leslie Hewitt
Amateur. *b:* 24.3.1871, Brighton, Sussex. *d:* 1.11.1949, Salcombe Regis, Sidmouth, Devon. Cousin of K. J. Key (Surrey). Lower order right-hand batsman, wicket-keeper. *Sch* Brighton and Marlborough. *Teams* Cambridge U (1891–93, blue 1892–93); Somerset (1894, 4 matches); Hampshire (1900, 9 matches). *Tour* Stoddart to Australia 1894/5. *Test* England (1894/5, 1 match).
Career batting
46–80–15–1005–60*–15.46–0–*ct* 69–*st* 20
Test batting
1–2–0–37–33–18.50–0–*ct* 3–*st* 1

His final first-class match was for MCC in 1904. A noted soccer player, he represented both Cambridge and England as goalkeeper.

Geary, Albert Charles Taylor
Professional. *b:* 11.9.1900, Croydon, Surrey. Lower order right-hand batsman, right-arm medium fast bowler. *Team* Surrey (1922–31, 88 matches).

Career batting
88–90–27–670–40–10.63–0–*ct* 33
Bowling 6068–198–30.64–6–1–6/50

Geary, Frederick William
Professional. *b:* 9.12.1887, Hinckley, Leics. *d:* 8.1.1980, Hinckley, Leics. Lower order batsman, bowler. *Team* Glamorgan (1923, 2 matches).
Career batting
2–4–0–3–2–0.75–0–*ct* 2
Bowling 24–0

Geary, George
Professional. *b:* 9.7.1893, Barwell, Leics. *d:* 6.3.1981, Leicester. Lower order right-hand batsman, right-arm fast medium bowler, good slip field. *Team* Leicestershire (1912–38, 456 matches). *Tours* Joel to South Africa 1924/5; MCC to India, Burma and Ceylon 1926/7, to South Africa 1927/8, to Australia 1928/9; Tennyson to Jamaica 1931/2. *Tests* England (1924–34, 14 matches).
Career batting
549–820–138–13504–122–19.80–8–*ct* 451
Bowling 41339–2063–20.03–125–30–10/18
Test batting
14–20–4–249–66–15.56–0–*ct* 13
Bowling 1353–46–29.41–4–1–7/70

He took 100 wickets in a season 11 times (best 152, av 19.60, in 1929). His best bowling in an innings was 10 for 18 for Leics v Glamorgan at Pontypridd in 1929.

Geeson, Frederic
Professional. *b:* 23.8.1862, Redmile, Leics. *d:* 2.5.1920, Johannesburg, South Africa. Lower order right-hand batsman, right-arm medium pace bowler also leg breaks, slip field. *Team* Leicestershire (1895–1902, 135 matches).
Career batting
150–250–55–3694–104*–18.94–1–*ct* 138
Bowling 12199–472–25.85–28–7–8/110

His first-class debut was for MCC in 1892, his County cricket originally being for Lincolnshire.

In 1901 he took 125 wickets, av 26.64. His bowling action had been condemned in 1900 and as a result he switched to spin.

Gehrs, Donald Raeburn Algernon
Amateur. *b:* 29.11.1880, Victoria Harbour, South Australia. *d:* 25.6.1953, King's Park, Adelaide, Australia. Middle order right-hand batsman, right-arm slow bowler. *Team* South Australia (1902/3 to 1920/1, 49 matches). *Tours* Australia to England 1905, to New Zealand 1904/05. *Tests* Australia (1903/4 to 1910/11, 6 matches).
Career batting
83–142–12–4377–170–33.66–13–*ct* 71–*st* 4
Bowling 416–8–52.00–0–0–2/9
Test batting
6–11–0–221–67–20.09–0–*ct* 6
Bowling 4–0

He had a very moderate tour of England in 1905.

Gemmill, William Neilson
Amateur. *b:* 14.6.1900, Thio, New Caledonia. Middle order right-hand batsman, right-arm medium fast bowler. *Sch* King's, Taunton. *Team* Glamorgan (1921–26, 47 matches).
Career batting
48–89–2–1243–77–14.28–0–*ct* 31
Bowling 104–0

Genders, William Roy
Amateur. *b:* 21.1.1913, Dore, Derbyshire. Middle order right-hand batsman, bowler. *Sch* King's School, Ely. *Teams* Derbyshire (1946, 3 matches); Worcestershire (1947–48, 5 matches); Somerset (1949, 2 matches).
Career batting
10–19–4–245–55*–16.33–0–*ct* 6
Bowling 98–3–32.66–0–0–2/43

He was the author of 'League Cricket in England'.

Gentry, Jack Sydney Bates
Amateur. *b:* 4.10.1899, Wanstead, Essex. *d:* 16.4.1978, Loxwood, Sussex. Lower order right-hand batsman, slow left-arm bowler. *Sch* Christ's Hospital. *Teams* Hampshire (1919, 1 match); Surrey (1922–23, 10 matches); Essex (1925, 1 match).
Career batting
12–12–4–68–23–8.50–0–*ct* 3
Bowling 794–36–22.05–0–0–4/36

George, Walter
Professional. *b:* 20.9.1847, Selling, Faversham, Kent. *d:* 2.11.1938, Sydenham, Kent. Tail end right-hand batsman, left-hand fast or medium round arm bowler. *Team* Kent (1875, 5 matches).
Career batting
5–8–5–4–2*–1.33–0–*ct* 1
Bowling 315–22–14.31–2–0–7/86

George, William
Professional. *b:* 29.6.1874, Shrewsbury. *d:* 4.12.1933, Birmingham. Hard hitting middle order right-hand batsman. *Team* Warwickshire (1901–06, 13 matches).
Career batting
13–18–2–342–71–21.37–0–*ct* 8

He also appeared for Wiltshire and Shropshire.
A noted soccer player, he kept goal for Aston Villa and England.

Gerds, George Fortunato
Amateur. *b:* 27.1.1866, Uitenhage, South Africa. *d:* 1914, South Africa. Lower order right-hand batsman, wicket-keeper. *Sch* Clifton. *Team* Cambridge U (1887).
Career batting
1–1–0–0–0–0.00–0–*ct* 1–*st* 1
He appeared occasionally for Hampshire (not first-class).
He was an athlete of some note and a useful rugby footballer.

German, Arthur Clive Johnson
Amateur. *b:* 28.6.1905, Ashby-de-la-Zouch, Leics. *d:* 2.2.1968, Aberdeen, Scotland. Middle order right-hand batsman. *Sch* Repton. *Teams* Leicestershire (1923–24, 3 matches).
Career batting
3–6–0–73–36–12.16–0–*ct* 2
He appeared in the Freshmen's Match at Oxford, but no first-class matches. A good soccer player, he captained Oxford in 1927 and appeared in the half back line for Corinthians and Nottingham Forest.

German, Harry
Amateur. *b:* 1865, Measham, Leics. *d:* 14.6.1945, London. Lower order right-hand batsman, wicket-keeper. *Team* Leicestershire (1896–98, 5 matches).
Career batting
5–9–0–69–13–7.66–0–*ct* 0

Gerrard, Ronald Anderson
Amateur. *b:* 26.1.1912, Hong Kong. *d:* 22.1.1943, near Tripoli, Libya. Middle order right-hand batsman. *Sch* Taunton. *Team* Somerset (1935, 3 matches).
Career batting
3–5–0–36–18–7.20–0–*ct* 1

Gethin, Stanley John
Amateur. *b:* 1875, Kidderminster, Worcs. *d:* 17.2.1950, Kidderminster, Worcs. Brother of W. G. (Worcs). Middle order right-hand batsman, right-arm medium pace bowler. *Team* Worcestershire (1900–01, 4 matches).
Career batting
4–7–0–86–41–12.28–0–*ct* 0
Bowling 49–1–49.00–0–0–1/25

Gethin, William George
Amateur. *b:* 1877, Kidderminster, Worcs. *d:* 4.11.1939, Kidderminster, Worcs. Brother of S. J. (Worcs). Lower order right-hand batsman, right-arm medium pace bowler. *Team* Worcestershire (1921, 1 match).
Career batting
1–2–0–20–19–10.00–0–*ct* 2
Bowling 38–0

Ghavri, Karson Devjibhai
Cricketer. *b:* 28.2.1951, Rajkot, India. Lower order left-hand batsman, left-arm medium, or slow, bowler. *Teams* Saurashtra (1969/70 to 1982/3); Bombay (1973/4 to 1981/2). *Tours* India to Sri Lanka 1973/4, to Australia 1977/8, to England 1979, to Pakistan 1978/9, to Australia and New Zealand 1980/1; CCI to Sri Lanka 1972/3; Wadekar to Sri Lanka 1975/6; International XI to Jamaica 1982/3. *Tests* India (1974/5 to 1980/1, 39 matches).
Career batting
151–192–47–4179–102–28.82–1–*ct* 56
Bowling 12734–448–28.42–20–2–7/34
Test batting
39–57–14–913–86–21.23–0–*ct* 16
Bowling 3656–109–33.54–4–0–5/33
He played in all four Tests on the 1979 tour to England, but his record in first-class matches was a modest one – 27 wickets, av 41.55.

Ghazali, Mohammad Ebrahim Zainuddin
Amateur. *b:* 15.6.1924, Gujerat, India. Middle/lower order left-hand batsman, off break bowler. *Teams* Maharastra (1942/3 to 1947/8); Muslims (1943/4 to 1945/6); Services (1953/4 to 1954/5). *Tours* Pakistan to England 1954; Pakistan Services to Ceylon 1953/4. *Tests* Pakistan (1954, 2 matches).
Career batting
46–68–7–1569–160–25.72–2–*ct* 17
Bowling 2053–61–33.65–2–0–5/28
Test batting
2–4–0–32–18–8.00–0–*ct* 0
Bowling 18–0
Although he appeared in two Tests on the 1954 tour of England, he achieved little in first-class matches either with bat or ball. His first-class debut in Pakistan was in 1948/9.

Ghorpade, Jaysinghrao Mansinghrao
Amateur. *b:* 2.10.1930, Panchgani, Maharashtra, India. *d:* 29.3.1978, Baroda, India, uncle of F. P., R. P. and S. P. Gaekwad (all Baroda). Middle order right-hand batsman, leg break and googly bowler, brilliant deep field. *Team* Baroda (1948/9 to 1965/6). *Tours* India to West Indies 1952/3, to England 1959. *Tests* India (1952/3 to 1959, 8 matches).

Career batting
82–116–13–2631–123–25.54–2–*ct* 33
Bowling 3515–114–30.83–4–0–6/19
Test batting
8–15–0–229–41–15.26–0–*ct* 4
Bowling 131–0

He failed to do himself justice on his single tour to England. At the time of his death he was Chairman of the Indian Selection Committee.

Ghulam Abbas
Cricketer. *b:* 1.5.1947, Delhi, India. Middle order left-hand batsman, slow left-arm bowler. *Teams* Karachi (1962/3 to 1970/1); National Bank (1971/2 to 1972/3); PIA (1973/4 to 1981/2). *Tours* Pakistan to England 1967, to Australia and New Zealand 1964/5, to Ceylon 1964/5; PIA to Zimbabwe 1981/2. *Test* Pakistan (1967, 1 match).
Career batting
100–162–18–5242–276–36.40–9–*ct* 83
Bowling 229–7–32.71–0–0–2/9
Test batting
1–2–0–12–12–12.00–0–*ct* 0

He hit 871 runs, av 34.84, on his 1967 tour to England and appeared in one Test. His highest score was 276 for PIA v Punjab B at Karachi in 1975/6.

Ghulam Ahmed
Amateur. *b:* 4.7.1922, Hyderabad, India. Tail end right-hand batsman, off break bowler. Uncle of Asif Iqbal Razvi (Pakistan and Kent). *Team* Hyderabad (1939/40 to 1958/9); Muslims (1945/6). *Tours* India to England 1952, to Pakistan 1954/5, to Ceylon 1956/7. *Tests* India (1948/9 to 1958/9, 22 matches).
Career batting
98–126–30–1341–90–13.96–0–*ct* 57
Bowling 9190–407–22.57–32–9–9/53
Test batting
22–31–9–192–50–8.72–0–*ct* 11
Bowling 2052–68–30.17–4–1–7/49

He was easily the most successful bowler on the 1952 tour of England, taking 15 wickets, av 24.73, in the Tests, and in all first-class matches 80 wickets, av 21.92. His best bowling was 9/53 for Hyderabad v Madras at Secunderabad in 1947/8.

Ghulam Mohammad
Amateur. *b:* 12.7.1898, India. *d:* 21.7.1966, Karachi, Pakistan. Lower order right-hand batsman, left-arm medium pace bowler. *Team* Muslims (1924/5 to 1931/2); Sind (1934/5 to 1938/9). *Tours* India to England 1932; Vizianagram to Ceylon 1930/1.
Career batting
40–59–5–644–74–11.92–0–*ct* 17
Bowling 2404–97–24.78–1–0–5/114

Although effective on matting wickets in India, he proved useless in England in 1932, taking only three wickets on the tour.

Gibaut, Russel Philip
Cricketer. *b*: 5.3.1963, St Saviour, Jersey. Right-hand batsman, right-arm medium pace bowler. *Team* Oxford U (1983).
Career batting
2–2–0–7–7–3.50–0–*ct* 0

Gibb, Frank
Professional. *b:* 1868, Ticehurst, Sussex. *d:* 23.3.1957, Tunbridge Wells, Kent. Lower order batsman, left-arm fast bowler. *Team* Sussex (1890, 10 matches).
Career batting
10–19–7–41–8–3.41–0–*ct* 2
Bowling 550–9–61.11–0–0–2/140

Gibb, Paul Antony
Amateur, turned professional in 1951. *b:* 11.7.1913, Brandsby, Yorkshire. *d:* 7.12.1977, Guildford, Surrey. Opening/middle order right-hand batsman, wicket-keeper. *Sch* St Edward's, Oxford. *Teams* Scotland (1934–38); Cambridge U (1935–38, blue all four years); Yorkshire (1935–46, 36 matches); Essex (1951–56, 145 matches). *Tours* Cahn to North America 1933 (not first-class); Yorkshire to Jamaica 1935/6; Tennyson to India 1937/8; MCC to South Africa 1938/9, to Australia 1946/7; Commonwealth to India 1953/4. *Tests* England (1938/9 to 1946/7, 8 matches).
Career batting
287–479–33–12520–204–28.07–19–*ct* 425–*st* 123
Bowling 161–5–32.20–0–0–2/40
Test batting
8–13–0–581–120–44.69–2–*ct* 3–*st* 1

His career is unusual in that he obtained a blue at Cambridge and later became a professional cricketer.

He hit 1,000 runs in a season five times (best 1,658, av 48.76, in 1938). His only double century was 204 for Cambridge U v Free Foresters in 1938. After leaving County cricket he was on the first-class umpires' list for 10 years.

Gibb, Richard Carver
Amateur. *b:* 30.8.1917, Christchurch, Hants. Lower order right-hand batsman, left-arm bowler. *Team* Cambridge U (1938).
Career batting
3–4–0–28–17–7.00–0–*ct* 2
Bowling 280–6–46.66–0–0–2/52

Gibbon, Rev John Houghton
Amateur. *b:* 21.8.1847, Woolton, Liverpool, Lancashire. *d:* 29.4.1883, Willersey, Gloucs.

Steady middle order right-hand batsman. *Sch* Harrow. *Team* Oxford U (1869, blue).
Career batting
4–6–0–31–17–5.16–0–*ct* 2
He played for Cheshire and Warwickshire (not first-class).

Gibbons, Herbert Gladstone
Professional *b:* 12.3.1905, Bradfield, Berkshire. *d:* 13.1.1963, Southampton, Hants. Lower order right-hand batsman, leg break and googly bowler. *Team* Hampshire (1925–28, 7 matches).
Career batting
7–8–1–70–27–10.00–0–*ct* 1
Bowling 92–0

Gibbons, Harold Harry Ian (Haywood)
Professional. *b:* 10.10.1904, Devonport, Devon. *d:* 16.2.1973, Worcester. Sound opening right-hand batsman, fine field. *Team* Worcestershire (1927–46, 380 matches).
Career batting
383–671–57–21087–212*–34.34–44–*ct* 156
Bowling 737–7–105.28–0–0–2/27
He hit 1,000 runs in a season 12 times going on to 2,000 on three occasions (best 2,654, av 52.03, in 1934). His two double hundreds were both for Worcs, the highest being 212* v Northants at Dudley in 1939.

Gibbs, Arthur Holland Dyer
Amateur. *b:* 1894, Axbridge, Somerset. *d:* 29.10.1963, Weston-super-Mare, Somerset. Lower order batsman, wicket-keeper. *Team* Somerset (1919–20, 3 matches).
Career batting
3–5–0–66–41–13.20–0–*ct* 4–*st* 2

Gibbs, Joseph Arthur
Amateur. *b:* 25.11.1867, London. *d:* 13.5.1899, Marylebone, London. Middle order right-hand batsman. *Sch* Eton. *Team* Somerset (1891–94, 5 matches). *Tour* Hawke to India 1892/3.
Career batting
10–18–1–162–75–9.52–0–*ct* 5
His final first-class match was for MCC in 1896. He was the author of a book on the care of cricket grounds.

Gibbs, Lancelot Richard
Professional. *b:* 29.9.1934, Georgetown, British Guiana. Cousin of C. H. Lloyd (Lancashire and West Indies). Lower order right-hand batsman, off break bowler. *Teams* British Guiana (1953/4 to 1974/5); Warwickshire (1967–72, 109 matches); South Australia (1969/70, 8 matches). *Tours* West Indies to India and Pakistan 1958/9, 1974/5, to Australia 1960/1, 1975/6, to England 1963, 1966, 1969, 1973, to India and Ceylon 1966/7, to Australia and New Zealand 1968/9; Rest of World to England 1970. *Tests* West Indies (1957/8 to 1975/6, 79 matches).
Career batting
330–352–150–1729–43–8.55–0–*ct* 203
Bowling 27878–1024–27.22–50–10–8/37
Test batting
79–109–39–488–25–6.97–0–*ct* 52
Bowling 8989–309–29.09–18–2–8/38
One of the greatest off spin bowlers, Gibbs was most successful on his first two tours (1963 and 1966) to England, but achieved only moderate figures on his later two visits. His best season with Warwickshire was 1971, when, in all first-class matches, he took 131 wickets, av 18.89.
He created a new Test career record in his last Test (v Australia 1975/6) by capturing his 308th wicket.

Gibbs, Peter John Keith
Cricketer. *b:* 17.8.1944, Buglawton, Cheshire. Opening right-hand batsman, off break bowler. *Teams* Oxford U (1964–66, blue all three years); Derbyshire (1966–72, 145 matches).
Career batting
178–319–14–8885–138*–29.13–11–*ct* 96
Bowling 321–4–80.25–0–0–2/54
He also played for Staffordshire.
He hit 1,000 runs in a season five times (best 1441, av 41.17, in 1970).

Gibbs, Wyatt
Amateur. *b:* 5.5.1830, West Itchenor, Sussex. *d:* 25.5.1891, Bagshot, Surrey. Lower order left-hand batsman, right-hand fast round arm bowler. *Team* Sussex (1864–65, 5 matches).
Career batting
5–7–3–42–18–10.50–0–*ct* 2
Bowling 180–7–25.71–0–0–3/49

Gibson, Arthur Buchwald Edgar
Amateur. *b:* 15.6.1863, Salford, Manchester, Lancashire. *d:* 11.3.1932, Cambridge. Middle order right-hand batsman, right-arm medium pace bowler. *Sch* Cheltenham. *Team* Lancashire (1887, 2 matches). *Tour* Hawke to India 1892/3.
Career batting
14–23–0–311–58–13.52–0–*ct* 4
Bowling 227–16–14.18–0–0–3/24
He emigrated to the colonies soon after his appearances for Lancashire.
His final first-class match was for MCC in 1896.
He also appeared for Lincolnshire.

Gibson, Arthur Cracroft
Amateur. *b:* 7.11.1863, Sittingbourne, Kent. *d:*

8.12.1895, Sittingbourne, Kent. Lower order right-hand batsman, right-arm medium pace bowler. *Team* Kent (1883–84, 5 matches).
Career batting
5–8–2–35–17*–5.83–0–*ct* 1
Bowling 50–0

Gibson, Arthur Kenneth
Amateur. *b*: 19.5.1889. *d*: 28.1.1950, Edinburgh, Scotland. Middle order batsman. *Team* Somerset (1919, 1 match).
Career batting
6–11–0–166–36–15.10–0–*ct* 0
Bowling 11–0
His first-class debut was for the Royal Navy in 1914 and final first-class match for the same team in 1924.

Gibson, Alfred Leonard
Professional. *b:* 13.2.1912, Devon, Jamaica. Hard hitting middle order right-hand batsman. *Team* Leicestershire (1946, 2 matches).
Career batting
2–3–0–17–11–5.66–0–*ct* 0

Gibson, Archibald Lesley
Amateur. *b:* 4.9.1877, Kingsclere, Hants. *d:* 29.7.1943, Nakuru, Kenya. Middle order right-hand batsman, right-arm slow bowler, good field. *Sch* Winchester. *Teams* Essex (1895–1910, 23 matches); Up-Country XI, Ceylon (1926/7).
Career batting
25–39–3–504–71–14.00–0–*ct* 9
Bowling 18–0
He resided in Russia 1897–98 and afterwards was a tea planter in Ceylon; his County cricket was therefore very limited.
His final first-class match in England was for P. F. Warner's XI in 1919.

Gibson, Clement Herbert
Amateur. *b:* 23.8.1900, Entre Rios, Argentina. *d:* 31.12.1976, Buenos Aires, Argentina. Lower order right-hand batsman, right-arm fast medium bowler. *Sch* Eton. *Teams* Sussex (1919–26, 26 matches); Cambridge U (1920–21, blue both years); Argentina (1926/7 to 1937/8). *Tours* South America to England 1932; MCC to Australia and New Zealand 1922/3.
Career batting
84–125–34–1369–64–15.04–0–*ct* 53
Bowling 7109–249–28.55–8–2–8/57
Spending most of his life in the Argentine, his appearances in County cricket were very limited.
His final first-class match was for MCC in 1939.

Gibson, David
Professional. *b:* 1.5.1936, Mitcham, Surrey. Middle/lower order right-hand batsman, right-arm fast medium bowler. *Team* Surrey (1957–69, 183 matches).
Career batting
185–211–45–3143–98–18.93–0–*ct* 76
Bowling 12266–552–22.22–26–1–7/26
He was also a useful rugby full back.

Gibson, Dr Ian
Amateur. *b:* 15.8.1936, Glossop, Derbyshire. *d:* 3.5.1963, Bowdon, Cheshire. Middle order right-hand batsman, leg break and googly bowler, good field. *Sch* Manchester GS. *Teams* Oxford U (1955–58, blue all four years); Derbyshire (1957–61, 7 matches).
Career batting
51–92–7–1697–100*–19.96–1–*ct* 29
Bowling 1959–51–38.41–2–0–5/29

Gibson, James Forbes
Amateur. *b:* 14.4.1888, Coatbridge, Lanarkshire, Scotland. *d:* 21.5.1960, Tunbridge Wells, Kent. Wicket-keeper. *Teams* Scotland (1912); Rangoon Gymkhana (1926/7).
Career batting
3–6–1–30–21–6.00–0–*ct* 2
Bowling 11–0

Gibson, Sir Kenneth Lloyd
Amateur. *b:* 11.5.1888, London. *d:* 14.5.1967, Marylebone, London. Middle order right-hand batsman, wicket-keeper. *Sch* Eton. *Team* Essex (1909–12, 36 matches). *Tour* MCC to Egypt 1909 (not first-class).
Career batting
42–63–6–959–75–16.82–0–*ct* 62–*st* 11
Bowling 9–1–9.00–0–0–1/9
His final first-class match was for the Army in 1920.

Gidney, Brian Bruce
Cricketer. *b:* 6.4.1938, Kingston, Surrey. *Sch* Kingston GS. *Team* Cambridge U (1963).
Career batting
1–2–0–16–9–8.00–0–*ct* 0

Giffen, George
Amateur. *b:* 27.3.1859, Adelaide, Australia. *d:* 29.11.1927, Adelaide, Australia. Brother of W. F. (South Australia). Hard hitting middle order right-hand batsman, right-arm medium slow bowler. *Team* South Australia (1877/8 to 1903/4, 64 matches). *Tours* Australia to England 1882, 1884, 1886, 1893 and 1896, to North America 1893, 1896. *Tests* Australia (1881/2 to 1896, 31 matches).

Career batting
251–421–23–11758–271–29.54–18–*ct* 195
Bowling 21782–1023–21.29–95–30–10/66
Test batting
31–53–0–1238–161–23.35–1–*ct* 24
Bowling 2791–103–27.09–7–1–7/117

He was most successful on his tours to England and on the last three performed the 'double', having his best record with both bat and ball in 1886 – 1,424 runs, av 26.86, and 154 wickets, av 17.36.

He performed the unique feat in first-class matches of hitting 271 and taking 16 wickets (for 166) in the same match – South Australia v Victoria at Adelaide in 1891/2. His best bowling in an innings was 10/66, Australian XI v Rest at Sydney in 1883/4. On nine occasions he performed the match 'double' of 100 runs and 10 wickets, though never in England. By many he was regarded as Australia's W. G. Grace.

Giffen, Walter Frank
Amateur. *b:* 20.9.1861, Adelaide, Australia. *d:* 28.6.1949, Unley, Adelaide, Australia. Brother of George (South Australia). Defensive right-hand batsman, good deep field. *Team* South Australia (1882/3 to 1901/2, 31 matches). *Tour* Australia to England and North America 1893. *Tests* Australia (1886/7 to 1891/2, 3 matches).
Career batting
47–80–6–1178–89–15.91–0–*ct* 23
Bowling 15–0
Test batting
3–6–0–11–3–1.83–0–*ct* 1

He did very little on his tour to England and was not required for the Tests.

Gifford, George Cooper
Amateur. *b:* 17.11.1891, Huntingdon. *d:* 16.9.1972, Huntingdon. Middle order right-hand batsman. *Team* Northants (1923–29, 14 matches).
Career batting
14–24–0–387–98–16.12–0–*ct* 5

He also played for Huntingdonshire.

Gifford, James
Amateur. *b:* 10.1.1864, Buenos Aires, Argentina. *d:* 18.4.1931, Buenos Aires, Argentina. Middle order right-hand batsman. *Sch* Christ College, Brecon. *Team* MCC (1897–98).
Career batting
5–10–2–143–37–17.87–0–*ct* 0

He played in the North v South series in Argentina.

Gifford, Norman, M.B.E.
Professional. *b*: 30.3.1940, Ulverston, Lancashire. Lower order left-hand batsman, slow left-arm bowler, gully field. *Teams* Worcestershire (1960–82, 541 matches); Warwickshire (1983, 22 matches). *Tours* MCC to India, Pakistan and Sri Lanka 1972/3; International XI to South Africa and Pakistan 1961/2; Worcestershire World Tour 1964/5; Commonwealth to Pakistan 1970/1; Rest of World to Australia 1971/2; International Wanderers to South Africa 1972/3. *Tests* England (1964–73, 15 matches).
Career batting
592–691–216–6503–89–13.69–0–*ct* 292
Bowling 41637–1824–22.82–86–14–8/28
Test batting
15–20–9–179–25*–16.27–0–*ct* 8
Bowling 1026–33–31.09–1–0–5/55

He took 100 wickets in a season four times (best 133, av 19.66, in 1961). From 1971 to 1980 he captained Worcestershire. He was appointed a Test Selector in 1982.

Gifkins, Charles John
Amateur. *b:* 19.2.1856, Thames Ditton, Surrey. Opening right-hand batsman, right-arm fast bowler. *Team* Yorkshire (1880, 2 matches).
Career batting
2–3–0–30–23–10.00–0–*ct* 1

Gilbert, Charles Arthur William
Amateur. *b:* 9.1.1855, Melton Mowbray, Leics. *d:* 28.9.1937, St John's Wood, London. Middle order right-hand batsman, right-arm fast or slow bowler, good field. *Team* Surrey (1877–78, 2 matches).
Career batting
2–4–1–25–17*–8.33–0–*ct* 0

He did not appear in first-class cricket whilst at Oxford, but was a noted athlete.

He also played for Staffordshire and Wiltshire.

Gilbert, George Henry Bailey
Amateur. *b:* 2.9.1829, Cheltenham, Gloucs. *d:* 16.6.1906, Summer Hill, New South Wales, Australia. Cousin of the Graces. Lower order right-hand batsman, right-hand medium pace round-arm bowler. *Teams* Middlesex (1851, 2 matches); New South Wales (1855/6 to 1874/5, 12 matches).
Career batting
18–34–0–283–31–8.32–0–*ct* 13
Bowling 160–16+12–10.00–2–1–6/65

He captained New South Wales in 1855/6.

Gilbert, Humphrey Adam
Amateur. *b:* 2.6.1886, Bombay, India. *d:* 19.7.1960, Bishopstone, Hereford. Lower order right-hand batsman, right-arm medium pace off break bowler. *Sch* Charterhouse. *Teams* Oxford

U (1907–09, blue all three years); Worcestershire (1921–30, 72 matches).
Career batting
118–180–65–811–35*–7.05–0–*ct* 59
Bowling 11268–476–23.67–38–8–8/48
He also appeared for Monmouthshire, Radnorshire and Wiltshire.

Gilbert, John
Professional. *b:* 7.3.1816, Mansfield, Notts. *d:* 22.11.1887, Mansfield, Notts. Middle order right-hand batsman. *Team* Nottinghamshire (1843–48, 3 matches).
Career batting
4–7–2–115–91–23.00–0–*ct* 4
He scored 91 on his debut, but did little in the few other Notts matches in which he played.

Gilbert, John
Professional. *b:* 1830. *d:* 28.11.1896, Newick, Sussex. Middle order batsman. *Team* Lord Sheffield's Team (1881).
Career batting
1–1–0–0–0–0.00–0–*ct* 0
He was aged 50 or 51 when he played in his only first-class match.

Gilbert, John Dudley Harwood
Amateur. *b:* 8.10.1910, Chellaston, Derbyshire. Opening/middle order right-hand batsman. *Sch* Repton. *Team* Derbyshire (1930–36, 11 matches).
Career batting
11–11–0–106–25–9.63–0–*ct* 2

Gilbert, William
Professional. *b:* 4.6.1856, Newick, Sussex. *d:* 4.1.1918, Holborn, London. Lower order right-hand batsman, right-hand fast round arm bowler, moderate field. *Team* Sussex (1879, 1 match).
Career batting
1–2–0–5–5–2.50–0–*ct* 1
Bowling 14–3–4.66–0–0–3/14

Gilbert, Walter Raleigh
Amateur. *b:* 16.9.1853, Strand, London. *d:* 26.7.1924, Calgary, Canada. Cousin of the Graces. Middle order right-hand batsman, right-hand slow round-arm bowler. *Teams* Middlesex (1873–74, 9 matches); Gloucestershire (1876–86, 108 matches). *Tour* Grace to Australia 1873/4 (not first-class).
Career batting
175–296–20–5290–205*–19.16–3–*ct* 160–*st* 6
Bowling 5291–295–17.93–15–1–7/28
In 1886 he emigrated to Canada, after a scandal involving some stealing from a dressing room.
His double century was 205* for an England XI v Cambridge U at Fenner's in 1876.

He played non-first-class cricket for Worcestershire and Northants.

Gilby, William
Professional. *b:* 26.7.1835, Leamington Spa, Warwickshire. *d:* 13.8.1903, Westminster London. Tail end right-hand batsman, lob bowler. *Team* Middlesex (1872, 1 match).
Career batting
1–2–1–9–5*–9.00–0–*ct* 0
Bowling 84–2–42.00–0–0–2/70

Gilchrist, Roy
Amateur. *b:* 28.6.1934, Seaforth, Jamaica. Tail end right-hand batsman, right-arm fast bowler. *Teams* Jamaica (1956/7 to 1961/2); Hyderabad (1962/3). *Tests* West Indies to England 1957, to India 1958/9. *Tests* West Indies (1957 to 1958/9, 13 matches).
Career batting
42–43–10–258–43*–7.81–0–*ct* 10
Bowling 4342–167–26.00–7–1–6/16
Test batting
13–14–3–60–12–5.45–0–*ct* 4
Bowling 1521–57–26.68–1–0–6/55
He was at his fastest on the 1957 tour to England and noted for the venom of his bouncers, but his figures were not impressive, his 37 wickets costing 31.78 runs each.

Gilchrist, Robert Selby
Amateur. *b:* 1822. *d:* 1905, Berwick-on-Tweed, Northumberland. Lower order batsman, bowler. *Team* Gentlemen of Middlesex (1865).
Career batting
1–2–0–2–2–1.00–0–*ct* 0
Bowling 19–0
He played for Northumberland.

Giles, Godwin Merryweather
Professional. *b:* 1876, Mere, Wiltshire. *d:* 1955, Middlesex. Middle order batsman, opening bowler. *Team* Gloucestershire (1903, 1 match).
Career batting
1–2–0–8–8–4.00–0–*ct* 1
Bowling 31–0

Giles, Ronald James
Professional. *b:* 17.10.1919, Chilwell, Notts. Opening right-hand batsman, slow left-arm bowler. *Team* Nottinghamshire (1937–59, 195 matches).
Career batting
195–310–19–7639–142–26.25–9–*ct* 65
Bowling 1318–23–57.30–0–0–3/1
He hit 1,000 runs in a season three times (best 1,293, av 34.94, in 1955).

Gilfillan, Andrew Douglas
Cricketer. *b:* 21.8.1959, Johannesburg, South Africa. Lower order right-hand batsman, leg break bowler. *Team* Oxford U (1982).
Career batting
3–4–1–40–31–13.33–0–*ct* 0
Bowling 218–2–109.00–0–0–2/177

Gill, Alan
Professional. *b:* 5.8.1940, Underwood, Notts. Middle order right-hand batsman, leg break bowler. *Team* Nottinghamshire (1960–65, 53 matches).
Career batting
53–98–7–1756–67–19.29–0–*ct* 18
Bowling 481–10–48.10–0–0–2/28

Gill, Ernest Harry
Professional. *b:* 1877, Mountsorrel, Leics. *d:* 1950, Hull, Yorkshire. Brother of G. C. (Leics and Somerset). Lower order right-hand batsman, right-arm fast medium bowler. *Team* Leicestershire (1901, 5 matches).
Career batting
5–5–3–23–11*–11.50–0–*ct* 3
Bowling 413–12–34.41–0–0–3/61

Gill, Fairfax
Professional. *b:* 3.9.1883, Wakefield, Yorkshire. *d:* 1.11.1917, Wimereux, France. He died of wounds. Opening/middle order batsman. *Team* Yorkshire (1906, 2 matches).
Career batting
2–4–0–18–11–4.50–0–*ct* 0

Gill, George Cooper
Professional. *b:* 18.4.1876, Mountsorrel, Leics. *d:* 21.8.1937, Leicester. Brother of E. H. (Leics). Middle/lower order right-hand batsman, right-arm fast medium bowler. *Teams* Somerset (1897–1902, 93 matches); London County (1902–03); Leicestershire (1903–06, 71 matches).
Career batting
171–290–31–4160–100–16.06–1–*ct* 74
Bowling 11793–465–25.36–26–3–9/89

He also played for Staffordshire. His best bowling was 9/89 for Leics v Warwickshire at Edgbaston in 1905.

Gill, James Rupert
Amateur. *b:* 24.9.1911, Dublin, Ireland. Right-hand batsman. *Team* Ireland (1948).
Career batting
1–2–0–106–106–53.00–1–*ct* 0

He made a century (106) in his only first-class match.

Gill, Peter Nigel
Cricketer. *b:* 12.11.1947, Stoke on Trent, Staffs. Middle order right-hand batsman, off break bowler. *Team* Minor Counties (1976–79). *Tour* Minor Counties to Kenya 1977/8 (not first-class).
Career batting
2–4–0–64–20–16.00–0–*ct* 1

His County cricket is for Staffordshire.

Gill, Roderick Ian
Amateur. *b:* 21.7.1919, Dublin, Ireland. *d:* 28.10.1983, Dublin. Right-hand batsman, right-arm medium pace bowler. *Team* Ireland (1947–50).
Career batting
3–6–1–72–37–14.40–0–*ct* 2
Bowling 128–3–42.66–0–0–2/19

Gillespie, Albert George
Amateur. *b:* 1912. *d:* 7.8.1938, Bury St Edmunds, Suffolk. Middle order batsman, useful bowler. *Team* Combined Services (1937).
Career batting
1–2–0–11–10–5.50–0–*ct* 0
Bowling 48–1–48.00–0–0–1/33

Gillespie, Derek William
Amateur. *b:* 26.4.1917, Aberford, Leeds, Yorkshire. *d:* 21.8.1981, Oxton, Tadcaster, Yorkshire. Lower order right-hand batsman, right-arm fast bowler. *Sch* Uppingham. *Team* Cambridge U (1938–39, blue 1939).
Career batting
10–15–3–155–60–12.91–0–*ct* 2
Bowling 683–22–31.04–0–0–4/48

Gillespie, Francis Sydney
Amateur. *b:* 26.3.1889, Croydon, Surrey. *d:* 18.6.1916, Ypres, Belgium. He died of wounds. Middle order left-hand batsman. *Sch* Dulwich. *Team* Surrey (1913, 6 matches).
Career batting
6–11–0–249–72–22.63–0–*ct* 2

Gillespie, Richard Henry
Amateur. *b:* 10.9.1878, Morpeth, Northumberland. *d:* 20.5.1952, Balham, London. Lower order batsman, bowler. *Sch* Uppingham. *Team* Leveson-Gower's Team (1909–11).
Career batting
3–4–0–10–8–2.50–0–*ct* 2
Bowling 209–3–69.66–0–0–3/89

He played for Northumberland.

Gillett, Charles Richard
Amateur. *b:* 24.8.1880, Compton, Surrey. *d:* 22.1.1964, Camberley, Surrey. Son of H. H.

(Oxford U). Middle order batsman. *Sch* St Edward's, Oxford. *Team* MCC (1920).
Career batting
1–2–0–5–3–2.50–0–*ct* 1

Gillett, Rev Hugh Hodgson
Amateur. *b:* 19.6.1836, Waltham, Melton Mowbray, Leics. *d:* 22.1.1915, Thornbury, Gloucs. Father of C. R. (MCC). Opening/middle order right-hand batsman, right-hand medium pace round-arm bowler, deep field. *Sch* Winchester. *Team* Oxford U (1857–58, blue both years).
Career batting
6–7–0–117–53–16.71–0–*ct* 3
Bowling 205–17–12.05–2–0–6/22

His final first-class match was for MCC in 1868.

His County cricket was for Leicestershire and Northants (neither first-class).

Gillhouley, Keith
Professional. *b:* 8.8.1934, Huddersfield, Yorkshire. Lower order right-hand batsman, slow left-arm bowler. *Teams* Yorkshire (1961, 24 matches); Nottinghamshire (1963–66, 83 matches).
Career batting
108–166–28–2051–75*–14.86–0–*ct* 60
Bowling 6922–255–27.14–8–0–7/82

Gilliat, Ivor Algernon Walter
Amateur. *b:* 8.1.1903, Eton, Bucks. *d:* 22.7.1967, Oxford. Lower order right-hand batsman, wicket-keeper. *Sch* Charterhouse. *Team* Oxford U (1922–25, blue 1925).
Career batting
13–21–4–435–70–25.58–0–*ct* 28–*st* 7
Bowling 17–0

An excellent soccer player, he appeared for Oxford U at inside right.

Gilliat, Richard Michael Charles
Cricketer. *b:* 20.5.1944, Ware, Herts. Middle order left-hand batsman, leg break bowler. *Sch* Charterhouse. *Teams* Oxford U (1964–67, blue all four years); Hampshire (1966–78, 220 matches). *Tour* MCC to Ceylon 1969/70 (no first-class matches).
Career batting
269–441–46–11589–223*–29.33–18–*ct* 221
Bowling 157–3–52.33–0–0–1/3

He captained Oxford in 1966 and Hampshire 1971 to 1978. He hit 1,000 runs in a season four times (best 1,386, av 39.60, in 1969). His only double hundred was 223* for Hants v Warwicks at Southampton in 1969.

A good soccer player he won his blue in 1964 and captained Oxford in 1966, thus having the unusual distinction of leading his University at both sports.

Gilligan, Arthur Edward (Robert)
Amateur. *b:* 23.12.1894, Denmark Hill, South London. *d:* 5.9.1976, Pulborough, Sussex. Brother of A. H. H. (Sussex) and F. W. (Essex). Middle/lower order right-hand batsman, right-arm fast medium bowler. brilliant field. *Sch* Dulwich. *Teams* Cambridge U (1919–20, blue both years); Surrey (1919, 3 matches); Sussex (1920–32, 227 matches). *Tours* MCC to South Africa 1922/3, to Australia 1924/5, to India and Ceylon 1926/7. *Tests* England (1922/3 to 1924/5, 11 matches).
Career batting
337–510–55–9140–144–20.08–12–*ct* 180
Bowling 20141–868–23.20–42–4–8/25
Test batting
11–16–3–209–39*–16.07–0–*ct* 3
Bowling 1046–36–29.05–2–1–6/7

He hit 1,000 runs in a season twice (best 1183, av 21.12, in 1923) and took 100 wickets three times (best 163, av 17.50, in 1923). He performed the 'double' once.

He captained England in nine Tests and MCC on the 1924/5 and 1926/7 tours. From 1922 to 1929 he led Sussex. After retiring from first-class cricket, he remained a major figure in Sussex cricket, being Chairman of the County Club for many years. In 1967 he was President of MCC.

Gilligan, Alfred (Herbert) Harold
Amateur. *b:* 29.6.1896, Denmark Hill, South London. *d:* 5.5.1978, Shamley Green, Surrey. Brother of A. E. R. (Sussex) and F. W. (Essex), father-in-law of P. B. H. May (Surrey). Opening/middle order right-hand batsman, leg break bowler, good cover point. *Sch* Dulwich. *Teams* Sussex (1919–31, 289 matches). *Tours* Joel to South Africa 1924/5; MCC to New Zealand and Australia 1929/30. *Tests* England (1929/30, 4 matches).
Career batting
321–525–31–8873–143–17.96–1–*ct* 123
Bowling 3872–115–33.66–0–0–4/13
Test batting
4–4–0–71–32–17.75–0–*ct* 0

He captained MCC and England on the tour of 1929/30 and Sussex in 1930. He hit 1,000 runs in a season three times (best 1,186, av 17.70, in 1923). In the same season he completed a record 70 innings.

Gilligan, Frank William
Amateur. *b:* 20.9.1893, Denmark Hill, South London. *d:* 4.5.1960, Wanganui, New Zealand, Brother of A. E. R. (Sussex) and A. H. H.

(Sussex). Middle order right-hand batsman, wicket-keeper. *Sch* Dulwich. *Teams* Oxford U (1919–20, blue both years); Essex (1919–29, 79 matches).
Career batting
129–174–46–3024–110–23.62–1–*ct* 153–*st* 69
Bowling 6–0
He emigrated to New Zealand and was headmaster of Wanganui Grammar School for 19 years.
His final first-class match was for MCC in 1935.

Gillingham, Rev Canon Frank Hay
Amateur. *b:* 6.9.1875, Tokyo, Japan. *d:* 1.4.1953, Monaco. Middle order right-hand batsman, wicket-keeper. *Sch* Dulwich. *Team* Essex (1903–28, 181 matches). *Tour* Tennyson to Jamaica 1926/7.
Career batting
210–352–24–10050–201–30.64–19–*ct* 111–*st* 1
Bowling 13–0
His best season was 1908 when he made 1,033 runs, av 39.73. His only double century was 201 for Essex v Middlesex at Lord's in 1904.
He was a noted preacher and after-dinner speaker. He commentated on some of the pre-1940 Test matches on the wireless.

Gillott, Eric Kenneth
Cricketer. *b:* 15.4.1951, Waiku, New Zealand. Tail end batsman, slow left-arm bowler. *Team* Northern Districts (1971/2 to 1978/9). *Tour* New Zealand to England 1973.
Career batting
31–37–17–172–22–8.60–0–*ct* 9
Bowling 2493–81–30.77–2–0–6/79
His bowling was completely ineffective on his 1973 tour to England and he did not appear in the Tests. He played for Buckinghamshire in 1976.

Gilman, James
Amateur. *b:* 17.3.1879, Marylebone, London. *d:* 14.9.1976, Shoreham by Sea, Sussex. Middle order right-hand batsman, right-arm slow bowler, good field. *Sch* St Paul's. *Teams* Middlesex (1900–01, 5 matches); Cambridge U (1901–02, blue 1902); London County (1900–04).
Career batting
41–67–8–977–72*–16.55–0–*ct* 21
Bowling 138–3–46.00–0–0–2/74
He also appeared for Northumberland.
A good athlete, he represented Cambridge in the mile.

Gilmour, Gary John
Cricketer. *b:* 26.6.1951, Waratah, New South Wales, Australia. Middle order left-hand batsman, left-arm fast medium bowler, excellent close field. *Team* New South Wales (1971/2 to 1979/80, 42 matches). *Tours* Australia to New Zealand 1973/4, 1976/7, to England 1975; International Wanderers to South Africa 1975/6. *Tests* Australia (1973/4 to 1976/7, 15 matches).
Career batting
75–120–18–3126–122–30.64–5–*ct* 68
Bowling 7345–233–31.52–6–0–6/85
Test batting
15–22–1–483–101–23.00–1–*ct* 8
Bowling 1406–54–26.03–3–0–6/85
Although he only appeared in one Test on the 1975 English tour, he performed usefully with both bat and ball.

Gilroy, George Bruce
Amateur. *b:* 16.9.1889, Cupar, Fife, Scotland. *d:* 15.7.1916, Longueval, France. He was mortally wounded. Lower order batsman, wicket-keeper. *Sch* Winchester. *Team* Oxford U (1909).
Career batting
1–1–1–2–2*–no av–0–*ct* 0

Gilson, Ronald Louis Desormeax
Amateur. *b:* 23.12.1907, South Africa. *d:* 9.10.1973, South Africa. Lower order batsman, useful bowler. *Team* Cambridge U (1930).
Career batting
2–3–1–38–17*–19.00–0–*ct* 4

Gimblett, Harold
Professional. *b:* 19.10.1914, Bicknoller, Somerset. *d:* 30.3.1978, Verwood, Dorset. Hard hitting opening right-hand batsman, right-arm medium pace bowler, good outfield. *Team* Somerset (1935–54, 329 matches). *Tour* Commonwealth to India and Ceylon 1950/1. *Tests* England (1936–39, 3 matches).
Career batting
368–673–37–23007–310–36.17–50–*ct* 247–*st* 1
Bowling 2124–41–51.80–0–0–4/10
Test batting
3–5–1–129–67*–32.25–0–*ct* 1
He hit 1,000 runs in a season 12 times plus once overseas, and reached 2,000 twice (best 2,134, av 39.51, in 1952). His highest innings was 310 for Somerset v Sussex at Eastbourne in 1948 and he exceeded 200 on one other occasion. On his first-class debut for Somerset v Essex at Frome he made 123 in 80 minutes, reaching his 100 in 63 minutes.
He also played for Dorset.

Gimson, Christopher
Amateur. *b:* 24.12.1886, Leicester. *d:* 8.11.1975, Leicester. Middle order right-hand batsman. *Sch*

Oundle. *Teams* Cambridge U (1908); Leicestershire (1921, 8 matches).
Career batting
9–17–1–175–40–10.93–0–*ct* 4
Bowling 52–1–52.00–0–0–1/20
He spent much of his life in the Indian Civil Service.

Gittings, Albert Edward
Professional. *b:* October 1897, Ormskirk, Lancashire. *d:* 1977, Birmingham. Lower order right-hand batsman, right-arm medium pace bowler. *Team* Warwickshire (1919, 2 matches).
Career batting
2–3–0–2–2–0.66–0–*ct* 1
Bowling 67–4–16.75–0–0–2/17
He is wrongly shown in Wisden as 'A. E. Giddings'.

Gladdon, Frederick
Professional. *b:* 9.6.1881. Lower order batsman, bowler. *Team* Hampshire (1905, 1 match).
Career batting
1–2–0–1–1–0.50–0–*ct* 0
Bowling 44–0

Gladwin, Christopher
Cricketer. *b*: 10.5.1962, East Ham, Essex. Opening left-hand batsman, right-arm medium pace bowler. *Team* Essex (1981–83, 10 matches).
Career batting
10–15–0–523–89–34.86–0–*ct* 4
Bowling 11–0

Gladwin, Clifford
Professional. *b:* 3.4.1916, Doe Lea, Derbyshire. Son of Joseph (Derbyshire). Lower order right-hand batsman, right-arm fast medium bowler. *Team* Derbyshire (1939–58, 332 matches). *Tour* MCC to South Africa 1948/9. *Tests* England (1947–49, 8 matches).
Career batting
374–510–148–6283–124*–17.35–1–*ct* 134
Bowling 30265–1653–18.30–101–18–9/41
Test batting
8–11–5–170–51*–28.33–0–*ct* 2
Bowling 571–15–38.06–0–0–3/21
He took 100 wickets in a season 12 times (best 152, av 19.19, in 1952). In 1949 he was only 86 runs short of performing the 'double'.
His most famous match was the Durban Test of 1948/9 when he ran a leg bye off the final ball of the game to bring England victory.

Gladwin, Joseph
Professional. *b:* 6.9.1890, Doe Lea, Derbyshire. *d:* 8.9.1962, Chesterfield, Derbyshire. Father of Clifford (Derbyshire). Lower order right-hand batsman, right-arm fast medium bowler. *Team* Derbyshire (1914–19, 3 matches).
Career batting
3–5–2–8–5*–2.66–0–*ct* 3
Bowling 20–1–20.00–0–0–1/15

Glassford, John
Cricketer. *b:* 20.7.1946, Sunderland, Co Durham. Lower order right-hand batsman, right-arm fast medium bowler. *Team* Warwickshire (1969, 2 matches).
Career batting
2–1–0–0–0–0.00–0–*ct* 1
Bowling 161–5–32.20–0–0–2/9
He also appeared for Durham.

Gleeson, John William
Cricketer. *b:* 14.3.1938, Wiangaree, New South Wales, Australia. Lower order right-hand batsman, leg break and googly bowler. *Teams* New South Wales (1966/7 to 1972/3, 35 matches); Eastern Province (1974/5). *Tours* Australia to New Zealand 1966/7, to England 1968, 1972, to Ceylon, India and South Africa 1969/70; Robins to South Africa 1973/4. *Tests* Australia (1967/8 to 1972, 29 matches).
Career batting
117–137–38–1095–59–11.06–0–*ct* 58
Bowling 10729–430–24.95–22–2–7/52
Test batting
29–46–8–395–45–10.39–0–*ct* 17
Bowling 3367–93–36.20–3–0–5/61
He did well in the first-class matches on the 1968 tour – 58 wickets, av 20.65, but managed little in the Tests. He was not so successful in 1972.

Glenister, Clement Edward
Amateur. *b:* 23.7.1897, Watford, Herts. *d:* 24.5.1968, Bovingdon, Herts. Lower order right-hand batsman, slow right-arm bowler. *Sch* Berkhamsted. *Team* Royal Navy (1924–29).
Career batting
5–9–0–104–49–11.55–0–*ct* 1
Bowling 245–9–27.22–0–0–2/39

Glenn, Michael
Cricketer. *b:* 14.6.1956, Belper, Derbyshire. Lower order right-hand batsman, right-arm fast medium bowler. *Team* Derbyshire (1975–76, 7 matches).
Career batting
7–7–4–23–11*–7.66–0–*ct* 1
Bowling 398–6–66.33–0–0–3/36

Glennie, Mervin Stephen
Amateur. *b:* 23.10.1918, Nantes, France.

Opening right-hand batsman, wicket-keeper. *Sch* Sherborne. *Team* Cambridge U (1939).
Career batting
3–5–0–19–11–3.80–0–*ct* 2–*st* 1
His final first-class match was for MCC in 1947.

Glennie, Rev Reginald Gerard
Amateur. *b:* 6.11.1864, Blore, Staffs. *d:* 24.10.1953, Worcester. Son of Rev J. D. (Cambridge U 1848). Opening/middle order right-hand batsman. *Sch* King's, Canterbury. *Team* Oxford U (1886).
Career batting
2–4–0–5–2–1.25–0–*ct* 1
He played for Staffordshire.

Glennon, Joseph Edward
Professional. *b:* 1889, Ashby-de-la-Zouch, Leicestershire. *d:* 26.6.1926, Moorhead, Sheffield, Yorkshire. Middle order batsman. *Team* Leicestershire (1921, 2 matches).
Career batting
2–4–0–12–7–3.00–0–*ct* 0
He played football for Sheffield United.

Glerum, Herman William
Amateur. *b:* 28.8.1911, Holland. Middle order batsman. *Team* Free Foresters (1957).
Career batting
1–2–0–1–1–0.50–0–*ct* 0
Bowling 32–3–10.66–0–0–2/16
He was a well-known cricketer in Holland.

Glover, Alfred Charles Stirrup
Amateur. *b:* 19.4.1872, Stoke on Trent, Staffs. *d:* 22.5.1949, Kenilworth, Warwickshire. Middle order right-hand batsman, right-arm medium pace bowler. *Sch* Repton. *Team* Warwickshire (1895–1909, 149 matches).
Career batting
151–230–28–5187–124–25.67–7–*ct* 81
Bowling 1578–49–32.20–1–0–5/21
He also played for Staffordshire. He hit 1,011 runs, av 40.44, in 1904.

Glover, Edward Robert Kenneth
Amateur. *b:* 19.7.1911, Worcester. *d:* 23.3.1967, Cardiff. Lower order right-hand batsman, fast medium bowler. *Sch* Sherborne. *Team* Glamorgan (1932–38, 47 matches).
Career batting
47–73–23–406–62–8.12–0–*ct* 18
Bowling 4284–118–36.30–3–0–5/79
He was also a useful rugby footballer with Glamorgan Wanderers and later a well-known sports journalist.

Glover, Trevor Richardson
Cricketer. *b:* 26.11.1951, Lancaster. Opening right-hand batsman, off break bowler. *Team* Oxford U (1973–75, blue all three years).
Career batting
22–42–1–769–117–18.75–2–*ct* 13
Bowling 12–0

Glynn, Brian Thomas
Professional. *b:* 27.4.1940, Birmingham. Middle order right-hand batsman, off break bowler. *Team* Warwickshire (1959–61, 2 matches).
Career batting
2–3–1–13–7–6.50–0–*ct* 0

Goatly, Edward Garnett
Professional. *b:* 3.12.1882, Twickenham, Middlesex. *d:* 12.2.1958, Brighton, Sussex. Middle order right-hand batsman, slow left-arm bowler. moderate field. *Team* Surrey (1901–14, 126 matches).
Career batting
126–198–21–4419–147*–24.96–3–*ct* 22
Bowling 733–19–38.57–0–0–4/48
He was the dressing room attendant at the Oval from 1919 to 1939.

Gobey, Stanley Clarke
Amateur. *b:* 18.6.1916, Stafford. Lower order left-hand batsman, right-arm medium pace bowler. *Team* Warwickshire (1946, 2 matches).
Career batting
2–3–0–2–2–0.66–0–*ct* 0
Bowling 9–0

Godambe, Shankarrao Ramachandra
Amateur. *b:* 1.3.1899, Bombay, India. *d:* 6.12.1969, Bombay, India. Lower order right-hand batsman, right-arm medium pace bowler. *Teams* Bombay (1926/7); Hindus (1920/1 to 1941/2); Gujerat (1934/5 to 1939/40). *Tours* India to England 1932; Bombay to Ceylon 1925/6; Vizianagram to Ceylon 1930/1.
Career batting
50–74–22–848–62–16.30–0–*ct* 49
Bowling 2346–103–22.77–4–1–6/32
He achieved almost nothing on his single tour to England.

Goddard, George Fergusson
Cricketer. *b:* 19.5.1938, Edinburgh, Scotland. Right-hand batsman, off-break bowler. *Team* Scotland (1960–80).
Career batting
22–33–5–371–39–13.25–0–*ct* 8
Bowling 1094–41–26.68–2–1–8/34

Goddard, John Douglas Claude
Amateur. *b:* 21.4.1919, Bridgetown, Barbados. Middle order left-hand batsman, right-arm medium pace off break bowler, excellent short leg. *Team* Barbados (1936/7 to 1957/8). *Tours* West Indies to England 1950, 1957, to Australia and New Zealand 1951/2, to India, Pakistan and Ceylon 1948/9, to New Zealand 1955/6. *Tests* West Indies (1947/8 to 1957, 27 matches).
Career batting
110–145–32–3769–218*–33.35–5–*ct* 94
Bowling 3845–146–26.33–4–0–5/20
Test batting
27–39–11–859–83*–30.67–0–*ct* 22
Bowling 1050–33–31.81–1–0–5/31
Goddard captained West Indies on both the 1950 and 1957 tours of England – on both he was more important as captain than as all-rounder, but performed usefully with bat and ball when required.
In all he led West Indies in 22 Tests. His only first-class double century was 218* for Barbados v Trinidad at Bridgetown in 1943/4.

Goddard, Trevor Leslie
Amateur. *b:* 1.8.1931, Durban, South Africa. Opening left-hand batsman, left-arm fast medium bowler. *Teams* Natal (1952/3 to 1969/70); N.E. Transvaal (1966/7 to 1967/8). *Tours* South Africa to England 1955, 1960, to Australia and New Zealand 1963/4. *Tests* South Africa (1955 to 1969/70, 41 matches).
Career batting
179–297–19–11279–222–40.57–26–*ct* 174
Bowling 11563–534–21.65–24–1–6/3
Test batting
41–78–5–2516–112–34.46–1–*ct* 48
Bowling 3226–123–26.22–5–0–6/53
On his 1955 tour of England he hit 1,163 runs, av 30.60, and took 60 wickets, av 21.85, and in 1960, 1,377 runs, av 37.21, and 73 wickets, av 19.71. Thus he was one of the leading all-rounders on both tours. He captained South Africa in 13 Tests and on the 1963/4 Tour.
His final first-class match in England was for MCC in 1962.

Goddard, Thomas William John
Professional. *b:* 1.10.1900, Gloucester. *d:* 22.5.1966, Gloucester. Lower order right-hand batsman, right-arm fast bowler until 1927, then off break for the remainder of his career. *Team* Gloucestershire (1922–52, 558 matches). *Tours* MCC to South Africa 1930/1, 1938/9. *Tests* England (1930–39, 8 matches).
Career batting
593–775–218–5234–71–9.39–*ct* 313
Bowling 59116–2979–19.84–251–86–10/113
Test batting
8–5–3–13–8–6.50–0–*ct* 3
Bowling 588–22–26.72–1–0–6/29
He took 100 wickets in a season 16 times and on four occasions went on to exceed 200 (best 248, av 16.76, in 1937). His 238, av 17.30, in 1947, when he was 46 years old, should also be noted.
His best bowling in an innings was 10/113 for Gloucs v Worcs at Cheltenham in 1937, and he took nine wickets in an innings an additional eight times (all for Gloucs).

Godfrey, Rev Charles John Melville
Amateur. *b:* 24.11.1862, Upper Clapton, Middlesex. *d:* 28.9.1941, Icknield, Great Chesterford, Essex. Lower order right-hand batsman, right-arm fast bowler. *Sch* Magdalen College School. *Teams* Oxford U (1882–85); Sussex (1885–92, 10 matches).
Career batting
18–34–7–179–20–6.62–0–*ct* 8
Bowling 801–33–24.27–2–0–5/22
He was a leading figure in London Club cricket in the 1890s.

Godfrey, John Frederick
Professional. *b:* 18.8.1917, Oxford. Tail end right-hand batsman, right-arm fast medium bowler. *Team* Hampshire (1939–47, 12 matches).
Career batting
12–19–5–61–25*–4.35–0–*ct* 1
Bowling 753–15–50.20–0–0–4/116
He also played for Oxfordshire and Cambridgeshire.

Godfrey, Sir William Wellington
Amateur. *b:* 2.4.1880, Newry, Ireland. *d:* 18.5.1952, Tavistock, Devon. Opening right-hand batsman. *Sch* Dulwich. *Team* Royal Navy (1912).
Career batting
1–2–0–30–30–15.00–0–*ct* 2–*st* 1

Godsell, Richard Thomas
Amateur. *b:* 9.1.1880, Stroud, Gloucs. *d:* 11.4.1954, Bromley, Kent. Opening right-hand batsman. *Sch* Clifton. *Teams* Cambridge U (1903, blue); Gloucestershire (1903–10, 51 matches). *Tours* MCC to North America 1905.
Career batting
61–115–5–1492–111–13.56–1–*ct* 24
Bowling 8–0

Godwin, Cuthbert Blair
Amateur. *b:* 16.10.1891, Frenchay, Bristol. *d:* 23.10.1969, Clifton, Bristol. Lower order right-hand batsman, slow right-arm bowler. *Sch* Winchester. *Team* Somerset (1926, 2 matches).
Career batting
2–4–0–8–5–2.00–0–*ct* 1
Bowling 72–1–72.00–0–0–1/66
He appeared for Canada v United States in 1909.

Gold, Cecil Argo
Amateur. *b:* 3.6.1887, London. *d:* 3.7.1916, Ovillers, France. He was killed in action. Middle order batsman. *Sch* Eton. *Team* Middlesex (1907, 1 match).
Career batting
1–2–1–0–0*–0.00–0–*ct* 0
He appeared in the Freshmen's Match at Oxford, but no first-class matches.
He also played for Berkshire.

Goldie, Christopher Frederick Evelyn
Cricketer. *b:* 2.11.1960, Johannesburg, South Africa. Lower order right-hand batsman, wicket-keeper. *Sch* St Pauls. *Teams* Cambridge U (1981–82, blue both years); Hampshire (1983, 1 match). *Tour* MCC to North America 1982 (not first-class).
Career batting
21–24–3–302–77–14.38–0–*ct* 32–*st* 7

Goldie, Kenneth Oswald
Amateur. *b:* 19.9.1882, Tongoo, Burma. *d:* 14.1.1938, Madras, India. Middle order right-hand batsman, right-arm fast bowler, good outfield. *Sch* Wellington. *Teams* Sussex (1900–11, 64 matches); London County (1901); Europeans (1913/14 to 1920/1); Gentlemen of India (1902/3). *Tour* MCC to North America 1907.
Career batting
86–139–7–3114–140–23.59–4–*ct* 90–*st* 2
Bowling 2205–65–33.92–2–0–5/80
Being in the Indian Army, his County cricket was fairly limited. He was a noted polo player.

Golding, Andrew Kenneth
Cricketer. *b:* 5.10.1963, Colchester, Essex. Lower order right-hand batsman, slow left-arm bowler. *Team* Essex (1983, 1 match).
Career batting
1–2–2–8–6*–no av–0–*ct* 0
Bowling 97–2–48.50–0–0–1/44

Goldney, G. H. (*see under* Hone-Goldney, G. H.)

Goldring, Stephen
Cricketer. *b:* 18.11.1932, Portsmouth, Hants. Tail end right-hand batsman, right-arm fast bowler. *Team* Combined Services (1964).
Career batting
1–2–2–23–14*–no av–0–*ct* 0
Bowling 43–0

Goldsmith, George
Amateur. *b:* 7.8.1850, Brighton, Sussex. *d:* 5.4.1916, Hanwell, Middlesex. Lower order right-hand batsman, right-hand fast bowler. *Teams* Sussex (1878–79, 2 matches); Kent (1875, 1 match).
Career batting
3–6–4–9–3*–4.50–0–*ct* 2
Bowling 71–1–71.00–0–0–1/38
He was Secretary to Sussex CCC 1881 to 1888.

Goldstein, Frederick Steven
Cricketer. *b:* 14.10.1944, Rhodesia. Opening right-hand batsman, off break bowler. *Teams* Oxford U (1966–69, blue all four years); Northants (1969, 10 matches); Transvaal (1969/70 to 1970/1); Western Province (1971/2 to 1977/8).
Career batting
89–163–4–4810–155–30.25–2–*ct* 62
Bowling 53–1–53.00–0–0–1/3

Gomes, Hilary Angelo
Cricketer. *b:* 13.7.1953, Arima, Trinidad. Brother of S. A. (Trinidad). Middle order left-hand batsman, right-arm medium pace bowler, good field. *Teams* Trinidad (1971/2 to 1982/3); Middlesex (1973–76, 42 matches). *Tours* West Indies to England 1976, to India and Sri Lanka 1978/9, to Australia and New Zealand 1979/80, to Pakistan 1980/1, to Australia 1981/2. *Tests* West Indies (1976 to 1982/3, 27 matches).
Career batting
163–266–33–9809–200*–42.09–24–*ct* 57
Bowling 3187–81–39.34–0–0–4/22
Test batting
27–40–2–1596–126–42.00–5–*ct* 7
Bowling 469–8–58.62–0–0–2/20
On the 1976 tour to England he hit 1,393 runs, av 48.03, and played in two Tests (1,435, av 47.83, in all first-class matches).

Gomez, Gerald Ethridge
Amateur. *b:* 10.10.1919, Woodbrook, Port of Spain, Trinidad. Middle order left-hand batsman, right-arm medium pace bowler. *Teams* Trinidad (1937/8 to 1955/6). *Tours* West Indies to England 1939, 1950, to Australia and New Zealand 1951/2, to India, Pakistan and Ceylon 1948/9. *Tests* West Indies (1939 to 1953/4, 29 matches).

Career batting
126–182–27–6764–216*–43.63–14–*ct* 92
Bowling 5052–200–25.26–5–2–9/24
Test batting
29–46–5–1243–101–30.31–1–*ct* 18
Bowling 1590–58–27.41–1–1–7/55

He had a modest tour of England in 1939, but in 1950 was second only to Worrell as the all-rounder of the side and hit 1,116 runs, av 42.92, in addition to taking 55 wickets, av 25.58. His highest score was 216* for Trinidad v Barbados at Port of Spain in 1942/3 and his best bowling 9/24 for West Indies v South Zone at Madras in 1948/9.

His final first-class match in England was for MCC in 1957.

He was an active member of the West Indies Board of Control and also in emergency umpired in one Test.

Gomm, Brian Arthur
Amateur. *b:* 24.6.1918, Castle Cary, Somerset. Lower order right-hand batsman, left-arm medium pace bowler. *Team* Somerset (1939, 2 matches).
Career batting
2–3–0–7–5–2.33–0–*ct* 2
Bowling 21–0

Gooch, Graham Alan
Cricketer. *b*: 23.7.1953, Leytonstone, Essex. Aggressive opening right-hand batsman, right-arm medium pace bowler, slip field. *Teams* Essex (1973–83, 179 matches); Western Province (1982/3). *Tours* England to Australia 1978/9, to Australia and India 1979/80, to West Indies 1980/1, to India and Sri Lanka 1981/2; SAB to South Africa 1981/2. *Tests* England (1975 to 1981/2, 42 matches).
Career batting
259–435–35–15789–205–39.47–37–*ct* 240
Bowling 3610–99–36.46–2–0–7/14
Test batting
42–75–4–2540–153–35.77–4–*ct* 36
Bowling 348–8–43.50–0–0–2/12

He hit 1,000 runs in a season seven times (best 1,632, av 44.10, in 1982). His only double century was 205 for Essex v Cambridge U at Fenner's in 1980. He captained the SAB England team in the 1981/2 matches against South Africa.

Gooch, Peter Alan
Cricketer. *b:* 2.5.1949, Timperley, Cheshire. Lower order left-hand batsman, right-arm fast medium bowler. *Teams* Lancashire (1970, 4 matches).
Career batting
4–3–1–0–0*–0.00–0–*ct* 3
Bowling 252–6–42.00–0–0–4/52

He appeared for Cheshire in 1971 and Buckinghamshire commencing 1976.

Good, Antony John
Cricketer. *b:* 10.11.1952, Kumasi, Gold Coast. Tail end right-hand batsman, right-arm fast medium bowler. *Sch* Worksop. *Team* Lancashire (1973–76, 8 matches).
Career batting
8–8–2–10–6–1.66–0–*ct* 1
Bowling 482–17–28.35–1–0–5/62

He appeared for Cheshire commencing 1977.

Good, Bartholomew
Professional. *b:* 20.1.1812, Market Rasen, Lincs. *d:* 12.3.1848, London, of consumption. Middle order left-hand batsman, left-hand slow round-arm bowler. *Teams* Nottinghamshire (1831–43, 16 matches); Hampshire (1844, 1 match).
Career batting
68–124–14–1154–82–10.49–0–*ct* 26
Bowling 207–6+21–34.50–0–0–3/84

His final first-class match was for MCC in 1847.

Good, Dennis Cunliffe
Amateur. *b:* 29.8.1926, Leeds, Yorkshire. Lower order right-hand batsman, right-arm fast medium bowler. *Sch* Denstone. *Teams* Worcestershire (1946, 1 match); Glamorgan (1947, 3 matches).
Career batting
4–7–3–54–21–13.50–0–*ct* 1
Bowling 300–8–37.50–0–0–2/34

Goodacre, William Bennett
Amateur. *b:* 26.2.1873, Nottingham. *d:* 29.6.1948, Sproxton, Leics. Middle order right-hand batsman, useful bowler. *Team* Nottinghamshire (1898–1903, 43 matches).
Career batting
43–66–4–1169–104*–18.85–1–*ct* 27
Bowling 440–12–36.66–0–0–3/30

Goodall, Harry Hornby
Amateur. *b:* 17.1.1877, Nottingham. *d:* 20.2.1961, Beeston, Notts. Middle order right-hand batsman. *Team* Nottinghamshire (1902–05, 5 matches).
Career batting
5–7–1–92–26–15.33–0–*ct* 1

An architect, he designed the Dixon Memorial Gates at Trent Bridge.

Goodall, John
Professional. *b:* 19.6.1863, London. *d:* 20.5.1942,

Watford, Herts. Middle order batsman. *Team* Derbyshire (1895–96, 2 matches).
Career batting
2–3–0–38–32–12.66–0–*ct* 2
He also played for Hertfordshire.
He was a noted soccer player, appearing for Preston North End, Derby County, New Brighton and Glossop.

Goodden, Cecil Phelips
Amateur. *b:* 12.11.1879, Compton, Sherborne, Dorset. *d:* 5.11.1969, Shaftesbury, Dorset. Middle order right-hand batsman, moderate field. *Sch* Harrow. *Teams* MCC (1900–03).
Career batting
3–5–0–27–9–5.40–0–*ct* 1
Bowling 37–0
He did not appear in first-class cricket whilst at Cambridge. His County cricket was for Dorset.

Gooder, Leonard Montague H.
Professional. *b:* 11.2.1876, Paddington, London. *d:* 1928, Willesden, London. Lower order right-hand batsman, slow right-arm bowler. *Team* Surrey (1901–05, 19 matches).
Career batting
19–29–2–312–35–11.55–0–*ct* 7
Bowling 1862–54–34.48–3–1–5/66

Goodfellow, Anthony
Amateur. *b:* 8.1.1940, Seale, Surrey. Middle order left-hand batsman. *Sch* Marlborough. *Team* Cambridge U (1960–62, blue 1961–62).
Career batting
21–42–1–941–81–22.95–0–*ct* 6
Bowling 4–0

Goodfellow, G.
Professional. Middle order batsman, change bowler. *Team* London United (1879).
Career batting
1–2–0–4–4–2.00–0–*ct* 0
Bowling 31–1–31.00–0–0–1/24

Goodhew, William
Professional. *b:* 24.5.1828, Chislehurst, Kent. *d:* 1.5.1897, Canterbury, Kent. Hard hitting middle order right-hand batsman, right-hand medium pace round-arm bowler. *Team* Kent (1854–66, 69 matches).
Career batting
86–160–19–1616–70–11.46–0–*ct* 40
Bowling 434–26–16.69–1–0–7/40

Goodland, Edward Stanley
Amateur. *b:* 22.9.1883, Taunton, Somerset. *d:* 12.1.1974, Bicknoller, Somerset. Middle order right-hand batsman. *Sch* Taunton. *Team* Somerset (1908–09, 4 matches).
Career batting
4–6–1–47–42*–9.40–0–*ct* 2

Goodliffe, Guy Vernon
Amateur. *b:* 17.9.1883, Kensington. *d:* 29.5.1963, Burnfoot, Co Donegal. Lower order batsman, bowler. *Sch* Charterhouse. *Team* Oxford U (1904).
Career batting
1–1–0–0–0–0.00–0–*ct* 1
Bowling 21–2–10.50–0–0–1/0

Goodman, Percy Arnold
Amateur. *b:* 3.10.1874, Barbados. *d:* 25.4.1935, Barbados. Brother of C. E., G. A. and W. E. (all Barbados). Middle order right-hand batsman, right-arm bowler. *Team* Barbados (1891/2 to 1912/3). *Tours* West Indies to England 1900 (not first-class), 1906.
Career batting
40–66–7–1824–180–30.91–5–*ct* 47
Bowling 1155–85+3–13.58–5–1–7/18
He was the leading all-rounder in Barbados at the turn of the century and on the 1906 tour to England he headed the tourists first-class batting averages with 607 runs, av 31.94.

Goodreds, William Arthur
Amateur. *b:* 3.11.1920, Pensnett, Dudley, Worcs. Lower order right-hand batsman, right-arm fast medium bowler. *Team* Worcestershire (1952, 1 match).
Career batting
1–1–1–4–4*–no av–0–*ct* 0
Bowling 48–0

Goodson, Donald
Amateur. *b:* 15.10.1932, Eastwell, Leics. Lower order right-hand batsman, right-arm medium pace bowler. *Team* Leicestershire (1950–53, 9 matches).
Career batting
9–13–4–36–22*–4.00–0–*ct* 1
Bowling 394–7–56.28–0–0–3/43

Goodway, Cyril Clement
Amateur. *b:* 10.7.1909, Smethwick, Staffs. Lower order right-hand batsman, wicket-keeper. *Team* Warwickshire (1937–47, 40 matches). *Tours* Cahn to Ceylon 1936/7, to New Zealand 1938/9 (no first-class matches in either tour).
Career batting
40–66–12–434–37*–8.03–0–*ct* 43–*st* 22
He also played for Staffordshire. He was chairman of Warwickshire CCC.

Goodwin, Douglas Edward
Cricketer. *b:* 2.5.1938, Dublin, Ireland. Right-hand batsman, right-arm fast medium bowler. *Team* Ireland (1965–73).
Career batting
11–16–2–188–39–13.42–0–*ct* 2
Bowling 583–20–29.15–1–0–5/46

Goodwin, Frederick
Professional. *b:* 28.6.1933, Heywood, Lancashire. Lower order right-hand batsman, right-arm fast medium bowler. *Team* Lancashire (1955–56, 11 matches).
Career batting
11–10–4–47–21*–7.83–0–*ct* 7
Bowling 715–27–26.48–1–0–5/35

He played soccer for Manchester United at left half.

Goodwin, Francis Herbert
Professional. *b:* 4.1.1866, Rainhill, Lancashire. *d:* 20.1.1931, Garston, Lancashire. Lower order left-hand batsman, slow left-arm bowler. *Team* Lancashire (1894, 3 matches).
Career batting
3–6–1–14–10–2.80–0–*ct* 0
Bowling 47–0

Goodwin, George William
Amateur. *b:* 7.9.1898, Chesterton, Staffs. Lower order batsman, slow left-arm bowler. *Sch* Rossall. *Team* Derbyshire (1921, 8 matches).
Career batting
8–16–1–224–53–14.93–0–*ct* 1
Bowling 205–7–29.28–0–0–4/23

Goodwin, Harold James
Amateur. *b:* 31.1.1886, Edgbaston, Warwickshire. *d:* 24.4.1917, Arras, France. He was killed in action. Middle order right-hand batsman, leg break bowler, excellent field. *Sch* Marlborough. *Teams* Cambridge U (1906–08, blue 1907–08); Warwickshire (1907–12, 19 matches).
Carrer batting
39–67–4–1255–101–19.92–1–*ct* 33
Bowling 2092–86–24.32–5–1–7/33

A noted hockey player, he appeared for Cambridge U and England.

Goodwin, Harry Smyth
Amateur. *b:* 30.9.1870, Merthyr-Tydfil, Glamorgan. *d:* 13.11.1955, Christ's Hospital, Horsham, Sussex. Middle order right-hand batsman. *Sch* Rossall. *Team* Gloucestershire (1896–1807, 31 matches).
Career batting
31–50–6–546–46–12.40–*ct* 20

Goodwin, Keith
Cricketer. *b:* 25.6.1938, Oldham, Lancashire. Lower order right-hand batsman, wicket-keeper. *Team* Lancashire (1960–74, 122 matches). *Tour* Rest of World XI to Pakistan 1973/4.
Career batting
124–153–43–636–23–5.78–*ct* 229–*st* 28

Goodwin, Thomas Jeffrey
Professional. *b:* 22.1.1929, Bignall End, Staffs. Nephew of A. Lockett (Minor Counties). Lower order left-hand batsman, left-arm fast medium bowler, good close field. *Team* Leicestershire (1950–59, 136 matches).
Career batting
136–167–80–474–23*–5.44–0–*ct* 40
Bowling 1010–335–30.17–15–2–8/81

Goodwyn, Canon Frederick Wyldman
Amateur. *b:* 20.1.1850, Calicut, India. *d:* 23.4.1931, St Leonards-on-Sea, Sussex. Middle order right-hand batsman, excellent deep field. *Sch* Clifton. *Team* Gloucestershire (1871–73, 3 matches).
Career batting
3–3–0–69–38–23.00–0–*ct* 0

He did not appear in any first-class matches whilst at Oxford, but rowed for his College.

He played non-first-class cricket for Somerset.

Goonasekera, Yohan
Cricketer. *b*: 8.11.1957, Colombo, Ceylon. Middle order left-hand batsman, left-arm medium, or slow, bowler. *Team* Sri Lanka (1980/1 to 1982/3). *Tours* Sri Lanka to India 1980/1, to England 1981, to Australia and New Zealand 1982/3. *Tests* Sri Lanka (1982/3, 2 matches).
Career batting
11–16–2–429–79*–30.64–0–*ct* 12
Bowling 38–1–38.00–0–0–1/17
Test batting
2–4–0–48–23–12.00–0–*ct* 6

Goonatilleke, Hettiarachige Mahes
Cricketer. *b*: 16.8.1952, Kandy, Ceylon. Solid opening right-hand batsman, wicket-keeper. *Team* Sri Lanka (1975/6 to 1982/3). *Tours* Sri Lanka to India 1975/6, 1976/7, 1982/3, to England 1981, to Pakistan 1981/2; Sri Lanka XI to South Africa 1982/3. *Tests* Sri Lanka (1981/2 to 1982/3, 5 matches).
Career batting
26–39–7–430–56–13.43–0–*ct* 36–*st* 18
Test batting
5–10–2–177–56–22.12–0–*ct* 10–*st* 3

Goonesena, Gamini
Professional, then amateur from 1954. *b:* 16.2.1931, Colombo, Ceylon. Middle order right-hand batsman, leg break bowler, good outfield. *Teams* Ceylon (1947/8 to 1961/2); Nottinghamshire (1952–64, 94 matches); Cambridge U (1954–57, blue all four years); New South Wales (1960/1 to 1963/4, 7 matches). *Tours* Ceylon to Pakistan 1949/50; Swanton to West Indies 1955/6; Cavaliers to West Indies 1964/5; International XI to India, Pakistan and Ceylon 1967/8.
Career batting
194–304–37–5751–211–21.53–3–*ct* 108
Bowling 16431–674–24.37–41–8–8/39

He hit 1,000 runs in a season twice (best 1,380, av 28.75, in 1955) and took 100 wickets in a season twice (best 134, av 21.05, in 1955). He achieved the 'double' twice. His only double century was for Cambridge U v Oxford U at Lord's in 1957.

His final first-class match was for Free Foresters in 1968, when he took 10 for 87 in the match.

Gopalan, Morappakam Joysam
Amateur. *b:* 6.6.1909, Morappakam, India. Middle/lower order right-hand batsman, right-arm fast medium bowler. *Teams* Madras (1926/7 to 1951/2); Hindus (1934/5). *Tour* India to England 1936. *Test* India (1933/4, 1 match).
Career batting
78–133–16–2916–101*–24.92–1–*ct* 49
Bowling 4695–194–24.20–9–3–7/57
Test batting
1–2–1–18–11*–18.00–0–*ct* 3
Bowling 39–1–39.00–0–0–1/39
Madras and Ceylon/Sri Lanka compete annually for the Gopalan Trophy.

Gopinath, Coimbatarao Doraikannu
Amateur. *b:* 1.3.1930, Madras, India. Middle order right-hand batsman, right-arm medium pace off break bowler. *Team* Madras (1949/50 to 1962/3). *Tours* India to England 1952, to Pakistan 1954/5; Madras to Ceylon 1953/4, 1956/7, 1958/9. *Tests* India (1951/2 to 1959/60, 8 matches).
Career batting
83–119–18–4259–234–42.16–9–*ct* 50
Bowling 389–14–27.78–0–0–3/15
Test batting
8–12–1–242–50*–22.00–0–*ct* 2
Bowling 11–1–11.00–0–0–1/11

On his single tour to England he found conditions difficult and had a very modest return.

His highest score was 234 for Madras v Mysore at Coimbatore in 1958/9.

Gordon, Alan
Cricketer. *b:* 29.3.1944, Coventry, Warwickshire. Middle order right-hand batsman, right-arm slow medium bowler, good slip field. *Team* Warwickshire (1966–71, 34 matches).
Career batting
34–59–4–891–65–16.20–0–*ct* 35
Bowling 1–0

Gordon, Charles
Amateur. *b:* 25.12.1814, London. *d;* 27.7.1899, Bedford. Opening/middle order right-hand batsman, slow round-arm bowler, good field. *Team* Middlesex (1851–62, 3 matches).
Career batting
27–46–5–493–33*–12.02–0–*ct* 13
Bowling 1 wicket, no analysis

He was noted cricketer in London for some 20 years and the 'crack of the once-famous Clapton Club'.

His first-class debut was for Gentlemen of England 1844.

Gordon, Brig-Gen Charles Steward
(later Gordon-Steward)
Amateur. *b:* 8.9.1849, Oakleaze, Gloucs. *d:* 24.3.1930, Nottington, Dorset. Opening right-hand batsman, slow under-arm bowler. *Sch* Marlborough. *Teams* Victoria (1869/70, 1 match); Gloucestershire (1870–75, 13 matches).
Career batting
14–21–0–504–121–24.00–1–*ct* 8
Bowling 202–8–25.25–0–0–3/67

His single first-class match (in which he scored 121) in Australia occurred when he was stationed there with his regiment.

He also played for Dorset.

Gordon, Herbert Pritchard
Amateur. *b:* 13.9.1898, Bridgnorth, Salop. *d:* 17.10.1965, Elm Grove, Brighton, Sussex. Middle order right-hand batsman, right-arm medium pace bowler. *Sch* Malvern. *Team* Worcestershire (1923–24, 7 matches).
Career batting
7–13–1–157–68*–13.08–0–*ct* 6

Gordon, John Harvey
Amateur. *b:* 15.6.1886, Reigate, Surrey. *d:* 23.4.1933, Charlottesville, Pennsylvania, USA. Middle order right-hand batsman, change bowler. *Sch* Winchester. *Teams* Oxford U (1906–07, blue both years); Surrey (1906–07, 3 matches).
Career batting
21–39–1–796–117–20.94–1–*ct* 12
Bowling 117–2–58.50–0–0–2/8

He emigrated to the United States about 1908, and appeared for USA v Canada in 1911.

Gordon-Lennox, Lord Bernard Charles
Amateur. *b:* 1.5.1878, London. *d:* 10.11.1914, Kleinzillebeke, Belgium. He was killed in action. Third son of the Duke of Richmond. Middle order batsman. *Sch* Eton. *Team* Middlesex (1903, 1 match). *Tour* I Zingari to Egypt 1914 (not first-class).
Career batting
1–1–0–0–0–0.00–0–*ct* 1
He scored many runs in military cricket.

Gordon-Walker, Rupert Adam
Cricketer. *b*: 10.8.1961, Moniaive, Dumfries, Scotland. Lower order left-hand batsman, wicket-keeper. *Team* Oxford U (1981).
Career batting
3–5–1–19–12–4.75–0–*ct* 3–*st* 2

Gore, Adrian Clements
Amateur. *b:* 14.5.1900, Dunoon, Scotland. Lower order right-hand batsman, right-arm fast medium bowler. *Sch* Eton. *Team* Army (1921–32).
Career batting
16–20–5–142–32*–9.46–0–*ct* 11
Bowling 1139–52–21.90–3–0–8/46

Gore, Francis William George
Amateur. *b:* 22.6.1855, Newton St Loe, Somerset. *d:* 17.7.1938, Westminster, London. Middle order batsman. *Sch* Harrow. *Team* I Zingari (1881).
Career batting
1–2–1–0–0*–0.00–0–*ct* 2

Gore, Hugh Edmond Ivor
Cricketer. *b:* 18.6.1953, St John's, Antigua. Lower order right-hand batsman, left-arm fast medium bowler. *Teams* Leeward Is (1972/3 to 1978/9); Somerset (1980, 11 matches).
Career batting
34–41–12–382–67–13.17–0–*ct* 14
Bowling 1917–57–33.63–1–0–5/66

Gore, Spencer William
Amateur. *b:* 10.3.1850, Wimbledon, Surrey. *d:* 19.4.1906, Ramsgate, Kent. Nephew of Lord Bessborough (Cambridge U 1836) and S. Ponsonby-Fane. Middle order right-hand batsman, right-hand fast round-arm bowler, good cover point. *Sch* Harrow. *Team* Surrey (1874–75, 2 matches).
Career batting
5–9–1–75–36–9.37–0–*ct* 3
Bowling 93–1–93.00–0–0–1/9
His final first-class match was for Gentlemen of the South in 1879. He also played for Dorset and Wiltshire. He was well-known as a lawn tennis player, being English Champion in 1877.

Gorell, Lord R. (*see under* Barnes, R. G.)

Gornall, James Parrington
Amateur. *b:* 22.9.1899, Farnborough, Hants. *d:* 13.11.1983, Lower Froyle, Hants. Middle order right-hand batsman, right-arm medium pace bowler. *Sch* Christ's Hospital. *Teams* Hampshire (1923, 1 match); Royal Navy (1921–24).
Career batting
4–8–0–149–33–18.62–0–*ct* 1
Bowling 16–0
He appeared in the Freshmen's Match at Cambridge, but no first-class matches.

Gorringe, Allan Lindsay
Amateur. *b:* 20.1.1884, Eastbourne, Sussex. *d:* 22.11.1918, Repton, Derbyshire. Middle order batsman. *Team* Sussex (1905, 4 matches).
Career batting
4–6–0–46–16–7.66–0–*ct* 0
He also played for Cambridgeshire.

Gorringe, Hubert Maurice
Amateur. *b:* 1886, Eastbourne. *d:* 28.8.1958, Hove, Sussex. Middle order batsman. *Team* Sussex (1920, 2 matches).
Career batting
2–4–1–49–29–16.33–0–*ct* 1

Goschen, Sir William Edward
Amateur. *b:* 18.7.1847, Oberlosnitz, Saxony. *d:* 20.5.1924, Chelsea, London. Middle order right-hand batsman, wicket-keeper. *Sch* Rugby. *Team* Oxford U (1868–69).
Career batting
3–5–0–10–4–2.00–0–*ct* 1

Gosling, Cecil Henry
Amateur. *b:* 22.2.1910, Dunmow, Essex. *d:* 19.5.1974, Hatfield-Broad Oak, Essex. Nephew of R. C. (Essex). Middle order right-hand batsman. *Sch* Eton. *Teams* Oxford U (1929); Essex (1930, 2 matches).
Career batting
5–8–0–132–37–16.50–0–*ct* 3
He was Deputy Lieutenant of Essex in 1949.

Gosling, Robert Cunliffe
Amateur. *b:* 15.6.1868, Farnham, Essex. *d:* 8.4.1922, Farnham, Essex. Uncle of C. H. (Essex). Stylish middle order right-hand batsman, right-arm slow bowler, good field. *Sch* Eton. *Teams* Cambridge U (1888–90, blue all three years); Essex (1894–96, 4 matches).

Career batting
26–48–5–584–61–13.58–0–*ct* 18
Bowling 11–0

A noted all-round sportsman, he also won his blue for soccer and went on to play for England. He was donor of the Arthur Dunn Cup.

Gothard, Edward James
Amateur. *b:* 1.10.1904, Burton-on-Trent. *d:* 17.1.1979, Birmingham. Lower order right-hand batsman, right-arm medium pace bowler. *Team* Derbyshire (1947–48, 45 matches).
Career batting
45–63–19–543–50–12.34–0–*ct* 10
Bowling 730–18–40.55–0–0–3/84

He captained Derbyshire in 1947 and 1948 and was later Hon Secretary to the County Club. He also played County cricket for Staffordshire.

Goudge, Rev William Henry
Amateur. *b:* 29.10.1877, Highworth, Wilts. *d:* 31.5.1967, Cheltenham. Opening right-hand batsman. *Sch* Bath College. *Team* Royal Navy (1919–23).
Career batting
5–10–0–191–58–19.10–0–*ct* 3

His County cricket was for Wiltshire.

Gough-Calthorpe, Hon F. S.
(*see under* Calthorpe, Hon F. S. G.)

Gould, Anthony Victor Endersby
Cricketer. *b:* 22.2.1944, Windsor, Berks. Opening/middle order right-hand batsman. *Team* Cambridge U (1964–66).
Career batting
13–24–0–241–38–10.04–0–*ct* 3
Bowling 16–1–16.00–0–0–1/10

Gould, Ian James
Cricketer. *b*: 19.8.1957, Taplow, Bucks. Middle or lower order left-hand batsman, wicket-keeper. *Teams* Middlesex (1975–80, 88 matches); Sussex (1981–83, 58 matches); Auckland (1979/80). *Tours* England to Australia and New Zealand 1982/3 (New Zealand not first-class); Middlesex to Zimbabwe 1980/1; International XI to Pakistan 1980/1.
Career batting
160–218–30–4253–128–22.62–1–*ct* 320–*st* 56
Bowling 35–0

Gould, Thomas
Professional. *b:* 26.9.1863, Brassington, Derbyshire. *d:* 30.3.1948, Burton-on-Trent. Lower order batsman, change bowler. *Team* Derbyshire (1896–97, 7 matches).
Career batting
7–10–2–63–16*–7.87–0–*ct* 5
Bowling 225–9–25.00–0–0–4/45

Goulder, Alfred
Professional. *b:* 16.8.1907, Sheffield, Yorkshire. Lower order left-hand batsman, slow left-arm bowler. *Team* Yorkshire (1929, 2 matches).
Career batting
2–1–0–3–3–3.00–0–*ct* 0
Bowling 90–3–30.00–0–0–2/21

Goulding, Sir William Basil
Amateur. *b:* 4.11.1909, Dublin, Ireland. *d:* 16.1.1982, Dargle, Enniskerry, Co Wicklow. Right-hand batsman, wicket-keeper. *Sch* Winchester. *Team* Ireland (1934).
Career batting
1–2–1–0–0*–0.00–0–*ct* 0

An all-round sportsman, he represented Ireland at squash and was awarded his blue for soccer.

Gouldsworthy, William Robert
Amateur. *b:* 20.5.1892, Bristol. *d:* 4.2.1969, Westbourne, Bournemouth, Hants. Lower order right-hand batsman, right-arm medium pace bowler. *Team* Gloucestershire (1921–29, 26 matches).
Career batting
26–44–10–277–65*–8.14–0–*ct* 11
Bowling 1729–62–27.88–4–1–6/47

Gover, Alfred Richard
Professional. *b:* 29.2.1908, Epsom, Surrey. Lower order right-hand batsman, right-arm fast bowler. *Team* Surrey (1928–47, 336 matches). *Tour* Tennyson to India 1937/8. *Tests* England (1936–46, 4 matches).
Career batting
362–414–167–2312–41*–9.36–0–*ct* 171
Bowling 36753–1555–23.63–95–17–8/34
Test batting
4–1–1–2–2*–no av–0–*ct* 1
Bowling 359–8–44.87–0–0–3/85

He took 100 wickets in a season eight times, going on to 200 in two seasons (best 201, av 18.98, in 1937). His final first-class match was for an England XI v Glamorgan in 1948. For many years he was proprietor of an Indoor Cricket School in South London. He was a noted goalkeeper in amateur football.

Govindraj, Devraj Devendraraj
Cricketer. *b:* 2.1.1947, Hyderabad, India. Lower order right-hand batsman, right-arm fast medium bowler. *Team* Hyderabad (1964/5 to 1974/5). *Tours* Hyderabad Blues to Ceylon 1966/7; State

Bank of India to Ceylon 1968/9; India to England 1971, to West Indies 1970/1.
Career batting
93–107–18–1202–72–13.50–0–*ct* 36
Bowling 5256–190–27.66–5–2–6/38

He achieved very little on his tour to England and did not appear in the Tests.

Gowans, James
Amateur. *b:* 23.4.1872, Westhoe, Co Durham. *d:* 14.3.1936, Rosherville, Johannesburg, South Africa. Lower order right-hand batsman, wicket-keeper. *Sch* Harrow. *Team* MCC (1891).
Career batting
1–1–0–40–40–40.00–0–*ct* 0

Whilst at Cambridge he appeared in the Freshmen's Match, but no first-class matches.

An excellent rugby footballer, he represented Cambridge and Scotland.

Gower, David Ivon
Cricketer. *b:* 1.4.1957, Tunbridge Wells, Kent. Excellent middle order left-hand batsman, off break bowler, good field. *Sch* King's, Canterbury. *Team* Leicestershire (1975–83, 109 matches). *Tours* England to Australia 1978/9, to Australia and India 1979/80, to West Indies 1980/1, to India and Sri Lanka 1981/2, to Australia and New Zealand 1982/3; Robins to Sri Lanka 1977/8. *Tests* England (1978–83, 53 matches).
Career batting
209–334–32–11886–200*–39.35–24–*ct* 125
Bowling 180–4–45.00–0–0–3/47
Test batting
53–93–8–3742–200*–44.02–7–*ct* 34
Bowling 2–1–2.00–0–0–1/1

He hit 1,000 runs in a season five times (best 1,530, av 46.36, in 1982). His only double century was 200* for England v India at Edgbaston in 1979. He captained England in one Test in 1982 and is regarded as the most accomplished English batsman of his generation.

Graburn, William Turbett
Amateur. *b:* 16.3.1865, Filey, Yorkshire. *d:* 13.12.1944, West Molesey, Surrey. Middle order right-hand batsman, slow right-arm bowler. *Sch* Repton. *Team* Surrey (1894, 1 match).
Career batting
2–3–0–63–39–21.00–0–*ct* 0

His debut in first-class matches was for the Hurst Park Club v Australians in 1890.

Commencing in 1892 he was Cricket Instructor to Surrey CCC.

Grace, Dr Alfred Henry
Amateur. *b:* 10.3.1866, Chipping Sodbury, Gloucs. *d:* 16.9.1929, Iron-Acton, Gloucs. Nephew of W. G., E. M., Henry and G. F. (Gloucs), cousin of W. G. jun (Gloucs), C. B. (London County) and N. V. (Royal Navy). Hard hitting right-hand batsman, right-arm medium pace bowler. *Sch* Epsom. *Teams* Gloucestershire (1886–91, 2 matches).
Career batting
2–3–0–5–4–1.66–0–*ct* 1
Bowling 42–1–42.00–0–0–1/42

Grace, Charles Butler
Amateur. *b:* 26.3.1882, Bristol. *d:* 6.6.1938, Bexhill, Sussex, whilst playing cricket. Son of W. G., brother of W. G. jun, nephew of E. M., Henry and G. F., cousin of A. H. (all Gloucs) and N. V. (Royal Navy). Tail end right-hand batsman, lob bowler. *Sch* Clifton. *Team* London County (1900).
Career batting
4–5–0–42–36–8.40–0–*ct* 3
Bowling 92–3–30.66–0–0–3/62

His final first-class match was for W. G. Grace's XI in 1906.

Grace, Dr Edward Mills
Amateur. *b:* 28.11.1841, Downend, Bristol. *d:* 20.5.1911, Thornbury, Gloucs. Brother of G. F., Henry and W. G. (Gloucs), father of N. V. (Navy), uncle of A. H., W. G. jun (Gloucs) and C. B. (London County). Opening right-hand batsman, right-hand fast round-arm, later slow under-arm bowler, brilliant point. *Team* Gloucestershire (1870–95, 253 matches). *Tour* Parr to Australia 1863/4. *Test* England (1880, 1 match).
Career batting
314–555–18–10025–192*–18.66–5–*ct* 369–*st* 1
Bowling 6213–305–20.37–17–2–10/69
Test batting
1–2–0–36–36–18.00–0–*ct* 1

Although his first-class record does not match that of W. G., E. M. was a great cricketer in his own right and a formidable figure in local cricket – even in 1909 he took 119 wickets, though his batting was handicapped by his lameness. His greatest feat in first-class matches was to score 192* and take 10 wickets in an innings in the same match – MCC v Gentlemen of Kent in 1862.

His first-class debut was for MCC in 1862.

Grace, George Frederick
Amateur. *b:* 13.12.1850, Downend, Bristol. *d:* 22.9.1880, Basingstoke, Hants, of congestion of the lungs. Brother of E. M., Henry and W. G. (Gloucs), uncle of A. H., W. G. jun (Gloucs), C. B. (London County) and N. V. (Royal Navy). Middle order right-hand batsman, right-hand fast round-arm bowler, good field. *Team* Gloucester-

shire (1870–80, 85 matches). *Test* England (1880, 1 match).
Career batting
194–316–40–6910–189*–25.03–8–*ct* 170–*st* 3
Bowling 6599–329–20.05–17–5–8/43
Test batting
1–2–0–0–0–0.00–0–*ct* 2

He was only 15 years and 159 days old when he made his first-class debut for Gentlemen of England v Oxford U in 1866.

He was taken ill and died whilst on his way to Winchester to play in a match.

Grace, Dr Henry
Amateur. *b:* 31.1.1833, Downend, Bristol. *d:* 13.11.1895, Honiton, Devon. Brother of E. M., G. F. and W. G. (Gloucs), uncle of A. H., W. G. jun (Gloucs), C. B. (London County) and N. V. (Royal Navy). Middle order right-hand batsman, right-hand medium pace round-arm bowler. *Team* Gloucestershire (1871, 2 matches).
Career batting
3–3–0–4–4–1.33–0–*ct* 0
Bowling 85–3–28.33–0–0–3/48

He was the eldest of the five Grace brothers, most of his cricket being played before Gloucestershire became first-class.

Grace, Norman Vere
Amateur. *b:* 31.7.1894, Thornbury, Gloucs. *d:* 20.2.1975, Amberley, Gloucs. Son of E. M. (Gloucs), nephew of W. G., Henry and G. F. (Gloucs), cousin of A. H., W. G. jun (Gloucs) and C. B. (London County). Middle order right-hand batsman, right-arm slow bowler. *Team* Royal Navy (1920–27).
Career batting
3–5–0–25–24–5.00–0–*ct* 1
Bowling 114–7–16.28–1–0–5/69

Grace, Dr William Gilbert
Amateur. *b:* 18.7.1848, Downend, Bristol. *d:* 23.10.1915, Mottingham, Kent. Brother of E. M., G. F. and Henry (Gloucs), father of W. G. jun (Gloucs) and C. B. (London County), uncle of A. H. (Gloucs) and N. V. (Royal Navy). Opening right-hand batsman, right-hand medium pace round-arm bowler, excellent field. *Teams* Gloucestershire (1870–99, 360 matches); Kent (1877, 1 match, given man); London County (1900–04). *Tours* FitzGerald to North America 1872 (not first-class); Grace to Australia 1873/4 (not first-class); Sheffield to Australia 1891/2. *Tests* England (1880–99, 22 matches).
Career batting
869–1478–104–54211–344–39.45–124–*ct* 874–*st* 5
Bowling 50982–2808–18.15–240–64–10/49
Test batting
22–36–2–1098–170–32.29–2–*ct* 39
Bowling 236–9–26.22–0–0–2/12

The most famous of all cricketers, W. G. Grace dominated the game from 1871 until the turn of the century. With his brothers he made Gloucestershire a first-class cricketing county and was the captain from the beginning until 1899, when he resigned owing to a dispute. His final years were mainly at Crystal Palace where he played for London County.

During his long career he broke, or perhaps created would be a more appropriate description, many first-class records. He hit the first first-class triple century: 344 for MCC v Kent in 1876, and a few days later hit 318 for Gloucs v Yorkshire at Clifton. Despite these innings he was unable to match, in 1876, the formidable run aggregate he had compiled in 1871 with 2,739 runs (av 78.25) – this was the first time any player had reached 2,000 runs in a first-class season. In 1874 he became the first player to perform the 'double' and in 1876 the first to achieve 2,000 runs and 100 wickets in a single season.

In all he made 1,000 runs in 28 seasons, going on to 2,000 five times. In nine summers he reached 100 wickets (best 191, av 12.94, in 1875) and in seven seasons achieved the 'double'. Around 1890 he seemed to be losing his appetite for records, but in 1895, at the age of 47, he came back to hit 1,000 runs in the month of May, the first time this rare feat had been achieved. His best bowling was 10/49 for MCC v Oxford U at Oxford in 1886.

His career record both in terms of runs scored and centuries remained unbeaten for many years – he was the first to hit 100 first-class centuries.

His record in Test cricket spanned 20 seasons, but as he only visited Australia with one Test playing side, he appeared in just 22 Tests, being captain in 13. He hit the first English Test hundred and created another record with his 170 in 1886. Altogether his was the most remarkable of all cricket careers. His final first-class match was for Gentlemen of England in 1908.

Grace, William Gilbert (jun)
Amateur. *b:* 6.7.1874, South Kensington, London. *d:* 2.3.1905, East Cowes, Isle of Wight, after an appendicitis operation. Son of W. G. (Gloucs), brother of C. B. (London County), nephew of E. M., Henry and G. M. (Gloucs), cousin of A. H. (Gloucs) and N. V. (Royal Navy). Middle order right-hand batsman, right-arm fast medium bowler. *Sch* Clifton. *Teams*

Gloucestershire (1893–98, 29 matches); Cambridge U (1894–96, blue 1895–96); London County (1900–03).
Career batting
57–91–4–1324–79–15.21–0–*ct* 43
Bowling 1657–42–39.45–1–0–6/79

Gracey, Peter Bosworth Kirkwood
Amateur. *b:* 12.12.1921, Bannu, India. Middle order right-hand batsman. *Sch* Wellington. *Teams* Oxford U (1947–48); Europeans (1945/6).
Career batting
5–9–1–176–61–22.00–0–*ct* 7
Bowling 54–2–27.00–0–0–2/21

Graf, Shaun Francis
Cricketer. *b:* 19.5.1957, Melbourne, Australia. Lower order left-hand batsman, right-arm fast medium bowler. *Teams* Victoria (1979/80 to 1982/3, 28 matches); Hampshire (1980, 15 matches).
Career batting
43–61–13–1090–100*–22.70–1–*ct* 20
Bowling 3067–88–34.85–1–0–5/95
He played for Wiltshire in 1979.

Graham, David
Amateur. *b:* 13.3.1922, Belfast, Ireland. Right-hand batsman, right-arm fast medium bowler. *Team* Ireland (1948).
Career batting
1–2–0–13–7–6.50–0–*ct* 0
Bowling 20–1–20.00–0–0–1/13

Graham, Godfrey Richard
Amateur. *b:* 23.8.1936, Dublin, Ireland. Right-hand batsman, leg break and googly bowler. *Team* Ireland (1954).
Career batting
1–1–1–1–1*–no av–0–*ct* 1
Bowling 100–2–50.00–0–0–2/100

Graham, Henry
Amateur. *b:* 22.11.1870, Carlton, Victoria, Australia. *d:* 7.2.1911, Dunedin, New Zealand. Middle order right-hand batsman, leg break bowler, good field. *Teams* Victoria (1892/3 to 1902/3, 43 matches); Otago (1903/4 to 1906/7). *Tours* Australia to England and North America 1893, 1896. *Tests* Australia (1893–96, 6 matches).
Career batting
114–201–9–5054–124–26.32–7–*ct* 87
Bowling 235–6–39.16–0–0–4/39
Test batting
6–10–0–301–107–30.10–2–*ct* 3
He was successful on his 1893 tour of England, hitting 1,119 runs, av 24.87, and scoring 107 in the Lord's Test, but in 1896 was dogged by ill-health.

Graham, Henry Canning
Professional. *b:* 31.5.1914, Belfast, Ireland. *d:* March 1982, Telford, Shropshire. Middle order right-hand batsman. *Team* Leicestershire (1936–37, 23 matches).
Career batting
23–38–4–589–75–17.32–0–*ct* 13
Bowling 37–1–37.00–0–0–1/9

Graham, John
Amateur. *b:* 10.10.1870, London. *d:* 26.8.1893, Norway. He was drowned while on holiday. Lower order batsman, wicket-keeper. *Sch* Clifton. *Team* Cambridge U (1892).
Career batting
1–1–0–3–3–3.00–0–*ct* 0–*st* 1

Graham, James McGill
Amateur. *b:* 2.11.1874, Ayr, Scotland. *d:* circa 1955. Right-hand batsman, leg break and googly bowler. *Team* Scotland (1924).
Career batting
1–2–1–3–3*–3.00–0–*ct* 1
Bowling 89–1–89.00–0–0–1/89

Graham, John Norman
Cricketer. *b:* 8.5.1943, Hexham, Northumberland. Tail end right-hand batsman, right-arm medium pace bowler. *Team* Kent (1964–77, 186 matches). *Tour* Kent to West Indies 1972/3 (not first-class).
Career batting
189–178–73–404–23–3.84–0–*ct* 40
Bowling 13722–614–22.34–26–3–8/20
He took 104 wickets, av 13.90, in 1967.
Since 1980 he has played for Northumberland.

Graham, James Robert
Amateur. *b:* 1908, Dublin, Ireland. *d:* 14.1.1942, Dublin, Ireland. Right-hand batsman, off break bowler. *Team* Ireland (1936–39).
Career batting
6–12–1–50–12*–4.54–0–*ct* 3
Bowling 389–13–29.92–0–0–3/76

Graham, Leonard
Professional. *b:* 20.8.1901, Leyton, Essex. Middle order batsman. *Team* Essex (1926, 2 matches).
Career batting
2–3–1–14–12–7.00–0–*ct* 2
He played football for Millwall.

Graham, Ogilvie Blair
Amateur. *b:* 8.7.1891, Ireland. *d:* 30.5.1971, Lower Quinton, Warwickshire. Lower order

batsman, bowler. *Sch* Harrow. *Teams* Free Foresters (1923); Europeans (1926/7).
Career batting
4–6–0–31–16–5.16–0–*ct* 2
Bowling 165–10–16.50–0–0–4/12

Graham, Peter Arthur Onslow
Amateur. *b:* 27.12.1920, Kurseong, Darjeeling, India. Lower order right-hand batsman, right-arm fast bowler. *Sch* Tonbridge. *Teams* Somerset (1948, 6 matches).
Career batting
6–11–2–82–33–9.11–0–*ct* 3
Bowling 316–7–45.14–0–0–3/47

Graham, Robert
Amateur. *b:* 16.9.1877, Grahamstown, South Africa. *d:* 21.4.1946, Eastbourne, Sussex. Lower order right-hand batsman, right-arm medium pace bowler. *Team* Western Province (1897/8 to 1898/9). *Tour* South Africa to England 1901. *Tests* South Africa (1898/9, 2 matches).
Career batting
18–33–9–260–63*–10.83–0–*ct* 22
Bowling 1406–61–23.04–5–1–8/90
Test batting
2–4–0–6–4–1.50–0–*ct* 2
Bowling 127–3–42.33–0–0–2/22

Graham-Brown, James Martin Hilary
Cricketer. *b:* 11.7.1951, Thetford, Norfolk. Middle order right-hand batsman, right-arm medium pace bowler. *Sch* Sevenoaks. *Teams* Kent (1974–76, 13 matches); Derbyshire (1977–78, 17 matches).
Career batting
30–37–7–368–43–12.26–0–*ct* 8
Bowling 696–12–58.00–0–0–2/23
He has played for Cornwall since 1981.

Grainge, Clifford Marshall
Amateur. *b:* 21.7.1927, Heckmondwike, Yorkshire. Tail end right-hand batsman, right-arm fast medium bowler. *Team* Oxford U (1950–52).
Career batting
14–15–6–47–14*–5.22–0–*ct* 4
Bowling 1090–25–43.60–1–0–5/127

Grainger, Charles Edward
Amateur. *b:* 22.11.1858, London. *d:* 19.9.1934, Kensington, London. Middle order right-hand batsman. *Sch* Marlborough. *Team* Cambridge U (1879).
Career batting
1–2–1–2–2*–2.00–0–*ct* 2

Grainger, George
Professional. *b:* 11.11.1887, Morton, Derbyshire. *d:* 17.8.1977, Walton, Chesterfield, Derbyshire. Lower order left-hand batsman, left-arm slow or medium bowler. *Team* Derbyshire (1909–21, 5 matches).
Career batting
5–9–3–36–10*–6.00–0–*ct* 1
Bowling 348–7–49.71–0–0–4/91

Grant, Christopher Robert Wellsley
Cricketer. *b:* 19.12.1935, Lincoln. Middle order left-hand batsman. *Team* Nottinghamshire (1968, 3 matches).
Career batting
3–6–0–125–48–20.83–0–*ct* 0

Grant, Edward
Amateur. *b:* 16.6.1874, Stockbridge, Hants. *d:* 12.1.1953, Bath, Somerset. Lower order batsman, slow bowler. *Team* Somerset (1899–1901, 5 matches).
Career batting
5–8–2–66–14–11.00–0–*ct* 6
Bowling 144–4–36.00–0–0–2/19
He also appeared for Wiltshire.

Grant, George Copeland
Amateur. *b:* 9.5.1907, Port of Spain, Trinidad. *d:* 26.10.1978, Cambridge. Brother of R. S. (Cambridge U and West Indies) and F. G. (Trinidad). Lower order right-hand batsman, right-arm fast medium bowler. *Teams* Cambridge U (1928–30, blue 1929–30); Trinidad (1933/4 to 1934/5); Rhodesia (1931/2). *Tours* West Indies to Australia 1930/1, to England 1933. *Tests* West Indies (1930/1 to 1934/5, 12 matches).
Career batting
81–136–17–3831–115–32.19–4–*ct* 71
Bowling 969–19–51.00–0–0–3/24
Test batting
12–21–5–413–71*–25.81–0–*ct* 10
Bowling 18–0
He captained West Indies in all the Tests in which he played. His first-class debut in West Indies was for G. C. Grant's XI in 1932/3. He hit 1,195 runs, av 30.64, in 1933.

Grant, Rolph Stewart
Amateur. *b:* 15.12.1909, Port of Spain, Trinidad. *d:* 18.10.1977, Canada. Brother of G. C. (Cambridge U and West Indies) and F. G. (Trinidad). Lower order right-hand batsman, off break bowler, brilliant close field. *Teams* Cambridge U (1932–33, blue 1933); Trinidad (1933/4 to 1938/9). *Tour* West Indies to England 1939. *Tests* West Indies (1934/5 to 1939, 7 matches).

Career batting
48–74–8–1883–152–28.53–1–*ct* 66
Bowling 1989–79–25.17–0–0–4/41
Test batting
7–11–1–220–77–22.00–0–*ct* 13
Bowling 353–11–32.09–0–0–3/68

He was awarded his blue at Cambridge mainly on account of his fielding. In 1939 he captained the West Indies tourists in England.

Grant, Trevor John Duncan
Amateur. *b:* 24.5.1926, Reigate, Surrey. *d:* 10.10.1957, Shotley, Suffolk. Opening right-hand batsman. *Teams* Sussex (1946, 1 match).
Career batting
1–2–0–6–6–3.00–0–*ct* 1

Grant, William St Clair
Amateur. *b:* 8.9.1894, Bhagalpur, India. *d:* 26.9.1918, near Passchendaele, Belgium. He was killed in action. Hard hitting batsman, medium pace bowler, fair field. *Sch* Clifton. *Team* Gloucestershire (1914, 4 matches).
Career batting
4–7–0–55–16–7.85–0–*ct* 1
Bowling 22–0

Grant-Asher, A. G. *(see under* Asher, A. G. G.)

Granville, Richard St Leger
Amateur. *b:* 24.4.1907, King's Worthy, Hants. *d:* 8.8.1972, Banbury, Oxon. Middle order right-hand batsman. *Sch* Eton. *Team* Warwickshire (1934, 1 match).
Career batting
1–2–0–9–7–4.50–0–*ct* 0

Grasett, Geoffrey William
Amateur. *b:* 28.7.1890, Hereford. *d:* 31.10.1934, Cranham, Gloucs. Lower order batsman, bowler. *Team* Oxford U (1912).
Career batting
1–2–1–2–2*–2.00–0–*ct* 0
Bowling 35–2–17.50–0–0–2/19

He played for Herefordshire.

Grass, Arthur Conrad
Amateur. *b:* October 1897, Denmark Hill, London. Middle order right-hand batsman, right-arm medium pace bowler, good cover point. *Sch* City of London. *Tour* South Americans to England 1932.
Career batting
3–6–4–60–24*–30.00–0–*ct* 0

Graveney, David Anthony
Cricketer. *b*: 2.1.1953, Bristol. Son of J. K. R. (Gloucs); nephew of T. W. (Gloucs and Worcs). Lower order right-hand batsman, slow left-arm bowler. *Sch* Millfield. *Team* Gloucestershire (1972–83, 239 matches).
Career batting
239–325–82–4657–119–19.16–2–*ct* 116
Bowling 15562–540–28.81–25–4–8/85

He has captained Gloucestershire since 1981.

Graveney, John Kenneth Richard
Professional. *b:* 16.12.1924, Hexham, Northumberland. Brother of T. W. (Gloucs and Worcs); father of D. A. (Gloucs). Lower order left-hand batsman, right-arm fast medium bowler. *Sch* Bristol Grammar School. *Team* Gloucestershire (1947–64, 110 matches).
Career batting
111–167–26–2034–62–14.42–0–*ct* 52
Bowling 4819–173–27.86–6–1–10/66

He retired owing to a back injury in 1951, but returned to captain Gloucestershire in 1963 and 1964. His outstanding performance was taking all ten wickets (for 66) for Gloucs v Derbyshire at Chesterfield in 1949.

Graveney, Thomas William, OBE
Professional. *b:* 16.6.1927, Riding Mill, Northumberland. Brother of J. K. R. (Gloucs), uncle of D. A. (Gloucs). Brilliant middle order right-hand batsman, leg break bowler. *Sch* Bristol Grammar School. *Teams* Gloucestershire (1948–60, 296 matches); Worcestershire (1961–70, 208 matches); Queensland (1969/70 to 1971/2, 7 matches). *Tours* MCC to Australia and New Zealand 1954/5, 1958/9, to Australia 1962/3, to West Indies 1953/4, 1967/8, to Ceylon, India and Pakistan 1951/2, to Ceylon and Pakistan 1968/9; Norfolk to West Indies 1956/7; Swanton to West Indies 1955/6; Cavaliers to West Indies 1963/4, to South Africa 1960/1; Commonwealth to South Africa 1959/60, to Pakistan 1963/4; Howard to India 1956/7; Worcs World Tour 1964/5; Rest of World to Barbados 1966/7; International XI to Pakistan, New Zealand and South Africa 1961/2. *Tests* England (1951–69, 79 matches).
Career batting
732–1223–159–47793–258–44.91–122–*ct* 549–*st* 1
Bowling 3037–80–37.96–1–0–5/28
Test batting
79–123–13–4882–258–44.38–11–*ct* 80
Bowling 167–1–167.00–0–0–1/34

Scoring over 1,000 runs in an English season no less than 20 times and going on to 2,000 seven times, Graveney was the equal in consistency of any of his contemporaries in County cricket. His runs were made in a most attractive style and he appeared the complete batsman, yet for over half his career he was unable to command a regular place in the England side. It was not until he had left Gloucestershire – over a disagreement concerning the captaincy – and re-established himself in the Worcestershire side that he really matured as an International cricketer.

His greatest innings for England were both made late in his career : 96 at Lord's against the West Indies in 1966 and 118 at Port of Spain on the 1967/8 tour. The most runs he scored in a season were 2,397, av 49.93, in 1956. Of his seven double centuries, five were for Gloucestershire, one for MCC and the highest, 258, for England against West Indies at Trent Bridge in 1957. He captained Gloucestershire in 1959 and 1960, Worcestershire 1968–70 and England in one Test in 1968. He was banned from Test cricket in 1969, when he played in a benefit match on a Sunday in the middle of a Test Match in which he was appearing.

After retiring from first-class cricket he became well-known as a commentator on the game. Apart from cricket he was a talented golfer.

Graves, Sir Cecil George
Amateur. *b:* 4.3.1892, Kensington, London. *d:* 12.1.1957, West Cults, Aberdeenshire. Lower order batsman, opening bowler. *Sch* Gresham's Holt. *Team* MCC (1920).
Career batting
1–2–0–48–33–24.00–0–*ct* 0
Bowling 81–0

Graves, Nelson Zwingluis
Amateur. *b:* 10.8.1880, Philadelphia, USA. *d:* 31.3.1918, Germantown, Philadelphia, USA. Opening/middle order right-hand batsman. *Team* Philadelphia (1898–1908). *Tours* Philadelphia to England 1903, 1908.
Career batting
33–62–3–1133–103*–19.20–1–*ct* 21
Bowling 57–1–57.00–0–0–1/13

He was described as being of first-class County standard on the 1903 tour to England and came second in the tourists' batting averages, but in 1908 he failed to find his form. He appeared for United States v Canada, making a century on his debut in this series in 1898.

Graves, Peter John
Cricketer. *b:* 19.5.1946, Hove, Sussex. Middle order left-hand batsman, slow left-arm bowler. *Teams* Sussex (1965–80, 270 matches); Orange Free State (1969/70 to 1976/7).
Career batting
292–502–51–12076–145–26.77–14–*ct* 223
Bowling 797–15–53.13–0–0–3/69

He hit 1,000 runs in a season five times (best 1,282, av 38.84, in 1974).

He was also a useful soccer player.

Gravett, Mark
Professional. *b:* 11.2.1865, Milford, Surrey. *d:* 8.2.1938, Godalming, Surrey. Lower order batsman, slow left-arm bowler. *Team* Hampshire (1899–1900, 4 matches).
Career batting
4–7–1–41–17*–6.83–0–*ct* 4
Bowling 445–15–29.66–1–0–5/50

He also played for Wiltshire and Staffordshire.

Gray, Cyril Douglas
Amateur. *b:* 26.4.1895, Hampstead, North London. *d:* 20.2.1969, Woking, Surrey. Middle order right-hand batsman. *Sch* Harrow and Westminster. *Team* Middlesex (1925–27, 15 matches).
Career batting
15–25–1–563–81–23.45–0–*ct* 7
Bowling 30–2–15.00–0–0–2/7

A well known golfer, he represented England.

Gray, David Anthony Athelstan
Amateur. *b:* 19.6.1922, London. Lower order right-hand batsman, slow left-arm bowler. *Sch* Winchester. *Teams* Cambridge U (1947); Essex (1947, 1 match).
Career batting
3–5–0–22–8–4.40–0–*ct* 1
Bowling 182–3–60.66–0–0–2/67

Gray, Euan John
Cricketer. *b*: 18.11.1954, Wellington, New Zealand. Right-hand batsman, slow left-arm bowler. *Team* Wellington (1975/6 to 1982/3). *Tour* New Zealand to England 1983. *Tests* New Zealand (1983, 2 matches).
Career batting
68–108–20–2398–126–27.25–2–*ct* 53
Bowling 4404–167–26.37–2–0–6/53
Test batting
2–4–0–38–17–9.50–0–*ct* 0
Bowling 128–4–32.00–0–0–3/73

Gray, Frank Davis
Amateur. *b:* 2.7.1873, Leicester. *d:* 23.2.1947, Leicester. Middle order batsman. *Sch* Mill Hill. *Teams* Leicestershire (1895, 1 match).
Career batting
1–2–0–17–9–8.50–0–*ct* 0

Gray, Rev Horace
Amateur. *b:* 29.11.1874, Chesterton, Cambridge. *d:* 21.1.1938, Bredfield, Suffolk. Lower order right-hand batsman, right-arm fast bowler. *Sch* Perse. *Team* Cambridge U (1894–96, blue 1894–95).

Career batting
18–27–11–97–10–6.06–0–*ct* 6
Bowling 2026–89–22.76–8–1–7/48

He played County cricket for Cambridgeshire and Devon.

Gray, John Dennis
Cricketer. *b:* 9.10.1948, Coventry, Warwickshire. Lower order left-hand batsman, left-arm medium fast bowler. *Team* Warwickshire (1968–69, 7 matches).
Career batting
7–6–3–34–18–11.33–0–*ct* 1
Bowling 534–21–25.42–1–0–5/2

He took five wickets for two runs in the first innings of his debut match – Warwickshire v Scotland 1968.

He is also a useful rugby footballer.

Gray, James Roy
Professional. *b:* 19.5.1926, Southampton, Hants. Opening right-hand batsman, right-arm medium pace bowler, brilliant field. *Sch* King Edward VI School, Southampton. *Team* Hampshire (1948–66, 453 matches).
Career batting
458–818–81–22650–213*–30.73–30–*ct* 352
Bowling 13719–457–30.01–11–1–7/52

He reached 1,000 runs in a season 13 times, going on to 2,000 on three occasions (best 2,224, av 40.43, in 1962). His only double century is 213* for Hants v Derbyshire at Portsmouth in 1962.

He played soccer for Arsenal.

Gray, Lawrence Herbert
Professional. *b:* 16.12.1915, Tottenham, North London. *d:* 3.1.1983, Langdon Hills, Essex. Lower order right-hand batsman, right-arm fast medium bowler. *Team* Middlesex (1934–51, 204 matches).
Career batting
219–252–130–901–35*–7.38–0–*ct* 125
Bowling 16014–637–25.13–26–3–8/59

He took 102 wickets, av 18.43, in 1946.

After retiring from first-class cricket, he became a County umpire.

Gray, Roger Ibbotson
Amateur. *b:* 16.6.1921, Leeds, Yorkshire. Lower order right-hand batsman, right-arm medium pace bowler. *Sch* Wycliffe. *Team* Oxford U (1947).
Career batting
1–2–0–11–11–5.50–0–*ct* 1
Bowling 57–0

Gray, Walter (*see under* Bunting, W. H.)

Gray, William Johns
Amateur. *b:* 26.11.1864, Chelmsford, Essex. *d:* 18.12.1898, Chelmsford, Essex. Opening batsman. *Sch* Mill Hill. *Team* Essex (1894, 1 match).
Career batting
1–2–0–4–3–2.00–0–*ct* 0

Grayland, Albert Victor
Professional. *b:* 24.3.1900, Aston, Birmingham. *d:* 3.2.1963, Birmingham. Lower order right-hand batsman, right-arm fast medium bowler. *Team* Warwickshire (1922–30, 4 matches).
Career batting
4–6–1–15–6–3.00–0–*ct* 0
Bowling 204–2–102.00–0–0–1/23

Grayson, Sir Henry Mulleneux
Amateur. *b:* 26.9.1865, Liverpool. *d:* 27.10.1951, Marylebone, London. Brother of J. H. F. (Liverpool and District). Middle order right-hand batsman, wicket-keeper. *Sch* Winchester. *Team* Liverpool and District (1889–90).
Career batting
2–4–0–66–42–16.50–0–*ct* 0

His County cricket was for Cheshire.

Grayson, John Herbert FitzHenry
Amateur. *b:* 17.6.1871, West Derby, Liverpool. *d:* 31.5.1936, Eastbourne, Sussex. Brother of H. M. (Liverpool and District). Middle order right-hand batsman, right-arm medium pace bowler. *Sch* Radley. *Team* Liverpool and District (1891–93).
Career batting
2–4–0–46–36–11.50–0–*ct* 0

His County cricket was for Cheshire.

Greasley, Douglas George
Professional. *b:* 20.1.1926, Hull, Yorkshire. Middle order right-hand batsman, slow left-arm bowler. *Team* Northants (1950–55, 58 matches).
Career batting
58–85–11–1659–104*–22.41–1–*ct* 22
Bowling 573–16–35.81–0–0–4/36

Greatorex, Joseph Edward Alfred
Amateur. *b:* 7.3.1863, Kensington, London. *d:* 16.12.1940, Uppingham, Rutland. Brother of Theophilus (Middlesex). Middle order right-hand batsman, slow bowler, good field. *Sch* Harrow. *Team* MCC (1882–84).
Career batting
2–3–0–18–12–6.00–0–*ct* 0

Greatorex, Rev Canon Theophilus
Amateur. *b:* 14.12.1864, Hyde Park, Westminster. *d:* 27.7.1933, London. Brother of

J. E. A. (MCC). Middle order right-hand batsman, right-arm medium pace bowler. *Sch* Harrow. *Team* Middlesex (1883–92, 6 matches); Cambridge U (1884–86).
Career batting
19–32–1–338–44*–10.90–0–*ct* 7
Bowling 61–6–10.16–0–0–3/4
A broken finger at Cambridge in 1884 possibly deprived him of his blue.

Green, Allan Michael
Cricketer. *b*: 28.5.1960, Pulborough, Sussex. Middle order right-hand batsman, right-arm medium pace bowler. *Sch* Brighton. *Team* Sussex (1980–83, 34 matches).
Career batting
34–62–3–1435–99–24.32–0–*ct* 18
Bowling 522–12–43.50–0–0–2/30

Green, Charles Ernest
Amateur. *b:* 26.8.1846, Walthamstow, Essex. *d:* 4.12.1916, Theydon Grove, Essex. Middle order right-hand batsman, right-hand fast round-arm bowler. *Sch* Uppingham. *Teams* Cambridge U (1865–68, blue all four years); Middlesex (1868–79, 33 matches); Sussex (1869, 1 match).
Career batting
94–162–15–2488–72–16.92–0–*ct* 46
Bowling 1357–65+1–20.87–2–0–8/66
He was appointed captain of Essex in 1882 and was the leading spirit behind that county's cricket for many years. In 1905 he was President of MCC.
A noted huntsman, he was Master of the Essex Hunt for many years. His final first-class match was for Over 30s in 1881.

Green, David John
Amateur. *b:* 18.12.1935, Burton on Trent. Opening right-hand batsman. *Teams* Derbyshire (1953–60, 37 matches); Cambridge U (1957–59, blue all three years). *Tours* MCC to Canada 1959 (not first-class).
Career batting
87–152–7–2929–134–20.20–1–*ct* 61
Bowling 99–1–99.00–0–0–1/19
His final first-class match was for Free Foresters in 1961.

Green, David Michael
Amateur. *b:* 10.11.1939, Llanengan, Caernarvon. Opening right-hand batsman, right-arm medium pace off break bowler. *Sch* Manchester GS. *Teams* Oxford U (1959–61, blue all three years); Lancashire (1959–67, 135 matches); Gloucestershire (1968–71, 81 matches). *Tour* International XI to South Africa 1972/3.
Career batting
266–479–15–13381–233–28.83–14–*ct* 96
Bowling 4460–116–38.44–1–0–5/61
He hit 1,000 runs in a season seven times, going on to 2,000 twice (best 2,137, av 40.32, in 1968). In 1965 he reached 2,000 runs without the aid of a single hundred. His highest score was 233 for Gloucs v Sussex at Hove in 1968.

Green, George
Professional. *b:* 13.4.1880, Hasland, Derbyshire. *d:* 25.11.1940, Chesterfield, Derbyshire. Lower order batsman, left-arm medium pace bowler. *Team* Derbyshire (1903–07, 6 matches).
Career batting
6–11–0–39–20–3.54–0–*ct* 2
Bowling 236–6–39.33–0–0–2/31

Green, Joseph Fletcher
Amateur. *b:* 28.4.1846, West Ham, Essex. *d:* 28.8.1923, Leeds, Yorkshire. Middle order batsman, bowler, excellent field. *Sch* Rugby. *Team* MCC (1870).
Career batting
2–3–1–23–12–11.50–0–*ct* 1
He also appeared for the Gentlemen of the South in 1870.

Green, John Herbert
Amateur. *b:* 9.5.1908, Kenilworth, Warwickshire. Lower order right-hand batsman, slow left-arm bowler. *Sch* Brighton. *Team* Warwickshire (1927, 1 match).
Career batting
1–1–1–0–0*–no av–0–*ct* 0
Bowling 16–0

Green, John James
Professional. *b:* 1897, Marylebone, London. *d:* 25.10.1960, London. Tail end right-hand batsman, right-arm medium fast bowler. *Team* Middlesex (1919, 1 match).
Career batting
1–1–0–3–3–3.00–0–*ct* 1
Bowling 129–2–64.50–0–0–2/97

Green, Leonard
Amateur. *b:* 1.2.1890, Whalley, Lancashire. *d:* 2.3.1963, Whalley, Lancashire. Middle order right-hand batsman, good field. *Sch* Bromsgrove. *Team* Lancashire (1922–35, 152 matches). *Tours* Tennyson to Jamaica 1926/7; Cahn to Argentina 1929/30.
Career batting
160–185–29–3981–110*–25.51–2–*ct* 39
Bowling 406–12–33.83–0–0–2/2

He captained Lancashire 1926 to 1928 – winning the Championship in each of the three seasons.

A good hockey and rugby player, he represented Lancashire at both sports.

Green, Michael Arthur
Amateur. *b:* 3.10.1891, Bristol. *d:* 28.12.1971, Kensington, London. Middle order right-hand batsman. *Teams* Gloucestershire (1912–28, 91 matches); Europeans (1922/3): Essex (1930, 2 matches). *Tours* Manager of MCC to South Africa 1948/9 and joint-manager of MCC to Australia and New Zealand 1950/1.
Career batting
107–183–20–2629–127–16.12–1–*ct* 55
Bowling 65–0

He was Secretary of Worcestershire CCC 1945–51. His final first-class match was for Free Foresters in 1934.

A noted footballer, he appeared for the Army and Surrey both at soccer and rugby.

Green, Robert Lawrence Herbert
Amateur. *b:* 11.12.1894, Chippenham, Wiltshire. *d:* 13.9.1969, Pulverbatch, Salop. Middle order batsman. *Sch* Cheltenham. *Team* Gloucestershire (1924, 1 match).
Career batting
1–2–0–5–3–2.50–0–*ct* 0

Green, W.
Professional. Right-arm medium pace bowler. *Team* Surrey (1883, 1 match).
Career batting
1–2–0–2–2–1.00–0–*ct* 1

Green, William Barham
Amateur. *b:* 1852. *d:* 18.1.1924, Chailey, Sussex. Opening batsman. *Sch* Eton. *Team* MCC (1880–84).
Career batting
4–6–0–53–21–8.83–0–*ct* 0

His County cricket was for Hertfordshire.

Green-Price, Rev Alfred Edward
(changed name from Price in 1861)
Amateur. *b:* 11.2.180, Knighton, Radnor. *d:* 29.6.1940, Presteigne, Radnor. Right-hand batsman. *Team* H. K. Foster's XI (1919).
Career batting
1–2–0–10–10–5.00–0–*ct* 1

His County cricket was for Herefordshire. He was aged 59 when he played in his only first-class match.

Greene, Alan Douglas
Amateur. *b:* 15.4.1856, Brandeston, Suffolk. *d:* 18.6.1928, Tunbridge Wells, Kent. Middle order right-hand batsman, lob bowler, good field. *Sch* Clifton. *Teams* Oxford U (1877–80, blue all four years); Gloucestershire (1876–86, 21 matches).
Career batting
40–69–6–661–93*–10.49–0–*ct* 24
Bowling 55–1–55.00–0–0–1/34

He appeared in non-first-class cricket for Somerset in 1877.

A good rugby footballer, he represented Gloucestershire.

Greene, Frank Awl
Amateur. *b:* 14.3.1878, Philadelphia, USA. *d:* 20.4.1961, Philadelphia, USA. Lower order batsman, left-arm bowler. *Team* Philadelphia (1908–12). *Tour* Philadelphia to England 1908.
Career batting
9–17–4–160–49*–12.30–0–*ct* 4
Bowling 346–17–20.35–0–0–4/27

He did not achieve anything out of the ordinary on his tour to England in 1908 and the best performance of his career was his bowling for Germantown against the Australians in 1913, when he took 8 for 66 in the match.

Greene, Robin Morton
Amateur. *b:* 1.11.1930, Durban, South Africa. Lower order right-hand batsman, right-arm fast bowler. *Teams* South African XI (1949/50); Gloucestershire (1951, 1 match).
Career batting
2–4–3–59–26*–59.00–0–*ct* 1
Bowling 79–1–79.00–0–0–1/56

Greenfield, Rev Frederick Francis John
Amateur. *b:* 10.5.1850, Gorakhpur, India. *d:* 25.10.1900, Near Dundee, Natal, South Africa. Opening/middle order right-hand batsman, right-hand slow round arm bowler *Sch* Hurstpierpoint. *Teams* Sussex (1873–83, 62 matches); Cambridge U (1874–76, blue all three years).
Career batting
85–155–3–2549–126–16.76–2–*ct* 81
Bowling 1979–110+1–17.99–4–1–7/26
He captained Sussex 1876–78 and 1881–82.

He was also a noted athlete, being captain of Cambridge in 1876. He was taken prisoner by the Boers, 'robbed of everything,' and died of pleurisy.

Greenfield, George Price
Amateur. *b:* 24.1.1843, Winchester. *d:* 3.9.1917, Ealing, Middlesex. Lower order right-hand batsman, right-hand fast round-arm bowler. *Teams* Surrey (1867–69, 3 matches); Hampshire (1875, 1 match).

Career batting
5–7–1–120–102–20.00–1–*ct* 0
Bowling 99–5–19.80–0–0–3/38

His first-class debut was for Gentlemen of the South in 1866.

Greenhalgh, Eric Washington
Professional. *b:* 18.5.1910, Sale, Cheshire. Middle order right-hand batsman, right-arm medium bowler. *Team* Lancashire (1935–38, 14 matches).
Career batting
14–18–5–366–53*–28.15–0–*ct* 2
Bowling 282–3–94.00–0–0–2/75

Greenhill, Hubert Maclean
Amateur. *b:* 18.9.1881, Christchurch, Hants. *d:* 22.1.1926, near Bockhampton, Dorset. He was found dead in a wood. Lower order right-hand batsman, slow left arm bowler. *Sch* Sherborne. *Team* Hampshire (1901, 2 matches).
Career batting
2–3–0–15–6–5.00–0–*ct* 0
Bowling 77–3–25.66–0–0–3/39

Most of his county cricket was for Dorset; he was also well known in military matches.

Greenhill, Walter
Amateur. *b:* 19.6.1849, St John's Wood, London. *d:* 26.6.1913, Warsash, Hants. Middle order right-hand batsman. *Team* Sussex (1868, 2 matches).
Career batting
2–4–0–24–15–6.00–0–*ct* 2

Greenhough, Thomas
Professional. *b:* 9.11.1931, Rochdale, Lancashire. Lower order right-hand batsman, leg break and googly bowler. *Team* Lancashire (1951–66, 241 matches). *Tours* Norfolk to Jamaica 1956/7; MCC to West Indies 1959/60. *Tests* England (1959–60, 4 matches).
Career batting
255–313–86–1913–76*–8.42–0–*ct* 84
Bowling 16802–751–22.37–34–5–7/56
Test batting
4–4–1–4–2–1.33–0–*ct* 1
Bowling 357–16–22.31–1–0–5/35

He took 100 wickets in a season twice (best 122, av 22.37, in 1959).

Greenidge, Cuthbert Gordon
(born as C.G. Lavine)
Cricketer. *b*: 1.5.1951, Black Bess, St Peter, Barbados. Aggressive opening right-hand batsman, right-arm medium or off break bowler, good slip field. *Teams* Hampshire (1970–83, 225 matches); Barbados (1972/3 to 1982/3). *Tours* West Indies to India, Sri Lanka and Pakistan 1974/5, to Australia 1975/6, 1981/2, to England 1976, 1980, to Australia and New Zealand 1979/80, to Pakistan 1980/1. *Tests* West Indies (1974/5 to 1982/3, 41 matches).
Career batting
347–598–45–24255–273*–43.86–54–*ct* 371
Bowling 438–16–27.37–1–0–5/49
Test batting
41–70–5–2962–154*–45.56–6–*ct* 43
Bowling 4–0

He hit 1,000 runs in a season twelve times (best 1,952, av 55.77), in 1976); his form in English limited overs cricket has been quite outstanding and he held three records, namely the highest innings in the Gillette Cup – 177 v Glamorgan at Southampton in 1975, the highest innings in the John Player League – 163* v Warwickshire at Edgbaston in 1979 and the highest innings in the B & H Competition, 173* v Minor Counties South at Amersham in 1973.

He was most successful on the 1976 tour to England scoring 592 runs, av 65.77, in the five Tests and also scoring most runs in first-class matches on the tour (see 1976 details above). In 1980 he also played in the five Tests, but only had modest returns.

Greenidge, Geoffrey Alan
Cricketer. *b:* 26.5.1948, Bridgetown, Barbados. Opening right-hand batsman, leg break and googly bowler. *Teams* Barbados (1966/7 to 1975/6); Sussex (1968–75, 152 matches). *Tours* D. H. Robins to South Africa 1974/5; International XI to South Africa 1975/6. *Tests* West Indies (1971/2 to 1972/3, 5 matches).
Career batting
182–332–22–9112–205–29.39–16–*ct* 95
Bowling 948–13–72.92–1–0–7/124
Test batting
5–9–2–209–50–29.85–0–*ct* 3
Bowling 75–0

He hit 1,000 runs in a season five times (best 1,334, av 26.68, in 1971). His only double century was 205 for Barbados v Jamaica at Bridgetown in 1966/7.

Barbados were refused entry into Guyana in 1974/5 because the former included Greenidge, who had played in South Africa.

Greening, Thomas
Amateur. *b:* 1883, Scotland. *d:* 25.3.1956, Leamington Spa, Warwickshire. Lower order batsman, right-arm medium off break bowler. *Team* Warwickshire (1912, 2 matches).
Career batting
2–2–1–26–14–26.00–0–*ct* 0
Bowling 91–1–91.00–0–0–1/35

Greenlees, Weir Loudon
Amateur. *b:* 26.12.1882, Islington, London. *d:* 10.1.1975, Marylebone, London. Middle/lower order batsman, wicket-keeper. *Sch* Harrow. *Team* Oxford U (1904); London County (1904).
Career batting
2–4–1–68–39*–22.66–0–*ct* 1

Greensmith, William Thomas
Professional. *b:* 16.8.1930, Middlesbrough, Yorkshire. Middle/lower order right-hand batsman, leg break and googly bowler. *Team* Essex (1947–63, 371 matches).
Career batting
379–566–151–8249–138*–19.87–1–*ct* 149
Bowling 21206–733–28.93–21–2–8/59

Greenstock, John Wilfrid
Amateur. *b:* 15.5.1905, Great Malvern, Worcs. Son of William (Worcs). Lower order right-hand batsman, slow left-arm bowler. *Sch* Malvern. *Teams* Worcestershire (1924–27, 13 matches); Oxford U (1925–27, blue all three years).
Career batting
46–68–14–507–43–9.38–0–*ct* 31
Bowling 3662–139–26.34–4–0–5/36
His final first-class match was for Leveson-Gower's XI in 1929.

Greenstock, William
Amateur. *b:* 15.1.1865, Keiskama Hoek, Cape Province, South Africa. *d:* 13.11.1944, Dogmersfield, Hants. Father of J. W. (Worcs). Middle order right-hand batsman, off break bowler. *Sch* Fettes. *Teams* Worcestershire (1899–1919, 4 matches); Cambridge U (1886).
Career batting
7–12–1–165–49–15.00–0–*ct* 3
Bowling 26–0

Greensword, Stephen
Cricketer. *b:* 6.9.1943, Gateshead, Co. Durham. Middle order right-hand batsman, right-arm medium pace bowler. *Team* Leicestershire (1963–66, 39 matches).
Career batting
41–71–8–1025–84*–16.26–0–*ct* 29
Bowling 917–28–32.75–0–0–3/22
He also appeared for Northumberland and Durham and has played in first-class matches for the Minor Counties XI (last in 1981).

Greenway, Cleveland Edmund
Amateur. *b:* 29.10.1864, *d:* 17.6.1934, Beckenham, Kent. Opening/middle order right-hand batsman, good field. *Sch* Cheltenham. *Team* Somerset (1882, 1 match). *Tour* Incogniti to USA 1913 (not first-class).
Career batting
2–4–0–31–18–7.75–0–*ct* 0
His final first-class match was for MCC in 1895.
He was stationed in India for some years and was a leading batsman with the Calcutta Club.
He also played for Northumberland.

Greenway, Charles H.
Professional. *b:* 1862. *d:* 1949, London. Tail end batsman, opening bowler. *Team* Gloucestershire (1890–91, 3 matches).
Career batting
3–6–0–8–6–1.33–0–*ct* 1
Bowling 196–4–49.00–0–0–2/40

Greenwood, Andrew
Professional. *b:* 20.8.1847, Cowmes Lepton, Huddersfield, Yorkshire. *d:* 12.2.1889, Huddersfield, Yorkshire. Nephew of Luke Greenwood (Yorkshire). Opening/middle order right-hand batsman, good deep field. *Team* Yorkshire (1869–80, 94 matches). *Tours* Grace to Australia 1873/4 (not first-class); Lillywhite to Australia 1876/7. *Tests* England (1876/7, 2 matches).
Career batting
141–249–14–4307–111–18.32–1–*ct* 70
Bowling 9–0
Test batting
2–4–0–77–49–19.25–0–*ct* 2

Greenwood, Charles William
Amateur. *b:* 23.7.1847, London. *d:* 14.9.1907, Westgate-on-Sea, Kent. Brother of G. G. (Hants). Middle order batsman. *Sch* Eton. *Team* MCC (1875).
Career batting
1–2–0–4–3–2.00–0–*ct* 0

Greenwood, Edward
Amateur. *b:* 19.1.1845, St John's Wood, Middlesex. *d:* 25.1.1899, Smithwood, Cranleigh, Surrey. Opening/middle order batsman. *Team* Kent (1873, 1 match).
Career batting
1–2–0–13–13–6.50–0–*ct* 0

Greenwood, Frank Edwards
Amateur. *b:* 28.9.1905, Huddersfield, Yorkshire. *d:* 30.7.1963, Huddersfield, Yorkshire. Middle order right-hand batsman, bowler. *Sch* Oundle. *Team* Yorkshire (1929–32, 57 matches).
Career batting
57–66–8–1558–104*–26.86–1–*ct* 37
Bowling 36–2–18.00–0–0–1/1
He captained Yorkshire in 1931 and 1932.

Greenwood, Sir Granville George
Amateur. *b:* 3.1.1850, London. *d:* 27.10.1928, Kensington, London. Brother of C.W. (MCC). Batsman. *Sch* Eton. *Team* Hampshire (1875, 1 match).
Career batting
1–2–0–2–1–1.00–0–*ct* 1

Greenwood, Henry William
Professional. *b:* 4.9.1909, East Preston, Sussex. *d:* 24.3.1979, Bromley, Kent. Opening right-hand batsman, right-arm slow bowler, wicket-keeper. *Teams* Sussex (1933–36, 19 matches); Northants (1938–46, 60 matches).
Career batting
79–133–4–2590–115–20.07–1–*ct* 55–*st* 13
Bowling 37–0

He also played for Durham.

His obituary was incorrectly included in Wisden in 1984.

Greenwood, John Frederick
Professional. *b:* 10.3.1851, Epsom, Surrey. *d:* 31.8.1935, Lewes, Sussex. Middle order right-hand batsman, right-arm medium pace bowler. *Team* Surrey (1874, 3 matches).
Career batting
3–5–0–17–8–3.40–0–*ct* 3

Greenwood, Luke
Professional. *b:* 13.7.1834, Cowmes Lepton, Huddersfield, Yorkshire. *d:* 1.11.1909, Morley, Yorkshire. Uncle of Andrew Greenwood (Yorkshire). Middle order right-hand batsman, right-hand fast round-arm bowler, good field. *Team* Yorkshire (1861–74, 51 matches).
Career batting
69–122–18–1244–83–11.96–0–*ct* 31
Bowling 2066–113–18.28–6–1–8/35

He was a noted umpire after retiring from first-class matches. His final first-class match was for United North in 1875.

Greenwood, Leonard Warwick
Amateur. *b:* 25.3.1899, Liverpool. *d:* 20.7.1982, Astley, Stourport, Worcs. Middle order right-hand batsman. *Sch* Winchester. *Teams* Oxford U (1919); Somerset (1920, 1 match); Worcestershire (1922–26, 3 matches).
Career batting
5–7–0–51–25–7.28–0–*ct* 2

Greenwood, Peter
Professional. *b:* 11.9.1924, Todmorden, Yorkshire. Middle order right-hand batsman, right-arm medium fast or off break bowler, good field. *Team* Lancashire (1948–52, 75 matches).
Career batting
75–92–15–1270–113–16.49–1–*ct* 20
Bowling 5090–208–24.47–9–1–6/35

He played soccer for Chester at wing half or inside forward.

Greetham, Christopher Herbert Millington
Professional. *b:* 28.8.1936, Wargrave, Berkshire. Middle order right-hand batsman, right-arm medium pace bowler. *Team* Somerset (1957–66, 205 matches).
Career batting
205–332–26–6723–151*–21.97–5–*ct* 95
Bowling 5529–195–28.35–5–1–7/56

He hit 1,000 runs in a season twice (best 1,186, av 28.23, in 1963). He also played for Devon.

Gregg, Thomas
Professional. *b:* 18.11.1859, Wilford, Notts. *d:* 25.3.1938, Gotham, Notts. Lower order right-hand batsman, right-arm fast bowler. *Teams* Somerset (1883, 1 match); Gloucestershire (1884–89, 32 matches).
Career batting
35–59–4–494–62–8.98–0–*ct* 23
Bowling 1540–55–28.00–1–0–6/47

Gregory, Benjamin Bridge
Professional. *b:* 6.10.1863, Eastwood, Notts. *d:* 27.1.1951, Kilton, Worksop, Notts. Lower order batsman, right-arm medium pace bowler. *Team* Nottinghamshire (1895–97, 5 matches).
Career batting
5–8–3–9–4*–1.80–0–*ct* 6
Bowling 321–9–35.66–0–0–4/48

He always appeared, both for Notts and during his pro engagements in Lancashire, under the surname Gregory, though registered at birth and death as Simpson.

Gregory, Dove
Professional. *b:* 9.2.1840, Sutton in Ashfield, Notts. *d:* 21.5.1873, Derby. Lower order right-hand batsman, right-hand fast round-arm bowler, good slip field. *Team* Derbyshire (1871–72, 4 matches).
Career batting
4–7–3–19–10–4.75–0–*ct* 3
Bowling 255–25–10.20–3–0–6/9

His first-class career was very brief owing to the fact that Derbyshire did not enter first-class cricket until 1871, and he died tragically young in 1873.

Gregory, David William
Amateur. *b:* 15.4.1845, Fairy Meadow, New South Wales, Australia. *d:* 4.8.1919, Turramurra, New South Wales, Australia. Brother of A. H., E. J., and C. W. (all NSW). Middle order right-hand batsman. right-hand fast round-arm bowler. *Team* New South Wales (1866/7 to 1882/3, 19

matches). *Tour* Australia to England and North America 1878. *Tests* Australia (1876/7 to 1878/9, 3 matches).
Career batting
41–68–7–889–85–14.57–0–*ct* 35
Bowling 553–29–19.06–1–0–5/55
Test batting
3–5–2–60–43–20.00–0–*ct* 0
Bowling 9–0
He captained Australia in the first three Tests and also on the 1878 tour to England, but on the tour had little success with the bat.

Gregory, George Robert
Amateur. *b:* 27.8.1878, Pilsley, Derbyshire. *d:* 28.11.1958, Scarborough, Yorkshire. Opening/middle order right-hand batsman, leg break bowler. *Team* Derbyshire (1899–1910, 15 matches).
Career batting
15–22–2–174–23–8.70–0–*ct* 5
Bowling 267–12–22.25–0–0–4/70

Gregory, Henry V.
Professional. *b:* 18.1.1936, Manchester, Lancashire. Lower order right-hand batsman, leg-break bowler. *Team* Sussex (1960, 1 match).
Career batting
1–2–0–18–14–9.00–0–*ct* 0
Bowling 46–0

Gregory, John Constable
Amateur. *b:* 17.8.1842, Marylebone, Middlesex. *d:* 28.6.1894, Weymouth, Dorset. Dashing middle order right-hand batsman, good field. *Teams* Middlesex (1865, 3 matches); Surrey (1870–71, 19 matches).
Career batting
23–42–5–760–70–20.54–0–*ct* 8
Bowling 12–0
Playing for Surrey v Sussex in 1871 he ruptured one of the arteries in his right leg and this ended his career in first-class matches. For several years he appeared in more matches than, perhaps, any other player in England and on some days played in no less than three matches, though of an inferior description.
In 1868 it was stated that he belonged to 18 separate London cricket clubs!

Gregory, Jack Morrison
Amateur. *b:* 14.8.1895, North Sydney, New South Wales, Australia. *d:* 7.8.1973, Bega, New South Wales, Australia. Son of C. S. (NSW). Opening/middle order left-hand batsman, right-arm fast bowler. *Teams* New South Wales (1920/1 to 1928/9, 17 matches). *Tours* Australia to England 1921, 1926, to South Africa 1921/2; AIF to England and South Africa 1919. *Tests* Australia (1920/1 to 1928/9, 24 matches).
Career batting
129–173–18–5661–152–36.52–13–*ct* 195
Bowling 10580–504–20.99–33–8–9/32
Test batting
24–34–3–1146–119–36.96–2–*ct* 37
Bowling 2648–85–31.15–4–0–7/69
His fast bowling partnership with McDonald on the 1921 tour of England was the equal of any pair of Test opening bowlers. Gregory took 116 wickets, av 16.58, on that tour and on the AIF tour of 1919 took 131 wickets, av 18.19. He was at this period of his career Australia's leading all-rounder. In 1926 however his bowling was not so effective and during the 1928/9 series in Australia injury brought his career to a premature close.
On the 1921 tour he hit 1,135 runs, av 36.61, thus performing the 'double'. His best bowling was 9/32 for AIF v Natal at Durban in 1919/20.

Gregory, John Thomas
Professional. *b:* 1887, Chesterfield, Derbyshire. *d:* 27.11.1914, near Zonnebeke, Belgium. He was killed in action. Lower order batsman, slow left-arm bowler. *Team* Hampshire (1913, 1 match).
Career batting
1–1–0–0–0–0.00–0–*ct* 0
Bowling 87–0

Gregory, Robert James
Professional. *b:* 26.8.1902, Selsdon. Surrey. *d:* 6.10.1973, Wandsworth, South London. Opening/middle order right-hand batsman, leg break bowler. *Team* Surrey (1925–47, 414 matches). *Tour* MCC to India and Ceylon 1933/4.
Career batting
431–646–78–19495–243–34.32–39–*ct* 301
Bowling 14122–437–32.31–11–1–6/21
He hit 1,000 runs in a season nine times, going on to 2,000 twice (best 2,379, av 51.71, in 1934). His only double century was 243 for Surrey v Somerset at the Oval in 1938.
A good soccer player, he appeared as full back for Norwich and Fulham.

Gregory, Sydney Edward
Amateur. *b:* 14.4.1870, Randwick, New South Wales, Australia. *d:* 1.8.1929, Randwick, New South Wales, Australia. Brother of C. W. (NSW), son of E. J. (NSW), brother-in-law of H. Donnan (NSW). Middle order right-hand batsman, right-arm bowler, brilliant cover point. *Team* New South Wales (1889/90 to 1911/2, 80 matches). *Tours* Australia to England 1890, 1893, 1896, 1899, 1902, 1905, 1909, 1912; to South Africa 1902/3, to New Zealand 1904/5, to North

America 1893, 1896, 1912. *Tests* Australia (1890–1912, 58 matches).
Career batting
368–587–55–15192–201–28.55–25–*ct* 174
Bowling 394–2–197.00–0–0–1/8
Test batting
58–100–7–2282–201–24.53–4–*ct* 25
Bowling 33–0

He hit over 1,000 runs on four of his tours to England, his best being 1,464, av 31.95, in 1896. He captained the 1912 team and altogether led Australia in six Tests. He hit two double centuries, the most noteworthy being 201 in the first Test of the 1894/5 series at Sydney.

Gregory, William Robert
Amateur. *b:* 20.5.1881, Gort, Co Galway, Ireland. *d:* 23.1.1918, Near Grossa, Padua, Italy. Right-hand batsman, leg break and googly bowler. *Sch* Harrow. *Team* Ireland (1912).
Career batting
1–2–0–0–0–0.00–0–*ct* 0
Bowling 92–9–10.22–1–0–8/80

Gregson, William Russell
Professional. *b:* 5.8.1878, Lancaster. *d:* 18.6.1963, Lancaster. Lower order right-hand batsman, right-arm fast bowler. *Team* Lancashire (1906, 5 matches).
Career batting
5–7–1–62–26–10.33–0–*ct* 0
Bowling 428–24–17.83–1–0–5/8

He had startling figures in his second first-class match 9.3–6–8–5 (for Lancs v Leics at Blackpool), including the hat-trick.

Greig, Anthony William
Cricketer. *b:* 6.10.1946, Queenstown, South Africa. Brother of I. A. (Sussex). Middle order right-hand batsman, right-arm medium off break bowler. *Teams* Border (1965/6 to 1969/70); Sussex (1966–78, 209 matches); Eastern Province (1970/1 to 1971/2). *Tours* International XI to India, Pakistan and Ceylon 1967/8; D. H. Robins to South Africa 1974/5; Norfolk to West Indies 1969/70; Rest of World to Australia 1971/2; MCC to India, Pakistan and Sri Lanka 1972/3, to West Indies 1973/4, to Australia and New Zealand 1974/5, to India, Sri Lanka and Australia 1976/7. *Tests* England (1972–77, 58 matches).
Career batting
350–579–45–16660–226–31.19–26–*ct* 345
Bowling 24702–856–28.85–33–8–8/25
Test batting
58–93–4–3599–148–40.43–8–*ct* 87
Bowling 4541–141–32.20–6–2–8/86

Qualifying for Sussex in 1967 at the age of 20, Greig made an immediate impact with a century (v Lancashire) in his first Championship match. From this he went on to record 1,299 runs and take 67 wickets in the season. By 1970 he was in the England side for the unofficial Tests against the Rest of the World and his appointment as captain of Sussex in 1973 was followed by the England captaincy in 1975. He was by this time the leading all-round cricketer in England. In 1976/77 he led the MCC team to India with its final match as the Centenary Test in Melbourne in March 1977.

During this tour the scheme to create Kerry Packer's World Series cricket was evolved and Greig acted as the leader of the English players in league with Packer. Though the subsequent court case between the TCCB and Greig and his colleagues went in favour of the latter, Greig's involvement with World Series Cricket effectively ended his role in first-class and Test cricket and thus his short, but brilliant, career ceased soon after he was 30.

He hit 1,000 runs in a season seven times (best 1,699, av 47.19, in 1975) and captained England in 14 out of his 58 Tests. His only double century was 226 for Sussex v Warwickshire at Hastings in 1975. After 1978 he went to live permanently in Australia.

Greig, Geoffrey George Fenner
Amateur. *b:* 15.8.1897, Blything, Suffolk. *d:* 24.10.1960, Ewhurst, Surrey. Lower order right-hand batsman, right-arm fast bowler. *Sch* Westminster. *Teams* Oxford U (1920); Worcestershire (1920–25, 18 matches).
Career batting
20–38–8–238–37–7.93–0–*ct* 7
Bowling 1347–34–39.61–1–0–7/86

Greig, Ian Alexander
Cricketer. *b:* 8.12.1955, Queenstown, South Africa. Brother of A. W. (Sussex). Middle order right-hand batsman, right-arm medium pace bowler, slip field. *Teams* Border (1974/5 to 1979/80); Cambridge U (1977–79, blue all three years); Sussex (1980–83, 58 matches); Griqualand West (1975/6). *Tests* England (1982, 2 matches).
Career batting
97–131–14–2926–147*–25.00–3–*ct* 58
Bowling 5899–214–27.56–7–2–7/43
Test batting
2–4–0–26–14–6.50–0–*ct* 0
Bowling 114–4–28.50–0–0–4/53

He gained his blue for rugby.

Greig, Canon John Glennie
Amateur. *b:* 24.10.1871, Mhow, India. *d:* 24.5.1958, Milford, Surrey. Opening right-hand batsman, slow right-arm bowler. *Sch* Downside.

Teams Europeans (1893/4 to 1920/1); Hampshire (1901–22, 77 matches).
Career batting
125–219–17–7348–249*–36.37–15–*ct* 102
Bowling 3238–138–23.46–8–2–7/35

His first-class debut in England was for MCC in 1898.

In the regular army stationed in India before the First World War, his County cricket was limited, though in 1901 he hit 1,277 runs, av 41.19. His highest score was 249* for Hampshire v Lancashire at Liverpool in 1901. He was secretary of Hampshire from 1921 to 1930 and in 1935 was ordained in Rome as a Catholic priest.

Greive, John
Amateur. *b:* 26.6.1886, Selkirk, Scotland. *d:* 7.6.1971, Selkirk, Scotland. Brother of Walter and William (Scotland). Right-hand batsman, right-arm medium pace bowler. *Team* Scotland (1911–26).
Career batting
5–9–1–208–58–26.00–0–*ct* 6
Bowling 22–0

Greive, Walter
Amateur. *b:* 10.2.1891, Selkirk, Scotland. *d:* 27.2.1918. He was killed in action. Brother of John and William (Scotland). Right-hand batsman, right-arm medium pace bowler. *Team* Scotland (1912–14).
Career batting
2–4–0–28–18–7.00–0–*ct* 0
Bowling 73–0

Greive, William
Amateur. *b:* 1.3.1888, Selkirk, Scotland. *d:* 17.7.1916, Bailleul, France. Brother of John and Walter (Scotland). Right-hand batsman. *Team* Scotland (1910).
Career batting
1–2–0–6–6–3.00–0–*ct* 0
Bowling 21–0

Gresson, Francis Henry
Amateur. *b:* 18.2.1868, Worthing, Sussex. *d:* 31.1.1949, Eastbourne, Sussex. Opening left-hand batsman, left-arm fast medium bowler. *Sch* Winchester. *Teams* Oxford U (1887–89, blue all three years); Sussex (1887–1901, 21 matches).
Career batting
47–80–5–1241–114–16.54–1–*ct* 23
Bowling 836–30–27.86–1–0–5/50

A school master by profession, his County cricket was very limited, and between 1890 and 1899 he did not appear in the ranks of Sussex.

Greswell, Ernest Arthur
Amateur. *b:* 8.6.1885, Cuddalore, Madras, India. *d:* 15.1.1962, Bicknoller, Somerset. Brother of W.T. (Somerset). Middle order right-hand batsman, right-arm slow bowler. *Sch* Repton. *Team* Somerset (1903–10, 12 matches).
Career batting
12–22–1–246–44–11.71–0–*ct* 4
Bowling 89–2–44.50–0–0–1/5

Greswell, William Territt
Amateur. *b:* 15.10.1889, Cuddalore, Madras, India. *d:* 12.2.1971, Bicknoller, Somerset. Brother of E. A. (Somerset). Middle order right-hand batsman, right-arm slow medium bowler. *Sch* Repton. *Teams* Somerset (1908–30, 115 matches); Ceylon (1925/6); Europeans (1926/7).
Career batting
134–200–27–2580–100–14.91–1–*ct* 103
Bowling 11516–540–21.32–37–7–9/62

He took 132 wickets, av 17.78, in 1912, and his best bowling was 9/62 for Somerset v Hampshire at Weston in 1928.

In 1909 he went out to Ceylon to work in the family business and his appearances in County cricket were therefore very limited. He was regarded as the leading cricketer in Ceylon and whilst there captained both the Ceylonese hockey and soccer teams.

His final first-class match was for Free Foresters in 1933.

Grevett, Robert Gordon
Amateur. *b:* 24.11.1914, Eastbourne, Sussex. Middle order right-hand batsman, off break bowler. *Team* Sussex (1939, 1 match).
Career batting
1–2–0–0–0–0.00–0–*ct* 0

Grevett, William Sydney Gordon
Amateur. *b:* 1892, Eastbourne, Sussex. *d:* 26.7.1967, Eastbourne, Sussex. Middle order batsman. *Team* Sussex (1922, 1 match).
Career batting
1–2–0–13–9–6.50–0–*ct* 0

Grewcock, George
Professional. *b:* 1862, Barwell, Leics. *d:* August, 1922, Toxteth, Liverpool. Lower order left-hand batsman, left-arm fast medium bowler. *Team* Leicestershire (1899, 3 matches).
Career batting
3–6–0–4–1–0.66–0–*ct* 1
Bowling 308–8–38.50–0–0–4/93

Gribble, Herbert Willis Reginald
Amateur. *b:* 23.12.1860, Clifton, Gloucs. *d:* 12.6.1943, Teddington, Middlesex. Middle order

right-hand batsman, good point. *Sch* Clifton. *Team* Gloucestershire (1878–82, 29 matches).
Career batting
29–40–7–342–37–10.36–0–*ct* 20

Grierson, Henry
Amateur. *b:* 26.8.1891, Chertsey, Surrey. *d:* 29.1.1972, Surrey. Lower order batsman, left-arm medium pace bowler. *Sch* Bedford GS. *Team* Cambridge U (1911–12, blue 1911).
Career batting
11–18–5–89–24–6.84–0–*ct* 6
Bowling 500–21–23.80–0–0–4/27

His County cricket was for Bedfordshire.

He was a well-known writer and after-dinner speaker and founded the Forty Club in 1936.

A good rugby footballer, he appeared for Bedford, Rosslyn Park and Leicester.

Grieve, Charles Frederick
Amateur. *b:* 1.10.1913, Manila, Philippines. Middle order right-hand batsman. *Team* Oxford U (1936).
Career batting
1–2–0–8–6–4.00–0–*ct* 1
Bowling 24–0

Grieves, Kenneth John
Professional. *b:* 27.8.1925, Sydney, Australia. Middle order right-hand batsman, leg break and googly bowler, brilliant slip field. *Teams* New South Wales (1945/6 to 1946/7, 10 matches); Lancashire (1949–64, 452 matches). *Tour* Commonwealth to India and Ceylon 1950/1
Career batting
490–746–79–22454–224–33.66–*ct* 608–*st* 4
Bowling 7209–242–29.78–8–0–6/60

He hit 1,000 runs in a season 13 times, plus once in India, and once went on to 2,000 – 2,253, av 41.72, in 1959. His three double centuries were all for Lancashire, the highest being 224 v Cambridge U at Fenner's in 1957.

He captained Lancashire in 1963–64.

A useful soccer player, he kept goal for Bury and Bolton Wanderers.

Griffin, Arthur Wilfrid Michael Stewart
Amateur. *b:* 19.2.1887, Iquique, Chile. *d:* 29.6.1962, East Grinstead, Sussex. Lower order right-hand batsman, right-arm fast medium bowler. *Sch* Harrow. *Team* Cambridge U (1910); Middlesex (1910, 1 match).
Career batting
2–4–0–14–8–3.50–0–*ct* 1
Bowling 90–0

After leaving Cambridge he went to Northern Rhodesia as Commissioner.

Griffin, Geoffrey Merton
Amateur. *b:* 12.6.1939, Greytown, South Africa. Lower order right-hand batsman, right-arm fast bowler. *Teams* Natal (1957/8 to 1960/1); Rhodesia (1961/2 to 1962/3). *Tour* South Africa to England 1960. *Tests* South Africa (1960, 2 matches).
Career batting
42–58–8–895–73–17.90–0–*ct* 19
Bowling 2324–108–21.51–4–1–7/11
Test batting
2–4–0–25–14–6.25–0–*ct* 0
Bowling 192–8–24.00–0–0–4/87

He was no-balled for throwing 28 times on his tour to England – the first time in first-class cricket that a bowler touring England had been called. He achieved the hat-trick in the second Test, but was no-balled during the match and did not bowl in the remaining first-class matches on the tour.

Griffin, Gerard Sandiforth Featherstone
Amateur. *b:* 1882, Fulham, Middlesex. *d:* 1950, Amersham, Bucks. Middle order right-hand batsman, good field. *Team* Middlesex (1900–03, 15 matches).
Career batting
20–29–2–452–88*–16.74–0–*ct* 13

Griffin, Harry
Professional. *b:* 1873, Wells, Somerset. *d:* 26.9.1938, Bristol. Middle/lower order left-hand batsman, slow left-arm bowler. *Team* Somerset (1898–99, 4 matches).
Career batting
4–7–0–69–23–9.85–0–*ct* 2
Bowling 217–14–15.50–1–0–6/40

Griffin, Neville (Fetherstone)
Cricketer. *b:* 17.12.1933, Croydon, Surrey. Middle order right-hand batsman, right-arm medium pace bowler. *Team* Surrey (1963, 1 match).
Career batting
1–2–1–90–83*–90.00–0–*ct* 0
Bowling 45–0

Griffith, Charles Christopher
Amateur. *b:* 14.12.1938, Pie Corner, Barbados. Tail end right-hand batsman, right-arm fast bowler. *Team* Barbados (1959/60 to 1965/66). *Tours* West Indies to England 1963, 1966, to Australia and New Zealand 1968/9, to India 1966/67; President's XI to India 1963/4; Commonwealth to Pakistan 1963/4. *Tests* West Indies (1959/60 to 1968/9, 28 matches).

Career batting
96–119–32–1502–98–17.26–0–*ct* 39
Bowling 7172–332–21.60–17–1–8/23
Test batting
28–42–10–530–54–16.56–0–*ct* 16
Bowling 2683–94–28.54–5–0–6/36

He was the success of the 1963 tour to England taking 119 wickets, av 12.83, in first-class matches and 32 wickets, av 16.21, in the Tests. On his second tour in 1966, his bowling came in for much criticism and he was no-balled for throwing. This affected his form and he was nothing like as successful as in 1963, though he still headed the first-class averages for the tour.

His final first-class match in West Indies was in 1967/8.

Griffith, George
Amateur. *b:* 20.12.1833, Ripley, Surrey. *d:* 3.5.1879, Stoke-next-Guildford, Surrey. Lower order left-hand batsman, left-hand fast round-arm, also (from 1862) slow under-arm bowler, brilliant field. *Team* Surrey (1856–71, 165 matches). *Tours* Stephenson to Australia 1861/2; Willsher to North America 1868 (not first-class).
Career batting
243–423–27–6314–142–15.94–2–*ct* 201–*st* 3
Bowling 11309–670–16.87–52–9–9/130

A brilliant hitter, he hit the ball out of the ground four times in succession at Hastings in 1864 for the United Eleven (not first-class). His best bowling was 9/130 for Surrey v Lancashire at the Oval in 1867.

Griffith, George Hugh Clarence
Amateur. *b:* 21.8.1929, Bridgetown, Barbados. Son of H. C. (West Indies), brother of H.L.V. (Barbados) and E.H.C (Barbados). Tail end right-hand batsman, leg break bowler. *Team* Cambridge U (1949–51).
Career batting
5–6–0–62–33–10.33–0–*ct* 3
Bowling 177–2–88.50–0–0–1/27

Griffith, Herman Clarence
Amateur. *b:* 1.12.1893, Trinidad. *d:* 18.3.1980, Bellevue, Bridgetown, Barbados. Father of G. H. C. (Cambridge U), E. H. C. and H. L. V. (Barbados). Lower order right-hand batsman, right-arm fast medium bowler. *Team* Barbados (1921/2 to 1940/1). *Tours* West Indies to England 1928, 1933, to Australia 1930/1. *Tests* West Indies (1928–33, 13 matches).
Career batting
79–108–28–1204–84–15.05–0–*ct* 36
Bowling 7294–258–28.27–12–2–7/38
Test batting
13–23–5–91–18–5.05–0–*ct* 4
Bowling 1243–44–28.25–2–0–6/103

He was the most successful bowler for West Indies in the 1928 Tests with 11 wickets, av 22.72, and in all first-class matches took 76 wickets, av 27.89. On the 1933 visit he was not so successful.

Griffith, Kevin
Cricketer. *b:* 17.1.1950, Warrington, Lancashire. Lower order right-hand batsman, off break bowler. *Sch* Worcester RGS. *Team* Worcestershire (1967–72, 44 matches).
Career batting
44–61–8–795–59–15.00–0–*ct* 17
Bowling 1753–50–35.06–1–0–7/41

Griffith, Mike Grenville
Cricketer. *b:* 25.11.1943, Beaconsfield, Bucks. son of S. C. (Surrey and Sussex). Middle order right-hand batsman, wicket-keeper. *Sch* Marlborough. *Teams* Sussex (1962–74, 232 matches); Cambridge U (1963–65, blue all three years). *Tours* MCC to South America 1964/5 (not first class); Norfolk to West Indies 1969/70; Swanton to West Indies 1963/4; MCC to East Africa 1973/4.
Career batting
276–455–90–8890–158–24.35–5–*ct* 268–*st* 20
Bowling 28–1–28.00–0–0–1/4

He hit 1,144 runs, av 30.10, in 1964. He captained Sussex jointly with J. M. Parks in 1968 and alone 1969 to 1972.

An excellent hockey player, he represented Cambridge and England and was also awarded his blue for rackets.

Griffith, Stewart Cathie, CBE
Amateur. *b:* 16.6.1914, Wandsworth, Surrey. Father of M. G. (Sussex). Lower order right-hand batsman, wicket-keeper. *Sch* Dulwich. *Teams* Cambridge U (1934–36, blue 1935); Surrey (1934, 1 match); Sussex (1937–54, 122 matches). *Tours* MCC to Australia and New Zealand 1935/6, to India 1939/40 (cancelled), to West Indies 1947/8, to South Africa 1948/9, to East Africa 1958/9 (not first-class). *Tests* England (1947/8 to 1948/9, 3 matches).
Career batting
215–336–41–4846–140–16.42–3–*ct* 328–*st* 80
Bowling 23–0
Test batting
3–5–0–157–140–31.40–1–*ct* 5

He captained Sussex in 1946 and was Secretary

to the County Club 1946 to 1950. Secretary of MCC 1962 to 1974 and President 1979/80.

Griffiths, Alan
Cricketer. *b*: 18.9.1957, Newcastle-under-Lyme, Staffs. Lower order right-hand batsman, wicket-keeper. *Team* Minor Counties (1981).
Career batting
1–1–0–26–26–26.00–0–*ct* 0
He has played for Staffordshire since 1979.

Griffiths, Algernon Sidney
Amateur. *b:* 23.5.1847, London. *d:* 18.4.1899, West Kensington, London. Middle order right-hand batsman, good point field. *Team* Middlesex (1871–72, 2 matches).
Career batting
6–11–1–121–36–12.10–0–*ct* 0
His first-class debut was for Gentlemen of the South in 1867 and his final first-class match for Gentlemen of MCC in 1873.

Griffiths, Brian James
Cricketer. *b*: 13.6.1949, Wellingborough, Northants. Tail end right-hand batsman, right-arm medium pace bowler. *Team* Northamptonshire (1974–83, 136 matches).
Career batting
136–102–35–207–16–3.08–0–*ct* 27
Bowling 9908–348–28.47–10–0–8/50
He had the misfortune to record ten consecutive first-class innings without a run.

Griffiths, Colin
Amateur. *b:* 9.12.1930, Upminster, Essex. Middle order right-hand batsman, right-arm medium pace bowler. *Sch* Brentwood. *Teams* Essex (1951–53, 27 matches).
Career batting
27–41–3–615–105–16.18–1–*ct* 4
Bowling 22–0

Griffiths, Edward Llewellyn
Amateur. *b:* 17.3.1862, Winchcombe, Gloucs. *d:* 20.4.1893, Cleeve, Cheltenham, Gloucs. Middle order right-hand batsman. *Sch* Rossall. *Teams* Gloucestershire (1885–89, 30 matches).
Career batting
30–52–9–499–40*–11.60–0–*ct* 14
Bowling 11–0

Griffiths, Gordon Craven
Amateur. *b:* 19.6.1905, Birmingham. Lower order right-hand batsman, wicket-keeper. *Sch* Malvern. *Teams* Worcestershire (1932–35, 5 matches).
Career batting
5–10–0–42–16–4.20–0–*ct* 2–*st* 1

Griffiths, Herbert Tyrrell
Amateur. *b:* 10.8.1853, Ryde, IOW. *d:* 3.11.1905, Preston-Candover, Hants. Middle order right-hand batsman, good deep field. *Sch* Eton. *Team* MCC (1876–78).
Career batting
2–3–1–84–68*–42.00–0–*ct* 1
He was not in the eleven whilst at Cambridge.

Griffiths, John Thomas
(registered at birth as James Griffiths)
Professional. *b:* 27.1.1863, Long Eaton, Derbyshire. Middle order batsman. *Team* Nottinghamshire (1891, 1 match).
Career batting
1 match, did not bat–*ct* 0

Griffiths, John Vesey Claude
Professional. *b:* 19.1.1931, Blackheath, Kent. *d:* 18.2.1982, Wedmore, Somerset. Tail end left-hand batsman, slow left-arm bowler. *Team* Gloucestershire (1952–57, 34 matches).
Career batting
34–53–10–396–32–9.20–0–*ct* 15
Bowling 1167–48–24.31–0–0–4/74
He was appointed a first-class umpire in 1979.

Griffiths, Peter David
Cricketer. *b*: 13.7.1961, Bulawayo, Rhodesia. Lower order right-hand batsman, slow left-arm bowler. *Team* Cambridge U (1982).
Career batting
1–2–0–1–1–0.50–0–*ct* 0
Bowling 39–0

Griffiths, Shirley
Professional. *b:* 11.7.1930, Barbados. Lower order right-hand batsman, right-arm fast bowler. *Team* Warwickshire (1956–58, 27 matches).
Career batting
27–26–12–76–17*–5.42–0–*ct* 3
Bowling 1827–74–25.22–4–0–7/62

Griffiths, Sir William Hugh
Amateur. *b:* 26.9.1923, London. Tail end right-hand batsman, right-arm fast medium bowler. *Sch* Charterhouse. *Teams* Cambridge U (1946–48, blue all three years); Glamorgan (1946–48 8 matches).
Career batting
38–48–13–137–19–3.91–0–*ct* 7
Bowling 3210–102–31.43–3–0–6/129
His final first-class match was for Free Foresters in 1949.

Grimmett, Clarence Victor
Amateur. *b:* 25.12.1891, Dunedin, New Zealand. *d:* 2.5.1980, Adelaide, Australia. Lower order

right-hand batsman, brilliant leg break and googly bowler. *Teams* Wellington (1911/2 to 1913/4); Victoria (1918/9 to 1923/4, 5 matches); South Australia (1924/5 to 1940/1, 105 matches). *Tours* Australia to England 1926, 1930 and 1934, to New Zealand 1927/8, to South Africa 1935/6. *Tests* Australia (1924/5 to 1935/6, 37 matches).
Career batting
248–321–54–4720–71*–17.67–0–*ct* 139
Bowling 31740–1424–22.28–127–33–10/37
Test batting
37–50–10–557–50–13.92–0–*ct* 17
Bowling 5231–216–24.21–21–7–7/40
Taking over 100 wickets in first-class matches on each of his three tours to England (best 144, av 16.85, in 1930), Grimmett had three most successful trips. In 1930 he took all 10 wickets (for 37) in an innings v Yorkshire at Bramall Lane and was the first bowler to claim over 200 wickets in a Test career.

Grimsdell, Arthur
Amateur. *b:* 23.3.1894, Watford, Herts. *d:* 13.3.1963, Watford, Herts. Middle order right-hand batsman, wicket-keeper. *Team* East of England (1927).
Career batting
1–2–0–43–40–21.50–0–*ct* 1
His County cricket was for Hertfordshire.
A noted soccer player, he appeared at left half for Tottenham Hotspur and England.

Grimshaw, Charles Henry
Professional. *b:* 12.5.1880, Calverley, Yorkshire. *d:* 25.9.1947, Calverley, Yorkshire. Opening left-hand batsman, right-arm medium bowler. *Team* Yorkshire (1904–08, 54 matches).
Career batting
54–75–7–1219–85–17.92–0–*ct* 42
Bowling 221–7–31.57–0–0–2/23

Grimshaw, George Henry
Amateur. *b:* 1838, Ashton, Lancashire. *d:* 21.1.1898, Grafton, Herts. Middle order batsman. *Team* Lancashire (1868, 1 match).
Career batting
1–2–0–11–11–5.50–0–*ct* 0

Grimshaw, Irwin
Professional. *b:* 4.5.1857, Farsley, Leeds, Yorkshire. *d:* 19.1.1911, Farsley, Leeds, Yorkshire. Middle order right-hand batsman. *Team* Yorkshire (1880–87, 125 matches).
Career batting
138–216–17–3682–129*–18.50–4–*ct* 85–*st* 3
He also excelled at the game of knurr and spell.

Grimshaw, James William Travis
Amateur. *b:* 17.2.1912, Darlington, Co Durham. *d:* 26.9.1944, Arnhem, Holland. Tail end right-hand batsman, slow left-arm bowler. *Sch* King William's, IOM. *Teams* Cambridge U (1932–35, blue 1934–35); Kent (1934, 2 matches).
Career batting
29–40–14–355–40–13.65–0–*ct* 20
Bowling 1760–65–27.02–1–0–5/92
His final first-class match was for MCC in 1936.

Grimshaw, Norman
Professional. *b:* 5.5.1912, Leeds, Yorkshire. Middle order right-hand batsman, right-arm slow bowler, good field. *Teams* Northants (1933–38, 78 matches).
Career batting
78–147–6–2445–92–17.34–0–*ct* 21
Bowling 427–6–71.16–0–0–2/60

Grimshaw, Vernon
Professional. *b:* 15.4.1916, Leeds, Yorkshire. Opening right-hand batsman, leg break bowler. *Team* Worcestershire (1936–38, 19 matches).
Career batting
19–32–2–418–103–13.93–1–*ct* 8
Bowling 46–2–23.00–0–0–1/2
He also played for Bedfordshire.

Grimston, Hon and Rev Edward Harbottle
Amateur. *b:* 2.4.1812, Mayfair, London. *d:* 4.5.1881, Pebmarsh, Essex. Brother of 2nd Earl of Verulam (Gentlemen), Hon F. S. (Cambridge U), Hon Robert (Middlesex), father of W. E. (Southgate). Stylish opening right-hand batsman, under-arm medium pace bowler. *Sch* Harrow. *Teams* Oxford U (1836, blue); MCC (1832–49).
Career batting
30–54–5–669–74–13.65–0–*ct* 5
Bowling 10 wickets, no analyses
One of the best amateur bats of his day, he gave up serious cricket on entering the Church in 1843. He played non-first-class cricket for Essex and Hertfordshire. He was MP for St Albans 1835–41.

Grimston, Hon and Rev Francis Sylvester
Amateur. *b:* 8.12.1822, Gorhambury, Herts. *d:* 28.10.1865, Wakes Colne, Essex. Brother of 2nd Earl of Verulam (Gentlemen), Hon E. H. (Oxford U), Hon Robert (Middlesex), uncle of W. E. (Southgate). Middle order batsman, wicket-keeper. *Sch* Harrow. *Team* Cambridge U (1843–45, blue all 3 years).
Career batting
18–30–1–172–20–5.93–0–*ct* 5–*st* 13

His final first-class match was for MCC in 1851 and his County cricket for Essex (pre-first-class) and Hertfordshire.

Grimston, George Sylvester
Amateur. *b:* 2.4.1905, Rawalpindi, India. Lower order right-hand batsman, right-arm medium fast or leg break bowler. *Sch* Winchester. *Teams* Sussex (1924–30, 18 matches); South Punjab (1926/7).
Career batting
26–43–5–826–104–21.73–1–*ct* 9
Bowling 419–11–38.09–1–0–5/40

He was a notable figure in Army cricket in the 1930s and his final first-class match was for the Army in 1939.

He was Secretary to Sussex CCC from 1950 to 1964.

Grimston, Viscount James Walter
(in 1845 succeeded as 2nd Earl of Verulam)
Amateur. *b:* 22.2.1809, Mayfair, London. *d:* 27.7.1895, Gorhambury, St. Albans. Brother of Hon E. H. (Oxford U), Hon F. S. (Cambridge), Hon Robert (Middlesex), uncle of W. E. (Southgate). Opening right-hand batsman. *Sch* Harrow. *Teams* Gentlemen (1836–39); MCC (1830–43)
Career batting
21–37–2–371–48–10.60–0–*ct* 3

He was at Oxford 1828–30, but there being only one match of note by the University in those three years, he did not appear in recorded matches for Oxford.

His final first-class match was for Married v Single in 1849.

He played County cricket for Hertfordshire. He was MP for St Albans 1830–1; Newport, Cornwall 1831–2; Hertfordshire 1832–45.

Grimston, Hon Robert
Amateur. *b:* 18.9.1816, Mayfair, London. *d:* 7.4.1884, Gorhambury, Herts. Brother of 2nd Earl of Verulam (Gentlemen), Hon E. H. (Oxford U), Hon F. S. (Cambridge U), uncle of W. E. (Southgate). Opening right-hand batsman, moderate field. *Sch* Harrow. *Teams* Oxford U (1838–40, blue 1838); Middlesex (1850–51, 3 matches); MCC (1836–55).
Career batting
63–116–4–1124–76–10.03–0–*ct* 7

According to Haygarth, when playing in a match against A. Mynn's bowling, Grimston took two bats to the wicket, a larger one to face Mynn and a standard one for the other bowlers!

He was on the MCC Committee for many years.

He also played for Hertfordshire.

Grimston, Walter Edward
Amateur. *b:* 16.5.1844, Pebmarsh, Essex. *d:* 28.7.1932, Earls Colne, Essex. Son of Hon E.H. (Oxford U), nephew of 2nd Earl of Verulam (Gentlemen), Hon F. S. (Cambridge U), Hon Robert (Middlesex). Hard hitting middle order right-hand batsman, wicket-keeper. *Sch* Harrow. *Team* Southgate (1868).
Career batting
1–2–0–8–5–4.00–0–*ct* 0

His County cricket was for Essex (non-first-class), Suffolk and Hertfordshire.

Grimwood, Alfred Stanley
Professional. *b:* 8.9.1905, West Ham, Essex. Middle order left-hand batsman. *Team* Essex (1925, 4 matches).
Career batting
4–6–0–26–15–4.33–0–*ct* 0
Bowling 5–0

Grinter, Trayton Golding
Amateur. *b:* 12.12.1885, Leytonstone, Essex. *d:* 21.4.1966, Frinton, Essex. Middle order right-hand batsman, right-arm fast medium bowler. *Team* Essex (1909–21, 8 matches).
Career batting
8–13–1–201–49*–16.75–0–*ct* 2

Despite being severely wounded in the left arm, he continued to play in good class cricket after the First World War, including some County matches, batting virtually one handed.

It was estimated that he scored over 200 centuries in all.

Gripper, Raymond Arthur
Amateur. *b:* 7.7.1938, Salisbury, Rhodesia. Middle order right-hand batsman. *Team* Rhodesia (1957/8 to 1971/2). *Tour* SA Fezala to England 1961.
Career batting
83–154–11–4353–279*–30.44–7–*ct* 58

Grisewood, Frederick Henry
Amateur. *b:* 11.4.1888, Daylesford, Worcs. *d:* 15.11.1972, Hindhead, Surrey. Middle order right-hand batsman. *Sch* Radley. *Team* Worcestershire (1908, 1 match).
Career batting
1–2–1–7–6*–7.00–0–*ct* 0

He appeared in the Freshmen's Match at Oxford, but no first-class matches. He became a well-known broadcaster and for many years chairman of the BBC Radio programme 'Any Questions?'.

Groome, Jeremy Jonathan
Cricketer. *b:* 7.4.1955, Bognor Regis, Sussex.

Middle order right-hand batsman, right-arm medium pace bowler. *Sch* Seaford. *Teams* Sussex (1974–78, 40 matches).
Career batting
40–74–3–1120–86–15.77–0–*ct* 19
Bowling 0–0

Grose, Daniel Charles Evans
Amateur. *b:* 3.4.1903, South Stoneham, Hants. *d:* 14.11.1971, Tonbridge, Kent. Middle order right-hand batsman, wicket-keeper. *Sch* Felsted. *Team* Army (1925–27).
Career batting
4–8–0–113–35–14.12–0–*ct* 3

Gross, Frederick Albert
Amateur, turned professional in 1930. *b:* 17.9.1902, Southampton. *d:* 11.3.1975, Birmingham. Lower order right-hand batsman, leg break and googly bowler. *Sch* King Edward VI School, Southampton. *Teams* Hampshire (1924–29, 34 matches); Warwickshire (1934, 1 match).
Career batting
35–45–17–202–32*–7.21–0–*ct* 18
Bowling 1926–51–37.76–1–0–5/53

Groube, Thomas Underwood
Amateur. *b:* 2.9.1857, Taranaki, New Zealand. *d:* 5.8.1927, Glenferrie, Victoria, Australia. Middle order right-hand batsman, right-arm medium pace bowler, excellent deep field. *Team* Victoria (1878/9 to 1881/2, 2 matches). *Tour* Australia to England 1880. *Test* Australia (1880, 1 match).
Career batting
13–23–2–179–61–8.52–0–*ct* 2
Test batting
1–2–0–11–11–5.50–0–*ct* 0

Considering that he played in all 37 matches on the 1880 tour to England his career in first-class cricket was remarkably brief and his fame rests with his batting for East Melbourne CC.

Grout, Arthur Theodore Wallace
Amateur. *b:* 20.3.1927, Mackay, Queensland, Australia. *d:* 9.11.1968, Wickham Terrace, Brisbane, Australia. Lower order right-hand batsman, wicket-keeper. *Team* Queensland (1946/7 to 1965/6, 94 matches). *Tours* Australia to South Africa 1957/8, to Pakistan and India 1959/60, 1964/5, to England 1961, 1964, to West Indies 1964/5; Rest of World to England 1965. *Tests* Australia (1957/8 to 1965/6, 51 matches).
Career batting
183–253–24–5168–119–22.56–4–*ct* 473–*st* 114
Bowling 115–3–38.33–0–0–1/22
Test batting
51–67–8–890–74–15.08–0–*ct* 163–*st* 24

In 1961 in England he played in all five Tests and by securing 23 victims behind the wicket set up a new record. In 1964 he again played in all five Tests and his ability behind the wicket was such that he was regarded as one of the greatest of all Australian wicketkeepers.

Grove, Charles William
Professional. *b:* 16.12.1912, Birmingham. *d:* 15.2.1982, Solihull, Warwickshire. Lower order right-hand batsman, right-arm medium fast bowler. *Teams* Warwickshire (1938–53, 201 matches); Worcestershire (1954, 15 matches).
Career batting
217–310–37–3161–104*–11.57–1–*ct* 91
Bowling 16866–744–22.66–28–5–9/39

He took 100 wickets in a season twice (best 118, av 17.13, in 1952). His best bowling was 9/39 for Warwickshire v Sussex at Edgbaston in 1952.

Grove, Lancelot Townley
Amateur. *b:* 22.8.1905, Satra, India. *d:* 9.2.1943, Newfoundland, in an air crash. Opening batsman. *Sch* Charterhouse. *Team* Army (1937–38).
Career batting
4–7–0–332–106–47.42–1–*ct* 1
Bowling 22–1–22.00–0–0–1/11

Grover, John Nelson
Amateur. *b:* 21.10.1915, Hexham, Northumberland. Middle order right-hand batsman, right-arm medium pace bowler. *Sch* Winchester. *Teams* Oxford U (1936–38, blue all three years).
Career batting
33–52–2–1188–121–23.96–3–*ct* 12
Bowling 9–0

His County cricket was for Northumberland.

Groves, Charles
Amateur. *b:* 13.1.1896, Leith, Midlothian, Scotland. *d:* 14.12.1969, Danby, Whitby, Yorkshire. Right-hand batsman, right-arm medium pace bowler. *Team* Scotland (1923–28).
Career batting
4–8–0–150–64–18.75–0–*ct* 1
Bowling 284–9–31.55–0–0–3/83

Groves, George Jasper
Amateur. *b:* 19.10.1868, Nottingham. *d:* 18.2.1941, Newmarket, Suffolk, as the result of an air-raid. Middle order right-hand batsman. *Team* Nottinghamshire (1899–1900, 17 matches).
Career batting
17–29–4–584–56*–23.36–0–*ct* 12
Bowling 6–0

His father was a well-known sporting journalist, G. T. Groves, editor of Whittam's 'Modern Cricket'.

Groves, Michael Godfrey Melvin
Amateur. *b:* 14.1.1943, Taihape, Wellington, New Zealand. Middle order right-hand batsman, right-arm fast medium bowler. *Teams* Western Province (1960/1); Oxford U (1963–66, blue 1964–66); Somerset (1965, 7 matches).
Career batting
55–97–10–2541–86–29.20–0–*ct* 33
Bowling 374–7–53.42–0–0–3/33
His first first-class match in England was for Free Foresters in 1962, and his last for Free Foresters in 1968. He hit 1,048 runs, av 29.11, in 1965.

Grundy, George Graham Stewart
Amateur. *b:* 24.6.1859, Manchester. *d:* 4.3.1945, Hunstanton, Norfolk. Middle order left-hand batsman, right-arm bowler. *Sch* Harrow. *Team* Sussex (1880, 2 matches).
Career batting
2–4–0–45–20–11.25–0–*ct* 0

Grundy, James
Professional. *b:* 5.3.1824, New Radford, Nottingham. *d:* 24.11.1873, Carrington, Nottingham. Father of John (An England XI, 1886), father-in-law of Charles Clifton (Notts). Middle order right-hand batsman, right-hand fast round-arm bowler, good field. *Team* Nottinghamshire (1851–67, 53 matches). *Tour* Parr to North America 1859 (not first-class).
Career batting
298–506–40–5898–95–12.65–0–*ct* 233–*st* 2
Bowling 11292–881+245–12.81–83–23–9/19
He took 114 wickets in 1851.
His first-class debut was for Under 35s in 1850 and his final first-class match for MCC in 1869. His best bowling was 9/19 for Notts v Kent at Trent Bridge in 1864.

Grundy, John
Professional. *b:* 25.6.1859, Carrington, Notts. *d:* 28.4.1909, Nottingham. Son of James (Notts). Lower order right-hand batsman, wicket-keeper. *Team* An England Eleven (1886).
Career batting
1–1–0–2–2–2.00–0–*ct* 0–*st* 2
His County cricket was for Warwickshire (not first-class)

Guard, David Radclyffe
Amateur. *b:* 19.5.1928, Romsey, Hants. *d:* 12.12.1978, Hartfield, Sussex. Middle order right-hand batsman. *Sch* Winchester. *Team* Hampshire (1946–49, 15 matches).
Career batting
16–29–1–430–89–15.35–0–*ct* 8

Guest, Melville Richard John
Cricketer. *b:* 18.11.1943, Rhodesia. Middle order right-hand batsman, right-arm medium pace bowler. *Sch* Rugby. *Team* Oxford U (1964–66, blue all three years).
Career batting
23–37–3–576–77–16.94–0–*ct* 10
Bowling 882–22–40.09–0–0–2/25
His County cricket was for Wiltshire.

Guggisberg, Brig Gen Sir Frederick Gordon
Amateur. *b:* 20.7.1869, Toronto, Canada. *d:* 21.4.1930, Bexhill on Sea, Sussex. Middle order batsman. *Team* MCC (1905).
Career batting
1–1–0–0–0–0.00–0–*ct* 1
Bowling 8–0
He wrote several interesting pieces on cricket.
From 1919 to 1927 he was Governor of the Gold Coast and afterwards Governor of British Guiana.

Guha, Subroto
Cricketer. *b:* 31.1.1946, Calcutta, India. Lower order right-hand batsman, right-arm medium fast bowler. *Team* Bengal (1965/6 to 1976/7). *Tours* India to England 1967; State Bank to Ceylon 1968/9. *Tests* India (1967 to 1969/70, 4 matches).
Career batting
85–102–18–1067–75–12.70–0–*ct* 46
Bowling 6068–299–20.29–18–4–7/18
Test batting
4–7–2–17–6–3.40–0–*ct* 2
Bowling 311–3–103.66–0–0–2/55
He had a very modest tour of England, but appeared in one Test.

Guise, John Lindsay
Amateur. *b:* 29.11.1903, Calcutta, India. Brother of J.L.T. (Free Foresters). Middle order right-hand batsman, right-arm medium pace bowler. *Sch* Winchester. *Teams* Middlesex (1922–34, 57 matches); Oxford U (1923–25, blue 1924–25); Europeans (1926/7 to 1927/8). *Tour* Martineau to Egypt 1934 (not first-class).
Career batting
94–156–12–3775–154*–26.21–4–*ct* 53
Bowling 1771–63–28.11–0–0–4/19
His most noteworthy innings was 278 for Winchester v Eton in 1921. From 1926 to 1929 he resided in India.
He also played for Cornwall.

Guise, James Louis Theodore
Amateur. *b:* 26.8.1910, Calcutta, India. Brother

of J. L. (Oxford U and Middlesex). Middle order right-hand batsman, slow left-arm bowler. *Sch* Winchester. *Team* Free Foresters (1937).
Career batting
1–2–0–18–11–9.00–0–*ct* 0
He did not appear in any first-class matches for the University, whilst at Oxford.

Gul Mohammad
Amateur. *b:* 15.10.1921, Lahore, India. Middle order left-hand batsman, left-arm medium pace bowler, brilliant cover point. *Teams* Northern India (1938/9 to 1943/4); Muslims (1941/2 to 1944/5); Baroda (1943/4 to 1950/1); Hyderabad (1951/2 to 1954/5); Lahore (1955/6 to 1958/9). *Tours* India to England 1946, to Australia 1947/8. *Tests* India (1946 to 1952/3, 8 matches); Pakistan (1956/7, 1 match).
Career batting
118–187–21–5614–319–33.81–12–*ct* 60
Bowling 2910–107–27.19–3–0–6/60
Test batting
9–17–1–205–34–12.81–0–*ct* 3
Bowling 24–2–12.00–0–0–2/21
On his 1946 tour to England he was unable to come to terms with English wickets and had a moderate tour, appearing in only one Test.
His most celebrated innings was 319 for Baroda v Holkar in 1946/7 at Baroda, adding a record 577 for the 4th wicket with V. S. Hazare.
His last first-class match in England was for Commonwealth in 1954.

Gunary, William Charles
Amateur. *b:* 5.8.1895, Dagenham, Essex. *d:* 26.1.1969, Upminster, Essex. Tail end right-hand batsman, left-arm fast medium bowler. *Team* Essex (1929, 1 match).
Career batting
1–1–0–0–0–0.00–0–*ct* 1
Bowling 58–0

Gunasekara, Dr Churchill Hector
Amateur. *b:* 27.7.1894, Colombo, Ceylon. *d:* 16.5.1969, Colombo, Ceylon. Lower order right-hand batsman, right-arm medium pace bowler. *Teams* Middlesex (1919–22, 39 matches); Ceylon (1926/7 to 1932/3). *Tour* Ceylon to India 1932/3.
Career batting
51–74–13–957–88*–15.68–0–*ct* 32
Bowling 2875–90–31.94–4–0–5/15
One of the leading Ceylonese cricketers, he captained Ceylon in 1930.
His final first-class match was for Indian University Occasionals in 1935/6.

Gunatilleke, Frederick Ranjan Manilal de Silva
Cricketer. *b*: 15.8.1951, Colombo, Ceylon. Lower order right-hand batsman, right-arm fast bowler. *Team* Sri Lanka (1973/4 to 1979). *Tours* Sri Lanka to India 1976/7, to England 1979.
Career batting
11–12–4–130–60*–16.25–0–*ct* 0
Bowling 688–16–43.00–1–0–5/79

Gunn, Brian George Herbert
Professional. *b:* 19.9.1921, Gravesend, Kent. Middle order batsman. *Team* Kent (1946, 4 matches).
Career batting
4–7–0–105–39–15.00–0–*ct* 7

Gunn, George
Professional. *b:* 13.6.1879, Hucknall Torkard, Notts. *d:* 29.6.1958, Tylers Green, Cuckfield, Sussex. Brother of J. R. (Notts), father of G.V. (Notts), nephew of William (Notts). Opening right-hand batsman, right-arm bowler, good slip field. *Team* Nottinghamshire (1902–32, 583 matches). *Tours* MCC to Australia 1907/8, 1911/12, to West Indies 1929/30. *Tests* England (1907/8 to 1929/30, 15 matches).
Career batting
643–1061–82–35208–220–35.96–62–*ct* 473
Bowling 2355–66–35.68–1–0–5/50
Test batting
15–29–1–1120–122*–40.00–2–*ct* 15
Bowling 8–0
He hit 1,000 runs in a season 20 times (best 1,933, av 40.27, in 1928). His only double century was 220 for Notts v Derbyshire at Trent Bridge in 1923. He and W. W. Whysall hit 40 century first wicket partnerships for Notts. Regarded by some as one of the greatest batsmen of his generation, his rather eccentric approach to the game meant that he only once appeared for England in England.

Gunn, George Vernon
Professional. *b:* 21.7.1905, West Bridgford, Nottingham. *d:* 15.10.1957, Shrewsbury, following a motor cycle accident. Son of George (Notts), nephew of J. R. (Notts). Middle order right-hand batsman, leg break bowler. *Sch* Nottingham HS. *Teams* Nottinghamshire (1928–50, 264 matches).
Career batting
266–395–43–10337–184–29.36–11–*ct* 115
Bowling 10026–281–35.67–9–1–7/44
He hit 1,000 runs in a season five times (best 1,763, av 44.07, in 1937).

Gunn, John Richmond
Professional. *b:* 19.7.1876, Hucknall Torkard, Notts. *d:* 21.8.1963, Basford, Nottingham. Brother of George (Notts), nephew of William (Notts), uncle of G. V. (Notts). Middle order

left-hand batsman, left-arm medium or slow bowler. *Teams* Nottinghamshire (1896–1925, 489 matches); London County (1904). *Tours* MacLaren to Australia 1901/2; Cahn to Argentina 1929/30. *Tests* England (1901/2 to 1905, 6 matches).
Career batting
535–845–105–24557–294–33.18–40–*ct* 248
Bowling 30463–1242–24.52–82–17–8/65
Test batting
6–10–2–85–24–10.62–0–*ct* 3
Bowling 387–18–21.50–1–0–5/76

He hit 1,000 runs in a season 11 times (best 1,665, av 42.69, in 1903) and took 100 wickets in a season five times (best 123, av 25.27, in 1904). He performed the 'double' four times.

His only double century was 294 for Notts v Leics at Trent Bridge in 1903.

Gunn, Lewis James Hamilton
Amateur. *b:* 1919, Scotland. Middle order right-hand batsman. *Team* Canada (1951–54). *Tour* Canada to England 1954.
Career batting
2–2–0–47–46–23.50–0–*ct* 0

Rain virtually washed out the only first-class match in which he appeared on the 1954 tour, but in fact he achieved very little in the minor matches of the visit.

Gunn, Terry
Professional. *b:* 27.9.1935, Barnsley, Yorkshire. Lower order right-hand batsman, wicket-keeper. *Team* Sussex (1961–67, 41 matches).
Career batting
41–54–19–179–19*–5.11–0–*ct* 109–*st* 4

Gunn, Thomas William
Professional. *b:* 10.7.1843, Croydon, Surrey. *d:* 4.5.1908, Croydon, Surrey. Middle order right-hand batsman, right-hand slow round arm bowler. *Team* Surrey (1863–69, 6 matches).
Career batting
6–11–3–52–13–6.50–0–*ct* 1

According to Haygarth his height was 5ft 1½ in only – one of the shortest men to appear in first-class cricket.

Gunn, William
Professional. *b:* 4.12.1858, Nottingham. *d:* 29.1.1921, Nottingham. Uncle of George (Notts) and J. R. (Notts). Middle order right-hand batsman, slow right-arm bowler, occasionally lobs. *Team* Nottinghamshire (1880–1904, 363 matches). *Tour* Shaw, Shrewsbury and Lillywhite to Australia 1886/7. *Tests* England (1886/7 to 1899, 11 matches).
Career batting
521–850–72–25791–273–33.15–48–*ct* 333–*st* 1
Bowling 1800–76–23.68–2–1–6/48
Test batting
11–20–2–392–102*–21.77–1–*ct* 5

He hit 1,000 runs in a season 12 times (best 2,057, av 42.85, in 1893). In all he hit eight double centuries, six for Notts, one for MCC and one for Players v Gentlemen. His highest score was 273 for Notts v Derbyshire at Derby in 1901.

A noted soccer player, he appeared for Nottingham Forest and Notts County and at outside left for England.

He was co-founder of the sports goods firm of Gunn and Moore.

Gunner, Charles Richards
Amateur. *b:* 7.1.1853, Bishops Waltham, Hants. *d:* 4.2.1934, Bishops Waltham, Hants. Father of J. H. (Hants). *Sch* Marlborough. *Teams* Hampshire (1878, 1 match).
Career batting
1 match, did not bat–*ct* 1

Gunner, John Hugh
Amateur. *b:* 17.5.1884, Bishops Waltham, Hants. *d:* 9.8.1918, Kemmel, Belgium. He died of wounds. Son of C. R. (Hants). Middle order batsman. *Sch* Marlborough. *Team* Hampshire (1906–07, 6 matches).
Career batting
6–9–1–65–32–8.12–0–*ct* 4

He did not appear in first-class cricket at Oxford.

Gupte, Subhashchandra Pandhrinath
Amateur. *b:* 11.12.1929, Bombay, India. Brother of B. P. (India). Lower order right-hand batsman, leg break and googly bowler. *Teams* Bombay (1948/9 to 1958/9); Bengal (1953/4 to 1957/8); Rajasthan (1960/1 to 1962/3); Trinidad (1963/4). *Tours* India to West Indies 1952/3, to Pakistan 1954/5, to England 1959. *Tests* India (1951/2 to 1961/2, 36 matches).
Career batting
115–125–32–761–47–8.18–0–*ct* 52
Bowling 12567–530–23.71–36–11–10/78
Test batting
36–42–13–183–21–6.31–0–*ct* 14
Bowling 4403–149–29.55–12–1–9/102

On his 1959 visit to England he took most wickets – 95, av 26.58, but was in fact not as successful as had been expected.

For Bombay v Pakistan Services and Bahawalpur at Bombay in 1954/5 he took all 10 wickets in an innings for 78 runs.

His debut in English first-class cricket was for a Commonwealth XI in 1957.

He emigrated to the West Indies in 1963.

Gurney, Edward Richmond
Amateur. *b:* 16.4.1868, Kidderminster, Worcs. *d:* 17.6.1938, Hove, Sussex. Opening batsman. *Team* Gloucestershire (1911, 1 match).
Career batting
1–2–0–10–8–5.00–0–*ct* 0

Gurr, David Roberts
Cricketer. *b:* 27.3.1956, Whitchurch, Bucks. Lower order right-hand batsman, right-arm fast medium bowler. *Teams* Oxford U (1976–77, blue both years); Somerset (1976–79, 24 matches).
Career batting
41–48–23–410–46*–16.40–0–*ct* 9
Bowling 3079–110–27.99–5–0–6/82

Guthrie, James Shields
Amateur. *b:* 14.12.1931, Kandy, Ceylon. Tail end right-hand batsman, off break bowler. *Team* Cambridge U (1953).
Career batting
1–2–0–1–1–0.50–0–*ct* 0
Bowling 30–0

Gutteres, Rev George Gilbert
Amateur. *b:* 11.10.1859, Kensington, London. *d:* 2.3.1898, Algiers. Opening right-hand batsman, brilliant cover point. *Sch* Winchester. *Teams* Oxford U (1881); Hampshire (1882, 1 match).
Career batting
3–5–2–111–34*–37.00–0–*ct* 4

He also played for Devon.

Guttridge, Frank (Herbert)
Professional. *b:* 12.4.1866, Nottingham. *d:* 13.6.1918, Nottingham. Lower order right-hand batsman, right-arm fast bowler. *Teams* Nottinghamshire (1889–1900, 58 matches); Sussex (1892–94, 49 matches).
Career batting
107–174–19–2190–114–14.12–1–*ct* 46
Bowling 5279–176–29.99–6–1–7/35

His obituary was erroneously published in 1906.

Guy, Joseph
Professional. *b:* 30.7.1814, Nottingham. *d:* 15.4.1873, Nottingham. Middle order right-hand batsman, occasional wicket-keeper, good point. *Team* Nottinghamshire (1837–54, 32 matches).
Career batting
148–267–14–3395–98–13.41–0–*ct* 102–*st* 14

He was one of the leading batsmen of his day, noted for the elegance of his style.

Guy, John Bernard
Amateur. *b:* 16.5.1916, Ramsgate, Kent. Opening right-hand batsman, left-arm medium pace bowler. *Sch* Chatham House, Ramsgate. *Teams* Oxford U (1938–39); Kent (1938, 1 match); Warwickshire (1950, 2 matches).
Career batting
9–16–0–130–45–8.12–0–*ct* 4

Guy, John Williams
Professional. *b:* 29.8.1934, Nelson, New Zealand. Attractive opening left-hand batsman. *Teams* Central Districts (1953/4 to 1962/3); Northants (1958, 2 matches); Canterbury (1957/8 to 1958/9); Otago (1959/60); Wellington (1960/1); Northern Districts (1964/5 to 1972/3). *Tours* New Zealand to India and Pakistan 1955/6, to Australia and South Africa 1961/2. *Tests* New Zealand (1955/6 to 1961/2, 12 matches).
Career batting
90–165–13–3923–115–25.80–3–*ct* 32
Bowling 82–1–82.00–0–0–1/0
Test batting
12–23–2–440–102–20.95–1–*ct* 2

Gwynn, Arthur Percival
Amateur. *b:* 11.6.1874, Ramelton, Co Donegal, Ireland. *d:* 14.2.1898, Rangoon, Burma. Brother of L. H. (Ireland) and R. M. (Dublin). Right-hand batsman, wicket-keeper. *Team* Dublin University (1895).
Career batting
4–8–0–267–130–33.37–1–*ct* 5–*st* 1

He played rugby for Ireland.

Gwynn, John David
Amateur. *b:* 13.7.1907, Clontarf, Co Dublin, Ireland. Right-hand batsman. *Team* Dublin University (1926).
Career batting
1–2–1–11–11*–11.00–0–*ct* 0

Gwynn, Lucius Henry
Amateur. *b:* 5.5.1873, Ramelton, Co Donegal, Ireland. *d:* 23.12.1902, Davos Platz, Switzerland. Brother of A. P. and R. M. (Dublin). Right-hand batsman. *Teams* Ireland (1902); Dublin University (1895); Gentlemen of England (1895–96).
Career batting
8–16–3–577–153*–44.38–2–*ct* 10
Bowling 410–18–22.77–0–0–4/81

He was regarded as a most accomplished batsman and would have played regularly in first-class County cricket if he had resided in England.

A noted rugby footballer, he was a three quarter for Monkstown and Ireland.

Gwynn, Rev Robert Malcolm
Amateur. *b:* 26.4.1877, Ramelton, Co Donegal, Ireland. *d:* 2.6.1962, Dublin, Ireland. Brother of A. P. (Dublin) and L. H. (Ireland). Right-hand batsman, right-arm slow bowler. *Team* Dublin University (1895).
Career batting
4–7–2–52–23*–10.40–0–*ct* 2
Bowling 274–8–34.25–0–0–3/21

Gwynne, David Graham Pugsley
Amateur. *b:* 8.12.1904, Swansea. *d:* 11.12.1934, Swansea. Middle order right-hand batsman. *Sch* Llandovery College. *Team* Glamorgan (1922–23, 3 matches).
Career batting
3–6–0–20–12–3.33–0–*ct* 1

HACK, EDWARD JOHN
Amateur. *b:* 1.10.1913, Long Ashton, Somerset. Middle order right-hand batsman. *Team* Somerset (1937, 1 match).
Career batting
1–1–0–6–6–6.00–0–*ct* 1

Hacker, Peter John
Cricketer. *b:* 16.7.1952, Lenton Abbey, Nottingham. Lower order right-hand batsman, left-arm fast medium bowler. *Teams* Nottinghamshire (1974–81, 61 matches); Orange Free State (1979/80); Derbyshire (1982, 8 matches).
Career batting
71–77–30–449–35–9.55–0–*ct* 16
Bowling 4792–153–31.32–4–0–6/35
He also played for Lincolnshire commencing 1983.

Hacker, William Stamford
Professional. *b:* 8.12.1876, Chipping Sodbury, Gloucs. *d:* 8.12.1925, Bristol. Lower order right-hand batsman, right-arm fast medium bowler. *Teams* Gloucestershire (1899–1901, 3 matches); Glamorgan (1921–23, 21 matches).
Career batting
25–40–12–222–27–8.60–0–*ct* 8
Bowling 2110–91–23.18–4–1–7/84
He also appeared for Herefordshire.

Hacking, John Kenneth
Amateur. *b:* 21.3.1909, Kenilworth, Warwickshire. *Sch* Warwick. Middle order right-hand batsman, right-arm medium pace bowler. *Team* Warwickshire (1946, 1 match).
Career batting
1–2–0–17–14–8.50–0–*ct* 2

Hadden, Sidney
Professional. *b:* 26.8.1877, Hastings, Sussex. *d:* 1934, West Ham, London. Lower order batsman, wicket-keeper. *Team* Essex (1912–20, 6 matches).
Career batting
6–5–2–29–17*–9.66–0–*ct* 5–*st* 1

Haden, J. V.
Professional. Opening/middle order batsman. *Team* Surrey (1882, 7 matches).
Career batting
7–10–0–42–22–4.20–0–*ct* 2

Hadfield, George Hugh
Amateur. *b:* 1880, Edmonton, Middlesex. *d:* 30.11.1935, Lambeth, South London. Tail end right-hand batsman, right-arm medium pace bowler. *Team* Surrey (1903–04, 4 matches).
Career batting
5–6–2–53–27*–13.25–0–*ct* 3
Bowling 526–17–30.94–1–0–5/52
His final first-class match was for W. G. Grace's XI in 1906.

Hadi, Syed Mohammad
Amateur. *b:* 12.8.1899, India. *d:* 14.7.1971, Hyderabad, India. Brother of S. M. Hussain (Hyderabad). Middle order right-hand batsman. *Teams* Hyderabad (1930/1 to 1940/1); Madras (1933/4). *Tour* India to England 1936.
Career batting
24–42–10–1043–132*–32.59–2–*ct* 9
On the 1936 tour he appeared in emergency in two matches only. He was the first cricketer to score a century in the Ranji Trophy Competition.

Hadingham, Anthony Wallace Gwynne
Amateur. *b:* 1.3.1913, Mentone, France. Opening right-hand batsman. *Sch* St Paul's. *Teams* Cambridge U (1932–33, blue 1932); Surrey (1932, 1 match). *Tour* Martineau to Egypt 1935 (not first-class).
Career batting
19–32–1–554–80–17.87–0–*ct* 4
Bowling 6–0

Hadlee, Dayle Robert
Cricketer. *b:* 6.1.1948, Christchurch, New Zealand. Son of W. A. (New Zealand), brother of R. J. (New Zealand) and B. G. (Canterbury). Lower order right-hand batsman, right-arm

medium fast bowler. *Team* Canterbury (1969/70 to 1982/3). *Tours* New Zealand to England 1969, 1973, 1978, to Australia 1973/4, 1969/70, to India and Pakistan 1969/70. *Tests* New Zealand (1969 to 1977/8, 26 matches).
Career batting
105–147–39–1973–109*–18.26–1–*ct* 39
Bowling 8566–334–25.64–11–3–7/55
Test batting
26–42–5–530–56–14.32–0–*ct* 8
Bowling 2389–71–33.64–0–0–4/30

Only on the second of his three tours to England did he have much success. On the first visit his inexperience told against him and on the 1978 tour he broke down after one match. His first-class debut was for New Zealand Under 23s in 1966/7.

Hadlee, Richard John
Cricketer. *b* 3.7.1951, Christchurch, New Zealand. Son of W. A. (New Zealand), brother of D. R. (New Zealand) and B. G. (Canterbury). Aggressive middle order left-hand batsman, right-arm fast bowler. *Teams* Canterbury (1971/2 to 1982/3); Nottinghamshire (1978–83, 71 matches); Tasmania (1979/80, 6 matches). *Tours* New Zealand to England 1973, 1978, 1983, to Australia 1972/3, 1973/4, 1980/1, to Pakistan and India 1976/7. *Tests* New Zealand (1972/3 to 1983, 44 matches).
Career batting
197–276–45–6228–142*–26.96–7–*ct* 103
Bowling 16109–815–19.76–47–6–7/23
Test batting
44–77–11–1601–103–24.25–1–*ct* 22
Bowling 5164–200–25.82–15–0–7/23

On his first tour to England 1973, he played in one Test and had a modest record both as batsman and bowler, but on his two subsequent visits he has been most successful; in 1978 he headed the bowling averages for both Test and first-class matches with 13 wickets, av 20.76, and 41, av 17.41, respectively. In 1983 he took 21 Test wickets, av 26.61, and also topped the Test batting averages with 301 runs, av 50.16. He is the first New Zealander to capture 200 Test wickets. His best season for Nottinghamshire was 1981 with 105 wickets, av 14.89.

Hadlee, Walter Arnold
Amateur. *b:* 4.6.1915, Lincoln, Canterbury, New Zealand. Father of D. R. (New Zealand), R. J. (New Zealand) and B. G. (Canterbury). Middle order right-hand batsman, good deep field. *Teams* Canterbury (1933/4 to 1951/2); Otago (1945/6 to 1946/7). *Tours* New Zealand to England 1937, 1949, to Australia 1937/8. *Tests* New Zealand (1937 to 1950/1, 11 matches).
Career batting
116–202–17–7421–198–40.11–17–*ct* 67
Bowling 293–6–48.83–0–0–3/14
Test batting
11–19–1–543–116–30.16–1–*ct* 6

He scored 1,225 runs, av 29.87, on the 1937 tour and 1,439, av 35.97, on the 1949 visit, being captain of the latter. In all he led New Zealand in eight Tests. Since retiring from first-class cricket he has been an important figure in the New Zealand Cricket Council.

Hadley, Robert John
Cricketer. *b:* 22.10.1951, Neath, Glamorgan. Tail end right-hand batsman, left-arm fast medium bowler. *Teams* Cambridge U (1971–73, blue all three years); Glamorgan (1971, 2 matches). *Tour* Oxford and Cambridge U to Malaysia 1972/3 (not first-class).
Career batting
28–36–16–65–17–3.25–0–*ct* 8
Bowling 1647–56–29.41–3–0–5/31

Hadow, Alexander Astell
Amateur. *b:* 1.6.1853, London. *d:* 1.6.1894, Neuenahr, Rhenish Prussia, Germany. Brother of E. M., P. F. and W. H. (Middlesex). Middle order right-hand batsman, round-arm or under-arm medium pace bowler. *Sch* Harrow. *Team* Middlesex (1872, 1 match).
Career batting
1–2–0–27–18–13.50–0–*ct* 1
Bowling 24–2–12.00–0–0–2/24

He was also a noted rackets player. Business prevented him from taking part in County matches regularly.

Hadow, Edward Maitland
Amateur. *b:* 13.3.1863, Sudbury Hill, Middlesex. *d:* 20.2.1895, Cannes, France. Brother of A. A., P. F. and W. H. (Middlesex). Hard hitting middle order batsman, right-arm fast bowler, good field. *Sch* Harrow. *Team* Middlesex (1883–93, 54 matches).
Career batting
77–133–10–1933–75–15.71–0–*ct* 38
Bowling 1189–50–23.78–0–0–4/24

He was also a good rackets player.

Hadow, Patrick Francis
Amateur. *b:* 24.1.1855, London. *d:* 29.6.1946, Bridgwater, Somerset. Brother of A. A., E. M. and W. H. (Middlesex). Middle order right-hand batsman, good field. *Sch* Harrow. *Team* Middlesex (1873–74, 4 matches).
Career batting
7–13–1–134–37–11.16–0–*ct* 4

His cricket career was very limited as he became

a planter in Ceylon. He was Amateur Lawn Tennis Champion at Wimbledon in 1878 and also a noted racquets player.

Hadow, Walter Henry
Amateur. *b:* 25.9.1849, London. *d:* 15.9.1898, Dupplin, Perthshire. Brother of A. A., E. M. and P. F. (Middlesex). Hard hitting middle order right-hand batsman, right-hand slow round-arm bowler. *Sch* Harrow. *Teams* Oxford U (1869–72, blue 1870–72); Middlesex (1870–79, 37 matches). *Tour* Fitzgerald to North America 1872 (not first-class).
Career batting
97–168–11–3071–217–19.56–2–*ct* 84
Bowling 2327–158+1–16.86–9–3–8/35

His only double century was 217 for Middlesex v MCC in 1871. He also played for Brecon and Shropshire. His final first-class match was for MCC in 1884. He was a champion racquets player at Oxford, a good tennis player and rowed for his college.

Hafeez, A. (*see under* Kardar, A.H.)

Haggas, Stell
Professional. *b:* 18.4.1856, Keighley, Yorkshire. *d:* 14.3.1926, Oldham, Lancashire. Father of W. (Lancashire). Middle order right-hand batsman, good long stop, occasional wicket-keeper. *Teams* Yorkshire (1878–82, 31 matches); Lancashire (1884–85, 3 matches).
Career batting
34–52–3–537–43–10.95–0–*ct* 10

Haggas, W.
Professional. Son of Stell (Yorkshire and Lancashire). Lower order batsman, wicket-keeper. *Team* Lancashire (1903, 2 matches).
Career batting
2–2–0–6–4–3.00–0–*ct* 3

Haggett, Norman Louis
Amateur. *b:* 8.7.1926, Lewisham, Kent. Opening right-hand batsman. *Team* Combined Services (1962–64).
Career batting
4–8–0–204–71–25.50–0–*ct* 4

Haggo, David John
Cricketer. *b:* 13.4.1964, Ayr, Scotland. Right-hand batsman, wicket-keeper. *Team* Scotland (1983).
Career batting
1–2–0–9–9–4.50–0–*ct* 1

Haig, Nigel Esmé
Amateur. *b:* 12.12.1887, Kensington. *d:* 27.10.1966, Eastbourne. Nephew of Lord Harris (Kent). Middle order right-hand batsman, right-arm fast medium bowler, good field. *Sch* Eton. *Team* Middlesex (1912–34, 417 matches). *Tour* MCC to West Indies (1929/30). *Tests* England (1921 to 1929/30, 5 matches).
Career batting
513–779–51–15220–131–20.90–12–*ct* 221
Bowling 30698–1117–27.48–47–2–7/33
Test batting
5–9–0–126–47–14.00–0–*ct* 4
Bowling 448–13–34.46–0–0–3/73

He hit 1,000 runs in a season six times (best 1,552, av 25.02, in 1929) and took 100 wickets five times (best 129, av 24.17, in 1929). He performed the 'double' three times. From 1929 to 1934 he captained Middlesex, in the last two years jointly with H. J. Enthoven. He also played tennis, rackets, squash and golf to a high standard. His final first-class match was for Leveson-Gower's XI in 1936.

Haigh, Charles Henry
Amateur. *b:* 26.9.1854, Rochdale, Lancashire. *d:* 15.3.1915, Bollington, Cheshire. Middle order right-hand batsman. *Sch* Bromsgrove. *Team* Lancashire (1879–87, 24 matches).
Career batting
24–33–3–435–80–14.50–0–*ct* 11

Haigh, Schofield
Professional. *b:* 19.3.1871, Berry Brow, Huddersfield, Yorkshire. *d:* 27.2.1921, Lockwood, Yorkshire. Middle/lower order right-hand batsman, right-arm fast medium bowler. *Team* Yorkshire (1895–1913, 513 matches). *Tours* Hawke to South Africa 1898/9; MCC to South Africa 1905/06. *Tests* England (1898/9 to 1912, 11 matches).
Career batting
561–747–119–11715–159–18.65–4–*ct* 298
Bowling 32091–2012–15.94–135–30–9/25
Test batting
11–18–3–113–25–7.53–0–*ct* 8
Bowling 622–24–25.91–1–0–6/11

He once exceeded 1,000 runs in a season – 1,055, av 26.37, in 1904. He took 100 wickets in a season 11 times (best 174, av 14.59, in 1906). His best bowling was 9/25 for Yorkshire v Gloucs at Leeds in 1912. In 1904 he performed the 'double'. He never made his mark in Test cricket, but played with success in County cricket, his batting perhaps being under-estimated.

Hailey, Henry
Amateur. *b:* 1851, Bow, Middlesex. *d:* 24.9.1932, Southend-on-Sea, Essex. Middle order right-hand batsman. *Team* Essex (1894–95, 13 matches).

Career batting
13–22–5–301–66*–17.70–0–*ct* 5

Haines, Alfred Hubert
Amateur. *b:* 27.8.1877, Long Sutton, Lincs. *d:* 30.5.1935, Ashford, Kent. Father of C. V. G. (Glamorgan). Middle order right-hand batsman. *Sch* Merchant Taylors. *Team* Gloucestershire (1901–10, 7 matches).
Career batting
7–13–2–117–23–10.63–0–*ct* 4

Haines, Claude Vincent Godby
Amateur. *b:* 17.1.1906, Bristol. *d:* 28.1.1965, Lower Cwmtwrch, Glamorgan. Son of A. H. (Gloucs). Middle order right-hand batsman. *Sch* King's, Canterbury. *Team* Glamorgan (1933–34, 12 matches).
Career batting
12–20–2–350–59–19.44–0–*ct* 3
Bowling 33–1–33.00–0–0–1/15
He also played for Devon.

Haines, Harold Attlee
Amateur. *b:* 17.11.1878, USA. *d:* 28.11.1970, Chestnut Hill, Pennsylvania, USA. Hard hitting middle order batsman, excellent field. *Team* Philadelphia (1903). *Tour* Philadelphia to England 1903.
Career batting
8–13–1–78–20*–6.50–0–*ct* 7
Bowling 45–0
He met with little success on his visit to England, but fared well for United States v Canada, appearing in four matches between 1901 and 1911.

Haines, John
Amateur. *b: circa* 1825, St Pancras, Middlesex. *d:* 1894, St Pancras, London. Middle order batsman. *Team* Middlesex (1865–67, 2 matches).
Career batting
2–4–0–13–5–3.25–0–*ct* 3

Hake, George John Gordon
Amateur. *b:* 24.8.1918, Sutton, Surrey. Middle order right-hand batsman, right-arm fast medium bowler. *Sch* Bromsgrove. *Team* Middlesex (1948, 1 match).
Career batting
1–1–0–2–2–2.00–0–*ct* 0
Bowling 84–1–84.00–0–0–1/84

Hake, Herbert Denys
Amateur. *b:* 8.11.1894, Bournemouth, Hants. *d:* 12.4.1975, Sydney, Australia. Attractive middle order right-hand batsman, good field, occasional wicket-keeper. *Sch* Haileybury. *Teams* Hampshire (1920–25, 21 matches); Cambridge U (1920–21).
Career batting
26–38–3–557–94–15.91–0–*ct* 6–*st* 1
Bowling 24–0

Hale, Harold
Amateur. *b:* 27.3.1867, Perth, Australia. *d:* 2.8.1947, Melbourne, Australia. Lower order right-hand batsman, right-arm medium pace off break bowler. *Teams* Gloucestershire (1886–89, 19 matches); Cambridge U (1887–90, blue 1887, 1889 and 1890); Tasmania (1883/4 to 1910/11, 13 matches). *Tour* Tasmania to New Zealand 1883/4.
Career batting
57–101–13–1067–53–12.12–0–*ct* 24
Bowling 2295–99–23.18–6–0–7/42

Hale, Ivor Edward
Amateur. *b:* 6.10.1922, Worcester. Middle order right-hand batsman, off break bowler. *Sch* Royal Grammar School, Worcester. *Teams* Gloucestershire (1947–48, 13 matches); Sussex (1946, 3 matches).
Career batting
16–28–3–314–61–12.56–0–*ct* 8
Bowling 65–2–32.50–0–0–1/18

Hale, John Hinde
Amateur. *b:* 16.9.1830, East Grinstead, Sussex. *d:* 11.7.1878, Notting Hill, London. Brother of T. W. (Oxford U). Middle order right-hand batsman, good deep field. *Sch* Rugby. *Team* Sussex (1853–65, 35 matches).
Career batting
49–94–1–1242–61–13.35–0–*ct* 37–*st* 1
He was regarded as the fastest scoring batsman of his day, 'though not possessing an elegant style'. For some years he was on the Committee of Sussex CCC. He also played for Buckinghamshire.

Hale, Percy William
Amateur. *b:* 1874, Kensington, London. *d:* 8.1.1933, Harrow, Middlesex. Middle order batsman. *Team* Middlesex (1900, 1 match).
Career batting
1–2–0–29–26–14.50–0–*ct* 2

Hale, Terrance Saville
Cricketer. *b:* 8.10.1936, Waterbeach, Cambs. Middle order left-hand batsman. *Team* Minor Counties (1965).
Career batting
1–2–0–8–8–4.00–0–*ct* 0
His County cricket was for Cambridgeshire commencing 1960, being captain in 1977–78.

Hale, Walter Henry
Professional. *b:* 6.3.1870, West Bromwich, Staffs. *d:* 12.8.1956, Bishopston, Bristol. Middle order right-hand batsman, right-arm slow bowler. *Teams* Gloucestershire (1895–1909, 60 matches); Somerset (1892, 8 matches).
Career batting
69–119–7–2124–135–18.96–2–*ct* 39
Bowling 414–9–46.00–0–0–2/16

A noted rugby footballer he appeared for Bristol as well as Gloucestershire and Somerset.

Hale, Warren Stormes
Amateur. *b:* 1862, Sudbury, Middlesex. *d:* 5.2.1934, Highgate, London. Middle order batsman. *Team* Middlesex (1893, 4 matches).
Career batting
5–9–1–86–36–10.75–0–*ct* 1

He was a prolific scorer in London Club cricket, notably for Hampstead. His final first-class match was for MCC in 1897.

Hales, John
Amateur. *b:* 16.9.1833, Charmouth, Dorset. *d:* 25.1.1915, Bournemouth, Hants. Steady opening right-hand batsman, right-hand fast medium round-arm bowler. *Sch* Rugby. *Teams* Cambridge U (1855–59, blue 1855 and 1856); Surrey Club (1865).
Career batting
8–15–0–69–19–4.60–0–*ct* 5

Hales, Lloyd Archibald
Amateur. *b:* 27.6.1921, Leicester. Middle order right-hand batsman, right-arm medium off break bowler. *Sch* Wyggeston and Bristol GS. *Team* Leicestershire (1947, 2 matches).
Career batting
2–4–0–76–62–19.00–0–*ct* 0
Bowling 38–0

Halford, John
Amateur. *b:* 1846, Newent, Gloucs. *d:* 1901, Gloucester. Middle order right-hand batsman. *Team* Gloucestershire (1870–74, 10 matches).
Career batting
10–15–2–150–42–11.53–0–*ct* 8–*st* 1
Bowling 12–0

Halfyard, David John
Professional. *b:* 3.4.1931, Winchmore Hill, Middlesex. Lower order right-hand batsman, right-arm fast medium or medium bowler. *Teams* Kent (1956–64, 185 matches); Nottinghamshire (1968–70, 77 matches).
Career batting
264–348–51–3242–79–10.91–0–*ct* 113
Bowling 24822–963–25.77–55–13–9/39

He also played for Durham, Northumberland and Cornwall. In 1967, having retired from first-class cricket due to injury he was appointed to the first-class umpires' list, but after one year resumed County cricket with Notts. He returned to the umpires' list in 1977. He took 100 wickets in a season five times (best 135, av 20.39, in 1958). His best bowling was 9/39 for Kent v Glamorgan at Neath in 1957.

Hall, Alfred Ewart
Professional. *b:* 23.1.1896, Bolton, Lancashire. *d:* 1.1.1964, Johannesburg, South Africa. Tail end right-hand batsman, left-arm fast medium bowler. *Teams* Transvaal (1920/1 to 1930/1); Lancashire (1923–24, 9 matches). *Tests* South Africa (1922/3 to 1930/1, 7 matches).
Career batting
46–57–21–134–22–3.44–0–*ct* 13
Bowling 4501–234–19.23–21–6–8/80
Test batting
7–8–2–11–5–1.83–0–*ct* 4
Bowling 886–40–22.15–3–1–7/63

Hall, Bert
Professional. Middle order batsman. *Team* Derbyshire (1902, 1 match).
Career batting
1–2–0–10–7–5.00–0–*ct* 0

Hall, Brian
Professional. *b:* 16.9.1929, Morley, Yorkshire. Tail end right-hand batsman, right-arm medium fast bowler. *Team* Yorkshire (1952, 1 match).
Career batting
1–2–0–14–10–7.00–0–*ct* 1
Bowling 55–1–55.00–0–0–1/55

Hall, Brian Charles
Professional. *b:* 2.3.1934, Marylebone, London. Lower order right-hand batsman, right-arm medium pace bowler. *Team* Worcestershire (1956–57, 3 matches).
Career batting
3–4–1–34–21–11.33–0–*ct* 1
Bowling 97–3–32.33–0–0–2/11

Hall, Charles
Professional. *b:* 16.10.1842, Islington, Middlesex. *d:* 1900, London. Lower order right-hand batsman, right-hand fast round-arm bowler. *Team* Middlesex (1867, 1 match).
Career batting
1–2–0–12–7–6.00–0–*ct* 0

Hall, Clifford Geoffrey
Amateur. *b:* 19.1.1902, Breamore, Hants. *d:* 9.7.1982, Breamore, Hants. Middle order right-

hand batsman. *Team* Hampshire (1933–35, 5 matches).
Career batting
5–7–0–77–37–11.00–0–*ct* 1
He also played for Wiltshire.

Hall, Charles Henry
Professional. *b:* 5.4.1906, York. *d:* 11.12.1976, Upper Poppleton, Yorks. Lower order right-hand batsman, right-arm medium fast bowler. *Team* Yorkshire (1928–34, 23 matches).
Career batting
23–22–9–67–15*–5.15–0–*ct* 11
Bowling 1226–45–27.24–2–0–6/71

Hall, Charles John
Professional. *b:* 12.8.1848, Kingston-on-Thames, Surrey. *d:* 18.11.1931, Heybridge, Essex. Middle/lower order right-hand batsman, right-hand fast round-arm bowler. *Team* Surrey (1868–73, 8 matches).
Career batting
8–13–1–71–15–5.91–0–*ct* 1
Bowling 13–1–13.00–0–0–1/4

Hall, Derek
Professional. *b:* 21.2.1932, Bolsover, Derbyshire. *d:* 13.3.1983, San Jose, California, USA. Tail end right-hand batsman, right-arm fast medium bowler. *Team* Derbyshire (1955–58, 20 matches).
Career batting
20–29–16–43–10*–3.30–0–*ct* 6
Bowling 1386–48–28.87–0–0–4/57

Hall, E.
Amateur. Middle order right-hand batsman, wicket-keeper. *Team* Hampshire (1880–85, 11 matches).
Career batting
11–21–2–198–22–10.42–0–*ct* 11–*st* 3

Hall, Egerton Hawkesley
Amateur. *b:* 25.4.1861. *d:* 8.2.1919, Axbridge, Somerset. Lower order batsman, useful bowler. *Team* Somerset (1884–85, 3 matches).
Career batting
3–6–1–43–23–8.60–0–*ct* 1
Bowling 145–3–48.33–0–0–2/67

Hall, Frederick Harrison
Amateur. *b:* 15.8.1892, Blackrock, Co Cork, Ireland. *d:* 4.1.1947, Virginia Water, Surrey. Right-hand batsman. *Sch* Dover. *Teams* Ireland (1925–26); Dublin U (1924).
Career batting
3–5–0–71–34–14.20–0–*ct* 2

Hall, Geoffrey Harold
Professional. *b:* 1.6.1941, Colne, Lancashire. Tail end right-hand batsman, right-arm fast bowler. *Team* Somerset (1961–65, 48 matches).
Career batting
48–51–26–90–12*–3.60–0–*ct* 9
Bowling 3425–111–30.85–2–0–6/60

Hall, Henry George Hamlet
Amateur. *b:* 24.12.1857, Bedminster, Somerset. *d:* 1934, Bristol. Lower order batsman, useful bowler. *Team* Somerset (1882–85, 2 matches).
Career batting
2–4–1–2–2–0.66–0–*ct* 1
Bowling 57–1–57.00–0–0–1/47

Hall, Harold St Alban
Amateur. *b:* 1875. *d:* 17.5.1915, Farnham, Surrey. Middle order batsman. *Team* Northants (1907, 1 match).
Career batting
1–2–0–12–7–6.00–0–*ct* 0

Hall, Ian William
Professional. *b:* 27.12.1939, Sutton Scarsdale, Derbyshire. Opening right-hand batsman, right-arm medium pace bowler. *Team* Derbyshire (1959–72, 270 matches).
Career batting
270–483–32–11666–136*–25.86–9–*ct* 189
Bowling 23–0
He hit 1,000 runs in a season five times (best 1,449, av 33.69, in 1971). A well-known soccer player, he appeared for Derby County and Mansfield Town at inside right.

Hall, John
Professional. *b:* 11.11.1815, Nottingham. Middle order right-hand batsman. *Team* Yorkshire (1844–63, 4 matches).
Career batting
4–7–1–49–28*–8.16–0–*ct* 6
Bowling 37–9+3–4.11–1–0–5/18
He appeared for Leicester in 1839 and moving to Bradford in 1841 was for many years the leading batsman of that town.

Hall, John Bernard
Amateur. *b:* 17.6.1903, Worksop, Notts. *d:* 27.5.1979, Retford, Notts. Father of M. J. (Notts). Lower order right-hand batsman, right-arm medium pace bowler. *Sch* Bloxham. *Team* Nottinghamshire (1935–46, 5 matches). *Tour* Cahn to Ceylon and Malaya (1936/7).
Career batting
7–13–1–114–24–9.50–0–*ct* 3
Bowling 516–21–24.57–1–0–6/75

Hall, John Edwin
Cricketer. *b:* 5.1.1950, Basutoland. Middle order right-hand batsman. *Sch* Ardingly. *Team* Cambridge U (1969–70, blue 1969).
Career batting
14–26–0–385–69–14.80–0–*ct* 3

Hall, John Keith
Amateur. *b:* 29.7.1934, West Wickham, Kent. Lower order right-hand batsman, right-arm fast medium bowler. *Sch* Lancing. *Teams* Surrey (1958–62, 13 matches); Sussex (1960, 1 match). *Tours* Surridge to Bermuda 1961 (not first-class); Brown to East Africa 1961/2 (not first-class).
Career batting
21–22–6–57–22–3.56–0–*ct* 9
Bowling 1532–54–28.37–1–0–5/30
He was also a good middle distance runner.

Hall, John Peter
Professional. *b:* 20.8.1874, Worksop, Notts. *d:* 9.11.1925, Worksop, Notts. Lower order right-hand batsman, right-arm fast medium bowler. *Team* Derbyshire (1895–97, 4 matches).
Career batting
4–7–1–3–2–0.50–0–*ct* 3
Bowling 112–3–37.33–0–0–1/12

Hall, J.W.C. *(see under* Cressy-Hall, J. W.)

Hall, Louis
Professional. *b:* 1.11.1852, Batley, Yorkshire. *d:* 19.11.1915, Morecambe, Lancashire. Steady opening right-hand batsman, right-hand slow round arm or lob bowler, brilliant close field. *Team* Yorkshire (1873–94, 279 matches).
Career batting
315–544–63–11095–160–23.06–12–*ct* 195
Bowling 927–22–42.13–0–0–4/51
He hit 1,000 runs in a season four times (best 1,240, av 38.75, in 1887). He carried his bat through a completed innings no less than 15 times and on many occasions batted with remarkable slowness; for Yorkshire v Kent at Canterbury in 1885 he lasted 165 minutes for 12. He captained Yorkshire often in the absence of Lord Hawke.

Hall, Maurice James
Amateur. *b:* 22.9.1849, Whatton, Notts. *d:* 24.7.1914, Middleburg, Cape Province. Middle order batsman. *Sch* Uppingham. *Team* Gentlemen of South (1870).
Career batting
1–1–0–9–9–9.00–0–*ct* 0
He appeared in emergency for Gentlemen of the South, being in fact a member of the Notts Gentlemen's Club, on which ground his only first-class match was played.

Hall, Michael John
Professional. *b:* 29.5.1935, Worksop, Notts. Son of J. B. (Notts). Middle order right-hand batsman, good field. *Team* Nottinghamshire (1958–59, 17 matches).
Career batting
17–30–1–430–72–14.82–0–*ct* 17
He was a leading batsman in Bassetlaw League cricket for 25 years.

Hall, Peter James
Amateur. *b:* 4.12.1927, Hong Kong. Middle/lower order right-hand batsman, right-arm medium pace bowler. *Teams* Cambridge U (1948–49, blue 1949); Otago (1955/6).
Career batting
12–14–3–235–49–21.36–0–*ct* 5
Bowling 1045–28–37.32–1–0–5/51

Hall, Patrick Martin
Amateur. *b:* 14.3.1894, Portsmouth, Hants. *d:* 5.8.1941, Fareham, Hants. Opening/middle order right-hand batsman. *Sch* Winchester. *Teams* Oxford U (1919); Hampshire (1919–26, 11 matches).
Career batting
14–23–1–292–101–13.27–1–*ct* 3

Hall, Thomas Auckland
Amateur. *b:* 19.8.1930, Durham. *d:* 21.4.1984, Rockland St Mary, Norfolk. Lower order right-hand batsman, right-arm fast medium bowler. *Sch* Uppingham. *Teams* Derbyshire (1949–52, 28 matches); Somerset (1953–54, 23 matches).
Career batting
66–103–23–892–69*–11.15–0–*ct* 29
Bowling 5108–183–27.91–4–0–5/50
His final first-class match was for Free Foresters in 1958. He also played for Norfolk.

Hall, Walter
Professional. *b:* 27.11.1861, Whitfield, Derbyshire. *d:* 23.4.1919, Halifax, Yorkshire. Lower order right-hand batsman, right-arm medium pace bowler. *Team* Derbyshire (1882–86, 11 matches).
Career batting
11–17–4–146–43–11.23–0–*ct* 9
Bowling 376–14–26.85–1–0–6/47

Hall, William
Professional. *b: circa* 1881, Bedworth, Warwickshire. *d: circa* 1930, Bedworth, Warwickshire. Lower order right-hand batsman, right-arm fast bowler. *Team* Warwickshire (1905, 2 matches).
Career batting
2–3–0–11–8–3.66–0–*ct* 2
Bowling 66–0

Hall, William Fletcher
Professional. *b:* 1853, Lindfield, Sussex. *d:* 1911, East Grinstead, Sussex. Lower order batsman, bowler. *Team* Sussex (1874, 1 match).
Career batting
1–2–0–19–18–9.50–0–*ct* 1
Bowling 57–1–57.00–0–0–1/57

Hall, Wesley Winfield
Amateur. *b:* 12.9.1937, Christchurch, Barbados. Hard hitting lower order right-hand batsman, right-arm fast bowler, good deep field, originally wicket-keeper. *Teams* Barbados (1955/6 to 1970/1); Trinidad (1966/7 to 1969/70); Queensland (1961/2 to 1962/3, 17 matches). *Tours* West Indies to England 1957, 1963, 1966, to India and Pakistan 1958/9, to India and Ceylon 1966/7, to Australia 1960/1, to Australia and New Zealand 1968/9; Commonwealth to South Africa 1962/3; Rest of the World to England 1965, 1968. *Tests* West Indies (1958/9 to 1968/9, 48 matches).
Career batting
170–215–38–2673–102*–15.10–1–*ct* 58
Bowling 14273–546–26.14–19–2–7/51
Test batting
48–66–14–818–50*–15.73–0–*ct* 11
Bowling 5066–192–26.38–9–1–7/69

Of his three Test tours to England, Hall achieved little in 1957, was at his peak in 1963 with 74 wickets, av 20.35, and in 1966 reserved his greatest efforts for the Tests. On the twin tour of India and Pakistan in 1958/9 he took no less than 48 wickets in the Tests. His bowling is chiefly associated with his partnership with C. C. Griffith, the pair being for a time the most feared fast bowling combination in the world.

Hallam, Albert William
Professional. *b:* 12.11.1869, East Leake, Notts. *d:* 24.7.1940, Loughborough, Leics. Lower order right-hand batsman, right-arm medium pace bowler. *Teams* Lancashire (1895–1900, 71 matches); Nottinghamshire (1901–10, 194 matches).
Career batting
273–365–100–2606–57–9.83–0–*ct* 171
Bowling 19255–1012–19.02–63–10–8/63

He took 100 wickets in a season three times (best 168, av 12.69, in 1907). He also appeared in non-first-class cricket for Leicestershire.

Hallam, Maurice Raymond
Professional. *b:* 10.9.1931, Leicester. Opening right-hand batsman, good close field. *Team* Leicestershire (1950–70, 493 matches).
Career batting
504–905–56–24488–210*–28.84–32–*ct* 451
Bowling 142–4–35.50–0–0–1/12

He hit 1,000 runs in a season thirteen times, going on to 2,000 in three seasons (best 2,262, av 39.68, in 1961). He made four double centuries, all for Leics, the highest being 210* v Glamorgan at Leicester in 1959. In that match he also made a century, and against Sussex at Worthing in 1961 again performed the rare feat of 200 and 100 in the same match. He captained Leics 1963–65 and in 1968.

Hallam, Thomas Haydn
Professional. *b:* 12.4.1881, Pilsley, Derbyshire. *d:* 24.11.1958, Christchurch, New Zealand. Opening/middle order right-hand batsman. *Team* Derbyshire (1906–07, 10 matches).
Career batting
10–19–0–224–68–11.78–0–*ct* 5

Halliday, Harry
Professional. *b:* 9.2.1920, Pudsey, Yorkshire. *d:* 27.8.1967, Wakefield, Yorkshire. Stylish middle order right-hand batsman, off break bowler, good slip field. *Team* Yorkshire (1938–53, 182 matches).
Career batting
187–287–18–8556–144–31.80–12–*ct* 144
Bowling 3201–107–29.91–2–0–6/79

He hit 1,000 runs in a season four times (best 1,484, av 38.05, in 1950). He also played for Cumberland.

Halliday, John Gordon
Amateur. *b:* 4.7.1915, Cockermouth, Cumberland. *d:* 3.12.1945, Rochefort, France. He was killed in an air crash. Opening right-hand batsman, right-arm medium pace bowler. *Sch* City of Oxford. *Teams* Oxford U (1934–37, blue 1935); Minor Counties (1934).
Career batting
26–42–8–848–87–24.94–0–*ct* 8
Bowling 747–21–35.57–0–0–3/11

His County cricket was for Oxfordshire, whom he captained in 1938.

Halliday, Michael
Cricketer. *b:* 20.8.1948, Dublin, Republic of Ireland. Right-hand batsman, off break bowler. *Team* Ireland (1970–83).
Career batting
10–9–4–75–30–15.00–0–*ct* 4
Bowling 594–27–22.00–1–0–5/39

Halliday, Simon John
Cricketer. *b:* 13.7.1960, Haverfordwest, Pembroke. Middle order right-hand batsman. *Sch* Downside. *Team* Oxford U (1980–82, blue 1980).

Career batting
9–14–2–348–113*–29.00–1–*ct* 3
His County cricket is for Dorset.

Halliday, Thomas Maxwell
Professional. *b:* 1.7.1904, Leyland, Lancashire. *d:* 28.2.1977, Leyland, Lancashire. Middle order right-hand batsman. *Team* Lancashire (1925–29, 41 matches).
Career batting
41–55–11–996–109*–22.63–1–*ct* 12
Bowling 16–0

Halliley, Charles
Professional. *b:* 5.12.1852, Earlsheaton, Dewsbury, Yorkshire. *d:* 1929, Dewsbury, Yorkshire. Middle order right-hand batsman, good field. *Team* Yorkshire (1872, 3 matches).
Career batting
3–5–0–27–17–5.40–0–*ct* 2

Halliwell, Ernest Austin
Amateur. *b:* 7.9.1864, Ealing, Middlesex. *d:* 2.10.1919, Johannesburg, South Africa. Son of R. B. (Middlesex). Middle order right-hand batsman, wicket-keeper. *Teams* Middlesex (1901, 1 match); London County (1901); Transvaal (1892/3 to 1908/9). *Tours* South Africa to England 1894 (not first-class), 1901, 1904. *Tests* South Africa (1891/2 to 1902/3, 8 matches).
Career batting
60–96–8–1702–92–19.34–0–*ct* 75–*st* 37
Bowling 175–3–58.33–0–0–2/49
Test batting
8–15–0–188–57–12.53–0–*ct* 9–*st* 2
His single appearance for Middlesex was made whilst he was a member of the 1901 South African touring team to England. He was the principal wicket-keeper on his three visits to England and also proved useful with the bat. Vice-captain of the 1904 side, he led South Africa in three Tests at home. He emigrated to the Gold Coast in 1882 and then moved to India, where he played much club cricket, before settling in South Africa in 1891.

Halliwell, Richard Bisset
Amateur. *b:* 30.11.1842, Bloomsbury, Middlesex. *d:* 9.11.1881, St Pancras, Middlesex. Father of E. A. (Middlesex and South Africa). Very hard hitting lower order right-hand batsman, wicket-keeper. *Team* Middlesex (1865–71, 20 matches).
Career batting
43–60–8–502–38*–9.65–0–*ct* 35–*st* 41
His final first-class match was Gentlemen v Players in 1873. He played most of his first-class cricket under various aliases.

Hallows, Charles
Professional. *b:* 4.4.1895, Little Lever, Lancashire. *d:* 10.11.1972, Bolton, Lancashire. Nephew of James (Lancashire). Opening left-hand batsman, slow left-arm bowler, good deep field. *Team* Lancashire (1914–32, 370 matches). *Tests* England (1921–28, 2 matches)
Career batting
383–586–66–20926–233*–40.24–55–*ct* 140
Bowling 784–19–41.26–0–0–3/28
Test batting 2–2–1–42–26–42.00–0–*ct* 0
He hit 1,000 runs in a season eleven times, going on to 2,000 on three occasions (best 2,645, av 64.51, in 1928). His three double centuries were all for Lancashire, the highest being 233* v Hampshire at Liverpool in 1927. In 1928 he hit exactly 1,000 runs (av 125.00) in the month of May. After retiring from first-class cricket he was chief coach at Worcester for five years and then held the same post at Old Trafford.

Hallows, James
Professional. *b:* 14.11.1873, Little Lever, Lancashire. *d:* 20.5.1910, Farnworth, Lancashire. Uncle of Charles (Lancashire). Middle order left-hand batsman, originally fast left-arm bowler, but changed to medium in 1897. *Team* Lancashire (1898–1907, 138 matches).
Career batting
139–203–27–5065–137*–28.77–8–*ct* 57
Bowling 6677–287–23.26–14–5–9/37
His great season was 1904 when he performed the 'double', taking 108 wickets, av 19.37, and scoring 1,071 runs, av 39.66. He hit 1,000 runs in a season twice (best 1,170, av 31.62, in 1901). His best bowling was 9/37 for Lancashire v Gloucs at Gloucester in 1904. He suffered from epilepsy and his career was marred by ill health.

Halsey, Sir Thomas Edgar
Amateur. *b:* 28.11.1898, South Mimms, Herts. *d:* 30.8.1970, Hemel Hempstead, Herts. Middle order right-hand batsman, right-arm fast bowler. *Sch* Eton. *Teams* Cambridge U (1920); Royal Navy (1920–28).
Career batting
12–23–5–685–102*–38.05–1–*ct* 5
Bowling 388–7–55.42–0–0–2/78
His County cricket was for Hertfordshire.

Hamblin, Christopher Bryan
Cricketer. *b:* 14.4.1952, Kenley, Surrey. Lower order right-hand batsman, right-arm medium pace bowler. *Sch* King's, Canterbury. *Team* Oxford U (1971–73, blue all three years).
Career batting
29–45–10–693–123*–19.80–1–*ct* 13
Bowling 1696–38–44.63–0–0–4/32

Hambling, Montague Leslie
Amateur. *b:* 6.12.1893, Croydon, Surrey. *d:* 22.8.1960, Stoke Bishop, Gloucs. Middle order right-hand batsman, right-arm fast bowler. *Team* Somerset (1920–27, 18 matches).
Career batting
18–30–4–350–59–13.46–0–*ct* 16
Bowling 493–24–20.54–1–0–6/31
He was also a good soccer player and golfer.

Hamence, Ronald Arthur
Amateur. *b:* 25.11.1915, Hindmarsh, Adelaide, Australia. Middle order right-hand batsman, good outfield. *Team* South Australia (1935/6 to 1950/1, 69 matches). *Tours* Australia to New Zealand 1945/6, to England 1948. *Tests* Australia (1946/7 to 1947/8, 3 matches).
Career batting
99–155–15–5285–173–37.75–11–*ct* 34
Bowling 239–8–29.87–0–0–2/13
Test batting 3–4–1–81–30*–27.00–0–*ct* 1
Owing to the success of the principal batsmen, Hamence had little opportunity to shine on his tour to England and was not required for the Tests.

Hamer, Arnold
Professional. *b:* 8.12.1916, Huddersfield, Yorkshire. Sound opening right-hand batsman, off break bowler. *Teams* Yorkshire (1938, 2 matches); Derbyshire (1950–60, 290 matches).
Career batting
295–515–19–15465–227–31.17–19–*ct* 164
Bowling 2363–71–33.28–0–0–4/27
He hit 1,000 runs in a season 10 times (best 1,850, av 36.27, in 1959). His only double century was 227 for Derbyshire v Notts at Trent Bridge in 1955. A useful soccer player, he appeared for York City.

Hamilton, Andrew Carodoc
Cricketer. *b:* 23.9.1953, Ardingly, Sussex. Opening left-hand batsman, slow left-arm bowler. *Sch* Charterhouse. *Team* Oxford U (1975–76, blue 1975).
Career batting
12–24–0–308–45–12.83–0–*ct* 2
Bowling 6–0

Hamilton, Blayney Balfour
Amateur. *b:* 13.6.1872, Mellifont, Collon, Co Louth. *d:* 16.12.1946, Dublin. Brother of W. D. (Oxford). Middle order right-hand batsman, slow left-arm bowler. *Sch* Haileybury. *Team* Ireland (1907).
Career batting
1–2–0–4–4–2.00–0–*ct* 2
Bowling 21–0

Hamilton, Cyril Penn
Amateur. *b:* 12.8.1909, Adelaide, Australia. *d:* 10.2.1941, Cheren, Eritrea. Opening right-hand batsman, right-arm slow bowler. *Sch* Wellington. *Teams* Army (1932–36); Kent (1935, 2 matches).
Career batting
8–13–1–475–121–39.58–2–*ct* 8
Bowling 203–6–33.83–1–0–5/83

Hamilton, Lord George Francis
Amateur. *b:* 17.12.1845, Brighton, Sussex. *d:* 22.9.1927, Marylebone, London. Lower order right-hand batsman, right-hand fast under-arm bowler, good field. *Sch* Harrow. *Team* MCC (1864).
Career batting
1–2–0–7–5–3.50–0–*ct* 0
Bowling 12–0
First Lord of the Admiralty for six years, then Secretary of State for India for eight years, he was MP for County of Middlesex 1868–85, and for Ealing Division 1885–1906. He was President of the MCC 1881, being a member for 64 years.

Hamilton, Canon the Rev Hamilton Anne
(in 1875 he assumed the name Douglas-Hamilton)
Amateur. *b:* 28.5.1853, Simla, India. *d:* 22.8.1929, Marlesford, Suffolk. Middle/lower order right-hand batsman, right-hand fast round-arm bowler, wicket-keeper. *Sch* Wellington. *Team* Cambridge U (1873–75, blue 1873, 1875).
Career batting
15–26–9–204–37–12.00–0–*ct* 12–*st* 7
Bowling 269–8–31.12–0–0–4/80
He also represented Cambridge at rugby football.

Hamilton, Leonard Alison Hall
Amateur. *b:* 23.12.1862, Mt Abu, India. *d:* 14.3.1957, Umberleigh, Devon. Middle order right-hand batsman. *Sch* Tonbridge. *Team* Kent (1890–92, 20 matches).
Career batting
21–37–2–645–117*–18.42–1–*ct* 7
Bowling 50–2–25.00–0–0–2/24
His final first-class match was for MCC in 1893.

Hamilton, William Drummond
Amateur. *b:* 4.5.1859, Mellifont, Collon, Co Louth. *d:* 4.3.1914, Oxford. Brother of B. B. (Ireland). Middle order left-hand batsman. *Sch* Haileybury. *Team* Oxford U (1882, blue).
Career batting
9–17–2–310–54–20.66–0–*ct* 5
He was so nervous when appearing at Lord's

in the University Match that when called for a run, he started off in the wrong direction! His final first-class match was for MCC in 1883.

Hammersley, William Josiah
Amateur. *b:* 25.9.1826, Ash, Surrey. *d:* 15.11.1886, Fitzroy, Victoria, Australia. Lower order right-hand batsman, right-hand medium pace round-arm bowler. *Teams* Cambridge U (1847, blue); Surrey (1848–59, 4 matches); Victoria (1856/7 to 1860/1, 5 matches).
Career batting
34–60–5–567–46–10.30–0–*ct* 23–*st* 1
Bowling 42–9+41–4.66–2–1–6/?
He was Editor of Cricketers' Register for Australia. His last first-class match in England was for Gentlemen in 1854.

Hammond, Charles James
Professional. *b:* 6.9.1818, Storrington, Sussex. *d:* July 1901, Storrington. Son of John (Sussex), uncle of Ernest (Sussex). Opening/middle order right-hand batsman. *Teams* Sussex (1841–54, 40 matches).
Career batting
49–89–8–1045–92–12.90–0–*ct* 19
Bowling 4–0+2–no av–0–0–2/?
A noted batsman, he made only restricted appearances in important matches due to poor fielding.

Hammond, Ernest
Professional. *b:* 29.7.1850, Storrington, Sussex. *d:* 31.7.1921, Storrington, Sussex. Nephew of C. J. (Sussex), grandson of John (Sussex). Middle order right-hand batsman, right-hand slow round-arm bowler. *Team* Sussex (1870, 5 matches).
Career batting
5–8–1–16–5–2.28–0–*ct* 2
Owing to ill-health his County cricket was very limited.

Hammond, Herbert Edward
Professional. *b:* 7.11.1907, Brighton, Sussex. Steady opening/middle order right-hand batsman, right-arm medium pace bowler. *Team* Sussex (1928–46, 196 matches).
Career batting
196–267–40–4251–103*–18.72–1–*ct* 170
Bowling 12290–428–28.73–16–1–8/76
He was a noted inside forward with Fulham FC.

Hammond, John
Professional. *b:* 15.1.1769, Pulborough, Sussex. *d:* 15.10.1844, Storrington, Sussex. Father of C. J. (Sussex), grandfather of Ernest (Sussex). Hard hitting middle order left-hand batsman, right-hand slow semi-round arm bowler, wicket-keeper. *Teams* Sussex (1790–1816); Kent (1806).
Career batting
51–90–6–1490–108–17.73–1–*ct* 47–*st* 62
Bowling 45 wickets, no analyses
He was regarded as one of the best all-round cricketers of his day, though many of his best performances no doubt are unrecorded. His first important match (after 1800) was for England in 1801.

Hammond, Jeffrey Roy
Cricketer. *b:* 19.4.1950, East Torrens, Adelaide, Australia. Lower order right-hand batsman, right-arm fast medium bowler. *Team* South Australia (1969/70 to 1980/1, 46 matches). *Tours* Australia to England 1972, to West Indies 1972/3. *Tests* Australia (1972/3, 5 matches).
Career batting
69–87–31–922–53–16.46–0–*ct* 36
Bowling 5315–184–28.88–8–0–6/15
Test batting
5–5–2–28–19–9.33–0–*ct* 2
Bowling 488–15–32.53–0–0–4/38
A strained back prevented him bowling at his best on his 1972 tour to England and he was not required for the Tests.

Hammond, Reginald Joseph Leslie
Amateur. *b:* 16.12.1909, Battersea, London. Opening right-hand batsman, wicket-keeper. *Team* Combined Services (1948).
Career batting
6–11–0–199–46–18.09–0–*ct* 6–*st* 3

Hammond, Walter Reginald
Professional, changed to amateur at start of 1938 season. *b:* 19.6.1903, Dover, Kent. *d:* 1.7.1965, Durban, South Africa. Middle order right-hand batsman, right-arm medium fast bowler, brilliant close field. *Teams* Gloucestershire (1920–51, 405 matches); South African Air Force (1942/3). *Tours* MCC to West Indies 1925/6, 1934/5, to South Africa 1927/8, 1930/1, 1938/9, to Australia 1928/9, to Australia and New Zealand 1932/3, 1936/7, 1946/7. *Tests* England (1927/8 to 1946/7, 85 matches).
Career batting
634–1005–104–50551–336*–56.10–167–*ct* 819–*st* 3
Bowling 22389–732–30.58–22–3–9/23
Test batting
85–140–16–7249–336*–58.45–22–*ct* 110
Bowling 3138–83–37.80–2–0–5/36
The greatest English batsman of his generation, Hammond statistically dominated County cricket during the 1930s and his achievement of heading the first-class batting averages for eight successive summers (1933–46) has never been equalled. He

completed 1,000 runs in 17 English seasons plus five overseas ones, on twelve occasions went on to top 2,000 and three times exceeded 3,000. His best year was 1933 with 3,323 runs, av 67.81. In no less than five seasons he hit over ten centuries and his tally of 36 double centuries in his career is a figure not remotely approached by another English cricketer. Of his triple centuries, three were for Gloucestershire, but the highest was 336* for England v New Zealand at Auckland in 1932/3, which created a Test record.

His career was rather slow to mature. First he was prevented from appearing in County Championship matches for Gloucestershire because he was not properly qualified, then in 1926 illness prevented him playing any first-class cricket. The following season however he had great success and being picked to go with MCC to South Africa won a place in the England team, which he held until his retirement from regular County cricket, after the 1946 season. He was to appear in a single match in 1950 and make a final appearance in 1951.

In 1928, for Gloucs v Surrey, he took ten catches, a first-class record except for wicket-keepers. In the same match he scored a century in each innings, a feat he performed seven times in all. His best bowling was 9/23 for Gloucs v Worcs at Cheltenham in 1928.

In 1938, when he became an amateur, he was chosen to captain England and led his country in 20 Tests and the MCC on two major overseas tours (1938/9 and 1946/7). He also captained Gloucestershire in 1939 and 1946.

Apart from his batting he was a brilliant slip field and a very useful bowler.

He played football for Bristol Rovers.

Hammond-Chambers-Borgnis, R. P.
(see under Borgnis, R. P.)

Hampshire, Alan Wesley
Cricketer. *b:* 18.10.1950, Rotherham, Yorkshire. Son of John (Yorkshire), brother of J. H. (Yorkshire and Derbyshire). Middle order right-hand batsman, right-arm medium pace bowler. *Team* Yorkshire (1975, 1 match).
Career batting
1–2–0–18–17–9.00–0–*ct* 1

Hampshire, John
Professional. *b:* 5.10.1913, Goldthorpe, Yorkshire. Father of A. W. (Yorkshire) and J. H. (Yorkshire and Derbyshire). Lower order right-hand batsman, right-arm fast bowler. *Team* Yorkshire (1937, 3 matches).
Career batting
3–2–0–5–5–2.50–0–*ct* 1
Bowling 109–5–21.80–0–0–2/22
He played football for Bristol City.

Hampshire, John Harry
Professional. *b* 10.2.1941, Thurnscoe, Yorkshire. Son of John (Yorks), brother of A.W. (Yorkshire). Attacking middle order right-hand batsman, leg break bowler, good field. *Teams* Yorkshire (1961–81, 456 matches); Tasmania (1967/8 to 1978/9, 15 matches); Leicestershire (1980/1, 3 matches); Derbyshire (1982–83, 37 matches). *Tours* MCC to Ceylon 1969/70, to Australia and New Zealand 1970/1; Cavaliers to West Indies 1964/5; Commonwealth to Pakistan 1967/8; Robins to South Africa 1972/3, to West Indies 1974/5 (not first-class); Leicestershire to Zimbabwe 1980/1. *Tests* England (1969–75, 8 matches).
Career batting
556–892–108–27267–183*–34.77–42–*ct* 426
Bowling 1637–30–54.56–2–0–7/52
Test batting
8–16–1–403–107–26.86–1–*ct* 9
He hit 1,000 runs in a season 15 times (best 1,596, av 53.20, in 1978). In 1979 and 1980 he captained Yorkshire.

Hampson, Arthur Harry
Professional. *b:* 1878, Earl Shilton, Leics. *d:* 24.11.1952, Earl Shilton, Leics. Lower order right-hand batsman, wicket-keeper. *Team* Leicestershire (1905–06, 11 matches).
Career batting
11–18–4–100–23–7.14–0–*ct* 9–*st* 7

Hampson, James Frederick
Amateur. *b:* 19.12.1877, Altrincham, Cheshire. *d:* 26.1.1931, Withington, Lancashire. Lower order batsman, bowler. *Sch* Rugby. *Team* London County (1901).
Career batting
2–2–0–18–17–9.00–0–*ct* 1
Bowling 29–2–24.50–0–0–1/1

Hampton, William Marcus
Amateur. *b:* 20.1.1903, Bromsgrove, Worcs. *d:* 7.4.1964, Ogdens, Fordingbridge, Hants. Middle order right-hand batsman, off break bowler. *Sch* Clifton. *Teams* Warwickshire (1922, 1 match); Worcestershire (1925–26, 12 matches).
Career batting
13–25–1–332–57–13.83–0–*ct* 8
Bowling 26–1–26.00–0–0–1/11

Hanbury, Edwin Charles
Amateur. *b:* 23.6.1848, Clapham Park, Surrey.

d: 1914, Thanet, Kent. Middle order right-hand batsman. *Team* Surrey (1871, 3 matches).
Career batting
3–6–2–44–17–11.00–0–*ct* 0

Hanbury, T. P.
Amateur. *Team* MCC (1882).
Career batting
1–1–1–0–0*–no av–0–*ct* 0

Hancock, Joseph (William)
Professional. *b:* 26.11.1876, Old Tupton, Derbyshire. *d:* 23.5.1939, Rotherham, Yorkshire. Lower order left-hand batsman, left-arm medium pace bowler. *Teams* Derbyshire (1897–1900, 47 matches); Scotland (1906).
Career batting
48–77–19–459–43*–7.91–0–*ct* 21
Bowling 2795–94–29.73–1–0–5/61

Hancock, Leslie Frank
Amateur. *b:* 25.10.1899, Jamnagar, India. *d:* 12.7.1944, Normandy, France. Middle/lower order right-hand batsman, right-arm medium fast bowler. *Sch* Cheltenham. *Team* MCC (1926).
Career batting
2–2–0–24–23–12.00–0–*ct* 3
Bowling 24–1–24.00–0–0–1/4

Hancock, Ralph Escott
Amateur. *b:* 20.12.1887, Cardiff. *d:* 29.10.1914, Festubert, France. Middle order right-hand batsman, change bowler. *Sch* Rugby. *Team* Somerset (1907–14, 9 matches).
Career batting
9–17–0–206–34–12.11–0–*ct* 0
Bowling 29–0

Hancock, William Ilbert
Amateur. *b:* 10.4.1873, Wiveliscombe, Somerset. *d:* 26.1.1910, Marylebone, London. Middle order batsman. *Sch* Dulwich. *Team* Somerset (1892, 1 match).
Career batting
1–2–0–7–7–3.50–0–*ct* 0

Handford, Alick
Professional. *b:* 3.5.1869, Wilford, Notts. *d:* 15.10.1935, Tavistock, Devon. Lower order right-hand batsman, right-arm medium pace bowler. *Teams* Nottinghamshire (1894–98, 15 matches); Southland (1914/5).
Career batting
25–36–9–262–24*–9.70–0–*ct* 16
Bowling 1664–59–28.20–5–0–7/39

His final first-class match in England was for MCC in 1901.

Handford, James
Professional. *b:* 1.2.1890, Hayfield, Derbyshire. *d:* 14.8.1948, Stockport, Cheshire. Middle order right-hand batsman. *Team* Derbyshire (1910, 9 matches).
Career batting
9–17–3–137–23–9.78–0–*ct* 4
Bowling 31–0

Hands, Barry Onslow
Amateur. *b:* 26.9.1916, Moseley, Birmingham. Lower order left-hand batsman, right-arm off break bowler. *Team* Warwickshire (1946–47, 3 matches).
Career batting
3–2–0–13–9–6.50–0–*ct* 0
Bowling 137–4–34.25–0–0–3/76

Hands, Kenneth Charles Myburgh
Amateur. *b:* 22.3.1892, Stellenbosch, South Africa. *d:* 18.11.1954, Darys, Orange Free State, South Africa. Brother of P. A. M. and R. H. M. (South Africa). Middle order right-hand batsman. *Teams* Oxford U (1912); Western Province (1921/2 to 1930/1).
Career batting
31–60–7–1543–171*–29.11–3–*ct* 12
Bowling 568–17–33.29–0–0–4/25

A noted rugby footballer, he was awarded his blue at Oxford.

Hands, Philip Albert Myburgh
Amateur. *b:* 18.3.1890, Claremont, Cape Town, South Africa. *d:* 27.4.1951, Paris, France. Brother of K. C. M. (Oxford U) and R. H. M. (South Africa). Middle order right-hand batsman. *Team* Western Province (1906/7 to 1926/7). *Tour* South Africa to England 1924. *Tests* South Africa (1913/14 to 1924, 7 matches).
Career batting
52–86–5–2034–119–25.11–3–*ct* 20
Bowling 84–5–16.80–0–0–3/9
Test batting
7–12–0–300–83–25.00–0–*ct* 3
Bowling 18–0

He had a very moderate tour to England in 1924, appearing in only one Test.

Hands, William Cecil
Amateur. *b:* 20.12.1886, Birmingham. *d:* 31.8.1974, Northwood, Middlesex. Lower order right-hand batsman, right-arm medium fast bowler. *Sch* KES Birmingham. *Team* Warwickshire (1909–20, 60 matches).
Career batting
60–91–23–856–63–12.58–0–*ct* 36
Bowling 3509–142–24.71–3–0–5/10

Business prevented him appearing regularly in County cricket.

Hanif Mohammad
Amateur. *b:* 21.12.1934, Junagadh, India. Brother of Wazir, Mushtaq and Sadiq (Pakistan) and Raees (Karachi), father of Shoaib (PIA and Pakistan), uncle of Shahid and Asif (PIA). Steady opening right-hand batsman, off break bowler, occasional wicket-keeper. *Teams* Karachi (1954/5 to 1968/9); Bahawalpur (1953/4); PIA (1960/1 to 1975/6). *Tours* Pakistan to England 1954, 1962, 1967, to Australia and New Zealand 1964/5, to India 1952/3, 1960/1, to West Indies 1957/8; Rest of World to England 1968; International XI to South Africa 1961/2; Rest of the World to England 1965, 1966. *Tests* Pakistan (1952/3 to 1969/70, 55 matches).
Career batting
238–370–44–17059–499–52.32–55–*ct* 178–*st* 12
Bowling 1509–53–28.50–0–0–3/4
Test batting
55–97–8–3915–337–43.98–12–*ct* 40
Bowling 95–1–95.00–0–0–1/1

He scored over 1,000 runs in 1954 and 1962 in England (best 1,623, av 36.88, in 1954), but considering his reputation, he never really succeeded in England and in the five 1962 Tests was in fact a complete failure. He captained the 1967 tourists in England and altogether led Pakistan in 11 Tests. His highest score is the world record 499 for Karachi v Bahawalpur at Karachi in 1958/9 and his highest Test score 337 v West Indies at Bridgetown in 1957/8. None of his seven scores over 200 were made in England. His first-class debut was for Karachi and Bahawalpur in 1951/2.

Hankey, Reginald
Amateur. *b:* 3.11.1832, Marylebone, Middlesex. *d:* 25.8.1886, Brighton, Sussex. Middle order right-hand batsman, right-hand medium round-arm bowler. *Sch* Harrow. *Teams* Oxford U (1853–55, blue 1853 and 1855); Surrey (1855, 1 match).
Career batting
18–34–1–489–70–14.81–0–*ct* 9
Bowling 200–10+12–20.00–0–0–4/?

He was regarded as one of the best amateur bats of his day, but business restricted his appearances in important cricket. He also played for Oxfordshire. His final first-class match was for MCC in 1860.

Hanley, Rupert William
Cricketer. *b* 29.1.1952, Port Elizabeth, South Africa. Tail end right hand batsman, right-arm fast bowler. *Teams* Eastern Province (1970/1 to 1974/5); D.H. Robins XI (1974); Orange Free State (1975/6); Transvaal (1976/7 to 1982/3).
Career batting
83–65–35–174–18–5.80–0–*ct* 32
Bowling 6436–326–19.74–18–2–6/27

His single appearance in English first-class cricket was for D.H. Robins' XI in 1974.

Hanna, Michael
Amateur. *b:* 6.6.1926, London. Lower order right-hand batsman, wicket-keeper. *Team* Somerset (1951–54, 2 matches).
Career batting
2–3–1–5–4*–2.50–0–*ct* 0

He was a noted rugby scrum-half with Bath and Somerset.

Hannay, Charles Scott
Amateur. *b:* 2.11.1879, West Derby, Liverpool. *d:* 27.6.1955, Aigburgh, Liverpool. Middle order right-hand batsman, right-arm medium pace bowler, good field. *Sch* Rugby. *Team* Oxford U (1901).
Career batting
1–2–0–24–20–12.00–0–*ct* 0

Hansell, Thomas Michael Geoffrey
Cricketer. *b:* 24.8.1954, Sutton Coldfield, Warwickshire. Middle order left-hand batsman, slow left-arm bowler. *Sch* Millfield. *Team* Surrey (1975–77, 14 matches).
Career batting
14–26–5–319–54–15.19–0–*ct* 2
Bowling 0–0

Hanson, Raymond Leslie
Cricketer. *b:* 12.4.1951, Chesterfield, Derbyshire. Lower order right-hand batsman, wicket-keeper. *Team* Derbyshire (1973, 1 match).
Career batting
1–1–1–1–1*–no av–0–*ct* 1

He also played for Lincolnshire.

Hanumant Singh
(Maharajkumar of Banswara)
Amateur. *b:* 29.3.1939, Banswara, India. Middle order right-hand batsman, leg break bowler. *Teams* Madhya Bharat (1956/7); Rajasthan (1957/8 to 1978/9). *Tour* India to England 1967. *Tests* India (1963/4 to 1969/70, 14 matches).
Career batting
206–331–50–12338–213*–43.90–29–*ct* 110
Bowling 2293–56–40.94–1–0–5/48
Test batting
14–24–2–686–105–31.18–1–*ct* 11
Bowling 51–0

He looked a better player than his figures with the bat (554, av 29.35) indicated on his single tour to England, and appeared in two Tests. His highest score was 213* for Rajasthan v Bombay at Bombay in 1966/7. He hit 1,000 runs in India in three seasons (best 1,586 av 68.95, in 1966/7).

Harben, Henry Eric Southey
Amateur. *b:* 1.8.1900, Farnham, Surrey. *d:* 1.10.1971, Malta. Middle order right-hand batsman, change bowler. *Sch* Eton. *Team* Sussex (1919, 4 matches).
Career batting
4–8–2–126–34–21.00–0–*ct* 1
Bowling 36–0

Harber, John
Professional. *b:* 1889, Worcestershire. *d:* 11.8.1962, Croome, Worcestershire. Lower order right-hand batsman, bowler. *Team* Worcestershire (1914, 1 match).
Career batting
1–2–0–3–3–1.50–0–*ct* 0
Bowling 46–3–15.33–0–0–2/24

Harbin, Dr Leonard
Amateur. *b:* 30.4.1915, Trinidad. Lower order right-hand batsman, off break bowler. *Teams* Trinidad (1935/6 to 1940/1); Gloucestershire (1949–51, 4 matches).
Career batting
12–18–1–337–89–19.82–*ct* 11
Bowling 633–25–25.32–1–0–5/80

Harbinson, William Kenneth
Amateur. *b:* 11.7.1906, Kilwaughter, Co Antrim. Steady middle order right-hand batsman, right-arm medium fast bowler, fine extra cover. *Sch* Marlborough. *Team* Cambridge U (1926–29, blue 1929).
Career batting
14–22–2–604–130–30.20–2–*ct* 6
Bowling 91–2–45.50–0–0–1/14

Harbord, William Edward
Amateur. *b:* 15.12.1908, Oakham, Rutland. Opening/middle order right-hand batsman, change bowler. *Sch* Eton. *Teams* Yorkshire (1929–35, 16 matches); Oxford U (1930). *Tours* Martineau to Egypt 1934 (not first-class); MCC to West Indies 1934/5.
Career batting
21–29–1–512–109–18.28–1–*ct* 9
Bowling 15–0

He was for many years on the Yorkshire CCC Committee.

Harbottle, Michael Neale
Amateur. *b:* 7.2.1917, Littlehampton, Sussex. Middle order left-hand batsman, slow left-arm bowler. *Sch* Marlborough. *Team* Army (1938).
Career batting
1–1–0–156–156–156.00–1–*ct* 0

His first-class career is noteworthy because he hit 156 in his only innings.

His County cricket was for Dorset.

Harcombe, John Dowie
Amateur. *b:* 1884, South Africa. *d:* 19.7.1954, Taunton, Somerset. Middle order right-hand batsman, right-arm slow bowler. *Sch* Taunton. *Team* Somerset (1905–19, 7 matches).
Career batting
7–12–2–76–29–7.60–0–*ct* 2
Bowling 132–3–44.00–0–0–3/51

Harcourt, Aubrey
Amateur. *b:* 16.8.1852. *d:* 22.3.1904, Monte Carlo, Monaco. *Sch* Eton. *Team* Lord Sheffield XI (1891).
Career batting
1–1–0–0–0–0.00–0–*ct* 0

Harcourt, Arthur Bryan
Amateur. *b:* 14.11.1917, South Africa. Lower order right-hand batsman, wicket-keeper. *Team* Oxford U (1947).
Career batting
4–8–2–76–25*–12.66–0–*ct* 4–*st* 3

Hardcastle, Ven Edward Hoare
Amateur. *b:* 6.3.1862, Manchester, Lancashire. *d:* 20.5.1945, Brighton, Sussex. Lower order left-hand batsman, left-arm fast bowler. *Sch* Winchester. *Team* Kent (1883–84, 2 matches).
Career batting
2–2–0–12–7–6.00–0–*ct* 4
Bowling 64–3–21.33–0–0–3/29

He also appeared for Worcestershire (not first-class), but whilst at Cambridge U did not play in the eleven.

Hardcastle, Frank
Amateur. *b:* 12.5.1844, Bolton, Lancashire. *d:* 6.11.1908, Lancaster Gate, London. Middle order batsman. *Sch* Repton. *Team* Lancashire (1868–69, 2 matches).
Career batting
2–4–1–17–9–5.66–0–*ct* 1

He was MP for Westhoughton from 1885 to 1892.

Hardcastle, Walter Mitchell
Amateur. *b:* 1843, Bolton, Lancashire. *d:* 27.4.1901, Bolton, Lancashire. Middle order

right-hand batsman, right-arm fast bowler. *Team* Lancashire (1869–74, 4 matches).
Career batting
4–7–0–33–11–4.71–0–*ct* 1

Hardie, Brian Ross
Cricketer. *b* 14.1.1950, Stenhousemuir, Stirlingshire, Scotland. Brother of K. M. (Scotland). Middle order right-hand batsman, right-arm medium pace bowler, close field. *Teams* Scotland (1970–72); Essex (1973–83, 230 matches).
Career batting
234–383–44–11502–162–33.92–14–*ct* 214
Bowling 80–2–40.00–0–0–2/39

He hit 1,000 runs in a season eight times (best 1,522, av 43.48, in 1975).

Hardie, J.
Amateur. *Team* Australians in England (in emergency) (1886).
Career batting
1–1–0–0–0–0.00–0–*ct* 0

Hardie, Keith Millar
Cricketer. *b:* 13.5.1947, Larbert, Stirlingshire, Scotland. Brother of B. R. (Essex). Right-hand batsman, slow left-arm bowler. *Team* Scotland (1966–76).
Career batting
10–11–4–158–65*–22.57–0–*ct* 1
Bowling 626–35–17.88–0–0–4/23

Harding, Kenneth
Amateur. *b:* 12.2.1892, Greenwich, Kent. *d:* 30.11.1977, Eastbourne, Sussex. Middle order right-hand batsman. *Sch* St Edward's, Oxford. *Team* Sussex (1928, 3 matches).
Career batting
3–6–1–91–55*–18.20–0–*ct* 0

Despite losing part of his right hand in the First World War, he was a most successful batsman in Sussex Club cricket in the 1920s and gained a trial for the County.

Harding, Norman Walter
Professional. *b:* 19.3.1916, Woolston, Hants. *d:* 25.9.1947, Abingdon, Berkshire. Lower order right-hand batsman, right-arm fast bowler. *Sch* Reading. *Team* Kent (1937–47, 83 matches).
Career batting
84–123–22–966–71–9.56–0–*ct* 55
Bowling 6531–229–28.51–9–1–5/31

He appeared as an amateur for Berkshire before joining Kent. For Kent 2nd XI v Wiltshire at Swindon in 1936 he took 18 wickets for 100 (nine in each innings), a feat unique in Minor County Championship cricket.

Hardinge, Harold Thomas William
Professional. *b:* 25.2.1886, Greenwich, Kent. *d:* 8.5.1965, Cambridge, Kent. Opening right-hand batsman, slow left-arm bowler. *Team* Kent (1902–33, 606 matches). *Test* England (1921, 1 match).
Career batting
623–1021–103–33519–263*–36.51–75–*ct* 297
Bowling 9825–371–26.48–8–1–7/64
Test batting
1–2–0–30–25–15.00–0–*ct* 0

He hit 1,000 runs in a season eighteen times, going on to 2,000 five times (best 2,446, av 59.65, in 1928). His four double centuries were all for Kent, his highest being 263* v Gloucs at Gloucester in 1928.

An inside-left, he was a noted soccer player with Newcastle United, Sheffield United and Arsenal, and was capped for England in 1910. He was employed for many years by the sports goods firm, John Wisden and Co.

Hardisty, Charles Henry
Professional. *b:* 10.12.1885, Wharfedale, Yorkshire. *d:* 2.3.1968, Leeds, Yorkshire. Middle order right-hand batsman, moderate field. *Team* Yorkshire (1906–09, 38 matches).
Career batting
39–57–5–998–84–19.19–0–*ct* 20

He also played for Northumberland.

Hardstaff, Joseph (sen)
Professional. *b:* 9.11.1882, Kirkby-in-Ashfield, Notts. *d:* 2.4.1947, Nuncargate, Notts. Father of Joseph jun (Notts), grandfather of Joseph (Free Foresters). Middle order right-hand batsman, right-arm fast medium bowler, excellent outfield. *Team* Nottinghamshire (1902–24, 340 matches). *Tour* MCC to Australia 1907/8. *Tests* England (1907/8, 5 matches).
Career batting
377–620–73–17146–213*–31.34–26–*ct* 187–*st* 2
Bowling 2244–58–38.68–1–0–5/133
Test batting
5–10–0–311–72–31.10–0–*ct* 1

He hit 1,000 runs in a season seven times plus once overseas (best 1,547, av 45.50, in 1911). His only double century was 213* for Notts v Sussex at Hove in 1914. His final first-class match was for MCC in 1926. He became well-known as an umpire, going with MCC to West Indies in that capacity in 1929/30, and officiated in Test Matches until the inclusion of his son in the England side prevented this. He played football for Nottingham Forest.

Hardstaff, Joseph (jun)
Professional. *b:* 3.7.1911, Nuncargate, Notts. Son

of Joseph sen (Notts), father of Joseph (Free Foresters). Middle order right-hand batsman, right-arm medium pace bowler, excellent outfield. *Teams* Nottinghamshire (1930–55, 408 matches); Services in India (1943/4 to 1944/5); Europeans (1944/5); Auckland (1948/9 to 1949/50). *Tours* MCC to Australia and New Zealand 1935/6, 1936/7, 1946/7, to West Indies 1947/8; Tennyson to India 1937/8; Cahn to New Zealand 1938/9. *Tests* England (1935–48, 23 matches).
Career batting
517–812–94–31847–266–44.35–83–*ct* 123
Bowling 2141–36–59.47–0–0–4/43
Test batting
23–38–3–1636–205*–46.74–4–*ct* 9

Regarded as the most elegant batsman of his generation, Hardstaff rarely failed in County cricket, scoring over 1,000 runs in an English season 13 times and going on to 2,000 four times. His highest season's aggregate was 2,540, av 57.72, in 1937, but his best year was 1949 when he was the leading batsman in the country with 2,251 runs, av 72.61. In all he hit ten double centuries, eight of which were for Notts, including the highest – 266 v Leicestershire at Leicester in 1937. Of the other two, one was for England v India at Lord's in 1946 and the second for Lord Tennyson's Team in India in 1937/38.

He was a regular member of the England team in the three seasons before the Second World War, but failed to regain a permanent Test place after 1946.

His appearance for Auckland in 1949/50 caused some controversy, since it was claimed that in playing for Notts and Auckland he was representing two 'counties' in the same year.

Hardstaff, Joseph
Amateur. *b:* 28.2.1935, Kirkby-in-Ashfield, Notts. Grandson of Joseph sen, son of Joseph jun (both Notts). Middle order right-hand batsman, right-arm medium pace bowler. *Team* Free Foresters (1961–62).
Career batting
2–4–0–57–36–14.25–0–*ct* 0
Bowling 32–1–32.00–0–0–1/32

A well-known player in Services cricket, he captained the RAF.

Hardstaff, Richard (Green)
Professional. *b:* 12.1.1863, Selston, Notts. *d:* 18.4.1932, Selston, Notts. Lower order left-hand batsman, left-arm medium pace bowler. *Team* Nottinghamshire (1887–99, 30 matches).
Career batting
30–41–10–252–60–8.12–0–*ct* 17
Bowling 1988–100–19.88–8–3–8/53

His County career ended in 1899 when he was no-balled for throwing.

Hardy, David
Professional. *b:* 1878, Northampton. *d:* 22.1.1951, Northampton. Lower order right-hand batsman, right-arm medium pace bowler. *Team* Northants (1907–24, 37 matches).
Career batting
37–62–13–499–37–10.18–0–*ct* 15
Bowling 584–14–41.71–1–0–6/11

Hardy, Donald Wrightson
Cricketer. *b:* 24.3.1926, East Boldon, Co Durham. Middle order right-hand batsman, right-arm medium pace bowler. *Team* Minor Counties (1965).
Career batting
1–2–0–29–29–14.50–0–*ct* 1

His County cricket was for Durham commencing 1948.

Hardy, Evan Michael Pearce
Amateur. *b:* 13.11.1927, Meerut, India. Middle order right-hand batsman. *Sch* Ampleforth. *Team* Combined Services (1959).
Career batting
1–2–0–15–15–7.50–0–*ct* 1

An excellent rugby footballer he was capped for England.

Hardy, Frederick Percey
Professional. *b:* 26.6.1880, Blandford, Dorset. *d:* 9.3.1916, London. He was found dead at King's Cross Station. Middle order left-hand batsman, right-arm medium pace bowler. *Team* Somerset (1902–14, 99 matches).
Career batting
100–176–8–2743–91–16.32–0–*ct* 41
Bowling 3216–91–35.34–2–0–6/82

He also played for Dorset.

Hardy, Michael John
Amateur. *b:* 30.7.1929, Hendon, Middlesex. Hard hitting middle order batsman. *Sch* Oundle. *Team* D. R. Jardine's XI (1958).
Career batting
1–2–0–15–15–7.50–0–*ct* 0
Bowling 35–1–35.00–0–0–1/35

He played for Buckinghamshire.

Hardy, Norman
Amateur. *b:* 1892, Norton-Malreward, Somerset. *d:* 17.11.1923, Fishponds, Bristol. He died of heart failure whilst playing football. Lower order right-hand batsman, right-arm fast medium bowler. *Team* Somerset (1912–21, 11 matches).

Career batting
11–19–7–169–38–14.08–0–*ct* 6
Bowling 747–34–21.97–0–0–4/22

Hardy, N. W.
Amateur. Lower order batsman, opening bowler. *Team* Leveson-Gower XI (1932).
Career batting
1–2–1–14–8*–14.00–0–*ct* 2
Bowling 91–4–22.75–0–0–3/48

Hardy, Silas
Professional. *b:* 30.4.1867, Ilkeston, Derbyshire. *d:* 27.6.1905, Kimberley, Notts. Lower order batsman, right-arm fast medium bowler. *Team* Nottinghamshire (1893–95, 5 matches).
Career batting
5–8–3–45–12*–9.00–0–*ct* 2
Bowling 274–4–68.50–0–0–2/100
He is not to be confused with Solomon Hardy (Derbyshire) although volume 15 of Scores and Biographies states, in error, that Silas Hardy played for both Nottinghamshire and Derbyshire.

Hardy, Solomon
Professional. *b:* 18.5.1863, Ilkeston, Derbyshire. *d:* 5.7.1931, Ilkeston, Derbyshire. Lower order right-hand batsman, wicket-keeper. *Team* Derbyshire (1898, 1 match).
Career batting
1–2–0–10–9–5.00–0–*ct* 2

Hare, John Hugh Montague
Amateur. *b:* 31.5.1857, Docking, Norfolk. *d:* 1.8.1935, King's Lynn, Norfolk. Middle order right-hand batsman, right-arm medium pace bowler, good field. *Sch* Uppingham. *Team* Oxford U (1879–80, blue 1879).
Career batting
8–16–5–126–38*–11.45–0–*ct* 6
Bowling 12–1–12.00–0–0–1/5
He played for Norfolk.

Hare, Peter Macduff Christian
Amateur. *b:* 12.3.1920, Wokingham, Berkshire. Lower order right-hand batsman, wicket-keeper. *Sch* Canford. *Team* Oxford U (1947).
Career batting
1–1–0–39–39–39.00–0–*ct* 2

Hare, Steriker Norman
Amateur. *b:* 31.3.1900, Tottenham, London. *d:* 30.9.1977, Meadle, Bucks. Middle order right-hand batsman. *Sch* Chigwell. *Team* Essex (1921, 3 matches).
Career batting
3–5–0–117–98–23.40–0–*ct* 1

Hare, Sir Thomas
Amateur. *b:* 27.7.1930, London. Middle order right-hand batsman, right-arm fast medium bowler. *Sch* Eton. *Team* Cambridge U (1953).
Career batting
10–17–1–218–47–13.62–0–*ct* 5
Bowling 754–19–39.68–1–0–5/35
His final first-class match was for Free Foresters in 1954 and his County cricket was for Norfolk.

Hare, William Henry
Cricketer. *b:* 29.11.1952, Newark, Notts. Middle order right-hand batsman, right-arm medium bowler. *Team* Nottinghamshire (1971–77, 10 matches).
Career batting
10–18–4–171–36–12.21–0–*ct* 5
Bowling 18–0
A well-known rugby full back, he has appeared for Newark, East Midlands, Leicester and England.

Harenc, Charles Joseph
Amateur. *b:* 3.8.1811, Foots Cray, Kent. *d:* 14.12.1877, Bedford. Brother of A. R. (Kent). Lower order right-hand batsman, right-hand fast under-arm bowler, later slow round arm. *Sch* Harrow. *Teams* Kent (1834–48, 14 matches); Oxford U (1832).
Career batting
56–99–12–830–68–9.54–0–*ct* 34
Bowling 154–6+124–25.66–7–2–8/?
In the period 1830 to 1834 he was considered one of the best bowlers in England. His final first-class match was for Gentlemen of Kent in 1849, his debut being for the same team in 1830.

Harfield, Lewis
Professional. *b:* 16.8.1905, Cheriton, Hants. Middle order right-hand batsman, right-arm medium pace bowler. *Team* Hampshire (1925–31, 80 matches).
Career batting
80–133–10–2460–89–20.00–0–*ct* 37
Bowling 649–14–46.35–0–0–3/35
He hit 1,216 runs, av 26.43, in 1929.

Harford, Noel Sherwin
Amateur. *b:* 30.8.1930, Winton, New Zealand. *d:* 30.3.1981, Auckland, New Zealand. Attractive middle order right-hand batsman, right-arm slow medium bowler. *Teams* Central Districts (1953/4 to 1958/9); Auckland (1963/4 to 1966/7). *Tours* New Zealand to India and Pakistan 1955/6, to England 1958. *Tests* New Zealand (1955/6 to 1958, 8 matches).

Career batting
74–122–8–3149–158–27.62–3–*ct* 39
Bowling 478–18–26.55–0–0–3/19
Test batting
8–15–0–229–93–15.26–0–*ct* 0

He appeared in four Tests on the 1958 tour, but in eight innings made only 41 runs. In first-class matches however he hit 1,067 runs, av 26.02.

Hargreave, Sam
Professional. *b:* 22.9.1875, Rusholme, Lancashire. *d:* 1.1.1929, Stratford-on-Avon, Warwickshire. Lower order left-hand batsman, left-arm slow medium bowler, good field. *Team* Warwickshire (1899–1909, 188 matches). *Tour* Hawke to Australia and New Zealand 1902/3.
Career batting
206–263–63–1932–45–9.66–0–*ct* 155
Bowling 20079–919–21.84–74–18–9/35

Injury prematurely ended his County cricket. He took 100 wickets in a season five times (best 134, av 14.02, in 1903). His best bowling was 9/35 for Warwickshire v Surrey at the Oval in 1903.

Hargreaves, Frederick William
Amateur. *b:* 1858, Blackburn, Lancashire. *d:* 5.4.1897, Wilpshire, Blackburn, Lancashire. Middle order batsman. *Sch* Malvern. *Team* Lancashire (1881, 1 match).
Career batting
1–1–0–0–0–0.00–0–*ct* 2

Hargreaves, Herbert S.
Professional. *b:* 22.3.1913, Anston, Yorkshire. Lower order right-hand batsman, right-arm fast medium bowler. *Team* Yorkshire (1934–38, 18 matches).
Career batting
19–22–6–53–9–3.31–0–*ct* 5
Bowling 1251–59–21.20–1–0–5/93

He also played for Suffolk.

Hargreaves, James Henry
(played under the alias J. Smith)
Professional. *b:* 1859. *d:* 11.4.1922, Portsmouth, Hants. Middle order batsman. *Team* Hampshire (1884–85, 2 matches).
Career batting
2–4–0–15–14–3.75–0–*ct* 0

Hargreaves, Reginald Gervis
Amateur. *b:* 13.10.1852, Accrington, Lancashire. *d:* 13.2.1926, Lyndhurst, Hants. Middle order right-hand batsman, lob bowler. *Sch* Eton. *Team* Hampshire (1875–85, 12 matches).
Career batting
25–47–8–544–46–13.94–0–*ct* 17
Bowling 426–15–28.40–0–0–4/55

He married Alice Liddell, the inspiration for Lewis Carroll's 'Alice in Wonderland'.

Hargreaves, William Henry
Amateur. *b:* 1873, Hitchin, Herts. *d:* 19.4.1948, Gravesend, Kent. Middle order batsman, bowler. *Team* Kent (1893, 1 match).
Career batting
1–2–0–10–10–5.00–0–*ct* 1

Harilal R. Shah
Cricketer. *b:* 1943, Kenya. Right-hand batsman, right-arm medium pace bowler. *Tour* East Africa to England 1975.
Career batting
1–2–0–92–59–46.00–0–*ct* 0
Bowling 7–0

Harington, Herbert Henry
Amateur. *b:* 14.8.1868, Chichester, Sussex. *d:* 1.1.1948, Eastbourne, Sussex. Middle order right-hand batsman. *Sch* Cheltenham. *Team* Kent (1897, 2 matches).
Career batting
2–4–0–49–34–12.25–0–*ct* 1

In 1893/4 he went with the Straits Settlements team on their tour of Ceylon.

Harkness, Donald Peter
Professional. *b:* 13.2.1931, Sydney, Australia. Middle order left-hand batsman, right-arm medium fast bowler. *Team* Worcestershire (1954, 13 matches).
Career batting
13–19–0–488–163–25.68–1–*ct* 9
Bowling 274–6–45.66–0–0–3/29

Harman, George Richard Uniacke
Amateur. *b:* 6.6.1874, Crosshaven, Co Cork, Ireland. *d:* 14.12.1975, Downderry, Torpoint, Cornwall. Middle order right-hand batsman. *Team* Dublin University (1895).
Career batting
1–2–1–2–2*–2.00–0–*ct* 0

He was an Irish rugby international.

Harman, Roger
Professional. *b:* 28.12.1941, Hersham, Surrey. Lower order right-hand batsman, slow left-arm bowler. *Team* Surrey (1961–68, 141 matches).
Career batting
144–147–52–947–34–9.96–0–*ct* 85
Bowling 8975–378–23.74–18–3–8/12

He took 136 wickets, av 21.01, in 1964.

Harman, William Ronayne
Amateur. *b:* 29.5.1869, Co Cork, Ireland. *d:* 4.7.1962, Co Cork, Ireland. Middle order batsman. *Team* Ireland (1907).
Career batting
1–2–0–2–2–1.00–0–*ct* 1

Harold, Frederick Vere
Professional. *b:* 1888, New Forest, Hants. *d:* 17.2.1964, Southall, Middlesex. Lower order batsman, bowler. *Team* Hampshire (1909–12, 2 matches).
Career batting
2–2–0–16–16–8.00–0–*ct* 1
Bowling 15–0

Haroon Rashid Dar
Cricketer. *b* 25.3.1953, Karachi, Pakistan. Brother of Mahmood Rashid (UBL). Attacking middle order right-hand batsman. *Teams* Karachi (1971/2); National Bank (1972/3 to 1975/6); PIA (1976/7); United Bank (1977/8 to 1982/3). *Tours* Pakistan to Sri Lanka 1975/6, to West Indies 1976/7, to Australia 1976/7, to England 1978, 1982, to Australia and New Zealand 1978/9. *Tests* Pakistan (1976/7 to 1982/3, 23 matches).
Career batting
132–209–24–6751–153–36.49–15–*ct* 113
Bowling 253–8–31.62–0–0–3/34
Test batting
23–36–1–1217–153–34.77–3–*ct* 16
Bowling 3–0
He had a most disappointing tour to England in 1978, though he played in three Tests; in 1982 he had a better record in first-class matches, but scored only one run in his single Test innings.

Harper, George (Minto)
Amateur. *b:* 30.8.1865, London. Middle order right-hand batsman, right-arm medium pace bowler. *Sch* Rugby. *Team* Lancashire (1883, 1 match).
Career batting
1–1–0–1–1–1.00–0–*ct* 0

Harper, Herbert
Amateur. *b:* 1.2.1889, Birmingham. *d:* 6.8.1983, Birmingham. Middle order right-hand batsman, leg break bowler. *Team* Worcestershire (1920, 1 match).
Career batting
1–2–0–10–7–5.00–0–*ct* 0

Harper, Sir Kenneth Brand
Amateur. *b:* 8.8.1891, South Kensington, London. *d:* 21.1.1961, Abinger Hammer, Surrey. Middle order right-hand batsman. *Sch* Uppingham. *Teams* Middlesex (1910, 3 matches); Bengal Governor's XI (1917/18).
Career batting
4–7–0–37–28–5.28–0–*ct* 1

Harper, Leonard Vyse
Amateur. *b:* 12.12.1880, Balham. *d:* 13.1.1924, Balham. Hard hitting middle order right-hand batsman, brilliant field. *Sch* Rossall. *Teams* Cambridge U (1901–03, blue all three years); Surrey (1904, 6 matches).
Career batting
34–61–2–988–84–16.74–0–*ct* 14
He also represented Cambridge at hockey.

Harper, Nicholas John
Amateur. *b:* 11.4.1939, Forest Hill, London. Lower order left-hand batsman, left-arm medium pace bowler. *Team* Cambridge U (1961).
Career batting
1–1–0–1–1–1.00–0–*ct* 0
Bowling 39–1–39.00–0–0–1/39

Harper, Roger Andrew
Cricketer. *b* 17.3.1963, Georgetown, British Guiana. Brother of L. S. (Guyana) and M. A. (Guyana). Right-hand batsman, off-break bowler. *Teams* Guyana (1979/80 to 1982/3); D. B. Close's XI (1983).
Career batting
20–31–1–382–38–12.73–0–*ct* 30
Bowling 2001–72–27.79–4–0–5/33

Harpur, Thomas
Cricketer. *b:* 16.5.1944, Omagh, Co Tyrone, Ireland. Right-hand batsman. *Team* Ireland (1980–81).
Career batting
2–2–0–10–6–5.00–0–*ct* 2
Bowling 5–0

Harragin, Alfred Ernest Albert
Amateur. *b:* 4.5.1877, Trinidad. *d:* 21.5.1941, Trinidad. Middle order right-hand batsman, good field. *Team* Trinidad (1896/7 to 1931/2). *Tour* West Indies to England 1906.
Career batting
39–67–3–1585–123–24.76–2–*ct* 32
He finished second in the first-class batting averages on his single visit to England with 412 runs, av 31.69.

Harries, Sir Douglas
Amateur. *b:* 30.3.1892. *d:* 6.12.1972, Crondale, Surrey. Middle order batsman. *Team* Free Foresters (1919–20).
Career batting
4–8–1–112–34–16.00–0–*ct* 3

Harrington, William
Amateur. *b:* 27.12.1869, Templeogue, Co Dublin, Ireland. *d:* 2.1.1940, Templeogue, Co Dublin, Ireland. Right-hand batsman, off break bowler. *Team* Ireland (1902–21).
Career batting
13–21–4–115–28–6.76–0–*ct* 3
Bowling 848–49–17.30–4–1–7/76

Harrington, William John Roy
Professional. *b:* 30.1.1915, St John's Wood, London. Lower order right-hand batsman, right-arm fast bowler. *Team* Middlesex (1946–48, 9 matches).
Career batting
12–19–2–143–45–8.41–0–*ct* 3
Bowling 376–16–23.50–1–0–6/57
His final first-class match was for MCC in 1951.

Harris, Alwyn
Professional. *b:* 31.1.1936, Aberdylais, Glamorgan. Middle order left-hand batsman. *Team* Glamorgan (1960–64, 49 matches).
Career batting
49–91–3–1698–110–19.29–2–*ct* 19
Bowling 0–0
He hit 1,048 runs, av 23.81, in 1962.

Harris, Archibald John
Amateur. *b:* 22.12.1892, Rugby, Staffs. *d:* 10.4.1955, Lymington, Hants. Brother of W. H. (Warwickshire). Middle order right-hand batsman. *Sch* Rugby. *Team* Warwickshire (1919, 1 match).
Career batting
1–2–0–18–14–9.00–0–*ct* 1

Harris, Charles Bowmar
Professional. *b:* 6.12.1907, Underwood, Notts. *d:* 8.8.1954, Nottingham. Brother of G. J. (Glamorgan). Opening right-hand batsman, right-arm medium or slow bowler. *Team* Nottinghamshire (1928–51, 362 matches).
Career batting
362–601–64–18823–239*–35.05–30–*ct* 164
Bowling 8395–196–42.83–3–0–8/80
He hit 1,000 runs in a season eleven times (best 1,891, av 38.59, in 1934). His two double centuries were both for Notts, the highest being 239* v Hampshire at Trent Bridge in 1950. With W. W. Keeton he shared in 46 century partnerships for the first wicket.

Harris, Christopher Robin
Cricketer. *b:* 16.10.1942, Buckingham. Lower order right-hand batsman, right-arm fast medium bowler. *Team* Oxford U (1964–65, blue 1964).
Career batting
12–16–6–48–14–4.80–0–*ct* 5
Bowling 896–17–52.70–1–1–6/83
His County Cricket was for Buckinghamshire.

Harris, David
Professional. *b:* 1755, Elvetham, Hants. *d:* 19.5.1803, Crookham, Hants. Lower order left-hand batsman, right-hand fast under-arm bowler, moderate field. *Team* Hampshire (1782–98).
The greatest bowler of the Hambledon Club, it is impossible to gauge his real success owing to lack of bowling analyses. During the latter part of his career he was much troubled by gout and used to arrive at the ground on crutches. His illness prevented him playing after 1798.

Harris, Dennis Frank
Amateur. *b:* 18.4.1911, Birmingham. *d:* 17.12.1959, Moseley, Birmingham. Middle order right-hand batsman. *Sch* KES Birmingham. *Team* Warwickshire (1946, 1 match).
Career batting
1–1–0–2–2–2.00–0–*ct* 0

Harris, Earlston Joseph
Cricketer. *b:* 3.11.1952, Lodge Village, St Kitts. Lower order right-hand batsman, right-arm medium pace bowler. *Team* Warwickshire (1975, 4 matches).
Career batting
4–5–2–26–16–8.66–0–*ct* 3
Bowling 295–9–32.77–0–0–3/66

Harris, Edwin Lawson J.
Amateur. *b:* 1891, East Preston, Sussex. *d:* 1961, Worthing, Sussex. Middle order right-hand batsman, right-arm medium pace bowler. *Team* Sussex (1922–24, 9 matches).
Career batting
9–15–1–208–51*–14.85–0–*ct* 3
Bowling 59–3–19.66–0–0–2/3

Harris, Frank Albert
Professional. *b:* 19.3.1907, Bristol. *d:* 21.2.1936, Greenbank, Bristol. Middle order right-hand batsman, change bowler. *Team* Gloucestershire (1929–31, 10 matches).
Career batting
10–13–1–68–33–5.66–0–*ct* 2
Bowling 33–0

Harris, George Cecil
Professional. *b:* 1906, Droitwich, Worcs. Lower order batsman, left-arm fast bowler. *Team* Worcestershire (1925, 4 matches).
Career batting
4–8–3–6–4–1.20–0–*ct* 1
Bowling 120–2–60.00–0–0–2/40

Harris, George Joseph
Amateur. *b:* 22.11.1904, Underwood, Notts. Brother of C. B. (Notts). Opening right-hand batsman, right-arm medium pace bowler, slip field. *Team* Glamorgan (1932, 1 match).
Career batting
1–1–0–0–0–0.00–0–*ct* 1

He was a professional until 1929, but on joining the police force played later as an amateur. A good soccer player, he appeared for Mansfield Town and Swansea as goalkeeper.

Harris, Hon George Robert Canning
(succeeded as 4th Lord Harris in 1872)
Amateur. *b:* 3.2.1851, St Anne's, Trinidad. *d:* 24.3.1932, Belmont, Faversham, Kent. Nephew of Hon W. M. Jervis (Derbyshire), uncle of N. E. Haig (Middlesex). Middle order right-hand batsman, right-hand fast round-arm bowler, good field. *Sch* Eton. *Teams* Oxford U (1871–74, blue 1871, 1872 and 1874); Kent (1870–1911, 157 matches). *Tours* Fitzgerald to North America 1872 (not first-class); Harris to Australia 1878/9. *Tests* England (1878/9 to 1884, 4 matches).
Career batting
224–395–23–9990–176–26.85–11–*ct* 190
Bowling 1758–70+5–25.11–1–0–5/57
Test batting
4–6–1–145–52–29.00–0–*ct* 2
Bowling 29–0

One of the most influential personalities involved in cricket, Lord Harris virtually controlled the Kent County Club for a period of about 50 years. Being appointed captain of the County in 1871 he gradually improved its fortunes, which had been at a very low point for many years. Apart from the leadership, which he held until 1889, he was President of the County in 1875, Hon Secretary 1875 to 1880 and for most of his life a Committee member. He hit 1,417 runs, av 33.73, in 1884.

He held various offices with the MCC, generally on the financial side, being a Trustee from 1906 to 1916 and Hon Treasurer from 1916 to his death. He was President in 1895.

He was a great believer in the correct administration of the Laws of cricket and was the prime mover in the stamping out of the 'throwing' epidemic which plagued the game in the 1880s. Although he was noted for the fairness of his judgment in all matters, his hot temper made him a fearsome opponent.

He captained England in all the four Tests in which he took part, including the first Test ever played in England, but various political offices restricted his first-class cricket after 1884. In the following year he was appointed Under-Secretary for India and later Under-Secretary for War. He spent five years in India as Governor of Bombay and assisted in the development of the game there.

Harris, George Woodrouffe
Amateur. *b:* 6.8.1880, Chelsea. *d:* 10.7.1954, Chorley Wood, Herts. Sound middle order right-hand batsman, good field. *Sch* Uppingham. *Team* Hampshire (1899, 1 match).
Career batting
1–2–0–10–10–5.00–0–*ct* 0

Harris, Henry Edward
Amateur. *b:* 6.8.1854, Brighton, Sussex. *d:* 8.12.1923, Littlehampton, Sussex. Middle order right-hand batsman, good field at point. *Team* Hampshire (1880, 3 matches).
Career batting
3–5–0–53–28–10.60–0–*ct* 1

Harris, John Humphrey
Professional. *b:* 13.2.1936, Taunton, Somerset. Lower order left-hand batsman, right-arm fast medium bowler. *Team* Somerset (1952–59, 15 matches).
Career batting
15–18–4–154–41–11.00–0–*ct* 6
Bowling 609–19–32.05–0–0–3/29

After his retirement, he was on the first-class umpires' list.

Harris, Kenrick Henry
Professional. *b:* 1888, Newport, Monmouthshire. Middle order batsman, bowler. *Team* Wales (1925).
Career batting
1–1–0–14–14–14.00–0–*ct* 0
Bowling 135–6–22.50–1–0–6/112

He played for Monmouthshire.

Harris, Leslie John
Amateur. *b:* 20.7.1915, Cardiff. Lower order right-hand batsman, right-arm medium pace bowler. *Team* Glamorgan (1947, 3 matches).
Career batting
3–4–2–7–5–3.50–0–*ct* 1
Bowling 183–5–36.60–0–0–3/39

Harris, Michael John
Cricketer. *b:* 25.5.1944, St Just-in-Roseland, Cornwall. Opening right-hand batsman, leg break bowler, wicket-keeper. *Teams* Middlesex (1964–68, 72 matches); Nottinghamshire (1969–82, 261 matches); Eastern Province (1971/2); Wellington (1975/6). *Tour* Robins to West Indies 1974/5 (not first-class).
Career batting
344–581–58–19196–201*–36.70–41–*ct* 288–*st* 14
Bowling 3459–79–43.78–0–0–4/16

He hit 1,000 runs in a season eleven times,

going on to 2,000 once – 2,238 av 50.86 in 1971. His only double century is 201* for Notts v Glamorgan at Trent Bridge in 1973.

Harris, Stanley Shute
Amateur. *b:* 19.7.1881, Clifton, Bristol. *d:* 4.5.1926, Farnham, Surrey. Middle order right-hand batsman. *Sch* Westminster. *Teams* Cambridge U (1902–04); Gloucestershire (1902, 1 match); Surrey (1904, 1 match); London County (1904); Sussex (1919, 3 matches).
Career batting
16–28–2–375–76–14.42–0–*ct* 4
Bowling 25–0
An excellent soccer player he captained Cambridge and went on to appear for Corinthians and England.

Harris, Thomas
Amateur. *b:* 9.5.1845, Bellary, India. *d:* 28.3.1918, Bedford Park, Chiswick, Middlesex. Lower order right-hand batsman, right-hand round-arm bowler. *Team* Kent (1864, 1 match).
Career batting
2–4–0–4–3–1.00–0–*ct* 1
Bowling 184–10–18.40–1–0–6/81

Harris, Terence Anthony
Amateur. *b:* 27.8.1916, Kimberley, South Africa. Forcing right-hand middle order batsman, excellent field. *Teams* Griqualand West (1933/4 to 1934/5); Transvaal (1936/7 to 1948/9). *Tour* South Africa to England 1947. *Tests* South Africa (1947 to 1948/9, 3 matches).
Career batting
55–80–7–3028–191*–41.47–6–*ct* 52
Bowling 33–0
Test batting
3–5–1–100–60–25.00–0–*ct* 1
He only performed moderately on his tour of England, but appeared in two of the five Tests. A noted rugby fly-half, he represented South Africa.

Harris, William
Professional. *b:* 21.11.1861, Greasbrough, Yorkshire. *d:* 23.5.1923, Longsight, Manchester. Middle order left-hand batsman. *Team* Yorkshire (1884–87, 4 matches).
Career batting
4–8–2–45–25–7.50–0–*ct* 1
Bowling 18–0

Harris, William
Professional. *b:* 17.6.1864, Kimberley, Notts. *d:* 18.6.1949, Sydenham, London. Middle order right-hand batsman, right-arm off break bowler. *Team* Nottinghamshire (1886, 1 match).
Career batting
1–1–0–2–2–2.00–0–*ct* 0
He also played for Surrey (but not in a first-class match). He was for many years groundsman at Guy's Hospital.

Harris, Wilfred Ernest
Amateur. *b:* 24.4.1919, Cardiff. Middle order right-hand batsman, right-arm medium pace bowler. *Team* Glamorgan (1938–47, 5 matches).
Career batting
5–8–0–59–25–7.37–0–*ct* 1
Bowling 43–0

Harris, William Henry
Amateur. *b:* 30.12.1883, Rugby. *d:* 14.10.1967, Rhodesia. Brother of A. J. (Warwickshire). Lower order right-hand batsman, wicket-keeper. *Team* Warwickshire (1904–19, 12 matches).
Career batting
12–18–1–204–42–12.00–0–*ct* 11–*st* 2
He played football for West Bromwich Albion.

Harris
Professional. Lower order batsman, wicket-keeper. *Team* Essex (1905, 2 matches).
Career batting
2–3–1–0–0*–0.00–0–*ct* 4

Harrison, Aelfric Milton
Amateur. *b:* 1889, Blandford, Dorset. *d:* 2.6.1958, Clifton, Bristol. Middle order right-hand batsman, right-arm bowler. *Sch* Christ's Hospital. *Team* Sussex (1913, 2 matches).
Career batting
3–5–0–32–14–6.40–0–*ct* 3
Bowling 33–1–33.00–0–0–1/33
He also played for Dorset. His last first-class match was for the West in 1927.

Harrison, Bernard Reginald Stanhope
Amateur. *b:* 28.9.1934, Worcester. Opening right-hand batsman, right-arm medium pace bowler. *Team* Hampshire (1957–62, 14 matches).
Career batting
14–24–2–519–110–23.59–1–*ct* 8
Bowling 65–1–65.00–0–0–1/34
A useful soccer player, he appeared for Crystal Palace, Southampton and Exeter City.

Harrison, Rev Christopher
Amateur. *b:* 24.3.1847, Brandesburton, Yorkshire. *d:* 23.2.1932, Bishop Norton, Lincs. Middle order right-hand batsman, right-arm slow bowler, good field. *Sch* Shrewsbury. *Team* Nottinghamshire (1878, 1 match).

Career batting
1–2–0–3–3–1.50–0–*ct* 0
He did not appear in any first-class matches whilst at Cambridge U. He also played for Lincolnshire.

Harrison, Cyril Stanley
Amateur. *b:* 11.11.1915, Droitwich, Worcs. Middle/lower order left-hand batsman, slow left-arm bowler. *Sch* Worcester RGS. *Team* Worcestershire (1934–35, 17 matches).
Career batting
17–29–2–166–28–6.14–0–*ct* 11
Bowling 1043–25–41.72–1–0–7/51

Harrison, Dominic Stephen
Cricketer. *b:* 15.1.1963, Tittensor, Staffordshire. Right-hand batsman, wicket-keeper. *Sch* Ampleforth. *Team* Oxford U (1983).
Career batting
1–2–0–9–8–4.50–0–*ct* 1

Harrison, Deryck William
Cricketer. *b:* 3.11.1943, Lurgan, Co Armagh, Ireland. Brother of G. D., James and Roy (Ireland). Right-hand batsman. *Team* Ireland (1978–79).
Career batting
2–1–0–0–0–0.00–0–*ct* 2

Harrison, Edward Ernest
Amateur. *b:* 25.5.1910, Chichester, Sussex. Lower order right-hand batsman, right-arm fast medium bowler. *Sch* Harrow. *Team* Sussex (1946–47, 10 matches).
Career batting
10–17–5–120–23–10.00–0–*ct* 3
Bowling 498–17–29.29–0–0–2/28

Harrison, E. E. *(see under* Ward, E. E.)

Harrison, F.
Professional. Lower order batsman, leg break bowler. *Team* Lancashire (1936, 3 matches).
Career batting
3–3–1–4–2*–2.00–0–*ct* 3
Bowling 118–4–29.50–0–0–2/30
He also played for Cornwall.

Harrison, George Benjamin
Professional. *b:* 1895, Askam, Lancashire. Middle order batsman. *Team* Glamorgan (1924–25, 9 matches).
Career batting
9–17–0–109–34–6.41–0–*ct* 2
Bowling 10–0

Harrison, George Crawford
Amateur. *b:* 27.6.1860, Maida Hill, Middlesex. *d:* 16.3.1900, Fettes College, Edinburgh. Lower order right-hand batsman, slow right-arm bowler. *Sch* Malvern and Clifton. *Team* Oxford U (1880–81, blue both years).
Career batting
18–31–3–237–28–8.46–0–*ct* 18
Bowling 1230–64–19.21–4–0–7/69
He played for Herefordshire.

Harrison, Gerald Cartmell
Amateur. *b:* 8.10.1883. *d:* 10.8.1943, Blyth, Notts. Middle order right-hand batsman. *Sch* Eton. *Teams* Royal Navy (1912–20); Hampshire (1914–20, 22 matches).
Career batting
33–57–3–1401–111–25.94–1–*ct* 12

Harrison, Garfield David
Cricketer. *b* 8.5.1962, Lurgan, Co Armagh. Brother of D.W. (Ireland), James (Ireland) and Roy (Ireland). Middle order batsman, change bowler. *Team* Ireland (1983).
Career batting
1–2–1–107–86–107.00–0–*ct* 0
Bowling 40–2–20.00–0–0–2/30

Harrison, George Puckrin
Professional. *b:* 11.2.1862, Scarborough, Yorkshire. *d:* 14.9.1940, Scarborough, Yorkshire. Lower order right-hand batsman, right-arm very fast, but after 1884 medium-fast bowler. *Team* Yorkshire (1883–92, 61 matches).
Career batting
67–100–31–484–28–6.72–0–*ct* 39
Bowling 3910–249–15.70–14–3–7/43
He took 100 wickets, av 13.26, in 1883, which was his debut season.
He was a noted umpire after ceasing to play in first-class cricket.

Harrison, Harold
Professional. *b:* 24.1.1885, Yeadon, Yorkshire. *d:* 11.2.1962, Wharfedale, Yorkshire. Tail end batsman, slow left-arm bowler. *Team* Yorkshire (1907, 2 matches).
Career batting
2–1–1–4–4*–no av–0–*ct* 1
Bowling 39–2–19.50–0–0–2/15

Harrison, Hugh Robert Edward
Amateur. *b:* 16.4.1875, Forden, Montgomeryshire. *d:* 19.5.1912, Elham, Kent. Lower order right-hand batsman, right-arm fast bowler. *Sch* Eton. *Team* MCC (1896–97).

Career batting
4–8–1–123–55–17.57–0–*ct* 1
Bowling 73–2–36.50–0–0–2/47
He played for Shropshire.

Harrison, Henry Starr
Professional. *b:* 12.4.1883, Cheam, Surrey. *d:* 8.12.1971, Bognor Regis, Sussex. Steady middle order right-hand batsman, slow right-arm bowler, good slip. *Team* Surrey (1909–23, 164 matches).
Career batting
165–255–33–5237–155*–23.59–2–*ct* 117
Bowling 726–20–36.30–0–0–2/14
He hit 1,293 runs, av 40.40, in 1913.

Harrison, Isaac Marshall
Professional. *b:* 8.6.1880, Calverton, Notts. *d:* 25.2.1909, Calverton, Notts. Middle order batsman, excellent field. *Team* Nottinghamshire (1901, 7 matches).
Career batting
7–12–2–143–33–14.30–0–*ct* 1

Harrison, James
Cricketer. *b:* 3.5.1941, Lurgan, Co Armagh, Ireland. Brother of D. W., G. D. and Roy (Ireland). Right-hand batsman. *Team* Ireland (1969–77).
Career batting
8–15–1–309–100*–22.07–1–*ct* 3

Harrison, Leo
Professional. *b:* 5.6.1922, Mudeford, Hants. Middle order right-hand batsman, wicket-keeper. *Team* Hampshire (1939–66, 387 matches).
Career batting
396–606–100–8854–153–17.49–6–*ct* 579–*st* 103
Bowling 166–0
He hit 1,000 runs in a season twice (best 1,191, av 27.06, in 1952).

Harrison, Nigel Sydney Augustine
Amateur. *b:* 29.11.1878, Maidstone, Kent. *d:* 13.11.1947, Norton, Stockton-on-Tees. Middle order right-hand batsman, right-arm fast medium bowler. *Sch* Haileybury. *Team* London County (1900).
Career batting
4–7–1–37–18–6.16–0–*ct* 3
His County cricket was for Durham.

Harrison, Percy
Professional. *b:* 15.10.1878, Mansfield Woodhouse, Notts. *d:* 11.4.1935, Worksop, Notts. Opening/middle order batsman, change bowler. *Team* Nottinghamshire (1899, 1 match).
Career batting
1–2–0–13–11–6.50–0–*ct* 0
Bowling 25–0

Harrison, Richard
Professional. Middle order right-hand batsman, right-arm bowler. *Team* Minor Counties (1912).
Career batting
1–1–1–8–8*–no av–0–*ct* 0
He played for Durham.

Harrison, Roy
Cricketer. *b:* 30.8.1939, Lurgan, Co Armagh, Ireland. Brother of D. W., G. D. and James (Ireland). Left-hand batsman. *Team* Ireland (1968).
Career batting
1–2–0–16–12–8.00–0–*ct* 2

Harrison, Stuart Charles
Cricketer. *b:* 21.9.1951, Cwmbran, Monmouthshire. Lower order right-hand batsman, right-arm fast medium bowler. *Team* Glamorgan (1971–77, 5 matches).
Career batting
5–6–0–32–15–5.40–0–*ct* 1
Bowling 314–7–44.85–0–0–3/55

Harrison, Rev William Bealey
Amateur. *b:* 16.1.1838, Norton Canes, Staffs. *d:* 23.12.1912, Lichfield, Staffs. Lower order batsman, useful bowler. *Sch* Rugby. *Team* Gentlemen of the North (1861–62).
Career batting
2–4–0–6–5–1.50–0–*ct* 2
Bowling 60–1–60.00–0–0–1/31

Harrison, William Henry
Professional. *b:* 29.5.1863, Bradford, Yorkshire. *d:* 15.7.1939, Bradford, Yorkshire. Middle order batsman, bowler. *Team* Yorkshire (1888, 3 matches).
Career batting
3–6–1–12–7–2.40–0–*ct* 0

Harrison, William Henry
Amateur. *b:* 1866. *d:* 23.12.1936, Salisbury, Wilts. Middle order batsman. *Team* Hampshire (1902, 1 match).
Career batting
1–2–1–12–12*–12.00–0–*ct* 0

Harrison, William Philip
Amateur. *b:* 13.11.1885, Church End, Finchley, Middlesex. *d:* 7.9.1964, Rudding Park, Harrogate. Middle order right-hand batsman, leg break bowler. *Sch* Rugby. *Teams* Kent (1904–05, 7 matches); Cambridge U (1905–07, blue 1907);

Middlesex (1906–11, 29 matches). *Tour* MCC to New Zealand 1906/7.
Career batting
56–90–10–1896–156–23.70–2–*ct* 29
Bowling 201–7–28.71–0–0–4/61

Harrold, James George William
Professional. *b:* 1892. *d:* 7.10.1950, Epsom, Surrey. Lower order right-hand batsman, off break bowler. *Team* Essex (1923–28, 11 matches).
Career batting
11–19–3–88–17–5.50–0–*ct* 13
Bowling 123–3–41.00–0–0–1/15

Harron, Dawson Gascoigne
Professional. *b:* 12.9.1921, Langley, Co Durham. Opening right-hand batsman. *Team* Leicestershire (1951, 10 matches).
Career batting
10–14–2–186–53–15.50–0–*ct* 2
He also played for Durham.

Harrop, Douglas John
Cricketer. *b:* 16.4.1947, Cosby, Leics. Lower order left-hand batsman, wicket-keeper. *Team* Leicestershire (1972, 1 match).
Career batting
1–2–1–11–11*–11.00–0–*ct* 3

Harrop, J.
Amateur. Lower order batsman, bowler. *Sch* Bramham College, Tadcaster. *Team* Lancashire (1874, 1 match).
Career batting
1–2–0–5–5–2.50–0–*ct* 0
Bowling 14–0

Harry, Frank
Professional, but became amateur after 1914/18 war. *b:* 22.12.1876, Torquay, Devon. *d:* 27.10.1925, Great Malvern, Worcs. Lower order right-hand batsman, right-arm medium pace bowler. *Teams* Lancashire (1903–08, 69 matches); Worcestershire (1919–20, 7 matches).
Career batting
76–117–11–1605–88–15.14–0–*ct* 40
Bowling 4089–215–19.01–14–1–9/44
His best bowling was 9/44 for Lancashire v Warwickshire at Old Trafford in 1906.
He also appeared for Durham and Cheshire. A noted rugby footballer, he played for Broughton Rangers.

Harry, John
Professional. *b:* 1.8.1857, Ballarat, Victoria, Australia. *d:* 27.10.1919, Canterbury, Victoria, Australia. Middle order right-hand batsman, off break bowler, wicket-keeper. *Teams* Victoria (1883/4 to 1897/8, 28 matches); MCC (1896). *Tests* Australia (1894/5, 1 match).
Career batting
32–60–3–1466–114–25.71–2–*ct* 18–*st* 3
Bowling 618–26–23.76–0–0–4/15
Test batting
1–2–0–8–6–4.00–0–*ct* 1

Hart, Eustace John Hewitt
Amateur. *b:* 14.11.1907, Poona, India. *d:* 4.2.1972, Swainswick, Bath. Middle order right-hand batsman. *Sch* Monkton Combe. *Team* Somerset (1930, 3 matches).
Career batting
3–6–1–45–16–9.00–0–*ct* 1

Hart, George Edmead
Professional. *b:* 13.1.1902, Harlington, Middlesex. Opening right-hand batsman, right-arm medium pace bowler. *Team* Middlesex (1926–39, 194 matches).
Career batting
198–309–31–5786–121–20.81–4–*ct* 60
Bowling 1082–21–51.52–0–0–3/64
He was also a useful soccer player.

Hart, Herbert William
Amateur. *b:* 21.9.1859, Hull, Yorkshire. *d:* 4.12.1895, Hull, Yorkshire. Lower order batsman, left-arm fast bowler. *Team* Yorkshire (1888, 1 match).
Career batting
1–2–0–6–6–3.00–0–*ct* 0
Bowling 32–2–16.00–0–0–2/19

Hart, Martin De Lisle
Amateur. *b:* 17.11.1927, Ealing, Middlesex. Lower order right-hand batsman, leg break bowler. *Sch* Sherborne. *Team* Oxford U (1951).
Career batting
4–5–0–8–4–1.60–0–*ct* 4
Bowling 330–6–55.00–0–0–2/77

Hart, Philip Richard
Cricketer. *b:* 12.1.1951, Seamer, Yorkshire. Lower order right-hand batsman, slow left-arm bowler. *Team* Yorkshire (1981, 3 matches).
Career batting
3–5–0–23–11–4.60–0–*ct* 1
Bowling 140–2–70.00–0–0–1/22

Hart, Thomas Mure
Amateur. *b:* 1.3.1909, Glasgow, Scotland. Middle/lower order right-hand batsman, right-arm fast medium bowler, good field. *Sch* Strathallan. *Teams* Oxford U (1931–32, blue both years); Scotland (1933–34).

Career batting
12–19–3–318–57–19.87–0–*ct* 5
Bowling 465–9–51.66–0–0–3/26
He played rugby for Scotland.

Harté, Christopher Charles John
Cricketer. *b:* 23.2.1949, Belfast, Ireland. Right-hand batsman. *Sch* Belfast Royal Academy. *Team* Ireland (1973–81).
Career batting
2–3–0–82–40–27.33–0–*ct* 0

Hartigan, Gerald Patrick Desmond
Amateur. *b:* 30.12.1884, Kingwilliamstown, South Africa. *d:* 7.1.1955, Durban, South Africa. Brother of E. M. (Border). Middle order right-hand batsman, leg break bowler, good field. *Team* Border (1903/4 to 1926/7). *Tour* South Africa to England 1912. *Tests* South Africa (1912 to 1913/14, 5 matches).
Career batting
37–62–9–1544–176*–29.13–3–*ct* 19
Bowling 1940–92–21.08–4–0–7/44
Test batting
5–10–0–114–51–11.40–0–*ct* 0
Bowling 141–1–141.00–0–0–1/72
He was moderately successful on the 1912 tour of England, but called upon for only 12 matches.

Hartigan, Roger Joseph
Amateur. *b:* 12.12.1879, Sydney, Australia. *d:* 7.6.1958, Brisbane, Australia. Brother of T. J. (NSW). Opening right-hand batsman. *Teams* Queensland (1905/06 to 1920/1, 19 matches); New South Wales (1903/04, 1 match). *Tour* Australia to England 1909. *Tests* Australia (1907/8, 2 matches).
Career batting
45–80–4–1901–116–25.01–2–*ct* 36
Bowling 361–9–40.11–0–0–3/27
Test batting
2–4–0–170–116–42.50–1–*ct* 1
Bowling 7–0
He failed to find his form on the 1909 tour to England and was not selected for the Tests.

Hartill, William Norman
Amateur. *b:* 13.12.1911, Dudley, Worcs. *d:* 3.3.1971, Martley, Worcs. Middle order right-hand batsman. *Team* Worcestershire (1935, 1 match).
Career batting
1–1–0–2–2–2.00–0–*ct* 0

Hartington, Harry Edmondson
Professional. *b:* 18.9.1881, Dewsbury, Yorkshire. *d:* 16.2.1950, Pontefract, Yorkshire. Lower order right-hand batsman, right-arm fast medium bowler. *Team* Yorkshire (1910–11, 10 matches).
Career batting
10–10–4–51–16–8.50–0–*ct* 2
Bowling 764–23–33.21–1–0–5/81

Hartley, Alfred
Amateur. *b:* 11.4.1879, New Orleans, USA. *d:* 9.10.1918, near Maissemy, France. He was killed in action. Brother of C. R. (Lancashire), son of George (Lancashire). Defensive opening right-hand batsman. *Team* Lancashire (1907–14, 112 matches).
Career batting
116–191–9–5049–234–27.74–6–*ct* 39
Bowling 61–1–61.00–0–0–1/39
He hit 1,000 runs in a season three times (best 1,585, av 36.86, in 1910). His only double century was 234 for Lancs v Somerset at Old Trafford in 1910.

Hartley, Charles Robert
Amateur. *b:* 13.2.1873, New Orleans, USA. *d:* 14.11.1927, Brooklands, Cheshire. Brother of Alfred (Lancashire), son of George (Lancashire). Sound middle order right-hand batsman. *Team* Lancashire (1897–1909, 106 matches).
Career batting
106–168–11–3729–139–23.75–4–*ct* 56
Bowling 53–0
His best season was 1900 when he hit 1,084 runs, av 30.11. He was a noted rugby footballer playing for Cheshire, as full back.

Hartley, Frank
Amateur. *b:* 1896, Shipton under Wychwood, Oxon. *d:* 20.10.1965, Shipton under Wychwood, Oxon. Middle order right-hand batsman, right-arm bowler. *Team* Minor Counties (1930).
Career batting
2–3–0–15–13–5.00–0–*ct* 2
Bowling 156–3–52.00–0–0–2/72
He played for Oxfordshire. An excellent soccer player, he appeared in seven England amateur internationals, after having appeared in a full England international in 1923. He also played for Corinthians and Tottenham Hotspur. A good hockey player, he played in several trials for England.

Hartley, Fred
Amateur. *b:* 24.4.1906. Lower order batsman, slow left-arm bowler. *Team* Lancashire (1924–45, 2 matches).
Career batting
2–1–0–2–2–2.00–0–*ct* 0
Bowling 44–1–44.00–0–0–1/44

Hartley, George
Amateur. *b:* 17.3.1849, Heywood, Lancashire. *d:* 9.12.1909, Timperley, Cheshire. Father of Alfred and C. R. (Lancashire). Middle order right-hand batsman, wicket-keeper. *Sch* Rossall. *Team* Lancashire (1871–72, 3 matches).
Career batting
3–3–0–37–24–12.33–0–*ct* 2

Hartley, George Edward
Amateur. *b:* 23.7.1909, Walsden, Yorkshire. Middle order right-hand batsman, slow right-arm bowler. *Sch* Rydal. *Team* MCC (1946).
Career batting
1–2–0–6–3–3.00–0–*ct* 0

Hartley, John Cabourn
Amateur. *b:* 15.11.1874, Lincoln. *d:* 8.3.1963, Woodhall Spa, Lincs. Middle/lower order right-hand batsman, right-arm slow leg break bowler, good field. *Sch* Tonbridge and Marlborough. *Teams* Oxford U (1895–97, blue 1896–97); Sussex (1895–98, 31 matches). *Tours* Mitchell to North America 1895; MCC to South Africa 1905/06, to Australia and New Zealand 1922/3. *Tests* England (1905/06, 2 matches).
Career batting
83–126–19–1366–84*–12.76–0–*ct* 52
Bowling 5626–221–25.45–12–4–8/161
Test batting
2–4–0–15–9–3.75–0–*ct* 2
Bowling 115–1–115.00–0–0–1/62
His final first-class match was for MCC in 1926.

Hartley, John D'Arcy
Amateur. *b:* 4.12.1855, Otley, Yorkshire. *d:* 24.12.1936, Billesdon, Leics. Middle order batsman. *Sch* Harrow. *Team* MCC (1878).
Career batting
1–2–0–6–6–3.00–0–*ct* 0

Hartley, Peter John
Cricketer. *b:* 18.4.1960, Keighley, Yorkshire. Lower order right-hand batsman, right-arm medium pace bowler. *Team* Warwickshire (1982, 3 matches).
Career batting
3–4–1–31–16–10.33–0–*ct* 1
Bowling 215–2–107.50–0–0–2/45

Hartley, Stuart Neil
Cricketer. *b:* 18.3.1956, Shipley, Yorkshire. Middle order right-hand batsman, right-arm medium pace bowler. *Teams* Yorkshire (1978–83, 70 matches); Orange Free State (1981/2 to 1982/3).
Career batting
79–123–17–2533–114–23.89–2–*ct* 35
Bowling 1193–27–44.18–0–0–3/40

Hartley-Smith, Hartley
(changed name from Hartley Smith in March 1881)
Amateur. *b:* 1852, Kensington. *d:* 1905, Weymouth, Dorset. Lower order batsman, wicket-keeper. *Teams* Surrey (1880, 1 match); Sussex (1889, 1 match).
Career batting
2–4–0–27–11–6.75–0–*ct* 2–*st* 1

Hartopp, Edward Samuel Evans
Amateur. *b:* 7.9.1820, Thurnby, Leics. *d:* 5.10.1894, South Pickenham Hall, Swaffham, Norfolk. Defensive middle order batsman, brilliant longstop. *Sch* Eton. *Teams* Cambridge U (1841–42, blue both years); Nottinghamshire (1843, 1 match).
Career batting
69–120–16–442–22–4.25–0–*ct* 16
Bowling 1 wicket, no analysis
He was a member of the MCC Committee and auditor to the Club from 1876 to his death. His final first-class match was for Gentlemen of England in 1857.

Harvey, Edmund
Amateur. *b:* 1850, Islington, Middlesex. *d:* 23.2.1902, Falmouth, Cornwall. Lower order batsman, left-arm fast bowler. *Sch* Radley. *Teams* Middlesex (1872, 1 match); Cambridge U (1872).
Career batting
4–6–0–17–7–2.83–0–*ct* 3
Bowling 143–12–11.91–2–0–5/22

Harvey, Rev Frank Northam
Amateur. *b:* 19.12.1864, Southampton, Hants. *d:* 10.11.1939, Southampton, Hants. Lower order right-hand batsman, wicket-keeper. *Team* Hampshire (1899–1900, 3 matches).
Career batting
3–4–0–20–7–5.00–0–*ct* 2–*st* 1
He also played under the alias of 'F. H. Northam'.

Harvey, John Frank
Professional. *b:* 27.9.1939, Cambridge. Middle order right-hand batsman, off break bowler. *Team* Derbyshire (1963–72, 204 matches).
Career batting
206–344–32–7538–168–24.16–4–*ct* 87
Bowling 21–1–21.00–0–0–1/0
He hit 1,000 runs in a season three times (best

1,226, av 32.26, in 1971). His first-class debut was for MCC in 1961. He also appeared for Cambridgeshire and Berkshire.

Harvey, Jonathan Robert William
Amateur. *b:* 3.2.1944, Yeovil, Somerset. Tail end right-hand batsman, right-arm fast medium bowler. *Sch* Marlborough. *Team* Cambridge U (1963–65, blue 1965).
Career batting
6–8–2–5–3–0.83–0–*ct* 1
Bowling 431–17–25.35–1–0–5/28

Harvey, Peter Fairfield
Professional. *b:* 15.1.1923, Linby, Notts. Lower order right-hand batsman, leg break and googly bowler, slip field. *Team* Nottinghamshire (1947–58, 173 matches).
Career batting
175–244–46–3645–150–18.40–2–*ct* 116
Bowling 11908–335–35.54–13–3–8/122

Harvey, Peter Vernon
Amateur. *b:* 6.1.1926, Wallington, Surrey. Middle order left-hand batsman. *Sch* Epsom. *Team* Oxford U (1949).
Career batting
1–1–0–9–9–9.00–0–*ct* 0

Harvey, Ronald Charles
Professional. *b:* 7.5.1934, Ingatestone, Essex. Lower order left-hand batsman, right-arm fast medium bowler. *Team* Essex (1952, 1 match).
Career batting
1–2–2–12–12*–no av–0–*ct* 0
Bowling 88–3–29.33–0–0–3/88

Harvey, Robert Neil
Amateur. *b:* 8.10.1928, Fitzroy, Victoria, Australia. Brother of C. E., M. R. and Raymond (all Victoria). Brilliant middle order left-hand batsman, off break bowler, excellent field. *Teams* Victoria (1946/7 to 1956/7, 64 matches); New South Wales (1958/9 to 1962/3, 30 matches). *Tours* Australia to England 1948, 1953, 1956, 1961, to South Africa 1949/50, 1957/8, to West Indies 1954/5, to India and Pakistan 1956/7, 1959/60, to New Zealand 1956/7; Commonwealth to Ceylon 1951/2. *Tests* Australia (1947/8 to 1962/3, 79 matches).
Career batting
306–461–35–21699–231*–50.93–67–*ct* 228
Bowling 1106–30–36.86–0–0–4/8
Test batting
79–137–10–6149–205–48.41–21–*ct* 64
Bowling 120–3–40.00–0–0–1/8
He hit 1,000 runs on his 1948 and 1961 tours to England and 2,040, av 65.80, in 1953, which was easily his best tour. He also reached 1,000 runs in Australia four times and in South Africa once. Of his seven double centuries, two were hit in Tests – v S Africa and West Indies – and two in England. His highest score was 231* for New South Wales v South Australia at Sydney in 1962/3.

Harvey, Rev Thomas Arnold
Amateur. *b:* 17.4.1878, Marsh's Library, Dublin, Ireland. *d:* 25.12.1966, Dublin, Ireland. Right-hand batsman, right-arm medium pace bowler. *Sch* Ellesmere College. *Team* Ireland (1902).
Career batting
2–4–0–113–62–28.25–*ct* 1
Bowling 78–2–39.00–0–0–2/67
He was later Bishop of Cashel.

Harvey, William Henry
Amateur. *b:* 12.4.1896, Freemantle, Southampton. Middle order right-hand batsman, right-arm medium pace bowler. *Team* Warwickshire (1927, 1 match).
Career batting
1–1–0–24–24–24.00–0–*ct* 0
A noted soccer player, he appeared for England in an amateur international, and for Sheffield Wednesday and Birmingham City.

Harvey-Walker, Ashley John
Cricketer. *b:* 21.7.1944, East Ham, Essex. Middle order right-hand batsman, right-arm medium pace off break bowler. *Sch* Strathallan. *Team* Derbyshire (1971–78, 81 matches).
Career batting
81–143–10–3186–117–23.95–3–*ct* 31
Bowling 1150–34–33.82–1–1–7/35
He scored 110 in the second innings of his debut match – Derbyshire v Oxford U at Burton on Trent 1971.

Harwood, Baron
Professional. *b:* 14.8.1852, Darwen, Lancashire. *d:* 16.12.1915, Moses Gate, Lancashire. Tail end right-hand batsman, right-arm fast bowler. *Team* Lancashire (1877, 1 match).
Career batting
1–2–2–0–0*–no av–0–*ct* 2
Bowling 16–1–16.00–0–0–1/16

Harwood, Frederick
Professional. *b:* 1.6.1828, Mitcham, Surrey. *d:* 11.12.1887, Mitcham, Surrey. Lower order right-hand batsman, right-hand fast round arm bowler. *Team* Surrey (1851–65, 4 matches).
Career batting
4–5–1–8–5–2.00–0–*ct* 3
Bowling 158–7–22.57–0–0–3/39

Hasan Jamil
Cricketer. *b:* 25.7.1952, Karachi, Pakistan. Middle order batsman, right-arm medium pace bowler. *Teams* Kalat (1969/70); Karachi (1969/70 to 1971/2); Universities (1972/3 to 1974/5); PIA (1975/6 to 1982/3). *Tours* Pakistan Under 25s to Sri Lanka 1973/4; Pakistan to Sri Lanka 1975/6, to England 1978; PIA to Zimbabwe 1981/2.
Career batting
109–160–28–3892–172–29.48–4–*ct* 54
Bowling 5633–180–31.29–5–0–5/38
He played in one first-class match on the 1978 tour to England in emergency.

Haseeb Ahsan
Amateur. *b:* 15.7.1939, Peshawar, India. Lower order right-hand batsman, off break bowler. *Teams* Peshawar (1956/7 to 1959/60); PIA (1960/1 to 1962/3); Karachi (1961/2 to 1962/3). *Tours* Pakistan to England 1962, to West Indies 1957/8, to India 1960/1; Pakistan Eaglets to England 1963. *Tests* Pakistan (1957/8 to 1961/2, 12 matches).
Career batting
49–59–16–242–36–5.62–0–*ct* 9
Bowling 3931–142–27.68–13–2–8/23
Test batting
12–16–7–61–14–6.77–0–*ct* 1
Bowling 1330–27–49.25–2–0–6/202
Owing to injury he appeared in only three matches on the 1962 tour to England, but his bowling action was also suspect.

Haskett-Smith, Algernon
Amateur. *b:* 4.7.1856, London. *d:* 21.11.1887, Paddington, London, from a gun accident. Opening right-hand batsman, good field. *Sch* Eton. *Team* Oxford U (1879, blue).
Career batting
5–8–1–114–38–16.28–0–*ct* 2
He also played for the Gentlemen of Kent in 1879.

Haslip, Shearman Montague
Amateur. *b:* 13.5.1897, Twickenham, Middlesex. *d:* 4.7.1968, Weymouth, Dorset. Lower order right-hand batsman, right-arm fast medium bowler. *Sch* Rugby. *Team* Middlesex (1919, 5 matches).
Career batting
9–12–0–91–20–7.58–0–*ct* 4
Bowling 592–18–32.88–0–0–3/12
His final first-class match was for MCC in 1920.

Haslop, Peter
Amateur. *b:* 17.9.1941, Midhurst, Sussex. Lower order right-hand batsman, right-arm medium pace bowler, good field. *Team* Hampshire (1962, 1 match).
Career batting
1–1–1–2–2*–no av–0–*ct* 1
Bowling 82–2–41.00–0–0–2/82
He re-appeared for Hampshire in a John Player League match in 1972.

Hassall, Frederick
Professional. *b:* 1868, Nantwich, Cheshire. *d:* 1945, Leicester. Hard hitting middle order right-hand batsman, right-arm medium pace bowler. *Team* Leicestershire (1894, 4 matches).
Career batting
4–7–0–57–20–8.14–0–*ct* 1
Bowling 25–0
He also played for Staffordshire.

Hassan, Frederick
Professional. *b:* circa 1860. *d:* 15.4.1940, Tooting Bec, London. Lower order batsman, bowler. *Team* Kent (1879, 1 match).
Career batting
1–2–0–0–0–0.00–0–*ct* 0
Bowling 12–1–12.00–0–0–1/5

Hassan, Sheikh Basharat
Cricketer. *b:* 24.3.1944, Nairobi, Kenya. Sound opening right-hand batsman, right-arm medium pace bowler, occasional wicket-keeper. *Teams* East Africa (1963/4 to 1964/5); Nottinghamshire (1966–83, 309 matches).
Career batting
312–517–49–13786–182*–29.45–14–*ct* 281–*st* 1
Bowling 407–6–67.83–0–0–3/33
His first-class debut was for East Africa in 1963/4 and he also played for Kenya. He hit 1,000 runs in a season five times (best 1,395, av 32.44, in 1970).
He is a useful hockey player.

Hassan, Syed Farooq Azim
Cricketer. *b:* 17.10.1941, Lahore, India. Lower order batsman, bowler. *Teams* Oxford U (1962–63); Pakistan Universities (1959/60).
Career batting
11–14–6–44–17–5.50–0–*ct* 3
Bowling 664–15–44.26–0–0–2/15

Hassett, Arthur Lindsay
Amateur. *b:* 28.8.1913, Geelong, Victoria, Australia. Brother of R. J. (Victoria). Middle order right-hand batsman, right-arm medium pace bowler. *Team* Victoria (1932/3 to 1952/3, 73 matches). *Tours* Australia to England 1938, 1948, 1953, to New Zealand 1945/6, to South Africa 1949/50; Australian Services to England, India

and Ceylon 1945. *Tests* Australia (1938–53, 43 matches).
Career batting
216–322–32–16890–232–58.24–59–*ct* 170
Bowling 703–18–39.05–0–0–2/10
Test batting
43–69–3–3073–198*–46.56–10–*ct* 30
Bowling 78–0

He hit 1,000 runs on each of his three Test tours to England with 1,589, av 54.79, in 1938 and 1,563, av 74.42, in 1948, whilst in 1953, when he captained the side, he headed the Test batting averages. In all he led Australia in 24 Tests. He also hit 1,000 twice in a season in Australia.

Of his eight double centuries, six, including his highest of 232 v MCC at Melbourne in 1950/51, were for Victoria and two were for the Australians in England.

His final first-class match was for A. L. Hassett's XI in 1953/4.

Hastie, James Henderson
Amateur. *b:* 20.6.1920, Glasgow, Scotland. Middle order left-hand batsman, slow left-arm bowler. *Team* Minor Counties (1953).
Career batting
1–2–0–37–22–18.50–0–*ct* 0

His County cricket was for Buckinghamshire.

Hastilow, Cyril Alexander Frederick
Amateur. *b:* 31.5.1895, Birmingham. *d:* 30.9.1975, Moseley, Birmingham. Lower order right-hand batsman, right-arm slow bowler. *Team* Warwickshire (1919, 2 matches).
Career batting
2–3–0–26–14–8.66–0–*ct* 0
Bowling 72–2–36.00–0–0–2/56

Hastings, Alfred Gardiner
Amateur. *b:* 29.10.1847, Glasgow, Scotland. *d:* 26.12.1916, Hammersmith, London. Steady middle order right-hand batsman, good field. *Sch* Winchester. *Team* MCC (1869).
Career batting
1–2–0–1–1–0.50–0–*ct* 0

He did not appear in first-class cricket whilst at Oxford U.

Hastings, Brian Frederick
Amateur. *b:* 23.3.1940, Wellington, New Zealand. Middle order right-hand batsman. *Teams* Wellington (1957/8); Central Districts (1960/1); Canterbury (1961/2 to 1976/7). *Tours* New Zealand to England 1969, 1973, to Australia 1969/70, 1973/4, to West Indies 1971/2, to India and Pakistan 1969/70. *Tests* New Zealand (1968/9 to 1975/6, 31 matches).
Career batting
163–273–32–7686–226–31.89–15–*ct* 112
Bowling 139–4–34.75–0–0–1/0
Test batting
31–56–6–1510–117*–30.20–4–*ct* 23
Bowling 9–0

He appeared in all three Tests on both his tours to England and was one of the leading batsmen, scoring in first-class matches 708 runs av 35.00, in 1969 and 662, av 38.94, in 1973. His highest score was 226 for Canterbury v New Zealand Under 23s at Christchurch in 1964/5.

Hatch, Peter George
Amateur. *b:* 3.7.1938, Kirkee, India. Hard hitting middle order right-hand batsman. *Teams* Combined Services (1960); Free Foresters (1961).
Career batting
5–7–0–60–15–8.57–0–*ct* 2

Hatfeild, Charles Eric
Amateur. *b:* 11.3.1887, Margate, Kent. *d:* 21.9.1918, Cambrai, France. He was killed in action. Middle order batsman, slow left-arm bowler. *Sch* Eton. *Teams* Oxford U (1907–09, blue 1908); Kent (1910–14, 45 matches). *Tour* MCC to the Argentine 1911/12.
Career batting
65–101–8–1498–74–16.10–0–*ct* 45
Bowling 1475–64–23.04–2–0–5/48

He gained his place in the Eton Eleven as a bowler, but won his blue as a batsman.

Hathorn, Christopher Maitland Howard
Amateur. *b:* 7.4.1878, Pietermaritzburg, South Africa. *d:* 17.5.1920, Johannesburg, South Africa. Middle order right-hand batsman. *Teams* Transvaal (1897/8 to 1906/7); London County (1901–04). *Tours* South Africa to England 1901, 1904, 1907, to Australia 1910/11. *Tests* South Africa (1902/3 to 1910/11, 12 matches).
Career batting
87–142–9–3541–239–26.62–9–*ct* 17
Bowling 52–1–52.00–0–0–1/16
Test batting
12–20–1–325–102–17.10–1–*ct* 5

He was most successful on his first two tours to England, heading the first-class batting averages in 1901 and in 1904 completing 1,000 runs – 1,317, av 36.58. His 1907 tour was not so successful. His highest score was 239 for South Africans v Cambridge U at Cambridge in 1901. His final first-class match in South Africa was for Wanderers Club in 1908/9.

Hatteea, Saeed Ahmed
Cricketer. *b:* 2.2.1950, Bombay, India. Tail end right-hand batsman, right-arm fast-medium

bowler. *Sch* City of London. *Team* Bombay (1969/70 to 1970/1); Rest of World (1970).
Career batting
8–5–0–1–1–0.20–0–*ct* 6
Bowling 764–27–28.29–1–0–5/33

Hattersley-Smith, Rev Percy
Amateur. *b:* 19.5.1847, Merton Hall, Cambridge. *d:* 19.1.1918, Cheltenham. Middle order batsman. *Sch* Perse, Cambridge. *Team* Gloucestershire (1878–79, 11 matches).
Career batting
11–15–2–198–56–15.23–0–*ct* 3
He also played for Cambridgeshire.

Hatton, Anthony George
Professional. *b:* 25.3.1937, Leeds, Yorkshire. Lower order left-hand batsman, right-arm fast bowler. *Team* Yorkshire (1960–61, 3 matches).
Career batting
3–1–1–4–4*–no av–0–*ct* 1
Bowling 202–6–33.66–0–0–2/27

Hatton, John
Amateur. *b:* 1858, Monmouth. *d:* 25.4.1915, Gloucester. Middle order batsman, wicket-keeper. *Team* Gloucestershire (1884, 3 matches).
Career batting
3–6–1–28–11*–5.60–0–*ct* 1

Haughton, William Edward
Amateur. *b:* 31.10.1923, Bray, Co Wicklow, Ireland. Right-hand batsman. *Team* Ireland (1953).
Career batting
1–2–0–0–0–0.00–0–*ct* 0

Hawes, George Howard
Amateur. *b:* 1881, Kettering, Northants. *d:* 26.10.1934, Desborough, Northants. Lower order right-hand batsman, right-arm medium pace bowler. *Team* Northants (1919, 2 matches).
Career batting
2–3–1–16–12*–8.00–0–*ct* 1
Bowling 87–1–87.00–0–0–1/43

Hawke, Christopher Richard John
Amateur. *b:* 12.4.1934, Portsmouth. Middle/lower order right-hand batsman, wicket-keeper. *Sch* Harrow. *Team* Oxford U (1953).
Career batting
1–2–1–31–23*–31.00–0–*ct* 1

Hawke, Hon Martin Bladen
(succeeded as 7th Baron Hawke in 1887)
Amateur. *b:* 16.8.1860, Willingham Rectory, Gainsborough, Lincs. *d:* 10.10.1938, Randolph Crescent, Edinburgh. Middle order right-hand batsman, good deep field. *Sch* Eton. *Teams* Cambridge U (1882–85, blue 1882, 1883 and 1885); Yorkshire (1881–1911, 513 matches). *Tours* Vernon to Australia 1887/8, to India 1889/90 (not first-class); Hawke to North America 1891, to India 1892/3, to North America 1894, to South Africa 1895/6, to West Indies 1896/7, to South Africa 1898/9; MCC to Argentine 1911/12. *Tests* England (1895/6 to 1898/9, 5 matches).
Career batting
633–936–105–16749–166–20.15–13–*ct* 209
Bowling 16–0
Test batting
5–8–1–55–30–7.85–0–*ct* 3
He captained Yorkshire from 1883 to 1910 and England in four of the five Tests in which he played, as well as his various touring teams overseas. President of Yorkshire from 1898 to his death, he virtually controlled the County's affairs for most of those years. He is credited with introducing Winter Pay for professionals, and at the same time he weeded out players who belonged to the 'hard drinking' variety. Owing to his suggestion Test selectors were introduced for home internationals and all in all his influence was much in evidence in the modernisation of first-class cricket. He hit 1,078 runs, av 23.95, in 1895.

Hawke, Neil James Napier
Amateur. *b:* 27.6.1939, Cheltenham, South Australia. Lower order right-hand batsman, right-arm medium fast bowler. *Teams* Western Australia (1959/60, 7 matches); South Australia (1960/1 to 1967/8, 60 matches); Tasmania (1968/9, 2 matches). *Tours* Australia to England 1964, 1968, to India and Pakistan 1964/5, to West Indies 1964/5, to South Africa 1966/7; Commonwealth to Pakistan 1970/1; Rest of World to West Indies 1966/7; Cavaliers in England 1969. *Tests* Australia (1962/3 to 1968, 27 matches).
Career batting
145–198–57–3383–141*–23.99–1–*ct* 85
Bowling 12088–458–26.39–23–5–8/61
Test batting
27–37–15–365–45*–16.59–0–*ct* 9
Bowling 2677–91–29.41–6–1–7/105
He had a most successful tour of England in 1964 taking 83 wickets, av 19.80, including 18 in Tests, but in 1968 his bowling was of little account and he took only one Test wicket. His final first-class match in England was for Cavaliers in 1969.

Hawker, Sir Frank Cyril
Amateur. *b:* 21.7.1900, Epping, Essex. Grandson of John Bastow (Middlesex); brother-in-law of T. N. Pearce (Essex). Middle order batsman. *Sch* City of London. *Team* Essex (1937, 1 match).

Career batting
1–2–0–26–16–13.00–0–*ct* 0
He was President of MCC 1970/1.

Hawkey, Richard Bladworth
Amateur. *b:* 7.8.1923, Teddington, Middlesex. Opening right-hand batsman, right-arm medium pace bowler. *Sch* Merchant Taylors. *Team* Cambridge U (1949).
Career batting
3–6–0–42–13–7.00–0–*ct* 0
Bowling 139–1–139.00–0–0–1/40
His first-class debut was for Free Foresters in 1948.

Hawkins, Charles
Professional. *b:* 20.6.1817, Cosham, Hants. *d:* 9.9.1846, Fittleworth, Petworth, Sussex. Middle order right-hand batsman, brilliant field. *Team* Sussex (1839–44, 25 matches).
Career batting
56–104–7–1198–95–12.35–0–*ct* 50–*st* 6
Bowling 1 wicket, no analysis
Regarded as the best point field of his day and would have developed perhaps into the best bat if he had not died so young. 'He had a most curious way of taking guard. He would make his block, or guard, within about an inch only of the stumps; then, when the bowler advanced to deliver the ball, he too would come forward, raising his bat over his shoulder.' His final first-class match was for Petworth in 1845.

Hawkins, Christopher G.
Professional. *b:* 31.8.1938, Slough, Bucks. Stylish middle order right-hand batsman, right-arm medium pace bowler, wicket-keeper. *Team* Warwickshire (1957, 4 matches).
Career batting
4–5–2–16–11*–5.33–0–*ct* 7–*st* 2

Hawkins, Derek Graham
Professional. *b:* 18.5.1935, Alveston, Gloucs. Middle order right-hand batsman, off break bowler. *Team* Gloucestershire (1952–62, 134 matches).
Career batting
134–220–14–3755–106–18.23–3–*ct* 79
Bowling 1153–38–30.34–1–0–6/81
He hit 1,021 runs, av 21.72, in 1961.

Hawkins, Frederick Albert
Amateur. *b:* 11.12.1888, Wandsworth, London. *d:* 12.9.1975, Elstead, Surrey. Middle order right-hand batsman, right-arm medium pace bowler. *Team* Middlesex (1927, 2 matches).
Career batting
2–2–1–19–19–19.00–0–*ct* 0

Hawkins, Henry
Amateur. *b:* 15.1.1876, Kegworth, Leics. *d:* 12.8.1930, Everdon Hall, Daventry. Hard hitting lower order right-hand batsman, right-arm fast medium bowler. *Sch* Taunton. *Team* Northants (1905–09, 26 matches).
Career batting
26–44–9–350–33–10.00–0–*ct* 10
Bowling 767–24–31.91–0–0–2/12

Hawkins, Herbert Hervey Baines
Amateur. *b:* 9.1.1876, Streatham Hill, London. *d:* 1.1.1933, Trincomalee, Ceylon. Middle order right-hand batsman, right-arm medium pace bowler. *Sch* Whitgift. *Team* Cambridge U (1896–99, blue 1898 and 1899).
Career batting
20–31–11–159–15*–7.95–0–*ct* 14
Bowling 1143–48–24.22–2–0–7/45

Hawkins, Laurence Cyril
Amateur. *b:* 15.5.1907, Birmingham. Middle order right-hand batsman, leg break bowler. *Team* Somerset (1928–37, 46 matches).
Career batting
46–81–8–1252–96–17.15–0–*ct* 21
Bowling 1067–22–48.50–0–0–4/39

Hawkwood, Clifford
Professional. *b:* 16.11.1909, Nelson, Lancashire. *d:* 15.5.1960, Burnley, Lancashire. Middle order right-hand batsman. *Team* Lancashire (1931–35, 24 matches).
Career batting
24–26–5–596–113–28.38–1–*ct* 9
Bowling 92–1–92.00–0–0–1/63

Hawley, Frank
Professional. *b:* 19.7.1877, Nottingham. *d:* 23.8.1913, Sutton in Ashfield, Notts. Lower order batsman, fast medium bowler. *Team* Nottinghamshire (1897, 1 match).
Career batting
1–1–0–1–1–1.00–0–*ct* 0
Bowling 67–1–67.00–0–0–1/31

Haworth, William Barratt
Amateur. *b:* 18.3.1884, Oldham, Lancashire. *d:* 27.1.1975, St Annes, Lancashire. Lower order right-hand batsman, leg break bowler, good close field. *Team* Gentlemen (1924).
Career batting
1–2–0–1–1–0.50–0–*ct* 0
Bowling 9–0
He was for many years the mainstay of the Blackpool Club.

Hawtin, Alfred Powell Rawlins
Amateur. *b:* 1.2.1883, Bugbrooke, Northants. *d:* 15.1.1975, Northampton. Brother of R. W. R. (Northants). Sound opening right-hand batsman. *Team* Northants (1908–30, 85 matches).
Career batting
86–151–5–3595–135–24.62–3–*ct* 31
During the Second World War he more or less single-handed kept the Northants County Club in existence, and after the war was the Club's Chairman.

Hawtin, Roger William Rawlins
Amateur. *b:* 30.9.1880, Bugbrooke, Northants. *d:* 7.9.1917, Northampton. Brother of A. P. R. (Northants). Steady middle order right-hand batsman, right-arm medium pace bowler. *Team* Northants (1905–08, 19 matches).
Career batting
19–37–4–508–65–15.39–0–*ct* 11
Bowling 663–22–30.13–2–0–5/33

Hawtin, Walter
Professional. *b:* 1906, Aston, Warwickshire. *d:* March, 1940, in an accident whilst working on munitions. Middle order right-hand batsman, right-arm medium pace bowler. *Team* Northants (1929–34, 4 matches).
Career batting
4–8–1–51–24–7.28–0–*ct* 4
Bowling 23–1–23.00–0–0–1/9

Hawtrey, Edward Montague
Amateur. *b:* 10.10.1847, Windsor, Berkshire. *d:* 14.8.1916, Westgate-on-Sea, Kent. Middle order batsman, bowler. *Sch* Eton. *Team* MCC (1880–82).
Career batting
2–4–0–1–1–0.25–0–*ct* 1
Bowling 64–2–32.00–0–0–2/50

Hay, David Osborne
Amateur. *b:* 29.11.1916, Barwon Heads, New South Wales, Australia. Hard hitting middle order right-hand batsman. *Team* Oxford U (1936–38).
Career batting
4–6–0–129–96–21.50–0–*ct* 1

Hay, George
Professional. *b:* 28.1.1851, Staveley, Derbyshire. *d:* 4.10.1913, Staveley, Derbyshire. Lower order right-hand batsman, right-hand fast medium round-arm bowler, good cover field. *Team* Derbyshire (1875–86, 47 matches).
Career batting
55–94–16–669–49–8.57–0–*ct* 34
Bowling 2444–148–16.51–8–1–6/16
His final first-class match was for the North in 1887. He joined the MCC Ground staff in 1882 and remained until 1912.

Hay, Thomas Douglas Baird
Amateur. *b:* 31.8.1876, Auckland, New Zealand. *d:* 19.4.1967, Auckland, New Zealand. Middle order right-hand batsman, useful change bowler. *Team* Auckland (1893/4 to 1906/7). *Tour* New Zealand to England 1927.
Career batting
25–47–5–689–144–16.40–1–*ct* 9
Bowling 444–19–23.36–1–0–5/10
He was manager of the 1927 team to England, but appeared in one first-class match.

Hay, William Harrington
Amateur. *b:* 21.1.1849, London. *d:* 3.3.1925, Great Bowden, Leics. Middle order right-hand batsman, good longstop. *Sch* Eton. *Team* MCC (1877).
Career batting
3–5–1–57–26*–14.25–0–*ct* 4
His first-class debut was for Gentlemen of England in 1875. His County cricket was for Leicestershire (not first-class).

Haycraft, James Samuel
Amateur. *b:* 1865, Islington, Middlesex. *d:* 26.3.1942, St Pancras, London. Opening right-hand batsman. *Sch* University College School. *Team* Middlesex (1885, 1 match).
Career batting
1–2–0–5–5–2.50–0–*ct* 0
A brilliant bat in London club cricket, notably for Stoics, Nondescripts and Pallingswick, he failed to do himself justice in his single County match.

Haye, William
Cricketer. *b:* 15.9.1948, St Catherine, Jamaica. *Team* Jamaica (1970/1 to 1971/2). *Tour* Jamaica to England 1970.
Career batting
7–8–0–198–60–24.75–0–*ct* 1
Bowling 287–6–47.83–0–0–1/8
He only appeared in one first-class match on the 1970 Jamaica tour to England.

Hayes, Ernest George
Professional before First World War, amateur 1919–23, professional from 1924. *b:* 6.11.1876, Peckham, Surrey. *d:* 2.12.1953, West Dulwich, London. Excellent middle order right-hand batsman, leg break bowler, brilliant slip field. *Teams* Surrey (1896–1919, 500 matches); London County (1903); Leicestershire (1926, 5 matches). *Tours* Brackley to West Indies 1904/5; MCC to

South Africa 1905/6, to Australia 1907/8. *Tests* England (1905/6 to 1912, 5 matches).
Career batting
560–896–48–27318–276–32.21–48–*ct* 609–*st* 2
Bowling 13754–515–26.70–12–2–8/22
Test batting
5–9–1–86–35–10.75–0–*ct* 2
Bowling 52–1–52.00–0–0–1/28

He hit 1,000 runs in a season six times, twice going on to 2,000 (best 2,309, av 45.27, in 1906). His four double centuries were all for Surrey with his highest being 276 v Hants at the Oval in 1909. He achieved very little for England and fared so poorly during the 1907/8 tour to Australia that he was not selected for any of the Tests in that series. He was chief coach at Leicester 1923–28 and at the Oval 1929–34.

Hayes, Frank Charles
Cricketer. *b:* 6.12.1946, Preston, Lancashire. Attractive middle order right-hand batsman, right-arm medium pace bowler, good cover field. *Teams* Lancashire (1970-83, 227 matches). *Tours* MCC to West Indies 1973/4; Robins to South Africa 1972/3, 1975/6; International Wanderers to South Africa 1975/6; Overseas XI to India 1980/1; International XI to Pakistan 1981/2. *Tests* England (1973–76, 9 matches).
Career batting
271–420–58–13007–187–35.93–23–*ct* 176
Bowling 15–0
Test batting
9–17–1–244–106*–15.25–1–*ct* 7

He hit 1,000 runs in a season six times (1,311, av 35.43, in 1974). He hit 34 off one over from M.A. Nash, Lancashire v. Glamorgan, Swansea, 1977. From 1978 to 1980 he captained Lancashire.

Hayes, John Arthur
Amateur. *b:* 11.1.1927, Auckland, New Zealand. Lower order right-hand batsman, right-arm fast bowler. *Teams* Auckland (1946/7 to 1958/9); Canterbury (1950/1 to 1954/5). *Tours* New Zealand to England 1949, 1958, to India and Pakistan 1955/6. *Tests* New Zealand (1950/1 to 1958, 15 matches).
Career batting
78–100–36–611–36–9.54–0–*ct* 29
Bowling 6759–292–23.14–12–3–7/28
Test batting
15–22–7–73–19–4.86–0–*ct* 3
Bowling 1217–30–40.56–0–0–4/36

Owing to illness he had a very moderate tour of England in 1949, but in 1958, though achieving little in the Tests, he headed the first-class bowling averages with 62 wickets, av 20.20. His final first-class match was Governor-General's XI v MCC in 1960/1.

Hayes, Kevin Anthony
Cricketer. *b:* 26.9.1962, Thurnscoe, Yorkshire. Middle order right-hand batsman, right-arm medium pace bowler. *Teams* Lancashire (1980–83, 11 matches); Oxford U (1981–83, blue all three years).
Career batting
29–47–3–1059–152–24.06–1–*ct* 8
Bowling 253–8–31.62–1–0–6/58

He also gained his blue for soccer.

Hayes, Peter James
Cricketer. *b:* 20.5.1954, Crowborough, Sussex. Lower order right-hand batsman, right-arm medium pace bowler. *Sch* Brighton. *Team* Cambridge U (1974–77, blue 1974, 1975 and 1977).
Career batting
27–44–11–343–56*–10.39–0–*ct* 19
Bowling 1832–51–35.92–1–0–5/48

His County cricket was for Suffolk.

Haygarth, Arthur
Amateur. *b:* 4.8.1825, Hastings, Sussex. *d:* 1.5.1903, Westminster, London. Cousin of E. B. (Gloucs and Hants) and J. W. (Oxford U). Defensive opening/middle order right-hand batsman. *Sch* Harrow. *Teams* Middlesex (1850–51, 3 matches); MCC (1844–61); Sussex (1848–60, 3 matches).
Career batting
136–247–14–3042–97–13.05–0–*ct* 65
Bowling 145–19–7.63–3–1–6/36

His lasting memorial is the set of 15 'Cricket Scores and Biographies' volumes, the first four published by F. Lillywhite and the remainder by MCC. This work contains the most comprehensive collection ever published of match scores and cricketers' biographies up to the year 1878.

Haygarth, Edward Brownlow
Amateur. *b:* 26.4.1854, Cirencester, Gloucs. *d:* 14.4.1915, Siddington, Gloucs. Brother of J. W. (Oxford U); cousin of Arthur (Middlesex and Sussex). Lower order right-hand batsman, wicket-keeper, lob bowler. *Sch* Lancing. *Teams* Gloucestershire (1883, 2 matches); Hampshire (1875, 1 match).
Career batting
3–5–0–18–7–3.60–0–*ct* 0–*st* 1

He also played for Berkshire.

Haygarth, John William
Amateur. *b:* 3.12.1842, Rodmarton, Gloucs. *d:* 31.3.1923, Korralbye, Ipswich, Queensland, Australia. Brother of E. B. (Gloucs and Hants), cousin of Arthur (Middlesex and Sussex). Hard hitting lower order right-hand batsman, excellent

wicket-keeper. *Sch* Winchester. *Team* Oxford U (1862–64, blue all three years).
Career batting
10–14–2–81–17–6.75–0–*ct* 12–*st* 12
He emigrated to Australia in 1865 and thus took no part in English cricket after leaving Oxford.

Hayhurst, Albert
Professional. *b:* 17.9.1905, Birdwell, Yorkshire. Lower order right-hand batsman, right-arm fast medium bowler. *Team* Warwickshire (1934–35, 7 matches).
Career batting
7–8–0–98–42–12.25–0–*ct* 2
Bowling 457–12–38.08–0–0–4/120
He also played for Buckinghamshire. An excellent soccer player, he was centre half for Reading and Luton Town.

Hayles, Basil Ratcliffe Marshall
Amateur. *b:* 29.10.1916, Andover, Hants. Lower order right-hand batsman, wicket-keeper. *Sch* Haileybury. *Teams* Combined Services (1947–49); Army (1938–39).
Career batting
7–10–1–69–40–7.66–0–*ct* 6–*st* 2
He played for Norfolk.

Hayley, Harry
Professional. *b:* 22.2.1860, Heath, Wakefield, Yorkshire. *d:* 3.6.1922, Wakefield, Yorkshire. Middle/lower order right-hand batsman, right-arm medium pace bowler. *Team* Yorkshire (1884–98, 7 matches).
Career batting
7–12–1–122–24–11.09–0–*ct* 3
Bowling 48–0

Hayman, Herbert Bailey
Amateur. *b:* 5.10.1873, Hendon, Middlesex. *d:* 31.7.1930, Winslow, Bucks. Hard hitting opening right-hand batsman, excellent outfield. *Team* Middlesex (1893–1901, 86 matches).
Career batting
105–191–15–4663–165–26.49–4–*ct* 46
Bowling 138–4–34.50–0–0–2/9
He was mainly connected with Hampstead CC, being a prolific scorer in London Club cricket.

Hayman, Rev Henry Telford
Amateur. *b:* 20.11.1853, West Malling, Kent. *d:* 8.2.1941, Cheltenham, Gloucs. Middle order right-hand batsman, good longstop. *Sch* Bradfield. *Team* Kent (1873, 2 matches).
Career batting
2–4–0–37–29–9.25–0–*ct* 2
He was not in the Eleven whilst at Cambridge.

Haynes, Carleton
Amateur. *b:* 7.2.1858, Newcastle, Barbados. *d:* 20.11.1945, Woodlands, Southampton. Hard hitting lower order right-hand batsman, right-arm fast bowler, good field. *Sch* Clifton. *Team* Gloucestershire (1878–79, 5 matches).
Career batting
5–10–2–76–21–9.50–0–*ct* 3
Bowling 38–1–38.00–0–0–1/8

Haynes, Desmond Leo
Cricketer. *b:* 15.2.1956, Holders Hill, St James, Barbados. Attacking opening right-hand batsman, right-arm leg break and googly bowler, good field. *Team* Barbados (1976/7 to 1982/3). *Tours* West Indies to Australia and New Zealand 1979/80, to England 1980, to Pakistan 1980/1, to Australia 1981/2; Young West Indies to Zimbabwe 1981/2. *Tests* West Indies (1977/8 to 1980/1, 24 matches).
Career batting
87–143–11–5413–184–41.00–8–*ct* 49
Bowling 21–1–21.00–0–0–1/2
Test batting
24–38–1–1431–184–38.67–3–*ct* 13
Bowling 8–1–8.00–0–0–1/2
On the 1980 tour to England he hit 874 runs, av 46.00, and was successful in the Tests with 308 runs, av 51.33. His last first-class match in England was for D.B. Close's XI in 1982.

Haynes, Denis Marshall
Amateur. *b:* 29.12.1923, Stoke-on-Trent, Staffs. Middle order right-hand batsman, right-arm medium pace bowler. *Sch* Denstone. *Team* MCC (1956).
Career batting
1–2–0–8–8–4.00–0–*ct* 1
He played for Staffordshire.

Haynes, John Perigoe
Amateur. *b:* 27.11.1926, Canterbury, Kent. Lower order right-hand batsman, right-arm medium pace bowler. *Sch* Dauntsey's. *Team* Cambridge U (1946).
Career batting
1–2–0–0–0–0.00–0–*ct* 1
Bowling 34–0

Haynes, Michael William
Professional. *b:* 19.5.1936, Nottingham. Middle order right-hand batsman. *Team* Nottinghamshire (1959–61, 9 matches).
Career batting
9–16–1–119–23–7.93–0–*ct* 6

Haynes, Richard William
Professional. *b:* 27.8.1913, Shipston-on-Stour, Warwickshire. *d:* 16.10.1976, Oxford. Opening

right-hand batsman, slow left-arm bowler. *Team* Gloucestershire (1930–39, 74 matches).
Career batting
74–121–6–1673–89–14.54–0–*ct* 40
Bowling 815–15–54.33–0–0–4/76

He also played for Oxfordshire. He was a useful hockey player.

Hays, David Leslie
Cricketer. *b:* 5.11.1944, Finchley, London. Middle order right-hand batsman, wicket-keeper. *Sch* Highgate. *Teams* Cambridge U (1965–68, blue 1966 and 1968); Scotland (1980).
Career batting
25–47–1–751–72–16.32–0–*ct* 26–*st* 2
Bowling 5–0

Hayter, Ernest F.
Professional. *b:* 8.9.1914, Southampton, Hants. Lower order right-hand batsman, leg break bowler. *Team* Hampshire (1935–37, 3 matches).
Career batting
3–6–1–36–17–7.20–0–*ct* 0
Bowling 29–0

Hayter, Montague William
Professional. *b:* 1871, Ringwood, Hants. *d:* 6.5.1948, Christchurch, Hants. Middle order right-hand batsman. *Team* Hampshire (1904, 7 matches).
Career batting
7–12–0–166–82–13.83–0–*ct* 3

Hayward, Arthur John
Professional. *b:* 12.9.1905, Christchurch, Hants. Lower order right-hand batsman, leg break and googly bowler. *Team* Hampshire (1925–26, 4 matches).
Career batting
4–4–0–17–10–4.25–0–*ct* 0

Hayward, Daniel (sen)
Professional. *b:* 25.8.1808, Mitcham, Surrey. *d:* 29.5.1852, Cambridge. Father of Daniel jun (Surrey and Cambridgeshire) and Thomas (Cambridgeshire), grandfather of T. W. (Surrey). Middle order right-hand batsman, wicket-keeper. *Teams* Surrey (1839–47, 3 matches); Cambridge Town Club (1832–51).
Career batting
24–42–4–420–53–11.05–0–*ct* 9–*st* 9
Bowling 5 wickets, no analyses

Hayward, Daniel (jun)
Professional. *b:* 19.10.1832, Chatteris, Cambs. *d:* 30.5.1910, Cambridge. Son of Daniel sen (Surrey), father of T. W. (Surrey), brother of Thomas (Cambridgeshire). Middle order right-hand batsman, good long stop. *Teams* Cambridge Town Club (1852–60); Cambridgeshire (1861–69, 31 matches); Surrey (1854, 1 match).
Career batting
43–77–8–690–59–10.00–0–*ct* 18

His single appearance for Surrey was played under the mistaken impression that he was born in Mitcham.

Hayward, David Russell
Amateur. *b:* 7.6.1920, Australia. *d:* 21.4.1945, Lasham, Hants. Lower order right-hand batsman, leg break and googly bowler. *Sch* Harrow. *Teams* Oxford U (1939); Middlesex (1939, 1 match).
Career batting
9–13–7–36–14–6.00–0–*ct* 2
Bowling 591–20–29.55–1–0–6/79

Hayward, James Gordon Rotherham
Professional. *b:* 31.12.1926, Bridlington, Yorkshire. Lower order left-hand batsman, right-arm fast medium bowler. *Team* Nottinghamshire (1951, 1 match).
Career batting
1 match, did not bat–*ct* 0
Bowling 78–2–39.00–0–0–2/78

Hayward, Richard Edward
Cricketer. *b:* 15.2.1954, Ickenham, Middlesex. Middle order left-hand batsman, left-arm medium pace bowler. *Teams* Hampshire (1981–82, 13 matches); Central Districts (1982/3).
Career batting
17–28–5–521–101*–22.65–1–*ct* 8
Bowling 6–0

He appeared for Buckinghamshire 1978–80 and made his first-class debut for Minor Counties in 1979.

Hayward, Thomas
Professional. *b:* 21.3.1835, Chatteris, Cambs. *d:* 21.7.1876, Cambridge. Son of Daniel sen (Surrey), brother of Daniel jun (Surrey), uncle of T. W. (Surrey). Opening/middle order right-hand batsman, right-hand medium pace round-arm bowler, excellent cover point. *Teams* Cambridgeshire (1857–71, 35 matches). Cambridge Town Club (1854–58); Yorkshire (1858). *Tours* Parr to North America 1859 (not first-class), to Australia 1863/4.
Career batting
118–200–11–4790–132–25.34–6–*ct* 62
Bowling 3840–242+25–15.86–19–1–9/30

He was for a few years regarded as the equal of any batsman in England, but most of his famous feats were performed for the AEE in odds matches. His final first-class match was for MCC in 1872. His best bowling was 9/30 for England v 16 of Kent at Lord's in 1860.

Hayward, Thomas Walter
Professional. *b:* 29.3.1871, Cambridge. *d:* 19.7.1939, Cambridge. Son of Daniel junior (Cambridgeshire and Surrey), grandson of Daniel senior (Surrey), nephew of Thomas (Cambridgeshire). Very sound opening right-hand batsman, right-arm medium pace bowler, good field. *Team* Surrey (1893–1914, 593 matches). *Tours* Hawke to South Africa 1895/96; Stoddart to Australia 1897/8; MCC to Australia 1901/02, 1903/04. *Tests* England (1895/6 to 1909, 35 matches).
Career batting
712–1138–96–43551–315*–41.79–104–*ct* 492
Bowling 11042–481–22.95–19–2–8/89
Test batting
35–60–2–1999–137–34.46–3–*ct* 19
Bowling 514–14–36.71–0–0–4/22

One of the most reliable of batsmen during the twenty years prior to the First World War, Hayward originally went in first wicket down for Surrey, but was promoted to open the innings about 1900, initially with R. Abel. Later he became associated with J. B. Hobbs and the pair produced a century stand for the first wicket on 40 occasions, with their highest partnership realising 352 runs against Warwickshire at the Oval in 1909. Hayward also assisted in six century first wicket stands for England.

For twenty successive seasons, commencing 1895, he reached 1,000 runs, going on to 2,000 in ten seasons and thence to 3,000 twice. His best year – 1906 – produced 3,518 runs, av 66.37, which created a new English first-class aggregate record that stood until 1947. In 1900 he reached the 1,000-run mark on the last day of May.

Eight times Hayward hit over 200 runs in an innings, his highest score being 315* for Surrey v Lancashire at the Oval in 1898.

In his early days he was a very useful bowler and in 1897 took 114 wickets, av 18.21, thus achieving the 'double' for the only time in his career. After 1904 he scarcely bowled at all.

All his tours to Australia were successful. In 1903/4 he topped the batting averages and in 1901/2 came second to A. C. MacLaren.

Hayward, William Irvine Dudley
Amateur. *b:* 15.4.1930, Adelaide, Australia. Middle/lower order right-hand batsman, right-arm medium fast bowler, excellent field. *Team* Cambridge U (1950–53, blue 1950, 1951 and 1953).
Career batting
27–33–4–309–57–10.65–0–*ct* 23
Bowling 1948–68–28.64–4–0–6/89

His final first-class match was for MCC in 1954.

Haywood, David Charles
Cricketer. *b:* 20.3.1945, Hucknall, Notts. Middle order left-hand batsman, right-arm medium pace bowler. *Sch* Nottingham High School. *Team* Cambridge U (1968, blue).
Career batting
9–15–0–284–62–18.93–0–*ct* 5

Haywood, Esme Thomas Lancelot Reed
Amateur. *b:* 23.8.1900, East Preston, Sussex. Middle order right-hand batsman. *Sch* Cheltenham. *Team* Somerset (1925–27, 8 matches).
Career batting
8–16–0–137–38–8.56–0–*ct* 1

Haywood, John William
Professional. *b:* 17.4.1878, Harby, Leics. *d:* 2.2.1963, Oakham. Lower order right-hand batsman, right-arm medium pace bowler. *Team* Leicestershire (1901–03, 3 matches).
Career batting
3–5–0–37–16–7.40–0–*ct* 1
Bowling 240–4–60.00–0–0–2/81

Haywood, Paul Raymond
Cricketer. *b:* 30.3.1947, Leicester. Middle order right-hand batsman, right-arm medium pace bowler, good cover point. *Sch* Wyggeston. *Team* Leicestershire (1969–73, 54 matches).
Career batting
54–82–8–1570–100*–21.22–1–*ct* 15
Bowling 324–9–36.00–0–0–4/60

A good hockey player, he represented Leics.

Haywood, Robert Allnutt
Professional. *b:* 16.9.1887, Eltham, Kent. *d:* 1.6.1942, Edinburgh. Father of R. O. (Scotland), son of R. J. (Kent). Middle order right-hand batsman, right-arm medium pace bowler. *Team* Northants (1908–24, 172 matches).
Career batting
172–306–15–8373–198–28.77–20–*ct* 85
Bowling 1466–34–43.11–0–0–3/73

He hit 1,000 runs in a season three times (best 1,909, av 42.42, in 1921). After the 1921 season he demanded better financial remuneration from the Northants Club; his request being turned down, he went as coach to Fettes and henceforth only appeared in the school holidays – a great loss to the County.

Haywood, Robert John
Professional. *b:* 3.3.1858, Eltham, Kent. *d:* 9.5.1922, Eltham, Kent. Father of R. A. (Northants), grandfather of R. O. (Scotland). Lower order batsman, bowler. *Team* Kent (1878, 1 match).
Career batting
1–2–1–0–0*–0.00–0–*ct* 1
Bowling 15–0

Haywood, Robert Oliver
Amateur. *b:* 22.4.1917, Northampton. *d:* 21.12.1963, Edinburgh. Son of R. A. (Northants), grandson of R. J. (Kent). Right-hand batsman. *Team* Scotland (1949).
Career batting
1–2–0–12–12–6.00–0–*ct* 0

Haywood, William John
Professional. *b:* 25.2.1842, Sheffield, Yorkshire. *d:* 1912, Sheffield, Yorkshire. Lower order right-hand batsman, right-arm fast medium bowler. *Team* Yorkshire (1878, 1 match).
Career batting
1–2–0–7–7–3.50–0–*ct* 0
Bowling 14–1–14.00–0–0–1/14

Hayzelden, Allan Frederick George
Amateur. *b:* 10.1.1904, Leytonstone, Essex. *d:* 10.4.1955, Harefield, Middlesex. Lower order right-hand batsman, right-arm fast bowler. *Sch* Merchant Taylors. *Team* Essex (1929–31, 2 matches).
Career batting
2–3–1–5–4*–2.50–0–*ct* 3
Bowling 110–6–18.33–0–0–3/30

Hazare, Vijay Samuel
Amateur. *b:* 11.3.1915, Sangli, Maharashtra, India. Brother of Vivekanand Samuel (Mysore), father of Ranjit (Baroda), uncle of Vikram Vivek Hazare and Sanjay Hazare (both Baroda). Middle order right-hand batsman, right-arm medium pace bowler, good slip field. *Teams* Maharashtra (1934/5 to 1940/1); Central India (1935/6 to 1938/9); Baroda (1941/2 to 1960/1). *Tours* India to England 1946, 1952, to Australia 1947/8, to West Indies 1952/3, to Ceylon 1944/5. *Tests* India (1946 to 1952/3, 30 matches).
Career batting
239–369–46–18754–316*–58.06–60–*ct* 166
Bowling 14648–595–24.61–27–3–8/90
Test batting
30–52–6–2192–164*–47.65–7–*ct* 11
Bowling 1220–20–61.00–0–0–4/29

He hit 1,000 runs on both his tours of England (best 1,344, av 49.77, in 1946) and appeared in all the Tests on both visits, leading India on the 1952 tour. He hit 1,000 runs five times in a season in India (best 1,480, av 87.05, in 1949/50) and once in Australia.

In all he has hit 10 scores over 200, including two over 300 (316* for Maharashtra v Baroda at Poona in 1939/40 highest). His highest innings in England is 244* v Yorkshire at Bramall Lane in 1946.

His partnership of 577 with Gul Mahomed for the 4th wicket in the match Baroda v Holkar at Baroda in 1946/7 created a new world first-class record. His final first-class match was his benefit for President's XI v West Indies in 1966/7.

Hazell, Horace Leslie
Professional. *b:* 30.9.1909, Brislington, Somerset. Hard hitting lower order left-hand batsman, slow left-arm bowler, good close field. *Team* Somerset (1929–52, 350 matches).
Career batting
350–507–228–2280–43–8.17–0–*ct* 249
Bowling 22941–957–23.97–57–7–8/27

He took 100 wickets in a season twice (best 106, av 19.48, in 1949). For Somerset v Gloucs at Taunton in 1949 he bowled 105 balls (including 17 successive maidens) without conceding a run.

Hazelton, Edwin Hills
Amateur. *b:* 16.12.1861, Southampton, Hants. *d:* 25.7.1916, Simla, India. Middle order batsman. *Team* Hampshire (1883, 3 matches).
Career batting
3–5–0–83–50–16.60–0–*ct* 0

Hazelton, Edward Wyndham
Amateur. *b:* 1894, Buckingham. *d:* 13.3.1958, Dunmow, Essex. Middle/lower order right-hand batsman, right-arm medium or leg break bowler. *Sch* Wellingborough. *Team* Essex (1919, 1 match).
Career batting
8–16–4–77–43–6.41–0–*ct* 6
Bowling 621–23–27.00–2–1–6/45

He also appeared for Buckinghamshire for many years. His final first-class match was for MCC in 1930.

Hazlerigg, Sir Arthur Grey, Bart
(created 1st Baron Hazlerigg in 1945)
Amateur. *b:* 17.11.1878, Ayr, Scotland. *d:* 25.5.1949, London. Father of Lord A. G. Hazlerigg (Leics), 2nd Baron. Lower order right-hand batsman, lob bowler. *Sch* Eton. *Team* Leicestershire (1907–10, 65 matches).
Career batting
65–108–28–866–55*–10.82–0–*ct* 36
Bowling 44–0

He captained Leics 1907 to 1910 and was President of the County Club in 1930. Whilst at Cambridge U he did not appear in any first-class matches.

Hazlerigg, Sir Arthur Grey
(succeeded as 2nd Baron Hazlerigg in 1949)
Amateur. *b:* 24.2.1910, South Kensington, London. Son of Lord A. G. Hazlerigg (Leics). Opening right-hand batsman, right-arm medium slow off break bowler, good slip field. *Sch* Eton. *Teams* Cambridge U (1930–32, blue all three years); Leicestershire (1930–34, 34 matches). *Tour* Martineau to Egypt 1935 (not first-class).
Career batting
66–106–9–2515–135–25.92–3–*ct* 75
Bowling 3476–112–31.03–1–0–6/27
He captained Cambridge U in 1932 and Leics in 1934. He hit 1,010 runs, av 36.07, in 1932.

Hazlitt, Gervys Rignold
Amateur. *b:* 4.9.1888, Enfield, New South Wales, Australia. *d:* 30.10.1915, Parramatta, New South Wales, Australia. Lower order right-hand batsman, right-arm medium pace off break bowler. *Teams* Victoria (1905/06 to 1910/11, 16 matches); New South Wales (1911/12 to 1912/13, 6 matches). *Tours* Australia to England 1912; Waddy to Ceylon 1913/14 (not first-class). *Tests* Australia (1907/8 to 1912, 9 matches).
Career batting
57–83–14–876–82*–12.69–0–*ct* 32
Bowling 4906–188–26.09–8–0–7/25
Test batting
9–12–4–89–34*–11.12–0–*ct* 4
Bowling 623–23–27.08–1–0–7/25
He had a very successful tour of England, taking, in all matches, 101 wickets, av 18.96; though his bowling action came in for some criticism.

Head, Francis Somerville
Amateur. *b:* 30.6.1846, Kensington, London. *d:* 2.4.1941, Bushey, Herts. Middle order batsman. *Sch* Marlborough. *Team* Lancashire (1868–69, 6 matches).
Career batting
7–12–0–80–24–6.66–0–*ct* 3
His final first-class match was for MCC in 1881.

Head, John Reginald
Amateur. *b:* 15.7.1868, Hackney, Middlesex. *d:* 15.5.1949, Folkestone, Kent. Middle order right-hand batsman, right-arm medium pace bowler. *Sch* Clifton. *Team* Middlesex (1892–98, 5 matches). *Tour* Warner to USA 1897.
Career batting
8–14–2–242–101–20.16–1–*ct* 3
Bowling 60–3–20.00–0–0–3/22
He also played for Suffolk.

Head, Timothy John
Cricketer. *b:* 22.9.1957, Hammersmith, London. Lower order right-hand batsman, wicket-keeper. *Sch* Lancing. *Team* Sussex (1976–81, 22 matches).
Career batting
22–26–6–335–52*–16.75–0–*ct* 54–*st* 6

Headlam, Cecil
Amateur. *b:* 19.9.1872, London. *d:* 12.8.1934, Charing, Kent. Lower order right-hand batsman, wicket-keeper. *Sch* Rugby. *Teams* Oxford U (1895); Middlesex (1902–06, 8 matches). *Tour* Oxford Univ Authentics in India 1902/3.
Career batting
23–35–7–287–44–10.25–0–*ct* 34–*st* 12
He played for Oxfordshire 1893–1901. A noted author his major cricket work was a book on his 1902/3 tour of India 'Ten Thousand Miles through India and Burma'.

Headley, George Alphonso
Amateur. *b:* 30.5.1909, Panama. *d:* 30.11.1983, Kingston, Jamaica. Father of R. G. A. (Worcs and West Indies). Brilliant middle order right-hand batsman, right-arm slow bowler, good field. *Team* Jamaica (1927/8 to 1953/4). *Tours* West Indies to Australia 1930/1, to England 1933, 1939, to India and Pakistan 1948/9. *Tests* West Indies (1929/30 to 1953/4, 22 matches).
Career batting
103–164–22–9921–344*–69.86–33–*ct* 76
Bowling 1842–51–36.11–1–0–5/33
Test batting
22–40–4–2190–270*–60.83–10–*ct* 14
Bowling 230–0
He was the outstanding batsman on both his tours to England, heading the first-class averages each year – 2,320, av 66.28, in 1933 and 1,745, av 72.70, in 1939. These successes merely confirmed that he was the outstanding West Indian batsman of the 1930s. He also scored 1,000 in an Australian season.
His highest innings was 344* for Jamaica v Lord Tennyson's XI at Kingston in 1931/2 and of his other scores over 200, two were in Tests against England – 223* at Kingston in 1929/30 and 270* at the same venue in 1934/5. He hit two double centuries on his 1933 visit to England and another two in 1939. His final first-class match was for the Commonwealth XI in 1954.

Headley, Ronald George Alphonso
Professional. *b:* 29.6.1939, Rollington Town,

Kingston, Jamaica. Son of G. A. (West Indies). Opening/middle order left-hand batsman, leg break bowler. *Teams* Jamaica (1965/6 to 1973/4); Worcestershire (1958–74, 403 matches). *Tours* West Indies to England 1973; Worcs World Tour 1964/5, to Jamaica 1965/6; Commonwealth to Pakistan 1970/1; Cavaliers to West Indies 1964/5. *Tests* West Indies (1973, 2 matches).
Career batting
423–758–61–21695–187–31.12–32–*ct* 357
Bowling 588–12–49.00–0–0–4/40
Test batting
2–4–0–62–42–15.50–0–*ct* 2
He hit 1,000 runs in a season thirteen times, going on to 2,000 once – 2,040, av 31.87, in 1961. He played for Derbyshire in one-day matches commencing 1975.

Heal, Michael George
Cricketer. *b:* 7.9.1948, Bristol. Middle order right-hand batsman, right-arm medium pace bowler. *Team* Oxford U (1969–72, blue 1970 and 1972).
Career batting
22–41–1–637–124*–15.92–1–*ct* 10
Bowling 3–0
He was awarded his rugby blue.

Heale, William Henry
Amateur. *b:* 27.4.1859, Hemel Hempstead, Hertfordshire. *d:* 24.4.1907, Westminster, London. Opening/middle order right-hand batsman, right-arm medium pace bowler. *Sch* Harrow. *Team* Oxford U (1881).
Career batting
1–2–0–10–9–5.00–0–*ct* 0
His County cricket was for Hertfordshire.

Healey, Robert Dennis
Cricketer. *b:* 10.2.1934, Plymouth, Devon. Lower order right-hand batsman, right-arm fast medium bowler. *Team* Combined Services (1964).
Career batting
2–4–0–14–7–3.50–0–*ct* 0
Bowling 146–0
He played for Devon.

Healing, John Alfred
Amateur. *b:* 14.6.1873, Tewkesbury, Gloucs. *d:* 4.7.1933, Caister-on-Sea, Norfolk. Stylish middle order left-hand batsman. *Sch* Clifton. *Teams* Cambridge U (1894); Gloucestershire (1899–1906, 10 matches).
Career batting
12–20–0–195–37–9.75–0–*ct* 10
He also played for Bedfordshire.

Healing, Percival
Amateur. *b:* 16.7.1878, Tewkesbury, Gloucs. *d:* 1.2.1915, Marylebone, London. Steady middle order right-hand batsman. *Sch* Cheltenham. *Team* Gloucestershire (1911, 1 match).
Career batting
1–2–0–38–30–19.00–0–*ct* 0

Heane, George Frank Henry
Amateur. *b:* 2.1.1904, Worksop, Notts. *d:* 24.10.1969, Skendleby, Lincs. Middle order left-hand batsman, right-arm medium pace bowler. *Team* Nottinghamshire (1927–51, 172 matches). *Tours* Cahn to Argentina 1929/30, to New Zealand 1938/9.
Career batting
189–268–24–6183–138–25.34–9–*ct* 100
Bowling 7307–222–32.91–5–1–6/52
He captained Notts 1935 to 1946, jointly with S. D. Rhodes in the first year. He hit 1,000 runs in a season three times (best 1,627, av 37.83, in 1939). He also appeared for Lincolnshire. A useful soccer player, he represented Notts.

Heap, John Garsden
Amateur. *b:* 1857, Haslingden, Lancashire. *d:* 1931, Fylde, Lancashire. Middle order batsman. *Team* Lancashire (1884, 2 matches).
Career batting
2–2–0–0–0–0.00–0–*ct* 2
Bowling 4–0

Heap, James Sutcliffe
Professional. *b:* 12.8.1882, Lowerhouse, Burnley, Lancashire. *d:* 30.1.1951, Stoneclough, Bolton, Lancashire. Lower order left-hand batsman, slow left-arm bowler. *Team* Lancashire (1903–21, 210 matches).
Career batting
210–312–41–5146–132*–18.98–1–*ct* 76
Bowling 9513–412–23.08–25–5–9/43
His best bowling was 9/43 for Lancashire v Northants at Northampton in 1910.

Heard, Hartley
Cricketer. *b:* 29.10.1947, Bristol. Tail end right-hand batsman, right-arm medium pace bowler. *Team* Oxford U (1967–70, blue 1969–70).
Career batting
30–45–14–273–31–8.80–0–*ct* 5
Bowling 2048–49–41.79–1–0–6/78

Hearn, Peter
Professional. *b:* 25.11.1925, Tunbridge Wells, Kent. Nephew of S. G. (Kent). Middle order left-hand batsman, slow left-arm bowler, good cover. *Team* Kent (1947–56, 196 matches).

Career batting
200–351–32–8138–172–25.81–7–*ct* 66
Bowling 1245–22–56.59–0–0–3/34

He hit 1,000 runs in a season three times (best 1,413, av 30.06, in 1954).

Hearn, Sidney George
Professional. *b:* 28.7.1899, Harbledown, Kent. *d:* 23.8.1963, Chartham, Kent. Uncle of Peter (Kent). Middle order left-hand batsman, slow left-arm bowler. *Team* Kent (1922–26, 31 matches).
Career batting
32–44–7–465–54*–12.56–0–*ct* 20
Bowling 399–22–18.13–0–0–3/15

Hearn, William
Professional. *b:* 30.11.1849, Essendon, Herts. *d:* 30.1.1904, Barnet, Herts. Middle order right-hand batsman, right-hand medium pace round-arm bowler, excellent cover point. *Team* MCC (1878–91).
Career batting
41–72–5–806–91–12.02–0–*ct* 27
Bowling 57–0

He was on the ground staff at Lord's from 1878 until his death, and latterly was a well known umpire. His County cricket was for Hertfordshire.

Hearne, Alec
Professional. *b:* 22.7.1863, Ealing, Middlesex. *d:* 16.5.1952, Beckenham, Kent. Son of George (Middlesex), brother of G. G. (Kent) and Frank (Kent), nephew of Thomas (Middlesex), cousin of G. F. (MCC), uncle of G. A. L. (South Africa). Steady middle order right-hand batsman, right-arm slow bowler, good slip. *Team* Kent (1884–1906, 403 matches). *Tours* Read to South Africa 1891/2; Kent to USA 1903. *Test* England (1891/2, 1 match).
Career batting
488–833–78–16436–194–21.65–15–*ct* 404
Bowling 23120–1160–19.93–52–9–8/15
Test batting
1–1–0–9–9–9.00–0–*ct* 1

He hit 1,000 runs in a season four times (best 1,477, av 29.54, in 1895). His final first-class match was for MCC in 1910.

Hearne, Frank
Professional. *b:* 23.11.1858, Ealing, Middlesex. *d:* 14.7.1949, Cape Town, South Africa. Son of George (Middlesex), brother of G. G. (Kent) and Alec (Kent), father of G. A. L. (South Africa), nephew of Thomas (Middlesex), cousin of G. F. (MCC). Sound opening right-hand batsman, right-hand fast round-arm bowler, good cover point. *Teams* Kent (1879–89, 125 matches); Western Province (1890/1 to 1903/4). *Tours* Warton to South Africa 1888/9; South Africa to England 1894 (not first-class). *Tests* England (1888/9, 2 matches); South Africa (1891/2 to 1895/6, 4 matches).
Career batting
161–285–20–4760–144–17.96–4–*ct* 111
Bowling 1346–58–23.20–2–0–5/45
Test batting
6–10–0–168–30–16.80–0–*ct* 3
Bowling 40–2–20.00–0–0–2/40

He emigrated to South Africa in 1889, opening a sports outfitters in Cape Town.

Hearne, George
Professional. *b:* 15.5.1829, Chalfont St Peter, Bucks. *d:* 9.12.1904, Catford, Kent. Brother of Thomas (Middlesex); father of G. G. (Kent), Frank (Kent) and Alec (Kent), grandfather of G. A. L. (South Africa), uncle of G. F. (Middlesex). Hard hitting middle order right-hand batsman, longstop. *Team* Middlesex (1861–68, 18 matches).
Career batting
20–32–6–550–72–21.15–0–*ct* 15–*st* 2

He was groundsman at the Private Banks Ground at Catford Bridge for a period of some thirty years. He also played for Buckinghamshire.

Hearne, George Alfred Lawrence
Amateur. *b:* 27.3.1888, Catford, Kent. *d:* 13.11.1978, Barberton, East Transvaal, South Africa. Son of Frank (Kent), grandson of George (Middlesex), nephew of Alec (Kent) and G. G. (Kent). Opening/middle order right-hand batsman, bowler. *Team* Western Province (1901/2 to 1926/7). *Tour* South Africa to England 1924. *Tests* South Africa (1922/3 to 1924, 3 matches).
Career batting
41–72–2–1981–138–28.30–2–*ct* 38–*st* 2
Bowling 401–14–28.64–0–0–3/9
Test batting
3–5–0–59–28–11.80–0–*ct* 3

He only appeared in one Test on the 1924 tour to England and his batting in first-class matches attained only modest success.

Hearne, George Francis
Professional. *b:* 18.10.1851, Stoke Poges, Bucks. *d:* 30.5.1931, St Albans, Herts. Son of Thomas (Middlesex), father of T. J. (Middlesex), nephew of George (Middlesex), cousin of Alec, G. G. and Frank (all Kent). Lower order right-hand batsman, change bowler, longstop. *Team* MCC (1882).
Career batting
1–1–0–26–26–26.00–0–*ct* 0
Bowling 23–0

Hearne, George Gibbons
Professional. *b:* 7.7.1856, Ealing, Middlesex. *d:* 13.2.1932, Denmark Hill, London. Son of George (Middlesex), brother of Frank (Kent) and Alexander (Kent), nephew of Thomas (Middlesex), uncle of G. A. L. (South Africa). Middle/lower order left-hand batsman, left-hand medium pace round-arm bowler. *Team* Kent (1875–95, 252 matches). *Tour* Read to South Africa 1891/2. *Test* England (1891/2, 1 match).
Career batting
328–571–56–9020–126–17.51–5–*ct* 214
Bowling 11506–685–16.79–40–12–8/21
Test batting
1–1–0–0–0–0.00–0–*ct* 0

He hit 1,000 runs in 1886 – 1,125, av 28.84, and took 100 wickets in a season twice (best 119, av 13.13, in 1878). His final first-class match was for MCC in 1903.

Hearne, Herbert
Professional. *b:* 15.3.1862, Chalfont St Giles, Bucks. *d:* 13.6.1906, Chalfont St Giles. Brother of Walter (Kent) and J. T. (Middlesex). Lower order right-hand batsman, right-arm fast bowler, good field. *Team* Kent (1884–86, 25 matches).
Career batting
25–36–9–252–36–9.33–0–*ct* 16
Bowling 1415–57–24.82–3–0–5/27

He also played for Buckinghamshire.

Hearne, John Thomas
Professional. *b:* 3.5.1867, Chalfont St Giles, Bucks. *d:* 17.4.1944, Chalfont St Giles, Bucks. Brother of Herbert (Kent) and Walter (Kent). Lower order right-hand batsman, right-arm medium pace bowler, slip field. *Team* Middlesex (1888–1923, 453 matches). *Tours* Read to South Africa 1891/2; Stoddart to Australia 1897/8. *Tests* England (1891/2 to 1899, 12 matches).
Career batting
639–919–318–7205–71–11.98–0–*ct* 426
Bowling 54352–3061–17.75–255–64–9/32
Test batting
12–18–4–126–40–9.00–0–*ct* 4
Bowling 1082–49–22.08–4–1–6/41

He took 100 wickets in a season fifteen times, going on to 200 on three occasions, (best 257, av 14.28, in 1896). He took nine wickets in an innings no less than eight times – five for MCC and three for Middlesex, his best figures being 9 for 32 for Middlesex v Notts at Trent Bridge in 1891. For six winters he went to India as a coach, but did not appear in any first-class matches whilst there.

Hearne, John William
Professional. *b:* 11.2.1891, Hillingdon, Middlesex. *d:* 14.9.1965, West Drayton, Middlesex. He was not closely related to the Hearnes of Middlesex and Kent. Stylish middle order right-hand batsman, leg break and googly bowler. *Team* Middlesex (1909–36, 465 matches). *Tours* MCC to West Indies 1910/11, to Australia 1911/12, 1920/1, 1924/5, to South Africa 1913/14. *Tests* England (1911/12 to 1926, 24 matches).
Career batting
647–1025–116–37252–285*–40.98–96–*ct* 348
Bowling 44926–1839–24.42–107–23–9/61
Test batting
24–36–5–806–114–26.00–1–*ct* 13
Bowling 1462–30–48.73–1–0–5/49

One of the leading all-rounders of his day, J. W. Hearne achieved the 'double' five times and on three of those occasions had the added distinction of exceeding 2,000 runs. In all he hit 1,000 runs in a season nineteen times, going on to 2,000 four times with 2,151, av 43.89, in 1932 as his best aggregate. He took over 100 wickets in a season five times (best 142, av 17.83, in 1930).

All eleven of his double centuries were for Middlesex, the highest being 285* v Essex at Leyton in 1929. His best bowling was 9/61 for Middlesex v Derbyshire at Chesterfield in 1933.

He went to Australia with the MCC on three tours, but only managed a moderate record – the best opportunity he had was in 1920/21, when unfortunately he was taken ill in the early stages of the tour and was unable to appear in the majority of matches. In fact ill-health to some extent affected his career and made him a much more cautious batsman than he might otherwise have been.

Hearne, Thomas
Professional. *b:* 4.9.1826, Chalfont St Peter, Bucks. *d:* 13.5.1900, Ealing, Middlesex. Brother of George (Middlesex), father of G. F. (MCC), grandfather of T. J. (Middlesex), uncle of Alec, G. G. and Frank (all Kent). Middle order right-hand batsman, right-hand medium pace round-arm bowler, good point. *Team* Middlesex (1859–75, 59 matches). *Tour* Stephenson to Australia 1861/2.
Career batting
173–292–20–5048–146–18.55–4–*ct* 116–*st* 7
Bowling 3994–283+9–14.11–16–2–6/12

His first-class debut was for MCC in 1857 and his final first-class match was for the same club in 1876. He also played for Hertfordshire and Buckinghamshire. From 1872 he was manager of the ground bowlers at Lord's, not resigning until 1897.

Hearne, Thomas John
Professional. *b:* 3.7.1887, Ealing, Middlesex. Grandson of Thomas (Middlesex), son of G. F. (Middlesex). Lower order batsman, left-arm medium pace bowler. *Team* Middlesex (1908, 1 match).
Career batting
1 match, did not bat–*ct* 0
He also played for Berkshire.

Hearne, Walter
Professional. *b:* 15.1.1864, Chalfont St Giles, Bucks. *d:* 2.4.1925, Canterbury, Kent. Brother of Herbert (Kent) and J. T. (Middlesex). Lower order right-hand batsman, right-arm fast, later medium, bowler. *Team* Kent (1887–96, 55 matches).
Career batting
55–92–19–553–34*–7.57–0–*ct* 23
Bowling 4349–273–15.93–28–10–8/40
He took 116 wickets, av 13.29, in 1894 and his career came to a sudden end in 1896 when he seriously injured his knee.

Hearsum, John
Amateur. *b:* 2.11.1852, Chelsea. *d:* 21.7.1931, Chelmsford, Essex. Middle order right-hand batsman, right-hand fast round arm bowler. *Team* Surrey (1871, 2 matches).
Career batting
2–4–0–43–25–10.75–0–*ct* 0
Bowling 59–0

Heartfield, James
Professional. *b:* 19.1.1823, Mitcham, Surrey. *d:* 1891, Greenwich, Kent. Tail end right-hand batsman, right-hand fast round-arm bowler. *Team* Surrey (1860–67, 9 matches).
Career batting
10–14–2–29–10*–2.41–0–*ct* 5
Bowling 338–21–16.09–2–0–6/28

Heaslip, John Ganly
Amateur. *b:* 26.11.1899, Dublin, Ireland. *d:* 23.5.1966, Twickenham, Middlesex. Middle order right-hand batsman, off break bowler. *Teams* Ireland (1920–29); Dublin U (1922–24).
Career batting
10–19–1–389–92*–21.61–0–*ct* 4
Bowling 610–25–24.40–2–0–5/67

Heasman, Dr William Gratwicke
Amateur. *b:* 9.12.1862, Angmering, Sussex. *d:* 25.1.1934, Eastbourne, Sussex. Middle order right-hand batsman, right-arm fast bowler, good point. *Team* Sussex (1885–95, 15 matches). *Tour* Philadelphians to Bermuda 1907 (not first-class).
Career batting
15–26–0–566–66–21.76–0–*ct* 7
Bowling 46–0
He also played for Berkshire and Norfolk.

Heath, Allan Borman
Amateur. *b:* 19.1.1865, East Woodhay, Hants. *d:* 21.6.1913, Cullompton, Devon. Stylish middle order right-hand batsman, right-arm fast medium bowler, good cover point. *Sch* Cheltenham. *Team* Hampshire (1883–85, 7 matches).
Career batting
7–14–0–132–42–9.42–0–*ct* 2
Bowling 28–2–14.00–0–0–2/28
He appeared for Hants with still a full year to go at school.

Heath, Arthur Howard
Amateur. *b:* 29.5.1856, Newcastle-under-Lyme, Staffs. *d:* 24.4.1930, Marylebone, London. Brother of Sir James (MCC). Middle order right-hand batsman, right-hand fast round-arm, or lob bowler. *Sch* Clifton. *Teams* Oxford U (1876–79, blue all four years); Gloucestershire (1875, 6 matches); Middlesex (1878, 2 matches).
Career batting
44–77–4–969–71–13.27–0–*ct* 26
Bowling 381–26–14.65–1–0–6/11
His final first-class match was for MCC in 1894. He was chiefly associated with Staffordshire, playing for that County from 1879 to 1898, being captain 1884 to 1893, but he also appeared for Cheshire occasionally.
A noted rugby footballer, he played for Oxford and England. He was Conservative MP for Hanley 1900–06 and Leek in 1910.

Heath, David Michael William
Amateur. *b:* 14.12.1931, Birmingham. Opening right-hand batsman. *Team* Warwickshire (1949–53, 16 matches).
Career batting
19–28–1–580–149–21.48–1–*ct* 15
He batted well for Combined Services in 1951 and 1952.

Heath, Frederick Rhead
Amateur. *b:* 30.10.1894, Swadlincote, Derbyshire. *d:* 19.9.1967, Seaford, Sussex. Brother of J. S. (Derbyshire). Middle order batsman. *Team* Derbyshire (1924, 3 matches).
Career batting
3–4–0–59–17–14.75–0–*ct* 1
Bowling 47–3–15.66–0–0–2/4

Heath, George Edward Mansel
Professional. *b:* 20.2.1913, The Peak, Hong Kong. Tail end right-hand batsman, right-arm fast

medium bowler. *Team* Hampshire (1937–49, 132 matches).
Career batting
132–188–83–586–34*–5.58–0–*ct* 49
Bowling 11359–404–28.11–23–2–7/49
His best season was 1938 when he took 97 wickets, av 23.77.

Heath, Rev Henry Francis Trafford
Amateur. *b:* 19.12.1885, Kadina, South Australia. *d:* 9.9.1967, Edinburgh. Lower order batsman, left-arm bowler. *Team* South Australia (1923/4, 2 matches). *Tour* AIF to England 1919.
Career batting
3–4–1–35–21–11.66–0–*ct* 3
Bowling 225–7–32.14–1–0–5/43

Heath, Sir James
Amateur. *b:* 26.1.1852, Newcastle-under-Lyme. *d:* 24.12.1942, Westminster, London. Brother of A. H. (Middlesex). Middle order right-hand batsman, right-hand medium pace round-arm bowler. *Sch* Clifton. *Team* MCC (1882).
Career batting
1–1–0–16–16–16.00–0–*ct* 0
His County cricket was for Staffordshire. He was MP for North West Staffordshire from 1892 to 1906.

Heath, John
Professional. *b:* 12.11.1807, Lambeth, Surrey. *d:* 7.11.1878, London. Steady middle order right-hand batsman, brilliant longstop. *Team* Surrey (1846–54, 19 matches).
Career batting
25–46–5–294–35–7.17–0–*ct* 23
Owing to the paucity of Surrey matches in the 1830s, he had little opportunity to appear in County cricket. His first-class debut was for England in 1842.

Heath, Jeremy Richard Percy
Cricketer. *b:* 26.4.1959, Turner's Hill, Sussex. Middle order left-hand batsman. *Team* Sussex (1980–83, 17 matches).
Career batting
17–31–4–611–101*–22.62–1–*ct* 6
Bowling 58–0

Heath, John Stanley
Amateur. *b:* 30.8.1891, Swadlincote, Derbyshire. *d:* 1.9.1972, Trentham, Staffs. Brother of F. R. (Derbyshire). Middle order right-hand batsman, leg break bowler. *Team* Europeans (India) (1918/9); Derbyshire (1924–25, 7 matches).
Career batting
12–21–3–227–34–12.61–0–*ct* 8
Bowling 832–30–27.73–3–0–5/33
His first-class debut in England was for Leveson-Gower's XI in 1921. He also played for Staffordshire.

Heath, Malcolm
Professional. *b:* 9.3.1934, Bournemouth, Hants. Tail end left-hand batsman, right-arm fast medium bowler. *Team* Hampshire (1954–62, 143 matches).
Career batting
143–163–66–569–33–5.86–0–*ct* 42
Bowling 13237–527–25.11–18–5–8/43
He took 100 wickets in a season once – 126, av 16.42, in 1958.

Heath, Thomas
Professional. *b:* 10.12.1806, Sutton in Ashfield, Notts. *d:* 16.10.1872, Sutton in Ashfield. Middle order right-hand batsman, good deep field. *Team* Nottinghamshire (1828–48, 18 matches).
Career batting
20–36–2–324–35–9.52–0–*ct* 7
He was a noted single-wicket player.

Heath, Walter
Amateur. *b:* 1860, Tewkesbury, Gloucs. *d:* 7.3.1937, Evesham, Worcs. Tail end batsman, wicket-keeper. *Team* Gloucestershire (1886, 1 match).
Career batting
1–1–0–0–0–0.00–0–*ct* 2

Heath, Walter Hodsoll Gordon
Amateur. *b:* 3.12.1897, Streatham, Surrey. *d:* 4.12.1965, Kingswear, Devon. Middle/lower order batsman, wicket-keeper. *Sch* Haileybury. *Team* Surrey (1919, 3 matches).
Career batting
7–11–2–170–58*–18.88–0–*ct* 8–*st* 1
His final first-class match was for Leveson-Gower's XI in 1924. He also appeared in matches for the RAF.

Heathcoat-Amory, Sir John
Amateur. *b:* 2.5.1894, London. *d:* 22.11.1972, Knightshayes Court, Somerset. Forcing middle order right-hand batsman, right-arm fast medium bowler. *Sch* Eton. *Team* Oxford U (1914).
Career batting
6–8–3–137–67*–27.40–0–*ct* 1
Bowling 357–15–23.80–0–0–4/52
His County cricket was for Devon, whom he captained for seven years; his final first-class match was for Minor Counties in 1928.

Heathcoat-Amory, Ludovic
Amateur. *b:* 11.5.1881, London. *d:* 25.8.1918, Bayonvillers, France. Lower order right-hand

batsman, right-arm fast bowler. *Sch* Eton. *Team* Oxford U (1902–03).
Career batting
6–11–0–76–26–6.90–0–*ct* 8
Bowling 165–9–18.33–0–0–4/55
He played for Devonshire.

Heatley, Arthur Edward
Amateur. *b:* 1866, Brighton, Sussex. *d:* 1.7.1941, Brentwood, Essex. Middle order batsman. *Team* Essex (1894, 1 match).
Career batting
1–2–1–20–13*–20.00–0–*ct* 4
Bowling 10–0

Heaven, Raymond Maurice
Professional. *b:* 8.10.1918, Shoreham-by-Sea, Sussex. Right-hand batsman, leg break bowler. *Team* Essex (1939, 1 match).
Career batting
1–1–1–5–5*–no av–0–*ct* 4

Hebden, Geoffrey George Lockwood
Amateur. *b:* 14.7.1918, London. Son of G. L. (Middlesex). Middle/lower order right-hand batsman, right-arm fast medium bowler. *Sch* King's Bruton. *Team* Hampshire (1937–51, 6 matches).
Career batting
6–11–3–69–22*–8.62–0–*ct* 1
Bowling 172–3–57.33–0–0–1/11
He also played for Dorset.

Hebden, George Lockwood
Amateur. *b:* 16.12.1879, Brentford, Middlesex. *d:* 11.6.1946, Bournemouth, Hants. Father of G. G. L. (Hants). Middle order right-hand batsman. *Team* Middlesex (1908–19, 28 matches).
Career batting
28–44–7–677–101–18.29–1–*ct* 13
Bowling 96–0

Hebert, Martyn Carthew
Amateur. *b:* 1841, Clapham, Surrey. *d:* 1905, Hampstead, London. Middle order batsman, change bowler. *Sch* Rossall. *Team* Middlesex (1862, 1 match).
Career batting
1–2–0–14–14–7.00–0–*ct* 0
Bowling 35–3–11.66–0–0–2/25

Hector, Patrick Anthony
Cricketer. *b:* 29.7.1958, Islington, London. Lower order right-hand batsman, right-arm medium pace bowler. *Team* Essex (1977, 3 matches).
Career batting
3–5–1–75–40–18.75–0–*ct* 0
Bowling 190–7–27.14–0–0–3/56

Hedges, Bernard
Professional. *b:* 10.11.1927, Pontypridd, Glamorgan. Opening right-hand batsman, fine outfield. *Team* Glamorgan (1950–67, 422 matches).
Career batting
422–744–41–17733–182–25.22–21–*ct* 199
Bowling 260–3–86.66–0–0–1/16
He hit 1,000 runs in a season nine times, going on to 2,000 once – 2,026, av 32.15, in 1961. He was a noted rugby footballer with Pontypridd and Swansea.

Hedges, Lionel Paget
Amateur. *b:* 13.7.1900, Streatham, London. *d:* 12.1.1933, Cheltenham, Gloucs. Middle order right-hand batsman, fine cover point. *Sch* Tonbridge. *Teams* Kent (1919–24, 52 matches); Oxford U (1920–22, blue all three years); Gloucestershire (1926–29, 30 matches).
Career batting
120–196–6–4219–130–22.20–4–*ct* 69
Bowling 60–1–60.00–0–0–1/23
His best season in first-class cricket was 1921 when he hit 1,138 runs, av 34.48. However, he never fully realised the potential he had shown as a schoolboy – in 1919 he hit 1,038 runs, av 86.50, for Tonbridge.

Hedley, Sir Walter Coote
Amateur. *b:* 12.12.1865, Taunton, Somerset. *d:* 27.12.1937, Sunningdale, Berkshire. Son-in-law of J. Fellowes (Hants and Kent). Middle order right-hand batsman, right-arm fast medium bowler. *Sch* Marlborough. *Teams* Kent (1888, 3 matches); Somerset (1892–1904, 84 matches); Hampshire (1905, 3 matches).
Career batting
103–181–17–2834–102–17.28–2–*ct* 76
Bowling 6628–343–19.32–23–5–8/18
In 1900 his bowling action was condemned by the Captains of the first-class Counties by eleven votes to one. He later played for Devonshire.

Heggie, William Robert
Amateur. *b:* 10.8.1914, Cupar, Fife, Scotland. Right-hand batsman. *Team* Scotland (1937–47).
Career batting
5–10–0–123–44–12.30–0–*ct* 3

Heighes, Bernard Roy
Cricketer. *b:* 16.1.1947, Brentford, Middlesex. Lower order batsman, useful bowler. *Team* MCC (1967).

Career batting
1–1–1–6–6*–no av–0–*ct* 0
Bowling 61–2–30.50–0–0–1/27

Heine, Peter Samuel
Amateur. *b:* 28.6.1928, Winterton, Natal, South Africa. Lower order right-hand batsman, right-arm fast bowler. *Teams* North East Transvaal (1951/2 to 1952/3); Orange Free State (1953/4 to 1954/5); Transvaal (1955/6 to 1964/5). *Tour* South Africa to England 1955. *Tests* South Africa (1955 to 1961/2, 14 matches).
Career batting
61–97–14–1255–67–15.52–0–*ct* 34
Bowling 5924–277–21.38–20–4–8/92
Test batting
14–24–3–209–31–9.95–0–*ct* 8
Bowling 1455–58–25.08–4–0–6/58
The most hostile of the fast bowlers on the 1955 tour of England, he was surprisingly omitted from the first Test, but thereafter bowled extremely well – in first-class matches he took 74 wickets, av 19.86, and had 21 wickets av 23.52, in the Tests.

Hellard, John Alexander
Amateur. *b:* 20.3.1882, Williton, Somerset. *d:* 2.7.1916, near Beaumont Hamel, France. Middle order right-hand batsman, right-arm fast medium bowler. *Sch* King's Canterbury. *Team* Somerset (1907–10, 2 matches).
Career batting
2–3–0–18–15–6.00–0–*ct* 0

Hellawell, Michael Stephen
Professional. *b:* 30.6.1938, Keighley, Yorkshire. Middle order right-hand batsman, right-arm medium pace bowler. *Team* Warwickshire (1962, 1 match).
Career batting
1–2–2–59–30*–no av–0–*ct* 0
Bowling 114–6–19.00–0–0–4/54
A good soccer player, he appeared at outside left for Birmingham City, Q.P.R., Sunderland, Huddersfield and Peterborough.

Hellmuth, Leon
Amateur. *b:* 14.8.1934, Blackheath, Kent. Lower order left-hand batsman, slow left-arm bowler. *Sch* Haberdashers Aske's School. *Team* Kent (1951–52, 7 matches).
Career batting
7–13–1–34–11–2.83–0–*ct* 8
Bowling 383–8–47.87–0–0–2/11

Helm, Dr George Frederick
Amateur. *b:* 11.1.1838, Worthing, Sussex. *d:* 31.3.1898, Marazion, Cornwall. Middle order right-hand batsman, left-hand medium pace round-arm bowler, short-slip. *Sch* Marlborough. *Teams* Sussex (1860, 2 matches); Cambridge U (1861–63, blue 1862 and 1863).
Career batting
5–6–1–21–11–4.20–0–*ct* 1
Bowling 76–5+8–15.20–1–0–6/?
He also played for Cambridgeshire.

Hemingway, George Edward
Amateur. *b:* Jan 1872, Sutton, Macclesfield, Cheshire. *d:* 11.3.1907, Rangoon, Burma. Brother of R. E. (Notts) and W. M. (Gloucs). Hard hitting middle order right-hand batsman, left-arm bowler. *Sch* Uppingham. *Team* Gloucestershire (1898, 1 match).
Career batting
1–2–0–0–0–0.00–0–*ct* 1

Hemingway, Ralph Eustace
Amateur. *b:* 15.12.1877, Sutton, Macclesfield, Cheshire. *d:* 15.10.1915, Loos, France. He was killed in action. Brother of G. E. (Gloucs) and W. M. (Gloucs). Middle order right-hand batsman. *Sch* Rugby. *Team* Nottinghamshire (1903–05, 30 matches).
Career batting
32–50–2–976–85–20.33–0–*ct* 17
Bowling 6–0
He was also a noted rugby footballer.

Hemingway, William McGregor
Amateur. *b:* 12.11.1873, Sutton, Macclesfield, Cheshire. *d:* 11.2.1967, Paignton, Devon. Brother of G. E. (Gloucs) and R. E. (Notts). Middle order right-hand batsman. *Sch* Uppingham. *Teams* Gloucestershire (1893–1900, 48 matches); Cambridge U (1895–96, blue both years). *Tours* Mitchell to North America 1895; Warner to North America 1897.
Career batting
69–118–3–1952–104–16.97–1–*ct* 28

Hemming, Sir Augustus William Lawson
Amateur. *b:* 2.9.1841, London. *d:* 27.3.1907, Cairo, Egypt. Lower order right-hand batsman, right-hand fast round-arm bowler, good field. *Sch* Epsom and Godolphin. *Teams* MCC (1866–74); Jamaica and United Services (1901/02).
Career batting
6–9–2–56–16–8.00–0–*ct* 3
Bowling 127–6–21.16–1–0–5/69
He was a founder member of the Incogniti and commencing 1871 the Hon Secretary of that Club.
His last first-class match in England was for MCC in 1878 and his next and final first-class match for Jamaica and United Services in 1901/2 – 23 years separating the two games.

In 1896 and 1897 he was Governor of British Guiana and from 1898 to 1904 Governor of Jamaica.

Hemming, Leonard Ernest Gerald
Amateur. *b:* 30.9.1916, Enfield, Middlesex. Right-hand batsman, off break bowler. *Team* Minor Counties (1951).
Career batting
1–2–0–28–14–14.00–0–*ct* 0
Bowling 60–1–60.00–0–0–1/60
He played for Oxfordshire.

Hemmings, Edward Ernest
Cricketer. *b:* 20.2.1949, Leamington Spa, Warwickshire. Lower order right-hand batsman, right-arm medium, later off break bowler. *Teams* Warwickshire (1966–78, 177 matches); Nottinghamshire (1979–83, 108 matches). *Tours* England to Australia and New Zealand 1982/3 (not first-class in New Zealand); Robins to South Africa 1974/5; International XI to Pakistan 1981/2, to Jamaica 1982/3. *Tests* England (1982 to 1982/3, 5 matches).
Career batting
298–412–88–6600–127*–20.37–1–*ct* 143
Bowling 24415–838–29.13–38–10–10/175
Test batting
5–10–1–198–95–22.00–0–*ct* 4
Bowling 558–12–46.50–0–0–3/68
His best season was 1981 with 90 wickets, av 20.63, and his best bowling in an innings was 10/175 for an International XI v West Indian XI at Kingston 1982/3.

Hemsley, Edward John Orton
Cricketer. *b:* 1.9.1943, Norton, Stoke on Trent, Staffs. Middle order right-hand batsman, right-arm medium pace bowler. *Team* Worcestershire (1963–82, 243 matches).
Career batting
243–389–57–9740–176*–29.33–8–*ct* 180
Bowling 2497–70–35.67–0–0–3/5
He hit 1,168 runs, av 38.93, in 1978. A noted soccer player, he appeared for Shrewsbury, Sheffield United and Doncaster Rovers.

Hemsley, Philip David
Cricketer. *b:* 23.11.1959, Buxted, Sussex. Lower order right-hand batsman, right-arm medium pace bowler. *Team* Cambridge U (1980–81).
Career batting
3–5–2–26–12*–8.66–0–*ct* 1
Bowling 143–1–143.00–0–0–1/4

Hemsted, Edward
Amateur. *b:* 10.10.1846, Whitchurch, Hants. *d:* 12.3.1884, Weymouth, Dorset. Middle order right-hand batsman, right-hand fast round-arm bowler, slip field. *Sch* Chatham House, Ramsgate. *Team* Hampshire (1866–69, 7 matches).
Career batting
8–15–1–220–39–15.71–0–*ct* 3
Bowling 139–10–13.90–1–0–5/14
His first-class debut was for Gentlemen of Kent in 1863.

Henderson, Andrew Arthur
Cricketer. *b:* 14.7.1941, Chadwell Heath, Essex. Lower order right-hand batsman, right-arm medium pace bowler. *Team* Sussex (1972, 1 match).
Career batting
1–2–0–11–9–5.50–0–*ct* 0
Bowling 132–5–26.40–0–0–3/65

Henderson, Andrew William
Amateur. *b:* 23.1.1922, Selkirk, Scotland. Right-hand batsman, right-arm medium pace bowler. *Team* Scotland (1953).
Career batting
1–1–0–2–2–2.00–0–*ct* 0
Bowling 10–0

Henderson, Derek
Amateur. *b:* 9.3.1926, Bexhill, Sussex. Father of S. P. (Worcs and Glamorgan). Lower order right-hand batsman, right-arm medium fast bowler. *Sch* St Edward's, Oxford. *Team* Oxford U (1949–50, blue 1950).
Career batting
16–20–8–131–21*–10.91–0–*ct* 3
Bowling 1039–34–30.55–0–0–4/39
His final first-class match was for Free Foresters in 1954.

Henderson, James Douglas
Amateur. *b:* 13.10.1918, Kelso, Scotland. Left-hand batsman, left-arm medium pace bowler. *Team* Scotland (1946–56).
Career batting
14–22–3–429–121–22.57–1–*ct* 7
Bowling 650–29–22.41–1–0–5/27

Henderson, Matthew
Amateur. *b:* 2.8.1895, Auckland, New Zealand. *d:* 17.6.1970, Lower Hutt, New Zealand. Lower order left-hand batsman, left-arm fast medium bowler. *Team* Wellington (1921/2 to 1931/2). *Tours* New Zealand to England 1927, to Australia 1927/8. *Test* New Zealand (1929/30, 1 match).

Career batting
41–57–22–495–47–14.14–0–*ct* 12
Bowling 3200–107–29.90–5–0–6/70
Test batting
1–2–1–8–6–8.00–0–*ct* 1
Bowling 64–2–32.00–0–0–2/38

He only obtained modest results on the 1927 tour of England, his bowling being somewhat wayward.

Henderson, Robert
Amateur. *b:* 3.5.1851, Fulham, Middlesex. *d:* 22.9.1895, Sedgewick Park, Horsham, Sussex. Lower order right-hand batsman, right-hand slow round-arm bowler, point field. *Sch* Harrow. *Team* Middlesex (1872–78, 16 matches).
Career batting
24–41–5–349–42–9.69–0–*ct* 15
Bowling 2503–151–16.57–17–3–8/46

Henderson, Robert
Professional. *b:* 30.3.1865, Newport, Monmouthshire. *d:* 28.1.1931, Wallington, Surrey. Middle order right-hand batsman, slow right-arm bowler. *Team* Surrey (1883–96, 141 matches).
Career batting
148–230–30–3701–106–18.50–1–*ct* 88
Bowling 1278–60–21.30–1–0–6/17

Owing to ill-health he played very little in the three seasons 1884 to 1886 and was twice sent overseas at the expense of the Surrey Club for health reasons.

Henderson, Stephen Peter
Cricketer. *b:* 24.9.1958, Oxford. Son of Derek (Oxford U). Middle order left-hand batsman, right-arm medium pace bowler. *Sch* Downside. *Team* Worcestershire (1977–81, 24 matches); Cambridge U (1982–83, blue both years); Glamorgan (1983, 10 matches). *Tour* MCC to North America 1982 (not first-class).
Career batting
53–87–12–1818–209*–24.24–2–*ct* 39
Bowling 185–3–61.66–0–0–2/48

His highest innings was 209* for Cambridge U v Middlesex at Fenner's in 1982.

Henderson, Dr Thomas Bonhote
Amateur. *b:* 3.1.1875, Kensington, London. *d:* 19.4.1920, East Harnham, Wiltshire. Middle order right-hand batsman, right-arm fast medium bowler, good field. *Sch* Winchester. *Team* Oxford U (1897).
Career batting
8–13–1–220–49–18.33–0–*ct* 10
Bowling 207–7–29.57–0–0–3/39

His final first-class match was for MCC in 1901.

Hendren, Denis
Professional. *b:* 25.9.1882, Chiswick, Middlesex. *d:* 29.5.1962, Paddington, London. Brother of E. H. (Middlesex). Middle order right-hand batsman, slow right-arm bowler. *Team* Middlesex (1905–19, 9 matches).
Career batting
9–16–2–109–23–7.78–0–*ct* 5
Bowling 104–3–34.66–0–0–1/19

His first-class cricket effectively ended in 1907 and he appeared for Durham from 1910 to 1914; later he was on the first-class umpires' list.

Hendren, Elias Henry
Professional. *b:* 5.2.1889, Turnham Green, Middlesex. *d:* 4.10.1962, Tooting Bec, London. Brother of Denis (Middlesex). Middle order right-hand batsman, right-arm slow bowler, excellent deep field. *Team* Middlesex (1907–37, 581 matches). *Tours* MCC to Australia 1920/1, 1924/5, 1928/9, to West Indies 1929/30, 1934/5, to South Africa 1930/1. *Tests* England (1920/1 to 1934/5, 51 matches).
Career batting
833–1300–166–57611–301*–50.80–170–*ct* 754
Bowling 2574–48–53.62–1–0–5/43
Test batting
51–83–9–3525–205*–47.63–7–*ct* 33
Bowling 31–1–31.00–0–0–1/27

The leading middle order batsman in English cricket during the 1920s, 'Patsy' Hendren was equally at home overseas and had tremendous success on all his MCC tours. His greatest triumph was the visit to West Indies in 1929/30. Hendren hit no less than four double centuries during the tour and a total of 1,765 runs, av 135.76 – a record which still stands. On each of his three trips to Australia he exceeded 1,000 runs with an average over 60.00 and he was almost as successful on his single tour to South Africa.

In English cricket he hit over 3,000 runs in a season three times, his highest aggregate being 3,311, av 70.44, in 1928. On twelve other occasions he exceeded 2,000 and on another six occasions he exceeded 1,000 runs.

His highest innings was 301* for Middlesex v Worcestershire at Dudley in 1933. In all he hit 22 first-class innings of 200 or more – only W. R. Hammond and D. G. Bradman scored more.

In Test cricket his highest innings was 205* v West Indies at Port of Spain in 1929/30 and of his contemporaries only J. B. Hobbs made more runs. No England team was representative if it lacked Hendren during the decade following the First World War.

His last first-class match was for an England XI in 1938.

He was an excellent soccer player, appearing

for Brentford, Queens Park Rangers, Manchester City and Coventry as a wing forward.

Hendrick, Michael
Cricketer. *b:* 22.10.1948, Darley Dale, Derbyshire. Lower order right-hand batsman, right-arm fast medium bowler, slip field. *Teams* Derbyshire (1969–81, 167 matches); Nottinghamshire (1982–83, 31 matches). *Tours* MCC to West Indies 1973/4, to Australia and New Zealand 1974/5, to Pakistan and New Zealand 1977/8, to Australia 1978/9, 1979/80; Robins to South Africa 1975/6; SAB to South Africa 1981/2. *Tests* England (1974–81, 30 matches).
Career batting
264–307–109–1601–46–10.13–0–*ct* 174
Bowling 15699–762–20.60–29–3–8/45
Test batting
30–35–15–128–15–6.40–0–*ct* 25
Bowling 2248–87–25.83–0–0–4/28
His best seasons were 1975 with 68 wickets, av 15.83, and 1977 with 67, av 15.94. His bowling, with its nagging accuracy, is particularly effective in limited overs cricket.

Hendriks, John Leslie
Amateur. *b:* 21.12.1933, Kingston, Jamaica. Lower order right-hand batsman, wicket-keeper. *Team* Jamaica (1953/4 to 1966/7). *Tours* West Indies to India and Pakistan 1958/9, to India 1966/7, to Australia 1960/1, to Australia and New Zealand 1968/9, to England 1966, 1969. *Tests* West Indies (1961/2 to 1969, 20 matches).
Career batting
83–113–23–1568–82–17.42–0–*ct* 140–*st* 50
Bowling 61–0
Test batting
20–32–8–447–64–18.62–0–*ct* 42–*st* 5
After missing the first two Tests of the 1966 England tour due to injury, he he was in fine form behind the wicket for the remainder of the tour. In 1969 however, though starting as the principal wicket-keeper, he lost his Test place to Findlay.

Hendry, Hunter Scott Thomas Laurie
Amateur. *b:* 24.5.1895, Woollahra, New South Wales, Australia. Middle/lower order right-hand batsman, right-arm fast medium bowler. *Teams* New South Wales (1918/9 to 1923/4, 38 matches); Victoria (1924/5 to 1932/3, 41 matches). *Tours* Australia to England 1921, 1926, to South Africa 1921/2, to India and Ceylon 1935/6; New South Wales to New Zealand 1923/4. *Tests* Australia (1921 to 1928/9, 11 matches).
Career batting
140–206–25–6799–325*–37.56–14–*ct* 151
Bowling 6647–229–29.02–6–1–8/33
Test batting
11–18–2–335–112–20.93–1–*ct* 10
Bowling 640–16–40.00–0–0–3/36
He played in four of the five Tests in England in 1921, but batted very low in the order and bowled only in order to rest the main attack; in 1926 he was struck down with scarlet fever early on the tour and missed all the Tests, thus his record in English cricket was very modest. In Australia however he proved a most accomplished all-rounder. His only innings over 200 was 325* for NSW v New Zealanders at Melbourne in 1925/6.

Hendy, A. S.
Amateur. *d:* 1910. *d:* 1965, British Columbia. Lower order left-hand batsman, slow left-arm bowler. *Team* Canada (1951–54). *Tour* Canada to England 1954.
Career batting
4–6–0–46–22–7.66–0–*ct* 2
Bowling 222–10–22.20–0–0–4/73

Henery, Perceval Jeffery Thornton
Amateur. *b:* 6.6.1859, London. *d:* 10.8.1938, Washford, Somerset. Hard hitting middle order right-hand batsman, right-hand slow round-arm bowler, brilliant field. *Sch* Harrow. *Teams* Middlesex (1879–94, 72 matches); Cambridge U (1881–83, blue 1882–83); British Guiana (1883/4).
Career batting
94–152–11–2229–138*–15.80–1–*ct* 53
Bowling 209–12–17.41–1–0–5/56

Henfrey, Arthur George
Amateur. *b:* 1868, Wellingborough, Northants. *d:* 17.10.1929, Finedon, Northants. Middle order right-hand batsman. *Sch* Wellingborough. *Team* Cambridge U (1890).
Career batting
1–2–0–17–11–8.50–0–*ct* 0

Henley, Anthony Alfred
Amateur. *b:* 1846, Sherborne, Dorset. *d:* 14.12.1916, Woodbridge, Suffolk. Brother of Robert (Hants). Middle order batsman. *Sch* Sherborne. *Team* Hampshire (1866, 1 match).
Career batting
1–2–0–16–9–8.00–0–*ct* 0
He also played for Dorset.

Henley, David Francis
(changed name to Henley-Welch 1948)
Amateur. *b:* 21.7.1923, Melton, Suffolk. Lower

order right-hand batsman, right-arm fast medium bowler. *Sch* Harrow. *Team* Oxford U (1946–48, blue 1947).
Career batting
17–30–4–558–58–21.46–0–*ct* 13
Bowling 931–23–40.47–0–0–3/28
His County cricket was for Suffolk and his final first-class match was for Minor Counties in 1949.

Henley, Francis Anthony Hoste
Amateur. *b:* 11.2.1884, Woodbridge, Suffolk. *d:* 26.6.1963, Wheathampstead, Herts. Lower order right-hand batsman, right-arm fast bowler. *Sch* Forest. *Teams* Oxford U (1903–05, blue 1905); Middlesex (1908, 3 matches). *Tour* MCC to North America (1905).
Career batting
15–26–3–257–52*–11.17–0–*ct* 14
Bowling 1106–41–26.97–0–0–4/39
He also played for Suffolk.

Henley, Robert
Amateur. *b:* 10.6.1851, Sherborne, Dorset. *d:* 21.3.1889, Ovington, Hants. Brother of A. A. (Hants). *Sch* Sherborne. *Team* Hampshire (1875, 1 match).
Career batting
1–1–0–14–14–14.00–0–*ct* 0
Bowling 14–0
He also played for Dorset.

Henry, Denis Philip
Amateur. *b:* 7.7.1907, London. Lower order right-hand batsman, leg break bowler. *Team* Free Foresters (1948).
Career batting
1–1–0–1–1–1.00–0–*ct* 0
Bowling 16–0

Henry, F.
Professional. Tail end batsman, opening bowler. *Team* Middlesex (1882, 1 match).
Career batting
1–2–1–5–5*–5.00–0–*ct* 1
Bowling 52–2–26.00–0–0–2/16

Henry, Ian Clifford
Amateur. *b:* 23.10.1914, London. Middle order right-hand batsman, leg break bowler. *Sch* Uppingham. *Team* Free Foresters (1937).
Career batting
1–2–0–84–80–42.00–0–*ct* 1

Henslow, Edward Lancelot Wall
Amateur. *b:* 19.3.1879, Mere, Wilts. *d:* 12.3.1947, Salisbury, Wilts. Middle order batsman, bowler. *Team* Army (1912).
Career batting
1–2–0–0–0–0.00–0–*ct* 0
Bowling 22–1–22.00–0–0–1/22
He played for Wiltshire.

Henson, Richard
Professional. *b:* 10.10.1864, Ruddington, Notts. *d:* 29.11.1929, Ruddington, Notts. Lower order batsman, left-arm slow medium bowler. *Team* Liverpool and District (1894).
Career batting
1–2–0–19–17–9.50–0–*ct* 0
Bowling 5–2–2.50–0–0–2/5

Henson, William Walker
Professional. *b:* 7.12.1872, Nottingham. *d:* 7.9.1922, Dumfries, Scotland. Lower order right-hand batsman, right-arm fast medium bowler. *Team* Nottinghamshire (1897–98, 13 matches).
Career batting
13–16–5–110–35*–10.00–0–*ct* 7
Bowling 835–24–34.79–0–0–4/82

Henty, Edward
Professional. *b:* 11.8.1839, Hawkhurst, Kent. *d:* 20.1.1900, Lewisham, Kent. Very steady lower order right-hand batsman, excellent wicket-keeper. *Team* Kent (1865–81, 116 matches).
Career batting
119–209–64–1153–72–7.95–0–*ct* 136–*st* 66
Bowling 10–1–10.00–0–0–1/3

Henwood, Pelham Peter
Cricketer. *b:* 22.5.1946, Durban, South Africa. Lower order right-hand batsman, slow left-arm bowler. *Teams* Orange Free State (1965/6); Natal (1966/7 to 1979/80). *Tour* South African Universities to England 1967.
Career batting
79–102–22–769–46–9.61–0–*ct* 26
Bowling 5877–212–27.72–9–1–7/34

Herbert, Allen William Henry
Amateur. *b:* 20.10.1852, Hythe, Kent. *d:* 14.9.1897, Belgravia, London. Middle order right-hand batsman. *Teams* Kent (1874, 1 match); Middlesex (1875, 1 match).
Career batting
11–19–2–239–63–14.05–0–*ct* 6
His first-class debut in 1872 and his final first-class match in 1876 were both for MCC. He also played for Wiltshire and Essex (non-first-class).

Herbert, Eric James
Professional. *b:* 1908, Rushden, Northants. *d:* 14.10.1963, Wellingborough, Northants. Steady lower order right-hand batsman, right-arm

medium pace bowler. *Team* Northants (1937–39, 35 matches).
Career batting
35–57–24–291–20–8.81–0–*ct* 11
Bowling 2322–69–33.65–1–0–5/103

Herbert, Herbert Henry Moore
Amateur. *b:* 1863, Kensington, London. *d:* 1884, St Pancras, London. *Team* Middlesex (1883, 1 match).
Career batting
1–2–1–1–1–1.00–0–*ct* 1

Herbert, Hon Mervyn Robert Howard Molyneux
Amateur. *b:* 27.11.1882, Kingsclere, Hants. *d:* 26.5.1929, Rome, Italy. Opening/middle order right-hand batsman. *Sch* Eton. *Teams* Nottinghamshire (1901–02, 6 matches); Somerset (1903–24, 31 matches); Oxford U (1904).
Career batting
42–74–3–854–78–12.02–0–*ct* 18
Bowling 28–0

Herbert, Percy
Amateur. *b:* 1878, Steyning, Sussex. *d:* 24.1.1958, Hove, Sussex. Uncle of P. G. H. Fender (Surrey). *Team* Gentlemen of the South (1920).
Career batting
1 match, did not bat–*ct* 0

Herbert, Reuben
Cricketer. *b:* 1.12.1957, Cape Town, South Africa. Middle order right-hand batsman, off break bowler. *Team* Essex (1976–80, 6 matches).
Career batting
6–9–1–62–14*–7.75–0–*ct* 5
Bowling 148–3–49.33–0–0–3/64

Herkes, Robert
Cricketer. *b:* 30.6.1957, Lincoln. Tail end right-hand batsman, right-arm medium pace bowler. *Team* Middlesex (1978–79, 3 matches).
Career batting
3–5–3–0–0*–0.00–0–*ct* 0
Bowling 93–6–15.50–1–0–6/60
He also played for Lincolnshire.

Herman, Oswald William
Professional. *b:* 18.9.1907, Horsepath, Oxon. Father of R. S. (Hants and Middlesex). Lower order right-hand batsman, right-arm fast medium bowler. *Team* Hampshire (1929–48, 321 matches).
Career batting
322–496–105–4336–92–11.08–0–*ct* 123
Bowling 28222–1045–27.00–58–6–8/49
He took 100 wickets in a season five times (best 142, av 22.07, in 1937). He also played for Wiltshire. He was later on the first-class umpires' list.

Herman, Robert Stephen
Cricketer. *b:* 30.11.1946, Southampton, Hants. Son of O. W. (Hampshire). Lower order right-hand batsman, right-arm fast medium bowler. *Teams* Middlesex (1965–71, 92 matches); Hampshire (1972–77, 89 matches); Border (1972/3); Griqualand West (1974/5).
Career batting
189–189–49–1426–56–10.18–0–*ct* 74
Bowling 13348–506–26.37–14–0–8/42
He also played for Dorset.
He was appointed a first-class umpire in 1980.

Hermiston, William
Amateur. *b:* 4.2.1913, Makerston, Roxburghshire, Scotland. Right-hand batsman, right-arm fast medium bowler. *Team* Scotland (1949).
Career batting
2–4–0–35–21–8.75–0–*ct* 1
Bowling 84–2–42.00–0–0–2/21

Heron, George Allen
Amateur. *b:* 19.2.1877, Marylebone, Middlesex. *d:* 22.7.1948, Pevensey Bay, Sussex. Middle order right-hand batsman, right-arm medium pace bowler. *Sch* Merchant Taylors and St Pauls. *Team* MCC (1899).
Career batting
1–2–0–37–31–18.50–0–*ct* 0

Heron, Jack Gunner
Cricketer. *b:* 8.11.1948, Salisbury, Rhodesia. Middle order right-hand batsman. *Team* Rhodesia/Zimbabwe (1967/8 to 1982/3). *Tour* Zimbabwe to England 1982.
Career batting
60–113–5–2830–175–26.20–5–*ct* 39
Bowling 17–0
He also represented Rhodesia at hockey.

Heroys, Nicholas
Amateur. *b:* 1.4.1937, Marylebone. Middle order right-hand batsman, right-arm medium pace bowler. *Sch* Tonbridge. *Team* Cambridge U (1960).
Career batting
1–2–0–10–10–5.00–0–*ct* 0
Bowling 35–0

Herring, Sir Edward Francis
Amateur. *b:* 2.9.1892, Maryborough, Victoria,

Australia. Nephew of L. L. (Western Australia). Opening right-hand batsman. *Team* Oxford U (1913).
Career batting
2–4–0–65–21–16.25–0–*ct* 1

Herringshaw, John Percy
Professional. *b:* 22.5.1892, Derby. *d:* 13.11.1974, Yapton, Sussex. Lower order left-hand batsman, slow left-arm bowler. *Team* Essex (1921–22, 9 matches).
Career batting
9–14–5–94–18–10.44–0–*ct* 7
Bowling 498–9–55.33–0–0–2/48

Herriot, Thomas Pearson
Amateur. *b:* 11.5.1887, Berwick-on-Tweed, Northumberland. *d:* 20.10.1949, Berwick-on-Tweed, Northumberland. Middle order batsman. *Sch* Fettes. *Team* Scotland (1911).
Career batting
1–1–0–80–80–80.00–0–*ct* 1
He played for Northumberland.

Herting, Frederick J.
Professional. *b:* 1940, Uxbridge, Middlesex. Lower order batsman, opening bowler. *Team* Somerset (1960, 5 matches).
Career batting
5–7–2–44–16*–8.80–0–*ct* 1
Bowling 506–7–72.28–0–0–4/85

Hervey-Bathurst, Sir Frederick Hutchinson
Amateur. *b:* 6.6.1807. *d:* 29.10.1881, Clarendon Park, Wilts. Father of Sir F. T. A. (Hants). Slogging right-hand batsman, fast right-hand round-arm bowler. *Sch* Winchester. *Team* Hampshire (1842–61).
Career batting
93–159–21–817–46–5.92–*ct* 41
Bowling 977–74+275–13.20–32–8–7/?
Regarded as one of the finest of all fast bowlers, he played regularly for the Gentlemen v Players between 1831 and 1854. His debut was for England in 1831. He also appeared for Devon and Wiltshire. He was on the Committee of MCC and President of the Club in 1857.

Hervey-Bathurst, Sir Frederick Thomas Arthur
Amateur. *b:* 13.3.1833, London. *d:* 20.5.1900, Westminster, London. Son of Sir F. H. (Hants). Hard-hitting lower order batsman, fast round-arm or slow under-arm bowler. *Sch* Eton. *Team* Hampshire (1865–66, 3 matches).
Career batting
13–24–2–187–49–8.50–0–*ct* 2
Bowling 44–2–22.00–0–0–1/17
His debut was for MCC in 1852 and he also played County cricket for Devon and Wiltshire. He was MP for Wiltshire and he fought in the Crimean War.

Hervey-Bathurst, Lionel
(later Paston-Cooper)
Amateur. *b:* 7.7.1849, Clarendon, Wiltshire. *d:* 4.5.1908, Hemel Hempstead, Herts. Opening batsman, wicket-keeper. *Sch* Rugby. *Team* Hampshire (1875, 2 matches).
Career batting
2–4–0–30–14–7.50–0–*ct* 1–*st* 1
Bowling 8–0

Heseltine, Christopher
Amateur. *b:* 26.11.1869, London. *d:* 13.6.1944, Walhampton, Lymington, Hants. Lower order right-hand batsman, right-arm fast bowler. *Sch* Eton. *Team* Hampshire (1895–1904, 52 matches). *Tours* Hawke to India 1892/3, to South Africa 1895/6, to West Indies 1896/7. *Tests* England (1895/6, 2 matches).
Career batting
79–121–8–1390–77–12.30–0–*ct* 54
Bowling 4171–170–24.53–7–0–7/106
Test batting
2–2–0–18–18–9.00–0–*ct* 3
Bowling 84–5–16.80–1–0–5/38
He did not play first-class cricket whilst at Cambridge, but was awarded his soccer blue in 1891/2. His debut in first-class cricket was for MCC in 1892 and his final first-class match for the same Club in 1914.

Heseltine, Phillip John
Cricketer. *b:* 21.6.1960, Skipton, Yorkshire. Middle order right-hand batsman, right-arm medium or off break bowler. *Team* Oxford U (1983, blue).
Career batting
6–10–1–176–40–19.55–0–*ct* 5

Hesketh-Prichard, Hesketh Vernon
Amateur. *b:* 17.11.1876, Jhansi, India. *d:* 14.6.1922, Gorhambury, Herts. Lower order right-hand batsman, right-arm fast bowler. *Sch* Fettes. *Teams* Hampshire (1900–13, 60 matches); London County (1902–04). *Tours* Brackley to West Indies 1904/5; MCC to North America 1907.
Career batting
86–135–38–724–37–7.46–0–*ct* 44
Bowling 7586–339–22.37–25–5–8/32
In 1904 he took 106 wickets, av 21.92. He was a well-known traveller and writer.

Heslop, Gerald Gwydyr
Amateur. *b:* 1879, Kingston, Surrey. *d:* 1913,

Norwich. Opening batsman. *Sch* Norwich. *Team* Cambridge U (1898).
Career batting
2–4–0–19–14–4.75–0–*ct* 1
His County cricket was for Norfolk.

Hettiaratchy, Nirmal Dilhan Peter
Cricketer. *b:* 30.9.1951, Colombo. Opening right-hand batsman, wicket-keeper. *Team* Sri Lanka (1970/1 to 1982/3). *Tours* Sri Lanka to India 1974/5, to England 1981; Sri Lanka XI to South Africa 1982/3.
Career batting
20–32–1–686–80–22.12–0–*ct* 14

Hever, Harold Lawrence
Professional. *b:* 23.6.1895, Southborough, Kent. *d:* 18.7.1958, Pembury, Kent. Lower order left-hand batsman, slow left-arm bowler. *Team* Kent (1921–25, 6 matches).
Career batting
7–11–6–25–11*–5.00–0–*ct* 4
Bowling 391–15–26.06–0–0–3/57

Hever, Norman George
Professional. *b:* 17.12.1924, Marylebone, London. Tail end right-hand batsman, right-arm fast medium bowler. *Teams* Middlesex (1947, 9 matches); Glamorgan (1948–53, 133 matches).
Career batting
144–177–81–897–40–9.34–0–*ct* 63
Bowling 7901–333–23.72–12–0–7/55

Hewan, Gethyn Elliot
Amateur. *b:* 23.12.1916, Edinburgh, Scotland. Middle order right-hand batsman, off break bowler. *Sch* Marlborough. *Team* Cambridge U (1938, blue).
Career batting
6–9–0–187–88–20.77–0–*ct* 2
Bowling 725–20–36.25–2–0–6/91
He played for Berkshire.

Hewetson, Edward Pearson
Amateur. *b:* 27.5.1902, Birmingham. *d:* 26.12.1977, Bampton, Oxon. Hard hitting lower order right-hand batsman, right-arm fast bowler. *Sch* Shrewsbury. *Teams* Warwickshire (1919–27, 29 matches); Oxford U (1922–25, blue 1923–25).
Career batting
66–94–10–1213–66–14.44–0–*ct* 41
Bowling 4169–163–25.58–6–1–5/16
His final first-class match was for Free Foresters in 1934. He appeared for Warwickshire in 1919 with two full years at school still to complete.

Hewetson, General Sir Reginald Hackett
Amateur. *b:* 4.8.1908, Shortlands, Kent. Middle order right-hand batsman. *Sch* Repton. *Teams* Army (1935–37); Europeans (1929/30).
Career batting
6–11–1–115–25–11.50–0–*ct* 3

Hewett, Herbert Tremenheere
Amateur. *b:* 25.5.1864, Norton-Fitzwarren, Somerset. *d:* 4.3.1921, Hove, Sussex. Hard hitting opening left-hand batsman, medium pace bowler. *Sch* Harrow. *Teams* Somerset (1884–93, 50 matches); Oxford U (1886, blue). *Tours* Hawke to North America 1891, to South Africa 1895/6 (no first-class matches).
Career batting
104–182–8–5099–201–29.30–7–*ct* 49
Bowling 240–2–120.00–0–0–2/40
He captained Somerset from 1891 to 1893, in which year he resigned because he felt that his authority during the match against the Australians had been unwarrantably overruled. After that season he rarely appeared in first-class matches, this being a great loss to the game, since he was one of the most remarkable batsmen of his time. He hit 1,000 runs in a season twice (best 1,407, av 35.17, in 1892). His only double century was 201 for Somerset v Yorkshire at Taunton in 1892. His final first-class match was for MCC in 1896.

Hewitson, Joseph
Professional. *b:* 1865, Bolton, Lancashire. *d:* 1925, Bolton, Lancashire. Lower order left-hand batsman, slow left-arm bowler. *Team* Lancashire (1890, 4 matches).
Career batting
4–5–0–99–56–19.80–0–*ct* 1
Bowling 235–14–16.78–1–1–6/57

Hewitt, Eric Joseph
Amateur. *b:* 19.12.1935, Erdington, Birmingham. Middle order right-hand batsman, leg break and googly bowler. *Team* Warwickshire (1954, 1 match).
Career batting
2–3–0–55–40–18.33–0–*ct* 1
Bowling 60–1–60.00–0–0–1/20
His final first-class match was for Combined Services in 1957.

Hewitt, Francis Stanley Arnot
Cricketer. *b:* 13.3.1936, Belfast, Ireland. Right-hand batsman, right-arm fast medium or off break bowler. *Sch* Royal Belfast Academical Institute. *Team* Ireland (1966).
Career batting
1–2–0–53–36–26.50–0–*ct* 1
Bowling 44–0

Hewitt, Steven Guy Paul
Cricketer. *b:* 6.4.1963, Radcliffe, Lancashire. Tail end right-hand batsman, wicket-keeper. *Team* Cambridge U (1983, blue).
Career batting
6–7–2–9–6–1.80–0–*ct* 6–*st* 1

Hewitt, W.
Amateur. Lower order batsman, useful bowler. *Team* Gentlemen of North (1877).
Career batting
1–2–0–1–1–0.50–0–*ct* 0
Bowling 16–1–16.00–0–0–1/16

Hewlett, Reginald James
Amateur. *b:* 12.8.1885, Bristol. *d:* 7.5.1950, Bristol. Middle order right-hand batsman. *Team* Gloucestershire (1909–22, 5 matches).
Career batting
5–10–0–80–24–8.00–0–*ct* 2

Heygate, Harold John
Amateur. *b:* 4.8.1884, Wellingborough, Northants. *d:* 27.6.1937, Guildford, Surrey. Brother of R. B. (Sussex). Stylish opening right-hand batsman. *Sch* Epsom and Wellingborough. *Team* Sussex (1903–1919, 6 matches).
Career batting
6–11–1–250–80–25.00–0–*ct* 0

He appeared for Canada v United States in 1908.

He was judged out by the umpire when he failed to appear at the wicket when the statutory two minutes had elapsed, the only example of such a dismissal in first-class cricket. The match was Sussex v Somerset at Taunton in 1919.

Heygate, Dr Reginald Beaumont
Amateur. *b:* 13.5.1883, Wellingborough, Northants. *d:* 24.4.1956, Crieff, Perthshire. Brother of H. J. (Sussex). Middle order right-hand batsman, useful change bowler. *Sch* Epsom and Wellingborough. *Teams* Sussex (1902–11, 70 matches); London County (1903).
Career batting
73–111–12–2818–136–28.46–3–*ct* 38
Bowling 102–4–25.50–0–0–2/28

He hit 1,000 runs in a season twice (best 1,062, av 35.40, in 1909).

Heymann, William Goodall
Amateur. *b:* 26.10.1885, West Bridgford, Notts. *d:* 27.11.1969, Long Clawson, Leics. Lower order right-hand batsman, left-arm medium pace bowler. *Sch* Haileybury. *Team* Nottinghamshire (1905, 1 match).
Career batting
1 match did not bat–*ct* 0
Bowling 48–2–24.00–0–0–2/37

Heys, William
Professional. *b:* 19.2.1931, Oswaldtwistle, Lancashire. Lower order right-hand batsman, wicket-keeper. *Team* Lancashire (1957, 5 matches).
Career batting
5–7–0–74–46–10.57–0–*ct* 5–*st* 3

Hibbard, Henry
Professional. *b:* 1854. *d:* 12.2.1902, Liverpool. Lower order batsman, bowler. *Team* Lancashire (1884, 1 match).
Career batting
1–2–0–7–4–3.50–0–*ct* 0
Bowling 54–2–27.00–0–0–2/35

Hibbard, John Arthur
Amateur. *b:* 7.9.1863, Chatham, Kent. *d:* 17.10.1905, Gillingham, Kent. Lower order batsman, wicket-keeper. *Team* Kent (1893, 4 matches).
Career batting
4–7–3–19–7–4.75–0–*ct* 10

Hibberd, George
Professional. *b:* 1845, Sheffield, Yorkshire. *d:* 1911, Worksop, Notts. Tail end batsman, right-arm fast bowler. *Team* Lancashire (1867, 1 match).
Career batting
1–2–1–4–3*–4.00–0–*ct* 1
Bowling 37–0

Hibberd, H.
Amateur. Middle order batsman, wicket-keeper. *Team* Surrey Club (1866).
Career batting
1–1–0–0–0–0.00–0–*ct* 0

Hibbert, Hugh Washington
Amateur. *b:* 4.10.1911, Kensington, London. Middle order right-hand batsman. *Sch* Downside. *Team* Northants (1931, 1 match).
Career batting
1–2–0–11–10–5.50–0–*ct* 1

Hibbert, John Calvert
Amateur. *b:* 4.8.1853, Chalfont, Bucks. *d:* 23.3.1929, Toulon, France. Middle order right-hand batsman, wicket-keeper. *Team* MCC (1881–82).
Career batting
2–3–0–0–0–0.00–0–*ct* 0

His County cricket was for Lincolnshire.

Hibbert, William John
Professional. *b:* 11.7.1873, Nottingham. *d:* 1934, Lincoln. Middle order left-hand batsman, bowler. *Team* Lancashire (1900–01, 14 matches).
Career batting
14–22–4–445–79–24.72–0–*ct* 5
Bowling 116–3–38.66–0–0–2/41

Hichens, Andrew Lionel
Amateur. *b:* 24.8.1936, Westminster, London. Lower order right-hand batsman, right-arm fast medium bowler. *Sch* Winchester. *Team* Oxford U (1957–59).
Career batting
3–2–0–4–4–2.00–0–*ct* 0
Bowling 270–6–45.00–0–0–4/97

Hickinbottom, Geoffrey Alfred
Professional. *b:* 15.11.1932, Leicester. Tail end right-hand batsman, wicket-keeper. *Team* Leicestershire (1959, 5 matches).
Career batting
5–7–5–6–4*–3.00–0–*ct* 4–*st* 3

Hickley, Anthony North
Amateur. *b:* 10.3.1906, Marylebone, London. *d:* 5.9.1972, Scotland. Middle order batsman, slow left-arm bowler. *Sch* Winchester. *Team* Middlesex (1930, 1 match).
Career batting
1–2–0–27–22–13.50–0–*ct* 0

Hickley, Charles Lushington
Amateur. *b:* 19.11.1862. *d:* 2.7.1935, Bayswater, London. Lower order right-hand batsman, right-arm fast medium bowler, moderate field. *Sch* Winchester. *Team* Oxford U (1883).
Career batting
1–2–0–29–15–14.50–0–*ct* 0
Bowling 25–0

Hickley, Admiral Cecil Spencer
Amateur. *b:* 22.1.1865, Bridgwater, Somerset. *d:* 1.5.1941, Kensington, London. Middle order batsman. *Teams* Western Province (1890/1); Somerset (1898–99, 5 matches).
Career batting
7–13–0–149–45–11.46–0–*ct* 0

Hickley, Frank
Amateur. *b:* 14.12.1895, Leicester. *d:* 28.10.1972, Leicester. Middle order right-hand batsman, change bowler. *Team* Leicestershire (1921, 2 matches).
Career batting
2–3–0–34–27–11.33–0–*ct* 0
Bowling 18–1–18.00–0–0–1/8

Hickman, George
Professional. *b:* 17.1.1909, Lanchester, Co Durham. Middle order right-hand batsman. *Team* Warwickshire (1929, 2 matches).
Career batting
4–6–0–26–17–4.33–0–*ct* 2

His final first-class match was for Minor Counties in 1935 and he appeared for some years for Durham. A useful soccer player, he represented Halifax Town.

Hickman, Malcolm Francis
Professional. *b:* 30.6.1936, Market Harborough, Leics. Middle order right-hand batsman, good deep field. *Team* Leicestershire (1954–57, 12 matches).
Career batting
12–22–2–232–40–11.60–0–*ct* 5

Hickmott, Edward
Professional. *b:* 20.3.1850, Maidstone, Kent. *d:* 7.1.1934, West Malling, Kent. Uncle of W. E. (Kent and Lancashire). Hard hitting lower order right-hand batsman, wicket-keeper. *Team* Kent (1875–88, 10 matches).
Career batting
10–15–2–85–44–6.53–0–*ct* 16–*st* 3

Hickmott, William Edward
Professional. *b:* 10.4.1893, Boxley, Kent. *d:* 16.1.1968, West Malling, Kent. Nephew of Edward (Kent). Lower order right-hand batsman, left-arm medium slow bowler. *Teams* Kent (1914–21, 3 matches); Lancashire (1923–24, 34 matches).
Career batting
37–40–11–301–31*–10.37–0–*ct* 25
Bowling 2360–92–25.65–2–0–5/20

He created a Central Lancashire League record by taking 140 wickets in a season for Rochdale in 1927.

Hicks, John
Professional. *b:* 10.12.1850, York. *d:* 10.6.1912, York. Middle order right-hand batsman, good field, right-arm fast bowler. *Team* Yorkshire (1872–76, 15 matches).
Career batting
21–36–4–423–66–13.21–0–*ct* 13
Bowling 70–3–23.33–0–0–2/53

Hickson, John Arnold Einem
Amateur. *b:* 1864, Edmonton, Middlesex. *d:* 2.1.1945, Surbiton, Surrey. Lower order batsman, wicket-keeper. *Teams* Transvaal (1889/90); Middlesex (1894–96, 3 matches).
Career batting
4–5–1–11–11–2.75–0–*ct* 8–*st* 1

Hickton, William
Professional. *b:* 14.12.1842, Hardstoft, Derbyshire. *d:* 27.2.1900, Lower Broughton, Manchester. Father of W. H. (Worcs). Lower order right-hand batsman, right-hand fast round-arm bowler, good slip. *Teams* Lancashire (1867–71, 22 matches); Derbyshire (1871–78, 34 matches).
Career batting
60–103–17–1054–63–12.25–0–*ct* 32
Bowling 4019–284–14.15–24–7–10/46
His feat of taking all 10 wickets in an innings (for 46) was for Lancashire v Hampshire at Old Trafford in 1870.

Hickton, William Henry
Professional. *b:* 28.8.1885, Lower Broughton, Lancashire. *d:* 8.4.1942, Leeds, Yorkshire. Son of William (Lancashire). Tail end right-hand batsman, slow left-arm bowler. *Team* Worcestershire (1909, 5 matches).
Career batting
5–9–0–41–17–4.55–0–*ct* 2
Bowling 104–2–52.00–0–0–1/9

Hiddleston, Douglas Stuart
Amateur. *b:* 2.3.1910, Johannesburg, South Africa. Right-hand batsman, leg break and googly bowler. *Team* Scotland (1930–34).
Career batting
5–8–1–65–15–9.28–0–*ct* 0
Bowling 414–27–15.33–2–0–7/69

Hide, Arthur Bollard
Professional. *b:* 7.5.1860, Eastbourne, Sussex. *d:* 5.11.1933, Denmark Hill, Surrey. Brother of J. B. (Sussex). Lower order left-hand batsman, left-arm medium pace bowler, good close field. *Team* Sussex (1882–90, 113 matches).
Career batting
115–196–40–1132–45–7.25–0–*ct* 73
Bowling 7736–403–19.19–20–1–7/44

Hide, Jesse Bollard
Professional. *b:* 12.3.1857, Eastbourne, Sussex. *d:* 19.3.1924, Edinburgh. Brother of A. B. (Sussex). Middle order right-hand batsman, right-hand fast round-arm bowler. *Teams* Sussex (1876–93, 155 matches); South Australia (1880/1 to 1882/3, 4 matches).
Career batting
176–323–20–4824–173–15.92–4–*ct* 112
Bowling 9573–441–21.70–19–4–8/47
He went to South Australia for a three year engagement, his services being lost to Sussex during that period commencing 1878. He also appeared for Cornwall.

Higginbotham, Charles Ernest
Amateur. *b:* 4.7.1866, Milngavie, Dunbartonshire, Scotland. *d:* 11.3.1915, near Neuve Chapelle, France. Son-in-law of James Round (MCC). Middle order right-hand batsman. *Sch* Rugby. *Teams* Army (1912); Army in South Africa (1905/06).
Career batting
2–4–1–45–40*–15.00–0–*ct* 1
His County cricket was for Devon.

Higgins, George Frederick
Amateur. *b:* 1868, Hackney, Middlesex. *d:* 16.8.1951, Woodford, Essex. Middle order right-hand batsman. *Team* Essex (1894–95, 9 matches).
Career batting
9–17–0–306–118–18.00–1–*ct* 2

Higgins, Harry Leslie
Amateur. *b:* 24.2.1894, Bournville, Warwickshire. *d:* 19.9.1979, Malvern, Worcs. Brother of J. B. (Worcs). Middle order right-hand batsman. *Sch* KES Birmingham. *Team* Worcestershire (1920–27, 97 matches).
Career batting
98–181–13–3437–137*–20.45–4–*ct* 54
He hit 1,000 runs in a season twice (best 1,182, av 28.82, in 1921).

Higgins, James
Professional. *b:* 13.3.1877, Birstal, Yorkshire. *d:* July 1954, Wibsey, Yorkshire. Lower order right-hand batsman, wicket-keeper. *Team* Yorkshire (1901–05, 9 matches).
Career batting
9–14–5–93–28*–10.33–0–*ct* 10–*st* 3

Higgins, John Bernard
Amateur. *b:* 31.12.1885, Harborne, Warwickshire. *d:* 3.1.1970, Malvern, Worcs. Brother of H. L. (Worcs). Middle order right-hand batsman, slow left-arm bowler. *Sch* KES Birmingham. *Teams* Worcestershire (1912–30, 111 matches); Europeans (1922/3 to 1928/9).
Career batting
121–223–11–4149–123–19.57–3–*ct* 59
Bowling 1604–30–53.46–1–0–5/72
He hit 1,041 runs, av 30.61, in 1928. He also played for Staffordshire.

Higgins, William Charles
Amateur. *b:* 12.12.1850, London. *d:* 8.4.1926, Chelsea, London. Lower order right-hand batsman, right-hand slow round-arm bowler, short-slip. *Sch* Eton. *Team* MCC (1870–73).
Career batting
6–10–2–66–20*–8.25–0–*ct* 2
He did not obtain his blue whilst at Oxford.

Higginson, J. D.
Amateur. *b:* Jan 1885, Worcester. *d:* Sept 1940, Wolverhampton. Lower order batsman, bowler. *Team* Worcestershire (1912, 1 match).
Career batting
1–1–1–0–0*–no av–0–*ct* 0
Bowling 20–0

Higginson, Thomas William
Amateur. *b:* 6.11.1936, Esher, Surrey. Lower order right-hand batsman, right-arm medium pace bowler. *Team* Middlesex (1960, 3 matches).
Career batting
4–4–2–50–20–25.00–0–*ct* 5
Bowling 24–1–24.00–0–0–1/24

Higgs, James Donald
Cricketer. *b:* 11.7.1950, Kyabram, Victoria, Australia. Tail end right-hand batsman, leg break and googly bowler. *Team* Victoria (1970/1 to 1982/3, 83 matches). *Tours* Australia to England 1975, to West Indies 1977/8, to India 1979/80. *Tests* Australia (1977/8 to 1980/1, 22 matches).
Career batting
122–131–60–384–21–5.40–0–*ct* 43
Bowling 11838–399–29.66–19–3–8/66
Test batting
22–36–16–111–16–5.55–0–*ct* 3
Bowling 2057–66–31.16–2–0–7/143

Only required for eight first-class matches on the 1975 tour to England, he did not appear in any Tests and had a very modest bowling return in the other games. He was dismissed by the only ball he faced during the tour!

Higgs, Kenneth
Professional. *b:* 14.1.1937, Kidsgrove, Staffs. Tail end left-hand batsman, right-arm fast, later medium pace, bowler. *Teams* Lancashire (1958–69, 306 matches); Leicestershire (1972–82, 165 matches). *Tours* MCC to Australia and New Zealand 1965/6, to West Indies 1967/8. *Tests* England (1965–68, 15 matches).
Career batting
509–528–206–3637–98–11.29–0–*ct* 311
Bowling 36196–1531–23.64–49–5–7/19
Test batting
15–19–3–185–63–11.56–0–*ct* 4
Bowling 1473–71–20.74–2–0–20.74

He also played for Staffordshire. He took 100 wickets in a season five times (best 132, av 19.42, in 1960). He captained Leicestershire in 1979 and is the present coach. With R. Illingworth he added 228 for the 10th wicket – Leics v Northants (Leicester) 1977 and with J.A. Snow added 128 for the 10th wicket – England v West Indies (Oval) 1966).

A good soccer player, he appeared as half-back for Port Vale.

Higgs, Kenneth Alan
Amateur. *b:* 5.10.1886, Haywards Heath, Sussex. *d:* 21.1.1959, Haywards Heath, Sussex. Middle order right-hand batsman. *Team* Sussex (1920–27, 41 matches).
Career batting
41–69–3–1693–111–25.65–2–*ct* 21
Bowling 131–4–32.75–0–0–2/15

He scored 101 for Sussex v Worcs at Hove in 1920 on his first-class debut.

Higgs-Walker, James Arthur
Amateur. *b:* 31.7.1892, Clent, Worcs. *d:* 3.9.1979, Midhurst, Sussex. Tail end right-hand batsman, right-arm fast bowler. *Sch* Repton. *Team* Worcestershire (1913–19, 2 matches).
Career batting
2–3–1–44–44–22.00–0–*ct* 0
Bowling 89–1–89.00–0–0–1/69

Highton, Edward Frederick William
Professional. *b:* 29.8.1924, Formby, Lancashire. Lower order right-hand batsman, right-arm fast medium bowler. *Team* Lancashire (1951, 1 match).
Career batting
2–3–0–34–26–11.33–0–*ct* 1
Bowling 162–7–23.57–0–0–4/87

His first-class debut was for Minor Counties in 1950.

Hignell, Antony Francis
Amateur. *b:* 6.7.1928, Kroonstad, Orange Free State, South Africa. Father of A. J. (Gloucs). Lower order right-hand batsman, right-arm medium pace bowler. *Sch* Denstone. *Team* Gloucestershire (1947, 1 match).
Career batting
1–1–0–7–7–7.00–0–*ct* 1
Bowling 48–0

Hignell, Alastair James
Cricketer. *b:* 4.9.1955, Cambridge. Son of A.F. (Gloucs). Middle order right-hand batsman, leg break bowler. *Sch* Denstone. *Teams* Cambridge U (1975–78, blue for all four years); Gloucestershire (1974–83, 137 matches).
Career batting
170–289–36–7459–149*–29.48–11–*ct* 150
Bowling 230–3–76.66–0–0–2/13

He hit 1,000 runs in a season three times (best 1,140, av 30.81, in 1976).

A noted rugby footballer, he played for Cambridge and England.

Higson, Peter
Amateur. *b:* 11.2.1905, Bramhall, Cheshire. Son of T. A. (Derbyshire and Lancashire), brother of

T. A. jun (Derbyshire and Lancashire). Middle order right-hand batsman. *Team* Lancashire (1928–31, 3 matches).
Career batting
4–4–2–51–29–25.50–0–*ct* 2
Bowling 18–0
His final first-class match was for Minor Counties in 1933.

Higson, Thomas Atkinson
Amateur. *b:* 18.11.1873, Stockport. *d:* 3.8.1949, Grange-over-Sands, Lancashire. Father of Peter (Lancashire) and T. A. jun (Lancashire and Derbyshire). Middle order right-hand batsman, off break bowler. *Sch* Rossall. *Teams* Oxford U (1892); Derbyshire (1899–1910, 21 matches); Lancashire (1905–23, 5 matches).
Career batting
29–50–4–584–46–12.69–0–*ct* 12
Bowling 1165–41–28.41–0–0–4/74
He also appeared for Cheshire. From 1931 to 1934 he was a member of the Test Selection Committee. For 49 years he was on the Lancashire CCC Committee, being for eight years Hon Treasurer and then Chairman. He was also a useful soccer and hockey player.

Higson, Thomas Atkinson (jun)
Amateur. *b:* 25.3.1911, Whaley Bridge, Derbyshire. Son of T. A. (Lancashire and Derbyshire), brother of Peter (Lancashire). Middle order left-hand batsman, right-arm medium pace bowler. *Sch* Cheltenham. *Teams* Derbyshire (1932–35, 6 matches); Lancashire (1936–46, 20 matches).
Career batting
26–32–1–326–51–10.51–0–*ct* 8
Bowling 302–6–50.33–0–0–1/14

Hilder, Alan Lake
Amateur. *b:* 8.10.1901, Beckenham, Kent. *d:* 2.5.1970, St Leonards, Sussex. Hard hitting middle order right-hand batsman. *Sch* Lancing. *Team* Kent (1924–29, 14 matches). *Tours* Tennyson to Jamaica 1926/7, 1927/8; Cahn to Jamaica 1928/9 (not first-class); Martineau to Egypt 1932 (not first-class).
Career batting
21–36–5–451–103*–14.54–1–*ct* 12
Bowling 536–13–41.23–0–0–3/77
He scored 103* for Kent v Essex at Gravesend in 1924 on his first-class debut. His final first-class match was for MCC in 1930.

Hilditch, Thomas Arthur
Amateur. *b:* 10.1.1885, Sandbach, Cheshire. *d:* 7.8.1957, Attleborough, Warwickshire. Lower order right-hand batsman, right-arm fast medium bowler. *Team* Warwickshire (1907–13, 8 matches).
Career batting
8–11–1–42–17–4.20–0–*ct* 3
Bowling 319–9–35.44–0–0–3/41
He also played for Shropshire and Cheshire.

Hildyard, Rev Lyonel D'Arcy
Amateur. *b:* 5.2.1861, Bury, Lancashire. *d:* 22.4.1931, Rowley Rectory, Hull, Yorkshire. Middle order right-hand batsman, good point field. *Teams* Somerset (1882–83, 7 matches); Oxford U (1884–86, blue all three years); Lancashire (1884–85, 8 matches).
Career batting
32–56–9–811–62*–17.25–0–*ct* 26
Bowling 24–0

Hill, Alan
Cricketer. *b:* 29.6.1950, Buxworth, Derbyshire. Opening right-hand batsman, off break bowler. *Teams* Derbyshire (1972–83, 194 matches); Orange Free State (1976/7).
Career batting
199–349–35–9233–160*–29.40–13–*ct* 72
Bowling 152–5–30.40–0–0–3/5
He hit 1,000 runs in a season three times (best 1,311, av 37.45, in 1983).

Hill, Allen
Professional. *b:* 14.11.1843, Kirkheaton, Huddersfield, Yorkshire. *d:* 29.8.1910, Leyland, Lancashire. Lower order right-hand batsman, right-hand fast round-arm bowler. *Team* Yorkshire (1871–82, 139 matches). *Tours* Lillywhite to Australia 1876/7. *Tests* England (1876/7, 2 matches).
Career batting
193–312–35–2478–49–8.94–0–*ct* 142
Bowling 10686–744+5–14.36–57–10–8/48
Test batting
2–4–2–101–49–50.50–0–*ct* 1
Bowling 130–7–18.57–0–0–4/27
He took 100 wickets in a season three times (best 116, av 15.45, in 1875). His final first-class match was for North v South in 1883. He took the first wicket in Test cricket.

Hill, Anthony Ewart Ledger
Amateur. *b:* 14.7.1901, Sparsholt, Hants. Son of A. J. L. (Hampshire). Middle order right-hand batsman. *Sch* Marlborough. *Team* Hampshire (1920–30, 18 matches).
Career batting
19–29–2–204–24–7.55–0–*ct* 7

Hill, Alfred John (Bostock)
Amateur. *b:* 8.4.1887, Solihull, Warwickshire. *d.* 20.8.1959, Okehampton, Devon. Lower order

batsman, right-arm bowler. *Team* Warwickshire (1920, 1 match).
Career batting
1–2–0–4–4–2.00–0–*ct* 0
Bowling 22–0

Hill, Arthur James Ledger
Amateur. *b:* 26.7.1871, Bassett, Hants. *d:* 6.9.1950, Sparsholt, near Romsey, Hants. Father of A. E. L. (Hants). Middle order right-hand batsman, originally right-arm fast medium bowler, later lobs, good slip field. *Sch* Marlborough. *Teams* Hampshire (1895–1921, 161 matches); Cambridge U (1890–93, blue all four years). *Tours* Hawke to India 1892/3, to North America 1894, to South Africa 1895/6; MCC to Argentine 1911/12. *Tests* England (1895/6, 3 matches).
Career batting
221–396–26–10353–199–27.98–19–*ct* 143
Bowling 8537–305–27.99–4–1–7/36
Test batting
3–4–0–251–124–62.75–1–*ct* 1
Bowling 8–4–2.00–0–0–4/8
He also played for Wiltshire. A splendid all-round sportsman, he captained Hampshire at rugby football and hockey and was also well known as a rackets player and boxer.

Hill, Alfred William
Professional. *b:* 1866, Little Rissington, Gloucs. *d:* 27.5.1936, Bourton-on-the-Water, Gloucs. Lower order left-hand batsman, off break bowler. *Team* Gloucestershire (1904–05, 2 matches).
Career batting
2–2–1–30–29*–30.00–0–*ct* 0
Bowling 54–1–54.00–0–0–1/47

Hill, Barrington Julian Warren
Amateur. *b:* 31.7.1915, Broadstairs, Kent. Lower order right-hand batsman, off break bowler. *Sch* St Lawrence College, Ramsgate. *Team* Oxford U (1935–37).
Career batting
4–5–0–46–28–9.20–0–*ct* 7
Bowling 129–5–25.80–0–0–2/48

Hill, Clement
Amateur. *b:* 18.3.1877, Adelaide, South Australia. *d:* 5.9.1945, Melbourne, Australia. Excellent middle order left-hand batsman, slow bowler. *Team* South Australia (1892/3 to 1922/3, 87 matches). *Tours* Australia to England 1896, 1899, 1902, 1905, to South Africa 1902/3, to North America 1896, to New Zealand 1904/5. *Tests* Australia (1896 to 1911/2, 49 matches).
Career batting
252–416–21–17213–365*–43.57–45–*ct* 168–*st* 1
Bowling 323–10–32.30–0–0–2/6
Test batting
49–89–2–3412–191–39.21–7–*ct* 33
He hit 1,000 runs on three of his English tours (best 1,722, av 38.26, in 1905) and on all four visits was most successful, though not so formidable as in Australia – all his four double centuries were scored for South Australia, the highest being 365* v New South Wales at Adelaide in 1900/01. His batting was more suited to hard wickets, but he was also very much a man for the big occasion and rarely failed in Test matches. He also hit 1,000 runs twice in a season in Australia. His final first-class match was for an Australian XI in 1924/5.

Hill, Charles Merrin
Amateur. *b:* 18.7.1903, Dublin, Ireland. *d:* 7.7.1982, Dublin, Ireland. Right-hand batsman. *Team* Ireland (1927).
Career batting
1–1–0–5–5–5.00–0–*ct* 0

Hill, Denys Vivian
Amateur. *b:* 13.4.1896, Edmonton, London. *d:* 15.5.1971, Barton on Sea, Hants. Lower order right-hand batsman, right-arm fast bowler. *Team* Worcestershire (1927–29, 28 matches).
Career batting
42–65–13–469–38–9.01–0–*ct* 23
Bowling 3487–130–26.82–6–0–6/59
He made his first-class debut for the Army in 1922. He also played for Oxfordshire.

Hill, Eric
Professional. *b:* 9.7.1923, Taunton, Somerset. Stylish opening right-hand batsman, good outfield. *Sch* Taunton. *Team* Somerset (1947–51, 72 matches).
Career batting
72–138–5–2118–85–15.92–0–*ct* 26
Bowling 55–1–55.00–0–0–1/25

Hill, Eustace Tickell
Amateur. *b:* 13.4.1869, Llandaff, Glamorgan. *d:* 11.1.1933, Ruthin, Denbighshire. Brother of V. T. (Somerset), uncle of E. V. L. (Somerset) and M. L. (Glamorgan and Somerset). Hard hitting right-hand batsman, useful change bowler. *Sch* Winchester. *Team* Somerset (1898–1901, 2 matches).
Career batting
2–4–0–70–31–17.50–0–*ct* 3

Hill, Evelyn Vernon Llewellyn
Amateur. *b:* 18.4.1907, Cardiff. *d:* 25.10.1953, Weston-super-Mare, Somerset. Son of V. T. (Somerset), brother of M. L. (Glamorgan and Somerset), nephew of E. T. (Somerset). Lower

order right-hand batsman, right-arm fast bowler. *Sch* Eton. *Team* Somerset (1926–29, 13 matches).
Career batting
13–16–8–134–32–16.75–0–*ct* 9
Bowling 1055–33–31.96–2–0–5/36

Hill, Rev Frederick Henry
Amateur. *b:* 29.11.1848, Bradfield, Berkshire. *d:* 28.7.1913, Kempston, Beds. Lower order right-hand batsman, right-hand medium pace round-arm bowler. *Sch* Bradfield. *Team* Oxford U (1867–70, blue 1867, 1869 and 1870).
Career batting
11–19–2–360–73–21.17–0–*ct* 9
Bowling 270–9–30.00–0–0–2/2
His final first-class match was for MCC in 1871. He played for Buckinghamshire, Bedfordshire, Northants and Worcestershire (not first-class).

Hill, Francis John
Amateur. *b:* 1.10.1862, Timsbury, Bath. *d: circa* 1935, Saskatoon, Canada. Brother of R. E. (Somerset). Middle order right-hand batsman. *Sch* Marlborough. *Team* Somerset (1882, 1 match).
Career batting
1–2–0–31–29–15.50–0–*ct* 0

Hill, Gerald
Professional. *b:* 15.4.1913, Totton, Hants. Middle order right-hand batsman, off break bowler, fine outfield. *Team* Hampshire (1932–54, 371 matches).
Career batting
371–595–94–9085–161–18.13–4–*ct* 169
Bowling 18464–617–29.92–18–3–8/62
He hit 1,000 runs in a season twice (best 1,051, av 22.36, in 1946); in 1935 he took 93 wickets, av 24.49.

Hill, Geoffrey Harry
Professional. *b:* 17.9.1934, Halesowen, Worcs. Lower order left-hand batsman, slow left-arm bowler. *Team* Warwickshire (1958–60, 41 matches).
Career batting
42–48–6–247–23–5.88–0–*ct* 26
Bowling 3195–108–29.58–3–0–8/70
His first-class debut was for Combined Services in 1957.

Hill, Henry
Amateur. *b:* 29.11.1858, Thornhill, Dewsbury, Yorkshire. *d:* 14.8.1935, Headingley, Leeds, Yorkshire. Hard hitting middle order right-hand batsman, excellent deep field. *Team* Yorkshire (1888–91, 14 matches).
Career batting
14–27–2–337–34–13.48–0–*ct* 10

Hill, Henry Barratt Grosvenor
Amateur. *b:* 23.7.1861, Handsworth, Warwickshire. *d:* 4.6.1913, Handsworth, Warwickshire. Brother of J. E. (Warwickshire). Lower order right-hand batsman, slow left-arm bowler. *Sch* KES Birmingham. *Team* Warwickshire (1894–1900, 5 matches).
Career batting
5–7–1–41–13–6.83–0–*ct* 3
Bowling 248–5–49.60–0–0–3/15
He was founder of the Birmingham and District League.

Hill, Henry James
Amateur. *b:* 8.4.1851, London. *d:* 7.5.1905, Bayswater, London. Opening right-hand batsman, right-hand medium pace round-arm bowler. *Team* MCC (1880–83).
Career batting
4–7–0–31–17–4.42–0–*ct* 1

Hill, Herbert James
Amateur. *b:* 12.2.1867, Kingston-on-Thames, Surrey. *d:* 27.2.1946, Sheringham, Norfolk. Right-hand batsman. *Sch* Harrow. *Team* MCC (1900–01).
Career batting
2–4–0–90–54–22.50–0–*ct* 0
His County cricket was for Hertfordshire.

Hill, John Charles
Amateur. *b:* 25.6.1923, Murrumbeena, Victoria, Australia. *d:* 11.8.1974, Caulfield, Victoria, Australia. Lower order right-hand batsman, leg break and googly bowler. *Team* Victoria (1945/6 to 1955/6, 38 matches). *Tours* Australia to England 1953, to West Indies 1954/5. *Tests* Australia (1953 to 1954/5, 3 matches).
Career batting
69–78–24–867–51*–16.05–0–*ct* 63
Bowling 5040–218–23.11–9–1–7/51
Test batting
3–6–3–21–8*–7.00–0–*ct* 2
Bowling 273–8–34.12–0–0–3/35
He took 63 wickets, av 20.98, on the 1953 tour to England, but did not impress in the Tests.

Hill, John Ernest
Amateur. *b:* 27.9.1867, Handsworth, Warwickshire. *d:* 2.12.1963, Smethwick, Staffs. Brother of H. B. G. (Warwickshire). Middle order right-hand batsman. *Sch* KES Birmingham. *Team* Warwickshire (1894–98, 25 matches).

Career batting
27–38–7–737–139*–23.74–1–*ct* 20
Bowling 14–0

Being the Public Prosecutor for Birmingham, his County cricket was very restricted.

Hill, John William
Amateur. *b:* 10.6.1920, Coleraine, Co Londonderry, Ireland. Right-hand batsman, off break bowler. *Team* Ireland (1946–51).
Career batting
7–12–7–82–18*–16.40–0–*ct* 1
Bowling 367–17–21.58–0–0–3/16

Hill, Lewis Gordon
Amateur. *b:* 22.11.1860, Bradford, Yorkshire. *d:* 27.8.1940, Heaton, Yorkshire. Middle order right-hand batsman. *Team* Yorkshire (1882, 1 match).
Career batting
1–2–0–13–8–6.50–0–*ct* 1

Hill, Leonard Winston
Cricketer. *b:* 14.4.1942, Caerleon, Monmouthshire. Middle order right-hand batsman, occasional wicket-keeper, good cover. *Team* Glamorgan (1964–76, 76 matches).
Career batting
76–130–20–2690–96*–24.45–0–*ct* 40–*st* 1
Bowling 44–0

He played soccer at right half for Newport County and Swansea.

Hill, Maurice
Professional. *b:* 14.9.1935, Scunthorpe, Lincs. Attractive middle order right-hand batsman, leg break bowler, good deep field. *Teams* Nottinghamshire (1953–65, 237 matches); Derbyshire (1966–67, 32 matches); Somerset (1970–71, 22 matches).
Career batting
272–484–39–10722–137*–24.09–7–*ct* 151
Bowling 311–5–62.20–0–0–2/60

He hit 1,000 runs in a season six times (best 1,416, av 27.76, in 1964).

Hill, Michael John
Cricketer. *b:* 1.7.1951, Harwell, Berks. Lower order left-hand batsman, wicket-keeper. *Team* Hampshire (1973–76, 6 matches).
Career batting
6–8–4–68–27*–17.00–0–0–*ct* 9

Hill, Mervyn Llewellyn
Amateur. *b:* 23.6.1902, Cardiff. *d:* 28.2.1948, London. Son of V. T. (Oxford U and Somerset), brother of E. V. L. (Somerset), nephew of E. T. (Somerset). Lower order right-hand batsman, wicket-keeper. *Sch* Eton. *Teams* Cambridge U (1923–24); Somerset (1921–32, 42 matches); Glamorgan (1923, 3 matches) *Tour* MCC to India, Burma and Ceylon (1926/7).
Career batting
64–95–29–864–60–13.09–0–*ct* 58–*st* 31

His first-class debut was for Gentlemen of England in 1920. He also played for Devon.

Hill, Norman William
Professional. *b:* 22.8.1935, Holbeck, Notts. Opening left-hand batsman, slip field. *Team* Nottinghamshire (1953–68, 280 matches).
Career batting
283–518–32–14303–201*–29.43–23–*ct* 224
Bowling 261–2–130.50–0–0–1/28

He hit 1,000 runs in a season eight times, going on to 2,000 twice (best 2,239, av 39.98, in 1961). His only double century was 201* for Notts v Sussex at Shireoaks in 1961. He captained Notts in 1966 and 1967.

Hill, Richard Ernest
Amateur. *b:* 12.8.1861, Timsbury, Bath. *d:* 1924, London. Brother of F. J. (Somerset). Lower order right-hand batsman, left-arm fast bowler. *Sch* Marlborough. *Team* Somerset (1882, 1 match).
Career batting
1–2–1–7–7*–7.00–0–*ct* 0
Bowling 21–1–21.00–0–0–1/21

Hill, Robert Gribben
Amateur. *b:* 15.7.1938, Kilmarnock, Scotland. Left-hand batsman. *Team* Scotland (1963–69).
Career batting
6–9–0–105–50–11.66–0–*ct* 2

Hill, Richard Hamilton
Amateur. *b:* 28.11.1900, Kensington, London. *d:* 5.10.1959, Hosey Hill, Westerham, Kent. Opening right-hand batsman. *Sch* Winchester. *Team* Middlesex (1921–31, 42 matches).
Career batting
45–59–4–861–71–15.65–0–*ct* 16

He appeared in the Freshmen's and Seniors' Matches at Cambridge but no first-class games; however he represented the University at royal tennis and rackets. For many years he reported both tennis and cricket for *The Times*.

Hill, Rupert Knight
Cricketer. *b:* 14.8.1954, Jamaica. Tail end right-hand batsman, right-arm medium pace bowler. *Team* Glamorgan (1975, 1 match).
Career batting
1 match, did not bat–*ct* 0
Bowling 58–1–58.00–0–0–1/34

Hill, Rowland Wright Davenport
Amateur. *b:* 5.9.1851, Hajepoor, India. *d:* 29.8.1912, Gladesville, New South Wales, Australia. Middle order right-hand batsman, wicket-keeper. *Team* Lancashire (1871, 1 match).
Career batting
1–2–0–8–5–4.00–0–*ct* 1

Hill, Vernon Tickell
Amateur. *b:* 30.1.1871, Llandaff, Glamorgan. *d:* 29.9.1932, Woodspring Priory, Somerset. Brother of E. T. (Somerset), father of E. V. L. (Somerset) and M. L. (Somerset and Glamorgan). Hard hitting middle order left-hand batsman, right-arm fast medium bowler. *Sch* Winchester. *Teams* Somerset (1891–1912, 121 matches); Oxford U (1892–93, blue 1892). *Tours* Mitchell to North America 1895; Warner to North America 1898.
Career batting
139–238–8–4501–116–19.56–2–*ct* 124
Bowling 875–29–30.17–0–0–4/20
He also played non-first-class cricket for Glamorgan.

Hill, William Aubrey
Professional. *b:* 27.4.1910, Carmarthen. Sound opening right-hand batsman, right-arm medium pace bowler. *Team* Warwickshire (1929–48, 169 matches).
Career batting
169–279–22–6423–147*–24.99–6–*ct* 51
Bowling 27–1–27.00–0–0–1/9
He hit 1,000 runs in a season twice (best 1,197, av 24.42, in 1947).

Hill, W. H.
Amateur. Middle order batsmen. *Team* Worcestershire (1900, 2 matches).
Career batting
2–4–1–46–13*–15.33–0–*ct* 0

Hillary, Anthony Aylmer
Amateur. *b:* 28.8.1926, Shenfield, Essex. Middle order right-hand batsman, off break bowler. *Team* Cambridge U (1951).
Career batting
1–1–0–49–49–49.00–0–*ct* 0

Hiller, Robert
Cricketer. *b:* 14.10.1942, Woking, Surrey. Lower order left-hand batsman, right-arm fast medium bowler. *Team* Oxford U (1966, blue).
Career batting
8–11–1–87–64–8.70–0–*ct* 6
Bowling 494–17–29.05–0–0–4/53
He played rugby for England.

Hillkirk, John Ritson
Amateur. *b:* 25.6.1845, Manchester. *d:* 1921, Isle of Wight. Hard hitting middle order right-hand batsman, right-hand medium pace round-arm bowler. *Sch* Ardwick School. *Team* Lancashire (1871–77, 30 matches).
Career batting
31–48–4–607–56*–13.79–0–*ct* 18–*st* 1
He was also a noted athlete.

Hills, Henry
Amateur. Lower order batsman, useful bowler. *Team* Cambridgeshire (1866–68, 5 matches).
Career batting
5–10–0–39–9–3.90–0–*ct* 3
Bowling 80–3–26.66–0–0–2/18

Hills, Harry Mountford
Professional. *b:* 28.9.1886, Mayland, Essex. Lower order right-hand batsman, leg break bowler. *Team* Essex (1912–19, 14 matches).
Career batting
14–21–4–139–26–8.17–0–*ct* 7
Bowling 738–15–49.20–1–0–5/63

Hills, Joseph John
Professional. *b:* 14.10.1897, Plumstead, Kent. *d:* 21.9.1969, Westbourne, Bournemouth, Hants. Middle order right-hand batsman, good field, occasional wicket-keeper. *Team* Glamorgan (1926–31, 104 matches).
Career batting
107–170–9–3474–166–21.57–7–*ct* 93–*st* 5
After retiring from first-class cricket he became a County umpire. A good soccer player, he was goalkeeper for Cardiff City, Swansea and Fulham.

Hills, Robert Savi
Amateur. *b:* 8.5.1837, St Johns Wood, Middlesex. *d:* 5.1.1909, Inverurie, Aberdeenshire, Scotland. Middle order batsman. *Sch* Rugby. *Team* MCC (1867–76).
Career batting
2–4–0–17–8–4.25–0–*ct* 1

Hills, Richard William
Cricketer. *b:* 8.1.1951, Borough Green, Kent. Lower order right-hand batsman, right-arm medium pace bowler. *Team* Kent (1973–80, 85 matches).
Career batting
85–95–25–995–45–14.21–0–*ct* 33
Bowling 4494–161–27.91–2–0–6/64

Hill-Wood, Sir Basil Samuel Hill
(formerly Wood)
Amateur. *b:* 5.2.1900, Chelsea, London. *d:* 3.7.1954, Farley Hill, Berkshire. Son of S. H.,

brother of C. K. H., D. J. C. H. and W. W. H. (Derbyshire). Lower order right-hand batsman, right-arm fast medium bowler. *Sch* Eton. *Team* Derbyshire (1919–25, 22 matches). *Tour* MCC to Australia and New Zealand 1922/3 (not in first-class matches).
Career batting
22–35–4–505–61–16.29–0–*ct* 8
Bowling 1406–45–31.24–1–0–6/74
He did not appear in first-class matches whilst at Cambridge.

Hill-Wood, Charles Kerrison Hill
(formerly Wood)
Amateur. *b:* 5.6.1907, Hoxne, Suffolk. Son of S. H., brother of B. S. H., D. J. C. H. and W. W. H. (Derbyshire). Lower order right-hand batsman, fast medium left-arm bowler. *Sch* Eton. *Teams* Derbyshire (1928–30, 18 matches); Oxford U (1928–30, blue all three years); Europeans (1935/6).
Career batting
58–77–13–1256–72–19.62–0–*ct* 20
Bowling 5547–185–29.98–10–1–7/68
His final first-class match in England was for Free Foresters in 1932.

Hill-Wood, Denis John Charles Hill
(formerly Wood)
Amateur. *b:* 25.6.1906, Hoxne, Suffolk. *d:* 4.5.1982, Hartley-Wintney, Hants. Son of S. H., brother of B. S. H., C. K. H. and W. W. H. (Derbyshire). Steady opening right-hand batsman, change bowler. *Sch* Eton. *Teams* Derbyshire (1928–29, 5 matches); Oxford U (1928, blue).
Career batting
12–21–1–453–85–22.65–0–*ct* 6
Bowling 123–3–41.00–0–0–1/4
He was a useful soccer player, obtaining his blue at Oxford; for some years he was Chairman of Arsenal FC.

Hill-Wood, Peter Denis
Amateur. *b:* 25.2.1936, Kensington, London. Middle order batsman, bowler. *Team* Free Foresters (1960).
Career batting
1–1–0–30–30–30.00–0–*ct* 1
Bowling 20–1–20.00–0–0–1/4
He is Chairman of Arsenal FC.

Hill-Wood, S. H. *(see under* Wood, S. H.)

Hill-Wood, Sir Wilfred William Hill
(formerly Wood)
Amateur. *b:* 8.9.1901, Chelsea, London. *d:* 10.10.1980, Kensington. Son of S. H., brother of B. S. H., C. K. H. and D. J. C. H. (Derbyshire). Solid opening right-hand batsman, slow right-arm spin bowler. *Sch* Eton. *Teams* Derbyshire (1919–36, 35 matches); Cambridge U (1921–22, blue 1922); Viceroy's XI (1932/3). *Tour* MCC to Australia and New Zealand 1922/3.
Career batting
63–107–4–2848–122*–27.65–3–*ct* 34
Bowling 2237–65–34.41–1–0–5/62
He hit 1,082 runs, av 36.06, in 1923.
His final first-class match was for MCC in 1939.

Hillyard, George Whiteside
Amateur. *b:* 6.2.1864, Hanwell, Middlesex. *d:* 24.3.1943, Pulborough, Sussex. Lower order right-hand batsman, right-arm fast medium bowler. *Teams* Middlesex (1886, 3 matches); Leicestershire (1894–96, 32 matches). *Tours* Hawke to North America 1891, 1894.
Career batting
49–89–12–707–36–9.18–0–*ct* 63
Bowling 3144–145–21.68–9–1–6/74
He appeared for Herts in 1891. A noted lawn tennis player, he represented England in the Olympic Games of 1908; in addition he excelled at golf and billiards.

Hillyer, Charles
Professional. *b:* 4.8.1845, Biddenden, Kent. *d:* 4.10.1872, Woodchurch, Kent. Middle order batsman, bowler. *Team* Kent (1868, 1 match).
Career batting
1–2–0–6–6–3.00–0–*ct* 1
Bowling 34–1–34.00–0–0–1/6

Hillyer, William Richard
Professional. *b:* 5.3.1813, Leybourne, Kent. *d:* 8.1.1861, Maidstone, Kent. Middle order right-hand batsman, right-hand medium fast round-arm bowler, excellent slip. *Teams* Kent (1835–53, 82 matches); Surrey (1849, 2 matches).
Career batting
230–411–68–2655–83–7.74–0–*ct* 203
Bowling 4148–376+1099–11.03–148–54–8/26
Described by some as 'the best of all bowlers', he was at his most brilliant about 1845. He took 100 wickets in a season seven times (best 174 in 1845). Owing to ill-health he was forced to give up cricket in 1855 and died aged 47 after a long and painful illness.
He was the first cricketer known to have performed the match 'double' of 100 runs and 10 wickets in first-class cricket, when he scored 26 and 83 and took 7 and 6 wickets for MCC v Oxford U at Oxford in 1847.

Hilton, Albert Walter
Professional. *b:* 9.7.1862, Alfriston, Sussex. *d:*

4.9.1935, Brighton, Sussex. Lower order batsman, left-arm medium pace bowler. *Team* Sussex (1891–95, 29 matches).
Career batting
29–37–9–182–28–6.50–0–*ct* 17
Bowling 2284–89–25.66–4–1–7/47

Hilton, Colin
Professional. *b:* 26.9.1937, Atherton, Lancs. Tail end right-hand batsman, right-arm fast bowler. *Teams* Lancashire (1957–63, 91 matches); Essex (1964, 24 matches)
Career batting
115–133–43–665–36–7.38–0–*ct* 41
Bowling 9040–321–28.16–8–1–6/38
His best season was 1962 when he took 92 wickets, av 26.62.

Hilton, James
Professional. *b:* 29.12.1930, Chadderton, Lancashire. Brother of M. J. (Lancashire). Lower order right-hand batsman, off break bowler, good outfield. *Teams* Lancashire (1952–53, 8 matches); Somerset (1954–57, 71 matches).
Career batting
79–129–29–1093–61*–10.93–0–*ct* 53
Bowling 3675–135–27.22–7–0–7/98

Hilton, John (jun)
Professional. *b:* 1838, Mansfield. *d:* 8.5.1910, Stafford. Son of John sen (Notts 1830). Opening batsman. *Team* Nottinghamshire (1865, 1 match).
Career batting
1–1–0–7–7–7.00–0–*ct* 0

Hilton, Malcolm Jameson
Professional. *b:* 2.8.1928, Chadderton, Lancashire. Brother of James (Lancashire and Somerset). Lower order right-hand batsman, slow left-arm bowler. *Team* Lancashire (1946–61, 241 matches). *Tour* MCC to India, Pakistan and Ceylon 1951/2. *Tests* England (1950 to 1951/2, 4 matches).
Career batting
270–324–42–3416–100*–12.11–1–*ct* 202
Bowling 19542–1006–19.42–51–8–8/19
Test batting
4–6–1–37–15–7.40–0–*ct* 1
Bowling 477–14–34.07–1–0–5/61
He took 100 wickets in a season four times (best 158, av 13.96, in 1956).

Hilton, Philip
Amateur. *b:* 10.3.1840, Selling, Faversham, Kent. *d:* 26.5.1906, St Pancras, London. Middle order right-hand batsman, good deep field. *Sch* Cheltenham. *Team* Kent (1865–73, 26 matches).
Career batting
33–56–1–621–74–11.29–0–*ct* 19
He was Treasurer of Kent CCC 1867–1871. His final first-class match was for MCC in 1874. It is assumed that 'H. Peters', who played for Kent in one match is an alias for Philip Hilton.

Hincks, R. H.
Amateur. Middle order batsman, change bowler. *Team* Leicestershire (1895, 2 matches).
Career batting
2–4–0–15–14–3.75–0–*ct* 1
Bowling 29–2–14.50–0–0–1/3

Hind, Amos
Professional. *b:* 1.2.1849, Calverton, Notts. *d:* 27.4.1931, Calverton, Notts. Brother of Samuel (Notts). Middle order right-hand batsman, right-hand medium pace round-arm bowler, deep field. *Team* Derbyshire (1876–77, 16 matches).
Career batting
16–30–0–392–77–13.06–0–*ct* 4
Bowling 419–24–17.45–0–0–4/9

Hind, Alfred Ernest
Amateur. *b:* 7.4.1878, Preston, Lancashire. *d:* 21.3.1947, Oadby, Leics. Lower order right-hand batsman, right-arm medium pace bowler, slip field. *Sch* Uppingham. *Teams* Cambridge U (1898–1901, blue all four years); Nottinghamshire (1901, 1 match).
Career batting
37–62–14–681–54*–14.18–0–*ct* 37
Bowling 2148–80–26.85–3–0–7/30
An excellent rugby footballer, he won his blue and went on to represent England.

Hind, Benjamin James
Amateur. *b:* 22.12.1882, Nottingham. *d:* 1974, Nottingham. Lower order right-hand batsman, leg break bowler. *Team* Nottinghamshire (1911, 1 match).
Career batting
1–2–0–28–23–14.00–0–*ct* 0
Bowling 42–0

Hind, Samuel
Professional. *b:* 14.12.1850, Calverton, Notts. *d:* 28.3.1923, Calverton, Notts. Brother of Amos (Derbyshire). Middle order right-hand batsman, left-hand fast round-arm bowler, good field. *Team* Nottinghamshire (1877–78, 6 matches).
Career batting
6–10–0–90–22–9.00–0–*ct* 2
Bowling 51–0

Hinde, Frank Langford
Amateur. *b:* 1869, Dublin, Ireland. *d:* 22.8.1931,

Reigate, Surrey. Middle order right-hand batsman. *Team* Gloucestershire (1895, 1 match).
Career batting
1–2–0–5–3–2.50–0–*ct* 0
He played with success in the Cambridge Freshmen's Match of 1893, but in no first-class matches whilst at the University. He also played for Lincolnshire.

Hinde, Harold Montague
Amateur. *b:* 24.8.1895, Portsmouth, Hants. *d:* 16.11.1965, Santa Margherita, Liguse, Italy. Lower order right-hand batsman, right-arm fast bowler. *Sch* Wellington and Blundells. *Team* Minor Counties (1924).
Career batting
1–2–1–0–0*–0.00–0–*ct* 0
Bowling 138–9–15.33–1–0–8/77
His County cricket was for Berkshire.

Hindlekar, Dattaram Dharmaji
Amateur. *b:* 1.1.1909, Bombay, India. *d:* 30.3.1949, Bombay, India. Originally opening, later lower order right-hand batsman, wicket-keeper. *Teams* Bombay (1934/5 to 1946/7; Hindus (1935/6 to 1945/6). *Tours* India to England 1936, 1946. *Tests* India (1936–46, 4 matches).
Career batting
94–148–8–2416–135–17.25–1–*ct* 125–*st* 58
Test batting
4–7–2–71–26–14.20–0–*ct* 3
Injury and blurred vision on the 1936 tour to England meant that he had very restricted opportunities. In 1946 he again was injured and in the absence of a competent deputy kept wicket when not fully fit.

Hine-Haycock, Rev Trevitt Reginald
Amateur. *b:* 3.12.1861, Old Charlton, Kent. *d:* 2.11.1953, Bedford. Steady opening right-hand batsman. *Sch* Wellington. *Teams* Oxford U (1882–84, blue 1883–84); Kent (1885–86, 6 matches). *Tours* Sanders to North America 1885, 1886.
Career batting
30–55–5–945–85–18.90–0–*ct* 23
Bowling 12–1–12.00–0–0–1/5
He appeared for Devon 1882–84.

Hings, John Preston
Amateur. *b:* 22.12.1910, Leicester. Middle order right-hand batsman. *Team* Leicestershire (1934, 2 matches).
Career batting
2–4–0–18–10–4.50–0–*ct* 2
Bowling 4–0

Hinkly, Edmund
Professional. *b:* 12.1.1817, Benenden, Kent. *d:* 8.12.1880, Walworth, London. Tail end left-hand batsman, left-hand fast round-arm bowler, moderate field. *Teams* Kent (1846–58, 34 matches); Surrey (1848–53, 2 matches).
Career batting
43–77–27–318–24–6.36–0–*ct* 22
Bowling 1303–87+102–14.97–18–7–10/?
On his debut at Lord's, playing for Kent v England, he took all ten wickets in England's second innings (in addition to six in the first). His career can be regarded as short but brilliant.

Hinks, Simon Graham
Cricketer. *b:* 12.10.1960, Northfleet, Kent. Middle order left-hand batsman, left-arm medium pace bowler, wicket-keeper. *Team* Kent (1982–83, 8 matches).
Career batting
8–14–1–288–87–22.15–0–*ct* 3
Bowling 5–0

Hinwood, John William James
Amateur. *b:* 8.4.1894, Wilton, Wilts. *d:* 14.5.1971, Swansea. Lower order right-hand batsman, right-arm fast medium bowler. *Team* Glamorgan (1923, 1 match).
Career batting
1–2–0–0–0–0.00–0–*ct* 0
Bowling 25–0

Hipkin, Augustus Bernard
Professional. *b:* 8.8.1900, Brancaster, Norfolk. *d:* 11.2.1957, Carluke, Lanarkshire. Lower order left-hand batsman, slow left-arm bowler, good field. *Team* Essex (1923–31, 231 matches).
Career batting
232–326–55–4239–108–15.64–2–*ct* 210
Bowling 13435–522–25.73–18–3–8/71
His best season was 1924 when he took 116 wickets, av 20.80. After leaving Essex he went to Scotland and appeared for Scotland in one non-first-class match. He played football for Charlton Athletic.

Hippisley, Harold Edwin
Amateur. *b:* 3.9.1890, Wells, Somerset. *d:* 23.10.1914, Langemark, Belgium. He was killed in action. Middle order right-hand batsman. *Sch* Kings, Bruton. *Team* Somerset (1909–13, 7 matches).
Career batting
7–13–1–114–40*–9.50–0–*ct* 2
He was an excellent hockey player.

Hird, Sydney Francis
Professional. *b:* 7.1.1910, Balmain, New South

Wales, Australia. *d:* 20.12.1980, Bloemfontein, South Africa. Middle order right-hand batsman, leg break and googly bowler. *Teams* New South Wales (1931/2 to 1932/3, 14 matches); Lancashire (1939, 1 match); Eastern Province (1945/6 to 1948/9); Border (1950/1).
Career batting
32–49–5–1453–130–33.02–5–*ct* 8
Bowling 1684–59–28.54–3–0–6/56

In 1934 he emigrated to England, becoming a professional in the Lancashire League – he neither batted or bowled in his single match for Lancs, the game being ruined by rain. His first-class debut in England was for Sir L. Parkinson's XI in 1935.

Hirsch, John Gauntlett
Amateur. *b:* 20.2.1883, South Africa. *d:* March 1958, Cape Town, South Africa. Middle order batsman, bowler. *Sch* Shrewsbury. *Teams* Cambridge U (1903–04); London County (1903–04).
Career batting
6–11–0–166–56–15.09–0–*ct* 4
Bowling 93–1–93.00–0–0–1/41

A noted rugby footballer, he toured England with the 1906 Springbok rugby team as centre three-quarter.

Hirst, Christopher Halliwell
Cricketer. *b:* 27.5.1947, Bradford, Yorkshire. Opening right-hand batsman, off break bowler. *Team* Cambridge U (1967).
Career batting
1–2–1–8–6*–8.00–0–*ct* 0

His County cricket was for Buckinghamshire.

Hirst, Edward Theodore
Amateur. *b:* 6.5.1857, Huddersfield, Yorkshire. *d:* 26.10.1914, Barnwood, Gloucs. Brother of E. W. (Yorkshire). Middle order right-hand batsman, good field. *Sch* Rugby. *Teams* Yorkshire (1877–88, 21 matches); Oxford U (1878–80, blue all three years).
Career batting
39–65–3–778–114–12.54–1–*ct* 17

An excellent rugby footballer, he gained his blue at Oxford.

Hirst, Ernest William
Amateur. *b:* 27.2.1855, Huddersfield, Yorkshire. *d:* 24.10.1933, Dorchester, Dorset. Brother of E. T. (Oxford U and Yorkshire). Middle order batsman. *Team* Yorkshire (1881, 2 matches).
Career batting
2–3–0–33–28–11.00–0–*ct* 0
Bowling 3–0

Hirst, George Herbert
Professional. *b:* 7.9.1871, Kirkheaton, Yorkshire. *d:* 10.5.1954, Lindley, near Huddersfield, Yorkshire. Aggressive middle order right-hand batsman, left-arm medium fast bowler, excellent field. *Teams* Yorkshire (1891–1929, 718 matches); Europeans (1921/2). *Tours* Stoddart to Australia 1897/8; MCC to Australia 1903/4. *Tests* England (1897/8 to 1909, 24 matches).
Career batting
826–1217–152–36356–341–34.13–60–*ct* 607
Bowling 51371–2742–18.73–184–40–9/23
Test batting
24–38–3–790–85–22.57–0–*ct* 18
Bowling 1770–59–30.00–3–0–5/48

Achieving the unique feat in English first-class cricket of scoring 2,000 runs and taking 200 wickets in the same season, Hirst must rank among the greatest of all cricketers. No less than 19 times did he hit 1,000 runs in a season, going on to 2,000 three times, with 2,501, av 54.36, in 1904 as his highest aggregate. In 15 seasons he topped 100 wickets and once exceeded 200 – 208, av 16.50, in 1906.

Apart from his 2,000 runs and 200 wickets in a season, he made 2,000 runs and took 100 wickets in two other years and in all performed the 'double' fourteen times.

His highest innings was 341 for Yorkshire v Leicestershire at Leicester in 1905, and his three other scores over 200 were also for Yorkshire. To him is attributed the perfection of seam and swing bowling – he possessed the knack of making the ball dip into the batsman very late in its flight. His match winning performances with both bat and ball for Yorkshire are numerous, yet curiously he achieved very little for England and was among the 'also-rans' on both his tours to Australia. His best bowling was 9/23 for Yorkshire v Lancashire at Headingly in 1910.

He appeared in County cricket until 1929, but after 1921, when he began his 18-year engagement at Eton College, his first-class matches were very few.

Hirst, Thomas Henry
Professional. *b:* 21.5.1865, Meltham Mills, Yorkshire. *d:* 3.4.1927, Meltham, Huddersfield, Yorkshire. Lower order batsman, bowler. *Teams* Yorkshire (1899, 1 match); Scotland (1905).
Career batting
2–3–1–66–33–33.00–0–*ct* 1
Bowling 44–0

In the Yorks v Somerset match of 1899 he was not part of the Yorkshire Eleven, but came on as substitute when C. E. M. Wilson was injured, and was allowed to both bat and bowl with the consent of the Somerset captain.

Hitch, John William
Professional. *b:* 7.5.1886, Radcliffe, Lancashire. *d:* 7.7.1965, Rumney, Cardiff. Hard hitting lower order right-hand batsman, right-arm fast bowler, brilliant short-leg. *Team* Surrey (1907–25, 305 matches). *Tours* MCC to Australia 1911/2, 1920/1. *Tests* England (1911/2 to 1921, 7 matches).
Career batting
350–480–51–7643–107–17.81–3–*ct* 230
Bowling 29915–1387–21.56–101–24–8/38
Test batting
7–10–3–103–51*–14.71–0–*ct* 4
Bowling 325–7–46.42–0–0–2/31
He took 100 wickets in a season seven times (best 174, av 18.55, in 1913). A great bowler for Surrey, he achieved very little on his appearances in Tests or on either of his two tours to Australia. He hit 1,061 runs, av 31.20, in 1921.

Hitchcock, Lt Gen Sir Basil Ferguson Burnett
(also known as Burnett-Hitchcock)
Amateur. *b:* 3.3.1877, Medway, Kent. *d:* 23.11.1938, Westminster, London. *Sch* Harrow and Brighton. *Team* Hampshire (1896, 2 matches).
Career batting
2–3–0–33–21–11.00–0–*ct* 0

Hitchcock, Raymond Edward
Professional. *b:* 28.11.1929, Christchurch, New Zealand. Middle order left-hand batsman, leg break and googly bowler. *Teams* Canterbury (1947/8); Warwickshire (1949–64, 319 matches).
Career batting
322–517–71–12442–153*–27.99–13–*ct* 113
Bowling 5749–194–29.63–7–1–7/76
He hit 1,000 runs in a season five times (best 1,840, av 34.07, in 1961). A good rugby scrum half, he appeared for Nuneaton.

Hoad, Edward Lisle Goldsworthy
Amateur. *b:* 29.1.1896, Richmond, near Bridgetown, Barbados. Opening right-hand batsman, right-arm leg break and googly bowler. *Team* Barbados (1921/2 to 1937/8). *Tours* West Indies to England 1928, 1933. *Tests* West Indies (1928 to 1933, 4 matches).
Career batting
63–104–13–3502–174*–38.48–8–*ct* 26
Bowling 1923–53–36.28–1–0–5/84
Test batting
4–8–0–98–36–12.25–0–*ct* 1
He topped the first-class batting averages for the 1928 tour (765, av 36.42) but was not so successful in 1933 though he hit 1,083 runs, av 27.76. He failed in both the Tests in which he took part.

Hoadley, Stephen John
Cricketer. *b:* 7.7.1955, Pembury, Kent. Brother of S. P. (Sussex). Middle order right-hand batsman, off break bowler. *Team* Sussex (1975–76, 7 matches).
Career batting
7–13–2–202–58–18.36–0–*ct* 3
Bowling 22–0

Hoadley, Simon Peter
Cricketer. *b:* 16.8.1956, Eridge, Sussex. Brother of S. J. (Sussex). Middle order right-hand batsman, off break bowler. *Team* Sussex (1978–79, 12 matches).
Career batting
12–19–0–329–112–17.31–1–*ct* 5

Hoar, Charles James
Amateur. *b:* 1862, Hambledon, Hants. *d:* June 1913, Ash, Farnham, Surrey. Middle order right-hand batsman. *Team* Sussex (1885, 1 match).
Career batting
1–2–1–12–8–12.00–0–*ct* 0
Bowling 28–0

Hoare, Arthur
Amateur. *b:* 16.9.1840, Withyham, Sussex. *d:* 26.12.1896, Edenbridge, Kent. Middle order right-hand batsman, bowler. *Teams* Sussex (1869–73, 2 matches); Kent (1871, 1 match).
Career batting
3–6–0–87–39–14.50–0–*ct* 1
Bowling 37–1–37.00–0–0–1/37

Hoare, Arthur Robertson
Amateur. *b:* 17.10.1871, Stibbard, Norfolk. *d:* 18.3.1941, Thetford, Norfolk. Right-hand batsman, right-arm medium pace bowler. *Sch* Eton. *Team* MCC (1903).
Career batting
1–2–0–45–41–22.50–0–*ct* 2
Bowling 19–0
He also played for Norfolk and Northumberland.

Hoare, Charles Arthur Richard
Amateur. *b:* 18.5.1847, Blackfriars, London. *d:* 22.5.1908, West Meon, Hants. Middle order right-hand batsman. *Team* Kent (1872, 1 match).
Career batting
1–2–0–18–14–9.00–0–*ct* 0
He founded and maintained the training ship *Mercury* on the Hamble.

Hoare, Charles Twysden
Amateur. *b:* 10.11.1851, Mitcham, Surrey. *d:* 22.1.1935, Bignell, Bicester, Oxon. Son of C. H. (Surrey). Middle order right-hand batsman,

excellent field. *Sch* Eton. *Teams* Surrey (1871–74, 4 matches); Middlesex (1875, 1 match).
Career batting
10–18–0–139–35–7.72–0–*ct* 4

He was not in the eleven whilst at Oxford. He also played for Devon. His final first-class match was for MCC in 1878.

Hoare, Ernest Stanley
Amateur. *b:* 21.6.1903, Andover, Hants. Middle order right-hand batsman. *Sch* Dean Close. *Team* Gloucestershire (1929, 3 matches).
Career batting
3–4–0–16–10–4.00–0–*ct* 1

Hoare, Henry William
(later Hamilton-Hoare)
Amateur. *b:* 1.4.1844. *d:* 7.9.1931, Westminster, London. Brother of H. N. (Sussex 1853). Opening/middle order batsman. *Sch* Eton. *Team* Oxford U (1865).
Career batting
5–6–0–43–33–7.16–0–*ct* 0

His final first-class match was for MCC in 1867.

Hoare, William
Amateur. *b:* 15.9.1847, Westminster, London. *d:* 22.7.1925, Benenden, Kent. Useful batsman. *Sch* Eton. *Team* Gentlemen of Kent (1879).
Career batting
1–1–0–9–9–9.00–0–*ct* 3

Hoare, Wilfred Norman Stewart
Amateur. *b:* 23.10.1909, Gloucester. Lower order right-hand batsman, wicket-keeper. *Team* Cambridge U (1931).
Career batting
1–2–1–15–11*–15.00–0–*ct* 1–*st* 1

Hobbs, John Anthony David
Amateur. *b:* 30.11.1935, Liverpool, Lancashire. Opening right-hand batsman. *Sch* Liverpool College. *Team* Oxford U (1956–58, blue 1957).
Career batting
18–36–1–614–95–17.20–0–*ct* 18

He represented Lancashire at hockey.

Hobbs, Sir John Berry
Professional. *b:* 16.12.1882, Cambridge. *d:* 21.12.1963, Hove, Sussex. Brilliant opening right-hand batsman, right-arm medium pace bowler, excellent cover. *Team* Surrey (1905–34, 598 matches). *Tours* MCC to Australia 1907/8, 1911/12, 1920/1, 1924/5, 1928/9, to South Africa 1909/10, 1913/14; Vizianagram's XI to India and Ceylon 1930/1. *Tests* England (1907/8 to 1930, 61 matches).
Career batting
834–1325–106–61760–316*–50.66–199–*ct* 339
Bowling 2704–108–25.04–3–0–7/56
Test batting
61–102–7–5410–211–56.94–15–*ct* 17
Bowling 165–1–165.00–0–0–1/19

'The Master' certainly earned his sobriquet. Although his figures as a batsman were later dwarfed by Bradman's achievements, many still ranked Hobbs the better of the two, stating that Hobbs scored his runs in a more attractive manner and was more capable on difficult wickets. Certainly he was recognised as the finest English batsman of his generation and for most of his career an essential part of the England side. He holds the record for the most runs scored in a first-class career as well as the most centuries. In 24 English seasons he completed 1,000 runs, going on to 2,000 17 times and in 1925 reaching 3,000 for the only time – 3,024, av 70.32. In 1926 he averaged 77.60 and the following year 82.00. He also hit 1,000 in a season in South Africa twice.

His highest score was 316* for Surrey v Middlesex at Lord's in 1926, but he made 15 other scores of 200 or more.

As an opening batsman he was fortunate to be associated with three distinguished partners; with Hayward he added a century for the first wicket on 40 occasions, with Sandham on 66 occasions and with Sutcliffe for England on 11 occasions. In all he was involved in 166 first-wicket three-figure partnerships.

He rarely failed in Test cricket, being the first batsman to reach a Test aggregate of 5,000 runs, and he was equally successful on his five consecutive Test tours to Australia.

He was an active member of Surrey CCC Committee from his retirement to his death and was knighted for his services to the game in 1953. Before appearing for Surrey he represented Cambridgeshire.

Hobbs, Norman Frederick Charles
Professional. *b:* 1900, Cheltenham. *d:* 6.4.1966, Coombe Down, Somerset. Middle order batsman. *Team* Gloucestershire (1924, 6 matches).
Career batting
6–10–1–53–28–5.88–0–*ct* 5

Hobbs, Robin Nicholas Stuart
Professional. *b:* 8.5.1942, Chippenham, Wilts. Lower order right-hand batsman, leg break and googly bowler. *Teams* Essex (1961–75, 325 matches); Glamorgan (1979–81, 41 matches). *Tours* MCC to East Africa 1963/4, to South Africa 1964/5, to Pakistan 1966/7, 1968/9, to West Indies 1967/8; Cavaliers to Jamaica 1963/4;

Norfolk to West Indies 1969/70; Robins to South Africa 1972/3; Commonwealth to Pakistan 1970/1; Rest of World to Pakistan 1973/4. *Tests* England (1967–71, 7 matches).
Career batting
440–546–138–4940–100–12.10–2–*ct* 295
Bowling 29776–1099–27.09–50–8–8/63
Test batting
7–8–3–34–15*–6.80–0–*ct* 8
Bowling 481–12–40.08–0–0–3/25

He took 100 wickets in a season twice (best 102, av 21.40, in 1970). For Essex v Australians at Chelmsford in 1975 he hit 100 in 44 minutes. In 1979 he captained Glamorgan. He also appeared for Suffolk 1976–78 and from 1982.

Hobgen, Arthur
Amateur. *b;* 3.9.1849, Siddlesham, Chichester, Sussex. *d:* 26.3.1886, Appledram, Chichester, Sussex. Left-hand batsman, right-hand slow round-arm bowler, good deep field. *Team* Sussex (1872–73, 3 matches).
Career batting
3–5–1–31–12–7.75–0–*ct* 1
Bowling 25–2–12.50–0–0–2/22

Hobson, Barry Sinton
Amateur. *b:* 22.11.1925, Dunmurry, Co Antrim, Ireland. Lower order right-hand batsman, right-arm medium pace bowler. *Sch* Taunton. *Team* Cambridge U (1946, blue).
Career batting
7–14–3–50–16*–4.54–0–*ct* 1
Bowling 460–10–46.00–0–0–3/60

He also played for Wiltshire.

Hockey, George William
Professional. *b:* 1.1.1905, Ipswich. Middle order right-hand batsman, right-arm medium pace bowler. *Sch* Ipswich. *Team* Essex (1928–31, 19 matches).
Career batting
19–33–5–305–23–10.88–0–*ct* 4
Bowling 20–0

He also played for Suffolk.

Hodder, Francis Samuel
Amateur. *b:* 11.2.1906. *d:* 6.9.1943, on active service. Lower order right-hand batsman, right-arm bowler. *Team* RAF (1931).
Career batting
1–2–2–11–10*–no av–0–*ct* 1
Bowling 69–1–69.00–0–0–1/69

Hodge, Robert Stevenson
Amateur. *b:* 5.11.1914, Greenock, Scotland. Lower order right-hand batsman, right-arm fast medium bowler. *Team* Scotland (1938–51).
Career batting
10–16–0–178–38–11.12–0–*ct* 2
Bowling 817–30–27.23–1–0–5/82

He appeared with success for Under 33 v Over 33 at Lord's in 1945.

Hodges, Aubrey Davis
Amateur. *b:* 3.2.1912. *d:* 27.5.1944, Minna, Nigeria. Opening right-hand batsman, good field. *Sch* Epsom. *Team* MCC (1936).
Career batting
1–2–0–44–34–22.00–*ct* 0

Hodges, Albert Edward
Amateur. *b:* 1905, Newport, Monmouthshire. Middle order right-hand batsman. *Teams* Wales (1930); Glamorgan (1936, 1 match).
Career batting
2–4–0–14–8–3.50–0–*ct* 0
Bowling 23–0

Hodges, Harold Augustus
Amateur. *b:* 22.1.1886, Mansfield Woodhouse, Notts. *d:* 22.3.1918, near Roye, France. He was killed in action. Middle order batsman. *Sch* Sedbergh. *Team* Nottinghamshire (1911–12, 3 matches).
Career batting
3–4–1–141–62–47.00–0–*ct* 1

He did not appear in first-class cricket whilst at Oxford. A noted rugby footballer, he played for Oxford U and England.

Hodgkins, Henry Joseph Jordan
Amateur. *b:* 11.11.1868, Cheltenham, Gloucs. *d:* 24.6.1952, Dorchester, Dorset. Middle order left-hand batsman, left-arm medium pace bowler. *Sch* Trent College. *Team* Gloucestershire (1900–01, 10 matches).
Career batting
10–17–1–209–44–13.06–0–*ct* 4
Bowling 183–5–36.60–0–0–3/68
He also played for Bedfordshire.

Hodgkins, John Seymour
Amateur. *b:* 2.1.1916, West Bridgford, Notts. Middle/lower order right-hand batsman, right-arm fast medium bowler. *Sch* Nottingham High School. *Team* Nottinghamshire (1938–51, 3 matches).
Career batting
3–5–0–106–44–21.20–0–*ct* 0
Bowling 238–3–79.33–0–0–1/55

Hodgkinson, Gilbert Frank
Amateur. *b:* 19.2.1913, Derby. Middle order right-hand batsman, good field. *Team* Derbyshire (1935–46, 19 matches).

Career batting
19–32–0–472–44–14.75–0–*ct* 10
He captained Derbyshire in 1946.

Hodgkinson, Canon George Langton
Amateur. *b:* 13.10.1837, Kentish Town, Middlesex. *d:* 16.2.1915, Wotton-under-Edge, Gloucs. Middle order right-hand batsman, good field. *Sch* Harrow. *Teams* Oxford U (1857–59, blue all three years); Middlesex (1861, 1 match).
Career batting
11–18–1–129–22–7.58–0–*ct* 4
Bowling 61–13–4.67–2–0–5/6

Hodgkinson, Gerard William
Amateur. *b:* 19.2.1883, Clifton, Bristol. *d:* 6.10.1960, Wookey Hole, Somerset. Middle order right-hand batsman. *Sch* Eton. *Team* Somerset (1904–11, 19 matches).
Career batting
19–35–1–515–99*–15.14–0–*ct* 6

Hodgkinson, J.
Professional. Lower order batsman, bowler. *Team* Derbyshire (1882, 1 match).
Career batting
1–2–0–5–5–2.50–0–*ct* 1
Bowling 83–1–83.00–0–0–1/83

Hodgson, Alan
Cricketer. *b:* 27.10.1951, Moorside, Consett, Co Durham. Lower order left-hand batsman, right-arm fast medium bowler. *Team* Northants (1970–79, 99 matches).
Career batting
99–118–24–909–41*–9.67–0–*ct* 31
Bowling 5964–206–28.95–2–0–5/30

Hodgson, Craig Andrew Thornton
Cricketer. *b:* 13.7.1955, East London, South Africa. Hard hitting middle order right-hand batsman. *Team* Zimbabwe (1979/80 to 1982/3). *Tour* Zimbabwe to England 1982.
Career batting
7–12–1–248–87–22.54–0–*ct* 5
Bowling 3–0

Hodgson, Gordon
Professional. *b:* 16.4.1904, Johannesburg, South Africa. *d:* 14.6.1951, Stoke-on-Trent, Staffs. Lower order right-hand batsman, right-arm fast bowler. *Team* Lancashire (1928–33, 56 matches).
Career batting
56–52–17–244–20–6.97–0–*ct* 37
Bowling 4107–148–27.75–4–0–6/77
A well-known soccer player, he appeared as a forward for Liverpool, Aston Villa and Leeds United, as well as for England

Hodgson, Gordon
Cricketer. *b:* 24.7.1938, Huddersfield, Yorkshire. Lower order right-hand batsman, wicket-keeper. *Teams* Yorkshire (1964, 1 match); Lancashire (1965, 1 match).
Career batting
2–2–0–5–4–2.50–0–*ct* 3–*st* 2

Hodgson, Herbert William
Amateur. *b:* 23.5.1891, Toxteth Park, Liverpool. *d:* 30.4.1964, Chingford, Essex. Middle order right-hand batsman. *Team* Minor Counties (1924–27).
Career batting
2–4–0–79–45–19.75–0–*ct* 1
He also played for Cheshire.

Hodgson, Isaac
Professional. *b:* 15.11.1828, Bradford, Yorkshire. *d:* 24.11.1867, Bradford, Yorkshire. Lower order right-hand batsman, left-hand slow round-arm bowler. *Team* Yorkshire (1852–66, 31 matches).
Career batting
39–65–21–329–32–7.47–0–*ct* 30
Bowling 2749–174–15.79–9–2–7/23
He also played for Northumberland. He was also a noted knurr and spell player.

Hodgson, Kenneth Ian
Cricketer. *b:* 24.2.1960, Port Elizabeth, South Africa. Lower order right-hand batsman, right-arm medium pace bowler. *Sch* Oundle. *Team* Cambridge U (1981–83, blue all three years).
Career batting
27–34–9–633–50–25.32–0–*ct* 4
Bowling 2093–55–38.05–1–1–8/68
He has played for Buckinghamshire since 1980.
He also represented Cambridge at squash rackets.

Hodgson, Philip
Professional. *b:* 21.9.1935, Todmorden, Yorkshire. Lower order right-hand batsman, right-arm fast medium bowler. *Team* Yorkshire (1954–56, 13 matches).
Career batting
17–11–4–65–26–9.28–0–*ct* 7
Bowling 946–39–24.25–1–0–5/41
His final first-class match was for Combined Services in 1957.

Hodgson, Rev Richard Greaves
Amateur. *b:* 9.3.1845, Manchester, Lancashire. *d:* 1.11.1931, Canterbury, Kent. Middle order right-hand batsman, point field. *Team* Kent (1871–74, 3 matches).
Career batting
3–6–0–77–47–12.83–0–*ct* 3

Hodson, James
Professional. *b:* 30.10.1808, Streat-Place, Ditchling, Sussex. *d:* 17.3.1879, Hunston Mill, Sussex. Hard-hitting right-hand batsman, right-hand medium pace round-arm bowler. *Team* Sussex (1838–54, 51 matches).
Career batting
54–95–16–620–44–7.84–0–*ct* 48
Bowling 454–29+66–15.65–3–0–8/?
One of the leading Sussex players of his day, he was no-balled for bowling with his arm above his shoulder at Lord's in 1839, one umpire considering his delivery fair, whilst the other was of the contrary opinion.

Hodson, Richard Philip
Cricketer. *b:* 26.4.1951, Wakefield, Yorkshire. Right-hand batsman, off break bowler. *Sch* Queen Elizabeth GS, Wakefield. *Team* Cambridge U (1971–73, blue 1972–73).
Career batting
19–36–3–687–111–20.81–1–*ct* 8
Bowling 766–29–26.41–0–0–4/54

Hoffman, Dr Myer
Amateur. *b:* 1902, Leeds, Yorkshire. *d: circa* 1965, Parow, South Africa. Right-hand batsman, right-arm medium pace bowler. *Team* Dublin University (1925).
Career batting
1–2–1–6–6*–6.00–0–*ct* 0
Bowling 18–0

Hofmeyr, Murray Bernard
Amateur. *b:* 9.12.1925, Pretoria, South Africa. Sound opening right-hand batsman. *Teams* Oxford U (1949–51, blue all three years); North East Transvaal (1951/2 to 1953/4).
Career batting
44–81–10–3178–161–44.76–7–*ct* 29
Bowling 12–1–12.00–0–0–1/0
He hit 1,063 runs, av 55.94, in 1950.
A noted rugby footballer, he obtained his blue and went on to represent England as full-back.

Hogan, Charles Ronald
Amateur. *b:* 10.1.1939, Paisley, Scotland. Right-hand batsman, right-arm fast/medium bowler. *Team* Scotland (1962–64).
Career batting
6–6–0–25–7–4.16–0–*ct* 2
Bowling 415–24–17.29–2–0–6/36

Hogan, Raymond P.
Professional. *b:* 8.5.1932, Temora, New South Wales, Australia. Hard-hitting right-hand batsman, right-arm fast medium bowler. *Team* Northants (1954–55, 3 matches).
Career batting
3–4–0–18–8–4.50–0–*ct* 2
Bowling 218–3–72.66–0–0–2/16
A good rugby footballer, he played for Northampton.

Hogg, Arthur
Professional. *b:* 20.6.1877, Ripley, Derbyshire. *d:* 21.4.1956, Ripley, Derbyshire. Middle order right-hand batsman. *Team* Derbyshire (1905–06, 3 matches).
Career batting
3–6–0–5–4–0.83–0–*ct* 0

Hogg, Rodney Malcolm
Cricketer. *b:* 5.3.1951, Melbourne, Australia. Lower order right-hand batsman, right-arm fast bowler. *Team* South Australia (1975/6 to 1982/3, 34 matches). *Tours* Australia to India 1979/80, to Sri Lanka 1980/1, 1982/3, to England 1981. *Tests* Australia (1978/9 to 1982/3, 26 matches).
Career batting
74–104–17–819–42–9.41–0–*ct* 19
Bowling 6213–273–22.75–15–4–7/53
Test batting
26–41–7–272–36–8.00–0–*ct* 5
Bowling 2277–94–24.22–5–2–6/74
In the 1978/9 series against England, when the leading Australian players were appearing in World Series Cricket, he created a sensation by taking a record 41 wickets, av 12.85, but on the 1981 tour to England he only played in two Tests and in first-class matches took 27 wickets, av 24.33.

Hogg, Vincent Richard
Cricketer. *b:* 3.7.1952, Salisbury, Rhodesia. Lower order right-hand batsman, right-arm fast medium bowler. *Team* Rhodesia/Zimbabwe (1971/2 to 1982/3). *Tour* Zimbabwe to England 1982.
Career batting
42–54–21–181–30–5.48–0–*ct* 12
Bowling 3169–119–26.63–3–0–6/26

Hogg, William
Cricketer. *b:* 12.7.1955, Ulverston, Lancashire. Lower order right-hand batsman, right-arm fast bowler. *Teams* Lancashire (1976–80, 44 matches); Warwickshire (1981–83, 50 matches).
Career batting
96–90–25–394–31–6.06–0–*ct* 19
Bowling 6437–222–28.99–6–1–7/84

Hoggarth, Francis Harry
Amateur. *b:* 1876, Whitby, Yorkshire. *d:*

7.1.1961, Aberdeen, Scotland. *Team* Scotland (1906).
Career batting
1–2–0–38–22–19.00–0–*ct* 0

Hogsflesh, William
Professional. *b:* 1744. *d:* April 1818, Southwick, Hampshire. Lower order batsman, excellent bowler. *Team* Hampshire (1769–75).

He was one of the most famous bowlers connected with the Hambledon Club, but his career seems to have been a short one, ending when he was only 32 years of age.

Holbech, William Hugh
Amateur. *b:* 18.8.1882, Canada. *d:* 1.11.1914, Kruiseecke, Belgium. He died of wounds. Middle order right-hand batsman. *Sch* Eton. *Team* Warwickshire (1910, 1 match).
Career batting
3–6–0–28–21–4.66–0–*ct* 1

His first-class debut was for MCC in 1908.

Holden, Cecil
Amateur. *b:* 1.6.1865, West Derby, Liverpool. *d:* 22.8.1928, Claughton, Cheshire. Hard-hitting middle order right-hand batsman, right-arm medium pace bowler, good slip. *Team* Lancashire (1890, 3 matches).
Career batting
8–14–1–136–45–10.46–0–*ct* 6
Bowling 63–1–63.00–0–0–1/29

Most of his County cricket was for Cheshire and he captained Birkenhead Park for 20 years. He also appeared for Liverpool and District (1886–91).

Holden, Stanley Mitton
Professional. *b:* 25.1.1886, Chesterfield, Derbyshire. *d:* 10.5.1971, Coventry, Warwickshire. Lower order right-hand batsman, left-arm fast medium bowler. *Team* Derbyshire (1910–20, 4 matches).
Career batting
4–6–2–13–6*–3.25–0–*ct* 1
Bowling 111–3–37.00–0–0–3/72

Holder, John Wakefield
Cricketer. *b:* 19.3.1945, St George, Barbados. Lower order right-hand batsman, right-arm fast medium bowler. *Team* Hampshire (1968–72, 47 matches).
Career batting
47–49–14–374–33–10.68–0–*ct* 12
Bowling 3415–139–24.56–5–1–7/79

He joined the umpires' list in 1983.

Holder, Vanburn Alonza
Cricketer. *b:* 8.10.1945, Bridgetown, Barbados. Lower order right-hand batsman, right-arm fast medium bowler. *Teams* Barbardos (1966/7 to 1977/8); Worcestershire (1968–80, 181 matches). *Tours* West Indies to England 1969, 1973, 1976, to India, Sri Lanka and Pakistan 1974/5, to Australia 1975/6, to India and Sri Lanka 1978/9; Rest of World to Pakistan 1973/4. *Tests* West Indies (1969 to 1978/9, 40 matches).
Career batting
311–354–81–3559–122–13.03–1–*ct* 98
Bowling 23183–948–24.45–38–3–7/40
Test batting
40–59–11–682–42–14.20–0–*ct* 16
Bowling 3627–109–33.27–3–0–6/28

The most successful of his three tours to England was in 1976 when he took 52 wickets, av 19.30. He also played for Shropshire 1981.

Holding, Michael Anthony
Cricketer. *b:* 16.2.1954, Half Way Tree, Kingston, Jamaica. Lower order-right hand batsman, right-arm fast bowler. *Teams* Jamaica (1972/3 to 1982/3); Lancashire (1981, 7 matches); Derbyshire (1983, 6 matches); Tasmania (1982/3, 7 matches). *Tours* West Indies to Australia 1975/6, 1981/2, to England 1976, 1980, to Australia and New Zealand 1979/80, to Pakistan 1980/1; International XI to Pakistan 1981/2. *Tests* West Indies (1975/6 to 1982/3, 36 matches).
Career batting
105–132–23–1521–67–13.82–0–*ct* 40
Bowling 9129–380–24.02–23–3–8/92
Test batting
36–49–8–461–58*–11.24–0–*ct* 12
Bowling 3696–151–24.47–10–2–8/92

On his first tour to England in 1976 he headed the first-class and Test bowling averages with 55 wickets, av 14.38, and 28, av 12.71, respectively. In 1980 he again played in all the Tests, but proved more expensive, his record in the Tests being 20 wickets, av 31.60.

Holdship, William Ernest Johnstone
Amateur. *b:* 15.2.1872, Auckland, New Zealand. Brother of A. R. (Wellington). Middle order batsman. *Sch* Cheltenham. *Team* Middlesex (1894, 3 matches).
Career batting
3–5–0–21–15–4.20–0–*ct* 2

Holdsworth, Romilly Lisle
Amateur. *b:* 25.2.1899, Mysore, India. *d:* 20.6.1976, Blagdon Hill, Somerset. Sound middle order right-hand batsman. *Sch* Repton. *Teams* Oxford U (1919–22, blue all four years); Warwickshire (1919–21, 30 matches); Sussex (1925–29, 36 matches); Northern India (1934/5); NWFP (1937/8 to 1941/2).

Career batting
109–197–17–4716–202–26.20–8–*ct* 51
Bowling 78–1–78.00–0–0–1/4

He hit 1,021 runs, av 26.17, in 1921. His only double century was 202 for Oxford U v Free Foresters at Oxford in 1921. Being in the scholastic profession his cricket after leaving Oxford was restricted and he later moved to India, where he was headmaster of Doon School, Dehra Dun.

Holdsworth, William Edgar Newman
Professional. *b:* 17.9.1928, Leeds, Yorkshire. Lower order right-hand batsman, right-arm fast medium bowler. *Team* Yorkshire (1952–53, 27 matches).
Career batting
27–26–12–111–22*–7.92–0–*ct* 7
Bowling 1598–53–30.01–2–0–6/58

Hole, Graeme Blake
Amateur. *b:* 6.1.1931, Concord West, New South Wales, Australia. Middle order right-hand batsman, off break bowler. *Teams* New South Wales (1949/50, 1 match); South Australia (1950/1 to 1957/8, 51 matches); Commonwealth in Ceylon 1951/2. *Tour* Australia to England 1953. *Tests* Australia (1950/1 to 1954/5, 18 matches).
Career batting
98–166–12–5647–226–36.66–11–*ct* 82
Bowling 2686–61–44.03–1–0–5/109
Test batting
18–33–2–789–66–25.45–0–*ct* 21
Bowling 126–3–42.00–0–0–1/9

Although he played in all five Tests on the 1953 tour to England, he had only moderate success and in all first-class matches hit 1,118 runs, av 33.87. His highest score was 226 for South Australia v Queensland at Adelaide in 1953/4.

Hole, Gilbert Lindsay Douglas
Amateur. *b:* 28.6.1882, Edinburgh, Scotland. *d:* 10.11.1967, Edinburgh, Scotland. Right-hand batsman, right-arm medium pace bowler. *Sch* Edinburgh Academy. *Team* Scotland (1910–26).
Career batting
10–17–2–260–37–17.33–0–*ct* 2
Bowling 450–27–16.66–2–0–5/20

Holford, David Anthony Jerome
Cricketer. *b:* 16.4.1940, Bridgetown, Barbados. Cousin of G. St. A. Sobers (West Indies and Notts). Middle order right-hand batsman, leg break bowler. *Teams* Trinidad (1962/3); Barbados (1960/1 to 1978/9). *Tours* West Indies to England 1966, to India 1966/7, to Australia and New Zealand 1968/9; Barbados to England 1969. *Tests* West Indies (1966 to 1976/7, 24 matches).
Career batting
99–149–27–3821–111–31.31–3–*ct* 83
Bowling 8096–253–32.00–8–2–8/52
Test batting
24–39–5–768–105*–22.58–1–*ct* 18
Bowling 2009–51–39.39–1–0–5/23

He proved a most useful all-rounder on the 1966 tour to England and played in all five Tests – in first-class matches he hit 759 runs, av 37.95, and took 51 wickets, av 28.60.

Holgate, Gideon
Professional. *b:* 23.6.1839, Sawley, Yorkshire. *d:* 11.7.1895, Accrington, Lancashire. Middle order right-hand batsman, wicket-keeper. *Teams* Yorkshire (1865–67, 12 matches); Lancashire (1866-67, 8 matches).
Career batting
20–34–1–455–65–13.78–0–*ct* 24–*st* 10

Holland, Frederick Charles
Professional, *b:* 10.2.1876, Battersea, Surrey. *d:* 5.2.1957, Beckenham, Kent. Middle order right-hand batsman, slow right-arm bowler. *Team* Surrey (1894–1908, 282 matches).
Career batting
284–429–29–10384–171–25.96–12–*ct* 232
Bowling 570–13–43.84–0–0–2/20

He hit 1,000 runs in a season four times (best 1,129, av 23.52, in 1903).

Holland, John
Professional. *b:* 7.4.1869, Nantwich, Chgeshire. *d:* 22.8.1914, Bury, Lancashire. Middle order right-hand batsman. *Teams* Lancashire (1900–02, 12 matches); Leicestershire (1894–96, 42 matches).
Career batting
54–101–7–1650–65–17.55–0–*ct* 25
Bowling 54–0

He also appeared for Cheshire.

Holland, Kenneth
Amateur. *b:* 29.3.1911, Leicester. Lower order right-hand batsman, right-arm fast medium bowler. *Team* Leicestershire (1935, 2 matches).
Career batting
2–2–0–2–2–1.00–0–*ct* 1
Bowling 146–3–48.66–0–0–1/9

Holland, Lawrence Edward
Amateur. *b:* 13.1.1887, Tinsley, Sheffield, Yorkshire. *d:* 3.7.1956, Desborough, Northants. Middle order right-hand batsman, slow right-arm bowler. *Team* Northants (1912–20, 10 matches).
Career batting
10–19–0–202–63–10.63–0–*ct* 1
Bowling 193–6–32.16–0–0–3/26

Holland-Martin, Admiral Sir Deric Douglas Eric
(Holland to 1917)
Amateur. *b:* 10.4.1906, Kensington, London. *d:* 6.1.1977, Kemerton, Gloucs. Lower order right-hand batsman, wicket-keeper. *Teams* Royal Navy (1928); Combined Services (1937).
Career batting
2–4–0–25–16–6.25–0–*ct* 7

Hollands, Sydney
Professional. *b:* 1866, East Grinstead, Sussex. *d:* 1949, Croydon, Surrey. *Team* Sussex (1887–93, 11 matches).
Career batting
11–21–0–154–21–7.33–0–*ct* 6

Hollick, Alexander Francis George Philip
Amateur. *b:* 13.2.1936, Cairo, Egypt. Right-hand batsman. *Sch* Royal Belfast Academical Institute. *Team* Ireland (1957).
Career batting
1–2–0–0–0–0.00–0–*ct* 1

Holliday, David Charles
Cricketer. *b:* 20.12.1958, Cambridge. Lower order right-hand batsman, leg break bowler. *Sch* Oundle. *Team* Cambridge U (1979–81, blue all three years).
Career batting
29–37–8–522–76*–18.00–0–*ct* 15
Bowling 400–6–66.66–0–0–2/23
His County cricket was for Cambridgeshire.

Hollies, William Eric
Professional. *b:* 5.6.1912, Old Hill, Staffs. *d:* 16.4.1981, Chinley, Derbyshire. Tail end right-hand batsman, leg break and googly bowler. *Team* Warwickshire (1932–57, 476 matches). *Tours* MCC to West Indies 1934/5, to Australia and New Zealand 1950/1. *Tests* England (1934/5 to 1950, 13 matches).
Career batting
515–616–282–1673–47–5.00–*ct* 179
Bowling 48656–2323–20.94–182–40–10/42
Test batting
13–15–8–37–18*–5.28–0–*ct* 2
Bowling 1332–44–30.27–5–0–7/50
He took 100 wickets in a season 14 times (best 184, av 15.60, in 1946); his outstanding analysis was for Warwickshire v Notts at Edgbaston in 1946 when he took all ten wickets in the innings at a cost of 49 runs. His most famous wicket was that of Bradman, when the great Australian was making his final appearance in Test cricket (at the Oval in 1948); Hollies bowled him before he had scored a run. He also played for Staffordshire.

Hollingdale, Reginald Allen
Professional. *b:* 6.3.1906, Burgess Hill, Sussex. Lower order right-hand batsman, right-arm fast medium bowler. *Teams* Sussex (1925–30, 78 matches); Scotland (1938).
Career batting
79–115–35–1071–57–13.38–0–*ct* 38
Bowling 2644–84–31.47–2–0–5/23

Hollings, Herbert John Butler
Amateur. *b:* 18.6.1855, Manningham, Yorkshire. *d:* 6.3.1922, Bournemouth, Hants. Middle order right-hand batsman, right-arm off break bowler. *Sch* Winchester. *Team* Oxford U (1877).
Career batting
1–2–0–0–0–0.00–0–*ct* 0

Hollington, Hugh Basil
Cricketer. *b:* 14.8.1949, Harpenden, Herts. Opening left-hand batsman. *Team* Minor Counties (1972).
Career batting
1–2–0–21–12–10.50–0–*ct* 0
He also played for Hertfordshire.

Hollingworth, Thomas Vernon
Amateur. *b:* 27.7.1907. *d:* 2.10.1973, Topsham, Devon. Middle order right-hand batsman, bowler. *Sch* Bromsgrove. *Teams* Hampshire (1929, 2 matches); Europeans (1932/3 to 1933/4).
Career batting
4–7–1–58–17–9.66–0–*ct* 0
Bowling 123–4–30.75–0–0–4/92
He also played for Devonshire.

Hollins, Sir Arthur Meyrick
Amateur. *b:* 16.7.1876, Preston, Lancashire. *d:* 30.7.1938, Walton-le-Dale, Lancashire. Brother of F. H. and J. C. H. L. (Lancashire). Middle order right-hand batsman, excellent deep field. *Sch* Eton. *Team* Oxford U (1899–1900, blue 1899). *Tour* Bosanquet to North America in 1901.
Career batting
12–20–2–389–63–21.61–0–*ct* 6
Bowling 249–3–83.00–0–0–1/19
A noted athlete, he ran in the 440 yards for Oxford in three seasons.

Hollins, Sir Frank Hubert
Amateur. *b:* 31.10.1877, Bowness-on-Windermere, Westmorland. *d:* 31.1.1963, Paddington, London. Brother of A. M. (Oxford U) and J. C. H. L. (Lancashire). Middle order right-hand batsman. *Sch* Eton. *Teams* Oxford U (1900–01, blue 1901); Lancashire (1902–04, 12 matches). *Tours* Bennett to West Indies 1901/2; OU Authentics to India 1902/3.

Career batting
35–58–5–1114–114–21.01–1–*ct* 33
Bowling 87–3–29.00–0–0–2/39

He also played for Cumberland. His first-class debut was for G. J. V. Weigall's XI in 1898 and his final first-class match for MCC in 1927.

Hollins, John Chard Humphrey Lancelot
Amateur. *b:* 3.6.1890, Preston, Lancashire. *d:* 13.11.1938, Whittle-le-Woods, Lancashire. Brother of A. M. (Oxford U) and F. H. (Oxford U and Lancashire). Opening right-hand batsman. *Sch* Eton. *Team* Lancashire (1914–19, 20 matches).
Career batting
20–30–0–454–65–15.13–0–*ct* 8
Bowling 99–1–99.00–0–0–1/45

He appeared in the Freshmen's match at Oxford, but no first-class games.

Hollinshead, Cyril
Amateur. *b:* 26.5.1902, Timberland, Lincs. Lower order left-hand batsman, left-arm fast medium bowler. *Team* Gloucestershire (1946, 1 match).
Career batting
1 match, did not bat –*ct* 0
Bowling 7–0

He also played for Lincolnshire.

Holloway, Bernard Henry
Amateur. *b:* 13.1.1888, Wandsworth, London. *d:* 27.9.1915, Loos, France. He was killed in action. Brother of N. J. (Cambridge U). Middle order right-hand batsman, right-arm fast medium bowler. *Sch* The Leys. *Team* Sussex (1911–14, 8 matches). *Tour* MCC to West Indies 1910/11.
Career batting
19–33–2–701–100–22.61–1–*ct* 13

He appeared in the Seniors' Match at Cambridge but no first-class matches. He was a noted rugby footballer, appearing for Cambridge, and also excelled at lacrosse, appearing for both Cambridge and England.

Holloway, George James Warner Sinclair
Amateur. *b:* 26.4.1884, Stroud, Gloucs. *d:* 22.9.1966, Cheltenham, Gloucs. Middle order left-hand batsman. *Sch* Clifton. *Team* Gloucestershire (1908–11, 10 matches).
Career batting
10–20–1–187–34*–9.84–0–*ct* 4

Holloway, Norman James
Amateur. *b:* 11.11.1889, Wandsworth, London. *d:* 17.8.1964, Walton-on-the-Hill, Surrey. Brother of B. H. (Sussex). Lower order right-hand batsman, right-arm fast bowler. *Sch* The Leys. *Teams* Cambridge U (1910–12, blue all three years); Sussex (1911–25, 67 matches).
Career batting
102–161–49–1227–55–10.95–0–*ct* 40
Bowling 8046–324–24.83–16–3–8/99

His final first-class match was for Free Foresters in 1928.

Holloway, Reginald Frederick Price
Amateur. *b:* 31.10.1904, Dursley, Gloucs. *d:* 12.2.1979, Bristol. Opening right-hand batsman. *Sch* Clifton. *Team* Gloucestershire (1923–26, 7 matches).
Career batting
7–12–3–108–28*–12.00–0–*ct* 4
Bowling 19–0

He appeared in the Freshmen's and Seniors' matches at Oxford, but no first-class games.

Holloway, William Octavius
Amateur. *b:* 15.9.1870, Chipping Norton, Oxfordshire. *d:* 2.12.1907, Farnborough, Hants. Tail end batsman, useful bowler. *Team* Sussex (1890, 1 match).
Career batting
4–5–2–36–18*–12.00–0–*ct* 1
Bowling 98–3–32.66–0–0–3/60

His final first-class match was for MCC in 1902.

Holman, John Charles
Amateur. *b:* 5.4.1938, Calcutta, India. Middle order right-hand batsman, wicket-keeper. *Sch* Tonbridge. *Team* Combined Services (1962–64).
Career batting
2–4–1–39–17–13.00–0–*ct* 3

Holmes, Albert John
Amateur. *b:* 30.6.1899, Thornton Heath, Surrey. *d:* 21.5.1950, Hollington, Hastings, Sussex. Father of J. R. R. (Sussex). Middle order right-hand batsman. *Sch* Repton. *Team* Sussex (1922–39, 203 matches). *Tours* Manager of MCC to South Africa 1938/9; Proposed captain MCC to India 1939/40 (tour cancelled).
Career batting
208–320–24–6282–133*–21.22–6–*ct* 122
Bowling 425–8–53.12–0–0–1/2

He hit 1,000 runs in a season twice (best 1,134, av 24.65, in 1937). He was Chairman of the Test Match Selection Committee 1946 to 1949, and a member of the Committee in 1939. Serving in the RAF from 1925 to 1935, his important cricket was very restricted during this period. He captained Sussex 1936–39.

Holmes, Errol Reginald Thorold
Amateur. *b:* 21.8.1905, Calcutta, India. *d:*

16.8.1960, Marylebone, London. Hard-hitting middle order right-hand batsman, right-arm fast, later medium pace bowler. *Sch* Malvern. *Teams* Oxford U (1925–27, blue all three years); Surrey (1924–55, 198 matches). *Tours* Tennyson to Jamaica 1926/7; MCC to West Indies 1934/5, to Australia and New Zealand 1935/6. *Tests* England (1934/5 to 1935, 5 matches).
Career batting
301–465–51–13598–236–32.84–24–*ct* 192
Bowling 9531–283–33.67–4–0–6/16
Test batting
5–9–2–114–85*–16.28–0–*ct* 4
Bowling 76–2–38.00–0–0–1/10

He hit 1,000 runs in a season six times (best 1,925, av 41.84, in 1935). Of his two double centuries, the highest was 236 for Oxford U v Free Foresters at Oxford in 1927 and the other for Surrey. He played very little important cricket from 1928 to 1933 owing to business, but in 1934 was appointed captain of Surrey, continuing until 1938 and again in 1947–48. He also led MCC on the 1935/6 tour of Australia and New Zealand. A good soccer player, he obtained his blue at Oxford as a Freshman.

Holmes, Geoffrey Clarke
Cricketer. *b:* 16.9.1958, Newcastle-on-Tyne. Middle order right-hand batsman, right-arm medium pace bowler. *Team* Glamorgan (1978–83, 54 matches).
Career batting
54–85–22–1396–100*–22.15–1–*ct* 19
Bowling 1017–26–39.11–1–0–5/86

Holmes, Henry
Professional. *b:* 11.11.1833, Romsey, Hants. *d:* 6.1.1913, Southampton, Hants. Opening/middle order right-hand batsman, right-hand medium pace round-arm bowler. *Team* Hampshire (1861–78, 28 matches).
Career batting
32–58–4–798–77–14.77–0–*ct* 14–*st* 1
Bowling 762–28–27.21–2–0–5/57

He also played for Wiltshire.

Holmes, John Rodney Reay
Amateur. *b:* 24.4.1924, Hastings, Sussex. *d:* 3.2.1980, Cervinia, Italy. He was killed by an avalanche. Son of A. J. (Sussex). Lower order right-hand batsman, wicket-keeper. *Sch* Repton. *Team* Sussex (1950–51, 2 matches).
Career batting
3–4–0–41–24–10.25–0–*ct* 6–*st* 1

His first-class debut was for Free Foresters in 1949.

Holmes, John Trevor
Professional. *b:* 16.11.1939, Holmfirth, Yorkshire. Lower order right-hand batsman, wicket-keeper. *Team* Somerset (1969, 1 match).
Career batting
1–2–0–8–8–4.00–0–*ct* 1

Holmes, Percy
Professional. *b:* 25.11.1886, Oakes, Huddersfield, Yorkshire. *d:* 3.9.1971, Huddersfield, Yorkshire. Very sound opening right-hand batsman, excellent field. *Team* Yorkshire (1913–33, 485 matches). *Tours* Joel to South Africa 1924/5; MCC to West Indies 1925/6, to South Africa 1927/8. *Tests* England (1921–32, 7 matches).
Career batting
555–810–84–30573–315*–42.11–67–*ct* 336
Bowling 185–2–92.50–0–0–1/5
Test batting
7–14–1–357–88–27.46–0–*ct* 3

He hit 1,000 runs in a season 14 times, going on to 2,000 seven times (best 2,453, av 57.04, in 1925). His highest innings was 315* for Yorkshire v Middlesex at Lord's in 1925; he hit a second triple hundred for his County in 1920 and ten other scores over 200. He was associated with H. Sutcliffe in 69 century partnerships for the first wicket, including the record 555 for Yorkshire v Essex at Leyton in 1932. He also hit 1,000 runs in a season in South Africa. His final first-class match was for Sir L. Parkinson's XI in 1935.

Holmes, William
Professional. b: 29.10.1885, Eastwood, Notts. *d:* 6.12.1951, Doncaster, Yorkshire. Lower order right-hand batsman, right-arm medium pace bowler, good deep field. *Team* Nottinghamshire (1919, 2 matches).
Career batting
2–2–0–33–19–16.50–0–*ct* 1
Bowling 105–4–26.25–0–0–2/50

Holroyd, Edwin
Amateur. *b:* 27.10.1855, Halifax, Yorkshire. *d:* 1914, Rochdale, Lancashire. Middle order right-hand batsman, right-arm medium pace bowler, good field. *Team* Lancashire (1878, 1 match).
Career batting
1–2–0–6–4–3.00–0–*ct* 1

Holroyd, John
Professional. *b:* 15.4.1907, Oldham, Lancashire. *d:* 1975, Whitehaven, Cumberland. Tail end left-hand batsman, slow left-arm bowler. *Team* Lancashire (1927–33, 11 matches).

Career batting
11–9–5–33–18*–8.25–0–*ct* 2
Bowling 652–23–28.34–2–0–5/47

Holt, Alfred
Amateur. *b:* 1862, London. *d:* 3.2.1942, Battersea, London. Middle order left-hand batsman, left-arm fast bowler. *Team* MCC (1883).
Career batting
2–4–0–39–31–9.75–0–*ct* 0
His first-class debut was for Gentlemen of England in 1881. He also played for Wiltshire.

Holt, Arthur George
Professional. *b:* 8.4.1911, Southampton, Hants. Opening/middle order right-hand batsman, off break bowler. *Team* Hampshire (1935–48, 79 matches).
Career batting
79–140–13–2853–116–22.46–2–*ct* 32
Bowling 47–1–47.00–0–0–1/24
After retiring from first-class cricket he became coach to Hampshire CCC. A noted soccer player, he captained Southampton.

Holt, Ernest Gerald
Amateur. *b:* 2.7.1904, Burnham-on-Sea, Somerset. *d:* 27.8.1970, Brent Knoll, Somerset. Middle order right-hand batsman. *Sch* Marlborough. *Team* Somerset (1930, 2 matches).
Career batting
2–3–0–12–8–4.00–0–*ct* 0
Bowling 15–0

Holt, John Kenneth (sen)
Amateur. *b:* 1885, Jamaica. *d:* 5.8.1968, Kingston, Jamaica. Father of J. K. jun (Jamaica). Middle order right-hand batsman, right-arm medium bowler, occasional wicket-keeper. *Team* Jamaica (1905/6 to 1929/30). *Tour* West Indies to England 1923.
Career batting
36–60–2–1600–142–27.58–4–*ct* 25–*st* 1
Bowling 1054–26–40.53–0–0–3/34
He achieved very little on his tour of England.

Holt, Richard Anthony Appleby
Amateur. *b:* 11.3.1920, London. Middle order right-hand batsman. *Sch* Harrow. *Team* Sussex (1938–39, 5 matches).
Career batting
6–9–1–60–30–7.50–0–*ct* 1
His final first-class match was for Free Foresters in 1947.

Holyoake, Ronald Hubert
Amateur. *b:* 1894. Droitwich, Worcs. *d:* 8.11.1966, Droitwich, Worcs. Middle order left-hand batsman. *Team* Worcestershire (1924, 3 matches).
Career batting
3–6–0–47–22–7.83–0–*ct* 0

Homer, Herbert Wesley Farmer
Amateur. *b:* 6.10.1895, Dudley, Worcs. *d:* 10.2.1977, Old Hill, West Midlands. Opening right-hand batsman. *Team* Minor Counties (1928–31).
Career batting
4–6–0–185–71–30.83–0–*ct* 1
He was a mainstay of Staffordshire for many years and later served on the Warwickshire CCC Committee for 25 years.

Hone, Sir Brian William
Amateur. *b:* 1.7.1907, Semaphore, South Australia. *d:* 28.5.1978, Paris, France. Father of D. J. (Oxford U). Opening/middle order right-hand batsman. *Teams* South Australia (1928/9 to 1929/30, 11 matches); Oxford U (1931–33, blue all three years).
Career batting
44–75–6–2768–170–40.11–9–*ct* 25
Bowling 7–0
He appeared for Wiltshire until 1939. A noted tennis player, he was awarded his blue.

Hone, David Jeremy
Cricketer. *b:* 30.6.1946, Australia. Son of B. W. (Oxford U and South Australia). Right-hand batsman, right-arm medium pace bowler. *Team* Oxford U (1970).
Career batting
3–5–0–26–13–5.20–0–*ct* 1
Bowling 284–1–284.00–0–0–1/82

Hone, Leland
Amateur. *b:* 30.1.1853, Dublin, Ireland. *d:* 31.12.1896, Dublin, Ireland. Uncle of W. P. (Ireland). Middle order right-hand batsman, occasional wicket-keeper. *Team* MCC (1878–80). *Tour* Harris to Australia 1878/9. *Test* England (1878/9, 1 match).
Career batting
8–13–1–85–27–7.08–0–*ct* 10–*st* 2
Test batting
1–2–0–13–7–6.50–0–*ct* 2
A noted figure in Irish cricket, he went on Lord Harris's 1878/9 tour to Australia and was pressed into service as a wicket-keeper – the team not possessing one!

Hone, Nathaniel Thomas
Amateur. *b:* 21.6.1861, Monkstown, Co Dublin, Ireland. *d:* 1.8.1881, Limerick, Ireland, from drinking carbolic acid in error. Lower order right-

hand batsman, wicket-keeper. *Sch* Rugby. *Team* Cambridge U (1881, blue).
Career batting
3–5–3–2–1–1.00–0–*ct* 6–*st* 2

Hone, William
Amateur. *b:* 9.5.1842, Dublin. *d:* 20.3.1919, Dublin. Middle order right-hand batsman. Trinity College, Dublin. *Team* MCC (1864–77).
Career batting
9–15–2–266–76–20.46–0–*ct* 6
Bowling 64–3–21.33–0–0–3/41
Most of his cricket was played in Ireland, where he had considerable success.

Hone, William Patrick
Amateur. *b:* 28.8.1886, Monkstown, Co Dublin, Ireland. *d:* 28.2.1976, Clondalkin, Co Dublin, Ireland. Nephew of Leland (MCC). Right-hand batsman, wicket-keeper. *Sch* Wellington. *Team* Ireland (1910–28).
Career batting
4–8–0–140–92–17.50–0–*ct* 5

Hone-Goldney, George Hone
(formerly Goldney)
Amateur. *b:* 24.1.1851, Southborough, Kent. *d:* 28.3.1921, Winchester, Hants. Lower order right-hand batsman, right-arm medium pace bowler. *Sch* Eton. *Team* Cambridge U (1873, blue). *Tour* Vernon to India 1889/90 (not first-class).
Career batting
3–6–1–20–10–4.00–0–*ct* 2
Bowling 88–4–22.00–0–0–2/16
His final first-class match was for MCC in 1876.

Hone-Foster, J. B. (*see under* Foster, J. B.)

Hood, Ernest Hugo Meggeson
Amateur. *b:* 27.8.1915, Pocklington, Yorkshire. *d:* 1.8.1968, Scarborough, Yorkshire. Lower order batsman, left-arm bowler. *Sch* Wellington. *Team* Somerset (1935, 1 match).
Career batting
1–2–0–6–4–3.00–0–*ct* 0
Bowling 43–0
He was a well-known player in military matches.

Hood, John Antony
Cricketer. *b:* 2.1.1952, Napier, New Zealand. Right-hand batsman, off break bowler. *Team* Oxford U (1977).
Career batting
2–3–0–9–7–3.00–0–*ct* 1

Hood, Rev John Shapland Elliott
(changed to Cockburn-Hood in April 1866)
Amateur. *b:* 16.1.1844, Sydney, Australia. *d:* 30.8.1902, Catterick Bridge, Yorkshire, as the result of a bicycle accident. Hard-hitting middle order right-hand batsman, useful right-hand round-arm bowler, excellent deep field. *Sch* Rugby. *Team* Cambridge U (1864–67, blue 1865 and 1867).
Career batting
19–29–2–433–117–16.03–1–*ct* 6
Bowling 322–12–26.83–0–0–3/19
He played little cricket after leaving Cambridge, except for a few non-first-class matches for Free Foresters. His final first-class match was for Gentlemen of England in 1869.

Hood, Hon William Nelson
Amateur. *b:* 6.1.1848, London. *d:* 25.10.1921, Fulham, London. Middle order batsman. *Team* MCC (1875–80).
Career batting
2–4–0–13–6–3.25–0–*ct* 1
He played for Somerset (pre-first-class).

Hook, Rev Arthur James
Amateur. *b:* 12.2.1877, Porlock, Somerset. *d:* 12.2.1957, Bridgwater, Somerset. Middle order left-hand batsman. *Sch* Blundells. *Team* Somerset (1897–1906, 2 matches).
Career batting
2–4–1–43–15*–14.33–0–*ct* 1

Hook, John Stanley
Cricketer. *b:* 27.5.1954, Weston-super-Mare, Somerset. Lower order right-hand batsman, off break bowler. *Team* Somerset (1975, 1 match).
Career batting
1–2–1–7–4*–7.00–0–*ct* 0
Bowling 29–0

Hooker, Ronald William
Professional. *b:* 22.2.1935, Lower Clapton, London. Middle order right-hand batsman, right-arm medium pace bowler. *Team* Middlesex (1956–69, 300 matches).
Career batting
300–442–71–8222–137–22.16–5–*ct* 301
Bowling 13457–490–27.46–16–0–7/18
He hit 1,000 runs in a season twice (best 1,449, av 30.18, in 1959). He also played for Buckinghamshire.

Hooker, William
Professional. *b:* 17.5.1779, Midhurst, Sussex. *d* 27.12.1867, Midhurst, Sussex. Steady middle order right-hand batsman, wicket-keeper. *Team* Sussex (1823–33).

Career batting
26–46–4–517–92–12.30–0–*ct* 15–*st* 1
Bowling 1 wicket, no analysis

He was for a few seasons one of the leading batsmen in England, but did not play in great matches for long.

Hookes, David William
Cricketer. *b:* 3.5.1955, Mile End, Adelaide, Australia. Attacking middle order left-hand batsman, left-arm medium, or slow, bowler. *Team* South Australia (1975/6 to 1982/3, 45 matches). *Tours* Australia to England 1977, to Pakistan 1979/80, to Sri Lanka 1982/3. *Tests* Australia (1976/7 to 1982/3, 14 matches).
Career batting
74–122–7–5090–193–44.26–12–*ct* 60
Bowling 575–10–57.50–0–0–1/8
Test batting
14–24–2–923–143*–41.95–1–*ct* 6
Bowling 35–0

On the 1977 tour to England he hit 804 runs, av 32.16, and played in all five Tests. When scoring 107 for South Australia v Victoria at Adelaide in 1982/3 he reached 100 in 34 balls, believed to be the fastest century in terms of balls received ever scored in first-class cricket.

Hool, Nathan Bernard
Amateur. *b:* 28.1.1924, Dublin, Ireland. Right-hand batsman, slow left-arm bowler. *Team* Ireland (1947–61).
Career batting
9–16–8–132–27–16.62–0–*ct* 4
Bowling 601–18–33.38–1–0–5/73

Hooman, Charles Victor Lisle
Amateur. *b:* 3.10.1887, Ditton, Kent. *d:* 20.11.1969, Palm Beach, Florida, USA. Middle order right-hand batsman, right-arm medium pace bowler. *Sch* Charterhouse. *Teams* Oxford U (1907–10, blue 1909–10); Kent (1910, 15 matches).
Career batting
38–64–2–1758–117–28.41–3–*ct* 33
Bowling 59–0

He also played for Devon. He hit 1,070 runs, av 29.72, in 1910. A brilliant golfer, he gained his blue and went on the play for England in the Walker Cup. He also obtained his blue for rackets.

Hooper, Andrew James Mendez
Cricketer. *b:* 17.9.1945, Denmark Hill, London. Lower order right-hand batsman, slow left-arm bowler. *Team* Kent (1966–69, 13 matches).
Career batting
13–13–4–70–35–7.77–0–*ct* 7
Bowling 493–16–30.82–1–0–6/92

Hooper, John Michael Mackenzie
Cricketer. *b:* 23.4.1947, Milford, Surrey. Middle order right-hand batsman, right-arm medium pace bowler. *Sch* Charterhouse. *Team* Surrey (1967–71, 21 matches).
Career batting
21–36–10–406–41*–15.61–0–*ct* 14
Bowling 10–1–10.00–0–0–1/10

He was also a useful soccer player.

Hope, Arthur Oswald James
(later Baron Rankeillour)
Amateur. *b:* 7.5.1897, London. *d:* 26.5.1958, Chelsea, London. *Sch* Oratory. *Team* Army (1926).
Career batting
1–2–0–25–23–12.50–0–*ct* 0

He was MP for Nuneaton 1924–29 and for Aston 1931–39.

Hope, Kenneth William
Amateur. *b:* 3.5.1939, Portarlington, Co Leix, Ireland. Right-hand batsman, off break bowler. *Team* Ireland (1958–66).
Career batting
9–14–3–75–21–6.81–0–*ct* 5
Bowling 339–12–28.25–1–0–6/59

Hope, Philip Palmer
Amateur. *b:* 10.2.1889, Hartlepool. *d:* 19.5.1962, Clifton, Bristol. Middle order right-hand batsman, right-arm fast medium bowler. *Sch* Sedbergh and Sherborne. *Team* Somerset (1914–25, 41 matches).
Career batting
41–71–2–1048–77–15.18–0–*ct* 15
Bowling 145–1–145.00–0–0–1/17

He also played for Dorset.

Hopkins, Albert John Young
Amateur. *b:* 3.5.1874, Sydney, Australia. *d:* 25.4.1931, North Sydney, Australia. Opening/middle order right-hand batsman, right-arm fast medium bowler. *Team* New South Wales (1896/7 to 1914/5, 52 matches). *Tours* Australia to England 1902, 1905, 1909, to South Africa 1902/3, to New Zealand 1904/5, 1909/10. *Tests* Australia (1901/2 to 1909, 20 matches).
Career batting
162–240–21–5563–218–25.40–8–*ct* 87
Bowling 6613–271–24.40–10–0–7/10
Test batting
20–33–2–509–43–16.42–0–*ct* 11
Bowling 696–26–26.76–0–0–4/81

He produced his best form on his first visit to England scoring 1,100 runs, av 23.91, and taking 34 wickets. Although he appeared in 10 Tests in England he never really played up to his Australian reputation. His highest score was 218 for NSW v South Australia in 1908/9.

Hopkins, David Charles
Cricketer. *b:* 11.2.1957, Birmingham. Lower order right-hand batsman, right-arm medium pace bowler. *Team* Warwickshire (1977–81, 37 matches).
Career batting
36–44–12–332–34*–10.37–0–*ct* 8
Bowling 2021–53–38.13–1–0–6/67
He also played for Buckinghamshire.

Hopkins, Frank Jesse
Professional. *b:* 30.6.1875, Birmingham. *d:* 15.1.1930, Southampton, Hants. Tail end batsman, left-arm medium pace bowler. *Teams* Warwickshire (1898–1903, 11 matches); Hampshire (1906–11, 3 matches).
Career batting
14–22–6–44–13–2.75–0–*ct* 3
Bowling 940–29–32.41–1–0–5/10
He was appointed groundsman at Southampton in 1904 and thus qualified for Hampshire.

Hopkins, Dr Herbert Oxley
Amateur. *b:* 6.7.1895, Australia. *d:* 23.2.1972, Milverton, Somerset. Middle order right-hand batsman. *Teams* Oxford U (1921–23, blue 1923); Worcestershire (1921–31, 63 matches).
Career batting
85–152–9–3204–142*–22.40–4–*ct* 29
Bowling 202–4–50.50–0–0–2/23
He went to the Malay States and thus appeared in little County cricket after 1924.

Hopkins, John Anthony
Cricketer. *b:* 16.6.1953, Maesteg, Glamorgan. Brother of J.D. (Middlesex). Opening right-hand batsman, occasional wicket-keeper. *Teams* Glamorgan (1970–83, 207 matches); Eastern Province (1981/2).
Career batting
213–376–22–9805–230–27.69–14–*ct* 155–*st* 1
Bowling 50–0
He hit 1,000 runs in a season six times (best 1,371, av 33.43, in 1978). His only double century was 230 for Glamorgan v Worcestershire at Worcester in 1977.

Hopkins, Jeffris David
Cricketer. *b:* 23.8.1950, Bridgend, Glamorgan. Brother of J. A. (Glamorgan). Tail end right-batsman, wicket-keeper. *Team* Middlesex (1969–72, 4 matches).
Career batting
4–5–0–8–4–1.60–0–*ct* 9

Hopkins, Victor
Professional. *b:* 21.1.1911, Dumbleton, Gloucs. Lower order right-hand batsman, wicket-keeper. *Team* Gloucestershire (1934–48, 139 matches).
Career batting
139–210–34–2608–83*–14.81–0–*ct* 138–*st* 44

Hopley, Frederick John Vanderbyl
Amateur. *b:* 27.8.1883, Grahamstown, South Africa. *d:* 16.8.1951, Marandellas, Rhodesia. Brother of G. W. V. (Cambridge U). Hard-hitting middle order right-hand batsman, right-arm fast bowler. *Sch* Harrow. *Teams* Cambridge U (1904–06, blue 1904); Western Province (1909/10). *Tours* MCC to North America 1905; Leveson-Gower to Rhodesia 1909/10.
Career batting
27–47–5–599–55–14.26–0–*ct* 17
Bowling 1620–48–33.75–1–1–6/37
His final first-class match in England was for Leveson-Gower's XI in 1907. An excellent rugby footballer, he won his blue and went on to represent England; he was also regarded as the best amateur heavyweight boxer of his day.

Hopley, Geoffrey William Vanderbyl
Amateur. *b:* 9.9.1891, Kimberley, Griqualand West, South Africa. *d:* 12.5.1915, Boulogne, France. He died of wounds. Brother of F. J. V. (Cambridge U). Middle order right-hand batsman. *Sch* Harrow. *Team* Cambridge U (1911–14, blue 1912).
Career batting
15–29–4–309–42–12.36–0–*ct* 23
Bowling 21–1–21.00–0–0–1/21
In 1912 he won the heavyweight boxing title for Cambridge.

Hopwood, John Anthony
Amateur. *b:* 23.10.1926, Blean, Kent. Opening batsman. *Team* Free Foresters (1951).
Career batting
1–2–0–9–8–4.50–0–*ct* 1

Hopwood, John Leonard
Professional. *b:* 30.10.1903, Newton Hyde, Cheshire. Defensive opening/middle order right-hand batsman, left-arm medium pace bowler. *Team* Lancashire (1923–39, 397 matches). *Tests* England (1934, 2 matches).

Career batting
400–575–55–15548–220–29.90–27–*ct* 198
Bowling 15110–673–22.45–35–6–9/33
Test batting
2–3–1–12–8–6.00–0–*ct* 0
Bowling 155–0

He hit 1,000 runs in a season eight times (best 1,972, av 46.95, in 1933) and took 100 wickets twice (best 111, av 20.69, in 1934). He performed the 'double' in 1934 and 1935. His only double century was 220 for Lancs v Gloucs at Bristol in 1934. His best bowling was 9/33 for Lancashire v Leicestershire at Old Trafford in 1933. He also appeared for Cheshire.

Hopwood, Reginald Arthur
Amateur. *b:* 1903, London. d: 3.6.1969, Tangier. Tail end batsman, opening bowler. *Sch* Eton. *Team* Gloucestershire (1924, 1 match).
Career batting
1–2–0–2–2–1.00–0–*ct* 0
Bowling 8–0

Horan, Thomas Patrick
Amateur. *b:* 8.3.1854, Midleton, Co Cork, Ireland. *d:* 16.4.1916, Malvern, Victoria, Australia. Father of J. F. (Victoria) and T. I. B. (Victoria). Defensive middle order right-hand batsman, right-hand fast medium round-arm bowler. *Team* Victoria (1874/5 to 1891/2, 42 matches). *Tours* Australia to England 1878, 1882, to North America 1878. *Tests* Australia (1876/7 to 1884/5, 15 matches).
Career batting
106–187–14–4027–141*–23.27–8–*ct* 39
Bowling 829–35–23.68–2–0–6/40
Test batting
15–27–2–471–124–18.84–1–*ct* 6
Bowling 143–11–13.00–1–0–6/40

He was most successful on his 1882 visit to England, scoring over 1,000 runs in all matches and coming second to Murdoch in the averages.

Hordern, Herbert Vivian
Amateur. *b:* 10.2.1883, North Sydney, New South Wales, Australia. *d:* 17.6.1938, Darlinghurst, New South Wales, Australia. Lower order right-hand batsman, leg break and googly bowler. *Teams* Philadelphia (1907 to 1908/9); New South Wales (1905/6 to 1912/13, 10 matches). *Tours* Philadelphia to England 1908, to Jamaica 1908/09. *Tests* Australia (1910/11 to 1911/12, 7 matches).
Career batting
33–53–9–721–64–16.38–0–*ct* 38
Bowling 3640–217–16.77–23–9–8/31
Test batting
7–13–2–254–50–23.09–0–*ct* 6
Bowling 1075–46–23.36–5–2–7/90

He was, after J. B. King, the principal bowler on the 1908 tour to England and in all matches took 74 wickets, av 17.09. The previous season he had visited England with the Pennsylvania University team and returned figures of 110 wickets, av 9.68 (not first-class).

Hore, Fraser Salter
Amateur. *b: circa* 1835, Wimbledon, Surrey. *d:* 7.7.1903, Christchurch, Hants. Middle order right-hand batsman, right-hand medium pace round-arm bowler. *Sch* Tonbridge. *Team* Surrey (1861, 1 match).
Career batting
5–8–2–32–9–5.33–0–*ct* 1

His final first-class match was for MCC in 1866.

Horlick, Sir James Nockells
Amateur. *b:* 22.3.1886, Brooklyn, New York, USA. *d:* 31.12.1972, Achamore, Isle of Gigha, Argyll. Lower order right-hand batsman, slow left-arm bowler. *Sch* Eton. *Teams* Oxford U (1906); Gloucestershire (1907–10, 2 matches).
Career batting
3–5–1–24–9–6.00–0–*ct* 2
Bowling 48–0

Hornby, Albert Henry
Amateur. *b:* 29.7.1877, Nantwich, Cheshire. *d:* 6.9.1952, North Kilworth, Rugby. Son of A. N. (Lancs), nephew of C. L. (Lancs). Middle order right-hand batsman. *Sch* Harrow. *Teams* Cambridge (1898); Lancashire (1899–1914, 283 matches). *Tour* OU Authentics to India 1902/3.
Career batting
292–439–41–9781–129–24.57–8–*ct* 217–*st* 2
Bowling 269–3–89.66–0–0–1/13

He hit 1,000 runs in a season once : 1,336, av 28.42, in 1913. From 1908 to 1914 he captained Lancashire.

Hornby, Albert Neilson
Amateur. *b:* 10.2.1847, Blackburn, Lancashire. *d:* 17.12.1925, Nantwich, Cheshire. Father of A. H. (Lancs), brother of C. L. (Lancs). Opening right-hand batsman, bowled both right and left arm, brilliant cover point. *Sch* Harrow. *Team* Lancashire (1867–99, 292 matches). *Tours* Fitzgerald to North America 1872 (not first-class); Harris to Australia 1878/9. *Tests* England (1878/9 to 1884, 3 matches).
Career batting
437–710–41–16109–188–24.07–16–*ct* 313–*st* 3
Bowling 258–11–23.45–0–0–4/40
Test batting
3–6–0–21–9–3.50–0–*ct* 0
Bowling 0–1–0.00–0–0–1/0

He hit 1,000 runs in a season twice (best 1,534, av 40.36,in 1881). He captained Lancashire from 1880 to 1893 and 1897 and 1898. His final first-class match was for an England XI in 1906. A noted rugby footballer, he was capped nine times for England.

Hornby, Cecil Lumsden
Amateur. *b:* 25.7.1843, Blackburn, Lancashire. *d:* 27.2.1896, Leamington Spa, Warwickshire. Brother of A. N. (Lancs), uncle of A. H. (Lancs). Opening right-hand batsman, good field. *Sch* Harrow. *Team* Lancashire (1877, 1 match).
Career batting
2–3–0–27–23–9.00–0–*ct* 0
Bowling 3–1–3.00–0–0–1/3

His cricket was confined mainly to military matches. He made his first-class debut for Gentlemen of England in 1874 and also appeared occasionally for Cheshire and Shropshire.

Hornby, Edgar Christian
Amateur. *b:* 14.9.1863, Liverpool, Lancahire. *d:* 2.4.1922, Claygate, Surrey. Cousin of A. N. (Lancs) and C. L. (Lancs). Middle order left-hand batsman, slow left-arm bowler. *Sch* Winchester. *Team* Lancashire (1885–87, 9 matches).
Career batting
13–20–1–360–82–18.94–0–*ct* 9
Bowling 177–6–29.50–0–0–2/23

He was principally connected with Liverpool CC and appeared in the Liverpool and District XI, his final first-class match being for that side in 1894.

Hornby, Gerald Frederick
Amateur. *b:* 9.6.1862, Liverpool, Lancashire. *d:* 9.2.1890, Tarporley, Cheshire. Lower order right-hand batsman, right-arm fast bowler. *Sch* Winchester. *Team* Oxford U (1882).
Career batting
1–2–0–1–1–0.50–0–*ct* 0
Bowling 35–0

Hornby, Thomas Whitfield
Professional. *b:* 2.10.1831, Stockton-on-Tees, Durham. *d:* 1.4.1900, Stockton-on-Tees. Middle order left-hand batsman. *Team* Yorkshire (1858–61, 2 matches).
Career batting
3–6–0–65–22–10.83–0–*ct* 1

His final first-class match was for an England XI in 1864. He also played for Durham.

Horncastle, William Allen
Amateur. *b:* 1864, Edmonton, Middlesex. *d:* 1917, West Ham, Essex. Lower order right-hand batsman, right-arm medium pace bowler. *Team* Middlesex (1883, 1 match).
Career batting
1–2–0–11–8–5.50–0–*ct* 1
Bowling 72–3–24.00–0–0–2/39

Horner, Charles Edward
Amateur. *b:* 9.4.1857, Dulwich Common, Surrey. *d:* 4.9.1925, Regent's Park, London. Tail end right-hand batsman, right-arm fast medium bowler. *Sch* Cheltenham. *Teams* Oxford U (1877–80); Surrey (1882–86, 53 matches). *Tour* Sanders to North America (1885).
Career batting
65–103–31–546–37*–7.58–0–*ct* 22
Bowling 4470–252–17.73–15–3–8/35

He took 107 wickets, av 14.97, in 1884, which was easily his best season in first-class cricket. He was on the Surrey CCC Committee for many years. A noted amateur billiards player, he was a prominent member of the Billiards Control Club.

Horner, Sir John Francis Fortescue
Amateur. *b:* 28.12.1842, Mells, Somerset. *d:* 31.3.1927, Westminster, London. Lower order batsman, left-arm medium fast bowler. *Sch* Eton. *Team* MCC (1867).
Career batting
5–10–2–19–7–2.37–0–*ct* 4
Bowling 124–9–13.77–0–0–4/24

His first-class debut was for Southgate in 1866 and his final first-class match for Gentlemen of England in 1873. His County cricket was for Somerset (not first-class).

Horner, Norman Frederick
Professional. *b:* 10.5.1926, Queensbury, Yorkshire. Sound opening right-hand batsman. *Teams* Yorkshire (1950, 2 matches); Warwickshire (1951–65, 357 matches).
Career batting
362–656–34–18533–203*–29.79–25–*ct* 130
Bowling 78–0

He hit 1,000 runs in a season 12 times (best 1,902, av 33.36, in 1960). His only double century was 203* for Warwickshire v Surrey at The Oval in 1960; with K. Ibadulla he created a record Warwickshire first-wicket partnership of 377* in the same match.

Hornibrook, Percival Mitchell
Amateur. *b:* 27.7.1899, Obi Obi, Queensland, Australia. *d:* 25.8.1976, Brisbane, Queensland, Australia. Lower order left-hand batsman, left-arm medium or slow bowler. *Team* Queensland (1919/20 to 1933/4, 28 matches). *Tours* Australia to New Zealand 1920/1, to England 1930. *Tests* Australia (1928/9 to 1930, 6 matches).

Career batting
71–91–21–754–59*–10.77–0–*ct* 66
Bowling 6648–279–23.82–17–6–8/60
Test batting
6–7–1–60–26–10.00–0–*ct* 7
Bowling 664–17–39.05–1–0–7/92

He was considered unlucky not to be chosen for either the 1921 or 1926 Australian tours to England. In 1930, on his only visit, he took 96 wickets, av 18.77, in first-class matches but succeeded in only the fifth Test.

Hornsby, John Henry James
Amateur. *b:* 18.4.1860, Grantham, Lincs. *d:* 9.7.1926, Cuckfield Park, Sussex. Lower order right-hand batsman, slow left-arm bowler, good field. *Sch* Fettes. *Team* Middlesex (1893, 1 match). *Tours* Vernon to India 1889/90 (not first-class); Hawke to North America 1891, to India 1892/93.
Career batting
31–54–4–678–56–13.56–0–*ct* 22
Bowling 891–52–17.13–3–2–8/40

His first-class debut was for the Gentlemen at Scarborough in 1887, and his final first-class match was for MCC in 1898.

Horrex, Graham Wade
Amateur. *b:* 27.12.1932, Goodmayes, Essex. Opening right-hand batsman. *Sch* Brentwood. *Team* Essex (1956–57, 7 matches).
Career batting
7–13–0–141–41–10.84–0–*ct* 0

A noted squash player, he represented Essex.

Horridge, Leonard
Professional. *b:* 18.8.1907, Chorley, Lancashire. *d:* 1976, Preston, Lancashire. Right-hand batsman, off break bowler. *Team* Lancashire (1927–29, 3 matches).
Career batting
5–6–1–57–15–11.40–0–*ct* 4
Bowling 79–3–26.33–0–0–2/46

His final first-class match was for Minor Counties in 1930.

Horrocks, Richard
Professional. *b:* 29.8.1857, Church, Lancashire. *d:* 19.6.1926, Church, Lancashire. Middle order right-hand batsman, good field. *Team* Lancashire (1880–82, 6 matches).
Career batting
7–12–0–121–61–10.08–0–*ct* 1

Horrocks, William John
Professional. *b:* 18.6.1905, Warrington, Lancashire. Middle order right-hand batsman. *Teams* Lancashire (1931–33, 15 matches); Western Australia (1926/7 to 1936/7, 11 matches).
Career batting
29–44–6–1255–148*–33.02–3–*ct* 9
Bowling 51–0

Horsey, Frank Lankester
Amateur. *b:* 22.1.1884, Woodbridge, Suffolk. *d:* 19.8.1956, Hyde Stile, Surrey. Middle order right-hand batsman, right-arm fast medium bowler. *Sch* King Edward, Southampton. *Team* Royal Navy (1914).
Career batting
1–2–0–23–15–11.50–0–*ct* 1
Bowling 17–2–8.50–0–0–2/17

Horsfall, Richard
Professional. *b:* 26.6.1920, Todmorden, Yorkshire. *d:* 25.8.1981, Halifax, Yorkshire. Middle order right-hand batsman, good field. *Teams* Essex (1947–55, 207 matches); Glamorgan (1956, 5 matches).
Career batting
214–361–25–9777–206–29.09–17–*ct* 87
Bowling 41–1–41.00–0–0–1/4

He hit 1,000 runs in a season four times (best 1,731, av 37.63, in 1953). His only double century was 206 for Essex v Kent at Blackheath in 1951.

Horsley, Albert Beresford
Amateur. *b:* 1880, Hartlepool, Co Durham. *d:* October 1924, West Hartlepool. Father of R. H. (Oxford U). Lower order batsman, useful bowler. *Sch* Leys. *Team* London County (1904).
Career batting
1–1–0–24–24–24.00–0–*ct* 0
Bowling 22–0

His County cricket was for Durham.

Horsley, James
Professional. *b:* 4.1.1890, Melbourne, Derbyshire. *d:* 13.2.1976, Derby. Lower order right-hand batsman, right-arm fast medium bowler. *Teams* Nottinghamshire (1913, 3 matches); Derbyshire (1914–25, 84 matches).
Career batting
87–132–32–1367–66–13.67–0–*ct* 47
Bowling 5412–267–20.26–19–3–7/48

Horsley, Norman
Amateur. *b:* 20.8.1922, Leicester. Lower order right-hand batsman, right-arm fast bowler. *Team* Nottinghamshire (1947, 3 matches).
Career batting
3–1–0–0–0–0.00–0–*ct* 1
Bowling 249–6–41.50–0–0–2/27

Horsley, Rupert Harry
Amateur. *b:* 18.12.1905, West Hartlepool. Son of A. B. (London County). Lower order right-hand batsman, wicket-keeper. *Sch* Winchester. *Team* Oxford U (1927).
Career batting
3–5–1–78–25–19.50–0–*ct* 9–*st* 1

Horton, Henry
Professional. *b:* 18.4.1923, Colwall, Herefordshire. Brother of Joseph (Worcs). Middle order right-hand batsman, slow left-arm bowler. *Teams* Worcestershire (1946–49, 11 matches); Hampshire (1953–57, 405 matches).
Career batting
417–744–84–21669–160*–32.83–32–*ct* 264
Bowling 194–3–64.66–0–0–2/0

He hit 1,000 runs in a season 12 times, going on to 2,000 in three seasons (best 2,428, av 47.60, in 1959). After retiring he was on the first-class umpires' list. A good soccer player, he appeared for Blackburn Rovers, Southampton and Bradford.

Horton, Joseph
Professional. *b:* 12.8.1916, Colwall, Herefordshire. Brother of Henry (Worcs and Hants). Middle order right-hand batsman, right-arm medium pace bowler. *Team* Worcestershire (1934–38, 62 matches).
Career batting
62–103–12–1258–70–13.82–0–*ct* 33
Bowling 362–5–72.40–0–0–2/3

He also played for Herefordshire.

Horton, Martin John
Professional. *b:* 21.4.1934, Worcester. Opening right-hand batsman, off break bowler. *Teams* Worcestershire (1952–66, 376 matches); Northern Districts (1967/8 to 1970/1). *Tours* Worcestershire World Tour 1964/5, to Jamaica 1965/6. *Tests* England (1959, 2 matches).
Career batting
410–724–49–19945–233–29.54–23–*ct* 166
Bowling 22226–825–26.94–40–7–9/56
Test batting
2–2–0–60–58–30.00–0–*ct* 2
Bowling 59–2–29.50–0–0–2/24

He hit 1,000 runs in a season 11 times, going on to 2,000 once : 2,468, av 44.87, in 1959. His two double centuries were both for Worcs, the highest being 233 v Somerset at Worcester in 1962. He took 100 wickets in a season twice (best 103, av 27.38, in 1955) and performed the 'double' twice. In 1967 he was appointed New Zealand national coach and therefore retired from County cricket. His best bowling was 9/56 for Worcs v South Africa at Worcester in 1955.

Horton, R.
Professional. Lower order batsman, slow left-arm bowler. *Team* Gloucestershire (1925, 3 matches).
Career batting
3–5–2–13–7–4.33–0–*ct* 1
Bowling 149–1–149.00–0–0–1/97

Horton, Thomas
Amateur. *b:* 16.5.1871, Edgbaston, Birmingham. *d:* 18.6.1932, Bilton House, Rugby. Forcing right-hand middle order batsman, good field. *Sch* Repton. *Team* Northants (1905–06, 26 matches).
Career batting
29–55–7–581–53–12.10–0–*ct* 18
Bowling 4–0

He captained Northants in 1905 and 1906. His first-class debut was for MCC in 1900.

Horton, William Herbert Francis Kenneth
Amateur. *b:* 25.4.1906, Brentford, Middlesex. Middle order right-hand batsman. *Sch* Stonyhurst. *Teams* Middlesex (1927, 2 matches); Europeans (1929/30 to 1934/5).
Career batting
4–7–0–59–38–8.42–0–*ct* 1

Horwood, Charles
Amateur. *b:* 8.12.1839, Berkhamsted, Herts. *d:* 7.1.1870, Broadwater, Worthing, Sussex. Lower order right-hand batsman, right-hand round-arm bowler. *Sch* Highgate. *Team* Sussex (1864–65, 3 matches).
Career batting
3–4–1–23–12*–7.66–0–*ct* 3

Horwood, Stanley Ebden
Amateur. *b:* 22.7.1877, Port Elizabeth, South Africa. *d:* 15.8.1959, Cape Town, South Africa. Middle order right-hand batsman. *Team* Western Province (1902/3 to 1909/10). *Tour* South Africa to England 1904.
Career batting
22–35–1–484–74–14.23–0–*ct* 8

His single visit to England proved to be a very modest affair. His first-class debut was for Cape Colony in 1898/99.

Hosen, Roger Wills
Cricketer. *b:* 12.6.1933, Helston, Cornwall. Lower order right-hand batsman, right-arm fast medium bowler. *Team* Minor Counties (1965).
Career batting
1–2–0–2–2–1.00–0–*ct* 0
Bowling 73–1–73.00–0–0–1/55

He played County cricket for Cornwall. He was an English rugby international.

Hosie, Alexander Lindsay
Amateur. *b:* 6.8.1890, Wenchow, China. *d:* 11.6.1957, Totton, Southampton. Hard-hitting middle order right-hand batsman, right-arm medium pace bowler. *Sch* St Lawrence College, Ramsgate. *Teams* Hampshire (1913–35, 80 matches); Oxford U (1913); Europeans (1921/2 to 1929/30); Bengal (1935/6 to 1937/8). *Tour* Tennyson to India (1937/8) – as an emergency.
Career batting
133–232–8–6195–200–27.65–8–*ct* 85
Bowling 500–11–45.45–0–0–4/35
He hit 1,000 runs in a season twice (best 1,331, av 30.25, in 1928). His only double century was 200 for Europeans v Hindus at Bombay in 1924/5. His first-class debut in India was for Bengal Governor's XI in 1917/8. His final first-class match was for MCC in 1938.

Hoskin, Worthington Wynn
Amateur. *b:* 8.5.1885, South Africa. *d:* 4.3.1956, East London, South Africa. Lower order batsman, useful bowler. *Teams* Oxford U (1907); Gloucestershire (1912, 5 matches).
Career batting
6–11–0–90–28–8.18–0–*ct* 7
Bowling 103–1–103.00–0–0–1/13
A noted rugby footballer, he played in the University match for four seasons.

Hoskyns, Sir John Chevallier
Amateur. *b:* 23.5.1926, Cambridge. *d:* 12.4.1956, Worcester. Opening left-hand batsman. *Sch* Marlborough. *Team* Cambridge U (1949).
Career batting
2–4–1–63–42*–21.00–0–*ct* 0

Hossack, Anthony Henry
Amateur. *b:* 2.5.1867, Walsall. *d:* 24.1.1925, Torquay. Lower order batsman, useful bowler. *Sch* Chigwell. *Team* Cambridge (1889).
Career batting
1–1–0–3–3–3.00–0–*ct* 0
Bowling 14–0
His County cricket was for Essex, commencing 1891 (not first-class). A noted soccer player, he obtained his blue at Cambridge and appeared for Corinthians and England at wing-half.

Hossell, John Johnson
Amateur. *b:* 25.5.1914, Birmingham. Middle order left-hand batsman, slow left-arm bowler. *Team* Warwickshire (1939–47, 35 matches).
Career batting
35–62–5–1217–83–21.35–0–*ct* 12
Bowling 370–7–52.85–0–0–3/24

Hotchkin, Neil Stafford
Amateur. *b:* 4.2.1914, Horncastle, Lincs. Opening right-hand batsman. *Sch* Eton. *Teams* Cambridge U (1934-35, blue 1935); Middlesex (1939–48, 6 matches); Services in India (1944/5); Europeans (1944/5).
Career batting
23–37–2–736–74–21.02–0–*ct* 4
Bowling 4–0
He also played for Lincolnshire.

Hotham, Admiral Sir Alan Geoffrey
Amateur. *b:* 3.10.1876, Edinburgh, Scotland. *d:* 10.7.1965, London. Middle order right-hand batsman. *Team* Hampshire (1901, 1 match).
Career batting
1–2–0–16–11–8.00–0–*ct* 0
Bowling 6–0
He also played for Devonshire.

Hotham, Rev Frederick William
Amateur. *b:* 17.1.1844, Bath, Somerset. *d:* 23.6.1908, Cricket-Malherbie, Somerset. Middle order right-hand batsman. *Sch* Eton. *Team* Somerset (1882, 1 match).
Career batting
2–4–0–18–7–4.50–0–*ct* 1
He also played for Hertfordshire. His final first-class match was for MCC in 1883.

Hough, Charles Henry
Amateur. *b:* March 1855, Cambridge. *d:* 15.10.1933, Victoria Park, Manchester. Middle order batsman. *Sch* Uppingham. *Team* MCC (1883).
Career batting
1–2–1–12–10–12.00–0–*ct* 0

Hough, Edwin John
Cricketer. *b:* 29.7.1957, Rusape, Rhodesia. Lower order right-hand batsman, right-arm fast-medium bowler. *Team* Zimbabwe (1981/2 to 1982/3). *Tour* Zimbabwe to England 1982.
Career batting
4–3–1–13–9–6.50–0–*ct* 0
Bowling 287–12–23.91–0–0–4/48

Hough, Gerald De Lisle
Amateur. *b:* 14.5.1894, Kensington, London. *d:* 29.9.1959, Canterbury, Kent. Hard-hitting middle order right-hand batsman, off break bowler. *Sch* Winchester. *Team* Kent (1919–20, 14 matches).
Career batting
15–20–5–444–87*–29.60–0–*ct* 5
Bowling 21–1–21.00–0–0–1/7
He was appointed manager of Kent in 1936 and later secretary, resigning through ill-health in 1949.

Houghton, David Laud
Cricketer. *b:* 23.6.1957, Salisbury, Rhodesia. Brother of W. J. (Rhodesia). Opening, or middle order right-hand batsman, wicket-keeper. *Team* Rhodesia/Zimbabwe (1978/9 to 1982/3). *Tour* Zimbabwe to England 1982.
Career batting
30–54–3–1261–87–24.72–0–*ct* 59–*st* 8

Houghton, William Eric
Amateur. *b:* 29.6.1910, Billingborough, Lincs. Middle order right-hand batsman, right-arm medium pace bowler. *Team* Warwickshire (1946–47, 7 matches).
Career batting
7–11–0–165–41–15.00–0–*ct* 2
He also played for Lincolnshire. He played football for Aston Villa and Notts County.

Houldsworth, William Harry
Amateur. *b:* 6.4.1873, Levenshulme, Manchester, Lancashire. *d:* 1909, Barton, Lancashire. Middle order batsman. *Team* Lancashire (1893–94, 10 matches).
Career batting
10–16–1–156–21–10.40–0–*ct* 2

Houlton, Gerard
Professional. *b:* 25.4.1939, St Helens, Lancashire. Middle order right-hand batsman, left-arm fast medium bowler. *Team* Lancashire (1961–63, 20 matches).
Career batting
20–33–2–688–86–22.19–0–*ct* 5
Bowling 6–0

Hounsfield, Thomas Douglas
Amateur. *b:* 28.4.1910, Hackenthorpe, Yorkshire. Middle order right-hand batsman. *Team* Derbyshire (1938–39, 16 matches).
Career batting
16–24–3–274–56–13.04–0–*ct* 7

House, Biron Howe
Professional. *b:* 1885, Langport, Somerset. *d:* 3.6.1930, Creech St Michael, Somerset. Tail end batsman, wicket-keeper. *Team* Somerset (1912–14, 3 matches).
Career batting
3–4–1–30–19*–10.00–0–*ct* 3

Houseman, Edward Outram
Professional. *b:* 19.3.1869, Dronfield, Derbyshire. *d:* 10.4.1942, Westhoughton, Lancashire. Middle order right-hand batsman. *Team* Derbyshire (1897, 1 match).
Career batting
1–2–0–4–4–2.00–0–*ct* 2

Housley, Richard
Professional. *b:* 8.5.1849, Mansfield Woodhouse, Notts. *d:* 23.4.1881, Mansfield Woodhouse, Notts. Middle order right-hand batsman, good field. *Team* Nottinghamshire (1870, 1 match).
Career batting
1–2–0–3–2–1.50–0–*ct* 0

Howard, Arthur
Amateur. *b:* 1882, Ashby-de-la-Zouch, Leics. *d:* 5.8.1946, Leicester. Father of Jack (Leics) and A. R. (Glamorgan). Middle order right-hand batsman. *Team* Leicestershire (1921, 3 matches).
Career batting
3–6–0–60–27–10.00–0–*ct* 0

Howard, Alan Raymond
Professional. *b:* 11.12.1910, Leicester. Brother of J. H. (Leics), son of Arthur (Leics). Middle order left-hand batsman, left-arm medium pace bowler. *Teams* Glamorgan (1928–33, 59 matches); Wales (1930).
Career batting
60–99–2–1181–63–12.17–0–0–*ct* 35
Bowling 70–0

Howard, Arthur Stanley
Amateur. *b:* 14.11.1936, South Africa. Lower order right-hand batsman, off break bowler. *Team* Cambridge U (1961).
Career batting
3–2–0–0–0–0.00–0–*ct* 1
Bowling 352–8–44.00–0–0–3/100

Howard, Barry John
Amateur. *b:* 21.5.1926, Preston, Lancashire. Brother of N. D. (Lancs), son of Rupert (Lancs). Sound middle order right-hand batsman. *Sch* Rossall. *Team* Lancashire (1947–51, 32 matches).
Career batting
35–51–3–1232–114–25.66–3–*ct* 26

Howard, Charlie
Professional. *b:* 27.9.1854, Chichester, Sussex. *d:* 20.5.1929, Chichester, Sussex. Middle order right-hand batsman. *Team* Sussex (1874–82, 22 matches).
Career batting
23–39–3–588–106–16.33–1–*ct* 6
Bowling 8–0

Howard, Cecil Geoffrey
Amateur. *b:* 14.2.1909, Hampstead Garden Suburb, Middlesex. Middle order right-hand batsman.
Team Middlesex (1930, 3 matches).
Career batting
3–6–0–25–12–4.16–0–*ct* 2

He was Secretary of Lancashire CCC from 1949 to 1964 and of Surrey CCC from 1965 to 1975.

Howard, Charles William Henry
Professional. *b:* 1904, Bromley, Kent. Middle order right-hand batsman, right-arm medium pace bowler. *Sch* Tonbridge. *Team* Middlesex (1931, 9 matches).
Career batting
9–12–2–123–29–12.30–0–*ct* 2

Howard, Jack
Professional. *b:* 24.11.1917, Leicester. Son of Arthur (Leics), brother of A. R. (Glamorgan). Middle order left-hand batsman, wicket-keeper. *Team* Leicestershire (1946–48, 41 matches).
Career batting
41–66–14–589–38*–11.32–0–*ct* 17
Bowling 5–0

Howard, Joseph
Amateur. *b:* 12.1.1871, Epsom, Surrey. *d:* 25.1.1951, Evenlode, Gloucs. Middle order right-hand batsman. *Sch* Haileybury. *Team* Worcestershire (1900–01, 5 matches).
Career batting
5–10–0–85–28–8.50–0–*ct* 1

Howard, Kenneth
Professional. *b:* 2.6.1941, Manchester, Lancashire. Lower order left-hand batsman, off break bowler. *Team* Lancashire (1960–66, 61 matches).
Career batting
61–82–35–395–23–8.40–0–*ct* 57
Bowling 3175–104–30.52–3–0–7/33

Howard, Nigel David
Amateur. *b:* 18.5.1925, Preston, Lancashire. *d:* 31.5.1979, Douglas, Isle of Man. Son of Rupert (Lancs), brother of B. J. (Lancs). Attractive right-hand batsman, fine cover field. *Sch* Rossall. *Team* Lancashire (1946–53, 170 matches). *Tour* MCC to India and Pakistan 1951/2. *Tests* England (1951/2, 4 matches).
Career batting
198–279–30–6152–145–24.70–3–*ct* 155
Bowling 52–1–52.00–0–0–1/14
Test batting
4–6–1–86–23–17.20–0–*ct* 4

He captained MCC on the tour in 1951/2 and England in his four Tests; also Lancashire 1949 to 1953. He hit 1,000 runs in a season once : 1,174, av 36.68, in 1950. His final first-class match was for MCC in 1954.

Howard, Rupert
Amateur. *b:* 17.4.1890, Ashton-under-Lyne, Lancashire. *d:* 10.9.1967, Manchester. Father of B. J. (Lancs) and N. D. (Lancs). Middle order right-hand batsman. *Team* Lancashire (1922–33, 8 matches). *Tours* Manager of MCC to Australia and New Zealand 1936/7 and 1946/7 (he played in non-first-class matches on the former).
Career batting
8–9–2–166–88*–23.71–0–*ct* 4
Bowling 18–0

He was Secretary of Lancashire CCC 1932 to 1948.

Howard, Thomas Charles
Professional. *b:* 19.7.1781, Hartley Witney, Hampshire. *d:* 18.5.1864, Hartford Bridge, Hartley Row, Hampshire. Middle order right-hand batsman, right-hand fast under-arm bowler, wicket-keeper. *Team* Hampshire (1803–28).
Career batting
88–161–17–1539–54*–10.68–0–*ct* 73–*st* 64
Bowling 326 wickets, no analyses

He was remarkable for excelling both as a bowler and a wicket-keeper. His final first-class match was for Players in 1829.

Howard-Smith, Gerald
Amateur. *b:* 21.1.1880, London. *d:* 29.3.1916, Merville St Vaast, France. Middle order right-hand batsman, right-arm fast bowler. *Sch* Eton. *Team* Cambridge U (1901–03, blue 1903).
Career batting
20–33–16–189–23*–11.11–0–*ct* 15
Bowling 1279–29–44.72–1–0–6/23

His first-class debut was for MCC in 1900. He also played for Staffordshire.

Howarth, Geoffrey Philip
Cricketer. *b:* 29.3.1951, Auckland, New Zealand. Brother of H.J. (New Zealand). Attractive opening or middle-order right-hand batsman, off break bowler, good field. *Teams* Surrey (1971–83, 164 matches); Auckland (1972/3 to 1973/4); Northern Districts (1974/5 to 1982/3). *Tours* New Zealand to Pakistan and India 1976/7, to England 1978, 1983, to Australia 1980/1, 1982/3; Robins to South Africa 1975/6, to Sri Lanka 1977/8. *Tests* New Zealand (1974/5 to 1983, 34 matches).
Career batting
280–486–38–15111–183–33.72–30–*ct* 197
Bowling 3378–109–30.99–1–0–5/32
Test batting
34–62–5–2014–147–35.33–6–*ct* 22
Bowling 236–3–78.66–0–0–1/13

On the 1978 tour to England he headed both the Test and first-class batting averages with 296 runs, av 74.00, and 816 runs, av 45.33. He captained the 1983 side to England, but was not so successful in the Tests, though in the first-class matches he hit 697 runs, av 41.00. In all he hit 1,000 runs in an English season four times (best 1,554, av 37.90, in 1976). He has captained New Zealand in 17 Tests, including the four on the 1983 tour. His first-class debut was for New Zealand Under 23s in 1968/9.

Howarth, Hedley John
Cricketer. *b:* 25.12.1945, Auckland, New Zealand. Brother of G. P. (New Zealand). Lower order left-hand batsman, slow left-arm bowler. *Teams* Auckland (1963/4 to 1978/9). *Tours* New Zealand to England 1969, 1973, to Australia 1969/70, 1970/1, to India and Pakistan 1969/70, to West Indies 1971/2. *Tests* New Zealand (1969 to 1976/7, 30 matches).
Career batting
145–179–58–1668–61–13.78–0–*ct* 138
Bowling 13674–541–25.27–31–6–8/75
Test batting
30–42–18–291–61–12.12–0–*ct* 33
Bowling 3178–86–36.95–2–0–5/34

He headed the first-class bowling averages on the 1969 tour to England with 57 wickets, av 19.75, and played in all three Tests; on his 1973 tour he was not so successful. His first-class debut was for New Zealand Under 23s in 1962/3.

Howarth, John S.
Cricketer. *b:* 26.3.1945, Stockport, Cheshire. Lower order right-hand batsman, right-arm fast medium bowler. *Team* Nottinghamshire (1966–67, 13 matches).
Career batting
13–7–3–0–0*–0.00–0–*ct* 3
Bowling 642–19–33.78–0–0–3/30

He also played for Cheshire 1976–78.

Howarth, Thomas
Professional. *b:* 10.5.1845. *d:* 12.10.1897, Fylde, Lancashire. Middle order batsman. *Team* Derbyshire (1873, 1 match).
Career batting
1–2–0–7–5–3.50–0–*ct* 1

Howat, Michael Gerald
Cricketer. *b:* 2.3.1958, Tavistock, Devon. Right-hand batsman, right-arm medium fast bowler. *Sch* Abingdon. *Team* Cambridge U (1977–80, blue 1977 and 1980).
Career batting
26–22–3–194–32–10.21–0–*ct* 7
Bowling 1560–26–60.00–0–0–3/39

Howcroft, Albert
Professional. *b:* 27.12.1882, Cliffe, Yorkshire. *d:* 7.3.1955, Belper, Derbyshire. Middle order left-hand batsman. *Team* Derbyshire (1908–10, 4 matches).
Career batting
4–8–0–46–19–5.75–0–*ct* 2

Howe, Richard
Amateur. *b:* 17.2.1853, Denton, Manchester, Lancashire. *d:* 21.1.1914, Alderley Edge, Cheshire. Hard-hitting middle order right-hand batsman, good cover point. *Team* Lancashire (1876–77, 3 matches).
Career batting
4–7–0–38–14–5.42–0–*ct* 4
Bowling 6–0

Howell, Albert Louis
Professional. *b:* 26.7.1898, Birmingham. *d:* 26.7.1958, Newcastle on Tyne. Brother of Henry (Warwickshire). Lower order right-hand batsman, right-arm medium fast bowler. *Team* Warwickshire (1919–22, 34 matches).
Career batting
35–57–16–249–26–6.07–0–*ct* 14
Bowling 2019–56–36.05–1–0–5/65

He also played for Durham. His final first-class match was for Minor Counties in 1929.

Howell, Henry
Professional. *b:* 29.11.1890, Birmingham. *d:* 9.7.1932, Birmingham. Brother of A. L. (Warwickshire). Lower order right-hand batsman, right-arm fast bowler. *Team* Warwickshire (1913–28, 198 matches). *Tours* MCC to Australia 1920/1, 1924/5. *Tests* England (1920/1 to 1924, 5 matches).
Career batting
227–326–111–1679–36–7.80–0–*ct* 67
Bowling 20700–975–21.23–75–18–10/51
Test batting
5–8–6–15–5–7.50–0–*ct* 0
Bowling 559–7–79.85–0–0–4/115

He took 100 wickets in a season six times (best 161, av 17.91, in 1920). In 1923 he took all ten wickets in an innings (for 51 runs) for Warwickshire v Yorkshire at Edgbaston. A useful soccer player, he appeared for Wolverhampton Wanderers and Accrington.

Howell, Leonard Sidgwick
Amateur. *b:* 6.8.1848, Dulwich. *d:* 7.9.1895, Lausanne, Switzerland. Middle order right-hand batsman. *Sch* Winchester. *Team* Surrey (1869–80, 13 matches).
Career batting
19–34–6–519–96–18.53–0–*ct* 9

An excellent soccer player for Wanderers and Surrey, he represented England in 1873, as well as appearing on the winning side in the FA Cup in the same season.

Howell, Miles
Amateur. *b:* 9.9.1893, Thames Ditton, Surrey. *d:* 23.2.1976, Worplesdon, Surrey. Son of Reginald (Surrey). Opening right-hand batsman, brilliant outfield. *Sch* Repton. *Teams* Oxford U (1914 and 1919, blue both years); Surrey (1919–25, 36 matches).
Career batting
96–160–17–4621–170–32.31–8–*ct* 32
Bowling 26–1–26.00–0–0–1/5

A noted soccer player, he captained Oxford in 1919, played also for the Corinthians and won several amateur international caps for England. His final first-class match was for Free Foresters in 1939.

Howell, Reginald
Amateur. *b:* 16.4.1856, Streatham. *d:* 3.8.1912, Esher, Surrey. Father of Miles (Oxford U and Surrey). Middle order right-hand batsman, right-hand slow round-arm bowler, good cover field. *Sch* Tonbridge. *Team* Surrey (1878–79, 3 matches).
Career batting
3–5–1–31–10–7.75–0–*ct* 0

Howell, Robert George Dunnett
Amateur. *b:* 23.1.1877, Edmonton, London. *d:* 27.9.1942, Sydenham, London. Opening batsman. *Sch* Felsted. *Teams* Cambridge U (1898); Sussex (1900, 1 match).
Career batting
3–5–0–14–7–2.80–0–*ct* 0

Howell, William Peter
Amateur. *b:* 29.12.1869, Penrith, New South Wales, Australia. *d:* 14.7.1940, Castlereagh, New South Wales, Australia. Nephew of E. Evans (NSW), father of W. H. (NSW). Lower order left-hand batsman, right-arm medium pace bowler. *Team* New South Wales (1894/5 to 1904/5, 48 matches). *Tours* Australia to England 1899, 1902 and 1905, to South Africa 1902/3, to New Zealand 1904/5. *Tests* Australia (1897/8 to 1903/4, 18 matches).
Career batting
141–201–51–2228–128–14.85–1–*ct* 126
Bowling 11157–519–21.49–30–5–10/28
Test batting
18–27–6–158–35–7.52–0–*ct* 12
Bowling 1407–49–28.71–1–0–5/81

He was most successful on his first visit to England in 1899, playing in all five Tests, and against Surrey at the Oval taking all ten wickets for 28. Neither of his other tours to England proved as profitable, and in 1902 he appeared in only one Test, whilst in 1905 he was not required for any. He took 117 wickets, av 20.35, in 1899.

Howgego, James Alan
Cricketer. *b:* 3.8.1948, Folkestone, Kent. Middle order right-hand batsman, leg break bowler. *Team* Kent (1977, 1 match).
Career batting
1–2–0–91–52–45.00–0–*ct* 0

Howick, Nicholas Keith
Cricketer. *b:* 14.3.1954, St Peter Port, Guernsey. Right-hand batsman, right-arm medium pace bowler. *Sch* Elizabeth College, Guernsey. *Team* Oxford U (1974).
Career batting
5–10–0–51–14–5.10–0–*ct* 1

Howitt, George
Professional. *b:* 14.3.1843, Old Lenton, Notts. *d:* 19.12.1881, Nottingham. Tail end left-hand batsman, left-hand fast round-arm bowler. *Teams* Nottinghamshire (1866-70, 8 matches); Middlesex (1865-76, 43 matches).
Career batting
79–129–29–483–49–4.83–0–*ct* 64
Bowling 5520–347+1–15.90–26–7–7/19

He also played for Lincolnshire.

Howitt, Richard Holmes
Amateur. *b:* 21.7.1864, Farnsfield, Notts. *d:* 10.1.1951, Farndon, Notts. Middle order right-hand batsman, medium pace bowler, good field. *Team* Nottinghamshire (1893–1901, 28 matches).
Career batting
28–50–2–492–119–10.25–1–*ct* 17
Bowling 337–8–42.12–0–0–2/25

He was on the committee of Notts CCC 1899 to 1934.

Howland, Christopher Burfield
Amateur. *b:* 6.2.1936, Whitstable, Kent. Brother of P. C. (Cambridge U). Middle/lower order right-hand batsman, wicket-keeper. *Sch* Dulwich. *Teams* Cambridge U (1958–60, blue all three years); Sussex (1960, 4 matches); Kent (1965, 2 matches). *Tours* MCC to South America 1958/9, to North America 1959 (neither first-class).
Career batting
64–104–8–1629–124–16.96–1–*ct* 130–*st* 21
Bowling 11–0

His first-class debut was for Combined Services in 1956 and his final first-class match for MCC in 1968.

Howland, Peter Charles
Cricketer. *b:* 9.3.1947, Orpington, Kent. Brother

of C. B. (Kent and Sussex). Right-hand batsman, off break bowler. *Sch* Dulwich. *Team* Cambridge U (1969).
Career batting
6–11–1–104–21–10.40–0–*ct* 4
Bowling 7–0

Howlett, Bernard
Amateur. *b:* 18.12.1898, Stoke Newington, Middlesex. *d:* 29.11.1943, Santa Maria, Imbaro, Italy. He was killed in action. Lower order right-hand batsman, right-arm fast bowler. *Sch* St Edmund's, Canterbury. *Teams* Kent (1922–28, 26 matches); Europeans (1925/6 to 1928/9); Bombay (1926/7).
Career batting
42–55–21–319–58–9.38–0–*ct* 23
Bowling 3156–108–29.22–3–0–6/35
He was a well-known player in military cricket and his final first-class match was for MCC in 1931.

Howman, John
Amateur. *b:* 26.4.1895, Stow-on-the-Wold, Gloucs. *d:* 4.4.1958, Oxford. Middle order right-hand batsman. *Team* Gloucestershire (1922–23, 13 matches).
Career batting
13–21–1–128–23–6.40–0–*ct* 4

Howorth, Richard
Professional. *b:* 26.4.1909, Bacup, Lancashire. *d:* 2.4.1980, Worcester. Middle/lower order left-hand batsman, slow left-arm bowler. *Teams* Worcestershire (1933–51, 348 matches); Europeans (1944/5). *Tour* MCC to West Indies 1947/8. *Tests* England (1947 to 1947/8, 5 matches).
Career batting
372–611–56–11479–114–20.68–4–*ct* 197
Bowling 29425–1345–21.87–74–7–7/18
Test batting
5–10–2–145–45*–18.12–0–*ct* 2
Bowling 635–19–33.42–1–0–6/124
He took 100 wickets in a season nine times (best 164, av 17.85, in 1947) and hit 1,000 runs in a season four times (best 1,510, av 26.03, in 1947), three times performing the 'double'.

Howsin, Dr Edward Arthur
Amateur. *b:* 26.7.1838, North Muskham, Notts. *d:* 27.2.1921, Boscombe, Hants. Middle order right-hand batsman, medium pace bowler. *Team* Nottinghamshire (1863, 2 matches).
Career batting
4–8–1–114–48*–16.28–0–*ct* 3–*st* 2
Bowling 42–2–21.00–0–0–1/14
His first-class debut was for Gentlemen of the South in 1862.

Hoyer Millar, Gurth Christian
Amateur. *b:* 13.12.1929, London. Lower order right-hand batsman, wicket-keeper. *Sch* Harrow. *Team* Oxford U (1952).
Career batting
2–3–1–17–10–8.50–0–*ct* 4
He played rugby for Scotland.

Hoyle, Theodore Hind
Professional. *b:* 19.3.1884. *d:* 2.6.1953, Kingston-on-Hull, Yorkshire. Lower order batsman, wicket-keeper. *Team* Yorkshire (1919, 1 match).
Career batting
1–2–0–7–7–3.50–0–*ct* 0–*st* 1

Huband, Ralph Croft
Amateur. *b:* 2.6.1902, Killiskey, Co Wicklow, Ireland. *d:* 7.11.1964, Lambeth, London. Opening/middle order right-hand batsman, wicket-keeper. *Sch* Winchester. *Team* Cambridge U (1923).
Career batting
2–4–2–64–61*–32.00–0–*ct* 0

Hubback, Theodore Rathbone
Amateur. *b:* 1873, Liverpool, Lancashire. *d:* 1942, Malaya. He was killed prior to the fall of Singapore. Middle order batsman, wicket-keeper. *Team* Lancashire (1892, 4 matches).
Career batting
6–10–1–140–67–15.55–0–*ct* 3–*st* 2
His final first-class match was for Liverpool and District in 1893.

Hubbard, George Cairns
Amateur. *b:* 23.11.1867, Benares, India. *d:* 18.12.1931, Eltham, Kent. Middle order right-hand batsman, right-arm medium pace bowler. *Sch* Tonbridge. *Team* Kent (1895, 3 matches).
Career batting
3–4–0–61–36–15.25–0–*ct* 4
Bowling 25–1–25.00–0–0–1/25
An excellent rugby footballer, he appeared for Blackheath and England.

Hubble, Harold John
Professional. *b:* 3.10.1904, Headcorn, Kent. Nephew of J. C. (Kent). Middle order right-hand batsman, leg break bowler. *Team* Kent (1929–31, 13 matches).
Career batting
13–21–3–285–50–15.83–0–*ct* 3
Bowling 33–1–33.00–0–0–1/5

Hubble, John Charlton
Professional. *b:* 10.2.1881, Wateringbury, Kent. *d:* 26.2.1965, St Leonards on Sea, Sussex. Uncle of H. J. (Kent). Middle/lower order right-hand

batsman, wicket-keeper. *Team* Kent (1904–29, 343 matches). *Tours* MCC to South Africa 1927/8 (in emergency).
Career batting
360–528–64–10939–189–23.57–5–*ct* 437–*st* 221
Bowling 27–0
He hit 1,000 runs in a season once : 1,282, av 33.73, in 1914. He took over as the regular County wicket-keeper only after the First World War.

Hubble, William George
Amateur. *b:* 20.6.1898, Leyton, Essex. *d:* 1978, Bishops Waltham, Hants. Left-hand batsman, slow left-arm bowler. *Team* Essex (1923, 1 match).
Career batting
1–1–0–0–0–0.00–0–*ct* 0
Bowling 60–2–30.00–0–0–2/3

Huddleston, William
Professional. *b:* 27.2.1873, Earlestown, Lancashire. *d:* 21.5.1962, Warrington, Lancashire. Lower order right-hand batsman, right-arm medium pace off break bowler. *Team* Lancashire (1899–1914, 183 matches).
Career batting
185–258–32–2765–88–12.23–0–*ct* 149
Bowling 12042–685–17.57–42–14–9/36
He took 100 wickets in a season once : 113, av 19.68, in 1913. His best bowling was 9/36 for Lancashire v Notts at Liverpool in 1906.

Hudleston, Sir Edmund Cuthbert
Amateur. *b:* 30.12.1908, Perth, Australia. Opening right-hand batsman. *Team* RAF (1929–31).
Career batting
4–7–0–97–38–13.85–0–*ct* 1

Hudson, Bennett
Professional. *b:* 29.6.1851, Sheffield, Yorkshire. *d:* 1901, Wortley, Yorkshire. Lower order right-hand batsman, right-arm fast bowler. *Teams* Yorkshire (1880, 3 matches); Lancashire (1886–88, 5 matches).
Career batting
8–10–0–220–98–22.00–0–*ct* 2
Bowling 59–3–19.66–0–0–2/14

Hudson, Eric Vaughan Hamilton
Amateur. *b:* 30.6.1900, Bihar, India. *d:* 6.2.1974, Churston-Ferrers, Devon. Brother of R. E. H. (Army). Right-hand batsman, right-arm fast bowler. *Sch* Haileybury. *Team* Army (1930).
Career batting
1–2–0–7–7–3.50–0–*ct* 0
Bowling 86–4–21.50–0–0–3/55
His County cricket was for Hertfordshire.

Hudson, Frederick John
Amateur. *b:* 22.11.1878, Bottesford, Leics. *d:* 7.10.1966, Bottesford, Leics. Middle order right-hand batsman, change bowler. *Team* Leicestershire (1901, 1 match).
Career batting
1–2–0–1–1–0.50–0–*ct* 0
Bowling 38–0
He also played for Lincolnshire.

Hudson, Gideon Dacre
Cricketer. *b:* 8.11.1944, Salisbury, Wilts. Right-hand batsman, wicket-keeper. *Team* Oxford U (1964).
Career batting
1–2–0–6–6–3.00–0–*ct* 2
His County cricket was for Buckinghamshire.

Hudson, George Neville
Amateur. *b:* 12.7.1905, Clitheroe, Lancashire. *d:* 24.11.1981, Preston, Lancashire. Lower order batsman, slow right-arm bowler. *Team* Lancashire (1936, 2 matches).
Career batting
2–2–1–1–1–1.00–0–*ct* 1
Bowling 82–0

Hudson, Reginald Eustace Hamilton
Amateur. *b:* 22.8.1904, Bihar, India. Brother of E. V. H. (Army). Opening right-hand batsman, right-arm medium pace bowler. *Sch* Haileybury. *Teams* Army (1925–38); Europeans (1926/7 to 1929/30).
Career batting
27–49–4–1807–217–40.15–5–*ct* 7
Bowling 14–0
His highest score was 217 for Army v RAF at the Oval in 1932. His County cricket was for Devon.

Huey, Samuel Scott Johnston
Amateur. *b:* 21.12.1923, Ture, Co Donegal, Ireland. Right-hand batsman, slow left-arm bowler. *Team* Ireland (1951–66).
Career batting
20–30–4–135–23*–5.19–0–*ct* 14
Bowling 1203–66–18.22–5–1–8/48

Huggett, Arthur
Professional. *b:* 1861, Godstone, Surrey. *d:* 14.4.1945, Tunbridge Wells, Kent. Lower order batsman, bowler. *Team* Sussex (1883–85, 3 matches).

Huggins

Career batting
3–5–1–14–5*–3.50–0–*ct* 1
Bowling 10–0

Huggins, Henry James
Professional. *b:* 15.3.1877, Headington, Oxon. *d:* 20.11.1942, Stroud, Gloucs. Hard-hitting lower order right-hand batsman, right-arm fast medium bowler. *Team* Gloucestershire (1901–21, 200 matches).
Career batting
200–347–44–4375–92–14.43–0–*ct* 47
Bowling 16957–584–29.03–24–5–9/34
His best bowling was 9/34 for Gloucs v Sussex at Bristol in 1904.

Hughes, David Garfield
Amateur. *b:* 21.5.1934, Taunton, Somerset. Lower order right-hand batsman, wicket-keeper. *Sch* Taunton. *Team* Somerset (1955, 1 match).
Career batting
1–1–0–2–2–2.00–0–*ct* 1–*st* 1

Hughes, David Paul
Cricketer. *b:* 13.5.1947, Newton-le-Willows, Lancashire. Hard hitting middle order right-hand batsman, slow left-arm bowler. *Teams* Lancashire (1967–83, 314 matches); Tasmania (1975/6 to 1976/7, 2 matches). *Tour* Robins to South Africa 1972/3.
Career batting
325–415–81–7495–153–22.44–6–*ct* 221
Bowling 17967–605–29.69–20–2–7/24
He hit 1,000 runs in a season twice (best 1,303, av 48.25, in 1982).

Hughes, Donald Wynn
Amateur. *b:* 12.7.1910, Monmouthshire. *d:* 12.8.1967, Welwyn Garden City, Herts. He was killed in a road accident. Lower order right-hand batsman, right-arm fast medium bowler. *Team* Glamorgan (1935–38, 22 matches).
Career batting
22–33–8–274–70*–10.96–0–*ct* 6
Bowling 1692–52–32.53–2–0–5/70
He also played for Monmouthshire and Dorset.

Hughes, Gwyn
Cricketer. *b:* 26.3.1941, Cardiff. Lower order right-hand batsman, slow left-arm bowler, excellent short-leg. *Sch* Cardiff High School. *Teams* Cambridge U (1965, blue); Glamorgan (1962–64, 17 matches).
Career batting
27–41–4–457–92–12.35–0–*ct* 22
Bowling 1368–31–44.12–0–0–4/31

Hughes, John
Professional. *b:* 2.7.1825, Hertford. *d:* 29.1.1907, Hertford. Lower order right-hand batsman, right-hand slow round-arm bowler, close field. *Team* South (1874).
Career batting
1–2–0–8–8–4.00–0–*ct* 1
Bowling 94–9–10.44–1–0–7/46
He played for Hertfordshire for about 30 years and was very successful for the county.

Hughes, Kimberley John
Cricketer. *b:* 26.1.1954, Margaret River, Western Australia. Stylish middle order right-hand batsman. *Team* Western Australia (1975/6 to 1982/3, 47 matches). *Tours* Australia to New Zealand 1976/7, 1981/2, to England 1977, 1980, 1981, to West Indies 1977/8, to India 1979/80, to Pakistan 1979/80, 1982/3, to Sri Lanka 1980/1. *Tests* Australia (1977 to 1982/3, 56 matches).
Career batting
146–247–12–8920–213–37.95–19–*ct* 104
Bowling 55–2–27.50–0–0–1/0
Test batting
56–100–6–3744–213–39.82–8–*ct* 40
Bowling 28–0
His 1977 tour to England produced modest results, and he played in only one Test. In the 1980 Centenary Test he hit 117 and 84, being the highest scorer in the match. He captained Australia on the 1981 tour, playing in all six Tests and scoring 300 runs, av 25.00. He has now led Australia in 16 Tests, and captained them in the 1983 World Cup.

Hughes, Lewis Patrick
Cricketer. *b:* 10.4.1943, Blackrock, Co Dublin, Ireland. Right-hand batsman, right-arm fast medium bowler. *Team* Ireland (1965–72).
Career batting
5–8–3–55–35–11.00–0–*ct* 6
Bowling 439–9–48.77–0–0–3/77

Hughes, Mervyn Gregory
Cricketer. *b:* 23.11.1961, Euroa, Victoria, Australia. Right-hand batsman, right-arm fast medium bowler. *Teams* Victoria (1981/2 to 1982/3, 9 matches); Essex (1983, 1 match).
Career batting
10–12–5–48–17–6.85–0–*ct* 2
Bowling 1332–38–38.05–0–0–4/69

Hughes, Noel
Professional. *b:* 6.4.1929, Sydney, Australia. Middle order right-hand batsman, off break bowler. *Team* Worcestershire (1953–54, 21 matches).

Career batting
21–32–6–651–95–25.03–0–*ct* 13–*st* 3
Bowling 317–10–31.70–0–0–4/19

Hughes, Owen
Amateur. *b:* 7.7.1889, Reigate, Surrey. *d:* 4.6.1972, Beaumont, St Peters, Jersey. Middle order right-hand batsman. *Sch* Malvern. *Team* Cambridge U (1910, blue).
Career batting
6–9–1–168–65–21.00–0–*ct* 7

Hughes, Richard Clive
Professional. *b:* 30.9.1926, Watford, Herts. Lower order right-hand batsman, left-arm medium fast bowler. *Team* Worcestershire (1950–51, 11 matches).
Career batting
11–10–2–47–21–5.87–0–*ct* 2
Bowling 694–15–46.26–0–0–3/38

Hughes, Simon Peter
Cricketer. *b:* 20.12.1959, Kingston-upon-Thames, Surrey. Lower order right-hand batsman, right-arm fast medium bowler. *Sch* Latymer. *Teams* Middlesex (1980–83, 42 matches); Northern Transvaal (1982/3). *Tours* Middlesex to Zimbabwe 1980/1; Overseas XI to India 1980/1.
Career batting
50–50–25–130–18–5.20–0–*ct* 11
Bowling 3938–149–26.42–6–1–6/32

Hughes, Walter Laurence
Amateur. *b:* 9.9.1917. Lower order batsman, bowler. *Team* Oxford U (1947).
Career batting
1–1–0–3–3–3.00–0–*ct* 2
Bowling 28–0

Hughes-Hallett, Norton Montrésor
Amateur. *b:* 18.4.1895, Melbourne, Derbyshire. Middle order right-hand batsman, leg break bowler. *Sch* Haileybury. *Teams* Derbyshire (1913–14, 6 matches); Europeans (1925/6 to 1926/7).
Career batting
10–17–1–255–67–15.93–0–*ct* 4
Bowling 312–17–18.35–2–1–8/81

Hugo, Stephanus Gideon
Cricketer. *b:* 20.7.1945, Caledon, South Africa. Lower order right-hand batsman, right-arm medium fast bowler. *Team* Western Province (1966/7 to 1977/8). *Tour* South African Universities to England 1967.
Career batting
22–29–6–584–68*–25.39–0–*ct* 12
Bowling 951–48–19.81–0–0–4/31

He achieved useful all-round figures on the 1967 tour and hit 57 in his only first-class innings as well as taking 5 wickets at moderate cost.

Hugonin, Francis Edgar
Amateur. *b:* 16.8.1897, London. *d:* 5.3.1967, Stainton-in-Cleveland, North Yorkshire. Lower order right-hand batsman, wicket-keeper. *Sch* Eastbourne. *Team* Essex (1927–28, 6 matches).
Career batting
14–19–6–167–44–12.84–*ct* 26–*st* 6

He appeared in many military matches and his final first-class match was for the Army in 1937. He also played for Berkshire.

Huish, Francis Edward
Professional. *b:* 9.12.1867, Clapham, Surrey. *d:* 1955, California, USA. Brother of F. H. (Kent). Middle order left-hand batsman, left-arm medium pace bowler. *Team* Kent (1895, 5 matches).
Career batting
5–8–4–32–12–8.00–0–*ct* 3
Bowling 433–11–39.36–1–0–5/52

He appeared for Surrey in 1888, but not in first-class matches.

Huish, Frederick Henry
Professional. *b:* 15.11.1869, Clapham, Surrey. *d:* 16.3.1957, Northiam, Sussex. Brother of F. E. (Kent). Lower order right-hand batsman, wicket-keeper. *Teams* Kent (1895–1914, 469 matches); London County (1900). *Tour* Kent to North America 1903.
Career batting
497–726–139–7547–93–12.85–0–*ct* 933–*st* 377
Bowling 87–0

He exceeded 100 dismissals in a season once : 102 in 1913, and in 1911 obtained exactly 100.

Hull, Rear Admiral Herbert Richard Barnes
Amateur. *b:* 27.10.1886, Chippenham, Wilts. *d:* 31.5.1970, Westminster, London. Tail end batsman, useful bowler. *Sch* Bath College. *Team* Royal Navy (1924).
Career batting
1–1–1–1–1*–no av–0–*ct* 0
Bowling 56–0

Hulls, Charles Henry
Amateur. *b:* 1861, Luton, Beds. *d:* 19.12.1912, Southend, Essex. Middle order batsman. *Team* Somerset (1885, 1 match).

Career batting
2–4–0–38–30–9.50–0–*ct* 1
Bowling 5–0
His final first-class match was for MCC in 1896. He also played for Oxfordshire.

Hulme, Joseph Harold Anthony
Professional. *b:* 26.8.1904, Stafford. Middle order right-hand batsman, right-arm medium bowler, good deep field. *Team* Middlesex (1929–39, 223 matches).
Career batting
225–350–45–8103–143–26.56–12–*ct* 110
Bowling 3240–89–36.40–0–0–4/44
He hit 1,000 runs in a season three times (best 1,258, av 34.94, in 1934). A well-known soccer player, he appeared for Blackburn Rovers, Arsenal, Huddersfield Town and England at outside right.

Hulme, John Joseph
Professional. *b:* 30.6.1862, Church Gresley, Derbyshire. *d:* 11.7.1940, Nelson, Lancashire. Lower order left-hand batsman, left-arm medium fast bowler. *Team* Derbyshire (1887–1903, 133 matches).
Career batting
142–229–32–2433–59–12.35–0–*ct* 80
Bowling 13364–557–23.99–34–9–9/27
His best bowling was 9/27 for Derbyshire v Yorkshire at Sheffield in 1894.

Hulse, Charles Westrow
Amateur. *b:* 25.11.1860, Breamore, Hants. *d:* 4.6.1901, Braklaagte, South Africa. Middle order batsman. *Sch* Winchester and Radley. *Team* MCC (1885).
Career batting
1–1–0–22–22–22.00–0–*ct* 0

Hulton, Campbell Arthur Grey
Amateur. *b:* 16.3.1846, Manchester, Lancashire. *d:* 23.6.1919, Marylebone, London. Middle order batsman. *Sch* Rossall. *Team* Lancashire (1869–82, 8 matches).
Career batting
8–12–3–80–19–8.88–0–*ct* 6
He also played for Cheshire.

Hulton, Rev Campbell Blethyn
(registered at birth as Campbell Grey Hulton)
Amateur. *b:* 30.5.1877, Chorlton, Lancashire. *d:* 10.4.1947, Mentmore, Bucks. Brother of J. M. (MCC). Middle order batsman. *Sch* Charterhouse. *Team* MCC (1903).
Career batting
1–2–0–4–4–2.00–0–*ct* 2

Hulton, Harrington Arthur Harrop
Amateur. *b:* 9.11.1846, Ashton-under-Lyne, Lancashire. *d:* 28.1.1923, Cheltenham, Gloucs. Middle order batsman. *Sch* Rossall. *Team* Lancashire (1868, 2 matches).
Career batting
2–4–1–13–6–4.33–0–*ct* 0

Hulton, John Meredith
Amateur. *b:* 8.1.1882, Chorlton, Lancashire. *d:* 13.7.1942, Poole, Dorset. Brother of C. B. (MCC). Middle order right-hand batsman. *Sch* Charterhouse. *Team* MCC (1903–05).
Career batting
3–5–0–127–65–25.40–0–*ct* 1
Bowling 36–0

Human, John Hanbury
Amateur. *b:* 13.1.1912, Castle Ward, Northumberland. Brother of R. H. C. (Worcs). Middle order right-hand batsman, leg break bowler. *Sch* Repton. *Teams* Cambridge U (1932–34, blue all three years); Middlesex (1935–38, 41 matches). *Tours* MCC to India and Ceylon 1933/4, to Australia and New Zealand 1935/6.
Career batting
105–161–14–5246–158*–35.68–15–*ct* 66
Bowling 2499–73–34.23–3–0–7/119
He hit 1,000 runs in a season twice (best 1,399, av 53.80, in 1934). He also played for Berkshire.

Human, Roger Henry Charles
Amateur. *b:* 11.5.1909, Newcastle-on-Tyne. *d:* 21.11.1942, Bangalore, India. Brother of J. H. (Middlesex). Forcing middle order right-hand batsman, right-arm medium pace bowler. *Sch* Repton. *Teams* Cambridge (1930–31, blue both years); Worcestershire (1934–39, 39 matches).
Career batting
59–95–4–2236–81–24.57–0–*ct* 34
Bowling 1947–51–38.17–0–0–4/42
He also played for Berkshire and Oxfordshire.

Humble, Rev William John
(changed name to Humble-Crofts in May 1879)
Amateur. *b:* 9.12.1846, Sutton Scarsdale, Derbyshire. *d:* 1.7.1924, Waldron, Sussex. Middle order right-hand batsman, good cover field. *Team* Derbyshire (1873–77, 6 matches).
Career batting
6–10–1–77–19*–8.55–0–*ct* 6
He did not appear in first-class cricket whilst at Oxford.

Hume, Edward
Amateur. *b:* 25.9.1841, Scaldwell, Northants. *d:* 24.10.1921, Totland Bay, Isle of Wight. Middle order right-hand batsman. *Sch* Marlborough.

Team Oxford U (1861–63, blue 1861 and 1862).
Career batting
8–14–2–102–26*–8.50–0–*ct* 4

He was on the MCC Committee and his final first-class match was for an England Eleven in 1879.

Humfrey, Stuart Harold Guise
Amateur. *b:* 17.2.1894, Thorpe-Mandeville, Northamptonshire. *d:* 9.6.1975, Dallington, Northampton. Hard-hitting middle order right-hand batsman, right-arm medium pace bowler. *Sch* Oakham. *Team* Northants (1913–26, 21 matches).
Career batting
21–36–2–477–61*–14.02–0–*ct* 4
Bowling 135–1–135.00–0–0–1/40

He was also a noted rugby centre three quarter.

Humpage, Geoffrey William
Cricketer. *b:* 24.4.1954, Birmingham. Middle order right-hand batsman, wicket-keeper, occasional right-arm medium pace bowler. *Teams* Warwickshire (1974–83, 191 matches); Orange Free State (1981/2). *Tour* England SAB XI to South Africa 1981/2.
Career batting
197–320–37–9987–254–35.28–18–*ct* 341–*st* 41
Bowling 387–8–48.37–0–0–2/13

He hit 1,000 runs in a season six times (best 1,701, av 50.02, in 1981). His only double century was 254 for Warwickshire v Lancashire at Southport in 1982, in the course of which he created with A.I. Kallicharran a new first-class English 4th wicket record partnership of 470.

Humpherson, Victor William
Amateur. *b:* 15.7.1896, Bewdley on Severn, Worcs. *d:* 19.10.1978, Rowfant, Sussex. Lower order right-hand batsman, right-arm medium pace bowler. *Team* Worcestershire (1921–23, 13 matches).
Career batting
13–25–5–154–16–7.70–0–*ct* 10
Bowling 500–16–31.25–1–0–5/50

Humphrey, Richard
Professional. *b:* 12.12.1848, Mitcham, Surrey. *d:* 28.2.1906. He was drowned in the River Thames. Brother of Thomas (Surrey) and William (Surrey and Hants). Opening right-hand batsman. *Team* Surrey (1870–81, 145 matches). *Tour* Grace to Australia 1873/4 (not first-class).
Career batting
194–355–23–5614–116*–16.90–1–*ct* 106

He hit 1,072 runs, av 23.82, in 1872, which was his best season. At the time of his death he had been in very poor circumstances for some years.

Humphrey, Richard George
Cricketer. *b:* 17.9.1936, Hampstead, London. Lower order right-hand batsman, wicket-keeper. *Team* Surrey (1964–70, 2 matches).
Career batting
2–2–1–63–58–63.00–0–*ct* 4–*st* 1

He also played for Buckinghamshire.

Humphrey, Thomas
Professional. *b:* 16.1.1839, Mitcham, Surrey. *d:* 3.9.1878, Brookwood, Surrey. Brother of Richard (Surrey) and William (Surrey and Hants). Splendid opening right-hand batsman, right-hand slow round-arm bowler, excellent deep field. *Team* Surrey (1862–74, 159 matches). *Tour* Willsher to North America 1868 (not first-class).
Career batting
212–381–18–6687–144–18.42–4–*ct* 95
Bowling 2461–114+2–21.58–6–0–6/29

He hit 1,223 runs, av 29.82, in 1865 and about that time was regarded as one of the leading batsmen in England, being known as the 'Pocket Hercules'. His final first-class match was for the South of England in 1876. He also appeared for Northants (not first-class).

Humphrey, William
Professional. *b:* 15.9.1843, Mitcham, Surrey. *d:* 24.2.1918, Norwich. Brother of Thomas (Surrey) and Richard (Surrey). Lower order right-hand batsman, right-hand fast round-arm bowler. *Teams* Surrey (1864, 4 matches); Hampshire (1864, 4 matches).
Career batting
8–14–1–99–25–7.61–0–*ct* 1
Bowling 248–6–41.33–0–0–3/61

He also played for Norfolk.

Humphreys, Edward
Professional. *b:* 24.8.1881, West Hoathly, Sussex. *d:* 6.11.1949, Maidstone, Kent. Opening right-hand batsman, slow left-arm bowler. *Team* Kent (1899–1920, 366 matches); Canterbury (1908/09). *Tour* MCC to West Indies 1912/13.
Career batting
393–639–45–16603–208–27.95–22–*ct* 229
Bowling 9314–379–24.57–12–2–7/33

He hit 1,000 runs in a season eight times (best 1,777, av 40.38, in 1911). Both his double centuries were for Kent, his highest being 208 v Gloucs at Catford in 1909.

Humphreys, George Thomas
Professional. *b:* 28.3.1845, Brighton, Sussex. *d:* 18.12.1894, Brighton, as the result of breaking a

blood vessel. Brother of W. A. (Sussex), uncle of W. A. jun (Sussex). Good middle order right-hand batsman, originally wicket-keeper, excellent field. *Team* Sussex (1869–86, 32 matches).
Career batting
32–60–7–545–58–10.28–0–*ct* 21–*st* 3

Humphreys, Walter Alexander
Professional. *b:* 28.10.1849, Southsea, Hants. *d:* 23.3.1924, Brighton, Sussex. Brother of G. T. (Sussex), father of W. A. jun (Sussex). Middle/lower order right-hand batsman, right-hand under-arm lob bowler, good field. *Teams* Sussex (1871–96, 248 matches); Hampshire (1900, 2 matches). *Tour* Stoddart to Australia (1894/5).
Career batting
273–485–96–6268–117–16.11–1–*ct* 213
Bowling 15457–718–21.52–51–8–8/83
He took 100 wickets in a season once : 150, av 17.32, in 1893. No lob bowler since has achieved such figures in first-class cricket.

Humphreys, Walter Alexander (jun)
Professional. *b:* 1878, Brighton, Sussex. *d:* 1.1.1960, Hove, Sussex. Son of W. A. sen (Sussex and Hants), nephew of G. T. (Sussex). Lower order right-hand batsman, right-hand slow under arm bowler. *Team* Sussex (1898–1900, 14 matches).
Career batting
14–20–6–81–27–5.78–0–*ct* 9
Bowling 1353–48–28.18–2–0–5/107

Humphries, Cedric Alfred
Amateur. *b:* 26.12.1914, Kidderminster, Worcs. *d:* 18.11.1944, Holland. Brother of G. H. and N. H. (Worcs). Middle order right-hand batsman, right-arm medium pace bowler. *Team* Worcestershire (1934–35, 13 matches).
Career batting
13–24–3–328–44–15.61–*ct* 3

Humphries, David John
Cricketer. *b:* 6.8.1953, Alveley, Shropshire. Lower order left-hand batsman, wicket-keeper. *Teams* Leicestershire (1974–76, 5 matches); Worcestershire (1977–83, 147 matches).
Career batting
152–219–36–4410–111*–24.09–2–*ct* 255–*st* 53
He also played for Shropshire.

Humphries, Gerald Harvey
Amateur. *b:* 8.12.1908, Kidderminster, Worcs. *d:* 3.2.1983, Rock, near Kidderminster. Brother of C. A. and N. H. (Worcs). Middle order right-hand batsman, right-arm medium pace bowler. *Team* Worcestershire (1932–34, 2 matches).
Career batting
2–3–0–66–36–22.00–0–*ct* 0
Bowling 13–0

Humphries, Henry Hurl
Amateur. *b:* 8.9.1879, Warkworth, Ontario, Canada. *d:* 12.10.1964, Bath, Somerset. Middle order left-hand batsman. *Teams* Somerset (1906, 1 match); Combined USA/Canada (1913).
Career batting
2–3–0–56–49–18.66–0–*ct* 0
Bowling 32–0

Humphries, Joseph
Professional. *b:* 19.5.1876, Stonebroom, Derbyshire. *d:* 7.5.1946, Chesterfield, Derbyshire. Lower order right-hand batsman, wicket-keeper. *Teams* Derbyshire (1899–1914, 276 matches). *Tour* MCC to Australia 1907/8. *Tests* England (1907/8, 3 matches).
Career batting
302–514–129–5464–68–14.19–0–*ct* 564–*st* 110
Bowling 43–3–14.33–0–0–1/5
Test batting
3–6–1–44–16–8.80–0–*ct* 7

Humphries, Norman Hampton
Amateur. *b:* 19.5.1917, Kidderminster, Worcs. Brother of C. A. and G. H. (Worcs). Middle order right-hand batsman, leg break bowler. *Team* Worcestershire (1946, 7 matches).
Career batting
7–11–1–137–22–13.70–0–*ct* 1
Bowling 52–0
He also played for Devonshire.

Humphrys, Sir Francis Henry
Amateur. *b:* 24.4.1879, Oswestry, Shropshire. *d:* 28.8.1971, Hampstead-Marshall, Berks. Lower order right-hand batsman, right-arm fast bowler, good field. *Sch* Shrewsbury. *Team* Oxford U (1899-1900).
Career batting
4–5–1–18–12–4.50–0–*ct* 3
Bowling 253–13–19.46–0–0–4/16
He appeared frequently for Free Foresters, Harlequins and I Zingari. His County cricket was for Wiltshire.

Hunt, Alma Victor
Professional. *b:* 1.10.1910, Bermuda. Left-hand batsman, right-arm fast medium bowler. *Teams* Scotland (1938); G. C. Grant's XI (West Indies 1932/3).
Career batting
2–4–0–65–31–16.25–0–*ct* 3
Bowling 71–2–35.50–0–0–1/15
He was the leading cricketer in Bermuda and

has continued as a major figure in the administration of cricket in Bermuda.

Hunt, Frederick Hunt
Professional. *b:* 13.9.1875, Aldworth, Berks. *d:* 31.3.1967, Worcester. Lower order right-hand batsman, right-arm medium pace bowler. *Teams* Kent (1897–98, 6 matches); Worcestershire (1900–22, 53 matches).
Career batting
59–97–21–806–40*–10.60–0–*ct* 17
Bowling 1635–51–32.05–0–0–4/36
For many years he was the groundsman at Worcester.

Hunt, George Edward
Professional. *b:* 30.9.1896, Pill, Somerset. *d:* 22.1.1959, Bristol. Brother of Hubert (Somerset). Middle order right-hand batsman, right-arm medium pace bowler, good short leg. *Team* Somerset (1921–31, 233 matches).
Career batting
233–381–60–4952–101–15.42–1–*ct* 197
Bowling 12691–386–32.87–11–1–7/61

Hunt, George Rupert
Amateur. *b:* 23.3.1873, Bath, Somerset. *d:* 22.8.1960, Old Burlesdon, Hants. Father of Kenneth (Gloucestershire). Middle order right-hand batsman, right-arm medium pace bowler. *Sch* Sutton Valence. *Team* Somerset (1898, 1 match).
Career batting
1–2–0–4–3–2.00–0–*ct* 1

Hunt, Hubert
Professional. *b:* 18.11.1911, Long Ashton, Somerset. Brother of George (Somerset). Lower order right-hand batsman, right-arm off break bowler. *Team* Somerset (1936, 11 matches).
Career batting
11–16–3–100–22–7.69–0–*ct* 2
Bowling 285–15–19.00–1–0–7/49
He also played for Cornwall.

Hunt, J. H. (*see under* Husey-Hunt, J. H.)

Hunt, John Henry Sneyd
Amateur. *b:* 24.11.1874, Kensington, London. *d:* 16.9.1916, near Ginchy, France. Middle order right-hand batsman, right-arm medium pace bowler. *Sch* Winchester. *Team* Middlesex (1902–12, 44 matches).
Career batting
46–71–6–1393–128–21.43–1–*ct* 29
Bowling 2137–80–26.71–2–0–5/60

Hunt, Kenneth
Amateur. *b:* 4.12.1902, Bristol. *d:* 16.3.1971, Chalford, Stroud. Son of G. R. (Somerset). Middle order right-hand batsman. *Sch* Dover. *Teams* Royal Navy (1925); Gloucestershire (1926, 1 match).
Career batting
2–4–0–11–7–2.75–0–*ct* 2

Hunt, Louis Edward
Amateur. *b:* 9.11.1908, Prestatyn, Flintshire. Lower order right-hand batsman, wicket-keeper. *Sch* Bradfield. *Teams* Cambridge U (1929); Bengal (1935/6); Europeans (1940/1).
Career batting
3–4–0–21–10–5.25–0–*ct* 2

Hunt, Robert Geoffrey
Amateur. *b:* 13.4.1915, Horsham, Sussex. Middle order right-hand batsman, off break bowler. *Sch* Aldenham. *Teams* Cambridge U (1935–37, blue 1937); Sussex (1936–47, 11 matches); Services (1943/4).
Career batting
27–46–4–831–117–19.78–1–*ct* 21
Bowling 959–31–30.93–2–0–5/51

Hunt, Robert Norman
Amateur. *b:* 24.9.1903, Worsley, Lancashire. *d:* 13.10.1983, Chichester, Sussex. Lower order right-hand batsman, right-arm fast medium bowler. *Team* Middlesex (1926–28, 8 matches).
Career batting
8–10–3–138–81*–19.71–0–*ct* 3
Bowling 453–5–90.60–0–0–3/32

Hunt, Samuel Walter
Professional. *b:* 9.1.1909, Doe Lea, Derbyshire. *d:* 2.8.1963, Rochdale, Lancashire. Middle order right-hand batsman, leg break bowler. *Team* Derbyshire (1936, 5 matches).
Career batting
5–5–0–48–17–9.60–0–*ct* 0
Bowling 3–0
He also played for Northumberland. He played football for Lincoln City, Mansfield, Torquay, Rochdale, Stockport, Accrington and Carlisle.

Hunt, Thomas
Professional. *b:* 2.9.1819, Chesterfield, Derbyshire. *d:* 11.9.1858, Rochdale, Lancashire. He was run over by a train. Stylish opening right-hand batsman, right-hand fast round-arm bowler, wicket-keeper. *Teams* Yorkshire (1845–51); Lancashire (1849).
Career batting
39–66–5–922–102–15.11–1–*ct* 33–*st* 9
Bowling 234–18+49–13.00–5–1–7/?

One of the best batsmen in the North of England, he was also a noted single wicket player. His final important match was for Manchester in 1858.

Hunte, Conrad Cleophas
Amateur. *b:* 9.5.1932, Belleplaine, Barbados. Sound right-hand opening batsman, right-arm medium bowler, brilliant outfield. *Teams* Barbados (1950/1 to 1966/7); Prime Minister's XI in India (1963/4). *Tours* West Indies to England 1963, 1966, to Australia 1960/1, to India and Pakistan 1958/9, to India 1966/7; Commonwealth in England 1956. *Tests* West Indies (1957/8 to 1966/7, 44 matches).
Career batting
132–222–19–8916–263–43.92–16–*ct* 68–*st* 1
Bowling 644–17–37.88–0–0–3/5
Test batting
44–78–6–3245–260–45.06–8–*ct* 16
Bowling 110–2–55.00–0–0–1/17
On his 1963 tour to England he hit 1,367 runs, av 44.09, and performed brilliantly in the five Tests, heading the batting averages; he was vice-captain of the tourists. Though not as prolific in 1966, he still appeared in all five Tests and only just missed scoring 1,000 runs in first-class matches. He hit 206 v Somerset at Taunton on the latter tour, his highest innings in England. His highest in all first-class matches was 263 for Barbados v Jamaica at Georgetown in 1961/2. He hit 1,000 in a season in India and Pakistan.

Hunter, Charles Herbert
Amateur. *b:* 18.4.1867, Lee, Kent. *d:* 2.4.1955, Budleigh Salterton, Devon. Hard-hitting lower order right-hand batsman, wicket-keeper. *Sch* Uppingham. *Teams* Cambridge U (1889); Kent (1895, 2 matches).
Career batting
3–5–1–29–16–7.25–0–*ct* 2–*st* 1

Hunter, Charles Michael Geoffrey
Cricketer. *b:* 11.9.1937, St Helens, Lancashire. Middle order right-hand batsman, right-arm medium pace bowler. *Team* Minor Counties (1971).
Career batting
1–2–1–50–41–50.00–0–*ct* 0
Bowling 52–0
He also played for Dorset.

Hunter, C. V.
Amateur. Middle order right-hand batsman. *Team* British Guiana (1912/13 to 1922/3). *Tour* West Indies to England 1923.
Career batting
7–12–0–275–66–22.91–0–*ct* 0
Bowling 16–0
On the 1923 tour he was mainly confined to minor matches, playing only two first-class innings. His first-class debut was for a West Indian XI in 1910/11.

Hunter, David
Professional. *b:* 23.2.1860, Scarborough, Yorkshire. *d:* 11.1.1927, Scarborough, Yorkshire. Brother of Joseph (Yorkshire). Lower order right-hand batsman, wicket-keeper. *Team* Yorkshire (1888–1909, 521 matches).
Career batting
552–728–351–4536–58*–12.03–0–*ct* 914–*st* 351
Bowling 43–0

Hunter, Frederic Cecil
Amateur. *b:* 23.8.1886, Glossop, Derbyshire. *d:* 21.7.1926, Australia. Middle/lower order right-hand batsman, leg break bowler. *Team* Derbyshire (1905–07, 28 matches).
Career batting
28–49–3–564–51–12.26–0–*ct* 8
Bowling 684–17–40.23–0–0–2/18
He also played for Cheshire.

Hunter, Joseph
Professional. *b:* 3.8.1855, Scarborough, Yorkshire. *d:* 4.1.1891, Rotherham, Yorkshire. Brother of David (Yorkshire). Tail end right-hand batsman, wicket-keeper. *Team* Yorkshire (1878–88, 143 matches). *Tours* Lillywhite, Shaw and Shrewsbury to Australia 1884/5. *Tests* England (1884/5, 5 matches).
Career batting
162–240–71–1330–60*–7.86–0–*ct* 234–*st* 122
Test batting
5–7–2–93–39*–18.60–0–*ct* 8–*st* 3

Hunter, William Raymond
Amateur. *b:* 3.4.1938, Belfast, Ireland. Right-hand batsman, right-arm medium pace bowler. *Team* Ireland (1958–65).
Career batting
11–18–0–201–39–11.16–0–*ct* 11
Bowling 445–19–23.42–1–0–5/22
He was an Irish rugby international.

Hurd, Alan
Amateur. *b:* 7.9.1937, Ilford, Essex. Tail end left-hand batsman, off break bowler. *Sch* Chigwell. *Teams* Cambridge U (1958–60, blue all three years); Essex (1958–60, 35 matches).
Career batting
90–106–36–376–21–5.37–0–*ct* 16
Bowling 7671–249–30.80–13–1–6/15

Hurd, William Sydney
Amateur. *b:* September 1908, Ashby-de-la-

Zouch, Leics. Lower order batsman, bowler. *Team* Leicestershire (1932–34, 3 matches).
Career batting
3–4–0–7–5–1.75–0–*ct* 0
Bowling 28–0

Hurst, Alan George
Cricketer. *b:* 15.7.1950, Altona, Victoria, Australia. Lower order right-hand batsman, right-arm fast bowler. *Team* Victoria (1972/3 to 1980/1, 50 matches). *Tours* Australia to England 1975, to New Zealand 1976/7, to India 1979/80; International Wanderers to South Africa 1976. *Tests* Australia (1973/4 to 1979/80, 12 matches).
Career batting
77–88–30–504–27*–8.68–0–*ct* 26
Bowling 7360–280–26.28–11–1–8/84
Test batting
12–20–3–102–26–6.00–0–*ct* 3
Bowling 1200–43–27.90–2–0–5/28
He took 21 wickets, av 31.38, on the 1975 tour to England and did not appear in the Tests.

Hurst, Christopher Salkeld
Amateur. *b:* 20.7.1886, Beckenham, Kent. *d:* 18.12.1963, Dorking, Surrey. Free scoring middle order right-hand batsman. *Sch* Uppingham. *Teams* Oxford U (1907–09, blue all three years); Kent (1908–27, 19 matches).
Career batting
47–82–6–1787–124–23.51–3–*ct* 41
Bowling 96–3–32.00–0–0–2/26
A noted hockey player, he represented Oxford.

Hurst, Geoffrey Charles
Professional. *b:* 8.12.1941, Ashton-under-Lyme, Lancashire. Lower order right-hand batsman, brilliant field, wicket-keeper. *Team* Essex (1962, 1 match).
Career batting
1–2–1–0–0*–0.00–0–*ct* 1
A well-known soccer player, he appeared as centre-forward for West Ham United, WBA, Stoke City and England, scoring a hat-trick in the World Cup Final of 1966.

Hurst, Gordon T.
Professional. *b:* 26.8.1920, Kenley, Surrey. Lower order right-hand batsman, off break bowler. *Team* Sussex (1947–49, 9 matches).
Career batting
9–13–4–27–9–3.00–0–*ct* 0
Bowling 760–28–27.14–2–0–6/80

Hurst, Robert Jack
Professional. *b:* 29.12.1933, Hampton Hill, Middlesex. Lower order right-hand batsman, slow left-arm bowler. *Team* Middlesex (1954–61, 100 matches).
Career batting
105–128–56–721–62–10.01–0–*ct* 56
Bowling 6189–255–24.27–6–1–8/65

Hurt, Colin Noel Bickley
Amateur. *b:* 16.12.1893, Darley Dale, Derbyshire. *d:* 31.12.1972, Bexhill, Sussex. Middle order right-hand batsman, right-arm medium pace bowler. *Sch* Malvern. *Team* Derbyshire (1914, 3 matches).
Career batting
3–5–0–23–13–4.60–0–*ct* 1
Bowling 6–0

Hurwood, Alexander
Amateur. *b:* 17.6.1902, Redland Bay, Brisbane, Australia. *d:* 26.9.1982, Cleveland, Brisbane, Australia. Lower order right-hand batsman, right-arm medium off break bowler. *Team* Queensland (1925/6 to 1931/2, 18 matches). *Tour* Australia to England 1930. *Tests* Australia (1930/1, 2 matches).
Career batting
43–56–5–575–89–11.27–0–*ct* 29
Bowling 3132–113–27.62–5–1–6/80
Test batting
2–2–0–5–5–2.50–0–*ct* 2
Bowling 170–11–15.45–0–0–4/22
For some reason he was given very little opportunity on the 1930 tour and did not appear in any Tests – on the occasions when he did bowl he looked impressive and economical.

Husey-Hunt, James Hubert
(originally J. H. Senior)
Amateur. *b:* 20.4.1853, Castle Cary, Somerset. *d:* 13.5.1924, Hove, Sussex. Right hand batsman. *Sch* Marlborough. *Team* Gloucestershire (1880, 2 matches).
Career batting
3–5–0–20–6–4.00–0–*ct* 1
His first-class debut was for MCC in 1878.

Huskinson, Geoffrey Mark Clement
Amateur. *b:* 25.9.1935, Langar, Notts. Son of G. N. B. (Notts). Middle order right-hand batsman, leg break bowler. *Sch* Ampleforth. *Team* Free Foresters (1959).
Career batting
1–2–0–10–7–5.00–0–*ct* 0

Huskinson, Geoffrey Neville Bayley
Amateur. *b:* 1.2.1900, Locarno, Switzerland. *d:* 17.6.1982, Hinton Waldrist, Berkshire. Father of G. M. C. (Free Foresters). Middle order right-hand batsman, leg break bowler. *Sch* Oundle.

Team Nottinghamshire (1922, 2 matches). *Tour* Martineau to Egypt 1933 (not first-class).
Career batting
2–2–0–33–33–16.50–0–*ct* 0

He was on the Notts CCC Committee 1943-58 and President 1959-60. Whilst at Oxford U he did not appear in any first-class matches. A noted rugby footballer, he played for Notts, East Midlands and Harlequins.

Hussain, Syed Mohammad
Amateur. *b:* 8.12.1909, India. *d:* 2.7.1982, Hyderabad, India. Brother of S. M. Hadi (India). Middle order batsman. *Teams* Madras (1926/7 to 1933/4); Hyderabad (1930/1 to 1942/3); Muslims (1927/8 to 1936/7). *Tour* India to England 1936.
Career batting
42–73–6–1626–94–24.26–0–*ct* 22
Bowling 90–3–30.00–0–0–2/35

He achieved modest success on the 1936 tour and did not appear in the Tests.

His first-class debut was for Indians v Europeans in 1925/6.

Hussey, John Allen
Amateur. *b:* 17.4.1897, Axbridge, Somerset. *d:* 18.8.1969, Wimbledon. Middle order right-hand batsman. *Team* Royal Navy (1929).
Career batting
1–1–0–54–54–54.00–0–*ct* 1

Hutchings, Frederick Vaughan
Amateur. *b:* 3.6.1880, Southborough, Kent. *d:* 6.8.1934, Hamburg, Germany. Brother of K. L. (Kent) and W. E. C. (Kent and Worcs). Sound middle order right-hand batsman, good cover point. *Sch* Tonbridge. *Team* Kent (1901–05, 3 matches).
Career batting
4–6–0–89–31–14.83–0–*ct* 0

Hutchings, Kenneth Lotherington
Amateur. *b:* 7.12.1882, Southborough, Kent. *d:* 3.9.1916, Ginchy, France. He was killed in action. Brother of F. V. (Kent) and W. E. C. (Kent and Worcs). Excellent middle order right-hand batsman, right-hand fast bowler, brilliant field. *Sch* Tonbridge. *Team* Kent (1902–12, 163 matches). *Tours* Kent to North America 1903; MCC to Australia 1907/8. *Tests* England (1907/8 to 1909, 7 matches).
Career batting
207–311–12–10054–176–33.62–22–*ct* 179
Bowling 938–24–39.08–0–0–4/15
Test batting
7–12–0–341–126–28.41–1–*ct* 9
Bowling 81–1–81.00–0–0–1/5

He hit 1,000 runs in a season six times (best 1,697, av 36.10, in 1909). His most notable asset was his driving, the force with which he hit the ball being quite remarkable.

Hutchings, William Edward Colebrooke
Amateur. *b:* 31.5.1879, Southborough, Kent. *d:* 8.3.1948, Prees, near Whitchurch, Salop. Brother of F. V. and K. L. (Kent). Middle order right-hand batsman. *Sch* Tonbridge. *Teams* Kent (1899, 2 matches); Worcestershire (1905–06, 22 matches).
Career batting
24–42–3–845–21.66–0–*ct* 20

He also played for Berkshire.

Hutchins, Gilbert William
Professional. *b:* 28.2.1858, Knebworth, Herts. *d:* 1902, Bedford. Lower order right-hand batsman, slow right-arm bowler. *Team* Middlesex (1890, 1 match).
Career batting
1–2–0–9–7–4.50–0–*ct* 0
Bowling 25–0

He also played for Bedfordshire, Huntingdonshire, Hertfordshire and Monmouth.

Hutchinson, James (Metcalf)
Professional. *b:* 29.11.1896, New Tupton, Derbyshire. Middle order right-hand batsman, right-arm medium pace off break bowler, brilliant cover point. *Team* Derbyshire (1920-31, 255 matches).
Career batting
256–416–38–7055–143–18.66–5–*ct* 97–*st* 2
Bowling 1238–31–39.93–0–0–3/44

His best year was 1928 with 990 runs, av 22.50.

Hutchinson, Leonard Staughton
Professional. *b:* 16.4.1901, Anstey, Leics. *d:* 2.10.1976, Glenfield, Leicester. Middle order right-hand batsman, bowler. *Team* Leicestershire (1923–25, 8 matches).
Career batting
8–15–1–65–14–4.64–0–*ct* 8
Bowling 64–1–64.00–0–0–1/9

Hutchinson, Major General William Francis Moore
Amateur. *b:* 3.2.1841. *d:* 22.4.1917, Eastbourne, Sussex. Middle order batsman. *Team* MCC (1869).
Career batting
1–1–0–1–1–1.00–0–*ct* 0

He also played for Devon and Norfolk.

Huth, Henry
Amateur. *b:* 1856, Huddersfield, Yorkshire. *d:* 1929. Middle order batsman. *Team* Gentlemen of the North (1877).

Career batting
1–2–0–7–7–3.50–0–*ct* 0

An excellent rugby footballer, he was capped for England.

Hutson, Andrew Massey
Cricketer. *b:* 18.3.1952, Tamworth, Staffs. Right-hand batsman, right-arm medium pace bowler. *Team* Cambridge U (1972).
Career batting
1–1–1–0–0*–no av–0–*ct* 0
Bowling 54–0

Hutson, Henry Wolseley
Amateur. *b:* 1866, Demerara, British Guiana. *d:* 25.3.1916, Wimbledon, Surrey. Middle order batsman. *Team* Cambridge U (1886).
Career batting
1–2–0–20–20–10.00–0–*ct* 1
Bowling 4–0

He also played for Berkshire.

Hutton, George
Amateur. *b:* 20.8.1942, Paisley, Scotland. Right-hand batsman, right-arm fast medium bowler. *Team* Scotland (1966–67).
Career batting
2–2–1–0–0*–0.00–0–*ct* 1
Bowling 56–2–28.00–0–0–2/16

Hutton, Sir Leonard
Professional. *b:* 23.6.1916, Fulneck, Pudsey, Yorkshire. Father of R. A. (Yorkshire), brother-in-law of F. Dennis (Yorkshire), uncle of S. J. Dennis (Yorkshire). Excellent opening right-hand batsman, leg break bowler, fine field. *Team* Yorkshire (1934–55, 341 matches). *Tours* Yorkshire to Jamaica 1935/6; MCC to South Africa 1938/9, 1948/9, to Australia and New Zealand 1946/7, 1950/1, 1954/5, to West Indies 1947/8, 1953/4. *Tests* England (1937 to 1954/5, 79 matches).
Career batting
513–814–91–40140–364–55.51–129–*ct* 400
Bowling 5106–173–29.51–4–1–6/76
Test batting
79–138–15–6971–364–56.67–19–*ct* 57
Bowling 232–3–77.33–0–0–1/2

Hutton succeeded Hobbs as the greatest opening batsman in England, and though forced in the second half of his career, especially for his country, to adopt a dour and unsmiling attitude to batting, he was also an attractive attacking player with a wide range of strokes. He placed himself above the ordinary by his innings of 364 for England against Australia at the Oval in 1938 and he remained for the rest of his career – nearly two decades – an outstanding player.

His best season in England was 1949 when he hit 3,429 runs, av 68.58. He exceeded 2,000 runs in a season in England eight other times and in all hit at least 1,000 runs 12 times, plus five times overseas.

Apart from his famous 364 he scored three double centuries for England – two being against the West Indies and one against New Zealand – and his total number of innings over 200 was 11.

His three MCC tours to Australia were all successes, in particular the 1950/1 visit when he carried the batting almost single handed. Called in emergency to reinforce the MCC in West Indies in 1947/8 midway through the tour, he ended by heading the batting averages.

Despite being a professional he was selected to captain England in 1953 and won back the Ashes; he then led England in the West Indies and managed to draw the series, two matches each, and on the 1954/5 tour to Australia won the series three matches to one. He retired from Test cricket after that series.

His post-war career was made that much more difficult by an accident to his arm during the war, which meant that his left arm was slightly shorter than his right.

He was knighted for his services to cricket in 1956; and served as a Test selector in 1975 and 1976.

His final first-class match was for L. C. Steven's XI in 1960.

Hutton, Richard Anthony
Cricketer. *b:* 6.9.1942, Pudsey, Yorkshire. Son of Leonard (Yorkshire), cousin of S. J. Dennis (Yorkshire). Middle order right-hand batsman, right-arm fast medium bowler. *Sch* Repton. *Teams* Yorkshire (1962-74, 208 matches); Cambridge U (1962–64, blue all three years); Transvaal (1975/6). *Tours* MCC to Pakistan 1966/7; Rest of World to Australia 1971/2; Swanton to West Indies 1963/4. *Tests* England (1971, 5 matches).
Career batting
281–410–58–7561–189–21.48–5–*ct* 216
Bowling 15008–625–24.01–21–3–8/50
Test batting
5–8–2–219–81–36.50–0–*ct* 9
Bowling 257–9–28.55–0–0–3/72

He hit 1,000 runs in a season twice (best 1,122, av 27.36, in 1963).

Hutton, Wilfred Noel Maxwell
Amateur. *b:* 5.6.1901, Dublin, Ireland. *d:* 12.9.1978, Carrigaline, Co Cork, Ireland. Right-hand batsman. *Sch* Shrewsbury. *Team* Dublin University (1922).
Career batting
1–2–0–2–2–1.00–0–*ct* 0

Huxford, Peter Nigel
Cricketer. *b:* 17.2.1960, Enfield, Middlesex. Tail end left-hand batsman, wicket-keeper. *Team* Oxford U (1980–81, blue 1981).
Career batting
7–9–4–27–10–5.40–0–*ct* 3–*st* 2

Huxter, Rupert James Alexander
Cricketer. *b:* 29.10.1959, Abingdon, Berkshire. Lower order right-hand batsman, right-arm medium pace bowler. *Sch* Magdalen College School. *Team* Cambridge U (1981, blue).
Career batting
4–5–0–34–20–6.80–0–*ct* 0
Bowling 224–5–44.80–0–0–2/49

Huyshe, Oliver Francis
Amateur. *b:* 26.7.1885, Wimborne Minster, Dorset. *d:* 23.8.1960, Exeter, Devon. Lower order batsman, wicket-keeper. *Sch* King's Canterbury. *Team* Oxford U (1907).
Career batting
1–1–1–0–0*–no av–0–*ct* 0
He also played for Dorset.

Hyde, Alfred John
Professional. *b:* 1884, Axbridge, Somerset. *d:* 13.4.1954, Clybach, Glamorgan. Lower order batsman, slow left-arm bowler. *Team* Warwickshire (1905–07, 2 matches).
Career batting
2–1–1–2–2*–no av–0–*ct* 0
Bowling 121–2–60.50–0–0–1/22

Hyde, Edward
Amateur. *b:* 1881, Wellingborough, Northants. *d:* 9.10.1941, Cambridge. *Team* Northants (1907, 1 match).
Career batting
1–2–1–3–3*–3.00–0–*ct* 2

Hyde, Lord Edward Hyde Villiers
(succeeded to the Earldom of Clarendon in June 1870)
Amateur. *b:* 11.2.1846, Grosvenor Crescent, London. *d:* 2.10.1914, Watford, Herts. Middle order right-hand batsman, fast round-arm bowler. *Sch* Harrow. *Team* Cambridge U (1864).
Career batting
1–2–0–8–7–4.00–0–*ct* 1
He also played for Hertfordshire and was on the Committee both of MCC and the Prince's Club. He was President of the MCC 1871.

Hyland, Frederick James
Professional. *b:* 1894, Battle, Sussex. *d:* 27.2.1964, Hartford, Cheshire. *Team* Hampshire (1924, 1 match).
Career batting
1 match, did not bat–*ct* 0

Hylton, Leslie George
Amateur. *b:* 29.3.1905, Kingston, Jamaica. *d:* 17.5.1955, Kingston, Jamaica. He was hanged for the murder of his wife. Lower order right-hand batsman, right-arm fast bowler. *Team* Jamaica (1926/7 to 1938/9). *Tour* West Indies to England 1939. *Tests* West Indies (1934/5 to 1939, 6 matches).
Career batting
40–54–9–843–80–18.73–0–*ct* 31
Bowling 3075–120–25.62–3–0–5/24
Test batting
6–8–2–70–19–11.66–0–*ct* 1
Bowling 418–16–26.12–0–0–4/27
Although he appeared in two Tests on the 1939 tour, he achieved very little and in all first-class matches took only 39 wickets, av 27.71.

Hylton-Stewart, Bruce De la Coeur
Amateur. *b:* 27.11.1891, New Brighton, Cheshire. *d:* 1.10.1972, London. Hard-hitting middle order right-hand batsman, right-arm fast medium bowler. *Sch* Bath College. *Teams* Somerset (1912–14, 33 matches); Cambridge U (1912).
Career batting
36–63–6–1003–110–17.59–1–*ct* 17
Bowling 1665–58–28.70–2–0–5/3
He also played for Hertfordshire.

Hyman, William
Amateur, changed to professional in 1902. *b:* 7.3.1875, Radstock, Bath, Somerset. *d:* February 1959, St Austell, Cornwall. Hard-hitting middle order batsman, right-arm medium pace bowler. *Team* Somerset (1900–14, 38 matches).
Career batting
38–68–4–1000–110–15.62–1–*ct* 10
He played an incredible innings of 359 not out for the Bath Cricket Association v Thornbury in 1902. The innings included 32 sixes off the bowling of E. M. Grace. He was also a noted local soccer player.

Hyndman, Henry Mayers
Amateur. *b:* 7.3.1842, Hyde Park Square, London. *d:* 22.11.1921, Hampstead, London. Middle order right-hand batsman, good field. *Teams* Cambridge U (1864); Sussex (1864–65, 9 matches).
Career batting
13–20–1–309–62–16.26–0–*ct* 3
He was a well-known Socialist politician.

Hyndson, James Gerard Wyndham
Amateur. *b:* 25.4.1892, Cape Town, South Africa. *d:* 23.2.1935, Holborn, London. Brother of R. W. J. G. (Essex). Lower order right-hand batsman, left-arm fast medium bowler. *Team* Surrey (1927, 2 matches).
Career batting
13–19–6–224–33–17.23–0–*ct* 6
Bowling 953–35–27.22–4–1–5/25
His first-class debut was for the Army in 1921 and much of his cricket was for MCC or in military matches.

Hyndson, Robert Wilberforce James Gerard
Amateur. *b:* 1894, Cape Town, South Africa. *d:* 27.9.1943, Bradford, Yorkshire. Brother of J. G. W. (Surrey). Middle order batsman, change bowler. *Team* Essex (1919, 1 match).
Career batting
1–2–0–7–6–3.50–0–*ct* 0
Bowling 71–0

Hyslop, Hector Henry
Professional. *b:* 13.12.1840, Southampton, Hants. *d:* 11.9.1920, Cosham, Hants. Opening right-hand batsman, wicket-keeper. *Team* Hampshire (1876–77, 7 matches). *Tours* Australia to England 1878 (not first-class) and 1886.
Career batting
9–16–1–121–34–8.06–0–*ct* 7–*st* 11
Bowling 31–2–15.50–0–0–2/12
He appeared in emergency for both the 1878 and 1886 Australians in England, it being thought that he was born in Australia.

I'ANSON, JOHN
Professional. *b:* 26.10.1869, Scorton, Yorkshire. *d:* 14.9.1936, Chester. Middle order right-hand batsman, right-arm fast medium pace bowler. *Team* Lancashire (1896–1908, 57 matches).
Career batting
57–76–9–986–110*–14.71–1–*ct* 29
Bowling 3072–148–20.75–7–2–7/31

Ibadulla, Khalid
Professional. *b:* 20.12.1935, Lahore, India. Father of K. B. K. (Otago). Opening right-hand batsman, right-arm medium off break bowler. *Teams* Punjab (1953/4); Warwickshire (1954–72, 377 matches); Otago (1964/5 to 1966/7); Tasmania (1970/1 to 1971/2, 4 matches). *Tours* Pakistan to India 1952/3, to New Zealand 1964/5, to England 1967; Commonwealth to Pakistan 1963/4; International XI to India, Pakistan and Ceylon 1967/8. *Tests* Pakistan (1964/5 to 1967, 4 matches).
Career batting
416–702–78–17039–171–27.30–22–*ct* 337
Bowling 14264–462–30.87–6–0–7/22
Test batting
4–8–0–253–166–31.62–1–*ct* 3
Bowling 99–1–99.00–0–0–1/42
He hit 1,000 runs in a season six times, going on to 2,000 once: best 2,098, av 33.83, in 1962. With N. F. Horner he created a new Warwickshire first wicket record partnership of 377* v Surrey at the Oval in 1960 and with R. B. Kanhai created a County fourth wicket record of 402 v Notts at Trent Bridge in 1968. He was on the first-class umpires' list.

Iddison, Roger
Professional. *b:* 15.9.1834, Bedale, Yorkshire. *d:* 19.3.1890, York. Brother of W. H. (Lancashire). Middle order right-hand batsman, right-hand fast round-arm, later lob bowler, excellent point. *Teams* Yorkshire (1853–76, 74 matches); Lancashire (1865–70, 16 matches). *Tour* Stephenson to Australia 1861/2.
Career batting
134–232–30–3791–112–18.76–2–*ct* 133
Bowling 3498–209+2–16.73–11–2–7/30
For several seasons in the 1860s he was among the leading batsmen in England. He was the principal organiser of the United North of England Eleven, which began in 1869, and in 1874 was co-secretary of the newly formed Yorkshire United Eleven. He also played for Cheshire.

Iddison, William Holdsworth
Professional until 1866. *b:* 5.2.1840, Bedale, Yorkshire. *d:* 1898, Chorlton, Lancashire. Brother of Roger (Yorkshire and Lancashire). Middle order right-hand batsman. *Team* Lancashire (1867–68, 4 matches).
Career batting
4–8–0–46–19–5.75–0–*ct* 1
Bowling 95–1–95.00–0–0–1/33

Iddon, John
Professional. *b:* 8.1.1902, Mawdesley, Lancashire. *d:* 17.4.1946, Madeley, Staffs. He was killed in a car accident. Middle order right-hand batsman, slow left-arm bowler. *Team* Lancashire (1924–45, 483 matches). *Tours* Cahn to Jamaica 1928/9; MCC to West Indies 1934/5. *Tests* England (1934/5 to 1935, 5 matches).

Career batting
504–712–95–22681–222–36.76–46–*ct* 217
Bowling 14823–551–26.90–14–2–9/42
Test batting
5–7–1–170–73–28.33–0–*ct* 0
Bowling 27–0

He hit 1,000 runs in a season 13 times, once going on to 2,000 : 2,381, av 52.91 in 1934. His five double centuries were all for Lancashire, the highest being 222 v Leics at Liverpool in 1929. His best bowling was 9/42 for Lancashire v Yorkshire at Sheffield in 1937.

Ijaz Butt
Amateur. *b:* 10.3.1938, Sialkot, India. Opening right-hand batsman, wicket-keeper. *Teams* Punjab (1955/6 to 1957/8); Lahore (1959/60 to 1967/8); Universities (1958/9 to 1959/60); Rawalpindi (1959/60 to 1961/2); Multan (1963/4). *Tours* Pakistan to England 1962, to West Indies 1957/8, to India 1960/1; PIA Eaglets to Ceylon 1960/1. *Tests* Pakistan (1958/9 to 1962, 8 matches).
Career batting
67–120–8–3842–161–34.30–7–*ct* 52–*st* 19
Bowling 146–3–48.66–0–0–1/21
Test batting
8–16–2–279–58–19.92–0–*ct* 5

He hit 1,016 runs, av 28.22, on the 1962 tour to England and, although the reserve wicket-keeper, gained a place in the Test side as a batsman – in the Oval Test, Pakistan's batting was opened in both innings by the two wicket-keepers, Imtiaz Ahmed and Ijaz Butt.

Ijaz Hussain
Cricketer. Opening right-hand batsman, wicket-keeper. *Teams* Bahawalpur (1956/7 to 1959/60); Multan (1961/2 to 1962/3); Railways (1963/4 to 1967/8); Karachi (1968/9); PWD (1968/9 to 1969/70); National Bank (1969/70 to 1975/6); Sind (1973/4). *Tour* Pakistan Eaglets to England 1963.
Career batting
82–141–6–4580–173–33.92–8–*ct* 122–*st* 38
Bowling 400–16–25.00–1–0–5/37

He appeared in only three first-class matches on the 1963 Eaglets tour to England.

Ikin, John Thomas
Professional. *b:* 7.3.1918, Bignall End, Staffs. Father of M. J. (Minor Counties). Middle order left-hand batsman, leg break and googly bowler, brilliant short leg. *Team* Lancashire (1939–57, 288 matches). *Tours* MCC to Australia and New Zealand 1946/7, to West Indies 1947/8; Commonwealth to India and Ceylon 1950/51. *Tests* England (1946–55, 18 matches).
Career batting
365–554–66–17968–192–36.81–27–*ct* 419
Bowling 10262–339–30.27–11–1–6/21
Test batting
18–31–2–606–60–20.89–0–*ct* 31
Bowling 354–3–118.00–0–0–1/38

He hit 1,000 runs in a season 10 times plus once overseas (best 1,912, av 45.52, in 1952). He played for Staffordshire 1934 to 1938 and returned in 1958. His first-class debut was for Minor Counties in 1938 and his final first-class match was for MCC in 1964.

Ikin, Michael John
Cricketer. *b:* 31.12.1946, Bignall End, Staffs. Son of J. T. (Lancashire). Middle order left-hand batsman, off break bowler. *Team* Minor Counties (1972–79).
Career batting
2–3–0–40–31–13.33–0–*ct* 0
Bowling 112–0

His County cricket was for Staffordshire commencing 1967.

Ikram Elahi
Amateur. *b:* 3.3.1933, Quetta, India. Hard-hitting lower order right-hand batsman, right-arm fast medium bowler. *Teams* Sind (1953/4); East Pakistan (1954/5); Karachi (1954/5 to 1961/2); PWD (1969/70). *Tours* Pakistan to England 1954, to West Indies 1957/8.
Career batting
47–59–5–1058–73–19.59–0–*ct* 19
Bowling 2403–107–23.39–4–0–6/25

He achieved little on his 1954 tour to England and did not appear in the Tests. His first-class debut was for Rest of Pakistan in 1952/3

Iles, John Henry
Amateur. *b:* 17.9.1871, Bristol. *d:* 29.5.1951, Birchington, Kent. Lower order batsman, bowler. *Team* Gloucestershire (1890–91, 3 matches).
Career batting
3–6–1–13–7–2.60–0–*ct* 3
Bowling 152–3–50.66–0–0–3/79

Illingworth, Edward Arnold
Professional. *b:* 1896, Dewsbury, Yorkshire. *d:* 2.4.1924, Barnsley, Yorkshire. Lower order left-hand batsman, slow left-arm bowler. *Team* Warwickshire (1920, 6 matches).
Career batting
6–12–3–17–8*–1.88–0–*ct* 2
Bowling 312–8–39.00–0–0–2/18

Illingworth, Nigel John Bartle
Cricketer. *b:* 23.11.1960, Chesterfield, Derby-

shire. Lower order right-hand batsman, right-arm medium pace bowler. *Sch* Denstone. *Team* Nottinghamshire (1981–83, 15 matches).
Career batting
15–20–5–207–49–13.80–0–*ct* 8
Bowling 694–16–43.37–1–0–5/89

Illingworth, Raymond, CBE
Professional. *b:* 8.6.1932, Pudsey, Yorkshire. Solid middle order right-hand batsman, off break bowler. *Teams* Yorkshire (1951–83, 496 matches); Leicestershire (1969–78, 176 matches). *Tours* MCC to West Indies 1959/60, to Australia and New Zealand 1962/3, 1970/1; Cavaliers to South Africa 1960/1. *Tests* England (1958–73, 61 matches).
Career batting
787–1073–213–24134–162–28.06–22–*ct* 446
Bowling 42023–2072–20.28–104–11–9/42
Test batting
61–90–11–1836–113–23.24–2–*ct* 45
Bowling 3807–122–31.20–3–0–6/29

One of the most complete cricketers of his generation, his career is divided into three parts. From 1951 to 1968 he was a Yorkshire and England all rounder who completed the 'double' six times – 1957, 1959 to 1962 and 1964. He appeared with success in 29 Tests, but only had a modest record on his major tour to Australia in 1962/3.

A difference between himself and the Yorkshire Club at the end of 1968 led to his appointment as captain of Leicestershire for 1969 and an injury to M.C. Cowdrey meant that he also captained England in the six Tests of 1969. In 1970 he continued to lead England in the series against the Rest of the World and the following winter was captain of the MCC team to Australia and New Zealand. In all he captained his country in 31 Tests ending in 1973. In 1975 he took Leicestershire to the top of the County Championship – in his initial season with his new County he headed both batting and bowling averages, but latterly went in very low down the order and concentrated more on captaincy and bowling.

The third phase of his career began in 1979 when he retired from first-class cricket and took over as manager of Yorkshire. The internal differences within that County Club continued to grow and midway through 1982 he returned to first-class cricket as Yorkshire's captain, a role from which he resigned at the close of 1983.

In all he hit 1,000 runs in a season eight times (best 1,726, av 46.64, in 1959) and took 100 wickets ten times (best 131, av 14.36, in 1968). His best innings analysis was 9 for 42 for Yorkshire v Worcestershire at Worcester in 1957. He was awarded the CBE in the 1973 New Year's Honours list.

Illingworth, Richard Keith
Cricketer. *b:* 23.8.1963, Greengates, Bradford, Yorkshire. Lower order right-hand batsman, slow left-arm bowler. *Team* Worcestershire (1982–83, 36 matches).
Career batting
36–51–10–464–55–11.31–0–*ct* 12
Bowling 2641–66–40.01–1–0–5/26

Ilsley, Stanley Thomas
Professional. *b:* 18.6.1938, Marylebone, London. Left-arm bowler. *Team* MCC (1956).
Career batting
2–2–0–8–8–4.00–0–*ct* 0
Bowling 137–5–27.40–0–0–3/39

Imlay, Alan Durant
Amateur. *b:* 14.2.1885, Bristol. *d:* 3.7.1959, Brent Knoll, Somerset. Lower order right-hand batsman, wicket-keeper. *Sch* Clifton. *Teams* Gloucestershire (1905–11, 7 matches); Cambridge U (1906–07, blue 1907).
Career batting
12–21–0–166–26–7.90–0–*ct* 16–*st* 1

Imran Khan Niazi
Cricketer. *b:* 25.11.1952, Lahore, Pakistan. Cousin of Majid Jahangir Khan (Pakistan) and Javed Burki (Pakistan). Attacking middle order right-hand batsman, right-arm fast bowler, excellent outfield. *Sch* Worcester RGS. *Teams* Lahore (1969/70 to 1970/1); Worcestershire (1971–76, 42 matches); Oxford U (1973–75, blue all three years); PIA (1975/6 to 1980/1); Sussex (1977–83, 102 matches). *Tours* Pakistan to England 1971, 1974, 1982, to Sri Lanka 1975/6, to Australia and West Indies 1976/7, to New Zealand and Australia 1978/9, to India 1979/80, to Australia 1981/2. *Tests* Pakistan (1971 to 1982/3, 49 matches).
Career batting
286–445–69–13105–170–34.85–22–*ct* 93
Bowling 21999–995–22.10–56–11–8/58
Test batting
49–73–11–1853–123–29.88–2–*ct* 16
Bowling 5318–232–22.92–16–4–8/58

His first tour to England was in 1971, when he played in one Test at the age of 18. In 1974 he joined the touring team only after coming down from Oxford and achieved little, though appearing in the three Tests. In 1982 he captained the tourists and had an outstanding series, hitting 212 runs, av 53.00, and taking 21 wickets, av 18.57. In all he has hit 1,000 runs in a season in England four times (best 1,339, av 41.84, in 1978).

His best bowling in a season in England was 1979 with 73 wickets, av 14.94. He is, at the present time, Pakistan's leading all-round cricketer.

Imtiaz Ahmed
Amateur. *b:* 5.1.1928, Lahore, India. Sound opening right-hand batsman, wicket-keeper. *Teams* Northern India (1944/5 to 1946/7); Punjab (1947/8 to 1948/9); Services (1953/4 to 1964/5); PAF (1969/70 to 1972/3). *Tours* Pakistan to England 1954, 1962, to India 1952/3, 1960/1, to Ceylon 1948/9, 1964/5, to West Indies 1957/8; Services to India and Ceylon 1954/5. *Tests* Pakistan (1952/3 to 1962, 41 matches).
Career batting
179–309–32–10323–300*–37.26–22–*ct* 314–*st* 77
Bowling 166–4–41.50–0–0–2/12
Test batting
41–72–1–2079–209–29.28–3–*ct* 77–*st* 16
Bowling 0–0
The principal Pakistan wicket-keeper during the country's first years in Test cricket, he appeared in every one of the initial 39 Tests involving Pakistan. He was successful on both tours to England, hitting 1,105 runs, av 29.07, in 1954 and 1,140 runs, av 30.00, in 1962 in addition to being a splendid wicket-keeper. He captained Pakistan in four Tests, including three v England in 1961/2. His final first-class match was for NWFP XI in 1973/4. His highest score was 300* for Prime Minister's XI v Commonwealth at Bombay in 1950/1. He hit 1,142 runs, av 49.65, in Pakistan in 1961/2.

Ince, Harry Wakefield
Amateur. *b:* 7.4.1893, Bridgetown, Barbados. *d:* 11.5.1978, Barbados. Middle order left-hand batsman. *Team* Barbados (1912/3 to 1929/30). *Tour* West Indies to England 1923.
Career batting
35–52–6–1352–167–29.39–3–*ct* 13
Bowling 242–5–48.40–0–0–3/34

Inchmore, John Darling
Cricketer. *b:* 22.2.1949, Ashington, Northumberland. Lower order right-hand batsman, right-arm fast medium bowler. *Teams* Worcestershire (1973–83, 167 matches); Northern Transvaal (1976/7).
Career batting
169–205–41–2687–113–16.38–1–*ct* 55
Bowling 12007–420–28.58–18–1–8/58

Indrajitsinhji, Kumar Shri Madhavsinhji Jadeja
Amateur. *b:* 15.6.1937, Jamnagar, India. Lower order right-hand batsman, wicket-keeper. *Teams* Saurashtra (1954/5 to 1971/2); Delhi (1958/9 to 1960/1); L. C. Steven's XI (1960). *Tour* India to Australia and New Zealand 1967/8. *Tests* India (1964/5 to 1969/70, 4 matches).
Career batting
90–146–8–3694–124–26.76–5–*ct* 134–*st* 80
Bowling 61–0
Test batting
4–7–1–51–23–8.50–0–*ct* 6–*st* 3
His only first-class match in England was for L. C. Steven's XI in 1960. His final first class match was for Ufoam in India in 1972/3.

Inge, William Walter
Amateur. *b:* 29.11.1907, Holmwood, Surrey. Middle/lower order right-hand batsman, wicket-keeper. *Sch* Winchester. *Teams* Oxford U (1930); Minor Counties (1930).
Career batting
3–4–2–20–9*–10.00–0–*ct* 2–*st* 4
His County cricket was for Oxfordshire.

Ingham, Peter Geoffrey
Cricketer. *b:* 28.9.1956, Sheffield, Yorkshire. Middle order right-hand batsman, right-arm medium pace bowler. *Team* Yorkshire (1979–81, 8 matches).
Career batting
8–14–0–290–64–20.71–0–*ct* 0

Ingle, Reginald Addington
Amateur. *b:* 5.11.1903, Bodmin, Cornwall. Middle order right-hand batsman. *Sch* Oundle. *Teams* Somerset (1923–39, 309 matches); Cambridge U (1924–25)
Career batting
325–543–19–9829–119*–18.75–10–*ct* 129
Bowling 26–0
He hit 1,000 runs in a season twice (best 1,083, av 24.06, in 1932). From 1932 to 1937 he captained Somerset.

Ingleby, Charles Willis
Professional. *b:* 1870, Leeds, Yorkshire. *d:* 15.11.1939, Eccleshill, Bradford. Middle order batsman, useful bowler. *Team* Lancashire (1899, 1 match).
Career batting
1–2–1–40–29–40.00–0–*ct* 0
Bowling 17–0
He also played for Cumberland.

Ingleby-Mackenzie, Alexander Colin David
Amateur. *b:* 15.9.1933, Dartmouth, Devon. Forcing middle order left-hand batsman, off break bowler, occasional wicket-keeper. *Sch* Eton. *Team* Hampshire (1951–65, 309 matches). *Tours* Swanton to West Indies 1955/6, to India 1963/4;

Norfolk to Jamaica 1956/7, Cavaliers to South Africa 1959/60, 1962/3, to Jamaica 1963/4, to West Indies 1964/5.
Career batting
343–574–64–12421–132*–24.35–11–*ct* 205–*st* 1
Bowling 35–0
He hit 1,000 runs in a season five times (best 1,613, av 25.68, in 1959). From 1958 to 1965 he captained Hampshire.

Inglis, Alfred Markham
Amateur. *b:* 24.9.1857, Rugby. *d:* 17.6.1919, Westerham, Kent. Brother of J. F. (Kent), uncle of C. T. (Essex), G. (Worcs), P. (Essex), and H. Ashton (Essex). Hard-hitting middle order right-hand batsman, fine field. *Sch* Rugby. *Team* Kent (1887, 1 match).
Career batting
2–4–0–35–12–8.75–0–*ct* 0
He did not appear in any first-class matches whilst at Oxford U. His first-class debut was for MCC in 1885.

Inglis, John Frederic
Amateur. *b:* 16.7.1853, Peshawar, India. *d:* 27.2.1923, Littleham, Devon. Brother of A. M. (Kent), uncle of C. T. (Essex), G. (Worcs), P. (Essex), and H. Ashton (Essex). Middle order batsman. *Sch* Charterhouse. *Team* Kent (1883, 1 match).
Career batting
1–1–0–19–19–19.00–0–*ct* 0

Inglis, Russell
Cricketer. *b:* 13.6.1936, Crook Hall, Co Durham. *d:* 28.4.1982, Chester-le-Street, Co Durham. Sound right-hand batsman, right-arm medium pace bowler. *Team* Minor Counties (1965–69).
Career batting
3–6–1–91–43–18.20–0–*ct* 5
Bowling 24–2–12.00–0–0–2/2
His County cricket was for Durham from 1956 to 1973.

Ingram, Edward
Amateur. *b:* 14.8.1910, Dublin, Ireland. *d:* 13.3.1973, Basingstoke, Hants. Lower order right-hand batsman, right-arm medium/leg break bowler. *Teams* Ireland (1928–53); Middlesex (1938–49, 12 matches).
Career batting
31–55–4–766–64–15.01–0–*ct* 14
Bowling 1896–79–24.00–1–0–5/48

Ingram, Isaac
Professional. *b:* 14.5.1855, Leigh, Tonbridge, Kent. *d:* 19.11.1947, Leigh, Tonbridge, Kent. Lower order right-hand batsman, wicket-keeper. *Team* Kent (1878–79, 12 matches).
Career batting
12–20–1–112–25–5.89–0–*ct* 8–*st* 7

Ingram, John Barkly
Amateur. *b:* 1857. *d:* 23.7.1924, Dewsbury, Yorkshire. Middle order batsman. *Team* England XI (1878).
Career batting
1–1–0–7–7–7.00–0–*ct* 0

Ingram, Dr Peter Robert
Amateur. *b:* 1869. *d:* 8.12.1955, Perranport, Cornwall. Lower order left-hand batsman, left-arm bowler. *Team* Somerset (1910, 2 matches).
Career batting
2–4–0–16–7–4.00–0–*ct* 1
Bowling 69–0

Inman, Clive Clay
Professional. *b:* 29.1.1936, Colombo, Ceylon. Middle order left-hand batsman, off break bowler. *Teams* Ceylon (1956/7 to 1966/7); Leicestershire (1961–71, 242 matches). *Tours* Ceylon to Pakistan 1966/7, to India 1957/8.
Career batting
255–422–42–13112–178–34.50–21–*ct* 108
Bowling 89–1–89.00–0–0–1/30
He hit 1,000 runs in a season eight times (best 1,735, av 36.91, in 1968). He hit 51 in eight minutes for Leics v Notts at Trent Bridge in 1965, the fastest fifty in first-class cricket.

Innes, Andrew David
Amateur. *b:* 3.5.1905, Glasgow, Scotland. *d:* 23.2.1968, Milngavie, Dunbartonshire, Scotland. Right-hand batsman, off break bowler. *Team* Scotland (1925–34).
Career batting
6–11–1–164–48–16.40–0–*ct* 6
Bowling 26–1–26.00–0–0–1/12

Inniss, Sir Clifford de Lisle
Amateur. *b:* 26.10.1910, Barbados. Middle order right-hand batsman. *Team* Barbados (1927/8 to 1938/9). *Tour* West Indies in England 1933.
Career batting
10–18–1–474–80–27.88–0–*ct* 4
Bowling 50–1–50.00–0–0–1/17
An undergraduate at Oxford he appeared in the Seniors' Match of 1933 and then assisted the West Indian tourists in two first-class matches. He played for Oxfordshire.

Inns, John Herbert
Professional. *b:* 30.3.1876, Writtle, Essex. *d:* 14.6.1905, Writtle, Essex. Lower order batsman, wicket-keeper. *Team* Essex (1898–1904, 10 matches).

Career batting
10–14–3–73–28–6.63–*ct* 8
Bowling 15–0

Insole, Douglas John, CBE
Amateur. *b:* 18.4.1926, Clapton, London. Sound middle order right-hand batsman, right-arm medium pace bowler, excellent all-round fielder, occasional wicket-keeper. *Teams* Cambridge U (1947–49, blue all three years); Essex (1947–63, 345 matches). *Tours* MCC to South Africa 1956/7; Manager of England to Australia 1978/9, 1982/3. *Tests* England (1950–57, 9 matches).
Career batting
450–743–72–25241–219*–37.61–54–*ct* 366–*st* 6
Bowling 4680–138–33.95–1–0–5/22
Test batting
9–17–2–408–110*–27.20–1–*ct* 8

He hit 1,000 runs in a season 13 times, going on to 2,000 three times (best 2,427, av 42.57, in 1955). His only double century is 219* for Essex v Yorkshire at Colchester in 1949. He captained Essex 1950 to 1960. He was appointed a Test Selector in 1959 and was Chairman of the TCCB 1975 to 1978. He was awarded the CBE for his services to cricket. A noted soccer player, he won his blue and also played for Southend United and Corinthian Casuals, appearing in the FA Amateur Cup Final in 1955/6.

Intikhab Alam Khan
Amateur. *b:* 28.12.1941, Hoshiarpur, India. Middle order right-hand batsman, leg break and googly bowler. *Teams* Karachi (1957/8 to 1970/1); PIA (1960/1 to 1974/5); PWD (1967/8 to 1969/70); Surrey (1969–81, 232 matches); Sind (1973/4); Punjab (1975/6). *Tours* Pakistan to India 1960/1, to England 1962, 1967, 1971, 1974, to Ceylon 1964, to Australia and New Zealand 1964/5, 1972/3, to Australia and West Indies 1976/7; Pakistan Eaglets to England 1963; PIA to East Africa 1964; Rest of World to Australia 1971/2. *Tests* Pakistan (1959/60 to 1976/7, 47 matches).
Career batting
489–725–78–14331–182–22.14–9–*ct* 228
Bowling 43472–1571–27.67–85–13–8/54
Test batting
47–77–10–1493–138–22.28–1–*ct* 20
Bowling 4494–125–35.95–5–2–7/52

He took 104 wickets, av 28.36, in 1971. He led Pakistan in 17 Tests and his most successful tour of England was as captain in 1974; he also captained the 1971 tour to England. He was appointed manager of Pakistan in 1982.

His last first-class match in Pakistan was for Pakistan in 1976/7 and last first-class match in England for D.B. Close's XI in 1982.

Intin, John Wilfred
Amateur. *b:* 8.7.1886, Hull, Yorkshire. *d:* 11.4.1970, Grangemouth, Stirlingshire, Scotland. Right-hand batsman, right-arm medium pace bowler. *Team* Scotland (1920).
Career batting
1–1–0–14–14–14.00–0–*ct* 0
Bowling 42–2–21.00–0–0–2/25

Inverarity, Robert John
Cricketer. *b:* 31.1.1944, Perth, West Australia. Son of Mervyn (Western Australia). Opening right-hand batsman, slow left-arm bowler, good slip. *Teams* Western Australia (1962/3 to 1978/9, 119 matches); South Australia (1979/80 to 1982/3, 33 matches). *Tours* Australia to England 1968, 1972, to New Zealand 1969/70. *Tests* Australia (1968–72, 6 matches).
Career batting
203–346–42–10995–187–36.16–26–*ct* 237
Bowling 4873–160–30.45–4–0–5/28
Test batting
6–11–1–174–56–17.40–0–*ct* 4
Bowling 93–4–23.25–0–0–3/26

Although he appeared in some Tests on both his tours to England, his first-class batting records were quite modest. On the 1968 tour he bowled only 8 overs, but in 1972 his spin bowling was used much more often.

Iqbal Qasim, Mohammad
Cricketer. *b:* 6.8.1953, Karachi, Pakistan. Lower order left-hand batsman, slow left-arm bowler, good close field. *Teams* Karachi (1971/2); National Bank (1972/3 to 1982/3); Sind (1972/3). *Tours* Pakistan to Australia and West Indies 1976/7, to England 1978, 1982, to Australia and New Zealand 1978/9, to India 1979/80, to Australia 1981/2. *Tests* Pakistan (1976/7 to 1982/3, 36 matches).
Career batting
135–133–35–1275–61–13.01–0–*ct* 102
Bowling 11718–528–22.19–34–8–9/80
Test batting
36–41–12–269–56–9.27–0–*ct* 27
Bowling 3426–115–29.79–4–2–7/49

Although he appeared in three Tests on the 1978 tour to England his record was very moderate. On the 1982 visit he did not play in the Tests.

Iredale, Francis Adams
Amateur. *b:* 19.6.1867, Surry Hills, New South Wales, Australia. *d:* 15.4.1926, North Sydney, New South Wales, Australia. Nephew of F.

Adams (NSW). Sound opening right-hand batsman, good deep field. *Team* New South Wales (1888/9 to 1901/2, 56 matches). *Tours* Australia to England 1896, 1899, to North America 1896. *Tests* Australia (1894/5 to 1899, 14 matches).
Career batting
133–214–12–6794–196–33.63–12–*ct* 111
Bowling 211–6–35.16–0–0–3/1
Test batting
14–23–1–807–140–36.68–2–*ct* 16
Bowling 3–0

After a poor start, he batted well during the 1896 tour to England and hit 1,328 runs, av 27.66, including a century in the Old Trafford Test. In 1899 he did not fair quite so well – 1,039 runs, av 29.68 – and was left out of two Tests.

Ireland, Arthur
Amateur. *b:* 1850, Brighton, Sussex. *d:* 1895, London. *Team* MCC (1881).
Career batting
1–1–0–1–1–1.00–0–*ct* 1

Ireland, Frederick Schomberg
Amateur. *b:* 6.4.1860, Port Louis, Mauritius. *d:* 16.3.1937, Mentone, France. Middle order right-hand batsman, round-arm fast right-hand bowler, close field. *Team* Kent (1878–87, 4 matches).
Career batting
4–8–1–125–87–17.85–0–*ct* 1
Bowling 44–3–14.66–0–0–3/27

Owing to his profession, as a solicitor, his appearances in first-class cricket were limited. He also played for Devon. He was also a good golfer.

Ireland, John Frederick
Amateur. *b:* 12.8.1888, Port Louis, Mauritius. *d:* 21.10.1970, Uckfield, Sussex. Middle order right-hand batsman, right-arm medium pace bowler. *Sch* Marlborough. *Team* Cambridge U (1908–11, blue all four years).
Career batting
27–50–3–1355–123–28.82–3–*ct* 21
Bowling 787–37–21.27–2–0–5/25

A brilliant schoolboy batsman, he scarcely bowled until his final year at Cambridge, when he performed the hat-trick against Oxford. His County cricket was for Suffolk. His final first-class match was for MCC in 1912. He also represented Cambridge at golf and hockey.

Iremonger, Albert
Professional. *b:* 15.6.1884, Wilford, Notts. *d:* 9.3.1958, Nottingham. Brother of James (Notts). Lower order right-hand batsman, right-arm medium pace bowler. *Team* Nottinghamshire (1906–10, 14 matches).
Career batting
14–19–3–261–60*–16.31–0–*ct* 17
Bowling 296–10–29.60–1–0–5/83

A noted goalkeeper, he appeared for Notts County from 1905 to 1926, and for Lincoln City in 1926/7.

Iremonger, James
Professional. *b:* 5.3.1876, Norton, Yorkshire. *d:* 25.3.1956, West Bridgford, Notts. Brother of Albert (Notts). Opening right-hand batsman, right-arm medium pace bowler. *Team* Nottinghamshire (1899–1914, 315 matches). *Tour* MCC to Australia 1911/12.
Career batting
334–534–60–16622–272–35.06–31–*ct* 191
Bowling 14224–619–22.97–35–8–8/21

He hit 1,000 runs in a season nine times (best 1,983, av 60.09, in 1904). All his four double centuries were for Notts, the highest being 272 v Kent at Trent Bridge in 1904. He exceeded 100 wickets in a season once : 101, av 26.10, in 1911. He was Notts CCC coach from 1921 to 1938. An excellent soccer player, he appeared as full back for Nottm Forest from 1895 to 1909 and for England.

Irish, Arthur Frank
Professional. *b:* 23.11.1918, Dudley, Worcs. Middle order right-hand batsman, right-arm medium pace bowler. *Team* Somerset (1950, 16 matches).
Career batting
16–29–4–629–76–25.16–0–*ct* 5
Bowling 206–3–68.66–0–0–2/5

He also played for Devon.

Irvin, Rev Arthur John Edward
Amateur. *b:* 10.3.1848, Hackness, Scarborough, Yorkshire. *d:* 22.7.1945, Basingstoke, Hants. Lower order right-hand batsman, wicket-keeper. *Sch* Rossall. *Team* Oxford U (1868–71).
Career batting
2–3–1–18–12–9.00–0–*ct* 4–*st* 1

Irvine, Brian Lee
Cricketer. *b:* 9.3.1944, Durban, South Africa. Middle order left-hand batsman, right-arm medium pace bowler, wicket-keeper. *Teams* Essex (1968–69, 54 matches); Natal (1965/6 to 1968/9); Transvaal (1969/70 to 1976/7). *Tests* South Africa (1969/70, 4 matches).
Career batting
157–271–26–9919–193–40.48–21–*ct* 240–*st* 7
Bowling 142–1–142.00–0–0–1/39
Test batting
4–7–0–353–102–50.42–1–*ct* 2

He scored over 1,000 runs in both his seasons

in English first-class cricket (best 1,439, av 32.70, in 1968). His first class debut was for a Western Province Invitation XI in 1962/3.

Irvine, Leonard George
Amateur. *b:* 11.1.1906, Bombay, India. *d:* 27.4.1973, Canterbury, Kent. Lower order right-hand batsman, slow leg break bowler. *Sch* Taunton. *Teams* Cambridge U (1926–28, blue 1926–27); Kent (1927, 1 match).
Career batting
28–35–16–154–14*–8.10–0–*ct* 13
Bowling 2287–98–23.33–7–2–7/79

Irwin, Philip Hastings
Amateur. *b:* 1884, Chorlton, Lancashire. *d:* 12.1.1958, St Peter Port, Guernsey. Opening right-hand batsman. *Sch* Forest. *Team* Royal Navy (1914–19).
Career batting
4–8–0–207–80–25.87–0–*ct* 0
His County cricket was for Cornwall. His final first-class match was for MCC in 1924.

Isaac, Arthur Whitmore
Amateur. *b:* 4.10.1873, Powick, Worcs. *d:* 7.7.1916, Contalmaison, France. He was killed in action. Brother of J. E. V. (Worcs), father of H. W. (Worcs). Middle order right-hand batsman, excellent field. *Sch* Harrow. *Team* Worcestershire (1899–1911, 52 matches).
Career batting
53–89–5–1155–60–13.75–0–*ct* 10
He did not play in first-class cricket whilst at Oxford U. His final first-class match was for H. K. Foster's XII in 1913.

Isaac, Herbert Whitmore
Amateur. *b:* 11.12.1899, Worcester. *d:* 26.4.1962, Chisekesi, Northern Rhodesia. Son of A. W. (Worcs), nephew of J. E. V. (Worcs). Lower order batsman, bowler. *Sch* Harrow. *Team* Worcestershire (1919, 3 matches).
Career batting
3–3–0–32–27–10.66–0–*ct* 0
Bowling 22–0

Isaac, John Edmund Valentine
Amateur. *b:* 14.2.1880, Upton, Worcs. *d:* 9.5.1915, Rouge Bancs, Armentieres, France. He was killed in action. Brother of A. W. (Worcs), uncle of H. W. (Worcs). Middle order right-hand batsman. *Sch* Harrow. *Teams* Worcestershire (1907, 4 matches); Orange Free State (1906/07).
Career batting
9–15–1–121–34*–8.64–0–*ct* 1
Bowling 0–0

He also played for Northumberland. His first-class debut was for the Army in South Africa in 1905/06. A well known gentleman jockey, he rode the winner of the 1911 Cairo Grand National.

Isherwood, F.
Professional. Middle order batsman. *Team* Lancashire (1881, 1 match).
Career batting
1–1–0–0–0–0.00–0–*ct* 0

Isherwood, Francis William Ramsbottom
Amateur. *b:* 16.10.1852. *d:* 30.4.1888, Southsea, Hants. Middle/lower order right-hand batsman, right-hand fast medium round-arm bowler, good field. *Sch* Rugby. *Team* Oxford U (1872, blue).
Career batting
5–8–2–71–19*–11.83–0–*ct* 1
Bowling 221–7–31.57–0–0–4/52
He played rugby for England.

Isherwood, Lionel Charles Ramsbottom
Amateur. *b:* 13.4.1891, Portsmouth, Hants. *d:* 30.9.1970, Merrow, Surrey. Middle order right-hand batsman, right-arm medium pace bowler. *Sch* Eton. *Teams* Hampshire (1919–23. 26 matches); Sussex (1925–27, 28 matches). *Tour* MCC to Argentine (1926/7).
Career batting
60–101–8–1529–75*–16.44–0–*ct* 25
Bowling 24–1–24.00–0–0–1/16
He also played for Buckinghamshire.

Isles, Derek
Cricketer. *b:* 14.10.1943, Bradford, Yorkshire. Lower order batsman, wicket-keeper. *Team* Worcestershire (1967, 1 match).
Career batting
1–2–2–21–17*–no av–0–*ct* 1–*st* 1

Ives, George Cecil
Amateur. *b:* 1867. *d:* 4.6.1950, Hampstead, London. Useful batsman. *Team* MCC (1902).
Career batting
1–2–0–9–7–4.50–0–*ct* 0
He was the adopted son of The Hon Mrs Emma Ives.

Ivey, Alfred Michael
Amateur. *b:* 11.7.1928, Leeds, Yorkshire. Opening right-hand batsman, right-arm medium pace bowler. *Sch* Leeds Grammar School. *Team* Oxford U (1949–51).
Career batting
7–12–0–220–40–18.33–0–*ct* 11
Bowling 160–2–80.00–0–0–1/7

Izzard, Wilfred Cyril
Amateur. *b:* 25.2.1892, Northampton. *d:* 15.9.1977, Northampton. Opening right-hand batsman. *Team* Northants (1919–20, 12 matches).
Career batting
12–20–0–206–51–10.30–0–*ct* 8

Jackman, Frederick
Professional. *b:* 15.5.1841, Fareham, Hants. *d:* 1891, Catherington, Hants. Middle/lower order right-hand batsman, right-hand fast round-arm bowler, slip field. *Team* Hampshire (1875–77, 2 matches).
Career batting
2–4–2–26–16–13.00–0–*ct* 0
Bowling 42–1–42.00–0–0–1/21

Jackman, Robin David
Cricketer. *b:* 13.8.1945, Simla, India. Lower order right-hand batsman, right-arm fast medium bowler. *Sch* St. Edmund's, Canterbury. *Teams* Surrey (1964–82, 338 matches); Western Province (1971/2); Rhodesia (1972/3 to 1979/80). *Tours* England to West Indies 1980/1, to Australia 1982/3; Robins to South Africa 1972/3. *Tests* England (1980/1 to 1982, 4 matches).
Career batting
399–478–157–5681–92*–17.69–0–*ct* 177
Bowling 31978–1402–22.80–67–8–8/40
Test batting
4–6–0–42–17–7.00–0–*ct* 0
Bowling 445–14–31.78–0–0–4/110
He took 121 wickets, av 15.40, in 1980. His inclusion in the England team to tour West Indies in 1980/1 caused the abandonment of the Georgetown Test, because the Guyanan Government objected to Jackman's previous connections with South Africa.

Jackson, Archibald (Alexander)
Amateur. *b:* 5.9.1909, Rutherglen, Scotland. *d:* 16.2.1933, Brisbane, Australia, of tuberculosis. Brilliant middle order right-hand batsman, good deep field. *Team* New South Wales (1926/7 to 1930/1, 28 matches). *Tours* Australia to New Zealand 1927/8, to England 1930. *Tests* Australia (1928/9 to 1930/1, 8 matches).
Career batting
70–107–11–4383–182–45.65–11–*ct* 26
Bowling 49–0
Test batting
8–11–1–474–164–47.40–1–*ct* 7
On his single tour to England he hit 1,097 runs, av 34.28. He had arrived in England with a brilliant reputation as a batsman, but failed to live up to it. His final years were marred by ill-health.

Jackson, Albert Brian
Professional. *b:* 21.8.1933, Kettleshulme, Cheshire. Lower order right-hand batsman, right-arm fast medium bowler. *Team* Derbyshire (1963–68, 148 matches).
Career batting
149–160–83–647–27–8.40–0–*ct* 29
Bowling 8656–457–18.94–17–4–8/18
He took 120 wickets, av 12.42, in 1965. He also played for Cheshire commencing 1956.

Jackson, Sir Anthony Henry Mather
(also known as Mather-Jackson)
Amateur. *b:* 9.11.1899, London. *d:* 11.10.1983, Kirklington, Notts. Cousin of G. L. (Derbyshire) and G. R. (Derbyshire). Middle order right-hand batsman, right-arm fast medium bowler. *Sch* Harrow. *Team* Derbyshire (1920–27, 64 matches).
Career batting
64–96–15–1199–75–14.80–0–*ct* 15
Bowling 1311–44–29.79–1–0–5/84

Jackson, Arnold Kenneth
Amateur. *b:* 21.6.1903, Edgbaston, Birmingham. *d:* 31.5.1971, Halstenbeck, West Germany. Lower order right-hand batsman, right-arm fast medium bowler. *Team* Warwickshire (1928–31, 2 matches).
Career batting
2–3–2–5–3*–5.00–0–*ct* 0
Bowling 73–0
He was on the Warwickshire CCC Committee from 1959 to his death.

Jackson, Alfred Louis Stewart
Amateur. *b:* 28.2.1904, Vina del Mar, Chile. *d:* 23.7.1982, Valparaiso, Chile. Brother of J. A. S. (Somerset). Opening right-hand batsman, wicket-keeper. *Sch* Cheltenham. *Team* Argentina (1937/8). *Tour* South Americans to England 1932.
Career batting
8–15–1–349–78–28.22–0–*ct* 3–*st* 1
He headed the batting averages, for all matches, on the 1932 tour.

Jackson, Charles Henry
Amateur. *b:* 6.6.1839, Chatham, Kent. Middle order batsman. *Team* Gentlemen of Kent (1865).
Career batting
1–2–1–10–6–10.00–0–*ct* 0

Jackson, Edward
Amateur. *b:* 17.3.1849, Lancaster. Brother of J. (Lancashire). Tail end right-hand batsman, wicket-keeper. *Team* Lancashire (1871–85, 15 matches).
Career batting
15–23–4–105–11–5.52–0–*ct* 21–*st* 14

Jackson, Edward John Wycliffe
Cricketer. *b:* 26.3.1955, Singapore. Middle order right-hand batsman, left-arm medium fast bowler. *Sch* Winchester. *Team* Cambridge U (1974–76, blue all three years).
Career batting
28–51–6–762–63–16.93–0–*ct* 4
Bowling 2215–43–51.51–1–1–7/98

Jackson, Rt Hon Sir Frank Stanley
(also known as Francis Stanley Jackson)
Amateur. *b:* 21.11.1870, Chapel Allerton, Leeds, Yorkshire. *d:* 9.3.1947, Hyde Park Hotel, Knightsbridge, London. Stylish middle order right-hand batsman, right-arm fast medium bowler, good field. *Sch* Harrow. *Teams* Cambridge U (1890–93, blue all four years); Yorkshire (1890–1907, 207 matches). *Tour* Hawke to India 1892/3. *Tests* England (1893–1905, 20 matches).
Career batting
309–505–35–15901–160–33.83–31–*ct* 197
Bowling 15767–774–20.37–42–6–8/54
Test batting
20–33–4–1415–144*–48.79–5–*ct* 10
Bowling 799–24–33.29–1–0–5/52

The epitome of the 'Golden Age' of cricket – the Edwardian era – Jackson captained England in the 1905 series of Tests v Australia, which England won two matches to nil; he also played a major part in the 1902 series, but pressure of business prevented him from going on tour to Australia.

At his best he was a brilliant all rounder, though he only achieved the 'double' once – in 1898 – this lack of statistical success again being due to the fact that he rarely managed to play a full season of first-class cricket in England.

In all he hit 1,000 runs in a season ten times, with his best year being 1899: 1,847 runs, av 45.04. He took 104 wickets, av 15.67, in 1898.

Although he had the unusual distinction of captaining Cambridge for two seasons and going on to lead England in five Tests, he did not captain his County.

He saw active service in the Boer War which meant his absence for two years from County cricket and later became a well-known politician, being MP for the Howdenshire Division of Yorkshire from 1915 to 1926, Financial Secretary to the War Office in 1922 and Chairman of the Unionist Party in 1923. Later he was appointed Governor of Bengal, where he narrowly escaped assassination.

Jackson, Finlay William
Amateur. *b:* 21.11.1901, Belfast, Ireland. *d:* 13.3.1941, Belfast, Ireland. Brother of Harold (Ireland). Right-hand batsman, leg break bowler. *Team* Ireland (1924–25).
Career batting
3–5–1–154–71–38.50–0–*ct* 0

He was an Irish rugby international.

Jackson, Geoffrey Laird
Amateur. *b:* 10.1.1894, Birkenhead, Cheshire. *d:* 9.4.1917, Faimpoux, Arras, Belgium. Brother of G. R. (Derbyshire), cousin of A. H. M. (Derbyshire). Middle order right-hand batsman, right-arm medium pace bowler, good cover-point. *Sch* Harrow. *Teams* Derbyshire (1912–14, 4 matches); Oxford U (1914).
Career batting
7–12–0–150–50–12.50–0–*ct* 4
Bowling 238–10–23.80–0–0–3/52

Jackson, Guy Rolfe
Amateur. *b:* 23.6.1896, Ankerbold, Tupton, Derbyshire. *d:* 21.2.1966, Chesterfield, Derbyshire. Brother of G. L. (Derbyshire), cousin of A. H. M. (Derbyshire). Middle order right-hand batsman. *Sch* Harrow. *Team* Derbyshire (1919–36, 260 matches). *Tours* MCC to Argentine 1926/7; Selected to captain MCC to South Africa 1927/8, but forced to decline through ill health.
Career batting
280–468–22–10291–140–23.07–9–*ct* 110
Bowling 208–3–69.33–0–0–1/10

He hit 1,000 runs in a season four times (best 1,278, av 26.62, in 1925). From 1922 to 1930 he captained Derbyshire.

Jackson, Harold
Amateur. *b:* September 1888, Belfast. *d:* 17.12.1979, Belfast. Brother of F. W. (Ireland). Left-hand batsman. *Team* Ireland (1923).
Career batting
1–2–1–65–62*–65.00–0–*ct* 0
Bowling 35–1–35.00–0–0–1/35

Jackson, Herbert Leslie
Professional. *b:* 5.4.1921, Whitwell, Derbyshire. Lower order right-hand batsman, right-arm fast bowler. *Team* Derbyshire (1947–63, 394 matches). *Tour* Commonwealth to India 1950/1. *Tests* England (1949–61, 2 matches).
Career batting
418–489–153–2083–39*–6.19–0–*ct* 136
Bowling 30101–1733–17.36–115–20–9/17
Test batting
2–2–1–15–8–15.00–0–*ct* 1
Bowling 155–7–22.14–0–0–2/26
He took 100 wickets in a season 10 times (best 160, av 13.61, in 1960). His best bowling performance in an innings was 9/17 for Derbyshire v Cambridge U at Fenner's in 1959.

Jackson, J.
Amateur. Brother of Edward (Lancashire). *Team* Lancashire (1867, 1 match).
Career batting
1–2–0–6–3–3.00–0–*ct* 0

Jackson, John
Professional. *b:* 21.5.1833, Bungay, Suffolk. *d:* 4.11.1901, Brounlow Hill, Liverpool. Hard-hitting right-hand batsman, right-hand fast round-arm bowler. *Teams* Nottinghamshire (1855–66, 33 matches); Kent (1858, 2 matches as given man). *Tours* Parr to North America 1859 (not first-class), to Australia and New Zealand 1863/4.
Career batting
115–191–33–1993–100–12.61–1–*ct* 106
Bowling 7490–650+5–11.52–59–20–9/27
He took 100 wickets in a season twice (best 109, av 9.20, in 1860). For several seasons he was regarded as the leading fast bowler in England. His best bowling was 9/27 for Kent v England at Lord's in 1858. His final first-class match was for the AEE in 1867.

Jackson, John Alfred Stewart
Amateur. *b:* 27.12.1898, Valparaiso, Chile. *d:* 13.3.1958, Santiago, Chile. Brother of A. L. S. (South America). Middle order right-hand batsman, leg break bowler. *Sch* Cheltenham. *Teams* Cambridge U (1920); Somerset (1920, 14 matches).
Career batting
19–34–1–739–106–22.39–1–*ct* 1
Bowling 38–0

Jackson, John Frederick Cecil
Amateur. *b:* 1880, North Aylesford, Kent. *d:* 1968, Blakedown, Worcs. Middle order batsman. *Sch* Tonbridge. *Team* Worcestershire (1907, 1 match).
Career batting
1–2–0–6–6–3.00–0–*ct* 0

Jackson, Kenneth Leslie Tattersall
Amateur. *b:* 17.11.1913, Shanghai, China. *d:* 21.3.1982, Hinton St George, Somerset. Lower order right-hand batsman, right-arm fast medium bowler. *Sch* Rugby. *Team* Oxford U (1934–35, blue 1934).
Career batting
9–16–2–181–33–12.92–0–*ct* 4
Bowling 874–29–30.13–1–0–5/66
His County cricket was for Berkshire. A noted rugby footballer, he was capped for Scotland.

Jackson, Leonard
Professional. *b:* 8.4.1848, Norton Woodseats, Yorkshire. *d:* 21.3.1887, Sheffield, Yorkshire. Lower order right-hand batsman, right-hand fast round-arm bowler, close field. *Team* Derbyshire (1877–82, 5 matches).
Career batting
7–12–1–109–28–9.90–0–*ct* 4
Bowling 198–10–19.80–0–0–3/9
His debut was for the North in 1875.

Jackson, Lionel
Amateur. *b:* 12.9.1877, Epsom, Surrey. *d:* 13.6.1949, Dorking, Surrey. Wicket-keeper. *Sch* Dulwich. *Team* London County (1901).
Career batting
1–2–0–50–26–15.00–0–*ct* 0–*st* 3

Jackson, McIvor Tindall
Professional. *b:* 24.5.1880, Merton, Surrey. *d:* 15.6.1936, Southwark. Lower order left-hand batsman, left-arm medium pace bowler. *Team* Surrey (1903–07, 11 matches).
Career batting
11–17–8–21–9–2.33–0–*ct* 6
Bowling 660–33–20.00–3–0–7/96

Jackson, Paul Brian
Cricketer. *b:* 9.12.1959, Belfast, Ireland. Lower order right-hand batsman, wicket-keeper. *Team* Ireland (1981–83).
Career batting
3–4–1–96–46–32.00–0–*ct* 4–*st* 1

Jackson, Percy Frederick
Professional. *b:* 11.5.1911, Aberfeldy, Perthshire. Lower order right-hand batsman, right-arm medium pace off break bowler. *Team* Worcestershire (1929–50, 383 matches).
Career batting
385–549–208–2052–40–6.01–0–*ct* 194
Bowling 30501–1159–26.31–61–11–9/45
He took 100 wickets in a season four times

(best 125, av 23.70, in 1947). His best bowling was 9/45 for Worcs v Somerset at Dudley in 1935.

Jackson, Roger Frank
Cricketer. *b:* 5.1.1939, Woolwich, Kent. Tail end right-hand batsman, right-arm fast bowler. *Team* Oxford U (1962).
Career batting
2–3–2–8–5*–8.00–0–*ct* 0
Bowling 126–0

Jackson, Samuel Robinson
Amateur. *b:* 15.7.1859, Sheffield, Yorkshire. *d:* 19.7.1941, Leeds, Yorkshire. Middle order right-hand batsman, right-arm fast bowler, good deep field. *Team* Yorkshire (1891, 1 match).
Career batting
1–2–0–9–9–4.50–0–*ct* 0

Jackson, Victor Edward
Professional. *b:* 25.10.1916, Sydney, Australia. *d:* 30.1.1965, near Manildra, New South Wales, Australia. He was killed in a level crossing accident. Hard-hitting middle order right-hand batsman, right-arm medium pace off break bowler, slip field. *Teams* New South Wales (1936/7 to 1940/1, 20 matches); Leicestershire (1938–56, 322 matches). *Tour* Cahn to New Zealand 1938/9.
Career batting
354–605–53–15698–170–28.43–21–*ct* 253
Bowling 23874–965–24.73–43–7–8/43

He hit 1,000 runs in a season 11 times (best 1,582, av 29.29, in 1955); took 100 wickets in a season once : 112, av 21.71, in 1955, achieving the 'double' that year. His final first-class match was for a Commonwealth XI in 1958.

Jacob, Norman Ernest
Amateur. *b:* 9.7.1901, Neath, Glamorgan. *d:* 12.3.1970, Grimsby, Lincs. Opening/middle order right-hand batsman, change bowler. *Sch* Tonbridge. *Team* Glamorgan (1922, 7 matches).
Career batting
7–13–0–79–19–6.07–0–*ct* 2
Bowling 42–0

Jacobs, Arnold Leslie
Amateur. *b:* 12.11.1892, Buenos Aires, Argentina. *d:* 9.8.1974, Buenos Aires, Argentina. Tail end right-hand batsman, wicket-keeper. *Tours* South America to England 1932.
Career batting
2–3–0–19–10–6.33–0–*ct* 3

Jacobs, J.
Amateur. Middle order right-hand batsman, occasional wicket-keeper. *Team* Canterbury (1927/8 to 1937/8). *Tour* New Zealand Services to England 1945.
Career batting
12–21–1–464–69–23.20–0–*ct* 5–*st* 1

Jacobson, Louis Collins
Amateur. *b:* 26.1.1918, Dublin, Ireland. Right-hand batsman. *Team* Ireland (1948–52).
Career batting
4–7–2–153–101*–30.60–1–*ct* 1

Jacques, Tom
Professional. Lower order right-hand batsman, right-arm medium pace bowler. *Team* Lancashire (1937, 2 matches).
Career batting
2–2–0–4–2–2.00–0–*ct* 1
Bowling 70–1–70.00–0–0–1/45

Jacques, Thomas Alec
Amateur turning professional in 1928. *b:* 19.2.1905, Cliffe, Yorkshire. Lower order right-hand batsman, right-arm fast bowler. *Team* Yorkshire (1927–36, 28 matches).
Career batting
30–22–9–168–35*–12.92–0–*ct* 14
Bowling 1935–62–31.20–2–0–5/33

Jaffey, Isaac Mervyn
(now known as Mervyn Jeffries)
Amateur. *b:* 9.9.1929, Dublin, Ireland. Right-hand batsman, wicket-keeper. *Team* Ireland (1953).
Career batting
1 match, did not bat – *ct* 1–*st* 1

Jagger, Samuel Thornton
Amateur. *b:* 30.6.1904, Llangollen, Denbigh, *d:* 30.5.1964, Hove, Sussex. Lower order right-hand batsman, right-arm medium pace bowler. *Sch* Malvern. *Teams* Worcestershire (1922–23, 5 matches); Cambridge U (1923–26, blue 1925 and 1926); Sussex (1931, 3 matches); Wales (1927–29).
Career batting
44–64–11–599–58–11.30–0–*ct* 38
Bowling 3040–90–33.77–4–0–5/24

He also played for Denbighshire.

He represented Cambridge U at fives.

Jahangir Khan, Dr Mohammad
Amateur. *b:* 1.2.1910, Jullundur, India. Father of Majid (Pakistan). Fast scoring middle/lower order right-hand batsman, right-arm fast medium bowler. *Teams* Cambridge U (1933–36, blue all 4 years); Muslims (1928/9 to 1939/40); Northern India (1940/1 to 1945/6); South Punjab (1946/7);

Punjab Governor's XI (1947/8); Punjab (1951/2 to 1955/6). *Tours* India to England 1932, 1936. *Tests* India (1932–36, 4 matches).
Career batting
111–175–25–3319–133–22.12–4–*ct* 79
Bowling 8197–326–25.06–12–2–8/33
Test batting
4–7–0–39–13–5.57–0–*ct* 4
Bowling 255–4–63.75–0–0–4/60

He appeared in the Tests on both his tours to England, but his figures were only modest ones and his days of success infrequent.

His final first-class match in England was for MCC in 1939.

Jai, Laxmidas Purshottamdas
Amateur. *b:* 1.4.1902, Bombay, India. *d:* 29.1.1968, Bombay, India. Middle order right-hand batsman. *Teams* Hindus (1920/1 to 1941/2); Bombay (1926/7 to 1941/2). *Tour* India to England 1936. *Test* India (1933/4, 1 match).
Career batting
67–108–7–3235–156–32.02–6–*ct* 27
Bowling 134–3–44.66–0–0–1/6
Test batting
1–2–0–19–19–9.50–0–*ct* 0

His general form in England in 1936 did not reflect the reputation he had acquired for himself in India.

Jaidka, Rattan Chand
Amateur. *b: circa* 1904, Malaya. Lower order batsman, bowler. *Team* Gloucestershire (1927, 2 matches).
Career batting
2–1–0–5–5–5.00–0–*ct* 1
Bowling 160–2–80.00–0–0–1/57

He played for Gloucestershire whilst at Bristol University.

Jaisimha, Motganhalli Laxmanarsu
Amateur. *b:* 3.3.1939, Secunderabad, India. Father of Vivek (Hyderabad). Opening/middle order right-hand batsman, right-arm medium off break bowler. brilliant field. *Team* Hyderabad (1954/5 to 1976/7). *Tours* India to England 1959, to West Indies 1961/2, 1970/1, to Australia and New Zealand 1967/8; Indian Starlets to Pakistan 1959/60; Hyderabad Blues to Ceylon 1966/7. *Tests* India (1959 to 1970/1, 39 matches).
Career batting
245–387–27–13515–259–37.54–33–*ct* 157
Bowling 12873–431–29.86–18–3–7/45
Test batting
39–71–4–2056–129–30.68–3–*ct* 17
Bowling 829–9–92.11–0–0–2/54

His only visit to England was very early in his career and though he showed much promise he accomplished very little and appeared in only one Test. His highest score was 259 for Hyderabad v Bengal at Hyderabad in 1964/5. He hit 1,000 runs in a season in India three times (best 1,293, av 41.70, in 1964/5).

Jakeman, Frederick
Professional. *b:* 10.1.1920, Holmfirth, Yorkshire. Father of R.S. (Northants). Aggressive middle order left-hand batsman, good outfield. *Teams* Yorkshire (1946–47, 10 matches); Northants (1949–54, 119 matches).
Career batting
134–205–19–5952–258*–32.00–11–*ct* 42
Bowling 162–5–32.40–0–0–2/8

He hit 1,000 runs in a season twice (best 1,989, av 56.82, in 1951). His only double century, 258* for Northants v Essex at Northampton in 1951, was a new county record. After retiring he was on the first-class umpires list.

Jakeman, Ronald Stuart
Cricketer. *b:* 20.9.1943, Holmfirth, Yorkshire. Son of Frederick (Yorkshire and Northants). Middle order left-hand batsman. *Team* Northants (1962–63, 3 matches).
Career batting
3–4–0–31–13–7.75–0–*ct* 1

He also played for Cumberland.

Jakobson, Tonu Robert
Amateur. *b:* 17.12.1937, London. Lower order right-hand batsman, right-arm fast medium bowler. *Sch* Charterhouse. *Team* Oxford U (1960–61, blue 1961).
Career batting
14–19–7–112–20–9.33–0–*ct* 10
Bowling 1184–37–32.00–1–0–5/61

Jalal-ud-din
Cricketer. *b:* 25.4.1959, Karachi, Pakistan. Lower order right-hand batsman, right-arm fast-medium bowler. *Teams* Railways (1975/6); PWD (1977/8); Karachi (1978/9); Industrial Development Bank (1979/80 to 1981/2); Allied Bank (1982/3). *Tour* Pakistan to England 1982. *Tests* Pakistan (1982/3, 3 matches).
Career batting
42–55–18–592–60*–16.00–0–*ct* 10
Bowling 3324–154–21.58–9–2–7/43
Test batting
3–2–2–1–1*–no av–0–*ct* 0
Bowling 244–7–34.85–0–0–3/77

He came to England as a replacement during the 1982 tour, but did not appear in the Tests.

James, Albert Edward
Professional. *b:* 7.8.1924, Newton Longville,

Bucks. Lower order right-hand batsman, right-arm medium pace bowler. *Team* Sussex (1948–60, 299 matches).
Career batting
299–414–135–3411–63*–12.22–0–*ct* 111
Bowling 22841–843–27.09–27–2–9/60

He took 100 wickets in a season twice (best 111, av 21.31, in 1955). His best bowling in an innings was 9 for 60 for Sussex v Yorkshire at Hove in 1955.

He also played for Buckinghamshire.

James, Brian
Professional. *b:* 23.4.1934, Darfield, Barnsley, Yorkshire. Lower order batsman, left-arm fast medium, bowler. *Team* Yorkshire (1954, 4 matches).
Career batting
4–5–3–22–11*–11.00–0–*ct* 0
Bowling 228–8–28.50–0–0–4/54

James, Burnet George
Amateur. *b:* 26.10.1886, Stoke Bishop, Bristol. *d:* 26.9.1915, Langemark, Belgium. Middle order left-hand batsman, slow left-arm bowler. *Sch* Charterhouse. *Team* Gloucestershire (1914, 3 matches).
Career batting
3–6–1–27–10–5.40–0–*ct* 1

James, Charles Cecil
Professional. *b:* 14.9.1885, New Basford, Notts. *d:* 28.7.1950, Bulwell, Nottingham. Middle order right-hand batsman, right-arm medium pace bowler. *Team* Nottinghamshire (1906–21, 20 matches).
Career batting
20–34–3–355–43–11.45–0–*ct* 7

He also played for Northumberland.

James, David Harry
Amateur. *b:* 3.3.1921, Briton-Ferry, Glamorgan. Son of E.H. (Glamorgan). Lower order right-hand batsman, right-arm medium fast bowler. *Team* Glamorgan (1948, 1 match).
Career batting
1–1–0–17–17–17.00–0–*ct* 1
Bowling 59–1–59.00–0–0–1/59

James, David John Gwynne
Amateur. *b:* 12.6.1937, Pembroke Dock, Pembroke. Middle order right-hand batsman, right-arm medium fast bowler. *Sch* Cheltenham. *Team* Free Foresters (1961).
Career batting
1–2–0–40–29–20.00–0–*ct* 0

James, Edward Hugh
Amateur. *b:* 14.4.1896, Briton-Ferry, Glamorgan. *d:* 15.3.1975, Briton-Ferry, Glamorgan. Father of D.H. (Glamorgan). Lower order left-hand batsman, slow left-arm bowler. *Team* Glamorgan (1922, 3 matches).
Career batting
3–6–0–13–4–2.16–0–*ct* 1
Bowling 209–7–29.85–0–0–4/79

James, Evan Llewellyn
Amateur. *b:* 10.5.1918, Barry, Glamorgan. Middle order right-hand batsman, right-arm medium pace bowler. *Team* Glamorgan (1946–47, 9 matches).
Career batting
9–12–4–232–62*–29.00–0–*ct* 10
Bowling 45–1–45.00–0–0–1/8

James, F. W.
Amateur. Middle order batsman. *Team* Gentlemen of England (1905).
Career batting
1–1–1–11–11*–no av–0–*ct* 0

James, J.
Professional. Lower order batsman, useful bowler. *Team* Northants (1906, 2 matches).
Career batting
2–3–0–2–1–0.66–0–*ct* 0
Bowling 125–2–62.50–0–0–1/14

James, Kenneth Cecil
Amateur turned professional in 1935. *b:* 12.3.1904, Wellington, New Zealand. *d:* 21.8.1976, Palmerston North, New Zealand. Middle/lower order right-hand batsman, wicket-keeper. *Teams* Wellington (1923/4 to 1946/7); Northants (1935–39, 101 matches). *Tours* New Zealand to Australia 1925/6, to England 1927, 1931; New Zealand Services to England 1945. *Tests* New Zealand (1929/30 to 1932/3, 11 matches).
Career batting
204–330–41–6413–109*–22.19–7–*ct* 311–*st* 112
Bowling 17–0
Test batting
11–13–2–52–14–4.72–0–*ct* 11–*st* 5

He hit 1,000 runs in a season once : 1,032, av 23.45, in 1938.

On both tours with New Zealand to England, he was the visitors' outstanding wicket-keeper.

James, Kevin David
Cricketer. *b:* 18.3.1961, Lambeth, London. Lower order left-hand batsman, left-arm medium pace bowler. *Teams* Middlesex (1980–83, 11 matches); Wellington (1982/3).

Career batting
13–14–5–190–34–21.11–0–*ct* 3
Bowling 388–21–18.47–1–0–5/28

James, P.
Amateur. *Team* H. K. Foster's XI (1919).
Career batting
1–1–0–11–11–11.00–0–*ct* 0

James, Ronald Michael
Amateur. *b:* 2.10.1934, Wokingham, Berkshire. Hard hitting middle order right-hand batsman, right-arm medium pace bowler. *Sch* St. John's, Leatherhead. *Teams* Cambridge U (1956–58, blue all three years); Wellington (1964/5).
Career batting
51–90–10–2208–168–27.60–4–*ct* 16
Bowling 1356–38–35.68–0–0–4/5

His County cricket was for Berkshire.

His final first-class match in England was for MCC in 1961.

James, William
Professional. Middle order batsman. *Team* Kent (1881, 1 match).
Career batting
1–2–0–0–0–0.00–0–*ct* 0

Jameson, Harold Gordon
Amateur. *b:* 25.1.1918, Dundrum, Co Dublin, Ireland. *d:* 26.8.1940, Eastney, Hants. Tail end right-hand batsman, right-arm fast medium bowler. *Sch* Monkton Combe. *Team* Cambridge U (1938).
Career batting
2–4–1–7–4–2.33–0–*ct* 0
Bowling 204–2–102.00–0–0–2/68

Jameson, John Alexander
Professional. *b:* 30.6.1941, Bombay, India. Brother of T.E.N. (Warwickshire). Forcing opening right-hand batsman, right-arm medium pace off break bowler, occasional wicket-keeper, good cover point. *Sch* Taunton. *Teams* Warwickshire (1960 to 1976, 345 matches). *Tours* Warwickshire to Uganda and Kenya 1967/8 (not first-class); MCC to West Indies 1973/4; Robins to West Indies 1974/5 (not first-class); International XI to South Africa 1972/3. *Tests* England (1971 to 1973/4, 4 matches).
Career batting
361–611–43–18941–240*–33.34–33–*ct* 255–*st* 1
Bowling 3782–89–42.49–0–0–4/22
Test batting
4–8–0–214–82–26.75–0–*ct* 0
Bowling 17–1–17.00–0–0–1/17

He hit 1,000 runs in a season 11 times (best 1,948, av 48.70 in 1973). Both his double centuries were for Warwickshire, the highest being 240* v Gloucs at Edgbaston in 1974; during the course of this innings he added 465* for the 2nd wicket with R.B. Kanhai, creating a new first-class world record.

Jameson, Thomas Edward Neville
Cricketer. *b:* 23.7.1946, Bombay, India. Brother of J.A. (Warwickshire). Lower order left-hand batsman, right-arm medium pace bowler. *Sch* Taunton. *Teams* Cambridge U (1970, blue); Warwickshire (1970, 1 match).
Career batting
10–17–2–181–32–12.06–0–*ct* 12
Bowling 531–10–53.10–0–0–2/21

Jameson, Thomas George Cairnes
Amateur. *b:* 6.4.1908, Bihar, India. Middle order right-hand batsman, right-arm medium or leg break bowler. *Team* Hampshire (1930–31, 3 matches).
Career batting
5–7–1–55–23*–9.16.0–*ct* 0
Bowling 25–0

His first-class debut was for the Navy in 1929.

Jameson, Tom Ormsby
Amateur. *b:* 4.4.1892, Clonsilla, Co Dublin, Ireland. *d:* 6.2.1965, Dun Laoghaire, Co Dublin, Ireland. Middle order right-hand batsman, leg break and googly bowler. good slip field. *Sch* Harrow. *Teams* Hampshire (1919–32, 53 matches); Ireland (1926–28). *Tours* Joel to South Africa 1924/5; MCC to West Indies 1925/6. to South America 1926/7; Tennyson to India 1937/8.
Career batting
124–198–22–4675–133–26.56–5–*ct* 102
Bowling 6057–252–24.03–11–2–7/92

A fine rackets player, he won the Army singles Championship three times and he also won the Amateur Squash Championship twice.

Jaques, Arthur
Amateur. *b:* 7.3.1888, Shanghai, China. *d:* 27.9.1915, Bois Hugo, Loos, France. He was killed in action. Lower order right-hand batsman, right-arm medium pace and leg break bowler. *Sch* Aldenham. *Team* Hampshire (1913–14, 49 matches). *Tour* MCC to West Indies 1912/13.
Career batting
60–99–22–982–68–12.75–0–*ct* 40
Bowling 3835–175–21.91–10–3–8/21

He took 117 wickets, av 18.69, in 1914.

Whilst at Cambridge he played in the Freshmen's and Seniors' Matches, but no first-class games.

Jaques, Peter Heath
Amateur. *b:* 20.11.1919, Aylestone, Leicester. Middle order right-hand batsman. *Sch* Wyggeston GS. *Team* Leicestershire (1949, 1 match).
Career batting
1–2–0–69–55–34.50–0–*ct* 0

Jardine, Douglas Robert
Amateur. *b:* 23.10.1900, Bombay, India. *d:* 18.6.1958, Montreux, Switzerland. Son of M.R. (Middlesex). Middle order right-hand batsman, leg break bowler. *Sch* Winchester. *Teams* Oxford U (1920–23, blue 1920, 1921 and 1923); Surrey (1921–33, 141 matches). *Tours* MCC to Australia 1928/9, to Australia and New Zealand 1932/3, to India and Ceylon 1933/4. *Tests* England (1928 to 1933/4, 22 matches).
Career batting
262–378–61–14848–214–46.83–35–*ct* 188
Bowling 1493–48–31.10–1–0–6/28
Test batting
22–33–6–1296–127–48.00–1–*ct* 26
Bowling 10–0

Captain of England on the 1932/3 tour to Australia, Jardine employed the controversial leg-theory bowling tactics in conjunction with Larwood and Voce. His captaincy caused much ill-feeling between England and Australia, but he proved successful winning the series by four matches to one. After taking the 1933/4 MCC team to India, Jardine retired from regular first-class cricket, though still at the height of his powers.

A determined batsman, he hit 1,000 runs in a season eight times, plus once overseas. His highest aggregate was 1,473, av 46.03, in 1926, but his best seasons were 1927 and 1928 when he headed the first-class averages with figures of 91.09 and 87.15 respectively. His only double century was 214 for MCC v Tasmania at Launceston in 1928/9. He led England in 15 Tests in all, losing only once, and also captained Surrey in 1932 and 1933.

His final first-class match was for England XI v Glamorgan in 1948.

He wrote a book on the 1932/3 tour and various other articles and commentaries on the game.

Jardine, James
Amateur. *b:* 6.6.1846, Dunstable Park, Bedfordshire. *d:* 6.1.1909, St Moritz, Switzerland. Opening right-hand batsman. *Sch* Dunstable. *Team* MCC (1870–74).
Career batting
4–7–0–53–21–7.57–0–*ct* 0

His County cricket was for Northumberland.

Jardine, Malcolm Robert
Amateur. *b:* 8.6.1869, Simla, India. *d:* 16.1.1947, South Kensington, London. Father of D.R. (Surrey). Middle order right-hand batsman, right-arm fast medium bowler, good deep field. *Sch* Fettes. *Teams* Oxford U (1889–92, blue all four years); Middlesex (1892, 6 matches); Europeans (1894/5 to 1902/03).
Career batting
46–84–3–1439–140–17.76–1–*ct* 42
Bowling 216–15–14.40–1–0–5/78

He spent most of his working life in India, rising to become Advocate-General of Bombay.

His final first-class match in England was for MCC in 1897.

Jarman, Barrington Noel
Amateur. *b:* 17.2.1936, Hindmarsh, Adelaide, Australia. Middle order right-hand batsman, wicket-keeper. *Team* South Australia (1955/6 to 1968/9, 94 matches). *Tours* Australia to New Zealand 1956/7, 1966/7, to South Africa 1957/8, to India and Pakistan 1959/60, 1964/5, to England 1961, 1964, 1968, to West Indies 1964/5. *Tests* Australia (1959/60 to 1968/9, 19 matches).
Career batting
191–284–37–5615–196–22.73–5–*ct* 431–*st* 129
Bowling 98–3–32.66–0–0–1/17
Test batting
19–30–3–400–78–14.81–0–*ct* 50–*st* 4

In 1961 and 1964 in England he acted as reserve wicket-keeper to Grout and was not required for the Tests, but in 1968 he was principal wicket-keeper as well as being vice-captain of the touring party, and played in all four Tests, one as captain.

Jarman, Harold James
Professional. *b:* 4.5.1939, Bristol. Middle order right-hand batsman, right-arm medium pace bowler. *Team* Gloucestershire (1961–71, 45 matches).
Career batting
45–74–18–1041–67*–18.58–0–*ct* 20
Bowling 131–0

A noted soccer player, he appeared for Bristol Rovers and Newport County.

Jarrett, David William
Cricketer. *b:* 19.4.1952, Bromsgrove, Worcs. Middle order right-hand batsman, right-arm medium pace bowler. *Sch* Wellington. *Teams* Oxford U (1974–75, blue 1975): Cambridge U (1976, blue).
Career batting
21–41–0–678–62–16.53–0–*ct* 12
Bowling 7–0

In 1976 he became the first cricketer ever to

gain a blue at both Oxford and Cambridge. His County cricket was for Bedfordshire.

Jarrett, Graham Maurice
Cricketer. *b:* 9.2.1937, Bedford. Tail end right-hand batsman, leg break bowler. *Team* Minor Counties (1971–74).
Career batting
3–4–2–32–24*–16.00–0–*ct* 0
Bowling 260–2–130.00–0–0–2/83
His County cricket was for Bedfordshire.

Jarrett, Harold Herman
Professional. *b:* 23.9.1907, Johannesburg, South Africa. *d:* 17.3.1983, Newport, Gwent. Father of K.S. (Glamorgan). Lower order right-hand batsman, leg break and googly bowler. *Sch* Highgate. *Teams* Warwickshire (1932–33, 14 matches); Glamorgan (1938, 1 match).
Career batting
15–16–1–228–45–15.20–0–*ct* 6
Bowling 1650–51–32.35–2–0–8/187

Jarrett, Keith Stanley
Cricketer. *b:* 18.5.1948, Newport, Monmouth. Son of H.H. (Warwickshire and Glamorgan). Middle order right-hand batsman, right-arm medium pace bowler, good outfield. *Team* Glamorgan (1967, 2 matches).
Career batting
2–3–1–27–18*–13.50–0–*ct* 0
Bowling 76–0
An excellent rugby full back or three quarter he played for Newport and for Wales, also toured South Africa with the Lions.

Jarvis, Arthur Harwood
Amateur. *b:* 19.10.1860, Hindmarsh, Adelaide, Australia. *d:* 15.11.1933, Hindmarsh, Adelaide, Australia. Father of H.S.C. (South Australia). Steady Middle/lower order right-hand batsman. *Team* South Australia (1877/8 to 1900/1, 42 matches). *Tours* Australia to England 1880, 1886, 1888 and 1893. *Tests* Australia (1884/5 to 1894/5, 11 matches).
Career batting
141–226–23–3161–98*–15.57–0–*ct* 114–*st* 83
Bowling 63–1–63.00–0–0–1/9
Test batting
11–21–3–303–82–16.83–0–*ct* 9–*st* 9
Since his career ran almost parallel to that of Blackham, he was always Australia's second choice wicket-keeper and his opportunities were therefore, in Test cricket, very limited, though his career with South Australia spanned over 20 years.

Jarvis, James Edward Frisby
Amateur. *b:* 1875, Leicester. *d:* 24.1.1962, Leicester. Lower order right-hand batsman, wicket-keeper. *Team* Leicestershire (1900, 1 match).
Career batting
1–2–1–0–0*–0.00–0–*ct* 1–*st* 1

Jarvis, Kevin Bertram Sidney
Cricketer. *b:* 23.4.1953, Dartford, Kent. Tail end right-hand batsman, right-arm fast medium bowler. *Team* Kent (1975–83, 177 matches). *Tours* Robins to Sri Lanka 1977/8; International XI to Jamaica 1982/3.
Career batting
182–125–52–234–14*–3.20–0–*ct* 44
Bowling 13930–471–29.57–14–3–8/97
Few players have attained such a poor batting record.

Jarvis, Lewis Kerrison
Amateur. *b:* 3.8.1857, Middleton Towers, Norfolk. *d:* 16.5.1938, Kensington, London. Excellent opening/middle order right-hand batsman, slow under-arm bowler, good deep field. *Sch* Harrow. *Team* Cambridge U (1877–79, blue all 3 years).
Career batting
23–35–2–504–47–15.27–0–*ct* 7
Bowling 49–4–12.25–0–0–2/7
He, together with his two brothers, played a major role in Norfolk cricket in the 1880s.
Whilst at Cambridge he was a triple blue, representing the University at soccer and the hurdles as well as cricket.
His final first-class match was for Cambridge University, Past and Present, in 1886.

Jarvis, Paul William
Cricketer. *b:* 29.6.1965, Redcar, Yorkshire. Lower order right-hand batsman, right-arm fast medium bowler. *Team* Yorkshire (1981–83, 9 matches).
Career batting
9–8–5–29–11*–9.66–0–*ct* 5
Bowling 663–11–60.27–0–0–2/24

Jarvis, Terrence Wayne
Cricketer. *b:* 29.7.1944, Auckland, New Zealand. Steady right-hand opening batsman, slip field. *Teams* Auckland (1964/5 to 1976/7); Canterbury (1969/70 to 1970/1). *Tours* New Zealand to England 1965, to India and Pakistan 1964/5, to Australia 1967/8, to West Indies 1971/2. *Tests* New Zealand (1964/5 to 1972/3, 13 matches).
Career batting
97–167–8–4666–182–29.34–6–*ct* 102
Bowling 89–0
Test batting
13–22–1–625–182–29.76–1–*ct* 3

Unfortunately he contracted an illness in India, just prior to the 1965 tour of England and was not really fit. He did not play in any of the Tests.

Jarvis, Victor Edmund
Amateur. *b:* 30.9.1898, Hampstead. *d:* 30.4.1975, Stokenchurch, Bucks. Middle order right-hand batsman, slow left-arm bowler. *Team* Essex (1925, 2 matches).
Career batting
2–4–0–44–37–11.00–0–*ct* 0
Bowling 23–0

Javed Akhtar
Amateur. *b:* 21.11.1940, Rawalpindi, India. Lower order right-hand batsman, off break bowler. *Team* Rawalpindi (1959/60 to 1975/6). *Tour* Pakistan to England 1962. *Test* Pakistan (1962, 1 match).
Career batting
51–63–10–835–88–15.75–0–*ct* 38
Bowling 3396–187–18.16–12–3–7/56
Test batting
1–2–1–4–2*–4.00–0–*ct* 0
Bowling 52–0

He was flown to England midway through the 1962 tour to replace the injured Haseeb Ahsan, appearing in seven matches, including the third Test.

Javed Burki *(see under* Burki, J.)

Javed Miandad Khan
Cricketer. *b:* 12.6.1957, Karachi, Pakistan. Brother of Anwar and Bashir (Karachi). Aggressive middle order right-hand batsman, leg break and googly bowler, good deep field. *Teams* Karachi (1973/4 to 1975/6); Sind (1973/4 to 1975/6); Sussex (1976–79, 40 matches); Habib Bank (1976/7 to 1982/3); Glamorgan (1980–83, 54 matches). *Tours* Pakistan to Sri Lanka 1975/6, to Australia and West Indies 1976/7, to England 1978, 1982, to New Zealand and Australia 1978/9, to India 1979/80, to Australia 1981/2. *Tests* Pakistan (1976/7 to 1982/3, 52 matches).
Career batting
263–424–69–18407–311–51.85–51–*ct* 260–*st* 3
Bowling 5924–181–32.72–6–0–7/39
Test batting
52–83–14–3992–280*–57.85–10–*ct* 48–*st* 1
Bowling 634–17–37.29–0–0–3/74

On the 1978 tour to England he appeared in all three Tests, but with little success; in 1982, however he hit 178 runs, av 35.60, in the Tests and 450, av 64.28, in first class matches. He has hit 1,000 runs in an English season three times going on to 2,000 once: 2,083, av 69.43, in 1981. A prolific batsman overseas he hit 1,000 runs in an overseas season six times and his highest innings was 311 for Karachi Whites v National Bank in 1974/5. He has hit two double centuries in England, namely 200* for Glamorgan v Somerset at Taunton in 1981 and 200* for Glamorgan v Essex at Colchester in 1981. He has captained Pakistan in ten Tests, but not in England. With Mudassar Nazar he equalled the record Test wicket partnership of 451 for Pakistan v India at Hyderabad in 1982/3.

Jawahir Shah
Cricketer. *b:* 1942, Kenya. Right-hand batsman. *Team* East Africa (1967/8 to 1975). *Tours* East Africa to England 1975.
Career batting
3–6–0–141–50–23.50–0–*ct* 2
Bowling 13–0

Jayantilal, Kenia Hirji
Cricketer. *b:* 13.1.1948, Hyderabad, India. Right-hand opening batsman. *Team* Hyderabad (1968/9 to 1978/9). *Tours* India to West Indies 1970/1, to England 1971; Indian Universities to Ceylon 1970/1. *Test* India (1970/1, 1 match).
Career batting
91–154–25–4687–197–36.33–8–*ct* 66
Bowling 311–6–51.83–0–0–3/47
Test batting
1–1–0–5–5–5.00–0–*ct* 0

He was most disappointing on the 1971 tour to England and did not appear in the Tests.

His first-class debut was for Hyderabad Blues in 1967/8.

Jayaram, Bangalore
Amateur. *b:* 23.4.1872, Bangalore, India. Middle order right-hand batsman, slow right-arm bowler. *Team* London County (1903–04). *Tour* India to England 1911.
Career batting
12–23–0–340–57–14.78–0–*ct* 5
Bowling 35–0

He did not appear in first-class matches in India.

Jayasekera, Rohan Stanley Amarasiriwardena
Cricketer. *b:* 7.12.1957, Colombo, Ceylon. Aggressive opening right-hand batsman, wicket-keeper. *Team* Sri Lanka (1979 to 1981/2). *Tour* Sri Lanka to England 1979, to India 1980/1, to Pakistan 1981/2. *Test* Sri Lanka (1981/2, 1 match).
Career batting
8–13–1–354–79*–29.50–0–*ct* 6–*st* 2
Bowling 8–0
Test batting
1–2–0–2–2–1.00–0–*ct* 0

Jayasinghe, Stanley
Professional. *b:* 19.1.1931, Badulla, Ceylon. Middle order right-hand batsman, off break bowler. *Team* Ceylon (1949/50 to 1968/9); Leicestershire (1961–65, 112 matches). *Tours* Ceylon to Pakistan 1949/50 and 1966/7, to India 1964/5.
Career batting
144–254–10–6811–135–27.91–6–*ct* 109
Bowling 1197–34–35.20–1–0–6/38

He hit 1,000 runs in a season four times (best 1,499, av 29.39 in 1962).

Jayasinghe, Sunil Asoka
Cricketer. *b:* 15.7.1955, Matugama, Ceylon. Middle order batsman, wicket-keeper. *Team* Sri Lanka (1979). *Tour* Sri Lanka to England 1979.
Career batting
6–7–1–183–64–30.50–0–*ct* 10–*st* 4

Jayes, Thomas
Professional. *b:* 17.4.1877, Ratby, Leics. *d:* 16.4.1913, Ratby, Leics., of consumption. Uncle of W.E.Astill (Leics). Hard hitting lower order right-hand batsman, right-arm fast bowler. *Team* Leicestershire (1903–11, 124 matches).
Career batting
128–210–20–2764–100–14.54–1–*ct* 116
Bowling 12832–535–23.98–41–9–9/78

He took 100 wickets in a season three times (best 109, av 20.61, in 1909). His best bowling was 9/78 for Leics v Derbyshire at Leicester in 1905.

He was selected to play for England v Australia in 1909, but dropped from the final eleven.

His health broke down in 1911 and though Leics CCC paid for him to go to Switzerland, he never recovered.

Jeacocke, Alfred
Amateur. *b:* 1.12.1892, Islington, London. *d:* 26.9.1961, Lewisham, Kent. Opening right-hand batsman, off break bowler, good slip. *Team* Surrey (1920–34, 132 matches).
Career batting
148–233–17–6228–201*–28.83–8–*ct* 111
Bowling 576–14–41.14–0–0–3/24

He hit 1,056 runs, av 42.24, in 1921 and his only double century was 201* for Surrey v Sussex at the Oval in 1922. In the same season Kent objected that he was unqualified for Surrey, the house in which he lived being in Kent, but the houses on the opposite side of the road were in Surrey!

However he resumed playing for Surrey in 1923.

Jeavons, Enoch Percy
Amateur. *b:* 1893, Dudley, Worcs. *d:* 1967, Dudley, Worcs. Middle order right-hand batsman. *Team* Worcestershire (1924, 1 match).
Career batting
1–2–1–1–1*–1.00–0–*ct* 2

Jeeves, Percy
Professional. *b:* 5.3.1888, Earlsheaton, Yorkshire. *d:* 22.7.1916, High Wood, Montauban, France. He was killed in action. Punishing lower order right-hand batsman, right-arm medium fast bowler. *Team* Warwickshire (1912–14, 49 matches).
Career batting
50–81–6–1204–86*–16.05–0–*ct* 49
Bowling 3987–199–20.03–12–1–7/34

He took 106 wickets, av 20.88, in 1913 and at the outbreak of war was regarded as one of the most promising young cricketers in England. His name was taken by P.G. Wodehouse, who saw him play in 1913, when Wodehouse wrote his first stories about the famous butler three years later.

Jeffares, Alfred Shaun
Amateur. *b:* 14.8.1906, Korngha, South Africa. Left-hand batsman, right-arm medium pace bowler. *Team* Dublin University (1926).
Career batting
1–2–0–15–13–7.50–0–*ct* 0
Bowling 72–2–36.00–0–0–2/72

Jefferies, Stephen Thomas
Cricketer. *b:* 8.12.1959, Cape Town, South Africa. Lower order left-hand batsman, left-arm fast medium bowler. *Teams* Western Province (1978/9 to 1982/3); Derbyshire (1982, 1 match); Lancashire (1983, 10 matches).
Career batting
49–59–14–1197–75*–26.60–0–*ct* 16
Bowling 4573–176–25.98–6–1–8/46

He represented South Africa in the unofficial 'Tests' v Sri Lanka and West Indies in 1982/3.

Jefferson, Julian
Amateur. *b:* 18.7.1899, Ripon, Yorkshire. *d:* 18.6.1966, Marylebone, London. Middle order batsman. *Sch* Gresham's Holt. *Teams* Army (1919); Combined Services (1922).
Career batting
2–4–0–84–26–21.00–0–*ct* 1
Bowling 168–5–33.60–0–0–4/129

Jefferson, Richard Ingleby
Amateur. *b:* 15.8.1941, Frimley, Surrey. Middle/lower order right-hand batsman, right-arm fast medium bowler. *Sch* Winchester. *Teams*

Cambridge U (1961, blue); Surrey (1961–66, 76 matches). *Tours* Brown to East Africa 1961/2 (not first-class); MCC to South America 1964/5 (not first-class).
Career batting
94–137–31–2094–136–19.75–2–*ct* 32
Bowling 7250–263–27.56–10–1–6/25
He also played for Norfolk and his final first-class match was for Minor Counties in 1969.
He played soccer for Corinthian Casuals.

Jeffery, George Ernest
Amateur. *b:* 9.2.1853, Eastbourne, Sussex. *d:* 8.4.1891, Streatham, London. Middle order right-hand batsman, slow round-arm bowler. good deep field. *Sch* Rugby. *Teams* Cambridge U (1872–74, blue 1873–74); Sussex (1872–74, 14 matches).
Career batting
31–55–5–808–127–16.16–1–*ct* 30
Bowling 1018–61+7–16.68–6–0–8/44

Jeffery, Howard William James
Cricketer. *b:* 5.5.1944, Cockermouth, Cumberland. Lower order right-hand batsman, right-arm fast medium bowler. *Team* Leicestershire (1964, 2 matches).
Career batting
2–3–1–6–6–3.00–0–*ct* 1
Bowling 103–2–51.50–0–0–2/77
He also played for Cumberland.

Jeffreys, Arthur Frederick
Amateur. *b:* 7.4.1848, London. *d:* 14.2.1906, Lasham, Hants. Middle order right-hand batsman, good cover point. *Sch* Eton. *Teams* New South Wales (1872/73, 1 match); Hampshire (1876–78, 10 matches).
Career batting
26–44–3–587–60–14.31–0–*ct* 9–*st* 1
His first-class debut was for MCC in 1872 and his final match for MCC in 1879.
He was MP for Northern Division, Hants, from 1887.

Jeffries, W.
Professional. Lower order batsman, bowler. *Teams* Gloucestershire (1919, 2 matches).
Career batting
2–4–1–0–0*–0.00–0–*ct* 0
Bowling 93–5–18.60–0–0–3/38

Jeganathan, Sridharan
Cricketer. *b:* 11.7.1951, Colombo, Ceylon. Middle order right-hand batsman, slow left-arm bowler. *Team* Sri Lanka (1973/4 to 1982/3). *Tours* Sri Lanka to Pakistan 1973/4, to England 1979, to Australia and New Zealand 1982/3, to Zimbabwe 1982/3. *Tests* Sri Lanka (1982/3, 2 matches).
Career batting
27–36–4–432–74–13.50–0–*ct* 14
Bowling 1425–47–30.31–1–0–5/34
Test batting
2–4–0–19–8–4.75–0–*ct* 0
Bowling 12–0

Jelf, Henry Francis Donhoff
Amateur. *b:* 27.8.1877, Aldershot, Hants. *d:* 18.4.1944, Southport, Lancashire. Middle order batsman. *Team* Derbyshire (1910–11, 10 matches).
Career batting
10–20–0–220–37–11.00–0–*ct* 3

Jelf, Hector Gordon
Amateur. *b:* 6.5.1917, Putney, London. Lower order right-hand batsman, wicket-keeper. *Sch* Marlborough. *Team* Oxford U (1938).
Career batting
2–3–0–48–35–16.00–0–*ct* 5–*st* 1

Jelf, Wilfrid Wykeham
Amateur. *b:* 22.7.1880, Halifax, Nova Scotia, Canada. *d:* 17.10.1933, Bridgwater, Somerset. Middle order right-hand batsman. *Sch* Eton. *Team* Leicestershire (1911, 3 matches).
Career batting
3–6–0–6–6–1.00–0–*ct* 3

Jellicoe, Rev Frederick Gilbert Gardiner
Amateur. *b:* 24.2.1858, Southampton, Hants. *d:* 29.7.1927, Southwark, London. Lower order right-hand batsman, left-hand medium slow round-arm bowler. *Sch* Haileybury. *Teams* Oxford U (1877–79, blue 1877 and 1879); Hampshire (1877–80, 4 matches).
Career batting
18–29–9–58–12–2.90–0–*ct* 8
Bowling 1164–78–14.92–5–1–8/36

Jellie, J. P. S. *(see under* Stephenson-Jellie, J. P.)

Jenkins, Huw
Cricketer. *b:* 24.10.1944, Swansea. Middle order left-hand batsman, right-arm medium pace bowler. *Team* Glamorgan (1970, 1 match).
Career batting
1–2–1–81–65–81.00–0–*ct* 1

Jenkins, Roland Oliver
Professional. *b:* 24.11.1918, Worcester. Sound middle/lower order right-hand batsman, leg break and googly bowler. *Team* Worcestershire (1938–58, 352 matches). *Tour* MCC to South

Africa (1948/9). *Tests* England (1948/9 to 1952, 9 matches).
Career batting
386–573–120–10073–109–22.23–1–*ct* 214
Bowling 30945–1309–23.64–92–20–8/62
Test batting
9–12–1–198–39–18.00–0–*ct* 4
Bowling 1098–32–34.31–1–0–5/116

He hit 1,000 runs in a season four times (best 1,356, av 27.12) and took 100 wickets in a season five times (best 183, av 21.19, in 1949). He performed the 'double' in 1949 and 1952.

Jenkins, Vivian Gordon James
Amateur. *b:* 2.11.1911, Port Talbot, Glamorgan. Lower order right-hand batsman, wicket-keeper. *Sch* Llandovery College. *Teams* Glamorgan (1931–37, 44 matches); Oxford U (1933, blue).
Career batting
53–84–10–1328–69–17.94–0–*ct* 17–*st* 7
Bowling 54–2–27.00–0–0–1/13

He was awarded his rugby blue and went on to appear for Wales as full back and three quarter. He later became well known as a sports commentator.

Jenkins, Wyndham Leslie Trevor
Amateur. *b:* 26.8.1898, Newport, Monmouth. *d:* 1971. Lower order right-hand batsman, wicket-keeper. *Sch* Malvern. *Team* Glamorgan (1921, 10 matches).
Career batting
10–20–1–155–39–8.15–0–*ct* 8–*st* 2

Jenkinson, Cecil Victor
Amateur. *b:* 15.5.1891, Ilford, Essex. *d:* 6.11.1980, Pembury, Kent. Lower order right-hand batsman, wicket-keeper. *Team* Essex (1922–23, 5 matches).
Career batting
5–6–2–9–8–2.25–0–*ct* 4–*st* 4

Jenner, Felix Donovan
Professional. *b:* 15.11.1892, Hastings, Sussex. *d:* 31.3.1953, Hampstead, London. Middle order right-hand batsman. *Team* Sussex (1919–21, 28 matches).
Career batting
28–50–1–595–55–12.14–0–*ct* 9
Bowling 66–2–33.00–0–0–2/34

He also played for Durham.

Jenner, Sir Herbert
(changed name to Jenner-Fust in 1864)
Amateur. *b:* 23.2.1806, St James's, London. *d* 30.7.1904, Hill Court, Falfield, Gloucestershire. Father of H. Jenner-Fust (Gloucs). Opening right-hand batsman, wicket-keeper, right-hand semi-under arm bowler. *Sch* Eton. *Teams* Cambridge U (1825–27, blue 1827); Kent (1828–36).
Career batting
36–63–3–842–75–14.03–0–*ct* 25–*st* 17
Bowling 74 wickets, no analyses

He was one of the best wicket-keepers of his day, but owing to his profession retired from serious cricket in 1836. He took a great interest in the game all his life, but 'he never took the trouble to see W.G. Grace play.' His final match was for Gentlemen of Kent in 1838.

Jenner-Fust, Herbert
(changed name from Jenner in 1864)
Amateur. *b:* 14.8.1841, Beckenham, Kent. *d:* 11.11.1940, Falfield, Gloucs. Son of H. Jenner-Fust (Cambridge U and Kent). *Sch* Eton. *Team* Gloucestershire (1875, 1 match).
Career batting
1–2–1–1–1–1.00–0–*ct* 0

Jennings, Claude Burrows
Amateur. *b:* 5.6.1884, East St Kilda, Victoria, Australia. *d:* 20.6.1950, Adelaide, Australia. Opening right-hand batsman. *Teams* South Australia (1902/3 to 1907/8, 21 matches): Queensland (1910/11 to 1911/12, 5 matches). *Tours* Australia to England 1912. *Tests* Australia (1912, 6 matches).
Career batting
60–103–7–2453–123–25.55–1–*ct* 38–*st* 3
Bowling 17–0
Test batting
6–8–2–107–32–17.83–0–*ct* 5

He hit 1,037 runs, av 22.54, on his 1912 tour to England and played some useful innings, despite the fact that the wet pitches told against him.

Jennings, David William
Professional. *b:* 4.6.1889, Kentish Town, London. *d:* 6.8.1918, Tunbridge Wells, Kent, after illness due to shell-shock. Brother of G.A. (Warwickshire), L.F. (RAF) and T.S. (Surrey). Middle order right-hand batsman. *Team* Kent (1909–14, 35 matches).
Career batting
35–48–4–1064–106–24.18–3–*ct* 28
Bowling 80–1–80.00–0–0–1/13

Jennings, Frank Leonard
Amateur. *b:* 1875, Bedminster, Somerset. Middle order batsman. *Team* Somerset (1895, 1 match).
Career batting
1–2–0–7–7–3.50–0–*ct* 0

Jennings, George Adolphus
Professional. *b:* 14.1.1895, Exeter, Devon. *d:* July

1959, Marlborough, Wilts. Brother of D.W. (Kent), L.F. (RAF) and T.S. (Surrey). Lower order right-hand batsman, slow left-arm bowler. *Team* Warwickshire (1923–25, 20 matches).
Career batting
20–27–5–243–41–11.04–0–*ct* 8
Bowling 916–23–39.82–1–0–5/92
He also played for Devon, and was coach at Marlborough College for over 30 years.

Jennings, Keith Francis
Cricketer. *b:* 5.10.1953, Wellington, Somerset. Lower order right-hand batsman, right-arm medium pace bowler. *Team* Somerset (1975–81, 68 matches).
Career batting
68–73–24–521–49–10.63–0–*ct* 48
Bowling 3403–96–35.44–1–0–5/18

Jennings, Leonard Frank
Amateur, *b:* 5.11.1903, Marlborough, Wilts. *d:* 28.3.1977, Battle, Sussex. Brother of D.W. (Kent), G.A. (Warwickshire) and T.S. (Surrey). Middle order batsman, change bowler. *Team* Royal Air Force (1929).
Career batting
2–3–1–55–45*–27.50–0–*ct* 1
Bowling 22–0

Jennings, Thomas Shepherd
Professional. *b:* 3.11.1896, Tiverton, Devon. *d:* 7.9.1972, Tiverton, Devon. Brother of D.W. (Kent), G.A. (Warwickshire) and L.F. (RAF). Lower order left-hand batsman, slow left-arm bowler. *Team* Surrey (1921–24, 18 matches).
Career batting
18–17–3–194–37*–13.85–0–*ct* 4
Bowling 1094–37–29.56–3–1–6/51
He also played for Devon.

Jephson, Digby Loder Armroid
Amateur. *b:* 23.2.1871, Clapham, Surrey. *d:* 19.1.1926, Cambridge. Opening/middle order right-hand batsman, right-arm fast bowler, changing to under-arm lobs about 1892. *Teams* Cambridge U (1890–92, blue all three years); Surrey (1894–1904, 165 matches).
Career batting
207–313–53–7973–213–30.66–11–*ct* 104
Bowling 7457–297–25.10–14–2–7/51
He hit 1,000 runs in a season four times (best 1,952, av 41.53, in 1900). His only double century was 213 for Surrey v Derbyshire at the Oval in 1900.
From 1900 to 1902 he captained Surrey.

Jephson, Selwyn Victor
Amateur. *b:* 24.5.1900, Beaminster, Dorset. *d:* 6.11.1978, Hambledon, Hants. Lower order right-hand batsman, right-arm fast medium bowler. *Team* Royal Navy (1924–28).
Career batting
4–7–0–49–14–7.00–0–*ct* 2
Bowling 421–6–70.16–0–0–2/73
He played for Dorset.

Jephson, Rev William Vincent
Amateur. *b:* 6.10.1873, Ayot St. Peter, Herts. *d:* 12.11.1956, Monkton Combe, Bath. Hard hitting right-hand batsman, wicket-keeper or slip. *Sch* Haileybury. *Team* Hampshire (1903–19, 57 matches).
Career batting
62–109–7–1791–114*–17.55–1–*ct* 39–*st* 1
Bowling 13–1–13.00–0–0–1/13
He also played for Hertfordshire and Dorset.
His final first-class match was for MCC in 1920.

Jepson, Arthur
Professional. *b:* 12.7.1915, Selston, Notts. Hard hitting lower order right-hand batsman, right-arm fast medium bowler. *Team* Nottinghamshire (1938–59, 390 matches).
Career batting
392–534–89–6369–130–14.31–1–*ct* 201
Bowling 30567–1051–29.08–40–6–8/45
He took 100 wickets in a season once : 115, av 27.78, in 1947.
A noted soccer player, he appeared in goal for Port Vale, Stoke City and Lincoln City.
Since 1960 he has been a first-class umpire and has stood in Tests.

Jerman, Lindsey Crawford Stapleton
Amateur. *b:* 23.4.1915, Old Fletton, Hunts. Lower order right-hand batsman, right-arm fast medium bowler. *Team* Essex (1950–51, 3 matches).
Career batting
3–2–0–8–8–4.00–0–*ct* 2
Bowling 222–1–222.00–0–0–1/39
He also played for Cambridgeshire.

Jerram, Nigel Martyn
Amateur. *b:* 9.3.1900, Weymouth. Dorset. *d:* 19.12.1968, Wadebridge, Cornwall. Middle order right-hand batsman. *Sch* Marlborough. *Team* Royal Air Force (1930).
Career batting
1–2–1–78–43*–78.00–0–*ct* 1

Jervis, Hon William Monk
Amateur. *b:* 25.1.1827, London. *d:* 25.3.1909, Quarndon, Derbyshire. Uncle of Lord Harris (Kent). Middle order right-hand batsman. *Sch*

Eton. *Teams* Derbyshire (1873, 1 match); Oxford U (1848).
Career batting
5–8–3–34–17–6.80–0–*ct* 3

He also played for Staffordshire, Warwickshire and Herefordshire.

He assisted in the establishment of Derbyshire CCC and was President of the County Club, 1871 to 1887.

Jervis, William Swynfen
Amateur. *b:* 18.11.1840, Stafford. *d:* 3.4.1920, Southsea, Hants. Middle order batsman, useful bowler. *Team* Lancashire (1874, 1 match).
Career batting
2–4–0–27–13–6.75–0–*ct* 0
Bowling 91–8–11.37–1–0–6/30

He also appeared for Warwickshire (not first-class) and Cheshire.

His first-class debut was for Gentlemen of Kent in 1865.

Jesson, Robert Wilfred Fairey
Amateur. *b:* 17.6.1886, Southampton, Hants. *d:* 22.2.1917, near Basra, Mesopotamia. Lower order right-hand batsman, slow leg break bowler. *Sch* Sherborne. *Teams* Hampshire (1907–10, 14 matches). Oxford U (1908).
Career batting
15–28–4–198–38–8.25–0–*ct* 8
Bowling 528–21–25.14–1–0–5/42

Jessop, Gilbert Laird
Amateur. *b:* 19.5.1874, Cheltenham, Gloucestershire. *d:* 11.5.1955, Fordington, Dorset. Father of G.L.O. (Hants), brother of O.W.T. (Gloucs). Brilliant middle order right-hand batsman, right-arm fast bowler, excellent deep field. *Teams* Gloucestershire (1894–1914, 345 matches); Cambridge U (1896–99, blue all four years); London County (1900–03). *Tours* Warner to USA 1897; Ranjitsinhji to North America 1899; MacLaren to Australia 1901/02. *Tests* England (1899–1912, 18 matches).
Career batting
493–855–37–26698–286–32.63–53–*ct* 463
Bowling 19904–873–22.80–42–4–8/29
Test batting
18–26–0–569–104–21.88–1–*ct* 11
Bowling 354–10–35.40–0–0–4/68

The most consistent of all fast scoring batsmen in first-class cricket, Jessop was known as 'The Croucher' from his stance at the wicket. Very quick on his feet and having a wonderful eye, he was able to come out to even the fastest bowlers and either straight drive them or pull them with incredible certainty. A few players have been able to hit the ball harder, but none excelled him in his all-round hitting.

Inevitably he would sometimes fail due to his determination to hit out almost from the start of an innings, but on many occasions his batting quickly turned the course of a match. His fielding at extra mid off was almost worth a place in a County side for the number of runs he saved and he was a notable fast bowler.

In all he hit 1,000 runs in a season 14 times, going on to 2,000 twice, with 2,323, av 40.75 in 1901 his best aggregate. Of his five double centuries, the highest was 286 for Gloucs v Sussex at Hove in 1903. In that innings he reached the 200 mark in 120 minutes – a record in first-class cricket, and three of his other double centuries came up in less than 2½ hours, a record totally without parallel. He took 100 wickets in a season twice (best 116, av 17.85, in 1897) and performed the 'double' twice, once including 2,000 runs.

His most famous innings came in the fifth Test against Australia at the Oval in 1902, when he scored 104 of 139 in 77 minutes, allowing England to recover from 48 for 5 and win by one wicket.

His name in fact dominates the 'Fast Scoring Record' section of the cricket press. Twice he reached fifty in 15 minutes and his fastest century came in 40 minutes, closely followed by another 42 minutes.

Jessop, Rev Gilbert Laird Osborne
Amateur. *b:* 6.9.1906, Kensington, London. Son of G.L. (Gloucs), nephew of O. W. T. (Gloucs). Middle order right-hand batsman, off break bowler. *Sch* Weymouth. *Team* Hampshire (1933, 3 matches).
Career batting
4–7–0–86–29–12.28–0–*ct* 2
Bowling 67–1–67.00–0–0–1/16

His debut in first-class matches was for MCC in 1929.

He also played for Cambridgeshire and Dorset.

Jessop, Hylton
Amateur. *b:* 1868, Cheltenham, Gloucs. *d:* 19.7.1924, Cheltenham, Gloucs. Father of W.H. (Gloucs). Hard hitting middle order batsman, slow bowler. *Team* Gloucestershire (1896, 3 matches).
Career batting
3–6–0–75–41–12.50–0–*ct* 5
Bowling 29–1–29.00–0–0–1/12

Jessop, Osman Walter Temple
Amateur. *b:* 3.1.1878, Cheltenham, Gloucs. *d:* 25.5.1941, Northwood, Middlesex. Brother of G.L. (Gloucs), uncle of G. L. O. (Hants). Middle

order batsman. *Team* Gloucestershire (1901–11, 2 matches).
Career batting
2–4–1–61–29–20.33–0–*ct* 1

Jessop, Walter Hylton
Amateur. *b:* 22.3.1899, Cheltenham, Gloucs. *d:* 25.12.1960, Charlton Kings, Gloucs. Son of Hylton (Gloucs). Middle order right-hand batsman. *Sch* Cheltenham. *Team* Gloucestershire (1920–21, 5 matches).
Career batting
5–10–1–118–25–13.11–0–*ct* 1

Jessopp, Neville Augustus
Amateur. *b:* 31.7.1898, Sleaford, Lincs. *d:* 13.7.1977, Claremont, Cape Province, South Africa. Lower order batsman, left-arm fast medium bowler. *Sch* Harrow. *Team* MCC (1919).
Career batting
2–3–1–2–2–1.00–0–*ct* 2
Bowling 150–7–21.42–0–0–3/64
He played County cricket for Norfolk in 1920, but then emigrated to British East Africa.

Jessup, Anthony
Amateur. *b:* 31.8.1928, Blindley Heath, Surrey. Lower order left-hand batsman, slow left-arm bowler. *Sch* Caterham. *Team* Oxford U (1950–51).
Career batting
7–10–7–18–7*–6.00–0–*ct* 4
Bowling 432–19–22.73–3–1–5/30

Jesty, Trevor Edward
Cricketer. *b:* 2.6.1948, Gosport, Hants. Middle order right-hand batsman, right-arm medium pace bowler. *Teams* Hampshire (1966–83, 315 matches); Border (1973/4); Griqualand West (1974/5 to 1980/1); Canterbury (1979/80). *Tours* International XI to Jamaica 1982/3; England to Australia and New Zealand 1982/3 (no first-class matches).
Career batting
341–540–71–14345–187–30.58–22–*ct* 197–*st* 1
Bowling 14397–536–26.86–18–0–7/75
He hit 1,000 runs in a season, six times (best 1,645, av 58.75, in 1982).

Jewell, Arthur North
Amateur. *b:* 1888, Iquique, Chile. *d:* 8.9.1922, Selsey, Sussex. Brother of M. F. S. (Worcs and Sussex) and J. E. (Orange Free State), uncle of J. M. H. (Worcs). Attractive middle order right-hand batsman, wicket-keeper. *Sch* Felsted. *Teams* Orange Free State (1910/11); Worcestershire (1919–20, 22 matches).
Career batting
29–56–0–946–128–16.89–3–*ct* 21–*st* 10

Jewell, Guy Alonzo Frederick William
Amateur. *b:* 6.10.1916, Axford Hants. *d:* 23.12.1965, Basingstoke, Hants. Left-hand batsman, slow left-arm bowler. *Team* Hampshire (1952, 1 match).
Career batting
1–2–0–1–1–0.50–0–*ct* 2
Bowling 52–1–52.00–0–0–1/38
He also played for Berkshire.

Jewell, John Mark Herbert
Amateur. *b:* 1917, Bloemfontein, South Africa. *d:* 29.10.1946, Durban, South Africa. Son of J. E. (Orange Free State), nephew of A. N. (Orange Free State and Worcs) and M. F. S. (Worcs and Sussex). Middle order right-hand batsman. *Sch* Felsted. *Team* Worcestershire (1939, 2 matches).
Career batting
2–4–0–30–24–7.50–0–*ct* 2

Jewell, Maurice Francis Stewart
Amateur. *b:* 15.9.1885, Iquique, Chile. *d:* 28.5.1978, Birdham, Sussex. Brother of A.N. (Worcs) and J. E. (Orange Free State), uncle of J. M. H. (Worcs). Attacking middle order right-hand batsman, slow left-arm bowler. *Sch* Marlborough. *Teams* Worcestershire (1909–33, 121 matches); Sussex (1914–19, 6 matches). *Tour* MCC to South America 1926/7.
Career batting
133–239–15–4114–125–18.36–2–*ct* 67
Bowling 3448–104–33.15–2–0–7/56
He appeared for both Sussex and Worcestershire in 1919, one of the few 20th century players to represent two first-class Counties in a single season. He captained Worcs 1920–21, 1926, 1928 and 1929 and was for many years one of the major figures behind the scenes at Worcester, ending as President from 1950 to 1956.

Jewell, William John
Amateur. *b:* 1855, Helston, Cornwall. *d:* 3.3.1927, Taunton. Opening batsman. *Team* Somerset (1884, 1 match).
Career batting
1–2–0–10–9–5.00–0–*ct* 0
Bowling 14–0

Jilani, Mohammad Baqa Khan
(*see under* Baqa Jilani)

Jobson, Edward Percy
Amateur. *b:* 20.3.1855, Wall Heath, Staffs. *d:* 20.4.1909, Himley, Staffs. Middle order right-hand batsman, right-hand medium pace round-

arm bowler, cover point. *Team* Worcestershire (1900–03, 7 matches).
Career batting
8–14–0–208–43–14.85–0–*ct* 1
Bowling 8–0
His first-class debut was for MCC in 1891 and most of his County cricket was played for Worcs before that side became first-class.

Joginder Singh
Amateur. *b:* 7.7.1904, Manakmasra, India. *d:* 1940, India. Attacking middle order right-hand batsman. *Teams* Sikhs (1925/6); South Punjab (1934/5 to 1938/9). *Tour* India to England 1932.
Career batting
22–41–6–561–79–16.02–0–*ct* 15–*st* 1
Bowling 101–2–50.50–0–0–2/101
He performed very modestly on his visit to England.

John, George
Amateur. *b: circa* 1883, St Vincent. *d:* 14.1.1944, Port of Spain, Trinidad. Lower order right-hand batsman, right-arm fast medium bowler. *Team* Trinidad (1909/10 to 1925/6). *Tour* West Indies to England 1923.
Career batting
29–42–9–466–111–14.12–1–*ct* 16
Bowling 2559–133–19.24–7–1–7/52
On his 1923 tour to England he headed the bowling averages of all matches, but was not quite so successful in strictly first-class games, taking 49 wickets, av 19.51.
His final first-class match was for Trinidad and Barbados in 1927/8.

John, Henry Celestine Robert
Amateur. *b:* 26.5.1862, Agra, India. *d:* 24.6.1941, Oxford. Lower order right-hand batsman, right-arm fast medium bowler. *Sch* Stonyhurst. *Teams* Lancashire (1881, 1 match); Europeans (1893/4 to 1903/4).
Career batting
6–9–5–65–15*–16.25–0–*ct* 8
Bowling 380–19–20.00–1–0–5/53

Johns, Alfred Edward
Amateur. *b:* 22.1.1868, Hawthorn, Victoria, Australia. *d:* 13.2.1934, Melbourne, Victoria, Australia. Lower order left-hand batsman, wicket-keeper. *Team* Victoria (1894/5 to 1898/9, 16 matches). *Tours* Australia to England 1896, 1899.
Career batting
37–54–16–429–57–11.28–0–*ct* 58–*st* 26
On both his visits to England he was the reserve wicket-keeper and did not appear in any Tests.

Johns, David Frank Victor
Amateur. *b:* 27.6.1921, Paddington, London. *d:* 20.11.1979, High Wycombe, Bucks. Middle order left-hand batsman, slow left-arm bowler. *Team* Minor Counties (1952).
Career batting
1–2–0–4–4–2.00–0–*ct* 1
Bowling 55–1–55.00–0–0–1/55
He appeared for Buckinghamshire from 1950 to 1965, being captain for three seasons.

Johns, John
Amateur. *b:* 15.10.1885, Briton-Ferry, Glamorgan. *d:* 10.1.1956, Briton-Ferry, Glamorgan. Lower order right-hand batsman, right-arm fast medium bowler. *Team* Glamorgan (1922, 1 match).
Career batting
1–2–1–4–3–4.00–0–*ct* 0
Bowling 62–2–31.00–0–0–2/29

Johns, Robert Leslie
(known as Robin Leslie Johns)
Cricketer. *b:* 30.6.1946, Southampton, Hants. Middle order right-hand batsman, off break bowler. *Teams* Oxford U (1970, blue); Northants (1971, 6 matches).
Career batting
14–22–2–335–61*–16.75–0–*ct* 9
Bowling 730–17–42.94–0–0–4/76
He appeared for Hertfordshire commencing 1975.

Johnson, Alexander Anthony
Cricketer. *b:* 30.3.1944, Loughborough, Leics. Lower order right-hand batsman, right-arm fast medium bowler. *Teams* Nottinghamshire (1963–66, 26 matches).
Career batting
27–37–4–289–45–8.75–0–*ct* 24
Bowling 1717–49–35.04–0–0–4/13
He also played for Northumberland and Durham. His final first-class match was for Minor Counties in 1974.

Johnson, Colin
Cricketer. *b:* 5.9.1947, Pocklington, Yorkshire. Middle order right-hand batsman, off break bowler. *Sch* Pocklington. *Team* Yorkshire (1969–79, 100 matches).
Career batting
100–152–14–2960–107–21.44–2–*ct* 50
Bowling 265–4–66.25–0–0–2/22

Johnson, Frederick
Professional. *b:* 14.3.1851, Rolvenden, Kent. *d:* 24.11.1923, Lambeth. Lower order left-hand batsman, left-arm fast medium bowler. *Team* Surrey (1878–83, 20 matches).

Career batting
20–32–8–158–21*–6.58–0–*ct* 14
Bowling 1302–51–25.52–4–1–6/42

Johnson, Frank Sidney Roland
Amateur. *b:* 4.8.1917, Simla, India. Middle order right-hand batsman. *Team* Combined Services (1947).
Career batting
1–2–0–11–11–5.50–0–*ct* 0

Johnson, George Henry
Amateur. *b:* 16.12.1894, Yorkshire. *d:* 20.1.1965, Uppingham, Rutland. Lower order right-hand batsman, wicket-keeper. *Team* Northants (1922–32, 18 matches).
Career batting
18–28–14–142–43*–10.14–0–*ct* 14–*st* 6
He served on Northants CCC Committee from 1926 to 1939.

Johnson, George James
Professional. *b:* 23.12.1907, Loddington, Northants. Lower order right-hand batsman, right-arm fast bowler. *Team* Northants (1929–35, 5 matches).
Career batting
5–8–1–49–28*–7.00–0–*ct* 1
Bowling 349–5–69.80–0–0–2/41

Johnson, Graham William
Cricketer. *b:* 8.11.1946, Beckenham, Kent. Opening or middle order right-hand batsman, off break bowler, good slip field. *Teams* Kent (1965–83, 340 matches); Transvaal (1981/2). *Tours* Kent to West Indies 1972/3 (not first-class); Robins to South Africa 1973/4, to West Indies 1974/5 (not first-class).
Career batting
349–543–68–11823–168–24.89–11–*ct* 280
Bowling 15838–516–30.69–19–3–7/76
He hit 1,000 runs in a season three times (best 1,438, av 31.26, in 1973 and 1,438, av 35.95, in 1975).

Johnson, Hophnie Hobah Hines
Amateur. *b:* 13.7.1910, Kingston, Jamaica. Vigorous tail end right-hand batsman, right-arm fast bowler, good slip. *Team* Jamaica (1934/5 to 1950/1). *Tour* West Indies to England 1950. *Tests* West Indies (1947/8 to 1950, 3 matches).
Career batting
28–30–12–316–39*–17.55–0–*ct* 13
Bowling 1589–68–23.36–5–1–5/33
Test batting
3–4–0–38–22–9.50–0–*ct* 0
Bowling 238–13–18.30–2–1–5/41
Not fully fit during the 1950 tour to England, he appeared in only two Tests and returned a modest record.

Johnson, Hubert Laurence
Amateur until 1950, professional from 1951. *b:* 8.11.1927, Barbados. Middle order right-hand batsman, off break bowler, fine cover field, occasional wicket-keeper. *Team* Derbyshire (1949–66, 350 matches).
Career batting
351–606–65–14286–154–26.40–16–*ct* 216–*st* 2
Bowling 822–21–39.14–0–0–3/12
He hit 1,000 runs in a season six times (best 1,872, av 37.44, in 1960).

Johnson, Ivan Nicholas
Cricketer. *b:* 27.6.1953, Nassau, Bahamas. Middle order left-hand batsman, slow left-arm bowler. *Sch* Malvern. *Team* Worcestershire (1972–75, 33 matches).
Career batting
33–43–10–716–69–21.69–0–*ct* 13
Bowling 1533–37–41.43–1–0–5/74

Johnson, Ian William
Amateur. *b:* 8.12.1918, North Melbourne, Victoria, Australia. Son of W.J. (Victoria). Lower order right-hand batsman, off break bowler. *Team* Victoria (1935/6 to 1955/6, 77 matches). *Tours* Australia to England 1948, 1956, to South Africa 1949/50, to West Indies 1954/5, to India and Pakistan 1956/7, to New Zealand 1945/6. *Tests* Australia (1945/6 to 1956/7, 45 matches).
Career batting
189–243–29–4905–132*–22.92–2–*ct* 137
Bowling 14423–619–23.30–27–4–7/42
Test batting
45–66–12–1000–77–18.51–0–*ct* 30
Bowling 3182–109–29.19–3–0–7/44
On his 1948 tour to England he took 85 wickets, av 18.37, in first-class matches, but proved ineffective in the Tests; in 1956 he was less successful, but as captain of the side proved an effective leader.

Johnson, Joseph
Professional. *b:* 16.5.1916, South Kirkby, Yorkshire. Lower order right-hand batsman, slow left-arm bowler. *Team* Yorkshire (1936–39, 3 matches).
Career batting
3–3–2–5–4*–5.00–0–*ct* 1
Bowling 27–5–5.40–1–0–5/16
He played soccer for Doncaster Rovers.

Johnson, Dr John Inchbald
Amateur. *b:* 1871, Great Ouseburn, Yorkshire. *d:*

20.10.1930, Culworth, Northants. Middle order batsman. *Team* Northants (1907, 1 match).
Career batting
1–1–0–0–0–0.00–0–*ct* 1

Johnson, John Stephen
Cricketer. *b:* 7.7.1944, Doncaster, Yorkshire. Opening right-hand batsman. *Team* Minor Counties (1979).
Career batting
1–2–1–170–146*–170.00–1–*ct* 0
He hit a century in his only first-class match.
He has appeared for Shropshire since 1968.

Johnson, Laurence Alan
Professional. *b:* 12.8.1936, West Horsley, Surrey. Lower order right-hand batsman, wicket-keeper. *Team* Northants (1958–72, 153 matches). *Tour* MCC to East Africa 1963/4.
Career batting
156–189–40–1573–50–10.55–0–*ct* 262–*st* 67
Bowling 61–1–61.00–0–0–1/60

Johnson, Mark
Cricketer. *b:* 23.4.1958, Gleadless, Sheffield, Yorkshire. Middle order right-hand batsman, right-arm medium or off break bowler. *Sch* Pocklington. *Team* Yorkshire (1981, 4 matches).
Career batting
4–4–2–2–2–1.00–0–*ct* 1
Bowling 301–7–43.00–0–0–4/48.

Johnson, Paul
Cricketer. *b:* 24.4.1965, Newark, Notts. Stylish middle order right-hand batsman, right-arm medium pace bowler. *Team* Nottinghamshire (1982–83, 20 matches).
Career batting
20–35–3–702–125–21.83–1–*ct* 9

Johnson, Peter David
Cricketer. *b:* 12.11.1949, Nottingham. Middle order right-hand batsmsn, leg break and googly bowler. *Sch* Nottingham High School. *Teams* Cambridge U (1970–72, blue all three years); Nottinghamshire (1970–77, 58 matches) *Tour* Minor Counties to East Africa 1982/3 (not first-class).
Career batting
89–149–14–3363–106*–24.91–2–*ct* 33
Bowling 972–11–83.36–0–0–3/34
His first-class debut was for D.H.Robins' XI in 1969. He hit 1,063 runs, av 32.21, in 1975.
He played for Lincolnshire 1978 to 1982, and for Cambridgeshire commencing 1983.
His final first-class match was for Minor Counties in 1982.

Johnson, Peter Lovell
Amateur. *b:* 22.8.1926, Liverpool. Middle order right-hand batsman, right-arm medium pace bowler. *Sch* Liverpool College. *Teams* Cambridge U (1947); Combined Services (1950).
Career batting
2–3–0–61–40–20.33–0–*ct* 1

Johnson, Peter Malcolm
Cricketer. *b:* 21.12.1947, London. Tail end right-hand batsman, wicket-keeper. *Team* Oxford U (1971).
Career batting
1–2–0–2–2–1.00–0–*ct* 0–*st* 1

Johnson, Peter Randall
Amateur. *b:* 5.8.1880, Wellington, New Zealand. *d:* 1.7.1959, Sidmouth, Devon. Son of G.R. (Cambridge U). Stylish right-hand opening batsman, right-arm fast bowler. *Sch* Eton. *Teams* Cambridge U (1900–01, blue 1901); Somerset (1901–27, 229 matches). *Tours* Bosanquet to North America 1901; Hawke to Australia and New Zealand 1902/03; MCC to New Zealand 1906/07.
Career batting
275–488–24–11931–164–25.71–18–*ct* 176
Bowling 777–20–38.85–0–0–4/99
He hit 1,000 runs in a season once : 1,012, av 28.91, in 1921.
He also played for Devonshire.

Johnson, Tyrell Francis
Amateur. *b:* 10.1.1917, Tunapuna, Trinidad. Lower order left-hand batsman, left-arm fast bowler. *Team* Trinidad (1935/6 to 1938/9). *Tour* West Indies to England 1939. *Test* West Indies (1939, 1 match).
Career batting
18–21–11–90–27–9.00–0–*ct* 8
Bowling 1075–50–21.50–1–0–6/41
Test batting
1–1–1–9–9*–no av–0–*ct* 1
Bowling 129–3–43.00–0–0–2/53
He looked a better bowler than his modest record in England showed, his physique being unable to stand the strain of constant first-class cricket.

Johnston, Andrew
Amateur. *b:* 26.2.1916, Linlithgow, West Lothian, Scotland. Right-hand batsman, off break bowler. *Team* Scotland (1947–51).
Career batting
2–4–1–82–50*–27.33–0–*ct* 2
Bowling 47–1–47.00–0–0–1/47

Johnston, Alexander Colin
Amateur. *b:* 26.1.1884, Derby. *d:* 27.12.1952, Knaphill, Woking, Surrey. Son of D.A. (Derbyshire). Opening right-hand batsman, leg break bowler. *Sch* Winchester. *Team* Hampshire (1902–1919, 108 matches).
Career batting
116–206–13–5966–175–30.91–10–*ct* 58–*st* 1
Bowling 805–18–44.72–0–0–4/21

A noted all-round sportsman, he played soccer and hockey for the Army and also was well known on the polo field. A permanent limp due to wounds received in the First World War did not prevent him from continuing to play cricket. He hit 1,000 runs in a season twice (best 1,158, av 36.18, in 1910).

His final first-class match was for Gentlemen of England in 1920.

Johnston, Arthur Sannox
Amateur. *b:* 16.3.1863, Hornsey, Middlesex. *d:* 8.8.1929, Eltham, London. Middle order right-hand batsman, right-arm medium pace bowler. *Sch* Mill Hill. *Teams* Middlesex (1886–87, 3 matches); Essex (1894–96, 7 matches).
Career batting
10–18–2–259–63–16.18–0–*ct* 5

Johnston, Sir Duncan Alexander
Amateur. *b:* 25.6.1847, Edinburgh, Scotland. *d:* 22.10.1931, Edinburgh, Scotland. Father of A.C. (Hampshire). Opening right-hand batsman. *Sch* Glenalmond. *Team* Derbyshire (1882, 4 matches).
Career batting
4–8–0–65–31–8.12–0–*ct* 0

Johnston, Donald Clark
Amateur. *b:* 2.12.1894, Shanghai, China. *d:* 1.8.1918, Beugneux, France. He died of wounds. Tail end batsman, bowler. *Sch* Malvern. *Team* Oxford U (1914).
Career batting
2–2–1–6–6–6.00–0–*ct* 2
Bowling 71–2–35.50–0–0–2/27

Johnston, Harry Grant Forsyth
Cricketer. *b:* 24.12.1949, Kirkwall, Orkney, Scotland. Left-hand batsman, slow left-arm bowler. *Team* Scotland (1975–81).
Career batting
2–3–0–24–12–8.00–0–*ct* 0
Bowling 86–3–28.66–0–0–2/60

He played football for Montrose.

Johnston, Robert Herbert
Amateur. *b:* 1.5.1865, Edinburgh, Scotland. *d:* 15.2.1910, Edinburgh, Scotland. Right-hand batsman, wicket-keeper. *Sch* Edinburgh Academy and Clifton. *Team* Scotland (1905).
Career batting
1–2–0–13–13–6.50–0–*ct* 2

Johnston, Robert Ian
Cricketer. *b:* 1.7.1948, Belfast. Right-hand batsman, right-arm medium pace bowler. *Team* Ireland (1979–83).
Career batting
3–5–2–86–34–28.66–0–*ct* 3
Bowling 3–0

Johnston, William Arras
Amateur. *b:* 26.2.1922, Beeac, Victoria, Australia. Lower order left-hand batsman, left-arm fast medium bowler or slow spin bowler. *Team* Victoria (1945/6 to 1954/5, 56 matches). *Tours* Australia to England 1948, 1953, to South Africa 1949/50, to West Indies 1954/5. *Tests* Australia (1947/8 to 1954/5, 40 matches).
Career batting
142–162–73–1129–38–12.68–0–*ct* 52
Bowling 12936–554–23.35–29–6–8/52
Test batting
40–49–25–273–29–11.37–0–*ct* 16
Bowling 3826–160–23.91–7–0–6/44

He had a most successful tour to England in 1948 taking 102 wickets, av 16.42, in first-class matches and 27 wickets in the Tests. In 1953 he was injured in a preliminary practice match and was never really fit, a fact that was reflected in his figures; he did however obtain a batting average of 102.00, by dint of being dismissed only once in 17 innings.

Johnstone, Conrad Powell, CBE
Amateur. *b:* 19.8.1895, Sydenham, Kent. *d:* 23.6.1974, Eastry, Kent. Opening left-hand batsman, right-arm medium pace bowler. *Sch* Rugby. *Teams* Cambridge U (1919–20, blue both years); Kent (1919–33, 36 matches); Europeans (1926/7 to 1947/8); Madras (1934/5 to 1944/5).
Career batting
110–190–11–5482–135–30.62–6–*ct* 105
Bowling 2798–102+1–27.43–3–0–6/28

He spent much of his life in India and was awarded the CBE for his efforts on behalf of cricket in Madras. His last first-class matches in England were for Free Foresters and for MCC in 1939. A noted golfer, he captained Cambridge in 1920.

Jolley, William Turner
Amateur. *b:* 3.8.1923, Smallthorne, Stoke-on-Trent, Staffs. Lower order right-hand batsman, right-arm fast bowler. *Team* Lancashire (1947, 2 matches).

Career batting
2–2–1–21–13–21.00–0–*ct* 5
Bowling 132–5–26.40–0–0–4/31
He also played for Staffordshire.

Jolliffe, Henry James
Amateur. *b:* 1867, Fordingbridge, Hants. *d:* 1909, Southampton, Hants. Middle order batsman. *Team* Hampshire (1902, 1 match).
Career batting
1–2–0–1–1–0.50–0–*ct* 1

Jolly, Norman William
Amateur. *b:* 5.8.1882, Adelaide, Australia. *d:* May 1954, Australia. Lower order batsman, wicket-keeper. *Team* Worcestershire (1907, 1 match).
Career batting
1–2–1–9–8–9.00–0–*ct* 3

Jones, Alan
Professional. *b:* 4.11.1938, Velindre, Glamorgan. Sound opening left-hand batsman, off break bowler. *Teams* Glamorgan (1957–83, 610 matches); Western Australia (1963/4, 9 matches); Northern Transvaal (1975/6); Natal (1976/7). *Tours* Glamorgan to West Indies 1969/70; MCC to Ceylon 1969/70.
Career batting
645–1168–72–36049–204*–32.89–56–*ct* 288
Bowling 333–3–111.00–0–0–1/24
He hit 1,000 runs in a season 23 times (best 1,865, av 34.53, in 1966). His only double century was 204* for Glamorgan v Hampshire at Basingstoke in 1980. He appeared for England v Rest of the World in 1970. From 1976 to 1978 he captained Glamorgan. He scored more runs in first-class cricket than any other non-Test player.

Jones, Allan Arthur
Cricketer. *b:* 9.12.1947, Horley, Surrey. Tail end right-hand batsman, right-arm fast medium bowler. *Sch* St John's, Horsham. *Teams* Sussex (1966–69, 18 matches); Somerset (1970–75, 118 matches); Northern Transvaal (1972/3); Middlesex (1976–79, 52 matches); Orange Free State (1976/7); Glamorgan (1980–81, 19 matches).
Career batting
214–216–68–799–33–5.39–0–*ct* 50
Bowling 15414–549–28.07–23–3–9/51
He was the first player since the rules governing County qualifications were introduced in 1873 to appear for four first-class Counties. His best bowling was 9/51 for Somerset v Sussex at Hove in 1972.

Jones, Alan Keith Colin
Cricketer. *b:* 20.4.1951, Solihull, Warwickshire. Opening right-hand batsman. *Sch* Solihull. *Teams* Warwickshire (1969–73, 4 matches); Oxford U (1971–73, blue all three years).
Career batting
35–65–1–1403–111–21.92–1–*ct* 13
Bowling 7–0
He appeared for Warwickshire in one match in 1969, then not again until 1973.

Jones, Alan Lewis
Cricketer. *b:* 1.6.1957, Alltwen, Glamorgan. Middle order left-hand batsman. *Team* Glamorgan (1973–83, 101 matches).
Career batting
101–179–16–3672–99–22.52–0–*ct* 56
Bowling 42–0.
He hit 1,036 runs, av 31.39, in 1983.

Jones, Adrian Nicholas
Cricketer. *b:* 22.7.1961, Woking, Surrey. Lower order left-hand batsman, right-arm fast medium bowler. *Teams* Sussex (1981–83, 14 matches); Border (1981/2).
Career batting
16–20–8–73–29–6.08–0–*ct* 1
Bowling 849–29–29.27–0–0–4/33

Jones, Arthur Owen
Amateur. *b:* 16.8.1872, Shelton, Notts. *d:* 21.12.1914, Dunstable, Beds. Opening right-hand batsman, leg break bowler, brilliant close field. *Sch* Bedford Modern. *Teams* Cambridge U (1892–93, blue 1893); Nottinghamshire (1892–1914, 397 matches); London County (1901). *Tours* MacLaren to Australia 1901/02; MCC to Australia 1907/08. *Tests* England (1899–1909, 12 matches).
Career batting
472–774–47–22935–296–31.54–34–*ct* 577–*st* 2
Bowling 10929–333–32.81–8–1–8/71
Test batting
12–21–0–291–34–13.85–0–*ct* 15
Bowling 133–3–44.33–0–0–3/73
He hit 1,000 runs in a season nine times, going on to 2,000 once : 2,292, av 46.77, in 1901. His four double centuries were all for Notts, the highest being 296 v Gloucs at Trent Bridge in 1903, a new County record.
He captained Notts from 1900 to 1914, though missing many matches in the last two years due to illness. He also led MCC to Australia in 1907/08 and captained England in two Tests.
He appeared occasionally for Bedfordshire.
A noted rugby footballer, he played as a three quarter for Leicester and later became a well-known referee.

Jones, Arthur Royston Gabe
(also known as Gabe-Jones)
Amateur. *b:* 25.11.1906, Clydach Vale, Glamorgan. *d:* 23.2.1965, Cardiff. Middle order batsman, useful bowler. *Sch* Blundell's. *Team* Glamorgan (1922, 1 match).
Career batting
1–1–1–6–6*–no av–0–*ct* 0
He was only 15 years and 9 months old on his appearance for Glamorgan v Leics at Cardiff in 1922, with still two seasons in front of him at school.

Jones, Archibald Trevor Maxwell
Amateur. *b:* 9.4.1920, Wells, Somerset. Middle order right-hand batsman, leg break bowler. *Team* Somerset (1938–48, 21 matches).
Career batting
21–35–0–399–106–11.40–1–*ct* 16
Bowling 132–3–44.00–0–0–1/3

Jones, Alfred William
Amateur. *b:* 6.8.1900, Tewkesbury, Gloucs. Middle order left-hand batsman, right-arm medium pace bowler. *Team* Northants (1933, 1 match).
Career batting
1–2–0–13–12–6.50–0–*ct* 0

Jones, Barry John Richardson
Cricketer. *b:* 2.11.1955, Shrewsbury, Salop. Opening left-hand batsman, right-arm medium pace bowler. *Sch* Wrekin College. *Team* Worcestershire (1976–80, 46 matches).
Career batting
46–81–3–1076–65–13.79–0–*ct* 19
He appeared for Shropshire commencing 1981.

Jones, Charles Ian McMillan
Amateur. *b:* 11.10.1934, Leeds, Yorkshire. Middle order right-hand batsman, right-arm medium pace bowler. *Team* Cambridge U (1959).
Career batting
2–3–0–44–44–14.66–0–*ct* 1
His County cricket was for Hertfordshire.

Jones, Charles Langton
Amateur. *b:* 27.11.1853, Liverpool, Lancashire. *d:* 2.4.1904, Toxteth Park, Liverpool, Lancashire. Opening right-hand batsman, useful bowler. *Team* Lancashire (1876–88, 5 matches).
Career batting
11–22–1–165–36–7.85–0–*ct* 0
Bowling 6–1–6.00–0–0–1/6
He was a noted player for Sefton and in Liverpool and District matches, his final first-class match being for Liverpool and District in 1890.

Jones, David
Professional. *b:* 9.4.1914, Hodthorpe, Derbyshire. Middle order right-hand batsman. *Team* Nottinghamshire (1935–39, 24 matches).
Career batting
24–38–5–594–60–18.00–0–*ct* 15
Bowling 7–1–7.00–0–0–1/7
A good soccer player, he appeared at right half for Bury.

Jones, David Alfred
Amateur. *b:* 9.3.1920, Aberkenfig, Glamorgan. Lower order right-hand batsman, right-arm medium pace bowler. *Sch* King's College, Taunton. *Team* Glamorgan (1938, 1 match).
Career batting
1–1–0–6–6–6.00–0–*ct* 0
Bowling 43–2–21.50–0–0–2/22

Jones, Ernest
Amateur. *b:* 30.9.1869, Auburn, South Australia. *d:* 23.11.1943, Adelaide, South Australia. Hard hitting lower order right-hand batsman, right-arm fast bowler, excellent mid off. *Teams* South Australia (1892/3 to 1902/03, 47 matches): Western Australia (1906/7 to 1907/8, 3 matches). *Tours* Australia to England 1896, 1899 and 1902, to South Africa 1902/03. *Tests* Australia (1894/5 to 1902/03, 19 matches).
Careeer batting
144–209–26–2421–82–13.22–0–*ct* 107
Bowling 14638–641–22.83–47–9–8/39
Test batting
19–26–1–126–20–5.04–0–*ct* 21
Bowling 1857–64–29.01–3–1–7/88
His great tour was in 1896 when he took 121 wickets, av 16.03; in 1899 he took 135 wickets, but his average increased to 21.10, whilst in 1902 he was definitely past his best. On his first visit his bowling action came in for considerable criticism, but later he modified his style. His deadliness with the ball came from his ability to make short-pitched deliveries rear up in a most alarming manner and at his height he was regarded by many as the greatest of all Australian fast bowlers.

Jones, Eddie Closs
Amateur, turned professional in 1937 season. *b:* 14.12.1912, Briton-Ferry, Glamorgan. Lower order right-hand batsman, off break bowler. *Team* Glamorgan (1934–46, 100 matches).
Career batting
101–142–30–2016–132–18.00–2–*ct* 44
Bowling 3345–103–32.47–6–1–7/79

Jones, Edward Cyril
Amateur. *b:* 11.3.96, Cardiff. *d:* 23.12.1978,

Cardiff. Middle order batsman. *Team* Glamorgan (1926, 1 match).
Career batting
1 match, did not bat –*ct* 1

Jones, Eifion Wyn
Professional. *b:* 25.6.1942, Velindre, Glamorgan. Brother of Alan (Glamorgan). Lower order right-hand batsman, wicket-keeper. *Team* Glamorgan (1961–83, 405 matches). *Tour* Glamorgan to West Indies 1969/70.
Career batting
405–591–119–8341–146*–17.67–3–*ct* 840–*st* 93
Bowling 5–0

Jones, Frederick Allan
Amateur. *b:* 23.2.1927, Macclesfield, Cheshire. Middle order right-hand batsman. *Teams* Oxford U (1951–52); Scotland (1954–61); Hyderabad (1962/3 to 1963/4).
Career batting
16–31–0–618–88–19.93–0–*ct* 11–*st* 3
Bowling 1–0

In the scholastic profession, he was teaching in Hyderabad when he appeared in Pakistan first-class cricket.

Jones, Frederick J.
Amateur. Tail end batsman, useful bowler. *Team* Liverpool and District (1889).
Career batting
1–2–0–15–12–7.50–0–*ct* 0
Bowling 71–4–17.75–0–0–4/71

Jones, F. M. (*see under* Meyrick-Jones, F. M.)

Jones, George Gregory
Professional. *b:* 8.1.1856, Mitcham, Surrey. *d:* 1.4.1936, Watford, Herts. Hard hitting lower order right-hand batsman, right-hand fast round-arm bowler, good mid off. *Team* Surrey (1875–88, 98 matches).
Career batting
102–162–23–1202–63–8.64–0–*ct* 61
Bowling 5566–323–17.23–15–2–7/20

Jones, George Leonard
Amateur. *b:* 11.2.1909, Lockerbie, Scotland. *d:* 6.6.1944, France. Middle order right-hand batsman. *Team* Hampshire (1937, 9 matches).
Career batting
9–16–4–169–37*–14.08–0–*ct* 3

He also played for Dorset.

Jones, Hugh
Amateur. *b:* 1889, Nass, Lydney, Gloucs. *d:* 10.11.1918, Chatham, Kent, of pneumonia. Middle order batsman. *Sch* Wycliffe. *Team* Gloucestershire (1914, 1 match).
Career batting
1–2–0–11–11–5.50–0–*ct* 0

Jones, Harry Ogwyn
Amateur. *b:* 6.10.1922, Llangennech, Carmarthen. Lower order right-hand batsman, right-arm medium pace bowler. *Team* Glamorgan (1946, 2 matches).
Career batting
2–3–3–10–7*–no av–0–*ct* 0
Bowling 53–0

Jones, Ivor Jeffrey
Professional. *b:* 10.12.1941, Dafen, Carmarthenshire. Tail end right-hand batsman, left-arm fast medium bowler. *Team* Glamorgan (1960–68, 157 matches). *Tours* MCC to East Africa 1963/4, to India 1963/4, to Australia and New Zealand 1965/6, to West Indies 1967/8. *Tests* England (1963/4 to 1967/8, 15 matches).
Career batting
198–213–84–513–21–3.97–0–*ct* 46
Bowling 13278–511–25.98–18–0–8/11
Test batting
15–17–9–38–16–4.75–0–*ct* 4
Bowling 1769–44–40.20–1–0–6/118

He took 100 wickets, av 19.49, in 1967. A serious injury to his arm ended his first-class career in 1968.

Jones, John
Professional. *b:* 18.9.1858, Birmingham. *d:* 18.9.1937, Chalfont St Giles, Bucks. Middle order right-hand batsman, right-arm medium pace bowler, good deep field. *Team* South (1884).
Career batting
3–4–0–173–125–43.25–1–*ct* 1

His County cricket was for Essex (pre first-class) and his final first-class match for Players of the South in 1885.

Jones, James Bruce
Amateur. *b:* 19.8.1910, Larbert, Stirlingshire, Scotland. *d:* 29.4.1943, near Enfidaville, Tunisia. Right-hand batsman. *Sch* Charterhouse. *Team* Scotland (1936–37).
Career batting
2–4–0–91–47–22.75–0–*ct* 0

Jones, James Forbes
Amateur. *b:* 9.1.1911, Larbert, Stirlingshire, Scotland. Right-hand batsman. *Sch* Fettes. *Team* Scotland (1930–39).
Career batting
10–18–1–404–91–23.76–0–*ct* 11
Bowling 38–1–38.00–0–0–1/38

Jones, James Lindley
Amateur. *b:* 1876, Liverpool. Lower order batsman, wicket-keeper. *Sch* Liverpool College. *Team* Lancashire (1910, 4 matches).
Career batting
4–5–4–10–7*–10.00–0–*ct* 5
He also played for Cheshire.

Jones, James M.
Professional. Opening/middle order left-hand batsman, wicket-keeper. *Teams* Somerset (1922–23, 17 matches); Glamorgan (1928–29, 8 matches); Wales (1929).
Career batting
27–48–3–846–75–18.80–0–*ct* 23–*st* 13

Jones, Keith Vaughan
Cricketer. *b:* 28.3.1942, Park Royal, Middlesex. Lower order right-hand batsman, right-arm medium pace bowler. *Team* Middlesex (1967–74, 117 matches).
Career batting
118–157–37–2064–57*–17.20–0–*ct* 49
Bowling 6603–242–27.28–7–0–7/52
He also played for Bedfordshire commencing 1975, his last first-class match being for Minor Counties in 1976.

Jones, Leslie Norman
Amateur. *b:* 1891, Chester, Cheshire. *d:* 8.1.1962, Chester, Cheshire. Middle order right-hand batsman, right-arm bowler. *Team* Minor Counties (1937).
Career batting
1–2–1–13–9*–13.00–0–*ct* 0
Bowling 22–7–3.14–1–0–5/8
He appeared for Cheshire for many years as a leading all-rounder – his brother, W.E. Jones, and his two sons, also represented the County.

Jones, Peter Charles Howard
Cricketer. *b:* 19.8.1948, Rhodesia. Middle order right-hand batsman, leg break bowler. *Team* Oxford U (1971–72, blue both years).
Career batting
26–45–8–521–67–14.08–0–*ct* 13
Bowling 525–13–40.38–0–0–3/51

Jones, Prior Erskine
Amateur. *b:* 6.6.1917, Princes Town, Trinidad. Lower order right-hand batsman, right-arm fast bowler, fine slip. *Team* Trinidad (1940/1 to 1950/1). *Tours* West Indies to India, Pakistan and Ceylon 1948/9, to England 1950, to Australia and New Zealand 1951/2. *Tests* West Indies (1947/8 to 1951/2, 9 matches).
Career batting
61–71–16–775–60*–14.09–0–*ct* 33
Bowling 4531–169–26.81–6–1–7/29
Test batting
9–11–2–47–10*–5.22–0–*ct* 4
Bowling 751–25–30.04–1–0–5/85
He had a very modest tour of England in 1950.

Jones, Peter Henry
Professional. *b:* 19.6.1935, Woolwich, Kent. Middle order left-hand batsman, slow left-arm bowler. *Team* Kent (1953–67, 140 matches).
Career batting
141–232–32–4196–132–20.98–2–*ct* 99
Bowling 6549–231–28.35–6–1–6/41
He hit 1,000 runs in a season twice (best 1,262, av 26.85, in 1961). He also played for Suffolk. He played soccer for Hastings United.

Jones, Ronald
Amateur. *b:* 9.9.1938, Wolverhampton. Middle order right-hand batsman, good cover point. *Team* Worcestershire (1955, 1 match).
Career batting
1–2–0–25–23–12.50–0–*ct* 0

Jones, Richard Henry
Amateur. *b:* 3.11.1916, Redditch, Worcs. Opening left-hand batsman, right-arm medium pace bowler. *Team* Warwickshire (1946, 1 match).
Career batting
1–2–0–32–23–16.00–0–*ct* 1
Bowling 27–0

Jones, Richard Stoakes
Amateur. *b:* 14.3.1857, Dymchurch, Kent. *d:* 9.5.1935, Dymchurch, Kent. Stylish middle order right-hand batsman, good deep field. *Sch* Chatham House, Ramsgate. *Team* Kent (1877–86, 49 matches); Cambridge U (1878–80, blue 1879–80).
Career batting
69–116–6–1887–124–17.15–1–*ct* 46

Jones, Richard Tyrrell
Amateur. *b:* 27.6.1871, Oswestry, Shropshire. *d:* 31.8.1940, Knolton Bryn, Flintshire. Steady middle order right-hand batsman, right-arm medium pace bowler. *Sch* Eton. *Teams* Oxford U (1890–92, blue 1892).
Career batting
10–20–0–310–63–15.50–0–*ct* 2
Bowling 13–0
He played for Shropshire and Staffordshire.

Jones, Samuel Percy
Amateur. *b:* 1.8.1861, Sydney, New South Wales,

Australia. *d:* 14.7.1951, Auckland, New Zealand. Opening/middle order right-hand batsman, right-arm fast medium bowler, brilliant field. *Teams* New South Wales (1880/1 to 1894/5, 31 matches); Queensland (1896/7 to 1899/1900, 8 matches); Auckland (1904/5 to 1908/9). *Tours* Australia to England 1882, 1886, 1888, 1890; Queensland to New Zealand 1896/7. *Tests* Australia (1881/2 to 1887/8, 12 matches).
Career batting
151–259–13–5193–151–21.10–5–*ct* 82
Bowling 1844–55–33.52–1–0–5/54
Test batting
12–24–4–432–87–21.60–0–*ct* 12
Bowling 112–6–18.66–0–0–4/47

His most successful tour to England was in 1886 when he hit 1,497 runs, av 24.95. On the 1888 tour he unfortunately contracted smallpox and missed over half the tour – the nature of his illness was not revealed in case it caused the tour to be cut shc

Jones, Thomas Babington
Amateur. *b:* 20.1.1851, Bridgend, Glamorgan. *d:* 6.8.1890, Brislington, Bristol. Lower order left-hand batsman, right-hand medium pace round-arm bowler, mid off. *Sch* Christ College, Brecon. *Team* Oxford U (1874, blue).
Career batting
6–10–1–146–40–16.22–0–*ct* 6
Bowling 267–19–14.05–1–1–6/26

He played for Breconshire. He was a rugby international for Wales.

Jones, Thomas Charles
Amateur. *b:* 1.4.1901, Pontypool, Monmouthshire. *d:* 19.7.1935, Westminster, London. Opening/middle order batsman, good cover point. *Sch* Shrewsbury. *Team* Glamorgan (1925–28, 3 matches).
Career batting
3–6–0–36–21–6.00–0–*ct* 0

Jones, Watkin Edward
Professional. *b:* 6.7.1917, Gwaun-cae-Gurwen, Glamorgan. Lower order right-hand batsman, right-arm fast medium bowler. *Team* Glamorgan (1946–47, 5 matches).
Career batting
5–1–0–0–0–0.00–0–*ct* 1
Bowling 342–13–26.30–1–0–7/92

Jones, Wilfred Edward
Professional. *b:* 2.2.1912, Pontardawe, Glamorgan. Lower order left-hand batsman, slow left-arm bowler. *Team* Glamorgan (1929–33, 50 matches).
Career batting
50–73–30–300–27–6.97–0–*ct* 21
Bowling 2754–77–35.76–3–0–6/93

Jones, William Edward
Amateur turned professional 1946. *b:* 31.10.1916, Carmarthen. Attractive middle order left-hand batsman, slow left-arm bowler, brilliant deep field. *Team* Glamorgan (1937–58, 340 matches).
Career batting
345–563–64–13535–212*–27.12–11–*ct* 120
Bowling 5782–192–30.11–3–0–5/50

He hit 1,000 runs in a season seven times (best 1,656, av 40.39, in 1948). Both his double centuries were for Glamorgan, the highest being 212* v Essex at Brentwood in 1948.

A noted rugby fly-half for Gloucester, he appeared for Wales in war-time internationals.

Jones, William Maxwell
Amateur. *b:* 11.2.1911, Alltwen, Glamorgan. *d:* December 1941, Denbigh. Middle order right-hand batsman, bowler. *Team* Glamorgan (1933–38, 11 matches).
Career batting
11–15–3–116–51*–9.66–0–*ct* 1
Bowling 214–6–35.66–0–0–3/11

Jones-Davies, Henry Mydrian Orford
(also known as Davies)
Amateur. *b:* 21.10.1910, Pontardawe, Glamorgan. *d:* 30.10.1976, Fairford, Gloucs. Lower order right-hand batsman, right-arm fast medium bowler. *Sch* St John's Leatherhead. *Team* Oxford U (1932).
Career batting
1–2–1–4–4*–4.00–0–*ct* 1
Bowling 38–0

Jordan, Henry Guy Bowen
Amateur. *b:* 10.6.1898, Buxton, Derbyshire. *d:* 5.10.1981, Tonbridge, Kent. Middle order right-hand batsman. *Sch* Marlborough. *Team* Derbyshire (1926, 1 match).
Career batting
1–2–0–0–0–0.00–0–*ct* 0

Jordan, John
Professional. *b:* 7.2.1932, Clough Fold, Rossendale, Lancashire. Lower order right-hand batsman, wicket-keeper. *Team* Lancashire (1955–57, 62 matches).
Career batting
62–75–7–754–39–11.08–0–*ct* 104–*st* 24

Jordan, Thomas
Professional. *b:* 15.10.1843, Stoke Newington, London. Son of David (Groundkeeper at Lord's,

1864–74). Lower order right-hand batsman, right-hand medium pace round-arm bowler, wicket-keeper or longstop. *Team* Players (1867).
Career batting
1–1–0–0–0–0.00–0–*ct* 0

Jordan, Thomas Carrick
Amateur. *b;* 10.2.1877, USA. *d:* 28.3.1925, USA. Lower order right-hand batsman, wicket-keeper. *Team* Philadephia (1901–13). *Tours* Philadelphia to England 1903, 1908.
Career batting
22–39–15–242–24*–10.08–0–*ct* 29–*st* 8

He is regarded as the best of all American wicket-keepers and was a great asset to the Philadelphians on his two tours to England, being able to cope with the bowling of J.B. King.

He represented USA v Canada in four matches commencing 1897.

Jorden, Anthony Mervyn
Cricketer. *b:* 28.1.1947, Radlett, Herts. Lower order right-hand batsman, right-arm fast medium bowler. *Sch* Monmouth. *Teams* Cambridge U (1968–70, blue all three years); Essex (1966–70, 60 matches).
Career batting
89–130–31–1112–67*–11.23–0–*ct* 47
Bowling 5347–176–30.38–1–0–5/95

He also played for Bedfordshire.

A noted rugby footballer, he won his blue and also played for Blackheath and England as full back.

Jose, Dr Anthony Douglas
Amateur. *b:* 17.2.1929, Adelaide, South Australia. *d:* 3.2.1972, Los Angeles, USA. Lower order right-hand batsman, right-arm fast medium bowler. *Teams* South Australia (1947/8, 3 matches); Oxford U (1950–51, blue both years); Kent (1951–52, 5 matches).
Career batting
29–44–8–269–39–7.47–0–*ct* 11
Bowling 2293–75–30.57–1–0–6/45

His final first-class match was for Free Foresters in 1953.

Joseph, Arthur Frederick
Amateur. *b:* 13.3.1919, Neath Abbey, Glamorgan. Middle order right-hand batsman, leg break and googly bowler. *Team* Glamorgan (1946, 1 match).
Career batting
1–2–0–8–8–4.00–0–*ct* 1

Josephs, John Michael
Amateur. *b:* 16.1.1924, Hendon, Middlesex. Lower order right-hand batsman, slow left-arm bowler. *Sch* Clifton. *Teams* Leicestershire (1946–53, 9 matches).
Career batting
9–14–2–116–25*–9.66–0–*ct* 1
Bowling 86–1–86.00–0–0–1/21

Joshi, Padmanabh Govind
Amateur. *b:* 27.10.1926, Baroda. Opening right-hand batsman, wicket-keeper. *Team* Maharashtra (1946/7 to 1964/5). *Tours* India to West India 1952/3, to England 1959. *Tests* India (1951/2 to 1960/1, 12 matches).
Career batting
78–111–10–1724–100*–17.06–1–*ct* 120–*st* 61
Bowling 13–0
Test batting
12–20–1–207–52*–10.89–0–*ct* 18–*st* 9

He was completely unable to find his batting form on his 1959 tour of England and in the last two Tests lost his place to the reserve wicket-keeper.

Joshi, Udaykumar Chaganlal
Cricketer. *b:* 23.12.1944, Rajkot, India. Lower order right-hand batsman, off break bowler. *Teams* Saurashtra (1965/6 to 1982/3); Railways (1967/8); Gujerat (1968/9 to 1979/80); Sussex (1970–74, 76 matches).
Career batting
186–238–55–2287–100*–12.49–1–*ct* 78
Bowling 16203–557–29.08–34–3–6/33

Joslin, Leslie Ronald
Cricketer. *b:* 13.12.1947, Yarraville, Victoria, Australia. Middle order left-hand batsman, left-arm medium pace bowler. *Team* Victoria (1966/7 to 1969/70, 30 matches). *Tour* Australia to England 1968. *Test* Australia (1967/8, 1 match).
Career batting
44–67–6–1816–126–29.77–2–*ct* 27
Bowling 73–1–73.00–0–0–1/14
Test batting
1–2–0–9–7–4.50–0–*ct* 0

He had a very moderate tour of England in 1968 and was not required for the Tests.

Jowett, David Colin Patrick Robert
Amateur. *b:* 24.1.1931, Bristol. Lower order left-hand batsman, off break bowler. *Sch* Sherborne. *Team* Oxford U (1952–55, blue all four years).
Career batting
50–73–25–578–57–12.04–0–*ct* 15
Bowling 4074–125–32.59–3–0–7/132

His County cricket was for Dorset.

His final first-class match was for MCC in 1958.

Jowett, George Edwin
Amateur. *b:* 20.8.1863, Roby, Prescot, Lancashire. *d:* 19.5.1928, Eccles, Lancashire. Middle order right-hand batsman, right-arm fast bowler. *Sch* King William's College, Isle of Man. *Team* Lancashire (1885–89, 19 matches).
Career batting
19–32–2–507–58–16.90–0–*ct* 11
Bowling 55–0
He was no-balled for throwing whilst playing for Lancashire.

Jowett, Richard Lund
Amateur. *b:* 29.4.1937, Rawdon, Yorkshire. Middle order right-hand batsman, off break bowler. *Sch* Bradford GS. *Team* Oxford U (1957–60, blue 1957–59).
Career batting
43–78–5–1499–122–20.53–2–*ct* 44
Bowling 802–20–40.10–0–0–4/67

Joy, Frank Douglas Howarth
Amateur. *b:* 26.9.1880, Sculcoates, Yorkshire. *d:* 17.2.1966, Winchester. Lower order right-hand batsman, left-arm fast medium bowler. *Sch* Winchester. *Teams* Europeans (1908/09; Somerset (1909–12, 11 matches).
Career batting
14–26–4–189–24–8.59–0–*ct* 9
Bowling 1353–57–23.73–3–2–7/24
He appeared in the Freshmen's match at Oxford, but no first-class matches. His daughter, Nancy Joy, wrote a history of women's cricket entitled 'Maiden Over'.

Joy, Jonathan
Professional. *b:* 29.12.1826, Preston Bottoms, Knaresborough, Yorkshire. *d:* 27.9.1889, Middlesbrough, Yorkshire. Middle order right-hand batsman, right-hand fast round-arm bowler, good point. *Team* Yorkshire (1849–67, 8 matches).
Career batting
11–20–0–283–74–14.15–0–*ct* 10
Bowling 56–1–56.00–0–0–1/16

Joy, Ronald Cecil Graham
Amateur. *b:* 30.7.1898, Colchester, Essex. *d:* 12.12.1974, Ditchingham, Norfolk. Son-in-law of F. Penn (Kent and England). Lower order right-hand batsman, right-arm fast medium bowler. *Sch* Winchester. *Teams* Essex (1922–28, 13 matches); Europeans (1929/30); Hyderabad (1931/2).
Career batting
21–29–4–315–36–12.60–0–*ct* 14
Bowling 916–41–22.34–1–0–5/70

Joyce, Francis Matthew
Amateur. *b:* 16.12.1886, Blackfordby, Leics. *d:* 23.9.1958, Earl's Court, London. Brother of J.H. and Ralph (Leics). Middle order right-hand batsman, right-arm fast medium bowler. *Sch* Bedford Grammar School. *Team* Leicestershire (1911–20, 16 matches).
Career bating
16–27–1–431–73–16.57–0–*ct* 7
Bowling 684–17–40.24–1–0–5/117

Joyce, John Hall
Amateur. *b:* 5.12.1868, Blackfordby, Leics. *d:* 17.4.1938, Vence, Nice, France. Brother of F.M. and Ralph (Leics). Middle order right-hand batsman, right-arm fast medium bowler. *Team* Leicestershire (1894, 1 match).
Career batting
1–1–0–18–18–18.00–0–*ct* 2
Bowling 47–2–23.50–0–0–2/33
He also played for Bedfordshire.

Joyce, Ralph
Amateur. *b:* 28.8.1878, Ashby-de-la-Zouch, Leics. *d:* 12.3.1908, Ashbourne, Derbyshire. Brother of F.M. and J.H. (Leics). Stylish middle order right-hand batsman, right-arm slow bowler. *Sch* Bedford Grammar School. *Team* Leicestershire (1896–1907, 48 matches).
Career batting
48–88–4–1586–102–18.88–1–*ct* 17
Bowling 590–11–53.63–0–0–2/36
He appeared in the Freshmen's match and Seniors' Match at Oxford, but no first-class games.

Joynson, William Reginald Hamborough
Amateur. *b:* 18.5.1917, Bickley, Kent. Middle order right-hand batsman. *Sch* Harrow. *Team* Oxford U (1939).
Career batting
2–4–0–30–11–7.50–0–*ct* 0

Joynt, Henry Walter
Amateur. *b:* 1.7.1931, St. Giles, Devon. Middle order right-hand batsman, right-arm medium pace bowler. *Sch* Bradfield. *Teams* Oxford U (1952–53): Madras (1957/8).
Career batting
12–23–4–280–42*–14.73–0–*ct* 9
Bowling 879–18–48.83–0–0–4/36

Juckes, Richard Humphrey
Amateur. *b:* 21.1.1902, Horsham, Sussex. *d:* 21.1.1981, Tredington, Gloucs. Middle order

right-hand batsman. *Sch* King's, Canterbury. *Team* Sussex (1924, 1 match).
Career batting
1–1–0–1–1–1.00–0–*ct* 0

Judd, Arthur Kenneth
Amateur. *b:* 1.1.1904, Staines, Middlesex. Middle order right-hand batsman, leg break bowler, good field. *Sch* St. Paul's. *Team* Hampshire (1925–35, 64 matches); Cambridge U (1927, blue). *Tour* Tennyson to Jamaica 1927/8.
Career batting
84–141–18–2624–124–21.33–2–*ct* 31
Bowling 1036–30–34.53–1–0–6/65
His appearances for Hampshire were restricted due to his posting in Nigeria during the 1930s.

Judd, Peter
Amateur. *b:* 29.4.1938, Balham, London. Lower order right-hand batsman, off break bowler. *Team* Surrey (1960, 1 match).
Career batting
1 match, did not bat–*ct* 1
Bowling 14–0

Judd, William George
Amateur. *b:* 23.10.1845, New Forest, Hants. *d:* 12.3.1925, Boscombe, Hants. Lower order batsman, bowler. *Team* Hampshire (1878, 1 match).
Career batting
1–2–0–8–7–4.00–0–*ct* 0
Bowling 50–1–50.00–0–0–1/22

Judge, Peter Francis
Amateur for Middlesex, professional for Glamorgan. *b:* 23.5.1916, Cricklewood, Middlesex. Lower order right-hand batsman, right-arm fast medium bowler. *Sch* St Pauls. *Team* Middlesex (1933–34, 8 matches); Glamorgan (1939–47, 54 matches); Bengal (1944/5 to 1945/6); Europeans (1944/5).
Career batting
68–90–31–454–40–7.69–0–*ct* 33
Bowling 4676–173–27.02–5–0–8/75
He also played for Buckinghamshire.

Judson, Albert
Professional. *b:* 10.7.1885, Keighley, Yorkshire. *d:* 8.4.1975, Bingley, Yorkshire. Lower order batsman, right-arm fast medium bowler. *Team* Yorkshire (1920, 1 match).
Career batting
1 match, did not bat–*ct* 0
Bowling 5–0

Julian, Raymond
Professional. *b:* 23.8.1936, Cosby, Leics. Lower order right-hand batsman, wicket-keeper. *Team* Leicestershire (1953–71, 192 matches).
Career batting
192–288–23–2581–51–9.73–0–*ct* 381–*st* 40
He is on the first-class umpires' list.

Julien, Bernard Denis
Cricketer. *b:* 13.3.1950, Carenage Village, Trinidad. Attacking lower order right-hand batsman, left-arm fast medium, or slow, bowler. *Teams* Trinidad (1968/9 to 1981/2); Kent (1970–77, 80 matches). *Tours* West Indies to England 1973, 1976, to India, Sri Lanka and Pakistan 1974/5, to Australia 1975/6; West Indies XI to South Africa 1982/3 (no first-class matches). *Tests* West Indies (1973 to 1976/7, 24 matches).
Career batting
192–267–35–5674–127–24.45–3–*ct* 124
Bowling 13656–479–28.50–15–1–9/97
Test batting
24–34–6–866–121–30.92–2–*ct* 14
Bowling 1868–50–37.36–1–0–5/57
He proved a useful all-rounder on the 1973 tour to England and appeared in all three Tests. On his second tour in 1976 he played well in the first-class matches but achieved little in the Tests. His best bowling in an innings was 9 for 97 for Trinidad v Jamaica at Port of Spain in 1981/2. His first-class debut was for North Trinidad in 1967/8.

Jumadeen, Raphick Rasif
Cricketer. *b:* 12.4.1948, Harmony Hall, Gasparillo, Trinidad. Brother of Shamshuddin (Trinidad). Lower order right-hand batsman, slow left-arm bowler. *Teams* Trinidad (1970/1 to 1980/1). *Tours* West Indies to England 1976, to India and Sri Lanka 1978/9. *Tests* West Indies (1971/2 to 1978/9, 12 matches).
Career batting
99–119–48–604–56–8.50–0–*ct* 45
Bowling 9686–347–27.91–16–3–6/30
Test batting
12–14–10–84–56–21.00–0–*ct* 4
Bowling 1141–29–39.34–0–0–4/72
He took 58 wickets, av 30.00, on the 1976 tour to England and played in one Test. His first-class debut was for South Trinidad in 1967/8.

Juniper, John William
Professional. *b:* 6.2.1862, Southwick, Brighton. Sussex. *d:* 20.6.1885, Southwick, of typhoid. Lower order batsman, left-arm fast bowler. *Team* Sussex (1880–85, 57 matches).
Career batting
57–97–24–490–31–6.71–0–*ct* 20
Bowling 3623–184–19.69–6–0–7/24

He suffered from the disability of having sight in only one eye. His death occurred just a few days after his final first-class match for Sussex.

Jupp, George Harman
Amateur. *b:* 26.2.1845, Brentford, Middlesex. *d:* 24.2.1930, Ealing, Middlesex. Hard hitting middle order right-hand batsman, slow round-arm bowler, good long stop. *Team* Middlesex (1867–68, 7 matches).
Career batting
8–14–0–181–49–12.92–0–*ct* 1
Bowling 49–2–24.50–0–0–2/49
He was also a noted athlete, especially excelling at the hurdles and 100 yards.

Jupp, George William
Amateur. *b:* 14.7.1873, Bloxwich, Staffs. *d:* 12.4.1945, Wolverhampton. Middle order right-hand batsman, bowler. *Teams* Somerset (1901–07, 5 matches); Scotland (1905–12).
Career batting
11–17–0–209–56–12.29–0–*ct* 6
Bowling 244–6–40.66–0–0–3/36

Jupp, Henry
Professional. *b:* 19.11.1841, Dorking, Surrey. *d:* 8.4.1889, Bermondsey. Cousin of W. T. (Surrey). Excellent opening right-hand batsman, right-hand fast round-arm bowler. wicket-keeper, good deep field. *Team* Surrey (1862–81, 252 matches). *Tours* Willsher to North America 1868 (not first-class); Grace to Australia 1873/4 (not first-class); Lillywhite to Australia 1876/7. *Tests* England (1876/7, 2 matches)
Career batting
378–692–48–15319–165–23.78–12–*ct* 229–*st* 19
Bowling 316–7–45.14–0–0–3/75
Test batting
2–4–0–68–63–17.00–0–*ct* 2
He hit 1,000 runs in a season eight times (best 1,275, av 36.42, in 1874). He was one of the most prolific batsmen of his day and owing to his great defensive powers known as 'Young Stonewall'.

Jupp, Vallance William Crisp
Professional, turned amateur in 1919. *b:* 27.3.1891, Burgess Hill, Sussex. *d:* 9.7.1960, Spratton, Northants. Middle order right-hand batsman, right-arm medium fast bowler, changed to off break in 1919, good cover field. *Teams* Sussex (1909–22, 173 matches); Northants (1923–38, 280 matches). *Tour* MCC to South Africa 1922/3. *Tests* England (1921–28, 8 matches).
Career batting
529–876–84–23296–217*–29.41–30–*ct* 222
Bowling 38166–1658–23.01–111–18–10/127
Test batting
8–13–1–208–38–17.33–0–*ct* 5
Bowling 616–28–22.00–0–0–4/37
He hit 1,000 runs in a season 13 times, going on to 2,000 once : 2,169, av 38.73, in 1921. His only double century was 217* for Sussex v Worcs at Worcester in 1914.
He took 100 wickets in a season 10 times (best 166, av 20.15, in 1928) and achieved the 'double' in each of those 10 seasons – twice whilst a Sussex player and eight times with Northants.
In 1921 he was appointed Secretary to Northants CCC and captained the County 1927 to 1931. He took all 10 wickets (for 127) in an innings for Northants v Kent at Tunbridge Wells in 1932.

Jupp, William Thomas
Professional. *b:* 11.11.1851, Dorking, Surrey. *d:* 3.8.1878, Chertsey, Surrey. Cousin of Henry (Surrey). Middle order right-hand batsman, right-hand fast round-arm bowler. *Team* Surrey (1876, 2 matches).
Career batting
3–5–1–27–11–6.75–0–*ct* 1
Bowling 57–0

KALAUGHER, WILFRED GEORGE
Amateur. *b:* 26.11.1904, Winchester, New Zealand. Lower order left-hand batsman, right-arm fast medium bowler. *Team* Oxford U (1928–31).
Career batting
8–10–3–27–10–3.85–0–*ct* 4
Bowling 641–20–32.05–1–0–5/87
He played for Oxfordshire.

Kallicharran, Alvin Isaac
Cricketer. *b:* 21.3.1949, Paidama, British Guiana. Brother of D. I. (Guyana). Attractive middle order left-hand batsman, slow right-arm bowler, good deep field. *Teams* Guyana (1966/7 to 1980/1); Warwickshire (1971–83, 192 matches); Queensland (1977/8, 7 matches); Transvaal (1981/2 to 1982/3). *Tours* West Indies to England 1973, 1976, 1980, to India, Sri Lanka and Pakistan 1974/5, to Australia 1975/6, to India and Sri Lanka 1978/9, to Australia and New Zealand 1979/80, to Pakistan 1980/1; World XI in Pakistan 1973/4; West Indies XI to South Africa 1982/3. *Tests* West Indies (1971/2 to 1980/1, 66 matches).
Career batting
385–624–66–25240–243*–45.23–65–*ct* 254
Bowling 3152–67–47.04–1–0–5/45
Test batting
66–109–10–4399–187–44.43–12–*ct* 51
Bowling 158–4–39.50–0–0–2/16
On the 1973 tour to England he hit 889 runs, av 46.78, in first-class matches and played in all three Tests. In 1976 he was not so successful and appeared in three out of the five Tests; in 1980, although playing in all five Tests, his form was again disappointing.
In England he hit 1,000 runs in a season nine times going on to 2,000 once: 2,120, av 66.25, in 1982. He hit five double centuries for Warwickshire, the highest being 243* v Glamorgan at Edgbaston in 1983.
He captained West Indies in nine Tests, but none in England.

Kaluperuma, Lalith Wasantha
Cricketer. *b:* 25.6.1949, Colombo, Ceylon. Lower order right-hand batsman, off break bowler. *Team* Sri Lanka (1970/1 to 1982/3). *Tours* Sri Lanka to India 1970/1, 1975/6, 1976/7, to Pakistan 1973/4, 1981/2, to England 1975; Sri Lanka XI to South Africa 1982/3. *Tests* Sri Lanka (1981/2, 2 matches).
Career batting
57–81–22–1023–96–17.33–0–*ct* 48
Bowling 3931–129–30.47–7–1–8/43
Test batting
2–4–1–12–11*–4.00–0–*ct* 2
Bowling 93–0

Kamm, Anthony
Amateur. *b:* 2.3.1931, Hampstead. Lower order right-hand batsman, wicket-keeper. *Sch* Charterhouse. *Teams* Oxford U (1952–55, blue 1954); Middlesex (1952, 2 matches).
Career batting
9–11–4–154–59*–22.00–0–*ct* 10–*st* 5
His final first-class match was for Free Foresters in 1956.

Kanga, Dr Hormasji Dorabji
Amateur. *b:* 9.4.1880, Bombay, India. *d:* 29.12.1945, Bombay, India. Brother of P.D. and D.D. (both Parsis). Opening right-hand batsman, right-arm medium pace bowler. *Team* Parsis (1899/1900 to 1921/2). *Tour* India to England 1911.
Career batting
43–77–6–1905–233–26.83–3–*ct* 32–*st* 4
Bowling 759–37–20.51–1–0–8/14
He was one of the more successful batsmen on the 1911 tour of England and scored 163 v Leicestershire to give the Indians their first ever win in a first-class match in England. His highest score was 233 for Parsis v Europeans at Poona in 1905/6.
His first-class debut in England was for Leveson-Gower's XI in 1909.

Kanhai, Rohan Babulal
Professional. *b:* 26.12.1935, Port Mourant, British Guiana. Attacking middle order right-hand batsman, right-arm medium pace bowler, wicket-keeper during the early part of his career. *Teams* British Guiana (1954/5 to 1973/4); Western Australia (1961/2, 8 matches); Warwickshire (1968–77, 173 matches); Tasmania (1969/70, 2 matches). *Tours* West Indies to England 1957, 1963, 1966, 1973, to India and Pakistan 1958/9, to Australia 1960/1, to India and Ceylon 1966/7, to Australia and New Zealand 1968/9; Commonwealth to South Africa 1962/3; Rest of World to England 1965, 1967,to Pakistan 1970/1, to Australia 1971/2; International XI to Pakistan 1973/4, 1981/2. *Tests* West Indies (1957 to 1973/4, 79 matches).
Career batting
416–669–82–28774–256–49.01–83–*ct* 318–*st* 7
Bowling 1009–18–56.05–0–0–2/5
Test batting
79–137–6–6227–256–47.53–15–*ct* 50
Bowling 85–0
He hit 1,000 runs in a season 10 times (best

1,894, av 57.39, in 1970). He also hit 1,000 in a season once in Australia and once in India and Pakistan. Of his seven double centuries the highest is 256 for West Indies v India at Calcutta in 1958/9; he scored another in Test cricket – 217 v Pakistan at Lahore in 1958/9; of the three he made for Warwickshire the highest is 253 v Notts at Trent Bridge in 1968. He created a new first-class world record with J.A. Jameson when the pair added 465* for the 2nd wicket for Warwickshire v Gloucs at Edgbaston in 1974.

He captained West Indies in 13 Tests including the tour of England in 1973.

Kapadia, Bahadur Edulji
Amateur. *b:* 9.4.1900, Bombay, India. *d:* 1.1.1973, Bombay, India. Brother of F.E. (Parsis and Bombay). Defensive lower order right-hand batsman, wicket-keeper. *Teams* Bombay (1925/6 to 1929/30); Parsis (1920/1 to 1929/30). *Tours* India to England 1932; Bombay to Ceylon 1925/6, 1929/30.
Career batting
30–44–6–522–59–13.73–0–*ct* 47–*st* 24

Travelling to England in 1932 as the reserve wicket-keeper, he appeared in only seven first-class matches.

His final first-class match was for Vizianagram's XI in 1935/6.

Kapil Dev Ramlal Nikhanj
Cricketer. *b:* 6.1.1959, Chandigarh, India. Attacking middle order right-hand batsman, right-arm fast medium bowler, good outfield. *Teams* Haryana (1975/6 to 1981/2); Northants (1981–83, 16 matches). *Tours* India to Pakistan 1978/9, 1982/3, to England 1979, 1982, to Australia and New Zealand 1980/1, to West Indies 1982/3. *Tests* India (1978/9 to 1982/3, 53 matches).
Career batting
131–182–18–4834–193–29.47–8–*ct* 83
Bowling 11657–418–27.88–24–2–8/38
Test batting
53–77–8–2253–126*–32.65–3–*ct* 19
Bowling 6082–206–29.52–15–1–8/85

On the 1979 tour to England he played in all four Tests and headed the Test bowling averages with 16 wickets, av 30.93. He appeared in all three Tests on the 1982 tour and as well as taking 10 wickets he hit 292 runs, av 73.00. He was the youngest player to take 100 Test wickets – 21 years 25 days – beating the record held by I. T. Botham.

Kardar, Abdul Hafeez
(played as Abdul Hafeez until 1947)
Amateur. *b:* 17.1.1925, Lahore, India. Attacking middle left-hand batsman, slow left-arm bowler. *Teams* Northern India (1943/4 to 1945/6); Muslims (1944/5); Services (1953/4 to 1954/5); Oxford U (1947–49, blue all three years); Warwickshire (1948–50, 45 matches). *Tours* India to England 1946; Pakistan to England 1954, to India 1952/3, to West Indies 1957/8; Services to India and Ceylon 1954/5. *Tests* India (1946, 3 matches); Pakistan (1952/3 to 1957/8, 23 matches).
Career batting
174–262–33–6832–173–29.83–8–*ct* 110
Bowling 8448–344–24.55–19–4–7/25
Test batting
26–42–3–927–93–23.76–0–*ct* 16
Bowling 954–21–45.42–0–0–3/34

His best playing season in England was 1949 when he took 92 wickets, av 19.31. He captained Pakistan in the country's first 23 Test matches.

His last first-class match was for Punjab Governor's XI 1965/6. After retiring from first-class cricket, he was President of the Pakistan Board of Control and a major force in the re-organisation of cricket in Pakistan.

Kasippillai, Mahendra
Amateur. *b:* 21.9.1927, Colombo, Ceylon. Middle order left-hand batsman, slow left-arm bowler. *Teams* Cambridge U (1956–57); Ceylon (1948/9 to 1951/2).
Career batting
11–21–2–277–62*–14.57–0–*ct* 4
Bowling 130–3–43.33–0–0–2/36

He played for Cambridgeshire.

Katinakis, George Demetrius
Amateur. *b:* 25.7.1873, London. *d:* 15.5.1943, Southwold, Suffolk. Opening batsman. *Team* Hampshire (1904–05, 4 matches).
Career batting
4–6–1–46–16*–9.20–0–*ct* 1
Bowling 27–0

Kay, Henry George
Amateur. *b:* 3.10.1851, Havant, Hants. *d:* 8.9.1922, Tottenham, London. Lower order right-hand batsman, wicket-keeper. *Sch* Cheltenham. *Team* Hampshire (1882, 2 matches).
Career batting
2–2–0–0–0–0.00–0–*ct* 0
Bowling 20–0

Kaye, Haven
Professional. *b:* 11.6.1846, Huddersfield, Yorkshire. *d:* 1892, Halifax, Yorkshire. Middle order

right-hand batsman, right-hand fast round-arm bowler. *Team* Yorkshire (1872–73, 8 matches).
Career batting
8–14–0–117–33–8.35–0–*ct* 3

Kaye, Harold Swift
Amateur. *b:* 9.5.1882, Mirfield, Yorkshire. *d:* 6.11.1953, Wakefield, Yorkshire. Middle order right-hand batsman, useful bowler. *Sch* Harrow. *Team* Yorkshire (1907–08, 18 matches). *Tour* Leveson-Gower to Rhodesia 1909/10.
Career batting
21–29–2–262–37–9.70–0–*ct* 9
Bowling 0–0

He appeared with much success for the Yorkshire Gentlemen; later he was for several years a member of Yorkshire CCC Committee.

Kaye, Dr Henry Wynyard
Amateur. *b:* 21.5.1875, London. *d:* 21.4.1922, Hatfield-Peverel, Essex. Opening/middle order right-hand batsman, good cover point. *Sch* Winchester. *Team* Middlesex (1900, 3 matches).
Career batting
3–5–0–117–76–23.40–0–*ct* 0

He appeared in the Freshmen's match at Oxford, but no first-class matches.

Kaye, James Levett
Amateur. *b:* 27.12.1861, Barnet, Herts. *d:* 17.11.1917, Chelsea, London. Lower order right-hand batsman, wicket-keeper. *Sch* Winchester. *Team* Hampshire (1881, 1 match).
Career batting
1–2–0–14–11–7.00–0–*ct* 0–*st* 1

He was for many years serving in India, being latterly in the Political Dept of the Government of India.

Kaye, Joseph Lowther
Professional. *b:* 1846, Huddersfield, Yorkshire. *d:* 12.10.1882, Whitefield, Bury, Lancashire. Middle order right-hand batsman, right-arm fast bowler. *Team* Lancashire (1867, 1 match).
Career batting
1–2–0–21–20–10.50–0–*ct* 0
Bowling 16–0

Kaye, Michael Arthur Chadwick Porter
Amateur. *b:* 11.1.1916, London. Hard hitting lower order right-hand batsman, right-arm medium fast bowler. *Sch* Harrow. *Team* Cambridge U (1937–38, blue 1938). *Tour* Oxford and Cambridge to Jamaica 1938/9.
Career batting
17–28–6–395–78–17.95–0–*ct* 11
Bowling 1244–31–40.12–1–0–5/89

His final first-class match was for Free Foresters in 1949.

Kayum, Donald Amrul
Cricketer. *b:* 13.10.1955, La Penitence, British Guiana. Right-hand middle order batsman, off break bowler. *Team* Oxford U (1977–78, blue both years).
Career batting
12–18–1–423–57–24.88–0–*ct* 8

Keay, George Alexander
Amateur. *b:* 14.3.1897. *d:* 8.8.1981, Swanage, Dorset. Lower order right-hand batsman, right-arm medium pace bowler. *Sch* Whitgift. *Team* Oxford U (1919–20).
Career batting
3–4–1–26–15–8.66–0–*ct* 3
Bowling 94–3–31.33–0–0–3/11

Kedward, Philip Morris
Amateur. *b:* 26.7.1909, Hull, Yorkshire. Middle order right-hand batsman, right-arm medium pace bowler. *Sch* Kingswood, Bath. *Team* Leveson-Gower's XI (1935).
Career batting
1–1–0–0–0–0.00–0–*ct* 0

Keeble, George
Professional. *b:* 26.9.1849, Southfleet, Kent. *d:* 26.5.1923, Dartford, Kent. Lower order right-hand batsman, right-hand fast round-arm bowler. *Team* Kent (1876, 1 match).
Career batting
1–2–1–8–6*–8.00–0–*ct* 0
Bowling 37–1–37.00–0–0–1/21

Keeler, John George
Professional. *b:* 2.5.1924, South Moor, Co Durham. Opening right-hand batsman, right-arm medium pace bowler. *Team* Minor Counties (1953).
Career batting
1–2–0–11–10–5.50–0–*ct* 0

His County cricket was for Durham commencing 1949.

Keeling, Harry Walter
Amateur. *b:* 8.11.1873, Hove, Sussex. *d:* 19.2.1898, Marylebone, London. Lower order right-hand batsman, off break bowler. *Sch* Hurstpierpoint. *Team* Kent (1893, 2 matches).
Career batting
2–3–0–40–24–13.33–0–*ct* 0
Bowling 48–0

Keeling, Michael Edward Allis
Amateur. *b:* 6.11.1925, London. Opening right-

hand batsman. *Sch* Eton. *Team* Oxford U (1948–49).
Career batting
5–6–0–175–40–12.50–0–*ct* 1
Bowling 5–0

Keen, Frederick Francis
Amateur. *b:* 14.7.1898, Larida, Argentine. Lower order left-hand batsman, left-arm fast medium bowler. *Team* Argentine (1926/7). *Tour* South America to England 1932.
Career batting
7–10–2–115–23–14.37–0–*ct* 2
Bowling 505–13–38.84–0–0–3/31

Keene, John William
Professional. *b:* 25.4.1873, Mitcham, Surrey. *d:* 3.1.1931, Crichton, Midlothian. Lower order left-hand batsman, left-arm slow medium bowler. *Teams* Surrey (1897, 2 matches); Worcestershire 1903–05, 24 matches); Scotland (1907).
Career batting
27–36–11–115–12–4.60–0–*ct* 12
Bowling 1580–66–23.93–5–1–6/22

Keeton, Frederick William
Professional. *b:* 26.10.1855, Mosbrough, Derbyshire. *d:* 27.11.1911, Bolton, Lancashire. Middle order right-hand batsman, right-hand medium pace round-arm bowler. *Team* Derbyshire (1876–80, 3 matches).
Career batting
3–6–0–33–9–5.50–0–*ct* 1

Keeton, William Walter
Professional. *b:* 30.4.1905, Shirebrook, Derbyshire. *d:* 10.10.1980, Forest Town, Notts. Attractive opening right-hand batsman, good deep field. *Team* Nottinghamshire (1926–52, 382 matches). *Tests* England (1934–39, 2 matches).
Career batting
397–657–43–24276–312*–39.53–54–*ct* 76
Bowling 103–2–51.50–0–0–2/16
Test batting
2–4–0–57–25–14.25–0–*ct* 0

He hit 1,000 runs in a season 12 times, going on to 2,000 six times (best 2,258, av 42.60, in 1933). His highest score was 312* for Notts v Middlesex at the Oval in 1939, a county record. He hit six other double centuries all for Notts. With C.B. Harris he recorded century partnerships for the first wicket on 45 occasions.

A good inside right, he played soccer for Sunderland and Nottingham Forest.

Keighley, William Geoffrey
Amateur. *b:* 10.1.1925, Nice, France. Sound opening right-hand batsman, right-arm medium pace bowler. *Sch* Eton. *Teams* Oxford U (1947–48, blue both years); Yorkshire (1947–51, 35 matches). *Tour* MCC to Canada 1951.
Career batting
65–102–8–2539–110–27.01–2–*ct* 16
Bowling 79–0

Keigwin, Henry David
Amateur. *b:* 14.5.1881, Colchester, Essex. *d:* 20.9.1916, nr Thiepval, France. He was killed in action. Brother of R.P. (Essex) and H.S. (London County and Rhodesia). Middle order right-hand batsman, left-arm medium pace bowler. *Sch* St. Paul's. *Teams* Cambridge U (1901); Essex (1906–07, 4 matches); Scotland (1907–09).
Career batting
11–18–0–351–77–19.50–0–*ct* 3
Bowling 472–15–31.46–1–0–5/83

Keigwin, Herbert Stanley
Amateur. *b:* 4.5.1878, Capel, Colchester, Essex. *d:* 11.3.1962, East London, South Africa. Brother of H.D. (Essex) and R.P. (Essex and Gloucs). Middle order right-hand batsman. *Sch* St Paul's. *Teams* Cambridge U (1901); London County (1901); Rhodesia (1909/10).
Career batting
8–15–1–296–111–21.14–1–*ct* 5

Keigwin, Richard Prescott
Amateur. *b:* 8.4.1883, Colchester, Essex. *d:* 26.11.1972, Polstead, Suffolk. Brother of H.D. (Essex) and H.S. (Cambridge U). Middle order right-hand batsman, slow right-arm bowler. *Sch* Clifton. *Teams* Cambridge U (1903–06, blue all four years); Essex (1903–19, 20 matches); Gloucestershire (1921–23, 9 matches).
Career batting
74–129–12–2316–116–19.79–1–*ct* 41
Bowling 2614–87–30.05–3–1–8/79

A noted all-round sportsman, he gained his blue for soccer, hockey and rackets and represented Essex at hockey as well as England.

He was a recognised authority on the works of Hans Christian Anderson.

Keith, Geoffrey Leyden
Professional. *b:* 19.11.1937, Winchester, Hants. *d:* 26.12.1975, Southampton, Hants. Middle order right-hand batsman, off break bowler, good slip. *Teams* Hampshire (1962–67, 60 matches); Somerset (1959–61, 15 matches); Western Province (1968/9).
Career batting
77–124–14–2108–101*–19.16–1–*ct* 79
Bowling 561–13–43.15–0–0–4/49

Keith, Headley James
Amateur. *b:* 25.10.1927, Dundee, South Africa. Forcing middle order left-hand batsman, slow left-arm bowler. *Teams* Natal (1950/1 to 1957/8). *Tours* South Africa to Australia and New Zealand 1952/3, to England 1954. *Tests* South Africa (1952/3 to 1956/7, 8 matches).
Career batting
74–113–8–3203–153–30.50–8–*ct* 61
Bowling 2174–79–27.51–2–0–5/27
Test batting
8–16–1–318–73–21.20–0–*ct* 9
Bowling 63–0
Although he appeared in four Tests on the 1955 tour of England, his record was only a modest one.

Kelland, Peter Alban
Amateur. *b:* 20.9.1926, Pinner, Middlesex. Tail end right-hand batsman, right-arm fast medium bowler. *Sch* Repton. *Teams* Cambridge U (1949–50, blue 1950); Sussex (1951–52, 3 matches).
Career batting
15–15–7–72–35–9.00–0–*ct* 4
Bowling 1053–27–39.00–0–0–3/24

Kelleher, Henry Robert Albert
Professional. *b:* 3.3.1929, Bermondsey, South London. Lower order left-hand batsman, right-arm fast medium bowler. *Teams* Surrey (1955, 3 matches); Northants (1956–58, 52 matches).
Career batting
55–51–17–256–25–7.52–0–*ct* 45
Bowling 3097–112–27.64–4–1–5/23

Kelleway, Charles
Amateur. *b:* 25.4.1886, Lismore, New South Wales, Australia. *d:* 16.11.1944, Lindfield, New South Wales, Australia. Sound opening right-hand batsman, right-arm fast medium bowler. *Team* New South Wales (1907/8 to 1928/9, 57 matches). *Tours* Australia to England and North America 1912, to New Zealand 1909/10; AIF to England 1919. *Tests* Australia (1910/11 to 1928/9, 26 matches).
Career batting
132–205–23–6389–168–35.10–15–*ct* 102
Bowling 8925–339–26.32–10–1–7/35
Test batting
26–42–4–1422–147–37.42–3–*ct* 24
Bowling 1683–52–32.36–1–0–5/33
He hit 1,281 runs, av 31.24, on his 1912 tour to England – his very defensive batting earning the comment 'one Kelleway in a side is well enough, two or three would be almost unbearable'.
He captained the AIF 1919 Team in England for the first few matches, then, for some unexplained reason, left the side.

Kelly, Augustine Patrick
Amateur. *b: circa* 1894, Dublin, Ireland. *d:* May 1960, Hackney, London. Right-hand batsman, wicket-keeper. *Sch* Ampleforth College. *Teams* Ireland (1920–30); Dublin University (1922).
Career batting
14–25–1–505–98–21.04–0–*ct* 17–*st* 6

Kelly, Acheson William Blake
Amateur. *b:* 5.8.1903, Dublin, Ireland. *d:* 6.10.1961, Bath, Somerset. Son of G.W.F.B. (Oxford U and Ireland), brother of G.N.B. (Ireland). Right-hand batsman, right-arm medium pace bowler. *Sch* Stonyhurst. *Teams* Dublin University (1924–26); Ireland (1926).
Career batting
4–8–0–92–35–11.50–0–*ct* 1
Bowling 59–3–19.66–0–0–3/29

Kelly, Edward Arthur
Professional. *b:* 26.11.1932, Bootle, Lancashire. Lower order right-hand batsman, right-arm bowler. *Team* Lancashire (1957, 4 matches).
Career batting
4–6–2–38–16*–9.50–0–*ct* 1
Bowling 248–4–12.00–0–0–3/77

Kelly, Gustavus Noel Blake
Amateur. *b:* 26.12.1901, Dublin, Ireland. *d:* 14.3.1980, Castlebar, Co Mayo, Ireland. Son of G.W.F.B. (Oxford U and Ireland), brother of A.W.B. (Ireland). Right-hand batsman, right-arm fast medium bowler. *Sch* Stonyhurst. *Teams* Dublin University (1922–26); Ireland (1922–26).
Career batting
7–14–5–275–76*–30.55–0–*ct* 5
Bowling 397–17–23.35–2–0–6/62

Kelly, Gustavus William Francis Blake
Amateur. *b:* 2.4.1877, Dublin, Ireland. *d:* 16.8.1951, Ballymoe, Co Roscommon, Ireland. Father of A.W.B. and G.N.B. (Ireland). Lower order right-hand batsman, right-arm fast bowler. *Sch* Stonyhurst. *Teams* Oxford (1901–02, blue both years); Ireland (1907–14).
Career batting
26–43–6–614–52–16.59–0–*ct* 10
Bowling 1257–55–22.85–2–0–5/32
He was a noted athlete, winning the long jump in the inter-University sports.

Kelly, James Joseph
Amateur. *b:* 10.5.1867, Port Melbourne, Victoria, Australia. *d:* 14.8.1938, Bellevue Hill, New South Wales, Australia. Lower order right-hand

batsman, wicket-keeper. *Team* New South Wales (1894/5 to 1904/5, 53 matches). *Tours* Australia to England 1896, 1899, 1902, 1905, to South Africa 1902/3, to New Zealand 1904/5, to North America 1896. *Tests* Australia (1896–1905, 36 matches).
Career batting
185–266–60–4108–108–19.94–3–*ct* 243–*st* 112
Bowling 16–0
Test batting
36–56–17–664–46*–17.02–0–*ct* 43–*st* 20

He was the principal wicket-keeper for the tourists on all his four visits to England – injury received during the 1905 tour compelled him to retire from first-class cricket.

His final first-class match was for Rest of Australia in 1906/7.

Kelly, John K.
Professional. *b:* 15.9.1930, Conisbrough, Yorkshire. Middle order left-hand batsman, slow left-arm bowler. *Team* Nottinghamshire (1953–57, 51 matches).
Career batting
51–72–11–1303–113–21.36–1–*ct* 29
Bowling 1844–38–48.52–0–0–4/25

He also played for Devon.

Kelly, John Martin
Professional. *b:* 19.3.1922, Bacup, Lancashire. *d:* 13.11.1979, Rochdale, Lancashire. Stylish opening right-hand batsman. *Teams* Lancashire (1947–49, 6 matches); Derbyshire (1950–60, 253 matches).
Career batting
259–437–29–9614–131–23.56–9–*ct* 122
Bowling 103–1–103.00–0–0–1/21

He hit 1,000 runs in a season five times (best 1,535, av 30.70, in 1957).

Kelsall, Robert Stuart
Cricketer. *b:* 29.6.1946, Stockport, Cheshire. Middle order right-hand batsman, off break bowler. *Teams* Nottinghamshire (1969, 1 match).
Career batting
1–1–1–8–8*–no av–0–*ct* 1
Bowling 6–1–6.00–0–0–1/6

He also played for Cheshire.

Kelsey, John Heneage
Amateur. *b:* 30.3.1867, Tunbridge Wells, Kent. *d:* 21.10.1945, Wadhurst, Sussex. Middle order right-hand batsman. *Sch* Repton. *Team* Sussex (1902, 1 match).
Career batting
1–1–0–1–1–1.00–0–*ct* 0

Kelson, George Mortimer
Amateur. *b:* 8.12.1835, Sevenoaks, Kent. *d:* 29.3.1920, Kingston-on-Thames, Surrey. Son of George (Kent 1828). Fine middle order right-hand batsman, right-hand fast round-arm bowler, occasional wicket-keeper, good deep field. *Team* Kent (1859–73, 69 matches).
Career batting
90–163–7–2240–122–14.35–1–*ct* 57–*st* 2
Bowling 1585–75+1–21.13–2–0–6/22

He also played for Buckinghamshire. He was a well-known writer on fishing.

Kember, Owen David
Amateur. *b:* 23.1.1943, Lingfield, Surrey. Lower order left-hand batsman, wicket-keeper. *Teams* Cambridge U (1963); Surrey (1962–63, 4 matches).
Career batting
6–9–2–61–19*–8.71–0–*ct* 6–*st* 3

Kemble, Arthur Twiss
Amateur. *b:* 3.2.1862, Sebergham, Carlisle, Cumberland. *d:* 13.3.1925, Crawley Down, Sussex. Middle/lower order right-hand batsman, wicket-keeper. *Team* Lancashire (1885–94, 76 matches).
Career batting
95–144–23–1347–50–11.13–0–*ct* 122–*st* 54

He also appeared for Cumberland, and was for several years Secretary of Liverpool CC.

His final first-class match was for West England in 1896.

An excellent rugby footballer, he represented Lancashire and England.

Kemmey, William
Professional. *b:* 21.7.1912, Atcham, Shropshire. Lower order right-hand batsman, wicket-keeper. *Team* Northants (1939, 5 matches).
Career batting
5–9–1–55–18–6.87–0–*ct* 4–*st* 2

Kemp, Arthur Fitch
Amateur. *b:* 1.8.1863, Hildenborough, Kent. *d:* 14.2.1940, Wentworth, Virginia Water, Surrey. Brother of C.W.M. (Kent) and M.C. (Kent). Lower order right-hand batsman, right-arm slow bowler. *Sch* Harrow. *Team* Kent (1884, 3 matches).
Career batting
5–9–1–40–13–5.00–0–*ct* 2
Bowling 54–1–54.00–0–0–1/26

His first-class debut was for an Oxford and Cambridge XI in 1883 and his final match for MCC in 1885.

Kemp, Arthur Lock
Amateur. *b:* 1869, London. *d:* 1929, Barnet, Herts. Middle/lower order batsman, bowler. *Sch* Denstone. *Team* Middlesex (1890–94, 2 matches).
Career batting
2–3–0–10–6–3.33–0–*ct* 0
Bowling 13–0

Kemp, Charles William Middleton
Amateur. *b:* 26.4.1856, Forest Hill, Sydenham, Kent. *d:* 15.5.1933, Ightham, Kent. Brother of A.F. (Kent) and M.C. (Kent). Middle order right-hand batsman, right-hand slow round-arm bowler, cover point. *Sch* Harrow. *Teams* Oxford U (1878, blue); Kent (1878, 1 match).
Career batting
4–7–2–58–17–11.60–0–*ct* 7
Bowling 8–0

He represented Oxford against Cambridge in the Athletics Meeting of 1878 and 1879, being victorious in the long jump.

Kemp, Sir George
(created Baron Rochdale in 1913)
Amateur. *b:* 9.6.1866, Rochdale, Lancashire. *d:* 24.3.1945, Keswick, Cumberland. Stylish middle order right-hand batsman, slow right-arm bowler, good mid off. *Sch* Mill Hill and Shrewsbury. *Teams* Cambridge U (1885–88, blue 1885, 1886 and 1888); Lancashire (1885–92, 18 matches).
Career batting
51–92–4–1641–125–18.64–3–*ct* 17
Bowling 3–0

His final first-class match was for A.J. Webbe's XI in 1899.

He also represented Cambridge at lawn tennis.

From 1895 to 1906 he was MP for the Heywood Division of Lancashire and from 1910 to 1912 for North West Division of Manchester, both as a Liberal.

Kemp, Sir Kenneth Hagar
Amateur. *b:* 21.4.1853, Erpingham, Norfolk. *d:* 22.4.1936, Sheringham, Norfolk. Useful right-hand middle order batsman. *Sch* Clergy Orphan School, Canterbury. *Team* Cambridge U (1873).
Career batting
4–7–1–105–41–17.50–0–*ct* 1
Bowling 7–0

His first-class debut was for MCC in 1872.

His County cricket was for Norfolk and Suffolk, and he was for some years Hon Secretary of the former County.

Kemp, Manley Colchester
Amateur. *b:* 7.9.1861, Sydenham, Kent. *d:* 30.6.1951, Aylesbury, Bucks. Brother of A.F. (Kent) and C.W.M. (Kent). Capital middle order right-hand batsman, wicket-keeper. *Sch* Harrow. *Teams* Kent (1880–95, 88 matches); Oxford U (1881–84, blue all four years).
Career batting
134–226–34–3040–175–15.83–1–*ct* 172–*st* 73

He captained Oxford for two seasons (1883 and 1884), which was unusual. His first-class debut was for Gentlemen of the South in 1879. An all-round sportsman, he also excelled at rackets, soccer and athletics.

Kemp, Nicholas John
Cricketer. *b:* 16.12.1956, Bromley, Kent. Lower order right-hand batsman; right arm fast medium bowler. *Sch* Tonbridge. *Teams* Kent (1977–81, 13 matches); Middlesex (1982, 5 matches).
Career batting
18–19–4–210–46*–14.00–0–*ct* 8
Bowling 801–16–50.06–1–0–6/119

Kemp, Percival Hepworth
Amateur. *b:* 2.7.1888, Luton, Beds. *d:* 14.2.1974, Islington, London. Middle order batsman. *Team* Middlesex (1919, 1 match).
Career batting
1–2–0–43–38–21.50–0–*ct* 1

Kempe, Cuthbert Reeves
Amateur. *b:* 1856, Bedminster, Bristol. *d:* 18.4.1953, Weston-super-Mare, Somerset. Middle order batsman. *Team* Gloucestershire (1877, 2 matches).
Career batting
2–3–0–28–15–9.33–0–*ct* 1

Kempe, Rev Wilfrid Noel
Amateur. *b:* 10.10.1887, Long Ashton, Somerset. *d:* 17.10.1958, Frenchay, Gloucs. Lower order batsman, wicket-keeper. *Sch* King's, Canterbury. *Team* Somerset (1919, 1 match).
Career batting
1–2–1–9–9–9.00–0–*ct* 0–*st* 1

Kempson, Simon Matthews Edwin
Amateur. *b:* 3.5.1831, Castle Bromwich, Birmingham. *d:* 20.6.1894, Uley, Gloucs. Hard hitting lower order right-hand batsman, right-hand medium pace round-arm bowler. *Sch* Cheltenham. *Team* Cambridge U (1851–56, blue 1851, and 1853).
Career batting
11–19–0–206–48–10.84–0–*ct* 11
Bowling 166–19+47–8.73–7–3–7/?

Illness prevented him playing against Oxford U in 1852.

He played little cricket after 1856 as he was in India until 1878.

His final first-class match was for MCC in 1865.

Kempster, James Francis
Amateur. *b:* 15.10.1892, Galway, Co Galway, Ireland. *d:* 21.4.1975, Kilternan, Co Dublin, Ireland. Right-hand batsman, right-arm medium pace bowler. *Team* Ireland (1920–22).
Career batting
2–4–0–55–33–13.75–0–*ct* 0
Bowling 18–0

Kemp-Welch, George Durant
Amateur. *b:* 4.8.1907, Chelsea, London. *d:* 18.6.1944, Chelsea. He died as a result of an air-raid. Attractive opening right-arm batsman, right-arm fast medium bowler. *Sch* Charterhouse. *Teams* Cambridge U (1929–31, blue all three years); Warwickshire (1927–35, 57 matches). *Tours* Tennyson to Jamaica 1927/8, 1931/2.
Career batting
114–182–14–4170–186–24.82–6–*ct* 50
Bowling 1716–41–41.85–0–0–4/41

He hit 1,561 runs, av 37.16, in 1931, the only season he exceeded 1,000 runs. His final first-class match was for Free Foresters in 1936.

He was son-in-law of Stanley Baldwin, the Prime Minister.

Kemsley, Jeremy Neil
Amateur. *b:* 28.9.1933, Melbourne, Australia. Right-hand batsman. *Team* Scotland (1955–57).
Career batting
8–14–0–285–103–20.35–1–*ct* 2

Kendall, Francis James
Professional. *b:* 1908, Northampton. *d:* 10.9.1966, Northampton. Tail end left-hand batsman, left-arm medium pace bowler. *Team* Northants (1930, 3 matches).
Career batting
3–6–1–1–1*–0.20–0–*ct* 0–*ct* 2
Bowling 172–6–28.66–0–0–2/26

His first-class batting record contains five consecutive ducks.

Kendall, John Thomas
Professional. *b:* 31.3.1921, Hawkesbury, Coventry, Warwickshire. Lower order right-hand batsman, wicket-keeper. *Team* Warwickshire (1948–49, 4 matches).
Career batting
4–4–1–26–18*–8.66–0–*ct* 5–*st* 4

Kendall, Michael Philip
Cricketer. *b:* 10.11.1949, Canterbury, Kent. Lower order right-hand batsman, left-arm medium pace bowler. *Team* Cambridge U (1971–72, blue 1972).
Career batting
12–16–4–60–13–5.00–0–*ct* 2
Bowling 852–23–37.04–1–0–6/43

Kenderdine, Derek Charles
Amateur. *b:* 1897, Bromley, Kent. *d:* 28.8.1947, Cambridge. Tail end right-hand batsman, right-arm medium fast bowler. *Team* Royal Navy (1921–22).
Career batting
2–4–1–7–6–2.33–0–*ct* 1
Bowling 121–2–60.50–0–0–1/46

Kendle, Charles Edward Compton
Amateur. *b:* 10.2.1875, Amesbury, Wilts. *d:* 3.1.1954, Hellingly, Sussex. Lower order right-hand batsman, wicket-keeper. *Team* Hampshire (1899, 2 matches).
Career batting
2–4–1–27–11–9.00–0–*ct* 2–*st* 1

He also played for Wiltshire.

Kendle, Rev William James
Amateur. *b:* 9.4.1847, Romsey, Hants. *d:* 30.1.1920, Woodsford, Dorset. Useful middle order right-hand batsman. *Sch* Sherborne. *Team* Hampshire (1869–78, 5 matches).
Career batting
5–9–0–66–29–7.33–0–*ct* 1

He appeared in the Cambridge Freshmen's match of 1867, but no first-class matches whilst at the University.

Kennard, John Adam Gaskell
Amateur. *b:* 8.11.1884, Chelsea, London. *d:* 6.4.1949, Hove, Sussex. Middle order batsman. *Sch* Harrow. *Team* Hampshire (1919, 2 matches).
Career batting
2–3–1–46–18–23.00–0–*ct* 0
Bowling 17–0

He also played for Oxfordshire.

Kennedy, Andrew
Cricketer. *b:* 4.11.1949, Blackburn, Lancashire. Opening left-hand batsman, right-arm medium pace bowler. *Team* Lancashire (1970–82, 149 matches). *Tour* Robins to South Africa 1975/6.
Career batting
150–243–20–6298–180–28.24–6–*ct* 85
Bowling 398–10–39.80–0–0–3/58

He hit 1,000 runs in a season three times (best 1,194, av 34.11, in 1980).

Kennedy, Alexander Stuart
Professional. *b:* 24.1.1891, Edinburgh, Scotland. *d:* 15.11.1959, Hythe, Southampton. Sound

opening/middle order batsman, right-arm medium pace inswing bowler. *Team* Hampshire (1907–36, 596 matches). *Tours* MCC to South Africa 1922/3; Joel to South Africa 1924/5. *Tests* England (1922/3, 5 matches).
Career batting
677–1025–130–16586–163*–18.53–10–*ct* 530
Bowling 61034–2874–21.23–225–45–10/37
Test batting
5–8–2–93–41*–15.50–0–*ct* 5
Bowling 599–31–19.32–2–0–5/76

He hit 1,000 runs in a season five times (best 1,437, av 26.61, in 1928) and took 100 wickets in a season 15 times, going on to 200 once : 205, av 16.80 in 1922. He performed the 'double' five times.

His best bowling in an innings was 10 for 37 for Players v Gentlemen at the Oval in 1927.

Kennedy, Charles Marshall
Amateur. *b:* 15.12.1849, Brighton, Sussex. *d:* 31.1.1906, Tunbridge Wells, Kent. Middle order right-hand batsman, wicket-keeper. *Sch* Brighton. *Team* Sussex (1872–78, 21 matches).
Career batting
23–43–7–284–37–7.88–0–*ct* 8–*st* 1

He did not play in any first-class matches whilst at Cambridge U.

Kennedy, David
Amateur. *b:* 10.7.1890, Uddington, Lanark, Scotland. *d:* 1.7.1916, The Somme, France. Right-hand batsman, wicket-keeper. *Team* Scotland (1914).
Career batting
1–2–0–11–10–5.50–0–*ct* 0

Kennedy, Derrick Edward de Vere
Amateur. *b:* 5.6.1904, Dublin, Ireland. *d:* 27.6.1976, Rathcoole, Co Dublin, Ireland. Right-hand batsman, right-arm fast medium bowler. *Sch* Clifton. *Team* Dublin University (1924): Ireland (1924).
Career batting
2–3–1–23–15*–11.50–0–*ct* 1
Bowling 89–1–89.00–0–0–1/65

Kennedy, Iain George
Cricketer. *b:* 28.5.1960, Paisley, Renfrewshire, Scotland. Opening right-hand batsman. *Team* Scotland (1983).
Career batting
1–2–0–15–12–7.50–0–*ct* 0

Kennedy, James Henry
Cricketer. *b:* 23.4.1949, Glasgow, Scotland. Right-hand batsman, left-arm fast medium bowler. *Team* Scotland (1970–71).
Career batting
2–2–1–7–6*–7.00–0–*ct* 0
Bowling 99–1–99.00–0–0–1/17

Kennedy, John Maxwell
Professional. *b:* 15.12.1931, Manchester, Lancashire. Middle order right-hand batsman. *Team* Warwickshire (1960–62, 31 matches).
Career batting
31–55–9–1188–94–25.82–0–*ct* 17
Bowling 1–2–0.5–0–0–2/1

Kenney, Edward Maxwell
(changed name to Kenney-Herbert, July 1875) Amateur. *b:* 10.12.1845, Bourton-on-Dunsmore, Warwickshire. *d:* 24.1.1916, Ealing, Middlesex. Free hitting lower order right-hand batsman, left-hand fast round-arm bowler. *Sch* Rugby. *Team* Oxford U (1865–68, blue 1866–68).
Career batting
17–25–3–204–64–9.27–0–*ct* 9
Bowling 903–60+6–15.01–5–1–8/68

His County cricket was for Warwickshire (pre-first-class) and Buckinghamshire.

He was also a noted rackets player.

Kennie, George
Professional. *b:* 17.5.1904, Bradford. Middle order right-hand batsman. *Team* Yorkshire (1927, 1 match).
Career batting
1–2–0–6–6–3.00–0–*ct* 1

Kenny, Charles John Michael
Amateur. *b:* 19.5.1929, Wellington, Surrey. Tail end right-hand batsman, right-arm fast medium bowler. *Sch* Ampleforth. *Teams* Essex (1950–53, 18 matches); Cambridge U (1952, blue); Ireland (1952–55).
Career batting
40–38–16–75–16–3.40–0–*ct* 17
Bowling 3348–117–28.61–6–1–7/45

His final first-class match was for Free Foresters in 1962.

Kenrick, Jarvis
Amateur. *b:* 13.11.1852, Chichester, Sussex. *d:* 29.1.1949, Blatchington, Sussex. Lower order right-hand batsman, left-arm medium pace bowler, slip field. *Sch* Lancing. *Team* Surrey (1876, 1 match).
Career batting
1–1–0–11–11–11.00–0–*ct* 0
Bowling 44–1–44.00–0–0–1/26

Kent, Humphrey Neild
Amateur. *b:* 2.11.1893, Watford, Herts. *d:* 19.4.1972, Upper Norwood, London. Lower

order batsman, bowler. *Sch* Clifton. *Team* Middlesex (1920, 2 matches).
Career batting
4–5–0–45–36–9.00–0–*ct* 2
Bowling 75–3–25.00–0–0–2/14
His final first-class match was for MCC in 1927.
He also played for Hertfordshire.

Kent, Kenneth Gwynne
Amateur. *b:* 10.12.1901, Birmingham. *d:* 29.12.1974, Fife, Scotland. Lower order right-hand batsman, right-arm fast medium bowler. *Sch* KES Birmingham. *Team* Warwickshire (1927–31, 9 matches).
Career batting
9–10–1–40–23*–4.44–0–*ct* 2
Bowling 639–10–63.90–0–0–3/91

Kent, Martin Francis
Cricketer. *b:* 23.11.1953, Mossman, Queensland, Australia. Opening or middle order right-hand batsman. *Team* Queensland (1974/5 to 1981/2, 49 matches). *Tours* Australia to Sri Lanka 1980/1, to England 1981; International Wanderers to South Africa 1975/6. *Tests* Australia (1981, 3 matches).
Career batting
64–110–11–3567–171–36.03–7–*ct* 60
Bowling 3–0
Test batting
3–6–0–171–54–28.50–0–*ct* 6
He hit 347 runs, av 23.13, on the 1981 tour and appeared in three of the six Tests.

Kent, Terence
Professional. *b:* 21.10.1939, Battersea. Lower order right-hand batsman, slow left-arm bowler. *Team* Essex (1960–62, 10 matches).
Career batting
10–10–4–74–23*–12.33–0–*ct* 5
Bowling 561–15–37.40–0–0–4/54
He played soccer for Millwall.

Kentfield, Richard William
Amateur. *b:* 1863, Bognor, Sussex. *d:* On or after 16.10.1904, his body being found in the River Ouse, Bedford. Lower order batsman, left-arm medium pace bowler. *Team* Lancashire (1888, 2 matches); Sussex (1894–96, 2 matches).
Career batting
4–8–0–49–18–6.12–0–*ct* 0
Bowling 232–10–23.20–1–0–6/45

Kentish, Esmond Seymour Maurice
Amateur. *b:* 21.11.1916, Cambridge, Jamaica. Tail end left-hand batsman, right-arm fast medium bowler. *Teams* Jamaica (1947/8 to 1956/7); Oxford U (1956, blue). *Tests* West Indies (1947/8 to 1953/4, 2 matches).
Career batting
27–29–21–109–15*–13.62–0–*ct* 6
Bowling 2084–78–26.71–4–0–5/36
Test batting
2–2–1–1–1*–1.00–0–*ct* 1
Bowling 178–8–22.25–1–0–5/49
He acted as manager of the West Indies team in England in 1973.
He is the oldest cricketer to be awarded his blue.

Kenward, Charles
Amateur. *b:* 7.9.1877, Rye, Sussex. *d:* 14.11.1948, Rye, Sussex. Brother of Richard (Derbyshire and Sussex). Middle order batsman. *Sch* Eastbourne. *Team* Gentlemen of England (1905).
Career batting
1–2–0–47–43–23.50–0–*ct* 2

Kenward, Richard
Amateur. *b:* 23.5.1875, Hastings, Sussex. *d:* 24.12.1957, Croydon, Surrey. Brother of Charles (Gentlemen of England). Middle order right-hand batsman. *Teams* Derbyshire (1899, 11 matches): Sussex (1902, 4 matches); London County (1902).
Career batting
17–27–0–387–56–14.33–0–*ct* 4
His final first-class match was for Gentlemen of England in 1905.

Kenyon, Donald
Professional. *b:* 15.5.1924, Wordsley, Staffs. Sound opening right-hand batsman, right-arm medium pace bowler, excellent field. *Team* Worcestershire (1946–67, 589 matches). *Tours* MCC to India, Pakistan and Ceylon 1951/52; Worcestershire World Tour 1964/5, to Jamaica 1965/6. *Tests* England (1951/2 to 1955, 8 matches).
Career batting
643–1159–59–37002–259–33.63–74–*ct* 327
Bowling 187–1–187.00–0–0–1/8
Test batting
8–15–0–192–87–12.80–0–*ct* 5
He hit 1,000 runs in a season 19 times, going on to 2,000 seven times (best 2,636, av 51.68, in 1954). His double centuries were all for Worcestershire, the highest being 259 v Yorkshire at Kidderminster in 1956. He captained Worcestershire 1959 to 1967 and was for several years a Test selector.

Kenyon, Myles Noel
Amateur. *b:* 25.12.1886, Bury, Lancashire. *d:* 21.11.1960, Birdham, Sussex. Middle/lower order

right-hand batsman. *Sch* Eton. *Team* Lancashire (1919–25, 91 matches).
Career batting
91–127–30–1435–61*–14.79–0–*ct* 20

He captained Lancashire 1919 to 1922 and was President of the County Club 1936 and 1937.

Kenyon-Slaney, Rt Hon William Stanley
Amateur. *b:* 24.8.1847, Rajkot, India. *d:* 24.4.1908, Hatton, Shifnal, Salop. Middle order right-hand batsman, good cover point. *Sch* Eton. *Team* MCC (1869–80).
Career batting
11–17–3–145–34–10.35–0–*ct* 2

He did not appear in any first-class matches whilst at Oxford U.

His County cricket was for Shropshire and he served on the MCC Committee for eight years.

At the time of his death he was Unionist MP for the Newport Division of Shropshire, having represented that constituency since 1886.

Ker, Andrew Burgher Michael
Cricketer. *b:* 16.10.1954, Kelso, Roxburghshire, Scotland. Brother of J.E. (Scotland). Right-hand batsman. *Team* Scotland (1981–83).
Career batting
3–5–1–170–65–42.50–0–*ct* 3

Ker, John Edward
Cricketer. *b:* 17.10.1952, Kelso, Roxburghshire, Scotland. Brother of A. B. M. (Scotland). Right-hand batsman, right-arm medium pace bowler. *Team* Scotland (1977–83).
Career batting
7–10–3–113–50–16.14–0–*ct* 3
Bowling 244–8–30.50–0–0–3/45

Kermode, Alexander
Professional. *b:* 15.5.1876, Sydney, New South Wales, Australia. *d:* 17.7.1934, Balmain, New South Wales, Australia. Lower order right-hand batsman, right-arm fast medium bowler. *Team* New South Wales (1901/2, 2 matches); Lancashire (1902–08, 76 matches); London County (1903).
Career batting
80–109–24–680–64*–8.00–0–*ct* 33
Bowling 7825–340–23.01–21–3–7/44

He took 100 wickets in a season once : 113, av 21.60, in 1905.

He came to England at the invitation of A.C. MacLaren specifically to qualify for Lancashire – a move that was severely criticised at the time by the traditionalists.

He also played for Cheshire.

Kerr, John
Amateur. *b:* 8.4.1885, Greenock, Scotland. *d:* 27.12.1972, Greenock, Scotland. Opening right-hand batsman, right-arm slow bowler, brilliant slip field. *Team* Scotland (1908–33).
Career batting
32–59–6–1975–178*–37.26–4–*ct* 31
Bowling 252–7–36.00–0–0–2/48

Regarded as one of Scotland's greatest cricketers, he hit 147 against the 1921 Australians at Edinburgh.

Kerr, John Lambert
Amateur. *b:* 28.12.1910, Dannevirke, New Zealand. Opening/middle order right-hand batsman, right-arm medium pace bowler, good field. *Team* Canterbury (1929/30 to 1939/40). *Tours* New Zealand to England 1931, 1937, to Australia 1937/8. *Tests* New Zealand (1931–37, 7 matches).
Career batting
89–157–7–4829–196–32.19–8–*ct* 28
Bowling 46–2–23.00–0–0–2/32
Test batting
7–12–1–212–59–19.27–0–*ct* 4

After a modest tour in 1931, he was one of the leading batsmen on the 1937 visit, scoring 1,205 runs, av 31.71.

His final first-class match was for New Zealand Army XI in 1942/3.

Kerr, James Reid
Amateur. *b:* 4.12.1883, Greenock, Scotland. *d:* 19.8.1963, Greenock, Scotland. Right-hand batsman. *Team* Scotland (1921).
Career batting
1–2–0–15–14–7.50–0–*ct* 2

Kerrigan, Michael
Amateur. *b:* 8.11.1931, Perth, Scotland. Left-hand batsman, slow left-arm bowler. *Team* Scotland (1954–61).
Career batting
12–18–4–84–18*–6.00–0–*ct* 4
Bowling 892–39–22.87–2–1–7/84

Kershaw, John Edward
Amateur. *b:* 12.1.1854, Heywood, Lancashire. *d:* 29.11.1903, Burnley, Lancashire, of consumption. Useful middle order right-hand batsman, wicket-keeper. *Team* Lancashire (1877–85, 33 matches).
Career batting
35–57–3–582–66–10.77–0–*ct* 15–*st* 1

Kerslake, Roy Cosmo
Amateur. *b:* 26.12.1942, Paignton, Devon. Lower order right-hand batsman, off break bowler, excellent field. *Sch* Kingswood. *Teams* Cambridge U (1962–64, blue 1963–64): Somerset (1962–68,

52 matches). *Tours* MCC to South America 1964/5 (not first-class).
Career batting
85–132–14–1939–80–16.43–0–*ct* 64
Bowling 2617–114–22.95–4–0–6/77
His final first-class match was for Minor Counties in 1976.
He captained Somerset in 1968.

Kersley, Tom
Professional. *b:* 9.2.1879, Surbiton, Surrey. *d:* 1927, Elham, Kent. Lower order batsman, opening bowler. *Team* Surrey (1899, 3 matches).
Career batting
3–4–1–23–15*–7.66–0–*ct* 1
Bowling 145–7–20.71–0–0–3/36

Kesteven, John
Professional. *b:* 8.7.1849, Sutton-in-Ashfield, Notts. Middle order right-hand batsman, right-hand medium pace round-arm bowler. *Team* Nottinghamshire (1876, 3 matches).
Career batting
3–4–0–24–12–6.00–0–*ct* 1

Kettle, Michael Keith
Cricketer. *b:* 18.3.1944, Stamford, Lincs. Lower order right-hand batsman, left-arm medium pace bowler. *Team* Northants (1963–70, 88 matches).
Career batting
88–105–20–1117–88–13.14–0–*ct* 63
Bowling 4800–179–26.81–5–0–6/67

Kettlewell, Henry Wildman
Amateur. *b:* 20.7.1876, East Harptree, Bath, Somerset. *d:* 28.4.1963, East Harptree, Bath, Somerset. Middle order right-hand batsman, right-arm fast bowler. *Sch* Eton. *Team* Somerset (1899, 1 match).
Career batting
1–2–1–7–6*–7.00–0–*ct* 0
Bowling 30–0

Kevan, Joseph Henry
Amateur. *b:* 13.9.1855, Bolton, Lancashire. *d:* 9.12.1891, Bolton, Lancashire. *Team* Lancashire (1875, 2 matches).
Career batting
2–4–0–12–12–3.00–0–*ct* 0

Kewley, Edward
Amateur. *b:* 20.6.1852, Eton, Bucks. *d:* 17.4.1940, Winchester, Hants. Middle order right-hand batsman. *Sch* Marlborough. *Team* Lancashire (1875, 1 match).
Career batting
1–2–0–3–3–1.50–0–*ct* 1
He played rugby for England.

Key, Sir Kingsmill James
Amateur. *b:* 11.10.1864, Streatham, Surrey. *d:* 9.8.1932, Wittersham, Kent, from blood poisoning after an insect bite. Cousin of L.H. Gay (Hants and Somerset). Attacking middle order right-hand batsman, right-arm slow off break bowler. *Sch* Clifton. *Teams* Surrey (1882–1904, 288 matches); Oxford U (1884–87, blue all four years). *Tours* Sanders to North America 1886; Hawke to North America 1891; Oxford Univ Authentics to India 1902/03.
Career batting
368–567–71–13008–281–26.22–13–*ct* 113
Bowling 337–12–28.08–0–0–2/32
He hit 1,000 runs in a season three times (best 1,684, av 43.17, in 1887). His only double century was 281 for Oxford U v Middlesex at Chiswick Park in 1887.
He led Surrey from 1894 to 1899 – 'a man of most original views, an always philosophic cricketer and an imperturbable captain'.
His final first-class match was in 1909 for Leveson-Gower's XI.
A noted rugby footballer, he gained his blue at Oxford.

Key, Laurence Henry
Amateur. *b:* 5.5.1895, Lincoln. *d:* 18.4.1971, Taunton. Lower order left-hand batsman, slow left-arm bowler. *Sch* Taunton. *Team* Somerset (1919–22, 8 matches).
Career batting
8–12–2–80–30–8.00–0–*ct* 5
Bowling 58–2–29.00–0–0–2/50

Key, Richard Leigh Troward
Amateur. *b:* 1844, St Pancras, Middlesex. *d:* 1875, Uxbridge, Middlesex. Middle order batsman. *Team* MCC (1866).
Career batting
1–2–0–5–5–2.50–0–*ct* 0

Khalid Hassan
Amateur. *b:* 14.7.1937, Peshawar, India. Lower order right-hand batsman, leg break and googly bowler. *Teams* Punjab (1953/4); East Pakistan (1956/7 to 1961/2); Lahore (1958/9). *Tour* Pakistan to England 1954. *Test* Pakistan (1954, 1 match).
Career batting
23–27–9–204–38–11.33–0–*ct* 3
Bowling 1389–32–43.40–0–0–3/29
Test batting
1–2–1–17–10–17.00–0–*ct* 0
Bowling 116–2–58.00–0–0–2/116
He was, according to his published birth date,

only 16 years and 352 days old when making his Test debut in the second Test of 1954; he achieved however only moderate results on the 1954 tour.

Khalid Ibadulla *(see under* Ibadulla, K.)

Khalid Wazir Ali
Amateur. *b:* 27.4.1936, Jullundur, India. Son of S. Wazir Ali (India). Middle order right-hand batsman, right-arm fast medium bowler. *Teams* Rest (1952/3); Hasan Mahmood's XI (1953/4). *Tour* Pakistan to England 1954. *Tests* Pakistan (1954, 2 matches).
Career batting
18–23–5–271–53–15.05–0–*ct* 12
Bowling 746–14–53.28–0–0–3/82
Test batting
2–3–1–14–9*–7.00–0–*ct* 0
He had very little success on his single tour to England, though appearing in two Tests.
After the 1954 tour he settled in England.

Khan, Asad Jahangir
Cricketer. *b:* 25.12.1945, Campbellpur, India. Opening right-hand batsman, off break bowler. *Teams* Oxford U (1967–69, blue 1968–69); Punjab Univ (1965/6); Lahore (1966/7 to 1970/1).
Career batting
40–64–5–1154–92–19.55–0–*ct* 44
Bowling 2030–53–38.30–2–0–7/84

Khan, M. J. *(see under* Majid J. Khan)

Khan Mohammad
Professional. *b:* 1.1.1928, Lahore, India. Lower order right-hand batsman, right-arm fast medium bowler, good short leg. *Teams* Northern India (1946/7); Punjab Univ (1947/8 to 1948/9); Somerset (1951, 1 match); Bahawalpur (1953/4); Karachi (1956/7); Lahore (1960/1). *Tours* Pakistan to Ceylon 1948/9, to India 1952/3, 1954/5, to England 1954, to West Indies 1957/8. *Tests* Pakistan (1952/3 to 1957/8, 13 matches).
Career batting
53–64–18–524–93–11.39–0–*ct* 20
Bowling 4939–212–23.29–16–1–7/56
Test batting
13–17–7–100–26*–10.00–0–*ct* 4
Bowling 1292–54–23.92–4–0–6/21
Playing in the Lancashire League he was drafted into the 1954 Pakistan touring team to England for five first-class matches, including two Tests.

Khanna, Bharatchand
Amateur. *b:* 22.6.1914, India. Middle order right-hand batsman, right-arm medium fast bowler. *Teams* Madras (1933/4); Cambridge Univ (1937, blue); Hyderabad (1937/8 to 1952/3).
Career batting
38–68–12–1285–75–22.94–0–*ct* 9
Bowling 2589–99–26.15–3–0–5/61

Khanna, Surinder Chamanlal
Cricketer. *b:* 3.6.1956, Delhi, India. Lower order right-hand batsman, wicket-keeper. *Team* Delhi (1976/7 to 1982/3). *Tour* India to England 1979.
Career batting
59–79–12–2618–143–37.84–8–*ct* 117–*st* 41
Bowling 21–0
The reserve wicket-keeper on the 1979 tour to England, he was not required for the Tests.

Kibble, George Herbert
Professional. *b:* 9.10.1865, Greenwich, Kent. *d:* 4.1.1923, Camberwell, London. Middle order batsman. *Team* Kent (1889, 1 match).
Career batting
1–2–0–9–6–4.50–0–*ct* 0

Kidd, Eric Leslie
Amateur. *b:* 18.10.1889, London. Attractive middle order right-hand batsman, slow leg break bowler, excellent field. *Sch* Wellington. *Teams* Cambridge U (1910–13, blue all four years); Middlesex (1910–28, 77 matches); Ireland (1921–28).
Career batting
147–218–13–5113–167–24.94–6–*ct* 129
Bowling 4581–186–24.62–8–1–8/49
His final first-class match was for Free Foresters in 1930.
His best season was 1913 when he hit 1,041 runs, av 49.57.

Kidd, Dr Percy Marmaduke
Amateur. *b:* 13.2.1851, Blackheath, Kent. *d:* 21.1.1942, Chalfont St Giles, Bucks. Middle order right-hand batsman, right-arm medium pace bowler. *Sch* Uppingham *Team* Kent (1874, 1 match).
Career batting
1–2–0–0–0–0.00–0–*ct* 0
Bowling 36–0

Kidman, Edward Arnold
Amateur. *b:* 9.10.1875, Edmonton, London. *d:* 30.4.1917, Calcutta, India. Opening/middle order batsman. *Sch* Liverpool College. *Team* Cambridge U (1897).
Career batting
1–2–0–25–23–12.50–0–*ct* 0

Kilbee, John Richard
Cricketer. *b:* 24.7.1947, Hong Kong. Middle

order right-hand batsman, right-arm medium pace bowler. *Sch* King's Canterbury. *Team* Oxford U (1968–69).
Career batting
8–12–4–70–18*–8.75–0–*ct* 4
Bowling 270–8–33.75–0–0–4/96

Kilburn, Sam
Professional. *b:* 16.10.1868, Huddersfield, Yorkshire. *d:* 25.9.1940, Huddersfield, Yorkshire. Middle order right-hand batsman. *Team* Yorkshire (1896, 1 match).
Career batting
1–1–0–8–8–8.00–0–*ct* 0

Killick, Anthony
Professional. *b:* 1829. *d:* 8.12.1881, Uckfield, Sussex. Brother of Henry (Sussex) and uncle of E.H. (Sussex). *Team* Sussex (1866, 1 match).
Career batting
1–1–0–0–0–0.00–0–*ct* 0

Killick, Ernest Harry
Professional. *b:* 17.1.1875, Horsham, Sussex. *d:* 29.9.1948, Hove, Sussex. Nephew of Anthony and Harry (Sussex). Free scoring middle order left-hand batsman, right-arm medium or slow bowler. *Team* Sussex (1893–1913, 450 matches).
Career batting
461–770–53–18768–200–26.17–22–*ct* 188
Bowling 19903–729–27.30–25–1–7/10

He hit 1,000 runs in a season 11 times (best 1,767, av 36.06, in 1906) and took 100 wickets once – 108, av 21.93, in 1905 – performing the 'double' that season. He had the misfortune to be hit for 34 off one over (including two no balls) when playing for Sussex v Notts at Hove in 1911; the batsman was E.B. Alletson. His highest score was 200 for Sussex v Yorkshire at Hove in 1901.

After retiring from County cricket he was for many years the Sussex scorer.

Killick, Rev Edgar Thomas
Amateur. *b:* 9.5.1907, Fulham, London. *d:* 18.5.1953, Northampton, whilst playing in a diocesan cricket match. Stylish opening right-hand batsman, good deep field. *Sch* St Paul's. *Teams* Middlesex (1926–39, 47 matches); Cambridge U (1927–30, blue 1928, 1929 and 1930). *Tests* England (1929, 2 matches).
Career batting
92–153–11–5730–206–40.35–15–*ct* 50
Bowling 229–3–76.33–0–0–1/20
Test batting
2–4–0–81–31–20.25–0–*ct* 2

He hit 1,000 runs in a season twice (best 1,384, av 44.64, in 1929). He scored only two double centuries for Cambridge, but his highest score was his only double century for Middlesex – 206 v Warwickshire at Lord's in 1931, curiously the only County Championship innings he played that season.

His final first-class match was for Free Foresters in 1946.

Owing to his calling he played little first-class cricket after leaving Cambridge.

He was also a good rugby footballer.

Killick, Harry
Professional. *b:* 13.7.1837, Crabtree, Horsham, Sussex. *d:* 22.11.1877, Brighton, Sussex. He dropped down dead having broken a blood vessel. Brother of Anthony (Sussex), uncle of E.H. (Sussex). Opening/middle order left-hand batsman, right-hand medium pace round-arm bowler, wicket-keeper. *Team* Sussex (1866–75, 40 matches).
Career batting
44–80–5–1097–78–14.62–0–*ct* 25
Bowling 219–6–36.50–0–0–3/37

Killick, William
Professional. *b:* 14.5.1855, Reigate, Surrey. *d:* 2.4.1938, Horley, Surrey. Middle order right-hand batsman, good field. *Team* Surrey (1876, 1 match).
Career batting
1–2–0–3–3–1.50–0–*ct* 0

Kilner, Norman
Professional. *b:* 21.7.1895, Wombwell, Yorkshire. *d:* 28.4.1979, Birmingham. Brother of Roy (Yorkshire), nephew of W. A. I. Washington (Yorkshire). Sound opening/middle order right-hand batsman, medium pace bowler. *Teams* Yorkshire (1919–23, 69 matches); Warwickshire (1924–37, 330 matches).
Career batting
403–619–42–17522–228–30.36–25–*ct* 184
Bowling 166–2–83.00–0–0–1/19

He hit 1,000 runs in a season 12 times, going on to 2,000 once – 2,159, av 44.97, in 1933. His only double century was 228 for Warwickshire v Worcestershire at Worcester in 1935.

After retiring he became coach and then groundsman at Edgbaston.

Kilner, Roy
Professional. *b:* 17.10.1890, Low Valley, Wombwell, Yorkshire. *d:* 5.4.1928, Kendray, Barnsley, Yorkshire, of enteric fever. Brother of Norman (Yorkshire), nephew of W. A. I. Washington (Yorkshire). Aggressive middle order left-hand batsman, slow left-arm bowler, good field. *Teams* Yorkshire (1911–27, 365 matches); Europeans (1922/3). *Tours* MCC to Australia 1924/5,

to West Indies 1925/6. *Tests* England (1924–26, 9 matches).
Career batting
416–546–56–14707–206*–30.01–18–*ct* 266
Bowling 18516–1003–18.46–48–10–8/26
Test batting
9–8–1–233–74–33.28–0–*ct* 6
Bowling 734–24–30.58–0–0–4/51

He hit 1,000 runs in a season 10 times (best 1,586, av 34.47, in 1913). His only double century was 206* for Yorkshire v Derbyshire at Bramall Lane in 1920.

He took 100 wickets in a season five times (best 158, av 12.91, in 1923) and achieved the 'double' four times - 1922, 1923, 1925 and 1926.

Kimbell, Ralph Raymond
Amateur. *b:* 12.6.1884, Brixworth, Northants. *d:* 4.8.1964, Ledbury, Herefordshire. Lower order batsman, bowler. *Team* Northants (1908, 1 match).
Career batting
1–2–0–4–4–2.00–0–*ct* 0
Bowling 45–2–22.50–0–0–2/45

Kimish, Arthur Edwards
Amateur. *b:* 5.7.1917, Southampton, Hants. Lower order right-hand batsman, wicket-keeper. *Team* Hampshire (1946, 3 matches).
Career batting
3–4–1–18–12*–6.00–0–*ct* 3–*st* 3

Kimmins, Simon Edward Anthony
Amateur. *b:* 26.5.1930, Belgravia, London. Middle order right-hand batsman, right-arm medium pace bowler, good coverpoint. *Sch* Charterhouse. *Teams* Kent (1950–51, 12 matches).
Career batting
16–29–3–563–81–21.65–0–*ct* 13
Bowling 996–24–41.50–1–0–5/42

His final first-class match was for Free Foresters in 1959.

Kimpton, Roger Charles MacDonald
Amateur. *b:* 21.9.1916, Toorak, Melbourne, Australia. Brother of S.M. (Oxford Univ). Middle order right-hand batsman, wicket-keeper. *Teams* Oxford Univ (1935–38, blue 1935, 1937 and 1938); Worcestershire (1937–49, 14 matches). *Tours* Oxford and Cambridge to Jamaica 1938/9; Swanton to West Indies 1955/6.
Career batting
62–109–8–3562–160–35.26–8–*ct* 57–*st* 14
Bowling 1336–28–47.71–0–0–2/20

He hit 1,568 runs, av 34.84, in 1937, the only season he exceeded 1,000 runs.

Kimpton, Stephen MacDonald
Amateur. *b:* 5.3.1914, Toorak, Melbourne, Australia. Brother of R.C.M. (Oxford U and Worcs). Middle order left-hand batsman, slow right-arm bowler. *Team* Oxford U (1935).
Career batting
4–7–1–112–31–18.66–0–*ct* 1
Bowling 384–9–42.66–0–0–4/65

Kinderman, Frederick Louis
Amateur. *b:* 1840, Liverpool. Middle order batsman. *Team* Gentlemen of North (1867).
Career batting
1–2–0–10–9–5.00–0–*ct* 1

King, Anthony Mountain
Professional. *b:* 8.10.1932, Laughton, Sheffield, Yorkshire. Middle order right-hand batsman. *Team* Yorkshire (1955, 1 match).
Career batting
1–1–0–12–12–12.00–0–*ct* 0

He played as stand-off half for Bradford RUFC.

King, Benjamin Philip
Professional. *b:* 22.4.1915, Leeds, Yorkshire. *d:* 31.3.1970, Bradford, Yorkshire. Aggressive middle order right-hand batsman, wicket-keeper. *Teams* Worcestershire (1935–39, 80 matches); Lancashire (1946–47, 37 matches).
Career batting
117–196–9–4124–145–22.05–6–*ct* 54–*st* 6
Bowling 4–0

He hit 1,000 runs in a season twice (best 1,177, av 22.63, in 1938). In 1946 he offered to play for Worcester without payment until he had reached 1,000 runs and to be paid £1 per run thereafter. The County turned down the offer and he joined Lancashire.

He later became a well-known sporting journalist.

King, Collis Llewellyn
Cricketer. *b:* 11.6.1951, Fairview, Christchurch, Barbados. Hard hitting middle order right-hand batsman, right-arm medium pace bowler. *Teams* Barbados (1972/3 to 1981/2); Glamorgan (1977, 16 matches); Worcestershire (1983, 2 matches). *Tours* West Indies to England 1976, 1980, to Australia and New Zealand 1979/80; West Indies XI to South Africa 1982/3; International XI to Pakistan 1981/2. *Tests* West Indies (1976 to 1980/1, 9 matches).

Career batting
99–160–22–5386–163–39.02–13–*ct* 87
Bowling 3621–115–31.48–1–0–5/91
Test batting
9–16–3–418–100*–32.15–1–*ct* 5
Bowling 282–3–94.00–0–0–1/30

On the 1976 tour he hit 1,320 runs, av 55.00, and played in three of the five Tests; in 1980 he was quite out of form and appeared in only one Test.

King, Edwin
Professional. *b:* 1884. *d:* 7.7.1952, Braunstone, Leicester. Lower order right-hand batsman, wicket-keeper. *Team* Leicestershire (1925, 2 matches).
Career batting
2–4–1–33–31*–11.00–0–*ct* 5–*st* 1

He also played soccer for Leicester City.

King, Edmund Hugh
Amateur. *b:* 26.3.1906, Birmingham *d:* 25.11.1981, Cropthorne, Worcs. He was killed in a road accident. Middle order right-hand batsman, off break bowler. *Sch* Ampleforth. *Team* Warwickshire (1928–32, 7 matches).
Career batting
7–10–0–84–24–8.40–0–*ct* 3
Bowling 15–0

He was Chairman of Warwickshire CCC 1962 to 1972 and a key figure in the formation of the TCCB, being Chairman of the TCCB Finance sub-committee from 1968 to 1980.

King, Edmund Poole
Amateur. *b:* 21.1.1907, Clifton, Bristol. Middle order right-hand batsman. *Sch* Winchester *Team* Gloucestershire (1927, 3 matches).
Career batting
3–4–0–14–6–3.50–0–*ct* 1

King, Frank
Amateur. *b:* 6.4.1911, London. Lower order right-hand batsman, right-arm fast medium bowler. *Sch* Dulwich. *Team* Cambridge U (1934–35, blue 1934).
Career batting
10–15–5–68–16*–6.80–0–*ct* 7
Bowling 615–22–27.95–2–0–6/64

He played for Dorset.

King, Frederick
Amateur. *b:* 12.11.1850, Harbledown, Kent. *d:* 16.6.1893, Hammersmith, London. Opening batsman. *Team* Kent (1871, 1 match).
Career batting
1–2–0–11–6–5.50–0–*ct* 0
Bowling 15–0

King, George Lionel
Amateur. *b:* 6.4.1857, Brighton, Sussex. *d:* 29.6.1944, Brighton, Sussex. Son of G.W. (Sussex). Middle order right-hand batsman, wicket-keeper. *Sch* Rugby. *Team* Sussex (1880–81, 6 matches).
Career batting
6–10–0–112–29–11.20–0–*ct* 2

He appeared in the Freshmen's and Seniors' matches at Cambridge, but no first-class matches.

King, George William
Amateur. *b:* 15.6.1822, London. *d:* 22.12.1881, Brighton, Sussex. Father of G.L. (Sussex). Defensive middle order left-hand batsman, good longstop. *Sch* Eton. *Teams* Cambridge U (1843); Sussex (1842–64, 18 matches).
Career batting
19–31–5–166–25–6.38–0–*ct* 4

He was Secretary of Sussex CCC for several years, resigning in 1880.

King, Harry
Amateur. *b:* 6.11.1881, Leicester. *d:* 30.6.1947, Leicester. Middle order right-hand batsman, right-arm medium pace bowler. *Team* Leicestershire (1912–20, 3 matches).
Career batting
3–6–1–29–11–5.80–0–*ct* 0
Bowling 64–0

King, Sir Henry Clark
Amateur. *b:* 20.6.1857, Durham. *d:* 23.7.1920, Hove, Sussex. Steady middle order right-hand batsman, right-arm medium pace bowler. *Sch* Durham and Marlborough. *Team* MCC (1895).
Career batting
1–1–0–0–0–0.00–0–*ct* 0

He lived in India for some years and appeared for Madras (not first-class).

A noted rugby footballer, he represented Midland Counties.

King, Horace David
Amateur. *b:* 10.2.1915, Brentford, Middlesex. *d:* 7.3.1974, Worthing, Sussex. Lower order right-hand batsman, wicket-keeper. *Sch* Taunton. *Teams* Europeans (1934/5); Middlesex (1936–46, 7 matches); Services (1943/4).
Career batting
9–13–4–104–26–11.55–0–*ct* 7–*st* 8

King, Ian Metcalf
Professional. *b:* 10.11.1931, Leeds, Yorkshire. Lower order left-hand batsman, slow left-arm bowler. *Teams* Warwickshire (1952–55, 53 matches); Essex (1957, 28 matches).

Career batting
81–96–39–476–33–8.35–0–*ct* 60
Bowling 3706–129–28.72–1–0–5/59

King, J.
Professional. Lower order left-hand batsman, left-arm fast bowler. *Teams* Kent (1881, 2 matches); Hampshire (1882, 1 match).
Career batting
3–5–1–39–16*–9.75–0–*ct* 3
Bowling 223–10–22.30–0–0–4/64

King, James
Professional. *b:* 3.5.1869, Lutterworth, Leics. *d:* 8.3.1948, Wisbech, Cambs. Brother of J.H. (Leics) and father of J.W. (Leics and Worcs). Sound middle order right-hand batsman, useful change bowler. *Team* Leicestershire (1899–1905, 7 matches).
Career batting
7–10–2–83–24*–10.37–0–*ct* 2
Bowling 146–2–73.00–0–0–2/71
He was also a good local rugby footballer.

King, John
Professional. *b:* 2.8.1845, Cambridge. Middle order batsman. *Team* Cambridge (1861–64, 4 matches).
Career batting
4–8–1–26–10*–3.71–0–*ct* 1

King, John Barton
Amateur. *b:* 19.10.1873, Philadelphia, USA. *d:* 17.10.1965, Philadelphia, USA. Middle order right-hand batsman, right-arm fast bowler. *Team* Philadelphia (1893–1912). *Tours* Philadelphia to England 1897, 1903 and 1908.
Career batting
62–111–9–2047–113*–20.06–1–*ct* 65
Bowling 6353–390–16.28–36–9–9/25
Regarded as the greatest bowler produced by Philadelphia, he proved his ability in 1908 when he took 87 wickets, av 11.01, in first-class matches and was the leading bowler in England that year. His best bowling was 9/25 for Philadelphia v Warner's XI at Belmont in 1897.

King, John Herbert
Professional. *b:* 16.4.1871, Lutterworth, Leics. *d:* 18.11.1946, Denbigh. Brother of James (Leics), uncle of J. W. (Leics and Worcs). Excellent middle order left-hand batsman, left-arm medium pace bowler, good slip field. *Team* Leicestershire (1895–1925, 502 matches). *Test* England (1909, 1 match).
Career batting
552–988–69–25122–227*–27.33–34–*ct* 340
Bowling 30312–1204–25.17–69–11–8/17
Test batting
1–2–0–64–60–32.00–0–*ct* 0
Bowling 99–1–99.00–0–0–1/99
He hit 1,000 runs in a season 14 times (best 1,788, av 38.04, in 1904) and took 100 wickets in a season twice (best 130, av 17.63, in 1912). He completed the 'double' in 1912.
Both his double centuries were for Leics, the highest being 227* v Worcs at Coalville in 1914 and the other being remarkable for the fact that it was scored in 1923, when King was aged 52 (205 v Hants at Leicester).

King, James Morris Roy
Cricketer. *b:* 15.9.1942, Bristol. Middle order batsman. *Team* Gloucestershire (1966, 3 matches).
Career batting
3–5–0–47–28–9.40–0–*ct* 2

King, John William
Professional. *b:* 21.1.1908, Leicester. *d:* 25.3.1953, Narborough, Leics. Son of James (Leics), nephew of J. H. (Leics). Sound right-hand batsman. *Teams* Leicestershire (1929, 8 matches); Worcestershire (1927–28, 40 matches).
Career batting
48–88–14–1169–91–15.79–0–*ct* 13

King, Kenneth Charles William
Amateur, turned professional midway through 1936 season. *b:* 4.12.1915, Beddington, Surrey. Lower order left-hand batsman, slow left-arm bowler. *Sch* KCS Wimbledon. *Team* Surrey (1936–38, 31 matches).
Career batting
32–40–8–361–64–11.28–0–*ct* 18
Bowling 1201–34–35.32–0–0–4/38
His final first-class match was for D.R. Jardine's XI in 1955.

King, Lester Anthony
Amateur. *b:* 27.2.1939, St Catherine Parish, Jamaica. Lower order right-hand batsman, right-arm fast bowler, good deep field. *Teams* Jamaica (1961/2 to 1967/8); Bengal (1962/3). *Tours* West Indies to England 1963, to India and Ceylon 1966/7, to Australia and New Zealand 1968/9. *Tests* West Indies (1961/2 to 1967/8, 2 matches).
Career batting
62–87–19–1404–89–20.64–0–*ct* 38
Bowling 4463–142–31.42–3–0–5/46
Test batting
2–4–0–41–20–10.25–0–*ct* 2
Bowling 154–9–17.11–1–0–5/46

He was overshadowed by W.W. Hall and C.C. Griffith on the 1963 tour to England and was not required for the Tests.

King, Percival
Professional. *b:* 9.12.1835, Stockwell, Surrey. *d:* 29.10.1910, Edinburgh, Scotland. Lower order right-hand batsman, right-hand round-arm bowler, either fast or slow, wicket-keeper. *Team* Surrey (1871, 1 match).
Career batting
1–2–0–16–13–8.00–0–*ct* 1
Bowling 18–0

He was prominently identified with cricket in Scotland, captaining the Players of Scotland against the Gentlemen, and was Editor of the 'Scottish Cricketers Guide' 1870/1 to 1887/8.

King, Robert Jasper Stuart
(also known as Stuart-King)
Amateur. *b:* 10.5.1909, Leigh-on-Sea, Essex. Lower order right-hand batsman, leg break bowler. *Sch* Felsted. *Team* Essex (1928, 1 match).
Career batting
1–1–0–3–3–3.00–0–*ct* 0
Bowling 20–0

King, Sidney
Amateur. *b:* 1885, Rushden, Northants. *d:* 1972, Rushden, Northants. Middle order batsman. *Team* Northants (1907–08, 4 matches).
Career batting
4–7–2–47–23–9.40–0–*ct* 2

King, William Robert
Amateur. *b:* 16.12.1902, Kilkishen, Co Clare, Ireland. Left-hand batsman, slow left-arm bowler. *Team* Dublin University (1922).
Career batting
1–2–0–15–8–7.50–0–*ct* 1
Bowling 36–0

Kingscote, Henry Bloomfield
Amateur. *b:* 28.2.1843, Kingscote, Gloucs. *d:* 1.8.1915, Belgravia, London. Nephew of H. R. (Surrey, Hants and Sussex). Hard hitting middle order right-hand batsman, wicket-keeper. *Teams* Kent (1867, 1 match); Gloucestershire (1877, 3 matches).
Career batting
12–18–2–91–44*–5.68–0–*ct* 12–*st* 8

His final first-class match was for MCC in 1878. He was principally connected with Army cricket, being a member of the Royal Artillery team from 1864 to 1881; from 1882 to 1889 he was stationed in India taking part in many matches there, and latterly selected the Army team to play the Bar in the annual match at Lord's.

Kingsford, Robert Kennett
Amateur. *b:* 23.12.1849, Sydenham, Kent. *d:* 14.10.1895, Adelaide, Australia. Free hitting middle order right-hand batsman, good deep field, occasional wicket-keeper. *Sch* Marlborough. *Team* Surrey (1872–74, 3 matches).
Career batting
3–5–0–80–30–16.00–0–*ct* 2

Kingsley, Sir Patrick Graham Toler
Amateur. *b:* 26.5.1908, Calcutta, India. Opening/middle order right-hand batsman, excellent slip field. *Sch* Winchester. *Team* Oxford (1928–30, blue all three years).
Career batting
47–78–2–2270–176–29.87–2–*ct* 41
Bowling 218–4–54.50–0–0–2/46

His County cricket was for Hertfordshire and Devon; his final first-class match being for Free Foresters in 1938.

Kingston, Rev Frederick William
Amateur. *b:* 24.12.1855, Oundle, Northants. *d:* 30.1.1933, Willington, Beds. Brother of J. P. (Warwicks), H. E. (Northants), W. H. (Northants), and C.A. (British Guiana). Lower order right-hand batsman, wicket-keeper. *Team* Cambridge U (1878, blue).
Career batting
6–9–0–141–61–15.66–0–*ct* 7–*st* 3

His final first-class match was for Cambridge University Past and Present in 1886.

Kingston, Graham Charles
Cricketer. *b:* 1.11.1950, Newport, Mon. Middle order right-hand batsman, right-arm medium pace bowler. *Team* Glamorgan (1967–71, 9 matches). *Tours* Glamorgan to West Indies 1969/70.
Career batting
9–15–2–161–26–12.38–0–*ct* 4
Bowling 210–4–52.50–0–0–2/18

He was also a good soccer and rugby footballer.

Kingston, Hubert Ernest
Amateur. *b:* 15.8.1876, Northampton. *d:* 9.6.1955, Long Buckby, Northants. Brother of W.H. (Northants), F.W. (Cambridge U), J.P. (Warwicks) and C.A. (British Guiana). Steady right-hand middle order batsman, right-arm slow bowler. *Sch* Blair Lodge. *Team* Northants (1905–06, 13 matches).
Career batting
13–25–4–335–68–15.95–0–*ct* 7
Bowling 246–6–41.00–0–0–2/8

Kingston, James Phillips
Amateur. *b:* 8.7.1857, Northampton. *d:* 14.3.1929, Italy. Brother of F.W. (Cambridge U), H.E. (Northants), W.H. (Northants) and C.A. (British Guiana). Opening right-hand batsman, leg break bowler, excellent point. *Team* Warwickshire (1894, 1 match).
Career batting
1–1–0–24–24–24.00–0–*ct* 0
Most of his County cricket was for Northants before that side became first-class. He was captain from 1877 to 1887 and in 1891, in which year he was also appointed Secretary.

Kingston, William Harold
Amateur. *b:* 12.8.1874, Northampton. *d:* 17.2.1956, Northampton. Brother of H.E. (Northants), F.W. (Cambridge U), J.P. (Warwicks) and C.A. (British Guiana). Sound right-hand opening batsman. *Team* Northants (1905–09, 77 matches).
Career batting
78–141–2–2599–83–18.69–0–*ct* 44
Bowling 25–2–12.50–0–0–2/5
His first-class debut was for the Gentlemen in 1904.

Kington, William Miles Nairn
Amateur. *b:* 24.9.1838, Clifton, Bristol. *d:* 21.4.1898, Montreux, Switzerland. Brother of P.O. (Victoria). Middle order right-hand batsman. *Sch* Harrow. *Team* Gloucestershire (1875–76, 2 matches).
Career batting
4–6–0–53–17–8.83–0–*ct* 0
He also played for Monmouthshire.
His first-class debut was for Manchester in 1858.

King-Turner, Dr Charles John
Amateur. *b:* 13.12.1904, Cirencester, Gloucs. *d:* 4.4.1972, Cirencester Gloucs. Good middle order right-hand batsman but too impatient, excellent cover point. *Sch* Cheltenham. *Team* Gloucestershire (1922, 6 matches).
Career batting
6–9–0–29–10–3.22–0–*ct* 3

Kinkead-Weekes, Roderick Calder
Cricketer. *b:* 15.3.1951, East London, South Africa. Lower order right-hand batsman, wicket-keeper. *Sch* Eton. *Teams* Oxford U (1972, blue); Middlesex (1976, 2 matches).
Career batting
6–9–2–76–25*–10.85–0–*ct* 7–*st* 3

Kinneir, Septimus (Paul)
Professional. *b:* 13.5.1871, Corsham, Wilts. *d:* 16.10.1928, Birmingham. Stylish opening left-hand batsman, slow left-arm bowler. *Team* Warwickshire (1898–1914, 302 matches). *Tour* MCC to Australia 1911/12. *Test* England (1911/2, 1 match).
Career batting
312–525–47–15641–268*–32.72–26–*ct* 181
Bowling 1492–48–31.08–0–0–3/13
Test batting
1–2–0–52–30–26.00–0–*ct* 0
He hit 1,000 runs in a season eight times (best 1,629, av 49.36, in 1911). Both his double centuries were for Warwickshire, the highest being 268* v Hampshire at Edgbaston in 1911.
He also played for Wiltshire.

Kinnersley, Kenneth Charles
Amateur. *b:* 13.3.1914, Apia, Samoa. Opening right-hand batsman, right-arm medium slow bowler. *Sch* Clifton. *Team* Somerset (1932–38, 10 matches).
Career batting
10–18–3–143–25*–9.53–0–*ct* 8
Bowling 436–17–25.64–0–0–3/40
He also played for Devon.

Kippax, Alan Falconer
Amateur. *b:* 25.5.1897, Sydney, New South Wales, Australia. *d:* 4.9.1972, Bellevue Hill, New South Wales, Australia. Stylish right-hand middle order batsman, leg break bowler. *Teams* New South Wales (1918/19 to 1935/6, 87 matches). *Tours* Australia to New Zealand 1920/1, 1927/8, to England 1930, 1934; NSW to New Zealand 1923/4. *Tests* Australia (1924/5 to 1934, 22 matches).
Career batting
175–256–33–12762–315*–57.22–43–*ct* 73
Bowling 1099–21–52.33–0–0–4/66
Test batting
22–34–1–1192–146–36.12–2–*ct* 13
Bowling 19–0
He was most successful on the 1930 tour to England with 1,451 runs, av 58.04, but in 1934 he suffered from illness and appeared in only one Test. His triple century was 315* for NSW v Queensland at Sydney in 1927/8; of his other scores over 200, the only one hit in England was 250 v Sussex at Hove in 1934. He was considered unlucky not to have been chosen for the Australian 1926 tour to England. He hit 1,000 runs in a season in Australia twice.

Kippax, Peter John
Professional. *b:* 15.10.1940, Huddersfield, Yorkshire. Middle order right-hand batsman, leg break and googly bowler. *Sch* Bedford Modern. *Team*

Yorkshire (1961–62, 4 matches). *Tour* Minor Counties to Kenya 1977/8 (not first-class).
Career batting
4–7–2–37–9–7.40–0–*ct* 0
Bowling 279–8–34.87–1–0–5/74
He also appeared for Northumberland and Durham.

Kirby, David
Amateur. *b:* 18.1.1939, Darlington, Co Durham. Opening/middle order right-hand batsman, off break bowler. *Sch* St Peter's, York. *Teams* Cambridge U (1959–61, blue all three years); Leicestershire (1959–64, 63 matches).
Career batting
117–218–9–4105–118–19.64–3–*ct* 51
Bowling 4251–113–37.61–1–0–5/76
He hit 1,000 runs in a season three times (best 1,158, av 23.63, in 1961). He captained Leicestershire in 1962.

Kirby, Geoffrey Norman George
Professional. *b:* 6.11.1923, Reading, Berks. Lower order right-hand batsman, wicket-keeper. *Team* Surrey (1948–53, 19 matches).
Career batting
23–21–8–168–32–12.92–0–*ct* 43–*st* 10
He made his first-class debut for South v North in 1947.
He also played for Berkshire.

Kirby, Henry Richard
Amateur. *b:* 19.3.1889, Bridge, Kent. *d:* 20.7.1976, Mayfield, Sussex. Middle order batsman. *Sch* Malvern. *Team* Sussex (1911, 1 match).
Career batting
1–2–0–9–7–4.50–0–*ct* 0

Kirby, John Edward Weston
Amateur. *b:* 4.2.1936, Newcastle-on-Tyne. Opening right-hand batsman, right-arm medium pace bowler. *Sch* Ampleforth. *Team* Oxford U (1956).
Career batting
3–6–0–78–28–13.00–0–*ct* 4

Kirk, Edwin
Amateur. *b:* 6.5.1866, Coventry, Warwickshire. *d:* 10.3.1957, Coventry, Warwickshire. Middle order right-hand batsman. *Team* Warwickshire (1898, 1 match).
Career batting
1–1–0–0–0–0.00–0–*ct* 1

Kirk, Ernest Charles
Amateur. *b:* 21.3.1884, Clapham, Surrey. *d:* 19.12.1932, Fulham, London, after an operation for appendicitis. Lower order left-hand batsman, left-arm medium fast bowler. *Team* Surrey (1906–21, 36 matches).
Career batting
40–57–8–495–43–10.10–0–*ct* 12
Bowling 3445–143–24.09–7–1–7/130
He was unable to find the time to appear regularly in County cricket, though worth his place in the Surrey Eleven.
His first-class debut was for Gentlemen of the South in 1905.

Kirk, John Alexander Wright
Amateur. *b:* 2.12.1888, Coatbridge, Lanarkshire, Scotland. *d:* 21.10.1961, Coatbridge, Lanarkshire, Scotland. Right-hand batsman, right-arm medium pace bowler. *Team* Scotland (1920–23).
Career batting
3–4–0–15–11–3.75–0–*ct* 3
Bowling 345–11–31.36–0–0–4/80

Kirk, Lionel
Amateur. *b:* 1.11.1884, Sheffield, Yorkshire. *d:* 27.2.1953, Nottingham. Middle order right-hand batsman. *Team* Nottinghamshire (1920–29, 14 matches).
Career batting
14–22–2–358–86–17.90–0–*ct* 6
Bowling 1–0
He was a member of Notts CCC Committee for many years and President of the County Club in 1951.
A good rugby footballer, he represented Notts.

Kirk, William
Professional. Middle order batsman. *Team* Nottinghamshire (1888, 1 match).
Career batting
1–1–0–4–4–4.00–0–*ct* 0

Kirkman, Frederick
Amateur. *b:* 13.7.1849, Croft, Lancashire. *d:* 8.12.1879, Croft, Lancashire. Lower order batsman, opening bowler. *Sch* Rossall. *Team* Cambridge U (1870).
Career batting
1–1–0–5–5–5.00–0–*ct* 0
Bowling 58–0
He played for Cheshire.

Kirkman, Michael
Cricketer. *b:* 11.2.1942, Bodmin, Cornwall. Tail end right-hand batsman, leg break bowler. *Sch* Dulwich. *Team* Cambridge U (1963, blue).
Career batting
11–15–11–28–7*–7.00–0–*ct* 2
Bowling 741–14–52.92–0–0–3/32

Kirkpatrick, Alexander Kennedy
Cricketer. *b:* 25.7.1938, Belfast. Left-hand batsman, off break bowler. *Team* Ireland (1962).
Career batting
1–2–1–31–30–31.00–0–*ct* 1
Bowling 46–0

Kirkpatrick, Sir James
Amateur. *b:* 22.3.1841, Closeburn, Dumfries, Scotland. *d:* 10.11.1899, Forest Hill, Kent. Lower order right-hand batsman, right-arm fast bowler. *Team* Gentlemen of South (1867).
Career batting
1–2–1–10–10*–10.00–0–*ct* 2
Bowling 48–3–16.00–0–0–3/36
A well-known soccer player, he captained Scotland in the first international against England in 1870.

Kirkwood, Euan MacMillan
Amateur. *b:* 7.12.1934, Paisley, Renfrewshire, Scotland. Right-hand batsman. *Sch* Merchiston. *Team* Scotland (1958).
Career batting
3–5–0–17–10–3.40–0–*ct* 5

Kirkwood, Henry Raphael
Amateur. *b:* 12.10.1886, Hartley Wintney, Hants. *d:* 14.4.1954, Folkestone, Kent. Lower order batsman, leg break bowler. *Team* Army (1923–28).
Career batting
5–9–1–127–50–15.87–0–*ct* 3
Bowling 362–12–30.16–1–0–5/100

Kirmani, Syed Mujtaba Hussein
Cricketer. *b:* 29.12.1949, Madras, India. Attacking middle order right-hand batsman, wicket-keeper. *Teams* Mysore/Karnataka (1967/8 to 1981/2). *Tours* India to England 1971, 1974, 1982, to West Indies 1975/6, 1982/3, to New Zealand 1975/6, 1980/1, to Australia 1977/8, 1980/1, to Pakistan 1978/9, 1982/3; Wadekar to Sri Lanka 1975/6. *Tests* India (1975/6 to 1982/3, 69 matches).
Career batting
198–277–52–5924–116–26.32–3–*ct* 270–*st* 88
Bowling 55–0
Test batting
69–99–14–2100–101*–24.70–1–*ct* 128–*st* 32
Bowling 0–0
He did not appear in any Tests in the 1971 and 1974 tours to England, but in 1982 played in all three.

Kirsten, Peter Noel
Cricketer. *b:* 14.5.1955, Pietermaritzburg, South Africa. Middle order right-hand batsman, off break bowler. *Teams* Western Province (1973/4 to 1982/3); Sussex (1975, 1 match); Derbyshire (1978–82, 106 matches).
Career batting
198–342–40–14071–228–46.89–38–*ct* 123
Bowling 2484–66–37.63–0–0–4/44
He hit 1,000 runs in a season five times (best 1,941, av 64.70, in 1982). In 1976/7 he hit six centuries in seven innings. His highest innings was 228 for Derbyshire v Somerset at Taunton in 1981. He played in 4 unofficial Tests for South Africa in 1982/3, captaining the team in each game.

Kirti Azad (*see under* Azad, K. B. J.)

Kirton, Harold Osborne
Amateur. *b:* 4.1.1894, London. *d:* 9.5.1974, Holland-on-Sea, Essex. Middle order right-hand batsman, right-arm medium pace bowler. *Team* Warwickshire (1925–29, 2 matches).
Career batting
2–3–0–82–52–27.33–0–*ct* 0

Kirwan, Rev John Henry
Amateur. *b:* 25.12.1816, Beaumaris, Anglesey. *d* 13.6.1899, St John, near Antony, Cornwall. Lower order batsman, right-hand fast round-arm bowler. *Sch* Eton. *Team* Cambridge U (1836–42, blue 1839).
Career batting
19–36–1–330–41–9.42–0–*ct* 3
Bowling 111 wickets, no analyses
His most notable bowling feat was to take 9 wickets in an innings, all bowled, (15, all bowled, in the match) for Cambridge U v Cambridge Town Club in 1836, though in the previous season he took all ten wickets for Eton v MCC at Lord's.

Kitcat, Sidney Austyn Paul
Amateur. *b:* 20.7.1868, Charlton, Tetbury, Gloucs. *d:* 17.6.1942, Esher, Surrey. Middle order right-hand batsman, right-arm medium pace bowler. *Sch* Marlborough. *Team* Gloucestershire (1892–1904, 50 matches).
Career batting
54–97–10–1899–95*–21.82–0–*ct* 38
Bowling 481–14–34.35–0–0–2/0
Owing to business his County cricket was restricted. His first-class debut was for MCC in 1890.
A talented hockey player, he represented Middlesex, Surrey and England.

Kitchen, Mervyn John
Professional. *b:* 1.8.1940, Nailsea, Somerset. Opening left-hand batsman, right-arm medium

pace bowler. *Team* Somerset (1960–79, 352 matches).
Career batting
354–612–32–15230–189–26.25–17–*ct* 157
Bowling 109–2–54.50–0–0–1/4
He hit 1,000 runs in a season seven times (best 1,730, av 36.04, in 1968).
He was appointed to the first-class umpires' list in 1982.

Kitchener, Frederick George
Professional. *b:* 2.7.1871, Hartley Row, Hants. *d:* 1948, Co Durham. Tail end right-hand batsman, right-arm fast medium bowler. *Team* Hampshire (1896–1903, 13 matches).
Career batting
13–19–3–80–16–5.00–0–*ct* 6
Bowling 630–28–22.50–2–0–6/59

Kitching, Ernest William
Amateur. *b:* 1851. *d:* 8.12.1902, Winson Green, Birmingham. *Team* Gentlemen of North (1877).
Career batting
1–1–0–0–0–0.00–0–*ct* 1
He appeared as a substitute in his only first-class match and was allowed to bat in the second innings.

Kitson, David Lees
Professional. *b:* 13.9.1925, Batley, Yorkshire. Opening right-hand batsman. *Team* Somerset (1952–54, 32 matches).
Career batting
32–60–3–886–69–15.54–0–*ct* 3

Kitson, Frederick
Professional. *b:* 1893, Marylebone, London. *d:* Feb 1925, Northampton. Tail end batsman, slow left-arm bowler. *Team* Northants (1919–20, 4 matches).
Career batting
4–6–3–31–13–10.33–0–*ct* 2
Bowling 192–3–64.00–0–0–3/63

Kline, Lindsay Francis
Amateur. *b:* 29.9.1934, Camberwell, Victoria, Australia. Lower order left-hand batsman, slow left-arm bowler. *Team* Victoria (1955/6 to 1961/2, 31 matches). *Tours* Australia to South Africa 1957/8, to India and Pakistan 1959/60, to England 1961, to New Zealand 1956/7. *Tests* Australia (1957/8 to 1960/1, 13 matches).
Career batting
88–96–31–559–37*–8.60–0–*ct* 55
Bowling 7562–276–27.39–11–0–7/75
Test batting
13–16–9–58–15*–8.28–0–*ct* 9
Bowling 776–34–22.82–1–0–7/75
He only had a moderate tour to England in 1961 and was not required to appear in any of the Tests.

Knapp, Edward Michael
Amateur. *b:* 28.4.1848, Bath, Somerset. *d:* 24.11.1903, Croydon, Surrey. Free hitting lower order right-hand batsman, right-hand fast round-arm bowler, good deep field. *Sch* Stonyhurst. *Team* Gloucestershire (1871–80, 12 matches).
Career batting
12–17–3–216–90*–15.42–0–*ct* 4
Bowling 48–2–24.00–0–0–2/27
He also played for Herefordshire.

Knapp, John Walter
Amateur. *b:* 8.3.1841, Paddington, London. *d:* 22.6.1881, St. Leonards, Sussex. Lower order batsman, right-arm fast bowler. *Sch* Merchant Taylors. *Team* Middlesex (1864, 1 match).
Career batting
1–1–0–3–3–3.00–0–*ct* 0
He also played for Dorset and Cornwall.

Knatchbull-Hugessen, Hon Cecil Marcus
(succeeded to the title 4th Lord Brabourne in 1915)
Amateur. *b:* 27.11.1863, Chelsea, London. *d:* 15.2.1933, at sea on SS *Caernarvon Castle* en route Cape Town to London. Nephew of W. W. (Kent). Middle order right-hand batsman, wicket-keeper. *Sch* Eton. *Teams* Cambridge U (1884–86, blue 1886); Kent (1884, 1 match).
Career batting
12–22–3–192–32–10.10–0–*ct* 10–*st* 1

Kneller, Arthur Harry
Amateur. *b:* 28.4.1894, Kingsclere, Hants. *d:* 19.7.1969, Chichester, Sussex. Middle order right-hand batsman. *Sch* Ardingly. *Team* Hampshire (1924–26, 8 matches).
Career batting
8–11–2–76–25*–8.44–0–*ct* 1
He spent many years in East Africa.

Knew, George Alan
Cricketer. *b:* 5.3.1954, Leicester. Son of G.F. (Leics). Middle order right-hand batsman. *Team* Leicestershire (1972–73, 4 matches).
Career batting
4–6–1–59–25–11.80–0–*ct* 0

Knew, George Frank
Professional. *b:* 13.10.1920, Leicester South. Father of G.A. (Leics). Stylish middle order right-

hand batsman. *Team* Leicestershire (1939, 5 matches).
Career batting
5–8–0–78–42–9.75–0–*ct* 2
Bowling 100–1–100.00–0–0–1/58

Knight, Albert Ernest
Professional. *b:* 8.10.1872, Leicester. *d:* 25.4.1946, Edmonton, London. Sound middle order right-hand batsman, excellent cover point. *Teams* Leicestershire (1895–1912, 367 matches); London County (1903–04). *Tour* MCC to Australia 1903/04. *Tests* England (1903/4, 3 matches).
Career batting
391–702–40–19357–229*–29.24–34–*ct* 132
Bowling 117–4–29.25–0–0–2/34
Test batting
3–6–1–81–70*–16.20–0–*ct* 1

He hit 1,000 runs in a season 10 times (best 1,834, av 45.85, in 1903). Both his double centuries were for Leics, the highest being 229* v Worcs at Worcester 1903.

He was the author of a notable book on the game entitled 'The Complete Cricketer' published in 1906.

Knight, Arthur Egerton
Amateur. *b:* 7.9.1887, Godalming, Surrey. *d:* 10.3.1956, Milton, Hants. Opening batsman. *Team* Hampshire (1913–23, 4 matches).
Career batting
4–7–0–41–29–5.85–0–*ct* 2
Bowling 17–1–17.00–0–0–1/17

He played football for Portsmouth.

Knight, Barry Rolfe
Professional. *b:* 18.2.1938, Chesterfield, Derbyshire. Middle order right-hand batsman, right-arm fast medium bowler. *Team* Essex (1955–66, 239 matches); Leicestershire (1967–69, 46 matches). *Tours* MCC to Pakistan, India and Ceylon 1961/2, to Australia and New Zealand 1962/3, 1965/6, to India 1963/4; Cavaliers to West Indies 1964/5; Commonwealth to India 1964/5. *Tests* England (1961/2 to 1969, 29 matches).
Career batting
379–602–83–13336–165–25.69–12–*ct* 263
Bowling 26203–1089–24.06–45–8–8/69
Test batting
29–38–7–812–127–26.19–2–*ct* 14
Bowling 2223–70–31.75–0–0–4/38

He hit 1,000 runs in a season five times (best 1,689, av 34.46, in 1962) and took 100 wickets in a season five times (best 140, av 21.72, in 1963). In all he achieved the 'double' in four seasons, 1962 to 1965 inclusive.

For Essex v Warwickshire at Edgbaston in 1962 he hit no less than 21 fours in an innings total of 88.

Knight, Donald John
Amateur. *b:* 12.5.1894, Sutton, Surrey. *d:* 5.1.1960, Marylebone, London. Stylish opening right-hand batsman, good close field. *Sch* Malvern. *Teams* Surrey (1911–37, 106 matches); Oxford U (1914 and 1919, blue both years). *Tests* England (1921, 2 matches).
Career batting
138–215–13–6231–156*–30.84–13–*ct* 74
Bowling 25–3–8.33–0–0–2/0
Test batting
2–4–0–54–38–13.50–0–*ct* 1

He hit 1,000 runs in a season twice (best 1,588, av 45.37, in 1919). Being in the scholastic profession limited his County cricket after he left Oxford.

Knight, George
Professional. *b:* 28.3.1835, Petworth, Sussex. *d:* 8.1.1901, Petworth, Sussex. Lower order right-hand batsman, wicket-keeper. *Team* Sussex (1860–74, 13 matches).
Career batting
13–24–4–125–21–6.25–0–*ct* 8–*st* 11
Bowling 43–1–43.00–0–0–1/25

Knight, George Thomas
Amateur. *b:* 22.11.1795, Goodnestone, Kent. *d* 25.8.1867, Hereford. Attacking lower order right-hand batsman, right-hand fast round-arm bowler. *Teams* Hampshire (1820–25); Kent (1827–28).
Career batting
23–43–2–282–36–6.87–0–*ct* 5–*st* 6
Bowling 22 wickets, no analyses

He was one of the first bowlers to defy the Law by bowling 'round-arm' and wrote strongly in favour of the new style of bowling. His final match was for Gentlemen in 1837.

Knight, John Mark
Cricketer. *b:* 16.3.1958, Oundle, Northants. Lower order right-hand batsman, right-arm fast medium bowler. *Sch* Oundle. *Team* Oxford U (1978–81, blue 1979).
Career batting
23–35–3–318–41*–9.93–0–*ct* 3
Bowling 1431–33–43.36–0–0–4/69

He appeared for Wiltshire commencing 1977.

Knight, Joseph William
Amateur. *b:* 20.9.1896, Highworth, Wilts. *d:* 3.3.1974, Childrey, Oxon. Lower order batsman, opening bowler. *Team* Cambridge U (1921).

Career batting
1–2–0–1–1–0.50–0–*ct* 0
Bowling 53–0
He played for Wiltshire.

Knight, Norman Spencer
Amateur. *b:* 30.3.1914, Eltham, Kent. Lower order left-hand batsman, wicket-keeper. *Sch* Uppingham. *Team* Oxford U (1933–35, blue 1934).
Career batting
11–15–1–189–87–13.50–0–*ct* 18–*st* 5

Knight, Philip Henry
Amateur. *b:* 25.8.1835, Chawton, Hants. *d:* 4.1.1882, Alton, Hants. Opening/middle order batsman. *Sch* Harrow. *Team* Cambridge U (1853).
Career batting
8–15–0–159–38–10.60–0–*ct* 4
His final first-class match was for Gentlemen of Kent in 1864.

Knight, Rev Richard
Amateur. *b:* 8.5.1892, South Molton, Devon. *d:* 9.1.1960, Weston-super-Mare, Somerset. Opening right-hand batsman. *Sch* St John's Leatherhead. *Team* Cambridge U (1912).
Career batting
4–7–1–101–66–16.83–0–*ct* 2
Bowling 177–8–22.12–0–0–4/23
He played for Devonshire.

Knight, Ronald
Professional. *b:* 12.5.1913, Northampton. Middle order right-hand batsman, right-arm fast bowler. *Team* Northants (1933–34, 10 matches).
Career batting
10–20–3–182–50–10.70–0–*ct* 4
Bowling 348–10–34.80–1–0–5/108

Knight, Roger David Verdon
Cricketer. *b:* 6.9.1946, Streatham, London. Middle order left-hand batsman, right-arm medium pace bowler. *Sch* Dulwich. *Teams* Cambridge U (1967–70, blue all four years); Surrey (1968–83, 153 matches); Gloucestershire (1971–75, 105 matches); Sussex (1976–77, 43 matches). *Tours* Robins to South Africa 1972/3; MCC to West Africa 1975/6 (not first-class); MCC to East Africa 1973/4; Overseas XI to India 1980/1.
Career batting
363–633–56–18264–165*–31.65–28–*ct* 275
Bowling 12327–342–36.04–4–0–6/44
He hit 1,000 runs in a season twelve times (best 1,350, av 38.57, in 1974). From 1978 to 1983 he captained Surrey.

Knight, Robert Francis
Amateur. *b:* 10.8.1879, Rushden, Northants. *d:* 9.1.1955, Kettering, Northants. Middle order right-hand batsman, leg break bowler. *Sch* Wellingborough. *Team* Northants (1905–21, 22 matches).
Career batting
22–37–3–408–67–12.00–0–*ct* 13
Bowling 667–21–31.76–1–0–6/90

Knight, Robert Lougher
Amateur. *b:* 21.4.1858, St Bride's Major, Glamorgan. *d:* 22.5.1938, Tythegston, Glamorgan. Lower order right-hand batsman, left-hand medium pace round-arm bowler, good close field. *Sch* Clifton. *Team* Oxford U (1878–80, blue 1878).
Career batting
8–14–2–100–36*–8.33–0–*ct* 6
Bowling 436–30–14.53–2–1–7/39
A good rugby footballer, he appeared for Oxford in 1880.

Knightley-Smith, William
Amateur. *b:* 1.8.1932, West Smithfield, London. *d:* 31.7.1962, Edinburgh, Scotland. He collapsed and died while playing tennis. Opening/middle order left-hand batsman. *Sch* Highgate. *Teams* Cambridge U (1953–55, blue 1953); Middlesex (1952, 26 matches); Gloucestershire (1955–57, 29 matches).
Career batting
87–155–10–2530–95–17.44–0–*ct* 28
Bowling 72–0
His final first-class match was for Free Foresters in 1961.
A good soccer player, he received his blue at Cambridge.

Knott, Alan Philip Eric
Cricketer. *b:* 9.4.1946, Belvedere, Kent. Middle order right-hand batsman, wicket-keeper, occasional off break bowler. *Teams* Kent (1964–83, 316 matches); Tasmania (1969/70, 2 matches). *Tours* MCC to Pakistan 1966/7, to West Indies 1967/8, 1973/4, to Ceylon and Pakistan 1968/9, to Australia and New Zealand 1970/1, 1974/5, to India, Sri Lanka and Pakistan 1972/3, to India, Sri Lanka and Australia 1976/7; Cavaliers to West Indies 1964/5; SAB to South Africa 1981/2. *Tests* England (1967–81, 95 matches).
Career batting
478–699–127–17431–156–30.47–17–*ct* 1129–*st* 131
Bowling 87–2–43.50–0–0–1/5
Test batting
95–149–15–4389–135–32.75–5–*ct* 250–*st* 19

He hit 1,000 runs in a season twice (best 1,209, av 41.68, in 1971). His best season as wicket-keeper was 1967 with 98 victims (90 ct, 8 st). For ten years he was regarded as the best wicket-keeper in England and commanded an automatic place in the Test side, but in 1977 he joined Packer's World Series Cricket and though he regained his England place after the agreement between Packer and the Australian Board, Knott later went on the SAB tour to South Africa and was banned from Test cricket for three years.

Knott, Charles Harold
Amateur. *b:* 20.3.1901, Tunbridge Wells, Kent. Brother of F. H. (Kent). Attacking middle order right-hand batsman, right-arm slow leg break bowler, excellent cover point. *Sch* Tonbridge. *Teams* Kent (1921–39, 104 matches); Oxford U (1922–24, blue all 3 years). *Tours* Martineau to Egypt 1929, 1930, 1931, 1933, 1934, 1936 (not first-class).
Career batting
136–206–27–5633–261*–31.46–9–*ct* 66
Bowling 660–24–27.50–0–0–4/24
His only double century was 261* for Harlequins v West Indians at Eastbourne in 1928.

Knott, Charles James
Amateur. *b:* 26.11.1914, Southampton, Hants. Lower order right-hand batsman, right-arm medium/off break bowler. *Team* Hampshire (1938–54, 166 matches).
Career batting
173–245–98–1023–27–6.95–0–*ct* 57
Bowling 15771–676–23.32–47–8–8/26
He took 100 wickets in a season four times (best 122, av 18.47, in 1946). His final first-class match was for MCC in 1957.

Knott, Frederick Hammett
Amateur. *b:* 30.10.1891, Tunbridge Wells, Kent. *d:* 10.2.1972, Woking, Surrey. Brother of C.H. (Kent). Middle order right-hand batsman, right-arm slow medium leg break and googly bowler, cover point. *Sch* Tonbridge. *Teams* Kent (1910–14, 11 matches); Oxford U (1911–14, blue 1912–14); Sussex (1926, 1 match).
Career batting
44–77–7–1800–116–25.71–3–*ct* 32–*st* 1
Bowling 103–4–25.75–0–0–3/65
A brilliant schoolboy cricketer, he was later handicapped by eye-trouble, which considerably affected his career in County cricket.
A good soccer player, he represented Oxford as a half-back.

Knowles, Arthur
Amateur. *b:* 10.4.1858, Pendlebury, Manchester, Lancashire. *d:* 10.7.1929, Alvaston, Cheshire. Middle order right-hand batsman, right-arm medium pace bowler. *Sch* Rugby. *Team* Lancashire (1888, 1 match).
Career batting
5–10–0–83–16–8.30–0–*ct* 2
His final first-class match was for MCC in 1896.

Knowles, Joseph
Professional. *b:* 25.3.1910, Nottingham. Middle order right-hand batsman, right-arm slow bowler. *Team* Nottinghamshire (1935–46, 125 matches).
Career batting
125–188–18–4194–114–24.67–2–*ct* 39
Bowling 1441–34–42.37–0–0–3/55
He hit 1,179 runs, av 25.08, in 1938.

Knowles, William Lancelot
Amateur. *b:* 27.11.1871, Twineham Grange, Henfield, Sussex. *d:* 1.12.1943, Ditchling, Sussex. Middle order right-hand batsman, good cover point. *Sch* Hurstpierpoint. *Teams* Kent (1892–1903, 34 matches); Sussex (1905, 1 match).
Career batting
37–65–2–1439–127–22.84–2–*ct* 13
He was Secretary of Sussex CCC for 22 years, resigning shortly before his death.
For several years he was Master of the Brighton foot beagles.

Knox, Frank Pery
Amateur. *b:* 23.1.1880, Clapham, Surrey. *d:* 1.2.1960, Hove, Sussex. Brother of N.A. (Surrey). Very patient opening left-hand batsman, right-arm medium pace bowler. *Sch* Dulwich. *Teams* Oxford U (1899–1901, blue all three years); Surrey (1899–1902, 7 matches).
Career batting
31–50–9–1281–198–31.24–2–*ct* 19
Bowling 2414–87–27.74–1–0–5/73

Knox, Gerald Keith
Cricketer. *b:* 22.4.1937, North Shields, Northumberland. Opening right-hand batsman, right-arm medium pace bowler, cover point. *Team* Lancashire (1964–67, 52 matches).
Career batting
52–92–3–1698–108–19.07–3–*ct* 38
Bowling 161–2–80.50–0–0–1/10
He also played for Northumberland.

Knox, John
Amateur. *b:* 4.10.1904, Buenos Aires, Argentina. *d:* 6.4.1966, Buenos Aires, Argentina. Middle order right-hand batsman, good field. *Team* Argentine (1926/7 to 1937/8). *Tour* South America to England 1932.

Career batting
12–22–4–575–110*–31.94–1–*ct* 9
Bowling 87–1–87.00–0–0–1/46

Knox, Neville Alexander
Amateur. *b:* 10.10.1884, Clapham, Surrey. *d:* 3.3.1935, Surbiton, Surrey. Brother of F.P. (Surrey). Lower order right-hand batsman, right-arm fast bowler. *Sch* Dulwich. *Team* Surrey (1904–10, 73 matches). *Tests* England (1907, 2 matches).
Career batting
88–129–40–905–45*–10.16–0–*ct* 32
Bowling 8860–411–21.55–38–9–8/48
Test batting
2–4–1–24–8*–8.00–0–*ct* 0
Bowling 105–3–35.00–0–0–2/39
He took 100 wickets in a season twice (best 144, av 19.63, in 1906). His career was brief but brilliant, his bowling being regarded as the equal of any fast bowler in England, but lameness ended his County cricket in 1910.
His final first-class match was for the Army in 1919.

Knox, William
Amateur. *b:* 20.11.1903, Paisley, Renfrewshire, Scotland. *d:* 11.6.1954, Paisley, Renfrewshire, Scotland. Right-hand batsman. *Team* Scotland (1938).
Career batting
1–2–0–0–0–0.00–0–*ct* 1

Knutton, Herbert John
Professional. *b:* 14.6.1867, Coventry, Warwickshire. *d:* 12.12.1946, Heaton, Bradford, Yorkshire. Lower order right-hand batsman, right-arm fast bowler. *Team* Warwickshire (1894, 1 match).
Career batting
2–3–0–17–8–5.66–0–*ct* 0
Bowling 178–10–17.80–1–1–9/100
Although a talented bowler he preferred League cricket to the first-class game and made just one first-class County appearance; in 1902 however he created a small sensation by taking 9 for 100 in the first innings of a match between an Eleven of England and the Australians at Bradford – it was his final first-class match.

Kok, Myron
Amateur. *b:* 7.12.1932, Johannesburg, South Africa. Tail end right-hand batsman, right-arm medium pace bowler. *Sch* Harrow. *Team* Cambridge U (1953).
Career batting
2–2–0–14–8–7.00–0–*ct* 2
Bowling 68–2–14.00–0–0–2/38

Konig, Peter Hans
Amateur. *b:* 16.10.1931, Vienna, Austria. Lower order right-hand batsman, wicket-keeper. *Team* Leicestershire (1949, 1 match).
Career batting
1–1–0–3–3–3.00–0–*ct* 1–*st* 1

Kortright, Charles Jesse
Amateur. *b:* 9.1.1871, Ingatestone, Essex. *d:* 12.12.1952, South Weald, Essex. Punishing middle order right-hand batsman, right-arm fast bowler. *Sch* Brentwood and Tonbridge. *Team* Essex (1894–1907, 160 matches).
Career batting
170–271–21–4404–131–17.61–2–*ct* 176
Bowling 10294–489–21.05–39–8–8/57
His debut in first-class matches was for MCC in 1833.
Regarded as the fastest bowler of his day, and by some as the fastest ever to appear in first-class County cricket, his best season was 1895 when he took 76 wickets, av 15.83, though in 1898 he took 96 wickets, but at an average of 19.19.

Kotze, Johannes Jacobus
Amateur. *b:* 7.8.1879, Hopefield, Cape Province, South Africa. *d:* 8.7.1931, Cape Town, South Africa. Tail end right-hand batsman, right-arm fast bowler, poor field. *Teams* Transvaal (1902/03); Western Province (1903/04 to 1910/11); London County (1904). *Tours* South Africa to England 1901, 1904 and 1907. *Tests* South Africa (1902/3 to 1907, 3 matches).
Career batting
72–105–25–688–60–8.60–0–*ct* 31
Bowling 6217–348–17.86–30–9–8/18
Test batting
3–5–0–2–2–0.40–0–*ct* 3
Bowling 243–6–40.50–0–0–3/64
Of his three visits to England, his most successful in first-class matches was 1904 when he took 104 wickets, av 20.50 – on that tour he also appeared for London County and in all first-class matches took 121, av 19.85. He was regarded as the fastest bowler ever to appear in first-class cricket in South Africa.

Krikken, Brian Egbert
Cricketer. *b:* 26.8.1946, Horwich, Lancashire. Lower order right-hand batsman, wicket-keeper. *Teams* Lancashire (1966–67, 2 matches); Worcestershire (1969, 1 match).
Career batting
3–3–0–8–4–2.66–0–*ct* 7

Kripal Singh, Amritsar Govindsingh
Amateur. *b:* 6.8.1933, Madras, India. Son of A.G. Ram Singh (Madras), brother of A.G.

Milka Singh and A.G. Satwender Singh (both Madras). Middle order right-hand batsman, right-arm off break bowler, moderate field. *Teams* Madras (1950/1 to 1964/5); Hyderabad (1965/6). *Tours* India to Ceylon 1956/7, to England 1959; Madras to Ceylon 1953/4, 1956/7, 1958/9, 1960/1, 1963/4. *Tests* India (1955/6 to 1964/5, 14 matches).
Career batting
96–143–22–4947–208–40.88–10–*ct* 57
Bowling 5029–177–28.41–3–1–6/14
Test batting
14–20–5–422–100*–28.13–1–*ct* 4
Bowling 584–10–58.40–0–0–3/43

Owing to injury he performed only moderately on his single tour to England, appearing in one Test. His highest score was 208 for Madras v Travancore-Cochin at Ernakulam in 1954/5.

Krishamurthy, Pochiah
Cricketer. *b:* 12.7.1947, Hyderabad, India. Lower order right-hand batsman, wicket-keeper. *Team* Hyderabad (1967/8 to 1978/9). *Tours* India to West Indies 1970/71, to England 1971, to Ceylon 1973/4, to New Zealand and West Indies 1975/6; Hyderabad Blues to Ceylon 1966/7. *Tests* India (1970/1, 5 matches).
Career batting
108–130–25–1559–82–14.84–0–*ct* 150–*st* 68
Bowling 32–0
Test batting
5–6–0–33–20–5.50–0–*ct* 7–*st* 1

He was almost superfluous during the 1971 tour to England, since F.M. Engineer was co-opted into the team as wicket-keeper for the Tests and S.M.H. Kirmani was also on the tour.

His first-class debut was for Indian Starlets in 1966/7.

Kumbleben, John Michael
Amateur. *b:* 26.5.1933, Bloemfontein, South Africa. Middle order right-hand batsman. *Teams* Oxford U (1956–57); Orange Free State (1957/8 to 1960/1).
Career batting
29–50–2–955–100–19.89–1–*ct* 16

Kunderan, Budhisagar Krishnappa
(changed from Kunderam in 1964)
Amateur. *b:* 2.10.1939, Mangalore, India. Attractive right-hand opening batsman, wicket-keeper. *Teams* Railways (1959/60 to 1964/5); Mysore (1965/6 to 1969/70). *Tours* India to West Indies 1961/2, to England 1967, to East Africa 1967; International XI to South Africa 1975/6; State Bank of India to Ceylon 1966/7, 1968/9. *Tests* India (1959/60 to 1967, 18 matches).
Career batting
129–217–20–5708–205–28.97–12–*ct* 175–*st* 85
Bowling 160–3–53.33–0–0–2/15
Test batting
18–34–4–981–192–32.70–2–*ct* 23–*st* 7
Bowling 13–0

Although going to England as reserve wicket-keeper to F.M. Engineer, Kunderan gained a place in two of the three Tests as a batsman and seemed equally at home either opening the innings or going lower down. His highest score was 205 for Railways v Jammu and Kashmir at Delhi in 1959/60. He hit 1,079 runs, av 38.53, in 1963/4 in India.

His first-class debut was for Cricket Club of India in 1958/9.

He represented Scotland in limited-overs matches.

Kynaston, Roger
Amateur. *b:* 5.11.1805, London. *d:* 21.6.1874, Marylebone, London. Middle order right-hand batsman, excellent longstop. *Sch* Eton. *Teams* MCC (1830–54); Middlesex (1850, 2 matches).
Career batting
167–304–17–2618–54–9.12–0–*ct* 42

He also played for Norfolk. 'When in position for batting he stood with his legs as far away from the wicket as possible'.

He was Secretary of MCC from 1842 to 1858 and Treasurer until 1866.

LACEY, SIR FRANCIS EDEN
Amateur. *b:* 19.10.1859, Wareham, Dorset. *d:* 26.5.1946, Sutton Veny, Wiltshire. Middle order right-hand batsman, right-hand slow round-arm bowler, good field. *Sch* Sherborne. *Teams* Hampshire (1880–97, 33 matches); Cambridge U (1882, blue).
Career batting
50–89–10–2589–211–32.77–4–*ct* 34
Bowling 1123–52–21.59–3–1–7/149

His only double century was 211 for Hampshire v Kent at Southampton in 1884.

He hit 323* for Hampshire v Norfolk in 1887 – the record score for a Minor County.

In 1878 he played for Dorset.

For 28 years commencing 1898, he was Secretary to MCC; in 1926 he was knighted for his services to the game.

Lacy-Scott, David Geffrey
Amateur. *b:* 18.8.1920, Calcutta, India. Opening right-hand batsman, right-arm fast medium bowler. *Sch* Marlborough. *Teams* Cambridge U (1946, blue); Kent (1946, 1 match).
Career batting
11–21–0–294–36–14.00–0–*ct* 0
Bowling 268–9–29.77–1–0–5/35

His final first-class match was for Free Foresters in 1948.

Lagden, Reginald Bousfield
Amateur. *b:* 15.4.1893, Maseru, Basutoland. *d:* 20.10.1944, Karachi, India. He was killed in an air crash. Brother of R. O. (Oxford U). Middle order right-hand batsman, right-arm off break bowler. *Sch* Marlborough. *Teams* Cambridge U (1912–14, blue all three years); Surrey (1912, 1 match); Europeans (1926/7).
Career batting
32–56–1–1751–153–31.83–6–*ct* 18
Bowling 343–11–31.18–0–0–2/22

A good half back, he played hockey for Cambridge U and England.

After the First World War he moved to India where he played both cricket and hockey extensively.

Lagden, Ronald Owen
Amateur. *b:* 21.11.1889, Maseru, Basutoland. *d:* 1.3.1915, St Eloi, Belgium. He was killed in action. Brother of R. B. (Surrey). Hard hitting middle order right-hand batsman, right-arm fast bowler. *Sch* Marlborough. *Team* Oxford U (1909–12, blue all four years).
Career batting
31–54–7–1197–99*–25.46–0–*ct* 18
Bowling 1406–56–25.10–1–0–6/57

An all-round sportsman he represented Oxford at rugby football, rackets and hockey, later gaining an England cap for rugby.

Laidlaw, William Kennedy
Amateur. *b:* 26.8.1912, Edinburgh, Scotland. Lower order right-hand batsman, leg break and googly bowler. *Teams* Scotland (1938–53); Minor Counties (1950).
Career batting
17–27–9–132–25–7.33–0–*ct* 8
Bowling 1225–42–29.16–2–0–7/70

He appeared for Durham from 1948 to 1952.

Laidlay, William James
Amateur. *b:* 12.8.1846, Calcutta, India. *d:* 25.10.1912, Freshwater, Isle of Wight. Lower order batsman, useful bowler. *Sch* Loretto. *Team* North (1875).
Career batting
1–2–0–14–11–7.00–0–*ct* 0
Bowling 105–3–35.00–0–0–2/85

Laing, James Gordon Brodie
Cricketer. *b:* 10.1.1938, Meigle, Perthshire, Scotland. Brother of J. R. (Scotland). Middle order right-hand batsman. *Team* Scotland (1964–74).
Career batting
19–32–4–655–93–23.39–0–*ct* 11

Laing, John Ralph
Cricketer. *b:* 27.8.1942, Meigle, Perthshire, Scotland. Brother of J. G. B. (Scotland). Middle order left-hand batsman. *Team* Scotland (1969–79).
Career batting
8–15–1–301–127*–21.50–1–*ct* 6

Laird, Bruce Malcolm
Cricketer. *b:* 21.11.1950, Lawley, Western Australia. Opening right-hand batsman. *Teams* Western Australia (1972/3 to 1982/3, 52 matches). *Tours* Australia to England 1975, 1980, to Pakistan 1979/80, 1982/3, to New Zealand 1981/2. *Tests* Australia (1979/80 to 1982/3, 21 matches).
Career batting
91–166–10–5379–171–34.48–8–*ct* 74
Bowling 63–0
Test batting
21–40–2–1341–92–35.28–0–*ct* 16
Bowling 12–0

He played in only nine first-class matches on the 1975 tour to England and was not required for the Tests. On the brief 1980 Centenary tour he appeared in the only Test, but was unfit for selection for the 1981 visit to England.

Laitt, David James
Amateur. *b:* 3.5.1931, Oxford. Lower order

right-hand batsman, right-arm medium pace bowler. *Sch* Magdalen College School, Oxford. *Team* Minor Counties (1959–60).
Career batting
2–3–1–25–10–12.50–0–*ct* 2
Bowling 186–6–31.00–0–0–4/58
His County cricket was for Oxfordshire.

Lake, Graham J.
Professional. *b:* 15.5.1935, Croydon, Surrey. Lower order right-hand batsman, right-arm fast medium bowler. *Team* Gloucestershire (1956–58, 13 matches).
Career batting
13–18–4–106–18–7.57–0–*ct* 6
Bowling 464–17–27.29–0–0–4/39

Lake, Ronald Dewé
Amateur. *b:* 9.5.1891, Bury St Edmunds, Suffolk. *d:* 28.7.1950, Winkton, Hampshire. Middle order right-hand batsman. *Sch* Uppingham. *Team* Northants (1922, 2 matches).
Career batting
2–4–1–48–30–16.00–0–*ct* 1
He also played for Suffolk.

Laker, James Charles
Professional for Surrey, amateur for Essex in 1962. *b:* 9.2.1922, Frizinghall, Bradford, Yorkshire. Lower order right-hand batsman, accurate off break bowler. *Teams* Surrey (1946–59, 309 matches); Essex (1962–64, 30 matches). *Tours* MCC to West Indies 1947/8, 1953/4, to South Africa 1956/7, to Australia and New Zealand 1958/9; Cavaliers to Jamaica 1963/4, to West Indies 1964/5. *Tests* England (1947/8 to 1958/9, 46 matches).
Career batting
450–548–108–7304–113–16.60–2–*ct* 271
Bowling 35791–1944–18.41–127–32–10/53
Test batting
46–63–15–676–63–14.08–0–*ct* 12
Bowling 4101–193–21.24–9–3–10/53
The most accomplished English off spin bowler of his generation, Laker was one of the principal architects of Surrey's great team which won the County Championship in seven successive seasons 1952 to 1958. He first played for England in the West Indies in 1947/8 and was the most successful bowler on the tour, in both the Tests and first-class games. The English Test selectors nonetheless showed little faith in him during the next eight years and he was never sure of a place in the England side. In 1956 however he completely demoralised the Australians, taking no less than 46 wickets in the series at a cost of 9.60 and at Old Trafford creating a unique record with 19 wickets for 90 runs. He caused controversy by at first declining a place in the team to tour Australia in 1958/59, although he later accepted. In 1960 he wrote his book 'Over to Me', which caused some ill-feeling. He had retired from Surrey at the close of the 1959 season, but re-appeared for Essex from 1962 to 1964.
In all he took 100 wickets in a season 11 times, his best total being 166 wickets, av 15.32, in 1950. Twice he achieved the feat of all 10 wickets in an innings, once for England (for 53 runs) in the 1956 Manchester Test noted previously, and once for Surrey, in the same year, also v Australians (for 88 runs at the Oval).
Since leaving first-class cricket, he has become well-known as a commentator on the game.

Laker, Peter Guy
Professional. *b:* 5.12.1926, Hurstpierpoint, Sussex. Lower order right-hand batsman, leg break bowler. *Team* Sussex (1948–49, 2 matches).
Career batting
2–2–1–14–8*–14.00–0–*ct* 1
Bowling 70–0
He is a well-known journalist on the *Daily Mirror*.

Lall Singh Narainsingh
Amateur. *b:* 16.12.1909, Kuala Lumpar, Malaya. Dashing middle order right-hand batsman, right-arm slow medium bowler, brilliant field. *Teams* Southern Punjab (1933/4 to 1935/6); Hindus (1934/5 to 1935/6). *Tour* India to England 1932. *Test* India (1932, 1 match).
Career batting
32–51–6–1123–107*–24.95–1–*ct* 23
Bowling 59–1–59.00–0–0–1/9
Test batting
1–2–0–44–29–22.00–0–*ct* 1
The most noteworthy feature of his cricket on the 1932 tour was his fielding. His first-class debut was in the Indian Trial matches of 1931/2.

Lamason, John Rider
Amateur. *b:* 29.10.1905, Wellington, New Zealand. *d:* 25.6.1961, Wellington, New Zealand. Middle order right-hand batsman, right-arm bowler. *Team* Wellington (1927/8 to 1946/7). *Tours* New Zealand to England 1937, to Australia 1937/8.
Career batting
60–106–7–2065–127–20.85–2–*ct* 61
Bowling 1476–45–32.80–1–0–5/67
He quite failed to reproduce his New Zealand form when visiting England in 1937 and was not required for the Tests.

Lamb, Arthur
Amateur. *b:* 1869, Cheltenham, Gloucs. *d:*

26.7.1908, Margate, Kent. Lower order batsman, useful bowler. *Team* Gloucestershire (1895–96, 2 matches).
Career batting
2–4–0–24–10–6.00–0–*ct* 0
Bowling 32–0

Lamb, Allan Joseph
Cricketer. *b:* 20.6.1954, Langebaanweg, Cape Province, South Africa. Middle order right-hand batsman, right-arm medium pace bowler. *Teams* Western Province (1972/3 to 1981/2); Northants (1978–83, 110 matches). *Tours* England to Australia and New Zealand 1982/3 (New Zealand not first-class). *Tests* England (1982–83, 15 matches).
Career batting
190–325–60–13542–178–51.10–34–*ct* 138
Bowling 93–4–23.25–0–0–1/1
Test batting
15–29–3–1061–137*–40.80–3–*ct* 16
Bowling 0–0

He hit 1,000 runs in a season five times, going on to 2,000 once: 2,049, av 60.26, in 1981. He made his debut for England soon after becoming qualified by residence in 1982.

Lamb, Bruce
Amateur. *b:* 25.8.1878, Andover, Hants. *d:* 21.3.1932, Andover, Hants. Middle order batsman. *Sch* Marlborough. *Team* Hampshire (1898–1901, 4 matches).
Career batting
4–7–0–29–8–4.14–0–*ct* 2

Lamb, Henry John Hey
Amateur. *b:* 3.5.1912, Kettering, Northants. Hard hitting middle order right-hand batsman, wicket-keeper. *Sch* Winchester. *Team* Northants (1934–38, 38 matches).
Career batting
38–69–5–1085–91*–16.95–0–*ct* 23–*st* 1

Lamb, Hon Timothy Michael
Cricketer. *b:* 24.3.1953, Hartford, Cheshire. Lower order right-hand batsman, right-arm medium pace bowler. *Sch* Shrewsbury. *Teams* Oxford U (1973–74, blue both years); Middlesex (1974–77, 36 matches); Northants (1978–83, 108 matches).
Career batting
160–163–61–1274–77–12.49–0–*ct* 40
Bowling 10459–361–28.97–10–0–7/56

Lambert, George Ernest Edward
Professional. *b:* 11.5.1919, London. Aggressive lower order right-hand batsman, right-arm fast medium bowler. *Teams* Gloucestershire (1938–57, 334 matches); Somerset (1960, 3 matches).
Career batting
340–489–61–6375–100*–14.89–1–*ct* 194
Bowling 26189–917–28.56–37–5–8/35

He took 100 wickets in a season once : 113, av 22.75, in 1952. About 1949 he was regarded as the fastest bowler in English County cricket.

Lambert, Noel Hamilton
Amateur. *b:* 5.6.1910, Dublin, Ireland. Son of R. J. H. (Ireland), nephew of S. D. (Ireland). Middle order right-hand batsman. *Sch* Rossall. *Team* Ireland (1932–47).
Career batting
9–17–2–213–69*–14.20–0–*ct* 5

Lambert, Reginald Everitt
Amateur. *b:* 25.9.1882, Telham, Sussex. *d:* 23.1.1968, Shaftesbury, Dorset. Middle order batsman, right-arm medium pace bowler. *Sch* Harrow. *Teams* Sussex (1904, 1 match); Cambridge U (1903–04).
Career batting
4–6–0–72–30–12.00–0–*ct* 1
Bowling 164–3–54.66–0–0–3/53

Lambert, Robert James Hamilton
Amateur. *b:* 18.7.1874, Rathmines, Dublin, Ireland. *d:* 24.3.1956, Rathfarnham, Dublin, Ireland. Brother of S. D. (Ireland), father of N. H. (Ireland). Middle order right-hand batsman, right-arm off break bowler. *Teams* Ireland (1902–28); London County (1903).
Career batting
25–45–6–1121–103*–28.74–1–*ct* 19
Bowling 1686–70–24.08–4–1–7/11

He was regarded as Ireland's greatest all-round cricketer and in three successive seasons achieved the feat of scoring over 2,000 runs and taking over 200 wickets. He captained Ireland in 13 matches and was for many years a selector of Irish teams, being in addition President of the Irish Cricket Union twice.

A noted badminton player, he represented Ireland.

Lambert, Septimus Drummond
Amateur. *b:* 3.8.1876, Rathmines, Dublin, Ireland. *d:* 21.4.1959, Dublin, Ireland. Brother of R. J. H. (Ireland), uncle of N. H. (Ireland). *Team* Ireland (1902–21).
Career batting
7–10–2–184–60*–23.00–0–*ct* 3

Lambert, William
Professional. *b:* 1779, Burstow, Surrey. *d:* 19.4.1851, Nutfield, Surrey. Excellent middle

order right-hand batsman, slow under-arm bowler. *Teams* Surrey (1801–17); Kent (1806); Sussex (1817); Hampshire (1806–07).
Career batting
64–114–5–3013–157–27.64–4–*ct* 62–*st* 26
Bowling 187 wickets, no analyses
He was regarded as one of the best all-round cricketers of his day and was an excellent single-wicket player. He was the first batsman to hit a century in both innings of an important match, scoring 107* and 157 for Sussex v Epsom at Lord's in 1817. He did not appear in matches at Lord's after 1817 because, it is said, that he 'sold' the England v Nottingham match of that year.

Lambert, William
Professional. *b:* 19.4.1843, Hatfield, Herts. *d:* 4.3.1927, St Fagan's, Cardiff, Wales. Middle order right-hand batsman, right-hand medium pace round-arm bowler, slip field. *Team* Middlesex (1874–77, 7 matches).
Career batting
7–14–3–112–34*–10.18–0–*ct* 9
Bowling 54–1–54.00–0–0–1/14
He also played for Hertfordshire.
His brother was George Lambert, the Tennis Master at Lord's, who was regarded as the leading player in England between 1871 and 1885.

Lampard, Albert Wallis
Amateur. *b:* 3.7.1885, Richmond, Victoria, Australia. *d:* 11.1.1984, St Kilda, Melbourne, Australia. Middle order right-hand batsman, leg break and googly bowler, wicket-keeper. *Team* Victoria (1908/9 to 1921/2, 18 matches). *Tours* AIF to England 1919, to South Africa 1919/20; Australia to New Zealand 1920/1.
Career batting
63–96–12–2597–132–30.91–3–*ct* 30–*st* 4
Bowling 3492–134–26.05–7–1–9/42
Without doing anything outstanding, he was a distinctly useful all-rounder on the 1919 tour of England. His best bowling was 9/42 for AIF v Lancashire at Old Trafford in 1919.

Lancashire, Oswald Philip
Amateur. *b:* 10.12.1857, Newton Heath, Manchester. *d:* 23.7.1934, West Didsbury, Manchester. Hard hitting middle order right-hand batsman, good field. *Sch* Lancing. *Teams* Cambridge U (1878–80, blue 1880); Lancashire (1878–88, 97 matches).
Career batting
122–197–18–2349–76*–13.12–0–*ct* 45
He was President of Lancashire CCC 1923–24.
A noted soccer player, he appeared three times for Cambridge v Oxford.

Lancashire, Walter
Amateur. *b:* 28.10.1903, Hemsworth, Yorkshire. *d:* 7.6.1981, Dorchester. Lower order right-hand batsman, right-arm medium pace bowler. *Sch* Taunton. *Team* Hampshire (1935–37, 18 matches).
Career batting
18–29–1–471–66–16.82–0–*ct* 7
Bowling 357–7–51.00–0–0–2/49
He also played for Dorset.

Lancaster, Thomas
Professional. *b:* 11.2.1863, Dalton, Huddersfield, Yorkshire. *d:* 12.12.1935, Blackburn, Lancashire. Brother of W. W. (Yorkshire). Lower order left-hand batsman, slow left-arm bowler. *Team* Lancashire (1894–99, 27 matches).
Career batting
27–40–11–554–66–19.10–0–*ct* 6
Bowling 1456–66–22.06–5–0–7/25
He played for Yorkshire in a non-first-class match in 1891.

Lancaster, William Whiteley
Professional. *b:* 4.2.1873, Dalton, Huddersfield, Yorkshire. *d:* 30.12.1938, Huddersfield, Yorkshire. Brother of Thomas (Lancashire). Middle order right-hand batsman, right-hand fast round-arm bowler. *Team* Yorkshire (1895, 7 matches).
Career batting
7–10–0–163–51–16.30–0–*ct* 1
Bowling 29–0

Lance, Herbert Roy
Amateur. *b:* 6.6.1940, Pretoria, South Africa. Opening or middle order right-hand batsman, right-arm medium pace bowler. *Teams* North East Transvaal (1958/9 to 1960/1); Transvaal (1961/2 to 1970/1); Northern Transvaal (1971/2). *Tour* South Africa to England 1965. *Tests* South Africa (1961/2 to 1969/70, 13 matches).
Career batting
103–171–18–5336–169–34.87–11–*ct* 101
Bowling 4284–167–25.65–2–0–6/55
Test batting
13–22–1–591–70–28.14–0–*ct* 7
Bowling 479–12–39.91–0–0–3/30
He played in all three Tests on the 1965 tour, but prospered more when not opening the batting in the latter half of the visit.

Lanchbury, Robert John
Cricketer. *b:* 11.2.1950, Evesham, Worcs. Middle order right-hand batsman. *Teams* Gloucestershire (1971, 5 matches); Worcestershire (1973–74, 8 matches).
Career batting
13–22–3–357–50*–18.78–0–*ct* 2

Landon, Charles Whittington
Amateur. *b:* 30.5.1850, Bromley, Kent. *d:* 5.3.1903, Ledston, Yorkshire. Middle order right-hand batsman, right-hand medium pace round-arm bowler, excellent cover point. *Sch* Bromsgrove. *Teams* Lancashire (1874–75, 6 matches); Yorkshire (1878–82, 9 matches).
Career batting
15–23–0–172–47–7.47–0–*ct* 8
Bowling 143–2–71.50–0–0–1/10
He was the leading figure in the Yorkshire Gentlemen's side for many years.

Lane, Albert Frederick
Amateur. *b:* 29.8.1885, Rowley Regis, Staffs. *d:* 29.1.1948, Upper Fulbrook, Warwickshire. He was killed in a road accident. Middle order right-hand batsman, off break bowler. *Teams* Worcestershire (1914–32, 45 matches); Warwickshire (1919–25, 12 matches).
Career batting
57–97–11–1422–76–16.53–0–*ct* 27
Bowling 1892–46–41.13–0–0–4/56
He also played for Staffordshire.

Lane, Rev Charlton George
Amateur. *b:* 11.6.1836, Kennington, Surrey. *d:* 2.11.1892, Little Gaddesden, Herts. Brother of W. W. C. (Surrey). Hard hitting middle order right-hand batsman, good outfield. *Sch* Westminster. *Teams* Oxford U (1856–60, blue 1856, 1858, 1859, 1860); Surrey (1856–61, 18 matches).
Career batting
46–82–4–1021–72–13.08–0–*ct* 14
Bowling 63–3–21.00–0–0–3/31
His first-class debut was for Gentlemen of England in 1854 and his final first-class match for Gentlemen of Surrey and Sussex in 1867.
He also played for Worcestershire, Buckinghamshire and Hertfordshire.
He was a rowing blue in 1858 and 1859.

Lane, George
Professional. *b:* 25.7.1852, Kimberley, Notts. *d:* 31.7.1917, Haverford, Philadelphia, USA. Lower order left-hand batsman, left-arm medium pace bowler. *Team* Nottinghamshire (1881, 3 matches).
Career batting
3–6–3–28–19*–9.33–0–*ct* 2
Bowling 87–6–14.50–0–0–4/32
For some years he was one of the leading professional cricketers in Philadelphia.

Lane, Sivell
Amateur. *b:* 21.8.1881, Ledbury, Herefordshire. *d:* 10.2.1961, Toronto, Canada. Lower order batsman, useful bowler. *Team* Gloucestershire (1901, 3 matches).
Career batting
3–5–1–16–8–4.00–0–*ct* 2
Bowling 296–7–42.28–1–0–5/139
He also played for Herefordshire.

Lane, William Ward Claypon
(assumed the name Lane-Claypon in 1875)
Amateur. *b:* 1.8.1845, Kennington, Surrey. *d:* 31.3.1939, Wheathampstead, Herts. Brother of C. G. (Surrey). Lower order right-hand batsman, right-hand slow round-arm bowler. *Sch* Westminster. *Teams* Cambridge U (1866–67); Surrey (1868–70, 2 matches).
Career batting
5–9–0–69–36–7.66–0–*ct* 0
Bowling 37–1–37.00–0–0–1/23
He also played for Lincolnshire.

Lang, Arthur Horace
Amateur. *b:* 25.10.1890, Malabar Hill, Bombay, India. *d:* 25.1.1915, Cuinchy, France. He was posted missing, believed killed in action. Sound middle order right-hand batsman, wicket-keeper. *Sch* Harrow. *Teams* Sussex (1911–13, 13 matches); Cambridge U (1912–13, blue 1913).
Career batting
22–40–3–830–141–22.45–2–*ct* 17–*st* 16
His final first-class match was for L. Robinson's XI in 1914.
He appeared for Suffolk from 1907 to 1911.

Lang, J. M.
Professional. Lower order left-hand batsman, slow left-arm bowler. *Team* Worcestershire (1923–24, 8 matches).
Career batting
8–14–8–27–9*–4.50–0–*ct* 4
Bowling 412–8–51.50–0–0–2/21

Lang, Thomas William
Amateur. *b:* 22.6.1854, Selkirk, Scotland. *d:* 30.5.1902, Virginia Water, Surrey. Opening/middle order right-hand batsman, right-hand medium pace round-arm bowler. *Sch* Clifton. *Teams* Gloucestershire (1872–74, 8 matches); Oxford U (1874–75, blue both years).
Career batting
18–26–3–303–54–13.17–0–*ct* 9
Bowling 1104–76–14.52–5–1–6/27
He also played for Northumberland.
His brother was Andrew Lang, the well-known writer.

Langdale, George Richmond
Amateur. *b:* 11.3.1916, Thornaby-on-Tees, Yorkshire. Forcing middle order left-hand

batsman, right-arm off break bowler. *Teams* Derbyshire (1936–37, 4 matches); Somerset (1946–49, 20 matches).
Career batting
25–42–3–709–146–18.17–1–*ct* 7
Bowling 939–23–40.82–1–0–5/30

His final first-class match was for Minor Counties in 1953; he also played County cricket for Berkshire and in 1953 took all 10 wickets (for 25) for that County v Dorset at Reading, and he also played for Norfolk.

Langdon, Rev George Leopold
Amateur. *b:* 11.2.1818, Winchester, Hants. *d:* 2.1.1894, St Paul's Cray, Kent. Middle order left-hand batsman. *Team* Sussex (1839–42, 8 matches)
Career batting
15–29–1–224–38–8.00–0–*ct* 9

He was regarded as one of the most promising players of his day, but retired from important matches on entering the Church.

In 1839 he was Hon Secretary of Sussex CCC.

Langdon, Thomas
Professional. *b:* 8.1.1879, Brighton, Sussex. *d:* 30.11.1944, Nuneaton, Warwickshire. Steady opening right-hand batsman, slow left-arm bowler. *Team* Gloucestershire (1900–14, 279 matches).
Career batting
282–519–14–10723–156–21.23–6–*ct* 207–*st* 3
Bowling 839–22–38.13–0–0–3/4

He hit 1,000 runs in a season three times (best 1,369, av 30.42, in 1907).

Langford, Brian Anthony
Professional. *b:* 17.12.1935, Birmingham. Lower order right-hand batsman, right-arm off break bowler. *Team* Somerset (1953–74, 504 matches).
Career batting
510–720–162–7588–68*–13.59–0–*ct* 230
Bowling 34964–1410–24.79–83–15–9/26

He took 100 wickets in a season five times (best 116, av 18.28, in 1958); his best bowling in an innings was 9 for 26 for Somerset v Lancashire at Weston-super-Mare in 1958.

He created a sensation when he first appeared for Somerset, by taking 26 wickets for 308 runs in his first three matches.

From 1969 to 1971 he captained Somerset.

For Somerset in the John Player League he bowled eight overs in a match without conceding a run – a record for the competition.

Langford, William Thomas
Professional. *b:* 5.10.1875, New Forest, Hants. *d:* 20.2.1957, Faversham, Kent. Lower order right-hand batsman, right-arm fast medium bowler. *Team* Hampshire (1902–08, 93 matches).
Career batting
93–153–25–1663–62*–12.99–0–*ct* 67
Bowling 5781–215–26.88–5–2–8/82

Langhorne, Alfred Robert Maskell
Amateur. *b:* 20.12.1845. *d:* 4.6.1930, Watford, Hertfordshire. Middle order batsman. *Sch* Rugby. *Team* MCC (1880).
Career batting
1–2–0–16–15–8.00–*ct* 0

Langley, Colin Kendall
Amateur. *b:* 11.7.1888, Narborough, Leics. *d:* 26.6.1948, Leamington Spa, Warwickshire. Lower order right-hand batsman, right-arm fast medium bowler. *Sch* Radley. *Team* Warwickshire (1908–14, 33 matches).
Career batting
33–52–4–455–61*–9.48–0–*ct* 12
Bowling 1391–54–25.75–3–0–8/29

He played in the Seniors' Match at Oxford, but no first-class matches.

At the time of his death he was Hon Secretary and Chairman of Warwickshire CCC.

Langley, Gilbert Roche Andrews
Amateur. *b:* 14.9.1919, North Adelaide, South Australia. Uncle of J. N. (Queensland). Stolid lower order right-hand batsman, wicket-keeper. *Team* South Australia (1945/6 to 1956/7, 55 matches). *Tours* Australia to England 1953, 1956, to West Indies 1954/5, to Pakistan and India 1956/7, to South Africa 1949/50. *Tests* Australia (1951/2 to 1956/7, 26 matches).
Career batting
122–165–39–3236–160*–25.68–4–*ct* 292–*st* 77
Bowling 2–0
Test batting
26–37–12–374–53–14.96–0–*ct* 83–*st* 15

He appeared in four out of the five Tests on the 1953 tour of England and three out of five in 1956 – in the latter Test series he dismissed 19 of the 44 batsmen to fall whilst he was wicket-keeper.

He dismissed nine batsmen (8 ct, 1 st) for Australia v England at Lord's in 1956, a Test record at the time.

Langley, Henry Fitzroy James
Amateur. *b:* 8.12.1846, London. *d:* 20.11.1884, Buenos Aires, Argentina. Middle order batsman. *Sch* Eton. *Team* I Zingari (1866).
Career batting
2–4–2–4–4–2.00–0–*ct* 1

Langley, John Douglas Algernon
Amateur. *b:* 25.4.1918, Northwood, Middlesex.

Middle order right-hand batsman. *Sch* Stowe. *Teams* Middlesex (1937, 1 match); Cambridge U (1938–39, blue 1938).
Career batting
14–22–0–442–119–20.09–1–*ct* 9

Langridge, James
Professional. *b:* 10.7.1906, Newick, Sussex. *d:* 10.9.1966, Brighton, Sussex. Brother of J. G. (Sussex), father of R. J. (Sussex). Middle order left-hand batsman, slow left-arm bowler, safe field. *Teams* Sussex (1924–53, 622 matches); Auckland (1927/8). *Tours* MCC to India and Ceylon 1933/4, Australia and New Zealand 1935/6, 1946/7; Tennyson to India 1937/8. *Tests* England (1933–46, 8 matches).
Career batting
695–1058–157–31716–167–35.20–42–*ct* 384
Bowling 34524–1530–22.56–90–14–9/34
Test batting
8–9–0–242–70–26.88–0–*ct* 6
Bowling 413–19–21.73–2–0–7/56

He hit 1,000 runs in a season 20 times, going on to 2,000 once : 2,082, av 40.82, in 1937. He took 100 wickets in a season six times (best 158, av 16.56, in 1933) and performed the 'double' six times – 1930, 1931, 1932, 1933, 1935 and 1937. His best bowling was 9/34 for Sussex v Yorkshire at Sheffield in 1934. From 1950 to 1952 he captained Sussex, and from 1953 to 1959 was County coach.

Langridge, John George, MBE
Professional. *b:* 10.2.1910, Chailey, Sussex. Brother of James (Sussex) and uncle of R. J. (Sussex). Fine opening right-hand batsman, right-arm medium bowler, excellent slip field. *Team* Sussex (1928–55, 567 matches). *Tours* MCC to India 1939/40 (selected, but tour was cancelled due to outbreak of war).
Career batting
574–984–66–34380–250*–37.45–76–*ct* 784
Bowling
1848–44–42.00–0–0–3/19

He hit 1,000 runs in a season 17 times going on to 2,000 11 times (best 2,914, av 60.70, in 1949). All his eight double centuries were for Sussex, the highest being 250* v Glamorgan at Hove in 1933.

With E. H. Bowley he added 490 for the first wicket for Sussex v Middlesex at Hove in 1933.

After retiring, he became a well-known umpire, standing in Test matches and was awarded the MBE for his services to cricket in 1979.

Langridge, Richard James
Professional. *b:* 13.4.1939, Brighton, Sussex. Son of James (Sussex), nephew of J. G. (Sussex). Middle order left-hand batsman, off break bowler. *Team* Sussex (1957–71, 207 matches). *Tour* MCC to East Africa 1963/4.
Career batting
212–391–28–8310–137*–22.89–5–*ct* 188
Bowling 91–0

He hit 1,000 runs in a season four times (best 1,885, av 30.90, in 1962). He did not play regularly after 1966 (except in 1970) in County cricket.

Langridge, William
Amateur. *Team* Hambledon XII (1908).
Career batting
1–1–0–2–2–2.00–0–*ct* 0
Bowling 42–1–42.00–0–0–1/42

Langton, Arthur Beaumont Chudleigh
Amateur. *b:* 2.3.1912, Isipingo, Natal. *d:* 27.11.1942, Accra, Gold Coast. He was killed in an air accident. Lower order right-hand batsman, right-arm fast medium or medium bowler. *Team* Transvaal (1931/2 to 1941/2). *Tour* South Africa to England 1935. *Tests* South Africa (1935 to 1938/9, 15 matches).
Career batting
52–74–13–1218–73*–19.96–0–*ct* 41
Bowling 4969–193–25.74–9–2–6/53
Test batting
15–23–4–298–73*–15.68–0–*ct* 8
Bowling 1827–40–45.67–1–0–5/58

He was most effective on his single tour to England, taking 115 wickets, av 21.16.

Langton, Samuel Thomas
Professional. *b:* 24.1.1886, Parkgate, Doncaster, Yorkshire. *d:* 10.7.1918, Bentley, Doncaster, Yorkshire. Middle order right-hand batsman, change bowler. *Team* Derbyshire (1909–10, 3 matches).
Career batting
3–5–0–14–6–2.80–0–*ct* 1
Bowling 42–0

Lapham, Arthur William Edwards
Amateur. *b:* 1879. *d:* 9.2.1964, Portsmouth, Hants. Middle order batsman, useful bowler. *Team* Essex (1921, 3 matches).
Career batting
3–5–0–31–16–6.20–0–*ct* 0
Bowling 90–5–18.00–0–0–2/25

He also played for Wiltshire.

Larkham, William Trevor
Amateur. *b:* 10.11.1929, Kidderminster, Worcs. Lower order right-hand batsman, leg break

bowler, good field. *Team* Worcestershire (1952, 1 match).
Career batting
1–2–0–13–13–6.50–0–*ct* 0
Bowling 64–1–64.00–0–0–1/64

Larking, John Gordon
Amateur. *b:* 4.11.1921, Maidstone, Kent. Middle order right-hand batsman. *Sch* Charterhouse. *Team* Kent (1946, 3 matches).
Career batting
3–6–1–15–8–3.00–0–*ct* 2

Larkins, Wayne
Cricketer. *b:* 22.11.1953, Roxton, Bedfordshire. Attractive opening right-hand batsman, right-arm medium pace bowler, fine field. *Teams* Northants (1972–83, 202 matches); Eastern Province (1982/3). *Tours* England to Australia and India 1979/80; SAB to South Africa 1981/2; Overseas XI to India 1980/1. *Tests* England (1979/80 to 1981, 6 matches).
Career batting
231–395–24–12640–252–34.07–29–*ct* 111
Bowling 1175–32–36.71–0–0–4/30
Test batting
6–11–0–176–34–16.00–0–*ct* 3

He hit 1,000 runs in a season six times (best 1,863, av 45.43, in 1982). Both his double centuries are for Northants, the highest being 252 v Glamorgan at Cardiff in 1983.

Larmour, Sir Edward Noel
Amateur. *b:* 25.12.1916, Belfast, Ireland. Middle order right-hand batsman. *Sch* Royal Belfast Academical Institution. *Team* Ireland (1938).
Career batting
1–2–0–45–34–22.50–0–*ct* 0

Larter, John David Frederick
Professional. *b:* 24.4.1940, Inverness, Scotland. Tail end right-hand batsman, right-arm fast medium bowler. *Sch* Framlingham. *Team* Northants (1960–69, 134 matches). *Tours* MCC to New Zealand 1960/1, to Australia and New Zealand 1962/3, 1965/6, to East Africa 1963/4, to India 1963/4; International XI to South Africa and Pakistan 1961/2. *Tests* England (1962–65, 10 matches).
Career batting
182–162–57–639–51*–6.08–0–*ct* 56
Bowling 13013–666–19.53–27–5–8/28
Test batting
10–7–2–16–10–3.20–0–*ct* 5
Bowling 941–37–25.43–2–0–5/57

He took 100 wickets in a season twice (best 121, av 16.76, in 1963). His promising career was marred by injury.

Larwood, Harold
Professional. *b:* 14.11.1904, Nuncargate, Notts. Hard hitting lower order right-hand batsman, devastating right-arm fast bowler. *Teams* Nottinghamshire (1924–38, 300 matches); Europeans (1936/7). *Tours* MCC to Australia 1928/9, 1932/3. *Tests* England (1926 to 1932/3, 21 matches).
Career batting
361–438–72–7290–102*–19.91–3–*ct* 234
Bowling 24994–1427–17.51–98–20–9/41
Test batting
21–28–3–485–98–19.40–0–*ct* 15
Bowling 2212–78–28.35–4–1–6/32

Controversy and ill-feeling reduced the Test career of Larwood, regarded as the greatest fast bowler of the inter-war period, to just over six years. His name is inevitably linked with the English 1932/3 tour to Australia, when the 'Bodyline' battle was at its height. In all first-class matches on that tour he took 49 wickets, av 16.66, and in the Tests alone 33 wickets, av 19.51, being the leading bowler in both. England won the series by four matches to one, but the outcome was that Larwood never again played for England and the subsequent rows in 1934/35 caused much heated argument in Nottingham.

Larwood took 100 wickets in a season eight times, with 162 wickets, av 12.86, in 1932 as his best year. His best bowling in an innings was 9 for 41 for Notts v Kent at Trent Bridge in 1931 and five times, in 1927, 1928, 1931, 1932 and 1936, he headed the season's first-class bowling averages.

Owing to injury, he retired from County cricket in 1938 and in 1949 emigrated to Australia. His memoirs were published in 1933, 'Bodyline?' and again in 1965, 'The Larwood Story'.

Lashbrooke, Albert Edward
Professional. *b:* 30.11.1883, West Ham, Essex. *d:* 1963, Oldham, Lancashire. Lower order batsman, opening bowler. *Team* Essex (1908, 1 match).
Career batting
1–2–0–9–9–4.50–0–*ct* 0
Bowling 61–1–61.00–0–0–1/26

Lashley, Patrick Douglas
(known as Peter)
Amateur. *b:* 11.2.1937, Maxwell, Christchurch, Barbados, West Indies. Steady middle order left-hand batsman, right-arm medium pace bowler, good field. *Team* Barbados (1957/8 to 1974/5). *Tours* West Indies to Australia 1960/1, to England 1966; Barbados to England 1969. *Tests* West Indies (1960/1 to 1966, 4 matches).

Career batting
85–132–13–4932–204–41.44–8–*ct* 66
Bowling 958–27–35.48–0–0–3/15
Test batting
4–7–0–159–49–22.71–0–*ct* 4
Bowling 1–1–1.00–0–0–1/1

On the 1966 tour to England he appeared in two Tests, but in all first-class matches had only a modest return with 647 runs, av 29.40. His highest score was 204 for Barbados v Guyana at Georgetown in 1966/7.

Latchford, John Richard
Professional. *b:* 16.6.1909, Delph, Yorkshire. *d:* 30.4.1980, Omagh, Co Tyrone, Ireland. Middle order right-hand batsman, right-arm medium pace bowler. *Team* Lancashire (1930–32, 7 matches).
Career batting
7–10–0–154–63–15.40–0–*ct* 4
Bowling 181–4–45.25–0–1/6

He also played for Durham.

Latchman, Amritt Harrichand
(known as Harry Chand Latchman)
Cricketer. *b:* 26.7.1943, Kingston, Jamaica. Lower order right-hand batsman, leg break and googly bowler. *Teams* Middlesex (1965–73, 170 matches); Nottinghamshire (1974–76, 40 matches). *Tour* International XI to Ceylon and India 1967/8.
Career batting
213–240–64–2333–96–13.25–0–*ct* 107
Bowling 13588–487–27.90–22–1–7/65

He played for Cambridgeshire 1977 and 1978.

Latham, Geoffrey Chitty
Amateur. *b:* 15.3.1887, Shanghai, China. *d:* 23.9.1980, Waverley, Farnham, Surrey. Son of Thomas (Cambridge U). Middle order right-hand batsman. *Sch* Winchester. *Team* Oxford U (1907).
Career batting
1–2–0–25–22–12.50–0–*ct* 1

Latham, Hubert Joseph
Amateur. *b:* 13.9.1932, Winson Green, Birmingham. Lower order right-hand batsman, right-arm fast bowler. *Team* Warwickshire (1955–59, 10 matches).
Career batting
10–13–2–129–26–11.72–0–*ct* 2
Bowling 751–27–27.81–1–0–6/49

Latham, Michael Edward
Professional. *b:* 14.1.1939, Birmingham. Lower order right-hand batsman, right-arm fast medium bowler. *Team* Somerset (1961–62, 18 matches).
Career batting
18–21–12–133–21*–14.77–0–*ct* 10
Bowling 888–29–30.63–2–0–5/20

He also played for Northumberland.

Latham, Percy Holland
Amateur. *b:* 3.2.1873, Llandudno, North Wales. *d:* 22.6.1922, Haileybury School, Herts. Attacking middle order right-hand batsman, right-arm slow bowler, good cover point. *Sch* Malvern. *Teams* Cambridge U (1892–94, blue all three years); Sussex (1898–1906, 40 matches).
Career batting
63–106–7–2580–172–26.06–1–4–*ct* 31
Bowling 99–2–49.50–0–0–1/0

He also played for Worcestershire (pre first-class).

Latham, Roger Done
Amateur. *b:* 1900, Chelsea, London. *d:* 24.11.1971, Onchan, Isle of Man. *Sch* Wellington. *Team* MCC (1920).
Career batting
1–2–2–16–16*–no av–0–*ct* 0

He was a well-known actor under the stage name 'Roger Maxwell'.

Latham, Richard Lockhart
Amateur. *b:* 5.1.1908, Sao Paulo, Brazil. *d:* 4.2.1953, Sao Paulo, Brazil. Sound middle order right-hand batsman, wicket-keeper. *Sch* Repton. *Tour* South America to England 1932.
Career batting
5–9–1–120–58–15.00–0–*ct* 6

He was one of the leading cricketers in Brazil.

Latham, Thomas
Amateur. *b:* 22.6.1847, St Pancras, London. *d:* 13.1.1926, West Folkestone, Kent. Father of G.C. (Oxford U). Stylish middle order right-hand batsman, good deep field. *Sch* Winchester. *Team* Cambridge U (1873–74, blue both years).
Career batting
9–17–1–293–48–18.31–0–*ct* 5

He played County cricket for Cheshire.

Laver, Frank
Amateur. *b:* 7.12.1869, Castlemaine, Victoria, Australia. *d:* 24.9.1919, East Melbourne, Victoria, Australia. Middle order right-hand bat with ungainly style, right-arm medium pace bowler, splendid point. *Team* Victoria (1891/2 to 1911/2, 78 matches). *Tours* Australia to England 1899, 1905, 1909, to New Zealand 1904/5, 1913/4. *Tests* Australia (1899–1909, 15 matches).

Career batting
163–255–38–5431–164–25.02–6–*ct* 147
Bowling 9990–404–24.72–19–5–8/31
Test batting
15–23–6–196–45–11.52–0–*ct* 8
Bowling 964–37–26.05–2–0–8/31

He was most successful as a bowler on the tour of 1905 and 1909, heading the first-class averages for each tour and in 1905 taking 115 wickets, av 18.19.

He acted as player-manager of the 1905 and 1909 visits to England, as well as the two tours to New Zealand. He was author of 'An Australian Cricketer on Tour', published in 1905.

His death was hastened through privations sustained whilst exploring the interior of Australia.

Lavers, Alan Braden
Amateur. *b:* 6.9.1912, Melbourne, Australia. Middle order right-hand batsman, off break bowler. *Sch* Chigwell. *Teams* Essex (1937–53, 25 matches).
Career batting
26–46–3–734–42*–17.06–0–*ct* 6
Bowling 497–13–38.23–0–0–4/68

Lavis, George
Professional. *b:* 17.8.1908, Sebastopol, Monmouth. *d:* 29.7.1956, Pontypool, Monmouth. Steady middle order right-hand batsman, right-arm medium fast bowler. *Team* Glamorgan (1928–49, 206 matches).
Career batting
206–312–43–4957–154–18.42–3–*ct* 71
Bowling 7768–156–49.79–0–0–4/55

He was coach to Glamorgan from 1946 until ill health forced him to retire.

Law, Alfred
Professional. *b:* 16.12.1862, Birmingham. *d:* 19.5.1919, Handsworth, Birmingham. Sound middle order right-hand batsman, good deep field. *Team* Warwickshire (1894–99, 52 matches).
Career batting
52–81–5–1459–89–19.19–0–*ct* 21

Law, Alexander Patrick
Amateur. *b:* 14.1.1832, North Repps, Norfolk. *d:* 30.10.1895, Richmond, Surrey. Stylish middle order right-hand batsman, right-hand medium pace round-arm bowler. *Sch* Rugby. *Teams* Oxford U (1855–57, blue 1857).
Career batting
19–35–4–488–59–15.74–0–*ct* 6
Bowling 516–19–27.15–1–0–5/72

He usually played under the name of 'Infelix'.

His first-class debut was for Gentlemen of England in 1851 and his final match for MCC in 1864.

His County cricket was for Norfolk.

Law, George
Amateur. *b:* 17.4.1846, Rochdale, Lancashire. *d:* 30.7.1911, Marylebone, London. Brother of William (Yorkshire). Middle order right-hand batsman, right-hand fast medium round-arm bowler. *Sch* Radley. *Team* Middlesex (1881, 3 matches).
Career batting
11–16–1–160–54–10.66–0–*ct* 6

His first-class debut was for Gentlemen of England in 1871.

He also played for Essex and Norfolk.

Law, John Alexander Gordon Charles
Amateur. *b:* 25.3.1923, Bangalore, India. Middle order right-hand batsman, wicket-keeper. *Sch* Edinburgh Academy. *Teams* Madras (1940/1 to 1941/2); Europeans (1944/5); Oxford U (1949).
Career batting
9–17–0–194–35–11.41–0–*ct* 17–*st* 3

Law, Rev William
Amateur. *b:* 9.4.1851, Rochdale, Lancashire. *d:* 20.12.1892, Rotherham, Yorkshire, of pleurisy. Brother of George (Middlesex). Hard hitting middle order right-hand batsman, right-arm fast bowler, brilliant cover point. *Sch* Harrow. *Teams* Oxford U (1871–74, blue all four years); Yorkshire (1871–73, 4 matches).
Career batting
28–47–0–501–39–10.65–0–*ct* 17
Bowling 353–14–25.21–0–0–4/83

His last first-class match was for Gentlemen of England in 1883.

He was also a good footballer.

Lawley, Rt Hon Beilby
(succeeded to the title 3rd Lord Wenlock in 1880)
Amateur. *b:* 12.5.1849, London. *d:* 15.1.1912, Marylebone, London. Opening batsman. *Sch* Eton. *Team* I Zingari (1880).
Career batting
1–1–0–3–3–3.00–0–*ct* 1

He was not in the Eleven at Cambridge.

In 1885 he was President of MCC.

He was appointed Governor of Madras in 1890 and took an active interest in the development of cricket in India.

He was MP for Chester, April to July, 1880, when he was unseated.

Lawlor, Peter John
Cricketer. *b:* 8.5.1960, Gowerton, Glamorgan.

Right-hand batsman, off break bowler. *Team* Glamorgan (1981, 1 match).
Career batting
1–2–0–8–8–4.00–0–*ct* 1
Bowling 50–1–50.00–0–0–1/36

Lawrence, Arthur Alfred Kenneth
Professional. *b:* 3.11.1930, Marlborough, Wiltshire. Middle order right-hand batsman, leg break bowler. *Team* Sussex (1952–56, 28 matches).
Career batting
28–44–7–632–63*–17.08–0–*ct* 28
Bowling 40–1–40.00–0–0–1/14

Lawrence, Anthony Sackville
Amateur. *b:* 25.3.1911, London. *d:* 17.3.1939, Westminster, London. Sound middle order right-hand batsman, left-arm medium pace bowler, good cover. *Sch* Harrow. *Team* Cambridge U (1933, blue).
Career batting
14–24–2–575–80–26.13–0–*ct* 7
Bowling 527–9–58.55–0–0–3/33
His final first-class match was for the Army in 1935.

Lawrence, Charles
Professional. *b:* 16.12.1828, Hoxton, Middlesex. *d:* 20.12.1916, Canterbury, Victoria, Australia. Middle order right-hand batsman, right-hand medium pace round-arm bowler. *Teams* Surrey (1854–57, 2 matches); Middlesex (1861, 1 match); New South Wales (1862/3 to 1869/70, 5 matches). *Tours* Stephenson to Australia 1861/2; Australian Aboriginals to England 1868 (not first-class).
Career batting
9–15–0–227–78–15.13–0–*ct* 7
Bowling 416–38–10.94–4–2–7/25
Having travelled to Australia with the 1861/2 English Team, he remained in that country when the tour ended and as a coach was largely responsible for the improvement of cricket in Australia in the 1860s.

Lawrence, C.
Amateur. *Team* MCC (1898).
Career batting
1 match, did not bat–*ct* 0

Lawrence, Douglas Rosyth
Amateur. *b:* 20.10.1929, Edinburgh, Scotland. Lower order right-hand batsman, right-arm fast medium bowler. *Team* Scotland (1956–58).
Career batting
7–12–4–32–10–4.00–0–*ct* 1
Bowling 491–12–40.91–0–0–4/56

Lawrence, David Valentine
Cricketer. *b:* 28.1.1964, Gloucester. Lower order right-hand batsman, right-arm fast medium bowler. *Team* Gloucestershire (1981–83, 10 matches).
Career batting
10–9–4–22–9–4.40–0–*ct* 1
Bowling 773–9–85.88–0–0–3/62

Lawrence, Hervey Major
Amateur. *b:* 24.3.1881, Hadlow, Kent. *d:* 17.9.1975, Ely, Cambridgeshire. Lower order right-hand batsman, right-arm fast medium bowler, good slip. *Team* Kent (1899, 4 matches).
Career batting
7–12–4–49–23–6.12–0–*ct* 1
Bowling 539–13–41.46–0–0–4/37
His final first-class match was Army in 1914.
He also played for Suffolk.

Lawrence, John
Professional. *b:* 29.3.1914, Carlton, Leeds, Yorkshire. Father of J.M. (Somerset). Middle order right-hand batsman, leg break and googly bowler. *Team* Somerset (1946–55, 281 matches).
Career batting
283–500–52–9183–122–20.49–3–*ct* 262
Bowling 19927–798–24.97–40–4–8/41
He hit 1,000 runs in a season three times (best 1,128, av 22.11,in 1955) and took 100 wickets twice (best 115, av 18.90, in 1950).

Lawrence, John Fortune
Amateur. *b:* 9.9.1904, Dublin, Ireland. Middle order right-hand batsman. *Team* Dublin University (1926).
Career batting
1–2–0–7–6–3.50–0–*ct* 0

Lawrence, John Miles
Professional. *b:* 7.11.1940, Rothwell, Yorkshire. Son of John (Somerset). Middle order right-hand batsman, leg break bowler. *Team* Somerset (1959–61, 18 matches).
Career batting
18–33–9–372–41–15.50–0–*ct* 7
Bowling 363–9–40.33–0–0–3/44

Lawrence, Mark Philip
Cricketer. *b:* 6.5.1962, Warrington, Lancashire. Left-hand batsman, slow left-arm bowler. *Sch* Manchester GS. *Team* Oxford U (1982–83).
Career batting
5–5–2–20–18–6.66–0–*ct* 1
Bowling 402–2–201.00–0–0–1/32

Lawrence, Patrick J.
Cricketer. *b:* 3.10.1942, Roseau, Dominica.

Lower order right-hand batsman, right-arm fast medium bowler. *Team* Middlesex (1964, 4 matches).
Career batting
4–4–1–19–14*–6.33–0–*ct* 0
Bowling 186–6–31.00–0–0–3/52

He was no-balled for throwing during the match between Middlesex and Sussex at Lord's in 1964 and did not play again in first-class cricket.

Lawrence, Terence Patrick
Amateur. *b:* 26.4.1910, Waltham Abbey, Essex. Middle order right-hand batsman, leg break bowler. *Sch* Uppingham. *Team* Essex (1933–35, 7 matches).
Career batting
7–14–0–133–39–9.50–0–*ct* 3

He played in the Freshmen's and Seniors' matches at Cambridge but no first-class games.

He also played for Berkshire and Hertfordshire.

Lawrence, Walter Nicholas Murray
Amateur. *b:* 8.2.1935, Marylebone, London. Opening right-hand batsman. *Sch* Winchester. *Team* Oxford U (1954).
Career batting
3–3–0–2–1–0.66–0–*ct* 3

Lawrie, Percy Edward
Amateur. *b:* 12.12.1902, Kensington, London. Middle order right-hand batsman. *Sch* Eton. *Teams* Hampshire (1921–28, 28 matches); Oxford U (1922–24).
Career batting
33–53–2–1084–107–21.25–1–*ct* 13

Lawry, William Justus
Cricketer. *b:* 24.4.1940, St Just, Cornwall. Lower order left-hand batsman, wicket-keeper. *Team* Minor Counties (1965–69).
Career batting
3–4–3–13–9–13.00–0–*ct* 8

His County cricket was for Cornwall, commencing 1958.

Lawry, William Morris
Amateur. *b:* 11.2.1937, Thornbury, Victoria, Australia. Very sound left-hand opening batsman, left-arm medium pace bowler. *Team* Victoria (1955/6 to 1971/2, 99 matches). *Tours* Australia to England 1961, 1964, 1968, to India and Pakistan 1964/5, to South Africa 1966/7, 1969/70, to West Indies 1964/5, to India and Sri Lanka 1969/70; Rest of World to Barbados 1966/7. *Tests* Australia (1961 to 1970/1, 67 matches).
Career batting
249–417–49–18734–266–50.90–50–*ct* 121
Bowling 188–5–37.60–0–0–1/3
Test batting
67–123–12–5234–210–47.15–13–*ct* 30
Bowling 6–0

His greatest success in England came on his first visit in 1961, when he topped both first-class and Test batting averages with figures of 2,019, av 61.18, and 420, av 52.50; he exceeded 1,000 runs in first-class matches on the 1964 tour, but a broken finger in 1968, when he captained the side, forced him to miss a number of games and his aggregate did not reach four figures. None of his four double centuries was made in England, where his highest innings was 165 v Surrey at the Oval in 1961. He captained Australia in 25 Tests, including 9 against England. His highest score was 266 for Victoria v NSW at Sydney in 1960/1. He hit 1,000 runs in an Australian season four times.

Laws, Michael Lutener
Amateur. *b:* 12.8.1926, Finchley, Middlesex. Lower order right-hand batsman, wicket-keeper. *Sch* Highgate. *Team* Middlesex (1948–50, 5 matches).
Career batting
8–8–3–19–12–3.80–0–*ct* 10–*st* 5

His first-class debut was for Combined Services in 1946.

Lawson, Geoffrey Francis
Cricketer. *b:* 7.12.1957, Wagga Wagga, New South Wales, Australia. Lower order right-hand batsman, right-arm fast bowler. *Teams* New South Wales (1977/8 to 1982/3, 42 matches); Lancashire (1979, 1 match). *Tours* Australia to India 1979/80, to Pakistan 1979/80, 1982/3, to Sri Lanka 1980/1, to England 1981. *Tests* Australia (1980/1 to 1982/3, 13 matches).
Career batting
68–85–20–864–57*–13.29–0–*ct* 35
Bowling 5993–256–23.41–12–1–7/81
Test batting
13–22–4–244–57*–13.55–0–*ct* 4
Bowling 1402–59–23.76–5–1–7/81

Owing to injury, he appeared in only three of the six Tests on the 1981 tour to England. In all first-class matches he took 25 wickets, av 26.08.

Lawson, Howard Maurice
Amateur. *b:* 22.5.1914, Bournemouth, Hants. Son of M.B. (Hants). Lower order right-hand batsman, right-arm fast medium bowler. *Team* Hampshire (1935–37, 45 matches).

Career batting
46–70–14–560–53–10.00–0–*ct* 18
Bowling 2573–71–36.23–2–0–5/91

Lawson, Joseph Frank
Amateur. *b:* 13.11.1893, Stroud, Gloucs. *d:* 1970, Wellington, New Zealand. Middle order batsman. *Sch* Wycliffe. *Team* Gloucestershire (1914, 1 match).
Career batting
1–2–0–4–3–2.00–0–*ct* 0

Lawson, Maurice Bertie
Amateur. *b:* 28.2.1885, Christchurch, Hants. *d:* 8.8.1961, Alton, Hants. Father of H.M. (Hants). Lower order right-hand batsman, right-arm fast medium bowler. *Team* Hampshire (1907–19, 7 matches).
Career batting
7–11–1–122–36–12.20–0–*ct* 2
Bowling 170–5–34.00–0–0–2/45

Lawson, Thomas Morrison
Amateur. *b:* 16.9.1890, Cumberland. *d:* 8.2.1967, Church Village, Glamorgan. Right-hand batsman. *Team* Scotland (1923–24).
Career batting
3–6–0–59–22–9.83–0–*ct* 0

Lawton, Albert Edward
Amateur. *b:* 31.3.1879, Dukinfield, Cheshire. *d:* 25.12.1955, Manchester. Hard hitting middle order right-hand batsman. right-arm medium slow bowler. *Sch* Rugby. *Teams* Derbyshire (1900–10, 131 matches); London County (1901–04); Lancashire (1912–14, 12 matches).
Career batting
182–314–11–7509–168–24.78–11–*ct* 125–*st* 1
Bowling 3607–113–31.92–0–0–4/19
He hit 1,000 runs in a season twice (best 1,064, av 22.63, in 1901). He also appeared for Cheshire.

Lawton, William
Professional. *b:* 4.6.1920, Ashton-under-Lyne, Lancashire. Lower order batsman, useful bowler. *Team* Lancashire (1948, 2 matches).
Career batting
2–2–0–3–3–1.50–0–*ct* 1
Bowling 64–1–64.00–0–0–1/0
He also played for Cumberland. A good soccer player, he appeared for Oldham Athletic and Chester.

Laxton, William John
Professional. *b:* 17.8.1849, Cambridge. *d:* 1882, Cambridge. Lower order right-hand batsman, right-hand fast round-arm bowler. *Team* All England Eleven (1872–73).
Career batting
2–3–1–49–36–24.50–0–*ct* 0
Bowling 69–2–34.50–0–0–2/49
He played County cricket for Wiltshire.

Laycock, David Allen
Cricketer. *b:* 2.9.1947, Woolwich, Kent. Middle order right-hand batsman. *Team* Kent (1969–73, 10 matches).
Career batting
10–16–2–266–58–19.00–0–*ct* 2

Layman, Alfred Richard
Amateur. *b:* 24.4.1858, Norwood. *d:* 8.11.1940, Beckenham, Kent. Lower order right-hand batsman, wicket-keeper. *Sch* Hurstpierpoint. *Team* Kent (1893, 1 match).
Career batting
1–2–0–1–1–0.50–0–*ct* 1

Layne, Oliver H.
Professional. *b:* 2.7.1876, Barbados, West Indies. *d:* August 1932. Middle order right-hand batsman, right-arm medium pace bowler. *Team* Barbados (1901/2 to 1904/5); British Guiana (1909/10 to 1912/13). *Tour* West Indies to England 1906.
Career batting
27–48–2–1023–106–22.23–1–*ct* 19
Bowling 2035–91–22.36–6–2–9/19
He proved a useful all-rounder on the 1906 tour to England. His best bowling was 9/19 for British Guiana v Shepherd's XI at Georgetown in 1909/10.

Leach, Clive William
Professional. *b:* 4.12.1934, Almudabad, Bombay, India. Opening right-hand batsman, slow left-arm bowler. *Team* Warwickshire (1955–58, 39 matches).
Career batting
39–64–6–1025–67–17.67–0–*ct* 28
Bowling 657–26–25.26–0–0–3/19
He also played for Buckinghamshire.
He was also a noted local soccer player.

Leach, Edward Leach Cecil
Professional. *b:* 28.11.1896, Featherstall, Lancashire. *d:* 4.1.1973, Nailsea, Somerset. Middle order batsman. *Teams* Lancashire (1923–24, 12 matches); Somerset (1924–28, 8 matches).
Career batting
20–29–1–250–79–8.92–0–*ct* 6
Bowling 87–1–87.00–0–0–1/62
He appeared for both Lancashire and Somerset in 1924, but not in a County Championship match for the latter.

Leach, George
Professional. *b:* 18.7.1881, Malta. *d:* 10.1.1945, Rawtenstall, Lancashire. Free hitting middle order right-hand batsman, right-arm fast bowler. *Team* Sussex (1903–14, 225 matches).
Career batting
226–352–42–5870–113*–18.93–2–*ct* 106
Bowling 11543–413–27.94–19–1–8/48
He hit 1,016 runs, av 24.78, in 1906 and in 1909 took 106 wickets, av 20.06.

Leach, Harold
Amateur. *b:* 13.3.1862, Rochdale, Lancashire. *d:* 15.2.1928, Bath, Somerset. Brother of John, Robert, R. C. and W. E. (all Lancashire). Middle order right-hand batsman, slow right-arm bowler, good field. *Team* Lancashire (1881, 1 match).
Career batting
3–5–1–101–46–25.25–0–*ct* 2
Bowling 4–0
His final first-class match was for Liverpool and District XI in 1891.

Leach, John
Amateur. *b:* 17.10.1846, Rochdale, Lancashire. *d:* 1.2.1893, Rochdale, Lancashire. Brother of Harold, Robert, R. C. and W. E. (all Lancashire). Opening right-hand batsman. *Sch* Marlborough. *Team* Lancashire (1866–77, 5 matches).
Career batting
5–9–0–103–34–11.44–0–*ct* 1

Leach, Rev Robert
Amateur. *b:* 18.12.1849, Rochdale, Lancashire. *d:* 10.9.1939, Newport Pagnell, Buckinghamshire. Brother of Harold, John, R. C. and W. E. (all Lancashire). Middle order right-hand batsman. *Sch* Marlborough. *Team* Lancashire (1868–76, 3 matches).
Career batting
3–5–0–35–14–7.00–0–*ct* 0

Leach, Roger Chadwick
Amateur. *b:* 21.9.1853, Rochdale, Lancashire. *d:* 21.4.1889, Salta, Argentine. Brother of Harold, John, Robert and W. E. (all Lancashire). Middle order right-hand batsman. *Sch* Marlborough. *Team* Lancashire (1885, 1 match).
Career batting
1–2–0–49–39–24.50–0–*ct* 0

Leach, William Edmund
Amateur. *b:* 7.11.1851, Rochdale, Lancashire. *d:* 30.11.1932, Ivinghoe, Bedfordshire. Brother of Harold, John, Robert and R. C. (all Lancashire). Middle order right-hand batsman, right-hand under-arm bowler, good field. *Sch* Marlborough. *Teams* Lancashire (1885, 5 matches); Canterbury (1876/7).
Career batting
6–11–1–235–56–23.50–0–*ct* 1
Bowling 11–0
He played in the North v South series in the Argentine.

Leach, William Robert Ronald
Amateur. *b:* 3.4.1883, Kensington, London. *d:* 1.11.1969, Eastbourne, Sussex. Lower order right-hand batsman, slow left-arm bowler. *Team* Royal Navy (1913).
Career batting
1–2–0–13–12–6.50–0–*ct* 1
Bowling 61–3–20.33–0–0–3/61

Leadbeater, Barrie
Cricketer. *b:* 14.8.1943, Harehills, Leeds, Yorkshire. Sound opening right-hand batsman, right-arm medium pace bowler. *Team* Yorkshire (1966–79, 144 matches). *Tour* Norfolk to West Indies 1969/70.
Career batting
147–241–29–5373–140*–25.34–1–*ct* 82
Bowling 5–1–5.00–0–0–1/1
He was appointed to the first-class umpires' list in 1981.

Leadbeater, Edric
Professional. *b:* 15.8.1927, Huddersfield, Yorkshire. Lower order right-hand batsman, leg break and googly bowler. *Team* Yorkshire (1949–56, 81 matches); Warwickshire (1957–58, 27 matches). *Tour* MCC to India and Ceylon 1951/2. *Tests* England (1951/2, 2 matches).
Career batting
118–138–36–1548–116–15.17–1–*ct* 74
Bowling 7947–289–27.49–11–2–8/83
Test batting
2–2–0–40–38–20.00–0–*ct* 3
Bowling 218–2–109.00–0–0–1/38

Leadbeater, Harry
Amateur. *b:* 31.12.1863, Scarborough, Yorkshire. *d:* 9.10.1928, Scarborough, Yorkshire. Attacking middle order left-hand batsman, left-arm medium pace bowler. *Team* Yorkshire (1884–90, 6 matches).
Career batting
10–15–2–218–65–16.76–0–*ct* 11
Bowling 93–3–31.00–0–0–2/42

Leadbeater, Stanley Albert
Amateur. *b:* 22.5.1939, Stanion, Northants. Middle order right-hand batsman. *Team* Combined Services (1956–57).

Career batting
3–6–1–112–46–22.40–*ct* 0
Bowling 15–0

Leaf, Herbert
Amateur. *b:* 10.10.1854, Norwood, Surrey. *d:* 13.2.1936, Marlborough, Wiltshire. Middle order right-hand batsman, good deep field. *Sch* Harrow. *Teams* Cambridge U (1876); Surrey (1877, 1 match).
Career batting
5–8–1–60–18–8.57–0–*ct* 3
He also played for Wiltshire. A noted tennis player, he represented Cambridge U.

Leaf, Henry Meredith
Amateur. *b:* 18.10.1862, Scarborough, Yorkshire. *d:* 23.4.1931, Westminster, London. Middle order right-hand batsman, right-arm slow off break bowler, good point field. *Sch* Marlborough and Clifton. *Teams* MCC (1884); G.J.V. Weigall's Team (1904).
Career batting
2–3–0–17–10–5.66–0–*ct* 1
His County cricket was for Essex (pre-first-class) and Wiltshire. Whilst at Cambridge he did not play in any first-class matches.

Leaf, James Gordon
Amateur. *b:* 18.10.1900, Shipston-on-Stour, Warwickshire. *d:* 8.12.1972, Osmaston, Ashbourne, Derbyshire. Middle order batsman. *Team* Army (1937).
Career batting
1–2–0–5–4–2.50–0–*ct* 0

Leaney, Edwin
Professional. *b:* 3.6.1860, Woolwich, Kent. *d:* 1.9.1904, Greenwich, Kent, as the result of an operation. Lower order right-hand batsman, wicket-keeper. *Team* Kent (1892, 6 matches). *Tour* Read to South Africa 1891/2 (he did not appear in first-class matches).
Career batting
6–11–3–76–33*–9.50–0–*ct* 4–*st* 1

Learmond, George Cyril
Amateur. *b:* 4.7.1875, Demerara, British Guiana. Father of Arnold (British Guiana), grandfather of G. S. Camacho (West Indies). Opening right-hand batsman. *Teams* Barbados (1894/5 to 1895/6); British Guiana (1896/7 to 1899/1900); Trinidad (1900/1 to 1906/7). *Tours* West Indies to England 1900 (not first-class), 1906.
Career batting
45–78–3–1700–120–22.66–1–*ct* 27–*st* 2
Bowling 69–2–34.50–0–0–1/4
Although successful in the West Indies, he was totally unable to make runs in England on either of his visits.

Leary, Stuart Edward
Professional. *b:* 30.4.1933, Cape Town, South Africa. Middle order right-hand batsman, leg break bowler, good close field. *Team* Kent (1951–71, 381 matches).
Career batting
387–627–96–16517–158–31.10–18–*ct* 362
Bowling 4935–146–33.80–2–0–5/22
He hit 1,000 runs in a season nine times (best 1,440, av 38.91, in 1961).
A noted soccer player, he appeared as centre forward for Charlton Athletic and Queen's Park Rangers.

Leat, Charles (William)
Professional. *b:* 6.12.1855, Ringwood, Hants. *d:* 1937, Christchurch, Hants. Lower order right-hand batsman, right-hand fast round-arm bowler, wicket-keeper. *Team* Hampshire (1878–85, 16 matches).
Career batting
16–29–1–323–63–11.53–0–*ct* 21–*st* 1
Bowling 49–2–24.50–0–0–2/10

Leat, Edwin John
Amateur. *b:* 24.4.1885, Wellington, Somerset. *d:* 8.6.1918, near Beaumont Hamel, France. He was killed in action. Middle order batsman. *Team* Somerset (1908–10, 2 matches).
Career batting
2–3–0–18–11–6.00–0–*ct* 3
He also played for Buckinghamshire.

Leatham, Albert Edward
Amateur. *b:* 9.8.1859, Heath, Wakefield, Yorkshire. *d:* 13.7.1948, Christchurch, New Zealand. Cousin of G. A. B. (Yorkshire). Lower order right-hand batsman, left-arm medium slow bowler. *Sch* Eton. *Team* Gloucestershire (1883–84, 7 matches). *Tours* Vernon to India and Ceylon 1889/90 (not first-class); Hawke to India 1892/3, to West Indies 1896/7, to New Zealand 1902/3.
Career batting
53–84–17–672–52–10.02–0–*ct* 22
Bowling 1104–47–23.48–2–0–7/54
His final first-class match in England was for MCC in 1897.

Leatham, Gerald Arthur Buxton
Amateur. *b:* 30.4.1851, Hemsworth Hall, Pontefract, Yorkshire. *d:* 19.6.1932, Padstow, Cornwall. Cousin of A. E. (Gloucs). Lower order right-hand batsman, wicket-keeper. *Sch*

Uppingham. *Team* Yorkshire (1874–86, 12 matches).
Career batting
32–51–18–173–20–5.24–0–*ct* 47–*st* 20
Bowling 0–0
His final first-class match was for A.J. Webbe's XI in 1887.
He was also an excellent golfer.

Leatham, Hugh William
Amateur. *b:* 14.6.1891, Pontefract, Yorkshire. *d:* 22.12.1973, Godalming, Surrey. Lower order batsman, right-hand slow under-arm bowler. *Sch* Charterhouse. *Team* G.J.V. Weigall's XI (1914).
Career batting
1–2–0–0–0–0.00–0–*ct* 1
Bowling 31–1–31.00–0–0–1/31
He was the last boy to be chosen for the Public Schools Match at Lord's purely on the strength of his 'lob' bowling.
He played in the Freshmen's and Seniors' Matches at Cambridge.
He was a noted rackets player.

Leather, Roland Sutcliffe
Amateur. *b:* 17.8.1880, Leeds, Yorkshire. *d:* 31.1.1913, Heliopolis, Egypt. Middle order right-hand batsman, good field. *Sch* Marlborough. *Team* Yorkshire (1906, 1 match).
Career batting
1–2–0–19–16–9.50–0–*ct* 0
He did not play in first-class cricket whilst at Oxford U.

Le Bas, Reginald Vincent
Amateur. *b:* 26.7.1856, Barnet, Hertfordshire. *d:* 7.7.1938, Winsford, Somerset. Middle order batsman. *Sch* Charterhouse. *Team* MCC (1882).
Career batting
1–2–0–0–0–0.00–0–*ct* 0

Le Couteur, Philip Ridgeway
Amateur. *b:* 26.6.1885, Kyneton, Victoria, Australia. *d:* 30.6.1958, Gunnedah, New South Wales, Australia. Attacking middle order right-hand batsman, leg break and googly bowler. *Team* Oxford U (1909–11, blue all three years); Victoria (1918/9, 3 matches).
Career batting
30–50–4–982–160–21.34–1–*ct* 31
Bowling 2633–138–19.07–10–4–8/99

Ledden, Peter Robert Varville
Professional. *b:* 12.7.1943, Scarborough, Yorkshire. Middle order left-hand batsman, right-arm medium pace bowler. *Team* Sussex (1961–67, 35 matches).
Career batting
35–56–6–756–98–15.12–0–*ct* 18
Bowling 338–8–42.25–1–0–5/43

Lee, Rev Arthur George
Amateur. *b:* 31.8.1849, Chelsea, London. *d:* 11.7.1925, Westminster, London. Middle order right-hand batsman, wicket-keeper. *Sch* Westminster. *Team* Oxford U (1868–71).
Career batting
4–6–1–22–16*–4.40–0–*ct* 6
His County cricket was for Berkshire, Worcestershire (pre-first-class) and Suffolk.

Lee, Arthur Michael
Amateur. *b:* 22.8.1913, Liphook, Hants. *d:* 14.1.1983, Midhurst, Sussex. Son of E. C. (Hampshire). Middle order right-hand batsman, slow left-arm bowler. *Sch* Winchester. *Teams* Hampshire (1933, 1 match); Oxford U (1934–35).
Career batting
4–6–0–64–24–10.66–0–*ct* 1

Lee, Charles
Professional. *b:* 17.3.1924, Rotherham, Yorkshire. Opening right-hand batsman, right-arm medium pace bowler. *Teams* Yorkshire (1952, 2 matches); Derbyshire (1954–64, 268 matches).
Career batting
271–472–16–12129–150–26.59–8–*ct* 202
Bowling 721–21–34.33–0–0–2/9
He hit 1,000 runs in a season eight times (best 1,503, av 37.57, in 1962). He captained Derbyshire in 1963 and 1964.
A useful soccer player, he appeared for Hull City.

Lee, Edward Cornwall
Amateur. *b:* 18.6.1877, Torquay, Devon. *d:* 16.6.1942, Petersfield, Hants. Father of A. M. (Hampshire). Lower order right-hand batsman, right-arm fast medium bowler. *Sch* Winchester. *Teams* Hampshire (1896–1909, 46 matches); Oxford U (1897–1900, blue 1898). *Tours* Warner to North America 1898 (no first-class matches); Bennett to West Indies 1901/2.
Career batting
85–138–14–1764–66*–14.22–0–*ct* 59
Bowling 1254–39–32.15–2–0–6/42
He played both golf and ice hockey for Oxford U v Cambridge U.

Lee, Frederick
Amateur. *b:* 11.8.1840, Finsbury Square, London. *d:* 13.11.1922, Streatham, South London. Half-brother of J. M. (Surrey). Lively middle order right-hand batsman, excellent field. *Sch* Rugby. *Teams* Cambridge U (1860–62, blue

1860); Surrey (1861, 1 match); Middlesex (1863–68, 4 matches).
Career batting
17–26–1–357–35–14.28–0–*ct* 9
Bowling 140–5–28.00–0–0–2/26

He was a member of the Committee of Surrey CCC for many years, resigning shortly before his death; he also served two terms on the MCC Committee.

Lee, Frederick
Professional. *b:* 18.11.1856, Baildon, Bradford, Yorkshire. *d:* 13.9.1896, Baildon, Bradford, Yorkshire. Middle order right-hand batsman, point field, occasional wicket-keeper. *Team* Yorkshire (1882–90, 106 matches).
Career batting
114–195–10–3953–165–21.36–3–*ct* 58–*st* 1

Lee, Frederick George
Professional. *b:* 24.5.1905, Chard, Somerset. *d:* 19.11.1977, Taunton, Somerset. Lower order batsman, bowler. *Team* Somerset (1925–27, 10 matches).
Career batting
10–13–6–21–8–3.00–0–*ct* 7
Bowling 439–11–39.90–0–0–3/103

Lee, Frederick Marshall
Amateur. *b:* 8.1.1871, Kensington, London. *d:* 18.11.1914, Wonford, Devon. Middle order right-hand batsman, slow left-arm bowler. *Sch* Uppingham. *Teams* Kent (1895, 2 matches); Somerset (1902–07, 77 matches).
Career batting
79–136–20–2253–83–19.42–0–*ct* 58
Bowling 190–4–42.50–0–0–3/7

Lee, Frank Stanley
Professional. *b:* 24.7.1905, St John's Wood, London. *d:* 30.3.1982, Westminster, London. Brother of H. W. (Middlesex) and J. W. (Middlesex and Somerset). Solid opening left-hand batsman, right-arm medium pace bowler. *Teams* Middlesex (1925, 2 matches); Somerset (1929–47, 328 matches).
Career batting
331–586–38–15310–169–27.93–23–*ct* 158–*st* 12
Bowling 862–25–34.48–1–0–5/53

He hit 1,000 runs in a season eight times, going on to 2,000 once: 2,019, av 44.86, in 1938.

From 1948 to 1963 he was a first-class umpire and stood in 29 Tests – his most notable decision being to no-ball Griffin, the fast bowler of the 1960 South African Touring Team to England.

Lee, George Henry
Professional. *b:* 24.8.1854, Lockwood, Yorkshire. *d:* 4.10.1919, Lockwood, Yorkshire. Brother of Herbert (Yorkshire). Opening batsman. *Team* Yorkshire (1879, 1 match).
Career batting
1–2–0–13–9–6.50–0–*ct* 0

Lee, Garnet Morley
Professional. *b:* 7.6.1887, Calverton, Notts. *d:* 29.2.1976, Hawtonville, Newark, Notts. Opening/middle order right-hand batsman, leg break and googly bowler. *Teams* Nottinghamshire (1910–22, 140 matches); Derbyshire (1925–33, 229 matches). *Tour* Tennyson to Jamaica 1927/8.
Career batting
373–624–47–14858–200*–25.75–22–*ct* 156
Bowling 11133–397–28.04–19–1–7/67

He hit 1,000 runs in a season seven times (best 1,279, av 28.42, in 1928). His only double century was 200* for Notts v Leics at Trent Bridge in 1913.

A useful soccer player, he appeared for Notts County.

Lee, Herbert
Professional. *b:* 2.7.1856, Lockwood, Yorkshire. *d:* 4.2.1908, Lockwood, Yorkshire. Brother of G. H. (Yorkshire). Middle order right-hand batsman. *Team* Yorkshire (1885, 5 matches).
Career batting
5–6–0–20–12–3.33–0–*ct* 2

Lee, Horace Cedric
Amateur. *b:* 14.3.1909, Tynemouth, Northumberland. *d:* 1981, Tyneside, Northumberland. Middle order right-hand batsman. *Team* Minor Counties (1936–37).
Career batting
2–4–0–112–61–28.00–0–*ct* 1

His County cricket was for Northumberland.

Lee, Henry (William)
Professional. *b:* 26.10.1890, Marylebone, London. *d:* 21.4.1981, Westminster, London. Brother of F. S. (Middlesex and Somerset) and J. W. (Middlesex and Somerset). Solid opening right-hand batsman, right-arm slow medium off break bowler. *Teams* Middlesex (1911–34, 401 matches); Cooch-Behar's XI (1917/18); England (in India) (1918/19). *Tour* MCC to South Africa 1930/1 (co-opted, whilst coaching in South Africa). *Test* England (1930/1, 1 match).
Career batting
437–722–49–20158–243*–29.95–38–*ct* 181
Bowling 12237–400+2–30.59–12–3–8/39
Test batting
1–2–0–19–18–9.50–0–*ct* 0

He hit 1,000 runs in a season 13 times (best

1,995, av 37.64, in 1929). His four double centuries were all for Middlesex, the highest being 243* v Notts at Lord's in 1921.

Lee, Jack
Amateur. *b:* 4.11.1920, Sileby, Leics. Lower order right-hand batsman, right-arm medium pace bowler. *Team* Leicestershire (1947, 1 match).
Career batting
1–2–0–3–3–1.50–0–*ct* 2
Bowling 13–1–13.00–0–0–1/13
The only wicket he took in first-class cricket was obtained with the first ball he bowled. He played soccer for Leicester City, Derby County and Coventry City.

Lee, James Edward
Amateur. *b:* 1838, Dewsbury, Yorkshire. *d:* 1880, Dewsbury, Yorkshire. Middle order batsman. *Team* Yorkshire (1867, 2 matches).
Career batting
2–3–0–9–6–3.00–0–*ct* 0

Lee, Canon John Morley
Amateur. *b:* 12.10.1825, Chelsea, London. *d:* 20.1.1903, Botley, Hants. Half-brother of Frederick (Surrey and Middlesex). Middle order right-hand batsman, right-hand medium fast round-arm bowler, good field. *Sch* Oundle. *Teams* Cambridge U (1845–49, blue 1846–48); Surrey (1847–50, 7 matches).
Career batting
36–57–6–678–110–13.29–1–*ct* 24
Bowling 25–3+94–8.33–7–3–7/?

Lee, John William
Professional. *b:* 1.2.1902, Marylebone, London. *d:* 20.6.1944, Normandy, France. He was killed in action. Brother of F. S. (Middlesex and Somerset) and H. W. (Middlesex). Opening right-hand batsman, leg break bowler. *Teams* Middlesex (1923, 1 match); Somerset (1925–36, 241 matches).
Career batting
243–418–44–7856–193*–21.00–6–*ct* 123
Bowling 14723–495–29.35–19–2–7/45
He hit 1,000 runs in a season three times (best 1,465, av 31.37, in 1934).
He played football for Arsenal, Chesterfield and Aldershot.

Lee, Nevill Bernard
Professional. *b:* 13.8.1898, Barlestone, Leics. *d:* 21.7.1978, Blackpool, Lancashire. Nephew of H. Whitehead (Leics). Middle order right-hand batsman. *Team* Leicestershire (1922–24, 8 matches).
Career batting
8–12–1–117–62–10.63–0–*ct* 4
Bowling 6–0

Lee, Peter Granville
Cricketer. *b:* 27.8.1945, Arthingworth, Northants. Lower order right-hand batsman, right-arm fast medium bowler. *Teams* Northants (1967–71, 44 matches); Lancashire (1972–82, 152 matches). *Tours* Robins to South Africa 1973/4, 1975/6.
Career batting
202–164–68–779–8.11–0–*ct* 29
Bowling 15339–599–25.60–29–7–8/34
He took 100 wickets in a season twice (best 112, av 18.45, in 1975). His best innings analysis was 8 for 34 for Lancashire v Oxford U at Oxford in 1980. He appeared for Durham in 1983.

Lee, Richard John
Cricketer. *b:* 6.3.1950, Ryde, New South Wales, Australia. Attacking opening right-hand batsman, right-arm medium pace bowler. *Team* Oxford U (1972–74, blue all three years).
Career batting
24–45–1–951–130–21.61–1–*ct* 14
Bowling 1081–29–37.27–0–0–4/56

Lee, Ronald Outram
Amateur. *b:* 26.12.1876, Thame, Oxfordshire. *d:* 12.3.1940, Oxford. Tail end right-hand batsman, right-arm fast bowler. *Sch* Haileybury. *Team* Cambridge U (1899).
Career batting
1–1–0–0–0–0.00–0–*ct* 1
Bowling 79–3–26.33–0–0–2/59
His County cricket was for Oxfordshire.

Leech, Andrew David
Cricketer. *b:* 9.3.1952, Farnworth, Lancashire. Lower order right-hand batsman, right-arm medium pace bowler. *Team* Oxford U (1972).
Career batting
9–11–4–24–8*–3.42–0–*ct* 3
Bowling 521–12–43.41–0–0–3/40

Leech, Colin
Amateur. *b:* 30.8.1889, Hayfield, Derbyshire. *d:* 6.3.1961, Frome, Somerset. Middle order right-hand batsman. *Team* Derbyshire (1922, 1 match).
Career batting
1–2–0–38–36–19.00–0–*ct* 1

Lees, Geoffrey William
Amateur. *b:* 1.7.1920, Chorlton, Manchester. Middle order right-hand batsman, leg break bowler. *Sch* King's, Rochester. *Teams* Cambridge U (1947); Sussex (1951, 1 match).

Career batting
3–5–0–28–15–5.60–0–*ct* 1

Lees, John
Amateur. *b:* 11.9.1861, Ashton-under-Lyne, Lancashire. *d:* 20.12.1934, Brenchley, Kent. Sound opening right-hand batsman, slow right-arm bowler. *Sch* Uppingham. *Team* Cambridge U (1881). *Tour* West Indies to USA 1886 (not first-class).
Career batting
1–2–0–15–9–7.50–0–*ct* 0
Bowling 10–0

His County cricket was for Cambridgeshire. He later appeared for Jamaica in non-first-class matches.

An excellent rugby footballer he represented Cambridge U.

Lees, Robin Douglas
Cricketer. *b:* 19.5.1949, Cranleigh, Surrey. Lower order right-hand batsman, right-arm medium bowler. *Team* Oxford U (1970).
Career batting
3–6–2–29–17*–7.25–0–*ct* 0
Bowling 144–1–144.00–0–0–1/53

Lees, Warren Kenneth
Cricketer. *b:* 19.3.1952, Dunedin, New Zealand. Middle order right-hand batsman, wicket-keeper. *Team* Otago (1972/3 to 1982/3). *Tours* New Zealand to India and Pakistan 1976/7, to Australia 1980/1, 1982/3, to England 1983. *Tests* New Zealand (1976/7 to 1983, 21 matches).
Career batting
106–184–32–3616–152–23.78–4–*ct* 207–*st* 28
Bowling 63–1–63.00–0–0–1/34
Test batting
21–37–4–778–152–23.57–1–*ct* 57–*st* 7
Bowling 4–0

He played in two Tests on the 1983 tour of England. His first-class debut was for New Zealand Under 23s in 1970/1.

Lees, Walter Scott
Professional. *b:* 25.12.1875, Sowerby Bridge, Yorkshire. *d:* 10.9.1924, West Hartlepool. Free hitting lower order right-hand batsman, right-arm medium fast bowler. *Teams* Surrey (1896–1911, 343 matches); London County (1903). *Tour* MCC to South Africa 1905/6. *Tests* England (1905/6, 5 matches).
Career batting
364–522–76–7642–137–17.13–2–*ct* 125
Bowling 30008–1402–21.40–97–20–9/81
Test batting
5–9–3–66–25*–11.00–0–*ct* 2
Bowling 467–26–17.96–2–0–6/78

He took 100 wickets in a season seven times (best 193, av 18.01, in 1905); his best bowling in an innings was 9 for 81 for Surrey v Sussex at Eastbourne in 1905.

Leese, Charles Philip
Amateur. *b:* 22.5.1889, Manchester. *d:* 19.1.1947, Hope-Bagot, Shropshire. Son of Ernest (Lancashire), nephew of J. F. (Lancashire). Opening right-hand batsman. *Sch* Wellington. *Teams* Oxford U (1908–10); Lancashire (1911, 1 match).
Career batting
16–29–1–341–48–12.25–0–*ct* 3

Leese, Ernest
Amateur. *b:* 30.11.1854, Bowdon, Cheshire. *d:* 15.11.1913, Southport, Lancashire. Brother of J. F. (Lancashire), father of C. P. (Lancashire), uncle of W. H. (MCC); V. F. (Cambridge U); and Neville (MCC). Middle order right-hand batsman, good field. *Sch* Cheltenham. *Team* Lancashire (1880–84, 8 matches).
Career batting
8–11–1–146–62–14.60–0–*ct* 1

Leese, Sir Joseph Francis
Amateur. *b:* 28.2.1845, Manchester. *d:* 29.7.1914, Sutton Park, Guildford, Surrey. Brother of Ernest (Lancashire), father of W. H. (MCC), V. F. (Cambridge U) and Neville (MCC), uncle of C. P. (Lancashire). Hard hitting middle order right-hand batsman, good point. *Team* Lancashire (1865–81, 24 matches).
Career batting
25–44–1–561–44–13.04–0–*ct* 14
Bowling 94–5–18.80–0–0–3/49

He was MP for Accrington from 1892 to 1909.

Leese, Neville
Amateur. *b:* 23.3.1872, Preston, Lancashire. *d:* 22.6.1948, Zeals, Wiltshire. Son of J. F. (Lancashire), brother of W. H. (MCC) and V. F. (Cambridge U), nephew of Ernest (Lancashire). Middle order batsman. *Sch* Winchester. *Team* MCC (1895).
Career batting
6–12–0–226–59–18.83–0–*ct* 3

Leese, Vernon Francis
Amateur. *b:* 20.2.1870, Kensington, London. *d:* 3.8.1926, Alassio, Italy. Son of J. F. (Lancashire), brother of W. H. (MCC) and Neville (MCC), nephew of Ernest (Lancashire). *Sch* Winchester. *Team* Cambridge U (1892).
Career batting
7–12–0–171–44–14.25–0–*ct* 3

His final first-class match was for MCC in 1879. He played County cricket for Devonshire.

Leese, Sir William Hargreaves
Amateur. *b:* 24.8.1868, Send, Woking, Surrey. *d:* 17.1.1937, Sidmouth, Devon. Son of J. F. (Lancashire), brother of V. F. (Cambridge U), and Neville (MCC), nephew of Ernest (Lancashire). Middle order right-hand batsman. *Sch* Winchester. *Team* MCC (1889–90).
Career batting
2–4–0–57–35–14.25–0–*ct* 3
He played in the Seniors' match whilst at Cambridge.

Leeson, Patrick George
Amateur. *b:* 17.7.1915, Darjeeling, India. Middle order right-hand batsman, off break bowler. *Sch* Malvern. *Team* Worcestershire (1936, 1 match).
Career batting
1–2–0–7–7–3.50–0–*ct* 1

Leeston-Smith, F. A.
(*see under* Smith, F. A. L.)

Le Fleming, John
Amateur. *b:* 23.10.1865, Tonbridge, Kent. *d:* 7.10.1942, Montreux, Switzerland. Brother of L. J. (Kent). Stylish middle order right-hand batsman, slow right-arm bowler, good deep field. *Sch* Tonbridge. *Team* Kent (1889–99, 40 matches).
Career batting
40–65–2–1201–134–19.06–1–*ct* 25
Bowling 120–3–40.00–0–0–2/44
He did not appear in any first-class matches whilst at Cambridge U.
A well-known rugby footballer he played for Cambridge, Blackheath and England as a three-quarter; he also won the hurdles for Cambridge and was English Champion. His other achievements were in skating, winning various championships.

Le Fleming, Lawrence Julius
Amateur. *b:* 3.6.1879, Tonbridge, Kent. *d:* 21.3.1918, Maissemy, France. He was killed in action. Brother of John (Kent). Middle order right-hand batsman. *Sch* Tonbridge. *Team* Kent (1897–99, 12 matches).
Career batting
13–18–0–240–40–13.33–0–*ct* 3
Bowling 20–0
His final first-class match was for the Army in 1912.

Legard, Alfred Digby
Amateur. *b:* 19.6.1878, Scarborough, Yorkshire. *d:* 15.8.1939, Newquay, Cornwall. Opening right-hand batsman, slow right-arm bowler. *Sch* Eton. *Team* Yorkshire (1910, 4 matches).
Career batting
6–8–1–68–27–9.71–0–*ct* 1
Bowling 33–0
His first-class debut was for MCC in 1904.

Legard, Antony Ronald
Amateur. *b:* 17.1.1912, Sialkot, India. Lower order right-hand batsman, right-arm medium pace bowler. *Sch* Winchester. *Teams* Oxford U (1932–35, blue 1932 and 1935); Worcestershire (1935, 1 match); Europeans (1943/4).
Career batting
36–52–10–234–38–5.57–0–*ct* 17
Bowling 2793–93–30.03–3–0–7/36
His final first-class match was for MCC in 1952.

Legard, Edwin
Professional. *b:* 23.8.1935, Barnsley, Yorkshire. Lower order right-hand batsman, wicket-keeper. *Team* Warwickshire (1962–68, 20 matches).
Career batting
20–24–11–144–21–11.07–0–*ct* 33–*st* 9

Leggatt, Logie Colin
Amateur. *b:* 24.9.1894, St John's Hill, Bangalore, India. *d:* 31.7.1917, Pilckem Ridge, Belgium. He was killed in action. Opening right-hand batsman, leg break bowler. *Sch* Eton. *Team* Cambridge U (1914).
Career batting
1–2–0–9–6–4.50–0–*ct* 0

Leggatt, William Murray
Amateur. *b:* 2.9.1900, Crail, Fife, Scotland. *d:* 11.8.1946, Westminster, London. Middle order right-hand batsman, right-arm fast bowler. *Sch* Winchester. *Team* Kent (1926, 5 matches).
Career batting
11–16–0–479–92–29.93–0–*ct* 9
He played in many military matches and in India for South Punjab (not first-class); his final first-class match was for the Army in 1933.

Legge, Geoffrey Bevington
Amateur. *b:* 26.1.1903, Bromley, Kent. *d:* 21.11.1940, Brampford Speke, Devon. He was killed whilst flying with the Fleet Air Arm. Stylish middle order right-hand batsman, right-arm slow bowler, good slip field. *Sch* Malvern. *Teams* Kent (1924–31, 114 matches); Oxford U (1925–26, blue both years). *Tours* MCC to South Africa 1927/8, to Australia and New Zealand 1929/30. *Tests* England (1927/8 to 1929/30, 5 matches).

Career batting
147–210–11–4955–196–24.89–7–*ct* 121
Bowling 181–8–22.62–0–0–3/23
Test batting
5–7–1–299–196–49.83–1–*ct* 1
Bowling 34–0

His highest score was 196 for England v New Zealand at Auckland in 1929/30. For three years, 1928–30, he captained Kent.

Le Gros, Philip Walter
Amateur. *b:* 3.10.1892, Reigate, Surrey. *d:* 27.2.1980, Richmond, Surrey. Attacking middle order right-hand batsman, right-arm fast bowler. *Sch* Rugby. *Teams* MCC (1921–22).
Career batting
4–7–1–94–51–15.66–0–*ct* 1
Bowling 24–0

His first-class debut was for the Gentlemen in 1920 and his final first-class match for Minor Counties in 1924.

His County cricket was for Buckinghamshire.

Leigh, James
Amateur. *b:* December 1862, West Leigh, Lancashire. *d:* 25.9.1925, Shepperton-on-Thames, Middlesex. Stylish middle order right-hand batsman, good field. *Sch* Uppingham. *Team* Lancashire (1887, 1 match). *Tour* Priestley to West Indies 1896/7.
Career batting
10–16–0–157–26–9.81–0–*ct* 5
Bowling 14–0

His final first-class match was for MCC in 1900.

Leigh, Spencer Austen
Amateur. *b:* 17.2.1834, Speen, Newbury, Berkshire. *d:* 9.12.1913, Alfriston, Sussex. Brother of C. E. A. (MCC), C. A. (MCC) and A. H. A. (Gentlemen of England). Hard hitting right-hand batsman, good deep field. *Sch* Harrow. *Team* Sussex (1862–66, 10 matches).
Career batting
13–21–2–209–42–11.00–0–*ct* 4
Bowling 14–1–14.00–0–0–1/9

He also appeared for Berkshire.

His first-class debut was for Gentlemen of England in 1857. His three brothers were all notable cricketers, but played mainly for Berkshire.

Leiper, John Morton
Amateur. *b:* 17.2.1921, Woodford Green, Essex. Father of R. J. (Essex). Attacking lower order left-hand batsman, right-arm fast medium bowler, occasional wicket-keeper. *Sch* Chigwell. *Team* Essex (1950, 2 matches).
Career batting
2–4–0–50–44–12.50–0–*ct* 1
Bowling 79–1–79.00–0–0–1/38

Leiper, Robert James
Cricketer. *b:* 30.8.1961, Woodford Green, Essex. Son of J.M. (Essex). Middle order left-hand batsman, right-arm medium pace bowler. *Sch* Chigwell. *Team* Essex (1981–82, 2 matches).
Career batting
2–4–0–53–49–13.25–0–*ct* 2

Lemmy, Brian Allen
Professional. *b:* 6.1.1937, Brentford, Middlesex. Lower order right-hand batsman, right-arm bowler. *Team* MCC (1958).
Career batting
1–2–2–12–7*–no av–0–*ct* 1
Bowling 117–3–39.00–0–0–2/92

Leney, Frederick Barcham
Amateur. *b:* 29.11.1876, Maidstone, Kent. *d:* 25.7.1921, Galway, Ireland. Nephew of Herbert (Kent). Middle order right-hand batsman, right-arm medium fast bowler. *Sch* Bradfield. *Team* Kent (1905, 1 match).
Career batting
1–2–0–39–30–19.50–0–*ct* 1
Bowling 23–1–23.00–0–0–1/0

Leney, Herbert
Amateur. *b:* 8.9.1850, Wateringbury, Kent. *d:* 18.11.1915, West Farleigh, Kent. Uncle of F. B. (Kent). Middle order right-hand batsman, right-hand fast round-arm bowler, good mid-off. *Sch* Chatham House. *Team* Kent (1873–77, 4 matches).
Career batting
4–6–1–58–33–11.60–0–*ct* 0
Bowling 7–0

He was not in the Eleven whilst at Oxford U.

Leng, Denis
Cricketer. *b:* 26.11.1934, Pudsey, Yorkshire. Lower order right-hand batsman, right-arm fast medium bowler. *Team* Ireland (1966).
Career batting
1–2–1–1–1–1.00–0–*ct* 1
Bowling 36–1–36.00–0–0–1/36

Lenham, Leslie John
Professional. *b:* 24.5.1936, Lancing, Sussex. Opening right-hand batsman, off break bowler. *Team* Sussex (1956–70, 300 matches).
Career batting
300–539–50–12796–191*–26.16–7–*ct* 110
Bowling 306–6–51.00–0–0–2/24

He hit 1,000 runs in a season six times, going

on to 2,000 once : 2,016, av 32.51, in 1961. After his first-class career ended he was coach to Sussex CCC.

Lennox, Hon Charles
(succeeded as Duke of Richmond in 1806)
Amateur. *b:* 9.9.1764. *d:* 28.8.1819, Montreal, Canada, of hydrophobia, having been bitten by a pet dog. Middle order right-hand batsman, wicket-keeper. *Teams* Surrey (1802); MCC (pre-1800).
Career batting
1–2–0–6–5–3.00–0–*ct* 0

One of the leading amateur cricketers of his day, he was a great patron of all athletic sports.

In 1789 he fought a notorious duel with the Duke of York (brother of King George III) on Wimbledon Common. At the time of his death he was Governor-General of Canada.

Le Peton, Howard Guerin
Amateur. *b:* 19.1.1895, Pwllheli, Caernarvonshire. *d:* 1981, Cambridgeshire. Middle order right-hand batsman. *Team* Ireland (1921).
Career batting
1–1–0–16–16–16.00–0–*ct* 0

Le Roux, Garth Stirling
Cricketer. *b:* 4.9.1955, Kenilworth, Cape Town, South Africa. Lower order right-hand batsman, right-arm fast bowler. *Teams* Western Province (1975/6 to 1982/3); Sussex (1978–83, 68 matches).
Career batting
128–162–47–2908–83–25.28–0–*ct* 52
Bowling 9807–496–19.77–27–3–8/107

His best season in England was 1981, with 81 wickets, av 19.53.

Leroy, Philip Newbold
Amateur. *b:* 25.9.1880. *d: circa* 1950. Lower order batsman, bowler. *Team* Philadelphia (1901 to 1908/9). *Tours* Philadelphia to England 1903, to Jamaica 1908/9.
Career batting
13–23–2–199–35–9.47–0–*ct* 11
Bowling 377–10–37.70–0–0–4/62

He had very little success on his single tour to England.

Leslie, Charles Frederick Henry
Amateur. *b:* 8.12.1861, London. *d:* 12.2.1921, Westminster, London. Father of John (Oxford U). Hard hitting middle order right-hand batsman, right-arm fast bowler, good cover point. *Sch* Rugby. *Teams* Oxford U (1881–83, blue all three years); Middlesex (1881–86, 20 matches). *Tour* Bligh to Australia 1882/3. *Tests* England (1882/3, 4 matches).
Career batting
48–86–5–1860–144–22.96–4–*ct* 18
Bowling 165–8–20.62–0–0–3/31
Test batting
4–7–0–106–54–15.14–0–*ct* 1
Bowling 44–4–11.00–0–0–3/31

His final first-class match was for Oxford University (Past and Present) v Australians in 1888. He also played for Shropshire.

He excelled at rackets and soccer, representing Oxford at both sports.

Leslie, John
Amateur. *b:* 26.8.1888, London. *d:* 1.10.1965, Brancaster, Norfolk. Son of C. F. H. (Oxford U and Middlesex). Opening/middle order right-hand batsman, right-arm slow bowler. *Sch* Winchester. *Team* Oxford U (1908).
Career batting
3–5–0–42–23–8.40–0–*ct* 4
Bowling 42–0

Lester, Edward
Professional. Lower order right-hand batsman, right-arm medium pace bowler. *Team* Middlesex (1929–30, 7 matches).
Career batting
7–11–4–41–13–5.85–0–*ct* 0
Bowling 10–0

Lester, Edward Ibson
Amateur, turned professional in 1948. *b:* 18.2.1923, Scarborough, Yorkshire. Aggressive middle order right-hand batsman, off-break bowler. *Team* Yorkshire (1945–56, 228 matches).
Career batting
232–347–28–10912–186–34.20–25–*ct* 108
Bowling 160–3–53.33–0–0–1/7

He hit 1,000 runs in a season six times (best 1,801, av 37.52, in 1949). He later became the Yorkshire scorer.

Lester, Gerald
Professional. *b:* 27.12.1915, Long Whatton, Leics. Sound opening or middle order right-hand batsman, leg break and googly bowler. *Team* Leicestershire (1937–58, 373 matches).
Career batting
373–649–54–12857–143–21.60–9–*ct* 159
Bowling 10882–307–35.44–7–1–6/42

He hit 1,000 runs in a season five times (best 1,599, av 33.31, in 1949). In 1959 he was appointed coach to Leicestershire, retiring in 1966.

Lester, John Ashby
Amateur. *b:* 1.8.1871, Penrith, Cumberland. *d:*

3.9.1969, Haverford, Philadelphia, USA. Middle order right-hand batsman, right-arm slow bowler, good slip. *Sch* Haverford College. *Team* Philadelphia (1896–08). *Tours* Philadelphia to England, 1897, 1903, 1908.
Career batting
47–84–7–2552–126*–33.14–2–*ct* 15
Bowling 1267–57–22.22–3–1–7/33
He headed the batting averages for both the 1897 and 1903 tours to England and was regarded for some years as the best batsman in the United States, playing for United States v Canada in 1901 and 1906.

L'Estrange, Michael Gerard
Cricketer. *b:* 12.10.1952, Sydney, New South Wales, Australia. Middle order left-hand batsman, occasional right-arm medium pace bowler. *Team* Oxford U (1977–79, blue 1977 and 1979).
Career batting
23–37–3–521–63–15.32–0–*ct* 18

Lethbridge, Christopher
Cricketer. *b:* 23.6.1961, Castleford, Yorkshire. Middle order right-hand batsman, right-arm medium pace bowler. *Team* Warwickshire (1981–83, 32 matches).
Career batting
32–38–9–625–87*–21.55–0–*ct* 10
Bowling 1746–42–41.57–1–0–5/68
He dismissed G. Boycott with his first delivery in first-class cricket.

Leventon, Edwin Charles
Amateur. *b:* 1845. *d:* 21.8.1909, Roby, Lancashire. Lower order batsman, useful bowler. *Team* Lancashire (1867, 1 match).
Career batting
1–2–0–6–6–3.00–0–*ct* 0
Bowling 24–2–12.00–0–0–2/24

Lever, Colin
Cricketer. *b:* 4.8.1939, Todmorden, Yorkshire. Brother of Peter (Lancashire). Middle order right-hand batsman, right-arm medium pace bowler. *Team* Minor Counties (1965).
Career batting
1–2–0–20–12–10.00–0–*ct* 0
Bowling 23–2–11.50–0–0–1/5
His County cricket was for Buckinghamshire, commencing 1962.

Lever, John Kenneth
Cricketer. *b:* 24.2.1949, Stepney, London. Lower order right-hand batsman, left-arm fast medium bowler. *Teams* Essex (1967–83, 330 matches); Natal (1982/3). *Tours* MCC to India, Sri Lanka and Australia 1976/7; England to Pakistan and New Zealand 1977/8, to Australia 1978/9, to Australia and India 1979/80, to India and Sri Lanka 1981/2; Robins to South Africa 1972/3, 1973/4, to Sri Lanka 1977/8; Overseas XI to India 1980/1; SAB to South Africa 1981/2. *Tests* England (1976/7 to 1981/2, 20 matches).
Career batting
418–431–114–2885–91–10.80–0–*ct* 159
Bowling 31850–1342–23.73–65–9–8/49
Test batting
20–29–4–306–53–12.24–0–*ct* 11
Bowling 1785–67–26.64–3–1–7/46
He took 100 wickets in a season three times: 106, av 15.18, in 1978, 106, av, 17.30, in 1979, and 106, av 16.28, in 1983.

Lever, Peter
Professional. *b:* 17.9.1940, Todmorden, Yorkshire. Brother of Colin (Minor Counties). Lower order right-hand batsman, right-arm fast medium bowler. *Teams* Lancashire (1960–76, 268 matches); Tasmania (1971/2, 1 match). *Tours* MCC to Australia and New Zealand 1970/1, 1974/5. *Tests* England (1970/1 to 1975, 17 matches).
Career batting
301–314–66–3534–88*–14.25–0–*ct* 106
Bowling 20377–796–25.59–28–2–7/70
Test batting
17–18–2–350–88*–21.87–0–*ct* 11
Bowling 1509–41–36.80–2–0–6/38
In 1974/5 when playing for England v New Zealand, one of his deliveries hit the New Zealand tail-ender, Chatfield, in the face. The batsman was taken unconscious to hospital and for some time his life was in danger. Happily, Chatfield fully recovered. Lever is joint Lancashire coach.

Leveson-Gower, Rev Frederick Archibald Gresham
Amateur. *b:* 20.2.1871, Titsey, Surrey. *d:* 3.10.1946, Folkestone, Kent. Brother of H. D. G. (Surrey). Middle order right-hand batsman, wicket-keeper. *Sch* Winchester. *Teams* Oxford U (1894); Hampshire (1899–1900, 2 matches).
Career batting
16–30–3–424–86–15.70–0–*ct* 11–*st* 1
Bowling 53–0
His final first-class match was for H. D. G. Leveson-Gower's XI in 1909.

Leveson-Gower, Sir Henry Dudley Gresham
Amateur. *b:* 8.5.1873, Titsey, Surrey. *d:* 1.2.1954, Kensington, London. Brother of F. A. G. (Hants). Middle order right-hand batsman, leg break bowler, cover field. *Sch*

Winchester. *Teams* Oxford U (1893–96, blue all four years); Surrey (1895–1920, 122 matches). *Tours* Hawke to West Indies 1896/7; Warner to USA 1897; MCC to South Africa 1905/6, 1909/10; Leveson-Gower to Rhodesia 1909/10. *Tests* England (1909/10, 3 matches).
Career batting
277–400–78–7638–155–23.72–4–*ct* 103
Bowling 1378–46–29.95–3–0–6/49
Test batting
3–6–2–95–31–23.75–0–*ct* 1

His final first-class match was for his own Team v Cambridge U in 1931. He captained Surrey 1908 to 1910, and the MCC Team to South Africa 1909/10, leading England in three Tests on that tour.

A noted cricket administrator, he joined the Test Selection Committee in 1909 and was Chairman for several years. He was also on the Committees of MCC and Surrey.

In 1953 he was knighted for his services to cricket.

Levett, William Howard Vincent
Amateur. *b:* 25.1.1908, Goudhurst, Kent. Lower order right-hand batsman, wicket-keeper. *Sch* Brighton. *Team* Kent (1930–47, 142 matches). *Tour* MCC to India and Ceylon 1933/4. *Test* England (1933/4, 1 match).
Career batting
175–264–58–2524–76–12.25–0–*ct* 283–*st* 195
Bowling 6–0
Test batting
1–2–1–7–5–7.00–0–*ct* 3

Levick, Deryck Cyril
Amateur. *b:* 27.5.1929, Acton, London. Aggressive middle order right-hand batsman, good field. *Team* Essex (1950–51, 3 matches).
Career batting
3–6–0–14–6–2.33–0–*ct* 1

Levy, Solomon
Professional. *b:* 18.5.1886, Stroud, Gloucs. Lower order right-hand batsman, off break bowler. *Team* Gloucestershire (1910–11, 4 matches).
Career batting
4–8–2–43–22–7.16–0–*ct* 0
Bowling 147–4–36.75–0–0–2/41

Lewin, Charles la Primaudaye
Amateur. *b:* 22.8.1874, Greenwich, Kent. *d:* 14.9.1952, St Helier, Jersey. Opening batsman. *Team* Royal Navy (1920).
Career batting
1–2–0–52–37–26.00–0–*ct* 0

Lewington, Peter John
Cricketer. *b:* 30.1.1950, Finchampstead, Berkshire. Lower order right-hand batsman, off break bowler. *Team* Warwickshire (1970–82, 69 matches). *Tours* Robins to South Africa 1972/3; MCC to Bangladesh 1978/9 (not first-class).
Career batting
72–73–21–383–34–7.36–0–*ct* 31
Bowling 5705–191–29.86–6–0–7/52

He also played for Berkshire.

He did not play for Warwickshire, 1977 to 1981.

Lewis, Anthony Charles Wilson
Amateur. *b:* 29.9.1932, Stoke on Trent, Staffs. Middle order right-hand batsman. *Sch* Repton. *Team* Cambridge U (1952–53).
Career batting
6–9–0–83–55–9.22–0–*ct* 0

He was an excellent tennis player.

Lewis, Albert Edward
Professional. *b:* 20.1.1877, Bedminster, Somerset. *d:* 22.2.1956, Redland, Bristol. Middle order right-hand batsman, right-arm fast medium bowler. *Team* Somerset (1899–1914, 208 matches).
Career batting
210–388–27–7745–201*–21.45–9–*ct* 106
Bowling 12091–522–23.16–39–5–8/103

He went out to India as coach in 1920, but did not play in any first-class matches. An excellent soccer player he appeared as goalkeeper for Sunderland, Sheffield United, West Bromwich, Leicester Fosse and Bristol City. His highest score was 201* for Somerset v Kent at Taunton in 1909.

Lewis, Arthur Hamilton
Amateur. *b:* 16.9.1901, Maseru, Basutoland. *d:* 23.8.1980, Heavitree, Devon. Hard hitting middle order right-hand batsman, brilliant cover point. *Sch* King William's College, IOM. *Team* Hampshire (1929, 1 match).
Career batting
1–1–0–20–20–20.00–0–*ct* 1

He also appeared for Berkshire.

Lewis, Anthony Robert
Amateur. *b:* 6.7.1938, Swansea, Glamorgan. Middle order right-hand batsman, leg break bowler. *Teams* Glamorgan (1955–74, 315 matches); Cambridge U (1960–62, blue all three years). *Tours* MCC to South America 1964/5 (not first-class), to Ceylon 1969/70, to India, Pakistan and Sri Lanka 1972/3; Glamorgan to West Indies 1969/70. *Tests* England (1972/3 to 1973, 9 matches).

Career batting
409–708–76–20495–223–32.42–30–*ct* 193
Bowling 432–6–72.00–0–0–3/18
Test batting
9–16–2–457–125–32.64–1–*ct* 0

He hit 1,000 runs in a season 11 times, going on to 2,000 twice (best 2,190, av 41.32, in 1966). His only double century was 223 for Glamorgan v Kent at Gravesend in 1966. He captained MCC on the 1972/3 tour, including eight Tests, and also led Glamorgan from 1967 to 1972.

Since retiring from first-class cricket he has become a well-known writer on the game.

Lewis, Brian
Cricketer. *b:* 18.7.1945, Maesteg, Glamorgan. Lower order right-hand batsman, off break bowler. *Team* Glamorgan (1965–68, 37 matches).
Career batting
37–45–5–333–38–8.32–0–*ct* 29
Bowling 2001–82–24.40–6–1–7/28

Lewis, Claude
Professional. *b:* 27.7.1908, Sittingbourne, Kent. Lower order left-hand batsman, slow left-arm bowler. *Team* Kent (1933–53, 128 matches).
Career batting
128–187–72–738–27–6.41–0–*ct* 61
Bowling 8198–301–27.23–14–4–8/58

In 1983 he was scorer to Kent CCC, having been connected with the County Club for 55 years, as player, coach and scorer.

Lewis, Charles Prytherch
Amateur. *b:* 20.8.1853, Llwen-Celn, Llangadog, Carmarthenshire. *d:* 28.5.1923, Llandingat, Llandovery, Carmarthenshire. Lower order right-hand batsman, right-arm fast bowler. *Sch* Llandovery College. *Team* Oxford U (1876, blue).
Career batting
5–7–0–76–33–10.85–0–*ct* 2
Bowling 501–17–29.47–1–0–7/35

A noted rugby footballer, he represented Wales.

Lewis, David John
Amateur. *b:* 27.7.1927, Bulawayo, Rhodesia. Middle order right-hand batsman. *Team* Rhodesia (1945/6 to 1963/4); Oxford U (1949–51, blue 1951).
Career batting
86–146–16–3662–170*–28.16–8–*ct* 39
Bowling 457–11–41.54–0–0–2/19

Lewis, Desmond Michael
Cricketer. *b:* 21.2.1946, Kingston, Jamaica. Middle order right-hand batsman, wicket-keeper. *Team* Jamaica (1970 to 1975/6). *Tour* Jamaica to England 1970. *Tests* West Indies (1970/1, 3 matches).
Career batting
36–56–5–1623–96–31.82–0–*ct* 67–*st* 11
Test batting
3–5–2–259–88–86.33–0–*ct* 8

Lewis, David Wyndham
Amateur. *b:* 18.12.1940, Cardiff. Lower order right-hand batsman, leg break bowler. *Sch* Wycliffe College. *Teams* Glamorgan (1960–69, 12 matches); Transvaal (1972/3).
Career batting
14–20–7–122–29*–9.38–0–*ct* 3
Bowling 958–21–45.61–0–0–4/42

He did not appear in first-class County cricket 1963 to 1967 inclusive.

Lewis, Esmond Burman
Amateur. *b:* 5.1.1918, Shirley, Solihull, Warwickshire. *d:* 19.10.1983, Dorridge, Solihull. Lower order right-hand batsman, wicket-keeper. *Team* Warwickshire (1949–58, 43 matches).
Career batting
47–56–12–533–51–12.56–0–*ct* 93–*st* 26

He was a member of Warwickshire CCC Committee.

Lewis, Euros John
Professional. *b:* 31.1.1942, Llanelly, Carmarthenshire. Middle order left-hand batsman, off break bowler. *Teams* Glamorgan (1961–66, 95 matches); Sussex (1967–69, 86 matches).
Career batting
182–276–28–3487–80–14.06–0–*ct* 131
Bowling 9286–341–27.23–13–2–8/89

Lewis, Frederick Stafford
Amateur. *b:* 12.4.1879. Edmonton, London. *d:* 22.5.1967, Chiddingfold, Surrey. Middle order right-hand batsman, right-arm medium pace bowler. *Sch* Marlborough. *Team* MCC (1903).
Career batting
1–1–0–1–1–1.00–0–*ct* 0

Lewis, Kenneth Humphrey
Professional. *b:* 10.11.1928, Newtown, Monmouthshire. Lower order right-hand batsman, right-arm fast medium bowler. *Team* Glamorgan (1950–56, 36 matches).
Career batting
36–48–14–312–34–9.17–0–*ct* 15
Bowling 2044–55–37.16–0–0–4/25

Lewis, Leslie Keith
Amateur. *b:* 25.9.1929, Finchley, North London. Middle order right-hand batsman, off break

bowler, cover field. *Sch* Taunton. *Team* Cambridge U (1952–53, blue 1953).
Career batting
6–11–1–155–53*–15.50–0–*ct* 2

An excellent hockey player, he appeared for Cambridge U.

Lewis, Reginald Chester Vale
Amateur. *b:* 4.10.1927, Cape Town, South Africa. Lower order right-hand batsman, leg break bowler. *Team* Oxford U (1949–50).
Career batting
4–6–2–65–34–16.25–0–*ct* 0
Bowling 222–8–27.75–0–0–3/31

He played County cricket for Oxfordshire.

Lewis, Roy Markham
Cricketer. *b:* 29.6.1948, Bromley, Kent. Middle order right-hand batsman, right-arm medium pace bowler. *Team* Surrey (1968–73, 38 matches).
Career batting
38–68–9–1746–87–29.59–0–*ct* 26
Bowling 7–0

Lewis, Richard Percy
Amateur. *b:* 10.3.1874, Marylebone, London. *d:* 7.9.1917, Ypres, Belgium. He died of wounds received in battle. Lower order right-hand batsman, wicket-keeper. *Sch* Winchester. *Teams* Oxford U (1894–96, blue all three years); Middlesex (1898, 2 matches). *Tour* Priestley to West Indies 1896/7.
Career batting
36–58–21–134–27*–3.62–0–*ct* 55–*st* 21

His final first-class match was for MCC in 1907. He was a notable figure in military cricket, both in England and overseas.

In 1892 he played for Surrey, but not in first-class matches.

Lewis, Richard Victor
Cricketer. *b:* 6.8.1947, Winchester, Hants. Middle order right-hand batsman, leg break bowler. *Team* Hampshire (1967–76, 103 matches).
Career batting
105–190–14–3471–136–19.72–2–*ct* 65
Bowling 104–1–104.00–0–0–1/59

He also played for Dorset commencing 1977 and his final first-class match was for the Minor Counties in 1981.

Lewis, William Ian
Amateur. *b:* 29.9.1935, Dublin, Ireland. Middle order right-hand batsman. *Team* Ireland (1956–72).
Career batting
5–10–0–67–20–6.70–0–*ct* 2

Lewis-Barclay, Harry Samuel
(originally H.S. Lewis)
Amateur. *b:* 7.11.1892, Shoreditch, London. *d:* 20.4.1956, Barnet, Hertfordshire. Lower order left-hand batsman, slow bowler. *Teams* Southern Punjab (1926/7); Army (1928).
Career batting
4–6–3–32–14*–10.66–0–*ct* 1
Bowling 316–9–35.11–0–0–3/75

Lewisham, Viscount William Heneage Legge
(succeeded to the title 6th Earl of Dartmouth in 1891)
Amateur. *b:* 6.5.1851, London W. *d:* 11.3.1936, Patshull, Staffs. Lower order right-hand batsman, right-hand slow round-arm bowler, long stop. *Sch* Eton. *Team* MCC (1877).
Career batting
1–2–2–29–24*–no av–0–*ct* 0

He was not in the Eleven whilst at Oxford.

He held office as President of Kent, of MCC (1893) and for 40 years of Staffordshire.

In 1878 he was elected MP for West Kent and in 1885 for Lewisham.

He played for Shropshire and Staffordshire.

Leyland, Morris
(known as Maurice)
Professional. *b:* 20.7.1900, Newpark, Harrogate, Yorkshire. *d:* 1.1.1967, Scotton Banks, Harrogate, Yorkshire. Brilliant middle order left-hand batsman, slow left-arm bowler. *Teams* Yorkshire (1920–47, 548 matches); Patiala (1926/7). *Tours* MCC to India 1926/7 (in emergency), to Australia and New Zealand 1928/9, 1932/3, 1936/7, to South Africa 1930/1, to West Indies 1934/5; Yorkshire to Jamaica 1935/6. *Tests* England (1928–38, 41 matches).
Career batting
686–932–101–32660–263–40.50–80–*ct* 246
Bowling 13659–466–29.31–11–1–8/63
Test batting
41–65–5–2764–187–46.06–9–*ct* 13
Bowling 585–6–97.50–0–0–3/91

One of the greatest of Yorkshire's batsmen, he hit over 1,000 runs for the County each season from 1923 to 1939, but had to wait until his eighth season in first-class cricket before winning a Test cap. Having however gained an England place he remained a major force in international cricket for eight seasons. He had three successful tours to Australia, his batting average exceeding 40 on each tour, and of the regular England players of his time only Hammond and Sutcliffe can boast better Test batting records.

In all he hit 1,000 runs in a season 17 times, going on to 2,000 three times, with his best 2,317, av 50.36, in 1933. All his five double centuries were for Yorkshire, the highest being 263 v Essex at Hull in 1936. He helped to break no less than three Yorkshire partnership records : 346 for the 2nd wicket with W. Barber v Middlesex at Bramall Lane in 1932; 323 for the 3rd wicket with H. Sutcliffe v Glamorgan at Huddersfield in 1928 and 276 for the 6th wicket with E. Robinson v Glamorgan at Swansea in 1926.

His slow bowling was at times most effective and he is reputed to have invented the term 'Chinaman' to denote his left-arm off breaks. He was a brilliant fielder in the deep.

His final first-class match was for an England XI in 1948. After retiring from first-class cricket he was coach to Yorkshire for 12 seasons until 1963.

Liaqat Ali Khan
Cricketer. *b:* 21.5.1955, Karachi, Pakistan. Lower order right-hand batsman, left-arm medium pace bowler. *Teams* Karachi (1970/1 to 1974/5); Sind (1974/5); Habib Bank (1975/6 to 1982/3); PIA (1981/2). *Tours* Pakistan to England 1978; PIA to Zimbabwe 1981/2. *Tests* Pakistan (1974/5 to 1978, 5 matches).
Career batting
135–135–52–643–51–7.74–0–*ct* 51
Bowling 9555–397–24.06–19–2–8/44
Test batting
5–7–3–28–12–7.00–0–*ct* 1
Bowling 359–6–59.83–0–0–3/80

On the 1978 tour to England he took 18 wickets, av 28.33, in first-class matches and appeared in two Tests.

Liddell, Allan Graham
Professional. *b:* 2.5.1908, Northampton. *d:* 17.2.1970, Northampton. Father of A. W. G. (Northants). Stylish middle order right-hand batsman, slow right-arm bowler. *Team* Northants (1927–34, 91 matches).
Career batting
91–161–7–2355–120–15.29–3–*ct* 66
Bowling 563–9–62.55–0–0–4/59

Liddell, Alan W. Graham
Amateur. *b:* 2.8.1930, Northampton. Son of A. G. (Northants). Lower order right-hand batsman, right-arm medium pace bowler. *Team* Northants (1952–55, 18 matches).
Career batting
18–20–6–201–38*–14.35–0–*ct* 4
Bowling 1399–24–58.29–0–0–3/62

Liebenrood, Fitzhardinge Hancock
(changed to Fitzhardinge Hancock in 1921)
Amateur. *b:* 14.9.1885, Dartford, Kent. *d:* 11.5.1969, Poole, Dorset. Middle order batsman. *Sch* Wellington. *Team* MCC (1905–07).
Career batting
7–12–1–125–26–11.36–0–*ct* 6
Bowling 44–2–22.00–0–0–1/9

Light, Elisha Edward
Professional. *b:* 1.9.1873, Winchester, Hants. *d:* 12.3.1952, Llanelly, Carmarthenshire. Brother of W. F. (Hants). Lower order left-hand batsman, slow left-arm bowler. *Team* Hampshire (1898–1900, 13 matches).
Career batting
13–22–6–168–35–10.50–0–*ct* 6
Bowling 263–5–52.60–0–0–2/22

He also played for Carmarthenshire.

Light, William Frederick
Professional. *b:* 1.3.1880, St Faiths, Hants. *d:* 10.11.1930, Exeter. Brother of E. E. (Hants). Lower order left-hand batsman, left-arm medium pace bowler. *Team* Hampshire (1897–98, 12 matches).
Career batting
12–19–2–101–41–5.94–0–*ct* 9
Bowling 343–10–34.30–0–0–3/32

He also played for Devon.

Lightfoot, Albert
Professional. *b:* 8.1.1936, Woore, Salop. Middle order left-hand batsman, right-arm medium pace bowler. *Team* Northants (1953–70, 290 matches).
Career batting
294–495–61–12000–174*–27.64–12–*ct* 161
Bowling 6192–172–36.00–4–0–7/25

He hit 1,000 runs in a season four times (best 1,878, av 41.73, in 1962). With R. Subba Row he created a new Northants partnership record by adding 376 for the 6th wicket v Surrey at the Oval in 1958.

Lilford, Lord John
(originally John Powys, succeeded as 5th Baron in 1882)
Amateur. *b:* 12.1.1863, Lilford-cum-Wigsthorpe, Northants. *d:* 17.12.1945, Kettering, Northants. *Sch* Harrow. *Team* Northants (1911, 1 match).
Career batting
1–1–0–4–4–4.00–0–*ct* 0

President of Northants CCC from 1904 to 1921 and a member of the County Committee until 1936, Lord Lilford was the major benefactor of the County Club in its early years in first-class cricket. Although a very moderate player himself he was invited to play for Northants v Indians in 1911, in appreciation of his work for the County.

Lillee, Dennis Keith
Cricketer. *b:* 18.7.1949, Subiaco, Western Australia. Lower order right-hand batsman, right-arm fast bowler. *Teams* Western Australia (1969/70 to 1982/3, 68 matches). *Tours* Australia to New Zealand 1969/70, 1976/7, 1981/2, to England 1972, 1975, 1980, 1981, to West Indies 1972/3, to Pakistan 1979/80, to Sri Lanka 1982/3; International Wanderers to South Africa 1975/6. *Tests* Australia (1970/1 to 1982/3, 65 matches).
Career batting
171–210–61–2134–73*–14.32–0–*ct* 57
Bowling 17804–786–22.65–46–13–8/29
Test batting
65–86–22–874–73*–13.65–0–*ct* 21
Bowling 7860–335–23.46–22–7–7/83

The outstanding fast bowler of his generation, he has taken more wickets in Test cricket than any other bowler, despite missing several series whilst he played for Packer's World Series Cricket.

He headed the Test bowling averages on his first tour to England in 1972 with 31 wickets, av 17.67, and also took most wickets in first-class matches: 53, av 22.58. In 1975 he was again the principal wicket taker with 21, av 21.90, in Tests and 41, av 21.60, in all first-class matches. On his 1981 visit he took 39 wickets, av 22.30, in the Tests and 47, av 21.87, in first-class matches.

Lilley, Arthur Frederick Augustus
Professional. *b:* 28.11.1866, Holloway Head, Birmingham. *d:* 17.11.1929, Brislington, Bristol. Middle order right-hand batsman, wicket-keeper, occasional right-arm medium pace bowler. *Teams* Warwickshire (1894–1911, 321 matches); London County (1900–01). *Tours* MacLaren to Australia 1901/2; MCC to Australia 1903/4. *Tests* England (1896–1909, 35 matches).
Career batting
416–639–46–15597–171–26.30–16–*ct* 717–*st* 194
Bowling 1485–41–36.21–1–0–6/46
Test batting
35–52–8–903–84–20.52–0–*ct* 70–*st* 22
Bowling 23–1–23.00–0–0–1/23

He hit 1,000 runs in a season three times (best 1,399, av 34.97, in 1895). His first-class debut was for North v South at Edgbaston in 1891.

He was for some ten years regarded as the best wicket-keeper in England.

Lilley, Alan William
Cricketer. *b:* 8.5.1959, Ilford, Essex. Middle order right-hand batsman, wicket-keeper. *Team* Essex (1978–83, 30 matches).
Career batting
30–48–2–1175–100*–25.54–1–*ct* 16
Bowling 10–0

He hit 100* in the second innings on his first-class debut for Essex v Nottinghamshire at Trent Bridge in 1978.

Lilley, Ben
Professional. *b:* 11.2.1895, Kimberley, Notts. *d:* 4.8.1950, Nottingham. Middle order right-hand batsman, wicket-keeper. *Team* Nottinghamshire (1921–37, 369 matches). *Tour* Cahn to Jamaica 1928/9.
Career batting
373–513–79–10496–124–24.18–7–*ct* 657–*st* 132
Bowling 27–0

He hit 1,000 runs in a season twice (best 1,074, av 27.53, in 1928).

Lillington, George
Amateur. Lower order batsman, wicket-keeper. *Team* Somerset (1883–85, 2 matches).
Career batting
2–3–1–2–1*–1.00–0–*ct* 3–*st* 3

Lillywhite, Frederick William
Professional. *b:* 13.6.1792, Westhampnett, Sussex. *d:* 21.8.1854, Islington, Middlesex. He died of cholera. Father of Frederick (Cricket reporter), John (Middlesex and Sussex) and James (Middlesex and Sussex), uncle of James, jun (Sussex). Lower order right-hand batsman, right-hand slow medium round-arm bowler. *Teams* Sussex (1825–53, 70 matches); Middlesex (1850–51, 3 matches); Surrey (1829, 2 matches); Hampshire (1842–45, 3 matches).
Career batting
245–416–93–2350–44*–7.27–0–*ct* 140
Bowling 2342–215+1355–10.89–154–54–10/?

He was regarded as one of the leading bowlers of his day, though he did not appear in important matches until he was over 30.

He took 100 wickets in a season four times (best 115 wickets, in 1844). He took ten wickets in an innings for Players v 18 Gentlemen at Lords in 1837.

Lillywhite, James, sen
Professional. *b:* 29.10.1825, Hove, Sussex. *d* 24.11.1882, Cheltenham, Gloucs. Son of F. W. (Sussex and Middlesex), brother of John (Sussex and Middlesex), cousin of James, jun (Sussex). Lower order right-hand batsman, right-hand medium pace round-arm bowler. *Teams* Sussex (1850–60, 18 matches); Middlesex (1851, 2 matches).
Career batting
20–33–6–169–33–6.25–0–*ct* 11
Bowling 324–21+10–15.42–0–0–3/11

He was the senior partner in the London sporting firm of James Lillywhite, Frowd and Co of the Haymarket.

Lillywhite, James, jun
Professional. *b:* 23.2.1842, Westhampnett, Sussex. *d:* 25.10.1929, Westerton, Chichester, Sussex. Nephew of F. W. (Middlesex and Sussex), cousin of James (Sussex) and John (Sussex and Middlesex). Lower order left-hand batsman, slow medium left-arm bowler. *Teams* Sussex (1862–83, 157 matches). *Tours* Willsher to North America 1868 (non-first-class); Grace to Australia 1873/4 (non-first-class); Lillywhite to Australia 1876/7; Lillywhite, Shaw and Shrewsbury to Australia 1881/2, 1884/5, 1886/7 (did not play in first-class matches on these 3 tours). *Tests* England (1876/7, 2 matches).
Career batting
256–445–59–5523–126*–14.30–2–*ct* 109
Bowling 18436–1210–15.23–96–22–10/129
Test batting
2–3–1–16–10–8.00–0–*ct* 1
Bowling 126–8–15.75–0–0–4/70

He took 100 wickets in a season once : 110, av 13.34, in 1873.

He took 10 wickets in an innings (for 129) for South v North at Canterbury in 1872. He also took 9 for 29 on his first-class debut for Sussex v MCC at Lord's in 1862.

He captained England in the first two Test matches.

His final first-class match was for Lord Sheffield's XI in 1885.

Lillywhite, John
Professional. *b:* 10.11.1826, Hove, Sussex. *d:* 27.10.1874, Euston Sq, St Pancras, London. Son of F. W. (Sussex and Middlesex), brother of James sen (Sussex and Middlesex), cousin of James jun (Sussex). Middle order right-hand batsman, originally right-hand fast round-arm, but latterly slow bowler. *Teams* Sussex (1850–69, 100 matches); Middlesex (1851–64, 6 matches).
Career batting
185–323–29–5127–138–17.43–2–*ct* 94
Bowling 2402–210+131–11.43–12–2–8/54

His final first-class match was for W.G. Grace's XI v Kent in 1873; his first-class debut having been for Manchester in 1848.

Limb, Thomas
Professional. *b:* 25.2.1850, Eastwood, Notts. *d:* 21.2.1901, Eastwood, Notts. Lower order right-hand batsman, right-hand medium pace round-arm bowler. *Team* Derbyshire (1878, 1 match).
Career batting
1–2–0–0–0–0.00–0–*ct* 0

Limbdi, Kumar Shri Ghanshyamshinhji Daulatsinhji Jhalla
Amateur. *b:* 23.10.1902, Limbdi, India. Brother-in-law of Maharaja of Porbandar (India). Middle order right-hand bat. *Sch* The Leys. *Team* Western Indian States (1932/3 to 1942/3). *Tour* India to England 1932.
Career batting
19–31–2–505–57–17.41–0–*ct* 11

He was vice-captain of the 1932 Indian touring team, but found batting in England not easy. His first-class debut was for Rest of India in 1930/1.

Linaker, Lewis
Professional. *b:* 8.4.1885, Huddersfield, Yorkshire. *d:* 17.11.1961, Huddersfield, Yorkshire. Lower order batsman, useful bowler. *Team* Yorkshire (1909, 1 match).
Career batting
1–2–0–0–0–0.00–0–*ct* 0
Bowling 28–1–28.00–0–0–1/28

Linathan, Douglas Valentine
Professional. *b:* 29.5.1885, Woodhouse, Sheffield, Yorkshire. *d:* 17.12.1932, Derby. Middle/lower order left-hand batsman, slow left-arm bowler. *Team* Derbyshire (1920, 3 matches).
Career batting
3–6–1–35–14*–7.00–0–*ct* 2
Bowling 78–1–78.00–0–0–1/15

Lindley, Leonard Oscroft
Amateur. *b:* 22.2.1861, Nottingham. *d:* 3.5.1915, King's Norton, Warwickshire. Brother of Tinsley (Notts). Middle order batsman. *Sch* Nottingham High School. *Team* North (1884).
Career batting
2–3–0–28–22–9.33–0–*ct* 2

Lindley, Tinsley
Amateur. *b:* 27.10.1865, Nottingham. *d:* 31.3.1940, Nottingham. Brother of L. O. (North). Middle order right-hand batsman, right-arm slow medium bowler. *Sch* The Leys and Nottingham High School. *Teams* Cambridge U (1885); Nottinghamshire (1888, 4 matches).
Career batting
10–16–1–150–40–10.00–0–*ct* 6
Bowling 220–9–24.44–0–0–3/44

His final first-class match was for Oxford and Cambridge (Past and Present) v Australians in 1893.

A noted soccer player, he appeared as centre forward for Nottingham Forest, Cambridge U, and England. He also represented Notts at rugby football.

Lindo, Cleveland Vincent
Professional. *b:* 6.6.1936, St Elizabeth County, Jamaica. Lower order right-hand batsman, right-arm fast bowler. *Teams* Nottinghamshire (1960, 1 match); Somerset (1963, 1 match).
Career batting
2–3–1–65–24–32.50–0–*ct* 0
Bowling 162–8–20.25–1–0–8/88
He also played for Staffordshire.

Lindop, Hubert Harry
Amateur. *b:* 21.8.1907, Walsall, Staffordshire. *d:* 30.5.1982, Stafford. Opening/middle order batsman. *Sch* Rossall. *Team* MCC (1936).
Career batting
1–2–1–25–19*–25.00–0–*ct* 0
His County cricket was for Staffordshire.

Lindsay, Alexander
Amateur. *b:* 13.2.1883, Broughty Ferry, Angus, Scotland. *d:* 26.1.1941, Dundee, Scotland. Middle order right-hand batsman, leg break and googly bowler. *Sch* Fettes. *Team* Scotland (1909).
Career batting
1–2–0–7–7–3.50–0–*ct* 1
Bowling 6–0

Lindsay, Denis Thomson
Amateur. *b:* 4.9.1939, Benoni, South Africa. Son of J. D. (South Africa), grandson of N. V. (South Africa). Middle order right-hand batsman, wicket-keeper. *Team* North East Transvaal (1958/9 to 1973/4). *Tours* SA Fezela to England 1961; South Africa to England 1965, to Australia and New Zealand 1963/4; Rest of World XI to England 1967 and 1968. *Tests* South Africa (1963/4 to 1969/70, 19 matches).
Career batting
124–214–15–7074–216–35.54–12–*ct* 292–*st* 41
Bowling 14–0
Test batting
19–31–1–1130–182–37.66–3–*ct* 57–*st* 2
The principal wicket-keeper on the 1965 tour to England, he appeared in all three of the Tests.
In the match between Fezela XI and Essex at Chelmsford in 1961 he hit five sixes off consecutive balls to end the match. His highest score was 216 for NE Transvaal v Transvaal 'B' at Johannesburg in 1966/7.
He hit 1,014 runs in the 1966/7 South African season.

Lindsay, John Dixon
Amateur. *b:* 8.9.1909, Barkly East, South Africa. Son of N. V. (South Africa), father of D. T. (South Africa). Lower order right-hand batsman, wicket-keeper. *Teams* Transvaal (1933/4 to 1936/7); NE Transvaal (1937/8 to 1948/9). *Tour* South Africa to England 1947. *Tests* South Africa (1947, 3 matches).
Career batting
29–45–14–346–51–11.16–0–*ct* 39–*st* 16
Test batting
3–5–2–21–9*–7.00–0–*ct* 4–*st* 1
He began the 1947 tour as the principal wicket-keeper but lost his place after the third Test to Fullerton.
He played football for Huddersfield Town.

Lindsay, William
Amateur. *b:* 3.8.1847, India. *d:* 15.2.1923, Rochester, Kent. Stylish middle order right-hand batsman, excellent cover field. *Sch* Winchester. *Team* Surrey (1876–82, 33 matches).
Career batting
33–62–5–987–74–17.31–0–*ct* 17
He also played for Devonshire.
An excellent soccer player, he represented England as full back and was in the winning FA Cup side three years in succession for Wanderers.

Lindsay, Sir William O'Brien
Amateur. *b:* 8.10.1909, Canterbury, Kent. *d:* 20.10.1975, Nairobi, Kenya. Determined opening right-hand batsman, wicket-keeper. *Sch* Harrow. *Teams* Oxford U (1929–32, blue 1931); Kent (1931, 2 matches); Scotland (1929).
Career batting
17–28–1–531–63–19.66–0–*ct* 10–*st* 2
Bowling 18–0
He had a distinguished career in the Sudan, becoming Chief Justice.

Lindsey, Peter John
Professional. *b:* 29.5.1944, Matlock, Derbyshire. Tail end right-hand batsman, off break bowler, outfield. *Team* Essex (1964, 1 match).
Career batting
1–1–1–7–7*–no av–0–*ct* 0
Bowling 50–1–50.00–0–0–1/8

Lindwall, Raymond Russell
Amateur. *b:* 3.10.1921, Mascot, New South Wales, Australia. Hard hitting lower order right-hand batsman, brilliant right-arm fast bowler. *Teams* New South Wales (1941/2 to 1953/4, 50 matches); Queensland (1954/5 to 1959/60, 34 matches). *Tours* Australia to England 1948, 1953, 1956, to South Africa 1949/50, to West Indies 1954/5, to New Zealand 1945/6, to Pakistan and India 1956/7, 1959/60; Swanton to West Indies 1960/1; Commonwealth to Rhodesia, India and Pakistan 1961/2. *Tests* Australia (1945/6 to 1959/60, 61 matches)

Career batting
228–270–39–5042–134*–21.82–5–*ct* 123
Bowling 16956–794–21.35–34–2–7/20
Test batting
61–84–13–1502–118–21.15–2–*ct* 26
Bowling 5251–228–23.03–12–0–7/38

The outstanding fast bowler of the decade immediately following the Second World War, he headed both the Test and first-class bowling averages on both the 1948 and 1953 tours to England. In 1948 he took 86 wickets, av 15.68, and in 1953, 85 wickets, av 16.40, his figures in the two Test series being 27, av 19.62, and 26, av 18.84, respectively. He captained Australia in one Test v India in 1956/7.

Lineham, Edwin
Amateur. *b:* 1879, Portsmouth, Hants. *d:* 12.8.1949, Portsmouth, Hants. Middle order batsman. *Team* Hampshire (1898, 1 match).
Career batting
1–2–1–0–0*–0.00–0–*ct* 0

His name was incorrectly given as 'Lynam' in the printed scores of his only first-class match.

Linehan, Alphonsus James
Cricketer. *b:* 20.4.1940, Dublin, Ireland. Middle order right-hand batsman. *Team* Ireland (1972–74).
Career batting
2–4–0–29–16–7.25–0–*ct* 2

Lines, Steven John
Cricketer. *b:* 16.3.1963, Luton, Bedfordshire. Right-hand batsman, right-arm medium pace bowler. *Team* Northants (1983, 1 match). *Tour* Minor Counties to East Africa 1982/3 (not first-class).
Career batting
1–1–0–29–29–29.00–0–*ct* 1

He also played for Bedfordshire commencing 1980.

Ling, Anthony John Patrick
Amateur. *b:* 10.8.1910, Skewen, Glamorgan. Middle order left-hand batsman. *Sch* Stowe. *Teams* Glamorgan (1934–36, 9 matches); Somerset (1939, 5 matches).
Career batting
14–19–3–256–41*–16.00–0–*ct* 2
Bowling 12–0

He also played for Wiltshire.

Ling, David John
Cricketer. *b:* 2.7.1946, Enfield, Middlesex. Middle order right-hand batsman, right-arm medium pace bowler. *Team* Middlesex (1966–68, 14 matches).
Career batting
14–15–3–174–40–14.50–0–*ct* 6
Bowling 386–7–55.14–0–0–3/24

Linnell, Herbert James
Amateur. *b:* 7.3.1909, Paddington, London. *d:* 8.2.1968, Sturry, Canterbury, Kent. Aggressive middle order right-hand batsman, right-arm fast bowler. *Sch* St Lawrence, Ramsgate. *Team* Oxford U (1929–32).
Career batting
4–6–0–34–11–5.66–0–*ct* 3
Bowling 310–8–38.75–0–0–4/57

Linnell, Michael Gerald
Amateur. *b:* 13.1.1876, Reigate, Surrey. *d:* 2.8.1959, Salisbury, Rhodesia. Lower order right-hand batsman, right-arm medium fast bowler. *Sch* St Lawrence, Ramsgate. *Teams* Rhodesia (1904/5); H. D. G. Leveson-Gower's XI (1909).
Career batting
2–4–1–36–15–12.00–0–*ct* 1
Bowling 33–0

Linney, Charles Keith
Professional. *b:* 26.8.1912, Hobart, Tasmania. Son of G. F. (Tasmania). Middle order left-hand batsman, left-arm medium pace bowler. *Team* Somerset (1931–37, 32 matches).
Career batting
32–49–9–576–60–14.40–0–*ct* 9
Bowling 119–2–59.50–0–0–1/9

Linton, James Edward Fryer
Amateur. *b:* 7.5.1909, Llandaff, Glamorgan. Middle order right-hand batsman, right-arm medium fast bowler. *Sch* Charterhouse. *Team* Glamorgan (1932, 2 matches).
Career batting
2–4–0–3–2–0.75–0–*ct* 0
Bowling 82–1–82.00–0–0–1/34

Lipscomb, Frank
Amateur. *b:* 13.3.1863, East Peckham, Kent. *d:* 25.9.1951, Randwick, New South Wales, Australia. Son of Robert (Kent). Hard hitting lower order right-hand batsman, right-arm fast bowler. *Team* Kent (1882–84, 16 matches).
Career batting
18–31–5–158–28–6.07–0–*ct* 8
Bowling 1178–52–22.65–1–0–5/19

He emigrated to Australia after the 1884 season and therefore did not again appear in County cricket.

Lipscomb, Francis Wallis
Amateur. *b:* 20.7.1834. *d:* 3.10.1906, Southsea, Hants. Middle order right-hand batsman, slow

round-arm bowler. *Team* Hampshire (1881–82, 3 matches).
Career batting
5–9–1–121–53–15.12–0–*ct* 2
Bowling 103–2–51.50–0–0–2/46
His first first-class match was for Gentlemen of England in 1857.

Lipscomb, Robert
Amateur. *b:* 28.2.1837, Penshurst, Kent. *d:* 8.1.1895, Tudeley, Kent. Father of Frank (Kent). Lower order right-hand batsman, right-hand fast round-arm bowler, good slip. *Team* Kent (1862–73, 48 matches).
Career batting
60–105–19–428–22–4.97–0–*ct* 23
Bowling 4608–271–17.00–19–3–9/88
His best bowling was 9 for 88 for Kent v MCC at Lord's in 1871.

Lipscomb, William Henry
Amateur. *b:* 20.11.1846, Winchester, Hants. *d:* 9.4.1918, Clapham, South London. Lower order right-hand batsman, right-hand medium pace round-arm bowler, good close field. *Sch* Marlborough. *Teams* Hampshire (1866–67, 4 matches); Oxford U (1868, blue).
Career batting
7–13–2–154–34–14.00–0–*ct* 3
Bowling 100–3–33.33–0–0–2/26
He was a noted oarsman.

Lister, Benjamin
Professional. *b:* 9.12.1850, Birkenshaw, Yorkshire. *b:* 3.12.1919, Bradford, Yorkshire. Lower order right-hand batsman, wicket-keeper. *Team* Yorkshire (1874–78, 6 matches).
Career batting
7–12–2–46–19*–4.60–0–*ct* 2
Although paid to play in County cricket, he did not accept engagements as a professional.

Lister, Derek John
Amateur. *b:* 25.8.1930, Salisbury, Wiltshire. Middle order right-hand batsman. *Sch* Cranleigh. *Team* Cambridge U (1954).
Career batting
1–2–0–35–31–17.50–0–*ct* 0
He played for Wiltshire.

Lister, Joseph
Amateur. *b:* 14.5.1930, Thirsk, Yorkshire. Middle order right-hand batsman. *Sch* Cheltenham. *Teams* Yorkshire (1954, 2 matches); Worcestershire (1954–59, 21 matches).
Career batting
24–43–4–796–99–20.41–0–*ct* 14
His first-class debut was for Combined Services in 1951. He appeared for both Yorkshire and Worcestershire in 1954.
He was Secretary of Worcestershire CCC until 1971 and in 1972 was appointed Secretary to Yorkshire CCC.
He also played hockey for Yorkshire.

Lister, John Wilton
Cricketer. *b:* 1.4.1959, Darlington, Co Durham. Opening right-hand batsman. *Team* Derbyshire (1978–79, 5 matches).
Career batting
5–10–0–205–48–20.50–0–*ct* 1
He played for Durham in 1983.

Lister, William Hubert Lionel
Amateur. *b:* 11.10.1911, Formby, Lancashire. Middle order right-hand batsman. *Sch* Malvern. *Teams* Cambridge U (1933); Lancashire (1933–39, 158 matches).
Career batting
162–218–17–3709–104*–18.45–2–*ct* 73–*st* 2
Bowling 87–1–87.00–0–0–1/10
He captained Lancashire from 1936 to 1939.
A noted soccer half back, he appeared for Cambridge and for England in Amateur Internationals.

Lister-Kaye, Sir Kenelm Arthur
Amateur. *b:* 27.3.1892, Kensington, London. *d:* 28.2.1955, Cape Town, South Africa. Lower order right-hand batsman, left-arm medium pace bowler. *Sch* Eton. *Teams* Oxford U (1912); Yorkshire (1928, 2 matches); Europeans (1920/1 to 1922/3).
Career batting
12–18–5–149–35–11.45–0–*ct* 8
Bowling 966–37–26.10–2–1–7/118

Lithgow, William Samuel Plenderleath
Amateur. *b:* 18.2.1920, London. Sound middle order right-hand batsman, off break bowler, good field. *Sch* Harrow. *Team* Oxford U (1939).
Career batting
3–5–1–69–27–17.25–0–*ct* 2
His County cricket was for Oxfordshire.

Litteljohn, Dr Arthur Rieusett
Amateur. *b:* 1.4.1881, Hanwell, Middlesex. *d:* 8.12.1919, London. Brother of E. S. (Middlesex). Middle order right-hand batsman, right-arm slow medium leg break bowler. *Sch* St. Paul's. *Team* Middlesex (1905–14, 31 matches).
Career batting
33–45–8–683–76*–18.45–0–*ct* 15
Bowling 1798–86–20.83–7–2–8/69
Owing to his profession his first-class cricket was very limited.

Litteljohn, Dr Edward Salterne
Amateur. *b:* 24.9.1878, Hanwell, Middlesex. *d:* 22.1.1955, Beaconsfield, Bucks. Brother of A. R. (Middlesex). Middle order right-hand batsman. *Sch* St. Paul's. *Team* Middlesex (1900–14, 74 matches).
Career batting
74–120–9–2832–141*–25.51–5–*ct* 34
Bowling 25–1–25.00–0–0–1/11

Little, Charles William
Amateur. *b:* 22.5.1870, Tonbridge, Kent. *d:* 20.5.1922, Winchester, Hants. Lower order right-hand batsman, wicket-keeper. *Sch* Winchester. *Teams* Kent (1893, 5 matches); Oxford U (1890).
Career batting
11–16–1–160–28–10.66–0–*ct* 16–*st* 2
He also played for Shropshire.

Littlehales, Rev Charles Gough
Amateur. *b:* 20.5.1871, Bulphan, Essex. *d:* 28.8.1945, Wickham Bishops, Essex. Lower order right-hand batsman, wicket-keeper. *Sch* Forest School. *Teams* Essex (1896–1904, 6 matches).
Career batting
6–10–1–109–23–12.11–0–*ct* 4–*st* 1
He did not play in any first-class matches whilst at Oxford U.

Littlewood, David John
Cricketer. *b:* 28.10.1955, Holloway, London. Lower order right-hand batsman, wicket-keeper. *Sch* Enfield GS. *Team* Cambridge U (1977–78, blue 1978).
Career batting
10–10–3–95–51–13.57–0–*ct* 12–*st* 6

Littlewood, George Hubert
Professional. *b:* 12.5.1882, Friarmere, Yorkshire. *d:* 20.12.1917, Oldham, Lancashire. Son of G. W. (Lancashire). Lower order batsman, slow left-arm bowler. *Team* Lancashire (1902–04, 14 matches).
Career batting
14–19–5–129–42–9.14–0–*ct* 12
Bowling 1123–58–19.32–5–1–7/49

Littlewood, George William
Professional. *b:* 10.5.1857, Holmfirth, Huddersfield, Yorkshire. *d:* 5.3.1928, Oldham, Lancashire. Father of G. H. (Lancashire). Lower order right-hand batsman, wicket-keeper. *Team* Lancashire (1885, 3 matches).
Career batting
3–6–1–28–8*–5.60–0–*ct* 4–*st* 3

Littlewood, Herbert Dell
(changed name to Littlewood-Clarke in 1894)
Amateur. *b:* 18.12.1858, Macclesfield, Cheshire. *b:* 31.12.1925, Ramsgate, Kent. Middle order right-hand batsman, deep field. *Team* MCC (1887–96).
Career batting
5–10–1–86–35–9.55–0–*ct* 1
His County cricket was for Cheshire commencing 1888.

Littlewood, Jesse
Professional. *b:* 8.4.1878, Yorkshire. *d:* 27.10.1942, Kidderminster, Worcs. Tail end batsman, bowler. *Team* Essex (1905, 1 match).
Career batting
1–1–1–5–5*–no av–0–*ct* 1
Bowling 36–0

Littlewood, John
Professional. *b:* 12.5.1852, Scissett, Huddersfield, Yorkshire. *d:* 22.3.1932, Harrogate, Yorkshire. Lower order left-hand batsman, slow left-arm bowler. *Team* An England XI (1888).
Career batting
1–2–2–2–2*–no av–0–*ct* 1
Bowling 14–0

Livesay, Brig-Gen Robert O'Hara
Amateur. *b:* 27.6.1876, Old Brompton, London. *d:* 23.3.1946, Magham Down, Sussex. Attractive middle order right-hand batsman, right-hand medium bowler, good field. *Sch* Wellington. *Team* Kent (1895–1904, 26 matches).
Career batting
26–46–3–986–78–22.93–0–*ct* 8
Bowling 7–0
A noted rugby footballer, he appeared as a half back for Blackheath and England.

Livingston, Leonard
Professional. *b:* 3.5.1920, Sydney, New South Wales, Australia. Forcing middle order left-hand batsman, slow left-arm bowler, occasional wicket-keeper, excellent cover field. *Teams* New South Wales (1941/2 to 1946/7, 5 matches); Northants (1950–57, 198 matches). *Tours* Commonwealth to India, Pakistan and Ceylon 1949/50; Howard to India 1956/7.
Career batting
236–384–45–15260–210–45.01–34–*ct* 148–*st* 23
Bowling 50–4–12.50–0–0–2/22
He hit 1,000 runs in a season seven times, going on to 2,000 three times (best 2,269, av 55.34, in 1954). He also hit 1,000 on the 1949/50 tour. His four double centuries were all for Northants,

the highest being 210 v Somerset at Weston-super-Mare in 1951. His final first-class match was for MCC in 1964.

Livingstone, David
Amateur. *b:* 23.2.1927, Glasgow, Scotland. Lower order right-hand batsman, off break bowler. *Team* Scotland (1957–66).
Career batting
18–26–10–102–16*–6.37–0–*ct* 5
Bowling 1255–50–25.10–4–1–6/33

Livingstone, Daintes Abbia
Professional. *b:* 21.9.1933, St John's, Antigua, West Indies. Middle order left-hand batsman, right-arm medium pace bowler, good slip field. *Team* Hampshire (1959–72, 299 matches).
Career batting
301–519–63–12722–200–27.89–16–*ct* 243–*st* 2
Bowling 93–1–93.00–0–0–1/31

He hit 1,000 runs in a season six times (best 1,817, av 37.08, in 1962); his only double century was 200 for Hants v Surrey (Southampton) 1962, when he shared in a County 9th wicket record partnership of 230 with A. T. Castell.

Livock, Gerald Edward
Amateur. *b:* 11.7.1897, Newmarket, Suffolk. Lower order right-hand batsman, wicket-keeper. *Sch* Cheltenham. *Team* Middlesex (1925–27, 5 matches). *Tour* Martineau to Egypt 1934 (not first-class).
Career batting
13–20–4–403–65–25.18–0–*ct* 19–*st* 5

His first-class debut was for Lord Cowdray's XI at Hastings in 1923 and his final first-class match for Gentlemen of England in 1934.

He also played for Cambridgeshire.

Livock, Michael Denzil
Amateur. *b:* 26.7.1936, Surbiton, Surrey. Lower order right-hand batsman, right-arm fast bowler. *Sch* Charterhouse. *Team* Free Foresters (1960).
Career batting
2–2–0–21–16–10.50–0–*ct* 1
Bowling 235–8–29.37–0–0–4/71

Livsey, Walter Herbert
Professional. *b:* 23.9.1893, Todmorden, Yorkshire. *d:* 12.9.1978, Merton Park, London. Lower order right-hand batsman, wicket-keeper. *Teams* Hampshire (1913–29, 309 matches); England XI in India (1915/6 to 1918/19); Cooch Behar's XI (1917/18). *Tour* MCC to South Africa 1922/3 (he did not play in any first-class matches owing to injury).
Career batting
320–455–137–4940–110*–15.53–2–*ct* 384–*st* 265

He was to a large extent responsible for the incredible recovery by Hampshire against Warwickshire at Edgbaston in 1922. Hampshire were dismissed for 15 in their first innings and were 186 for 6 having followed on. Livsey came in at number ten and hit 110*, adding 177 for the 9th wicket and then 70 for the 10th wicket; eventually Hampshire won the game by 155 runs.

Llewellyn, Charles Bennett
Professional. *b:* 26.9.1876, Pietermaritzburg, South Africa. *d:* 7.6.1964, Chertsey, Surrey. Attacking middle order left-hand batsman, left-arm slow medium bowler, excellent mid off. *Teams* Natal (1894/5 to 1897/8); Hampshire (1899–1910, 196 matches); London County (1901–03). *Tours* South Africa to England 1904, 1912, to Australia 1910/11; Ranjitsinhji to North America 1899. *Tests* South Africa (1895/6 to 1912, 15 matches).
Career batting
267–461–34–11425–216–26.75–18–*ct* 175
Bowling 23715–1013–23.41–82–20–9/55
Test batting
15–28–1–544–90–20.14–0–*ct* 7
Bowling 1421–48–29.60–4–1–6/92

He hit 1,000 runs in a season six times (best 1,347, av 28.06, in 1908) and took 100 wickets in a season four times (best 170, av 18.61, in 1902). In 1901, 1908 and 1910 he achieved the 'double'.

His only double century was 216 for Hampshire v South Africans at Southampton in 1901. His best bowling was 9/55 for London County v Cambridge U at Crystal Palace in 1902.

He left Hampshire due to a disagreement over terms and after touring Australia with the 1910/11 South Africans came back to play League cricket in England. He was co-opted into the South African side in England in 1912, playing in five Tests and one other first-class match.

Llewellyn, Michael John
Cricketer. *b*: 27.11.1953, Clydach, Glamorgan. Hard hitting middle order left-hand batsman, off break bowler. *Team* Glamorgan (1970–82, 136 matches).
Career batting
136–215–30–4288–129*–23.17–3–*ct* 87
Bowling 615–23–26.73–0–0–4/35

Llewelyn, William Dillwyn
(also known as Dillwyn-Llewelyn)
Amateur. *b:* 1.4.1868, Ynisygerwn, Glamorgan. *d:* 24.8.1893, Penllergaer, Swansea. He died as the result of a shooting accident. Middle order right-hand batsman, right-arm fast medium bowler. *Sch* Eton. *Team* Oxford U (1890–91, blue both years).

Career batting
20–39–2–834–116–22.54–1–*ct* 15
Bowling 44–0

He played for Glamorgan (pre-first-class).

His final first-class match was for MCC in 1893.

Lloyd, Barry John
Cricketer. *b*: 6.9.1953, Neath, Glamorgan. Lower order right-hand batsman, off break bowler. *Team* Glamorgan (1972–83, 147 matches).
Career batting
147–184–47–1631–48–11.90–0–*ct* 87
Bowling 10133–247–41.02–3–0–8/70

Lloyd, Clive Hubert
Cricketer. *b*: 31.8.1944, Queenstown, Georgetown, British Guiana. Cousin of L.R. Gibbs (West Indies). Excellent middle order left-hand batsman, right-arm medium pace bowler, good outfield. *Teams* British Guiana/Guyana (1963/4 to 1982/3); Lancashire (1968–83, 250 matches). *Tours* West Indies to India and Ceylon 1966/7, to Australia and New Zealand 1968/9, 1979/80, to England 1969, 1973, 1976, 1980, to Sri Lanka, India and Pakistan 1974/5, to Australia 1975/6, 1981/2, to Pakistan 1980/1; Rest of World to Pakistan 1970/1, 1973/4, to Australia 1971/2. *Tests* West Indies (1966/7 to 1982/3, 90 matches).
Career batting
447–674–87–28660–242*–48.82–74–*ct* 345
Bowling 4104–114–36.00–0–0–4/48
Test batting
90–149–10–6238–242*–44.87–16–*ct* 68
Bowling 622–10–62.20–0–0–2/13

By the end of the 1982/3 Test series he had captained West Indies in no less than 54 Tests – a record for any Test captain – and for almost twenty years he has been one of the leading batsman in the world, despite a knee injury which has threatened to end his career on several occasions.

His four tours with the West Indies team in England have all seen him in excellent form, his best record being on the 1976 tour with 1,363 runs, av 61.95. He played in all Tests on each tour except in 1980 when he missed one match through injury. He captained the tourists both in 1976 and 1980. On his Test debut against England in 1966/7 and against Australia in 1968/9 he scored centuries. A leading member of Packer's World Series Cricket, he was at odds with the West Indian Board of Control in 1977/8 and missed several Tests as a consequence.

His first first-class match in England was for the Rest of the World in 1967. In all he has hit 1,000 runs in a season in England ten times, his best being 1,603, av 47.14, in 1970; in addition he reached 1,000 runs in four overseas seasons. His highest innings is 242* for West Indies v India at Bombay in 1974/5 and his highest in England 217* for Lancashire v Warwickshire at Old Trafford in 1971. He reached 200 in 120 minutes for West Indies v Glamorgan at Swansea in 1976 to equal G.L. Jessop's record for the fastest 200.

In 1981 he was appointed captain of Lancashire.

Lloyd, David
Cricketer. *b*: 18.3.1947, Accrington, Lancashire. Stylish opening or middle order left-hand batsman, slow left-arm bowler, excellent short leg field. *Team* Lancashire (1965–83, 370 matches). *Tours* MCC to Australia 1974/5; Robins to South Africa 1975/6. *Tests* England (1974 to 1974/5, 9 matches).
Career batting
407–652–74–19269–214*–33.33–38–*ct* 334
Bowling 7172–237–30.26–5–1–7/38
Test batting
9–15–2–552–214*–42.46–1–*ct* 11
Bowling 17–0

He hit 1,000 runs in a season eleven times (best 1,510, av 47.18, in 1972). His highest innings was 214* for England v India at Edgbaston in 1974. He was captain of Lancashire, 1973–77.

Lloyd, Edward Wynell Mayow
Amateur. *b:* 19.3.1845, Benares, India. *d:* 27.9.1928, Hartley Wintney, Hants. Middle order right-hand batsman. *Sch* Rugby. *Team* Cambridge U (1866–68).
Career batting
4–6–2–63–20*–15.75–0–*ct* 1

He played County cricket for Shropshire and Somerset (pre-first-class).

Lloyd, J. G.
Amateur. Middle order batsman. *Team* W.G. Grace's XI (1871).
Career batting
1–1–0–4–4–4.00–0–*ct* 1

Lloyd, John Maurice Edward
Amateur. *b:* 7.5.1844, Montgomery. *d:* 21.1.1910, Montgomery. Middle order batsman. *Sch* Marlborough. *Team* Oxford U (1866).
Career batting
1–1–0–6–6–6.00–0–*ct* 1

Lloyd, Martyn Frederick Dafydd
Cricketer. *b:* 6.6.1954, Oxford. Middle order right-hand batsman, occasional right-arm medium pace bowler. *Sch* Magdalen College School. *Team* Oxford U (1974–75, blue 1974).

Career batting
6–11–0–74–36–6.72–0–*ct* 2

His County cricket was for Oxfordshire, commencing 1974, and Dorset, commencing 1981.

Lloyd, Richard Averill
Amateur. *b:* 4.8.1891, Dungannon, Co Tyrone, Ireland. *d:* 23.12.1950, Belfast, Ireland. Middle order right-hand batsman. *Teams* Ireland (1911–12); Lancashire (1921–22, 3 matches).
Career batting
6–10–0–202–51–20.20–0–*ct* 5

He also played for Denbighshire.

A noted rugby footballer, he appeared at half back for Lancashire, Ulster and Ireland.

Lloyd, Timothy Andrew
Cricketer. *b*: 5.11.1956, Oswestry, Shropshire. Middle order left-hand batsman, right-arm medium pace bowler. *Teams* Warwickshire (1977–83, 128 matches); Orange Free State (1978/9 to 1979/80).
Career batting
138–244–28–7775–208*–35.99–13–*ct* 83
Bowling 699–8–87.37–0–0–2/29

He hit 1,000 runs in a season four times (best 1,673, av 45.21, in 1983). His only double century is 208* for Warwickshire v Gloucestershire at Edgbaston in 1983.

Lloyds, Jeremy William
Cricketer. *b*: 17.11.1954, Penang, Malaya. Middle order left-hand batsman, off break bowler. *Team* Somerset (1979–83, 80 matches).
Career batting
80–132–10–3224–132*–26.42–4–*ct* 62
Bowling 3937–119–33.08–6–1–7/88

Loader, Peter James
Professional. *b:* 25.10.1929, Wallington, Surrey. Lower order right-hand batsman, right-arm fast bowler. *Teams* Surrey (1951–63, 298 matches); Western Australia (1963/4, 1 match). *Tours* MCC to Australia and New Zealand 1954/5, 1958/9, to South Africa 1956/7; Commonwealth to India 1953/4, South Africa 1962/3; Surrey to Rhodesia 1959/60; Brown to East Africa 1961/2 (not first-class). *Tests* England (1954 to 1958/9, 13 matches).
Career batting
371–382–110–2314–81–8.50–0–*ct* 120
Bowling 25260–1326–19.04–70–13–9/17
Test batting
13–19–6–76–17–5.84–0–*ct* 2
Bowling 878–39–22.51–1–0–6/36

He took 100 wickets in a season seven times (best 133, av 15.47, in 1957). Twice he obtained nine wickets in an innings, his best being 9/17 for Surrey v Warwickshire at the Oval in 1958. He performed the hat-trick in the Headingley Test against the West Indies in 1957.

Lobb, Bryan
Professional. *b:* 11.1.1931, Birmingham. Tail end right-hand batsman, right-arm fast medium bowler. *Sch* KES, Birmingham. *Teams* Warwickshire (1953, 1 match); Somerset (1955–69, 115 matches).
Career batting
116–170–50–624–42–5.20–0–*ct* 24
Bowling 8760–370–23.67–15–2–7/43

He took 110 wickets, av 19.48, in 1957.

After 1958 he ceased to appear regularly in first-class cricket, having gone into the scholastic profession.

Lobban, H. W. Kenneth
Professional. *b:* 9.5.1924, Jamaica. Lower order right-hand batsman, right-arm fast bowler. *Team* Worcestershire (1952–54, 17 matches).
Career batting
17–23–11–81–18–6.75–0–*ct* 4
Bowling 1452–47–30.89–4–0–6/51

Lock, Bernard Henry
Amateur. *b:* 8.6.1915, Exeter. Middle order right-hand batsman, slip field. *Sch* Sherborne. *Team* Kent (1952, 1 match).
Career batting
2–4–0–69–57–17.25–0–*ct* 1

He also played for Devon.

His last first-class match was for MCC in 1955.

A good rugby footballer, he represented Exeter and Ulster.

Lock, Edward John
Amateur. *b:* 21.11.1868, Taunton, Somerset. *d:* 3.5.1949, Taunton, Somerset. Middle order batsman. *Team* Somerset (1891–93, 2 matches).
Career batting
2–4–1–16–10–5.33–0–*ct* 0

Lock, Graham Anthony Richard
Professional. *b:* 5.7.1929, Limpsfield, Surrey. Lower order right-hand batsman, brilliant slow medium left-arm bowler, excellent close field. *Teams* Surrey (1946–63, 385 matches); Leicestershire (1965–67, 65 matches); Western Australia (1962/3 to 1970/1, 74 matches). *Tours* MCC to West Indies 1953/4, 1967/8, to Pakistan 1955/6, to South Africa 1956/7, to Australia and New Zealand 1958/9, to India, Pakistan and Ceylon 1961/2; Surrey to Rhodesia 1959/60. *Tests* England (1952 to 1967/8, 49 matches).

Career batting
654–812–161–10342–89–15.88–9–*ct* 831
Bowling 54709–2844–19.23–196–50–10/54
Test batting
49–63–9–742–89–13.74–0–*ct* 59
Bowling 4451–174–25.58–9–3–7/35

The epitome of ebullience, Lock found great success with each of the four major sides for whom he played : England, Surrey, Western Australia and Leicestershire. Initially a slow bowler, he developed into almost medium pace about 1950, but this faster delivery led to his being called for 'throwing' and throughout the 1950s he was on the borderline between bowling and throwing, being no-balled several times by various umpires. He then reverted to his former slower style and during the last ten years of his first-class career was free from criticism.

He took 100 wickets in a season 14 times, going on to 200 twice, his best year being 1955 with 216 wickets, av 14.39. His most outstanding bowling performance was taking all ten wickets in an innings (for 54) for Surrey v Kent at Blackheath in 1956.

In 1962/3, when he was surprisingly omitted from the MCC team to tour Australia, he went to that country and played for Western Australia. In the opinion of many, his nine years with that State were the best of his career and he led them to the Sheffield Shield title. In 1965 he appeared for Leicestershire and the following two seasons captained that County, taking them to second place in the County Championship in 1967, the best season they had ever enjoyed to that date.

Lock, Herbert Christmas
Professional. *b:* 8.5.1903, East Molesey, Surrey. *d:* 19.5.1978, Honor Oak, London. Lower order right-hand batsman, right-arm medium pace bowler. *Team* Surrey (1926–32, 32 matches). *Tour* Tennyson to Jamaica 1926/7.
Career batting
35–31–9–93–20*–4.22–0–*ct* 10
Bowling 2658–81–32.81–0–0–4/34

After leaving the Surrey staff he played for Devon and his final first-class appearance was for the Minor Counties in 1935.

He was in later years the head groundsman at the Oval and Official Inspector of pitches for the TCCB.

Lock, Norman William
Professional. *b:* 13.3.1912, Ham Common, Surrey. Lower order right-hand batsman, right-arm medium pace bowler. *Team* Surrey (1934, 1 match).
Career batting
1–2–1–1–1–1.00–0–*ct* 0

Selected as scorer for Surrey, he played in emergency due to Sandham being taken ill just prior to the match.

Lock, Walter George
Amateur. *b:* 11.10.1907, Bristol. *d:* 10.3.1980, Taunton, Somerset. Middle order batsman. *Sch* Taunton. *Team* Somerset (1928, 1 match).
Career batting
1–1–0–2–2–2.00–0–*ct* 0

Locker, William
Professional. *b:* 16.2.1866, Long Eaton, Derbyshire. *d:* 15.8.1952, Derby. Opening right-hand batsman. *Team* Derbyshire (1894–1903, 16 matches).
Career batting
16–30–0–511–76–17.03–0–*ct* 4

A noted soccer player, he appeared for Notts County, taking part in the FA Cup final of 1891.

Lockett, Aaron
Professional. *b:* 1892, Newcastle-under-Lyme, Staffs. *d:* 10.2.1965, Bignall End, Staffs. Middle order right-hand batsman, right-arm bowler. *Team* Minor Counties (1928–29).
Career batting
2–4–1–197–154–65.66–1–*ct* 2
Bowling 71–2–35.50–0–0–1/14

His County cricket was for Staffordshire, but he was also a noted figure in the Central Lancashire League, appearing for Oldham for 12 years.

His first-class debut was for Minor Counties v West Indies at Exeter in 1928. The Minor Counties were made to follow on, being 181 behind on the first innings. Lockett hit a brilliant 154 in the second innings and Minor Counties went on to win the match.

An excellent inside forward, he played soccer for Port Vale and Stoke City.

Lockhart, J. H. B.
(*see under* Bruce-Lockhart, J. H.)

Lockhart, R. B. B.
(*see under* Bruce-Lockhart, R. B.)

Locks, George Melbourne
Amateur. *b:* 1898, Leytonstone, Essex. *d:* 17.9.1965, Redbridge, Essex. Lower order batsman, useful bowler. *Team* Essex (1928, 2 matches).
Career batting
2–4–2–5–3*–2.50–0–*ct* 0
Bowling 227–3–75.66–0–0–2/86

Lockton, John Henry
Amateur. *b:* 22.5.1892, Peckham, Surrey. *d:*

29.6.1972, Thornton Heath, Surrey. Attacking lower order right-hand batsman, right-arm fast medium bowler. *Sch* Dulwich. *Team* Surrey (1919–26, 32 matches).
Career batting
32–34–9–409–77*–16.36–0–*ct* 26
Bowling 2071–78–26.55–1–0–5/80

He represented London University at both cricket and soccer and went on to play soccer as inside forward for Nottingham Forest and Crystal Palace; later he became a noted soccer referee.

Lockwood, Arthur Leslie
Amateur. *b:* 1.4.1903, Romiley, Cheshire. *d:* 8.11.1933, Llandudno, Caernarvonshire. Lower order right-hand batsman, right-arm bowler. *Team* Wales (1926).
Career batting
1–1–0–5–5–5.00–0–*ct* 1
Bowling 84–1–84.00–0–0–1/34

Lockwood, Ephraim
Professional. *b:* 4.4.1845, Lascelles Hall, Huddersfield, Yorkshire. *d:* 19.12.1921, Huddersfield, Yorkshire. Brother of Henry (Yorkshire), nephew of John Thewlis (Yorkshire). Sound opening/middle order right-hand batsman, right-hand slow medium round-arm bowler. *Team* Yorkshire (1868–84, 213 matches). *Tour* Daft to North America 1879 (not first-class).
Career batting
328–569–39–12512–208–23.60–8–*ct* 232–*st* 3
Bowling 3458–206+1–16.78–7–1–7/35

He hit 1,000 runs in a season four times (best 1,261, av 32.33, in 1876). His only double century was 208 for Yorkshire v Kent at Gravesend in 1883.

In the late 1870s he captained Yorkshire.

Lockwood, Henry
Professional. *b:* 5.11.1855, Lascelles Hall, Huddersfield, Yorkshire. *d:* February 1930, Huddersfield, Yorkshire. Brother of Ephraim (Yorkshire), nephew of John Thewlis (Yorkshire). Middle order right-hand batsman, right-hand fast round-arm bowler. *Team* Yorkshire (1877–82, 16 matches).
Career batting
16–27–2–408–90–16.32–0–*ct* 8
Bowling 37–0

Lockwood, William (Henry)
Professional. *b:* 25.3.1868, Old Radford, Notts. *d:* 26.4.1932, Radford, Notts. Middle/lower order right-hand batsman, right-arm fast bowler. *Teams* Nottinghamshire (1886–87, 5 matches); Surrey (1889–1904, 305 matches). *Tour* Stoddart to Australia 1894/5. *Tests* England (1893–1902, 12 matches).
Career batting
362–531–45–10673–165–21.96–15–*ct* 140
Bowling 25247–1376–18.34–121–29–9/59
Test batting
12–16–3–231–52*–17.76–0–*ct* 4
Bowling 884–43–20.55–5–1–7/71

Regarded as one of the most effective fast bowlers of his day, Lockwood's particular asset was the ability to bowl a slower ball without a noticeable change in his action. In the early 1890s he was a major force in English cricket, but he failed on the 1894/5 tour to Australia, and within a couple of years looked likely to drop out of County cricket. In 1898, however, not only did his bowling form return but his batting improved, and in both 1899 and 1900 he performed the 'double'. His best Test series came in 1902, when he took 11 for 76 in the fourth Test.

He took 100 wickets in a season seven times (best 151, av 13.60, in 1892), and hit 1,000 runs twice (best 1,367 runs, av 32.54, in 1900). His best bowling was 9/59 for Surrey v Essex at Leyton in 1902.

Lockyer, Thomas
Professional. *b:* 1.11.1826, Old Town, Croydon, Surrey. *d:* 22.12.1869, Croydon, Surrey. He died of consumption. Middle order right-hand batsman, right-hand fast medium round-arm bowler, excellent wicket-keeper. *Team* Surrey (1849–66, 124 matches). *Tours* Parr to North America 1859 (not first-class), to Australia 1863/4.
Career batting
223–361–51–4917–108*–15.86–1–*ct* 301–*st* 123
Bowling 1986–99+20–20.06–10–1–6/33

He was regarded as the equal of any wicket-keeper in England about 1860.

Lodge, Joe Thomas
Professional. *b:* 16.4.1921, Huddersfield, Yorkshire. Middle order right-hand batsman, change bowler. *Team* Yorkshire (1948, 2 matches).
Career batting
2–3–0–48–30–16.00–0–*ct* 0
Bowling 17–0

Lodge, Lewis Vaughan
Amateur. *b:* 21.12.1872, Darlington, Co Durham. *d:* 21.10.1916, Burrage, Derbyshire. He was found drowned in a pond. Middle order batsman. *Sch* Durham. *Team* Hampshire (1900, 3 matches).
Career batting
3–4–0–6–4–1.50–0–*ct* 0
Bowling 6–0

He also played for Durham. Whilst at

Cambridge he played in the Freshmen's and Seniors' Matches, but no first-class games.

A noted soccer player, he won his blue and went on to represent England, and played (once) for Birmingham City.

Logan, Hugh
Amateur. *b:* 10.5.1885, Market Harborough, Leics. *d:* 24.2.1919, Tournai, Belgium. Middle order right-hand batsman, brilliant deep field. *Sch* Westminster. *Team* Leicestershire (1903, 1 match).
Career batting
1–2–0–13–12–6.50–0–*ct* 0

He appeared in the Freshmen's Match at Cambridge, but no first-class games.

Logan, James Douglas, jun
Amateur. *b:* 24.6.1880, Cape Town, South Africa. *d:* 3.1.1960, Matjesfontein, South Africa. Middle order batsman. *Tour* South Africa to England 1901.
Career batting
4–8–0–100–35–12.50–0–*ct* 3
Bowling 20–0

His father, the Hon J. D. Logan, financed the 1901 tour to England. He never appeared in first-class cricket in South Africa.

Logan, William Ross
Amateur. *b:* 24.11.1909, Edinburgh, Scotland. Lower order batsman, wicket-keeper. *Sch* Merchiston. *Team* Scotland (1932).
Career batting
1–1–0–1–1–1.00–0–*ct* 5

He played rugby for Scotland.

Lohmann, George Alfred
Professional. *b:* 2.6.1865, Kensington, London. *d:* 1.12.1901, Matjesfontein, South Africa. Lower order right-hand batsman, right-arm medium fast bowler, excellent slip. *Teams* Surrey (1884–96, 186 matches); Western Province (1894/5). *Tours* Lillywhite, Shaw and Shrewsbury to Australia 1886/7, 1887/8; Sheffield to Australia 1891/2; Hawke to South Africa 1895/6. *Tests* England (1886–96, 18 matches).
Career batting
293–427–39–7247–115–18.67–3–*ct* 337
Bowling 25295–1841–13.73–176–57–9/28
Test batting
18–26–2–213–62*–8.87–0–*ct* 28
Bowling 1205–112–10.75–9–5–9/28

The leading wicket-taker in England for several successive seasons, Lohmann had much to do with the rise in Surrey's fortunes in the 1880s. He was equally successful in Australia on each of his three tours and in 1887/8 took 63 wickets in first-class matches at a cost of 11.98 runs each. On his tour to South Africa he proved altogether too much for the opposition and produced some startling performances in the Tests, including 9 for 28 at Johannesburg, which was the best innings analysis of his career. His best in England was 9 for 67 for Surrey v Essex at Hove in 1889.

He took 100 wickets in a season eight times and went on to 200 three times with 220, av 13.62, in 1890 as his best.

Owing to ill-health his career was relatively short and he emigrated to South Africa in the hope that the climate might benefit him. His final first-class match was for A. Bailey's XI in South Africa in 1897/8. In 1901 he came back to England as assistant manager of the South African team, but died of consumption later in the same year.

Lomas, John Millington
Amateur. *b:* 12.12.1917, Epsom, Surrey. *d:* 4.12.1945, Westminster, London. Opening right-hand batsman. *Sch* Charterhouse. *Team* Oxford U (1938–39, blue both years).
Career batting
23–43–1–1460–138–34.76–2–*ct* 10

Lomax, Ian Raymond
Amateur. *b:* 30.7.1931, Fulham, London. Stylish middle order right-hand batsman, right-arm fast medium bowler. *Sch* Eton. *Team* Somerset (1962, 6 matches). *Tour* Surridge to Bermuda 1961 (not first-class).
Career batting
12–21–1–370–83–18.50–0–*ct* 6
Bowling 229–4–57.25–0–0–2/45

His first-class debut was for Free Foresters in 1952 and his final first-class match for MCC in 1965.

Most of his County cricket was for Wiltshire.

Lomax, James Geoffrey
Professional. *b:* 5.5.1925, Rochdale, Lancashire. Middle order right-hand batsman, right-arm fast medium bowler. *Teams* Lancashire (1949–53, 57 matches); Somerset (1954–62, 211 matches).
Career batting
269–463–23–8672–104*–19.70–2–*ct* 238
Bowling 10773–316–34.09–4–0–6/75

He hit 1,000 runs in a season twice (best 1,298, av 24.96, in 1959).

Loney, Escott Frith
Amateur. *b:* 21.7.1903, Bristol. *d:* 19.6.1982, Toronto, Canada. Middle/lower order right-hand batsman, left-arm medium fast bowler. *Sch* Derby School. *Team* Derbyshire (1925–27, 25 matches).

Career batting
25–37–7–511–39*–17.03–0–*ct* 18
Bowling 650–20–32.50–0–0–4/27

He also appeared for Canada in non-first-class matches.

Loney, Joseph Kevin
Cricketer. *b:* 30.8.1951, Lurgan, Co Armagh, Ireland. Middle order left-hand batsman, occasional right-arm medium pace bowler. *Team* Cambridge U (1974).
Career batting
2–2–0–4–2–2.00–0–*ct* 0

Long, Arnold
Professional. *b:* 18.12.1940, Cheam, Surrey. Lower order left-hand batsman, wicket-keeper. *Teams* Surrey (1960–75, 352 matches); Sussex (1976–80, 97 matches). *Tour* Robins to South Africa 1972/3.
Career batting
452–537–131–6801–92–16.75–0–*ct* 921–*st* 124
Bowling 2–0

He created a first-class record by taking 11 catches in the match for Surrey v Sussex at Hove in 1964.

From 1978 to 1980 he captained Sussex.

An excellent soccer player, he appeared for Corinthian Casuals.

Long, Edmund James
Amateur. *b:* 28.3.1883, Darlinghurst, New South Wales, Australia. *d:* 8.12.1947, Leichardt, New South Wales, Australia. Lower order right-hand batsman, wicket-keeper. *Team* New South Wales (1911/12, 1 match). *Tours* AIF to England and South Africa 1919; Waddy to Ceylon 1913/4 (not first-class).
Career batting
18–22–10–135–24–11.25–0–*ct* 20–*st* 12

Long, Rev Henry James
Amateur. *b:* 14.8.1859, Henlow, Bedfordshire. *d:* 18.6.1902, Marylebone, London. Middle order batsman. *Sch* King's, Canterbury. *Team* MCC (1880).
Career batting
1–2–0–8–5–4.00–0–*ct* 0

Long, Robert
Professional. *b:* 9.11.1846, Richmond, Surrey. *d:* 6.8.1924, Enfield, Middlesex. Lower order right-hand batsman, right-arm fast bowler. *Team* Surrey (1870, 2 matches).
Career batting
2–4–0–0–0–0.00–0–*ct* 0
Bowling 20–0

Longcroft, Okeover Butler
Amateur. *b:* March, 1850, Havant, Hants. *d:* 7.9.1871, Havant, Hants. Opening right-hand batsman, wicket-keeper. *Sch* Bradfield. *Team* Hampshire (1869–70, 2 matches).
Career batting
2–4–0–28–12–7.00–0–*ct* 1–*st* 1
Bowling 75–8–9.37–0–0–3/15

Longdon, Albert
Professional. *b:* 1.11.1865, Watnall Greasley, Notts. *d:* 13.5.1937, Bentley, Doncaster, Yorkshire. Middle order right-hand batsman, right-arm medium pace bowler. *Team* Nottinghamshire (1895, 2 matches).
Career batting
2–4–1–28–20*–9.33–0–*ct* 1

Longfield, Geoffrey Phelps
Amateur. *b:* 4.12.1909, High Halstow, Kent. *d:* 25.2.1943, Rennes, France. He was killed during air operations. Brother of T. C. (Kent). Middle order right-hand batsman, right-arm bowler. *Sch* Aldenham. *Team* RAF (1931–32).
Career batting
2–4–0–36–26–9.00–0–*ct* 0
Bowling 138–2–69.00–0–0–2/51

Longfield, Thomas Cuthbert
Amateur. *b:* 12.5.1906, High Halstow, Kent. *d:* 21.12.1981, Ealing, London. Brother of G. P. (RAF), father-in-law of E. R. Dexter (Sussex). Middle order right-hand batsman, right-arm medium pace bowler, good field. *Sch* Aldenham. *Teams* Cambridge U (1927–28, blue both years); Kent (1927–39, 30 matches); Europeans (1929/30 to 1944/5); Bengal (1935/6 to 1938/9).
Career batting
82–127–18–2446–120–22.44–2–*ct* 49
Bowling 6416–195–32.90–7–0–6/12

Going to India after leaving Cambridge, he could only play for Kent very infrequently.

His final first-class match was for Free Foresters in 1951.

Longland, Harry
Amateur. *b:* 1881, Leicester. *d:* September, 1911, Piddington, Northants. Middle order batsman. *Team* Northants (1907, 1 match).
Career batting
1 match, did not bat–*ct* 0

Longman, George Henry
Amateur. *b:* 3.8.1852, Farnborough, Hants. *d:* 19.8.1938, Wimbledon. Father of H. K. (Middlesex). Stylish opening right-hand batsman, brilliant deep field. *Sch* Eton. *Teams* Cambridge

U (1872–75, blue all four years); Hampshire (1875–85, 27 matches).
Career batting
68–121–2–2448–98–20.57–0–*ct* 41–*st* 4
Bowling 180–3–60.00–0–0–1/1

He was President of Surrey CCC 1926–28 and Hon Treasurer from 1929 to his death.

A good footballer, he represented Middlesex.

Longman, Henry Kerr
Amateur. *b:* 8.3.1881, Kensington, London. *d:* 7.10.1958, Pyrford, Surrey. Son of G. H. (Cambridge U). Opening right-hand batsman, good field. *Sch* Eton. *Teams* Cambridge U (1901, blue); Surrey (1901–08, 5 matches); Middlesex (1919–20, 11 matches).
Career batting
32–58–2–1148–150–20.50–1–*ct* 24
Bowling 50–0

His final first-class match was for H. D. G. Leveson-Gower's XI in 1921

Longmore, Andrew Nigel Murray
Cricketer. *b:* 24.9.1953, Woolwich, Kent. Lower order right-hand batsman, wicket-keeper. *Sch* Winchester. *Team* Oxford U (1973–75).
Career batting
2–4–1–28–15–9.33–0–*ct* 3

He is the Assistant Editor of *The Cricketer* magazine.

Longrigg, Edmund Fallowfield
Amateur. *b:* 16.4.1906, Bath, Somerset. *d:* 23.7.1974, Bath, Somerset. Sound middle order left-hand batsman, right-arm slow bowler, good close field. *Sch* Rugby. *Teams* Somerset (1925–47, 219 matches); Cambridge U (1926–28, blue 1927 and 1928).
Career batting
248–407–25–9416–205–24.64–10–*ct* 143
Bowling 100–1–100.00–0–0–1/7

He hit 1,000 runs in a season twice (best 1,567, av 30.72, in 1930); his only double century was 205 for Somerset v Leics at Taunton in 1930.

From 1938 to 1946 he captained Somerset.

Being in the legal profession his appearances in first-class cricket were limited and he played little between 1931 and 1937.

Also a noted hockey player, he represented Somerset.

Lord, Albert
Professional. *b:* 28.8.1888, Barwell, Leics. *d:* 29.3.1969, Barwell, Leics. Sound opening right-hand batsman, right-arm medium pace bowler. *Team* Leicestershire (1910–26, 131 matches).
Career batting
130–235–12–3864–102–17.32–1–*ct* 73
Bowling 1060–39–27.17–2–0–5/40

He always appeared for Leicestershire under his 'cricketing name' of A. Lord. The story behind his pseudonym is that he arrived on the Leicestershire staff to find one cricketer called 'King' and another called 'Knight', so thought he should also join the aristocracy. His real name was Albert Callington.

Lord, Gordon John
Cricketer. *b:* 25.4.1961, Birmingham. Middle order left-hand batsman, slow left-arm bowler. *Team* Warwickshire (1983, 3 matches).
Career batting
3–3–0–91–61–30.33–0–*ct* 1
Bowling 12–0

Lord, John Carr
Amateur. *b:* 17.8.1844, Hobart, Tasmania. *d:* 25.5.1911, Antill Ponds, Tasmania. Middle order right-hand batsman. *Teams* Hampshire (1864, 1 match); Tasmania (1872/3, 1 match).
Career batting
2–4–1–29–11–9.66–0–*ct* 1

Lord, Reginald Arthur
Amateur. *b:* 29.1.1905, Beckenham, Kent. Opening right-hand batsman, slow left-arm bowler. *Sch* Marlborough. *Team* Oxford U (1924).
Career batting
3–6–0–57–21–9.50–0–*ct* 0

His final first-class match was for H. D. G. Leveson-Gower's XI in 1926.

Lord, Thomas
Professional *b:* 23.11.1755, Thirsk, Yorkshire. *d:* 13.1.1832, West Meon, Hampshire. Father of Thomas, jun (Surrey and Middlesex). Lower order right-hand slow under-arm bowler. *Teams* Middlesex (1801); Epsom (1815).
Career batting
2–2–1–12–10*–12.00–0–*ct* 0
Bowling 1 wicket, no analysis

His memorial is Lord's Cricket Ground, which he originally laid out where Dorset Square now stands in 1787. He moved to North Bank, Regent's Park and in 1813/14 to the present site in St John's Wood, Marylebone.

Lord, William Alston
Professional. *b:* 8.8.1873, Washwood Heath, Birmingham. *d:* 16.6.1906, Gravelly Hill North, Erdington, Birmingham. Lower order left-hand batsman, left-arm fast medium bowler. *Team* Warwickshire (1897–99, 13 matches).

Career batting
13–18–8–69–10*–6.90–0–*ct* 4
Bowling 811–26–31.19–1–0–5/73

Lord, Wilfrid Fraser
Amateur. *b:* 1.8.1888, Kolhapur, India. *d:* 19.9.1960, Hove, Sussex. Tail end right-hand batsman, right-arm fast bowler. *Sch* Tonbridge. *Teams* Oxford U (1911–12); Middlesex (1919, 2 matches).
Career batting
9–15–8–121–44*–12.10–0–*ct* 4
Bowling 543–12–45.25–0–0–4/107

Lorimer, James
Amateur. *b:* 1860, Victoria, Australia. Lower order batsman, bowler. *Team* Oxford U (1883).
Career batting
1–2–2–7–4*–no av–0–*ct* 0
Bowling 22–0

Lorrimer, Alexander
Amateur. *b:* 9.1.1859, Aylestone, Leicester. *d:* 2.2.1947, Leicester. Brother of David (Leics). Middle order right-hand batsman. *Team* Leicestershire (1894–96, 6 matches).
Career batting
6–12–0–174–46–14.50–0–*ct* 3
He hit a century on his debut for Leicestershire (v Surrey in 1890) – not a first-class match.

Lorrimer, David
Amateur. *b:* 16.1.1865, Aylestone, Leicester. *d:* 12.11.1925, Boscombe, Hants. Brother of Alexander (Leics). Middle order right-hand batsman, good point. *Team* Leicestershire (1894–95, 9 matches).
Career batting
9–16–0–194–46–12.12–0–*ct* 6

Louden, George Marshall
Amateur. *b:* 6.9.1885, Forest Gate, Essex. *d:* 28.12.1972, Amersham, Bucks. Lower order right-hand batsman, right-arm fast medium bowler. *Team* Essex (1912–27, 82 matches).
Career batting
94–140–39–931–74–9.21–0–*ct* 62
Bowling 10081–451–22.35–36–5–8/36

Loudon, William David Grafton
Cricketer. *b:* 22.5.1954, Lanark, Scotland. Right-hand batsman, right-arm medium pace bowler. *Sch* Edinburgh Acadamy. *Team* Scotland (1982).
Career batting
1–1–0–21–21–21.00–0–*ct* 1
Bowling 11–3–3.66–0–0–3/4

Loughery, William Gordon Ridley
Amateur. *b:* 1.11.1907, Belfast, Ireland. *d:* 1.8.1977, Abbey Dore, Herefordshire. Middle order right-hand batsman. *Sch* Campbell College. *Team* Ireland (1929–33).
Career batting
2–4–1–34–18*–11.33–0–*ct* 1

Love, Geoffrey Robert Stuart
Amateur. *b:* 19.4.1889, Islington, Middlesex. *d:* 6.2.1978, Balquhidder, Perthshire. Lower order left-hand batsman, slow left-arm bowler. *Team* Middlesex (1920, 1 match).
Career batting
1–2–0–2–2–1.00–0–*ct* 0
Bowling 39–0

Love, Harry
Professional. *b:* 30.5.1871, Hastings, Sussex. *d:* 26.3.1942, Hastings, Sussex. Opening right-hand batsman, right-arm slow medium bowler. *Team* Sussex (1892–94, 5 matches).
Career batting
5–10–1–110–30–12.22–0–*ct* 3
Bowling 7–0

Love, Hampden Stanley Bray
Amateur. *b:* 10.8.1895, Lilyfield, New South Wales, Australia. *d:* 22.7.1969, Mosman, New South Wales, Australia. Middle order right-hand batsman, wicket-keeper. *Teams* New South Wales (1920/1 to 1932/3, 21 matches); Victoria (1922/3 to 1926/7, 16 matches). *Tours* AIF to England 1919; Australia to India 1935/6. *Test* Australia (1932/3, 1 match).
Career batting
54–90–7–2906–192–35.01–7–*ct* 73–*st* 29
Bowling 19–0
Test batting
1–2–0–8–5–4.00–0–*ct* 3
He appeared in only one match for AIF in England.

Love, James Derek
Cricketer. *b:* 22.4.1955, Leeds, Yorkshire. Middle order right-arm batsman, right-arm medium pace bowler. *Team* Yorkshire (1975–83, 141 matches).
Career batting
143–236–36–6301–170*–31.50–10–*ct* 78
Bowling 233–1–233.00–0–0–1/46
He hit 1,000 runs in a season twice (best 1,203, av 33.41, in 1981). He represented England in One-day Internationals.

Love, Raymond Henry Arnold Davison
Amateur. *b:* 11.5.1888, Chatham, Kent. *d:* 12.10.1962, Woking, Surrey. Lower order right-hand batsman, right-arm medium pace bowler.

Sch Marlborough. *Team* Hampshire (1932, 2 matches).
Career batting
2–3–1–15–13*–7.50–0–*ct* 2
Bowling 6–0

Loveday, Francis Alfred
Professional. *b:* 14.9.1892, Hackney, London. *d:* 18.10.1954, North Walsham, Norfolk. Middle order left-hand batsman. *Sch* City of London. *Teams* Essex (1921–23, 7 matches).
Career batting
7–14–0–321–81–22.92–0–*ct* 2
He also played for Cambridgeshire.

Loveitt, Frank Russell
Amateur. *b:* 24.4.1871, Rugby. *d:* 1.9.1939, Coventry, Warwickshire. Middle order right-hand batsman. *Team* Warwickshire (1898–1905, 25 matches).
Career batting
25–42–6–846–110–23.50–1–*ct* 7
He was a noted rugby footballer with Coventry.

Lovell-Hewitt, William
Amateur. *b:* 7.11.1901, Trowbridge, Wiltshire. Lower order right-hand batsman, right-arm medium pace bowler. *Sch* King's, Bruton. *Team* Minor Counties (1938–39).
Career batting
3–5–0–175–92–35.00–0–*ct* 1
Bowling 55–0
His County cricket was for Wiltshire.

Lowe, Charles
Professional. *b:* 23.6.1890, Whitwell, Derbyshire. Tail end batsman, right-arm fast medium bowler. *Team* Derbyshire (1909–12, 5 matches).
Career batting
5–8–2–25–17–4.16–0–*ct* 0
Bowling 90–2–45.00–0–0–1/20

Lowe, George
Amateur. *b:* 25.5.1915, Mastin Moor, Derbyshire. Middle order right-hand batsman. *Team* Derbyshire (1949–53, 2 matches).
Career batting
2–3–0–43–22–14.33–0–*ct* 3
He played soccer for Chesterfield.

Lowe, George Emanuel
Professional. *b:* 12.1.1878. *d:* 15.8.1932, Middlesbrough. Lower order batsman, wicket-keeper. *Team* Yorkshire (1902, 1 match).
Career batting
1–1–1–5–5*–no av–0–*ct* 1

Lowe, H. F.
Amateur. Middle order batsman. *Team* Hampshire (1882, 1 match).
Career batting
1–1–0–0–0–0.00–0–*ct* 0

Lowe, John Claude Malcolm
Amateur. *b:* 21.2.1888, Coventry, Warwickshire. *d:* 27.7.1970, Hastings, Sussex. Lower order right-hand batsman, right-arm fast medium bowler. *Sch* Uppingham. *Teams* Oxford U (1907–10, blue 1907, 1908 and 1909), Warwickshire (1907, 1 match).
Career batting
35–59–20–300–46–7.69–0–*ct* 33
Bowling 2767–106–26.10–7–0–8/144
He was also a good hockey player, obtaining his blue at Oxford.

Lowe, Peter John
Cricketer. *b:* 7.1.1935, Sutton Coldfield. Lower order right-hand batsman, wicket-keeper. *Team* Warwickshire (1964, 1 match).
Career batting
1 match, did not bat–*ct* 2

Lowe, Richard
Professional. *b:* 18.6.1869, Kirkby-in-Ashfield, Notts. *d:* 3.7.1946, Kirby-in-Ashfield, Notts. Brother of Tom (Notts) and Sam (Notts). Lower order right-hand batsman, left-arm medium pace bowler. *Team* Sussex (1893–94, 14 matches).
Career batting
15–25–8–183–34*–10.76–0–*ct* 5
Bowling 578–22–26.27–0–0–4/26
He played in one non-first-class match for Notts in 1891 and from 1897 to 1901 for Glamorgan (pre-first-class).
His first-class debut was for Lord Sheffield's XI in 1891.

Lowe, Ronald Francis
Professional. *b:* 28.7.1905, Shepherd's Bush, London. *d:* 29.8.1960, Colchester, Essex. Tail end right-hand batsman, slow left-arm bowler. *Team* Surrey (1923, 10 matches).
Career batting
10–11–3–15–7–1.87–0–*ct* 3
Bowling 557–26–21.42–1–0–5/15

Lowe, Richard Geoffrey Harvey
Amateur. *b:* 11.6.1904, Wimbledon, London. Middle order left-hand batsman, right-arm fast medium bowler. *Sch* Westminster. *Teams* Cambridge U (1925–27, blue all three years); Kent (1926, 2 matches).

Career batting
33–44–7–697–83–18.83–0–*ct* 16
Bowling 1837–70–26.24–3–0–5/31

Lowe, Sam
Professional. *b:* 1867, Kirkby-in-Ashfield, Notts. *d:* March 1947, Kirkby-in-Ashfield, Notts. Brother of Richard (Sussex) and Tom (Notts). Lower order right-hand batsman, right-arm fast bowler. *Team* Nottinghamshire (1894, 1 match).
Career batting
1–2–0–8–8–4.00–0–*ct* 0
Bowling 19–0

He also played for Glamorgan (pre-first-class).

Lowe, Tom
Professional. *b:* 25.7.1859, Kirkby-in-Ashfield, Notts. *d:* 29.8.1934, Kirkby-in-Ashfield, Notts. Brother of Richard (Sussex) and Sam (Notts). Lower order right-hand batsman, right-arm medium pace bowler. *Team* Nottinghamshire (1894, 1 match).
Career batting
1–1–1–0–0*–no av–0–*ct* 0
Bowling 41–0

He also played for Northants (pre-first-class).

Lowe, Walter George Hassall
Amateur. *b:* 26.8.1870, Bretby, Derbyshire. *d: circa* 1935, California, USA. Middle order batsman. *Team* Nottinghamshire (1895, 1 match).
Career batting
1–2–1–29–15*–29.00–0–*ct* 1

He emigrated to USA about 1910 and became a fruit farmer.

Lowe, William Walter
Amateur. *b:* 17.11.1873, Stamford, Lincs. *d:* 26.5.1945, Hartley Wintney, Hants. Lower order right-hand batsman, right-arm fast bowler. *Sch* Malvern. *Teams* Cambridge U (1895–96, blue 1895); Worcestershire (1899–1911, 39 matches). *Tour* Mitchell to North America 1895.
Career batting
53–88–11–1711–154–22.22–4–*ct* 17
Bowling 2097–74–28.33–4–0–6/15

A noted soccer player, he played for Cambridge U and Corinthians.

Lowles, George William
Professional. *b:* 1865, Whitechapel, Middlesex. *d:* 1940, Lambeth, South London. Lower order batsman, wicket-keeper. *Teams* Surrey (1887, 1 match); Middlesex (1889, 1 match).
Career batting
2–4–1–4–3–1.33–0–*ct* 0

Lowndes, William Geoffrey Lowndes Frith
(formerly W. G. L. Frith)
Amateur. *b:* 24.1.1898, Wandsworth. *d:* 23.5.1982, Newbury, Berks. Son of W. F. L. Frith (London County). Fast scoring middle order right-hand batsman, right-arm medium fast bowler, good close field. *Sch* Eton. *Teams* Oxford U (1921, blue); Hampshire (1924–35, 41 matches). *Tours* Martineau to Egypt 1930, 1931 and 1932 (not first-class).
Career batting
79–138–4–32344–216–24.02–5–*ct* 38
Bowling 3003–78–38.50–0–0–3/5

His only double century was 216 for Oxford U v H. D. G. Leveson-Gower's XI in 1921 at Eastbourne.

His final first-class match was for Free Foresters in 1936.

Lowry, Thomas Coleman
Amateur. *b:* 17.2.1898, Fernhill, Napier, New Zealand. *d:* 20.7.1976, Hastings, New Zealand. Brother-in-law to A. P. F. Chapman (Kent) and R. H. B. Bettington (New South Wales). Attacking right-hand batsman, right-arm slow medium bowler, wicket-keeper. *Teams* Auckland (1917/8); Cambridge U (1921–24, blue 1923–24); Wellington (1926/7 to 1932/3); Somerset (1921–24, 46 matches). *Tours* MCC to Australia and New Zealand 1922/3; New Zealand to England 1927, 1931, 1937, to Australia 1937/8. *Tests* New Zealand (1929/30 to 1931, 7 matches).
Career batting
198–322–20–9421–181–31.19–18–*ct* 189–*st* 48
Bowling 1323–49–27.00–0–0–3/13
Test batting
7–8–0–223–80–27.87–0–*ct* 8
Bowling 5–0

His first-class debut in England was for Leveson-Gower's XI in 1919.

He hit 1,000 runs in a season three times (best 1,564, av 35.54, in 1923). He captained the New Zealand tourists on their 1927 and 1931 tours to England and was manager of the 1937 tour; he also led New Zealand in seven Tests.

Lowson, Frank Anderson
Professional. *b:* 1.7.1925, Bradford, Yorkshire. Sound opening right-hand batsman, good outfield. *Team* Yorkshire (1949–58, 252 matches). *Tour* MCC to India, Pakistan and Ceylon 1951/2. *Tests* England (1951–55, 7 matches).
Career batting
277–449–37–15321–259*–37.18–31–*ct* 190
Bowling 31–0
Test batting
7–13–0–245–68–18.84–0–*ct* 5

He hit 1,000 runs in a season eight times, going on to 2,000 once : 2,152, av 42.19, in 1950. His only double century was 259* for Yorkshire v Worcs at Worcester in 1953. He also hit 1,000 runs on the 1951/2 tour.

Loxley-Firth, E. (*see under* Firth, E. L.)

Loxton, Colin Cameron
Amateur. *b:* 1.1.1914, Brisbane, Australia. Father of J. F. C. (Queensland). Lower order right-hand batsman, right-arm fast medium bowler. *Teams* Cambridge U (1935); Queensland (1937/8, 4 matches).
Career batting
5–10–1–100–36*–11.11–0–*ct* 4
Bowling 299–8–37.37–0–0–2/27

Loxton, Samuel John Everett
Amateur. *b:* 29.3.1921, Albert Park, Victoria, Australia. Fine driving middle order right-hand batsman, right-arm fast medium bowler, good field. *Team* Victoria (1946/7 to 1957/8, 77 matches). *Tours* Australia to England 1948, to South Africa 1949/50; Commonwealth to India 1953/4; Australia to India and Pakistan 1959/60 (manager, but played in one match). *Tests* Australia (1947/8 to 1950/1, 12 matches).
Career batting
140–192–23–6249–232*–36.97–13–*ct* 83
Bowling 5971–232–25.73–3–0–6/49
Test batting
12–15–0–554–101–36.93–1–*ct* 7
Bowling 349–8–43.62–0–0–3/55
Although hitting 973 runs, av 57.23, in first-class matches during the 1948 Australian tour to England, he could only find a place in three of the five Tests. His highest score was 232* for Victoria v Queensland at Melbourne in 1946/7.

Loyd, Sir Henry Charles
Amateur. *b:* 21.2.1891, London. *d:* 11.11.1973, Bungay, Suffolk. Middle order batsman, wicket-keeper. *Sch* Eton. *Team* Army (1914–20).
Career batting
3–5–1–100–63*–25.00–0–*ct* 2–*st* 1

Luard, Arthur John Hamilton
Amateur. *b:* 3.9.1861, Watlair, India. *d:* 22.5.1944, Guildford, Surrey. Hard hitting middle order right-hand batsman, excellent cover point. *Sch* Denstone and Cheltenham. *Teams* Gloucestershire (1892–1907, 45 matches); Hampshire (1897, 5 matches).
Career batting
52–92–2–1218–75*–13.53–0–*ct* 29
He was stationed in India from 1882 to 1890 and therefore not available for County cricket.

Lubbock, Alfred
Amateur. *b:* 31.10.1845, London. *d:* 17.7.1916, Kilmarth Manor, Par, Cornwall. Brother of Nevile (Kent) and Edgar (Kent). Excellent free hitting middle order right-hand batsman, good deep field. *Sch* Eton. *Team* Kent (1863–75, 4 matches). *Tour* Fitzgerald to North America 1872 (not first-class).
Career batting
28–51–7–1043–129–23.70–2–*ct* 14
Bowling 92–4–23.00–0–0–2/62
He was regarded as one of the most promising of young players, but owing to his profession as a banker he played little County cricket.

Lubbock, Christopher William Stuart
Amateur. *b:* 4.1.1920, London. Middle order right-hand batsman, right-arm medium or leg break bowler. *Sch* Charterhouse. *Teams* Northants (1938–39, 6 matches); Oxford U (1939).
Career batting
9–15–1–189–69–13.50–0–*ct* 1
Bowling 372–25–14.88–0–0–4/44
He also played for Suffolk.

Lubbock, Edgar
Amateur. *b:* 22.2.1847, London. *d:* 9.9.1907, Chelsea, London. Brother of Alfred (Kent) and Nevile (Kent). Middle order right-hand batsman, right-hand fast under-arm bowler. *Sch* Eton. *Team* Kent (1871, 1 match). *Tour* Fitzgerald to North America 1872 (not first-class).
Career batting
3–5–0–77–54–15.40–0–*ct* 1
Bowling 27–1–27.00–0–0–1/4
His first-class debut was for Gentlemen of Kent in 1866.

Lubbock, Sir Nevile
Amateur. *b:* 31.3.1839, Pimlico, London. *d:* 12.9.1914, Bromley Common, Kent. Brother of Alfred (Kent) and Edgar (Kent). Steady middle order right-hand batsman, good close field. *Sch* Eton. *Team* Kent (1860, 2 matches).
Career batting
6–10–1–135–42–15.00–0–*ct* 2
His first-class debut was for Gentlemen of Kent in 1858.

Lucas, Sir Arthur Charles
Amateur. *b:* 22.5.1853, Lowestoft, Suffolk. *d:* 14.6.1915, Marylebone, London. Stylish opening or middle order right-hand batsman, good point. *Sch* Harrow. *Teams* Surrey (1874, 1 match); Middlesex (1877, 2 matches).

Career batting
5–9–0–140–29–15.55–0–*ct* 4

His final first-class match was for Gentlemen of England in 1879.

Lucas, Alfred George
Amateur. *b:* 26.10.1854, Wandsworth, Surrey. *d:* 4.5.1941, Hove, Sussex. Brother of C. J. (Sussex), F. M. (Sussex) and M. P. (Sussex), uncle of C. E. (Sussex). Middle order batsman. *Team* MCC (1879).
Career batting
1–1–0–46–46–46.00–0–*ct* 0

Lucas, Alfred Perry
Amateur. *b:* 20.2.1857, Westminster, London. *d:* 12.10.1923, Great Waltham, Essex. Cousin of C. F. (Hants). Stylish opening right-hand batsman, right-hand slow round-arm bowler, good field. *Sch* Uppingham. *Teams* Surrey (1874–82, 41 matches); Cambridge U (1875–78, blue all four years); Middlesex (1883–88, 11 matches); Essex (1894–1907, 98 matches). *Tour* Harris to Australia 1878/9. *Tests* England (1878/9 to 1884, 5 matches).
Career batting
256–435–46–10263–145–26.38–8–*ct* 152
Bowling 2849–155–18.38–4–0–6/10
Test batting
5–9–1–157–55–19.62–0–*ct* 1
Bowling 54–0

He captained Essex 1892 to 1894, but his County cricket was fairly limited throughout his long career.

Lucas, Charles Eric
Amateur. *b:* 16.4.1885, London. *d:* 4.4.1967, Warnham, Sussex. Son of C. J. (Middlesex and Sussex), nephew of A. G. (MCC), F. M. (Sussex) and M. P. (Sussex). Middle order right-hand batsman, right-arm slow bowler. *Sch* Eton. *Teams* Sussex (1906, 3 matches); Cambridge U (1908).
Career batting
5–8–1–78–22–11.14–0–*ct* 3
Bowling 197–11–17.91–2–1–5/74

Lucas, Charles Frank
Amateur. *b:* 25.11.1843, Stowe, Staffs. *d:* 27.9.1919, Carshalton, Surrey. Cousin of A. P. (Surrey). Middle order right-hand batsman, excellent long stop. *Team* Hampshire (1864–80, 14 matches).
Career batting
17–31–1–650–135–21.66–1–*ct* 10

Lucas, Charles James
Amateur. *b:* 25.2.1853, Clapham Common, Surrey. *d:* 17.4.1928, Westminster, London. Brother of A. G. (MCC), F. M. and M. P. (Sussex), father of C. E. (Sussex). Lower order right-hand batsman, right-hand fast round-arm bowler. *Sch* Harrow. *Teams* Middlesex (1876–77, 3 matches); Sussex (1880–82, 8 matches).
Career batting
12–23–3–137–38–11.85–0–*ct* 7
Bowling 165–7–23.57–0–0–3/17

Lucas, Frederick Charles
Professional. *b:* 29.9.1933, Slade Green, Kent. Middle order right-hand batsman, off break bowler. *Team* Kent (1954, 2 matches)
Career batting
2–4–0–62–38–15.50–0–*ct* 1
Bowling 17–0

He played football for Charlton Athletic.

Lucas, Frederick Murray
Amateur. *b:* 3.2.1860, Clapham Common, Surrey. *d:* 7.11.1887, Surat, India. He died of choleraic diarrhoea. Brother of A. G. (MCC), C. J. (Middlesex and Sussex) and M. P. (Sussex), uncle of C. E. (Sussex). Hard hitting middle order left-hand batsman, medium pace bowler, good deep field. *Sch* Marlborough. *Teams* Sussex (1880–87, 18 matches); Cambridge U (1881–82).
Career batting
28–45–3–1291–215*–30.73–2–*ct* 10
Bowling 32–0

He captained Sussex in 1886. He hit 215* for Sussex v Gloucs at Hove in 1885.

He also appeared for Suffolk.

A noted rackets player, he represented Cambridge U.

Lucas, John H.
Amateur. *b:* 1922, Barbados. Middle order right-hand batsman, off break bowler. Brother of N. S. (Barbados). *Teams* Barbados (1945/6 to 1949/50); Canada (1951/2 to 1954). *Tour* Canada to England 1954.
Career batting
15–25–5–1074–216*–53.70–2–*ct* 11
Bowling 484–15–32.66–0–0–4/88

He achieved very little on the 1954 visit to England. His highest score was 216* for Barbados v Trinidad at Bridgetown in 1948/9.

Lucas, Morton Peto
Amateur. *b:* 24.11.1856, Clapham Common, Surrey. *d:* 9.7.1921, Westminster, London. Brother of A. G. (MCC), C. J. (Middlesex and Sussex) and F. M. (Sussex), uncle of C. E. (Sussex). Middle order right-hand batsman, right-hand fast round-arm bowler, good cover point. *Sch* Harrow. *Team* Sussex (1877–90, 23 matches).

Career batting
27–49–2–940–131–20.00–1–*ct* 18
Bowling 263–7–37.57–0–0–3/35

He also appeared for Warwickshire (pre-first-class).

Lucas, Robert Slade
Amateur. *b:* 17.7.1867, Teddington, Middlesex. *d:* 5.1.1942, Haywards Heath, Sussex. Middle order right-hand batsman, right-arm medium pace bowler. *Sch* Merchant Taylors. *Team* Middlesex (1891–1900, 73 matches). *Tours* Hawke to North America 1894; Lucas to West Indies 1894/5.
Career batting
93–153–9–2685–185–18.64–1–*ct* 42
Bowling 366–6–61.00–0–0–2/44

He was also a well-known hockey player, being captain of Teddington for many years.

Luce, Frank Mowbray
Amateur. *b:* 26.4.1878, Gloucester. *d:* 9.9.1962, Reading, Berkshire. Middle order right-hand batsman, left-arm bowler. *Sch* Cheltenham. *Team.* Gloucestershire (1901–11, 25 matches).
Career batting
25–46–5–754–57–18.39–0–*ct* 19
Bowling 20–0

Luck, Arthur
Professional. *b:* 1914, Northampton. Lower order right-hand batsman, right-arm medium pace bowler. *Team* Northants (1937–38, 2 matches).
Career batting
2–4–0–52–18–13.00–0–*ct* 0
Bowling 155–2–77.50–0–0–1/34

Luckes, Walter Thomas
Professional. *b:* 1.1.1901, London. *d:* 27.10.1982, Bridgwater, Somerset. Lower order right-hand batsman, wicket-keeper. *Team* Somerset (1924–49, 365 matches).
Career batting
365–564–212–5710–121*–16.28–1–*ct* 586–*st* 240

Owing to ill health he played little during the three seasons 1929 to 1931.

Luckhurst, Brian William
Professional. *b:* 5.2.1939, Sittingbourne, Kent. Solid opening right-hand batsman, slow left-arm bowler. *Team* Kent (1958–76, 335 matches). *Tours* MCC to Australia and New Zealand 1970/1, 1974/5; Commonwealth to Pakistan 1967/8; Cavaliers to West Indies 1969/70; Kent to West Indies 1972/3 (not first-class). *Tests* England (1970/1 to 1974/5, 21 matches).
Career batting
388–660–76–22293–215–38.17–48–*ct* 391
Bowling 2744–64–42.87–0–0–4/32
Test batting
21–41–5–1298–131–36.05–4–*ct* 14
Bowling 32–1–32.00–0–0–1/9

He hit 1,000 runs in a season 14 times (best 1,914, av 47.85, in 1969); both his double centuries were for Kent, the highest being 215 v Derbyshire at Derby in 1973. He is the present manager of Kent CCC.

Luckin, Roger Alfred Geoffrey
Amateur. *b:* 25.11.1939, High Easter, Pleshey, Essex. Middle order left-hand batsman, moderate field. *Sch* Felsted. *Team* Essex (1962–63, 29 matches).
Career batting
29–46–3–735–82–17.09–0–*ct* 8

He also played for Cambridgeshire.

Luckin, Verner Valentine
Professional. *b:* 14.2.1892, Woking, Surrey. *d:* 28.11.1931, Froxfield, Hants. Lower order left-hand batsman, leg break and googly bowler. *Teams* Hampshire (1910–12, 10 matches); Warwickshire (1919, 9 matches).
Career batting
19–28–14–212–59*–15.14–0–*ct* 9
Bowling 845–24–35.20–0–0–3/19

Luddington, Henry Tansley
Amateur. *b:* 9.12.1854, Littleport, Cambs. *d:* 14.4.1922, Ashdon, Essex. Tail end right-hand batsman, right-hand fast round-arm bowler. *Sch* Uppingham. *Team* Cambridge U (1876–77, blue both years).
Career batting
11–15–4–65–25–6.90–0–*ct* 4
Bowling 832–42–19.80–3–0–5/28

His County cricket was for Norfolk and Cambridgeshire.

His final first-class match was for Gentlemen of England in 1878.

Luddington, Richard Simon
Cricketer. *b:* 8.4.1960, Kingston-upon-Thames, Surrey. Lower order right-hand batsman, wicket-keeper. *Sch* KCS, Wimbledon. *Team* Oxford U (1982, blue).
Career batting
10–14–1–290–65–22.30–0–*ct* 5–*st* 1

An all-round sportsman, he also gained blues for rugby football and hockey.

Luff, Alfred
Professional. *b:* 5.4.1846, Kew, Surrey. *d:* 1925, Horsham, Sussex. Stylish middle order right-hand

batsman, right-hand fast round-arm bowler. *Team* Surrey (1867, 3 matches).
Career batting
3–6–1–25–8–5.00–0–*ct* 0
Bowling 111–2–55.50–0–0–1/25
He was a noted coursing slipper.

Lulham, Edwin Percy Habberton
Amateur. *b:* 1865, Norwich. *d:* 27.6.1940, Hurstpierpoint, Sussex. Lower order batsman, useful bowler. *Team* Sussex (1894, 1 match).
Career batting
1–2–0–6–5–3.00–0–*ct* 0
Bowling 25–3–8.33–0–0–3/25

Lumb, Edward
Amateur. *b:* 12.9.1852, Dalton, Huddersfield, Yorkshire. *d:* 5.4.1891, Westminster, London. He died of pleurisy. Very steady opening right-hand batsman, cover point. *Team* Yorkshire (1872–86, 14 matches).
Career batting
17–28–5–356–70*–15.47–0–*ct* 7
Owing to illness he was unable to appear in County cricket as often as his ability merited, missing the whole of 1884 and 1885 seasons for that reason.

Lumb, Richard Graham
Cricketer. *b:* 27.2.1950, Doncaster, Yorkshire. Opening right-hand batsman, right-arm medium pace bowler. *Team* Yorkshire (1970–83, 229 matches).
Career batting
235–389–28–11189–159–30.99–20–*ct* 129
He hit 1,000 runs in a season five times (best 1,532, av 41.40, in 1975).

Lumsden, Ian James Michael
Amateur. *b:* 6.4.1923, Edinburgh, Scotland. Middle order right-hand batsman. *Sch* George Watson's College. *Teams* Scotland (1946–48); Combined Services (1948–49).
Career batting
7–14–0–379–66–27.07–0–*ct* 3
An excellent rugby footballer, he was capped for Scotland.

Lumsden, Vincent Roy
Amateur. *b:* 19.7.1930, Buff Bay, Jamaica. Hard hitting middle order right-hand batsman, off break bowler, occasional wicket-keeper. *Teams* Jamaica (1949/50 to 1959/60); Cambridge U (1953–56, blue 1953–55).
Career batting
57–102–5–2699–107–27.82–1–*ct* 36
Bowling 355–11–32.36–0–0–4/20
He played for Cambridgeshire.

Lund, Edward Victor
Amateur. *b:* 28.4.1902, Eton, Bucks. *d:* 20.2.1971, Cippenham, Bucks. Lower order right-hand batsman, right-arm medium pace bowler. *Team* Minor Counties (1937).
Career batting
1–2–0–5–4–2.50–0–*ct* 0
Bowling 94–3–31.33–0–0–2/78
He appeared for Buckinghamshire from 1929 to 1946.
He was also a useful soccer player.

Lupton, Arthur William
Amateur. *b:* 23.2.1879, Bradford, Yorkshire. *d:* 14.4.1944, Carlton, Guiseley, Yorkshire. Hard hitting lower order left-hand batsman, right-arm fast medium bowler. *Sch* Sedbergh. *Team* Yorkshire (1908–27, 104 matches).
Career batting
109–88–18–724–43*–10.34–0–*ct* 30
Bowling 455–14–32.50–0–0–4/109
Although he made his Yorkshire debut in 1908, his first-class career was to all intents and purposes confined to the three seasons 1925 to 1927, when he captained the County.

Lush, John Grantley
Amateur. *b:* 14.10.1913, Prahan, Victoria, Australia. Lower order right-hand batsman, right-arm fast bowler. *Team* New South Wales (1933/4 to 1946/7, 18 matches). *Tour* Cahn to New Zealand 1938/9 (no first-class matches).
Career batting
20–33–5–554–54–19.78–0–*ct* 10
Bowling 1346–50–26.92–3–1–7/72
His only first-class match in England was for Sir Julien Cahn's Team in 1938.

Lushington, Algernon Hay
Amateur. *b:* 29.9.1847, Lyndhurst, Hants. *d:* 13.9.1930, Shanklin, Isle of Wight. Middle order right-hand batsman. *Sch* Rugby. *Team* Hampshire (1870–77, 3 matches).
Career batting
3–6–0–48–21–8.00–0–*ct* 1
Bowling 98–3–32.66–0–0–2/48

Luther, Alan Charles Grenville
Amateur. *b:* 17.9.1880, Kensington, London. *d:* 23.6.1961, Curland, Somerset. Middle order right-hand batsman, good point field. *Sch* Rugby. *Team* Sussex (1908, 9 matches). *Tour* MCC to Egypt 1909 (not first-class).
Career batting
17–26–3–383–42–16.65–0–*ct* 7
His final first-class match was for MCC in 1911. He was a noted cricketer in military matches and later became Secretary to Berkshire CCC.

Also a well-known rackets player, he was runner-up in the Amateur Singles Championship of 1907.

Lutterlock, Edward
Professional. *b:* 26.2.1852, Stockwell, Surrey. *d:* 1938, St. Albans, Herts. Free hitting middle order right-hand batsman, right-hand fast round-arm bowler, long stop. *Team* Surrey (1874, 3 matches).
Career batting
3–6–0–23–8–3.83–0–*ct* 0

Luxton, Rev Charles Henry
Amateur. *b:* 19.1.1861, Okehampton, Devon. *d:* 17.10.1918, St. Pancras, London. Tail end batsman, useful bowler. *Team* Cambridge U (1881–82).
Career batting
2–4–0–10–9–2.50–0–*ct* 0
Bowling 94–4–23.50–0–0–2/60
He played for Devonshire.

Luyt, Sir Richard Edmonds
Amateur. *b:* 8.11.1915, Cape Town, South Africa. Son of R. R. (Western Province). Middle order right-hand batsman, wicket-keeper. *Team* Oxford U (1938).
Career batting
3–5–1–71–32–17.75–0–*ct* 9–*st* 4

Lyall, Charles Ross
Amateur. *b:* 3.10.1880, Calcutta, India. *d:* 4.6.1950, Basingstoke, Hants. Middle order right-hand batsman. *Sch* Edinburgh Academy. *Team* Somerset (1911, 2 matches).
Career batting
2–4–2–55–21*–27.50–0–*ct* 0

Lyle, Sir Archibald Moir Park
Amateur. *b:* 5.2.1884, Greenock, Renfrewshire, Scotland. *d:* 4.12.1946, London. Middle order batsman, bowler. *Sch* Fettes. *Teams* Oxford U (1904–06); Scotland (1912).
Career batting
3–6–0–77–27–12.83–0–*ct* 2
Bowling 30–0
An all-round sportsman, he represented Oxford against Cambridge in the 120 yards hurdles and putting the weight, as well as being in the rugby XV for three seasons.

Lynas, George Goulton
Professional. *b:* 7.9.1832, Coutham, Cleveland, Yorkshire. *d:* 8.12.1896, Guisborough, Yorkshire. Lower order right-hand batsman, wicket-keeper, occasional right-hand fast round-arm bowler. *Team* Yorkshire (1867, 2 matches).
Career batting
2–3–1–4–4*–2.00–0–*ct* 2

Lynch, Monte Alan
Cricketer. *b:* 21.5.1958, Georgetown, British Guiana. Middle order right-hand batsman, right-arm medium or off break bowler. *Teams* Surrey (1977–83, 99 matches), Guyana (1982–3). *Tours* International XI to Pakistan 1981/2.
Career batting
109–187–24–5035–141*–30.88–9–*ct* 67
Bowling 574–11–52.18–0–0–3/6
He hit 1,558 runs, av 53.72 in 1983.

Lynch, Ronald Victor
Amateur. *b:* 22.5.1923, Stratford, East London. Tail end right-hand batsman, slow left-arm bowler. *Sch* St Paul's. *Team* Essex (1954, 3 matches).
Career batting
3–3–2–7–6*–7.00–0–*ct* 2
Bowling 107–4–26.75–0–0–4/64

Lynes, John
Professional. *b:* 6.6.1872, Coleshill, Warwickshire. Lower order right-hand batsman, right-arm fast medium bowler. *Team* Warwickshire (1897–1905, 8 matches).
Career batting
8–8–0–79–26–9.87–0–*ct* 6
Bowling 576–15–38.40–0–0–3/54

Lyness, George Edward Given
Amateur. *b:* 16.12.1937, Dunmurry, Belfast, Ireland. Right-hand batsman, off break bowler. *Team* Ireland (1961).
Career batting
1–2–0–12–9–6.00–0–*ct* 2
Bowling 90–8–11.25–1–0–6/39

Lynn, George Henry
Professional. *b:* 31.3.1848, East Grinstead, Sussex. *d:* 21.9.1921, East Grinstead, Sussex. Free hitting right-hand middle order batsman, deep field. *Team* Sussex (1872–73, 8 matches).
Career batting
8–13–0–128–25–9.84–0–*ct* 1
Bowling 8–1–8.00–0–0–1/8

Lynn, Joseph
Professional. *b:* 1856, London. *d:* 1927, Southampton, Hants. Lower order batsman, fair bowler. *Team* Hampshire (1875, 1 match).
Career batting
1–2–1–4–4*–4.00–0–*ct* 1
Bowling 34–2–17.00–0–0–2/25

Lyon, Beverley Hamilton
Amateur. *b:* 19.1.1902, Caterham, Surrey. *d:* 22.6.1970, Balcombe, Sussex. Brother of M. D. (Somerset). Hard hitting middle order right-hand batsman, excellent close field. *Sch* Rugby. *Teams* Gloucestershire (1921–47, 238 matches); Oxford U (1922–23, blue both years); Europeans (1924/5 to 1945/6). *Tour* Cahn to Ceylon 1936/7 (no first-class matches).
Career batting
267–448–20–10694–189–24.98–16–*ct* 263
Bowling 2341–52–45.02–1–0–5/72

He hit 1,000 runs in a season four times (best 1,576, av 38.43, in 1930). From 1929 to 1934 he captained Gloucestershire and in 1931 was the instigator of the 'freak' declaration, whereby a County declared their first innings closed, after a nominal single ball, when rain had reduced the playing time, in order to have the chance of gaining maximum points. He was also among the first to advocate County cricket on Sunday.

His final first-class match was for West v East in the 1948 Kingston Festival.

He also played for Wiltshire.

Lyon, Brigadier-General Charles Harry
Amateur. *b:* 18.3.1878, Rocester, Staffs. *d:* 3.12.1959, Ightfield, Salop. Middle order right-hand batsman. *Sch* Newton College. *Team* Derbyshire (1902, 2 matches).
Career batting
2–2–0–6–4–3.00–0–*ct* 0
Bowling 6–0

Lyon, Admiral Sir George Hamilton D'Oyly
Amateur. *b:* 3.10.1883, Bankipore, India. *d:* 19.8.1947, Eastshaw, Midhurst, Sussex. Middle order right-hand batsman, right-arm pace bowler. *Sch* King's School, Bruton. *Teams* Hampshire (1907, 2 matches); Royal Navy (1911–22).
Career batting
4–7–0–185–90–26.42–0–*ct* 4
Bowling 140–7–20.00–0–0–4/51

An excellent rugby full back, he represented Surrey and England.

Lyon, Gordon William Francis
Amateur. *b:* 22.5.1905, Bradford on Avon, Wiltshire. *d:* 22.12.1932, Steyning, Sussex. Opening right-hand batsman. *Sch* Brighton. *Team* Oxford U (1925–27, blue 1925).
Career batting
9–17–1–262–52–16.37–0–*ct* 7
Bowling 5–1–5.00–0–0–1/5

Lyon, Herbert
Amateur. *b:* 29.4.1867, Valparaiso, Chile. *d:* 7.12.1951, Woking, Surrey. Attacking lower order right-hand batsman, wicket-keeper. *Sch* Winchester. *Team* Oxford U (1887–90).
Career batting
3–6–2–13–9*–3.25–0–*ct* 1

Lyon, John
Cricketer. *b:* 17.5.1951, St. Helens, Lancashire. Lower order right-hand batsman, wicket-keeper. *Team* Lancashire (1973–79, 84 matches). *Tour* Robins to South Africa 1974/5.
Career batting
86–91–18–1016–123–13.91–1–*ct* 159–*st* 12

Lyon, Malcolm Douglas
Amateur. *b:* 22.4.1898, Caterham, Surrey. *d:* 17.2.1964, St. Leonards-on-Sea, Sussex. Brother of B. H. (Gloucs). Forcing middle order right-hand batsman, wicket-keeper. *Sch* Rugby. *Teams* Somerset (1920–38, 123 matches); Cambridge U (1920–22, blue 1921–22).
Career batting
158–265–16–7294–219–29.29–14–*ct* 149–*st* 43
Bowling 574–8–71.75–0–0–3/43

He hit 1,000 runs in a season twice (best 1,298, av 34.15, in 1923); both his double centuries were for Somerset, the highest being 219 v Derbyshire at Burton upon Trent in 1924.

He was regarded as one of the best batsmen not to be capped by England; the fact that he was rather a controversial cricketer perhaps swayed the selectors.

His County cricket virtually ended in 1932 when he was appointed a magistrate in Gambia; from 1948 to 1957 he was Chief Justice in the Seychelles and later Puisne Judge in Uganda. He also played for Wiltshire.

Lyons, Godrey Louis
Amateur. *b:* 23.5.1853, Fleetwood, Lancashire. *d:* 1931, Brighton, Sussex. Right-hand middle order batsman, deep field. *Team* Surrey (1880, 1 match).
Career batting
1–2–0–8–8–4.00–0–*ct* 0

Lyons, John James
Amateur. *b:* 21.5.1863, Gawler, South Australia. *d:* 21.7.1927, Adelaide, Australia. Fine attacking opening right-hand batsman, right-arm medium pace bowler. *Team* South Australia (1894/5 to 1899/1900, 47 matches). *Tours* Australia to England 1888, 1890, 1893, to North America 1893. *Tests* Australia (1886/7 to 1897/8, 14 matches).

Career batting
153–275–11–6752–149–25.57–11–*ct* 60
Bowling 3225–107–30.14–5–0–6/38
Test batting
14–27–0–731–134–27.07–1–*ct* 3
Bowling 149–6–24.83–1–0–5/30

He hit 1,000 runs on the tours of 1890 and 1893, being seen at his best in the latter season with 1,377 runs, av 28.10.

Lyons, Kevin James
Cricketer. *b:* 18.12.1946, Cardiff. Middle order right-hand batsman, right-arm medium pace bowler. *Team* Glamorgan (1967–77, 62 matches). *Tour* Glamorgan to West Indies 1969/70.
Career batting
62–99–14–1673–92–19.68–0–*ct* 27
Bowling 252–2–126.00–0–0–1/36

Lyons, Reginald William
Amateur. *b:* 12.7.1922, Dublin, Ireland. *d:* 12.9.1976, Worthing, Sussex. Lower order right-hand batsman, wicket-keeper. *Team* Ireland (1947).
Career batting
1–1–1–0–0*–no av–0–*ct* 0–*st* 4

Lyttelton, Hon Alfred
Amateur. *b:* 7.2.1857, London. *d:* 5.7.1913, Marylebone, London. He died following an operation. Son of 4th Lord Lyttelton (Cambridge U), brother of Edward (Middlesex), C. G. (Cambridge U), R. H. (MCC), A. T. (MCC), G. W. S. (Cambridge U), uncle of C. J. (Worcs). Fine middle order right-hand batsman, wicket-keeper, occasional right-hand under-arm bowler. *Sch* Eton. *Teams* Cambridge U (1876–79, blue all four years); Middlesex (1877–87, 35 matches). *Tests* England (1880–84, 4 matches).
Career batting
101–171–12–4429–181–27.85–7–*ct* 134–*st* 70
Bowling 172–4–43.00–0–0–4/19
Test batting
4–7–1–94–31–15.66–0–*ct* 2
Bowling 19–4–4.74–0–0–4/19

He was President of MCC in 1898 and a member of the Committee 1881–85 and 1899–1903. He appeared also for Worcestershire (not first-class).

Owing to his work at the Bar, he gave up first-class cricket in 1887.

An excellent soccer player, he represented England in 1877 and the Old Etonians in the FA Cup Final of 1876. He also represented Cambridge at Real Tennis, rackets and athletics.

From 1895 to 1906 he was MP for Warwick and from 1906 to his death MP for St George's, Hanover Square.

Lyttelton, Right Rev the Hon Arthur Temple
Amateur. *b:* 7.1.1852, London. *d:* 19.2.1903, Petersfield, Hants. Son of 4th Lord Lyttelton (Cambridge U), brother of Alfred (Middlesex), C. G. (Cambridge U), Edward (Middlesex), R. H. (MCC), G. W. S. (Cambridge U), uncle of C. J. (Worcs). Middle order right-hand batsman, good deep field. *Sch* Eton. *Team* MCC (1872).
Career batting
1–2–0–4–4–2.00–0–*ct* 0

At the time of his death he was Bishop of Southampton.

He was not in the Eleven whilst at Cambridge.

Lyttelton, Rev Hon Charles Frederick
Amateur. *b:* 26.1.1887, London. *d:* 3.10.1931, Paddington, London. Lower order right-hand batsman, right-arm fast bowler. *Sch* Eton. *Teams* Worcestershire (1906–10, 9 matches); Cambridge U (1907–09, blue 1908–09).
Career batting
31–48–15–304–25*–9.21–0–*ct* 16
Bowling 2155–86–25.05–2–0–5/33

Curiously he was unable to find a place in the eleven at Eton, but still won his blue at Cambridge.

Lyttelton, Hon Charles George
(succeeded as 8th Viscount Cobham in 1888)
Amateur. *b:* 27.10.1842, Hagley Hall, Stourbridge, Worcs. *d:* 9.6.1922, Hagley Hall, Stourbridge, Worcs. Son of 4th Lord Lyttelton (Cambridge U), brother of Alfred (Middlesex), Edward (Middlesex), R. H. (MCC), A. T. (MCC), G. W. S. (Cambridge U), father of C. J. (Worcs). Hard hitting middle order right-hand batsman, right-hand fast medium round-arm bowler, also under-arm lobs, occasional wicket-keeper. *Sch* Eton. *Teams* Cambridge U (1861–64, blue all four years).
Career batting
35–54–1–1439–129–27.15–2–*ct* 33–*st* 5
Bowling 547–28+1–19.53–0–0–4/19

His final first-class match was for Southgate in 1867.

Lyttelton, Hon Charles John
(succeeded as 10th Viscount Cobham in 1949)
Amateur. *b:* 8.8.1909, London. *d:* 20.3.1977, Marylebone, London. Son of 9th Viscount Cobham (Worcs). Hard hitting middle order right-hand batsman, right-arm medium pace bowler. *Sch* Eton. *Team* Worcestershire (1932–39, 93 matches). *Tours* MCC to Australia and New Zealand 1935/6; Norfolk to Jamaica 1956/7 (he did not play in first-class matches).

Career batting
104–171–14–3181–162–20.26–1–*ct* 52
Bowling 1318–32–41.18–0–0–4/83

His final first-class match was for Governor-General's XI v MCC in New Zealand in 1960/1 – he was Governor-General from 1957 to 1962.

In 1954 he was President of MCC and Treasurer in 1963.

From 1936 to 1939 he captained Worcestershire.

Lyttelton, Rev the Hon Edward
Amateur. *b:* 23.7.1855, London. *d:* 26.1.1942, Lincoln. Son of 4th Lord Lyttelton (Cambridge U), brother of Alfred (Middlesex), C. G. (Cambridge U), R. H. (MCC), A. T. (MCC), G. W. S. (Cambridge U), uncle of C. J. (Worcs). Middle order right-hand batsman, good deep field. *Sch* Eton. *Teams* Cambridge U (1875–78, blue all four years); Middlesex (1878–82, 13 matches).
Career batting
57–95–5–2013–113–22.36–1–*ct* 43
Bowling 50–1–50.00–0–0–1/4

He also played for Worcestershire (pre-first-class), and Hertfordshire.

He excelled at football, fives and athletics.

From 1905 to 1916 he was Headmaster of Eton.

Lyttelton, Hon George William Spencer
Amateur. *b:* 12.6.1847, London. *d:* 5.12.1913, Westminster, London. Son of 4th Lord Lyttelton, brother of Alfred (Middlesex), A. T. (MCC), C. G. (Cambridge U), Edward (Middlesex), R. H. (MCC), uncle of C. J. (Worcs). Middle order right-hand batsman, right-hand fast round-arm bowler, good field. *Sch* Eton. *Team* Cambridge U (1866–67, blue both years).
Career batting
18–29–1–581–114–20.75–1–*ct* 11–*st* 6
Bowling 781–33–23.66–2–1–7/33

His final first-class match was for Gentlemen of England in 1872.

He played County cricket for Worcestershire, Shropshire and Northants.

He was chief private secretary to W. E. Gladstone 1892–94.

Lyttelton, Hon J. C.
(*see under* Cobham, 9th Viscount)

Lyttelton, Hon Robert Henry
Amateur. *b:* 18.1.1854, St. James's Square, London. *d:* 7.11.1939, North Berwick. Son of 4th Lord Lyttelton (Cambridge U), brother of Alfred (Middlesex), C. G. (Cambridge U), Edward (Middlesex), A. T. (MCC), G. W. S. (Cambridge U), uncle of C. J. (Worcs). Middle order right-hand batsman, slow under-arm bowler. *Sch* Eton. *Team* MCC (1873).
Career batting
7–12–1–67–27–6.09–0–*ct* 2
Bowling 31–1–31.00–0–0–1/27

He was not in the eleven whilst at Cambridge, but represented the University at tennis.

Although not a famous cricketer, he was a noted student and critic of the game, contributing several well-known essays on various aspects of cricket.

His final first-class match was for I Zingari in 1880.

Lywood, Lewis William
Professional. *b:* 23.12.1906, Walthamstow, Essex. *d:* 31.10.1971, Caterham, Surrey. Lower order right-hand batsman, right-arm fast medium bowler. *Teams* Surrey (1927–28, 2 matches); Essex (1930, 2 matches).
Career batting
4–5–0–19–7–3.80–0–*ct* 0
Bowling 260–3–86.66–0–0–1/7

He was for many years a noted club cricketer in South London.

MAARTENSZ, SYDNEY GRATIEN ADAIR
Amateur. *b:* 14.4.1882, Colombo, Ceylon. *d:* 10.9.1967, Pyrford, Surrey. Lower order right-hand batsman, wicket-keeper. *Team* Hampshire (1919, 12 matches).
Career batting
12–17–2–283–60–18.86–0–*ct* 21–*st* 4

Maazullah Khan
Cricketer. *b:* 1.9.1947, Peshawar, Pakistan. Lower order right-hand batsman, off break bowler. *Teams* Peshawar (1965/6 to 1979/80); Railways (1971/2). *Tour* Pakistan to England 1974.
Career batting
45–71–7–1312–130–20.50–2–*ct* 20
Bowling 2766–120–23.05–4–1–8/97
He played in only four first-class matches on the 1974 tour.

McAdam, Keith Paul William James
Cricketer. *b:* 13.8.1945, Edinburgh, Scotland. Opening left-hand batsman, right-arm bowler. *Sch* Millfield. *Team* Cambridge U (1965–66, blue both years).
Career batting
21–39–0–815–63–20.89–0–*ct* 10
Bowling 2–0
His final first-class match was for MCC in 1967. His County cricket was for Buckinghamshire.

McAdam, William James
Cricketer. *b:* 3.10.1944, Springs, Transvaal. Brother of S. J. (Eastern Province). Middle order right-hand batsman. *Teams* Western Province (1966/7 to 1968/9); Eastern Province (1971/2). *Tour* South African Universities to England 1967.
Career batting
19–30–1–668–129–23.03–1–*ct* 7
Bowling 3–0
His first-class debut was for South African Universities in 1966/7.

McAlister, Peter Alexander
Amateur. *b:* 11.7.1869, Williamstown, Victoria, Australia. *d:* 10.5.1938, Richmond, Victoria, Australia. Stylish opening right-hand batsman. *Team* Victoria (1898/9 to 1910/11, 55 matches). *Tour* Australia to England 1909. *Tests* Australia (1903/4 to 1909, 8 matches).
Career batting
85–148–9–4552–224–32.74–9–*ct* 91
Bowling 56–3–18.66–0–0–1/0
Test batting
8–16–1–252–41–16.80–0–*ct* 10
A good batsman, he came to England too late in his career and it was unfortunate for him that the selectors made a controversial decision in choosing him as vice-captain of the tourists over the heads of Trumper and Armstrong. His highest score was 224 for Victoria v New Zealand at Melbourne in 1898/9.

McAllister, Alexander Eric
Amateur. *b:* 19.12.1920, Paisley, Renfrewshire, Scotland. Middle order right-hand batsman. *Team* Scotland (1950).
Career batting
1–2–0–13–9–6.50–0–*ct* 1

McAlpine, Kenneth
Amateur. *b:* 11.4.1858, Leamington, Warwickshire. *d:* 10.2.1923, Loose, Maidstone, Kent. Opening right-hand batsman. *Sch* Haileybury. *Team* Kent (1885–86, 3 matches). *Tours* Hawke to North America 1891, 1894 (he did not play in first-class matches).
Career batting
4–7–1–30–10–5.00–0–*ct* 2
He was a great supporter of Kent cricket and President of the County Club in 1922.

Macan, George
Amateur. *b:* 9.9.1853, Greenmount Castle, Bellingham, Co Louth, Ireland. *d:* 2.11.1943, Wimbledon Common, South London. Lower order right-hand batsman, right-hand slow round-arm bowler. *Sch* Harrow. *Team* Cambridge U (1872–75, blue 1874–75).
Career batting
18–33–6–391–57–14.48–0–*ct* 6

Macartney, Charles George
Amateur. *b:* 27.6.1886, West Maitland, New South Wales, Australia. *d:* 9.9.1958, Sydney, New South Wales, Australia. Grandson of G. Moore (New South Wales). Attacking middle order right-hand batsman, slow left-arm bowler, fine field. *Team* New South Wales (1905/6 to 1926/7, 81 matches). *Tours* Australia to England 1909, 1912, 1921, 1926, to South Africa 1921/2, to North America 1913, to India and Ceylon 1935/6. *Tests* Australia (1907/8 to 1926, 35 matches).
Career batting
249–360–32–15019–345–45.78–49–*ct* 102
Bowling 8781–419–20.95–17–1–7/58
Test batting
35–55–4–2131–170–41.78–7–*ct* 17
Bowling 1240–45–27.55–2–1–7/58
His outstanding tour to England was in 1921 when he hit 2,317 runs, av 59.42, but he also scored over 2,000 runs in 1912 when he in addition headed the bowling averages; in 1926 he easily topped 1,000 runs. On his first visit he was regarded more as a bowler than a batsman, taking

64 wickets, av 17.85. His most famous innings was 345 against Notts at Trent Bridge in 1921 – the entire innings was completed on the first day, a record in first-class cricket. He hit three other double centuries, including one v Essex in 1912.

Macaulay, George Gibson

Professional. *b:* 7.12.1897, Thirsk, Yorkshire. *d:* 14.12.1940, Church Fenton, Yorkshire. Lower order right-hand batsman, originally right-arm fast, but in 1921 altered to medium pace bowler, brilliant close field. *Sch* Barnard Castle. *Team* Yorkshire (1920–35, 445 matches). *Tours* MCC to South Africa 1922/3). *Tests* England (1922/3 to 1933, 8 matches).

Career batting
468–460–125–6056–125*–18.07–3–*ct* 374
Bowling 32440–1837–17.65–126–31–8/21
Test batting
8–10–4–112–76–18.66–0–*ct* 5
Bowling 662–24–27.58–1–0–5/64

He took 100 wickets in a season ten times including over 200 once – 211, av 15.48, in 1925. An injury to his finger in 1934 caused him to retire from first-class cricket earlier than would otherwise have been the case.

Macaulay, Michael John

Amateur. *b:* 19.4.1939, Durban, South Africa. Lower order right-hand batsman, left-arm medium pace bowler. *Teams* Transvaal (1957/8 to 1965/6); Western Province (1960/1); NE Transvaal (1966/7 to 1968/9); Orange Free State (1963/4 to 1964/5); Eastern Province (1977/8 to 1978/9). *Tour* South Africa to England 1965. *Test* South Africa (1964/65, 1 match).

Career batting
69–91–23–888–59–13.05–0–*ct* 45
Bowling 5357–234–22.89–16–4–7/49
Test batting
1–2–0–33–21–16.50–0–*ct* 0
Bowling 73–2–36.50–0–0–1/10

Although he bowled usefully on the 1965 tour to England, he was not required for any of the Tests.

McBride, Walter Nelson

Amateur. *b:* 27.11.1904, Croydon, Surrey. *d:* 30.1.1974, Ealing, Middlesex. Lower order left-hand batsman, right-arm medium pace bowler. *Sch* Westminster. *Teams* Hampshire (1925–29, 31 matches); Oxford U (1925–27, blue 1926).

Career batting
47–67–16–656–51–12.86–0–*ct* 31
Bowling 1791–56–31.98–2–0–5/57

He also played for Dorset. A good goalkeeper, he obtained his soccer blue in 1927.

MacBryan, John Crawford William

Amateur. *b:* 22.7.1892, Box, Wiltshire. *d:* 14.7.1983, London. Stylish middle order right-hand batsman. *Sch* Cheltenham. *Teams* Somerset (1911–31, 156 matches); Cambridge U (1919–20, blue 1920). *Tour* Joel to South Africa 1924/5. *Test* England (1924, 1 match).

Career batting
206–363–12–10322–164–29.49–18–*ct* 128
Bowling 61–0
Test batting
1 match, did not bat–*ct* 0

He hit 1,000 runs in a season four times (best 1,831, av 35.90, in 1923). His final first-class match was for MCC in 1936.

McCabe, Stanley Joseph

Amateur. *b:* 16.7.1910, Grenfell, New South Wales, Australia. *d:* 25.8.1968, Beauty Point, Mosman, New South Wales, Australia. Brilliant middle order right-hand batsman, right-arm medium pace bowler. *Team* New South Wales (1928/9 to 1941/2, 55 matches). *Tours* Australia to England 1930, 1934, 1938, to South Africa 1935/6. *Tests* Australia (1930–38, 39 matches).

Career batting
182–262–20–11951–240–49.38–29–*ct* 139
Bowling 5362–159–33.72–1–0–5/36
Test batting
39–62–5–2748–232–48.21–6–*ct* 41
Bowling 1543–36–42.86–0–0–4/13

His greatest innings in England was his 232 in the Trent Bridge Test of 1938 – regarded by many as one of the all time exhibitions of batsmanship. Curiously he had a very moderate tour otherwise and scored only 1,124 runs. In 1934 he hit 2,078, av 69.26, and in 1930, 1,012 av 32.64, so that in terms of figures 1934 was easily his most rewarding visit. His highest score was 240 for Australians v Surrey at the Oval in 1934.

McCall, Barney Ernest Wilford

Amateur. *b:* 13.5.1913, Bristol. *d:* 27.11.1982, Cambridge. Middle order left-hand batsman, left-arm bowler. *Sch* Weymouth. *Teams* Army (1936); Minor Counties (1937); Combined Services (1948).

Career batting
3–6–0–56–31–9.33–0–*ct* 4
Bowling 35–1–35.00–0–0–1/34

His County cricket was for Dorset. A noted rugby footballer, he was capped for Wales.

McCall, Hugh Con

Cricketer. *b:* 29.3.1940, Holywood, Co Down, Ireland. Middle order right-hand batsman, slow left-arm bowler. *Sch* Campbell College. *Team* Ireland (1964–68).

Career batting
7–14–1–308–81–23.69–0–*ct* 3
Bowling 1–0

McCanlis, George
Professional. *b:* 3.12.1847, Landguard, Suffolk. *d:* 18.10.1937, Upper Norwood, London. Brother of William (Kent). Middle order right-hand batsman, right-hand medium pace round-arm bowler. *Team* Kent (1873–78, 17 matches).
Career batting
17–31–2–364–60–12.55–0–*ct* 8
Bowling 117–3–39.00–0–0–1/9

McCanlis, Maurice Alfred
Amateur. *b:* 17.6.1906, Quetta, India. Middle order right-hand batsman, right-hand medium pace bowler. *Sch* Cranleigh. *Teams* Oxford U (1926–28, blue all three years); Surrey (1926–27, 2 matches); Gloucestershire (1929, 1 match); Rajputana (1938/9 to 1939/40).
Career batting
30–45–13–493–40*–15.40–0–*ct* 19
Bowling 2642–82–32.22–4–0–5/42
A noted rugby footballer, he was capped for England.

McCanlis, William
Professional. *b:* 30.10.1840, Woolwich, Kent. *d:* 19.11.1925, Westcombe Park, Kent. Brother of George (Kent). Hard hitting middle order right-hand batsman. *Team* Kent (1862–77, 45 matches).
Career batting
45–86–4–1113–67–13.57–0–*ct* 20
Bowling 496–18–27.55–0–0–4/67
He appeared in some matches under the alias of 'Willis'.

McCarthy, Charles Henry Florence D'Arcy
Amateur. *b:* 29.6.1899, Coimbatore, India. *d:* 24.7.1977, Nassau, Bahamas. Sound middle order right-hand batsman, leg break bowler, good field. *Sch* Rugby. *Teams* Army (1921); Burma/Rangoon (1926/7).
Career batting
3–6–1–75–48–15.00–0–*ct* 0
Bowling 33–1–33.00–0–0–1/33
He played occasionally for Devon.

McCarthy, Cuan Neil
Amateur. *b:* 24.3.1929, Pietermaritzburg, South Africa. Tail end right-hand batsman, right-arm fast bowler. *Teams* Natal (1947/8 to 1950/1); Cambridge U (1952, blue). *Tour* South Africa to England 1951. *Tests* South Africa (1948/9 to 1951, 15 matches).
Career batting
60–68–35–141–23*–4.27–0–*ct* 23
Bowling 4551–176–25.85–8–1–8/36
Test batting
15–24–15–28–5–3.11–0–*ct* 6
Bowling 1510–36–41.94–2–0–6/43
He was not too successful on the 1951 tour to England, taking 59 wickets, av 23.96, in first-class matches, but he appeared in all five Tests. In 1952 he easily headed the Cambridge University bowling averages, but was no-balled for throwing, and he did not appear in first-class cricket after 1952. He played County cricket for Dorset. A good boxer, he was awarded his blue whilst at Cambridge.

MacCarthy-Morrogh, William Charles Frederick
Amateur. *b:* 19.11.1870, Kerry, Ireland. *d:* 15.9.1939, Falmouth, Cornwall. Left-hand batsman, slow left-arm bowler. *Sch* Stonyhurst. *Team* Dublin U (1895).
Career batting
1–2–0–3–2–1.50–0–*ct* 1
Bowling 50–0

McCaskie, Norman
Amateur. *b:* 23.3.1911, Kensington, London. *d:* 1.7.1968, Theale, Berkshire. Middle order left-hand batsman, left-arm medium pace bowler. *Sch* Winchester. *Teams* Middlesex (1931–32, 3 matches); Oxford U (1932).
Career batting
4–6–0–55–26–9.16–0–*ct* 1
Bowling 22–0

McCaughey, Samuel
Amateur. *b:* 27.11.1892, Coree, New South Wales, Australia. *d:* 29.1.1955, Deniliquin, New South Wales, Australia. Lower order batsman, right-arm medium and leg break bowler. *Sch* Haileybury. *Team* Cambridge U (1913).
Career batting
2–3–0–10–9–3.33–0–*ct* 3
Bowling 123–9–13.66–1–0–7/46

McCausland, Charles Edward
Amateur. *b:* 4.10.1898, Dublin, Ireland. *d:* 12.11.1965, Folkestone, Kent. Middle order right-hand batsman, right-arm fast medium bowler. *Sch* Winchester. *Teams* Dublin U (1922–25); Ireland (1922–24).
Career batting
5–10–0–139–26–13.90–0–*ct* 4
Bowling 175–3–58.33–0–0–2/38

McCay, David Lawrence
Cricketer. *b:* 18.11.1943, Cape Town, South

Africa. Lower order right-hand batsman, right-arm medium pace bowler. *Team* Western Province (1966/7 to 1973/4). *Tour* South African Universities to England 1967.
Career batting
17–25–3–345–82–15.68–0–*ct* 12
Bowling 1071–49–21.85–2–1–8/76

McClintock, William Kerr
Amateur. *b:* 7.3.1896, Newcastle on Tyne, Northumberland. *d:* 30.3.1946, Bow, London. Middle order right-hand batsman. *Sch* Harrow. *Team* Gloucestershire (1920–21, 8 matches).
Career batting
8–13–0–98–24–7.53–0–*ct* 4

McCloughin, Kenelm Rees
Amateur. *b:* 18.8.1884, Bombay, India. *d:* 30.11.1915, near Bethune, France. Opening or middle order batsman. *Sch* Dulwich. *Teams* Europeans (1909/10); Army (1914); L. Robinson's XI (1914); Free Foresters (1914).
Career batting
5–9–0–158–57–17.55–0–*ct* 2
Bowling 52–1–52.00–0–0–1/4

McCloy, Thomas
Amateur. *b:* 31.8.1927, Lambeg, Co. Antrim, Ireland. Middle order right-hand batsman, right-arm medium pace bowler. *Team* Ireland (1952–65).
Career batting
12–24–0–374–53–15.58–0–*ct* 6
Bowling 15–0

MacColl, René
Amateur. *b:* 12.1.1905, Brentford, Middlesex. *d:* 20.5.1971, Crowborough, Sussex. Opening or middle order batsman, change bowler. *Sch* University College School. *Team* Oxford U (1924).
Career batting
1–2–0–4–4–2.00–0–*ct* 0
He was a well-known journalist.

McConnon, James (Edward)
Professional. *b:* 21.6.1922, Burnopfield, Co Durham. Lower order right-hand batsman, right-arm off break bowler. *Team* Glamorgan (1950–61, 243 matches). *Tours* MCC to Australia 1954/5; Commonwealth to India 1953/4. *Tests* England (1954, 2 matches).
Career batting
256–366–42–4661–95–14.38–0–*ct* 152
Bowling 16285–819–19.88–49–12–8/36
Test batting
2–3–1–18–11–9.00–0–*ct* 4
Bowling 74–4–18.50–0–0–3/19

He took 100 wickets in a season three times (best 136, av 16.07, in 1951). His best innings analysis was 8 for 36 for Glamorgan v Notts at Trent Bridge in 1953. He also played for Cheshire. A good soccer player, he was centre half for Aston Villa.

McCool, Colin Leslie
Professional. *b:* 9.12.1915, Sydney, Australia. Father of R. J. (Somerset). Middle order right-hand batsman, leg break bowler, good slip field. *Teams* New South Wales (1939/40 to 1940/1, 7 matches); Queensland (1945/6 to 1952/3, 47 matches); Somerset (1956–60, 138 matches). *Tours* Australia to England 1948, to South Africa 1949/50, to New Zealand 1945/6; Howard to India 1956/7. *Tests* Australia (1945/6 to 1949/50, 14 matches).
Career batting
251–412–34–12421–172–32.85–18–*ct* 262–*st* 2
Bowling 16542–602–27.47–34–2–8/74
Test batting
14–17–4–459–104*–35.30–1–*ct* 14
Bowling 958–36–26.61–3–0–5/41
Although he was a useful all-rounder he did not appear in any of the Tests on the 1948 tour – as a bowler he took 57 wickets, av 17.82. During his seasons with Somerset he hit 1,000 runs four times (best 1,967, av 37.82, in 1956).

McCool, Russel John
Cricketer. *b:* 4.12.1959, Taunton, Somerset. Son of C.L. (Somerset, Queensland and NSW). Right-hand batsman, leg break and googly bowler. *Team* Somerset (1982, 1 match).
Career batting
1–2–0–19–12–9.50–0–*ct* 1
Bowling 63–0

McCorkell, Neil Thomas
Professional. *b:* 23.3.1912, Portsmouth, Hants. Opening right-hand batsman, wicket-keeper. *Team* Hampshire (1932–51, 383 matches). *Tour* Tennyson to India 1937/8.
Career batting
396–696–67–16107–203–25.60–17–*ct* 532–*st* 184
Bowling 117–1–117.00–0–0–1/73
He hit 1,000 runs in a season nine times (best 1,871, av 38.18, in 1949). His only double century was 203 for Hants v Gloucs at Gloucester in 1951.

McCormick, Edward James
Amateur. *b:* 1.11.1862, Hastings, Sussex. *d:* 31.12.1941, Templemore, Co. Tipperary, Ireland. Middle order right-hand batsman, right-arm medium pace bowler, good deep field. *Team* Sussex (1880–90, 46 matches).

Career batting
50–91–4–1346–73–15.47–0–*ct* 26
Bowling 338–9–37.55–0–0–2/36

He was for many years a noted figure in Hastings cricket, but owing to his profession (he was a banker), was unable to appear often in County matches.

McCormick, Ernest Leslie
Amateur. *b:* 16.5.1906, North Carlton, Victoria, Australia. Tail end left-hand batsman, right-arm fast bowler. *Team* Victoria (1929/30 to 1938/9, 43 matches). *Tours* Australia to South Africa 1935/6, to England 1938. *Tests* Australia (1935/6 to 1938, 12 matches).
Career batting
85–98–31–582–77*–8.68–0–*ct* 46
Bowling 6686–241–27.74–6–1–9/40
Test batting
12–14–5–54–17*–6.00–0–*ct* 8
Bowling 1079–36–29.97–0–0–4/101

Described at the time as the most over-rated bowler ever to tour England, he tried to bowl too fast and suffered from being no-balled for over-stepping the crease on many occasions. His results were very moderate, with 34 wickets, av 33.41, in first-class matches. His best bowling was 9/40 for Victoria v South Australia at Adelaide in 1936/7.

McCormick, Rev Canon Joseph
Amateur. *b:* 29.10.1834, Liverpool, Lancashire. *d:* 9.4.1914, Westminster, London. Fine punishing middle order right-hand batsman, right-hand slow round-arm bowler. *Sch* Liverpool College. *Team* Cambridge U (1854–56, blue 1854 and 1856).
Career batting
19–35–0–561–137–16.82–1–*ct* 11–*st* 1
Bowling 490–35+31–14.00–5–1–7/?

He played little important cricket after leaving Cambridge. His final first-class match was for MCC in 1868. He was in the Cambridge boat in 1856 and was also a noted boxer.

McCormick, Rev William Patrick Glyn
Amateur. *b:* 14.6.1877, Hull, Yorkshire. *d:* 16.10.1940, Westminster, London. Middle order right-hand batsman, slow left-arm bowler. *Team* MCC (1907).
Career batting
1–2–0–17–17–8.50–0–*ct* 0
Bowling 5–0

McCorquodale, Alastair
Amateur. *b:* 5.12.1925, Glasgow, Scotland. Lower order left-hand batsman, right-arm fast bowler. *Sch* Harrow. *Team* Middlesex (1951, 3 matches). *Tour* MCC to Canada 1951 (not in a first-class match).
Career batting
6–6–2–34–21–8.50–0–*ct* 1
Bowling 399–4–99.75–0–0–2/62

His first-class debut was for MCC in 1948.

A noted athlete, he came fourth in the 100 metres in the 1948 Olympic Games.

McCorquodale, Edmund George
Amateur. *b:* 23.7.1881, Weybridge, Surrey. *d:* 24.5.1904, Tulchan Lodge, Morayshire, Scotland. He died of appendicitis. Lower order right-hand batsman, right-arm medium pace bowler, moderate field. *Sch* Harrow. *Team* Cambridge U (1901).
Career batting
2–1–1–3–3*–no av–0–*ct* 1
Bowling 82–1–82.00–0–0–1/27

His County cricket was for Hertfordshire.

McCosker, Richard Bede
Cricketer. *b:* 11.12.1946, Inverell, New South Wales, Australia. Sound opening right-hand batsman. *Team* New South Wales (1973/4 to 1982/3, 75 matches). *Tours* Australia to England 1975, 1977, to New Zealand 1976/7. *Tests* Australia (1974/5 to 1979/80, 25 matches).
Career batting
116–209–24–8260–168–44.64–26–*ct* 129
Bowling 119–2–59.50–0–0–2/28
Test batting
25–46–5–1622–127–39.56–4–*ct* 21

His great match of the 1977 tour to England was the third Test, when he hit 51 and 107. He played in all the other Tests, but with little success, nor did he score many runs in the other first-class matches.

McCulloch, John Wyndham Hamilton
Amateur. *b:* 4.12.1894, Calcutta, India. *d:* 21.10.1915, Bailleul, Lille, France. He died of wounds. Middle order right-hand batsman. *Sch* Westminster. *Team* Middlesex (1914, 2 matches).
Career batting
2–3–0–18–14–6.00–0–*ct* 0

He was also a talented soccer player.

McCurdy, Rodney John
Cricketer. *b:* 30.12.1959, Melbourne, Australia. Lower order right-hand batsman, right-arm fast medium bowler. *Teams* Derbyshire (1979, 1 match); Tasmania (1980/1, 7 matches); Victoria (1981/2 to 1982/3, 15 matches). *Tour* Young Australia to Zimbabwe 1982/3.

Career batting
25–36–6–246–32–8.20–0–*ct* 8
Bowling 2642–90–29.35–5–0–7/91
He played for Shropshire in 1979.

McDermott, Enda Anthony
Cricketer. *b:* 1.12.1945, Dublin. Left-hand batsman. *Team* Ireland (1982).
Career batting
1–2–0–18–18–9.00–0–*ct* 1

McDonagh, Samuel Wilfred
Amateur. *b:* 8.8.1899, Armagh, Ireland. Right-hand batsman, wicket-keeper. *Team* Ireland (1930).
Career batting
1–2–0–61–48–30.50–0–*ct* 0

McDonald, Colin Campbell
Amateur. *b:* 17.11.1928, Glen Iris, Victoria, Australia. Brother of I. H. (Victoria). Sound opening right-hand batsman. *Team* Victoria (1947/8 to 1962/3, 60 matches). *Tours* Australia to England 1953, 1956, 1961, to South Africa 1957/8, to West Indies 1954/5, to India and Pakistan 1956/7, 1959/60; International XI to South Africa and Pakistan 1961/2. *Tests* Australia (1951/2 to 1961, 47 matches).
Career batting
192–307–26–11375–229–40.48–24–*ct* 55–*st* 2
Bowling 192–3–64.00–0–0–1/10
Test batting
47–83–4–3107–170–39.32–5–*ct* 14
Bowling 3–0
In 1953 he had a very modest tour and did not appear in the Tests, but in 1956 he hit 1,202 runs, av 34.34, and was the main opening bat. His last tour to England was not a success and after a poor start he was handicapped by injury. His highest score was 229 for Victoria v South Australia at Adelaide in 1953/4.

MacDonald, Donald
Amateur. *b:* 22.2.1887, Chard, Somerset. *d:* 29.6.1961, Southbourne, Hampshire. Lower order batsman, slow left-arm bowler. *Sch* Taunton. *Team* Scotland (1913).
Career batting
1–1–0–6–6–6.00–0–*ct* 1
Bowling 148–6–24.66–1–0–5/51

McDonald, Edgar Arthur
Professional. *b:* 6.1.1891, Launceston, Tasmania. *d:* 22.7.1937, Blackrod, Bolton, Lancashire. He was killed in a road accident. Lower order right-hand batsman, right-arm fast bowler. *Teams* Lancashire (1924–31, 217 matches); Tasmania (1909/10 to 1910/11, 2 matches); Victoria (1911/12 to 1921/2, 22 matches). *Tours* Australia to England 1921, to South Africa 1921/2. *Tests* Australia (1920/1 to 1921/2, 11 matches).
Career batting
281–302–47–2663–100*–10.44–1–*ct* 98
Bowling 28966–1395–20.76–119–31–8/41
Test batting
11–12–5–116–36–16.57–0–*ct* 3
Bowling 1431–43–33.27–2–0–5/32
Coming to England with the 1921 Australians, he proved to be the outstanding bowler of the tour, heading the Test averages and in first-class matches taking 138 wickets, av 16.55. He later returned to England to qualify for Lancashire and in 1925 took 205 wickets, av 18.66 – the only time he exceeded 200 wickets in a season, though he achieved over 100 seven times. His final first-class match was for Sir L. Parkinson's XI in 1935. In Australia he was also a noted footballer, both rugby and association.

MacDonald, Harry Lindsay Sumerlid
Amateur. *b:* 2.8.1861, Westminster, London. *d:* 18.8.1936, Bathford, Somerset. Middle order batsman. *Sch* Charterhouse. *Team* Somerset (1896, 1 match).
Career batting
1–2–1–22–22*–22.00–0–*ct* 2

MacDonald, James
Amateur. *b:* 17.9.1906, Comber, Co Down, Ireland. *d:* 8.3.1969, Bangor, Co Down, Ireland. Brother of T. J. (Ireland). Middle order left-hand batsman, slow left-arm bowler. *Team* Ireland (1926–39).
Career batting
14–27–1–622–108*–23.92–1–*ct* 5
Bowling 891–35–25.45–1–0–5/33

McDonald, John Archibald
Amateur. *b:* 29.5.1882, Belper, Derbyshire. *d:* 4.6.1961, Blackburn, Lancashire. Middle order right-hand batsman. *Team* Derbyshire (1905–06, 3 matches).
Career batting
3–6–0–57–21–9.50–0–*ct* 0

MacDonald, Dr Robert
Amateur. *b:* 28.2.1870, Melbourne, Australia. *d:* May 1945, Victoria, British Columbia. Middle order right-hand batsman, leg break bowler. *Teams* Queensland (1893/4 to 1903/4, 14 matches); Leicestershire (1899–1902, 33 matches). *Tour* Queensland to New Zealand 1896/7.
Career batting
48–80–15–2068–147*–31.81–4–*ct* 34
Bowling 181–3–60.33–0–0–3/49

MacDonald, Thomas John
Amateur. *b:* 27.12.1908, Comber, Co Down, Ireland. Brother of James (Ireland). Middle order right-hand batsman, leg break bowler. *Teams* Ireland (1928–36); Cambridge U (1929).
Career batting
7–14–0–291–132–20.78–1–*ct* 4
Bowling 32–0
He played for Lincolnshire.

MacDonald-Watson, Alistair
Amateur. *b:* 29.1.1909, Croydon, Surrey. Tail end right-hand batsman, right-arm fast bowler. *Team* Somerset (1932–33, 4 matches).
Career batting
4–6–1–2–1–0.40–0–*ct* 1
Bowling 219–8–27.37–1–0–5/27

McDonell, Harold Clark
Amateur. *b:* 19.9.1882, Wimbledon, Surrey. *d:* 23.7.1965, Onich, Fort William, Inverness, Scotland. Lower order right-hand batsman, leg break bowler, good field. *Sch* Winchester. *Teams* Cambridge U (1902–05, blue 1903–05); Surrey (1901–04, 13 matches); Hampshire (1908–21, 78 matches). *Tour* MCC to North America 1905.
Career batting
129–210–19–3005–78–15.73–0–*ct* 124
Bowling 9710–443–21.91–22–3–8/83

MacDonnell, James Edward
Amateur. *b:* 23.4.1841, Ireland. *d:* 26.11.1891, Brighton, Sussex. Middle order batsman. *Team* Gloucestershire (1881, 1 match).
Career batting
1–1–0–0–0–0.00–0–*ct* 0

McDonnell, Percy Stanislaus
Amateur. *b:* 13.11.1858, Kensington, London. *d:* 24.9.1896, Brisbane, Australia. He died of consumption. Fine attacking opening right-hand batsman, brilliant slip. *Teams* Victoria (1877/8 to 1884/5, 14 matches); New South Wales (1885/6 to 1891/2, 17 matches); Queensland (1894/5 to 1895/6, 3 matches). *Tours* Australia to England 1880, 1882, 1884 and 1888. *Tests* Australia (1880–88, 19 matches).
Career batting
166–285–10–6470–239–23.52–7–*ct* 98
Bowling 247–2–123.50–0–0–1/7
Test batting
19–34–1–950–147–28.78–3–*ct* 6
Bowling 53–0
He was most successful on the 1888 tour to England, hitting 1,331 runs, av 23.35. He captained the side on this visit. He led Australia in six Tests, but was on the losing side in five of them. His only double century was 239 for New South Wales v Victoria at Melbourne in 1886/7.

McDougall, John Robson
Amateur. *b:* 2.3.1886, Galashiels, Selkirkshire, Scotland. *d:* 1.4.1971, Ayr, Scotland. Right-hand batsman, wicket-keeper. *Team* Scotland (1912).
Career batting
1–2–0–15–12–7.50–0–*ct* 1

McDowall, James Ian
Cricketer. *b:* 9.12.1947, Sutton Coldfield, Warwickshire. Opening/middle order right-hand batsman, wicket-keeper. *Sch* Rugby. *Teams* Cambridge U (1969–70, blue 1969); Warwickshire (1969–73, 12 matches).
Career batting
29–53–5–811–89–16.89–0–*ct* 50–*st* 3
His father was Hon Treasurer of Warwickshire CCC in 1970.

McEntyre, Kenneth Brinsley
Cricketer. *b:* 24.3.1944, Chester. Middle order right-hand batsman, good field. *Team* Surrey (1965–66, 3 matches).
Career batting
3–3–0–33–15–11.00–0–*ct* 0

McEvoy, Michael Stephen Anthony
Cricketer. *b:* 25.1.1956, Jorhat, Assam, India. Opening right-hand batsman, right-arm medium pace bowler. *Teams* Essex (1976–81, 43 matches); Worcestershire (1983, 16 matches). *Tour* Minor Counties to East Africa 1982/3 (not first-class).
Career batting
59–100–2–1940–103–19.79–1–*ct* 59
Bowling 103–3–34.33–0–0–3/20
He also played for Cambridgeshire.

McEwan, Kenneth Scott
Cricketer. *b:* 16.7.1952, Bedford, South Africa. Middle order right-hand batsman, right-arm off break bowler, occasional wicket-keeper. *Teams* Eastern Province (1972/3 to 1978/9); Essex (1974–83, 229 matches); Western Australia (1979/80 to 1980/1, 18 matches); Western Province (1981/2 to 1982/3).
Career batting
322–534–45–19716–218–40.31–53–*ct* 290–*st* 7
Bowling 309–4–77.25–0–0–1/0
His first-class debut in England was for T. N. Pearce's XI in 1973. He hit 1,000 runs in a season ten times, going on to 2,000 once – 2,176, av 64.00, in 1983. His highest score is 218 for Essex v Sussex at Chelmsford in 1977.

McEwen, John William
Amateur. *b:* 25.11.1862, Dalston, Middlesex. *d:* 16.2.1902, Stepney, London. Lower order right-hand batsman, right-arm fast bowler. *Team* Middlesex (1884, 3 matches).
Career batting
3–5–0–13–8–2.60–0–*ct* 1
Bowling 126–4–31.50–0–0–3/37

MacFadyen, Air Marshal Sir Douglas
Amateur. *b:* 8.8.1902, Newcastle upon Tyne. *d:* 26.7.1968, Sherlock Row, Berkshire. Lower order batsman, useful bowler. *Sch* Royal Grammar School, Newcastle. *Team* RAF (1929–31).
Career batting
2–4–0–11–9–2.75–0–*ct* 0
Bowling 63–2–31.50–0–0–2/59

McFarlane, Andrew
Amateur. *b:* 21.6.1899, Sion Mills, Co. Tyrone, Ireland. *d:* 14.6.1972, Londonderry, Ireland. Middle order right-hand batsman, off break bowler. *Team* Ireland (1937).
Career batting
1–2–0–23–23–11.50–0–*ct* 1

McFarlane, Leslie Leopold
Cricketer. *b:* 19.8.1952, Portland, Jamaica. Tail end right-hand batsman, right-arm medium pace bowler. *Teams* Northants (1979, 8 matches); Lancashire (1982–83, 23 matches).
Career batting
31–21–11–74–12*–7.40–0–*ct* 7
Bowling 2257–55–41.03–1–0–6/59
He also played for Bedfordshire.

MacFarlane, Robert
Amateur. *b:* 29.4.1908, Uddingston, Lanarkshire, Scotland. Middle order right-hand batsman, right-arm medium pace bowler. *Team* Scotland (1939).
Career batting
1–2–0–70–48–35.00–0–*ct* 0

McGahey, Charles Percy
Amateur. *b:* 12.2.1871, Hackney, Middlesex. *d:* 10.1.1935, Whipps Cross, Essex. He died of septic poisoning. Attacking middle order right-hand batsman, slow right-arm leg break bowler. *Teams* Essex (1894–1921, 400 matches); London County (1901–04). *Tour* MacLaren to Australia 1901/2. *Tests* England (1901/2, 2 matches).
Career batting
437–751–65–20723–277–30.20–31–*ct* 151
Bowling 10300–330–31.21–12–3–7/27
Test batting
2–4–0–38–18–9.50–0–*ct* 1
He hit 1,000 runs in a season ten times (best 1,838, av 48.36, in 1901). His three double centuries were all for Essex, the highest being 277 v Derbyshire at Leyton in 1905. He captained Essex 1907 to 1910 and was for several years Assistant Secretary. From 1930 he was the County Scorer. A good full-back he played soccer for Tottenham Hotspur, Clapton Orient, Arsenal and Sheffield United, as well as captaining representative teams of London and Middlesex.

McGaw, Alfred Joseph Thoburn
Amateur. *b:* 1.4.1900, Haslemere, Surrey. *d:* 8.2.1984, Jersey, Channel Islands. Lower order right-hand batsman, slow right-arm bowler. *Sch* Charterhouse. *Teams* Sussex (1928, 2 matches); Punjab Governor's XI (1929/30).
Career batting
7–11–1–170–52–17.00–0–*ct* 3
Bowling 274–8–34.25–0–0–4/17
His final first-class match was for the Army in 1932, and he was a noted figure in military cricket in the 1930s.

MacGibbon, Anthony Roy
Amateur. *b:* 28.8.1924, Christchurch, New Zealand. Lower order right-hand batsman, right-arm fast medium bowler. *Team* Canterbury (1947/8 to 1961/2). *Tours* New Zealand to Australia and South Africa 1953/4, to India and Pakistan 1955/6, to England 1958. *Tests* New Zealand (1950/1 to 1958, 26 matches).
Career batting
123–204–20–3611–94–19.62–0–*ct* 82
Bowling 9227–352–26.21–8–0–7/56
Test batting
26–46–5–814–66–19.85–0–*ct* 13
Bowling 2160–70–30.85–1–0–5/64
He was easily the best bowler on the 1958 tour to England, taking 20 wickets av 19.45, in the Tests – no other New Zealand bowler captured more than six wickets. In all first-class matches his record was 73, av 21.35.

McGibbon, Charles Edward
Amateur. *b:* 1880, Portsmouth, Hampshire. *d:* 2.4.1954, Hamble, Hampshire. Lower order batsman, useful bowler. *Team* Hampshire (1919, 1 match).
Career batting
1–2–1–1–1*–1.00–0–*ct* 0
Bowling 10–0

McGibbon, Lewis
Professional. *b:* 8.10.1931, Newcastle upon Tyne. Lower order right-hand batsman, right-arm medium pace in-swing bowler. *Team* Northants (1957–59, 13 matches).

Career batting
13–11–5–17–4–2.83–0–*ct* 2
Bowling 858–33–26.00–0–0–4/42
He also played for Northumberland.

MacGinty, Raphael Joseph Anthony
Amateur. *b:* 22.3.1927, London. Tail end right-hand batsman, off break bowler. *Team* Cambridge U (1952).
Career batting
6–8–1–32–18–4.57–0–*ct* 4
Bowling 504–17–29.64–0–0–4/58
His County cricket was for Cambridgeshire.

McGirr, Herbert Mendelson
Amateur. *b:* 5.11.1891, Wellington, New Zealand. *d:* 14.4.1964, Nelson, New Zealand. Son of W. P. (Wellington). Middle order right-hand batsman, right-arm medium pace bowler. *Team* Wellington (1913/14 to 1932/3). *Tours* New Zealand to England 1927, to Australia 1927/8. *Tests* New Zealand (1929/30, 2 matches).
Career batting
88–146–7–3992–141–28.71–5–*ct* 54
Bowling 6571–239–27.49–9–1–7/45
Test batting
2–1–0–51–51–51.00–0–*ct* 0
Bowling 115–1–115.00–0–0–1/65
On his visit to England he took 49 wickets, av 27.67, and scored 737 runs.

McGlew, Derrick John
Amateur. *b:* 11.3.1929, Pietermaritzburg, South Africa. Stubborn opening right-hand batsman, leg break bowler, brilliant cover field. *Team* Natal (1947/8 to 1966/7). *Tours* South Africa to England 1951, 1955, 1960, to Australia and New Zealand 1952/3. *Tests* South Africa (1951 to 1961/2, 34 matches).
Career batting
190–299–34–12170–255*–45.92–27–*ct* 103
Bowling 932–35–26.62–0–0–2/4
Test batting
34–64–6–2440–255*–42.06–7–*ct* 18
Bowling 23–0
He topped 1,000 runs in each of his three tours to England (best 1,871, av 58.46, in 1955). In 1955 he also headed the Test batting averages. He was vice-captain of the 1955 tourists and captain in 1960.
He holds a curious record. During the Natal v Transvaal match at Durban in 1963/4, he performed a hat-trick, with two wickets in one innings and another in the other, yet at no time in his career did he capture more than two wickets in a single innings. His highest score was 255* for South Africa v New Zealand at Wellington in 1952/3.

MacGregor, Gregor
Amateur. *b:* 31.8.1869, Merchiston, Edinburgh, Scotland. *d:* 20.8.1919, Marylebone, London. Lower order right-hand batsman, wicket-keeper. *Sch* Uppingham. *Teams* Middlesex (1892–1907, 184 matches); Cambridge U (1888–91, blue all four years); Scotland (1905). *Tours* Sheffield to Australia 1891/2; MCC to North America 1907. *Tests* England (1890–93, 8 matches).
Career batting
265–412–58–6381–141–18.02–3–*ct* 411–*st* 148
Test batting
8–11–3–96–31–12.00–0–*ct* 14–*st* 3
He captained Middlesex from 1899 to 1907. A brilliant rugby footballer, he represented Cambridge and Scotland.

Machin, Reginald Stanley
Amateur. *b:* 16.4.1904, Weybridge, Surrey. *d:* 3.11.1968, Wellingborough, Northants. Lower order right-hand batsman, wicket-keeper. *Sch* Lancing. *Teams* Cambridge U (1926–27, blue 1927); Surrey (1927–30, 8 matches).
Career batting
32–33–6–300–57–11.11–0–*ct* 57–*st* 14
His final first-class match was in 1934 for Gentlemen.

McHugh, Francis Prest
Professional. *b:* 15.11.1925, Leeds, Yorkshire. Lower order right-hand batsman, right-arm fast medium bowler. *Teams* Yorkshire (1949, 3 matches); Gloucestershire (1952–56, 92 matches).
Career batting
95–111–43–179–18–2.63–0–*ct* 24
Bowling 6857–276–24.84–15–4–7/32
His best season was 1954 when he took 92 wickets, av 20.00.

McIlwaine, Richard Johnston
Cricketer. *b:* 16.3.1950, Portsmouth, Hants. Lower order right-hand batsman, right-arm medium pace bowler. *Team* Hampshire (1969–70, 4 matches).
Career batting
4–3–1–29–17–14.50–0–0–*ct* 1
Bowling 273–4–68.25–0–0–2/40

McIlwraith, John
Amateur. *b:* 7.9.1857, Collingwood, Victoria, Australia. *d:* 5.7.1938, Camberwell, Victoria, Australia. Attacking middle order right-hand batsman. *Team* Victoria (1884/5 to 1889/90, 13 matches). *Tour* Australia to England 1886. *Test* Australia (1886, 1 match).

Career batting
44–68–7–1468–133–24.06–2–*ct* 24
Test batting
1–2–0–9–7–4.50–0–*ct* 1
He achieved very little on his single tour to England.

Macindoe, David Henry
Amateur. *b:* 1.9.1917, Eton, Buckinghamshire. Lower order right-hand batsman, right-arm medium fast bowler. *Sch* Eton. *Team* Oxford U (1937–39 and 1946, blue all four years).
Career batting
42–64–12–747–51–14.17–0–*ct* 38
Bowling 4339–152–28.53–5–1–6/61
His County cricket was for Buckinghamshire.

McInerny, James Jeremy
Amateur. *b:* 12.4.1933, Paddington, London. Middle order right-hand batsman. *Sch* Christs Hospital. *Team* Oxford U (1955–56).
Career batting
2–3–0–25–22–8.33–0–*ct* 1

McIntosh, Robert Ian Fanshawe
Amateur. *b:* 19.8.1907, Darjeeling, India. Tail end right-hand batsman, right-arm medium fast bowler. *Sch* Uppingham. *Teams* Oxford U (1927–29, blue 1927 and 1928); Madras (1933/4).
Career batting
24–32–18–161–23–11.50–0–*ct* 9
Bowling 2273–69–32.94–2–0–5/52
His County cricket was for Devon.

McIntyre, Arthur John William
Professional. *b:* 14.5.1918, Kennington, London. Middle/lower order right-hand batsman, right-arm leg break bowler, wicket-keeper. *Team* Surrey (1938–63, 377 matches). *Tours* MCC to Australia and New Zealand 1950/1; Surrey to Rhodesia 1959/60. *Tests* England (1950–55, 3 matches).
Career batting
391–567–79–11145–143*–22.83–7–*ct* 639–*st* 156
Bowling 180–4–45.00–0–0–1/10
Test batting
3–6–0–19–7–3.16–0–*ct* 8
He hit 1,000 runs in a season three times (best 1,200, av 24.48, in 1949). He was appointed County coach to Surrey after the 1958 season, but continued to appear in first-class matches occasionally until 1963.

McIntyre, Arthur Seymour
Amateur. *b:* 29.5.1889, Hartley-Wintney, Hampshire. *d:* 14.3.1945, Nottingham. Middle order right-hand batsman. *Sch* Blundells. *Team* Hampshire (1920–23, 28 matches).

Career batting
28–45–2–493–55–11.46–0–*ct* 15
Bowling 36–0

McIntyre, Evan James
Cricketer. *b:* 16.12.1951, Edinburgh, Scotland. Right-hand batsman, off break bowler. *Team* Scotland (1981–83).
Career batting
2–3–1–7–6–3.50–0–*ct* 1
Bowling 39–0

McIntyre, Hugh
Professional. *b:* 27.6.1855, Glasgow, Scotland. *d:* 1918, Liverpool, Lancashire. Lower order batsman, wicket-keeper. *Team* Lancashire (1884, 1 match).
Career batting
1–1–1–1–1*–no av–0–*ct* 1–*st* 2
A noted soccer player, he represented Glasgow Rangers and Scotland.

McIntyre, John McLachlan
Cricketer. *b:* 4.7.1944, Auckland, New Zealand. Lower order left-hand batsman, slow left-arm bowler. *Teams* Auckland (1961/2 to 1982/3); Canterbury (1965/6 to 1968/9). *Tour* New Zealand to England 1978.
Career batting
113–148–55–1668–87*–17.93–0–*ct* 46
Bowling 7917–336–23.56–10–1–6/84
He achieved only modest results on the 1978 tour of England and did not appear in the Tests.

McIntyre, Martin
Professional. *b:* 15.8.1847, Eastwood, Notts. *d:* 28.2.1885, Moor Green, Notts. Brother of Michael (Notts) and William (Notts and Lancashire). Middle order right-hand batsman, right-hand fast round-arm bowler. *Team* Nottinghamshire (1868–77, 45 matches). *Tour* Grace to Australia 1873/74 (not first-class).
Career batting
77–127–5–1992–88*–16.32–0–*ct* 33
Bowling 3374–194–17.34–12–2–9/33
His final first-class match was for an England XI v Cambridge U in 1878. He took 9 for 33 for Notts v Surrey at the Oval in 1872.

McIntyre, Michael
Professional. *b:* 13.11.1839, Nottingham. *d:* 9.10.1888, Basford, Notts. Brother of Martin (Notts) and William (Notts and Lancashire). Lower order batsman, useful bowler. *Team* Nottinghamshire (1864, 1 match).

Career batting
3–5–1–44–23–11.00–0–*ct* 0
Bowling 78–4–19.50–0–0–2/30
His first-class debut was for the North v Surrey in 1863.

McIntyre, Terence Frank
Amateur. *b:* 2.7.1930, Hendon, Middlesex. Lower order right-hand batsman, wicket-keeper. *Team* Combined Services (1959–64).
Career batting
5–9–0–87–36–9.66–0–*ct* 5–*st* 2

McIntyre, William
Professional. *b:* 24.5.1844, Eastwood, Notts. *d:* 13.9.1892, Prestwich, Lancashire. Brother of Martin (Notts) and Michael (Notts). Lower order right-hand batsman, right-arm fast bowler. *Teams* Nottinghamshire (1869–71, 14 matches); Lancashire (1872–80, 72 matches).
Career batting
97–151–24–1323–99–10.41–0–*ct* 70
Bowling 6432–510–12.60–53–14–8/31
He headed the first-class bowling averages for three seasons – 1872, 41 wickets, av 5.65; 1873, 63, av 8.38; 1876, 89, av 11.41, being for a few years one of the best bowlers in England.

McIver, Colin Donald
Amateur. *b:* 23.1.1881, Hong Kong. *d:* 13.5.1954, Worcester College, Oxford, whilst on a visit. Middle order right-hand batsman, slow right-arm bowler, wicket-keeper. *Sch* Forest. *Teams* Essex (1902–22, 59 matches); Oxford U (1903–04, blue both years).
Career batting
134–227–18–4651–134–22.25–5–*ct* 98–*st* 24
Bowling 40–1–40.00–0–0–1/4
He hit 1,197 runs, av 30.69, in 1914. His final first-class match was for MCC in 1934; he continued to play in club matches for MCC until over 60. A good soccer player he was centre-forward for Essex and won an England amateur international cap.

Mack, Andrew James
Cricketer. *b:* 14.1.1956, Aylsham, Norfolk. Lower order left-hand batsman, left-arm medium pace bowler. *Teams* Surrey (1976–77, 10 matches); Glamorgan (1978–80, 21 matches).
Career batting
31–32–10–102–18–4.63–0–*ct* 4
Bowling 1889–44–42.93–0–0–4/28

Mackay, Claude Lysaght
Amateur. *b:* 29.10.1894, Satara, India. *d:* 7.6.1915, Boulogne, France. He died of wounds received in action. Middle order right-hand batsman, right-arm fast medium bowler. *Sch* Clifton. *Team* Gloucestershire (1914, 1 match).
Career batting
1–2–0–28–15–14.00–0–*ct* 1
Bowling 24–0
He was a noted athlete and represented the public schools as a heavyweight boxer.

Mackay, Daniel Alexander
Amateur. *b:* 12.3.1894, Glasgow, Scotland. *d:* 13.5.1951, Pollockshaws, Glasgow, Scotland. Right-hand batsman, right-arm medium pace bowler. *Team* Scotland (1923–30).
Career batting
8–14–0–203–68–14.50–0–*ct* 2
Bowling 40–3–13.33–0–0–3/35

Mackay, Kenneth Donald
Amateur. *b:* 24.10.1925, Windsor, Queensland, Australia. *d:* 13.6.1982, Stradbroke Island, Queensland, Australia. Very stubborn middle order left-hand batsman, right-arm medium pace bowler. *Team* Queensland (1946/7 to 1963/4, 109 matches). *Tours* Australia to England 1956, 1961, to South Africa 1957/8, to India 1956/7, to India and Pakistan 1959/60. *Tests* Australia (1956 to 1962/3, 37 matches).
Career batting
201–294–46–10823–223–43.64–23–*ct* 84
Bowling 8363–251–33.31–7–0–6/42
Test batting
37–52–7–1507–89–33.48–0–*ct* 16
Bowling 1721–50–34.42–2–0–6/42
On his 1956 tour to England he headed the first-class batting averages, 1,103 runs, av 52.52, but failed utterly in the Tests. He had only a modest tour in 1961, though appearing in all five Tests. His highest score was 223 for Queensland v Victoria at Brisbane in 1953/4.

Mackay, William Gilfellon
Amateur. *b:* 1892. *d:* 8.8.1962, Heaton, Newcastle upon Tyne. Middle order right-hand batsman. *Team* Minor Counties (1929).
Career batting
1 match, did not bat–*ct* 0
His County cricket was for Northumberland.

McKee, William A.
Amateur. *b:* 27.8.1923, Belfast, Ireland. Right-hand batsman, right-arm fast medium bowler. *Team* Ireland (1946).
Career batting
1–1–0–16–16–16.00–0–*ct* 2
Bowling 57–0

McKelvey, James Moorhead
Amateur. *b:* 2.4.1933, Belfast, Ireland. Left-hand

batsman. *Sch* Campbell College. *Team* Ireland (1954).
Career batting
2–4–0–25–9–6.25–0–*ct* 1
A noted rugby footballer, he was capped for Ireland.

McKelvey, Patrick George
Professional. *b:* 25.12.1935, Barnet, Herts. Lower order right-hand batsman, slow left-arm bowler. *Team* Surrey (1959–60, 2 matches).
Career batting
2 matches, did not bat–*ct* 1
Bowling 19–1–19.00–0–0–1/7

McKelvie, Robert Douglas
Amateur. *b:* 1.7.1912, Blofield, Norfolk. Lower order batsman, wicket-keeper. *Team* Free Foresters (1948).
Career batting
1–2–0–22–12–11.00–0–*ct* 1

Mackenna, Robert Ogilvie
Amateur. *b:* 21.3.1913, Paisley, Renfrewshire, Scotland. Lower order right-hand batsman, right-arm fast medium bowler. *Team* Scotland (1938–46).
Career batting
2–4–1–8–4*–2.66–0–*ct* 0
Bowling 129–2–64.50–0–0–1/20

MacKenzie, Lord Charles Kincaid
Amateur. *b:* 9.3.1857, Edinburgh, Scotland. *d:* 1.4.1938, Scotland. Father of M. K. (Oxford U). Lower order right-hand batsman, useful bowler. *Sch* Repton. *Team* Oxford U (1876).
Career batting
1–2–1–10–8*–10.00–0–*ct* 0
Bowling 3–0

MacKenzie, Frederick Finch
Amateur. *b:* 14.7.1849, Kensington, London. *d:* 17.7.1934, Hove, Sussex. Middle order right-hand batsman, right-hand medium round-arm bowler. *Sch* Wellington. *Team* Kent (1880, 2 matches).
Career batting
2–3–0–6–4–2.00–0–*ct* 2
He did not play in first-class matches whilst at Oxford.

McKenzie, Graham Douglas
Amateur. *b:* 24.6.1941, Cottesloe, Perth, Western Australia. Son of E. N. (Western Australia), nephew of D. C. (Western Australia). Lower order right-hand batsman, right-arm medium fast bowler. *Teams* Western Australia (1959/60 to 1973/4, 81 matches); Leicestershire (1969–75, 151 matches). *Tours* Australia to England 1961, 1964, 1968, to South Africa 1966/7, 1969/70, to West Indies 1964/5, to India and Pakistan 1964/5, to Ceylon and India 1969/70; Rest of World to West Indies 1966/7, to England 1966, 1967; Cavaliers to India and South Africa 1962/3; International XI to South Africa 1972/3, 1974/5. *Tests* Australia (1961 to 1970/1, 60 matches).
Career batting
383–471–109–5662–76–15.64–0–*ct* 201
Bowling 32868–1219–26.96–49–5–8/71
Test batting
60–89–12–945–76–12.27–0–*ct* 34
Bowling 7328–246–29.78–16–3–8/71
Of his three tours to England easily his best was in 1964 when he took 88 wickets, av 22.45, in first-class matches and headed the Test averages with 29 wickets, av 22.55. He was at the time the youngest player ever to achieve the milestones of 100, 150 and 200 Test wickets in a career.

Mackenzie, K. A. M.
(*see under* Muir-Mackenzie, K. A.)

MacKenzie, Mark Kincaid
Amateur. *b:* 22.8.1888, Edinburgh, Scotland. *d:* 25.9.1914, Soupir, Soissons, France. He was killed in action. Son of C. K. (Oxford U). Lower order batsman, left-arm fast medium bowler. *Sch* Winchester. *Team* Oxford U (1910).
Career batting
3–5–1–65–48*–16.25–0–*ct* 3
Bowling 185–6–30.83–0–0–2/65

MacKenzie, Percy Alec
Professional. *b:* 5.10.1918, Canterbury, Kent. Middle order right-hand batsman, leg break and googly bowler. *Team* Hampshire (1938–39, 22 matches).
Career batting
22–36–3–652–76–19.75–0–*ct* 11
Bowling 605–17–35.58–0–0–4/34
He also played for Berkshire.

Mackenzie, Robert Theodore Hope
Amateur. *b:* 8.10.1886, Poona, India. *d:* 20.3.1934, New Delhi, India. Forcing middle order right-hand batsman, right-arm fast bowler. *Sch* Cheltenham. *Teams* Gloucestershire (1907, 2 matches); Cambridge U (1907–08).
Career batting
4–7–0–38–21–5.42–0–*ct* 2
Bowling 84–3–28.00–0–0–2/30
He also played for Devon.

MacKenzie, William Forbes
Amateur. *b:* 5.6.1907, Salisbury, Rhodesia. *d:* 1.8.1980, Salisbury, Rhodesia. Tail end right-

hand batsman, right-arm fast medium bowler. *Sch* Merchiston. *Team* Cambridge U (1927).
Career batting
1–1–0–1–1–1.00–0–*ct* 0
Bowling 150–9–16.66–1–0–5/50

Mackeson, William James
Amateur. *b:* 7.12.1856, Kensington, London. *d:* 21.7.1925, Atcham, Shropshire. Middle order batsman. *Sch* Harrow. *Team* MCC (1883).
Career batting
1–2–0–8–7–4.00–0–*ct* 0
His County cricket was for Shropshire.

Mackessack, Douglas
Amateur. *b:* 7.10.1903, Alves, Morayshire, Scotland. Brother of Kenneth (Army). Right-hand batsman, useful bowler. *Sch* Rugby. *Team* Scotland (1927).
Career batting
1–2–0–27–14–13.50–0–*ct* 2
Bowling 51–0

Mackessack, Kenneth
Amateur. *b:* 24.10.1902, Alves, Morayshire, Scotland. *d:* 18.10.1982, Elgin, Morayshire, Scotland. Brother of Douglas (Scotland). Tail end batsman, good bowler. *Sch* Rugby. *Teams* Army (1926); Northern Punjab (1926/7); Europeans (1927/8).
Career batting
4–5–2–34–20*–11.33–0–*ct* 2
Bowling 200–8–25.00–0–0–3/42

McKibbin, David Gordon Robinson
Amateur. *b:* 16.6.1912, Comber, Co Down, Ireland. Right-hand batsman, leg break bowler. *Team* Ireland (1937).
Career batting
1–2–0–46–31–23.00–0–*ct* 0

McKibbin, Thomas Robert
Amateur. *b:* 10.12.1870, Raglan, Bathurst, New South Wales, Australia. *d:* 15.12.1939, Bathurst, New South Wales, Australia. Lower order left-hand batsman, right-arm medium, or off break, bowler, good slip field. *Team* New South Wales (1894/5 to 1898/9, 25 matches). *Tour* Australia to England and North America 1896. *Tests* Australia (1894/5 to 1897/8, 5 matches).
Career batting
57–92–24–683–75–10.04–0–*ct* 46
Bowling 6297–320–19.67–28–11–9/68
Test batting
5–8–2–88–28–14.66–0–*ct* 4
Bowling 496–17–29.17–0–0–3/35
He was the leading bowler on the 1896 tour to England, taking 101 wickets, av 14.26, but the fairness of his delivery was questioned by some. His best bowling was 9 for 68 for New South Wales v Queensland in 1894/5.

McKiddie, Gavin Thomson
Cricketer. *b:* 17.5.1940, Forfar, Scotland. Right-hand batsman, off break bowler. *Team* Scotland (1977).
Career batting
1–2–0–10–8–5.00–0–*ct* 1
Bowling 41–2–20.50–0–0–1/3

McKinna, Gordon Hayden
Amateur. *b:* 2.8.1930, Sale, Cheshire. Lower order right-hand batsman, right-arm medium pace bowler. *Sch* Manchester Grammar School. *Team* Oxford U (1951–53, blue 1953).
Career batting
6–8–2–40–18–6.66–0–*ct* 1
Bowling 391–17–23.00–0–0–4/39
His final first-class match was for Combined Services in 1955. His County cricket was for Cheshire.

McKinnon, Atholl Henry
Amateur. *b:* 20.8.1932, Port Elizabeth, South Africa. *d:* 2.12.1983, Durban, South Africa. Lower order right-hand batsman, slow left-arm bowler. *Teams* Eastern Province (1952/3 to 1962/3); Transvaal (1963/4 to 1968/9). *Tours* South Africa to England 1960, 1965. *Tests* South Africa (1960 to 1966/67, 8 matches).
Career batting
111–152–39–1687–62–14.92–0–*ct* 32
Bowling 9937–470–21.14–38–9–7/37
Test batting
8–13–7–107–27–17.83–0–*ct* 1
Bowling 925–26–35.57–0–0–4/128
On the 1960 tour, he appeared in one Test and ought to have been given more opportunities early in the season; he took 53 wickets, av 20.88, in first-class matches. On the short tour of 1965 he appeared in two Tests and proved to be most effective.

MacKinnon, Donald William
Amateur. *b:* 3.3.1842, Bangalore, India. *d:* 19.11.1931, Waterlooville, Hampshire. Middle order batsman, useful bowler. *Team* Lancashire (1870–71, 3 matches).
Career batting
4–7–0–112–42–16.00–0–*ct* 4
Bowling 132–7–18.85–0–0–3/13

MacKinnon of MacKinnon, Francis Alexander
Amateur. *b:* 9.4.1848, Kensington, London. *d:* 27.2.1947, Drumduan, Forres, Morayshire, Scotland. Steady middle order right-hand batsman. *Sch* Harrow. *Teams* Kent (1875–85, 78 matches);

Cambridge U (1870, blue). *Tour* Harris to Australia 1878/9. *Test* England (1878/9, 1 match).
Career batting
88–163–16–2318–115–15.76–2–*ct* 38
Test batting
1–2–0–5–5–2.50–0–*ct* 0

MacKinnon, James Curdie
Amateur. *b:* 10.1.1865, Terang, Victoria, Australia. *d:* 4.7.1957, Australia. Lower order right-hand batsman, slow left-arm bowler. *Team* Cambridge U (1886–88).
Career batting
5–8–2–31–11*–5.16–0–*ct* 3
Bowling 236–4–59.00–0–0–2/39

Mackinnon, Malcolm
Amateur. *b:* 11.5.1891, Toward Point, Argyll, Scotland. *d:* 13.2.1975, Sunningdale, Berkshire. Middle order right-hand batsman, right-arm off break bowler. *Teams* Essex (1927, 3 matches); Europeans (1927/8 to 1934/5).
Career batting
6–10–0–122–31–12.20–0–*ct* 3

He did not appear in first-class cricket whilst at Oxford.

Mackintosh, David Stewart
Cricketer. *b:* 18.2.1947, Paisley, Renfrewshire, Scotland. Middle order right-hand batsman. *Team* Scotland (1972).
Career batting
1–2–0–66–57–33.00–0–*ct* 0

Mackintosh, Kevin Scott
Cricketer. *b:* 30.8.1957, Surbiton, Surrey. Lower order right-hand batsman, right-arm fast medium bowler. *Teams* Nottinghamshire (1978–80, 19 matches); Surrey (1981–83, 14 matches).
Career batting
33–33–17–303–31–18.93–0–*ct* 14
Bowling 2092–59–35.45–1–0–6/61

MacLachlan, Andrew
Amateur. *b:* 27.2.1941, Anglesey. Lower order right-hand batsman, useful bowler. *Team* Oxford U (1962).
Career batting
5–10–3–99–28–14.14–0–*ct* 1
Bowling 239–3–79.66–0–0–1/49

McLachlan, Angus Alexander
Cricketer. *b:* 11.11.1944, Adelaide, South Australia. Brother of I. M. (South Australia and Cambridge U). Lower order right-hand batsman, leg break googly bowler. *Team* Cambridge U (1964–65, blue both years).
Career batting
17–28–3–232–27–9.28–0–*ct* 8
Batting 1198–32–37.43–0–0–4/36

McLachlan, Ian Murray
Amateur. *b:* 2.10.1936, Adelaide, South Australia. Brother of A. A. (Cambridge U). Opening right-hand batsman, useful bowler. *Teams* Cambridge U (1956–58, blue 1957 and 1958); South Australia (1960/1 to 1963/4, 31 matches). *Tour* Swanton to West Indies 1960/1.
Career batting
72–128–10–3743–188*–31.72–9–*ct* 41
Bowling 382–6–63.66–0–0–2/33

MacLachlan, Norman
Amateur. *b:* 12.10.1858, Darlington, Co. Durham. *d:* 18.2.1928, Torquay, Devon. Tail end right-hand batsman, right-arm fast medium bowler, good deep field. *Sch* Loretto. *Team* Oxford U (1879–82, blue all four years).
Career batting
20–34–4–252–27–8.40–0–*ct* 15
Bowling 675–38–17.76–1–0–6/40

His County cricket was for Cheshire. He was also a noted rugby footballer, being awarded his blue as a back.

MacLaren, Archibald Campbell
Amateur. *b:* 1.12.1871, Whalley Range, Manchester. *d:* 17.11.1944, Warfield Park, Bracknell, Berkshire. Brother of J. A. and G. (both Lancashire). Attacking opening right-hand batsman, right-arm fast bowler, good slip field. *Sch* Harrow. *Team* Lancashire (1890–1914, 308 matches). *Tours* Stoddart to Australia 1894/5, 1897/8; MacLaren to Australia 1901/2; Ranjitsinhji to North America 1899; MCC to South America 1911/12, to New Zealand and Australia 1922/3. *Tests* England (1894/5 to 1909, 35 matches).
Career batting
424–703–52–22237–424–34.15–47–*ct* 452
Bowling 267–1–267.00–0–0–1/44
Test batting
35–61–4–1931–140–33.87–5–*ct* 29

Holder of the highest innings record in first-class English cricket with 424 for Lancashire against Somerset at Taunton in 1895, MacLaren is also regarded by some contemporaries as England's best captain. Everyone is agreed that he was a great tactical expert, but whilst he led his country he was criticised for his part in the selection of some of the England teams. At the end of his career however he silenced his critics by choosing a side to meet the strong 1921 Australian team and, against all odds, beating them when everyone else had failed.

On his three tours to Australia – he captained

the 1897/8 and 1901/2 Test sides there – he batted quite brilliantly, but in England the damper climate aggravated his lumbago, so that he was not such a prolific scorer. In spite of this he hit 1,000 runs in a season eight times, the best year being 1903 with 1,886 runs, av 42.86. Apart from his 424 he hit three other scores above 200 for Lancashire and one each in Australia and New Zealand. He also hit 1,000 runs in an Australian season.

From 1894 to 1896 and from 1899 to 1907 he captained Lancashire. At the end of its life he managed the weekly magazine '*Cricket*', which ceased publication in 1914. His final first-class match in England was for L. Robinson's XI in 1921.

McLaren, Frederick Albert
Amateur. *b:* 19.8.1874, Farnham, Surrey. *d:* 23.9.1952, Dartford, Kent. Lower order batsman, useful bowler. *Team* Hampshire (1908, 2 matches).
Career batting
2–3–0–4–4–1.33–0–0–*ct* 1
Bowling 114–4–28.50–0–0–2/30

MacLaren, Frederic Grahame
Amateur. *b:* 5.11.1875, Worsley, Manchester, Lancashire. *d:* 10.5.1952, Bowden, Cheshire. Middle order batsman, useful bowler, good slip field. *Sch* Fettes. *Team* Lancashire (1903, 1 match).
Career batting
1–2–0–19–19–9.50–0–*ct* 0
Bowling 7–0
He also played for Cheshire.

MacLaren, Geoffrey
Amateur. *b:* 28.2.1883, Whalley Range, Manchester, Lancashire. *d:* 14.9.1966, Bexhill-on-Sea, Sussex. Brother of A. C. (Lancashire) and J. A. (Lancashire). Lower order batsman, useful bowler. *Sch* Harrow. *Team* Lancashire (1902, 2 matches).
Career batting
2–4–0–7–3–1.75–0–*ct* 0
Bowling 13–2–6.50–0–0–1/5

MacLaren, Dr James Alexander
Amateur. *b:* 4.1.1870, Whalley Range, Manchester, Lancashire. *d:* 8.7.1952, Salisbury, Wiltshire. Brother of A. C. and Geoffrey (both Lancashire). Hard hitting middle order right-hand batsman, slip field. *Sch* Harrow. *Team* Lancashire (1891–94, 4 matches).
Career batting
4–4–0–9–6–2.25–0–*ct* 4

McLaren, John William
Amateur. *b·* 24.12.1887, Toowong, Queensland, Australia. *d:* 17.11.1921, Highgate Hill, Queensland, Australia. Lower order right-hand batsman, right-arm fast bowler. *Team* Queensland (1906/7 to 1914/15, 18 matches). *Tour* Australia to England and North America 1912. *Test* Australia (1911/2, 1 match).
Career batting
34–59–14–564–43*–12.53–0–*ct* 7
Bowling 2862–107–26.74–3–0–5/55
Test batting
1–2–2–0–0*–no av–0–*ct* 0
Bowling 70–1–70.00–0–0–1/23
He was very much one of the reserves on the 1912 tour of England, his record in first-class matches being a modest one.

McLaren, Robert Stewart
Amateur. *b:* 10.5.1919, Perth, Scotland. Lower order right-hand batsman, wicket-keeper. *Team* Scotland (1947–49).
Career batting
6–10–2–23–7–2.87–0–*ct* 6–*st* 7

McLean, Douglas Hamilton
Amateur. *b:* April 1863, Queensland, Australia. *d:* 5.2.1901, Johannesburg, South Africa. Middle order batsman. *Sch* Eton. *Team* Somerset (1896, 1 match).
Career batting
1–2–1–13–9*–13.00–0–*ct* 0

MacLean, John Francis
Amateur. *b:* 1.3.1901, Alnwick, Northumberland. Middle order right-hand batsman, wicket-keeper. *Sch* Eton. *Teams* Worcestershire (1922–24, 45 matches); Gloucestershire (1930–32, 6 matches). *Tour* MCC to Australia and New Zealand 1922/3.
Career batting
69–113–15–1812–121–18.48–1–*ct* 61–*st* 43
His first-class debut was in 1919 for H. K. Foster's XI.

McLean, Leslie Eric
Amateur. *b:* 19.4.1918, Lynton, Devon. Opening right-hand batsman. *Sch* Bishop's Stortford. *Team* Oxford U (1939).
Career batting
3–6–0–79–51–13.16–0–*ct* 3
His County cricket was for Hertfordshire.

MacLean, Montague Francis
Amateur. *b:* 12.9.1870, London. *d:* 14.1.1951, Ross, Herefordshire. Middle order batsman, change bowler. *Team* MCC (1893). *Tour* Hawke to India 1892/3.

Career batting
5–8–5–65–25–21.66–0–*ct* 3
Bowling 31–0

McLean, Roy Alastair
Amateur. *b:* 9.7.1930, Pietermaritzburg, South Africa. Aggressive middle order right-hand batsman. *Team* Natal (1949/50 to 1965/6). *Tours* South Africa to England 1951, 1955, 1960, to Australia and New Zealand 1952/3; SA Fezela to England 1961; Commonwealth to New Zealand 1961/2. *Tests* South Africa (1951 to 1964/5, 40 matches).
Career batting
200–318–19–10969–207–36.68–22–*ct* 132
Bowling 122–2–61.00–0–0–2/22
Test batting
40–73–3–2120–142–30.28–5–*ct* 23
Bowling 1–0
He hit 1,000 runs on both the 1955 and 1960 visits (best 1,516, av 37.90, in 1960). Possibly his most noteworthy innings in England was 142 in the Lord's Test of 1955, the runs being hit out of 196. His highest score was 207 for South Africans v Worcestershire at Worcester in 1960.

McLellan, Alan James
Cricketer. *b:* 2.9.1958, Ashton-under-Lyne, Lancashire. Lower order right-hand batsman, wicket-keeper. *Team* Derbyshire (1978–79, 26 matches).
Career batting
26–24–8–99–41–6.18–0–*ct* 41–*st* 2

MacLeod, Alastair
Amateur. *b:* 12.11.1894, Kensington, London. *d:* 24.4.1982, Broomfield, Essex. Middle order right-hand batsman. *Sch* Felsted. *Team* Hampshire (1914–38, 12 matches).
Career batting
12–18–0–271–87–15.05–0–*ct* 5

McLeod, Charles Edward
Amateur. *b:* 24.10.1869, Port Melbourne, Victoria, Australia. *d:* 26.11.1918, Toorak, Victoria, Australia. Brother of R. W. (Victoria) and D. H. (Victoria). Opening right-hand batsman, right-arm medium pace bowler. *Team* Victoria (1893/4 to 1903/4, 41 matches). *Tours* Australia to England 1899, 1905, to New Zealand 1904/5. *Tests* Australia (1894/5 to 1905, 17 matches).
Career batting
114–179–23–3321–112–21.28–2–*ct* 63
Bowling 8123–334–24.32–22–4–7/34
Test batting
17–29–5–573–112–23.87–1–*ct* 9
Bowling 1325–33–40.15–2–0–5/65
He put in some useful performances on both tours to England, but achieved nothing outstanding.

MacLeod, Kenneth Grant
Amateur. *b:* 2.2.1888, Liverpool. *d:* 7.3.1967, St James, Cape Province, South Africa. Middle/lower order right-hand batsman, right-arm fast bowler. *Sch* Fettes. *Teams* Cambridge U (1908–09, blue both years); Lancashire (1908–13, 75 matches).
Career batting
94–161–16–3458–131–23.84–6–*ct* 107
Bowling 2748–103–26.67–2–1–6/29
He hit 1,361 runs, av 28.95, in 1911.
His final first-class match was for Free Foresters in 1914. A noted rugby footballer, he represented both Cambridge and Scotland as a wing threequarter; he also appeared for his University as a 100 yards sprinter and in the long jump.

McLeod, Robert William
Amateur. *b:* 19.1.1868, Port Melbourne, Victoria, Australia. *d:* 14.6.1907, Middle Park, Victoria, Australia. Brother of C. E. (Victoria) and D. H. (Victoria). Correct middle order left-hand batsman, right-arm medium pace bowler. *Team* Victoria (1889/90 to 1899/1900, 26 matches). *Tour* Australia to England and North America 1893. *Tests* Australia (1891/2 to 1893, 6 matches).
Career batting
57–95–19–1701–101–22.38–1–*ct* 39
Bowling 3206–141–22.73–7–2–7/24
Test batting
6–11–0–146–31–13.27–0–*ct* 3
Bowling 384–12–32.00–1–0–5/55
He achieved modest success on the 1893 tour, and appeared in all three Tests.

McMahon, John William Joseph
Professional. *b:* 28.12.1917, Balaklava, South Australia. Lower order left-hand batsman, slow left-arm bowler. *Teams* Surrey (1947–53, 84 matches); Somerset (1954–57, 115 matches).
Career batting
201–285–125–989–24–6.18–0–*ct* 109
Bowling 16289–590–27.60–30–2–8/46
His best season was 1956 when he took 103 wickets, av 25.57, and twice he took 8 for 46 in an innings – for Surrey v Northants at the Oval in 1948 and for Somerset v Kent at Yeovil in 1955.

McMahon, William John Alexander
Amateur. *b:* 13.7.1894, Richhill, Co. Armagh, Ireland. *d:* December 1974, Dublin, Ireland. Lower order batsman, useful bowler. *Team* Dublin U (1925–26).

Career batting
3–6–1–23–18–4.60–0–*ct* 4
Bowling 178–2–89.00–0–0–2/92

McMaster, Michael
Amateur. *b:* 1896, Williton, Somerset. *d:* 29.3.1965, Brook, Isle of Wight. Lower order batsman, useful bowler. *Team* Royal Navy (1920).
Career batting
1–2–1–13–7*–13.00–0–*ct* 1
Bowling 73–1–73.00–0–0–1/55

McMillan, Quintin
Amateur. *b:* 23.6.1904, Germiston, Transvaal, South Africa. *d:* 3.7.1948, Randfontein, Transvaal, South Africa. Hard hitting right-hand batsman, leg break and googly bowler. *Team* Transvaal (1928/9 to 1929/30). *Tours* South Africa to England 1929, to Australia and New Zealand 1931/2. *Tests* South Africa (1929 to 1931/2, 13 matches).
Career batting
50–76–16–1607–185*–26.78–1–*ct* 30
Bowling 5033–189–26.62–12–2–9/53
Test batting
13–21–4–306–50*–18.00–0–*ct* 8
Bowling 1243–36–34.52–2–0–5/66
On the 1929 tour he took most first-class wickets – 91, av 25.45 – but was ineffective in the Tests. He retired from important cricket early for business reasons, his final first-class match in South Africa being in 1930/1. His best bowling was 9/53 for South Africans v South Australians at Adelaide in 1931/2.

McMillan, Stuart Thomas
Professional. *b:* 17.9.1896, Leicester. *d:* 27.9.1963, Ashbourne, Derbyshire. Lower order right-hand batsman, right-arm medium fast bowler. *Team* Derbyshire (1922–24, 4 matches).
Career batting
4–6–2–30–24–7.50–0–*ct* 0
Bowling 14–0
A noted soccer player, he appeared for Derby County, Gillingham, Wolverhampton Wanderers, Bristol City, Nottingham Forest and Leyton Orient.

McMorris, Easton Dudley Ashton St John
Amateur. *b:* 4.4.1935, Kingston, Jamaica. Sound opening right-hand batsman, off break bowler. *Team* Jamaica (1956/7 to 1971/2). *Tours* West Indies to England 1963, 1966; Jamaica to England 1970. *Tests* West Indies (1957/8 to 1966, 13 matches).
Career batting
95–158–18–5906–218–42.18–18–*ct* 36
Bowling 107–0
Test batting
13–21–0–564–125–26.85–1–*ct* 5
Apart from an innings of 190* v Middlesex, he achieved very little on the 1963 tour, though he appeared in two Tests. His experience in 1966 was curiously similar, he again doing little in the two Tests for which he was selected. His highest score was 218 for Jamaica v Guyana at Georgetown in 1966/7.

McMurray, Alfred
Amateur. *b:* 4.11.1914, Belfast, Ireland. Brother of Thomas (Surrey). Right-hand batsman. *Team* Ireland (1939).
Career batting
1–2–0–9–5–4.50–0–*ct* 1

McMurray, Thomas
Professional. *b:* 24.7.1911, Belfast, Ireland. *d:* 24.3.1964, Belfast, Ireland. Brother of Alfred (Ireland). Middle order right-hand batsman, wicket-keeper. *Team* Surrey (1933–39, 33 matches).
Career batting
33–54–6–892–62–18.58–0–*ct* 14
Bowling 23–1–23.00–0–0–1/3
He was a noted soccer forward, appearing for Tranmere Rovers, Millwall and Rochdale.

McNab, Alexander
Amateur. *b:* 11.1.1887, Uddingston, Lanarkshire, Scotland. *d: circa* 1925, Philadelphia, USA. Right-hand batsman, right-arm medium pace bowler. *Team* Scotland (1910).
Career batting
1–2–1–0–0*–0.00–0–*ct* 0
Bowling 43–0

MacNab, Maurice Ronald
Amateur. *b:* May 1902, Elham, Kent. *d:* 12.4.1962, Marianglas, Anglesey. Lower order left-hand batsman, left-arm bowler. *Sch* Malvern and St Edward's, Oxford. *Team* Wales (1930).
Career batting
1–2–0–3–2–1.50–0–*ct* 0
Bowling 16–1–16.00–0–0–1/16

McNab, William
Amateur. *b:* 2.10.1916, Edinburgh, Scotland. Right-hand batsman, wicket-keeper. *Sch* George Watson's College. *Team* Scotland (1947).
Career batting
1–2–0–10–10–5.00–0–*ct* 2

MacNairy, Roy
Professional. *b:* 1904, Barrow-in-Furness, Lancashire. *d:* 5.9.1962, Bradley, Huddersfield, Yorkshire. Lower order batsman, useful bowler. *Team* Lancashire (1925, 1 match).
Career batting
1–1–1–4–4*–no av–0–*ct* 0
Bowling 73–1–73.00–0–0–1/23

McNamara, Francis Knyvett
Amateur. *b:* 30.4.1912, Missouri, India. Opening right-hand batsman, left-arm medium pace bowler. *Sch* Marlborough. *Team* Free Foresters (1952).
Career batting
1–2–0–18–16–9.00–0–*ct* 0

McNamara, N. F.
Amateur. Middle order batsman, useful bowler. *Team* Ireland (1913).
Career batting
1–2–1–54–30–54.00–0–*ct* 1
Bowling 49–0

McNeil, Alastair Simpson Bell
Amateur. *b:* 28.6.1915, Edinburgh, Scotland. *d:* 26.1.1944, Anzio, Italy. Lower order batsman, slow left-arm bowler. *Sch* George Watson's College. *Team* Scotland (1937).
Career batting
1–2–0–28–23–14.00–0–*ct* 0
He played rugby football for Scotland.

McNeill, Rt Hon Ronald John
(created Baron Cushendun in 1927)
Amateur. *b:* 30.4.1861, Crays, Belfast, Ireland. *d:* 12.10.1934, Cushendun, Co Antrim, Ireland. Tail end right-hand batsman, useful underarm bowler, brilliant field. *Sch* Harrow. *Team* MCC (1885).
Career batting
1–1–0–2–2–2.00–0–*ct* 0
He was at both Cambridge and Oxford, but in the eleven at neither. In 1911 he became MP for East Kent and in 1918 for Canterbury. In 1922 and 1924 he was Under-Secretary of State for Foreign Affairs.

Macniven, Edward
Amateur. *b:* 21.6.1827, Offley, Herts. *d:* 4.1.1858, Perrysfield, Godstone, Surrey. He was killed when his dog-cart overturned. Hard hitting middle order right-hand batsman. *Sch* Eton. *Teams* Cambridge U (1846–48, blue 1846); Surrey (1851, 1 match).
Career batting
12–21–4–407–88*–23.94–0–*ct* 6
Bowling 2 wickets, no analyses
An excellent oarsman, he was in the eight at Eton and Cambridge.

McPate, William Adamson
Cricketer. *b:* 22.7.1951, Baillieston, Lanarkshire, Scotland. Right-hand batsman, right-arm fast medium bowler. *Team* Scotland (1983).
Career batting
1–1–1–5–5*–no av–0–*ct* 0
Bowling 45–1–45.00–0–0–1/8

McPhail, Angus William
Cricketer. *b:* 25.5.1956, Ipswich, Suffolk. Lower order right-hand batsman, wicket-keeper. *Sch* Abingdon. *Team* Oxford U (1977).
Career batting
4–8–1–63–37–9.00–0–*ct* 6

Macpherson, Moray Charles Livingstone
Cricketer. *b:* 4.11.1959, Barton-on-Sea, Hampshire. Lower order right-hand batsman, wicket-keeper. *Sch* Winchester. *Team* Oxford U (1980).
Career batting
5–10–1–52–22–5.77–0–*ct* 8–*st* 1

McPherson, Thomas Ian
Cricketer. *b:* 14.10.1942, Scone, Perthshire, Scotland. Lower order right-hand batsman, slow left-arm bowler. *Team* Scotland (1977–79).
Career batting
5–7–3–83–28–20.75–0–*ct* 0
Bowling 230–10–23.00–0–0–4/74

Macpherson, William Douglas Lawson
Amateur. *b:* 1841, Cheltenham, Gloucs. *d:* 24.2.1920, Silverton, Devon. Useful right-hand batsman, wicket-keeper. *Team* Gloucestershire (1870–71, 3 matches).
Career batting
3–4–1–7–5–2.33–0–*ct* 0

McQuilken, Archibald Lynn
Amateur. *b:* 27.9.1933, Muckamore, Co Antrim, Ireland. *d:* 16.10.1983, Belfast, Ireland. Right-hand batsman, leg break and googly bowler. *Team* Ireland (1962).
Career batting
2–4–0–140–42–35.00–0–*ct* 0
Bowling 60–5–12.00–1–0–5/37

McRae, Dr Foster Moverley
Amateur. *b:* 12.2.1916, Buenos Aires, Argentine. *d:* 25.2.1944. He died at sea aboard HMS *Mahratta* in the Barents Sea. Middle order right-

hand batsman. *Sch* Christ's Hospital. *Team* Somerset (1936–39, 25 matches).
Career batting
25–45–5–972–107–24.30–1–*ct* 9

McTavish, Alastair Kenneth
Amateur. *b:* 22.12.1904, Rothiemay, Banff, Scotland. *d:* 23.3.1961, Newton-Mearns, Renfrewshire. Right-hand batsman, wicket-keeper. *Team* Scotland (1929–39).
Career batting
15–26–0–675–109–25.96–1–*ct* 9–*st* 4

McVeagh, Trevor George Brooke
Amateur. *b:* 14.9.1906, Athboy, Co. Meath, Ireland. *d:* 5.6.1968, Dublin, Ireland. Sound left-hand batsman. *Teams* Dublin U (1925–26); Ireland (1926–34).
Career batting
12–23–2–814–109–38.76–2–*ct* 11

MacVicar, Angus David Lees
Cricketer. *b:* 25.8.1955, Sheffield, Yorkshire. Lower order right-hand batsman, right-arm fast medium bowler. *Sch* Rugby. *Team* Cambridge U (1977).
Career batting
1 match, did not bat–*ct* 0
Bowling 141–2–70.50–0–0–2/82

McVicker, Norman Michael
Cricketer. *b:* 4.11.1940, Radcliffe, Lancashire. Lower order right-hand batsman, right-arm fast medium bowler. *Teams* Warwickshire (1969–72, 104 matches); Leicestershire (1974–76, 67 matches).
Career batting
173–210–53–3108–83*–19.79–0–*ct* 48
Bowling 11567–453–25.53–19–0–7/29

He appeared for Lincolnshire from 1963 to 1968 and made his first-class debut for Minor Counties in 1965.

McVittie, Charles Arthur Blake
Amateur. *b:* 30.7.1908, Rugeley, Staffordshire. *d:* 4.9.1973, Stowting Common, Kent. Middle order right-hand batsman, wicket-keeper. *Sch* Bedford. *Teams* Cambridge U (1929); Kent (1929, 1 match).
Career batting
4–4–2–58–30–29.00–0–*ct* 3–*st* 2

Madan Lal Udhouram Sharma
Cricketer. *b* 20.3.1951, Amritsar, India. Attractive middle order right-hand batsman, right-arm medium-fast bowler. *Teams* Punjab (1968/9 to 1971/2); Delhi (1972/3 to 1982/3). *Tours* India to Sri Lanka 1973/4, to England 1974, 1972, to West Indies and New Zealand 1975/6, to Australia 1977/8, to West Indies 1982/3, to Pakistan 1982/3. *Tests* India (1974/5 to 1982/3, 31 matches).
Career batting
173–258–73–8036–223–43.43–18–*ct* 109
Bowling 12126–476–25.47–23–4–9/31
Test batting
31–49–12–762–55*–20.59–0–*ct* 14
Bowling 2365–64–36.95–4–0–5/23

He had very modest figures on the 1974 tour to England, though he appeared in two Tests. In 1982 he showed greatly improved form, hitting 309 runs, av 61.80, and taking 22 wickets, av 34.68, and played in all three Tests. His highest score is 223 for Delhi v Rajasthan at Delhi in 1977/8 and his best bowling is 9/31 for Delhi v Haryana at Delhi in 1979/80.

Madden, John Charles Pengelly
(also known as Madden-Gaskell)
Amateur. *b:* 1.3.1896, Pontypool, Monmouthshire. *d:* 4.2.1975, Lowertown, Helston, Cornwall. Middle order right-hand batsman. *Sch* Haileybury. *Teams* Somerset (1928–30, 9 matches); Glamorgan (1922, 1 match).
Career batting
10–19–0–300–63–15.78–0–*ct* 5
Bowling 8–0

Maddocks, Leonard Victor
Amateur. *b:* 24.5.1926, Beaconsfield, Victoria, Australia. Brother of R. I. (Victoria), father of I. L. (Victoria). Middle order right-hand batsman, wicket-keeper. *Teams* Victoria (1946/7 to 1961/2, 66 matches); Tasmania (1962/3 to 1967/8, 6 matches). *Tours* Australia to England 1956, to West Indies 1954/5, to India 1956/7, to New Zealand 1959/60; Cavaliers to South Africa 1960/1. *Tests* Australia (1954/5 to 1956/7, 7 matches).
Career batting
112–158–33–4106–122*–32.84–6–*ct* 209–*st* 68
Bowling 4–1–4.00–0–0–1/4
Test batting
7–12–2–177–69–17.70–0–*ct* 19–*st* 1

He played in two Tests on the 1956 tour to England, standing in for the injured Langley. He was manager of the 1977 Australian team to England.

Madugalle, Ranjan Senerath
Cricketer. *b:* 22.4.1959, Kandy, Ceylon. Middle order right-hand batsman, off break bowler, good field. *Team* Sri Lanka (1979 to 1982/3). *Tours* Sri Lanka to England 1979, to India 1980/1, 1982/3, to Pakistan 1981/2, to Australia and New Zealand 1982/3, to Zimbabwe 1982/3. *Tests* Sri Lanka (1981/2 to 1982/3, 8 matches).

Career batting
35–50–2–1377–142*–28.68–1–*ct* 25
Bowling 32–0
Test batting
8–16–1–431–91*–28.73–0–*ct* 5

Magee, Brian Robert Boyd
Amateur. *b:* 4.5.1918, Canada. Lower order batsman, useful bowler. *Sch* Radley. *Team* Canada to England 1954.
Career batting
1–2–0–16–13–8.00–0–*ct* 0
Bowling 40–1–40.00–0–0–1/22

Magee, James Mary
Amateur. *b:* 1874, Rathmines, Co. Dublin, Ireland. *d:* February 1949, Greystones, Co. Wicklow, Ireland. Right-hand batsman. *Team* Ireland (1907).
Career batting
1–2–0–26–14–13.00–0–*ct* 0
He was a noted rugby footballer

Magill, Michael Desmond Ponsonby
Amateur. *b:* 28.9.1915, Sevenoaks, Kent. *d:* 5.9.1940, Cheshire. Middle order right-hand batsman, right-arm fast medium bowler. *Sch* Eton. *Teams* Oxford U (1938); Army (1939). *Tour* Oxford and Cambridge to Jamaica 1938/9.
Career batting
6–9–2–160–80–22.85–0–*ct* 3
Bowling 291–7–41.57–1–0–5/57
His County cricket was for Berkshire.

Magnay, Sir Christopher Boyd William
Amateur. *b:* 27.3.1884, Marylebone, London. *d:* 4.9.1960, Great Saxham, Suffolk. Middle order right-hand batsman. *Sch* Harrow. *Teams* Middlesex (1906–11, 3 matches); Cambridge U (1904).
Career batting
12–21–0–308–73–14.66–0–*ct* 5
Bowling 2–0
His County cricket was for Suffolk.

Maguire, Keith Robert
Cricketer. *b:* 20.3.1961, Marston Green, Birmingham. Right-hand batsman, right-arm medium pace bowler. *Team* Warwickshire (1982, 3 matches).
Career batting
3–3–0–3–2–1.00–0–*ct* 0
Bowling 123–1–123.00–0–0–1/32

Mahaffy, John Pentland
Amateur. *b:* 18.6.1906, Suva, Fiji. *d:* 8.12.1937, Mundesley-on-Sea, Norfolk. Middle order batsman. *Team* MCC (1934).
Career batting
1–1–0–8–8–8.00–0–*ct* 0

Maher, Bernard Joseph Michael
Cricketer. *b:* 11.2.1958, Hillingdon, Middlesex. Lower order right-hand batsman, wicket-keeper. *Team* Derbyshire (1981–83, 20 matches).
Career batting
20–26–8–205–52–11.38–0–*ct* 32–*st* 5

Mahmood Hussain
Amateur. *b:* 2.4.1932, Lahore, India. Lower order right-hand batsman, right-arm fast medium bowler. *Teams* Universities (1949/50); West Punjab (1951/2); Karachi (1953/4 to 1961/2); East Pakistan (1955/6). *Tours* Pakistan to India 1952/3, 1960/1, to England 1954, 1962, to West Indies 1957/8. *Tests* Pakistan (1952/3 to 1962, 27 matches).
Career batting
95–115–12–1107–50–10.74–0–*ct* 29
Bowling 8073–322–25.07–19–3–8/95
Test batting
27–39–6–336–35–10.18–0–*ct* 5
Bowling 2628–68–38.64–2–0–6/67
On his 1954 visit to England he took 72 wickets, av 21.30, and though not so successful in 1962 he headed the first-class averages with 44 wickets, av 23.45. His final first-class match was for the National Tyre and Rubber Co. 1968/9.

Mahmoodul Hasan
Cricketer. Middle order batsman, useful bowler. *Teams* East Pakistan (1966/7 to 1967/8); Karachi (1959/60 to 1970/1); PWD (1964/5 to 1971/2); Dacca (1964/5 to 1965/6). *Tour* Pakistan Eaglets to England 1963.
Career batting
63–95–7–3199–196–36.35–6–*ct* 41
Bowling 337–4–84.25–0–0–1/1

Mahony, Noel Cameron
Amateur. *b:* 15.1.1913, Fermoy, Co. Cork, Ireland. Right-hand batsman. *Team* Ireland (1948–53).
Career batting
5–10–0–116–29–11.60–0–*ct* 3

Maidlow, William John
Cricketer. *b:* 15.7.1949, Bristol. Right-hand batsman. *Team* Oxford U (1972).
Career batting
2–4–0–53–45–13.25–0–*ct* 2

Mailey, Arthur Alfred
Amateur. *b:* 3.1.1886, Waterloo, New South Wales, Australia. *d:* 31.12.1967, Kirrawee, New South Wales, Australia. Tail end right-hand

batsman, leg break and googly bowler. *Team* New South Wales (1912/13 to 1929/30, 67 matches). *Tours* Australia to England 1921, 1926, to South Africa 1921/2, to New Zealand 1913/14, to North America 1913; NSW to New Zealand 1923/4. *Tests* Australia (1920/1 to 1926, 21 matches).
Career batting
158–186–62–1529–66–12.33–0–*ct* 157
Bowling 18774–779–24.10–61–16–10/66
Test batting
21–29–9–222–46*–11.10–0–*ct* 14
Bowling 3358–99–33.91–6–2–9/121

On his first visit to England in 1921 he took 134 wickets, av 19.36, and in 1926, 126, av 19.34. His bowling was much more difficult to master than it appeared. His outstanding success was to take 10 for 66 v Gloucestershire in 1921, but he also took 9 for 121 against England in the Test at Melbourne in 1920/1. His final first-class match was for the Rest of Australia in 1930/1. He was a talented writer and cartoonist.

Mainprice, Humphrey
Amateur. *b:* 27.11.1882, Ashley, Cheshire. *d:* 24.11.1958, Penmere, Cornwall. Lower order right-hand batsman, leg break bowler. *Sch* Blundell's. *Teams* Gloucestershire (1905, 1 match); Cambridge U (1905–06, blue 1906).
Career batting
15–23–2–381–60–18.14–0–*ct* 9
Bowling 686–21–32.66–0–0–4/34

He also played for Cheshire.

Mains, Geoffrey
Professional *b:* 24.1.1934, Mangotsfield, Gloucs. Lower order right-hand batsman, right-arm fast medium bowler. *Team* Gloucestershire (1951–54, 6 matches).
Career batting
6–10–1–19–8–2.11–0–*ct* 2
Bowling 305–6–50.83–0–0–2/42

Mair, Norman George Robertson
Amateur. *b:* 7.10.1928, Edinburgh, Scotland. Left-hand batsman, slow left-arm bowler. *Sch* Merchiston. *Team* Scotland (1952).
Career batting
1–1–1–4–4*–no av–0–*ct* 0

An excellent rugby player, he represented Scotland.

Maitland, Reginald Paynter
Amateur. *b:* 6.3.1851, Portsea, Hampshire. *d:* 10.4.1926, Bartley, Hampshire. Middle order batsman. *Team* MCC (1885).
Career batting
1–1–0–0–0–0.00–0–*ct* 0

Maitland, William Fuller
(also known as Fuller-Maitland)
Amateur. *b:* 6.5.1844, Stansted, Essex. *d:* 15.11.1932, Brighton, Sussex. Hard hitting lower order right-hand batsman, right-arm slow bowler. *Sch* Harrow. *Team* Oxford U (1864–67, blue all four years).
Career batting
38–62–5–790–61–13.85–0–*ct* 28
Bowling 1631–103+20–15.87–9–3–8/48

He was able to get an exceptional amount of spin on the ball and often obtained wickets with deliveries which the batsman regarded as too wide to be dangerous. His County cricket was for Oxfordshire and Essex (pre-first-class). His final first-class match was for MCC in 1870.

A noted athlete, he represented Oxford in both the high and long jump as well as rackets. From 1875 to 1895 he was MP for Breconshire.

Maitland, William James
Amateur. *b:* 22.7.1847, Edinburgh, Scotland. *d:* 8.5.1919, Marylebone, London. Middle order right-hand batsman, deep field. *Sch* Edinburgh Academy. *Team* MCC (1868–69).
Career batting
3–3–0–71–57–23.66–0–*ct* 2

He lived for many years in India, where he took a prominent part in cricket. He played occasionally for Devon.

Majendie, Nicholas Lionel
Amateur. *b:* 9.6.1942, Cheltenham, Gloucs. Lower order right-hand batsman, wicket-keeper. *Sch* Winchester. *Teams* Oxford U (1961–63, blue 1962–63); Surrey (1963, 8 matches).
Career batting
26–33–6–313–54–11.59–0–*ct* 64–*st* 4

Majendie, Vivian Henry Bruce
Amateur. *b:* 20.4.1886, Ipplepen, Devon. *d:* 13.1.1960, Watford, Hertfordshire. Son of H. W. (Oxford U, 1860). Middle order right-hand batsman, wicket-keeper. *Sch* Winchester. *Team* Somerset (1907–10, 2 matches).
Career batting
2–4–0–55–28–13.75–0–*ct* 2–*st* 4

He also played for Devon.

Majid Jahangir Khan
Cricketer. *b:* 28.9.1946, Ludhiana, India. Son of M. Jahangir Khan (Cambridge U and India), cousin of Imran Khan (Pakistan) and Javed Burki (Pakistan). Attacking middle order, later opening, right-hand batsman, right-arm medium, or off break, bowler, good close field. *Teams* Lahore (1961/2 to 1982/3); Punjab (1964/5 to 1967/8); PIA (1968/9 to 1980/1); Glamorgan

(1968–76, 154 matches); Cambridge U (1970–72, blue all three years); Queensland (1973/4, 9 matches). *Tours* Pakistan to England 1967, 1971, 1974, 1982, to Australia, New Zealand and Ceylon 1972/3, to Australia and New Zealand 1978/9, to Australia 1976/7, 1981/2, to West Indies 1976/7, to India 1979/80; Pakistan Eaglets to England 1963. *Tests* Pakistan (1964/5 to 1982/3, 63 matches).
Career batting
407–697–60–27328–241–42.90–73–*ct* 408
Bowling 7197–224–32.12–4–0–6/67
Test batting
63–106–5–3931–167–38.92–8–*ct* 70
Bowling 1456–27–53.92–0–0–4/45

Of his four tours to England the most successful was 1974 when he hit 1,000 runs, av 50.00, in first-class matches and 262, av 43.66, in the Tests. On the 1971 tour he appeared in just two games, both Tests, whilst in 1982 his form was such that he only played in one Test.

In all he hit 1,000 runs in an English season eight times, going on to 2,000 once: 2,074, av 61.00 in 1972. His highest innings in England was 204 for Glamorgan v Surrey at the Oval in 1972 and his other English double century was for Cambridge in the 1970 University match. His highest score was 241 for Lahore Greens v Bahawalpur at Lahore in 1965/6.

Major, John
Professional. *b:* 6.2.1861, Seaford, Sussex. *d:* 1931, Wakefield, Yorkshire. Middle order right-hand batsman, right-arm medium pace bowler. *Team* Sussex (1888–89, 11 matches).
Career batting
12–23–2–363–106–17.28–1–*ct* 2
Bowling 53–3–17.66–0–0–2/10

He also played for Warwickshire (pre-first-class). A good soccer player, he appeared for West Bromwich Albion.

Major, Lionel Hugh
Amateur. *b:* 21.4.1883, Wembdon, Somerset. *d:* 25.6.1965, Exmouth, Devon. Lower order batsman, useful bowler. *Team* Somerset (1903, 1 match).
Career batting
1–2–0–17–11–8.50–*ct* 0
Bowling 5–1–5.00–0–0–1/5

Makepeace, Joseph William Henry
Professional. *b:* 22.8.1881, Middlesbrough, Yorkshire. *d:* 19.12.1952, Spital, Bebington, Cheshire. Stubborn opening right-hand batsman, slow leg break bowler, excellent cover point. *Team* Lancashire (1906–30, 487 matches). *Tour* MCC to Australia 1920/1. *Tests* England (1920/1, 4 matches).
Career batting
499–778–66–25799–203–36.23–43–*ct* 194
Bowling 1971–42–46.92–0–0–4/33
Test batting
4–8–0–279–117–34.87–1–*ct* 0

He hit 1,000 runs in a season thirteen times, going on to 2,000 twice (best 2,340, av 48.75, in 1926). Both his double centuries were for Lancashire, the highest being 203 v Worcs at Worcester in 1923. For 20 years up to 1951, he was chief coach at Old Trafford. A noted soccer player, he appeared as right half for Everton and England, thus being a double international.

Makinson, Joseph
Amateur. *b:* 25.8.1836, Higher Broughton, Lancashire. *d:* 14.3.1914, Sale, Cheshire. Brother of Charles (Victoria). Attacking middle order right-hand batsman, right-hand medium pace round-arm bowler, good field. *Teams* Cambridge U (1856–58, blue all three years); Cambridgeshire (1857–58, 3 matches); Lancashire (1865–73, 5 matches).
Career batting
27–50–2–862–66–17.95–0–*ct* 23–*st* 2
Bowling 566–39+7–15.29–2–1–7/38

He was for some years Chairman of Lancashire CCC

Malalasekera, Vijaya Prasanna
Cricketer. *b:* 8.8.1945, Colombo, Ceylon. Middle order right-hand batsman. *Team* Cambridge U (1966–68, blue 1966–67).
Career batting
27–50–1–699–80–14.26–0–*ct* 11
Bowling 9–0

Malcolm, Henry John James
Professional. *b:* 4.7.1914, Richmond, Surrey. Middle order right-hand batsman, right-arm fast medium bowler. *Team* Middlesex (1948, 4 matches).
Career batting
4–6–1–139–76*–27.80–0–*ct* 1
Bowling 6–0

Malden, Ernest
Amateur. *b:* 10.10.1870, Sheldwich, Kent. *d:* 13.9.1955, Salisbury, Rhodesia. Cousin of Eustace (Kent). Fast scoring middle order right-hand batsman, right-arm medium pace bowler, close field. *Sch* Clergy School, Canterbury. *Team* Kent (1893, 1 match).
Career batting
1–2–0–22–22–11.00–0–*ct* 1
Bowling 15–0

Malden, Rev Eustace
Amateur. *b:* 19.8.1863, Brighton, Sussex. *d:* 3.12.1947, Rottingdean, Sussex. Cousin of Ernest (Kent), father of W. J. (Sussex). Lower order right-hand batsman, wicket-keeper. *Sch* Haileybury. *Team* Kent (1892–93, 12 matches).
Career batting
13–21–1–133–27–6.65–0–*ct* 7–*st* 5
He played for Hertfordshire 1887.

Malden, William Jack
Amateur. *b:* 14.5.1899, Ticehurst, Sussex. *d:* 23.11.1963, Newbury, Berkshire. Son of Eustace (Kent). Opening/middle order right-hand batsman, fine field. *Sch* Haileybury. *Teams* Sussex (1920–22, 23 matches); Cambridge U (1921).
Career batting
24–36–1–624–100–17.85–1–*ct* 12

Malet, Alexander George William
Amateur. *b:* 25.10.1845, Portsmouth, Hants. *d:* 11.1.1922, Marylebone, London. Steady middle order right-hand batsman, wicket-keeper. *Sch* Cheltenham. *Team* Gentlemen of England (1865).
Career batting
1–2–0–23–12–11.50–0–*ct* 1
He played for Dorset and Cheshire.

Malhotra, Ashok Omprakash
Cricketer. *b:* 26.1.1957, Amritsar, India. Attractive middle order right-hand batsman, right-arm medium pace bowler. *Team* Haryana (1973/4 to 1982/3). *Tours* India to England 1982, to West Indies 1982/3. *Tests* India (1981/2 to 1982, 3 matches).
Career batting
74–117–17–4655–228–46.55–11–*ct* 34
Bowling 79–1–79.00–0–0–1/37
Test batting
3–4–0–36–31–9.00–0–*ct* 2
He hit 462 runs, av 33.00, on the 1982 tour to England and played in one Test. His highest score is 228 for Haryana v Services at Delhi in 1982/3.

Malik, Hardit Singh
Amateur. *b:* 30.11.1894, Rawalpindi, India. Middle order right-hand batsman. *Sch* Eastbourne. *Teams* Sussex (1914–21, 9 matches); Oxford U (1921); Sikhs (1922/3 to 1928/9); Hindus (1929/30).
Career batting
18–32–0–636–106–19.87–2–*ct* 8
Bowling 151–3+1–50.33–0–0–2/92

Mallalieu, Albert Edward
Amateur. *b:* 13.1.1904, Delph, Yorkshire. Opening right-hand batsman. *Sch* Leys. *Team* Wales (1924–30).
Career batting
6–8–0–137–66–17.12–0–*ct* 2
His County cricket was for Caernarvonshire.

Mallam, Charles George Cave
Amateur. *b:* 4.8.1859, Oxford. *d:* 8.12.1950, Brentwood, Essex. Lower order right-hand batsman, right-arm slow bowler. *Sch* Uppingham. *Team* Oxford U (1882).
Career batting
1–2–1–4–2*–4.00–0–*ct* 2
Bowling 39–0
His County cricket was for Rutland, Oxfordshire and Devon.

Mallender, Neil Alan
Cricketer. *b:* 13.8.1961, Kirk Sandall, Yorkshire. Lower order right-hand batsman, right-arm medium pace bowler. *Team* Northants (1980–83, 69 matches).
Career batting
69–70–26–568–71*–12.90–0–*ct* 27
Bowling 5065–163–31.07–5–1–7/41

Mallett, Ashley Alexander
Cricketer. *b:* 13.7.1945, Chatswood, New South Wales, Australia. Lower order right-hand batsman, off break bowler. *Team* South Australia (1967/8 to 1980/1, 91 matches). *Tours* Australia to England 1968, 1972, 1975, 1980, to Ceylon and India 1969/70, to South Africa 1969/70, to New Zealand 1973/4; International Wanderers to South Africa 1975/6. *Tests* Australia (1968/9 to 1980, 38 matches).
Career batting
183–230–59–2326–92–13.60–0–*ct* 105
Bowling 18208–693–26.27–33–5–8/59
Test batting
38–50–13–430–43*–11.62–0–*ct* 30
Bowling 3940–132–29.84–6–1–8/59
He appeared in some Tests on all his major tours to England, but achieved only modest results.

Mallett, Anthony William Haward
Amateur. *b:* 29.8.1924, Dulwich, South London. Father of N. V. H. (Oxford U). Attacking middle order right-hand batsman, right-arm fast medium bowler. *Sch* Dulwich. *Teams* Oxford U (1947–48, blue both years); Kent (1946–53, 33 matches). *Tour* MCC to Canada 1951.
Career batting
75–108–14–1764–97–18.76–0–*ct* 61
Bowling 5748–213–26.98–9–0–6/42
His first-class debut was for the Under-33 XI in 1945 at Lord's.

Mallett, Nicholas Vivian Haward
Cricketer. *b:* 30.10.1956, Haileybury, Hertfordshire. Son of A. W. H. (Kent). Lower order right-hand batsman, right-arm medium pace bowler. *Team* Oxford U (1980–81, blue 1981).
Career batting
11–20–2–237–52–13.16–0–*ct* 3
Bowling 841–19–44.26–1–0–5/52

Mallett, Richard Henry
Amateur. *b:* 14.10.1858, Louth, Lincolnshire. *d:* 29.11.1939, Ickenham, Middlesex. Opening right-hand batsman, right-arm medium pace bowler. *Team* MCC (1901).
Career batting
1–1–0–8–8–8.00–0–*ct* 0
Bowling 28–0
He appeared for Durham.

Malone, Michael Francis
Cricketer. *b:* 9.10.1950, Perth, Australia. Lower order right-hand batsman, right-arm fast medium bowler. *Teams* Western Australia (1974/5 to 1981/2, 45 matches); Lancashire (1979–80, 19 matches). *Tours* Australia to England 1977, to Pakistan 1979/80. *Test* Australia (1977, 1 match).
Career batting
73–79–22–914–46–16.03–0–*ct* 30
Bowling 6441–260–24.77–13–1–7/88
Test batting
1–1–0–46–46–46.00–0–*ct* 0
Bowling 77–6–12.83–1–0–5/63
He took 32 wickets, av 26.15, on the 1977 tour of England and made a successful Test debut on that tour, but his signing for World Series Cricket ended a possibly fruitful Test career.

Malone, Steven John
Cricketer. *b:* 19.10.1953, Chelmsford, Essex. Lower order right-hand batsman, right-arm medium pace bowler. *Sch* King's School, Ely. *Teams* Essex (1975–78, 2 matches); Hampshire (1980–83, 43 matches).
Career batting
45–38–14–174–23–7.25–0–*ct* 9
Bowling 3378–99–34.12–2–1–7/55

Maltby, George
Professional. *b:* 1.10.1876, South Normanton, Derbyshire. *d:* 30.7.1924, Huthwaite, Notts. Middle order right-hand batsman. *Team* Derbyshire (1905, 3 matches).
Career batting
3–6–1–22–7*–4.40–0–*ct* 1
Bowling 20–0

Maltby, Norman
Cricketer. *b:* 16.7.1951, Marske-by-the-Sea, Yorkshire. Lower order left-hand batsman, right-arm medium pace bowler. *Team* Northants (1972–74, 9 matches).
Career batting
9–14–4–185–59–18.50–0–*ct* 2
Bowling 97–2–48.50–0–0–2/43

Malthouse, Samuel
Professional. *b:* 13.10.1857, Whitwell, Derbyshire. *d:* 7.2.1931, Whitwell, Derbyshire. Father of W. N. (Derbyshire). Lower order left-hand batsman, right-arm medium pace off break bowler. *Team* Derbyshire (1894–95, 9 matches).
Career batting
9–12–2–118–38–11.80–0–*ct* 3
Bowling 67–0

Malthouse, William Norman
Professional. *b:* 16.12.1890, Whitwell, Derbyshire. *d:* 10.5.1961, South Kirkby, Yorkshire. Son of Samuel (Derbyshire). Middle order right-hand batsman, right-arm off break bowler. *Team* Derbyshire (1919–20, 7 matches).
Career batting
7–13–1–116–30–9.66–0–*ct* 2
Bowling 69–0

Manasseh, Maurice
Amateur. *b:* 12.1.1943, Calcutta, India. Middle order right-hand batsman, right-arm medium pace off break bowler. *Sch* Epsom. *Teams* Middlesex (1964–67, 7 matches); Oxford U (1962–64, blue 1964).
Career batting
42–73–11–1607–129*–25.91–2–*ct* 19
Bowling 2557–61–41.92–2–0–5/51

Manjrekar, Vijay Laxman
Amateur. *b:* 26.9.1931, Bombay, India. *d:* 18.10.1983, Madras, India. Stylish middle order right-hand batsman, off break bowler, excellent field. *Teams* Bombay (1949/50 to 1955/6); Bengal (1953/4); Andhra (1956/7); Uttar Pradesh (1957/8); Rajasthan (1958/9 to 1965/6); Maharashtra (1966/7 to 1967/8). *Tours* India to England 1952, 1959, to West Indies 1952/3, 1961/2, to Pakistan 1954/5, to Ceylon 1956/7. *Tests* India (1951/2 to 1964/5, 55 matches).
Career batting
198–295–38–12832–283–49.92–38–*ct* 72–*st* 6
Bowling 657–20–32.85–0–0–4/21
Test batting
55–92–10–3208–189*–39.12–7–*ct* 19–*st* 2
Bowling 44–1–44.00–0–0–1/16
On the 1952 tour to England he hit 1,059 runs, av 39.22, his highest score of 133 coming in the

first Test at Headingley. In 1959 he was much handicapped by injury, but batted well when available. His final first-class match was for Kerala Chief Minister's XI in 1972/3. His highest score was 283 for Vizianagram's XI v Tata S. C. XI at Hyderabad in 1963/4. He hit 1,077 runs in the 1963/4 Indian season.

Mankad, Ashok Vinoo Mulwantrai
Cricketer. *b:* 12.10.1946, Bombay, India. Son of M.H. (India), brother of R.V. (Bombay). Opening or middle order right-hand batsman, right-arm medium pace bowler. *Team* Bombay (1963/4 to 1982/3). *Tours* India to West Indies 1970/1, to England 1971, 1974, to Sri Lanka 1973/4, to Australia 1977/8; CCI to Sri Lanka 1972/3. *Tests* India (1969/70 to 1977/8, 22 matches).
Career batting
218–326–71–12980–265–50.90–31–*ct* 126
Bowling 3277–72–45.51–2–0–5/21
Test batting
22–42–3–991–97–25.41–0–*ct* 12
Bowling 43–0

On his 1971 tour to England he hit 795 runs, av 41.84, and played in all three Tests, though with no success. In 1974 he played in only one Test and in first-class matches hit 611 runs, av 38.18. His highest score was 265 for Bombay v Delhi at Bombay in 1980/1

Mankad, Mulwantrai Himatlal
(known as 'Vinoo')
Amateur. *b:* 12.4.1917, Jamnagar, India. *d:* 21.8.1978, Bombay, India. Father of A. V. M. (India) and R. V. (Bombay). Talented opening right-hand batsman, slow left-arm bowler. *Teams* Western India (1935/6); Nawanagar (1936/7 to 1941/2); Hindus (1936/7 to 1945/6); Maharashtra (1943/4); Gujerat (1944/5 to 1950/1); Bengal (1948/9); Bombay (1951/2 to 1955/6); Rajasthan (1956/7 to 1961/2). *Tours* India to Ceylon 1944/5, to England 1946, 1952, to Australia 1947/8, to West Indies 1952/3, to Pakistan 1954/5. *Tests* India (1946 to 1958/9, 44 matches).
Career batting
232–359–27–11566–231–34.83–26–*ct* 188
Bowling 19159–781–24.53–38–9–8/35
Test batting
44–72–5–2109–231–31.47–5–*ct* 33
Bowling 5236–162–32.32–8–2–8/52

The leading Indian all-rounder of his generation, he performed the 'double' on his 1946 tour to England, hitting 1,120 runs, av 28.00, and taking 129 wickets, av 20.76. In 1952 he was engaged by a League Club and released only for the Tests. Between 1950 and 1958 he appeared for a Commonwealth XI in several Festival matches in England. His highest score was 231 for India v New Zealand at Bombay in 1955/6.

Mann, Eric William
Amateur. *b:* 4.3.1882, Sidcup, Kent. *d:* 15.2.1954, Rye, Kent. Hard hitting middle order right-hand batsman, right-hand fast medium bowler. *Sch* Harrow. *Teams* Kent (1902–03, 6 matches); Cambridge U (1903–05, blue all three years). *Tour* MCC to North America, 1905.
Career batting
43–81–4–1932–157–25.09–2–*ct* 43
Bowling 744–19–39.15–0–0–4/25

Mann, Francis George
Amateur. *b:* 6.9.1917, Byfleet, Surrey. Son of F. T. (Middlesex), brother of J. P. (Middlesex). Middle order right-hand batsman. *Sch* Eton. *Teams* Cambridge U (1938–39, blue both years); Middlesex (1937–54, 54 matches). *Tour* MCC to South Africa 1948/9. *Tests* England (1948/9 to 1949, 7 matches).
Career batting
166–262–17–6350–136*–25.91–7–*ct* 72
Bowling 389–3–129.66–0–0–2/16
Test batting
7–12–2–376–136*–37.60–1–*ct* 3

He hit 1,000 runs in a season three times (best 1,311, av 24.73, in 1949). He captained MCC in South Africa in 1948/9 and England in all the seven Tests in which he played. In 1948 and 1949 he was captain of Middlesex. His final first-class match was for Free Foresters in 1958. He is Chairman of the TCCB.

Mann, Francis Thomas
Amateur. *b:* 3.3.1888, Winchmore Hill, Middlesex. *d:* 6.10.1964, Milton-Lilbourne, Wiltshire. Father of F. G. and J. P. (both Middlesex). Attacking middle order right-hand batsman, slow right-arm bowler, brilliant outfield. *Sch* Malvern. *Teams* Cambridge U (1909–11, blue all three years); Middlesex (1909–31, 314 matches). *Tour* MCC to South Africa 1922/3. *Tests* England (1922/3, 5 matches).
Career batting
398–612–47–13235–194–23.42–9–*ct* 174
Bowling 249–3–83.00–0–0–1/7
Test batting
5–9–1–281–84–35.12–0–*ct* 4

He captained Middlesex in 1921–28, MCC in South Africa 1922/3 and England in all five matches on the tour. In 1930 he was a Test selector. He hit 1,000 runs in a season three times (best 1,343, av 26.33, in 1923). His final first-class match was for H. D. G. Leveson-Gower's XI in 1933.

Mann, Sir Horatio
Amateur. *b:* 2.2.1744, Kent. *d:* 2.4.1814, Margate, Kent. *Sch* Charterhouse. *Team* Kent (1773–82).
Career batting
not applicable – pre-first-class

One of the greatest patrons of the game, his last recorded match was in 1782 and no doubt the details of most of his cricket have been lost. He was MP for Maidstone 1774–84 and for Sandwich from 1790 to 1807, but 'his life was rather dedicated to pleasure than business.' A number of great matches were staged at his estate at Dandelion, near Margate, and at Bourne House, Bishopsbourne, near Canterbury.

Mann, Ian Rutherford
Amateur. *b:* 4.5.1906, Melbourne, Australia. Middle order right-hand batsman. *Team* Cambridge U (1927).
Career batting
1–1–0–26–26–26.00–0–*ct* 0

Mann, James Elliot Furneaux
Amateur. *b:* 2.12.1903, Melbourne, Australia. Middle order right-hand batsman. *Team* Cambridge U (1924, blue).
Career batting
6–10–1–219–114–24.33–1–*ct* 6

Mann, John Pelham
Amateur. *b:* 13.6.1919, Byfleet, Surrey. Brother of F. G. (Middlesex), son of F. T. (Middlesex). Middle order right-hand batsman, leg break bowler. *Sch* Eton. *Team* Middlesex (1939–47, 15 matches).
Career batting
21–32–3–608–77–20.96–0–*ct* 18
Bowling 366–6–61.00–0–0–3/71

Mann, Noah
Professional. *b:* 15.11.1756, Northchapel, Sussex. *d:* December 1789, Northchapel. Whilst sleeping in front of a fire his clothes caught alight and he died of burns. Father of Noah jun (MCC). Hard hitting left-hand batsman, left-hand under-arm bowler, good field. *Team* Hampshire (1777–89).
Career batting
not applicable – pre-first-class

For about 10 years he was one of the principal cricketers of the Hambledon Club.

Mann, Norman Bertram Fleetwood
Amateur. *b:* 28.12.1920, Brakpan, Transvaal, South Africa. *d:* 31.7.1952, Johannesburg, South Africa. Hard hitting lower order right-hand batsman, slow left-arm bowler. *Teams* Natal (1939/40 to 1945/6); Eastern Province (1946/7 to 1950/1). *Tours* South Africa to England 1947, 1951. *Tests* South Africa (1947–51, 19 matches).
Career batting
73–99–16–1446–97–17.42–0–*ct* 25
Bowling 5952–251–23.71–14–3–8/59
Test batting
19–31–1–400–52–13.33–0–*ct* 3
Bowling 1920–58–33.10–1–0–6/59

Although at Cambridge, he was not tried in any first-class matches for the University and instead gained a golfing blue. On the 1947 tour he appeared in all five Tests and headed the Test bowling averages. In 1951 he repeated this feat, but his form was already being affected by the illness from which he died only a year later.

Mann, William Horace
Amateur. *b:* 28.7.1878, Melksham, Wiltshire. *d:* 24.2.1938, Canford Cliffs, Dorset. Middle order right-hand batsman. *Sch* Marlborough. *Team* Worcestershire (1924, 1 match).
Career batting
1–2–0–7–4–3.50–0–*ct* 0

Manners, Dunlop Crawford John
Amateur. *b:* 24.8.1916, Kuala Lumpur, Malaya. Lower order right-hand batsman, right-arm fast bowler. *Sch* Lancing. *Team* Army (1939).
Career batting
1–1–1–33–33*–no av–0–*ct* 1
Bowling 83–1–83.00–0–0–1/83

Manners, Herbert Cecil
Amateur. *b:* 16.4.1877, Hartley-Wintney, Hampshire. *d:* 30.12.1955, Worthing, Sussex. Lower order right-hand batsman, wicket-keeper. *Sch* Cheltenham. *Team* Gloucestershire (1902–11, 5 matches).
Career batting
5–8–0–60–32–7.50–0–*ct* 1

Manners, John Errol
Amateur. *b:* 25.9.1914, Exeter, Devon. Aggressive middle order right-hand batsman. *Team* Hampshire (1936–48, 7 matches).
Career batting
21–37–0–1162–147–31.40–4–*ct* 4
Bowling 16–0

His final first-class match was for the Combined Services in 1953 and his County cricket was restricted due to his being an officer in the Royal Navy.

Mannes, Charles Turnbull
Amateur. *b:* 25.10.1863, Glasgow, Scotland. *d:* 29.12.1937, Airdrie, Lanarkshire, Scotland.

Right-hand batsman, right-arm medium pace bowler. *Team* Scotland (1906–08).
Career batting
3–6–0–129–62–21.50–0–*ct* 1

Manning, John Stephen
Professional. *b:* 11.6.1924, Adelaide, Australia. Lower order left-hand batsman, left-arm slow bowler. *Teams* South Australia (1951/2 to 1953/4, 19 matches); Northants (1954–60, 117 matches).
Career batting
146–207–31–2766–132–15.71–1–*ct* 77
Bowling 11662–513–22.73–25–4–8/43
He took 100 wickets in a season three times (best 116, av 20.68, in 1956).

Manning, Thomas Edgar
Amateur. *b:* 2.9.1884, Northampton. *d:* 22.11.1975, Dallington, Northants. Middle order right-hand batsman, wicket-keeper. *Sch* Wellingborough. *Team* Northants (1906–22, 53 matches).
Career batting
53–93–15–1026–57–13.15–0–*ct* 29–*st* 3
He appeared in the Seniors match whilst at Cambridge, but no first-class matches. He captained Northants from 1908 to 1910 and was President from 1948 to 1955.

Mannings, George
Amateur. *b:* 13.10.1843, Downton, Wiltshire. *d:* 28.11.1876, Downton, Wiltshire. Middle order batsman. *Sch* Marlborough. *Team* Hampshire (1864, 1 match).
Career batting
1–2–0–7–5–3.50–0–*ct* 1
He also played for Wiltshire.

Mansell, Alan William
Cricketer. *b:* 19.5.1951, Redhill, Surrey. Middle order right-hand batsman, wicket-keeper. *Team* Sussex (1969–75, 58 matches).
Career batting
58–93–21–1098–72*–15.25–0–*ct* 108–*st* 7

Mansell, Percy Neville Frank
Amateur. *b:* 16.3.1920, St George's, Salop. Brother of A. J. M. (Rhodesia). Middle order right-hand batsman, leg break bowler or right-arm medium pace. *Team* Rhodesia (1936/7 to 1961/2). *Tours* South Africa to England 1951, 1955, to Australia and New Zealand 1952/3. *Tests* South Africa (1951–55, 13 matches).
Career batting
113–172–17–4598–154–29.66–5–*ct* 156
Bowling 7798–299–26.08–21–5–7/43
Test batting
13–22–2–355–90–17.75–0–*ct* 15
Bowling 736–11–66.90–0–0–3/58
Without achieving anything of real note, he proved a useful all-rounder on both tours to England – curiously none of his 13 Tests took place at home.

Manser, Robert Marsack
Amateur. *b:* 10.10.1880, Tonbridge, Kent. *d:* 15.2.1955, Parkstone, Dorset. Middle order right-hand batsman. *Sch* Tonbridge. *Team* Hampshire (1904, 1 match).
Career batting
1–2–0–1–1–0.50–0–*ct* 1
He also played for Dorset.

Mansfield, Hon James William
Amateur. *b:* 12.2.1862, Bombay, India. *d:* 17.6.1932, Westminster, London. Middle order right-hand batsman. *Sch* Winchester. *Team* Cambridge U (1883–84, blue both years).
Career batting
17–31–2–437–117–15.06–1–*ct* 10
Bowling 17–0
His County cricket was for Norfolk commencing 1882. His first-class debut was for XI of England in 1882 and his final match for MCC in 1888.

Mansoor Akhtar
Cricketer. *b:* 25.12.1956, Karachi, Pakistan. Opening or middle order right-hand batsman, excellent outfield. *Teams* Karachi (1974/5 to 1976/7); Sind (1976/7 to 1977/8); United Bank (1977/8 to 1982/3). *Tours* Pakistan to Australia 1981/2, to England 1982. *Tests* Pakistan (1980/1 to 1982/3, 13 matches).
Career batting
75–126–13–4419–224*–38.76–6–*ct* 56–*st* 2
Bowling 205–3–68.33–0–0–1/16
Test batting
13–22–3–484–111–25.47–1–*ct* 7
In 1976/7, with Waheed Mirza, he created a new first-class first wicket record partnership of 561 for Karachi Whites v Quetta at Karachi. On the 1982 tour to England he scored 595 runs, av 39.66, and played in all three Tests.

Mansur Ali Khan
(see under Pataudi, Nawab of)

Mantell, David Norman
Professional. *b:* 22.7.1934, Acton, Middlesex. Lower order right-hand batsman, wicket-keeper. *Team* Sussex (1954–58, 25 matches).
Career batting
25–31–6–150–34–6.00–0–*ct* 28–*st* 2

Mantle, Thomas Allen
Professional. *b:* 31.1.1840, Kates Hill, Worcs. *d:* 29.4.1884, Wandsworth Common, Surrey. Lower order right-hand batsman, right-arm

medium pace bowler. *Team* Middlesex (1864–72, 22 matches).
Career batting
27–48–3–503–46–11.17–0–*ct* 13
Bowling 651–29–22.44–0–0–4/30
His final first-class match was for Players of the South in 1873.

Manton, Joseph
Amateur. *b:* 4.12.1871, West Bromwich, Staffs. *d:* 9.12.1958, Henham, Essex. Middle order right-hand batsman, right-arm fast bowler. *Team* Warwickshire (1898, 1 match).
Career batting
1–2–0–5–5–2.50–0–*ct* 0
Bowling 51–1–51.00–0–0–1/51
He also played for Bedfordshire and Staffordshire.

Mantri, Madhav Krishnaji
Amateur. *b:* 1.9.1921, Nasik, India. Opening right-hand batsman, wicket-keeper. Uncle of S. M. Gavaskar (India). *Teams* Maharashtra (1942/3); Bombay (1941/2 to 1956/7). *Tours* India to England 1952, to Pakistan 1954/55; ACC to Pakistan 1961/2. *Tests* India (1951/2 to 1954/5, 4 matches).
Career batting
95–141–11–4403–200–37.86–7–*ct* 136–*st* 56
Bowling 121–3–40.33–0–0–2/38
Test batting
4–8–1–67–39–9.57–0–*ct* 8–*st* 1
He appeared in two Tests on the 1952 tour to England, but achieved little with the bat. His only double century was 200 for Bombay v Maharashtra in 1948/9. His final first-class match was for Goa Chief Minister's XI in 1967/8.

Manville, David W.
Professional. *b:* 18.8.1934, Brighton, Sussex. Lower order right-hand batsman, wicket-keeper. *Team* Sussex (1956, 3 matches).
Career batting
3–5–0–13–8–2.60–0–*ct* 1

Maqsood Ahmed
Amateur. *b:* 26.3.1925, Amritsar, India. Middle order right-hand batsman, right-arm medium pace bowler. *Teams* South Punjab (1944/5 to 1946/7); Bahawalpur (1953/4); Karachi (1956/7); Rawalpindi (1960/1 to 1963/4). *Tours* Pakistan to India 1952/3, to England 1954. *Tests* Pakistan (1952/3 to 1955/6, 16 matches).
Career batting
81–125–9–3716–144–32.03–6–*ct* 46
Bowling 3412–120–28.43–6–1–7/39
Test batting
16–27–1–507–99–19.50–0–*ct* 13
Bowling 191–3–63.66–0–0–2/12
He hit 1,314 runs, av 34.57, in first-class matches on the 1954 tour to England and appeared in all four Tests. His first-class debut in Pakistan was for Punjab Governor's XI in 1947/8; he first played in England for a Commonwealth XI in 1952.

Marchant, Francis
Amateur. *b:* 22.5.1864, Matfield, Kent. *d:* 13.4.1946, Roehampton, London. Stylish middle order right-hand batsman. *Sch* Eton and Rugby. *Teams* Cambridge U (1884–87, blue, all four years); Kent (1883–1905, 226 matches).
Career batting
267–451–16–9124–176–20.97–8–*ct* 130
Bowling 609–20–30.45–0–0–2/11
His best seasons were 1889 with 669 runs, av 29.08, and 1891 with 660 runs, av 27.50.

Marchbank, Walter James
Professional. *b:* 1840, Preston, Lancashire. *d:* 1893, Preston, Lancashire. *Team* Lancashire (1869–70, 4 matches).
Career batting
4–7–1–20–15–3.33–0–*ct* 1–*st* 2

Mardall, James Henry Thrale
Amateur. *b:* 7.11.1899, Harpenden, Hertfordshire. Middle order right-hand batsman, slow right-arm bowler. *Sch* Aldenham. *Team* Army (1931).
Career batting
1–2–0–1–1–0.50–0–*ct* 2
His County cricket was for Hertfordshire.

Mare, John Matthew
Amateur. *b:* 22.2.1854, Paddington, London. *d:* 11.12.1909. Hard hitting middle order right-hand batsman. *Team* Sussex (1870–78, 26 matches).
Career batting
26–47–3–616–97–14.00–0–*ct* 9

Margrett, Charles Henry
Amateur. *b:* 1862, Cheltenham, Gloucs. *d:* 22.11.1941, Cheltenham, Gloucs. *Team* Gloucestershire (1886, 1 match).
Career batting
1–2–0–14–14–7.00–0–*ct* 0
He played only in emergency for Gloucestershire in the absence of W. R. Gilbert.

Marie, Gregory Vincent
Cricketer. *b:* 17.2.1945, Perth, Australia. Lower order right-hand batsman, right-arm medium pace bowler. *Team* Oxford U (1978–79, blue 1978).

Career batting
10–13–2–104–27–9.45–0–*ct* 1
Bowling 666–20–33.30–1–0–5/46
Appointed captain of Oxford in 1979, injury prevented him playing against Cambridge.

Mariner, Edward Charles
Amateur. *b:* 1877, Winchester, Hants. *d:* 10.5.1949, Portsmouth, Hants. Lower order batsman, useful bowler. *Sch* Cranleigh. *Team* Hampshire (1896, 1 match).
Career batting
1–2–0–0–0–0.00–0–*ct* 0
Bowling 20–0

Marks, Alfred Edwin
Amateur. *b:* 15.5.1924, Belfast, Ireland. Right-hand batsman, wicket-keeper. *Team* Ireland (1953–55).
Career batting
3–6–0–35–17–5.83–0–*ct* 5–*st* 2

Marks, Christopher Peter
Cricketer. *b:* 17.7.1946, Hanley, Staffs. Lower order right-hand batsman, right-arm medium pace bowler. *Sch* Worksop. *Team* Derbyshire (1967–69, 14 matches).
Career batting
14–21–2–216–39–11.36–0–*ct* 6
He also played for Staffordshire.

Marks, Frederick David
Amateur. *b:* 1867, Stoke-Damerel, Devon. Lower order right-hand batsman, right-arm fast bowler. *Team* Somerset (1884, 1 match).
Career batting
1–2–1–2–2–2.00–0–*ct* 0
Bowling 3–0
He also played for Wiltshire.

Marks, Geoffrey
Amateur. *b:* 15.11.1864, Croydon, Surrey. *d:* 25.8.1938, Nately-Scures, Hants. Lower order batsman, wicket-keeper. *Sch* Whitgift. *Team* Middlesex (1894–95, 2 matches).
Career batting
2–4–2–31–17–15.50–0–*ct* 3

Marks, M.
Amateur. Middle order batsman. *Team* W. G. Grace's XI (1873).
Career batting
1–1–0–1–1–1.00–0–*ct* 0

Marks, Oliver
Amateur. *b:* 10.9.1866, Croydon, Surrey. *d:* 24.5.1940, Kensington, London. Lower order batsman, useful bowler. *Team* MCC (1901).
Career batting
1–1–0–1–1–1.00–0–*ct* 0
Bowling 36–0

Marks, Victor James
Cricketer. *b:* 25.6.1955, Middle Chinnock, Somerset. Middle order right-hand batsman, off break bowler. *Sch* Blundell's. *Teams* Oxford U (1975–78, blue all four years); Somerset (1975–83, 135 matches). *Tour* England to Australia and New Zealand 1982/3 (New Zealand not first-class). *Tests* England (1982–83, 2 matches).
Career batting
179–275–38–6234–105–26.30–1–*ct* 78
Bowling 13381–395–33.87–17–0–7/51
Test batting
2–4–1–25–12*–8.33–0–*ct* 0
Bowling 109–4–27.25–0–0–3/78
He also represented Oxford at rugby fives.

Marlar, Robin Geoffrey
Amateur. *b:* 2.1.1931, Eastbourne, Sussex. Lower order right-hand batsman, off break bowler. *Sch* Harrow. *Teams* Cambridge U (1951–53, blue all three years); Sussex (1951–68, 223 matches). *Tour* Swanton to West Indies 1955/6.
Career batting
289–379–67–3033–64–9.72–0–*ct* 136
Bowling 24469–970–25.22–66–15–9/46
He took 100 wickets in a season four times (best 139, av 21.55, in 1955). His best bowling in an innings was 9 for 46 for Sussex v Lancs at Hove in 1955. From 1955 to 1959 he captained Sussex – after 1959 he played very little first-class cricket. He is a well-known writer and commentator on the game.

Marlow, Christopher Roderick James
Cricketer. *b:* 30.9.1949, Bexhill-on-Sea, Sussex. Middle order left-hand batsman, right-arm medium pace bowler. *Sch* Uppingham. *Team* Cambridge U (1973).
Career batting
3–6–1–29–15–5.80–0–*ct* 2
Bowling 7–1–7.00–0–0–1/7

Marlow, Francis William
Professional. *b:* 8.10.1867, Tamworth, Staffs. *d:* 7.8.1952, Hove, Sussex. Stylish opening right-hand batsman, right-arm medium bowler, brilliant field. *Team* Sussex (1891–1904, 211 matches).
Career batting
218–379–23–7890–155–22.16–7–*ct* 58
Bowling 196–4–49.00–0–0–2/18
He played for Staffordshire 1887 to 1890. His first-class debut was for an England XI in 1890. He hit 1,054 runs, av 25.09, in 1895.

Marlow, Joseph
Professional. *b:* 12.12.1854, Bulwell, Notts. *d:* 8.6.1923, Bulwell, Notts. Middle order right-hand batsman, right-arm medium pace bowler. *Team* Derbyshire (1879–86, 24 matches).
Career batting
24–45–5–317–25–7.92–0–*ct* 23
Bowling 1237–60–20.61–5–1–7/46

Marlow, Thomas
Professional. *b:* 1879, Anstey, Leics. *d:* 15.8.1954, Leicester. Lower order left-hand batsman, slow medium left-arm bowler. *Team* Leicestershire (1900–03, 15 matches).
Career batting
15–22–8–46–10*–3.28–0–*ct* 7
Bowling 846–31–27.29–2–0–6/50

Marlow, William Henry
Professional. *b:* 13.2.1900, Wigston, Leics. *d:* 16.12.1975, Leicester. Lower order left-hand batsman, left-arm medium pace bowler. *Team* Leicestershire (1931–36, 109 matches).
Career batting
109–158–33–1117–64–8.93–0–*ct* 77
Bowling 7615–261–29.17–12–2–7/90

Marner, Peter Thomas
Professional. *b:* 31.3.1936, Oldham, Lancashire. Middle order right-hand batsman, right-arm medium pace bowler. *Teams* Lancashire (1952–64, 236 matches); Leicestershire (1965–70, 165 matches). *Tour* Commonwealth to Pakistan 1967/8.
Career batting
414–680–62–17513–142*–28.33–18–*ct* 378
Bowling 11385–360–31.62–13–1–7/29
He hit 1,000 runs in a season twelve times (best 1,685, av 38.29, in 1958).

Marple, George (Smith)
Amateur. *b:* 14.8.1868, Chester, Cheshire. *d:* 12.8.1932, Sheffield, Yorkshire. *Team* Derbyshire (1901, 1 match).
Career batting
1–1–0–6–6–6.00–0–*ct* 0
Bowling 17–1–17.00–0–0–1/17

Marples, George
Professional. *b:* 30.5.1883, Attercliffe, Yorkshire. *d:* 30.12.1947, Chesterfield, Derbyshire. Tail end batsman, left-arm medium fast bowler. *Team* Derbyshire (1905, 2 matches).
Career batting
2–4–0–11–6–2.75–0–*ct* 1
Bowling 116–1–116.00–0–0–1/53

Marriott, Charles
Amateur. *b:* 18.10.1848, Cotesbach, Leicestershire. *d:* 9.7.1918, Cotesbach, Leicestershire. Brother of G. S. (Oxford U). Middle order right-hand batsman, slow right-arm bowler. *Sch* Bradfield and Winchester. *Team* Oxford U (1870–71, blue 1871).
Career batting
31–50–6–628–48–14.27–0–*ct* 23
Bowling 57–0+1–no av–0–0–1/?
His final first-class match was for I Zingari in 1882. He was a major figure in Leicestershire cricket before the County was raised to first-class status and County captain for about 15 years. He was also on the MCC Committee.

Marriott, Charles Stowell
Amateur. *b:* 14.9.1895, Heaton Moor, Lancashire. *d:* 13.10.1966, Dollis Hill, Middlesex. Tail end right-hand batsman, leg break and googly bowler. *Sch* St Columba's. *Teams* Lancashire (1919–21, 12 matches); Cambridge U (1920–21, blue both years); Kent (1924–37, 101 matches). *Tours* Joel to South Africa 1924/5; MCC to India and Ceylon 1933/4. *Test* England (1933, 1 match).
Career batting
159–178–48–574–21–4.41–0–*ct* 47
Bowling 14304–711–20.11–48–10–8/98
Test batting
1–1–0–0–0–0.00–0–*ct* 1
Bowling 96–11–8.72–2–1–6/59
Throughout the 1920s and early 1930s he was one of the leading bowlers in first-class County cricket, but being a master at Dulwich College most of his appearances were in August. His best season was 1931 with 76 wickets, av 14.61. His final first-class match was for Free Foresters in 1938.

Marriott, Dennis Alston
Cricketer. *b:* 29.11.1939, Amity Hall, Jamaica. Lower order right-hand batsman, left-arm fast medium bowler. *Teams* Surrey (1965–67, 19 matches); Middlesex (1972–74, 11 matches).
Career batting
30–26–13–139–24*–10.69–0–*ct* 5
Bowling 1990–67–29.70–1–0–5/71

Marriott, Rev George Strickland
Amateur. *b:* 7.10.1855, Cotesbach, Leics. *d:* 21.10.1905, Sigglesthorne, Yorkshire. Brother of Charles (Oxford U). Middle order right-hand batsman, right-hand fast round-arm bowler. *Sch* Winchester. *Team* Oxford U (1878, blue).

Career batting
3–6–0–21–11–3.50–0–*ct* 0
Bowling 87–0
He appeared occasionally for Leicestershire 1874 to 1885 (not first-class).

Marriott, Harold Henry
Amateur. *b:* 20.1.1875, Leicester. *d:* 15.11.1949, Kensington, London. Middle order right-hand batsman, right-arm medium pace bowler. *Sch* Malvern. *Teams* Leicestershire (1894–1902, 40 matches); Cambridge U (1895–98, blue all four years). *Tours* Mitchell to North America 1895 (he did not play in first-class matches); Warner to North America 1897.
Career batting
87–151–4–3266–146*–22.21–5–*ct* 65
Bowling 296–8–37.00–0–0–4/60
His final first-class match was for MCC in 1919.

Marriott, William
Professional. *b:* 6.1.1850, Hucknall under Huthwaite, Notts. *d:* 28.8.1887, Huyton, Lancashire. Middle order right-hand batsman, useful bowler. *Team* Nottinghamshire (1880–81, 2 matches).
Career batting
2–3–0–27–14–9.00–0–*ct* 0
Bowling 10–2–5.00–0–0–2/10

Marrison, Fernley
Amateur. *b:* 16.10.1891, Medway, Kent. *d:* 13.2.1967, Farnborough, Hampshire. Lower order right-hand batsman, right-arm fast bowler. *Teams* Army (1914–20); Europeans (1925/6).
Career batting
8–11–3–85–20*–10.62–0–*ct* 6
Bowling 537–16–33.56–1–0–6/44
His final first-class match in England was for H. D. G. Leveson-Gower's XI in 1925.

Marsden, Arthur
Amateur. *b:* 28.10.1880, Buxton, Derbyshire. *d:* 31.7.1916, St Pancras, London. He died of wounds received on the Somme. Opening right-hand batsman. *Sch* Cheethams School, Manchester. *Team* Derbyshire (1910, 1 match).
Career batting
1–2–0–6–6–3.00–0–*ct* 1

Marsden, Edmund
Amateur. *b:* 18.4.1881, Madras, India. *d:* 26.5.1915, Myitkina, Burma. Middle order batsman. *Sch* Cheltenham. *Team* Gloucestershire (1909, 2 matches).
Career batting
2–4–0–79–38–19.75–0–*ct* 0

Marsden, Edward Leverson
Amateur. *b:* 25.7.1870, Hampstead, Middlesex. *d:* 2.7.1946, Hampstead, Middlesex. Lower order left-hand batsman, left-arm fast bowler. *Team* Middlesex (1897, 1 match).
Career batting
1–1–0–3–3–3.00–0–*ct* 0
Bowling 68–1–68.00–0–0–1/45

Marsden, George Allen
Amateur. *b:* 28.6.1869, Wirksworth, Derbyshire. *d:* 7.1.1938, Diep River, Cape Province, South Africa. Middle order right-hand batsman, leg break bowler. *Sch* Denstone College. *Team* Derbyshire (1894–98, 30 matches).
Career batting
30–46–6–417–37–10.42–0–*ct* 12

Marsden, Keith
Amateur. *b:* 24.7.1931, Carlisle, Cumberland. Lower order right-hand batsman, right-arm medium pace bowler. *Team* Cambridge U (1952).
Career batting
1 match, did not bat–*ct* 0
Bowling 56–0

Marsden, Robert
Cricketer. *b:* 2.4.1959, Kensington, London. Middle order right-hand batsman, off break bowler. *Sch* Merchant Taylors. *Team* Oxford U (1979–82, blue 1982).
Career batting
13–23–1–507–60–23.04–0–*ct* 6

Marsden, Thomas
Professional. *b:* 1805, Sheffield, Yorkshire. *d:* 27.2.1843, Sheffield, Yorkshire. Attacking middle order left-hand batsman, left-hand fast under-arm, or slow round-arm, bowler. *Teams* Sheffield (1827–30); Yorkshire (1833–35).
Career batting
55–99–3–1724–227–17.95–2–*ct* 45
Bowling 96 wickets, no analyses
His most famous innings was 227 for the combined Sheffield and Leicester eleven v Nottingham at Darnall, Sheffield in 1826, being his debut. His final match was for MCC in 1841.

Marsh, Eric
Amateur. *b:* 30.5.1940, Greenwich, South London. Middle order right-hand batsman, leg break bowler. *Sch* St Dunstan's. *Team* Oxford U (1962).
Career batting
10–20–3–419–50–24.64–0–*ct* 4
His County cricket was for Shropshire.

Marsh, Edward Caldecot
Amateur. *b:* 7.5.1865, Belgaum, Bombay, India. *d:* 27.11.1926, Kendal, Westmorland. Middle order right-hand batsman. *Sch* Malvern. *Team* Somerset (1885, 2 matches).
Career batting
2–4–0–18–15–4.50–0–*ct* 1
He also played for Devon.

Marsh, Frederick Eric
Professional. *b:* 17.7.1920, Bolsover, Derbyshire. Nephew of T. S. Worthington (Derbyshire). Lower order left-hand batsman, slow left-arm bowler. *Team* Derbyshire (1946–49, 66 matches).
Career batting
66–109–20–1627–86–18.28–0–*ct* 32
Bowling 1698–44–38.59–1–0–6/37

Marsh, John Frederick
Amateur. *b:* 11.5.1875, Thame, Oxfordshire. *d:* 30.10.1927, Higham-on-the-Hill, Leics. Stubborn opening right-hand batsman. *Sch* Amersham Hall. *Team* Cambridge U (1901–04, blue 1904).
Career batting
8–16–3–548–172*–42.15–2–*ct* 7
Bowling 18–0
He played for Oxfordshire commencing 1892 and at one time captained the County.

Marsh, Rev James William
Amateur. *b:* 16.10.1872, Thame, Oxfordshire. *d:* 26.3.1930, Ludlow, Shropshire. Middle order right-hand batsman, wicket-keeper. *Team* Cambridge U (1901).
Career batting
8–15–2–145–29*–11.15–0–*ct* 5–*st* 5
His final first-class match was for J. Bamford's XI in 1907. He played County cricket for Oxfordshire.

Marsh, Paul
Cricketer. *b:* 5.12.1939, South Africa. Middle order right-hand batsman, off break bowler. *Team* Cambridge U (1965).
Career batting
1–2–0–25–23–12.50–0–*ct* 1
Bowling 22–0

Marsh, Reginald Bert
Professional. *b:* 11.8.1897, Wells, Somerset. *d:* 25.4.1969, Bristol. Lower order right-hand batsman, right-arm medium pace bowler. *Team* Somerset (1928–34, 4 matches).
Career batting
4–5–1–42–24*–10.50–0–*ct* 1
Bowling 197–2–98.50–0–0–2/121

Marsh, Rodney William
Cricketer. *b:* 11.11.1947, Armadale, Western Australia. Attacking middle order left-hand batsman, wicket-keeper. *Teams* Western Australia (1968/9 to 1982/3, 89 matches). *Tours* Australia to England 1972, 1975, 1977, 1980, 1981, to West Indies 1972/3, to New Zealand 1973/4, 1976/7, 1981/2, to Pakistan 1979/80, 1982/3. *Tests* Australia (1970/1 to 1982/3, 91 matches).
Career batting
244–379–37–10607–236–31.01–11–*ct* 749–*st* 61
Bowling 74–1–74.00–0–0–1/0
Test batting
91–144–11–3558–132–26.75–3–*ct* 322–*st* 12
Bowling 51–0
Apart from the period which he spent with World Series Cricket, he has been Australia's principal wicket-keeper since his debut and has not missed a single Test on his five tours to England. He holds the record for the most Test victims by a wicket-keeper.

Marsh, Steven Andrew
Cricketer. *b:* 27.1.1961, Westminster, London. Lower order right-hand batsman, wicket-keeper. *Team* Kent (1982–83, 3 matches),
Career batting
3–3–1–15–10*–7.50–0–*ct* 6

Marsh, William
Amateur. *b:* 10.9.1917, Newbridge, Glamorgan. *d:* 6.2.1978, Newbridge, Glamorgan. Lower order batsman, right-arm fast medium bowler. *Team* Glamorgan (1947, 4 matches).
Career batting
4–6–1–39–13–7.80–0–*ct* 2
Bowling 290–8–36.25–0–0–3/70

Marshal, Alan
Amateur, turned professional in 1906. *b:* 12.6.1883, Warwick, Queensland, Australia. *d:* 23.7.1915, Imtarfa Military Hospital, Malta. He died of enteric fever. Hard hitting middle order right-hand batsman, right-arm fast medium bowler, brilliant catcher, excellent all-round field. *Teams* Queensland (1903/04 to 1913/14, 11 matches); Surrey (1907–10, 98 matches).
Career batting
119–198–13–5177–176–27.98–8–*ct* 114
Bowling 2718–119–22.84–7–1–7/41
He hit 1,000 runs in a season three times (best 1,931, av 40.22, in 1908). He came to England in 1904 and qualified by residence for Surrey. After two successful seasons, he was suspended in 1909 by the Surrey Committee and in 1910 returned to Australia. His first-class debut in England was for Gentlemen of England in 1905.

Marshal, Henry Worgan
Amateur. *b:* 27.6.1900, Santa Maria, Colombia. *d:* 6.1.1970, Ullesthorpe, Leicestershire. Opening right-hand batsman, wicket-keeper. *Sch* Oundle. *Team* Argentine (1926/7 to 1929/30). *Tour* South America to England 1932.
Career batting
10–18–1–487–153–28.64–2–*ct* 11
He was expected to be the outstanding batsman of the 1932 tour and in the first first-class match – v Oxford U – hit an excellent 153, but he achieved very little in the later first-class matches.

Marshall, Alexander
Amateur. *b:* 31.10.1820, Godalming, Surrey. *d:* 28.9.1871, Godalming, Surrey. Brother of Frederic (MCC) and Henry (Surrey). Very steady middle order right-hand batsman. *Team* Surrey (1849–57, 14 matches).
Career batting
26–43–6–221–23*–5.97–0–*ct* 13
His final first-class match was in 1860 for Gentlemen of the South.

Marshall, Amos
Professional. *b:* 10.7.1849, Yeadon, Yorkshire. *d:* 3.8.1891, Yeadon, Yorkshire. Lower order right-hand batsman, left-arm medium pace bowler, slip field. *Team* Yorkshire (1874, 1 match).
Career batting
2–4–1–18–13–6.00–0–*ct* 0
Bowling 18–1–18.00–0–0–1/7
His final first-class match was for the North in 1875. He also played for Northumberland.

Marshall, Alan George
Amateur. *b:* 17.4.1895, Tripatur, Madras, India. *d:* 14.5.1973, Deben, Norfolk. Brother of L. P. (Somerset). Lower order right-hand batsman, slow right-arm bowler, wicket-keeper. *Sch* Taunton. *Team* Somerset (1914–31, 44 matches).
Career batting
44–67–9–592–37–10.20–*ct* 34–*st* 9
Bowling 333–10–33.00–0–0–3/51

Marshall, Anthony Granville
Professional. *b:* 10.9.1932, Isleworth, Middlesex. Lower order right-hand batsman, right-arm medium fast bowler. *Sch* Chatham House, Ramsgate. *Team* Kent (1950–54, 5 matches).
Career batting
6–11–1–37–7–3.70–0–*ct* 1
Bowling 399–13–30.69–1–0–6/53
His final first-class match was for Minor Counties in 1967; he also played for Wiltshire.

Marshall, Bertie
Professional. *b:* 5.5.1902, Sutton-in-Ashfield, Notts. Lower order right-hand batsman, right-arm fast bowler. *Team* Notts (1923–29, 4 matches).
Career batting
4–5–1–61–36–15.25–0–*ct* 3
Bowling 203–5–40.60–0–0–2/39
He played for Perthshire from 1927 to 1937 and appeared for Scotland but not in first-class matches. In 1939 he played as an amateur for Staffordshire.

Marshall, Charles
Amateur. *b:* 20.2.1843, Cricklewood, Middlesex. *d:* 25.2.1904, Putney. Middle order right-hand batsman, right-arm medium pace bowler. *Sch* Rugby. *Teams* Middlesex (1866, 2 matches); Cambridgeshire (1866–68, 5 matches).
Career batting
7–11–0–209–50–19.00–0–*ct* 3
He also played for Norfolk and Huntingdonshire.

Marshall, Charles
Professional. *b:* 1.10.1863, Woodville, Leicestershire. *d:* 20.11.1948, Birmingham. Lower order right-hand batsman, wicket-keeper. *Team* Surrey (1893–99, 43 matches).
Career batting
43–60–13–341–42–7.25–0–*ct* 82–*st* 15
He also played for Leicestershire (pre-first-class).

Marshall, David Alexander Cadman
Amateur. *b:* 29.12.1935, Sheffield, Yorkshire. Middle order right-hand batsman, leg break bowler. *Sch* Rugby. *Team* Oxford U (1957).
Career batting
1–2–2–68–54*–no av–0–*ct* 1

Marshall, Edwin Alfred
Amateur. *b:* 21.8.1904, Nottingham. *d:* 28.1.1970, Nottingham. Lower order right-hand batsman, right-arm fast bowler. *Sch* Nottingham High School. *Team* Notts (1937–38, 4 matches).
Career batting
4–5–0–19–13–3.80–0–*ct* 4
Bowling 167–3–0–55.66–0–0–2/43
He collapsed and died during the 1970 Notts CCC AGM, being a member of the County Committee from 1942 and President in 1964–65.

Marshall, Sir Frederic
Amateur. *b:* 26.7.1830, Godalming, Surrey. *d:* 8.6.1900, Westminster, London. Brother of Alexander (Surrey) and Henry (Surrey). Middle order

right-hand batsman. *Sch* Eton. *Team* MCC (1854–65).
Career batting
21–35–4–244–31–7.87–0–*ct* 12

Marshall, Francis William
Amateur. *b:* 30.1.1888, Rugby, Warwickshire. *d:* 24.5.1955, Kensington, London. Middle order right-hand batsman. *Team* Warwickshire (1922, 2 matches).
Career batting
2–2–0–14–10–7.00–0–*ct* 0
He also played for Montgomeryshire.

Marshall, Gordon Alex
Amateur. *b:* 12.3.1935, Birmingham. Lower order right-hand batsman, right-arm fast medium bowler. *Sch* King's Norton GS. *Team* Warwickshire (1961–63, 4 matches).
Career batting
4–5–3–24–18*–12.00–0–*ct* 3
Bowling 221–9–24.55–1–0–5/22

Marshall, Henry
Amateur. *b:* 22.4.1831, Godalming, Surrey. *d:* 30.4.1914, Ipswich, Suffolk. Brother of Alexander (Surrey) and Frederic (MCC). Middle order right-hand batsman. *Sch* Winchester. *Team* Surrey (1853–54, 2 matches).
Career batting
17–31–1–200–33–6.66–0–*ct* 10
His final first-class match was for MCC in 1863.

Marshall, Hugh Dykes Ferguson
Cricketer. *b:* 11.1.1942, Ashford, Kent. Middle order right-hand batsman, right-arm medium pace bowler. *Team* Oxford U (1966).
Career batting
3–5–0–86–48–17.20–0–*ct* 1

Marshall, Herbert Menzies
Amateur. *b:* 1.8.1841, Outwood Hall, Leeds, Yorkshire. *d:* 2.3.1913, South Kensington, London. Middle order right-hand batsman, brilliant long stop. *Sch* Westminster. *Team* Cambridge U (1861–64, blue all four years).
Career batting
15–25–2–317–76*–13.78–0–*ct* 9
He was a well-known artist, being especially noted as a water-colourist.

Marshall, Joseph
Professional. *b:* 25.7.1862, Mosbrough, Yorkshire. *d:* 15.1.1913, Derby. Middle order right-hand batsman. *Team* Derbyshire (1887, 2 matches).
Career batting
2–4–0–50–31–12.50–0–*ct* 1
A useful soccer player, he appeared for Derby County.

Marshall, John Campbell
Amateur *b:* 30.1.1929, Sheffield, Yorkshire. Opening right-hand batsman. *Sch* Rugby. *Team* Oxford U (1951–53, blue 1953).
Career batting
16–27–0–710–111–26.29–1–*ct* 10

Marshall, Rev John Hannah
Amateur. *b:* 1.10.1837, Cambridge. *d:* 2.2.1879, Kaiteriteri, Riwaka, Nelson, New Zealand. Brother of J. W. (Cambridge U). Middle order right-hand batsman, good deep field. *Sch* KES, Birmingham. *Teams* Cambridge Town Club (1857); Cambridgeshire (1861–67, 7 matches); Cambridge U (1859, blue).
Career batting
12–20–4–240–47*–15.00–0–*ct* 9
Bowling 5–0
He also played for Suffolk and he represented Cambridge at rackets.

Marshall, John Maurice Alex
Amateur. *b:* 26.10.1916, Kenilworth, Warwickshire. Middle order right-hand batsman, leg break bowler. *Team* Warwickshire (1946–50, 28 matches).
Career batting
29–51–4–812–47–17.27–0–*ct* 14
Bowling 1604–47–34.12–2–0–5/65
A master at Warwick School, his first-class County cricket was very restricted. His final first-class match was for MCC in 1956.

Marshall, Kenneth Walker
Amateur. *b:* 23.7.1911, Kimberley, South Africa. Right-hand batsman. *Sch* Edinburgh Academy. *Team* Scotland (1931–32).
Career batting
2–4–0–50–19–12.50–0–*ct* 1
An excellent rugby footballer, he represented Scotland.

Marshall, Leslie Phillips
Amateur. *b:* 25.1.1894, Tripatur, Madras, India. *d:* 28.2.1978, Taunton, Somerset. Brother of A. G. (Somerset). Middle order right-hand batsman. *Sch* Taunton. *Team* Somerset (1913–31, 11 matches).
Career batting
11–20–1–162–37–8.52–0–*ct* 6
Bowling 16–1–16.00–0–0–1/7

Marshall, Malcolm Denzil
Cricketer. *b:* 18.4.1958, Pine, Bridgetown, Barbados. Lower order right-hand batsman, right-arm fast bowler. *Teams* Barbados (1977/8 to 1982/3); Hampshire (1979–83, 79 matches). *Tours* West Indies to India and Sri Lanka 1978/9, to Australia and New Zealand 1979/80, to England 1980, to Pakistan 1980/1, to Australia 1981/2; Young West Indies to Zimbabwe 1981/2. *Tests* West Indies (1978/9 to 1982/3, 17 matches).
Career batting
145–186–24–3552–116*–21.92–4–*ct* 56
Bowling 11199–614–18.23–38–6–8/71
Test batting
17–22–2–200–45–10.00–0–*ct* 7
Bowling 1579–55–28.70–1–0–5/37
He took 134 wickets, av 15.73, in 1982. On the 1980 tour to England he took 49 wickets, av 17.63, and played in four of the five Tests.

Marshall, Nariman Darabsha
Amateur. *b:* 3.1.1905, Bombay, India. *d:* 29.8.1979, Jaipur, India. Stylish middle order right-hand batsman, right-arm medium slow bowler, occasional wicket-keeper. *Teams* Parsis (1928/9 to 1934/5); Western India (1933/4 to 1934/5); Nawanagar (1936/7 to 1937/8). *Tour* India to England 1932.
Career batting
27–48–4–906–120–20.59–2–*ct* 12
Bowling 337–12–28.08–0–0–3/17
For no obvious reason he appeared in only six first-class matches on the 1932 tour, scoring 268 runs, av 26.80.

Marshall, Roy Edwin
Professional. *b:* 25.4.1930, Farmers Plantation, St Thomas, Barbados. Brother of N. E. (West Indies). Attractive opening right-hand batsman, off break bowler. *Teams* Barbados (1945/6 to 1951/2); Hampshire (1953–72, 504 matches). *Tours* West Indies to England 1950, to Australia and New Zealand 1951/2; Norfolk to Jamaica 1956/7; Brown to East Africa 1961/2 (not first-class); Cavaliers to Jamaica 1963/4, to West Indies 1964/5; Commonwealth to India 1953/4; International XI to Pakistan, New Zealand and South Africa 1961/2; Commonwealth to South Africa 1959/60, 1960/1. *Tests* West Indies (1951/2, 4 matches).
Career batting
602–1053–59–35725–228*–35.94–68–*ct* 294
Bowling 5092–176–28.93–5–0–6/36
Test batting
4–7–0–143–30–20.42–0–*ct* 1
Bowling 15–0
He scored 1,000 runs in a season eighteen times, going on to 2,000 six times (best 2,607, av 43.45, in 1961). His three double centuries were all for Hampshire, the highest being 228* v Pakistan at Bournemouth in 1962. On his 1950 tour to England he hit 1,117 runs, av 39.89, but was not selected for any Test matches. He captained Hampshire 1966 to 1970.

Marshall, Roger Philip Twells
Cricketer. *b:* 28.2.1952, Horsham, Sussex. Lower order right-hand batsman, left-arm fast medium bowler. *Sch* Charterhouse. *Team* Sussex (1973–78, 24 matches).
Career batting
24–37–15–315–37–14.31–0–*ct* 6
Bowling 1927–49–39.32–0–0–4/37

Marshall, Thomas Roger
Amateur. *b:* 26.6.1849, Chatton Park, Northumberland. *d:* 27.6.1913, Kingfield, Surrey. Opening right-hand batsman. *Sch* Edinburgh Academy. *Team* MCC (1884–86).
Career batting
5–9–2–250–80–35.71–0–*ct* 2
A noted rugby footballer, he represented Scotland.

Marshall, Walter
Professional. *b:* 27.10.1853, Hyson Green, Nottingham. *d:* 15.1.1943, West Bridgford, Nottingham. Middle order batsman, left-arm medium pace bowler. *Team* Notts (1889–91, 3 matches).
Career batting
3–4–0–42–26–10.50–0–*ct* 1
He was appointed coach to Notts CCC in 1897 and continued as groundsman from 1922 until 1936. He also played for Lincolnshire.

Marsham, Algernon James (Bullock)
Amateur. *b:* 14.8.1919, Chart Sutton, Kent. Son of C. H. B. (Oxford U and Kent), grandson of C. D. B. (Oxford U), nephew of F. W. B. (MCC). Lower order left-hand batsman, right-arm leg break bowler. *Sch* Eton. *Teams* Oxford U (1939, blue); Kent (1946–47, 6 matches).
Career batting
17–26–4–362–74*–16.45–0–*ct* 6
Bowling 1381–35–39.45–1–0–5/136

Marsham, Rev Cloudesley Dewar (Bullock)
Amateur. *b:* 30.1.1835, Merton College, Oxford. *d:* 2.3.1915, Harrietsham, Maidstone, Kent. Brother of C. J. B. (Oxford U) and R. H. B. (Oxford U), father of C. H. B. (Kent) and F. W. B. (MCC), grandfather of A. J. B. (Oxford U and Kent). Lower order right-hand batsman, right-hand medium fast round-arm bowler. *Team* Oxford U (1854–58, blue all five years).

Career batting
34–61–9–602–39*–11.57–0–*ct* 26
Bowling 2095–171+9–12.25–14–4–9/64

His best bowling was 9/64 for Gentlemen of England v Gentlemen of MCC at Lord's in 1855. He was regarded as the best amateur bowler of his day, appearing ten times for the Gentlemen against Players at Lord's. After 1862 he rarely played in important matches, but occasionally for Buckinghamshire, Oxfordshire and Northants. His final first-class match was for Gentlemen of England in 1866.

Marsham, Cloudesley Henry (Bullock)
Amateur. *b:* 10.2.1879, Stoke-Lyne, Bicester, Oxfordshire. *d:* 19.7.1928, Wrotham Heath, Kent. Son of C. D. B. (Oxford U), nephew of C. J. B. (Oxford U) and R. H. B. (Oxford U), brother of F. W. B. (MCC), father of A. J. B. (Oxford U and Kent). Sound middle order batsman. *Sch* Eton. *Teams* Oxford U (1900–02, blue all three years); Kent (1900–22, 141 matches).
Career batting
175–283–23–5879–161*–22.61–7–*ct* 88
Bowling 175–2–87.50–0–0–1/0

He captained Kent from 1904 to 1908, but after 1908 only played occasionally for the County. He hit 1,000 runs in a season twice (best 1,070, av 28.91, in 1904). He also played for Shropshire.

Marsham, Charles Jacob (Bullock)
Amateur. *b:* 18.1.1829, Merton College, Oxford. *d:* 20.8.1901, Westminster, London. Brother of C. D. B. (Oxford U) and R. H. B. (Oxford U), uncle of C. H. B. (Oxford U and Kent) and F. W. B. (MCC). Attacking middle order right-hand batsman, slip field. *Team* Oxford U (1851–52, blue 1851).
Career batting
38–70–5–782–50–12.03–0–*ct* 10
Bowling 6 wickets, no analyses

His final first-class match was for MCC in 1867. He played County cricket for Oxfordshire, Northants and Buckinghamshire.

Marsham, Francis William (Bullock)
Amateur. *b:* 13.7.1883, Stoke-Lyne, Bicester, Oxfordshire. *d:* 22.12.1971, Salen, Isle of Mull. Son of C. D. B. (Oxford U), nephew of C. J. B. (Oxford U) and R. H. B. (Oxford U), brother of C. H. B. (Kent), uncle of A. J. B. (Oxford U and Kent). Middle order batsman. *Sch* Eton. *Team* MCC (1905).
Career batting
1–2–0–9–6–4.50–0–*ct* 0

Marsham, George
Amateur. *b:* 10.4.1849, Allington, Kent. *d:* 2.12.1927, Hayle, Maidstone, Kent. Lower order right-hand batsman, slow under-arm bowler, wicket-keeper. *Sch* Eton. *Team* Kent (1876–77, 3 matches).
Career batting
3–5–2–36–20–12.00–0–*ct* 2–*st* 2

He was President of Kent CCC in 1886.

Marsham, Hon Rev John
Amateur. *b:* 25.7.1842, Boxley, Kent. *d:* 16.9.1926, Roehampton, London. Lower order right-hand batsman, right-hand fast round-arm bowler. *Sch* Eton. *Team* Kent (1873, 2 matches).
Career batting
2–4–0–5–3–1.25–0–*ct* 1

He was not in the eleven whilst at Oxford. He played occasionally for Northants.

Marsham, Robert Henry (Bullock)
Amateur. *b:* 3.9.1833, Merton College, Oxford. *d:* 5.4.1913, Bifrons, Canterbury, Kent. Brother of C. D. B. (Oxford U) and C. J. B. (Oxford U), uncle of C. H. B. (Oxford U and Kent) and F. W. B. (MCC). Opening right-hand batsman, right-hand medium slow round-arm bowler. *Team* Oxford U (1854–56, blue 1856).
Career batting
15–28–4–253–42–10.54–0–*ct* 8
Bowling 284–35–8.11–2–2–8/27

He appeared for Oxfordshire, Buckinghamshire and Northants. His final first-class match was for MCC in 1863.

Marsland, Geoffrey Peter
Amateur. *b:* 17.5.1932, Ashton-under-Lyne, Lancashire. Opening/middle order right-hand batsman, off break bowler, good outfield. *Sch* Rossall. *Team* Oxford U (1953–54, blue 1954).
Career batting
17–31–3–448–74–16.00–0–*ct* 7
Bowling 138–2–69.00–0–0–2/68

Marson, Lionel Frederick
Amateur. *b:* 15.6.1895, Wandsworth, London. *d:* 31.3.1960, Melrose, Roxburghshire, Scotland. Middle order right-hand batsman. *Sch* Haileybury. *Team* Army (1930).
Career batting
1–2–0–56–53–28.00–0–*ct* 1

He played County cricket for Wiltshire.

Marston, John William
Amateur. *b:* 25.10.1893, Rosario, Argentina. *d:* 9.7.1938, Lambeth, London. Lower order right-hand batsman, leg break and googly bowler. *Sch* Haileybury. *Team* Essex (1923–24, 2 matches).

Career batting
2–4–1–12–6–4.00–0–*ct* 1
Bowling 112–2–56.00–0–0–2/47

Marten, George Nisbet
Amateur. *b:* 20.6.1840, Ghazeepoor, Bengal, India. *d:* 25.8.1905, Crowborough, Sussex. Middle order right-hand batsman. *Sch* Harrow. *Team* MCC (1864–69).
Career batting
4–6–1–50–26–10.00–0–*ct* 2
His County cricket was for Hertfordshire.

Marten, William George
Professional. *b:* 5.9.1845, Tunbridge Wells, Kent. *d:* 25.11.1907, Stoke Newington, London. Lower order right-hand batsman, right-hand fast round-arm bowler, good slip. *Teams* Kent (1865–71, 15 matches); Surrey (1871–72, 24 matches).
Career batting
45–80–23–312–27*–5.47–0–*ct* 27
Bowling 2543–114–22.30–4–2–6/11
He also appeared for Essex (pre-first-class).

Martin, Arthur Dalby
Amateur. *b:* 1888, Hackney, Middlesex. *d:* 1958, Harrow, Middlesex. Lower order batsman, useful bowler. *Team* Essex (1920–21, 3 matches).
Career batting
3–3–0–0–0–0.00–0–*ct* 1
Bowling 210–5–42.00–0–0–3/43

Martin, Barry Robert
Cricketer. *b:* 18.7.1950, Hampton Court, Middlesex. Lower order right-hand batsman, right-arm medium fast bowler. *Sch* Kingston GS. *Team* Cambridge U (1971–73).
Career batting
6–10–1–36–14–4.00–0–*ct* 2
Bowling 400–9–44.44–0–0–2/42

Martin, Charles
Professional. *b:* 6.8.1836, Breamore, Hampshire. *d:* 28.3.1878, Hilsea, Hampshire. Tail end left-hand batsman, left-hand fast round-arm bowler, slip field. *Team* Hampshire (1869–70, 4 matches).
Career batting
5–10–1–11–3–1.22–0–*ct* 3
Bowling 168–9–18.66–0–0–3/38

Martin, Eric
Amateur. *b:* 20.5.1894, Barnet, Herts. *d:* 2.5.1924, Duxford, Cambs. He was killed in a flying accident. Middle order batsman. *Team* Middlesex (1919–23, 16 matches).
Career batting
17–26–4–325–64–14.77–*ct* 16

Martin, Eric Gordon
Amateur. *b:* 4.2.1907, Rock Ferry, Cheshire. *d:* 27.1.1978, Chelsea, London. Middle order right-hand batsman, right-arm medium pace bowler. *Sch* Birkenhead. *Team* Essex (1928, 2 matches).
Career batting
2–4–0–25–13–6.25–0–*ct* 1
Bowling 140–2–70.00–0–0–1/63

Martin, Evelyn George
Amateur. *b:* 22.3.1881, Upton-on-Severn, Worcs. *d:* 27.4.1945, Hadleigh, Suffolk. Lower order right-hand batsman, right-arm fast bowler. *Sch* Eton. *Teams* Oxford U (1903–06, blue all four years); Worcestershire (1903–07, 3 matches).
Career batting
29–51–10–519–56–12.65–0–*ct* 10
Bowling 2516–107–23.51–5–0–7/81

Martin, Eric James
Professional. *b:* 17.8.1925, Lambley, Notts. Middle order right-hand batsman. *Team* Notts (1949–59, 125 matches).
Career batting
125–199–20–4086–133*–22.82–3–*ct* 53
His best season was 1954 with 977 runs, av 30.53.

Martin, Frederick
Professional. *b:* 12.10.1861, Dartford, Kent. *d:* 13.12.1921, Dartford, Kent. Half-brother of A. Blackman (Surrey, Sussex and Kent). Lower order left-hand batsman, left-arm medium pace bowler. *Team* Kent (1885–99, 229 matches). *Tour* Read to South Africa 1891/2. *Tests* England (1890 to 1891/2, 2 matches).
Career batting
317–492–118–4545–90–12.15–0–*ct* 120
Bowling 22901–1317–17.38–95–23–8/45
Test batting
2–2–0–14–13–7.00–0–*ct* 2
Bowling 141–14–10.07–2–1–6/50
He took 100 wickets in a season six times (best 190, av 13.05, in 1890). His final first-class match was for MCC in 1900.

Martin, Frank Reginald
Amateur. *b:* 12.10.1893, Jamaica. *d:* 23.11.1967, Kingston, Jamaica. Opening/middle order left-hand batsman, slow left-arm bowler. *Team* Jamaica (1924/5 to 1929/30). *Tours* West Indies to England 1928 and 1933, to Australia 1930/1. *Tests* West Indies (1928 to 1930/1, 9 matches).
Career batting
65–108–13–3589–204*–37.77–6–*ct* 19
Bowling 3149–74–42.55–1–0–5/90
Test batting
9–18–1–486–123*–28.58–1–*ct* 2
Bowling 619–8–77.37–0–0–3/91

On his 1928 visit to England he hit 1,370 runs, av 32.61, and headed the Test batting averages – his was a very difficult wicket to obtain. In 1933 he was injured after playing in six matches and the strain proved so serious that he did not play again on the tour. His highest score was 204* for Jamaica v L. H. Tennyson's XI at Kingston in 1926/7.

Martin, G.
Amateur. Lower order batsman, useful bowler. *Team* Glamorgan (1921, 1 match).
Career batting
1–2–0–2–2–1.00–0–*ct* 1
Bowling 77–1–77.00–0–0–1/77

Martin, George
Professional. *b:* 29.11.1875, Tail end batsman, useful bowler. *Team* Hampshire (1898–99, 4 matches).
Career batting
4–7–5–19–6*–9.50–0–0–*ct* 3
Bowling 321–8–40.12–0–0–3/64

Martin, George Need
Professional. *b:* 25.7.1845, Nottingham. *d:* 2.9.1900, Nottingham. Lower order right-hand batsman, wicket-keeper. *Team* Notts (1870, 1 match).
Career batting
2–4–0–15–14–3.75–0–*ct* 0
His final first-class match was for the All England XI in 1874.

Martin, Herbert
Amateur. *b:* 4.5.1927, Lisburn, Co Antrim, Ireland. Brother of Thomas (Ireland). Middle order right-hand batsman. *Sch* Royal Belfast Academical Institution. *Team* Ireland (1949–68).
Career batting
19–38–3–671–88–19.17–0–*ct* 17

Martin, J.
Professional. *Team* Hampshire (1904, 1 match).
Career batting
1–2–0–66–39–33.00–0–*ct* 3
Bowling 166–5–33.20–0–0–4/100
His career in first-class County cricket is a curiosity in that he batted at No. 11 in his only match, adding 76 for the 10th wicket in the first innings and 48 for the 10th wicket in the second innings.

Martin, James David
Amateur. *b:* 1.7.1901, Edinburgh, Scotland. Middle order right-hand batsman. *Sch* George Watson's College. *Team* Scotland (1926–29).
Career batting
3–4–0–101–88–25.25–0–*ct* 1

Martin, John Donald
Cricketer. *b:* 23.12.1941, Oxford. Tail end right-hand batsman, right-arm fast medium bowler. *Sch* Magdalen College School. *Teams* Oxford U (1962–65, blue 1962, 1963 and 1965); Somerset (1964–65, 2 matches). *Tour* MCC to South America 1964/5 (not first-class).
Career batting
40–52–14–148–14*–3.89–0–*ct* 13
Bowling 2701–93–29.04–4–0–7/26
He also played for Berkshire.

Martin, John Newton
Amateur. *b:* 1867, St Austell, Cornwall. *d:* 31.8.1942, Torquay, Devon. Middle order batsman. *Team* MCC (1891).
Career batting
1–2–1–30–29*–30.00–0–*ct* 0
His County cricket was for Devon.

Martin, John Stapleton
Amateur. *b:* 15.3.1846, Holborn, London. *d:* 26.9.1922, Norton juxta Kempsey, Worcs. Middle order right-hand batsman, good field. *Sch* Wimbledon. *Team* MCC (1871).
Career batting
3–5–2–107–51*–35.66–0–*ct* 1
He did not play in any first-class matches whilst at Cambridge U.

Martin, John Wesley
Amateur. *b:* 28.7.1931, Wingham, New South Wales, Australia. Lower order left-hand batsman, slow left-arm bowler. *Teams* New South Wales (1956/7 to 1967/8, 78 matches); South Australia (1958/9, 9 matches). *Tours* Australia to England 1964, to Pakistan and India 1964/5, to South Africa 1966/7, to New Zealand 1956/7, 1959/60; Cavaliers to India and South Africa 1962/3. *Tests* Australia (1960/1 to 1966/7, 8 matches).
Career batting
135–193–26–3970–101–23.77–1–*ct* 114
Bowling 13872–445–31.17–17–1–8/97
Test batting
8–13–1–214–55–17.83–0–*ct* 5
Bowling 832–17–48.94–0–0–3/56
He had little success in England in 1964 and did not appear in the Tests.

Martin, John William
Amateur. *b:* 16.2.1917, Catford, London. Lower order right-hand batsman, right-arm fast bowler. *Team* Kent (1939–53, 33 matches). *Test* England (1947, 1 match).

Career batting
44–69–15–623–40–11.53–0–*ct* 32
Bowling 3888–162–24.00–8–1–7/53
Test batting
1–2–0–26–26–13.00–0–*ct* 0
Bowling 129–1–129.00–0–0–1/111

A noted figure in London Club cricket, he could not afford the time for regular County matches and appeared in only a handful each season.

Martin, Marcus Trevelyan
Amateur. *b:* 29.4.1842, Barrackpore, Calcutta, India. *d:* 5.6.1908, Marylebone, London. He died of appendicitis. Middle order right-hand batsman, wicket-keeper. *Sch* Rugby. *Teams* Cambridge U (1862–64, blue 1862 and 1864); Middlesex (1870, 1 match).
Career batting
9–12–1–208–63–18.90–0–*ct* 8–*st* 6

His first-class debut was for Gentlemen of the North in 1861. He also played non-first-class cricket for Warwickshire and Huntingdonshire.

Martin, Robert Harold
Amateur. *b:* 7.10.1918, Liverpool. Lower order right-hand batsman, right-arm medium bowler. *Sch* Oundle. *Team* Combined Services (1951).
Career batting
1–2–0–4–4–2.00–0–*ct* 0
Bowling 91–1–91.00–0–0–1/29

Martin, Sidney Hugh
Professional. *b:* 11.1.1909, Durban, South Africa. Middle order right-hand batsman, left-arm medium bowler. *Teams* Natal (1925/6 to 1946/7); Worcestershire (1931–39, 236 matches); Rhodesia (1947/8 to 1949/50).
Career batting
267–457–31–11511–191*–27.02–13–*ct* 159
Bowling 15063–532–28.31–21–6–8/24

He hit 1,000 runs in a season seven times (best 1,705, av 31.57, in 1935). His first-class debut in England was for MCC in 1929. He took 100 wickets in a season twice (best 114, av 20.25, in 1937) and achieved the 'double' in 1937 and 1939.

Martin, Thomas
Amateur. *b:* 31.8.1909, Hamburg, Germany. Lower order right-hand batsman, wicket-keeper. *Sch* Cheltenham. *Team* Cambridge U (1928).
Career batting
2–4–0–5–2–1.25–0–*ct* 1–*st* 1

Martin, Thomas
Amateur. *b:* 15.1.1911, Lisburn, Co. Antrim, Ireland. *d:* 7.12.1937, Lisburn, Co. Antrim, Ireland. Brother of Herbert (Ireland). Right-hand batsman, right-arm fast medium bowler. *Team* Ireland (1934).
Career batting
1–2–1–7–7–7.00–0–*ct* 0
Bowling 49–0

Martin, William
Professional. *b:* 19.2.1844, Nursling, Hants. *d:* 27.5.1871, Southampton, Hants. Middle order right-hand batsman, right-arm medium pace bowler. *Team* Hampshire (1867, 1 match).
Career batting
1–2–0–2–1–1.00–0–*ct* 0

Martindale, Emanuel Alfred
Amateur. *b:* 25.11.1909, Barbados. *d:* 17.3.1972, Ashton Hall, Barbados. Hard hitting lower order right-hand batsman, attacking right-arm fast bowler. *Team* Barbados (1929/30 to 1935/6). *Tours* West Indies to England 1933, 1939. *Tests* West Indies (1933–39, 10 matches).
Career batting
59–84–20–972–134–15.18–1–*ct* 29
Bowling 5205–203–25.64–11–1–8/32
Test batting
10–14–3–58–22–5.27–0–*ct* 5
Bowling 804–37–21.72–3–0–5/22

The outstanding bowler of the 1933 tour – he took 103 wickets, av 20.98 – he was the only regular bowler to average less than 30.00 and in the Tests the only bowler to achieve respectable figures. He was however criticised for employing leg-theory bowling in the Tests. He totally failed to find his form on the 1939 tour.

Martineau, Alfred
Amateur. *b:* 11.11.1868, Esher, Surrey. *d:* 2.2.1940, Aberdeen, Scotland. Lower order right-hand batsman, right-arm slow bowler, good slip field. *Sch* Uppingham. *Team* Cambridge U (1889).
Career batting
2–3–0–4–2–1.33–0–*ct* 0
Bowling 65–1–65.00–0–0–1/65

Martineau, Hubert Melville
Amateur. *b:* 24.10.1891, London. *d:* 11.9.1976, Westminster, London. Son of P. H. (MCC), cousin of Lionel (Surrey). Lower order right-hand batsman, slow left-arm bowler. *Sch* Eton. *Team* Leveson-Gower's XI (1931–32). *Tours* He managed and captained his own team to Egypt for eleven successive years, 1929–39 (not first-class).
Career batting
3–6–2–44–19*–11.00–0–*ct* 0
Bowling 95–0

From 1924 to 1939 he ran his own team based at his country house, Holyport Lodge, near Maidenhead.

Martineau, Lionel
Amateur. *b:* 19.2.1867, Esher, Surrey. *d:* 17.11.1906, Esher, Surrey. Cousin of H. M. (Leveson-Gower's XI), cousin of P. H. (MCC). Middle order right-hand batsman, right-arm slow bowler, fine field. *Sch* Uppingham. *Team* Cambridge U (1887–88, blue 1887).
Career batting
11–19–5–277–109–19.78–1–*ct* 8
Bowling 542–17–31.88–0–0–4/59

Martineau, Sir Philip Hubert
Amateur. *b:* 28.10.1862, London. *d:* 7.10.1944, Sunningdale, Berkshire. Father of H. M. (Leveson-Gower's XI), uncle of Lionel (Cambridge U). Lower order batsman, left-arm fast medium bowler, good field. *Sch* Harrow. *Team* MCC (1883).
Career batting
2–4–0–27–14–6.75–0–*ct* 0
He did not appear in any first-class matches whilst at Cambridge.

Martingell, William
Professional. *b:* 20.8.1818, Nutfield, Surrey. *d:* 29.9.1897, Eton Wick, Bucks. Son of Russell (Surrey). Hard hitting middle/lower order right-hand batsman, right-hand medium pace round-arm bowler. *Teams* Kent (1841–52, 49 matches); Hampshire (1845, 1 match); Surrey (1839–59, 51 matches).
Career batting
182–308–46–2401–49–9.16–0–*ct* 129
Bowling 3852–333+196–11.56–36–4–8/37
His final first-class match was in 1860 for MCC. One of the great bowlers of his day he appeared for the Players v Gentlemen from 1844 to 1858 and in the 1853 match took 7 for 19 – possibly the best performance of his career.

Martyn, Henry
Amateur. *b:* 16.7.1877, Lifton, Devon. *d:* 8.8.1928, Dawlish, Devon. Middle/lower order right-hand batsman, wicket-keeper. *Teams* Oxford U (1899–1900, blue both years); Somerset (1901–08, 74 matches).
Career batting
97–158–6–3740–130*–24.60–1–*ct* 113–*st* 48
Bowling 143–2–71.50–0–0–1/19
He hit 1,005 runs, av 31.40, in 1906. He also appeared for Devon and Cornwall. Regarded as one of the best wicket-keepers of his day, he was unfortunate not to represent England.

Martyn, Oswald
Amateur. *b:* 1887, Wandsworth, London. *d:* 14.9.1959, Patcham, Sussex. Middle order batsman. *Team* Essex (1922, 1 match).
Career batting
1–1–0–0–0–0.00–0–*ct* 1

Maru, Rajesh Jamnadass
Cricketer. *b:* 28.10.1962, Nairobi, Kenya. Lower order right-hand batsman, slow left-arm bowler. *Team* Middlesex (1980–82, 16 matches). *Tour* Middlesex to Zimbabwe 1980/1.
Career batting
16–16–3–147–25–11.30–0–*ct* 14
Bowling 766–23–33.30–0–0–4/30

Maslin, Martin
Cricketer. *b:* 14.3.1942, Grimsby, Lincs. Opening right-hand batsman, right-arm medium pace bowler, occasional leg breaks. *Team* Minor Counties (1967–74).
Career batting
5–10–1–274–66*–30.44–0–*ct* 2
Bowling 44–0
His County cricket was for Lincolnshire, commencing 1959.

Mason, Alan
Professional. *b:* 2.5.1921, Addingham, Yorkshire. Lower order left-hand batsman, slow left-arm bowler. *Team* Yorkshire (1947–50, 18 matches).
Career batting
18–19–3–105–22–6.56–0–*ct* 6
Bowling 1473–51–28.88–1–0–5/56

Mason, Andrew Lindsey
Cricketer. *b:* 22.9.1943, Birmingham. Lower order right-hand batsman, wicket-keeper. *Team* Oxford U (1963–65).
Career batting
15–23–4–213–47–11.21–0–*ct* 12–*st* 5

Mason, Charles Eagleton Stuart
Amateur. *b:* 6.6.1871, Woolwich, Kent. *d:* 29.4.1945, Blackheath, Kent. Middle order batsman. *Team* MCC (1896).
Career batting
1–2–0–8–8–4.00–0–*ct* 0

Mason, Henry
Amateur. *b:* 1841, Fulbourn, Cambridgeshire. Middle order batsman, bowler. *Team* Cambridgeshire (1869–71, 2 matches).
Career batting
2–4–0–19–12–4.75–0–*ct* 0
Bowling 60–5–12.00–0–0–3/48

Mason, James Ernest
Amateur. *b:* 29.10.1876, Blackheath, Kent. *d:* 8.2.1938, Wallington, Surrey. Brother of J. R. (Kent). Middle order right-hand batsman, good cover field. *Sch* Tonbridge. *Team* Kent (1900, 1 match).
Career batting
1–1–0–1–1–1.00–0–*ct* 0
He also played for Berkshire.

Mason, John Richard
Amateur. *b:* 26.3.1874, Blackheath, Kent. *d:* 15.10.1958, Cooden, Sussex. Brother of J. E. (Kent). Stylish middle order right-hand batsman, right-arm fast medium bowler, good slip field. *Sch* Winchester. *Team* Kent (1893–1914, 300 matches). *Tours* Stoddart to Australia, 1897/8; Kent to the United States, 1903. *Tests* England (1897/8, 5 matches).
Career batting
339–557–36–17337–183–33.27–34–*ct* 390
Bowling 18989–848–22.39–35–9–8/29
Test batting
5–10–0–129–32–12.90–0–*ct* 3
Bowling 149–2–74.50–0–0–1/8
He hit 1,000 runs in a season eight times (best 1,561, av 36.30, in 1901). In the same season he took 100 wickets for the only time – 118, av 20.44, thus completing the 'double'. His final first-class match was for L. Robinson's XII in 1919.

Mason, Percy
Professional. *b:* 19.11.1873, East Bridgford, Notts. *d:* 27.11.1952, Gunthorpe, Nottingham. Lower order right-hand batsman, right-arm fast bowler. *Team* Notts (1896–1901, 43 matches).
Career batting
43–64–10–879–80–16.27–0–*ct* 7
Bowling 402–10–40.20–0–0–2/20
He played for Cheshire from 1909 to 1912.

Masood Iqbal Qureshi
Cricketer. *b:* 17.4.1952, Lahore, Pakistan. Lower order right-hand batsman, wicket-keeper. *Teams* Lahore (1969/70 to 1974/5); Punjab U (1971/2); Punjab (1973/4 to 1975/6); Habib Bank (1976/7 to 1982/3). *Tours* Pakistan to Australia and New Zealand 1972/3, to England 1978.
Career batting
118–175–29–2127–69–14.56–0–*ct* 251–*st* 46
Bowling 134–3–44.66–0–0–1/12
He appeared in only one first-class match on the 1978 tour.

Massey, Joseph
Amateur. Middle order right-hand batsman. *Team* Sir L. Parkinson's XI (1933–35).
Career batting
2–4–0–65–25–16.25–0–*ct* 0

Massey, John Alfred
Amateur. *b:* 1899, Hendon, Middlesex. *d:* 1963, Colchester, Essex. Middle order batsman. *Team* Middlesex (1927, 1 match).
Career batting
1–1–0–17–17–17.00–0–*ct* 0

Massey, William Morton
Amateur. *b:* 11.4.1846, Scotland. *d:* 19.4.1899, New York, USA. *Teams* Somerset (1882, 1 match); Lancashire (1883, 1 match).
Career batting
2–4–0–10–5–2.50–0–*ct* 1
He also played for Devon.

Massie, Hugh Hamon
Amateur. *b:* 11.4.1854, near Belfast, Victoria, Australia. *d:* 12.10.1938, Point Piper, New South Wales, Australia. Father of R. J. A. (New South Wales). Opening right-hand batsman, good field. *Team* New South Wales (1877/8 to 1887/8, 17 matches). *Tour* Australia to England 1882. *Tests* Australia (1881/2 to 1884/5, 9 matches).
Career batting
64–113–5–2485–206–23.00–1–*ct* 35
Bowling 60–2–30.00–0–0–2/39
Test batting
9–16–0–249–55–15.56–0–*ct* 5
He had a successful tour to England in 1882, hitting 1,360 runs, av 25.66, in first-class matches, including 206 v Oxford U at Oxford, which was his only double century. His final first-class matches were in England in 1895 for MCC and for Gentlemen of England. Business commitments prevented him appearing more often in important matches.

Massie, Robert Arnold Lockyer
Cricketer. *b:* 14.4.1947, Subiaco, Perth, Australia. Lower order left-hand batsman, right-arm medium fast bowler. *Teams* Western Australia (1965/6 to 1974/5, 28 matches); Ranji's XI in India 1972/3. *Tours* Australia to England 1972, to West Indies 1972/3. *Tests* Australia (1972 to 1972/3, 6 matches).
Career batting
52–54–14–385–42–9.62–0–*ct* 8
Bowling 4446–179–24.83–6–2–8/53
Test batting
6–8–1–78–42–11.14–0–*ct* 1
Bowling 647–31–20.87–2–1–8/53
He was an outstanding success on his tour to England, taking 23 wickets, av 17.78, in the Tests and 50 wickets, av 17.02, in first-class matches, including 16 in his first Test match (at Lord's). His exceptional ability to swing the ball in humid

conditions accounted for his success, but he found that this knack faded and he soon dropped out of first-class cricket.

Master, A. W. C.
(*see under* Chester-Master, A. W.)

Master, E. C. (*see under* Chester-Master, E.)

Masterman, Sir John Cecil
Amateur. *b:* 12.1.1891, Kingston-on-Thames, Surrey. *d:* 6.6.1977, Oxford. Sound middle order left-hand batsman, right-arm medium pace bowler. *Teams* Leveson-Gower's XI (1926); Harlequins (1927); Free Foresters (1927–30). *Tours* Free Foresters to Canada 1923 (not first-class); Martineau to Egypt 1930, 1931 (not first-class); MCC to Canada 1937 (not first-class).
Career batting
4–6–2–77–36*–19.25–0–*ct* 7
Bowling 236–4–59.00–0–0–2/124

His County cricket was for Oxfordshire. For many years he was on the Committees of I Zingari and Free Foresters. He wrote several delightful pieces on cricket.

A noted all-round games player, he represented Oxford and England at hockey and lawn tennis, as well as winning the University high jump.

Masters, Kevin David
Cricketer. *b:* 19.5.1961, Chatham, Kent. Left-hand batsman, right-arm medium fast bowler. *Team* Kent (1983, 2 matches).
Career batting
2–4–0–1–1–0.25–0–*ct* 2
Bowling 121–2–60.50–0–0–2/26

Masterton, Albert Edward George William
Professional. *b:* 19.5.1843, Cambridge. *d:* 1887, Epping, Essex. Lower order batsman, bowler. *Team* Cambridgeshire (1867–71, 3 matches).
Career batting
3–5–1–13–5–3.25–0–*ct* 1

Matheson, Alexander Malcolm
Amateur. *b:* 27.2.1906, Omaha, Auckland, New Zealand. Lower order right-hand batsman, right-arm medium pace bowler. *Teams* Auckland (1926/7 to 1939/40); Wellington (1944/5 to 1946/7). *Tour* New Zealand to England 1931. *Tests* New Zealand (1929/30 to 1931, 2 matches).
Career batting
69–97–19–1844–112–23.64–1–*ct* 44
Bowling 5534–194–28.52–2–0–5/50
Test batting
2–1–0–7–7–7.00–0–*ct* 2
Bowling 136–2–68.00–0–0–2/7

His 44 wickets on the 1931 tour of England cost 23.81 runs each and he only appeared in one of three Tests.

Matheson, Edward
Amateur. *b:* 14.6.1865, Charlton, Kent. *d:* 26.2.1945, Uffculme, Tiverton, Devon. Middle order right-hand batsman, right-arm bowler. *Sch* Clergy Orphan School, Canterbury. *Team* Warwickshire (1899, 1 match).
Career batting
2–4–0–21–9–5.25–0–*ct* 1

His first-class debut was for the South of England in 1886.

Matheson, John Alexander
Cricketer. *b:* 26.10.1950, Dunedin, New Zealand. Lower order right-hand batsman, wicket-keeper. *Team* Oxford U (1977).
Career batting
1 match, did not bat–*ct* 0

Mathews, Ernest
Amateur. *b:* 17.5.1847, London. *d:* 25.11.1930, Amersham, Bucks. Lower order right-hand batsman, right-hand slow round-arm bowler. *Sch* Harrow. *Team* Oxford U (1867–69, blue 1868–69).
Career batting
11–18–0–179–44–9.94–0–*ct* 9
Bowling 167–7–23.85–0–0–3/57

He played County cricket for Hertfordshire.

Mathews, Frederick John
Professional. *b:* 7.3.1861, Thames Ditton, Surrey. *d:* 9.2.1950, Surbiton, Surrey. Middle order batsman. *Team* Surrey (1883, 2 matches).
Career batting
2–3–0–14–9–4.66–0–*ct* 0

Mathews, John Kenneth
Amateur. *b:* 6.2.1884, Epping, Essex. *d:* 6.4.1962, Worthing, Sussex. Father of K. P. A. (Sussex). Forcing middle order right-hand batsman. *Sch* Felsted. *Team* Sussex (1909–30, 40 matches).
Career batting
40–61–4–778–78–13.64–0–*ct* 11
Bowling 98–0

He also played for Wiltshire. A noted hockey player, he represented England.

Mathews, Kenneth Patrick Arthur
Amateur. *b:* 10.5.1926, Worthing, Sussex. Son of J. K. (Sussex). Sound opening right-hand batsman, right-arm medium pace bowler. *Sch* Felsted. *Teams* Sussex (1950–51, 6 matches); Cambridge U (1951, blue).

Career batting
21–30–1–796–77–27.44–0–*ct* 7
Bowling 19–0

His final first-class match was for Free Foresters in 1956. He also was awarded his blue for golf and hockey, and appeared for Sussex and England at the latter sport.

Mathews, Leslie Henry Staverton
Amateur. *b:* 1.3.1875, Kensington, London. *d:* 7.4.1946, Fulham, London. Lower order batsman, wicket-keeper. *Sch* St Paul's. *Team* Oxford U (1897).
Career batting
2–3–0–9–9–3.00–0–*ct* 1

He represented Oxford as a heavyweight boxer.

Mathews, Michael John Anderson
Amateur. *b:* 6.1.1934, Durban, South Africa. Lower order right-hand batsman, leg break bowler. *Team* Oxford U (1957).
Career batting
2–4–0–9–5–2.25–0–*ct* 1
Bowling 77–6–12.83–1–0–5/58

Mathews, William
Professional. *b:* 23.3.1793, Crondall, Hampshire. *d:* 20.8.1858, Woodbridge, Suffolk. Lower order batsman, right-hand slow round-arm bowler. *Teams* Surrey (1828–29); Hampshire (1829).
Career batting
31–55–2–329–33–6.20–0–*ct* 26
Bowling 79 wickets, no analyses

During his short career in great matches, he was one of the best bowlers in England. His debut was for Godalming in 1821 and his final important match for Suffolk in 1830.

Mathias, Frederick William
Amateur. *b:* 7.8.1898, Radyr, Glamorgan. *d:* 19.4.1955, Radyr, Glamorgan. Middle order right-hand batsman, slow right-arm bowler. *Sch* Clifton. *Teams* Glamorgan (1922–30, 28 matches); Wales (1926).
Career batting
29–47–5–522–65–12.42–0–*ct* 8
Bowling 126–3–42.00–0–0–2/23

Mathie-Morton, Alexander Fullarton
Amateur. *b:* 7.6.1880, Ayr, Scotland. *d:* 16.1.1965, Ayr, Scotland. Middle order right-hand batsman. *Sch* Blair Lodge. *Team* Scotland (1922).
Career batting
1–2–0–16–9–8.00–0–*ct* 0

Mathwin, Henry
Amateur. *b:* 23.8.1852, Bolton-le-Moors, Lancashire. *d:* 31.12.1911, Birkdale, Lancashire. Middle order batsman. *Team* Cambridge U (1874).
Career batting
1–2–1–18–17–18.00–0–*ct* 2

Matthews, Austin David George
Professional. *b:* 3.5.1904, Penarth, Glamorgan. *d:* 29.7.1977, Penrhyn Bay, Gwynedd. Lower order right-hand batsman, right-arm fast medium bowler. *Sch* St David's, Lampeter. *Teams* Northants (1927–36, 224 matches); Glamorgan (1937–47, 51 matches). *Test* England (1937, 1 match).
Career batting
281–447–70–5909–116–15.67–2–*ct* 124
Bowling 19099–816–23.40–45–6–7/57
Test batting
1–1–1–2–2*–no av–0–*ct* 1
Bowling 65–2–32.50–0–0–1/13

His best season was 1946 when he took 93 wickets, av 14.29. A noted rugby footballer, he played for Northampton, Penarth, East Midlands and had a trial for Wales. He also represented Wales at table tennis.

Matthews, Alan Ivor
Professional. *b:* 3.5.1913, Keynsham, Somerset. Lower order right-hand batsman, right-arm fast medium bowler. *Team* Gloucestershire (1933–38, 16 matches).
Career batting
16–25–6–185–51–9.73–0–*ct* 10
Bowling 980–14–70.00–0–0–4/81

Matthews, Albert J.
Cricketer. *b:* 29.4.1944, Fearn, Inverness, Scotland. Lower order right-hand batsman, off break bowler. *Team* Leicestershire (1965–68, 16 matches).
Career batting
16–20–3–167–32–9.82–0–*ct* 8
Bowling 786–24–32.75–0–0–4/87

Matthews, Colin S.
Professional. *b:* 17.10.1929, Worksop, Notts. Tail end right-hand batsman, left-arm medium pace bowler. *Team* Notts (1950–59, 84 matches).
Career batting
85–103–36–493–41–7.35–0–*ct* 38
Bowling 5433–147–36.95–4–0–6/65

Matthews, Dudley Muir
Amateur. *b:* 11.9.1916, Prescot, Lancashire. *d:* 1967. Middle order left-hand batsman. *Sch* Felsted. *Team* Lancashire (1936–38, 7 matches).
Career batting
7–8–0–130–46–16.25–0–*ct* 1

Matthews, Frank Cyril (Leonard)
Professional. *b:* 15.8.1892, Willoughby-on-the-Wolds, Notts. *d:* 11.1.1961, Nottingham. Tail end right-hand batsman, right-arm fast bowler. *Team* Notts (1920–27, 82 matches).
Career batting
82–94–24–500–34–7.14–0–*ct* 42
Bowling 5331–261–20.42–14–2–9/50
His great season was 1923 when he took 115 wickets, av 15.30, and against Northants at Trent Bridge he took 17 wickets for 89, a County record.

Matthews, John Duncan
Amateur. *b:* 19.9.1921, Rainhill, Lancashire. Middle order left-hand batsman. *Sch* Shrewsbury. *Team* Scotland (1951–55).
Career batting
5–7–0–81–29–11.57–0–*ct* 0

Matthews, John Leonard
Amateur. *b:* 2.8.1847, Clifton, Gloucs. *d:* 25.9.1912, Maidenhead, Berks. Brother of T. G. (Gloucs). *Sch* Cheltenham. *Team* Gloucestershire (1872, 1 match).
Career batting
1 match, did not bat–*ct* 0
The only match in which he appeared for Gloucestershire was almost completely washed out by rain.

Matthews, Michael Harrington
Amateur. *b:* 26.4.1914, Wandsworth, London. *d:* 29.5.1940, Dunkirk. He was killed in action on a destroyer off the coast. Attacking lower order right-hand batsman, wicket-keeper. *Sch* Westminster. *Team* Oxford U (1934–37, blue 1936–37).
Career batting
23–33–3–393–68–13.10–0–*ct* 32–*st* 6
He also achieved success as a sprinter and as a boxer whilst at Oxford.

Matthews, Robin Birkby
Cricketer. *b:* 30.1.1944, Stockton-on-Tees, Co Durham. Lower order right-hand batsman, right-arm medium pace bowler. *Team* Leicestershire (1971–73, 25 matches).
Career batting
25–18–8–89–16*–8.90–0–*ct* 8
Bowling 1338–48–27.88–1–0–7/51

Matthews, Thomas Gadd
Amateur. *b:* 9.12.1845, Bristol, Gloucs. *d:* 5.1.1932, Newport, Gloucs. Brother of J. L. (Gloucs). Hard hitting opening right-hand batsman. *Team* Gloucestershire (1870–78, 29 matches).
Career batting
29–47–0–769–201–16.36–1–*ct* 13
His only double century was 201 for Gloucs v Surrey at Clifton in 1871 – he being the first cricketer to perform such a feat for Gloucestershire.

Matthews, Thomas James
Amateur. *b:* 3.4.1884, Williamstown, Victoria, Australia. *d:* 14.10.1943, Caulfield, Victoria, Australia. Stubborn lower order right-hand batsman, leg break bowler. *Team* Victoria (1906/7 to 1914/15, 32 matches). *Tour* Australia to England and North America 1912. *Tests* Australia (1911/2 to 1912, 8 matches).
Career batting
67–99–13–2149–93–24.98–0–*ct* 56
Bowling 4507–177–25.46–8–1–7/46
Test batting
8–10–1–153–53–17.00–0–*ct* 7
Bowling 419–16–26.18–0–0–4/29
At Old Trafford for Australia v South Africa in 1912 he performed one hat-trick in each innings – the only time such a feat has been achieved in Test matches. Although his performances on the rest of the tour did not match this, he was a very useful bowler.

Matts, Alfred Shipley
Professional. *b:* 2.4.1893, Barrow-on-Soar, Leics. *d:* 20.6.1970, Anstey, Leics. Lower order left-hand batsman, left-arm bowler. *Team* Leicestershire (1921, 1 match).
Career batting
1–2–0–3–3–1.50–0–*ct* 0
Bowling 54–1–54.00–0–0–1/54

Maturin, Dr Henry
Amateur. *b:* 5.4.1842, Fanetglebe, Clondevaddock, Co Donegal, Ireland. *d:* 24.2.1920, Hartley-Wintney, Hampshire. Lower order right-hand batsman, right-hand fast round-arm bowler. *Sch* Marlborough. *Teams* Middlesex (1863, 1 match); Hampshire (1864–82, 9 matches).
Career batting
12–19–1–178–28–9.88–0–*ct* 7
Bowling 201–6+2–33.50–0–0–4/68

Maude, Edmund
Amateur. *b:* 31.12.1839. *d:* 2.7.1876, Headingley, Leeds, Yorkshire. Middle order batsman. *Team* Yorkshire (1866, 2 matches).
Career batting
2–2–0–17–16–8.50–0–*ct* 0

Maude, Frederick William
Amateur. *b:* 28.2.1857, Plumstead, Kent. *d:* 9.2.1923, St Pancras, London. Right-hand

batsman, right-arm medium pace bowler, good slip. *Team* Middlesex (1890–96, 2 matches).
Career batting
13–26–0–323–60–12.42–0–*ct* 8
Bowling 325–9–36.11–1–0–6/90
His first-class debut was for MCC in 1883 and his final first-class match was for MCC in 1897. He stood four times for Parliament but was not returned. He was a Baron of Cinque Ports.

Maude, John
Amateur. *b:* 17.3.1850, Millfield, Yorkshire. *d:* 17.11.1934, Oberhofen, Switzerland. Lower order batsman, left-arm medium pace bowler. *Sch* Eton. *Team* Oxford U (1873, blue).
Career batting
5–7–3–25–12*–6.25–0–*ct* 2
Bowling 255–23–11.08–2–0–6/14
He appeared for Warwickshire commencing 1870 (pre-first-class).

Maudsley, Ronald Harling
Amateur. *b:* 8.4.1918, Lostock-Gralam, Cheshire. *d:* 29.9.1981, San Diego, California, USA. Sound middle order right-hand batsman, right-arm medium pace bowler. *Sch* Malvern. *Teams* Oxford U (1946–47, blue both years); Warwickshire (1946–51, 45 matches).
Career batting
67–116–5–2676–130–24.10–4–*ct* 48
Bowling 1470–52–28.26–2–0–6/54
He was joint captain of Warwickshire in 1948.

Maul, Rev John Broughton
Amateur. *b:* 28.11.1857, Newport Pagnell, Bucks. *d:* 5.11.1931, Banbury, Oxfordshire. Middle order right-hand batsman, right-hand slow round-arm bowler, excellent field. *Sch* Uppingham. *Team* Cambridge U (1878).
Career batting
1–1–0–0–0–0.00–0–*ct* 0
Bowling 8–1–8.00–0–0–1/8

Maundrell, Rev William Herbert
Amateur. *b:* 5.11.1876, Nagasaki, Japan. *d:* 17.6.1958, Deal, Kent. Middle order right-hand batsman. *Sch* King's, Canterbury. *Team* Hampshire (1900, 1 match).
Career batting
1–1–0–0–0–0.00–0–*ct* 0

Maw, Michael Trentham
Amateur. *b:* 1912, Reigate, Surrey. *d:* 13.8.1944, on air operations over Germany. Tail end right-hand batsman, right-arm medium pace bowler. *Sch* Oundle. *Team* Cambridge U (1933–34).
Career batting
3–5–2–19–9–6.33–0–*ct* 0
Bowling 141–3–47.00–0–0–1/15

Mawle, Henry Edward
Professional. *b:* 1871, Battle, Sussex. *d:* 1943, Totnes, Devon. Lower order batsman, wicket-keeper. *Team* Sussex (1896, 1 match).
Career batting
1–1–0–0–0–0.00–0–*ct* 0
He also played for Devon.

Maxwell, Cecil Reginald Napp
Amateur. *b:* 21.5.1913, London. *d:* 25.9.1973, Taunton, Somerset. Hard hitting middle order right-hand batsman, wicket-keeper. *Sch* Brighton. *Teams* Nottinghamshire (1936–39, 16 matches); Middlesex (1946, 4 matches); Worcestershire (1948–51, 7 matches). *Tours* Cahn to North America 1933 (not first-class), to Ceylon 1936/7, to New Zealand 1938/9.
Career batting
44–67–7–1564–268–26.06–1–*ct* 70–*st* 25
His first-class debut was for Sir J. Cahn's XI in 1932, and his most notable innings was 268 for the same team v Leicestershire at Loughborough Road, West Bridgford, in 1935. Whilst at Brighton he was regarded as the outstanding schoolboy batsman-wicketkeeper of his generation.

Maxwell, James
Professional. *b:* 13.1.1884, Taunton, Somerset. *d:* 27.12.1967, Taunton, Somerset. Lower order right-hand batsman, right-arm fast medium bowler. *Team* Somerset (1906–08, 10 matches).
Career batting
11–18–5–218–67*–16.76–0–*ct* 6
Bowling 917–24–38.20–1–0–5/63
His final first-class match was for South Wales in 1912.

Maxwell, Lawrence Evan
Cricketer. *b:* 17.1.1941, Barbados. Right-hand tail end batsman, off break bowler. *Team* Barbados (1968/9 to 1978/9). *Tour* Barbados to England 1969.
Career batting
16–23–11–90–19–7.50–0–*ct* 2
Bowling 1261–34–36.52–1–0–5/73

Maxwell, Dr Patrick Arthur
Amateur. *b:* 10.7.1869, Dublin, Ireland. Middle order batsman. *Team* Dublin U (1895).
Career batting
4–8–0–105–39–13.12–0–*ct* 1

Maxwell, Thomas Stanislaus Alfred Charles Joseph
Amateur. *b:* 15.3.1903, London. *d:* 27.3.1970, Camberwell, London. Middle order right-hand batsman, right-arm bowler. *Team* Minor Counties (1937–38).
Career batting
2–4–2–79–78*–39.50–0–*ct* 0
Bowling 108–2–54.00–0–0–1/11
He appeared for Surrey 2nd XI.

Maxwell-Heron, John Heron
Amateur. *b:* 5.9.1836, Port Louis, Mauritius. *d:* 26.1.1899, Westminster, London. Middle order batsman, left-hand round-arm bowler. *Sch* Harrow. *Team* Gentlemen of England (1865).
Career batting
1–1–0–3–3–3.00–0–*ct* 1
Bowling 44–2–22.00–0–0–2/32
He was MP for Kirkcudbright from 1880 to 1885.

Maxwell, W.
Amateur. *Team* MCC (1890).
Career batting
1–1–0–0–0–0.00–0–*ct* 0

May, Barry
Cricketer. *b:* 1.11.1944, Johannesburg, South Africa. Middle order right-hand batsman. *Team* Oxford U (1970–72, blue all three years).
Career batting
22–40–1–703–103–18.02–1–*ct* 12

May, Frank Boyd
Amateur. *b:* 24.10.1862, London. *d:* 1.6.1907, Hurley, Marlow, Bucks. He died by his own hand having been declared a defaulter on the Stock Exchange. Middle order batsman. *Sch* Clifton. *Team* MCC (1898–1906).
Career batting
4–7–1–12–7–2.00–0–*ct* 2

May, John
Professional. *b:* 26.9.1845, Southampton, Hants. Lower order right-hand batsman, right-arm fast bowler. *Team* Hampshire (1867–70, 4 matches).
Career batting
4–8–2–71–28–11.83–0–*ct* 0
Bowling 165–6–27.50–0–0–4/80

May, Peter Barker Howard
Amateur. *b:* 31.12.1929, Reading, Berkshire. Son-in-law of A. H. H. Gilligan (Sussex). Polished middle order right-hand batsman. *Sch* Charterhouse. *Teams* Surrey (1950–63, 208 matches); Cambridge U (1950–52, blue all three years). *Tours* MCC to West Indies 1953/4, 1959/60, to Australia and New Zealand 1954/5, 1958/9, to South Africa 1956/7. *Tests* England (1951–61, 66 matches).
Career batting
388–618–77–27592–285*–51.00–85–*ct* 282
Bowling 49–0
Test batting
66–106–9–4537–285*–46.77–13–*ct* 42
The most talented English batsman of his generation, May first came to the public eye whilst at Charterhouse, where he was in the Eleven for four years – heading the school's batting averages at the age of 14. In 1946 he represented Berkshire and at the age of 17 hit a brilliant 146 for the Public Schools against Combined Services at Lord's. His first-class debut was for Combined Services in 1948, and having ended his National Service he went up to Cambridge, where he had an outstanding three years. In the vacation of 1950 he made his Surrey debut and the following season celebrated his England debut with an innings of 138 v South Africa at Headingley; in the same year he topped the first-class averages, completing 2,000 runs for the first of five times. In all he exceeded 1,000 runs in an English season eleven times (best 2,554, av 51.08, in 1953). He also hit 1,000 runs in a season once in Australia and once in South Africa.
He remained an automatic choice for England until the demands of business coupled with ill health forced him to retire from regular first-class cricket after the 1961 season. He was appointed captain of Surrey in 1957, a post he held until 1962, and led England in 41 Tests commencing in 1955, and including the MCC tours to South Africa 1956/7, Australia and New Zealand 1958/9 and West Indies 1959/60. On the last named tour ill health forced him to return to England after the third Test.
Of his five double centuries the highest was 285* for England v West Indies at Edgbaston in 1957. He hit two double centuries for Surrey, one for Cambridge and one for MCC in Rhodesia.
In 1982 he was appointed Chairman of the English Test Selection Committee.

May, Percy Robert
Amateur. *b:* 13.3.1884, Chertsey, Surrey. *d:* 6.12.1965, Moor Green, Eastleigh, Hants. Lower order right-hand batsman, right-arm fast bowler. *Teams* Surrey (1902–09, 12 matches); London County (1902–04); Cambridge U (1903–06, blue 1905–06). *Tour* MCC to New Zealand 1906/7.
Career batting
72–112–39–1037–51*–14.20–0–*ct* 36
Bowling 6094–247–24.67–14–3–7/41
His final first-class match was in 1926 for Free

Foresters. He was for some years well-known in Ceylon cricket. He also obtained his soccer blue at Cambridge.

Mayall, James
Professional. *b:* 1856, Oldham, Lancashire. *d:* 1916, Oldham, Lancashire. Lower order batsman, wicket-keeper. *Team* Lancashire (1885, 1 match).
Career batting
1–1–0–0–0–0.00–0–*ct* 1–*st* 2

Mayer, Joseph Herbert
Professional. *b:* 2.3.1902, Audley, Staffs. *d:* 6.9.1981, Kingsbury, Warwickshire. Useful lower order right-hand batsman, right-arm fast medium bowler. *Team* Warwickshire (1926–39, 332 matches).
Career batting
333–409–115–2839–74*–9.65–0–*ct* 184
Bowling 25404–1144–22.20–71–9–8/62
He took 100 wickets in a season twice (best 126, av 22.35, in 1929). He also played for Staffordshire.

Mayes, Richard
Professional. *b:* 7.10.1922, Littlebourne, Kent. Stylish middle order right-hand batsman, good cover field. *Team* Kent (1947–53, 80 matches).
Career batting
80–144–7–2689–134–19.62–4–*ct* 28
Bowling 46–0
He also played for Suffolk.

Mayes, T.
Professional. Lower order batsman, wicket-keeper. *Team* Sussex (1889, 7 matches).
Career batting
7–12–3–51–15–5.66–0–*ct* 11–*st* 3
He also played for Monmouthshire.

Mayes, William Henry James
Amateur. *b:* 17.7.1885, Marylebone, London. *d:* 5.2.1946, Esher, Surrey. Lower order right-hand batsman, right-arm fast bowler. *Team* Essex (1914, 1 match).
Career batting
1–2–0–2–2–1.00–0–*ct* 0
Bowling 69–0

Mayhew, John Francis Nicholas
Amateur. *b:* 6.12.1909, Mungumbankum, India. Lower order right-hand batsman, wicket-keeper. *Sch* Eton. *Team* Oxford U (1929–31, blue 1930).
Career batting
14–21–9–115–26*–9.58–0–*ct* 8–*st* 4
He played for Buckinghamshire.

Maynard, Christopher
Cricketer. *b:* 8.4.1958, Haslemere, Surrey. Middle order right-hand batsman, wicket-keeper. *Teams* Warwickshire (1978–82, 24 matches); Lancashire (1982–83, 38 matches). *Tour* Robins to Australia (not first-class) and New Zealand 1979/80.
Career batting
64–76–12–1211–85–18.92–0–*ct* 86–*st* 12
He appeared for both Warwickshire and Lancashire in 1982.

Maynard, Edmund Anthony Jefferson
Amateur. *b:* 10.2.1861, Chesterfield, Derbyshire. *d:* 10.1.1931, Hoon, Hilton, Derbyshire. Middle order right-hand batsman, slow right-arm bowler. *Sch* Harrow. *Teams* Derbyshire (1880–87, 37 matches); Cambridge U (1881–83).
Career batting
47–85–4–720–84–8.88–0–*ct* 18
Bowling 53–2–26.50–0–0–2/34

Mayne, Edgar Richard
Amateur. *b:* 4.7.1884, Jamestown, South Australia. *d:* 26.10.1961, Carrum, Victoria, Australia. Opening right-hand batsman. *Teams* South Australia (1906/7 to 1914/5, 37 matches); Victoria (1918/19 to 1925/6, 43 matches). *Tours* Australia to England 1912, 1921, to New Zealand 1909/10, to North America 1912, 1913; Victoria to New Zealand 1924/5. *Tests* Australia (1912 to 1921/2, 4 matches).
Career batting
141–243–10–7624–209–32.72–14–*ct* 80
Bowling 440–13–33.84–0–0–3/6
Test batting
4–4–1–64–25*–21.33–0–*ct* 2
Bowling 1–0
He achieved little on his two tours to England – in 1921 his opportunities were very limited and he did not appear in the Tests. His highest score was 209 for Victoria v Queensland at Melbourne in 1923/4.

Mayo, Charles Thomas Worsfold
Amateur. *b:* 5.2.1903, Victoria, British Columbia. *d:* 10.4.1943. He was killed in action in the Middle East. Middle order right-hand batsman. *Sch* Eton. *Team* Somerset (1928, 6 matches).
Career batting
6–9–0–193–60–21.44–0–*ct* 3

Mayo, Henry Edward
Amateur. *b:* 13.11.1847, South Lambeth, Surrey. *d:* 30.10.1891, Brixton, Surrey. Middle order

right-hand batsman, right-hand fast round-arm bowler. *Team* Surrey (1868–70, 14 matches).
Career batting
14–27–1–246–53–9.46–0–*ct* 8
Bowling 112–4–28.00–0–0–2/13

Mead, Charles Philip
Professional. *b:* 9.3.1887, Battersea, London. *d:* 26.3.1958, Boscombe, Hants. Sound middle order left-hand batsman, slow left-arm bowler. *Team* Hampshire (1905–36, 700 matches). *Tours* MCC to Australia 1911/2, 1928/9, to South Africa 1913/4, 1922/3; Tennyson to Jamaica (1927/8. *Tests* England (1911/12 to 1928/9, 17 matches).
Career batting
814–1340–185–55061–280*–47.67–153–*ct* 671
Bowling 9613–277–34.70–5–0–7/18
Test batting
17–26–2–1185–182*–49.37–4–*ct* 4

He hit 1,000 runs in a season 27 times, going on 2,000 nine times and 3,000 twice, (best 3,179, av 69.10, in 1921).

He scored 13 double centuries, 11 of them for Hampshire, the highest being 280* v Notts at Southampton in 1921.

In the opinion of many he was considered unlucky not to obtain a regular place in the England team.

He appeared for Suffolk in 1938 and 1939. Though blind for the last ten years of his life he continued to attend Hampshire matches.

Mead, Harold
Professional. *b:* 13.6.1895, Walthamstow, Essex. *d:* April 1921, Epping, Essex. Son of Walter (Essex). Tail end right-hand batsman, slow left-arm bowler. *Team* Essex (1913–14, 4 matches).
Career batting
4–8–2–19–8*–3.16–0–*ct* 3
Bowling 194–3–64.66–0–0–2/84

Mead, Walter
Professional. *b:* 25.3.1868, Clapton, Middlesex. *d:* 18.3.1954, Chipping Ongar, Essex. Father of Harold (Essex). Lower right-hand batsman, slow medium off break, and occasional leg break bowler. *Teams* Essex (1894–1913, 332 matches); London County (1904). *Test* England (1899, 1 match).
Career batting
429–618–148–4991–119–10.61–1–*ct* 194
Bowling 36388–1916–18.99–152–39–9/40
Test batting
1–2–0–7–7–3.50–0–*ct* 1
Bowling 91–1–91.00–0–0–1/91

He took 100 wickets in a season ten times (best 179, av 14.55, in 1895); three times he took nine wickets in an innings for Essex, his best analysis being 9 for 40 v Hampshire at Southampton in 1900. His first-class debut was for MCC in 1892.

Mead-Briggs, Richard
Amateur. *b:* 25.3.1902, St Dunstan, Sturry, Kent. *d:* 15.1.1956, Harborne, Birmingham. Middle order right-hand batsman, right-arm medium fast bowler. *Sch* King's, Canterbury. *Team* Warwickshire (1946, 2 matches).
Career batting
2–2–1–46–44*–46.00–0–*ct* 3
Bowling 96–1–96.00–0–0–1/44

He was a noted all-rounder in Midlands Club cricket for over 30 years.

Meaden, H. J. B.
Amateur. Middle order batsman. *Team* Hampshire (1881, 3 matches).
Career batting
3–6–1–20–9*–4.00–0–0–*ct* 2

Meads, Eric Alfred
Professional. *b:* 17.8.1916, Nottingham. Tail end right-hand batsman, wicket-keeper. *Team* Notts (1939–53, 205 matches).
Career batting
205–240–90–1475–56*–9.83–0–*ct* 364–*st* 83
Bowling 5–0

Meads, James Wilford
(known as James Wilfred)
Professional. *b:* 28.10.1877, Calverton, Notts. *d:* 3.11.1957, Calverton, Notts. Lower order batsman, slow right-arm bowler. *Team* Surrey (1905, 3 matches).
Career batting
3–4–0–9–4–2.25–0–*ct* 0
Bowling 135–7–19.28–0–0–4/36

Meakin, Bernard
Amateur. *b:* 5.3.1885, Stone, Staffs. *d:* 17.2.1964, Dunsfold, Surrey. Middle order left-hand batsman, leg break bowler. *Sch* Clifton. *Teams* Gloucestershire (1906, 1 match); Cambridge U (1906–07).
Career batting
8–13–2–109–60–9.90–0–*ct* 4

He was a leading cricketer for Staffordshire, captaining the County from 1911–21 and President from 1946–56.

His final first-class match was for Free Foresters in 1922.

Meakin, Douglas
Amateur. *b:* 28.3.1929, Swadlincote, Derbyshire. Lower order right-hand batsman, right-arm fast bowler. *Team* Combined Services (1959–62).

Career batting
4–6–3–55–16–18.33–0–*ct* 0
Bowling 206–10–20.60–0–0–4/56

Meale, Trevor
Amateur. *b:* 11.11.1928, Auckland, New Zealand. Opening left-hand batsman. *Team* Wellington (1951/2 to 1953/4). *Tour* New Zealand to England 1958. *Tests* New Zealand (1958, 2 matches).
Career batting
32–54–5–1352–130–27.59–2–*ct* 17
Bowling 3–0
Test batting
2–4–0–21–10–5.25–0–*ct* 0
He was a surprise choice for the 1958 tour to England, and though appearing in two Tests achieved very little.
His final first-class match in New Zealand was for an Eleven of New Zealand in 1957/8.

Meares, George Brooke
Amateur. *b:* 26.10.1841, Glandovey Castle, Cardiganshire. *d:* 21.8.1894, Kneller Hall, Middlesex. Middle order right-hand batsman, good bowler. *Sch* Bedford GS. *Team* MCC (1874–76).
Career batting
4–7–1–52–23–8.66–0–*ct* 5
Bowling 163–7–23.78–0–0–4/18
He appeared for Hampshire and Essex (both pre-first-class).
For some considerable time he was stationed in India.

Mechen, William
Professional. *b:* 8.1.1852, Southwick, Sussex. *d:* March 1880, Southwick, Sussex. Middle order right-hand batsman. *Team* Sussex (1876–79, 4 matches).
Career batting
4–8–0–43–20–5.37–0–*ct* 7

Medhurst, Roy
Professional. *b:* 30.4.1922, East Chiltington, Sussex. Tail end right-hand batsman, right-arm fast medium bowler. *Team* Sussex (1948, 3 matches).
Career batting
3–3–2–17–15*–17.00–0–*ct* 1
Bowling 233–3–77.66–0–0–1/11

Medlicott, Walter Sandfield
Amateur. *b:* 28.8.1879, Potterne, Wiltshire. *d:* 24.6.1970, Hawick, Roxburghshire, Scotland. Steady middle order right-hand batsman, good field. *Sch* Harrow. *Team* Oxford U (1901–02, blue 1902).
Career batting
13–20–2–423–81–23.50–0–*ct* 13
His County cricket was for Wiltshire.
His final first-class match for MCC in 1911.

Mee, Robert John
Professional. *b:* 25.9.1867, Shelford, Notts. *d:* 6.2.1941, Shelford, Notts. Lower order right-hand batsman, right-arm fast bowler. *Team* Notts (1887–96, 37 matches).
Career batting
41–66–20–366–35–7.95–0–*ct* 25
Bowling 3207–133–24.11–4–1–9/54
His best bowling was 9/54 for Notts v Sussex at Trent Bridge in 1893. He also played for Monmouthshire and Staffordshire.

Meek, Henry Edgar
Amateur. *b:* 8.10.1857, Devizes, Wiltshire. *d:* 23.6.1920, Gullane, East Lothian, Scotland. Middle order right-hand batsman. *Sch* Harrow. *Team* MCC (1878).
Career batting
1–1–0–0–0–0.00–0–*ct* 1

Meers, William Simons
Amateur. *b:* 27.3.1844, Stoke, Kent. *d:* 12.7.1902, Horsham, Sussex. Middle order batsman. *Sch* Chatham House, Ramsgate. *Team* Kent (1866, 1 match).
Career batting
1–1–0–11–11–11.00–0–*ct* 0

Meeson, Martin Stewart
Amateur. *b:* 6.11.1933, London. Middle order left-hand batsman. *Sch* Bedford. *Team* Cambridge U (1957).
Career batting
1–2–0–25–21–12.50–0–*ct* 0

Meggitt, Frank Claxton
Amateur. *b:* 17.2.1901, Barry, Glamorgan. *d:* 9.10.1945, Radyr, Glamorgan. Lower order right-hand batsman, wicket-keeper. *Sch* Mill Hill. *Team* Glamorgan (1923, 1 match).
Career batting
1–2–0–4–4–2.00–0–*ct* 0

Meherhomji, Khershed Rustomji
Amateur. *b:* 9.8.1911, Bombay, India. *d:* 10.2.1982, Bombay, India. Nephew of R.P. (India). Tail end right-hand batsman, wicket-keeper. *Teams* Bombay (1933/4); Western India (1934/5 to 1935/6); Parsis (1933/4 to 1945/6). *Tour* India to England 1936. *Test* India (1936, 1 match).

Career batting
29–45–4–646–71–15.75–0–*ct* 59–*st* 10
Test batting
1–1–1–0–0*—no av–0–*ct* 1

He was the reserve wicket-keeper on the 1936 tour.

Meherhomji, Rustomji Perozsha
Amateur. *b:* 4.3.1877, Bombay, India. *d:* 14.11.1943, Bombay, India. Uncle of K.R. (Bombay). Opening right-hand batsman, right-arm fast bowler. *Team* Parsis (1901/2 to 1916/17). *Tour* India to England 1911.
Career batting
39–69–1–1777–102–26.13–2–*ct* 9
Bowling 10–0

On the 1911 tour, he was the only batsman to complete 1,000 runs in all matches, and in first-class matches hit 684, av 24.42.

Mehta, Praful
Cricketer. *b:* 1941, Tanganyika. Left-hand batsman, wicket-keeper. *Team* East Africa (1975). *Tour* East Africa to England 1975.
Career batting
1–2–0–29–17–14.50–0–*ct* 4

Meintjes, Douglas James
Amateur. *b:* 9.6.1890, Pretoria, South Africa. *d:* 17.7.1979, South Africa. Lower order right-hand batsman, right-arm fast medium bowler. *Team* Transvaal (1910/1 to 1925/6). *Tour* South Africa to England 1924. *Tests* South Africa (1922/3, 2 matches).
Career batting
52–78–7–1146–87–16.14–0–*ct* 25
Bowling 2698–91–29.64–1–1–8/63
Test batting
2–3–0–43–21–14.33–0–*ct* 3
Bowling 115–6–19.16–0–0–3/38

He had little success on his single visit to England and was not required for the Tests.

Meldon, Dr George Edward Pugin
Amateur. *b:* 12.9.1875, Dublin, Ireland. *d:* 2.7.1950, Dublin, Ireland. Right-hand batsman. *Team* Dublin University (1895).
Career batting
4–8–2–93–33–15.50–0–*ct* 2

Meldon, Dr George James
Amateur. *b:* 18.1.1885, Dublin, Ireland. *d:* 27.11.1951, Stourbridge, Worcs. Brother of L. A. (Ireland). Right-hand batsman. *Sch* Stonyhurst. *Team* Ireland (1907–12).
Career batting
10–18–0–263–41–14.61–0–*ct* 4

Meldon, John Michael
Amateur. *b:* 29.9.1869, Dublin, Ireland. *d:* 12.12.1954, Tunbridge Wells, Kent. Right-hand batsman, right-arm bowler. *Sch* Beaumont. *Team* Ireland (1902–10).
Career batting
5–10–1–55–14–6.11–0–*ct* 1

Meldon, Louis Albert
Amateur. *b:* 10.10.1886, Dublin, Ireland. *d:* 21.2.1956, Dun Laoghaire, Co Dublin, Ireland. Brother of G. J. (Ireland). Right-hand batsman, right-arm medium pace bowler. *Sch* Stonyhurst. *Team* Ireland (1909–12).
Career batting
4–6–0–151–47–25.16–0–*ct* 3
Bowling 15–1–15.00–0–0–1/4

Meldon, Philip Albert
Amateur. *b:* 18.12.1874, Dublin, Ireland. *d:* 8.4.1942, Marylebone, London. Brother of W. W. (Warwickshire). Lower order batsman, bowler. *Team* MCC (1911).
Career batting
2–3–0–14–7–4.66–0–*ct* 1
Bowling 83–3–27.66–0–0–2/83

He played for Ireland from 1899 to 1905, but not in a first-class match.

A brilliant soccer player, he represented Ireland.

Meldon, William Waltrude
Amateur. *b:* 9.4.1879, Dublin, Ireland. *d:* 23.5.1957, Putney, London. Brother of P. A. (MCC). Middle order right-hand batsman, right-arm fast medium bowler. *Sch* Beaumont College. *Teams* Warwickshire (1909–10, 5 matches); Ireland (1911–14).
Career batting
8–14–1–208–44–16.00–0–*ct* 4
Bowling 338–14–24.14–1–0–5/53

He also appeared for Northumberland and Durham.

Melhuish, Francis
Amateur. *b:* 17.5.1857, Birkenhead, Cheshire. Middle order right-hand batsman. *Sch* Marlborough. *Team* Lancashire (1877, 3 matches).
Career batting
3–6–0–32–13–5.33–0–*ct* 0

Melle, Dr Basil George von Brandis
Amateur. *b:* 31.3.1891, Somerset, Cape Province, South Africa. *d:* 8.1.1966, Johannesburg, South Africa. Father of M.G. (South Africa). Middle order right-hand batsman, right-arm medium, later slow leg break, bowler, good field. *Teams* Western Province (1908/9); Oxford U (1913–14,

blue both years); Hampshire (1914–21, 27 matches); Transvaal (1923/4). *Tour* Incogniti to USA 1913 (not first-class).
Career batting
62–101–9–2535–145–27.55–3–*ct* 33
Bowling 2931–114–25.71–9–1–7/48

His best season as a bowler was 1913 with 55 wickets, av 15.90 – a broken finger the following year deprived his bowling of its bite and he was played more for his batting. He hit 1,021 runs, av 35.20, in 1919.

Melle, Michael George
Amateur. *b:* 3.6.1930, Johannesburg, South Africa. Son of B.G. von B. (Hampshire). Lower order right-hand batsman, right-arm fast bowler. *Teams* Transvaal (1948/9 to 1951/2); Western Province (1953/4). *Tours* South Africa to England 1951, to Australia and New Zealand 1952/3. *Tests* South Africa (1949/50 to 1952/3, 7 matches).
Career batting
52–68–20–544–59–11.33–0–*ct* 22
Bowling 3990–160–24.93–6–2–9/22
Test batting
7–12–4–68–17–8.50–0–*ct* 4
Bowling 851–26–32.73–2–0–6/71

He headed the first-class bowling averages on the 1951 tour (50 wkts, av 20.68), but injury forced him to miss many matches.

Bowling for Transvaal v Griqualand West at Johannesburg in 1950/1 he took 8 for 8. His best bowling was 9/22 for South Africans v Tasmania at Launceston in 1952/3.

Mellin, Eric Lawrence
Amateur. *b:* 27.7.1886, West Wickham, Kent. *d:* 8.9.1968, Maresfield Park, Sussex. Hard hitting opening or middle order batsman, useful bowler. *Sch* Malvern. *Team* Cambridge U (1907).
Career batting
1–1–0–13–13–13.00–0–*ct* 0

Melling, John
Professional. *b:* 6.4.1848, Clayton-le-Moors, Lancashire. *d:* 31.1.1881, Burnley, Lancashire. Right-hand batsman. *Team* Lancashire (1874–76, 3 matches).
Career batting
3–5–0–39–20–7.80–0–*ct* 4
Bowling 16–0

Mellon, Charles William
Amateur. *b:* 9.2.1915, Dublin, Ireland. Right-hand batsman, right-arm medium pace bowler. *Team* Ireland (1937–38).
Career batting
2–4–0–48–30–12.00–0–*ct* 1
Bowling 2–0

Mellor, Alan John
Cricketer. *b:* 4.7.1959, Horninglow, Staffs. Tail end right-hand batsman, slow left-arm bowler. *Team* Derbyshire (1978–80, 13 matches).
Career batting
13–15–6–26–10*–2.88–0–*ct* 4
Bowling 653–17–38.41–1–0–5/52

Mellor, Francis Hamilton
Amateur. *b:* 13.5.1854, Bloomsbury, London. *d:* 27.4.1925, Paris. Stylish middle order right-hand batsman, slow under-arm bowler, good outfield. *Sch* Cheltenham. *Teams* Cambridge U (1874–77, blue 1877); Kent (1877–78, 4 matches).
Career batting
12–22–1–211–46–10.04–0–*ct* 7

Mellor, Horace
Amateur. *b:* 21.2.1851, Paddington, London. *d:* 27.2.1942, Castletown, Isle of Man. Middle order right-hand batsman. *Sch* Cheltenham. *Team* Lancashire (1874–75, 2 matches).
Career batting
2–4–0–28–17–7.00–0–*ct* 0

Mellor, James Philip
Cricketer. *b:* 19.1.1953, Oxford. Middle order right-hand batsman, off break bowler. *Sch* Rydal. *Team* Cambridge U (1973).
Career batting
3–5–0–27–22–5.40–0–*ct* 1

Melluish, Gordon Christopher
Amateur. *b:* 25.8.1906, Walthamstow, Essex. *d:* 14.4.1977, Bushey Heath, Herts. Tail end right-hand batsman, slow left-arm bowler. *Sch* Haberdashers' Aske's. *Team* Essex (1926, 4 matches).
Career batting
4–3–1–18–16*–9.00–0–*ct* 0
Bowling 115–3–38.33–0–0–1/17

Melluish, Michael Edward Lovelace
Amateur. *b:* 13.6.1932, Westcliff on Sea, Essex. Lower order right-hand batsman, wicket-keeper. *Sch* Rossall. *Teams* Cambridge U (1954–56, blue all three years); Middlesex (1957, 1 match).
Career batting
49–67–17–524–36–10.48–0–*ct* 80–*st* 35

His final first-class match was for MCC in 1959.

Melsome, Robert George William
Amateur. *b:* 16.1.1906, Christchurch, Hants. Lower order right-hand batsman, right-arm medium pace bowler. *Sch* Lancing. *Team* Gloucestershire (1925–34, 16 matches).

Career batting
27–42–4–500–60–13.15–0–*ct* 22
Bowling 1098–45–24.40–3–0–8/103

His final first-class match was for the Army in 1938.

Melville, Alan
Amateur. *b:* 19.5.1910, Carnarvon, Cape Province, South Africa. *d:* 18.4.1983, Kruger National Park, Transvaal, South Africa. Fluent stroke making opening right-hand batsman, leg break and googly bowler. *Teams* Natal (1928/9 to 1929/30); Oxford U (1930–33, blue all four years); Sussex (1932–36, 86 matches); Transvaal (1936/7 to 1948/9). *Tour* South Africa to England 1947. *Tests* South Africa 1938/9 to 1948/9, 11 matches).
Career batting
190–295–15–10598–189–37.85–25–*ct* 156
Bowling 3959–132–29.99–7–0–5/17
Test batting
11–19–2–894–189–52.58–4–*ct* 8

He captained Oxford U in 1931 and 1932, Sussex in 1934 and 1935, and South Africa in 10 Tests as well as on the 1947 tour to England.

He hit 1,000 runs in a season three times (best 1,904, av 40.51, in 1935).

Melville, Dr Charles
Amateur. *b:* 9.4.1896, Falkirk, Lanarkshire, Scotland. *d:* 25.3.1954, Dumfries, Scotland. Right-hand batsman, useful bowler. *Team* Scotland (1928–29).
Career batting
3–5–0–50–24–10.00–0–*ct* 0
Bowling 150–3–50.00–0–0–2/72

Melville, Christopher Duncan McLean
Amateur. *b:* 4.10.1935, Pietermaritzburg, South Africa. Middle order right-hand batsman, right-hand medium bowler. *Team* Oxford U (1956–57, blue 1957).
Career batting
12–22–3–758–142–39.89–2–*ct* 10
Bowling 368–6–61.33–0–0–1/19

Melville, Colin McLean
Amateur. *b:* 13.7.1903, South Africa. Middle order right-hand batsman. *Team* Oxford U (1928).
Career batting
1–2–0–29–28–14.50–0–*ct* 1

Melville, James
Amateur. *b:* 15.3.1909, Barrow in Furness, Lancashire. *d:* 2.8.1961, Coventry, Warwickshire. Lower order right-hand batsman, slow left-arm bowler. *Team* Warwickshire (1946, 2 matches).
Career batting
2–3–0–14–13–4.66–0–*ct* 1
Bowling 84–5–16.80–0–0–3/34

He played soccer for Blackburn Rovers, Hull City and Northampton.

Melville, James Edward
Cricketer. *b:* 3.3.1936, Streatham, London. Lower order right-hand batsman, right-arm fast medium bowler. *Team* Kent (1962–63, 6 matches).
Career batting
6–8–4–20–6–5.00–0–*ct* 4
Bowling 422–14–30.14–0–0–4/78

Melville, John Hutchison
Amateur. *b:* 19.6.1895, Cowdenbeath, Fife, Scotland. *d:* 22.9.1951, Aylesbury, Bucks. Right-hand batsman, slow left-arm bowler. *Team* Scotland (1932–37).
Career batting
6–11–3–32–9*–2.62–0–*ct* 4
Bowling 559–33–16.93–3–0–6/32

He played for Buckinghamshire.

Mence, Michael David
Cricketer. *b:* 13.4.1944, Newbury, Berkshire. Middle order left-hand batsman, right-arm medium pace bowler. *Sch* Bradfield. *Teams* Warwickshire (1962–65, 31 matches); Gloucestershire (1966–67, 22 matches). *Tours* MCC to West Africa 1975/6, to Bangladesh 1976/7 (neither first-class).
Career batting
54–78–15–949–78–15.06–0–*ct* 23
Bowling 3050–86–35.46–2–0–5/26

He played for Berkshire in 1961 and again after retiring from first-class cricket.

Mendis, Gehan Dixon
Cricketer. *b:* 20.4.1955, Colombo, Ceylon. Opening right-hand batsman, occasional wicket-keeper. *Team* Sussex (1974–83, 153 matches). *Tours* International XI to Pakistan 1981/2, to Jamaica 1982/3.
Career batting
158–284–25–8724–204–33.68–14–*ct* 74–*st* 1
Bowling 11–0

He hit 1,000 runs in a season four times (best 1,624, av 40.60, in 1983). His highest score is 204 for Sussex v Northants at Eastbourne in 1980.

Mendis, Louis Rohan Duleep
Cricketer. *b:* 25.8.1952, Moratuwa, Ceylon. Middle order right-hand batsman, right-arm medium pace bowler, occasional wicket-keeper.

Team Sri Lanka (1971/2 to 1982/3). *Tours* Sri Lanka to India 1972/3, 1974/5, 1975/6, 1976/7, 1982/3, to Pakistan 1973/4, 1981/2, to England 1975, 1979, 1981, to Australia and New Zealand 1982/3, to Zimbabwe 1982/3. *Tests* Sri Lanka (1981/2 to 1982/3, 6 matches).
Career batting
72–122–11–4056–194–36.54–8–*ct* 35–*st* 1
Bowling 30–1–30.00–0–0–1/4
Test batting
6–12–0–450–105–37.50–2–*ct* 4
He captained Sri Lanka in two Test matches.

Mendl, Derek Francis
Amateur. *b:* 1.8.1914, Hurlingham, Argentine. Brother of J.F. (Scotland and MCC). Middle order right-hand batsman, wicket-keeper. *Sch* Repton. *Teams* Free Foresters (1951); MCC (1951).
Career batting
2–4–0–59–26–14.75–0–*ct* 2

Mendl, Jack Francis
Amateur. *b:* 6.12.1911, Hurlingham, Argentine. Brother of D.F. (MCC). Opening right-hand batsman. *Sch* Repton. *Teams* Minor Counties (1949); Scotland (1953–55); MCC (1957).
Career batting
7–13–2–269–65–24.45–0–*ct* 0

Menzies, Dr Henry
Amateur. *b:* 28.3.1867, Lambeth, Surrey. *d:* 7.3.1936, Farnborough, Hants. Lower order right-hand batsman, wicket-keeper. *Sch* St Pauls. *Team* Middlesex (1891–93, 5 matches).
Career batting
5–7–3–47–18*–11.75–0–*ct* 6–*st* 2

Mercer, Charles Frederick
Amateur. *b:* 1896, Hackney, Middlesex. *d:* 1965, Brentwood, Essex. Middle order left-hand batsman. *Team* Essex (1929, 2 matches).
Career batting
2–4–0–26–8–6.50–0–*ct* 0

Mercer, Ian Pickford
Cricketer. *b:* 30.5.1930, Oldham, Lancashire. Middle order right-hand batsman, right-arm medium pace bowler. *Team* Minor Counties (1965).
Career batting
1–2–0–1–1–0.50–0–*ct* 1
His County cricket was for Norfolk.

Mercer, John
Professional. *b:* 22.4.1895, Southwick, Sussex. Lower order right-hand batsman, right-arm fast medium bowler. *Teams* Sussex (1919–21, 12 matches); Glamorgan (1922–39, 412 matches); Wales (1923–30); Northants (1947, 1 match). *Tours* MCC to India, Burma and Ceylon 1926/7; Cahn to Jamaica 1928/9.
Career batting
457–628–112–6076–72–11.77–0–*ct* 144
Bowling 37210–1591–23.38–104–17–10/51
He took 100 wickets in a season nine times (best 145, av 20.88, in 1929); his best bowling in an innings was 10 for 51 for Glamorgan v Worcestershire at Worcester in 1936.
He was appointed Northants County coach in 1947 and became County scorer.

Mercer, William Norman
Amateur. *b:* 30.5.1922, Prescot, Lancashire. Right-hand batsman, leg break and googly bowler. *Teams* Sussex (1948–56, 2 matches); South African Air Force (1942/3).
Career batting
3–4–1–40–24–13.33–0–*ct* 2
Bowling 103–6–17.16–0–0–3/31

Merchant, Vijaysingh Madhavji
Amateur. *b:* 12.10.1911, Bombay, India. Brother of U.M. (Bombay). Stylish opening right-hand batsman, right-arm medium pace bowler. *Teams* Hindus (1929/30 to 1945/6); Bombay (1933/4 to 1950/1. *Tours* Indian University Occasionals to Ceylon 1935/6; India to England 1936, 1946, to Ceylon 1944/5. *Tests* India (1933/4 to 1951/2, 10 matches).
Career batting
148–232–45–13340–359*–71.33–44–*ct* 115
Bowling 2088–65–32.12–1–0–5/73
Test batting
10–18–0–859–154–47.72–3–*ct* 7
Bowling 40–0
He was the most accomplished batsman of the 1936 tour, heading the averages with 1,745 runs, av 51.32. In 1946 he was even more successful with 2,385 runs, av 74.53. His highest innings was 359* for Bombay v Maharastra at Bombay in 1943/4 and of his other 10 scores over 200, two were made in England, the highest being 242* v Lancashire at Old Trafford in 1946. He also hit 1,000 runs in a season in India. In the 1951/2 series of Tests in India, a shoulder injury ended his career.
After retiring he became well-known as an administrator of cricket in India.

Meredith, Henry Chase
Amateur. *b:* 8.10.1881, Richmond, Surrey. *d:* 21.9.1957, Ludlow, Shropshire. Lower order

batsman, useful bowler. *Sch* Eton. *Team* H.K. Foster's XI (1919).
Career batting
2–3–0–35–34–11.66–0–*ct* 2
Bowling 28–0
His County cricket was for Shropshire.

Mermagen, Patrick Hassell Frederick
Amateur. *b:* 8.5.1911, Colyton, Devon. Middle order right-hand batsman, right-arm fast medium bowler. *Sch* Sherborne. *Team* Somerset (1930, 8 matches).
Career batting
8–10–0–114–35–11.40–0–*ct* 4
Bowling 26–0

Merrall, John Edwin
Amateur. *b:* 7.1.1909, Shipley, Yorkshire. Lower order right-hand batsman, right-arm fast medium bowler. *Team* Surrey (1932–33, 2 matches).
Career batting
3–2–0–10–5–5.00–0–*ct* 3
Bowling 202–6–33.66–0–0–3/24
His final first-class match was for Minor Counties in 1934.

Merrick, Horace
Amateur. *b:* 21.12.1887, Clifton, Gloucs. *d:* 16.8.1961, Clifton, Gloucs. Middle order right-hand batsman. *Team* Gloucestershire (1909–11, 12 matches).
Career batting
12–23–5–257–58–14.27–0–*ct* 4

Merritt, William Edward
Professional. *b:* 18.8.1908, Sumner, Christchurch, New Zealand. *d:* 9.6.1977, Christchurch, New Zealand. Lower order right-hand batsman, leg break and googly bowler. *Teams* Canterbury (1926/7 to 1935/6); Northants (1938–46, 41 matches). *Tours* New Zealand to England 1927, 1931, to Australia 1927/8. *Tests* New Zealand (1929/30 to 1931, 6 matches).
Career batting
125–191–33–3147–87–19.91–0–*ct* 58
Bowling 13669–536–25.50–37–8–8/41
Test batting
6–8–1–73–19–10.42–0–*ct* 2
Bowling 617–12–51.41–0–0–4/104
On the 1927 tour to England he was the most successful bowler taking 107 wickets, av 23.64, and in 1931 he took 99 wickets, av 26.48. He played in the Lancashire League as a professional and qualified for Northants in 1939.

Merry, Cyril Arthur
Amateur. *b:* 20.1.1911, Scarborough, Tobago, West Indies. *d:* 19.4.1964, St Clair, Port of Spain, Trinidad. Brother of David (Trinidad). Middle order right-hand batsman, useful bowler. *Team* Trinidad (1929/30 to 1938/9). *Tour* West Indies to England 1933. *Tests* West Indies (1933, 2 matches).
Career batting
37–64–7–1547–146–27.14–1–*ct* 33
Bowling 746–33–22.60–0–0–3/13
Test batting
2–4–0–34–13–8.50–0–*ct* 1
Although playing in two Tests on the 1933 tour, he only achieved modest results on the visit – 856 runs, av 28.53; 13 wickets, av 32.30.

Merry, William Gerald
Cricketer. *b:* 8.8.1955, Newbury, Berkshire. Lower order right-hand batsman, right-arm medium pace bowler. *Team* Middlesex (1979–82, 26 matches). *Tours* MCC to Bangladesh 1978/9, to East Africa 1981/2, to North America 1982 (none first-class); Robins to New Zealand 1979/80; Middlesex to Zimbabwe 1980/1.
Career batting
27–11–42–14*–7.00–0–*ct* 6
Bowling 1554–49–31.71–0–0–4/24
He played for Hertfordshire 1976 to 1978.

Merson, Ronald David
Amateur. *b:* 25.7.1925, Stockton-on-Tees, Co Durham. Right-hand batsman. *Sch* Merchiston. *Team* Scotland (1947).
Career batting
1–2–0–16–15–8.00–0–*ct* 0

Meston, Alexander Hubert
Professional. *b:* 1.6.1898, Leytonstone, Essex. *d:* 1980, Camborne, Cornwall. Brother of S.P. (Essex and Gloucs). Lower order right-hand batsman. *Team* Essex (1926–27, 12 matches).
Career batting
12–17–4–143–41–11.00–0–*ct* 9
Bowling 352–4–88.00–0–0–2/18

Meston, Samuel Paul
Amateur. *b:* 19.11.1882, Loughton, Essex. *d:* 9.1.1960, Vancouver, Canada. Brother of A.H. (Essex). Middle order right-hand batsman, right-hand medium bowler. *Teams* Gloucestershire (1906, 3 matches); Essex (1907–08, 17 matches).
Career batting
20–35–2–516–130–15.63–1–*ct* 11
Bowling 65–1–65.00–0–0–1/10

Metcalfe, Ashley Anthony
Cricketer. *b:* 25.12.1963, Horsforth, Yorkshire. Right-hand batsman, off break bowler. *Team* Yorkshire (1983, 1 match).

Career batting
1–2–0–129–122–64.50–1–*ct* 1
Bowling 6–0
He hit 122 on his debut for Yorkshire v Notts at Bradford in 1983.

Metcalfe, Stanley Gordon
Amateur. *b:* 20.6.1932, Horsforth, Yorkshire. Middle order right-hand batsman, good deep field. *Sch* Leeds Grammar School. *Team* Oxford U (1954–56, blue 1956).
Career batting
27–50–3–1200–153*–25.53–2–*ct* 11
Bowling 352–9–39.11–0–0–2/32
He appeared regularly for Free Foresters, his final first-class match being for that side in 1968.

Metcalfe, Vivian Alderson
Amateur. *b:* 1906, Saltburn, Yorkshire. *d:* 28.12.1967, Addlestone, Surrey. Middle order right-hand batsman. *Teams* Wales (1928); Ireland (1936).
Career batting
4–8–0–81–36–10.12–0–*ct* 0

Metson, Colin Peter
Cricketer. *b:* 2.7.1963, Cuffley, Hertfordshire. Right-hand batsman, wicket-keeper. *Team* Middlesex (1981, 1 match).
Career batting
1–1–1–38–38*–no av–0–*ct* 1

Meunier, James Brown
Professional. *b:* 1885. *d:* 30.9.1957, Loughborough, Leics. Lower order batsman, right-arm fast bowler. *Team* Warwickshire (1920, 2 matches).
Career batting
2–3–0–12–9–4.00–0–*ct* 1
Bowling 38–0
He also played for Lincolnshire.
A good soccer player, he appeared for Everton and Lincoln City.

Meyer, Barrie John
Professional. *b:* 21.8.1932, Bournemouth, Hants. Lower order right-hand batsman, leg break bowler, wicket-keeper. *Team* Gloucestershire (1957–71, 406 matches). *Tour* Gloucestershire to Bermuda, 1962 (not first-class).
Career batting
406–569–191–5367–63–14.19–0–*ct* 709–*st* 118
Bowling 28–0
He was appointed a first-class umpire in 1973 and has umpired in Test Matches since 1978. A noted soccer player, he appeared as inside left for Bristol Rovers, Plymouth Argyle, Newport County and Bristol City.

Meyer, Rollo John Oliver
Amateur. *b:* 15.3.1905, Clophill, Bedfordshire. Attacking middle order right-hand batsman, right-arm slow medium bowler. *Sch* Haileybury. *Teams* Cambridge U (1924–26, blue all three years); Western India (1930/1 to 1934/5); Bombay (1926/7); Somerset (1936–49, 65 matches); Europeans (1926/7 to 1934/5).
Career batting
127–210–15–4621–202*–23.69–2–*ct* 85
Bowling 10328–408–25.39–25–3–9/160
His final first-class match was for MCC in 1950.
His only double century was 202* for Somerset v Lancashire at Taunton in 1936 and his best bowling was 9/160 for Europeans v Muslims at Bombay in 1927/8.
He captained Somerset in 1947.

Meyer, William Eustace
Amateur. *b:* 12.1.1883, Redland, Bristol. *d:* 1.10.1953, Falmouth, Cornwall. Middle order right-hand batsman, right-arm fast medium bowler. *Team* Gloucestershire (1909–10, 9 matches).
Career batting
9–16–0–136–43–8.50–0–*ct* 5

Meyrick-Jones, Frederic Meyrick
(changed name from Jones in 1893)
Amateur. *b:* 14.1.1867, Blackheath, Kent. *d:* 25.10.1950, Shaftesbury, Dorset. Hard hitting middle order right-hand batsman, slow right-arm bowler, good deep field or wicket-keeper. *Sch* Marlborough. *Team* Cambridge U (1887–88, blue 1888); Kent (1893–96, 6 matches).
Career batting
18–32–5–512–67–18.96–0–*ct* 9–*st* 2
Bowling 87–2–43.50–0–0–1/3
He also appeared for Hampshire (not first-class) and Norfolk.

Michell, Charles
Amateur. *b:* 17.2.1849, York. *d:* 25.1.1900, Forcett, Yorkshire. Brother of E.J. (Hampshire). Lower order right-hand batsman, wicket-keeper. *Sch* Haileybury. *Team* MCC (1875).
Career batting
1–1–0–1–1–1.00–0–*ct* 1
He was 'The first boy to enter Haileybury School'.

Michell, Edward John
Amateur. *b:* 15.6.1853, Steyning, Sussex. *d:* 5.5.1900, New Zealand. Brother of Charles (MCC). Middle order right-hand batsman. *Sch*

Harrow and Haileybury. *Team* Hampshire (1880, 1 match).
Career batting
1–1–0–7–7–7.00–0–*ct* 1

Micklem, Leonard
Amateur. *b:* 12.3.1845, Henley-on-Thames, Oxfordshire. *d:* 7.7.1919, Elstree, Hertfordshire. Middle order right-hand batsman, excellent deep field. *Sch* Eton. *Team* MCC (1869).
Career batting
1–1–0–9–9–9.00–0–*ct* 0

He did not appear in first-class matches whilst at Oxford. His County cricket was for Berkshire.

Micklethwait, William Henry
Amateur. *b:* 12.11.1885, Rotherham, Yorkshire. *d:* 7.10.1947, Rotherham, Yorkshire. Middle order batsman. *Team* Yorkshire (1911, 1 match).
Career batting
1–1–0–44–44–44.00–0–*ct* 0

Middlebrook, Willie
Professional. *b:* 23.5.1858, Morley, Yorkshire. *d:* 26.4.1919, Dewsbury, Yorkshire. Lower order right-hand batsman, right-arm fast bowler. *Team* Yorkshire (1888–89, 17 matches).
Career batting
19–29–7–96–19*–4.36–0–*ct* 20
Bowling 1071–54–19.83–1–0–5/59

His final first-class match was for L. Hall's XI in 1891.

Middlemost, Livingston
Amateur. *b:* 1839, South Shields, Co Durham. *d:* 28.10.1897, Sedgefield, Huddersfield, Yorkshire. Middle order batsman. *Teams* North (1860); Players of the North (1877).
Career batting
2–3–0–21–17–7.00–0–*ct* 1

Although an amateur, he appeared for the Players in 1877.

Middleton, Cecil
Amateur. *b:* 26.5.1911, Leeds, Yorkshire. Middle order right-hand batsman, right-arm medium pace bowler. *Sch* Charterhouse. *Team* Oxford U (1933).
Career batting
4–6–0–128–44–21.33–0–*ct* 1
Bowling 201–4–50.25–0–0–3/60

Middleton, Charles
Professional. *b:* 21.12.1869, Leeds, Yorkshire. *d:* 5.2.1938, Chesterfield, Derbyshire. Middle order right-hand batsman, leg break bowler. *Team* Derbyshire (1896–1903, 4 matches).
Career batting
4–8–1–47–21–6.71–0–*ct* 0
Bowling 21-0

Middleton, James
Professional. *b:* 30.9.1865, Chester-le-Street, Co Durham. *d:* 28.12.1913, Newlands, Cape Town, South Africa. Attacking lower order batsman, slow medium left-arm bowler. *Team* Western Province (1890/1 to 1903/4). *Tours* South Africa to England 1894 (not first-class) and 1904. *Tests* South Africa (1895/6 to 1902/03, 6 matches).
Career batting
31–50–21–176–32–6.06–0–*ct* 14
Bowling 2523–140–18.02–10–4–7/64
Test batting
6–12–5–52–22–7.42–0–*ct* 1
Bowling 442–24–18.41–2–0–5/51

He took 83 wickets, av 15.79, in the non first-class tour of 1894, but was not very effective in 1904.

He was bought out of the Army by Cape Town CC in order to become their professional.

Middleton, John William
Professional. *b:* 26.10.1890, Stoney Stanton, Leics. *d:* 16.9.1966, Stoney Stanton, Leics. Opening right-hand batsman. *Team* Leicestershire (1914–21, 14 matches).
Career batting
24–45–0–478–37–10.62–0–*ct* 7
Bowling 60–0

Middleton, Samuel Henry Windrush
Amateur. *b:* 27.9.1901, Greystones, Co Wicklow, Ireland. *d:* 6.1.1949, Dublin, Ireland. Right-hand batsman, off break bowler. *Team* Dublin University (1922).
Career batting
1–2–1–0–0*–0.00–0–*ct* 0
Bowling 22–0

Middleton, William George
Amateur. *b:* 16.4.1846. *d:* 9.4.1892, Kineton, Warwickshire. His neck was broken in a fall during a point-to-point race. Middle order batsman, useful bowler. *Team* MCC (1870–78).
Career batting
12–20–1–123–22–6.47–0–*ct* 3
Bowling 92–3–30.66–0–0–2/39

His final first-class match was for I Zingari in 1882.

He played County cricket for Cheshire.

Midgley, Charles Augustus
Amateur. *b:* 11.11.1877, Wetherby, Yorkshire.

d: 24.6.1942, Bradford, Yorkshire. Lower order right-hand batsman, right-arm fast bowler. *Team* Yorkshire (1906, 4 matches).
Career batting
4–6–2–115–59*–28.75–0–*ct* 3
Bowling 149–8–18.62–0–0–2/13

Midwinter, William (Evans)
Professional. *b:* 19.6.1851, St Briavels, Gloucs. *d:* 3.12.1890, Kew, Melbourne, Australia. In June 1890 he became insane and was confined to Kera Asylum, the loss of his wife and two children having unhinged his mind. Excellent middle order right-hand batsman, right-hand medium pace round-arm bowler, good deep field. *Teams* Victoria (1874/5 to 1886/7, 13 matches); Gloucestershire (1877–82, 58 matches). *Tours* Australia to England 1878, 1884; Lillywhite, Shaw and Shrewsbury to Australia 1881/2. *Tests* Australia (1876/7 to 1886/7, 8 matches); England (1881/2, 4 matches).
Career batting
160–264–27–4534–137*–19.13–3–*ct* 122
Bowling 7298–419–17.41–27–3–7/27
Test batting
12–21–1–269–37–13.45–0–*ct* 10
Bowling 605–24–25.20–1–0–5/78
Halfway through the 1878 tour of England, he was persuaded by W.G. Grace to leave the touring party and appear for Gloucestershire for whom he had played the season before.
He is the only cricketer to represent England in Australia and Australia in England.

Mignon, Edward
Professional. *b:* 1.11.1885, Kilburn, Middlesex. *d:* 14.5.1925, Southwark, South London. He died of pneumonia. Lower order right-hand batsman, right-arm fast bowler with ungainly action. *Team* Middlesex (1905–13, 140 matches).
Career batting
149–200–78–1080–34–8.85–0–*ct* 83
Bowling 11471–439–26.12–27–8–7/28
His final first-class match was for MCC in 1914.

Milbank, Sir Mark Vane
Amateur. *b:* 11.1.1907, Kington, Herefordshire. *d:* 4.4.1984, Barningham, Richmond, Yorkshire. Lower order right-hand batsman, medium slow left-arm bowler. *Sch* Eton. *Team* Army (1930).
Career batting
1–1–0–1–1–1.00–0–*ct* 1
Bowling 40–1–40.00–0–0–1/8

Milburn, Barry Douglas
Cricketer. *b:* 24.11.1943, Dunedin, New Zealand. Lower order right-hand batsman, wicket-keeper. *Team* Otago (1963/4 to 1982/3). *Tours* New Zealand to England 1969, to India and Pakistan 1969/70. *Tests* New Zealand (1968/9, 3 matches).
Career batting
75–97–33–737–103–11.51–1–*ct* 176–*st* 19
Test batting
3–3–2–8–4*–8.00–0–*ct* 6–*st* 2
The reserve wicket-keeper on the 1969 tour of England, he appeared in only eight matches.

Milburn, Colin
Professional. *b:* 23.10.1941, Burnopfield, Co Durham. Attacking opening right-hand batsman, right-arm medium pace bowler. *Teams* Northants (1960–74, 196 matches); Western Australia (1966/7 to 1968/9, 17 matches). *Tours* MCC to East Africa 1963/4, to West Indies 1967/8, to Pakistan 1968/9. *Tests* England (1966 to 1968/9, 9 matches).
Career batting
255–435–34–13262–243–33.07–23–*ct* 224
Bowling 3171–99–32.03–1–0–6/59
Test batting
9–16–2–654–139–46.71–2–*ct* 7
He hit 1,000 runs in a season six times (best 1,861, av 48.97, in 1966). His highest innings was 243 for Western Australia v Queensland at Brisbane in 1968/9 and his only other double century was for Northants.
He tragically lost an eye in a road accident on 23 May 1969 and this more or less ended his career in first-class cricket, although he reappeared for Northants in 1973–74.
He played for Durham before joining Northants.

Mildmay, Sir Henry Paulet St John
Amateur. *b:* 28.4.1853, London. *d:* 24.4.1916, Dogmersfield, Hants. Middle order right-hand batsman, useful bowler. *Sch* Eton. *Team* Hampshire (1881–84, 7 matches).
Career batting
7–13–1–137–26–11.41–0–*ct* 4
Bowling 51–1–51.00–0–0–1/26

Miles, Audley Charles
Amateur. *b:* 6.9.1855, Clifton, Bristol. *d:* 6.9.1919, Polmaise, Stirling, Scotland. Brother of C.N. (MCC). Middle order right-hand batsman, good field. *Sch* Eton. *Team* MCC (1876).
Career batting
1–1–0–0–0–0.00–0–*ct* 0
He did not appear in any first-class matches whilst at Oxford.

Miles, Charles Napier
Amateur. *b:* 9.4.1854, Clifton, Bristol. *d:*

25.5.1918, Malmesbury, Wilts. Brother of A.C. (MCC). Middle order right-hand batsman. *Sch* Eton. *Team* MCC (1874).
Career batting
1–1–0–8–8–8.00–0–*ct* 0
He was a well-known figure in military cricket.

Miles, Harold Philip
Amateur. *b:* 31.1.1899, Rosario, Argentine. *d:* 21.7.1957, Barnstaple, Devon. Middle order right-hand batsman, off break bowler. *Sch* Shrewsbury. *Teams* Army (1920–31); Minor Counties (1928); Free Foresters (1930–36); Europeans (1937/8). *Tour* MCC to South America 1926/7.
Career batting
23–32–4–613–107–21.89–1–*ct* 8
Bowling 1180–38–31.05–2–0–5/74
His County cricket was for Devon.

Miles, Othneil
Cricketer. *b:* 23.9.1939, Jamaica. *d:* February 1982, Kingston, Jamaica. Lower order right-hand batsman, off break bowler. *Team* Jamaica (1967/8 to 1975/6). *Tour* Jamaica to England 1970.
Career batting
21–22–6–214–43*–13.37–0–*ct* 15
Bowling 1588–58–27.37–2–0–7/71

Miles, Philip William Herbert
Amateur. *b:* 7.1.1848, Bingham, Notts. *d:* 4.12.1933, Bude, Cornwall. Brother of R.F. (Gloucs). Middle order right-hand batsman, right-hand fast round-arm bowler, slip field. *Sch* Marlborough. *Team* Nottinghamshire (1868–77, 3 matches).
Career batting
3–6–0–65–23–10.83–0–*ct* 0
Bowling 16–1–16.00–0–0–1/11

Miles, Robert Fenton
Amateur. *b:* 24.1.1846, Bingham, Nottinghamshire. *d:* 26.2.1930, Cifton, Bristol. Brother of P.W.H. (Notts). Tail end right-hand batsman, slow left-arm bowler. *Sch* Marlborough. *Teams* Gloucestershire (1870–79, 59 matches); Oxford U (1867–69, blue all three years).
Career batting
69–96–23–577–79–7.90–0–*ct* 28
Bowling 3335–216–15.43–15–2–7/38

Millard, David Edward Shaxson
Cricketer. *b:* 3.4.1931, South Africa. *d:* 30.1.1978, Cape Town, South Africa. Middle order right-hand batsman, right-arm bowler. *Teams* Western Province (1951/2 to 1954/5); Eastern Province (1952/3 to 1953/4); Oxford U (1965).
Career batting
14–26–2–497–73–20.70–0–*ct* 4
Bowling 448–15–29.86–1–0–6/68

Millard, William Henry
Professional. *b:* 25.5.1856, New Swindon, Wiltshire. *d:* 20.7.1923, Tenby, Pembrokeshire. Middle order right-hand batsman, bowler, good deep field. *Team* Sussex (1879–80, 5 matches).
Career batting
5–8–0–54–26–6.75–0–*ct* 3
Bowling 44–2–22.00–0–0–2/32
He also appeared for Wiltshire. He played under a handicap, having only one eye.

Millener, David John
Cricketer. *b:* 2.5.1944, Auckland, New Zealand. Tail end right-hand batsman, right-arm medium fast bowler. *Team* Auckland (1964/5 to 1967/8); Oxford U (1969–70, blue both years).
Career batting
26–30–12–176–24–9.77–0–*ct* 9
Bowling 1958–57–34.35–0–0–4/97

Miller, Andrew John Trevor
Cricketer. *b:* 30.5.1963, Chesham, Buckinghamshire. Opening left-hand batsman. *Sch* Haileybury. *Teams* Oxford U (1982–83, blue 1983); Middlesex (1983, 6 matches).
Career batting
16–28–3–1022–127*–40.88–1–*ct* 1
He hit 1,002 runs, av 43.56, in 1983.

Miller, Audley Montague
Amateur. *b:* 19.10.1869, Westbury-on-Trym, Gloucs. *d:* 26.6.1959, Clifton, Bristol. Middle order right-hand batsman, right-arm medium fast bowler. *Sch* Eton. *Team* MCC (1896–1903). *Tour* Hawke to South Africa 1895/6. *Test* England (1895/6, 1 match).
Career batting
5–9–2–105–36–15.00–0–*ct* 0
Bowling 49–1–49.00–0–0–1/1
Test batting
1–2–2–24–20*–no av–0–*ct* 0
His County cricket was for Wiltshire, which side he captained for 25 years, also being Hon Secretary.
His first-class debut was for England v South Africa in 1895/6.

Miller, E.
Professional. Lower order left-hand batsman, left-arm fast bowler. *Team* Sussex (1878, 1 match).
Career batting
1–2–0–2–1–1.00–0–*ct* 0
Bowling 7–0

Miller, Frank Joseph
Amateur. *b:* 2.10.1916, Cork, Ireland. Lower order right-hand batsman, wicket-keeper. *Team* Ireland (1949–54).
Career batting
7–11–6–44–18*–8.80–0–*ct* 8–*st* 7

Miller, F. N.
Amateur. Opening batsman. *Teams* Lancashire (1904, 1 match); Natal (1909/10).
Career batting
2–4–0–64–37–16.00–0–*ct* 2

Miller, Frederick Peel
Amateur. *b:* 29.7.1828, Clapham, Surrey. *d:* 22.11.1875, Chilworthy, Somerset. Brother of W.H. (Surrey Club). Attacking right-hand opening batsman, right-hand medium pace round-arm, also slow under-arm, bowler, good deep field. *Team* Surrey (1851–67, 80 matches).
Career batting
137–235–20–3117–133–14.49–2–*ct* 86
Bowling 4865–237+19–20.52–6–0–6/36

He captained Surrey from 1851 to 1857 and his final first-class match was for Gentlemen of the South in 1868. He also played for Bedfordshire and Herefordshire.

He was responsible for the retailing of Volumes 3 and 4 of *Scores and Biographies* and when sales were poor, he burnt all the copies still in stock.

Miller, Frank Samuel
Amateur. *b:* 26.6.1851, Ayr, Scotland. *d:* 1930, Chelmsford, Essex. Brother of W.H. (MCC). Middle order right-hand batsman. *Team* MCC (1877).
Career batting
2–3–0–12–8–4.00–0–*ct* 2

Miller, Geoffrey
Cricketer. *b:* 8.9.1952, Chesterfield, Derbyshire. Middle order right-hand batsman, off break bowler. *Team* Derbyshire (1973–83, 179 matches). *Tours* England to India, Sri Lanka and Australia 1976/7, to Pakistan and New Zealand 1977/8, to Australia 1978/9, 1979/80, to West Indies 1980/1, to Australia and New Zealand (New Zealand not first-class) 1982/3. *Tests* England (1976 to 1982/3, 32 matches).
Career batting
250–372–61–8496–98*–27.31–0–*ct* 172
Bowling 15536–606–25.63–27–6–8/70
Test batting
32–47–4–1171–98*–27.23–0–*ct* 15
Bowling 1717–59–29.10–1–0–5.44

He captained Derbyshire 1979 to 1981.

His best season was 1977 with 87 wickets, av 17.82.

Miller, George
Amateur. *b:* 19.8.1929, Edinburgh, Scotland. Left-hand batsman, right-arm fast medium bowler. *Team* Scotland (1955).
Career batting
1–2–1–8–6*–8.00–0–*ct* 0
Bowling 50–0

Miller, Henry
Amateur. *b:* 18.9.1859, Liverpool, Lancashire. *d:* 11.4.1927, Walton-on-Thames, Surrey. Lower order right-hand batsman, right-arm fast bowler. *Sch* Uppingham. *Team* Lancashire (1880–81, 5 matches).
Career batting
5–8–0–84–27–10.50–0–*ct* 1
Bowling 202–10–20.20–1–0–5/46

Miller, Hamish David Sneddon
Cricketer. *b:* 20.4.1943, Blackpool, Lancashire. Lower order right-hand batsman, right-arm medium fast bowler. *Teams* Western Province (1962/3); Glamorgan (1963–66, 27 matches); Orange Free State (1969/70 to 1970/1).
Career batting
38–58–7–589–81–11.54–0–*ct* 23
Bowling 2200–76–28.94–1–0–7/48

He was also a useful rugby full back.

Miller, Harry Rayment
Amateur. *b:* 22.2.1907, Gravesend, Kent. Lower order batsman, right-arm medium pace bowler. *Team* Warwickshire (1928, 1 match).
Career batting
1–1–0–8–8–8.00–0–*ct* 1
Bowling 38–1–38.00–0–0–1/15

Miller, Keith Ross
Amateur. *b:* 28.11.1919, Sunshine, Victoria, Australia. Attacking middle order right-hand batsman, right-arm fast bowler. *Teams* Victoria (1937/8 to 1946/7, 18 matches); New South Wales (1947/8 to 1955/6, 50 matches); Nottinghamshire (1959, 1 match). *Tours* Australia to England 1948, 1953, 1956, to South Africa 1949/50, to West Indies 1954/5, to New Zealand 1945/6, to Pakistan 1956/7; Australian Services to England, India and Ceylon 1945. *Tests* Australia (1945/6 to 1956/7, 55 matches).
Career batting
226–326–36–14183–281*–48.90–41–*ct* 136
Bowling 11087–497–22.30–16–1–7/12
Test batting
55–87–7–2958–147–36.97–7–*ct* 38
Bowling 3906–170–22.97–7–1–7/60

A brilliant all-rounder of the immediate post-war period, he hit 1,000 runs on the 1948 and 1953 tours to England (best 1,433, av 51.17, in

1953). He also hit 1,000 runs in an Australian season twice. In 1956 he topped the bowling averages for the tour with 50 wickets, av 19.60. Four of his double centuries were scored in England, included the highest : 281* v Leics at Leicester in 1956. He hit a century on his single appearance for Notts in 1959.

After retiring from first-class cricket he became a well-known journalist.

Miller, Lawrence Somerville Martin
Amateur. *b:* 31.3.1923, New Plymouth, New Zealand. Hard hitting opening left-hand batsman. *Teams* Central Districts (1950/1 to 1952/3); Wellington (1954/5 to 1959/60). *Tours* New Zealand to South Africa and Australia 1953/4, to England 1958. *Tests* New Zealand (1952/3 to 1958).
Career batting
82–142–15–4777–144–37.61–5–*ct* 33
Bowling 75–3–25.00–0–0–1/7
Test batting
13–25–0–346–47–13.84–0–*ct* 1
Bowling 1–0

On his tour to England he hit 1,148 runs, av 30.21, playing in four Tests.

Miller, Martin Ellis
Cricketer. *b:* 15.12.1940, Lytham, Lancashire. Lower order batsman, slow left-arm bowler. *Team* Cambridge U (1963, blue).
Career batting
12–15–5–48–21*–4.80–0–*ct* 4
Bowling 770–33–23.33–2–0–6/89

Miller, Neville
Amateur. *b:* 27.8.1874, Shanghai, China. *d:* 3.3.1967, Tooting Bec, South London. Opening right-hand batsman, useful bowler. *Sch* Dulwich. *Team* Surrey (1899–1903, 9 matches).
Career batting
9–12–1–346–124–31.45–1–*ct* 1
Bowling 114–1–114.00–0–0–1/28

He scored 124 on his debut for Surrey v Sussex in 1899.

He was for many years a notable figure in London Club cricket and played for Streatham for 42 years.

Miller, Roger
Amateur. *b:* April 1857, Reading, Berkshire. *d:* 1912, Mutford, Suffolk. Middle order right-hand batsman, right-arm medium pace bowler. *Sch* Somerset College and Uppingham. *Team* Cambridge U (1881).
Career batting
7–12–1–261–73–23.72–0–*ct* 2
Bowling 24–0

His final first-class match was for MCC in 1884.

Miller, Roland
Professional. *b:* 6.1.1941, Houghton-le-Spring, Co Durham. Lower order right-hand batsman, slow left-arm bowler. *Team* Warwickshire (1961–68, 133 matches).
Career batting
133–166–34–1658–72–12.55–0–*ct* 144
Bowling 7289–241–30.24–6–0–6/28

He also appeared for Durham.

Miller, Robert Alexander Tamplin
Amateur. *b:* 12.11.1895, Lockwood, Travancore, India. *d:* 10.7.1941, North Africa. Lower order right-hand batsman, wicket-keeper. *Sch* Uppingham. *Team* Sussex (1919, 12 matches).
Career batting
12–22–2–191–39–9.55–0–*ct* 10–*st* 10

Miller, Roger Simon
Amateur. *b:* 16.2.1938, Hailsham, Sussex. Tail end left-hand batsman, left-arm bowler. *Sch* Harrow. *Team* MCC (1959).
Career batting
1–2–2–1–1*–no av–0–*ct* 1
Bowling 91–5–18.20–0–0–3/41

Miller, Thomas
Amateur. *b:* 8.3.1883, St Vicente, Cape Verde Islands. *d:* 20.10.1962, Goring, Oxfordshire. Lower order right-hand batsman, right-arm fast bowler. *Sch* Clifton. *Team* Gloucestershire (1902–14, 18 matches).
Career batting
18–32–1–406–35–13.09–0–*ct* 8
Bowling 253–4–63.25–0–0–2/5

Miller, William Henry
Amateur. *b:* 14.5.1848, Ayr, Scotland. *d:* 12.12.1909, Ealing, Middlesex. Brother of F. S. (MCC). Opening right-hand batsman, good close field. *Team* MCC (1876).
Career batting
1–2–1–11–8*–11.00–0–*ct* 0

Milles, Hon Henry Augustus
(changed to Milles-Lade in 1900)
Amateur. *b:* 24.11.1867, Lees Court, Faversham, Kent. *d:* 30.7.1937, Nash Court, Faversham. Brother of Viscount Throwley (Kent). Middle order right-hand batsman, off break bowler. *Sch* Eton. *Team* Kent (1888–97, 2 matches). *Tour* Hawke to North America 1891.

Career batting
4–5–0–24–11–4.80–0–*ct* 1
Bowling 99–3–33.00–0–0–1/16
He was at Cambridge, but not in the eleven.

Millett, Frederick William
Amateur. *b:* 30.3.1928, Macclesfield, Cheshire. Opening right-hand batsman, off break bowler. *Team* Minor Counties (1960–73).
Career batting
7–13–3–312–102*–31.20–1–*ct* 2
Bowling 106–2–53.00–0–0–1/4
His County cricket was for Cheshire.

Milligan, Frank William
Amateur. *b:* 19.3.1870, Aldershot, Hants. *d:* 31.3.1900, Ramathelabama, South Africa. He fell in action whilst with the forces trying to relieve Mafeking. Hard hitting middle/lower order right-hand batsman, right-arm fast bowler, good field. *Sch* Eton. *Team* Yorkshire (1894–98, 81 matches). *Tours* Mitchell to North America 1895; Hawke to South Africa 1898/9. *Tests* England (1898/9, 2 matches).
Career batting
94–133–10–2226–74–18.09–0–*ct* 52
Bowling 3324–142–23.40–6–2–7/61
Test batting
2–4–0–58–38–14.50–0–*ct* 1
Bowling 29–0
He also played for Staffordshire.

Milligan, William Laidlaw
Amateur. *b:* 2.12.1906, Scotland. *d:* 31.3.1977, Edinburgh, Scotland. Lower order batsman, slow left-arm bowler. *Sch* Merchiston. *Team* Cambridge U (1928).
Career batting
3–2–2–3–3*–no av–0–*ct* 3
Bowling 191–4–47.75–0–0–2/55

Milling, David Alexander Hyndman
Amateur. *b:* 8.10.1872, Comber, Co Down, Ireland. *d:* 26.4.1929, Upper Rathmines, Co Dublin, Ireland. Lower order right-hand batsman, wicket-keeper. *Team* Ireland (1912–14).
Career batting
2–4–1–17–8–5.66–0–*ct* 1–*st* 2

Millman, Geoffrey
Professional. *b:* 2.10.1934, Bedford. Opening or middle order right-hand batsman, wicket-keeper. *Team* Nottinghamshire (1957–65, 257 matches). *Tours* MCC to India, Pakistan and Ceylon (he did not play in first-class match in Ceylon) 1961/2. *Tests* England (1961/2 to 1962, 6 matches).
Career batting
282–471–59–7771–131*–18.86–3–*ct* 559–*st* 97
Bowling 32–0
Test batting
6–7–2–60–32*–12.00–0–*ct* 13–*st* 2
His first-class debut was for Combined Services in 1956. He hit 1,000 runs in a season twice (best 1,350, av 22.50 in 1961). From 1963 to 1965 he captained Notts.
He also appeared for Bedfordshire.

Millner, David
Professional. *b:* 24.7.1938, Dove Holes, Derbyshire. Middle order right-hand batsman, off break bowler. *Team* Derbyshire (1960–63, 31 matches).
Career batting
31–56–1–701–80–12.74–0–*ct* 6
Bowling 27–0

Mills, A. H.
Professional. Lower order batsman, useful bowler. *Team* Gloucestershire (1939–48, 4 matches).
Career batting
4–5–0–81–39–16.20–0–*ct* 1
Bowling 62–3–20.66–0–0–2/28
He also played for Wiltshire.

Mills, Charles Henry
Professional. *b:* 26.11.1867, Peckham, Surrey. *d:* 26.7.1948, Southwark, South London. Lower order right-hand batsman, right-arm medium pace bowler. *Teams* Surrey (1888, 2 matches); Kimberley (1889/90); Western Province (1892/3 to 1894/5). *Tour* South Africa to England 1894 (not first-class). *Test* South Africa (1891/2, 1 match).
Career batting
8–13–0–160–31–12.30–0–*ct* 11
Bowling 451–29–15.55–3–0–5/36
Test batting
1–2–0–25–21–12.50–0–*ct* 2
Bowling 83–2–41.50–0–0–2/83
He went out to South Africa as coach to the Cape Town Club.

Mills, David Cecil
Amateur. *b:* 23.4.1937, Camborne, Cornwall. Opening right-hand batsman, right-arm medium pace bowler. *Sch* Clifton. *Team* Gloucestershire (1958, 1 match).
Career batting
2–2–0–19–17–9.50–0–*ct* 1
Bowling 25–0
His final first-class match was for Free Foresters in 1960. He did not appear in any first-

class matches for Cambridge U, but was awarded his blue for rugby and represented Cornwall and the Harlequins.

Mills, Edwin
Professional. *b:* 6.3.1857, Coddington, Notts. *d:* 25.1.1899, Cossall, Notts. Brother of John (Notts). Lower order left-hand batsman, left-arm fast bowler. *Teams* Nottinghamshire (1878–84, 29 matches); Surrey (1885–87, 7 matches).
Career batting
43–68–8–919–74–15.31–0–*ct* 31
Bowling 1778–87–20.43–4–1–7/97

Mills, Frederick
Professional. *b:* 1898, Leicester. *d:* 4.11.1929, Leicester. Middle order left-hand batsman, slow left-arm bowler. *Team* Leicestershire (1921–23, 5 matches).
Career batting
5–7–2–69–30*–13.80–0–*ct* 0

Mills, George Thomas
Amateur. *b:* 12.9.1923, Redditch, Worcs. *d:* 15.9.1983, Bromsgrove, Worcs. Lower order right-hand batsman, wicket-keeper. *Team* Worcestershire (1953, 2 matches).
Career batting
2–4–0–46–23–11.50–0–*ct* 5–*st* 4

Mills, Henry Maynard
Amateur. *b:* 1847, Kensington, London. *d:* 13.4.1915, Buenos Aires, Argentine. Lower order batsman, wicket-keeper. *Team* Middlesex (1881, 1 match).
Career batting
4–7–0–27–10–3.85–0–*ct* 4–*st* 1
His first-class debut was for the Gentlemen of England in 1879. He also played in the North v South series in the Argentine.

Mills, John
Amateur. *b:* 1848. *d:* 14.4.1935, Obcrwil, Basle, Switzerland. Middle order batsman. *Team* Gloucestershire (1870, 1 match).
Career batting
1–2–0–17–15–8.50–0–*ct* 1

Mills, John
Professional. *b:* 28.1.1855, Coddington, Notts. *d:* 27.6.1932, Ilkeston, Derbyshire. He died whilst watching Notts playing Derbyshire. Brother of Edwin (Notts and Surrey). Middle order right-hand batsman, right-hand fast round-arm bowler. *Team* Nottinghamshire (1875–81, 11 matches).
Career batting
13–19–2–140–24–8.23–0–*ct* 12
Bowling 7–0
His final first-class match was for the Hon M.B. Hawke's XI in 1885.

Mills, Josiah
Professional. *b:* 25.10.1862, Oldham, Lancashire. *d:* 23.11.1929, Oldham, Lancashire. Tail end right-hand batsman, wicket-keeper. *Team* Lancashire (1889, 1 match).
Career batting
1–1–0–1–1–1.00–0–*ct* 1–*st* 1

Mills, John Ernest
Amateur. *b:* 3.9.1905, Carisbrook, Dunedin, New Zealand. *d:* 11.12.1972, Hamilton, New Zealand. Son of George, nephew of Edward, Isaac and William (all Auckland). Attractive opening left-hand batsman. *Team* Auckland (1924/5 to 1937/8). *Tours* New Zealand to England 1927, 1931, to Australia 1927/8. *Tests* New Zealand (1929/30 to 1932/3, 7 matches).
Career batting
97–161–8–5025–185–32.84–11–*ct* 30
Bowling 123–4–30.75–0–0–2/57
Test batting
7–10–1–241–117–26.77–1–*ct* 1
He batted well on both his tours to England, scoring 1,251 runs, 37.90, in 1927 and 1,368, av 31.81, in 1931.

Mills, John Michael
Amateur. *b:* 27.7.1921, Birmingham. Father of J.P.C. (Northants). Lower order right-hand batsman, leg break and googly bowler. *Sch* Oundle. *Teams* Cambridge U (1946–48, blue all three years); Warwickshire (1946, 4 matches).
Career batting
38–60–10–743–44–14.86–0–*ct* 13
Bowling 2743–95–30.95–5–0–7/69

Mills, John Peter Crispin
Cricketer. *b:* 6.12.1958, Kettering, Northants. Son of J. M. (Warwickshire). Opening/middle order right-hand batsman, right-arm medium pace bowler. *Sch* Oundle. *Teams* Cambridge U (1979–82, blue all four years); Northants (1981, 3 matches).
Career batting
41–68–2–1585–111–24.01–1–*ct* 14
Bowling 5–0
He captained Cambridge U in the 1982 University match when the elected captain, D. R. Pringle, chose to play for England on the same dates.

Mills, Percy Thomas
Professional. *b:* 7.5.1879, Cheltenham, Gloucestershire. *d:* 8.12.1950, Abingdon, Berks. Lower

order right-hand batsman, right-arm medium pace bowler. *Team* Gloucestershire (1902–29, 346 matches).
Career batting
347–548–117–5051–95–11.71–0–*ct* 186
Bowling 20764–825–25.16–39–5–7/30

He took 100 wickets in a season once : 101, av 23.55, in 1926. In the Gloucs v Somerset match at Bristol in 1928 he returned the remarkable analysis of 6.4–6–0–5.

He also played for Berkshire.

Mills, Walter George
Amateur. *b:* 1852, Hackney, Middlesex. *d:* January 1902, Chorlton, Lancashire. Lower order right-hand batsman, right-hand fast round-arm bowler. *Team* Lancashire (1871–77, 6 matches).
Career batting
6–11–1–57–26–5.70–0–*ct* 4
Bowling 97–6–16.16–0–0–3/52

Millward, Arthur
Professional *b:* 4.7.1858, Kidderminster, Worcs. *d:* 21.1.1933, Eastbourne, Sussex. Middle order right-hand batsman, right-arm off break bowler. *Team* North (1900).
Career batting
1–2–1–19–19*–19.00–0–*ct* 0
Bowling 32–0

He appeared for Worcestershire and Cheshire, assisting the former in its second class days, commencing 1881.

Milman, Sir Dermot Lionel Kennedy
Amateur. *b:* 24.10.1912, Eltham, Kent. Lower order right-hand batsman, slow left-arm bowler, excellent close field. *Sch* Uppingham and Bedford. *Team* Cambridge U (1932–33).
Career batting
2–4–2–15–7*–7.50–0–*ct* 0
Bowling 142–4–35.50–0–0–3/55

His County cricket was for Bedfordshire. A noted rugby footballer, he played for Cambridge and England.

Milman, George Alderson
Amateur. *b:* 11.10.1830, Westminster, London. *d:* 29.12.1898, Heavitree, Devon. Opening or middle order right-hand batsman, right-hand medium pace round-arm bowler, slip field. *Team* MCC (1863–69).
Career batting
3–5–0–48–31–9.60–0–*ct* 2
Bowling 144–15–9.60–2–1–7/65

Whilst serving in Ceylon, he was accidently shot in the shoulder during an elephant hunt, but returning to England in 1858 he continued to play cricket, batting in military matches with much success, using a small bat with his good arm.

Milne, George Taylor
Professional. *b:* 1877, Newcastle-upon-Tyne. *d:* 3.11.1968, Newcastle-upon-Tyne. Middle order left-hand batsman, left-arm bowler. *Team* Minor Counties (1912).
Career batting
1–1–1–9–9*–no av–0–*ct* 0

His County cricket was for Northumberland.

Milne, Robert Oswald
Amateur. *b:* 10.9.1852, Manchester, Lancashire. *d:* 6.9.1927, Leamington Spa, Warwickshire. Middle order batsman. *Sch* Rugby. *Team* Lancashire (1882, 1 match).
Career batting
1–1–1–7–7*–no av–0–*ct* 0

Milner, Joseph
Professional. *b:* 22.8.1937, Johannesburg, South Africa. Forcing middle order right-hand batsman. *Team* Essex (1957–61, 66 matches).
Career batting
67–119–12–2767–135–25.85–3–*ct* 57
Bowling 14–0

He hit 1,387 runs, av 28.49, in 1961.

Milner, Marcus Henry
Amateur. *b:* 16.4.1864, Bedford. *d:* 16.1.1939, Liverpool. Lower order left-hand batsman, left-arm medium pace bowler. *Sch* Wellington. *Team* Cambridge U (1884).
Career batting
2–4–0–28–20–7.00–0–*ct* 0
Bowling 161–5–32.20–0–0–3/79

His County cricket was for Cambridgeshire.

Milton, Clement Arthur
Professional. *b:* 10.3.1928, Bristol, Gloucestershire. Attractive opening right-hand batsman, right-arm medium bowler, good close field. *Team* Gloucestershire (1948–74, 585 matches). *Tours* MCC to Ceylon, Australia and New Zealand (he did not play in first-class matches in Ceylon or New Zealand) 1958/59; Gloucestershire to Bermuda 1962 (not first-class); Gloucestershire in Zambia 1971/72 (not first-class). *Tests* England (1958–59, 6 matches).
Career batting
620–1078–125–32150–170–33.73–56–*ct* 758
Bowling 3630–79–45.94–1–0–5/64
Test batting
6–9–1–204–104*–25.50–1–*ct* 5
Bowling 12–0

He hit 1,000 runs in a season 16 times, going on to 2,000 once : 2,089, av 46.42, in 1967. In 1956 he held 63 catches in the field.

He captained Gloucestershire in 1968.

A well-known soccer player, he appeared at outside right for Arsenal and Bristol City and was capped for England in 1951/2.

Milton, Harold Aubrey
Amateur. *b:* 15.1.1882, Hackney Downs, Middlesex. *d:* 14.3.1970, Islington, London. Middle order right-hand batsman. *Sch* University College, London. *Team* Middlesex (1907, 3 matches).
Career batting
3–5–0–52–45–10.40–0–*ct* 4

Minnett, Dr Roy Baldwin
Amateur. *b:* 13.6.1888, St Leonards, New South Wales, Australia. *d:* 21.10.1955, Manly, New South Wales, Australia. Brother of L.A. (New South Wales) and R.V. (New South Wales). Middle order right-hand batsman, right-arm fast medium bowler. *Team* New South Wales (1906/07 to 1914/15, 19 matches). *Tours* Australia to England 1912; Waddy to Ceylon 1913/4 (not first-class). *Tests* Australia (1911/12 to 1912, 9 matches).
Career batting
54–83–8–2142–216*–28.94–2–*ct* 17
Bowling 2152–86–25.02–3–1–8/50
Test batting
9–15–0–391–90–26.06–0–*ct* 0
Bowling 290–11–26.36–0–0–4/34

He had a disappointing tour of England in 1912, the wet wickets being totally against his style of batting. His highest score was 216* for NSW v Victoria at Sydney in 1911/12.

Minnett, Rupert Villiers
Amateur. *b:* 2.9.1884, St Leonards, New South Wales, Australia. *d:* 24.6.1974, Cremorne, New South Wales, Australia. Brother of L.A. (New South Wales) and R.B. (New South Wales). Middle order right-hand batsman. *Team* New South Wales (1909/10 to 1914/5, 5 matches).
Career batting
6–10–1–331–169–36.77–1–*ct* 4

His single match in England was for L. Robinson's XI in 1912.

Minney, John Henry
Amateur. *b:* 25.4.1939, Finedon, Northants. Middle order right-hand batsman. *Sch* Oundle. *Teams* Cambridge U (1959–61); Northants (1961–67, 5 matches).
Career batting
19–33–3–572–58–19.06–0–*ct* 10
Bowling 7–0

He did not appear in any first-class matches 1962 to 1966 for Northants.

Minnis, Arnold
Amateur. *b:* 26.10.1891, Wortley, Yorkshire. *d:* 26.9.1972, Cirencester, Gloucs. Tail end right-hand batsman, slow left-arm bowler. *Team* Army (1930–32).
Career batting
4–5–2–10–5*–3.33–0–*ct* 0
Bowling 348–23-15.14–1–0–7/48

Minns, Robert Ernest Frederick
Amateur. *b:* 18.11.1940, Penang, Malaya. Middle order right-hand batsman. *Sch* King's School, Canterbury. *Teams* Kent (1959–63, 2 matches); Oxford U (1962–63, blue both years).
Career batting
20–38–3–947–81–27.05–0–*ct* 12

Minshull, John
Professional. *b:* 1741. *d:* October 1793. Excellent batsman. *Teams* Kent (1773); Surrey (1779).
Career batting
not applicable–pre-1800

For the Duke of Dorset's XI v Wrotham on 31 August 1769 he scored 107 – the first recorded instance of a player making a century.

Minton, Robert Samuel
Amateur. *b:* 4.1.1899, Kensington, London. *d:* 1928, East Grinstead, Sussex. Middle order batsman. *Team* Sussex (1919, 1 match).
Career batting
1–2–0–24–24–12.00–0–*ct* 0

Mirehouse, George Tierney
Amateur. *b:* 11.5.1863, Easton-in-Gordano, Somerset. *d:* 5.3.1923, Turramurra, New South Wales, Australia. Tail end right-hand batsman, right-arm medium fast bowler. *Sch* Westminster. *Teams* Cambridge U (1884–85); Somerset (1884–85, 4 matches).
Career batting
13–22–4–74–20–4.11–0–*ct* 4
Bowling 606–22–27.54–0–0–4/51

His final first-class match was for MCC in 1896.

Mirehouse, William Edward
Amateur. *b:* 29.10.1844, Hambrook, Bristol. *d:* 16.6.1925, Hambrook, Bristol. Sound middle order right-hand batsman, useful bowler, good deep field. *Sch* Harrow. *Team* Gloucester (1872, 1 match).
Career batting
1 match, did not bat–*ct* 0

He appeared for Cambridge University in non-first-class matches only in 1864.

Mischler, Norman Martin
Amateur. *b:* 9.10.1920, Paddington, London. Lower order right-hand batsman, wicket-keeper. *Sch* St Paul's. *Teams* Europeans (1941/2 to 1943/4); Cambridge U (1946–47, blue both years).
Career batting
24–38–1–568–76–15.35–0–*ct* 35–*st* 10
His final first-class match was for Free Foresters in 1951.

Misselbrook, Henry
Professional. *b:* 16.12.1832, Otterbourne, Hants. *d:* 11.7.1895, Winchester, Hants. Middle order batsman, useful bowler. *Team* Hampshire (1869, 1 match).
Career batting
1–2–0–3–3–1.50–0–*ct* 0
Bowling 39–6–6.50–0–0–4/18

Missen, Edward Sebley
Amateur. *b:* 1875, Cambridge. *d:* 17.11.1927, Colchester, Essex. Middle order batsman, right-arm medium pace bowler. *Team* Essex (1928, 1 match).
Career batting
1–2–0–20–12–10.00–0–*ct* 0
He also played for Cambridgeshire.

Misson, Francis Michael
Amateur. *b:* 19.11.1938, Darlinghurst, New South Wales, Australia. Lower order right-hand batsman, right-arm fast medium bowler. *Team* New South Wales (1958/9 to 1963/4, 42 matches). *Tours* Australia to New Zealand 1959/60, to England 1961. *Tests* Australia (1960/1 to 1961, 5 matches).
Career batting
71–77–17–1052–51*–17.53–0–*ct* 58
Bowling 5511–177–31.13–1–0–6/75
Test batting
5–5–3–38–25*–19.00–0–*ct* 6
Bowling 616–16–38.50–0–0–4/58
He played in two Tests on the 1961 tour of England, but his returns were only modest.

Mistry, Kekhashru Maneksha
Amateur. *b:* 7.11.1874, Bombay, India. *d:* 22.7.1959, Bombay, India. Opening or middle order left-hand batsman, left-arm medium pace bowler. *Teams* Parsis (1893/4 to 1927/8); South Punjab (1926/7). *Tour* India to England 1911.
Career batting
38–69–1–1600–95–23.52–0–*ct* 32
Bowling 1370–103–13.30–6–2–7/26
Owing to other duties he was only available to play in three first-class matches on the 1911 tour – a great loss to the team.

Mitchell, Arthur
Professional. *b:* 13.9.1902, Baildon, Yorkshire. *d:* 25.12.1976, Bradford, Yorkshire. Steady middle order right-hand batsman, slow right-arm bowler, excellent close field. *Team* Yorkshire (1922–45, 401 matches). *Tours* MCC to India and Ceylon 1933/4; Yorkshire to Jamaica 1935/6. *Tests* England (1933/4 to 1936, 6 matches).
Career batting
426–593–72–19523–189–37.47–44–*ct* 438
Bowling 327–7–46.71–0–0–3/49
Test batting
6–10–0–298–72–29.80–0–*ct* 9
Bowling 4–0
He hit 1,000 runs in a season 10 times (2,300 av 58.97, in 1933 was the only time he exceeded 2,000).
From 1945 to 1970 he was Yorkshire County Coach.
His final first-class match was for the North in 1947.

Mitchell, Bruce
Amateur. *b:* 8.1.1909, Johannesburg, South Africa. Stylish opening right-hand batsman, right-arm slow bowler, slip field. *Team* Transvaal (1925/6 to 1949/50). *Tours* South Africa to England 1929, 1935, 1947, to Australia and New Zealand 1931/2. *Tests* South Africa (1929 to 1948/9, 42 matches).
Career batting
173–281–30–11395–195–45.39–30–*ct* 228
Bowling 6382–249–25.63–15–2–6/33
Test batting
42–80–9–3471–189*–48.88–8–*ct* 56
Bowling 1380–27–51.11–1–0–5/87
He was most successful on all three of his tours to England with first-class aggregates of 1,615, av 32.95, in 1929; 1,451, av 45.34, in 1935; and 2,014, av 61.03, in 1947. In 1935 he topped the Test averages with 488 runs, av 69.71.

Mitchell, Clement
Amateur. *b:* 20.2.1862, Cambridge. *d:* 6.10.1937, Hove, Sussex. Dangerous middle order left-hand batsman, fine field. *Sch* Felsted. *Team* Kent (1890–92, 8 matches).
Career batting
8–14–1–126–38*–9.69–0–*ct* 6
He was a noted cricketer in Calcutta in the 1880s.

Mitchell, Colin Gerald
Amateur. *b:* 27.1.1929, Brislington, Somerset. Lower order right-hand batsman, right-arm fast medium bowler. *Team* Somerset (1952–54, 30 matches).

Career batting
30–45–20–186–26*–7.44–0–*ct* 9
Bowling 2035–53–38.39–2–1–6/62

A useful soccer player, he represented Gloucestershire.

Mitchell, Frank
Amateur. *b:* 13.8.1872, Market Weighton, Yorkshire. *d:* 11.10.1935, Blackheath, Kent. Father of T.F. (Kent). Attacking middle order right-hand batsman, right-arm medium pace bowler. *Sch* St Peter's, York. *Teams* Cambridge U (1894–97, blue all four years); Yorkshire (1894–1904, 83 matches); London County (1901); Transvaal (1902/3 to 1903/4). *Tours* Mitchell to North America 1895; Warner to North America 1898; Hawke to South Africa 1898/9; Bosanquet to North America 1901; South Africa to England 1904, 1912. *Tests* England (1898/9, 2 matches); South Africa (1912, 3 matches).
Career batting
198–304–19–9117–194–31.98–17–*ct* 147–*st* 2
Bowling 828–35–23.65–1–0–5/57
Test batting
5–10–0–116–41–11.60–0–*ct* 2

In 1899 he hit 1,748 runs, av 31.78 – then after serving in the Boer War he returned in 1901 to score 1,807 runs, av 44.07, these being the only two seasons he had as a regular County cricketer. He also reached 1,000 runs in 1904. He captained both the 1904 and 1912 South African tourists and led South Africa in three Tests.

His final first-class match was for MCC in 1914.

A brilliant all-round sportsman he also gained his blues for rugby football (later gaining six England caps) and putting the weight. He also played soccer, keeping goal for Sussex. Later he was a noted sports writer.

Mitchell, Sir Frank Herbert
Amateur. *b:* 13.6.1878, Eton, Bucks. *d:* 27.11.1951, Crowborough, Sussex. Son of R.A.H. (Oxford U). Middle order right-hand batsman, right-hand slow round-arm or under-arm bowler. *Sch* Eton. *Team* Oxford U (1898).
Career batting
3–4–0–23–9–5.75–0–*ct* 0
Bowling 114–5–22.80–1–0–5/32

His County cricket was for Buckinghamshire.

A noted golfer, he represented Oxford and England.

He was for some time Assistant Private Secretary to George VI.

Mitchell, Frank Rawlinson
Professional. *b:* 3.6.1922, Sydney, New South Wales, Australia. *d:* 4.4.1984, Warwick. Lower order right-hand batsman, right-arm medium pace off break bowler. *Team* Warwickshire (1946–48, 17 matches).
Career batting
17–29–2–224–43–8.29–0–*ct* 7
Bowling 856–22–38.90–0–0–4/69

He also played for Cornwall.

A noted half-back, he played soccer of Birmingham City, Chelsea and Watford.

Mitchell, George Frederick
Professional. *b:* March 1897, West Ham, Essex. Tail end left-hand batsman, useful bowler. *Team* Essex (1926, 1 match).
Career batting
1–1–0–4–4–4.00–0–*ct* 0
Bowling 45–1–45.00–0–0–1/25

Mitchell, Horace
Professional. *b:* 19.1.1858, West Tarring, Worthing, Sussex. *d:* 4.1.1951, West Tarring, Worthing, Sussex. Lower order right-hand batsman, right-arm medium fast bowler, slip field. *Team* Sussex (1882–91, 8 matches).
Career batting
8–14–3–44–9–4.00–0–*ct* 0
Bowling 355–19–18.68–1–0–5/35

He appeared for Sussex in 1882 and 1891, but not in the intervening years.

Mitchell, Ian Norman
Amateur. *b:* 17.4.1925, Bristol, Gloucestershire. Middle order right-hand batsman. *Sch* Harrow. *Teams* Gloucestershire (1950–52, 9 matches); Cambridge U (1949).
Career batting
11–19–1–160–27–8.88–0–*ct* 5

Mitchell, James Stanley Lyons
Cricketer. *b:* 19.10.1946, Londonderry, Ireland. Middle order left-hand batsman. *Team* Ireland (1974).
Career batting
1–2–0–29–27–14.50–0–*ct* 1

Mitchell, Kenneth James
Amateur. *b:* 5.12.1924, Old Hill, Staffs. Middle order left-hand batsman. *Team* Worcestershire (1946, 1 match).
Career batting
1–2–0–10–10–5.00–0–*ct* 1

Mitchell, Richard Arthur Henry
Amateur. *b:* 22.1.1843, Enderby Hall, Leicester. *d:* 19.4.1905, Woking, Surrey. Father of F. H. (Oxford U). Fine powerful middle order right-hand batsman, right-hand medium pace round-

arm bowler, good point field. *Sch* Eton. *Team* Oxford U (1862–65, blue all four years).
Career batting
57–90–6–2517–125*–29.96–2–*ct* 36–*st* 10
Bowling 403–15+7–26.86–0–0–4/30

His first-class debut was for Gentlemen of the North in 1861, and his final first-class match was for MCC in 1883. He also played for Buckinghamshire, Leicestershire and Warwickshire (non-first-class).

He captained Oxford against Cambridge for three successive matches 1863–65.

An assistant master at Eton from 1866, his appearances in first-class cricket were very limited, though he was regarded as one of the best batsman of his day.

Mitchell, Richard William Gordon Lewis
Amateur. *b:* 27.2.1913, Grenada, West Indies. Middle order right-hand batsman, right-arm fast medium bowler. *Team* Oxford U (1935).
Career batting
1–1–1–9–9*–no av–0–*ct* 0

Mitchell, Thomas Bignall
Profesional. *b:* 4.9.1902, Creswell, Derbyshire. Lower order right-hand batsman, leg break and googly bowler. *Team* Derbyshire (1928–39, 303 matches). *Tour* MCC to Australia and New Zealand 1932/3. *Tests* England (1932/3 to 1935, 5 matches).
Career batting
328–412–107–2431–57–7.97–0–*ct* 132
Bowling 30543–1483–20.59–118–30–10/64
Test batting
5–6–2–20–9–5.00–0–*ct* 1
Bowling 498–8–62.25–0–0–2/49

He took 100 wickets in a season 10 times (best 171, av 20.16, in 1935).

His best bowling in an innings was 10 for 64 for Derbyshire v Leicestershire at Leicester in 1935.

He was known as the 'merry-hearted' cricketer.

Mitchell, Thomas Frank
Amateur. *b:* 22.10.1907, Johannesburg, South Africa. *d:* 20.5.1960, Marylebone, London. Son of Frank (Yorkshire). Steady middle order right-hand batsman, off break bowler. *Sch* Tonbridge. *Team* Kent (1928–34, 24 matches).
Career batting
31–50–3–711–64–15.12–0–*ct* 15
Bowling 247–2–123.50–0–0–1/48

Mitchell, William Henry
Amateur. *b:* 1859, Worthing, Sussex. *d:* 1929, Horsham, Sussex. Middle order batsman. *Team* Sussex (1886, 2 matches).
Career batting
2–4–0–8–4–2.00–0–*ct* 0

Mitchell, William MacFarlane
Amateur. *b:* 15.8.1929, Lewisham, London. Middle/lower order right-hand batsman, leg break and googly bowler. *Sch* Dulwich. *Team* Oxford U (1951–53, blue 1951 and 1952).
Career batting
26–40–8–480–48–15.00–0–*ct* 12
Bowling 1998–35–57.08–1–0–5/107

Mitchell-Innes, Norman Stewart
Amateur. *b:* 7.9.1914, Calcutta, India. Stylish middle order right-hand batsman, right-arm fast, later medium, bowler. *Sch* Sedbergh. *Teams* Somerset (1931–49, 69 matches); Oxford U (1934–37, blue all four years); Scotland (1937). *Tour* MCC to Australia and New Zealand 1935/6. *Test* England (1935, 1 match).
Career batting
132–239–18–6944–207–31.42–13–*ct* 152
Bowling 2846–82–34.70–0–0–4/65
Test batting
1–1–0–5–5–5.00–0–*ct* 0

He hit 1,000 runs in a season three times (best 1,438, av 44.93, in 1936). After leaving University he joined the Sudan Civil Service, thus restricting his appearances in first-class cricket. In 1948 he was joint-captain of Somerset. His highest score was 207 for Oxford U v Leveson-Gower's XI at Reigate in 1936.

Mitra, Avijit
Cricketer. *b:* 6.7.1953, Calcutta, India. Opening right-hand batsman, off break bowler. *Sch* KES, Birmingham. *Team* Oxford U (1974–75).
Career batting
6–12–0–157–30–13.08–0–*ct* 2

Mitten, John
Professional. *b:* 30.3.1941, Manchester, Lancashire. Right-hand batsman, wicket-keeper. *Team* Leicestershire (1961–63, 14 matches).
Career batting
14–23–2–259–50*–12.33–0–*ct* 23

A noted soccer player, he appeared for Mansfield, Newcastle United, Leicester City, Coventry, Plymouth and Exeter.

Mitton, John
Professional. *b:* 7.11.1895, Todmorden, Yorkshire. *d:* November 1981. Tail end batsman, bowler. *Team* Somerset (1920, 2 matches).

Career batting
2–3–2–15–6–15.00–0–*ct* 0
Bowling 100–1–100.00–0–0–1/47
He played football for Exeter City, Sunderland and Wolverhampton.

Moan, Raymond
Cricketer. *b:* 12.1.1951, Sion Mills, Co Tyrone, Ireland. Right-hand batsman, off break bowler. *Team* Ireland (1970).
Career batting
1–1–1–0–0*–no av–0–*ct* 0
Bowling 58–1–58.00–0–0–1/58

Moberly, John (Cornelius)
Amateur. *b:* 22.4.1848, Winchester, Hampshire. *d:* 29.1.1928, Bassett, Hampshire. Middle order right-hand batsman, right-arm medium pace bowler. *Sch* Winchester. *Team* Hampshire (1877, 1 match).
Career batting
1–2–0–31–27–15.50–0–*ct* 0
He played in the Oxford Freshmen's match of 1867.

Moberley, William Octavius
Amateur. *b:* 14.11.1850, Shoreham, Sussex. *d:* 2.2.1914, Mullion, Cornwall. Middle order right-hand batsman, wicket-keeper. *Sch* Rugby. *Teams* Gloucestershire (1876–87, 64 matches); Oxford U (1870).
Career batting
66–105–7–2104–121–21.46–3–*ct* 48–*st* 16
He also played for Warwickshire and Leicestershire (pre-first-class).
A noted rugby footballer, he obtained his blue and went on to represent England.

Mobey, Gerald Spencer
Professional. *b:* 5.3.1904, Surbiton, Surrey. Lower order right-hand batsman, wicket-keeper. *Team* Surrey (1930–48, 77 matches).
Career batting
81–112–19–1684–75–18.10–0–*ct* 130–*st* 11

Mocatta, John Edward Abraham
Amateur. *b:* 6.5.1936, London. Middle order right-hand batsman, leg break bowler. *Sch* Clifton. *Team* Oxford U (1958).
Career batting
4–8–0–106–37–13.25–0–*ct* 2

Modi, Rusi Sheriyar
Amateur. *b:* 11.11.1924, Bombay, India. Sound middle order right-hand batsman, right-arm medium pace bowler. *Teams* Parsis (1941/2 to 1945/6); Bombay (1943/4 to 1959/60). *Tours* India to Ceylon 1944/5, to England 1946; ACC to Pakistan 1961/2. *Tests* India (1946 to 1952/3, 10 matches).
Career batting
105–154–12–7529–245*–53.02–20–*ct* 29
Bowling 1226–32–38.31–1–0–5/25
Test batting
10–17–1–736–112–46.00–1–*ct* 3
Bowling 14–0
A consistent batsman on the 1946 tour with 1,196 runs, av 37.37, he was a prolific scorer in India. Three of his four double centuries were hit in the 1944/5 season, when he scored 1,386 runs, av 115.50. His highest score was 245* for Bombay v Baroda at Baroda in 1944/5.

Moeller, David
Amateur. *b:* 2.3.1941, Cardiff. Middle order right-hand batsman. *Sch* Haileybury. *Team* Oxford U (1961).
Career batting
1–2–0–25–24–12.50–0–*ct* 0

Moffat, Douglas
Amateur. *b:* 31.7.1843, Cawnpore, India. *d:* 27.3.1922, Paddington, London. Father of N.J.D. (Middlesex). Lower order batsman, bowler. *Team* Middlesex (1864, 1 match).
Career batting
2–3–0–31–25–10.33–0–*ct* 0
He made his first-class debut in 1863 for MCC. He also played County cricket for Northumberland.
Whilst at Oxford he did not play in the Eleven, but represented the University as a boxer.

Moffat, Norman John Douglas
Amateur. *b:* 13.9.1883, Edenhall, Roxburgh, Scotland. *d:* 11.10.1972, Dartford, Kent. Son of Douglas (Middlesex). Middle order right-hand batsman. *Team* Middlesex (1921–25, 11 matches).
Career batting
16–26–4–552–92–25.09–0–*ct* 8
His final first-class match was for MCC in 1926.

Moffatt, Neil Thomas
Cricketer. *b:* 10.5.1946, Oxford. Middle order left-hand batsman. *Team* Cambridge U (1969).
Career batting
1–2–0–6–4–3.00–0–*ct* 1

Mohamed, Timur
Cricketer. *b:* 7.6.1957, Georgetown, British Guiana. Opening left-hand batsman, leg break bowler. *Team* Guyana (1975/6 to 1981/2). *Tours* West Indies to England 1980; Young West Indies to Zimbabwe 1981/2.

Career batting
23–37–3–1232–193–36.23–4–*ct* 9
Bowling 36–0

He was co-opted into the 1980 West Indian touring team for two matches. Commencing 1979 he played County cricket for Suffolk.

Mohammad Aslam Khokhar
Amateur. *b:* 5.1.1920, Lahore, India. Middle order right-hand batsman, leg break bowler, good outfield. *Teams* Muslims (1938/9); Northern India (1941/2 to 1946/7); Railways (1953/4 to 1963/4). *Tour* Pakistan to England 1954. *Test* Pakistan (1954, 1 match).
Career batting
45–73–8–1700–103–26.15–1–*ct* 18
Bowling 630–21–30.00–1–0–6/26
Test batting
1–2–0–34–18–17.00–0–*ct* 0

He had a modest tour of England in 1954, playing in only 12 first-class matches and one Test.

Mohammad Farooq
Amateur. *b:* 8.4.1938, Junagadh, India. Hard hitting tail end right-hand batsman, right-arm fast medium bowler. *Team* Karachi (1959/60 to 1964/5). *Tours* Pakistan to India 1960/1, to England 1962. *Tests* Pakistan (1960/1 to 1964/5, 7 matches).
Career batting
33–31–17–173–47–12.35–0–*ct* 7
Bowling 3319–123–26.98–5–1–6/87
Test batting
7–9–4–85–47–17.00–0–*ct* 1
Bowling 682–21–32.47–0–0–4/70

Although perhaps the best of the seam bowlers on the 1962 tour of England, he achieved only modest results.

Mohammad Ilyas
Cricketer. *b:* 19.3.1946, Lahore, India. Attacking opening right-hand batsman, leg break and googly bowler. *Teams* Lahore (1961/2 to 1963/4); Punjab Univ (1964/5); PIA (1966/7 to 1971/2). *Tours* Pakistan to Australia and New Zealand 1964/5, to England 1967, to Ceylon and Australia 1972/3; International XI to South Africa 1975/6. *Tests* Pakistan (1964/5 to 1968/9, 10 matches).
Career batting
82–139–10–4607–154–35.71–12–*ct* 48
Bowling 1643–53–31.00–3–0–6/66
Test batting
10–19–0–441–126–23.21–1–*ct* 6
Bowling 63–0

His Test career ended on a controversial note during the 1972/3 tour to Australia and he remained in Australia after the season ended.

Mohammad Munaf
Amateur. *b:* 2.11.1935, Bombay, India. Lower order right-hand batsman, right-arm fast medium bowler. *Teams* Sind (1953/4 to 1955/6); Karachi (1956/7 to 1963/4); PIA (1961/2 to 1970/1). *Tours* Pakistan Eaglets to England 1963; Pakistan to West Indies 1957/8, to India 1960/1. *Tests* Pakistan (1959/60 to 1961/2, 4 matches).
Career batting
71–90–13–1356–76–17.61–0–*ct* 47
Bowling 4360–180–24.22–6–1–8/84
Test batting
4–7–2–63–19–12.60–0–*ct* 0
Bowling 341–11–31.00–0–0–4/42

Mohammad Nazir
Cricketer. *b:* 8.3.1946, Rawalpindi, India. Lower order right-hand batsman, off break bowler. *Team* Railways (1964/5 to 1982/3). *Tours* Pakistan to England 1971, 1974. *Tests* Pakistan (1969/70 to 1980/1, 8 matches).
Career batting
136–193–46–3474–113*–23.63–2–*ct* 68
Bowling 12101–604–20.03–43–9–7/35
Test batting
8–11–7–89–29*–22.55–0–*ct* 2
Bowling 635–26–24.42–2–0–7/99

He was a late replacement on the 1971 tour of England, but headed the first-class bowling averages with 20 wickets, av 19.80 – on his return in 1974 he achieved very little. He did not appear in any Tests in England.

Mohammad Saeed
Professional. *b:* 31.8.1910, Lahore, India *d:* 23.8.1979, Lahore, Pakistan. Father of Yawar Saeed (Somerset). Middle order right-hand batsman. *Teams* Muslims (1929/30 to 1934/5); Patiala (1932/3); Southern Punjab (1933/4 to 1945/6); Northern India (1944/5 to 1946/7); Punjab (1953/4 to 1954/5). *Tour* Pakistan to Ceylon 1948/9.
Career batting
51–81–2–2338–175–29.59–3–*ct* 31
Bowling 268–5–53.60–0–0–1/6

His only match in England was for a Commonwealth XI in 1952.

Mohammad Younis *(see under* Younis Ahmed)

Mohan, Keith Frederick
Professional. *b:* 11.6.1935, Glossop, Derbyshire. Middle order right-hand batsman. *Team* Derbyshire (1957–58, 10 matches).
Career batting
10–17–2–163–49–10.86–0–*ct* 4
Bowling 23–0

Mohol, Sadanand Namdeo
Amateur. *b:* 6.10.1938, Bassein, Thana, India. Lower order right-hand batsman, right-arm medium fast bowler. *Team* Maharashtra (1959/60 to 1970/1). *Tour* India to England and East Africa 1967.
Career batting
48–55–12–554–40–12.88–0–*ct* 22
Bowling 3659–174–21.02–10–2–8/42
He appeared in only seven matches on the 1967 tour owing to injury.

Mohsin Hasan Khan
Cricketer. *b:* 15.3.1955, Karachi, Pakistan. Elegant opening right-hand batsman, right-arm medium pace bowler. *Teams* Railways (1970/1 to 1971/2); Karachi (1972/3 to 1974/5); Universities (1973/4); Sind (1974/5 to 1975/6); Habib Bank (1975/6 to 1982/3). *Tours* Pakistan to West Indies 1976/7, to England 1978, 1982, to Australia and New Zealand 1978/9, to India 1979/80, to Australia 1981/2. *Tests* Pakistan (1977/8 to 1982/3, 22 matches).
Career batting
155–257–28–9467–246–41.34–27–*ct* 111
Bowling 482–14–34.42–0–0–2/13
Test batting
22–35–4–1516–200–48.90–4–*ct* 18
Bowling 6–0
He played in all three Tests on the 1978 tour to England, but had only a modest first-class record; in 1982 however he hit 1,248 runs, av 73.41, and headed the Test batting averages with 310 runs, av 62.00, including 200 v England in the second Test at Lord's. He also scored 203* v Leicestershire at Leicester. His highest score is 246 for Habib Bank v PIA at Karachi in 1976/7.

Moir, Alexander McKenzie
Amateur. *b:* 17.7.1919, Dunedin, New Zealand. Attacking lower order right-hand batsman, leg break and googly bowler. *Team* Otago (1949/50 to 1961/2). *Tours* New Zealand to India and Pakistan 1955/6, to England 1958. *Tests* New Zealand (1950/1 to 1958/9, 17 matches).
Career batting
97–150–22–2102–70–16.42–0–*ct* 44
Bowling 9040–368–24.56–25–5–8/37
Test batting
17–30–8–327–41*–14.86–0–*ct* 2
Bowling 1418–28–50.64–2–0–6/155
He showed modest returns on his 1958 tour to England, but played in the last two Tests.

Moir, Dallas Gordon
Cricketer. *b:* 13.4.1957, Imtarfa, Malta. Lower order right-hand batsman, slow left-arm bowler. *Teams* Scotland (1980); Derbyshire (1981–83, 43 matches).
Career batting
44–49–5–456–53–10.36–0–*ct* 39
Bowling 3742–122–30.67–6–0–6/63

Mold, Arthur (Webb)
Professional. *b:* 27.5.1863, Middleton Cheney, Northants. *d:* 29.4.1921, Middleton Cheney. Tail end right-hand batsman, right-arm fast bowler. *Team* Lancashire (1889–1901, 260 matches). *Tests* England (1893, 3 matches).
Career batting
287–389–130–1850–57–7.14–0–*ct* 111
Bowling 26010–1673–15.54–152–56–9/29
Test batting
3–3–1–0–0*–0.00–0–*ct* 1
Bowling 234–7–33.42–0–0–3/44
He took 100 wickets in a season nine times, going on to 200 twice (best 213, av 15.96, in 1895). He captured nine wickets in an innings four times, his best being 9 for 29 for Lancashire v Kent at Tonbridge in 1892.
Throughout his career the fairness of his delivery was questioned, but not until 1900 was he no-balled for throwing. He was again no-balled in 1901 and this ended his County career.

Moline, Charles Henry
Amateur. *b:* June 1863, Laibach, Austria. *d:* 23.5.1927, Weston-super-Mare, Somerset. Brother of E.R. (Gloucs). Lower order right-hand batsman, slow right-arm bowler. *Sch* Bristol GS. *Team* Cambridge U (1886).
Career batting
2–3–1–22–16–11.00–0–*ct* 2
Bowling 76–1–76.00–0–0–1/15

Moline, Edgar Robert
Amateur. *b:* 2.1.1855, Austria. *d:* 16.12.1943, Lynton, Devon. Brother of C.H. (Cambridge U). Middle order right-hand batsman, right-arm medium, or slow under-arm, bowler. *Sch* Bristol GS. *Team* Gloucestershire (1878, 2 matches).
Career batting
2–3–0–31–28–10.33–0–*ct* 0

Molineux, George King
Amateur. *b:* 15.4.1887, Eastbourne, Sussex. *d:* 5.5.1915, near Ypres, Belgium. He was killed in action. Lower order right-hand batsman, slow bowler. *Sch* Winchester. *Team* Oxford U (1907).
Career batting
4–7–1–127–78*–21.16–0–*ct* 2
Bowling 308–11–28.00–0–0–4/62
His final first-class match was for Gentlemen of England in 1908.

Moloney, Denis Andrew Robert
Amateur. *b:* 11.8.1910, Dunedin, New Zealand.

d: 15.7.1942, El Alamein, Egypt. Middle order right-hand batsman, good bowler. *Teams* Otago (1927/8 to 1939/40); Wellington (1935/6 to 1937/8); Canterbury (1940/1). *Tours* New Zealand to England 1937, to Australia 1937/8. *Tests* New Zealand (1937, 3 matches).
Career batting
64–119–7–3219–190–28.74–2–*ct* 35
Bowling 3151–95–33.16–3–0–5/23
Test batting
3–6–0–156–64–26.00–0–*ct* 3
Bowling 9–0

He hit 1,463 runs, av 34.83, on the 1937 tour to England and appeared in all three Tests.

Molony, Trevor James
Amateur. *b:* 6.7.1897, Kensington, London. *d:* 3.9.1962, Cannes, France. Lower order right-hand batsman, right-hand slow under-arm bowler. *Sch* Repton. *Team* Surrey (1921, 3 matches).
Career batting
3–4–0–2–2–0.50–0–*ct* 0
Bowling 89–4–22.25–0–0–3/11

He appeared in the Cambridge Freshmen's Match of 1920, but no first-class matches for the University.

It is believed that he was the last player to be chosen for a County Championship match purely on his merits as an under-arm bowler.

Molyneux, Paul Seymour Morthier
Amateur. *b:* 12.1.1906, Wells, Somerset. Middle order right-hand batsman, off break bowler. *Sch* Allhallows. *Team* Somerset (1937, 6 matches).
Career batting
6–10–0–94–25–9.40–0–*ct* 2

Monckton, Walter Turner
(created Viscount Monckton of Brenchley in 1958)
Amateur. *b:* 17.1.1891, Plaxtol, Kent. *d:* 9.1.1965, Folkington, Sussex. Lower order batsman, wicket-keeper. *Sch* Harrow. *Team* Combined Oxford and Cambridge U (1911).
Career batting
1–2–1–72–43–72.00–0–*ct* 1–*st* 1

He appeared in the Freshmen's and Seniors' matches at Oxford but no first-class matches.

In 1956 he was President of MCC and from 1950 to 1952, and 1959 to 1965, President of Surrey.

After a distinguished career as a barrister, he was Attorney-General (at the time of the abdication of Edward VIII), Solicitor-General, Minister of Defence, Paymaster-General and Minister of Labour.

Money, David Charles
Amateur. *b:* 5.10.1918, Oxford. Lower order right-hand batsman, wicket-keeper. *Team* Oxford U (1947).
Career batting
1–1–1–27–27*–no av–0–*ct* 1–*st* 1

His County cricket was for Bedfordshire.

Money, Rev Walter Baptist
Amateur. *b:* 27.7.1848, Sternfield, Suffolk. *d:* 1.3.1924, Edgbaston, Warwickshire. Middle order right-hand batsman, slow under-arm left arm lobs, good field. *Sch* Harrow. *Teams* Kent (1867, 1 match); Cambridge U (1868–71, blue all four years); Surrey (1869, 2 matches).
Career batting
29–52–4–1154–134–24.04–2–*ct* 34
Bowling 1452–82–17.70–8–2–6/24

His first-class debut was for Gentlemen of Kent in 1866, when he had the unusual distinction of bowling unchanged through the first innings, taking 5 for 35.

He also appeared for Suffolk.

After entering the Church in 1871, he gave up serious cricket.

A noted rackets player, he represented Cambridge.

Monkhouse, Graham
Cricketer. *b:* 26.4.1954, Carlisle, Cumberland. Lower order right-hand batsman, right-arm medium pace bowler. *Team* Surrey (1981–83, 30 matches).
Career batting
30–34–14–465–63*–23.25–0–*ct* 13
Bowling 1659–66–25.13–1–0–7/51

He also played for Cumberland. A good soccer player, he appeared for Carlisle United and Workington.

Monkland, Francis George
Amateur. *b:* 8.10.1854, Trichinopoly, India. *d:* 15.1.1915, Regent's Park, London. Middle order right-hand batsman, right-hand slow under-arm bowler, good deep field. *Sch* Repton. *Team* Gloucestershire (1874–79, 26 matches).
Career batting
31–45–6–534–59–13.69–0–*ct* 11
Bowling 30–0

Monks, Clifford Ivon
Amateur, but turned professional in 1936. *b:* 4.3.1912, Bristol, Gloucestershire. *d:* 23.1.1974, Coalpit Heath, Bristol. Sound middle order right-hand batsman, right-arm medium pace bowler, good deep field. *Team* Gloucestershire (1935–52, 65 matches).

Career batting
65–101–17–1589–120–18.91–1–*ct* 31
Bowling 1629–36–45.25–0–0–4/70

Monks, George D.
Professional. *b:* 3.9.1929, Sheffield, Yorkshire. Lower order batsman, wicket-keeper. *Team* Yorkshire (1952, 1 match).
Career batting
1–1–0–3–3–3.00–0–*ct* 1

Montagu, Admiral Sir Victor Alexander
Amateur. *b:* 20.4.1841. *d:* 30.1.1915, Westminster, London. Middle order batsman. *Team* MCC (1868).
Career batting
2–3–0–4–3–1.33–0–*ct* 0
His County cricket was for Huntingdonshire and Dorset.
He joined the Navy at the age of 12.

Monteith, James Dermott
Cricketer. *b:* 2.6.1943, Lisburn, Co Antrim, Ireland. Middle order right-hand batsman, slow left-arm bowler. *Teams* Ireland (1965–83); Middlesex (1981–82, 9 matches).
Career batting
27–38–5–435–78–13.18–0–*ct* 23
Bowling 1836–92–19.95–7–1–7/38

Montgomerie, Robert David
Amateur. *b:* 26.9.1937, Watford, Hertfordshire. Middle order right-hand batsman.
Career batting
1–2–0–16–15–8.00–0–*ct* 0
His County cricket was for Hertfordshire.

Montgomery, Hugh Ferguson
Amateur. *b:* 6.5.1880, Umbala, Bengal, India. *d:* 10.12.1920, Bray, Co Dublin, Ireland. Middle order right-hand batsman, good field. *Sch* Marlborough. *Team* Somerset (1901–09, 12 matches).
Career batting
17–30–0–416–50–13.86–0–*ct* 10
Bowling 267–5–53.40–0–0–2/17
His final first-class match was for the Navy in 1912.

Montgomery, Rt Rev Henry Hutchinson
Amateur. *b:* 3.10.1847, Cawnpore, India. *d:* 25.11.1932, Moville, Co Donegal, Ireland. Opening right-hand batsman, excellent point field. *Sch* Harrow. *Team* Cambridge U (1867–69).
Career batting
5–9–1–112–43*–14.00–0–*ct* 1
He was the father of Field Marshal Lord Montgomery of Alamein.

Montgomery, Stanley William
Amateur. *b:* 7.7.1920, West Ham, Essex. Sound middle order right-hand batsman. *Team* Glamorgan (1949–53, 29 matches).
Career batting
29–43–2–763–117–18.60–1–*ct* 9
Bowling 99–6–16.50–0–0–3/29
A useful soccer player he appeared at centre half for Cardiff City, Southend, Newport and Hull City.

Montgomery, William
Professional. *b:* 4.3.1878, Staines, Middlesex. *d:* 14.11.1952, Peterborough, Northants. Lower order right-hand batsman, right-arm fast bowler. *Teams* Surrey (1901–04, 14 matches); Somerset (1905–07, 10 matches).
Career batting
24–39–4–234–50–6.68–0–*ct* 13
Bowling 687–25–27.48–0–0–4/17
He also played for Wiltshire, Cheshire and Hertfordshire.

Montresor, Welby Francis
Amateur. *b:* 3.10.1849, Kishnagar, India. *d:* 27.1.1909, Kensington, London. Middle order batsman. *Sch* Eton. *Team* MCC (1880).
Career batting
2–4–0–22–7–5.50–0–*ct* 0

Moon, Sir Cecil Ernest
Amateur. *b:* 2.9.1867, Cassio Bridge, Hertfordshire. *d:* 22.2.1951, Chapel-en-le-Frith, Derbyshire. Middle order batsman. *Team* London County (1900).
Career batting
1–2–0–29–17–14.50–0–*ct* 0

Moon, Leonard James
Amateur. *b:* 9.2.1878, London. *d:* 23.11.1916, near Karasouli, Salonica, Greece. He died of wounds. Brother of W.R. (Middlesex). Forcing opening right-hand batsman, wicket-keeper. *Sch* Westminster. *Teams* Cambridge U (1897–1900, blue 1899 and 1900); Middlesex (1899–1909, 63 matches). *Tours* MCC to North America 1905, to South Africa 1905/6. *Tests* England (1905/6, 4 matches).
Career batting
96–163–8–4166–162–26.87–7–*ct* 72–*st* 13
Bowling 55–1–55.00–0–0–1/5
Test batting
4–8–0–182–36–22.75–0–*ct* 4
His final first-class match was for L. Robinson's XI in 1913.

Moon, William Robert
Amateur. *b:* 7.6.1868, Maida Vale, Middlesex. *d:*

9.1.1943, Hendon, Middlesex. Brother of L.J. (Middlesex). Hard hitting middle order right-hand batsman, wicket-keeper. *Sch* Westminster. *Team* Middlesex (1891, 2 matches).
Career batting
2–1–1–17–17*–no av–0–*ct* 2
A well-known soccer player, he kept goal for Corinthians and England.

Mooney, Francis Leonard Hugh
Amateur. *b:* 26.5.1921, Wellington, New Zealand. Opening right-hand batsman, wicket-keeper. *Team* Wellington (1941/2 to 1954/5). *Tours* New Zealand to England 1949, to South Africa and Australia 1953/4. *Tests* New Zealand (1949 to 1953/4, 14 matches).
Career batting
90–148–14–3134–180–23.38–2–*ct* 164–*st* 51
Bowling 0–0
Test batting
14–22–2–343–46–17.15–0–*ct* 22–*st* 8
Bowling 0–0
Going in fairly low down the order during the 1949 tour of England, he batted soundly and kept wicket in three Tests.

Mooney, William McCartan
Amateur. *b:* 5.10.1890, Blanchardstown, Co Dublin. *d:* 1968, Ballsbridge, Co Dublin, Ireland. Right-hand batsman. *Sch* Beaumont. *Team* Ireland (1912).
Career batting
1–2–1–23–23*–23.00–0–*ct* 0

Moor, David Child
Amateur. *b:* 18.12.1934, Faversham, Kent. Middle order left-hand batsman. *Sch* King's, Canterbury. *Team* Oxford U (1956).
Career batting
3–6–1–42–22–8.40–0–*ct* 0

Moorcroft, William
Amateur. Lower order batsman, good bowler. *Team* Hampshire (1911, 1 match).
Career batting
1 match, did not bat–*ct* 0
Bowling 68–0

Moore, Denis Neville
Amateur. *b:* 26.9.1910, Tewkesbury, Gloucs. Opening right-hand batsman, right-arm fast bowler. *Sch* Shrewsbury. *Teams* Oxford U (1930–31, blue 1930): Gloucestershire (1930–36, 31 matches).
Career batting
51–77–6–2307–206–32.49–4–*ct* 22
Bowling 252–6–42.00–0–0–3/39
He hit 1,000 runs in a season once : 1,317, av 41.15, in 1930. His only double century was 206 made on his debut for Gloucestershire – v Oxford U at Oxford in 1930. In 1931 he was captain of Oxford, but could not play in the University match due to illness.

Moore, Frederic James Stevenson
Amateur. *b:* 26.2.1873, Leominster, Herefordshire. *d:* 1.3.1947, Sherborne, Dorset. Opening or middle order right-hand batsman, slow left-arm bowler. *Sch* St George's, Harpenden. *Team* Cambridge U (1896).
Career batting
1–1–0–61–61–61.00–0–*ct* 2
His County cricket was for Herefordshire.

Moore, Frederick W.
Professional. *b:* 17.1.1931, Rochdale, Lancashire. Lower order right-hand batsman, right-arm medium pace bowler. *Team* Lancashire (1954–58, 24 matches).
Career batting
24–26–7–151–18–7.94–0–*ct* 11
Bowling 1516–54–28.07–2–1–6/45

Moore, Harry Ian
Cricketer. *b:* 28.2.1941, Sleaford, Lincs. Middle order right-hand batsman, right-arm medium pace bowler. *Team* Nottinghamshire (1962–69, 176 matches).
Career batting
177–299–29–6765–206*–25.05–7–*st* 106
Bowling 144–5–28.80–0–0–2/37
He hit 1,000 runs in a season three times (best 1,188, av 24.75, in 1965). His only double century was 206* for Notts v Indians at Trent Bridge in 1967.
His final first-class match was for Minor Counties in 1973 – before and after playing for Notts, he appeared for Lincolnshire.

Moore, John William
Professional. *b:* 29.4.1891, Winchfield, Hants. *d:* 23.6.1980, Basingstoke, Hants. Middle order right-hand batsman, right-arm medium pace bowler. *Team* Hampshire (1910–13, 15 matches).
Career batting
15–25–6–256–30–13.47–0–*ct* 4
Bowling 72–0

Moore, Kenneth Francis
Professional. *b:* 4.1.1940, Croydon, Surrey. Tail end right-hand batsman, left-arm medium fast bowler. *Team* Essex (1961, 1 match).
Career batting
1–1–0–2–2–2.00–0–*ct* 2
Bowling 43–4–10.75–0–0–4/21

Moore, Nigel Harold
Amateur. *b:* 20.4.1930, Norwich. Middle order right-hand batsman, right-arm fast medium bowler. *Sch* Norwich. *Team* Cambridge U (1952).
Career batting
4–6–0–139–59–23.16–0–*ct* 2
His County cricket was for Norfolk, and his final first-class match for Minor Counties in 1960.

Moore, Richard Henry
Amateur. *b:* 14.11.1913, Bournemouth, Hants. Opening right-hand batsman, right-arm medium pace bowler. *Team* Hampshire (1931–39, 129 matches).
Career batting
137–239–8–6026–316–26.08–10–*ct* 116
Bowling 978–25–39.11–0–0–3/46
He hit 1,000 runs in a season three times (best 1,569, av 30.17, in 1934). His only score over 200 was 316 for Hampshire v Warwickshire at Bournemouth in 1937.
He also played for Denbighshire.

Moore, Robert William
Amateur. *b:* 15.8.1905, Brooklands, USA. *d:* 27.10.1945, Sudden, Rochdale, Lancashire. Right-hand batsman, slow left-arm bowler. *Team* Ireland (1926).
Career batting
2–3–0–51–22–17.00–0–*ct* 0
Bowling 17–0

Moore, William Frederic Powell
(also known as Powell-Moore)
Amateur. *b:* 1846, London. *d:* 1919, Islington, London. Lower order batsman, wicket-keeper. *Team* MCC (1870).
Career batting
2–4–1–21–19*–7.00–0–*ct* 2
His final first-class match was for Gentlemen of England in 1879.

Moore-Gwyn, Howell Gwyn
(formerly Moore)
Amateur. *b:* 7.7.1886, Dyffryn Clydach, Glamorgan. *d:* 31.7.1956, Eastbourne, Sussex. Middle order right-hand batsman. *Sch* Winchester. *Teams* Army (1923); Punjab Governor's XI (1929/30).
Career batting
2–4–1–91–58–30.33–0–*ct* 1
Bowling 67–0

Moores, Peter
Cricketer. *b:* 18.12.1962, Macclesfield, Cheshire. Lower order right-hand batsman, wicket-keeper. *Team* Worcestershire (1983, 7 matches).
Career batting
7–11–1–154–30–15.40–0–*ct* 11–*st* 2

Moorhouse, Edward
Amateur. *b:* 1851, Haslingden, Lancashire. *d:* 1927, Manchester, Lancashire. Lower order batsman, wicket-keeper. *Team* Lancashire (1873–75, 5 matches).
Career batting
5–9–3–75–34–12.50–0–*ct* 8–*st* 3

Moorhouse, Fred
Professional. *b:* 25.3.1880, Berry Brow, Huddersfield, Yorkshire. *d:* 7.4.1933, Dudley, Worcs. Brother of Robert (Yorkshire). Lower order right-hand batsman, right-arm medium pace bowler. *Team* Warwickshire (1900–08, 117 matches).
Career batting
117–154–37–1549–75–13.23–0–*ct* 54
Bowling 6232–260–23.96–8–2–7/53
He also played for Cheshire.

Moorhouse, Sir Harry Claude
Amateur. *b:* 30.1.1872, Bombay, India. *d:* 16.12.1934, Newbury, Berkshire. Middle order batsman. *Sch* Brighton. *Team* MCC (1901–07).
Career batting
4–6–0–77–44–12.83–0–*ct* 1

Moorhouse, Robert
Professional. *b:* 7.9.1866, Berry Brow, Huddersfield, Yorkshire. *d:* 7.1.1921, Berry Brow, Huddersfield, Yorkshire. Brother of Fred (Warwickshire). Middle/lower order right-hand batsman, right-arm medium pace bowler, good field. *Team* Yorkshire (1888–99, 209 matches).
Career batting
217–331–46–5337–113–18.72–3–*ct* 95
Bowling 1376–49–28.08–0–0–4/40
He hit 1,096 runs, av 32.23, in 1895.
His final first-class match was for MCC in 1900.

Moorsom, Lewis Henry
Amateur. *b:* 1835. *d:* 10.3.1914, Moordown, Bournemouth, Hampshire. Middle order batsman, useful bowler. *Teams* Lancashire (1865, 1 match); Trinidad (1868/9).
Career batting
3–6–0–41–15–6.83–0–*ct* 1
Bowling 22–0

Morant, Edward John Harry Eden
Amateur. *b:* 29.1.1868, London. *d:* 20.1.1910, Brockenhurst, Hants. Lower order batsman, bowler. *Team* MCC (1895).

Career batting
1–2–2–3–3*–no av–0–*ct* 0
Bowling 34–2–17.00–0–0–2/34

Morby-Smith, Lynton
Amateur. *b:* 27.5.1936, Durban, South Africa. Brother of Grahame (Natal). Middle order right-hand batsman, slow right-arm off break bowler. *Teams* Natal (1958/9 to 1960/1); Western Province (1963/4 to 1966/7). *Tour* SA Fezela to England 1961.
Career batting
35–55–4–1743–127–34.17–2–*ct* 19
Bowling 33–2–16.50–0–0–1/0

Morcom, Dr Alfred Farr
Amateur. *b:* 16.2.1885, Dunstable, Beds. *d:* 12.2.1952, Westminster, London. Lower order right-hand batsman, right-arm fast medium bowler. *Sch* Repton. *Team* Cambridge U (1905–07, blue all three years).
Career batting
23–36–14–257–29–11.68–0–*ct* 10
Bowling 2322–97–23.95–5–1–7/76
His County cricket was for Bedfordshire.
His final first-class match was for MCC in 1911.

Mordaunt, David John
Amateur. *b:* 24.8.1937, Chelsea, London. Middle/lower order right-hand batsman, right-arm medium fast bowler. *Sch* Wellington. *Team* Sussex (1958–60, 19 matches). *Tours* MCC to North America 1959 (not first-class), to South America 1964/5 (not first-class).
Career batting
20–29–3–599–96–23.03–0–*ct* 15
Bowling 601–24–25.04–1–0–5/42
His final first-class match was for MCC in 1964; he also played for Berkshire.

Mordaunt, Eustace Charles
Amateur. *b:* 6.9.1870, Wellesbourne, Warwickshire. *d:* 21.6.1938, Marylebone, London. Son of J.M. (MCC 1863), brother of H.J. (Middlesex and Hants) and G.J. (Kent), nephew of Osbert (MCC). Lower order right-hand batsman, right-arm fast bowler. *Sch* Wellington. *Teams* Middlesex (1891–94, 4 matches); Kent (1896–97, 6 matches).
Career batting
11–18–0–132–21–7.33–0–*ct* 3
Bowling 136–4–34.00–0–0–1/4
He also appeared for Hampshire (non-first-class).
His final first-class match was for I Zingari in 1904.

Mordaunt, Gerald John
Amateur. *b:* 20.1.1873, Wellesbourne, Warwickshire. *d:* 5.3.1959, Hayling Island, Hants. Son of J.M. (MCC 1863), brother of H.J. (Middlesex) and E.C. (Middlesex), nephew of Osbert (MCC). Middle order right-hand batsman, slow ambidextrous under-arm bowler. *Sch* Wellington. *Teams* Oxford U (1893–96, blue all four years); Kent (1895–97, 16 matches). *Tour* Hawke to North America 1894.
Career batting
60–107–5–2675–264*–26.22–2–*ct* 72
Bowling 13–0
His highest score was 264* for Oxford v Sussex at Hove in 1895.
His final first-class match was for Gentlemen of England in 1904. A noted athlete, he represented Oxford in the long-jump.

Mordaunt, Sir Henry John
Amateur. *b:* 12.7.1867, Westminster, London. *d:* 15.1.1939, Westminster. Son of J.M. (MCC 1863), brother of E.C. (Middlesex and Kent) and G.J. (Kent), nephew of Osbert (MCC). Middle order right-hand batsman, right-arm fast, later slow, bowler. *Sch* Eton. *Teams* Hampshire (1885, 1 match); Cambridge U (1888–89, blue both years); Middlesex (1889–93, 7 matches).
Career batting
27–48–1–729–127–15.51–1–*ct* 13
Bowling 1037–49–21.16–1–0–5/17
His final first-class match was for MCC in 1896.

Mordaunt, Canon Osbert
Amateur. *b:* 4.12.1842, Walton, Warwickshire. *d:* 25.9.1923, Hampton Lucy, Warwickshire. Brother of J.M. (MCC 1863), uncle of H. J. (Middlesex), E. C. (Middlesex) and G. J. (Kent). Middle order right-hand batsman, lob bowler, delivering with either hand, good close field. *Sch* Eton. *Team* MCC (1866).
Career batting
1–2–0–11–6–5.50–0–*ct* 0
His County cricket was for Warwickshire (pre-first-class), Shropshire and Staffordshire.

Mordaunt, Osbert Cautley
Amateur. *b:* 26.5.1876, Flax Bourton, Somerset. *d:* 20.10.1949, Yew Green, Sussex. Lower order right-hand batsman, right-arm slow bowler. *Team* Somerset (1905–10, 14 matches).
Career batting
17–30–8–148–23–6.72–0–*ct* 12
Bowling 1115–42–26.55–1–0–5/68
His final first-class match was for L. Robinson's XI in 1914.

More, Hamish Kenneth
Cricketer. *b:* 30.5.1940, Edinburgh, Scotland. Middle or lower order right-hand batsman, wicket-keeper. *Team* Scotland (1966–76).
Career batting
18–36–2–639–89–18.79–0–*ct* 29–*st* 2
He played his final first-class match for T.N. Pearce's XI in 1976.

More, Richard Edwardes
Amateur. *b:* 3.1.1879, Linley, Salop. *d:* 24.11.1936, Cairo, Egypt. Attacking middle order right-hand batsman, right-arm medium pace bowler. *Sch* Westminster. *Teams* Oxford U (1898–1901, blue last two years); Middlesex (1901–10, 36 matches). *Tour* Bosanquet to North America 1901.
Career batting
57–92–12–1671–133–20.88–3–*ct* 38
Bowling 3430–124–27.66–4–2–6/28
His final first-class match was for G.J.V. Weigall's XI in 1914. He also played for Shropshire.
Being in the Egyptian Civil Service limited his opportunites for County cricket.

Morfee, Percival Ernest
Professional. *b:* 2.5.1886, Ashford, Kent. *d:* 1954. Lower order right-hand batsman, right-arm fast bowler. *Team* Kent (1910–12, 11 matches).
Career batting
11–17–7–132–32–13.20–0–*ct* 12
Bowling 934–28–33.35–1–0–5/47
He played for Scotland in a non-first-class match in 1913.

Morgan, Andrew Howard
Cricketer. *b:* 30.11.1945, Hastings, Sussex. Middle order left-hand batsman, wicket-keeper. *Team* Oxford U (1966–69, blue 1969).
Career batting
11–20–4–381–59*–23.81–0–*ct* 9

Morgan, Aubrey Neil
Amateur. *b:* 30.1.1904, Llandaff, Glamorgan. Brother of J.T. (Glamorgan). Lower order right-hand batsman, right-arm medium fast bowler. *Sch* Charterhouse. *Teams* Glamorgan (1928–29, 5 matches); Wales (1929).
Career batting
6–11–0–95–35–8.63–0–*ct* 1
Bowling 336–6–56.00–0–0–2/37

Morgan, Bertie Francis
Professional. *b:* 1886, Islington, Middlesex. *d:* 1959, Co Durham. Lower order right-hand batsman, left-arm bowler. *Team* Somerset (1909–10, 6 matches).
Career batting
6–11–0–63–23–5.72–0–*ct* 3
Bowling 175–2–87.50–0–0–1/19
He also played for Staffordshire.

Morgan, Charles
Amateur. *b:* 29.1.1839, Greenwich, Kent. *d:* 17.7.1904, Clapham, South London. Father of C.L. (Surrey, non-first-class). Lower order right-hand batsman, left-hand fast round-arm bowler. *Team* Surrey (1871, 4 matches).
Career batting
5–8–0–60–29–7.50–0–*ct* 2
Bowling 220–4–55.00–0–0–1/22
His first-class debut was for the Gentlemen of England in 1865.

Morgan, Charles
Professional. *b:* 7.2.1917, Clay Cross, Derbyshire. Lower order right-hand batsman, off break bowler. *Team* Nottinghamshire (1946, 1 match).
Career batting
1–2–0–13–13–6.50–0–*ct* 0
Bowling 94–0

Morgan, Derek Clifton
Professional. *b:* 26.2.1929, Muswell Hill, London. Middle order right-hand batsman, right-arm fast medium bowler, good close field. *Sch* Berkhamsted. *Team* Derbyshire (1950–69, 540 matches).
Career batting
556–882–146–18356–147–24.94–9–*ct* 572
Bowling 31302–1248–25.08–35–5–7/33
He hit 1,000 runs in a season eight times (best 1,669, av 46.36, in 1962). His best season with the ball was 1957 with 94 wickets, av 23.04.
He captained Derbyshire from 1965 to 1969.

Morgan, David Lindsay
Amateur. *b:* 5.11.1888, Tientsin, China. *d:* 22.1.1969, Pasadena, California, USA. Middle order batsman. *Sch* Clifton and Mill Hill. *Team* Gloucestershire (1907, 2 matches).
Career batting
2–4–0–3–2–0.75–0–*ct* 6

Morgan, Edward Noel
Amateur. *b:* 22.12.1905, Garnant, Carmarthenshire. *d:* 27.8.1975, Cardiff. Brother of W.G. (Glamorgan). Middle order right-hand batsman. *Team* Glamorgan (1934, 1 match).
Career batting
1–1–0–1–1–1.00–0–*ct* 0

Morgan, Henry Randolph
Amateur. *b:* 6.7.1907, Belfast, Ireland. Right-

hand batsman, right-arm fast medium bowler. *Team* Ireland (1931–38).
Career batting
4–8–3–54–21–10.80–0–*ct* 2
Bowling 187–18–10.39–1–1–7/41

Morgan, Howard William
Professional. *b:* 29.6.1931, Maesteg, Glamorgan. Lower order right-hand batsman, off break bowler. *Team* Glamorgan (1958, 2 matches).
Career batting
2–3–1–11–5–5.50–0–*ct* 0
Bowling 58–2–29.00–0–0–1/27

Morgan, John Trevil
Amateur. *b:* 7.5.1907, Llandaff, Glamorgan. *d:* 18.12.1976, Bristol. Brother of A.N. (Glamorgan). Middle order left-hand batsman, right-arm medium pace bowler, wicket-keeper. *Sch* Charterhouse. *Teams* Glamorgan (1925–34, 39 matches); Cambridge U (1927–30, blue last three years); Wales (1928).
Career batting
83–124–13–2339–149–21.07–4–*ct* 60–*st* 12
Bowling 1343–26–51.65–0–0–3/16

Morgan, Michael
Professional. *b:* 21.5.1936, Ynyshir, Glamorgan. Lower order right-hand batsman, off break bowler. *Team* Nottinghamshire (1957–61, 61 matches).
Career batting
61–86–16–488–56*–6.97–0–*ct* 24
Bowling 5287–146–36.21–3–0–6/50

Morgan, Michael Naunton
Amateur. *b:* 15.5.1932, Marylebone, London. Lower order right-hand batsman, right-arm fast medium bowler. *Sch* Marlborough. *Team* Cambridge U (1951–54, blue 1954).
Career batting
14–14–9–49–11*–9.80–0–*ct* 4
Bowling 1062–30–35.40–1–0–5/58

His final first-class match was for MCC in 1957. His County cricket was for Berkshire.

Morgan, Philip Richard Llewelyn
Amateur. *b:* 11.3.1927, Derby. Lower order right-hand batsman, leg break bowler. *Sch* St John's, Leatherhead. *Team* Oxford U (1946).
Career batting
1–1–0–1–1–1.00–0–*ct* 0
Bowling 38–0

Morgan, Rurie Tranton
Amateur. *b:* 30.7.1912, Wellington, New Zealand. *d:* 4.1.1980, Wellington, New Zealand. Middle order right-hand batsman, right-arm bowler. *Team* Wellington (1932/3 to 1940/1). *Tour* New Zealand Services to England 1945.
Career batting
11–20–2–374–81–20.77–0–*ct* 12
Bowling 384–12–32.00–0–0–2/34

Morgan, Ross Winston
Cricketer. *b:* 12.2.1941, Auckland, New Zealand. Middle order right-hand batsman, off break bowler. *Team* Auckland (1957/8 to 1976/7). *Tours* New Zealand to India and Pakistan 1964/5, to England 1965, to Australia 1969/70, 1970/1, to West Indies 1971/2. *Tests* New Zealand (1964/5 to 1971/2, 20 matches).
Career batting
136–229–13–5940–166–27.50–8–*ct* 85–*st* 1
Bowling 3558–108–32.94–4–0–6/40
Test batting
20–34–1–734–97–22.24–0–*ct* 12
Bowling 609–5–121.80–0–0–1/16

He played in all three Tests on the 1965 tour and in first-class matches scored 645 runs, av 23.88.

Morgan, Samuel Augustus
Cricketer. *b:* 7.8.1950, Half Way Tree, Kingston, Jamaica. Middle order batsman. *Team* Jamaica (1969/70 to 1973/4). *Tour* Jamaica to England 1970.
Career batting
22–35–3–998–126–31.18–1–*ct* 10
Bowling 82–1–82.00–0–0–1/16

Morgan, Thomas R.
Amateur. *b:* 1893. Middle order right-hand batsman. *Team* Glamorgan (1921–25, 39 matches).
Career batting
39–73–5–1044–87*–15.35–0–*ct* 5
Bowling 10–0

Morgan, William
Amateur. *b:* 1862. *d:* 22.10.1914, Porthleven, Cornwall. Lower order batsman, useful bowler. *Teams* Liverpool and District XI (1889); West of England (1894).
Career batting
3–5–0–34–24–6.80–0–*ct* 2
Bowling 32–3–10.66–0–0–2/21

Morgan, William Guy
(later Stewart-Morgan)
Amateur. *b:* 26.12.1907, Garnant, Carmarthenshire. *d:* 29.7.1973, Carmarthen. Brother of E.N. (Glamorgan). Middle order right-hand batsman, right-arm medium pace bowler. *Sch* Brecon. *Teams* Cambridge U (1927–28); Glamorgan (1927–38, 45 matches); Wales (1929).

Career batting
49–73–12–1071–91*–17.55–0–*ct* 8
Bowling 257–3–85.66–0–0–1/15
A noted rugby footballer, he played for Swansea, Cambridge and Wales.

Morgan, William Percival
Amateur. *b:* 1.1.1905, Abercrave, Brecon. *d:* 3.3.1983, Neath, Glamorgan. Middle order right-hand batsman, right-arm medium pace bowler. *Sch* Brecon. *Team* Glamorgan (1925, 1 match).
Career batting
1–2–0–4–4–2.00–0–*ct* 0
Bowling 0–0

Morkel, Denys Paul Beck
Amateur. *b:* 25.1.1906, Cape Town, South Africa. *d:* 6.10.1980, Nottingham. Brother of R.K.B. (Western Province). Attacking middle order right-hand batsman, right-arm fast medium bowler, slip field. *Team* Western Province (1924/5 to 1929/30). *Tours* South Africa to England 1929, to Australia and New Zealand 1931/32; Cahn to North America 1933 (not first-class), to Ceylon 1936/7. *Tests* South Africa (1927/8 to 1931/2, 16 matches).
Career batting
86–143–12–4494–251–34.30–8–*ct* 67
Bowling 4973–174–28.58–6–0–8/13
Test batting
16–28–1–663–88–24.55–0–*ct* 13
Bowling 821–18–45.61–0–0–4/93
He showed excellent all-round form on his 1929 tour to England, hitting 1,443 runs, av 34.35, and taking 69 wickets, av 26.01, in first-class matches and coming second in both the batting and bowling tables in the Tests. His highest innings was 251 for Cahn's XI v South Americans at Nottingham in 1932, his other double century being for Western Province.
He emigrated to England and appeared regularly for Sir J. Cahn's XI from 1932 to 1939. He also played for Bedfordshire. His last first-class match was for Sir J. Cahn's XI in 1938.

Morley, Frederick
Professional. *b:* 16.12.1850, Sutton-in-Ashfield, Notts. *d:* 28.9.1884, Sutton-in-Ashfield, Notts. Cousin of Thomas (Notts). Tail end left-hand batsman, left-arm fast bowler. *Team* Nottinghamshire (1872–83, 113 matches). *Tour* Bligh to Australia 1882/3. *Tests* England (1880 to 1882/3, 4 matches).
Career batting
232–355–95–1404–31–5.20–0–*ct* 107
Bowling 17103–1273+1–13.43–119–36–8/26
Test batting
4–6–2–6–2*–1.50–0–*ct* 4
Bowling 296–16–18.50–1–0–5/56
He took 100 wickets in a season seven times (best 197, av 12.11, in 1878).
On the sea voyage to Australia with Bligh's Team he was seriously injured when the ship was in collision with another and he never fully recovered from the accident.
His first-class debut was for the United North in 1871.

Morley, Henry
Professional. *b:* 1852, Edwinstowe, Notts. *d:* 16.8.1924, Edwinstowe, Notts. Lower order batsman, right-arm fast bowler. *Team* Nottinghamshire (1884, 1 match).
Career batting
1–1–0–0–0–0.00–0–*ct* 0
Bowling 29–2–14.50–0–0–1/9

Morley, Jeremy Dennis
Cricketer. *b:* 20.10.1950, Newmarket, Suffolk. Middle order left-hand batsman. *Team* Sussex (1971–76, 72 matches).
Career batting
72–131–12–2752–127–23.12–2–*ct* 26–*st* 1
Bowling 2–0

Morley, James Henry
Amateur. *b:* 20.12.1835, Herne Hill, London. *d:* 7.4.1904, Hove, Sussex. Lower order batsman, wicket-keeper. *Sch* Merchant Taylors'. *Team* Middlesex (1865, 1 match).
Career batting
1–2–1–25–19–25.00–0–*ct* 1–*st* 2

Morley, Thomas
Professional. *b:* 10.3.1863, Sutton-in-Ashfield, Notts. *d:* 28.10.1919, Thorpe St Andrew, Norwich. Cousin of Frederick (Notts). Stylish middle/lower order right-hand batsman, right-arm fast bowler. *Team* Nottinghamshire (1887, 1 match).
Career batting
1–2–0–17–12–8.50–0–*ct* 0
Bowling 5–0
He appeared for Norfolk from 1888 to 1900.
A useful soccer player, he represented Norfolk as a goalkeeper.

Mornement, Robert Harry
Amateur. *b:* 15.8.1873, Wayland, Norfolk. *d:* 16.4.1948, Chatham, Kent. Opening right-hand

batsman, right-arm medium pace bowler. *Team* Hampshire (1906, 3 matches).
Career batting
5–8–0–121–73–15.12–0–*ct* 4
Bowling 259–9–28.77–0–0–3/62

He played for the Combined Army and Navy Team in 1910 and 1911.

He also played for Norfolk.

Morres, Hugh Frederick Michael
Amateur. *b:* 8.7.1876, Wokingham, Berkshire. *d:* 28.1.1934, Wareham, Dorset. Middle order right-hand batsman, right-arm fast medium bowler. *Sch* Winchester. *Team* Oxford U (1898).
Career batting
2–3–0–29–28–9.66–0–*ct* 1
Bowling 10–0

His County cricket was for Berkshire and Dorset.

Morrill, Nicholas David
Cricketer. *b:* 9.12.1957, Ryde, Isle of Wight. Middle/lower order right-hand batsman, off break bowler. *Sch* Millfield. *Team* Oxford U (1978–79, blue 1979).
Career batting
14–21–3–241–45–13.38–0–*ct* 5
Bowling 741–12–61.75–0–0–3/53

Morris, Alan
Cricketer. *b:* 23.8.1953, Staveley, Derbyshire. Middle order right-hand batsman, leg break bowler. *Teams* Derbyshire (1974–78, 47 matches); Griqualand West (1979/80).
Career batting
49–81–5–1188–74–15.63–0–*ct* 31
Bowling 118–0

Morris, Alfred
Professional. *b:* 1874, West Hartlepool, Co Durham. *d:* 29.3.1961, Lancaster Moor, Lancashire. Lower order batsman, right-arm medium pace bowler. *Teams* Minor Counties (1912); England XI (1912).
Career batting
2–2–0–7–4–3.50–0–*ct* 0
Bowling 80–10–8.00–0–0–4/50

He played for Durham from 1905 to 1914.

Morris, Arthur Robert
Amateur. *b:* 19.1.1922, Dungog, New South Wales, Australia. Excellent opening left-hand batsman, slow left-arm bowler. *Team* New South Wales (1940/1 to 1954/5, 50 matches). *Tours* Australia to England 1948, 1953, to South Africa 1949/50, to West Indies 1954/5; Cavaliers to India and South Africa 1962/3; Presidents XI (Defence Fund Match) in India 1963/4. *Tests* Australia (1946/7 to 1954/5, 46 matches).
Career batting
162–250–15–12614–290–53.67–46–*ct* 73
Bowling 592–12–49.33–0–0–3/36
Test batting
46–79–3–3533–206–46.48–12–*ct* 15
Bowling 50–2–25.00–0–0–1/5

He had a splendid first tour of England in 1948, topping the Test batting averages with 696 runs, av 87.00, and in all first-class matches hitting 1,922 runs, av 71.18, including his highest innings of 290 v Gloucs at Bristol. He was not so successful in 1953, but in first-class matches hit 1,303 runs, av 38.29. He hit 1,000 runs in an Australian season three times and once in South Africa.

His most outstanding record was the scoring of a century in each innings of his first-class debut match : 148 and 111 for New South Wales v Queensland at Sydney in 1940/1.

Morris, Charles Anthony
Amateur. *b:* 9.5.1939, Cambridge. Middle order left-hand batsman, leg break bowler. *Sch* Marlborough. *Team* Cambridge U (1960).
Career batting
4–6–1–23–8–4.60–0–*ct* 3
Bowling 47–0

A useful rugby footballer, he appeared at scrum half for Rosslyn Park.

Morris, Charles Christopher
Amateur. *b:* 30.6.1882, USA. *d:* 17.6.1971, Villanova, Pennsylvania, USA. Middle order right-hand batsman, leg break and googly bowler, good close field. *Team* Philadelphia (1901-13). *Tours* Philadelphians to England 1903, 1908.
Career batting
35–62–2–1251–164–20.85–1–*ct* 22

Although he hit the highest score on the 1903 tour, his batting was on the whole disappointing. In 1908 his batting was again not up to the standard he displayed at home. He represented USA v Canada in 5 matches. The cricket library at Haverford College was named in his honour.

Morris, Charles Richard
Amateur. *b:* 26.8.1880, Nottingham. *d:* 10.8.1947, Hampstead, London. Middle order right-hand batsman. *Sch* Oakham. *Team* Nottinghamshire (1902–04, 5 matches).
Career batting
5–8–1–63–24*–9.00–0–*ct* 5

Morris, Edward Silvester
Amateur. *b:* 1849, Bedminster, Gloucs. *d:* 1928,

Rochdale, Lancashire. Useful batsman. *Team* Gloucestershire (1870, 2 matches).
Career batting
2–2–0–30–17–15.00–0–*ct* 0

Morris, Hugh
Cricketer. *b:* 5.10.1963, Canton, Cardiff. Middle order left-hand batsman. *Sch* Blundell's. *Team* Glamorgan (1981–83, 13 matches).
Career batting
13–22–6–462–63–28.87–0–*ct* 8
Bowling 23–0

Morris, Huson
Amateur. *b:* 22.5.1848, Kensington, London. *d:* 14.2.1924, St Jean de Luz, France. Middle order right-hand batsman, right-hand fast medium round-arm bowler. *Sch* Lancing and Dulwich. *Team* MCC (1868).
Career batting
1–1–0–0–0–0.00–0–*ct* 1

Morris, Harold Marsh
Amateur. *b:* 16.4.1898, Wanstead, Essex. Middle order right-hand batsman, right-arm medium pace bowler. *Sch* Repton. *Team* Essex (1919–32, 240 matches). *Tour* Tennyson to Jamaica 1926/7.
Career batting
246–393–30–7086–166–19.52–3–*ct* 80
Bowling 885–16–55.31–0–0–2/16
He captained Essex 1929 to 1932.

Morris, Ian
Cricketer. *b:* 27.6.1946, Maesteg, Glamorgan. Middle order right-hand batsman, slow left-arm bowler, close field. *Team* Glamorgan (1966–68, 14 matches).
Career batting
14–25–2–253–38–11.00–0–*ct* 15
Bowling 141–4–35.25–0–0–2/30

Morris, John Edward
Cricketer. *b:* 1.4.1964, Crewe, Cheshire. Middle order right-hand batsman, right-arm medium pace bowler. *Team* Derbyshire (1982–83, 11 matches).
Career batting
11–22–1–379–58–18.04–0–*ct* 4
Bowling 0–0

Morris, John Frederick
Amateur. *b:* 14.10.1880, Ampthill, Bedfordshire. *d:* 23.3.1960, Norwich. Lower order right-hand batsman, slow right-arm bowler. *Sch* Wellingborough. *Team* Cambridge U (1902).
Career batting
1–2–2–9–7*–no av–0–*ct* 0
His County cricket was for Bedfordshire.

Morris, Leonard John
Amateur. *b:* 26.9.1898, Birmingham. *d:* 9.3.1984, Dorridge, Warwickshire. Middle order left-hand batsman, right-arm medium pace bowler. *Team* Warwickshire (1925–26, 7 matches).
Career batting
7–11–0–262–76–23.81–0–*ct* 4
Bowling 70–3–23.33–0–0–2/41

Morris, Norman
Amateur. *b:* 1849, Peckham. *d:* 20.1.1874, Ford, Lingfield, Surrey. Middle order right-hand batsman, wicket-keeper. *Sch* Tonbridge. *Teams* Kent (1870–72, 10 matches); Surrey (1873, 5 matches).
Career batting
17–33–0–473–64–14.33–0–*ct* 7–*st* 4
Bowling 14–0

Morris, Philip Edward
Amateur. *b:* 26.11.1877, Kennington, London. *d:* 6.7.1945, Hove, Sussex. Lower order batsman, leg break bowler. *Sch* Mill Hill and Bancrofts. *Team* Essex (1909–24, 28 matches).
Career batting
28–43–5–418–55*–11.00–0–*ct* 13
Bowling 1848–83–22.24–6–1–8/106

Morris, P. J.
Amateur. Middle order batsman. *Team* Worcestershire (1914, 1 match).
Career batting
1–2–0–74–71–37.00–0–*ct* 1
Bowling 13–0

Morris, Ray
Amateur. *b:* 20.6.1929, Hartlebury, Worcs. Lower order right-hand batsman, wicket-keeper. *Team* Worcestershire (1958, 2 matches).
Career batting
2–3–0–7–7–2.33–0–*ct* 8

Morris, Robert John
Amateur. *b:* 27.11.1926, Swansea, Glamorgan. Son of W.P. (Glamorgan). Sound opening right-hand batsman, off break bowler. *Sch* Blundell's. *Teams* Kent (1950, 2 matches); Cambridge U (1949–51, blue 1949).
Career batting
22–36–2–778–96–22.88–0–*ct* 7
Bowling 192–2–96.00–0–0–1/38

Morris, Vernon Leslie
Amateur. *b:* 13.6.1894, Neath, Glamorgan. *d:* 11.1.1973, Exmouth, Devon. Opening right-hand batsman. *Team* Glamorgan (1921–29, 18 matches).
Career batting
18–33–1–407–42–12.71–0–*ct* 9

Morris, William
Amateur. *b:* 23.11.1873, Lee, Kent. *d:* 6.5.1945, Kensington, London. Steady middle order right-hand batsman. *Team* Kent (1896, 2 matches).
Career batting
2–4–0–14–6–3.50–0–*ct* 0

Morris, William Bancroft
Professional. *b:* 28.5.1917, Kingston, Jamaica. Middle order right-hand batsman, slow leg break bowler. *Team* Essex (1946–50, 48 matches).
Career batting
48–78–10–1219–68–17.92–0–*ct* 18
Bowling 1975–43–45.93–0–0–4/90
He also played for Cambridgeshire.

Morris, William Percy
Professional. *b:* 19.6.1881, Swansea, Glamorgan. *d:* 30.7.1975, Swansea. Father of R.J. (Kent). Opening or middle order right-hand batsman, right-arm medium pace bowler. *Team* Glamorgan (1921–25, 8 matches).
Career batting
9–18–1–159–30–9.35–0–*ct* 6
Bowling 99–2–49.50–0–0–1/11
His first-class debut was for South Wales in 1912.

Morrison, Charles Stuart
Amateur. *b:* 27.5.1883, Jamaica. *d:* 25.11.1948, Kingston, Jamaica. Lower order right-hand batsman, right-arm slow medium bowler. *Team* Jamaica (1904/5 to 1925/6). *Tour* West Indies to England 1906.
Career batting
25–44–10–396–54–11.64–0–*ct* 13
Bowling 1236–60–20.60–2–1–7/44
Although quite effective in the minor matches of the 1906 tour, his bowling return was modest in first-class matches.

Morrison, Ewart Gladstone
Amateur. *b:* 7.10.1899, Ceylon. Middle order left-hand batsman, left-arm medium pace bowler. *Team* Gloucestershire (1926–33, 20 matches).
Career batting
20–34–1–340–59–10.30–0–*ct* 12
Bowling 209–3–69.66–0–0–1/30

Morrison, George Charles
Amateur. *b:* 27.6.1915, Downpatrick, Co Down, Ireland. Right-hand batsman. *Team* Ireland (1947).
Career batting
2–4–0–48–16–12.00–0–*ct* 0
Bowling 32–0

Morrison, John Stanton Fleming
Amateur. *b:* 17.4.1892, Newcastle-upon-Tyne. *d:* 28.1.1961, Farnham, Surrey. Middle order right-hand batsman, wicket-keeper. *Sch* Charterhouse. *Teams* Cambridge U (1912–19, blue 1912, 1914 and 1919); Somerset (1920, 1 match).
Career batting
38–67–2–1982–233*–30.49–4–*ct* 21–*st* 4
Bowling 6–1–6.00–0–0–1/6
His final first-class match was for Combined Universities in 1922. He also played for Northumberland. His highest score was 233* for Cambridge U v MCC at Cambridge in 1914.
A useful soccer player he appeared for Sunderland.

Morrogh, W. C. F. M.
(*see under* MacCarthy-Morrogh, W. C. F.)

Morrow, George Alexander
Amateur. *b:* 1877, Ireland. *d:* 15.11.1914, Ranelagh, Dublin, Ireland. Middle order right-hand batsman. *Team* Ireland (1907–12).
Career batting
6–10–0–149–49–14.90–0–*ct* 3
A noted badminton player, he represented Ireland.

Mortensen, Ole Henrek
Cricketer. *b:* 29.1.1958, Vejle, Jutland, Denmark. Lower order right hand batsman, right-arm fast medium bowler. *Team* Derbyshire (1983, 18 matches).
Career batting
18–23–15–76–14*–9.50–0–*ct* 5
Bowling 1605–66–24.31–3–1–6/27
He represented Denmark commencing 1975.

Morter, Frank William
Amateur. *b:* 14.8.1897, Down, Kent. *d:* 20.12.1958, Birmingham. Lower order right-hand batsman, right-arm medium fast bowler. *Team* Warwickshire (1922, 3 matches).
Career batting
3–5–2–13–8–4.33–0–*ct* 0
Bowling 138–3–46.00–0–0–2/5

Mortimer, Harry
Professional. *b:* 1872, Sculcoates, Yorkshire. *d:* 1953, Birmingham. Lower order batsman,

wicket-keeper. *Team* Worcestershire (1904, 1 match).
Career batting
1–2–0–11–7–5.50–0–*ct* 0

Mortimer, John
Amateur. *b:* 13.1.1911, Peterculter, Aberdeenshire, Scotland. *d:* 22.3.1967, Aberdeen, Scotland. Right-hand batsman, off break bowler. *Team* Scotland (1932–33).
Career batting
2–3–0–20–18–6.66–0–*ct* 3
Bowling 154–8–19.25–0–0–3/67

Mortimer, Sir Ralph George Elphinstone
Amateur. *b:* 7.7.1869, Newcastle-upon-Tyne. *d:* 3.5.1955, Melbourne, Northumberland. Middle order right-hand batsman. *Sch* Harrow. *Team* Lancashire (1891, 1 match).
Career batting
1–1–1–22–22*–no av–0–*ct* 0

He did not appear in any first-class matches whilst at Cambridge. He also assisted Northumberland, commencing 1893.

Mortimore, John Brian
Professional. *b:* 14.5.1933, Bristol. Lower order right-hand batsman, off break bowler. *Team* Gloucestershire (1950–75, 594 matches). *Tours* MCC to Australia and New Zealand 1958/9, to India 1963/4, to East Africa 1963/4; Brown to East Africa, 1961/2 (not first-class); Gloucestershire to Bermuda, 1962 (not first-class). *Tests* England (1958/9 to 1964, 9 matches).
Career batting
640–989–122–15891–149–18.32–4–*ct* 348
Bowling 41904–1807–23.18–75–8–8/59
Test batting
9–12–2–243–73*–24.30–0–*ct* 3
Bowling 733–13–56.38–0–0–3/36

He hit 1,000 runs in a season five times (best 1,425, av 26.88, in 1963) and took 100 wickets in a season three times (best 113, av 18.28, in 1959). He achieved the 'double' in three seasons.

He captained Gloucestershire 1965 to 1967.

Mortlock, Harry Clive
Amateur. *b:* 13.10.1892, Hackney, Middlesex. *d:* 29.3.1963, Brentwood, Essex. Lower order batsman, slow left-arm bowler. *Sch* Brentwood and Felsted. *Team* Essex (1912–21, 4 matches).
Career batting
4–4–0–32–26–8.00–0–*ct* 6
Bowling 380–7–54.28–1–0–5/104

Mortlock, William
Professional. *b:* 18.7.1832, Kennington, Surrey. *d:* 23.1.1884, Brixton, Surrey. Opening/middle order right-hand batsman, right-arm medium, later lob, bowler, long stop. *Team* Surrey (1851–70, 138 matches). *Tour* Stephenson to Australia 1861/2.
Career batting
191–330–35–5528–106–18.73–3–*ct* 85
Bowling 2615–147–17.78–7–2–7/42

Morton, Arthur
Professional. *b:* 27.3.1882, Salford, Lancashire. *d:* 21.2.1970, Sheffield, Yorkshire. Right-hand batsman, right-arm fast medium bowler. *Team* Derbyshire (1901, 1 match).
Career batting
1–2–0–0–0–0.00–0–*ct* 0
Bowling 14–0

Morton, Arthur
Professional. *b:* 7.5.1883, Mellor, Derbyshire. *d:* 19.12.1935, Hayfield, Derbyshire. Middle order right-hand batsman, right-arm medium pace off break bowler. *Team* Derbyshire (1903–26, 350 matches).
Career batting
357–623–56–10957–131–19.32–6–*ct* 128
Bowling 22352–981–22.78–63–11–9/71

He hit 1,000 runs in a season once : 1,089, av 25.32, in 1914 and took 100 wickets in a season twice (best 116, av 22.67, in 1910). His best bowling was 9/71 for Derbyshire v Notts at Blackwell in 1911.

After leaving County cricket he umpired in first-class matches and in several Tests.

Morton, A. F. M.
(*see under* Mathie-Morton, A. F.)

Morton, Geoffrey Dalgleish
Professional. *b:* 27.7.1922, Acton, Middlesex. Lower order right-hand batsman, right-arm medium fast bowler. *Team* Middlesex (1950, 2 matches).
Career batting
3–3–2–1–1–1.00–0–*ct* 3
Bowling 146–0

His final first-class match was for MCC in 1952.

An excellent soccer player, he kept goal for Watford and Southend.

Morton, John
Amateur. *b:* 1895, Coventry, Warwickshire. *d:* 28.5.1966, Leamington Spa, Warwickshire. Middle order right-hand batsman. *Team* Warwickshire (1929–30, 9 matches).
Career batting
9–14–0–162–38–11.57–0–*ct* 4

Morton, Malcolm James Henry
Amateur. *b:* 13.5.1910, West Southbourne, Hants. Opening/middle order right-hand batsman, slow left-arm bowler. *Sch* Marlborough. *Team* Cambridge U (1931).
Career batting
1–2–0–3–2–1.50–0–*ct* 0

Morton, Philip Howard
Amateur. *b:* 20.6.1857, Tatterford, Norfolk. *d:* 13.5.1925, Boscombe, Hants. Lower order right-hand batsman, right-arm fast bowler, good close field. *Sch* Rossall. *Teams* Cambridge U (1877–80, blue 1878, 1879 and 1880); Surrey (1884, 2 matches).
Career batting
31–45–18–346–39*–12.81–0–*ct* 14
Bowling 2019–139–14.53–14–2–7/45

His final first-class match was for Cambridge University Past and Present in 1886. He also appeared for Norfolk.

Being in the scholastic profession limited his appearances in first-class matches after leaving Cambridge.

Morton, William
Cricketer. *b:* 21.4.1961, Stirling, Scotland. Left-hand batsman, slow left-arm bowler. *Team* Scotland (1982–83).
Career batting
2–2–0–8–5–4.00–0–*ct* 3
Bowling 216–9–24.00–0–0–4/40

Moseley, Ezra Alphonsa
Cricketer. *b:* 5.1.1958, Christ Church, Barbados. Lower order right-hand batsman, right-arm fast medium bowler. *Teams* Glamorgan (1980–81, 29 matches); Barbados (1981/2). *Tour* West Indies to South Africa 1982/3.
Career batting
35–42–10–714–70*–22.31–0–*ct* 11
Bowling 2870–125–22.96–5–0–6/23

Moseley, Hallam Reynold
Cricketer. *b:* 28.5.1948, Providence, Barbados. Lower order right-hand batsman, right-arm fast medium bowler. *Teams* Barbados (1969 to 1971/2); Somerset (1971–82, 205 matches). *Tour* Barbados to England 1969.
Career batting
213–217–94–1533–67–12.46–0–*ct* 78
Bowling 13668–557–24.53–16–1–6/34

Moses, Eric Claude
(changed name to Murray)
Amateur. *b:* 18.7.1893, Johannesburg, South Africa. *d:* 10.7.1971, Durban, South Africa. Middle order right-hand batsman, off break bowler. *Sch* Repton. *Teams* Derbyshire (1911, 3 matches); Transvaal (1912/3 to 1922/3).
Career batting
11–18–1–125–31–7.35–0–*ct* 10
Bowling 291–17–17.11–0–0–4/32

He played for Derbyshire with still another season ahead of him at Repton.

Moses, Geoffrey Haydn
Cricketer. *b:* 24.9.1952, Mountain Ash, Glamorgan. Tail end left-hand batsman, right-arm fast medium bowler. *Team* Cambridge U (1974, blue).
Career batting
3–4–2–37–24*–18.50–0–*ct* 0
Bowling 176–9–19.55–1–0–5/31

Mosey, Stuart David Houlden
Amateur. *b:* 28.11.1937, Keighley, Yorkshire. Lower order right-hand batsman, right-arm fast medium bowler. *Team* Cambridge U (1959).
Career batting
2–2–1–17–17*–17.00–0–*ct* 0
Bowling 203–1–203.00–0–0–1/42

Mosley, Henry
Professional. *b:* 8.3.1850, Kildwick, Skipton, Yorkshire. *d:* 1933, Huddersfield, Yorkshire. Lower order right-hand batsman, left-arm fast bowler. *Team* Yorkshire (1881, two matches).
Career batting
3–5–1–1–1–0.25–0–*ct* 1
Bowling 65–4–16.25–0–0–3/12

Moss, Alan Edward
Professional. *b:* 14.11.1930, Tottenham, North London. Tail end right-hand batsman, right-arm fast medium bowler. *Team* Middlesex (1950–63, 307 matches). *Tours* MCC to West Indies 1953/4, 1959/60, to Pakistan 1955/6; Norfolk to Jamaica 1956/7; Howard to India 1956/7; Cavaliers to South Africa 1960/1. *Tests* England (1953/4 to 1960, 9 matches).
Career batting
382–410–171–1671–40–6.99–0–*ct* 143
Bowling 27035–1301–20.78–65–13–8/31
Test batting
9–7–1–61–26–10.16–0–*ct* 1
Bowling 626–21–29.80–0–0–4/35

He took 100 wickets in a season five times (best 136, av 13.72, in 1960).

His final first-class match was for Free Foresters in 1968.

Moss, Ernest
Professional. Lower order batsman, useful bowler. *Team* Glamorgan (1923, 1 match).

Career batting
1–2–0–15–10–7.50–0–*ct* 1
Bowling 70–2–35.00–0–0–2/70

Moss, Edward Henry
Amateur. *b:* 25.5.1911, Godden Green, Kent. *d:* 31.3.1944. He was killed during a raid on Leipzig, Germany. Attacking middle order right-hand batsman, good field. *Sch* Malvern. *Team* Oxford U (1933–34).
Career batting
5–10–0–206–50–20.60–0–*ct* 2
His County cricket was for Berkshire.
He represented Oxford at golf.

Moss, John
Professional. *b:* 7.2.1864, Clifton, Notts. *d:* 10.7.1950, Keyworth, Notts. Middle order right-hand batsman, right-arm medium pace bowler. *Team* Nottinghamshire (1892, 1 match). *Tours* Brackley to West Indies 1904/5 (as umpire); MCC to New Zealand 1906/7 (as umpire).
Career batting
1–2–0–2–1–1.00–0–*ct* 0
He was a County umpire from 1889 to 1924 and stood in four Test series.

Moss, Rev Reginald Heber
Amateur. *b:* 24.2.1868, Huyton, Lancashire. *d:* 19.3.1956, Bridport, Dorset. Lower order right-hand batsman, right-arm fast, later medium, bowler. *Sch* Radley. *Teams* Oxford U (1887–89, blue 1889); Worcestershire (1925, 1 match).
Career batting
16–28–10–123–18*–6.83–0–*ct* 11
Bowling 886–25–35.44–0–0–4/19
His first-class career is a curiosity – his final match was for Worcs v Gloucs in May 1925, but his penultimate game had taken place in August 1893 – Liverpool and District v Australians.
He also played for Bedfordshire and Herefordshire.

Motley, Arthur
Amateur. *b:* 5.2.1858, Osmondthorpe, Yorkshire. *d:* 29.9.1897, New Zealand. Middle/lower order right-hand batsman, right-arm fast bowler. *Teams* Yorkshire (1879, 2 matches); Wellington (1886/7 to 1888/9).
Career batting
7–10–2–106–58*–13.25–0–*ct* 1
Bowling 135–7–19.28–0–0–4/48
He was regarded as one of the fastest bowlers in England, but by some his bowling was looked upon as a pure throw.
He emigrated to Australia in the autumn of 1879 and later to New Zealand.

Mottram, Thomas James
Cricketer. *b:* 7.9.1945, Liverpool. Tail end right-hand batsman, right-arm medium pace bowler. *Team* Hampshire (1972–76, 35 matches).
Career batting
35–35–18–95–15*–5.58–0–*ct* 11
Bowling 2671–111–24.11–4–0–6/63

Motz, Richard Charles
Amateur. *b:* 12.1.1940, Christchurch, New Zealand. Aggressive lower order right-hand batsman, right-arm fast bowler. *Team* Canterbury (1957/8 to 1968/9). *Tours* New Zealand to South Africa 1961/2, to Australia 1961/2, 1967/8 to England 1965 and 1969, to India and Pakistan 1964/5. *Tests* New Zealand (1961/2 to 1969, 32 matches).
Career batting
142–225–21–3494–103*–17.12–1–*ct* 41
Bowling 11767–518–22.71–23–4–8/61
Test batting
32–56–3–612–60–11.54–0–*ct* 9
Bowling 3148–100–31.48–5–0–6/63
On his first tour of England in 1965, he headed the Test bowling averages and took most wickets in first-class matches – 54, av 22.98; in 1969 he was suffering from a displaced vertebra and although appearing in all three Tests, achieved little. His injury resulted in his retirement from first-class cricket after the tour.

Moulder, John Hardie
Professional. *b:* 29.9.1881, Richmond, Surrey. *d:* 13.10.1933, South Africa. Middle order right-hand batsman, right-arm off break bowler. *Teams* Surrey (1902–06, 24 matches); London County (1904); Transvaal (1909/10 to 1912/13).
Career batting
36–52–6–757–70–16.45–0–*ct* 13
Bowling 413–14–29.50–0–0–3/33

Moulding, Roger Peter
Cricketer. *b:* 3.1.1958, Enfield, Middlesex. Middle order right-hand batsman, leg break bowler. *Sch* Haberdashers' Aske's. *Teams* Middlesex (1977, 1 match); Oxford U (1978–83, blue all six years).
Career batting
47–79–9–1344–80*–19.20–0–*ct* 17
Bowling 22–0

Moule, Alfred Samuel
Professional. *b:* 31.7.1894, West Ham, Essex. *d:* 5.2.1973, Shoreham by Sea, Sussex. Middle order right-hand batsman. *Team* Essex (1921–24, 17 matches).

Career batting
17–31–5–317–64–12.19–0–*ct* 5
Bowling 6–0
He also played for Devon.
A good soccer player, he appeared for Millwall, Norwich City and Watford.

Moule, Harry George
Amateur. *b:* 23.12.1921, Kidderminster, Worcs. Attractive opening right-hand batsman. *Team* Worcestershire (1952, 1 match).
Career batting
1–2–0–102–57–51.00–0–*ct* 0

Moule, Judge William Henry
Amateur. *b:* 31.1.1858, Brighton, Victoria, Australia. *d:* 24.8.1939, St Kilda, Victoria, Australia. Lower order right-hand batsman, right-arm medium pace bowler, good deep field. *Team* Victoria (1878/9 to 1885/6, 4 matches). *Tour* Australia to England 1880. *Test* Australia (1880, 1 match).
Career batting
9–15–3–137–34–11.41–0–*ct* 7
Bowling 106–5–21.20–0–0–3/23
Test batting
1–2–0–40–34–20.00–0–*ct* 1
Bowling 23–3–7.66–0–0–3/23
Although he played very little first-class cricket, he batted and bowled well in the Oval Test of 1880.

Mounsey, Joseph Thomas
Professional. *b:* 30.8.1871, Heeley, Sheffield. *d:* 6.4.1949, Godalming, Surrey. Steady middle order right-hand batsman, right-arm medium pace bowler. *Team* Yorkshire (1891–97, 94 matches).
Career batting
94–147–21–1963–64–15.57–0–*ct* 45
Bowling 476–13–36.61–0–0–3/58

Mounteney, Arthur
Professional. *b:* 11.2.1883, Belgrave, Leicester. *d:* 1.6.1933, Leicester. Attractive middle order right-hand batsman. *Team* Leicestershire (1911–24, 144 matches).
Career batting
144–267–12–5306–153–20.80–6–*ct* 53
Bowling 504–17–29.64–0–0–3/38
A noted soccer player, he appeared for Leicester Fosse, Birmingham City, Preston North End and Grimsby Town.

Mountford, Peter Neville George
Amateur. *b:* 21.6.1940, Birmingham. Lower order right-hand batsman, right-arm medium fast bowler. *Sch* Bromsgrove. *Team* Oxford U (1962–63, blue 1963).
Career batting
18–27–11–111–22*–6.93–0–*ct* 5
Bowling 1606–40–40.15–1–0–7/47

Moxon, Howard
Amateur. *b:* 23.3.1940, Elsecar, Yorkshire. Middle order right-hand batsman, right-arm medium pace bowler. *Team* Cambridge U (1960).
Career batting
1–2–0–24–23–12.00–0–*ct* 0

Moxon, Martyn Douglas
Cricketer. *b:* 4.5.1960, Barnsley, Yorkshire. Middle order right-hand batsman, right-arm medium pace bowler. *Teams* Yorkshire (1981–83, 25 matches); Griqualand West (1982/3).
Career batting
31–58–1–1888–153–33.12–4–*ct* 17
Bowling 174–1–174.00–0–0–1/25
He scored 116 in the second innings of his first-class debut, Yorkshire v Essex at Headingley in 1981.

Moylan, Adrian Charles David
Cricketer. *b:* 26.6.1955, Weston-super-Mare, Somerset. Opening left-hand batsman, slow left-arm bowler. *Sch* Clifton. *Team* Cambridge U (1976–77, blue 1977).
Career batting
5–9–0–176–29–19.55–0–*ct* 1
Bowling 3–0

Moylan-Jones, Roger Charles
Cricketer. *b:* 18.4.1940, Torquay, Devon. Middle order right-hand batsman, off break bowler. *Team* Combined Services (1964).
Career batting
1–2–0–34–31–17.00–0–*ct* 0
Bowling 36–2–18.00–0–0–2/36
His County cricket was for Devon.

Mubarak, Aziz Mohamed
Cricketer. *b:* 4.7.1951, Colombo, Ceylon. Opening right-hand batsman, right-arm medium off break bowler. *Team* Cambridge U (1978–80, blue all three years).
Career batting
24–38–2–765–105–21.25–1–*ct* 14
Bowling 6–0

Mucklow, Peter
Cricketer. *b:* 5.11.1949, Warwick. Middle order right-hand batsman. *Team* Oxford U (1970).
Career batting
2–4–0–48–32–12.00–0–*ct* 1

Mudassar Nazar
Cricketer. *b:* 6.4.1956, Lahore, India. Son of Nazar Mohammad (Pakistan). Sound opening

right-hand batsman, right-arm medium pace bowler. *Teams* Lahore (1971/2 to 1974/5); Universities (1974/5); Habib Bank (1975/6); PIA (1975/6 to 1977/8); United Bank (1978/9 to 1982/3). *Tours* Pakistan to Sri Lanka 1975/6, Australia 1976/7, 1981/2, Australia and New Zealand 1978/9, England 1978, 1982. *Tests* Pakistan (1976/7 to 1982/3, 35 matches).
Career batting
144–238–25–10119–241–47.50–31–*ct* 96
Bowling 2598–86–30.20–1–0–6/32
Test batting
35–54–5–2138–231–43.63–6–*ct* 23
Bowling 839–25–33.56–1–0–6/32

On his first tour to England in 1978 he hit 677 runs, av 33.85, in first-class matches and appeared in all three Tests, though not being successful in these. This pattern was repeated in 1982 when he topped the first-class averages with 825 runs, av 82.50, but scored few runs in the Tests; in the second Test however he took 6 wickets for 32 in the second innings and with ten wickets in the series headed the bowling table. He hit 1,000 in a season in Pakistan three times (best 1,110, av 85.38, in 1982/3). He scored the slowest 100 in first-class cricket (557 minutes) for Pakistan v England at Lahore in 1977/8. He also played for Cheshire.

Muddiah, Ventappa Musandra
Amateur. *b:* 8.6.1929, Bangalore, India. Tail end right-hand batsman, right-arm medium off break bowler. *Teams* Services (1949/50 to 1960/1); Hyderabad (1953/4). *Tour* India to England 1959. *Tests* India (1959/60 to 1960/1, 2 matches).
Career batting
61–71–13–805–67–13.87–0–*ct* 62
Bowling 4159–175–23.76–10–1–8/54
Test batting
2–3–1–11–11–5.50–0–*ct* 0
Bowling 134–3–44.66–0–0–2/40

He achieved very little on his tour to England, being unable to adapt to turf wickets and also missing many matches through illness.

His final first-class match was for Indian Air Force in 1962/3.

Mudge, Harold
Professional. *b:* 14.2.1914, Stanmore, New South Wales, Australia. Middle order right-hand batsman, leg break and googly bowler. *Teams* New South Wales (1935/6 to 1939/40, 14 matches); Leicestershire (1937, 1 match). *Tours* Cahn to Ceylon 1936/7, to New Zealand 1938/9 (not in first-class matches).
Career batting
18–34–2–1060–118–33.12–1–*ct* 15
Bowling 1106–25–44.24–2–0–6/42

His last first-class match in England was for Sir J. Cahn's XI in 1938.

Mudie, William
Professional. *b:* 26.4.1836, Kennington, Surrey. *d:* 25.1.1871, Vauxhall, Surrey. He died of paralysis of the brain. Steady middle order right-hand batsman, right-hand slow round-arm or under-arm bowler. *Team* Surrey (1856–65, 37 matches). *Tour* Stephenson to Australia 1861/2.
Career batting
41–64–11–666–79–12.56–0–*ct* 28
Bowling 760–47+1–16.17–3–0–7/61

Mugliston, Francis Hugh
Amateur. *b:* 7.6.1886, Singapore. *d:* 3.10.1932, Marylebone, London. Lower order right-hand batsman, right-arm slow medium bowler. *Sch* Rossall. *Teams* Lancashire (1906–08, 7 matches); Cambridge U (1906–08, blue last two years).
Career batting
33–55–1–874–109–16.18–1–*ct* 16
Bowling 301–4–75.25–0–0–3/32

His final first-class match was for H.D.G. Leveson-Gower's XI in 1911.

A noted soccer player, he appeared as left back for Oxford and the Corinthians. He also represented Oxford at golf.

Muir-Mackenzie, Sir Kenneth Augustus
Amateur. *b:* 29.6.1845, Scotland. *d:* 22.5.1930, Regent's Park, London. Middle order batsman. *Sch* Charterhouse. *Team* MCC (1870).
Career batting
1–2–0–21–17–10.50–0–*ct* 0

Mulholland, Hon Godfrey John Arthur Murray Lyle
Amateur. *b:* 3.10.1892, Monkstown, Ireland. *d:* 1.3.1948, St Pancras, London. Brother of H.G.H. (Cambridge U). Middle order batsman. *Sch* Eton. *Team* Cambridge U (1912).
Career batting
1–2–1–9–6–9.00–0–*ct* 1

Mulholland, Hon Sir Henry George Hill
Amateur. *b:* 20.12.1888, Monkstown, Ireland. *d:* 5.3.1971, Bellaghy, Co Derry, Ireland. Brother of G.J.A.M.L. (Cambridge U). Middle order right-hand batsman, slow right-arm bowler. *Sch* Eton. *Teams* Cambridge U (1911–14, blue 1911, 1912 and 1913); Ireland (1911). *Tour* Incogniti to USA 1913 (not first-class).
Career batting
32–55–1–1642–153–30.40–4–*ct* 37
Bowling 1217–51–23.66–2–0–5/9

It was intended that he should play in the 1914 University Match, but in deference to an agreement of some 50 years previous he stood down.

He was an MP and Speaker of the Northern Ireland House of Commons from 1929 to 1945.

Mulla, Hormasji Furdunji
Amateur. *b:* 4.5.1885, Bombay, India. Middle order right-hand batsman, wicket-keeper. *Team* Parsis (1907/8 to 1915/16). *Tour* India to England 1911.
Career batting
28–46–1–781–151–17.35–1–*ct* 26–*st* 13
He achieved very little on his visit to England.

Mumford, George
Professional. *b:* 1.2.1845, Ealing, Middlesex. *d:* 12.11.1877, Ealing, Middlesex. He died of consumption. Lower order right-hand batsman, left-hand fast round-arm bowler. *Team* Middlesex (1867–72, 2 matches).
Career batting
4–7–1–12–4*–2.00–0–*ct* 1
Bowling 39–1–39.00–0–0–1/6

Muncer, Bernard Leonard
Professional. *b:* 23.10.1913, Hampstead, North London. *d:* 18.1.1982, Camden, London. Aggressive middle order right-hand batsman, leg break and googly bowler, changed to off breaks about 1947, good slip. *Teams* Middlesex (1933–46, 82 matches); Glamorgan (1947–54, 224 matches).
Career batting
317–478–64–8646–135–20.88–4–*ct* 144
Bowling 15783–755–20.90–44–8–9/62
He hit 1,000 runs in a season once – 1,097, av 24.37, in 1952, in which year he also completed the 'double'. He took 100 wickets in a season five times (best 159, av 17.27, in 1948). His final first-class match was for MCC in 1957. His best bowling was 9/62 for Glamorgan v Essex at Brentwood at 1948.
After retiring from first-class cricket he became Head Coach at Lord's.

Muncey, George
Professional. *b:* 27.12.1835, Mildenhall, Suffolk. *d:* 14.3.1883, Cambridge. Middle order right-hand batsman, right-hand slow under-arm bowler, long stop. *Team* Cambridgeshire (1861–66, 8 matches).
Career batting
11–20–1–197–37–10.36–0–*ct* 1
Bowling 174–9+1–19.33–0–0–4/27
His first-class debut was for Cambridge Town Club in 1860.

Munden, Donald Francis Xavier
Professional. *b:* 17.10.1934, Leicester. Brother of P.A. and V.S. (both Leicestershire). Lower order right-hand batsman, leg break bowler. *Team* Leicestershire (1960–61, 7 matches).
Career batting
7–13–0–98–34–7.53–0–*ct* 2
Bowling 13–0

Munden, Marwood Mintern
Amateur. *b:* 13.6.1885, Ilminster, Somerset. *d:* 8.3.1952, Eastcombe, Gloucs. Middle order batsman. *Sch* Weymouth. *Team* Somerset (1908, 3 matches).
Career batting
3–5–0–31–11–6.20–0–*ct* 0

Munden, Paul Anthony
Professional. *b:* 5.11.1938, Leicester. Brother of D.F.X. and V.S. (Leicestershire). Lower order left-hand batsman, off break bowler. *Team* Leicestershire (1957–64, 47 matches).
Career batting
47–85–6–1193–77–15.10–0–*ct* 17

Munden, Victor Stanislaus
Professional. *b:* 2.1.1928, Leicester. Brother of P.A. and D.F.X. (Leicestershire). Middle order left-hand batsman, slow left-arm bowler. *Team* Leicestershire (1946–57, 228 matches).
Career batting
232–376–43–5786–102–17.37–2–*ct* 82
Bowling 10603–371–28.57–14–1–6/33
He hit 1,259 runs, av 29.97, in 1952. Between 1951 and 1956 he appeared in 159 consecutive matches for Leicestershire.

Munds, Arthur Edward
Professional. *b:* 20.1.1870, Lydd, Kent. *d:* 19.7.1940, High Wycombe, Bucks. Brother of Raymond (Kent). Lower order left-hand batsman, left-arm medium pace bowler. *Team* Kent (1896, 1 match).
Career batting
1–2–0–10–9–5.00–0–*ct* 0
Bowling 16–0

Munds, Raymond
Professional. *b:* 28.12.1882, Lydd, Kent. *d:* 29.7.1962, Folkestone, Kent. Brother of A.E. (Kent). Lower order left-hand batsman, right-arm slow bowler, wicket-keeper. *Team* Kent (1902–08, 7 matches).
Career batting
7–11–1–121–29–12.10–0–*ct* 3

Mungrue, Altaff Ali
Cricketer. *b:* 25.8.1934, Port of Spain, Trinidad. Middle order right-hand batsman, right-arm

medium pace and off break bowler. *Team* Combined Services (1964).
Career batting
2–4–0–102–51–25.50–0–*ct* 0
Bowling 129–8–16.12–0–0–4/58

Munir Malik
Amateur. *b:* 10.7.1934, Leih, India. Lower order right-hand batsman, right-arm fast medium bowler. *Teams* Punjab (1956/7 to 1957/8); Rawalpindi (1958/9 to 1964/5); Services (1962/3 to 1963/4); Karachi (1965/6). *Tours* Pakistan Eaglets to Ceylon 1960/1; Pakistan to England 1962. *Tests* Pakistan (1959/60 to 1962, 3 matches).
Career batting
49–71–10–675–72–11.06–0–*ct* 23
Bowling 4285–197–21.75–14–4–8/154
Test batting
3–4–1–7–4–2.33–0–*ct* 1
Bowling 358–9–39.77–1–0–5/128
Although he appeared in two Tests on the 1962 tour, his bowling achieved only modest results – in first-class matches 43 wickets, av 39.93.

Munn, John Shannon
Amateur. *b:* 6.6.1880, St John's, Newfoundland. *d:* 14.2.1918. He was lost on board SS *Florizel* between Newfoundland and New York. Lower order batsman, left-arm bowler. *Sch* Forest School. *Team* Oxford U (1900–01, blue 1901).
Career batting
10–13–7–55–13*–9.66–0–*ct* 2
Bowling 711–24–29.62–0–0–4/39

Munn, Reginald George
Amateur. *b:* 20.8.1869, Madresfield, Worcs. *d:* 12.4.1947, Virginia Water, Surrey. Middle order batsman. *Sch* Haileybury. *Team* Worcestershire (1900, 1 match).
Career batting
1–1–0–2–2–2.00–0–*ct* 0

Munnion, Henry
Professional. *b:* 23.1.1849, Ardingly, Sussex. *d:* 24.6.1904, Ardingly, Sussex. Lower order right-hand batsman, left-arm medium pace bowler. *Team* Sussex (1877–80, 2 matches).
Career batting
2–3–0–0–0–0.00–0–*ct* 1
Bowling 28–2–14.00–0–0–2/15

Munro, Hector Campbell
Amateur. *b:* 24.10.1920, Calcutta, India. Middle order right-hand batsman. *Sch* Rugby. *Team* Oxford U (1947).
Career batting
1–2–0–0–0–0.00–0–*ct* 1

Munt, Harry Raymond
Amateur. *b:* 31.10.1902, Paddington, West London. *d:* 27.12.1965, Derby. He died following a road accident. Middle order right-hand batsman, right-arm fast bowler. *Sch* Westminster. *Team* Middlesex (1923, 1 match). *Tours* Cahn to Argentine 1929/30, to North America 1933 (not first-class).
Career batting
2–1–0–0–0–0.00–0–*ct* 0
Bowling 64–1–64.00–0–0–1/28
He was for some years on the Committee of Notts CCC.

Murch, Stewart Nigel Clifford
Cricketer. *b:* 27.6.1944, Warrnambool, Victoria, Australia. Lower order right-hand batsman, right-arm fast bowler. *Teams* Victoria (1966/7 to 1969/70, 9 matches); Northants (1968, 1 match).
Career batting
10–15–3–215–64–17.91–0–*ct* 5
Bowling 868–17–51.05–0–0–3/49

Murch, William
Professional. *b:* 18.11.1867, Bristol, Gloucs. *d:* 1.5.1928, Bristol, Gloucs. Lower order right-hand batsman, right-arm medium pace bowler, good deep field. *Teams* Gloucestershire (1889–03, 77 matches); London County (1901–04).
Career batting
88–147–14–1337–58–10.05–0–*ct* 40–*st* 1
Bowling 5103–207–24.65–11–4–8/68
His final first-class match was for W. G. Grace's XI in 1906.
He also played for Wiltshire.

Murdin, John Vernon
Professional. *b:* 16.8.1891, Wollaston, Northants. *d:* 11.4.1971, Stonehouse, Gloucs. Tail end right-hand batsman, right-arm fast bowler. *Team* Northants (1913–27, 171 matches).
Career batting
173–279–69–1800–90*–8.57–0–*ct* 111
Bowling 12324–455–27.08–28–4–8/81

Murdoch, William Lloyd
Amateur. *b:* 18.10.1854, Sandhurst, Victoria, Australia. *d:* 18.2.1911, Melbourne, Australia. He was seized with apoplexy whilst attending a Test Match between Australia and South Africa. Stylish middle order right-hand batsman, wicket-keeper. *Teams* New South Wales (1875/6 to 1893/4, 19 matches); Sussex (1893–99, 137 matches); London County (1901–04). *Tours* Australia to England 1878, 1880, 1882, 1884, 1890, to North America 1878; Read to South Africa 1891/2. *Tests* Australia (1876/7 to 1890, 18 matches); England (1891/2, 1 match).

Career batting
391–679–48–16953–321–26.86–19–*ct* 218–*st* 25
Bowling 430–10–43.00–0–0–2/11
Test batting
19–34–5–908–211–31.31–2–*ct* 12–*st* 2

He was most successful on his tours to England, being the equal of any of the batsmen on each tour and three times exceeding 1,000 runs (best 1,582, av 31.64, in 1882). In all he exceeded 1,000 runs in an English season seven times. His highest score in England was 286* for Australians v Sussex 1882, but he hit 211 for Australia in the Oval Test of 1884 and his highest score of 321 for NSW v Victoria at Sydney in 1881/2.

He captained the Australians on the tours of 1880, 1882, 1884 and 1890 and led Australia in 16 Tests.

He captained Sussex from 1893 to 1899, dropping out of the side midway through the last season.

Murdoch-Cozens, Alan James
(formerly Murdoch)
Amateur. *b:* 17.9.1893, Wallingford, Berkshire. *d:* 23.7.1970, Malvern, Worcs. Middle order right-hand batsman. *Sch* Brighton. *Team* Sussex (1919, 4 matches).
Career batting
4–7–0–124–56–17.71–0–*ct* 0

Murdock, Ernest George
Amateur. *b:* 14.11.1864, Keynsham, Somerset. *d:* 18.5.1926, Bower Ashton, Somerset. He died whilst waiting to bat in a local club match. Middle/lower order right-hand batsman, occasional bowler, wicket-keeper. *Teams* Somerset (1885, 2 matches); Gloucestershire (1889, 3 matches).
Career batting
5–10–1–40–14–4.44–0–*ct* 4
Bowling 11–1–11.00–0–0–1/11

Murgatroyd, Henry
Professional. *b:* 19.9.1853, New Swindon, Wilts. *d:* 15.3.1905, Portsmouth, Hants. Lower order right-hand batsman, right-arm fast bowler. *Team* Hampshire (1883, 1 match).
Career batting
1–2–1–2–1*–2.00–0–*ct* 0
Bowling 7–0

Murley, Anthony Jonathan
Cricketer. *b:* 7.8.1957, Radlett, Herts. Middle order right-hand batsman, right-arm medium pace bowler. *Sch* Oundle. *Team* Cambridge U (1981).
Career batting
6–11–0–152–48–13.81–0–*ct* 2
Bowling 1–0

He played for Hertfordshire commencing 1979.

He represented Cambridge at golf and rugby fives.

Murphy, Desmond James
Amateur. *b:* 6.7.1896, Armagh, Ireland. *d:* February 1982, Cabinteely, Co Dublin, Ireland. Right-hand batsman, leg break and googly bowler. *Team* Ireland (1920).
Career batting
1–2–0–0–0–0.00–0–*ct* 0
Bowling 49–0

Murphy, Edward Gordon
Amateur. *b:* 6.12.1921, Sheffield, Yorkshire. Middle order right-hand batsman, right-arm medium pace bowler. *Team* Combined Services (1948).
Career batting
2–4–0–24–11–6.00–0–*ct* 1

Murphy, Patrick
Amateur. Right-hand batsman, right-arm medium pace bowler. *Team* Ireland (1909–12).
Career batting
2–4–2–26–10–13.00–0–*ct* 1
Bowling 117–4–29.25–0–0–2/92

Murray, Athol Leslie
Amateur. *b:* 29.6.1901, Mill Hill, Middlesex. *d:* 10.1.1981, Grasmere, Cumbria. Middle order right-hand batsman, right-arm medium fast bowler. *Team* Warwickshire (1922, 11 matches).
Career batting
11–17–0–161–33–9.47–0–*ct* 3
Bowling 49–2–24.50–0–0–2/29

He appeared in the Seniors' Match whilst at Oxford, but no first-class matches.

An excellent golfer, he represented the University.

Murray, Anton Ronald Andrew
Amateur. *b:* 30.4.1922, Grahamstown, South Africa. Middle order right-hand batsman, right-arm slow medium bowler. *Team* Eastern Province (1947/8 to 1955/6). *Tours* South Africa to Australia and New Zealand 1952/3, to England 1955. *Tests* South Africa (1952/3 to 1953/4, 10 matches).
Career batting
64–100–10–2685–133–29.83–4–*ct* 31
Bowling 4683–188–24.90–8–2–7/30
Test batting
10–14–1–289–109–22.23–1–*ct* 3
Bowling 710–18–39.44–0–0–4/169

He bowled usefully on his 1955 tour to England, but had limited opportunities and did not appear in the Tests.

Murray, Bruce Alexander Grenfell
Amateur. *b:* 18.9.1940, Wellington, New Zealand. Sound opening right-hand batsman, leg break bowler, good field. *Team* Wellington (1958/9 to 1972/3). *Tours* New Zealand to Australia 1967/8, to England 1969, to India and Pakistan 1969/70. *Tests* New Zealand (1967/8 to 1970/1, 13 matches).
Career batting
102–187–11–6257–213–35.55–6–*ct* 124
Bowling 868–30–28.93–0–0–4/43
Test batting
13–26–1–598–90–23.92–0–*ct* 21
Bowling 0–1–0.00–0–0–1/0

He topped the first-class batting averages on the 1969 tour with 800 runs, av 40.00, but achieved little in the Tests. His highest score was 213 for Wellington v Otago at Dunedin in 1968/9.

Murray, David Anthony
Cricketer. *b:* 29.5.1950, Carrington, Bridgetown, Barbados. Middle order right-hand batsman, wicket-keeper. *Team* Barbados (1970/1 to 1981/2). *Tours* West Indies to England 1973, 1980, to India, Pakistan and Sri Lanka 1974/5, to Australia 1975/6, 1979/80, 1981/2, to Pakistan 1980/1, to New Zealand 1979/80, to India and Sri Lanka 1978/9, to South Africa 1982/3. *Tests* West Indies (1977/8 to 1981/2, 19 matches).
Career batting
105–161–27–4200–206*–31.34–7–*ct* 258–*st* 31
Bowling 11–0
Test batting
19–31–3–601–84–21.46–0–*ct* 57–*st* 5

He came to England in 1973 as reserve wicket-keeper and did not play in any Tests; in 1980 he came in the same capacity and played in only six first-class matches and no Tests. His highest score was 206* for West Indies v East Zone at Jamshedpur in 1978/9.

Murray, Deryck Lance
Amateur. *b:* 20.5.1943, Port of Spain, Trinidad. Sound middle order right-hand batsman, occasional leg break bowler, wicket-keeper. *Teams* Trinidad (1960/1 to 1980/1); Cambridge U (1965–66, blue both years); Nottinghamshire (1966–69, 97 matches); Warwickshire (1972–75, 58 matches). *Tours* West Indies to England 1963, 1973, 1976, 1980, to India and Ceylon 1966/7, to India, Pakistan and Sri Lanka 1974/5, to Australia 1975/6, 1979/80, to New Zealand 1979/80. *Tests* West Indies (1963–80, 62 matches).
Career batting
367–554–85–13291–166*–28.33–10–*ct* 741–*st* 108
Bowling 367–5–73.40–0–0–2/50
Test batting
62–96–9–1993–91–22.90–0–*ct* 181–*st* 8

He hit 1,000 runs in a season three times (best 1,358, av 30.17, in 1966). He appeared in all the Tests on each of his four tours to England, being the principal wicket-keeper – he batted usefully on each visit but played no major innings.

He was the first Secretary of the West Indian Cricketers Association and an influential figure at the time of Packer's World Series Cricket.

Murray, E. C. (*see under* Moses, E. C.)

Murray, John Congreve
Amateur. *b:* 21.8.1882, Edinburgh, Scotland. *d:* 23.9.1917, near Poelcappelle, Belgium. Middle order batsman. *Sch* Edinburgh Academy. *Team* Scotland (1909–13).
Career batting
3–5–0–78–34–15.60–0–*ct* 2

Murray, John Matthew
Amateur. *b:* 1878, Auckland, Co Durham. *d:* 31.5.1916, aboard HMS *Queen Mary* at the Battle of Jutland. Middle order right-hand batsman, right-arm fast bowler. *Team* Royal Navy (1913).
Career batting
1–2–0–29–29–14.50–0–*ct* 0

Murray, John Thomas
Professional. *b:* 1.4.1935, North Kensington, London. Lower order right-hand batsman, right-arm medium pace bowler, wicket-keeper. *Team* Middlesex (1952–75, 508 matches). *Tours* MCC to New Zealand 1960/1, to India and Pakistan 1961/2, to Australia and New Zealand 1962/3, 1965/6, to South Africa 1963/4, to Ceylon and Pakistan 1968/9; Cavaliers to Jamaica 1963/4, 1969/70; Rest of World to Barbados 1966/7; Robins to South Africa 1972/3, 1973/4. *Tests* England (1961–67, 21 matches).
Career batting
635–936–136–18872–142–23.59–16–*ct* 1270–*st* 257
Bowling 243–6–40.50–0–0–2/10
Test batting
21–28–5–506–112–22.00–1–*ct* 52–*st* 3

He hit 1,000 runs in a season six times (best 1160, av 28.29, in 1965). In 1957 he took 104 dismissals as a wicket-keeper thus completing the 'double' of 1000 runs and 100 dismissals in a season. He also exceeded 100 dismissals in 1960. On his retirement he held the record for the most dismissals in first-class cricket.

Murray, John Tinline
Amateur. *b:* 1.12.1892, Australia. *d:* 8.9.1974, Stirling, South Australia. Middle order right-hand batsman. *Team* South Australia (1911/12 to 1925/6, 17 matches). *Tours* AIF to England 1919, to South Africa 1919/20.
Career batting
48–79–5–1964–152–26.54–4–*ct* 38
Bowling 694–12–57.83–0–0–2/63
He hit 793 runs, av 24.03, during 1919 with the Australian Forces.

Murray, Michael Patrick
Amateur. *b:* 14.5.1930, Westminster, London. Sound opening right-hand batsman. *Team* Middlesex (1952–53, 5 matches).
Career batting
10–19–1–216–44–12.00–0–*ct* 7
Bowling 3–0
His first-class debut was for Combined Services in 1949 and his final first-class match was for MCC in 1963.

Murray-Willis, Peter E.
Amateur. *b:* 14.7.1910, Aston, Birmingham. Opening/middle order right-hand batsman. *Sch* St Georges, Harpenden. *Teams* Worcestershire (1935–36, 7 matches); Northants (1938–46, 22 matches).
Career batting
29–47–2–467–54–10.37–0–*ct* 3
He captained Northants in 1946.

Murray-Wood, William
Amateur. *b:* 30.6.1917, Dartford, Kent. *d:* 21.12.1968, Southwark, London. Hard hitting middle order right-hand batsman, leg break bowler. *Sch* Mill Hill. *Teams* Oxford U (1936–38, blue 1936); Kent (1936–53, 77 matches). *Tours* Combined Oxford and Cambridge Team to Jamaica 1938/9; Surridge to Bermuda 1961 (not first-class).
Career batting
106–177–15–2262–107–13.96–3–*ct* 45
Bowling 3850–100–38.50–2–0–6/29
He captained Kent in 1952 and 1953. His last first-class match was for MCC in 1956.

Murrell, Harry Robert
Professional. *b:* 19.11.1879, Hounslow, Middlesex. *d:* 15.8.1952, West Wickham, Kent. Lower order right-hand batsman, left-arm bowler, wicket-keeper. *Teams* Kent (1899–1905, 27 matches); Middlesex (1905–26, 342 matches).
Career batting
378–528–62–6663–96*–14.29–0–*ct* 565–*st* 269
Bowling 174–0
A noted soccer player, he appeared for Arsenal.

Murrills, Timothy James
Cricketer. *b:* 22.12.1953, Sheffield, Yorkshire. Middle order right-hand batsman, right-arm medium pace bowler, wicket-keeper. *Sch* The Leys. *Team* Cambridge U (1973–76, blue 1973, 1974 and 1976).
Career batting
37–69–4–996–67–15.32–0–*ct* 18
Bowling 4–0
His County cricket was for Dorset commencing 1974.

Murtagh, Andrew Joseph
Cricketer. *b:* 6.5.1949, Dublin, Ireland. Lower order right-hand batsman, right-arm medium pace bowler. *Teams* Hampshire (1973–77, 26 matches); Eastern Province (1973/4).
Career batting
27–47–5–640–65–15.23–0–*ct* 9
Bowling 489–6–81.50–0–0–2/46

Musgrave, John Musgrave
(also known as Tattersall-Musgrave)
Amateur. *b:* 1845, Armley, Yorkshire. *d:* 12.3.1885, Beverley, Yorkshire. Lower order right-hand batsman, right-hand fast round-arm bowler. *Sch* Pocklington. *Team* Cambridge U (1868).
Career batting
1–1–0–0–0–0.00–0–*ct* 2
Bowling 19–1–19.00–0–0–1/19

Musgrove, Henry Alfred
Amateur. *b:* 27.11.1858, Surbiton, Surrey. *d:* 2.11.1931, Darlinghurst, New South Wales, Australia. Middle order right-hand batsman. *Team* Victoria (1881/2 to 1887/8, 3 matches). *Tours* Australia to England 1896 (acting as manager, but he played in 2 matches). *Test* Australia (1884/5, 1 match).
Career batting
7–12–0–99–62–8.25–0–*ct* 3
Bowling 18–0
Test batting
1–2–0–13–9–6.50–0–*ct* 0

Mushet, John A.
Amateur. Middle order batsman. *Team* Scotland (1912).
Career batting
1–2–0–3–2–1.50–0–*ct* 0

Mushtaq Ali, Syed Yacubali
Amateur. *b:* 17.12.1914, Indorè, India. Brother of S. Ishtiaq Ali (Holkar), father of S. Gulrez Ali (Madhya Pradesh). Opening or middle order right-hand batsman, slow left-arm bowler. *Teams* Central India (1934/5 to 1939/40); Muslims (1935/6 to 1944/5); Maharashtra (1940/1); Gujerat (1940/1); Holkar (1941/2 to 1954/5); Madhya Bharat (1955/6); Uttar Pradesh (1956/7);

Madhya Pradesh (1957/8); *Tours* Vizianagram to India and Ceylon 1930/1; India to England 1936, 1946, to Ceylon 1944/5; Holkar to Ceylon 1947/8. *Tests* India (1933/4 to 1951/2, 11 matches).
Career batting
224–382–16–13130–233–35.87–30–*ct* 160
Bowling 4601–156–29.49–6–2–7/108
Test batting
11–20–1–612–112–32.21–2–*ct* 7
Bowling 202–3–67.33–0–0–1/45

On the 1936 tour he hit 1,078 runs, av 25.06, and in 1946 673 runs, av 24.03. A brilliant batsman on his day, he was very inconsistent in England – his 1936 aggregate contained four centuries, including one in the Second Test.

His highest score was 233 for Holkar v United Provinces at Indore in 1947/8.

His first-class debut was for Indians v Europeans in Madras in 1930/1 and his final match for Bombay Chief Minister's XI in 1963/4.

Mushtaq Mohammad
Amateur. *b:* 22.11.1943, Junagadh, India. Brother of Hanif, Sadiq and Wazir (Pakistan) and Raees (Karachi), uncle of Shoaib, Asif and Shahid (PIA). Versatile middle order right-hand batsman, leg break and googly bowler. *Teams* Karachi (1956/7 to 1967/8); PIA (1960/1 to 1979/80); Northants (1964–77, 262 matches). *Tours* Pakistan to India 1960/1, to England 1962, 1967, 1971, 1974; Pakistan Eaglets to England 1963; Pakistan to Ceylon 1972/3, to Australia and New Zealand 1972/3, 1978/9, to Australia and West Indies 1976/7; PIA to Zimbabwe 1981/2; Rest of World to West Indies 1966/7; Cavaliers to West Indies 1969/70; Commonwealth to India 1964/5. *Tests* Pakistan (1958/9 to 1978/9, 57 matches).
Career batting
500–840–104–31044–303*–42.17–72–*ct* 346
Bowling 22758–936–24.31–39–2–7/18
Test batting
57–100–7–3643–201–39.17–10–*ct* 42
Bowling 2309–79–29.22–3–0–5/28

Of his four Test tours to England the outstanding one was his first in 1962, when he headed both Test and first-class averages with 401 runs, av 44.55, and 1,614 runs, av 41.38. In both 1967 and 1971 his appearances were virtually confined to the Tests, since he remained with Northants for each season. In all he hit 1,000 runs in a season in England 12 times (best 1,949, av 59.06, in 1972) as well as three times overseas. His highest score was 303* for Karachi Blues v Karachi University at Karachi in 1967/8 and of his four double centuries the only one in England was 204* for Northants v Hampshire at Northampton in 1976. If his published date of birth is correct, he was the youngest Test cricketer at 15 years 124 days in 1958/9. He captained Northants in 1975 to 1977 and Pakistan in 19 Tests, but none in England.

He also played for Northumberland and Staffordshire.

Musson, Major-General Alfred Henry
Amateur. *b:* 14.8.1900, Clitheroe, Lancashire. Brother of F.W. (Lancashire) and R.G. (Combined Services). Middle order right-hand batsman, right-arm medium pace bowler. *Sch* Tonbridge. *Team* Army (1925).
Career batting
1–2–0–51–27–25.50–0–*ct* 0
Bowling 42–0

Musson, Francis William
Amateur. *b:* 31.5.1894, Clitheroe, Lancashire. *d:* 2.1.1962, Chatham, Kent. Brother of A.H. (Army) and R.G. (Combined Services). Middle order right-hand batsman, wicket-keeper. *Sch* Tonbridge. *Team* Lancashire (1914–21, 16 matches).
Career batting
19–31–1–539–75–11.96–0–*ct* 13–*st* 4
Bowling 57–0

He played in the Cambridge Freshmen's match of 1914.

His final first-class match was for Civil Service in 1927.

Musson, Rowland Gascoigne
Amateur. *b:* 7.2.1912, Clitheroe, Lancashire. *d:* 24.8.1943, Clovely, Devonshire. He was killed whilst serving with Coastal Command. Brother of A.H. (Army) and F.W. (Lancashire). Middle order batsman, useful bowler. *Sch* Tonbridge. *Team* Combined Services (1937).
Career batting
1–1–0–24–24–24.00–0–*ct* 0

He appeared for Lancashire in some non-first-class wartime matches and in the 1930s in service matches in Egypt.

A well-known pilot, he made several world record flights.

Muzzell, Robert Kendal
Cricketer. *b:* 23.12.1945, Stutterheim, South Africa. Brother of P.J. (Border). Lower order right-hand batsman, leg break bowler. *Teams* Transvaal (1968/9 to 1976/7); Western Province (1964/5 to 1967/8); Eastern Province (1974/5). *Tour* South African Universities to England 1967.

Career batting
75–128–12–4052–238*–34.93–7–*ct* 49
Bowling 2028–61–33.24–1–0–6/69

His highest score was 238* for Transvaal 'B' v Natal 'B' at Johannesburg in 1967/70.

Myburgh, Claude John
Amateur. *b:* 4.7.1911, Cheltenham, Gloucs. Lower order right-hand batsman, right-arm fast medium bowler. *Sch* St Lawrence College, Ramsgate. *Team* Army (1933).
Career batting
1–1–1–13–13*–no av–0–*ct* 1
Bowling 70–1–70.00–0–0–1/12

His County cricket was for Devon.

Mycroft, Frank
Professional. *b:* 30.6.1873, Furnace, Shirland, Derbyshire. *d:* 26.9.1900, Leicester. Tail end left-hand batsman, wicket-keeper. *Team* Derbyshire (1894–95, 2 matches).
Career batting
2–4–0–7–4–1.75–0–*ct* 4

Mycroft, Thomas
Professional. *b:* 28.3.1848, Brimington, Derbyshire. *d:* 13.8.1911, Mickleover, Derbyshire. Half brother of William (Derbyshire). Lower order left-hand batsman, right-arm medium pace bowler, wicket-keeper. *Team* Derbyshire (1877–85, 16 matches).
Career batting
24–46–14–249–24*–7.78–0–*ct* 43–*st* 16
Bowling 16–0

He was on the ground staff at Lord's for 22 years and umpired in many first-class matches, his last first-class match being for MCC in 1887.

Mycroft, William
Professional. *b:* 1.2.1841, Brimington, Derbyshire. *d:* 19.6.1894, Derby. Half brother of Thomas (Derbyshire). Lower order right-hand batsman, left-arm fast bowler. *Team* Derbyshire (1873–85, 78 matches).
Career batting
138–234–86–791–44*–5.34–0–*ct* 94
Bowling 10442–863–12.09–87–28–9/25

He took 100 wickets in a season twice (157, av 12.27, in 1877 being his highest aggregate). His best season was 1875 when he topped the bowling averages with 90 wickets, av 7.38. By some his action was regarded as doubtful, especially when he bowled his fast yorker, which gained him many wickets. His best bowling was 9/25 for Derbyshire v Hampshire at Southampton in 1876. His final first-class match was for MCC in 1886.

He umpired in first-class matches after retiring from County cricket.

Myers, Dr Arthur Thomas
Amateur. *b:* 16.4.1851, Keswick, Cumberland. *d:* 10.1.1894, Marylebone, London. Middle order right-hand batsman. *Sch* Cheltenham. *Team* Cambridge U (1870).
Career batting
1–2–0–13–7–6.50–0–*ct* 0

Myers, Edwin Bertram
Professional. *b:* 5.7.1888, Blackheath, Kent. *d:* 15.9.1916, near Adanac, France. He was killed in action. Middle order right-hand batsman, slow left-arm bowler. *Team* Surrey (1910–14, 11 matches).
Career batting
11–17–1–217–40–13.56–0–*ct* 3
Bowling 211–3–70.33–0–0–1/10

Myers, Hubert
Professional. *b:* 2.1.1875, Yeadon, Yorkshire. *d:* 12.6.1944, Hobart, Tasmania. Lower order right-hand batsman, right-arm medium pace bowler. *Teams* Yorkshire (1901–10, 201 matches); Tasmania (1913/4 to 1924/5, 4 matches).
Career batting
210–304–48–4753–91–18.56–0–*ct* 110
Bowling 7664–303–25.29–13–1–8/81

After losing his place in the Yorkshire side he emigrated to Tasmania and was for many years coach to the Tasmanian Cricket Association.

Myers, Matthew
Professional. *b:* 12.4.1847, Yeadon, Yorkshire. *d:* 8.12.1919, Yeadon, Yorkshire. Middle order right-hand batsman, right-hand fast or slow round-arm bowler, deep field. *Team* Yorkshire (1876–78, 21 matches).
Career batting
24–44–6–600–49–15.78–0–*ct* 11
Bowling 20–0

Mynn, Alfred
Amateur. *b:* 19.1.1807, Goudhurst, Kent. *d:* 1.11.1861, Southwark, London. Brother of W.P. (Kent). Fine, powerful right-hand middle order batsman, right-hand fast round-arm bowler. *Teams* Kent (1834–59, 90 matches); Sussex (1839–47, 4 matches).
Career batting
212–395–26–4955–125*–13.42–1–*ct* 125
Bowling 2989–292+741–10.23–91–33–9/?

The greatest all-rounder of his day 'it was considered one of the grandest sights at cricket to see Mynn advance and deliver the ball' (*Scores and Biographies*). He appeared for the Gentlemen against the Players in twenty matches, being for many years the mainstay of the former team. His best bowling was 9 wickets in an innings for

Gentlemen of Kent v Gentlemen of England at Lord's in 1842

His first-class debut was for Gentlemen of Kent in 1832.

Mynn, Walter Parker
Amateur. *b:* 24.11.1805, Goudhurst, Kent. *d:* 17.10. 1878, Peckham, Surrey. Brother of Alfred (Kent). Steady opening right-hand batsman, good long stop. *Team* Kent (1835–48, 45 matches).
Career batting
76–141–9–1107–41–8.38–0–*ct* 29
Bowling 17–1+1–17.00–0–0–1/17

His final first-class match was for Gentlemen of Kent in 1852, his debut having been for the same team in 1833.

NADEN, JAMES RUPERT
Amateur. *b:* 13.7.1889, Tipton, Staffs. *d:* 14.6.1963, Sedgley, Worcs. Lower order right-hand batsman, right-arm fast medium bowler. *Team* Worcestershire (1922, 2 matches).
Career batting
2–3–2–23–16*–23.00–0–*ct* 2
Bowling 136–2–68.00–0–0–2/11

Nadkarni, Rameshchandra Gangaram
Amateur. *b:* 4.4.1932, Nasik, India. Middle order left-hand batsman, slow left-arm bowler, good close field. *Teams* Maharashtra (1951/2 to 1959/60); Bombay (1960/1 to 1967/8). *Tours* India to Ceylon 1956/7, to England 1959, to West Indies 1961/2, to Australia and New Zealand 1967/8; ACC to Pakistan, 1961/2. *Tests* India (1955/6 to 1967/8, 41 matches).
Career batting
191–266–46–8880–283*–40.36–14–*ct* 140
Bowling 10686–500–21.37–19–1–6/17
Test batting
41–67–12–1414–122*–25.70–1–*ct* 22
Bowling 2559–88–29.07–4–1–6/43

He proved a useful all-rounder of the 1959 tour, appearing in four Tests and in first-class matches hitting 945 runs, av 23.62, and taking 55 wickets, av 28.41. His three double centuries were all scored in India, the highest being 283* for Bombay v Delhi at Bombay in 1960/61. His final first-class match was for ACC in 1971/2. He hit 1,190 runs, av 70.00, in India in 1962/3.

Naeem Ahmed
Cricketer. *b:* 20.9.1952, Karachi, Pakistan. Middle order right-hand batsman, slow left-arm bowler. *Teams* Karachi (1969/70 to 1971/2); Universities (1972/3 to 1974/5); National Bank (1974/5); PIA (1975/6 to 1982/3); United Bank (1977/8). *Tours* Pakistan to Sri Lanka 1975/6, to England 1978; PIA to Zimbabwe 1981/2.
Career batting
111–139–37–2932–127–28.74–3–*ct* 52
Bowling 9237–347–26.61–20–3–8/49

He played in only two first-class matches on the 1978 tour to England.

Nagenda, John
Cricketer. *b:* 1938, Uganda. Lower order right-hand batsman, right-arm fast medium bowler. *Team* East Africa (1975). *Tour* East Africa to England 1975.
Career batting
1–2–2–5–5*–no av–0–*ct* 1
Bowling 91–3–30.33–0–0–2/17

Naik, Sudhir Sakharam
Cricketer. *b:* 21.2.1945, Bombay, India. Steady opening/middle order right-hand batsman. *Team* Bombay (1966/7 to 1977/8). *Tours* India to England 1974; CCI to Ceylon 1972/3. *Tests* India (1974 to 1974/5, 3 matches).
Career batting
85–139–15–4376–200*–35.29–7–*ct* 42
Bowling 52–3–17.33–0–0–1/0
Test batting
3–6–0–141–77–23.50–0–*ct* 0

He hit 730 runs, av 40.55, on the 1974 tour to England, but played in only one Test. His highest score was 200* for Bombay v Baroda at Bombay in 1973/4.

Nana, P. G.
Cricketer. *b:* 1933, Northern Rhodesia. Lower order right-hand batsman, slow left-arm bowler. *Team* East Africa (1973/4 to 1975). *Tour* East Africa to England 1975.
Career batting
2–4–0–21–16–5.25–0–*ct* 1
Bowling 170–4–42.50–0–0–3/61

Nanan, Nirmal
Cricketer. *b:* 19.8.1951, Preysal Village, Couva, Trinidad. Uncle of Ranjie (West Indies). Middle order right-hand batsman, leg break and googly bowler. *Team* South Trinidad (1969/70); Central Trinidad (1972/3); Nottinghamshire (1971–80, 32 matches).

Career batting
34–62–5–900–72–15.78–0–*ct* 22
Bowling 322–9–35.77–0–0–3/12

Naoomal Jaoomal Makhija
Amateur. *b:* 17.4.1904, Karachi, India. *d:* 28.7.1980, Bombay, India. Father of Hari Naoomal (Karachi). Steady opening right-hand batsman, slow left-arm bowler. *Teams* Northern India (1926/7); Hindus (1927/8 to 1936/7); Sind (1932/3 to 1944/5). *Tours* India to England 1932; Vizianagram's XI to India and Ceylon 1930/1. *Tests* India (1932 to 1933/4, 3 matches).
Career batting
82–139–16–4093–203*–33.27–7–*ct* 43
Bowling 2835–105–27.00–6–0–5/18
Test batting
3–5–1–108–43–27.00–0–*ct* 0
Bowling 68–2–34.00–0–0–1/4
He batted well on his 1932 visit to England scoring 1,297 runs, av 30.88. His only double century was 203* for Sind v Nawanagar at Karachi in 1938/9. After the partition of India he was appointed National Coach to Pakistan.

Napier, Duncan Robertson
Amateur. *b:* 6.10.1871, Croydon, Surrey. *d:* 24.10.1898, India. He died of wounds whilst serving on the North West Frontier. Middle order left-hand batsman, slow left-arm bowler, good deep field. *Sch* Harrow. *Team* MCC (1892).
Career batting
2–3–0–50–33–16.66–0–*ct* 1

Napier, Guy Greville
Amateur. *b:* 26.1.1884, London. *d:* 25.9.1915, Loos, France. He died of wounds. Tail end right-hand batsman, right-arm medium pace bowler. *Sch* Marlborough. *Teams* Cambridge U (1904–07, blue all four years); Middlesex (1904–13, 21 matches); Europeans (1907–10). *Tour* MCC to North America 1905.
Career batting
81–127–29–854–59–8.71–0–*ct* 84
Bowling 7787–365–21.33–23–5–9/17
He had a splendid record in the University match, taking 31 wickets, av 17.55, in his four appearances. After leaving Cambridge he took up a Government appointment in Quetta, India and his County cricket was therefore very restricted. His best bowling was 9/17 for Europeans v Parsis at Poona in 1909/10.

Napier, Rev John Russell
Amateur. *b:* 5.1.1859, Preston, Lancashire. *d:* 12.3.1939, Bexhill, Sussex. Lower order right-hand batsman, right-hand fast round-arm bowler, good mid off. *Sch* Marlborough. *Teams* Cambridge U (1881); Lancashire (1888, 2 matches).
Career batting
4–5–1–72–37–18.00–0–*ct* 1
Bowling 245–17–14.41–0–0–4/0
Injury prevented him from obtaining his blue at Cambridge and later he would probably have achieved much in County cricket, had he been able to afford the time.

Napier, Ronald Stuart
Amateur. *b:* 23.10.1935, South Africa. Lower order right-hand batsman, leg break bowler. *Team* Oxford U (1956)
Career batting
1–1–0–0–0–0.00–0–*ct* 1
Bowling 18–0

Napper, Edwin
Amateur. *b:* 26.1.1815, Wisborough Green, Sussex. *d:* 8.3.1895, Rudgwick, Sussex. Brother of William (Sussex). Attacking middle order left-hand batsman, right-hand round arm bowler. *Team* Sussex (1839–62, 92 matches).
Career batting
128–242–8–2645–83*–11.30–0–*ct* 51
Bowling 330–21+18–15.71–1–0–6/27
He was on the Committees of both Sussex and Surrey Cricket Clubs. He captained Sussex, 1847–62.

Napper, William
Amateur. *b:* 25.8.1816, Wisborough Green, Sussex. *d:* 13.7.1897, Brighton, Sussex. Brother of Edwin (Sussex). Middle order left-hand batsman, right-hand slow round-arm bowler. *Team* Sussex (1842–60, 53 matches).
Career batting
63–114–5–945–67–8.66–0–*ct* 34
Bowling 431–24+9–17.95–1–0–5/19

Napper, William Henry
Amateur. *b:* 5.11.1880, Co Wexford, Ireland. *d:* August 1967, Ganges Harbour, Salt Spring Island, British Columbia, Canada. Lower order batsman, slow left-arm bowler. *Sch* Shrewsbury. *Team* Ireland (1908–09).
Career batting
3–6–0–16–10–2.66–0–*ct* 2
Bowling 81–3–27.00–0–0–3/79

Narayan, Prince Kumar Hitendra Singh
Amateur. *b:* 1.7.1890, Cooch Behar, India. *d:* 7.11.1920, Darjeeling, India. He died of influenza. Son of HH the Maharajah of Cooch Behar. Middle order right-hand batsman. *Sch* Eton. *Teams* Somerset (1909–10, 4 matches); Cooch Behar's XI (1918/19).

Naseer Malik

Career batting
7–11–2–60–16–6.66–0–*ct* 2
Bowling 50–0

He did not appear in any first-class matches whilst at Cambridge.

Naseer Malik
Cricketer. *b:* 1.2.1950, Lyallpur, Pakistan. Lower order right-hand batsman, right-arm fast medium bowler. *Teams* Khairpur (1969/70 to 1972/3); Sind (1972/3 to 1973/4); Karachi (1973/4); National Bank (1974/5 to 1981/2). *Tours* Pakistan to England 1974; Pakistan Under 25 Team to Sri Lanka 1973/4.
Career batting
72–81–12–765–55–11.08–0–*ct* 46
Bowling 5053–203–24.89–15–0–8/49

He played in only seven matches on the 1974 tour of England, taking 20 wickets, av 26.90.

Nash, Albert (Jack)
Professional. *b:* 18.9.1873, Blean, Kent. *d:* 6.12.1956, Battersea, London. Lower order right-hand batsman, off break bowler. *Team* Glamorgan (1921–22, 36 matches).
Career batting
36–65–9–315–28–5.62–0–*ct* 6
Bowling 2901–133–21.81–11–2–9/93

He was easily the best bowler for Glamorgan on their debut in the County Championship in 1921, taking 91 wickets, av 18.57; most of his cricket however was played before the County became first-class. His best bowling was 9/93 for Glamorgan v Sussex at Swansea in 1922.

Nash, Edward Montague
Amateur. *b:* 12.4.1902, Swindon, Wilts. Lower order right-hand batsman, wicket-keeper. *Team* Minor Counties (1936–37).
Career batting
2–4–3–62–45*–62.00–0–*ct* 3

His County cricket was for Wiltshire.

Nash, George
Professional. *b:* 1.4.1850, Oving, Aylesbury, Bucks. *d:* 13.11.1903, Aylesbury, Bucks. Tail end right-hand batsman, slow left-arm bowler, slip field. *Team* Lancashire (1879–85, 54 matches).
Career batting
58–88–28–347–30–5.78–0–*ct* 37
Bowling 2866–232–12.35–17–5–8/14

He achieved very good bowling figures for Lancashire from 1880 to 1883 (best 62 wickets, av 10.58, in 1882), but his delivery was considered illegal by some and he dropped out of first-class County cricket in 1885, though he appeared for Buckinghamshire afterwards.

Nash, Malcolm Andrew
Cricketer. *b:* 9.5.1945, Abergavenny, Monmouth. Lower order left-hand batsman, left-arm medium pace bowler. *Team* Glamorgan (1966–83, 335 matches). *Tour* Glamorgan to West Indies 1969/70.
Career batting
336–469–67–7129–130–17.73–2–*ct* 148
Bowling 25698–993–25.87–45–5–9/56

He captained Glamorgan in 1980 and 1981. He suffered the misfortune of being hit for 36 off a single six-ball over, the batsman being G. St A. Sobers for Notts v Glamorgan at Swansea in 1968. His best innings analysis was 9 for 56 for Glamorgan v Hampshire at Basingstoke in 1975.

Nash, Philip Geoffrey Elwin
Amateur. *b:* 20.9.1906, Accrington, Lancashire. *d:* 8.12.1982, Old Basing, Hants. Middle order right-hand batsman, right-arm medium pace bowler. *Sch* St Paul's. *Team* Oxford U (1928).
Career batting
1–2–0–16–14–8.00–0–*ct* 0
Bowling 39–0

His County cricket was for Berkshire.

Nash, Rev William Wallace Hayward
Amateur. *b:* 22.9.1884, Gloucester. *d:* 24.7.1971, Minchinhampton, Gloucs. Middle order batsman. *Sch* King's, Bruton. *Team* Gloucestershire (1905–06, 3 matches).
Career batting
3–6–1–81–34–16.20–0–*ct* 0

He appeared in the Freshmen's and Seniors' matches at Cambridge, but no first-class games.

Nasim-ul-Ghani
Amateur. *b:* 14.5.1941, Delhi, India. Steady middle order left-hand batsman, left-arm medium or slow bowler. *Teams* Karachi (1956/7 to 1972/3); Universities (1958/9); Dacca (1965/6); East Pakistan (1966/7 to 1967/8); PWD (1966/7 to 1971/2); National Bank (1973/4 to 1974/5). *Tours* Pakistan to England 1962, 1967, to Australia and New Zealand 1964/5, to West Indies 1957/8, to India 1960/1, to Australia 1972/3. *Tests* Pakistan (1957/8 to 1972/3, 29 matches).
Career batting
117–175–17–4490–139–28.41–7–*ct* 104
Bowling 8630–343–25.16–23–2–6/24
Test batting
29–50–5–747–101–16.60–1–*ct* 11
Bowling 1959–52–37.66–2–0–6/67

Although appearing in all five Tests on the 1962 tour of England, his returns were modest, his one day of real success being his 101 in the Lord's Test. On the 1967 tour he was not a member of the main touring party, but, being engaged in League cricket in England, he appeared in three matches, including two Tests. If his published date of birth is correct, he made his first-class debut at 15 and his Test debut at 16. He has also appeared for Staffordshire and played in a first-class match for Minor Counties in 1972.

Nasiruddin, Shaikh Mohammed
Amateur. *b:* 9.8.1916, Mangrol, India Son of Abdul Khaliq (Western India), uncle of K. S. Zahid (Saurashtra). Stylish middle order right-hand batsman. *Teams* Northants (1938–39, 5 matches); Western Indian States (1940/1 to 1941/2); Muslims (1940/1).
Career batting
9–15–1–263–64–18.78–0–*ct* 0
Bowling 7–0
He did not appear in any first-class matches whilst at Cambridge U.

Nasir Zaidi, Syed Mohammad
Cricketer. *b:* 25.3.1961, Karachi, Pakistan. Lower order right-hand batsman, leg break bowler. *Team* Lancashire (1983, 13 matches).
Career batting
13–16–6–215–51–21.50–0–*ct* 9
Bowling 530–16–33.12–0–0–3/27

Nason, John William Washington
Amateur. *b:* 4.8.1889, Corse Grange, Gloucs. *d:* 26.12.1916, near Vlamertinghe, Belgium. Opening/middle order right-hand batsman, slow right-arm bowler. *Teams* Sussex (1906–10, 22 matches); Cambridge U (1909–10, blue both years); Gloucestershire (1913–14, 19 matches).
Career batting
57–98–6–1649–139–17.92–1–*ct* 35
Bowling 395–10–39.50–0–0–2/24
He first represented Sussex with two seasons at school still ahead of him – on his first-class debut v Warwickshire at Hastings in 1906, he came into the side as a substitute, but was allowed to bat.

Naumann, Charles Cecil
Amateur. *b:* August 1897, Croydon, Surrey. *d:* 16.12.1946, St Pancras, London. Brother of F. C. G. (Surrey) and J. H. (Sussex). Middle order right-hand batsman. *Sch* Malvern. *Team* Cambridge U (1919).
Career batting
1–1–0–5–5–5.00–0–*ct* 0

Naumann, Frank Charles Gordon
Amateur. *b:* 9.4.1892, Lewisham, Kent. *d:* 30.10.1947, Cranleigh, Surrey. Brother of C. C. (Cambridge U) and J. H. (Sussex). Middle order right-hand batsman, right-arm medium pace bowler. *Sch* Malvern. *Teams* Oxford U (1912–14, 1919, blue 1914 and 1919); Surrey (1919–21, 11 matches).
Career batting
51–84–8–1454–118*–19.13–2–*ct* 22
Bowling 2804–85–32.99–4–1–6/81
In the 1919 University match he appeared for Oxford whilst his brother played for Cambridge. His final first-class match was for H. D. G. Leveson-Gower's XI in 1926.

Naumann, John Harold
Amateur. *b:* 9.9.1893, Lewisham, Kent. *d:* 6.12.1964, New York, USA. Brother of C. C. (Cambridge U) and F. C. G. (Oxford U and Surrey). Middle order right-hand batsman, left-arm slow medium bowler. *Sch* Malvern. *Teams* Cambridge U (1913–19, blue 1913 and 1919); Sussex (1925, 17 matches).
Career batting
44–73–8–1391–134*–21.40–1–*ct* 23
Bowling 1142–36–31.72–0–0–4/37
His brother F. C. G. Naumann was opposed to him in the 1919 University match. His final first-class match was for H. D. G. Leveson-Gower's XI in 1928.

Naushad Ali
Amateur. *b:* 1.10.1943, Gowaliar, India. Opening right-hand batsman, wicket-keeper. *Teams* Karachi (1960/1 to 1974/5); East Pakistan (1966/7 to 1967/8); Rawalpindi (1967/8 to 1969/70); Peshawar (1967/8 to 1972/3); Punjab (1976/7); Services (1976/7 to 1979/80). *Tours* Pakistan Eaglets to England 1963; Pakistan to Australia and New Zealand 1964/5, to England 1971. *Tests* Pakistan (1964/5, 6 matches).
Career batting
85–135–16–4406–158–37.02–9–*ct* 136–*st* 34
Bowling 5–0
Test batting
6–11–0–156–39–14.18–0–*ct* 9
As reserve wicket-keeper on the 1971 tour of England he was only required for eight matches.

Navle, Janardan Gyanoba
Amateur. *b:* 7.12.1902, Fulgaon, India. *d:* 7.9.1979, Pune, India. Opening or middle order right-hand batsman, wicket-keeper. *Teams* Hindus (1918/9 to 1934/5); Rajputana (1926/7); Central India (1935/6); Holkar (1942/3); Gwalior (1943/4). *Tour* India to England 1932. *Tests* India (1932 to 1933/4, 3 matches).
Career batting
65–107–4–1976–96–19.18–0–*ct* 101–*st* 36
Test batting
2–4–0–42–13–10.50–0–*ct* 1
He was highly praised for his wicket-keeping on the 1932 tour of England and appeared in the single Test.

Nayak, Surendra Vithal
Cricketer. *b:* 20.10.1954, Bombay, India. Stylish middle order right-hand batsman, right-arm medium pace bowler, good cover point. *Team* Bombay (1976/7 to 1982/3). *Tour* India to England 1982. *Tests* India (1982, 2 matches).
Career batting
48–61–17–1406–100*–31.95–2–*ct* 19
Bowling 2831–85–33.30–4–1–6/65
Test batting
2–3–1–19–11–9.50–0–*ct* 1
Bowling 132–1–132.00–0–0–1/16
He had a modest tour of England in 1982, but appeared in two Tests.

Naylor, John E.
Professional. *b:* 11.12.1930, Thurcroft, Yorkshire. Lower order batsman, slow left-arm bowler. *Team* Yorkshire (1953, 1 match).
Career batting
1 match, did not bat –*ct* 1
Bowling 88–0

Naylor, W.
Professional. Lower order batsman, wicket-keeper. *Team* Essex (1906, 1 match).
Career batting
1–2–0–2–2–1.00–0–*ct* 2

Nayudu, Cottari Kanakaiya
Amateur. *b:* 31.10.1895, Nagpur, India. *d:* 14.11.1967, Indore, India. Brother of C. S. (India), C. L. (Hindus), father of Prakash (Madhya Pradesh), grandfather of V. K. (Madhya Pradesh). Hard hitting middle order right-hand batsman, right-arm medium slow bowler, good field. *Teams* Hindus (1916/7 to 1939/40); Rajputana (1926/7); CP and Berar (1932/3 to 1933/4); Central India (1934/5 to 1937/8); Holkar (1941/2 to 1952/3); Andhra (1953/4); United Provinces (1956/7). *Tours* India to England 1932, 1936; Vizianagram to India and Ceylon 1930/1; Bombay to Ceylon 1925/6; Holkar to Ceylon 1947/8. *Tests* India (1932–36, 7 matches).
Career batting
207–344–15–11825–200–35.94–26–*ct* 170–*st* 1
Bowling 12029–411–29.26–12–2–7/44
Test batting
7–14–0–350–81–25.00–0–*ct* 4
Bowling 386–9–42.88–0–0–3/40
He hit 1,000 runs on both tours to England (best 1,618, av 40.45, in 1932), and led India in their first Test Match (at Lord's in 1932) – he captained India in four Tests in all. His highest score was 200 for Holkar v Baroda at Indore in 1945/6. He was later an Indian Test Selector and Vice-President of the Indian Cricket Board of Control. His final first-class match was for Maharashtra Governor's XI in 1963/4 when he was aged 68. He was also a noted soccer and hockey player.

Nayudu, Cottari Subbanna
Amateur. *b:* 18.4.1914, Nagpur, India. Brother of C. K. (India), C. L. (Hindus), uncle of Prakash (Madhya Pradesh). Lower order right-hand batsman, leg break and googly bowler, good deep field. *Teams* Central India (1934/5 to 1935/6); Hindus (1934/5 to 1944/5); Baroda (1939/40 to 1943/4); Holkar (1944/5 to 1949/50); Bengal (1950/1 to 1951/2); Andhra (1953/4 to 1959/60); Uttar Pradesh (1956/7 to 1958/9); Madhya Pradesh (1960/1); Central Provinces & Berar (1932/3 to 1933/4). *Tours* India to England 1936, 1946, to Australia 1947/8, to Ceylon 1944/5; Holkar to Ceylon 1947/8. *Tests* India (1933/4 to 1951/2, 11 matches).
Career batting
174–267–25–5786–127–23.90–4–*ct* 143
Bowling 17174–647–26.54–50–13–8/93
Test batting
11–19–3–147–36–9.18–0–*ct* 3
Bowling 359–2–179.50–0–0–1/19
In 1936 he joined the side in June as a late reinforcement, but achieved little. On the 1946 tour, he appeared in two Tests, but was too erratic to be very economical. His first-class debut was in a Trial Match in 1931/2. He played for Durham in 1956.

Nazir Ali, Syed
Amateur. *b:* 8.6.1906, Jullundur, India. *d:* 18.2.1975, Lahore, Pakistan. Brother of S. Wazir Ali (India), uncle of Khalid Wazir (Pakistan). Attacking opening right-hand batsman, right-hand fast medium bowler. *Teams* Muslims (1923/4 to 1939/40); Southern Punjab (1926/7 to 1941/2); Sussex (1927, 1 match); Patiala (1932/3). *Tour* India to England 1932. *Tests* India (1932 to 1933/4, 2 matches).
Career batting
74–121–8–3416–197–30.23–7–*ct* 47
Bowling 4012–157–25.55–6–0–7/93
Test batting
2–4–0–30–13–7.50–0–*ct* 0
Bowling 83–4–20.75–0–0–4/83
He resided in England for several years commencing 1927 and played much club cricket in the London area. He batted successfully on the 1932 tour to England hitting 1,020 runs, av 31.87, but his bowling was ineffective in first-class matches. His final first-class match was for Punjab Governor's XI in 1947/8.

Neal, John Howard
Amateur. *b:* 18.10.1926, Ditchling, Sussex.

Right-hand batsman, wicket-keeper. *Sch* Hurstpierpoint. *Team* Sussex (1951, 1 match).
Career batting
1–2–0–28–23–14.00–0–*ct* 0

Neal, Reginald George
Amateur. *b:* 1901, Bristol. *d:* 2.10.1964, Bournemouth, Hants. Middle order batsman, useful bowler. *Team* Gloucestershire (1922, 1 match).
Career batting
1–1–1–2–2*–no av–0–*ct* 0

Neale, George Henry
Amateur. *b:* 31.1.1869, Reigate, Surrey. *d:* 28.9.1915, near Loos, France. He was killed in action. Stylish middle order batsman. *Sch* Lancing. *Team* MCC (1902).
Career batting
1–2–0–0–0–0.00–0–*ct* 0
He was for some years stationed in India and took part in many matches there; in 1902/03 he hit 55 and 124* for Peshawar v the Oxford Authentics touring team.

Neale, Maurice West
Amateur. *b:* 1849, Thakeham, Sussex. *d:* 1935, Surrey. Middle order batsman. *Team* W. G. Grace's XI (1871).
Career batting
1–1–0–0–0–0.00–0–*ct* 1

Neale, Phillip Anthony
Cricketer. *b:* 5.6.1954, Scunthorpe, Lincs. Middle order right-hand batsman, right-arm medium pace bowler. *Team* Worcestershire (1975–83, 172 matches).
Career batting
173–298–34–8808–163*–33.36–14–*ct* 71
Bowling 190–1–190.00–0–0–1/15
He hit 1,000 runs in a season five times (best 1,521, av 41.10, in 1983). In 1983 he was appointed captain of Worcestershire. He also appeared for Lincolnshire. A useful soccer player, he appeared for Lincoln City.

Neale, William Legge
Amateur to 1928 then professional. *b:* 3.3.1904, Berkeley, Gloucs. *d:* 26.10.1955, Gloucester. Sound middle order batsman, slow right-arm bowler, good deep field. *Team* Gloucestershire (1923–48, 452 matches).
Career batting
452–700–79–14752–145*–23.75–14–*ct* 227
Bowling 3970–100–39.70–1–0–6/9
He hit 1,000 runs in a season six times (best 1,488, av 29.76, in 1938).

Neame, Arthur Rex Beale
Amateur. *b:* 14.6.1936, Faversham, Kent. Middle order right-hand batsman, right-arm medium pace bowler. *Sch* Harrow. *Team* Kent (1956–57, 4 matches).
Career batting
10–18–0–234–69–13.00–0–*ct* 8
Bowling 170–4–42.50–0–0–2/4
His final first-class match was for D. R. Jardine's XI in 1958.

Neate, Francis Webb
Amateur. *b:* 13.5.1940, Newbury, Berks. Brother of P. W. (Oxford U). Middle order right-hand batsman. *Sch* St Paul's. *Team* Oxford U (1960–62, blue 1961–62).
Career batting
17–30–6–914–112–38.08–1–*ct* 7
His County cricket was for Berkshire, being captain 1971 to 1975.

Neate, Patrick Whistler
Cricketer. *b:* 2.5.1946, Newbury, Berks. Brother of F. W. (Oxford U). Lower order left-hand batsman, right-arm medium pace bowler. *Sch* St Paul's. *Team* Oxford U (1966).
Career batting
1–1–0–3–3–3.00–0–*ct* 2
Bowling 53–0
His County cricket was for Berkshire.

Neblett, James M.
Amateur. *b:* 13.11.1901, Barbados. Middle order left-hand batsman, left-arm medium pace bowler. *Team* British Guiana (1925/6 to 1938/9). *Tour* West Indies to England 1928. *Test* West Indies (1934/5, 1 match).
Career batting
20–33–5–526–61–18.78–0–*ct* 15
Bowling 1205–29–41.55–0–0–4/82
Test batting
1–2–1–16–11*–16.00–0–*ct* 0
Bowling 75–1–75.00–0–0–1/44
He had a very modest tour of England in 1928 and appeared in only eight first-class matches. He represented 'Barbados-born' in 1927/8, but never played for the full Barbados team in a first-class match.

Needham, Andrew
Cricketer. *b:* 23.3.1957, Calow, Derbyshire. Middle/lower order right-hand batsman, off break bowler. *Team* Surrey (1977–83, 36 matches).
Career batting
36–48–9–497–134*–12.74–1–*ct* 14
Bowling 2138–51–41.92–3–0–6/30

Needham, Ernest
Professional. *b:* 21.1.1873, Newbold Moor, Chesterfield, Derbyshire. *d:* 8.3.1936, Chesterfield, Derbyshire. Sound opening left-hand batsman, right-arm medium pace bowler, occasional wicket-keeper. *Team* Derbyshire (1901–12, 186 matches).
Career batting
186–340–15–6550–159–20.15–7–*ct* 135–*st* 1
Bowling 82–0
His best season was 1908 when he hit 1,178 runs, av 28.73. A notable soccer player, he appeared as half back for Sheffield United and England, gaining 16 caps.

Needham, Frank
Professional. *b:* 27.8.1861, Arnold, Notts. *d:* 15.10.1923, Arnold, Notts. Tail end batsman, left-arm slow medium bowler. *Team* Nottinghamshire (1890–91, 5 matches).
Career batting
8–15–3–49–13–4.08–0–*ct* 4
Bowling 442–24–18.42–1–0–5/44
His final first-class match was for MCC in 1901 – he was on the staff at Lord's from 1891 until his death in 1923.

Needham, Joseph
Professional. *b:* 9.1.1862, Flagg, Derbyshire. *d:* 30.8.1889, Taddington, Derbyshire. Middle order right-hand batsman. *Team* Derbyshire (1883, 1 match).
Career batting
1–2–1–9–6*–9.00–0–*ct* 0

Needham, Patrick John Easthorpe
Cricketer. *b:* 6.12.1951, Cardiff. Middle order left-hand batsman, right-arm medium pace bowler, wicket-keeper. *Sch* Harrow. *Team* Glamorgan (1975, 1 match).
Career batting
1–1–0–4–4–4.00–0–*ct* 1
Bowling 105–2–52.50–0–0–1/49

Needham, Rowland
Professional. *b:* 1878, Huncote, Leics. *d:* 28.4.1963, Leicester. Lower order left-hand batsman, left-arm medium pace bowler. *Team* Leicestershire (1911, 1 match).
Career batting
1–2–1–31–16–31.00–0–*ct* 0
Bowling 75–2–37.50–0–0–2/75

Nelson, Alfred Leonard
Amateur. *b:* 13.11.1871, Kenilworth, Warwickshire. *d:* 2.5.1927, Holly Green, Worcs. Middle order right-hand batsman, wicket-keeper, change bowler. *Sch* Radley. *Team* Warwickshire (1895, 1 match).
Career batting
1–2–0–0–0–0.00–0–*ct* 0
He hit a century in the Oxford Freshmen's Match of 1891, but never appeared in any first-class matches for the University.

Nelson, Guy Montague (Blyth)
Amateur. *b:* 8.8.1900, Warwick. *d:* 13.1.1969, Great Bourton, Banbury, Oxfordshire. Lower order right-hand batsman, right-arm fast medium bowler. *Sch* Rugby. *Team* Warwickshire (1921–22, 13 matches).
Career batting
13–21–8–97–23–7.46–0–*ct* 2
Bowling 746–22–33.90–0–0–4/53

Nelson, J.
Amateur. *b: circa* 1890, near Blackpool, Lancashire. *d:* during the 1914–18 War. Middle order batsman. *Team* Lancashire (1913, 1 match).
Career batting
1–2–0–7–5–3.50–0–*ct* 0
His name appears on the Old Trafford War Memorial to the 1914–18 War, but there are over 70 of this name and initials in the War Deaths and it has not been possible to identify him.

Nelson, Peter John Mytton
Amateur. *b:* 16.5.1918, Finchley, Middlesex. Middle order left-hand batsman, left-arm medium pace bowler. *Sch* St George's, Harpenden. *Teams* Northants (1938, 1 match); Kent (1946, 1 match).
Career batting
2–4–1–55–32–18.33–0–*ct* 0
Bowling 51–2–25.50–0–0–1/9

Nelson, Peter Maurice
Amateur. *b:* 22.3.1913, Bradfield, Berkshire. Stylish middle order right-hand batsman, right-arm slow off break bowler. *Sch* Marlborough. *Team* Army (1939).
Career batting
1–1–0–62–62–62.00–0–*ct* 2
Bowling 63–1–63.00–0–0–1/63
His County cricket was for Oxfordshire.

Nelson, Robert Prynne
Amateur. *b:* 7.8.1912, Fulham, London. *d:* 29.10.1940, Deal, Kent. He was killed while serving with the Royal Marines. Opening/middle order right-hand batsman, slow left-arm bowler. *Sch* St Albans and St George's, Harpenden. *Teams* Middlesex (1932–33, 9 matches); Cambridge U (1934–36, blue 1936); Northants (1937–39, 50 matches).

Career batting
77–136–12–3394–123*–27.37–2–*ct* 35
Bowling 2208–62–35.61–0–0–3/7
He hit 1,000 runs in a season twice (best 1,264, av 26.89, in 1938). In 1938 and 1939 he captained Northants. He also appeared for Hertfordshire.

Nepean, Augustus Adolphus St John Marriott
Amateur. *b:* 24.6.1849, London. *d:* 24.1.1933, Westminster, London. Brother of C. E. B. (Middlesex), uncle of E. A. (Middlesex). Middle order left-hand batsman, right-hand fast round-arm bowler. *Team* Middlesex (1876–77, 3 matches).
Career batting
7–11–3–187–51–23.37–0–*ct* 3
Bowling 66–2–33.00–0–0–1/13

Nepean, Rev Charles Edward Burroughs
Amateur. *b:* 5.2.1851, Mayfair, London. *d:* 26.3.1903, Lenham, Kent. Brother of A. A. St J. M. (Middlesex), uncle of E. A. (Middlesex). Middle order right-hand batsman, slow under-arm bowler, wicket-keeper. *Sch* Charterhouse. *Teams* Oxford U (1870–73, blue 1873); Middlesex (1873–74, 2 matches).
Career batting
10–17–1–290–50–18.12–0–*ct* 7–*st* 6
He also played for Dorset and was later on the Committee of Kent CCC.

Nepean, Evan Alcock
Amateur. *b:* 13.9.1865, Mitcham, Surrey. *d:* 20.1.1906, Windsor, Berks. Nephew of A. A. St J. M. (Middlesex) and C. E. B. (Middlesex). Middle order right-hand batsman, right-arm fast, later leg break, bowler. *Sch* Sherborne. *Teams* Oxford U (1887–88, blue both years); Middlesex (1887–95, 45 matches).
Career batting
89–152–21–2439–71–18.61–0–*ct* 28
Bowling 5307–264–20.10–12–1–8/48
His final first-class match was for MCC in 1902. He also played for Dorset.

Nesbitt, Arnold Stearns
Amateur. *b:* 16.10.1878, Chertsey, Surrey. *d:* 7.11.1914, Ploegsteert Wood, Belgium. He was killed in action. Lower order right-hand batsman, wicket-keeper. *Sch* Bradfield. *Team* Worcestershire (1914, 1 match).
Career batting
1–2–1–5–3–5.00–0–*ct* 1

Neser, Justice Vivian Herbert
Amateur. *b:* 16.6.1894, Klerksdorp, Transvaal. *d:* 22.12.1956, Pretoria, South Africa. Middle order right-hand batsman. *Teams* Oxford U (1919–21, blue 1921); Transvaal (1921/2 to 1924/5).
Career batting
18–29–2–743–90–27.51–0–*ct* 28–*st* 15
He was also awarded his blue for rugby football.

Nesfield, Edward Roy
Amateur. *b:* 7.3.1900, Armthorpe, Yorkshire. Lower order right-hand batsman, off break bowler. *Sch* King's, Worcester. *Team* Worcestershire (1919–20, 3 matches).
Career batting
3–4–0–27–16–6.75–0–*ct* 0
Bowling 10–0

Neve, John Tanner
Amateur. *b:* 2.10.1902, Cranbrook, Kent. *d:* 7.7.1976, Woodcutts, Wilts. Hard-hitting lower order right-hand batsman, right-arm medium pace bowler. *Sch* Cheltenham. *Team* MCC (1936). *Tour* MCC to Canada 1937 (not first-class).
Career batting
1–2–0–14–9–7.00–0–*ct* 1
Bowling 66–2–33.00–0–0–1/32

Nevell, William Thomas
Professional. *b:* 13.6.1916, Balham, South London. *d:* 25.8.1978, Worthing, Sussex. Hard-hitting lower order right-hand batsman, right-arm medium fast bowler. *Teams* Middlesex (1936–38, 13 matches); Surrey (1939, 1 match); Northants (1946–47, 36 matches).
Career batting
51–81–9–671–55*–9.31–0–*ct* 18
Bowling 3488–105–33.21–0–0–4/11

Nevile, Bernard Philip
Amateur. *b:* 1.8.1888, Wellingore, Lincs. *d:* 11.2.1916, near Ypres, Belgium. He was killed in action. Middle/lower order batsman, right-arm fast bowler. *Sch* Downside. *Team* Worcestershire (1913, 5 matches).
Career batting
6–10–2–65–17*–8.12–0–*ct* 1
Bowling 149–7–21.28–0–0–4/53
He appeared in the Freshmen's and Seniors' Matches at Cambridge, but no first-class matches. His first-class debut was for Free Foresters in 1912. He also played for Lincolnshire. A good golfer, he was awarded his blue.

Neville, Patrick Augustine
Amateur. *b:* 22.6.1920, Donabate, Co Dublin,

Ireland. *d:* 16.11.1977, Dublin, Ireland. Right-hand batsman. *Team* Ireland (1956–60).
Career batting
4–8–0–143–38–17.87–0–*ct* 4

Nevin, Michael Robert Spencer
Cricketer. *b:* 5.4.1950, London. Lower order right-hand batsman, right-arm fast medium bowler. *Sch* Winchester. *Team* Cambridge U (1969, blue).
Career batting
8–12–8–34–14*–8.50–0–*ct* 1
Bowling 407–5–81.40–0–0–2/50

Nevinson, John Harcourt
Amateur. *b:* 2.11.1910, Lausanne, Switzerland. Tail end right-hand batsman, right-arm fast medium bowler. *Sch* Eton. *Teams* Oxford U (1929–31); Middlesex (1933, 6 matches).
Career batting
15–18–10–56–20*–7.00–0–*ct* 8
Bowling 1113–21–53.00–0–0–4/15
His final first-class match was for Free Foresters in 1935.

New, Frank Chandler
Amateur. *b:* 25.12.1859, Southwick, Sussex. *d:* 1924, Steyning, Sussex. Very steady middle order right-hand batsman, right-arm medium pace bowler. *Team* Sussex (1890, 3 matches).
Career batting
3–6–0–63–43–10.50–0–*ct* 1

Newbery, Arthur Leonard
Amateur. *b:* 6.1.1905, Battle, Sussex. *d:* 17.12.1976, Ightham, Kent. Middle order right-hand batsman. *Team* Sussex (1925, 3 matches).
Career batting
3–6–1–58–50*–11.60–0–*ct* 0
He was a director of John Wisden and Co and Manager of Gray-Nicolls.

Newbolt, Robert Henry
Amateur. *b:* 29.4.1833. *d:* 10.8.1885, Dresden, Germany. Middle order batsman. *Team* Gentlemen of England (1865).
Career batting
1–1–0–10–10–10.00–0–*ct* 0

Newburn, Thomas
Amateur. *b:* 10.8.1918, Belfast. Lower order batsman, right-arm fast medium bowler. *Team* Ireland (1949).
Career batting
1–2–0–12–8–6.00–0–*ct* 1
Bowling 31–3–10.33–0–0–3/23

Newcomb, Alfred Edwin
Professional. *b:* 1873, Market Harborough, Leics. *d:* 4.2.1932, Market Harborough, Leics. Lower order right-hand batsman, right-arm fast medium, later slow, bowler. *Team* Leicestershire (1911, 1 match).
Career batting
1–2–0–1–1–0.50–0–*ct* 0
Bowling 74–1–74.00–0–0–1/26

Newcombe, Charles Niel
Amateur. *b:* 16.3.1891, Yarmouth. *d:* 27.12.1915, Fleuraix, France. He was killed in action. Lower order right-hand batsman, left-arm slow medium bowler. *Team* Derbyshire (1910, 1 match).
Career batting
1–2–0–1–1–0.50–0–*ct* 0
Bowling 32–0

Newhall, William Price
Amateur. Son of G. M. (Philadelphia), nephew of R. S., D. S. and C. A. (Philadelphia). Middle order batsman, good cover. *Teams* Philadelphia (1908–12); US and Canada (1913). *Tours* Philadelphia to England 1908, to Jamaica 1908/9.
Career batting
6–11–0–232–57–21.09–0–*ct* 4
Bowling 63–2–31.50–0–0–2/30
He played in only two first-class matches on the 1908 tour and in 1912 represented the United States v Canada. He was the son of one of several brothers who played a prominent part in Philadelphian cricket.

Newham, William
Amateur. *b:* 12.12.1860, Shrewsbury. *d:* 26.6.1944, Hove, Sussex. Attractive fast scoring middle order right-hand batsman. *Sch* Ardingly. *Team* Sussex (1881–1905, 334 matches). *Tour* Lillywhite, Shaw and Shrewsbury to Australia 1887/8. *Test* England (1887/8, 1 match).
Career batting
368–643–43–14657–201*–24.42–19–*ct* 183
Bowling 615–10–61.50–0–0–3/57
Test batting
1–2–0–26–17–13.00–0–*ct* 0
He hit 1,000 runs in a season four times (best 1,183, av 31.97, in 1896). His only double century was 201* for Sussex v Somerset at Hove in 1896. He captained Sussex in 1889 and 1891 and was Secretary to the County Club, as well as being the manager.

Newland, Frederick
Professional. *b:* 14.1.1850, Henfield, Sussex. *d:* 1921, Steyning, Sussex. Lower order right-hand batsman, right-hand fast round-arm bowler. *Team* Sussex (1875–79, 3 matches).

Career batting
3–4–1–11–7*–3.66–0–*ct* 1
Bowling 79–2–39.50–0–0–2/46

Newland, Philip Mesner
Amateur. *b:* 2.2.1875, Adelaide, South Australia. *d:* 11.8.1916, Australia. Lower order batsman, wicket-keeper. *Team* South Australia (1899/1900 to 1905/6, 16 matches). *Tours* Australia to New Zealand 1904/5, to England 1905.
Career batting
28–46–13–599–77–18.15–0–*ct* 30–*st* 18
He came to England in 1905 as reserve wicket-keeper, and did not appear in any Tests.

Newland, Richard
Amateur. *b:* 1718. *d:* 29.5.1791, Bath, Somerset. Left-hand batsman. *Team* Slindon.
Career batting
not applicable, pre-1800
His most famous innings was 88 for England v Kent in 1745 – most of his records are lost, but he was regarded as the finest batsman in England.

Newman, Arthur William
Professional. *b:* 1883, Westbury, Wilts. *d:* 16.3.1966, Melksham, Wilts. Middle order batsman, useful bowler. *Team* MCC (1907–19).
Career batting
5–6–1–39–15*–7.80–0–*ct* 4
Bowling 57–2–28.50–0–0–1/12
His final first-class match was for West of England in 1927. His County cricket was for Wiltshire.

Newman, Charles
Professional. *b:* 7.8.1839, Cambridge. *d:* 23.4.1883, Cambridge. Hard-hitting middle order right-hand batsman. *Team* Cambridgeshire (1861–69, 15 matches).
Career batting
17–32–2–195–32–6.16–0–*ct* 8
His first-class debut was for the Cambridge Town Club in 1860.

Newman, Douglas Leonard
Amateur. *b:* 25.6.1920, Harringay, London. *d:* 11.9.1959, St Pancras, London. Middle order right-hand batsman. *Team* Middlesex (1948–51, 11 matches).
Career batting
12–19–1–256–29–14.22–0–*ct* 5
His final first-class match was for MCC in 1953. A noted club cricketer in London, he captained Winchmore Hill.

Newman, Frederick Charles William
Amateur. *b:* 2.2.1896, Luton, Beds. *d:* 1.1.1966, Malpas, Truro, Cornwall. Middle order right-hand batsman, bowler. *Sch* Bedford Modern. *Team* Surrey (1919–21, 5 matches). *Tours* Cahn to Jamaica 1928/9 (did not play in first-class matches), to Argentine 1929/30.
Career batting
13–20–1–442–101–23.26–1–*ct* 4
Bowling 80–1–80.00–0–0–1/31
He was appointed Private Secretary to Julien Cahn in 1926, a post he retained until Cahn's death, and he was responsible for arranging Cahn's tours overseas. His final first-class match was for Sir Julien Cahn's XI in 1936. He also played for Bedfordshire.

Newman, George Christopher
Amateur. *b:* 26.4.1904, London. *d:* 13.10.1982, Braintree, Essex. Middle order right-hand batsman, right-arm medium pace bowler. *Sch* Eton. *Teams* Oxford U (1926–27, blue both years); Middlesex (1929–36, 50 matches). *Tour* MCC to Canada 1937 (not first-class).
Career batting
73–116–10–2742–112–28.86–3–*ct* 27
Bowling 670–17–39.41–0–0–3/48
A noted athlete, he represented Oxford in the high jump and hurdles.

Newman, H. J.
Amateur. Middle order batsman. *Team* Northants (1905, 1 match).
Career batting
1–2–0–5–5–2.50–0–*ct* 0

Newman, John Alfred
Professional. *b:* 12.11.1884, Southsea, Hants. *d:* 21.12.1973, Cape Town, South Africa. Opening/middle order right-hand batsman, right-arm fast medium bowler. *Teams* Hampshire (1906–30, 506 matches); England XI in India (1915/6); Cooch Behar's XI (1917/8 to 1918/9); Canterbury (1927/8 to 1928/9).
Career batting
541–841–129–15364–166*–21.57–10–*ct* 320
Bowling 51427–2054–25.03–134–35–9/131
He hit 1,000 runs in a season six times (best 1,474, av 29.48, in 1928) and took 100 wickets nine times (best 177, av 21.56, in 1921). In all he achieved the 'double' five times. His best bowling in an innings was 9/131 for Hampshire v Essex at Bournemouth in 1921. During the Hants v Notts match at Trent Bridge in 1922 he was ordered off the field for indiscipline by his captain, Lord Tennyson.

Newman, Paul Geoffrey
Cricketer. *b:* 10.1.1959, Evington, Leicester. Lower order right-hand batsman, right-arm fast

medium bowler. *Team* Derbyshire (1980–83, 43 matches).
Career batting
45–46–11–371–39*–10.60–0–*ct* 13
Bowling 3329–101–32.96–1–0–5/51

Newman, Robert Grant
Amateur. *b:* 23.12.1933, Bristol. Attractive middle order right-hand batsman. *Sch* Clifton. *Team* Cambridge U (1955–57).
Career batting
4–7–0–133–44–19.00–0–*ct* 1

Newman, William
Amateur. *b:* 1837, Cambridge. Lower order batsman, bowler. *Team* Cambridgeshire (1867–71, 5 matches).
Career batting
5–10–0–34–9–3.40–0–*ct* 0
Bowling 124–6–20.66–0–0–3/19

Newnham, Arthur Tristram Herbert
Amateur. *b:* 17.1.1861, Dharwar, India. *d:* 29.12.1941, Wolborough, Devon. Middle/lower order right-hand batsman, right-arm fast bowler. *Sch* Malvern. *Teams* Gloucestershire (1887–94, 16 matches); Europeans (1892/3 to 1898/9).
Career batting
23–37–5–337–56–10.53–0–*ct* 11
Bowling 1127–59+1–19.10–4–0–6/64
Commencing in 1883 he was stationed in India, which restricted his opportunities in County cricket.

Newnham, Stanley William
Amateur. *b:* 7.4.1910, New Cross, Kent. Middle order right-hand batsman, slow left-arm bowler. *Team* Surrey (1932, 1 match).
Career batting
1–1–0–4–4–4.00–0–*ct* 1
Bowling 13–2–6.50–0–0–2/13
He also played for Denbighshire.

Newport, George Bernard
Amateur. *b:* 29.3.1876, Muttum, India. *d:* 12.7.1953, Exeter, Devon. Lower order right-hand batsman, wicket-keeper. *Sch* Bishop's Stortford. *Team* Somerset (1902–04, 2 matches).
Career batting
2–4–0–27–16–6.75–0–*ct* 4

Newport, Philip John
Cricketer. *b:* 11.10.1962, High Wycombe, Bucks. Lower order right-hand batsman, right-arm fast medium bowler. *Team* Worcestershire (1982–83, 7 matches).
Career batting
7–9–2–110–41*–15.71–0–*ct* 1
Bowling 356–9–39.55–0–0–4/76
He played for Buckinghamshire in 1981.

Newsom, David John
Amateur. *b:* 5.10.1937, Plymouth, Devon. Opening batsman. *Sch* Haileybury. *Team* Combined Services (1960–61).
Career batting
2–2–0–33–23–16.50–0–*ct* 2

Newstead, John Thomas
Professional. *b:* 8.9.1877, Martin-in-Cleveland, Yorkshire. *d:* 25.3.1952, Blackburn, Lancashire. Steady middle order right-hand batsman, right-arm medium off break bowler. *Team* Yorkshire (1903–13, 96 matches).
Career batting
109–150–20–2104–100*–16.18–1–*ct* 83
Bowling 5947–310–19.18–13–4–7/10
He took 140 wickets, av 16.50, in 1908.

Newton, Arthur Edward
Amateur. *b:* 12.9.1862, Barton Grange, near Taunton, Somerset. *d:* 15.9.1952, Dipford, Trull, Somerset. Free hitting lower order right-hand batsman, excellent wicket-keeper. *Sch* Eton. *Teams* Oxford U (1885, blue); Somerset (1891–1914, 197 matches). *Tours* Sanders to North America 1885; Vernon to Australia 1887/8.
Career batting
217–360–73–3614–77–12.59–0–*ct* 319–*st* 128
Bowling 4–0
He played club cricket until he was 81. Having made his debut for Somerset in 1880 (before the County were first-class), his career for that side lasted 35 seasons.

Newton, Edward
Professional. *b:* 31.10.1871. *d:* 9.5.1906, Edinburgh, Scotland. He died of pneumonia. Middle order batsman, brilliant field. *Team* Hampshire (1900, 17 matches).
Career batting
17–32–1–568–69–18.32–0–*ct* 8

Newton, Frederick Arthur
Professional. *b:* 16.9.1890, Denaby Main, Yorkshire. *d:* 8.8.1924, Warsop, Notts. He was killed in a colliery accident. Middle order right-hand batsman, leg break bowler, good field. *Team* Derbyshire (1909–19, 20 matches).
Career batting
20–37–6–422–87–13.61–0–*ct* 7
Bowling 21–0

Newton, Harry
Cricketer. *b:* 2.5.1935, Little Lever, Bolton, Lancashire. Lower order right-hand batsman, right-arm fast medium bowler. *Team* Sussex (1966, 2 matches).
Career batting
2–4–2–16–16*–8.00–0–*ct* 0
Bowling 141–6–23.50–1–0–5/54

Newton, Harold Maurice
Amateur. *b:* 5.9.1918, Overstone, Northants. Middle order right-hand batsman. *Sch* Gresham's Holt. *Team* Northants (1938, 1 match).
Career batting
1–2–0–2–2–1.00–0–*ct* 0

Newton, Stephen Cox
Amateur. *b:* 21.4.1853, Nailsea, Somerset. *d:* 16.8.1916, Ipswich, Suffolk. Attacking middle order right-hand batsman, brilliant cover point. *Sch* Victoria College, Jersey. *Teams* Cambridge U (1876, blue); Somerset (1882–84, 16 matches); Middlesex (1885, 3 matches).
Career batting
33–59–3–1137–86–20.30–0–*ct* 20
Bowling 185–2–92.50–0–0–2/54

His final first-class match was for MCC in 1890. He also represented Huntingdonshire and Suffolk.

Newton-Thompson, Christopher Lawton
Amateur. *b:* 14.2.1919, Kensington, London. Brother of J. O. (Oxford U). Middle order right-hand batsman, wicket-keeper. *Team* Cambridge U (1939).
Career batting
1–2–0–16–8–8.00–0–*ct* 1

Newton-Thompson, John Oswald
Amateur. *b:* 2.12.1920, London. *d:* 3.4.1974, near Luderitz, South West Africa. He was killed in an air crash. Brother of C. L. (Cambridge U). Middle order right-hand batsman, right-arm slow bowler. *Teams* Oxford U (1946, blue); Western Province (1948/9).
Career batting
9–18–1–281–78–16.52–0–*ct* 6
Bowling 125–0

A noted rugby footballer, he was awarded his blue and went on to play for England in 1947. He entered the South African Parliament in 1961, as a member of the United Party.

Niaz Ahmed
Cricketer. *b:* 11.11.1945, Benares, India. Lower order right-hand batsman, right-arm fast medium bowler. *Teams* Dacca (1965/6); PWD (1965/6 to 1973/4); East Pakistan (1967/8 to 1968/9); Railways (1970/1). *Tour* Pakistan to England 1967. *Tests* Pakistan (1967 to 1968/9, 2 matches).
Career batting
39–48–16–466–71*–14.56–0–*ct* 31
Bowling 2384–62–38.45–1–0–5/86
Test batting
2–3–3–17–16*–no av–0–*ct* 1
Bowling 94–3–31.33–0–0–2/72

He appeared in one Test on the 1967 tour of England, but his performances were very moderate.

Nice, Ernest Herbert Leonard
Professional. *b:* 1.8.1875, Earlswood, Surrey. *d:* 6.6.1946, Redhill, Surrey. Lower order right-hand batsman, right-arm fast medium bowler. *Team* Surrey (1895–1905, 69 matches).
Career batting
69–96–10–1247–66–14.50–0–*ct* 34
Bowling 4394–174–25.25–5–1–8/83

Nichol, David
Amateur. *b:* 25.8.1914, Galashiels, Selkirkshire, Scotland. Brother of R. J. and William (both Scotland). Right-hand batsman, slow left-arm bowler. *Team* Scotland (1952).
Career batting
1–2–0–6–4–3.00–0–*ct* 1
Bowling 61–2–30.50–0–0–2/61

Nichol, Maurice
Professional. *b:* 10.9.1904, Hetton, Co Durham. *d:* 21.5.1934, Chelmsford, Essex. Stylish middle order right-hand batsman. *Team* Worcestershire (1928–34, 135 matches).
Career batting
136–234–16–7484–262*–34.33–17–*ct* 64
Bowling 1281–21–61.00–0–0–2/6

He hit 1,000 runs in a season four times, going on to 2,000 once: 2,154, av 43.95, in 1933. His only double century was 262* for Worcs v Hants at Bournemouth in 1930. He also played for Durham.

On the second morning of the Worcestershire v Essex match at Chelmsford in 1934, in which he was playing, he was found dead in bed. He had not enjoyed the best of health for several years, but his end was very unexpected.

Nichol, Robert John
Amateur. *b:* 14.3.1924, Galashiels, Selkirkshire, Scotland. Brother of David and William (Scotland). Lower order right-hand batsman, right-

arm fast medium bowler. *Team* Scotland (1951–55).
Career batting
7–10–2–67–19–8.37–0–*ct* 5
Bowling 505–12–42.08–1–0–5/87

Nichol, William
Amateur. *b:* 3.12.1912, Galashiels, Selkirkshire, Scotland. *d;* 1.6.1973, Paisley, Renfrewshire, Scotland. Brother of David and R. J. (Scotland). Left-hand batsman, slow left-arm bowler. *Team* Scotland (1938–56).
Career batting
26–43–3–931–139*–23.27–2–*ct* 13
Bowling 1395–55–25.36–3–1–7/39

Nicholas, Frederick William Herbert
Amateur. *b:* 25.7.1893, Federated Malay States. *d:* 20.10.1962, Kensington, London. Middle order right-hand batsman, wicket-keeper. *Sch* Forest. *Team* Essex (1912–29, 63 matches). *Tours* Joel to South Africa 1924/5; Cahn to Jamaica 1928/9, to Argentine 1929/30.
Career batting
76–122–5–2634–140–22.51–1–*ct* 51–*st* 16
He appeared in the Oxford Freshmen's Match of 1913, but no first-class matches for the University. From 1927 to 1931 he was a regular cricketer with Sir Julien Cahn's XI and in 1929 scored over 2,000 runs for that side. He also appeared for Bedfordshire.

Nicholas, Mark Charles Jefford
Cricketer. *b:* 29.9.1957, London. Middle order right-hand batsman, right-arm medium pace bowler. *Sch* Bradfield. *Team* Hampshire (1978–83, 94 matches).
Career batting
94–160–23–4444–206*–32.43–9–*ct* 61
Bowling 859–29–29.62–1–0–5/45
He hit 1,000 runs in a season twice (best 1,418, av 37.31 in 1983). His only double century was 206* for Hampshire v Oxford U at Oxford in 1982.

Nicholl, Kenneth Iltyd
Amateur. *b:* 13.2.1885, Marylebone, London. *d:* 2.3.1952, Famagusta, Cyprus. Stylish opening right-hand batsman. *Sch* Eton. *Team* Middlesex (1904, 2 matches).
Career batting
6–11–0–254–62–23.09–0–*ct* 2
He did not appear in any first-class matches whilst at Oxford, but played some County cricket with Berkshire. His final first-class match was for Free Foresters in 1921.

Nicholls, Benjamin Ernest
Amateur. *b:* 4.10.1864, Byfleet, Surrey. *d:* 6.6.1945, Kirdford, Sussex. Hard-hitting lower order right-hand batsman, right-arm slow bowler, excellent slip field. *Sch* Winchester. *Teams* Sussex (1883–88, 4 matches); Oxford U (1884–85, blue 1884).
Career batting
16–25–6–192–44–10.10–0–*ct* 23
Bowling 666–31–21.40–1–0–5/46
His final first-class match was for MCC in 1901.

Nicholls, Cecil Burleigh
Amateur. *b:* 21.12.1880. *d:* 1.6.1943, Folkestone, Kent. Lower order batsman, bowler. *Sch* Chigwell. *Team* W. G. Grace's XI (1906).
Career batting
1–2–0–20–19–10.00–0–*ct* 0
Bowling 42–0

Nicholls, David
Professional. *b:* 8.12.1943, East Dereham, Norfolk. Attacking opening left-hand batsman, off break bowler, often wicket-keeper in later years of his career. *Team* Kent (1960–77, 201 matches).
Career batting
202–342–24–7072–211–22.23–2–*ct* 326–*st* 13
Bowling 23–2–11.50–0–0–1/0
He hit 1,000 runs, av 32.25 in 1971. His only double century was 211 for Kent v Derbyshire at Folkestone in 1963.

Nicholls, Ronald Bernard
Professional. *b:* 4.12.1933, Sharpness, Gloucs. Sound opening right-hand batsman, off break bowler, good cover field, occasional wicket-keeper. *Team* Gloucestershire (1951–75, 534 matches).
Career batting
534–954–52–23607–217–26.17–18–*ct* 283–*st* 1
Bowling 719–11–65.36–0–0–2/19
He hit 1,000 runs in a season 15 times, going on to 2,000 once : 2,059, av 36.76, in 1962. His only double century was 217 for Gloucs v Oxford U at Oxford in 1962, during which innings he set up a County record 1st wicket partnership of 395 with D. M. Young. A well-known soccer player, he kept goal for Bristol Rovers, Cardiff City, Fulham and Bristol City.

Nicholls, Richard William
Amateur. *b:* 23.7.1875, Crouch End, Middlesex. *d:* 22.1.1948, Eastbourne, Sussex. Middle order right-hand batsman, good field. *Sch* Rugby. *Team* Middlesex (1896–1904, 65 matches).

Career batting
72–113–10–1732–154–16.81–1–*ct* 31

With W. Roche he added 230 for the last Middlesex wicket v Kent at Lord's in 1899, creating a new record.

Nichols, George Benjamin
Amateur for Gloucs, but professional for Somerset. *b:* 14.6.1862, Fishponds, Bristol. *d:* 19.2.1911, Dublin. He died of pneumonia. Lower order right-hand batsman, right-arm fast medium bowler, good slip. *Teams* Gloucestershire (1883–85, 5 matches); Somerset (1891–99, 134 matches).
Career batting
143–248–31–2958–74*–13.63–0–*ct* 65
Bowling 7138–299–23.87–7–0–6/75

He appeared for Devon in 1900 and 1901. He was also a playwright of some note.

Nichols, John Bowes
Amateur. *b:* 1.1.1931, Latchford, Cheshire. Lower order right-hand batsman, slow left-arm bowler. *Team* Cambridge U (1953).
Career batting
5–5–0–33–16–6.60–0–*ct* 0
Bowling 81–0

Nichols, John Ernest
Professional. *b:* 20.4.1878, Acle, Norwich. *d:* 29.2.1952, Thorpe, Norwich. Middle order batsman. *Team* Worcestershire (1902–04, 5 matches).
Career batting
6–10–1–45–13–5.00–0–*ct* 3
Bowling 13–0

His final first-class match was for Minor Counties in 1912. He played for Staffordshire and Norfolk.

Nichols, Morris Stanley
Professional. *b:* 6.10.1900, Stondon Massey, Essex. *d:* 26.1.1961, Newark, Notts. Attacking middle order left-hand batsman, right-arm fast bowler. *Team* Essex (1924–39, 418 matches). *Tours* Cahn to Jamaica 1928/9; MCC to Australia and New Zealand 1929/30, to India and Ceylon 1933/4; Tennyson to Jamaica 1931/2; selected for MCC to India 1939/40 (cancelled because of war). *Tests* England (1929/30 to 1939, 14 matches).
Career batting
483–756–85–17827–205–26.56–20–*ct* 325
Bowling 39666–1833–21.63–118–23–9/32
Test batting
14–19–7–355–78*–29.58–0–*ct* 11
Bowling 1152–41–28.09–2–0–6/35

One of the leading all-round cricketers of his day, he performed the 'double' eight times, including five seasons in succession. In all he hit 1,000 runs in a season nine times (best 1,460, av 30.41, in 1933) and took 100 wickets eleven times (best 171, av 19.92, in 1938). His only double century was 205 for Essex v Hampshire at Southend in 1936. His best bowling was 9/32 for Essex v Notts at Trent Bridge in 1936. A useful soccer player, he kept goal for Queen's Park Rangers.

Nichols, Thomas
Professional. *b:* 25.5.1844, Dorking, Surrey. Lower order right-hand batsman, right-hand fast medium round-arm bowler. *Team* Players (1867).
Career batting
1–1–0–0–0–0.00–0–*ct* 0

Nichols, Rev Thomas Bartrup
Amateur. *b:* 1848, Cambridge. *d:* 7.3.1915, Kineton, Warwickshire. Middle order batsman. *Team* Cambridgeshire (1868, 1 match).
Career batting
1–2–1–16–15*–16.00–0–*ct* 0

He also played for Staffordshire.

Nicholson, Anthony George
Professional. *b:* 25.6.1938, Dewsbury, Yorkshire. Lower order right-hand batsman, right-arm medium pace bowler. *Team* Yorkshire (1962–75, 282 matches). *Tour* English Counties XI to West Indies 1974/5 (not first-class).
Career batting
283–268–126–1669–50–11.75–0–*ct* 85
Bowling 17371–879–19.76–40–3–9/62

He took 100 wickets in a season twice (best 113, av 15.50, in 1966). His best bowling in an innings was 9 for 62 for Yorkshire v Sussex at Eastbourne in 1967. He was chosen to tour South Africa with MCC in 1964/5, but prevented from going due to injury.

Nicholson, John Simmonds
Professional. *b:* 1903. *d:* 18.3.1950, Bedford. Lower order right-hand batsman, right-arm medium pace bowler. *Team* Northants (1924–28, 63 matches).
Career batting
64–103–19–778–45–9.26–0–*ct* 54
Bowling 3221–93–34.63–3–0–5/40

Nicholson, Thomas Brinsley
Amateur. *b:* 15.3.1876, Madras, India. *d:* 3.10.1939, Cambridge. Hard-hitting middle order right-hand batsman, good deep field. *Sch* Clifton. *Teams* London County (1904); Jamaica (1908/9 to 1910/11).
Career batting
12–22–2–470–73*–23.50–0–*ct* 10

Nicholson, William
Amateur. *b:* 7.5.1909, Kirn, Argyllshire, Scotland. Right-hand batsman. *Sch* Loretto. *Team* Scotland (1929–33).
Career batting
10–18–2–396–101–24.75–1–*ct* 6

Nicholson, William
Amateur. *b:* 2.9.1824, Upper Holloway, Middlesex. *d:* 25.7.1909, Westminster, London. Brother of John (Cambridge U, 1845). Attacking middle order right-hand batsman, wicket-keeper. *Sch* Harrow. *Team* Middlesex (1850–65, 5 matches).
Career batting
148–261–11–3447–86–13.78–0–*ct* 110–*st* 89
His first-class debut was for Gentlemen of England in 1845 and his final match for MCC in 1869. In 1866 his financial support saved Lord's from the builders. He was on the MCC Committee and President of the Club in 1879. From 1866 to 1874 he was Liberal MP for Petersfield and from 1880 to 1885 Conservative for the same constituency.

Nicoll, Henry Russell
Amateur. *b:* 27.2.1883, Mains, Angus, Scotland. *d:* 25.9.1948, Dundee, Scotland. Lower order batsman, good bowler. *Team* Scotland (1914).
Career batting
1–2–1–0–0*–0.00–0–*ct* 0
Bowling 144–8–18.00–1–0–7/64

Nicolson, John Fairless William
Amateur. *b:* 19.7.1899, Durban, South Africa. *d:* 13.12.1935, Kilkeel, Co Down, Northern Ireland. Sound opening left-hand batsman. *Teams* Oxford U (1923); Natal (1923/4 to 1929/30). *Tests* South Africa (1927/8, 3 matches).
Career batting
28–44–3–1543–252*–37.63–3–*ct* 8
Bowling 205–3–68.33–0–0–2/36
Test batting
3–5–0–179–78–35.80–0–*ct* 0
Bowling 17–0
His most noteworthy innings was 252* for Natal v Orange Free State at Bloemfontein in 1926/7, when, with I. J. Siedle, he set up a new record of 424 for the 1st wicket. In 1932 he moved to Ireland where he took up a scholastic post.

Nightingale, James
Professional. *b:* 10.8.1840, Reigate, Surrey. *d:* 9.2.1917, Reigate, Surrey. Lower order batsman, useful bowler. *Team* Surrey (1868, 1 match).
Career batting
1–1–1–2–2*–no av–0–*ct* 1
Bowling 8–0

Nimbalkar, Raosaheb Babashaheb
Amateur. *b:* 1.12.1915, Kolhapur, India. *d:* 1.6.1965, Jalna, India. Brother of B. B. (Baroda), uncle of S. B. (Maharashtra). Middle order right-hand batsman, leg break bowler, wicket-keeper. *Teams* Maharashtra (1934/5 to 1940/1); Hindus (1938/9); Baroda (1938/9 to 1952/3). *Tours* India to Ceylon 1944/5, to England 1946.
Career batting
63–94–5–2687–132–30.19–4–*ct* 82–*st* 41
Bowling 179–3–59.66–0–0–1/8
Owing to a fractured thumb he appeared in just seven first-class matches on the 1946 tour to England and no Tests.

Nissar Mohammad, Laheem Shaheem Mohammad
Amateur. *b:* 1.8.1910, Hoshiarpur, India. *d:* 11.3.1963, Lahore, Pakistan. Tail end right-hand batsman, right-arm fast medium bowler. *Teams* Patiala (1932/3 to 1933/4); Southern Punjab (1933/4 to 1940/1); Muslims (1934/5 to 1939/40); Uttar Pradesh (1945/6). *Tours* India to England 1932, 1936. *Tests* India (1932–36, 6 matches).
Career batting
89–130–34–1015–49–10.51–0–*ct* 60
Bowling 6972–389–17.92–32–3–6/17
Test batting
6–11–3–55–14–6.87–0–*ct* 2
Bowling 707–25–28.28–3–0–5/90
His first-class debut was in a Trial Match in 1931/2. In 1932 he headed the tourists' first-class bowling averages with 71 wickets, av 18.09, and in 1936 took most wickets : 66, av 25.13. His last first-class match was for the C-in-C XI in 1949/50.

Niven, Robert Andrew
Cricketer. *b:* 28.4.1948, Felixstowe, Suffolk. Lower order right-hand batsman, left-arm medium pace bowler. *Sch* Berkhamsted. *Team* Oxford U (1968–69 and 1973, blue all 3 years).
Career batting
25–31–14–182–24*–10.70–0–*ct* 6
Bowling 1806–53–34.07–2–0–5/60

Nixon, George Tait St Aubyn
Amateur. *b:* 11.8.1850, Neermuck, Rajputana, India. *d:* February 1913, Lintlaw, Saskatchewan, Canada. Middle order right-hand batsman, right-hand slow round-arm bowler, wicket-keeper. *Sch* Rossall. *Teams* Middlesex (1868–70, 3 matches); Cambridge U (1870).
Career batting
6–10–0–113–54–11.30–0–*ct* 5–*st* 6

Nixon, Harry
Professional. *b:* 1.2.1878. Middle order batsman, left-arm bowler. *Team* Scotland (1906).
Career batting
1–2–0–53–41–26.50–0–*ct* 1
Bowling 195–5–39.00–0–0–3/106

Nixon, Henry
Professional. *b:* 1.5.1852, Cambridge. *d:* 1915, Cambridge. Lower order right-hand batsman, right-hand medium pace round-arm bowler. *Team* MCC (1873).
Career batting
1–1–1–15–15*–no av–0–*ct* 0

He was generally given the initial 'G' to distinguish him from T. H. Nixon in match scores. His County cricket was for Huntingdonshire and Shropshire, but he was best known as an umpire.

Nixon, Thomas
Professional. *b:* 4.6.1815, Nottingham. *d:* 20.7.1877, Chelford, Cheshire. Father of T. H. (MCC). Tail end right-hand batsman, right-hand slow round-arm bowler. *Team* Nottinghamshire (1841–54, 7 matches).
Career batting
54–88–18–339–34–4.84–0–*ct* 22
Bowling 1290–129+135–10.00–23–7–9/?

He was on the staff at Lord's 1851 to 1859 and at that time one of the leading bowlers in England. He took 9 wickets in an innings for MCC v Middlesex at Lord's in 1851. Later he appeared for Oxfordshire and Cheshire. He invented cork pads in 1841, open pads and cane-handled bats in 1853, also about 1862 a mechanical round-arm bowling machine. His final first-class match was for MCC in 1859.

Nixon, Thomas Henry
Professional. *b:* 24.4.1843, Sneinton, Notts. *d:* 23.1.1907, Hillingdon East, Middlesex. Son of Thomas (Notts). Lower order right-hand batsman, right-hand slow medium round-arm bowler, slip field. *Team* MCC (1862–67).
Career batting
2–3–0–15–9–5.00–0–*ct* 0
Bowling 76–4–19.00–0–0–2/26

He was engaged by MCC for 12 seasons and was best known as an umpire.

Noble, Charles
Amateur. *b:* 9.2.1850, Kennington, Surrey. *d:* 1927, Melksham, Wilts. Brother of J. W. (Surrey). Middle order right-hand batsman, right-hand slow round-arm bowler, deep field. *Team* Surrey (1868, 4 matches).
Career batting
5–9–0–72–17–8.00–0–*ct* 3

His first-class debut was for Gentlemen of the South in 1867, when he replaced his brother who was injured.

Noble, John Wilson
Amateur. *b:* 4.8.1845, Kennington, Surrey. *d:* April 1889. Chelsea, London. Brother of Charles (Surrey). Lower order right-hand batsman, right-hand slow under-arm bowler, deep field. *Team* Surrey (1866–69, 26 matches).
Career batting
31–51–2–554–71–11.30–0–*ct* 5
Bowling 392–18–21.77–0–0–4/36

Noble, Montague Alfred
Amateur. *b:* 28.1.1873, Sydney, New South Wales, Australia. *d:* 22.6.1940, Randwick, New South Wales, Australia. Brother of E. G. (New South Wales). Defensive right-hand middle order batsman, right-arm medium off break bowler, brilliant point field. *Team* New South Wales (1893/4 to 1919/20, 77 matches). *Tours* Australia to England 1899, 1902, 1905, 1909, to South Africa 1902/03, to New Zealand 1904/05, 1913/14; New South Wales to New Zealand 1893/4. *Tests* Australia (1897/8 to 1909, 42 matches).
Career batting
248–377–34–13975–284–40.74–37–*ct* 191
Bowling 14445–625–23.11–33–7–8/48
Test batting
42–73–7–1997–133–30.25–1–*ct* 26
Bowling 3025–121–25.00–9–2–7/17

He hit 1,000 runs on all four of his tours to England, going on to 2,000 once : 2,053, av 46.65, in 1905. Of his seven double centuries the highest was 284 for Australians v Sussex at Hove in 1896. His bowling proved effective on his first two visits to England, but latterly he bowled little. He captained the 1909 Team and led Australia in a total of 15 Tests. He also hit 1,000 in an Australian season once. He was the author of several notable books on cricket.

Noble, Norman Doncaster
Amateur. *b:* 2.3.1881, Lucknow, India. *d:* 21.9.1955, Hartlip, Kent. Middle order batsman. *Sch* Edinburgh Academy. *Team* Scotland (1922).
Career batting
1–2–0–53–38–26.50–0–*ct* 2
Bowling 8–0

Noblet, Geoffrey
Amateur. *b:* 14.9.1916, Adelaide, South Australia. Lower order right-hand batsman, right-arm medium pace bowler. *Team* South Australia (1945/6 to 1952/3, 49 matches). *Tour* Australia to

South Africa 1949/50. *Tests* Australia (1949/50 to 1952/3, 3 matches).
Career batting
71–99–29–975–55*–13.92–0–*ct* 44
Bowling 5432–282–19.26–13–2–7/29
Test batting
3–4–1–22–13*–7.33–0–*ct* 1
Bowling 183–7–26.14–0–0–3/21
His only first-class match in England was for a Commonwealth XI in 1956.

Nolan, Geoffrey John
Cricketer. *b:* 6.10.1937, Colchester, Essex. Middle order right-hand batsman. *Team* Essex (1968, 1 match).
Career batting
1–2–0–14–11–7.00–0–*ct* 0
He was also a useful hockey player.

Norbury, Duncan Victor
Professional. *b:* 3.8.1887, Bartley, Hants. *d:* 23.10.1972, Sutton, Surrey. Hard-hitting middle order right-hand batsman, slow right-arm bowler. *Teams* Hampshire (1905–06, 11 matches); Lancashire (1919–22, 14 matches).
Career batting
26–44–2–806–100–19.19–1–*ct* 8
Bowling 996–30–33.20–0–0–4/28
His last first-class match was for Sir L. Parkinson's XI in 1935. He also played for Northumberland.

Norley, Frederick
Professional. *b:* 23.2.1846, Canterbury, Kent. Brother of James (Kent and Gloucs). Lower order right-hand batsman, right-hand fast medium round-arm bowler. *Team* Kent (1864–65, 7 matches).
Career batting
8–15–4–69–12–6.27–0–*ct* 2
Bowling 233–10–23.30–1–0–5/52

Norley, James
Professional. *b:* 5.1.1847, Canterbury, Kent. *d:* 24.10.1900, Eastville, Bristol. Brother of Frederick (Kent). Middle/lower order right-hand batsman, right-hand medium pace round-arm bowler. *Teams* Kent (1870–71, 8 matches); Gloucestershire (1877, 1 match).
Career batting
9–17–3–60–21*–4.28–0–*ct* 8
Bowling 108–3–36.00–0–0–1/16

Norman, Charles Lloyd
Amateur. *b:* 10.3.1833, Bromley Common, Kent. *d:* 17.2.1889, San Remo, Italy. Son of G. W. (Kent), brother of F. H. (Kent) and Philip (Gentlemen of Kent). Middle order right-hand batsman. *Sch* Eton. *Teams* Cambridge U (1852–53, blue both years); Kent (1853, 1 match).
Career batting
13–24–2–200–34–9.09–0–*ct* 4
His final first-class match was for Gentlemen of Kent in 1854.

Norman, Frederick Henry
Amateur. *b:* 23.1.1839, Bromley, Kent. *d:* 6.10.1916, Mayfair, London. Son of G. W. (Kent) and brother of C. L. (Cambridge U and Kent) and Philip (Gentlemen of Kent). Stylish middle order right-hand batsman, good deep field. *Sch* Eton. *Teams* Cambridge U (1858–60, blue all three years); Kent (1858–64, 10 matches); Cambridgeshire (1858, 1 match).
Career batting
26–44–2–782–103–18.61–2–*ct* 11
His final first-class match was for R. D. Walker's XI in 1866. He served on the Committees of both MCC and Kent CCC.

Norman, George
Amateur. *b:* 23.8.1890, London. *d:* 24.11.1964, Virginia Water, Surrey. Middle order batsman. *Sch* Bancroft's. *Team* Essex (1920, 4 matches).
Career batting
4–5–1–44–21–11.00–0–*ct* 1
Bowling 18–0

Norman, John William
Amateur. *b:* 22.8.1936, Maidstone, Kent. Lower order right-hand batsman, wicket-keeper. *Team* Cambridge U (1957).
Career batting
2–3–0–12–9–4.00–0–*ct* 3

Norman, Michael Eric John Charles
Professional. *b:* 19.1.1933, Northampton. Opening right-hand batsman, right-arm leg break bowler. *Teams* Northamptonshire (1952–65, 202 matches); Leicestershire (1966-75, 151 matches). *Tour* MCC to Bangladesh 1976/7 (not first-class).
Career batting
363–640–44–17441–221*–29.26–24–*ct* 161
Bowling 164–2–82.00–0–0–2/0
He hit 1,000 runs in a season eight times (best 1,964, av 33.86, in 1960). His only double century was 221* for Leics v Cambridge U at Fenner's in 1967. After the 1969 season he became a teacher and his County cricket was restricted.

Norman, Newman Frederick
Amateur. *b:* 2.2.1884, Camberwell, Surrey. *d:* 28.8.1954, Westcliff-on-Sea, Essex. Middle order right-hand batsman. *Sch* City of London. *Teams*

London County (1902–03); Northants (1905–09, 11 matches).
Career batting
18–32–1–258–32–8.32–0–*ct* 8

Norman, Philip
Amateur. *b:* 9.7.1842, Bromley, Kent. *d* 17.5.1931, London. Son of G. W. (Kent), brother of C. L. (Kent) and F. H. (Kent). Middle order right-hand batsman. *Sch* Eton. *Team* Gentlemen of Kent (1865).
Career batting
1–2–0–1–1–0.50–0–*ct* 2
He published many books on antiquarian and topographical subjects and also wrote several cricket books.

Norman, Dr Ralph Oliver Geoffrey
Amateur. *b:* 30.7.1911, Southend, Essex. *d:* 26.7.1983, Thorpe Bay, Essex. Middle order right-hand batsman, left-arm medium pace bowler. *Sch* Rugby. *Team* Essex (1932, 1 match).
Career batting
1–2–0–20–10–10.00–0–*ct* 0
He played in the Cambridge Seniors' match of 1932, but no first-class matches for the University.

Nornable, Charles Ernest
Professional. *b:* 25.12.1886, Norton, Derbyshire. *d:* 21.4.1970, Sheffield, Yorkshire. Lower order right-hand batsman, right-arm fast medium bowler. *Team* Derbyshire (1909, 1 match).
Career batting
1–1–0–8–8–8.00–0–*ct* 0
Bowling 72–5–14.40–0–0–3/24

Norris, David William Worsley
Cricketer. *b:* 1.5.1946, Hampstead, London. Middle order right-hand batsman, wicket-keeper. *Sch* Harrow. *Team* Cambridge U (1967–68, blue both years).
Career batting
20–33–2–307–43–9.90–0–*ct* 21–*st* 3

Norris, Graham Walter
Amateur. *b:* 17.10.1905, Brackley, Northants. *d:* 6.12.1933, Banbury, Oxon. Lower order right-hand batsman, right-arm medium slow bowler. *Sch* Eton. *Team* Northants (1925–26, 5 matches).
Career batting
5–8–0–38–16–4.75–0–*ct* 3
Bowling 154–7–22.00–0–0–3/48
He did not play in any first-class matches whilst at Oxford.

Norris, Oswald Thomas
Amateur. *b:* 1.7.1883, Chipstead, Surrey. *d:* 22.3.1973, Tilgate, Sussex. Father-in-law of M. J. C. Allom (Surrey). Sound middle order right-hand batsman, slow right-arm bowler. *Sch* Charterhouse. *Team* Oxford U (1904–05).
Career batting
11–20–0–413–87–20.65–0–*ct* 7
Bowling 272–4–68.00–0–0–2/109
He was in the Eleven selected to play Cambridge in 1904, but forced to stand down due to injury. A useful soccer player, he captained Oxford.

North, Albert Edward Charles
Professional. *b:* 1878, Bedminster, Bristol. *d:* 4.6.1933, Bristol. Lower order batsman, right-arm fast bowler. *Teams* Somerset (1903–09, 15 matches); Gloucestershire (1912, 2 matches).
Career batting
17–26–11–182–30*–12.13–0–*ct* 6
Bowling 929–25–37.16–0–0–4/47

North, Ernest John
Professional. *b:* 23.9.1895, Burton-on-Trent, Derbyshire. *d:* 24.8.1955, Havant, Hants. Tail end right-hand batsman, right-arm slow medium bowler. *Team* Middlesex (1923–27, 24 matches).
Career batting
27–34–9–247–80–9.88–0–*ct* 10
Bowling 1414–49–28.65–0–0–4/18
He was a noted soccer player, appearing for Arsenal, Reading, Gillingham, Norwich and Watford.

Northcote, Dr Percy
Amateur. *b:* 18.9.1866, Islington, Middlesex. *d:* 3.3.1934, Marylebone, London. Free scoring middle order right-hand batsman, slow left-arm bowler. *Sch* Cranbrook. *Teams* Middlesex (1888, 2 matches); Kent (1889–95, 3 matches).
Career batting
7–12–3–105–27*–11.66–0–*ct* 3
Bowling 156–2–78.00–0–0–1/31
His final first-class match was for MCC in 1903.

Northcote-Green, Simon Roger
Cricketer. *b:* 30.8.1954, Worksop, Notts. Opening/middle order right-hand batsman, right-arm medium pace bowler. *Sch* St Edward's, Oxford. *Team* Oxford U (1974 and 1979).
Career batting
9–16–2–138–38*–9.85–0–*ct* 3

Northway, Edward George
Amateur. *b:* 1902, Ceylon. *d:* 4.8.1966, Marylebone, London. Brother of R. P. (Somerset and Northants). Middle order batsman. *Team* Somerset (1925–26, 8 matches).

Career batting
11–18–4–265–83–18.92–0–*ct* 4
His final first-class match was for the RAF in 1928.

Northway, Reginald Philip
Amateur. *b:* 14.8.1906, Ceylon. *d:* 26.8.1936, Kibworth, Leics. He was killed in a road accident. Brother of E. G. (Somerset). Steady opening right-hand batsman, brilliant deep field. *Sch* Oratory. *Teams* Somerset (1929–33, 17 matches); Northants (1936, 17 matches).
Career batting
34–57–5–806–75*–15.50–0–*ct* 5

Norton, Bradbury
Amateur. *b:* 23.8.1834, Town Malling, Kent. *d:* 21.2.1917, Porta De Taltal, Chile. Brother of W. S. (Kent) and Selby (Kent), cousin of W. O. J. (Kent). Middle order right-hand batsman. *Team* Kent (1858–66, 10 matches).
Career batting
10–18–2–181–56–11.31–0–*ct* 7

Norton, Ernest Willmott
Amateur. *b:* 19.6.1889, Birmingham. *d:* 1972, Birmingham. Lower order right-hand batsman, leg break and googly bowler. *Teams* Warwickshire (1920, 2 matches); Worcestershire (1922–23, 6 matches).
Career batting
8–11–4–108–26*–15.42–0–*ct* 2
Bowling 357–7–51.00–0–0–3/74

Norton, Gerald Ivor Desmond
Amateur. *b:* 19.5.1919, Earl Shilton, Leics. Middle order right-hand batsman, slow left-arm bowler. *Sch* Malvern. *Team* MCC (1958–60).
Career batting
2–3–2–4–2*–4.00–0–*ct* 3
Bowling 133–17–7.82–2–0–6/57

Norton, Ian David
Amateur. *b:* 21.10.1937, Stamford, Lincs. Middle order right-hand batsman. *Team* Oxford U (1959).
Career batting
1–1–0–30–30–30.00–0–*ct* 2

Norton, William South
Amateur. *b:* 8.6.1831, Town Malling, Kent. *d:* 19.3.1916, Charterhouse, London. Brother of Bradbury (Kent) and Selby (Kent), cousin of W. O. J. (Kent). Very steady middle order right-hand batsman, right-hand medium pace round-arm bowler, point field. *Team* Kent (1849–70, 62 matches).
Career batting
87–161–16–2010–120*–13.86–1–*ct* 64
Bowling 1030–61+23–16.88–6–0–7/57
He was Hon Secretary of Kent CCC commencing 1859, and captained the County for some seasons.

Notley, Bernarr
Amateur. *b:* 31.8.1918, Mapperley, Nottingham. Lower order right-hand batsman, off break bowler. *Team* Nottinghamshire (1949, 1 match).
Career batting
1–1–0–0–0–0.00–0–*ct* 0
Bowling 90–1–90.00–0–0–1/90

Nott, Arthur Samuel
Professional. *b:* 1881, Bristol. *d:* 1959, Nuneaton, Warwickshire. Lower order right-hand batsman, wicket-keeper. *Team* Gloucestershire (1903–12, 15 matches).
Career batting
15–25–3–182–44*–8.27–0–*ct* 9–*st* 4
Bowling 77–0

Nourse, Arthur Dudley
Amateur. *b:* 12.11.1910, Durban, South Africa. *d:* 14.8.1981, Durban, South Africa. Son of A. W. (South Africa). Sound middle order right-hand batsman, excellent field. *Team* Natal (1931/2 to 1952/3). *Tours* South Africa to England 1935, 1947, 1951. *Tests* South Africa (1935–51, 34 matches).
Career batting
175–269–27–12472–260*–51.53–41–*ct* 135
Bowling 124–0
Test batting
34–62–7–2960–231–53.81–9–*ct* 12
Bowling 9–0
He hit 1,681 runs, av 41.00, on the 1935 tour: 1,453, av 42.73, in 1947, but did not reach 1,000 runs in 1951 owing to a broken thumb. Two of his six double centuries were scored in England, the highest being 208 in the Trent Bridge Test of 1951. He was vice-captain of the 1947 tourists and captain in 1951; in all he led South Africa in 15 Tests.

Nourse, Arthur William
(known as A. D. Nourse)
Amateur. *b:* 26.1.1879, Thornton Heath, Surrey. *d:* 8.7.1948, Port Elizabeth, South Africa. Father of A. D. (Natal and South Africa). Steady middle order left-hand batsman, left-arm medium or slow bowler, good slip field. *Teams* Natal (1896/7 to 1924/5); Transvaal (1925/6 to 1926/7); Western Province (1927/8 to 1935/6). *Tours* South Africa

to England 1907, 1912, 1924, to Australia 1910/11. *Tests* South Africa (1902/03 to 1924, 45 matches).
Career batting
228–371–39–14216–304*–42.81–38–*ct* 171
Bowling 7125–305–23.36–13–1–6/33
Test batting
45–83–8–2234–111–29.78–1–*ct* 43
Bowling 1553–41–37.87–0–0–4/25

He hit 1,000 runs on each of his three visits to England (best 1,928, av 39.14, in 1924). His only double century in England was 213* v Hants at Bournemouth in 1912; his triple century was 304* for Natal v Transvaal at Johannesburg in 1919/20. He also hit 1,000 runs in an Australian season. He went to South Africa with the Army in 1895 and settled there. Spanning forty seasons – 1896/7 to 1935/6 – his first-class career was one of the longest on record and he was familiarly known as the 'Grand Old Man' of South African cricket.

Noyes, Francis
Amateur. *b:* 1817. Stylish middle order batsman. *Team* Nottinghamshire (1842–48, 9 matches).
Career batting
21–40–3–402–50–10.86–0–*ct* 11

The unique feature of his cricketing career is that he was allowed to bat twice in each innings for Notts v Hampshire at Southampton in 1843 – one of the Notts eleven having been injured on the journey from Nottingham.

Nugent, Brig-General Frank Henry
(later Burnell-Nugent)
Amateur. *b:* 5.9.1880, Basingstoke, Hants. *d:* 12.3.1942, Kingsclere, Hants. Lower order right-hand batsman, wicket-keeper. *Sch* Winchester. *Team* Hampshire (1904, 1 match).
Career batting
1–2–0–0–0–0.00–0–*ct* 1

Nunes, Robert Karl
Amateur. *b:* 7.6.1894, Kingston, Jamaica. *d:* 23.7.1958, Paddington, London. Opening/middle order left-hand batsman, wicket-keeper. *Sch* Dulwich. *Team* Jamaica (1924/5 to 1931/2). *Tours* West Indies to England 1923, 1928. *Tests* West Indies (1928 to 1929/30, 4 matches).
Career batting
61–94–8–2695–200*–31.33–6–*ct* 31–*st* 8
Bowling 83–3–27.66–0–0–2/49
Test batting
4–8–0–245–92–30.62–0–*ct* 2

He was vice-captain of the 1923 tourists and captain in 1928, leading West Indies in that team's first four Tests. His highest score was 200* for Jamaica v Tennyson's XI at Kingston in 1926/7. He was a founder member of the Jamaican Cricket Board of Control and President of the West Indies Board of Control from 1945 to 1952.

Nunley, Harold
Professional. *b:* 12.1.1912, Raunds, Northants. Lower order left-hand batsman, slow left-arm bowler. *Team* Northants (1931, 3 matches).
Career batting
3–5–2–20–12–6.66–0–*ct* 0
Bowling 92–0

Nunn, John Ayscough
Amateur. *b:* 19.3.1906, Hadley, Herts. Middle order right-hand batsman, right-arm fast bowler, excellent field. *Sch* Sherborne. *Teams* Oxford U (1926–28, blue 1926–27); Middlesex (1926, 3 matches).
Career batting
22–36–2–641–98–18.85–0–*ct* 10

His final first-class match was for Free Foresters in 1946.

Nupen, Eiulf Peter
Amateur. *b:* 1.1.1902, Johannesburg, South Africa. *d:* 29.1.1977, Johannesburg, South Africa. Lower order right-hand batsman, right-arm fast medium bowler. *Team* Transvaal (1920/1 to 1936/7). *Tour* South Africa to England 1924. *Tests* South Africa (1922/3 to 1935/6, 17 matches).
Career batting
74–105–14–1635–89–17.96–0–*ct* 34
Bowling 6077–334–18.19–32–12–9/48
Test batting
17–31–7–348–69–14.50–0–*ct* 9
Bowling 1788–50–35.76–5–1–6/46

On his tour to England he found himself unable to adapt to turf wickets and though appearing in two Tests, achieved very little. His best bowling was 9/48 for Transvaal v Griqualand West at Johannesburg in 1931/2. He lost an eye in an accident when four years old.

Nurse, Seymour MacDonald
Amateur. *b:* 10.11.1933, Bayville, Bridgetown, Barbados. Middle order right-hand batsman, off break bowler, excellent close field. *Team* Barbados (1958/9 to 1971/2). *Tours* West Indies to Australia 1960/1, to Australia and New Zealand 1968/9, to England 1963, 1966, to India and Sri Lanka 1966/7; Commonwealth to Pakistan 1963/4; Rest of World to England 1967, 1968; Barbados to England 1969. *Tests* West Indies (1959/60 to 1968/9, 29 matches).

Career batting
141–235–19–9489–258–43.93–26–*ct* 116
Bowling 389–12–32.41–0–0–3/36
Test batting
29–54–1–2523–258–47.60–6–*ct* 21
Bowling 7–0

He was most successful on his 1966 tour to England, scoring 1,105 runs, av 44.20, in first-class matches and 501, av 62.62, in the five Tests, including two centuries. Three of his four double centuries were scored in West Indies, but the highest, 258,was made for West Indies v New Zealand at Christchurch in 1968/9. On his 1963 tour to England he achieved little due to an injury early on.

Nuttall, Henry
Professional. *b:* 6.2.1855, Erith. *d:* 8.10.1945, Goudhurst, Kent. Lower order right-hand batsman, wicket-keeper. *Team* Kent (1889–94, 14 matches).
Career batting
14–19–6–39–8–3.00–0–*ct* 12–*st* 6

Nutter, Albert Edward
Professional. *b:* 28.6.1913, Burnley, Lancashire. Sound middle/lower order right-hand batsman, right-arm medium fast bowler, good slip. *Teams* Lancashire (1935–45, 70 matches); Northants (1948–53, 145 matches).
Career batting
224–294–47–4828–109*–19.54–1–*ct* 161
Bowling 15739–600–26.23–29–2–7/52

His best season was 1938, when he hit 1,156 runs, av 32.11, and took 91 wickets, av 24.64. He exceeded 100 wickets in a season once: 105, av 22.88, in 1948.

Nutter, Ezra
Professional. *b:* 1859, Nelson, Lancashire. *d:* November, 1903, Nelson, Lancashire. Middle order batsman. *Team* Lancashire (1885, 1 match).
Career batting
1–1–0–18–18–18.00–0–*ct* 0

Nye, John Kent
Professional. *b:* 23.5.1914, Isfield, Sussex. Lower order right-hand batsman, right-arm fast bowler. *Team* Sussex (1934–47, 99 matches).
Career batting
99–136–33–885–51–8.59–0–*ct* 35
Bowling 10407–304–34.23–10–0–6/95

He took 110 wickets, av 30.60, in 1939. He had emigrated to Australia in 1926 and spent several years there, before returning to Sussex.

Nyren, John
Professional. *b:* 15.12.1764, Hambledon, Hants. *d:* 28.6.1837, Bromley-by-Bow, Middlesex. Son of Richard (Hampshire). Middle order left-hand batsman. *Teams* Homerton (1808); England (1802–05).
Career batting
12–20–1–159–50*–8.36–0–*ct* 7

His final first-class match was for F. Beauclerk's XI in 1817. Although a useful cricketer in his day, he is remembered principally as the author of 'The Young Cricketer's Tutor' published in 1833. The book was edited by C. C. Clarke and contained an account of the Hambledon Club and its players.

Nyren, Richard
Professional. *b:* 1734 or 1735. *d:* 25.4.1797, Lee or Leigh, Kent. Father of John (England). Hard-hitting left-hand batsman, left-hand under-arm bowler. *Team* Hampshire (1772–84).
Career batting
Not applicable, pre-1800

He was landlord of the Bat and Ball Inn at Hambledon and later the George Inn, Hambledon, and looked after the cricket grounds used by the Hambledon Club, being perhaps the major figure of that Club.

OAKDEN, ROBERT PATRICK
Professional. *b:* 9.5.1938, Kirkby-in-Ashfield, Notts. Tail end right-hand batsman, right-arm fast medium bowler. *Team* Nottinghamshire (1960–61, 8 matches).
Career batting
8–10–3–68–24–9.71–0–*ct* 4
Bowling 728–17–42.82–0–0–4/78

Oakes, Charles
Professional. *b:* 10.8.1912, Horsham, Sussex. Brother of J. Y. (Sussex). Forceful middle order right-hand batsman, leg break and googly bowler. *Team* Sussex (1935–54, 285 matches).
Career batting
288–474–40–10893–160–25.09–14–*ct* 160
Bowling 14326–458–31.27–16–0–8/147
He hit 1,000 runs in a season five times (best 1,607, av 29.21, in 1949).

Oakes, Dennis Raymond
Cricketer. *b:* 10.4.1946, Bedworth, Warwickshire. Middle order right-hand batsman, leg break bowler, close field. *Team* Warwickshire (1965, 5 matches).
Career batting
5–8–1–81–33–11.57–0–*ct* 7
Bowling 1–0
A useful soccer player, he appeared for Notts County and Peterborough.

Oakes, John Ypres
Professional. *b:* 29.3.1916, Horsham, Sussex. Brother of Charles (Sussex). Hard-hitting middle order right-hand batsman, off break bowler. *Team* Sussex (1937–51, 128 matches).
Career batting
128–218–19–4410–151–22.16–2–*ct* 84
Bowling 6508–166–39.20–6–0–7/64
He hit 1,157 runs, av 22.68, in 1950. He also played for Northumberland.

Oakley, Leonard
Professional. *b:* 11.1.1916, Stourbridge, Worcs. Lower order batsman, slow left-arm bowler. *Team* Worcestershire (1935–48, 8 matches).
Career batting
8–13–4–43–11–4.77–0–*ct* 2
Bowling 393–12–32.75–1–0–6/64

Oakley, William
Professional. *b:* 6.5.1868, Shrewsbury. Lower order batsman, left-arm medium pace bowler. *Team* Lancashire (1893–94, 20 matches).
Career batting
24–38–10–144–24–5.14–0–*ct* 21
Bowling 973–55–17.69–5–1–6/50
His first-class debut was for Liverpool and District XI in 1892. He also played for Shropshire.

Oakman, Alan Stanley Myles
Professional. *b:* 20.4.1930, Hastings, Sussex. Middle order right-hand batsman, off break bowler, excellent slip. *Team* Sussex (1947–68, 497 matches). *Tours* Swanton to West Indies 1955/6; MCC to South Africa 1956/7. *Tests* England (1956, 2 matches).
Career batting
538–912–79–21800–229*–26.17–22–*ct* 594
Bowling 20343–736–27.63–31–2–7/39
Test batting
2–2–0–14–10–7.00–0–*ct* 7
Bowling 21–0
He hit 1,000 runs in a season nine times, going on to 2,000 twice (best 2,307, av 36.61, in 1961). He took 99 wickets, av 20.97, in 1954. His only double century was 229* for Sussex v Notts at Worksop in 1961. After retiring from first-class cricket he took up an appointment as coach to Warwickshire CCC. A useful soccer player, he kept goal for Hastings United.

Oates, Archer Williamson
Professional. *b:* 9.12.1908, Doncaster, Yorkshire. *d:* 31.12.1968, Nottingham. Nephew of T. W. (Notts). Lower order right-hand batsman, right-arm fast medium bowler. *Team* Nottinghamshire (1931–33, 7 matches).
Career batting
7–7–2–21–12–4.20–0–*ct* 3
Bowling 465–8–58.12–0–0–2/38

Oates, Thomas William
Professional. *b:* 9.8.1875, Eastwood, Notts. *d:* 18.6.1949, Eastwood, Notts. Uncle of A. W. (Notts). Lower order right-hand batsman, wicket-keeper. *Teams* Nottinghamshire (1897–1925, 420 matches); London County (1900).
Career batting
434–577–111–5976–88–12.82–0–*ct* 758–*st* 235
Bowling 20–0

Oates, William
Professional. *b:* 2.1.1852, Wentworth, Yorkshire. *d:* 9.12.1940, Rotherham, Yorkshire. Lower order right-hand batsman, wicket-keeper. *Team* Yorkshire (1874–75, 7 matches).
Career batting
7–13–7–34–14*–5.66–0–*ct* 5–*st* 1

Oates, William Coape
Amateur. *b:* 7.7.1862, Besthorpe, Notts. *d:* 20.2.1942, Lincoln. Opening/middle order right-

hand batsman. *Sch* Harrow. *Team* Nottinghamshire (1881–82, 4 matches).
Career batting
5–8–0–124–39–15.50–0–*ct* 4

His final first-class match was for MCC in 1895. His chief claim to cricketing fame rests with his innings of 313 not out for the 1st Royal Munster Fusiliers v Army Service Corps at the Curragh in 1895, when, with F. Fitzgerald, he added 623 for the 2nd wicket – the match was described as 'a farce'.

Oates, William Farrand
Professional. *b:* 11.6.1929, Aston, Sheffield, Yorkshire. Attacking middle order right-hand batsman, right-arm medium off break bowler. *Teams* Yorkshire (1956, 3 matches); Derbyshire (1959–65, 121 matches).
Career batting
124–214–14–4588–148*–22.94–2–*ct* 54
Bowling 577–13–44.38–1–0–6/47

He hit 1,000 runs in a season twice (best 1,288, av 33.02, in 1961).

O'Bree, Arthur
Amateur. *b:* 31.5.1886, Poona, India. *d:* 27.12.1943, Baragwanath, Johannesburg, South Africa. Middle order right-hand batsman, right-arm medium pace bowler. *Team* Glamorgan (1921–23, 18 matches).
Career batting
18–34–1–431–42*–13.06–0–*ct* 9

O'Brien, Brendan Anthony
Cricketer. *b:* 2.9.1942, Galway, Co Galway. Right-hand batsman. *Team* Ireland (1966–81).
Career batting
11–17–1–319–45–19.93–0–*ct* 6

O'Brien, Hon Donough
Amateur. *b:* 29.8.1879, Holyhead, Anglesey. *d:* 23.9.1953, Ras-El-Soda, Alexandria, Egypt. Cousin of A. P., R. M., and L. H. Gwynn (Ireland). Middle order right-hand batsman. *Sch* Winchester. *Teams* Ireland (1902); MCC (1906–07).
Career batting
3–6–1–77–57–15.40–0–*ct* 1

O'Brien, Francis Patrick
Professional. *b:* 11.2.1911, Canterbury, New Zealand. Attacking middle order right-hand batsman, right-arm medium pace bowler. *Teams* Canterbury (1932/3 to 1945/6); Northants (1938–39, 40 matches).
Career batting
66–113–5–2649–164–24.52–4–*ct* 34
Bowling 655–14–46.78–0–0–2/14

O'Brien, Gerard Peter
Cricketer. *b:* 12.11.1942, Dublin. Right-hand batsman. *Team* Ireland (1976–77).
Career batting
2–4–0–22–11–5.50–0–*ct* 3

O'Brien, John George
Amateur. *b:* 10.1.1866, Dublin. *d:* 15.8.1920, Dublin. Brother of Sir T. C. (Middlesex). Middle order batsman. *Team* Ireland (1910).
Career batting
1–2–0–7–4–3.50–0–*ct* 1

He also played for Herefordshire.

O'Brien, Neil Terence
Cricketer. *b:* 9.3.1945, Heaton Moor, Lancashire. Middle order right-hand batsman, right-arm medium pace bowler. *Team* Minor Counties (1979–81).
Career batting
2–2–0–27–14–13.50–0–*ct* 1
Bowling 101–1–101.00–0–0–1/23

His County cricket is for Cheshire, making his debut in 1970.

O'Brien, Robin
Amateur. *b:* 20.11.1932, Shillong, India. *d:* 26.8.1959, Biddenden, Kent. Opening right-hand batsman, off break bowler. *Sch* Wellington. *Teams* Cambridge U (1954–56, blue 1955–56); Ireland (1954–58).
Career batting
40–74–3–1609–146–22.66–2–*ct* 10
Bowling 4–0

He also was awarded his blue for golf.

O'Brien, Sir Timothy Carew
Amateur. *b:* 5.11.1861, Dublin. *d:* 9.12.1948, Ramsey, Isle of Man. Brother of J. G. (Ireland), brother-in-law of C. E. de Trafford (Leics). Attractive middle order right-hand batsman, left-arm bowler. *Sch* Downside. *Teams* Middlesex (1881–98, 156 matches); Oxford U (1884–85, blue both years); Ireland (1902–07). *Tours* Vernon to Australia 1887/8; Hawke to South Africa 1895/6. *Tests* England (1884 to 1895/6, 5 matches).
Career batting
266–452–30–11397–202–27.00–15–*ct* 173–*st* 2
Bowling 340–4–85.00–0–0–1/10
Test batting
5–8–0–59–20–7.37–0–*ct* 4

He hit 1,000 runs in a season three times (best 1,150, av 27.38, in 1884). His only double century was 202 for Middlesex v Sussex at Hove in 1895. He captained England in one Test. His final first-class match was for L. Robinson's XI in 1914, when he had the satisfaction of scoring 90 and 111.

O'Brien-Butler, Paget Terence
Amateur. *b:* 1.8.1911, Vanowrie, India. *d:* 22.6.1952, Ballynure, Co Wicklow. Middle order batsman. *Sch* Clifton. *Team* Ireland (1936).
Career batting
1–2–0–33–18–16.50–0–*ct* 0

O'Byrne, William Francis Thomas
Amateur. *b:* 30.4.1908, Bromley, Kent. *d:* 23.10.1951, St Leonards-on-Sea, Sussex. Middle order right-hand batsman. *Team* Sussex (1935, 1 match).
Career batting
1–2–0–34–26–17.00–0–*ct* 1

Ochse, Arthur Lennox
Amateur. *b:* 11.10.1899, Graaff-Reinet, Cape Province, South Africa. *d:* 6.5.1949, Middleburg, Cape Province, South Africa. Lower order right-hand batsman, right-arm fast bowler. *Team* Eastern Province (1921/2 to 1937/8). *Tour* South Africa to England 1929. *Tests* South Africa (1927/8 to 1929, 3 matches).
Career batting
45–66–12–564–41–10.44–0–*ct* 20
Bowling 3967–140–28.33–7–1–6/37
Test batting
3–4–1–11–4*–3.66–0–*ct* 1
Bowling 362–10–36.20–0–0–4/79
Although the best of the fast bowlers on the 1929 tour to England, he returned only moderate figures, topping the Test averages with 10 wickets, av 31.70. He was very erratic in some of the County matches.

O'Connor, Jack
Professional. *b:* 6.11.1897, Cambridge. *d:* 22.2.1977, Buckhurst Hill, Essex. Son of John (Derbyshire), nephew of H. A. Carpenter (Essex). Middle order right-hand batsman, slow right-arm leg break and off break bowler. *Team* Essex (1921–39, 516 matches). *Tours* Tennyson to Jamaica 1926/7; Cahn to Jamaica 1928/9; MCC to West Indies 1929/30. *Tests* England (1929 to 1929/30, 4 matches).
Career batting
540–903–79–28764–248–34.90–72–*ct* 226–*st* 1
Bowling 18325–557–32.89–18–2–7/52
Test batting
4–7–0–153–51–21.85–0–*ct* 2
Bowling 72–1–72.00–0–0–1/31
He hit 1,000 runs in a season 16 times going on to 2,000 four times (best 2,350, av 55.95, in 1934). Both his double centuries were for Essex, the highest being 248 v Surrey at Brentwood 1934. He represented Buckinghamshire in 1946 and 1947.

O'Connor, John
Professional. *b:* 23.2.1867, Pinxton, Derbyshire. *d:* 13.7.1936, Cambridge. Father of Jack (Essex), brother-in-law of H. A. Carpenter (Essex). Tail end right-hand batsman, right-arm medium off break bowler. *Team* Derbyshire (1900, 9 matches).
Career batting
9–14–5–55–17–6.11–0–*ct* 4
Bowling 619–24–25.79–2–1–5/56
He also played for Cambridgeshire.

O'Connor, John Denis Alphonsus
Amateur. *b:* 9.9.1875, Sydney, Australia. *d:* 23.8.1941, Lewisham, New South Wales, Australia. Lower order left-hand batsman, right-arm medium pace bowler. *Teams* New South Wales (1904/5 to 1905/6, 8 matches); South Australia (1906/7 to 1909/10, 15 matches). *Tour* Australia to England 1909. *Tests* Australia (1907/8 to 1909, 4 matches).
Career batting
50–77–18–695–54–11.77–0–*ct* 32
Bowling 5255–224–23.45–18–5–7/36
Test batting
4–8–1–86–20–12.28–0–*ct* 3
Bowling 340–13–26.15–1–0–5/40
Regarded as one of the principal bowlers of the 1909 touring team, he took a long time to adapt to English wickets and played in only one Test.

O'Connor, Valentine R.
Amateur. *b:* 1878, Ireland. *d:* 1956, Paddington, London. Middle order right-hand batsman, slow right-arm bowler. *Sch* Prior Park College. *Team* Middlesex (1908–09, 3 matches).
Career batting
3–4–0–40–30–10.00–0–*ct* 2
Bowling 62–1–62.00–0–0–1/62

Odams, Frederick Williams
Professional. *b:* 5.1.1843, Cambridge. *d:* 30.1.1879, Cambridge. Lower order right-hand batsman, right-hand slow round-arm bowler, wicket-keeper. *Team* Cambridgeshire (1867, 2 matches).
Career batting
2–4–0–3–3–0.75–0–*ct* 0

Odell, Edwin Freame
Amateur. *b:* 2.12.1883, Leicester. *d:* 11.3.1960, Yardley, Birmingham. Brother of W. W. (Leics). Lower order left-hand batsman, left-arm medium pace bowler. *Team* Leicestershire (1912, 1 match).
Career batting
1–1–0–0–0–0.00–0–*ct* 0
Bowling 42–2–21.00–0–0–2/42

Odell, William Ward
Amateur. *b:* 5.11.1881, Smethwick, Staffs. *d:* 4.10.1917, near Passchendaele, Belgium. He was killed in action. Brother of E. F. (Leics). Lower order right-hand batsman, right-arm medium pace bowler. *Sch* KES, Birmingham. *Teams* Leicestershire (1901–14, 172 matches); London County (1902–04).
Career batting
193–299–53–3368–75–13.69–0–*ct* 88
Bowling 17416–737–23.63–45–6–8/20
He took 100 wickets in a season four times (best 112, av 25.08, in 1904).

Odendaal, André
Cricketer. *b:* 4.5.1954, Queenstown, South Africa. Middle order right-hand batsman, off break bowler. *Teams* Cambridge U (1980–83, blue 1980); Boland (1980/1 to 1981/2).
Career batting
22–37–3–659–61–19.38–0–*ct* 16
He is a well known writer on cricket.

Ogilvy, Geoffrey Littlejohn
Amateur. *b:* 25.1.1906, Lewisham, Kent. *d:* 20.1.1962, Maughold, Isle of Man. Middle order right-hand batsman. *Sch* St Bees. *Team* Somerset (1936, 2 matches).
Career batting
2–3–0–44–29–14.66–0–*ct* 1
He also played for Dorset.

O'Gorman, Joseph George
Amateur. *b:* 24.7.1890, Walworth, London. *d:* 26.8.1974, Addlestone, Surrey. Lower order right-hand batsman, right-arm slow medium bowler. *Team* Surrey (1927, 3 matches).
Career batting
3–4–3–106–42*–106.00–0–*ct* 1
Bowling 167–4–41.75–0–0–2/49
With his brother, Dave, he formed a famous comedy act and his theatrical engagements prevented him from appearing in much County cricket.

O'Halloran, James Patrick
Professional. *b:* 12.1.1872, Richmond, Victoria, Australia. *d:* 28.4.1943, East Melbourne, Australia. Middle order right-hand batsman, right-arm medium pace bowler. *Teams* Victoria (1896/7, 3 matches); MCC (1897–98).
Career batting
9–15–3–243–128*–20.25–1–*ct* 4
Bowling 523–11–47.54–0–0–3/92

O'Keeffe, Kerry James
Cricketer. *b:* 25.11.1949, Hurstville, New South Wales, Australia. Lower order right-hand batsman, leg break and googly bowler. *Teams* New South Wales (1968/9 to 1979/80, 65 matches); Somerset (1971–72, 46 matches). *Tours* Australia to England 1977, to West Indies 1972/3, to New Zealand 1969/70, 1973/4, 1976/7. *Tests* Australia (1970/1 to 1977, 24 matches).
Career batting
169–233–73–4169–99*–26.05–0–*ct* 112
Bowling 13382–476–28.11–24–5–7/38
Test batting
24–34–9–644–85–25.76–0–*ct* 15
Bowling 2018–53–38.07–1–0–5/101
Although he played in three Tests on the 1977 tour of England his bowling record was a modest one – 36 wickets, av 28.75, in all first-class matches. His best season in England was 1972 when he took 77 wickets, av 23.57.

Old, Alan Gerald Bernard
Cricketer. *b:* 23.9.1945, Middlesbrough, Yorkshire. Brother of C. M. (Yorkshire and Warwickshire). Middle order right-hand batsman, right-arm fast medium bowler. *Team* Warwickshire (1969, 1 match).
Career batting
1–1–0–34–34–34.00–0–*ct* 1
Bowling 93–1–93.00–0–0–1/64
He also played for Durham. An excellent rugby footballer, he has represented England and the British Lions at fly-half and on one occasion was playing rugby for England on the same day as his brother represented England in a Test.

Old, Christopher Middleton
Cricketer. *b:* 22.12.1948, Middlesbrough, Yorkshire. Brother of A. G. B. (Warwickshire). Hard-hitting lower order left-hand batsman, right-arm fast medium bowler. *Teams* Yorkshire (1966–82, 222 matches); Northern Transvaal (1981/2 to 1982/3); Warwickshire (1983, 22 matches). *Tours* Norfolk to West Indies 1969/70; MCC to India, Pakistan and Sri Lanka 1972/3, to West Indies 1973/4, 1980/1, to Australia and New Zealand 1974/5, to India, Sri Lanka and Australia 1976/7; England to Pakistan and New Zealand 1977/8, to Australia 1978/9; International Wanderers to South Africa 1975/6. *Tests* England (1972/3 to 1981, 46 matches).
Career batting
353–434–85–7241–116–20.74–6–*ct* 205
Bowling 23309–1012–23.03–35–1–7/20
Test batting
46–66–9–845–65–14.82–0–*ct* 22
Bowling 4020–143–28.11–4–0–7/50
Originally coming to Yorkshire as a batsman who could bowl, Old found himself succeeding Trueman as the County's principal opening bowler. So successful was he that he gained a

regular place in the England team in 1973, despite the fact that serious knee injuries had necessitated operations both in 1970 and 1971. In 1972 he took 54 wickets, av 17.24, and in 1974, 72 wickets, av 18.97. In 1976, however, he was once again dogged by knee trouble, which meant that he played little first-class cricket at all that season. He proved his fitness in a dramatic manner in 1977 by hitting a century in 37 minutes for Yorkshire v Warwickshire at Edgbaston and the following summer was perhaps the best of his career. In the Tests v Pakistan his 13 wickets cost 14.69 runs each and in the Edgbaston Test he took four wickets in five balls. His first-class record for the year was 64 wickets, av 17.31, and his best all-round performance came in the Roses Match at Old Trafford, when he not only took 9 wickets but hit a century.

In 1981 he was appointed captain of the troubled Yorkshire side, but in the middle of the following year was dismissed and in rather acrimonious circumstances left the County at the end of 1982. He made his debut for Warwickshire in 1983, taking 62 wickets, av 29.41, in that season.

Before joining Yorkshire he appeared occasionally for Durham.

Oldfield, Christopher Campbell
Amateur. *b:* 30.10.1838, Patna, India. *d:* 14.5.1916, Westminster, London. Tail end batsman, good bowler. *Sch* Eton. *Team* Gentlemen of Kent (1864).
Career batting
4–7–2–24–19–4.80–0–*ct* 1
Bowling 137–9–15.22–0–0–4/45

His final first-class match was for MCC in 1873.

Oldfield, Norman
Professional. *b:* 5.5.1911, Dukinfield, Cheshire. Stylish opening right-hand batsman, good field at gully. *Teams* Lancashire (1935–39, 151 matches); Northants (1948–54, 159 matches). *Tours* Cahn to New Zealand 1938/9; Commonwealth to India, Pakistan and Ceylon 1949/50. *Test* England (1939, 1 match).
Career batting
332–521–51–17811–168–37.89–38–*ct* 96
Bowling 121–2–60.50–0–0–1/0
Test batting
1–2–0–99–80–49.50–0–*ct* 0

He hit 1,000 runs in a season 11 times going on to 2,000 once : 2,192, av 49.81, in 1949. After retiring he joined the first-class umpires' list.

Oldfield, Peter Carlton
Amateur. *b:* 27.2.1911, Leeds, Yorkshire. Lower order right-hand batsman, wicket-keeper. *Sch* Repton. *Team* Oxford U (1931–33, blue 1932–33).
Career batting
24–31–7–237–36–9.87–0–*ct* 26–*st* 33

His final first-class match was for MCC in 1934.

Oldfield, William Albert Stanley, MBE
Amateur. *b:* 9.9.1894, Alexandria, New South Wales, Australia. *d:* 10.8.1976, Killara, New South Wales, Australia. Lower order right-hand batsman, brilliant wicket-keeper. *Team* New South Wales (1919/20 to 1937/8, 82 matches). *Tours* AIF to England and South Africa 1919; Australia to England 1921, 1926, 1930, 1934, to South Africa 1921/2, 1935/6, to New Zealand 1927/8; New South Wales to New Zealand 1923/4. *Tests* Australia (1920/1 to 1936/7, 54 matches).
Career batting
245–315–57–6135–137–23.77–6–*ct* 399–*st* 262
Test batting
54–80–17–1427–65*–22.65–0–*ct* 78–*st* 52

On the 1921 tour to England he was the reserve wicket-keeper and appeared in only one Test, but on his three subsequent visits he appeared in all fifteen Tests and built up a reputation as one of the greatest of all wicket-keepers and the best of his generation.

Oldham, Stephen
Cricketer. *b:* 26.7.1948, High Green, Sheffield, Yorkshire. Tail end right-hand batsman, right-arm fast medium bowler. *Teams* Yorkshire (1974–79, 49 matches); Derbyshire (1980–83, 70 matches).
Career batting
119–90–37–555–50–10.47–0–*ct* 35
Bowling 8114–251–32.32–4–0–7/78

Oldknow, James
Professional. *b:* 12.3.1873, Denby, Derbyshire. *d:* 10.9.1944, Belper, Derbyshire. Tail end right-hand batsman, right-arm medium pace bowler. *Team* Derbyshire (1901, 2 matches).
Career batting
2–4–1–7–4*–2.33–0–*ct* 2
Bowling 162–4–40.50–0–0–3/123

Oldroyd, Edgar
Professional. *b:* 1.10.1888, Healey, Batley, Yorkshire. *d:* 27.12.1964, Truro, Cornwall. Sound middle order right-hand batsman, right-arm medium pace off break bowler. *Team* Yorkshire (1910–31, 383 matches).

Career batting
384–511–58–15925–194–35.16–36–*ct* 203
Bowling 1658–42–39.47–0–0–4/14
He hit 1,000 runs in a season ten times (best 1,690, av 43.33, in 1922).

O'Linn, Sydney
Professional. *b:* 5.5.1927, Cape Town, South Africa. Middle order left-hand batsman, wicket-keeper, excellent field. *Teams* Western Province (1945/6 to 1946/7); Kent (1951–54, 26 matches); Transvaal (1957/8 to 1965/6). *Tours* South Africa to England 1960. *Tests* South Africa (1960 to 1961/2, 7 matches).
Career batting
92–156–29–4525–120*–35.62–4–*ct* 97–*st* 6
Bowling 119–2–59.50–0–0–2/14
Test batting
7–12–1–297–98–27.00–0–*ct* 4
He hit 1,000 runs in a season twice – once for Kent in 1952 and once for the South African tourists in 1960 (best 1,080, av 29.18, in 1952). On the 1960 tour he proved one of the most reliable batsmen, playing in all five Tests. He played soccer for Charlton Athletic.

Oliphant, Patrick James
Amateur. *b:* 19.3.1914, Edinburgh, Scotland. *d:* 1.1.1979, Edinburgh, Scotland. Right-hand batsman. *Sch* Edinburgh Academy. *Team* Scotland (1937).
Career batting
1–2–0–15–15–7.50–0–*ct* 0

Olive, Martin
Cricketer. *b:* 18.4.1958, Watford, Herts. Middle order right-hand batsman, right-arm medium pace bowler. *Sch* Millfield. *Team* Somerset (1977–81, 17 matches).
Career batting
17–32–2–467–50–15.56–0–*ct* 9
He also played for Devon.

Oliver, Charles Joshua
Amateur. *b:* 1.11.1905, Wanganui, New Zealand. *d:* 25.9.1977, Brisbane, Australia. Hard-hitting middle order right-hand batsman, good outfield. *Team* Canterbury (1923/4 to 1935/6). *Tours* New Zealand to Australia 1925/6, 1927/8, to England 1927.
Career batting
35–61–5–1301–91–23.23–0–*ct* 20
Bowling 169–1–169.00–0–0–1/35
He had very little success on the 1927 tour to England. His final first-class match was for NZ Air Force XI in 1942/3. A noted rugby footballer, he represented New Zealand.

Oliver, Frederick William
Amateur. *b:* 4.1.1836, Mayfair, London. *d:* 7.7.1899, Earls Court, London. Opening/middle order right-hand batsman, right-hand fast medium round-arm bowler, slip field. *Sch* Westminster. *Teams* Surrey (1855–56, 2 matches); Oxford U (1856–57, blue both years).
Career batting
10–19–0–247–32–13.00–0–*ct* 5–*st* 2
Bowling 77–3–25.66–0–0–3/43
He was the mainstay of the Wimbledon Club for many years.

Oliver, John Archibald Ralph
Amateur. *b:* 25.11.1918, Whitwell, Herts. Opening right-hand batsman, right-arm medium fast, or off break, bowler. *Sch* Aldenham. *Team* Minor Counties (1951).
Career batting
1–2–1–93–84*–93.00–0–*ct* 0
He played for Bedfordshire.

Oliver, Leonard
Amateur. *b:* 18.10.1886, Glossop, Derbyshire. *d:* 22.1.1948, Glossop, Derbyshire. Opening left-hand batsman, right-arm medium pace bowler. *Sch* Manchester GS. *Team* Derbyshire (1908–24, 174 matches).
Career batting
174–322–13–6303–170–20.39–6–*ct* 69
Bowling 328–5–65.60–0–0–2/20
He was joint captain of Derbyshire in 1920.

Oliver, Philip Robert
Cricketer. *b:* 9.5.1956, West Bromwich, Staffs. Middle order right-hand batsman, off break bowler. *Team* Warwickshire (1975–82, 89 matches).
Career batting
89–128–20–2679–171*–24.80–2–*ct* 46
Bowling 2115–27–78.33–0–0–2/28
He also played for Shropshire.

Olivier, Eric
Amateur. *b:* 24.11.1888, Oudtshoorn, Cape Province, South Africa. *d:* 1.6.1928, Cape Town, South Africa. Tail end right-hand batsman, right-arm fast medium bowler. *Sch* Repton. *Teams* Cambridge U (1908–09, blue both years); Hampshire (1911, 7 matches).
Career batting
22–38–11–302–43–11.18–0–*ct* 9
Bowling 2036–90–22.62–8–4–8/51
He played in South Africa against MCC in 1913/14, but not in first-class matches.

Olivier, Sidney Richard
Amateur. *b:* 1.3.1870, Wilton, Wilts. *d:*

21.1.1932, Horton, Dorset. Middle order batsman. *Team* Hampshire (1895, 1 match).
Career batting
1–1–0–0–0–0.00–0–*ct* 3
He also played for Wiltshire.

Olley, Martin William Charles
Cricketer. *b:* 27.11.1963, Romford, Essex. Right-hand batsman, wicket-keeper. *Sch* Felsted. *Team* Northamptonshire (1983, 1 match).
Career batting
1–1–0–8–8–8.00–0–*ct* 3

Ollis, Richard Leslie
Cricketer. *b:* 14.1.1961, Clifton, Gloucs. Middle order left-hand batsman, right-arm medium pace bowler. *Team* Somerset (1981–83, 16 matches).
Career batting
16–28–2–579–99*–22.26–0–*ct* 5
Bowling 2–0

Ollivant, Alfred
Amateur. *b:* 1839, Chorlton, Lancashire. *d:* 26.5.1906, Bowden, Cheshire. Middle order batsman. *Team* Lancashire (1873–74, 2 matches).
Career batting
2–3–1–36–24*–18.00–0–*ct* 0

Ollivierre, Charles Augustus
Amateur. *b:* 20.7.1876, Kingstown, St Vincent. *d:* 25.3.1949, Pontefract, Yorkshire. Brother of Helon (Trinidad) and R. C. (West Indies). Attractive opening right-hand batsman, good field. *Teams* Trinidad (1894/5); Derbyshire (1901–07, 110 matches). *Tour* West Indies to England 1900 (not first-class).
Career batting
114–209–4–4830–229–23.56–3–*ct* 109
Bowling 664–29–22.89–3–1–6/51
After the 1900 tour of England, he remained behind in order to qualify for Derbyshire. He hit 1,268, av 34.27, in 1904; this included his only double century – 229 for Derbyshire v Essex at Chesterfield. His final first-class match in the West Indies was for A. B. St Hill's XII in 1898/9.

Ollivierre, Richard Cordice
Amateur. *b:* 1880, Kingstown, St Vincent. *d:* 5.6.1937, New York, USA. Brother of C. A. (Derbyshire) and Helon (Trinidad). Middle or lower order right-hand batsman, right-arm bowler. *Teams* W. Shepherd's XI (1909/10); A. B. St Hill's XII (1898/9 to 1900/1). *Tour* West Indies to England 1906.
Career batting
25–49–0–878–67–17.91–0–*ct* 22–*st* 2
Bowling 1867–88–21.21–4–1–7/23
He proved to be a useful all-rounder on the 1906 tour. His final first-class match was for a West Indies XI in 1912/13.

Olton, Michael Francis
Cricketer. *b:* 20.6.1938, San Fernando, Trinidad. Middle order right-hand batsman, off break bowler. *Teams* Trinidad (1959/60); Kent (1962, 1 match).
Career batting
3–6–1–98–28–19.60–0–*ct* 0
Bowling 199–2–99.50–0–0–2/86

O'Maille, Ciaran
Amateur. *b:* 14.6.1925, Dublin. *d:* 4.3.1977, Dublin. Right-hand batsman. *Team* Ireland (1953–60).
Career batting
2–3–1–10–5–5.00–0–*ct* 2

O'Meara, Joseph Anthony
Cricketer. *b:* 24.6.1943, Dublin. Right-hand batsman, off break bowler. *Team* Ireland (1963).
Career batting
1–2–0–0–0–0.00–0–*ct* 3
Bowling 14–1–14.00–0–0–1/14

O'Neill, Norman Clifford
Amateur. *b:* 19.2.1937, Carlton, New South Wales, Australia. Father of M. D. (Western Australia). Attacking middle order right-hand batsman, right-arm medium, or leg break, bowler, excellent deep field. *Team* New South Wales (1955/6 to 1966/7, 70 matches). *Tours* Australia to England 1961, 1964, to West Indies 1964/5, to New Zealand 1956/7, 1966/7, to India and Pakistan 1959/60; Cavaliers to South Africa 1960/1, to India and South Africa 1962/3. *Tests* Australia (1958/9 to 1964/5, 42 matches).
Career batting
188–306–34–13859–284–50.95–45–*ct* 104
Bowling 4060–99–41.01–0–0–4/40
Test batting
42–69–8–2779–181–45.55–6–*ct* 21
Bowling 667–17–39.23–0–0–4/41
Coming to England in 1961 with a big reputation, he took some time to master English wickets, but latterly was most successful and in first-class matches hit 1,981 runs, av 60.03. He played in all five Tests hitting 117 in the fifth Match at the Oval. A knee injury affected his form on the 1964 tour, but in first-class matches he made 1,369 runs, av 45.63; he appeared in four of the five Tests, failing to reach 50 in any of his six innings. His highest score was 284 for Australians v President's XI at Ahmedabad in 1959/60 and he twice hit 1,000 runs in an Austra-

lian season. His final first-class match was for the Prime Minister's XI in the Koyna Relief Fund Match in India in 1967/8.

Onslow, Denzil Roberts
Amateur. *b:* 12.6.1839, Chittore, Madras, India. *d:* 21.3.1908, Westminster, London. Grandson of D. Onslow (Kent, Surrey and Hants). Attacking middle order right-hand batsman, right-hand fast bowler. *Sch* Brighton. *Teams* Cambridge U (1859–61, blue 1860–61); Sussex (1860–69, 6 matches).
Career batting
23–40–0–426–53–10.65–0–*ct* 6
Bowling 257–14+6–18.35–2–0–6/?
His final first-class match was for MCC in 1873. He was in India for some years, being Private Secretary to the Finance Minister and played for Calcutta. Commencing 1874 he was MP for Guildford until the borough was disfranchised in 1885.

Ontong, Rodney Craig
Cricketer. *b:* 9.9.1955, Johannesburg, South Africa. Middle order right-hand batsman, right-arm fast medium bowler. *Teams* Border (1972/3 to 1982/3); Glamorgan (1975–83, 145 matches); Transvaal (1976/7 to 1977/8); Northern Transvaal (1978/9 to 1981/2).
Career batting
209–355–37–8547–152*–26.87–14–*ct* 97
Bowling 13658–443–30.83–16–2–7/60
He hit 1,000 runs in a season three times (best 1,310, av 38.52, in 1983).

Opatha, Antony Ralph Marinon
Cricketer. *b:* 5.8.1947, Colombo, Ceylon. Lower order right-hand batsman, right-arm medium pace bowler. *Team* Sri Lanka (1969/70 to 1982/3). *Tours* Sri Lanka to Pakistan 1973/4, to England 1975, 1979, to India 1975/6; Sri Lanka XI to South Africa 1982/3.
Career batting
39–53–7–790–65–17.17–0–*ct* 24
Bowling 3413–111–30.74–2–0–6/91
He acted as a manager on the 1982/3 tour to South Africa.

Openshaw, William Edward
Amateur. *b:* 5.2.1852. *d:* 7.2.1915, Haydock, Newton-le-Willows, Lancashire. Sound middle order right-hand batsman. *Sch* Harrow. *Team* Lancashire (1879–82, 4 matches).
Career batting
4–5–0–29–16–5.80–0–*ct* 1
He also played for Cheshire. A noted rugby footballer, he represented England.

Ord, John Douglas
Professional. *b:* 1.2.1907, Backworth, Northumberland. Brother of J. S. (Warwickshire). Middle order left-hand batsman, slow left-arm bowler. *Team* Minor Counties (1934).
Career batting
1–2–0–42–35–21.00–0–*ct* 0
He played for Northumberland.

Ord, James Simpson
Professional. *b:* 12.7.1912, Backworth, Northumberland. Brother of J. D. (Minor Counties). Middle order right-hand batsman, right-arm medium pace bowler, excellent outfield. *Team* Warwickshire (1933–53, 273 matches).
Career batting
273–459–35–11788–187*–27.80–16–*ct* 78
Bowling 244–2–122.00–0–0–1/0
He hit 1,000 runs in a season six times (best 1,577, av 39.42, in 1948).

Orders, Jonathan Oliver Darcy
Cricketer. *b:* 12.8.1957, Beckenham, Kent. Middle order left-hand batsman, left-arm medium pace bowler. *Sch* Winchester. *Team* Oxford U (1978–81, blue all four years).
Career batting
27–49–3–1072–79–23.30–0–*ct* 9
Bowling 656–11–59.63–0–0–2/16

O'Reilly, Peter Mark
Cricketer. *b:* 23.7.1964, Dublin. Tail end right-hand batsman, right-arm fast bowler. *Team* Ireland (1982).
Career batting
1–2–1–1–1*–1.00–0–*ct* 0
Bowling 14–1–14.00–0–0–1/14

O'Reilly, William Joseph
Amateur. *b:* 20.12.1905, White Cliffs, New South Wales, Australia. Lower order left-hand batsman, leg break and googly bowler. *Team* New South Wales (1927/8 to 1945/6, 54 matches). *Tours* Australia to England 1934, 1938, to South Africa 1935/6, to New Zealand 1945/6. *Tests* Australia (1931/2 to 1945/6, 27 matches).
Career batting
135–167–41–1655–56*–13.13–0–*ct* 65
Bowling 12850–774–16.60–63–17–9/38
Test batting
27–39–7–410–56*–12.81–0–*ct* 7
Bowling 3254–144–22.59–11–3–7/54
The outstanding success of the 1934 tour to England, he headed the first-class averages with 109 wickets, av 17.04, and the Test averages with 28, av 24.92. His ability to vary his pace and turn the ball either way, plus the knack he had of making the ball lift unexpectedly, proved the

downfall of many leading English batsmen. He was just as deadly in 1938 with 104 wickets, av 16.59, in first-class matches and 22, av 27.72, in Tests, again heading both tables. By the end of the 1938 visit he was described as one of the greatest bowlers of all time. His best bowling was 9/38 for Australians v Somerset at Taunton in 1934. After retiring he became a well-known cricket writer.

Orford, Lewis Alfred
Amateur. *b:* 12.3.1865, Cheetham Hill, Manchester, Lancashire. *d:* 18.1.1948, Crumpsall, Manchester, Lancashire. Lower order right-hand batsman, wicket-keeper. *Sch* Uppingham. *Team* Cambridge U (1886–87, blue both years).
Career batting
7–12–1–205–76–18.63–0–*ct* 13–*st* 3

O'Riordan, Alex John
Amateur. *b:* 20.7.1940, Dublin. Right-hand batsman, left-arm fast medium bowler. *Team* Ireland (1958–77).
Career batting
25–44–5–614–117–15.74–1–*ct* 19
Bowling 1604–75–21.38–2–0–6/35

Orman, Charles Edward Linton
Amateur. *b:* 6.9.1859, Roorkee, India. *d:* 11.2.1927, Epping, Essex. Middle order batsman. *Sch* Felsted. *Team* Essex (1896, 2 matches).
Career batting
2–2–0–16–12–8.00–0–*ct* 1
He also played for Bedfordshire.

Ormerod, Sir Cyril Berkeley
Amateur. *b:* 3.10.1897, Edmonton, London. *d:* 1.11.1983, London. Lower order batsman, bowler. *Sch* St Pauls. *Team* MCC (1927).
Career batting
1–1–1–1–1*–no av–0–*ct* 0
Bowling 101–3–33.66–0–0–2/56
He played for Oxfordshire.

Ormrod, Joseph Alan
Cricketer. *b:* 22.12.1942, Ramsbottom, Lancashire. Middle order right-hand batsman, off break bowler. *Team* Worcestershire (1962–83, 465 matches). *Tours* Worcestershire to Jamaica 1965/6; MCC to Pakistan 1966/7.
Career batting
473–799–92–21952–204*–31.04–31–*ct* 386
Bowling 1094–25–43.76–1–0–5/27
He hit 1,000 runs in a season 12 times (best 1,535, av 45.14, in 1978). Both his double centuries were for Worcs, the highest being 204* v Kent at Dartford in 1973.

O'Rourke, Christopher
Cricketer. *b:* 30.3.1945, Widnes, Lancashire. Lower order right-hand batsman, wicket-keeper. *Team* Warwickshire (1968, 1 match).
Career batting
1–1–1–23–23*–no av–0–*ct* 3

Orr, Frank William
Amateur. *b:* 6.3.1879, Marylebone, London. *d:* 18.6.1967, Wandsworth, London. Opening right-hand batsman, leg break bowler. *Sch* Tonbridge. *Team* P. F. Warner's XI (1903).
Career batting
1–2–0–30–28–15.00–0–*ct* 0

Orr, Hugh James
Amateur. *b:* 21.1.1878, Deniliquin, New South Wales, Australia. *d:* 19.4.1946, Putney, London. Lower order batsman, good bowler. *Team* Hampshire (1902–07, 6 matches).
Career batting
7–14–2–85–13–7.08–0–*ct* 2
Bowling 468–19–24.63–1–0–7/74
His final first-class match was for the Royal Navy in 1912.

Orr, Herbert Richard
Amateur. *b:* 3.2.1865, London. *d:* 22.5.1940, Sevenoaks, Kent. Stylish middle order right-hand batsman, right-arm slow bowler, good field. *Sch* Bedford Grammar. *Teams* Cambridge U (1886–87); Western Australia (1892/3, 2 matches).
Career batting
4–8–0–98–44–12.25–0–*ct* 2
Bowling 56–0
He played for Bedfordshire and Northants (pre-first-class).

Orr, James Harper
Amateur. *b:* 18.10.1878, Glasgow, Scotland. *d:* 19.3.1956, Old Polmont, Stirlingshire, Scotland,. Middle order batsman. *Sch* Loretto. *Team* Scotland (1912–13).
Career batting
3–5–1–91–34–22.75–0–*ct* 0

Orton, Charles Talbot
Amateur. *b:* 9.8.1910, Farnham, Surrey. *d:* 28.5.1940, Dunkirk, France. Lower order batsman, slow left-arm bowler. *Sch* Tonbridge. *Teams* Army (1937); Europeans (1938/9).
Career batting
4–8–6–55–20*–27.50–0–*ct* 1
Bowling 318–12–26.50–1–0–7/51

Osbaldeston, George
Amateur. *b:* 26.12.1786, Westminster, London. *d:* 1.8.1866, St John's Wood, London. Hard-

hitting middle order right-hand batsman, right-hand fast under-arm bowler. *Sch* Eton. *Teams* MCC (1808–30); Surrey (1815–17); Sussex (1815–17).
Career batting
33–61–8–1002–112–18.90–2–*ct* 16–*st* 5
Bowling 45 wickets, no analyses
A controversial figure, he was one of the best all-rounders of his day, but at the height of his career, in 1818, he resigned from the MCC on a matter of principle and scarcely played again in important matches. He was a crack shot and a famous rider.

Osborn, Frederick
Professional. *b:* 10.11.1889, Leicester. *d:* 11.10.1954, Leicester. Middle order batsman. *Team* Leicestershire (1911–13, 2 matches).
Career batting
2–3–0–14–14–4.66–0–*ct* 2
A good soccer player, he appeared for Leicester Fosse and Preston North End.

Osborn, George Newland
Professional. *b:* 1851, Romford, Essex. *d:* 3.3.1913, Westminster, London. Lower order right-hand batsman, right-arm fast bowler. *Team* Middlesex (1881, 3 matches).
Career batting
3–4–1–9–6–3.00–0–*ct* 0
Bowling 105–4–26.25–0–0–2/32

Osborne, David Robert
Amateur. *b:* 29.9.1879, Perth, Australia. *d:* 1954, Bahamas, West Indies. Lower order batsman, right-arm medium pace bowler. *Teams* Cambridge U (1905); Middlesex (1911, 1 match).
Career batting
4–6–1–62–35*–12.40–0–*ct* 0
Bowling 225–5–45.00–0–0–2/79
His final first-class match was for MCC in 1914.

Osborne, Ernest Charles
Amateur. *b:* 1873, Melbourne, Australia. *d:* 25.3.1926, Cardinia, Victoria, Australia. Lower order batsman, opening bowler. *Team* Cambridge U (1894).
Career batting
3–5–0–6–5–1.20–0–*ct* 1
Bowling 227–5–45.40–0–0–3/46

Osborne, George
Professional. Middle order batsman, bowler. *Team* Derbyshire (1879–83, 7 matches).
Career batting
8–15–1–60–14–4.28–0–*ct* 3
Bowling 39–1–39.00–0–0–1/23
His first-class debut was for Players of the North in 1877.

Osborne, Michael John
Amateur. Middle order right-hand batsman, off break bowler. *Team* Combined Services XI (1961–62).
Career batting
3–6–0–155–60–25.83–0–*ct* 3
Bowling 81–2–40.50–0–0–2/65

Osborne, W. G.
Amateur. Middle order batsman. *Team* Combined Oxford and Cambridge XI (1922).
Career batting
1–2–0–49–37–24.50–0–*ct* 0

Oscroft, Donald Straker
Amateur. *b:* 12.4.1908, London. *d:* 19.2.1944, Milltimber, Aberdeenshire, Scotland. Son of P. W. (Notts). Opening/middle order right-hand batsman, right-arm medium pace bowler. *Sch* Uppingham. *Teams* Leicestershire (1928, 4 matches); Cambridge U (1929).
Career batting
5–9–1–105–50–13.12–0–*ct* 0
He also played for Hertfordshire.

Oscroft, Eric
Professional. *b:* 20.4.1933, Sutton-in-Ashfield, Notts. Tail end right-hand batsman, left-arm fast medium bowler. *Team* Nottinghamshire (1950–51, 9 matches).
Career batting
9–8–3–8–7*–1.60–0–*ct* 1
Bowling 707–13–54.38–0–0–4/88

Oscroft, John Thomas
Professional. *b:* 24.3.1846, Arnold, Notts. *d:* 15.6.1885, Arnold, Notts. Brother of William (Notts). Hard-hitting middle order right-hand batsman, right-hand fast round-arm bowler. *Team* Nottinghamshire (1867–74, 14 matches).
Career batting
18–31–0–244–51–7.87–0–*ct* 10
Bowling 160–3–53.33–0–0–1/6
He also played for Northants (pre-first-class).

Oscroft, Percy William
Amateur. *b:* 27.11.1872, Nottingham. *d:* 8.12.1933, St John's Wood, London. Father of D. S. (Leics). Steady middle order right-hand batsman, left-arm medium pace bowler, excellent slip. *Sch* Nottingham High School. *Team* Nottinghamshire (1894–1900, 18 matches).

Career batting
18–31–2–409–40–14.10–0–*ct* 9
Bowling 37–2–18.50–0–0–1/10

He did not appear in any first-class matches whilst at Cambridge.

Oscroft, William
Professional. *b:* 16.12.1843, Arnold, Notts. *d:* 10.10.1905, Nottingham. Brother of J. T. (Notts). Excellent opening right-hand batsman, right-hand fast round-arm bowler, good field. *Team* Nottinghamshire (1864–82, 167 matches). *Tours* Grace to Australia 1873/4; Daft to North America 1879 (neither first-class).
Career batting
244–419–21–7596–140–19.08–2–*ct* 169–*st* 1
Bowling 1588–76–20.89–2–0–5/34

He was for some years one of the leading batsmen in England and in 1865 topped the first-class batting averages with 518 runs, av 43.16. He captained Notts in 1881 and 1882.

O'Shaughnessy, Edward
Professional. *b:* 16.11.1860, Canterbury, Kent. *d:* 6.8.1885, Marylebone, London. He died of rapid consumption. Hard-hitting middle order batsman, right-hand slow round-arm bowler, good field. *Team* Kent (1879–85, 59 matches).
Career batting
62–109–9–1193–98–11.93–0–*ct* 47
Bowling 1607–80–20.08–5–1–7/16

O'Shaughnessy, Steven Joseph
Cricketer. *b:* 9.9.1961, Bury, Lancashire. Hard-hitting opening right-hand batsman, right-arm medium pace bowler. *Team* Lancashire (1980–83, 47 matches).
Career batting
47–70–14–1559–105–27.83–2–*ct* 11
Bowling 1955–64–30.54–0–0–4/66

For Lancashire v Leicestershire at Old Trafford in 1983 he hit 101* in 35 minutes (105 in all) to equal the fastest time for a century in first-class cricket – the innings was made in farcical conditions.

Osman, Wayne Miles
Cricketer. *b:* 19.8.1950, Athens, Greece. Middle order left-hand batsman, left-arm medium pace bowler. *Team* Northants (1970–71, 9 matches).
Career batting
9–16–0–287–60–17.94–0–*ct* 6

Since 1972 he has appeared for Hertfordshire.

O'Sullivan, David Robert
Cricketer. *b:* 16.11.1944, Palmerston North, New Zealand. Lower order right-hand batsman, slow left-arm bowler. *Teams* Hampshire (1971–73, 26 matches); Central Districts (1972/3 to 1982/3). *Tours* New Zealand to Australia 1972/3, 1973/4, to India and Pakistan 1976/7. *Tests* New Zealand (1972/3 to 1976/7, 11 matches).
Career batting
121–172–41–1992–70*–15.20–0–*ct* 45
Bowling 11766–454–25.91–24–3–6/26
Test batting
11–21–4–158–23*–9.29–0–*ct* 2
Bowling 1221–18–67.83–1–0–5/148

He also played for Durham.

Oswald, Denis Geoffrey
Amateur. *b:* 12.11.1910, Port Stanley, Falkland Islands. Opening/middle order right-hand batsman. *Sch* St Lawrence College. *Team* Oxford U (1931).
Career batting
2–2–1–21–16–21.00–0–*ct* 0

Ottaway, Cuthbert John
Amateur. *b:* 20.7.1850, Dover, Kent. *d:* 2.4.1878, Westminster, London. Sound middle order right-hand batsman, wicket-keeper. *Sch* Eton. *Teams* Kent (1869–70, 2 matches); Oxford U (1870–73, blue all four years); Middlesex (1874–76, 7 matches). *Tour* Fitzgerald to North America 1872 (not first-class).
Career batting
37–67–5–1691–112–27.27–2–*ct* 22–*st* 1

He was one of the best amateur batsmen of his day, but retired on being called to the bar. An all-round sportsman, he represented Oxford at racquets and tennis as well as receiving his soccer blue. A good forward, he appeared for England in two International soccer matches.

Ottley, David George
Cricketer. *b:* 23.6.1944, Worcester Park, Surrey. Middle order right-hand batsman. *Sch* Tiffin. *Team* Middlesex (1967, 7 matches).
Career batting
7–9–1–109–30–13.62–0–*ct* 3

He also played for Hertfordshire.

Outschoorn, Ladislaw
Professional. *b:* 26.9.1918, Colombo, Ceylon. Stylish middle order right-hand batsman, right-arm medium pace bowler. *Team* Worcestershire (1946–59, 341 matches).
Career batting
346–595–53–15496–215*–28.59–25–*ct* 277
Bowling 2030–33–61.51–0–0–2/15

He hit 1,000 runs in a season nine times (best 1,761, av 35.93, in 1951). Both his double centuries were for Worcs, the highest being 215* v Northants at Worcester in 1949.

Ovenstone, Douglas McPherson
Amateur. *b:* 31.7.1921, Cape Town, South Africa. Middle order right-hand batsman, wicket-keeper. *Team* Western Province (1946/7 to 1947/8). *Tour* South Africa to England 1947.
Career batting
20–32–2–437–52–14.56–0–*ct* 40–*st* 15
South Africa's decision to include three wicket-keepers in the 1947 touring party meant that he would have few opportunities to prove his ability; as it was a broken finger prevented him for playing for half the season and he was not selected for any Tests. His first-class debut was for 1st South African Division XI in 1942/3.

Overton, William
Professional. *b:* 28.3.1873, Swindon, Wilts. *d:* August 1949, Paddington, London. Lower order right-hand batsman, slow right-arm bowler. *Team* MCC (1898–1908).
Career batting
8–12–4–63–19–7.87–0–*ct* 5
Bowling 340–21–16.19–0–0–4/22
He played for Wiltshire.

Owen, Hugh Glendwr Palmer
Amateur. *b:* 19.5.1859, Bath, Somerset. *d:* 20.10.1912, Landwick, Dengie, Essex. Sound opening right-hand batsman, right-arm medium pace bowler. *Teams* Cambridge U (1882); Essex (1894–1902, 133 matches).
Career batting
136–228–17–4510–134–21.37–3–*ct* 38
Bowling 332–9–36.88–0–0–2/37
His career with Essex began in 1880 and most of his best batting for the County was performed during its pre-first-class period. He captained Essex from 1895 to 1902. He played soccer for Notts County.

Owen, Joseph Glyn
Professional for Surrey, but amateur for Bedfordshire. *b:* 23.1.1909, Llanelly, Glamorgan. *d:* 17.2.1978, Eastbourne, Sussex. Middle order left-hand batsman, slow left-arm bowler. *Team* Surrey (1930–33, 15 matches).
Career batting
18–19–3–361–57–22.56–0–*ct* 8
Bowling 837–16–52.31–0–0–3/15
He appeared for Bedfordshire from 1939 to 1957 and his final first-class match was for Minor Counties in 1951.

Owen, Norman William
Professional. *b:* 16.3.1915, Shepherds Bush, London. *d:* 9.9.1977, Darlington, Co Durham. Right-hand batsman, right-arm medium fast or off break bowler. *Team* Minor Counties (1951).
Career batting
1–2–0–26–14–13.00–0–*ct* 0
Bowling 33–1–33.00–0–0–1/33
His County cricket was for Durham.

Owen-Smith, Dr Harold Geoffrey (Owen)
Amateur. *b:* 18.2.1909, Rondebosch, Cape Town, South Africa. Adventurous middle order right-hand batsman, slow leg break bowler, brilliant outfield. *Teams* Western Province (1927/8 to 1949/50); Oxford U (1931–33, blue all three years); Middlesex (1935–37, 28 matches). *Tours* South Africa to England 1929. *Tests* South Africa (1929, 5 matches).
Career batting
101–162–11–4059–168*–26.88–3–*ct* 93
Bowling 7410–319–23.22–20–3–7/153
Test batting
5–8–2–252–129–42.00–1–*ct* 4
Bowling 113–0
He was most successful on the 1929 tour to England, hitting 1,168 runs, av 35.39, and taking 30 wickets, av 25.80. An all-round sportsman, he was awarded his blue for rugby and boxing and went on the captain England at the former.

Owen-Thomas, Dudley Richard
Cricketer. *b:* 20.9.1948, Mombasa, Kenya. Middle order right-hand batsman, off break bowler. *Sch* KCS, Wimbledon. *Teams* Cambridge U (1969–72, blue all four years); Surrey (1970–75, 73 matches). *Tours* MCC to Bangladesh 1976/7 (not first-class), to East Africa 1973/4.
Career batting
112–188–20–4891–182*–29.11–8–*ct* 48
Bowling 798–20–39.90–0–0–3/20
He hit 1,065 runs, av 34.35, in 1971.

Oxley, John Haywood
Amateur. *b:* 1850, Rotherham, Yorkshire. *d:* 1917, Staines, Middlesex. Lower order batsman, wicket-keeper. *Team* Middlesex (1883, 2 matches).
Career batting
2–4–0–10–5–2.50–0–*ct* 2–*st* 2

Oyston, Charles
Professional. *b:* 12.5.1869, Armley, Yorkshire. *d:* 15.7.1942, Leeds, Yorkshire. Lower order left-hand batsman, slow left-arm bowler. *Team* Yorkshire (1900–09, 15 matches).
Career batting
15–21–8–96–22–7.38–0–*ct* 3
Bowling 872–31–28.12–0–0–3/30

PACKE, CHARLES WILLIAM CHRISTOPHER
Amateur. *b:* 2.5.1909, Pietermaritzburg, South Africa. *d:* 1.7.1944, Normandy. He was killed in action. Brother of M. St J. and R. J. (Leics). Forcing middle order right-hand batsman, right-arm medium pace bowler, brilliant field. *Sch* Eton. *Team* Leicestershire (1929–34, 21 matches).
Career batting
26–41–0–1013–176–24.71–2–*ct* 17
Bowling 75–3–25.00–0–0–2/33
His final first-class match was for the Army in 1939 and military service very much restricted his appearances in County cricket. He captained Leicestershire in 1932.

Packe, Michael St John
Amateur. *b:* 21.8.1916, Eastbourne, Sussex. *d:* 20.12.1978, St Anne's, Alderney. Brother of C. W. C. and R. J. (Leics). Forcing middle order right-hand batsman. *Sch* Wellington. *Teams* Cambridge U (1936); Leicestershire (1936–39, 35 matches).
Career batting
41–64–3–1151–118–18.86–1–*ct* 30
Bowling 14–1–14.00–0–0–1/0
He captained Leicestershire in 1939.

Packe, Robert Julian
Amateur. *b:* 8.7.1913, Hounslow, Middlesex. *d:* 24.10.1935, Ahmednagar, India. He died of dysentery. Brother of C. W. C. and M. St J. (Leics). Lower order right-hand batsman, slow left-arm bowler. *Sch* Stowe. *Team* Leicestershire (1933, 3 matches).
Career batting
3–5–2–25–12–8.33–0–*ct* 2
Bowling 68–1–68.00–0–0–1/31

Packer, Admiral Sir Herbert Annesley
Amateur. *b:* 9.10.1894, Cressage, Shropshire. *d:* 23.9.1962, Bishopscourt, Wynberg, South Africa. Lower order batsman, wicket-keeper. *Team* Royal Navy (1920).
Career batting
1–2–0–3–3–1.50–0–*ct* 2

Padgett, Douglas Ernest Vernon
Professional. *b:* 20.7.1934, Idle, Yorkshire. Opening or middle order right-hand batsman, right-arm medium pace bowler. *Team* Yorkshire (1951–71, 487 matches). *Tours* MCC to New Zealand 1960/1; Yorkshire to North America 1964 (not first-class). *Tests* England (1960, 2 matches).
Career batting
506–806–67–21124–161*–28.58–32–*ct* 261
Bowling 216–6–36.00–0–0–1/2
Test batting
2–4–0–51–31–12.75–0–*ct* 0
Bowling 8–0
He hit 1,000 runs in a season twelve times, going on to 2,000 once : 2,181, av 41.15, in 1959.
He is the Yorkshire coach.

Padgett, Grenville Hubert
Professional. *b:* 9.10.1931, Silkstone, Barnsley, Yorkshire. Forcing middle order right-hand batsman, right-arm medium pace bowler, good field. *Team* Yorkshire (1952, 6 matches).
Career batting
6–7–4–56–32*–18.66–0–*ct* 5
Bowling 336–4–84.00–0–0–2/37

Padgett, John
Professional. *b:* 21.11.1860, Scarborough, Yorkshire. Middle order right-hand batsman. *Team* Yorkshire (1882–89, 6 matches).
Career batting
7–11–0–130–25–11.81–0–*ct* 2

Padley, William
Professional. *b:* 11.4.1842, Moor Green, Notts. *d:* 21.7.1904, Bagthorpe, Notts. Lower order right-hand batsman, right-hand medium pace round-arm bowler, wicket-keeper. *Team* Nottinghamshire (1876, 1 match).
Career batting
1–2–1–15–10–15.00–0–*ct* 0

Padmore, A. Hal
Amateur. *b:* West Indies. Lower order right-hand batsman, right-arm medium pace bowler. *Team* Canada (1951–54). *Tour* Canada to England 1954.
Career batting
3–5–1–34–15*–8.50–0–*ct* 1
Bowling 312–14–22.28–1–0–5/47
He proved quite effective on the 1954 visit.

Padmore, Albert Leroy
Cricketer. *b:* 17.12.1946, St James, Barbados. Tail end right-hand batsman, off break bowler. *Team* Barbados (1972/3 to 1981/2). *Tours* West Indies to India, Pakistan and Sri Lanka 1974/5, to Australia 1975/6, to England 1976. *Tests* West Indies (1975/6 to 1976, 2 matches).
Career batting
65–63–21–544–79–12.95–0–*ct* 27
Bowling 5503–188–29.27–8–2–6/69
Test batting
2–2–1–8–8*–8.00–0–*ct* 0
Bowling 135–1–135.00–0–0–1/36
He took 59 wickets, av 23.40, on the 1976

tour to England, appearing in one Test, the fast bowlers dominating the series. He was manager of the West Indies team to South Africa in 1982/3.

Page, Sir Arthur
Amateur. *b:* 9.3.1876, London. *d:* 1.9.1958, Hildenborough, Kent. Opening or middle order right-hand batsman, good deep field. *Sch* Harrow. *Team* Oxford U (1899).
Career batting
9–13–2–180–48–16.36–0–*ct* 4
He was in India for some years and later became Chief Justice of Burma. He played for MCC between 1898 and 1904.

Page, Charles Carew
Amateur. *b:* 25.4.1884, Barnet, Herts. *d:* 10.4.1921, Hook Heath, Woking, Surrey. Opening or middle order right-hand batsman, good outfield. *Sch* Malvern. *Teams* Cambridge U (1905–06, blue both years); Middlesex (1905–09, 36 matches). *Tour* MCC to New Zealand 1906/7.
Career batting
71–115–4–2919–164*–26.29–2–*ct* 30
Bowling 53–1–53.00–0–0–1/25
A noted soccer player, he gained his blue and also appeared for the Corinthians.

Page, Dallas Alexander Chancellor
Amateur. *b:* 11.4.1911, Cheltenham, Gloucs. *d:* 2.9.1936, Cirencester, Gloucs. He died as the result of a road accident. Son of H. V. (Gloucs and Oxford U). Hard hitting middle order right-hand batsman, brilliant cover point. *Sch* Cheltenham. *Team* Gloucestershire (1933–36, 106 matches).
Career batting
106–167–7–2993–116–18.70–1–*ct* 75
Bowling 45–0
He hit 1,059 runs, av 20.36, in 1935. In 1935 and 1936 he captained Gloucestershire and was travelling home from the County's match with Nottinghamshire when the fatal accident occurred.

Page, E. W.
Amateur. Lower order batsman, useful bowler. *Team* Somerset (1885, 1 match).
Career batting
1–2–1–1–1*–1.00–0–*ct* 0
Bowling 67–0

Page, Edgar Wells
Amateur. *b:* 31.12.1884, Wolverhampton. *d:* 12.5.1956, Wolverhampton, Staffordshire. Middle order right-hand batsman. *Sch* Repton. *Team* Minor Counties (1924).
Career batting
1–2–0–26–26–13.00–0–*ct* 0
His County cricket was for Staffordshire. A noted hockey player, he represented England.

Page, Herbert Vivian
Amateur. *b:* 30.10.1862, Lancaster, Lancashire. *d:* 1.8.1927, Cheltenham, Gloucs. Father of D. A. C. (Gloucs). Sound middle order right-hand batsman, right-arm medium pace off break bowler. *Sch* Cheltenham. *Teams* Oxford U (1883–86, blue all four years); Gloucestershire (1883–95, 102 matches).
Career batting
146–247–22–4005–116–17.80–1–*ct* 111–*st* 14
Bowling 4929–212–23.25–5–0–6/28
An all-round sportsman, he was awarded his blue for rugby and also played for Gloucestershire. He captained East Gloucestershire Hockey Club for 22 years.

Page, John Colin Theodore
Professional. *b:* 20.5.1930, Mereworth, Kent. Tail end right-hand batsman, right-arm medium pace, later off break bowler. *Team* Kent (1950–63, 198 matches).
Career batting
198–273–124–818–23–5.48–0–*ct* 74
Bowling 14967–521–28.72–22–2–8/117
After retiring he became Manager of Kent.

Page, Julian Thomas
Cricketer. *b:* 1.5.1954, Clifton, Bristol. Lower order left-hand batsman, left-arm medium pace bowler. *Team* Cambridge U (1974).
Career batting
2–4–0–31–11–7.75–0–*ct* 0
Bowling 95–1–95.00–0–0–1/14
He appeared for Gloucestershire in one John Player League match.

Page, Michael Harry
Cricketer. *b:* 17.6.1941, Blackpool, Lancashire. Middle order right-hand batsman, off break bowler. *Team* Derbyshire (1964–75, 254 matches).
Career batting
254–451–47–11538–162–28.55–9–*ct* 248
Bowling 527–7–75.28–0–0–1/0
He hit 1,000 runs in a season six times (best 1,344, av 40.72, in 1970).

Page, Milford Laurenson
Amateur. *b:* 8.5.1902, Littelton, New Zealand. Steady middle order right-hand batsman, right-arm slow bowler, good slip field. *Team* Canterbury (1920/1 to 1936/7). *Tours* New Zealand to England 1927, 1931, 1937, to Australia

1927/8, 1937/8. *Tests* New Zealand (1929/30 to 1937, 14 matches).
Career batting
132–213–17–5857–206–29.88–9–*ct* 117
Bowling 2365–73–32.39–0–0–4/10
Test batting
14–20–0–492–104–24.60–1–*ct* 6
Bowling 231–5–46.20–0–0–2/21

He exceeded 1,000 runs only on the 1927 tour to England: 1,154, av 34.96. Captain of New Zealand in seven Tests, he led the 1937 touring party. His first first-class match was for New Zealand Army XI in 1942/3. His highest score was 206 for Canterbury v Wellington at Wellington in 1931/2. He also played rugby for New Zealand.

Page, Richard Kennett
Amateur. *b:* 24.1.1910, Burlesdon, Hants. Middle order right-hand batsman, leg break bowler. *Sch* Marlborough. *Team* Army (1937).
Career batting
1–2–0–12–12–6.00–0–*ct* 0
Bowling 25–0

Page, Thomas Heritage
Amateur. *b:* 28.5.1872, Canterbury, Kent. *d:* 7.12.1953, Swanage, Dorset. Lower order batsman, bowler. *Sch* St Edward's, Oxford. *Team* Hampshire (1900, 2 matches).
Career batting
2–4–1–77–61*–25.66–0–*ct* 3
Bowling 198–4–49.50–0–0–4/115

Page, William
Professional. *b:* 29.4.1847, Caverswall, Staffs. *d:* 27.9.1904, Derby. Middle order right-hand batsman. *Team* Derbyshire (1881–82, 3 matches).
Career batting
3–6–0–50–19–8.33–0–*ct* 0

An accident which deprived him of the sight of one eye prematurely ended his cricket career.

Pai, Mukundrao Damodar
Amateur. *b:* 21.6.1883, Bombay. *d:* 5.8.1948, Bombay. Middle order right-hand batsman. *Team* Hindus (1906/7 to 1920/1). *Tour* India to England 1911.
Career batting
22–37–3–640–107–18.82–1–*ct* 14

He achieved very little on the 1911 tour to England.

Pain, Edwin Llewellyn
Amateur. *b:* 1891, Swansea, Glamorgan. *d* 14.7.1947, Plymouth, Devon. Tail-end right-hand batsman, right-arm medium pace bowler. *Team* Royal Navy (1926).
Career batting
1–2–0–18–17–9.00–0–*ct* 2
Bowling 99–3–33.00–0–0–3/90

His County cricket was for Devon.

Paine, George Alfred Edward
Professional. *b:* 11.6.1908, Paddington, London. *d:* 30.3.1978, Solihull. Lower order right-hand batsman, slow left-arm bowler, good slip field. *Teams* Middlesex (1926, 5 matches); Warwickshire (1929–47, 240 matches). *Tour* MCC to West Indies 1934/5. *Tests* England (1934/5, 4 matches).
Career batting
258–349–62–3430–79–11.95–0–*ct* 160
Bowling 23334–1021–22.85–74–13–8/43
Test batting
4–7–1–97–49–16.16–0–*ct* 5
Bowling 467–17–27.47–1–0–5/168

He took 100 wickets in a season five times (best 156, av 17.07, in 1934). Rheumatism hampered his bowling from 1936 and a disagreement over terms in 1938 virtually ended his County cricket.

Paine, John Gosling
Amateur. *b:* 10.11.1829, Brighton, Sussex. *d:* 1.11.1859, Brighton, Sussex. He died suddenly of apoplexy. Hard hitting middle order right-hand batsman, wicket-keeper. *Team* Sussex (1851–59, 5 matches).
Career batting
13–22–2–224–47–11.20–0–*ct* 7–*st* 3

A most promising cricketer, he died before he could fulfil expectations.

Painter, John Richard
Professional. *b:* 11.11.1856, Bourton-on-the-Water, Gloucs. *d:* 16.9.1900, Bourton-on-the-Water, Gloucs. Middle order right-hand batsman, right-arm fast bowler, good field. *Team* Gloucestershire (1881–97, 192 matches).
Career batting
198–353–16–5927–150–17.58–5–*ct* 151
Bowling 1232–46–26.78–2–1–8/67

His best season was 1890 when he scored 683 runs, av 25.29.

Pairaudeau, Bruce Hamilton
Professional. *b:* 14.4.1931, Georgetown, British Guiana. Stylish opening right-hand batsman. *Teams* British Guiana (1946/7 to 1957/8); Northern Districts (1958/9 to 1966/7). *Tours* West Indies to New Zealand 1955/6, to England 1957. *Tests* West Indies (1952/3 to 1957, 13 matches).

Career batting
89–159–5–4930–163–32.01–11–*ct* 64
Bowling 82–0
Test batting
13–21–0–454–115–21.61–1–*ct* 6
Bowling 3–0

His debut in English first-class cricket was for a Commonwealth XI in 1950. Although he appeared in two Tests on the 1957 tour to England, his figures in first-class matches were very modest. He emigrated to New Zealand in 1958.

Paish, Arthur James
Professional. *b:* 5.4.1874, Gloucester. *d:* 16.8.1948, Gloucester. Tail end batsman, slow left-arm bowler. *Team* Gloucestershire (1898–1903, 79 matches).
Career batting
79–123–38–967–66–11.37–0–*ct* 79
Bowling 8610–354–24.32–27–7–8/68

His best season was 1899 when he took 137 wickets, av 18.54.

Palairet, Henry Hamilton
Amateur. *b:* 1845, Bradford-on-Avon, Wilts. *d:* 20.3.1923, Cattistock, Dorset. Father of L. C. H. and R. C. N. (Somerset). Middle order batsman. *Sch* Eton. *Team* MCC (1868–69).
Career batting
2–4–1–28–14*–9.33–0–*ct* 2

He was for many years the Champion Archer of England.

Palairet, Lionel Charles Hamilton
Amateur. *b:* 27.5.1870, Grange-over-Sands, Lancashire. *d:* 27.3.1933, Exmouth, Devon. Son of H. H. (MCC), brother of R. C. N. (Somerset). Stylish opening right-hand batsman, right-arm medium pace bowler and occasionally under arm lobs. *Sch* Repton. *Teams* Oxford U (1890–93, blue all four years); Somerset (1891–1909, 222 matches). *Tests* England (1902, 2 matches).
Career batting
267–488–19–15777–292–33.63–27–*ct* 248–*st* 15
Bowling 4849–143–33.90–2–0–6/84
Test batting
2–4–0–49–20–12.25–0–*ct* 2

He hit 1,000 runs in a season seven times (best 1,906, av 57.75, in 1901). Both his double centuries were for Somerset, the highest being 292 v Hampshire at Southampton in 1896. He was Captain of Somerset in 1906 and President of Somerset CCC in 1929. An all-round sportsman he played soccer for the Corinthians and represented Oxford in the three miles.

Palairet, Richard Cameron North
Amateur. *b:* 25.6.1871, Grange-over-Sands, Lancashire. *d:* 11.2.1955, Knowle, Budleigh Salterton, Devon. Son of H. H. (MCC), brother of L. C. H. (Somerset). Graceful opening right-hand batsman, good field. *Sch* Repton. *Teams* Oxford U (1893–94, blue both years); Somerset (1891–1902, 85 matches). *Tour* Priestley to West Indies 1896/7.
Career batting
112–198–9–4000–156–21.16–2–*ct* 108
Bowling 167–3–55.66–0–0–1/19

He was Secretary of Surrey CCC from 1920 to 1932 and in 1932/3 was joint-manager of the MCC Team to Australia. From 1937 to 1946 he was President of Somerset. He was awarded his soccer blue as an inside-forward.

Palfreman, Anthony Brian
Cricketer. *b:* 27.8.1946, Ravenshead, Notts. Lower order right-hand batsman, right-arm fast medium bowler. *Sch* Nottingham High School. *Team* Cambridge U (1966–68, blue 1966).
Career batting
16–31–3–432–67–15.42–0–*ct* 11
Bowling 1158–31–37.35–1–0–5/63

Palia, Phiroze Edulji
Amateur. *b:* 5.9.1910, Bombay, India. *d:* 9.9.1981, Bangalore, India. Attractive middle order left-hand batsman, slow left-arm bowler, good field. *Teams* Parsis (1928/9 to 1945/6); Madras (1933/4); United Provinces (1934/5 to 1942/3); Bombay (1937/8); Mysore (1944/5 to 1953/4); Bengal (1948/9). *Tours* India to England 1932, 1936; Vizianagram's XI to India and Ceylon 1930/1; Indian University Occasionals to Ceylon 1935/6. *Tests* India (1932–36, 2 matches).
Career batting
100–162–22–4536–216–32.40–8–*ct* 39
Bowling 5038–208–24.22–7–0–7/109
Test batting
2–4–1–29–16–9.66–0–*ct* 0
Bowling 13–0

Although he appeared in a Test on each of the tours to England, his success in terms of figures was very modest. His only double century was 216 for the United Provinces v Maharashtra at Poona in 1939/40.

Paling, George
Professional. *b:* 29.11.1836, Nottingham. *d:* 18.12.1879, Nottingham. Hard hitting middle order right-hand batsman, right-hand medium pace round-arm bowler, good deep field. *Team* Nottinghamshire (1865–67, 7 matches).
Career batting
8–14–3–148–41*–13.45–0–*ct* 3

Pallett, Henry James
Professional. *b:* 2.1.1863, Birmingham. *d:* 18.6.1917, Aston, Birmingham. Steady lower order right-hand batsman, right-arm slow bowler. *Team* Warwickshire (1894–98, 73 matches).
Career batting
77–104–21–929–55*–11.19–0–*ct* 21
Bowling 6580–305–21.57–21–7–9/55

His debut for Warwickshire was in 1883 and his best seasons for the County occurred before they became first-class. He played for Staffordshire in 1903. His first-class debut was for an Eleven of England v Australians in 1886. His best bowling was 9/55 for Warwickshire v Essex at Leyton in 1894

Palmer, Clayton
Amateur. *b:* 14.7.1885, London. *d:* April 1956, Uckfield, Sussex. Middle order right-hand batsman. *Sch* Uppingham. *Teams* Middlesex (1904–12, 19 matches); Cambridge U (1905–07, blue 1907).
Career batting
35–58–6–767–55*–14.75–0–*ct* 12

Palmer, Cecil Howard
Amateur. *b:* 14.7.1873, Eastbourne, Sussex. *d:* 26.7.1915, near Hill Q, Gallipoli. He was killed in action. Middle order right-hand batsman, excellent field. *Sch* Radley. *Teams* Hampshire (1899–1907, 8 matches); Worcestershire (1904, 1 match).
Career batting
9–18–2–380–75*–23.75–0–*ct* 2

A regular soldier, his County cricket was very restricted, but in 1904 he had the curious experience of appearing both for Hampshire and Worcestershire in first-class matches. He also played for Barbados (not first-class).

Palmer, Charles Henry
Amateur. *b:* 15.5.1919, Old Hill, Staffs. Sound middle order right-hand batsman, right-arm medium, or very slow, bowler. *Teams* Worcestershire (1938–49, 66 matches); Leicestershire (1950–59, 231 matches); Europeans (1945/6). *Tours* MCC to South Africa 1948/9, to West Indies 1953/4. *Test* England (1953/4, 1 match).
Career batting
336–588–38–17458–201–31.74–33–*ct* 147
Bowling 9183–365–25.15–5–0–8/7
Test batting
1–2–0–22–22–11.00–0–*ct* 0
Bowling 15–0

He hit 1,000 runs in a season eight times going on to 2,000 once : 2,071, av 39.82, in 1952. His only double century was 201 for Leics v Northants at Northampton in 1953. He returned the remarkable analysis of 14–12–7–8 for Leics v Surrey at Grace Road, Leicester in 1955. From 1950 to 1957 he was captain of Leicestershire, also acting as Secretary to the County. He was later Chairman of Leicestershire and in 1978/9 President of MCC.

Palmer, Eric John
Amateur. *b:* 16.6.1931, Romford, Essex. Tail end left-hand batsman, right-arm fast medium bowler. *Team* Essex (1957, 4 matches).
Career batting
4–6–5–39–11*–39.00–0–*ct* 1
Bowling 225–7–32.14–0–0–2/35

Palmer, George Arthur
Amateur. *b:* 5.6.1897, Hopsford, Withybrook, Warwickshire. *d:* 1.6.1962, Higham-on-the-Hill, Warwickshire. Lower order right-hand batsman, right-arm fast medium bowler. *Team* Warwickshire (1928, 9 matches).
Career batting
9–12–2–87–20–8.70–0–*ct* 7
Bowling 450–8–56.25–0–0–2/21

Palmer, George Eugene
Amateur. *b:* 22.2.1860, Mulwala, Albury, New South Wales, Australia. *d:* 22.8.1910, Baddaginnie, Victoria, Australia. Lower order right-hand batsman, right-arm medium off break bowler. *Teams* Victoria (1878/9 to 1894/5, 19 matches); Tasmania (1896/7, 1 match). *Tours* Australia to England 1880, 1882, 1884, 1886. *Tests* Australia (1880–86, 17 matches).
Career batting
133–200–31–2728–113–16.14–1–*ct* 108
Bowling 10520–594–17.71–54–16–8/48
Test batting
17–25–4–296–48–14.09–0–*ct* 13
Bowling 1678–78–21.51–6–2–7/65

He took 100 wickets in a season on three of his four tours to England (best 132, av 16.43, in 1884). With less matches in 1880 he took 66 wickets, av 11.69.

Palmer, George Harry
Amateur. *b:* 24.10.1917, Ibstock, Leics. Son of John (Leics). Lower order right-hand batsman, right-arm medium pace bowler. *Team* Leicestershire (1938–39, 5 matches).
Career batting
5–6–1–31–14*–6.20–0–*ct* 3
Bowling 320–12–26.66–0–0–3/36

Palmer, Gary Vincent
Cricketer. *b:* 15.11.1965, Taunton, Somerset. Son of K. E. (Somerset), nephew of Roy (Somerset). Lower order right-hand batsman, right-arm

medium pace bowler. *Team* Somerset (1982–83, 11 matches).
Career batting
11–15–2–152–78–11.69–0–*ct* 8
Bowling 687–20–34.35–1–0–5/38

Palmer, Harold James
Amateur. *b:* 30.8.1890, Epping, Essex. *d:* 12.2.1967, Battle, Sussex. Tail end right-hand batsman, right-arm fast medium, or leg break, bowler. *Team* Essex (1924–32, 53 matches).
Career batting
58–74–27–278–25*–5.91–0–*ct* 21
Bowling 4053–160–25.33–7–0–6/68
His final first-class match was for MCC in 1936.

Palmer, John
Professional. *b:* 1881, Ibstock, Leics. *d:* 14.6.1928, Ibstock. Father of G. H. (Leics). Lower order right-hand batsman, right-arm medium pace bowler. *Team* Leicestershire (1906, 3 matches).
Career batting
3–6–1–27–13–5.40–0–*ct* 2
Bowling 209–8–26.12–0–0–3/14

Palmer, Kenneth Ernest
Professional. *b:* 22.4.1937, Winchester, Hants. Brother of Roy (Somerset), father of G. V. (Somerset). Middle order right-hand batsman, right-arm fast medium bowler. *Team* Somerset (1955–69, 302 matches). *Tours* MCC to South Africa 1964/5 – in an emergency (he was coaching there); Commonwealth to Pakistan 1963/4; Cavaliers to West Indies 1963/4. *Test* England (1964/5, 1 match).
Career batting
314–481–105–7771–125*–20.66–2–*ct* 156
Bowling 18485–866–21.34–46–5–9/57
Test batting
1–1–0–10–10–10.00–0–*ct* 0
Bowling 189–1–189.00–0–0–1/113
He took 100 wickets in a season four times (best 139, av 16.07, in 1963) and in 1961 hit 1,036 runs, av 25.90, achieving the 'double' that season. His best bowling was 9/57 for Somerset v Notts at Trent Bridge in 1963. Appointed to the first class umpires' list in 1972, he has officiated in Tests.

Palmer, Richard
Professional. *b:* 13.9.1848, Hadlow, Kent. *d:* 2.3.1939, Lower Halstow, Kent. Lower order right-hand batsman, right-hand medium pace round-arm bowler, wicket-keeper. *Team* Kent (1873–82, 13 matches).
Career batting
13–25–6–104–20–5.47–0–*ct* 5–*st* 7
Bowling 20–0
He also played for Staffordshire.

Palmer, Roy
Cricketer. *b:* 12.7.1942, Devizes, Wilts. Brother of K. E. (Somerset), uncle of G. V. (Somerset). Lower order right-hand batsman, right-arm fast medium bowler. *Team* Somerset (1965–70, 74 matches).
Career batting
74–110–32–1037–84–13.29–0–*ct* 25
Bowling 5439–172–31.62–4–0–6/45
He joined the first-class umpires' list in 1980.

Palmer, Rodney Howell
Amateur. *b:* 24.11.1907, Basingstoke, Hants. Tail end right-hand batsman, right-arm fast bowler. *Sch* Harrow. *Teams* Cambridge U (1929); Hampshire (1930–33, 3 matches).
Career batting
4–2–0–0–0–0.00–0–*ct* 1
Bowling 292–9–32.44–1–0–5/93
He also played for Berkshire.

Palmer, Robert William Michael
Cricketer. *b:* 4.6.1960, Hong Kong. Right-hand batsman, left-arm medium pace bowler. *Sch* Bedford School. *Team* Cambridge U (1981–83, blue 1982).
Career batting
11–9–5–20–12–5.00–0–*ct* 4
Bowling 954–16–59.62–0–0–4/96

Palmer, Septimus
Amateur. *b:* 23.8.1858, Australia. *d:* 14.12.1935, Kensington, London. Middle order batsman. *Sch* Stonyhurst. *Team* Lancashire (1879–80, 6 matches).
Career batting
6–9–0–28–8–3.11–0–*ct* 4
Bowling 11–0

Palmer, William Thomas
Professional. *b:* 5.1.1847, Canterbury, Kent. *d:* 2.9.1906, Southfields, London. Hard hitting middle order right-hand batsman, right-hand medium pace round-arm bowler, good deep field. *Teams* Kent (1867–70, 17 matches); Surrey (1872–76, 19 matches).
Career batting
39–72–1–654–54–9.21–0–*ct* 15
Bowling 29–1–29.00–0–0–1/8
His final first-class match was for the South v North in 1877.

Palmes, Manfred Jerome
Amateur. *b:* 5.2.1887, Naburn, York. *d:* 5.5.1968, Murdoch Valley, Simonstown, Cape Province, South Africa. Lower order batsman, useful bowler. *Team* Royal Navy (1919–20).
Career batting
2–4–1–10–6–3.33–0–*ct* 0
Bowling 97–0

Pank, Philip Esmond Durrell
Amateur. *b:* 22.4.1892, Jaypore, India. *d:* 15.2.1966, Colchester, Essex. Middle order batsman, slow left-arm bowler. *Sch* Wellington. *Teams* Europeans (1918/9); Army (1925).
Career batting
4–8–2–79–29–13.16–0–*ct* 3
Bowling 113–9–12.55–1–0–7/12

Pape, Arthur Albert Brinkley
Amateur. *b:* 1890, Cirencester, Gloucs. *d:* 11.8.1945, Hartlepool, Co Durham. Middle order batsman. *Team* Somerset (1912, 1 match).
Career batting
1–2–0–0–0–0.00–0–*ct* 0
He also played for Durham.

Papillon, Godfrey Keppel
Amateur. *b:* 24.9.1867, Lexden, Essex. *d:* 14.8.1942, Hexham, Northumberland. Middle order right-hand batsman, wicket-keeper. *Sch* Marlborough. *Team* Gentlemen (1892).
Career batting
1–1–0–10–10–10.00–0–*ct* 1
He played for Northants (pre-first-class).

Parfitt, Judge James John Alexander
Amateur. *b:* 23.12.1857, Slwch Villa near Brecon. *d:* 17.5.1926, Wimbledon, Surrey. Lower order right-hand batsman, right-arm fast medium bowler, slip field. *Sch* Prior Park College. *Teams* Surrey (1881–82, 8 matches); Somerset (1883–85, 6 matches).
Career batting
14–27–3–222–41*–9.25–0–*ct* 4
Bowling 932–38–24.52–1–1–7/33
He appeared for Warwickshire in 1886 (pre-first-class). In the legal profession he became a County Court Judge.

Parfitt, Peter Howard
Professional. *b:* 8.12.1936, Billingford, Fakenham, Norfolk. Sound middle order left-hand batsman, right-arm medium, or off break, bowler, excellent field. *Teams* Middlesex (1956–72, 387 matches); President's XI in India (1963/4). *Tours* MCC to India, Pakistan and Ceylon 1961/2, to Australia and New Zealand 1962/3, 1965/6, to East Africa 1963/4, 1973/4, to India 1963/4. to South Africa 1964/5. *Tests* England (1961/2 to 1972, 37 matches).
Career batting
498–845–104–26924–200*–36.33–58–*ct* 564
Bowling 8401–277–30.32–5–0–6/45
Test batting
37–52–6–1882–131*–40.91–7–*ct* 42
Bowling 574–12–47.83–0–0–2/5
One of the leading batsman in England in the 1960s, he played in 37 Test matches, but never managed to secure an unassailable position in the England side. Coming to the top in 1961 with over 2,000 runs, he gained a place in the MCC side to India that winter and in 1962 not only headed the Test batting averages, but hit 2,121 runs (av 45.12) in first-class matches – in all he completed 1,000 runs in a season fourteen times, plus once overseas and went on to 2,000 three times. A poor tour in Australia in 1962/3 however lost him his Test place and although he was to be given several other opportunities in the England team, he never made many runs. His final Test appearances came in his last summer with Middlesex, when he was batting well, but once more at Test level he could show only moderate form.
His only double century was 200* for Middlesex v Notts at Trent Bridge in 1964. Before appearing for Middlesex he played for Norfolk.
A useful soccer player, he appeared for Norwich City.

Paris, Alexander
Amateur. *b:* 29.8.1908, Torphichen, West Lothian, Scotland. Right-hand batsman, right-arm medium pace bowler. *Team* Scotland (1937–38).
Career batting
3–6–1–40–24–8.00–0–*ct* 2
Bowling 210–12–17.50–1–0–6/35

Paris, Cecil Gerard Alexander
Amateur. *b:* 20.8.1911, Kirkee, India. Middle order right-hand batsman. *Sch* King's, Canterbury. *Team* Hampshire (1933–48, 98 matches).
Career batting
100–172–9–3730–134*–22.80–2–*ct* 75
Bowling 216–4–54.00–0–0–1/10
He hit 1,058, av 23.51, in 1938. An important figure in cricket administration he was Chairman of the T. C. C. B.

Paris, William
Professional. *b:* 29.4.1840, Old Alresford, Hants. *d:* 12.1.1915, Winchester. Attacking lower order

right-hand batsman, right-hand round-arm bowler. *Team* Hampshire (1875–81, 6 matches).
Career batting
6–11–1–81–51*–8.10–0–*ct* 0
Bowling 52–5–10.40–0–0–3/28

Parkar, Ghulam Ahmed Hassan Mohammad
Cricketer. *b:* 25.10.1955, Kaluste, India. Brother of Z.A.H.M. (Bombay). Opening right-hand batsman. *Team* Bombay (1978/9 to 1982/3). *Tour* India to England 1982. *Test* India (1982, 1 match).
Career batting
44–72–7–2640–156–40.61–8–*ct* 23–*st* 1
Bowling 62–2–31.00–0–0–1/5
Test batting
1–2–0–7–6–3.50–0–*ct* 1
He hit 433 runs, av 36.08, on the 1982 tour to England and played in one Test.

Parke, Elliot Anderson
Amateur. *b:* 19.7.1850, Belgravia, London. *d:* 22.6.1923, South Kensington, London. Middle order right-hand batsman, right-hand fast round-arm bowler, deep field. *Sch* Harrow. *Team* Kent (1874, 1 match).
Career batting
8–13–2–110–47–10.00–0–*ct* 4
Bowling 33–1–33.00–0–0–1/30
He did not appear in any first-class matches whilst at Oxford. Much of his cricket was for MCC and his final first-class match was for that Club in 1884.

Parke, Walter Evelyn
Amateur. *b:* 27.7.1891, Moreton Heath, Dorset. *d:* 13.10.1914, Hazebrouck, France. Middle order left-hand batsman. *Sch* Winchester. *Team* Army (1914).
Career batting
1–2–0–18–11–9.00–0–*ct* 1
He played for Dorset.

Parker, Cyril Brien Dennis
Amateur. *b: circa* 1900, Ireland. *d:* December 1962, Ireland. Right-hand batsman. *Team* Dublin U (1922).
Career batting
1–2–0–42–29–21.00–0–*ct* 0

Parker, Charles Warrington Leonard
Professional. *b:* 14.10.1882, Prestbury, Gloucs. *d:* 11.7.1959, Cranleigh, Surrey. Lower order right-hand batsman, slow left-arm bowler. *Team* Gloucestershire (1903–35, 602 matches). *Tour* Joel to South Africa 1924/5. *Test* England (1921, 1 match).
Career batting
635–954–195–7951–82–10.47–0–*ct* 248
Bowling 63817–3278–19.46–277–91–10/79
Test batting
1–1–1–3–3*–no av–0–*ct* 0
Bowling 32–2–16.00–0–0–2/32
He took 100 wickets in a season sixteen times, going on to 200 five times (best 222, av 14.91, in 1925). His best bowling in an innings was 10 for 79 for Gloucs v Somerset at Bristol in 1920; in addition he took nine wickets in an innings on eight other occasions. For Gloucs v Yorkshire at Bristol in 1922 (his benefit match) he hit the stumps with five consecutive deliveries – unfortunately the second was a no-ball. He was also an excellent golfer.

Parker, Frederick Anthony Vivian
Amateur. *b:* 11.2.1913, London. Son of W. M. (Army). Opening or middle order right-hand batsman, right-arm medium pace bowler. *Sch* Winchester. *Team* Hampshire (1946, 2 matches).
Career batting
5–9–0–147–116–16.33–1–*ct* 2
He also played for Devonshire.

Parker, George Macdonald
Professional. *b:* 27.5.1899, Cape Town, South Africa. *d:* 1.5.1969, Thredbo, New South Wales, Australia. Lower order right-hand batsman, right-arm fast bowler. *Team* South Africa (1924). *Tour* South Africa to England 1924. *Tests* South Africa (1924, 2 matches).
Career batting
3–4–2–3–2*–1.50–0–*ct* 0
Bowling 307–12–25.58–1–0–6/152
Test batting
2–4–2–3–2*–1.50–0–*ct* 0
Bowling 273–8–34.12–1–0–6/152
A professional in the Bradford League he was co-opted into the 1924 team for two Tests only, and one other first-class game. He never appeared in first-class matches in South Africa.

Parker, Grahame Wilshaw
Amateur. *b:* 11.2.1912, Gloucester. Sound opening right-hand batsman, bowler, excellent field. *Teams* Gloucestershire (1932–50, 70 matches); Cambridge U (1934–35, blue both years).
Career batting
89–147–12–2956–210–21.90–5–*ct* 73
Bowling 2291–57–40.19–2–0–5/57
He hit 210 for Gloucs v Kent at Dover in 1937. He was Secretary-Manager of Gloucs CCC until 1976. He also played for Devon. A noted rugby footballer, he appeared as full back for Cambridge and England.

Parker, Irvine Theodore
Amateur. *b:* 26.3.1890, Newton-on-Ayr, Ayrshire, Scotland. *d:* 14.5.1961, Kilmarnock, Scotland. Right-hand batsman. *Team* Scotland (1920–26).
Career batting
2–2–0–62–62–31.00–0–*ct* 1

Parker, J. E.
Amateur. *b:* 2.7.1872. Tail end batsman, slow bowler. *Team* British Guiana (1905/6 to 1909/10). *Tour* West Indies to England 1906.
Career batting
8–15–1–61–15–4.35–0–*ct* 4
Bowling 281–5–56.20–0–0–2/28
He played in only five first-class matches on the 1906 visit to England, achieving very little.

Parker, John Frederick
Professional. *b:* 23.4.1913, Battersea, London. *d:* 26.1.1983, Bromley, Kent. Attacking middle order right-hand batsman, right-arm medium pace bowler, good slip field. *Team* Surrey (1932–52, 334 matches). *Tour* Selected to go with MCC to India 1939/40 (tour abandoned due to outbreak of war).
Career batting
340–523–71–14272–255–31.57–20–*ct* 330
Bowling 15677–543–28.87–8–0–6/34
He hit 1,000 runs in a season nine times (best 1,789, av 40.65 in 1949). Both his double centuries were for Surrey, the highest being 255 v New Zealanders at the Oval in 1949.

Parker, John Morton
Cricketer. *b:* 21.2.1951, Dannevirke, Hawke's Bay, New Zealand. Brother of N. M. (New Zealand) and K. J. (Auckland). Determined opening or middle order right-hand batsman, leg break and googly bowler, occasional wicket-keeper, good field. *Teams* Worcestershire (1971–75, 61 matches); Northern Districts (1972/3 to 1982/3). *Tours* New Zealand to England 1973, 1978, to Australia 1973/4, 1980/1, to India and Pakistan 1976/7. *Tests* New Zealand (1972/3 to 1980/1, 36 matches).
Career batting
198–345–37–10748–195–34.89–20–*ct* 171–*st* 5
Bowling 645–14–46.02–0–0–3/26
Test batting
36–63–2–1498–121–24.55–3–*ct* 30
Bowling 24–1–24.00–0–0–1/24
He hit 1,000 runs in a season twice (best 1,182, av 32.83, in 1973). On his 1973 tour to England he was very disappointing; playing in all three Tests he scored only 23 runs, av 4.60. On the 1978 tour he showed little improvement in the Tests, but hit 549 runs, av 36.60, in all first-class matches. He captained New Zealand in one Test v Pakistan in 1976/7.

Parker, John Palmer
Amateur. *b:* 29.11.1902, Portsmouth, Hants. Middle order right-hand batsman. *Team* Hampshire (1926–33, 44 matches). *Tour* Tennyson to Jamaica (1926/7).
Career batting
47–72–8–1117–156–17.45–1–*ct* 22
Bowling 258–6–43.00–0–0–2/14

Parker, Paul William Giles
Cricketer. *b:* 15.1.1956, Bulawayo, Rhodesia. Middle order right-hand batsman, right-arm medium pace or leg break bowler, brilliant field. *Teams* Cambridge U (1976–78, blue all three years); Sussex (1976–83, 137 matches). Natal (1980/1). *Test* England (1981, 1 match).
Career batting
178–303–44–8559–215–33.04–18–*ct* 109
Bowling 501–8–62.62–0–0–2/23
Test batting
1–2–0–13–13–6.50–0–*ct* 0
He hit 1,000 runs in a season five times (best 1,412, av 45.54, in 1981). His highest innings is 215 for Cambridge U v Essex at Fenner's in 1976. A good rugby footballer, he was chosen for Cambridge but had to withdraw due to injury.

Parker, Roland John
Amateur. *b:* 19.7.1925, Pudsey, Yorkshire. Middle order right-hand batsman, off break bowler. *Sch* Uppingham. *Team* Combined Services (1947).
Career batting
2–3–0–36–18–12.00–0–*ct* 0

Parker, W.
Amateur. Middle order batsman, opening bowler. *Team* Lancashire (1904, 2 matches).
Career batting
2–3–0–66–40–22.00–0–*ct* 0
Bowling 175–4–43.75–0–0–2/47

Parker, William Mackworth
Amateur. *b:* 1.9.1886, Belgaum, India. *d:* 30.7.1915, Hooge, Belgium. He was killed in action. Father of F. A. V. (Hants). Stylish middle order right-hand batsman, bowler. *Sch* Winchester. *Teams* MCC (1913); Army (1914).
Career batting
2–4–0–34–11–8.50–0–*ct* 2
Bowling 81–4–20.25–0–0–3/64
From 1906 when he was in the Sandhurst XI he was considered one of the best military batsmen.

Parkes, Howard Roderick
Amateur. *b:* 31.5.1877, Aston, Birmingham. *d:* 28.5.1920, Studland, Dorset. Stylish opening or middle order right-hand batsman, excellent cover point. *Sch* Uppingham. *Teams* Warwickshire (1898, 1 match); London County (1900).
Career batting
7–10–0–79–21–7.90–0–*ct* 3
He appeared in the Freshmen's and Seniors' Matches at Oxford, but no first-class games.

Parkes, John Leonard
Amateur. *b:* 23.6.1938, Leamington Spa, Warwickshire. Lower order left-hand batsman, leg break bowler. *Sch* Warwick. *Team* Free Foresters (1960).
Career batting
1–2–0–0–0–0.00–0–*ct* 0
Bowling 61–1–61.00–0–0–1/61

Parkhouse, Richard John
Amateur. *b:* 1910, Clydach, Neath, Glamorgan. Middle order right-hand batsman. *Team* Glamorgan (1939, 2 matches).
Career batting
2–1–0–0–0–0.00–0–*ct* 0

Parkhouse, William Gilbert Anthony
Professional. *b:* 12.10.1925, Swansea. Stylish opening right-hand batsman, right arm medium pace bowler, good close field. *Sch* Wycliffe. *Team* Glamorgan (1948–64, 435 matches). *Tour* MCC to Australia and New Zealand 1950/1. *Tests* England (1950–59, 7 matches).
Career batting
455–791–49–23508–201–31.68–32–*ct* 324
Bowling 125–2–62.50–0–0–1/4
Test batting
7–13–0–373–78–28.69–0–*ct* 3
He hit 1,000 runs in a season fifteen times, going on to 2,000 once : 2,243, av 48.76, in 1959. His only double century was 201 for Glamorgan v Kent at Swansea in 1956.

Parkin, Cecil Harry
Professional. *b:* 18.2.1886, Eaglescliffe, Co Durham. *d:* 15.6.1943, Elizabeth St, Manchester. Father of R. H. (Lancashire). Useful lower order right-hand batsman, right-arm slow bowler, off break and leg break. *Teams* Yorkshire (1906, 1 match); Lancashire (1914–26, 157 matches). *Tour* MCC to Australia 1920/1. *Tests* England (1920/1 to 1924, 10 matches).
Career batting
197–239–33–2425–57–11.77–0–*ct* 126
Bowling 18434–1048–17.58–93–27–9/32
Test batting
10–16–3–160–36–12.30–0–*ct* 3
Bowling 1128–32–35.25–2–0–5/38
He took 100 wickets in a season four times, going on to 200 twice (best 209, av 16.94, in 1923). His best bowling in an innings was 9 for 32 for Lancashire v Leicestershire at Ashby-de-la-Zouch in 1924. Following a single appearance for Yorkshire it was discovered that he was not qualified to represent the County, being born 20 yards over the border. Most of his cricket was in the Leagues and his relatively brief career with Lancashire was brought to a premature close due to a disagreement with the Committee. He played also for Durham. His non-stop humour earned him the title of 'Cricket's comedian'.

Parkin, John Maurice
Cricketer. *b:* 16.10.1944, Kimberley, Notts. Middle order right-hand batsman. *Team* Nottinghamshire (1966–68, 28 matches).
Career batting
28–39–8–349–53–11.25–0–*ct* 9

Parkin, Reginald Henry
Professional. *b:* 25.7.1909, Tunstall, Staffordshire. Son of C. H. (Lancashire and Yorkshire). Middle order right-hand batsman, off break bowler. *Team* Lancashire (1931–39, 20 matches).
Career batting
21–19–4–286–60–19.06–0–*ct* 4
Bowling 880–23–38.26–0–0–3/52
He also played for Staffordshire.

Parkins, William Richard
Amateur. *b:* 20.8.1925, Glenfield, Leicester. *d:* 1.11.1969, Leicester. Aggressive middle order right-hand batsman. *Sch* Wyggeston GS. *Team* Leicestershire (1950, 5 matches).
Career batting
5–10–0–125–39–12.50–0–*ct* 2

Parkinson, Ernest William
Amateur. *b:* 28.4.1894, Sileby, Leics. *d:* 14.4.1978, Leicester. Lower order right-hand batsman, useful bowler. *Team* Leicestershire (1920, 2 matches).
Career batting
2–4–0–26–18–6.50–0–*ct* 0
Bowling 100–0

Parkinson, Herbert Black
Professional. *b:* 11.9.1892, Barrow-in-Furness, Lancashire. *d:* 27.4.1947, Barrow-in-Furness, Lancashire. Tail end right-hand batsman, wicket-

keeper. *Team* Lancashire (1922–23, 15 matches).
Career batting
15–18–5–34–8–2.61–0–*ct* 14–*st* 3

Parkinson, Leonard Wright
Professional. *b:* 15.9.1908, Salford, Manchester. *d:* 16.3.1969, Manchester. Attacking middle or lower order right-hand batsman, leg break bowler, good field. *Team* Lancashire (1932–36, 88 matches).
Career batting
88–112–13–2132–93–21.55–0–*ct* 45
Bowling 5654–192–29.44–7–0–6/112

He also played for Cheshire.

Parks, Henry William
Professional. *b:* 18.7.1906, Haywards Heath, Sussex. *d:* 7.5.1984, Taunton, Somerset. Brother of J. H. (Sussex), uncle of J. M. (Sussex and Somerset). Sound opening or middle order right-hand batsman, right-arm medium bowler. *Team* Sussex (1926–48, 480 matches). *Tour* Commonwealth to India 1949/50 (1 match).
Career batting
483–745–98–21725–200*–33.57–42–*ct* 196
Bowling 705–13–54.23–0–0–2/37

He hit 1,000 runs in a season fourteen times going on to 2,000 once : 2,122, av 38.58, in 1947. His only double century was 200* for Sussex v Essex at Chelmsford in 1931.

Parks, James Horace
Professional. *b:* 12.5.1903, Haywards Heath, Sussex. *d:* 21.11.1980, Cuckfield, Sussex. Brother of H. W. (Sussex), father of J. M. (Sussex and Somerset), grandfather of R. J. (Hants). Sound opening or middle order right-hand batsman, right-arm slow medium bowler. *Teams* Sussex (1924–39, 434 matches); Canterbury (1946/7). *Tours* MCC to Australia and New Zealand 1935/6; Tennyson to India 1937/8. *Test* England (1937, 1 match).
Career batting
468–758–63–21369–197–30.74–41–*ct* 325
Bowling 22789–852–26.74–24–1–7/17
Test batting
1–2–0–29–22–14.50–0–*ct* 0
Bowling 36–3–12.00–0–0–2/26

He hit 1,000 runs in a season twelve times and in the only summer he exceeded 2,000, actually reached 3,003, av 50.89. In that same season, 1937, he took 101 wickets, av 25.83, thus achieving an unique 'double'. He reached 100 wickets in one other season, 103, av 19.57, in 1935. From 1953 to 1957 he was coach to Nottinghamshire CCC.

Parks, James Michael
Professional. *b:* 21.10.1931, Haywards Heath, Sussex. Son of J. H. (Sussex), father of R. J. (Hants), nephew of H. W. (Sussex). Attacking middle order right-hand batsman, leg break bowler, wicket-keeper, good cover point. *Teams* Sussex (1949–72, 563 matches); Somerset (1973–76, 27 matches). *Tours* MCC to Pakistan 1955/6, to South Africa 1956/7, 1964/5, to West Indies 1959/60, 1967/8, to New Zealand 1960/1, to India 1963/4, to Australia and New Zealand 1965/6. *Tests* England (1954 to 1967/8, 46 matches).
Career batting
739–1227–172–36673–205*–34.76–51–*ct* 1088–*st* 93
Bowling 2235–51–43.82–0–0–3/23
Test batting
46–68–7–1962–108*–32.16–2–*ct* 103–*st* 11
Bowling 51–1–51.00–0–0–1/43

Although remembered as a batsman-wicket-keeper, Parks played County cricket for almost ten years as a batsman and brilliant cover point and had been capped by England and had travelled on two MCC tours before he was made the regular Sussex wicket-keeper midway through the 1958 season. His first full year behind the stumps – 1959 – was one of continuous success. He hit 2,313 runs – one run less than in 1955, but with an average of 51.40 compared with 42.07 – and claimed 93 victims behind the wicket. Joining the 1959/60 MCC side in the West Indies following the illness of P. B. H. May, he was most successful and it looked as if his future as England's wicket-keeper was secure, but illness and lack of form meant that over the next few seasons he shared the Test wicket-keeping place with J. T. Murray.

In all he hit 1,000 runs in a season twenty times, going on to 2,000 three times. His only double century was 205* for Sussex v Somerset at Hove in 1955.

He was made captain of Sussex in 1967, but resigned midway through the following summer and at the close of the 1972 season left Sussex for Somerset under controversial circumstances.

Parks, Robert James
Cricketer. *b:* 15.6.1959, Cuckfield, Sussex. Grandson of J. H. (Sussex) and son of J. M. (Sussex and Somerset). Lower order right-hand batsman, wicket-keeper. *Team* Hampshire (1980–83, 80 matches).
Career batting
80–87–18–1093–64*–15.84–0–*ct* 182–*st* 23
Bowling 0–0

Parnaby, Alan Herring
Amateur. *b:* 2.9.1916, Durham. *d:* 25.11.1974, Camberley, Surrey. Attractive opening right-

hand batsman. *Teams* Minor Counties (1939); Combined Services (1949–53).
Career batting
8–16–0–433–101–27.06–1–*ct* 3
Bowling 10–0
His County cricket was for Durham commencing 1936 and he was for some years one of the leading cricketers in the Army side.

Parnell, William Henry
Amateur. *b:* 7.10.1837, Marylebone, London. *d:* 4.5.1879, Westminster, London. Attacking lower order right-hand batsman, right-hand fast round-arm bowler. *Sch* Rugby. *Team* MCC (1859–70).
Career batting
17–28–2–144–26–5.53–0–*ct* 10
Bowling 199–13–15.30–1–0–5/42
He was elected to the Committee of MCC in 1874.

Parnham, John Thomas
Professional. *b:* 6.9.1856, Bottesford, Leics. *d:* 18.2.1908, Church, Lancashire. Lower order batsman, slow left-arm bowler, slip field. *Team* MCC (1883–89).
Career batting
8–11–2–178–90*–19.77–0–*ct* 3
Bowling 294–16–18.37–2–1–7/25
His first-class debut was for the United Eleven v Australians in 1882 when he created a sensation by taking 12 wickets for 126 in the match. In the North v South match in 1886 he added 157 runs for the last wicket with J. White. His County cricket was for Leicestershire 1881 to 1886 (pre-first-class); he also appeared for Caernarvonshire in 1882. After retiring he became a County umpire.

Parr, Butler
Professional. *b:* 9.11.1810, Martin, Lincolnshire. *d:* 16.3.1872, Radcliffe-on-Trent, Notts. Father-in-law of Richard Daft. Middle order right-hand batman, wicket-keeper. *Team* Nottinghamshire (1835–54, 18 matches).
Career batting
23–40–2–418–61*–11.00–0–*ct* 14–*st* 6
He was on the Nottinghamshire CCC Committee from 1865 until his death.

Parr, Francis D.
Professional. *b:* 1.6.1928, Wallasey, Cheshire. Lower order left-hand batsman, wicket-keeper. *Team* Lancashire (1951–54, 48 matches).
Career batting
49–53–11–507–42–12.07–0–*ct* 71–*st* 20

Parr, George
Professional. *b:* 22.5.1826, Radcliffe-on-Trent, Notts. *d:* 23.6.1891, Radcliffe-on-Trent, Notts. Brother of H. J. (Notts) and Samuel (Notts). Excellent middle order right-hand batsman, right-hand under-arm lob bowler, good field. *Teams* Kent (1854–58, 3 matches); Nottinghamshire (1845–70, 54 matches); Surrey (1852, 1 match); Sussex (1853–54, 2 matches). *Tours* Parr to North America 1859 (not first-class), to Australia and New Zealand 1863/4.
Career batting
207–358–30–6626–130–20.20–1–*ct* 126
Bowling 445–29–15.34–1–0–6/42
About 1860 he was regarded as the best batsman in England. From 1856 to 1870 he captained Nottinghamshire and also was captain and manager of the All England Eleven. He led the pioneering touring team to North America and the second touring team to Australia, having declined to go on the first. His first-class debut was for Players of Notts in 1844.

Parr, Henry Bingham
Amateur. *b:* 6.6.1845, Grappenhall Hayes, Lancashire. *d:* 24.3.1930, Liverpool. Stubborn middle order right-hand batsman, bowler, deep field. *Sch* Cheltenham. *Team* Lancashire (1872–76, 10 matches).
Career batting
11–16–0–180–61–11.25–0–*ct* 4
He also played for Cheshire.

Parr, Henry John
Professional. *b:* 7.1.1838, Radcliffe-on-Trent, Notts. *d:* 24.4.1863, Radcliffe-on-Trent, Notts. Brother of George (Notts) and Samuel (Notts). Middle order right-hand batsman. *Team* Nottinghamshire (1856–58, 3 matches).
Career batting
3–6–1–55–13–11.00–0–*ct* 2

Parr, Percivall Chase
Amateur. *b:* 2.12.1859, Belgaum, India. *d:* 3.9.1912, Bromley, Kent. Lower order right-hand batsman, right-arm fast bowler. *Sch* Winchester. *Team* Gentlemen of Kent (1880).
Career batting
1–1–1–0–0*–no av–0–*ct* 0
Bowling 71–1–71.00–0–0–1/71

Parr, Samuel
Professional. *b:* 2.5.1820, Radcliffe-on-Trent, Notts. *d:* 12.5.1873, Nottingham. Brother of George (Notts) and H. J. (Notts). Middle order right-hand batsman, good deep field. *Team* Nottinghamshire (1840–55, 17 matches).

Career batting
25–44–4–533–53–13.32–0–*ct* 16
Bowling 18–1–18.00–0–0–1/18

He achieved notoriety amongst his fellow cricketers due to his practical jokes.

Parratt, John
Professional. *b:* 24.3.1859, Dewsbury, Yorkshire. *d:* 6.5.1905, Morley, Yorkshire. Lower order batsman, useful bowler. *Team* Yorkshire (1888–90, 2 matches).
Career batting
2–2–0–11–11–5.50–0–*ct* 4
Bowling 75–1–75.00–0–0–1/12

Parrington, William Ferguson
Amateur. *b:* 1.11.1889, Sunderland, Co Durham. *d:* 7.5.1980, Northallerton, Yorkshire. Middle order right-hand batsman, right-arm medium pace bowler. *Sch* Rossall. *Team* Derbyshire (1926, 6 matches).
Career batting
6–11–1–148–47–14.80–0–*ct* 1

He also played for Durham.

Parris, Frederick
Professional. *b:* 20.9.1867, Ringmer, Sussex. *d:* 17.1.1941, Cuckfield, Sussex. Lower order left-hand batsman, right-arm slow medium bowler. *Team* Sussex (1890–1901, 105 matches).
Career batting
105–177–24–2222–77–14.52–0–*ct* 59
Bowling 7539–291–25.56–20–5–8/28

After retiring he was for many years on the first-class umpires' list.

Parry, Cecil Wynne
Amateur. *b:* 6.8.1866, Clifton, Bristol. *d:* 4.1.1901, York. Stylish middle order right-hand batsman, right-arm medium pace bowler. *Sch* Charterhouse. *Team* Cambridge U (1889).
Career batting
1–2–0–16–9–8.00–0–*ct* 0
Bowling 25–0

He played for Buckinghamshire.

Parry, Donald Morris
Amateur. *b:* 8.2.1911, Hatch End, Middlesex. Middle order right-hand batsman, right-arm medium pace bowler. *Sch* Merchant Taylors. *Team* Cambridge U (1931–32, blue 1931).
Career batting
17–31–5–574–87*–22.09–0–*ct* 6

Parry, Derick Ricaldo
Cricketer. *b:* 22.12.1954, Nevis, Leeward Islands. Middle order right-hand batsman, off break bowler. *Team* Leeward Islands (1975/6 to 1981/2). *Tours* West Indies to India and Sri Lanka 1978/9, to Australia and New Zealand 1979/80, to England 1980, to Pakistan 1980/1; West Indies XI to South Africa 1982/3. *Tests* West Indies (1977/8 to 1979/80, 12 matches).
Career batting
72–110–21–2345–96–26.34–0–*ct* 47
Bowling 6878–240–28.65–12–1–9/76
Test batting
12–20–3–381–65–22.41–0–*ct* 4
Bowling 936–23–40.69–1–0–5/15

He did not play in any Tests on the 1980 tour to England. His best innings analysis was 9 for 76 for Combined Islands v Jamaica at Kingston in 1979/80. He also played for Cambridgeshire.

Parry, Matthew Croose
Amateur. *b:* 11.12.1885, Birley, Herefordshire. *d:* 5.2.1931, Carrigrohane, Co Cork. Middle order right-hand batsman. *Teams* Warwickshire (1908–10, 2 matches); Ireland (1925).
Career batting
4–7–0–211–124–30.14–1–*ct* 2
Bowling 71–2–35.50–0–0–2/31

He also played for Herefordshire.

Parslow, Leonard Frederick
Amateur. *b:* 11.11.1909, London. *d:* 6.8.1963, Rochford, Essex. Middle order right-hand batsman. *Team* Essex (1946, 1 match).
Career batting
1–2–0–9–5–4.50–0–*ct* 0

Parsons, Arthur Brian Douglas
Amateur, turned professional on joining Surrey staff in 1958. *b:* 20.9.1933, Guildford, Surrey. Steady opening or middle order right-hand batsman, leg break bowler. *Sch* Brighton. *Teams* Cambridge U (1954–55, blue both years); Surrey (1958–63, 119 matches).
Career batting
152–263–22–6376–125–26.45–3–*ct* 69
Bowling 23–0

He hit 1,000 runs in a season three times (best 1,415, av 32.15, in 1961).

Parsons, Austin Edward Werring
Cricketer. *b:* 9.1.1949, Glasgow, Scotland. Sound middle order right-hand batsman, leg break bowler. *Teams* Auckland (1973/4 to 1982/3); Sussex (1974–75, 21 matches).
Career batting
82–156–10–3847–141–26.34–4–*ct* 44
Bowling 183–2–91.50–0–0–1/26

His first-class debut was for New Zealand Under 23s XI in 1971/2. In 1975 for Sussex he hit 977 runs, av 25.71.

Parsons, David Joseph
Cricketer. *b:* 28.10.1954, Accrington, Lancashire. Lower order right hand batsman, left-arm medium fast bowler. *Team* Minor Counties (1981).
Career batting
1–1–0–1–1–1.00–0–*ct* 0
Bowling 53–1–53.00–0–0–1/53
His County cricket is for Cumberland, making his debut in 1981.

Parsons, Gordon James
Cricketer. *b:* 17.10.1959, Slough, Bucks. Lower order left-hand batsman, right-arm medium pace bowler. *Team* Leicestershire (1978–83, 78 matches). *Tour* Leics to Zimbabwe 1980/1.
Career batting
78–93–22–1019–56–14.35–0–*ct* 25
Bowling 5340–164–32.56–2–0–5/25

Parsons, Canon John Henry
Professional to 1914; amateur 1919 to 1923; professional 1924 to 1928; then amateur from 1929 onwards. *b:* 30.5.1890, Oxford. *d:* 2.2.1981, Plymouth, Devon. Attacking middle order right-hand batsman, right-arm medium pace bowler, slip field. *Teams* Warwickshire (1910–34, 312 matches); Europeans (1919/20 to 1921/2). *Tour* MCC to India, Burma and Ceylon 1926/7.
Career batting
355–555–52–17969–225–35.72–38–*ct* 260
Bowling 2405–83–28.97–3–1–7/41
He hit 1,000 runs in a season in England ten times (best 1,700, av 50.00, in 1927). His only double century was 225 for Warwickshire v Glamorgan at Edgbaston in 1927. His final first-class match was for MCC in 1936. He also hit 1,000 runs in an Indian season.

Parsons, Walter Dyett
Professional. *b:* 1861, Southampton. *d:* 24.12.1939, East Wellow, Hants. Lower order batsman, useful bowler. *Team* Hampshire (1882, 2 matches).
Career batting
2–4–2–31–12*–15.50–0–*ct* 1
Bowling 72–1–72.00–0–0–1/23

Parthasarathi, Gopalaswami
Amateur. *b:* 7.7.1912, Madras, India. Middle order right-hand batsman, leg break and googly bowler. *Teams* Oxford U (1933–35); Madras (1936/7 to 1943/4); Indians (1929/30 to 1947/8).
Career batting
25–43–2–879–87–21.43–0–*ct* 17
Bowling 1473–62–23.75–2–1–6/49

Parton, John Wesley
Professional. *b:* 31.1.1863, Wellington, Shropshire. *d:* 30.1.1906, Rotherham, Yorkshire. Lower order batsman, useful bowler. *Team* Yorkshire (1889, 1 match).
Career batting
1–2–0–16–14–8.00–0–*ct* 0
Bowling 4–1–4.00–0–0–1/4
He also played for Shropshire.

Partridge, Brian John Macpherson
Cricketer. *b:* 21.1.1956, Haddington, East Lothian, Scotland. Tail end right-hand batsman, right-arm medium fast bowler. *Sch* Loretto. *Team* Oxford U (1977).
Career batting
4–6–4–5–4–2.50–0–*ct* 0
Bowling 170–4–42.50–0–0–2/38

Partridge, Cyril
Amateur. *b:* 1896, Wellingborough, Northants. *d:* 23.2.1945, Shillington, Bedfordshire. Middle order right-hand batsman. *Sch* Wellingborough. *Team* Northants (1921, 1 match).
Career batting
1–2–0–1–1–0.50–0–*ct* 0

Partridge, Martin David
Cricketer. *b:* 25.10.1954, Birdlip, Gloucs. Middle or lower order left-hand batsman, right-arm medium pace bowler. *Team* Gloucestershire (1976–80, 46 matches).
Career batting
46–66–21–1202–90–26.71–0–*ct* 16
Bowling 2076–41–50.63–1–0–5/29

Partridge, Norman Ernest
Amateur. *b:* 10.8.1900, Great Barr, Staffs. *d:* 10.3.1982, Aberystwyth. Middle order right-hand batsman, right-arm medium fast bowler. *Sch* Malvern. *Teams* Warwickshire (1921–37, 100 matches); Cambridge U (1920, blue).
Career batting
112–164–18–2719–102–18.62–1–*ct* 109
Bowling 9047–393–23.02–19–2–7/66
An outstanding schoolboy cricketer, he was invited to play for the Gentlemen in 1919, his final summer at Malvern, but the school authorities would not grant permission.

Partridge, Reginald Joseph
Professional. *b:* 11.2.1912, Wollaston, Northants. Defensive opening or middle order right-hand batsman, right-arm medium, later off break or leg break bowler. *Team* Northants (1929–48, 277 matches).

Career batting
280–462–122–3922–70–11.47–0–*ct* 105
Bowling 19946–638–31.26–22–2–9/66

His best season was 1938 with 94 wickets, av 25.70, and his best bowling in an innings 9 for 66 for Northants v Warwickshire at Kettering in 1934.

Parvez Jamil Mir
Cricketer. *b:* 24.9.1953, Dacca, Pakistan. Middle order right-hand batsman, right-arm medium fast bowler. *Teams* Rawalpindi (1970/1); Lahore (1971/2 to 1982/3); Punjab (1972/3 to 1975/6); Universities (1973/4 to 1974/5); Derbyshire (1975, 1 match); Habib Bank (1975/6 to 1980/1); Glamorgan (1979, 1 match). *Tour* Pakistan to Sri Lanka 1975/6.
Career batting
71–122–13–3353–155–30.76–5–*ct* 61
Bowling 4266–164–26.01–9–1–6/31

He also played for Norfolk.

Parvin, Alfred William
Amateur. *b:* 1860, Southampton. *d:* 1916, Brighton, Sussex. Middle order batsman. *Sch* Ipswich. *Team* Hampshire (1885, 1 match).
Career batting
1–2–0–11–11–5.50–0–*ct* 1

Pascall, Victor S.
Amateur. *b:* 1886, Diego Martin, Trinidad. *d:* 7.7.1930, Port of Spain, Trinidad. Uncle of L. N. Constantine (West Indies), brother-in-law of L. S. Constantine (West Indies). Lower order left-hand batsman, slow left-arm bowler. *Team* Trinidad (1905/6 to 1926/7). *Tour* West Indies to England 1923.
Career batting
49–77–14–859–92–13.63–0–*ct* 31
Bowling 3435–171–20.08–6–1–6/26

In first-class matches on the 1923 tour he took 52 wickets, av 24.28. His final first-class match was a trial match in West Indies in 1927/8.

Pascoe, Charles Henry
Professional. *b:* 1877, Shoreditch, Middlesex. *d:* 26.1.1957, Walthamstow, Essex. Tail end batsman, slow left-arm bowler. *Team* Essex (1909, 1 match).
Career batting
1–1–1–3–3*–no av–0–*ct* 0
Bowling 16–0

Pascoe, Leonard Stephen
(formerly Durtanovich)
Cricketer. *b:* 13.2.1950, Bridgetown, Western Australia. Lower order right-hand batsman, right-arm fast bowler. *Team* New South Wales (1974/5 to 1982/3, 48 matches). *Tours* Australia to England 1977, 1980, to New Zealand 1981/2. *Tests* Australia (1977 to 1981/2, 14 matches).
Career batting
74–77–25–472–51*–9.07–0–*ct* 22
Bowling 7314–289–25.30–10–2–8/41
Test batting
14–19–9–106–30*–10.60–0–*ct* 2
Bowling 1668–64–26.06–1–0–5/59

On the 1977 tour he took 41 wickets, av 21.78, and played in three Tests. On the brief 1980 visit he took 17 wickets, av 26.17, and bowled well in the Centenary Test.

Pasqual, Sudath Prajiv
Cricketer. *b:* 15.10.1961, Colombo, Ceylon. Middle order left-hand batsman, right-arm medium pace bowler. *Team* Sri Lanka (1979). *Tour* Sri Lanka to England 1979.
Career batting
7–9–2–250–101*–35.71–1–*ct* 3
Bowling 144–2–72.00–0–0–1/22

His only first-class cricket was in England in 1979, when he proved a useful all-rounder.

Passey, Michael Francis William
Amateur. *b:* 6.6.1937, Crossway Green, Worcs. Lower order right-hand batsman, off break bowler. *Team* Worcestershire (1953, 1 match).
Career batting
1–1–0–1–1–1.00–0–*ct* 0
Bowling 57–1–57.00–0–0–1/57

Passmore, George
Professional. *b:* 1852, Plympton, Devon. *d:* 8.2.1935, Croston, Devon. Tail end batsman, wicket-keeper. *Team* Hampshire (1896, 1 match).
Career batting
1–1–0–0–0–0.00–*ct* 2–*st* 1

Pataudi, Nawab of, Iftikhar Ali Khan
Amateur. *b:* 16.3.1910, Pataudi, India. *d:* 5.1.1952, New Delhi, India. He died of a heart attack while playing polo. Father of Nawab of Pataudi (India, Sussex and England). Attractive middle order right-hand batsman. *Teams* Oxford U (1928–31, blue 1929, 1930 and 1931); Patiala (1931/2); Worcestershire (1932–38, 37 matches); Western India States (1943/4); Southern Punjab (1945/6). *Tours* MCC to Australia 1932/3; India to England 1946. *Tests* England (1932/3 to 1934, 3 matches); India (1946, 3 matches).
Career batting
127–204–24–8750–238*–48.61–29–*ct* 58
Bowling 529–15–35.26–1–0–6/111
Test batting
6–10–0–199–102–19.90–1–*ct* 0

He had three outstanding seasons in English first-class cricket. In 1934 he headed the first-class averages with 945 runs, av 78.75; in 1931 he came second with 1,454 runs, av 69.23, and 1933 was his most prolific season with 1,754 runs, av 48.72.

His 238* for Oxford U v Cambridge U at Lord's in 1931 was a new record for the University match; his other three double centuries were all for Worcestershire.

He captained the Indian touring team to England in 1946 and led the side in the three Tests.

Pataudi, Nawab of, Mansur Ali Khan
Amateur. *b:* 5.1.1941, Bhopal, India. Son of Nawab of Pataudi (Worcs and India). Attacking middle order right-hand batsman, right-arm medium pace bowler, good field. *Sch* Winchester. *Teams* Sussex (1957–70, 88 matches); Oxford U (1960–63, blue 1960 and 1963); Delhi (1960/1 to 1964/5); Hyderabad (1965/6 to 1975/6). *Tours* India to West Indies 1961/2, to England 1967, to Australia and New Zealand 1967/8, to East Africa 1967; Swanton to West Indies 1960/1; Rest of World to England 1968. *Tests* India (1961/2 to 1974/5, 46 matches).
Career batting
310–499–41–15425–203*–33.67–33–*ct* 208
Bowling 776–10–77.60–0–0–1/0
Test batting
46–83–3–2793–203*–34.91–6–*ct* 27
Bowling 88–1–88.00–0–0–1/10

He hit 1,000 runs in a season in England four times (best 1,290, av 32.25, in 1963) and three times overseas (best 1,416, av 59.00, in 1964/5). Both his double centuries were made in India, the highest being 203* for India v England at Delhi in 1963/4. He captained Sussex in 1966 and India in 40 Tests, including the 1967 tour of England. In 1961 he was seriously injured in a road accident, which damaged his eyesight and caused him to miss the 1961 University match, when he would have captained Oxford.

Patel, Ashok Sitaram
Cricketer. *b:* 23.9.1956, Nairobi, Kenya. Middle or lower order left-hand batsman, slow left-arm bowler. *Team* Middlesex (1978, 2 matches).
Career batting
2–3–1–56–25*–28.00–0–*ct* 1
Bowling 55–2–27.50–0–0–2/55

He also played for Durham.

Patel, Brijesh Pursuram
Cricketer. *b:* 24.11.1952, Baroda, India. Nephew of B. R., K. R., M. R., cousin of Y. B. (all Mysore). Stylish middle order right-hand batsman, off break bowler. *Teams* Mysore/Karnataka (1969/70 to 1982/3). *Tours* India to England 1974, 1979, to West Indies 1975/6, to New Zealand 1975/6, to Sri Lanka 1973/4, to Australia 1977/8. *Tests* India (1974 to 1977/8, 21 matches).
Career batting
173–264–37–9763–216–43.00–29–*ct* 80
Bowling 215–7–30.71–0–0–1/0
Test batting
21–38–5–972–115*–29.45–1–*ct* 17

He appeared in two Tests on the 1974 tour but none in 1979, and his record in England was a modest one. His highest score was 216 for Karnataka v Baroda at Bangalore in 1978/9. He hit 1,000 runs in a season in India four times.

Patel, Dipak Narshibhai
Cricketer. *b:* 25.10.1958, Nairobi, Kenya. Middle order right-hand batsman, off break bowler. *Team* Worcestershire (1976–83, 161 matches). *Tour* Robins to New Zealand 1979/80.
Career batting
163–254–18–6515–138–27.60–12–*ct* 101
Bowling 8704–239–36.41–10–0–7/46

He emigrated to England in 1967. He hit 1,000 runs in a season three times (best 1,615, av 38.45, in 1983).

Paterson, Arthur William Sibbald
Amateur. *b:* 28.2.1878, Weston-super-Mare, Somerset. *d:* 13.11.1937, Burnham, Somerset. Middle order batsman. *Sch* Malvern. *Team* Somerset (1903, 2 matches).
Career batting
2–3–0–38–19–12.66–0–*ct* 1

Paterson, Charles Strathern
Amateur. *b:* 18.11.1882, Edinburgh, Scotland. *d:* 23.7.1973, Edinburgh, Scotland. Right-hand batsman, right-arm medium pace bowler. *Team* Scotland (1913–27).
Career batting
7–10–3–188–49–26.85–0–*ct* 2
Bowling 244–10–24.40–0–0–4/33

Paterson, Joseph
Amateur. *b:* 27.12.1923, Coatbridge, Ayrshire, Scotland. Right-hand batsman, right-arm medium pace bowler. *Team* Scotland (1956).
Career batting
1–2–0–1–1–0.50–0–*ct* 0

Paterson, Robert Fraser Troutbeck
Amateur. *b:* 8.9.1916, Stansted, Essex. *d:* 29.5.1980, Edinburgh, Scotland. Middle order right-hand batsman, right-arm medium pace bowler, occasional wicket-keeper. *Sch* Brighton. *Team* Essex (1946, 25 matches).
Career batting
28–45–5–884–88–22.10–0–*ct* 16–*st* 3
Bowling 464–13–35.69–0–0–4/98

His final first-class match was for MCC in 1958. From 1947 to 1950 he was Secretary to Essex CCC.

Pathmanathan, Gajanand
Cricketer. *b:* 23.1.1954, Colombo, Ceylon. Hard hitting middle order right-hand batsman, leg break bowler. *Teams* Sri Lanka (1972/3 to 1978/9); Oxford U (1975–78, blue all four years); Cambridge U (1983, blue). *Tours* Sri Lanka to India 1972/3; to Pakistan 1973/4.
Career batting
44–77–3–1553–82–20.98–0–*ct* 35
Bowling 26–0

Patiala, Maharaja of, H. H. Bhupendrasingh Rajindersingh
Amateur. *b:* 12.10.1891, Patiala, India. *d:* 23.3.1938, Patiala, India. Father of Yuvraj (later Maharaja) of Patiala (India) and M. K. B. Singh (Cambridge U). Hard hitting middle order right-hand batsman, good field. *Teams* Hindus (1915/6 to 1921/2); Sikhs (1922/3 to 1924/5); Northern India (1926/7); Patiala (1931/2 to 1937/8); Southern Punjab (1933/4 to 1934/5). *Tours* India to England 1911; MCC to India 1926/7 (co-opted); Australia to India 1935/6 (co-opted).
Career batting
27–40–3–643–83–17.37–0–*ct* 4
Bowling 60–2–30.00–0–0–2/40

A very keen patron of cricket in India, poor health limited his own participation in first-class matches. He was President of the Cricket Club of India at the time of his death.

Patil, Sandeep Madhusudan
Cricketer. *b:* 18.8.1956, Bombay, India. Son of M. S. (Bombay). Middle order right hand batsman, right-arm medium pace bowler. *Team* Bombay (1976/7 to 1982/3). *Tours* India to Australia and New Zealand 1980/1, to England 1982, to Pakistan 1982/3; Wadekar to Sri Lanka 1975/6. *Tests* India (1979/80 to 1982/3, 20 matches).
Career batting
64–99–7–3806–210–41.37–10–*ct* 32
Bowling 1277–34–37.55–0–0–4/58
Test batting
20–33–4–1254–174–43.24–3–*ct* 8
Bowling 238–9–26.44–0–0–2/28

His highest score is 210 for Bombay v Saurashtra at Bombay in 1979/80.

Paton, J.
Amateur. Lower order batsman, good bowler. *Team* Scotland (1914).
Career batting
1–2–0–2–2–1.00–0–*ct* 1
Bowling 88–5–17.60–0–0–4/48

Patten, Mark
Amateur. *b:* 28.7.1901, Edinburgh, Scotland. Lower order right-hand batsman, wicket-keeper. *Sch* Winchester. *Teams* Oxford U (1922–23, blue both years); Scotland (1922–25).
Career batting
27–41–7–407–58–11.97–0–*ct* 36–*st* 3

His final first-class match was for Free Foresters in 1929.

Pattenden, Edward Peter
Professional. *b:* 31.10.1842, Brighton, Sussex. *d:* 3.6.1879, Brighton, Sussex. Lower order right-hand batsman, useful bowler. *Team* Sussex (1874–75, 4 matches).
Career batting
4–5–1–6–3*–1.50–0–*ct* 1
Bowling 33–0

Patterson, George Stuart
Amateur. *b:* 10.10.1868, Philadelphia, USA. *d:* 7.5.1943, Philadelphia, USA. Stylish opening right-hand batsman, right-arm medium pace bowler. *Sch* Haverford College. *Team* Philadelphia (1885–97). *Tours* Philadelphia to England 1889 (not first-class), 1897.
Career batting
25–41–4–1205–162–32.56–2–*ct* 11
Bowling 1020–35–29.14–0–0–4/14

He was one of the principal batsmen in the United States and captained the 1897 team to England, when, despite injury, he came second in the batting averages.

Patterson, Rev John Irwin
Amateur. *b:* 11.3.1860, Sandhurst, Berkshire. *d:* 22.9.1943, Woking, Surrey. Brother of W. H. (Kent). Defensive lower order right-hand batsman, slow left-arm bowler, good field. *Sch* Chatham House School. *Teams* Kent (1881–82, 6 matches); Oxford U (1882, blue).
Career batting
7–11–3–38–9–4.75–0–*ct* 7
Bowling 197–12–16.41–1–0–5/12

In a minor match for St Lawrence v Dover in 1880 he took seven wickets in seven consecutive balls.

Patterson, William Henry
Amateur. *b:* 11.3.1859, Sandhurst, Berkshire. *d:* 3.5.1946, Hove, Sussex. Brother of J. I. (Kent). Sound opening or middle order right-hand batsman, right-hand medium or slow round-arm bowler, good field, occasional wicket-keeper. *Sch*

Harrow. *Teams* Oxford U (1878–81, blue 1880–81); Kent (1880–1900, 152 matches).
Career batting
176–311–23–7570–181–26.28–10–*ct* 122
Bowling 1043–31–33.64–0–0–4/13

He was joint captain of Kent 1890 to 1893, but owing to his profession was unable to play regularly in County cricket. His final first-class match was for G. J. V. Weigall's XI in 1904. He was later President of Kent CCC and served on the MCC Committee.

Patterson, William Seeds
Amateur. *b:* 19.3.1854, Mossley Hill, Liverpool, Lancashire. *d:* 20.10.1939, Hook Heath, Woking, Surrey. Attractive middle order right-hand batsman, right-arm slow bowler. *Sch* Uppingham. *Teams* Cambridge U (1874–77, blue last three years); Lancashire (1874–82, 7 matches).
Career batting
39–63–5–1059–105*–18.25–1–*ct* 18
Bowling 2279–152+5–14.99–16–5–7/30

Patteson, Canon Charles
Amateur. *b:* 11.11.1891, Upper Norwood, London. *d:* 9.12.1957, Howden, Yorkshire. Opening right-hand batsman. *Sch* Marlborough. *Team* Cambridge U (1912).
Career batting
5–9–2–157–57–22.42–0–*ct* 5
Bowling 36–1–36.00–0–0–1/12

Pattisson, Hoel Carlos
Amateur. *b:* 5.9.1905, West Byfleet, Surrey. *d:* 10.7.1979, Rye Foreign, Sussex. Attacking middle order batsman. *Sch* Rugby. *Team* Free Foresters (1937).
Career batting
1–2–0–20–20–20.00–0–*ct* 0

Pattisson, Walter Badeley
Amateur. *b:* 27.8.1854, Witham, Essex. *d:* 6.11.1913, Beckenham, Kent. Middle order right-hand batsman, good deep field. *Sch* Tonbridge. *Team* Kent (1876–87, 12 matches).
Career batting
13–22–1–230–38–10.95–0–*ct* 6

He served on the Committee of Kent CCC for several years. A noted rugby footballer, he appeared as a three-quarter in some England trials.

Paul, Arthur George
Professional. *b:* 24.7.1864, Belfast. *d:* 14.1.1947, Didsbury, Lancashire. Middle order right-hand batsman, right-arm slow bowler, occasional wicket-keeper. *Sch* Victoria College, IOM. *Team* Lancashire (1889–1900, 95 matches).
Career batting
96–152–15–2796–177–21.72–4–*ct* 73–*st* 1
Bowling 146–2–73.00–0–0–1/7

After retiring from first-class cricket due to ill-health he became coach at Old Trafford. A good all-round sportsman, he toured Australia with the 1888 English rugby football team and as a soccer player kept goal for Blackburn Rovers.

Paul, Edmund Parris
Amateur. *b:* 1882, Taunton, Somerset. *d:* 26.4.1966, Taunton, Somerset. Lower order right-hand batsman, wicket-keeper. *Team* Somerset (1907–10, 4 matches).
Career batting
4–8–0–37–12–4.62–0–*ct* 2

Paul, James Hugh
Amateur. *b:* 10.2.1888. *d:* 27.2.1937, Earlswood, Surrey. Middle order right-hand batsman. *Sch* Malvern. *Teams* Leveson-Gower's XI (1934–35); Argentine (1926/7 to 1929/30). *Tour* South America to England 1932.
Career batting
9–15–0–272–39–18.13–0–*ct* 2
Bowling 315–9–35.00–0–0–2/23

Paul, Nigel Aldridge
Amateur. *b:* 31.3.1933, Esher, Surrey. Forcing middle order right-hand batsman, left-arm fast medium bowler. *Sch* Cranleigh. *Team* Warwickshire (1954–55, 4 matches).
Career batting
7–10–0–157–40–15.70–0–*ct* 6
Bowling 196–3–65.33–0–0–1/5

His final first-class match was for D. R. Jardine's XI in 1958.

Pauline, Duncan Brian
Cricketer. *b:* 15.12.1960, Aberdeen, Scotland. Middle order right-hand batsman, right-arm medium pace bowler. *Team* Surrey (1979–83, 26 matches).
Career batting
26–42–3–1044–115–26.76–1–*ct* 5
Bowling 22–0

Paull, Richard Kenyon
Cricketer. *b:* 20.2.1944, Bridgwater, Somerset. Middle order right-hand batsman, leg break bowler. *Sch* Millfield. *Teams* Cambridge U (1967, blue); Somerset (1963–64, 6 matches).
Career batting
13–20–1–257–37–13.52–0–*ct* 3
Bowling 104–1–104.00–0–0–1/12

Pauncefote, Bernard
Amateur. *b:* 28.6.1848, Cuddalore, India. *d:*

24.9.1882, Blackheath, Kent. Stylish middle order right-hand batsman, right-hand medium pace round-arm bowler, good deep field. *Sch* Rugby. *Teams* Oxford U (1868–71, blue all four years); Middlesex (1868–72, 8 matches).
Career batting
32–55–3–1141–123–21.94–2–*ct* 21
Bowling 322–18–17.88–1–0–5/43

He went to China in 1872 and then to Ceylon, where he was in business. His County career was therefore very brief.

Paver, Kenneth Edwin
Amateur. *b:* 4.10.1903, Dover, Kent. *d:* 20.11.1975, Ringwood, Hants. Middle order batsman. *Team* Hampshire (1925–26, 2 matches).
Career batting
2–4–0–52–26–13.00–0–*ct* 2

Paver, Roland George Lyall
Cricketer. *b:* 4.4.1950, Johannesburg, South Africa. Lower order right-hand batsman, wicket-keeper. *Team* Oxford U (1972–74, blue 1973–74).
Career batting
16–26–2–290–34–12.08–0–*ct* 33–*st* 5

Pavri, Dr Mehallasha Edulji
Amateur. *b:* 10.10.1866, Nausari, near Bombay, India. *d:* 19.4.1946, Bombay, India. Opening or middle order right-hand batsman, right-arm fast bowler. *Teams* Parsis (1892/3 to 1912/3); Middlesex (1895, 1 match). *Tour* Parsis to England 1888 (not first-class).
Career batting
26–39–1–589–69–15.50–0–*ct* 19
Bowling 891–44–20.25–2–0–6/36

He was most successful on the 1888 Parsi tour to England taking in all matches 170 wickets, and was all in all the greatest of the 19th century Parsi cricketers. Later he wrote an interesting book on Indian cricket.

Pavy, C. S.
Amateur. *Team* MCC (1882).
Career batting
1–1–0–2–2–2.00–0–*ct* 0

Pawle, John Hanbury
Amateur. *b:* 18.5.1915, Widford, Herts. Middle order right-hand batsman. *Sch* Harrow. *Teams* Cambridge U (1935–37, blue 1936–37); Essex (1935–38, 6 matches).
Career batting
34–59–4–1544–125–28.07–3–*ct* 14
Bowling 13–0

His final first-class match was for Free Foresters in 1947. He also played for Hertfordshire.

Pawley, Tom Edward
Amateur. *b:* 21.1.1859, Farningham, Kent. *d:* 3.8.1923, Canterbury, Kent. Middle order right-hand batsman, right-arm fast, later lob, bowler. *Sch* Tonbridge. *Team* Kent (1880–87, 4 matches).
Career batting
4–7–1–23–10–3.83–0–*ct* 1
Bowling 11–3–3.66–0–0–3/11

He was manager of the Kent team for many years and in 1903 acted in that capacity for the Kent tour to America, and in 1911/12 for the MCC tour to Australia. He died very suddenly whilst making arrangements for the 1923 Canterbury Cricket Festival.

Pawling, Sydney Southgate
Amateur. *b:* 6.2.1862, Wallingford, Berkshire. *d:* 23.12.1922, Eastbourne, Sussex. Lower order right-hand batsman, right-arm fast bowler. *Sch* Mill Hill. *Team* Middlesex (1894, 3 matches).
Career batting
3–4–1–5–3–1.66–0–*ct* 1
Bowling 219–9–24.33–1–0–5/60

He was a noted figure in North London Club cricket for many years. From 1919 to his death he was Hon Treasurer of Middlesex CCC.

Pawson, Arthur Clive
Amateur. *b:* 5.1.1882, Bramley, Leeds, Yorkshire. *d:* 14.8.1969, Nynehead, Wellington, Somerset. Brother of A. G. (Oxford U and Worcs), uncle of H. A. (Oxford U and Kent). Sound middle order right-hand batsman, good field. *Sch* Winchester. *Team* Oxford U (1903, blue).
Career batting
8–13–1–177–51–14.75–0–*ct* 5

Pawson, Albert Guy
Amateur. *b:* 30.5.1888, Bramley, Yorkshire. Brother of A. C. (Oxford U), father of H. A. (Oxford U and Kent). Lower order right-hand batsman, wicket-keeper. *Sch* Winchester. *Teams* Oxford U (1908–11, blue all four years); Worcestershire (1908, 1 match).
Career batting
28–50–13–448–41*–12.10–0–*ct* 30–*st* 16

Pawson, Henry Anthony
Amateur. *b:* 22.8.1921, Chertsey, Surrey. Son of A. G. (Worcs), nephew of A. C. (Oxford U). Stylish middle order right-hand batsman, off break bowler, good outfield. *Sch* Winchester. *Teams* Kent (1946–53, 43 matches); Oxford U (1947–48, blue both years).
Career batting
69–113–11–3807–150–37.32–7–*ct* 36
Bowling 280–7–40.00–0–0–2/26

He hit 1,000 runs in a season twice (best 1,312, av 38.58, in 1947). A good soccer player, he was awarded his blue and later played for Charlton Athletic. He was also noted in fishing circles.

Payn, Leslie William
Amateur. *b:* 6.5.1915, Umzinto, Natal, South Africa. Lower order right-hand batsman, left-arm slow medium bowler. *Team* Natal (1936/7 to 1952/3). *Tour* South Africa to England 1947.
Career batting
51–51–5–657–103–14.28–1–*ct* 30
Bowling 3893–151–25.78–4–2–8/89
He achieved very little on the 1947 tour and did not appear in the Tests.

Payne, Albert
Professional. *b:* 1885, Leicester. *d:* 7.5.1908, Leicester. He died of consumption. Tail end right-hand batsman, wicket-keeper. *Team* Leicestershire (1906–07, 5 matches).
Career batting
5–9–3–15–7*–2.50–0–*ct* 6–*st* 1

Payne, Rev Alfred
Amateur. *b:* 7.12.1831, Leicester. *d:* 25.6.1874, Westminster, London. Twin brother of A. F. (Oxford U). Lower order left-hand batsman, left-hand round-arm bowler. *Team* Oxford U (1852–56, blue 1852, 1854, 1855 and 1856).
Career batting
25–44–8–479–40–13.30–0–*ct* 17
Bowling 1024–84+27–12.19–8–1–7/42
His final first-class match was for Gentlemen in 1864. He played County cricket for Leicestershire (pre-first-class), Oxfordshire and Staffordshire.

Payne, Alfred
Professional. *b:* 28.4.1858, East Grinstead, Sussex. *d:* 23.7.1943, Uckfield, Sussex. Brother of William (Sussex), nephew of Charles, J. S. (Sussex and Kent) and Richard (Sussex). Sound, steady middle order right-hand batsman, wicket-keeper. *Team* Sussex (1880–86, 17 matches).
Career batting
18–34–4–275–42–9.16–0–*ct* 8–*st* 1
Bowling 18–0

Payne, Arnold Cyril
Amateur. *b:* 3.10.1897, Northampton. *d:* 13.2.1973, Northampton. Lower order right-hand batsman, wicket-keeper. *Sch* Wycliffe. *Team* Northants (1931–34, 3 matches).
Career batting
3–5–1–27–22*–6.75–0–*ct* 6–*st* 4

Payne, Rev Alfred Ernest
Amateur. *b:* 29.12.1849, Oswestry, Shropshire. *d:* 30.6.1927, Ruabon, Denbighshire. Middle order batsman. *Team* MCC (1883–84).
Career batting
8–15–1–75–16–5.35–0–*ct* 2
Bowling 2–0
He played for Shropshire.

Payne, Arthur Frederick
Amateur. *b:* 7.12.1831, Leicester. *d:* 23.6.1910, Brighton, Sussex. Twin brother of Alfred (Oxford U). Middle order right-hand batsman. *Team* Oxford U (1854–55, blue 1855).
Career batting
10–18–1–102–21–6.00–0–*ct* 5
His final first-class match was for MCC in 1867.

Payne, Alan Undy
Amateur. *b:* 28.1.1903, Witney, Oxon. *d:* 16.8.1977, Felsted, Essex. Middle order right-hand batsman, right-arm medium fast bowler, good field. *Sch* St Edmund's, Canterbury. *Team* Cambridge U (1925, blue).
Career batting
7–9–1–86–27*–10.75–0–*ct* 2
Bowling 63–1–63.00–0–0–1/36
His County cricket was for Buckinghamshire – he was awarded his blue at Cambridge on account of his fielding, a decision which was much criticised at the time.

Payne, Charles
Professional. *b:* 12.5.1832, East Grinstead, Sussex. *d:* 18.2.1909, Tonbridge, Kent. Brother of J. S. (Sussex and Kent) and Richard (Sussex), uncle of Alfred (Sussex) and William (Sussex). Fine middle order right-hand batsman, good close field. *Teams* Sussex (1857–70, 50 matches); Kent (1863–70, 26 matches).
Career batting
88–162–20–2702–137–19.02–2–*ct* 69
Bowling 223–7–31.85–0–0–3/13
His final first-class match was for the North in 1875. He also umpired in first-class matches.

Payne, Cecil Arthur Lynch
Amateur. *b:* 30.8.1885, Dacca, India. *d:* 21.3.1976, Vancouver, Canada. Cousin of M. W. (Middlesex). Opening or middle order right-hand batsman, right-arm medium pace bowler. *Sch* Charterhouse. *Teams* Middlesex (1905–09, 13 matches); Oxford U (1906–07, blue both years).
Career batting
29–49–0–1001–101–20.42–1–*ct* 10
Bowling 59–0
His first-class debut was for MCC v Derbyshire

at Lord's in 1905, when he hit 101. About 1910 he emigrated to Canada, thus ending his County cricket. He was a noted golfer and billiards player.

Payne, Christopher John
Cricketer. *b:* 30.12.1947, Hatfield, Herts. Middle order right-hand batsman, occasional wicket-keeper. *Team* Middlesex (1968–70, 5 matches).
Career batting
5–8–0–40–22–5.00–0–*ct* 0

Payne, Ian Roger
Cricketer. *b:* 9.5.1958, Kennington, London. Middle or lower order right-hand batsman, right-arm medium pace bowler. *Sch* Emanuel. *Team* Surrey (1977–83, 27 matches).
Career batting
27–34–5–308–43–10.62–0–*ct* 26
Bowling 1025–23–44.56–1–0–5/13

Payne, James
Professional. Lower order batsman, useful bowler. *Team* Lancashire (1898, 1 match).
Career batting
1–2–0–0–0–0.00–0–*ct* 0
Bowling 48–0

Payne, John Henry
Amateur. *b:* 19.3.1858, Broughton, Lancashire. *d:* 24.1.1942, Manchester. Son of J. B. (Gentlemen of North 1860). Middle order right-hand batsman, wicket-keeper. *Sch* Cheltenham. *Teams* Cambridge U (1880); Lancashire (1883, 9 matches).
Career batting
11–19–3–166–33–10.37–0–*ct* 7–*st* 4
A noted rugby footballer, he played for England.

Payne, Joseph Spencer
Professional. *b:* 29.4.1829, East Grinstead, Sussex. *d:* 12.4.1880, Greenwich, Kent. Brother of Charles (Sussex and Kent) and Richard (Sussex), uncle of Alfred and William (Sussex). Lower order right-hand batsman, left-hand medium pace round-arm bowler. *Teams* Sussex (1861, 2 matches); Kent (1864, 1 match).
Career batting
3–6–1–35–32–7.00–0–*ct* 3
Bowling 150–13–11.53–1–0–8/73

Payne, Meyrick Whitmore
Amateur. *b:* 10.5.1885, London. *d:* 2.6.1963, Little Easton, Essex. Cousin of C. A. L. (Middlesex). Attacking opening right-hand batsman, right-arm fast bowler, wicket-keeper. *Sch* Wellington. *Teams* Cambridge U (1904–07, blue all four years); Middlesex (1904–09, 25 matches). *Tour* MCC to North America 1905.
Career batting
86–152–9–3547–24.80–5–*ct* 116–*st* 33
Bowling 130–3–43.33–0–0–2/27
His final first-class match was for Free Foresters in 1929.

Payne, Richard
Professional. *b:* 9.6.1827, East Grinstead, Sussex. *d:* 11.4.1906, East Grinstead, Sussex. Brother of Charles (Sussex and Kent) and J. S. (Sussex and Kent), uncle of Alfred and William (Sussex). Lower order right-hand batsman, right-hand medium round-arm, or under-arm, bowler. *Team* Sussex (1853–66, 7 matches).
Career batting
7–12–0–81–28–6.75–0–*ct* 4
Bowling 50–3–16.66–0–0–2/23

Payne, Richard Bethune Tripp Selwyn
Amateur. *b:* 18.9.1885, Rangoon, Burma. *d:* 1.2.1949, Exmouth, Devon. Middle order batsman. *Sch* Malvern. *Team* Somerset (1906, 1 match).
Career batting
1–1–0–15–15–15.00–0–*ct* 0

Payne, S.
Professional. Lower order batsman, bowler. *Team* Sussex (1869, 1 match).
Career batting
1–2–0–4–4–2.00–0–*ct* 1
Bowling 7–0

Payne, William
Professional. *b:* 6.8.1854, East Grinstead, Sussex. *d:* 25.6.1909, East Grinstead, Sussex. Brother of Alfred (Sussex), nephew of Charles, J. S. (Sussex and Kent) and Richard (Sussex). Lower order right-hand batsman, right-arm medium pace bowler, good cover point. *Team* Sussex (1877–83, 17 matches).
Career batting
18–33–7–189–39*–7.26–0–*ct* 9
Bowling 488–25–19.52–0–0–3/34

Payne-Gallwey, William Thomas
Amateur. *b:* 25.3.1881. *d:* 14.9.1914, Vendress, Troyon, France. He was killed in action. Tail end batsman, right-arm fast bowler. *Sch* Eton. *Teams* Army (1912); MCC (1912).
Career batting
2–4–2–37–16–18.50–0–*ct* 1
Bowling 55–2–27.50–0–0–1/10

Paynter, Edward
Professional. *b:* 5.11.1901, Oswaldwistle, Lancashire. *d:* 5.2.1979, Keighley, Yorkshire. Attacking opening or middle order left-hand

batsman, right-arm medium pace bowler, brilliant outfield. *Team* Lancashire (1926–45, 293 matches). *Tours* MCC to Australia and New Zealand 1932/3, to South Africa 1938/9; Commonwealth to India 1950/1. *Tests* England (1931–39, 20 matches).
Career batting
352–533–58–20075–322–42.26–45–*ct* 160
Bowling 1371–30–45.70–0–0–3/13
Test batting
20–31–5–1540–243–59.23–4–*ct* 7

Playing in seven Tests for England v Australia, he hit 591 runs, average 84.42, a quite remarkable statistic, and his overall record in Tests is equalled by few. His Test career and indeed his first-class career were relatively brief, for he did not gain a regular place in the Lancashire side until 1931, the year of his England debut, and the outbreak of the Second World War effectively ended his first-class career.

He hit 1,000 runs in a season nine times, going on to 2,000 four times, his best year being 1937 with 2,904 runs, average 53.77. His highest score was 322 for Lancashire v Sussex at Hove in 1937; of his six other scores over 200, four were for his County and two for England. His best remembered innings came in the fourth Test of the 1932/3 series, when he left his hospital bed – being laid low with tonsilitis – and scored 83 in four hours.

Although he lost the top joints of two fingers in an accident early in life, he was a brilliant fieldsman and actually kept wicket most efficiently in one innings of the 1938 Lord's Test. His final first-class matches in England came in the 1947 Harrogate Festival, when he had innings of 154, 73 and 127, though he had played in only one first-class match since 1939.

Payton, Albert Ivan
Professional. *b:* 20.1.1898, Stapleford, Notts. *d:* 27.9.1967, Sandiacre, Derbyshire. Brother of W. R. D. (Notts), uncle of W. E. G. (Notts and Derbyshire). Middle order right-hand batsman, right-arm medium pace bowler. *Team* Nottinghamshire (1922, 1 match).
Career batting
1–2–0–16–15–8.00–0–*ct* 0

Payton, Ven Wilfred Ernest Granville
Amateur. *b:* 27.12.1913, Beeston, Notts. Son of W. R. D. (Notts), nephew of A. I. (Notts). Sound opening right-hand batsman, good deep field. *Sch* Nottingham High School. *Teams* Nottinghamshire (1935, 1 match); Cambridge U (1937, blue); Derbyshire (1949, 2 matches).
Career batting
27–52–4–995–98–20.72–0–*ct* 11

Most of his cricket was for the RAF, and his final first-class match was for Combined Services in 1953.

Payton, Wilfred Richard Daniel
Professional. *b:* 13.2.1882, Stapleford, Notts. *d:* 2.5.1943, Beeston, Notts. Brother of A. I. (Notts), father of W. E. G. (Notts and Derbyshire). Middle order right-hand batsman, good outfield. *Team* Nottinghamshire (1905–31, 489 matches).
Career batting
491–770–126–22132–169–34.36–39–*ct* 147
Bowling 68–1–68.00–0–0–1/18

He hit 1,000 runs in a season nine times (best 1,864, av 47.79, in 1926).

Peacey, Rev Canon John Raphael
Amateur. *b:* 16.7.1896, Steyning, Sussex. *d:* 31.10.1971, Hurstpierpoint, Sussex. Middle order batsman. *Sch* St Edmund's School, Canterbury. *Team* Sussex (1920–22, 4 matches).
Career batting
4–7–1–54–26–9.00–0–*ct* 0

Peach, Charles William
Professional. *b:* 3.1.1900, Cale Hill, Kent. *d:* 27.2.1977, Coxheath, Maidstone, Kent. Lower order right-hand batsman, right-arm medium fast bowler. *Team* Kent (1930–31, 19 matches).
Career batting
19–25–10–108–20–7.20–0–*ct* 9
Bowling 830–30–27.66–0–0–4/38

Owing to some doubts as to the fairness of his bowling action, he did not have an extended trial in County cricket.

Peach, Frederick George
Amateur. *b:* 2.11.1882, Repton, Derbyshire. *d:* 15.1.1965, Stapenhill, Staffs. Middle order right-hand batsman, leg break bowler. *Team* Derbyshire (1907–25, 12 matches).
Career batting
12–24–1–258–61*–11.21–0–*ct* 3
Bowling 170–4–42.50–0–0–3/50

Peach, Herbert Alan
Professional. *b:* 6.10.1890, Maidstone, Kent. *d:* 8.10.1961, North End, Hampshire. Lower order right-hand batsman, right-arm medium pace bowler, good field. *Team* Surrey (1919–31, 324 matches). *Tour* Cahn to Jamaica 1928/9.
Career batting
338–428–51–8940–200*–23.71–4–*ct* 182
Bowling 21136–795–26.58–30–1–8/60

For Surrey v Sussex at the Oval in 1924 he took 4 wickets in 4 balls. His only double century was

200* for Surrey v Northants at Northampton in 1920. He also played for Berkshire. From 1935 to 1939 he was coach to Surrey CCC.

Peach, Roy Alan
Amateur. *b:* 19.10.1937, London. Right-hand batsman, right-arm medium pace bowler. *Team* Combined Services (1960).
Career batting
2–1–1–6–6*–no av–0–*ct* 2
Bowling 13–0

Peach, William
Professional. *b:* 6.5.1875, Timberland, Lincs. *d:* 29.1.1959, Chesterfield, Derbyshire. Lower order right-hand batsman, right-arm fast medium bowler. *Team* Derbyshire (1905, 1 match).
Career batting
1–2–0–10–10–5.00–0–*ct* 1
Bowling 46–4–11.50–0–0–4/46

Peacock, Horace Ogilvie
Amateur. *b:* 26.9.1869, Greatford, Lincs. *d:* 5.6.1940, Greatford, Lincs. Middle order right-hand batsman. *Sch* Harrow. *Team* MCC (1896–99).
Career batting
6–10–0–124–38–12.40–0–*ct* 5
His County cricket was for Lincolnshire.

Peacocke, Joseph Reginald Hyde
Amateur. *b:* 23.3.1904, Dublin. *d:* December 1961, Umtali, Southern Rhodesia. Right-hand batsman. *Sch* Rossall. *Teams* Dublin U (1925); Ireland (1926).
Career batting
2–4–0–86–48–21.50–0–*ct* 0

Peake, Rev Edward
Amateur. *b:* 29.3.1860, Tidenham, Gloucs. *d:* 3.1.1945, Huntingdon. Tail end right-hand batsman, right-arm fast bowler, close field. *Sch* Marlborough. *Teams* Oxford U (1880–83, blue 1881–83); Gloucestershire (1881–89, 26 matches).
Career batting
46–80–11–902–53–13.07–0–*ct* 27
Bowling 2551–116–21.99–6–1–7/39
He also played for Berkshire.

Peake, Rev George Eden Frederick
Amateur. *b:* 1846, Taunton, Somerset. *d:* 24.6.1901, Newquay, Cornwall. Middle order batsman. *Team* Somerset (1885, 1 match).
Career batting
1–2–0–6–6–3.00–0–*ct* 0

Peake, Kenneth George
Amateur. *b:* 24.7.1920, Leicester. Lower order right-hand batsman, right-arm fast medium bowler. *Team* Leicestershire (1946, 1 match).
Career batting
1–2–1–2–1*–2.00–0–*ct* 0
Bowling 52–0

Pearce, George Smart
Professional. *b:* 27.10.1908, Horsham, Sussex. Lower order right-hand batsman, right-arm medium pace bowler. *Team* Sussex (1928–36, 54 matches).
Career batting
54–79–10–1295–80–18.76–0–*ct* 23
Bowling 2588–89–29.07–3–0–5/34

Pearce, Harold Edgar
Amateur. *b:* 1.4.1884, Barnet, Herts. *d:* 19.5.1939, Chichester, Sussex. Middle order batsman. *Team* Middlesex (1905–07, 5 matches).
Career batting
5–9–1–169–46*–21.12–0–*ct* 4
Bowling 16–0
He was a well-known actor.

Pearce, Jonathan Peter
Cricketer. *b:* 18.4.1957, Newcastle-on-Tyne. Lower order right-hand batsman, slow left-arm bowler. *Sch* Ampleforth. *Team* Oxford U (1978–79, blue 1979).
Career batting
7–11–5–22–8*–3.66–0–*ct* 2
Bowling 501–11–45.54–0–0–4/94

Pearce, Stanley Herbert Hicks
Amateur. *b:* 21.9.1863, Lopperwood, Totton, Hants. *d:* 5.4.1929, Oswestry, Shropshire. Middle order batsman. *Sch* Winchester. *Team* Hampshire (1885, 1 match).
Career batting
1–2–0–18–18–9.00–0–*ct* 0

Pearce, Thomas Albert
Professional. *b:* 11.5.1847, Essendon, Hertfordshire. *d:* 20.8.1898, St Albans, Hertfordshire. Lower order right-hand batsman, wicket-keeper, occasional right-hand slow round-arm bowler. *Team* MCC (1874–76).
Career batting
5–8–0–35–21–4.37–0–*ct* 4
His first-class debut was for the South of England in 1872 and his County cricket for Hertfordshire, commencing 1867.

Pearce, Thomas Alexander
Amateur. *b:* 18.12.1910, Hong Kong. *d:* 11.8.1982, Tunbridge Wells. Middle order right-hand batsman, off break bowler, brilliant field.

Sch Charterhouse. *Team* Kent (1930–46, 52 matches).
Career batting
55–82–8–1213–106–16.39–1–*ct* 23
Bowling 22–1–22.00–0–0–1/22

In 1933 he left England to return to Hong Kong and his appearances in County cricket were therefore very sparse. After coming back to England in 1946 he served on the Kent CCC Committee and was President of the Club in 1978.

Pearce, Thomas Neill
Amateur. *b:* 3.11.1905, Stoke Newington, London. Very sound middle order right-hand batsman, right-arm medium pace bowler. *Sch* Christ's Hospital. *Team* Essex (1929–50, 231 matches). *Tour* Martineau to Egypt 1939 (not first-class).
Career batting
250–406–54–12061–211*–34.26–22–*ct* 153
Bowling 927–15–61.80–0–0–4/12

He hit 1,000 runs in a season six times (best 1,826, av 49.35, in 1948). His only double century was 211* for Essex v Leics at Westcliff in 1948. He was joint-captain of Essex 1933 to 1938 and 1950, and sole captain 1946 to 1949. In 1949 and 1950 he was a Test Selector. His final first-class match was for a Commonwealth XI in 1952. For many years he selected a team to play in the Scarborough Festival each September. A noted rugby referee, he officiated in international matches.

Pearce, Sir William
Amateur. *b:* 18.3.1853, Poplar, Middlesex. *d:* 24.8.1932, Walmer, Kent. Middle order right-hand batsman. *Team* Kent (1878, 3 matches).
Career batting
3–6–0–50–14–8.33–0–*ct* 2
Bowling 88–6–14.66–0–0–3/16

He also appeared for Essex in non-first-class matches. He was MP for Limehouse, 1906 to 1922.

Pearce, Walter Kennedy
Amateur. *b:* 2.4.1893, Bassett, Hants. *d:* 31.7.1960, Romsey, Hants. Middle order right-hand batsman. *Sch* Malvern. *Team* Hampshire (1923–26, 9 matches).
Career batting
9–10–3–127–63–18.14–0–*ct* 1

Peare, William George
Professional, but amateur after 1926. *b:* 25.6.1905, Waterford, Ireland. *d:* 16.11.1979, St Lukes, Co Cork, Ireland. Lower order right-hand batsman, right-arm medium fast bowler. *Team* Warwickshire (1926, 7 matches).
Career batting
8–11–7–19–12*–4.75–0–*ct* 3
Bowling 213–8–26.62–0–0–3/45

His final first-class match was for MCC in 1936.

Pearman, Hugh
Cricketer. *b:* 1.6.1945, Birmingham. Brother of Roger (Middlesex). Opening right-hand batsman, slow left-arm bowler. *Teams* Cambridge U (1969, blue); Middlesex (1969–72, 5 matches).
Career batting
12–17–1–294–61–18.37–0–*ct* 7
Bowling 578–16–36.12–0–0–4/56

Pearman, Roger
Amateur. *b:* 13.2.1943, Lichfield, Staffs. Brother of Hugh (Middlesex). Middle order right-hand batsman, off break bowler, close field. *Team* Middlesex (1962–64, 8 matches).
Career batting
8–13–3–264–72*–26.40–*ct* 4

He was appointed Chief Executive to Derbyshire CCC in 1982.

Pearsall, Richard Devenish
Amateur. *b:* 15.1.1921, Kenilworth, Warwickshire. Lower order right-hand batsman, right-arm medium pace bowler. *Sch* Oundle. *Team* Cambridge U (1947–48).
Career batting
15–19–4–230–80*–15.33–0–*ct* 12
Bowling 982–27–36.37–0–0–4/51

Pearse, Allan Arthur
Amateur. *b:* 22.4.1915, Watchet, Somerset. *d:* 14.6.1981, Watchet, Somerset. Middle order right-hand batsman, good field. *Team* Somerset (1936–38, 9 matches).
Career batting
9–15–1–81–20–5.78–0–*ct* 1
Bowling 3–0

Pearse, Gerald Vyvyan
Amateur. *b:* 7.9.1891, South Africa. *d:* 19.12.1956, Marylebone, London. Middle order right-hand batsman, right-arm bowler. *Teams* Natal (1910/1); Oxford U (1919).
Career batting
14–23–5–413–67*–22.94–0–*ct* 12
Bowling 932–27–34.51–0–0–4/57

His final first-class match was for Free Foresters in 1927.

Pearson, Alexander (Gillespie)
Amateur. *b:* 21.1.1856, Edinburgh, Scotland. *d:* 24.1.1931, Locarno, Switzerland. Opening or middle order right-hand batsman, right-hand

medium pace round-arm bowler, good field. *Sch* Rugby and Loretto. *Team* Oxford U (1876–77, blue both years).
Career batting
12–21–1–163–35–8.15–0–*ct* 5
Bowling 289–16–18.06–0–0–3/10
He also played for Scotland (non-first-class).

Pearson, Anthony John Grayhurst
Amateur. *b:* 30.12.1941, Harrow, Middlesex. Tail end right-hand batsman, right-arm fast medium bowler. *Sch* Downside. *Teams* Cambridge U (1961–63, blue all three years); Somerset (1961–63, 6 matches).
Career batting
42–51–11–355–30–8.87–0–*ct* 29
Bowling 3918–139–28.18–2–1–10/78
He took 10 wickets in a single innings (for 78), for Cambridge U v Leics at Loughborough in 1961.

Pearson, Dr Cecil Joseph Herbert
Amateur. *b:* 22.1.1888, Poplar, London. *d:* 14.9.1971, Porthcawl, Glamorgan. Middle order right-hand batsman, slow right-arm bowler. *Team* Glamorgan (1922, 1 match).
Career batting
1–2–0–9–9–4.50–0–*ct* 0
Bowling 12–0
He also played for Devonshire.

Pearson, Derek Brooke
Professional. *b:* 29.3.1937, Stourbridge, Worcs. Lower order right-hand batsman, right-arm fast medium bowler. *Team* Worcestershire (1954–61, 74 matches).
Career batting
76–107–21–734–49–8.53–0–*ct* 35
Bowling 5540–210–26.38–9–1–6/70
He was no-balled for throwing in 1959 and 1960.

Pearson, Frederick Albert
Professional. *b:* 23.9.1880, Brixton, London. *d:* 10.11.1963, Droitwich, Worcs. Opening right-hand batsman, right-arm slow bowler. *Teams* Worcestershire (1900–26, 445 matches); Auckland (1910/11).
Career batting
454–811–38–18735–167–24.23–22–*ct* 162
Bowling 24716–853–28.97–38–4–9/41
He hit 1,000 runs in a season eight times (best 1,498, av 36.53, in 1921) and in 1923 took 111 wickets, av 22.89, completing the 'double' for the only time in his career. His best bowling was for H. K. Foster's XI v Oxford U at Oxford in 1914.

Pearson, George Timothy
Amateur. *b:* 21.7.1921, London. *d:* 24.7.1983, Cuxham, Oxford. Lower order right-hand batsman, wicket-keeper. *Sch* Radley. *Team* Free Foresters (1948–59).
Career batting
2–3–2–54–28–54.00–0–*ct* 3

Pearson, Harry Eyre
Professional. *b:* 7.8.1851, Attercliffe, Sheffield, Yorkshire. *d:* 8.7.1903, Nether Edge, Sheffield, Yorkshire. Tail end right-hand batsman, right-hand fast, later slow, round-arm bowler, deep field. *Team* Yorkshire (1878–80, 4 matches).
Career batting
4–7–5–31–10*–15.50–0–*ct* 1
Bowling 90–5–18.00–0–0–3/37

Pearson, Joseph Garside
Professional. *b:* 26.3.1860, Worksop, Notts. *d:* 18.1.1892, Boughton, Notts. Middle order batsman. *Team* Nottinghamshire (1883, 1 match).
Career batting
1–1–0–1–1–1.00–0–*ct* 0
Bowling 1–3–0.33–0–0–3/1
His curious bowling record can be regarded as a fluke, since he played purely as a batsman, and even in local cricket, very rarely bowled.

Pearson, John Henry
Professional. *b:* 14.5.1915, Scarborough, Yorkshire. Hard hitting opening right-hand batsman. *Team* Yorkshire (1934–36, 3 matches).
Career batting
3–3–0–54–44–18.00–0–*ct* 0

Pearson, James W.
Professional. Tail end left-hand batsman, left-arm bowler. *Team* Northants (1932, 1 match).
Career batting
1–2–1–1–1–1*–1.00–0–*ct* 0
Bowling 43–0

Pearson, Kenneth
Cricketer. *b:* 30.8.1951, Bedlington, Northumberland. Sound opening right-hand batsman. *Team* Minor Counties (1976).
Career batting
1–2–0–13–9–6.50–0–*ct* 1
He has played for Northumberland since 1972.

Pearson, Kenneth R.
Professional. Lower order batsman, bowler. *Team* MCC (1946).
Career batting
1–2–0–26–17–13.00–0–*ct* 0
Bowling 74–2–37.00–0–0–2/42

Pearson, Lawrence Ivor
Professional. *b:* 25.1.1922, Darnall, Sheffield, Yorkshire. Middle order left-hand batsman. *Team* Derbyshire (1946, 2 matches).
Career batting
2–4–0–24–18–6.00–0–*ct* 0

Pearson, Sir Robert Barclay
Amateur. *b:* 20.11.1871, Scotland. *d:* 12.2.1954, Marylebone, London. Neat lower order right-hand batsman, right-arm slow bowler. *Sch* Loretto. *Team* Oxford U (1894).
Career batting
1–2–0–48–44–24.00–0–*ct* 0
Bowling 35–0

A noted all-round sportsman, he represented Oxford at rugby football and golf, as well as having a trial in the rowing eight. He was for many years Chairman of the London Stock Exchange.

Pearson, Thomas Sherwin
(later Pearson-Gregory)
Amateur. *b:* 20.6.1851, Barwell, Leics. *d:* 25.11.1935, Harlaxton, Lincs. Father of P. J. S. Pearson-Gregory (Notts). Attacking middle order right-hand batsman, right-arm slow bowler, wicket-keeper. *Sch* Rugby. *Teams* Oxford U (1872); Middlesex (1878–85, 66 matches).
Career batting
122–202–14–3347–121–17.80–1–*ct* 130–*st* 5
Bowling 1008–38–26.52–1–0–5/36

He also appeared for Leicestershire, Warwickshire (both pre-first-class) and Bedfordshire. His final first-class match was for Gentlemen of England in 1891. In 1902 he was President of Nottinghamshire CCC. He represented Oxford at real tennis and was also a useful rackets player.

Pearson-Gregory, Philip John Sherwin
Amateur. *b:* 26.3.1888, Harlaxton, Lincs. *d:* 12.6.1955, St Pancras, London. Son of T. S. Pearson (Middlesex). Middle order right-hand batsman, slip field. *Sch* Eton. *Team* Nottinghamshire (1910–14, 3 matches).
Career batting
3–2–0–119–71–59.50–0–*ct* 3

He appeared in the Freshmen's and Seniors' matches at Oxford, but no first-class games.

Peat, Charles Urie
Amateur. *b:* 28.2.1892, London. *d:* 27.10.1979, Wycliffe, Barnard Castle, Co Durham. Lower order right-hand batsman, right-arm fast bowler. *Sch* Sedbergh. *Teams* Oxford U (1913, blue); Middlesex (1914, 6 matches).
Career batting
23–35–12–186–30–8.08–0–*ct* 8
Bowling 1696–54–31.40–2–0–6/51

His final first-class match was for Free Foresters in 1922. He was Conservative MP for Darlington 1931 to 1945.

Peate, Edmund
Professional. *b:* 2.3.1856, Holbeck, Leeds, Yorkshire. *d:* 11.3.1900, Newlay, Leeds, Yorkshire. Tail end left-hand batsman, slow left-arm bowler. *Team* Yorkshire (1879–87, 154 matches). *Tour* Lillywhite, Shaw and Shrewsbury to Australia 1881/2. *Tests* England (1881/2 to 1886, 9 matches).
Career batting
209–312–88–2384–95–10.64–0–*ct* 132
Bowling 14515–1076–13.48–93–27–8/5
Test batting
9–14–8–70–13–11.66–0–*ct* 2
Bowling 682–31–22.00–2–0–6/85

He took 100 wickets in a season six times, going on to 200 once : 214, av 11.52, in 1882.

His sudden departure from County cricket whilst in his prime was caused by Lord Hawke's determination to rid the Yorkshire team of its more unruly elements. His final first-class match was for the North in 1890.

Peatfield, Albert Edward
Amateur. *b:* 1874, Retford, Notts. *d:* 12.12.1953, Retford, Notts. Middle order right-hand batsman. *Team* England XI (1906).
Career batting
1–2–1–18–10–18.00–0–*ct* 0

He appeared for Glamorgan (pre-first-class).

Peck, David Arthur
Amateur. *b:* 3.5.1940, Rushden, Northants. Brother of R. L. (Combined Services). Lower order right-hand batsman, wicket-keeper. *Sch* Wellingborough. *Team* Cambridge U (1960).
Career batting
1–1–0–0–0–0.00–0–*ct* 2

Peck, Ian George
Cricketer. *b:* 18.10.1957, Great Staughton, Huntingdonshire. Opening right-hand batsman, wicket-keeper. *Sch* Bedford School. *Teams* Cambridge U (1978–81, blue 1980 and 1981); Northants (1980–81, 2 matches).
Career batting
25–36–4–410–45–12.81–0–*ct* 12–*st* 1

He also played for Bedfordshire.

An excellent rugby footballer he was awarded his blue and toured with England.

Peck, Richard Leslie
Amateur. *b:* 27.5.1937, Rushden, Northants. Brother of D. A. (Cambridge U). Middle order right-hand batsman. *Team* Combined Services (1960).
Career batting
2–2–0–24–19–12.00–0–*ct* 1
Bowling 1–2–0.50–0–0–2/1

Pedder, Guy Richard
Amateur. *b:* 7.7.1892, London. *d:* 6.4.1964, Hoxne, Suffolk. Tail end right-hand batsman, wicket-keeper. *Sch* Repton. *Team* Gloucestershire (1925, 1 match).
Career batting
5–5–1–120–82–30.00–0–*ct* 7–*st* 2
Most of his County cricket was for Norfolk and his first-class debut was in 1924 for the Minor Counties. His last first-class match took place in 1931 for Free Foresters.

Peden, David Murray
Cricketer. *b:* 4.11.1946, Edinburgh, Scotland. *d:* 12.3.1978, Dunfermline, Scotland. Right-hand batsman, right-arm medium pace bowler. *Team* Scotland (1973–76).
Career batting
3–5–0–108–45–21.60–0–*ct* 0
Bowling 74–2–37.00–0–0–2/53

Pedley, William Everard
Amateur. *b:* 16.6.1858, Wingerworth, Derbyshire. *d:* 9.7.1920, Riverside, California, USA. Lower order right-hand batsman, right-arm medium pace bowler. *Sch* Eastbourne. *Team* Sussex (1879, 2 matches).
Career batting
2–4–1–45–16*–15.00–0–*ct* 0
Bowling 138–10–13.80–1–0–7/36
He appeared for Derbyshire in non-first-class matches in 1888. An engineer, he spent many years in India and thus was not afforded much opportunity for County cricket.

Peebles, Ian Alexander Ross
Amateur. *b:* 20.1.1908, Aberdeen, Scotland. *d:* 28.2.1980, High Wycombe, Bucks. Lower order right-hand batsman, leg break bowler. *Sch* Glasgow Academy. *Teams* Middlesex (1928–48, 165 matches); Oxford U (1930, blue); Scotland (1937). *Tours* MCC to South Africa 1927/8, 1930/1; Cahn to Ceylon 1936/7 (he did not play in first-class matches); Tennyson to India 1937/8. *Tests* England (1927/8 to 1931, 13 matches).
Career batting
251–330–101–2213–58–9.66–0–*ct* 172
Bowling 19738–923–21.38–62–15–8/24
Test batting
13–17–8–98–26–10.88–0–*ct* 5
Bowling 1391–45–30.91–3–0–6/63
He took 100 wickets in a season three times (best 139, av 18.51, in 1931). In 1939 he captained Middlesex. His first-class debut was for the Gentlemen in 1927. The loss of an eye in an air-raid during the Second World War more or less ended his first-class career. He later became a well-known cricket writer and journalist.

Peel, Bertram Lennox
Amateur. *b:* 19.4.1881, Derby. *d:* 19.1.1945, Colinton, Edinburgh, Scotland. Brother of D. H. (Oxford U). Opening or middle order right-hand batsman, slow right-arm bowler. *Sch* Bedford Grammar School. *Teams* Oxford U (1903); Scotland (1905–12).
Career batting
10–18–0–288–74–16.00–0–*ct* 4
Bowling 249–10–24.90–0–0–4/123

Peel, Denis Heywood
Amateur. *b:* 1.2.1886, Liverpool, *d:* 25.10.1927, Montana, Switzerland. Brother of B. L. (Scotland). Lower order batsman, bowler. *Sch* Bedford Grammar School. *Team* Oxford U (1907).
Career batting
3–5–0–9–6–1.80–0–*ct* 1
Bowling 161–3–53.66–0–0–1/32
He played for Bedfordshire.

Peel, Robert
Professional. *b:* 12.2.1857, Churwell, Leeds, Yorkshire. *d:* 12.8.1941, Morley, Leeds, Yorkshire. Middle or lower order left-hand batsman, slow left-arm bowler. *Team* Yorkshire (1882–97, 321 matches). *Tours* Lillywhite, Shaw and Shrewsbury to Australia 1884/5; Vernon to Australia 1887/8; Sheffield to Australia 1891/2; Stoddart to Australia 1894/5. *Tests* England (1884/5 to 1896, 20 matches).
Career batting
436–693–66–12191–210*–19.44–7–*ct* 214
Bowling 28758–1776–16.19–123–34–9/22
Test batting
20–33–4–427–83–14.72–0–*ct* 17
Bowling 1715–102–16.81–6–2–7/31
He took 100 wickets in a season eight times, (best 180, av 14.97, in 1895) and hit 1,000 runs once : 1,206, av 30.15, in 1896, completing the 'double' in the same summer. His only double century was 210* for Yorkshire v Warwickshire at Edgbaston in 1896, and his best bowling in an innings 9 for 22 for Yorkshire v Somerset at

Headingley in 1895. Regarded as the best bowler of his type in England, his County career came to a premature end when Lord Hawke dismissed him because of his inebriate habits. His final first-class match was for an England XI in 1899.

Pegler, Sidney James
Amateur. *b:* 28.7.1888, Durban, South Africa. *d:* 9.9.1972, Cape Town, South Africa. Lower order right-hand batsman, right-arm medium pace leg break bowler. *Team* Transvaal (1908/09 to 1912/13). *Tours* South Africa to Australia 1910/11, to England 1912, 1924. *Tests* South Africa (1909/10 to 1924, 16 matches).
Career batting
103–150–18–1677–79–12.70–0–*ct* 56
Bowling 8324–425–19.58–32–5–8/54
Test batting
16–28–5–356–35*–15.47–0–*ct* 5
Bowling 1572–47–33.44–2–0–7/65

He was the outstanding success of the 1912 South African tour, taking 189 wickets, av 15.26, heading both Test and first-class averages. On his 1924 tour he again took over 100 wickets. He spent a number of summers in England and appeared in a few first-class matches, the final one being for MCC in 1930. A South African Test selector after the Second World War, he was Manager of the 1951 touring team.

Pelham, Anthony George
Amateur. *b:* 4.9.1911, Minehead, Somerset. *d:* 10.3.1969, Dorking, Surrey. Grandson of F. G. (Cambridge U and Sussex). Lower order right-hand batsman, right-arm medium pace bowler. *Sch* Eton. *Teams* Sussex (1930–33, 10 matches); Cambridge U (1932–34, blue 1934); Somerset (1933, 2 matches).
Career batting
35–47–16–339–40*–10.93–0–*ct* 19
Bowling 2610–84–31.05–2–0–5/37

Pelham, Hon Francis Godolphin
(succeeded as the 5th Earl of Chichester in 1901)
Amateur. *b:* 18.10.1844, Stanmer Park, Lewes, Sussex. *d:* 21.4.1905, Stanmer Park, Lewes, Sussex. Cousin of Sidney (Oxford U), grandfather of A. G. (Sussex). Middle order right-hand batsman, right-hand slow round-arm bowler, slip field. *Sch* Eton. *Teams* Cambridge U (1864–67, blue all four years); Sussex (1865–68, 8 matches).
Career batting
25–47–5–637–78–15.16–0–*ct* 24
Bowling 1731–88+4–19.67–7–0–7/26

He also played for Devonshire. He was also a noted athlete, winning many races whilst at Cambridge.

Pelham, Ven Archdeacon Sidney
Amateur. *b:* 16.5.1849, Brighton, Sussex. *d:* 14.7.1926, Norwich. Cousin of F. G. (Cambridge U and Sussex). Lower order right-hand batsman, right-hand slow round-arm bowler. *Sch* Harrow. *Team* Oxford U (1871–72, blue 1871).
Career batting
7–9–4–24–14*–4.80–0–*ct* 6
Bowling 314–20+1–15.70–1–0–6/51

He played for Norfolk, commencing 1871.

Pell, Godfrey Arnold
Amateur. *b:* 11.3.1928, Sunderland. Lower order right-hand batsman, leg break and googly bowler. *Sch* KES Birmingham. *Team* Warwickshire (1947, 1 match).
Career batting
1–2–1–24–16*–24.00–0–*ct* 1
Bowling 31–4–7.75–0–0–2/9

Pellew, Clarence Everard
Amateur. *b:* 21.9.1893, Port Pirie, South Australia. *d:* 9.5.1981, Adelaide, South Australia. Attacking middle order right-hand batsman, brilliant outfield. *Team* South Australia (1913/14 to 1928/9, 23 matches). *Tours* AIF to England 1919, to South Africa 1919/20; Australia to England 1921, to South Africa 1921/2. *Tests* Australia (1920/1 to 1921/2, 10 matches).
Career batting
91–147–12–4536–271–33.60–9–*ct* 45
Bowling 849–12–70.75–0–0–3/119
Test batting
10–14–1–484–116–37.23–2–*ct* 4
Bowling 34–0

He hit 1,260 runs, av 38.18, in 1919, but was not so successful in 1921, though he played in all five Tests due in part to his outstanding fielding. His highest score was 271 for South Australia v Victoria at Adelaide in 1919/20.

Pelly, John Noel
Amateur. *b:* 15.6.1888, Witham, Essex. *d:* 6.6.1945, Hove, Sussex. Middle or lower order batsman. *Sch* Bradfield. *Team* Royal Navy (1926).
Career batting
1–2–0–5–5–2.50–0–*ct* 0

Pember, Francis William
Amateur. *b:* 16.8.1862, Hatfield, Herts. *d:* 19.1.1954, Cambridge. Middle order right-hand batsman. *Sch* Harrow. *Team* Hampshire (1885, 2 matches).
Career batting
5–9–2–112–47*–16.00–0–*ct* 5

He played in the 1881 Freshmen's Match at Oxford, but no first-class matches for the University. His first-class debut was for MCC in 1882.

Pember, John Devereaux Dubricious
Amateur. *b:* 8.6.1940, Creaton, Northants. Tail end left-hand batsman, right-arm fast medium bowler. *Sch* Wellingborough. *Team* Leicestershire (1968–71, 24 matches).
Career batting
24–25–10–271–53–18.06–0–*ct* 11
Bowling 1370–43–31.86–1–0–5/45
He played rugby football for Northampton.

Pemberton, Ralph Hylton
Amateur. *b:* 17.7.1864, Sunderland. *d:* 11.1.1931, Lurgashall, Sussex. Opening right-hand batsman. *Sch* Eton. *Team* Oxford U (1885).
Career batting
3–5–0–65–40–13.00–0–*ct* 0
He played for Durham.

Pemberton, William Cecil
Amateur. *b:* 15.11.1898, Dublin. *d:* 25.12.1978, Dublin, Ireland. Lower order right-hand batsman, left-arm fast medium bowler. *Team* Ireland (1923–28).
Career batting
4–7–3–55–31–13.75–0–*ct* 1
Bowling 263–5–52.60–0–0–3/40

Penduck, Arthur E.
Professional. *b:* 1885. *d:* 1924, Bristol. Lower order right-hand batsman, right-arm fast bowler. *Team* Gloucestershire (1908–09, 5 matches).
Career batting
5–8–2–18–8–3.00–0–*ct* 0
Bowling 294–6–49.00–0–0–3/98

Penfold, Alexander George
Amateur. *b:* 14.5.1901, Kenley, Surrey. *d:* 28.9.1982, Isfield, Sussex. Lower order right-hand batsman, right-arm fast medium bowler. *Teams* Madras (1926/7); Europeans (1924/5 to 1929/30); Surrey (1929, 3 matches).
Career batting
12–19–7–78–17*–6.50–0–*ct* 2
Bowling 1007–62–16.24–3–1–8/43
Being employed by the Bank of India, his opportunities for County cricket were very limited.

Penn, Alfred
Amateur. *b:* 6.1.1855, Lewisham, Kent. *d:* 18.10.1889, Lee, Kent. Brother of Frank and William (Kent), uncle of E. F. (Cambridge U) and Frank jun (Kent). Lower order left-hand batsman, left-hand slow round-arm bowler. *Team* Kent (1875–84, 41 matches).
Career batting
48–82–13–538–66–7.79–0–*ct* 20
Bowling 3580–223–16.05–20–3–8/34

Penn, Christopher
Cricketer. *b:* 19.6.1963, Dover, Kent. Left-hand batsman, right-arm fast medium bowler. *Team* Kent (1982–83, 9 matches).
Career batting
9–9–4–78–30–15.60–0–*ct* 5
Bowling 443–9–49.22–0–0–2/11

Penn, Eric Frank
Amateur. *b:* 17.4.1878, London. *d:* 18.10.1915, Hohenzollern, Loos, France. He was killed in action. Son of William (Kent), nephew of Frank (Kent) and Alfred (Kent), cousin of Frank (Kent). Middle order right-hand batsman, right-arm slow bowler. *Sch* Eton. *Team* Cambridge U (1899–1902, blue 1899 and 1902). *Tour* Warner to North America 1898 (he did not play in first-class matches).
Career batting
22–36–6–449–51*–14.96–0–*ct* 13
Bowling 1076–34–31.64–1–0–5/47
His first-class debut was for MCC in 1898; in 1899 he left Cambridge in order to serve in the Boer War, resuming his place at the University in 1901. His final first-class match was for MCC in 1903. He played for Norfolk, commencing 1899.

Penn, Frank
Amateur. *b:* 7.3.1851, Lewisham, Kent. *d:* 26.12.1916, Bifrons, Canterbury, Kent. Brother of Alfred (Kent) and William (Kent), father of Frank jun (Kent), uncle of E. F. (Cambridge U). Attacking middle order right-hand batsman, right-hand slow round-arm bowler, deep field. *Team* Kent (1875–81, 62 matches). *Tour* Harris to Australia 1878/9. *Test* England (1880, 1 match).
Career batting
98–172–14–4291–160–27.15–6–*ct* 49
Bowling 370–10–37.00–0–0–3/36
Test batting
1–2–1–50–27*–50.00–0–*ct* 0
Bowling 2–0
Regarded as one of the most brilliant batsman of his day, he was forced to retire from important cricket in 1881 on medical advice.

Penn, Frank (jun)
Amateur. *b:* 18.8.1884, Owsden, Suffolk. *d:* 23.4.1961, Bawdsey, Woodbridge, Suffolk. Son of Frank sen (Kent), nephew of Alfred (Kent) and William (Kent), cousin of E. F. (Cambridge U).

Middle order right-hand batsman. *Team* Kent (1904–05, 5 matches).
Career batting
5–9–0–130–43–14.44–0–*ct* 3
He made a name for himself in military matches.

Penn, William
Amateur. *b:* 29.8.1849, Lewisham, Kent. *d:* 15.8.1921, Westminster, London. Brother of Alfred (Kent) and Frank (Kent), father of E. F. (Cambridge U), uncle of Frank jun (Kent). Opening right-hand batsman, right-hand fast round-arm bowler, good deep field. *Sch* Harrow. *Team* Kent (1870–78, 18 matches).
Career batting
22–37–1–402–39–11.16–0–*ct* 12

Pennington, George Arthur Adam Septimus Carter Trenchard Sale
Amateur. *b:* 28.4.1899, Cote Brook, Cheshire. *d:* 15.9.1933, Armthorpe, Doncaster, Yorkshire. He was killed in a flying accident. Middle order right-hand batsman, useful bowler. *Team* Northants (1927, 12 matches).
Career batting
12–19–0–259–47–13.63–0–*ct* 6
Bowling 8–0
He was the pilot of a plane which took off from Armthorpe Aerodrome and crashed in an adjoining field – amongst the survivors were the jockey, Gordon Richards, and the Gloucestershire cricketer and racehorse trainer, Herbert Blagrave.

Pennington, Harry
Professional. *b:* 1880, Salford, Manchester. *d:* 1961, Manchester. Lower order batsman, wicket-keeper. *Team* Lancashire (1900, 4 matches).
Career batting
4–5–1–41–29*–10.25–0–*ct* 2–*st* 3
He played football for Notts County.

Pennington, John Henry
Professional. *b:* 24.6.1881, Sutton-on-Trent, Notts. *d:* 2.1.1942, Newark, Notts. Lower order batsman, left-arm medium pace bowler. *Team* Nottinghamshire (1902–05, 18 matches).
Career batting
18–24–8–89–18–5.56–0–*ct* 8
Bowling 1345–41–32.80–3–0–7/223

Penny, Joshua Hudson
Professional. *b:* 29.9.1857, Yeadon, Yorkshire. *d:* 1902, Dewsbury, Yorkshire. Lower order left-hand batsman, slow left-arm bowler. *Team* Yorkshire (1891, 1 match).
Career batting
1–1–1–8–8*–no av–0–*ct* 1
Bowling 31–2–15.50–0–0–1/7

Penny, Thomas Simpson
Amateur. *b:* 15.7.1929, Bristol. *d:* 26.7.1983, Casterton, Cumbria. Sound middle order right-hand batsman, off break bowler. *Sch* Clifton. *Team* Oxford U (1951–52).
Career batting
5–5–2–73–34–24.33–0–*ct* 1
Bowling 400–11–36.36–0–0–4/75

Pennycuick, John
Amateur. *b:* 15.1.1841, Poona, India. *d:* 9.3.1911, Camberley, Surrey. Middle order right-hand batsman, right-arm medium pace bowler. *Sch* Cheltenham. *Team* MCC (1883).
Career batting
1–2–2–21–20*–no av–0–*ct* 0
He spent most of his life in India and was a major figure in the promotion of cricket in that sub-continent.

Pentecost, John
Professional. *b:* 15.10.1857, Brighton, Sussex. *d:* 23.2.1902, St John's Wood, London. Lower order right-hand batsman, wicket-keeper. *Team* Kent (1882–90, 63 matches).
Career batting
66–102–26–573–38–7.53–0–*ct* 95–*st* 32
Bowling 20–1–20.00–0–0–1/19
Failing eyesight forced him to retire from County cricket earlier than would otherwise have been the case.

Pepall, George
Professional. *b:* 29.2.1876, Stow-on-the-Wold, Gloucs. *d:* 8.1.1953, Bourton-on-the-Water, Gloucs. Tail end right-hand batsman, right-arm fast bowler. *Team* Gloucestershire (1896–1904, 14 matches).
Career batting
14–24–7–99–45–5.82–0–*ct* 8
Bowling 725–20–36.25–1–0–5/63

Pepper, Charles (Beardmore)
Professional. *b:* 25.11.1875, Pinxton, Derbyshire. *d:* 13.9.1917, near La Clytte, Belgium. Defensive middle order right-hand batsman, right-arm medium pace bowler. *Team* Nottinghamshire (1900–01, 7 matches).
Career batting
7–12–3–162–40*–18.00–0–*ct* 2
Bowling 72–3–24.00–0–0–3/23
He also played for Bedfordshire in 1903.

Pepper, Cecil George
Professional. *b:* 15.9.1918, Forbes, New South Wales, Australia. Middle order right-hand batsman, leg break and googly bowler. *Teams* New South Wales (1938/9 to 1940/1, 16 matches); Commonwealth XI (in England) (1956–57). *Tours* Australian Services to England 1945, to India and Ceylon 1945/6; Commonwealth to India and Pakistan 1949/50.
Career batting
44–72–7–1927–168–29.64–1–*ct* 41
Bowling 5019–171–29.35–7–0–6/33
From 1964 to 1979 he was on the English first-class umpires' list.

Pepper, John
Amateur. *b:* 21.10.1922, Wimbledon, London. Middle order right-hand batsman, good field. *Sch* The Leys. *Team* Cambridge U (1946–48, blue all three years).
Career batting
29–49–1–1108–185–23.08–1–*ct* 5
He played for Denbighshire.

Pepys, Rev John Alfred
Amateur. *b:* 16.4.1838, Marylebone, London. *d* 22.3.1924, Bexhill-on-Sea, Sussex. Forceful middle order right-hand batsman, good cover point. *Sch* Eton. *Teams* Oxford (1861, blue); Kent (1859–69, 13 matches).
Career batting
30–50–1–592–55–12.08–0–*ct* 19
Bowling 25–1–25.00–0–0–1/25

Percival, John Douglas
Amateur. *b:* 5.8.1902, Kensington, London. *d:* 5.3.1983, Roehampton, London. Hard hitting opening right-hand batsman. *Sch* Westminster. *Teams* Oxford U (1922); Gloucestershire (1923, 1 match).
Career batting
3–6–0–38–17–6.33–0–*ct* 0

Percival, W. Alan
Amateur. *b:* 1923, Canada. Middle order right-hand batsman, wicket-keeper. *Team* Canada (1951–54). *Tour* Canada to England 1954.
Career batting
5–7–0–61–23–8.62–0–*ct* 9–*st* 1

Pereira, Aloysius Stanislaus
Amateur. *b:* 30.12.1859, Calcutta, India. *d:* 11.11.1935, Dehra Dun, India. Lower order batsman, bowler. *Sch* Stonyhurst. *Team* Cambridge U (1880).
Career batting
1–2–0–10–7–5.00–0–*ct* 2
Bowling 44–1–44.00–0–0–1/44

Pereira, Eustace Lorenz
Amateur. *b:* 4.7.1939, Colombo, Ceylon. Middle order left-hand batsman, off break bowler. *Team* Cambridge U (1962–63).
Career batting
2–2–1–11–8*–11.00–0–*ct* 0

Pereira, Rev Edward Thomas
Amateur. *b:* 26.9.1866, Colwich, Staffs. *d:* 25.2.1939, Edgbaston, Birmingham. Forcing middle order right-hand batsman, right-arm fast bowler, excellent field. *Sch* Oratory. *Team* Warwickshire (1895–96, 5 matches).
Career batting
7–12–1–177–34–16.09–0–*ct* 4
Bowling 13–0
His Warwickshire debut was in 1886, but he did not appear again for the County until 1895. His final first-class match was for MCC in 1900.

Perkins, Arthur Lionel Bertie
Amateur. *b:* 19.10.1905, Swansea, Glamorgan. Middle order right-hand batsman. *Sch* Bromsgrove. *Team* Glamorgan (1925–33, 6 matches).
Career batting
6–10–3–102–26*–14.57–0–*ct* 4

Perkins, Charles Meigh
Amateur. *b:* 1854, Foleshill, Warwickshire. *d:* 1912, Steyning, Sussex. Middle order right-hand batsman. *Team* Sussex (1884, 1 match).
Career batting
1–2–1–12–11–12.00–0–*ct* 0

Perkins, George
Professional. *b:* 1864, Ealing, Middlesex. *d:* 1933, Ealing, Middlesex. Middle order right-hand batsman, right-arm medium pace bowler. *Team* Middlesex (1884, 1 match).
Career batting
1–2–0–0–0–0.00–0–*ct* 0

Perkins, George Cyril
Professional. *b:* 4.6.1911, Wollaston, Northants. Middle order right-hand batsman, left-arm medium, later slow, bowler. *Team* Northants (1934–37, 56 matches).
Career batting
57–95–23–589–29–8.18–0–*ct* 30
Bowling 3359–93–36.11–5–0–6/54
He also played for Suffolk. His final first-class match was for Minor Counties in 1951.

Perkins, Henry
Amateur. *b:* 10.12.1832, Thriplow, Cambs. *d:* 6.5.1916, New Barnet, Hertfordshire. Brother of John (Cambridgeshire). Hard slashing middle

order right-hand batsman, right-hand slow under-arm bowler, good mid wicket. *Sch* Bury St Edmunds. *Teams* Cambridge U (1854, blue); Cambridgeshire (1857–66, 9 matches).
Career batting
28–48–8–370–36–9.25–0–*ct* 15
Bowling 428–23+7–18.60–2–0–5/48

He also played for Hertfordshire. His final first-class match was for MCC in 1868. He was Secretary of MCC from October 1876 to December 1897 – an easy-going autocrat.

Perkins, Hubert George
Professional. *b:* 18.6.1907, Attleborough, Warwickshire. *d:* 4.5.1935, Nuneaton, Warwickshire. Tail end left-hand batsman, slow left-arm bowler. *Team* Warwickshire (1926–27, 4 matches).
Career batting
4–5–2–10–6*–3.33–0–*ct* 1
Bowling 55–1–55.00–0–0–1/30

Perkins, John
Amateur. *b:* 17.5.1837, Sawston, Cambridgeshire. *d:* 30.4.1901, East Hatley, Cambs. Brother of Henry (Cambridge U and Cambridgeshire). Steady middle order right-hand batsman, deep field. *Sch* Bury St Edmunds. *Team* Cambridgeshire (1861–67, 11 matches).
Career batting
15–25–1–440–67–18.33–0–*ct* 5

He appeared occasionally for Cambridge U, but not in first-class matches. In 1866 he was appointed Hon Secretary to Cambridgeshire CCC. His final first-class match was for MCC in 1868.

Perkins, Thomas Tosswill Norwood
Amateur. *b:* 19.12.1870, Strood, Kent. *d:* 26.7.1946, Stone, Tonbridge, Kent. Sound middle order right-hand batsman, right-arm fast bowler, good deep field. *Sch* St John's, Leatherhead. *Teams* Cambridge U (1893–94, blue both years); Kent (1893–1900, 25 matches).
Career batting
46–77–6–1675–109–23.59–1–*ct* 27
Bowling 198–2–99.00–0–0–1/15

He also appeared for Hertfordshire and Wiltshire, but had little time for serious cricket on taking up a scholastic appointment. A good soccer player, he was awarded his blue.

Perks, Reginald Thomas David
Professional. *b:* 4.10.1911, Hereford. *d:* 22.11.1977, Worcester. Hard hitting lower order left-hand batsman, right-arm fast medium bowler. *Team* Worcestershire (1930–55, 561 matches). *Tour* MCC to South Africa 1938/9. *Tests* England (1938/9 to 1939, 2 matches).
Career batting
595–884–150–8956–75–12.20–0–*ct* 240
Bowling 53770–2233–24.07–143–24–9/40
Test batting
2–2–2–3–2*–no av–0–*ct* 1
Bowling 355–11–32.27–2–0–5/100

He also played for Herefordshire and Monmouth. He took 100 wickets in a season sixteen times (best 159, av 19.22, in 1939). Twice he had nine wickets in an innings, the best being 9/40 for Worcs v Glamorgan at Stourbridge in 1939. After retiring he was elected to the Committee of Worcestershire CCC.

Perks, T. W.
Professional. Lower order batsman. Wicket-keeper. *Team* MCC (1902).
Career batting
1–2–0–16–11–8.00–0–*ct* 1–*st* 3
Bowling 31–0

Perrin, Percival Albert
Amateur. *b:* 26.5.1876, Hackney, Middlesex. *d:* 20.11.1945, Hickling, Norfolk. Sound middle order right-hand batsman, slow right-arm bowler, moderate field. *Teams* Essex (1896–1928, 525 matches); London County (1902)
Career batting
538–918–91–29709–343*–35.92–66–*ct* 293
Bowling 753–16–47.06–0–0–3/13

He hit 1,000 runs in a season eighteen times (best 1,893, av 47.32, in 1906). His highest innings was 343* for Essex v Derbyshire at Chesterfield in 1904 (Essex lost) and he scored two double centuries for the County. He was a Test Selector in 1926 and again in 1931 and 1939, being Chairman of the Selectors in 1939.

Perry, Ernest Harvey
Amateur. *b:* 16.1.1908, Chaddesley Corbett, Worcs. Lower order right-hand batsman, right-arm fast bowler. *Team* Worcestershire (1933–46, 10 matches).
Career batting
10–16–0–148–46–9.25–0–*ct* 3
Bowling 732–22–33.27–1–0–5/42

Perry, Harry
Amateur. *b:* 1895, Stourbridge, Worcs. *d:* 28.2.1961, Stourbridge, Worcs. Middle or lower order right-hand batsman, right-arm medium pace bowler. *Team* Worcestershire (1927–28, 5 matches).
Career batting
5–8–1–109–40–15.57–0–*ct* 0
Bowling 46–1–46.00–0–0–1/38

Perry, Horace Thomas
Professional. *b:* 1906, Bristol. *d:* 1962, Bristol. Middle order right-hand batsman, right-arm fast bowler. *Team* Somerset (1927, 1 match).
Career batting
1–2–0–9–9–4.50–0–*ct* 0

Perry, Neil James
Cricketer. *b:* 27.5.1958, Sutton, Surrey. Tail end right-hand batsman, slow left-arm bowler. *Team* Glamorgan (1979–81, 13 matches).
Career batting
13–12–4–19–6–2.37–0–*ct* 9
Bowling 920–21–43.80–0–0–3/51

Perry, William
Professional. *b:* 12.8.1830, Oxford. *d:* 1913, Newbury, Berkshire. Lower order batsman, good bowler. *Team* Lancashire (1865, 1 match).
Career batting
2–3–1–27–16–13.50–0–*ct* 3–*st* 1
Bowling 29–0
He also played for Oxfordshire and Berkshire. His first-class debut was for the North of England in 1856.

Perryman, Stephen Peter
Cricketer. *b:* 22.10.1955, Yardley, Birmingham. Lower order right-hand batsman, right-arm medium pace bowler. *Teams* Warwickshire (1974–81, 130 matches); Worcestershire (1982–83, 26 matches).
Career batting
156–162–68–872–43–9.27–0–*ct* 58
Bowling 11337–358–31.66–19–3–7/49

Pershke, William Jack
Amateur. *b:* 8.8.1918, Richmond, Surrey. *d:* January 1944. He died on active service. Lower order right-hand batsman, right-arm fast medium bowler. *Sch* Uppingham. *Team* Oxford U (1938, blue).
Career batting
8–10–5–57–17*–11.40–0–*ct* 5
Bowling 752–28–26.85–3–0–6/46

Persse, Henry Wilfred
Amateur. *b:* 19.9.1885, Southampton. *d:* 28.6.1918, near St Omer, France. He died of wounds. Lower order right-hand batsman, right-arm fast bowler. *Team* Hampshire (1905–09, 51 matches).
Career batting
51–84–8–889–71–11.69–0–*ct* 40
Bowling 3813–127–30.02–3–0–6/64
His County cricket ended in 1909 when he was posted abroad.

Pervez Sajjad Hassan
Cricketer. *b:* 30.8.1942, Lahore, India. Brother of Waqar Hassan (Pakistan). Tail end right-hand batsman, slow left-arm bowler. *Teams* Lahore (1961/2 to 1967/8); PIA (1967/8 to 1973/4); Karachi (1968/9). *Tours* Pakistan Eaglets to England 1963; Pakistan to England 1967, 1971, to Australia and New Zealand 1964/5, to Ceylon 1964/5, to Ceylon, Australia and New Zealand 1972/3; PIA to England 1969 (not first-class). *Tests* Pakistan (1964/5 to 1972/3, 19 matches).
Career batting
133–128–53–786–56*–10.48–0–*ct* 57
Bowling 10750–493–21.80–28–6–8/89
Test batting
19–20–11–123–24–13.66–0–*ct* 9
Bowling 1410–59–23.89–3–0–7/74
He did not appear in any Tests on the 1967 tour to England, and when more was expected of him in 1971, he unfortunately missed several matches through injury, though playing in all three Tests.

Pestell, Kenneth Frederick
Amateur. *b:* 7.5.1931, Edmonton, London. Middle order right-hand batsman, right-arm medium pace bowler. *Team* D. R. Jardine's XI (1957).
Career batting
1–2–0–37–21–18.50–0–*ct* 0
Bowling 17–0

Petchey, Michael David
Cricketer. *b:* 16.12.1958, London. Right-hand batsman, right-arm medium pace bowler. *Sch* Latymer Upper. *Team* Oxford U (1983, blue).
Career batting
6–6–0–21–18–3.50–0–*ct* 3
Bowling 804–12–67.00–0–0–2/70

Peters, Richard Charles
Amateur. *b:* 12.9.1911, Chew Magna, Somerset. Right-hand batsman, right-arm fast bowler. *Team* Somerset (1946, 1 match).
Career batting
1–2–1–5–3–5.00–0–*ct* 0
Bowling 18–0

Pether, Stewart
Amateur. *b:* 15.10.1916, Oxford. Lower order right-hand batsman, right-arm medium fast bowler. *Sch* Magdalen College School, Oxford. *Team* Oxford U (1939, blue).
Career batting
10–14–2–103–20*–8.58–0–*ct* 3
Bowling 622–31–20.06–2–0–5/7
His County cricket was for Oxfordshire.

Petrie, Eric Charlton
Amateur. *b:* 22.5.1927, Ngaruawahia, New Zealand. Opening or middle order right-hand batsman, wicket-keeper. *Teams* Auckland (1950/1 to 1955/6); Northern Districts (1956/7 to 1966/7); Gentlemen (1958). *Tours* New Zealand to England 1958, to India and Pakistan 1955/6. *Tests* New Zealand (1955/6 to 1965/6, 14 matches).
Career batting
115–189–34–2788–151–17.98–2–*ct* 197–*st* 37
Bowling 16–0
Test batting
14–25–5–258–55–12.90–0–*ct* 25
He was most successful on the 1958 tour to England, playing in all five Tests and appearing for the Gentlemen v Players.

Pettiford, John
Professional. *b:* 29.11.1919, Freshwater, Sydney, Australia. *d:* 11.10.1964, North Sydney, Australia. Middle order right-hand batsman, leg break and googly bowler. *Teams* New South Wales (1946/7 to 1947/8, 16 matches); Kent (1954–59, 153 matches). *Tours* Australian Services to England 1945, to India and Ceylon 1945/6; Commonwealth to India and Pakistan 1949/50.
Career batting
201–324–48–7077–133–25.64–4–*ct* 99
Bowling 9259–295–31.38–7–1–6/134
He hit 1,000 runs in a season twice (best 1,336, av 28.42, in 1955).

Pettit, David William
Amateur. *b:* 24.3.1937, Canterbury, Kent. Tail end right-hand batsman, right-arm fast medium bowler. *Sch* St Edmund's, Canterbury. *Team* Oxford U (1958–59).
Career batting
5–7–4–33–22–11.00–0–*ct* 0
Bowling 432–6–72.00–0–0–2/72

Pevensey, Viscount, Henry North Holroyd
(later 3rd Earl of Sheffield)
Amateur. *b:* 18.1.1832, London. *d:* 21.4.1909, Beaulieu, Hampshire. Middle order batsman. *Sch* Eton. *Team* Sussex (1854, 1 match).
Career batting
1–2–0–0–0–0.00–0–*ct* 0
He was the greatest patron Sussex cricket ever had, being President of the County Club from 1879 to 1897 and 1904. In 1891/2 he financed the English tour to Australia and opened his private ground at Sheffield Park in 1864. The Sheffield Shield was named after him. He was MP for East Sussex, 1857 to 1865.

Pewtress, Alfred William
Amateur. *b:* 27.8.1891, Rawtenstall, Lancashire. *d:* 21.9.1960, Brighton, Sussex. Middle order right-hand batsman, bowler. *Sch* Christ's Hospital. *Team* Lancashire (1919–25, 50 matches).
Career batting
50–73–5–1483–89–21.80–0–*ct* 16
Bowling 10–1–10.00–0–0–1/10

Phadkar, Dattatraya Gajanan
Professional. *b:* 12.12.1925, Kalhapur, Poona, India. Attacking middle order right-hand batsman, right-arm fast medium, or off break, bowler. *Teams* Maharashtra (1942/3 to 1943/4); Bombay (1944/5 to 1951/2); Hindus (1944/5 to 1945/6); Bengal (1954/5 to 1957/8); Railways (1958/9 to 1959/60); Combined XI in Ceylon 1949/50. *Tours* India to Australia 1947/8, to England 1952, to West Indies 1952/3, to Pakistan 1954/5. *Tests* India (1947/8 to 1958/9, 31 matches).
Career batting
133–178–29–5377–217–36.08–8–*ct* 92
Bowling 10271–466–22.04–31–3–7/26
Test batting
31–45–7–1229–123–32.34–2–*ct* 21
Bowling 2285–62–36.85–3–0–7/159
Although he played in all four Tests on the 1952 tour of England, his all-round record was a modest one. His only double century was 217 for Bombay v Maharashtra at Bombay in 1950/1. His final first-class match in England was for a Commonwealth XI in 1957.

Pheasant, Steven Thomas
Cricketer. *b:* 25.6.1951, Borough, London. Lower order right-hand batsman, left-arm medium pace bowler. *Team* Sussex (1971, 1 match).
Career batting
1–2–1–2–2*–2.00–0–*ct* 2
Bowling 121–4–30.25–0–0–4/88

Phebey, Arthur Henry
Professional. *b:* 1.10.1924, Catford, Kent. Stylish opening right-hand batsman, good field. *Team* Kent (1946–61, 320 matches).
Career batting
327–599–34–14643–157–25.91–13–*ct* 205
Bowling 4–0
He hit 1,000 runs in a season nine times (best 1,800, av 33.33, in 1959). His final first-class match was for MCC in 1964. A good soccer player, he appeared at inside right for Dulwich Hamlet and Hendon and was a schoolboy international.

Phelan, Patrick John
Professional. *b:* 9.2.1938, Chingford, Essex.

Lower order left-hand batsman, off break bowler. *Team* Essex (1958–65, 154 matches).
Career batting
160–199–71–1693–63–13.22–0–*ct* 67
Bowling 9006–314–28.68–17–2–8/109

Phelps, Peter Horsley
Amateur. *b:* 5.2.1909, Malvern, Worcs. Lower order right-hand batsman, right-arm medium pace bowler. *Sch* Felsted. *Team* Worcestershire (1931–32, 3 matches).
Career batting
3–4–0–25–11–6.25–0–*ct* 1

Philips, Stanley Ian
Amateur. *b:* 4.2.1920, Tunbridge Wells, Kent. Stylish middle order right-hand batsman, right-arm medium pace bowler. *Sch* Brighton. *Teams* Northants (1938–39, 6 matches); Europeans (1941/2).
Career batting
7–14–3–156–42–14.18–0–*ct* 3
Bowling 15–0
He appeared in wartime matches for Oxford University. On his first-class debut for Northants he still had another year at school to complete.

Philipson, Hylton
Amateur. *b:* 8.6.1866, Tynemouth, Northumberland. *d:* 4.12.1935, Westminster, London. Middle or lower order right-hand batsman, wicket-keeper. *Sch* Eton. *Teams* Oxford U (1887–89, blue all three years); Middlesex (1895–98, 10 matches). *Tours* Vernon to Ceylon and India 1889/90 (not first-class); Sheffield to Australia 1891/2; Stoddart to Australia 1894/5. *Tests* England (1891/2 to 1894/5, 5 matches).
Career batting
85–139–27–1951–150–17.41–2–*ct* 103–*st* 47
Test batting
5–8–1–63–30–9.00–0–*ct* 8–*st* 3
His final first-class match was for A. J. Webbe's XI in 1899. He also played for Northumberland. An all-round sportsman, he represented Oxford at rackets, tennis and soccer, being a full back in 1889.

Phillip, Norbert
Cricketer. *b:* 22.6.1949, Bioche, Dominica, West Indies. Hard hitting middle order right-hand batsman, right-arm fast medium bowler. *Teams* Windward Islands (1969/70 to 1982/3); Essex (1978–83, 127 matches). *Tour* West Indies to India and Sri Lanka 1978/9. *Tests* West Indies (1977/8 to 1978/9, 9 matches).
Career batting
202–299–35–6278–134–23.78–1–ct 66
Bowling 15058–619–24.32–27–2–7/33
Test batting
9–15–5–297–47–29.70–0–*ct* 5
Bowling 1041–28–37.17–0–0–4/48
His best season was 1982 with 82 wickets, av 22.46.

Phillips, Alan Geoffrey
Amateur. *b:* 27.3.1931, Blackburn, Lancashire. Middle order right-hand batsman, leg break bowler. *Team* Oxford U (1953–54).
Career batting
3–5–0–71–31–14.20–0–*ct* 1

Phillips, Edmund Frederick
Professional. *b:* 12.1.1932, Bridgnorth, Salop. Middle order right-hand batsman. *Team* Leicestershire (1957–59, 32 matches).
Career batting
32–54–7–629–55–13.38–0–*ct* 10

Phillips, Edward Stone
Amateur. *b:* 18.1.1883, Maindee, Newport, Monmouthshire. *d:* 8.5.1915, near Ypres, Belgium. Brother of N. C. (MCC). Middle order right-hand batsman. *Sch* Marlborough. *Team* Cambridge U (1903–04, blue 1904).
Career batting
10–18–0–422–107–23.44–1–*ct* 3
He played for Monmouthshire.

Phillips, Francis Ashley
Amateur. *b:* 11.4.1873, Crumlin, Monmouthshire. *d:* 5.3.1955, Holmer, Hereford. Free-scoring middle order right-hand batsman, right-arm medium pace bowler, fine deep field. *Sch* Rossall. *Teams* Oxford U (1892–95, blue 1892, 1894 and 1895); Somerset (1897–1911, 67 matches). *Tour* Mitchell to North America 1895.
Career batting
107–191–7–4277–163–23.24–4–*ct* 65–*st* 2
Bowling 390–7–55.71–0–0–2/8
He also appeared for Essex in 1892 (pre-first-class), Monmouthshire and Brecon. His final first-class match was for H. K. Foster's XI in 1919.

Phillips, Henry
Professional. *b:* 14.10.1844, Hastings, Sussex. *d:* 3.7.1919, Clive Vale, Hastings, Sussex. Brother of James (Sussex). Middle order right-hand batsman, left-hand slow round-arm bowler, excellent wicket-keeper. *Team* Sussex (1868–91, 195 matches).

Career batting
216–366–75–2998–111–10.30–1–*ct* 341–*st* 195
Bowling 283–14–20.21–0–0–4/33

Phillips, Hugh Raymond
Amateur. *b:* 8.4.1929, Kuala Lumpur, Malaya. Middle order right-hand batsman. *Team* Warwickshire (1951, 1 match).
Career batting
1–1–0–3–3–3.00–0–*ct* 0

Phillips, Howard William
Professional. *b:* 20.4.1872, Isle of Wight. *d:* 17.3.1960, East London, South Africa. Opening batsman, useful bowler. *Teams* Hampshire (1899–1902, 5 matches); Border (1908/09 to 1913/14).
Career batting
17–31–2–276–47–9.51–0–*ct* 12
Bowling 162–2–81.00–0–0–1/10

Phillips, James
Professional. *b:* 1.9.1860, Pleasant Creek, Victoria, Australia. *d:* 21.4.1930, Burnaby, Vancouver, Canada. Lower order right-hand batsman, right-arm medium pace bowler, good cover point. *Teams* Victoria (1885/6 to 1895/6, 17 matches); Middlesex (1890–98, 90 matches); Canterbury (1898/9).
Career batting
124–203–58–1826–110*–12.59–1–*ct* 50
Bowling 7102–355–20.00–30–7–8/69

He was best known as an umpire and due to his actions, above all, the prevalence of 'throwing' among bowlers in the 1890s was stamped out – notably he no-balled the Australian, Ernest Jones, for throwing in 1897/8 and later, in England, A. W. Mold of Lancashire.

Phillips, James
Professional. *b:* 26.9.1849, Hastings, Sussex. *d:* 31.1.1905, Hastings, Sussex. Brother of Henry (Sussex). Middle order right-hand batsman, good field. *Team* Sussex (1871–86, 64 matches).
Career batting
73–137–6–1931–89–14.74–0–*ct* 67

His final first-class match was for an England XI in 1888.

Phillips, John Brydon Mills
Amateur. *b:* 19.11.1933, Canterbury, Kent. Tail end right-hand batsman, right-arm fast medium bowler. *Sch* King's, Canterbury. *Teams* Oxford U (1955–57, blue 1955); Kent (1955, 4 matches).
Career batting
32–43–15–151–25–5.39–0–*ct* 9
Bowling 2567–72–35.65–1–0–5/62

Phillips, Joseph Evelyn
Amateur. *b:* 30.7.1891, St John's, Barbados. *d:* 10.12.1958, Edinburgh, Scotland. Right-hand batsman, right-arm medium pace bowler. *Teams* Scotland (1923); Barbados (1919/20).
Career batting
4–6–0–52–25–8.66–0–*ct* 4
Bowling 118–2–59.00–0–0–1/15

Phillips, Joseph Herbert
Amateur. *b:* 2.12.1881, Ansley, Warwickshire. *d:* 15.1.1951, Oldbury, Nuneaton, Warwickshire. Lower order right-hand batsman, right-arm fast bowler. *Team* Warwickshire (1904–11, 6 matches).
Career batting
6–7–0–35–16–5.00–0–*ct* 5
Bowling 159–1–159.00–0–0–1/30

Phillips, Leslie Jack
Amateur. *b:* 20.1.1899, Leyton, Essex. *d:* 22.4.1979, Woodford Wells, Essex. Middle order right-hand batsman, slow left-arm bowler. *Sch* Forest. *Team* Essex (1919–22, 4 matches).
Career batting
4–5–1–38–19–9.50–0–*ct* 0
Bowling 31–0

Phillips, Noel Clive
Amateur. *b:* 30.7.1883, Maindee, Newport, Monmouthshire. *d:* 15.8.1961, Colwall, Worcs. Brother of E. S. (Cambridge U). Attacking middle order right-hand batsman. *Sch* Marlborough. *Teams* MCC (1908); South Wales (1912).
Career batting
6–11–0–188–62–17.09–0–*ct* 4

His final first-class match was for Free Foresters in 1921. He played for Monmouthshire.

Phillips, Raymond L.
Amateur. Lower order right-hand batsman, slow right-arm bowler. *Team* Jamaica (1925/6 to 1927/8). *Tour* West Indies to England 1923.
Career batting
7–5–1–69–38–17.25–0–*ct* 3
Bowling 622–24–25.91–1–0–5/68

Owing to injury he played in only one first-class match on the 1923 tour.

Phillips, Reginald Maurice
Amateur. *b:* 19.10.1897, Newport, Monmouthshire. *d:* 7.6.1963, Budleigh Salterton, Devon. *Sch* Shrewsbury. *Team* Wales (1925).
Career batting
1–2–0–13–11–6.50–0–*ct* 0

He played for Monmouthshire.

Phillips, Roy Wycliffe
Cricketer. *b:* 8.4.1941, Holders Hill, St James, Barbados. Middle order right-hand batsman, leg break bowler. *Teams* Barbados (1966/7); Gloucestershire (1968–70, 16 matches).
Career batting
18–28–0–529–92–18.89–0–*ct* 11
Bowling 6–0

Phillips, Walter
Amateur. *b:* 1.4.1881, West Malling, Kent. *d:* 21.6.1948, Mereworth, Kent. Middle order batsman. *Sch* Eastbourne. *Team* Kent (1903, 1 match).
Career batting
2–4–0–83–55–20.75–0–*ct* 2
His final first-class match was for H. D. G. Leveson-Gower's XI in 1912.

Phillips, William
Professional. Lower order batsman, wicket-keeper. *Team* Lancashire (1904–08, 10 matches).
Career batting
10–18–3–109–18–7.26–0–*ct* 17–*st* 2
He played also for Cheshire.

Phillipson, Christopher Paul
Cricketer. *b:* 10.2.1952, Vrindaban, India. Tail end, originally, but from about 1975 middle order right-hand batsman, right-arm medium pace bowler. *Sch* Ardingly. *Team* Sussex (1970–83, 167 matches).
Career batting
167–225–61–3046–87–18.57–0–*ct* 135
Bowling 5213–153–34.07–4–0–6/56

Phillipson, William Edward
Professional. *b:* 3.12.1910, North Reddish, Cheshire. Middle order right-hand batsman, right-arm fast medium bowler. *Team* Lancashire (1933–48, 158 matches). *Tour* Cahn to New Zealand 1938/9.
Career batting
162–208–49–4096–113–28.76–2–*ct* 82
Bowling 13722–555–24.72–29–6–8/100
He took 100 wickets in a season twice (best 133, av 22.33, in 1939). He also played for Northumberland. He was appointed to the first-class umpires' list in 1956 and officiated in 12 Test matches.

Phipps, Douglas David
Cricketer. *b:* 27.7.1934, Edmonton, London. Middle order batsman, bowler. *Team* Combined Services (1964).
Career batting
1–2–0–15–15–7.50–0–*ct* 1
Bowling 53–1–53.00–0–0–1/53

Phipps, Herbert Gould
Amateur. *b:* 8.8.1845, Shepton Mallet, Somerset. *d:* 19.10.1899, Tientsin, China. Twin brother of W. T. (Southgate). Lower order right-hand batsman, right-hand slow medium round-arm bowler, excellent deep field. *Sch* Harrow. *Team* MCC (1865).
Career batting
2–3–1–9–6*–4.50–0–*ct* 0
A merchant in Foochow, China, from about 1870 he had no opportunities to appear in first-class cricket.

Phipps, Walter Tudway
Amateur. *b:* 8.8.1845, Shepton Mallet, Somerset. *d:* 28.4.1902, Shanghai, China. Twin brother of H. G. (MCC). Middle order right-hand batsman, right-hand slow round-arm or fast under-arm bowler. *Sch* Harrow. *Team* Southgate (1867–68).
Career batting
2–3–1–44–30–22.00–0–*ct* 1
He did not appear in any first-class matches whilst at Oxford U.

Piachaud, James Daniel
Amateur. *b:* 1.3.1937, Colombo, Ceylon. Lower order right-hand batsman, off break bowler, good close field. *Teams* Oxford U (1958–61, blue all four years); Hampshire (1960, 12 matches); Ceylon (1968/9). *Tours* MCC to North America 1959 (non-first-class), to Bangladesh 1976/7 (non-first-class); Swanton to India 1963/4.
Career batting
71–103–18–1037–40–12.20–0–*ct* 53
Bowling 5070–205–24.73–8–1–8/72

Pick, Robert Andrew
Cricketer. *b:* 19.11.1963, Nottingham. Lower order left-hand batsman, right-arm medium fast bowler. *Team* Nottinghamshire (1983, 6 matches).
Career batting
6–8–2–84–25*–14.00–0–*ct* 0
Bowling 500–7–71.42–0–0–2/50

Pickeman, Douglas C.
Amateur. *b:* *circa* 1900, Ireland. *d:* June 1965, Ireland. Right-hand batsman, leg break bowler. *Team* Ireland (1926).
Career batting
1–2–0–2–2–1.00–0–*ct* 1

Pickering, Arthur
Amateur. *b:* 1878, Ashton, Bristol. *d:* 15.12.1939, Cotham, Bristol. Middle order batsman. *Teams* London County (1901); Gloucestershire (1908, 1 match).

Career batting
2–4–0–10–4–2.50–0–*ct* 0
Bowling 20–0

Pickering, Rev Edward Hayes
Amateur. *b:* 21.5.1807, Clapham, Surrey. *d:* 19.5.1852, Eton, Buckinghamshire. Brother of W. P. (Cambridge U and Surrey), uncle of F. P. U. (Sussex). Stylish middle order right-hand batsman. *Sch* Eton. *Teams* Cambridge U (1827–29, blue 1827 and 1829); Surrey (1844, 1 match).
Career batting
15–26–3–274–72*–11.91–0–*ct* 4
Bowling 15 wickets, no analyses
A schoolmaster at Eton College, he was unable to spare the time for much cricket after leaving Cambridge.

Pickering, Francis Percy Umfreville
Amateur. *b:* 4.8.1851, Shipton, York. *d:* 11.3.1879, West Chiltington, Sussex. Nephew of E. H. (Surrey) and W. P. (Surrey). Middle order right-hand batsman, right-hand fast under-arm bowler. *Sch* Eton. *Teams* Oxford U (1873); Sussex (1874–75, 3 matches). *Tour* Fitzgerald to North America 1872 (not first-class).
Career batting
5–7–0–87–24–12.42–0–*ct* 7
Bowling 64–8–8.00–0–0–4/16

Pickering, Harry Gordon
Amateur. *b:* 18.1.1917, Hackney, London. *d:* 4.3.1984, Seaford, Sussex. Middle order right-hand batsman, slow right-arm bowler. *Teams* Essex (1938, 3 matches); Leicestershire (1947, 5 matches).
Career batting
8–16–0–297–79–18.56–0–*ct* 0

Pickering, Peter Barlow
Professional. *b:* 24.3.1926, York. Middle order right-hand batsman, good close field. *Team* Northants (1953, 1 match).
Career batting
1–2–0–59–37–29.50–0–*ct* 0
He became a first-class umpire in South Africa. A well-known soccer player he kept goal for Chelsea, York City and Northampton.

Pickering, William Percival
Amateur. *b:* 25.10.1819, Clapham, Surrey. *d:* 16.8.1905, Vancouver, Canada. Brother of E. H. (Cambridge U and Surrey), uncle of F. P. U. (Sussex). Middle order right-hand batsman, left-hand medium pace round-arm bowler, brillant cover point. *Sch* Eton. *Teams* Cambridge U (1840–42, blue 1840 and 1842); Surrey (1844–48, 3 matches).
Career batting
30–53–6–544–76*–11.57–0–*ct* 17
Bowling 35–0+7–no av–0–0–3/?
He could throw in with either hand. He emigrated to Montreal in 1852 and was the chief organiser of the 1859 pioneering tour by the English side to Canada.

Pickett, Christopher Arthur
Amateur. *b:* 26.8.1926, Hedgerley, Bucks. Lower order left-hand batsman, left-arm fast, or slow, bowler. *Team* Minor Counties (1953).
Career batting
1–2–1–10–7*–10.00–0–*ct* 0
Bowling 54–0
His County cricket was for Buckinghamshire.

Pickett, Henry
Professional. *b:* 26.3.1862, Stratford, Essex. *d:* 3.10.1907, Aberavon, Glamorgan. He disappeared from his home and his body was found on the beach in December. Lower order right-hand batsman, right-arm fast bowler. *Team* Essex (1894–97, 52 matches).
Career batting
62–94–37–450–35–7.89–0–*ct* 25
Bowling 3269–134–24.39–4–1–10/32
His career with Essex began in 1881 and he made his first-class debut in 1884 for MCC. His best bowling in an innings was 10 for 32 for Essex v Leics at Leyton in 1895.

Pickles, David
Professional. *b:* 16.11.1935, Halifax, Yorkshire. Lower order right-hand batsman, right-arm fast medium bowler. *Team* Yorkshire (1957–60, 41 matches).
Career batting
41–40–20–74–12–3.70–0–*ct* 10
Bowling 2062–96–21.45–4–1–7/61

Pickles, Lewis
Professional. *b:* 17.9.1932, Wakefield, Yorkshire. Opening right-hand batsman, off break bowler, close field. *Team* Somerset (1955–58, 47 matches).
Career batting
47–88–5–1702–87–20.50–0–*ct* 21
Bowling 65–1–65.00–0–0–1/22
He hit 1,136 runs, av 24.69, in 1956.

Picknell, George
Professional. *b:* 29.11.1813, Chalvington, Sussex. *d:* 26.2.1863, Chalvington, Sussex. He died following the amputation of his leg. Brother of Robert (Sussex). Powerful middle order right-hand batsman, right-hand fast round-arm bowler. *Team* Sussex (1836–54, 63 matches).

Career batting
81–146–16–1661–79–12.77–0–*ct* 48
Bowling 498–33+35–15.09–4–0–6/?

Picknell, Robert
Professional. *b:* 2.6.1816, Chalvington, Sussex. *d:* 7.2.1869, Eastbourne, Sussex. Brother of George (Sussex). Middle order right-hand batsman, excellent cover point. *Team* Sussex (1837–45, 16 matches).
Career batting
18–34–1–182–23–5.51–0–*ct* 5

Pickthall, Harold
Professional. *b:* 1896, Burnley, Lancashire. *d:* 8.8.1965, Preston, Lancashire. Lower order batsman, good bowler. *Team* MCC (1928–35).
Career batting
12–16–6–109–29*–10.90–0–*ct* 3
Bowling 772–25–30.88–0–0–4/30
He played for Monmouthshire.

Pickup, James Kenneth
Cricketer. *b:* 25.9.1952, Stalybridge, Cheshire. Middle order right-hand batsman, wicket-keeper. *Team* Oxford U (1973–75).
Career batting
3–6–0–19–14–3.16–0–*ct* 1
His County cricket was for Cheshire, commencing 1972.

Pidcock, Charles Alexander
Amateur. *b:* 27.8.1850, Bareilly, India. *d:* 28.10.1901, Hastings, Sussex. Lower order right-hand batsman, wicket-keeper. *Sch* Harrow. *Team* An England XI (1872).
Career batting
1–1–0–12–12–12.00–0–*ct* 0
He was for some years a Civil Commissioner in Matabeleland, Rhodesia.

Pieris, Percival Ian
Amateur. *b:* 14.3.1933, Colombo, Ceylon. Middle order right-hand batsman, right-arm medium pace bowler. *Teams* Cambridge U (1956–58, blue 1957–58); Ceylon (1964/5 to 1966/7). *Tours* Ceylon to India 1966/7, to Pakistan 1966/7.
Career batting
44–66–13–917–55*–17.30–0–*ct* 14
Bowling 3530–101–34.95–4–1–6/30

Pierpoint, Frederick George
Professional. *b:* 24.4.1915, Walworth, London. Lower order right-hand batsman, right-arm fast medium bowler. *Team* Surrey (1936–46, 8 matches).
Career batting
8–11–7–15–4–3.75–0–*ct* 3
Bowling 592–13–45.54–0–0–3/60
He also played for Norfolk and Devonshire.

Pierre, Lance Richard
Amateur. *b:* 5.6.1921, Woodbrook, Port of Spain, Trinidad. Tail end right-hand batsman, right-arm fast medium bowler. *Team* Trinidad (1940/1 to 1949/50). *Tour* West Indies to England 1950. *Test* West Indies (1947/8, 1 match).
Career batting
35–35–14–131–23–6.23–0–*ct* 14
Bowling 2522–102–24.72–4–0–8/51
Test batting
1 match, did not bat – *ct* 0
Bowling 28–0
Due to injury he played only 12 first-class matches on the 1950 tour and no Tests.

Pigg, Charles
Amateur. *b:* 4.9.1856, Buntingford, Hertfordshire. *d:* 28.2.1929, Cheltenham, Gloucs. Twin brother of Herbert (Cambridge U). Free hitting lower order right-hand batsman, right-hand slow round-arm bowler. *Team* Cambridge U (1878).
Career batting
17–27–5–300–48–13.63–0–*ct* 10
Bowling 151–6–25.16–0–0–1/0
His first-class debut was for An England Eleven in 1876, and his last first-class match was for MCC in 1901. For Hertfordshire v Northants in 1880 he took all ten wickets (for 13). His County cricket was for Hertfordshire, Northants (pre-first-class) and Cambridgeshire.

Pigg, Herbert
Amateur. *b:* 4.9.1856, Buntingford, Herts. *d:* 8.6.1913, Manitoba, Canada. Twin brother of Charles (Cambridge U). Lower order right-hand batsman, right-arm fast round-arm bowler. *Team* Cambridge U (1877–78, blue 1877).
Career batting
15–29–4–363–59–14.52–0–*ct* 8
Bowling 579–28–20.67–1–1–7/55
He played for Northants in 1874 and 1875 and Hertfordshire 1876 to 1897. His final first-class match was for the Gentlemen in 1891. The brothers were generally known as Hot and Cold Pigg.

Piggott, Julian Ito
Amateur. *b:* 25.3.1888, Tokyo, Japan. *d:* 23.1.1965, Coldharbour, Dorking, Surrey. Middle order right-hand batsman. *Sch* Cheltenham. *Team* Surrey (1910–13, 3 matches).

Career batting
3–5–1–153–84–38.25–0–*ct* 5
He appeared in the Freshmen's and Seniors' matches at Cambridge but no first-class games.

Pigot, David Richard
Amateur. *b:* 14.1.1900, Dublin. *d:* 10.8.1965, Dublin. Brother of J. P. M. (Dublin University), father of D. R. jun (Ireland). Right-hand batsman, right-arm fast medium bowler. *Teams* Dublin University (1922–26); Ireland (1922–39).
Career batting
11–22–0–338–51–15.36–0–*ct* 4
Bowling 29–0

Pigot, David Richard (jun)
Cricketer. *b:* 18.7.1929, Dublin. Son of D. R. (Ireland), nephew of J. P. M. (Dublin University). Middle order right-hand batsman. *Team* Ireland (1966–75).
Career batting
11–21–0–406–88–19.33–0–*ct* 8

Pigot, James Poole Maunsell
Amateur. *b:* 31.1.1901, Dublin. *d:* 20.7.1980, Dublin, Ireland. Brother of D. R. (Ireland), uncle of D. R. jun (Ireland). Lower order right-hand batsman, leg break and googly bowler. *Teams* Dublin University (1924–25); Europeans (1925/6 to 1929/30).
Career batting
5–9–1–67–50–8.37–0–*ct* 3
Bowling 184–4–46.00–0–0–3/71

Pigott, Anthony Charles Shackleton
Cricketer. *b:* 4.6.1958, London. Lower order right-hand batsman, right-arm fast medium bowler. *Sch* Harrow. *Teams* Sussex (1978–83, 73 matches); Wellington (1982/3). *Tour* Robins to New Zealand 1979/80.
Career batting
81–94–20–1131–63–15.28–0–*ct* 34
Bowling 5864–216–27.14–10–1–7/74

Pike, Arthur
Professional. *b:* 25.12.1862, Keyworth, Notts. *d:* 15.11.1907, Keyworth, Notts. Lower order right-hand batsman, wicket-keeper. *Team* Nottinghamshire (1894–99, 65 matches).
Career batting
66–101–20–1128–66–13.92–0–*ct* 102–*st* 30
His final first-class match was for MCC in 1901. From 1902 to 1905 he was on the first-class umpires' list, but then was compelled by ill-health to retire.

Pilch, Fuller
Professional. *b:* 17.3.1804, Horningtoft, Norfolk. *d:* 1.5.1870, Canterbury, Kent. Brother of Nathaniel and William (Norfolk), uncle of William (Kent). Brilliant middle order right-hand batsman, right-hand slow round-arm bowler. *Teams* Norfolk (1820–36); Kent (1836–54, 84 matches); Hampshire (1842–45, 5 matches); Surrey (1830–44, 2 matches); Sussex (1840–42, 3 matches); Cambridge Town Club (1832).
Career batting
229–416–32–7147–153*–18.61–3–*ct* 121
Bowling 109–6+136–18.16–3–0–7/?
For a period of about 15 years commencing in the early 1830s, Pilch was the premier batsman in England. Haygarth, writing in 1862, described Pilch as 'the best batsman that has ever yet appeared'. Haygarth went on: 'his style of batting was very commanding, extremely forward, and he seemed to crush the best bowling by his long forward plunge before it had time to shoot, or rise, or do mischief by catches.'

Pilch, William
Professional. *b:* 18.6.1820, Brinton, Norfolk. *d:* 11.1.1882, Canterbury. Son of Nathaniel (Norfolk), nephew of Fuller (Kent) and William (Norfolk). Middle order right-hand batsman, useful bowler, excellent long-stop. *Team* Kent (1840–54, 45 matches).
Career batting
52–100–11–718–38–8.06–0–*ct* 33
Bowling 32–5+12–6.40–0–0–3/7
He won his place in the County side mainly due to his long-stopping. His final first-class match was in 1857 for Kent and Sussex. He also played for Norfolk.

Pilkington, Alfred Frederick
Professional. *b:* 22.4.1901, Camberwell, London. Tail end batsman, good bowler. *Team* Surrey (1926, 1 match).
Career batting
1–1–0–4–4–4.00–0–*ct* 0
Bowling 29–1–29.00–0–0–1/29

Pilkington, Charles Carlisle
Amateur. *b:* 13.12.1876, Woolton, Lancashire. *d:* 8.1.1950, South Warnborough, Hampshire. Brother of H. C. (Middlesex). Stylish middle order right-hand batsman, right-arm medium pace bowler. *Sch* Eton. *Teams* Lancashire (1895, 2 matches); Oxford U (1896, blue); Middlesex (1903, 2 matches).
Career batting
13–20–1–468–86–24.63–0–*ct* 6
Bowling 370–9–41.11–0–0–3/70
Regarded as a most gifted all-rounder, he played very rarely in first-class cricket. His final first-class match was for Gentlemen of England in 1919.

Pilkington, Hubert Carlisle
Amateur. *b:* 23.10.1879, Woolton, Liverpool, Lancashire. *d:* 17.6.1942, Letchworth, Herts. Brother of C. C. (Lancashire and Middlesex). Stylish middle order right-hand batsman, right-arm slow bowler, good field. *Sch* Eton. *Teams* Oxford U (1899–1900, blue both years); Middlesex (1903–04, 4 matches).
Career batting
20–30–2–688–93–24.57–0–*ct* 7
Bowling 16–0

Pillans, Albert Alexander
Amateur. *b:* 25.2.1869, Ceylon. *d:* 28.11.1901, Maskeliya, Ceylon. He died of peritonitis. Middle/lower order batsman, good bowler, moderate field. *Team* Hampshire (1896, 3 matches).
Career batting
3–6–2–82–32*–20.50–0–*ct* 0
Bowling 151–6–25.16–0–0–2/31

Pilling, Harry
Cricketer. *b:* 23.2.1943, Ashton-under-Lyne, Lancashire. Sound middle order right-hand batsman, off break bowler. *Team* Lancashire (1962–80, 323 matches). *Tours* Robins to the Far East 1977/8 (first-class in Sri Lanka); Commonwealth to Pakistan 1970/1; Rest of World to Pakistan 1973/4.
Career batting
333–542–68–15279–149*–32.23–25–*ct* 89
Bowling 195–1–195.00–0–0–1/42
He hit 1,000 runs in a season eight times (best 1,606 runs, av 36.50, in 1967).

Pilling, Richard
Professional. *b:* 5.7.1855, Bedford. *d:* 28.3.1891, Old Trafford, Lancashire. Brother of William (Lancashire). Lower order right-hand batsman, splendid wicket-keeper. *Team* Lancashire (1877–89, 177 matches). *Tours* Lillywhite, Shaw and Shrewsbury to Australia 1881/2, 1887/8. *Tests* England (1881/2 to 1888, 8 matches).
Career batting
250–372–111–2572–78–9.85–0–*ct* 461–*st* 206
Test batting
8–13–1–91–23–7.58–0–*ct* 10–*st* 4
He was regarded for several years as the equal of any wicket-keeper in England; his career was brought to an early end when he had inflammation of the lungs following a football match in 1889/90. He was sent to Australia at the expense of Lancashire CCC during the winter of 1890/1, but died six days after returning home.

Pilling, William
Professional. *b: circa* 1858. *d:* 27.3.1924, Stretford, Lancashire. Brother of Richard (Lancashire). Lower order batsman, wicket-keeper. *Team* Lancashire (1891, 1 match).
Career batting
1–1–1–9–9*–no av–0–*ct* 1–*st* 1

Pinch, Francis Brewster
Amateur. *b:* 24.2.1891, Bodmin, Cornwall. *d:* 8.10.1961, Ashford, Kent. Middle order right-hand batsman, right-arm medium pace bowler. *Teams* Glamorgan (1921–26, 41 matches); Wales (1924).
Career batting
42–73–5–1082–138*–15.91–1–*ct* 25
Bowling 1265–39–32.43–0–0–4/48
On his first-class debut, for Glamorgan v Worcs at Swansea in 1921, he hit 138*.

Pinder, George
(real name George Pinder Hattersley)
Professional. *b:* 15.7.1841, Ecclesfield, Sheffield, Yorkshire. *d:* 15.1.1903, Hickleton, Yorkshire. Hard hitting lower order right-hand batsman, slow under-arm bowler, wicket-keeper. *Team* Yorkshire (1867–80, 124 matches). *Tour* Daft to North America 1879 (not first-class).
Career batting
179–286–66–2415–78–10.97–0–*ct* 220–*st* 137
Bowling 481–23–20.91–0–0–4/56
His final first-class match was for T. Emmett's XI in 1881.

Pinfield, Reginald Gordon C.
Amateur. *b:* 31.12.1894, Chippenham, Wiltshire. *d:* 1972, Bournemouth, Hants. Middle order batsman. *Team* Sussex (1922, 4 matches).
Career batting
4–7–1–97–42*–16.16–0–*ct* 6
He also played for Wiltshire.

Pink, Alfred
Professional. *b:* 1.6.1855, Fratton Bridge, Portsmouth. *d:* 1931, Portsmouth, Hants. Middle/lower order right-hand batsman, right-arm medium pace bowler, close field. *Team* Hampshire (1885, 1 match).
Career batting
1–2–0–54–39–27.00–0–*ct* 0
Bowling 15–1–15.00–0–0–1/15

Pink, Hubert Selwyn
Amateur. *b:* 12.11.1878, Chapel-en-le-Frith, Derbyshire. *d:* 25.11.1946, Chapel-en-le-Frith, Derbyshire. Middle order right-hand batsman.

Sch St Edmunds, Canterbury. *Team* Derbyshire (1900, 3 matches).
Career batting
3–5–0–24–11–4.80–0–*ct* 0
Bowling 33–0

Pinner, William Gladstone
Amateur. *b:* 1877, West Bromwich, Staffordshire. *d:* 1944, Wednesbury, Staffordshire. Lower order batsman, useful bowler. *Team* Northants (1908, 1 match).
Career batting
1–2–1–26–24–26.00–0–*ct* 0
Bowling 17–0

Pinnock, Renford Augustus
Cricketer. *b:* 26.9.1937, St Catherine, Jamaica. Middle order right-hand batsman, wicket-keeper. *Team* Jamaica (1963/4 to 1974/5). *Tour* Jamaica to England 1970.
Career batting
44–71–5–2662–176–40.33–6–*ct* 26–*st* 5
Bowling 52–1–52.00–0–0–1/25
He was most successful on the 1970 tour with 321 runs, av 80.25.

Pitchford, Harry
Professional. *b:* 11.2.1891, Wing, Bucks. *d:* July 1965, Wing, Bucks. Brother of Leonard (Glamorgan). Middle order right-hand batsman, right-arm slow bowler. *Team* Minor Counties (1928).
Career batting
1–2–0–36–24–18.00–0–*ct* 0
Bowling 9–0
His County cricket was for Buckinghamshire.

Pitchford, Leonard
Professional. *b:* 4.12.1900, Wing, Bucks. Brother of Harry (Minor Counties). Middle order right-hand batsman. *Team* Glamorgan (1935, 2 matches).
Career batting
2–3–1–24–14*–12.00–0–*ct* 0
Bowling 4–0
He also played for Monmouthshire.

Pithey, Anthony John
Amateur. *b:* 17.7.1933, Umtali, Southern Rhodesia. Brother of D. B. (Northants and South Africa). Sound opening right-hand batsman. *Teams* Rhodesia (1950/1 to 1968/9); Western Province (1955/6 to 1957/8). *Tours* South Africa to England 1960, to Australia and New Zealand 1963/4. *Tests* South Africa (1956/7 to 1964/5, 17 matches).
Career batting
124–213–16–7073–170–35.90–13–*ct* 59
Bowling 17–0
Test batting
17–27–1–819–154–31.50–1–*ct* 3
Bowling 5–0
He appeared in two Tests on the 1960 tour to England and in first-class matches scored 614 runs, av 27.90.

Pithey, David Bartlett
Amateur. *b:* 4.10.1936, Salisbury, Rhodesia. Brother of A. J. (South Africa). Forceful opening or middle order right-hand batsman, off break bowler. *Teams* Western Province (1957/8); Natal (1966/7); Transvaal (1967/8); Rhodesia (1956/7 to 1965/6); Oxford U (1960–62, blue 1961 and 1962); Northants (1962, 3 matches). *Tour* South Africa to Australia and New Zealand 1963/4. *Tests* South Africa (1963/4 to 1966/7, 8 matches).
Career batting
99–160–13–3420–166–23.26–3–*ct* 55
Bowling 7388–240–30.78–13–1–7/47
Test batting
8–12–1–138–55–12.54–0–*ct* 6
Bowling 577–12–48.08–1–0–6/58
His best season in England was 1961 with 824 runs, av 26.58.

Pitman, Raymond Walter Charles
Professional. *b:* 21.2.1933, Bartley, Hants. Middle order right-hand batsman, right-arm medium fast bowler. *Team* Hampshire (1954–59, 50 matches).
Career batting
50–76–8–926–77–13.61–0–*ct* 42
Bowling 68–1–68.00–0–0–1/4

Pitt, James Albert
Amateur. *b:* 14.9.1921, Birmingham. Middle order right-hand batsman, bowler. *Team* Combined Services (1957).
Career batting
1–2–1–36–26*–36.00–0–*ct* 1
Bowling 4–0

Pitt, Thomas Alfred
Amateur. *b:* 1892, Hardingstone, Northants. *d:* 22.4.1957, Northampton. Lower order right-hand batsman, right-arm medium pace bowler. *Team* Northants (1932–35, 25 matches).
Career batting
25–43–14–207–31*–7.13–0–*ct* 6
Bowling 1563–43–36.34–0–0–4/65

Pitts, George James Stuart
Amateur. *b:* 6.10.1878, St John's, Newfoundland. *d:* 27.7.1939, Margate, Kent. Tail end right-

hand batsman, right-arm fast bowler. *Sch* Merchant Taylors. *Team* Middlesex (1914, 2 matches).
Career batting
2–2–1–14–14–14.00–0–*ct* 0
Bowling 165–6–27.50–0–0–3/36

Place, Winston
Professional. *b:* 7.12.1914, Rawtenstall, Lancashire. Sound opening, later middle order, batsman, good field. *Team* Lancashire (1937–55, 298 matches). *Tours* MCC to West Indies 1947/8; Commonwealth to India, Pakistan and Ceylon 1949/50. *Tests* England (1947/8, 3 matches).
Career batting
324–487–49–15609–266*–35.63–36–*ct* 190
Bowling 42–1–42.00–0–0–1/2
Test batting
3–6–1–144–107–28.80–1–*ct* 0
He hit 1,000 runs in a season eight times, going on to 2,000 once : 2,501, av 62.52, in 1947. His three double centuries were all for Lancashire, the highest being 266* v Oxford U at Oxford in 1947.

Platt, George (John) William
Professional. *b:* 9.6.1881, Richmond, Surrey. *d:* 14.4.1955, Old Hill, Staffs. Tail end right-hand batsman, right-arm medium, later off break, bowler. *Team* Surrey (1906–14, 33 matches).
Career batting
35–53–9–421–49–9.56–0–*ct* 28
Bowling 2253–111–20.29–6–1–6/61
For Surrey 2nd XI v Dorset at Dorchester in 1908 he created a Minor Counties Competition record by taking all 10 wickets in a single innings for 15 runs.

Platt, Robert Kenworthy
Professional. *b:* 26.12.1932, Holmfirth, Yorkshire. Lower order right-hand batsman, right-arm medium pace bowler. *Teams* Yorkshire (1955–63, 96 matches); Northants (1964, 2 matches).
Career batting
101–107–49–424–57*–7.31–0–*ct* 38
Bowling 6799–301–22.58–10–3–7/40

Platts, John Thomas Brown Dumelow
Professional. *b:* 23.11.1848, Chellaston, Derbyshire. *d:* 6.8.1898, Derby. Middle order left-hand batsman, right-hand fast, later slow, round-arm bowler. *Team* Derbyshire (1871–84, 90 matches).
Career batting
97–180–6–2237–115–12.85–1–*ct* 56
Bowling 3673–195–18.83–7–0–6/39
His first-class debut was for MCC in 1870 v Notts at Lord's and during this match a delivery from Platts hit Summers on the head. The batsman subsequently died from the accident and Platts was so affected by the tragedy that he changed from fast bowler to slow. For some years he was a County umpire.

Playle, William Rodger
Amateur. *b:* 1.12.1938, Palmerston North, New Zealand. Stylish middle order right-hand batsman. *Teams* Auckland (1956/7 to 1963/4); Western Australia (1965/6 to 1967/8, 17 matches). *Tour* New Zealand to England 1958. *Tests* New Zealand (1958 to 1962/3, 8 matches).
Career batting
85–145–13–2888–122–21.87–4–*ct* 82
Bowling 94–1–94.00–0–0–1/11
Test batting
8–15–0–151–65–10.06–0–*ct* 4
Although he played in all five Tests on the 1958 tour, he achieved very little.

Pleass, James Edward
Amateur in 1947, turned professional 1948. *b:* 21.5.1923, Cardiff. Sound middle order right-hand batsman, fine outfield. *Team* Glamorgan (1947–56, 171 matches).
Career batting
171–253–31–4293–102*–19.30–1–*ct* 77
Bowling 15–0

Plimsoll, John Bruce
Amateur. *b:* 27.10.1917, Cape Town, South Africa. Father of J. B., jun (Natal). Tail end right-hand batsman, left-arm medium fast bowler. *Teams* Western Province (1939/40 to 1947/8); Natal (1948/9 to 1949/50). *Tour* South Africa to England 1947. *Test* South Africa (1947, 1 match).
Career batting
39–47–13–386–51–11.35–0–*ct* 9
Bowling 3581–155–23.10–9–3–7/35
Test batting
1–2–1–16–8*–16.00–0–*ct* 0
Bowling 143–3–47.66–0–0–3/128
He took 68 wickets, av 23.32, in first-class matches on the 1947 tour, but was only effective on pitches which suited him and appeared in just a single Test.

Plowden, Sir Henry Meredyth
Amateur. *b:* 26.9.1840, Sylhet, India. *d:* 8.1.1920, Sunninghill, Berkshire. Stylish middle or lower order right-hand batsman, right-hand slow off break round-arm bowler. *Sch* Harrow. *Teams* Cambridge U (1860–63, blue all four years); Hampshire (1865, 1 match).
Career batting
15–25–6–248–69*–13.05–0–*ct* 10
Bowling 552–43+13–12.83–5–0–7/25
He went to India and from 1877 to 1894 was Judge of the Chief Court in the Punjab; his first-

class cricket career was therefore very brief. His final first-class match was for MCC in 1866. He was also a noted rackets player.

Plowright, Arthur Vincent
Amateur. *b:* 6.10.1916, Edinburgh, Scotland. Right-hand batsman. *Team* Scotland (1937).
Career batting
1–2–0–36–29–18.00–0–*ct* 1

Plumb, Stephen George
Cricketer. *b:* 17.1.1954, Wimbish, Essex. Middle order right-hand batsman, right-arm medium pace bowler. *Team* Essex (1975–77, 2 matches). *Tour* MCC to Bangladesh 1980/81 (not first-class).
Career batting
3–5–1–97–37*–24.25–0–*ct* 1
Bowling 60–2–30.00–0–0–2/47

He appeared for Norfolk commencing 1978. His final first-class match was for Minor Counties in 1981.

Plumb, Thomas
Professional. *b:* 26.7.1833, Aylesbury, Bucks. *d:* 29.3.1905, Northampton. Middle or lower order right-hand batsman, right-hand medium pace bowler, wicket-keeper. *Teams* North (1866–74); South (1879).
Career batting
26–47–10–474–67–12.81–0–*ct* 27–*st* 15
Bowling 35–3–11.66–0–0–3/35

He played for Northamptonshire from 1850 to 1884 and occasionally for Buckinghamshire and Bedfordshire. He died in very poor circumstances.

Plummer, Peter John
Cricketer. *b:* 28.1.1947, Nottingham. Lower order right-hand batsman, slow left-arm bowler. *Team* Nottinghamshire (1969–72, 33 matches).
Career batting
33–37–7–386–46–12.86–0–*ct* 16
Bowling 2016–63–32.00–2–0–7/71

He also played for Buckinghamshire commencing 1973.

Pocknee, John
Professional. *b:* 1860, Brighton, Sussex. *d:* 1938, Kilburn, London. Lower order batsman, wicket-keeper. *Team* Middlesex (1884, 1 match).
Career batting
1–2–0–8–5–4.00–0–*ct* 1

Pocock, Howard John
Amateur. *b:* 8.4.1921, Maidstone, Kent. Middle order right-hand batsman. *Team* Kent (1947–49, 7 matches).
Career batting
7–11–1–118–34–11.80–0–*ct* 3
Bowling 70–1–70.00–0–0–1/53

He is the present chairman of Kent CCC.

Pocock, Nicholas Edward Julian
Cricketer. *b:* 15.12.1951, Maracaibo, Venezuela. Middle order right-hand batsman, left-arm medium pace bowler. *Sch* Shrewsbury. *Team* Hampshire (1976–83, 114 matches). *Tours* MCC to Far East 1981, to United States 1982 (neither first-class).
Career batting
114–168–20–3476–164–23.48–2–*ct* 111
Bowling 335–4–83.75–0–0–1/4

He has captained Hampshire since 1980.

Pocock, Patrick Ian
Cricketer. *b:* 24.9.1946, Bangor, Caernarvonshire. Lower order right-hand batsman, off break bowler. *Teams* Surrey (1964–83, 423 matches); Northern Transvaal (1971/2). *Tours* MCC to Pakistan 1966/7, to West Indies 1967/8, 1973/4, to Ceylon and Pakistan 1968/9, to Ceylon 1969/70, to India, Pakistan and Sri Lanka 1972/3; Rest of World in Pakistan 1970/1. *Tests* England (1967/8 to 1976, 17 matches).
Career batting
481–517–132–4431–75*–11.50–0–*ct* 167
Bowling 37368–1443–25.89–56–6–9/57
Test batting
17–27–2–165–33–6.60–0–*ct* 13
Bowling 2023–47–43.04–3–0–6/79

He took 112 wickets, av 18.22, in 1967. His best bowling in an innings is 9 for 57 for Surrey v Glamorgan at Sophia Gardens, Cardiff in 1979. He created a sensation during the Surrey v Sussex match at Eastbourne in 1972 by taking four wickets in four balls, then five in six, six in nine and finally seven wickets in eleven balls.

Poidevin, Dr Leslie Oswald Sheridan
Amateur. *b:* 5.11.1876, Merrila, New South Wales, Australia. *d:* 18.11.1931, Bondi, New South Wales, Australia. Defensive middle order right-hand batsman, right-arm slow bowler, good field. *Teams* New South Wales (1895/6 to 1904/5, 13 matches); London County (1902–04); Lancashire (1904–08, 105 matches). *Tour* New South Wales to New Zealand 1895/6.
Career batting
149–234–21–7022–179–32.96–14–*ct* 163
Bowling 1927–46–41.89–2–0–8/66

He hit 1,000 runs in a season twice (best 1,433, av 39.80, in 1905). Latterly he was a noted cricket writer.

Poland, Rev Frederick William
Amateur. *b:* 10.10.1858, Shepherd's Bush, London. *d:* 1940, Mount Royal, Montreal, Canada. Middle order right-hand batsman, wicket-keeper. *Sch* Newton College. *Team* Cambridge U (1881).
Career batting
1–1–1–4–4*–no av–0–*ct* 2–*st* 3
He played for Devonshire and Hertfordshire.

Pollard, David
Professional. *b:* 7.8.1835, Comus Lepton, Yorkshire. *d:* 26.3.1909, Lepton, Yorkshire. He was found dead in bed. Lower order right-hand batsman, right-arm medium pace bowler, slip field. *Team* Yorkshire (1865, 1 match).
Career batting
2–3–0–6–3–2.00–0–*ct* 1
Bowling 124–2–62.00–0–0–2/75
His final first-class match was for An England Eleven in 1872.

Pollard, Richard
Professional. *b:* 19.6.1912, Westhoughton, Lancashire. Hard hitting lower order right-hand batsman, right-arm fast medium bowler. *Team* Lancashire (1933–50, 266 matches). *Tour* MCC to Australia and New Zealand 1946/7. *Tests* England (1946–48, 4 matches).
Career batting
298–328–63–3522–63–13.29–0–*ct* 225
Bowling 25314–1122–22.56–60–10–8/33
Test batting
4–3–2–13–10*–13.00–0–*ct* 3
Bowling 378–15–25.20–1–0–5/24
He took 100 wickets in a season seven times (best 149, av 21.58, in 1938). His final first-class match was for a Commonwealth XI in 1952.

Pollard, Victor
Cricketer. *b:* 7.9.1945, Burnley, Lancashire. Middle order right-hand batsman, off break bowler. *Teams* Central Districts (1964/5 to 1968/9); Canterbury (1969/70 to 1974/5). *Tours* New Zealand to England 1965, 1969, 1973, to India and Pakistan 1964/5, 1969/70, to Australia 1967/8. *Tests* New Zealand (1964/5 to 1973, 32 matches).
Career batting
130–207–33–5314–146–30.54–6–*ct* 81
Bowling 6931–224–30.94–6–1–7/65
Test batting
32–59–7–1266–116–24.34–2–*ct* 19
Bowling 1853–40–46.32–0–0–3/3
After two modest tours to England in 1965 and 1969, he was most successful in 1973, and with two Test centuries headed the Test batting averages with 302 runs, av 100.66.

Polley, Vivian Ralph
Amateur. *b:* 22.12.1880, Fulham, Middlesex. *d:* 12.2.1967, Brighton, Sussex. Lower order right-hand batsman, right-arm fast bowler. *Team* Middlesex (1913, 5 matches).
Career batting
5–8–4–18–5–4.50–0–*ct* 2
Bowling 382–10–38.20–0–0–3/49

Pollitt, George
Professional. *b:* 3.6.1874, Chickenley, Yorkshire. Middle order batsman. *Team* Yorkshire (1899, 1 match).
Career batting
1–1–0–51–51–51.00–0–*ct* 1
He also played for Bedfordshire.

Pollitt, Tom Urquhart
Amateur. *b:* 14.7.1900, Farnham, Surrey. *d:* 13.8.1979, Ely, Cambridgeshire. Opening left-hand batsman. *Team* RAF (1931).
Career batting
1–2–0–20–14–10.00–0–*ct* 2

Pollock, Angus John
Cricketer. *b:* 19.4.1962, Liversedge, Yorkshire. Lower order right-hand batsman, right-arm medium pace bowler. *Sch* Shrewsbury. *Team* Cambridge U (1982–83, blue both years).
Career batting
17–17–4–101–19–7.76–0–*ct* 4
Bowling 1233–35–35.22–2–0–5/107

Pollock, John Stuart
Amateur. *b:* 5.6.1920, Belfast. Son of William (Ireland). Middle order right-hand batsman, off break bowler. *Sch* Campbell College. *Team* Ireland (1939–57).
Career batting
23–43–2–1036–129–25.26–1–*ct* 17
Bowling 2–0
His final first-class match was for Free Foresters in 1958. He represented Ireland at squash.

Pollock, Peter Maclean
Amateur. *b:* 30.6.1941, Pietermaritzburg, Natal, South Africa. Son of A. M. (Orange Free State), brother of R. G. (Eastern Province). Lower order right-hand batsman, right-arm fast bowler. *Team* Eastern Province (1958/9 to 1971/2). *Tours* SA Fezela to England 1961; South Africa to England 1965, to Australia and New Zealand 1963/4; Rest of World to Australia 1971/2, to England 1966, 1967, 1968 and 1970. *Tests* South Africa (1961/2 to 1969/70, 28 matches).

Career batting
127–177–43–3028–79–22.59–0–*ct* 54
Bowling 10620–485–21.89–27–2–7/19
Test batting
28–41–13–607–75*–21.67–0–*ct* 9
Bowling 2806–116–24.18–9–1–6/38

The most successful bowler on the 1965 tour of England he headed both the Test and first-class averages and played in all three Tests.

Pollock, Robert Graeme
Cricketer. *b:* 27.2.1944, Durban, Natal, South Africa. Son of A. M. (Orange Free State), brother of P. M. (Eastern Province). Attacking middle order left-hand batsman, leg break bowler. *Teams* Eastern Province (1961/2 to 1977/8); Transvaal (1978/9 to 1982/3). *Tours* South Africa to England 1965, to Australia and New Zealand 1963/4; Rest of the World to England 1966, 1967, 1968 and 1970. *Tests* South Africa (1963/4 to 1969/70, 23 matches).
Career batting
226–380–50–18352–274–55.61–56–*ct* 214
Bowling 2062–43–47.95–0–0–3/46
Test batting
23–41–4–2256–274–60.97–7–*ct* 17
Bowling 204–4–51.00–0–0–2/50

Most successful on the 1965 tour to England, he headed both Test and first-class batting averages, in the latter scoring 1,147 runs, av 57.35. He also hit 1,000 runs in a South African season four times and once in Australia. Regarded by many as the equal of any batsman in the World during the 1970s, his first-class cricket has been almost entirely confined to domestic matches in South Africa. His highest score was 274 for South Africa v Australia at Durban in 1969/70.

Pollock, William
Amateur. *b:* 28.8.1886, Belfast. *d:* 24.11.1972, Belfast. Father of J. S. (Ireland). Right-hand batsman, right-arm fast bowler. *Sch* Campbell College, Belfast. *Team* Ireland (1909–23).
Career batting
5–9–0–312–144–34.66–1–*ct* 0
Bowling 200–9–22.22–0–0–3/42

Pomfret, Rear Admiral Arnold Ashworth
Amateur. *b:* 1.6.1900, Blackpool, Lancashire. *d:* 3.4.1984, Taunton, Somerset. Tail end right-hand batsman, right-arm fast medium bowler. *Team* Royal Navy (1929).
Career batting
3–5–1–5–5–1.25–0–*ct* 1
Bowling 291–12–24.37–1–0–6/39

Ponniah, Charles Edward Manoharan
Cricketer. *b:* 3.5.1943, Ceylon. Sound opening right-hand batsman, leg break bowler. *Teams* Cambridge U (1967–69, blue all three years); Ceylon (1963/4 to 1964/5). *Tour* Ceylon to India 1964/5.
Career batting
45–87–8–1978–101*–25.03–1–*ct* 12
Bowling 82–6–13.66–1–0–5/20

Ponsford, William Harold
Amateur. *b:* 19.10.1900, North Fitzroy, Victoria, Australia. Sound opening right-hand batsman. *Team* Victoria (1920/1 to 1933/4, 55 matches). *Tours* Australia to England 1926, 1930 and 1934, to New Zealand 1927/8. *Tests* Australia (1924/5 to 1934, 29 matches).
Career batting
162–235–23–13819–437–65.18–47–*ct* 71
Bowling 41–0
Test batting
29–48–4–2122–266–48.22–7–*ct* 21

A record-breaking batsman with 13 innings over 200 to his name, including two triple centuries and two over 400, his highest being 437 for Victoria v Queensland at Melbourne in 1927/8, he was relatively unsuccessful on two of his three visits to England. In 1926 tonsilitis laid him low, in 1930 he hit 1,425 runs, av 49.13, and only in 1934 did he really demonstrate his full talents with 1,784 runs, av 77.56, including 266 for Australia v England at the Oval. He twice hit 1,000 runs in an Australian season. His final first-class match was for W. M. Woodfull's XI in 1934/5.

Ponsonby, Cecil Brabazon
Amateur. *b:* 26.12.1892, London. *d:* 11.5.1945, St John's Wood, London. Lower order right-hand batsman, wicket-keeper. *Sch* Eton. *Team* Worcestershire (1911–28, 74 matches).
Career batting
76–131–26–844–50*–8.03–0–*ct* 73–*st* 11

He played in the Oxford Freshmen's Match of 1912, but no first-class matches for the University. In 1927 he captained Worcestershire.

Ponsonby, John Henry
(changed name to Ponsonby Fane in 1875)
Amateur. *b:* 21.7.1848, Westminster, London. *d:* 11.9.1916, Brympton, Somerset. Son of S. C. B. (Surrey and Middlesex), nephew of 6th Earl of Bessborough (Cambridge U). Steady lower order right-hand batsman, right-hand slow under-arm bowler, wicket-keeper. *Sch* Harrow. *Team* MCC (1870).
Career batting
7–9–1–161–53–20.12–0–*ct* 9–*st* 2
Bowling 209–13–16.07–1–0–5/51

Playing for I Zingari v School of Gunnery at Shoeburyness in 1874 he took 19 of the 22 wickets (the match being 12 a side).

Ponsonby, Rt Hon Sir Spencer Cecil Brabazon
(changed name to Ponsonby Fane in 1875)
Amateur. *b:* 14.3.1824, Mayfair, London. *d:* 1.12.1915, Brympton, Yeovil. Brother of 6th Earl of Bessborough (Cambridge U), father of J. H. (MCC). Lively opening or middle order right-hand batsman, good deep field. *Teams* Surrey (1844–53, 3 matches); Middlesex (1862, 1 match).
Career batting
62–117–3–1359–108–11.92–1–*ct* 30–*st* 2
Bowling 48–2+12–24.00–1–0–5/?
His first important match was in 1841 and his last in 1864 (both for MCC). He was on the MCC Committee 1866–68, 1870–73, 1875–78, Treasurer 1879 to his death and Trustee from 1900; he was a founder member of the Surrey Committee and President of Somerset CCC from 1890. With his brother and J. L. Baldwin he founded I Zingari in 1845 and was Hon Secretary and Governor of the Club.
Apart from his cricket connections he held many important posts including Private Secretary to Lord Palmerston, the Earl of Clarendon and Earl Granville, also Comptroller of the Lord Chamberlain's Office, Gentleman Usher of the Sword and Bath King of Arms.

Pont, Ian Leslie
Cricketer. *b:* 28.8.1961, Brentwood, Essex. Brother of K. R. (Essex). Middle order right-hand batsman, right-arm medium pace bowler. *Sch* Brentwood. *Team* Nottinghamshire (1982, 4 matches).
Career batting
4–7–1–32–16–5.33–0–*ct* 1
Bowling 302–3–100.66–0–0–2/107
He played for Buckinghamshire in 1983.

Pont, Keith Rupert
Cricketer. *b:* 16.1.1953, Wanstead, Essex. Brother of I. L. (Notts). Middle order right-hand batsman, right-arm medium pace bowler. *Team* Essex (1970–83, 179 matches).
Career batting
179–274–40–6061–125*–25.90–7–*ct* 86
Bowling 2689–83–32.39–2–0–5/17
His best season was 1983 with 802 runs, av 34.86.

Pontifex, Rev Alfred
Amateur. *b:* 17.3.1842, London. *d:* 25.8.1930, Weston, Bath, Somerset. Middle order batsman. *Team* Gloucestershire (1871, 1 match).
Career batting
1–2–1–12–6*–12.00–0–*ct* 1
Whilst at Cambridge he appeared in some Trial Matches, but no first-class contests. He also played for Somerset (pre-first-class), Norfolk and Suffolk.

Pontifex, Dudley David
Amateur. *b:* 12.2.1855, Bath, Somerset. *d:* 27.9.1934, Dulwich, London. Opening or middle order right-hand batsman. *Sch* Bath College. *Teams* Somerset (1882, 1 match); Surrey (1881, 9 matches).
Career batting
17–27–1–357–89–13.73–0–*ct* 3
Bowling 13–0
He played in the 1875 Freshmen's Match at Cambridge, but no first-class games whilst at the University. His first-class debut was for the Gentlemen of England in 1878 and his final appearance for MCC in 1896.

Pool, Charles James Tomlin
Amateur. *b:* 21.1.1876, Northampton. *d:* 13.10.1954, Epsom, Surrey. Attractive middle order right-hand batsman. *Team* Northants (1905–10, 94 matches).
Career batting
94–177–6–4350–166–25.43–4–*ct* 51
Bowling 227–5–45.40–0–0–4/53
He made his debut for Northants in 1893 and spent three years in Australia at the turn of the century. A good hockey player he represented Northants.

Poole, Arthur Bertram
Amateur. *b:* 30.6.1907, Bedford. *d:* 22.11.1979, Hammersmith, London. Hard hitting middle order right-hand batsman. *Sch* Bedford Modern. *Team* Minor Counties (1936).
Career batting
1–2–1–92–91*–92.00–0–*ct* 0
He played for Bedfordshire from 1925 to 1951, being captain from 1946 to 1951 and later Chairman and President of the County Club.

Poole, Cyril John
Professional. *b:* 13.3.1921, Forest Town, Mansfield, Notts. Attacking middle order left-hand batsman, left-arm medium pace bowler, excellent deep field, occasional wicket-keeper. *Team* Nottinghamshire (1948–62, 366 matches). *Tour* MCC to India and Ceylon 1951/2. *Tests* England (1951/2, 3 matches).

Career batting
383–637–42–19364–222*–32.54–24–*ct* 224–*st* 5
Bowling 347–4–86.75–0–0–1/8
Test batting
3–5–1–161–69*–40.25–0–*ct* 1
Bowling 9–0

He hit 1,000 runs in a season twelve times (best 1,860, av 33.21, in 1961). Both his double centuries were for Notts, the highest being 222* v Indians at Trent Bridge in 1952. A good soccer player, he appeared for Gillingham and Mansfield Town.

Poole, Kenneth John
Professional. *b:* 27.4.1934, Thurgarton, Notts. Middle order right-hand batsman, right-arm medium fast bowler. *Team* Nottinghamshire (1955–57, 26 matches).
Career batting
26–44–5–612–58–15.69–0–*ct* 21
Bowling 1361–21–64.80–0–0–2/10

A farming accident in October 1957, which resulted in him losing three fingers of his right hand, ended his career in County cricket. He played football for Northampton Town.

Pooley, Edward
Professional. *b:* 13.2.1838, Richmond, Surrey. *d:* 18.7.1907, Lambeth, London. Brother of F. W. (Surrey). Hard hitting middle order right-hand batsman, wicket-keeper. *Teams* Surrey (1861–83, 256 matches); Middlesex (1864–65, 7 matches). *Tours* Willsher to North America 1868 (not first-class); Lillywhite to Australia and New Zealand 1876/7 (not first-class in New Zealand).
Career batting
370–645–56–9345–125–15.86–1–*ct* 496–*st* 358
Bowling 390–6–65.00–0–0–2/39

One of the greatest wicket-keepers of his day, especially to slow bowling, his record of 12 dismissals in a match (ct 8, st 4 for Surrey v Sussex at the Oval in 1868) still stands unchallenged in English first-class cricket. He hit 1,084 runs, av 23.06, in 1870. Faults of a personal nature marred his otherwise brilliant career and he ended his days in the workhouse.

Pooley, Frederick William
Professional. *b:* 7.4.1852, Richmond, Surrey. *d:* 14.9.1905, West Ham, Essex. Brother of E. (Surrey and Middlesex). Middle order right-hand batsman, wicket-keeper. *Team* Surrey (1876–77, 3 matches).
Career batting
4–6–0–16–11–2.66–0–*ct* 5

Poore, Brigadier-General Robert Montagu
Amateur. *b:* 20.3.1866, Carysfort, Dublin. *d:* 14.7.1938, Bournemouth, Hants. Attacking middle order right-hand batsman, right-arm slow bowler, fine field. *Teams* Europeans (1892/3 to 1913/4); South Africa (1895/6); Hampshire (1898–06, 36 matches). *Tests* South Africa (1895/6 3 matches).
Career batting
55–98–9–3441–304–38.66–11–*ct* 38
Bowling 252–13–19.38–0–0–2/10
Test batting
3–6–0–76–20–12.66–0–*ct* 3
Bowling 4–1–4.00–0–0–1/4

He created a sensation in 1899, the only English season in which he appeared regularly in County cricket, by hitting 1,551 runs, av 91.23, including 304 for Hampshire v Somerset at Taunton. He was easily the leading batsman of the summer.

He was a prolific batsman in India in the early 1890s and appeared in non-first-class matches for Natal with such success that he gained a place in the South African team.

A noted all-round sportsman he was a fine swordsman, a first-rate polo player and a good tennis player.

Pope, Andrew Noble
Amateur. *b:* 14.11.1881, Clifton, Bristol. *d:* 18.4.1942, Cheltenham, Gloucs. Middle order batsman. *Sch* Harrow. *Team* Gloucestershire (1911, 2 matches).
Career batting
2–4–0–46–29–11.50–0–*ct* 1

Pope, Alfred Vardy
Professional. *b:* 15.8.1909, Tibshelf, Derbyshire. Brother of G. H. and Harold (Derbyshire). Hard hitting lower order right-hand batsman, right-arm fast medium, or off break, bowler. *Team* Derbyshire (1930–39, 211 matches).
Career batting
214–316–46–4963–103–18.38–1–*ct* 98
Bowling 12512–555–22.54–22–3–7/84

His best season was 1936, when he took 99 wickets, av 18.13.

Pope, Charles George
Amateur. *b:* 21.1.1872, Sandy, Bedfordshire. *d:* 31.1.1959, New Milton, Hants. Lower order right-hand batsman, right-arm medium fast bowler. *Sch* Harrow. *Team* Cambridge U (1892–95, blue 1894).
Career batting
11–18–5–136–26*–10.46–0–*ct* 8
Bowling 497–20–24.85–1–0–5/39

He played for Bedfordshire from 1892 to 1901.

Pope, Dudley Fairbridge
Professional. *b:* 28.10.1906, Barnes, London. *d:*

8.9.1934, Writtle, Essex. He was killed in a road accident. Defensive opening right-hand batsman, excellent deep field. *Teams* Gloucestershire (1925–27, 11 matches); Essex (1928–34, 148 matches).
Career batting
159–268–19–6557–161–26.33–7–*ct* 38
Bowling 272–4–68.00–0–0–1/11
He hit 1,000 runs in a season four times (best 1,750, av 34.31, in 1934); his final first-class innings was 108 for Essex v Gloucs at Gloucester.

Pope, George Henry
Professional. *b:* 27.1.1911, Tibshelf, Derbyshire. Brother of A. V. and Harold (Derbyshire). Middle order right-hand batsman, right-arm fast medium bowler. *Team* Derbyshire (1933–48, 169 matches). *Tours* Tennyson to India 1937/8; Commonwealth to India, Pakistan and Ceylon 1949/50. *Test* England (1947, 1 match).
Career batting
205–312–44–7518–207*–28.05–8–*ct* 157
Bowling 13488–677–19.92–40–7–8/38
Test batting
1–1–1–8–8*–no av–0–*ct* 0
Bowling 85–1–85.00–0–0–1/49
He hit 1,000 runs in a season four times (best 1,464, av 31.82, in 1939), and took 100 wickets twice (best 114, av 18.38, in 1947). In 1948 he completed the 'double'. His highest score was 207* for Derbyshire v Hampshire at Portsmouth in 1948. He retired from County cricket after the 1948 season owing to the health of his wife, and was later a first-class umpire.

Pope, Harold
Professional. *b:* 10.5.1919, Chesterfield, Derbyshire. Brother of A. V. and G. H. (Derbyshire). Lower order right-hand batsman, leg break bowler. *Team* Derbyshire (1939–46, 10 matches).
Career batting
10–16–3–81–24*–6.23–0–*ct* 3
Bowling 599–15–39.93–0–0–3/80

Pope, Dr Roland James
Amateur. *b:* 18.2.1864, Sydney, New South Wales, Australia. *d:* 27.7.1952, Manly, New South Wales, Australia. Neat middle order right-hand batsman, right-hand slow under-arm bowler, good deep field. *Teams* New South Wales (1884/5, 3 matches); MCC (1889–91). *Tours* Assisted the Australians in England 1886, 1890, 1902. *Test* Australia (1884/5, 1 match).
Career batting
20–33–7–318–47–12.23–0–*ct* 13
Bowling 19–0
Test batting
1–2–0–3–3–1.50–0–*ct* 0

He came to Britain to study medicine and remained for some years.

Popham, Reginald Francis
Amateur. *b*: 8.1.1892, Kensington, London. *d:* 9.9.1975, Warnham, Sussex. Steady middle order right-hand batsman. *Sch* Repton. *Team* MCC (1919).
Career batting
5–6–1–151–52*–30.20–0–*ct* 0
Bowling 10–0
His County cricket was for Norfolk, commencing in 1910. A noted soccer player he captained Oxford and went on to win three amateur international caps for England.

Popplewell, Nigel Francis Mark
Cricketer. *b:* 8.8.1957, Chislehurst, Kent. Son of O. B. (Cambridge U). Attacking middle order right-hand batsman, right-arm medium pace bowler. *Sch* Radley. *Teams* Cambridge U (1977–79, blue all three years); Somerset (1979–83, 78 matches). *Tour* MCC to Bangladesh 1976/7 (not first-class).
Career batting
103–148–23–2890–143–23.12–2–*ct* 73
Bowling 3914–95–41.20–1–0–5/33
He appeared for Buckinghamshire in 1975 and 1978.

Popplewell, Oliver Bury
Amateur. *b:* 15.8.1927, Northwood, Middlesex. Father of N. F. M. (Cambridge U and Somerset). Lower order right-hand batsman, wicket-keeper. *Sch* Charterhouse. *Team* Cambridge U (1949–51, blue all three years).
Career batting
41–56–13–881–74*–20.48–0–*ct* 63–*st* 16
Bowling 10–0
His final first-class match was for Free Foresters in 1960.

Porbandar, H. H. the Maharaja of, Rana Saheb Shri Natvarsinhji Bhavsinhji
Amateur. *b:* 30.6.1901, Porbandar, India. *d:* 4.10.1979, Porbandar, India. Brother-in-law of K. S. Limbdi (Western India States). Steady middle order right-hand batsman. *Teams* Roshanara Club (1931/2); Viceroys's XI (1932/3). *Tour* India to England 1932.
Career batting
6–7–0–42–22–6.00–0–*ct* 0
He came forward to captain the 1932 touring team, when the Maharaja of Patiala was forced to stand down. His abilities as a batsman were not up to first-class cricket and he played in very few matches on the tour and did not appear in the Test match.

Porch, Robert Bagehot
Amateur. *b:* 3.4.1875, Weston-super-Mare, Somerset. *d:* 29.10.1962, Great Malvern, Worcs. Middle order right-hand batsman, leg break bowler, excellent field. *Sch* Malvern. *Team* Somerset (1895–1910, 27 matches).
Career batting
27–50–7–665–85*–15.46–0–*ct* 10
Bowling 61–0
He appeared in the Seniors Match at Oxford but no first-class matches – a schoolmaster, his opportunities for County cricket were limited.

Portal, Sir Gerald Herbert
Amateur. *b:* 13.3.1858, Laverstoke, Hants. *d:* 25.1.1894, Westminster, London. He died of typhoid fever. Middle order right-hand batsman, left-arm fast bowler. *Sch* Eton. *Team* I Zingari (1885).
Career batting
1–1–0–6–6–6.00–0–*ct* 1
Bowling 55–4–13.75–0–0–4/55
At the time of his death he was Consul General at Zanzibar and was preparing an official report on Uganda, having been on a special mission to that country.

Porteous, Thomas Wilkie
Cricketer. *b:* 22.1.1948, Glasgow, Scotland. Right-hand batsman. *Team* Scotland (1973–74).
Career batting
2–4–0–18–18–4.50–0–*ct* 5

Porter, Arthur
Amateur. *b:* 25.3.1914, Enfield, Lancashire. Steady middle order right-hand batsman. *Team* Glamorgan (1936–49, 38 matches).
Career batting
38–64–7–1292–105–22.66–2–*ct* 16
Bowling 480–16–30.00–0–0–4/25

Porter, Rev Albert Lavington
Amateur. *b:* 20.1.1864, Croydon, Surrey. *d:* 14.12.1937, Tiverton, Devon. Middle order batsman. *Sch* Marlborough. *Teams* Somerset (1883, 2 matches); Hampshire (1895, 1 match).
Career batting
4–5–0–19–7–3.80–0–*ct* 3
Bowling 20–0
He appeared in the Cambridge Freshmen's Match, but no first-class matches whilst at the University.

Porter, Andrew Marshall
Amateur. *b:* 6.1.1874, Dublin. *d:* 5.6.1900, Ladywood, Lindley, Orange Free State, South Africa. Right-hand batsman, wicket-keeper. *Sch* Harrow. *Team* Dublin University (1895).
Career batting
4–8–0–87–44–10.87–0–*ct* 2
Bowling 9–0

Porter, Edward Horatio
Amateur. *b:* 13.10.1846, Liverpool. *d:* 31.10.1918, Hooton, Cheshire. Hard hitting middle order right-hand batsman, right-hand medium pace round-arm bowler. *Team* Lancashire (1874–82, 17 matches).
Career batting
20–34–1–374–61–11.33–0–*ct* 13
Bowling 48–3–16.00–0–0–3/28
His final first-class match was for a Combined Lancashire and Yorkshire XI in 1883.

Porter, George
Professional. *b:* 3.12.1861, Kilburn, Derbyshire. *d:* 15.7.1908, Spondon, Derbyshire. He died of sunstroke. Lower order right-hand batsman, right-arm fast medium bowler, moderate field. *Team* Derbyshire (1881–96, 36 matches).
Career batting
37–56–15–386–93–9.41–0–*ct* 26
Bowling 2795–130–21.50–7–1–7/49
His career ended abruptly due to a back injury in 1896; he afterwards umpired in County matches.

Porter, Hugh Lachlan
Amateur. *b:* 25.1.1911, London. *d:* 8.1.1982, Ealing, Middlesex. Middle order right-hand batsman, right-arm slow bowler. *Sch* Winchester. *Team* Minor Counties (1935).
Career batting
2–2–0–42–38–21.00–0–*ct* 0
He played for Suffolk.

Porter, Simon Robert
Cricketer. *b:* 9.8.1950, Oxford. Lower order right-hand batsman, off break bowler. *Team* Oxford U (1973, blue). *Tour* Minor Counties to East Africa 1982/3 (not first-class).
Career batting
7–12–2–76–20–7.60–0–*ct* 2
Bowling 600–18–33.33–0–0–4/26
His County cricket was for Oxfordshire, commencing 1971.

Porthouse, Stanley Clive
Amateur. *b:* 14.8.1910, Redditch, Worcs. Middle order right-hand batsman. *Team* Worcestershire (1934–35, 5 matches).
Career batting
5–8–1–70–27–10.00–0–*ct* 0
Bowling 4–0

Portman, Francis John
Amateur. *b:* 24.3.1878, Corton Denham, Somerset. *d:* 2.5.1905, Ajmer, India. He died of typhoid. Middle or lower order right-hand batsman, right-arm fast medium bowler. *Sch* Radley. *Team* Somerset (1897–99, 2 matches).
Career batting
2–4–1–12–8–4.00–0–*ct* 2
Bowling 68–3–22.66–0–0–2/38
He appeared in the Oxford Freshmen's Match of 1897.

Posnett, Charles Edward
Amateur. *b:* 29.5.1914, Belfast. Right hand batsman. *Team* Ireland (1947).
Career batting
1–2–0–46–26–23.00–0–*ct* 1

Posno, Bernard (Maurice)
Amateur. *b:* 1850, Barnet, Herts. *d:* 24.2.1901, Paris, France. Middle order batsman. *Team* An England Eleven (1878–79).
Career batting
2–4–0–5–2–1.25–0–*ct* 0

Posthuma, C. J.
Amateur. *b:* 11.1.1868, Haarlem, Holland. *d:* 21.12.1939, near Haarlem, Holland. Middle order left-hand batsman, left-arm fast bowler. *Team* London County (1903).
Career batting
5–6–0–45–29–7.50–0–*ct* 1
Bowling 346–23–15.04–2–1–7/68
He was regarded as the 'W. G. Grace' of Dutch cricket.

Potbury, Frederick John
Amateur. *b:* 1862, Honiton, Devon. *d:* 4.4.1943, Honiton, Devon. Middle order batsman. *Team* Somerset (1882, 1 match).
Career batting
1–2–0–0–0–0.00–0–*ct* 0

Pothecary, Arthur Ernest
Professional. *b:* 1.3.1906, Southampton, Hampshire. Nephew of S.G. (Hampshire). Sound middle or lower order left-hand batsman, slow left-arm bowler. *Team* Hampshire (1927–46, 271 matches).
Career batting
271–445–39–9477–130–23.34–9–*ct* 146
Bowling 2140–52–41.15–0–0–4/47
He hit 1,000 runs in a season four times (1,357, av 27.14, in 1938 best).

Pothecary, James Edward
Amateur. *b:* 6.12.1933, Cape Town, South Africa. Lower order right-hand batsman, right-arm medium pace bowler. *Team* Western Province (1954/5 to 1964/5). *Tour* South Africa to England 1960. *Tests* South Africa (1960, 3 matches).
Career batting
54–77–11–1039–81*–15.74–0–*ct* 42
Bowling 4054–143–28.34–2–0–5/29
Test batting
3–4–0–26–12–6.50–0–*ct* 2
Bowling 354–9–39.33–0–0–4/58
He played in three Tests on the 1960 tour and in first-class matches took 53 wickets, av 29.52 – a disappointing return.

Pothecary, Sidney George
Professional. *b:* 26.9.1886, Southampton. *d:* 1976, Southampton. Uncle of A. E. (Hampshire). Lower order left-hand batsman, left-arm medium pace bowler. *Team* Hampshire (1912–20, 12 matches).
Career batting
12–16–6–103–22*–10.30–0–*ct* 5
Bowling 257–4–64.25–0–0–3/43

Potter, Charles Warren
Professional in 1869, but amateur from 1870. *b:* 18.4.1851, Albury, Surrey. *d:* 6.6.1895, Shamley Green, Surrey. Steady middle order right-hand batsman, good deep field. *Team* Surrey (1869–71, 17 matches).
Career batting
17–31–3–385–31–13.75–0–*ct* 3
Bowling 17–1–17.00–0–0–1/17

Potter, George
Amateur. *b:* 3.10.1878, Oldham, Lancashire. Middle order right-hand batsman. *Team* Lancashire (1902, 10 matches).
Career batting
10–17–1–449–86–28.06–0–*ct* 3
He also played for Cheshire.

Potter, Gordon
Professional. *b:* 26.10.1931, Dormans Land, Surrey. Middle order right-hand batsman, leg break bowler. *Team* Sussex (1949–57, 55 matches).
Career batting
55–84–11–1313–88–19.35–0–*ct* 34
Bowling 863–19–44.89–0–0–3/29

Potter, Ian Caesar
Amateur. *b:* 2.9.1938, Woking, Surrey. Tail end right-hand batsman, right-arm medium pace bowler. *Sch* King's, Canterbury. *Teams* Kent (1959–61, 3 matches); Oxford U (1960–62, blue 1961–62).

Career batting
19–24–10–124–34–8.85–0–*ct* 11
Bowling 1300–45–28.88–2–0–6/74

Potter, Jack
Amateur. *b:* 13.4.1938, Melbourne, Australia. Attacking middle order right-hand batsman, leg break and googly bowler. *Team* Victoria (1956/7 to 1967/8, 81 matches). *Tours* Australia to England 1964, to New Zealand 1959/60.
Career batting
104–169–20–6142–221–41.22–14–*ct* 85
Bowling 1287–31–41.51–0–0–4/20
He hit 751 runs, av 31.29, on the 1964 tour of England, but was not required for any of the Tests. His highest score was 221 for Victoria v NSW at Melbourne 1965/6.

Potter, Joseph
Professional. *b:* 13.1.1839, Northampton. *d:* 2.6.1906, Northampton. Lower order right-hand batsman, right-arm medium pace bowler. *Teams* Kent (1871, 2 matches); Surrey (1875–81, 35 matches).
Career batting
38–68–14–357–27*–6.61–0–*ct* 32
Bowling 2111–100–21.11–7–3–7/31
He also appeared for Northants (pre-first-class) and Wiltshire. After retiring from County cricket he became an umpire.

Potter, Laurie
Cricketer. *b:* 7.11.1962, Bexleyheath, Kent. Opening right-hand batsman, left-arm medium pace bowler. *Team* Kent (1981–83, 21 matches).
Career batting
21–38–3–1132–118–32.34–2–*ct* 10
Bowling 47–2–23.50–0–0–1/9
He played for both Young Australia and Young England.

Potter, Thomas Owen
Amateur. *b:* 10.9.1844, Calcutta, India. *d:* 27.4.1909, Hoylake, Cheshire. Brother of W. H. (Lancashire). Middle order batsman. *Team* Lancashire (1866, 1 match).
Career batting
1–2–0–39–39–19.50–0–*ct* 0

Potter, Wilfred
Professional. *b:* 2.5.1910, Swinecliffe, Harrogate, Yorkshire. Lower order right-hand batsman, leg break bowler. *Team* Warwickshire (1932, 1 match).
Career batting
1–2–0–0–0–0.00–0–*ct* 1
Bowling 31–1–31.00–0–0–1/19

Potter, William Henry
Amateur. *b:* 20.8.1847, Gufsey, India. *d:* 10.4.1920, Boreham Wood, Hertfordshire. Brother of T.O. (Lancashire). Middle order batsman. *Team* Lancashire (1870, 1 match).
Career batting
1–2–0–23–12–11.50–0–*ct* 0
He also played for Herefordshire.

Potts, Henry James
Amateur. *b:* 23.1.1925, Carlisle. Middle order right-hand batsman. *Team* Oxford U (1949–50, blue 1950).
Career batting
9–14–1–290–50–22.30–0–*ct* 6
He played football for Northampton Town.

Pougher, Arthur Dick
Professional. *b:* 19.4.1865, Leicester. *d:* 20.5.1926, Leicester. Middle order right-hand batsman, right-arm fast medium bowler, good field. *Team* Leicestershire (1894–1901, 88 matches). *Tours* Lillywhite, Shaw and Shrewsbury to Australia 1887/8; Read to South Africa 1891/2. *Test* England (1891/2, 1 match).
Career batting
164–275–30–4553–114–18.58–5–*ct* 99
Bowling 10175–535–19.01–31–7–9/34
Test batting
1–1–0–17–17–17.00–0–*ct* 2
Bowling 26–3–8.66–0–0–3/26
His first-class debut was for North v South at Lord's in 1886. He had made his debut for Leicestershire in 1885 and in 1887 became a member of the Lord's groundstaff, remaining there 20 years. His last first-class match was for MCC in 1902. He hit 1,121 runs, av 29.50, in 1896 and the previous year took 112 wickets, av 19.39. His best bowling in an innings 9 for 34 for an England XI v Surrey at the Oval in 1895.

Poulet, Roger John
Cricketer. *b:* 18.7.1942, Sheen, Staffs. Middle order right-hand batsman. *Team* Cambridge U (1968).
Career batting
1–2–0–6–6–3.00–0–*ct* 2

Poulter, Stephen John
Cricketer. *b:* 9.9.1956, Hornsey, London. Middle order right-hand batsman. *Team* Middlesex (1978, 3 matches).
Career batting
3–3–0–47–36–15.66–0–*ct* 0

Pountain, Francis Robert
Professional. *b:* 23.4.1941, Eastleigh, Hampshire. Middle or lower order right-hand batsman, right-

arm medium pace bowler. *Team* Sussex (1960–65, 76 matches).
Career batting
76–119–16–1920–96–18.64–0–*ct* 43
Bowling 3054–86–35.51–1–0–5/91

Povey, Arthur
Professional. *b:* 16.5.1886, West Bromwich, Staffordshire. *d:* 13.2.1946, Tonbridge, Kent. Tail end right-hand batsman, wicket-keeper. *Team* Kent (1921–22, 5 matches).
Career batting
5–8–4–64–21*–16.00–0–*ct* 5–*st* 1

Powell, Adam Gordon
Amateur. *b:* 17.8.1912, Boxted, Essex. *d:* 7.6.1982, Sandwich, Kent. Lower order right-hand batsman, wicket-keeper. *Sch* Charterhouse. *Teams* Essex (1932–37, 23 matches); Cambridge U (1933–34, blue 1934). *Tours* MCC to Australia and New Zealand 1935/6, to Canada 1937 (not first-class), 1951 (did not play in first-class match); Martineau to Egypt 1937, 1938, 1939 (not first-class).
Career batting
53–82–12–1149–79–16.41–0–*ct* 75–*st* 19

His final first-class match was for Free Foresters in 1957. He appeared for Suffolk, commencing 1938.

Powell, Albert James
Amateur. *b:* 8.12.1893, Presteigne, Radnorshire, Wales. *d:* 15.2.1979, Liskeard, Cornwall. Lower order right-hand batsman, right-arm medium pace bowler. *Team* Worcestershire (1921, 1 match).
Career batting
1–2–0–10–9–5.00–0–*ct* 0
Bowling 8–0

Powell, Alfred Peter
Amateur. *b:* 19.8.1909, Marylebone, London. Opening batsman, bowler. *Sch* Mill Hill. *Team* Middlesex (1927, 1 match).
Career batting
1–2–0–0–0–0.00–0–*ct* 1

He also played for Buckinghamshire.

Powell, Ernest Ormsby
Amateur. *b:* 19.1.1861, Liverpool, Lancashire. *d:* 29.3.1928, Stafford. Sound middle order right-hand batsman, good cover point. *Sch* Charterhouse. *Teams* Cambridge U (1883–84); Hampshire (1884–85, 11 matches); Surrey (1882, 4 matches).
Career batting
21–39–2–1024–140–27.67–1–*ct* 10

His final first-class match was for MCC in 1895.

Powell, James Alfred
Professional. *b:* 5.5.1899, Bloomsbury, London. *d:* 1973, Chelsea, London. Lower order right-hand batsman, leg break and googly bowler. *Team* Middlesex (1926–30, 29 matches).
Career batting
32–37–13–97–8*–4.04–0–*ct* 9
Bowling 2150–77–27.92–3–0–8/72

His final first-class match was for MCC in 1931.

Powell, Louis St Vincent
Amateur. *b:* 13.11.1902, Kingstown, St Vincent, West Indies. Lower order right-hand batsman, right-arm fast bowler. *Team* Somerset (1927–38, 10 matches).
Career batting
10–15–1–153–52–10.92–0–*ct* 5
Bowling 376–5–75.20–0–0–3/63

Powell, Tyrone Lyndon
Cricketer. *b:* 17.6.1953, Bargoed, Glamorgan. Opening right-hand batsman, off break bowler. *Teams* New Zealand Under 23s XI (1971/2); Glamorgan (1976, 1 match).
Career batting
2–4–0–24–14–6.00–0–*ct* 0

He also played for Norfolk.

Powell, William Allan
Amateur. *b:* 19.1.1885, Blundellsands, Lancashire. *d:* 1.1.1954, Earls Court, London. Middle order right-hand batsman, right-arm slow bowler. *Team* Kent (1912–21, 12 matches).
Career batting
15–20–3–187–48–11.00–0–*ct* 8
Bowling 559–19–29.42–1–0–5/40

His first-class debut was for H. D. G. Leveson-Gower's XI in 1909.

Powell-Moore, W. F.
(*see under* Moore, W. F. P.)

Powell-Williams, R. (*see under* Williams, R. P.)

Power, Dr George Edward
Amateur. *b:* 16.5.1849, Highgate, London. *d:* 29.10.1904, Hucknall Torkard, Notts. Middle order right-hand batsman. *Team* Nottinghamshire (1876, 1 match).
Career batting
1–1–0–3–3–3.00–0–*ct* 1

A spectator in the Notts v Surrey match at Trent Bridge in 1876, he went on the field as a substitute for the injured Tolley and was subsequently allowed to bat.

Power, Richard Wood
Amateur. *b:* 2.2.1896, Dublin. *d:* 3.3.1978, Fownhope, Herefordshire. Right-hand batsman, wicket-keeper. *Team* Ireland (1920–26).
Career batting
4–6–0–78–30–13.00–0–*ct* 1

Powers, John
Amateur. *b:* 1868, Barwell, Leics. *d:* 9.11.1939, Leicester Forest East. Powerful middle order right-hand batsman. *Team* Leicestershire (1895–96, 9 matches).
Career batting
9–17–1–195–25–12.18–0–*ct* 4

Powys, Walter Norman
Amateur. *b:* 28.7.1849, Titchmarsh, Northants. *d:* 7.1.1892, Nottingham. Tail end left-hand batsman, left-hand fast round-arm bowler, slip field. *Teams* Cambridge U (1871–74, blue 1871, 1872 and 1874); Hampshire (1877–78, 2 matches).
Career batting
27–42–7–244–30–6.97–0–*ct* 9
Bowling 1372–95+3–14.44–6–3–9/42
He did not appear for Cambridge in 1873, being in the United States. His final first-class match was for MCC in 1879. His best bowling was on his debut, namely 9/42 for Cambridge U v MCC at Cambridge in 1871.

Powys-Keck, Horatio James
Amateur. *b:* 7.3.1873, Switzerland. *d:* 30.1.1952, Kensington, London. Tail end batsman, left-arm fast bowler. *Sch* Malvern and Monkton Combe. *Team* Worcestershire (1903–07, 3 matches). *Tours* Oxford Authentics to India 1902/3; Brackley to West Indies 1904/5.
Career batting
9–14–5–69–25*–7.66–0–*ct* 0
Bowling 439–23–19.08–1–0–5/27
His greatest success came on the Authentics tour of India when, in all matches, he took 69 wickets, av 11.03. He did not appear in any trials whilst at Oxford.

Powys-Maurice, Canon Lionel Selwyn
(formerly L. S. Maurice)
Amateur. *b:* 7.5.1899, Brighton, Sussex. Middle order right-hand batsman. *Sch* Haileybury. *Team* Northants (1922–23, 11 matches).
Career batting
11–19–0–156–65–8.21–0–*ct* 1

Poynder, Charles Eustace Hadden
Amateur. *b:* 15.7.1910, Barnstaple, Devon. Middle order right-hand batsman. *Sch* Newton College. *Team* Minor Counties (1937).
Career batting
1–2–0–6–3–3.00–0–*ct* 0
His County cricket was for Devon.

Poynton, Dr Frederic John
Amateur. *b:* 26.6.1869, Kelston, Somerset. *d:* 29.10.1943, Weston, Bath, Somerset. Stylish middle order right-hand batsman, good field. *Sch* Marlborough. *Team* Somerset (1891–96, 25 matches).
Career batting
25–48–6–575–57–13.69–0–*ct* 7
Bowling 38–2–19.00–0–0–1/6
His County cricket was limited, due to his profession.

Poyntz, Edward Stephen Massey
Amateur. *b:* 27.10.1883, Chelmsford, Essex. *d:* 26.12.1934, Minehead, Somerset. Brother of H. S. (Somerset). Hard hitting middle order right-hand batsman, good field. *Sch* Haileybury. *Team* Somerset (1905–19, 102 matches).
Career batting
105–190–7–3127–114–17.08–1–*ct* 95
Bowling 317–8–39.62–1–0–5/36
He captained Somerset in 1913 and 1914.

Poyntz, Hugh Stainton
Amateur. *b:* 17.9.1877, Basford, Notts. *d:* 22.6.1955, Harestock, Hants. Brother of E. S. M. (Somerset). Middle order right-hand batsman, leg break bowler. *Sch* Eastbourne. *Teams* Somerset (1904–21, 37 matches); Orange Free State (1912/13).
Career batting
40–70–3–1288–85–19.22–0–*ct* 27
Bowling 182–5–36.40–0–0–3/37
A regular army officer, his County cricket was very restricted. He was also a good soccer player and captained the Army in 1907.

Prasanna, Erapalli Anatharao Srinivas
Amateur. *b:* 22.5.1940, Bangalore, India. Lower order right-hand batsman, off break bowler. *Team* Mysore/Karnataka (1961/2 to 1978/9). *Tours* India to West Indies 1961/2, 1970/1, 1975/6, to England 1967, 1971, 1974, to Australia and New Zealand 1967/8, to Australia 1977/8, to New Zealand 1975/6, to Pakistan 1978/9, to East Africa 1967/8. *Tests* India (1961/2 to 1978/9, 49 matches).
Career batting
235–275–67–2476–81–11.90–0–*ct* 127
Bowling 22442–957–23.45–56–9–8/50
Test batting
49–84–20–735–37–11.48–0–ct 18
Bowling 5742–189–30.38–10–2–8/76
His results on the three tours to England did

not match his ability and he was overshadowed by India's three other slow bowlers. He appeared in all three Tests on the 1967 tour, none in 1971 and two in 1974.

Pratt, David
Professional. *b:* 20.7.1938, Watford, Herts. Tail end right-hand batsman, slow left-arm bowler. *Teams* Worcestershire (1959, 8 matches); Nottinghamshire (1962, 7 matches).
Career batting
18–23–7–50–14–3.12–0–*ct* 4
Bowling 1141–23–49.60–1–0–5/54
He played for Hertfordshire in 1957.

Pratt, Derek Edward
Professional. *b:* 31.10.1925, Balham, London. Brother of R. C. E. (Surrey). Sound middle order right-hand batsman, leg break bowler. *Team* Surrey (1954–57, 9 matches).
Career batting
9–12–4–171–33–21.37–0–*ct* 4
Bowling 392–13–30.15–1–0–6/119

Pratt, Donald Montague McVeagh
Amateur. *b:* 9.7.1935, Dublin. Middle order left-hand batsman. *Team* Ireland (1963–66).
Career batting
6–12–0–171–58–14.25–0–*ct* 0

Pratt, John
Professional. *b:* 4.2.1834, Mitcham, Surrey. *d:* 6.6.1886, Merton, Surrey. Brother-in-law of James Southerton (Surrey). Lower order right-hand batsman, right-hand medium pace round-arm bowler, slip field. *Team* Surrey (1868, 1 match).
Career batting
1–2–0–10–9–5.00–0–*ct* 2
Bowling 12–0

Pratt, Richard
Professional. *b:* 23.6.1896, Lower Broughton, Manchester. *d:* 10.10.1982, Derby. Lower order right-hand batsman, wicket-keeper. *Team* Derbyshire (1923–24, 5 matches).
Career batting
5–10–1–73–17*–8.11–0–*ct* 3

Pratt, Ronald Charles Ernest
Professional. *b:* 5.5.1928, Balham, London. *d:* 1.6.1977, Banstead, Surrey. Brother of D. E. (Surrey). Stylish middle order left-hand batsman, off break bowler, good slip. *Team* Surrey (1952–59, 69 matches).
Career batting
69–102–14–1900–120–21.59–1–*ct* 53
Bowling 138–3–46.00–0–0–1/8

He hit over 1,000 runs for Surrey 2nd XI in the Minor Counties Competition in 1952, but never was able to command a regular place in the full County side.

Pratt, Rodney Lynes
Professional. *b:* 15.11.1938, Stoney Stanton, Leics. Lower order right-hand batsman, right-arm fast medium bowler. *Team* Leicestershire (1955–64, 99 matches).
Career batting
102–158–22–1824–80–13.41–0–*ct* 69
Bowling 6726–259–25.96–11–2–7/47

Pratt, William Ewart
Amateur. *b:* 2.7.1895, Hinckley, Leics. *d:* 27.5.1974, Leicester. Middle order right-hand batsman. *Team* Leicestershire (1920–30, 9 matches).
Careeer batting
9–17–1–166–29*–10.37–0–*ct* 2
Bowling 52–0

Pratten, Frederick Leslie
Professional. *b:* 13.2.1904, Weston-super-Mare, Somerset. *d:* 23.2.1967, Midsomer-Norton, Somerset. Lower order right-hand batsman, wicket-keeper. *Team* Somerset (1930–31, 12 matches).
Career batting
12–18–9–71–16–7.88–0–*ct* 6–*st* 5

Preece, Charles Richard
Professional. *b:* 15.12.1887, Broadheath, Worcs. *d:* 5.2.1976, Oldbury, Worcs. Lower order right-hand batsman, right-arm medium pace bowler. *Team* Worcestershire (1920–27, 88 matches).
Career batting
89–161–23–1601–69–11.60–0–*ct* 53
Bowling 4174–140–29.81–5–0–7/35
His first-class debut was for H. K. Foster's XI in 1919. His obituary was incorrectly published in Wisden ten years prior to his actual demise.

Preece, Henry Charles
Amateur. *b:* 27.10.1867, Weobley, Herefordshire. *d:* 17.9.1937, Highgate, Middlesex. Middle order batsman. *Team* Essex (1895, 2 matches).
Career batting
2–4–0–74–49–18.50–0–*ct* 0
He played for Cheshire in 1893. He lost his sight relatively early in life, but continued his profession as a lecturer at King's College, London.

Preece, Trevor
Professional. *b:* 1882, Bridgend, Glamorgan. *d:*

21.9.1965, Whitchurch, Glamorgan. Opening batsman. *Team* Glamorgan (1923, 1 match).
Career batting
1–2–0–8–4–4.00–0–*ct* 1

Prentice, Christopher Norman Russell
Cricketer. *b:* 5.9.1954, London. Middle order right-hand batsman, right-arm medium off break bowler. *Sch* Shrewsbury. *Team* Oxford U (1974).
Career batting
1–2–0–23–19–11.50–0–*ct* 0

Prentice, Francis Thomas
Professional until 1950, amateur 1951. *b:* 22.4.1912, Knaresborough, Yorkshire. *d:* 10.7.1978, Headingley, Leeds, Yorkshire. Consistent middle order right-hand batsman, off break bowler. *Team* Leicestershire (1934–51, 241 matches).
Career batting
241–421–24–10997–191–27.70–17–*ct* 75
Bowling 5847–117–49.97–2–0–5/46

He hit 1,000 runs in a season five times (best 1,742, av 38.71, in 1949). After the 1949 season he retired from regular County cricket to concentrate on his business interests.

Prentice, Leslie Roff Vincent
Amateur. *b:* 1887, Melbourne, Australia. *d:* 13.8.1928, Harrold, Bedfordshire. Lower order right-hand batsman, slow right-arm bowler. *Team* Middlesex (1920–23, 12 matches).
Career batting
18–24–1–147–42*–6.39–0–*ct* 9
Bowling 1032–31–33.29–1–0–6/95

Presland, Edward Robert
Professional. *b:* 27.3.1943, High Beech, Essex. Lower order right-hand batsman, right-arm medium off break bowler. *Team* Essex (1962–70, 30 matches).
Career batting
30–41–4–625–51–16.89–0–*ct* 24
Bowling 761–13–58.53–0–0–2/19

A noted soccer player, he has appeared for West Ham United, Crystal Palace and Colchester.

Pressdee, James Stuart
Professional. *b:* 19.6.1933, Mumbles, Glamorgan. Middle order right-hand batsman, slow left-arm bowler, good close field. *Teams* Glamorgan (1949–65, 322 matches); North East Transvaal (1965/6 to 1969/70).
Career batting
347–583–88–14267–150*–28.82–13–*ct* 371
Bowling 10666–481–22.17–21–5–9/43

He hit 1,000 runs in a season six times (best 1,911, av 34.74, in 1962) and took 100 wickets in a season twice (best 106, av 21.62, in 1963). In 1963 and 1964 he performed the 'double'. His best bowling was 9/43 for Glamorgan v Yorkshire at Swansea in 1965. He emigrated to South Africa in the autumn of 1965. A good soccer player, he was a schoolboy international and appeared at left back for Swansea Town.

Prest, Charles Henry
Amateur. *b:* 9.12.1841, York. *d:* 4.3.1875, Gateshead. Brother of Edward (Cambridge U) and William (Yorkshire 1853). Attacking opening or middle order right-hand batsman, good field. *Sch* St Peter's, York. *Teams* Yorkshire (1864, 2 matches); Middlesex (1870, 1 match).
Career batting
5–10–0–132–57–13.20–0–*ct* 3

His first-class debut was for Gentlemen of the North in 1861. A noted amateur actor he appeared on the London stage under the name of 'Mr Peveril'.

Prest, Harold Edward Westray
Amateur. *b:* 9.1.1890, Beckenham, Kent. *d:* 5.1.1955, Shalford, Surrey. Stylish middle order right-hand batsman, good field. *Sch* Malvern. *Teams* Cambridge U (1909–11, blue 1909 and 1911); Kent (1909–22, 19 matches).
Career batting
32–45–4–1156–133*–28.19–1–*ct* 22
Bowling 4–1–4.00–0–0–1/4

He also was awarded his blue for soccer and golf.

Preston, Benjamin
Amateur. *b:* 20.4.1846, Lowestoft, Suffolk. *d:* 1.6.1914, Lowestoft, Suffolk. Stylish opening right-hand batsman, deep field. *Sch* Westminster. *Team* Cambridge U (1869–70, blue 1869).
Career batting
8–14–2–124–28–10.33–0–*ct* 4

He played for Norfolk and Suffolk.

Preston, Derek John
Amateur. *b:* 12.1.1936, Leyton, Essex. Middle order right-hand batsman, slow left-arm bowler. *Sch* Bancrofts. *Team* Sussex (1959, 12 matches).
Career batting
12–15–2–154–54–11.84–0–*ct* 8
Bowling 562–13–43.23–0–0–3/45

Preston, Henry John Berridge
Professional. *b:* 25.10.1883, Bareilly, India. *d:* 23.4.1964, Hastings, Sussex. Lower order right-hand batsman, right-arm medium pace bowler. *Team* Kent (1907–13, 19 matches).

Career batting
19–27–14–84–18–6.46–0–*ct* 4
Bowling 865–43–20.11–1–0–5/23

He appeared for Scotland in a representative non-first-class match in 1936. His career in club cricket was a long one and would have been even more extensive if he had not lost an arm in an accident with a mowing machine.

Preston, Joseph Merritt
Professional. *b:* 22.8.1864, Yeadon, Yorkshire. *d:* 26.11.1890, Windhill, Yorkshire. He died of a chill. Stylish middle or lower order right-hand batsman, right-arm fast bowler. *Team* Yorkshire (1885–89, 80 matches). *Tour* Lillywhite, Shaw and Shrewsbury to Australia 1887/8.
Career batting
95–157–14–2131–93–14.90–0–*ct* 43
Bowling 3761–211–17.82–9–5–9/28

His best season was 1887 with 52 wickets, av 18.73. His best bowling in an innings was 9 for 28 for Yorkshire v MCC at Scarborough in 1888.

Preston, Kenneth Charles
Professional. *b:* 22.8.1925, Goodmayes, Essex. Lower order right-hand batsman, right-arm fast medium bowler. *Team* Essex (1948–64, 391 matches).
Career batting
397–468–169–3053–70–10.21–0–*ct* 350
Bowling 30533–1160–26.32–37–2–7/55

He took 140 wickets, av 20.35, in 1957.

Preston, Stephen
Professional. *b:* 11.8.1905, Heywood, Lancashire. Lower order right-hand batsman, right-arm medium pace bowler. *Team* Lancashire (1928–30, 5 matches).
Career batting
5–4–2–46–33–23.00–0–*ct* 1
Bowling 212–6–35.33–0–0–2/42

Pretlove, John Frederick
Amateur. *b:* 23.11.1932, Camberwell, London. Determined middle order left-hand batsman, slow left-arm bowler. *Sch* Alleyns. *Teams* Cambridge U (1954–56, blue all three years); Kent (1955–59, 85 matches). *Tour* MCC to North America 1959 (not first-class).
Career batting
124–212–21–5115–137–26.78–10–*ct* 70–*st* 2
Bowling 1319–43–30.67–1–0–5/55

He hit 1,191 runs, av 25.89, in 1957. He was Assistant Secretary to Kent CCC, 1955 to 1957. His final first-class match was for MCC in 1968. An all-round sportsman, he gained his blue for soccer and rugby fives.

Pretty, Dr Harold Cooper
Amateur. *b:* 23.10.1875, Fressingfield, Suffolk. *d:* 30.5.1952, Kettering, Northants. Punishing middle order right-hand batsman, off break bowler. *Sch* Epsom. *Teams* Surrey (1899, 8 matches); Northants (1906–07, 8 matches).
Career batting
16–26–0–696–200–26.76–2–*ct* 9
Bowling 138–5–27.60–0–0–3/39

He hit 124 for Surrey v Notts at the Oval in 1899 on his first-class debut and his only other three-figure innings was 200 for Northants v Derbyshire at Chesterfield in 1906.

Price, Alfred
Professional. *b:* 5.1.1862, Ruddington, Notts. *d:* 21.3.1942, Oldham, Lancashire. Son of Walter (Notts), brother of William (Liverpool) and Frederick (North). Defensive middle order right-hand batsman. *Teams* Lancashire (1885, 1 match); Nottinghamshire (1887, 3 matches).
Career batting
7–12–0–110–37–9.16–0–*ct* 7

His first-class debut was for North v South at Lord's in 1884.

Price, Charles F. T.
Amateur. *b:* 1918, New South Wales, Australia. Right-hand batsman, right-arm bowler. *Team* Australian Services (1945 to 1945/6). *Tours* Australian Services to England 1945, to India and Ceylon 1945/6.
Career batting
14–20–3–327–55–19.23–0–*ct* 11
Bowling 643–24–26.79–0–0–4/33

Price, Charles John
Amateur. *b:* 1890, Newent, Gloucs. Middle order batsman. *Team* Gloucestershire (1919, 1 match).
Career batting
1–2–0–19–13–9.50–0–*ct* 0

Price, David Howe
Cricketer. *b:* 25.7.1955, Gloucester. Middle order right-hand batsman, right-arm medium pace bowler. *Sch* Malvern. *Team* Oxford U (1975–78).
Career batting
5–10–0–104–27–10.40–0–*ct* 4
Bowling 174–2–87.00–0–0–1/22

Price, Eric
Professional. *b:* 27.10.1918, Middleton, Lancashire. Lower order left-hand batsman, slow left-arm bowler. *Teams* Lancashire (1946–47, 35 matches); Essex (1948–49, 43 matches).
Career batting
80–95–31–558–54–8.71–0–*ct* 40
Bowling 5722–215–26.61–10–2–8/125

Price, Frederick
Professional. *b:* 24.12.1857, Ruddington, Notts. *d:* January 1927, Nottingham. Son of Walter (Notts), brother of Alfred (Notts) and William (Liverpool). Lower order batsman, right-arm medium pace bowler. *Team* North (1887).
Career batting
1–1–1–9–9*–no av–0–*ct* 0

Price, Frederic Richard
Amateur. *b:* 2.2.1840, Llewes Hall, Denbigh. *d:* 1895, at sea between USA and Britain. Middle order right-hand batsman, slow under-arm bowler, point field. *Sch* Cheltenham. *Teams* Oxford U (1861); Gloucestershire (1872, 2 matches).
Career batting
6–10–2–90–33–11.25–0–*ct* 8–*st* 3
Bowling 99–6–16.50–0–0–3/33
His first-class debut was for Gentlemen of the North in 1859. He also played for Monmouth, Cheshire and Denbigh. He emigrated to the United States, becoming a farmer in Iowa.

Price, Rev Frederic William Stephen
Amateur. *b:* 1852, Lutterworth, Leics. *d:* December 1937, Worthing, Sussex. Middle order right-hand batsman, right-arm medium pace bowler. *Team* Cambridge U (1873).
Career batting
4–7–1–13–5–2.16–0–*ct* 3
Bowling 37–1–37.00–0–0–1/10
His final first-class match was for An England Eleven in 1874. He played for Berkshire.

Price, Herbert Leo
Amateur. *b:* 21.6.1899, Sutton, Surrey. *d:* 18.7.1943, Manchester. He died following an operation. Brother of V.R. (Surrey). Middle order right-hand batsman. *Sch* Bishop's Stortford. *Team* Oxford U (1920–22).
Career batting
2–4–1–46–32*–15.33–0–*ct* 1
An all-round sportsman, he represented Oxford at rugby football, hockey and water polo, going on to be capped for England as a rugby wing forward and a hockey centre-half.

Price, John
Amateur. *b:* 6.7.1908, Worcester. Brother of W. H. (Worcs). Lower order right-hand batsman, right-arm fast medium bowler. *Team* Worcestershire (1927–29, 11 matches).
Career batting
11–18–4–81–33–5.78–0–*ct* 4
Bowling 611–12–50.91–0–0–2/35

Price, John Sidney Ernest
Professional. *b:* 22.7.1937, Harrow, Middlesex. Lower order left-hand batsman, right-arm fast medium bowler. *Team* Middlesex (1961–75, 242 matches). *Tours* MCC to India 1963/4, to South Africa 1964/5. *Tests* England (1963/4 to 1972, 15 matches).
Career batting
279–223–91–1108–53*–8.39–0–*ct* 103
Bowling 19221–817–23.52–26–4–8/48
Test batting
15–15–6–66–32–7.33–0–*ct* 7
Bowling 1401–40–35.02–1–0–5/73
His best season was 1966 with 94 wickets, av 18.74. Injury restricted his cricket during several seasons.

Price, Vincent Rains
Amateur. *b:* 22.5.1895, Sutton, Surrey. *d:* 29.5.1973, Bexhill, Sussex. Brother of H. L. (Oxford U). Lower order right-hand batsman, right-arm fast medium bowler. *Sch* Bishop Stortford. *Teams* Oxford U (1919–22, blue all four years); Surrey (1919, 1 match).
Career batting
38–59–12–745–76*–15.85–0–*ct* 24
Bowling 3394–131–25.90–7–1–8/30
He created a stir by taking 14 wickets for 112 for Oxford U v Gentlemen in the first first-class match played after the 1914–18 war, but he scarcely lived up to expectations in his later appearances. His final first-class match was for Leveson-Gower's XI in 1924. A good rugby footballer, he appeared for Oxford three times.

Price, Walter
Professional. *b:* 9.10.1834, Ruddington, Notts. *d:* 4.9.1894, Ruddington, Notts. Father of Alfred (Lancashire and Notts), Frederick (North) and William (Liverpool). Middle order right-hand batsman, right-hand medium pace round-arm bowler. *Team* Nottinghamshire (1869–70, 5 matches).
Career batting
35–56–5–625–57–12.21–0–*ct* 14
Bowling 301–15–20.06–1–0–5/66
His first-class debut was for MCC in 1868 and his final first-class match for the same Club in 1882. He was a first-class umpire for many years, being on the staff at Lord's until his death.

Price, William
Professional. *b:* Ruddington, Notts. Son of Walter (Notts), brother of Alfred (Lancashire and Notts) and Frederick (North). *Team* Liverpool and District (1889).
Career batting
2–4–2–29–26*–14.50–0–*ct* 1
Bowling 113–10–11.30–1–0–6/51

Price, Wilfred Frederick Frank
Professional. *b:* 25.4.1902, Westminster, London. *d:* 13.1.1969, Hendon, Middlesex. Sound opening or middle order right-hand batsman, wicket-keeper. *Team* Middlesex (1926–47, 382 matches). *Tours* MCC to West Indies 1929/30; Brinckman to Argentine 1937/8. *Test* England (1938, 1 match).
Career batting
402–590–97–9035–111–18.32–3–*ct* 666–*st* 321
Test batting
1–2–0–6–6–3.00–0–*ct* 2
He hit 1,000 runs in a season once : 1,298, av 25.96, in 1934. From 1950 to 1967 he was a first-class umpire and caused a sensation by no-balling G. A. R. Lock for throwing.

Price, William Harry
Amateur. *b:* 28.5.1900, Worcester. *d:* 15.4.1982, Worcester. Brother of John (Worcs). Lower order right-hand batsman, right-arm fast medium bowler. *Sch* Royal Grammar School, Worcester. *Team* Worcestershire (1923, 1 match).
Career batting
1–1–1–0–0*–no av–0–*ct* 0
Bowling 12–0

Price, Walter Longsdon
Amateur. *b:* 2.2.1886, Toxteth Park, Liverpool. *d:* 26.12.1943, Lechlade, Gloucs. Lower order batsman, left-arm medium pace bowler. *Sch* Repton. *Team* Worcestershire (1904, 3 matches).
Career batting
3–3–0–12–7–4.00–0–*ct* 1
Bowling 284–8–35.50–0–0–4/86
He appeared for Canada v USA in 1912.

Price, William Leslie
Amateur. *b:* 19.3.1881, Taunton, Somerset. *d:* 6.2.1958, Taunton, Somerset. Lower order batsman, wicket-keeper. *Team* Somerset (1901, 1 match).
Career batting
1–2–0–10–10–5.00–0–*ct* 0

Prichard, Hubert Cecil
(also known as Collins-Prichard)
Amateur. *b:* 6.2.1865, Clifton, Bristol. *d:* 12.11.1942, Pwllywrach, Cowbridge, Glamorgan. Middle order batsman. *Sch* Clifton. *Team* Gloucestershire (1896, 2 matches).
Career batting
2–4–0–46–23–11.50–0–*ct* 1

Priddy, James
Amateur. *b:* 3.12.1909, Chard, Somerset. Lower order batsman, useful bowler. *Team* Somerset (1933–39, 7 matches).
Career batting
7–10–2–104–27–13.00–0–*ct* 3
Bowling 241–4–60.25–0–0–2/114

Pride, Thomas
Professional. *b:* 23.7.1864, York. *d:* 16.2.1919, Canobie, Dumfries-shire, Scotland. Lower order right-hand batsman, wicket-keeper. *Team* Yorkshire (1887, 1 match).
Career batting
1–1–0–1–1–1.00–0–*ct* 4–*st* 3

Prideaux, Roger Malcolm
Amateur. *b:* 13.7.1939, Chelsea, London. Sound right-hand opening batsman, right-arm medium pace bowler. *Sch* Tonbridge. *Teams* Cambridge U (1958–60, blue all three years); Kent (1960–61, 33 matches); Northants (1962–70, 234 matches); Sussex (1971–73, 65 matches); Orange Free State (1971/2 to 1974/5). *Tours* MCC to North America 1959 (not first-class), to New Zealand 1960/1, to Ceylon and Pakistan 1968/9; Commonwealth to Pakistan 1967/8. *Tests* England (1968 to 1968/9, 3 matches).
Career batting
446–808–75–25136–202*–34.29–41–*ct* 302
Bowling 176–3–58.66–0–0–2/13
Test batting
3–6–1–102–64–20.40–0–*ct* 0
Bowling 0–0
He hit 1,000 runs in a season thirteen times (best 1,993, av 41.52, in 1968). His only double century was 202* for Northants v Oxford U at Oxford in 1963. In 1961 he hit a century in 52 minutes for North v South at Blackpool. From 1967 to 1970 he captained Northants.

Pridgeon, Alan Paul
Cricketer. *b:* 22.2.1954, Wall Heath, Staffs. Lower order right-hand batsman, right-arm medium pace bowler. *Team* Worcestershire (1972–83, 163 matches).
Career batting
163–162–68–821–34–8.73–0–*ct* 48
Bowling 12277–351–34.97–6–1–7/35

Pridmore, Reginald George
Amateur. *b:* 29.4.1886, Birmingham. *d:* 13.3.1918, near Piave River (North of Venice), Italy. He was killed in action. Middle order batsman. *Team* Warwickshire (1909–12, 14 matches).
Career batting
14–26–1–315–49–12.60–0–*ct* 7
He also played for Hertfordshire.

Priestley, Sir Arthur Alexander
Amateur. *b:* 9.11.1865, Kensington, London. *d:*

10.4.1933, Monaco. Middle order right-hand batsman. *Team* MCC (1895). *Tours* Lucas to West Indies 1894/5; Priestley to West Indies 1896/7; Ranjitsinhji to North America 1899 (he did not play in first-class matches); Bosanquet to North America 1901 (he did not play in first-class matches).
Career batting
18–27–2–183–36–7.32–0–*ct* 11
He was MP for Grantham from 1900 to 1918.

Priestley, Donald Lacey
Amateur. *b:* 28.7.1887, Tewkesbury, Gloucs. *d:* 30.10.1917, Passchendale, Belgium. He was killed in action. Middle order right-hand batsman, right-arm medium pace bowler. *Team* Gloucestershire (1909–10, 7 matches).
Career batting
7–13–1–154–51–12.83–0–*ct* 2

Priestley, Hugh William
Amateur. *b:* 19.9.1887, Marylebone, London. *d:* 6.1.1932, Marylebone, London. Father of R. H. (Free Foresters). Opening right-hand batsman, right-arm medium pace bowler. *Sch* Uppingham. *Team* MCC (1911).
Career batting
1–2–0–33–31–16.50–0–*ct* 0
Bowling 16–1–16.00–0–0–1/16
He appeared in the Oxford Freshmen's Match of 1907, but no first-class matches for the University. His County cricket was for Buckinghamshire.

Priestley, Neil
Cricketer. *b:* 23.6.1961, Blyborough, Lincolnshire. Lower order left-hand batsman, wicket-keeper. *Team* Northants (1981, 1 match).
Career batting
1–1–1–20–20*–no av–0–*ct* 1–*st* 2
He also played for Lincolnshire.

Priestley, Robert Hugh
Amateur. *b:* 23.11.1911, Maida Vale, London. Son of H. W. (MCC). Opening right-hand batsman, off break bowler. *Sch* Winchester. *Team* Free Foresters (1932).
Career batting
1–2–0–16–16–8.00–0–*ct* 0

Prince, Charles Frederick Henry
Amateur. *b:* 11.9.1874, Boshof, Orange Free State, South Africa. *d:* 5.3.1948, near Cape Town, South Africa. Middle order right-hand batsman, wicket-keeper. *Teams* Western Province (1894/5 to 1904/5); Border (1897/8); Eastern Province (1902/3 to 1903/4); London County (1901). *Tour* South Africa to England 1901. *Test* South Africa (1898/9, 1 match).
Career batting
24–41–0–730–61–17.80–0–*ct* 14–*st* 14
Bowling 28–0
Test batting
1–2–0–6–5–3.00–0–*ct* 0
He played in few matches on the 1901 tour, but made a fleeting appearance for London County.

Prince, William
Professional. *b:* 28.3.1868, Somercotes, Derbyshire. *d:* 1.6.1948, Ollerton, Notts. Lower order right-hand batsman, right-arm medium fast bowler. *Team* Derbyshire (1898, 1 match).
Career batting
1–1–1–2–2*–no av–0–*ct* 0
Bowling 38–0

Pringle, Derek Raymond
Cricketer. *b:* 18.9.1958, Nairobi, Kenya. Middle order right-hand batsman, right-arm medium pace bowler. Son of Don (East Africa). *Sch* Felsted. *Teams* Essex (1978–83, 44 matches); Cambridge U (1979–82, blue 1979–81). *Tour* England to Australia 1982/3. *Tests* England (1982 to 1982/3, 7 matches).
Career batting
93–133–28–3307–127*–31.49–6–*ct* 44
Bowling 5528–196–28.20–5–1–7/32
Test batting
7–11–2–166–47*–18.44–0–*ct* 0
Bowling 495–11–45.00–0–0–2/16
In 1982 he took the unprecedented step of standing down from the University match, having been chosen as captain, in order to play for England.

Prior, Ian David
Cricketer. *b:* 26.7.1930, Battersea, London. Middle order right-hand batsman, wicket-keeper. *Team* Minor Counties (1967).
Career batting
1–2–0–21–21–10.50–0–*ct* 3
His County cricket was for Suffolk.

Prior, John Andrew
Cricketer. *b:* 14.6.1960, Dublin, Ireland. Right-hand batsman, right-arm medium pace bowler. *Team* Ireland (1981–83).
Career batting
3–5–0–99–55–19.80–0–*ct* 1
Bowling 80–0

Pritchard, Graham Charles
Cricketer. *b:* 14.1.1942, Farnborough, Hants. Lower order right-hand batsman, right-arm fast medium bowler. *Sch* King's, Canterbury. *Teams*

Cambridge U (1962–64, blue 1964); Essex (1965–66, 10 matches).
Career batting
35–42–15–111–18–4.11–0–*ct* 13
Bowling 2058–56–36.75–2–0–6/51

Pritchard, Jack Mervyn
Amateur. *b:* 19.5.1895. *d:* 17.11.1936, South Kensington, London. Lower order batsman, good bowler. *Sch* Charterhouse. *Team* Oxford U (1919).
Career batting
2–3–1–36–22*–18.00–0–*ct* 2
Bowling 177–7–25.28–0–0–4/45

Pritchard, Thomas Leslie
Amateur. *b:* 10.3.1917, Kaupokonui, New Zealand. Fierce hitting lower order right-hand batsman, right-arm fast, later fast medium, bowler. *Teams* Wellington (1937/8 to 1940/1); Warwickshire (1946–55, 170 matches); Kent (1956, 4 matches).
Career batting
200–293–41–3363–81–13.34–0–*ct* 82
Bowling 19062–818–23.30–48–11–8/20

He took 100 wickets in a season four times (best 172, av 18.75, in 1948). His final first-class match in New Zealand was for North Island Army in 1942/3.

Procter, Michael John
Cricketer. *b:* 15.9.1946, Durban, South Africa. Son of W. C. (Eastern Province), brother of A. W. (Natal). Attacking middle order right-hand batsman, right-arm fast, or off break, bowler. *Teams* Gloucestershire (1965–81, 259 matches); Natal (1965/6 to 1982/3); Western Province (1969/70); Rhodesia (1970/1 to 1975/6). *Tests* South Africa (1966/7 to 1969/70, 7 matches).
Career batting
393–656–56–21748–254–36.24–47–*ct* 321
Bowling 26775–1395–19.19–69–15–9/71
Test batting
7–10–1–226–48–25.11–0–*ct* 4
Bowling 616–41–15.02–1–0–6/73

One of the most dynamic cricketers of the 1970s, he captained Gloucestershire from 1977 to 1981, but was forced to retire from County cricket in 1981 due to a knee injury. He hit 1,000 runs in a season nine times (best 1,786, av 45.79, in 1971) and took 100 wickets in a season twice (best 109, av 18.04, in 1977). His highest score in England was 203 for Gloucs v Essex at Gloucester in 1978. In 1970/71 he hit six hundreds in six consecutive innings for Rhodesia. His highest score was 254 for Rhodesia v Western Province at Salisbury in 1970/1; his best bowling was 9/71 for Rhodesia v Transvaal at Bulawayo in 1972/3.

Prodger, John Michael
Professional. *b:* 1.9.1935, Forest Hill, London. Opening right-hand batsman, excellent slip field. *Team* Kent (1956–67, 151 matches).
Career batting
151–259–22–4831–170*–20.38–3–*ct* 170
Bowling 14–1–14.00–0–0–1/14

Proffitt, Stanley
Professional. *b:* 8.10.1910, Oldham, Lancashire. Opening left-hand batsman, slow left-arm bowler. *Team* Essex (1937, 7 matches).
Career batting
7–14–0–170–39–12.14–0–*ct* 1
Bowling 32–0

He was English table tennis champion.

Prosser, William Henry
Amateur. *b:* 16.7.1870, Devauden Green, Monmouthshire. *d:* 30.6.1952, Snettisham, Norfolk. Lower order batsman, right-arm fast medium bowler. *Team* Cambridge U (1893).
Career batting
1–1–0–0–0–0.00–0–*ct* 1
Bowling 32–0

He played for Monmouthshire.

Prothero, Rowland Edmund
(created 1st Lord Ernle in 1919)
Amateur. *b:* 6.9.1851, Clifton-upon-Teme, Worcs. *d:* 1.7.1937, Ginge, Berks. Middle order right-hand batsman, right-arm medium bowler. *Sch* Marlborough. *Team* Hampshire (1875–83, 4 matches).
Career batting
6–10–4–190–110–31.66–1–*ct* 7
Bowling 181–10–18.10–1–0–5/34

His first-class debut was for Gentlemen of England in 1872.

Proud, Roland Barton
Amateur. *b:* 29.9.1919, Bishop Auckland, Co Durham. *d:* 27.10.1961, Bishop Auckland, Co Durham. Dashing middle order right-hand batsman, right-arm medium pace bowler. *Sch* Winchester. *Teams* Hampshire (1938–39, 7 matches); Oxford U (1939, blue).
Career batting
18–33–1–681–87–21.28–0–*ct* 7

He captained Durham from 1948 to 1955, and his last first-class match was for the Minor Counties in 1950.

Prouton, Ralph Oliver
Professional. *b:* 1.3.1926, Southampton. Sound

opening or middle order right-hand batsman, wicket-keeper. *Team* Hampshire (1949–54, 52 matches).
Career batting
52–79–11–982–90–14.44–0–*ct* 84–*st* 13
He played football for Swindon Town.

Pruett, Harry George
Amateur. *b:* 1890. *d:* 22.1.1948, Bristol. Tail end batsman, left-arm bowler. *Team* Somerset (1921–26, 2 matches).
Career batting
2–4–0–7–5–1.75–0–*ct* 0
Bowling 49–0

Pryer, Barry James Keith
Amateur. *b:* 1.2.1925, Plumstead, London. Lower order right-hand batsman, leg break bowler. *Sch* City of London. *Teams* Kent (1947–49, 2 matches); Cambridge U (1948–49, blue 1948).
Career batting
27–37–10–252–75*–9.33–0–*ct* 9
Bowling 1888–48–39.33–0–0–4/25
His first-class debut was for Combined Services in 1946 and his final first-class match for Free Foresters in 1950.

Pryor, Frederick Charles
Professional. *b:* 10.11.1844, Cambridge. Son of Charles (Cambridge TC). Hard hitting middle order right-hand batsman, right-hand fast round-arm bowler, wicket-keeper. *Team* Cambridgeshire (1863–71, 22 matches).
Career batting
25–46–2–486–69–11.04–0–*ct* 16–*st* 3
His first-class debut was for Cambridge Town Club in 1861.

Pryor, Ronald McDonell
Amateur. *b:* 1901, Brazil. *d:* 24.12.1977, Brazil. Tail end batsman, slow left-arm bowler. *Sch* Tonbridge. *Team* South America (1932). *Tour* South America to England 1932.
Career batting
1–2–0–0–0–0.00–0–*ct* 0
Bowling 13–0
He had little success on the 1932 tour and appeared in only a single first-class match.

Puckeridge, Anthony
Cricketer. *b:* 5.4.1943, Bickley, Worcs. Lower order right-hand batsman, wicket-keeper. *Team* Oxford U (1963).
Career batting
1–1–0–1–1–1.00–0–*ct* 2

Puddefoot, Sydney Charles
Professional. *b:* 17.10.1894, Limehouse, London. *d:* 2.10.1972, Rochford, Essex. Lower order right-hand batsman, left-arm medium pace bowler. *Team* Essex (1922–23, 8 matches).
Career batting
8–8–2–101–42–16.83–0–*ct* 2
Bowling 105–1–105.00–0–0–1/34
An excellent soccer player, he was inside right for West Ham United, Falkirk, Blackburn Rovers and appeared twice for England.

Pugh, Charles Thomas Michael
Amateur. *b:* 13.3.1937, Marylebone, London. Nephew of J. G. (Warwickshire). Steady opening right-hand batsman, right arm slow bowler. *Sch* Eton. *Team* Gloucestershire (1959–62, 76 matches).
Career batting
80–142–9–2469–137–18.56–1–*ct* 42
Bowling 30–1–30.00–0–0–1/12
He hit 1,011 runs, av 21.51, in 1960. He captained Gloucestershire in 1961 and 1962.

Pugh, John Geoffrey
Amateur. *b:* 22.1.1904, Coventry, Warwickshire. *d:* 14.2.1964, Hastings, Barbados. Uncle of C. T. M. (Gloucs). Attacking middle order right-hand batsman, bowler. *Sch* Rugby. *Team* Warwickshire (1922–27, 9 matches).
Career batting
9–9–0–82–41–9.11–0–*ct* 3
Bowling 206–6–34.33–0–0–4/100

Pullan, Cecil Douglas Ayrton
Amateur. *b:* 26.7.1910, Mahoba, India. *d:* 24.6.1970, Tongaat Beach, Natal, South Africa. Middle order right-hand batsman, right-arm medium fast bowler. *Sch* Malvern. *Teams* Oxford U (1932); Worcestershire (1935–38, 25 matches).
Career batting
33–58–9–1049–84–21.40–0–*ct* 20
Bowling 357–8–44.62–0–0–2/26
He captained the Oxford U boxing team.

Pullan, David Anthony
Cricketer. *b:* 1.5.1944, Farsley, Yorkshire. Lower order right-hand batsman, wicket-keeper. *Team* Nottinghamshire (1970–74, 95 matches).
Career batting
95–106–36–613–34–8.75–0–*ct* 206–*st* 28
He was General Manager of Nottinghamshire CCC 1980 to 1982.

Pullan, Peter
Professional. *b:* 29.3.1857, Guiseley, Yorkshire. *d:* 1901, Guiseley, Yorkshire. Lower order right-

hand batsman, right-arm slow bowler. *Team* Yorkshire (1884, 1 match).
Career batting
1–1–0–14–14–14.00–0–*ct* 1
Bowling 5–0

Pullar, Geoffrey
Amateur, turned professional in 1956. *b:* 1.8.1935, Swinton, Lancashire. Stylish opening left-hand batsman, leg break bowler, good outfield. *Teams* Lancashire (1954–68, 312 matches); Gloucestershire (1969–70, 25 matches). *Tours* MCC to West Indies 1959/60, to India, Pakistan and Ceylon 1961/2, to Australia and New Zealand 1962/3; Cavaliers to South Africa 1960/1. *Tests* England (1959 to 1962/3, 28 matches).
Career batting
400–672–63–21528–175–35.34–41–*ct* 125
Bowling 387–10–38.70–0–0–3/91
Test batting
28–49–4–1974–175–43.86–4–*ct* 2
Bowling 37–1–37.00–0–0–1/1

Originally a middle order batsman, Pullar was promoted to open the innings in order to fulfil the needs of England, and with M. C. Cowdrey formed a splendid partnership on the 1959/60 tour to West Indies. A wrist injury hampered him in 1960, but again in 1961 and on the Indian subcontinent in 1961/2 he proved most reliable. On his visit to Australia, however, he came home early due to an injured knee and for the remainder of his career he never really was able to avoid injury for long – arthritis finally forced him to retire in 1970.

He hit 1,000 runs in a season nine times (plus once overseas) and went on to 2,000 twice, his best summer being 1959 with 2,647 runs, av 55.14. His highest innings was only 175 for England v South Africa at the Oval in 1960, but the keynote to his batsmanship was reliability, as can be seen by the fact that his Test batting average is 43.86, despite having only four Test hundreds to his name.

Pullen, William Wade Fitzherbert
Amateur. *b:* 24.6.1866, Itchington, Gloucs. *d:* 9.8.1937, Southampton, Hants. Attacking middle order right-hand batsman, good field, occasional wicket-keeper. *Team* Gloucestershire (1882–92, 91 matches).
Career batting
94–167–8–2765–161–17.39–1–*ct* 63–*st* 4
Bowling 93–3–31.00–0–0–1/11

He made his County debut for Somerset in a non-first-class match v Hampshire in 1881, being only 15 years and 2 months old, and made his first-class debut for Gloucestershire the following year. In 1895 he began to assist Glamorgan (pre-first-class).

Pullinger, George Richard
Amateur. *b:* 14.3.1920, Islington, London. Lower order right-hand batsman, right-arm fast medium bowler. *Team* Essex (1949–50, 18 matches).
Career batting
18–20–11–53–14*–5.88–0–*ct* 14
Bowling 1557–41–37.97–1–0–5/54

Pulman, Rev William Walker
Amateur. *b:* 14.11.1852, Wellington, Somerset. *d:* 22.8.1936, Wellington, Somerset. Hard hitting middle order right-hand batsman, good field. *Sch* Marlborough. *Team* Oxford U (1874–75, blue both years).
Career batting
10–17–2–271–46–18.06–0–*ct* 4

His County cricket was for Somerset and Worcestershire (both pre-first-class).

Purchase, Richard
Professional. *b:* 24.9.1756, Liss, Hampshire. *d:* 1.4.1837, Liss, Hampshire. Opening or middle order right-hand batsman, medium pace under-arm bowler. *Team* Hampshire (1773–1803).
Career batting
1–1–0–0–0–0.00–0–*ct* 1
Bowling 2 wickets, no analyses

In a minor match (details lost), he and William Harding hit up 200 runs for the first wicket, the first time a double century partnership had been recorded (*circa* 1780).

Purdy, Henry Fox
Professional. *b:* 17.1.1883, Brimington, Derbyshire. *d:* 21.2.1943, Chesterfield, Derbyshire. Nephew of J. H. (Derbyshire). Lower order right-hand batsman, right-arm fast medium bowler. *Team* Derbyshire (1906–19, 16 matches).
Career batting
16–30–4–170–21–6.53–0–*ct* 5
Bowling 661–26–25.42–1–0–6/84

Purdy, John Henry
(also known as Perdew)
Professional. *b:* 23.9.1871, Brimington, Derbyshire. *d:* 19.5.1938, Mansfield, Notts. Uncle of H. F. (Derbyshire). Lower order right-hand batsman, right-arm fast medium bowler. *Team* Derbyshire (1896–1906, 9 matches).
Career batting
9–13–4–39–10–4.33–0–*ct* 4
Bowling 310–9–34.44–0–0–3/53

Purves, James Hamilton
Amateur. *b:* 4.12.1937, Hemel Hempstead, Herts. Middle order left-hand batsman, right-arm medium pace bowler. *Sch* Uppingham. *Team* Essex (1960–61, 5 matches).
Career batting
11–19–0–474–74–24.94–0–*ct* 5
His final first-class match was for Free Foresters in 1964.

Putner, Frank William
Professional. *b:* 26.9.1912, Greenwich, Kent. Middle order right-hand batsman, right-arm bowler. *Team* Middlesex (1933–34, 11 matches).
Career batting
13–19–2–192–80–11.29–0–*ct* 4
Bowling 96–2–48.00–0–0–2/42
His final first-class match was for MCC in 1938.

Puttock, Eric Clarence
Amateur. *b:* 2.3.1900, Billingshurst, Sussex. *d:* 14.12.1969, Slinfold, Sussex. Middle order batsman. *Sch* Dover. *Team* Sussex (1921, 2 matches).
Career batting
2–4–0–9–5–2.25–0–*ct* 1

Pycroft, Andrew John
Cricketer. *b:* 6.6.1956, Salisbury, Rhodesia. Middle order right-hand batsman, off break bowler. *Teams* Western Province (1975/6 to 1976/7); Rhodesia/Zimbabwe (1979/80 to 1982/3). *Tour* Zimbabwe to England 1982.
Career batting
33–60–7–2062–133–38.90–3–*ct* 24
Bowling 47–1–47.00–0–0–1/0

Pyemont, Christopher Patrick
Cricketer. *b:* 17.1.1948, Etchingham, Sussex. Middle order right-hand batsman, slow left-arm bowler. *Sch* Marlborough. *Team* Cambridge U (1967, blue).
Career batting
14–25–2–516–61–22.43–0–*ct* 1
Bowling 83–3–27.66–0–0–2/7
A good hockey player, he represented Cambridge.

Pye-Smith, Dr Edward John
Amateur. *b:* 24.2.1901, Sheffield, Yorkshire. *d:* 6.3.1983, Bishop Monkton, Harrogate, Yorkshire. Middle order right-hand batsman, right-arm medium pace bowler. *Sch* Cheltenham. *Team* Cambridge U (1922).
Career batting
1–1–0–32–32–32.00–0–*ct* 1

QUAIFE, BERNARD WILLIAM
Amateur. *b:* 24.11.1899, Olton, Warwickshire. Son of William (Warwickshire), nephew of Walter (Sussex and Warwickshire). Stolid middle order right-hand batsman, wicket-keeper. *Sch* Solihull. *Teams* Warwickshire (1920–26, 48 matches); Worcestershire (1928–37, 271 matches).
Career batting
319–528–49–9594–136*–20.02–3–*ct* 186–*st* 54
Bowling 297–9–33.00–0–0–2/5
He hit 1,000 runs in a season twice (best 1,167, av 26.52, in 1935).

Quaife, Frank Cyril
Professional. *b:* 1905, Hastings, Sussex. *d:* 27.8.1968, Eastbourne, Sussex. Lower order left-hand batsman, slow left-arm bowler. *Team* Sussex (1928, 2 matches).
Career batting
2–1–0–0–0–0.00–0–*ct* 0
Bowling 47–1–47.00–0–0–1/19

Quaife, Walter
Professional. *b:* 1.4.1864, Newhaven, Sussex. *d:* 18.1.1943, Norwood, Surrey. Brother of William (Warwickshire), uncle of B. W. (Warwickshire and Worcs). Stylish opening right-hand batsman, right-arm medium pace bowler. *Teams* Sussex (1884–91, 90 matches); Warwickshire (1894–1901, 121 matches).
Career batting
226–396–23–8536–156*–22.88–10–*ct* 85
Bowling 463–15–30.86–0–0–4/35
He hit 1,219 runs, av 34.82, in 1895. He also played for Suffolk.

Quaife, William (George)
Professional. *b:* 17.3.1872, Newhaven, Sussex. *d:* 13.10.1951, Edgbaston, Birmingham. Brother of Walter (Sussex and Warwickshire), father of B. W. (Warwickshire and Worcs). Sound middle order right-hand batsman, right-arm medium pace, or leg break, bowler, excellent cover point. *Teams* Warwickshire (1894–1928, 665 matches) London County (1900–03); Griqualand West (1912/3). *Tours* MacLaren to Australia 1901/2.

Tests England (1899 to 1901/2, 7 matches).
Career batting
718–1203–185–36012–255*–35.37–72–*ct* 349–*st* 1
Bowling 25443–931–27.32–32–2–7/76
Test batting
7–13–1–228–68–19.00–0–*ct* 4
Bowling 6–0

He hit 1,000 runs in a season 24 times, going on to 2,000 once : 2,060, av 54.21, in 1905. His four double centuries were all for Warwickshire, the highest being 255* v Surrey at the Oval in 1905. He played for Sussex in one non-first-class match in 1891.

Quentin, Rev George Augustus Frederick
Amateur. *b:* 3.11.1848, Kirkee, India. *d:* 6.5.1928, St Leonards on Sea, Sussex. Middle order right-hand batsman, right-hand fast round-arm bowler. *Sch* Shrewsbury. *Team* Gloucestershire (1874, 1 match).
Career batting
1–1–0–22–22–22.00–0–*ct* 0

He did not play in first-class matches whilst at Oxford U, being handicapped by ill-health.

Quick, Arnold Bertram
Amateur. *b:* 10.2.1915, Clacton, Essex. Middle order right-hand batsman. *Team* Essex (1936–52, 19 matches).
Career batting
20–33–1–439–57–13.74–0–*ct* 13
Bowling 10–0

He also played for Suffolk.

Quick, Ian William
Amateur. *b:* 5.11.1933, Geelong, Victoria, Australia. Aggressive tail end right-hand batsman, slow left-arm bowler. *Team* Victoria (1956/7 to 1961/2, 34 matches). *Tours* Australia to England 1961, to New Zealand 1959/60.
Career batting
63–71–13–816–61*–14.06–0–*ct* 32
Bowling 5922–195–30.36–7–1–7/20

He had only modest success on the 1961 tour of England and failed to gain a place in the Test side.

Quin, Stanley Edgar Vivian
Amateur. *b:* 3.4.1896, Bishops Glen, Orange Free State, South Africa. *d:* 9.4.1970, Bishops Glen, Orange Free State, South Africa. Middle order right-hand batsman, right-arm medium pace off break bowler. *Teams* Essex (1924, 1 match); Orange Free State (1931/2).
Career batting
3–5–0–3–3–0.60–0–*ct* 0
Bowling 60–0

Quinlan, Dr Bernard Gerald
Amateur. *b: circa* 1885, Perth, Australia. *d: circa* 1950, Perth, Australia. Brother of P. F. (Ireland). Lower order right-hand batsman, leg break and googly bowler. *Team* Ireland (1911).
Career batting
1 match, did not bat – *ct* 0
Bowling 49–3–16.33–0–0–2/36

Quinlan, Patrick Francis
Amateur. *b:* 17.3.1891, Perth, Australia. *d:* 15.8.1935, Perth, Australia. Brother of B. G. (Ireland). Opening right-hand batsman, right-arm medium pace bowler. *Teams* Ireland (1912–14); Western Australia (1925/6 to 1928/9, 8 matches).
Career batting
13–22–2–530–80–26.50–0–*ct* 8
Bowling 530–10–53.00–0–0–2/38

Quinn, Francis Michael
Amateur. *b:* 8.12.1915, Gort, Co Galway. Brother of G. J. and K. J. (Ireland). Right-hand batsman, right-arm medium pace bowler. *Team* Ireland (1936–48).
Career batting
7–14–0–227–140–16.21–1–*ct* 6
Bowling 22–0

Quinn, Gerard Joseph
Amateur. *b:* 10.9.1917, Gort, Co Galway. *d:* 20.11.1968, Dublin. Brother of F. M. and K. J. (Ireland). Right-hand batsman. *Team* Ireland (1937).
Career batting
1–2–0–14–12–7.00–0–*ct* 1

Quinn, Kevin Joseph
Amateur. *b:* 14.3.1923, Gort, Co Galway. Brother of F. M. and G. J. (Ireland). Right-hand batsman, slow left-arm bowler. *Team* Ireland (1957–59).
Career batting
3–5–0–49–25–9.80–0–*ct* 0
Bowling 14–0

He played rugby for Ireland.

Quinn, Neville Anthony
Amateur. *b:* 21.2.1908, Tweefontein, Orange Free State, South Africa. *d:* 5.8.1934, Kimberley, South Africa. Lower order right-hand batsman, left-arm medium fast bowler. *Teams* Griqualand West (1927/8 to 1932/3); Transvaal (1933/4). *Tours* South Africa to England 1929, to Australia and New Zealand 1931/2. *Tests* South Africa (1929 to 1931/2, 12 matches).

Career batting
51–63–15–438–32–9.12–0–*ct* 10
Bowling 3866–186–20.78–12–3–8/37
Test batting
12–18–3–90–28–6.00–0–*ct* 1
Bowling 1145–35–32.71–1–0–6/92

On his 1929 tour to England he headed the first-class bowling averages with 65 wickets, av 23.89.

Quinney, David Henry
Cricketer. *b:* 28.7.1950, Basford, Notts. Right-hand batsman. *Team* Cambridge U (1971).
Career batting
1–2–0–4–4–2.00–0–*ct* 1

Quinton, Brigadier General Francis William Drummond
Amateur. *b:* 27.12.1865, Fyzabad, India. *d:* 5.11.1926, Marylebone, London. Brother of J. M. (Hants). Hard hitting middle order right-hand batsman, slow under-arm bowler, good outfield. *Sch* Marlborough. *Team* Hampshire (1895–1900, 45 matches).
Career batting
51–94–8–2393–178–27.82–2–*ct* 46
Bowling 855–30–28.50–1–0–5/93

His first-class debut was for C. I. Thornton's XI in 1885. He also played for Devon commencing 1882.

Quinton, James Maurice
Amateur. *b:* 12.5.1874, Simla, India. *d:* 22.12.1922, Reading, Berkshire. Brother of F. W. D. (Hants). Attacking middle order right-hand batsman, right-arm fast bowler, good field. *Sch* Cheltenham. *Teams* Hampshire (1895–99, 4 matches); Oxford U (1895–96).
Career batting
6–10–2–79–22–9.87–0–*ct* 4
Bowling 111–1–111.00–0–0–1/14

He shot himself (through unnecessary worry) in a Great Western Railway express.

Quintrell, Robert N.
Amateur. *b:* 1931, Australia. Opening right-hand batsman. *Team* Canada (1954). *Tour* Canada to England 1954.
Career batting
4–6–0–76–29–12.66–0–*ct* 2
Bowling 43–0

RABONE, GEOFFREY OSBOURNE
Amateur. *b:* 6.11.1921, Gore, New Zealand. Free scoring middle order right-hand batsman, right-arm slow off break, or leg break bowler. *Teams* Wellington (1945/6 to 1950/1); Auckland (1951/2 to 1959/60). *Tours* New Zealand to England 1949, to South Africa 1953/4. *Tests* New Zealand (1949 to 1954/5, 12 matches).
Career batting
82–135–14–3425–125–28.30–3–*ct* 76
Bowling 4835–173–27.94–9–0–8/66
Test batting
12–20–2–562–107–31.22–1–*ct* 5
Bowling 635–16–39.68–1–0–6/68

He hit 1,021 runs, av 32.93, and took 50 wickets, av 35.70, on the 1949 tour, appearing in all four Tests. His final first-class match was for the Governor-General's XI in 1960/1 in New Zealand.

Racionzer, Terence Beverley
Cricketer. *b:* 18.12.1943, Maidenhead, Berks. Middle order right-hand batsman, off break bowler. *Teams* Sussex (1967–69, 26 matches); Scotland (1965–83).
Career batting
44–78–9–1494–115–21.65–1–*ct* 35
Bowling 52–2–26.00–0–0–2/11

Radcliffe, Sir Everard Joseph Reginald Henry
Amateur. *b:* 27.1.1884, Tiverton, Devon. *d:* 23.11.1969, Richmond, Yorkshire. Lower order right-hand batsman, useful bowler. *Sch* Downside. *Team* Yorkshire (1909–11, 64 matches).
Career batting
64–89–13–826–54–10.86–0–*ct* 21
Bowling 134–2–67.00–0–0–1/15

He captained Yorkshire in 1911, having acted as Lord Hawke's deputy in 1909 and 1910.

He also appeared for Shropshire.

Radcliffe, George
Professional. *b:* 25.9.1877, Ormskirk, Lancashire. *d:* 27.10.1951, Dukinfield, Cheshire. Opening right-hand batsman. *Team* Lancashire (1903–06, 7 matches).
Career batting
7–11–0–171–60–15.54–0–*ct* 2

He also played for Cheshire. Although a

professional when playing for Lancashire he appeared in the Central Lancashire League as an amateur for Stalybridge.

Radcliffe, Lees
Professional. *b:* 23.11.1865, Smithy Bridge, Rochdale, Lancashire. *d:* 1928, Manchester, Lancashire. Lower order right-hand batsman, wicket-keeper. *Team* Lancashire (1897–1905, 50 matches).
Career batting
50–67–22–275–25–6.11–0–*ct* 69–*st* 34
He also played for Durham.

Radcliffe, Octavius Goldney
Amateur. *b:* 20.10.1859, North Newnton, Wilts. *d:* 13.4.1940, Cherhill, Calne, Wiltshire. Steady opening right-hand batsman, off break bowler. *Teams* Gloucestershire (1885–93, 119 matches); Somerset (1885, 5 matches). *Tour* Sheffield to Australia 1891/2.
Career batting
144–264–7–5406–117–21.03–5–*ct* 60
Bowling 3050–103–29.61–2–0–5/43
He also played for Wiltshire.

Radcliffe, Stephen Tempest Adair
Amateur. *b:* 24.8.1904, Ballybrittas, Queen's County. *d:* 25.4.1982, Netherbury, Dorset. Right-hand batsman, right-arm medium pace bowler. *Sch* Oratory. *Team* Dublin University (1925–26).
Career batting
2–4–0–28–14–7.00–0–*ct* 1
Bowling 11–1–11.00–0–0–1/11

Radford, Henry William
Amateur. *b:* 19.6.1896, Derby. *d:* 29.11.1972, Banbury, Oxon. Tail end batsman, left-arm medium pace bowler. *Team* Derbyshire (1920, 3 matches).
Career batting
3–6–2–23–14–5.75–0–*ct* 0
Bowling 86–4–21.50–0–0–2/18

Radford, Neal Victor
Cricketer. *b:* 7.6.1957, Luanshya, Northern Rhodesia. Lower order right-hand batsman, right-arm fast medium bowler. *Teams* Lancashire (1980–83, 20 matches); Transvaal (1978/9 to 1982/3).
Career batting
55–65–14–1073–76*–21.03–0–*ct* 28
Bowling 4632–154–30.07–6–1–6/41

Radley, Clive Thornton
Cricketer. *b:* 13.5.1944, Hertford. Middle order right-hand batsman, leg break bowler, good close field. *Team* Middlesex (1964–83, 434 matches). *Tours* Robins to South Africa 1972/3, 1974/5; England to Pakistan and New Zealand 1977/8, to Australia 1978/9; Middlesex to Zimbabwe 1980/1. *Tests* England (1977/8 to 1978, 8 matches).
Career batting
474–758–106–22829–171–35.01–39–*ct* 464
Bowling 117–6–19.50–0–0–1/0
Test batting
8–10–0–481–158–48.10–2–*ct* 4
He hit 1,000 runs in a season 14 times (best 1,491, av 57.34, in 1980). Although very reliable in County cricket, he was unable to command a regular place in the England team.

Rae, Allan Fitzroy
Amateur. *b:* 30.9.1922, Kingston, Jamaica. Son of E. A. (West Indies). Steady opening left-hand batsman. *Team* Jamaica (1946/7 to 1959/60). *Tours* West Indies to India, Pakistan and Ceylon 1948/9, to England 1950, to Australia and New Zealand 1951/2. *Tests* West Indies (1948/9 to 1952/3, 15 matches).
Career batting
80–128–7–4798–179–39.65–17–*ct* 42
Bowling 26–0
Test batting
15–24–2–1016–109–46.18–4–*ct* 10
He hit 1,330 runs, av 39.11, in first-class matches on the 1950 tour and 377, av 62.83, in the four Tests. He also hit 1,000 runs in a season on the Indian Sub-continent.
In 1982/3 he was President of the West Indies Cricket Board of Control.

Rae, Ernest Allan
Amateur. *b:* 8.11.1897, St Andrew, Jamaica. *d:* 28.6.1969, Mona, Kingston, Jamaica. Father of A. F. (West Indies). Hard hitting middle order right-hand batsman, leg break bowler, good deep field. *Team* Jamaica (1924/5 to 1935/6). *Tour* West Indies to England 1928.
Career batting
29–43–6–1118–121–30.21–1–*ct* 27
Bowling 368–10–36.80–0–0–4/50
He achieved nothing of note on the 1928 tour.

Rae, Robert Burns
Professional. *b:* 23.7.1912, Littleborough, Lancashire. Middle order right-hand batsman, right-arm fast bowler. *Team* Lancashire (1945, 1 match).
Career batting
1–1–0–74–74–74.00–0–*ct* 0
Bowling 29–0

Raffety, Cairns Vezey
Amateur. *b:* 9.8.1906, Orpington, Kent. Middle

order left-hand batsman, slow left-arm bowler. *Sch* Cranleigh. *Team* Minor Counties (1931).
Career batting
1–1–0–16–16–16.00–0–*ct* 1
His County cricket was for Buckinghamshire.

Raikes, Douglas Charles Gordon
Amateur. *b:* 26.1.1910, Bristol, Gloucestershire. Lower order right-hand batsman, wicket-keeper. *Sch* Shrewsbury. *Teams* Oxford U (1931, blue); Gloucestershire (1932, 5 matches); Kent (1948, 2 matches).
Career batting
12–12–2–76–37–7.60–0–*ct* 21–*st* 8

Raikes, Rev George Barkley
Amateur. *b:* 14.3.1873, Carleton-Forehoe, Norfolk. *d:* 18.12.1966, Shepton Mallet, Somerset. Lower order right-hand batsman, right-arm medium pace bowler. *Sch* Shrewsbury. *Teams* Oxford U (1893–95, blue 1894–95); Hampshire (1900–02, 9 matches).
Career batting
30–53–5–816–77–17.00–0–*ct* 30
Bowling 1733–71–24.40–2–0–6/62
He played for Norfolk from 1890–97. His final first-class match was for an England XI in 1912.
An excellent goalkeeper, he gained his blue at Oxford and went on to play for England.

Raikes, Kenneth Cochrane
Amateur. *b:* 9.5.1889, Malpas, Newport, Monmouthshire. *d:* 29.11.1973, Hatfield, Herts. Middle order right-hand batsman, good bowler. *Sch* Shrewsbury. *Team* Wales (1925–29).
Career batting
6–8–0–135–50–16.87–0–*ct* 5
Bowling 502–18–27.88–1–0–7/28
He played County cricket for Monmouthshire.

Raikes, Thomas Barkley
Amateur. *b:* 16.12.1902, Bombay, India. *d:* 2.3.1984, Rickinghall Superior, Suffolk. Middle order right-hand batsman, right-arm medium-fast bowler. *Sch* Winchester. *Team* Oxford U (1922–25, blue 1922–24).
Career batting
38–58–15–554–44–12.88–0–*ct* 24
Bowling 3305–132–25.03–7–2–9/38
His County cricket was for Norfolk. His best bowling was 9/38 for Oxford U v Army at Oxford in 1924.

Raison, Max
Amateur. *b:* 7.11.1901, Wanstead, Essex. Middle order right-hand batsman, right-arm medium pace bowler. *Sch* Forest. *Team* Essex (1928–30, 17 matches).
Career batting
17–27–2–451–57–18.04–0–*ct* 6
Bowling 575–14–41.07–1–0–5/104

Rait-Kerr, Rowan Scrope
Amateur. *b:* 13.4.1891, Bray, Co Wicklow. *d:* 7.4.1961, Constantine Bay, Cornwall. Middle order right-hand batsman. *Sch* Rugby. *Teams* Army (1931); Europeans (1913/14 to 1920/1).
Career batting
6–12–0–89–24–7.41–0–*ct* 3
He was Secretary of MCC from 1936 to 1952 and mainly responsible for the revised code of Laws of Cricket in 1947, after which he published a book tracing the history of the Laws. His daughter Miss Diana Rait-Kerr, was for many years the Librarian at Lord's.

Rajkot, Thakore Saheb Sir Lakhaji Raj Bawaji Raj
(played cricket in England as Prince Chakorsab)
Amateur. *b:* 17.12.1885, India. *d:* 2.2.1930, India. Lower order right-hand batsman, fast bowler. *Teams* Gentlemen of England (1908); Hindus (1912/13); Combined Hindus and Muslims XI (1922/3).
Career batting
3–6–0–41–14–6.83–0–*ct* 2
Bowling 187–4–46.75–0–0–3/77

Ralph, Louis Henry Roy
Amateur, turned professional in 1958. *b:* 22.5.1920, East Ham, Essex. Lower order right-hand batsman, right-arm medium pace bowler. *Team* Essex (1953–61, 174 matches).
Career batting
174–262–39–3763–73–16.88–0–*ct* 143
Bowling 11053–460–24.02–19–3–7/42
His best season was 1957 with 102 wickets, av 22.00.

Ralston, Francis William
Amateur. *b:* 7.6.1867, Philadelphia, USA. *d:* 7.10.1920, Charleston, USA. Lower order right-hand batsman, wicket-keeper. *Team* Philadelphia (1886–97). *Tour* Philadelphia to England 1897.
Career batting
22–37–5–417–53–13.03–0–*ct* 27–*st* 1
He proved an excellent wicket-keeper on the 1897 tour to England, but did little with the bat.

Ramadhin, Sonny
Professional. *b:* 1.5.1929, Esperance Village, Trinidad. Tail end right-hand batsman, off break bowler. *Teams* Trinidad (1949/50 to 1952/3); Lancashire (1964–65, 33 matches). *Tours* West Indies to England 1950, 1957, to Australia and New Zealand 1951/2, to New Zealand 1955/6, to

Australia 1960/1, to India and Pakistan 1958/9; International XI to India, Pakistan, South Africa, New Zealand 1961/2; Commonwealth to India and Ceylon 1950/1, to India 1953/4. *Tests* West Indies (1950 to 1960/1, 43 matches).
Career batting
184–191–65–1092–44–8.66–0–*ct* 38
Bowling 15345–758–20.24–51–15–8/15
Test batting
43–58–14–361–44–8.20–0–*ct* 9
Bowling 4579–158–28.98–10–1–7/49

Coming to England in 1950 as a totally unknown cricketer he created a sensation by playing a major role in winning the rubber for West Indies. He headed the first-class bowling averages with 135 wickets, av 14.88, and took 26 wickets, av 23.23, in the Tests. In 1957 he again headed the first-class averages with 119 wickets, av 13.98, but was not so effective in the Tests.

He was fairly successful for Lancashire in 1964, but in 1965 lost his place in the County side.

He also played for Lincolnshire.

Ramage, Alan
Cricketer. *b:* 29.11.1957, Guisborough, Yorkshire. Left-hand batsman, right-arm fast medium bowler. *Team* Yorkshire (1979–83, 23 matches).
Career batting
23–22–9–219–52–16.84–0–*ct* 1
Bowling 1649–44–37.47–1–0–5.65

He played football for Middlesbrough.

Ramage, Paul Frederick
Amateur. *b:* 13.3.1940, Leamington Spa, Warwickshire. Lower order right-hand batsman, slow left-arm bowler. *Sch* Warwick. *Team* Cambridge U (1962–63).
Career batting
13–22–7–252–50–16.80–0–*ct* 5
Bowling 613–17–36.05–0–0–4/65

His County cricket was for Buckinghamshire.

Ramaswami, Cotar
Amateur. *b:* 16.6.1896, Madras, India. Sound middle order left-hand batsman, right-arm bowler. *Teams* Indians (1915/6 to 1939/40); Madras (1926/7 to 1941/2). *Tour* India to England 1936. *Tests* India (1936, 2 matches).
Career batting
53–92–9–2400–127*–28.91–2–*ct* 33
Bowling 992–30–33.06–0–0–4/29
Test batting
2–4–1–170–60–56.66–0–*ct* 0

After an uncertain start, he proved one of the most reliable batsmen on the 1936 tour, heading the Test averages, and in first-class matches scoring 737 runs, av 30.70. He represented India in the Davis Cup.

Ramchand, Gulabrai Sipahimalani
Professional. *b:* 26.7.1927, Karachi, India. Aggressive middle order right-hand batsman, right-arm medium fast bowler. *Teams* Sind (1945/6 to 1946/7); Bombay (1948/9 to 1965/6). *Tours* India to England 1952, to West Indies 1952/3, to Pakistan 1954/5, to Ceylon 1956/7. *Tests* India (1952 to 1959/60, 33 matches).
Career batting
145–202–36–6027–230*–36.30–16–*ct* 105
Bowling 7518–255–29.48–9–0–8/12
Test batting
33–53–5–1180–109–24.58–2–*ct* 20
Bowling 1899–41–46.31–1–0–6/49

He hit 644 runs, av 24.76, and took 64 wickets, av 25.85, on the 1952 tour to England, but failed to make any impression in the Tests, though playing in all four. He also played in England for a Commonwealth XI in 1953 and 1957. His highest score was 230* for Bombay v Maharashtra at Bombay in 1950/1. His final first-class match was for Dungarpur XI in India in 1967/8.

Rammell, Arthur William
Amateur. *b:* 21.9.1868, Blean, Kent. *d:* 10.3.1956, Eastbourne, Sussex. Middle order batsman. *Team* MCC (1896).
Career batting
1–2–0–5–5–2.50–0–*ct* 0

Ramnarace, Randolph
Cricketer. *b:* 25.7.1941, Berbice, British Guiana. Lower order batsman, good bowler. *Team* British Guiana (1965/6 to 1972/3). *Tour* Rest of World to England 1968.
Career batting
28–46–3–972–71–22.60–0–*ct* 15
Bowling 2336–75–31.14–1–0–6/101

His first-class debut was for Berbice in 1960/1 and his final match for the same side in 1973/4.

Ramsamooj, Donald
Professional. *b:* 5.7.1932, San Fernando, Trinidad. Middle order right-hand batsman, right-arm off break bowler. *Teams* Northamptonshire (1958–64, 71 matches); Trinidad (1952/3 to 1956/7).
Career batting
79–143–9–2755–132–20.55–4–*ct* 36
Bowling 178–3–59.33–0–0–1/28

Ramsay, Marmaduke Francis
Amateur. *b:* 8.12.1860, Cheltenham, Gloucs. *d:* 31.12.1947, Lee, Canterbury, Kent. Brother of R. C. (Cambridge U and Somerset). Lower order right-hand batsman, right-arm medium pace bowler, good point field. *Sch* Harrow. *Teams*

MCC (1894); Queensland (1892/3 to 1899/1900, 3 matches).
Career batting
4–8–0–170–58–21.25–0–*ct* 3
Bowling 182–9–20.22–0–0–4/61

He was for some years a sheep farmer in Australia.

He also played for Somerset (pre-first-class).

Ramsay, Robert Christian
Amateur. *b:* 20.12.1861, Cheltenham, Gloucestershire. *d:* 25.6.1957, Bekesbourne, Kent. Brother of M. F. (Queensland). Lower order right-hand batsman, right-arm slow bowler. *Sch* Harrow. *Teams* Cambridge U (1881–82, blue 1882); Somerset (1882, 4 matches).
Career batting
15–26–4–303–71–13.77–0–*ct* 11
Bowling 1230–69–17.82–5–2–7/22

Whilst bowling for Cambridge U v Lancashire at Old Trafford in 1882 he had the mortifying experience of seeing the batsman dropped off every ball of one four-ball over.

In the 1880s he emigrated to Australia and spent most of his adult life there. He played for Queensland but not in first-class matches.

Ramsbotham, Wilfrid Hubert
Amateur. *b:* 20.12.1888. *d:* 7.11.1978, Kensington, London. Middle order right-hand batsman. *Sch* Uppingham. *Teams* Cambridge U (1908–09); Sussex (1908–10, 7 matches).
Career batting
9–15–0–245–56–16.33–0–*ct* 2

Ramsbottom, Henry John
Professional. *b:* 21.10.1846, Enfield, Lancashire. *d:* 1905, Blackburn, Lancashire. Opening right-hand batsman, right-arm medium pace bowler. *Team* Lancashire (1868, 1 match).
Career batting
1–2–0–1–1–0.50–0–*ct* 0
Bowling 11–0

Ramsden, Frederick William
Amateur. *b:* 11.1.1911, Leeds, Yorkshire. Right-hand batsman. *Team* Scotland (1937–39).
Career batting
4–8–0–108–29–13.50–0–*ct* 1

Ranasinghe, Anura Nandana
Cricketer. *b:* 12.10.1956, Diyatalawa, Ceylon. Attacking middle order right-hand batsman, left-arm medium, or slow, bowler. *Team* Sri Lanka (1974/5 to 1982/3). *Tours* Sri Lanka to India 1974/5, 1975/6, 1980/1, 1982/3, to England 1981, to Pakistan 1981/2, Sri Lanka XI to South Africa 1982/3. *Tests* Sri Lanka (1981/2 to 1982/3, 2 matches).
Career batting
33–58–6–1253–77–24.09–0–*ct* 22
Bowling 1656–39–42.46–1–0–5/65
Test batting
2–4–0–88–77–22.00–0–*ct* 0
Bowling 69–1–69.00–0–0–1/23

Randall, Derek William
Cricketer. *b:* 24.2.1951, Retford, Nottinghamshire. Attacking middle order right-hand batsman, right-arm medium pace bowler, brilliant cover field. *Team* Nottinghamshire (1972–83, 211 matches). *Tours* English Counties XI to West Indies 1974/5 (not first-class); Robins to South Africa 1975/6; MCC to India, Sri Lanka and Australia 1976/7; England to Pakistan and New Zealand 1977/8, to Australia 1978/9, 1979/80, 1982/3. *Tests* England (1976/7 to 1983, 40 matches).
Career batting
291–496–43–16296–209–35.97–26–*ct* 200
Bowling 142–3–47.33–0–0–3/15
Test batting
40–68–5–2073–174–32.90–5–*ct* 28
Bowling 3–0

He hit 1,000 runs in a season eight times (best 1,546, av 42.94, in 1976). Both his double centuries were for Notts, the highest being 209 v Middlesex at Trent Bridge in 1979 – he also scored 146 in the same match.

His most famous innings was 174 scored in the Centenary Test Match in Melbourne in 1976/7.

Randall, James
Amateur. *b:* 9.5.1876, London. *d:* 8.9.1954, Guethary, Basses Pyrenees, France. Lower order batsman, useful bowler. *Sch* Sedbergh. *Team* MCC (1904).
Career batting
1–2–0–0–0–0.00–0–*ct* 0
Bowling 40–0

Randir Singh Baldevsingh
Cricketer. *b:* 16.8.1957, Delhi, India. Tail end right-hand batsman, right-arm fast medium bowler. *Teams* Orissa (1978/9 to 1979/80); Bihar (1980/1 to 1982/3). *Tour* India to England 1982.
Career batting
27–30–11–155–15–8.15–0–*ct* 6
Bowling 2550–66–38.63–2–0–6/141

He achieved very little on the 1982 tour to England.

Randolph, Bernard Montgomery
Amateur. *b:* 10.4.1834, Much Hadham, Herts. *d:* 3.7.1857, Christ Church College, Oxford. Brother of L. C. (Oxford U 1845). Middle order batsman. *Sch* Charterhouse. *Teams* Oxford U

(1855–57, blue 1855 and 1856); Sussex (1856, 1 match).
Career batting
7–13–0–207–61–15.92–0–*ct* 4
Bowling 20–1–20.00–0–0–1/6

He also played for Cheshire and Herefordshire.

He appeared for Oxford U v MCC on 18 and 19 June 1857, was too ill to play in the University match the following week and died on 3 July.

Randolph, Rev John
Amateur. *b:* 15.5.1821, Sanderstead, Surrey. *d:* 11.7.1881, Sanderstead, Surrey. Lower order right-hand batsman, useful bowler, good long stop. *Sch* Westminster. *Team* Oxford U (1842–44, blue 1843).
Career batting
11–22–3–45–10–2.36–0–*ct* 8
Bowling 19–1–19.00–0–0–1/19

His final first-class match was for MCC in 1864. His County cricket was for Northants (pre-first-class), Buckinghamshire and Bedfordshire. From 1875 to his death he was Auditor to the MCC.

Randon, Frederick sen
Professional. *b:* 24.6.1845, Stapleford, Notts. *d:* 19.2.1883, Hathern, Leics. Father of Frederick, jun (Leics). Lower order right-hand batsman, right-hand fast round-arm bowler. *Team* MCC (1874–76).
Career batting
15–26–10–104–23*–6.50–0–*ct* 6
Bowling 655–37–17.70–2–0–6/54

He played for Nottinghamshire in non-first-class matches.

Randon, Frederick jun
Professional. *b:* 18.11.1873, Hathern, Leics. *d:* 15.1.1949, Hathern, Leics. Son of Frederick sen (MCC). Lower order left-hand batsman, left-arm medium pace bowler. *Team* Leicestershire (1894, 3 matches).
Career batting
3–5–2–5–5–1.66–0–*ct* 1
Bowling 128–4–32.00–0–0–3/20

Ranjitsinhji, Kumar Shri
(later H. H. Shri Sir Ranjitsinhji Vibhaji, Jam Sahib of Nawanagar)
Amateur. *b:* 10.9.1872, Sarodar, India. *d:* 2.4.1933, Jamnagar, India. Brother of K. S. Digvijaysinhji (Western India), uncle of K. S. Duleepsinhji (Cambridge U and Sussex), K. S. Himmatsinhji (Rajputana) and M. S. Samarsinhji (Nawanagar). Fine middle order right-hand batsman, slow right-arm bowler. *Teams* Cambridge U (1893–94, blue 1893); Sussex (1895–1920, 211 matches); London County (1901–04). *Tours* Stoddart to Australia 1897/8; Ranjitsinhji to North America 1899. *Tests* England (1896–1902, 15 matches).
Career batting
307–500–62–24692–285*–56.37–72–*ct* 233
Bowling 4601–133–34.59–4–0–6/53
Test batting
15–26–4–989–175–44.95–2–*ct* 13
Bowling 39–1–39.00–0–0–1/23

After a modest career at Cambridge, Ranjitsinhji developed quickly into one of the foremost batsman in England – in fact in terms of statistics he was the best from 1899 to 1904. He hit 3,159 runs, av 63.18, in 1899 and the following year 3,065, av 87.57. These were his most prolific years, but he exceeded 2,000 runs in three other seasons and over 1,000 on six other occasions, also once in Australia. Fourteen times he compiled double centuries, all of which were for Sussex, the highest being 285* v Somerset at Taunton in 1901. He appeared in four Test series against Australia and was successful in all but the 1902 Tests.

He captained Sussex from 1899 to 1903 and left England in 1904 to return to India. Thereafter his appearances in County cricket were limited. He played in the summer of 1908 and again in 1912, in both years exceeding 1,000 runs. A shooting accident resulted in his losing one eye and this virtually ended his first-class career, though he played a little in 1920.

In 1907 he became the Maharaja Jam Sahib of Nawanagar and was increasingly involved in the administration of his State. He was also a delegate to the League of Nations after the First World War.

Ransford, Vernon Seymour
Amateur. *b:* 20.3.1885, South Yarra, Victoria, Australia. *d:* 19.3.1958, Brighton, Victoria, Australia. Sound middle order left-hand batsman, slow left-arm bowler, good deep field. *Team* Victoria (1903/04 to 1927/8, 76 matches). *Tours* Australia to England 1909, to New Zealand 1913/4, 1920/1; Victoria to New Zealand 1924/5. *Tests* Australia (1907/8 to 1911/12, 20 matches).
Career batting
142–219–24–8268–190–42.40–25–*ct* 74
Bowling 888–29–30.62–1–0–6/38
Test batting
20–38–6–1211–143*–37.84–1–*ct* 10
Bowling 28–1–28.00–0–0–1/9

He was very successful on his only tour to England, hitting 1,736 runs, av 43.40. He appeared in all five Tests and easily topped the batting with 353, av 58.83.

Ransom, Victor Joseph
Amateur. *b:* 17.5.1917, New Malden, Surrey. Hard hitting lower order right-hand batsman,

right-arm fast medium bowler. *Teams* Hampshire (1947–50, 34 matches); Surrey (1951–55, 2 matches).
Career batting
40–58–11–455–58–9.68–0–*ct* 22
Bowling 3469–98–35.39–3–0–5/50

Raper, James Rhodes Stanley
Amateur. *b:* 9.8.1909, Bradford, Yorkshire. Lower order right-hand batsman, right-arm medium pace bowler. *Sch* Leys. *Team* Yorkshire (1936–47, 3 matches). *Tour* Yorkshire to Jamaica 1935/6 (he did not play in first-class matches).
Career batting
3–4–0–24–15–6.00–0–*ct* 0

Raphael, Geoffrey Lewis
Amateur. *b:* 10.1.1910, Westminster, London. Lower order right-hand batsman, right-arm medium pace bowler. *Sch* Harrow. *Team* Middlesex (1928, 1 match).
Career batting
1–1–0–1–1–1.00–0–*ct* 0
Bowling 36–0

Raphael, John Edward
Amateur. *b:* 30.4.1882, Brussels, Belgium. *d:* 11.6.1917, Reny, Belgium, He died of wounds. Attacking middle order right-hand batsman, slow medium right-arm bowler. *Sch* Merchant Taylors. *Teams* London County (1901–02); Oxford U (1903–05, blue all three years); Surrey (1903–09, 39 matches).
Career batting
76–128–8–3717–201–30.97–5–*ct* 36
Bowling 411–3–137.00–0–0–1/34

He hit 1,695 runs, av 39.41, in 1904 and in the same year hit 201 for Oxford U v Yorkshire at Oxford. His final first-class match was for MCC in 1913. An excellent three-quarter back he obtained his blue and was capped nine times for England. He stood as Liberal candidate for Croydon but was not elected.

Raphael, Richard Henry
Amateur. *b:* 1872, Steyning, Sussex. *d:* 23.1.1910, Westminster, London. Middle order right-hand batsman. *Sch* Wellington. *Team* G.J.V. Weigall's XI (1904). *Tour* Oxford University Authentics to India 1902/3.
Career batting
4–8–1–246–111–35.14–1–*ct* 0
Bowling 18–0

Rashleigh, Canon William
Amateur. *b:* 7.3.1867, Farningham, Kent. *d:* 13.2.1937, Balcombe, Sussex. Stylish opening right-hand batsman, slow right-arm bowler. *Sch* Tonbridge. *Teams* Kent (1885–1901, 96 matches); Oxford U (1886–89, blue all four years).
Career batting
127–220–6–5379–163–25.13–9–*ct* 56
Bowling 29–0

A useful rugby footballer, he played as full back against Cambridge in 1887 and 1888.

Raspin, Peter Hugh
Cricketer. *b:* 26.11.1951, Bolton, Lancashire. Lower order right-hand batsman, slow left-arm bowler. *Sch* Birkenhead. *Team* Oxford U (1973).
Career batting
2–2–1–15–10–15.00–0–*ct* 0
Bowling 117–3–39.00–0–0–2/69

Ratcliff, John
Amateur. *b:* 31.12.1848, Richmond, Surrey. *d:* 11.8.1925, Twickenham, Middlesex. Lower order right-hand batsman, wicket-keeper. *Team* Surrey (1876, 4 matches).
Career batting
4–8–0–69–27–8.62–0–*ct* 1

Ratcliffe, Alan
Amateur. *b:* 31.3.1909, Dulwich. *d:* 21.8.1967, Toronto, Canada. Opening right-hand batsman. *Sch* Rydal. *Teams* Wales (1928–30); Cambridge U (1930–32, blue all three years); Surrey (1932–33, 7 matches).
Career batting
49–82–7–1969–201–26.25–5–*ct* 40
Bowling 22–0

He created a new University record by scoring 201 for Cambridge in 1931 – he was chosen for the match only at the last moment due to the injury of J. G. W. Davies. He also played for Denbighshire and Buckinghamshire. His final first-class match was for Over 33s in 1945.

Ratcliffe, David Philip
Professional. *b:* 11.5.1939, Hall Green, Birmingham. Opening right-hand batsman. *Team* Warwickshire (1957–68, 20 matches).
Career batting
20–33–2–603–79–19.45–0–*ct* 18

Ratcliffe, Edgar
Amateur. *b:* 1863, Liverpool. *d:* 29.7.1915, Aston, Birmingham. Middle order batsman. *Team* Lancashire (1884, 1 match).
Career batting
4–7–0–67–28–9.57–0–*ct* 2
Bowling 43–1–43.00–0–0–1/10

His final first-class match was for Liverpool and District XI in 1889.

Ratcliffe, George
Amateur. *b:* 1856, Ilkeston, Derbyshire. *d:* 7.3.1928, Nottingham. Attacking middle order left-hand batsman. *Team* Derbyshire (1887, 5 matches).
Career batting
5–10–0–145–64–14.50–0–*ct* 0
Bowling 8–0
He appeared for Nottinghamshire in non-first-class matches.

Ratcliffe, George
Professional. *b:* November 1885. *d:* 31.12.1952, Ollerton, Notts. Tail end right-hand batsman, good bowler. *Team* Derbyshire (1919, 1 match).
Career batting
1–2–1–8–5*–8.00–0–*ct* 2
Bowling 10–1–10.00–0–0–1/10

Ratcliffe, Robert Malcolm
Cricketer. *b:* 29.11.1951, Accrington, Lancashire. Lower order right-hand batsman, right-arm medium pace bowler. *Team* Lancashire (1972–80, 82 matches).
Career batting
82–84–22–1011–101*–16.48–1–*ct* 23
Bowling 5411–205–26.39–15–2–7/58

Ratliff, Thomas
Amateur. *b:* 31.3.1836, Camberwell, Surrey. Middle order right-hand batsman, right-hand slow under-arm bowler, good cover point. *Team* Middlesex (1869–73, 3 matches).
Career batting
4–6–1–50–18–10.00–0–*ct* 0
Bowling 29–3–9.66–0–0–3/21
His first-class debut was for Gentlemen of the North in 1862. He played for Warwickshire from 1863 to 1876 (pre-first-class).

Ratnayeke, Joseph Ravindran
Cricketer. *b:* 2.5.1960, Colombo, Ceylon. Lower order right-hand batsman, right-arm fast medium bowler. *Team* Sri Lanka (1980/1 to 1982/3). *Tours* Sri Lanka to India 1980/1, 1982/3, to England 1981, to Pakistan 1981/2, to Zimbabwe 1982/3, to Australia and New Zealand 1982/3. *Tests* Sri Lanka (1981/2 to 1982/3, 5 matches).
Career batting
19–28–9–352–64*–18.52–0–*ct* 5
Bowling 1232–34–36.23–1–0–5/120
Test batting
5–10–2–102–29*–13.75–0–*ct* 0
Bowling 450–9–50.00–0–0–3/93

Rattenbury, Gilbert Leach
Amateur. *b:* 28.2.1878, Cardiff. *d:* 14.8.1958, Penarth, Glamorgan. Middle order right-hand batsman, right-arm fast bowler. *Team* Gloucestershire (1902–09, 2 matches).
Career batting
2–4–0–7–7–1.75–0–*ct* 0
Bowling 129–1–129.00–0–0–1/54
He also played for Glamorgan (pre-first-class).

Rattigan, Cyril Stanley
Amateur. *b:* 5.8.1884, Camberwell, London. *d:* 13.11.1916, near Beaucourt, France. He was killed in action. Middle order right-hand batsman, right-arm medium pace bowler. *Sch* Harrow. *Team* Cambridge U (1906–07).
Career batting
7–11–2–183–42–20.33–0–*ct* 3
Bowling 217–5–43.40–0–0–3/61
His final first-class match was for MCC in 1908.

Raven, John Earle Reynolds
Amateur. *b:* 23.2.1851, Broughton Astley, Leicestershire. *d:* 3.4.1940, Nutfield, Surrey. Tail end right-hand batsman, right-arm fast medium bowler. *Sch* Lancing. *Team* Sussex (1874, 1 match).
Career batting
1–2–0–14–10–7.00–0–*ct* 0
Bowling 37–0

Raven, Reginald Owen
Amateur. *b:* 26.11.1884, Baldock, Herts. *d:* 4.4.1936, Eastbourne, Sussex. Lower order right-hand batsman, bowler. *Sch* Wellingborough. *Team* Northamptonshire (1905–21, 31 matches).
Career batting
31–58–2–766–59–13.67–0–*ct* 10
Bowling 59–1–59.00–0–0–1/15
He captained Northants in 1920–21.
He also represented Northants at hockey.

Ravenhill, Edward Harry Goring
Amateur. *b:* 11.11.1845. *d:* 1.3.1924, Brentwood, Essex. Middle order batsman. *Team* MCC (1882).
Career batting
1–2–0–9–6–4.50–0–*ct* 0

Ravenhill, Frederick Henry Harvey
Amateur. *b:* 25.7.1837, Littlehampton, Sussex. *d:* 4.8.1897, Hove, Sussex. Middle order right-hand batsman. *Sch* Brighton. *Team* Sussex (1863–67, 2 matches).
Career batting
2–3–0–10–7–3.33–0–*ct* 1
He did not appear in first-class matches whilst at Oxford.

Ravenscroft, Joseph
Amateur. *b:* 19.3.1858, Birkenhead. *d:* 28.4.1913,

North Birkenhead, Cheshire. Middle order right-hand batsman. *Sch* Rugby. *Team* Liverpool and District XI (1888–94).
Career batting
2–4–0–0–0–0.00–0–*ct* 1
His County cricket was for Cheshire.

Raw, George David
Cricketer. *b:* 14.11.1944, Ossett, Yorkshire. Middle order right-hand batsman. *Team* Cambridge U (1967–68).
Career batting
6–10–0–82–21–8.20–0–*ct* 0

Raw, Roland
Amateur. *b:* 16.7.1884. *d:* 7.8.1915, Hill 10, Suvla Bay, Gallipoli. Middle order batsman. *Sch* Clifton. *Team* Gentlemen of England (1905).
Career batting
2–2–0–48–47–24.00–0–*ct* 0

Rawlence, John Rooke
Amateur. *b:* 23.9.1915, Lymington, Hants. *d:* 17.1.1983, Ascot, Berks. Middle order right-hand batsman. *Sch* Wellington. *Team* Hampshire (1934, 2 matches).
Career batting
5–6–0–87–38–14.50–0–*ct* 3
His final first-class match was for Combined Services in 1950.

Rawlin, Eric Raymond
Professional. *b:* 4.10.1897, Rotherham, Yorkshire. *d:* 11.1.1943, Rotherham, Yorkshire. Son of J. T. (Yorkshire and Middlesex). Lower order left-hand batsman, right-hand fast medium bowler. *Team* Yorkshire (1927–36, 8 matches).
Career batting
8–10–1–72–35–8.00–0–*ct* 2
Bowling 498–21–23.71–0–0–3/28

Rawlin, John Thomas
Professional. *b:* 10.11.1856, Greasbrough, Rotherham, Yorkshire. *d:* 19.1.1924, Greasbrough, Rotherham, Yorkshire. Father of E. R. (Yorkshire). Lower order right-hand batsman, right-arm fast medium bowler. *Teams* Yorkshire (1880–85, 27 matches); Middlesex (1889–1909, 229 matches). *Tour* Vernon to Australia 1887/8.
Career batting
315–493–44–7651–122*–17.04–2–*ct* 200
Bowling 16689–811–20.57–46–12–8/29
He took 104 wickets, av 14.53, in 1894.

Rawlins, Frederick
Amateur. *b:* 1907, Biggleswade, Bedfordshire. *d:* 27.12.1968, Biddenham, Bedfordshire. Middle order right-hand batsman. *Sch* Wellingborough. *Team* Minor Counties (1930–34).
Career batting
2–3–0–110–74–36.66–0–*ct* 0
His County cricket was for Bedfordshire.

Rawlinson, Elisha Barker
Professional. *b:* 10.4.1837, Yeadon, Yorkshire. *d:* 17.2.1892, Sydney, Australia. He died of jaundice. Middle order right-hand batsman, right-hand fast round-arm bowler, cover point. *Teams* Yorkshire (1867–75, 37 matches); Lancashire (1867, 1 match).
Career batting
45–80–7–1120–55–15.34–0–*ct* 23
Bowling 79–8–9.87–0–0–4/41
His County cricket ended in 1875 as in April 1876 he emigrated to Australia.

Rawlinson, Henry Thomas
Cricketer. *b:* 21.1.1963, Edgware, Middlesex. Brother of J. L. (Oxford U). Lower order right-hand batsman, right-arm medium pace bowler. *Sch* Eton. *Team* Oxford U (1982–83, blue 1983).
Career batting
12–15–2–121–24–9.30–0–*ct* 3
Bowling 1061–19–55.84–1–0–5/123

Rawlinson, John Baldwin
Amateur. *b:* 1.5.1867, Whitehaven, Cumberland. *d:* 12.5.1945, Kensington, London. Lower order right-hand batsman, right-arm fast bowler. *Sch* Malvern. *Team* Oxford U (1887).
Career batting
1–1–0–0–0–0.00–0–*ct* 1
Bowling 45–1–45.00–0–0–1/45

Rawlinson, John Lawrence
Cricketer. *b:* 4.8.1959, Edgware, Middlesex. Brother of H. T. (Oxford U). Middle order right-hand batsman. *Sch* Eton. *Team* Oxford U (1979–80).
Career batting
9–16–2–112–19–8.00–0–*ct* 5

Rawlinson, William
Professional. *b:* 5.9.1850, Burnley, Lancashire. Middle order batsman. *Team* Lancashire (1870–71, 3 matches).
Career batting
3–6–0–24–10–4.00–0–*ct* 1

Rawson, Major General Geoffrey Grahame
Amateur. *b:* 2.12.1887, Shirmadavy, India. *d:* 14.1.1979, Kensington, London. Opening right-hand batsman. *Sch* Cheltenham. *Team* Army (1921).
Career batting
3–5–0–69–39–13.80–0–*ct* 5

Rawson, Herbert Edward
Amateur. *b:* 3.9.1852, Port Louis, Mauritius. *d:* 18.10.1924, Westminster, London. Lower order right-hand batsman, wicket-keeper. *Sch* Westminster. *Team* Kent (1873, 1 match).
Career batting
1–2–0–0–0–0.00–0–*ct* 1–*st* 3
In 1874 he was posted overseas and therefore had no opportunity for County cricket.

Rawson, Peter Walter Edward
Cricketer. *b:* 25.5.1957, Salisbury, Rhodesia. Lower order right-hand batsman, right-arm fast medium bowler. *Team* Zimbabwe (1982 to 1982/3). *Tour* Zimbabwe to England 1982.
Career batting
6–8–2–88–63*–14.66–0–*ct* 2
Bowling 578–32–18.06–4–1–7/55

Rawstorne, George (Streynsham)
Amateur. *b:* 22.1.1895, Croston, Lancashire. *d:* 15.7.1962, Rovie, Rogart, Sutherland. Middle order batsman. *Sch* Eton. *Team* Lancashire (1919, 1 match).
Career batting
1–1–0–2–2–2.00–0–*ct* 0

Ray, Donald William Garnham
Amateur. *b:* 2.7.1903, Wimborne, Dorset. *d:* 12.7.1944, Normandy, France. Lower order batsman, wicket-keeper. *Sch* Wellington. *Team* MCC (1931).
Career batting
1–2–0–2–2–1.00–0–*ct* 1–*st* 2

Raybould, John Griffith
Amateur. *b:* 26.7.1934, Middlesbrough, Yorkshire. Lower order left-hand batsman, leg break and googly bowler. *Sch* Leeds GS. *Team* Oxford U (1957–59, blue 1959).
Career batting
18–32–10–281–81*–12.77–0–*ct* 8
Bowling 1302–34–38.29–0–0–4/31
His final first-class match was for Free Foresters in 1962.

Rayment, Alan William Harrington
Professional. *b:* 29.5.1928, Finchley, Middlesex. Middle order right-hand batsman. *Team* Hampshire (1949–58, 198 matches).
Career batting
199–340–28–6338–126–20.31–4–*ct* 86
Bowling 772–19–40.63–0–0–4/75
He hit 1,000 runs in a season twice (best 1,056, av 23.46, in 1952). His first-class debut was for Combined Services in 1947.

Raynbird, Robert
Amateur. *b:* 29.6.1851, Whitchurch, Hants. *d:* 28.12.1920, Basingstoke, Hants. Brother of Walter (Hampshire). Lower order batsman, bowler. *Sch* Framlingham. *Team* Hampshire (1878, 1 match).
Career batting
1–2–0–0–0–0.00–0–*ct* 0
Bowling 15–0

Raynbird, Walter
Amateur. *b:* 1.6.1854, Basingstoke, Hants. *d:* 6.5.1891, Hackwood Park, Hants. Brother of Robert (Hampshire). Middle order batsman. *Team* Hampshire (1880–81, 2 matches).
Career batting
2–4–1–25–13–8.33–0–*ct* 0
Bowling 14–0

Rayner, Dr Howard Luscombe
Amateur. *b:* 12.3.1896, Glenelg, South Australia. *d:* 13.6.1975, Twickenham, Middlesex. Middle order batsman. *Team* P. F. Warner's XI (1919).
Career batting
1–2–1–23–21*–23.00–0–*ct* 1

Raynes, Thomas Arthur
Amateur. *b:* 18.7.1835, Ripe, Sussex. *d:* 6.3.1914, Cockington, Torquay, Devon. Attacking middle order right-hand batsman, good point field. *Sch* Marlborough. *Team* Sussex (1854–64, 7 matches).
Career batting
10–19–2–207–59–12.17–0–*ct* 5

Raynor, Rev George Sydney
Amateur. *b:* 9.10.1852, Sandsend, Lythe, Yorkshire. *d:* 1.9.1887, Croydon, Surrey. Lower order right-hand batsman, right-arm fast bowler. *Sch* Winchester. *Team* Cambridge U (1872–73, blue 1872).
Career batting
7–10–1–66–37*–7.33–0–*ct* 5
Bowling 370–17–21.76–1–0–5/44
His County cricket was for Essex (pre-first-class).

Raynor, Kenneth
Amateur. *b:* 23.5.1886, Wellington, Berkshire. *d:* 15.4.1973, Greendale, Rhodesia. Middle order right-hand batsman, leg break and googly bowler. *Sch* Ipswich. *Teams* Oxford U (1906–08); Leicestershire (1923, 1 match).
Career batting
7–14–1–125–31–9.61–0–*ct* 4
Bowling 12–1–12.00–0–0–1/12
He also played for Suffolk.

Razzell, Edward Timothy
Cricketer. *b:* 12.6.1943, London. Lower order right-hand batsman, right-arm medium off break bowler. *Sch* St. Paul's. *Team* Oxford U (1964).
Career batting
6–9–4–57–25*–11.40–0–*ct* 3
Bowling 396–13–30.46–0–0–3/44

Read, Arnold Holcombe
Amateur. *b:* 24.1.1880, Snaresbrook, Essex. *d:* 20.5.1957, Englefield Green, Surrey. Father of H. D. (Essex). Lower order right-hand batsman, right-arm slow medium bowler. *Sch* Winchester. *Team* Essex (1904–10, 22 matches).
Career batting
22–30–6–419–70–17.45–0–*ct* 7
Bowling 1192–38–31.36–1–0–7/75

Read, Ernest George
Amateur. *b:* 8.10.184, Portsmouth, Hants. *d:* 21.3.1921, Wandsworth, London. Nephew of H. W. R. Bencraft (Hants). Middle order right-hand batsman, wicket-keeper. *Sch* St Edward's, Oxford. *Teams* Hampshire (1903, 3 matches); Sussex (1904–06, 4 matches).
Career batting
7–11–0–113–44–10.27–0–*ct* 7

Read, Frederick Hurrell
Professional. *b:* 26.12.1855, Thames Ditton, Surrey. *d:* 4.5.1933, Hounslow, Middlesex. Brother of J. M. (Surrey), nephew of H. H. Stephenson (Surrey). Middle order batsman. *Team* Surrey (1881, 1 match).
Career batting
1–1–0–4–4–4.00–0–*ct* 0

Read, Holcombe Douglas
Amateur. *b:* 28.1.1910, Woodford Green, Essex. Son of A. H. (Essex). Tail end right-hand batsman, right-arm fast bowler. *Sch* Winchester. *Teams* Essex (1933–35, 32 matches); Surrey (1933, 2 matches). *Tours* Martineau to Egypt 1933 (not first-class); MCC to Australia and New Zealand 1935/6. *Test* England (1935, 1 match).
Career batting
54–70–27–158–25*–3.67–0–*ct* 21
Bowling 5022–219–22.93–13–2–7/35
Test batting
1 match, did not bat–*ct* 0
Bowling 200–6–33.33–0–0–4/136

In 1935 he took 97 wickets, av 22.16. His final first-class match was for MCC in 1948. He played for both Surrey and Essex in 1933.

Read, Henry Marvelle
Amateur. *b:* 8.11.1888, Roscrea, Co Tipperary. *d:* 6.12.1972, Dalkey, Co Dublin. Right-hand batsman. *Team* Ireland (1912).
Career batting
1–2–0–2–2–1.00–0–*ct* 0

He played rugby for Ireland.

Read, John Maurice
Professional. *b:* 9.2.1859, Thames Ditton, Surrey. *d:* 17.2.1929, Winchester, Hants. Brother of F. H. (Surrey), nephew of H. H. Stephenson (Surrey). Middle order right-hand batsman, right-arm fast medium bowler. *Team* Surrey (1880–95, 278 matches). *Tours* Lillywhite, Shaw and Shrewsbury to Australia 1884/5, 1886/7, 1887/8; Warton to South Africa 1888/9; Sheffield to Australia 1891/2. *Tests* England (1882–93, 17 matches).
Career batting
380–611–43–14010–186*–24.66–11–*ct* 215
Bowling 1807–73–24.75–1–0–6/41
Test batting
17–29–2–463–57–17.14–0–*ct* 8

He hit 1,000 runs in a season three times (best 1,364, av 34.97, in 1886). He retired whilst still worth his place in the County side, in order to take up an appointment on the Tichborne estate.

Read, Walter William
Amateur. *b:* 23.11.1855, Reigate, Surrey. *d:* 6.1.1907, Addiscombe, Surrey. Excellent middle order right-hand batsman, right-hand fast round-arm, later slow under-arm bowler, excellent point field. *Team* Surrey (1873–97, 366 matches). *Tours* Bligh to Australia 1882/3; Vernon to Australia 1887/8; W. W. Read to South Africa 1891/2. *Tests* England (1882/3 to 1893, 18 matches).
Career batting
467–749–52–22349–338–32.06–38–*ct* 381–*st* 20
Bowling 3483–108–32.25–1–0–6/24
Test batting
18–27–1–720–117–27.69–1–*ct* 16
Bowling 63–0

He hit 1,000 runs in a season nine times (best 1,880, av 44.76, in 1885). His highest innings was 338 for Surrey v Oxford U at the Oval in 1880; he also made two double centuries for Surrey. He was regarded as one of the best batsman in England during the 1880s, his most famous innings being 117 for England v Australia at the Oval in 1884, when he went in at No 10 and saved the match for his side.

Reader-Blackton, Walter
(formerly Reader)
Professional in 1914, amateur in 1920 and 1921. *b:* 4.7.1895, Shirland, Derbyshire. *d:* 1.1.1976, Derby. Middle order right-hand batsman, right-

arm medium pace bowler. *Team* Derbyshire (1914–21, 8 matches).
Career batting
8–15–1–107–31*–7.64–0–*ct* 6
Bowling 81–5–16.20–0–0–3/40

Reading, Major General Arnold Hughes Eagleton
Amateur. *b:* 3.4.1896, Heilbron, South Africa. *d:* 4.1.1975, Sellicks Green, Taunton, Somerset. Middle order batsman. *Sch* Cranleigh. *Team* Royal Navy (1929).
Career batting
1–2–0–19–12–9.50–0–*ct* 0

Reason, David Jordan
Amateur. *b:* 1897, Neath, Glamorgan. *d:* 17.2.1955, Blackheath, Kent. Middle order batsman, wicket-keeper. *Team* Glamorgan (1921–22, 2 matches).
Career batting
2–3–0–3–2–1.00–0–*ct* 3–*st* 1

Reason, Dr Thomas Francis
Amateur. *b:* 1890, Neath, Glamorgan. *d:* 15.2.1935, Skewen, Glamorgan. Lower order batsman, useful bowler. *Team* Glamorgan (1923, 1 match).
Career batting
1–2–0–13–10–6.50–0–*ct* 0
Bowling 34–0

Reay, Gilbert Martin
Amateur. *b:* 24.1.1887, Wallington, Surrey. *d:* 31.1.1967, Croydon, Surrey. Brother of W. F. (Gentlemen). Hard hitting lower order right-hand batsman, right-arm fast bowler. *Team* Surrey (1913–23, 27 matches).
Career batting
28–36–4–423–54–13.21–0–*ct* 13
Bowling 1961–91–21.54–3–0–5/22
He played for Beddington CC for 42 years.

Reay, Wilfrid Francis
Amateur. *b:* 12.6.1891, Wallington, Surrey. *d:* 8.10.1915, near Thiepval, France. Brother of G. M. (Surrey). Excellent fast medium bowler. *Team* Gentlemen of England (1910).
Career batting
1–2–2–5–5*–no av–0–*ct* 0
Bowling 51–1–51.00–0–0–1/51

Recordon, Lionel Walther
Amateur. *b:* 25.2.1907, Anerley, South London. Middle order right-hand batsman, leg break and googly bowler. *Sch* Brighton. *Team* Kent (1927–29, 11 matches).
Career batting
11–16–3–242–64*–18.61–0–*ct* 9
Bowling 86–0

Reddick, Tom Bokenham
Amateur. *b:* 17.2.1912, Shanghai, China. *d:* 1.6.1982, Cape Town, South Africa. Middle order right-hand batsman, leg break bowler. *Sch* KCS Wimbledon. *Teams* Middlesex (1931, 2 matches); Nottinghamshire (1946–47, 50 matches); Western Province (1950/1). *Tours* Cahn to North America and Bermuda 1933 (not first-class), Ceylon 1936/7.
Career batting
62–99–11–2688–139–30.54–2–*ct* 15
Bowling 468–6–78.00–0–0–1/4
He hit 1,231 runs, av 35.17, in 1947. After being coach to Nottinghamshire CCC in 1946 and 1947, he took a similar post in Cape Town and remained in South Africa for most of the rest of his life.

Reddish, John
Professional. *b:* 22.12.1904, Nottingham. Middle order right-hand batsman, leg break and googly bowler. *Team* Nottinghamshire (1930, 1 match).
Career batting
1–1–1–2–2*–no av–0–*ct* 1
Bowling 125–0
A noted soccer player, he was full back for Tottenham Hotspur and Lincoln City.

Reddy, Bharath
Cricketer. *b:* 12.11.1954, Madras, India. Lower order right-hand batsman, wicket-keeper. *Team* Tamil Nadu (1973/4 to 1982/3). *Tours* India to Sri Lanka 1973/4, to Australia 1977/8, to Pakistan 1978/9, to England 1979, to Australia and New Zealand 1981/2; Tamil Nadu to Sri Lanka 1975/6, 1982/3. *Tests* India (1979, 4 matches).
Career batting
78–96–17–1368–88–17.31–0–*ct* 145–*st* 41
Test batting
4–5–1–38–21–9.50–0–*ct* 9–*st* 2
The principal wicket-keeper on the 1979 tour to England, he played in all four Tests.

Reddy, Francis James Anthony
Amateur. *b:* 15.6.1906, Dublin. Right-hand batsman. *Team* Ireland (1931–39).
Career batting
7–14–2–202–50*–16.83–0–*ct* 11

Reddy, Nayini Santosh Kumar
(known in India as Santosh Reddy)
Amateur. *b:* 22.10.1938, Madras, India. Middle order left-hand batsman. *Teams* Cambridge U

(1959–61, blue all three years); Hyderabad (1966/7 to 1970/1).
Career batting
61–102–8–2284–113*–24.29–2–*ct* 37
Bowling 306–5–61.20–0–0–3/26

Redfearn, John
Professional. *b:* 13.5.1860, Lascelles Hall, Yorkshire. *d:* 27.2.1942, Harrogate, Yorkshire. Middle order batsman. *Team* Yorkshire (1890, 1 match).
Career batting
1–1–0–5–5–5.00–0–*ct* 0

Redgate, Oliver
Amateur. *b:* 16.2.1863, Nottingham. *d:* 11.2.1913, Sherwood, Nottingham. Middle order right-hand batsman, bowler. *Team* Nottinghamshire (1889–94, 8 matches).
Career batting
12–20–2–205–37–11.39–0–*ct* 6
Bowling 130–7–18.57–0–0–3/8

Redgate, Samuel
Professional. *b:* 27.7.1810, Arnold, Notts. *d:* 13.4.1851, Old Radford, Nottinghamshire. Lower order right-hand batsman, right-hand fast round-arm bowler. *Teams* Nottinghamshire (1830–45, 24 matches); Cambridge Town Club (1839).
Career batting
78–138–22–1011–41–8.71–0–*ct* 60–*st* 2
Bowling 800–67+367–11.94–30–10–8/?

For a few years he was regarded as one of the best round-arm bowlers, his bowling being 'very fast and ripping', but he was obliged to give up important cricket in 1846 owing to ill-health. His final first-class match was for the North in 1846.

Redgewell, Louis J.
Professional. *b:* 13.10.1894, Battersea, London. *d:* 1966, Wandsworth, London. Lower order right-hand batsman, wicket-keeper. *Team* Surrey (1922–23, 3 matches).
Career batting
3–4–2–5–4–2.50–0–*ct* 4–*st* 1

Redhouse
Professional. Lower order batsman, useful bowler. *Team* Hampshire (1900, 1 match).
Career batting
1–2–0–4–4–2.00–0–*ct* 1
Bowling 13–0

Redman, James
Professional. *b:* 1.3.1926, Bath, Somerset. *d:* 24.9.1981, Salisbury, Wilts. Lower order right-hand batsman, right-arm fast medium bowler. *Team* Somerset (1948–53, 65 matches).
Career batting
65–105–23–1013–45–12.34–0–*ct* 20
Bowling 4169–117–35.63–4–0–7/23

He also played for Wiltshire.

Redmond, Rodney Ernest
Cricketer. *b:* 29.12.1944, Whangarei, New Zealand. Aggressive opening left-hand batsman, slow left-arm bowler. *Teams* Wellington (1966/7 to 1967/8); Auckland (1969/70 to 1975/6). *Tours* New Zealand to Australia 1972/3, to England 1973. *Tests* New Zealand (1972/3, 1 match).
Career batting
53–100–7–3134–141*–33.69–4–*ct* 31
Bowling 481–17–28.29–1–1–6/56
Test batting
1–2–0–163–107–81.50–1–*ct* 0

He hit 483 runs, av 28.41, on the 1973 tour, not playing in any Tests. His first-class debut was for New Zealand Under 23s in 1963/4. He had the unusual distinction of scoring a century in his only Test match.

Redpath, Ian Ritchie
Amateur. *b:* 11.5.1941, Geelong, Victoria, Australia. Sound opening right-hand batsman, right-arm medium pace bowler, good short leg field. *Team* Victoria (1961/2 to 1975/6, 92 matches). *Tours* Australia to England 1964, 1968, to South Africa 1966/7, 1969/70, to West Indies 1972/3, to India and Pakistan 1964/5, to India and Ceylon 1969/70, to New Zealand 1973/4. *Tests* Australia (1963/4 to 1975/6, 66 matches).
Career batting
226–391–34–14993–261–41.99–32–*ct* 211
Bowling 466–13–35.84–0–0–3/24
Test batting
66–120–11–4737–171–43.45–8–*ct* 83
Bowling 41–0

On the 1964 tour to England he hit 1,075 runs, av 32.57, and played in all five Tests; in 1968 he hit 1,474 runs, av 43.35 and again appeared in all five Tests, scoring his runs much more fluently than on his first visit. His highest score was 261 for Victoria v Queensland at Melbourne in 1962/3. He hit 1,000 in an Australian season once.

Reece, Courtenay Walton
Amateur. *b:* 4.12.1899, Barbados. Lower order batsman, good bowler. *Teams* Oxford U (1925); Barbados (1926/7 to 1929/30).
Career batting
4–5–1–4–3–1.00–0–*ct* 4
Bowling 433–13–33.30–0–0–4/72

His County cricket was for Oxfordshire.

Reed, Albert Adams
Professional. *b:* 16.11.1847, Sompting, Sussex. *d:*

1931, East Preston, Sussex. Brother of W. B. (Sussex) Middle order right-hand batsman, right-hand medium pace round-arm bowler, mid off. *Team* Sussex (1867–73, 25 matches).
Career batting
27–47–5–620–70*–14.76–0–*ct* 17
Bowling 389–23–16.91–1–0–5/28

Reed, Basil Duck
Amateur. *b:* 1895, Malmesbury, Wiltshire. *d:* 1968, Swindon, Wiltshire. Lower order right-hand batsman, right-arm medium pace bowler. *Team* Royal Navy (1921).
Career batting
1–2–1–8–8*–8.00–0–*ct* 1
Bowling 83–1–83.00–0–0–1/56
His County cricket was for Wiltshire.

Reed, Barry Lindsay
Amateur. *b:* 17.9.1937, Southsea, Hants. Opening right-hand batsman. *Sch* Winchester. *Team* Hampshire (1958–70, 122 matches). *Tour* MCC to Bangladesh 1978/9 (not first-class).
Career batting
123–215–11–4962–138–24.32–2–*ct* 61
Bowling 0–0
He hit 1,000 runs in a season three times (best 1,136, av 24.17, in 1967).

Reed, Rev Francis
Amateur. *b:* 24.10.1850, Ottery St Mary, Devon. *d:* 30.4.1912, London. Middle order right-hand batsman, right-arm medium pace bowler, slip field. *Team* Somerset (1882–84, 10 matches).
Career batting
10–18–1–198–57*–11.64–0–*ct* 4
Bowling 380–12–31.66–0–0–4/35
He did not appear in any first-class matches whilst at Oxford University.

Reed, George H.
Professional. *b:* 1901. Tail end right-hand batsman, left-arm fast medium bowler. *Team* Glamorgan (1934–38, 25 matches).
Career batting
25–25–12–65–11–5.00–0–*ct* 6
Bowling 1941–62–31.30–1–0–5/30

Reed, Henry Albert
Amateur. *b:* 1892, Bristol. *d:* 3.5.1963, Bristol. Middle order batsman. *Team* Gloucestershire (1921–23, 6 matches).
Career batting
6–12–0–110–45–9.16–0–*ct* 1

Reed, Herbert F.
Amateur. *b:* 1858. *d:* 1913, Paddington, London. Middle order right-hand batsman, good field. *Team* Somerset (1882–85, 7 matches).
Career batting
8–15–1–161–33–11.50–0–*ct* 4
Bowling 61–2–30.50–0–0–1/6

Reed, Walter Bartlett
Professional. *b:* 4.2.1839, Sompting, Sussex. *d:* 1880, Thakeham, Sussex. Brother of A. A. (Sussex). Middle order right-hand batsman, left-hand fast round-arm bowler. *Team* Sussex (1860, 6 matches).
Career batting
6–10–1–38–10*–4.22–0–*ct* 0
Bowling 103–2–51.50–0–0–1/8

Rees, Alan
Professional. *b:* 17.2.1938, Port Talbot, Glamorgan. Middle order right-hand batsman, right-arm medium pace bowler, fine field. *Team* Glamorgan (1955–68, 216 matches).
Career batting
216–372–53–7681–111*–24.07–2–*ct* 113
Bowling 398–6–63.00–0–0–3/68
He hit 1,000 runs in a season four times (best 1,206, av 30.15, in 1964). A noted rugby footballer, he was capped for Wales in 1961/2 and then turned professional for Leeds in the Rugby League.

Rees-Davies, William Rupert
Amateur. *b:* 19.11.1916, Bridgend, Glamorgan. Lower order right-hand batsman, right-arm fast medium bowler. *Sch* Eton. *Team* Cambridge U (1936–38, blue 1938).
Career batting
15–23–12–37–7–3.36–0–*ct* 6
Bowling 1433–33–43.42–0–0–4/21
He was elected Conservative MP for the Isle of Thanet in 1953.

Reese, Daniel
Amateur. *b:* 26.1.1879, Christchurch, New Zealand. *d:* 12.6.1953, Christchurch, New Zealand. Brother of T. W. (Canterbury). Forcing middle order left-hand batsman, left-arm slow medium bowler. *Teams* Essex (1906, 8 matches); Canterbury (1895/6 to 1920/1); London County (1903). *Tours* New Zealand to Australia 1898/9, 1913/14.
Career batting
72–134–8–3182–148–25.25–4–*ct* 36
Bowling 3893–196–19.86–11–1–7/53
He captained the New Zealand touring team in Australia and also Canterbury. He was later President of the New Zealand Cricket Council and wrote his memoirs 'Was it all Cricket?' in 1948.

Reeve, Dermot Alexander
Cricketer. *b:* 2.4.1963, Kowloon, Hong Kong. Lower order right-hand batsman, right-arm medium pace bowler. *Team* Sussex (1983, 17 matches).
Career batting
17–20–5–192–42*–12.80–0–*ct* 7
Bowling 1233–42–29.35–0–0–4/15
He played for Hong Kong in the 1982 ICC Trophy.

Reeves, Edmund
Amateur. *b:* 1821, Kennington, Surrey. *d:* 10.12.1906, Wimbledon, Surrey. Stylish middle order right-hand batsman, right-arm medium fast bowler. *Teams* Surrey (1848–52, 9 matches); Middlesex (1851, 1 match).
Career batting
21–35–3–368–57–11.50–0–*ct* 2
Bowling 6 wickets, no analyses
He played for the Gentlemen and was one of the best cricketers of his time, but his career in important matches was very brief.

Reeves, William
Professional. *b:* 22.6.1875, Cambridge. *d:* 22.3.1944, Hammersmith, London. Lower order right-hand batsman, right-arm medium pace bowler. *Team* Essex (1897–1921, 271 matches).
Career batting
280–436–35–6656–135–16.59–3–*ct* 121
Bowling 16526–601–27.49–38–5–7/33
He hit 1,174 runs, av 29.35, in 1905 and took 106 wickets, av 26.16, in 1904. After retiring from County cricket he was a well-known umpire and stood in several Test matches.

Regan, Charles
Professional. *b:* 11.5.1842, Barnsley, Yorkshire. *d:* 17.5.1921, Southend on Sea, Essex. Lower order right-hand batsman, wicket-keeper. *Team* Derbyshire (1877, 5 matches).
Career batting
5–10–0–90–22–9.00–0–*ct* 1
He also played for Essex (pre-first-class).

Reid, Allan
Amateur. *b:* 1.10.1877, Cape Town, South Africa. *d:* 31.10.1948, Cape Town, South Africa. Brother of Norman (South Africa). Middle order right-hand batsman. *Team* Western Province (1896/7 to 1908/9). *Tour* South Africa to England 1901.
Career batting
32–54–4–894–101*–17.88–1–*ct* 13
He was only moderately successful on the 1901 tour.

Reid, John Richard, OBE
Amateur. *b:* 3.6.1928, Auckland, New Zealand. Father of R. B. (Wellington and Transvaal). Attacking middle order right-hand batsman, right-arm fast medium, later off break bowler, good close field, occasional wicket-keeper. *Teams* Otago (1956/7 to 1957/8); Wellington (1947/8 to 1964/5). *Tours* New Zealand to England 1949, 1958, 1965, to South Africa and Australia 1953/4, 1961/2, to India and Pakistan 1955/6, 1964/5; Cavaliers to South Africa 1962/3; Rest of World to England 1965. *Tests* New Zealand (1949–65, 58 matches).
Career batting
246–418–28–16128–296–41.35–39–*ct* 240–*st* 7
Bowling 10535–466–22.60–15–1–7/20
Career batting
58–108–5–3428–142–33.28–6–*ct* 43–*st* 1
Bowling 2835–85–33.35–1–0–6/60
On his 1949 visit to England he developed into the most useful all-rounder of the party and hit 1,488 runs, av 41.33, and played in the last two Tests. In 1958 he topped the batting averages with 1,429 runs, av 39.69, but in 1965, coming as captain, he could only score 799 runs, av 31.96, but was handicapped by a knee injury. He led New Zealand in all three Tests in 1965 and on 34 occasions in all. For Wellington v Northern Districts at Wellington in 1962/3, he created a new first-class record by hitting 15 sixes in his innings of 296. None of his four double centuries was made in England. In the 1961/2 season, playing in Australia and South Africa, he hit 2,083 runs.

Reid, Keith Patrick
Cricketer. *b:* 24.7.1951, Port Elizabeth, South Africa. Middle order right-hand batsman, right-arm medium pace bowler. *Teams* Eastern Province (1970/1 to 1980/1); Northamptonshire (1973, 1 match).
Career batting
57–97–20–1518–109–19.71–1–*ct* 28
Bowling 2335–78–29.93–3–0–7/50

Reid, Leonard John
Amateur. *b:* 14.1.1888, Chesterton, Cambridgeshire. *d:* 25.10.1938, New York, USA. Middle order batsman. *Sch* Aldenham. *Team* MCC (1913).
Career batting
1–2–0–10–6–5.00–0–*ct* 1
His County cricket was for Hertfordshire. He was for some time City Editor of the *Daily Telegraph*.

Reid, Robert Threshie
(created 1st Earl Loreburn in 1906)
Amateur. *b:* 3.4.1846, Kerkira, Corfu, Ionian

Isles. *d:* 30.11.1923, Dover, Kent. Lower order right-hand batsman, wicket-keeper. *Sch* Cheltenham. *Team* Oxford U (1865–68, blue 1866–68).
Career batting
15–23–4–97–23–5.10–0–*ct* 17–*st* 5

He represented Oxford at rackets in 1865 and 1867. In 1907 he was President of the MCC and also of Kent. He was MP for Hereford 1880–85 and for Dumfries from 1886 to 1906. In 1894 he became Solicitor-General, then Attorney-General, and from 1906 to 1912 he was Lord Chancellor.

Reid, William Hamilton
Amateur. *b:* 25.7.1893, Uddingston, Lanarkshire, Scotland. *d:* 17.1.1949, Glasgow, Scotland. Lower order right-hand batsman, off break bowler. *Team* Scotland (1923).
Career batting
1–2–1–0–0*–0.00–0–*ct* 0
Bowling 52–4–13.00–0–0–4/29

Reid-Kerr, J. (*see under* Kerr, J. R.)

Reidy, Bernard Wilfrid
Cricketer. *b:* 18.9.1953, Bramley Meade, Whalley, Lancashire. Middle order left-hand batsman, left-arm medium pace bowler. *Sch* St Mary's College, Blackburn. *Team* Lancashire (1973–82, 107 matches).
Career batting
107–162–26–3641–131*–26.77–2–*ct* 65
Bowling 2508–60–41.80–1–0–5/61

He also played for Cumberland.

Reiner, Charles Frederick
Amateur. *b:* 15.2.1884, Sutton, Surrey. *d:* 9.1.1947, Maida Vale, London. Opening batsman. *Sch* Dulwich. *Team* Surrey (1906, 1 match).
Career batting
2–4–0–82–26–20.50–0–*ct* 0

Reith, Michael Stevens
Cricketer. *b:* 2.5.1948, Lurgan, Co Armagh. Left-hand batsman, right-arm medium pace bowler. *Team* Ireland (1970–80).
Career batting
9–16–0–346–82–21.62–0–*ct* 5
Bowling 56–1–56.00–0–0–1/24

Relf, Albert Edward
Professional. *b:* 26.7.1874, Brightling, Sussex. *d:* 26.3.1937, Wellington College, Berkshire. He shot himself in a fit of depression. Brother of E. H. (Sussex) and R. R. (Sussex). Middle order right-hand batsman, right-arm medium pace off break bowler, excellent slip field. *Teams* Sussex (1900–21, 448 matches); London County (1904); Auckland (1907/8 to 1909/10). *Tours* MCC to Australia 1903/4, to South Africa 1905/6, 1913/4, to West Indies 1912/13. *Tests* England (1903/4 to 1913/14, 13 matches).
Career batting
565–900–70–22238–189*–26.79–26–*ct* 537
Bowling 39724–1897–20.94–114–23–9/95
Test batting
13–21–3–416–63–23.11–0–*ct* 14
Bowling 624–25–24.96–1–0–5/85

He hit 1,000 runs in a season 11 times (best 1,846, av 31.82, in 1913) and took 100 wickets in a season 11 times (best 158, av 19.67, in 1910). He achieved the 'double' eight times. Before appearing for Sussex he played for Norfolk and Berkshire. His best bowling was 9/95 for Sussex v Warwickshire at Hove in 1910.

Relf, Ernest Herbert
Professional. *b:* 1889, Sandhurst, Berkshire. *d:* 27.7.1918, Leicester. Brother of A. E. (Sussex) and R. R. (Sussex). Lower order right-hand batsman, right-arm medium pace bowler. *Team* Sussex (1912–14, 12 matches).
Career batting
12–23–3–232–36–11.60–0–*ct* 5
Bowling 212–8–26.50–0–0–2/24

Relf, Robert Richard
Professional. *b:* 1.9.1883, Sandhurst, Berkshire. *d:* 28.4.1965, Reading, Berkshire. Brother of A. E. (Sussex) and E. H. (Sussex). Solid right-hand opening batsman, right-arm fast medium bowler. *Teams* Sussex (1905–24, 283 matches); P. W. Sherwell's XI (1913/14). *Tour* MCC to South Africa 1913/14 (he was co-opted).
Career batting
302–529–18–14522–272*–28.41–24–*ct* 300
Bowling 8715–317–27.49–12–2–8/79

He hit 1,000 runs in a season six times (best 1,804, av 32.21, in 1912). His three double centuries were all for Sussex, the highest being 272* v Worcs at Eastbourne in 1909. He played for Berkshire before appearing for Sussex and in 1923 re-appeared for his native County. In 1924 he began to play in the Sussex v Surrey match at the Oval, but was objected to by the Surrey captain, as not qualified. Relf withdrew from the match, rejoined Berkshire, and was instrumental in that County winning the Minor Counties Championship the same year. His final first-class match was for Minor Counties in 1933.

Remnant, Ernest Richard
Professional. *b:* 1.5.1881, Croydon, Surrey. *d:* 18.3.1969, Harrow, Middlesex. Son of G. H.

(Kent). Lower order right-hand batsman, slow left-arm bowler. *Teams* Hampshire (1908–22, 121 matches); England XI in India (1915/16); Europeans (1916/17).
Career batting
124–200–32–2877–115*–17.12–1–*ct* 60
Bowling 4701–172–27.33–7–0–8/61

Remnant, George Henry
Professional. *b:* 20.11.1846, Rochester, Kent. *d:* 24.2.1941, Rochester, Kent. Father of E. R. (Hampshire). Middle order right-hand batsman, right-hand fast round-arm bowler. *Team* Kent (1868–78, 42 matches).
Career batting
42–79–8–564–62–7.94–0–*ct* 23
Bowling 325–19–17.10–1–0–5/24

Remnant, Hon Peter Farquharson
Amateur. *b:* 21.9.1897, Paddington, London. *d:* 31.1.1968, Ipsden, Oxon. Brother of R. J. F. (Minor Counties). Opening right-hand batsman. *Sch* Eton. *Team* Minor Counties (1929).
Career batting
1–2–0–62–62–31.00–0–*ct* 0

He did not appear in any first-class matches whilst at Oxford. His County cricket was for Berkshire. From 1950 to 1959 he was Conservative MP for Wokingham.

Remnant, Hon Robert John Farquharson
(succeeded to the title 2nd Baron Remnant in 1933)
Amateur. *b:* 29.3.1895, Westminster, London. *d:* 4.6.1967, Bear Ash, Berkshire. Brother of P. F. (Minor Counties). Middle order right-hand batsman, right-arm medium fast bowler. *Sch* Eton. *Team* Minor Counties XI (1931–36).
Career batting
3–5–1–113–47–28.25–0–*ct* 1
Bowling 189–5–37.80–0–0–3/80

His County cricket was for Berkshire.

Render, George William Armitage
Professional. *b:* 5.1.1887, Dewsbury, Yorkshire. *d:* 17.9.1922, Hanging-Heaton, Yorkshire. Middle order batsman. *Team* Yorkshire (1919, 1 match).
Career batting
1–1–0–5–5–5.00–0–*ct* 0

Renneberg, David Alexander
Cricketer. *b:* 23.9.1942, Balmain, New South Wales, Australia. Tail end right-hand batsman, right-arm fast bowler. *Team* New South Wales (1964/5 to 1970/1, 54 matches). *Tours* Australia to England 1968, to South Africa 1966/7, to New Zealand 1969/70. *Tests* Australia (1966/7 to 1967/8, 8 matches).
Career batting
90–109–43–466–26–7.06–0–*ct* 35
Bowling 8527–291–29.30–13–1–8/72
Test batting
8–13–7–22–9–3.66–0–*ct* 2
Bowling 830–23–36.08–2–0–5/39

Although he bowled with some success in the first-class matches, he was not chosen for any Tests in the 1968 tour to England.

Renny-Tailyour, Henry Waugh
Amateur. *b:* 9.10.1849, Missouri, North West Provinces, India. *d:* 15.6.1920, Newmanswalls, Montrose, Scotland. Hard hitting middle order right-hand batsman, right-hand fast round-arm bowler, good cover point. *Sch* Cheltenham. *Team* Kent (1873–83, 19 matches).
Career batting
28–48–5–818–124–19.02–1–*ct* 16
Bowling 87–5–17.40–0–0–2/28

He was a noted batsman in military matches, and among his many large innings for the Royal Engineers was 331* in 330 minutes v Civil Service in 1880. An excellent soccer player he represented Scotland as a forward and played in three of the first four FA Cup finals for the Royal Engineers including the victory in 1875. He also played rugby for Scotland in 1872.

Renshaw, Alfred George
Amateur. *b:* 8.9.1844, Islington, Middlesex. *d:* 14.7.1897, Svenningdal, Nordland, Norway. Middle order batsman. *Team* MCC (1871).
Career batting
1–1–0–0–0–0.00–0–*ct* 0

Reoch, Earl Clark
Cricketer. *b:* 5.3.1942, Monifieth, Angus, Scotland. Right-hand batsman, slow left-arm bowler. *Team* Scotland (1973).
Career batting
1–2–0–7–7–3.50–0–*ct* 1

Reunert, Clive
Amateur. *b:* 7.12.1887, Johannesburg, South Africa. *d:* 11.4.1953, Johannesburg, South Africa. Brother of John (Cambridge U). Opening batsman, bowler. *Sch* Harrow. *Team* Cambridge U (1908).
Career batting
3–6–1–60–28*–12.00–0–*ct* 1
Bowling 138–4–34.50–0–0–3/89

Reunert, John
Amateur. *b:* 1.4.1886, Johannesburg, South Africa. *d:* 25.7.1946, Johannesburg, South Africa.

Brother of Clive (Cambridge U). Lower order left-hand batsman, left-arm fast bowler. *Sch* Harrow. *Team* Cambridge U (1908).
Career batting
5–9–1–65–19–8.12–0–*ct* 3
Bowling 393–9–43.66–1–0–5/100

Revill, Alan Chambers
Professional. *b:* 27.3.1923, Sheffield, Yorkshire. Son of T. F. (Derbyshire). Middle order right-hand batsman, off break bowler, brilliant short leg. *Team* Derbyshire (1946–57, 321 matches); Leicestershire (1958–60, 64 matches). *Tour* Surridge to Bermuda 1961 (not first-class).
Career batting
387–654–53–15917–156*–26.48–16–*ct* 396
Bowling 1924–49–39.26–0–0–3/12
He hit 1,000 runs in a season nine times (best 1,643, av 35.71, in 1950).

Revill, Thomas Frederick
Professional. *b:* 9.5.1892, Bolsover, Derbyshire. *d:* 29.3.1979, Mansfield, Notts. Father of A. C. (Derbyshire). Middle order left-hand batsman, leg break and googly bowler. *Team* Derbyshire (1913–20, 11 matches).
Career batting
11–20–4–231–65*–14.43–0–*ct* 6

Reynolds, Alan Boyd
Amateur. *b:* 12.3.1879, Islington, Middlesex. *d:* 2.6.1940, Marylebone, London. Lower order right-hand batsman, wicket-keeper. *Team* Oxford U (1900).
Career batting
4–4–0–34–21–8.50–0–*ct* 0
His final first-class match was for MCC in 1903 and his County cricket for Hertfordshire.

Reynolds, Brian Leonard
Professional. *b:* 10.6.1932, Kettering, Northamptonshire. Middle order right-hand batsman, off break bowler, wicket-keeper. *Team* Northamptonshire (1950–70, 426 matches).
Career batting
429–737–65–18824–169–28.01–21–*ct* 302–*st* 20
Bowling 284–4–71.00–0–0–1/0
He hit 1,000 runs in a season ten times (best 1,843, av 35.44, in 1962). After retiring he was coach to the County. A useful soccer player, he appeared for Kettering Town.

Reynolds, Frederick Reginald
Professional. *b:* 7.8.1834, Bottisham, Cambridgeshire. *d:* 18.4.1915, Chorlton-cum-Hardy, Lancashire. Hard hitting tail end right-hand batsman, right-hand fast round-arm, later slow under-arm bowler. *Teams* Cambridgeshire (1857–67, 16 matches); Lancashire (1865–74, 38 matches); Cambridge Town Club (1854–60).
Career batting
65–106–26–444–34*–5.55–0–*ct* 52
Bowling 3028–172+36–17.60–11–0–6/58
From 1860 to 1908 he was manager of Old Trafford cricket ground.

Reynolds, Graham Edward Arthur
Cricketer. *b:* 23.9.1937, Newport, Monmouthshire. Lower order left-hand batsman, right-arm medium pace bowler. *Team* Glamorgan (1970–71, 2 matches).
Career batting
2–3–2–37–23*–37.00–0–*ct* 0
Bowling 75–2–37.50–0–0–2/24

Reynolds, Henry Smith
Professional. *b:* 6.1.1844, Ollerton, Notts. *d:* 21.4.1894, Burnley, Lancashire. He died of dropsy. Middle order right-hand batsman, right-arm fast bowler, good mid off. *Team* Nottinghamshire (1872–75, 13 matches).
Career batting
17–26–4–319–70*–14.50–0–*ct* 8
Bowling 65–1–65.00–0–0–1/30
His final first-class match was for An Eleven of England in 1876.

Reynolds, James Francis
Amateur. *b:* 2.5.1866, Tonbridge, Kent. *d:* 6.9.1950, West Malling, Kent. Lower order right-hand batsman, right-arm medium pace bowler. *Team* Kent (1890–97, 2 matches).
Career batting
2–2–0–21–13–10.50–0–*ct* 1
Bowling 63–3–21.00–0–0–3/63

Rhind, Peter Alan
Cricketer. *b:* 20.6.1945, Dundee, Scotland. Lower order right-hand batsman, right-arm fast medium bowler. *Team* Scotland (1968–82).
Career batting
6–7–4–23–10–7.66–0–*ct* 3
Bowling 332–6–55.33–0–0–3/62

Rhodes, Albert
Amateur. *b:* 9.4.1889, Saddleworth, Yorkshire. *d:* 10.3.1970, Blackpool, Lancashire. Middle order right-hand batsman, right-arm slow medium bowler. *Team* Lancashire (1922–24, 17 matches).
Career batting
17–25–3–382–70–17.36–0–*ct* 9
Bowling 475–15–31.66–0–0–2/24

Rhodes, Arthur Cyril
Professional. *b:* 14.10.1906, Headingley, Leeds,

Yorkshire. *d:* 21.5.1957, Headingley, Leeds, Yorkshire. Lower order right-hand batsman, right-arm fast medium pace bowler. *Team* Yorkshire (1932–34, 61 matches).
Career batting
61–70–19–917–64*–17.98–0–*ct* 45
Bowling 3026–107–28.28–5–0–6/19

Rhodes, Albert Ennion Groucott
Professional. *b:* 10.10.1916, Tintwhistle, Cheshire. *d:* 17.10.1983, Barlow, Derbyshire. Father of H. J. (Derbyshire). Middle order right-hand batsman, right-arm fast medium or leg break bowler. *Team* Derbyshire (1937–54, 267 matches). *Tour* MCC to India 1951/2.
Career batting
275–422–34–7363–127–18.97–4–*ct* 85
Bowling 18660–661–28.22–29–4–8/162

He hit 1,156 runs, av 25.68, in 1949 and took 130 wickets, av 22.19, in 1950. Owing to injury he played in only three matches on the tour of India. Appointed a first-class umpire in 1959, he stood in eight Test matches.

Rhodes, Cecil A.
Amateur, turned professional in 1938. *b:* 1906. Tail end batsman, slow left-arm bowler. *Team* Lancashire (1937–38, 8 matches).
Career batting
8–10–4–11–6–1.83–0–*ct* 1
Bowling 619–22–28.13–0–0–4/37

He also played for Berkshire.

Rhodes, Herbert Edward
Amateur. *b:* 11.1.1852, Hennerton, Berkshire. *d:* 10.9.1889, Dover, Kent. Stylish right-hand middle order batsman, wicket-keeper. *Sch* Eton. *Team* Yorkshire (1878–83, 10 matches).
Career batting
25–40–3–424–64–11.45–0–*ct* 14–*st* 2

He did not appear in first-class matches for the University whilst at Cambridge, but was in the University Eight for four years. He was among the players down to go on Vernon's tour to India in 1889/90, but died suddenly in September 1889, from the effects of a fall. He also played for Staffordshire.

Rhodes, Harold James
Professional. *b:* 22.7.1936, Hadfield, Glossop, Derbyshire. Son of A. E. G. (Derbyshire). Tail end right-hand batsman, right-arm fast bowler. *Team* Derbyshire (1953–75, 288 matches). *Tours* International XI to South Africa, New Zealand, India and Pakistan 1961/2, to India, Pakistan and Ceylon 1967/8; Commonwealth to South Africa 1959/60; Swanton to West Indies 1960/1. *Tests* England (1959, 2 matches).
Career batting
322–399–143–2427–48–9.48–0–*ct* 86
Bowling 21145–1073–19.70–42–4–7/38
Test batting
2–1–1–0–0*–no av–0–*ct* 0
Bowling 244–9–27.11–0–0–4/50

He took 100 wickets in a season three times (best 119, av 11.04, in 1965). In 1960, 1961 and 1965 he was no-balled for throwing, but in 1966 the MCC sub-committee ruled that his action was fair. In spite of this he was again reported as having a suspect action. The TCCB in December 1968 reconsidered his case and after deliberation decided his bowling to be legal. In 1970 he appeared for Nottinghamshire in John Player League matches.

Rhodes, James
Amateur. *b:* 1866. *d:* 26.8.1939, Solihull, Warwickshire. Middle order right-hand batsman. *Team* Warwickshire (1895, 3 matches).
Career batting
3–6–0–89–64–14.83–0–*ct* 2

Rhodes, Stuart Denzil
Amateur. *b:* 24.3.1910, Sneinton, Nottingham. Middle order right-hand batsman, right-arm medium pace bowler. *Sch* Dean Close. *Team* Notunghamshire (1930–35, 19 matches). *Tours* Cahn to the Argentine 1929/30, to North America and Bermuda 1933 (not first-class), to Ceylon and Malaya 1936/7.
Career batting
24–32–3–599–70–20.65–0–*ct* 7
Bowling 57–0

His final first-class match in England was for J. Cahn's XI in 1936.

He was joint-captain of Nottinghamshire in 1935. In 1946 he appeared in the Hertfordshire side. A useful hockey player, he represented Notts at left back.

Rhodes, Steven John
Cricketer. *b:* 17.6.1964, Bradford, Yorkshire. Son of W. E. (Notts). Lower order right-hand batsman, wicket-keeper. *Team* Yorkshire (1981, 1 match).
Career batting
1 match, did not bat–*ct* 0

Rhodes, Thomas Basil
Amateur. *b:* 13.8.1874, Uttoxeter, Staffs. *d:* 26.5.1936, Worthing, Sussex. Lower order right-hand batsman, wicket-keeper. *Sch* Malvern. *Team* Warwickshire (1899, 4 matches).

Career batting
4–7–1–105–55–17.50–0–*ct* 3

He also played for Worcestershire (pre-first-class).

Rhodes, Wilfred
Professional. *b:* 29.10.1877, Kirkheaton, Yorkshire. *d:* 8.7.1973, Branksome, Dorset. Excellent right-hand batsman, slow left-arm bowler. *Teams* Yorkshire (1898–1930, 883 matches); Patialia (1926/7); Europeans (1921/2 to 1922/3). *Tours* MCC to Australia 1903/4, 1907/8, 1911/12, 1920/1, to South Africa 1909/10, to South Africa 1913/14, to the West Indies 1929/30. *Tests* England (1899 to 1929/30, 58 matches).
Career batting
1110–1534–237–39969–267*–30.58–58–*ct* 766
Bowling 70322–4204–16.72–287–68–9/24
Test batting
58–98–21–2325–179–30.19–2–*ct* 60
Bowling 3425–127–26.96–6–1–8/68

The sudden departure of Peel from the Yorkshire side created a vacancy for a slow left-arm bowler in 1898. Rhodes played in the opening match, took six for 63, and by the end of the summer had captured 154 wickets and stood second in the first-class averages, an astonishing opening to a record breaking career. The following summer he was capped for England. No less than 23 times he was to take 100 wickets in a season – easily a record – and three times he went to 200, with 261, av 13.81, in 1900 his best. His tally of 4,204 wickets, av 16.72, stands alone, no one else having topped 4,000.

These bowling details place him among the greatest of all bowlers, but this was only one side of his talent. Although he began as a lower order batsman, within a few seasons he had developed into one of the principal batsmen in England. Twenty times he exceeded 1,000 runs in a season – plus once in Australia – and twice he went on to 2,000, with 2,261, av 38.32, in 1911 his best. In sixteen seasons he achieved the 'double' – another record unlikely to be beaten.

His highest innings was 267* for Yorkshire v Leics at Headingley in 1921 and of his two other double centuries, one was for Yorkshire and the other for MCC. His best bowling in an innings was 9 for 24 for C. I. Thornton's XI v Australians at Scarborough in 1899.

On retiring from first-class cricket he became coach at Harrow School. After the Second World War when his sight failed, he still regularly attended important matches, and he took a keen interest in the game until the end.

Rhodes, William
Professional. *b:* 4.3.1885, Leeds, Yorkshire. *d:* 5.8.1941, Leeds, Yorkshire. Tail end right-hand batsman, right-arm fast bowler. *Team* Yorkshire (1911, 1 match).
Career batting
1–1–1–1–1*–no av–0–ct 0
Bowling 40–0

Rhodes, William Ernest
Professional. *b:* 5.8.1936, Bradford, Yorkshire. Father of S. J. (Yorkshire). Middle order right-hand batsman, wicket-keeper. *Team* Nottinghamshire (1961–64, 36 matches).
Career batting
38–66–6–1207–132–20.11–1–*ct* 41–*st* 1

Rhys, Hubert Ralph John
Amateur. *b:* 31.8.1897, Aberdare, Glamorgan. *d:* 18.3.1970, Llandaff, Glamorgan. Sound middle order right-hand batsman. *Sch* Shrewsbury. *Teams* Glamorgan (1929–30, 7 matches); Wales (1929–30).
Career batting
10–19–1–383–149–21.27–1–*ct* 5

His first-class debut was for Free Foresters v Cambridge U at Fenner's in 1929, when he hit 149.

Riaz-ur-Rehman
Amateur. *b:* 1940, India. *d:* 10.7.1966, Loughborough, Leics. He was killed in a road accident. Middle order right-hand batsman. *Teams* Lahore (1958/9); Rawalpindi-Peshawar (1960/1); Karachi (1961/2); Leicestershire (1966, 1 match).
Career batting
7–12–0–354–70–29.50–0–*ct* 4
Bowling 10–0

Rice, Alan Sedgwick
Amateur. *b:* 29.8.1929, Leicester. Middle order left-hand batsman, right-arm fast medium bowler. *Sch* Wyggeston GS. *Team* Leicester (1954, 3 matches).
Career batting
3–2–0–15–13–7.50–0–*ct* 1
Bowling 269–8–33.62–0–0–3/34

He was also a useful rugby full back.

Rice, Clive Edward Butler
Cricketer. *b:* 23.7.1949, Johannesburg, South Africa. Grandson of P. S. S. Bower (Oxford U). Attacking middle order right-hand batsman, right-arm fast medium bowler. *Teams* Transvaal (1969/70 to 1982/3); Nottinghamshire (1975–83, 196 matches).
Career batting
312–501–74–17056–246–39.94–30–*ct* 243
Bowling 14601–679–21.50–20–1–7/62

He hit 1,000 runs in a season nine times (best

1,871, av 66.82, in 1978). His three double centuries have all been for Nottinghamshire, the highest being 246 v Sussex at Hove in 1976. His first-class debut in England was for D. H. Robins' XI in 1973. He was appointed captain of Nottinghamshire for 1978, but just prior to the start of the season he signed a contract for Packer's World Series Cricket and his appointment was cancelled; he was re-appointed County captain in July 1979.

Rice, Dr David
Amateur. *b:* 8.4.1914, Hellesdon, Norfolk. Lower order right-hand batsman, right-arm medium pace bowler. *Sch* Lancing. *Team* L. C. Steven's XI (1960–61).
Career batting
2–3–1–32–23–16.00–0–*ct* 2
Bowling 84–1–84.00–0–0–1/37

Rice, John Michael
Cricketer. *b:* 23.10.1949, Chandlers Ford, Hants. Opening right-hand batsman, right-arm medium pace bowler. *Team* Hampshire (1971–82, 168 matches).
Career batting
168–271–22–5091–161*–20.44–2–*ct* 153
Bowling 7707–230–33.50–3–0–7/48
He also played for Wiltshire.

Rice, Reginald William
Amateur. *b:* 14.11.1868, Tewkesbury, Gloucestershire. *d:* 11.2.1938, Bedford. Steady opening right-hand batsman, right-arm slow bowler. *Teams* Gloucestershire (1890–1903, 123 matches); Oxford U (1892–94, blue 1893).
Career batting
135–237–19–4376–111–20.07–2–*ct* 67
Bowling 4–0
He also played for Bedfordshire.

Rice, Father William Ignatius
Amateur. *b:* 15.3.1883, Birmingham. *d:* 22.4.1955, Douai Abbey, Woolhampton, Reading, Berkshire. Middle order right-hand batsman, right-arm medium pace bowler. *Team* Warwickshire (1920, 2 matches).
Career batting
2–4–0–15–9–3.75–0–*ct* 1
Headmaster of Douai School from 1915 to 1952, he was a member of the Order of St Benedict and perhaps the only monk to play County Championship cricket.

Richards, Arthur Carew
Amateur. *b:* 20.2.1865, Grays, Essex. *d:* 29.11.1930, Nottingham. Son of W. H. (MCC). Hard hitting middle order right-hand batsman, slow right-arm bowler, good slip field. *Sch* Eton. *Team* Hampshire (1884–1904, 4 matches).
Career batting
4–6–0–104–47–17.33–0–*ct* 2
Bowling 112–3–37.33–0–0–3/45
In a minor military match in South Africa he scored 101* and 185 out of a combined total for the two innings of 311, no other batsman exceeding 6!

Richards, Barry Anderson
Cricketer. *b:* 21.7.1945, Durban, South Africa. Brilliant opening right-hand batsman, off break bowler. *Teams* Natal (1964/5 to 1982/3); Gloucestershire (1965, 1 match); Hampshire (1968–78, 204 matches); South Australia (1970/1, 10 matches); Transvaal (1970/1). *Tests* South Africa (1969/70, 4 matches).
Career batting
339–576–58–28358–356–54.74–80–*ct* 367
Bowling 2886–77–37.48–1–0–7/63
Test batting
4–7–0–508–140–72.57–2–*ct* 3
Bowling 26–1–26.00–0–0–1/12
He hit 1,000 runs in a season in England nine times, going on to 2,000 once: 2,395, av 47.90, in 1968. He scored three double centuries for Hampshire, the highest being 240 v Warwickshire at Coventry in 1973, but his most famous innings was 356 for South Australia v Western Australia at Perth in 1970/1, when he made 325* on the opening day of the match. He appeared in all five matches for the Rest of the World v England in 1970. He also hit 1,000 in a South African season five times and in Australia once. One of the outstanding batsmen of the 1970s, he was very successful with World Series Cricket in Australia.

Richards, Charles Herbert
Amateur. *b:* 20.8.1873, Dolgelley, Merioneth. *d:* 21.9.1925, Ruthin, Denbigh. Middle order batsman. *Sch* Winchester. *Team* London County (1903).
Career batting
2–3–0–12–8–4.00–0–*ct* 3
Bowling 28–0

Richards, Clifton James
Cricketer. *b:* 10.8.1958, Penzance, Cornwall. Lower order right-hand batsman, wicket-keeper. *Team* Surrey (1976–83, 150 matches). *Tours* Robins to Australia and New Zealand 1979/80; England to India and Sri Lanka 1981/2; International XI to Jamaica 1982/3.
Career batting
161–197–46–3214–117*–21.28–1–*ct* 302–*st* 44
Bowling 24–0

Richards, Cyril James Ridding
Amateur. *b:* 14.7.1870, Andover, Hants. *d:* 27.10.1933, Cluny, Aberdeenshire. Middle order left-hand batsman, left-arm fast bowler, good field. *Sch* Lancing. *Team* Hampshire (1895, 1 match).
Career batting
1–2–0–48–43–24.00–0–0–*ct* 0
Whilst at Oxford he played in some Trials but no first-class matches. He also played for Shropshire.

Richards, Dick Stanley
Professional. *b:* 10.9.1908, Bognor Regis, Sussex. Middle order right-hand batsman, slow left-arm bowler. *Team* Sussex (1927–35, 18 matches).
Career batting
18–27–5–220–23–10.00–0–*ct* 7
Bowling 205–1–205.00–0–0–1/8

Richards, Gwyn
Cricketer. *b:* 29.11.1951, Maesteg, Glamorgan. Middle order right-hand batsman, off break bowler. *Team* Glamorgan (1971–79, 107 matches).
Career batting
107–174–26–3370–102*–22.77–1–*ct* 36
Bowling 2257–48–47.02–1–0–5/55

Richards, Ian Michael
Cricketer. *b:* 9.12.1957, Stockton on Tees, Co Durham. Middle order left-hand batsman, right-arm medium pace bowler. *Team* Northamptonshire (1976–79, 23 matches).
Career batting
23–25–4–467–50–22.23–0–*ct* 5
Bowling 201–7–28.71–0–0–4/57
He played for Durham, commencing 1981.

Richards, Isaac Vivian Alexander
Cricketer. *b:* 7.3.1952, St Johns, Antigua. Brother of Donald and Mervin (Leeward Is). Brilliant middle order right-hand batsman, right-arm medium or off break bowler. *Teams* Leeward Islands (1971/2 to 1982/3); Somerset (1974–83, 154 matches); Queensland (1976/7, 5 matches). *Tours* West Indies to India, Pakistan and Sri Lanka 1974/5, to Australia 1975/6, 1979/80, 1981/2, to England 1976, 1980, to Pakistan 1980/1. *Tests* West Indies (1974/5 to 1982/3, 52 matches).
Career batting
298–490–35–22630–291–49.73–69–*ct* 282–*st* 1
Bowling 5728–136–42.11–1–0–5/88
Test batting
52–80–4–4411–291–58.03–14–*ct* 56
Bowling 790–14–56.57–0–0–2/20
He was the outstanding batsman of the 1976 tour to England, scoring 1,724 runs, av 71.83, in first-class matches and 829 runs, av 118.42, in the Tests, including his highest innings of 291 in the fifth Test at the Oval. On the 1980 tour he again topped both first-class and Test batting averages with 911 runs, av 56.93, and 379 runs, av 63.16. He captained West Indies in one Test on this tour. In all he has scored 1,000 runs in a season in England ten times, going on to 2,000 once : 2,161, av 65.48, in 1977. He has hit five double centuries for Somerset. He has also reached 1,000 runs in an overseas season three times.

Richards, James Henry
Professional. *b:* 1855, Brixton, Surrey. *d:* 24.8.1923, Brixton. Lower order batsman, useful bowler. *Team* Surrey (1881, 2 matches).
Career batting
2–4–0–9–8–2.25–0–*ct* 0
Bowling 89–2–0–44.50–0–0–2/40

Richards, John Lawson
Amateur. *b: circa* 1920, Australia. Tail end batsman, useful bowler. *Sch* Monmouth. *Team* Cambridge U (1939).
Career batting
1–2–0–0–0–0.00–0–*ct* 0
Bowling 50–0

Richards, Robert John
Cricketer. *b:* 5.6.1934, Winchester, Hants. Lower order right-hand batsman, wicket-keeper. *Team* Essex (1970, 1 match).
Career batting
1 match, did not bat–*ct* 0

Richards, Walter
Professional. *b:* 28.9.1865, Balsall Heath, Worcs. *d:* 14.10.1917, Birmingham. Stylish middle order right-hand batsman, right-arm off break bowler, good field. *Team* Warwickshire (1895–96, 7 matches).
Career batting
7–11–1–112–61*–11.20–0–*ct* 4
He made his debut for Warwickshire in 1883; thus most of his County career took place before Warwickshire became first-class.

Richards, Rev William Henry
Amateur. *b:* 26.6.1833, Keevil, Wiltshire. *d:* 22.9.1912, St Helens, Isle of Wight. Father of A. C. (Hampshire). Middle order batsman. *Team* MCC (1866).
Career batting
2–3–1–39–20*–19.50–0–*ct* 0
His County cricket was for Essex (pre-first-class).

Richardson, Alan
Professional. *b:* 28.10.1926, Woodborough, Notts. Tail end right-hand batsman, right-arm fast medium bowler. *Team* Nottinghamshire (1949–51, 28 matches).
Career batting
28–31–16–73–7*–4.86–0–*ct* 10
Bowling 1819–40–45.47–0–0–4/24

Richardson, Alfred Graham
Amateur. *b:* 24.7.1875, Sandy, Bedfordshire. *d:* 17.12.1934, Umtata, Cape Province, South Africa. Opening or middle order right-hand batsman. *Sch* King's, Canterbury. *Teams* Somerset (1895, 1 match); Gloucestershire (1897–1901, 20 matches); Cambridge U (1897); Orange Free State (1906/7 to 1913/14).
Career batting
29–48–1–698–89–14.85–0–*ct* 10
Bowling 112–2–56.00–0–0–1/23
He also played for Bedfordshire.

Richardson, Arthur John
Amateur. *b:* 24.7.1888, Seven Hills, South Australia. *d:* 23.12.1973, Adelaide, Australia. Opening right-hand batsman, right-arm medium pace off break bowler. *Teams* South Australia (1918/9 to 1926/7, 45 matches); Western Australia (1927/8 to 1929/30, 4 matches). *Tour* Australia to England 1926. *Tests* Australia (1924/5 to 1926, 9 matches).
Career batting
86–139–13–5238–280–41.57–13–*ct* 33
Bowling 6555–209–31.36–7–1–6/28
Test batting
9–13–0–403–100–31.00–1–*ct* 1
Bowling 521–12–43.41–0–0–2/20
He was a useful all-rounder on the 1926 tour hitting 728 runs, av 33.09, and taking 49 wickets, av 19.71. He played in all five Tests. His final first-class match was for Sir L. Parkinson's XI in 1933. His highest score was 280 for South Australia v MCC at Adelaide in 1922/3.

Richardson, Arthur Walker
Amateur. *b:* 4.3.1907, Quarndon, Derbyshire. *d:* 29.7.1983, Ednaston, Derbyshire. Father of G. W. (Derbyshire). Middle order right-hand batsman. *Sch* Winchester. *Team* Derbyshire (1928–36, 159 matches).
Career batting
159–239–30–3982–90–19.05–0–*ct* 58
Bowling 34–0
He hit 1,258 runs, av 29.95, in 1932.
He captained Derbyshire from 1931 to 1936.

Richardson, Brian Anthony
Cricketer. *b:* 24.2.1944, Kenilworth, Warwickshire. Brother of D. W. (Worcs) and P. E. (Worcs and Kent). Opening left-hand batsman, leg break bowler. *Sch* Malvern. *Team* Warwickshire (1963–67, 40 matches).
Career batting
40–72–4–1323–126–19.45–2–*ct* 28
Bowling 157–1–157.00–0–0–1/32

Richardson, Bertram Harold
Professional. *b:* 12.3.1932, Ashton-under-Lyne, Lancashire. Lower order left-hand batsman, slow left-arm bowler, good outfield. *Team* Derbyshire (1950–53, 27 matches).
Career batting
27–36–11–279–29–11.16–0–*ct* 14
Bowling 1003–33–30.39–0–0–4/39

Richardson, Charles Stewart
Amateur. *b:* 23.3.1885, Terling, Essex. *d:* 5.4.1948, Great Totham, Essex. Middle order left-hand batsman. *Team* Essex (1914, 1 match).
Career batting
1–1–0–15–15–15.00–0–*ct* 1

Richardson, Derek Walter
Amateur, turned professional for 1956 season. *d:* 3.11.1934, Hereford. Brother of B. A. (Warwickshire) and P. E. (Worcs and Kent). Middle order left-hand batsman, left-arm medium pace bowler, good close field. *Team* Worcestershire (1952–67, 371 matches). *Tours* Worcestershire World Tour 1964/5, to Jamaica 1965/6. *Test* England (1957, 1 match).
Career batting
383–660–65–16303–169–27.40–16–*ct* 419
Bowling 354–8–44.25–0–0–2/11
Test batting
1–1–0–33–33–33.00–0–*ct* 1
He hit 1,000 runs in a season nine times (best 1,830, av 32.67, in 1957).

Richardson, George William
Amateur. *b:* 26.4.1938, Marylebone, London. Son of A. W. (Derbyshire). Middle order right-hand batsman, left-arm fast medium bowler. *Sch* Winchester. *Team* Derbyshire (1959–65, 62 matches).
Career batting
69–107–15–1460–91–15.86–0–*ct* 12
Bowling 4072–147–27.70–5–2–8/54

Richardson, Henry
Professional. *b:* 4.10.1857, Bulwell, Nottinghamshire. *d:* 20.3.1940, Bulwell, Nottinghamshire. Lower order right-hand batsman, right-arm medium pace bowler. *Team* Nottinghamshire (1887–90, 53 matches).

Career batting
65–91–14–663–55–8.61–0–*ct* 44
Bowling 2545–185–13.75–10–1–7/24
His final first-class match was for MCC in 1894.

Richardson, Henry Adair
Amateur. *b:* 31.7.1846, Bayswater, London. *d:* 17.9.1921, Hastings, Sussex. Forceful middle order right-hand batsman, wicket-keeper. *Sch* Tonbridge. *Teams* Cambridge U (1867–69, blue all three years); Middlesex (1868–69, 2 matches); Kent (1866–68, 11 matches).
Career batting
37–63–7–1166–143–20.82–0–*ct* 26–*st* 13
Bowling 65–4–16.25–0–0–2/19
His best season was 1868 when he hit 431 runs, av 28.73, coming fourth in the first-class averages. His last first-class match was for the Gentlemen of the South in 1871. An excellent billiards player he represented Cambridge in 1868, 1869 and 1870.

Richardson, Harold Bamford
Amateur. *b:* 10.3.1873. Middle order right-hand batsman, slow right-arm bowler. *Sch* Clifton. *Team* Surrey (1899, 22 matches).
Career batting
22–31–5–585–72–22.50–0–*ct* 8
Bowling 1–0
He was in business in San Francisco until 1906 when his name can be found in street directories – after the earthquake there is no further trace of him and he may therefore have been killed in the 1906 earthquake.

Richardson, John
Professional. *b:* 17.3.1856, Duckmanton, Derbyshire. *d:* 19.2.1940, Brimington, Derbyshire. Tail end right-hand batsman, right-arm fast bowler. *Team* Derbyshire (1878–83, 11 matches).
Career batting
11–21–4–117–18–6.88–0–*ct* 9
Bowling 517–32–16.15–1–0–7/76

Richardson, John Alan
Amateur. *b:* 4.8.1908, Sleights, Yorkshire. Stylish middle order right-hand batsman, off break bowler. *Team* Yorkshire (1936–47, 7 matches).
Career batting
8–14–3–343–61–31.18–0–*ct* 4
Bowling 108–2–54.00–0–0–2/23
He was a major force in Yorkshire Council cricket. His first-class debut was for the Gentlemen in 1934.

Richardson, John Charles
Amateur. *b:* 5.12.1912, Carron, Morayshire. Right-hand batsman, right-arm medium pace bowler. *Team* Scotland (1953).
Career batting
2–3–0–32–24–10.66–0–*ct* 1

Richardson, John Maunsell
Amateur. *b:* 12.6.1846, Great Limber, Caistor, Lincs. *d:* 22.1.1912, Westminster, London. Middle order right-hand batsman, right-hand slow round-arm bowler, good deep field. *Sch* Harrow. *Team* Cambridge U (1866–68, blue all three years).
Career batting
18–31–1–347–58–11.56–0–*ct* 10
Bowling 35–1–35.00–0–0–1/21
His final first-class match was for MCC in 1874 and his County cricket was for Cheshire and Lincolnshire. A famous amateur jockey, he won the Grand National in 1873 and 1874 and was regarded as the leading amateur rider of his day. He was MP for Brigg in 1894 and 1895.

Richardson, James Vere
Amateur. *b:* 16.12.1903, Heswall, Cheshire. Middle order right-hand batsman, right-arm medium bowler. *Sch* Uppingham. *Teams* Essex (1924–26, 14 matches); Oxford U (1924–25, blue 1925).
Career batting
35–53–9–1038–89–23.59–0–*ct* 21
Bowling 838–27–31.03–0–0–3/25
A noted rugby footballer he was awarded his blue at Oxford and went on to be capped for England.

Richardson, Peter Edward
Amateur. *b:* 4.7.1931, Hereford. Brother of D. W. (Worcs) and B. A. (Worcs). Forceful opening left-hand batsman, excellent cover point. *Sch* Cathedral School, Hereford. *Teams* Worcestershire (1949–58, 161 matches); Kent (1959–65, 162 matches). *Tours* MCC to Pakistan 1955/6, to South Africa 1956/7, to East Africa 1957/8 (not first-class), to Australia and New Zealand 1958/9, to India, Pakistan and Ceylon 1961/2; Cavaliers to Jamaica 1963/4; Commonwealth to Pakistan 1963/4, to India 1964/5. *Tests* England (1956–63, 34 matches).
Career batting
454–794–41–26055–185–34.60–44–*ct* 220
Bowling 499–11–45.36–0–0–2/10
Test batting
34–56–1–2061–126–37.47–5–*ct* 6
Bowling 48–3–16.00–0–0–2/10
In his second full season of first-class County cricket, he hit 2,294 runs, av 39.55, and although he was to reach over 2,000 runs in three other seasons and in all top 1,000 runs eleven times in

England, he never improved on his 2,294 of 1953. He also hit 1,000 runs on the 1961/2 tour. In 1956 he made his England debut, playing in all five Tests against the Australians and opening the innings with Cowdrey in each match. Richardson was also successful the following winter in South Africa and in the 1957 series against the West Indies. His place in the England side looked firmly established, but he failed completely on the 1958/9 tour to Australia, perhaps due to the problems he encountered as captain of Worcestershire. He left the County in controversial circumstances after the 1958 season and was forced to spend an idle summer qualifying for Kent.

For several seasons he was back at his best with his new County, but apart from the 1961/2 tour to India and Pakistan, received only one further England cap – v West Indies in 1963. He retired from County cricket at the close of the 1965 season.

Richardson, Percy John
Amateur. *b:* 2.4.1891, West Ham, Essex. *d:* 23.3.1964, Reigate, Surrey. Middle order batsman. *Sch* Clifton. *Teams* Essex (1912, 2 matches); Cambridge U (1912).
Career batting
3–4–0–44–21–11.00–0–*ct* 2
Bowling 12–0

Richardson, Richard Taswell
Amateur. *b:* 9.8.1852, Broughton, Hants. *d:* 16.5.1930, Capenhurst, near Chester. Middle order right-hand batsman. *Sch* Marlborough. *Team* MCC (1876–77).
Career batting
5–7–0–160–48–22.85–0–*ct* 0

Richardson, Samuel
Amateur. *b:* 24.5.1844, Derby. *d:* 18.1.1938, Madrid, Spain. Middle order right-hand batsman, wicket-keeper. *Team* Derbyshire (1871–78, 14 matches).
Career batting
15–27–0–202–25–7.48–0–*ct* 8–*st* 1
Bowling 43–1–43.00–0–0–1/43

He captained Derbyshire from 1871 to 1875 and was assistant secretary to the County club until 1890, when he absconded with about £1,000 of the Club's money and went to live under an assumed name in Spain.

Richardson, Stanley Hugh
Amateur. *b:* 2.7.1890, Marston Green, Warwickshire. *d:* 24.1.1958, Cambridge. Middle order right-hand batsman. *Teams* Nottinghamshire (1925, 1 match); Warwickshire (1920, 2 matches).
Career batting
3–5–1–22–8*–5.50–0–*ct* 0

Richardson, Thomas
Professional. *b:* 11.8.1870, Byfleet, Surrey. *d:* 2.7.1912, St Jean d'Arvey, France. He died of congestion of the brain. Lower order right-hand batsman, right-arm fast bowler. *Teams* Somerset (1905, 1 match); Surrey (1892–1904, 305 matches); London County (1904). *Tours* Stoddart Australia 1894/5, 1897/8. *Tests* England (1893 to 1897/8, 14 matches).
Career batting
358–479–124–3424–69–9.64–0–*ct* 126
Bowling 38794–2104–18.43–200–72–10/45
Test batting
14–24–8–177–25*–11.06–0–*ct* 5
Bowling 2220–88–25.22–11–4–8/94

He was regarded as the greatest English fast bowler of his generation, though his period at the very peak of his form lasted just five seasons. He made his Surrey debut in 1892 and the following year gained his England cap, taking 174 wickets, av 15.40, in first-class matches. In 1894 he was the leading bowler in England with 196 wickets, av 10.32. Going to Australia that winter he topped the bowling averages for the tour, and returning home exceeded 200 wickets for the first of three times – 290, av 14.37. In all he took 100 wickets in a season 10 times. His best bowling was 10 for 45 for Surrey v Essex at the Oval in 1894 and he took nine wickets in an innings on three other occasions.

After his second visit to Australia his increasing weight gradually reduced his effectiveness and he lost his place in the Surrey side in 1904.

Richardson, Thomas Geoffrey
Amateur. *b:* 7.3.1907, Worsley, Manchester. *d:* 13.7.1928, Worsley, Manchester. Middle order batsman. *Sch* Manchester GS. *Team* Oxford U (1927).
Career batting
1–2–1–4–4*–4.00–0–*ct* 0–*st* 1

Richardson, Thomas Haden
Amateur. *b:* 4.7.1865, Tutbury, Staffs. *d:* 10.12.1923, Tutbury, Staffs. Middle order right-hand batsman. *Team* Derbyshire (1895, 3 matches).
Career batting
4–7–0–49–15–7.00–0–*ct* 5

His first-class debut was for an England XI in 1888. He also played for Staffordshire.

Richardson, Victor York
Amateur. *b:* 7.9.1894, Unley, Adelaide, Australia. *d:* 29.10.1969, Fullarton Park, Adelaide, Australia. Grandfather of G. S. Chappell, I. M. Chappell and T. M. Chappell (Australia). Forceful middle order right-hand batsman, excellent field. *Team* South Australia (1918/9 to 1937/8, 104 matches). *Tours* Australia to England 1930, to South Africa 1935/6, to New Zealand 1920/1, 1927/8. *Tests* Australia (1924/5 to 1935/6, 19 matches).
Career batting
184–297–12–10727–231–37.63–27–*ct* 213–*st* 4
Bowling 545–8–68.12–0–0–3/22
Test batting
19–30–0–706–138–23.53–1–*ct* 24
His batting was very disappointing on the 1930 tour to England. He was vice-captain of the side and later captained Australia in five Tests, all against South Africa. His highest score was 231 for South Australia v MCC at Adelaide in 1928/9. An all-round sportsman he also excelled at tennis, lacrosse and basketball. After retiring he became a well-known radio commentator.

Richardson, William Ethelbert
Amateur. *b:* 23.12.1894, St Helens, Lancashire. *d:* 5.11.1971, Hartlebury, Worcs. Lower order right-hand batsman, right-arm fast bowler. *Team* Worcestershire (1920–28, 30 matches).
Career batting
30–57–17–269–24–6.72–0–*ct* 9
Bowling 1865–44–42.38–1–0–6/48
A good rugby footballer he appeared for Moseley, Kidderminster and Bromsgrove.

Richardson, William Percival
Amateur. *b:* 25.2.1861, Great Barford, Bedfordshire. *d:* 13.6.1933, Littlestone-on-Sea, Kent. Lower order right-hand batsman, wicket-keeper. *Sch* Clifton. *Team* Cambridge U (1882).
Career batting
1–2–0–8–8–4.00–0–*ct* 1

Riches, John Dansey Hurry
Amateur. *b:* 30.12.1920, Cardiff. Son of N. V. H. (Glamorgan). Middle order right-hand batsman, slow left-arm bowler. *Sch* Repton. *Team* Glamorgan (1947, 1 match).
Career batting
1–2–0–5–4–2.50–0–*ct* 0

Riches, Norman Vaughan Hurry
Amateur. *b:* 9.6.1883, Cardiff. *d:* 6.11.1975, Cyncoed, Cardiff. Father of J. D. H. (Glamorgan). Sound opening right-hand batsman, occasional wicket-keeper. *Teams* Glamorgan (1921–34, 82 matches); Wales (1923–30).
Career batting
104–175–12–5750–239*–35.27–9–*ct* 49–*st* 6
Bowling 112–4–28.00–0–0–4/21
His debut for Glamorgan was in 1901. He captained the County in 1921 and jointly in 1929. After retiring he was for many years on the Committee and at one time President. He hit 1,080 runs, av 43.20, in 1921, which was his only full season in first-class cricket. His only double century was 239* for Wales v Ireland in 1926. His first-class debut was for South Wales in 1912.

Richmond, Sir Bruce Lyttelton
Amateur. *b:* 12.1.1871, Kensington, London. *d:* 1.10.1964, Islip, Oxfordshire. Opening or middle order right-hand batsman. *Sch* Westminster. *Team* Oxford U (1892).
Career batting
2–3–0–12–11–4.00–0–*ct* 0

Richmond, Thomas Leonard
Professional. *b:* 23.6.1890, Radcliffe on Trent, Notts. *d:* 29.12.1957, Saxondale, Notts. Tail end right-hand batsman, leg break and googly bowler. *Team* Nottinghamshire (1912–28, 245 matches). *Tour* Cahn to South America 1929/30. *Test* England (1921, 1 match).
Career batting
252–281–116–1644–70–9.96–0–*ct* 39
Bowling 24959–1176–21.22–90–19–9/21
Test batting
1–2–0–6–4–3.00–0–*ct* 0
Bowling 86–2–43.00–0–0–2/69
He took 100 wickets in a season seven times (best 169, av 13.48, in 1922); his best bowling in an innings was 9 for 21 for Notts v Hampshire at Trent Bridge in 1922. His final first-class match was for Sir Julien Cahn's XI in 1932.

Richmond, William
Professional. *b:* 1843, Burnley, Lancashire. *d:* 11.11.1912, Burnley, Lancashire. Middle order batsman, wicket-keeper. *Team* Lancashire (1868, 1 match).
Career batting
1–2–0–1–1–0.50–0–*ct* 0

Rickards, Kenneth Roy
Amateur. *b:* 22.8.1923, Rollington Town, Kingston, Jamaica. Attractive middle order right-hand batsman, leg break bowler. *Teams* Essex (1953, 1 match); Jamaica (1945/6 to 1958/9). *Tours* West Indies to Australia and New Zealand 1951/2, to India, Pakistan and Ceylon 1948/9. *Tests* West Indies (1947/8 to 1951/2, 2 matches).

Career batting
37–60–7–2065–195–38.96–2–*ct* 10
Bowling 128–1–128.00–0–0–1/66
Test batting
2–3–0–104–67–34.66–0–*ct* 0

His English first-class debut was for a Commonwealth XI in 1952.

Ricketts, Arthur James
Professional. *b:* 27.8.1913, Farmborough, Somerset. Lower order left-hand batsman, slow left-arm bowler. *Team* Somerset (1936, 1 match).
Career batting
1 match, did not bat–*ct* 0

Ricketts, George William
Amateur. *b:* 2.6.1864, Allahabad, India. *d:* 16.6.1927, South Kensington, London. Aggressive middle order right-hand batsman, right-arm medium bowler, good point field. *Sch* Winchester. *Teams* Oxford U (1887, blue); Surrey (1887, 3 matches). *Tour* Hawke to North America 1891.
Career batting
13–21–1–385–92–19.25–0–*ct* 5
Bowling 79–3–26.33–0–0–2/21

He was for several years on the MCC Committee. His final first-class match was for MCC in 1902. Twice in 1910 he stood unsuccessfully as Liberal candidate for Winchester.

Ricketts, James
Professional. *b:* 9.2.1842, Manchester, Lancashire. *d:* 5.6.1894, Altrincham, Cheshire. Fine opening right-hand batsman, right-hand slow round-arm bowler, short leg. *Team* Lancashire (1867–77, 34 matches).
Career batting
42–79–5–1226–195*–16.56–1–*ct* 28–*st* 1
Bowling 284–12–23.66–0–0–4/40

He had a remarkable debut in first-class cricket, scoring 195 not out for Lancashire v Surrey at the Oval in 1867 and carrying his bat through the completed Lancashire innings.

Ricketts, Michael Rodney
Amateur. *b:* 27.9.1923, King's Norton, Warwickshire. Middle order right-hand batsman. *Sch* Sherborne. *Team* Free Foresters (1948).
Career batting
1–1–0–1–1–1.00–0–*ct* 0

His County cricket was for Suffolk.

Rickman, Reginald Binns
Amateur. *b:* 6.5.1881, Doncaster, Yorkshire. *d:* 22.11.1940, Chelsea, London. Lower order right-hand batsman, right-arm medium pace bowler. *Sch* Sherborne. *Team* Derbyshire (1906–11, 65 matches).
Career batting
65–118–8–1262–68–11.47–0–*ct* 7
Bowling 1967–62–31.72–1–0–5/80

He also played for Devon.

Rickman, William
Amateur. *b:* 1849, South Yarra, Victoria, Australia. *d:* 6.6.1911, Frankston, Victoria, Australia. Middle order right-hand batsman, right-arm fast bowler. *Teams* Lancashire (1876, 1 match); Victoria (1880/1, 1 match).
Career batting
2–3–0–29–19–9.66–0–*ct* 1
Bowling 7–0

Riddell, David Adams
Amateur. *b:* 30.9.1899, Glasgow, Scotland. *d:* 3.4.1957, Australia. Right-hand batsman. *Sch* Fettes. *Team* Scotland (1921–22).
Career batting
3–5–0–56–32–11.20–0–*ct* 2

Riddell, Edward Mitford Hutton
Amateur. *b:* 31.10.1845, Carlton-on-Trent, Notts. *d:* 22.10.1898, Lincoln. Lower order right-hand batsman, right-arm medium fast bowler. *Sch* Uppingham. *Team* MCC (1870–71).
Career batting
4–8–1–89–36–12.71–0–*ct* 2
Bowling 125–2–62.50–0–0–1/33

He played for Nottinghamshire in one non-first-class match in 1873, most of his major cricket being for the Gentlemen of that County.

Riddell, Neil Anthony
Cricketer. *b:* 16.7.1947, Staindrop, Co Durham. Middle order left-hand batsman, right-arm medium pace bowler. *Team* Minor Counties (1976). *Tour* Minor Counties to Kenya 1977/8 (not first-class).
Career batting
1–2–0–34–20–17.00–0–*ct* 0

His County cricket has been for Durham, commencing 1972.

Riddell, Victor Horsley Hume
Amateur. *b:* 23.7.1905, Rotherham, Yorkshire. *d:* 9.8.1976, Stratford on Avon, Warwickshire. Lower order right-hand batsman, wicket-keeper. *Sch* Clifton. *Team* Cambridge U (1926, blue).
Career batting
5–8–2–48–13*–8.00–0–*ct* 3–*st* 3

Ridding, Rev Charles Henry
Amateur. *b:* 26.11.1825, Winchester, Hants. *d:* 13.3.1905, Fareham, Hants. Brother of William

(Hampshire) and Arthur (Oxford U 1846–50). Steady middle order right-hand batsman, excellent long stop. *Sch* Winchester. *Teams* Oxford U (1845–49, blue all five years); Hampshire (1861–64, 3 matches).
Career batting
29–50–9–492–33–12.00–0–*ct* 11
Bowling 1 wicket, no analyses
He also played for Oxfordshire, 1859 to 1864, and for Wiltshire

Ridding, Rev William
Amateur. *b:* 23.11.1830, Winchester, Hants. *d:* 1.5.1900, Clapton, London. Brother of C. H. (Hampshire) and Arthur (Oxford U 1846–50). Attacking right-hand batsman, wicket-keeper. *Sch* Winchester. *Teams* Oxford U (1849–53, blue 1849, 1850, 1852 and 1853); Hampshire (1861, 1 match).
Career batting
17–25–4–326–53–15.52–0–*ct* 10–*st* 17
He also played for Oxfordshire, Wiltshire and Monmouthshire.

Riddington, Anthony
Professional. *b* 22.12.1911, Countesthorpe, Leicester. Opening or middle order left-hand batsman, left-arm slow medium, or medium bowler. *Team* Leicestershire (1931–50, 128 matches).
Career batting
128–214–17–3650–104*–18.52–1–*ct* 53
Bowling 3232–83–38.93–1–0–5/34

Ridge, Stuart Peter
Cricketer. *b:* 23.11.1961, Beaconsfield, Bucks. Lower order right-hand batsman, right-arm medium pace bowler. *Team* Oxford U (1981–82).
Career batting
11–15–6–71–22–7.88–0–*ct* 3
Bowling 894–14–63.85–0–0–4/128
He also played for Buckinghamshire.

Ridgway, Frederick
Professional. *b:* 10.8.1923, Stockport, Cheshire. Lower order right-hand batsman, right-arm fast medium bowler. *Team* Kent (1946–61, 298 matches). *Tours* Commonwealth to India and Ceylon 1950/51; MCC to India, Pakistan and Ceylon 1951/2. *Tests* England (1951/2, 5 matches).
Career batting
341–486–115–4081–94–11.00–0–*ct* 235
Bowling 25381–1069–23.74–41–6–8/39
Test batting
5–6–0–49–24–8.16–0–*ct* 3
Bowling 379–7–54.14–0–0–4/83
He took 105 wickets, av 23.32, in 1949.

Riding, Henry Wadsworth
Amateur. *b:* 19.9.1899, Epping, Essex. *d:* 21.5.1923, Chingford, Essex. Middle order batsman. *Sch* Bancrofts. *Team* Essex (1921, 1 match).
Career batting
1–2–0–23–16–11.50–0–*ct* 0

Ridland, James David
Amateur. *b:* 17.1.1923, New Plymouth, New Zealand. *d:* 4.2.1978, New Plymouth, New Zealand. Middle order right-hand batsman, wicket-keeper. *Tour* New Zealand Services to England 1945.
Career batting
1–2–0–62–44–31.00–0–*ct* 1
He did not appear in first-class matches in New Zealand.

Ridley, Alfred Bayley
Amateur. *b:* 14.12.1859, Hollington, Hants. *d:* 26.3.1898, Lambeth, London. Brother of A. W. (Hampshire). Lower order right-hand batsman, right-hand fast round-arm bowler. *Sch* Eton. *Team* Hampshire (1884–85, 2 matches).
Career batting
2–4–0–43–41–10.75–0–*ct* 1
Bowling 35–2–17.50–0–0–2/30

Ridley, Arthur William
Amateur. *b:* 11.9.1852, Newbury, Berkshire. *d:* 10.8.1916, Westminster, London. Brother of A. B. (Hampshire). Stylish middle order right-hand batsman, excellent lob bowler. *Sch* Eton. *Teams* Oxford U (1872–75, blue all four years); Hampshire (1875–78, 10 matches); Middlesex (1882–85, 16 matches); Kent (1877, 1 match).
Career batting
96–167–11–3150–136–20.19–4–*ct* 77–*st* 2
Bowling 3375–222–15.20–19–5–7/21

Ridley, Christopher Jonathan Ben
Cricketer. *b:* 17.6.1946, Bulawayo, Rhodesia. Brother of G. N. S. (Kent). Lower order right-hand batsman, right-arm medium fast bowler. *Team* Oxford U (1971).
Career batting
6–10–2–88–23–11.00–0–*ct* 4
Bowling 356–3–118.66–0–0–2/70

Ridley, Giles Nicholas Spencer
Cricketer. *b:* 27.11.1944, Bulawayo, Rhodesia. Brother of C. J. B. (Oxford U). Lower order right-hand batsman, slow left-arm bowler. *Teams*

Kent (1965, 1 match); Oxford U (1965–68, blue all four years).
Career batting
45–68–8–889–50*–14.81–0–*ct* 40
Bowling 3051–123–24.80–2–0–7/110
He also played for Oxfordshire, and his final first-class match was for Minor Counties in 1972.

Ridley, Gerald Vernon Newport
Amateur. *b:* 23.10.1897, Felsted, Essex. *d:* 12.11.1953, Chignal St James, Essex. Middle order right-hand batsman, right-arm medium bowler. *Sch* Marlborough. *Team* Essex (1922–26, 6 matches).
Career batting
6–11–0–113–54–10.27–0–*ct* 3
From 1929 to his death he was on the Committee of Essex CCC.

Ridley, Robert Michael
Cricketer. *b:* 8.1.1947, Oxford. Opening right-hand batsman. *Sch* Clifton. *Teams* Oxford U (1967–70, blue 1968–70); Ireland (1968).
Career batting
23–42–1–994–79–24.24–0–*ct* 9
Bowling 0–0
His County cricket was for Berkshire.

Ridley, Rev Thomas Glynn
Amateur. *b:* July 1858, Cullercoats, Northumberland. *d:* 30.6.1945, Cape Town, South Africa. Opening or middle order right-hand batsman, right-hand slow round-arm bowler. *Sch* Uppingham. *Team* Gentlemen of England (1881).
Career batting
1–2–0–33–32–16.50–0–*ct* 0
He appeared in the Freshmen's and Seniors' matches at Oxford. His County cricket was for Northumberland.

Righton, Edward Grantham (sen)
Amateur. *b:* 23.11.1885, Evesham, Worcs. *d:* 3.1.1964, Evesham, Worcs. Father of E. G. jun (Worcestershire). Middle order right-hand batsman, right-arm medium pace bowler. *Sch* Dean Close. *Team* Worcestershire (1911–13, 4 matches).
Career batting
4–4–0–60–48–15.00–0–*ct* 1
Bowling 21–1–21.00–0–0–1/21

Righton, Edward Grantham (jun)
Amateur. *b:* 24.9.1912, Evesham, Worcs. Son of E. G. sen (Worcestershire). Right-hand batsman. *Sch* Dean Close. *Team* Worcestershire (1934–36, 4 matches).
Career batting
4–7–0–27–19–3.85–0–*ct* 1

Rigley, William
Professional. *b:* 24.3.1852, Eastwood, Notts. *d:* 15.3.1897, Nottingham. Opening or middle order right-hand batsman, right-arm medium pace bowler. *Team* Derbyshire (1873–82, 57 matches).
Career batting
62–115–0–1449–69–12.60–0–*ct* 22
Bowling 30–3–10.00–0–0–2/10

Riley, Edwin
Professional. *b:* 1867, Stoney Stanton, Leics. *d:* 4.5.1936, Stoney Stanton, Leics. Father of Harold (Leics). Lower order batsman, bowler. *Team* Leicestershire (1895, 2 matches).
Career batting
2–3–1–13–8*–6.50–0–*ct* 0
Bowling 7–0

Riley, Harold
Professional. *b:* 3.10.1902, Stoney Stanton, Leicestershire. Son of Edwin (Leicestershire). Middle order right-hand batsman, off break bowler, good cover point. *Team* Leicestershire (1928–37, 94 matches).
Career batting
94–147–11–2346–101–17.25–1–*ct* 30
Bowling 173–5–34.60–0–0–2/32
He was a useful soccer inside forward.

Riley, Harry
Professional. *b:* 17.8.1875, Thackley, Yorkshire. *d:* 6.11.1922, Bradford, Yorkshire. Lower order batsman, left-arm medium pace bowler. *Team* Yorkshire (1895–1900, 4 matches).
Career batting
4–5–1–36–25*–9.00–0–*ct* 1
Bowling 54–1–54.00–0–0–1/17

Riley, James
Professional. *b:* 11.12.1860, Kirkby in Ashfield. *d:* 8.11.1937, Derby. Lower order right-hand batsman, right-arm medium pace bowler. *Team* Nottinghamshire (1898, 2 matches).
Career batting
2–1–0–3–3–3.00–0–*ct* 1
Bowling 49–0

Riley, J.
b: Lancashire. Lower order batsman, bowler. *Team* Worcestershire (1953, 1 match).
Career batting
1–1–0–1–1–1.00–0–*ct* 1
Bowling 48–3–16.00–0–0–3/25

Riley, John Christopher William
Amateur. *b:* 6.4.1934, Esher, Surrey. Tail end

right-hand batsman, wicket-keeper. *Sch* Uppingham. *Team* Cambridge U (1955–56).
Career batting
2–3–1–0–0*–0.00–0–*ct* 3–*st* 1

Riley, Martin
Amateur. *b:* 5.4.1851, Cleckheaton, Yorkshire. *d:* 1.6.1899, Harrogate, Yorkshire. Hard hitting middle order right-hand batsman, right-hand fast round-arm bowler. *Team* Yorkshire (1878–82, 17 matches).
Career batting
20–34–1–381–92–11.54–0–*ct* 5
Bowling 10–0
His final first-class match was for A. Shaw's Australian XI at Harrogate in 1885.

Riley, Terence Michael Noel
Cricketer. *b:* 25.12.1939, Birmingham. Opening right-hand batsman, leg break bowler. *Teams* Gloucestershire (1964, 11 matches); Warwickshire (1961–64, 12 matches).
Career batting
23–43–2–678–84–16.53–0–*ct* 5
Bowling 15–0
He played for both Gloucs and Warwickshire in 1964.

Riley, William
Professional. *b:* 11.8.1888, Newstead, Notts. *d:* 9.8.1917, near Coxyde, Belgium. He was killed by a shell splinter. Tail end left-hand batsman, slow left-arm medium bowler. *Team* Nottinghamshire (1909–14, 80 matches).
Career batting
80–110–24–740–48–8.60–0–*ct* 69
Bowling 5497–235–23.39–10–2–7/80

Riley, William Nairn
Amateur. *b:* 24.11.1892, Appleby Magna, Leicestershire. *d:* 20.11.1955, Hove, Sussex. Right-hand batsman, right-arm fast medium bowler. *Teams* Leicestershire (1911–14, 32 matches); Cambridge U (1912–14, blue 1912).
Career batting
55–91–1–1620–121–18.00–2–*ct* 31
Bowling 314–7–44.85–0–0–2/12

Rilstone, Thomas Melville
Amateur. *b:* 12.1.1918, Wallaroo, South Australia. Lower order left-hand batsman, right-arm leg break and googly bowler. *Team* Canada (1951–54). *Tour* Canada to England 1954.
Career batting
3–3–0–54–38–18.00–0–*ct* 0
Bowling 150–0

Rimbault, Geoffrey Acworth
Amateur. *b:* 17.4.1908, Wandsworth, London. Middle order right-hand batsman. *Teams* Europeans (1934/5); Army (1938).
Career batting
2–3–0–31–16–10.33–0–*ct* 0

Rimell, Anthony Geoffrey Jordan
Amateur. *b:* 29.8.1928, Kasauli, India. Stylish middle order left-hand batsman, off break bowler. *Sch* Charterhouse. *Teams* Hampshire (1946–50, 2 matches); Cambridge U (1949–50, blue both years).
Career batting
23–35–5–854–160–28.46–1–*ct* 13
Bowling 1445–40–36.12–1–0–6/100

Rimmer, Joseph
Professional. *b:* 26.1.1925, Langwith, Derbyshire. Tail end right-hand batsman, right-arm medium pace bowler. *Team* Derbyshire (1949, 3 matches).
Career batting
3–3–2–1–1*–1.00–0–*ct* 0
Bowling 264–5–52.80–0–0–2/71

Ring, Douglas Thomas
Amateur. *b:* 14.10.1918, Hobart, Tasmania. Lower order right-hand batsman, leg break and googly bowler. *Team* Victoria (1938/9 to 1952/3, 67 matches). *Tours* Australia to England 1948, 1953, to New Zealand 1949/50. *Tests* Australia (1947/8 to 1953, 13 matches).
Career batting
129–169–22–3418–145–23.25–1–*ct* 93
Bowling 12847–451–28.48–21–2–7/88
Test batting
13–21–2–426–67–22.42–0–*ct* 5
Bowling 1305–35–37.28–2–0–6/72
Although he played little part in the Tests either in 1948 or 1953, he proved useful in the other first-class matches.

Ring, John
Professional. *b:* 1758, Darenth, Kent. *d:* 25.10.1800, Bridge, Kent. He died following an injury while playing cricket. Brother of George (England 1796). Steady middle order right-hand batsman, good cover point. *Team* Kent (1782–96).
Career batting
not applicable, pre 1800
He was for sometime regarded as the 'crack' batsman in Kent – his play being scientific.
Beldham stated that Ring was partially responsible for the passing of the lbw law, since he was

'shabby enough' to use his legs to defend his wicket, but Beldham was in error, since the lbw law was passed before Ring played for Kent.

Ringrose, William
Professional. *b:* 2.9.1871, Ganton, Yorkshire. *d:* 14.9.1943, Cross Gates, Leeds, Yorkshire. Tail end left-hand batsman, right-arm fast medium bowler. *Teams* Yorkshire (1901–06, 57 matches); Scotland (1908–12).
Career batting
61–74–11–377–23–5.98–0–*ct* 27
Bowling 3568–175–20.38–10–2–9/76

He was Yorkshire scorer from 1923 to 1939.

His outstanding bowling analysis of 9 for 76 was performed for Yorkshire v Australians in 1905 at Bradford.

Ripley, Roderic George
Amateur. *b:* 1900, Weekley, Kettering, Northants. *d:* January 1931, South Africa. Middle order right-hand batsman. *Teams* Northants (1922, 4 matches); Eastern Province (1928/9).
Career batting
6–11–1–94–23–9.40–0–*ct* 1
Bowling 25–0

Rippon, Albert Dudley Eric
Amateur. *b:* 29.4.1892, Kensington, London. *d:* 16.4.1963, Wallingford, Berks. Twin brother of A. E. S. (Somerset). Solid opening right-hand batsman, right-arm medium pace bowler. *Sch* King's College, Taunton. *Team* Somerset (1914–20, 31 matches).
Career batting
31–56–4–1043–134–20.05–2–*ct* 30
Bowling 1110–37–30.00–1–0–5/107

Soon after the First World War he was compelled to retire from County cricket owing to ill-health.

Rippon, Arthur Ernest Sydney
Amateur. *b:* 29.4.1892, Kensington. *d:* 13.4.1966, Kingston, Surrey. Twin brother of A. D. E. (Somerset). Opening right-hand batsman, right-arm slow bowler. *Sch* King's College, Taunton. *Team* Somerset (1914–37, 102 matches).
Career batting
104–185–8–3823–133–21.59–6–*ct* 44
Bowling 121–3–40.33–0–0–1/6

Rippon, Thomas John
Professional. *b:* 6.7.1918, Swansea, Glamorgan. Lower order right-hand batsman, wicket-keeper. *Team* Glamorgan (1947–48, 3 matches).
Career batting
3–4–2–45–30–22.50–0–*ct* 0–*st* 3

Rist, Frank Henry
Professional. *b:* 30.3.1914, Wandsworth, London. Middle order right-hand batsman, right-arm medium bowler, wicket-keeper. *Team* Essex (1934–53, 65 matches).
Career batting
65–108–9–1496–62–15.11–0–*ct* 35–*st* 5
Bowling 8–1–8.00–0–0–1/8

He was appointed coach to Essex CCC in 1949.

A good soccer player, he appeared at centre half for Charlton Athletic.

Ritchie, David Mawdsley
Amateur. *b:* 12.8.1892, Toxteth Park, Liverpool. *d:* 10.9.1974, Stevenage, Herts. Lower order right-hand batsman, right-arm fast bowler. *Sch* Loretto. *Team* Lancashire (1924, 1 match).
Career batting
4–5–1–27–12–6.75–0–*ct* 4
Bowling 252–9–28.00–0–0–3/44

His first-class debut was for Free Foresters in 1922, and his final first-class match for the same club in 1926.

Rivett-Carnac, Ernest Henry
Amateur. *b:* 30.6.1857, Steyning, Sussex. *d:* 4.9.1940. Middle order batsman. *Sch* Harrow. *Team* MCC (1900).
Career batting
1–1–0–10–10–10.00–0–*ct* 0

Rix, David William
Cricketer. *b:* 7.12.1939, Bulawayo, Rhodesia. Lower order right-hand batsman, left-arm fast medium bowler. *Team* Oxford U (1964).
Career batting
1–2–0–0–0–0.00–0–*ct* 1
Bowling 90–3–30.00–0–0–3/90

Rixon, Stephen John
Cricketer. *b:* 25.2.1954, Albury, New South Wales, Australia. Lower order right-hand batsman, wicket-keeper. *Team* New South Wales (1974/5 to 1982/3, 85 matches). *Tours* Australia to West Indies 1977/8, to England 1981, to Sri Lanka 1980/1. *Tests* Australia (1977/8, 10 matches).
Career batting
109–160–27–2895–128–21.76–4–*ct* 278–*st* 46
Bowling 20–0
Test batting
10–19–3–341–54–21.31–0–*ct* 31–*st* 4

He went to England on the 1981 tour as reserve wicket-keeper and had few opportunities, not playing in any Tests.

Roach, Clifford Archibald
Amateur. *b:* 13.3.1904, Port of Spain, Trinidad.

Attractive opening right-hand batsman, bowler, excellent cover point. *Team* Trinidad (1923/4 to 1937/8). *Tours* West Indies to England 1928, 1933, to Australia 1930/1. *Tests* West Indies (1928 to 1934/5, 16 matches).
Career batting
98–177–4–4851–209–28.04–5–*ct* 43
Bowling 526–5–105.20–0–0–1/18
Test batting
16–32–1–952–209–30.70–2–*ct* 5
Bowling 103–2–51.50–0–0–1/18

In 1928 he played in all three Tests and in first-class matches hit 1,222 runs, av 26.56. On his second English tour he hit 1,286 runs, av 25.72, the highlight being his 180 v Surrey at the Oval which was regarded as the innings of the visit. His highest score was 209 for West Indies v England at Georgetown in 1929/30.

Robathan, George Lionel
Amateur. *b:* 1878, Brighton, Sussex. *d:* 3.8.1951, Lower Bourne, Surrey. Middle order right-hand batsman. *Sch* Epsom. *Team* Gloucestershire (1922, 3 matches).
Career batting
3–6–0–118–42–19.66–0–*ct* 1

Roberson, Benjamin
Professional. *b:* 12.9.1832, Ware, Herts. *d:* 6.4.1874, Upper Holloway, Middlesex. Middle order right-hand batsman. *Team* Middlesex (1865–66, 2 matches).
Career batting
2–3–0–19–13–6.33–0–*ct* 1–*st* 1

He also played occasionally for Hertfordshire.

Roberts, Arthur C.
Amateur. Lower order batsman, useful bowler. *Team* Auckland (1947/8). *Tour* New Zealand Services to England 1945.
Career batting
2–3–1–26–12–13.00–0–*ct* 0
Bowling 182–4–45.50–0–0–3/83

Roberts, Anderson Montgomery Everton
Cricketer. *b:* 29.1.1951, Urlings Village, Antigua. Lower order right-hand batsman, right-arm fast bowler. *Teams* Leeward Islands (1969/70 to 1982/3); Hampshire (1973–78, 58 matches); New South Wales (1976/7, 2 matches); Leicestershire (1981–83, 28 matches). *Tours* West Indies to India, Pakistan and Sri Lanka 1974/5, to Australia 1975/6, 1979/80, 1981/2, to England 1976, 1980, to New Zealand 1979/80. *Tests* West Indies (1973/4 to 1982/3, 45 matches).
Career batting
208–266–60–3074–63–14.92–0–*ct* 49
Bowling 17181–824–20.85–43–6–8/47
Test batting
45–60–10–694–54–13.88–0–*ct* 9
Bowling 5026–197–25.51–11–2–7/54

On the 1976 tour to England he took 28 wickets, av 19.17, in the five Tests and 44 wickets, av 24.75, in first-class matches. In 1980 he was handicapped by injury and appeared in three of the five Tests, but only nine first-class matches altogether.

His best season in England was 1974 when he took 119 wickets, av 13.62.

Roberts, Albert William
Amateur. *b:* 20.8.1909, Christchurch, New Zealand. *d:* 13.5.1978, Clyde, New Zealand. Steady middle order right-hand batsman, right-arm medium pace bowler, good slip. *Teams* Canterbury (1927/8 to 1940/1); Otago (1944/5 to 1950/1). *Tours* New Zealand to England 1937, to Australia 1937/8. *Tests* New Zealand (1929/30 to 1937, 5 matches).
Career batting
84–135–17–3645–181–30.88–3–*ct* 78
Bowling 4762–167–28.51–3–0–5/47
Test batting
5–10–1–248–66*–27.55–0–*ct* 4
Bowling 209–7–29.85–0–0–4/101

He was a useful all-round cricketer on the 1937 tour with 510 runs, av 25.50, and 62 wickets, av 26.20.

Roberts, Arthur Wilson
Amateur. *b:* 23.9.1874, Malegaon, India. *d:* 27.6.1961, Hastings, Sussex. Brother of F. B. (Gloucestershire). Middle order right-hand batsman, right-arm fast medium bowler. *Sch* Rossall. *Team* Gloucestershire (1909–13, 28 matches).
Career batting
29–46–3–807–90–18.77–0–*ct* 17
Bowling 405–12–33.75–0–0–2/20

He also played for Oxfordshire and Buckinghamshire.

Roberts, Christopher Paul
Cricketer. *b:* 12.10.1951, Cleethorpes, Lincs. *d:* 9.6.1977, Raven Crag, Coombe Gliyl, Borrowdale, Cumberland. He was killed in a climbing accident. Right-hand batsman, right-arm medium pace bowler. *Team* Worcestershire (1974, 1 match).
Career batting
1–1–1–0–0*–0–*ct* 0
Bowling 40–1–40.00–0–0–1/34

He also played for Lincolnshire.

Roberts, Desmond
Amateur. *b:* 5.2.1894, Hampstead, London. *d:* 11.1.1968, Eastbourne, Sussex. Middle order left-hand batsman, right-arm medium pace bowler. *Sch* St Bees. *Team* Surrey (1921, 1 match).
Career batting
12–19–2–255–56–15.00–0–*ct* 3
Bowling 438–9–48.66–0–0–3/49

His first-class debut was for Leveson-Gower's XI in 1920 and his final first-class match for MCC in 1936.

Roberts, David John
Cricketer. *b:* 1.10.1942, Middle order batsman. *Team* MCC (1963).
Career batting
1–1–0–6–6–6.00–0–*ct* 0

Roberts, Edward A.
Professional. Lower order right-hand batsman, slow left-arm bowler. *Teams* MCC (1931–39); Minor Counties (1936–39).
Career batting
9–15–5–82–32–8.20–0–*ct* 4
Bowling 577–15–38.46–0–0–3/36

His County cricket was for Hertfordshire.

Roberts, Edward Stanley
Amateur. *b:* 6.5.1890, Oswestry, Shropshire. *d:* September 1964, Rhodesia. Middle order batsman. *Team* Worcestershire (1925, 3 matches).
Career batting
3–6–0–23–12–3.83–0–*ct* 2

Roberts, Frederick
Professional. *b:* 24.9.1848, Kennington, Surrey. *d:* 1903, Bermondsey, London. Lower order right-hand batsman, right-hand fast round-arm bowler. *Team* Surrey (1867–68, 4 matches).
Career batting
4–7–2–20–7–4.00–0–*ct* 1
Bowling 159–9–17.66–1–0–7/72

Roberts, Francis Bernard
Amateur. *b:* 20.5.1882, Anjini Hill, Nasik, India. *d:* 8.2.1916, St Julien, Ypres, Belgium. He was killed in action. Brother of A. W. (Gloucestershire). Middle order right-hand batsman, right-arm fast bowler. *Sch* Rossall. *Teams* Cambridge U (1903–04, blue 1903); Gloucestershire (1906–14, 67 matches).
Career batting
80–138–12–2566–157–20.36–5–*ct* 66
Bowling 3005–88–34.15–1–0–5/69

He appeared occasionally for Oxfordshire.

He also obtained his blue for hockey.

Roberts, Frederick Charles
Amateur. *b:* 1881, Bridgwater, Somerset. Lower order batsman, bowler. *Team* Somerset (1899, 1 match).
Career batting
1–1–0–3–3–3.00–0–*ct* 0
Bowling 11–0

Roberts, Frederick George
Professional. *b:* 1.4.1862, Mickleton, Gloucestershire. *d:* 7.4.1936, Bristol. Tail end left-hand batsman, left-arm fast bowler. *Team* Gloucestershire (1887–1905, 260 matches).
Career batting
261–412–151–1927–38–7.38–0–*ct* 98
Bowling 21303–970–21.96–62–8–8/40

He took 119 wickets, av 22.70, in 1901.

From 1906 to 1919 he stood as a first-class umpire.

Roberts, Harry Edmund
Professional. *b:* 5.6.1924, Coventry. Opening left-hand batsman, right-arm medium pace bowler. *Team* Warwickshire (1949–50, 5 matches).
Career batting
5–8–0–52–30–6.50–0–*ct* 3

Roberts, Henry Edmund
Professional. *b:* 8.2.1888, East Preston, Sussex. *d:* 28.6.1963, Farnborough, Hampshire. Lower order right-hand batsman, right-arm medium pace bowler. *Team* Sussex (1911–25, 157 matches).
Career batting
157–249–76–2302–124*–13.30–1–*ct* 70
Bowling 8267–342–24.17–18–2–7/32

He also played for Devon.

Roberts, Harley James
Professional, changed to amateur in 1935. *b:* 24.5.1912, Bearwood, Staffs. Middle order right-hand batsman, right-arm medium pace bowler. *Team* Warwickshire (1932–37, 17 matches).
Career batting
17–27–4–348–61–15.13–0–*ct* 11
Bowling 407–9–45.22–0–0–3/6

Roberts, Jack
Professional. *b:* 4.3.1933, Bolton, Lancashire. Lower order right-hand batsman, right-arm medium fast bowler. *Team* Lancashire (1957, 2 matches).
Career batting
2–4–2–5–5–2.50–0–*ct* 0
Bowling 90–0

Roberts, James Brown
Amateur. *b:* 11.10.1933, Dundee, Scotland. Right-hand batsman, right-arm fast medium bowler. *Team* Scotland (1956–59).
Career batting
10–17–5–154–31*–12.83–0–*ct* 4
Bowling 434–13–33.38–0–0–3/70

Roberts, John Frederick
Amateur. *b:* 24.2.1913, Pontardawe, Glamorgan. Middle order left-hand batsman. *Team* Glamorgan (1934–36, 5 matches).
Career batting
8–11–1–204–52–20.40–0–*ct* 7
His final first-class match was for Combined Services in 1949.

Roberts, James Harry
Amateur. *b:* July 1864, Anfield, Liverpool. *d:* 11.8.1911, Bexhill, Sussex. Attacking middle order left-hand batsman, bowler, good field. *Sch* Uppingham. *Team* Middlesex (1892, 1 match). *Tour* Warton to South Africa 1888/9 (he did not play in first-class matches).
Career batting
1–1–0–35–35–35.00–0–*ct* 1
He also played for Buckinghamshire.

Roberts, John Kelvin
Cricketer. *b:* 9.10.1949, Liverpool. Tail end right-hand batsman, left-arm medium pace bowler. *Team* Somerset (1969–70, 8 matches).
Career batting
8–9–6–3–2*–1.00–0–*ct* 2
Bowling 485–15–32.33–0–0–4/38

Roberts, Lambert Lloyd
Amateur. *b:* 13.3.1878, Brentford, Middlesex. *d:* 26.6.1919, Sekondi, Gold Coast. Middle order batsman. *Sch* Harrow. *Team* Gloucestershire (1900, 2 matches).
Career batting
2–3–0–4–4–1.33–0–*ct* 2

Roberts, General Sir Ouvry Lindfield
Amateur. *b:* 3.4.1898, Bogawantalawa, Ceylon. Middle order right-hand batsman, wicket-keeper. *Sch* Cheltenham. *Team* Cambridge U (1925).
Career batting
3–6–0–38–10–6.33–0–*ct* 4–*st* 1
His final first-class match was for Free Foresters in 1926.

Roberts, Pascall
Amateur. *b:* 15.12.1937, Port of Spain, Trinidad. Lower order right-hand batsman, left-arm fast, later slow, bowler. *Team* Trinidad (1960/1 to 1971/2). *Tour* West Indies to England 1969.
Career batting
67–83–20–871–105*–13.82–1–*ct* 32
Bowling 5286–211–25.05–7–1–6/17
He achieved very little on the 1969 tour and did not appear in the Tests; earlier his bowling action had been criticised and he was no-balled for throwing in the West Indies in 1966/7. His final first-class match was for North Trinidad in 1978/9.

Roberts, R.
Amateur. Middle order batsman. *Team* Lancashire (1872–74, 10 matches).
Career batting
10–16–0–100–20–6.25–0–*ct* 9–*st* 5

Roberts, Simon Nicholas
Amateur. *b:* 11.9.1926, Durban, South Africa. Opening or middle order right-hand batsman, leg break bowler. *Team* Cambridge U (1947–49).
Career batting
6–11–1–158–49*–15.80–0–*ct* 0
Bowling 21–0

Roberts, William Braithwaite
Professional. *b:* 27.9.1914, Kirkham, Lancashire. *d:* 23.8.1951, Bangor, North Wales. Tail end right-hand batsman, slow left-arm bowler. *Team* Lancashire (1939–49, 114 matches).
Career batting
119–120–39–865–51–10.67–0–*ct* 61
Bowling 8296–392–21.16–25–3–8/50
He took 123 wickets, av 19.34, in 1946.

Robertson, Frank
Cricketer. *b:* 25.2.1944, Aberdeen, Scotland. Right-hand batsman, right-arm fast medium bowler. *Team* Scotland (1971–81).
Career batting
12–17–1–163–51–10.18–0–*ct* 3
Bowling 743–36–20.63–2–0–6/58

Robertson, Frederick Marrant
Amateur. *b:* 1843, Ramble, Jamaica. *d:* 28.3.1920, Kensington, London. Lower order batsman, right-arm medium pace bowler. *Sch* Rossall. *Team* Surrey (1877, 1 match).
Career batting
1–2–1–7–4–7.00–0–*ct* 0
Bowling 49–2–0–24.50–0–0–2/32

Robertson, George André
Amateur. *b:* 3.9.1929, St Jean-de-Luz, France. Lower order right-hand batsman, right-arm

medium pace bowler. *Sch* Ampleforth. *Team* Cambridge U (1950).
Career batting
2–2–1–7–7*–7.00–0–*ct* 0
Bowling 106–3–35.33–0–0–2/53

Robertson, George Pringle
Amateur. *b:* 23.8.1842, Hobart, Tasmania. *d:* 23.6.1895, Colac, Melbourne, Victoria, Australia. Middle order right-hand batsman. *Sch* Rugby *Teams* Oxford U (1866, blue); Victoria (1866/7 to 1871/2, 4 matches).
Career batting
9–14–1–234–53–18.00–0–*ct* 2
His County cricket was for Warwickshire.

Robertson, James
(changed to Robertson-Walker in 1893)
Amateur. *b:* 10.11.1850, Edinburgh, Scotland. *d:* 21.3.1927, Kensington, London. Lower order right-hand batsman, right-arm fast bowler, good slip. *Sch* Edinburgh Academy. *Team* Middlesex (1878–91, 102 matches).
Career batting
156–247–42–2102–62–10.25–0–*ct* 110
Bowling 9065–405–22.38–19–2–8/48
His first-class debut was for an England Eleven in 1877 and his final first-class match for MCC in 1892.
Whilst at Oxford University he did not appear in any first-class matches. He was on the MCC Committee.

Robertson, John David Benbow
Professional. *b:* 22.2.1917, Chiswick, Middlesex. Stylish opening right-hand batsman, right-arm off break bowler, good field. *Team* Middlesex (1937–59, 423 matches). *Tours* MCC to West Indies 1947/8, to India, Pakistan and Ceylon 1951/2. *Tests* England (1947 to 1951/2, 11 matches).
Career batting
509–897–46–31914–331*–37.50–67–*ct* 349
Bowling 2536–73–34.73–0–0–4/37
Test batting
11–21–2–881–133–46.36–2–*ct* 6
Bowling 58–2–29.00–0–0–2/17
He hit 1,000 runs in a season 14 times in England and once overseas, going on to 2,000 runs nine times (best 2,917, av 56.09, in 1951). His highest score was 331* for Middlesex v Worcs at Worcester in 1949 and he made three double centuries, all for his county.

Robertson, James Richard
Amateur. *b:* 18.6.1844, Hollingbourne, Kent. *d:* 6.8.1877, Folkestone, Kent. Son of J.C. (Oxford U 1829). *Sch* Cheltenham. *Team* Gentlemen of Kent (1863–64).
Career batting
2–4–1–39–13*–13.00–0–*ct* 1
Bowling 43–0

Robertson, L. G.
Amateur. Tail end batsman, bowler. *Team* D. R. Jardine's XI (1955).
Career batting
1–1–1–2–2*–no av–0–*ct* 2
Bowling 60–5–12.00–0–0–4/44

Robertson, William Parish
Amateur. *b:* 5.9.1879, Lima, Peru. *d:* 7.5.1950, Debden, Essex. Middle order right-hand batsman, wicket-keeper. *Sch* Harrow. *Teams* Middlesex (1900–19, 99 matches); Cambridge U (1901, blue). *Tour* Ranjitsinhji to USA 1899.
Career batting
116–187–13–4510–130–25.91–4–*ct* 61–*st* 15
Bowling 27–0
He hit 1,102 runs, av 27.55, in 1901. His first-class debut was for A. J. Webbe's XI in 1899.

Robertson-Glasgow, Raymond Charles
Amateur. *b:* 15.7.1901, Edinburgh, Scotland. *d:* 4.3.1965, Buckhold, Berks. He died by his own hand. Opening, later lower order, right-hand batsman, right-arm fast medium bowler. *Sch* Charterhouse. *Teams* Oxford U (1920–23, blue all four years); Somerset (1920–35, 77 matches).
Career batting
144–223–64–2102–80–13.22–0–*ct* 89
Bowling 11959–464–25.77–28–5–9/38
His final first-class match was for Free Foresters in 1937. He took 108 wickets, av 17.40, in 1923; his best bowling in an innings was 9 for 38 for Somerset v Middlesex at Lord's in 1924.
He was one of the most distinguished of cricket writers, both as a journalist for *The Morning Post* and other English newspapers and as an author of some notable books on the game.

Robins, Derrick Harold
Amateur. *b:* 27.6.1914, Bexleyheath, Kent. Lower order right-hand batsman, wicket-keeper. *Team* Warwickshire (1947, 2 matches).
Career batting
5–7–3–70–29*–17.50–0–*ct* 4
His final first-class match was for his own XI v Indians in 1971.
A great patron of cricket, he has taken teams of English cricketers regularly on overseas tours, including each winter from 1972/3 to 1979/80.

Robins, Glen Lello
Amateur. *b:* 23.10.1922, Kingston-on-Thames,

Surrey. Lower order batsman, left-arm slow bowler. *Sch* Merchant Taylors. *Team* Cambridge U (1947).
Career batting
1–2–1–0–0*–0.00–0–*ct* 0
Bowling 104–2–52.00–0–0–2/60

Robins, Robert Victor Charles
Amateur. *b:* 13.3.1935, Burnham, Bucks. Son of R. W. V. (Middlesex), nephew of W. V. H. (Army). Lower order right-hand batsman, leg break bowler. *Sch* Eton. *Team* Middlesex (1953–60, 44 matches). *Tours* MCC to East Africa 1957/8, to South America 1958/9; McAlpine to South Africa 1968/9 (none of these tours was first-class).
Career batting
60–92–9–1055–49–12.72–0–*ct* 19
Bowling 3597–107–33.61–3–0–7/78
His final first-class match was for MCC in 1962.

Robins, Robert Walter Vivian
Amateur. *b:* 3.6.1906, Stafford. *d:* 12.12.1968, Marylebone, London. Father of R. V. C. (Middlesex), brother of W. V. H. (Army). Middle order right-hand batsman, leg break bowler. *Sch* Highgate. *Teams* Cambridge U (1926–28, blue all three years); Middlesex (1925–51, 258 matches). *Tours* Cahn to Argentine 1929/30, to North America and Bermuda 1933 (not first-class); MCC to Australia 1936/7, to Canada 1951. *Tests* England (1929–37, 19 matches).
Career batting
379–565–39–13884–140–26.39–11–*ct* 221
Bowling 22580–969–23.30–54–4–8/69
Test batting
19–27–4–612–108–26.60–1–*ct* 12
Bowling 1758–64–27.46–1–0–6/32
He hit 1,000 runs in a season four times (best 1,397, av 31.04, in 1946) and in 1929 took 162 wickets, av 21.53, achieving the 'double' that season. His best bowling in an innings was 9 for 69 for Middlesex v Gloucs at Lord's in 1929. He captained Middlesex from 1935 to 1938, 1946, 1947 and 1950 and was a Test Selector in 1947 and 1948, then again 1962 to 1964, being Chairman in the last three years. He captained the MCC side to Canada in 1951 and was manager of the 1959/60 side to West Indies. A good soccer player, he was inside left for Cambridge and Nottm Forest.

Robins, William Vernon Harry
Amateur. *b:* 29.5.1907, Stafford. Brother of R. W. V. (Middlesex), uncle of R. V. C. (Middlesex). Middle order left-hand batsman, leg break and googly bowler. *Sch* University College School, London. *Teams* Army (1931–37); Madras (1937/8 to 1938/9).
Career batting
8–13–1–207–60–17.25–0–*ct* 3
Bowling 563–15–37.53–0–0–4/36

Robinson, Arthur
Amateur. *b:* 1855. *d:* 24.2.1913, Lawrence Weston, Gloucestershire. Father of D. C. and V. J. (Gloucs). Lower order right-hand batsman, right-arm slow bowler. *Team* Gloucestershire (1878, 3 matches).
Career batting
3–4–3–38–34*–38.00–0–*ct* 2

Robinson, Albert George
Professional. *b:* 22.3.1917, Leicester. Lower order right-hand batsman, right-arm fast medium pace bowler. *Sch* Wyggeston GS. *Team* Northamptonshire (1937–46, 24 matches).
Career batting
24–37–12–167–32–6.68–0–*ct* 13
Bowling 1464–35–41.82–1–0–5/37
He also played for Cambridgeshire and Berkshire.

Robinson, Arthur Herbert
Amateur. *b: circa* 1896, Dublin. *d:* 1937. Right-hand batsman. *Teams* Ireland (1924–29); Dublin University (1924).
Career batting
7–12–0–155–32–12.91–0–*ct* 3

Robinson, Arthur Leslie
Cricketer. *b:* 17.8.1946, Brompton, Yorkshire. Tail end left-hand batsman, left-arm fast medium bowler. *Team* Yorkshire (1971–77, 84 matches).
Career batting
84–69–31–365–30*–9.60–0–*ct* 46
Bowling 4927–196–25.13–7–0–6/61

Robinson, A. W.
Amateur. Middle order batsman. *Team* Worcestershire (1920–26, 6 matches).
Career batting
6–11–1–95–37–9.50–0–*ct* 2

Robinson, Canon Cyril Deason
Amateur. *b:* 18.7.1873, Durban, South Africa. *d:* 26.8.1948, Kearsney, Natal, South Africa. Lower order right-hand batsman, wicket-keeper. *Teams* Cambridge U (1895–96); Natal (1905/6 to 1910/11). *Tours* Mitchell to North America 1895; South Africa to England 1907.
Career batting
29–49–8–505–41–12.31–0–*ct* 31–*st* 17

He played in only six first-class matches on the 1907 tour, being the reserve wicket-keeper. He played County cricket for Buckinghamshire.

Robinson, Crescens James
Amateur. *b:* 21.5.1864, Gloucester. *d:* 8.6.1941, Chelsea, London. Brother of Theodore (Somerset). Middle order right-hand batsman. *Sch* Mill Hill. *Team* Somerset (1885–96, 31 matches).
Career batting
32–51–8–547–55–12.71–0–*ct* 19
Bowling 3–0
He also played for Suffolk.

Robinson, Douglas Charles
Amateur. *b:* 20.4.1884, Bristol. *d:* 30.7.1963, Charlton Kings, Gloucestershire. Son of Arthur, brother of V. J. (Gloucs). Lower order right-hand batsman, wicket-keeper. *Sch* Marlborough. *Teams* Essex (1908, 7 matches); Gloucestershire (1905–26, 124 matches). *Tour* Tennyson to Jamaica 1927/8 (he did not play in first-class matches).
Career batting
155–267–14–4376–150*–17.29–1–*ct* 123–*st* 39
He captained Gloucestershire from 1924 to 1926.

Robinson, Edward
Amateur. *b:* 19.12.1862, Yorkshire. *d:* 3.9.1942, Clifton, Bristol. *Team* Yorkshire (1887, 1 match).
Career batting
1–2–1–23–23*–23.00–0–*ct* 0

Robinson, Emmott
Professional. *b:* 16.11.1883, Keighley, Yorkshire. *d:* 17.11.1969, Hinckley, Leics. Middle order right-hand batsman, right-arm fast medium bowler, good cover point. *Team* Yorkshire (1919–31, 413 matches).
Career batting
416–460–78–9744–135*–25.50–7–*ct* 323
Bowling 19890–902–22.05–36–5–9/36
He hit 1,000 runs in a season twice (best 1,104, av 29.83, in 1921) and took 100 wickets once : 113, av 22.83, in 1928. His best bowling was 9 for 36 for Yorkshire v Lancashire at Bradford in 1920.

Robinson, Ellis P.
Professional. *b:* 10.8.1911, Denaby Main, Yorkshire. Nephew of G. L. (Notts). Attacking lower order left-hand batsman, off break bowler, excellent close field. *Teams* Somerset (1950–52, 90 matches); Yorkshire (1934–49, 208 matches). *Tour* Yorkshire to Jamaica 1935/6.
Career batting
301–388–71–3492–75*–11.01–0–*ct* 266
Bowling 22784–1009–22.58–61–12–8/35
He took 100 wickets in a season five times (best 167, av 14.95, in 1946).

Robinson, Sir Foster Gotch
Amateur. *b:* 19.9.1880, Sneyd Park, Bristol. *d:* 31.10.1967, East Harptree, Somerset. Brother of P. G. and father of J. F. (both Gloucestershire). Middle order right-hand batsman, wicket-keeper. *Sch* Clifton. *Teams* London County (1900); Gloucestershire (1903–23, 68 matches).
Career batting
71–122–2–2121–144–17.67–2–*ct* 47–*st* 28
He appeared in the Oxford Freshmen's Match in 1900. From 1919 to 1921 he captained Gloucestershire. A member of the Jockey Club, he was a noted owner-breeder.

Robinson, Geoffrey
Cricketer. *b:* 13.1.1944, Bridlington, Yorkshire. Attacking middle order left-hand batsman, slow left-arm bowler, wicket-keeper. *Team* Minor Counties (1971–72).
Career batting
2–4–0–100–36–25.00–0–*ct* 0
His County cricket is for Lincolnshire commencing 1965.

Robinson, George Adrian
Cricketer. *b:* 3.11.1949, Preston, Lancashire. Steady opening left-hand batsman, wicket-keeper. *Team* Oxford U (1970–71, blue 1971).
Career batting
14–25–0–573–62–22.92–0–*ct* 19–*st* 1

Robinson, George Edward
Amateur. *b:* 13.3.1861, Deytheur, Oswestry, Shropshire. *d:* 30.11.1944, Acton, Staffordshire. Lower order batsman, left-arm fast bowler. *Team* Oxford U (1881–83, blue all three years).
Career batting
17–30–11–168–28–8.84–0–*ct* 7
Bowling 1376–80–17.20–4–0–7/47
His County cricket was for Shropshire.

Robinson, George Lutha
(known as George Luther Robinson)
Professional. *b:* 22.2.1873, Ruddington, Nottinghamshire. *d:* 23.3.1930, Conisbrough, Yorkshire. Uncle of E. P. (Yorkshire and Somerset). Lower order right-hand batsman, leg break bowler. *Team* Nottinghamshire (1896, 5 matches).
Career batting
5–9–2–58–17–8.28–0–*ct* 2
Bowling 24–1–24.00–0–0–1/14

Robinson, George William
Professional until 1935, amateur in 1936. *b:*

15.2.1908, Kirkby in Ashfield, Notts. *d:* 16.7.1967, Basford, Notts. Lower order right-hand batsman, slow left-arm bowler. *Team* Nottinghamshire (1930–36, 21 matches).
Career batting
21–20–7–39–10–3.00–0–*ct* 4
Bowling 1196–46–26.00–0–0–4/54

A useful soccer player he appeared for Mansfield Town.

Robinson, Henry
Professional. *b:* 12.5.1858, Yorkshire. *d:* 14.12.1909. Lower order batsman, useful bowler. *Team* Yorkshire (1879, 1 match).
Career batting
1–2–0–5–4–2.50–0–*ct* 0
Bowling 20–1–20.00–0–0–1/20

Robinson, Henry
Professional. *b:* 13.11.1863, Nottingham. Middle order batsman. *Team* Nottinghamshire (1889, 1 match).
Career batting
1–2–0–0–0–0.00–0–*ct* 0

Robinson, Henry Basil Oswin
Amateur. *b:* 3.3.1919, Eastbourne, Sussex. Lower order right-hand batsman, right-arm slow off break bowler. *Teams* Oxford U (1947–48, blue both years); Canada (1951–54). *Tour* Canada to England 1954.
Career batting
24–31–7–325–51–13.54–0–*ct* 16
Bowling 1442–53–27.20–3–0–6/55

He captained the 1954 Canadian touring team to England.

Robinson, Jethro Frederick
Amateur. *b:* 10.8.1914, St Pancras, London. Lower order batsman, slow left-arm bowler. *Sch* King's, Canterbury. *Teams* Sussex (1935–36, 2 matches); Cambridge U (1936).
Career batting
3–4–0–11–5–2.75–0–*ct* 3
Bowling 166–8–20.75–1–0–5/47

Robinson, John Foster
Amateur. *b:* 2.2.1909, Bristol, Gloucestershire. Son of F. G. (Gloucestershire), nephew of P. G. (Gloucs). Lower order right-hand batsman, leg break and googly bowler. *Sch* Harrow. *Team* Gloucestershire (1929, 1 match).
Career batting
1 match, did not bat–*ct* 0
Bowling 50–0

He did not appear in any first-class matches for the University whilst at Oxford.

Robinson, John James
Amateur. *b:* 28.6.1872, Burton-on-Trent, Staffs. *d:* 3.1.1959, Headingley, Leeds, Yorkshire. Middle order right-hand batsman, right-arm bowler. *Team* Cambridge U (1894).
Career batting
10–18–6–173–29–14.41–0–*ct* 6
Bowling 690–28–24.64–2–0–7/93

His first-class debut was for MCC in 1893. An excellent rugby footballer, he played for Cambridge and England.

Robinson, John Sandford
Amateur. *b:* 5.2.1868, Arnold, Notts. *d:* 21.4.1898, Worksop, Notts. He died after a fall from his horse. Middle order right-hand batsman, wicket-keeper. *Sch* Harrow. *Team* Nottinghamshire (1888–96, 35 matches). *Tours* Hawke to India 1892/3, to North America 1894.
Career batting
48–74–7–751–72–11.20–0–*ct* 41–*st* 2
Bowling 3–0

He appeared in the Freshmen's and Seniors' matches at Cambridge, but no first-class games.

Robinson, Keith
Amateur. *b:* 17.12.1933, Wakefield, Yorkshire. Middle order batsman. *Team* Combined Services (1961).
Career batting
1–1–0–18–18–18.00–0–*ct* 0

Robinson, Kenneth Mark Lefebvre
Amateur. *b:* 1897, South Stoneham, Hampshire. *d:* 9.1.1963, Riverstone, Hampshire. Middle order right-hand batsman, right-arm medium pace bowler. *Team* Royal Navy (1927).
Career batting
1–2–0–14–13–7.00–0–*ct* 0

Robinson, Lancelot Charles Digby
Amateur. *b:* 23.10.1905. *d:* 31.5.1935, Quetta, India. He was killed with his wife by an earthquake, which almost destroyed Quetta. Steady middle order right-hand batsman, right-arm slow bowler, good field. *Sch* Bedford. *Team* MCC (1934).
Career batting
1–1–0–39–39–39.00–0–*ct* 0

His County cricket was for Bedfordshire.

Robinson, Maurice
Amateur. *b:* 16.7.1921, Lisburn, Co Antrim. Sound middle order right-hand batsman, right-arm fast medium bowler. *Teams* Europeans (1942/3 to 1944/5); Hyderabad (1943/4); Madras (1944/5); Glamorgan (1946–50, 66 matches); Warwickshire (1951–52, 8 matches).

Career batting
83–134–11–2719–190–22.10–2–*ct* 23
Bowling 870–34–25.58–2–0–7/51

Robinson, Miles Trevor
Amateur. *b:* 13.12.1929, Eastbourne, Sussex. Lower order left-hand batsman, right-arm medium fast bowler. *Sch* Shrewsbury. *Team* Sussex (1947, 2 matches).
Career batting
2–2–0–4–4–2.00–0–*ct* 0
Bowling 157–0

Robinson, Paul Andrew
Cricketer. *b:* 16.7.1956, Boksburg, South Africa. Lower order right-hand batsman, right-arm fast medium bowler. *Teams* Northern Transvaal (1977/8 to 1982/3); Lancashire (1979, 1 match).
Career batting
20–29–6–239–25*–10.39–0–*ct* 7
Bowling 1440–48–30.00–0–0–3/33
He appeared for Cheshire in 1978.

Robinson, Percy Gotch
Amateur. *b:* 2.11.1881, Bristol, Gloucestershire. *d:* 29.1.1951, Queen Charlton, Somerset. Brother of F. G. (Gloucs), uncle of J. F. (Gloucs). Middle order right-hand batsman. *Sch* Clifton. *Team* Gloucestershire (1904–21, 26 matches).
Career batting
28–50–1–899–66–18.34–0–*ct* 23
Bowling 799–17–47.00–1–0–5/60

Robinson, Peter James
Cricketer. *b:* 9.2.1943, Worcester. Nephew of R. O. Jenkins (Worcs). Opening or middle order left-hand batsman, slow left-arm bowler. *Teams* Somerset (1965–77, 180 matches); Worcestershire (1963–64, 5 matches).
Career batting
185–287–55–4936–140–21.27–3–*ct* 170
Bowling 8101–297–27.27–10–1–7/10
He hit 1,158 runs, av 26.93 in 1970. He is the present Somerset coach. A useful soccer player, he appeared for Worcester City.

Robinson, Peter Michael Heasty
Amateur. *b:* 14.10.1929, Trinidad. Middle order right-hand batsman, right-arm medium pace off break bowler. *Sch* Lancing. *Team* L. C. Steven's XI (1961).
Career batting
1–2–0–19–12–9.50–0–*ct* 0
Bowling 41–0

Robinson, Robert
Professional. *b:* 1765, Ash, Surrey. *d:* 2.9.1822 or 2.10.1822, Ash, Surrey. Hard hitting middle order left-hand batsman. *Teams* Hampshire (1792–1816); Surrey (1794–1810); Kent (1795); Middlesex (1815).
Career batting
59–113–9–2168–93–20.84–0–*ct* 11
Bowling 22 wickets, no analyses
Early in life he damaged the fingers of one hand in a fire and had the handle of his bat especially grooved to fit the injured hand. He made himself 'pads' of two thin angled boards to protect his legs, but being laughed at dispensed with them. Another of his innovations was a spiked shoe. His final first-class match was for Players in 1819.

Robinson, Richard Daryl
Cricketer. *b:* 8.6.1946, East Melbourne, Victoria, Australia. Opening or middle order right-hand batsman, wicket-keeper. *Team* Victoria (1971/2 to 1981/2, 76 matches). *Tours* Australia to England 1975, 1977. *Tests* Australia (1977, 3 matches).
Career batting
97–153–33–4776–185–39.80–7–*ct* 289–*st* 40
Test batting
3–6–0–100–34–16.66–0–*ct* 4
Coming to England in 1975 as reserve wicket-keeper, he was given few opportunities; in 1977 he was drafted into the Test side as a batsman, due to various injuries, but made little impact on the series.

Robinson, Robert Geoffrey
Professional. *b:* 23.9.1924, Wellingborough, Northants. *d:* 21.12.1973, Wellingborough, Northants. Middle order batsman, useful bowler. *Team* Northants (1946, 4 matches).
Career batting
4–8–1–85–53–12.14–0–*ct* 0
Bowling 90–0

Robinson, Ralf Hubert
Amateur. *b:* 1885, West Ham, Essex. *d:* 23.8.1917, Westhoek Ridge, Ypres, Belgium. Lower order batsman, wicket-keeper. *Team* Essex (1912, 4 matches).
Career batting
4–7–2–25–11*–5.00–0–*ct* 9–*st* 4

Robinson, Sir Roy Lister
(created 1st Baron Robinson in 1947)
Amateur. *b:* 8.3.1883, Macclesfield, near Adelaide, Australia. *d:* 5.9.1952, Ottawa, Canada. Lower order right-hand batsman, right-arm fast bowler. *Team* Oxford U (1908–09, blue both years).
Career batting
13–22–1–256–51–12.19–0–*ct* 7
Bowling 998–44–22.66–4–0–6/90
His final first-class match was for Gentlemen

of England in 1910. He also represented the University at lacrosse. He died of pnuemonia whilst leading the British Delegation to a Conference on Forestry.

Robinson, Raymond Thomas
Cricketer. *b:* 15.9.1940, Charmouth, Dorset. Middle order right-hand batsman. *Team* Somerset (1964, 1 match).
Career batting
1–2–0–0–0–0.00–0–*ct* 0

Robinson, Robert Timothy
Cricketer. *b:* 21.11.1958, Sutton-in-Ashfield, Notts. Sound opening right-hand batsman, right-arm medium pace bowler. *Team* Nottinghamshire (1978–83, 82 matches).
Career batting
82–142–17–4085–207–32.68–4–*ct* 39
Bowling 94–2–47.00–0–0–1/22

He hit 1,545 runs, av 40.65, in 1983. His highest innings is 207 for Notts v Warwickshire at Trent Bridge in 1983.

Robinson, Theodore
Amateur. *b:* 16.2.1866, Beaminster, Dorset. *d:* 4.10.1959, West Town, Somerset. Brother of C. J. (Somerset). Middle order batsman, bowler. *Team* Somerset (1884–94, 10 matches).
Career batting
10–18–0–152–57–8.44–0–*ct* 3
Bowling 86–2–43.00–0–0–2/80

He was a member of the well-known family who fielded a complete team for some years.

Robinson, Thomas Lloyd
Amateur. *b:* 21.12.1912, Swansea, Glamorgan. Lower order right-hand batsman, right-arm medium fast bowler. *Sch* Wycliffe. *Team* Warwickshire (1946, 4 matches).
Career batting
4–7–1–27–13*–4.50–0–*ct* 0
Bowling 277–6–46.16–0–0–2/74

Robinson, Vivian John
Amateur. *b:* 16.5.1897, Bristol, Gloucestershire. *d:* 28.2.1979, Henford, Wilts. Son of Arthur (Gloucs), brother of D. C. (Gloucs). Lower order right-hand batsman, right-arm fast medium bowler. *Team* Gloucestershire (1923, 1 match).
Career batting
1–2–0–2–2–1.00–0–*ct* 1

Robinson, Walter
Professional. *b:* 29.11.1851, Greetland, Yorkshire. *d:* 14.8.1919. Hard hitting middle order right-hand batsman, right-hand medium pace round-arm bowler, cover point. *Team* Lancashire (1880–88, 115 matches); Yorkshire (1876–77, 7 matches).
Career batting
129–213–11–3902–154–19.31–4–*ct* 52
Bowling 61–0

Robotham, Reginald
Amateur. *b:* 14.7.1911, Alcester, Warwickshire. *d:* 31.1.1978, Hastings, Sussex. Middle order batsman. *Team* Sussex (1946, 1 match).
Career batting
1–2–0–31–21–15.50–0–*ct* 1

Robson, Charles
Amateur. *b:* 20.6.1859, Twickenham, Middlesex. *d:* 27.9.1943, Abingdon, Berks. Lower order right-hand batsman, slow right-arm bowler, wicket-keeper. *Teams* Middlesex (1881–83, 12 matches); Hampshire (1895–1906, 129 matches); London County (1903–04). *Tours* Ranjitsihji to North America 1899; MacLaren to Australia 1901/2.
Career batting
160–278–26–3840–101–15.23–1–*ct* 201–*st* 45
Bowling 165–2–82.50–0–0–1/2

He captained Hampshire 1900 to 1902.

Robson, Clayton Graeme Wynne
Amateur. *b:* 3.7.1901, Bareilly, India. Middle order right-hand batsman. *Sch* Malvern. *Teams* Middlesex (1926, 4 matches); Worcestershire (1921, 2 matches).
Career batting
6–10–1–136–46–15.11–0–*ct* 2

Robson, Ernest
Professional. *b:* 1.5.1870, Chapel Allerton, Leeds, Yorkshire. *d:* 23.5.1924, Bristol. He died following an operation. Middle order right-hand batsman, right-arm fast medium bowler. *Teams* Somerset (1895–1923, 424 matches); London County (1900).
Career batting
432–761–45–12620–163*–17.62–5–*ct* 258
Bowling 30337–1147–26.44–58–5–8/35

He hit 1,048 runs, av 31.75, in 1899. He played for Cheshire 1891 to 1893.

Robson, Henry
Professional. *b:* 1904, Chester-le-Street, Co Durham. *d:* 31.8.1968, Chester-le-Street, Co Durham. Lower order left-hand batsman, slow left-arm bowler. *Team* Minor Counties (1939).
Career batting
1–1–0–3–3–3.00–0–*ct* 0
Bowling 124–4–31.00–0–0–4/80

His County cricket was for Northumberland and Durham.

Roche, William
Professional. *b:* 20.7.1871, South Australia. *d:* 2.1.1950, East Brunswick, Victoria, Australia. Lower order right-hand batsman, slow right-arm bowler. *Teams* Victoria (1894/5 to 1897/8, 13 matches); Middlessex (1899–1900, 28 matches).
Career batting
62–96–33–924–77–14.66–0–*ct* 30
Bowling 4520–181–24.97–13–1–8/66
His first-class debut in England was for MCC in 1897.

Rochford, Peter
Professional. *b:* 27.8.1928, Halifax, Yorkshire. Lower order right-hand batsman, wicket-keeper. *Team* Gloucestershire (1952–57, 80 matches).
Career batting
80–113–22–479–31*–5.25–0–*ct* 118–*st* 34
He was a first-class umpire 1975–77.

Rock, Claude William
Amateur. *b:* 9.6.1863, Deloraine, Tasmania. *d:* 27.7.1950, Longford, Tasmania. Brother of N. V. (Tasmania), father of H. C. (New South Wales). Steady middle order right-hand batsman, right-hand medium pace round-arm bowler. *Teams* Cambridge U (1884–86, blue all three years); Tasmania (1888/9 to 1892/3, 3 matches).
Career batting
31–55–5–809–102–16.18–1–*ct* 38
Bowling 2350–142–16.54–13–5–8/36
He played County cricket for Warwickshire (pre-first-class).

Rock, David John
Cricketer. *b:* 20.4.1957, Southsea, Hampshire. Opening or middle order right-hand batsman, right-arm medium pace bowler. *Team* Hampshire (1976–79, 37 matches).
Career batting
37–65–1–1227–114–19.17–3–*ct* 19
Bowling 0–0

Rodger, Sir John Pickersgill
Amateur. *b:* 12.2.1851, Westminster, London. *d:* 19.9.1910, Mayfair, London. Brother of W. W. (Kent). Sound middle order right-hand batsman. *Sch* Eton. *Team* Kent (1870, 1 match).
Career batting
1–2–0–7–4–3.50–0–*ct* 0
He played in one or two trials at Oxford, but no first-class matches. For seven years he was Governor of the Gold Coast, retiring a few days before his death.

Rodger, Richard Gordon
Cricketer. *b:* 1.10.1947, Norwich. Middle order batsman, useful bowler. *Team* Scotland (1975).
Career batting
1–2–0–2–2–1.00–0–*ct* 0
Bowling 38–0
He also played for Cheshire.

Rodger, William Wallace
(changed his name to Rodger-Cunliffe in 1887) Amateur. *b:* 13.1.1847, Marylebone, London. *d:* 23.10.1888, Barming Heath, Kent. Brother of J. F. (Kent). Middle order right-hand batsman. *Sch* Eton. *Team* Kent (1867–73, 17 matches).
Career batting
19–35–2–304–32–9.21–0–*ct* 3
Bowling 20–0
He did not play in any first-class matches whilst at Oxford University. His first-class debut was for Gentlemen of Kent in 1865. One of the leading billiards players of his day, he won the Champion Cue at Oxford and represented Oxford against Cambridge three times, afterwards playing in several notable contests.

Rodriguez, Chevalier Epifanio
Amateur. *b:* 1855. *d:* 20.12.1912, Westminster, London. Middle order batsman. *Team* MCC (1900).
Career batting
1–2–1–1–1*–1.00–0–*ct* 0

Rodriguez, William Vincente
Amateur. *b:* 25.6.1934, Woodbrook, Port of Spain, Trinidad. Middle order right-hand batsman, leg break and googly bowler. *Team* Trinidad (1953/4 to 1969/70). *Tours* West Indies to India and Pakistan 1958/9, to England 1963. *Tests* West Indies (1961/2 to 1967/8, 5 matches).
Career batting
64–98–15–2061–105–24.83–1–*ct* 36
Bowling 3342–119–28.08–8–0–7/90
Test batting
5–7–0–96–50–13.71–0–*ct* 3
Bowling 374–7–53.42–0–0–3/51
He played in one Test on the 1963 tour, but his opportunites were restricted due to cartilage trouble.

Rodwell, William Hunter
Amateur. *b:* 18.4.1850, London. *d:* 3.8.1929, Amersham, Bucks. Middle order batsman. *Sch* Harrow. *Team* MCC (1882).
Career batting
1–2–0–32–31–16.00–0–*ct* 1
His County cricket was for Suffolk and Essex (pre-first-class).

Roe, Brian
Professional. *b:* 27.1.1939, Cleethorpes, Lincs.

Opening right-hand batsman. *Team* Somerset (1957–66, 131 matches).
Career batting
136–234–9–5010–128–22.26–4–*ct* 45
Bowling 104–2–52.00–0–0–1/43

He hit 1,000 runs in a season three times (best 1,552, av 26.30, in 1962). He also played for Devon.

Roe, William Nicholas
Amateur. *b:* 21.3.1861, Closworth, Somerset. *d:* 11.10.1937, Marylebone, London. Stylish middle order right-hand batsman, right-arm medium pace off break bowler, good deep field. *Sch* Clergy School, Canterbury. *Teams* Cambridge U (1882–83, blue 1883); Somerset (1882–99, 66 matches).
Career batting
83–141–8–2690–132–20.22–4–*ct* 35
Bowling 1005–32–31.40–0–0–3/17

He hit 415 not out for the Emmanuel Long Vacation Club v Caius Long Vacation Club in 1881.

Roebuck, Paul Gerrard Peter
Cricketer. *b:* 13.10.1963, Bath, Somerset. Brother of P.M. (Somerset). Lower order left-hand batsman, right-arm medium fast bowler. *Sch* Millfield. *Team* Cambridge U (1983).
Career batting
5–7–3–82–31*–20.50–0–*ct* 1
Bowling 269–6–44.83–0–0–2/44

Roebuck, Peter Michael
Cricketer. *b:* 6.3.1956, Oxford. Brother of P. G. P. (Cambridge U). Middle order right-hand batsman, off break bowler. *Sch* Millfield. *Teams* Somerset (1974–83, 153 matches); Cambridge U (1975–77, blue all three years).
Career batting
182–305–48–8288–158–32.24–6–*ct* 96
Bowling 2004–42–47.71–1–0–6/50

He hit 1,000 runs in a season three times (best 1,273, av 47.14, in 1979).

Rogers, Basil Leonard
Professional. *b:* 20.6.1896, Bedford. *d:* 1975, near Ripon, Yorkshire. Middle order batsman, useful bowler. *Team* Glamorgan (1923, 2 matches).
Career batting
2–4–1–46–16*–15.33–0–*ct* 0
Bowling 33–1–33.00–0–0–1/22

He also played for Bedfordshire and Oxfordshire.

Rogers, Francis Galpin
Amateur. *b:* 7.4.1897, Bristol. *d:* 28.7.1967, Dorchester, Dorset. Forcing middle order right-hand batsman. *Teams* Gloucestershire (1924–31, 26 matches); Europeans (1924/5 to 1932/3); Madras (1933/4).
Career batting
37–63–4–1309–154–22.18–1–*ct* 22

Rogers, George Howard
Professional. *b:* 1905, Camborne, Cornwall. *d:* 1958, Camborne, Cornwall. Middle order right-hand batsman. *Team* Minor Counties (1939).
Career batting
1–2–0–8–8–4.00–0–*ct* 0

His County cricket was for Cornwall.

Rogers, George John
Professional. *b:* 1.5.1815, Hackney, Middlesex. *d:* 2.9.1870, Holloway, Middlesex. Middle order right-hand batsman. *Team* Middlesex (1850–51, 3 matches).
Career batting
9–14–0–116–36–8.28–0–*ct* 9

His final first-class match was for the Surrey Club in 1854.

Rogers, George Russell
Amateur. *b:* 20.4.1847, West Brixton, Surrey. *d:* 14.12.1905, Kensington, London. Middle order right-hand batsman. *Team* Surrey (1870, 5 matches).
Career batting
5–10–1–34–18–3.77–0–*ct* 2

Rogers, Herbert James
Professional. *b:* 1893, Godalming, Surrey. Middle order left-hand batsman, off break bowler. *Team* Hampshire (1912–14, 7 matches).
Career batting
7–12–0–69–18–5.75–0–*ct* 0
Bowling 62–1–62.00–0–0–1/26

The Hampshire Year Book for many years carried a 'Roll of Honour' for the First World War which included Rogers – there are however a number of people of this name in the War Death records and it has not been possible to identify him.

Rogers, Harry Oliver
Professional. *b:* 21.1.1889, Hednesford, Staffs. *d:* 4.7.1956, Worcester. Lower order left-hand batsman, right-arm medium pace bowler. *Team* Worcestershire (1923–28, 86 matches).
Career batting
86–146–31–1683–118*–14.62–1–*ct* 32
Bowling 3705–138–26.84–5–1–8/85

Rogers, Joseph Alfred
Professional. *b:* 1.2.1908, Oxford. *d:* 25.3.1965, Chelmsford, Essex. Lower order right-hand

batsman, right-arm fast bowler. *Team* Gloucestershire (1929–33, 46 matches).
Career batting
46–56–2–461–59–8.53–0–*ct* 22
Bowling 1644–45–36.53–0–0–4/50
He also played for Oxfordshire.

Rogers, John Hickling
Amateur. *b:* 7.8.1910, Birkenhead, Cheshire. Middle order right-hand batsman. *Sch* Birkenhead. *Team* Oxford U (1932).
Career batting
3–5–0–26–9–5.20–0–*ct* 2
His County cricket was for Cheshire.

Rogers, James Julian
Cricketer. *b:* 20.8.1958, Kendal, Westmorland. Middle order right-hand batsman, right-arm slow bowler. *Sch* Sedbergh. *Team* Oxford U (1979–81, blue all three years).
Career batting
26–45–3–693–54–16.50–0–*ct* 7
Bowling 39–1–39.00–0–0–1/24
His County cricket was for Cumberland.

Rogers, John Phillips
Amateur. *b:* 1860, Hackney, Middlesex. Lower order batsman, wicket-keeper. *Team* Middlesex (1891, 1 match).
Career batting
1–2–1–7–7*–7.00–0–*ct* 1

Rogers, Neville Hamilton
Professional. *b:* 9.3.1918, Oxford. Sound opening right-hand batsman, excellent field. *Team* Hampshire (1946–55, 285 matches).
Career batting
298–529–28–16056–186–32.04–28–*ct* 197
Bowling 37–0
He hit 1,000 runs in a season nine times, going on to 2,000 once : 2,244, av 40.80, in 1952. He also played for Oxfordshire.

Rogers, Peter James
Cricketer. *b:* 28.12.1928, Swansea, Glamorgan. Lower order batsman, useful bowler. *Team* MCC (1967).
Career batting
1–2–1–24–24*–24.00–0–*ct* 0
Bowling 95–0

Rogers, Rupert Ashley Cave
(known as Cave-Rogers)
Amateur. *b:* 27.5.1902, Cannock, Staffs. *d:* 2.5.1976, Eastbourne, Sussex. Opening batsman. *Sch* Malvern. *Team* Worcestershire (1919, 1 match).
Career batting
1–1–0–3–3–3.00–0–*ct* 1
Bowling 25–0

Rogers, Stuart Scott
Amateur. *b:* 18.3.1923, Muswell Hill, Middlesex. *d:* 6.11.1969, Chartridge, Bucks. Attacking middle order right-hand batsman, excellent field. *Sch* Highgate. *Teams* Europeans (1946/7); Somerset (1948–53, 118 matches).
Career batting
119–202–11–3608–107*–18.89–3–*ct* 46
Bowling 145–2–72.50–0–0–2/13
He played for Cambridge U against Oxford in 1942 (not first-class). From 1950 to 1952 he was captain and secretary of Somerset. He hit 1,127 runs, av 25.61, in 1950.

Rogerson, George Henry
Amateur. *b:* 1896, Nantwich, Cheshire. *d:* 1961, Crewe, Cheshire. Middle order right-hand batsman. *Team* Lancashire (1923, 12 matches).
Career batting
12–20–1–340–47*–17.89–0–*ct* 3

Roll, Henry (Trevor)
Professional. *b:* 18.3.1905, Alloa, Scotland. *d:* 25.5.1967, Downend, Gloucs. Middle order right-hand batsman, right-arm medium pace bowler. *Team* Warwickshire (1927, 1 match).
Career batting
1–1–0–0–0–0.00–0–*ct* 1
Bowling 40–0
He was a noted batsman in London Club cricket for some years.

Roller, Charles Trevor
Amateur. *b:* 28.2.1865, Clapham Common, Surrey. *d:* 15.11.1912, Eastbourne, Sussex. Brother of W. E. (Surrey). Middle order right-hand batsman, right-arm medium pace bowler, third man. *Sch* Westminster. *Team* Surrey (1886, 1 match).
Career batting
1–2–0–15–14–7.50–0–*ct* 0

Roller, William Eyton
Amateur. *b:* 1.2.1858, Clapham Common, Surrey. *d:* 27.8.1949, Bayswater, London. Brother of C. T. (Surrey). Forceful middle order right-hand batsman, right-arm medium pace bowler, good field, occasional wicket-keeper. *Sch* Westminster. *Team* Surrey (1881–90, 102 matches). *Tours* Sanders to North America 1885, 1886.
Career batting
120–193–12–3820–204–21.10–7–*ct* 75
Bowling 3728–190–19.62–4–0–6/44

He did not appear in any first-class matches whilst at Cambridge – one of the best cricketers who was not awarded a blue. His highest score was 204 for Surrey v Sussex at the Oval in 1885. He was also a noted golfer.

Rollins, Herbert
Amateur. *b:* 29.12.1899, Dublin. *d:* 17.6.1921, Dublin. Right-hand batsman. *Team* Ireland (1920).
Career batting
1–2–0–11–8–5.50–0–*ct* 1

Romaines, Paul William
Cricketer. *b:* 25.12.1955, Bishop Auckland, Co Durham. Middle order right-hand batsman, right-arm medium pace bowler. *Teams* Northamptonshire (1975–76, 6 matches); Gloucestershire (1982–83, 37 matches).
Career batting
43–74–7–1951–186–29.11–4–*ct* 15
Bowling 9–0
He played for Durham 1977 to 1981. He hit 1,286 runs, av 34.75, in 1983.

Romans, George
Amateur. *b:* 30.11.1876, Gloucester. *d:* 2.1.1946, Bedminster, Somerset. Middle order right-hand batsman. *Team* Gloucestershire (1899–1903, 11 matches).
Career batting
11–19–3–218–62–13.62–0–*ct* 4
A good rugby footballer, he played full back for Gloucestershire.

Rome, David Aubrey Moberley
Amateur. *b:* 14.4.1910, Marylebone, London. *d:* 20.5.1970, Kennington. He died as the result of a fall at the Oval. Middle order right-hand batsman, right-arm medium pace bowler. *Sch* Harrow. *Team* Middlesex (1930–33, 4 matches). *Tours* Martineau to Egypt 1935, 1936 and 1937 (not first-class).
Career batting
4–6–0–56–32–9.33–0–*ct* 1
Bowling 11–0
He appeared in the Freshmen's and Seniors' matches at Cambridge and was later a major figure in the Free Foresters and I Zingari. For many years he was a member of Surrey CCC Committee.

Romney, Francis William
Amateur. *b:* 25.11.1873, Tewkesbury, Gloucestershire. *d:* 28.1.1963, Malvern, Worcestershire. Middle order right-hand batsman. *Sch* Malvern. *Team* Worcestershire (1900, 4 matches).
Career batting
4–7–3–39–20*–9.75–0–*ct* 0

Rooney, E. A.
Amateur. Middle order batsman. *Team* Ireland (1913–14).
Career batting
2–3–1–34–12*–17.00–0–*ct* 1

Roope, Graham Richard James
Cricketer. *b:* 12.7.1946, Fareham, Hants. Middle order right-hand batsman, right-arm medium pace bowler, brilliant slip field. *Sch* Bradfield. *Teams* Surrey (1964–82, 342 matches); Griqualand West (1973/4). *Tours* MCC to Ceylon and Far East 1969/70, to Pakistan, India and Sri Lanka 1972/3; Robins to South Africa 1973/4; England to Pakistan and New Zealand 1977/8; International XI to South Africa 1973/4, 1974/5, 1975/6. *Tests* England (1972/3 to 1978, 21 matches).
Career batting
401–644–129–19037–171–36.96–26–*ct* 599–*st* 2
Bowling 8395–225–37.31–4–0–5/14
Test batting
21–32–4–860–77–30.71–0–*ct* 35
Bowling 76–0
He hit 1,000 runs in a season eight times (best 1,641, av 44.35, in 1971). He appeared for Berkshire in 1963 and returned to that County in 1983. A useful soccer player, he kept goal for Corinthian Casuals.

Roopnaraine, Rupert
Cricketer. *b:* 31.1.1943, Georgetown, British Guiana. Lower order right-hand batsman, off break bowler. *Team* Cambridge U (1964–66, blue 1965–66).
Career batting
29–52–14–302–50*–7.94–0–*ct* 7
Bowling 2119–58–34.81–2–0–8/88

Root, Charles Frederick
Professional. *b:* 16.4.1890, Somercotes, Derbyshire. *d:* 20.1.1954, Wolverhampton, Staffs. Hard hitting lower order right-hand batsman, right-arm fast medium pace bowler. *Teams* Derbyshire (1910–20, 57 matches); Worcestershire (1921–32, 284 matches). *Tour* MCC to West Indies 1925/6. *Tests* England (1926, 3 matches).
Career batting
365–586–51–7911–107–14.78–1–*ct* 243
Bowling 31933–1512–21.11–125–33–9/23
Test batting
3 matches, did not bat–*ct* 1
Bowling 194–8–24.25–0–0–4/84
He took 100 wickets in a season nine times, going on to 200 once : 219, av 17.21, in 1925. In 1928 he hit 1,044 runs, av 20.88, and achieved the

'double' for the only time in his career. Three times he captured nine wickets in an innings, his best analysis being 9 for 23 for Worcs v Lancashire at Worcester in 1931. After retiring from first-class cricket he became well-known as a sporting journalist.

Roper, Arthur William
Amateur. *b:* 20.2.1917, Petersham, New South Wales, Australia. *d:* 4.9.1972, Woy Woy, New South Wales, Australia. Lower order right-hand batsman, right-arm fast medium bowler. *Team* New South Wales (1939/40, 2 matches). *Tours* Australian Services to England 1945, to India and Ceylon 1945/6.
Career batting
11–15–0–102–28–6.80–0–*ct* 11
Bowling 503–13–38.69–0–0–2/9

Roper, Arthur William Frederick
Amateur. *b:* 1890, Bedminster, Gloucester. *d:* 21.6.1956, Marylebone, London. Middle order batsman. *Team* Gloucestershire (1920–21, 13 matches).
Career batting
13–21–2–226–55–11.89–0–*ct* 7
Bowling 7–0

Roper, Colin
Professional. *b:* 25.7.1936, Dorchester, Dorset. Lower order right-hand batsman, wicket-keeper. *Team* Hampshire (1957, 1 match).
Career batting
1–1–0–7–7–7.00–0–*ct* 1
He also played for Dorset.

Roper, Donald George B.
Amateur. *b:* 14.12.1922, Botley, Hants. Middle order batsman. *Team* Hampshire (1947, 1 match).
Career batting
1–2–0–30–30–15.00–0–*ct* 0
A well-known soccer player, he appeared for Southampton and Arsenal.

Roper, Edward
Amateur. *b:* 8.4.1851, Richmond, Yorkshire. *d:* 24.4.1921, South Liverpool. He died after an appendicitis operation. Middle order right-hand batsman. *Sch* Clifton. *Teams* Lancashire (1876–86, 28 matches); Yorkshire (1878–80, 5 matches).
Career batting
36–59–3–715–68–12.76–0–*ct* 9
Bowling 6–1–6.00–0–0–1/6
His final first-class match was for Liverpool and District XI in 1893. He was for many years involved in the organisation of cricket in the Liverpool area.

Rose, Alfred
Professional. *b:* 15.2.1894, Glossop, Derbyshire. Middle order right-hand batsman. *Team* Derbyshire (1924, 1 match).
Career batting
1–1–0–0–0–0.00–0–*ct* 0

Rose, Brian Charles
Cricketer. *b:* 4.6.1950, Dartford, Kent. Opening left-hand batsman, left-arm medium pace bowler. *Team* Somerset (1969–83, 172 matches). *Tours* England to Pakistan and New Zealand 1977/8, to West Indies 1980/1. *Tests* England (1977/8 to 1980/1, 9 matches).
Career batting
228–379–40–11340–205–33.45–22–*ct* 113
Bowling 224–6–37.33–0–0–3/9
Test batting
9–16–2–358–70–25.57–0–*ct* 4
He hit 1,000 runs in a season eight times (best 1,624, av 46.40, in 1976). His only double century was 205 for Somerset v Northants at Weston-super-Mare in 1977. He captained Somerset from 1978 to 1983.

Rose, Edward McQueen
Amateur. *b:* 2.9.1936, Oxted, Surrey. Middle order left-hand batsman. *Sch* Rugby. *Team* Cambridge U (1958–60).
Career batting
24–47–2–700–57–15.55–0–*ct* 8
Bowling 19–1–19.00–0–0–1/9

Rose, John
Professional. *b:* 24.12.1853, Warwick. *d:* 6.11.1920, Tiddington, Warwickshire. Lower order right-hand batsman, slow right-arm bowler, wicket-keeper. *Team* Surrey (1878, 1 match).
Career batting
1–2–0–0–0–0.00–0–*ct* 0
Bowling 2–1–2.00–0–0–1/2
He also played for Warwickshire (pre-first-class).

Rose, Michael Harrison
Cricketer. *b:* 8.4.1942, Hereford. Middle order right-hand batsman, excellent outfield. *Sch* Pocklington. *Teams* Cambridge U (1962–64, blue 1963–64); Leicestershire (1963–64, 4 matches).
Career batting
31–52–4–808–86–16.83–0–*ct* 11
Bowling 0–0

Rose, Thomas Ginnever
Professional. *b:* 16.3.1901, Ilkeston, Derbyshire. *d:* 8.8.1979, St Ives, Cornwall. Lower order left-hand batsman, slow left-arm bowler. *Team* Worcestershire (1922, 6 matches).

Career batting
6–10–1–47–15–5.22–0–*ct* 1
Bowling 219–7–31.28–0–0–3/68

Rose, William Molyneux
Amateur. *b:* 20.9.1842, London. *d:* 13.1.1917, Wolston, Warwickshire. Lower order right-hand batsman, right-hand slow under-arm bowler. *Sch* Eton. *Team* MCC (1867–71). *Tour* Fitzgerald to North America 1872 (not first-class).
Career batting
7–10–2–35–12–4.37–0–*ct* 10
Bowling 219–23–9.52–2–1–8/71
His County cricket was for Buckinghamshire.

Ross, Alexander
Amateur. *b:* 3.1.1895, Arbroath, Angus, Scotland. *d:* 12.12.1972, Gosport, Hampshire. Tail end right-hand batsman, wicket-keeper. *Team* Civil Service (1927).
Career batting
1–2–1–1–1–1.00–0–*ct* 0

Ross, Arthur Annesley Somerset Luce
Amateur. *b:* 13.7.1869, Bathampton, Somerset. *d:* 9.4.1947, Hove, Sussex. Opening or middle order batsman. *Sch* Bath College. *Team* Cambridge U (1889).
Career batting
2–3–0–24–17–8.00–0–*ct* 0

Ross, Arthur Patrick Aloysius
Amateur. *b: circa* 1870, Dublin. Middle order batsman. *Sch* Downside. *Team* Dublin University (1895).
Career batting
2–4–0–22–11–5.50–0–*ct* 0

Ross, Charles Hoadley Ashe
Amateur. *b:* 22.7.1852, Bath, Somerset. *d:* 5.2.1911, Hove, Sussex. Brother of Hamilton (Middlesex and Somerset). Attacking opening right-hand batsman, right-arm fast bowler, wicket-keeper. *Team* Middlesex (1875, 2 matches).
Career batting
3–6–1–19–10–3.80–*ct* 2

Ross, Christopher Jonathan
Cricketer. *b:* 24.6.1954, Warri, Nigeria. Tail end right-hand batsman, right-arm medium pace bowler. *Teams* Wellington (1975/6); Oxford U (1978–80, blue all three years).
Career batting
31–41–13–132–23*–4.71–0–*ct* 8
Bowling 1938–55–35.23–0–0–4/34

Ross, Hamilton
Amateur. *b:* 26.8.1849, Grenada, West Indies. *d:* 29.3.1938, Grenada, West Indies. Brother of C. H. A. (Middlesex). Middle order right-hand batsman, wicket-keeper. *Teams* Middlesex (1876, 1 match); Somerset (1883–91, 5 matches).
Career batting
20–35–1–337–91–9.91–0–*ct* 9–*st* 2
His first-class debut was for the Gentlemen in 1874.

Ross, Nigel Douglas Carne
Amateur. *b:* 21.12.1882, Penzance, Cornwall. *d:* 27.1.1933, Manchester. Middle order batsman. *Sch* Uppingham. *Team* Cambridge U (1905).
Career batting
1–2–0–38–26–19.00–0–*ct* 2
His County cricket was for Buckinghamshire.

Ross, Nigel Patrick Dorai
Cricketer. *b:* 5.4.1953, Chelsea, London. Middle order right-hand batsman, wicket-keeper. *Team* Middlesex (1973–77, 25 matches).
Career batting
25–36–3–506–53–15.33–0–*ct* 21
Bowling 13–0

Ross, Nicholas Peter Gilbert
Cricketer. *b:* 2.10.1947, Edinburgh, Scotland. Lower order left-hand batsman, leg break and googly bowler. *Sch* Marlborough. *Team* Cambridge U (1969–70, blue 1969).
Career batting
8–14–6–224–68–28.00–0–*ct* 5
Bowling 261–9–29.00–0–0–2/22
He played County cricket for Cambridgeshire.

Ross, P. C.
Amateur. Right-hand batsman, useful bowler. *Team* Ireland (1912).
Career batting
1–2–0–29–26–14.50–0–*ct* 0
Bowling 99–2–49.50–0–0–2/99

Ross, Thomas Couland
Amateur. *b:* 14.2.1872, Belfast. *d:* 2.1.1947, Foxrock, Co Dublin. Right-hand batsman, off break bowler. *Team* Ireland (1902–10).
Career batting
10–19–3–320–89–20.00–0–*ct* 8
Bowling 901–46–19.58–5–0–7/82

Rotherham, Gerard Alexander
Amateur. *b:* 28.5.1899, Coventry, Warwickshire. Lower order right-hand batsman, right-arm medium pace bowler. *Sch* Rugby. *Teams*

Cambridge U (1919–20, blue 1919); Warwickshire (1919–21, 44 matches); Wellington (1928/9).
Career batting
65–107–11–1801–84*–18.76–0–*ct* 48
Bowling 5105–180–28.36–8–0–7/69

Rotherham, Hugh
Amateur. *b:* 16.3.1861, Coventry, Warwickshire. *d:* 24.2.1939, Coventry, Warwickshire. Lower order right-hand batsman, right-hand fast round-arm bowler, wicket-keeper. *Sch* Uppingham. *Team* Warwickshire (1903, 1 match). *Tour* Sanders to North America 1886.
Career batting
23–32–7–179–33–7.16–0–*ct* 21
Bowling 2004–101–19.84–8–2–8/57
His first-class debut was for An England XII in 1880. For several years in the 1880s he lived in Australia. A noted rugby three-quarter, he played for Coventry.

Rothery, James William
Professional. *b:* 5.9.1877, Staincliffe, Yorkshire. *d:* 2.6.1919, Leeds, Yorkshire. He died as the result of wounds received in the war. Stylish middle order right-hand batsman. *Team* Yorkshire (1903–10, 150 matches).
Career batting
151–238–18–4619–161–20.99–3–*ct* 45
Bowling 44–2–22.00–0–0–1/18
He also played for Durham.

Rothschild, Lord Nathaniel Mayer Victor
Amateur. *b:* 31.10.1910, Kensington, London. Stylish opening right-hand batsman, right-arm slow leg break bowler, good slip. *Sch* Harrow. *Teams* Northamptonshire (1929–31, 10 matches); Cambridge U (1930).
Career batting
11–19–1–282–63–15.66–0–*ct* 8
Bowling 53–0

Rought-Rought, Basil William
Amateur. *b:* 15.9.1904, Brandon, Suffolk. Brother of D. C. (Cambridge U) and R. C. (Cambridge U). Middle order left-hand batsman. *Team* Minor Counties (1937–38).
Career batting
4–8–0–229–61–28.62–0–*ct* 3
His County cricket was for Norfolk. His first-class debut was for H. D. G. Leveson-Gower's XI in 1933.

Rought-Rought, Desmond Charles
Amateur. *b:* 3.5.1912, Brandon, Suffolk. *d:* 7.1.1970, Cambridge. He died following a road accident. Brother of B. W. (Minor Counties) and R. C. (Cambridge U). Attacking middle order right-hand batsman, right-arm fast medium bowler. *Team* Cambridge U (1934–37, blue 1937).
Career batting
24–39–5–739–92–21.73–0–*ct* 16
Bowling 2129–74–28.77–3–1–7/100
His County cricket was for Norfolk and his final first-class match for Free Foresters in 1947.

Rought-Rought, Rodney Charles
Amateur. *b:* 17.2.1908, Brandon, Suffolk. *d:* 5.5.1979, Fulham, London. He died following an accident. Brother of D. C. (Cambridge U) and B. W. (Minor Counties). Hard hitting lower order right-hand batsman, fast medium bowler. *Team* Cambridge U (1930–32, blue 1930 and 1932).
Career batting
34–51–18–457–52–13.84–0–*ct* 17
Bowling 2892–122–23.70–6–2–7/36
His County cricket was for Norfolk and his final first-class match for Free Foresters in 1937.

Round, Charles James
Amateur. *b:* 3.9.1885, Kensington, London. *d:* 6.10.1945, Birch, Essex. Son of James (Oxford U). Lower order batsman, bowler. *Sch* Eton and Winchester. *Team* Essex (1921, 2 matches).
Career batting
2–4–0–9–8–2.25–0–*ct* 0
Bowling 62–1–62.00–0–0–1/49

Round, Rt Hon James
Amateur. *b:* 6.4.1842, Colchester, Essex. *d:* 24.12.1916, Birch Hall, Essex. Father of C. J. (Essex), father-in-law of C. E. Higginbotham (Army). Defensive lower order right-hand batsman, right-hand under-arm bowler, wicket-keeper. *Sch* Eton. *Team* Oxford U (1864).
Career batting
22–34–6–472–142–16.85–1–*ct* 20–*st* 14
His County cricket was for Essex (pre-first-class). His final first-class match was for MCC in 1869. For 38 years he represented East and North East Essex in the House of Commons.

Roundell, James
Cricketer. *b:* 23.10.1951, Nantwich, Cheshire. Tail end left-hand batsman, right-arm medium fast bowler. *Sch* Winchester. *Team* Cambridge U (1973, blue).
Career batting
10–14–9–36–10*–7.20–0–*ct* 1
Bowling 509–9–56.55–0–0–3/12

Rouse, Stephen John
Cricketer. *b:* 20.1.1949, Merthyr Tydfil, Glamorgan. Left-hand batsman, left-arm medium

pace bowler. *Team* Warwickshire (1970–81, 124 matches). *Tours* Robins to South Africa 1974/5, West Indies 1974/5 (not first-class).
Career batting
127–156–34–1924–93–15.77–0–*ct* 55
Bowling 8312–270–30.78–5–0–6/34

Routledge, Reginald
Professional. *b:* 12.6.1920, North Kensington, London. Aggressive middle order right-hand batsman, right-arm medium pace bowler. *Team* Middlesex (1946–54, 64 matches).
Career batting
65–98–18–1331–121–16.63–2–*ct* 38
Bowling 1604–38–42.21–0–0–4/29
He played for Devon in 1947.

Rowan, Athol Matthew Burchell
Amateur. *b:* 7.2.1921, Johannesburg, South Africa. Brother of E. A. B. (South Africa). Lower order right-hand batsman, off break bowler, good field. *Team* Transvaal (1939/40 to 1949/50). *Tours* South Africa to England 1947, 1951. *Tests* South Africa (1947–51, 15 matches).
Career batting
58–82–20–1492–100*–24.06–1–*ct* 25
Bowling 6408–273–23.47–20–7–9/19
Test batting
15–23–6–290–41–17.05–0–*ct* 7
Bowling 2084–54–38.59–4–0–5/68
He was the only tourist to take 100 wickets on the 1947 tour : 102, av 24.97, but was expensive in the Tests. In 1951 he was troubled with a knee injury and bowled less, though being more effective in the Tests. His best bowling was 9/19 for Transvaal v Australians at Johannesburg in 1949/50.

Rowan, Eric Alfred Burchell
Amateur. *b:* 20.7.1909, Johannesburg, South Africa. Brother of A. M. B. (South Africa). Sound opening right-hand batsman. *Teams* Transvaal (1929/30 to 1953/4); Eastern Province (1945/6). *Tours* South Africa to England 1935, 1951. *Tests* South Africa (1935–51, 26 matches).
Career batting
157–258–17–11710–306*–48.58–30–*ct* 83
Bowling 168–4–42.00–0–0–3/11
Test batting
26–50–5–1965–236–43.66–3–*ct* 14
Bowling 7–0
He scored more runs than any of his colleagues on the 1935 tour with 1,948, av 44.27, but was not so successful in the Tests. In 1951 he repeated his record with 1,852 runs, av 50.05, and also headed the Test averages with 515 runs, av 57.22. He hit two double centuries on the 1951 tour, including 236 v England at Headingley. His highest score was 306* for Transvaal v Natal at Johannesburg in 1939/40.

Rowbotham, Joseph
Professional. *b:* 8.7.1831, Highfield, Sheffield, Yorkshire. *d:* 22.12.1899, Morecambe, Lancashire. Fine middle order right-hand batsman. *Team* Yorkshire (1861–76, 100 matches). *Tours* Willsher to North America 1868 (not first-class).
Career batting
141–247–15–3694–113–15.92–3–*ct* 70–*st* 5
Bowling 37–3–12.33–0–0–3/37
His first-class debut was for Sheffield in 1854.

Rowden, George Henry
Amateur. *b:* 6.10.1914, Midsomer Norton, Somerset. Middle order right-hand batsman, off break bowler. *Team* Somerset (1936, 1 match).
Career batting
1–2–0–11–9–5.50–0–*ct* 0

Rowe, Charles James Castell
Cricketer. *b:* 27.11.1951, Hong Kong. Opening or middle order right-hand batsman, right-arm off break bowler. *Sch* King's School, Canterbury. *Teams* Kent (1974–81, 122 matches); Glamorgan (1982–83, 47 matches).
Career batting
169–266–41–6018–147*–26.74–6–*ct* 61
Bowling 4771–116–41.12–3–1–6/46
He hit 1,000 runs in a season twice (best 1,071, av 32.45, in 1982).

Rowe, Edmund John
Professional. *b:* 21.7.1920, Netherfield, Notts. Tail end right-hand batsman, wicket-keeper. *Team* Nottinghamshire (1949–57, 103 matches).
Career batting
103–122–68–295–16–5.46–0–*ct* 152–*st* 52

Rowe, Francis Coryndon Carpenter
Amateur. *b:* 27.7.1859, Colombo, Ceylon. *d:* 5.4.1897, at sea on a voyage from Australia to England. Middle order left-hand batsman, wicket-keeper. *Sch* Harrow. *Team* Cambridge U (1880–81, blue 1881).
Career batting
6–10–0–155–38–15.50–0–*ct* 3

Rowe, Francis Erskine
Amateur. *b:* 30.11.1864, Hartford End, Essex. *d:* 17.5.1928, Littlehampton, Sussex. Son of A. W. (Cambridge U 1859). Sound middle order right-hand batsman, occasional wicket-keeper. *Sch* Marlborough. *Team* Essex (1894–95, 3 matches).
Career batting
4–7–1–53–19–8.83–0–*ct* 2
He did not appear in any first-class matches

whilst at Cambridge U. He also appeared for Berkshire. His first-class debut was for Cambridge University, Past and Present in 1890.

Rowe, George Alexander
Amateur. *b:* 15.6.1874, Grahamstown, South Africa. *d:* 8.1.1959, Cape Town, South Africa. Tail end right-hand batsman, slow left-arm bowler. *Team* Western Province (1893/4 to 1906/7). *Tours* South Africa to England 1894 (not first-class), 1901. *Tests* South Africa (1895/6 to 1902/3, 5 matches).
Career batting
36–62–19–303–21*–7.04–0–*ct* 22
Bowling 3592–170–21.12–13–5–8/25
Test batting
5–9–3–26–13*–4.33–0–*ct* 4
Bowling 456–15–30.40–1–0–5/115

He was easily the most successful bowler on the non-first-class 1894 tour with 136 wickets, av 12.89. He repeated his success in 1901 with 136, av 18.54, and in first-class matches took 70 wickets, 25.00.

Rowe, Leonard Charles
Amateur. *b:* 23.1.1938, Northampton. Opening right-hand batsman. *Sch* Northampton GS. *Team* Oxford U (1958).
Career batting
5–10–2–61–35–7.62–0–*ct* 5

He played rugby football for Northampton.

Rowe, Lawrence George
Cricketer. *b:* 8.1.1949, Whitfield Town, Kingston, Jamaica. Attacking opening or middle order right-hand batsman, left-arm fast medium bowler. *Teams* Jamaica (1968/9 to 1981/2). Derbyshire (1974, 17 matches). *Tours* West Indies to England 1973, 1976, 1980, to India 1974/5, to Australia and New Zealand 1979/80; Jamaica to England 1970; West Indies XI to South Africa 1982/3. *Tests* West Indies (1971/2 to 1979/80, 30 matches).
Career batting
142–233–12–8372–302–37.88–17–*ct* 115
Bowling 224–2–112.00–0–0–1/19
Test batting
30–49–2–2047–302–43.55–7–*ct* 17
Bowling 44–0

His first-class debut in England was for the International Cavaliers in 1969. In 1974 he hit 1,059 runs, av 36.51; but on the 1976 tour to England he failed to reach 1,000 runs and appeared in only two Tests. On the tours of 1973 and 1980, he was dogged by injury and played little, missing all the Tests.

His principal claim to fame is his feat of scoring 214 and 100* for West Indies v New Zealand in 1971/2 on his Test debut. His highest innings is 302 for West Indies v England at Bridgetown in 1973/4. He captained the West Indies Team on the 1982/3 controversial tour to South Africa.

Rowell, William Irvine
Amateur. *b:* 18.6.1869, Singapore. *d:* 17.12.1916, Stansted, Essex. Opening right-hand batsman. *Sch* Marlborough. *Team* Cambridge U (1889–91, blue 1891).
Career batting
11–21–0–261–53–12.43–0–*ct* 3

Rowland, Cyril Arthur
Amateur. *b:* 9.6.1905, Colwyn Bay, Denbighshire. *d:* 30.6.1971, Great Horkesley, Essex. Brother of W. H. (Wales). Middle order right-hand batsman. *Sch* Westminster. *Team* Wales (1924–30). *Tour* Cahn to the Argentine 1929/30 (not in first-class matches).
Career batting
14–22–2–330–52*–16.50–0–*ct* 3

His County cricket was for Denbighshire.

Rowland, Daniel
Professional. *b:* 1826. *d:* 1891, Bury, Lancashire. Middle order batsman, useful bowler. *Team* Lancashire (1849–68, 2 matches).
Career batting
2–4–0–9–9–2.25–0–*ct* 0
Bowling 23–0

Rowland, William Harold
Amateur. *b:* 1904, Colwyn Bay, Denbighshire. *d:* 12.4.1942, Wilford, Notts. Brother of C.A (Wales). Middle order batsman. *Team* Wales (1925–30).
Career batting
6–9–4–25–11*–5.00–0–*ct* 4–*st* 1

His County cricket was for Denbighshire.

Rowlands, Frank
Amateur. *b:* 26.7.1889, Bristol, Gloucestershire. *d:* 6.9.1975, Sydenham, Kent. Brother of W. H. (Gloucestershire). Middle order right-hand batsman. *Team* Gloucestershire (1920–22, 11 matches).
Career batting
11–21–0–308–50–14.66–0–*ct* 9

Rowlands, Leslie Samuel
Professional. *b:* 29.8.1880, Birmingham. *d:* 1.10.1947, Clapham Common, London. Lower order right-hand batsman, right-arm medium pace bowler. *Team* Lancashire (1903–10, 6 matches).

Career batting
7–11–4–33–9–4.71–0–*ct* 2
Bowling 357–18–19.83–0–0–4/29
He also played for Cheshire.

Rowlands, William Henry
Amateur. *b:* 30.7.1883, Bristol, Gloucs. *d:* 29.6.1948, Bristol. Brother of Frank (Gloucestershire). Middle order right-hand batsman. *Team* Gloucestershire (1901–28, 138 matches).
Career batting
138–207–14–3248–113–16.82–2–*ct* 100
Bowling 280–10–28.00–0–0–1/0
He hit 1,014 runs, av 22.04, in 1921. In 1927 and 1928 he captained Gloucestershire.

Rowley, Alexander Butler
Amateur. *b:* 3.10.1837, Manchester, Lancashire. *d:* 9.1.1911, Dover, Kent. Brother of E. B. (Lancashire), uncle of E. B. jun (Lancashire). Forcing middle order right-hand batsman, left-hand slow medium round-arm bowler, short leg. *Sch* Rossall. *Team* Lancashire (1865–71, 12 matches).
Career batting
31–58–11–967–63*–20.57–0–*ct* 19
Bowling 1670–79–21.13–4–2–6/21
His first-class debut was for Manchester in 1854.
He took a prominent part in the formation of Lancashire County Cricket Club and was President from 1874 to 1879.
He also played for Cheshire.

Rowley, Charles Robert
Amateur. *b:* 29.12.1849, London. *d:* 5.4.1933, Kensington. Middle order right-hand batsman, right-hand slow under-arm bowler, wicket-keeper. *Sch* Harrow. *Team* Middlesex (1872, 1 match).
Career batting
9–17–3–177–49*–12.64–0–*ct* 5–*st* 2
His first-class debut was for MCC in 1870 and his final first-class match for the same Club in 1879.
He also played for Devon and Suffolk.

Rowley, Edmund Butler
Amateur. *b:* 4.5.1842, Manchester, Lancashire. *d:* 8.2.1905, Chorlton-on-Medlock, Lancashire. Father of E. B. jun (Lancashire), brother of A. B. (Lancashire). Hard hitting middle order right-hand batsman, slip field. *Sch* Rossall. *Team* Lancashire (1865–80, 81 matches).
Career batting
89–145–8–1853–78–13.52–0–*ct* 25–*st* 1
Bowling 31–1–31.00–0–0–1/14
His first-class debut was for Gentlemen of the North in 1860.
He captained Lancashire from 1866 to 1879 and was afterwards on the County Committee until his death.

Rowley, Ernest Butler
Amateur. *b:* 15.1.1870, Kersal, Manchester, Lancashire. *d:* 4.10.1962, Manchester, Lancashire. Son of E. B. (Lancashire), nephew of A. B. (Lancashire). Middle order right-hand batsman. *Sch* Clifton. *Team* Lancashire (1893–98, 16 matches).
Career batting
17–27–4–586–65–25.47–0–*ct* 4

Rowley, Sir George William
Amateur. *b:* 10.5.1896, Brabourne, Kent. *d:* 8.8.1953, Newlyn, Cornwall. Middle order right-hand batsman. *Sch* Repton. *Teams* Essex (1926, 5 matches); Central Provinces and Berar (1932/3).
Career batting
6–9–1–73–23–9.12–0–*ct* 0
Bowling 29–0

Rowley, John Vincent D'Alessio
Amateur. *b:* 12.9.1907, Graaff Reinet, South Africa. Lower order right-hand batsman, wicket-keeper. *Team* Oxford U (1927).
Career batting
2–3–1–4–2*–2.00–0–*ct* 1–*st* 1

Roy, Pankaj Khirodroy
Amateur. *b:* 31.5.1928, Calcutta, India. Uncle of Ambar (India), father of P. P. (India). Defiant opening right-hand batsman, right-arm medium pace bowler. *Team* Bengal (1946/7 to 1967/8). *Tours* India to England 1952, 1959, to West Indies 1952/3, to Pakistan 1954/5, to Ceylon 1956/7. *Tests* India (1951/2 to 1960/1, 43 matches).
Career batting
185–298–18–11868–202*–42.38–33–*ct* 75
Bowling 648–21–30.85–1–0–5/53
Test batting
43–79–4–2442–173–32.56–5–*ct* 16
Bowling 66–1–66.00–0–0–1/6
A successful batsman in India he was a complete failure on the 1952 tour to England, playing in all four Tests, but scoring only 54 runs. He was vice-captain of the 1959 side, but again failed in the Tests, though hitting 1,207 runs, av 28.73, in first-class matches.
He hit 112* for Bengal v United Provinces on his first-class debut in 1946/7. His highest score was 202* for Bengal v Orissa at Cuttack in 1963/4.

Roy, Pranab Pankaj
Cricketer. *b:* 10.2.1957, Calcutta, India. Son of P. K. (India), cousin of Ambar (India). Opening right-hand batsman, right-arm medium pace bowler. *Team* Bengal (1978/9 to 1982/3). *Tour* India to England 1982. *Tests* India (1981/2, 2 matches).
Career batting
33–61–5–1857–160*–33.16–6–*ct* 15
Bowling 49–1–49.00–0–0–1/3
Test batting
2–3–1–71–60*–35.50–0–*ct* 1
He hit 105 for Bengal v Assam on his first-class debut in 1978/9. On the 1982 tour to England he had a very modest record and did not appear in the Tests.

Royle, George Murray
Amateur. *b:* 9.1.1843, Nottingham. *d:* 26.2.1910, Sherwood Rise, Nottingham. Middle order right-hand batsman, slow right-arm bowler, good deep field. *Team* Nottinghamshire (1871–81, 3 matches).
Career batting
3–5–0–52–45–10.40–0–*ct* 2
Owing to business he was unable to play regularly in County cricket.

Royle, Rev Vernon Peter Fanshawe Archer
Amateur. *b:* 29.1.1854, Brooklands, Cheshire. *d:* 21.5.1929, Stanmore, Middlesex. Fine middle order right-hand batsman, right-hand slow round-arm bowler, brilliant cover point. *Sch* Rossall. *Teams* Oxford U (1875–76, blue both years); Lancashire (1873–91, 74 matches). *Tours* Harris to Australia 1878/9. *Test* England (1878/9, 1 match).
Career batting
102–165–15–2322–81–15.48–0–*ct* 19
Bowling 376–15–25.06–0–0–4/51
Test batting
1–2–0–21–18–10.50–0–*ct* 2
Bowling 6–0
He also played for Cheshire, and in 1929 was President of Lancashire CCC.

Roynon, Gavin Devonald
Amateur. *b:* 26.4.1936, Sutton, Surrey. Middle order right-hand batsman, leg break bowler. *Sch* Charterhouse. *Team* Oxford U (1958).
Career batting
9–15–2–188–58–14.46–0–*ct* 10
Bowling 6–0

Royston, Henry
Professional. *b:* 12.8.1819, Harrow on the Hill, Middlesex. *d:* 30.9.1873, St John's Wood, Middlesex. Lower order right-hand batsman, right-hand slow round-arm bowler, good field. *Team* Middlesex (1850–62, 4 matches).
Career batting
68–121–19–1065–60–10.44–0–*ct* 28
Bowling 658–55+55–11.96–6–1–8/44
His first-class debut was for MCC in 1843.

Ruane, John Davison
Amateur. *b:* 11.7.1919, Ely, Cambridgeshire. *d:* 3.11.1983, Bury St Edmunds, Suffolk. Lower order left-hand batsman, left-arm medium fast bowler. *Sch* Beaumont. *Team* Cambridge U (1938–39).
Career batting
2–3–0–27–19–9.00–0–*ct* 0
Bowling 166–3–55.33–0–0–2/41

Rubie, Claude Blake
Amateur. *b:* 25.3.1888, Lewes, Sussex. *d:* 3.11.1939, Hove, Sussex. He died following an operation. Lower order right-hand batsman, wicket-keeper. *Sch* Lancing. *Teams* Europeans (1919/20); Madras (1926/7); Sussex (1930, 4 matches).
Career batting
10–18–8–245–84–24.50–0–*ct* 16–*st* 7
Three months before his death he had been appointed Manager of the 1939/40 MCC team to India – war caused the tour to be abandoned.

Rucker, Charles Edward Sigismund
Amateur. *b:* 4.9.1894, Bromley, Kent. *d:* 24.11.1965, Blandford, Dorset. Brother of P. W. (Oxford U). Lower order right-hand batsman, right-arm fast bowler. *Sch* Charterhouse. *Team* Oxford U (1914, blue).
Career batting
5–8–3–66–26*–13.20–0–*ct* 1
Bowling 289–13–22.23–2–0–6/69
The loss of a leg during the First World War ended his cricket career, but he was Secretary at Oxford in 1919, in which year his younger brother P. W. Rucker, played against Cambridge.

Rucker, Patrick William
Amateur. *b:* 5.5.1900, Bromley, Kent. *d:* 20.5.1940, Amiens, France. Brother of C. E. S. (Oxford U). Lower order batsman, left-arm medium pace bowler. *Sch* Charterhouse. *Team* Oxford U (1919, blue).
Career batting
7–10–4–48–17–8.00–0–*ct* 2
Bowling 462–11–42.00–0–0–4/107

Rudd, Charles John Lockhart
Amateur. *b:* 12.3.1873, Cape Town, South Africa. *d:* 1.4.1950, Kingston-on-Thames, Surrey. Lower order left-hand batsman, left-arm

fast bowler. *Sch* Harrow. *Team* Cambridge U (1894).
Career batting
1–1–1–1–1*–no av–0–*ct* 0
Bowling 29–0

Rudd, Clifford Robin David
Amateur. *b:* 25.3.1929, Kenilworth, Cape Province, South Africa. Stylish middle order right-hand batsman. *Sch* Eton. *Team* Oxford U (1949–51, blue 1949). *Tour* MCC to Canada 1951.
Career batting
21–40–4–604–70–16.77–0–*ct* 11
His final first-class match was for MCC in 1960.

Rudd, George Boyd Franklin
Amateur. *b:* 3.7.1894, Leicester. *d:* 4.2.1957, Leicester. Son of G. E. (Leicestershire). Forcing middle order right-hand batsman, right-arm medium bowler, occasional wicket-keeper. *Sch* Westminster. *Team* Leicestershire (1913–32, 88 matches).
Career batting
88–159–7–2916–114–19.18–1–*ct* 37
Bowling 713–18–39.61–0–0–3/38
He did not appear in first-class matches whilst at Oxford. From 1947 he was Hon Secretary of Leicestershire CCC.

Rudd, George Edward
Amateur. *b:* 14.1.1866, York. *d:* 16.9.1921, Leicester. Father of G. B. F. (Leics). Middle order right-hand batsman, slow left-arm bowler. *Team* Leicestershire (1894–1901, 22 matches).
Career batting
22–36–6–379–47–12.63–0–*ct* 11
Bowling 537–12–44.75–1–0–5/118
He did not play in any first-class matches whilst at Oxford. From 1907 to 1921 he was Hon Secretary of Leicestershire CCC.

Rudd, William James
Professional. *b:* 29.6.1880, Little Amwell, Herts. *d:* 27.3.1971, Ipswich, Suffolk. Tail end left-hand batsman, left-arm medium pace bowler. *Team* Surrey (1904, 1 match).
Career batting
1–2–0–4–4–2.00–0–*ct* 0
He also played for Hertfordshire.

Ruddle, Marcus Poole
Amateur. *b:* 16.1.1905, Dublin. Right-hand batsman. *Team* Ireland (1937).
Career batting
1–2–1–0–0*–0.00–0–*ct* 0
Bowling 17–0

Rudge, Lloyd M.
Amateur. *b:* 11.2.1934, Walsall, Staffs. Hard hitting lower order right-hand batsman, right-arm fast bowler. *Team* Worcestershire (1952, 1 match).
Career batting
1–1–0–1–1–1.00–*ct* 0
Bowling 36–0

Rudston, Horace
Professional. *b:* 22.11.1878, Hessle, Yorkshire. *d:* April 1962, Holderness, Yorkshire. Opening or middle order right-hand batsman. *Team* Yorkshire (1902–07, 21 matches).
Career batting
22–31–0–631–164–20.35–1–*ct* 5

Ruggles-Brise, Major General Sir Harold Goodeve
Amateur. *b:* 17.3.1864, Finchingfield, Essex. *d:* 24.6.1927, Marylebone, London. He died of pneumonia contracted while playing tennis. Middle order right-hand batsman, right-arm medium pace bowler. *Sch* Winchester. *Team* Oxford U (1883, blue).
Career batting
8–15–0–278–73–18.53–0–*ct* 6
Bowling 32–1–32.00–0–0–1/11
He appeared occasionally for Essex, but mainly in military matches. His final first-class match was for MCC in 1884.

Rumbold, Jack Seddon
Amateur. *b:* 5.3.1920, New Zealand. Opening right-hand batsman. *Team* Oxford U (1946–47, blue 1946).
Career batting
7–14–0–175–25–12.50–0–*ct* 6

Rumsey, Frederick Edward
Professional. *b:* 4.12.1935, Stepney, London. Tail end right-hand batsman, left-hand fast medium bowler. *Teams* Worcestershire (1960–62, 13 matches); Somerset (1963–68, 153 matches); Derbyshire (1970, 1 match). *Tests* England (1964–65, 5 matches).
Career batting
180–204–84–1015–45–8.45–0–*ct* 92
Bowling 11773–580–20.29–30–5–8/26
Test batting
5–5–3–30–21*–15.00–0–0–*ct* 0
Bowling 461–17–27.11–0–0–4/25
He took 100 wickets in a season three times (best 119, av 16.18, in 1965). He joined Derbyshire CCC as the Public Relations Officer and played chiefly for the County in limited overs matches.

Rumsey, Robert Edwin
Professional. *b:* 17.2.1844, Greenwich, Kent. *d:* 12.6.1884, Greenwich, Kent. Lower order right-hand batsman, right-hand fast round-arm bowler, slip field. *Team* Kent (1875, 3 matches).
Career batting
3–5–1–20–13–5.00–0–*ct* 2
Bowling 140–7–20.00–1–0–5/48

Rushby, Thomas
Professional. *b:* 6.9.1880, Cobham, Surrey. *d:* 13.7.1962, Ewell, Surrey. Tail end right-hand batsman, right-arm fast medium bowler. *Team* Surrey (1903–21, 228 matches).
Career batting
229–289–129–1192–58*–7.45–0–*ct* 64
Bowling 19640–954–20.58–58–9–10/43
He took 100 wickets in a season four times (best 132, av 21.71, in 1911). His best bowling in an innings was 10 for 43 for Surrey v Somerset at Taunton in 1921.

Rushmere, Colin G.
Amateur. *b:* 16.4.1937, Port Elizabeth, South Africa. Middle order right-hand batsman, right-arm medium pace bowler. *Teams* Eastern Province (1956/7 to 1965/6), Western Province (1957/8 to 1960/1). *Tour* SA Fezela to England 1961.
Career batting
33–58–4–1245–153–23.05–2–*ct* 19
Bowling 576–20–28.80–0–0–4/29

Rushton, Frank
Professional. *b:* 21.4.1906, Bolton, Lancashire. *d:* 15.10.1975, Bolton, Lancashire. Lower order right-hand batsman, right-arm fast medium bowler. *Team* Lancashire (1928–29, 6 matches).
Career batting
6–5–0–59–28–11.80–0–*ct* 2
Bowling 362–10–36.20–0–0–4/30

Rushton, Thomas Henry
Amateur. *b:* 14.5.1845, Horwich, Lancashire. *d:* 1.7.1903, Garstang, Lancashire. Middle order batsman. *Team* Lancashire (1870, 1 match).
Career batting
1–1–0–7–7–7.00–0–*ct* 0

Rushworth, William Robert
Amateur. *b:* 4.11.1914, Dulwich, London. *d:* 19.1.1966, Bedford. Tail end batsman, opening bowler. *Sch* Alleyns. *Team* Surrey (1946, 1 match).
Career batting
1–1–0–0–0–0.00–0–*ct* 3
Bowling 86–2–43.00–0–0–1/15

Russel, John Somerville
Amateur. *b:* 19.3.1849, Edinburgh, Scotland. *d:* 12.9.1902, Blackhall, Banchory, Kincardine, Scotland. Opening right-hand batsman, good point field. *Sch* Royal High School, Edinburgh. *Team* MCC (1875–91).
Career batting
79–134–7–1641–83–12.92–0–*ct* 32
Bowling 14–0
His County cricket was for Northumberland.

Russel, Patrick
Amateur. *b:* 16.10.1857, Edinburgh, Scotland. *d:* 12.10.1917, City of London. Middle order batsman. *Sch* Fettes and Edinburgh Academy. *Team* MCC (1894).
Career batting
1–2–1–25–25*–15.00–0–*ct* 0

Russell, Alfred Edward
Professional. *b:* 9.1.1875, Lewisham, London. *d:* 8.9.1940, Whipps Cross, Essex. Brother of T. M. (Essex), uncle of C. A. G. (Essex). Lower order left-hand batsman, wicket-keeper. *Team* Essex (1898–1910, 130 matches).
Career batting
130–196–42–2025–100–13.14–1–*ct* 163–*st* 44

Russell, Charles Albert George
(also known as Albert Charles Russell)
Professional. *b:* 7.10.1887, Leyton, Essex. *d:* 23.3.1961, Whipps Cross, Essex. Son of T. M. (Essex), nephew of A. E. (Essex). Sound opening right-hand batsman, right-arm slow medium bowler, good slip field. *Team* Essex (1908–30, 379 matches). *Tours* MCC to Australia 1920/1, to South Africa 1922/3, Joel to South Africa 1924/5. *Tests* England (1920/1 to 1922/3, 10 matches).
Career batting
437–717–59–27358–273–41.57–71–*ct* 313
Bowling 7637–283–26.90–5–0–5/25
Test batting
10–18–2–910–140–56.87–5–*ct* 8
He hit 1,000 runs in a season 13 times, going on to 2,000 five times (best 2,575, av 54.78, in 1922). His highest innings was 273 for Essex v Northants at Leyton in 1921; his only other double century being for MCC in Australia. In the series between England and South Africa in 1922/3, he became the first English batsman to hit a century in each innings in a Test.

Russell, David Francis
Amateur. *b:* 29.10.1936, Ashtead, Surrey. Lower order right-hand batsman, off break bowler. *Sch* St John's, Leatherhead. *Team* Oxford U (1959).

Career batting
5–6–2–57–22–14.25–0–*ct* 3
Bowling 344–11–31.27–0–0–3/53

Russell, Denis Leslie
Amateur. *b:* 2.7.1909, Paddington, London. Lower order right-hand batsman, slow left-arm bowler. *Sch* Beaumont. *Teams* Middlesex (1928–32, 25 matches); Oxford U (1930–31).
Career batting
34–53–5–92–666–92–13.88–0–*ct* 11
Bowling 527–17–31.00–1–0–7/43

Russell, David Paul
Cricketer. *b:* 4.6.1951, St Helens, Lancashire. Middle order right-hand batsman, right-arm medium pace bowler. *Team* Cambridge U (1974–75, blue both years).
Career batting
16–30–4–514–56*–19.76–0–*ct* 7
Bowling 952–16–59.50–0–0–3/60

Russell, H. F.
Amateur. Middle order batsman. *Team* Hampshire (1884, 1 match).
Career batting
1–2–0–11–10–5.50–0–0–*ct* 0

Russell, John
Amateur. *b:* 8.4.1887, Liff, Angus, Scotland. *d:* 20.6.1965, Dundee, Scotland. Middle order right-hand batsman. *Team* Scotland (1923).
Career batting
1–2–0–58–29–29.00–0–*ct* 1

Russell, John Bernard
Amateur. *b:* 2.10.1883, Walsall, Staffs. *d:* 17.8.1965, Lichfield, Staffs. Lower order right-hand batsman, wicket-keeper. *Team* Warwickshire (1920, 1 match).
Career batting
1–2–0–31–23–15.50–0–*ct* 1–*st* 1
He also played for Staffordshire.

Russell, Philip Edgar
Cricketer. *b:* 9.5.1944, Ilkeston, Derbyshire. Lower order right-hand batsman, right-arm medium pace off break bowler. *Team* Derbyshire (1965–79, 167 matches).
Career batting
167–207–44–2015–72–12.36–0–*ct* 124
Bowling 10108–335–30.17–5–0–7/46
He was appointed Derbyshire CCC coach in 1976.

Russell, Robert Charles
Cricketer. *b:* 15.8.1963, Stroud, Gloucs. Lower order left-hand batsman, wicket-keeper. *Team* Gloucestershire (1981–83, 29 matches).
Career batting
29–39–11–589–64*–21.03–0–*ct* 57–*st* 20

Russell, Sidney Edward James
Professional. *b:* 4.10.1937, Feltham, Middlesex. Middle order right-hand batsman, right-arm medium pace bowler. *Teams* Gloucestershire (1965–68, 80 matches); Middlesex (1960–64, 61 matches).
Career batting
142–248–19–5464–130–23.86–4–*ct* 41
Bowling 121–2–60.50–0–0–1/8
He hit 1,000 runs in a season twice (best 1,256, av 25.12, in 1965). A useful soccer player, he played for Brentford.

Russell, Stephen George
Cricketer. *b:* 13.3.1945, Sutton, Surrey. Tail end right-hand batsman, right-arm fast medium bowler. *Sch* Tiffins. *Teams* Cambridge U (1965–67, blue all three years); Surrey (1967, 1 match).
Career batting
35–58–21–203–21*–5.48–0–*ct* 12
Bowling 2480–76–32.63–4–0–5/41

Russell, Thomas Marychurch
Professional. *b:* 6.7.1868, Lewisham, Kent. *d:* 28.2.1927, Leyton, Essex. Father of C. A. G. (Essex), brother of A. E. (Essex). Lower order right-hand batsman, wicket-keeper. *Team* Essex (1894–1905, 162 matches).
Career batting
170–260–46–3273–139–15.29–3–*ct* 251–*st* 89
He was for some years a first-class umpire.

Russell, William Cecil
Amateur. *b:* 25.4.1866, Rokewood, Victoria, Australia. *d:* 9.5.1929, Haremere, Etchingham, Sussex. Middle order batsman. *Sch* Eton. *Team* Hampshire (1898, 1 match).
Career batting
1–2–0–7–5–3.50–*ct* 0

Russell, William Eric
Professional. *b:* 3.7.1936, Dumbarton, Scotland. Opening right-hand batsman, right-arm medium pace bowler. *Team* Middlesex (1956–72, 400 matches). *Tours* MCC to New Zealand 1960/1, to India and Pakistan 1961/2, to Australia and New Zealand 1965/6. *Tests* England (1961/2 to 1967, 10 matches).

Career batting
448–796–64–25525–193–34.87–41–*ct* 304
Bowling 993–22–45.13–0–0–3/20
Test batting
10–18–1–362–70–21.29–0–*ct* 4
Bowling 44–0

He hit 1,000 runs in a season 13 times, going on to 2,000 three times (best 2,342, av 45.92, in 1964).

Russom, Neil
Cricketer. *b:* 3.12.1958, Finchley, London. Middle order right-hand batsman, right-arm medium bowler. *Teams* Cambridge U (1979–81, blue 1980–81); Somerset (1980–83, 4 matches).
Career batting
25–34–14–641–79*–32.05–0–*ct* 6
Bowling 1744–42–41.52–0–0–4/84

Rust, Thomas Henry
Amateur. *b:* 3.3.1881, Gloucester. *d:* 9.8.1962, Gloucester. Middle order right-hand batsman. *Team* Gloucestershire (1914, 1 match).
Career batting
1–2–0–2–2–1.00–0–*ct* 0

Rutherford, Arnold Page
Amateur. *b:* 2.9.1892, Highclere, Hants. *d:* 23.7.1980, Weybridge, Surrey. Brother of J. S. (Hampshire). Middle order right-hand batsman, right-arm medium pace bowler. *Sch* Repton. *Team* Hampshire (1912, 1 match).
Career batting
1–1–0–18–18–18.00–0–*ct* 0

Rutherford, Ian Alexander
Cricketer. *b:* 30.6.1957, Dunedin, New Zealand. Brother of K. R. (Otago). Right-hand batsman, right-arm medium pace, off break bowler. *Teams* Worcestershire (1976, 2 matches); Otago (1974/5 to 1982/3).
Career batting
76–139–3–3667–222–26.96–5–*ct* 46
Bowling 56–2–28.00–0–0–1/8

His highest score was 222 for Otago v Central Districts at New Plymouth in 1978/9.

Rutherford, John Robert Fulton
Amateur. *b:* 9.8.1935, Hawkhurst, Kent. Lower order right-hand batsman, right-arm medium pace bowler. *Sch* Nottingham HS. *Team* Cambridge U (1957–58).
Career batting
11–21–5–105–37*–6.56–0–*ct* 3
Bowling 555–10–55.50–0–0–3/53

Rutherford, John Seymour
Amateur. *b:* 27.2.1890, Highclere, Hants. *d:* 14.4.1943, Oxford. Brother of A. P. (Hampshire). Lower order right-hand batsman, right-arm medium pace bowler. *Sch* Repton. *Team* Hampshire (1913, 8 matches).
Career batting
8–15–1–128–33*–9.14–0–*ct* 1
Bowling 110–3–36.66–0–0–1/4

Rutherford, John Walter
Amateur. *b:* 25.9.1929, Bungulluping, Western Australia. Opening right-hand batsman, leg break bowler. *Team* Western Australia (1952/3 to 1960/1, 38 matches). *Tours* Australia to England 1956, to India 1956/7. *Test* Australia (1956/7, 1 match).
Career batting
67–115–9–3367–167–31.76–6–*ct* 53
Bowling 1313–29–45.27–0–0–3/12
Test batting
1–1–0–30–30–30.00–0–*ct* 0
Bowling 15–1–15.00–0–0–1/11

He had a modest tour of England in 1956 and did not appear in the Tests.

Rutter, Allen Edward Henry
Amateur. *b:* 24.12.1928, Bromley, Kent. Opening or middle order right-hand batsman. *Sch* Dauntsey's. *Team* Cambridge U (1953).
Career batting
3–4–0–49–45–2.25–0–*ct* 0

His County cricket was for Wiltshire. His final first-class match was for Free Foresters in 1955.

Rutter, Edward
Amateur. *b:* 3.8.1842, Hillingdon, Middlesex. *d:* 4.2.1926, Halliford, Middlesex. Brother of F. J. (Lancashire). Lower order right-hand batsman, slow left-arm bowler. *Sch* Rugby. *Team* Middlesex (1862–76, 32 matches).
Career batting
45–77–11–733–64–11.10–0–*ct* 29
Bowling 3172–180+2–17.62–15–5–7/47

He was a prominent member of the Free Foresters, being Hon Secretary of that Club for some years. A noted rugby footballer, he played for Richmond and was a member of the original Committee set up by the Rugby Union.

Rutter, Frederick John
Amateur. *b:* 12.9.1840, Hillingdon, Middlesex. *d:* 19.1.1907, Abbey Wood, Kent. Brother of Edward (Middlesex). Opening batsman. *Sch* Rugby. *Team* Lancashire (1868, 2 matches).
Career batting
2–4–1–15–8*–5.00–0–*ct* 0
Bowling 11–0

Rutter, Ronald Howard
Amateur. *b:* 13.7.1910, Amersham, Bucks. *d:* 8.8.1974, Beaconsfield, Bucks. He died after a long illness. Lower order right-hand batsman, right-arm fast medium bowler. *Sch* Tonbridge. *Teams* Minor Counties (1929–36); MCC (1932–33).
Career batting
6–9–3–66–37*–11.00–0–*ct* 3
Bowling 408–13–31.33–0–0–3/27

His County cricket was for Buckinghamshire. For Buckinghamshire v Oxfordshire at High Wycombe in 1932 he hit 106 in 45 minutes.

Rutty, Arthur William Forder
Amateur. *b:* 22.8.1872, Reading, Berkshire. *d:* 10.1.1932, Newcastle on Tyne, Northumberland. Lower order right-hand batsman, off break bowler. *Sch* St John's Leatherhead, Sherborne. *Team* Surrey (1910, 1 match).
Career batting
1–2–2–18–12*–no av–0–*ct* 1

Ryan, Francis Peter
Professional. *b:* 14.11.1888, New Jersey, USA. *d:* 5.1.1954, Leicester. Tail end left-hand batsman, left-arm slow bowler. *Sch* Bedford GS. *Teams* Hampshire (1919–20, 23 matches); Glamorgan (1922–31, 215 matches); Wales (1923–30).
Career batting
247–357–118–1908–52*–7.98–0–*ct* 103
Bowling 21311–1013–21.03–86–18–8/41

He took 100 wickets in a season five times (best 120, av 14.58, in 1924).

Ryan, James Henry Aloysius
Amateur. *b:* 15.9.1892, Roade, Northants. *d:* 25.9.1915, Loos, France. He was killed in action. Middle order right-hand batsman, right-arm medium pace bowler. *Sch* Downside. *Teams* Northants (1911–14, 8 matches); Ireland (1912).
Career batting
9–15–1–119–41–8.50–0–*ct* 2
Bowling 152–4–38.00–0–0–2/51

Ryan, Melville
Professional. *b:* 23.6.1933, Huddersfield, Yorkshire. Lower order right-hand batsman, right-arm fast medium bowler. *Team* Yorkshire (1954–65, 150 matches). *Tour* Yorkshire to North America and Bermuda 1964 (not first-class).
Career batting
150–149–58–682–26*–7.49–0–*ct* 59
Bowling 9466–413–22.92–12–2–7/45

Ryder, John
Amateur. *b:* 8.8.1889, Collingwood, Victoria, Australia. *d:* 3.4.1977, Fitzroy, Victoria, Australia. Aggressive middle order right-hand batsman, right-arm fast medium bowler. *Team* Victoria (1912/3 to 1931/2, 80 matches). *Tours* Australia to England 1921, 1926, to South Africa 1921/2; Australians to India and Ceylon 1935/6. *Tests* Australia (1920/1 to 1928/9, 20 matches).
Career batting
177–274–37–10499–295–44.29–24–*ct* 132
Bowling 7064–238–29.68–9–1–7/53
Test batting
20–32–5–1394–201*–52.62–3–*ct* 17
Bowling 743–17–43.70–0–0–2/20

His batting in England was a shadow of what he achieved at home – he did not reach 1,000 runs either in 1921 or 1926. In the former year he was not picked for any of the Tests, but in 1926 appeared in four, though only making 73 runs in them. His highest score was 295 for Victoria v NSW at Melbourne in 1926/7. He hit 1,045 runs, av 69.66, in the 1928/9 Australian season.

Ryder, Louis
Professional. *b:* 28.8.1900, Thirsk, Yorkshire. *d:* 24.1.1955, Summer Bridge, Yorkshire. Lower order right-hand batsman, right-arm fast bowler. *Team* Yorkshire (1924, 2 matches).
Career batting
2–2–1–1–1–1.00–0–*ct* 2
Bowling 151–4–37.75–0–0–2/75

Ryder, Reginald Talbot
Amateur. *b:* 18.6.1875, Crewe, Cheshire. *d:* 6.11.1923, Stockport, Cheshire. Middle order batsman. *Sch* Denstone. *Team* Derbyshire (1903, 1 match).
Career batting
1–1–0–10–10–10.00–0–*ct* 1

Rylott, Arnold
Professional. *b:* 18.2.1839, Grantham, Lincs. *d:* 17.4.1914, Sandy, Bedfordshire. Lower order right-hand batsman, left-arm fast bowler. *Team* MCC (1872–88).
Career batting
85–137–26–703–45–6.33–0–*ct* 64
Bowling 5333–456–11.69–39–14–9/30

His first-class debut was for Left Handed v Right Handed in 1870. He played County cricket for Leicestershire commencing 1875 and was on the ground staff at Lord's from 1872. His best bowling was 9/30 for MCC v Cambridge U at Cambridge in 1873. He also played for Staffordshire. He was author of a book of verse 'Our Bobby Rykitt when a Boy.'

Rymill, Kenneth James
Amateur. *b:* 30.8.1906, Northampton. *d:* 31.5.1977, Northampton. Middle order right-hand batsman. *Team* Northants (1926–32, 4 matches).
Career batting
4–6–0–35–28–5.83–0–*ct* 1

SABINE, PETER NOEL BARRINGTON
Cricketer. *b:* 21.9.1941, Cookham Dean, Berkshire. Middle order right-hand batsman, leg break bowler. *Sch* Marlborough. *Team* Oxford U (1962–63, blue 1963).
Career batting
12–23–3–420–56–21.00–0–*ct* 10
Bowling 553–15–36.86–0–0–4/51

Sadiq Mohammad
Cricketer. *b:* 5.5.1945, Junagadh, India. Brother of Hanif, Mushtaq and Wazir (Pakistan) and Raees (Karachi), uncle of Shoaib, Shahid and Asif (PIA). Opening left-hand batsman, leg break and googly bowler. *Teams* Karachi (1960/1 to 1972/3); PIA (1961/2 to 1966/7); Essex (1970, 1 match); Gloucestershire (1972–82, 193 matches); Tasmania (1974/5, 2 matches); United Bank (1976/7 to 1982/3). *Tours* Pakistan to England 1971, 1974, 1978, to Ceylon, Australia and New Zealand 1972/3, to Australia 1976/7, to West Indies 1976/7, to India 1979/80; Pakistan Eaglets to England 1963; PIA to East Africa 1964/5. *Tests* Pakistan (1969/70 to 1980/1, 41 matches).
Career batting
373–657–39–23140–203–37.44–48–*ct* 316
Bowling 7371–231–31.90–8–0–7/34
Test batting
41–74–2–2579–166–35.81–5–*ct* 28
Bowling 98–0

Of his three Test tours to England, his best was 1978 when he headed both Test and first-class batting averages, his figures for the latter being 675 runs, av 37.50. On the 1974 tour he completed 1,000 runs: 1,007, av 45.77. In all he hit 1,000 runs in an English season seven times (best 1,759, av 47.54, in 1976). He also hit 1,000 runs in a Pakistan season. His only double century in England is 203 for Gloucestershire v Sri Lanka in 1981. According to his published date of birth he was 14 years 9 months old when making his first-class debut, for Fazal Mahmood's XI in 1959/60.

Sadler, Thomas William
Professional. *b:* 15.1.1892, Chesterton, Cambridgeshire. *d:* 20.1.1973, Brandon, Suffolk. Lower order right-hand batsman, left-arm bowler. *Team* Wales (1930).
Career batting
1–2–1–18–17–18.00–0–*ct* 1
Bowling 55–3–18.33–0–0–3/55

His County cricket was for Cambridgeshire and Monmouthshire. In the Minor Counties match between Monmouthshire and Dorset in 1930 he took all ten wickets in an innings.

Sadler, William Cecil Holborn
Professional. *b:* 24.9.1896, Kings Cross, London. *d:* 12.2.1981, Wandsworth, London. Lower order right-hand batsman, right-arm fast bowler. *Team* Surrey (1923–25, 51 matches).
Career batting
51–65–22–646–68–15.02–0–*ct* 20
Bowling 3907–167–23.39–7–2–6/50

He also played for Durham.

Saeed Ahmed
Amateur. *b:* 1.10.1937, Jullundur, India. Brother of Younis (Pakistan). Attacking middle order right-hand batsman, off break bowler. *Teams* Punjab (1954/5 to 1957/8); Railways (1955/6); Universities (1958/9); Lahore (1959/60); PIA (1961/2 to 1962/3); Karachi (1961/2 to 1971/2); PWD (1971/2). *Tours* Pakistan to England 1962, 1967, 1971, to Australia and New Zealand 1964/5, 1972/3, to West Indies 1957/8, to India 1960/1; International XI to South Africa 1961/2; Rest of World to England 1968. *Tests* Pakistan (1957/8 to 1972/3, 41 matches).
Career batting
213–346–25–12847–203*–40.02–34–*ct* 122
Bowling 8217–332–24.75–15–2–8/41
Test batting
41–78–4–2991–172–40.41–5–*ct* 13
Bowling 802–22–36.45–0–0–4/64

On his 1962 tour to England he hit 1,294 runs, av 34.97, and appeared in all five Tests. In 1967, on the shortened tour, he made 845 runs, av 33.80, again playing in all the Tests. He was unable to find his form until late on in the 1971 visit and played only in the last Test. His only double century was 203* for Karachi v PWD at Karachi in 1970/1. He also hit 1,000 runs in a Pakistan season. Apart from his cricket for Pakistan, he played in England in 1966 for MCC and in 1968 for Rest of World. His final first-class match was for NWFP XI v England in 1977/8.

Saggers, Ronald Arthur
Amateur. *b:* 15.5.1917, Sydenham, New South Wales, Australia. Lower order right-hand batsman, wicket-keeper. *Team* New South Wales (1939/40 to 1950/1, 40 matches). *Tours* Australia to England 1948, to South Africa 1949/50. *Tests* Australia (1948 to 1949/50, 6 matches).
Career batting
77–93–14–1888–104*–23.89–1–*ct* 147–*st* 74
Test batting
6–5–2–30–14–10.00–0–*ct* 16–*st* 8
The reserve wicket-keeper to D. Tallon on the 1948 tour, he played in one Test.

Sainsbury, Edward
Amateur. *b:* 5.7.1851, Bath, Somerset. *d:* 28.10.1930, Weston super Mare, Somerset. Opening or middle order right-hand batsman, slow under-arm bowler. *Sch* Sherborne. *Teams* Gloucestershire (1891–92, 18 matches); Somerset (1882–85, 25 matches).
Career batting
46–85–4–1213–116–14.97–1–*ct* 20
Bowling 644–25–25.76–0–0–4/74
He captained Somerset in 1886, when the County was not first-class.

Sainsbury, Gary Edward
Cricketer. *b:* 17.1.1958, Wanstead, Essex. Tail end right-hand batsman, left-arm medium pace bowler. *Teams* Essex (1979–80, 3 matches); Gloucestershire (1983, 23 matches).
Career batting
26–25–10–72–13–4.80–0–*ct* 1
Bowling 2205–66–33.40–3–0–6/66

Sainsbury, John Popham
Amateur. *b:* 8.1.1927, Weston super Mare, Somerset. Attacking middle order right-hand batsman, good outfield. *Sch* Clifton. *Team* Somerset (1951, 2 matches).
Career batting
2–4–0–16–16–4.00–0–*ct* 0
He was a good rugby footballer, playing at left-wing for Somerset.

Sainsbury, Peter James
Professional. *b:* 13.6.1934, Chandlers Ford, Hants. Middle order right-hand batsman, slow left-arm bowler, excellent field. *Team* Hampshire (1954–76, 593 matches). *Tours* MCC to Pakistan, 1955/6; Robins to West Indies 1974/5 (not first-class); International XI to South Africa 1974/5.
Career batting
618–948–197–20176–163–26.86–7–*ct* 617
Bowling 31777–1316–24.14–36–5–8/76
He hit 1,000 runs in a season six times (best 1,533, av 30.05, in 1961) and took 100 wickets in a season twice (best 107, av 17.51, in 1971).

Saint, Norman Hunt
Amateur. *b:* 22.4.1901, Tollington Park, Islington, London. *d:* 15.8.1930, Whitechapel, London. Middle order right-hand batsman, left-arm medium bowler. *Sch* Merchant Taylors. *Team* Essex (1920–23, 44 matches).
Career batting
44–72–7–757–36–11.64–0–*ct* 10
Bowling 800–17–47.05–0–0–3/32

St Hill, Wilton H.
Amateur. *b:* 6.7.1893, Port of Spain, Trinidad. *d:* 1957, Trinidad. Brother of E. L. (West Indies). Entertaining middle order right-hand batsman, right-arm medium pace bowler. *Team* Trinidad (1911/12 to 1929/30). *Tour* West Indies to England 1928. *Tests* West Indies (1928 to 1929/30, 3 matches).
Career batting
43–74–3–1928–144–27.15–5–*ct* 14
Bowling 209–5–41.80–0–0–2/14
Test batting
3–6–0–117–38–19.50–0–*ct* 1
Bowling 9–0
He had a very moderate tour to England, being too anxious to attack the bowling from the start of each innings.

Salah-ud-din Mulla
Amateur. *b:* 14.2.1947, Aligarh, India. Middle order right-hand batsman, off break bowler. *Teams* Karachi (1964/5 to 1971/2); P.I.A. (1972/3 to 1979/80). *Tours* Pakistan Eaglets to England 1963; Pakistan to England 1967. *Tests* Pakistan (1964/5 to 1969/70, 5 matches).
Career batting
111–168–31–5729–256–41.81–14–*ct* 63
Bowling 4431–155–28.58–4–0–6/76
Test batting
5–8–2–117–34*–19.50–0–*ct* 3
Bowling 187–7–26.71–0–0–2/36
He achieved very little on the 1967 tour to England and did not appear in the Tests. His highest score was 256 for Karachi v East Pakistan at Karachi in 1968/9.

Salam-ud-din, Khan
Amateur. *b:* 16.10.1888, Basty Sheikh Darwesh, Jullundur, India. Middle order right-hand batsman, right-arm fast bowler. *Team* Muslims (1912/13). *Tour* India to England 1911.

Career batting
15–29–5–362–50–15.08–0–*ct* 17
Bowling 1143–36–31.75–3–0–6/64
He proved to be a useful all-rounder on the 1911 tour.

Sale, Henry George
Amateur. *b:* 26.3.1889, Shipston-on-Stour, Warwickshire. *d:* 30.8.1975, Shipston-on-Stour, Warwickshire. Middle order right-hand batsman. *Sch* Wellingborough. *Team* Worcestershire (1921–25, 4 matches).
Career batting
4–8–3–74–28*–14.80–0–*ct* 1

Sale, Richard (sen)
Amateur. *b:* 21.6.1889, Broughty Ferry, Angus, Scotland. *d:* 7.9.1970, East Hanney, Berkshire. Father of Richard (Derbyshire and Warwickshire). Middle order left-hand batsman, right-arm fast medium bowler. *Sch* Repton. *Teams* Oxford U (1909–11, blue 1910); Derbyshire (1908–12, 23 matches).
Career batting
39–70–2–961–69–14.13–0–*ct* 12
Bowling 471–10–47.10–0–0–2/25

Sale, Richard (jun)
Amateur. *b:* 4.10.1919, Shrewsbury, Shropshire. Son of Richard (Derbyshire). Stylish opening left-hand batsman, good field. *Sch* Repton. *Teams* Oxford U (1939 and 1946, blue both years); Derbyshire (1949–54, 24 matches); Warwickshire (1939–47, 19 matches).
Career batting
66–115–8–2923–157–27.32–3–*ct* 27
Bowling 4–1–4.00–0–0–1/4
He hit 1,047 runs, av 34.90, in 1946.

Saleem Altaf Bokhari
Cricketer. *b:* 23.3.1944, Lahore, India. Lower order right-hand batsman, right-arm fast medium bowler. *Teams* Lahore (1963/4); Punjab University (1964/5 to 1967/8); PIA (1967/8 to 1978/9). *Tours* Pakistan to England 1967, 1971, to Australia and New Zealand 1972/3, to Australia 1976/7, to West Indies 1976/7. *Tests* Pakistan (1967 to 1976/7, 21 matches).
Career batting
143–184–50–3067–111–22.88–1–*ct* 61
Bowling 9479–334–28.38–8–1–7/69
Test batting
21–31–12–276–53*–14.52–0–*ct* 3
Bowling 1710–46–37.17–0–0–4/11
He played in two Tests on both 1967 and 1971 tours, and proved a useful bowler, but in both years missed matches through injury or illness.

Saleem Yousuf
Cricketer. *b:* 7.12.1959, Karachi, Pakistan. Middle order right-hand batsman, wicket-keeper. *Teams* Karachi (1978/9); Sind (1978/9); Industrial Development Bank of Pakistan (1979/80 to 1981/2); Allied Bank (1982/3). *Tour* Pakistan to England 1982. *Test* Pakistan (1981/2, 1 match).
Career batting
44–71–4–2172–145*–32.41–5–*ct* 111–*st* 14
Bowling 16–1–16.00–0–0–1/16
Test batting
1–1–0–4–4–4.00–0–*ct* 5–*st* 2
The reserve wicket-keeper on the 1982 tour to England, he appeared in only four first-class matches.

Salim Malik
Cricketer. *b:* 16.4.1963, Lahore, Pakistan. Attractive middle order right-hand batsman, good field. *Teams* Lahore (1978/9 to 1981/2); Habib Bank (1982/3). *Tours* Pakistan to Australia 1981/2, to England 1982. *Tests* Pakistan (1981/2 to 1982/3, 8 matches).
Career batting
46–64–8–2556–126*–45.64–10–*ct* 29
Bowling 148–4–37.00–0–0–2/1
Test batting
8–8–1–261–107–37.28–2–*ct* 9
On the 1982 tour to England he played in five first-class matches, but no Tests.

Salim-ud-din
Amateur. *b: circa* 1939, India. Middle order batsman, useful bowler. *Team* Karachi (1957/8 to 1962/3). *Tour* Pakistan Eaglets to England 1963.
Career batting
9–13–0–467–137–35.92–1–*ct* 2
Bowling 40–1–40.00–0–0–1/16
His first-class debut was for Combined Schools in 1954/5.

Salmon, Edward Henry Pearse
Amateur. *b:* 24.12.1853, Madras, India. *d:* 1.2.1907, Cliftonville, Kent. Middle order right-hand batsman, wicket-keeper. *Sch* Victoria College, Jersey. *Team* Middlesex (1878–79, 9 matches).
Career batting
11–18–3–171–49–11.40–0–*ct* 13–*st* 15

Salmon, Gordon Hedley
Amateur. *b:* 1.8.1894, Leicester. *d:* 13.6.1978, Exmouth, Devon. Middle order right-hand batsman. *Sch* Wyggeston. *Team* Leicestershire (1913–24, 47 matches).

Career batting
47–86–5–1273–72–15.71–0–*ct* 12
Bowling 31–0

It was thought that an injury to his arm during the First World War would finish his cricket, but despite this disability he continued to bat successfully in both County and Club cricket.

Salter, George
Amateur. *b:* 18.4.1834. *d:* 15.8.1911, Chichester, Sussex. Opening batsman. *Team* Sussex (1864, 1 match).
Career batting
1–2–1–19–15–19.00–0–*ct* 1

He was scorer to Sussex CCC for many years.

Salter, Malcolm Gurney
Amateur. *b:* 10.5.1887, Cheltenham, Gloucestershire. *d:* 15.6.1973, Chesham Bois, Bucks. Middle order right-hand batsman. *Sch* Cheltenham. *Teams* Gloucestershire (1907–25, 34 matches); Oxford U (1908–10, blue 1909–10); Europeans (1913/4 to 1925/6); Rajputana (1926/7).
Career batting
65–119–4–2486–152–21.61–2–*ct* 44–*st* 1

Sampson, Richard King
Amateur. *b:* 1860, Lewes, Sussex. *d:* 12.7.1927, Ringmer, Sussex. Middle order right-hand batsman, wicket-keeper. *Team* Sussex (1886, 1 match).
Career batting
1–2–0–7–5–3.50–0–*ct* 1

Samson, Oswald Massey
Amateur. *b:* 8.8.1881, Taunton, Somerset. *d:* 17.9.1918, near Peronne, France. He died of wounds. Middle order left-hand batsman, slow left-arm bowler. *Sch* Cheltenham. *Teams* Oxford U (1902–03, blue 1903); Somerset (1900–13, 45 matches).
Career batting
49–85–5–1464–105–18.30–1–*ct* 32
Bowling 88–5–17.60–0–0–2/4

Samuel, Glyndwr Ninian Thomas Watkin
Amateur. *b:* 26.10.1917, Swansea, Glamorgan. Middle order right-hand batsman. *Sch* Uppingham. *Team* Glamorgan (1936, 3 matches).
Career batting
3–4–0–41–22–10.25–0–*ct* 0

Sandeman, George Amelius Crawshay
Amateur. *b:* 18.4.1883, London. *d:* 26.4.1915, Zonnebeke, Belgium. He was killed in action. Lower order left-hand batsman, slow left-arm bowler. *Sch* Eton. *Team* Hampshire (1913, 3 matches).
Career batting
6–11–7–18–5*–4.50–0–0–*ct* 3
Bowling 242–5–48.40–0–0–2/73

He played in the Oxford Freshmen's Match of 1903, but no first-class matches for the University. His final first-class match was for MCC in 1914.

Sanders, Arthur Thomas
Amateur. *b:* 21.12.1900, London. *d:* 22.11.1920, Westminster, London. Middle order batsman. *Sch* Harrow. *Team* Somerset (1919, 1 match).
Career batting
1–1–0–0–0–0.00–0–*ct* 0

Sanders, Wilfred
Professional. *b:* 4.4.1910, Chilvers-Coton, Warwickshire. *d:* May 1965, Nuneaton, Warwickshire. Lower order right-hand batsman, right-arm medium pace bowler. *Team* Warwickshire (1928–34, 84 matches).
Career batting
84–100–18–706–64–8.60–0–*ct* 46
Bowling 4663–119–39.18–0–0–4/44

Sanderson, Gerald Barry
Amateur. *b:* 12.5.1881, Toxteth Park, Liverpool. *d:* 3.10.1964, Westminster, London. Middle order right-hand batsman. *Sch* Malvern. *Teams* Warwickshire (1901, 1 match); Worcestershire (1923, 1 match).
Career batting
2–2–0–16–16–8.00–0–*ct* 0

Sanderson, John Frederick Waley
Cricketer. *b:* 10.9.1954, Highgate, Middlesex. Lower order right-hand batsman, right-arm medium pace bowler. *Sch* Westminster. *Team* Oxford U (1979–80, blue 1980).
Career batting
6–6–2–18–9–4.50–0–*ct* 2
Bowling 282–10–28.20–1–0–6/67

Sanderson, Sir Lancelot
Amateur. *b:* 24.10.1863, Lancaster, Lancashire. *d:* 9.3.1944, Ellel, Lancashire. Defensive lower order right-hand batsman, right-arm slow bowler, useful field. *Sch* Harrow. *Team* Lancashire (1884, 1 match).
Career batting
2–3–0–71–61–23.66–0–*ct* 1

He played in the Freshmen's Match at Cambridge, but no first-class matches for the University. His final first-class match was for MCC in 1888. From 1910 to 1915 he was MP for Appleby; he later went to India where he was the Chief Justice of Bengal.

Sanderson, Richard Withington Bromiley
Amateur. *b:* 15.1.1847, Cheetham Hill, Manchester. *d:* 1934, Tynemouth, Northumberland. Middle order batsman. *Team* Lancashire (1870, 1 match)
Career batting
1–2–0–7–6–3.50–0–*ct* 0

Sandford, John Douglas
Amateur. *b:* 3.8.1832, Chillingham, Northumberland. *d:* 26.5.1892, Windsor, Berkshire. Middle order batsman. *Sch* Rugby. *Team* Oxford U (1855–56).
Career batting
3–5–0–45–20–9.00–0–*ct* 1
His final first-class match was for MCC in 1869.

Sandford, Temple Charles Gabriel
Amateur. *b:* 16.5.1877, Landkey, Devon. *d:* 27.12.1942, Marlborough, Wiltshire. Son of E. G. (Oxford U 1859). Middle order right-hand batsman. *Team* Oxford U (1900).
Career batting
2–3–0–19–11–6.33–0–*ct* 1
His County cricket was for Wiltshire.

Sandham, Andrew
Professional. *b:* 6.7.1890, Streatham, Surrey. *d:* 20.4.1982, Westminster, London. Sound opening right-hand batsman. *Team* Surrey (1911–37, 525 matches). *Tours* MCC to South Africa 1922/3, 1930/1, to Australia 1924/5, to India, Burma and Ceylon 1926/7, to West Indies 1929/30; Cahn to Jamaica 1928/9; Brinckman to South America 1937/8. *Tests* England (1921 to 1929/30, 14 matches).
Career batting
642–1000–79–41284–325–44.82–107–*ct* 158
Bowling 560–18–31.11–0–0–3/27
Test batting
14–23–0–879–325–38.21–2–*ct* 4
He hit 1,000 runs in a season eighteen times in England and twice overseas, going on to 2,000 eight times (best 2,565, av 51.30, in 1929). His highest innings was 325 for England v West Indies at Kingston in 1929/30 and his highest in England 282* for Surrey v Lancashire at Old Trafford in 1928. He hit nine other double centuries, all for Surrey. On 63 occasions he assisted J. B. Hobbs to record a century partnership for the first wicket. From 1946 to 1958 he was coach to Surrey CCC and for the following 12 years was County scorer.

Sands, Jeremy Nigel
Cricketer. *b:* 9.1.1944, Carshalton, Surrey. Middle order right-hand batsman. *Sch* Edinburgh Academy. *Team* Scotland (1965).
Career batting
4–5–0–37–17–7.40–0–*ct* 1
His final first-class match was for MCC in 1967.

Sanger, Percival Bertram
Amateur. *b:* 19.10.1899, Reading, Berkshire. *d:* 17.9.1968, Avebury, Wiltshire. Lower order right-hand batsman, wicket-keeper. *Sch* Cheltenham. *Team* Army (1925).
Career batting
1–1–0–2–2–2.00–0–*ct* 2–*st* 1

Santall, Frederick Reginald
Amateur, turned professional in 1923. *b:* 12.7.1903, Acocks Green, Birmingham, Warwickshire. *d:* 3.11.1950, Cheltenham, Gloucestershire. Son of Sydney (Warwickshire). Hard hitting middle order right-hand batsman, right-arm medium pace bowler, excellent field. *Team* Warwickshire (1919–39, 496 matches). *Tour* Brinckman to South America 1937/8.
Career batting
500–797–86–17730–201*–24.93–21–*ct* 268
Bowling 12257–283–43.31–2–0–5/47
He hit 1,000 runs in a season seven times (best 1,727, av 46.67, in 1933). His only double century was 201* for Warwickshire v Northants at Northampton in 1933.

Santall, John Frank Eden
Professional. *b:* 3.12.1907, King's Heath, Birmingham. Middle order right-hand batsman, right-arm medium bowler. *Team* Worcestershire (1930, 8 matches).
Career batting
8–13–1–117–36*–9.75–0–*ct* 2
Bowling 124–2–62.00–0–0–2/29

Santall, Sydney
Professional. *b:* 10.6.1873, Peterborough, Northants. *d:* 19.3.1957, Ensbury Park, Bournemouth, Hampshire. Father of F. R. (Warwickshire). Lower order right-hand batsman, right-arm medium pace bowler. *Teams* Warwickshire (1894–1914, 371 matches); London County (1900).
Career batting
374–539–119–6516–73–15.51–0–*ct* 175
Bowling 29250–1220–23.97–63–5–8/23
He exceeded 100 wickets in a season once – 101, av 16.62, in 1907. Before appearing for Warwickshire he played occasionally as an amateur for Northants (pre-first-class).

Saravanamuttu, Sabdharatnajyoti
Amateur. *b:* 1898, Colombo, Ceylon. *d:* 17.7.1957, Colombo, Ceylon. Middle order right-hand batsman, right-arm medium fast bowler. *Teams* Cambridge U (1923); Ceylon (1926/7); Engineer's XI in India (1947/8).
Career batting
6–9–0–148–63–16.44–0–*ct* 2
Bowling 76–2–38.00–0–0–2/26

Sardesai, Dilip Narayan
Amateur. *b:* 8.8.1940, Margao, Goa, India. Stylish middle order right-hand batsman, good cover field. *Team* Bombay (1960/1 to 1972/3). *Tours* India to England 1967, 1971, to Australia and New Zealand 1967/8, to West Indies 1961/2, 1970/1; A.C.C. to Pakistan 1961/2. *Tests* India (1961/2 to 1972/3, 30 matches).
Career batting
179–271–26–10230–222–41.75–25–*ct* 85
Bowling 552–8–69.00–0–0–2/15
Test batting
30–55–4–2001–212–39.23–5–*ct* 4
Bowling 45–0

A broken finger resulted in him being sent home half way through the 1967 tour to England, but he played in one Test and had the best first-class batting average – 288 runs, av 41.14. He played some good innings on the 1971 visit, but his overall figures were not impressive. His highest score was 222 for ACC XI v Indian Starlets at Hyderabad in 1964/5. He hit 1,000 runs in an Indian season three times.

Sarel, William Godfrey Molyneux
Amateur. *b:* 15.12.1875, Dover, Kent. *d:* 5.4.1950, Whitechapel, London. Stylish middle order right-hand batsman, right-arm off break bowler. *Teams* Surrey (1904–09, 4 matches); Kent (1912–14, 9 matches); Sussex (1919–21, 12 matches); Trinidad (1904/5 to 1905/6).
Career batting
35–63–5–1313–103–22.63–1–*ct* 19
Bowling 197–3–65.66–0–0–1/1

He also played for Northumberland. From 1919 to 1922 he was Secretary to Sussex CCC.

Sarfraz Nawaz, Malik
Cricketer. *b:* 1.12.1948, Lahore, Pakistan. Attacking lower order right-hand batsman, right-arm fast medium bowler. *Teams* Lahore (1967/8 to 1982/3); Punjab Univ (1968/9 to 1971/2); Northamptonshire (1969–82, 151 matches); Punjab (1974/5); Railways (1975/6); United Bank (1976/7 to 1977/8). *Tours* Pakistan to England 1971, 1974, 1978, 1982, to Australia and New Zealand 1972/3, 1978/9, to Australia 1976/7, 1981/2, to West Indies 1976/7, to Ceylon 1972/3, 1975/6. *Tests* Pakistan (1968/9 to 1982/3, 49 matches).
Career batting
286–349–68–5417–90–19.27–0–*ct* 157
Bowling 23193–969–23.93–46–4–9/86
Test batting
49–62–9–827–55–15.60–0–*ct* 25
Bowling 5020–155–32.38–4–1–9/86

Owing to injury he appeared in only three matches on the 1971 Pakistan tour to England. In 1974 he played in all three Tests and headed the Test bowling averages. He was again injured in 1978, but when available was the most effective bowler in the side. His Test career has been affected by a number of disagreements with the Pakistan Board of Control. In 1975 he took 101 wickets, av 20.30. His best bowling in an innings was 9 for 86 for Pakistan v Australia at Melbourne in 1978/9; in a spell of 33 balls during that innings he took 7 wickets for one run.

Sargent, Arthur Harry Thomas
Professional. *b:* 24.3.1908, Northampton. Lower order right-hand batsman, right-arm medium pace off break bowler. *Team* Northamptonshire (1932, 4 matches).
Career batting
4–7–1–41–18–6.83–0–*ct* 3
Bowling 286–7–40.85–1–0–5/88

Sargent, Murray Alfred James
Professional. *b:* 23.8.1928, Adelaide, Australia. Middle order right-hand batsman, leg break bowler. *Teams* Leicestershire (1951–52, 13 matches); South Australia (1960/1, 9 matches).
Career batting
22–38–4–804–164–23.64–1–*ct* 5
Bowling 204–3–68.00–0–0–2/18

Sarwate, Chandrasekhar Trimbak
Amateur. *b:* 22.6.1920, Saugor, Vidarbha, India. Defensive middle order right-hand batsman, right-arm leg break, or occasional off break, bowler. *Teams* Central Provinces and Berar (1936/7); Maharashtra (1938/9 to 1946/7); Hindus (1941/2 to 1944/5); Bombay (1943/4); Holkar (1944/5 to 1954/5); Madhya Bharat (1955/6 to 1956/7); Madhya Pradesh (1958/9 to 1967/8); Vidarbha (1968/9). *Tours* Holkar to Ceylon 1947/8; India to England 1946, 1952, to Australia 1947/8. *Tests* India (1946 to 1951/2, 9 matches).
Career batting
171–257–30–7430–246–32.73–14–*ct* 91
Bowling 11633–494–23.54–26–3–9/61
Test batting
9–17–1–208–37–13.00–0–*ct* 0
Bowling 374–3–124.66–0–0–1/16

On the 1946 tour to England he assisted S. N.

Banerjee in a record 10th wicket partnership of 249 v Surrey at the Oval; this innings was in fact the only one of note he achieved during the visit. His bowling seemed to lack confidence. In 1952 he was completely out of form. His highest score was 246 for Holkar v Bengal at Calcutta in 1950/1 and his best bowling 9/61 for Holkar v Mysore at Indore in 1945/6.

Saunders, Sir Alan Arthur
Amateur. *b:* 15.12.1892, Brighton, Sussex. *d:* 26.2.1957, Hove, Sussex. Middle order right-hand batsman, useful bowler. *Team* Sussex (1922–23, 12 matches).
Career batting
12–20–4–186–36–11.62–0–*ct* 7
Bowling 129–2–64.50–0–0–1/6

Saunders, Christopher John
Cricketer. *b:* 7.5.1940, Worthing, Sussex. Lower order right-hand batsman, wicket-keeper. *Sch* Lancing. *Teams* Cambridge U (1962–63); Oxford U (1964, blue).
Career batting
12–14–8–69–21–11.50–0–*ct* 10–*st* 3
His County cricket was for Berkshire.

Saunders, Henry Banyard
Professional. *b:* 29.12.1841, Impingham, Cambridgeshire. *d:* 1904, West Derby, Liverpool. Attacking middle order right-hand batsman wicket-keeper. *Teams* Cambridgeshire (1865–66, 9 matches).
Career batting
9–15–0–151–39–10.06–0–*ct* 4–*st* 2
Bowling 47–1–47.00–0–0–1/47

Saunders, Henry William
Amateur. *b:* 1883. *d:* 24.4.1942, Weston-super-Mare, Somerset. Middle order left-hand batsman. *Team* Somerset (1911–22, 4 matches).
Career batting
4–8–1–50–17–7.14–0–*ct* 4

Saunders, James
Professional. *b:* 27.5.1802, Haslemere, Surrey. *d:* 27.3.1832, Haslemere, Surrey. He died of consumption. Cousin of William Searle (Kent and Surrey). Middle order left-hand batsman, wicket-keeper. *Teams* Sussex (1823–25); Kent (1827); Surrey (1828–30).
Career batting
54–97–7–2180–100*–24.22–1–*ct* 43–*st* 31
Bowling 2 wickets, no analyses
Haygarth in *Scores & Biographies* states: 'His career was short but most brilliant; and, considering the early age at which he died, his performances with the bat will be found exceeded by few, if, indeed, by any.' His first-class debut was for Godalming in 1822 and his final match for England in 1831.

Saunders, J.
Professional. Left-hand batsman. *Team* Middlesex (1891, 2 matches).
Career batting
2–3–1–16–7*–8.00–0–*ct* 0
He also played for Buckinghamshire.

Saunders, John Graham
Cricketer. *b:* 30.11.1936, South Africa. Lower order right-hand batsman, off break bowler. *Team* Oxford U (1966).
Career batting
2–4–1–48–47*–16.00–0–*ct* 1
Bowling 163–10–16.30–2–1–5/50

Saunders, John Victor
Amateur. *b:* 3.2.1876, Melbourne, Australia. *d:* 21.12.1927, Toorak, Victoria, Australia. Tail end left-hand batsman, left-arm medium pace spin bowler. *Teams* Victoria (1899/1900 to 1909/10, 51 matches); Wellington (1910/11 to 1913/14). *Tours* Australia to England 1902, to South Africa 1902/3. *Tests* Australia (1901/2 to 1907/8, 14 matches).
Career batting
107–170–47–586–29*–4.76–0–*ct* 71
Bowling 12064–553–21.81–48–9–8/106
Test batting
14–23–6–39–11*–2.29–0–*ct* 5
Bowling 1796–79–22.73–6–0–7/34
He was most successful on the 1902 tour to England, taking 123 wickets, av 16.95, a figure only bettered by Trumble. His bowling action however came in for some criticism.

Saunders, Martyn
Cricketer. *b:* 16.5.1958, Worcester. Lower order right-hand batsman, right-arm fast medium bowler. *Team* Worcestershire (1980, 3 matches).
Career batting
3–2–0–12–12–6.00–0–*ct* 0
Bowling 212–6–35.33–0–0–3/47

Saunders, Philip Frederick
Professional. *b:* 28.4.1929, Adelaide, Australia. Lower order right-hand batsman, right-arm fast or leg break bowler. *Team* Leicestershire (1951–52, 9 matches).
Career batting
9–11–4–93–30–13.28–0–*ct* 2
Bowling 190–6–31.66–0–0–3/57

Saunders, William
Amateur. *b:* 29.3.1840, Histon, Cambridgeshire.

d: 10.12.1923, Chesterton, Cambridgeshire. Brother of H. B. (Cambridgeshire). Lower order right-hand batsman, right-hand slow round-arm bowler, slip field. *Team* Cambridgeshire (1865, 3 matches).
Career batting
3–5–2–21–11*–7.00–0–*ct* 4
Bowling 183–10–18.30–0–0–4/50

Savage, John Scholes
Cricketer. *b:* 3.3.1929, Ramsbottom, Lancashire. Lower order right-hand batsman, off break bowler. *Teams* Leicestershire (1953–66, 281 matches); Lancashire (1967–69, 58 matches).
Career batting
347–460–161–2154–33–7.20–0–*ct* 98
Bowling 23777–965–24.63–46–7–8/50
He took 100 wickets in a season three times (best 122, av 18.93, in 1961). He is joint Lancashire coach.

Savage, Richard Le Quesne
Cricketer. *b:* 10.12.1955, Waterloo, London. Lower order right-hand batsman, right-arm off break bowler. *Sch* Marlborough. *Teams* Oxford U (1976–78, blue all three years); Warwickshire (1976–79, 23 matches).
Career batting
44–52–25–196–22*–7.25–0–*ct* 14
Bowling 3787–127–29.81–6–1–7/50

Savile, George
Amateur. *b:* 26.4.1847, Methley, Yorkshire. *d:* 4.9.1904, Tetbury, Gloucestershire. Excellent middle order right-hand batsman, good deep field. *Sch* Rossall and Eton. *Teams* Cambridge U (1867–68, blue 1868); Yorkshire (1867–74, 5 matches); Canterbury (1871/2).
Career batting
16–24–1–529–105–23.00–1–*ct* 10–*st* 1

Savill, Leslie Austin
Professional. *b:* 30.6.1935, Brentwood, Essex. Opening right-hand batsman. *Team* Essex (1953–61, 125 matches).
Career batting
125–200–16–3919–115–21.29–4–*ct* 50
Bowling 26–1–26.00–0–0–1/26
He hit 1,197 runs, av 32.35, in 1959.

Saville, Clifford Allen
Amateur. *b:* 5.2.1892, Tottenham, Middlesex. *d:* 8.11.1917, Fresnoy Le Grand, Aisne, France. He was killed in action. Brother of S. H. (Middlesex). Middle order right-hand batsman. *Sch* Marlborough. *Team* Middlesex (1914, 3 matches).
Career batting
3–5–0–57–32–11.40–0–*ct* 0

Saville, Graham John
Cricketer. *b:* 5.2.1944, Leytonstone, Essex. Middle order right-hand batsman, leg break and googly bowler, good slip field. *Team* Essex (1963–74, 124 matches).
Career batting
126–218–29–4474–126*–23.67–3–*ct* 103
Bowling 76–3–25.33–0–0–2/30
He left Essex in 1966 and appeared for Norfolk 1967 to 1969, returning to Essex in 1970. In 1970 he hit 1,133 runs, av 29.81. He was appointed Assistant Secretary to Essex CCC at the close of the 1973 season.

Saville, Stanley Herbert
Amateur. *b:* 21.11.1889, Tottenham, Middlesex. *d:* 22.2.1966, Eastbourne, Sussex. Brother of C. A. (Middlesex). Middle order right-hand batsman, slow right-arm bowler. *Sch* Marlborough. *Teams* Cambridge U (1911–14, blue all four years); Middlesex (1910–28, 50 matches).
Career batting
90–140–12–2784–141*–21.75–2–*ct* 60
Bowling 197–4–49.25–0–0–2/29
A fine hockey player at inside-right, he captained England and appeared in 37 internationals.

Savory, Henry Jarvis
Amateur. *b:* 4.3.1914, Chipping Sodbury, Gloucestershire. Middle order right-hand batsman, right-arm medium bowler. *Team* Gloucestershire (1937, 1 match).
Career batting
1–1–0–16–16–16.00–0–*ct* 0

Savory, Rev James Henry
Amateur. *b:* 20.3.1855, Binfield, Bracknell, Berkshire. *d:* 5.8.1903, Bayham Abbey, Sussex. Attacking middle order right-hand batsman, good cover point. *Sch* Winchester. *Team* Oxford U (1877–78, blue both years).
Career batting
13–24–1–231–36–10.04–0–*ct* 7
His last first-class match was for MCC in 1883. For many years he was a prominent member of the Free Foresters.

Sawyer, Charles Montague
Amateur. *b:* 1856, Broughton, Lancashire. *d:* 30.3.1921, Ormskirk, Lancashire. Lower order batsman, bowler. *Team* Lancashire (1884, 2 matches).
Career batting
2–2–1–21–11*–21.00–0–*ct* 0
Bowling 65–0
A brilliant rugby three-quarter he represented Lancashire and England.

Saxelby, Kevin
Cricketer. *b:* 23.2.1959, Worksop, Notts. Lower order right-hand batsman, right-arm fast bowler. *Team* Nottinghamshire (1978–83, 43 matches).
Career batting
43–52–11–475–59*–11.58–0–*ct* 8
Bowling 2631–101–26.04–2–0–5/52

Saxena, Ramesh Chand
Amateur. *b:* 12.9.1944, Delhi, India. Middle order right-hand batsman, leg break bowler. *Teams* Delhi (1960/1 to 1965/6); Bihar (1966/7 to 1981/2). *Tours* India to England 1967, to East Africa 1967, to Australia and New Zealand 1967/8; State Bank of India to Ceylon 1966/7. *Test* India (1967, 1 match).
Career batting
147–231–29–8255–202*–40.86–17–*ct* 65
Bowling 933–33–28.27–0–0–4/24
Test batting
1–2–0–25–16–12.50–0–*ct* 0
Bowling 11–0
A brilliant schoolboy batsman, he achieved little on the 1967 tour to England, though playing in one Test. His highest score was 202* for Bihar v Assam at Dhanbad in 1969/70.

Sayen, William Henry
Amateur. *b:* 1883, Philadelphia, USA. Tail end right-hand batsman, right-arm fast bowler. *Team* Gentlemen of England (1908). *Tour* Philadelphia to England 1908.
Career batting
7–13–2–136–29–12.36–0–*ct* 5
Bowling 406–12–33.83–0–0–4/44
He played for the USA v Canada in 1907. His reminiscences 'A Yankee Looks at Cricket' were published in 1956.

Sayer, David Michael
Amateur. *b:* 19.9.1936, Romford, Essex. Lower order right-hand batsman, right-arm fast bowler. *Sch* Maidstone. *Teams* Oxford U (1958–60, blue all three years); Kent (1955–76, 154 matches). *Tours* MCC to South America 1958/9 (not first-class), to New Zealand 1960/1.
Career batting
204–237–86–1252–62–8.29–0–*ct* 76
Bowling 14397–613–23.48–19–2–7/37

Sayer, John Druce
Amateur. *b:* 29.10.1920, Hong Kong. Lower order batsman, slow left-arm bowler, good slip field. *Sch* Shrewsbury. *Team* Combined Services (1950–52).
Career batting
4–7–0–81–49–11.57–0–*ct* 3
Bowling 274–7–39.14–0–0–4/38

Sayers, Denis
Cricketer. *b:* 17.3.1934, St Pancras, London. Lower order right-hand batsman, right-arm medium pace bowler. *Team* Essex (1967, 1 match).
Career batting
1–1–1–0–0*–no av–0–*ct* 0
Bowling 64–1–64.00–0–0–1/22

Sayres, Rev Edward
Amateur. *b:* 19.12.1815, North Stoke, Sussex. *d:* 11.1.1888, Cold-Ashton, Gloucs. Lower order right-hand batsman, right-hand slow round-arm bowler. *Teams* Cambridge U (1838–41, blue all four years); Sussex (1840, 1 match).
Career batting
24–43–9–103–19–3.02–0–*ct* 7
Bowling 100 wickets, no analyses
His final first-class match was for MCC in 1842.

Scattergood, Joseph Henry
Amateur. *b:* 26.1.1877, Philadelphia, USA. *d:* 1954, Philadelphia, USA. Brother of Alfred (USA v Canada). Tail end right-hand batsman, wicket-keeper. *Team* Philadelphia (1897–1903). *Tours* Philadelphia to England 1897, 1903.
Career batting
15–26–8–104–13–5.77–0–*ct* 25–*st* 9
He was the principal wicket-keeper on the 1897 tour, but in 1903 played in only four matches due to injury.

Schepens, Martin
Cricketer. *b:* 12.8.1955, Barrow-upon-Soar, Leicestershire. Middle order right-hand batsman, leg break bowler. *Team* Leicestershire (1973–80, 19 matches).
Career batting
19–28–5–407–57–17.69–0–*ct* 12
Bowling 13–0

Schofield, Dennis
Cricketer. *b:* 9.10.1947, Holmfirth, Yorkshire. Lower order right-hand batsman, right-arm medium pace bowler. *Team* Yorkshire (1970–74, 3 matches).
Career batting
3–4–4–13–6*–no av–0–*ct* 0
Bowling 112–5–22.40–1–0–5/42

Schofield, J.
Amateur. Lower order batsman, wicket-keeper. *Team* Lancashire (1876, 4 matches).
Career batting
4–6–2–27–11–6.75–0–*ct* 7–*st* 1

Scholey, John Colin
Professional. *b:* 28.9.1930, Beeston, Leeds, Yorkshire. Defensive lower order right-hand batsman, wicket-keeper. *Team* Worcestershire (1952–53, 10 matches).
Career batting
10–7–2–32–16–6.40–0–*ct* 21–*st* 4

Scholfield, Frank Beaumont
Amateur. *b:* 16.11.1886, Bury, Lancashire. *d:* 1.3.1950, Chelsea, London. Middle order batsman. *Sch* Sedbergh. *Team* Lancashire (1911, 1 match).
Career batting
1–2–1–17–17–17.00–0–*ct* 0
Bowling 2–0
He also played for Cheshire.

Schultz, Sandford Spence
(later Storey)
Amateur. *b:* 29.8.1857, Birkenhead, Cheshire. *d:* 18.12.1937, South Kensington, London. Lower order right-hand batsman, right-hand fast round-arm bowler, good slip field. *Sch* Uppingham. *Teams* Cambridge U (1876–77, blue 1877); Lancashire (1877–82, 9 matches). *Tour* Harris to Australia 1878/9. *Test* England (1878/9, 1 match).
Career batting
42–70–9–1046–90–17.14–0–*ct* 29
Bowling 1143–28–40.82–0–0–4/37
Test batting
1–2–1–20–20–20.00–0–*ct* 0
Bowling 26–1–26.00–0–0–1/16
His final match was for C. I. Thornton's XI in 1885. He also played for Huntingdonshire and Lincolnshire.

Schwann, Henry Sigismund
(later Henry Bagehot Swann)
Amateur. *b:* 19.11.1868, North Houghton, Stockbridge, Hampshire. *d:* 27.5.1931, Eastbourne, Sussex. Sound middle order right-hand batsman. *Sch* Clifton. *Team* Oxford U (1890, blue).
Career batting
6–11–0–204–70–18.54–0–*ct* 1

Schwarz, Reginald Oscar
Amateur. *b:* 4.5.1875, Lee, Kent. *d:* 18.11.1918, Etaples, France. He died of influenza. Attacking lower order right-hand batsman, originally right-arm medium pace, but later slow off break bowler with a leg break action. *Sch* St Paul's. *Teams* Transvaal (1902/3 to 1909/10); Middlesex (1901–05, 14 matches). *Tours* Bosanquet to North America 1901; MCC to North America 1907; South Africa to England 1904, 1907 and 1912, to Australia 1910/11. *Tests* South Africa (1905/06 to 1912, 20 matches).
Career batting
125–192–24–3798–102–22.60–1–*ct* 108
Bowling 7000–398–17.58–25–3–8/55
Test batting
20–35–8–374–61–13.85–0–*ct* 18
Bowling 1417–55–25.76–2–0–6/47
He played in the Freshmen's Match at Cambridge in 1894 and the Seniors' Match of 1895, but no first-class matches. On the 1904 South African tour to England he surprised everyone by taking 65 wickets, av 18.26, and topping the bowling table. In 1907 he was the leading bowler in England with 137 wickets, av 11.79; he achieved little on the 1912 tour. His last first-class match was for L. Robinson's XI in 1914. A noted rugby football full back he represented both Cambridge and England.

Sclater, Arthur William Bassett
Amateur. *b:* 27.7.1859, Awburn, Co Cavan, Ireland. *d:* 16.6.1882, River Titirau, Tortois Station, Otago, New Zealand. He died in a shooting accident. Middle order right-hand batsman, right-arm medium pace bowler, good point field. *Sch* Cheltenham. *Team* Sussex (1879–80, 9 matches).
Career batting
9–14–5–107–18*–11.88–0–*ct* 12
Bowling 687–35–19.62–1–1–7/45
He was 6 ft 6½ in tall, being, perhaps, the tallest cricketer of his day.

Scobell, Rev John Frederick
Amateur. *b:* 22.2.1844, Plymouth, Devon. *d:* 8.7.1898, St Leonards-on-Sea, Sussex. Hard hitting middle order right-hand batsman. *Sch* Marlborough. *Team* Oxford U (1865–67).
Career batting
4–7–1–73–44–12.16–0–*ct* 2
Bowling 10–0
His County cricket was for Devon, and in 1866 he hit 269 for that County v Dorset, but curiously was dismissed for 'a pair' in the next match. He lived in Cawnpore, India, for some years commencing about 1870.

Scobie, Charles Smith
Amateur. *b:* 21.2.1895, Edinburgh, Scotland. *d:* 2.9.1965, Trinity, Edinburgh, Scotland. Right-hand batsman, leg break and googly bowler. *Team* Scotland (1923–28).
Career batting
8–15–3–95–26–7.91–0–*ct* 4
Bowling 583–20–29.15–1–0–5/112

Scoggins, Roy
Amateur. *b:* 13.3.1908, West Ham, Essex. *d:* 19.1.1970, Middleton-on-Sea, Sussex. Lower order batsman, useful bowler. *Team* RAF (1932).
Career batting
1–2–0–1–1–0.50–0–*ct* 0
Bowling 112–5–22.40–1–0–5/112
His County cricket was for Buckinghamshire.

Scorer, Reginald Ivor
Amateur. *b:* 6.1.1892, Middlesbrough, Yorkshire. *d:* 19.3.1976, Birmingham. Middle order right-hand batsman, right-arm fast medium pace bowler. *Team* Warwickshire (1921–26, 29 matches).
Career batting
29–52–8–718–113–16.31–1–*ct* 9
Bowling 659–18–36.61–0–0–3/1
He also played for Staffordshire. He was a noted rugby footballer and was on the Committee of the Rugby Union for 16 years.

Scotland, Kenneth James Forbes
Amateur. *b:* 29.8.1936, Edinburgh, Scotland. Right-hand batsman. *Team* Scotland (1958).
Career batting
1–1–0–0–0–0.00–0–*ct* 0
A noted rugby footballer, he was capped for Scotland.

Scott, Arthur Avison
Amateur. *b:* 3.12.1883, Bootle, Lancashire. *d:* 6.1.1968, Attleborough, Norfolk. Son of A. T. (Cambridge U), brother of G. A. (Cambridge U). Lower order right-hand batsman, right-arm fast bowler. *Team* Royal Navy (1912).
Career batting
1–2–0–9–9–4.50–0–*ct* 1
Bowling 96–2–48.00–0–0–1/46

Scott, Andrew Archibald Steele
Amateur. *b:* 26.1.1918, Liberton, Midlothian, Scotland. Right-hand batsman. *Sch* Sedbergh. *Team* Scotland (1947).
Career batting
1–2–0–12–12–6.00–0–*ct* 0

Scott, Arthur Pickett
Amateur. *b:* 1.9.1885, Poplar, Middlesex. *d:* 3.6.1933, Boxgrove, Sussex. Middle order batsman, useful bowler. *Sch* Marlborough. *Team* MCC (1929).
Career batting
1–2–1–40–25–40.00–0–*ct* 0

Scott, Ven Avison Terry
Amateur. *b:* 18.7.1848, Cambridge. *d:* 18.6.1925, Marylebone, London. Father of A. A. (Royal Navy) and G. A. (Cambridge U). Middle order right-hand batsman. *Sch* Brighton. *Teams* Cambridgeshire (1867–71, 4 matches); Cambridge U (1870–71, blue both years).
Career batting
11–21–3–393–76–21.83–0–*ct* 8
He also played for Norfolk. Whilst at Cambridge he won the pole-jump and later became a noted golfer.

Scott, Christopher John
Cricketer. *b:* 16.9.1959, Swinton, Manchester. Lower order left-hand batsman, wicket-keeper. *Team* Lancashire (1977–82, 46 matches).
Career batting
46–51–13–262–27*–6.89–0–*ct* 94–*st* 10

Scott, Colin J.
Professional. *b:* 1.5.1919, Syston, Gloucs. Hard hitting lower order right-hand batsman, right-arm medium fast bowler. *Team* Gloucestershire (1938–54, 235 matches).
Career batting
235–326–43–3375–90–11.92–0–*ct* 193
Bowling 16766–531–31.57–22–2–8/90
He took 100 wickets in a season twice (best 121, av 22.89, in 1939).

Scott, Christopher William
Cricketer. *b:* 27.1.1964, Thorpe-on-the-Hill, Lincolnshire. Middle order right-hand batsman, wicket-keeper. *Team* Nottinghamshire (1981–83, 5 matches).
Career batting
5–6–1–125–78–25.00–0–*ct* 7–*st* 2

Scott, Donald Edward
Amateur. *b:* 5.6.1898, West Ham, Essex. *d:* 9.1.1981, Sturminster-Newton, Dorset. Middle order batsman. *Team* Somerset (1936, 1 match).
Career batting
1–2–1–12–11*–12.00–0–*ct* 0

Scott, Emanuel
Professional. *b:* 6.7.1834, Birkenshaw, Yorkshire. *d:* 3.12.1898, Birkenshaw, Yorkshire. Lower order right-hand batsman, right-hand medium pace round-arm bowler. *Team* Yorkshire (1864, 1 match).
Career batting
1–1–0–8–8–8.00–0–*ct* 1
Bowling 27–2–13.50–0–0–1/6

Scott, Dr Edward Keith
Amateur. *b:* 14.6.1918, Truro, Cornwall. Right-hand batsman, leg break bowler. *Sch* Clifton. *Teams* Gloucestershire (1937, 2 matches); Oxford U (1938). *Tour* MCC to Canada 1951.

Career batting
9–15–1–136–31–9.71–0–*ct* 4
Bowling 444–12–37.00–0–0–2/21

He also played for Cornwall and his last first-class match in England was for Minor Counties in 1949. A noted rugby footballer, he played for Oxford and England.

Scott, Rev George Arbuthnot
Amateur. *b:* 12.4.1879, Wimbledon, Surrey. *d:* 8.6.1927, Eastbourne, Sussex. Son of A. T. (Cambridge U), brother of A. A. (Royal Navy). Tail end right-hand batsman, right-arm fast bowler. *Sch* Tonbridge. *Team* Cambridge U (1900–01).
Career batting
5–7–1–40–10–6.66–0–*ct* 1
Bowling 265–8–33.12–1–0–5/72

His County cricket was for Norfolk.

Scott, Gary Michael
Cricketer. *b:* 8.3.1960, Bulawayo, Rhodesia. Middle order right-hand batsman, right-arm medium pace bowler. *Team* Rhodesia/Zimbabwe (1979/80 to 1982). *Tour* Zimbabwe to England 1982.
Career batting
2–2–0–31–21–15.50–0–*ct* 2

Scott, Lord George William Montagu-Douglas
Amateur. *b:* 31.8.1866. Bowhill, Selkirk, Scotland. *d:* 23.2.1947, Melrose, Roxburghshire, Scotland. Brother of H. F. M. (Philipson's XI) and Earl of Dalkeith (MCC). Middle order right-hand batsman, good deep field. *School* Eton. *Teams* Oxford U (1887–89, blue all three years); Middlesex (1888, 2 matches).
Career batting
27–44–4–882–100–22.05–1–*ct* 14
Bowling 12–0

His debut was for MCC in 1886 and his final first-class match was for MCC in 1905. Whilst serving in the Army in the Boer War, he ran up the Union Jack over Bloemfontein, when the town was captured.

Scott, Henry
Professional. *b:* 28.10.1851, Sutton-in-Ashfield, Notts. *d:* 11.11.1941, Sutton-in-Ashfield, Notts. Tail end right-hand batsman, right-arm slow off break bowler. *Team* Somerset (1882, 2 matches).
Career batting
2–4–1–12–6–4.00–0–*ct* 1
Bowling 99–2–49.50–0–0–2/49

Scott, Harold Eldon
Amateur. *b:* 4.9.1907, Crowborough, Sussex. Son of Osmund (Gloucestershire), brother of K. B. (Sussex). Middle order right-hand batsman, right-arm fast medium bowler. *Sch* Winchester. *Team* Sussex (1937, 2 matches).
Career batting
4–8–0–48–16–6.00–0–*ct* 2
Bowling 158–2–79.00–0–0–1/21

Scott, Lord Henry Francis Montagu-Douglas
Amateur. *b:* 15.1.1868, Bowhill, Selkirk, Scotland. *d:* 19.4.1945, Melrose, Roxburghshire, Scotland. Brother of G. W. M. (Middlesex) and Earl of Dalkeith (MCC). Middle order batsman. *Sch* Eton. *Team* H. Philipson's XI (1891).
Career batting
1–2–1–25–23*–25.00–0–*ct* 0

Scott, Dr Henry James Herbert
Amateur. *b:* 26.12.1858, Toorak, Victoria, Australia. *d:* 23.9.1910, Scone, New South Wales, Australia. Cautious middle order right-hand batsman, right-arm medium fast bowler, good field. *Team* Victoria (1877/8 to 1885/6, 12 matches). *Tours* Australia to England 1884 and 1886. *Tests* Australia (1884–86, 8 matches).
Career batting
85–141–15–2863–123–22.72–4–*ct* 56
Bowling 494–18–27.44–1–0–6/33
Test batting
8–14–1–359–102–27.61–1–*ct* 8
Bowling 26–0

He batted well on his 1884 tour to England, the highlight being his 102 in the Test at the Oval. In 1886 he captained the tourists and his responsibilities in that direction affected his batting. He led Australia in three Tests.

Scott, Hugh Wilson
Amateur. *b:* 18.12.1927, Belfast. Lower order right-hand batsman, right-arm medium pace bowler. *Team* Ireland (1958).
Career batting
1 match, did not bat–*ct* 0
Bowling 9–0

Scott, John Gordon Cameron
Amateur. *b:* 14.3.1888, Eastbourne, Sussex. *d:* 21.3.1946, Warsash, Southampton, Hants. Middle order right-hand batsman. *Sch* Marlborough. *Teams* Sussex (1907–10, 4 matches); Europeans (1914/5 to 1917/8).
Career batting
13–21–3–347–137–19.27–1–*ct* 5

In 1908 he played in the Freshmen's Match at Cambridge and in the Seniors' Matches of the two following years. On his first-class debut, for

Sussex v Oxford U in 1907, he hit 137. His final first-class match in England was for H. D. G. Leveson-Gower's XI in 1912.

Scott, Kenneth Bertram
Amateur. *b:* 17.8.1915, Uckfield, Sussex. *d:* 9.8.1943, Bronte, near Syracuse, Sicily. Son of Osmund (Gloucs), brother of H. E. (Sussex). Middle order right-hand batsman, right-arm medium pace bowler. *Sch* Winchester. *Teams* Oxford U (1935–37, blue 1937); Sussex (1937, 6 matches).
Career batting
14–22–4–274–56–15.22–0–*ct* 3
Bowling 715–12–59.58–0–0–2/13

Scott, Lothian Kerr
Amateur. *b:* 24.5.1841, Paris, France. *d:* 7.7.1919, Farnborough, Hampshire. Middle order right-hand batsman, right-hand medium pace round-arm bowler, deep field. *Sch* Winchester. *Team* Gentlemen of Kent (1864).
Career batting
1–2–0–16–16–8.00–0–*ct* 3
Bowling 22–0

He was most successful in military matches in the 1860s.

Scott, Michael David
Amateur. *b:* 14.11.1933, London. Middle order right-hand batsman, wicket-keeper. *Sch* Winchester. *Team* Oxford U (1956–57, blue 1957).
Career batting
21–38–5–499–52–15.12–0–*ct* 24–*st* 11

His final first-class match was for MCC in 1963.

Scott, Malcolm Ernest
Professional. *b:* 8.5.1936, South Shields, Co Durham. Lower order right-hand batsman, slow left-arm bowler. *Team* Northamptonshire (1959–69, 183 matches).
Career batting
185–253–63–2445–62–12.86–0–*ct* 92
Bowling 11397–461–24.72–20–4–7/32

He took 113 wickets, av 19.27, in 1964. His first-class debut was for Combined Services in 1958. From 1953 to 1956 he appeared for Durham. His bowling action was reported by the umpires in 1967 and he was temporarily banned from County cricket. A good soccer player, he was half back for Newcastle United and Darlington.

Scott, Mark Stephen
Cricketer. *b:* 10.3.1959, Muswell Hill, Middlesex. Middle order right-hand batsman. *Team* Worcestershire (1981–83, 32 matches).
Career batting
32–60–3–1383–109–24.26–1–*ct* 9
Bowling 37–0

Scott, Hon Osmund
Amateur. *b:* 24.3.1876, Wareham, Dorset. *d:* 9.9.1948, Marylebone, London. Father of H. E. (Sussex) and K. B. (Sussex). Right-hand batsman, slow left-arm bowler. *Sch* Winchester. *Team* Gloucestershire (1905, 2 matches).
Career batting
2–4–1–29–23*–9.66–0–*ct* 0
Bowling 11–0

A noted golfer, he represented England and was the losing finalist in the British Amateur championship of 1905.

Scott, Oscar Charles
Amateur. *b:* 25.8.1893, Jamaica. *d:* 15.6.1961, Kingston, Jamaica. Father of A. P. H. (West Indies). Middle order right-hand batsman, leg break bowler. *Team* Jamaica (1910/1 to 1934/5). *Tours* West Indies to England 1928, to Australia 1930/1. *Tests* West Indies (1928 to 1930/1, 8 matches).
Career batting
45–66–12–1317–94–24.38–0–*ct* 14
Bowling 5556–182–30.52–14–5–8/67
Test batting
8–13–3–171–35–17.10–0–*ct* 0
Bowling 925–22–42.04–1–0–5/266

He played in two Tests on the 1928 tour, but he was only moderately successful.

Scott, Peter Marriott Raleigh
Amateur. *b:* 1.2.1912, Paddington, London. *d:* 13.6.1944, Villers-Bocage, France. Brother of R. S. G. (Sussex). Hard hitting lower order left-hand batsman, left-arm fast bowler. *Team* Oxford U (1932–33).
Career batting
5–8–1–114–37–16.28–0–*ct* 1
Bowling 321–5–64.20–0–0–2/22

Scott, Robert Strickland Gilbert
Amateur. *b:* 26.4.1909, Paddington, London. *d:* 26.8.1957, Paddington, London. Brother of P. M. R. (Oxford U). Dashing middle order right-hand batsman, right-arm fast medium bowler. *Sch* Winchester. *Teams* Oxford U (1930–31, blue 1931); Sussex (1931–34, 66 matches).

Career batting
86–113–10–2042–116–19.82–2–*ct* 54
Bowling 3595–134–26.52–5–0–6/64

His final first-class match was for Free Foresters in 1939.

Scott, Stanley Winckworth
Amateur. *b:* 24.3.1854, Bombay, India. *d:* 8.12.1933, Beckenham, Kent. Middle order right-hand batsman, right-arm fast bowler. *Sch* Brentwood and Epsom. *Team* Middlesex (1878–93, 97 matches).
Career batting
104–192–19–4432–224–25.61–4–*ct* 61
Bowling 207–3–69.00–0–0–1/15

He hit 224 for Middlesex v Gloucestershire at Lord's in 1892, and in the same year scored 1,015 runs, av 39.03. After 1893 he gave up regular County cricket owing to business. He also played occasionally for Herefordshire.

Scott, Verdun John
Amateur. *b:* 31.7.1916, Devonport, Auckland, New Zealand. *d:* 2.8.1980, Devonport, Auckland, New Zealand. Solid opening right-hand batsman, good field. *Team* Auckland (1937/8 to 1952/3). *Tour* New Zealand to England 1949. *Tests* New Zealand (1945/6 to 1951/2, 10 matches).
Career batting
79–128–16–5575–204–49.77–16–*ct* 42
Bowling 205–5–41.00–0–0–3/22
Test batting
10–17–1–458–84–28.62–0–*ct* 7
Bowling 14–0

He played in all four Tests on the 1949 tour and in first-class matches hit 1,572 runs, av 40.30. His highest score in England was 203 v Combined Services at Gillingham, his highest in New Zealand being 204 for Auckland v Otago at Dunedin in 1947/8.

Scott, William Ainslie
Amateur. *b:* 1845. *d:* 17.6.1899, Bolton, Lancashire. Middle order batsman. *Team* Lancashire (1874, 1 match).
Career batting
1–2–1–14–9–14.00–0–*ct* 0

Scott, William Ernest Newnham
Amateur. *b:* 31.5.1903, Binstead, Isle of Wight. Lower order right-hand batsman, slow right-arm bowler. *Team* Hampshire (1927, 5 matches).
Career batting
5–7–2–102–35–20.40–0–*ct* 0
Bowling 131–4–32.75–0–0–2/66

Scott, Dr William Jerman
Amateur. *b:* 4.4.1864, Hartley-Wintney, Hants. *d:* 18.7.1920, Windsor, Berks. Middle order right-hand batsman. *Sch* Merchant Taylor's. *Team* Middlesex (1894–95, 3 matches).
Career batting
4–6–0–119–107–19.83–1–*ct* 2

Scott, William Martin
Amateur. *b:* 27.3.1870, Gateshead, Co Durham. *d:* 26.2.1944, Horsham, Sussex. Hard hitting opening or middle order right-hand batsman, right-arm medium pace bowler. *Team* Cambridge U (1891–92).
Career batting
6–11–0–158–56–14.36–0–*ct* 5
Bowling 140–3–46.66–0–0–2/47

His County cricket was for Northumberland. A noted rugby footballer, he played for Cambridge and England.

Scott-Chad, George Norman
(G. N. Chad at birth)
Amateur. *b:* 1.11.1899, Kensington, London. *d:* 4.7.1950, Paddington, London. Lower order right-hand batsman, useful bowler. *Sch* Eton. *Team* Army (1923–24). *Tour* Tennyson to Jamaica 1931/2 (he did not play in first-class matches).
Career batting
3–5–0–49–24–9.80–0–*ct* 4
Bowling 213–6–35.50–0–0–2/43

His County cricket was for Norfolk.

Scott-Malden, Christopher Edward
Amateur. *b:* 2.9.1890, Brighton, Sussex. *d:* 27.7.1956, Washington, Sussex. Lower order batsman, useful bowler. *Sch* Brighton. *Team* Sussex (1920, 2 matches).
Career batting
2–3–0–6–6–2.00–0–*ct* 0
Bowling 20–0

Scotton, William Henry
Professional. *b:* 15.1.1856, Nottingham. *d:* 9.7.1893, St John's Wood, London. He died by his own hand. Defensive opening left-hand batsman, left-arm fast medium bowler. *Team* Nottinghamshire (1875–90, 153 matches). *Tours* Lilleywhite, Shaw and Shrewsbury to Australia 1881/2, 1884/5, 1886/7. *Tests* England (1881/2 to 1886/7, 15 matches).
Career batting
237–377–33–6527–134–18.97–4–*ct* 124
Bowling 410–8–51.25–0–0–1/7
Test batting
15–25–2–510–90–22.17–0–*ct* 4
Bowling 20–0

His best season was 1886 with 979 runs, av 26.45, and his final first-class match was for MCC in 1891. He was noted for his defensive batting and on two occasions in first-class matches batted for an hour without scoring a single run.

Scoulding, Frederick John
Professional. *b:* 1887, Bow, Middlesex. *d:* 25.8.1928, Whitechapel, London. Lower order batsman, slow left-arm bowler. *Team* Essex (1912–20, 22 matches).
Career batting
22–28–11–92–21–5.41–0–*ct* 6
Bowling 1252–32–39.12–0–0–4/50
He also played for Monmouthshire.

Seabrook, Frederick James
Amateur. *b:* 9.1.1899, Gloucester. *d:* 7.8.1979, Cirencester, Gloucs. Brother of W. G. (Gloucestershire). Opening left-hand batsman, slow left-arm bowler. *Sch* Haileybury. *Teams* Cambridge U (1926–28, blue all three years); Gloucestershire (1919–35, 104 matches). *Tour* Tennyson to Jamaica 1927/8.
Career batting
143–225–15–5335–136–25.40–8–*ct* 82
Bowling 274–8–34.25–0–0–4/77
His best season was 1928 with 1,406 runs, av 40.17. He also completed 1,000 runs in one other season. A schoolmaster at Haileybury his County cricket was mainly confined to the school holidays.

Seabrook, Walter George
Amateur. *b:* 12.2.1904, Gloucester. Brother of F. J. (Gloucestershire). Left-hand batsman, left-arm fast medium bowler. *Sch* Haileybury. *Team* Gloucestershire (1928, 1 match).
Career batting
1–2–0–0–0–0.00–0–*ct* 0
Bowling 10–0

Seager, Christopher Paul
Cricketer. *b:* 5.4.1951, Salisbury, Rhodesia. Middle order right-hand batsman. *Team* Cambridge U (1971, blue).
Career batting
8–11–1–104–23–10.40–0–*ct* 2
His County cricket was for Berkshire.

Seal, Alfred
Professional. *b:* 1875, South Stoneham, Hampshire. *d:* 13.2.1961, South Chailey, Sussex. Lower order batsman, useful bowler. *Team* Sussex (1904, 2 matches).
Career batting
2–2–0–0–0–0.00–0–*ct* 1
Bowling 17–0

Sealey, Benjamin James
Amateur. *b:* 12.8.1899, St Joseph, Trinidad. *d:* 12.9.1963, Trinidad. Middle order right-hand batsman, right-arm medium pace bowler. *Team* Trinidad (1923/4 to 1940/1). *Tour* West Indies to England 1933. *Test* West Indies (1933, 1 match).
Career batting
51–84–12–2115–116–29.37–4–*ct* 22
Bowling 2026–78–25.97–2–0–5/22
Test batting
1–2–0–41–29–20.50–0–*ct* 0
Bowling 10–1–10.00–0–0–1/10
He hit 1,072 runs, av 39.70, on the 1933 tour and played in one Test.

Sealy, Arthur John Edmund
Amateur. *b:* 30.11.1903, Woolwich, Kent. *d:* 11.11.1944, Portsmouth, Hampshire. Lower order right-hand batsman, right-arm medium pace bowler. *Sch* Winchester. *Team* Oxford U (1924).
Career batting
8–11–7–62–17*–15.50–0–*ct* 6
Bowling 547–20–27.35–0–0–3/25

Sealy, James Edward Derek
Amateur. *b:* 11.9.1912, Barbados. *d:* 3.1.1982, St Patrick, Trinidad. Attractive hard-hitting medium order batsman, right-arm medium pace bowler, wicket-keeper. *Teams* Barbados (1928/9 to 1943/4); Trinidad (1935/6 to 1948/9). *Tours* West Indies to Australia 1930/1, to England 1939. *Tests* West Indies (1929/30 to 1939, 11 matches).
Career batting
80–134–8–3831–181–30.40–8–*ct* 67–*st* 13
Bowling 1802–63–28.60–2–1–8/8
Test batting
11–19–2–478–92–28.11–0–*ct* 6–*st* 1
Bowling 94–3–31.33–0–0–2/7
On his Test debut at Bridgetown in 1929/30 v England, he was the youngest cricketer to play in a Test – 17 years 122 days. His batting was rather uneven on the 1939 tour to England, but he played in all three Tests and took over as wicket-keeper in the Second and Third. He returned the remarkable analysis of 6.7–2–8–8 for Barbados v Trinidad at Bridgetown in 1941/2.

Seamer, John Wemyss
Amateur. *b:* 23.6.1913, Shapwick, Somerset. Steady middle order right-hand batsman. *Sch* Marlborough. *Teams* Oxford U (1934–36, blue all three years); Somerset (1932–48, 59 matches).
Career batting
81–134–12–2483–194–20.35–4–*ct* 44
Bowling 171–4–42.75–0–0–2/6

His final first-class match was for Free Foresters in 1949; he also played for Wiltshire. He gained a blue for hockey.

Searby, John Epton
Amateur. *b:* 1.11.1900, Croft, Lincolnshire. *d:* 12.10.1956, Croft, Lincolnshire. Opening right-hand batsman. *Sch* Magdalen College School. *Team* East of England (1927).
Career batting
1–2–0–17–10–8.50–0–*ct* 0
His County cricket was for Lincolnshire.

Searle, Cyril John
Amateur. *b:* 12.5.1921, Battersea, London. Lower order batsman, wicket-keeper. *Team* Essex (1947, 1 match).
Career batting
1–1–1–5–5*–no av–0–*ct* 1–*st* 1

Sears, Leslie Daniel
Amateur. *b:* 12.1.1901, Wokingham, Berkshire. Middle order left-hand batsman. *Team* Essex (1925, 2 matches).
Career batting
2–4–0–18–16–4.50–0–*ct* 0
He also played for Berkshire.

Seaton, Geoffrey Stuart
Amateur. *b:* 6.3.1926, Brighton, Sussex. Middle order right-hand batsman, slow left-arm bowler. *Sch* Denstone. *Teams* Cambridge U (1946–47); Oxford U (1957).
Career batting
8–15–2–196–51–15.07–0–*ct* 6

Seaton, John
Professional. *b:* 15.1.1844, Nottingham. *d:* 14.10.1918, Oldham, Lancashire. Right-hand batsman, right-arm medium pace bowler. *Team* Nottinghamshire (1872, 4 matches).
Career batting
4–7–0–80–27–11.42–0–*ct* 1
Bowling 12–1–12.00–0–0–1/12

Seddon, Rev Richard
Amateur. *b:* 11.2.1825, Leicester. *d:* 13.7.1884, Bournemouth, Hampshire. Middle order batsman. *Teams* Cambridge U (1846–47, blue both years); Nottinghamshire (1845, 1 match).
Career batting
14–24–0–165–26–6.87–0–*ct* 4
He played for Leicestershire (pre-first-class), but it is believed did not appear in any matches of note after leaving Cambridge.

Sedgley, John Brian
Professional. *b:* 17.2.1939, West Bromwich, Staffs. Middle order right-hand batsman. *Team* Worcestershire (1959–61, 15 matches).
Career batting
15–27–2–389–95–15.56–0–*ct* 7

Sedgwick, Herbert Amos
Professional. *b:* 8.4.1883, Richmond, Yorkshire. *d:* 28.12.1957, Stoke-on-Trent. Lower order right-hand batsman, right-arm fast bowler. *Team* Yorkshire (1906, 3 matches).
Career batting
3–5–2–53–34–17.66–0–*ct* 2
Bowling 327–16–20.43–1–0–5/8
He also played for Staffordshire.

Seeley, Gerald Henry
Amateur. *b:* 9.5.1903, Port Blair, Andaman Islands. *d:* 23.7.1941, at sea off Belgium. Right-hand batsman. *Sch* Marlborough. *Team* Worcestershire (1921, 1 match).
Career batting
1–1–0–7–7–7.00–0–*ct* 0

Seitz, John Arnold
Amateur. *b:* 19.9.1883, Carlton, Victoria, Australia. *d:* 1.5.1963, St Kilda, Victoria, Australia. Middle order right-hand batsman. *Teams* Oxford U (1909, blue); Victoria (1910/11 to 1912/13, 15 matches).
Career batting
20–35–1–981–120–28.85–3–*ct* 18
Bowling 12–1–12.00–0–0–1/7

Selby, John
Professional. *b:* 1.7.1849, Nottingham. *d:* 11.3.1894, Nottingham. Son of W. W. (Notts, 1848). Opening or middle order right-hand batsman, right-arm medium pace bowler. *Team* Nottinghamshire (1870–87, 164 matches). *Tours* Lillywhite to Australia 1876/7; Daft to North America 1879 (not first-class); Lillywhite, Shaw and Shrewsbury to Australia 1881/2. *Tests* England (1876/7 to 1881/2, 6 matches).
Career batting
222–355–25–6215–128*–18.83–4–*ct* 128–*st* 4
Bowling 188–5–37.60–0–0–2/27
Test batting
6–12–1–256–70–23.27–0–*ct* 1
His best season was 1878 with 938 runs, av 31.26 – he was the leading batsman in England.

Selby, Thomas Gothard
Professional. *b:* 19.2.1851, North Wingfield,

Derbyshire. *d:* 6.11.1924, Shirebrook, Derbyshire. Right-hand batsman, right-arm fast bowler. *Team* Derbyshire (1885, 1 match).
Career batting
1–2–0–3–2–1.50–0–*ct* 0
Bowling 7–0

Sellar, Kenneth Anderson
Amateur. *b:* 11.8.1906, London. Middle order right-hand batsman, useful change bowler. *Team* Sussex (1928, 8 matches).
Career batting
19–32–1–616–119–19.87–1–*ct* 12
Bowling 37–0
His first-class debut was for the Royal Navy in 1924 and his final first-class match for Leveson-Gower's XI in 1935. A noted rugby footballer, he represented the Royal Navy and England.

Sellers, Arthur
Amateur. *b:* 30.5.1870, Keighley, Yorkshire. *d:* 25.9.1941, Keighley, Yorkshire. Father of A. B. (Yorkshire). Aggressive opening right-hand batsman, good close field. *Team* Yorkshire (1890–99, 51 matches).
Career batting
53–95–2–1852–105–19.91–2–*ct* 47
Bowling 149–2–74.50–0–0–2/28
The demands of business restricted his first-class cricket. He was for many years a member of the Yorkshire Committee.

Sellers, Arthur Brian
Amateur. *b:* 5.3.1907, Keighley, Yorkshire. *d:* 20.2.1981, Eldwick, Bingley, Yorkshire. Son of Arthur (Yorkshire). Middle order right-hand batsman, brilliant close field. *Team* Yorkshire (1932–48, 334 matches).
Career batting
344–455–53–9273–204–23.04–4–*ct* 273
Bowling 676–9–75.11–0–0–2/10
He captained Yorkshire from 1933 to 1948. He hit 1,143 runs, av 27.21, in 1938 and his only double century was 204 for Yorkshire v Cambridge U at Cambridge in 1936. He was on the Yorkshire Committee until 1972 and often in the forefront of the storms to which Yorkshire was subjected in post-war years. He was also for several years a Test Selector.

Sellers, Arthur Ernest
Amateur. *b:* 23.2.1876, Mansfield, Notts. *d:* 9.2.1949, Edinburgh, Scotland. Right-hand batsman, right-arm medium pace bowler. *Team* Scotland (1920–22).
Career batting
2–3–0–29–17–9.66–0–*ct* 0
Bowling 153–8–19.12–1–0–5/22

Sellers, Reginald Hugh Durnford
Amateur. *b:* 20.8.1940, Bulsar, India. Lower order right-hand batsman, leg break and googly bowler. *Team* South Australia (1959/60 to 1966/7, 39 matches). *Tours* Australia to England 1964, to India 1964/5. *Test* Australia (1964/5, 1 match).
Career batting
53–80–20–1089–87–18.15–0–*ct* 41
Bowling 4653–121–38.45–4–1–5/36
Test batting
1–1–0–0–0–0.00–0–*ct* 1
Bowling 17–0
An injury before the team landed in England prevented him from making the most of the 1964 tour.

Sellick, Arthur Samuel
Professional. *b:* June 1878, Gloucester. *d:* 1958, Surrey. Middle order batsman. *Teams* Gloucestershire (1903–04, 11 matches); Somerset (1905, 6 matches).
Career batting
17–30–6–298–49–12.41–0–*ct* 8
Bowling 57–0
He also played for Wiltshire.

Sells, Hugh Michael
Amateur. *b:* 23.3.1922, Westcliff-on-Sea, Essex. *d:* 17.1.1978, Chelsea, London. Middle order left-hand batsman. *Sch* Malvern. *Team* RAF (1946).
Career batting
1–2–0–46–26–23.00–0–*ct* 1

Selvey, Michael Walter William
Cricketer. *b:* 25.4.1948, Chiswick, London. Lower order right-hand batsman, right-arm fast medium bowler. *Teams* Surrey (1968–71, 6 matches); Cambridge U (1971, blue); Middlesex (1972–82, 213 matches); Orange Free State (1973/4); Glamorgan (1983, 24 matches). *Tours* MCC to India and Australia 1976/7; Middlesex to Zimbabwe 1980/1; International XI to Pakistan 1981/2. *Tests* England (1976 to 1976/7, 3 matches).
Career batting
263–260–80–2294–67–12.74–0–*ct* 70
Bowling 19585–747–26.21–37–4–7/20
Test batting
3–5–3–15–5*–7.50–0–*ct* 1
Bowling 343–6–57.16–0–0–4/41
In 1978 he took 101 wickets, av 19.09. He was appointed captain of Glamorgan in 1983.

Selwood, Timothy
Cricketer. *b:* 1.9.1944, Prestatyn, Flint. Right-hand batsman, right-arm medium pace bowler. *Teams* Middlesex (1966–73, 18 matches); Central Districts (1972/3).

Career batting
20–35–4–603–89–19.45–0–*ct* 9
Bowling 1–0
He also played for Durham.

Semmence, Derek John
Professional. *b:* 20.4.1938, Worthing, Sussex. Right-hand batsman, right-arm medium bowler. *Teams* Essex (1962, 1 match); Sussex (1956–68, 35 matches).
Career batting
39–63–2–890–108–14.59–1–*ct* 24
Bowling 123–1–123.00–0–0–1/43
He played for Sussex until 1960, made a single appearance for Essex in a non-Championship match in 1962, then re-appeared for Sussex in 1967. He also played for Cambridgeshire.

Sen, Probir Kumar
Amateur. *b:* 31.5.1926, Comilla, India. *d:* 27.1.1970, South Calcutta, India. Defensive lower order right-hand batsman, wicket-keeper. *Team* Bengal (1943/4 to 1957/8). *Tours* India to Australia 1947/8, to England 1952. *Tests* India (1947/8 to 1952/3, 14 matches).
Career batting
82–118–7–2580–168–23.24–3–*ct* 107–*st* 36
Bowling 106–7–15.14–0–0–3/4
Test batting
14–18–4–165–25–11.78–0–*ct* 20–*st* 11
He played in the last two Tests of the 1952 series in England. A specialist wicket-keeper, he was put on to bowl in the second innings of the match between Bengal and Orissa at Cuttack in 1954/5 and performed the hat-trick.

Senescall, John
Professional. *b:* 31.5.1853, Greetham, Rutland. *d:* 1937, Holderness, Yorkshire. Lower order right-hand batsman, right-arm fast bowler, good field. *Team* Sussex (1882–83, 6 matches).
Career batting
6–10–1–26–8–2.88–0–*ct* 1
Bowling 274–18–15.22–1–0–6/23

Senghera, Ravindera
Cricketer. *b:* 25.1.1947, Delhi, India. Right-hand batsman, off break bowler. *Team* Worcestershire (1974–76, 23 matches).
Career batting
24–25–7–281–36*–15.61–0–*ct* 7
Bowling 2303–58–39–70–1–0–5/81

Senior, Eric Malcolm
Amateur. *b:* 6.10.1920, Shaftesbury, Dorset. *d:* 24.4.1970, Radnage, Buckinghamshire. Middle order batsman. *Team* Combined Services (1961).
Career batting
1–2–0–1–1–0.50–0–*ct* 0
His County cricket was for Lincolnshire.

Serjeant, Arthur Thomas
Amateur. *b:* 1856, Clifton, Gloucestershire. *d:* 1916, Bristol. Middle order batsman. *Team* Gloucestershire (1883, 3 matches).
Career batting
3–6–0–41–25–6.83–0–*ct* 1

Serjeant, Craig Stanton
Cricketer. *b:* 1.11.1951, Nedlands, Western Australia. Middle order right-hand batsman. *Team* Western Australia (1976/7 to 1982/3, 51 matches). *Tours* Australia to England 1977, to West Indies 1977/8. *Tests* Australia (1977 to 1977/8, 12 matches).
Career batting
80–134–19–4030–159–35.04–9–*ct* 90
Bowling 4–0
Test batting
12–23–1–522–124–23.72–1–*ct* 13
Although he appeared in three Tests on the 1977 tour, he was only moderately successful, and in all first-class matches hit 663 runs, av 33.15.

Serrurier, Louis Roy
Amateur. *b:* 7.2.1905, Sea Point, Cape Town, South Africa. Middle order right-hand batsman, right-arm medium bowler. *Teams* Oxford U (1925–27); Worcestershire (1927, 7 matches); Western Province (1927/8 to 1929/30); Transvaal (1931/2).
Career batting
30–46–8–1281–171–33.71–3–*ct* 17
Bowling 1127–42–26.83–1–0–5/103

Seshachari, Kilvidi
Amateur. *b:* 2.1.1876, Madras, India. *d:* 25.1.1917, Calcutta, India. Lower order right-hand batsman, wicket-keeper. *Team* Hindus (1905/6 to 1912/13). *Tour* India to England 1911.
Career batting
19–34–10–138–29–5.75–0–*ct* 20–*st* 16

Sethi, Ramesh Kumar
Cricketer. *b:* 4.9.1941, Kenya. Lower order right-hand batsman, off break bowler. *Team* East Africa (1975). *Tour* East Africa to England 1975.
Career batting
1–2–0–12–12–6.00–0–*ct* 1
Bowling 27–0
He appeared for Shropshire commencing 1976.

Seth-Smith, Derek John
Amateur. *b:* 11.8.1920, Hartley-Wintney, Hampshire. *d:* 24.6.1964, Chelsea, London.

Lower order batsman, useful bowler. *Sch* Charterhouse. *Team* Free Foresters (1950).
Career batting
1–2–0–3–3–1.50–0–*ct* 0
Bowling 23–0

Seton, Walter John
Amateur. *b:* 29.12.1864, Calcutta, India. *d:* 30.10.1912, Fleet, Hampshire. Middle order batsman. *Team* Oxford U (1894).
Career batting
1–2–1–1–1–1.00–0–*ct* 0

Severn, Arthur
Professional. *b:* 23.6.1893, Alfreton, Derbyshire. *d:* 10.1.1949, Stainforth, Yorkshire. Middle order batsman. *Team* Derbyshire (1919–20, 13 matches).
Career batting
13–24–2–342–73–15.54–0–*ct* 5

Sewell, Cyril Otto Hudson
Amateur. *b:* 19.12.1874, Pietermaritzburg, South Africa. *d:* 19.8.1951, Bexhill, Sussex. Son of J. J. (Middlesex). Hard hitting right-hand batsman, slow right-arm bowler, brilliant off side field. *Team* Gloucestershire (1895–1919, 158 matches). *Tours* Warner to North America 1898; South Africa to England 1894 (not first-class).
Career batting
173–303–13–7562–165–26.07–9–*ct* 118
Bowling 308–5–61.60–0–0–2/35

He hit 1,000 runs in a season twice (best 1,142, av 26.55 in 1914).

He captained Gloucestershire in 1913 and 1914, and was County Secretary from 1912 to 1914.

Sewell, Edward Humphrey Dalrymple
Amateur generally, but professional with Essex. *b:* 30.9.1872, Lingsugur, India. *d:* 20.9.1947, Paddington, London. Punishing right-hand batsman, right-arm medium pace bowler. *Sch* Bedford GS. *Teams* India (1892/3); London County (1900–04); Essex (1902–04, 55 matches).
Career batting
87–147–7–3430–181–24.50–5–*ct* 70
Bowling 807–17–47.47–0–0–3/73

He hit 1,080 runs, av 28.42 in 1904. His final first-class match was for MCC in 1922. He was at one time coach to Surrey CCC and later played for Bedfordshire and Buckinghamshire, also acting as the latter County's Secretary. He was a good rugby footballer, playing for Blackheath and Harlequins. The author of several books on cricket he also wrote for various newspapers on both cricket and rugby.

Sewell, Frederick Alexander Seymour
Amateur. *b:* 6.10.1881, Leamington Spa, Warwickshire. *d:* 5.6.1964, Parkstone, Dorset. Middle order right-hand batsman, slow right-arm bowler. *Sch* Weymouth. *Team* Cambridge U (1901–02).
Career batting
5–8–2–69–19*–11.50–0–*ct* 4
Bowling 213–6–35.50–0–0–3/71

His County cricket was for Bedfordshire and for Dorset from 1902 to 1913.

Sewell, Frederic John
Amateur. *b:* 29.9.1913, Stow on the Wold, Gloucestershire. Middle order left-hand batsman. *Sch* Cheltenham. *Team* Gloucestershire (1937, 4 matches).
Career batting
4–7–0–113–56–16.14–0–*ct* 3

Sewell, John Joseph
Amateur. *b:* 10.2.1844, Cirencester, Gloucs. *d:* 8.6.1897, Pietermaritzburg, Natal, South Africa. Father of C. O. H. (Gloucestershire). Attractive right-hand batsman, right-arm fast medium bowler. *Sch* Marlborough. *Team* Middlesex (1863–67, 9 matches).
Career batting
12–18–2–419–166–26.18–1–*ct* 4
Bowling 24–1–24.00–0–0–1/22

He emigrated to South Africa after the 1867 season and thus was lost to County cricket, though it was not clear what qualifications he had for representing Middlesex. He also played for Norfolk and Wiltshire.

Sewell, Robert Page
Amateur. *b:* 3.9.1866, Maldon, Essex. *d:* 7.2.1901, Surbiton, Surrey. Attacking middle order right-hand batsman, good field. *Sch* Blackheath. *Team* Kent (1884, 2 matches). *Tour* Lucas to West Indies 1894/5.
Career batting
10–15–1–281–77–20.07–0–*ct* 11
Bowling 189–11–17.18–0–0–4/29

He appeared for Essex (pre-first-class).

Sewell, Thomas (sen)
Professional. *b:* 5.5.1806, Mitcham, Surrey. *d:* 1.11.1888, Sevenoaks, Kent. Father of Thomas (Surrey and Kent). Middle order right-hand batsman, under-arm bowler, good field. *Teams* Surrey (1839–49, 9 matches); Kent (1852, 2 matches); Middlesex (1830, 2 matches).

Career batting
117–210–14–1956–66*–9.97–0–*ct* 56–*st* 4
Bowling 2–0+3–no av–0–0–2/?
His final first-class match was for a Combined Kent and Sussex XI in 1853.

Sewell, Thomas (jun)
Professional. *b:* 15.3.1830, Mitcham, Surrey. *d:* 13.6.1871, St John's, Sevenoaks, Kent. Son of Thomas (Surrey, Kent and Middlesex). Right-hand batsman, right-arm fast bowler. *Teams* Kent (1856–66, 20 matches); Surrey (1859–68, 109 matches). *Tour* Stephenson to Australia 1861/2.
Career batting
158–266–51–2542–62–11.82–0–*ct* 73
Bowling 6304–330+8–19.10–14–1–8/45

Seymour, Alfred
Amateur. *b:* 16.2.1843. *d:* 31.1.1897, Folkestone, Kent. *Sch* Rugby. *Teams* Lancashire (1869, 1 match); Hampshire (1870, 1 match).
Career batting
2–4–0–47–25–11.75–0–*ct* 1

Seymour, Charles Read
Amateur. *b:* 6.2.1855, Winchfield, Hants. *d:* 6.11.1934, Winchester, Hampshire. Middle order right-hand batsman. *Sch* Harrow. *Team* Hampshire (1880–85, 15 matches).
Career batting
16–31–3–485–77*–17.32–0–2–*ct* 12
His first-class debut was for MCC in 1879.

Seymour, Edward Neville
Amateur. *b:* 14.1.1906, Dublin. *d:* 12.2.1980, Dublin, Ireland. Right-hand batsman, right-arm fast medium bowler. *Team* Ireland (1927–28).
Career batting
3–5–0–9–3–1.80–0–*ct* 1
Bowling 147–4–36.75–0–0–2/26

Seymour, James
Professional. *b:* 25.10.1879, West Hoathly, Sussex. *d:* 30.9.1930, Marden, Kent. Brother of John (Sussex). Sound middle order right-hand batsman, left-arm medium pace bowler, excellent slip. *Teams* London County (1900–01); Kent (1902–26, 536 matches). *Tour* Kent to United States 1903.
Career batting
553–911–62–27237–218*–32.08–53–*ct* 675
Bowling 805–17–47.35–0–0–4/62
He reached 1,000 runs in a season sixteen times, going on to 2,000 once – 2,088, av 38.66, in 1913. His three double centuries were all for Kent, the highest being 218* v Essex at Leyton in 1911. His benefit match, Kent v Hampshire at Canterbury in 1920, was used as a test court case, which went to the House of Lords. The final ruling was that cricketers' benefit proceeds should not be subject to tax.

Seymour, John
Professional. *b:* 24.8.1881, Brightling, Sussex. *d:* 1.12.1967, Daventry, Warwickshire. Brother of James (Kent). Attacking middle order right-hand batsman, slow left-arm bowler. *Teams* Sussex (1904–07, 42 matches); Northamptonshire (1908–19, 94 matches).
Career batting
136–221–20–3430–136*–17.06–1–*ct* 104
Bowling 3231–113–28.59–3–0–6/58
He also played for Berkshire.

Shackle, Thomas
Amateur. *b:* 28.7.1834, Hillingdon, Middlesex. *d:* 12.3.1887, Hayes, Middlesex. Right-hand batsman, right-arm fast bowler. *Team* Middlesex (1868, 3 matches).
Career batting
3–5–1–67–41*–16.75–0–*ct* 1
He also played for Buckinghamshire.

Shackleton, Derek
Professional. *b:* 12.8.1924, Todmorden, Yorkshire. Father of J. H. (Gloucestershire). Lower order right-hand batsman, right-arm medium pace bowler. *Team* Hampshire (1948–69, 583 matches). *Tours* MCC to India, Pakistan and Ceylon 1951/2; Commonwealth to India and Ceylon 1950/1. *Tests* England (1950–63, 7 matches).
Career batting
647–852–197–9574–87*–14.61–0–*ct* 221
Bowling 53303–2857–18.65–194–38–9/30
Test batting
7–13–7–113–42–18.83–0–*ct* 1
Bowling 768–18–42.66–0–0–4/72
He took 100 wickets in a season twenty times (best 172, av 20.15, in 1962). His sequence of 20 consecutive seasons (1949 to 1968) with at least 100 wickets in each is a record. His best innings analysis was 9 for 30 for Hampshire v Warwickshire at Portsmouth in 1960; he also returned the remarkable figures of 8 wickets for 4 runs for Hampshire v Somerset at Weston-super-mare in 1955. He also played for Dorset. He became a first-class umpire.

Shackleton, Julian Howard
Cricketer. *b:* 29.1.1952, Todmorden, Yorkshire. Son of Derek (Hampshire). Lower order right-hand batsman, right-arm medium pace bowler. *Team* Gloucestershire (1971–78, 48 matches).
Career batting
48–64–20–596–41*–13.54–0–*ct* 36
Bowling 2242–49–45.75–0–0–4/38

Shackleton, William Allan
Professional. *b:* 9.3.1908, Keighley, Yorkshire. *d:* 16.11.1971, Bridlington, Yorkshire. Lower order right-hand batsman, right-arm medium pace or leg break bowler. *Team* Yorkshire (1928–34, 5 matches).
Career batting
5–6–0–49–25–8.16–0–*ct* 3
Bowling 130–6–21.66–0–0–4/18

Shacklock, Francis Joseph
Professional. *b:* 22.9.1861, Crich, Derbyshire. *d:* 3.5.1937, Christchurch, New Zealand. Lower order right-hand batsman, right-arm fast bowler. *Teams* Derbyshire (1884–85, 18 matches); Nottinghamshire (1883–93, 117 matches); Otago (1903/4 to 1904/5).
Career batting
156–231–26–2438–71–11.89–0–*ct* 92
Bowling 9458–497–19.03–39–8–8/32

His best season was 1889 with 80 wickets, av 14.60. He took four wickets in four balls for Nottinghamshire v Somerset at Trent Bridge in 1893.

Shaddick, Dr Rowland Allen
Amateur. *b:* 26.3.1920, Hackney, Middlesex. Lower order right-hand batsman, off break bowler. *Sch* City of London. *Team* Middlesex (1946–47, 7 matches).
Career batting
20–25–13–62–12*–5.16–0–*ct* 6
Bowling 1418–49–28.93–1–0–5/34

His final first-class match was for Free Foresters in 1955.

Shadwell, Francis Bradby
Amateur. *b:* 4.5.1851, Barnes, Surrey. *d:* 9.2.1915, Windsor, Berks. Middle order batsman, good bowler. *Sch* Uppingham. *Team* Surrey (1880, 1 match).
Career batting
3–5–1–58–18*–14.50–0–*ct* 1
Bowling 86–7–12.28–1–0–5/35

His final first-class match was for MCC in 1881.

Shafiq Ahmed
Cricketer. *b:* 28.3.1949, Lahore, Pakistan. Opening right-hand batsman, right-arm medium pace bowler. *Teams* Punjab University (1967/8 to 1971/2); Lahore (1968/9 to 1973/4); Punjab (1972/3 to 1977/8); National Bank (1974/5 to 1982/3). *Tours* Pakistan Under 25 to Sri Lanka 1973/4; Pakistan to England 1974, to Sri Lanka 1975/6. *Tests* Pakistan (1974 to 1980/1, 6 matches).
Career batting
162–276–35–12599–217*–52.27–39–*ct* 142
Bowling 2871–85–33.77–0–0–4/27
Test batting
6–10–1–99–27*–11.00–0–*ct* 0
Bowling 1–0

He hit 451 runs, av 50.11, in first-class matches on the 1974 tour, but after playing in the first Test, lost his place and was given few opportunities in later matches. His highest score was 217* for National Bank v MCB at Karachi in 1978/9. He hit 1,000 runs in Pakistan six times (best 1,409, av 82.88, in 1978/9).

Shafqat Hussain
Amateur. *b:* 17.7.1885, Meerut, India. Lower order right-hand batsman, useful bowler. *Tour* India to England 1911.
Career batting
8–16–3–80–21–6.15–0–*ct* 1
Bowling 282–4–70.50–0–0–2/73

He achieved very little on the 1911 tour to England. Curiously he did not appear in first-class matches in India.

Shafqat Rana
Amateur. *b:* 10.8.1943, Simla, India. Middle order right-hand batsman, off break bowler. *Tours* Pakistan Eaglets to Ceylon 1960/1, to England 1963; PIA to East Africa 1964/5, to England 1969 (not first-class); Pakistan to Australia and New Zealand 1964/5, to Ceylon 1964/5, to England 1971. *Tests* Pakistan (1964/5 to 1969/70, 5 matches).
Career batting
107–158–18–4947–174–35.33–9–*ct* 83
Bowling 560–16–35.00–0–0–2/8
Test batting
5–7–0–221–95–31.57–0–*ct* 5
Bowling 9–1–9.00–0–0–1/2

He achieved little on the 1971 tour to England and was not required for the Tests.

Shahid Mahmood
Amateur. *b:* 17.3.1939, Lucknow, India. Middle order left-hand batsman, left-arm medium pace bowler. *Teams* Karachi (1956/7 to 1969/70); Universities (1958/9); PWD (1964/5). *Tour* Pakistan to England 1962. *Test* Pakistan (1962, 1 match).
Career batting
66–107–9–3117–220–31.80–5–*ct* 25
Bowling 1931–89–21.69–3–1–10/58
Test batting
1–2–0–25–16–12.50–0–*ct* 0
Bowling 23–0

He was given only limited opportunities on the 1962 tour to England. His best bowling in an innings was 10 for 58 for Karachi Whites v Khairpur at Karachi in 1969/70. His highest score was 220 for Karachi U v Peshawar U at Karachi in 1958/9.

Shakespeare, William Harold Nelson
Amateur. *b:* 24.8.1893, Worcester. *d:* 10.7.1976, Whittington, Worcs. Middle order right-hand batsman. *Sch* Worcester RGS. *Team* Worcestershire (1919–31, 26 matches).
Career batting
26–44–4–789–67*–19.72–0–*ct* 11
Bowling 8–0
He was President of Worcestershire CCC at the time of his death.

Shakoor Ahmed
Amateur. *b:* 15.9.1928, Kampala, Uganda. Opening right-hand batsman, wicket-keeper. *Teams* Punjab University (1947/8 to 1948/9); Punjab (1951/2 to 1957/8); Multan (1958/9); Lahore (1959/60 to 1967/8). *Tours* Pakistan to England 1954; Pakistan Eaglets to Ceylon 1960/1.
Career batting
53–84–4–2958–280–36.97–8–*ct* 56–*st* 16
Bowling 8–0
He had few opportunities of the 1954 tour, playing in only 9 first-class matches. His highest score was 280 for Lahore Greens v Railways at Lahore in 1964/5.

Shalders, William Alfred
Amateur. *b:* 10.2.1880, Kimberley, South Africa. *d:* 18.3.1917, Cradock, Cape Province, South Africa. Opening right-hand batsman. *Teams* Griqualand West (1897/8); Cape Colony (1898/9); Transvaal (1902/3 to 1906/7); London County (1904). *Tours* South Africa to England 1904, 1907. *Tests* South Africa (1898/9 to 1907, 12 matches).
Career batting
88–152–8–3351–105–23.27–2–*ct* 38
Bowling 139–6–23.16–0–0–3/30
Test batting
12–23–1–355–42–16.13–0–*ct* 3
Bowling 6–1–6.00–0–0–1/6
Although having no outstanding innings to his name on either visit to England, he proved a most consistent batsman. His final first-class match was for Wanderers CC in 1908/9.

Shand, Francis Livingstone
Amateur. *b:* 23.6.1855, Old Charlton, Kent. *d:* 5.6.1921, Denham, Buckinghamshire. Lower order left-hand batsman, left-arm fast bowler, slip field. *Sch* Harrow. *Team* Gentlemen of England (1874–89). *Tours* Vernon to Ceylon and India 1889/90 (not first-class); Hawke to Ceylon and India 1892/3 (he played in emergency, but not in first-class matches).
Career batting
5–6–2–49–17–12.25–0–*ct* 2
Bowling 168–17–9.88–1–0–6/32
He resided for many years in Ceylon, being a noted figure in local cricket there. An excellent footballer, he represented Surrey.

Shantry, Brian Keith
Cricketer. *b:* 26.5.1955, Bristol. Tail end left-hand batsman, left-arm fast bowler. *Team* Gloucestershire (1978–79, 3 matches).
Career batting
3 matches, did not bat–*ct* 0
Bowling 167–3–55.66–0–0–2/63
He also played for Dorset.

Shapcott, Morton Swan
Amateur. *b:* 27.9.1901, Camberwell, London. *d:* 15.4.1977, St Pancras, London. Middle order right-hand batsman. *Sch* Alleyn's School, Dulwich. *Team* RAF (1927–32).
Career batting
4–8–1–246–68–35.14–0–*ct* 2

Shardlow, Bertie
Professional. *b:* 15.12.1909, Stone, Staffs. *d:* 30.4.1976, Stoke-on-Trent, Staffs. Lower order left-hand batsman, slow left-arm bowler. *Team* Minor Counties (1949–50).
Career batting
2–4–1–45–24*–15.00–0–*ct* 3
Bowling 89–6–14.83–1–0–5/25
His County cricket was for Staffordshire between 1936 and 1957.

Shardlow, Wilfred
Professional. *b:* 30.9.1902, Clowne, Derbyshire. *d:* 21.6.1956, Burton on Trent, Staffs. Lower order left-hand batsman, right-arm fast medium bowler. *Team* Derbyshire (1925–28, 38 matches).
Career batting
38–42–14–201–39*–7.17–0–*ct* 16
Bowling 1939–56–34.62–1–0–5/41

Sharland, Alfred Percival
Amateur. *b:* 1890, Croydon, Surrey. *d:* 18.7.1944, Farnborough, Kent. Lower order right-hand batsman, leg break bowler. *Team* Civil Service (1927).
Career batting
1–2–0–2–2–1.00–0–*ct* 0
Bowling 67–1–67.00–0–0–1/67

Sharman, Graham John
Amateur. *b:* 30.5.1938, London. Middle order

right-hand batsman, leg break and googly bowler. *Sch* Lancing. *Team* Oxford U (1958).
Career batting
2–4–0–9–6–2.25–0–*ct* 0
He was awarded his blue for squash.

Sharood, Arthur John
Amateur. *b:* 9.8.1856, Hurstpierpoint, Sussex. *d:* 31.3.1895, Axim, Gold Coast. He died of fever. Lower order right-hand batsman, right-arm fast medium bowler. *Sch* Hurstpierpoint. *Team* Sussex (1879, 1 match).
Career batting
1 match, did not bat–*ct* 0
Bowling 51–2–25.50–0–0–2/51
He did not appear in first-class matches whilst at Oxford University. He was for some years the Solicitor-General for the Gold Coast.

Sharp, Aubrey Temple
Amateur. *b:* 23.3.1889, Whitwick, Leicestershire. *d:* 15.2.1973, Leicester. He died following a road accident. Father of J. A. T. (Leicestershire). Middle order right-hand batsman. *Sch* Repton. *Team* Leicestershire (1908–35, 130 matches).
Career batting
131–230–25–5263–216–25.67–8–*ct* 66
Bowling 78–0
His only double century was 216 for Leicestershire v Derbyshire at Chesterfield in 1911. He captained Leicestershire in 1921.

Sharp, Charles
Amateur. *b:* 6.9.1848, Horsham, Sussex. *d:* 23.9.1903. Lower order left-hand batsman, slow left-arm bowler. *Team* Sussex (1873–79, 17 matches).
Career batting
17–31–0–345–54–11.12–0–*ct* 10
Bowling 214–14–15.14–1–0–6/34

Sharp, George
Cricketer. *b:* 12.3.1950, West Hartlepool, Co Durham. Lower order right-hand batsman, left-arm medium pace bowler, wicket-keeper. *Team* Northamptonshire (1968–83, 283 matches).
Career batting
284–371–80–5975–98–20.53–0–*ct* 534–*st* 185
Bowling 68–1–68.00–0–0–1/47

Sharp, Harry Philip Hugh
Professional. *b:* 6.10.1917, Kentish Town, London. Sound opening right-hand batsman, off break bowler. *Team* Middlesex (1946–55, 162 matches).
Career batting
167–276–30–6422–165–26.10–10–*ct* 61
Bowling 1670–52–32.11–1–0–5/52
He hit 1,000 runs in a season three times (best 1,564, av 32.58, in 1953). His final first-class match was for MCC in 1957.

Sharp, John
Professional to 1914, then amateur from 1919. *b:* 15.2.1878, Hereford. *d:* 28.1.1938, Wavertree, Liverpool, Lancashire. Attractive middle order right-hand batsman, left-arm fast medium bowler, brilliant cover point. *Team* Lancashire (1899–1925, 518 matches). *Tests* England (1909, 3 matches).
Career batting
534–805–75–22715–211–31.11–38–*ct* 236
Bowling 12088–441–27.41–18–3–9/77
Test batting
3–6–2–188–105–47.00–1–*ct* 1
Bowling 111–3–37.00–0–0–3/67
His only double century was 211 for Lancashire v Leicestershire at Old Trafford in 1912. He hit 1,000 runs in a season ten times, going on to 2,000 once – 2,099, av 40.36, in 1911. His best season as a bowler was 1901 with 112 wickets, av 22.43, and his best analysis 9 for 77 for Lancashire v Worcestershire at Worcester in the same season. He captained Lancashire from 1923 to 1925. He appeared occasionally for Herefordshire. A noted soccer player, he was outside right for Aston Villa, Everton and England.

Sharp, General Sir John Aubrey Taylor
Amateur. *b:* 6.8.1917, Blaby, Leicestershire. *d:* 15.1.1977, Oslo, Norway. Son of A. T. (Leicestershire). Middle order right-hand batsman, useful bowler. *Sch* Repton. *Teams* Leicestershire (1937–46, 4 matches); Cambridge U (1939).
Career batting
5–10–0–64–36–6.40–0–*ct* 0
Bowling 172–7–24.57–0–0–4/63
He was also a good hockey player.

Sharp, Kevin
Cricketer. *b:* 6.4.1959, Leeds, Yorkshire. Middle order left-hand batsman, off break bowler. *Teams* Yorkshire (1976–83, 80 matches); Griqualand West (1981/2 to 1982/3). *Tours* Robins to Australia and New Zealand 1979/80 (no first-class matches in Australia).
Career batting
96–161–13–4546–139–30.71–8–*ct* 36
Bowling 47–0

Sharp, Norman
Amateur. *b:* 15.4.1901, Derby. *d:* 14.7.1977,

Sutton Coldfield. Middle order right-hand batsman. *Team* Warwickshire (1923, 1 match).
Career batting
1–1–0–3–3–3.00–0–*ct* 1

Sharp, Robert Henry
Amateur. *b:* 11.6.1893, Doncaster, Yorkshire. *d:* 15.3.1961, Bradford on Avon, Wilts. Lower order right-hand batsman, right-arm fast medium bowler. *Team* Essex (1925–28, 16 matches).
Career batting
16–25–7–169–36*–9.38–0–*ct* 16
Bowling 696–16–43.50–1–0–5/66

Sharp, Thomas Murray
Amateur. *b:* 23.1.1916, Gisborne, New Zealand. Lower order right-hand batsman, leg break bowler. *Team* Canterbury (1936/7). *Tour* New Zealand Services in England 1945.
Career batting
4–7–2–94–28–18.80–0–*ct* 0
Bowling 222–6–37.00–0–0–3/65
His final first-class match was for North Island (New Zealand) in 1945/6.

Sharpe, Cloudesley Brereton
Amateur. *b:* 5.2.1904, Hampstead, London. Lower order right-hand batsman, slow left-arm medium bowler. *Sch* Sherborne. *Team* Middlesex (1923, 3 matches).
Career batting
3–5–1–5–3–1.25–0–*ct* 1
Bowling 109–1–109.00–0–0–1/18
He also played for Dorset.

Sharpe, Rev Charles Molesworth
Amateur. *b:* 6.9.1851, Cadicote, Hertfordshire. *d:* 25.6.1935, Ilkley, Yorkshire. Lower order right-hand batsman, slow right-hand round-arm bowler, good deep field. *Teams* Cambridge U (1875, blue); Yorkshire (1875, 1 match).
Career batting
9–12–3–129–29–14.33–0–*ct* 10
Bowling 945–67+3–14.10–9–4–7/43
He also played for Hertfordshire and Cambridgeshire. His first-class career is remarkable for the fact that in his nine appearances he took 70 wickets. A good soccer player he was awarded his blue.

Sharpe, Harry Wetherherd
Amateur. *b:* 14.8.1901, Wolstanton, Staffordshire. *d:* 8.7.1950, Portsmouth, Hampshire. Lower order right-hand batsman, wicket-keeper. *Team* Royal Navy (1929).
Career batting
3–5–0–35–17–7.00–0–*ct* 6–*st* 3

Sharpe, John William
Professional. *b:* 9.12.1866, Ruddington, Notts. *d:* 19.6.1936, Ruddington, Notts. Son of Samuel (Nottinghamshire). Lower order right-hand batsman, right-arm fast medium bowler. *Teams* Nottinghamshire (1894, 5 matches); Surrey (1889–93, 59 matches). *Tour* Sheffield to Australia 1891/2. *Tests* England (1890 to 1891/2, 3 matches).
Career batting
82–116–39–657–36–8.53–0–*ct* 48
Bowling 5430–338–16.06–22–7–9/47
Test batting
3–6–4–44–26–22.00–0–*ct* 2
Bowling 305–11–27.72–1–0–6/84
His best season was 1890 when he took 139 wickets, av 12.61; he also took over 100 wickets in 1891. He played soccer for Notts County. His best bowling was 9/47 for Surrey v Middlesex at the Oval in 1891.

Sharpe, Philip John
Cricketer. *b:* 27.12.1936, Baildon, Yorkshire. Aggressive opening right-hand batsman, off break bowler, brilliant slip field. *Sch* Bradford GS and Worksop. *Teams* Yorkshire (1958–74, 411 matches); Derbyshire (1975–76, 40 matches). *Tours* Cavaliers to South Africa 1962/3, to West Indies 1969/70; MCC to India 1963/4; Yorkshire to North America and Bermuda 1964 (not first-class); Duke of Norfolk XI to West Indies 1969/70. *Tests* England (1963–69, 12 matches).
Career batting
493–811–78–22530–228–30.73–29–*ct* 617
Bowling 197–3–65.66–0–0–1/1
Test batting
12–21–4–786–111–46.23–1–*ct* 17
His first-class debut was for Combined Services in 1956. He hit 1,000 runs in a season twelve times, going on to 2,000 once – 2,252, av 40.94, in 1962. He scored three double centuries, the highest being 228 for Derbyshire v Oxford U at Oxford in 1976. Commencing 1977, he played for Norfolk.

Sharpe, Samuel
Professional. *b:* 13.1.1839, Ruddington, Notts. *d:* 5.11.1924, Ruddington, Notts. Father of J. W. (Notts and Surrey). Right-hand batsman, right-arm medium pace bowler. *Team* Nottinghamshire (1868, 2 matches).
Career batting
2–3–0–29–13–9.66–0–*ct* 3

Sharples, J. E.
Amateur. Middle order batsman. *Team* Glamorgan (1922, 1 match).

Career batting
1–1–0–0–0–0.00–0–*ct* 0
Bowling 1–0

Sharpless, Dr Frederic Cope
Amateur. *b:* 1.10.1880, Haverford, Philadelphia, USA. *d:* 16.11.1971, West Chester, Pennsylvania, USA. Defensive middle order right-hand batsman. *Team* Philadelphia (1903–13). *Tour* Philadelphia to England 1903.
Career batting
13–23–1–383–54–17.40–0–*ct* 6
Bowling 232–5–46.40–0–0–2/7

Sharratt, J.
Professional. Middle order batsman, wicket-keeper. *Team* North (1880).
Career batting
1–2–0–6–5–3.00–0–*ct* 0–*st* 2

Shastri, Ravishankar Jayadritha
Cricketer. *b:* 27.5.1962, Bombay, India. Lower order, occasional opening, right-hand batsman, slow left-arm bowler. *Teams* Bombay (1979/80 to 1981/2). *Tours* India to New Zealand 1980/1, to England 1982, to West Indies 1982/3, to Pakistan 1982/3. *Tests* India (1980/1 to 1982/3, 19 matches).
Career batting
51–73–12–1817–134–29.78–3–*ct* 31
Bowling 4168–150–27.73–7–1–9/101
Test batting
19–27–5–669–128–30.40–2–*ct* 8
Bowling 1662–42–39.57–1–0–5/125

He looked most promising on the 1982 tour to England, but his figures were very modest. He played in all three Tests. His best bowling is 9 for 101 for Bombay v Rest of India at Poona, 1981/2.

Shaw, Alfred
Professional. *b:* 29.8.1842, Burton Joyce, Nottinghamshire. *d:* 16.1.1907, Gedling, Nottinghamshire. Lower order right-hand batsman, right-arm medium, later slow medium, bowler. *Teams* Nottinghamshire (1864–97, 193 matches); Sussex (1894–95, 10 matches). *Tours* Willsher to North America 1868 (not first-class); Lillywhite to Australia 1876/7; Daft to North America 1879 (not first-class); Lillywhite, Shaw and Shrewsbury to Australia 1881/2, 1884/5, 1886/7 (no first-class matches in last two); Sheffield to Australia 1891/2 (manager). *Tests* England (1876/7 to 1881/2, 7 matches).
Career batting
404–630–101–6585–88–12.83–0–*ct* 368
Bowling 24579–2027+1–12.12–177–44–10/73
Test batting
7–12–1–111–40–10.09–0–*ct* 4
Bowling 285–12–23.75–1–0–5/38

A master of line and length, he was the most economical bowler of his generation, bowling more overs than he conceded runs. He took 100 wickets in a season eight times going on to 200 once – 202, av 10.89, in 1878. His best innings analysis was 10 wickets for 73 runs for MCC v North at Lord's in 1874, but perhaps his most outstanding figures were 41.2–36–7–7 for Nottinghamshire v MCC in 1875, also at Lord's. He captained Nottinghamshire to four successive Championship titles – 1883 to 1886 – after which his connection with his native county virtually ended. For some years he was employed by Lord Sheffield to coach young Sussex cricketers and in 1894, having been absent from county cricket for six years, he turned out for Sussex at the age of 51 and ended the season at the top of the county averages.

A joint promoter of four tours to Australia, he captained the 1881/2 team to Australia and led England in four Tests. From 1898 to 1905 he umpired in first-class matches and he was for many years a partner in the sports goods firm of Shaw and Shrewsbury.

Shaw, Alexander Armstrong
Amateur. *b:* 7.9.1907, Shardlow, Derbyshire. *d:* 19.7.1945, New Delhi, India. Sound opening right-hand batsman, wicket-keeper. *Sch* Eastbourne. *Team* Sussex (1927, 1 match).
Career batting
1–1–0–6–6–6.00–0–*ct* 4–*st* 3

Shaw, Dennis G.
Professional. *b:* 16.2.1931, Salford, Lancashire. Right-hand batsman, leg break and googly bowler. *Team* Warwickshire (1949, 1 match).
Career batting
1–1–0–17–17–17.00–0–*ct* 0
Bowling 106–2–53.00–0–0–2/60

Shaw, Edward Alfred
Amateur. *b:* 16.5.1892, Bishops Stortford, Herts. *d:* 7.10.1916, Le Sars, France. He was killed in action. Son of E. D. (Middlesex), brother of R. J. (Royal Navy). Middle order right-hand batsman, wicket-keeper. *Sch* Marlborough. *Team* Oxford U (1912–14, blue 1912 and 1914).
Career batting
13–22–2–424–57*–21.20–0–*ct* 12–*st* 8

His County cricket was for Buckinghamshire from 1908 to 1914, when he scored a century in his last match.

Shaw, Rt Rev Edward Domett
Amateur. *b:* 5.10.1860, Passage West, Co Cork. *d:* 5.11.1937, Bisham, Berks. Father of E. A. (Oxford U) and R. J. (Royal Navy). Lower order right-hand batsman, right-arm fast or medium pace bowler. *Sch* Forest. *Teams* Oxford U (1882–83, blue 1882); Middlesex (1882, 1 match).
Career batting
11–21–1–315–78*–15.75–0–*ct* 3
Bowling 358–19–18.84–1–0–5/29
He also played for Essex (pre-first-class), Hertfordshire and Buckinghamshire. He was Bishop of Buckingham.

Shaw, Frederick Roland Studdert
Amateur. *b:* 29.2.1892, Dublin. *d:* 2.12.1935, K3 Pipe Line Station, near Haditha, Iraq. Lower order right-hand batsman, right-arm fast medium bowler. *Teams* Ireland (1913–14); Europeans (1922/3); Army (1923–24).
Career batting
7–12–1–193–65–17.54–0–*ct* 8
Bowling 290–21–13.80–2–1–7/30

Shaw, George
Professional. *b:* 20.5.1839, Sutton-in-Ashfield, Notts. *d:* 17.8.1905, Loose, Kent. Lower order batsman, left-hand fast round-arm bowler. *Team* Kent (1872, 2 matches).
Career batting
2–4–2–17–13*–8.50–0–*ct* 3
Bowling 178–11–16.18–1–0–5/89

Shaw, George Bernard
Professional. *b:* 24.10.1931, Treharris, Glamorgan. Lower order right-hand batsman, off break bowler. *Team* Glamorgan (1951–55, 16 matches).
Career batting
16–20–13–30–11–4.28–0–*ct* 4
Bowling 706–26–27.15–2–1–5/38

Shaw, Henry
Professional. *b:* 21.5.1854, Mansfield, Notts. *d:* 8.11.1932, Derby. Lower order right-hand batsman, right-hand medium round-arm bowler. *Team* Derbyshire (1875–84, 14 matches).
Career batting
14–25–7–121–22–6.72–0–*ct* 5
Bowling 158–10–15.80–1–0–5/34
He also played for Staffordshire and Lincolnshire.

Shaw, James
Professional. *b:* 12.3.1865, Linthwaite, Yorkshire. *d:* 22.1.1921, Armley, Leeds, Yorkshire. Lower order batsman, slow left-arm bowler. *Team* Yorkshire (1896–97, 3 matches).
Career batting
3–3–0–8–7–2.66–0–*ct* 2
Bowling 181–7–25.85–0–0–4/119
He also played for Durham.

Shaw, James Coupe
Professional. *b:* 11.4.1836, Sutton in Ashfield, Notts. *d:* 7.3.1888, New Cross, Sutton in Ashfield, Notts. Tail end right-hand batsman, left-hand fast round-arm bowler. *Team* Nottinghamshire (1865–75, 69 matches).
Career batting
115–176–66–467–18*–4.24–0–*ct* 62
Bowling 9181–636+5–14.43–59–18–9/86
In his debut season of 1865 he headed the first-class averages with 44 wickets, av 10.75; he took his most wickets in 1870 with 96, av 10.31. His best bowling was 9 for 84 for Nottinghamshire v Gloucestershire at Trent Bridge in 1871, though for XIV of Notts v England in 1870 he took 10 for 20 (non-first-class). He was generally regarded as the worst batsman in first-class county cricket about 1870.

Shaw, John Monson
Amateur. *b:* 1.10.1832, Rochester, Kent. *d:* 4.9.1912, Kirkley, Suffolk. Middle order right-hand batsman. *Sch* Eton. *Team* Kent (1865–66, 3 matches).
Career batting
3–6–0–31–13–5.16–0–*ct* 2

Shaw, Robert John
Amateur. *b:* 10.2.1900, High Wycombe, Buckinghamshire. Son of E. D. (Middlesex), brother of E. A. (Oxford U). Opening right-hand batsman, wicket-keeper. *Teams* Royal Navy (1926–28); Combined Services (1931–37).
Career batting
7–13–0–531–119–40.84–1–*ct* 4
Bowling 12–0

Shaw, Vero Kemball
(later Shaw-MacKenzie)
Amateur. *b:* 14.1.1854, Belgaum, Bombay, India. *d:* 18.12.1905, Hastings, Sussex. Lower order right-hand batsman, left-hand fast round-arm bowler, good field. *Sch* Haileybury. *Teams* Kent (1875–78, 25 matches); Cambridge U (1875–76, blue 1876).
Career batting
34–56–8–560–74–11.66–0–*ct* 36
Bowling 959–38+1–25.23–0–0–4/1

Shaw, William
Professional. *b:* 5.8.1827, Burton Joyce, Notts. *d:* February 1890, Burton Joyce, Notts. Right-hand batsman, right-arm medium pace bowler. *Team* Nottinghamshire (1866, 1 match).
Career batting
1–1–0–1–1–1.00–0–*ct* 0

Shawe, Charles
Amateur. *b:* 15.11.1878, Weddington, Warwickshire. *d:* 9.2.1951, Witham Friary, Frome, Somerset. Middle order batsman. *Sch* Eton. *Team* Leveson-Gower's XI (1919).
Career batting
1–1–0–0–0–0.00–0–*ct* 0
Bowling 32–0

Shea, Alfred James
Professional. *b:* 7.11.1898, Briton-Ferry, Glamorgan. *d:* May 1969, Briton-Ferry, Glamorgan. Father of W. D. (Glamorgan). Lower order right-hand batsman, right-arm medium pace bowler. *Team* Glamorgan (1928, 2 matches).
Career batting
2–3–0–22–10–7.33–0–*ct* 0
Bowling 171–1–171.00–0–0–1/130

Shea, William Dennis
Professional. *b:* 7.2.1924, Briton-Ferry, Glamorgan. *d:* 22.9.1982, Scarisbrick, Lancashire. Son of A. J. (Glamorgan). Lower order right-hand batsman, leg break and googly bowler. *Team* Glamorgan (1947–48, 3 matches).
Career batting
3–3–1–27–18*–13.50–0–*ct* 0
Bowling 180–5–36.00–0–0–4/68

Sheahan, Andrew Paul
Cricketer. *b:* 30.9.1946, Werribee, Victoria, Australia. Great-grandson of W. H. Cooper (Australia). Middle order right-hand batsman. *Team* Victoria (1965/6 to 1973/4, 47 matches). *Tours* Australia to England 1968, 1972; to India 1969/70; to South Africa 1970/1; New Zealand 1973/4. *Tests* Australia (1967/8 to 1973/4, 31 matches).
Career batting
133–206–33–7987–202–46.16–19–*ct* 89
Bowling 66–1–66.00–0–0–1/19
Test batting
31–53–6–1594–127–33.91–2–*ct* 17

Although he played in all five Tests on the 1968 tour to England, he scored only 817 runs, av 28.17, in first-class matches. In 1972 he hit 788, av 41.47, but appeared in just two of the Tests. His highest score was 202 for Victoria v South Australia at Melbourne in 1966/7, and he hit 1,002 runs, av 83.50, in 1972/3.

Shearer, Edgar Donald Reid
Amateur. *b:* 6.6.1909, Harrow, Middlesex. Middle order right-hand batsman. *Sch* Aldenham. *Team* Ireland (1933–52).
Career batting
14–27–1–628–72–24.15–0–*ct* 12

Shearwood, Kenneth Arthur
Amateur. *b:* 5.9.1921, Derby. Lower order right-hand batsman, wicket-keeper. *Sch* Shrewsbury. *Teams* Oxford U (1949–51); Derbyshire (1949, 1 match).
Career batting
5–6–1–45–28–9.00–0–*ct* 5–*st* 4

He also played for Cornwall. A noted soccer player, he played centre half for Oxford and Pegasus, playing in the FA Amateur Cup Final in 1950/1.

Sheepshanks, Ernest Richard
Amateur. *b:* 22.3.1910, Wharfedale, Yorkshire. *d:* 31.12.1937, Terval, Spain. He was killed whilst a journalist reporting on the civil war. Middle order right-hand batsman. *Sch* Eton. *Team* Yorkshire (1929, 1 match).
Career batting
1–1–0–26–26–26.00–0–*ct* 0

He was the Reuter correspondent in Spain at the time of his death, which occurred when his car was hit by a shell. A fellow journalist, who accompanied him and escaped with minor injuries, was Kim Philby.

Sheffield, Edward James
Professional. *b:* 20.6.1908, New Eltham, Kent. *d:* 28.4.1971, Chobham, Surrey. Lower order right-hand batsman, right-arm fast medium bowler. *Teams* Surrey (1930–32, 23 matches); Kent (1933, 5 matches).
Career batting
28–26–3–319–64*–13.86–0–*ct* 17
Bowling 1871–78–23.98–2–0–7/123

Sheffield, James Roy
Professional. *b:* 19.11.1906, Barking, Essex. Lower order right-hand batsman, wicket-keeper. *Teams* Essex (1929–36, 177 matches); Wellington (1938/9).
Career batting
180–277–40–3914–108–16.51–1–*ct* 196–*st* 54
Bowling 28–0

Sheldrake, Edgar Francis Talman
Amateur. *b:* 18.1.1864, Aldershot, Hampshire. *d:* 1950, Surrey. Right-hand batsman, right-arm fast bowler. *Team* Hampshire (1884–85, 3 matches).

Career batting
3–5–0–52–20–10.40–0–*ct* 0
Bowling 78–1–78.00–0–0–1/41

Shelmerdine, George Owen
Amateur. *b:* 7.9.1899, Pendleton, Manchester. *d:* 31.7.1967, Brighton, Sussex. Middle order right-hand batsman, right-arm medium fast bowler. *Sch* Cheltenham. *Teams* Lancashire (1919–25, 31 matches); Cambridge U (1920–22, blue 1922).
Career batting
53–77–8–1614–105–23.39–1–*ct* 19
Bowling 205–3–68.33–0–0–2/24

He was for many years on the Committee of Lancashire and was President at the time of his death. He was also Chairman of the Forty Club.

Shelmerdine, Norman
Amateur. *b:* 1922, Chorlton-cum-Hardy, Lancashire. *Team* RAF (1945).
Career batting
1 match, did not bat–*ct* 0

Shenton, John Charles L.
Amateur. *b:* 1862, Bethnal Green, Middlesex. *d:* 26.1.1900, Epping, Essex. Right-hand batsman. *Team* Middlesex (1888, 1 match).
Career batting
1–2–0–8–5–4.00–0–*ct* 0

Shenton, Peter Anthony
Professional. *b:* 5.5.1936, Redcar, Yorkshire. Lower order batsman, off break bowler. *Teams* Kent (1960, 7 matches); Northants (1958, 1 match).
Career batting
8–8–3–68–33–13.60–0–*ct* 1
Bowling 442–17–26.00–1–0–5/68

Shepherd, Donald Arthur
Amateur. *b:* 10.3.1916, Whitkirk, Yorkshire. Right-hand batsman, off break bowler. *Sch* Leeds GS. *Team* Yorkshire (1938, 1 match).
Career batting
1–1–0–0–0–0.00–0–*ct* 0

Shepherd, Donald John
Professional. *b:* 12.8.1927, Porteynon, Glamorgan. Lower order right-hand batsman, right-arm medium or off break bowler. *Team* Glamorgan (1950–72, 647 matches). *Tours* Brown to East Africa 1961/2 (not first-class); Glamorgan to West Indies 1969/70; MCC to Ceylon 1969/70; Commonwealth to Pakistan 1967/8, 1970/1; Gloucestershire to Zambia 1971/2 (not first-class).
Career batting
668–837–249–5696–73–9.68–0–*ct* 251
Bowling 47302–2218–21.32–123–28–9/47

He took 100 wickets in a season twelve times (best 177, av 15.36, in 1956) and was the first Glamorgan bowler to reach 2,000 wickets in a career. No other bowler has taken as many first-class wickets and yet failed to be selected for Test cricket. His best innings analysis was 9 for 47 for Glamorgan v Northants at Cardiff in 1954.

Shepherd, David Robert
Cricketer. *b:* 27.12.1940, Bideford, Devon. Middle order right-hand batsman, right-arm medium pace bowler. *Team* Gloucestershire (1965–79, 282 matches).
Career batting
282–476–40–10672–153–24.47–12–*ct* 95
Bowling 106–2–53.00–0–0–1/1

He hit 1,000 runs in a season twice (best 1,079, av 26.97, in 1970). He also played for Devon. In 1981 he joined the first-class umpires' list.

Shepherd, John Neil
Cricketer. *b:* 9.11.1943, Belleplaine, Barbados. Middle order right-hand batsman, right-arm medium pace bowler. *Teams* Barbados (1964/5 to 1970/1); Kent (1966–81, 303 matches); Rhodesia (1975/6); Gloucestershire (1982–83, 45 matches). *Tours* West Indies to England 1969; Kent to West Indies 1972/3 (not first-class); Robins to South Africa 1973/4, 1974/5, to West Indies 1974/5 (not first-class); International XI to South Africa 1974/5, 1975/6. *Tests* West Indies (1969 to 1970/1, 5 matches).
Career batting
397–572–99–12468–170–26.35–10–*ct* 277
Bowling 29710–1083–27.43–52–2–8/40
Test batting
5–8–0–77–32–9.62–0–*ct* 4
Bowling 479–19–25.21–1–0–5/104

His best English season was 1968, when he hit 1,157 runs, av 29.66, and took 96 wickets, av 18.72. He hit 1,000 runs in one other season.

Shepherd, Sydney George
Professional. *b:* 23.8.1908, York. Middle order right-hand batsman, right-arm medium fast bowler. *Team* Worcestershire (1936, 1 match).
Career batting
1–2–0–9–9–4.50–0–*ct* 0
Bowling 4–0

He also played for Cheshire.

Shepherd, Thomas Frederick
Professional. *b:* 5.12.1889, Headington Quarry, Oxon. *d:* 13.2.1957, Kingston on Thames, Surrey. Sound middle order right-hand batsman, right-arm medium pace bowler, excellent slip field. *Team* Surrey (1919–32, 354 matches).

Career batting
363–531–61–18715–277*–39.81–42–*ct* 274
Bowling 13678–445–30.73–12–0–6/78

He hit 1,000 runs in a season twelve times, going on to 2,000 once – 2,145, av 55.00, in 1927. His five double centuries were all for Surrey, the highest being 277* v Gloucestershire at the Oval in 1927.

Shepherd, William
Professional. *b:* 9.8.1841, Kennington, Surrey. *d:* 27.5.1919, Tooting, Surrey. Lower order left-hand batsman, left-arm medium pace bowler. *Team* Surrey (1864–65, 13 matches).
Career batting
13–17–6–56–18–5.09–0–*ct* 8
Bowling 709–38–18.65–2–0–8/49

Sheppard, Rt Rev David Stuart
Amateur. *b:* 6.3.1929, Reigate, Surrey. Stylish opening right-hand batsman, slow left-arm bowler, brilliant close field. *Sch* Sherborne. *Teams* Cambridge U (1950–52, blue all three years); Sussex (1947–62, 141 matches). *Tours* MCC to Australia and New Zealand 1950/1, 1962/3. *Tests* England (1950 to 1963/4, 22 matches).
Career batting
230–395–31–15838–239*–43.51–45–*ct* 195
Bowling 88–2–44.00–0–0–1/5
Test batting
22–33–2–1172–119–37.80–3–*ct* 12

Whilst at Cambridge he created a new record by hitting 1,281, with seven centuries, in 1952 and he scored a record 3,545 in his University career. He hit 1,000 runs in a season six times, going on to 2,000 three times (best 2,270, av 45.40, in 1953). He hit one double century for Sussex and two for Cambridge, his highest being 239* for Cambridge v Worcestershire at Worcester in 1952. He captained Sussex in 1953, but after that season ceased to play regular first-class cricket, though captaining England twice in 1954. From 1969 to 1975 he was Bishop Suffragan of Woolwich and from 1975 Bishop of Liverpool.

Sheppard, Edward Cecil J.
Amateur. *b:* 1891, Bristol, Gloucestershire. *d:* 23.12.1962, Bristol, Gloucestershire. Middle order batsman. *Team* Gloucestershire (1921–22, 5 matches).
Career batting
5–9–0–117–29–13.00–0–*ct* 3

Sheppard, Geoffrey Allan
Amateur. *b:* 18.12.1890. *d:* 22.5.1940, Hornwick, Newbury, Berkshire. Middle order batsman. *Sch* Charterhouse. *Team* Worcestershire (1919, 2 matches).
Career batting
2–4–0–18–11–4.50–0–*ct* 2

Sheppard, Harold Frederick
Amateur. *b:* 11.9.1917, Glasgow, Scotland. Son of H. H. (Scotland). Right-hand batsman. *Team* Scotland (1938–52).
Career batting
13–24–1–509–72–22.13–0–*ct* 11
Bowling 7–0

Sheppard, Harold Holmes
Amateur. *b:* 20.5.1889, Pewsey, Wiltshire. *d:* 28.7.1978, Sherborne, Dorset. Father of H. F. (Scotland). Right-hand batsman, left-arm medium pace bowler. *Team* Scotland (1924).
Career batting
1–2–0–15–9–7.50–0–*ct* 1
Bowling 63–0

Sheppard, Robert Alexander
Amateur. *b:* 24.8.1879, Croydon, Surrey. *d:* 28.1.1953, Carshalton, Surrey. Right-hand batsman, right-arm off break bowler. *Sch* Whitgift. *Team* Surrey (1904–05, 12 matches).
Career batting
14–18–1–403–82–23.70–0–*ct* 10
Bowling 602–22–27.36–0–0–4/33

Sheppard, Thomas Winter
(later Sheppard-Graham)
Amateur. *b:* 4.3.1873, Havant, Hampshire. *d:* 7.6.1954, Callander, Perthshire, Scotland. *Sch* Haileybury. *Teams* Hampshire (1905, 1 match); Worcestershire (1909, 1 match).
Career batting
2–3–0–53–22–17.66–0–*ct* 0

Shepperd, John
Professional. *b:* 8.5.1937, Willesden, Middlesex. Lower order right-hand batsman, right-arm fast medium bowler. *Team* Middlesex (1959–60, 3 matches).
Career batting
4–6–2–32–13–8.00–0–*ct* 0
Bowling 253–4–63.25–0–0–3/35

He also played for Norfolk.

Shepstone, George Harold
Amateur. *b:* 9.4.1876, Pietermaritzburg, South Africa. *d:* 3.7.1940, Johannesburg, South Africa. Middle order right-hand batsman, right-arm fast bowler. *Sch* Repton. *Teams* Transvaal (1897/8 to 1904/5); MCC (1904). *Tour* South Africa to England 1904. *Tests* South Africa (1895/6 to 1898/9, 2 matches).

Career batting
22–34–1–693–104–21.00–1–*ct* 11
Bowling 682–42–16.23–3–1–5/17
Test batting
2–4–0–38–21–9.50–0–*ct* 2
Bowling 47–0

He appeared in only six first-class matches on the 1904 tour. His first-class debut was for South Africa v England in 1895/6.

Sherman, Howard Richard
Cricketer. *b:* 15.6.1943, Seven Kings, Essex. Middle order right-hand batsman, off break bowler. *Sch* Chigwell. *Team* Essex (1967–69, 13 matches).
Career batting
13–21–3–448–66–24.88–0–*ct* 4
Bowling 23–0

Sherman, Thomas
Professional. *b:* 1.12.1825, Mitcham, Surrey. *d:* 10.10.1911, Mitcham, Surrey. Right-hand batsman, right-arm fast bowler. *Teams* Surrey (1847–70, 51 matches); Lancashire (1849, 2 matches).
Career batting
82–137–35–713–41–6.99–0–*ct* 61
Bowling 2438–168+176–14.51–29–8–8/?

His first-class debut was for Manchester in 1846. He also played for Cheshire and Herefordshire.

Sherrard, Patrick
Amateur. *b:* 7.1.1919, Burton on Trent, Staffs. Right-hand batsman. *Sch* Stowe. *Teams* Cambridge U (1938); Leicestershire (1938, 1 match).
Career batting
2–3–0–60–53–20.00–0–*ct* 0

He also played for Berkshire.

Sherwell, Noel Benjamin
Amateur. *b:* 16.3.1904, Hendon, Middlesex. *d:* 29.12.1960, Flims, near Chur, Switzerland. He was killed while ski-ing. Lower order right-hand batsman, wicket-keeper. *Sch* Tonbridge. *Teams* Cambridge U (1923–25, blue all three years); Middlesex (1925–26, 3 matches).
Career batting
36–56–10–670–53*–14.56–0–*ct* 36–*st* 25

His final first-class match was for Free Foresters in 1939.

Sherwell, Percy William
Amateur. *b:* 17.8.1880, Isipingo, Natal, South Africa. *d:* 17.4.1948, Bulawayo, Southern Rhodesia. Opening or middle order right-hand batsman, wicket-keeper. *Sch* Bedford County. *Team* Transvaal (1902/3 to 1906/7). *Tours* South Africa to England 1907, to Australia 1910/11; Leveson-Gower to Rhodesia 1909/10. *Tests* South Africa (1905/6 to 1910/11, 13 matches).
Career batting
58–91–16–1808–144–24.10–3–*ct* 67–*st* 52
Test batting
13–22–4–427–115–23.72–1–*ct* 20–*st* 16

He captained the 1907 South African touring team to England and hit 806 runs, av 23.02, his only innings of note being 115 in the first Test at Lord's. He lived in England for some years and played for Cornwall. His final first-class match was for P. W. Sherwell's XI in 1913/14.

Sherwin, Arthur West
Amateur. *b:* 22.7.1879, Derby. *d:* 10.10.1947, Duffield, Derbyshire. Brother of C. B. (Derbyshire). Right-hand batsman, right-arm medium bowler. *Team* Derbyshire (1908, 11 matches).
Career batting
11–21–2–152–24–8.00–0–*ct* 4

Sherwin, Charles Bakewell
Amateur. *b:* 9.8.1877, Derby. *d:* 8.6.1950, Derby. Brother of A. W. (Derbyshire). Right-hand batsman. *Team* Derbyshire (1907, 1 match).
Career batting
1–2–0–7–7–3.50–0–*ct* 0

Sherwin, Howard
Professional. *b:* 22.7.1911, Chesterfield, Derbyshire. Left-hand batsman. *Team* Derbyshire (1937, 1 match).
Career batting
1–2–2–12–9*–no av–0–*ct* 0
Bowling 32–0

Sherwin, Mordecai
Professional. *b:* 26.2.1851, Kimberley, Notts. *d:* 3.7.1910, Nottingham. Tail end right-hand batsman, occasional right-arm fast bowler, wicket-keeper. *Team* Nottinghamshire (1876–96, 206 matches). *Tour* Lillywhite, Shaw and Shrewsbury to Australia 1886/7. *Tests* England (1886/7 to 1888, 3 matches).
Career batting
328–454–147–2339–37–7.61–0–*ct* 611–*st* 225
Bowling 108–8–13.50–0–0–2/7
Test batting
3–6–4–30–21*–15.00–0–*ct* 5–*st* 2

He captained Nottinghamshire in 1887 and 1888. A good soccer player, he kept goal for Notts County.

Shield, Ian Noel Ridley
Amateur. *b:* 25.12.1914, Lymington, Hants. Lower order right-hand batsman, right-arm fast

medium bowler. *Sch* Rugby. *Team* Hampshire (1939, 4 matches).
Career batting
4–5–1–16–6–4.00–0–*ct* 0
Bowling 274–4–68.50–0–0–2/91

Shields, John
Amateur. *b:* 1.2.1882, Loudoun, Ayrshire, Scotland. *d:* 11.5.1960, Isley Walton, Leicestershire. Lower order right-hand batsman, wicket-keeper. *Team* Leicestershire (1906–23, 129 matches).
Career batting
133–215–44–1401–63–8.19–0–*ct* 176–*st* 60
Bowling 4–0

Shillingford, Grayson Cleophas
Cricketer. *b:* 25.9.1944, Macoucherie, Dublanc, Dominica. Cousin of I. T. (West Indies). Tail end left-hand batsman, right-arm fast medium bowler. *Team* Windward Islands (1967/8 to 1978/9). *Tours* West Indies to England 1969, 1973. *Tests* West Indies (1969 to 1971/2, 7 matches).
Career batting
81–106–28–791–42–10.14–0–*ct* 22
Bowling 5760–217–26.54–6–0–6/49
Test batting
7–8–1–57–25–8.14–0–*ct* 2
Bowling 537–15–35.80–0–0–3/63

He took 36 wickets, av 18.58, on the 1969 tour, playing in two Tests, but injury meant that he missed several matches. In 1973 he was ineffective and not selected for the Tests.

Shilton, John Edward
Professional. *b:* 2.10.1861, Horbury Junction, Yorkshire. *d:* 27.9.1899, Sedbergh, Yorkshire. Lower order right-hand batsman, slow left-arm bowler. *Team* Warwickshire (1894–95, 19 matches).
Career batting
24–32–10–203–30–9.22–0–*ct* 17
Bowling 1631–71–22.97–4–0–7/75

His first-class debut was for the North of England in 1884. He appeared for Yorkshire in 1883 in non-first-class cricket and also at various times for Durham, Northumberland and Worcestershire.

Shinde, Sadashiv Ganpatrao
Amateur. *b:* 18.8.1923, Bombay, India. *d:* 22.6.1955, Bombay, India. He died of typhoid. Attacking lower order right-hand batsman, leg break and googly bowler. *Teams* Maharashtra (1940/1 to 1949/50); Hindus (1945/6); Baroda (1947/8 to 1948/9); Bombay (1950/1 to 1954/5). *Tours* India to England 1946, 1952. *Tests* India (1946–52, 7 matches).
Career batting
79–95–33–871–50*–14.04–0–*ct* 16
Bowling 7496–230–32.59–12–0–8/162
Test batting
7–11–5–85–14–14.16–0–*ct* 0
Bowling 717–12–59.75–1–0–6/91

He was disappointing on both his tours to England, but appeared in both Test series.

Shine, Eustace Beverley
Amateur. *b:* 9.7.1873, Port of Spain, Trinidad. *d:* 11.11.1952, New Milton, Hants. Lower order right-hand batsman, right-arm fast bowler. *Teams* Cambridge U (1895–97, blue 1896–97); Kent (1896–99, 23 matches).
Career batting
46–68–13–576–49–10.47–0–*ct* 45
Bowling 3909–165–23.69–8–2–8/45

He played a major part in changing the follow-on law from being compulsory to being optional. In the University match of 1896 he deliberately bowled three deliveries to the boundary in order to concede 12 runs and avoid letting Oxford follow-on.

Shingler, George
Professional. *b:* 1882, Leicester. *d:* May 1946, Barrow upon Soar, Leicestershire. Right-hand batsman. *Team* Leicestershire (1920–21, 4 matches).
Career batting
4–8–0–76–26–9.50–0–*ct* 5
Bowling 85–0

Shipman, Alan Wilfred
Professional. *b:* 7.3.1901, Ratby, Leicestershire. *d:* 12.12.1979, Leicester. Brother of William (Leicestershire). Middle order right-hand batsman, right-arm fast bowler. *Team* Leicestershire (1920–36, 383 matches).
Career batting
386–661–72–13682–226–23.22–15–*ct* 97
Bowling 15394–607–25.36–16–0–7/62

He hit 1,000 runs in a season eight times (best 1,621, av 33.77, in 1928). His only double century was 226 for Leicestershire v Kent at Tonbridge in 1928.

Shipman, William
Professional. *b:* 1.3.1886, Ratby, Leicestershire. *d:* 26.8.1943, Ratby, Leicestershire. Brother of A. W. (Leicestershire). Lower order right-hand batsman, right-arm fast bowler. *Team* Leicestershire (1908–21, 111 matches).
Career batting
113–190–14–2497–69–14.18–0–*ct* 83
Bowling 10006–367–27.26–16–3–9/83

His best bowling was 9/83 for Leics v Surrey at the Oval in 1911. He took 110 wickets, av 26.95, in 1911.

Shippey, Peter Anthony
Amateur. *b:* 31.8.1939. Newton, Wisbech, Cambridgeshire. Middle order left-hand batsman. *Teams* MCC (1967); Minor Counties (1969–71).
Career batting
4–7–1–187–94*–31.16–0–*ct* 0
His County cricket was for Cambridgeshire, commencing 1957.

Shipston, Frank William
Professional. *b:* 29.7.1906, Bulwell, Notts. Middle order right-hand batsman, off break bowler. *Team* Nottinghamshire (1925–33, 49 matches).
Career batting
49–72–8–1183–118*–18.48–2–*ct* 13
He was coach to Nottinghamshire from 1957 to 1966.

Shipton, William Louis
Amateur. *b:* 19.3.1861, Buxton, Derbyshire. *d:* 21.10.1941, Buxton, Derbyshire. Right-hand batsman, right-arm fast bowler. *Sch* Repton. *Team* Derbyshire (1884, 1 match).
Career batting
1–2–0–4–3–2.00–0–*ct* 0
He did not play in first-class matches whilst at Cambridge University.

Shirley, William Robert de la Cour
Amateur. *b:* 13.10.1900, London. *d:* 23.4.1970, Bognor Regis, Sussex. Opening right-hand batsman, right-arm fast medium bowler. *Sch* Eton. *Teams* Cambridge U (1924, blue); Hampshire (1922–25, 49 matches).
Career batting
62–93–11–1458–90–17.77–0–*ct* 31
Bowling 1912–81–23.60–0–0–4/10

Shirreff, Alexander Campbell
Amateur. *b:* 12.2.1919, Ealing, Middlesex. Sound middle order right-hand batsman, right-arm medium pace bowler. *Sch* Dulwich. *Teams* Cambridge U (1939, blue); Hampshire (1946–47, 12 matches); Kent (1950–56, 46 matches); Somerset (1958, 2 matches).
Career batting
119–203–24–3887–115*–21.71–1–*ct* 89
Bowling 9575–304–31.49–11–0–8/111
Being in the RAF his County cricket was very intermittant, but he played frequently for Combined Services and for the RAF XI.

Shivram, Babaji Palwankar
Amateur. *b:* 6.3.1878, Bhuj, India. *d:* 28.12.1941, Bombay, India. Brother of P. Baloo, P. Ganpat, P. Vithal (Hindus). Middle order right-hand batsman, off break bowler. *Team* Hindus (1905/6 to 1924/5). *Tour* India to England 1911.
Career batting
39–67–7–1130–113*–18.83–1–*ct* 18
Bowling 1090–53–20.56–0–0–4/31
He hit 631 runs, av 28.68, on the 1911 tour, being second in the first-class averages.

Shoesmith, George
Professional. *b:* 19.10.1842, Storrington, Sussex. *d:* 27.7.1877, Sutton, Pulborough, Sussex. He died of bronchitis. Lower order left-hand batsman, right-hand fast round-arm bowler, slip field. *Team* Sussex (1869–71, 11 matches).
Career batting
11–20–7–91–17*–7.00–0–*ct* 5
Bowling 467–20–23.35–1–0–5/48

Shoosmith, Joseph
Professional. *b:* 1859, Brighton, Sussex. *d:* 1901, Brighton, Sussex. Lower order batsman, useful bowler. *Team* Sussex (1881, 1 match).
Career batting
1–2–1–2–2–2.00–0–*ct* 0
Bowling 23–1–23.00–0–0–1/23

Shooter, Thomas
Professional. *b:* 11.3.1845, Hucknall Torkard, Notts. *d:* 14.7.1919, Hucknall Torkard, Notts. Middle order right-hand batsman, right-arm fast bowler. *Team* Nottinghamshire (1881, 2 matches).
Career batting
2–4–1–23–15*–7.66–0–*ct* 1
Bowling 57–0

Shore, Charles
Professional. *b:* 21.11.1858, Sutton in Ashfield, Notts. *d:* 5.6.1912, Sutton in Ashfield, Notts. Lower order left-hand batsman, slow left-arm bowler. *Teams* Lancashire (1886, 1 match); Nottinghamshire (1881–85, 10 matches).
Career batting
13–21–9–159–42*–13.25–0–*ct* 9
Bowling 938–41–22.87–2–0–5/36
His final first-class match was for Liverpool and District XI in 1887. He played for Herefordshire in 1886 and Norfolk from 1889 to 1901.

Shore, Richard Graham
Amateur. *b:* 9.3.1941, Bournemouth, Hants. Lower order right-hand batsman, right-arm medium pace bowler. *Sch* Blundells. *Team* Oxford U (1962).

Career batting
4–8–2–46–24–7.66–0–*ct* 1
Bowling 395–10–39.50–0–0–3/57

Shorrocks, Ernest
Professional. *b:* 1875, Rhodes, Lancashire. *d:* 20.7.1916, Thiepval, France. He was killed in action. Lower order batsman, useful bowler. *Team* Somerset (1905, 1 match).
Career batting
1–2–1–16–16*–16.00–0–*ct* 0
Bowling 60–2–30.00–0–0–2/60

Short, Arthur Martin
Cricketer. *b:* 27.9.1947, Graaff-Reinet, South Africa. Opening right-hand batsman. *Teams* Eastern Province (1966/7 to 1974/5); Natal (1969/70 to 1972/3). *Tours* South African Universities to England 1967; selected for South Africa to England 1970 (cancelled).
Career batting
66–123–4–3318–118–27.88–2–*ct* 51
Bowling 62–3–20.66–0–0–2/2

Short, John David
Amateur. *b:* 13.6.1934, Chesterfield, Derbyshire. Middle order right-hand batsman, off break bowler. *Sch* Denstone. *Team* Derbyshire (1957–60, 11 matches).
Career batting
11–19–0–271–86–14.26–0–*ct* 6
Bowling 11–0

Short, John Francis
Cricketer. *b:* 12.4.1951, Cork. Right-hand batsman. *Team* Ireland (1974–83).
Career batting
10–17–2–518–114–34.53–1–*ct* 10

Short, Robert Leslie
Cricketer. *b:* 24.9.1948, Chesterfield, Derbyshire. Middle order right-hand batsman. *Sch* Denstone. *Team* Cambridge U (1969–70, blue 1969).
Career batting
11–20–1–355–58–18.68–0–*ct* 4

Shorter, Richard Nicholas
Amateur. *b:* 26.7.1906, Loughton, Essex. *d:* 20.1.1984, Co Meath, Ireland. Left-hand batsman, right-arm medium bowler. *Sch* Repton. *Team* Essex (1927–29, 23 matches).
Career batting
23–29–11–104–21–5.77–0–*ct* 12
Bowling 695–15–46.33–0–0–3/14

Shorting, Wilfred Lionel
Amateur. *b:* 12.3.1904, Tenbury, Worcestershire. *d:* 10.10.1982, Hastings, Sussex. Right-hand batsman. *Sch* King's, Worcester. *Team* Worcestershire (1922–26, 9 matches).
Career batting
9–17–1–165–27–10.31–0–*ct* 2

Shortland, Norman Arthur
Professional. *b:* 6.7.1916, Coventry, Warwickshire. *d:* 14.3.1973, Finham, Warwickshire. Middle order right-hand batsman, right-arm medium pace bowler. *Team* Warwickshire (1938–50, 23 matches).
Career batting
23–40–5–487–70–13.91–0–*ct* 4
Bowling 50–0

Shortt, Roland Henry
Amateur. *b:* 7.8.1898, Dublin. *d:* 8.8.1963, Dublin. Right-hand batsman, right-arm medium pace bowler. *Team* Ireland (1934).
Career batting
1–2–0–0–0–0.00–0–*ct* 0
Bowling 66–3–22.00–0–0–3/22

Shotton, William
Professional. *b:* 1.12.1840, Lascelles Hall, Yorkshire. *d:* 26.5.1909, Kirkheaton, Yorkshire. Opening right-hand batsman, right-hand medium pace round-arm bowler, good point field. *Team* Yorkshire (1865–74, 2 matches).
Career batting
2–4–0–13–7–3.25–0–*ct* 0

Shoubridge, Thomas
Professional. *b:* 8.9.1869. *d:* 22.10.1937, Prescot, Lancashire. Lower order batsman, right-hand fast round-arm bowler. *Team* Sussex (1890, 2 matches).
Career batting
3–6–2–14–10–3.50–0–*ct* 0
Bowling 77–1–77.00–0–0–1/35

Showers, Charles James
Amateur. *b:* 12.1.1848, Fort William, Calcutta, India. Opening right-hand batsman, right-hand medium pace round-arm bowler. *Sch* Cheltenham and Wellington. *Team* MCC (1881).
Career batting
3–5–0–82–39–16.40–0–*ct* 0
Bowling 48–1–48.00–0–0–1/48

He played for the United South of England Eleven during 1877, but later went to Assam as a tea planter. His first-class debut was for the South in 1877.

Shrewsbury, Arthur
Professional. *b:* 11.4.1856, New Lenton, Notts. *d:* 19.5.1903, Gedling, Notts. He died by his own

hand. Brother of William (Nottinghamshire), uncle of Arthur jun (Notts). Very sound opening right-hand batsman, good point field. *Team* Nottinghamshire (1875–1902, 357 matches). *Tours* Daft to North America 1879 (not first-class); Lillywhite, Shaw and Shrewsbury to Australia 1881/2, 1884/5, 1886/7, 1887/8. *Tests* England (1881/2 to 1893, 23 matches).
Career batting
498–813–90–26505–267–36.65–59–*ct* 376
Bowling 2–0
Test batting
23–40–4–1277–164–35.47–3–*ct* 29
Bowling 2–0

The principal professional batsman in England in the 1880s and early 1890s, he topped the first-class batting averages in 1886, 1887, 1890, 1891, 1892 and 1902. His most outstanding summer was 1887 when he hit 1,653 runs, av 78.71, which was then the highest average ever recorded by a batsman playing regular first-class cricket. In all he completed 1,000 runs in a season thirteen times. He hit ten double centuries, seven of which were for Nottinghamshire and three in Australia. Twice he made 267, both times for the County – v Middlesex at Trent Bridge in 1887 and v Sussex at Trent Bridge in 1890. In the latter match, with W. Gunn, he created a new first-class second wicket partnership record of 398 which stood for 44 years.

With Lillywhite and Shaw he sponsored several tours to Australia and captained the tourists in 1884/5 and 1886/7, also leading England in seven Test matches.

He committed suicide in 1903. This tragic act was due, at least in part, to the belief that ill-health would prevent him from continuing to play in first-class cricket – he had headed the batting averages in the previous season.

Shrewsbury, Arthur (jun)
Professional. *b:* 4.7.1874, Nottingham. *d:* 6.10.1917, Nottingham. Son of William (Nottinghamshire), nephew of Arthur (Nottinghamshire). Right-hand batsman, right-arm medium pace bowler. *Team* Nottinghamshire (1892, 3 matches).
Career batting
3–5–3–63–31*–31.50–0–*ct* 1
Bowling 31–0

Shrewsbury, William
Professional. *b:* 30.4.1854, New Lenton, Notts. *d:* 14.11.1931, Fiskerton, Nottinghamshire. Brother of Arthur (Nottinghamshire), father of Arthur, jun (Notts). Right-hand batsman, right-arm fast bowler. *Team* Nottinghamshire (1875–79, 9 matches).
Career batting
9–13–2–77–34–7.00–0–*ct* 5

Shrimpton, Herbert John Donald
Amateur. *b:* 12.4.1903, Worcester. *d:* 12.3.1979, Southwark, London. Right-hand batsman, leg break bowler. *Team* Gloucestershire (1923, 3 matches).
Career batting
3–6–1–26–14–5.20–0–*ct* 1

Shuckburgh, Sir Charles Gerald Stewkley
Amateur. *b:* 28.2.1911, Shuckburgh, Warwickshire. Middle order right-hand batsman. *Sch* Harrow. *Team* Warwickshire (1930, 1 match).
Career batting
1–1–0–0–0–0.00–*ct* 1

Shuja-ud-din Butt
Amateur. *b:* 10.4.1930, Lahore, India. Lower order right-hand batsman, slow left-arm bowler, good field. *Teams* Northern India (1946/7); Punjab U (1947/8); Services (1953/4 to 1963/4); Bahawalpur (1957/8 to 1969/70); Rawalpindi (1965/6). *Tours* Pakistan to England 1954, to India 1960/1. *Tests* Pakistan (1954 to 1961/2, 19 matches).
Career batting
98–156–21–3342–147–24.75–6–*ct* 68
Bowling 6714–298–22.53–15–3–8/53
Test batting
19–32–6–395–47–15.19–0–*ct* 8
Bowling 801–20–40.05–0–0–3/18

On the 1954 tour he took 67 wickets, av 28.85, and played in three Tests.

Shuja-ud-din Butt
Amateur. Lower order batsman, useful bowler. *Teams* Punjab (1953/4); Railways (1954/5 to 1959/60); Lahore (1959/60). *Tour* Pakistan to England 1962.
Career batting
18–32–6–633–77–24.34–0–*ct* 9
Bowling 440–9–48.88–0–0–2/49

He was co-opted into the 1962 touring team for one first-class match. His final first-class match in Pakistan was for Railways and Quetta in 1960/1.

Shuker, Abraham
Amateur. *b:* 6.7.1848, Stockton, Shropshire. *d:* 11.2.1909, Chell, Tunstall, Staffs. Steady middle order right-hand batsman. *Sch* Brewood. *Team* Derbyshire (1874–82, 22 matches).
Career batting
22–40–2–601–86–15.81–0–*ct* 12

He did not play in any first-class matches whilst at Cambridge University. He appeared occasionally for Staffordshire.

Shuldham, Walter Frank Quantock
Amateur. *b:* 17.6.1892, Stoke-sub-Hamdon, Somerset. *d:* 7.2.1971, Stoke-sub-Hamdon, Somerset. Middle order right-hand batsman. *Sch* Marlborough. *Teams* Somerset (1914–24, 6 matches); Rajputana (1926/7).
Career batting
8–13–1–126–25–10.50–0–*ct* 0

Shuter, John
Amateur. *b:* 9.2.1855, Thornton Heath, Surrey. *d:* 5.7.1920, Blackheath, Kent. Brother of L. A. (Surrey), uncle of L. R. W. A. (MCC). Stylish opening right-hand batsman, good field. *Sch* Winchester. *Teams* Kent (1874, 1 match); Surrey (1877–1909, 274 matches). *Test* England (1888, 1 match).
Career batting
306–503–23–10206–135–21.26–8–*ct* 157
Bowling 49–0
Test batting
1–1–0–28–28–28.00–0–*ct* 0

His best season was 1884 when he hit 968 runs, av 26.88. He captained Surrey from 1880 to 1893 and was appointed Secretary to the County Club in 1919, unfortunately dying before he had completed a year in office; he had been however a very active member of the Club from his retirement as captain in 1893.

Shuter, Leonard Allen
Amateur. *b:* 25.5.1852, Thornton Heath, Surrey. *d:* 13.7.1928, Eastbourne, Sussex. Brother of John (Surrey), father of L. R. W. A. (MCC). Middle order right-hand batsman, right-arm fast or slow left-arm bowler, good field. *Sch* Rugby. *Team* Surrey (1876–83, 37 matches).
Career batting
38–66–2–1074–89–16.78–0–*ct* 16
Bowling 75–1–75.00–0–0–1/10

Shuter, Leonard Robert Warner Allen
Amateur. *b:* 21.3.1887, Dartford, Kent. *d:* 21.11.1960, Aldeburgh, Suffolk. Son of L. A. (Surrey), nephew of John (Surrey). Opening batsman. *Sch* Tonbridge. *Team* MCC (1908).
Career batting
1–2–0–15–11–7.50–0–*ct* 0

Shutt, Albert
Cricketer. *b:* 21.9.1952, Stockton on Tees, Co Durham. Lower order right-hand batsman, right-arm medium fast bowler. *Team* Worcestershire (1972, 2 matches).
Career batting
2 matches, did not bat–*ct* 1
Bowling 181–2–90.50–0–0–1/36

He also played for Durham.

Shutt, Herbert
Professional. *b:* 1879, Chorlton, Lancashire. *d:* 1922, Whitehaven, Cumberland. Lower order batsman, good bowler. *Team* Hampshire (1906, 4 matches).
Career batting
4–5–3–7–6–3.50–0–*ct* 0
Bowling 231–8–28.87–0–0–4/29

He also played for Cumberland.

Shuttleworth, Guy Mitchell
Amateur. *b:* 6.11.1926, Blackburn, Lancashire. Middle order right-hand batsman. *Team* Cambridge U (1946–48, blue all three years).
Career batting
25–39–5–786–96–23.11–0–*ct* 7

Shuttleworth, Kenneth
Cricketer. *b:* 13.11.1944, St Helens, Lancashire. Lower order right-hand batsman, right-arm fast bowler. *Teams* Lancashire (1964–75, 177 matches); Leicestershire (1977–80, 41 matches). *Tours* Commonwealth to Pakistan 1967/8; MCC to Australia and New Zealand 1970/1. *Tests* England (1970/1 to 1971, 5 matches).
Career batting
239–241–85–2589–71–16.59–0–*ct* 128
Bowling 15270–623–24.51–21–1–7/41
Test batting
5–6–0–46–21–7.66–0–*ct* 1
Bowling 427–12–35.58–1–0–5/47

Sibbles, Frank Marshall
Amateur. *b:* 15.3.1904, Oldham, Lancashire. *d:* 20.7.1973, Wilmslow, Cheshire. Lower order right-hand batsman, right-arm medium pace off break bowler. *Team* Lancashire (1925–37, 308 matches).
Career batting
315–316–79–3478–71*–14.67–0–*ct* 181
Bowling 21087–940–22.53–41–4–8/24

He took 100 wickets in a season twice (best 131, av 18.25, in 1932). He was elected to the Committee of Lancashire CCC in 1950 and was Chairman for two years.

Siddons, Anthony
Professional. *b:* 29.12.1941, Nottingham. Tail end right-hand batsman, off break bowler. *Team* Nottinghamshire (1959–60, 5 matches).
Career batting
5–8–3–36–8–7.20–0–*ct* 1
Bowling 266–8–33.25–0–0–4/37

Sidebottom, Arnold
Cricketer. *b:* 1.4.1954, Barnsley, Yorkshire. Lower order right-hand batsman, right-arm fast medium bowler. *Teams* Yorkshire (1973–83, 118

matches); Orange Free State (1981/2). *Tour* SAB England XI to South Africa 1981/2 (he did not play in first-class matches).
Career batting
122–138–32–2306–124–21.75–1–*ct* 34
Bowling 7009–285–24.59–11–2–7/18

A good soccer player, he has appeared for Manchester United, Huddersfield Town and Halifax.

Sidgwick, Robert
Amateur. *b:* 7.8.1851, Embsay Kirk, Yorkshire. *d:* 1934, Kingston, Jamaica. Middle order right-hand batsman, brilliant field. *Sch* Wellington. *Teams* Yorkshire (1882, 9 matches); Jamaica (1894/5).
Career batting
10–15–0–72–17–4.80–0–*ct* 7

He emigrated to Jamaica in 1892, where he became a coffee planter.

Sidwell, Thomas Edgar
Professional. *b:* 30.1.1888, Belgrave, Leicestershire. *d:* 8.12.1958, Braunstone Frith, Leicester. Sound right-hand batsman, wicket-keeper. *Team* Leicestershire (1913–33, 388 matches).
Career batting
392–605–87–7929–105–15.30–3–*ct* 583–*st* 137

He hit 1,153 runs, av 29.56, in 1928.

Siedle, Ivan Julian
Amateur. *b:* 11.1.1903, Durban, South Africa. *d:* 24.8.1982, Durban, South Africa. Father of J. R. (Western Province). Solid opening right-hand batsman. *Team* Natal (1922/3 to 1936/7). *Tours* South Africa to England 1929, 1935. *Tests* South Africa (1927/8 to 1935/6, 18 matches).
Career batting
123–204–11–7730–265*–40.05–17–*ct* 57–*st* 1
Bowling 35–1–35.00–0–0–1/7
Test batting
18–34–0–977–141–28.73–1–*ct* 7
Bowling 7–1–7.00–0–0–1/7

In first-class matches on the 1929 tour he hit 1,579 runs, av 35.88, but failed in the Tests. In 1935 he hit 1,346 runs, av 39.58, but again had only a modest return in the Tests. His highest score was 265* for Natal v Orange Free State at Durban in 1929/30.

Sievwright, Robert Willis
Amateur. *b:* 16.6.1882, Arbroath, Angus, Scotland. *d:* 12.7.1947, Arbroath, Scotland. Left-hand batsman, slow left-arm bowler. *Team* Scotland (1912–30).
Career batting
13–19–6–98–13*–7.53–0–*ct* 2
Bowling 1298–65–19.96–5–1–7/71

Sikander Bakht
Cricketer. *b:* 25.8.1957, Karachi, Pakistan. Tail end right-hand batsman, right-arm medium pace bowler. *Teams* PWD (1974/5); Sind (1975/6); PIA (1975/6); United Bank (1975/6 to 1982/3). *Tours* Pakistan to Australia and West Indies 1976/7, to England 1978, 1982, to Australia and New Zealand 1978/9, to India 1979/80, to Australia 1981/2. *Tests* Pakistan (1976/7 to 1982/3, 26 matches).
Career batting
117–120–40–1169–67–14.61–0–*ct* 54
Bowling 9321–346–26.93–20–2–8/69
Test batting
26–35–12–146–22*–6.34–0–*ct* 7
Bowling 2411–67–35.98–3–1–8/69

He played in all three Tests on the 1978 tour, but only had a modest record. In 1982 he played in two Tests, and in all first-class matches took 27 wickets, av 35.51.

Silcock, Frank
Professional. *b:* 2.10.1838, Sawbridgeworth, Herts. *d:* 26.5.1897, High Ongar, Essex. Stylish middle order right-hand batsman, right-hand fast medium round-arm bowler, slip field. *Team* Players (1868–69).
Career batting
41–76–8–776–66–11.41–0–*ct* 31
Bowling 1629–79–20.62–5–0–7/132

He made his first-class debut for the South in 1864 and his final match for UEE in 1879. His County cricket was for Essex (pre-first-class) and for Hertfordshire.

Silcock, William
Professional. *b:* 1868, Chorley, Lancashire. *d:* 30.7.1933, Leyland, Lancashire. Lower order batsman, good bowler. *Team* Lancashire (1899–1902, 6 matches).
Career batting
6–7–1–82–43–13.66–0–*ct* 5
Bowling 367–5–73.40–0–0–2/62

Silk, Dennis Raoul Whitehall
Amateur. *b:* 8.10.1931, Eureka, California, USA. Opening right-hand batsman, right-arm leg break bowler. *Sch* Christ's Hospital. *Teams* Cambridge U (1952–55, blue 1953–55); Somerset (1956–60, 33 matches). *Tours* MCC to East Africa 1957/8, to South America 1958/9, to North America 1959 (none first-class), to New Zealand 1960/1.
Career batting
83–140–11–3845–126–29.80–7–*ct* 45
Bowling 240–1–240.00–0–0–1/22

He captained the MCC teams in North

America and in New Zealand. A good rugby footballer, he played for Cambridge and Sussex; he also represented the University at rugby fives.

Silkin, Rt Hon Samuel Charles
Amateur. *b:* 6.3.1918, Neath, Glamorgan. Lower order right-hand batsman, right-arm off break bowler. *Sch* Dulwich. *Teams* Cambridge U (1938); Glamorgan (1938, 1 match).
Career batting
2–3–0–4–2–1.33–0–*ct* 2
Bowling 119–2–59.50–0–0–1/27

In 1964 he was elected Labour MP for Camberwell; from 1974 to 1979 he served as Attorney-General, having previously been Chairman of the Council of Europe Legal Committee.

Silvester, Stephen
Cricketer. *b:* 12.3.1951, Hull, Yorkshire. Lower order right-hand batsman, right-arm fast medium bowler. *Team* Yorkshire (1976–77, 6 matches).
Career batting
6–7–4–30–14–10.00–0–*ct* 2
Bowling 313–12–26.08–0–0–4/86

Sim, Archibald Millar Robertson
Cricketer. *b:* 8.1.1942, Johannesburg, South Africa. Middle order right-hand batsman. *Teams* North Eastern Transvaal (1962/3); Northamptonshire (1964–66, 4 matches).
Career batting
7–12–1–196–66*–17.81–0–*ct* 2
Bowling 12–1–12.00–0–0–1/12

Sime, Judge William Arnold
Amateur. *b:* 8.2.1909, Wepener, Orange Free State, South Africa. *d:* 5.5.1983, Wymeswold, Leics. Attacking middle order right-hand batsman, slow left-arm bowler. *Sch* Bedford. *Teams* Nottinghamshire (1935–50, 91 matches); Oxford U (1931).
Career batting
96–138–17–2473–176*–20.43–1–*ct* 55
Bowling 2300–49–46.93–0–0–4/51

He also played for Bedfordshire commencing 1928 and made his first-class debut for the Minor Counties in 1929. Whilst in South Africa during the war he played in a single first-class match for the Air Force in 1942/3. He was on the Committee of Nottinghamshire and later President of the County Club. A noted rugby footballer he played for Bedford, Notts and East Midlands and had a trial for England. In the legal profession he was appointed a Judge in 1972.

Simmonds, Rev Arthur
Amateur. *b:* 1.2.1848, Godalming, Surrey. *d:* 2.8.1933, Ascot, Berks. Middle order right-hand batsman, point field. *Sch* Brighton. *Teams* Cambridge U (1871); Surrey (1872–73, 6 matches).
Career batting
7–14–0–183–50–13.07–0–*ct* 1

Simmonds, William Henry
Amateur. *b:* 1892, Bristol. *d:* 11.3.1957, Bishopston, Bristol. Middle order batsman. *Team* Gloucestershire (1924–25, 2 matches).
Career batting
2–3–0–57–44–19.00–0–*ct* 0

Simmons, C. H.
Professional. Lower order batsman, opening bowler. *Team* Sussex (1920, 1 match).
Career batting
1–2–0–0–0–0.00–0–*ct* 0
Bowling 42–1–42.00–0–0–1/18

Simmons, Jack
Cricketer. *b:* 28.3.1941, Clayton le Moors, Lancashire. Attacking lower order right-hand batsman, off break bowler. *Teams* Lancashire (1968–83, 323 matches); Tasmania (1972/3 to 1978/9, 20 matches). *Tour* Overseas XI to India 1980/1.
Career batting
344–420–112–7205–112–23.59–5–*ct* 269
Bowling 20838–759–27.45–26–3–7/59

He received £128,000 from his benefit in 1980.

Simms, Harry Lester
Amateur. *b:* 31.1.1888, Adelaide, South Australia. *d:* 9.6.1942, Weybridge, Surrey. Brother of R. K. (Sussex). Middle order right-hand batsman, right-arm fast bowler. *Teams* Sussex (1905–13, 79 matches); Europeans (1909/10 to 1916/17); Cooch-Behar's XI (1917/8); Bengal Governor's XI (1918/9); Warwickshire (1921–22, 5 matches).
Career batting
110–186–10–3154–126–17.92–1–*ct* 70
Bowling 4230–219+1–19.31–12–0–7/84

He performed the 'double' in 1912 with 1,099 runs, av 20.73, and 110 wickets, av 22.68.

Simms, Royston Knox
Amateur. *b:* 1.1.1894. *d:* 1978, Yeovil, Somerset. Brother of H. L. (Sussex and Warwickshire). Lower order batsman, useful bowler. *Sch* Lancing. *Team* Sussex (1912, 2 matches).
Career batting
2–2–0–5–4–2.50–0–*ct* 0
Bowling 64–2–32.00–0–0–1/23

Simons, Robert George
Amateur. *b:* 23.3.1922, Watford, Hertfordshire. Middle order right-hand batsman, wicket-keeper. *Sch* Berkhamsted. *Team* Minor Counties (1959).
Career batting
1–1–0–0–0–0.00–0–*ct* 1–*st* 1
His County cricket was for Hertfordshire.

Simpkins, David Paul
Cricketer. *b:* 28.3.1962, Chippenham, Wiltshire. Right-hand batsman, off break bowler. *Team* Gloucestershire (1982, 1 match).
Career batting
1–2–1–1–1*–1.00–0–*ct* 0
Bowling 15–0

Simpkins, Peter Anthony
Amateur. *b:* 27.11.1928, Dover, Kent. Lower order left-hand batsman, slow left-arm bowler. *Team* Free Foresters (1962).
Career batting
1 match, did not bat–*ct* 2
Bowling 114–3–38.00–0–0–3/69
His County cricket was for Berkshire.

Simpson, Alexander Russell
Amateur. *b:* 28.2.1905, Dunfermline, Fife, Scotland. *d:* 10.11.1975, Weston-super-Mare, Somerset. Lower order right-hand batsman, wicket-keeper. *Team* Scotland (1925–34).
Career batting
12–22–6–101–19*–6.31–0–*ct* 14–*st* 10

Simpson, B. B. (*see under* Gregory, B.)

Simpson, Cyril Charles
Amateur. *b:* 1874, Erpingham, Norfolk. *d:* 5.5.1953, Hove, Sussex. Lower order batsman, useful bowler. *Sch* Wellingborough. *Team* Northamptonshire (1908, 1 match).
Career batting
1–2–0–3–3–1.50–0–*ct* 0
Bowling 36–1–36.00–0–0–1/36

Simpson, Ernest Herbert
Amateur. *b:* 17.12.1875, Clapton, Middlesex. *d:* 2.10.1917, St Omer, France. Middle order right-hand batsman, good field. *Sch* Malvern. *Team* Kent (1896, 7 matches).
Career batting
7–14–0–219–94–15.64–0–*ct* 1

Simpson, Edward Thornhill Beckett
Amateur. *b:* 5.3.1867, Crofton, Wakefield, Yorkshire. *d:* 20.3.1944, Walton, Wakefield, Yorkshire. Middle order right-hand batsman. *Sch* Harrow. *Teams* Oxford U (1888, blue); Yorkshire (1889, 2 matches).
Career batting
11–19–3–205–82–12.81–0–*ct* 13

Simpson, Frank William
Amateur. *b:* 27.3.1909, Theberton, Suffolk. Opening right-hand batsman, right-arm medium pace bowler. *Sch* Merchant Taylors. *Teams* Army (1931); Combined Services (1948).
Career batting
2–4–0–92–40–23.00–0–*ct* 1

Simpson, Gerard Amyatt
Amateur. *b:* 29.3.1886, Edinburgh, Scotland. *d:* 22.2.1957, Chartham, Kent. Middle order batsman. *Sch* Wellington. *Teams* Kent (1929–31, 3 matches); Argentina (1911/2).
Career batting
4–6–1–50–26–10.00–0–*ct* 0

Simpson, George Hayward Thomas
(changed to Simpson-Hayward in 1898)
Amateur. *b:* 7.6.1875, Kenilworth, Warwickshire. *d:* 2.10.1936, Icomb, Gloucestershire. Forcing middle order right-hand batsman, right-hand slow under-arm bowler. *Sch* Malvern. *Teams* Cambridge U (1895–97); Worcestershire (1899–1914, 156 matches). *Tours* Oxford Authentics to India 1902/3; Brackley to West Indies 1904/5; MCC to New Zealand 1906/7, to North America 1907, to Egypt 1909 (not first-class), to South Africa 1909/10; Leveson-Gower to Rhodesia 1909/10. *Tests* England (1909/10, 5 matches).
Career batting
199–325–26–5556–130–18.58–3–*ct* 133
Bowling 10762–503–21.39–31–1–7/54
Test batting
5–8–1–105–29*–15.00–0–*ct* 1
Bowling 420–23–18.26–2–0–6/46
He was one of the last of the major under-arm bowlers to appear regularly in first-class cricket. His best season was 1908 when he took 68 wickets, av 18.61. A good soccer player, he appeared as full back for Cambridge.

Simpson, Harold Benjamin
Amateur. *b:* 27.1.1879, Higham Ferrers, Northants. *d:* March 1924, Chelveston, Northants. Middle order right-hand batsman, useful bowler. *Sch* Wellingborough. *Team* Northants (1905–11, 8 matches).
Career batting
8–15–1–128–44–9.14–0–*ct* 3
Bowling 413–9–45.88–0–0–4/29

Simpson, Jack
Amateur. *b:* 1.12.1920, Lisburn, Co Antrim.

Right-hand batsman, right-arm fast medium bowler. *Team* Ireland (1954).
Career batting
1–1–0–26–26–26.00–0–*ct* 0
Bowling 50–0

Simpson, Robert Baddeley
Amateur. *b:* 3.2.1936, Marrickville, New South Wales, Australia. Attractive right-hand opening batsman, leg break and googly bowler, brilliant slip field. *Teams* New South Wales (1952/3 to 1977/8, 67 matches); Western Australia (1956/57 to 1960/1, 24 matches). *Tours* Australia to England 1961, 1964, to South Africa 1957/8, 1966/7, to West Indies 1964/5, 1977/8, to India and Pakistan 1964/5, to New Zealand 1956/7, 1959/60; Commonwealth to South Africa 1959/60, to India, Pakistan and New Zealand 1961/2; Cavaliers to South Africa 1960/1; Rest of World to England 1966. *Tests* Australia (1957/8 to 1977/8, 62 matches).
Career batting
257–436–62–21029–359–56.22–60–*ct* 383
Bowling 13287–349–38.07–6–0–5/33
Test batting
62–111–7–4869–311–46.81–10–*ct* 110
Bowling 3001–71–42.26–2–0–5/57

On the 1961 tour to England he hit 1,947 runs, av 51.23, and played in all five Tests, but without any noteworthy innings. He captained the 1964 tourists to England and headed both Test and first-class averages with 458 runs, av 76.33, and 1,714 runs, av 57.13, respectively. His great innings was 311 in the fourth Test at Old Trafford, when he and W. M. Lawry added 201 for the first wicket. This innings was his only score over 200 in England, though he made ten other double centuries and one triple century, namely 359 for NSW v Queensland at Brisbane in 1963/4. He hit 1,000 runs in Australia four times and once in South Africa. He captained Australia in 39 Tests in all. He came out of retirement in 1977/8 to lead Australia when most of the side had joined the rival WSC organisation set up by Kerry Packer.

Simpson, Reginald Thomas
Amateur. *b:* 27.2.1920, Sherwood Rise, Nottingham. Attractive opening right-hand batsman, off break bowler. *Sch* Nottingham High. *Teams* Nottinghamshire (1946–63, 366 matches); Sind (1944/5 to 1945/6); Europeans (1944/5 to 1945/6). *Tours* MCC to South Africa 1948/9, to Australia and New Zealand 1950/1, 1954/5; Commonwealth to India 1953/4; Howard to India 1956/7. *Tests* England (1948/9 to 1954/5, 27 matches).
Career batting
495–852–55–30546–259–38.32–64–*ct* 193
Bowling 2227–59–37.74–0–0–3/22
Test batting
27–45–3–1401–156*–33.35–4–*ct* 5
Bowling 22–2–11.00–0–0–2/4

He hit 1,000 runs in England thirteen times, going on to 2,000 five times (best 2,576, av 62.82, in 1950). Of his ten double centuries, nine were for Nottinghamshire, but the highest was 259 for MCC v NSW at Sydney in 1950/1, and perhaps his most noteworthy innings was on the same tour, when he hit 156* for England v Australia at Melbourne in the fifth Test. He captained Nottinghamshire from 1951 to 1960 and since his retirement has been a member of the Nottinghamshire Committee.

Simpson, Thomas
Professional. *b:* 13.8.1879, Keyworth, Notts. *d:* 19.12.1961, Oldham, Lancashire. Middle order left-hand batsman, left-arm medium pace bowler. *Team* Nottinghamshire (1903–05, 5 matches).
Career batting
5–8–1–38–14–5.42–0–*ct* 0
Bowling 85–2–42.50–0–0–1/28

He also played for Cheshire. A useful soccer player, he appeared for Notts County and Everton.

Simpson, Valentine
Amateur. *b:* 1849, Newington, Middlesex. *d:* 2.11.1915, Fareham, Hants. Middle order batsman. *Teams* Hampshire (1885, 1 match).
Career batting
1–2–0–10–7–5.00–0–0–*ct* 2

Simpson-Hayward, G. H. T.
(*see under* Simpson, G. H. T.)

Sims, Rev Herbert Marsh
Amateur. *b:* 15.3.1853, Mount Tavy, Tavistock, Devon. *d:* 5.10.1885, Thorpe, Whitby, Yorkshire. Middle order right-hand batsman, right-arm fast bowler. *Sch* St Peter's, York. *Teams* Cambridge U (1873–75, blue all three years); Yorkshire (1875–77, 5 matches).
Career batting
23–40–8–484–71–15.12–0–*ct* 18
Bowling 1224–63+2–19.42–3–0–6/76

Sims, James Morton
Amateur. *b:* 13.5.1903, Leyton, Essex. *d:* 27.4.1973, Canterbury, Kent. Attacking lower order right-hand batsman, leg break bowler. *Team* Middlesex (1929–52, 381 matches). *Tours* MCC to Australia and New Zealand 1935/6, 1936/7; Brinckman to South America 1937/8.

Tests England (1935 to 1936/7, 4 matches).
Career batting
462–635–116–8983–123–17.30–4–*ct* 254
Bowling 39401–1581–24.92–98–21–10/90
Test batting
4–4–0–16–12–4.00–0–*ct* 6
Bowling 480–11–43.63–1–0–5/73

He took 100 wickets in a season eight times (best 159, av 20.30, in 1939). His best bowling in an innings was 10 for 90 for East v West at Kingston-upon-Thames in 1948. His final first-class match was for MCC in 1953.

Sinclair, Barry Whitley
Amateur. *b:* 23.10.1936, Wellington, New Zealand. Determined middle order right-hand batsman, excellent cover field. *Team* Wellington (1955/6 to 1970/1). *Tours* New Zealand to England 1965, to India and Pakistan 1964/5, to Australia 1967/8. *Tests* New Zealand (1962/3 to 1967/8, 21 matches).
Career batting
118–204–18–6114–148–32.87–6–*ct* 45
Bowling 86–2–43.00–0–0–2/32
Test batting
21–40–1–1148–138–29.43–3–*ct* 8
Bowling 32–2–16.00–0–0–2/32

He was second in the first-class averages of the 1965 tour with 807 runs, av 36.68, and appeared in all three Tests. He captained New Zealand in three Tests.

Sinclair, Erroll Hamish Lindsay Graeme
Amateur. *b:* 10.9.1904, Bradfield, Berkshire. *d:* 24.2.1954, at sea aboard SS *Orion*. Attractive middle order left-hand batsman,leg break bowler. *Sch* Winchester. *Teams* Oxford U (1924, blue); Ceylon (1926/7).
Career batting
7–11–1–126–37–12.60–0–*ct* 2
Bowling 639–19–33.63–0–0–4/56

Sinclair, Edward Wortley
Amateur. *b:* 4.1.1889, Paddington, London. *d:* 22.12.1966, Orpington, Kent. Lower order right-hand batsman, right-arm medium pace bowler. *Sch* Clifton. *Team* Royal Navy (1913–19).
Career batting
3–6–1–23–19–4.60–0–*ct* 1
Bowling 310–9–34.44–0–0–4/162

Sinclair, James Hugh
Amateur. *b:* 16.10.1876, Swellendam, South Africa. *d:* 23.2.1913, Yeoville, South Africa. Hard hitting middle order right-hand batsman, right-arm medium pace bowler. *Teams* Transvaal (1892/3 to 1911/12); London County (1901–04). *Tours* South Africa to England 1901, 1904 and 1907, to Australia 1910/11. *Tests* South Africa (1895/6 to 1910/11, 25 matches).
Career batting
129–214–6–4483–136–21.55–6–*ct* 65
Bowling 10527–491–21.43–33–10–8/32
Test batting
25–47–1–1069–106–23.23–3–*ct* 9
Bowling 1996–63–31.68–1–0–6/26

He was the most successful bowler of the 1901 tour to England taking 61 wickets, av 19.85; in 1904 he took 92, av 23.19 (98, av 23.76 in total), but on his final visit he was not so prominent.

Sinfield, Reginald Albert
Professional. *b:* 24.12.1900, Stevenage, Hertfordshire. Middle order right-hand batsman, slow right-arm bowler. *Team* Gloucestershire (1924–39, 423 matches). *Test* England (1938, 1 match).
Career batting
430–696–86–15674–209*–25.70–16–*ct* 178
Bowling 28734–1173–24.49–66–9–9/111
Test batting
1–1–0–6–6–6.00–0–*ct* 0
Bowling 123–2–61.50–0–0–1/51

He hit 1,000 runs in a season ten times (best 1,740, av 35.51, in 1935). He took 100 wickets in a season four times (best 161, av 19.14, in 1936) and completed the 'double' in 1934 and 1937. His only double century was 209* for Gloucestershire v Glamorgan at Cardiff in 1935, and his best bowling in an innings was 9 for 111 for Gloucestershire v Middlesex at Lord's in 1936. His first-class debut was for MCC in 1921 and he also played for Hertfordshire.

Singh, Dr Kanwar Shumshere
Amateur. *b:* 21.6.1879, Bahraich, Oud, India. *d:* 12.5.1975, New Delhi, India. Sound middle order right-hand batsman, good field. *Sch* Rugby. *Teams* Kent (1901–02, 4 matches); Cambridge U (1901).
Career batting
5–9–0–174–45–19.33–0–*ct* 4

Singh, Maharaj Kumar Bhalindra
Amateur. *b:* 9.10.1919, India. Son of Maharaja of Patiala, brother of Yuvraj of Patiala (India). Middle order right-hand batsman, slow right-arm bowler. *Teams* Cambridge U (1939); Southern Punjab (1939/40 to 1946/7); Patiala (1953/4).
Career batting
13–21–3–392–109–21.77–1–*ct* 4
Bowling 675–25–27.00–0–0–4/34

Singh, Swaranjit
Amateur. *b:* 18.7.1932, Amritsar, India. Middle order left-hand batsman, right-arm medium pace bowler. *Teams* Cambridge U (1954–56, blue

1955–56); Warwickshire (1956–62, 27 matches); East Punjab (1950/1 to 1958/9); Madras (1958/9); Bengal (1959/60 to 1961/2). *Tours* Madras to Ceylon 1958/9; Swanton to West Indies 1955/6.
Career batting
88–154–17–3709–146–27.07–4–*ct* 33
Bowling 5470–183–29.89–7–1–6/20

Singleton, Alexander Parkinson
Amateur. *b:* 5.8.1914, Repton, Derbyshire. Brother of G. M. (Worcestershire). Middle order right-hand batsman, slow left-arm bowler. *Sch* Shrewsbury. *Teams* Oxford U (1934–37, blue all four years); Worcestershire (1934–46, 58 matches); Rhodesia (1946/7 to 1949/50).
Career batting
114–191–21–4700–164–27.64–4–*ct* 90
Bowling 7317–240–30.48–8–1–6/44
He hit 1,773 runs, av 34.09, in 1946.

Singleton, George Michael
Amateur. *b:* 12.5.1913, Repton, Derbyshire. Brother of A. P. (Worcestershire). Lower order right-hand batsman, slow left-arm bowler. *Sch* Uppingham. *Team* Worcestershire (1946, 2 matches).
Career batting
3–5–1–34–23–8.50–0–*ct* 1
Bowling 146–5–29.20–0–0–1/1

Sinker, Nigel Dalcour
Cricketer. *b:* 19.4.1946, Writtle, Chelmsford, Essex. Lower order left-hand batsman, slow left-arm bowler. *Sch* Winchester. *Team* Cambridge U (1966–67, blue 1966).
Career batting
13–23–4–188–31*–9.89–0–*ct* 2
Bowling 711–22–32.31–0–0–4/10

Sismey, Stanley George
Amateur. *b:* 15.7.1916, Junee, New South Wales, Australia. Lower order right-hand batsman, wicket-keeper. *Teams* New South Wales (1938/9 to 1950/1, 20 matches); Scotland (1952). *Tours* Australian Services to England 1945, to Ceylon and India 1945/6.
Career batting
35–52–11–725–78–17.68–0–*ct* 88–*st* 18

Siviter, Kenneth
Cricketer. *b:* 10.12.1953, Southport, Lancashire. Lower order right-hand batsman, right-arm fast medium bowler. *Sch* Liverpool College. *Team* Oxford U (1974–77, blue 1976).
Career batting
16–28–9–138–26–7.26–0–*ct* 3
Bowling 964–25–38.56–0–0–4/67

Skala, Steven Michael
Cricketer. *b:* 6.10.1955, Brisbane, Australia. Lower order right-hand batsman, wicket-keeper. *Team* Oxford U (1979).
Career batting
2–3–0–18–11–6.00–0–*ct* 6–*st* 1

Skeet, Challen Hasler Lufkin
Amateur. *b:* 17.8.1895, Oamaru, Otago, New Zealand. *d:* 20.4.1978, Andover, Hants. Middle order right-hand batsman, right-arm fast bowler. *Sch* St Paul's. *Teams* Oxford U (1919–20, blue 1920); Middlesex (1920–22, 19 matches).
Career batting
33–55–10–945–106–21.00–1–*ct* 19
Bowling 27–0

Skelding, Alexander
Professional. *b:* 5.9.1886, Leicester. *d:* 18.4.1960, Westcoates, Leicester. Lower order right-hand batsman, right-arm fast bowler. *Team* Leicestershire (1912–29, 177 matches).
Career batting
177–257–92–1117–33–6.76–0–*ct* 48
Bowling 14630–593–24.67–35–4–8/44
His best season was 1927, when he took 102 wickets, av 20.80. He was appointed to the first-class umpires' list in 1931 and did not retire until 1958 at the age of 72. Noted for his eccentricities, he used his own system of umpiring signals and had a particular aversion to dogs on the cricket field.

Skene, Robert Warboys
Amateur. *b:* 20.5.1908, Belmont, Surrey. Sound middle order left-hand batsman, slow left-arm bowler. *Sch* Sedbergh. *Team* Oxford U (1928–30, blue 1928).
Career batting
21–32–7–644–105–25.76–1–*ct* 14
Bowling 1230–26–47.30–0–0–3/53

Skey, Dr Arthur Richard Harrie
Amateur. *b:* 13.2.1873, Lucknow, India. *d:* 13.7.1942, Haslar, Hampshire. Lower order right-hand batsman, slow left-arm bowler. *Sch* Dulwich. *Team* Royal Navy (1912).
Career batting
1–2–1–4–4–4.00–0–*ct* 0
Bowling 117–6–19.50–1–0–5/27

Skinner, Alan Frank
Amateur. *b:* 22.4.1913, Brighton, Sussex. *d:* 28.2.1982, Bury St Edmunds, Suffolk. Brother of D. A. (Derbyshire). Opening or middle order right-hand batsman. *Sch* Leys School. *Teams* Derbyshire (1931–38, 83 matches); Cambridge U (1934); Northants (1949, 1 match).

Career batting
86–142–7–3537–102–26.20–1–*ct* 60
Bowling 250–6–41.66–0–0–2/12
He hit 1,019 runs, av 27.54, in 1934.

Skinner, Alfred George
Amateur. *b:* 11.8.1910, Calcutta, India. Middle order right-hand batsman, off break bowler. *Sch* Oundle. *Teams* Minor Counties (1933); Bengal (1935/6 to 1938/9); Europeans (1935/6 to 1936/7); Services (1943/4).
Career batting
13–22–3–490–125–25.78–1–*ct* 10
Bowling 475–9–52.77–0–0–3/44
His County cricket was for Buckinghamshire.

Skinner, David Anthony
Amateur. *b:* 22.3.1920, Duffield, Derbyshire. Brother of A. F. (Derbyshire). Middle order right-hand batsman, off break bowler. *Sch* Leys. *Team* Derbyshire (1947–49, 23 matches).
Career batting
23–36–1–475–63–13.57–0–*ct* 11
Bowling 182–2–91.00–0–0–1/41
He captained Derbyshire in 1949.

Skinner, Edward Alfred
Professional. *b:* 18.1.1847, Mitcham, Surrey. *d:* 10.2.1919, Brighton, Sussex. Lower order right-hand batsman, right-hand fast round-arm bowler, slip field. *Team* Surrey (1871–81, 3 matches).
Career batting
3–6–1–37–10–7.40–0–*ct* 1
Bowling 112–3–37.33–0–0–2/33

Skinner, Ivor John
Professional. *b:* 1.4.1928, Walthamstow, Essex. Lower order right-hand batsman, right-arm fast medium bowler. *Team* Essex (1950, 13 matches).
Career batting
13–21–7–28–7*–2.00–0–*ct* 5
Bowling 808–21–38.47–0–0–4/56
He also played for Cornwall.

Skinner, John
Professional. *b:* 16.7.1850, Steyning, Sussex. *d:* 17.2.1926, Steyning, Sussex. Lower order right-hand batsman, left-hand fast round-arm bowler. *Team* Sussex (1873–82, 10 matches).
Career batting
10–20–4–41–10–2.56–0–*ct* 6
Bowling 479–16–29.93–0–0–4/95

Skinner, Lonsdale Ernest
Cricketer. *b:* 7.9.1950, Plaisance, British Guiana. Middle order right-hand batsman, wicket-keeper. *Teams* Surrey (1971–77, 71 matches); Guyana (1973/4 to 1976/7).
Career batting
79–127–17–2503–93–22.75–0–*ct* 119–*st* 16

Slack, Hiram
Professional. *b:* 23.7.1843, Bradford, Yorkshire. *d:* 1918, Prestwich, Lancashire. Nephew of Hiram (Nottingham 1831). Lower order right-hand batsman, right-hand medium pace round-arm bowler. *Team* North of England (1866).
Career batting
1–2–1–7–4–7.00–0–*ct* 0
His County cricket was for Warwickshire.

Slack, John Kenneth Edward
Amateur. *b:* 23.12.1930, Wembley, Middlesex. Middle order right-hand batsman. *Sch* University College School, London. *Team* Cambridge U (1954, blue). *Tour* Surridge to Bermuda 1961 (not first-class).
Career batting
7–14–0–434–135–31.00–1–*ct* 4
He hit 135 for Cambridge v Middlesex at Fenner's on his first-class debut in 1954. He played County cricket for Buckinghamshire. A useful rugby footballer, he represented Middlesex.

Slack, Wilfred Norris
Cricketer. *b:* 12.12.1954, Troumaca, St Vincent, Windward Islands. Opening left-hand batsman, right-arm medium pace bowler. *Teams* Middlesex (1977–83, 93 matches); Windward Islands (1981/2 to 1982/3). *Tours* Middlesex to Zimbabwe 1980/1; International XI to Pakistan 1981/2.
Career batting
104–173–15–5582–248*–35.32–8–*ct* 72
Bowling 386–18–21.44–0–0–3/17
He hit 1,000 runs three times (best 1,499, av 44.08, in 1982).
He also played for Buckinghamshire.

Slade, Douglas Norman Frank
Professional. *b:* 24.8.1940, Feckenham, Worcs. Lower order right-hand batsman, slow left-arm bowler. *Team* Worcestershire (1958–71, 266 matches). *Tours* Commonwealth to Pakistan 1963/4, 1970/1; Worcestershire World Tour 1964/5, to Jamaica 1965/6.
Career batting
280–395–103–5275–125–18.06–1–*ct* 191
Bowling 11785–502–23.47–14–1–7/47
His best season was 1960, when he took 97 wickets, av 19.83. He also played for Shropshire.

Slade, William Douglas
Professional. *b:* 27.9.1941, Briton-Ferry, Glamorgan. Lower order right-hand batsman,

right-arm medium bowler, fine close field. *Team* Glamorgan (1961–67, 67 matches).
Career batting
67–116–11–1482–73*–14.11–0–*ct* 100
Bowling 1493–32–46.65–0–0–4/144

Sladen, Arthur Redman
Professional. *b:* 1877, Bradford, Yorkshire. *d:* 25.7.1934, Lake Side, Lancashire. Lower order batsman, slow left-arm bowler. *Teams* London County (1901–02); Lancashire (1903–04, 2 matches).
Career batting
5–7–3–10–5–2.50–0–*ct* 2
Bowling 450–19–23.68–2–0–5/50

Slater, Archibald Gilbert
Professional. *b:* 22.11.1890, Pilsley, Derbyshire. *d:* 22.7.1949, Manchester, Lancashire. Son of Henry (Derbyshire), brother of Herbert (Derbyshire). Lower order right-hand batsman, right-arm medium bowler. *Team* Derbyshire (1911–31, 210 matches).
Career batting
211–327–28–5943–105–19.87–1–*ct* 124
Bowling 10548–500–21.09–28–2–8/24

He took 108 wickets, av 16.25, in 1931. His final first-class match was for Sir L. Parkinson's XI in 1933.

Slater, Henry
Professional. *b:* 23.2.1855, Heanor, Derbyshire. *d:* 20.11.1916, Worksop, Notts. Father of A. G. (Derbyshire) and Herbert (Derbyshire). Lower order right-hand batsman, right-arm medium bowler. *Team* Derbyshire (1882–87, 5 matches).
Career batting
5–9–3–22–11–3.66–0–*ct* 2
Bowling 185–3–61.66–0–0–1/35

Slater, Herbert
Professional. *b:* 11.11.1881, Langley Mill, Derbyshire. *d:* 2.12.1958, Creswell, Derbyshire. Brother of A. G. (Derbyshire), son of Henry (Derbyshire). Right-hand batsman, right-arm fast medium bowler, off break bowler. *Team* Derbyshire (1907, 5 matches).
Career batting
5–9–2–39–21–5.57–0–*ct* 0
Bowling 38–2–19.00–0–0–2/15

Slater, Leonard
Amateur. *b:* 11.10.1875, Barnstaple, Devon. *d:* 14.9.1914, Aisne, France. Middle order batsman. *Sch* Marlborough. *Team* Gentlemen of the South (1909).
Career batting
1–2–0–15–15–7.50–0–*ct* 0

Slater, Philip Hugh
Amateur. *b:* 1.4.1876, Canterbury, Kent. *d:* 20.8.1958, Fleet, Hants. Middle order batsman. *Sch* King's, Canterbury. *Team* Surrey (1911, 1 match).
Career batting
1–1–0–1–1–1.00–0–*ct* 0

Slater, R.
Amateur. Lower order right-hand batsman, right-hand fast round-arm bowler. *Team* Lancashire (1865, 1 match).
Career batting
1–2–0–0–0–0.00–0–*ct* 0
Bowling 3–0

Slatter, Air Marshal Sir Leonard Horatio
Amateur. *b:* 8.12.1894, Durban, South Africa. *d:* 14.4.1961, Uxbridge, Middlesex. Lower order right-hand batsman, right-arm bowler. *Team* RAF (1928).
Career batting
1–1–1–1–1*–no av–0–*ct* 2
Bowling 33–0

In his obituary published in Wisden 1962, his surname is incorrectly given as 'Slater'.

Slaven, Francis Ferguson
Amateur. *b:* 3.3.1931, Bulawayo, Southern Rhodesia. Middle order right-hand batsman, good cover field. *Team* Oxford U (1955).
Career batting
2–2–0–13–13–6.50–0–*ct* 2

Slight, James
Amateur. *b:* 20.10.1855, Ashby, Geelong, Victoria, Australia. *d:* 9.12.1930, Elsternwick, Victoria, Australia. Brother of William (Victoria). Sound middle order right-hand batsman, good field. *Team* Victoria (1874/5 to 1887/8, 14 matches). *Tour* Australia to England 1880. *Test* Australia (1880, 1 match).
Career batting
19–34–1–415–53–12.57–0–*ct* 4
Bowling 37–3–12.33–0–0–2/4
Test batting
1–2–0–11–11–5.50–0–*ct* 0

Owing to illness, his opportunities on the 1880 tour were restricted, but he did appear in the Test.

Slinger, Edward
Cricketer. *b:* 2.2.1938, Haslingden, Lancashire. Opening batsman. *Team* MCC (1967).
Career batting
1–1–1–12–12*–no av–0–*ct* 1

Slinn, William
Professional. *b:* 13.12.1826, Sheffield, Yorkshire.

d: 19.6.1888, Wortley, Sheffield, Yorkshire. Tail end right-hand batsman, right-hand fast round-arm bowler. *Team* Yorkshire (1860–64, 11 matches).
Career batting
19–31–8–46–11–2.00–0–*ct* 11
Bowling 1466–112–13.08–9–4–8/33

A brilliant bowler, his poor showing both as a batsman and fielder very much reduced his appearances in first-class cricket. His greatest bowling feat was to take all ten wickets in an innings when bowling for XXII of Scarborough against the All England Eleven in 1862.

Slocock, Ernest Frederick
Amateur. *b:* 7.3.1865, Winterbourne, Berkshire. *d:* 11.1.1940, Bolsterstone, Yorkshire. Lower order right-hand batsman, wicket-keeper. *Sch* Lancing. *Team* Cambridge U (1886).
Career batting
1–2–0–4–4–2.00–0–*ct* 2

Slocombe, Philip Anthony
Cricketer. *b:* 6.9.1954, Weston-super-Mare, Somerset. Middle order right-hand batsman, right-arm medium pace bowler. *Sch* Millfield. *Team* Somerset (1975–83, 135 matches). *Tour* Robins to South Africa 1975/6.
Career batting
139–233–29–5640–132–27.64–7–*ct* 65
Bowling 54–3–18.00–0–0–1/2

He hit 1,000 runs in a season twice (best 1,221, av 38.15, in 1978).

Sloman, William Henry
Professional. *b:* 1871, Launceston, Cornwall. *d:* 10.8.1926, South Molton, Devon. Middle order batsman, useful bowler. *Team* Somerset (1895–96, 4 matches).
Career batting
4–8–0–97–48–12.12–0–*ct* 2
Bowling 7–1–7.00–0–0–1/7

Sly, Gerald Brian
Professional. *b:* 21.10.1932, Ealing, Middlesex. Lower order batsman, useful fast medium bowler. *Team* Sussex (1953, 1 match).
Career batting
1 match, did not bat–*ct* 1
Bowling 29–1–29.00–0–0–1/24

Smail, Alastair Harold Kurt
Cricketer. *b:* 3.7.1964, Kingston-upon-Thames, Surrey. Lower order right-hand batsman, left-arm medium pace bowler. *Team* Oxford U (1983).
Career batting
6–6–1–24–13*–4.80–0–*ct* 1
Bowling 222–5–44.40–0–0–3/49

Smailes, Thomas Francis
Professional. *b:* 27.3.1910, Ripley, Yorkshire. *d:* 1.12.1970, Harrogate, Yorkshire. Lower order left-hand batsman, right-arm medium pace bowler. *Sch* Pocklington. *Team* Yorkshire (1932–48, 262 matches). *Tour* Yorkshire to Jamaica 1935/6. *Test* England (1946, 1 match).
Career batting
269–349–43–5892–117–19.25–3–*ct* 154
Bowling 17114–822–20.81–41–6–10/47
Test batting
1–1–0–25–25–25.00–0–*ct* 0
Bowling 62–3–20.66–0–0–3/44

He took 100 wickets in a season four times (best 130, av 17.54, in 1936). His best innings analysis was 10 for 47 for Yorkshire v Derbyshire at Bramall Lane in 1939. He hit 1,002 runs, av 25.05, in 1938.

Smales, Kenneth
Professional. *b:* 15.9.1927, Horsforth, Yorkshire. Lower order right-hand batsman, off break bowler. *Teams* Nottinghamshire (1951–58, 148 matches); Yorkshire (1948–50, 13 matches).
Career batting
161–229–55–2512–64–14.43–0–*ct* 60
Bowling 11946–389–30.70–20–5–10/66

His best bowling in an innings was 10 for 66 for Nottinghamshire v Yorkshire at Stroud in 1956 and his best season was 1955 with 117 wickets, av 24.12. After retiring from first-class cricket he became Secretary to Nottingham Forest FC.

Small, Gladstone Cleophas
Cricketer. *b:* 18.10.1961, St George, Barbados. Lower order right-hand batsman, right-arm fast medium bowler. *Team* Warwickshire (1980–83, 65 matches). *Tours* Robins to New Zealand 1979/80; International XI to Pakistan 1981/2.
Career batting
68–82–18–687–57*–10.73–0–*ct* 19
Bowling 4939–143–34.53–2–0–7/68

Small, John (sen)
Professional. *b:* 19.4.1737, Empshott, Hants. *d:* 31.12.1826, Petersfield, Hants. Father of John, jun (Hampshire) and Eli (Hampshire). Middle order right hand batsman, good field. *Team* Hampshire (1773–98).

He is said to have commenced playing in great matches in 1755, though no details of these early games have yet been discovered, and since his final important match was in 1798, his career was very long. An original member of the Hambledon Club, he was one of the leading batsmen of his day.

Small, Joseph A.
Amateur. *b:* 3.11.1892, Princes Town, Trinidad. *d:* 26.4.1958, Trinidad. Attractive middle order right-hand batsman, right-arm medium fast bowler, brilliant slip field. *Team* Trinidad (1909/10 to 1931/2). *Tours* West Indies to England 1923, 1928. *Tests* West Indies (1928 to 1929/30, 3 matches).
Career batting
77–128–11–3063–133–26.17–4–*ct* 72
Bowling 4589–165–27.81–7–0–7/49
Test batting
3–6–0–79–52–13.16–0–*ct* 3
Bowling 184–3–61.33–0–0–2/67
On the 1923 tour he hit 776 runs, av 31.04, but in 1928 his batting was not so successful, though his bowling greatly improved with 50 wickets, av 28.88.

Smalley, J.
Professional. Middle order batsman. *Team* Lancashire (1869, 2 matches).
Career batting
2–4–0–24–17–6.00–0–*ct* 0

Smart, Cyril Cecil
Professional. *b:* 23.7.1898, Lacock, Wiltshire. *d:* 21.5.1975, Abertillery, Glamorgan. Brother of J. A. (Warwickshire). Attacking middle order right-hand batsman, leg break bowler, good field. *Teams* Warwickshire (1920–22, 45 matches); Glamorgan (1927–46, 190 matches).
Career batting
236–383–46–8992–151*–26.68–9–*ct* 163
Bowling 7505–180–41.69–1–0–5/39
He hit 1,000 runs in a season five times (best 1,560, av 36.27, in 1935). He hit 32 runs off one over from G. Hill of Hampshire at Cardiff in 1935.

Smart, John Abbott
Professional. *b:* 12.4.1891, Forest Hill, Marlborough, Wiltshire. *d:* 3.10.1979, Bulkington, Nuneaton. Brother of C. C. (Warwickshire and Glamorgan). Lower order right-hand batsman, wicket-keeper, right-arm off break bowler. *Team* Warwickshire (1919–36, 238 matches).
Career batting
238–340–43–3425–68*–11.53–0–*ct* 317–*st* 107
Bowling 1262–22–57.36–0–0–2/13
From 1937 to 1948 he was on the first-class umpires' list.

Smedley, Michael John
Cricketer. *b:* 28.10.1941, Maltby, Yorkshire. Stylish middle order right-hand batsman. *Team* Nottinghamshire (1964–79, 357 matches).
Career batting
360–604–76–16482–149–31.21–28–*ct* 261
Bowling 4–0
He hit 1,000 runs in a season nine times (best 1,718, av 38.17, in 1971). From 1975 to June 1979 he captained Nottinghamshire.

Smethers, Michael Charles
Cricketer. *b:* 18.8.1947, London. Lower order right-hand batsman, wicket-keeper. *Sch* Highgate. *Team* Cambridge U (1967).
Career batting
2–3–0–19–14–6.33–0–*ct* 1–*st* 1

Smith, A.
Professional. Lower order batsman, opening bowler. *Team* Liverpool and District XI (1894).
Career batting
2–4–0–38–21–9.50–0–*ct* 1
Bowling 170–7–24.28–0–0–4/57

Smith, A.
Professional. *b:* 1892, Beckenham, Kent. Lower order batsman, left-arm medium pace bowler. *Team* G. J. V. Weigall's XI (1914).
Career batting
1–2–0–9–8–4.50–0–*ct* 0
Bowling 102–3–34.00–0–0–3/102

Smith, Alfort
Professional. *b:* 7.7.1846, Bank Lane, Bury, Lancashire. *d:* 21.12.1908, Glossop, Derbyshire. Lower order right-hand batsman, wicket-keeper. *Teams* Derbyshire (1873–80, 49 matches); Lancashire (1867–71, 4 matches).
Career batting
55–98–34–305–30–4.76–0–*ct* 70–*st* 12
Bowling 7–0

Smith, Alfred
Amateur. *b:* 6.11.1909, Kilmarnock, Ayrshire, Scotland. *d:* 28.2.1977, Fleet, Hants. Right-hand batsman, off break bowler. *Team* Scotland (1934–37).
Career batting
3–6–1–96–36*–19.20–0–*ct* 2
Bowling 114–3–38.00–0–0–1/3

Smith, Arthur
Amateur. *b:* 26.5.1851, Hurstpierpoint, Sussex. *d:* 8.3.1923, Amberley, Sussex. Brother of C. H. (Sussex). Lower order right-hand batsman, left-hand medium slow round-arm bowler. *Sch* Brighton. *Team* Sussex (1874–80, 19 matches).

Career batting
19–30–8–94–13–4.27–0–*ct* 7
Bowling 1084–61–17.77–3–1–7/47

Smith, Arthur
Professional. *b:* 1872, Barlestone, Leicestershire. *d:* 3.10.1952, Melton Mowbray, Leicestershire. Tail end right-hand batsman, right-arm fast bowler. *Team* Leicestershire (1897–1901, 4 matches).
Career batting
4–7–1–16–9–2.66–0–*ct* 0
Bowling 135–5–27.00–0–0–3/40

Smith, Alan Christopher
Amateur. *b:* 25.10.1936, Hall Green, Birmingham. Middle order right-hand batsman, occasional right-arm fast medium bowler, wicket-keeper. *Teams* Warwickshire (1958–74, 358 matches); Oxford U (1958–60, blue all three years). *Tours* MCC to North America 1959, (not first-class), to Australia and New Zealand 1962/3, to New Zealand 1974/5 (assistant manager, but played in emergency); Swanton to West Indies 1960/1. *Tests* England (1962/3, 6 matches).
Career batting
428–612–85–11027–145–20.92–5–*ct* 715–*st* 61
Bowling 3074–131–23.46–2–0–5/32
Test batting
6–7–3–118–69–29.50–0–*ct* 20
He hit 1,201 runs, av 31.60, in 1962, as well as dismissing 82 batsmen as wicket-keeper. For Warwickshire v Essex at Clacton in 1965, he was in the team as wicket-keeper, but was put on to bowl and performed the hat-trick. He captained Warwickshire 1968 to 1974 and is the present Secretary of the County Club. He was also on the Test Match Selection Committee.

Smith, Alfred Farrer
Amateur. *b:* 7.3.1847, Dewsbury, Yorkshire. *d:* 6.1.1915, Ossett, Yorkshire. Very steady opening right-hand batsman. *Team* Yorkshire (1868–74, 28 matches).
Career batting
29–51–4–796–99–16.93–0–*ct* 10

Smith, Arthur Frederick
Amateur. *b:* 13.5.1853, Regent's Park, London. *d:* 18.1.1936, South Africa. Middle order right-hand batsman, right-hand fast round-arm bowler. *Sch* Wellington and Harrow. *Teams* Cambridge U (1875, blue); Middlesex (1874–77, 6 matches).
Career batting
14–23–3–193–48*–9.65–0–*ct* 15
Bowling 30–0
His first-class debut was for An England XI in 1873 and his final first-class appearance for Gentlemen in 1878.

Smith, Anthony John Shaw
Cricketer. *b:* 8.12.1951, Johannesburg, South Africa. Middle order right-hand batsman, wicket-keeper. *Teams* Natal (1972/3 to 1982/3); D. H. Robins' XI (1974).
Career batting
98–161–23–3726–150*–27.00–2–*ct* 302–*st* 9
Bowling 28–1–28.00–0–0–1/4
His first-class debut was for South African Universities in 1971/2.

Smith, Sir Archibald Levin
Amateur. *b:* 27.8.1836, Salt Hill, Chichester, Sussex. *d:* 20.10.1901, Wester Elchies House, Aberlour, Morayshire, Scotland. Steady opening right-hand batsman, right-hand fast under-arm bowler. *Sch* Eton. *Team* MCC (1861–64).
Career batting
2–4–0–16–7–4.00–0–*ct* 0
Bowling 1 wicket, no analyses
He was not in the Eleven whilst at Cambridge, but rowed against Oxford, and in 1859 was a member of the Cambridge boat which sank. Unable to swim he was fortunate to be rescued with the aid of a lifebuoy. He was appointed a Lord Justice of Appeal in 1892 and Master of the Rolls in 1900.

Smith, Anthony Mervyn
Cricketer. *b:* 26.2.1930, Bristol. Middle order batsman, useful bowler. *Team* Minor Counties (1965).
Career batting
1–2–0–20–12–10.00–0–*ct* 0
His County cricket was for Wiltshire.

Smith, Arthur Price
Professional. *b:* 3.12.1857, Ruddington, Notts. *d:* 3.6.1937, Tottenham, London. Steady middle order right-hand batsman, right-arm medium pace bowler. *Teams* Nottinghamshire (1883, 2 matches); Lancashire (1886–94, 48 matches).
Career batting
50–79–5–1475–124–19.93–2–*ct* 31
Bowling 517–29–17.82–1–0–5/49

Smith, Alexander Victor
Cricketer. *b:* 11.5.1945, Dublin. Left-hand batsman. *Team* Ireland (1978–79).
Career batting
2–1–1–11–11*–no av–0–*ct* 1

Smith, Benjamin Charles
Professional. *b:* 10.7.1859, Daventry, Northants. *d:* 29.11.1942, Northampton. Lower order right-

hand batsman, wicket-keeper. *Team* Northamptonshire (1905–06, 31 matches).
Career batting
31–55–25–393–38*–13.10–0–*ct* 43–*st* 4
Bowling 2–0

Smith, Bertrand Nigel Bosworth
(known as Bosworth-Smith)
Amateur. *b:* 20.6.1873, Harrow, Middlesex. *d:* 19.2.1947, Hove, Sussex. Right-hand batsman, slow left-arm bowler. *Sch* Harrow. *Teams* Oxford U (1895–96); Middlesex (1895, 1 match); Europeans (1900/1); Gentlemen of India (1902/3).
Career batting
11–19–0–323–45–17.00–0–*ct* 6
Bowling 24–0
His final first-class match in England was for MCC in 1901. He also represented Dorset.

Smith, Charles
Professional. *b:* 24.8.1961, Calverley, Yorkshire. *d:* 2.5.1925, Calverley, Yorkshire. Lower order right-hand batsman, wicket-keeper. *Team* Lancashire (1893–1902, 167 matches).
Career batting
168–236–50–2251–81–12.10–0–*ct* 316–*st* 120
Bowling 18–1–18.00–0–0–1/18
He appeared for Yorkshire in a non-first-class match in 1885.

Smith, Sir Charles Aubrey
Amateur. *b:* 21.7.1863, City of London. *d:* 20.12.1948, Beverley Hills, California. Lower order right-hand batsman, right-arm fast bowler. *Sch* Charterhouse. *Team* Cambridge U (1882–85, blue all four years); Sussex (1882–96, 99 matches); Transvaal (1889/90). *Tours* Lillywhite, Shaw and Shrewsbury to Australia 1887/8; Warton to South Africa 1888/9. *Test* England (1888/9, 1 match).
Career batting
143–247–28–2986–85–13.63–0–*ct* 97
Bowling 7728–345–22.40–19–1–7/16
Test batting
1–1–0–3–3–3.00–0–*ct* 0
Bowling 61–7–8.71–1–0–5/19
He captained Sussex in 1887 and 1888 and also led the 1887/8 team to Australia. After the 1888/9 tour to South Africa he remained in that country setting up a business there, but much later he gained fame as an actor and, based in Hollywood, appeared in numerous films in the 1930s and 1940s.

Smith, Charles (Hamlin)
Amateur. *b:* 31.8.1838, Albourne, Sussex. *d:* 12.3.1909, Henfield, Sussex. Brother of Arthur (Sussex), father of C. L. A. (Sussex). Middle order right-hand batsman, good close field. *Team* Sussex (1861–74, 62 matches).
Career batting
63–111–7–1705–95–16.39–0–*ct* 45
Bowling 206–4–51.50–0–0–2/61
He captained Sussex from 1864 to 1874, jointly in the first and last of those seasons.

Smith, Cedric Ivan James
Professional. *b:* 25.8.1906, Corsham, Wilts. *d:* 9.2.1979, Mellor, Lancashire. Brother of W. A. (Minor Counties). Lower order right-hand batsman, right-arm fast bowler. *Team* Middlesex (1934–39, 152 matches). *Tour* MCC to West Indies 1934/35. *Tests* England (1934/5 to 1937, 5 matches).
Career batting
208–304–31–4007–101–14.67–1–*ct* 99
Bowling 16271–845–19.25–47–8–8/102
Test batting
5–10–0–102–27–10.20–0–*ct* 1
Bowling 393–15–26.20–1–0–5/16
His first-class debut was for the Minor Counties in 1930. He took 100 wickets in a season four times (best 172, av 18.88, in 1934). He was a noted big hitter and scored many sixes in first-class matches. He also played for Wiltshire.

Smith, Charles John
Amateur. *b:* 19.1.1849, London. *d:* 8.5.1930, Hendon, Middlesex. Stylish middle order right-hand batsman, right-hand fast round-arm bowler. *Sch* Harrow. *Team* Middlesex (1868–76, 3 matches).
Career batting
10–19–2–172–43–10.11–0–*ct* 3
Bowling 147–8–18.37–0–0–4/34
His first-class debut was for MCC in 1867. His final first-class match was for MCC in 1878. He was a talented athlete, specialising in the half mile and mile.

Smith, Clifford John
Professional. *b:* 1902, Stepney, London. *d:* 4.6.1959, Cambridge. Lower order left-hand batsman, left-arm medium pace bowler. *Team* Minor Counties (1937).
Career batting
1–2–0–29–21–14.50–0–*ct* 2
Bowling 39–2–19.50–0–0–1/18
His County cricket was for Cambridgeshire.

Smith, Christopher Lyall
Cricketer. *b:* 15.10.1958, Durban, South Africa. Brother of R. A. (Hampshire). Opening right-hand batsman, off break bowler. *Teams* Natal (1977/8 to 1982/3); Glamorgan (1979, 1 match);

Hampshire (1980–83, 50 matches). *Tests* England (1983, 2 matches).
Career batting
81–142–16–5124–193–40.66–13–*ct* 50
Bowling 952–21–45.33–0–0–3/35
Test batting
2–4–0–78–43–19.50–0–*ct* 2
Bowling 31–2–15.50–0–0–2/31

He hit 1,000 runs in a season twice (best 1,923, av 53.42, in 1983). In May 1983 he qualified as an English player.

Smith, Charles Lawrence Arthur
Amateur. *b:* 1.1.1879, Brighton, Sussex. *d:* 22.11.1949, Wineham, Henfield, Sussex. Son of C. H. (Sussex). Middle order right-hand batsman, right-arm medium fast bowler. *Sch* Brighton. *Team* Sussex (1898–1911, 218 matches).
Career batting
220–336–37–5844–103*–19.54–2–*ct* 149
Bowling 585–9–65.00–0–0–1/0

He hit 1,032 runs, av 24.57, in 1906. He captained Sussex in 1909, and during part of 1906 when C. B. Fry was injured.

Smith, Colin Milner
Amateur. *b:* 2.11.1936, Mottingham, Kent. Lower order right-hand batsman, wicket-keeper. *Sch* Tonbridge. *Team* Oxford U (1958).
Career batting
1–2–0–16–12–8.00–0–*ct* 1–*st* 1

Smith, Charles Neville Strode
Amateur. *b:* 26.12.1898, Axbridge, Somerset. *d:* 9.9.1955, Instow, Devon. Middle order batsman. *Team* Royal Navy (1929).
Career batting
1–2–0–54–47–27.00–0–*ct* 0

Smith, Colin Stansfield
Amateur. *b:* 1.10.1932, Didsbury, Manchester. Lower order right-hand batsman, right-arm fast medium bowler. *Sch* William Hulme's GS. *Teams* Lancashire (1951–57, 45 matches); Cambridge U (1954-57, blue all four years).
Career batting
106–153–28–2339–103*–18.71–1–*ct* 47
Bowling 7183–293–24.51–9–1–6/35

His final first-class match was for D. R. Jardine's XI in 1958.

Smith, Cameron Wilberforce
Amateur. *b:* 29.7.1933, Christchurch, Barbados. Opening right-hand batsman, wicket-keeper. *Team* Barbados (1951/2 to 1964/5). *Tours* West Indies to Australia 1960/1; West Indian XI in England 1964; Commonwealth in India 1964. *Tests* West Indies (1960/1 to 1961/2, 5 matches).
Career batting
37–64–3–2277–140–37.32–5–*ct* 32–*st* 3
Bowling 97–3–32.33–0–0–2/24
Test batting
5–10–1–222–55–24.66–0–*ct* 4–*st* 1

Smith, D.
Amateur. Lower order batsman, useful bowler. *Team* Combined Services (1947).
Career batting
1–2–0–23–22–11.50–0–*ct* 0
Bowling 50–0

Smith, Denis
Professional. *b:* 24.1.1907, Somercotes, Derbyshire. *d:* 12.9.1979, Derby. Sound opening left-hand batsman, right-arm medium bowler. *Team* Derbyshire (1927–52, 420 matches). *Tour* MCC to Australia and New Zealand 1935/6. *Tests* England (1935, 2 matches).
Career batting
443–753–63–21843–225–31.65–32–*ct* 379–*st* 5
Bowling 734–20–36.70–1–0–5/37
Test batting
2–4–0–128–57–32.00–0–*ct* 1

He hit 1,000 runs in a season twelve times, going on to 2,000 once : 2,175, av 39.54, in 1935. Both his double centuries were for Derbyshire, the highest being 225 v Hampshire at Chesterfield in 1935. From 1951 to 1971 he was coach to Derbyshire CCC.

Smith, David Bertram Miller
Amateur. *b:* 14.9.1884, Richmond, Victoria, Australia. *d:* 29.7.1963, Hawthorn, Victoria, Australia. Middle order right-hand batsman. *Team* Victoria (1908/9 to 1911/12, 19 matches). *Tours* Australia to New Zealand 1909/10, to England and North America 1912. *Tests* Australia (1912, 2 matches).
Career batting
46–77–3–1764–146–23.83–3–*ct* 16
Bowling 22–1–22.00–0–0–1/22
Test batting
2–3–1–30–24*–15.00–0–*ct* 0

Although he played in two Tests, he achieved little on the 1912 tour to England.

Smith, David Henry Kilner
Cricketer. 29.6.1940, Shipley, Yorkshire. Opening left-hand batsman, occasional wicket-keeper. *Team* Derbyshire (1965–70, 112 matches); Orange Free State (1976/7 to 1977/8).
Career batting
114–202–14–4995–136–26.56–4–*ct* 84
Bowling 23–1–23.00–0–0–1/1

He hit 1,000 runs in a season three times (best 1,397, av 28.51, in 1968).

Smith, David James
Cricketer. *b:* 28.4.1962, Brighton, Sussex. Lower order left-hand batsman, wicket-keeper. *Team* Sussex (1981–83, 11 matches).
Career batting
11–12–2–26–13–2.60–0–*ct* 15

Smith, Donald J.
Professional. *b:* 1.5.1929, Accrington, Lancashire. Lower order right-hand batsman, left-arm fast medium bowler. *Team* Lancashire (1951–52, 3 matches).
Career batting
3–4–0–26–14–6.50–0–*ct* 2
Bowling 205–4–52.25–0–0–1/19

Smith, Donald Joseph
Amateur. *b:* 19.10.1933, Stockport, Cheshire. Tail end left-hand batsman, right-arm fast medium bowler. *Sch* Stockport GS. *Team* Cambridge U (1955–57, blue 1955–56).
Career batting
28–37–21–128–18*–8.00–0–*ct* 6
Bowling 2297–73–31.49–2–0–7/55
His County cricket was for Cheshire.

Smith, Douglas James
Professional. *b:* 29.5.1873, Batley, Yorkshire. *d:* 16.8.1949, Grahamstown, South Africa. Brother of William (Somerset), son of John (Yorkshire and Lancashire). Middle order right-hand batsman, right-arm slow bowler. *Teams* Somerset (1896–98, 21 matches); Worcestershire (1901–04, 9 matches).
Career batting
30–52–4–558–62–11.62–0–*ct* 24–*st* 1
Bowling 24–0
He also played for Glamorgan (pre-first-class).

Smith, David Lind Addison
Amateur. *b:* 9.1.1873, Edinburgh, Scotland. *d:* 2.11.1937, Leith, Midlothian, Scotland. Lower order batsman, slow left-arm bowler. *Team* Scotland (1905).
Career batting
1–2–0–59–45–29.50–0–*ct* 2
Bowling 108–1–108.00–0–0–1/91

Smith, David Mark
Cricketer. *b:* 9.1.1956, Balham, London. Middle order left-hand batsman, right-arm medium pace bowler. *Team* Surrey (1973–83, 141 matches).
Career batting
141–215–48–5220–160–31.25–8–*ct* 96
Bowling 1463–27–54.18–0–0–3/40
He hit 1,065 runs, av 50.71, in 1982.

Smith, David Martin
Cricketer. *b:* 21.1.1962, Kersley, Coventry, Warwickshire. Lower order left-hand batsman, slow left-arm bowler. *Team* Warwickshire (1981–83, 4 matches).
Career batting
4–5–2–148–100*–49.33–1–*ct* 2
Bowling 201–2–100.50–0–0–1/44

Smith, Douglas Maxwell
Professional. *b:* 14.9.1915, Cuckfield, Sussex. Lower order right-hand batsman, right-arm fast bowler. *Team* Sussex (1938–46, 6 matches).
Career batting
6–10–2–55–34–6.87–0–*ct* 5
Bowling 401–19–21.11–1–0–5/25

Smith, David Robert
Professional. *b:* 5.10.1934, Bristol, Gloucestershire. Lower order right-hand batsman, right-arm medium pace bowler. *Team* Gloucestershire (1956–70, 357 matches). *Tours* MCC to New Zealand 1960/1, to India and Pakistan 1961/2; Gloucestershire to Bermuda 1962 (not first-class). *Tests* England (1961/2, 5 matches).
Career batting
386–520–116–4970–74–12.30–0–*ct* 292
Bowling 29654–1250–23.72–51–6–7/20
Test batting
5–5–1–38–34–9.50–0–*ct* 2
Bowling 359–6–59.83–0–0–2/60
He took 100 wickets in a season five times (best 143, av 20.30, in 1960). A good soccer player, he was outside right for Bristol City and Millwall.

Smith, Donald Victor
Professional. *b:* 14.6.1923, Broadwater, Sussex. Sound opening left-hand batsman, left-arm medium pace bowler. *Team* Sussex (1946–62, 360 matches). *Tour* Norfolk to Jamaica 1956/7. *Tests* England (1957, 3 matches).
Career batting
377–625–66–16960–206*–30.33–19–*ct* 234
Bowling 9670–340–28.44–6–1–7/40
Test batting
3–4–1–25–16*–8.33–0–*ct* 0
Bowling 97–1–97.00–0–0–1/12
He hit 1,000 runs in a season eight times, going on to 2,000 once: 2,088, av 42.61, in 1957. His only double century was 206* for Sussex v Nottinghamshire at Trent Bridge in 1950.

Smith, Edwin
Professional. *b:* 2.1.1934, Grassmoor, Chesterfield, Derbyshire. Lower order right-hand batsman, off break bowler. *Team* Derbyshire (1951–71, 497 matches).

Career batting
503–674–144–6998–90–13.01–0–*ct* 207
Bowling 31448–1217–25.84–51–4–9/46

His best season was 1955 when he took 105 wickets, av 17.65, and his best bowling in an innings 9 for 46 for Derbyshire v Scotland in the same year.

Smith, Edwin
Professional. *b:* 11.6.1860, Peatling Magna, Leics. *d:* 1939, Lutterworth, Leics. Lower order right-hand batsman, right-arm fast medium bowler. *Team* Liverpool & District XI (1893–94).
Career batting
4–8–1–86–32–12.28–0–*ct* 2
Bowling 162–5–32.40–0–0–4/83

He played for Leicestershire (pre-first-class) and Cheshire.

Smith, Ernest
Professional. *b:* 11.7.1888, Barnsley, Yorkshire. *d:* 2.1.1972, Blackburn, Lancashire. Lower order right-hand batsman, left-arm medium slow bowler. *Team* Yorkshire (1914–26, 16 matches).
Career batting
16–21–5–169–49–10.53–0–*ct* 5
Bowling 1090–46–23.69–2–0–6/40

He is generally referred to as E. Smith of Ossett, being associated with that Yorkshire team for many years.

Smith, Ernest
Amateur. *b:* 19.10.1869, Morley, Leeds, Yorkshire. *d:* 9.4.1945, Eastbourne, Sussex. Attacking middle order right-hand batsman, right-arm fast bowler. *Sch* Clifton. *Teams* Oxford U (1889-91, blue 1890 and 1891); Yorkshire (1888–1907, 154 matches).
Career batting
242–391–33–7686–164*–21.48–6–*ct* 173
Bowling 11666–454–25.69–22–3–7/40

A schoolmaster, his County cricket was confined mainly to August and he usually captained Yorkshire when Lord Hawke was absent. His final first-class match was for Leveson-Gower's XI in 1928. He was a useful golfer and rugby footballer.

Smith, Edwin George
Amateur. *b:* 29.8.1848, Cheltenham, Gloucestershire. *d:* 5.4.1880, Cheltenham, Gloucestershire. Middle order right-hand batsman, right-arm medium pace bowler. *Team* Gloucestershire (1875–76, 2 matches).
Career batting
2–3–0–26–14–8.66–0–*ct* 0

Smith, Ernest James
Professional. *b:* 6.2.1886, Birmingham, Warwickshire. *d:* 31.8.1979, Birmingham, Warwickshire. Sound opening right-hand batsman, wicket-keeper. *Team* Warwickshire (1904–30, 444 matches). *Tours* MCC to Australia 1911/12, to South Africa 1913/14, to West Indies 1925/6. *Tests* England (1911/2 to 1913/14, 11 matches).
Career batting
496–814–55–16997–177–22.39–20–*ct* 722–*st* 156
Bowling 102–2–51.00–0–0–1/0
Test batting
11–14–1–113–22–8.69–0–*ct* 17–*st* 3

He hit 1,000 runs in a season six times (best 1,477, av 31.42, in 1925). He was on the first-class umpires' list after retiring in 1930 and stood in Test matches. In 1946 he was appointed coach to Warwickshire, and remained at Edgbaston until 1970.

Smith, Rev Edward Paske
Amateur. *b:* 9.9.1854, Mussoorie, India. *d:* 2.1.1909, Seaford, Sussex. Lower order right-hand batsman, right-arm medium pace bowler. *Sch* Sherborne. *Team* Oxford U (1876).
Career batting
1–2–0–6–6–3.00–0–*ct* 0
Bowling 42–3–14.00–0–0–2/24

He was a missionary in Calgary and Saskatchewan.

Smith, Fred
Professional. *b:* 18.12.1879, Yeadon, Yorkshire. *d:* 20.10.1905, Nelson, Lancashire. He died of pneumonia caught whilst playing rugby football. Middle order left-hand batsman. *Team* Yorkshire (1903, 13 matches).
Career batting
13–19–1–292–55–16.22–0–*ct* 3

Smith, Fred
Professional. *b:* 26.12.1885, Idle, Yorkshire. Middle order batsman. *Team* Yorkshire (1911, 1 match).
Career batting
1–1–0–11–11–11.00–0–*ct* 0
Bowling 45–2–22.50–0–0–1/12

Smith, Frederick Aitken (Leeston)
(also known as Leeston-Smith)
Amateur. *b:* 10.5.1854, London. *d:* 17.1.1894, Poole, Dorset. Middle order right-hand batsman, right-arm fast bowler. *Sch* Malvern and Christ College, Brecon. *Team* Somerset (1884–85, 3 matches).
Career batting
3–6–0–130–37–21.66–0–*ct* 0

Smith, Frank Brunton
Amateur. *b:* 13.3.1922, Rangiora, New Zealand. Middle order right-hand batsman, good field. *Team* Canterbury (1946/7 to 1952/3). *Tour* New Zealand to England 1949. *Tests* New Zealand (1946/7 to 1951/2, 4 matches).
Career batting
48–83–5–2588–153–33.17–4–*ct* 21
Bowling 48–1–48.00–0–0–1/6
Test batting
4–6–1–237–96–47.40–0–*ct* 1

He hit 1,008 runs, av 28.00, on the 1949 tour, playing in two Tests. His great success was in the first Test when he scored 96 and 54*. His first-class debut was for South Island Army XI in New Zealand in 1942/3.

Smith, Frank Ernest
Professional. *b:* 13.5.1872, Bury St Edmunds, Suffolk. *d:* 3.12.1943, Sedbergh, Yorkshire. Lower order left-hand batsman, slow left-arm bowler. *Teams* Surrey (1893–1908, 56 matches); London County (1901–02); Transvaal (1906/7).
Career batting
68–87–28–578–45–9.79–0–*ct* 31
Bowling 3951–194–20.37–9–3–6/12

He took 95 wickets, av 13.94, in 1894.

He also played for Suffolk.

Smith, Geoffrey
Amateur. *b:* 30.11.1925, Huddersfield, Yorkshire. Lower order right-hand batsman, strong right-arm medium fast bowler. *Sch* Christ's Hospital. *Team* Kent (1951–58, 42 matches).
Career batting
42–71–12–728–60–12.33–0–*ct* 29
Bowling 3766–165–22.82–10–0–8/110

Smith, George
Professional. *b:* 17.12.1844, Cambridge. *d:* 22.9.1876, Cambridge. He died of a complication of disorders. Brother of John (Cambridgeshire). Lower order right-hand batsman, right-hand fast round-arm bowler. *Team* Cambridgeshire (1868–71, 4 matches).
Career batting
4–8–1–23–7–3.28–0–*ct* 2
Bowling 384–23–16.69–1–0–6/32

Smith, George
Professional. *b:* 13.1.1876. *d:* 16.1.1929, Thorp Arch, Boston Spa, Yorkshire. *Team* Yorkshire (1901–06, 2 matches).
Career batting
2–1–0–7–7–7.00–0–*ct* 3
Bowling 62–0

Smith, Geoffrey John
Professional. *b:* 2.4.1935, Braintree, Essex. Opening right-hand batsman, off break bowler. *Team* Essex (1955–66, 239 matches).
Career batting
243–419–30–8796–148–22.61–5–*ct* 133
Bowling 951–33–28.81–1–0–5/39

He hit 1,000 runs in a season four times (best 1,908, av 32.89, in 1961). He also played for Hertfordshire.

Smith, Gilbert Oswald
Amateur. *b:* 25.11.1872, Croydon, Surrey. *d:* 6.12.1943, Lymington, Hants. Middle order right-hand batsman, right-arm fast medium pace bowler. *Sch* Charterhouse. *Teams* Oxford U (1893–96, blue 1895–96); Surrey (1896, 3 matches).
Career batting
17–29–3–778–132–29.92–2–*ct* 11

He also played County cricket for Hertfordshire, but played little important cricket after leaving Oxford. Regarded as the greatest centre forward of his day, he represented Oxford v Cambridge four times and England in 20 internationals. He appeared in the FA Amateur Cup Final with Old Carthusians in 1895 and 1897 and later played for Corinthians.

Smith, Graham Stuart
Amateur. *b:* 4.7.1923, Leicester. Middle order right-hand batsman. *Sch* Bedford and Stoneygate. *Team* Leicestershire (1949, 1 match).
Career batting
1–2–0–29–22–14.50–0–*ct* 0

Smith, George William Oswald
Amateur. *b:* 7.3.1906, Halstead, Essex. Lower order right-hand batsman, wicket-keeper. *Sch* Bishop's Stortford. *Team* Essex (1929–30, 10 matches).
Career batting
10–18–3–206–39*–13.73–0–*ct* 2

He played in the the Seniors' match whilst at Cambridge. He also played for Suffolk.

Smith, Harry
Professional. *b:* 21.5.1891, Fishponds, Bristol. *d:* 12.11.1937, Downend, Bristol. Sound middle order right-hand batsman. *Team* Gloucestershire (1912–35, 393 matches). *Test* England (1928, 1 match).
Career batting
402–656–56–13413–149–22.35–0–*ct* 457–*st* 266
Bowling 7–0
Test batting
1–1–0–7–7–7.00–0–*ct* 1

He hit 1,000 runs in a season five times (best 1,573, av 28.08, in 1926). He also played soccer for Bolton Wanderers.

Smith, Haydon Arthur
Professional. *b:* 29.3.1901, Groby, Leicestershire. *d:* 7.8.1948, Groby, Leicestershire. Lower order right-hand batsman, right-arm fast bowler. *Team* Leicestershire (1925–39, 341 matches).
Career batting
341–500–82–4603–100*–11.01–1–*ct* 257
Bowling 27968–1076–25.99–66–11–8/40
He took 100 wickets in a season five times (best 150, av 19.66, in 1935).

Smith, Hamilton Augustus Haigh
(also known as Haigh-Smith)
Amateur. *b:* 21.10.1884, Sandown, Isle of Wight. *d:* 28.10.1955, Paddington, London. Middle order right-hand batsman, leg break and googly bowler. *Sch* Marlborough. *Team* Hampshire (1909–14, 27 matches).
Career batting
27–41–10–327–43*–10.54–0–*ct* 9
Bowling 574–14–41.00–0–0–3/95
A noted rugby footballer, he played for Barbarians and also represented Hampshire; he appeared for the County's hockey team as well.

Smith, Henry E.
Amateur. *b:* 21.4.1884, Gamtoos River, Cape Colony, South Africa. Brother of C. J. E. (South Africa). Middle order right-hand batsman. *Team* Transvaal (1905/6 to 1906/7). *Tour* South Africa to England 1907.
Career batting
15–23–2–395–53–18.80–0–*ct* 2
His final first-class match was for Wanderers CC in 1908/9.

Smith, Hugh Purefoy
Amateur. *b:* 16.10.1856, Lasham, Hampshire. *d:* 16.1.1939. Lower order right-hand batsman, right-arm medium pace bowler. *Sch* Bradfield. *Team* Sussex (1878, 1 match).
Career batting
1–2–0–10–10–5.00–0–*ct* 1
Bowling 82–1–82.00–0–0–1/82

Smith, Harry Turberville
(later Smith-Turberville, H. T.)
Amateur. *b:* 1848, London. *d:* 28.7.1934, Hove, Sussex. Lower order batsman, useful bowler. *Team* MCC (1886). *Tour* Lucas to West Indies 1894/5.
Career batting
2–4–1–31–14–10.33–0–*ct* 0
Bowling 28–1–28.00–0–0–1/28

Smith, Harry Thomas Oliver
Amateur. *b:* 5.3.1906, Warley, Essex. Lower order right-hand batsman, right-arm fast medium bowler. *Team* Essex (1929–35, 23 matches).
Career batting
25–40–5–400–38–11.42–0–*ct* 20
Bowling 1740–63–27.61–3–0–6/56
His final first-class match was for Leveson-Gower's XI in 1936.

Smith, Harry Watson
(also known as Watson-Smith)
Amateur. *b:* 30.9.1886, Chesterfield, Derbyshire. *d:* 24.6.1955, Ruthin, Denbighshire. Lower order right-hand batsman, wicket-keeper. *Sch* Worksop. *Teams* Derbyshire (1920, 1 match); Warwickshire (1912, 1 match).
Career batting
2–3–1–49–24*–24.50–0–*ct* 0

Smith, Harry William
Professional. *b:* 6.9.1890, Mile End, London. Lower order right-hand batsman, right-arm fast medium bowler. *Team* Essex (1912–22, 20 matches).
Career batting
20–31–12–195–22–10.26–0–*ct* 12
Bowling 1055–35–30.14–1–0–5/59

Smith, Ian David Stockley
Cricketer. *b:* 28.2.1957, Nelson, New Zealand. Lower order right-hand batsman, wicket-keeper *Team* Central Districts (1977/8 to 1982/3). *Tours* New Zealand to England 1983, to Australia 1981/2. *Tests* New Zealand (1980/1 to 1983, 9 matches).
Career batting
56–88–7–1788–145–22.07–3–*ct* 129–*st* 9
Bowling 6–0
Test batting
9–13–3–108–20–10.80–0–*ct* 29
He appeared in two of the four Tests on the 1983 visit to England.

Smith, Irving Wilmot
Amateur. *b:* 5.2.1884, Birmingham, Warwickshire. *d:* 21.10.1971, Sutton Coldfield, Warwickshire. Right-hand batsman, right-arm medium and leg break bowler. *Team* Warwickshire (1905, 1 match).
Career batting
1–1–0–1–1–1.00–0–*ct* 0
Bowling 13–0

Smith, Jack
Cricketer. *b:* 7.3.1936, Stotfold, Bedfordshire. Middle order right-hand batsman, off break

bowler. *Sch* Bedford School. *Team* Minor Counties (1965).
Career batting
1–2–0–17–17–8.50–0–*ct* 0
Bowling 99–4–24.75–0–0–2/47

His County cricket was for Bedfordshire, from 1959.

Smith, John
Professional. *b:* 23.3.1833, Yeadon, Yorkshire. *d:* 12.2.1909, Worcester. Father of D. J. (Somerset and Worcs) and William (Somerset). Lower order left-hand batsman, left-hand fast round-arm bowler. *Teams* Yorkshire (1865, 2 matches); Lancashire (1865-69, 6 matches).
Career batting
8–15–1–181–40*–12.92–0–*ct* 7
Bowling 362–18–20.11–0–0–4/46

From 1883 to 1897 he was a professional for Worcestershire, initially as player and later as groundsman.

Smith, John
Professional. *b:* 8.11.1835, Ruddington, Nottinghamshire. *d:* May 1888, Manchester, Lancashire. Middle order right-hand batsman, right-arm medium bowler. *Team* Nottinghamshire (1864, 2 matches).
Career batting
2–4–0–30–27–7.50–0–*ct* 1
Bowling 21–1–21.00–0–0–1/21

He umpired in first-class matches in the 1870s.

Smith, John
Amateur. *b:* 27.10.1841, Clifton, Derbyshire. *d:* 26.11.1898, Derby. Right-hand batsman, right-hand slow medium round-arm bowler. *Team* Derbyshire (1871–78, 22 matches).
Career batting
22–38–2–403–35–11.19–0–*ct* 14
Bowling 162–6–27.00–0–0–3/38

Smith, John
Professional. *b:* 20.11.1843, Cambridge. *d:* 15.4.1873, Stratford-by-Bow, Essex. Brother of George (Cambridgeshire). Attractive middle order right-hand batsman, brilliant cover point. *Team* Cambridgeshire (1863–71, 25 matches).
Career batting
75–135–2–2274–97–17.09–0–*ct* 36
Bowling 9–0

His final first-class match was for MCC in 1872

Smith, James Crosbie
Professional. *b:* 26.9.1894, Ledbury, Herefordshire. *d:* 19.2.1980, Ledbury, Herefordshire. Middle order left-hand batsman. *Team* Worcestershire (1923–25, 16 matches).
Career batting
16–27–1–313–70–12.03–0–*ct* 15
Bowling 10–0

Smith, John Willoughby Dixie
(also known as Dixie-Smith)
Amateur. *b:* 11.3.1882, Blaby, Leicestershire. *d:* 2.10.1959, Harrow-on-the-Hill, Middlesex. Middle order right-hand batsman. *Team* Leicestershire (1921, 2 matches).
Career batting
2–4–0–30–25–7.50–0–*ct* 0
Bowling 17–0

Smith, John Westwood Rowley
Amateur. *b:* 28.7.1924, Clarendon Park, Leicester. Lower order right-hand batsman, wicket-keeper. *Sch* Stoneygate and Repton. *Team* Leicestershire (1950–55, 3 matches).
Career batting
3–3–0–5–4–1.66–0–*ct* 1–*st* 1

Smith, Kevin Brian
Cricketer. *b:* 28.8.1957, Lewes, Sussex. Middle order left-hand batsman, slow left-arm bowler. *Team* Sussex (1978, 4 matches).
Career batting
4–8–1–90–43–12.85–0–*ct* 1

Smith, Kenneth David
Cricketer. *b:* 9.7.1956, Newcastle-upon-Tyne. Son of K. D. (Leicestershire), brother of P. A. (Warwickshire). Opening or middle order right-hand batsman. *Team* Warwickshire (1973–83, 171 matches).
Career batting
171–297–27–7922–140–29.34–9–*ct* 66
Bowling 3–0

He hit 1,000 runs in a season four times (best 1,582, av 36.79, in 1980).

Smith, Kenneth Desmond
Professional. *b:* 30.4.1922, Bishop Auckland, Co Durham. Father of K. D. (Warwickshire) and P. A. (Warwickshire). Middle order right-hand batsman. *Team* Leicestershire (1950–51, 26 matches).
Career batting
26–43–7–621–70*–17.25–0–*ct* 12
Bowling 103–3–34.33–0–0–2/37

He also played for Northumberland.

Smith, Lewis Alfred
Amateur. *b:* 12.7.1913, Brentford, Middlesex. *d:* October 1978, Ealing, Middlesex. Right-hand batsman, right-arm fast medium bowler. *Teams* Middlesex (1934–37, 3 matches); Northamptonshire (1947, 2 matches).

Career batting
5–8–2–92–55–15.33–0–*ct* 2
Bowling 397–11–36.09–0–0–4/55

Smith, Lemuel Strutt Tugby
Professional. *b:* 5.6.1880, Tibshelf, Derbyshire. *d:* 30.12.1927, South Kirkby, Yorkshire. Lower order right-hand batsman, wicket-keeper. *Team* Derbyshire (1909, 2 matches).
Career batting
2–3–0–9–5–3.00–0–*ct* 1

Smith, Michael Graham Milner
Amateur. *b:* 28.9.1941, Otford, Kent. Lower order right-hand batsman, wicket-keeper. *Sch* Tonbridge. *Team* Cambridge U (1961).
Career batting
1–2–1–24–18*–24.00–0–*ct* 1–*st* 1

Smith, Michael John
Professional. *b:* 4.1.1942, Enfield, Middlesex. Sound opening right-hand batsman, slow left-arm bowler. *Team* Middlesex (1959–80, 399 matches). *Tours* Robins to South Africa 1972/3, 1973/4, to West Indies 1974/5 (not first-class), to Sri Lanka 1977/8.
Career batting
422–704–78–19814–181–31.65–40–*ct* 218
Bowling 1866–57–32.73–0–0–4/13

He hit 1,000 runs in a season eleven times (best 1,705, av 39.65, in 1970).

Smith, Michael John Knight
Amateur. *b:* 30.6.1933, Leicester. Stylish middle order right-hand batsman, right-arm slow medium bowler, brilliant short leg field. *Sch* Stamford. *Teams* Leicestershire (1951–55, 28 matches); Oxford U (1954–56, blue all three years); Warwickshire (1956–75, 430 matches). *Tours* MCC to East Africa 1957/8 (not first-class), to South America 1958/9 (not first-class), to West Indies 1959/60, to India, Pakistan and Ceylon 1961/2, to East Africa 1963/4, to India 1963/4, to South Africa 1964/5, to Australia and New Zealand 1965/6; Cavaliers to South Africa 1960/1. *Tests* England (1958 to 1972, 50 matches).
Career batting
637–1091–139–39832–204–41.84–69–*ct* 592
Bowling 305–5–61.00–0–0–1/0
Test batting
50–78–6–2278–121–31.63–3–*ct* 52
Bowling 128–1–128.00–0–0–1/10

One of the most prolific scorers in post-war English cricket, he was most successful whilst at Oxford, hitting three centuries, including one double century against Cambridge, and went on to a long and brilliant career with Warwickshire. He reached 1,000 runs in a season 19 times, going to 2,000 six times and to 3,000 once: 3,245, av 57.94, in 1959. Apart from his double century for Oxford he hit 200* for Warwickshire v Worcestershire at Edgbaston in 1959 and 204 for Cavaliers v Natal at Durban in 1960/1.

He captained Warwickshire from 1957 to 1967 and led England in 25 Tests, also captaining the MCC on three Test tours – to India, to South Africa and to Australia and New Zealand.

He was also an excellent rugby footballer, gaining a blue as fly-half and being capped for England.

Smith, Neil
Cricketer. *b:* 1.4.1949, Dewsbury, Yorkshire. Lower order right-hand batsman, wicket-keeper. *Teams* Yorkshire (1970–71, 8 matches); Essex (1973–81, 178 matches).
Career batting
187–239–53–3336–126–17.93–2–*ct* 395–*st* 51

Smith, O'Neil Gordon
Amateur. *b:* 5.5.1933, Kingston, Jamaica. *d:* 9.9.1959, Stoke-on-Trent. He died following a motor-car accident. Middle order right-hand batsman, off break bowler, brilliant field. *Team* Jamaica (1954/5 to 1957/8). *Tours* West Indies to New Zealand 1955/6, to England 1957, to India and Pakistan 1958/9. *Tests* West Indies (1954/5 to 1958/9, 26 matches).
Career batting
70–112–12–4031–169–40.31–12–*ct* 39
Bowling 3754–121–31.02–2–0–5/63
Test batting
26–42–0–1331–168–31.69–4–*ct* 9
Bowling 1625–48–33.85–1–0–5/90

He headed the West Indies Test batting averages on the 1957 tour to England with 396 runs, av 39.60, and in all first-class matches hit 1,483 runs, av 41.19. Regarded as the most promising of young West Indian cricketers he tragically died after being injured in a car crash. About 60,000 people attended his funeral in Jamaica. His final first-class match in England was for a Commonwealth XI in 1958 – in 1958 and 1959 he was professional for Burnley.

Smith, Paul Andrew
Cricketer. *b:* 15.4.1964, Gosforth, Newcastle-upon-Tyne. Son of K. D. (Leicestershire), brother of K. D. (Warwickshire). Middle order right-hand batsman, right-arm medium pace bowler. *Team* Warwickshire (1982–83, 23 matches).
Career batting
23–33–4–841–114–29.00–1–*ct* 8
Bowling 1380–31–44.51–0–0–3/40

Smith, Peter Bruce
Cricketer. *b:* 18.3.1944, Oxford. Lower order right-hand batsman, right-arm medium pace bowler. *Team* Oxford U (1967).
Career batting
5–6–1–36–18–7.20–0–*ct* 0
Bowling 291–7–41.42–0–0–4/92
His County cricket was for Oxfordshire.

Smith, Peter Thomas
Professional. *b:* 5.10.1934, Leicester. Middle order right-hand batsman. *Team* Leicestershire (1956–57, 15 matches).
Career batting
15–24–2–152–40–6.90–0–*ct* 4

Smith, Raymond
Professional. *b:* 10.8.1914, Boreham, Essex. Cousin of T. P. B. Smith (Essex). Aggressive right-hand batsman, right-arm medium pace or off break bowler. *Team* Essex (1934–56, 419 matches). *Tour* Commonwealth to India, Ceylon and Pakistan 1949/50.
Career batting
445–682–88–12041–147–20.27–8–*ct* 191
Bowling 41265–1350–30.56–73–10–8/63
He hit 1,000 runs in a season four times (best 1,386, av 28.87, in 1947) and took 100 wickets in a season seven times (best 136, av 28.87, in 1952). He completed the 'double' in 1947, 1950 and 1952.

Smith, Dr Reginald
(also known as Starkey-Smith)
Amateur. *b:* 1.5.1868, Warrington, Lancashire. *d:* 5.10.1943, Scarborough, Yorkshire. Middle order batsman, useful bowler. *Team* Lancashire (1893, 1 match).
Career batting
1–1–0–6–6–6.00–0–*ct* 0
Bowling 11–0
He also played for Norfolk.

Smith, Rodney
Cricketer. *b:* 6.4.1944, Batley, Yorkshire. Middle order right-hand batsman, slow left-arm bowler. *Team* Yorkshire (1969–70, 5 matches).
Career batting
5–8–3–99–37*–19.80–0–*ct* 0

Smith, Ronald
Amateur. *b:* 16.2.1926, Dudley, Worcestershire. Lower order right-hand batsman, right-arm fast medium bowler. *Team* Northants (1954, 1 match).
Career batting
1–2–1–19–19*–19.00–0–*ct* 0
Bowling 38–1–38.00–0–0–1/38

Smith, Roy
Amateur. *b:* 20.1.1910, Wolstanton, Staffordshire. *d:* 19.10.1971, Fegg Hayes, Staffordshire. Middle order right-hand batsman. *Team* Minor Counties (1949).
Career batting
1–2–0–29–29–14.50–0–*ct* 1
His County cricket was for Staffordshire.

Smith, Roy
Professional. *b:* 14.4.1930, Taunton, Somerset. Middle order right-hand batsman, slow left-arm bowler. *Team* Somerset (1949–55, 96 matches).
Career batting
96–173–21–2600–100–17.10–1–*ct* 31
Bowling 1083–19–57.00–0–0–4/91
He hit 1,176 runs, av 26.13, in 1953.
He also played for Devon.

Smith, Robin Arnold
Cricketer. *b:* 13.9.1963, Durban, South Africa. Brother of C. L. (Glamorgan and Hampshire). Middle order right-hand batsman, leg break bowler. *Teams* Natal (1980/1 to 1982/3); Hampshire (1982–83, 8 matches).
Career batting
25–44–7–1266–104*–34.21–3–*ct* 9
Bowling 25–0

Smith, Raymond Charles
Professional. *b:* 3.8.1935, Duddington, Northants. Lower order right-hand batsman, slow left-arm bowler. *Sch* Stamford. *Team* Leicestershire (1956–64, 104 matches).
Career batting
104–156–37–1115–36–9.36–0–*ct* 28
Bowling 5514–203–27.16–11–1–7/54

Smith, Robert Posnett
(changed name to Stevens, September 1885)
Amateur. *b:* 1.11.1848, Sawley, Derbyshire. *d:* 1.5.1899, Staunton, Notts. Sound middle order right-hand batsman, right-hand fast round-arm, or slow under-arm bowler. *Team* Derbyshire (1871–84, 90 matches).
Career batting
103–190–3–2719–87–14.54–0–*ct* 74
Bowling 23–0
He captained Derbyshire from 1876 to 1883.

Smith, Stanley
Professional. *b:* 14.1.1929, Heywood, Lancashire. Middle order right-hand batsman. *Team* Lancashire (1952–56, 38 matches).
Career batting
44–66–5–1117–101*–18.31–1–*ct* 10
His first-class debut was for Combined Services in 1950.

Smith, S. C.
Amateur. Left-hand batsman. *Team* Ireland (1907–08).
Career batting
3–6–0–19–11–3.16–0–*ct* 2

Smith, Sydney Francis
Amateur. *b:* 1892, Northampton. Middle order batsman. *Team* Northamptonshire (1914, 2 matches).
Career batting
2–4–0–16–6–4.00–0–*ct* 0

Smith, Sydney Gordon
Amateur. *b:* 15.1.1881, San Fernando, Trinidad. *d:* 25.10.1963, Auckland, New Zealand. Fast scoring middle order left-hand batsman, slow left-arm bowler. *Teams* Trinidad (1899/1900 to 1905/6); Northants (1907–14, 119 matches); Auckland (1917/8 to 1925/6). *Tours* West Indies to England 1906; MCC to West Indies 1910/11, 1912/13.
Career batting
211–379–30–10920–256–31.28–14–*ct* 158
Bowling 17271–955–18.08–71–19–9/34

He hit 1,000 runs in a season four times (best 1,522, av 37.12, in 1913) and took 100 wickets in a season four times, performing the 'double' three times. His best season was 1909 with 115 wickets, av 19.51. He proved the best all-rounder on the 1906 West Indies tour to England and after the visit remained in England to qualify for Northants. He captained that County in 1913 and 1914. In 1915 he emigrated to New Zealand and played with much success there, appearing in the representative New Zealand team against English and Australian touring sides. His highest score was 256 for Auckland v Canterbury at Auckland in 1919/20, and his best bowling 9/34 for a West Indies XI v Bennett's XI at Port of Spain in 1901/2.

Smith, Thomas
Professional. *b:* 26.8.1848, Glossop, Derbyshire. Right-hand batsman, right-hand medium pace round-arm bowler, slip field. *Team* Lancashire (1867, 2 matches); Liverpool and District (1886–91).
Career batting
7–12–2–50–16–5.00–0–*ct* 5
Bowling 361–21–17.19–1–1–7/59

Smith, Thomas
Amateur. *b:* 6.4.1854, Guildford, Surrey. Middle order right-hand batsman, left-arm bowler. *Team* Surrey (1876, 1 match).
Career batting
1–2–0–16–13–8.00–0–*ct* 1
Bowling 20–0

Smith, Thomas George Harrison
Professional. *b:* 6.3.1905, Northampton. Middle order right-hand batsman. *Team* Northamptonshire (1931, 1 match).
Career batting
1–1–0–11–11–11.00–0–*ct* 0
Bowling 28–0

Smith, Thomas Michael
Amateur. *b:* 15.6.1899, Lambeth, London. *d:* 17.11.1965, Taunton, Somerset. Middle order batsman. *Team* Hampshire (1923–24, 9 matches).
Career batting
9–11–1–89–18–8.90–0–*ct* 3

Smith, Thomas Peter Bromley
Professional. *b:* 30.10.1908, Ipswich, Suffolk. *d:* 4.8.1967, Hyeres, France. He died following a fall whilst on holiday. Cousin of Raymond (Essex). Lower order right-hand batsman, leg break and googly bowler. *Team* Essex (1929–51, 434 matches). *Tours* Tennyson to India 1937/8; Cahn to New Zealand 1938/9; selected for MCC to India 1939/40 (cancelled due to war); MCC to Australia and New Zealand 1946/7. *Tests* England (1946 to 1946/7, 4 matches).
Career batting
465–690–123–10142–163–17.88–8–*ct* 346
Bowling 45059–1697–26.55–120–28–9/77
Test batting
4–5–0–33–24–6.60–0–*ct* 1
Bowling 319–3–106.33–0–0–2/172

He hit 1,000 runs in a season once – 1,065, av 23.66, completing the 'double' in the same year. He took 100 wickets in a season six times (best 172, av 27.13, in 1947). In the same year he hit 163 for Essex v Derbyshire at Chesterfield, adding 218 for the last wicket with F. H. Vigar – Smith came in as last man. His best bowling was 9/77 for Essex v Middlesex at Colchester in 1947.

Smith, Vivian Ian
Amateur. *b:* 23.2.1925, Durban, South Africa. Tail end right-hand batsman, leg break bowler. *Team* Natal (1945/6 to 1957/8). *Tours* South Africa to England 1947, 1955. *Tests* South Africa (1947 to 1957/8, 9 matches).
Career batting
97–114–61–547–37–10.32–0–*ct* 37
Bowling 8233–365–22.55–26–8–9/88
Test batting
9–16–6–39–11*–3.90–0–*ct* 3
Bowling 769–12–64.08–0–0–4/143

He headed the first-class bowling figures for the 1947 tour with 58 wickets, av 23.17, and against Derbyshire returned an analysis of 4.5–3–1–6; in 1955 he was overshadowed by Tayfield and given few opportunities. His best bowling was 9/88 for Natal v Border at Pietermaritzburg in 1946/7.

Smith, Walker
Professional. *b:* 14.8.1847, Bradford, Yorkshire. *d:* 1900, North Bierley, Yorkshire. Aggressive middle order right-hand batsman, mid-wicket field. *Team* Yorkshire (1874, 5 matches).
Career batting
5–9–0–152–59–16.88–0–*ct* 2

Smith, William
Professional. *b:* 1.11.1839, Darlington, Co Durham. Attacking middle order right-hand batsman. *Team* Yorkshire (1865–74, 11 matches).
Career batting
11–19–3–260–90–16.25–0–*ct* 8
He also played for Durham.

Smith, William
Professional. *b:* 23.4.1871, Batley, Yorkshire. Brother of D. J. (Somerset), son of John (Yorkshire and Lancashire). Middle order right-hand batsman, right-arm medium pace bowler. *Team* Somerset (1895–98, 6 matches).
Career batting
8–13–2–97–21–8.81–0–*ct* 1
Bowling 88–0
His final first-class match was for MCC in 1902. He also played for Wiltshire.

Smith, William
Amateur. *b:* 1875. *d:* 20.3.1942, Chittlehambolt, Devon. Middle order right-hand batsman, useful bowler. *Team* London County (1901–04).
Career batting
30–45–6–1191–143–30.54–2–*ct* 17
Bowling 67–2–33.50–0–0–1/6
His County cricket was for Oxfordshire.

Smith, Willie
Professional. *b:* 12.5.1885, Gringley-on-the-Hill, Nottinghamshire. *d:* 8.5.1964, Scawsby, Yorkshire. Middle order right-hand batsman. *Team* Derbyshire (1913, 2 matches).
Career batting
2–4–0–13–8–3.25–0–*ct* 0

Smith, Walter Alfred
Amateur. *b:* 23.2.1913, Leicester. Middle order right-hand batsman, slow right-arm bowler. *Sch* Wyggeston GS. *Team* Leicestershire (1930–46, 27 matches).
Career batting
27–44–4–754–125*–18.85–1–*ct* 13
Bowling 122–3–40.66–0–0–1/4

Smith, William Albert
Professional. *b:* 15.9.1937, Salisbury, Wiltshire. Middle order left-hand batsman, right-arm batsman, right-arm medium pace bowler. *Team* Surrey (1961–70, 144 matches).
Career batting
144–242–18–5024–103–22.42–2–*ct* 52
Bowling 1–0
He hit 1,002 runs, av 24.43, in 1968. He also played for Wiltshire.

Smith, William Alfred
Professional. *b:* 29.9.1900, Corsham, Wiltshire. Brother of C. I. J. (Middlesex). Lower order right-hand batsman, right-arm fast medium bowler. *Team* Minor Counties (1935–36).
Career batting
2–4–1–47–35–15.66–0–*ct* 1
Bowling 208–9–23.11–1–0–5/95
His County cricket was for Wiltshire.

Smith, William Alexander Bremner
Amateur. *b:* 22.7.1902, Greenock, Renfrewshire, Scotland. *d:* 21.12.1937, Kuala Lumpur, Malaya. Right-hand batsman, right-arm fast medium bowler. *Team* Scotland (1927).
Career batting
1–2–0–1–1–0.50–0–*ct* 1
Bowling 71–1–71.00–0–0–1/29

Smith, William Charles
Professional. *b:* 4.10.1877, Oxford. *d:* 15.7.1946, Bermondsey, London. Lower order right-hand batsman, right-arm off break bowler. *Teams* Surrey (1900–14, 229 matches); London County (1900). *Tour* MCC to West Indies 1912/13.
Career batting
245–343–71–3453–126–12.69–1–*ct* 157
Bowling 18910–1077–17.55–95–27–9/31
He took 100 wickets in a season three times, going on to 200 once : 247 av 13.05, in 1910. His best innings analysis was 9 for 31 for Surrey v Hampshire in 1904 at the Oval. Ill-health marred his career and his very sparse figure earned him the nickname 'Razor'. He also played for Oxfordshire.

Smith, Walter Frederick Sundius
Amateur. *b:* 8.2.1889, Steyning, Sussex. *d:* 30.12.1969, Hove, Sussex. Lower order batsman, useful bowler. *Sch* Oundle. Team Oxford U (1920).
Career batting
1–2–0–12–12–6.00–0–*ct* 0
Bowling 47–2–23.50–0–0–2/38

Smith, William John
Professional. *b:* 13.5.1882, Freasley, Warwick-

shire. Lower order right-hand batsman, right-arm fast medium bowler. *Team* Warwickshire (1906, 1 match).
Career batting
1–1–0–0–0–0.00–*ct* 0
Bowling 93–2–46.50–0–0–2/83

Smith-Barry, Arthur Hugh
(created 1st Lord Barrymore in 1902)
Amateur. *b:* 17.1.1843, Leamington, Warwickshire. *d:* 22.2.1925, Westminster, London. Middle order right-hand batsman, wicket-keeper. *Sch* Eton. *Team* MCC (1873–75).
Career batting
2–4–0–14–9–3.50–0–*ct* 1
He was not in the Eleven whilst at Oxford, but played County cricket for Warwickshire (pre-first-class) and Cheshire, also for Gentlemen of Ireland. He was MP for Co Cork from 1867 to 1874, and for South Huntingdonshire from 1886 to 1900.

Smith-Masters, William Allan
Amateur. *b:* 13.3.1850, Humber, Herefordshire. *d:* 27.8.1937, Meopham, Kent. Middle order batsman. *Sch* Marlborough. *Team* Kent (1875, 1 match).
Career batting
1–1–0–7–7–7.00–0–*ct* 0

Smithson, Gerald Arthur
Professional. *b:* 1.11.1926, Spofforth, Yorkshire. *d:* 6.9.1970, Abingdon, Berks. Middle order left-hand batsman. *Teams* Yorkshire (1946–50, 39 matches); Leicestershire (1951–56, 154 matches). *Tour* MCC to West Indies 1947/8. *Tests* England (1947/8, 2 matches).
Career batting
200–333–27–6940–169–22.67–8–*ct* 131
Bowling 117–1–117.00–0–0–1/26
Test batting
2–3–0–70–35–23.33–0–*ct* 0
He hit 1,351 runs, av 27.57, in 1952. He played for Hertfordshire from 1957 to 1962. He was a conscript in the mines in 1947 when he was selected to tour West Indies with MCC and after his case had been debated in the House of Commons he was granted permission by the Government to take part in the tour.

Smithurst, Isaiah
Professional. *b:* 6.11.1920, Hill Top, Eastwood, Nottinghamshire. Lower order left-hand batsman, slow left-arm bowler. *Team* Nottinghamshire (1946, 1 match).
Career batting
1–2–0–1–1–0.50–0–*ct* 0
Bowling 48–0

Smithyman, Michael James
Cricketer. *b:* 17.11.1945, Pietermaritzburg, South Africa. Steady middle order right-hand batsman, right-arm medium fast bowler. *Team* Natal (1965/6 to 1974/5). *Tour* South African Universities to England 1967.
Career batting
40–59–10–1162–73–23.71–0–*ct* 16
Bowling 2027–79–25.65–0–0–4/25
He was most successful on his visit to England, heading the batting and bowling averages in all matches with 562 runs, av 93.66, and 51 wickets, av 13.98.

Smoker, George
Professional. *b:* 1857, Winchester, Hampshire. *d:* 23.5.1925, Alresford, Hampshire. Middle order batsman. *Team* Hampshire (1885, 2 matches).
Career batting
2–4–1–17–13–5.66–0–*ct* 2

Smoker, Henry George
Professional. *b:* 1.3.1881, Alresford, Hampshire. *d:* 7.9.1966, Wallasey, Cheshire. Lower order left-hand batsman, right-arm medium fast bowler. *Team* Hampshire (1901–07, 31 matches).
Career batting
31–50–15–334–39*–9.54–0–*ct* 18
Bowling 733–33–22.21–2–0–7/35
He also played for Cheshire.

Smurthwaite, James
Professional. *b:* 17.10.1916, North Ormesby, Yorkshire. Tail end right-hand batsman, right-arm fast medium, or off break bowler. *Team* Yorkshire (1938–39, 7 matches).
Career batting
7–9–5–29–20*–7.25–0–*ct* 4
Bowling 237–12–19.75–1–0–5/7

Smyth, Richard Ian
Cricketer. *b:* 19.11.1951, Sunderland, Co Durham. Middle order right-hand batsman, leg break bowler. *Sch* Sedbergh. *Team* Cambridge U (1973–75, blue all three years).
Career batting
21–41–2–711–61–18.23–0–*ct* 4
His County cricket was for Durham.

Smyth, Richard Nicholas Paul
Cricketer. *b:* 27.6.1950, Chichester, Sussex. Middle order right-hand batsman. *Team* Sussex (1970, 3 matches).
Career batting
3–5–0–42–25–8.40–0–*ct* 0

Smythe, David
Amateur. *b:* 4.12.1889, Rockingham, Northants. *d:* 6.3.1962, Edinburgh, Scotland. Lower order

batsman, right-arm fast bowler. *Sch* Repton. *Team* Cambridge U (1912).
Career batting
3–3–0–15–12–5.00–0–*ct* 0
Bowling 149–6–24.83–0–0–2/43

Smythe, John W.
Amateur. *b:* 1849. *d:* 1937, Staines, Middlesex. Middle order batsman. *Team* MCC (1878–85).
Career batting
5–10–1–122–35–13.55–0–*ct* 3
Bowling 24–2–12.00–0–0–2/24

Snaith, John Collis
Amateur. *b:* 24.2.1876, Nottingham. *d:* 8.12.1936, Hampstead, London. Middle order left-hand batsman, left-arm medium pace bowler. *Team* Nottinghamshire (1900, 1 match).
Career batting
1–1–0–21–21–21.00–0–*ct* 1
A well-known popular novelist of his day, he wrote one noteworthy book on cricket 'Willow the King'.

Snape, Maurice Desmond
Professional. *b:* 7.7.1923, Creswell, Derbyshire. Middle order right-hand batsman. *Team* Derbyshire (1949, 2 matches).
Career batting
2–3–1–0–0*–0.00–0–*ct* 0

Snary, Horace Charles
Professional. *b:* 22.9.1897, Whissendine, Rutland. *d:* 26.12.1966, Whissendine, Rutland. Stubborn middle order right-hand batsman, right-arm medium-slow bowler. *Team* Leicestershire (1921–33, 183 matches).
Career batting
183–249–114–2156–124*–15.97–1–*ct* 115
Bowling 10170–419–24.27–12–1–7/31
He took 101 wickets, av 18.11, in 1931.

Snedden, Martin Colin
Cricketer. *b:* 23.11.1958, Auckland, New Zealand. Lower order left-hand batsman, right-arm medium fast bowler. *Team* Auckland (1977/8 to 1982/3). *Tours* New Zealand to Australia 1980/1, 1982/3, to England 1983. *Tests* New Zealand (1980/1 to 1983, 9 matches).
Career batting
45–50–12–775–69–20.39–0–*ct* 21
Bowling 3706–149–24.87–5–1–7/49
Test batting
9–10–2–120–32–15.00–0–*ct* 2
Bowling 690–23–30.00–0–0–3/21
He had only modest success on the 1983 tour to England and appeared in one Test.

Snell, Edward
Amateur. *b:* 22.4.1906, Steyning, Sussex. *d:* 6.9.1973, Hove, Sussex. Middle order right-hand batsman, slow right-arm bowler. *Sch* Winchester. *Team* Sussex (1927–28, 3 matches).
Career batting
3–3–0–13–13–4.33–0–*ct* 1

Snell, Harold Saxon
Amateur. *b:* 6.12.1876, Highworth, Wiltshire. *d:* 9.7.1942, Daventry, Northants. Middle order batsman. *Sch* Dean Close, Cheltenham. *Team* Northamptonshire (1909–13, 3 matches).
Career batting
3–5–0–119–52–23.80–0–*ct* 2
He also played for Wiltshire.

Snellgrove, Kenneth Leslie
Cricketer. *b:* 12.11.1941, Shepton-Mallet, Somerset. Middle order right-hand batsman. *Team* Lancashire (1965–74, 105 matches).
Career batting
106–172–16–3948–138–25.30–2–*ct* 36
Bowling 27–3–9.00–0–0–2/23
His best season was 1971 with 991 runs, av 31.96.

Snodgrass, David Lang
Cricketer. *b:* 21.1.1958, Partick Hill, Glasgow, Scotland. Lower order right-hand batsman, right-arm medium pace bowler. *Team* Scotland (1982).
Career batting
1–1–0–6–6–6.00–0–*ct* 1
Bowling 80–3–26.66–0–0–2/30

Snooke, Stanley Delacourtte
Amateur. *b:* 11.11.1878, St. Mark's, Temboland, South Africa. *d:* 4.4.1959, Cape Town, South Africa. Brother of S. J. (South Africa). Middle order right-hand batsman, bowler. *Teams* Western Province (1904/5 to 1910/11); Transvaal (1920/1). *Tour* South Africa to England 1907. *Test* South Africa (1907, 1 match).
Career batting
32–53–5–798–74–16.62–0–*ct* 31
Bowling 224–19–11.78–1–1–7/29
Test batting
1–1–0–0–0–0.00–0–*ct* 2
He achieved very little on the 1907 visit to England.

Snooke, Sibley John
Amateur. *b:* 1.2.1881, St Mark's Tembuland, South Africa. *d:* 14.8.1966, Port Elizabeth, South Africa. Brother of S. D. (South Africa). Middle order right-hand batsman, right-arm fast medium bowler. *Teams* Border (1897/8 to 1908/9); Western Province (1903/4 to 1907/8); MCC

(1907); Transvaal (1909/10 to 1923/4). *Tours* South Africa to England 1904, 1907, 1912, to Australia 1910/11; MCC to North America 1907. *Tests* South Africa (1905/6 to 1922/3, 26 matches).
Career batting
124–202–16–4821–187–25.91–7–*ct* 83
Bowling 3017–120–25.14–3–1–8/70
Test batting
26–46–1–1008–103–22.40–1–*ct* 24
Bowling 702–35–20.05–1–1–8/70
His most successful visit to England was in 1907 when he hit 943 runs, av 29.46, in first-class matches.

Snow, Albert Henry Percival
Amateur. *b:* 9.8.1852, Bedford. *d:* 5.4.1909, Gunnersbury, Middlesex. Lower order batsman, left-arm fast bowler. *Team* Middlesex (1875–76, 4 matches).
Career batting
4–8–3–9–3–1.80–0–*ct* 1
Bowling 308–22–14.00–2–0–5/35
He also played for Bedfordshire.

Snow, John Augustine
Professional. *b:* 13.10.1941, Peopleton, Worcestershire. Lower order right-hand batsman, right-arm fast medium bowler. *Sch* Christ's Hospital. *Team* Sussex (1961–77, 267 matches). *Tours* MCC to West Indies 1967/8, to Ceylon and Pakistan 1968/9, to Australia 1970/1; Robins to South Africa 1972/3; Cavaliers to West Indies 1969/70; International XI to South Africa 1975/6. *Tests* England (1965–76, 49 matches).
Career batting
346–451–110–4832–73*–14.17–0–*ct* 125
Bowling 26675–1174–22.72–56–9–8/87
Test bowling
49–71–14–772–73–13.54–0–*ct* 16
Bowling 5387–202–26.66–8–1–7/40
He took 100 wickets in a season twice (best 126, av 19.09, in 1966). A controversial cricketer, his greatest Test series were those in the West Indies in 1967/8 and in Australia in 1970/1; his best series in England being in 1975 against Australia. At his peak he was the leading fast bowler in England, but was too often at loggerheads with authority. When he signed for Kerry Packer's WSC his first-class cricket virtually ended. His autobiography was entitled 'Cricket Rebel'. He also published two volumes of poetry.

Snow, Philip Sidney
Amateur. *b:* 2.7.1907, Kendal, Westmoreland. Middle order right-hand batsman, right-arm medium off break bowler. *Sch* Shrewsbury. *Team* Oxford U (1928–29).
Career batting
2–4–0–41–22–10.25–0–*ct* 1
Bowling 119–5–23.80–0–0–2/31

Snowden, Arthur Owen
Amateur. *b:* 7.5.1885, Ramsgate, Kent. *d:* 22.5.1964, Canterbury, Kent. Middle order right-hand batsman, left-arm medium pace bowler. *Sch* Rugby. *Teams* Oxford U (1905); Kent (1911, 1 match).
Career batting
6–11–1–142–54–14.20–0–*ct* 2
Bowling 38–0
His final first-class match was for MCC in 1912.

Snowden, Alexander William
Amateur. *b:* 15.8.1913, Peterborough, *d:* 7.5.1981, Peterborough, Opening right-hand batsman, left-arm medium pace bowler, good short leg. *Sch* King's, Peterborough. *Team* Northamptonshire (1931–39, 136 matches).
Career batting
136–250–10–4343–128–18.09–2–*ct* 46
Bowling 22–2–11.00–0–0–1/5
He was originally a left-hand batsman, but persuaded at school to change to right. He hit 1,000 runs, av 20.40, in 1934

Snowden, William
Cricketer. *b:* 27.9.1952, Prescot, Lancashire. Opening right-hand batsman, right-arm medium pace bowler. *Sch* Merchant Taylor's, Crosby. *Team* Cambridge U (1972–75, blue all four years).
Career batting
37–69–3–1413–108*–21.40–3–*ct* 10
Bowling 13–0

Soames, Henry
Amateur. *b:* 18.1.1843, Brighton, Sussex. *d:* 30.8.1913, Salisbury, Wiltshire. Brother of W. A. (Sussex). Middle order batsman. *Sch* Brighton. *Team* Hampshire (1867, 1 match).
Career batting
1–2–0–54–52–27.00–0–*ct* 0

Soames, William Aldwin
Amateur. *b:* 10.7.1850, Brighton, Sussex. *d:* 27.12.1916, Bank Station, City of London. Brother of Henry (Hampshire). Middle order right-hand batsman, good deep field. *Sch* Brighton. *Team* Sussex (1875, 3 matches).
Career batting
3–5–0–17–11–3.40–0–*ct* 2

Soar, Thomas
Professional. *b:* 3.9.1865, Whitemoor, Notts. *d:* 17.5.1939, Llandovery, Carmarthenshire. Lower

order right-hand batsman, right-arm fast bowler. *Team* Hampshire (1895–1904, 101 matches).
Career batting
101–173–29–1927–95–13.38–0–*ct* 49
Bowling 7697–323–23.82–23–7–8/38

He made his debut for Hampshire in 1888, so that for several seasons he played only second-class County cricket. He also played for Carmarthenshire.

Sobers, Sir Garfield St Aubrun
Professional. *b:* 28.7.1936, Bay Land, Bridgetown, Barbados. Brilliant middle order left-hand batsman, left-arm medium or slow bowler, good field. *Teams* Barbados (1952/3 to 1973/4); South Australia (1961/2 to 1963/4, 26 matches); Nottinghamshire (1968–74, 107 matches). *Tours* West Indies to England 1957, 1963, 1966, 1969, 1973, to Australia 1960/1, 1968/9, to New Zealand 1955/6, 1968/9, to Ceylon and India 1966/7, to India and Pakistan 1958/9; Rest of World to Pakistan 1970/1, to Australia 1971/2; Swanton to India 1963/4; Cavaliers to West Indies and India 1962/3. *Tests* West Indies (1953/4 to 1973/4, 93 matches).
Career batting
383–609–93–28315–365*–54.87–86–*ct* 407
Bowling 28941–1043–27.74–36–1–9/49
Test batting
93–160–21–8032–365*–57.78–26–*ct* 109
Bowling 7999–235–34.03–6–0–6/73

The outstanding all-rounder of post war cricket, his records in Test cricket alone speak for themselves. He was the first Test cricketer to hit over 8,000 runs in his career, a total which included 365* for West Indies v Pakistan at Kingston in 1957/8, creating a new record for the highest individual innings in Test cricket. He is one of the few bowlers to capture over 200 Test wickets, and this fact, allied to his 109 catches demonstrates his standing amongst the greatest players of all time. He captained the West Indies in 39 Tests, which was, at the time, yet another record.

Of his five West Indian tours to England the outstanding visit came in 1966, when his Test record was quite incredible – 722 runs, av 103.14, and 20 wickets, av 27.25.

He joined Nottinghamshire as captain in 1968 and remained with the County until he retired in 1974. He hit 1,000 runs in a season in England nine times, his best season being 1970 with 1,742 runs, av 75.73, when he also captained the Rest of the World in five matches against England. His most famous feat in County cricket was to hit 6 sixes off a single six-ball over delivered by M. A. Nash of Glamorgan at Swansea in 1968. His best bowling was 9/49 for West Indies v Kent at Canterbury in 1966. He hit 1,000 runs in an overseas season five times.

On retiring from first-class cricket he was knighted for his services to the game.

Soden, Frederick Brewer
Amateur. *b:* 30.3.1846, Clapham Common, Surrey. *d:* 13.4.1877, Lambeth, Surrey. Right-hand batsman, right-hand round-arm medium bowler. *Sch* Brighton. *Team* Surrey (1870–71, 3 matches).
Career batting
3–6–1–35–18*–7.00–0–*ct* 1
Bowling 17–2–8.50–0–0–1/2

Soga, Dennis W.
Amateur. *b:* 1916, South Africa. *d: circa* 1945, South Africa. Right-hand batsman, off break bowler. *Team* Scotland (1936).
Career batting
1–2–0–25–24–12.50–0–*ct* 0

Sohoni, Sriranga Wasudeo
Amateur. *b:* 5.3.1918, Nimbosa, India. Lower order right-hand batsman, right-arm medium fast bowler. *Teams* Maharashtra (1935/6 to 1959/60); Hindus (1941/2 to 1945/6); Baroda (1948/9); Bombay (1951/2 to 1954/5). *Tours* India to England 1946, to Australia 1947/8. *Tests* India (1946 to 1951/2, 4 matches).
Career batting
108–164–14–4307–218*–28.71–8–*ct* 69
Bowling 7647–232–32.96–11–2–7/20
Test batting
4–7–2–83–29*–16.60–0–*ct* 2
Bowling 202–2–101.00–0–0–1/16

Although he appeared in two of the three Tests in England in 1946, his bowling was not very penetrative and in all first-class matches he took only 14 wickets, av 44.07. His final first-class match was for Bombay Governor's XI in 1963/4. His highest score was 218* for Maharashtra v Western India at Rajkot in 1940/1.

Solanky, John William
Cricketer. *b:* 20.6.1942, Dar-es-Salaam, Tanganyika. Middle order right-hand batsman, right-arm medium off break bowler. *Teams* Glamorgan (1972–76, 82 matches); East Africa (1963/4 to 1964/5).
Career batting
84–138–22–2374–73–20.46–0–*ct* 17
Bowling 4639–183–25.34–8–0–6/63

Solbé, Edward Philip
Amateur. *b:* 10.5.1902, Bromley, Kent. *d:* 29.12.1961, Nottingham. Son of F. de L. (Kent). Middle order right-hand batsman, left-arm

medium pace bowler. *Sch* Tonbridge. *Team* Kent (1921–24, 15 matches). *Tour* Cahn to North America 1933 (not first-class).
Career batting
15–24–2–371–66–16.86–0–*ct* 8
Bowling 6–0

Solbé, Frank de Lisle
Amateur. *b:* 1.6.1871, Che-foo, China. *d:* 12.1.1933, Bromley, Kent. Father of E. P. (Kent). Middle order right-hand batsman, slow under-arm bowler. *Sch* Dulwich and Blair Lodge. *Team* Kent (1891–92, 4 matches).
Career batting
5–7–0–14–9–2.00–0–*ct* 0
His final first-class match was for MCC in 1898.

Solkar, Eknath Dhondu
Cricketer. *b:* 18.3.1948, Bombay, India. Attractive middle order left-hand batsman, left-arm medium, or spin, bowler, excellent field. *Teams* Bombay (1966/7 to 1980/1); Sussex (1969, 1 match). *Tours* India to England 1971, 1974, to West Indies 1970/1, 1975/6, to Sri Lanka 1973/4, to New Zealand 1975/6. *Tests* India (1969/70 to 1976/7, 27 matches).
Career batting
189–270–36–6851–145*–29.27–8–*ct* 190
Bowling 8283–276–30.01–10–1–6/38
Test batting
27–48–6–1068–102–25.42–1–*ct* 53
Bowling 1070–18–59.44–0–0–3/28
He was most successful on the 1971 tour to England, being second in the batting averages for both the Test series and first-class matches, in the latter hitting 802 runs, av 44.55. He was not so useful in 1974. His first-class debut was for Vazir Sultan Colts XI in 1965/6.

Solly, Edward Walter
Professional. *b:* 7.5.1882, Eastry, Kent. *d:* 12.2.1966, Cefn Mably, Glamorgan. Lower order left-hand batsman, left-arm fast medium bowler. *Team* Worcestershire (1903–07, 8 matches).
Career batting
8–10–1–78–43–8.66–0–*ct* 1
Bowling 665–14–47.50–0–0–3/25

Solly, George Edward
Amateur. *b:* 27.3.1855, West Heath, Congleton, Cheshire. *d:* 10.3.1930, Mentone, France. Lower order batsman, useful bowler. *Sch* Winchester. *Team* Oxford U (1877).
Career batting
1–2–0–8–6–4.00–0–*ct* 0
Bowling 59–3–19.66–0–0–3/44
His County cricket was for Cheshire.

Solomon, Joseph Stanislaus
Amateur. *b:* 26.8.1930, Corentyne, British Guiana. Sound middle order right-hand batsman, leg break bowler. *Team* British Guiana (1956/7 to 1968/9). *Tours* West Indies to England 1963, 1966, to India and Pakistan 1958/9, to Australia 1960/1. *Tests* West Indies (1958/9 to 1964/5, 27 matches).
Career batting
104–156–28–5318–201*–41.54–12–*ct* 46
Bowling 1950–51–38.23–0–0–4/28
Test batting
27–46–7–1326–100*–34.00–1–*ct* 13
Bowling 268–4–67.00–0–0–1/20
His first-class career commenced in a spectacular fashion with three successive centuries for British Guiana – the first time a batsman had achieved such a feat. His figures on the 1963 tour to England were modest, but he was employed mainly in a defensive role as a foil to his more aggressive colleagues; he appeared in all five Tests. In 1966 he did not take part in any of the Tests. His only double century was 201* for Berbice v MCC at Blairmont in 1959/60. His throw, which ran out the last Australian batsman, led to the only tied Test at Brisbane in 1960.

Somers, Lord Arthur Herbert Tennyson
Amateur. *b:* 20.3.1887, Isle of Wight. *d:* 14.7.1944, Eastnor, Hereford. Middle order right-hand batsman. *Sch* Charterhouse. *Team* Worcestershire (1923–25, 16 matches).
Career batting
17–30–1–390–52–13.44–0–*ct* 10
Bowling 4–0
His first-class debut was for MCC in 1906.

Somerset, Arthur Plantagenet Francis Cecil
Amateur. *b:* 28.9.1889, East Preston, Sussex. *d:* 13.10.1957, Worthing, Sussex. Son of A. W. F. (Sussex). Middle order right-hand batsman, right-arm medium pace bowler. *Team* Sussex (1911–19, 9 matches). *Tours* MCC to West Indies 1910/11, 1912/13.
Career batting
29–52–10–439–39*–10.45–0–*ct* 10
Bowling 954–33–28.90–1–0–5/62

Somerset, Arthur William Fitzroy
Amateur. *b:* 20.9.1855, Brompton, Chatham, Kent. *d:* 8.1.1937, Castle Goring, Worthing, Sussex. Father of A. P. F. C. (Sussex). Middle order right-hand batsman, right-arm fast bowler, occasional wicket-keeper. *Sch* Wellington. *Teams* Sussex (1892–1905, 5 matches); London County (1900). *Tours* Brackley to West Indies 1904/5; MCC to West Indies 1910/11, 1912/13.

Career batting
48–80–19–1221–68*–20.01–0–*ct* 41–*st* 7
Bowling 53–2–26.50–0–0–2/37

His first-class debut was for Sheffield's XI in 1891, and his final first-class match in England for MCC in 1906. He captained the two MCC tours to West Indies. He was also a heavy-weight boxer of some note.

Somers-Smith, Ernest
Amateur. *b:* 1895, Sheffield, Yorkshire. *d:* 1950, Bradford, Yorkshire. Middle order right-hand batsman. *Team* Worcestershire (1921, 2 matches).
Career batting
2–4–0–33–22–8.25–0–*ct* 0

Somerville, Reginald James
Amateur. *b:* 9.10.1918, Camberwell, London. *d:* 13.8.1979, Lambeth, London. Middle order right-hand batsman, wicket-keeper. *Team* D. R. Jardine's XI (1955).
Career batting
1–1–0–3–3–3.00–0–*ct* 1

Soppitt, William James B.
Amateur. *b:* 1857, Maidstone, Kent. *d:* 1910, Fulham, London. Lower order right-hand batsman, right-arm fast medium bowler. *Team* Middlesex (1887, 1 match).
Career batting
2–4–0–15–10–3.75–0–*ct* 3
Bowling 159–5–31.80–1–0–5/159

Sorrie, James Webster
Amateur. *b:* 31.12.1885, Brechin, Angus, Scotland. *d:* 31.7.1955, Blackpool, Lancs. Right-hand batsman, useful change bowler. *Team* Scotland (1912–24).
Career batting
9–18–0–346–61–19.22–0–*ct* 4
Bowling 23–2–11.50–0–0–1/2

Souness, James McGill
Amateur. *b:* 9.11.1928, Leith, Midlothian, Scotland. Lower order right-hand batsman, right-arm fast medium bowler. *Team* Scotland (1954–55).
Career batting
3–5–0–11–7–2.20–0–*ct* 0
Bowling 301–4–75.25–0–0–2/63

Soutar, Kenneth Hannam
Amateur. *b:* 11.10.1888, Gloucester. *d:* 2.9.1914, Marylebone, London. Middle order batsman. *Sch* Marlborough. *Team* Gloucestershire (1908, 3 matches).
Career batting
3–5–0–59–16–11.80–0–*ct* 1

Souter, James Stewart
Amateur. *b:* 9.2.1944, Kanpur, India. Middle order right-hand batsman. *Sch* Haileybury. *Team* Oxford U (1948).
Career batting
3–2–0–47–30–23.50–0–*ct* 2

Southall, H.
Amateur. Middle order batsman. *Team* Worcestershire (1907, 1 match).
Career batting
1–1–0–11–11–11.00–0–*ct* 0

Southby, Sir Archibald Richard Charles
Amateur. *b:* 18.6.1910, Devonport, Devon. Opening right-hand batsman. *Sch* Eton. *Teams* Madras (1935/6 to 1936/7); Army (1939).
Career batting
7–12–0–158–33–13.16–0–*ct* 3

Southcombe, Richard
Amateur. *b:* 22.11.1909, Taunton, Somerset. Middle order right-hand batsman, off break bowler. *Team* Somerset (1936–37, 2 matches).
Career batting
2–4–0–20–10–5.00–0–*ct* 0

Southern, John Dunlop
Amateur. *b:* 5.11.1899, Derby. *d:* 7.2.1972, Melksham, Wilts. Middle order right-hand batsman. *Sch* Malvern. *Team* Derbyshire (1919–34, 5 matches).
Career batting
5–10–0–95–43–9.50–0–*ct* 0

Southern, John William
Cricketer. *b:* 2.9.1952, King's Cross, London. Lower order right-hand batsman, slow left-arm bowler. *Team* Hampshire (1975–83, 164 matches).
Career batting
164–179–71–1653–61*–15.30–0–*ct* 59
Bowling 12283–412–29.81–17–0–6/46

Southerton, James
Professional. *b:* 16.11.1827, Petworth, Sussex. *d:* 16.6.1880, Mitcham, Surrey. Tail end right-hand batsman, slow right-hand round-arm bowler. *Teams* Hampshire (1861–67, 13 matches); Sussex (1858–72, 50 matches); Surrey (1854–79, 152 matches). *Tours* Grace to Australia 1873/4 (not first-class); Lillywhite to Australia 1876/7. *Tests* England (1876/7, 2 matches).

Career batting
286–480–130–3159–82–9.02–0–*ct* 215–*st* 3
Bowling 24290–1681–14.45–192–59–9/30
Test batting
2–3–1–7–6–3.50–0–*ct* 2
Bowling 107–7–15.28–0–0–4/46

He took 100 wickets in a season ten times, going on to 200 once: 210, av 14.63, in 1870. His best innings analysis was 9 for 30 for South v North at Lord's in 1875. He had the curious experience of playing for three counties – Hampshire, Sussex and Surrey in the same season, but this was before the qualification rules were introduced.

Southwood, Albert Henry Howard
Amateur. *b:* July 1882, Taunton, Somerset. *d:* 13.7.1965, Taunton, Somerset. Middle order right-hand batsman, slow right-arm bowler. *Team* Somerset (1911-13, 3 matches).
Career batting
3–6–0–96–33–16.00–0–*ct* 0

Sowden, Abraham
Professional. *b:* 1.12.1853, Great Horton, Bradford, Yorkshire. *d:* 5.7.1921, Heaton, Bradford, Yorkshire. Middle order right-hand batsman, right-hand fast round-arm bowler. *Team* Yorkshire (1878–87, 8 matches).
Career batting
10–14–0–163–37–11.64–0–*ct* 1
Bowling 70–0

His final first-class match was for an England XI in 1902.

Sowter, Unwin
Amateur. *b:* 22.4.1839, Derby. *d:* 14.4.1910, Derby. Middle order right-hand batsman, good point field. *Sch* Derby School. *Team* Derbyshire (1871–76, 7 matches).
Career batting
7–11–1–128–47*–12.80–0–*ct* 7

He assisted in the founding of Derbyshire CCC and was for some years on the Committee.

Spanswick, John George
Professional. *b:* 30.9.1933, Folkestone, Kent. Lower order right-hand batsman, right-arm medium fast bowler. *Team* Kent (1955–56, 16 matches).
Career batting
16–22–1–135–24–6.42–0–*ct* 7
Bowling 1175–36–32.63–0–0–4/64

Sparkes, George
Professional. *b:* 1845, Westbourne, Sussex. *d:* 9.3.1908, Bosham, Sussex. Middle order batsman. *Team* Sussex (1875, 1 match).
Career batting
1–2–0–0–0–0.00–*ct* 0

Sparks, John Barnes
Amateur. *b:* 31.5.1873, Morar, India. *d:* 29.3.1920, Marylebone, London. Middle order right-hand batsman, wicket-keeper. *Team* Royal Navy (1913).
Career batting
1–2–0–17–13–8.50–0–*ct* 0

Sparling, John Trevor
Amateur. *b:* 24.7.1938, Auckland, New Zealand. Middle order right-hand batsman, off break bowler. *Team* Auckland (1956/7 to 1970/1). *Tours* New Zealand to England 1958, to South Africa and Australia 1961/2. *Tests* New Zealand (1958 to 1963/4, 11 matches).
Career batting
127–215–26–4606–105–24.37–2–*ct* 86
Bowling 7223–318–22.71–17–3–7/49
Test batting
11–20–2–229–50–12.72–0–*ct* 3
Bowling 327–5–65.40–0–0–1/9

He took 38 wickets, av 20.28, on the 1958 tour to England and played in three Tests.

Sparrow, Adolphus James
Amateur. *b:* 1869, Alverstoke, Hampshire. *d:* 1936, Sheppey, Kent. Middle order batsman. *Team* Hampshire (1902, 1 match).
Caree batting
1–1–0–1–1–1.00–0–*ct* 0

Sparrow, Guy Ratcliff
Amateur. *b:* 2.7.1877, Aston, Birmingham. *d:* 4.1.1958, Burton-on-Trent, Staffs. Middle order right-hand batsman. *Team* Derbyshire (1905, 2 matches).
Career batting
2–4–0–75–64–18.75–0–*ct* 0

Speak, Gary John
Cricketer. *b:* 26.4.1962, Chorley, Lancashire. Tail end right-hand batsman, right-arm fast medium bowler. *Team* Lancashire (1981–82, 5 matches).
Career batting
5–6–4–27–15*–13.50–0–*ct* 3
Bowling 230–1–230.00–0–0–1/78

Speak, Walter
Amateur. *b:* 20.2.1873, Ripon, Yorkshire. *d:* 21.6.1943, Victoria, British Columbia, Canada. Lower order left-hand batsman, leg break bowler. *Team* Nottinghamshire (1905, 3 matches).

Career batting
3–6–0–39–19–6.50–0–*ct* 0
Bowling 54–0

Speed, Andrew Watson
Amateur. *b:* 19.1.1899, Glasgow, Scotland. Lower order right-hand batsman, right-arm fast medium bowler. *Team* Warwickshire (1927–28, 8 matches).
Career batting
8–7–3–29–11*–7.25–0–*ct* 1
Bowling 538–29–18.55–2–0–6/81

Speed, Francis Elmer
Amateur. *b:* 28.2.1859, Paddington, London. *d:* 23.8.1928, Knowlton Court, Canterbury, Kent. Middle order right-hand batsman, wicket-keeper. *Sch* Rugby. *Team* MCC (1882–84).
Career batting
3–5–0–30–16–6.00–0–*ct* 0
He played some County cricket for Herefordshire.

Spelman, Guy Dennis
Cricketer. *b:* 18.10.1958, Westminster, London. Lower order left-hand batsman, right-arm medium pace bowler. *Sch* Sevenoaks. *Team* Kent (1980–82, 7 matches).
Career batting
7–7–1–9–4–1.50–0–*ct* 2
Bowling 357–10–35.70–0–0–2/27

Spence, Lawrence Arthur
Professional. *b:* 14.1.1932, Blaby, Leicestershire. Middle order right-hand batsman, leg break bowler, good outfield. *Team* Leicestershire (1952–54, 20 matches).
Career batting
20–34–6–326–44–11.64–0–*ct* 4
Bowling 9–0

Spencer, Alan Horace
Professional. *b:* 4.7.1936, Lee Green, London. Middle order right-hand batsman, off break bowler, slip field. *Team* Worcestershire (1957–61, 27 matches).
Career batting
27–52–1–934–85–18.31–0–*ct* 22
Bowling 23–0

Spencer, Charles Richard
Amateur. *b:* 21.6.1903, Llandough, Cardiff. *d:* 29.9.1941, Gosport, Hampshire. Lower order right-hand batsman, wicket-keeper. *Sch* Clifton. *Teams* Oxford U (1923); Glamorgan (1925, 1 match).
Career batting
4–6–2–46–17–11.50–0–*ct* 1–*st* 1

Spencer, Charles Terrance
Professional. *b:* 18.8.1931, Leicester. Lower order right-hand batsman, right-arm medium pace bowler. *Team* Leicestershire (1952–74, 496 matches).
Career batting
506–687–142–5871–90–10.77–0–*ct* 379
Bowling 36486–1367–26.69–47–6–9/63
He took 123 wickets, av 19.56, in 1961. His best innings analysis was 9 for 63 for Leicestershire v Yorkshire at Huddersfield in 1954. He became a first-class umpire.

Spencer, Harry
Professional. Middle order batsman. *Team* Derbyshire (1895, 1 match).
Career batting
1–1–0–0–0–0.00–0–*ct* 0

Spencer, Helm
Professional. *b:* 31.12.1891, Padiham, Lancashire. *d:* 1974, Burnley, Lancashire. Lower order right-hand batsman, right-arm fast bowler. *Teams* Lancashire (1914, 2 matches); Glamorgan (1923–25, 39 matches); Wales (1923–24).
Career batting
43–73–4–799–56–11.57–0–*ct* 40
Bowling 2517–111–22.67–4–0–7/33

Spencer, Harry Norman Ernest
Amateur. *b:* 1.10.1901, Shipston on Stour, Warwickshire. *d:* 13.8.1954, Hammersmith, London. Right-hand batsman, right-arm medium bowler. *Teams* Warwickshire (1930, 3 matches); Worcestershire (1927, 1 match).
Career batting
4–4–1–32–26–10.66–*ct* 3
Bowling 214–3–71.33–0–0–1/34

Spencer, John
Cricketer. *b:* 6.10.1949, Brighton, Sussex. Lower order right-hand batsman, right-arm medium pace bowler. *Teams* Sussex (1969–80, 186 matches), Cambridge U (1970–72, blue all three years).
Career batting
215–286–80–2787–79–13.52–0–*ct* 75
Bowling 14622–554–26.39–21–1–6/19

Spencer, Ralph
Amateur. *b:* 14.4.1861, Newburn-on-Tyne, Northumberland. *d:* 23.8.1926, Netherwitton Hall, Morpeth, Northumberland. Middle order right-hand batsman, right-arm fast bowler, slip field. *Sch* Harrow. *Team* Cambridge U (1881–82, blue 1881).

Career batting
12–20–0–181–57–9.05–0–*ct* 23
Bowling 461–19–24.26–0–0–3/19
He played County cricket for Northumberland.

Spencer, Thomas
Amateur. *b:* 10.6.1850. *d:* 1933, Newton Abbot, Devon. Middle order batsman. *Team* Somerset (1891–93, 3 matches).
Career batting
3–5–1–30–14–7.50–0–*ct* 5

Spencer, Thomas William
Professional. *b:* 22.3.1914, Deptford, London. Middle order right-hand batsman, right-arm medium pace bowler. *Team* Kent (1935–46, 76 matches).
Career batting
76–120–13–2152–96–20.11–0–*ct* 36
Bowling 19–1–19.00–0–0–1/19
He was appointed to the first-class umpires' list in 1950 and did not retire until 1980, standing in 17 Test matches.

Spencer, Walter Gordon
Amateur. *b:* 2.8.1912, Chingford, Essex. *d:* 20.7.1971, Chelmsford, Essex. Right-hand batsman, slow left-arm bowler. *Sch* Bancroft's. *Team* Essex (1938–48, 3 matches).
Career batting
3–5–1–52–25–13.00–0–*ct* 0
Bowling 8–1–8.00–0–0–1/8
He also played for Suffolk.

Spencer-Smith, Gilbert Joshua
Amateur. *b:* 17.12.1843, Brooklands, Hants. *d:* 4.2.1928, Burlesdon, Hampshire. Twin brother of Orlando (Hampshire). Middle order right-hand batsman, slow right-arm bowler. *Sch* Eton. *Team* Hampshire (1864, 1 match).
Career batting
1–2–0–20–11–10.00–0–*ct* 0

Spencer-Smith, Rev Orlando
Amateur. *b:* 17.12.1843, Brooklands, Hampshire. *d:* 23.11.1920, Swanwick, Southampton. Twin brother of G. J. (Hampshire). Middle order right-hand batsman, slow right-arm bowler. *Sch* Eton. *Teams* Hampshire (1866, 1 match); Oxford U (1866, blue).
Career batting
7–11–1–354–98–35.40–0–*ct* 0
Bowling 130–3–43.33–0–0–2/53
He also played for Dorset.

Spens, Major General James
Amateur. *b:* 30.3.1853, Subathoo, India. *d:* 19.6.1934, Folkestone, Kent. Middle order right-hand batsman, right-hand medium pace round-arm bowler, good cover point. *Sch* Rugby and Haileybury. *Team* Hampshire (1884–99, 10 matches).
Career batting
13–25–1–581–118*–24.20–1–*ct* 6
Bowling 16–0

Sperry, James
Professional. *b:* 19.3.1910, Thornton, Leicestershire. Lower order left-hand batsman, left-arm fast medium bowler. *Team* Leicestershire (1937–52, 187 matches).
Career batting
188–265–99–1193–35–7.18–0–*ct* 52
Bowling 13958–492–28.36–19–4–7/19
His best season was 1948 with 81 wickets, av 23.55.

Spicer, Norman
Amateur. *b:* 1879, Eltham, Kent. *d:* 1.9.1936, Regent's Park, London. Lower order batsman, useful bowler. *Sch* The Leys. *Team* Cambridge U (1901).
Career batting
1–2–0–7–6–3.50–0–*ct* 2
Bowling 52–2–26.00–0–0–1/1
An all-round athlete, he represented Cambridge at rugby football and athletics, as well as being a noted lacrosse player. He also played rugby for Kent.

Spicer, Peter Alfred
Professional. *b:* 11.5.1939, Ilford, Essex. *d:* 18.8.1969, Hainault, Essex. He was killed in a road accident. Middle order left-hand batsman, slow left-arm bowler. *Team* Essex (1962–63, 17 matches).
Career batting
17–29–2–526–86–19.48–0–*ct* 4
Bowling 55–2–27.50–0–0–2/1

Spicer, William Baldwin
Professional. *b:* 18.5.1846, Kensington, London. *d:* 1892, Lambeth, London. Lower order batsman, left-hand medium pace round-arm bowler, slip field. *Team* Surrey (1870, 1 match).
Career batting
1–2–0–16–14–8.00–0–*ct* 0
Bowling 17–1–17.00–0–0–1/17

Spiller, Cecil Willmington
Amateur. *b:* 19.8.1900, Cardiff. *d:* 1974, Cardiff. Lower order batsman, useful bowler. *Team* Glamorgan (1922, 2 matches).

Career batting
2–4–0–20–14–5.00–0–*ct* 0
Bowling 144–4–36.00–0–0–3/50

Spiller, William (John)
Amateur. *b:* 8.7.1886, Cardiff, Wales. *d:* 9.6.1970, Cardiff, Wales. Middle order right-hand batsman. *Team* Glamorgan (1921–23, 13 matches).
Career batting
13–22–0–411–104–18.68–1–*ct* 7
Bowling 31–0

A noted rugby footballer, he was a centre three-quarter for Cardiff and Wales.

Spillman, George
Professional. *b:* 24.10.1856, Strand, London. *d:* 18.4.1911, Brighton, Sussex. Middle order right-hand batsman, wicket-keeper. *Sch* King's College, London. *Team* Middlesex (1886, 10 matches).
Career batting
12–20–0–477–87–23.85–0–*ct* 14–*st* 3
Bowling 12–1–12.00–0–0–1/12

About 1902 he fell down the cabin stairs of a passenger steamer and so damaged his right leg that it had to be amputated, thus ending his cricket career – he was a coach in Jersey at the time.

Spilsbury, John William Edward
Amateur. *b:* 27.10.1933, Worcester. Right-hand batsman, right-arm fast medium bowler. *Team* Worcestershire (1952, 1 match).
Career batting
1–1–0–16–16–16.00–0–*ct* 1
Bowling 86–0

Spinks, Edwin Frederick
Professional. *b:* 3.8.1902. *d:* 19.10.1982, Grays, Essex. Lower order batsman, useful bowler. *Team*, Essex (1926, 2 matches).
Career batting
2–3–1–2–2–1.00–0–*ct* 1
Bowling 81–0

Spiro, Douglas Gray
Amateur. *b:* 21.12.1863, Melbourne, Australia. *d:* 16.1.1935, Westminster, London. Hard-hitting middle order right-hand batsman, right-arm medium pace bowler, good deep field. *Sch* Harrow. *Team* Cambridge U (1883–85, blue 1884).
Career batting
12–21–1–207–47–10.35–0–*ct* 3

Owing to an accident he played little cricket in 1883. His final first-class match was for MCC in 1890.

Spofforth, Frederick Robert
Amateur. *b:* 9.9.1853, Balmain, New South Wales, Australia. *d:* 4.6.1926, Ditton Hill Lodge, Long Ditton, Surrey. Hard-hitting lower order right-hand batsman, right-arm fast medium bowler. *Team* New South Wales (1874/5 to 1884/5, 12 matches); Victoria (1885/6 to 1887/8, 5 matches). *Tours* Australia to England 1878, 1880, 1882, 1884, 1886, to North America 1878. *Tests* Australia (1876/7 to 1886/7, 18 matches).
Career batting
155–236–41–1928–56–9.88–0–*ct* 83
Bowling 12760–853–14.95–84–32–9/18
Test batting
18–29–6–217–50–9.43–0–*ct* 11
Bowling 1731–94–18.41–7–4–7/44

His record on his tours to England was quite outstanding. In 1884 he took 207 wickets, av 12.82; in 1882, 157, av 13.24; and in 1878, 97, av 11.00. He was known as the 'Demon' bowler. In 1888 he emigrated to England and played for Derbyshire from 1889 to 1891 (not first-class). His best bowling was 9/18 for Australians v Oxford U at Oxford in 1886. He appeared regularly in the Scarborough Festival matches from 1888, and his final first-class match was for MCC v Yorkshire at Scarborough in 1897.

Spooner, Archibald Franklin
Amateur. *b:* 21.5.1886, Litherland, Lancashire. *d:* 11.1.1965, Dartmouth, Devon. Brother of R. H. (Lancashire). Stylish middle order right-hand batsman. *Sch* Haileybury. *Team* Lancashire (1906–09, 18 matches).
Career batting
18–33–1–500–83–15.62–0–*ct* 8

Spooner, Reginald Herbert
Amateur. *b:* 21.10.1880, Litherland, Lancashire. *d:* 2.10.1961, Lincoln. Brother of A. F. (Lancashire). Stylish opening right-hand batsman, slow right-arm bowler. *Sch* Marlborough. *Team* Lancashire (1899–1921, 170 matches). *Tests* England (1905–12, 10 matches).
Career batting
237–393–16–13681–247–36.28–31–*ct* 142
Bowling 582–6–97.00–0–0–1/5
Test batting
10–15–0–481–119–32.06–1–*ct* 4

He hit 1,000 runs in a season six times, going on to 2,000 once: 2,312, av 51.37, in 1911. Each of his five double centuries was for Lancashire, the highest being 247 v Nottinghamshire at Trent Bridge in 1903. His final first-class match was for MCC in 1923. He has come to be regarded as the supreme example of the amateur batsman of the 'Golden Age'. A noted rugby footballer, he was a centre three-quarter for Liverpool and England.

Spooner, Richard Thompson
Professional. *b:* 30.12.1919, Stockton-on-Tees, Co Durham. Forceful opening left-hand batsman, wicket-keeper. *Team* Warwickshire (1948–59, 312 matches). *Tours* MCC to India, Pakistan and Ceylon 1951/2, to West Indies 1953/4; Commonwealth to India 1950/1. *Tests* England 1951/2 to 1955, 7 matches).
Career batting
359–580–72–13851–168*–27.26–12–*ct* 589–*st* 178
Bowling 46–0
Test batting
7–14–1–354–92–27.23–0–3–*ct* 10–*st* 2
He hit 1,000 runs in a season six times (best 1,767, av 43.09, in 1951). He also played for Durham.

Spottiswoode, William Hugh
Amateur. *b:* 12.7.1864, Belgravia, London. *d:* 20.8.1915, Llandrindod Wells, Radnorshire. Hard-hitting middle order right-hand batsman, slow under-arm bowler. *Sch* Eton. *Team* Kent (1890, 2 matches).
Career batting
2–3–0–51–37–17.00–0–*ct* 1
He was a partner in the publishers, Eyre and Spottiswoode.

Spowart, Thomas
Amateur. *b:* 24.3.1903, Dunfermline, Fife, Scotland. *d:* 12.5.1971, Edinburgh, Scotland. Right-hand batsman. *Team* Scotland (1932–38).
Career batting
4–7–0–98–66–14.00–0–*ct* 0

Spray, Philip Henry
Cricketer. *b:* 28.9.1945, Bedford. Middle order right-hand batsman. *Sch* Bedford. *Team* Oxford U (1967–68).
Career batting
9–13–2–135–54–12.27–0–*ct* 4

Spring, Trevor Coleridge
Amateur. *b:* 6.2.1882, Kidderpore, Bengal, India. *d:* 13.3.1926, Westminster, London. He died suddenly after an operation. Middle order right-hand batsman, useful bowler. *Sch* Blundells. *Team* Somerset (1909–10, 8 matches).
Career batting
11–19–1–324–117–18.00–1–*ct* 3
Bowling 71–3–23.66–0–0–3/59
His final first-class match was for the Army in 1919. He also played for Devon and Northumberland.

Spring, William Amos
Professional. *b:* 17.5.1880, Dulwich, Surrey. *d:* 14.3.1958, Chase Side, Enfield, Middlesex. Middle order right-hand batsman, right-arm fast medium bowler. *Team* Surrey (1906–13, 68 matches).
Career batting
68–106–13–1968–135–21.16–2–*ct* 54
Bowling 2093–71–29.47–3–1–6/38

Springall, John Denis
Professional. *b:* 19.9.1932, Southwark, London. Opening or middle order right-hand batsman, right-arm medium pace bowler, occasional wicket-keeper. *Team* Nottinghamshire (1955–63, 119 matches).
Career batting
121–224–24–5176–107–25.88–2–*ct* 51
Bowling 3312–80–41.40–2–0–6/43
He hit 1,000 runs in a season twice (best 1,488, av 35.42, in 1959).

Sprinks, Henry Robert James
Amateur. *b:* 19.8.1905, Alexandria, Egypt. Lower order right-hand batsman, right-arm fast bowler. *Team* Hampshire (1925–29, 21 matches).
Career batting
21–27–9–167–40–9.27–0–*ct* 14
Bowling 1338–29–46.13–0–0–4/56

Sprot, Edward Mark
Amateur. *b:* 4.2.1872, Edinburgh, Scotland. *d:* 8.10.1945, Fareham, Hampshire. Forcing middle order right-hand batsman, right-arm medium pace bowler, good close field. *Sch* Harrow. *Team* Hampshire (1898–1914, 267 matches).
Career batting
270–458–28–12328–147–28.66–13–*ct* 228
Bowling 1865–55–33.90–1–0–5/28
He hit 1,000 runs in a season four times (best 1,272, av 33.47, in 1907). A talented all-round sportsman, he won the Army Rackets Challenge Cup, was a good golfer, a keen shot and fisherman and a noted billiards player.

Sproule, Wallace
Amateur. *b:* 17.4.1891, Killyleagh, Co Down. *d:* 10.5.1957, Belfast. Lower order right-hand batsman, right-arm medium pace bowler. *Team* Ireland (1923).
Career batting
1–2–0–1–1–0.50–0–*ct* 2
Bowling 83–6–13.83–0–0–4/64

Spry, Edward James
Professional. *b:* 31.7.1881, Bristol, Gloucs. *d:* 19.11.1958, Bristol, Gloucs. Lower order right-hand batsman, leg break bowler. *Team* Gloucestershire (1899–1921, 89 matches).

Career batting
89–154–24–1447–76–11.13–0–*ct* 44
Bowling 4307–149–28.90–13–3–8/52

Spurr, Harold
Amateur. *b:* 17.6.1889, Leytonstone, Essex. *d:* 21.12.1962, Dunmow, Essex. Middle order right-hand batsman. *Sch* Merchant Taylors'. *Team* Essex (1923, 1 match).
Career batting
1–2–0–13–9–6.50–0–*ct* 0

Spurway, Rev Edward Popham
Amateur. *b:* 4.4.1863, Heathfield, Somerset. *d:* 8.2.1914, Heathfield, Somerset. Brother of R. P. (Somerset). Middle order right-hand batsman. *Sch* Charterhouse. *Team* Somerset (1885–98, 2 matches).
Career batting
2–4–0–26–15–6.50–0–*ct* 1

Spurway, Rev Francis Edward
Amateur. *b:* 8.8.1894, Winchester, Hampshire. *d:* 30.12.1980, Halse, Taunton, Somerset. Lower order right-hand batsman, wicket-keeper. *Sch* King's Bruton. *Team* Somerset (1920–29, 23 matches).
Career batting
23–39–4–328–35–9.37–*ct* 29–*st* 14

Spurway, Michael Vyvyan
Amateur. *b:* 24.1.1909, Heathfield, Somerset. Lower order right-hand batsman, wicket-keeper. *Sch* St. Edward's, Oxford. *Team* Somerset (1929, 3 matches).
Career batting
3–5–2–22–10–7.33–0–*ct* 4–*st* 1

Spurway, Robert Popham
Amateur. *b:* 16.7.1866, Heathfield, Somerset. *d:* 4.12.1898, Woolwich, Kent. Brother of E. P. (Somerset). Middle order right-hand batsman, off break bowler. *Sch* Haileybury. *Teams* Natal (1889/90); Somerset (1893–98, 16 matches).
Career batting
19–34–3–578–108*–18.64–1–*ct* 3

Spyers, Thomas Roper
Amateur. *b:* 7.12.1868, Faversham, Kent. *d:* 19.2.1961, Chelsea, London. Middle order right-hand batsman, wicket-keeper. *Sch* Radley. *Team* MCC (1890).
Career batting
1–2–0–9–9–4.50–0–*ct* 0

In a very varied life he was an actor, a theatrical producer, schoolmaster and hotel proprietor.

Squire, Dick
Professional. *b:* 31.12.1864, Bradford, Yorkshire. *d:* 28.4.1922, Scholes, Yorkshire. Lower order batsman, slow left-arm bowler. *Team* Yorkshire (1893, 1 match).
Career batting
1–2–0–0–0–0.00–0–*ct* 0
Bowling 25–0

Squire, Samuel Gimson
Amateur. *b:* 14.1.1879, Leicester. *d:* 18.9.1962, Duston, Northants. Tail end batsman, useful bowler. *Sch* Wyggeston GS. *Team* Cambridge U (1900).
Career batting
1–2–0–12–12–6.00–0–*ct* 0
Bowling 61–2–30.50–0–0–2/61

Squires, Harry Stanley
Amateur, turned professional in 1930. *b:* 22.2.1909, Kingston-on-Thames, Surrey. *d:* 24.1.1950, Richmond, Surrey. Stylish middle order right-hand batsman, right-arm medium off break, or leg break, bowler. *Team* Surrey (1928–49, 402 matches).
Career batting
410–658–44–19186–236–31.24–37–*ct* 140
Bowling 10817–306–35.34–7–0–8/52

He hit 1,000 runs in a season eleven times (best 1,847, av 36.94, in 1947). His three double centuries were all for Surrey, the highest being 236 v Lancashire at the Oval in 1933.

Squires, Peter John
Cricketer. *b:* 4.8.1951, Ripon, Yorkshire. Middle order right-hand batsman. *Team* Yorkshire (1972–76, 49 matches).
Career batting
49–84–8–1271–70–16.72–0–*ct* 14
Bowling 32–0

A noted rugby footballer, he played for Harrogate, Yorkshire and England, touring South Africa in 1973.

Stacey, Charles Frederick
Professional. *b:* 27.4.1878, Chalfont St Giles, Buckinghamshire. *d:* 1950, Scotland. Lower order batsman, useful bowler. *Team* Surrey (1901, 1 match).
Career batting
1–1–1–0–0*–no av–0–*ct* 0
Bowling 148–1–148.00–0–0–1/78

Stackpole, Keith Raymond
Amateur. *b:* 10.7.1940, Collingwood, Victoria, Australia. Son of K. W. (Victoria). Excellent opening right-hand batsman, leg break bowler, good slip field. *Team* Victoria (1959/60 to 1973/4,

75 matches). *Tours* Australia to South Africa 1966/7, 1969/70, to India and Ceylon 1969/70, to England 1972, to West Indies 1972/3, to New Zealand 1973/4. *Tests* Australia (1965/6 to 1973/4, 43 matches).
Career batting
167–279–22–10100–207–39.29–22–*ct* 166
Bowling 5814–148–39.28–2–0–5/38
Test batting
43–80–5–2807–207–37.42–7–*ct* 47
Bowling 1001–15–66.73–0–0–2/33

On his only tour to England he topped the Test batting averages with 485 runs, av 53.88, and in first-class matches hit 1,309 runs, av 43.63, altogether being the success of the tour. His highest score was 207 for Australia v England at Brisbane in 1970/1. He hit 1,000 runs in an Australian season once.

Staddon, Ernest Henry
Amateur. *b:* 1883, Bristol, Gloucs. *d:* 23.7.1965, Bristol, Gloucs. Middle order batsman. *Team* Gloucestershire (1912, 1 match).
Career batting
1–2–0–16–12–8.00–0–*ct* 0

Stafford, James Pratt
Professional. *b:* 1844, Godalming, Surrey. *d:* 24.8.1919, Southsea, Hampshire. Lower order batsman, useful bowler. *Team* Surrey (1864, 1 match).
Career batting
1–2–0–0–0–0.00–0–*ct* 0
Bowling 31–0

Staines, Alfred
Professional. *b:* 22.5.1838, Charlton, Greenwich, Kent. *d:* 13.6.1910, Sydenham, Kent. Tail end right-hand batsman, wicket-keeper. *Team* Kent (1863–64, 5 matches).
Career batting
5–10–4–6–2–1.00–0–*ct* 4–*st* 5

Stainton, Robert George
Amateur. *b:* 23.5.1910, Whitstable, Kent. Middle order right-hand batsman, slow right-arm bowler. *Sch* Malvern. *Teams* Oxford U (1932–34, blue 1933); Sussex (1936–47, 45 matches).
Career batting
61–104–8–2330–89–24.27–0–*ct* 27
Bowling 25–1–25.00–0–0–1/12

Stallard, George
Amateur. *b:* 14.1.1856, Worcester. *d:* 21.8.1912, North Tawton, Devon. Middle order right-hand batsman. *Sch* Rossall. *Team* An England XI (1875).
Career batting
1 match, did not bat –*ct* 0

He was Chief Justice of Sierra Leone, 1897 to 1901.

Stallibrass, Michael James Dahl
Cricketer. *b:* 28.6.1951, Exeter, Devon. Lower order left-hand batsman, off break bowler. *Sch* Lancing. *Team* Oxford U (1972–74, blue 1974).
Career batting
21–31–7–194–24–8.08–0–*ct* 7
Bowling 993–22–45.13–1–0–5/80

Stanbury, Richard Vivian Macaulay
Amateur. *b:* 5.2.1916, Madras, India. Lower order right-hand batsman, wicket-keeper. *Sch* Shrewsbury. *Team* Somerset (1935–36, 2 matches).
Career batting
2–4–1–31–21–10.33–0–*ct* 2

Standen, James Alfred
Professional. *b:* 30.5.1935, Edmonton, London. Lower order right-hand batsman, right-arm medium pace bowler. *Team* Worcestershire (1959–70, 133 matches).
Career batting
133–174–28–2092–92*–14.32–*ct* 84
Bowling 7934–313–25.34–13–0–7/30

His best season was 1964, with 64 wickets, av 13.00. He also played for Hertfordshire. A noted goalkeeper, he played soccer for Arsenal, Luton, West Ham United, Millwall and Portsmouth and Detroit Cougars, and won an FA Cup Winners medal with West Ham in 1964.

Standing, David Kevin
Cricketer. *b:* 21.10.1963, Brighton, Sussex. Middle order right-hand batsman, off break bowler. *Team* Sussex (1983, 4 matches).
Career batting
4–8–3–240–60–48.00–0–*ct* 2
Bowling 32–0

Standring, Kenneth Brooks
Amateur. *b:* 17.2.1935, Clitheroe, Lancashire. Lower order left-hand batsman, right-arm fast bowler. *Team* Lancashire (1955–59, 8 matches).
Career batting
13–22–5–255–41–15.00–0–*ct* 2
Bowling 867–25–34.68–0–0–4/61

Stanford, Ross Milton
Amateur. *b:* 25.9.1917, Fulham, South Australia. Middle order right-hand batsman. *Team* South Australia (1935/6 to 1947/8, 10 matches). *Tours* Australian Services to England 1945, to India and Ceylon 1945/6.

Career batting
23–35–3–832–153–26.00–1–*ct* 4
Bowling 25–0

Stanhope, Rt Hon Edward
Amateur. *b:* 24.9.1840, Westminster, London. *d:* 21.12.1893, Chevening, Sevenoaks, Kent. Middle order right-hand batsman. *Sch* Harrow. *Team* Kent (1861, 1 match).
Career batting
3–6–1–44–17–8.80–0–*ct* 1
His final first-class match was for MCC in 1879. He was MP for Horncastle, Lincolnshire and held at one time the offices of Secretary of State for the Colonies and Secretary of State for War.

Stanley, Edward
Amateur. *b:* 29.6.1852, Wincanton, Somerset. *d:* 7.4.1896, Accra, Gold Coast. Middle order batsman. *Sch* Tonbridge. *Team* Somerset (1884, 1 match).
Career batting
1–1–0–0–0–0.00–0–*ct* 0

Stanley, Ernest A. W.
Professional. *b:* 27.9.1926, Leyton, Essex. Middle order right-hand batsman, off break bowler. *Team* Essex (1950–52, 13 matches).
Career batting
13–21–3–226–35–12.55–0–*ct* 2
Bowling 8–0

Stanley, Harry Cecil
Amateur. *b:* 16.2.1888, Rotherham, Yorkshire. *d:* 18.5.1934, Scarborough, Yorkshire. Middle order right-hand batsman. *Team* Yorkshire (1911–13, 8 matches).
Career batting
8–13–0–155–42–11.92–0–*ct* 6

Stanley, Henry Thomas
Amateur. *b:* 20.8.1873, London. *d:* 16.9.1900, Hekpoort, Transvaal, South Africa. He died whilst on active service in the Boer War. Middle order right-hand batsman. *Sch* Eton. *Team* Somerset (1894–99, 50 matches). *Tour* Priestley to West Indies 1896/7.
Career batting
63–117–4–1691–127–14.96–1–*ct* 27
Bowling 250–9–27.77–0–0–2/11

Stanley-Clarke, Arthur Christopher Lancelot
Amateur. *b:* 30.6.1886, Brighton, Sussex. *d:* 8.1.1983, Shiel Bailey, Co Dublin, Ireland. Middle order right-hand batsman. *Sch* Winchester. *Team* Army (1923–24).
Career batting
5–8–1–262–66–37.42–0–*ct* 1
His County cricket was for Dorset.

Stannard, George Arthur
Professional. *b:* 9.7.1892, Steyning, Sussex. *d:* 28.6.1971, Brighton, Sussex. Middle order right-hand batsman, right-arm slow medium bowler. *Team* Sussex (1914–25, 73 matches).
Career batting
73–121–14–1437–114–13.43–1–*ct* 15
Bowling 724–14–51.71–0–0–4/70

Stanning, Henry Duncan
Amateur. *b:* 14.11.1881, Leyland, Lancashire. *d:* 5.3.1946, Kampi-Ya-Moto, Kenya. Brother of John (Lancashire). Middle order right-hand batsman. *Sch* Rugby. *Team* Lancashire (33 matches).
Career batting
33–54–1–898–86–16.94–0–*ct* 10
Bowling 3–0

Stanning, John
Amateur. *b:* 10.10.1877, Leyland, Lancashire. *d:* 19.5.1929, Nakwin, Kenya. He died in a motor accident. Brother of H. D. (Lancashire). Sound opening or middle order right-hand batsman, good field. *Sch* Rugby. *Teams* Cambridge U (1900, blue); Lancashire (1900–03, 4 matches). *Tour* Hawke to Australia and New Zealand 1902/3.
Career batting
26–45–5–964–120–24.10–1–*ct* 19
Bowling 15–0
His first-class debut was for MCC in 1899. He also played for Cheshire.

Stanning, John
Amateur. *b:* 24.6.1919, Nairobi, Kenya. Middle order right-hand batsman. *Sch* Winchester. *Teams* Oxford U (1939, blue); Worcestershire (1939–46, 9 matches).
Career batting
16–22–3–403–56*–21.21–0–*ct* 7

Stanton, John Latham
Amateur. *b:* 8.3.1901, Bristol. *d:* 27.6.1973, Midhurst, Sussex. Middle order right-hand batsman. *Sch* Marlborough. *Team* Gloucestershire (1921–22, 4 matches).
Career batting
4–7–0–80–47–11.42–0–*ct* 0

Stanworth, John
Cricketer. *b:* 30.9.1960, Oldham, Lancashire.

Right-hand batsman, wicket-keeper. *Team* Lancashire (1983, 3 matches).
Career batting
3–6–2–90–31*–22.50–0–*ct* 2

Stanyard, Anthony Roy
Professional. *b:* 5.4.1938, West Ham, Essex. Middle order right-hand batsman, right-arm medium pace bowler. *Team* Essex (1960, 2 matches).
Career batting
2–3–0–47–26–15.66–0–*ct* 0

Stanyforth, Ronald Thomas
Amateur. *b:* 30.5.1892, Chelsea, London. *d:* 20.2.1964, Kirk Hammerton, Yorkshire. Lower order right-hand batsman, wicket-keeper. *Sch* Eton. *Teams* Oxford U (1914); Yorkshire (1928, 3 matches). *Tours* MCC to South America 1926/7, to South Africa 1927/8, to West Indies 1929/30. *Tests* England (1927/8, 4 matches).
Career batting
61–79–16–1092–91–17.33–0–*ct* 72–*st* 21
Test batting
4–6–1–13–6*–2.60–0–*ct* 7–*st* 2

He captained MCC on the 1927/8 tour to South Africa and led England in four Tests – an unusual appointment since, at that time, he had never appeared in first-class County cricket, most of his matches being military ones. His final first-class match was in 1933 for MCC.

Staples, Arthur
Professional. *b:* 4.2.1899, Newstead, Notts. *d:* 9.9.1965, Redhill, Notts. Brother of S. J. (Notts). Sound middle order right-hand batsman, right-arm medium pace bowler. *Team* Nottinghamshire (1924–38, 353 matches).
Career batting
358–512–59–12762–153*–28.17–12–*ct* 215
Bowling 18942–635–29.82–14–1–7/20

He hit 1,000 runs in a season seven times (best 1,531, av 38.27, in 1932). A useful soccer player, he kept goal for Mansfield Town.

Staples, Cyril V.
Amateur. *d*: 12.5.1937. Lower order batsman, wicket-keeper. *Teams*: W. G. Grace's XI (1906); Gentlemen of England (1908).
Career batting
4–6–2–35–14–8.75–0–*ct* 4–*st* 3

Staples, Samuel James
Professional. *b:* 18.9.1892, Newstead, Nottinghamshire. *d:* 4.6.1950, Nottingham. Brother of Arthur (Notts). Lower order right-hand batsman, off break bowler, good slip field. *Team* Nottinghamshire (1920–34, 368 matches). *Tours* MCC to South Africa 1927/8; to Australia 1928/9 (he returned without playing a first-class match, owing to illness). *Tests* England (1927/8, 3 matches).
Career batting
385–475–95–6470–110–17.02–1–*ct* 340
Bowling 30421–1331–22.85–72–11–9/141
Test batting
3–5–0–65–39–13.00–0–*ct* 0
Bowling 435–15–29.00–0–0–3/50

He took 100 wickets in a season five times (best 132, av 23.03, in 1927). His best innings analysis was 9 for 141 for Notts v Kent at Canterbury in 1927. He was coach to Hampshire CCC in 1939 and a first-class umpire in 1949.

Stapleton, Ernest
Professional. *b:* 15.1.1869, New Basford, Nottinghamshire. *d:* 14.12.1938, Nottingham. Opening right-hand batsman. *Team* Derbyshire (1902, 1 match).
Career batting
1–2–0–3–2–1.50–0–*ct* 0

Stapleton, James
Professional. *b:* 8.8.1879, Eastwood, Nottinghamshire. *d:* 10.7.1944, Brinsley, Nottinghamshire. Lower order right-hand batsman, wicket-keeper. *Team* Nottinghamshire (1899–1911, 10 matches).
Career batting
10–15–2–152–21–11.69–0–*ct* 22–*st* 3

Starkie, Sydney
Professional. *b:* 4.4.1926, Burnley, Lancashire. Lower order right-hand batsman, right-arm off break bowler, slip field. *Team* Northamptonshire (1951–56, 95 matches).
Career batting
95–110–30–857–60–10.71–0–*ct* 64
Bowling 5685–166–34.25–6–1–6/33

Starmer, Clement Edward
Professional. *b:* 2.12.1895, Cosby, Leicestershire. *d:* 25.7.1978, Preston Village, North Shields, Tyne and Wear. Middle order right-hand batsman. *Team* Leicestershire (1925, 3 matches).
Career batting
3–4–0–19–8–4.75–0–*ct* 0

Statham, John Brian, CBE
Professional. *b:* 17.6.1930, Gorton, Manchester, Lancashire. Lower order left-hand batsman, right-arm fast medium bowler. *Team* Lancashire (1950–68, 430 matches). *Tours* MCC to Australia and New Zealand 1950/1, 1954/5, 1958/9, 1962/3, to India, Pakistan and Ceylon 1951/2, to West Indies 1953/4, 1959/60, to South Africa 1956/7;

Cavaliers to South Africa 1960/1; President's XI to India 1967/8. *Tests* England (1950/1 to 1965, 70 matches).
Career batting
559–647–145–5424–62–10.80–0–*ct* 230
Bowling 36995–2260–16.36–123–11–8/34
Test batting
70–87–28–675–38–11.44–0–*ct* 28
Bowling 6261–252–24.84–9–1–7/39

For a period of about ten years between 1953 and 1963, he was one of England's opening bowlers; he headed the Test averages on the 1953/4 tour to West Indies, being partnered by Trueman, then on the 1954/5 tour to Australia he partnered Tyson, with equal success. This partnership continued in 1955 in England against South Africa. On the 1958/9 tour to Australia he completely outshone both Trueman and Tyson in the Test series. On his fourth visit to Australia in 1962/3, he had lost his nip off the wicket, but he ended the tour standing second in the list of those taking most wickets in a Test career.

He took 100 wickets in an English season 13 times, his best year being 1959 with 139 wickets, av 15.01. The best analysis of his career was 8 for 34 for Lancashire v Warwickshire at Coventry in 1957, when he took 15 for 89 in the match.

From 1965 to 1967 he captained Lancashire, and in 1966 was awarded the CBE for his services to cricket.

Staunton, Rev Harvey
Amateur. *b:* 21.11.1870, Staunton, Nottinghamshire. *d:* 14.1.1918, Arzizieh, Mesopotamia. Middle order right-hand batsman. *Sch* Bromsgrove. *Team* Nottinghamshire (1903–05, 16 matches).
Career batting
16–24–0–456–78–19.00–0–*ct* 8
Bowling 48–0

He also played for Bedfordshire.

Staveley, Miles
Professional. *b:* 12.8.1846, St Pancras, Middlesex. Lower order right-hand batsman, right-hand fast round-arm bowler. *Team* Surrey (1870, 1 match).
Career batting
1–2–0–3–3–1.50–0–*ct* 0
Bowling 51–1–51.00–0–0–1/24

Staziker, Michael William
Cricketer. *b:* 7.11.1947, Croston, Lancashire. Tail end right-hand batsman, right-arm medium fast bowler. *Team* Lancashire (1970, 2 matches).
Career batting
2–2–2–1–1*–no av–0–*ct* 0
Bowling 269–1–269.00–0–0–1/114

Stead, Barry
Professional. *b:* 21.6.1939, Leeds, Yorkshire. *d:* 15.4.1980, Drighlington, Yorkshire. Lower order left-arm batsman, left-arm fast medium bowler. *Teams* Essex (1962, 1 match); Nottinghamshire (1962–76, 215 matches); Yorkshire (1959, 2 matches): Northern Transvaal (1975/6).
Career batting
232–253–77–2166–58–12.30–0–*ct* 59
Bowling 18318–653–28.05–24–2–8/44

His best season was 1972 when he took 98 wickets, av 20.38. He is credited with a match for Essex in 1962, being shown in the scorecard as 'did not bat', but in fact he was not at the ground, as he was playing for Notts 2nd XI on the same day.

Stead, Peter
Amateur. *b:* 1930, Yorkshire. Tail end right-hand batsman, right-arm fast medium bowler. *Team* Canada (1954). *Tour* Canada to England 1954
Career batting
3–4–3–6–4*–6.00–0–*ct* 0
Bowling 177–9–19.66–0–0–4/52

Stedman, Fred
Professional. *b:* 4.3.1870. Cobham, Surrey. *d:* 5.2.1918, Bray, Co Wicklow. He was accidently killed on the railway. Lower order right-hand batsman, wicket-keeper. *Teams* Surrey (1899–1908, 134 matches); London County (1900–03); Ireland (1912).
Career batting
140–192–68–1535–62–12.37–0–*ct* 266–*st* 50
Bowling 53–0

He was a professional at Woodbrook in Ireland after leaving Surrey.

Stedman, Rev Henry Charles Plumer
Amateur. *b:* 11.10.1848, Great Budworth, Cheshire. *d:* 30.7.1904, Leire, Leicestershire. Lower order right-hand batsman, right-hand fast round-arm bowler, cover point. *Team* Cambridge U (1871, blue).
Career batting
4–8–1–98–22–14.00–0–*ct* 2

His County cricket was for Bedfordshire 1876 to 1882, Leicestershire (pre-first-class) and Cheshire.

Steel, Allan Gibson
Amateur. *b:* 24.9.1858, Liverpool. *d:* 15.6.1914, Hyde Park, London. Brother of H. B., D. Q. and E. E. (all Lancashire), father of A. I. (Middlesex). Attacking middle order right-hand batsman, right-arm slow medium, or occasionally fast medium bowler. *Sch* Marlborough. *Teams* Lancashire (1877–93, 47 matches); Cambridge U

(1878–81, blue all four years). *Tour* Bligh to Australia 1882/3. *Tests* England (1880–88, 13 matches).
Career batting
162–261–23–7000–171–29.41–8–*ct* 137
Bowling 11667–788–14.80–64–20–9/63
Test batting
13–20–3–600–148–35.29–2–*ct* 5
Bowling 605–29–20.86–0–0–3/27

He was outstandingly successful in 1878, his first full season in first-class cricket, taking 164 wickets, av 9.43, as well as hitting 537 runs, av 22.37. It was to prove the best season of his career, though he took 130 wickets, av 13.41, in 1881. His best innings bowling analysis was 9 for 63 for Lancashire v Yorkshire at Old Trafford in 1878.

He captained England in four Tests, including the three of 1886, when England won each match.

His final first-class match was for I Zingari in 1895.

Steel, Allan Ivo
Amateur. *b:* 27.9.1892, Toxteth Park, Liverpool. *d:* 8.10.1917, Langemark, Belgium. He was killed in action. Son of A. G. (Lancashire); nephew of H. B., D. Q. and E. E. (all Lancashire). Lower order right-hand batsman, slow right-arm bowler. *Sch* Eton. *Team* Middlesex (1912, 2 matches).
Career batting
5–8–0–116–26–14.50–0–*ct* 2
Bowling 39–0

He took up a business appointment in India on leaving Eton and played for Calcutta CC.

Steel, Douglas Quintin
Amateur. *b:* 19.6.1856, Liverpool. *d:* 2.12.1933, Upton, Cheshire. Brother of A. G., H. B., E. E. (all Lancashire), uncle of A. I. (Middlesex). Stylish middle order right-hand batsman, right-hand slow round-arm bowler, wicket-keeper. *Sch* Uppingham. *Teams* Cambridge U (1876–79, blue all four years); Lancashire (1876–87, 22 matches).
Career batting
57–89–3–1674–158–19.46–1–*ct* 28–*st* 4
Bowling 173–7–24.71–1–0–5/65

A noted footballer, he represented Cambridge at both rugby and association.

Steel, Ernest Eden
Amatuer. *b:* 25.6.1864, Liverpool, Lancashire. *d:* 14.7.1941, Southport, Lancashire. Brother of A. G., D. Q., H. B. (all Lancashire), uncle of A. I. (Middlesex). Middle order right-hand batsman, slow right-arm bowler, good field. *Sch* Marlborough. *Teams* Lancashire (1884–1903, 40 matches); Europeans (1892/3).
Career batting
47–69–4–1133–111–17.43–1–*ct* 42
Bowling 2877–129+2–22.30–11–2–6/69

In 1890 he went to live in Bombay and his County cricket was therefore very limited. His final first-class match was for I Zingari in 1904.

Steel, Harold Banner
Amateur. *b:* 9.4.1862, South Hill, Liverpool. *d:* 29.6.1911, Burnham, Somerset. Brother of A. G., D. Q., E. E. (all Lancashire), uncle of A. I. (Middlesex). Powerful middle order right-hand batsman, right-arm medium pace bowler. *Sch* Repton and Uppingham. *Team* Lancashire (1883–96, 22 matches).
Career batting
36–63–3–1042–100–17.36–1–*ct* 20
Bowling 83–1–83.00–0–0–1/15

He might have played more often for Lancashire, but preferred local club matches. Owing to a football injury he played no cricket whilst at Cambridge University.

Steele, Alexander
Cricketer. *b:* 25.2.1941, Salisbury, Rhodesia. Right-hand batsman, wicket-keeper. *Team* Scotland (1967–80).
Career batting
14–25–0–621–97–24.84–0–*ct* 11–*st* 2

Steele, Sir Charles Ronald
Amateur. *b:* 9.11.1897, Sheffield, Yorkshire. *d:* 14.2.1973, Cambridge. Middle order right-hand batsman. *Sch* Oundle. *Team* RAF (1929).
Career batting
2–3–0–147–63–49.00–0–*ct* 0

Steele, David Aubrey
Amateur. *b:* 3.6.1869, Southampton, Hampshire. *d:* 25.3.1935, Caterham, Surrey. Stubborn middle order right-hand batsman, slow right-arm bowler, wicket-keeper. *Team* Hampshire (1895–1906, 163 matches).
Career batting
164–279–33–3448–80–14.01–0–*ct* 133–*st* 4
Bowling 4628–135–34.28–4–0–5/32

Steele, David Stanley
Cricketer. *b:* 29.9.1941, Bradeley, Staffordshire. Brother of J. F. (Leicestershire), cousin of B. Crump (Northants). Sound middle order right-hand batsman, slow left-arm bowler, good close field. *Teams* Northamptonshire (1963–83, 391 matches); Derbyshire (1979–81, 64 matches); Leicestershire (1980/1, 3 matches). *Tours* Robins to South Africa 1975/6; Leicestershire to Zimbabwe 1980/1. *Tests* England (1975–76, 8 matches).

Career batting
475–773–111–21707–140*–32.79–30–*ct* 517
Bowling 13411–562–23.86–24–3–8/29
Test batting
8–16–0–673–106–42.06–1–*ct* 7
Bowling 39–2–19.50–0–0–1/1

He hit 1,000 runs in a season ten times (best 1,756, av 48.77, in 1975). He was appointed captain of Derbyshire when he joined the County at the beginning of the 1979 season, but resigned at the end of June. In 1982 he re-joined Northants.

He also played for Staffordshire.

Steele, Frederick
Professional. *b:* 14.5.1847, London. *d:* 22.1.1915, Hackney, London. Left-hand batsman, left-arm fast bowler. *Team* Middlesex (1877–79, 10 matches).
Career batting
13–23–3–33–6–1.65–0–*ct* 3
Bowling 751–43–17.46–1–0–5/22

He also played for Northumberland. His final first-class match was for MCC in 1880.

Steele, Howard Keith
Cricketer. *b:* 4.4.1951, New Zealand. Middle order right-hand batsman, right-arm medium pace bowler. *Teams* Cambridge U (1970–72, blue 1971–72); Auckland (1974/5).
Career batting
26–40–4–711–103*–19.75–1–*ct* 13
Bowling 1276–30–42.53–0–0–4/71

Steele, John Frederick
Cricketer. *b:* 23.7.1946, Brown Edge, Staffordshire. Brother of D. S. (Northants and Derbyshire), cousin of B. S. Crump (Northants). Opening right-hand batsman, slow left-arm bowler. *Teams* Leicestershire (1970–83, 312 matches); Natal (1973/4 to 1977/8). *Tour* Robins to South Africa 1974/5.
Career batting
331–535–65–13669–195–29.08–20–*ct* 360
Bowling 12762–496–25.72–12–0–7/29

He hit 1,000 runs in a season six times (best 1,347, av 31.32, in 1972). He also played for Staffordshire.

Steele, Rev John William Jackson
Amateur. *b:* 30.7.1905, Nantwich, Cheshire. Lower order right-hand batsman, right-arm medium pace bowler. *Team* Hampshire (1938–39, 17 matches).
Career batting
19–28–2–434–44–16.69–0–*ct* 9
Bowling 1710–66–25.90–3–0–6/62

He also played in military cricket.

Steeples, Albert
Professional. *b:* 28.7.1870, Somercotes, Derbyshire. *d:* 14.8.1945, Derby. Brother of Richard (Derbyshire). Lower order batsman, right-arm fast medium bowler. *Team* Derbyshire (1899, 1 match).
Career batting
1–2–0–18–16–9.00–0–*ct* 0
Bowling 21–0

Steeples, Richard
Professional. *b:* 30.4.1873, Somercotes, Derbyshire. *d:* 2.8.1946, Somercotes, Derbyshire. Brother of Albert (Derbyshire). Lower order batsman, right-arm fast medium bowler. *Team* Derbyshire (1897, 3 matches).
Career batting
3–5–0–20–16–4.00–0–*ct* 1
Bowling 214–9–23.77–0–0–4/73

He also played for Monmouthshire.

Stenton, John D.
Amateur. *b:* 26.10.1924, Sheffield, Yorkshire. Right-hand batsman, slow left-arm bowler. *Team* Somerset (1953, 1 match).
Career batting
1–2–0–19–18–9.50–0–*ct* 0
Bowling 44–1–44.00–0–0–1/44

Stephen, Norman Kenneth
Amateur. *b:* 24.6.1865, Kinloss, Morayshire. *d:* 4.7.1948, Hampstead, London. Middle order right-hand batsman, slow right-arm bowler. *Sch* Fettes. *Team* Cambridge U (1887).
Career batting
4–5–2–6–3*–2.00–0–*ct* 1
Bowling 261–15–17.40–1–0–5/52

Stephens, Eric James
Professional. *b:* 23.3.1909, Gloucester. Dashing middle order left-hand batsman, right-arm bowler, good field. *Team* Gloucestershire (1927–37, 216 matches).
Career batting
216–313–54–4593–92–17.73–0–*ct* 167
Bowling 1171–29–40.38–1–1–6/59

He hit 1,134 runs, av 28.35, in 1935. He played rugby football for Gloucester and soccer for Hereford Town and Bristol Rovers.

Stephens, Frederick
Amateur. *b:* 4.2.1836, Caversham, Berkshire. *d:* 1.4.1909, Chawton, Hampshire. Middle order batsman. *Sch* Winchester. *Team* MCC (1865).
Career batting
1–2–1–9–9*–9.00–0–*ct* 1

His County cricket was for Berkshire and Huntingdonshire.

Stephens, Frank Garfield
Amateur. *b:* 26.4.1889, Edgbaston, Birmingham. *d:* 9.8.1970, Birmingham. Twin brother of G. W. (Warwickshire). Middle order right-hand batsman, leg break bowler. *Sch* Rossall. *Team* Warwickshire (1907–12, 32 matches).
Career batting
32–50–7–1102–144–25.62–1–*ct* 17
Bowling 205–3–68.33–0–0–2/24
He was for some time on the Committee of Warwickshire CCC.

Stephens, Frederick Geoffrey Roger Byng
Amateur. *b:* 27.5.1887. *d:* 9.5.1967, Northallerton, Yorkshire. Lower order right-hand batsman, useful bowler. *Sch* Winchester. *Team* G. J. V. Weigall's XI (1908).
Career batting
1–2–1–8–4*–8.00–0–*ct* 0
Bowling 47–2–23.50–0–0–2/47
He did not play in any first-class matches whilst at Oxford.

Stephens, George William
Amateur. *b:* 26.4.1889, Edgbaston, Birmingham. *d:* 17.3.1950, Knowle, Solihull, Warwickshire. Twin brother of F. G. (Warwickshire). Middle order right-hand batsman, leg break bowler. *Sch* Rossall. *Team* Warwickshire (1907–25, 123 matches).
Career batting
127–209–15–4171–143–21.50–4–*ct* 51
Bowling 80–4–20.00–0–0–2/25
His final first-class match was for F. S. G. Calthorpe's XI in 1926.

Stephens, John Patrick Rhodes Felix
Cricketer. *b:* 6.8.1942, Cheltenham, Gloucestershire. Opening right-hand batsman. *Team* Oxford U (1966–67).
Career batting
3–6–0–73–27–12.16–0–*ct* 2

Stephenson, Edwin
Professional. *b:* 5.6.1832, Sheffield, Yorkshire. *d:* 5.7.1898, Liverpool, Lancashire. Very sound middle order right-hand batsman, right-hand fast round-arm bowler, wicket-keeper. *Team* Yorkshire (1858–73, 46 matches). *Tour* Stephenson to Australia 1861/2.
Career batting
82–142–11–1940–69–14.80–0–*ct* 57–*st* 48
Bowling 24–0
His first-class debut was for Sheffield in 1854.

Stephenson, Frederick
Professional. *b:* 24.4.1853, Todmorden, Lancashire. *d:* July 1927. Lower order left-hand batsman, left-hand fast round-arm bowler. *Team* Lancashire (1875–77, 2 matches).
Career batting
2–4–1–0–0*–0.00–0–*ct* 2
Bowling 17–1–17.00–0–0–1/17
At 5ft 2in tall, he was one of the smallest of all first-class cricketers.

Stephenson, Franklyn da Costa
Cricketer. *b:* 8.4.1959, Halls, Holders, St James, Barbados. Middle order right-hand batsman, right-arm fast bowler. *Teams* Tasmania (1981/2, 7 matches); Barbados (1981/2); Gloucestershire (1982–83, 9 matches). *Tour* West Indies to South Africa 1982/3.
Career batting
23–32–2–601–165–20.03–1–*ct* 14
Bowling 1874–95–19.72–6–1–6/19
He also played for Staffordshire.

Stephenson, George Robert
Cricketer. *b:* 19.11.1942, Derby. Lower order right-hand batsman, wicket-keeper. *Sch* Derby. *Teams* Derbyshire (1967–68, 9 matches); Hampshire (1969–80, 263 matches).
Career batting
272–357–66–4781–100*–16.42–1–*ct* 584–*st* 77
Bowling 39–0
His best season as wicket-keeper was 1970 when he had 80 dismissals (73*ct* 7*st*).
A good soccer player, he appeared for Derby County, Shrewsbury and Rochdale.

Stephenson, Heathfield Harman
Professional. *b:* 3.5.1833, Esher, Surrey. *d:* 17.12.1896, Uppingham, Rutland. Middle order right-hand batsman, right-hand fast round-arm bowler, wicket-keeper. *Team* Surrey (1853–71, 179 matches). *Tours* Parr to North America 1859 (not first-class); Stephenson to Australia 1861/2.
Career batting
256–452–41–7360–119–17.90–3–*ct* 152–*st* 25
Bowling 4920–300+2–16.40–17–4–8/28
His best season was 1864, when he came second in the first-class averages with 824 runs, av 39.23.
He captained the first English Team to Australia in 1861/2.

Stephenson, H. W. *(see under* Stephenson, W. H.)

Stephenson, John Stewart
Amateur. *b:* 10.11.1903, Brough, Yorkshire. *d:* 7.10.1975, Horsham, Sussex. Middle order right-hand batsman, right-arm medium pace bowler. *Sch* Shrewsbury. *Teams* Oxford U (1923–26, blue 1925 and 1926); Yorkshire (1923–26, 16 matches).

Career batting
35–53–5–949–72–19.77–0–*ct* 21
Bowling 521–11–47.36–0–0–3/44
He was also awarded his blue for soccer.

Stephenson, John William Arthur
Amateur. *b:* 1.8.1907, Hong Kong. *d:* 20.5.1982, Pulborough, Sussex. Attacking middle lower order right-hand batsman, right-arm fast medium bowler. *Teams* Europeans (1928/9 to 1929/30); Madras (1930/1); Essex (1934–39, 61 matches); Worcestershire (1947, 1 match).
Career batting
103–158–37–2582–135–21.33–2–*ct* 60
Bowling 7521–312–24.10–16–2–9/46
His first-class debut in England was for the Army in 1931 and his final first-class match for South of England in 1948. His best bowling in an innings was 9 for 46 for Gentlemen v Players at Lord's in 1936. His career in the Army prevented him from appearing regularly in County cricket. He played also for Buckinghamshire.

Stephenson, Robert Hearfield
Amateur. *b:* 3.6.1906, Beverley, Yorkshire. *d:* 9.11.1942. He was killed in action. Middle order right-hand batsman. *Team* Royal Navy (1927–28).
Career batting
3–6–0–122–75–20.33–0–*ct* 3

Stephenson, William Harold
(known as Harold William)
Professional. *b:* 18.7.1920, Haverton Hill, Co Durham. Middle order right-hand batsman, wicket-keeper. *Team* Somerset (1948–64, 428 matches). *Tour* Commonwealth to India and Ceylon 1950/1.
Career batting
462–747–91–13195–147*–20.11–7–*ct* 748–*st* 334
Bowling 135–1–135.00–0–0–1/0
He hit 1,000 runs in a season five times (best 1,143, av 21.56, in 1953).
From 1960 to 1964 he captained Somerset.
He also played for Durham and Dorset.

Stephenson-Jellie, James Parker
Amateur. *b:* 1875. *d:* 1960, Australia. Middle order batsman. *Team* Gloucestershire (1896–1908, 6 matches).
Career batting
6–10–0–88–27–8.80–0–*ct* 1

Stevens, Bertie Grosvenor
Amateur. *b:* 9.4.1886, Thingoe, Suffolk. *d:* March 1943, Wednesbury, Staffs. Right-hand batsman, wicket-keeper. *Sch* Cheltenham and Worcester R.G.S. *Team* Worcestershire (1905–14, 18 matches).
Career batting
19–33–2–379–41–12.22–0–*ct* 15
Bowling 18–0
His final first-class match was for H. K. Foster's XI in 1919.

Stevens, Edward
Professional, *b:* 1735, Send, Surrey. *d:* 7.9.1819, Walton-on-Thames, Surrey. Tail end right-hand batsman, right-hand medium pace under-arm bowler. *Team* Surrey (1773–89).
He was generally known under the appellation 'Lumpy' and was famous as a bowler in matches organized by the Hambledon Club 'being able to deliver more balls of a length than other men, and he never used to tire.'

Stevens, Geoffrey Alden
Amateur. *b:* 17.10.1890, Norwich. *d:* 24.3.1963, Norwich. Middle order right-hand batsman. *Team* Minor Counties (1912–24).
Career batting
3–5–0–56–20–11.20–0–*ct* 6
His County cricket was for Norfolk from 1906 to 1930. He hit 201 for Norfolk v Berkshire in the Minor Counties Championship Match of 1910, which resulted in Norfolk taking the title. From 1952 to 1961 he was Secretary of Norfolk CCC.

Stevens, Greville Thomas Scott
Amateur. *b:* 7.1.1901, Hampstead, Middlesex. *d:* 19.9.1970, Islington, London. Right-hand batsman, leg break bowler, good close field. *Sch* University College School. *Teams* Oxford U (1920–23, blue all four years); Middlesex (1919–32, 127 matches). *Tours* MCC to South Africa 1922/3, 1927/8, to West Indies 1929/30; Tennyson to Jamaica 1931/2. *Tests* England (1922/3 to 1929/30, 10 matches).
Career batting
243–387–36–10376–182–29.56–12–*ct* 213
Bowling 18364–684–26.84–29–5–8/38
Test batting
10–17–0–263–69–15.47–0–*ct* 9
Bowling 648–20–32.40–2–1–5/90
He created a sensation in 1919 when he hit 466 in a House match at school and was then selected to play for the Gentlemen v Players at Lord's. He hit 1,000 runs in a season twice (best 1,434, av 33.34, in 1923), but after leaving University he could not spare the time for regular County cricket.

Stevens, John
Amateur. *b:* 5.10.1854, Guildford, Surrey.

Middle order right-hand batsman, good deep field. *Team* Surrey (1874–75, 3 matches).
Career batting
3–4–0–36–16–9.00–0–*ct* 1

Stevens, John Elgar
Amateur. *b:* 21.3.1875, Salisbury, Wiltshire. *d:* April 1923, Guildford, Surrey. Capable middle order right-hand batsman, right-arm medium fast bowler. *Sch* Sherborne. *Team* MCC (1902).
Career batting
1–1–0–4–4–4.00–0–*ct* 0

He played in the Freshmen's match in 1895, but no first-class matches for Oxford. His County cricket was for Wiltshire, whom he represented for many years.

He was also a useful boxer, rugby footballer and steeplechase jockey.

Stevens, James Norman
Amateur. *b:* 4.6.1910, Bexhill-on-Sea, Sussex. Lower order right-hand batsman, right-arm fast medium bowler. *Sch* Northampton. *Team* Northamptonshire (1937, 5 matches).
Career batting
7–12–1–76–19–6.90–0–*ct* 1
Bowling 571–9–63.44–0–0–3/85

His final first-class match was for Free Foresters in 1953.

He also played for Wiltshire and Suffolk.

Stevens, Keith Brian Havelock
Amateur. *b:* 22.8.1942, Bombay, India. Middle order right-hand batsman. *Sch* Bradfield. *Team* Oxford U (1962).
Career batting
5–10–0–102–52–10.20–0–*ct* 4

Stevens, Roy Gilbert
Cricketer. *b:* 6.2.1933, Eastry, Kent. Middle order batsman. *Team* Combined Services (1962).
Career batting
1–2–0–38–29–19.00–0–*ct* 2
Bowling 47–2–23.50–0–0–1/23

He was Secretary of Somerset CCC 1975 to 1979 and of Sussex CCC 1980 to 1983.

Stevenson, Alexander James
Amateur. *b:* 15.7.1901, Edinburgh, Scotland. *d:* 2.9.1970, Edinburgh, Scotland. Middle order batsman, lob bowler. *Sch* Edinburgh Academy. *Team* Scotland (1925–28).
Career batting
4–7–0–190–54–27.14–0–*ct* 2
Bowling 15–0

Stevenson, David Craig
Amateur. *b:* 3.5.1890, Kilmarnock, Ayrshire, Scotland. *d:* 21.3.1977, Dundee, Scotland. Lower order left-hand batsman, slow left-arm bowler. *Team* Scotland (1922–25).
Career batting
6–11–0–96–35–8.72–0–*ct* 1
Bowling 161–4–40.25–0–0–2/29

He played County cricket for Cumberland and Northumberland.

Stevenson, Graham Barry
Cricketer. *b:* 16.12.1955, Ackworth, Yorkshire. Lower order right-hand batsman, right-arm medium pace bowler. *Team* Yorkshire (1973–83, 157 matches). *Tours* England to Australia and India 1979/80, to West Indies 1980/1. *Tests* England (1979/80 to 1980/1, 2 matches).
Career batting
167–204–30–3626–115*–20.83–2–*ct* 67
Bowling 12789–459–27.86–18–2–8/57
Test batting
2–2–1–28–27*–28.00–0–*ct* 0
Bowling 183–5–36.60–0–0–3/111

Stevenson, George Stanley
Professional. *b:* 20.7.1876, Derby. *d:* 25.7.1938, Fritchley, Derbyshire. Lower order batsman, useful bowler. *Team* Derbyshire (1904, 2 matches).
Career batting
2–4–0–10–9–2.50–0–*ct* 1
Bowling 92–1–92.00–0–0–1/79

Stevenson, Henry James
Amateur. *b:* 12.7.1867, Edinburgh, Scotland. *d:* 8.8.1945, Corstophine, Edinburgh, Scotland. Right-hand batsman, slow under-arm bowler. *Sch* Edinburgh Academy. *Team* Scotland (1905).
Career batting
5–9–0–104–35–11.55–0–*ct* 5
Bowling 269–4–67.25–0–0–3/77

His first-class debut was for MCC in 1901.

A noted rugby footballer he represented Scotland from 1888 to 1893.

Stevenson, James Alexander
Amateur. *b:* 24.6.1915, Edinburgh, Scotland. Middle order right-hand batsman, right-arm medium pace bowler. *Sch* Edinburgh Academy. *Team* Scotland (1937–51).
Career batting
4–8–2–127–45*–21.16–0–*ct* 2

Stevenson, John Francis
Amateur. *b:* 18.3.1888, Handsworth, Warwickshire, *d:* 5.12.1951, Birmingham, Warwickshire.

Right-hand batsman. *Team* Warwickshire (1919, 1 match).
Career batting
1–2–0–18–18–9.00–0–*ct* 0

Stevenson, Keith
Cricketer. *b:* 6.10.1950, Derby. Lower order right-hand batsman, right-arm fast medium bowler. *Teams* Derbyshire (1974–77, 47 matches); Hampshire (1978–83, 99 matches).
Career batting
146–167–58–1046–33–9.59–0–*ct* 48
Bowling 10536–355–29.67–16–0–7/22

Stevenson, Michael Hamilton
Amateur. *b:* 13.6.1927, Chinley, Derbyshire. Sound middle order right-hand batsman, slow left-arm bowler. *Sch* Rydal. *Teams* Cambridge U (1949–52, blue all four years); Derbyshire (1950–52, 3 matches); Ireland (1952–64).
Career batting
66–106–7–2467–122–24.91–4–*ct* 26
Bowling 1882–50–37.64–1–0–5/36

He also played for Staffordshire and Denbighshire. His final first-class match was for MCC in 1967.

He is a well-known sports journalist and commentator mainly associated with *The Daily Telegraph*.

Stevenson, R. C.
Amateur. Lower order right-hand batsman, off break bowler. *Team* Combined Services (1962).
Career batting
2–4–1–33–17*–11.00–0–*ct* 1
Bowling 230–3–76.66–0–0–3/86

Steward, Exley Anthony Whitefoord
Cricketer. *b:* 27.6.1941, Durban, South Africa. Middle order right-hand batsman, leg break bowler, wicket-keeper. *Teams* Essex (1964–65, 15 matches); Natal (1967/8).
Career batting
18–27–3–310–47–12.91–0–*ct* 20

Stewart, Alec James
Cricketer. *b:* 8.4.1963, Merton, Surrey. Son of M. J. (Surrey). Middle order right-hand batsman, wicket-keeper. *Team* Surrey (1981–83, 12 matches).
Career batting
12–21–4–560–118*–32.94–1–*ct* 11–*st* 1

Stewart, Rev Alexander Lamont
Amateur. *b:* 2.6.1858, Port of Spain, Trinidad. *d:* 17.2.1904, Marylebone, London. Brother of J. M. (Middlesex). Middle order right-hand batsman, right-arm fast bowler. *Sch* Clifton. *Teams* Middlesex (1880, 1 match); Oxford U (1883).
Career batting
4–8–2–27–12*–4.50–0–*ct* 5
Bowling 154–6–25.66–0–0–2/33

He also played for Norfolk.

Stewart, David
Amateur. *b:* 21.5.1924, Perth, Scotland. Right-hand batsman, right-arm medium pace bowler. *Team* Scotland (1950).
Career batting
1–2–1–7–5*–7.00–0–*ct* 0
Bowling 21–2–10.50–0–0–2/12

Stewart, David Ernest Robertson
Cricketer. *b:* 22.5.1948, Bombay, India. Opening right-hand batsman, off break bowler. *Teams* Scotland (1969–79); Worcestershire (1970–73, 23 matches).
Career batting
32–51–3–854–69–17.79–0–*ct* 17
Bowling 72–0

Stewart, Maj-Gen Sir Herbert
Amateur. *b:* 30.6.1843, Sparsholt, Hampshire. *d:* 16.2.1885, Gakdul, Sudan. He was wounded in the battle of Abu Klea and died from his injuries. Brother of W. A. (Hampshire). Lower order right-hand batsman, wicket-keeper. *Sch* Winchester. *Team* Hampshire (1869, 1 match).
Career batting
4–7–0–19–8–2.71–0–0–*ct* 2–*st* 1

Stewart, Haldane Campbell
Amateur. *b:* 28.2.1868, Notting Hill, London. *d:* 16.6.1942, Oxford. Stylish middle order right-hand batsman, useful bowler. *Team* Kent (1892–1903, 73 matches). *Tour* Kent to United States 1903.
Career batting
75–128–3–2829–142–22.63–2–*ct* 42
Bowling 97–3–32.33–0–0–1/2

He did not play in any first-class matches whilst at Oxford.

Stewart, Hugh Lambert
Amateur. *b:* 2.5.1907, Ceres, Fife, Scotland. Right-hand batsman, right-arm fast medium bowler. *Team* Scotland (1932).
Career batting
2–4–0–42–25–10.50–0–*ct* 2
Bowling 71–1–71.00–0–0–1/31

Stewart, Maj-Gen Sir James Marshall
Amateur. *b:* 9.8.1861, Glasgow, Scotland. *d:* 20.7.1943, Whitchurch, Devon. Brother of A. L. (Middlesex). Right-hand batsman, right-arm

medium pace bowler. *Sch* Clifton and Malvern. *Team* Middlesex (1880, 1 match).
Career batting
1–2–0–8–8–4.00–0–*ct* 0
Bowling 11–1–11.00–0–0–1/11

Stewart, Michael James
Professional. *b:* 16.9.1932, Herne Hill, London. Father of A. J. (Surrey). Neat opening right-hand batsman, right-arm medium pace bowler, brilliant close field. *Sch* Alleyn's. *Team* Surrey (1954–72, 498 matches). *Tours* Swanton to West Indies 1955/6; Surrey to Rhodesia 1959/60; MCC to East Africa 1963/4, to India 1963/4; International XI to India, Pakistan and Ceylon 1967/8; Cavaliers to South Africa and India 1962/3. *Tests* England (1962 to 1963/4, 8 matches).
Career batting
530–898–93–26492–227*–32.90–49–*ct* 634
Bowling 99–1–99.00–0–0–1/4
Test batting
8–12–1–385–87–35.00–0–*ct* 6

He hit 1,000 runs in a season 15 times, going on to 2,000 once : 2,045, av 44.45, in 1962. Both his double centuries were for Surrey, the highest being 227* v Middlesex at the Oval in 1964.

In 1957 he held 77 catches, and in the same year held 7 catches in an innings for Surrey v Northants at Northampton.

From 1963 to 1972 he captained Surrey and from 1979 he has been manager of the County Club.

A good soccer player he was inside right for Wimbledon, Hendon and Corinthian Casuals as an amateur, and was then professional with Charlton Athletic.

Stewart, Richard William
Cricketer. *b:* 28.2.1945, Portland, Jamaica. Lower order right-hand batsman, right-arm fast medium bowler. *Teams* Gloucestershire (1966, 1 match); Middlesex (1966–68, 51 matches).
Career batting
52–36–11–107–19–4.28–0–*ct* 17
Bowling 3133–131–23.91–5–0–6/65

He appeared for both Gloucestershire and Middlesex in 1966.

Stewart, Theophile Lecompte
Amateur. *b:* 9.5.1891, Brisbane, Australia. *d:* 14.12.1952, Morriston, Glamorgan. Middle order batsman. *Team* Glamorgan (1923, 1 match).
Career batting
1–2–0–4–4–2.00–0–*ct* 0

Stewart, Rev William Anthony
Amateur. *b:* 19.5.1847, Sparsholt, Hampshire. *d:* 31.7.1883, Twyford, Hampshire. Brother of Herbert (Hampshire). Right-hand batsman, wicket-keeper. *Sch* Winchester. *Teams* Oxford U (1869–70, blue both years); Hampshire (1869–78, 2 matches).
Career batting
9–17–5–46–12–3.83–0–*ct* 15–*st* 9

Stewart, William James Perver
Professional. *b:* 31.8.1934, Llanelly, Carmarthenshire. Middle order right-hand batsman, off break bowler. *Teams* Warwickshire (1955–69, 279 matches); Northants (1971, 1 match). *Tour* MCC to New Zealand 1960/1.
Career batting
290–491–56–14826–182*–34.08–25–*ct* 132
Bowling 15–2–7.50–0–0–2/4

He hit 1,000 runs in a season six times, going on to 2,000 once: 2,318, av 43.73, in 1962. A noted hitter of sixes, he hit ten in one innings of 155 for Warwickshire v Lancashire at Blackpool in 1959.

A useful rugby footballer, he was centre three quarter for Coventry.

Stewart-Brown, Philip Harman
Amateur. *b:* 30.4.1904, Wirral, Cheshire. *d:* 21.12.1960, Marylebone London. Opening or middle order right-hand batsman. *Sch* Harrow. *Team* Oxford U (1924–26, blue 1925 and 1926).
Career batting
17–31–1–845–99–28.16–0–*ct* 9

His final first-class match was for Leveson-Gower's XI in 1927.

Stileman-Gibbard, Leonard Gibbard
Amateur. *b:* 22.6.1856, Bombay, India. *d:* 19.9.1939, Sharnbrook, Bedfordshire. Middle order right-hand batsman, right-hand slow round-arm bowler. *Team* South of England (1886).
Career batting
1–2–0–55–46–27.50–0–*ct* 1

His County cricket was for Bedfordshire. Though at Cambridge, he did not appear for the University in any first-class matches.

Still, Stuart John
Cricketer. *b:* 14.12.1957, Hove, Sussex. Lower order right-hand batsman, right-arm medium pace bowler. *Team* Sussex (1975, 1 match).
Career batting
1–2–0–6–6–3.00–0–*ct* 0
Bowling 42–1–42.00–0–0–1/42

Stimpson, Peter John
Cricketer. *b:* 25.5.1947, Aberfan, Glamorgan. Middle order right-hand batsman, right-arm medium pace bowler. *Team* Worcestershire (1971–72, 30 matches).

Career batting
30–54–3–1327–103–26.01–1–*ct* 8
Bowling 19–0

Stinchcombe, Frederick William
Professional. *b:* 12.3.1930, Barnby Moor, Nottinghamshire. Lower order right-hand batsman, leg break and googly bowler. *Team* Nottinghamshire (1950–51, 6 matches).
Career batting
6–8–2–87–48–14.50–0–*ct* 1
Bowling 539–4–134.75–0–0–1/42

Stirling, Haycraft
Amateur. *b:* 8.2.1908, Barnet, Middlesex. *d:* 7.5.1952, Byfleet, Surrey. Lower order right-hand batsman, right-arm fast medium bowler. *Sch* Bishop's Stortford. *Team* Middlesex (1932–33, 2 matches).
Career batting
2–3–1–4–3–2.00–0–*ct* 1
Bowling 195–0

Stirling, William Stuart
Amateur. *b:* 20.3.1891, South Australia. *d:* 18.7.1971, Australia. Middle or lower order batsman, left-arm bowler. *Team* South Australia (1908/9 to 1920/1, 14 matches). *Tours* AIF to England 1919, to South Africa 1919/20.
Career batting
47–72–7–931–62–14.32–0–*ct* 32
Bowling 1891–61–31.00–3–0–5/26

He was a useful all-rounder for AIF in 1919.

Stockley, Anthony John
Cricketer. *b:* 4.4.1940, Kingston on Thames, Surrey. Right-hand batsman, right-arm off break bowler. *Team* Surrey (1968, 3 matches).
Career batting
3–2–0–5–5–2.50–0–*ct* 3
Bowling 194–10–19.40–0–0–4/74

Stocks, Edward William
Amateur. *b:* 27.5.1856, Norwich. *d:* 26.10.1876, Norwich. He died of typhoid fever. Attacking opening right-hand batsman, right-hand medium pace round-arm bowler, slip field. *Sch* Clergy Orphan School, Canterbury. *Team* Cambridge U (1875–76).
Career batting
4–5–0–18–11–3.60–0–*ct* 1
Bowling 22–0

He represented Cambridge in the athletic sports of 1875.

His County cricket was for Norfolk.

Stocks, Frederick
Professional. *b:* 23.5.1883, Shireoaks, Notts. *d:* 2.1.1954, Hucknall, Notts. Father of F. W. (Notts). Middle order batsman, useful bowler. *Team* Northants (1906, 2 matches)
Career batting
2–4–0–24–13–6.00–0–*ct* 1
Bowling 37–0

Stocks, Francis Wilfrid
Amateur. *b:* 10.12.1873, Market Harborough, Leicestershire. *d:* 21.5.1929, Framlingham, Suffolk. Lower order left-hand batsman, left-arm medium bowler, good field. *Sch* Lancing and Denstone. *Teams* Oxford U (1896–99, blue 1898 and 1899); Leicestershire (1894–1903, 44 matches). *Tour* Warner to United States 1897.
Career batting
63–102–19–834–58–10.04–0–*ct* 70
Bowling 5205–208–25.02–14–3–8/22

He also represented Oxford at hockey.

Stocks, Frederick Wilfred
Professional. *b:* 6.11.1918, Carcroft, Yorkshire. Son of Frederick (Northants). Attacking middle order left-hand batsman, right-arm medium pace bowler. *Team* Nottinghamshire (1946–57, 283 matches).
Career batting
284–430–45–11397–171–29.60–13–*ct* 158
Bowling 9794–223–43.91–6–0–6/37

He hit 1,000 runs in a season five times (best 1,396, av 34.04, in 1951).

He hit a century on his first-class debut in 1946 and took a wicket with his first ball (not in the same match).

Stoddart, Andrew Ernest
Amateur. *b:* 11.3.1863, Westoe, South Shields, Co Durham. *d:* 4.4.1915, St John's Wood, London. He shot himself through the head. Stylish opening right-hand batsman, right-arm medium pace bowler, excellent field. *Team* Middlesex (1885–1900, 170 matches). *Tours* Vernon to Australia 1887/8; Sheffield to Australia 1891/2; Stoddart to Australia 1894/5, 1897/8; Priestley to West Indies 1896/7; Ranjitsinhji to North America 1899. *Tests* England (1887/8 to 1897/8, 16 matches).
Career batting
309–537–16–16738–221–32.12–26–*ct* 257
Bowling 6571–278–23.63–10–2–7/67
Test batting
16–30–2–996–173–35.57–2–*ct* 6
Bowling 94–2–47.00–0–0–1/10

He hit 1,000 runs in a season six times, going on to 2,000 once : 2,072, av 42.28, in 1893. Both his double centuries were for Middlesex, the highest being 221 v Somerset at Lord's in 1900.

He took two teams to Australia, acting as captain on both tours and led England in eight Tests.

An excellent rugby footballer he played for Middlesex and England in the three-quarter line.

Stoddart, Peter Laurence Bowring
Amateur. *b:* 24.6.1934, London. Opening right-hand batsman. *Sch* Eton. *Team* MCC (1958).
Career batting
1–2–0–22–11–11.00–0–*ct* 0

Stoddart, Wilfred Bowring
Amateur. *b:* 27.4.1871, West Derby, Liverpool, Lancashire. *d:* 8.1.1935, Liverpool, Lancashire. Lower order right-hand batsman, slow right-arm leg break bowler. *Team* Lancashire (1898–99, 15 matches).
Career batting
19–32–5–410–43*–15.18–0–*ct* 7
Bowling 1122–48–23.37–3–0–6/121

He was a member of the Committee of Lancashire CCC.

A good forward, he played rugby football for Lancashire and England.

Stogdon, Rev Edgar
Amateur. *b:* 30.7.1870, Harrow, Middlesex. *d:* 30.6.1951, Northwood, Middlesex. Brother of J. H. (Middlesex). Middle order right-hand batsman. *Sch* Harrow. *Team* Cambridge U (1893).
Career batting
2–4–0–19–12–4.75–0–*ct* 1

Stogdon, John Hubert
Amateur. *b:* 25.4.1876, Harrow, Middlesex. *d:* 17.12.1944, Pinner, Middlesex. Brother of Edgar (Cambridge U). Middle order right-hand batsman. *Sch* Harrow. *Teams* Cambridge U (1896–99, blue 1897–99); Middlesex (1899–1907, 14 matches).
Career batting
44–78–1–1347–101–17.49–1–*ct* 49
Bowling 10–0

His final first-class match was for H. D. G. Leveson-Gower's XI in 1909.

Stokes, Dennis Wilfrid
Amateur. *b:* 26.1.1911, Reading. Berkshire. Opening right-hand batsman, wicket-keeper. *Sch* Wellingborough. *Team* Minor Counties (1937–38).
Career batting
2–4–0–47–39–11.75–0–*ct* 1

His County cricket was for Berkshire.

Stokes, Frederic
Amateur. *b:* 12.7.1850, Greenwich, Kent. *d:* 7.1.1929, Inhurst, Berkshire. Brother of Graham (Kent) and Lennard (Kent). Middle order right-hand batsman, right-hand fast round-arm bowler, long-stop. *Sch* Rugby. *Team* Kent (1871–75, 4 matches).
Career batting
8–12–1–167–65–15.18–0–*ct* 3
Bowling 335–13–25.76–0–0–3/36

A noted rugby footballer, he captained England v Scotland in 1872.

Stokes, Graham
Amateur. *b:* 22.3.1858, Greenwich, Kent. *d:* 19.12.1921, Blackheath, Kent. Brother of Frederic (Kent) and Lennard (Kent). Middle order batsman. *Team* Kent (1880–81, 4 matches).
Career batting
4–8–0–39–27–4.87–0–*ct* 3

Stokes, Dr Lennard
Amateur. *b:* 12.2.1856, Greenwich, Kent. *d:* 3.5.1933, Upton, Hampshire. Brother of Frederic (Kent) and Graham (Kent). Hard hitting lower order right-hand batsman, right-hand slow under-arm bowler. *Sch* Bath. *Team* Kent (1877–80, 4 matches).
Career batting
4–6–1–43–17–8.60–0–*ct* 2
Bowling 135–6–22.50–0–0–3/56

A noted rugby footballer, he played for Blackheath and England and in 1886 was President of the Rugby Football Union.

Stollmeyer, Jeffrey Baxter
Amateur. *b:* 11.4.1921, Santa Cruz, Trinidad. Brother of V. H. (West Indies). Elegant opening right-hand batsman, leg break and googly bowler. *Team* Trinidad (1938/9 to 1956/7). *Tours* West Indies to England 1939, 1950, to India, Pakistan and Ceylon 1948/9, to Australia and New Zealand 1951/2. *Tests* West Indies (1939 to 1954/5, 32 matches).
Career batting
117–194–16–7942–324–44.61–14–*ct* 93
Bowling 2482–55–45.12–0–0–3/32
Test batting
32–56–5–2159–160–42.33–4–*ct* 20
Bowling 507–13–39.00–0–0–3/32

In 1939 in England he hit 916 runs, av 30.53, and in 1950, 1,334 runs, av 37.05. He played in all Tests on both tours.

He captained West Indies in 13 Tests and afterwards became a noted member of the West Indies Board of Control and Test Selector.

His highest innings was 324 for Trinidad v British Guiana at Port of Spain in 1946/7 and of his four double centuries three were made in the West Indies and one in India. He also hit 1,000 runs on the 1948/9 tour.

Stollmeyer, Victor Humphrey
Amateur. *b:* 24.1.1916, Santa Cruz, Trinidad. Brother of J. B. (West Indies). Opening right-hand batsman, leg break and googly bowler. *Team* Trinidad (1935/6 to 1945/6). *Tour* West Indies to England 1939. *Test* West Indies (1939, 1 match).
Career batting
33–58–9–2096–139–42.77–77–4–*ct* 16
Bowling 612–15–40.80–0–0–3/38
Test batting
1–1–0–96–96–96.00–0–*ct* 0
Troubled by illness, he missed a number of matches in the 1939 tour and played in only one Test. In first-class games he hit 542 runs, av 30.11.

Stone, Charles Cecil
Amateur. *b:* 13.6.1865, Knighton, Leicester. *d:* 11.11.1951, Eastbourne. Middle order right-hand batsman, right-arm medium pace bowler. *Sch* Uppingham. *Team* Leicestershire (1895–96, 7 matches). *Tour* Priestley to West Indies 1896/7.
Career batting
14–28–3–203–55–8.12–0–*ct* 4
Bowling 8–0
His first-class debut was for MCC in 1894. He also played for Oxfordshire.

Stone, Donald H.
Professional. *b:* 9.1.1927, Clayton, Lancashire. Lower order left-hand batsman, right-arm fast medium bowler. *Team* Lancashire (1949–50, 6 matches).
Career batting
6–8–2–86–46–14.33–0–*ct* 1
Bowling 472–9–52.44–0–0–4/30

Stone, James
Professional. *b:* 29.11.1876, Southampton. *d:* 15.11.1942, Maidenhead, Berkshire. Middle order right-hand batsman, right-arm medium pace bowler, wicket-keeper. *Teams* Hampshire (1900–14, 274 matches); Glamorgan (1922–23, 27 matches).
Career batting
306–524–63–10341–174–22.43–6–*ct* 394–*st* 130
Bowling 104–1–104.00–0–0–1/77
He hit 1,000 runs in a season three times (best 1,249, av 25.48, in 1913).

Stoner, Arthur
Professional. *b:* 11.5.1871, Streatham, Surrey. Lower order batsman, useful bowler. *Team* Surrey (1899–1900, 6 matches).
Career batting
6–9–0–98–61–10.88–0–*ct* 2
Bowling 344–14–24.57–0–0–4/16
He also played for Durham.

Storer, Enoch
Professional. *b:* 18.5.1838, Clay Cross, Derbyshire. *d:* 1880, Chorlton-cum-Hardy, Lancashire. Lower order left-hand batsman, right-hand fast round-arm bowler, slip field. *Team* Lancashire (1865–78, 6 matches).
Career batting
6–11–5–46–23–7.66–0–*ct* 2
Bowling 245–15–16.33–1–0–5/12

Storer, Harry
Professional. *b:* 24.7.1870, Butterley, Derbyshire. *d:* 25.4.1908, Holloway, Derby. He died of consumption. Brother of William (Derbyshire), father of Harry jun (Derbyshire). Middle order right-hand batsman. *Team* Derbyshire (1895, 6 matches).
Career batting
6–10–1–92–35–10.22–0–*ct* 3
Bowling 13–0
A noted soccer player, he played for Liverpool and Arsenal.

Storer, Harry (jun)
Professional. *b:* 2.2.1898, West Derby, Liverpool, Lancashire. *d:* 1.9.1967, Derby. Son of Harry (Derbyshire), nephew of William (Derbyshire). Sound opening right-hand batsman, leg break bowler, occasional wicket-keeper. *Team* Derbyshire (1920–36, 302 matches).
Career batting
302–517–28–13513–232–27.63–18–*ct* 214–*st* 1
Bowling 7525–232–32.43–9–0–7/26
He hit 1,000 runs in a season six times (best 1,652, av 36.71, in 1929).
Both his double centuries were for Derbyshire, the highest being 232 v Essex at Derby in 1933.
An excellent wing-half he played soccer for Derby County, Grimsby, Burnley and England. He later managed several League clubs.

Storer, Richard Elliott Daniel
Cricketer. *b:* 9.5.1948, Nottingham. Lower order right-hand batsman, wicket-keeper. *Sch* Nottingham HS. *Team* Oxford U (1972).
Career batting
4–6–3–13–9–4.33–0–*ct* 2

Storer, William
Professional. *b:* 25.1.1867, Butterley, Derbyshire. *d:* 28.2.1912, Derby. Brother of Harry (Derbyshire), uncle of Harry jun (Derbyshire). Sound middle order right-hand batsman, leg break

bowler, wicket-keeper. *Teams* Derbyshire (1887–1905, 209 matches); London County (1900). *Tour* Stoddart to Australia, 1897/8. *Tests* England (1897/8 to 1899, 6 matches).
Career batting
289–490–41–12966–216–28.87–17–*ct* 376–*st* 55
Bowling 7863–232–33.89–4–0–5/20
Test batting
6–11–0–215–51–19.54–0–*ct* 11
Bowling 108–2–54.00–0–0–1/24

He hit 1,000 runs in a season seven times (best 1,548, av 41.43, in 1898). His only double century was 216* for Derbyshire v Leicestershire at Chesterfield in 1899. A useful soccer player he appeared for Derby County.

Storey, Stewart James
Professional. *b:* 6.1.1941, Worthing, Sussex. Middle order right-hand batsman, right-arm medium pace bowler, good close field. *Teams* Surrey (1960–74, 315 matches); Sussex (1978, 16 matches).
Career batting
332–492–62–10776–164–25.06–12–*ct* 325
Bowling 13175–496–26.56–11–2–8/22

He hit 1,000 runs in a season five times (best 1,184, av 35.87, in 1971). He took 104 wickets, av 18.39, in 1966, achieving the 'double' that season.

He is the Sussex coach.

Storrie, James
Amateur. *b:* 7.2.1885, Hawick, Roxburghshire, Scotland. *d:* 23.7.1951, Hawick, Scotland. Brother of Walter (Scotland). Right-hand batsman, off break bowler. *Team* Scotland (1911).
Career batting
2–3–0–53–26–17.66–0–*ct* 0
Bowling 86–1–86.00–0–0–1/10

Storrie, Walter
Amateur. *b:* 2.1.1875, Hawick, Roxburghshire, Scotland. *d:* 3.12.1945, Hawick, Roxburghshire, Scotland. Brother of James (Scotland). Right-hand batsman. *Team* Scotland (1911).
Career batting
1–2–0–8–8–4.00–0–*ct* 0

Story, William Frederick
Amateur. *b:* 3.4.1852, Stockport, Cheshire. *d:* 1.12.1939, Marylebone, London. Lower order right-hand batsman, right-arm fast bowler, wicket-keeper. *Sch* Repton. *Team* Nottinghamshire (1878–79, 6 matches).
Career batting
8–13–1–41–16–3.41–0–*ct* 6–*st* 4

His final first-class match was for MCC in 1883. He was at on the Committee of Nottinghamshire CCC in 1920 and President of the Club in 1929.

He was a well-known racehorse owner.

Stott, William Brian
Professional. *b:* 18.7.1934, Yeadon, Yorkshire. Aggressive opening left-hand batsman, off break bowler. *Team* Yorkshire (1952–63, 187 matches).
Career batting
190–314–20–9248–186–31.45–17–*ct* 91
Bowling 112–7–16.00–0–0–4/34

He hit 1,000 runs in a season five times (best 2,034, av 37.66 in 1959).

Stovold, Andrew Willis
Cricketer. *b:* 19.3.1953, Southmead, Bristol. Brother of M. W. (Gloucs). Opening or middle order right-hand batsman, wicket-keeper. *Teams* Gloucestershire (1973–83, 216 matches); Orange Free State (1974/5 to 1975/6).
Career batting
224–400–22–11768–212*–31.13–13–*ct* 220–*st* 43
Bowling 86–2–43.00–0–0–1/0

He hit 1,000 runs in a season five times (best 1,671, av 42.84, in 1983).

Stovold, Martin Willis
Cricketer. *b:* 28.12.1955, Almondsbury, Bristol. Brother of A. W. (Gloucestershire). Middle order left-hand batsman. *Team* Gloucestershire (1979–82, 25 matches).
Career batting
25–37–6–518–75*–16.70–0–*ct* 5
Bowling 19–0

Stow, Montague Haslam
Amateur. *b:* 21.7.1847, Whin Moor, Roundhay, Leeds, Yorkshire. *d:* 7.9.1911, Monifieth, Scotland. Stylish middle order right-hand batsman, wicket-keeper. *Sch* Harrow. *Team* Cambridge U (1867–69, blue all three years).
Career batting
16–26–3–303–41–13.17–0–*ct* 18–*st* 1

His final first-class match was for Gentlemen of the North in 1871.

He represented Cambridge at racquets in 1868 and 1870.

Stow, Vincent Aubrey Stewart
Amateur. *b:* 27.7.1883, Kensington, London. *d:* 21.4.1968, St Pancras, London. Lower order batsman, wicket-keeper. *Sch* Winchester. *Team* Oxford U (1904). *Tour* MCC to North America 1905.
Career batting
3–5–1–47–23–11.75–0–*ct* 2

His final first-class match in England was for Gentlemen of England in 1905.

Strachan, George
Amateur. *b:* 21.11.1850, Prestbury, Gloucs. *d:* 29.12.1901, Middleburg, Transvaal, South Africa. He died of fever. Lower order right-hand batsman, slow right-arm bowler. *Sch* Cheltenham. *Teams* Gloucestershire (1870–82, 13 matches); Middlesex (1870–71, 3 matches); Surrey (1872–80, 54 matches).
Career batting
99–159–17–2014–84–14.18–0–*ct* 94
Bowling 3346–179+3–18.69–7–0–6/31

Strachan, George Robson
Cricketer. *b:* 29.8.1932, Blackridge, West Lothian, Scotland. Right-hand batsman, right-arm medium pace bowler. *Team* Scotland (1965).
Career batting
2–1–1–17–17*–no av–0–*ct* 0
Bowling 34–2–17.00–0–0–1/14

Strachan, John Harold
Amateur. *b:* 8.3.1896, Chertsey, Surrey. Middle order right-hand batsman. *Sch* Charterhouse. *Team* Free Foresters (1926).
Career batting
1–2–0–53–53–26.50–0–*ct* 0

Straker, Arthur Coppin
Amateur. *b:* 12.8.1893, Hexham, Northumberland. *d:* 14.10.1961, Pawston, Northumberland. Middle order batsman. *Sch* Harrow. *Team* Cambridge U (1913).
Career batting
1–2–0–21–21–10.50–0–*ct* 0

Strang, Dr Robert
Amateur. *b:* 30.9.1901, Hornchurch, Essex. *d:* 15.3.1976, Tylers Green, Bucks. Right-hand batsman, right-arm medium pace bowler. *Sch* Whitgift. *Team* Scotland (1925).
Career batting
1–2–0–34–23–17.00–0–*ct* 0
Bowling 66–2–33.00–0–0–2/47
He played for Berkshire.

Stratford, Alfred Hugh
Amateur. *b:* 5.9.1853, Kensington, London. *d:* 2.5.1914, Newark, New Jersey, USA. Lower order right-hand batsman, slow right-arm bowler. *Sch* Malvern. *Team* Middlesex (1877–80, 18 matches).
Career batting
33–53–8–577–55*–12.82–0–*ct* 10
Bowling 1355–83–16.32–2–0–6/44
He also played for Herefordshire. He emigrated to the USA about 1890 and played much cricket for New York and other clubs there.
A good soccer player, he appeared for Wanderers when they won the FA Cup in 1876, 1877 and 1878.

Stratton, Henry Duncan
Amateur. *b:* 1870, Wolverhampton, Staffs. *d:* 1958, Battle, Sussex. Middle order right-hand batsman. *Team* MCC (1904–14).
Career batting
4–8–3–75–20–15.00–0–*ct* 1
His County cricket was for Staffordshire.

Stratton, John William
Amateur. *b:* 31.8.1875, Turweston, Buckinghamshire. *d:* 29.10.1919, Repton, Derbyshire. Lower order right-hand batsman, right-arm fast bowler. *Sch* Cheltenham. *Team* Oxford U (1896).
Career batting
1–2–0–8–7–4.00–0–*ct* 1
Bowling 93–3–31.00–0–0–3/93
His County cricket was for Buckinghamshire.

Stratton, Robert Arthur
Amateur. *b:* 10.10.1924, Birmingham. Tail end right-hand batsman, wicket-keeper. *Sch* St Peter's, York. *Team* Cambridge U (1946).
Career batting
3–4–3–23–12*–23.00–0–*ct* 0–*st* 1

Straw, David Sorby
Cricketer. *b:* 28.5.1935, South Croydon, Surrey. Middle order right-hand batsman, wicket-keeper. *Sch* Whitgift. *Team* MCC (1964).
Career batting
1–1–0–10–10–10.00–0–*ct* 0

Straw, Thomas
Professional. *b:* 1.9.1870, Hucknall Torkard, Notts. *d:* 5.9.1959, Hucknall Torkard, Notts. Lower order right-hand batsman, wicket-keeper. *Team* Worcestershire (1899–1907, 61 matches).
Career batting
61–94–38–600–32–10.71–0–*ct* 122–*st* 12
He was dismissed twice in first-class County matches 'obstructing field' – for Worcestershire against Warwickshire in 1899 and in 1901.

Streatfeild, Alexander McNeill
(changed name to Streatfeild-Moore in 1885)
Amateur. *b:* 17.10.1863, Charts Edge, Westerham, Kent. *d:* 30.12.1940, Newbury, Berkshire. Brother of E. C. (Surrey). Middle order right-hand batsman, slow right-arm bowler. *Sch* Charterhouse. *Team* Kent (1885–88, 7 matches).
Career batting
7–14–0–127–36–9.07–0–*ct* 5
He also played for Buckinghamshire.

Streatfeild, Edward Champion
Amateur. *b:* 16.6.1870, Nutfield, Surrey. *d:* 22.8.1932, Eastbourne, Sussex. Brother of A. M. (Kent). Sound middle order right-hand batsman, right-arm medium bowler, good slip field. *Sch* Charterhouse. *Teams* Cambridge U (1890–93, blue all four years); Surrey (1890–92, 9 matches).
Career batting
38–66–9–1414–145–24.80–2–*ct* 39
Bowling 2232–123–18.14–6–2–6/34
He was also awarded his soccer blue.

Streatfeild, Granville Gerald Champion
Amateur. *b:* 5.11.1904, Westerham, Kent. *d:* 28.9.1954, Kadam Valley, Kenya. Attractive middle order right-hand batsman, left-arm fast medium bowler. *Sch* Marlborough. *Teams* Cambridge U (1925); Burma and Rangoon Gymkhana (1926/7).
Career batting
5–7–1–72–18–12.00–0–*ct* 0

Street, Alfred Edward
Professional. *b:* 7.7.1869, Godalming, Surrey. *d:* 18.2.1951, Exmouth, Devon. Son of James (Surrey). Middle order right-hand batsman, right-arm medium pace bowler. *Team* Surrey (1892–98, 50 matches).
Career batting
50–66–6–1356–161*–22.60–1–*ct* 16
Bowling 393–15–26.20–0–0–3/44
He was for many years a first-class umpire and officiated in Test matches. Whilst umpiring at Taunton in 1919 he gave a Sussex batsman, Heygate, out for failing to reach the wicket within two minutes – a decision which caused much controversy at the time.

Street, Frank
Amateur. *b:* 31.5.1870, London. *d:* 7.7.1916, Ovilliers la Boiselle, France. Middle order right-hand batsman, right-arm medium pace bowler. *Sch* Westminster. *Team* Essex (1898–99, 9 matches).
Career batting
9–11–0–246–76–22.36–0–*ct* 4
Bowling 14–0
He did not play in first-class cricket whilst at Oxford, but was awarded his blue for soccer.

Street, Francis Edward
Amateur. *b:* 16.2.1851, Hampstead, Middlesex. *d:* 4.6.1928, Armidale, New South Wales, Australia. Opening right-hand batsman, good deep field. *Sch* Uppingham. *Team* Kent (1875–77, 4 matches).
Career batting
4–7–0–21–12–3.00–0–*ct* 2

Street, George Benjamin
Professional. *b:* 6.12.1889, Charlwood, Surrey. *d:* 24.4.1924, Portslade, Sussex. He was killed in a motor-cycle accident. Middle order right-hand batsman, wicket-keeper. *Team* Sussex (1909–23, 192 matches). *Tour* MCC to South Africa 1922/3. *Test* England (1922/3, 1 match).
Career batting
197–304–73–3984–109–17.24–1–*ct* 308–*st* 121
Bowling 66–3–22.00–0–0–3/26
Test batting
1–2–1–11–7*–11.00–0–*ct* 0–*st* 1
On the 1922/3 tour to South Africa, Livsey, the wicket-keeper, was injured and Street was sent out as a replacement, but only played in four first-class matches, including the third Test.

Street, Henry
Professional. *b:* 18.4.1863, Riddings, Derbyshire. *d:* 12.3.1953, Riddings, Derbyshire. Middle order right-hand batsman. *Team* Derbyshire (1887, 2 matches).
Career batting
2–4–1–24–15*–8.00–0–*ct* 1

Street, James
Professional. *b:* 10.3.1839, Cranleigh, Surrey. *d:* 17.9.1906, Godalming, Surrey. Father of A. E. (Surrey). Lower order right-hand batsman, right-hand fast round-arm bowler. *Team* Surrey (1863–78, 139 matches).
Career batting
143–247–73–1308–50–7.51–0–*ct* 74
Bowling 11578–540–21.44–36–6–7/141
His best season was 1872, when he took 60 wickets, av 15.11. He later umpired in first-class matches.

Street, Lawrence Charles
Professional. *b:* 4.2.1920, Erdington, Birmingham. Lower order right-hand batsman, right-arm fast medium bowler. *Team* Warwickshire (1946, 4 matches).
Career batting
4–7–2–17–8*–3.40–0–*ct* 2
Bowling 146–3–48.66–0–0–2/15

Street, Norman Kingsley
Amateur. *b:* 13.8.1881, Birmingham. *d:* 10.8.1915, Suvla Bay, Gallipoli Peninsula, Turkey. Middle order right-hand batsman. *Sch* Bromsgrove. *Team* Warwickshire (1908, 5 matches).
Career batting
5–9–0–43–14–4.77–0–*ct* 3

Stretton, Sidney
Professional. *b:* 1903, Stamford, Lincolnshire.

Left-hand batsman, left-arm fast bowler. *Team* Northamptonshire (1928, 1 match).
Career batting
1–2–0–1–1–0.50–0–*ct* 1
Bowling 120–2–60.00–0–0–2/120

Stretton, Terry Kevin
Cricketer. *b:* 23.5.1953, Cosby, Leicestershire. Lower order right-hand batsman, right-arm medium pace bowler. *Team* Leicestershire (1972–75, 6 matches).
Career batting
6–7–3–20–6*–5.00–0–*ct* 2
Bowling 338–4–84.50–0–0–2/71

Stricker, Louis Anthony
Amateur. *b:* 26.5.1884, Beaconsfield, Kimberley, South Africa. *d:* 5.2.1960, Cape Town, South Africa. Opening right-hand batsman. *Team* Transvaal (1906/7 to 1911/2). *Tours* South Africa to Australia 1910/11, to England 1912. *Tests* South Africa (1909/10 to 1912, 13 matches).
Career batting
60–96–4–2105–146–22.88–2–*ct* 29–*st* 2
Bowling 303–8–37.87–0–0–3/13
Test batting
13–24–0–342–48–14.25–0–*ct* 3
Bowling 105–1–105.00–0–0–1/36
He hit 875 runs, av 19.88, in all matches on the 1912 visit to England.

Stringer, Peter Michael
Cricketer. *b:* 23.2.1943, Leeds, Yorkshire. Lower order left-hand batsman, right-arm fast medium bowler. *Teams* Leicestershire (1970–72, 37 matches); Yorkshire (1967–69, 19 matches).
Career batting
56–63–21–333–22–7.92–0–*ct* 27
Bowling 2772–88–31.50–1–0–5/43

Stringer, Thomas
Professional. *b:* 1874, Yorkshire. Tail end batsman, leg break bowler. *Team* Worcestershire (1909, 1 match).
Career batting
1–2–1–0–0*–0.00–*ct* 0
Bowling 103–1–103.00–0–0–1/103

Stripp, David Arthur
Professional. *b:* 4.4.1935, Crawley Down, Sussex. Middle order right-hand batsman, right-arm fast medium bowler. *Team* Sussex (1956–57, 12 matches).
Career batting
12–20–3–183–32*–10.76–0–*ct* 10
Bowling 297–6–49.50–0–0–2/12

Stroud, Eric Gundry
Amateur. *b:* 11.7.1904, Caterham, Surrey. *d:* 14.8.1944, Haslemere, Surrey. Lower order right-hand batsman, right-arm medium bowler. *Team* Surrey (1930, 7 matches).
Career batting
10–13–3–157–24–15.70–0–*ct* 6
Bowling 832–38–21.89–2–0–7/92
His final first-class match was for H. D. G. Leveson-Gower's XI in 1932.

Strudwick, Herbert
Professional. *b:* 28.1.1880, Mitcham, Surrey. *d:* 14.2.1970, Shoreham, Sussex. Lower order right-hand batsman, excellent wicket-keeper. *Team* Surrey (1902–27, 554 matches). *Tours* MCC to Australia 1903/4, 1911/2, 1920/1, 1924/5, to South Africa 1909/10, 1913/14. *Tests* England (1909/10 to 1926, 28 matches).
Career batting
674–835–243–6445–93–10.88–0–*ct* 1242–*st* 254
Bowling 102–1–102.00–0–0–1/9
Test batting
28–42–13–230–24–7.93–0–*ct* 60–*st* 12
One of the best wicket-keepers of his day, he set up a career record for the most dismissals by a wicket-keeper, which stood for nearly 50 years, before being beaten by J. T. Murray.

Strutt, Hon Henry
(in 1880 succeeded to the title 2nd Lord Belper)
Amateur. *b:* 20.5.1840, Westminster, London. *d:* 26.7.1914, Kingston-upon-Soar, Notts. Hard hitting lower order right-hand batsman, wicket-keeper. *Sch* Harrow. *Team* Cambridge U (1862).
Career batting
5–7–1–97–31*–16.16–0–*ct* 1
He was President of MCC in 1882 and of Nottinghamshire CCC in 1885 and 1886. His final first-class match was for MCC in 1865.
When travelling in Greece in 1865 he was taken prisoner by brigands and forced to pay £1,000 ransom for his release.
He was MP for East Derbyshire 1868 to 1874 and Berwick-on-Tweed in 1880.

Strutton, Benjamin Thomas
Professional. *b:* 1892. *d:* 9.2.1968, Southwark, London. Lower order batsman, slow left-arm bowler. *Team* Essex (1914–19, 4 matches).
Career batting
4–6–1–64–19–12.80–0–*ct* 1
Bowling 197–0

Stuart, Pascoe William Grenfell
(changed name to Stuart-French in 1917)
Amateur. *b:* 25.10.1868, Woolwich, Kent. *d:* 5.2.1954, Cobh, Co Cork. Middle order right-

hand batsman. *Sch* Sherborne. *Team* London County (1904).
Career batting
3–5–0–67–50–13.40–0–*ct* 2
His final first-class match was for MCC in 1906.

Stuart, Robert Livingstone
Amateur. *b:* 30.12.1908, Buenos Aires, Argentina. Middle order right-hand batsman, right-arm medium pace bowler. *Sch* Highgate. *Team* Argentine (1929/30 to 1937/8). *Tour* South America to England 1932.
Career batting
9–17–1–405–133–25.31–1–*ct* 4
Bowling 58–1–58.00–0–0–1/35

Stuart, William Grant Spruell
Amateur. *b:* 1889, Scotland. *d:* 23.4.1917, Arras, France. He was killed in action. Middle order batsman. *Sch* George Watson's College. *Team* Scotland (1914).
Career batting
1–2–0–27–17–13.50–0–*ct* 2

Stuart-King, R. J. *(see under* King, R. J. S.)

Stubberfield, Henry
Professional. b: 16.3.1835, Brighton, Sussex. *d:* 14.2.1918, Brighton, Sussex. Lower order right-hand batsman, right-hand fast medium round-arm bowler, good slip field. *Team* Sussex (1857–74, 57 matches).
Career batting
61–99–27–518–40–7.19–0–*ct* 55
Bowling 2522–141–17.88–8–2–7/10
After retiring from County cricket, he became a well-known umpire.

Stubbings, James
Professional. *b:* 27.4.1856, Whitwell, Derbyshire. *d:* 17.7.1912, Huddersfield, Yorkshire. Brother of Walter (Derbyshire). Lower order right-hand batsman, right-arm fast bowler. *Team* Derbyshire (1880–85, 4 matches).
Career batting
5–10–3–26–10*–3.71–0–*ct* 1
Bowling 142–7–20.28–1–0–5/51
His first-class debut was for Players of North in 1877.

Stubbings, Walter
Professional. *b:* 4.9.1870, Whitwell, Derbyshire. *d:* 28.11.1949, Wakefield, Yorkshire. Brother of James (Derbyshire). Lower order batsman, useful bowler. *Team* Derbyshire (1900, 1 match).
Career batting
1–2–1–9–9*–9.00–0–*ct* 0
Bowling 80–0

Stubbs, Thomas Alfred
Amateur. *b:* 1872, West Derby, Liverpool. Middle order batsman. *Team* Liverpool & District (1893–94).
Career batting
4–8–1–168–43–24.00–0–*ct* 2

Stubbs, Thomas Walker
Amateur. *b:* 11.9.1856, Ashton-upon-Mersey, Cheshire. *d:* 5.6.1899, Stow-on-the-Wold, Gloucs. Hard hitting lower order right-hand batsman, right-hand fast round-arm bowler. *Sch* Clifton. *Team* Oxford U (1877).
Career batting
1–1–0–1–1–1.00–0–*ct* 0
Bowling 41–3–13.66–0–0–2/26
He appeared for Gloucestershire in non-first-class matches in 1889.

Stuchbury, Stephen
Cricketer. *b:* 22.6.1954, Sheffield, Yorkshire. Lower order left-hand batsman, left-arm fast medium bowler. *Team* Yorkshire (1978–81, 3 matches).
Career batting
3–3–2–7–4*–7.00–0–*ct* 0
Bowling 236–8–29.50–0–0–3/82

Studd, Arthur Haythorne
Amateur. *b:* 19.11.1863, Hallaton Hall, Billesden, Leics. *d:* 26.1.1919, Marylebone, London. Half brother of E. J. C. (MCC), brother of J. E. K. (Middlesex), G. B. (Middlesex), C. T. (Middlesex), H. W. (Hants and Middlesex) and R. A. (Hampshire). Opening or middle order right-hand batsman, right-arm slow bowler, good cover point. *Sch* Eton. *Team* MCC (1887–88).
Career batting
5–8–0–104–47–13.00–0–*ct* 4
Bowling 23–0
He played in the 1885 Cambridge Freshmen's Match, but no first-class games at the University. In 1888 he appeared for Hampshire (non-first-class).
His first-class debut was for A. J. Webbe's XI in 1885.

Studd, Charles Thomas
Amateur. *b:* 2.12.1860, Spratton, Northants. *d:* 16.7.1931, Ibambi, Belgian Congo. Half brother of E. J. C. (MCC), brother of A. H. (MCC), J. E. K. (Middlesex), G. B. (Middlesex), H. W. (Hants and Middlesex), R. A. (Hampshire). Stylish middle order right-hand batsman, right-

arm medium fast bowler. *Sch* Eton. *Teams* Middlesex (1879–84, 34 matches); Cambridge U (1880–83, blue all four years). *Tour* Bligh to Australia 1882/3. *Tests* England (1882 to 1882/3, 5 matches).
Career batting
99–167–23–4391–175*–30.49–8–*ct* 73
Bowling 7658–441+3–17.36–32–9–8/40
Test batting
5–9–1–160–48–20.00–0–*ct* 5
Bowling 98–3–32.66–0–0–2/35

The most talented of the Studd family, he topped the first-class batting averages in 1882 with 1,249 runs, av 32.86, and came second in 1883 with 1,193, av 41.13. He took 100 wickets in a season twice (best 128+3, av 16.38, in 1883) and performed the 'double' in both years. After 1884 however he left England to become a missionary in China, remaining there until ill-health forced him home in 1895. In 1900 he went out to India to do similar work and later went to the Belgian Congo where he stayed for the remainder of his life, despite numerous illnesses and hardship.

Studd, Edward Basil Turnour
Amateur. *b:* 20.10.1878, Dhoolie, Tirhoot, India. *d:* 2.3.1951, Cheltenham, Gloucestershire. Son of E. J. C. (MCC). Middle order right-hand batsman. *Sch* Harrow. *Teams* Europeans (1917/8); Gloucestershire (1919, 2 matches).
Career batting
3–6–0–69–25–11.50–0–*ct* 2

Studd, Edward John Charles
Amateur. *b:* 13.2.1849, Tirhoot, India. *d:* 1.3.1909, Folkestone, Kent. Elder half-brother of J. E. K. (Middlesex), G. B. (Middlesex), C. T. (Middlesex), A. H. (MCC), H. W. (Hants and Middlesex) and R. A. (Hants), father of E. B. T. (Gloucs). Middle order right-hand batsman, good field. *Sch* Cheltenham. *Team* MCC (1879–85).
Career batting
21–34–1–621–110–18.81–1–*ct* 17

His final first-class match was for C. I. Thornton's XI in 1888.

For 16 years he lived in India, being an indigo planter and therefore had little opportunity for good class cricket.

Studd, George Brown
Amateur. *b:* 20.10.1859, Netheravon, Wiltshire. *d:* 13.2.1945, Pasadena, California, USA. Half-brother of E. J. C. (MCC), brother of J. E. K. (Middlesex), C. T. (Middlesex), A. H. (MCC), H. W. (Hants and Middlesex), R. A. (Hampshire). Middle order right-hand batsman, brilliant field. *Sch* Eton. *Teams* Cambridge U (1879–82, blue all four years); Middlesex (1879–86, 29 matches). *Tour* Bligh to Australia 1882/3. *Tests* England (1882/3, 4 matches).
Career batting
87–142–10–2892–120–21.90–3–*ct* 74–*st* 1
Bowling 29–2–14.50–0–0–1/5
Test batting
4–7–0–31–9–4.42–0–*ct* 8

His best season was 1881 with 647 runs, av 30.90.

A good tennis player he represented Cambridge. After leaving University he became, like his brother C. T., a missionary in China and later in India and America.

Studd, Brig-Gen Herbert William
Amateur. *b:* 26.12.1870, Tidworth, Wiltshire. *d:* 8.8.1947, Bayswater, London. Half-brother of E. J. C. (MCC), brother of J. E. K. (Middlesex), C. T. (Middlesex), A. H. (MCC), G. B. (Middlesex), R. A. (Hampshire). Middle order right-hand batsman. *Sch* Eton. *Teams* Middlesex (1890, 1 match); Hampshire (1898, 4 matches).
Career batting
8–13–0–352–71–27.07–0–*ct* 5
Bowling 71–1–71.00–0–0–1/23

He played in the Freshmen's match of 1890, but no first-class matches for Cambridge.

Studd, Sir John Edward Kynaston
Amateur. *b:* 26.7.1858, Netheravon, Wiltshire. *d:* 14.1.1944, Marylebone, London. Half-brother of E. J. C. (MCC), brother of C. T. (Middlesex), A. H. (MCC), G. B. (Middlesex), H. W. (Middlesex and Hampshire), R. A. (Hampshire). Middle order right-hand batsman, right-arm fast bowler. *Sch* Eton. *Teams* Middlesex (1878–84, 11 matches); Cambridge U (1881–84, blue all four years).
Career batting
55–98–3–1691–154–17.80–1–*ct* 22
Bowling 322–12–26.83–0–0–3/32

His final first-class match was for MCC in 1885.

He took a prominent part in the founding and running of the London Polytechnic and was President from 1903 to his death. In 1928/9 he was Lord Mayor of London.

Studd, Sir Peter Malden
Amateur. *b:* 15.9.1916, Dublin. Attacking middle order right-hand batsman, good field. *Sch* Harrow. *Team* Cambridge U (1936–39, blue 1937–39).
Career batting
28–46–4–1075–80*–25.59–0–*ct* 12

He was Lord Mayor of London in 1970–71.

Studd, Reginald Augustus
Amateur. *b:* 18.12.1873, Tidworth, Wiltshire. *d:* 3.2.1948, Northampton. Half-brother of E. J. C. (MCC), brother of C. T. (Middlesex), A. H. (MCC), G. B. (Middlesex), H. W. (Middlesex and Hampshire) and J. E. K. (Middlesex). Middle order right-hand batsman. *Sch* Eton. *Teams* Cambridge U (1895, blue); Hampshire (1895, 3 matches). *Tour* Mitchell to North America 1895 (he did not play in first-class matches).
Career batting
14–24–2–585–96*–26.59–0–*ct* 3
His first-class debut was for MCC in 1894.

Sturgeon, S. M.
Amateur. Lower order batsman, wicket-keeper. *Team* Scotland (1922–23).
Career batting
2–3–0–1–1–0.33–0–*ct* 5–*st* 1

Sturman, Walter
Professional. *b:* 29.8.1882, Leicester. *d:* July 1958, Leicester. Lower order right-hand batsman, wicket-keeper. *Team* Leicestershire (1909–12, 24 matches).
Career batting
24–36–9–273–46–10.11–0–*ct* 27–*st* 5

Sturt, Montague Alfred Sliney
Amateur. *b:* 11.11.1876, Sunderland, Co Durham. *d:* 16.1.1961, Dover, Kent. Middle order right-hand batsman. *Sch* Taunton. *Team* Somerset (1896–1910, 10 matches).
Career batting
10–17–1–199–35–12.43–0–*ct* 3
Bowling 15–1–15.00–0–0–1/15
He also played for Devon.

Sturt, Michael Ormonde Cleasby
Amateur. *b:* 12.9.1940, Wembley, Middlesex. Lower order right-hand batsman, wicket-keeper. *Team* Middlesex (1961–78, 33 matches).
Career batting
33–35–9–202–26–7.76–0–*ct* 61–*st* 10

Style, Sir William Henry Marsham
Amateur. *b:* 3.9.1826, Bicester, Oxon. *d:* 31.1.1904, Folkestone, Kent. Lower order batsman, wicket-keeper. *Sch* Eton. *Team* Hampshire (1865, 1 match).
Career batting
1–2–0–1–1–0.50–0–*ct* 0–*st* 1
He also played for Wiltshire and Brecon.

Styler, Sidney William
Professional. *b:* 26.8.1908, Cotteridge, Warwickshire. *d:* 1980, Worcester. Lower order right-hand batsman, wicket-keeper. *Team* Worcestershire (1929–31, 18 matches).
Career batting
18–31–6–134–24–5.36–0–*ct* 23–*st* 3

Subba Row, Raman
Amateur. *b:* 29.1.1932, Streatham, Surrey. Sound opening or middle order left-hand batsman, slow leg break and googly bowler, excellent slip field. *Sch* Whitgift. *Teams* Cambridge U (1951–53, blue all three years); Surrey (1953–54, 41 matches); Northamptonshire (1955–61, 113 matches). *Tours* MCC to Australia and New Zealand 1958/9, to West Indies 1959/60; Commonwealth to India 1953/4; International XI to India and Pakistan 1961/2; President's XI in India 1967/8. *Tests* England (1958–61, 13 matches).
Career batting
260–407–65–14182–300–41.46–30–*ct* 176
Bowling 3363–87–38.65–2–0–5/21
Test batting
13–22–1–984–137–46.85–3–*ct* 5
Bowling 2–0
He hit 1,000 runs in a season six times (best 1,917, av 46.75, in 1959). His highest innings was 300 for Northants v Surrey at the Oval in 1958, he also hit one double century for Northants.
From 1958 to 1961 he captained Northants. In 1981/2 he was manager of the England team to India.
Chairman of Surrey, he also serves on several MCC Committees.

Subramanya, Venkataraman
Amateur. *b:* 16.7.1936, Bangalore, India. Middle order right-hand batsman, right-arm medium, or leg break and googly bowler, good close field. *Team* Mysore (1959/60 to 1969/70). *Tours* India to England 1967, to Australia and New Zealand 1967/8, to East Africa 1967/8; State Bank of India to Ceylon 1968/9. *Tests* India (1964/5 to 1967/8, 9 matches).
Career batting
101–150–16–4219–213*–31.48–8–*ct* 121
Bowling 3093–70–44.18–1–0–7/78
Test batting
9–15–1–263–75–18.78–0–*ct* 9
Bowling 201–3–67.00–0–0–2/32
He played in two Tests on the 1967 tour, but his overall figures were very modest. His highest score was 213* for Mysore v Madras at Madras in 1966/7.

Such, Peter Mark
Cricketer. *b:* 12.6.1964, Helensburgh, Scotland. Tail end right-hand batsman, off break bowler. *Team* Nottinghamshire (1982–83, 18 matches).

Career batting
18–24–7–16–5–0.94–0–*ct* 13
Bowling 1504–45–33.42–2–0–6/123

Suckling, Ernest
Professional. *b:* 27.3.1890, Birmingham. *d:* 24.2.1962, Blackpool, Lancashire. Middle order left-hand batsman, slow left-arm bowler. *Teams* Warwickshire (1919, 2 matches); Worcestershire (1923–24, 3 matches).
Career batting
5–8–1–130–58–18.57–*ct* 1
Bowling 129–4–32.25–0–0–4/71

Sueter, Thomas
Professional. *b:* 1750, Hambledon, Hampshire. *d:* 17.2.1827, Hambledon, Hampshire. Middle order left-hand batsman, wicket-keeper. *Teams* Hampshire (1772–86); Surrey (1788–89).
He was one of the leading batsmen of the Hambledon Club.

Sugden, Henry Emanuel
Amateur. *b:* 16.7.1859, Edmonton, Middlesex. *d:* 4.9.1935, Chilworth, Hampshire. Middle order right-hand batsman. *Team* Derbyshire (1882, 2 matches).
Career batting
2–4–0–13–9–3.25–0–*ct* 0
His brother, A. S. Sugden, played for Derbyshire in non-first-class matches.

Sugden, Mark
Amateur. *b:* 11.2.1902, Leek, Staffs. Right-hand batsman, right-arm fast medium bowler. *Sch* Denstone. *Teams* Dublin University (1922–26); Ireland (1924–30).
Career batting
8–16–1–263–51–17.53–0–*ct* 3
Bowling 255–6–42.50–0–0–3/98
A noted rugby footballer, he was capped for Dublin University and Ireland.

Sugden, Ronald Scott
Amateur. *b:* 25.5.1896, Aintree, Liverpool. *d:* 26.3.1971, Dinas Powys, Glamorgan. Lower order batsman, useful bowler. *Team* RAF (1929).
Career batting
2–3–0–17–12–5.66–0–*ct* 0
Bowling 33–0

Sugg, Frank Howe
Professional. *b:* 11.1.1862, Ilkeston, Derbyshire. *d:* 29.5.1933, Liverpool, Lancashire. Brother of Walter (Yorkshire and Derbyshire). Attacking middle order right-hand batsman, brilliant outfield. *Teams* Derbyshire (1884–86, 33 matches); Lancashire (1887–99, 235 matches); Yorkshire (1883, 8 matches). *Tests* England (1888, 2 matches).
Career batting
305–515–30–11859–220–24.45–16–*ct* 167–*st* 1
Bowling 273–10–27.30–0–0–2/12
Test batting
2–2–0–55–31–27.50–0–*ct* 0
He hit 1,000 runs in a season five times (best 1,439, av 31.26, in 1896). His only double century was 220 for Lancashire v Gloucestershire at Bristol in 1896.
A noted soccer player, he captained Sheffield Wednesday, Derby County and Burnley, also playing for Bolton Wanderers. Other sports at which he excelled were long distance swimming, billiards, rifle shooting, putting the shot and weight lifting.

Sugg, Walter
Amateur. *b:* 21.5.1860, Ilkeston, Derbyshire. *d:* 21.5.1933, Dore, Yorkshire. Brother of F. H. (Yorkshire, Derbyshire and Lancashire). Middle order right-hand batsman, right-arm medium bowler, good cover point. *Teams* Derbyshire (1884–1902, 128 matches); Yorkshire (1881, 1 match).
Career batting
129–218–16–3469–107–17.17–2–*ct* 64
Bowling 1560–50–31.20–0–0–4/61

Sulley, Joseph
Professional. *b:* 28.5.1850, Arnold, Nottinghamshire. *d:* 14.2.1932, Daybrook, Nottinghamshire. Lower order batsman, left-hand fast round-arm bowler. *Team* Nottinghamshire (1887–88, 2 matches).
Career batting
3–6–1–57–31–11.40–0–*ct* 2
Bowling 251–15–16.73–1–0–5/46
His first-class debut was as a given man for Gentlemen of the North in 1880.

Sullivan, Rev Arnold Moon
Amateur. *b:* 30.8.1878, Kirby Moorside, Yorkshire. *d:* 27.6.1943, Meads, Eastbourne, Sussex. Middle order right-hand batsman. *Sch* St Peter's, York. *Teams* Cambridge U (1899–1900); Sussex (1901, 4 matches).
Career batting
13–23–3–341–63–17.05–0–*ct* 10

Sullivan, Dennis
Professional. *b:* 28.1.1883, Mitcham, Surrey. *d:* 28.12.1968, Harold Wood, Essex. Lower order right-hand batsman, wicket-keeper. *Teams* Surrey (1914–21, 8 matches); Glamorgan (1922–28, 115

matches); Wales (1923–28). *Tours* Tennyson to Jamaica 1926/7, 1927/8.
Career batting
136–192–63–971–47*–7.52–0–*ct* 152–*st* 93

Sullivan, John
Cricketer. *b:* 5.2.1945, Stalybridge, Lancashire. Lower order right-hand batsman, right-arm medium pace bowler. *Team* Lancashire (1963–76, 154 matches).
Career batting
154–241–32–4286–81*–20.50–0–*ct* 85
Bowling 2216–76–29.15–0–0–4/19

Sullivan, Joseph Hubert Baron
Amateur. *b:* 21.9.1890, York. *d:* 8.2.1932, Parkgate, Chester. Sound opening batsman, useful bowler. *Sch* Rossall and St Peter's, York. *Teams* Yorkshire (1912, 1 match); Cambridge U (1912); Europeans (1921/2 to 1924/5).
Career batting
8–15–0–209–44–13.80–0–*ct* 3
Bowling 194–7–27.71–0–0–3/24

Sullivan, John Patrick
Cricketer. *b:* 11.3.1948, Bristol. Middle order right-hand batsman, occasional wicket-keeper. *Team* Gloucestershire (1968–77, 23 matches).
Career batting
23–40–1–480–53–12.30–0–*ct* 14
Bowling 50–2–25.00–0–0–2/50

Sully, Haydn
Professional. *b:* 1.11.1939, Watchet, Somerset. Lower order left-hand batsman, slow left-arm bowler. *Teams* Northamptonshire (1964–69, 110 matches); Somerset (1959–63, 12 matches).
Career batting
122–134–50–722–48–8.59–0–*ct* 63
Bowling 8686–314–27.66–16–2–7/29

He took 101 wickets, av 21.23, in 1966.

Sumar, Shiraz
Cricketer. *b:* 1950, Tanganyika. Middle order right-hand batsman. *Team* East Africa (1975). *Tour* East Africa to England 1975.
Career batting
1–2–0–25–15–12.50–0–*ct* 1

Summers, Douglas Walter Levi
Professional. *b:* 12.10.1911, Smethwick, Staffordshire. Son of F. T. (Worcestershire). Lower order right-hand batsman, slow left-arm bowler. *Team* Worcestershire (1930, 1 match).
Career batting
1–1–0–4–4–4.00–0–*ct* 0
Bowling 11–0

Summers, Francis Theodore
Professional. *b:* 25.1.1887, Alcester, Warwickshire. *d:* 27.10.1967, Inkberrow, Worcestershire. Father of D. W. L. (Worcestershire). Lower order right-hand batsman, wicket-keeper. *Team* Worcestershire (1921–28, 57 matches).
Career batting
57–91–27–409–36–6.39–0–*ct* 76–*st* 8

In a local club match he removed the first five batsman as a wicket-keeper and then took off his pads and dismissed the remaining five as a bowler.

Summers, George
Professional. *b:* 21.6.1844, Nottingham. *d:* 19.6.1870, Nottingham. Opening right-hand batsman. *Team* Nottinghamshire (1867–70, 18 matches).
Career batting
32–59–1–922–57–15.89–0–*ct* 15

Batting for Nottinghamshire v MCC at Lord's in 1870 he was hit on the head by a ball from Platts and died a few days later from the injury.

Summers, Gerald Frank
Amateur. *b:* 9.1.1905, Richmond, Surrey. *d:* 12.8.1983, Harrogate, Yorkshire. Attacking middle order right-hand batsman. *Team* Cahn's XI (1932–38). *Tours* Cahn to North America 1933 (not first-class), to Ceylon 1936/7.
Career batting
5–9–1–119–54*–14.87–0–*ct* 1
Bowling 213–6–35.50–0–0–3/18

He also played for Surrey 2nd XI.

Summers, Leonard Shelton Heath
Amateur. *b:* 25.6.1904, Fulham, London. *d:* 26.2.1977, Barnes, Surrey. Opening batsman, leg break bowler. *Sch* Emanuel. *Teams* Leveson-Gower's XI (1932); Minor Counties (1933).
Career batting
2–4–0–103–57–25.75–0–*ct* 1
Bowling 154–4–38.50–0–0–3/99

He was a noted club cricketer in the London area, being particularly associated with Dulwich and Surrey 2nd XI.

Summers, Rev W.
Amateur. Middle order batsman. *Team* Lord Sheffield's XI (1881).
Career batting
1–2–1–2–2*–2.00–0–*ct* 0

Sunnucks, Peter Regan
Professional. *b:* 22.6.1916, Boughton-Monchelsea, Kent. Middle order right-hand batsman. *Team* Kent (1934–46, 68 matches).
Career batting
68–121–8–2016–162–17.84–1–*ct* 11

Surendranath
Amateur. *b:* 4.1.1937, Meerut, India. Lower order right-hand batsman, right-arm medium pace bowler. *Team* Services (1955/6 to 1968/9). *Tour* India to England 1959. *Tests* India (1958/9 to 1960/1, 11 matches).
Career batting
88–115–29–1351–119–15.70–1–*ct* 32
Bowling 7055–278–25.37–15–1–7/14
Test batting
11–20–7–136–27–10.46–0–*ct* 4
Bowling 1053–26–40.50–2–0–5/75
On the 1959 tour he took 79 wickets, av 28.60, in first-class matches and headed the Test bowling with 16 wickets, av 26.62, but was heavily criticised for bowling very negatively down the leg side.

Surfleet, Dr Desmond Ford
Amateur. *b:* 5.2.1912, Dublin. Middle order right-hand batsman, right-arm medium pace bowler. *Sch* University College School. *Team* Middlesex (1931–33, 10 matches).
Career batting
14–21–1–337–86–16.85–0–*ct* 7
Bowling 34–0

Surman, Godfrey Pearce
Amateur. *b:* 18.7.1914, Uckington, Gloucs. Lower order right-hand basman, right-arm fast medium bowler. *Sch* Cheltenham. *Team* Gloucestershire (1936–37, 2 matches).
Career batting
2–4–3–11–5*–11.00–0–*ct* 0
Bowling 99–2–49.50–0–0–2/60

Surridge, David
Cricketer. *b:* 6.1.1956, Bishop's Stortford, Herts. Lower order right-hand batsman, right-arm fast medium bowler. *Team* Cambridge U (1979, blue); Gloucestershire (1980–82, 25 matches).
Career batting
34–28–16–103–14*–8.58–0–*ct* 7
Bowling 2599–87–29.87–1–0–5/78
He also played for Hertfordshire.

Surridge, John Giles Clive
Amateur. *b:* 10.8.1935, Sutton, Surrey. Middle order right-hand batsman, useful bowler. *Sch* Marlborough. *Team* Oxford U (1956).
Career batting
1–2–0–1–1–0.50–0–*ct* 1
Bowling 3–0

Surridge, Stuart Spicer
Cricketer. *b:* 28.10.1951, Westminster, London. Son of W. S. (Surrey). Lower order right-hand batsman, wicket-keeper. *Sch* Westminster. *Team* Surrey (1978, 1 match).
Career batting
1–1–1–2–2*–no av–0–*ct* 1

Surridge, Walter Stuart
Amateur. *b:* 3.9.1917, Herne Hill, London. Father of S. S. (Surrey). Lower order right-hand batsman, right-arm fast medium bowler, brilliant close field. *Sch* Emanuel. *Team* Surrey (1947–59, 254 matches). *Tours* Surrey to Rhodesia 1959/60; Surridge to Bermuda 1961 (not first-class).
Career batting
267–333–33–3882–87–12.94–0–*ct* 375
Bowling 14623–506–28.89–22–1–7/49
He captained Surrey from 1952 to 1956 and led the County to the Championship title in all five seasons.
His best bowling season was 1952 with 78 wickets, av 25.21.

Surti, Rusi Framroze
Amateur. *b:* 25.5.1936, Surat, India. Dashing middle order left-hand batsman, left-arm medium pace bowler, good outfield. *Teams* Gujerat (1956/7 to 1968/9); Rajasthan (1959/60 to 1960/1); Queensland (1968/9 to 1972/3, 35 matches). *Tours* India to England 1967, to Australia and New Zealand 1967/8, to West Indies 1961/2. *Tests* India (1960/1 to 1969/70, 26 matches).
Career batting
160–278–17–8066–246*–30.90–6–*ct* 121
Bowling 10529–284–37.07–10–0–5/42
Test batting
26–48–4–1263–99–28.70–0–*ct* 26
Bowling 1962–42–46.71–1–0–5/74
He appeared in two Tests on the 1967 tour to England, but made little impact – the very wet weather telling against him. His highest score was 246* for Rajasthan v Uttar Pradesh at Udaipur in 1959/60. His final first-class match in India was the first Test at Bombay in 1969/70.

Susskind, Manfred Julius
Amateur. *b:* 8.6.1891, Johannesburg, South Africa. *d:* 9.7.1957, Johannesburg, South Africa. He collapsed and died in the Stock Exchange. Steady middle order right-hand batsman. *Sch* University College School, London. *Teams* Middlesex (1909–10, 6 matches); Cambridge U (1910–12); Transvaal (1912/13 to 1936/7). *Tour* South Africa to England 1924. *Test* South Africa (1924, 5 matches).
Career batting
97–149–11–4775–171–34.60–11–*ct* 85–*st* 3
Bowling 81–1–81.00–0–0–1/13
Test batting
5–8–0–268–65–33.50–0–*ct* 1

He hit 1,413 runs, av 35.32, on the 1924 tour and came second in the Test batting averages.

Sutcliffe, Bert
Amateur. *b:* 17.11.1923, Ponsonby, Auckland, New Zealand. Excellent opening later middle order left-hand batsman, slow left-arm bowler, good field. *Teams* Auckland (1941/2 to 1948/9); Otago (1946/7 to 1961/2); Northern Districts (1962/3 to 1965/6). *Tours* New Zealand to England 1949, 1958, 1965, to South Africa and Australia 1953/4, to India and Pakistan 1955/6, 1964/5; Commonwealth to South Africa 1959/60. *Tests* New Zealand (1946/7 to 1965, 42 matches).
Career batting
232–405–39–17283–385–47.22–44–*ct* 158–*st* 1
Bowling 3264–86–37.95–2–0–5/19
Test batting
42–76–8–2727–230*–40.10–5–*ct* 20
Bowling 344–4–86.00–0–0–2/38

The outstanding New Zealand cricketer of his generation, he hit 2,627 runs, av 59.70, on the 1949 tour to England in first-class matches and 423, av 60.42, in Tests; in 1958 he hit 1,085 runs, av 31.00, in first-class matches; coming out of retirement for the 1965 tour he achieved little.

His highest score was 385 for Otago v Canterbury at Christchurch in 1952/3. He also hit 355 for Otago, but not one of his six double centuries was made in England. He hit 1,000 runs in an overseas season twice.

Sutcliffe, Herbert
Professional. *b:* 24.11.1984, Summer Bridge, Harrogate, Yorkshire. *d:* 22.1.1978, Crosshills, Yorkshire. Father of W. H. H. (Yorkshire). Excellent opening right-hand batsman. *Team* Yorkshire (1919–45, 602 matches). *Tours* MCC to Australia 1924/5, 1928/9, to Australia and New Zealand 1932/3, to South Africa 1927/8; Yorkshire to Jamaica 1935/6; Vizianagram to India and Ceylon 1930/1. *Tests* England (1924–35, 54 matches).
Career batting
754–1098–124–50670–313–52.02–150–*ct* 472
Bowling 563–14–40.21–0–0–3/15
Test batting
54–84–9–4555–194–60.73–16–*ct* 23

One of the greatest of all opening batsman, he had the technique and the determination to score runs even on the worst of wickets, and in fact became more determined as the bowler or the wicket grew more difficult. Unlike many obdurate players, however, he was equally at home when fast scoring and sixes were needed. His career began in 1919 and he completed 1,000 runs in every season from then until 1939, when he retired – though he made a brief appearance in 1945. He went on to reach 2,000 runs in fifteen seasons and then on to 3,000 three times, his best year being 1932 with 3,336 runs, av 74.13; his highest average, however, came the previous summer with 3,006 runs, av 96.96 – in both years he was the leading English player. He also hit 1,000 runs twice in Australia and once in South Africa.

His highest innings was 313 for Yorkshire v Essex at Leyton in 1932, in the course of which he and P. Holmes added a record-breaking 555 for the first wicket. He hit 16 double centuries, all but one for Yorkshire.

With Holmes, he put on a century partnership for the first wicket 74 times, and with Hobbs he compiled eleven century first wicket partnerships, including three in consecutive innings in Australia in 1924/5. Perhaps his most famous partnership with Hobbs was the one during the fifth Test at the Oval in 1926, which realised 172 runs and virtually won the Ashes for England. In that series Sutcliffe scored 472 runs, av 78.66. In the next home series against Australia in 1930 he hit 436 runs, av 87.20, and in his final series in 1934, 304 runs, av 50.66. He was equally at ease in Australia, his figures in first-class matches for his three tours being most impressive : 1924/5, 1,250, av 69.44; 1928/9, 852, av 53.25; 1932/3, 1,345, av 64.05.

Sutcliffe, James Frederick
Amateur. *b:* 12.12.1876, Medway, Kent. *d:* 14.7.1915, Gallipoli Peninsula, Turkey. Middle order batsman. *Team* Hampshire (1911, 1 match).
Career batting
1–2–0–24–16–12.00–0–*ct* 0

Sutcliffe, Richard John
Cricketer. *b:* 18.9.1954, Rochdale, Lancashire. Lower order right-hand batsman, right-arm medium pace bowler. *Team* Lancashire (1978, 1 match).
Career batting
1–2–2–10–10*–no av–0–*ct* 0
Bowling 37–1–37.00–0–0–1/37

Sutcliffe, Simon Paul
Cricketer. *b:* 22.5.1960, Watford, Herts. Lower order right-hand batsman, off break bowler. *Teams* Oxford U (1980–81, blue both years); Warwickshire (1981–83, 20 matches).
Career batting
38–47–11–141–20–3.91–0–*ct* 6
Bowling 4020–96–41.87–2–0–6/19

Sutcliffe, William Herbert Hobbs
Amateur. *b:* 10.10.1926, Pudsey, Yorkshire. Son of Herbert (Yorkshire). Forcing middle order

right-hand batsman, right-arm medium, or leg break bowler. *Sch* Rydal. *Team* Yorkshire (1948–57, 177 matches). *Tours* Commonwealth to India and Ceylon 1950/1, MCC to Pakistan 1955/6.
Career batting
210–326–41–7530–181–26.42–6–*ct* 90
Bowling 334–15–22.26–0–0–2/12
He hit 1,261 runs, av 33.18, in 1955. He was captain of Yorkshire in 1956 and 1957.
His final first-class match was for MCC in 1959.

Sutherland, Henry Boyd
Amateur. *b:* 4.12.1844, Croydon, Surrey. *d:* 27.8.1915, St Leonard's-on-Sea, Sussex. Tail end batsman, right-hand medium pace round-arm bowler, good point field. *Sch* Eton. *Team* Kent (1871, 1 match).
Career batting
2–3–0–29–22–9.66–0–*ct* 3
Bowling 55–2–27.50–0–0–2/32
His final first-class match was for MCC in 1873.
He also played for Cheshire.

Sutherland, Ian
Amateur. *b:* 7.7.1926, Leicester. Middle order right-hand batsman, leg break and googly bowler. *Sch* Wyggeston GS. *Team* Cambridge U (1949).
Career batting
1–1–0–9–9–9.00–0–*ct* 0
Bowling 23–0

Sutherland, Thomas
Professional. *b:* 17.2.1880. Lower order right-hand batsman, right-arm fast bowler. *Team* Hampshire (1898–99, 9 matches).
Career batting
9–14–9–74–21–14.80–0–*ct* 6
Bowling 446–11–40.54–1–0–6/111

Sutor, John Alan
Amateur. *b:* July 1909, Tenbury, Worcestershire. *d:* December 1966, Australia. Middle order right-hand batsman, right-arm medium pace bowler. *Sch* Uppingham. *Team* Worcestershire (1928, 1 match).
Career batting
1–2–0–3–2–1.50–0–*ct* 0

Sutthery, Arthur Melbourne
Amateur. *b:* 25.3.1864, Clifton-Reynes, Buckinghamshire. *d:* 15.5.1937, Chelsea, London. Aggressive opening or middle order right-hand batsman, right-arm fast medium bowler, good field. *Sch* Oundle and Uppingham. *Team* Cambridge U (1886–87, blue 1887).
Career batting
20–34–2–658–73–20.56–0–*ct* 11
Bowling 622–23–27.04–1–0–5/51
His County cricket was for Northants (pre-first-class), later for Devon and Shropshire.
His final first-class match was for an England XI in 1888.

Suttle, Kenneth George
Professional. *b:* 25.8.1928, Kensington, London. Attractive middle order left-hand batsman, slow left-arm bowler, brilliant outfield. *Team* Sussex (1949–71, 601 matches). *Tours* MCC to the West Indies 1953/4; International XI to India, Pakistan and Ceylon 1967/8.
Career batting
612–1064–92–30225–204*–31.09–49–*ct* 384–*st* 3
Bowling 8727–266–32.80–1–0–6/64
He hit 1,000 runs in a season 17 times, going on to 2,000 once : 2,326, av 39.42, in 1962. He appeared in 423 consecutive County Championship matches between August 1954 and July 1969. He hit 204* for Sussex v Kent at Tunbridge Wells in 1962.
He was a useful soccer player with Chelsea and Brighton and Hove Albion, later being player-manager to non-League clubs.

Sutton, Cecil Alfred Leonard
Amateur. *b:* 1886, Lambeth, London. *d:* 10.2.1965, Whatton, Nottinghamshire. Hard hitting lower order right-hand batsman, right-arm medium pace bowler. *Sch* Nottingham HS. *Team* Nottinghamshire (1907, 1 match).
Career batting
1–1–0–1–1–1.00–0–*ct* 0
Bowling 26–0
A well-known local architect he designed the pavilion of Sir Julien Cahn's ground in West Bridgford, Nottingham.

Sutton, Charles Henry
Amateur. *b:* 1907. *d:* 1945, Gosport, Hants. Lower order batsman, useful bowler. *Sch* Leys. *Team* South America (1932). *Tour* South Americans to England 1932.
Career batting
1–1–0–10–10–10.00–0–*ct* 0
Bowling 23–0
He only played in one first-class match on the 1932 tour.

Sutton, Charles Lexington Manners
Amateur. *b:* 26.4.1891, Chichester, Sussex. *d:* 8.10.1962, Mount Ephraim, Tunbridge Wells, Kent. Lower order batsman, useful bowler. *Team* Army (1920–23).

Career batting
5–8–5–90–30*–30.00–0–*ct* 4
Bowling 396–10–39.60–0–0–3/15

Sutton, Edmund George Gresham
Amateur. *b:* 12.10.1844, Marylebone. *d:* 7.10.1903, Tring, Herts. Middle order right-hand batsman. *Team* Middlesex (1868, 1 match).
Career batting
25–39–4–483–40–13.80–0–*ct* 26
Bowling 21–0
His debut in first-class cricket was for MCC in 1864, and his final match for MCC in 1873.
He also played for Buckinghamshire and Hertfordshire.

Sutton, George
Professional. Middle order batsman. *Team* Essex (1912, 1 match).
Career batting
1–1–0–0–0–0.00–0–*ct* 0

Sutton, John Arthur
Cricketer. *b:* 26.6.1939, Manchester, Lancashire. Middle order left-hand batsman, off break bowler. *Team* Minor Counties (1969–72).
Career batting
4–8–0–164–57–20.50–0–*ct* 2
Bowling 197–4–49.25–0–0–2/44
His County cricket is for Cheshire, commencing 1959.

Sutton, Leonard Cecil Leicester
Amateur. *b:* 14.4.1890, Half Way Tree, Jamaica. *d:* 3.6.1916. Middle order left-hand batsman, left-arm slow medium bowler. *Sch* King's Bruton. *Team* Somerset (1909–12, 17 matches).
Career batting
17–29–5–171–30–7.12–0–*ct* 10
Bowling 6–0

Sutton, Michael Antony
Amateur. *b:* 29.3.1921, Weymouth, Dorset. Lower order right-hand batsman, off break bowler. *Sch* Ampleforth. *Teams* Oxford U (1946–47, blue 1946); Somerset (1948, 1 match).
Career batting
19–26–8–144–30–8.00–0–*ct* 23
Bowling 1218–47–25.91–1–0–5/63

Sutton-Mattocks, Christopher John
Cricketer. *b:* 10.7.1951, London. Middle order left-hand batsman. *Sch* Winchester. *Team* Oxford U (1972–73).
Career batting
6–12–0–107–37–8.91–0–*ct* 2

Swaffer, John
Professional. *b:* 10.11.1852, Ruckinge, Kent. *d:* 26.7.1936, Orsett, Essex. Sound middle order right-hand batsman. *Team* Kent (1873, 1 match).
Career batting
1–2–0–18–18–9.00–0–*ct* 0

Swain, William
Professional. *b:* 8.9.1830, Burley, Otley, Yorkshire. *d:* 5.10.1910, East Brisbane, Australia. Stylish middle order right-hand batsman, right-hand fast, or slow, round-arm bowler. *Team* MCC (1864).
Career batting
2–4–2–22–13*–11.00–0–*ct* 0

Swallow, Ian Geoffrey
Cricketer. *b:* 18.12.1962, Barnsley, Yorkshire. Right-hand batsman, off break bowler. *Team* Yorkshire (1983, 2 matches).
Career batting
2–3–2–19–11*–19.00–0–*ct* 1
Bowling 82–2–41.00–0–0–1/15

Swallow, Raymond
Professional. *b:* 15.6.1935, Southwark, London. Middle order right-hand batsman, good cover field. *Team* Derbyshire (1959–63, 37 matches).
Career batting
38–68–2–1323–115–20.04–1–*ct* 13
Bowling 8–0
His first-class debut was for MCC in 1957.
A good soccer player he appeared at outside-right for Arsenal and Derby County.

Swalwell, Reginald Sawdon
Amateur. *b:* 25.6.1873, York. *d:* 20.9.1930, Sunningdale, Berkshire. Middle order left-hand batsman, useful bowler. *Team* Worcestershire (1907–20, 18 matches).
Career batting
26–45–2–665–72–15.46–0–*ct* 8
Bowling 156–3–52.00–0–0–3/49
His final first-class match was for MCC in 1925.
He also played for Dorset and Berkshire.

Swan, John James
Professional. *b:* 24.9.1848, Oadby, Leicestershire. *d:* 22.2.1924, Maidstone, Kent. Middle order right-hand batsman, right-hand medium pace round-arm bowler. *Team* Surrey (1870–76, 32 matches).
Career batting
35–65–5–662–62–11.03–0–*ct* 22
Bowling 83–2–41.50–0–0–1/15

Swan, Richard Gilroy
Cricketer. *b:* 6.12.1951, Duns, Berwickshire, Scotland. Middle order right-hand batsman. *Sch* Merchiston. *Team* Scotland (1980–83).
Career batting
4–8–1–180–66–25.71–0–*ct* 3
Bowling 0–0

Swann, Charles Frederick
Professional. *b:* 1883, West Ham, Essex. *d:* 7.3.1960, Leytonstone, Essex. Middle order right-hand batsman. *Team* Essex (1912, 1 match).
Career batting
1–1–0–0–0–0.00–0–*ct* 0

Swann, John Lassam
Amateur. *b:* 3.10.1926, Ealing, Middlesex. Lower order left-hand batsman, leg break bowler. *Team* Middlesex (1949–51, 4 matches).
Career batting
4–6–3–69–23*–23.00–0–*ct* 0
Bowling 220–6–36.66–0–0–3/39

Swann-Mason, Rev Richard Swann
Amateur. *b:* 4.3.1871, Haslingfield, Cambridgeshire. *d:* 21.2.1942, St Pancras, London. Middle order batsman. *Sch* Perse. *Team* MCC (1909–14).
Career batting
3–5–1–67–25–16.75–0–*ct* 4
Bowling 36–0

Swanton, Ernest William, OBE
Amateur. *b:* 11.2.1907, Forest Hill, London. Middle order right-hand batsman. *Sch* Cranleigh. *Team* Middlesex (1937–38, 3 matches). *Tour* Cahn to North America 1933 (not first-class).
Career batting
3–5–0–67–26–13.40–*ct* 1

He organised several tours in the 1950s to the West Indies.

One of the best-known cricket journalists and commentators, he wrote mainly for the London *Evening Standard* and *Daily Telegraph*. He is also the author of numerous books on cricket.

Swarbrook, Frederick William
Cricketer. *b:* 17.12.1950, Derby. Middle order left-hand batsman, slow left-arm bowler. *Teams* Derbyshire (1967–79, 199 matches); Griqualand West (1972/3 to 1982/3); Orange Free State (1979/80).
Career batting
231–340–89–5300–90–21.11–0–*ct* 141
Bowling 13998–467–29.97–15–2–9/20

His best bowling was 9/20 for Derbyshire v Sussex at Hove in 1975.

Swart, Peter Douglas
Cricketer. *b:* 27.4.1946, Bulawayo, Rhodesia. Middle order right-hand batsman, right-arm medium pace bowler. *Teams* Rhodesia (1965/6); Western Province (1967/8 to 1980/1); Boland (1981/2 to 1982/3); Glamorgan (1978–79, 44 matches).
Career batting
158–250–27–5652–122–25.34–6–*ct* 102
Bowling 9070–358–25.33–5–1–6/85

His debut in England was for International Cavaliers in 1969; he also played for D. H. Robins' XI in England in 1974.

In 1978 he hit 1,078 runs, av 31.70.

Swayne, Harry Walter
Amateur. *b:* 3.3.1869, Glastonbury, Somerset. *d:* 25.11.1911, Pertapur, India. Middle order batsman. *Sch* Winchester. *Team* Somerset (1894, 1 match).
Career batting
1–2–1–27–19*–27.00–0–*ct* 0

Sweet, Charles Francis Long
Amateur. *b:* 29.11.1860, Bath, Somerset. *d:* 24.1.1932, Teignmouth, Devon. Middle order batsman. *Sch* Winchester. *Team* Somerset (1882–83, 5 matches).
Career batting
5–9–5–67–19*–16.75–0–*ct* 3

He also played for Dorset and Wiltshire.

Sweet-Escott, Edward Rice
Amateur. *b:* 27.7.1879, Brompton-Ralph, Somerset. *d:* 1.7.1956, Penarth, Glamorgan. Middle order right-hand batsman. *Team* Glamorgan (1921, 1 match).
Career batting
1–2–0–13–13–6.50–0–*ct* 0

Sweetland, Edward Henry
Professional. *b:* 25.4.1903, London. *d:* 18.7.1978, Middleton-on-Sea, Sussex. Lower order batsman, wicket-keeper. *Team* Middlesex (1927, 2 matches).
Career batting
5–5–3–19–8*–9.50–0–*ct* 5

His final first-class match was for MCC in 1933.

Swetman, Roy
Professional. *b:* 25.10.1933, Westminster, London. Lower order right-hand batsman, wicket-keeper, occasional off break bowler. *Teams* Surrey (1954–61, 129 matches); Nottinghamshire (1966–67, 56 matches); Gloucestershire (1972–74, 45 matches). *Tours* MCC to Pakistan 1955/6, to Australia and New Zealand 1958/9, to

West Indies 1959/60; Surrey to Rhodesia 1959/60; Cavaliers to India and South Africa 1962/3; Commonwealth to South Africa 1962/3. *Tests* England (1958/9 to 1959/60, 11 matches).
Career batting
286–411–73–6495–115–19.21–2–*ct* 531–*st* 66
Bowling 69–1–69.00–0–0–1/10
Test batting
11–17–2–254–65–16.93–0–*ct* 24–*st* 2
His first-class debut was for Combined Services in 1953.

Swift, Brian Tennant
Amateur. *b:* 9.9.1937, Adelaide, South Australia. *d:* 8.3.1958, Higham, Suffolk. He died in a motor-car accident. Lower order right-hand batsman, wicket-keeper. *Team* Cambridge U (1957, blue).
Career batting
17–23–7–160–25–10.00–0–*ct* 37–*st* 10

Swinburne, John Warwick
Cricketer. *b:* 4.12.1939, Wath-on-Dearne, Yorkshire. Lower order right-hand batsman, off break bowler. *Team* Northamptonshire (1970–74, 29 matches).
Career batting
29–36–8–160–25–5.71–0–*ct* 13
Bowling 2281–83–27.48–4–1–6/57
He also played for Shropshire and Devon.

Swindell, Robert Stephen
Cricketer. *b:* 22.1.1950, Derby. Lower order right-hand batsman, off break bowler. *Team* Derbyshire (1972–77, 23 matches).
Career batting
23–32–11–242–38–11.52–0–*ct* 11
Bowling 1665–50–33.30–4–0–6/79

Swinford, Thomas Francis
Amateur. *b:* 9.5.1839, Margate, Kent. *d:* 23.1.1915, Eastbourne, Sussex. Opening right-hand batsman, good long-stop. *Sch* Blackheath. *Team* Kent (1874, 4 matches).
Career batting
4–8–0–89–50–11.12–0–*ct* 0
He also played for Northumberland.

Swinstead, Frank Hillyard
Amateur. *b:* 6.8.1862, Chelsea, Middlesex. *d:* 6.12.1937, Hornsey, Middlesex. Stylish middle order batsman. *Team* MCC (1900).
Career batting
2–4–0–37–15–9.25–0–*ct* 1
Bowling 22–0
His first-class debut was for Gentlemen of England in 1888. His County cricket was for Herefordshire.

Swire, Samuel Henry
Amateur. *b:* 3.1.1839, Ashton-under-Lyme, Lancashire. *d:* 29.12.1905, Southport, Lancashire. Middle order right-hand batsman, useful bowler, cover-point field. *Team* Lancashire (1865–68, 5 matches).
Career batting
5–9–1–93–18*–11.62–0–*ct* 1
Bowling 37–0
He was Honorary Secretary of Lancashire CCC from 1873 until his death in 1905.

Swyer, Basil James
Amateur. *b:* 6.6.1898, West Ham, Essex. *d:* 7.7.1964, Nottingham. Lower order batsman, right-arm medium pace bowler. *Sch* Bancroft's. *Team* Essex (1923, 1 match).
Career batting
1–2–0–12–7–6.00–0–*ct* 0
Bowling 56–0

Sydenham, David Alfred Donald
Professional. *b:* 6.4.1934, Surbiton, Surrey. Lower order right-hand batsman, left-arm fast medium bowler. *Team* Surrey (1957–72, 142 matches).
Career batting
145–133–65–487–24*–7.16–0–*ct* 52
Bowling 9732–487–19.98–26–3–9/70
He took 100 wickets in a season twice (best 115, av 17.65, in 1962). His best innings analysis was 9 for 70 for Surrey v Gloucestershire at the Oval in 1964. After 1965 he made only one further first-class appearance – in 1972.

Syed Hussain
Amateur. *b:* 1888, Moradabad, United Provinces, India. Middle order right-hand batsman, wicket-keeper. *Tour* India to England 1911.
Career batting
8–16–4–52–14–4.33–0–*ct* 2–*st* 2
He did not appear in first-class matches in India.

Syfret, Admiral Sir Edward Neville
Amateur. *b:* 20.6.1889, Cape Town, South Africa. *d:* 10.12.1972, Hornsey, Middlesex. Middle order right-hand batsman. *Team* Royal Navy (1912).
Career batting
1–2–0–30–30–15.00–0–*ct* 0

Sykes, Charles Percy
Amateur. *b:* 9.8.1862, Westminster, London. *d:* 17.6.1899, Chelsea, London. Middle order batsman. *Sch* Harrow. *Team* MCC (1890).
Career batting
1–2–0–14–12–7.00–0–*ct* 0

Sykes, Eric
Professional. *b:* 23.6.1906, Bolsover, Derbyshire. Son of E. C. Sykes (Hampshire). Middle order right-hand batsman. *Team* Derbyshire (1925–32, 5 matches).
Career batting
5–10–1–105–50–11.66–0–*ct* 0
Bowling 2–0

Sykes, Ernest Castle
Professional. *b:* 31.5.1869, Sheffield, Yorkshire. *d:* 30.11.1925, Bolsover, Derbyshire. Father of Eric (Derbyshire). Lower order right-hand batsman, wicket-keeper. *Team* Hampshire (1896, 1 match).
Career batting
1–2–2–5–5*–no av–0–*ct* 0

Sykes, James Frederick
Cricketer. *b:* 30.12.1965, Shoreditch, London. Right-hand batsman, off break bowler. *Team* Middlesex (1983, 1 match).
Career batting
1–1–0–4–4–4.00–0–*ct* 0
Bowling 54–1–54.00–0–0–1/32

Syme, Ian Alexander Hastie
Amateur. *b:* 29.12.1929, Stirling, Scotland. Right-hand batsman, right-arm fast medium bowler. *Sch* Edinburgh Academy. *Team* Scotland (1950).
Career batting
1–2–0–12–12–6.00–0–*ct* 0
Bowling 7–0

Symes-Thompson, Rev Francis
Amateur. *b:* 2.2.1875, Marylebone, London. *d:* 3.3.1948, Teignmouth, Devon. Brother of H. E. (Cambridge U). Lower order right-hand batsman, wicket-keeper. *Sch* Harrow. *Team* Oxford U (1898).
Career batting
1–1–1–7–7*–no av–0–*ct* 0
His County cricket was for Buckinghamshire.

Symes-Thompson, Dr Henry Edmund
Amateur. *b:* 22.6.1873, Marylebone, London. *d:* 18.1.1952, Oxford. Brother of Francis (Oxford U). Middle order right-hand batsman. *Sch* Winchester. *Team* Cambridge U (1894–95).
Career batting
8–16–1–174–31–11.60–0–*ct* 6
His final first-class match was for MCC in 1906.

Symington, Stuart Johnston
Amateur. *b:* 16.9.1926, Bexhill, Sussex. Right-hand batsman, right-arm fast medium pace bowler. *Sch* Canford. *Team* Leicestershire (1948–49, 23 matches).
Career batting
23–40–6–744–65–21.88–0–*ct* 13
Bowling 1448–36–40.22–1–0–5/45

Symonds, Henry George
Amateur. *b:* 24.6.1889, Cardiff. *d:* 1.1.1945, Canton, Cardiff. Middle order left-hand batsman, slow left-arm bowler. *Teams* Glamorgan (1921–25, 22 matches); Wales (1925–29).
Career batting
27–48–2–766–76–16.65–0–*ct* 5
Bowling 307–8–38.37–0–0
His first-class debut was for South Wales in 1912.

Syrée, Dr Anton Hugh
Amateur. *b:* 21.10.1859, Port Corrie, South Africa. *d:* 9.1.1924, Cheslyn Hay, Staffordshire. Middle order right-hand batsman, slow right-arm bowler. *Sch* St John's, Leatherhead. *Team* Kent (1879, 1 match).
Career batting
1–2–0–7–7–3.50–0–*ct* 0
Bowling 10–0

TABER, HEDLEY BRIAN
Cricketer. *b:* 29.4.1940, Wagga Wagga, New South Wales, Australia. Lower order right-hand batsman, leg break bowler, wicket-keeper. *Team* New South Wales (1964/5 to 1973/4, 73 matches). *Tours* Australia to England 1968, 1972, to South Africa 1966/7, 1969/70, to India and Sri Lanka 1969/70. *Tests* Australia (1966/7 to 1969/70, 16 matches).
Career batting
129–182–35–2648–109–18.01–0–*ct* 345–*st* 50
Bowling 6–0
Test batting
16–27–5–353–48–16.04–0–*ct* 56–*st* 4
He was the reserve wicket-keeper on both visits to England, but appeared in one Test in 1968.

Taberer, Henry Melville
Amateur. *b:* 7.10.1870, Keiskama Hoek, Cape Province, South Africa. *d:* 5.6.1932, Colesburg, South Africa. Middle order right-hand batsman, right-arm fast bowler, good field. *Teams* Oxford U (1891–92); Natal (1893/4 to 1894/5). *Test* South Africa (1902/3, 1 match).
Career batting
11–20–3–222–47*–13.05–0–*ct* 5
Bowling 446–22–20.27–0–0–4/14
Test batting
1–1–0–2–2–2.00–0–*ct* 0
Bowling 48–1–48.00–0–0–1/25
He played for Essex 1891 to 1893 (pre-first-class) and also Rhodesia and Transvaal in non-first-class matches. He captained South Africa in his only Test, which was also his final first-class match. A noted rugby footballer, he was awarded his blue at Oxford and also represented the University in the long-jump. At the time of his death he was a member of the South Africa Board of Control and vice-chairman of the South African Cricket Association.

Tabor, Alfred
Amateur. *b:* 24.2.1850, Trent, Middlesex. *d:* 16.12.1925, Eastbourne, Sussex. Brother of A. S. (Middlesex and Surrey). Sound defensive opening right-hand batsman, good field. *Sch* Harrow. *Team* Middlesex (1872, 1 match). *Tour* Ceylon to India 1884/5 (not first-class).
Career batting
1–2–0–49–42–24.50–0–*ct* 0
His opportunity for County cricket was very limited, since he went to Ceylon as a coffee planter in 1873, not returning until 1890. He did however play in Ceylon, being for some time captain of the Ceylon team. He did not appear in any first-class matches whilst at Cambridge, though he played in the Freshmen's match of 1870.

Tabor, Arthur Sydney
Amateur. *b:* 9.11.1852, Trent, Middlesex. *d:* 14.10.1927, Earl's Court, London. Brother of Alfred (Middlesex). Attractive opening right-hand batsman, good deep field. *Sch* Eton. *Teams* Cambridge U (1872–74, blue all three years); Middlesex (1872–74, 6 matches); Surrey (1878, 1 match).
Career batting
28–49–1–682–59–14.20–0–*ct* 9

Tagart, Noel Ongley
Amateur. *b:* 24.12.1878, Paddington, London. *d:* 8.10.1913, Molyneux Park, Tunbridge Wells, Kent. Opening right-hand batsman, point field. *Sch* Clifton. *Teams* Cambridge U (1900); Gloucestershire (1900–01, 6 matches).
Career batting
8–11–0–140–30–12.72–0–*ct* 4

Tahir Naqqash
Cricketer. *b:* 28.6.1959, Lahore, Pakistan. Brother of Arif Naqqash (Lahore). Lower order right-hand batsman, originally slow, later right-arm fast medium bowler. *Teams* Lahore (1975/6); Servis Industries (1976/7); Punjab (1975/6); Muslim Commercial Bank (1976/7 to 1982/3). *Tours* Pakistan to Australia 1981/2, to England 1982. *Tests* Pakistan (1981/2 to 1982/3, 10 matches).
Career batting
39–41–6–715–60–20.42–0–*ct* 19
Bowling 2772–85–32.61–3–0–9/45
Test batting
10–11–3–182–57–22.75–0–*ct* 1
Bowling 910–23–39.56–1–0–5/40
He played in two Tests on the 1982 tour, but his record in all first-class matches was only 15 wickets, av 35.80. His best bowling was 9/45 for MCB v Karachi at Karachi in 1980/1.

Tait, Alan
Cricketer. *b:* 27.12.1953, Washington, Co Durham. Opening left-hand batsman. *Teams* Northants (1971–75, 52 matches); Gloucestershire (1978, 11 matches).
Career batting
63–104–1–1897–99–18.41–0–*ct* 15
Bowling 0–0

Tait, John Robert
Amateur. *b:* 20.11.1886, Scotland. *d:* 13.4.1945, Clifton, Bristol. Aggressive middle order right-hand batsman. *Teams* Glamorgan (1921–26, 43 matches); Wales (1923).
Career batting
44–82–1–1477–96–18.35–0–*ct* 22
Bowling 87–1–87.00–0–0–1/5

Tait, Robert Garland Work
Amateur. *b:* 28.6.1885, Aberdeen, Scotland. *d:* 18.8.1973, Dundee, Scotland. Right-hand batsman. *Team* Scotland (1907–13).
Career batting
13–25–1–590–59–24.58–0–*ct* 9
Bowling 125–2–62.50–0–0–1/8

Tait, Thomas
Professional. *b:* 7.10.1872, Langley Moor, Co Durham. *d:* 6.9.1954, Hemsworth, Yorkshire. Opening or middle order batsman. *Team* Yorkshire (1898–99, 2 matches).
Career batting
2–3–1–7–3–3.50–0–*ct* 1

Talat Ali Malik
Cricketer. *b:* 29.5.1950, Lahore, Pakistan. Opening right-hand batsman, right-arm medium pace off break bowler. *Teams* Lahore (1967/8 to 1970/1); Punjab University (1969/70 to 1971/2); PIA (1973/4 to 1978/9); United Bank (1977/8). *Tours* Pakistan to England 1971, 1978, to Australia and New Zealand 1972/3, 1978/9; Pakistan Under-25 to Sri Lanka 1973/4. *Tests* Pakistan (1972/3 to 1978/9, 10 matches).
Career batting
115–205–15–7296–258–38.36–15–*ct* 42
Bowling 247–2–123.50–0–0–1/32
Test batting
10–18–2–370–61–23.12–0–*ct* 4
Bowling 7–0
He had only a modest tour of England in 1971, not appearing in the Tests; in 1978 he played in two Tests, but in first-class matches only hit 278 runs, av 25.27. His highest score was 258 for PIA v Rawalpindi at Rawalpindi in 1975/6. He hit 1,124 runs, av 34.06, in Pakistan in 1973/4.

Talbot, Basil Lynch
Amateur. *b:* 23.2.1903, Portsmouth, Hampshire. *d:* 18.2.1962, Wareham, Dorset. Lower order batsman, wicket-keeper. *Team* Sussex (1947, 1 match).
Career batting
1–2–0–35–25–17.50–0–*ct* 2

Talbot, Henry Lynch
Amateur. *b:* 1863, Greenwich, Kent. *d:* 1911, Perak, Malaya. Middle order right-hand batsman. *Sch* Wellington. *Team* MCC (1895).
Career batting
1–2–0–9–7–4.50–0–*ct* 1
His County cricket was for Bedfordshire.

Talbot, Hon Milo George
Amateur. *b:* 14.9.1854, Malahide Castle, Co Dublin. *d:* 3.9.1931, Bifrons, Canterbury, Kent. Opening right-hand batsman, right-hand medium pace round-arm bowler. *Sch* Wellington. *Team* Gentlemen of the South (1875).
Career batting
1–2–0–1–1–0.50–ct 2

Talbot, Rev Neville Stuart
Amateur. *b:* 21.8.1879, Headington, Oxfordshire. *d:* 3.4.1943, Henfield, Sussex. Lower order batsman, useful bowler. *Sch* Haileybury. *Team* Oxford U (1907).
Career batting
1–2–0–30–26–15.00–0–*ct* 0
Bowling 44–3–14.66–0–0–2/18

Talbot, Ronald Osman
Amateur. *b:* 26.11.1904, Christchurch, New Zealand. *b:* 5.1.1983, Auckland, New Zealand. Middle order right-hand batsman, right-arm medium pace bowler. *Team* Canterbury (1922/3 to 1935/6). *Tour* New Zealand to England 1931.
Career batting
51–86–7–1946–117–24.63–3–*ct* 31
Bowling 2005–54–37.12–1–0–5/106
On his tour to England he hit 759 runs, av 23.71, but proved ineffective as a bowler.

Tallon, Donald
Amateur. *b:* 17.2.1916, Bundaberg, Queensland, Australia. Brother of L. W. T. (Queensland). Lower order right-hand batsman, wicket-keeper. *Team* Queensland (1933/4 to 1953/4, 86 matches). *Tours* Australia to England 1948, 1953, to New Zealand 1945/6, 1949/50. *Tests* Australia (1945/6 to 1953, 21 matches).
Career batting
150–228–21–6034–193–29.14–9–*ct* 302–*st* 130
Bowling 202–0
Test batting
21–26–3–394–92–17.13–0–*ct* 50–*st* 8
He was the principal wicket-keeper of the 1948 Australian touring team, but lost his Test place to Langley on the 1953 visit.

Tamhane, Narendra Shankar
Amateur. *b:* 4.8.1931, Bombay, India. Lower order right-hand batsman, wicket-keeper. *Team* Bombay (1953/4 to 1963/4). *Tours* India to Pakistan 1954/5, to Ceylon 1956/7, to England 1959. *Tests* India (1954/5 to 1960/1, 21 matches).
Career batting
93–96–16–1459–109*–18.23–1–*ct* 175–*st* 78
Bowling 43–2–21.50–0–0–2/43
Test batting
21–27–5–225–54*–10.22–0–*ct* 35–*st* 16
He played in two of the four Tests on the

1959 tour. His first-class debut was for Indian Universities in 1951/2 and his final match for Bandokar's XI in 1968/9.

Tamplin, Cyril
Amateur. *b:* 27.5.1921, Cardiff. Lower order right-hand batsman, wicket-keeper. *Teams* Bengal (1942/3); Glamorgan (1947, 3 matches).
Career batting
4–5–2–56–40*–18.66–0–*ct* 8–*st* 2

Tancred, Augustus Bernard
Amateur. *b:* 20.8.1865, Port Elizabeth, South Africa. *d:* 23.11.1911, Cape Town, South Africa. He died after an operation. Brother of L. J. (South Africa) and V. M. (South Africa). Sound opening right-hand batsman. *Teams* Kimberley (1889/90 to 1890/1); Griqualand West (1890/1); Transvaal (1896/7 to 1898/9); MCC (1897). *Tests* South Africa (1888/9, 2 matches).
Career batting
11–21–1–708–106–35.40–1–*ct* 6
Bowling 220–8–27.50–0–0–3/22
Test batting
2–4–1–87–29–29.00–0–*ct* 2
Owing to business commitments he was unable to come to England with the 1894 South African touring team – his single appearance in England was for MCC in 1897. His first-class debut was in the first Test match v England in 1888/9.

Tancred, Louis Joseph
Amateur. *b:* 7.10.1876, Port Elizabeth, South Africa. *d:* 28.7.1934, Johannesburg, South Africa. Brother of A. B. and V. M. (South Africa). Steady opening right-hand batsman. *Teams* Transvaal (1896/7 to 1919/20); London County (1901). *Tours* South Africa to England 1901, 1904, 1907, 1912. *Tests* South Africa (1902/3 to 1912, 14 matches).
Career batting
130–219–12–5695–160–27.51–11–*ct* 73
Bowling 190–8–23.75–0–0–4/43
Test batting
14–26–1–530–97–21.20–0–*ct* 3
During his four tours to England he achieved the greatest success in 1904 with 1,217 runs, av 41.96 – he did not reach 1,000 runs on the other visits for South Africans, but in all first-class matches he scored 1,000 runs in a season twice (best 1,269, av 40.93, in 1904). He captained South Africa in three Tests in 1912.

Tandy, Brig-General Ernest Napper
Amateur. *b:* 13.5.1879, Axbridge, Somerset. *d:* 6.5.1953, St Pancras, London. Middle order right-hand batsman, good field. *Sch* Wellington. *Team* Somerset (1904–05, 2 matches).
Career batting
3–5–0–81–30–16.20–0–*ct* 1
His final first-class match was for MCC in 1908.

Tankerville, 4th Earl of, Charles Bennett
Amateur. *b:* 15.11.1743. *d:* 10.12.1822, Walton-on-Thames, Surrey. Middle order right-hand batsman. *Team* Surrey (1773–79).
Career batting
not applicable, pre-1800
He was a great patron of cricket and many matches were played under his auspices at Laleham-Burway. Among professional cricketers whom he employed on his estate were Lumpy Stevens and Bedster.

Tanner, Arthur Ralph
Amateur. *b:* 25.12.1889, Bromley, Kent. *d:* 16.8.1966, Hendon, Middlesex. Lower order right-hand batsman, left-arm medium or slow bowler. *Team* Middlesex (1920–27, 45 matches).
Career batting
47–68–10–764–81*–13.17–0–*ct* 56
Bowling 1969–71–27.73–1–0–5/13
His final first-class appearance was for Free Foresters in 1929.

Tanner, John Denys Parkin
Amateur. *b:* 2.7.1921, Harrogate, Yorkshire. Lower order left-hand batsman, wicket-keeper. *Sch* Charterhouse. *Team* Oxford U (1947–49).
Career batting
7–13–4–112–25*–12.44–0–*ct* 8–*st* 3
His final first-class match was for MCC in 1955. His County cricket was for Oxfordshire. He played soccer for Huddersfield Town.

Tanner, William
Professional. *b:* 11.4.1841, Weybridge, Surrey. Tail end right-hand batsman, right-hand fast round-arm bowler, mid-wicket field. *Team* Surrey (1866–68, 2 matches).
Career batting
3–6–2–2–1*–0.50–0–*ct* 1
Bowling 26–0
His first-class debut was for Players of Surrey in 1863. He also played for Devon.

Tapling, Thomas Keay
Amateur. *b:* 30.10.1855, Norwood, Surrey. *d:* 11.4.1891, Gumley Hall, Leics. Hard-hitting middle order right-hand batsman. *Sch* Harrow and Brighton. *Team* MCC (1886). *Tour* Vernon to India and Ceylon 1889/90 (not first-class).
Career batting
1–2–0–5–5–2.50–0–*ct* 0
He did not appear in first-class cricket whilst

at Cambridge. He was Conservative MP for the Harborough Division of Leicestershire from 1886 to his death.

Tapp, Theodore Arthur
Amateur. *b:* 5.4.1883, Bromley, Kent. *d:* 21.10.1917, nr Dozingham, Belgium. Middle order right-hand batsman, right-arm fast bowler. *Sch* Rugby. *Team* London County (1904).
Career batting
1–2–0–9–5–4.50–0–*ct* 0
Bowling 99–5–19.80–1–0–5/99

Tapsfield, Rev Hugh Alexander
Amateur. *b:* 31.1.1870, Windsor, Berkshire. *d:* 3.3.1945, Weybridge, Surrey. Middle order right-hand batsman. *Sch* Bradfield. *Team* Somerset (1892, 1 match).
Career batting
1–2–0–1–1–0.50–0–*ct* 0
He appeared in the Seniors Match at Oxford, but no first-class matches.

Tarbox, Charles Victor
Professional. *b:* 2.7.1891, Hemel Hempstead, Hertfordshire. *d:* 15.6.1978, Peacehaven, Sussex. Middle order right-hand batsman, right-arm medium pace bowler. *Team* Worcestershire (1921–29, 226 matches).
Career batting
226–398–31–5824–109–15.86–2–*ct* 121
Bowling 13256–375–35.34–11–1–7/55
He also played for Hertfordshire.

Tarilton, Percy Hamilton
Amateur. *b:* 6.2.1885, St Johns, Barbados. *d:* 18.2.1953, Paynes Bay, Barbados. Opening right-hand batsman. *Team* Barbados (1905/6 to 1929/30). *Tour* West Indies to England 1923.
Career batting
51–79–7–2777–304*–38.56–8–*ct* 33–*st* 5
Bowling 0–1–0.00–0–0–1/0
He hit 554 runs, av 21.30, on the 1923 tour. His innings of 304* for Barbados v Trinidad at Bridgetown in 1919/20 was a new first-class record for the West Indies.

Tarrant, Edward
Professional. *b:* 1846, Cambridge. *d*: 19.7.1885, Cambridge. Brother of G. F. (Cambridgeshire). Lower order batsman, useful bowler. *Team* Cambridgeshire (1866, 1 match).
Career batting
1–2–0–4–4–2.00–0–*ct* 1
Bowling 25–0

Tarrant, Francis Alfred
Professional. *b:* 11.12.1880, Fitzroy, Victoria, Australia. *d:* 29.1.1951, Upper Hawthorn, Victoria, Australia. Nephew of W. A. (Victoria). Cautious middle order right-hand batsman, left-arm slow medium bowler, good slip field. *Teams* Victoria (1898/9 to 1925/6, 13 matches); Middlesex (1904 to 1914, 206 matches); Europeans (1915/6 to 1936/7); Patiala (1926/7 to 1933/4). *Tour* Australians to India 1935/6.
Career batting
329–541–48–17952–250*–36.41–33–*ct* 304
Bowling 26391–1506+5–17.52–133–38–10/90
He hit 1,000 runs in a season nine times, going on to 2,000 once : 2,030, av 46.13, in 1911. Eight times he exceeded 100 wickets in a season (best 183, av 15.70, in 1907) – in all eight of these summers he achieved the 'double'. He was regarded by some as the greatest all-rounder of his generation, but as an Australian living in England was never selected for Test matches. Three of his four double centrues were for Middlesex, the other being for Victoria, and his highest innings was 250* for Middlesex v Essex at Leyton in 1914. He took nine wickets in an innings seven times, going on to take all ten once (for 90)– for Maharaja of Cooch Behar's XI v Lord Willingdon's XI at Poona in 1918/19; he also hit 182* in this match. His first-class debut in England was for MCC in 1903.

Tarrant, George Frederick
(his death was recorded as G. F. Wood)
Professional. *b:* 7.12.1838, Cambridge. *d:* 2.7.1870, Cambridge. He died of pleurisy. Brother of Edward (Cambridgeshire). Hard-hitting lower order right-hand batsman, right-hand fast round-arm bowler, good field. *Team* Cambridgeshire (1861–68, 31 matches). *Tours* Parr to Australia 1863/4; Willsher to North America 1868 (not first-class).
Career batting
71–119–9–1633–108–14.84–1–*ct* 58
Bowling 4792–410+11–11.68–41–16–10/40
His first-class debut was for AEE in 1860, and his final first-class match for AEE in 1869. He was for a few seasons perhaps the best fast bowler in England – in 1862 he took 96 wickets, av 10.07; in 1864 67 (av 8.80); in 1865 45 (av 14.15); in 1866 61 (av 13.26); and in 1867 44 (av 8.70). His best bowling was 10/40 for England v XIII of Kent at Lord's in 1863.

Tasker, Alfred George Ernest
Professional. *b:* 16.6.1934, Southwark, London. Lower order batsman, wicket-keeper. *Team* Worcestershire (1956, 1 match).
Career batting
1 match, did not bat – *ct* 1

Tasker, John
Amateur. *b:* 4.2.1887, South Kirkby, Yorkshire.

d: 24.8.1975, Greenham Common, Berkshire. Middle order right-hand batsman. *Team* Yorkshire (1912–13, 31 matches).
Career batting
33–47–4–644–67–14.97–0–*ct* 14
Bowling 16–0

His final first-class match was for the Army in 1919.

Tate, Cecil Frederick
Professional. *b:* 1.5.1908, Gillingham, Kent. Son of F. W. (Sussex), brother of M. W. (Sussex). Middle order right-hand batsman, slow left-arm bowler. *Teams* Derbyshire (1928, 4 matches); Warwickshire (1931–33, 7 matches).
Career batting
11–12–3–82–21–9.11–0–*ct* 5
Bowling 409–8–51.12–0–0–3/65

Tate, Edward
Professional. *b:* 30.8.1877, Lyndhurst, Hampshire. *d:* 4.1.1953, Malvern, Worcs. Lower order right-hand batsman, right-arm medium pace bowler. *Team* Hampshire (1898–1902, 29 matches).
Career batting
35–62–17–326–34*–7.24–0–*ct* 13
Bowling 2054–66–31.12–2–1–8/51

He also played for Devon. For fifty years he was cricket professional and manager of the college store at Malvern.

Tate, Frederick
Professional. *b:* 6.6.1844, Lyndhurst, Hampshire. *d:* 24.4.1935, Lyndhurst, Hampshire. Brother of H. W. (Hampshire). Lower order right-hand batsman, right-hand fast round-arm bowler, slip field. *Team* Hampshire (1870–76, 4 matches).
Career batting
4–8–3–50–18*–10.00–0–*ct* 5
Bowling 147–13–11.30–2–0–6/63

Tate, Frederick William
Professional. *b:* 24.7.1867, Brighton, Sussex. *d:* 24.2.1943, Burgess Hill, Sussex. Father of M. W. (Sussex) and C. F. (Derbyshire and Warwickshire). Tail end right-hand batsman, right-arm medium pace bowler, slip field. *Team* Sussex (1887–1905, 312 matches). *Test* England (1902, 1 match).
Career batting
320–458–150–2952–84–9.58–0–*ct* 236
Bowling 28691–1331–21.55–104–29–9/73
Test batting
1–2–1–9–5*–9.00–0–*ct* 2
Bowling 51–2–25.50–0–0–2/7

He took 100 wickets in a season five times (best 180, av 15.71, in 1902). His best analysis in an innings was 9 for 73 for Sussex v Leics at Leicester in 1902. On his only appearance in Test cricket (having been chosen instead of G. H. Hirst on the morning of the match), he went in to bat as England's last man with eight runs needed for victory – he was dismissed for 4 and England lost by three runs.

Tate, Harry Geroge
Amateur. *b:* 18.7.1862, East Knoyle, Wiltshire. *d:* 9.3.1949, Bishop's Hull, Somerset. Middle order batsman. *Team* Somerset (1882, 1 match).
Career batting
1–2–0–0–0–0.00–0–*ct* 1

Tate, Henry William
Professional. *b:* 4.10.1849, Lyndhurst, Hampshire. *d:* 9.5.1936, Richmond, Surrey. Brother of Frederick (Hants). Lower order right-hand batsman, right-hand fast round-arm bowler, good slip field. *Team* Hampshire (1869–85, 29 matches).
Career batting
29–54–9–499–61*–11.08–0–*ct* 26
Bowling 1744–96–18.16–6–1–6/51

He also played for Huntingdonshire.

Tate, Maurice William
Professional. *b:* 30.5.1895, Brighton, Sussex. *d:* 18.5.1956, Wadhurst, Sussex. Son of F. W. (Sussex), brother of C. F. (Derbyshire and Warwickshire). Hard-hitting middle order right-hand batsman, slow off break, changed in 1922 to right-arm fast medium, or medium pace, bowler. *Team* Sussex (1912–37, 525 matches). *Tours* MCC to Australia 1924/5, 1928/9, to Australia and New Zealand 1932/3, to India, Burma and Ceylon 1926/7, to South Africa 1930/1; Brinckman to South America 1937/8 (injured on outward voyage and did not play in a match). *Tests* England (1924–35, 39 matches).
Career batting
679–970–102–21717–203–25.01–23–*ct* 284
Bowling 50571–2784–18.16–195–44–9/71
Test batting
39–52–5–1198–100*–25.48–1–*ct* 11
Bowling 4055–155–26.16–7–1–6/42

Until 1922 an off break bowler, Tate then developed into the most effective medium fast bowler of his generation. He was the first bowler to thoroughly exploit the use of the seam and his deceptive swerve combined with his nip off the pitch troubled even the best batsmen. He took over 100 wickets in a season 13 times in England, plus once overseas, going on to 200 three times with his best being 228, av 14.97, in 1925. His best bowling in an innings was 9 for 71 for Sussex v Middlesex at Lord's in 1926. In Test cricket he was England's most effective bowler on two tours of Australia – in 1924/5 and 1928/9 – on the former visit he took 77 wickets, av 19.01. He hit 1,000 runs in a season 11 times and once overseas (when he performed the 'double').

Tate's batting was also most effective – in three seasons he achieved the exceptional 'double' of 1,000 runs and 200 wickets and the more ordinary 1,000 runs and 100 wickets in five other seasons. His best summer with the bat was 1927 with 1,713 runs, av 36.44, and his highest innings 203 for Sussex v Northants at Hove in 1921.

Tate, Walter William Giffard
Amateur. *b:* 1863, Axminster, Devon. Middle order batsman. *Team* Somerset (1882, 1 match).
Career batting
1–2–0–19–19–9.50–0–*ct* 0
Bowling 27–0

Tattersall, Geoffrey
Amateur. *b:* 21.4.1882, Ripon, Yorkshire. *d:* 29.6.1972, Harrogate, Yorkshire. Middle order batsman. *Team* Yorkshire (1905, 1 match).
Career batting
1–2–0–26–26–13.00–0–*ct* 0

Tattersall, J. M. *(see under* Musgrave, J. M.)

Tattersall, Keith
Cricketer. *b:* 6.3.1946, Tonbridge, Kent. Opening left-hand batsman. *Teams* Western Province (1965/6 to 1969/70); Rhodesia (1973/4 to 1975/6). *Tours* South African Universities to England 1967.
Career batting
33–58–2–1275–112–22.76–1–*ct* 39
Bowling 101–1–101.00–0–0–1/0

Tattersall, Roy
Professional. *b:* 17.8.1922, Bolton, Lancashire. Lower order left-hand batsman, off break bowler. *Team* Lancashire (1948–60, 277 matches). *Tours* MCC to Australia and New Zealand 1950/1, to India, Pakistan and Ceylon 1951/2. *Tests* England (1950/1 to 1954, 16 matches).
Career batting
328–369–151–2040–58–9.35–0–*ct* 146
Bowling 24692–1369–18.03–99–18–9/40
Test batting
16–17–7–50–10*–5.00–0–*ct* 8
Bowling 1513–58–26.08–4–1–7/52

He took 100 wickets in a season eight times (best 193, av 13.59, in 1950). His best analysis in an innings was 9 for 40, including the hat-trick, for Lancashire v Notts at Old Trafford in 1953. His final first-class match was for MCC in 1964.

Tattersall, Roger Hartley
Cricketer. *b:* 12.3.1952, Nelson, Lancashire. Lower order left-hand batsman, left-arm medium pace bowler. *Sch* The Leys. *Team* Lancashire (1971, 2 matches).
Career batting
2 matches, did not bat – *ct* 0
Bowling 219–1–219.00–0–0–1/44

Tavaré, Christopher James
Cricketer. *b:* 27.10.1954, Orpington, Kent. Sound opening or middle order right-hand batsman, right-arm medium pace bowler. *Sch* Sevenoaks. *Teams* Kent (1974–83, 140 matches); Oxford U (1975–77, blue all 3 years). *Tours* England to India and Sri Lanka 1981/2, Australia and New Zealand 1982/3 (no first-class matches in New Zealand). *Tests* England (1980–83, 26 matches).
Career batting
201–339–38–12058–168*–40.05–23–*ct* 200
Bowling 275–2–137.50–0–0–1/20
Test batting
26–48–1–1620–149–34.46–2–*ct* 17
Bowling 11–0

He hit 1,000 runs in a season seven times (best 1,770, av 53.63, in 1981). In 1983 he was appointed captain of Kent. For England v Australia at Manchester in 1981 he scored 147 in 710 minutes in the two innings (69 in 287 minutes and 78 in 423 minutes) – the slowest scoring in Test cricket.

Tayfield, Hugh Joseph
Amateur. *b:* 30.1.1928, Durban, South Africa. Lower order right-hand batsman, brilliant off break bowler. Brother of Arthur (Transvaal) and Cyril (Griqualand West). *Teams* Rhodesia (1947/8 to 1948/9); Natal (1945/6 to 1946/7); Transvaal (1956/7 to 1962/3). *Tours* South Africa to England 1951, 1955, 1960, to Australia and New Zealand 1952/3. *Tests* South Africa (1949/50 to 1960, 37 matches).
Career batting
187–259–47–3668–77–17.30–0–*ct* 149
Bowling 18890–864–21.86–67–16–9/113
Test batting
37–60–9–862–75–16.90–0–*ct* 26
Bowling 4405–170–25.91–14–2–9/113

He was flown in as a reinforcement for the 1951 touring team and did not play in the Tests. In 1955, however, he carried all before him, heading the first-class bowling table with 143 wickets, av 15.75, and in Tests 26 wickets, av 21.84. In 1960 he took over 100 first-class wickets, but was very expensive in the Tests. His best bowling was 9/113 for South Africa v England at Johannesburg in 1956/7.

Tayler, Frederick Ernest
Amateur. *b:* 18.7.1889, Aston-Blank, Gloucestershire. *d:* 30.4.1954, Cold Aston, Gloucestershire. Brother of H. W. (Gloucs and Glamorgan). Middle order batsman. *Sch* Wellingborough. *Team* Warwickshire (1910, 4 matches); Gloucestershire (1911, 4 matches).
Career batting
8–16–0–165–44–10.31–0–*ct* 0
Bowling 12–0

Tayler, Herbert William
Amateur. *b:* 6.12.1887, Aldsworth, Gloucestershire. *d:* 17.4.1984, Dawlish, Devon. Brother of F. E. (Warwickshire and Gloucs). Middle order right-hand batsman, right-arm medium pace bowler. *Sch* Wellingborough. *Teams* Gloucestershire (1914, 2 matches); Glamorgan (1921–27, 10 matches).
Career batting
12–23–4–344–44–18.10–0–*ct* 3

Tayler, Robert Frederick
Amateur. *b:* 17.3.1836, Wendover, Hastings, Sussex. *d:* 1.1.1888, Woking Village, Surrey. Solid opening right-hand batsman, good short leg. *Teams* Kent (1865, 2 matches); Hampshire (1866, 2 matches).
Career batting
5–10–0–107–42–10.70–0–*ct* 1

Taylor, Andrew
Professional. *b:* 20.4.1838, Camberwell, Surrey. *d:* 1901, Birmingham. Attacking middle order right-hand batsman, right-hand medium pace round-arm bowler, long stop. *Team* Surrey (1865, 1 match).
Career batting
1–1–0–1–1–1.00–0–*ct* 0
Bowling 13–1–13.00–0–0–1/13

Taylor, Arthur
Professional. *b:* 1880, Maltby, Yorkshire. *d:* 13.11.1956, Winson Green, Birmingham. Tail end right-hand batsman, right-arm medium fast bowler. *Team* Warwickshire (1913, 6 matches).
Career batting
6–11–2–83–17–9.22–0–*ct* 3
Bowling 137–4–34.25–0–0–2/10

Taylor, Albert Edward
Professional. *b:* 14.6.1894, Nuneaton, Warwickshire. *d:* 19.8.1960, Firbeck, Rotherham, Yorkshire. Lower order right-hand batsman, right-arm medium fast bowler. *Team* Warwickshire (1927, 1 match).
Career batting
1–1–0–0–0–0.00–0–*ct* 0
Bowling 7–0

Taylor, Alfred George
Amateur. *b:* 29.12.1891, West Ham, Essex. Lower order batsman, useful bowler. *Team* Essex (1923, 2 matches).
Career batting
2–3–0–7–7–2.33–0–*ct* 0
Bowling 77–1–77.00–0–0–1/40

Taylor, Brian
Professional. *b:* 19.6.1932, West Ham, Essex. Middle order left-hand batsman, wicket-keeper. *Team* Essex (1949–73, 539 matches). *Tours* MCC to South Africa 1956/7, to Bangladesh 1976/7 (not first-class).
Career batting
572–949–73–19094–135–21.79–9–*ct* 1081–*st* 213
Bowling 30–1–30.00–0–0–1/16

He hit 1,000 runs in a season eight times (best 1,837, av 30.61, in 1959). In 1962 he dismissed 91 batsmen (*ct* 81, *st* 10). Between 1961 and 1972 he appeared in 301 consecutive Championship matches for Essex. In 1973 he was appointed to the Test Selection Committee. He captained Essex 1967 to 1973. A good soccer player, he appeared at left back for Brentford.

Taylor, Bruce Richard
Amateur. *b:* 12.7.1943, Timaru, New Zealand. Forcing middle order left-hand batsman, right-arm fast medium bowler, good slip. *Team* Canterbury (1964/5 to 1969/70); Wellington (1970/1 to 1979/80). *Tours* New Zealand to England 1965, 1969, 1973, to West Indies 1971/2, to India and Pakistan 1964/5, 1969/70, to Australia 1967/8, 1969/70, 1970/1. *Tests* New Zealand (1964/5 to 1973, 30 matches).
Career batting
141–210–25–4579–173–24.75–4–*ct* 66
Bowling 10605–422–25.13–15–0–7/74
Test batting
30–50–6–898–124–20.40–2–*ct* 10
Bowling 2953–111–26.60–4–0–7/74

After a moderate tour in 1965, he headed the Test bowling in 1969 with 10 wickets, av 15.50. In 1973 however he was not so successful. His first-class debut was for New Zealand Under 25s in 1964/5.

Taylor, Benjamin (Williamson)
Professional. *b:* 16.6.1873, Kimberley, Notts. *d:* 24.8.1938, Eastwood, Notts. Lower order right-hand batsman, right-arm fast medium bowler. *Team* Nottinghamshire (1902–09, 31 matches).

Career batting
31–41–11–379–54*–12.63–0–*ct* 19
Bowling 2790–85–32.82–3–0–6/109

Taylor, Charles George
Amateur. *b:* 21.11.1816, Middlesex. *d:* 10.9.1869, Frensham Hill, Surrey. He died of apoplexy. Stylish opening right-hand batsman, right-hand slow round-arm bowler, good deep field. *Sch* Eton. *Teams* Cambridge U (1836–39, blue 1836, 1838 and 1839); Sussex (1838–54, 38 matches).
Career batting
125–227–11–3088–114–14.29–2–*ct* 71
Bowling 816–61+225–13.37–22–5–8/?
He was one of the first batsmen to move to the pitch of the ball and in addition the most polished amateur of his time. His final first-class match was for Gentlemen of England in 1859. He excelled at both billiards and tennis.

Taylor, Claude Hilary
Amateur. *b:* 6.2.1904, Leicester. *d:* 28.1.1966, Sherfield-on-Loddon, Hampshire. Solid, stylish middle order right-hand batsman, leg break and googly bowler. *Sch* Westminster. *Teams* Leicestershire (1922–27, 45 matches); Oxford U (1923–26, blue all four years).
Career batting
88–147–11–3378–123–24.83–9–*ct* 66
Bowling 920–21–43.80–0–0–2/6
He was the first Oxford Freshman to hit a century in the University match, in 1923. He also played for Buckinghamshire. With D. H. Macindoe, he was joint author of *Cricket Dialogue*.

Taylor, Charles James
Professional. *b:* 8.6.1881, Bristol. *d:* August, 1960, Leek, Staffordshire. Father of Frederick (Warwickshire). Lower order right-hand batsman, right-arm fast medium bowler. *Team* Warwickshire (1908–09, 3 matches).
Career batting
3–4–0–6–5–1.50–0–*ct* 1
Bowling 257–9–28.55–0–0–4/99
He also played for Staffordshire.

Taylor, C. J. *(see under* Taylor, J. C.)

Taylor, Chilton Richard Vernon
Cricketer. *b:* 3.10.1951, Birkenhead, Cheshire. Lower order right-hand batsman, wicket-keeper. *Teams* Warwickshire (1970, 1 match); Cambridge U (1971–73, blue all three years); Middlesex (1981, 2 matches).
Career batting
33–45–5–276–25–6.90–0–*ct* 56–*st* 9
He appeared for Middlesex without being registered and the County were penalized. He also played for Cheshire.

Taylor, Donald Dougald
Professional. *b:* 2.3.1923, Auckland, New Zealand. *d:* 5.12.1980, Epsom, Auckland, New Zealand. Attractive opening or middle order right-hand batsman, off break bowler. *Teams* Auckland (1946/7 to 1960/1); Warwickshire (1949–53, 45 matches). *Tests* New Zealand (1946/7 to 1955/6, 3 matches).
Career batting
93–164–6–3734–143–23.63–1–*ct* 61
Bowling 1019–30–33.97–0–0–4/24
Test batting
3–5–0–159–77–31.80–0–*ct* 2

Taylor, Derief David Samuel
Professional. *b:* 17.9.1918, Kingston, Jamaica. Middle order left-hand batsman, slow left-arm bowler. *Team* Warwickshire (1948–50, 16 matches).
Career batting
16–23–7–519–121–32.43–1–*ct* 4
Bowling 607–15–40.46–0–0–3/41
He was coach to Warwickshire after retiring.

Taylor, Derek John Somerset
Cricketer. *b:* 12.11.1942, Amersham, Bucks. Twin brother of M. N. S. (Notts and Hampshire). Middle or lower order, occasional opening, right-hand batsman, wicket-keeper. *Teams* Surrey (1966–69, 10 matches); Somerset (1970–82, 280 matches); Griqualand West (1970/1 to 1971/2).
Career batting
302–420–95–7404–179–22.78–4–*ct* 622–*st* 84
Bowling 16–0
He scored 1,121 runs, av 28.02, in 1975. He played soccer for Corinthian Casuals.

Taylor, Edward Fairfax
Amateur. *b:* 10.7.1845, Holborn, London. *d:* 27.1.1902, Ewell, Surrey. Lower order right-hand batsman, right-hand fast medium round-arm bowler, slip field. *Sch* Marlborough. *Team* Surrey (1865–67, 2 matches).
Career batting
2–4–0–48–27–12.00–0–*ct* 2
Bowling 135–7–19.28–0–0–4/59
Owing to his position at the House of Lords, where latterly he was Taxing Master, he was unable to appear often in County cricket.

Taylor, Edmund Judkin
Amateur. *b:* 30.12.1854, Bristol. *d:* 25.12.1936, Redland, Bristol. Middle order right-hand batsman, good cover field. *Sch* Clifton and

Rugby. *Team* Gloucestershire (1876–86, 24 matches).
Career batting
24–35–3–319–33–9.96–0–*ct* 7–*st* 1

Taylor, Frank
Amateur. *b:* 4.5.1855, Rochdale, Lancashire. *d:* 14.8.1936, Cheadle, Cheshire. Stylish middle order right-hand batsman, round-arm bowler, good deep field. *Sch* Clifton. *Teams* Gloucestershire (1873, 3 matches); Lancashire (1874–88, 52 matches).
Career batting
55–89–4–1492–96–17.55–0–*ct* 25
Bowling 73–3–24.33–0–0–1/4

Taylor, Fred
Professional. *b:* 1891, Oldham, Lancashire. *d:* 1968, Clitheroe, Lancashire. Lower order batsman, left-arm medium pace bowler. *Team* Lancashire (1920–22, 15 matches).
Career batting
15–18–6–188–29*–15.66–0–*ct* 7
Bowling 1026–40–25.65–3–0–6/65

Taylor, Frederick
Professional. *b:* 29.4.1916, Leek, Staffordshire. Son of C. J. (Warwickshire). Lower order right-hand batsman, right-arm fast medium bowler. *Team* Warwickshire (1939, 1 match).
Career batting
2–3–0–8–8–2.66–0–*ct* 3
Bowling 142–8–17.75–1–0–5/71

His final first-class match was for Minor Counties v Australians at Stoke in 1953. He also played for Staffordshire.

Taylor, Francis Henry
Amateur. *b:* 14.6.1890, Wirksworth, Derbyshire. *d:* 6.12.1963, Derby. Brother of W. T. (Derbyshire). Middle order right-hand batsman. *Team* Derbyshire (1908–11, 8 matches).
Career batting
8–16–1–95–18–6.33–0–*ct* 3

Taylor, George Rammell
Amateur. *b:* 25.11.1909, Havant, Hampshire. Middle order right-hand batsman. *Sch* Lancing. *Team* Hampshire (1935–39, 24 matches).
Career batting
24–37–4–306–41–9.27–0–*ct* 15
Bowling 21–1–21.00–0–0–1/8

Taylor, Harry
Professional. *b:* 18.12.1900, Yorkshire. Middle order right-hand batsman, right-arm medium pace bowler. *Team* Yorkshire (1924–25, 9 matches).
Career batting
9–13–0–153–36–11.76–0–*ct* 1

Taylor, Herbert
Amateur. *b:* 22.2.1911, Accrington, Lancashire. Tail end right-hand batsman, right-arm fast bowler. *Team* Middlesex (1933, 3 matches).
Career batting
3–4–0–11–6–2.75–0–*ct* 2
Bowling 181–3–60.33–0–0–1/17

Taylor, Howard
Amateur. *b:* 5.4.1908, Woolwich, Kent. Lower order right-hand batsman, right-arm bowler. *Sch* Mill Hill. *Team* Kent (1937, 3 matches).
Career batting
3–6–0–53–29–8.83–0–*ct* 0
Bowling 121–2–60.50–0–0–1/34

Taylor, Henry Blair Johnson
Amateur. *b:* 1.6.1875, Dalhousie, India. *d:* 29.5.1903, Bengeo, Herefordshire. Middle order right-hand batsman. *Sch* Newton College. *Team* Cambridge U (1897).
Career batting
2–2–0–3–3–1.50–0–*ct* 1

Taylor, Horace James
Amateur. *b:* 26.12.1895, Sevenoaks, Kent. *d:* 13.10.1961, Tunbridge Wells, Kent. Middle order right-hand batsman, right-arm medium pace bowler. *Sch* Sevenoaks. *Team* Kent (1922–25, 12 matches).
Career batting
12–13–3–181–33–18.10–0–*ct* 2

Taylor, Henry James Corbett
Cricketer. *b:* 16.4.1949, Solihull, Warwickshire. Middle order right-hand batsman, off break bowler. *Team* Cambridge U (1968–69).
Career batting
13–25–1–246–50–10.25–0–*ct* 4
Bowling 5–0

Taylor, Henry Storm
Professional. *b:* 11.12.1856, Scarborough, Yorkshire. *d:* 16.11.1896, Great Lever, Lancashire. Middle order right-hand batsman, close field. *Team* Yorkshire (1879, 3 matches).
Career batting
3–5–0–36–22–7.20–0–*ct* 0

Taylor, Henry Thomas
Amateur. *b:* 7.7.1911, Cardiff. *d:* 20.7.1970, Pontypridd, Glamorgan. Middle order batsman. *Team* Glamorgan (1932–34, 3 matches).

Career batting
3–4–1–17–16*–5.66–0–*ct* 1
Bowling 11–0

Taylor, Herbert Wilfred
Amateur. *b:* 5.5.1889, Durban, South Africa. *d:* 8.2.1973, Newlands, Cape Town, South Africa. Son of David, brother of David jun (Natal). Stylish opening right-hand batsman, bowler, splendid field. *Teams* Natal (1909/10 to 1934/5); Transvaal (1925/6 to 1930/1); Western Province (1935/6). *Tours* South Africa to England 1912, 1924, 1929, to Australia and New Zealand 1931/2. *Tests* South Africa (1912 to 1931/2, 42 matches).
Career batting
206–340–27–13105–250*–41.86–30–*ct* 75
Bowling 560–22–25.45–0–0–4/36
Test batting
42–76–4–2936–176–40.77–7–*ct* 19
Bowling 156–5–31.20–0–0–3/15

He exceeded 1,000 runs on each of his three tours to England and in both 1924 and 1929, each time as captain, he headed the batting averages – his best figures were in 1924 with 1,898 runs, av 42.17. He also played in England in 1919, having served in the First World War, and appeared for L. Robinson's XI v AIF. His highest score was 250* for Natal v Transvaal at Johannesburg in 1912/13. His final first-class match in England was for Rest of England in 1932. He captained South Africa in 18 Tests. A noted rugby half-back, he represented Natal.

Taylor, Harold William Frank
Amateur. *b:* 27.12.1909, Chesterton, Cambridgeshire. Middle order right-hand batsman. *Team* Minor Counties XI (1939).
Career batting
2–3–1–58–38–29.00–0–*ct* 2

His County cricket was for Cambridgeshire.

Taylor, James
Professional. *b:* 25.5.1846, Littleborough, Lancashire. *d:* 1915, Rochdale, Lancashire. Middle order right-hand batsman, right-hand fast round-arm bowler, point field. *Team* Lancashire (1871–73, 3 matches).
Career batting
3–6–0–52–33–8.66–0–*ct* 0
Bowling 13–0

Taylor, John
Professional, *b:* 2.7.1849, Beeston, Notts. *d:* 2.3.1921, Beeston, Notts. Middle order right-hand batsman, right-hand medium pace round-arm bowler. *Team* Nottinghamshire (1876, 1 match).
Career batting
1–2–0–2–2–1.00–0–*ct* 1

Taylor, John
Professional, *b:* 2.4.1850, Pudsey, Yorkshire. *d:* 27.5.1924, Boston Spa, Yorkshire. Steady middle order right-hand batsman, right-hand medium pace round-arm bowler. *Team* Yorkshire (1880–81, 9 matches).
Career batting
10–15–1–110–44–7.85–0–*ct* 4

His first-class debut was for North v South in 1875.

Taylor, James Alexander Simson
Amateur. *b:* 19.6.1917, Weston-super-Mare, Somerset. Middle order right-hand batsman, off break bowler. *Sch* Oakham. *Teams* Leicestershire (1937, 3 matches); Scotland (1952–54).
Career batting
9–10–0–198–78–19.80–0–*ct* 12
Bowling 58–1–58.00–0–0–1/11

Whilst at Cambridge he did not appear in any first-class matches for the University.

Taylor, Dr John Clifford
(Known as Clifford John Taylor)
Amateur. *b:* 1.8.1875, Clifton, Gloucs. *d:* 10.11.1952, Camberwell, London. Lower order batsman, useful bowler. *Sch* Edinburgh University. *Team* Gloucestershire (1899–1900, 4 matches).
Career batting
4–5–0–72–25–14.40–0–*ct* 0
Bowling 44–2–22.00–0–0–2/33

Taylor, John Dennis
Professional. *b:* 18.12.1923, Ipswich, Suffolk. Middle order right-hand batsman, right-arm medium pace bowler. *Team* Hampshire (1947–49, 4 matches).
Career batting
4–8–3–76–27*–15.20–0–*ct* 0
Bowling 24–0

Taylor, John Frederick
Professional. *b:* 9.6.1937, West Ham, London. Middle order right-hand batsman, wicket-keeper. *Team* Essex (1960–61, 14 matches).
Career batting
15–24–7–461–86–27.11–0–*ct* 22–*st* 5

His final first-class match was for MCC in 1967. A useful soccer player, he appeared for Grays Athletic.

Taylor, John Morris
Amateur. *b:* 10.10.1895, Stanmore, New South Wales, Australia. *d:* 12.5.1971, Turramurra, New

South Wales, Australia. Polished middle order right-hand batsman, brilliant cover point. *Team* New South Wales (1913/14 to 1926/7, 27 matches). *Tours* AIF to England 1919, to South Africa 1919/20; Australia to England 1921, 1926, to South Africa 1921/2. *Tests* Australia (1920/1 to 1926, 20 matches).
Career batting
135–195–7–6274–180–33.37–11–*ct* 68
Bowling 53–1–53.00–0–0–1/25
Test batting
20–28–0–997–108–35.60–1–*ct* 11
Bowling 45–1–45.00–0–0–1/25
He was probably at his best, so far as his three visits to England were concerned, in 1919, when he hit 1,187 runs, av 31.23. In 1921 he just reached 1,000 runs in first-class matches, but in 1926 showed little form in the important fixtures.

Taylor, James Robert Niven
Amateur. *b:* 11.8.1929, Calcutta, India. Right-hand batsman. *Teams* Scotland (1949); Bengal (1952/3).
Career batting
4–8–1–129–41–18.42–0–*ct* 0

Taylor, Kenneth
Professional. *b:* 21.8.1935, Huddersfield, Yorkshire. Father of N. S. (Yorkshire). Opening or middle order right-hand batsman, right-arm medium pace bowler. *Teams* Yorkshire (1953–68, 303 matches); Auckland (1963/4). *Tours* MCC to Bangladesh 1978/9 (not first-class); Swanton to India 1963/4. *Tests* England (1959–64, 3 matches).
Career batting
313–524–36–13053–203*–26.74–16–*ct* 150
Bowling 3763–131–28.72–1–0–6/75
Test batting
3–5–0–57–24–11.40–0–*ct* 1
Bowling 6–0
He hit 1,000 runs in a season six times (best 1,494, av 34.74, in 1961). His only double century was 203* for Yorkshire v Warwickshire at Edgbaston in 1961. He also played for Norfolk. A useful soccer player, he was centre half for Huddersfield Town and Bradford.

Taylor, Kenneth Alexander
Professional. *b:* 29.9.1916, Muswell Hill, London. Steady opening right-hand batsman, right-arm medium pace bowler. *Team* Warwickshire (1946–49, 87 matches).
Career batting
87–155–10–3145–102–21.68–1–*ct* 42
Bowling 33–1–33.00–0–0–1/18
He hit 1,259 runs, av 26.22, in 1947. He was on the Committee of Nottinghamshire CCC from 1963 to 1978, and since then Manager of the County Club.

Taylor, Leslie Brian
Cricketer. *b:* 25.10.1953, Earl Shilton, Leicestershire. Lower order right-hand batsman, right-arm fast medium bowler. *Teams* Leicestershire (1977–83, 111 matches); Natal (1981/2 to 1982/3). *Tours* Leics to Zimbabwe 1980/1; SAB English Team to South Africa 1981/2.
Career batting
129–110–48–636–47–10.25–0–*ct* 32
Bowling 9336–390–23.93–12–1–7/28
His best season was 1981 with 75 wickets, av 21.70.

Taylor, Malcolm Lees
Professional. *b:* 16.7.1904, Heywood, Lancashire. *d:* 14.3.1978, Wimborne, Dorset. Stylish middle order left-hand batsman. *Team* Lancashire (1924–31, 95 matches).
Career batting
96–112–15–2216–107*–22.91–1–*ct* 42
Bowling 26–0
From 1934 to 1948 he played for Dorset.

Taylor, Michael Norman Somerset
Cricketer. *b:* 12.11.1942, Amersham, Bucks. Twin brother of D. J. S. (Somerset). Middle or lower order right-hand batsman, right-arm medium pace bowler. *Teams* Nottinghamshire (1964–72, 230 matches); Hampshire (1973–80, 145 matches).
Career batting
375–518–116–8031–105–19.97–3–*ct* 213
Bowling 22016–830–26.52–24–0–7/23
His best bowling season was 1968 with 99 wickets, av 21.00. In 1961 and 1962 he appeared for Buckinghamshire.

Taylor, Neil Royston
Cricketer. *b:* 21.7.1959, Farnborough, Kent. Opening right-hand batsman, off break bowler. *Team* Kent (1979–83, 68 matches).
Career batting
69–120–16–3517–155*–33.81–9–*ct* 46
Bowling 234–5–46.80–0–0–2/58
He hit 1,000 runs in a season twice (best 1,340, av 34.35, in 1982). He hit 110 for Kent v Sri Lankans at Canterbury on his first-class debut.

Taylor, Nicholas Simon
Cricketer. *b:* 2.6.1963, Holmfirth, Yorkshire. Son of Kenneth (Yorkshire). Lower order right-hand batsman, right-arm fast medium bowler. *Team* Yorkshire (1982–83, 8 matches).

Career batting
8–6–1–10–4–2.00–0–*ct* 2
Bowling 720–22–32.72–1–0–5/49

Taylor, Paul Adrian
Professional. *b:* 9.3.1939, East Kirkby, Notts. Tail end left-hand batsman, left-arm fast medium bowler. *Team* Nottinghamshire (1958, 6 matches).
Career batting
6–10–5–34–13–6.80–0–*ct* 5
Bowling 335–7–47.85–0–0–2/82

Taylor, Philip Henry
Professional. *b:* 18.9.1917, Bristol. Middle order right-hand batsman. *Team* Gloucestershire (1938, 1 match).
Career batting
1–2–0–14–12–7.00–0–*ct* 0

He played soccer for Liverpool, captaining them in the 1950 FA Cup Final.

Taylor, Ronald Alfred
Professional. *b:* 25.3.1909, Nottingham. Cousin of George Duckworth (Lancashire). Opening or middle order right-hand batsman, right-arm medium or leg break bowler. *Team* Nottinghamshire (1932–35, 23 matches).
Career batting
23–35–2–599–107–18.15–1–*ct* 7–*st* 1
Bowling 1–0

Taylor, Robert Joseph
Professional. *b:* 1.11.1873, Liverpool, Lancashire. Lower order right-hand batsman, right-arm medium pace bowler. *Teams* Lancashire (1898, 2 matches); Worcestershire (1900, 1 match).
Career batting
3–5–0–7–6–1.40–0–*ct* 0
Bowling 137–2–68.50–0–0–1/25

Taylor, Reginald Minshall
Professional, amateur in 1946. *b:* 30.11.1909, Southend, Essex. Stylish middle order right-hand batsman, slow left-arm bowler. *Team* Essex (1931–46, 206 matches).
Career batting
206–349–21–6755–193–20.59–5–*ct* 185
Bowling 2933–92–31.88–3–0–7/99

He hit 1,000 runs in a season twice (best 1,181, av 24.10, in 1933).

Taylor, Robert William
Professional. *b:* 17.7.1941, Stoke-on-Trent, Staffs. Lower order right-hand batsman, right-arm medium pace bowler, brilliant wicket-keeper. *Team* Derbyshire (1961–83, 496 matches). *Tours* MCC to Ceylon 1969/70, to Australia and New Zealand 1970/1, 1974/5, to West Indies 1973/4; England to Pakistan and New Zealand 1977/8, to Australia 1978/9, to Australia and India 1979/80, to India and Sri Lanka 1981/2, to Australia and New Zealand 1982/3 (New Zealand not first-class); Rest of World to Australia 1971/2; International Wanderers to South Africa 1975/6. *Tests* England (1970/1 to 1983, 51 matches).
Career batting
609–843–159–11521–100–16.84–1–*ct* 1424–*st* 170
Bowling 52–0
Test batting
51–74–12–1073–97–17.30–0–*ct* 155–*st* 7
Bowling 6–0

He played for Staffordshire 1958–60, making his first-class debut for Minor Counties in 1960. In 1975–76 he captained Derbyshire. During the 1970s he vied with A. P. E. Knott as the leading wicket-keeper in England, but only gained a regular England Test place when Knott was banned. For England v India at Bombay in 1979/80, he made 7 dismissals in an innings and 10 in the match. He has made more dismissals in his first-class career than any other wicket-keeper.

Taylor, Stanley Shelbourne
Amateur. *b:* 2.3.1875, London. *d:* 22.7.1965, Basingstoke, Hampshire. Middle order batsman. *Sch* Aldenham. *Team* Middlesex (1901, 2 matches).
Career batting
2–3–0–24–16–8.00–0–*ct* 3

Taylor, Thomas
Professional. *Baptised:* 18.10.1753, Ropley, Hampshire. *d:* 29.4.1806, Alresford, Hampshire. Attacking right-hand batsman, useful bowler, fine field. *Team* Hampshire (1775–98).
Career batting
not applicable, pre-1800.

He was 'shabby enough to put his leg in front of his wicket', which caused the leg before wicket law to be instituted.

Taylor, Timothy John
Cricketer. *b:* 28.3.1961, Romiley, Cheshire. Lower order right-hand batsman, slow left-arm bowler. *Sch* Stockport GS. *Teams* Oxford U (1981–82, blue both years); Lancashire (1981–82, 4 matches).
Career batting
14–17–7–115–28*–11.50–0–*ct* 2
Bowling 1272–37–34.37–2–0–5/81

He also played for Cheshire.

Taylor, Tom Launcelot
Amateur. *b:* 25.5.1878, Headingley, Leeds, York-

shire. *d:* 16.3.1960, Chapel Allerton, Leeds, Yorkshire. Sound middle order right-hand batsman, wicket-keeper. *Sch* Uppingham. *Teams* Cambridge (1897–1900, blue 1898 to 1900); Yorkshire (1899–1906, 78 matches). *Tour* Hawke to New Zealand and Australia 1902/3.
Career batting
130–202–16–5968–156–32.08–13–*ct* 86–*st* 6
He hit 1,000 runs in a season three times (best 1,517, av 37.92, in 1902). He was President of Yorkshire CCC from 1956 until his death. He played hockey for Cambridge and was also a good tennis player.

Taylor, William
Cricketer. *b:* 24.1.1947, Manchester. Lower order right-hand batsman, right-arm fast medium bowler. *Team* Nottinghamshire (1971–77, 95 matches).
Career batting
95–97–39–374–26*–6.44–0–*ct* 14
Bowling 6291–211–29.81–6–1–6/42

Taylor, William Herbert
Amateur. *b:* 23.6.1885, Sale, Cheshire. *d:* 27.5.1959, Birlingham, Worcestershire. Lower order right-hand batsman, right-arm fast medium bowler. *Team* Worcestershire (1909–25, 107 matches).
Career batting
110–194–40–1792–59*–11.63–0–*ct* 35
Bowling 5877–164–35.83–5–0–7/64
He captained Worcestershire in 1914 and 1919 and at the time of his death was on the County Committee.

Taylor, W. H.
Professional. Lower order batsman, right-arm fast bowler. *Team* Somerset (1910–11, 18 matches).
Career batting
18–34–5–220–33–7.58–0–*ct* 8
Bowling 1704–52–32.77–2–0–6/82

Taylor, William Thomas
Amateur. *b:* 14.4.1885, Wirksworth, Derbyshire. *d:* 17.8.1976, Breadsall, Derbyshire. Brother of F. H. (Derbyshire). Lower right-hand batsman, right-arm medium pace bowler. *Team* Derbyshire (1905–10, 4 matches).
Career batting
4–8–1–53–11–7.57–0–*ct* 2
Bowling 56–2–28.00–0–0–1/9
He was Secretary to Derbyshire CCC from 1908 to 1959 – his tenure of 51 years being the longest served in that post in first-class County cricket.

Taylor-Jones, Rev Edward William Tetley
(changed name from Jones to Taylor-Jones in September 1891).
Amateur. *b:* 28.5.1866, Sydenham, Kent. *d:* 15.9.1956, Sittingbourne, Kent. Attacking middle order left-hand batsman, right-arm fast bowler, slip field. *Team* Kent (1894, 2 matches).
Career batting
3–6–0–22–11–3.66–0–*ct* 2
Bowling 12–0
His final first-class match was for MCC in 1901. He did not appear in any first-class matches whilst at Cambridge.

Teape, Arthur Stanley
Amateur. *b:* 28.1.1843, Blackheath, Kent. *d:* 1.3.1885, Haverstock Hill, London. Brother of C. A. (Middlesex). Tail end right-hand batsman, right-hand fast round-arm bowler, short leg. *Sch* Eton. *Team* Oxford U (1863–66, blue 1863–65).
Career batting
16–20–9–111–19–10.09–0–*ct* 8
Bowling 462–46+8–10.04–5–1–6/19

Teape, Charles Ashley
Amateur. *b:* 1844, Blackheath, Kent. *d:* 1.8.1925, Chelsea, London. Brother of A. S. (Oxford U). Lower order batsman, useful bowler. *Sch* Eton. *Team* Middlesex (1872, 1 match).
Career batting
1–2–1–2–2*–2.00–0–*ct* 1
Bowling 42–4–10.50–0–0–4/38
He played in some trials but no first-class matches whilst at Oxford.

Tebay, Henry
Professional. *b:* 5.10.1866, East Grinstead, Sussex. *d:* 1946, Bromley, Kent. Middle order right-hand batsman. *Team* Sussex (1886–90, 18 matches).
Career batting
18–36–0–265–43–7.36–0–*ct* 17

Tebay, Kevan
Professional. *b:* 2.2.1936, Bolton, Lancashire. Middle order right-hand batsman. *Team* Lancashire (1961–63, 15 matches).
Career batting
15–27–2–509–106–20.36–1–*ct* 3

Tebbitt, Gilbert George
Amateur. *b:* 13.9.1908, Welton, Northants. Middle order right-hand batsman, off break bowler. *Sch* Wellingborough. *Team* Northants (1934–38, 11 matches).
Career batting
11–21–3–248–41–13.77–0–*ct* 4
Bowling 29–0

Tebbs, Reginald Kearsley
Amateur. *b:* 8.5.1908, Leeds, Yorkshire. Lower order batsman, left-arm medium fast bowler. *Team* Cambridge U (1929).
Career batting
1–1–0–0–0–0.00–0–*ct* 1
Bowling 87–1–87.00–0–0–1/70
His County Cricket was for Berkshire.

Tebbut, Charles Mansfield
Amateur. *b:* 1840, West Ham, Essex. *d:* 27.9.1898, South Hampstead, Middlesex. Middle order batsman. *Team* Middlesex (1866–70, 6 matches).
Career batting
6–9–1–38–10–4.75–0–*ct* 0
A great patron of cricket, he was for many years on the Committees of both Middlesex and Essex and advanced a considerable sum of money to the latter County Club which saved it from extinction. A noted soccer player, he was one of the first to establish the game on a firm basis.

Tedder, Ernest Cranfield
Amateur. *b:* 5.9.1915, Woodford Green, Essex. *d:* 9.9.1972, Ipswich, Suffolk. Middle order right-hand batsman. *Sch* Chigwell. *Team* Essex (1946, 8 matches).
Career batting
8–14–0–208–55–14.85–0–*ct* 3

Tedstone, Geoffrey Alan
Cricketer. *b:* 19.1.1961, Southport, Lancashire. Lower order right-hand batsman, wicket-keeper. *Team* Warwickshire (1982–83, 16 matches).
Career batting
16–21–5–288–67*–18.00–0–*ct* 27–*st* 5

Teesdale, Hugh
Amateur. *b:* 12.2.1886, Staines, Middlesex. *d:* 31.3.1971, Hove, Sussex. Sound opening right-hand batsman. *Sch* Winchester. *Teams* Surrey (1906–08, 2 matches); Oxford U (1908, blue).
Career batting
12–21–0–637–149–30.33–2–*ct* 4
His final first-class match was for MCC in 1910.

Teggin, Alfred
Amateur. *b:* 1860, Salford, Lancashire. *d:* 1941, Fylde, Lancashire. Lower order right-hand batsman, leg break bowler. *Team* Lancashire (1886, 6 matches).
Career batting
6–8–0–31–9–3.87–0–*ct* 4
Bowling 176–16–11.00–2–1–6/53
A noted rugby footballer, he represented England.

Tennant, Peter Norie
Cricketer. *b:* 17.4.1942, Sutton Coldfield, Warwickshire. Lower order right-hand batsman, wicket-keeper. *Sch* Solihull. *Team* Warwickshire (1964, 1 match).
Career batting
1 match, did not bat –*ct* 3–*st* 1
He was also a useful hockey player.

Tennekoon, Anura Punchi Banda
Cricketer. *b:* 29.10.1946, Anuradhapura, Ceylon. *Team* Ceylon (1965/6 to 1979). *Tours* Ceylon/Sri Lanka to England 1975, 1979, to India 1966/7, 1968/9, 1970/1, 1975/6, to Pakistan 1966/7, 1973/4.
Career batting
61–107–11–3481–169*–36.26–5–*ct* 60
Bowling 60–2–30.00–0–0–2/23

Tennent, Hector Norman
Amateur. *b:* 6.4.1842, Hobart, Tasmania. *d:* 19.4.1904, Hanover Square, London W. Brother of J. P. (Victoria) and W. M. (Lancashire). Middle order right-hand batsman, cover point. *Sch* Merchiston Castle and Loretto. *Team* Lancashire (1865–70, 2 matches). *Tour* Australia to England 1878 (in emergency).
Career batting
19–31–3–344–45*–12.28–0–*ct* 8
Bowling 20–0
He was also noted as a sprinter, excelling in the 100 yards. At the time of his death he was Secretary of the Empire Theatre, Leicester Square, being a member of the well-known theatrical family.

Tennent, James M'William
Amateur. *b:* 7.9.1888, Glasgow, Scotland. *d:* 20.3.1955, Westminster, London. Right-hand batsman. *Sch* Merchiston. *Team* Scotland (1922–28).
Career batting
3–5–0–44–26–8.80–0–*ct* 3
A noted rugby footballer, he represented Scotland.

Tennent, William Middleton
Amateur. *b:* 6.10.1845, Hobart, Tasmania. *d:* 5.7.1883, Hastings, Sussex. Brother of H. N. (Lancashire) and J. P. (Victoria). Middle order batsman. *Sch* Merchiston. *Team* Lancashire (1867, 1 match).
Career batting
1–2–0–3–3–1.50–0–*ct* 0

Tennyson, Hon Lionel Hallam
(succeeded to the title the 3rd Baron Tennyson in 1928)
Amateur. *b:* 7.11.1889, Westminster, London. *d:* 6.6.1951, Bexhill-on-Sea, Sussex. Grandson of the poet. Attacking middle order right-hand batsman, right-arm fast bowler. *Sch* Eton. *Team* Hampshire (1913–35, 347 matches). *Tours* MCC to South Africa 1913/14, to West Indies 1925/6; Joel to South Africa 1924/5; Tennyson to Jamaica 1926/7, 1927/8, 1931/2; Cahn to Jamaica 1928/9; Tennyson to India 1937/8. *Tests* England (1913/4 to 1921, 9 matches).
Career batting
477–759–38–16828–217–23.33–19–*ct* 172
Bowling 2976–55–54.10–0–0–3/50
Test batting
9–12–1–345–74*–31.36–0–*ct* 6
Bowling 1–0

He hit 1,000 runs in a season seven times (best 1,335, av 30.34, in 1925). His only double century was 217 for Hampshire v West Indies at Southampton in 1928. He captained Hampshire from 1919 to 1933 and England in three Tests in 1921. As well as captaining his own touring sides, he led Joel's Team to South Africa in 1924/25. His final first-class match in England was for MCC in 1937.

Terry, Rev Francis William
Amateur. *b:* 26.10.1860, Wells, Somerset. *d:* 5.10.1936, Mimico, Ontario, Canada. Middle order right-hand batsman, right-arm medium pace bowler, wicket-keeper. *Sch* St Edward's, Oxford. *Team* Somerset (1882–85, 10 matches).
Career batting
10–18–1–552–121–32.47–1–*ct* 13–*st* 2

He played in the Oxford Freshmen's Match of 1881, but no first-class matches for the University. After leaving Oxford he emigrated to Canada and was for many years one of the leading cricketers there, playing against the United States between 1891 and 1907.

Terry, Vivian Paul
Cricketer. *b:* 14.1.1959, Osnabruck, West Germany. Middle order right-hand batsman, right-arm medium pace bowler. *Sch* Millfield. *Team* Somerset (1978–83, 39 matches).
Career batting
39–62–10–1465–115–28.17–3–*ct* 24
Bowling 39–0

He hit 1,096 runs, av 40.59, in 1983.

Tester, William Abraham
Professional. *b:* 8.6.1857, Brighton, Sussex. *d:* 9.6.1890, Brighton, Sussex. Middle order right-hand batsman, right-hand slow round-arm bowler. *Team* Sussex (1878–88, 100 matches).
Career batting
103–191–7–2675–130–14.53–2–*ct* 52
Bowling 3712–154–24.10–2–0–7/40

Tew, Anthony Martin
Amateur. *b:* 24.8.1908, Haxby, Yorkshire. Brother of J. E. (Oxford U). Right-hand batsman, right-arm fast medium bowler. *Sch* Winchester. *Team* Oxford U (1928).
Career batting
2–3–0–15–15–5.00–0–*ct* 1
Bowling 221–3–73.66–0–0–2/80

Tew, John Edward
Amateur. *b:* 3.9.1905, Haxby, Yorkshire. Brother of A. M. (Oxford U). Middle order right-hand batsman. *Sch* Eton. *Teams* Oxford U (1927–28); Europeans (1928/9 to 1947/8).
Career batting
11–21–0–334–76–15.90–0–*ct* 9

Thackara, Anthony Leonard Samuel Salter
Amateur. *b:* 14.3.1917, Portsmouth, Hampshire. Opening right-hand batsman. *Team* Combined Services (1949–55).
Career batting
4–6–0–112–42–18.66–0–*ct* 3

His County cricket was for Cornwall.

Thackeray, Peter Robert
Cricketer. *b:* 26.9.1950, Nairobi, Kenya. Middle order right-hand batsman, right-arm medium pace bowler. *Sch* St Edward's, Oxford. *Team* Oxford U (1974, blue).
Career batting
8–15–4–315–65*–28.63–0–*ct* 3
Bowling 1–0

His County cricket was for Devon.

Thain, Caryl
Amateur. *b:* 11.4.1895, Portsmouth, Hampshire. *d:* 24.9.1969, Lambeth, London. Lower order right-hand batsman, right-arm fast medium bowler. *Team* Surrey (1923, 2 matches).
Career batting
2–2–1–4–4*–4.00–0–*ct* 0
Bowling 88–3–29.33–00–0–3/38

He was a member of the Surrey Committee for 40 years, being Hon Treasurer and President. A useful soccer player, he appeared for Chelsea.

Tharp, Arthur Keane
Amateur. *b:* 15.9.1848, Chippenham, Cambs. *d:* 17.11.1928, Bitterne Park, Hampshire. Middle order right-hand batsman, right-hand medium pace round-arm bowler. *Sch* Haileybury. *Team* Cambridgeshire (1868–71, 3 matches).

Career batting
3–6–0–37–16–6.16–0–*ct* 3
He appeared in the Freshmen's Match at Cambridge in 1868, but no first-class matches for the University. He also played for Suffolk and Norfolk.

Thayer, Harry Chapman
Amateur. *b:* 31.12.1872, Stafford, Philadelphia, USA. *d:* 3.8.1936, Haverford, Philadelphia, USA. Brother of J. B. (Philadelphians to England 1884). Middle order right-hand batsman, wicket-keeper. *Team* Philadelphia (1891–99). *Tour* Philadelphia to England 1897.
Career batting
17–30–1–419–59–14.44–0–*ct* 4
He only achieved modest results on the 1897 tour. A noted American footballer, he appeared in the All American Team of 1892.

Theobald, F. A.
Amateur. Middle order batsman. *Team* H. K. Foster's XI (1919).
Career batting
1–1–0–4–4–4.00–0–*ct* 0
Bowling 28–0

Theobold, Harold Ernest
Amateur. *b:* 18.3.1896, Norwich. Middle order right-hand batsman. *Sch* Taunton. *Team* Minor Counties (1938).
Career batting
1–2–0–42–42–21.00–0–*ct* 1
His County cricket was for Norfolk.

Thesiger, Hon Frederic John Napier
(succeeded to the title 3rd Lord Chelmsford in 1905, created Viscount in 1921)
Amateur. *b:* 12.8.1868, London. *d:* 1.4.1933, Ardington, Berkshire. Attacking middle order right-hand batsman, slow round-arm bowler. *Sch* Winchester. *Teams* Oxford U (1888–91, blue 1888, 1890 and 1891); Middlesex (1888–92, 6 matches).
Career batting
33–58–3–870–88–15.81–0–*ct* 22
Bowling 154–8–19.25–0–0–3/6
He fielded before lunch on the first day of the 1891 University match, but injured his hand and retired, his place in the eleven being taken by T. B. Case. He appeared for Worcestershire in 1884 (not first-class). He was Governor of Queensland 1905 to 1909, Governor of New South Wales 1909 to 1913, Viceroy of India 1916 to 1921 and First Lord of the Admiralty in the Labour Government of 1924.

Thewlis, Herbert
Professional. *b:* 31.8.1865, Lascelles Hall, Yorkshire. *d:* 30.11.1920, Lascelles Hall, Yorkshire. Middle order batsman. *Team* Yorkshire (1888, 2 matches).
Career batting
2–4–1–4–2*–1.33–0–*ct* 2

Thewlis, John (sen)
Professional. *b:* 30.6.1828, Kirkheaton, Yorkshire. *d:* 29.12.1899, Huddersfield, Yorkshire. Uncle of John Thewlis junior (Yorkshire) and E. Lockwood (Yorkshire). Sound opening right-hand batsman, right-hand medium pace round-arm bowler, good long stop. *Team* Yorkshire (1862–75, 46 matches).
Career batting
56–104–4–1548–108–15.48–1–*ct* 30–*st* 1

Thewlis, John (jun)
Professional. *b:* 21.9.1850, Lascelles Hall, Yorkshire. *d:* 1901, Lascelles Hall, Yorkshire. Nephew of John Thewlis senior (Yorkshire), cousin of E. Lockwood (Yorkshire). Middle order right-hand batsman, right-hand round-arm bowler, good cover point. *Team* Yorkshire (1879, 3 matches).
Career batting
3–4–0–21–10–5.25–0–*ct* 0

Thewlis, Joseph
Amateur. *b:* 14.4.1939, Northumberland. Middle order right-hand batsman. *Team* Combined Services (1962).
Career batting
1–2–0–18–17–9.00–0–*ct* 0
His County cricket was for Northumberland.

Thomas, Alan
Cricketer. *b:* 7.1.1947, Bolton, Lancashire. Lower order right-hand batsman, off break bowler. *Team* Lancashire (1966, 1 match).
Career batting
1–2–0–4–4–2.00–0–*ct* 0
Bowling 7–0

Thomas, Albert Edward
Professional. *b:* 7.6.1893, Ruthin, Denbighshire. *d:* 21.3.1865, Kidderminster, Worcs. Hard hitting lower order right-hand batsman, right-arm fast medium bowler, good slip field. *Team* Northants (1919–33, 284 matches).
Career batting
288–467–106–4872–84–13.49–0–*ct* 121
Bowling 21237–832–25.52–30–5–9/30
His best season was 1928 with 101 wickets, av 25.36 and his best analysis 9 for 30 for Northants

v Yorkshire at Bradford in 1920. A useful soccer player, he appeared for Denbigh, Norwich City and Northampton Nomads as a forward.

Thomas, Arthur Emlyn
Amateur. *b:* 7.5.1895, Briton-Ferry, Glamorgan. *d:* 11.2.1953, Briton-Ferry, Glamorgan. Middle order right-hand batsman. *Team* Glamorgan (1925, 1 match).
Career batting
1–2–0–15–11–7.50–0–*ct* 0

Thomas, A. F.
Amateur. Middle order batsman. *Team* Gentlemen of England (1878).
Career batting
1–2–0–3–3–1.50–0–*ct* 0

Thomas, Dillwyn
Professional. *b:* 13.2.1905, Neath Abbey, Glamorgan. Lower order left-hand batsman, right-arm medium fast bowler. *Team* Glamorgan (1939, 2 matches).
Career batting
2–2–1–14–14*–14.00–0–*ct* 1
Bowling 99–5–19.80–1–0–5/64

Thomas, David James
Cricketer. *b:* 30.6.1959, Solihull, Warwickshire. Middle order left-hand batsman, left-arm medium pace bowler. *Teams* Surrey (1977–83, 78 matches); Northern Transvaal (1980/1).
Career batting
87–118–24–1947–119–20.71–2–*ct* 31
Bowling 6386–185–34.51–2–0–6/84

Thomas, David John
Amateur. *b:* 25.11.1911, Swansea, Glamorgan. Tail end right-hand batsman, right-arm medium pace bowler. *Team* Glamorgan (1932, 1 match).
Career batting
1–1–1–10–10*–no av–0–*ct* 0
Bowling 63–0

Thomas, Edgar Lang
Amateur. *b:* 2.11.1875, Clifton, Gloucs. *d:* 1936, Hammersmith, London. Brother of F. E. (Gloucs). Middle order right-hand batsman. *Sch* Clifton. *Team* Gloucestershire (1895–1907, 27 matches).
Career batting
27–45–0–571–109–12.68–1–*ct* 14

Thomas, Freeman
(changed to Freeman-Thomas in 1892; created 1st Lord Willingdon 1910)
Amateur. *b:* 12.9.1866, Ratton Park, Eastbourne, Sussex. *d:* 12.8.1941, Westminster, London. Son of F. F. Thomas (Sussex). Steady middle order right-hand batsman, slow under-arm bowler. *Sch* Eton. *Teams* Cambridge U (1886–89, blue all 4 years); Sussex (1886–90, 18 matches); England XII in India (1915/6); Willingdon's XI in India (1918/9).
Career batting
40–72–3–1587–114–23.00–1–*ct* 19
Bowling 13–0

He was Liberal MP for Hastings 1900–1906 and for Bodmin 1906–1910. From 1909 to 1912 he was Junior Lord of the Treasury; from 1913 to 1919 Governor of Bombay; from 1919 to 1924 Governor of Madras and from 1924 Governor-General of Canada. From 1931 to 1936 he was Viceroy of India.

Thomas, Frank Edgecumbe
Amateur. *b:* 5.4.1877, Clifton, Bristol. *d:* 20.5.1924, Clifton, Bristol. Brother of E. L. (Gloucs). Stylish middle order right-hand batsman, right-arm medium pace bowler, good field. *Sch* Clifton. *Team* Gloucestershsire (1901–06, 51 matches).
Career batting
51–87–3–1874–138–22.30–3–*ct* 31
Bowling 330–10–33.00–0–0–3/22

Thomas, Freeman Frederick
Amateur. *b:* 11.4.1838, Lymington, Hants. *d:* 1.12.1868, San Remo, Italy. He died of consumption. Father of 1st Lord Willingdon (Sussex). Lower order right-hand batsman, brilliant cover point. *Team* Sussex (1860–67, 9 matches).
Career batting
9–18–0–89–18–4.94–0–*ct* 6

Thomas, Frederick Oswald
Amateur. *b:* 19.11.1917, Corstorphine, Midlothian, Scotland. Right-hand batsman, right-arm fast medium bowler. *Team* Scotland (1951).
Career batting
1–2–0–21–21–10.50–0–*ct* 0

Thomas, Grahame
Cricketer. *b:* 21.3.1938, Croydon Park, New South Wales, Australia. Opening right-hand batsman. *Teams* New South Wales (1957/8 to 1965/6, 68 matches); Rest of World (Scarborough) (1966). *Tours* Australia to New Zealand 1959/60, to West Indies 1964/5, to South Africa 1966/7. *Tests* Australia (1964/5 to 1965/6, 8 matches).
Career batting
100–154–12–5726–229–40.32–17–*ct* 92–*st* 2
Bowling 30–0
Test batting
8–12–1–325–61–29.54–0–*ct* 3

His appearances in England were limited to one

for Rest of World XI at Scarborough in 1966. His highest score was 229 for NSW v Victoria at Melbourne in 1965/6. He hit 1,171 runs, av 58.55, in 1965/6.

Thomas, Gwyn
Amateur. *b:* 1892, Pontardawe, Glamorgan. *d:* 10.1.1984, Vero Beach, Florida, USA. Middle order batsman. *Team* Glamorgan (1922, 1 match).
Career batting
1–2–0–27–21–13.50–0–*ct* 0

Thomas, Gary Philip
Cricketer. *b:* 8.11.1958, Birmingham. Middle order right-hand batsman, right-arm medium pace bowler. *Team* Warwickshire (1978–81, 8 matches).
Career batting
8–15–1–277–52–19.78–0–*ct* 6

Thomas, J.
Amateur. Lower order batsman, useful bowler. *Team* Somerset (1901–05, 3 matches).
Career batting
3–4–1–27–23–9.00–0–*ct* 1
Bowling 130–1–130.00–0–0–1/63

Thomas, John Gregory
Cricketer. *b:* 12.8.1960, Garnswllt, Glamorgan. Lower order right-hand batsman, right-arm medium pace bowler. *Team* Glamorgan (1979–83, 24 matches).
Career batting
24–31–4–355–84–13.14–0–*ct* 8
Bowling 1530–52–29.42–3–0–5/61

Thomas, Leopold Ernest
Amateur. *b:* 16.2.1865. *d:* 28.5.1937, Marylebone, London. Lower order batsman, wicket-keeper. *Team* Middlesex (1893, 1 match).
Career batting
1–2–1–0–0*–0.00–0–*ct* 5

Thomas, Richard
Professional. *b:* 15.7.1867, Wales. *d:* 18.12.1918, Oldham, Lancashire. Lower order batsman, wicket-keeper. *Team* Lancashire (1894–1902, 20 matches).
Career batting
20–22–5–60–17–3.52–0–*ct* 22–*st* 8

Thomas, Richard James
Cricketer. *b:* 18.6.1944, Griffithstown, Monmouthshire. Lower order right-hand batsman, right-arm medium pace bowler. *Team* Glamorgan (1974, 1 match).
Career batting
1–1–1–8–8*–no av–0–*ct* 0
Bowling 40–1–40.00–0–0–1/40

Thomas, Rhodri James Alban
Cricketer. *b:* 13.3.1942, St Dogmaels, Pembroke. Opening or middle order right-hand batsman. *Sch* Radley. *Team* Oxford U (1963–65, blue 1965).
Career batting
15–28–2–622–135*–23.92–1–*ct* 9
Bowling 5–1–5.00–0–0–1/4

Thomas, William Owen
Amateur. *b:* 27.4.1921, Middlesbrough, Yorkshire. Lower order left-hand batsman, slow left-arm bowler. *Sch* Dulwich. *Team* Cambridge U (1948).
Career batting
4–5–4–44–19*–44.00–0–*ct* 2
Bowling 145–3–48.33–0–0–1/10
His final first-class match was for MCC in 1954. He played County cricket for Norfolk.

Thomas, Wyndham R.
Professional. Lower order batsman, useful bowler. *Team* Somerset (1928, 1 match).
Career batting
1 match, did not bat – *ct* 0

Thomas, William Richard Keay
Cricketer. *b:* 22.7.1960, Redditch, Worcs. Middle order right-hand batsman, right-arm medium pace bowler. *Sch* Dean Close. *Team* Worcestershire (1981, 1 match).
Career batting
1–2–1–57–44–57.00–0–*ct* 0
Bowling 54–0

Thompson, Arthur Paul
Amateur. *b:* 1.3.1914, Leicester. Neat middle order left-hand batsman, right-arm medium pace bowler. *Sch* Shrewsbury. *Team* Leicestershire (1937, 2 matches).
Career batting
2–4–1–11–5–3.66–0–*ct* 0

Thompson, Alexander Richard
Amateur. *b:* 1.12.1876, Stamford, Lincolnshire. *d:* 16.12.1951, Durban, South Africa. Reliable opening right-hand batsman. *Sch* Malvern. *Team* Northants (1905–08, 17 matches).
Career batting
17–29–2–358–48*–13.25–0–*ct* 8

Thompson, Alexander William
Professional. *b:* 17.4.1916, Liverpool, Lancashire. Attacking middle order right-hand batsman, good

outfield. *Team* Middlesex (1939–55, 195 matches).
Career batting
202–329–30–7915–158–26.47–5–*ct* 68
Bowling 831–12–69.25–0–0–2/35
He hit 1,000 runs in a season three times (best 1,245, av 31.92, in 1953).

Thompson, Eddie Clarke
Professional. *b:* 27.2.1907, Leyton, Essex. *d:* 18.3.1982, Torquay, Devon. Stylish middle order left-hand batsman, slow left-arm bowler. *Team* Essex (1926–29, 44 matches).
Career batting
44–61–17–696–45*–15.81–0–*ct* 10
Bowling 938–17–55.17–0–0–2/12

Thompson, Eric Richard
Cricketer. *b:* 6.10.1938, Kirkwall, Orkney. Lower order right-hand batsman, right-arm fast medium bowler. *Team* Scotland (1965–74).
Career batting
16–20–7–135–29*–10.38–0–*ct* 11
Bowling 1118–35–31.94–2–0–5/11

Thompson, George Joseph
Amateur in 1895, professional commencing 1897. *b:* 27.10.1877, Cogenhoe, Northampton. *d:* 3.3.1943, Clifton, Bristol. Steady middle order right-hand batsman, right-arm fast medium bowler, close field. *Sch* Wellingborough. *Teams* Northants (1905–22, 222 matches); Auckland (1911/12). *Tours* Hawke to New Zealand and Australia 1902/3; Brackley to West Indies 1904/5; MCC to South Africa 1909/10. *Tests* England (1909 to 1909/10, 6 matches).
Career batting
353–606–60–12018–131*–22.01–9–*ct* 251
Bowling 30058–1591–18.89–147–40–9/64
Test batting
6–10–1–273–63–30.33–0–*ct* 5
Bowling 638–23–27.73–0–0–4/50
He hit 1,000 runs in a season three times (best 1,080, av 31.76, in 1914), completing the 'double' in 1906 and 1910. In all he took 100 wickets eight times (best 163, av 14.67, in 1909). For a short time after the First World War, he was player-coach to Northants, but injury received in the war effectively ended his first-class career. His first-class debut was for MCC in 1897. His best bowling was 9/64 for Northants v Derbyshire at Northampton in 1906.

Thompson, Herbert
Professional. *b:* 6.12.1869, West Norwood, Surrey. *d:* 22.10.1947, Caterham, Surrey. Lower order right-hand batsman, leg break and googly bowler. *Team* Surrey (1894–1919, 12 matches).
Career batting
12–20–4–138–44*–8.62–0–*ct* 4
Bowling 663–31–21.38–2–1–5/59

Thompson, Herbert
Amateur. *b:* 14.5.1886, Leicester. *d:* 8.8.1941, Sevenoaks, Kent. Aggressive middle order right-hand batsman, good field. *Sch* Rugby. *Team* Leicestershire (1908–10, 10 matches).
Career batting
10–18–0–233–72–12.94–0–*ct* 4
He did not appear in first-class matches whilst at Oxford U. For many years he was Honorary Secretary to the Incogniti CC.

Thompson, Hugh Reginald Patrick
Amateur. *b:* 11.4.1934, Scunthorpe, Lincs. Lower order right-hand batsman, off break bowler. *Sch* Cheltenham. *Team* Hampshire (1953–54, 2 matches).
Career batting
2–1–0–16–16–16.00–0–*ct* 1
Bowling 259–2–129.50–0–0–2/106
He was also a useful hockey player.

Thompson, John Charles Peace
Amateur. *b:* 14.4.1870, Chester. *d:* 31.12.1945, Tarset, Northumberland. Middle order batsman. *Sch* Harrow. *Team* Liverpool and District XI (1892).
Career batting
1–1–0–14–14–14.00–0–*ct* 1
His County cricket was for Cheshire.

Thompson, John Ross
Amateur. *b:* 10.5.1918, Berkhamsted, Hertfordshire. Attractive opening right-hand batsman, off break bowler. *Sch* Tonbridge. *Teams* Cambridge U (1938–39, blue both years); Warwickshire (1938–54, 44 matches). *Tours* MCC to North America 1951, 1959 (not first-class).
Career batting
68–116–5–3455–191–31.12–6–*ct* 32
Bowling 13–0
He also played for Wiltshire.

Thompson, Leslie Baines
Amateur. *b:* 12.11.1908, Brentford, Middlesex. Lower order right-hand batsman, off break bowler. *Team* Middlesex (1946–49, 6 matches).
Career batting
6–4–2–16–13–8.00–0–*ct* 3
Bowling 248–5–49.60–0–0–3/50

Thompson, M.
Amateur. Middle order batsman. *Team* Middlesex (1866, 2 matches).
Career batting
2–3–1–9–5–4.50–0–*ct* 1

Thompson, Neil Powney
Amateur. *b:* 10.10.1938, Colombo, Ceylon. Tail end left-hand batsman, left-arm fast medium bowler. *Sch* Christ's Hospital. *Team* Oxford U (1961).
Career batting
7–7–3–16–4*–4.00–0–*ct* 3
Bowling 637–17–37.47–0–0–4/72

Thompson, Roland George
Professional. *b:* 26.9.1932, Binley, Coventry, Warwickshire. Lower order right-hand batsman, right-arm fast medium bowler. *Team* Warwickshire (1949–62, 157 matches).
Career batting
158–187–71–657–25*–5.66–0–*ct* 51
Bowling 10901–479–22.75–21–5–9/65
His best analysis in an innings was 9 for 65 for Warwickshire v Notts at Edgbaston in 1952.

Thompson, Thomas
Cricketer. *b:* 24.2.1934, Workington, Cumberland. Lower order right-hand batsman, off break bowler. *Team* Leicestershire (1963–64, 9 matches).
Career batting
9–14–5–43–12–4.77–0–*ct* 2
Bowling 497–17–29.23–0–0–3/53
He appeared for Cumberland from 1955 to 1974.

Thompson, W. H.
Amateur. Middle order batsman. *Team* Liverpool and District XI (1892).
Career batting
1–1–0–10–10–10.00–0–*ct* 0
Bowling 24–1–24.00–0–0–1/24

Thompson, William Holloway
Professional. *b:* 24.6.1882, Spondon, Derbyshire. *d:* 19.10.1954, Spondon, Derbyshire. Middle order right-hand batsman. *Team* Derbyshire (1908, 1 match).
Career batting
1–2–0–17–17–8.50–0–*ct* 0

Thomson, Alpin Erroll
Amateur. *b:* 14.5.1893, Perth, Australia. *d:* 6.3.1960, Hawridge, Buckinghamshire. Lower order right-hand batsman, useful bowler. *Team* Somerset (1922–23, 2 matches).
Career batting
3–5–3–7–7*–3.50–0–*ct* 1
Bowling 189–4–47.25–0–0–3/90
A noted rugby footballer, he represented Scotland.

Thomson, Edmund Peel
Amateur. *b:* 22.4.1874, Moss Side, Manchester, Lancashire. *d:* 21.12.1914, nr La Bassee, France. Middle order right-hand batsman. *Sch* Fettes. *Team* MCC (1913–14).
Career batting
6–12–1–201–53–18.27–0–*ct* 1
His County cricket was for Wiltshire.

Thomson, Graeme Bruce
Cricketer. *b:* 31.7.1951, Invercargill, New Zealand. Lower order left-hand batsman, left-arm medium pace bowler. *Team* Otago (1974/5 to 1980/1). *Tour* New Zealand to England 1978.
Career batting
47–59–22–340–34*–9.18–0–*ct* 23
Bowling 3180–110–28.90–3–1–6/41
He achieved very little on the 1978 visit and did not appear in the Tests.

Thomson, Henry Shepherd
Amateur. *b:* 4.6.1854, Ramsgate, Kent. Lower order left-hand batsman, left-hand fast round-arm bowler. *Sch* Hurstpierpoint. *Team* Kent (1876, 2 matches).
Career batting
2–3–0–44–27–14.66–0–*ct* 2
Bowling 86–3–28.66–0–0–1/14

Thomson, James
Amateur. *b:* 13.2.1940, Kilmarnock, Ayrshire, Scotland. Lower order right-hand batsman, leg break and googly bowler. *Team* Scotland (1962).
Career batting
1–1–1–1–1*–no av–0–*ct* 2
Bowling 38–0

Thomson, Jeffrey Robert
Cricketer. *b:* 16.8.1950, Greenacre, New South Wales, Australia. Lower order right-hand batsman, right-arm fast bowler. *Teams* New South Wales (1972/3 to 1973/4, 7 matches); Queensland (1974/5 to 1982/3, 50 matches); Middlesex (1981, 8 matches). *Tours* Australia to England 1975, 1977, 1980, to West Indies 1977/8, to New Zealand 1981/2, to Pakistan 1982/3. *Tests* Australia (1972/3 to 1982/3, 49 matches).

Career batting
140–171–41–1744–61–13.41–0–*ct* 53
Bowling 12995–518–25.08–22–3–7/33
Test batting
49–69–16–641–49–12.09–0–*ct* 19
Bowling 5326–197–27.03–8–0–6/46

On the 1975 tour, which followed his success against England in Australia, he played in all four Tests, but was very erratic. In 1977 with 23 wickets, av 25.34, in the five Tests, he took most wickets, but was troubled by injury. In 1980 he proved totally ineffective and did not play in the Test. During the 1981 season he was engaged by Middlesex, but due to injury played little. All in all he has not bowled up to his Australian form whilst in England.

Thomson, Norman Ian
Amateur 1952, turned professional 1953. *b:* 23.1.1929, Walsall, Staffordshire. Lower order right-hand batsman, right-arm medium pace bowler. *Sch* Forest. *Team* Sussex (1952–72, 403 matches). *Tours* MCC to Pakistan 1955/6, to South Africa 1964/5. *Tests* England (1964/5, 5 matches).
Career batting
425–583–100–7120–77–14.74–0–*ct* 135
Bowling 32867–1597–20.58–73–8–10/49
Test batting
5–4–1–69–39–23.00–0–*ct* 3
Bowling 568–9–63.11–0–0–2/55

He took 100 wickets in a season twelve times (best 134, av 20.98, in 1961). His best bowling analysis in an innings was 10 for 49 for Sussex v Warwickshire at Worthing in 1964. He retired after the 1965 season, but reappeared in 1972.

Thomson, Richard Harry
Amateur. *b:* 19.10.1938, Bexhill-on-Sea, Sussex. Middle order left-hand batsman. *Teams* Cambridge U (1961–62, blue both years); Sussex (1961, 2 matches).
Career batting
25–48–5–883–84–20.53–0–*ct* 15
Bowling 13–0

Thomson, Samuel Johnstone
Amateur. *b:* 27.5.1911, Johnstone, Renfrewshire, Scotland. Right-hand batsman, leg break and googly bowler. *Team* Scotland (1938–51).
Career batting
4–7–2–75–21*–15.00–0–*ct* 3
Bowling 246–17–14.47–1–0–5/54

Thorburn, Robert Murray
Amateur. *b:* 22.3.1883, Peebles, Peebleshire, Scotland. *d:* 8.5.1943, Edinburgh, Scotland. Middle order batsman, useful bowler. *Team* Scotland (1924).
Career batting
1–2–0–11–11–5.50–0–*ct* 0
Bowling 32–0

Thorburn, Walter Hunter
Amateur. *b:* 7.10.1884, Innerleithen, Peebleshire, Scotland. *d:* 27.3.1957, Peebles, Scotland. Middle order batsman. *Team* Scotland (1909–12).
Career batting
5–8–2–183–90*–30.50–0–*ct* 1
Bowling 21–0

Thorley, Joseph James
Amateur. *b:* 1894, Faringdon, Berkshire. *d:* 26.12.1962, Marylebone, London. Middle order right-hand batsman, right-arm medium pace bowler. *Sch* Tonbridge. *Teams* Gentlemen (1925); Tennyson's XI (1926).
Career batting
2–3–1–47–27–23.50–0–*ct* 0
Bowling 22–0

His County cricket was for Hertfordshire

Thorn, Hubert Wethered
Amateur. *b:* 21.4.1909, Tiptree, Essex. *d:* 20.5.1982, Colchester, Essex. Middle order batsman, useful bowler. *Team* Essex (1928, 1 match).
Career batting
1–2–0–12–7–6.00–0–*ct* 0
Bowling 42–1–42.00–0–0–1/42

Thorn, Philip Leslie
Cricketer. *b:* 17.11.1951, Bristol. Lower order right-hand batsman, slow left-arm bowler. *Team* Gloucestershire (1974, 4 matches).
Career batting
4–6–2–45–25–11.25–0–*ct* 4
Bowling 227–4–56.75–0–0–2/53

He also played for Wiltshire.

Thornber, Harry
Amateur. *b:* 1851, Manchester, Lancashire. *d:* July 1913, St Pancras, London. Sound middle order right-hand batsman. *Team* (Lancashire 1874, 1 match).
Career batting
1–2–0–0–0–0.00–0–*ct* 0

He played for Cheshire, being captain of the County for several seasons.

Thorne, David Anthony
Cricketer. *b:* 12.12.1964, Coventry, Warwickshire. Lower order right-hand batsman, left-arm medium pace bowler. *Team* Warwickshsire (1983, 5 matches).

Career batting
5–7–3–62–23*–15.50–0–*ct* 3
Bowling 189–2–94.50–0–0–1/21

Thorne, Major General Sir David Calthorpe
Cricketer. *b:* 13.12.1933, Hertford. Lower order batsman, left-arm bowler. *Team* Combined Services (1964).
Career batting
2–4–1–98–59–32.66–0–*ct* 0
Bowling 133–2–66.50–0–0–2/74

Thorne, Gordon Calthorpe
Amateur. *b:* 3.3.1897, Chelsea, London. *d:* 2.3.1942, at sea off the coast of Singapore. Middle order right-hand batsman. *Sch* Haileybury. *Team* Army (1927).
Career batting
1–2–0–24–17–12.00–0–*ct* 0
His County cricket was for Norfolk.

Thorne, Robert
Amateur. *b:* 1860, Southampton, Hants. *d:* 11.2.1930, Southampton, Hants. Opening batsman. *Team* Hampshire (1883, 2 matches).
Career batting
2–4–0–9–6–2.25–0–*ct* 0

Thorneycroft, Charles Bedford
Professional. *b:* 1879, Towcester, Northants. Lower order batsman, right-arm fast bowler. *Team* Northants (1907, 2 matches).
Career batting
2–4–0–5–3–1.25–0–*ct* 1
Bowling 50–2–25.00–0–0–1/14

Thornhill, Frederick
Professional. *b:* 25.9.1846, Beeston, Notts. *d:* 23.7.1876, Toton Sidings, Long Eaton, Derbyshire. He was killed crossing a railway line. Middle order batsman. *Team* Derbyshire (1876, 1 match).
Career batting
1–2–0–0–0–0.00–0–*ct* 0

Thornhill, Robert Victor
Amateur. *b:* 1904. *d:* 28.7.1963, Merton, Surrey. Middle order right-hand batsman. *Team* Leveson-Gower's XI (1934).
Career batting
1–2–0–64–52–32.00–0–*ct* 0

Thornton, A.
Professional. *b:* 20.7.1854. *d:* 19.4.1915. Middle order right-hand batsman. *Team* Yorkshire (1881, 3 matches).
Career batting
3–4–0–21–7–5.25–0–*ct* 2

Thornton, Albert James
Amateur. *b:* 17.1.1856, Folkestone, Kent. *d:* 14.6.1931, Kensington, London. Brother of R. T. (Kent) and W. A. (Oxford U). Free hitting middle order right-hand batsman, right-hand slow under-arm bowler. *Sch* Winchester. *Teams* Sussex (1880–81, 5 matches); Kent (1884–91, 21 matches). *Tour* Sanders to North America 1885.
Career batting
30–52–7–947–137–21.04–1–*ct* 13
Bowling 667–27–24.70–0–0–4/20
He did not appear in first-class matches whilst at Oxford, his first-class debut being for MCC in 1879. He also played for Devon and for the Gentlemen of Hampshire.

Thornton, Charles Inglis
Amateur. *b:* 20.3.1850, Llanwarne, Herefordshire. *d:* 10.12.1929, Marylebone, London. Cousin of P. M. Thornton (Middlesex). Very powerful middle order right-hand batsman, right-hand fast under-arm bowler, good long leg. *Sch* Eton. *Teams* Kent (1867–72, 18 matches); Middlesex (1875–85, 29 matches); Cambridge U (1869–72, blue all four years).
Career batting
216–374–16–6928–124–19.35–5–*ct* 119
Bowling 944–47–20.08–0–0–4/19
His first-class debut was for Gentlemen of Kent in 1866 and his final first-class appearance for his own Eleven v Cambridge U in 1897. He also played for Lincolnshire.
He was regarded as the greatest hitter of his day, his most effective stroke being the drive, during which he moved out to meet the ball, in contrast to the usual firm footed methods employed by his contemporaries. In practice he hit a ball 168 yards and 162 yards, and in a match at Canterbury 152 yards. He was for many years a leading figure in the Scarborough Festival.

Thornton, Edward
Amateur. *b:* 27.10.1893. *d:* 18.10.1970, Stockport, Cheshire. Middle order batsman. *Team* Combined Services (1922).
Career batting
1–2–0–59–38–29.50–0–*ct* 0

Thornton, Frank Kenneis
Amateur. *b:* 25.10.1898, Leicester. Middle order batsman. *Sch* Oakham. *Team* Northants (1937, 2 matches).
Career batting
2–4–1–27–13–9.00–0–*ct* 0

Thornton, Dr George
Amateur. *b:* 24.12.1867, Skipton, Yorkshire. *d:* 31.1.1939, Kensington, London. Father of P. A.

(Ireland and Border). Robust middle order left-hand batsman, slow left-arm bowler. *Teams* Yorkshire (1891, 3 matches); Middlesex (1893–99, 32 matches). *Tour* Ceylon to India 1909/10 (not first-class). *Test* South Africa (1902/3, 1 match).
Career batting
41–67–11–1263–161–22.55–1–*ct* 13
Bowling 1007–32–31.46–1–0–5/20
Test batting
1–1–1–1–1*–no av–0–*ct* 1
Bowling 20–1–20.00–0–0–1/20

He lived for several years in South Africa and played for Transvaal, though not in a first-class match. Later he moved to Ceylon and was President of the Colombo Cricket Club.

Thornton, John Arthur Curzon
Amateur. *b:* 24.2.1902, Leicester. Middle order right-hand batsman, right-arm fast medium bowler. *Sch* Uppingham. *Team* Leicestershsire (1921, 3 matches).
Career batting
3–5–3–53–19*–26.50–0–*ct* 1
Bowling 72–1–72.00–0–0–1/21

Thornton, James Richard
Amateur. *b:* 11.1.1861, Horsham, Sussex. *d:* 1.3.1916, Burgess Hill, Sussex. Lower order right-hand batsman, right-arm fast bowler, good field. *Team* Sussex (1880–83, 3 matches).
Career batting
3–5–0–73–29–14.60–0–*ct* 2
Bowling 42–1–42.00–0–0–1/30

Thornton, Dr Patrick Alban
Amateur. *b:* 4.5.1904, Cape Town, South Africa. *d:* 1.2.1961, East London, South Africa. Son of Dr G. (Yorkshire and Middlesex). Right-hand batsman, right-arm medium pace bowler. *Teams* Ireland (1928–29); Border (1933/4).
Career batting
6–11–1–119–37–11.70–0–*ct* 3
Bowling 212–10–21.20–0–0–4/64

Thornton, Percy Melville
Amateur. *b:* 29.12.1841, Mayfair, London. *d:* 8.1.1918, South Kensington, London. Cousin of C. I. (Middlesex). Lower order right-hand batsman, right-hand fast round-arm bowler, good long stop. *Sch* Harrow. *Teams* Cambridge U (1864); Middlesex (1872, 1 match).
Career batting
4–5–1–34–27*–8.50–0–*ct* 0
Bowling 3–0

Commencing 1870 he was Hon Secretary of Middlesex CCC, not retiring until 1898, though he continued on the County Committee. He was a noted athlete and as Hon Sec of the Cambridge University Athletic Club was one of the founders of the inter-University Sports in 1864. He was also MP for Clapham from 1892 to 1910.

Thornton, Rev Richard Thornton
Amateur. *b:* 28.3.1853, Folkestone, Kent. *d:* 30.5.1928, Eastbourne, Sussex. Brother of A. J. (Kent) and W. A. (Oxford U). Middle order right-hand batsman, right-hand slow round-arm, or under-arm, bowler. *Team* Kent (1881–88, 45 matches). *Tour* Sanders to North America 1885.
Career batting
66–112–11–2021–107–20.00–1–*ct* 42
Bowling 104–3–34.66–0–0–2/16

He did not appear in first-class cricket whilst at Oxford, but was awarded his soccer blue. His final first-class match was for MCC in 1893. He also appeared for Devon, Dorset and Wiltshire.

Thornton, Thomas
Amateur. *b:* 29.5.1922, Elland, Yorkshire. Opening right-hand batsman. *Team* RAF (1946).
Career batting
1–2–0–29–23–14.50–0–*ct* 0

Thornton, Walter Alfred
Amateur. *b:* 23.2.1858, London. *d:* 2.2.1915, Blakedown, Kidderminster. Brother of A. J. (Kent and Sussex) and R. T. (Kent). Middle order right-hand batsman, right-arm fast bowler. *Sch* Winchester. *Team* Oxford U (1879–82, blue all four years).
Career batting
24–47–2–843–70–18.73–0–*ct* 9
Bowling 561–27–20.77–0–0–4/29

His final first-class match was for MCC in 1883. His County cricket was for Devonshire commencing 1874.

Thornycroft, Guy Mytton
Amateur. *b:* 1.4.1917, Ulverston, Lancashire. Middle order right-hand batsman. *Sch* Shrewsbury. *Team* Worcestershire (1947, 1 match).
Career batting
1–2–0–3–3–1.50–0–*ct* 0

Thorp, Philip
Amateur. *b:* 6.5.1911, Kidderminster, Worcestershire. Middle order right-hand batsman. *Team* Worcestershire (1935, 2 matches).
Career batting
2–4–0–19–11–4.75–0–*ct* 0

Thorpe, Charles
Amateur. *b:* 11.8.1882, Fotheringhay, Northants. *d:* 5.5.1953, Fotheringhay, Northants. Middle

order right-hand batsman. *Sch* Oundle. *Team* Northants (1908–09, 9 matches).
Career batting
9–17–0–195–50–11.47–0–*ct* 1
Bowling 16–0

Thorpe, George
Professional. *b:* 20.2.1834, Sheffield, Yorkshire. *d:* 1899, Sheffield, Yorkshire. Middle order right-hand batsman. *Team* Yorkshire (1862–64, 2 matches).
Career batting
2–4–1–19–9*–6.33–0–*ct* 3
Bowling 4–0

Thorpe, Thomas
Professional. *b:* 19.5.1881, Attercliffe, Sheffield, Yorkshire. *d:* 28.9.1953, Worksop, Notts. Middle order batsman. *Team* Northants (1913, 3 matches).
Career batting
3–4–1–11–6–3.66–0–*ct* 2

A useful soccer player, he kept goal for Northampton Town.

Thoy, Reginald Ernest
Amateur. *b:* 12.5.1921, Singapore. Opening batsman. *Team* D. R. Jardine's XI (1955–57).
Career batting
2–3–0–24–13–8.00–0–*ct* 3

Threapleton, Joseph William
Professional. *b:* 20.7.1857, Pudsey, Yorkshire. *d:* 1918, North Bierley, Yorkshire. Sound lower order right-hand batsman, wicket-keeper. *Team* Yorkshire (1881, 1 match).
Career batting
1–1–1–8–8*–no av–0–*ct* 2–*st* 1

Thresher, Philip
Amateur. *b:* 1.3.1844, South Stoneham, Hampshire. *d:* 11.4.1883, Shepherd's Bush, London. Opening batsman. *Sch* Winchester. *Team* Hampshire (1865–69, 5 matches).
Career batting
5–9–1–93–47*–11.62–0–*ct* 0
Bowling 19–1–19.00–0–0–1/19

Whilst at Oxford University he played in some Trial matches, but no first-class contests.

Thresher, Ronald Stanley
Amateur. *b:* 31.12.1930, Tonbridge, Kent. Lower order right-hand batsman, right-arm fast bowler. *Team* Kent (1957, 2 matches).
Career batting
5–9–4–51–19–10.20–0–*ct* 0
Bowling 407–14–29.07–0–0–4/29

His final first-class match was for D. R. Jardine's XI in 1958.

Thring, Charles Henry Meredith
Amateur. *b:* 21.1.1861, Uppingham, Rutland. *d:* 11.4.1939, Chilcompton, Somerset. Middle order batsman. *Sch* Marlborough. *Team* MCC (1889).
Career batting
1–1–0–12–12–12.00–0–*ct* 0

He also played for Wiltshire and Bedfordshire.

Throwley, Viscount George Edward Milles
(succeeded to the title 2nd Earl Sondes in 1894)
Amateur. *b:* 11.5.1861, Lees Court, Faversham, Kent. *d:* 1.10.1907, Marylebone, London. He died after an operation. Brother of H. A. Milles (Kent). Middle order right-hand batsman, right-arm medium pace bowler. *Sch* Eton. *Team* Kent (1882–84, 6 matches). *Tour* Hawke to North America 1891.
Career batting
8–12–2–168–82–16.80–0–*ct* 7
Bowling 125–5–25.00–0–0–3/29

He did not appear in any first-class matches whilst at Cambridge.

Thursfield, John Hunt
Amateur. *b:* 16.6.1892, Alvechurch, Worcestershire. *d:* 26.4.1951, Shenstone, Lichfield, Staffordshire. Middle order right-hand batsman. *Sch* Shrewsbury. *Team* Worcestershire (1922–25, 3 matches).
Career batting
3–6–0–70–35–11.66–0–*ct* 1

Thursting, Laurence Denis
Professional. *b:* 9.9.1915, Lambeth, London. Opening or middle order right-hand batsman, slow left-arm bowler. *Team* Leicestershire (1938–47, 29 matches).
Career batting
29–45–10–882–94–25.20–0–*ct* 10
Bowling 660–13–50.76–0–0–3/34

Thwaites, Ian Guy
Cricketer. *b:* 4.3.1943, Brighton, Sussex. Middle order right-hand batsman. *Sch* Eastbourne. *Team* Cambridge U (1963–64, blue 1964).
Career batting
22–38–4–769–61–22.61–0–*ct* 3
Bowling 127–4–31.75–0–0–1/1

Tidy, Thomas
Professional. *b:* 6.10.1847, Hurstpierpoint, Sussex. *d:* 11.9.1918, Hildenborough, Kent.

Middle order right-hand batsman. *Team* Kent (1868, 1 match).
Career batting
1–2–0–21–16–10.50–0–*ct* 0

Tidy, Warwick Nigel
Cricketer. *b:* 10.2.1953, Birmingham. Tail end right-hand batsman, leg break and googly bowler. *Team* Warwickshire (1970–74, 36 matches).
Career batting
36–34–14–70–12*–3.50–0–*ct* 17
Bowling 2775–81–34.25–3–0–5/24

Tillard, Alfred Edmund
Amateur. *b:* 20.4.1847, Conington, Cambridgeshire. *d:* 9.8.1926, Tooting Bec, London. Middle order batsman. *Sch* Norwich. *Team* Cambridgeshire (1868, 1 match).
Career batting
1–2–1–27–14–27.00–0–*ct* 2
He also played for Lincolnshire.

Tillard, Charles
Amateur. *b:* 18.4.1851, Wimbledon, Surrey. *d:* 7.3.1944, Bathford, Somerset, Father of E. D. (Somerset). Lower order right-hand batsman, right-hand fast round-arm bowler, good cover point. *Sch* Repton. *Teams* Cambridge U (1871–73, blue 1873); Surrey (1874–75, 3 matches).
Career batting
16–26–2–328–62*–13.66–0–*ct* 6
Bowling 958–54–17.74–4–1–7/35
In 1868 he appeared for Norfolk. He was a good athlete, especially in the long and high jumps.

Tillard, Elliot Dowell
Amateur. *b:* 22.7.1880, Cheltenham, Gloucs. *d:* 19.2.1967, Bude, Cornwall. Son of Charles (Surrey). Middle order batsman, useful bowler. *Sch* Malvern. *Teams* Europeans (1907/8 to 1922/3); Somerset (1912, 9 matches).
Career batting
16–30–1–357–39–12.31–0–*ct* 3
Bowling 221–14–15.78–2–0–6/40

Tillard, John Robert
Amateur. *b:* 26.5.1924, London. Middle order right-hand batsman. *Sch* Winchester. *Team* Sussex (1949, 1 match).
Career batting
1–2–0–3–3–1.50–0–*ct* 0

Tilley, Eric Warrington
Amateur. *b:* 22.9.1913, Whatstandwell, Derbyshire. *d:* 1.12.1977, Leicester. Lower order right-hand batsman, right-arm fast medium bowler. *Team* Leicestershire (1946, 4 matches).
Career batting
4–3–0–3–2–1.00–0–*ct* 2
Bowling 256–10–25.60–0–0–3/33

Tilly, Henry William
Professional. b: 25.5.1932, Edmonton, Middlesex. Lower order right-hand batsman, right-arm fast medium bowler. *Team* Middlesex (1954–61, 59 matches).
Career batting
64–88–13–814–49*–10.85–0–*ct* 18
Bowling 3502–134–26.13–4–0–6/33
After leaving Middlesex he played for Hertfordshire and his final first-class appearance was for the Minor Counties in 1967.

Tilson, John
Professional. *b:* 27.3.1845, Ilkeston, Derbyshire. *d:* 4.11.1895, Ilkeston, Derbyshire. Middle order right-hand batsman, right-hand medium pace round-arm bowler. *Team* Derbyshire (1871–76, 3 matches).
Career batting
3–5–0–26–14–5.20–0–*ct* 0

Timmis, Peter John
Cricketer. *b:* 30.7.1942, Stoke-on-Trent, Staffs. Lower order right-hand batsman, right-arm fast medium bowler. *Team* Minor Counties (1971).
Career batting
1 match, did not bat–*ct* 0
Bowling 36–0
His County cricket was for Staffordshire commencing 1962.

Timms, Bryan Stanley Valentine
Professional. *b:* 17.12.1940, Ropley, Hampshire. Lower order right-hand batsman, wicket-keeper. *Teams* Hampshire (1959–68, 208 matches); Warwickshire (1969–71, 24 matches).
Career batting
232–306–74–3657–120–15.76–1–*ct* 456–*st* 70

Timms, Herbert Henry
Professional. *b:* 6.7.1890, Moreton-in-Marsh, Gloucs. *d:* 1.3.1973, Eynsham, Oxon. Middle order left-hand batsman, right-arm fast medium bowler. *Team* Gloucestershire (1911–12, 3 matches).
Career batting
3–6–0–33–12–5.50–0–*ct* 0

Timms, John Edward
Amateur, turned professional in 1927. *b:* 3.11.1906, Silverstone, Northants. *d:* 18.5.1980, Buckingham. Attractive middle order right-hand

batsman, right-arm medium pace bowler, excellent cover point. *Sch* Wellingborough. *Team* Northants (1925–49, 468 matches).
Career batting
472–848–30–20509–213–25.07–31–*ct* 153
Bowling 6626–149–44.46–2–0–6/18

He hit 1,000 runs in a season 11 times (best 1,632, av 34.72, in 1934). His only double century was 213 for Northants v Worcs at Stourbridge in 1934.

Timms, Wilfrid Walter
Amateur. *b:* 28.9.1902, Northampton. Sound opening right-hand batsman, leg break bowler. *Sch* Northampton County Grammar. *Teams* Northants (1921–32, 99 matches); Cambridge U (1925).
Career batting
106–196–15–4683–154*–22.55–4–*ct* 25
Bowling 175–0

He hit 1,008 runs, av 27.24, in 1925.

Tindall, Christian
Amateur. *b:* 1878, Leighton Buzzard, Bedfordshire. *d:* 13.4.1951, Littleham, Devon. Middle order batsman. *Sch* Malvern. *Team* London County (1904).
Career batting
1–2–1–10–9*–10.00–0–*ct* 0

Tindall, Rev Henry Charles Lenox
Amateur. *b:* 4.2.1863, Margate, Kent. *d:* 10.6.1940, Peasmarsh, Sussex. Brother of S. M. (Lancashire). Stylish middle order right-hand batsman, right-arm fast bowler, good field. *Team* Kent (1893–95, 3 matches).
Career batting
5–6–1–71–32–14.20–0–*ct* 3
Bowling 166–4–41.50–0–0–2/56

He did not appear in first-class cricket whilst at Cambridge, but was a noted athlete, obtaining his blue and winning the 880, 440 and 100 yards. In 1889 he won the 440 yards Amateur Championship. Also a good rugby footballer, he appeared for Rosslyn Park.

Tindall, Mark
Amateur. *b:* 31.3.1914, Marylebone, London. Father of R. M. (Northants). Middle order right-hand batsman, left-arm fast-medium bowler. *Sch* Harrow. *Teams* Middlesex (1933–38, 16 matches); Cambridge U (1935–37, blue all three years).
Career batting
51–92–3–2202–117–24.74–3–*ct* 15
Bowling 65–3–21.66–0–0–2/21

He hit 1,018 runs, av 29.08, in 1936.

Tindall, Ronald Albert Ernest
Professional. *b:* 23.9.1935, Streatham, London. Middle order right-hand batsman, off break bowler. *Team* Surrey (1956–66, 172 matches).
Career batting
173–257–38–5446–109*–24.86–2–*ct* 129
Bowling 4857–150–32.38–2–0–5/41

He hit 1,126 runs, av 28.15, in 1963.

A noted soccer player, he was centre forward for Chelsea, West Ham United, Reading and Portsmouth.

Tindall, Richard Geoffrey
Amateur. *b:* 20.2.1912, Sherborne, Dorset. *d:* 22.1.1942, Jadabia, Libya. Lower order right-hand batsman, right-arm fast bowler. *Sch* Winchester. *Team* Oxford U (1933–34, blue both years).
Career batting
18–30–3–610–113–22.96–1–*ct* 11
Bowling 1581–50–31.62–2–0–5/73

His County cricket was for Dorset.

Tindall, Robert Michael
Cricketer. *b:* 16.6.1959, Harrow-on-the-Hill, Middlesex. Son of Mark (Middlesex). Middle order left-hand batsman, slow left-arm bowler. *Sch* Harrow. *Team* Northants (1980–81, 14 matches).
Career batting
14–22–4–330–60*–18.33–0–*ct* 6
Bowling 331–4–82.75–0–0–2/1

Tindall, Sidney Maguire
Amateur. *b:* 18.2.1867, Margate, Kent. *d:* 19.9.1922, Sydney, Australia. He died after fracturing his skull whilst falling from a moving tram. Brother of H. C. L. (Kent). Attacking middle order right-hand batsman, good outfield. *Teams* Lancashire (1894–98, 42 matches); London County (1900–01).
Career batting
56–86–1–1304–86–15.34–0–*ct* 24
Bowling 69–2–34.50–0–0–1/11

He emigrated to Australia in 1911 and was for a short time Secretary of Melbourne CC. A noted hockey player, he was regarded as one of the best in England about 1890.

Tindill, Eric William Thomas
Amateur. *b:* 18.12.1910, Nelson, New Zealand. Opening or lower order left-hand batsman, wicket-keeper. *Team* Wellington (1932/3 to 1949/50). *Tours* New Zealand to England 1937, to Australia 1937/8. *Tests* New Zealand (1937 to 1946/7, 5 matches).

Career batting
68–114–13–3091–149–30.60–6–*ct* 93–*st* 33
Test batting
5–9–1–73–37*–9.12–0–*ct* 6–*st* 1

He kept wicket in all three Tests on the 1937 tour. A good rugby footballer, he represented New Zealand.

Tinkler, Edward W.
Amateur. *b:* 11.3.1921, Burnley, Lancashire. Stylish middle order right-hand batsman, right-arm medium pace bowler. *Sch* Worcester RGS. *Team* Worcestershire (1953, 1 match).
Career batting
3–5–0–15–7–3.00–0–*ct* 1
Bowling 14–0

His final first-class match was for MCC in 1961.

Tinley, Francis
Professional. *b:* 3.3.1819, Southwell, Notts. *d:* 2.6.1889, Birmingham. Brother of R. C. (Notts) and Vincent (Notts). Hard hitting lower order right-hand batsman, right-hand medium pace round-arm bowler. *Team* Nottinghamshire (1845–56, 13 matches).
Career batting
19–32–7–188–23*–7.52–0–*ct* 7
Bowling 589–63+2–9.34–5–1–6/29

His debut was for Players of Notts in 1844.

Tinley, Robert Crispin
Professional. *b:* 25.10.1830, Southwell, Notts. *d:* 11.12.1900, Burton-on-Trent, Staffs. Brother of Francis (Notts) and Vincent (Notts). Attacking lower order right-hand batsman, right-hand fast round-arm, but after 1858 slow under-arm bowler, good point field. *Team* Nottinghamshire (1847–69, 54 matches). *Tour* Parr to Australia 1863/4.
Career batting
117–199–23–2004–56–11.38–0–*ct* 143–*st* 2
Bowling 4248–294+15–14.44–22–5–8/12

His last first-class match was AEE v Yorkshire in 1874. He was for some years the leading exponent of 'lob' bowling in England. He umpired in important matches after retiring from first-class cricket.

Tinley, Vincent
Professional. *b:* 26.1.1828, Southwell, Notts. *d:* 19.11.1899, Nottingham. Brother of Francis (Notts) and R. C. (Notts). Middle order right-hand batsman, right-hand slow under-arm bowler, wicket-keeper. *Teams* Lancashire (1851, 2 matches); Nottinghamshire (1864, 1 match).
Career batting
3–5–1–41–13–10.25–0–*ct* 1

He also played for Devon and Lincolnshire.

Tinsley, Alfred
Professional. *b:* 12.3.1867, Welham, Malton, Yorkshire. *d:* 25.9.1933, Musselburgh, Midlothian, Scotland. Brother of H. J. (Lancashire and Yorkshire). Middle order right-hand batsman, good deep field. *Team* Lancashire (1890–95, 58 matches).
Career batting
58–91–10–1348–65–16.64–0–*ct* 27
Bowling 7–0

He played in one match for Yorkshire in 1887 (v Cheshire); and later for Staffordshire.

Tinsley, Henry James
Professional. *b:* 20.2.1865, Welham, Malton, Yorkshire. *d:* 10.12.1938, Heworth, Yorkshire. Brother of Alfred (Lancashire). Middle order right-hand batsman, right-arm fast bowler. *Teams* Yorkshire (1890–91, 9 matches); Lancashire (1894–96, 4 matches).
Career batting
14–21–0–122–18–5.80–0–*ct* 4
Bowling 57–4–14.25–0–0–3/15

Tipper, Benjamin Claude Cecil
Amateur. *b:* 7.7.1896, Birmingham. *d:* 11.7.1970, Norton-Lindsey, Warwickshire. Middle order right-hand batsman, bowler. *Sch* KES, Birmingham. *Team* Worcestershire (1919, 5 matches).
Career batting
5–10–1–137–43–15.22–0–*ct* 7
Bowling 80–4–20.00–0–0–2/0

Tissera, Michael Hugh
Cricketer. *b:* 23.3.1939, Colombo, Ceylon. Middle order right-hand batsman, leg break bowler. *Team* Ceylon (1958/9 to 1975). *Tours* Ceylon/Sri Lanka to India 1959/60, 1961/2, 1964/5, to Pakistan 1966/7, to England 1975.
Career batting
30–54–5–1394–122–28.44–2–*ct* 15
Bowling 856–27–31.70–1–0–5/95

He captained Sri Lanka in 1975.

Titchmarsh, Charles Harold
Amateur. *b:* 18.2.1881, Royston, Herts. *d:* 23.5.1930, Royston, Herts. He died following a stroke. Middle order right-hand batsman, wicket-keeper. *Sch* Bishop's Stortford. *Team* MCC (1920–28). *Tours* MCC to Australia and New Zealand 1922/3.

Career batting
42–72–6–2589–171–39.22–4–*ct* 16
Bowling 4–0

He played for Hertfordshire from 1906 to 1929 and proved the mainstay of that County. In 1921 and 1925 he was chosen to represent the Gentlemen v Players and would no doubt have made a name for himself in first-class cricket if he had forsaken Hertfordshire for one of the major counties.

Titchmarsh, Valentine Adolphus
Amateur, turned professional 1880. *b:* 14.2.1853, Royston, Hertfordshire. *d:* 11.10.1907, St Albans, Herts. He died of locomotor ataxy. Lower order left-hand batsman, right-arm fast bowler. *Team* MCC (1885–91).
Career batting
8–12–0–82–23–6.83–0–*ct* 5
Bowling 187–9–20.77–1–0–5/69

He made his first-class debut for South of England in 1880. His County cricket was for Hertfordshire. Commencing about 1890 he was one of the best known County umpires.

Titley, Edward George
Amateur. *b:* August 1911, Chilwell, Notts. *d:* 17.7.1943, while flying on active service. Lower order right-hand batsman, wicket-keeper. *Sch* Uppingham. *Team* Cambridge U (1932).
Career batting
2–4–0–4–3–1.00–0–*ct* 2

Titmus, Frederick John, MBE
Professional. *b:* 24.11.1932, Kentish Town, London. Middle or lower order right-hand batsman, right-arm medium off break bowler. *Teams* Middlesex (1949–82, 642 matches); Surrey (1978, 1 match); Orange Free State (1975/6). *Tours* MCC to Pakistan 1955/6, to Australia and New Zealand 1962/3, 1965/6, 1974/5, to India 1963/4, to South Africa 1964/5, to West Indies 1967/8; Robins to South Africa 1975/6; MCC to Far East 1981/2 (not first-class); Cavaliers to South Africa 1969/70. *Tests* England (1955 to 1974/5, 53 matches).
Career batting
792–1142–208–21588–137*–23.11–6–*ct* 473
Bowling 63313–2830–22.37–168–26–9/52
Test batting
53–76–11–1449–84*–22.29–0–*ct* 35
Bowling 4931–153–32.22–7–0–7/79

Although he made his debut in 1949, aged 16, it was not until 1953 that he really hit the headlines. In that year he took 100 wickets for the first of sixteen times. His best season came in 1955 with 191 wickets, av 16.31, and in that year he first appeared in Test cricket and achieved the 'double' for the first of eight times. His best season with the bat was 1961 with 1,703 runs, av 37.02, and he topped 1,000 runs in seven other seasons.

After his initial games for England in 1955, he did not re-appear until 1962, then played regularly until his visit to West Indies in 1967/8, when in a swimming accident he lost four toes. He recovered sufficiently to resume County cricket, but never played again in Test cricket in England, his only other Tests being in Australia in 1974/5.

His best bowling performances were both for Middlesex, namely 9 for 52 v Cambridge University in 1962 at Fenner's and 9 for 57 v Lancashire in 1964 at Lord's.

In 1965 he was chosen as captain of Middlesex, but his leadership did not prove a success and he resigned midway through the 1968 season. In 1977 he moved to the Oval as Surrey's coach, but again found the position uncomfortable and left in 1979 – he played once for Surrey. He reappeared for Middlesex in 1979, 1980 and 1982.

Tobin, Rev Frederic
Amateur. *b:* 5.7.1849, Liscard, Birkenshaw, Cheshire. *d:* 28.9.1914, West Folkestone, Kent. Middle order right-hand batsman, good field. *Sch* Rugby. *Team* Cambridge U (1870–72, blue all three years).
Career batting
13–24–2–369–77–16.77–0–*ct* 8

His County cricket was for Lincolnshire, Huntingdonshire and Warwickshire (pre-first-class).

Tod, Ben Ross
Amateur. *b:* 6.8.1908, Edinburgh, Scotland. *d:* 3.6.1967, Belmont, Surrey. Right-hand batsman, off break bowler. *Sch* Edinburgh Academy. *Team* Scotland (1930–39).
Career batting
11–20–3–387–143*–22.76–1–*ct* 5
Bowling 23–1–23.00–0–0–1/17

Todd, James Henry
Amateur. *b:* 16.12.1867, Forest Hill, Kent. *d:* 11.8.1956, Marylebone, London. Middle order right-hand batsman. *Sch* Mill Hill. *Team* London County (1901).
Career batting
3–6–0–66–24–11.00–0–*ct* 6

His final first-class match was for W. G. Grace's XI in 1906.

Todd, Leslie John
Professional. *b:* 19.6.1907, Catford, Kent. *d:* 20.8.1967, Buckland, Dover, Kent. Sound opening left-hand batsman, left-arm slow bowler,

changing to medium in 1933. *Team* Kent (1927–50, 426 matches).
Career batting
437–727–93–20087–174–31.68–38–*ct* 236
Bowling 15883–572–27.76–20–1–6/26

He hit 1,000 runs in a season ten times, going on to 2,000 once : 2,312, av 46.24, in 1947. He achieved the 'double' in 1936, when he took 100 wickets for the only time in his career (103 wickets, av 21.93). He was on the first-class umpires' list after retiring. He played soccer as an amateur for Dulwich Hamlet and represented England at table tennis.

Todd, Norman Douglas
Amateur. *b:* 11.6.1884, Hetton-le-Hole, Co Durham. *d:* 12.5.1959, Ruddington, Notts. Middle order batsman. *Team* Derbyshire (1906–08, 2 matches).
Career batting
2–4–0–6–6–1.50–0–*ct* 0

Todd, Paul Adrian
Cricketer. *b:* 12.3.1953, Morton, Southwell, Notts. Opening right-hand batsman, right-arm medium pace bowler. *Team* Nottinghamshire (1972–82, 156 matches).
Career batting
156–276–16–7168–178–27.56–8–*ct* 105
Bowling 3–0

He scored 1,000 runs in a season three times (best 1,181, av 29.52, in 1978).

Toft, David Penn
Cricketer. *b:* 1.3.1945, Tunbridge Wells, Kent. Opening right-hand batsman. *Sch* Tonbridge. *Team* Oxford U (1965–67, blue 1966 and 1967).
Career batting
27–48–4–1222–145–27.77–1–*ct* 10

Tolchard, Jeffrey Graham
Cricketer. *b:* 17.3.1944, Torquay, Devon. Brother of R. W. (Leics). Middle order right-hand batsman, right-arm medium pace bowler, occasional wicket-keeper. *Sch* Malvern. *Team* Leicestershire (1970–77, 77 matches).
Career batting
78–109–17–1865–78–20.27–0–*ct* 24
Bowling 5–0

He played for Devon 1963, 1966 to 1969 and again commencing 1979. His final first-class match was for Minor Counties in 1981. A good soccer player, he appeared for Torquay United and Exeter City.

Tolchard, Roger William
Cricketer. *b:* 15.6.1946, Torquay, Devon. Brother of J. G. (Leics). Middle order right-hand batsman, wicket-keeper. *Sch* Malvern. *Team* Leicestershire (1965–83, 431 matches). *Tours* International XI to Pakistan, India and Ceylon 1967/8; MCC to India, Pakistan and Sri Lanka 1972/3; Robins to South Africa 1973/4, 1974/5, 1975/6, to Sri Lanka 1977/8; International Wanderers to Rhodesia 1974/5, 1975/6; MCC to India, Sri Lanka and Australia 1976/7; England to Australia 1978/9; Leics to Zimbabwe 1980/1; Overseas XI to India 1980/1. *Tests* England (1976/7, 4 matches).
Career batting
483–680–189–15288–126*–31.13–12–*ct* 912–*st* 125
Bowling 34–1–34.00–0–0–1/4
Test batting
4–7–2–129–67–25.80–0–*ct* 5

His best season was 1970 with 998 runs, av 30.24. From 1981 to 1983 he captained Leicestershire. He played for Devon 1963 and 1964. A useful soccer player, he had a trial with Leicester City.

Tolfree, Edward
Professional. *b:* 12.7.1881, Southampton, Hants. *d:* 20.3.1966, Southampton, Hants. Lower order batsman, useful bowler. *Team* Hampshire (1906–19, 5 matches).
Career batting
5–8–2–53–22*–8.83–0–*ct* 0
Bowling 185–2–92.50–0–0–2/13

Tollemache, Hon Mortimer Granville
Amateur. *b:* 12.4.1872, Westminster, London. *d:* 27.3.1950, Sudbury, Suffolk. Middle order right-hand batsman. *Sch* Eton. *Team* Cambridge U (1891–93).
Career batting
9–16–1–151–28–10.06–0–*ct* 10

He played County cricket for Cheshire and Suffolk.

Toller, Montagu Henry
Amateur. *b:* February 1871, Barnstaple, Devon. *d:* 5.8.1948, Meon Beach, Titchfield, Hampshire. Middle order right-hand batsman, right-arm fast bowler. *Sch* Blundells. *Team* Somerset (1897, 6 matches).
Career batting
6–11–1–77–17–7.70–0–*ct* 1
Bowling 15–1–15.00–0–0–1/15

He also played for Devon.

Tolley, Robert
Amateur. *b:* 14.3.1849, Nottingham. *d:* 2.1.1901, Mapperley, Nottingham. Steady middle order right-hand batsman, right-hand fast, or slow, round-arm bowler. *Team* Nottinghamshire (1871–78, 29 matches).

Career batting
30–47–3–556–54–12.63–0–*ct* 20
Bowling 98–0

Tomblin, Charles Bryan
Professional. *b:* 29.6.1891, Brixworth, Northants. *d:* 1.6.1918, nr Sissonne, France. Middle order batsman. *Team* Northants (1914, 2 matches).
Career batting
2–4–0–8–3–2.00–0–*ct* 2

Tomkins, Eric Feltham
Amateur. *b:* 18.12.1892, Rushden, Northants. *d:* 20.7.1980, Rushden, Northants. Middle order right-hand batsman. *Team* Northants (1920–21, 13 matches).
Career batting
13–22–2–204–50*–10.20–0–*ct* 3

Tomkinson, Francis Martin
Amateur. *b:* 21.10.1883, Kidderminster, Worcs. *d:* 24.11.1963, Cleobury Mortimer, Salop. Brother of G. S. (Worcs). Middle order right-hand batsman. *Sch* Eton. *Team* Worcestershire (1902, 1 match).
Career batting
1–1–0–0–0–0.00–0–*ct* 1

Tomkinson, Sir Geoffrey Stewart
Amateur. *b:* 7.11.1881, Kidderminster, Worcs. *d:* 8.2.1963, Kidderminster, Worcs. Brother of F. M. (Worcs). Middle order batsman. *Sch* Winchester. *Team* Worcestershire (1903–26, 2 matches).
Career batting
2–3–0–12–10–4.00–0–*ct* 0
He did not appear in any first-class matches whilst at Cambridge. In 1956 he was President of Worcestershire CCC. A noted rugby footballer, he captained Kidderminster RFC.

Tomkinson, Robert Edward
Amateur. *b:* 14.8.1847, Chester. *d:* 27.7.1928, Burnham-on-Sea, Somerset. Robust opening right-hand batsman. *Sch* Marlborough. *Team* MCC (1873).
Career batting
3–6–1–81–52–16.20–0–*ct* 3
His County cricket was for Cheshire.

Tomlin, William
Professional. *b:* 15.9.1866, Broughton-Astley, Leics. *d:* 11.5.1910, Leicester. He died of cancer. Graceful middle order right-hand batsman, right-arm medium pace bowler, good field. *Team* Leicestershire (1894–99, 68 matches).
Career batting
68–127–11–2353–140–20.28–4–*ct* 30
Bowling 346–8–43.25–0–0–3/49
His best season was 1895 when he scored 787 runs, av 23.14.

Tomlins, Keith Patrick
Cricketer. *b:* 23.10.1957, Kingston-upon-Thames, Surrey. Middle order right-hand batsman, right-arm medium pace bowler. *Team* Middlesex (1977–83, 65 matches). *Tour* Middlesex to Zimbabwe 1980/1.
Career batting
65–90–12–2166–146–27.76–3–*ct* 49
Bowling 308–4–77.00–0–0–2/28

Tomlinson, Denis Stanley
Amateur. *b:* 4.9.1910, Umtali, Rhodesia. Brother of R. N. (Rhodesia). Lower order right-hand batsman, leg break and googly bowler. *Teams* Rhodesia (1927/8 to 1947/8); Border (1928/9). *Tour* South Africa to England 1935. *Test* South Africa (1935, 1 match).
Career batting
48–73–19–912–109–16.88–1–*ct* 17
Bowling 4418–156–28.32–9–1–6/56
Test batting
1–1–0–9–9–9.00–0–*ct* 0
Bowling 38–0

Tomlinson, Harry
Professional. *b:* 1886, Barwell, Leicestershire. *d:* 29.11.1944, Briton-Ferry, Glamorgan. Middle order left-hand batsman, off break bowler. *Team* Glamorgan (1921–23, 8 matches).
Career batting
8–16–0–244–36–15.25–0–*ct* 2
Bowling 163–1–163.00–0–0–1/30

Tomlinson, Dr John Derek (Williams)
Amateur. *b:* 26.3.1926, South Normanton, Derbyshire. Middle order right-hand batsman. *Team* Derbyshire (1946, 1 match).
Career batting
1–1–0–2–2–2.00–0–*ct* 1

Tomlinson, William James Vincent
Amateur. *b:* 10.8.1901, Winshill, Burton-on-Trent, Staffs. *d:* 16.5.1984, Elsing, Norfolk. Middle order right-hand batsman, right-arm medium pace bowler. *Sch* Felsted. *Teams* Derbyshire (1920–24, 26 matches); Cambridge U (1922–23, blue 1923).
Career batting
38–65–8–852–66–14.94–0–*ct* 10
Bowling 1870–58–32.24–1–0–5/53

Tompkin, Maurice
Professional. *b:* 17.2.1919, Countesthorpe, Leics.

d: 27.9.1956, Leicester. He died following an operation. Polished middle order right-hand batsman. *Team* Leicestershire (1938–56, 349 matches). *Tour* MCC to Pakistan 1955/6.
Career batting
378–655–29–19927–186–31.83–31–*ct* 113
Bowling 106–1–106.00–0–0–1/1

He hit 1,000 runs in a season ten times, going to 2,000 once : 2,190, av 37.11, in 1955. A useful soccer player, he appeared for Leicester City, Bury and Huddersfield at either outside or inside right.

Tonge, John Norton
Amateur. *b:* 9.7.1865, Otford, Kent. *d:* 8.7.1903, Morants Court, Chevening, Kent. Brother of W. C. (Gloucs). Sound middle order right-hand batsman, bowler. *Sch* Cheltenham. *Team* Kent (1884–97, 36 matches). *Tour* Warner to USA 1897.
Career batting
38–68–3–895–60–13.76–0–*ct* 7
Bowling 356–9–39.55–0–0–3/14

Tonge, William Corrie
Amateur. *b:* 14.4.1862, Starborough, Edenbridge, Kent. *d:* 2.5.1943, Fulmer, Bucks. Brother of J. N. (Kent). Middle order right-hand batsman, right-arm medium pace bowler, good field. *Sch* Tonbridge and Cheltenham. *Team* Gloucestershire (1880, 2 matches).
Career batting
2–2–0–8–5–4.00–0–*ct* 0

He played for Norfolk commencing 1895.

Tongue, Christopher Hugh
Cricketer. *b:* 2.4.1943, Uppingham, Rutland. Middle order batsman, useful bowler. *Team* Cambridge U (1963).
Career batting
1–2–0–20–13–10.00–0–*ct* 0
Bowling 23–0

Toogood, Giles John
Cricketer. *b:* 19.11.1961, West Bromwich, Staffs. Middle order right-hand batsman, off break bowler. *Team* Oxford U (1982–83, blue both years).
Career batting
14–24–4–440–83–22.00–0–*ct* 4
Bowling 22–0

Toogood, Thomas Hector
Professional. *b:* 1873, Clifton, Gloucs. *d:* September 1953, Bristol. Lower order right-hand batsman, right-arm slow medium bowler. *Team* Gloucestershire (1900–14, 8 matches).
Career batting
8–11–3–30–12–3.75–0–*ct* 5
Bowling 488–16–30.50–1–0–6/115

Tooker, E. W.
(*see under* Whalley-Tooker, E.)

Toole, Charles Laurence
Cricketer. *b:* 9.1.1939, London. Middle order right-hand batsman, right-arm medium fast bowler. *Team* MCC (1967). *Tour* MCC to Bangladesh 1978/9 (not first-class).
Career batting
1–2–0–78–54–39.00–0–*ct* 0
Bowling 56–1–56.00–0–0–1/31

Toon, Joseph
Professional. *b:* 1879, Market Bosworth, Leics. *d:* 7.3.1950, Braunstone, Leics. Lower order right-hand batsman, right-arm medium pace bowler. *Team* Leicestershire (1902–09, 10 matches).
Career batting
10–19–4–159–39–10.60–0–*ct* 6
Bowling 477–10–47.70–0–0–4/114

Toon, James Harry Cecil
Amateur. *b:* 17.1.1916, Oundle, Northants. Lower order batsman, useful bowler. *Team* Northants (1946, 1 match).
Career batting
1–2–0–1–1–0.50–0–*ct* 0
Bowling 126–4–31.50–0–0–3/79

Toone, Percy
Professional. *b:* 1883, Ealing, Middlesex. *d:* 1955, Colchester, Essex. Lower order right-hand batsman, right-arm fast bowler. *Team* Essex (1912–22, 29 matches).
Career batting
29–42–13–215–24–7.41–0–*ct* 23
Bowling 1954–62–31.51–2–1–6/51

Tootell, Dr Edward
Amateur. *b:* 22.11.1851, Maidstone, Kent. *d:* 20.3.1878, Jacobabad, Sind, India. Middle order right-hand batsman, right-arm medium pace bowler. *Sch* Chatham House. *Team* Kent (1872, 3 matches).
Career batting
3–6–0–42–24–7.00–0–*ct* 2
Bowling 55–2–27.50–0–0–1/27

Topham, Rev Harry Gillespie
Amateur. *b:* 17.2.1862, Ladbroke, Warwickshire. *d:* 28.2.1925, Middleham, Yorkshire. Lower order left-hand batsman, slow left-arm bowler, good slip field. *Sch* Repton. *Teams* Derbyshire (1881, 1 match); Cambridge U (1883–84, blue both years).

Career batting
16–28–12–95–12–5.93–0–*ct* 15
Bowling 1120–60–18.66–4–1–7/62

Topham, Robert Denham Nigel
Cricketer. *b:* 17.7.1952, Trowbridge, Wiltshire. Middle order right-hand batsman. *Sch* Shrewsbury. *Team* Oxford U (1976, blue).
Career batting
4–7–1–91–31–15.16–0–*ct* 2

Topley, Peter Aland
Cricketer. *b:* 29.8.1950, Canterbury, Kent. Lower order right-hand batsman, slow left-arm bowler. *Team* Kent (1972–75, 18 matches).
Career batting
19–19–4–184–38*–12.26–0–*ct* 19
Bowling 741–15–49.40–0–0–2/28

Toppin, Charles
Amateur. *b:* 9.8.1864, Musgrave Hall, Skelton, Cumberland. *d:* 8.6.1928, Great Malvern, Worcs. Father of C. G. and J. F. T. (Worcs), brother-in-law of A. P. and S. H. Day (Kent). Lower order right-hand batsman, right-arm fast bowler, good field. *Sch* Sedbergh. *Team* Cambridge U (1885–87, blue all three years).
Career batting
25–40–4–319–39–8.86–0–*ct* 14
Bowling 2059–81–25.43–2–0–7/51
His County cricket was for Cumberland and Worcestershire (pre-first-class). His final first-class match was for MCC in 1891. A master at Malvern College for 42 years, he was in charge of cricket there for 37 years and to him belongs the credit for developing a great many cricketers who subsequently became famous.

Toppin, Charles Graham
Amateur. *b:* 17.4.1906, Upton, Worcs. *d:* 20.5.1972, Leamington Spa, Warwickshire. Son of Charles (Cambridge U), brother of J. F. T. (Worcs), nephew of A. P. and S. H. Day (Kent). Attacking middle order right-hand batsman, slow off break bowler. *Sch* Malvern. *Team* Worcestershire (1927–28, 4 matches).
Career batting
4–5–0–17–10–3.40–0–*ct* 0

Toppin, John Fallowfield Townsend
Amateur. *b:* 25.2.1900, Malvern, Worcestershire. *d:* 22.11.1965, Ascot, Berkshire. Son of Charles (Cambridge U), brother of C. G. (Worcs), nephew of A. P. and S. H. Day (Kent). Lower order right-hand batsman, right-arm medium fast bowler. *Sch* Winchester. *Team* Worcestershire (1920, 1 match).
Career batting
1–2–0–8–6–4.00–0–*ct* 0
Bowling 5–0

Tordoff, Gerald George
Amateur. *b:* 6.12.1929, Whitwood, Yorkshire. Sound middle order left-hand batsman, right-arm medium pace bowler, good field. *Teams* Somerset (1950–55, 54 matches); Cambridge U (1952, blue).
Career batting
85–155–13–3975–156*–27.99–5–*ct* 47
Bowling 1959–40–48.97–0–0–4/43
He captained Somerset in 1955. His final first-class match was for Combined Services in 1962 and he was one of the leading Royal Navy cricketers for some years. He also played for Berkshire. He hit 1,000 runs in a season twice (best 1,196, av 22.56, in 1955). A useful soccer player, he gained his Blue at Cambridge.

Torkington, Harold Fleming
Cricketer. *b:* 4.12.1959, Poynton, Cheshire. Middle order right-hand batsman. *Sch* Stockport GS. *Team* Cambridge U (1981).
Career batting
1–2–0–9–9–4.50–0–*ct* 1
His County cricket was for Cheshire.

Torrens, Attwood Alfred
Amateur. *b:* 13.2.1874, Baston Manor, Hayes, Kent. *d:* 8.12.1916, Ovilliers La Boiselle, France. He was killed in action. Brother of W. M. (Kent), son of Alfred (MCC 1855). Middle order right-hand batsman, right-arm medium pace bowler, good deep field. *Sch* Eton. *Team* MCC (1907). *Tour* MCC to New Zealand 1906/7.
Career batting
9–13–0–183–87–14.07–0–*ct* 2
Bowling 335–11–30.45–0–0–3/41
His final first-class match was for Free Foresters in 1913.

Torrens, Robert
Cricketer. *b:* 17.5.1948, Londonderry. Right-hand batsman, right-arm fast medium bowler. *Team* Ireland (1966–82).
Career batting
6–8–1–42–17–6.00–0–*ct* 1
Bowling 402–26–15.46–2–0–7/40

Torrens, William Matt
Amateur. *b:* 19.10.1869, Hayes, Kent. *d:* 18.2.1931, Westminster, London. Brother of A. A. (MCC), son of Alfred (MCC 1855). Middle

order right-hand batsman, wicket-keeper. *Sch* Harrow. *Team* Kent (1890, 4 matches).
Career batting
4–7–1–86–43–14.33–0–*ct* 2

Tosetti, Gilbert
Amateur. *b:* 1.8.1879, Bromley, Kent. *d:* 16.4.1923, Eldoret, Kenya. Middle order right-hand batsman, right-arm medium pace bowler. *Sch* Bancroft's. *Team* Essex (1898–1905, 41 matches).
Career batting
41–63–6–1054–132*–18.49–1–*ct* 15
Bowling 891–16–55.68–0–0–3/67

Toshack, Ernest Raymond Herbert
Amateur. *b:* 15.12.1914, Cobar, New South Wales, Australia. Lower order right-hand batsman, left-arm medium pace bowler. *Team* New South Wales (1945/6 to 1949/50, 21 matches). *Tours* Australia to New Zealand 1945/6, to England 1948. *Tests* Australia (1945/6 to 1948, 12 matches).
Career batting
48–45–13–185–20*–5.78–0–*ct* 10
Bowling 3973–195–20.37–12–1–7/81
Test batting
12–11–6–73–20*–14.60–0–*ct* 4
Bowling 989–47–21.04–4–1–6/29

He broke down with cartilage trouble during the fourth Test of the 1948 tour, but until that point proved a most useful member of the attack, especially used as a bowler keeping down the run rate.

Toulmin, Evelyn Murrough O'Brien
Amateur. *b:* 13.8.1877, Hatfield-Peverel, Essex. *d:* 7.1.1945, Paris, France. Middle order left-hand batsman, slow right-arm bowler. *Sch* King's School, Canterbury. *Teams* Essex (1899–1912, 2 matches); Argentina (1911/12).
Career batting
5–8–0–134–59–16.75–0–*ct* 4
Bowling 250–17–14.70–1–1–6/60

Tovey, Gordon Charles
Amateur. *b:* 4.7.1912, Salisbury, Wiltshire. Middle order right-hand batsman. *Sch* Clifton. *Team* Cambridge U (1933).
Career batting
1–2–0–3–2–1.50–0–*ct* 0

His County cricket was for Dorset.

Tovey, Wilson Gardner
Amateur. *b:* 1874, Cirencester, Gloucs. *d:* 4.3.1950, Cirencester, Gloucs. Middle order batsman, useful bowler. *Sch* Wellingborough. *Team* Gloucestershire (1901, 1 match).
Career batting
1–2–0–8–8–4.00–0–*ct* 0
Bowling 42–2–21.00–0–0–2/42

Towell, Edgar Fremantle
Amateur. *b:* 5.7.1901, Kettering, Northants. *d:* 2.6.1972, Kettering, Northants. Lower order left-hand batsman, right-arm medium fast bowler. *Team* Northants (1923–34, 70 matches).
Career batting
70–111–17–1199–66–12.75–0–*ct* 11
Bowling 3379–102–33.12–0–0–4/42

Townsend, Alan
Professional. *b:* 26.8.1921, Stockton-on-Tees, Co Durham. Middle order right-hand batsman, right-arm medium pace bowler, good close field. *Team* Warwickshire (1948–60, 340 matches).
Career batting
342–553–70–12054–154–24.95–6–*ct* 413
Bowling 9374–325–28.84–7–1–7/84

He hit 1,000 runs in a season five times (best 1,227, av 29.92, in 1953). He appeared for Durham in 1947.

Townsend, Arnold Frederick
Professional. *b:* 29.3.1912, Long Eaton, Derbyshire. Brother of L. F. (Derbyshire). Sound opening right-hand batsman. *Teams* Derbyshire (1934–50, 116 matches); South African Air Force (1942/3).
Career batting
117–200–13–4327–142*–23.13–5–*ct* 30
Bowling 39–0

He hit 1,000 runs in a season twice (best 1,348, av 30.63, in 1947).

Townsend, Arthur Fenton Miles
Amateur. *b:* 1.8.1885, Clifton, Gloucs. *d:* 1948, Chelsea, London. Son of Frank (Gloucs), brother of C. L. (Gloucs) and F. N. (Gloucs), uncle of D. C. H. (Oxford U) and P. N. (Oxford U), great-uncle of J. R. A. (Oxford U). Middle order right-hand batsman, slow under-arm bowler. *Sch* Blair Lodge. *Teams* Gloucestershire (1903–06, 9 matches); Essex (1910, 1 match).
Career batting
10–14–0–200–28–14.28–0–*ct* 5
Bowling 171–3–57.00–0–0–1/23

Townsend, Charles Lucas
Amateur. *b:* 7.11.1876, Clifton, Gloucs. *d:* 17.10.1958, Elton, Stockton-on-Tees, Co Durham. Son of Frank (Gloucs), brother of A. F. M. (Gloucs) and F. N. (Gloucs), father of D. C. H. (Oxford U) and P. M. (Oxford U); grandfather of J. R. A. (Oxford U). Sound middle order left-hand batsman, right-arm slow off break

bowler, good close field. *Sch* Clifton. *Teams* Gloucestershire (1893–1922, 162 matches); London County (1900). *Tour* Ranjitsinhji to North America 1899. *Tests* England (1899, 2 matches).
Career batting
199–342–28–9512–224*–30.29–21–*ct* 194
Bowling 16761–725–23.11–67–18–9/48
Test batting
2–3–0–51–38–17.00–0–*ct* 0
Bowling 75–3–25.00–0–0–3/50

He created a sensation in 1895, when, on leaving Clifton College, he joined the Gloucestershire Eleven and ended the summer with 131 wickets, av 13.94, making him the bowler of the season. His best year with the ball was 1898 with 145 wickets, av 20.64. Altogether he took 100 wickets in a season four times. He hit 2,440 runs, av 51.91, in 1899, but only exceeded 1,000 runs in two other years. He performed the 'double' in 1898 and 1899. After 1900 he moved to Stockton-on-Tees and his first-class cricket was very limited. His highest score was 224* for Gloucs v Essex at Clifton in 1899 and his best bowling 9/48 for Gloucs v Middlesex at Lord's in 1898.

Townsend, David Charles Humphrey
Amateur. *b:* 20.4.1912, Norton-on-Tees, Co Durham. Son of C. L. (Gloucs), grandson of Frank (Gloucs), nephew of A. F. M. (Gloucs) and F. N. (Gloucs), brother of P. N. (Oxford U), father of J. R. A. (Oxford U). Attractive opening right-hand batsman, right-arm medium pace bowler. *Sch* Winchester. *Team* Oxford U (1933–34, blue both years). *Tours* MCC to West Indies 1934/5; Martineau to Egypt 1936 (not first-class). *Tests* England (1934/5, 3 matches).
Career batting
37–64–2–1801–195–29.04–4–*ct* 16
Bowling 501–6–83.50–0–0–2/31
Test batting
3–6–0–77–36–12.83–0–*ct* 1
Bowling 9–0

His County cricket was for Durham and his final first-class match for Free Foresters in 1948.

Townsend, Frank
Amateur. *b:* 17.10.1847, Clifton, Gloucs. *d:* 25.10.1920, Lambeth, London. Father of A. F. M. (Gloucs), C. L. (Gloucs) and F. N. (Gloucs); grandfather of D. C. H. (Oxford U) and P. N. (Oxford U), great grandfather of J. R. A. (Oxford U). Free scoring middle order right-hand batsman, right-hand slow under-arm bowler, good field. *Team* Gloucestershire (1870–91, 169 matches).
Career batting
179–288–19–5110–136–18.99–2–*ct* 131
Bowling 2550–101–25.24–2–0–6/31

Being in the scholastic profession his first-class cricket was restricted mainly to August.

Townsend, Frank Norton
Amateur. *b:* 16.9.1875, Clifton, Gloucs. *d:* 25.5.1901, Kimberley, South Africa. Son of Frank (Gloucs), brother of A. F. M. (Gloucs) and C. L. (Gloucs), uncle of D. C. H. (Oxford U) and P. N. (Oxford U), great-uncle of J. R. A. (Oxford U). Middle order right-hand batsman, wicket-keeper. *Sch* Blair Lodge and Marlborough. *Teams* Gloucestershire (1896–1900, 11 matches); Transvaal (1898/9).
Career batting
12–20–4–230–56–14.37–0–*ct* 13–*st* 3

Townsend, Jonathan Richard Arthur
Cricketer. *b:* 30.11.1942, Filkins, Gloucs. Great-grandson of Frank (Gloucs), grandson of C. L. (Gloucs), son of D. C. H. (Oxford U), nephew of P. N. (Oxford U), great-nephew of A. F. M. (Gloucs) and F. N. (Gloucs). Middle order right-hand batsman. *Sch* Winchester. *Team* Oxford U (1964–65).
Career batting
10–18–0–245–64–13.61–0–*ct* 1

His County cricket was for Durham in 1964, Wiltshire in 1967 and 1968, Suffolk in 1973.

Townsend, Leslie Fletcher
Professional. *b:* 8.6.1903, Long Eaton, Derbyshire. Brother of A. F. (Derbyshire). Middle order right-hand batsman, right-arm medium pace off break bowler. *Teams* Derbyshire (1922–39, 446 matches); Auckland (1934/5 to 1935/6). *Tours* MCC to West Indies 1929/30, to India and Ceylon 1933/4. *Tests* England (1929/30 to 1933/4, 4 matches).
Career batting
493–786–75–19555–233–27.50–22–*ct* 237
Bowling 22985–1088–21.12–51–16–8/26
Test batting
4–6–0–97–40–16.16–0–*ct* 2
Bowling 205–6–34.16–0–0–2/22

He hit 1,000 runs in a season nine times, going on to 2,000 once : 2,268, av 44.47, in 1933. He took 100 wickets in a season four times (best 117, av 18.45, in 1932). In the seasons 1928, 1932 and 1933 he performed the 'double'. His only double century was 233 for Derbyshire v Leicestershire at Loughborough in 1933. He also played for Northumberland.

Townsend, Peter Norton
Amateur. *b:* 15.2.1910, Stockton-on-Tees, Co

Durham. Son of C. L. (Gloucs), grandson of Frank (Gloucs), brother of D. C. H. (Oxford U), nephew of A. F. M. (Gloucs) and F. N. (Gloucs), uncle of J. R. A. (Oxford U). Lower order right-hand batsman, leg break bowler. *Sch* Winchester. *Team* Oxford U (1929).
Career batting
2–3–0–16–12–5.33–0–*ct* 1
Bowling 152–3–50.66–0–0–2/18

Townshend, Rev William
Amateur. *b:* 16.11.1849, Sehore, Bhopal, India. *d:* 19.7.1923, Kirkby Mallory, Leics. Attacking middle order right-hand batsman, good long stop. *Sch* Rossall. *Team* Oxford U (1870–72, blue all three years).
Career batting
16–31–2–460–55–15.86–0–*ct* 6

His final first-class match was for MCC in 1874. He played County cricket for Herefordshire, Leicestershire (pre-first-class), Cheshire, Denbighshire and Shropshire.

Townsley, Richard Andrew John
Cricketer. *b:* 24.6.1952, Castleford, Yorkshire. Middle order left-hand batsman, right-arm medium pace bowler. *Team* Yorkshire (1974–75, 2 matches).
Career batting
2–4–0–22–12–5.50–0–*ct* 1
Bowling 0–0

Toynbee, Geoffrey Percy Robert
Amateur. *b:* 18.5.1885, Paddington, London. *d:* 15.11.1914, Ploegstraete, Armentieres, France. He was killed in action. Opening right-hand batsman. *Sch* Winchester. *Team* Hampshire (1912, 2 matches).
Career batting
3–3–0–18–14–6.00–0–*ct* 1

He made many runs in military matches, first at Sandhurst and later for the Green Jackets.

Toynbee, Walter Turner
Amateur. *b:* 23.12.1852, Lincoln. *d:* 26.12.1930, Hyde Park, London. Middle order batsman. *Team* MCC (1879).
Career batting
1 match, did not bat–*ct* 0

His County cricket was for Lincolnshire and Huntingdonshire.

Toyne, Stanley Mease
Amateur. *b:* 13.6.1881, Bournemouth, Hampshire. *d:* 22.1.1962, Ware, Hertfordshire. Middle order right-hand batsman, slow under-arm bowler. *Sch* Haileybury. *Team* Hampshire (1905, 1 match).
Career batting
2–4–1–17–9–5.66–0–*ct* 2

His final first-class appearance was for MCC in 1928, 23 seasons after his previous first-class match.

Tracy, Sean Robert
Cricketer. *b:* 7.6.1963, Auckland, New Zealand. Lower order right-hand batsman, right-arm fast medium bowler. *Teams* Auckland (1982/3); Gloucestershire (1983, 1 match). *Tour* New Zealand to England 1983.
Career batting
8–9–1–17–5–2.12–0–*ct* 5
Bowling 666–22–30.27–1–0–5/29

He was co-opted into the 1983 New Zealand touring team for two matches.

Traicos, Athanasios John
Cricketer. *b:* 17.5.1947, Zabazib, Egypt. Lower order right-hand batsman, right-arm off break bowler, good field. *Team* Rhodesia/Zimbabwe (1967/8 to 1982/3). *Tours* South African Universities to England 1967; selected for South Africa to England 1970 (tour abandoned); Zimbabwe to England 1982. *Tests* South Africa (1969/70, 3 matches).
Career batting
71–105–47–787–43–13.56–0–*ct* 61
Bowling 5802–179–32.41–6–0–6/66
Test batting
3–4–2–8–5*–4.00–0–*ct* 4
Bowling 207–4–51.75–0–0–2/70

Traill, Major General George Balfour
Amateur. *b:* 20.6.1833, Lewisham, Kent. *d:* 20.11.1913, Battersea Park, Surrey. Brother of W. F. (Kent) and J. C. (Oxford U 1848). Middle order batsman. *Team* MCC (1864).
Career batting
1–2–1–5–4–5.00–0–*ct* 0

Traill, William Frederick
Amateur. *b:* 7.1.1838, Lewisham, Kent. *d:* 3.10.1905, South Hampstead, London. Brother of G. B. (MCC) and J. C. (Oxford U 1848). Lower order right-hand batsman, right-hand medium fast round-arm bowler, slip field. *Sch* Merchant Taylor's. *Teams* Oxford U (1858–60, blue all three years); Kent (1860–66, 11 matches).
Career batting
35–59–5–541–49–10.01–0–*ct* 17
Bowling 1245–66+6–18.86–6–1–6/35

His final first-class match was for the Gentlemen in 1867.

Tranter, Enoch
Professional. *b:* 27.4.1842, Old Park, Shropshire.

d: 1910, Newport, Shropshire. Lower order left-hand batsman, left-hand fast round-arm bowler. *Team* Lancashire (1875–76, 3 matches).
Career batting
3–5–0–9–5–1.80–0–*ct* 2
Bowling 94–3–31.33–0–0–2/11
He also played for Staffordshire.

Trapnell, Barry Maurice Waller
Amateur. *b:* 18.5.1924, London. Middle order right-hand batsman, right-arm medium pace bowler. *Sch* University College School. *Teams* Cambridge U (1946, blue); Middlesex (1946, 1 match).
Career batting
11–20–3–283–41–16.64–0–*ct* 4
Bowling 621–16–38.81–1–0–5/73

Trask, Dr John Ernest
Amateur. *b:* 27.10.1861, Yeovil, Somerset. *d:* 25.7.1896, Kosheh, Sudan. He died of cholera. Cousin of William (Somerset). Attacking middle order right-hand batsman, right-arm medium pace bowler, deep field. *Sch* Somerset College. *Teams* Somerset (1884–95, 9 matches); Europeans (1892/3 to 1894/5).
Career batting
16–29–2–515–78–19.07–0–*ct* 9
Bowling 9–0
He was stationed for 4½ years in India and played a great deal of cricket there, being largely responsible for instituting the inter-Presidency matches. At the time of his death he was a Surgeon-Captain in the Egyptian Army.

Trask, William
Amateur. *b:* 15.7.1859, Norton-sub-Hamdon, Ilminster, Somerset. *d:* 24.6.1949, Frome, Somerset. Cousin of J. E. (Somerset). Stylish middle order right-hand batsman, right-arm slow bowler. *Sch* Sherborne. *Team* Somerset (1882–1900, 47 matches).
Career batting
48–90–5–1225–76–14.41–0–*ct* 20
Bowling 454–12–37.83–0–0–3/33

Travers, Basil Holmes
Amateur. *b:* 7.7.1919, Sydney, Australia. Lower order right-hand batsman, right-arm medium pace bowler. *Team* Oxford U (1946–48, blue 1946 and 1948).
Career batting
24–37–9–718–65*–25.64–0–*ct* 27
Bowling 1450–48–30.20–0–0–4/65
His County cricket was for Oxfordshire. A noted rugby footballer, he played for Oxford and England

Tredcroft, Edward
Amateur. *b:* 15.12.1828, Horsham, Sussex. *d:* 8.4.1888, Westminster, London. Lower order right-hand batsman, right-hand under-arm fast, or slow, bowler, good long leg. *Sch* Eton. *Team* Sussex (1852–60, 19 matches).
Career batting
53–96–10–759–44*–8.82–0–*ct* 32–*st* 1
Bowling 161–5+6–32.20–0–0–3/?
His first-class debut was for Gentlemen of England in 1851 and his last first-class match was for MCC in 1865.

Treglown, Claude Jesse Helby
Amateur. *b:* 13.2.1893, Herne Bay, Kent. *d:* 7.5.1980, Worthing, Sussex. Opening or middle order right-hand batsman. *Sch* Norwich. *Team* Essex (1922–28, 34 matches).
Career batting
34–55–3–792–77–15.23–0–*ct* 11
He also played for Norfolk.

Trelor, (Arthur) Thomas Edward
Professional. *b:* 29.10.1846, St Austell, Cornwall. Lower order right-hand batsman, right-hand fast round-arm bowler. *Team* Middlesex (1872, 1 match).
Career batting
1–2–0–10–6–5.00–0–*ct* 0
Bowling 27–1–27.00–0–0–1/27
He was best known as the manager and captain of the 'Imperial Clown Cricketers', a travelling team of players who mixed serious cricket with circus tricks. In 1876 he took his team on tour to North America.

Trembath, Christopher Richard
Cricketer. *b:* 27.9.1961, Willesden, London. Lower order right-hand batsman, right-arm medium pace bowler. *Sch* Dulwich and Clifton. *Team* Gloucestershire (1982, 2 matches).
Career batting
2–1–1–8–8*–no av–0–*ct* 1
Bowling 219–6–36.50–1–0–5/91

Tremenheere, James Henry Apperley
Amateur. *b:* 30.10.1853, Poona, India. *d:* 28.10.1912, Inglismaldie, Edzell, Kincardine. Middle order right-hand batsman, right-hand medium pace round-arm bowler. *Sch* Lancing and Cheltenham. *Team* Gloucestershire (1872, 1 match).
Career batting
1–1–0–7–7–7.00–0–*ct* 0

Tremlett, Major General Erroll Arthur Edwin
Amateur. *b:* 22.12.1893, Brentford, Middlesex. *d:* 24.12.1982, Kenn, Devon. Right-hand batsman,

right-arm medium pace bowler. *Team* MCC (1929–34).
Career batting
2–4–0–35–23–8.75–0–*ct* 1
Bowling 31–1–31.00–0–0–1/1

Tremlett, Maurice Fletcher
Professional. *b:* 5.7.1923, Stockport, Cheshire. Father of T. M. (Hampshire). Attacking middle order right-hand batsman, right-arm fast medium bowler. *Teams* Somerset (1947–60, 353 matches); Central Districts (1951/2). *Tours* MCC to West Indies 1947/8, to South Africa 1948/9. *Tests* England (1947/8, 3 matches).
Career batting
388–681–49–16038–185–25.37–16–*ct* 257
Bowling 10778–351–30.70–11–0–8/31
Test batting
3–5–2–20–18*–6.66–0–*ct* 0
Bowling 226–4–56.50–0–0–2/98
He hit 1,000 runs in a season ten times, going on to 2,000 once : 2,101, av 35.61, in 1951. He captained Somerset 1956 to 1959.

Tremlett, Timothy Maurice
Cricketer. *b:* 26.7.1956, Wellington, Somerset. Son of M. F. (Somerset). Lower order right-hand batsman, right-arm medium pace bowler. *Team* Hampshire (1976–83, 87 matches).
Career batting
87–120–18–2078–88–20.37–0–*ct* 47
Bowling 3587–143–25.08–3–0–6/82

Tremlin, Bert
Professional. *b:* 18.9.1877, Bristol, Gloucs. *d:* 12.4.1936, Essex. Lower order right-hand batsman, right-arm medium pace bowler. *Team* Essex (1900–19, 132 matches).
Career batting
136–200–64–1843–61–13.55–0–*ct* 64
Bowling 12058–467–25.82–23–4–9/126
His best season was 1914 when he took 101 wickets, av 26.00. His best bowling was 9/126 for Essex v Derbyshire at Leyton in 1905. In 1923 and 1924 he was on the first-class umpires' list.

Trenerry, William Leo
Amateur. *b:* 29.11.1892, Queanbeyan, New South Wales, Australia. *d:* 4.9.1975, Mosman, New South Wales, Australia. Brother of Edwin (New South Wales). Opening or middle order right-hand batsman, leg break bowler. *Team* New South Wales (1920/1 to 1924/5, 3 matches). *Tours* AIF to England 1919, to South Africa 1919/20.
Career batting
38–61–3–1547–82–26.67–0–*ct* 22
Bowling 337–10–33.70–0–0–3/28
He proved a sound batsman in 1919 with 961 runs, av 28.26.

Tresawna, Dr William Samson
Amateur. *b:* 14.4.1880, Lamellyn, Probus, Cornwall. *d:* 21.8.1945, Abergavenny, Monmouth. Middle order right-hand batsman. *Team* H. K. Foster's XI (1919).
Career batting
1–2–0–76–55–38.00–0–*ct* 0
His County cricket was for Cornwall and Monmouthshire.

Trestrail, Alfred Ernest Yates
Amateur. *b:* 24.1.1876, Hallatrow, Somerset. *d:* 5.2.1935, New Milton, Hampshire. Middle order batsman. *Sch* Amersham Hall School. *Team* Somerset (1905, 1 match).
Career batting
1–2–0–7–4–3.50–0–*ct* 0
He did not appear in any first-class matches whilst at Cambridge.

Trestrail, Kenneth B.
Amateur. *b:* 26.11.1927, Trinidad. Brother of A. L. (Trinidad). Attacking middle order right-hand batsman. *Team* Trinidad (1943/4 to 1949/50). *Tours* West Indies to England 1950; Canada to England 1954.
Career batting
41–65–8–2183–161*–38.29–5–*ct* 22
Bowling 114–4–28.50–0–0–3/20
His opportunities were very limited on the 1950 tour and he did not appear in the Tests. In 1954 with the Canadians he scored freely and was the best batsman in the side.

Trevett, John Charles Pullman
Amateur. *b:* 30.7.1942, Surrey. Lower order batsman, useful bowler. *Team* Oxford U (1962).
Career batting
2–3–1–1–1–0.50–0–*ct* 0
Bowling 139–0

Trevor, Arthur Hill
Amateur. *b:* 14.11.1858, Calcutta, India. *d:* 27.9.1924, Newtown, Elvanfoot, Lanarkshire, Scotland. Free hitting opening or middle order right-hand batsman, slow under-arm bowler, good deep field. *Sch* Winchester. *Teams* Oxford U (1879–81, blue 1880 and 1881); Sussex (1880–82, 12 matches).
Career batting
31–61–2–1064–103–18.03–1–*ct* 18
Bowling 52–1–52.00–0–0–1/5
At Twickenham in 1882, he scored 338 for Orleans Club v Rickling Green and with G. F. Vernon added 603 runs for the second wicket. His final first-class match was for MCC in 1885.

Trevor, Frederick George Brunton
Amateur. *b:* 28.10.1838, India. *d:* 20.2.1925, Richmond, Surrey. Middle order batsman, useful bowler. *Sch* Marlborough and St Peter's, York. *Team* MCC (1864).
Career batting
1–2–0–12–8–6.00–0–*ct* 0
Bowling 5–0

Trevor, Brigadier General Herbert Edward
Amateur. *b:* 16.12.1871, India. *d:* 23.3.1939, Brighton, Sussex. Middle order batsman. *Sch* Winchester. *Teams* Bombay (1892/3); Sussex (1908, 2 matches).
Career batting
3–6–2–51–22*–12.75–0–*ct* 1

Tribe, George Edward
Professional. *b:* 4.10.1920, Yarraville, Victoria, Australia. Aggressive middle order left-hand batsman, left-arm slow off break and chinaman bowler. *Teams* Victoria (1945/6 to 1946/7, 13 matches); Northants (1951–59, 233 matches). *Tours* Commonwealth to India, Pakistan and Ceylon 1949/50, to India and Ceylon 1950/1; Howard to India 1956/7; Norfolk to Jamaica 1956/7. *Tests* Australia (1946/7, 3 matches).
Career batting
308–454–82–10177–136*–27.35–7–*ct* 242
Bowling 28321–1378–20.55–93–23–9/43
Test batting
3–3–1–35–25*–17.50–0–*ct* 0
Bowling 330–2–165.00–0–0–2/48

He hit 1,000 runs in a season seven times (best 1,260, av 36.00, in 1953) and took 100 wickets eight times (best 176, av 19.12, in 1955). He completed the 'double' seven times. His best bowling analysis in an innings were 9 for 43 Northants v Worcs at Northampton in 1958, 9 for 45 Victoria v Queensland at Brisbane in 1945/6 and 9 for 45 Northants v Yorkshire at Bradford in 1955.

Trick, Stanley Arthur
Amateur. *b:* 13.6.1884, Stoke Newington, London. *d:* 11.2.1958, Worcester Park, Surrey. Middle order right-hand batsman. *Sch* Merchant Taylor's. *Team* Essex (1905–19, 5 matches).
Career batting
5–9–0–69–26–7.66–0–*ct* 1

Trick, William Mervyn Stanley
Amateur. *b:* 31.10.1916, Briton-Ferry, Glamorgan. Lower order right-hand batsman, left-arm medium pace spin bowler. *Team* Glamorgan (1946–50, 19 matches).
Career batting
19–22–11–52–15–4.72–0–*ct* 9
Bowling 1087–56–19.41–4–2–6/29

Trim, Geoffrey Edward
Cricketer. *b:* 6.4.1956, Openshaw, Manchester. Middle order right-hand batsman, leg break bowler. *Team* Lancashire (1976–80, 15 matches).
Career batting
15–25–0–399–91–15.96–0–*ct* 10
Bowling 13–0

Trimborn, Patrick Henry Joseph
Cricketer. *b:* 18.5.1940, Durban, South Africa. Lower order right-hand batsman, right-arm fast bowler, good close field. *Team* Natal (1961/2 to 1975/6). *Tour* Selected for South Africa to England 1970 (tour abandoned). *Tests* South Africa (1966/7 to 1969/70, 4 matches).
Career batting
94–111–37–880–52–11.89–0–*ct* 79
Bowling 7102–314–22.61–12–1–6/36
Test batting
4–4–2–13–11*–6.50–0–*ct* 7
Bowling 257–11–23.36–0–0–3/12

His only appearance in England was for International Cavaliers in 1969.

Tripp, Graham Malcolm
Professional. *b:* 29.6.1932, Clevedon, Somerset. Middle order right-hand batsman, good outfield. *Team* Somerset (1955–59, 34 matches).
Career batting
34–62–7–700–62–12.72–0–*ct* 29
Bowling 10–0

Tristram, Henry Barrington
Amateur. *b:* 5.9.1861, Greatham, Co Durham. *d:* 1.10.1946, St Helier, Jersey. Middle order right-hand batsman, right-arm fast bowler, good cover point. *Sch* Loretto and Winchester. *Team* Oxford U (1883).
Career batting
1–2–0–7–6–3.50–0–*ct* 0

His County cricket was for Durham 1883 to 1893. A noted rugby footballer, he played for Oxford and England.

Tritton, Edward William
Amateur. *b:* 3.8.1844, London. *d:* 1.12.1901, Paignton, Devon. Sound middle order right-hand batsman. *Sch* Eton. *Teams* Middlesex (1864–67, 6 matches); Oxford U (1864–67, blue all four years).
Career batting
39–65–5–1000–114–16.66–2–*ct* 20
Bowling 50–1–50.00–0–0–1/34

His final first-class match was for MCC in

1875. He appeared for Surrey in 1864 in a non-first-class match. A talented athlete he took part in the 1865 inter-University athletic meeting.

Trodd, Thomas
Professional. *b:* 1852. *d:* 26.7.1908, Macclesfield, Cheshire. Lower order batsman, useful bowler. *Team* Surrey (1879–80, 4 matches).
Career batting
5–10–6–13–5–3.25–0–*ct* 1
Bowling 152–12–12.66–1–0–6/35

Trodd, William
Professional. *baptised* 7.8.1836, Stoke-next-Guildford, Surrey. *d:* 9.4.1880, Bow, Middlesex. Middle order batsman, useful bowler. *Team* Surrey (1869, 6 matches).
Career batting
6–11–0–65–16–5.90–0–*ct* 1
Bowling 146–3–48.66–0–0–2/38

Trollope, William Stapleton
Amateur. *b:* 31.7.1854, South Lambeth, London. *d:* 20.9.1895, Southampton, Hants. Attacking middle order right-hand batsman, right-hand medium pace round-arm bowler. *Sch* Westminster. *Team* Surrey (1877–82, 7 matches).
Career batting
7–14–0–154–35–11.00–0–*ct* 3
Bowling 99–4–24.75–0–0–2/2

Trott, Albert Edwin
Professional. *b:* 6.2.1873, Abbotsford, Victoria, Australia. *d:* 30.7.1914, Harlesden, Willesden, London. He shot himself, having been ill for some time with little hope of recovery. Brother of G. H. S. (Victoria). Very hard hitting middle order right-hand batsman, right-arm fast medium, or medium off break, bowler, good field. *Teams* Victoria (1892/3 to 1895/6, 13 matches); Middlesex (1898–1910, 223 matches); London County (1900–04); Hawke's Bay (1901/2). *Tours* Hawke to South Africa 1898/9, to Australia 1902/3 (co-opted). *Tests* Australia (1894/5, 3 matches); England (1898/9, 2 matches).
Career batting
375–602–53–10696–164–19.48–8–*ct* 452
Bowling 35317–1674–21.09–131–41–10/42
Test batting
5–9–3–228–85*–38.00–0–*ct* 4
Bowling 390–26–15.00–2–0–8/43

He hit 1,000 runs in a season twice (best 1,337, av 23.87, in 1900) – in 1899 and 1900 he achieved the feat of 1,000 runs and 200 wickets. In all he took 100 wickets in a season seven times, going on to 200 twice (best 239, av 17.09, in 1899). His best analysis in an innings was 10 for 42 for Middlesex v Somerset in 1900 at Taunton. Disappointed at not being selected to tour England with the 1896 Australians, he paid his own fare and then obtained a position on the ground-staff at Lord's. For MCC v Australians in 1899 he hit a ball from M. A. Noble over the pavilion at Lord's. His final first-class match was for MCC in 1911.

Trott, George Henry Stevens
Amateur. *b:* 5.8.1866, Collingwood, Victoria, Australia. *d:* 10.11.1917, Albert Park, Victoria, Australia. Brother of A. E. (Victoria and Middlesex). Excellent opening or middle order right-hand batsman, leg break bowler, good point field. *Team* Victoria (1885/6 to 1907/8, 59 matches). *Tours* Australia to England 1888, 1890, 1893, 1896, to North America 1893, 1896. *Tests* Australia (1888 to 1897/8, 24 matches).
Career batting
222–393–19–8804–186–23.54–9–*ct* 183
Bowling 9700–386–25.12–17–2–8/63
Test batting
24–42–0–921–143–21.92–1–*ct* 21
Bowling 1019–29–35.13–0–0–4/71

He proved a useful all-rounder on each of his tours to England, but his greatest distinction came in 1896 when he proved one of the best of all Australian captains – he was able to inspire even the most despondent of his team. Although Australia lost the 1896 Test series 2 to 1, Trott then led Australia to a 4–1 victory in the 1897/8 series, after which a serious illness compelled him to retire from regular first-class matches. He hit 1,000 runs in a season four times (best 1,297, av 26.51, in 1896)

Trotter, David North
Amateur. *b:* 24.5.1858, Forkhill, Co Down. *d:* 17.3.1912, Dublin. Middle order right-hand batsman, good point. *Team* North of England (1877). *Tours* Gentlemen of Ireland to North America 1879 (not first-class).
Career batting
1–2–0–42–33–21.00–0–*ct* 1

He played for Ireland 1875 to 1890 (not first-class).

Troughton, Lionel Holmes Wood
Amateur. *b:* 17.5.1879, Seaford, Sussex. *d:* 31.8.1933, Southwark, London. Cousin of M. A. (Kent). Resolute middle order right-hand batsman, good field. *Sch* Dulwich. *Team* Kent (1907–23, 164 matches). *Tour* MCC to Argentine 1911/12.
Career batting
180–265–31–4013–104–17.14–1–*ct* 80
Bowling 20–0

He captained Kent 1914 to 1923 and from 1924 to his death was General Manager of the County Club.

Troughton, Medhurst Albert
Amateur. *b:* 25.12.1839, Milton-next-Gravesend, Kent. *d:* 1.1.1912, Campden Hill, London. Cousin of L. H. W. (Kent). Middle order right-hand batsman, right-hand slow round or under-arm bowler, occasional wicket-keeper. *Team* Kent (1864–73, 39 matches).
Career batting
46–84–11–1197–87–16.39–0–*ct* 33
Bowling 218–10–21.80–1–0–5/70
His first-class debut was for Gentlemen of Kent in 1862.

Trouncer, Charles Albert
Amateur. *b:* 14.8.1866, Uckfield, Sussex. *d:* 13.3.1938, Benllech Bay, Anglesey. Opening left-hand batsman, left-arm medium pace bowler, wicket-keeper. *Sch* Cranbrook. *Teams* Cambridge U (1887–88); Surrey (1888, 3 matches).
Career batting
9–16–2–205–30*–14.64–0–*ct* 8
Bowling 54–0
His final first-class match was for Oxford and Cambridge, Past and Present v Australians in 1890.

Troup, Frank Colin
Amateur. *b:* 27.9.1896, Mussoorie, India. *d:* 19.1.1924, Murray Bridge, South Australia. Son of Walter (Gloucs). Middle order right-hand batsman. *Sch* Cheltenham. *Team* Gloucestershire (1914–21, 3 matches).
Career batting
3–5–0–10–7–2.00–0–*ct* 0

Troup, Gary Bertram
Cricketer. *b:* 3.10.1952, Taumarunui, New Zealand. Lower order right-hand batsman, left-arm fast medium bowler. *Team* Auckland (1974/5 to 1982/3). *Tours* Robins to South Africa 1975/6; New Zealand to India and Pakistan 1976/7, to England 1978, to Australia 1980/1, 1982/3. *Tests* New Zealand (1976/7 to 1981/2, 12 matches).
Career batting
68–77–28–570–58*–11.63–0–*ct* 28
Bowling 5168–180–28.71–2–1–6/48
Test batting
12–15–6–43–13*–4.77–0–*ct* 2
Bowling 1114–34–32.76–1–1–6/95
He was co-opted into the 1978 team to England for one match.

Troup, Walter
Amateur. *b:* 16.10.1869, Meerut, India. *d:* December 1940, Brentford, Middlesex. Father of F. C. (Gloucs). Defensive middle order right-hand batsman, good cover point. *Teams* Gloucestershire (1887–1911, 80 matches); All India (1892/3); Gentlemen of India (1902/03).
Career batting
85–144–15–3366–180–26.09–7–*ct* 26
Bowling 4–0
He hit 1,073 runs, av 29.00, in 1899.

Trubshaw, Ernest Brian
Amateur. *b:* 29.1.1924, Liverpool. Middle order batsman. *Sch* Winchester. *Team* RAF (1946).
Career batting
1–2–0–2–1–1.00–0–*ct* 0
He was a noted test pilot, and among the aircraft with which he was concerned was the Concorde.

Trueman, Frederick Sewards
Professional. *b:* 6.2.1931, Stainton, Yorkshire. Hard hitting lower order right-hand batsman, aggressive right-arm fast bowler. *Team* Yorkshire (1949–68, 459 matches). *Tours* MCC to West Indies 1953/4, 1959/60, to Australia and New Zealand 1958/9, 1962/3; Howard to India 1956/7; Cavaliers to South Africa 1960/1, to Jamaica 1963/4, 1964/5; Yorkshire to North America 1964 (not first-class). *Tests* England (1952–65, 67 matches).
Career batting
603–713–120–9231–104–15.56–3–*ct* 439
Bowling 42154–2304–18.29–126–25–8/28
Test batting
67–85–14–981–39*–13.81–0–*ct* 64
Bowling 6625–307–21.57–17–3–8/31
A fast bowler whose belligerence made him the most feared by batsmen in England in the 1950s and early 1960s, Trueman took 29 wickets in his first Test series v India in 1952 and finally ended his international career with a record (since broken) of 307 Test wickets. His reputation for being difficult to handle and outspoken caused him to miss a number of Tests, however.
He took 100 wickets in a season 12 times with 175, av 13.98, in 1960 best. Of his four hat-tricks in first-class cricket, curiously three were for Yorkshire against Notts. The best bowling figures in an innings were 8 for 28 for Yorkshire v Kent at Dover in 1954, all the wickets being taken before lunch on the first day. His last first-class appearance was for Cavaliers in 1969.
After leaving Yorkshire, he played for Derbyshire in John Player matches in 1972 and has since become a regular commentator on cricket and a notable television personality.

Truman, Thomas Archibald
Amateur. *b:* 1881, Newton Abbot, Devon. *d:* 14.9.1918, No. 1 Canadian Casualty Clearing Station, near Etrun, France. He died of pneumonia. Middle order batsman, useful bowler. *Team* Gloucestershire (1910–13, 4 matches).
Career batting
4–8–2–39–12*–6.50–0–*ct* 5
Bowling 11–1–11.00–0–0–1/10

Trumble, Frederick Hugh Geoffrey
Amateur. *b:* 1893, Isle of Wight. *d:* 10.5.1918, at sea on board HMS *Warwick*. Middle order right-hand batsman. *Team* Royal Navy (1914).
Career batting
1–2–0–8–8–4.00–0–*ct* 0

Trumble, Hugh
Amateur. *b:* 12.5.1867, Abbotsford, Victoria, Australia. *d:* 14.8.1938, Hawthorn, Victoria, Australia. Brother of J. W. (Victoria). Middle order right-hand batsman, right-arm medium pace off break bowler, good slip field. *Team* Victoria (1887/8 to 1903/4, 47 matches). *Tours* Australia to England 1890, 1893, 1896, 1899, 1902, to North America 1893, 1896, to South Africa 1902/3. *Tests* Australia (1890 to 1903/4, 32 matches).
Career batting
213–344–67–5395–107–19.47–3–*ct* 328
Bowling 17134–929–18.44–69–25–9/39
Test batting
32–57–14–851–70–19.79–0–*ct* 45
Bowling 3072–141–21.78–9–3–8/65

Except on his first visit in 1890, he was most successful in England, and his record reads: 1893, 108 wickets, av 16.61; 1896, 148, 15.81; 1899, 142, 18.43; and 1902, 137, 14.02. In 1899 he hit 1,183 runs, av 27.51, thus completing the 'double' that season. His best analysis in an innings was 9 for 39 v South of England at Bournemouth in 1902. In 1912 he was appointed Secretary of Melbourne CC, a position he held for some 20 years.

Trumble, John William
Amateur. *b:* 16.9.1863, Kew, Victoria, Australia. *d:* 17.8.1944, Brighton, Victoria, Australia. Brother of Hugh (Victoria). Stylish middle order right-hand batsman, right-arm off break bowler. *Teams* Victoria (1883/4 to 1889/90, 18 matches); Gentlemen of England (1893). *Tour* Australia to England 1886. *Tests* Australia (1884/5 to 1886, 7 matches).
Career batting
63–104–11–1761–87–18.93–0–*ct* 33
Bowling 2627–109–24.10–5–1–6/33
Test batting
7–13–1–243–59–20.25–0–*ct* 3
Bowling 222–10–22.20–0–0–3/29

He had only modest all-round success on the 1886 tour. In 1893 on a visit to England he played in some first-class matches.

Trumper, Victor Thomas
Amateur. *b:* 2.11.1877, Darlinghurst, New South Wales, Australia. *d:* 28.6.1915, Darlinghurst, New South Wales, Australia. He died of Bright's disease. Father of Victor (New South Wales). Brilliant opening right-hand batsman, right-arm medium pace bowler. *Team* New South Wales (1894/5 to 1913/4, 73 matches). *Tours* Australia to England 1899, 1902, 1905, 1909, to South Africa 1902/3, to New Zealand 1904/5, 1913/14. *Tests* Australia (1899 to 1911/12, 48 matches).
Career batting
255–401–21–16939–300*–44.57–42–*ct* 172
Bowling 2031–64–31.73–2–0–5/19
Test batting
48–89–8–3163–214*–39.04–8–*ct* 31
Bowling 317–8–39.62–0–0–3/60

Regarded by his contemporaries as the greatest of all Australian batsmen, his form in England, with the exception of the 1902 season, cannot be compared with that of Bradman. He reached 2,000 runs only in 1902 – 2,570, av 48.49 – and scored over 1,000 on each of the three other visits. In 1905 he was most disappointing, failing completely in the Tests. His highest score in England was 300* v Sussex at Hove in 1899, but not one of his seven double centuries was hit in England. He also hit 1,000 runs in an Australian season.

Truswell, John Richard
Amateur. *b:* 14.1.1841, Farnsfield, Notts. *d:* 6.8.1892, Farnsfield, Notts. Lower order right-hand batsman, right-hand slow round-arm bowler. *Team* Nottinghamshire (1868, 2 matches).
Career batting
2–4–0–18–9–4.50–0–*ct* 2
Bowling 51–6–8.50–1–0–5/45

Tryon, Richard
Amateur. *b:* 31.8.1837, Oundle, Northants. *d:* 12.12.1905, Marylebone, London. Middle order batsman. *Sch* Harrow. *Team* MCC (1871).
Career batting
1–1–0–7–7–7.00–0–*ct* 1

His County cricket was for Northants.

Tubb, Henry
Amateur. *b:* 16.6.1851, Bicester, Oxfordshire. *d:* 8.2.1924, Chesterton, Bicester. Middle order right-hand batsman, right-hand medium pace round-arm bowler. *Sch* Rugby. *Team* MCC (1873–77).
Career batting
5–9–0–93–24–10.33–0–*ct* 2
Bowling 22–0

His County cricket was for Oxfordshire and he captained the team for some years commencing 1894.

Tubb, Samson
Professional. *b:* 1839, East Dean, Hampshire. *d:* 27.1.1891, Southsea, Hampshire. Lower order right-hand batsman, left-hand fast round-arm bowler. *Team* Hampshire (1864–67, 10 matches).
Career batting
10–19–5–170–24*–12.14–0–*ct* 5
Bowling 746–37–20.16–2–0–7/32

He also played for Devon and Wiltshire.

Tuck, George Hustler
Amateur. *b:* 28.4.1843, Norwich. *d:* 13.12.1920, Bracondale, Norwich. Opening or middle order right-hand batsman, wicket-keeper. *Sch* Eton. *Team* Cambridge U (1863–66, blue all four years).
Career batting
18–32–0–375–51–11.71–0–*ct* 9–*st* 1

His County cricket was for Norfolk. His final first-class match was for MCC in 1876.

Tuck, Gerald Seymour
Amateur. *b:* 5.5.1902, Hartley Wintney, Hampshire. Middle order right-hand batsman. *Team* Royal Navy (1927–29).
Career batting
6–10–0–314–125–31.40–1–*ct* 2

His County cricket was for Northumberland.

Tuck, James Jeffry
Professional. *b:* 3.6.1853, Ringwood, Hampshire. *d:* 20.1.1918, Devizes, Wiltshire. Solid lower order right-hand batsman, right-hand medium pace round-arm bowler, good cover point. *Team* Hampshire (1877–82, 9 matches).
Career batting
9–17–2–166–32*–11.06–0–*ct* 4
Bowling 36–2–18.00–0–0–1/11

Playing football in the winter of 1882/3, he broke his knee cap and this ended his cricket, but he later became well-known as an umpire.

Tuckett, Lindsay
Amateur. *b:* 2.2.1919, Durban, South Africa. Son of L. R. (South Africa). Lower order right-hand batsman, right-arm medium fast bowler. *Team* Orange Free State (1934/5 to 1954/5). *Tours* South Africa to England 1947. *Tests* South Africa (1947 to 1948/9, 9 matches).
Career batting
61–101–16–1496–101–17.60–1–*ct* 38
Bowling 5191–225–23.07–18–2–8/32
Test batting
9–14–3–131–40*–11.90–0–*ct* 9
Bowling 980–19–51.57–2–0–5/68

He began the 1947 tour in good form, and despite a strain proved the best bowler of his type during the season. He played in all five Tests and came second in the Test bowling table with 15 wickets, av 44.26.

Tudor, Claud Lechmere St John
Amateur. *b:* 27.12.1888, Willingdon, Sussex. *d:* 3.8.1977, Halton, Oxford. Brother of R. G. (Sussex). Middle order right-hand batsman. *Sch* Eastbourne. *Team* Sussex (1910–11, 7 matches).
Career batting
19–34–4–640–116–21.33–1–*ct* 12
Bowling 16–0

His final first-class match was for the Army in 1927.

Tudor, Roland Grimston
Amateur. *b:* 4.12.1890, Willingdon, Sussex. *d:* 11.10.1973, Lewes, Sussex. Brother of C. L. St J. (Sussex). Middle order batsman. *Sch* Eastbourne. *Teams* Sussex (1912–19, 3 matches); Cambridge U (1913).
Career batting
5–10–1–94–25*–10.44–0–*ct* 2

Tudor, Richard Thornhill
Cricketer. *b:* 27.9.1948, Shrewsbury. Lower order right-hand batsman, right-arm medium pace bowler. *Sch* Shrewsbury. *Team* Warwickshire (1976, 1 match).
Career batting
1–1–0–6–6–6.00–0–*ct* 0
Bowling 42–0

Tudway, Hervey Robert Charles
Amateur. *b:* 23.9.1888, London. *d:* 18.11.1914, Kleinzillebeke, Belgium. Middle order batsman. *Sch* Eton. *Team* Somerset (1910, 1 match).
Career batting
1–2–0–12–6–6.00–0–*ct* 0

Tuff, Frank Noel
Amateur. *b:* 26.11.1889, Rochester, Kent. *d:* 5.11.1915, Imtarfa, Malta. He died of wounds. Lower order right-hand batsman, right-arm medium fast bowler. *Sch* Malvern. *Team* Oxford U (1910–11, blue 1910).

Career batting
11–20–7–190–35–14.61–0–*ct* 6
Bowling 670–25–26.80–2–0–7/47
His final first-class match was for Free Foresters in 1914. He played soccer for Oxford and the Corinthians.

Tufnell, Carleton Fowell
Amateur. *b:* 20.2.1856, Northfleet, Kent. *d:* 26.5.1940, Chelsea, London. Father of N. C. (Surrey). Middle order right-hand batsman, right-hand slow or medium pace round-arm bowler, good slip. *Sch* Eton. *Team* Kent (1878–79, 7 matches).
Career batting
8–13–3–108–26–10.80–0–*ct* 2
Bowling 285–15–19.00–0–0–3/31

Tufnell, Neville Charsley
Amateur. *b:* 13.6.1887, Simla, India. *d:* 3.8.1951, Whitechapel, London. Son of C. F. (Kent). Lower order right-hand batsman, right-arm slow bowler, wicket-keeper. *Sch* Eton. *Teams* Cambridge U (1908–10, blue 1909 and 1910); Surrey (1922, 1 match). *Tours* MCC to New Zealand 1906/7, to South Africa 1909/10, to Argentina 1911/12. *Test* England (1909/10, 1 match).
Career batting
70–120–14–1514–102–14.28–1–*ct* 59–*st* 40
Bowling 117–1–117.00–0–0–1/54
Test batting
1–1–0–14–14–14.00–0–*ct* 0–*st* 1
His final first-class match was for Free Foresters in 1924, his debut having been for MCC in 1907. He also played for Norfolk.

Tufton, Hon John Sackville Richard
(succeeded to the title 2nd Lord Hothfield in 1926)
Amateur. *b:* 8.11.1873, Hothfield, Kent. *d:* 21.12.1952, Bayswater, London. Middle order right-hand batsman. *Sch* Eton. *Team* Kent (1897–98, 8 matches).
Career batting
13–19–2–243–33*–14.29–0–*ct* 5
His final first-class match was for MCC in 1899.

Tuke, Dr Charles Molesworth
Amateur. *b:* 23.5.1857, Chiswick, Middlesex. *d:* 24.1.1925, Chiswick, Middlesex. Lower order right-hand batsman, right-arm fast bowler. *Sch* Merchant Taylor's. *Team* Middlesex (1882, 7 matches).
Career batting
8–12–4–29–8–3.62–0–*ct* 4
Bowling 505–15–33.66–0–0–3/38
His final first-class match was for the Gentlemen in 1890.

Tulk, Derek Thomas
Professional. *b:* 21.4.1934, Southampton, Hants. Lower order right-hand batsman, right-arm medium pace bowler. *Team* Hampshire (1956–57, 2 matches).
Career batting
2–2–2–8–8*–no av–0–*ct* 1
Bowling 70–0

Tunnicliffe, Colin John
Cricketer. *b:* 11.8.1951, Derby. Lower order right-hand batsman, left-arm fast medium bowler. *Team* Derbyshire (1973–83, 150 matches).
Career batting
150–176–30–2092–91–14.32–0–*ct* 65
Bowling 10265–319–32.17–6–0–7/36

Tunnicliffe, Howard Trevor
Cricketer. *b:* 4.3.1950, Derby. Middle or lower order right-hand batsman, right-arm medium pace bowler. *Sch* Malvern. *Team* Nottinghamshire (1973–80, 65 matches).
Career batting
65–110–27–2116–100*–25.49–1–*ct* 37
Bowling 1601–42–38.11–0–0–4/30

Tunnicliffe, John
Professional. *b:* 26.8.1866, Low Town, Pudsey, Yorkshire. *d:* 11.7.1948, Westbury Park, Bristol. Attacking opening right-hand batsman, slow right-arm bowler, brilliant slip field, occasional wicket-keeper. *Team* Yorkshire (1891–1907, 475 matches).
Career batting
498–811–59–20310–243–26.95–23–*ct* 694
Bowling 405–7–57.85–0–0–1/6
He hit 1,000 runs in a season 12 times (best 1,804, av 41.00, in 1898). His only double century was 243 for Yorkshire v Derbyshire at Chesterfield in 1898, when together with J. T. Brown he added a record 554 for the first wicket. Altogether he and J. T. Brown realised 26 century first-wicket partnerships. After retiring he was coach at Clifton College and later a member of Gloucestershire CCC Committee, his son being the Secretary to the County Club.

Tuppin, Alfred George
Professional. *b:* 17.12.1911, Brighton, Sussex. Lower order right-hand batsman, right-arm medium pace bowler. *Team* Sussex (1935–39, 23 matches).

Career batting
23–31–6–294–31*–11.77–0–*ct* 11
Bowling 1626–56–29.03–4–0–5/30

Turberville, H. T. S. *(see under* Smith, H. T.)

Turland, Herbert
Professional. *b:* 29.8.1894, Stapleford, Notts. Middle order right-hand batsman, left-arm medium pace bowler. *Teams* Derbyshire (1921, 1 match); Nottinghamshire (1924, 1 match).
Career batting
2–4–0–30–29–7.50–0–*ct* 0
Bowling 14–0

Turnbull, Bertrand
Amateur. *b:* 1887, Cardiff. *d:* 17.11.1943, Southerndown, Glamorgan. Middle order batsman, wicket-keeper. *Team* Gloucestershire (1911, 1 match).
Career batting
1–2–1–35–28*–35.00–0–*ct* 0–*st* 1
He also played for Glamorgan (pre-first-class).

Turnbull, Charles Lane
Amateur. *b:* 1851, Gloucester. *d:* 24.3.1920, Swindon, Wiltshire. Middle order batsman. *Team* Gloucestershire (1873, 1 match).
Career batting
1–1–0–0–0–0.00–0–*ct* 0

Turnbull, Jonathan Richard
Cricketer. *b:* 13.11.1962, Northwood, Middlesex. Lower order right-hand batsman, right-arm medium pace bowler. *Sch* Merchant Taylors'. *Team* Oxford U (1983).
Career batting
7–7–4–5–5*–1.66–0–*ct* 6
Bowling 424–12–35.33–0–0–4/61

Turnbull, Maurice Joseph Lawson
Amateur. *b:* 16.3.1906, Cardiff. *d:* 5.8.1944, near Montchamp, France. He was killed in action. Attractive middle order right-hand batsman. *Sch* Downside. *Teams* Glamorgan (1924–39, 314 matches); Cambridge U (1926–29, blue 1926, 1928 and 1929). *Tours* MCC to Australia and New Zealand 1929/30, to South Africa 1930/1. *Tests* England (1929/30 to 1936, 9 matches).
Career batting
388–626–37–17544–233–29.78–29–*ct* 280
Bowling 355–4–88.75–0–0–1/4
Test batting
9–13–2–224–61–20.36–0–*ct* 1
He hit 1,000 runs in a season ten times (best 1,650, av 33.00, in 1935). Each of his three double centuries was made for Glamorgan, the highest being 233 v Worcestershire at Swansea in 1937. In conjunction with M. J. C. Allom he wrote accounts of both his MCC tours. From 1930 to 1939 he captained Glamorgan. A noted rugby half back, he played for Cardiff and Wales.

Turnbull, Rivers Montagu
Amateur. *b:* 6.1.1855, Bullundshuhr, North West Provinces, India. *d:* 24.2.1927, Westminster, London. Lower order right-hand batsman, right-hand slow round-arm bowler. *Team* Sussex (1877–79, 2 matches).
Career batting
2–4–0–2–2–0.50–0–*ct* 1
Bowling 54–2–27.00–0–0–2/23

Turnbull, William Fleming
Amateur. *b:* 26.1.1879, Falkirk, Stirlingshire, Scotland. *d:* 26.12.1959, Edinburgh, Scotland. Right-hand batsman. *Team* Scotland (1911–12).
Career batting
4–7–1–78–41*–13.00–0–*ct* 1
Bowling 12–0

Turner, Alan
Cricketer. *b:* 23.7.1950, Camperdown, New South Wales, Australia. Opening left-hand batsman. *Team* New South Wales (1968/9 to 1977/8, 76 matches). *Tours* Australia to England 1975, to New Zealand 1969/70, 1976/7. *Tests* Australia (1975 to 1976/7, 14 matches).
Career batting
105–196–10–5744–156–30.88–7–*ct* 80
Bowling 10–1–10.00–0–0–1/6
Test batting
14–27–1–768–136–29.53–1–*ct* 15
On the 1975 tour to England he hit 654 runs, av 34.42, and played in three of the four Tests, but with little success.

Turner, Alban
Professional. *b:* 2.9.1885, Staincross, Yorkshire. *d:* 29.8.1951, Goldthorpe, Yorkshire. Middle order right-hand batsman. *Team* Yorkshire (1910–11, 9 matches).
Career batting
9–16–1–163–37–10.86–0–*ct* 7

Turner, Allen
Professional. b: 24.10.1891, Heath, Derbyshire. *d:* 15.1.1961, Holmwood, Derbyshire. Tail end right-hand batsman, right-arm fast medium bowler. *Team* Derbyshire (1920, 2 matches).
Career batting
2–4–0–4–2–1.00–0–*ct* 1
Bowling 138–6–23.00–0–0–3/66

Turner, Arthur Jervois
Amateur. *b:* 10.7.1878, Mussorie, India. *d:*

8.9.1952, Graffham, Sussex. Brother of W. M. F. (Essex) Middle order right-hand batsman, right-arm medium pace bowler, wicket-keeper. *Sch* Bedford Modern. *Team* Essex (1897–1910, 68 matches).
Career batting
77–134–15–4053–124–34.05–11–*ct* 31–*st* 2
Bowling 484–15–32.26–0–0–3/58

In his first season in first-class cricket he hit 590 runs, av 42.14, and in 1899, 804, av 40.20, but owing to military duties was not able to play regularly. His final first-class match was for Free Foresters in 1914. He also played for Bedfordshire. His father was a member of the Hong Kong team which was drowned in a ship wreck returning from the annual match with Shanghai. A noted rugby footballer he played for Blackheath and Kent.

Turner, Brian
Professional. *b:* 25.7.1938, Sheffield, Yorkshire. Lower order left-hand batsman, right-arm medium pace bowler. *Team* Yorkshire (1960–61, 2 matches).
Career batting
2–4–2–7–3*–3.50–0–*ct* 2
Bowling 47–4–11.75–0–0–2/9

Turner, Charles
Amateur. *b:* March 1862. *d:* 20.5.1926, Thatcham, Berkshire. Lower order batsman, useful bowler. *Sch* Uppingham. *Team* Gloucestershire (1886–89, 3 matches).
Career batting
3–5–0–33–17–6.60–0–*ct* 2
Bowling 119–3–39.66–0–0–1/16

From 1904 until his death he was Hon Secretary of Berkshire CCC.

Turner, Cyril
Professional. *b:* 11.1.1902, Wombwell, Yorkshire. *d:* 19.11.1968, Wath-on-Dearne, Yorkshire. Middle order left-hand batsman, right-arm medium pace bowler. *Team* Yorkshire (1925–46, 200 matches). *Tour* Yorkshire to Jamaica 1935/6.
Career batting
201–266–32–6132–130–26.20–2–*ct* 181
Bowling 5354–173–30.94–4–0–7/54

He hit 1,153 runs, av 28.82, in 1934.

Turner, Charles Thomas Biass
Amateur. *b:* 16.11.1862, Bathurst, New South Wales, Australia. *d:* 1.1.1944, Manly, New South Wales, Australia. Brother-in-law of A. E. A. Goldman (Queensland). Forcing middle order right-hand batsman, right-arm medium fast bowler. *Team* New South Wales (1882/3 to 1909/10, 43 matches). *Tours* Australia to England 1888, 1890, 1893. *Tests* Australia (1886/7 to 1894/5, 17 matches).
Career batting
155–261–13–3856–103–15.54–2–*ct* 85
Bowling 14147–993–14.24–102–35–9/15
Test batting
17–32–4–323–29–11.53–0–*ct* 8
Bowling 1670–101–16.53–11–2–7/43

On his first visit to England in 1888 he was immensely successful, taking 283 wickets, av 11.68. In 1890 he had 179, av 14.21 and in 1893, 148, av 13.63. On each tour he headed the Australians' bowling averages and in 1893 proved to be the leading bowler in first-class cricket. In Australia in 1887/8, he took 106 first-class wickets, av 13.59, a number which remains a seasonal record. His best innings analysis was 9 for 15 for Australians v An England XI at Stoke-on-Trent in 1888.

Turner, David Roy
Cricketer. *b:* 5.2.1949, Corsham, Wiltshire. Middle order left-hand batsman, right-arm medium pace bowler. *Teams* Hampshire (1966–83, 322 matches); Western Province (1977/8). *Tour* Robins to South Africa 1972/3.
Career batting
332–544–49–14070–181*–28.42–21–*ct* 165
Bowling 323–9–35.88–0–0–2/7

He hit 1,000 runs in a season six times (best 1,269, av 36.25, in 1976). He also played for Wiltshire.

Turner, Francis Gordon
Amateur. *b:* 1.3.1890, London. *d:* 21.11.1979, Deal, Kent. Middle order right-hand batsman, leg break bowler. *Sch* Westminster. *Team* Hampshire (1912, 1 match).
Career batting
1–1–0–14–14–14.00–0–*ct* 1

Turner, Frederick Harding
Amateur. *b:* 29.5.1888, Sefton Park, Liverpool, Lancashire. *d:* 10.1.1915, near Kemmel, Belgium. He was killed in action. Lower order batsman, useful bowler. *Sch* Sedbergh. *Team* Oxford U (1909).
Career batting
5–9–2–67–44–9.57–0–*ct* 2
Bowling 272–17–16.00–0–0–4/46

A noted rugby footballer, he was capped for Scotland.

Turner, Francis Irving
Amateur. *b:* 3.9.1894, Barnsley, Yorkshire. *d:* 18.10.1954, Killearn, Stirlingshire, Scotland.

Right-hand batsman, right-arm medium pace bowler. *Team* Yorkshire (1924, 5 matches).
Career batting
5–7–0–33–12–4.71–0–*ct* 2
He also played for Scotland (not first class).

Turner, Francis Michael
Professional. *b:* 8.8.1934, Leicester. Middle order right-hand batsman, leg break and googly bowler. *Team* Leicestershire (1954–59, 10 matches).
Career batting
10–16–5–196–28*–17.81–0–*ct* 2
Bowling 223–3–74.33–0–0–3/56
Since 1960 he has been Secretary of Leicestershire CCC.

Turner, Glenn Maitland
Cricketer. *b:* 26.5.1947, Dunedin, New Zealand. Very sound opening right-hand batsman, off break bowler. *Teams* Otago (1964/5 to 1982/3); Worcestershire (1967–82, 284 matches); Northern Districts (1976/7). *Tours* New Zealand to England 1969, 1973, to India and Pakistan 1969/70, 1976/7, to Australia 1969/70, 1973/4, to West Indies 1971/2; International XI to South Africa 1972/3, 1975/6. *Tests* New Zealand (1968/9 to 1982/3, 41 matches).
Career batting
455–792–101–34346–311*–49.70–103–*ct* 410
Bowling 189–5–37.80–0–0–3/18
Test batting
41–73–6–2991–259–44.64–7–*ct* 42
Bowling 5–0
He hit 1,000 runs in a season 15 times, going on to 2,000 three times (best 2,416, av 67.11, in 1973). In 1973 he hit 1,018 runs by May 31. He also completed 1,000 runs in three overseas seasons, including a New Zealand record of 1,244, av 77.75, in 1975/6. His highest innings of 311* for Worcs v Warwickshire at Worcester in 1982 was also his 100th century – he has hit nine other scores over 200. He captained Worcestershire in 1981 and 1982 and New Zealand in 10 Tests.

Turner, Harry
Professional. *b:* 6.4.1879, Birkenshaw, Yorkshire. *d:* 23.10.1939, Shrewsbury, Shropshire. Right-hand batsman, right-arm fast medium bowler. *Team* Scotland (1913).
Career batting
2–4–0–32–22–8.00–0–*ct* 5
Bowling 89–1–89.00–0–0–1/14

Turner, James
Professional. *b:* 23.7.1865, Teversal, Notts. *d:* 30.1.1945, Sutton-in-Ashfield, Notts. Lower order batsman, right-arm medium pace bowler. *Team* Nottinghamshire (1894, 2 matches).
Career batting
2–3–0–30–26–10.00–0–*ct* 3
Bowling 72–1–72.00–0–0–1/11

Turner, John
Amateur. *b:* 1854. *d:* 22.10.1912, Bexhill-on-Sea, Sussex. Opening right-hand batsman. *Team* MCC (1876–83).
Career batting
20–36–2–417–65–12.26–0–*ct* 9
His County cricket was for Northants and Bedfordshire.

Turner, John Alfred
Amateur. *b:* 10.4.1863, Leicester. *d:* 23.7.1924, Roehampton, Surrey. Steady middle order right-hand batsman, right-arm fast bowler, good field. *Sch* Uppingham. *Team* Cambridge U (1883–86, blue all four years). *Tours* Sanders to North America 1885, 1886.
Career batting
36–63–8–1060–174–19.27–2–*ct* 24
Bowling 1136–33–34.42–0–0–4/46
He played for Leicestershire 1883 to 1892 (pre-first-class). His final first-class match was for Cambridge Past and Present in 1890. His County cricket ended when he lost an eye whilst playing rackets.

Turner, John Bernard
Cricketer. *b:* 2.1.1949, Princes Risborough, Bucks. Opening right-hand batsman, slow left-arm bowler. *Team* Minor Counties (1974).
Career batting
1–2–0–127–106–63.50–1–*ct* 1
On his first-class debut and only first-class match, Minor Counties v Pakistan at Jesmond, 1974 he hit 106 in the second innings. His County cricket was for Buckinghamshire commencing 1968.

Turner, James William Cecil
Amateur. *b:* 2.10.1886, Bromley, Kent. *d:* 29.11.1968, Cambridge. Middle order right-hand batsman, useful bowler. *Team* Worcestershire (1911–21, 46 matches).
Career batting
48–91–6–1266–106–14.89–1–*ct* 13
Bowling 32–2–16.00–0–0–1/14

Turner, Lennox James
Amateur. *b:* 1863, Croydon, Surrey. *d:* 2.12.1914, Croydon, Surrey. Lower order batsman, useful bowler. *Sch* Whitgift. *Team* MCC (1896).
Career batting
1–2–0–17–11–8.50–0–*ct* 0
Bowling 15–0

Turner, Montague
Amateur. *b:* 21.9.1843, Acton, Middlesex. *d:* 25.1.1908, Cuckfield, Sussex. Lower order right-hand batsman, wicket-keeper. *Sch* Cheltenham. *Team* Middlesex (1863–78, 29 matches).
Career batting
53–93–14–952–82–12.05–0–*ct* 79–*st* 64
He served on the Committee of both MCC and Middlesex CCC. He also played for Lincolnshire.

Turner, Nigel Frederick
Amateur. *b:* 8.8.1914, Paddington, London. *d:* 31.1.1962, Swindon, Wiltshire. Lower order right-hand batsman, right-arm fast medium bowler. *Sch* Eton. *Team* Middlesex (1937, 1 match).
Career batting
1–1–0–0–0–0.00–0–*ct* 0
Bowling 43–2–21.50–0–0–2/38
He did not appear in any trials whilst at Cambridge University.

Turner, Noel Vernon Cyril
Amateur. *b:* 12.5.1887, Eastwood, Notts. *d:* 13.6.1941, Hungerford Park, Berkshire. Brother of R. H. T. (Notts). Middle order right-hand batsman. *Sch* Repton. *Team* Nottinghamshire (1906–09, 23 matches).
Career batting
24–38–2–553–73*–15.36–0–*ct* 11
His final first-class match was for Free Foresters in 1912. A good goalkeeper, he played for Corinthian Casuals and for England in an amateur international.

Turner, Ronald
Amateur. *b:* 1885, Medway, Kent. *d:* 15.8.1915, Suvla Bay, Gallipoli Peninsula, Turkey. Middle order batsman. *Sch* Hurstpierpoint. *Team* Gloucestershire (1906, 3 matches).
Career batting
3–6–0–30–19–5.00–0–*ct* 0

Turner, Richard Ernest
Professional. *b:* 4.5.1888, Mitcham, Surrey. *d:* 16.3.1967, Hastings, Sussex. Middle order right-hand batsman, right-arm medium pace bowler. *Team* Worcestershire (1909–22, 52 matches).
Career batting
52–96–8–1010–66–11.47–0–*ct* 29
Bowling 225–4–56.25–0–0–3/7

Turner, Robert Frewin
Professional. *b:* 15.7.1885, Leicester. *d:* 15.2.1959, Darlington, Co Durham. Middle order right-hand batsman, bowler. *Team* Leicestershire (1909–11, 20 matches).
Career batting
20–34–1–525–41–15.90–0–*ct* 7
Bowling 367–9–40.77–0–0–2/2
A good soccer player, he appeared for Leicester Fosse, Everton, Preston North End and Darlington.

Turner, Robert Harrison Tom
Amateur. *b:* 26.10.1888, Eastwood, Notts. *d:* 13.9.1947, Shipley, Derbyshire. Brother of N. V. C. (Notts). Stylish middle order right-hand batsman. *Sch* Repton. *Team* Nottinghamshire (1906–27, 26 matches).
Career batting
26–48–6–755–84–17.97–0–*ct* 6

Turner, Richard Vinson
Amateur. *b:* 6.4.1932, Torquay, Devon. Middle order right-hand batsman. *Sch* Clifton. *Team* Cambridge U (1953–54).
Career batting
10–16–4–213–113*–17.75–1–*ct* 3

Turner, Stuart
Cricketer. *b:* 18.7.1943, Chester. Middle or lower order right-hand batsman, right-arm fast medium bowler. *Teams* Essex (1965–83, 335 matches); Natal (1976/7 to 1977/8). *Tour* Robins to South Africa 1974/5.
Career batting
342–489–95–9064–121–23.00–4–*ct* 213
Bowling 20275–787–25.76–27–1–6/26

Turner, Walter Martin FitzHerbert
Amateur. *b:* 4.4.1881, Meerut, India. *d:* 1.2.1948, Harrow, Middlesex. Brother of A. J. (Essex). Middle order right-hand batsman, right-arm medium pace bowler. *Sch* Wellington. *Teams* Essex (1899–1926, 48 matches); Europeans (1910/11).
Career batting
51–86–7–2090–172–26.45–2–*ct* 62
Bowling 205–5–41.00–0–0–2/12

Turnour, Viscount Edward
(succeeded as 5th Earl of Winterton in 1879)
Amateur. *b:* 15.8.1837, Shillinglee Park, Petworth, Sussex. *d:* 5.9.1907, Shillinglee Park, Petworth, Sussex. Hard hitting middle order right-hand batsman, right-hand fast round-arm bowler, cover point. *Sch* Eton. *Team* Sussex (1862–67, 5 matches).
Career batting
7–13–1–49–27*–4.08–0–*ct* 6–*st* 1
He also played for Norfolk. He was on the Committee of MCC and of Sussex and President of MCC in 1884.

Turrall, Percy Wakeford
Amateur. *b:* 1883, Billericay, Essex. *d:* 17.5.1941, Chelmsford, Essex. Opening batsman. *Team* Essex (1927, 1 match).
Career batting
1–1–0–45–45–45.00–0–*ct* 0

Tweed, Thomas Edward
Amateur. *b:* 11.12.1904, Colombo, Ceylon. *d:* 23.3.1973, Colombo, Sri Lanka. Lower order right-hand batsman, right-arm medium pace bowler. *Team* Cambridge U (1925–26).
Career batting
4–6–1–97–24–19.40–0–*ct* 3
Bowling 177–5–35.40–0–0–2/30

Twining, Richard Haynes
Amateur. *b:* 3.11.1889, Paddington, London. *d:* 3.1.1979, Kensington, London. Opening right-hand batsman, wicket-keeper. *Sch* Eton. *Teams* Oxford U (1910–13, blue all four years); Middlesex (1910–28, 32 matches).
Career batting
78–137–8–2963–135–22.96–3–*ct* 40–*st* 10
Bowling 23–0

He served on the MCC Committee commencing 1933, was a Trustee of the Club from 1952 to 1969 and President in 1964, afterwards being elected a Life Vice-President. From 1950 to 1957 he was President of Middlesex CCC.

Tye, John
Professional. *b:* 10.7.1848, Bulwell, Notts. *d:* 19.11.1905, Rastrick, Yorkshire. Tail end right-hand batsman, right-hand fast round-arm bowler, slip field. *Teams* Derbyshire (1874, 3 matches); Nottinghamshire (1876–81, 17 matches).
Career batting
24–38–8–226–48–7.53–0–*ct* 20
Bowling 1102–45–24.48–2–0–5/41

Tylden, James Richard
Amateur. *b:* 26.4.1889, Milstead, Kent. *d:* 24.2.1949, Whitechapel, London. Middle order left-hand batsman. *Sch* Rugby. *Team* Kent (1923, 1 match).
Career batting
1–2–0–19–19–9.50–0–*ct* 0

He appeared in the Oxford Freshmen's Match of 1908 and the Seniors' Match of 1909.

Tyldesley, (George) Ernest
Professional. *b:* 5.2.1889, Roe Green, Worsley, Lancashire. *d:* 5.5.1962, Rhos-on-Sea, Denbighshire. Brother of J. T. (Lancashire). Excellent middle order right-hand batsman, slow medium right-arm bowler. *Team* Lancashire (1909–36, 573 matches). *Tours* Joel to South Africa 1924/5; Tennyson to Jamaica 1926/7; MCC to South Africa 1927/8, to Australia 1928/9. *Tests* England (1921 to 1928/9, 14 matches).
Career batting
648–961–106–38874–256*–45.46–102–*ct* 293
Bowling 346–6–57.66–0–0–3/33
Test batting
14–20–2–990–122–55.00–3–*ct* 2
Bowling 2–0

He hit 1,000 runs in a season 18 times in England and once in South Africa going on to 2,000 six times and thence to 3,000 once : 3,024, av 79.57, in 1928. All his seven double centuries were for Lancashire, the highest being 256* v Warwickshire at Old Trafford in 1930.

Tyldesley, Harry
Professional. *b:* 1893, Westhoughton, Lancashire. *d:* 30.8.1935, Sandylands, Morecambe, Lancashire. Brother of J. D. (Lancashire), R. K. (Lancashire) and W. K. (Lancashire). Lower order right-hand batsman, right-arm slow bowler. *Team* Lancashire (1914–22, 4 matches). *Tour* MCC to Australia and New Zealand 1922/3.
Career batting
9–15–3–102–33*–8.50–0–*ct* 7
Bowling 500–18–27.77–1–0–5/100

Tyldesley, James Derbyshire
Professional. *b:* 10.8.1889, Ashton-in-Makerfield, Lancashire. *d:* 31.1.1923, Bolton, Lancashire. Brother of Harry (Lancashire), R. K. (Lancashire) and W. K. (Lancashire). Middle order right-hand batsman, right-arm fast bowler. *Team* Lancashire (1910–22, 116 matches).
Career batting
116–169–16–2885–112*–18.85–3–*ct* 97
Bowling 8092–309–26.18–15–0–7/34

He also played for Cumberland.

Tyldesley, John Thomas
Professional. *b:* 22.11.1873, Roe Green, Worsley, Lancashire. *d:* 27.11.1930, Monton, Manchester, Lancashire. He collapsed and died whilst putting on his boots to go to work. Brother of G. E. (Lancashire). Attractive middle order right-hand batsman, excellent outfield. *Team* Lancashire (1895–1923, 507 matches). *Tours* Hawke to South Africa 1898/9; MacLaren to Australia 1901/2; MCC to Australia 1903/4. *Tests* England (1898/9 to 1909, 31 matches).
Career batting
608–994–62–37897–295*–40.66–86–*ct* 355
Bowling 211–3–70.33–0–0–1/4
Test batting
31–55–1–1661–138–30.75–4–*ct* 16

Appearing for Lancashire in the middle of the 1895 season, he hit 152* in his second game (v

Warwickshire) and almost at once established himself in the County side. In 1901 he scored 3,041 runs, av 55.29, which was to remain his best aggregate, but in all he exceeded 1,000 runs in a season 19 times and went on to 2,000 five times. All of his 13 double centuries were for Lancashire, his highest being 295* for Lancashire v Kent at Old Trafford in 1906.

Very quick on his feet, he could score all round the wicket, as well as having an excellent defence. For ten years he played regularly for England, with his best series in 1905 against the Australians, when he hit 424 runs, average 53.00. After retiring he became coach at Old Trafford until 1929.

Tyldesley, Richard Knowles
Professional. *b:* 11.3.1897, Westhoughton, Lancashire. *d:* 17.9.1943, Over Hulton, Bolton, Lancashire. Brother of Harry (Lancashire), J. D. (Lancashire) and W. K. (Lancashire). Lower order right-hand batsman, right-arm slow bowler. *Team* Lancashire (1919–31, 374 matches). *Tour* MCC to Australia 1924/5. *Tests* England (1924–30, 7 matches).
Career batting
397–464–54–6419–105–15.65–1–*ct* 337
Bowling 25980–1509–17.21–101–22–8/15
Test batting
7–7–1–47–29–7.83–0–*ct* 1
Bowling 619–19–32.57–0–0–3/50

He took 100 wickets in a season 10 times (best 184, av 13.98, in 1924). He was easily the leading Lancashire bowler during the 1931 season, but a disagreement over terms with the Lancashire Committee brought a sudden end to his County career. His final first-class match was for Sir L. Parkinson's XI in 1935.

Tyldesley, William Knowles
Professional. *b:* 10.8.1887, Aspull, Wigan, Lancashire. *d:* 26.4.1918, Kemmel, Belgium. He was killed in action. Brother of Harry (Lancashire), J. D. (Lancashire) and R. K. (Lancashire). Middle order left-hand batsman, left-arm medium fast bowler. *Team* Lancashire (1908–14, 87 matches).
Career batting
87–137–7–2979–152–22.91–3–*ct* 52
Bowling 383–8–47.87–0–0–2/0

Tylecote, Edward Ferdinando Sutton
Amateur. *b:* 23.6.1849, Marston Moretaine, Bedfordshire. *d:* 15.3.1938, New Hunstanton, Norfolk. Brother of H. G. (Oxford U). Middle order right-hand batsman, wicket-keeper. *Sch* Clifton. *Teams* Oxford U (1869–72, blue all four years); Kent (1875–83, 22 matches). *Tour* Bligh to Australia 1882/3. *Tests* England (1882/3 to 1886, 6 matches).
Career batting
93–158–10–3065–107–20.70–3–*ct* 128–*st* 57
Bowling 14–0
Test batting
6–9–1–152–66–19.00–0–*ct* 5–*st* 5

In 1868 he hit 404* for Classical v Modern at Clifton College, a record in any match at that date. He played some County cricket for Bedfordshire. His final first-class match was for MCC in 1886.

Tylecote, Henry Grey
Amateur. *b:* 24.7.1853, Marston Moretaine, Bedfordshire. *d:* 8.3.1935, Oxford. Brother of E. F. S. (Kent). Sound, patient middle order right-hand batsman, right-hand medium pace round-arm bowler, wicket-keeper. *Sch* Clifton. *Team* Oxford U (1874–77, blue all four years).
Career batting
29–46–9–442–54–11.94–0–*ct* 25–*st* 5
Bowling 776–45–17.24–3–0–8/51

His final first-class match was for MCC in 1886. He played for Bedfordshire from 1876 to 1883 and later for Hertfordshire. He took a prominent part in athletics at Oxford, being a noted middle distance runner.

Tyler, Arthur Wellesley
Amateur. *b:* 18.6.1907, Charlton, Kent. Middle order right-hand batsman, wicket-keeper. *Sch* Cheltenham. *Team* Army (1931–32).
Career batting
3–5–1–77–26–19.25–0–*ct* 4–*st* 2

His County cricket was for Norfolk.

Tyler, Bernard
Professional. *b:* 29.4.1902, Ridlington, Rutland. Lower order right-hand batsman, right-arm fast bowler. *Teams* Northants (1923–24, 9 matches); Leicestershire (1926–28, 5 matches).
Career batting
14–25–6–135–26–7.10–0–*ct* 9
Bowling 553–11–50.27–0–0–2/13

Tyler, Cyril
Amateur. *b:* 26.1.1911, Ossett, Yorkshire. Lower order right-hand batsman, leg break bowler. *Team* Gloucestershire (1936–38, 16 matches).
Career batting
16–22–4–113–22–6.27–0–*ct* 7
Bowling 1122–33–34.00–1–0–5/116

Tyler, Charles Herbert
Amateur. *b:* 13.9.1887, Northampton. *d:* 17.5.1942, Blackpool, Lancashire. Son of Frederick (Northants captain 1892). Middle order right-hand batsman, good field. *Team* Northants (1910–23, 27 matches).

Career batting
27–48–7–582–63–14.19–0–*ct* 21
He captained Northants in 1922.

Tyler, Edwin James
Professional. *b:* 13.10.1864, Kidderminster, Worcs. *d:* 25.1.1917, Taunton, Somerset. Lower order left-hand batsman, slow left-arm bowler, good field. *Team* Somerset (1891–1907, 177 matches). *Tour* Hawke to South Africa 1895/6. *Test* England (1895/6, 1 match).
Career batting
185–310–52–2952–66–11.44–0–*ct* 118
Bowling 19779–895–22.09–76–21–10/49
Test batting
1–1–0–0–0–0.00–0–*ct* 0
Bowling 65–4–16.25–0–0–3/49
He took 100 wickets in a season three times (best 124, av 22.58, in 1895). In 1900 he was no-balled for throwing. He appeared in non-first-class matches for Worcestershire before playing for Somerset. His best bowling was 10/49 for Somerset v Surrey at Taunton in 1895.

Tyrwhitt-Drake, Thomas William
Amateur. *b:* 5.11.1926, London. Opening right-hand batsman, wicket-keeper. *Sch* Haileybury. *Team* Cambridge U (1946–48).
Career batting
4–8–0–122–38–15.25–0–*ct* 1
His county cricket was for Hertfordshire. His final first-class match was for Free Foresters in 1957

Tyson, Cecil Thomas
Professional. *b:* 24.1.1889, Brompton, Scarborough, Yorkshire. *d:* 3.4.1940, Leeds, Yorkshire. Middle order left-hand batsman, left-arm bowler. *Teams* Yorkshire (1921, 3 matches); Glamorgan (1926, 2 matches).
Career batting
5–9–2–320–100*–45.71–1–*ct* 1
Bowling 32–0
He hit 100 not out for Yorkshire v Hampshire at Southampton on his first-class debut in 1921, but owing to a disagreement over terms, his County cricket was very limited.

Tyson, Frank Holmes
Professional. *b:* 6.6.1930, Farnworth, Lancashire. Lower order right-hand batsman, hostile right-arm fast bowler. *Team* Northants (1952–60, 170 matches). *Tours* MCC to Australia and New Zealand 1954/5, 1958/9, to West Indies 1955/6, to South Africa 1956/7; Commonwealth to South Africa 1959/60. *Tests* England (1954 to 1958/9, 17 matches).
Career batting
244–316–76–4103–82–17.09–0–*ct* 85
Bowling 16030–767–20.89–34–5–8/60
Test batting
17–24–3–230–37*–10.95–0–*ct* 4
Bowling 1141–76–18.56–4–1–7/27
He took 101 wickets, av 21.47, in 1957. His best bowling in an innings was 8 for 60 for Northants v Surrey at the Oval in 1957. For a few years the most aggressive fast bowler in England, his greatest triumphs were during the 1954/5 tour to Australia, when he took 28 wickets, av 20.82, in the Tests and 64 wickets, av 17.81, in all first-class matches. After retiring from County cricket he emigrated to Australia where he was appointed coach to the Victorian Cricket Association and also became a well-known sports commentator.

Tyssen, Rev Charles Amherst Daniel
Amateur. *b:* 11.12.1857, Sandgate, Kent. *d:* 26.12.1940, Sandgate, Kent. Opening batsman. *Sch* Harrow. *Team* Gentlemen of England (1877).
Career batting
1–2–0–2–2–1.00–0–*ct* 2
He played in the Freshmen's Match and Seniors' Match at Oxford.

Ubsdell, George
Professional. *b:* 4.4.1844, Southampton, Hants. *d:* 15.10.1905, Garston, Liverpool, Lancashire. Lower order right-hand batsman, right-arm medium bowler, wicket-keeper. *Team* Hampshire (1864–70, 15 matches).
Career batting
15–29–4–170–29–6.80–0–*ct* 4–*st* 13

Udal, Geoffrey Francis U.
Amateur. *b:* 23.2.1908, Holborn, London. *d:* 5.12.1980, Surrey. Tail end right-hand batsman, right-arm fast bowler. *Teams* Leicestershire (1946, 2 matches); Middlesex (1932, 1 match).
Career batting
4–8–3–4–2*–0.80–0–*ct* 2
Bowling 216–3–72.00–0–0–2/105

Udal, John Symonds
Amateur. *b:* 10.11.1848, Birmingham. *d:* 13.3.1925, St John's Wood, London. Father of N. R. (Oxford U). Middle order right-hand batsman, right-arm bowler. *Sch* Bromsgrove. *Team* MCC (1871–75). *Tour* Fiji to New Zealand 1894/5.
Career batting
9–17–1–215–50–13.43–0–*ct* 3
Bowling 5–0
He did not play in any first-class matches whilst at Oxford U. His County cricket was for Dorset and Somerset. As Attorney-General of Fiji he did much to promote cricket there, as later he did in the Leeward Islands when Chief Justice.

Udal, Nicholas Robin
Amateur. *b:* 16.10.1883, Richmond, Surrey. *d:* 27.2.1964, Pembury, Kent. Son of J. S. (MCC and Fiji). Lower order right-hand batsman, right-arm fast bowler. *Sch* Winchester. *Team* Oxford U (1904–06, blue 1905 and 1906).
Career batting
14–24–5–387–49*–20.36–0–*ct* 17
Bowling 1439–65–22.13–5–2–7/133
His final first-class match was for MCC in 1914. He played County cricket for Dorset and Devon. A member of the Sudan Civil Service from 1906 to 1930, his opportunities for first-class cricket were very limited.

Ufton, Derek Gilbert
Professional. *b:* 31.5.1928, Crayford, Kent. Sound lower order left-hand batsman, wicket-keeper. *Team* Kent (1949–62, 148 matches).
Career batting
149–244–48–3919–119*–19.99–1–*ct* 270–*st* 44
A good soccer player, he appeared for Charlton Athletic at centre-half.

Ullathorne, Charles Edward
Professional. *b:* 11.4.1845, Hull, Yorkshire. *d:* 3.5.1904, Manchester. Middle order right-hand batsman, right-hand fast round-arm bowler, splendid cover point. *Team* Yorkshire (1868–75, 27 matches).
Career batting
31–53–9–326–28–7.40–0–*ct* 23
He was also a noted athlete.

Ulyett, George
Professional. *b:* 21.10.1851, Pitsmoor, Sheffield, Yorkshire. *d:* 18.6.1898, Pitsmoor, Sheffield, Yorkshire. He died of pneumonia contracted whilst watching Yorkshire play Kent at Bramall Lane. Forceful opening right-hand batsman, right-hand fast round-arm bowler, good field. *Team* Yorkshire (1873–93, 359 matches). *Tours* Lillywhite to Australia 1876/7; Harris to Australia 1878/9; Daft to North America 1879 (not first-class); Lillywhite, Shaw and Shrewsbury to Australia 1881/2, 1884/5, 1887/8; Warton to South Africa 1888/9. *Tests* England (1876/7 to 1890, 25 matches).
Career batting
537–928–40–20823–199*–23.44–18–*ct* 367
Bowling 13157–653–20.14–23–3–7/30
Test batting
25–39–0–949–149–24.33–1–*ct* 18
Bowling 1020–50–20.40–1–0–7/36
He hit 1,000 runs in a season ten times (best 1,562, av 31.87, in 1883). At the time of his death he was regarded as the greatest batsman that Yorkshire had produced and was particularly noted for his opening partnerships with L. Hall.

Umrigar, Pahlan Ratanji
Amateur. *b:* 28.3.1926, Sholapur, Maharashtra, India. Attacking middle order right-hand batsman, right-arm medium off break bowler. *Teams* Parsis (1944/5 to 1945/6); Bombay (1946/7 to 1962/3); Gujerat (1950/1 to 1951/2). *Tours* India to England 1952, 1959, to West Indies 1952/3, 1961/2, to Pakistan 1954/5, to Ceylon 1956/7; ACC to Pakistan 1961/2. *Tests* India (1948/9 to 1961/2, 59 matches).
Career batting
243–350–41–16155–252*–52.28–49–*ct* 216
Bowling 8350–325–25.69–14–2–7/32
Test batting
59–94–8–3631–223–42.22–12–*ct* 33
Bowling 1473–35–42.08–2–0–6/74
Although he completely failed in the Tests on the 1952 tour, he was the leading batsman in first-class matches with 1,688 runs, av 48.22, including no less than three double centuries; on the 1959 tour he hit 1,826 runs, av 55.33, with another three double centuries and hit 118 in the Old

Trafford Test; owing to injury he missed the last part of the tour as well as the last Test. He captained India in eight Tests, though not in England. His highest score was 252* for Indians v Cambridge U at Cambridge in 1959. He also hit 1,000 runs in a season twice in India. His final first-class match was for Dungarpur XI in 1967/8.

Underdown, George
Amateur. *b:* 1859, Petersfield, Hampshire. *d:* 29.5.1895, Petersfield, Hampshire. Middle order batsman, useful bowler. *Team* Hampshire (1882–85, 9 matches).
Career batting
10–18–0–231–63–12.83–0–*ct* 3
Bowling 80–1–80.00–0–0–1/15

Underwood, Arthur Joseph
Professional. *b:* 21.9.1927, Wiseton, Nottinghamshire. Lower order right-hand batsman, left-arm medium pace bowler. *Team* Nottinghamshire (1949–54, 14 matches).
Career batting
16–15–4–109–39–9.90–0–*ct* 12
Bowling 907–10–90.70–0–0–2/72

Underwood, Derek Leslie
Cricketer. *b:* 8.6.1945, Bromley, Kent. Lower order right-hand batsman, left-arm spin, either slow-medium or medium, bowler. *Team* Kent (1963–83, 425 matches). *Tours* MCC to Pakistan 1966/7, to Ceylon and Pakistan 1968/9, to Australia and New Zealand 1970/1, 1974/5, to West Indies 1973/4, to India, Sri Lanka and Australia 1976/7; England to Australia and India 1979/80, to India and Sri Lanka 1981/2; International XI to Africa and Asia 1967/8; International Wanderers to South Africa 1975/6; SAB to South Africa 1981/2; Norfolk to West Indies 1969/70. *Tests* England (1966 to 1981/2, 86 matches).
Career batting
580–606–168–4132–80–9.43–0–*ct* 238
Bowling 44014–2224–19.79–148–45–9/28
Test batting
86–116–35–937–45*–11.56–0–*ct* 44
Bowling 7674–297–25.83–17–6–8/51

The leading spin bowler in England for some 20 years, his accuracy combined with his ability to vary the pace of his deliveries give him the edge over other left-arm spin bowlers of the present generation. But for the fact that he left Test cricket to join World Series Cricket in 1977 and then after the reconciliation between Packer and the Establishment he again left to tour South Africa with the 1981/2 SAB side, Underwood by now probably would have been the leading wicket-taker in Test cricket.

His career began in 1963 in sensational fashion when he became the youngest player to take 100 wickets in a debut season. He has now taken 100 wickets in a season ten times (best 157 wickets, av 13.80, in 1966). He reached the milestone of 1,000 wickets in a career at the age of 25 – only two cricketers have improved on this record. The best bowling analyses of his career are 9 for 28 for Kent v Sussex at Hastings in 1964 and 9 for 32 for Kent v Surrey at the Oval in 1978.

He was banned from Test cricket for three years commencing 1981/2.

Underwood, William
Professional. *b:* 26.2.1853, Ruddington, Nottinghamshire. *d:* 9.5.1914, Bradmore, Nottinghamshire. He died by his own hand. Middle order right-hand batsman, slow right-arm bowler. *Team* Nottinghamshire (1881, 1 match).
Career batting
1–1–0–10–10–10.00–0–*ct* 0

He also played for Devonshire.

Unsworth, James
Professional. *b:* 4.3.1844, Everton, Liverpool, Lancashire. *d:* 1.1.1893, Warrington, Lancashire. Lower order right-hand batsman, right-hand fast round-arm bowler. *Team* Lancashire (1871, 2 matches).
Career batting
2–3–0–25–23–8.33–0–*ct* 2
Bowling 75–3–25.00–0–0–3/52

Unwin, Ernest James
Amateur. *b:* 18.9.1912, Birdbrook, Essex. Brother of F. St G. (Essex). Middle order right-hand batsman, right-arm fast medium bowler. *Sch* Haileybury. *Team* Essex (1932–39, 7 matches).
Career batting
7–14–0–152–48–10.85–0–*ct* 2
Bowling 103–0

He also played for Suffolk. A noted rugby footballer, he played for Rosslyn Park and England.

Unwin, Frederick St George
Amateur. *b:* 23.4.1911, Halstead, Essex. Brother of E. J. (Essex). Forcing right-hand batsman, right-arm medium pace bowler. *Sch* Haileybury. *Team* Essex (1932–50, 52 matches). *Tour* Martineau to Egypt 1938 (not first-class).
Career batting
53–87–9–1138–60–14.58–0–*ct* 33
Bowling 41–0

He was joint captain of Essex in 1939. His final first-class match was for Free Foresters in 1951. He also played for Suffolk.

Upton, Mark
Cricketer. *b:* 30.6.1950, Poole, Dorset. Tail end

right-hand batsman, slow left-arm bowler. *Team* Sussex (1971, 1 match).
Career batting
1–1–1–2–2*–no av–0–*ct* 0
Bowling 120–1–120.00–0–0–1/72

Urquhart, John Rankin
Amateur. *b:* 29.5.1921, Chelmsford, Essex. Lower order right-hand batsman, right-arm medium fast bowler. *Team* Cambridge U (1948, blue).
Career batting
4–6–2–13–6*–3.25–0–*ct* 0
Bowling 231–15–15.40–0–0–4/21

Usher, John
Professional. *b:* 26.2.1859, Staincliffe, Yorkshire. *d:* 10.8.1905, Haslingden, Lancashire. Lower order left-hand batsman, slow left-arm bowler, slip field. *Team* Yorkshire (1888, 1 match).
Career batting
1–2–0–7–5–3.50–0–*ct* 1
Bowling 31–2–15.50–0–0–2/11

Utley, Father Richard Peter Hugh
Amateur. *b:* 11.2.1906, Havant, Hampshire. *d:* 28.8.1968, Ampleforth, Yorkshire. Lower order right-hand batsman, right-arm fast bowler. *Sch* Ampleforth. *Team* Hampshire (1927–28, 27 matches).
Career batting
31–38–9–210–30–7.24–0–*ct* 12
Bowling 2370–90–26.33–4–1–6/43

VALENTINE, ALFRED LEWIS
Amateur. *b:* 29.4.1930, Kingston, Jamaica. Tail end right-hand batsman, slow left-arm bowler. *Team* Jamaica (1949/50 to 1964/5). *Tours* West Indies to England 1950, 1957, 1963, to Australia and New Zealand 1951/2, to New Zealand 1955/6, to Australia 1960/1. *Tests* West Indies (1950 to 1961/2, 36 matches).
Career batting
125–142–48–470–24*–5.00–0–*ct* 45
Bowling 12451–475–26.21–32–6–8/26
Test batting
36–51–21–141–14–4.70–0–*ct* 13
Bowling 4215–139–30.32–8–2–8/104

He created a sensation on his first tour to England – completely unknown before the visit, he took 123 wickets, av 17.94, in first-class matches and was the leading bowler in the Tests with 33 wickets, av 20.42. On his second tour to England he took 60 wickets, av 19.66, but was unable to retain his Test place – playing two games against England without taking a wicket. On his third English tour he was not a success and did not play in the Tests.

Valentine, Bryan Herbert
Amateur. *b:* 17.1.1908, Blackheath, Kent. *d:* 2.2.1983, Otford, Kent. Forceful middle order right-hand batsman, right-arm medium pace bowler, good field. *Sch* Repton. *Teams* Kent (1927–48, 308 matches); Cambridge U (1928–29, blue 1929). *Tours* Tennyson to Jamaica 1931/2; Martineau to Egypt 1933 1935, 1938 (not first-class); MCC to India and Ceylon 1933/4, to South Africa 1938/9. *Tests* England (1933/4 to 1938/9, 7 matches).
Career batting
399–645–38–18306–242–30.15–35–*ct* 289
Bowling 1125–27–41.66–0–0–3/58
Test batting
7–9–2–454–136–64.85–2–*ct* 2

He hit 1,000 runs in a season nine times (best 1,738, av 33.42, in 1933). Both his double centuries were for Kent, the highest being 242 v Leicestershire at Oakham in 1938. He was joint captain of Kent in 1937 and sole captain from 1946 to 1948. His final first-class match was for Free Foresters in 1950. He was also an excellent lawn tennis player.

Valentine, Vincent A.
Amateur. *b:* 4.4.1908, Port Antonio, Jamaica. *d:* 6.7.1972, Kingston, Jamaica. Attacking lower order right-hand batsman, right-arm fast medium bowler. *Team* Jamaica (1931/2 to 1938/9). *Tour* West Indies to England 1933. *Tests* West Indies (1933, 2 matches).
Career batting
24–33–5–500–59*–17.85–0–*ct* 11
Bowling 1980–49–40.40–0–0–4/83
Test batting
2–4–1–35–19*–11.66–0–*ct* 0
Bowling 104–1–104.00–0–0–1/55

He played in two Tests on the 1933 tour but made little impression, and his wickets in the first-class games were terribly expensive – 36, av 42.80.

Valiant, James
Professional. *b:* 1884, West Derby, Liverpool, Lancashire. *d:* 28.10.1917, Gaza, Palestine. Lower order batsman, useful bowler. *Team* Essex (1912, 1 match).

Career batting
1–2–1–3–3–3.00–0–*ct* 0
Bowling 20–0

Van der Bijl, Pieter Gerhart Vintcent
Amateur. *b:* 21.10.1907, Cape Town, South Africa. *d:* 16.2.1973, Kalk Bay, Cape, South Africa. Son of V. A. W. (Western Province), father of V. A. P. (Middlesex). Steady opening right-hand batsman. *Teams* Oxford U (1931–32, blue 1932); Western Province (1925/6 to 1931/2). *Tests* South Africa (1938/9, 5 matches).
Career batting
44–76–9–2692–195–40.17–5–*ct* 36–*st* 2
Bowling 158–5–31.60–0–0–2/20
Test batting
5–9–0–460–125–51.11–1–*ct* 1
His final first-class match was for the lst South African Division XI in 1942/3.

Van der Bijl, Vintcent Adriaan Pieter
Cricketer. *b:* 19.3.1948, Cape Town, South Africa. Grandson of V. A. W. (Western Province), son of P. G. V. (South Africa). Lower order right-hand batsman, right-arm fast medium bowler. *Teams* Natal (1968/9 to 1981/2); Middlesex (1980–81, 21 matches); Transvaal (1982/3).
Career batting
156–188–48–2269–87–16.20–0–*ct* 51
Bowling 12692–767–16.54–46–12–8/35
His first-class debut was for South African Universities in 1967/8. He headed the averages in 1980, his single full year in County cricket.

Van der Bijl, Voltelin Albert William
Amateur. *b:* 1872, South Africa. *d:* 2.10.1941, Cape Town, South Africa. Father of P. G. V. (South Africa), grandfather of V. A. P. (Middlesex). Lower order batsman, useful bowler. *Teams* Western Province (1890/1 to 1895/6); G. J. V. Weigall's XI (1904).
Career batting
7–11–1–176–61–17.60–0–*ct* 5
Bowling 421–19–22.16–1–0–6/56

Vanderbyl, Philip Breda
Amateur. *b:* 11.11.1867, Kensington, London. *d:* 20.3.1930, Cairo, Egypt. Middle order batsman. *Team* MCC (1900).
Career batting
1–1–0–38–38–38.00–0–*ct* 0

Van der Gucht, Paul Ian
Amateur. *b:* 2.11.1911, Sparken, Worksop, Nottinghamshire. Lower order right-hand batsman, wicket-keeper. *Sch* Radley. *Teams* Gloucestershire (1932–33, 33 matches); Bengal (1935/6 to 1947/8); Europeans (1935/6 to 1936/7).
Career batting
51–80–11–1587–115–23.00–1–*ct* 74–*st* 25
Bowling 5–0
His final match in England was for MCC in 1939.

Van der Knapp, David Saunders
Cricketer. *b:* 7.9.1948, Johannesburg, South Africa. Lower order right-hand batsman, off break bowler. *Teams* Lancashire (1967, 1 match); Transvaal (1967/8 to 1978/9).
Career batting
43–43–16–289–44–10.70–0–*ct* 39
Bowling 3389–121–28.00–7–0–6/61

Van der Merwe, Edward Alexander
Amateur. *b:* 9.11.1904, Rustenburg, South Africa. *d:* 28.2.1971, Johannesburg, South Africa. Lower order right-hand batsman, wicket-keeper. *Team* Transvaal (1928/9 to 1937/8). *Tours* South Africa to England 1929, to Australia 1931/2. *Tests* South Africa (1929 to 1935/6, 2 matches).
Career batting
27–36–9–287–35*–10.62–0–*ct* 35–*st* 29
Test batting
2–4–1–27–19–9.00–0–*ct* 3
The reserve wicket-keeper on the 1929 tour to England, he appeared in one Test. A good rugby footballer, he represented Transvaal.

Van der Merwe, Peter Lawrence
Amateur. *b:* 14.3.1937, Paarl, nr Cape Town, South Africa. Steady middle order right-hand batsman, slow left-arm bowler, good field. *Teams* Western Province (1958/9 to 1965/6); Eastern Province (1966/7 to 1968/9). *Tours* SA Fezala to England 1961; South Africa to Australia and New Zealand 1963/4, to England 1965. *Tests* South Africa (1963/4 to 1966/7, 15 matches).
Career batting
94–152–12–4086–128–29.18–4–*ct* 73
Bowling 2108–82–25.70–3–0–6/40
Test batting
15–23–2–533–76–25.38–0–*ct* 11
Bowling 22–1–22.00–0–0–1/6
He captained the South Africans on the 1965 tour and played in all three Tests, but his batting only proved moderately successful with 363 runs, av 16.50, in first-class matches. In all he captained South Africa in eight Tests. His first-class debut was for South African Universities in 1956/7.

Vanderspar, George Augustus Hunter
Amateur. *b:* 1858. *d:* 23.5.1940, Bournemouth, Hampshire. Middle order right-hand batsman. *Sch* Southampton College. *Team* MCC (1893). *Tours* Ceylon to Calcutta 1884/5, to Madras 1885/6, 1891/2 (none first-class).

Career batting
1–1–0–7–7–7.00–0–*ct* 0
He played County cricket for Somerset 1880 (pre-first-class). From 1884 to 1908 he was the organiser and promoter of cricket in Ceylon.

Van Geloven, John
Professional. *b:* 4.1.1934, Guiseley, Yorkshire. Middle order right-hand batsman, right-arm medium pace bowler. *Teams* Leicestershire (1956–65, 244 matches); Yorkshire (1955, 3 matches).
Career batting
247–431–44–7522–157*–19.43–5–*ct* 137
Bowling 13912–486–28.62–14–1–7/56
He hit 1,000 runs in a season three times (best 1,324, av 23.22, in 1959). In 1962 he took 100 wickets, av 28.11, performing the 'double'. From 1966 to 1973 he played for Northumberland, and in 1977 was appointed to the first-class umpires' list.

Van Geyzel, Carl Theodore
Amateur. *b:* 19.12.1902, Colombo, Ceylon. *d:* 18.1.1971, Lunnwila, Sri Lanka. Stylish middle order right-hand batsman. *Sch* Royal College, Colombo. *Teams* Cambridge U (1924); Ceylon (1926/7).
Career batting
2–4–0–74–66–18.50–0–*ct* 3
He gained an athletics blue and established a new high jump record of 6 ft 1½ in.

Vann, Denis William Arthur
Amateur. *b:* 21.11.1916, Northampton. *d:* 20.1.1961, Kettering, Northants. Middle order right-hand batsman. *Team* Northamptonshire (1936–37, 4 matches).
Career batting
4–6–0–47–16–7.83–0–*ct* 1
Bowling 104–2–52.00–0–0–2/26

Van Ryneveld, Anthony John
Amateur. *b:* 12.11.1925, Cape Town, South Africa. Middle order right-hand batsman, right-arm fast medium bowler. *Team* Oxford U (1947).
Career batting
1–2–0–69–50–34.50–0–*ct* 0
Bowling 2–0

Van Ryneveld, Clive Berrange
Amateur. *b:* 19.3.1928, Cape Town, South Africa. Enterprising middle order right-hand batsman, leg break bowler, good field. *Teams* Oxford U (1947–50, blue 1948–50); Western Province (1946/7 to 1962/3). *Tour* South Africa to England 1951. *Tests* South Africa (1951 to 1957/8, 19 matches).
Career batting
101–171–12–4803–150–30.20–4–*ct* 71
Bowling 6230–206–30.24–9–0–8/48
Test batting
19–33–6–724–83–26.81–0–*ct* 14
Bowling 671–17–39.47–0–0–4/67
On the 1951 tour to England he hit 983 runs, av 29.78, and played in all five Tests. He later captained South Africa in eight Tests in South Africa. An outstanding rugby footballer he played at stand off half for Oxford and England. After retiring from active sport he was elected to the South African Parliament.

Van Straubenzee, Sir Casimir Cartwright
Amateur. *b:* 11.11.1867. *d:* 28.3.1956, Lansdown, Bath, Somerset. Middle order batsman. *Team* MCC (1899).
Career batting
1–1–0–20–20–20.00–0–*ct* 0

Van Straubenzee, Henry Hamilton
Amateur. *b:* 7.3.1914, Johannesburg, South Africa. Lower order right-hand batsman, slow left-arm bowler. *Sch* Winchester. *Team* Essex (1938, 1 match).
Career batting
4–4–2–56–38–28.00–0–*ct* 0
Bowling 185–10–18.50–0–0–4/96
His final first-class match was for the Army in 1939.

Varey, David William
Cricketer. *b:* 15.10.1961, Darlington, Co Durham. Twin brother of J. G. (Oxford U). Opening right-hand batsman. *Sch* Birkenhead. *Team* Cambridge U (1981–83, blue 1982 and 1983).
Career batting
22–42–5–971–156*–26.24–1–*ct* 11
Bowling 4–0
His County cricket was for Cheshire.

Varey, Jonathan Guy
Cricketer. *b:* 15.10.1961, Darlington, Co Durham. Twin brother of D. W. (Cambridge U). Middle order right-hand batsman, right-arm medium pace bowler. *Sch* Birkenhead. *Team* Oxford U (1982–83, blue both years).
Career batting
13–22–8–426–69*–30.42–0–*ct* 3
Bowling 866–6–144.33–0–0–3/69
His County cricket was for Cheshire.

Varley, P.
Professional. Middle order batsman. *Team* North of England (1866).
Career batting
1–2–1–15–8*–15.00–0–*ct* 0

Vasey, Percy Walter
Amateur. *b:* 29.7.1883, Highbury, Middlesex. *d:* 11.9.1952, Crediton, Devon. Middle order right-hand batsman, slow right-arm bowler. *Sch* Merchant Taylors'. *Team* Somerset (1913, 1 match).
Career batting
1–2–0–13–10–6.50–0–*ct* 0
He also played for Hertfordshire.

Vassall, Gilbert Claude
Amateur. *b:* 5.4.1876, Hardington-Mandeville, Somerset. *d:* 19.9.1941, Oxford. Middle order batsman, useful bowler. *Sch* Charterhouse. *Team* Somerset (1902–05, 6 matches).
Career batting
6–10–1–46–27*–5.11–0–*ct* 4
Bowling 72–1–72.00–0–0–1/56

Vassila, George Charles
Professional. *b:* 1857, Richmond, Surrey. *d:* 1915, Epsom, Surrey. Lower order right-hand batsman, right-arm fast bowler. *Team* Middlesex (1880, 1 match).
Career batting
1–2–1–0–0*–0.00–0–*ct* 0
Bowling 37–0

Vaughan, Richard Thomas
Amateur. *b:* 28.5.1908, Mazatlan, Mexico. *d:* 1.4.1966, Woodborough, Wiltshire. Lower order right-hand batsman, wicket-keeper. *Sch* Repton. *Team* Cambridge U (1928).
Career batting
2–3–0–16–13–5.33–0–*ct* 2
His County cricket was for Berkshire.

Vaughan-Thomas, Hugh Wyndham
Amateur. *b:* 13.5.1910, Swansea, Glamorgan. Middle order right-hand batsman. *Team* Glamorgan (1933, 1 match).
Career batting
1–1–0–3–3–3.00–0–*ct* 1

Vaulkhard, Patrick
Amateur. *b:* 15.9.1911, Nottingham. Attacking middle order right-hand batsman, leg break bowler, wicket-keeper. *Sch* Oakham. *Teams* Derbyshire (1946–52, 65 matches); Nottinghamshire (1934, 9 matches).
Career batting
77–122–7–2460–264–21.39–1–*ct* 64–*st* 4
Bowling 124–1–124.00–0–0–1/30
He hit 264 for Derbyshire v Nottinghamshire at Trent Bridge in 1946. In 1950 he captained Derbyshire. He appeared for Northumberland in 1939 and was also a prominent member of Sir Julien Cahn's XI. A useful amateur soccer player he represented Nottinghamshire.

Vavasour, Sir Geoffrey William
Amateur. *b:* 5.9.1914, Queenstown, Ireland. Middle order right-hand batsman. *Team* Combined Services (1947).
Career batting
1–2–0–14–8–7.00–0–*ct* 0

Veal, Charles Lewis
Amateur. *b:* 29.8.1876, Bridgend, Glamorgan. *d:* 1.6.1929, Kensington, London. Middle order batsman. *Sch* Charterhouse and Repton. *Team* MCC (1906–10).
Career batting
6–11–0–145–41–13.18–0–*ct* 4

Veivers, Thomas Robert
Amateur. *b:* 6.4.1937, Beenleigh, Queensland, Australia. Middle order left-hand batsman, off break bowler. *Team* Queensland (1958/9 to 1967/8, 55 matches). *Tours* Australia to England 1964, to India and Pakistan 1964/5, to South Africa 1966/7. *Tests* Australia (1963/4 to 1966/7, 21 matches).
Career batting
106–162–24–5100–137–36.95–4–*ct* 52
Bowling 7393–191–38.70–3–0–5/63
Test batting
21–30–4–813–88–31.26–0–*ct* 7
Bowling 1375–33–41.66–0–0–4/68
He proved to be a useful all-rounder on the 1964 visit to England, playing in all five Tests, and in first-class games hitting 725 runs, av 34.52, and taking 52 wickets, av 36.17.

Venables, Rowland George
Amateur. *b:* 18.1.1846, Truro, Cornwall. *d:* 9.3.1920, Oswestry, Shropshire. Lower order right-hand batsman, left-hand medium pace round-arm bowler, mid off field. *Sch* Rugby. *Team* Oxford U (1866–69).
Career batting
2–3–1–26–24*–13.00–0–*ct* 0
Bowling 92–4–23.00–0–0–3/25
He was a prominent member of the Free Foresters, his County cricket was for Shropshire and Cornwall.

Venes, Richard Stephen
Amateur. *b:* 1885, Wandsworth, Surrey. *d:* 10.6.1959, Northampton. Lower order right-hand batsman, leg break and googly bowler. *Team* Northamptonshire (1922, 4 matches).
Career batting
4–8–2–8–4*–1.33–0–*ct* 1
Bowling 105–5–21.00–0–0–4/60

Vengsarkar, Dilip Balwant
Cricketer. *b:* 6.4.1956, Bombay, India. Stylish opening or middle order right-hand batsman, right-arm medium pace bowler. *Team* Bombay (1975/6 to 1981/2). *Tours* India to England 1979, 1982, to Australia 1977/8, to Australia and New Zealand 1980/1, to West Indies 1975/6, 1982/3, to Pakistan 1978/9, 1982/3. *Tests* India (1975/6 to 1982/3, 63 matches).
Career batting
147–238–25–9521–210–44.69–24–*ct* 111
Bowling 69–0
Test batting
63–103–10–3484–157*–37.46–6–*ct* 44
Bowling 17–0

On the 1979 tour to England he hit 751 runs, av 41.72, in first-class matches and in the four Tests 249 runs, av 41.50. On his second tour his figures were 610, av 55.45, and 193, av 38.60, his best innings in England being 157 in the Lord's Test of 1982. His highest score was 210 for Bombay v Baroda at Baroda in 1979/80. He hit 1,000 runs in a season in India twice (best 1,495, av 57.50, in 1979/80).

Venkataraghavan, Srinivasaraghavan
Cricketer. *b:* 21.4.1945, Madras, India. Tail end right-hand batsman, off break bowler. *Teams* Tamil Nadu (formerly Madras) (1963/4 to 1982/3); Derbyshire (1973–75, 46 matches). *Tours* India to England 1967, 1971, 1974, 1979, to West Indies 1970/1, 1975/6, 1982/3, to Ceylon 1973/4, to New Zealand 1975/6, to Australia 1977/8, to Pakistan 1978/9; Madras to Ceylon 1965/6, 1967/8, 1969/70, 1971/2. *Tests* India (1964/5 to 1982/3, 55 matches).
Career batting
328–444–80–6528–137–17.93–1–*ct* 311
Bowling 32441–1337–24.26–81–20–9/93
Test batting
55–74–12–737–64–11.88–0–*ct* 44
Bowling 5530–155–35.67–3–1–8/72

Although coming to England on four Test playing tours, he only made much impression on the 1971 visit when he took 63 wickets, av 24.90, in first-class matches and 13, av 26.92, in the Tests, being second in both sets of bowling averages. He captained India on the 1979 tour. His best season with Derbyshire was 1975 with 68 wickets, av 21.42, and his best bowling analysis in England was 9 for 93 for Indians v Hampshire at Bournemouth in 1971.

Venn, Horace
Amateur. *b:* 4.7.1892, Coventry, Warwickshire. *d:* 23.11.1953, Keresley, Coventry, Warwickshire. Middle order right-hand batsman. *Team* Warwickshire (1919–25, 34 matches).
Career batting
34–60–0–1047–151–17.45–2–*ct* 14
Bowling 28–0

Vere Hodge, Nicholas
Amateur. *b:* 31.10.1912, Woodford Green, Essex. Middle order right-hand batsman, wicket-keeper. *Sch* Uppingham. *Team* Essex (1936–39, 23 matches).
Career batting
23–38–6–713–108–22.15–2–*ct* 11

He did not appear in any first-class matches whilst at Cambridge U.

Verelst, Harry William
Amateur. *b:* 2.7.1846, Claughton, Cheshire. *d:* 5.4.1918, Aston, Derbyshire. Middle order right-hand batsman, long stop. *Sch* Rugby. *Team* Yorkshire (1868–69, 3 matches).
Career batting
11–18–4–215–78–15.35–0–*ct* 3–*st* 2

His first-class debut was for Gentlemen of the North in 1867 and his last first-class match for I Zingari in 1878.

Verity, Hedley
Professional. *b:* 18.5.1905, Headingley, Leeds, Yorkshire. *d:* 31.7.1943, Caserta, Italy. He died of wounds. Lower order right-hand batsman, slow left-arm bowler, good short leg. *Team* Yorkshire (1930–39, 278 matches). *Tours* MCC to Australia and New Zealand 1932/3, 1936/7, to Ceylon and India 1933/4, to South Africa 1938/9; Yorkshire to Jamaica 1935/6. *Tests* England (1931–39, 40 matches).
Career batting
378–416–106–5603–101–18.07–1–*ct* 269
Bowling 29146–1956–14.90–164–54–10/10
Test batting
40–44–12–669–66*–20.90–0–*ct* 30
Bowling 3510–144–24.37–5–2–8/43

The best left-arm spin bowler in England in the 1930s, he took 100 wickets in a season nine times, going on to 200 three times (best 216, av 13.18, in 1936). His best analysis in an innings was a record 10 for 10 for Yorkshire v Notts at Headingley in 1931; he also took 10 for 36 for Yorkshire v Warwickshire at Headingley in 1931 and in addition had nine wickets in an innings seven times, all for Yorkshire.

Verity, Stuart Anthony
Cricketer. *b:* 1948, Bradford, Yorkshire. Lower order right-hand batsman, right-arm medium pace bowler. *Team* Oxford U (1970).
Career batting
4–7–2–55–15–11.00–0–*ct* 0
Bowling 260–4–65.00–0–0–3/42

Vernon, George Frederick
Amateur. *b:* 20.6.1856, London. *d:* 10.8.1902, Elmina, Gold Coast. He died of malarial fever. Attractive middle order right-hand batsman, occasional slow under-arm bowler, excellent deep field. *Sch* Rugby. *Team* Middlesex (1878–95, 103 matches). *Tours* Bligh to Australia 1882/3; Vernon to Australia 1887/8, to Ceylon and India 1889/90 (not first-class); Hawke to India 1892/3. *Test* England (1882/3, 1 match).
Career batting
239–391–21–7070–160–19.10–4–*ct* 171
Bowling 69–2–34.50–0–0–1/11
Test batting
1–2–1–14–11*–14.00–0–*ct* 0
He captained the 1887/8 team to Australia and the 1889/90 team to India. A noted rugby footballer, he played for Blackheath and England.

Vernon, John Michael
Amateur. *b:* 27.7.1922, Port Said, Egypt. Middle order right-hand batsman, right-arm medium pace bowler. *Sch* Tonbridge. *Team* Combined Services (1949–52).
Career batting
8–13–0–290–83–22.30–0–*ct* 5
Bowling 100–2–50.00–0–0–1/8

Vernon, Martin Jeffrey
Cricketer. *b:* 9.7.1951, Marylebone, London. Lower order right-hand batsman, right-arm fast medium bowler. *Teams* Gloucestershire (1977, 5 matches); Middlesex (1974–76, 16 matches).
Career batting
22–27–5–146–27–6.63–0–*ct* 5
Bowling 1198–31–38.64–2–1–6/58

Verrinder, Alan Otto Charles
Cricketer. *b:* 28.7.1955, Henley on Thames, Oxon. Lower order right-hand batsman, right-arm fast medium bowler. *Teams* Kent (1977, 1 match); Surrey (1974–76, 3 matches).
Career batting
4–4–1–24–23–8.00–0–*ct* 3
Bowling 144–4–36.00–0–0–2/42

Vials, George Alfred Turner
Amateur. *b:* 18.3.1887, Northampton. *d:* 26.4.1974, Northampton. Middle order right-hand batsman. *Sch* Wellingborough. *Team* Northamptonshire (1905–22, 122 matches).
Career batting
122–220–10–3808–129–18.15–2–*ct* 105
Bowling 19–0
He captained Northants from 1911 to 1913 and was President of the County Club from 1956 to 1968. He also played soccer for Northampton Town and hockey for the County.

Vickery, Anthony
Amateur. *b:* 26.8.1925, Taunton, Somerset. Middle order right-hand batsman. *Team* Somerset (1947–48, 6 matches).
Career batting
6–12–1–89–21–8.09–0–*ct* 2

Vidler, John Lionel Symonds
Amateur. *b:* 30.3.1890, Rye, Sussex. *d:* 15.10.1967, Rye, Sussex. Middle order right-hand batsman, right-arm medium pace bowler. *Sch* Repton. *Teams* Oxford U (1910–12, blue all three years); Sussex (1910–19, 7 matches).
Career batting
29–52–6–682–55–14.39–0–*ct* 21
Bowling 1861–81–22.97–3–1–7/23
He also played for Oxfordshire.

Vigar, Frank Henry
Professional. *b:* 14.7.1917, Bruton, Somerset. Sound middle order right-hand batsman, leg break bowler, good close field. *Team* Essex (1938–54, 256 matches).
Career batting
257–399–62–8858–145–26.28–12–*ct* 197
Bowling 9135–241–37.90–8–0–8/128
He hit 1,000 runs in a season three times (best 1,735, av 35.40, in 1947).

Vigar, Herbert Evelyn
Professional. *b:* 29.11.1883, Redhill, Surrey. *d:* 27.10.1946, Redhill, Surrey. Lower order right-hand batsman, wicket-keeper. *Team* Surrey (1906–11, 15 matches).
Career batting
15–21–2–226–33*–11.89–0–*ct* 21–*st* 2

Viljoen, Kenneth George
Amateur. *b:* 14.5.1910, Windsorton, Kimberley, South Africa. *d:* 21.1.1974, Johannesburg, South Africa. Sound right-hand middle order batsman, excellent outfield. *Teams* Griqualand West (1926/7 to 1930/1); Orange Free State (1933/4 to 1935/6); Transvaal (1936/7 to 1948/9). *Tours* South Africa to Australia and New Zealand 1931/2, to England 1935, 1947. *Tests* South Africa (1930/1 to 1948/9, 27 matches).

Career batting
133–209–25–7964–215–43.28–23–*ct* 49
Bowling 722–29–24.89–0–0–4/23
Test batting
27–50–2–1365–124–28.43–2–*ct* 5
Bowling 23–0

He headed the first-class batting averages on the 1935 tour with 1,454 runs, av 46.90, and in the Tests hit 244 runs, av 48.80. On his return in 1947 he had a very similar record with 1,441 runs, av 49.68, though he was not quite so successful in the Tests. His highest innings in England was 201 v Sussex at Hove in 1947. His two other double centuries were made in South Africa, the highest being 215 for Griqualand West v Western Province at Kimberley in 1929/30. After retiring he was President of the South African Cricket Association. He was manager of the South African touring sides to Australia and New Zealand in 1952/3 and 1963/4 and to England in 1955.

Vince, John
Professional. *b:* 31.12.1849, Hackbridge, Surrey. *d:* 1886, Croydon, Surrey. Lower order right-hand batsman, right-arm fast bowler. *Team* Surrey (1870, 11 matches).
Career batting
11–22–1–60–10*–2.85–0–*ct* 11
Bowling 454–15–30.26–0–0–4/58

Vincent, Cyril Leverton
Amateur. *b:* 16.2.1902, Johannesburg, South Africa. *d:* 24.8.1968, Durban, South Africa. Lower order right-hand batsman, slow left-arm bowler. *Team* Transvaal (1920/1 to 1930/1). *Tours* South Africa to England 1929, 1935, to Australia and New Zealand 1931/2. *Tests* South Africa (1927/8 to 1935, 25 matches).
Career batting
85–117–29–1582–83–17.97–0–*ct* 68
Bowling 7006–293–23.91–16–2–7/36
Test batting
25–38–12–526–60–20.23–0–*ct* 27
Bowling 2631–84–31.32–3–0–6/51

In England in 1929 he took 68 wickets, av 28.80, and appeared in four Tests. On his second tour he took 92 wickets, av 20.90, and again played in four Tests. His final first-class match was for the South African Air Force XI in 1942/3. He was Chairman of the South African Selection Committee, as well as being on the Transvaal Committee. A noted baseball player, he represented South Africa.

Vincent, Sir Harold Graham
Amateur. *b:* 13.11.1891, Hendon, Middlesex. *d:* 5.11.1981, Tonbridge, Kent. Middle order right-hand batsman. *Sch* Haileybury. *Team* Cambridge U (1914, blue).
Career batting
4–8–0–106–41–13.25–0–*ct* 11
Bowling 2–0

Vincett, John Herbert
Professional, but amateur in 1921. *b:* 24.5.1883, Hastings, Sussex. *d:* 28.12.1953, Lambeth, London. Lower order right-hand batsman, right-arm medium pace bowler. *Teams* Surrey (1921, 2 matches); Sussex (1907–19, 169 matches).
Career batting
172–260–49–3464–90*–16.41–0–*ct* 116
Bowling 8984–342–26.26–19–0–7/41

Vine, Joseph
Professional. *b:* 15.5.1875, Willingdon, Sussex. *d:* 25.4.1946, Hove, Sussex. Forcing right-hand batsman, leg break bowler. *Teams* Sussex (1896–1922, 506 matches); London County (1901–04). *Tours* MCC to Australia 1911/12. *Tests* England (1911/12, 2 matches).
Career batting
547–920–79–25171–202–29.92–34–*ct* 240
Bowling 19541–685–28.52–27–3–8/68
Test batting
2–3–2–46–36–46.00–0–*ct* 0

He hit 1,000 runs in a season fourteen times (best 1,871, av 34.01, in 1905). His only double century was 202 for Sussex v Northamptonshire at Hastings in 1920. He appeared in 421 consecutive matches for Sussex. In 1901 he took 113 wickets, av 29.72, and completed the 'double'.

Virgin, Roy Thomas
Professional. *b:* 26.8.1939, Taunton, Somerset. Opening right-hand batsman, leg break bowler, occasional wicket-keeper. *Teams* Northamptonshire (1973–77, 103 matches); Somerset (1957–72, 321 matches); Western Province (1972/3). *Tour* Commonwealth to Pakistan 1970/1.
Career batting
437–773–39–21930–179*–29.87–37–*ct* 414
Bowling 340–4–85.00–0–0–1/6

He hit 1,000 runs in a season twelve times, going on to 2,000 once : 2,223, av 47.29, in 1970. He was appointed County captain of Northants in 1975, but resigned midway through the season.

Viswanath, Gundappa Rangnath
Cricketer. *b:* 12.2.1949, Bhadravati, Mysore, India. Brother-in-law of S. M. Gavaskar (India). Attractive middle order right-hand batsman, leg break bowler. *Team* Karnataka (formerly Mysore) (1967/8 to 1982/3). *Tours* India to England 1971, 1974, 1979, 1982, to Sri Lanka 1973/4, to Australia 1977/8, to Australia and New

Zealand 1980/1, to West Indies 1970/1, 1975/6, New Zealand 1975/6, to Pakistan 1978/9, 1982/3; Wadekar to Sri Lanka 1975/6. *Tests* India (1969/70 to 1982/3, 91 matches).
Career batting
280–442–40–16513–247–41.07–40–*ct* 211
Bowling 685–15–45.66–0–0–2/21
Test batting
91–155–10–6080–222–41.93–14–*ct* 63
Bowling 46–1–46.00–0–0–1/11

He played in all the Tests on each of his four tours to England, his most successful visit being in 1982 when he hit 561 runs, av 62.33, in first-class matches and 189 runs, av 47.25, in the three Tests. In 1979 his figures were 757, av 50.46, and 341, av 48.71. In 1971 and 1974 his record was not so impressive. None of his double centuries was scored in England. His greatest feat was perhaps to score 230 on his first-class debut for Mysore v Andhra at Vijayawada in 1967/8, though he also hit a century on his Test debut, in the second innings v Australia at Kanpur in 1969/70. His highest score was 247 for Karnataka v Uttar Pradesh at Mohan Nagar in 1977/8. He hit 1,000 runs in a season in India three times (best 1,538, av 53.33, in 1974/5). He played in a record 87 consecutive Test matches.

Vivian, Graham Ellery
Cricketer. *b:* 28.2.1946, Auckland, New Zealand. Son of H. G. (New Zealand). Dashing middle order left-hand batsman, leg break bowler. *Team* Auckland (1966/7 to 1978/9). *Tours* New Zealand to India 1964/5, to England 1965, to Australia 1969/70, 1972/3, to West Indies 1971/2. *Tests* New Zealand (1964/5 to 1971/2, 5 matches).
Career batting
88–140–25–3259–137*–28.33–3–*ct* 41
Bowling 2128–56–38.00–1–0–5/59
Test batting
5–6–0–110–43–18.33–0–*ct* 3
Bowling 107–1–107.00–0–0–1/14

On the 1965 tour to England he played in only eight matches and no Tests. He made his first-class debut at Calcutta in the Second Test v India in 1964/5.

Vivian, Henry Gifford
Amateur. *b:* 4.11.1912, Auckland, New Zealand. *d:* 12.8.1983, Auckland, New Zealand. Father of G. E. (New Zealand). Attractive middle order left-hand batsman, slow left-arm bowler, good field. *Team* Auckland (1930/1 to 1938/9). *Tours* New Zealand to England 1931, 1937, to Australia 1937/8. *Tests* New Zealand (1931–37, 7 matches).
Careeer batting
85–143–15–4443–165–34.71–6–*ct* 71
Bowling 6160–223–27.62–12–2–6/49
Test batting
7–10–0–421–100–42.10–1–*ct* 4
Bowling 633–17–37.23–0–0–4/58

In 1931 he hit 1,002 runs, av 30.36, and played in two Tests, whilst in 1937 he made 1,118 runs, av 29.42, and appeared in all three Tests, his bowling also being useful.

Vizard, Walter Oswald
Amateur. *b:* 16.11.1861, Bellary, India. *d:* 10.1.1929, Bayswater, London. Lower order right-hand batsman, wicket-keeper. *Sch* Clifton. *Team* Gloucestershire (1882–90, 18 matches).
Career batting
18–32–2–256–49*–8.53–0–*ct* 11–*st* 1

Vizianagram, The Rajkumar of, Sir Vijay Anand
Amateur. *b:* 28.12.1905, Benares, India. *d:* 2.12.1965, Benares, India. Stylish middle order right-hand batsman. *Teams* Vizianagram's XI (1930/1 to 1935/6); Indians (Madras) (1930/1 to 1933/4); United Provinces (1934/5 to 1935/6). *Tours* India to England 1936; Vizianagram's XI to India and Ceylon 1930/1. *Tests* India (1936, 3 matches).
Career batting
47–73–7–1228–77–18.60–0–*ct* 18
Bowling 139–4–34.75–0–0–1/1
Test batting
3–6–2–33–19*–8.25–0–*ct* 1

He was a great patron of Indian cricket and organised his own Team, which played first-class matches. He captained the 1936 Indian side to England and led India in the three Tests. In first-class matches on the tour he scored 600 runs, av 16.21. During the tour he received a knighthood. From 1954 to 1956 he was President of the Indian Cricket Board of Control. He was also a member of the Indian Parliament. For several seasons he broadcast Test match commentaries.

Voce, William
Professional. *b:* 8.8.1909, Annesley Woodhouse, Notts. *d:* 6.6.1984, Nottingham. Attacking lower order right-hand batsman, left-arm fast medium, or slow medium, bowler. *Team* Nottinghamshire (1927–52, 345 matches). *Tours* MCC to West Indies 1929/30, to South Africa 1930/1, to Australia and New Zealand 1932/3, 1936/7, 1946/7. *Tests* England (1929/30 to 1946/7, 27 matches).
Career batting
426–525–130–7590–129–19.21–4–*ct* 286
Bowling 35961–1558–23.08–84–20–8/30
Test batting
27–38–15–308–66–13.39–0–*ct* 15
Bowling 2733–98–27.88–3–2–7/70

He took 100 wickets in a season six times (best

139, av 21.58, in 1935). He hit 1,020 runs, av 35.17, in 1933. His best remembered Test series was in 1932/3 in Australia when he partnered Larwood, but his best record came in the 1936/7 series when he was England's best bowler with 26 wickets, av 21.53. Because of the controversial 'bodyline' tour, he did not play for England for nearly four years between 1932/3 and the final Test of 1936. He retired from regular County cricket in 1947 and from then until 1952 was coach to Nottinghamshire CCC.

Vogler, Albert Edward Ernest
Professional in 1906, but reverted to amateur in 1907. *b:* 28.11.1876, Swartwater, nr Queenstown, South Africa. *d:* 9.8.1946, Pietermaritzburg, South Africa. Middle order right-hand batsman, leg break and googly bowler. *Teams* Natal (1903/4); Eastern Province (1905/6 to 1906/7); Transvaal (1904/5 to 1909/10); Middlesex (1906, 1 match). *Tours* South Africa to England 1907, to Australia 1910/11. *Tests* South Africa (1905/6 to 1910/11, 15 matches).
Career batting
83–136–19–2375–103–20.29–1–*ct* 81
Bowling 7182–393–18.27–31–7–10/26
Test batting
15–26–6–340–65–17.00–0–2–*ct* 20
Bowling 1455–64–22.73–5–1–7/94

On his tour to England in 1907 he took 119 wickets, av 15.62, in first-class matches and 15, av 19.66, in the Tests. The previous year he had been on the groundstaff at Lord's with the intention of qualifying for Middlesex, but returned to South Africa at the end of that season. His final first-class match was for Woodbrook C & G in 1912. His best innings analysis was 10 for 26 for Eastern Province v Griqualand West at Johannesburg in 1906/7. His final first-class match in South Africa was for Tancred's XI in 1911/12.

Von Ernsthausen, Adolph Christian Ernest
(changed to Howeson in 1914)
Amateur. *b:* 17.10.1880, Belsize Park, Middlesex. *d:* 29.5.1928, Ditton Hill, Surrey. Hard hitting lower order right-hand batsman, right-arm fast bowler. *Sch* Uppingham. *Teams* Surrey (1900–01, 2 matches); Oxford U (1902–04, blue all three years).
Career batting
30–49–7–506–45–12.04–0–*ct* 25
Bowling 2605–94–27.71–4–0–7/80

A skilled chess player, he represented Oxford v Cambridge from 1901 to 1904.

Voss, Ralph
Professional. *b:* 30.3.1860, Croydon, Surrey. *d:* 16.11.1900, Croydon, Surrey. Lower order right-hand batsman, useful bowler. *Team* Surrey (1883–86, 3 matches).
Career batting
3–5–2–10–7–3.33–0–*ct* 0
Bowling 53–2–26.50–0–0–2/31

Voss, Richard Zahn Hartwig
Amateur. *b:* 10.11.1880, Altrincham, Cheshire. *d:* 3.9.1948, Flixton, Lancashire. Middle order right-hand batsman. *Teams* Oxford U (1901–03); London County (1903).
Career batting
8–16–1–276–50–18.40–0–*ct* 2
Bowling 32–0

His County cricket was for Cheshire.

Voules, Rev Stirling Cookesley
Amateur. *b:* 4.1.1843, Middle Chinnock, Somerset. *d:* 6.5.1923, Maida Hill, London. Forcing middle order right-hand batsman, right-hand fast round-arm bowler. *Sch* Marlborough. *Team* Oxford U (1863–66, blue all four years).
Career batting
24–37–3–664–78–19.52–0–*ct* 24
Bowling 479–34+6–14.08–3–0–7/26

He retired from first-class cricket on entering the Church. His County cricket was for Somerset (pre-first-class), Devon, Dorset and Staffordshire. His first-class debut was for Gentlemen of the South in 1862 and his final first-class match for Southgate in 1867. A good athlete he was best known as a sprinter in the 100 and 440 yards.

Vowles, Roger Charles
Professional. *b:* 5.4.1932, Grimsby, Lincs. Middle order right-hand batsman, right-arm medium pace bowler. *Team* Nottinghamshire (1957–61, 16 matches).
Career batting
16–28–3–292–54–11.68–0–*ct* 7
Bowling 920–23–43.00–0–0–4/106

Vyse, Edmund Waller
Amateur. *b:* 20.2.1831, Luton, Bedfordshire. *d:* 11.4.1890, Westgate on Sea, Kent. Middle order right-hand batsman. *Team* Surrey (1857, 2 matches).
Career batting
13–22–4–116–24–6.44–0–*ct* 5

His first-class debut was for the Surrey Club in 1854 and his final match for Southgate in 1866. He also played for Bedfordshire and Buckinghamshire.

WADDINGTON, ABRAHAM (known as Abram) Professional. *b:* 4.2.1893, Clayton, Thornton, Yorkshire. *d:* 28.10.1959, Scarborough, Yorkshire. Tail end right-hand batsman, left-arm fast medium bowler. *Team* Yorkshire (1919–27, 255 matches). *Tour* MCC to Australia 1920/1. *Tests* England (1920/1, 2 matches).
Career batting
266–265–69–2527–114–12.89–1–*ct* 231
Bowling 16833–852–19.75–51–10–8/34
Test batting
2–4–0–16–7–4.00–0–*ct* 1
Bowling 119–1–119.00–0–0–1/35

He took 100 wickets in a season five times (best 141, av 16.79, in 1920). He kept goal for Bradford City and Halifax and was also a skilful golfer.

Waddington, John Ernest Walter
Amateur. *b:* 22.5.1910, Woodford Green, Essex. Middle order right-hand batsman. *Sch* Chigwell. *Team* Essex (1931, 1 match).
Career batting
1–1–0–8–8–8.00–0–*ct* 0

Waddy, Bernard Broughton
Amateur. *b:* 3.7.1911, Parramatta, New South Wales, Australia. *d:* 7.8.1981, Winchester, Hampshire. Son of P. S. (Oxford U), nephew of E. F. (Warwickshire and New South Wales) and E. L. (New South Wales). Lower order right-hand batsman, right-arm medium pace bowler. *Team* Oxford U (1932).
Career batting
4–6–0–49–26–8.16–0–*ct* 0
Bowling 206–7–29.42–0–0–2/11

His final first-class match was for MCC in 1936.

Waddy, Rev Ernest Frederick
Amateur. *b:* 5.10.1880, Morpeth, New South Wales, Australia. *d:* 23.9.1958, South Littleton, Evesham, Worcestershire. Brother of E. L. (New South Wales) and P. S. (Oxford U), uncle of B. B. (Oxford U). Middle order right-hand batsman. *Teams* New South Wales (1902/03 to 1910/11, 28 matches); Warwickshire (1919–22, 26 matches). *Tour* Waddy to Ceylon 1913/4 (not first-class).
Career batting
55–87–5–2326–129–28.36–4–*ct* 43
Bowling 23–0

Waddy, Canon Percival Stacy
Amateur. *b:* 8.1.1875, Morpeth, New South Wales, Australia. *d:* 8.2.1937, St Pancras, London. Brother of E. F. (New South Wales and Warwickshire) and E. L. (New South Wales), father of B. B. (Oxford U). Middle order right-hand batsman, right-arm medium pace bowler. *Team* Oxford U (1896–97, blue both years).
Career batting
13–20–3–400–107*–23.52–1–*ct* 13
Bowling 914–39–23.45–1–0–5/96

He was Secretary of the Society for the Propagation of the Gospel.

Wade, Herbert Frederick
Amateur. *b:* 14.9.1905, Durban, South Africa. *d:* 22.11.1980, Johannesburg, South Africa. Brother of W. W. (South Africa). Forceful opening or middle order right-hand batsman. *Team* Natal (1924/5 to 1936/7). *Tour* South Africa to England 1935. *Tests* South Africa (1935 to 1935/6, 10 matches).
Career batting
74–118–9–3858–190–35.39–9–*ct* 50
Test batting
10–18–2–327–40*–20.43–0–*ct* 4

He captained the 1935 touring team and led South Africa in the five Tests. He hit 1,042 runs, av 28.94.

Wade, Saul
Professional. *b:* 8.2.1858, Farsley, Leeds, Yorkshire. *d:* 5.11.1931, Oldham, Lancashire. Middle order right-hand batsman, slow right-arm off break bowler. *Team* Yorkshire (1886–90, 66 matches).
Career batting
70–120–24–1490–74*–15.52–0–*ct* 31
Bowling 2610–136–19.19–7–2–7/28

His first-class debut was for L. Hall's XI in 1885.

Wade, Thomas Henry
Professional. *b:* 24.11.1910, Maldon, Essex. Lower order left-hand batsman, off break bowler, neat wicket-keeper. *Team* Essex (1929–50, 318 matches). *Tour* MCC to Australia 1936/7 (co-opted for 2 matches).
Career batting
321–476–135–5024–96–14.73–0–*ct* 414–*st* 178
Bowling 1418–48–29.54–1–0–5/64

A useful soccer player, he appeared for Southend United.

Wadekar, Ajit Laxman
Amateur. *b:* 1.4.1941, Bombay, India. Stylish middle order left-hand batsman, left-arm medium, or slow, bowler. *Team* Bombay (1958/9 to 1974/5). *Tours* India to England 1967, 1971, 1974, to Australia and New Zealand 1967/8, to West Indies 1970/1, to Sri Lanka 1973/4, to East Africa 1967/8; State Bank of India to Ceylon

1966/7, 1968/9. *Tests* India (1966/7 to 1974, 37 matches).
Career batting
237–360–33–15380–323–47.03–36–*st* 271
Bowling 908–21–43.23–0–0–2/0
Test batting
37–71–3–2113–143–31.07–1–*ct* 46
Bowling 55–0

He batted well on all three visits to England, being captain in both 1971 and 1974. His best batting came in 1971 with 1,057 runs, av 40.65. In all he led India in 16 Tests. His highest innings was 323 for Bombay v Mysore at Bombay in 1966/7 and both his double centuries were scored in India. He hit 1,000 runs in India three times (best 1,321, av 60.40, in 1966/7).

Wadey, Alan Nigel Charles
Cricketer. *b:* 12.9.1950, Billingshurst, Sussex. Lower order right-hand batsman, right-arm medium pace bowler. *Sch* Seaford College. *Team* Sussex (1975, 1 match).
Career batting
1–2–2–0–0*–no av–0–*ct* 0
Bowling 44–1–44.00–0–0–1/44

Wadsworth, Ernest
Professional. *b:* 30.9.1850, Manchester, Lancashire. *d:* 7.1.1918, Bowden, Cheshire. Middle order right-hand batsman, right-hand fast round-arm bowler, long-leg. *Team* Lancashire (1871–79, 7 matches).
Career batting
7–13–0–69–30–5.30–0–*ct* 1
Bowling 13–0

Wadsworth, Kenneth John
Cricketer. *b:* 30.11.1946, Nelson, New Zealand. *d:* 19.8.1976, Nelson, New Zealand. He died of cancer. Middle order right-hand batsman, wicket-keeper, occasional slow medium right-arm bowler. *Teams* Central Districts (1968/9 to 1971/2); Canterbury (1972/3 to 1975/6). *Tours* New Zealand to England 1969, 1973, to Australia 1969/70, 1970/1, 1973/4, to India and Pakistan 1969/70, to West Indies 1971/2. *Tests* New Zealand (1969 to 1975/6, 33 matches).
Career batting
118–166–23–3664–117–25.62–2–*ct* 265–*st* 26
Bowling 10–0
Test batting
33–51–4–1010–80–21.48–0–*ct* 92–*st* 4

He was the principal wicket-keeper on both his tours to England and played in all Tests on both visits. He had only a modest batting record.

Wagener, Jack Gordon
Amateur. *b:* January, 1905, Eastbourne, Sussex. Lower order left-hand batsman, right-arm fast medium bowler. *Sch* Bradfield. *Teams* Cambridge U (1927); Sussex (1927–30, 9 matches).
Career batting
12–15–3–310–80*–25.83–0–*ct* 3
Bowling 476–8–59.50–0–0–3/74

His final first-class match was for the Gentlemen of England in 1931.

Waghorn, Leslie Arthur
Professional. *b:* 29.7.1906, Robertsbridge, Sussex. *d:* 22.8.1979, Robertsbridge, Sussex. Lower order left-hand batsman, slow left-arm bowler. *Team* Sussex (1926–27, 4 matches).
Career batting
5–8–1–14–7–2.00–0–*ct* 4
Bowling 263–4–65.75–0–0–2/34

His final first-class match was for MCC in 1928.

Wagstaff, Hugh
Professional. *b:* 15.10.1895, Romford, Essex. *d:* 2.3.1970, Hornchurch, Essex. Tail end batsman, right-arm medium pace bowler. *Team* Essex (1920–21, 5 matches).
Career batting
5–6–4–19–17*–9.50–0–*ct* 0
Bowling 135–2–67.50–0–0–1/19

Wagstaffe, Michael Christopher
Cricketer. *b:* 26.9.1945, Kohat, India. Lower order left-hand batsman, slow left-arm bowler. *Sch* Rossall. *Team* Oxford U (1972, blue).
Career batting
13–23–7–233–42–14.56–0–*ct* 5
Bowling 870–28–38.07–0–0–4/96

His County cricket was for Dorset commencing 1972.

Wainwright, Edward
Professional. *b:* 8.4.1865, Tinsley, Sheffield, Yorkshire. *d:* 28.10.1919, Sheffield, Yorkshire. He died after a long illness. Middle order right-hand batsman, right-arm medium off break bowler. *Team* Yorkshire (1888–1902, 356 matches). *Tour* Stoddart to Australia 1897/8. *Tests* England (1893 to 1897/8, 5 matches).
Career batting
392–607–32–12513–228–21.76–19–*ct* 350
Bowling 19536–1071–18.24–63–15–9/66
Test batting
5–9–0–132–49–14.66–0–*ct* 2
Bowling 73–0

He hit 1,000 runs in a season three times (best 1,612, av 35.82, in 1897) and he took 100 wickets in a season five times (best 166, av 12.73, in 1894). In 1897 he performed the 'double'. His only double century was 228 for Yorkshire v Surrey at the Oval in 1899 and his best innings analysis 9 for 66 for Yorkshire v Middlesex at Bramall Lane in 1894.

Wainwright, Thomas Dodsworth
Amateur. *b:* 12.11.1940, Bombay, India. Middle order right-hand batsman. *Sch* Eastbourne. *Team* L. C. Steven's XI (1961).
Career batting
1–2–0–37–28–18.50–0–*ct* 0

Wainwright, Walker
Professional. *b:* 21.1.1882, Rotherham, Yorkshire. *d:* 31.12.1961, Winchester, Hampshire. Middle order left-hand batsman, slow left-arm bowler. *Team* Yorkshire (1903–05, 24 matches).
Career batting
25–38–3–652–62–18.62–0–*ct* 21
Bowling 582–19–30.63–1–0–6/49
He was later a first-class umpire.

Wait, Owen John
Amateur. *b:* 2.8.1926, Dulwich, London. *d:* 26.4.1981, Bromley, Kent. Lower order right-hand batsman, right-arm fast medium bowler. *Sch* Dulwich. *Teams* Cambridge U (1949–51, blue 1949 and 1951); Surrey (1950–51, 7 matches).
Career batting
45–40–17–132–19–5.73–0–*ct* 17
Bowling 3280–125–26.24–6–1–6/18
His final first-class match was for MCC in 1961.
He was elected to the MCC Committee in 1977.

Waite, Anthony Charles
Professional. *b:* 29.5.1943, Pinner, Middlesex. Lower order right-hand batsman, right-arm fast medium bowler. *Team* Middlesex (1962–64, 11 matches).
Career batting
12–14–8–58–29–9.66–0–*ct* 1
Bowling 691–18–38.38–0–0–4/25
He also played for Buckinghamshire.

Waite, John Henry Bickford
Amateur. *b:* 19.1.1930, Johannesburg, South Africa. Sound defensive opening or middle order right-hand batsman, wicket-keeper. *Teams* Eastern Province (1948/9 to 1951/2); Transvaal (1953/4 to 1965/6). *Tours* South Africa to England 1951, 1955, 1960, to Australia and New Zealand 1952/3, 1963/4. *Tests* South Africa (1951 to 1964/5, 50 matches).
Career batting
199–314–34–9812–219–35.04–23–*ct* 426–*st* 84
Bowling 8–0
Test batting
50–86–7–2405–134–30.44–4–*ct* 124–*st* 17
Although he completed 1,000 runs only on his 1951 tour to England (1,011, av 33.70) he proved very effective in the Tests and actually topped the Test averages in 1960 with 267 runs, av 38.14. He missed only one of the 15 Tests which were played on the three tours and was the leading wicket-keeper-batsman of his day. His highest score was 219 for Eastern Province v Griqualand West at Kimberley in 1950/1.

Waite, Mervyn George
Amateur. *b:* 7.1.1911, Kent Town, South Australia. Middle or lower order right-hand batsman, right-arm medium pace bowler. *Team* South Australia (1930/1 to 1945/6, 72 matches). *Tour* Australia to England 1938. *Tests* Australia (1938, 2 matches).
Career batting
103–155–15–3888–137–27.77–1–*ct* 66
Bowling 6071–192–31.61–5–0–7/101
Test batting
2–3–0–11–8–3.66–0–*ct* 1
Bowling 190–1–190.00–0–0–1/150
He proved a useful all-rounder on the 1938 tour and appeared in two Tests.

Wake, William Robert
Amateur. *b:* 21.5.1852, Sheffield, Yorkshire. *d:* 14.3.1896, Norwood, Sheffield, Yorkshire. Son of Bernard (Yorkshire 1849–51). Middle order right-hand batsman, right-arm slow bowler. *Team* Yorkshire (1881, 3 matches).
Career batting
3–3–0–13–11–4.33–0–*ct* 2

Wakefield, Percy Harold
Amateur. *b:* 3.9.1888, Pill, Somerset. *d:* 20.12.1973, Worcester. Right-hand batsman, right-arm medium pace bowler. *Sch* Taunton. *Team* Worcestershire (1922, 1 match).
Career batting
1–2–0–8–8–4.00–0–*ct* 1
Bowling 13–0

Wakelin, Edwin
Professional. *b:* 1880, Oxford. *d:* 1925, Headington, Oxon. Middle order batsman. *Team* Worcestershire (1910, 1 match).
Career batting
1–1–0–6–6–6.00–0–*ct* 0
He also played for Oxfordshire.

Walcott, Clyde Leopold
Amateur. *b:* 17.1.1926, Bridgetown, Barbados.

Father of M. A. C. (Barbados). Attacking middle order right-hand batsman, right-arm fast medium bowler, wicket-keeper or slip field. *Teams* Barbados (1941/2 to 1955/6); British Guiana (1954/5 to 1963/4). *Tours* West Indies to India, Pakistan and Ceylon 1948/9, to England 1950, 1957, to Australia and New Zealand 1951/2. *Tests* West Indies (1947/8 to 1959/60, 44 matches).
Career batting
146–238–29–11820–314*–56.55–40–*ct* 174–*st* 33
Bowling 1269–35–36.25–1–0–5/41
Test batting
44–74–7–3798–220–56.68–15–*ct* 53–*st* 11
Bowling 408–11–37.09–0–0–3/50

On the 1950 tour he hit 1,674 runs, av 55.80, his highest innings being 168* in the Lord's Test. On his second visit he made 1,414 runs, av 45.61. His highest innings was 314* for Barbados v Trinidad in Port of Spain in 1945/6 and each of his three double centuries were also scored in the West Indies. He also hit 1,000 runs on the 1948/9 tour.

Walden, Frederick Ingram
Professional. *b:* 1.3.1888, Wellingborough, Northants. *d:* 3.5.1949, Northampton. Attacking middle order right-hand batsman, right-arm slow bowler, brilliant cover point. *Team* Northants (1910–29, 258 matches).
Career batting
259–436–36–7538–128–18.84–5–*ct* 132
Bowling 4276–119–35.93–0–0–4/35

Only 5 ft 2 in tall, he was one of the smallest players to appear in County cricket. After retiring he joined the first-class umpires' list and officiated in several Tests. A noted right-winger, he played soccer for Tottenham Hotspur, Northampton Town and England.

Waldock, Frederic Alexander
Amateur. *b:* 16.3.1898, Colombo, Ceylon. *d:* 4.7.1959, Taunton, Somerset. Brother of H. F. (Foster's XI). Middle order left-hand batsman, left-arm slow bowler. *Sch* Uppingham. *Teams* Oxford U (1919–20, blue both years); Somerset (1920–24, 17 matches); Ceylon (1926/7 to 1933/4).
Test batting
40–72–1–1634–85–23.01–0–*ct* 22
Bowling 924–24–34.33–1–0–7/46

He lived in Ceylon for many years and captained the Ceylon team. He was also a good rugby footballer at stand-off half.

Waldock, Harold Francis
Amateur. *b:* 17.5.1899, Colombo, Ceylon. *d:* 4.9.1923, Colombo, Ceylon. Brother of F. A. (Somerset). Middle order batsman. *Team* H. K. Foster's XI (1919).
Career batting
2–4–1–65–43*–21.66–0–*ct* 1
Bowling 45–0

Waldron, Alan Noel Edwin
Amateur. *b:* 23.12.1920, Portsmouth, Hampshire. Hard hitting lower order right-hand batsman, right-arm fast medium bowler. *Sch* St Edwards, Oxford. *Team* Hampshire (1948, 2 matches).
Career batting
4–7–0–91–52–13.00–0–*ct* 3
Bowling 204–3–68.00–0–0–2/66

Waldron, Patrick Henry Pearse
Amateur. *b:* 5.2.1917, Limerick, Co Limerick. Right-hand batsman. *Team* Ireland (1946–47).
Career batting
4–8–0–99–52–12.37–0–*ct* 0

Wales, Peter John
Amateur. *b:* 30.10.1928, Hove, Sussex. Opening right-hand batsman, right-arm medium pace bowler. *Team* Sussex (1951, 1 match).
Career batting
1–2–1–38–29–38.00–0–*ct* 1
Bowling 13–5–2.60–0–0–3/12

Walford, John Erskine Scott
Amateur. *b:* 14.8.1899, Hanbury, Worcestershire. *d:* 22.8.1961, Ravenscourt Park, London. Lower order right-hand batsman, right-arm fast medium bowler. *Sch* Malvern. *Team* Worcestershire (1923–30, 6 matches).
Career batting
11–18–0–198–31–11.00–0–*ct* 6
Bowling 468–29–16.13–2–0–6/27

His final first-class match was for the Army in 1932.

Walford, Michael Moore
Amateur. *b:* 27.11.1915, Norton-on-Tees, Co Durham. Attractive opening right-hand batsman, left-arm slow bowler, excellent cover point. *Sch* Rugby. *Teams* Oxford U (1935–38, blue 1936 and 1938); Somerset (1946–53, 52 matches). *Tours* Oxford and Cambridge to Jamaica 1938/9; MCC to Canada 1951.
Career batting
97–169–11–5327–264–33.71–9–*ct* 50
Bowling 249–8–31.12–1–0–6/49

His highest innings was 264 for Somerset v Hampshire at Weston-super-Mare at 1947; his only other double century was for Oxford U. A master at Sherborne School, his County cricket was confined mainly to August. He also played for Dorset and Durham. He was a triple blue at Oxford – rugby and hockey as well as cricket – and went on to captain the England hockey team, representing Great Britain in the 1948 Olympics.

Walkden, George Godfrey
Amateur. *b:* 10.3.1883, Derby. *d:* 16.5.1923, Derby. He died following a motor cycle accident. Middle order batsman. *Sch* Uppingham. *Team* Derbyshire (1905–06, 7 matches).
Career batting
7–13–0–114–33–8.76–0–*ct* 2

Walker, Alan
Cricketer. *b:* 7.7.1962, Emley, Yorkshire. Lower order left-hand batsman, right-arm fast medium bowler. *Team* Northants (1983, 6 matches).
Career batting
6–4–3–18–7*–18.00–0–*ct* 3
Bowling 578–22–26.27–0–0–4/61

Walker, Alfred
Amateur. *b:* 8.9.1827, Southgate, Middlesex. *d:* 4.9.1870, Margate, Kent. Brother of A. H. (Middlesex), Frederic (Middlesex), I. D. (Middlesex), John (Middlesex), R. D. (Middlesex) and V. E. (Middlesex). Hard hitting lower order right-hand batsman, right-hand fast under-arm 'daisy-cutter' bowler, good field. *Teams* Cambridge U (1846–48); Middlesex (1851–59, 4 matches).
Career batting
14–23–3–95–20–4.75–0–*ct* 10
Bowling 83–6+30–13.83–3–0–7/?
His final first-class match was for Gentlemen of the South in 1860. He also played for Buckinghamshire.

Walker, Ashley
Amateur. *b:* 22.6.1844, Bradford, Yorkshire. *d:* 26.5.1927, Harrold, Bedfordshire. Cousin of C. W. (Gentlemen of North). Stylish opening right-hand batsman, right-hand slow round-arm bowler, good deep field. *Sch* Westminster. *Teams* Yorkshire (1863–70, 9 matches); Cambridge U (1864–66, blue all three years).
Career batting
20–36–2–531–65–15.61–0–*ct* 5
Bowling 289–18–16.05–2–0–6/89
He lived for many years in Ceylon and captained Ceylon against Madras in 1885 and Bombay in 1886 (not first-class). He also played for Staffordshire.

Walker, Arthur Henry
Amateur. *b:* 30.6.1833, Southgate, Middlesex. *d:* 4.10.1878, Arnos Grove, Middlesex. Brother of Alfred (Middlesex), Frederic (Middlesex), I. D. (Middlesex), John (Middlesex), R. D. (Middlesex) and V. E. (Middlesex). Middle order right-hand batsman, right-hand round-arm bowler, good point field. *Sch* Harrow. *Team* Middlesex (1859–62, 4 matches).
Career batting
23–39–3–601–90–16.69–0–*ct* 21
Bowling 351–14–25.07–0–0–4/79
His first-class debut was for MCC in 1855. He suffered a badly broken leg whilst playing football in December 1862 and this ended his career in important cricket. He also played for Buckinghamshire.

Walker, Alan Keith
Professional. *b:* 4.10.1925, Manly, New South Wales, Australia. Attacking lower order right-hand batsman, left-arm fast bowler. *Teams* New South Wales (1948/9 to 1952/3, 26 matches); Nottinghamshire (1954–58, 49 matches). *Tour* Australia to South Africa 1949/50.
Career batting
94–118–26–1603–73–17.42–0–*ct* 37
Bowling 6072–221–27.47–9–0–7/56
He took four wickets in four balls for Notts v Leicestershire at Leicester in 1956, namely the last wicket of the first innings and a hat-trick with the first three deliveries of the second innings. A good rugby league footballer, he toured England with the 1947/8 Australian team.

Walker, Arthur Walton
Amateur. *b:* 10.9.1891, Belfast. *d:* 13.1.1968, Bangor, Co Down. Brother of Laurence (Ireland). Right-hand batsman. *Team* Ireland (1913).
Career batting
1–1–0–3–3–3.00–0–*ct* 0

Walker, Clifford
Professional. *b:* 26.6.1919, Huddersfield, Yorkshire. Sound middle order right-hand batsman, right-arm medium pace bowler, good slip field. *Teams* Yorkshire (1947–48, 5 matches); Hampshire (1949–54, 126 matches).
Career batting
131–224–34–5258–150*–27.67–8–*ct* 89
Bowling 2615–53–49.33–2–0–5/40
He hit 1,000 runs in a season four times (best 1,302, av 36.16, in 1953).

Walker, Charles William
Amateur. *b:* 11.1.1851, Bowling, Bradford, Yorkshire. *d:* 2.3.1915, Palmerston North, New Zealand. Cousin of Ashley (Yorkshire). Middle order right-hand batsman, slow right-arm bowler. *Sch* Harrow. *Team* Gentlemen of the North (1870).

Career batting
1–2–0–59–40–29.50–0–*ct* 0
Bowling 85–0
He went to Madras in 1871 and later moved to New Zealand.

Walker, Charles William
Amateur. *b:* 19.2.1909, Hindmarsh, Adelaide, Australia. *d:* 21.12.1942, on a flight over Germany. Lower order right-hand batsman, wicket-keeper. *Team* South Australia (1928/9 to 1940/1, 78 matches). *Tour* Australia to England 1930, 1938.
Career batting
109–152–35–1754–71–14.99–0–*ct* 171–*st* 149
He was the reserve wicket-keeper on the tours of 1930 and 1938 – on the latter tour he played in only nine first-class matches owing to injury. He did not appear in Test cricket.

Walker, David Frank
Amateur. *b:* 31.5.1913, Loddon, Norfolk. *d:* 7.2.1942. He was killed on a flight over Norway, and buried at Trondheim. Stylish right-hand opening batsman, slow left-arm bowler. *Sch* Uppingham. *Team* Oxford U (1933–35, blue all three years).
Career batting
37–66–2–1880–118–29.39–2–*ct* 18
Bowling 299–6–49.83–0–0–2/36
His County cricket was for Norfolk. His final first-class match was for P. F. Warner's XI in 1938.

Walker, Donald Frederick
Amateur with Surrey 2nd XI, turned professional 1937. *b:* 15.8.1912, Wandsworth Common, London. *d:* 18.6.1941. He was killed flying over Holland. Patient middle order left-hand batsman. *Sch* KCS, Wimbledon. *Team* Hampshire (1937–39, 73 matches).
Career batting
73–126–11–3004–147–26.12–4–*ct* 75–*st* 1
Bowling 22–0
He hit 1,149 runs, av 28.72, in 1939.

Walker, Edwin William
Amateur. *b:* 27.12.1909, Coalville, Leics. Lower order right-hand batsman, right-arm fast medium bowler. *Team* Leicestershire (1930, 1 match).
Career batting
1–2–1–2–1*–2.00–0–*ct* 0
Bowling 21–1–21.00–0–0–1/21

Walker, Frederic
Amateur. *b:* 4.12.1829, Southgate, Middlesex. *d:* 20.12.1889, Arnos Grove, Middlessex. Brother of Alfred (Middlesex), A. H. (Middlesex), I. D. (Middlesex), John (Middlesex), R. D. (Middlesex), V. E. (Middlesex). Aggressive middle order right-hand batsman, good point field. *Teams* Cambridge U (1849–52, blue all four years); Middlesex (1859, 2 matches).
Career batting
34–62–4–726–71–12.51–0–*ct* 20–*st* 2
Bowling 10–0+13–no av–2–0–6/?
Owing to illness he did not appear in important matches as frequently as his talents warranted. His final first-class match was for Gentlemen of the South in 1860.

Walker, Gilbert
Amateur. *b:* 15.2.1888, Solihull, Warwickshire. Middle order right-hand batsman. *Team* Warwickshire (1912, 1 match).
Career batting
1–2–0–13–13–6.50–0–*ct* 0

Walker, George Arthur
Professional. *b:* 25.1.1919, West Bridgford, Nottingham. Lower order right-hand batsman, right-arm fast medium bowler. *Team* Nottinghamshire (1937, 2 matches).
Career batting
2–4–3–24–10*–24.00–0–*ct* 1
Bowling 176–1–176.00–0–0–1/98
He played soccer for West Ham and Lincoln City.

Walker, George Glossop
Amateur. *b:* 14.6.1860, Harthill, Yorkshire. *d:* 11.1.1908, Whitwell, Derbyshire. Lower order left-hand batsman, left-arm slow, later fast, bowler. *Team* Derbyshire (1881–98, 70 matches).
Career batting
75–128–24–1141–66–10.97–0–*ct* 26
Bowling 5063–202–25.06–10–3–9/68
His best innings analysis was 9 for 68 for Derbyshire v Leicestershire at Leicester in 1895.

Walker, Harry
Professional. *b:* 1760, Churt, Surrey. *d:* July 1805, Brook, Surrey. Brother of Thomas (Surrey). Middle order left-hand batsman. *Teams* Hampshire (1784–93); Surrey (1788–1802).
Career batting
3–6–0–20–9–3.33–0–*ct* 5
A noted hard hitting batsman of his day, but he was not as famous as his brother.

Walker, H.
Amateur. Middle order batsman. *Team* Northants (1947, 1 match).
Career batting
1–2–0–8–7–4.00–0–*ct* 0

Walker, Isaac Donnithorne
Amateur. *b:* 8.1.1844, Southgate, Middlesex. *d:* 6.7.1898, Regent's Park, London. Brother of Alfred (Middlesex), A. H. (Middlesex), Frederic (Middlesex), John (Middlesex), R. D. (Middlesex), V. E. (Middlesex). Excellent stylish middle order right-hand batsman, right-hand fast, later slow, under-arm bowler, good deep field. *Sch* Harrow. *Team* Middlesex (1862–84, 144 matches).
Career batting
294–508–43–11400–179–24.51–7–*ct* 248–*st* 3
Bowling 4755–215+3–22.11–9–1–6/42

His best season was 1868 with 661 runs, av 34.78, which placed him second in the first-class batting averages, but he remained one of the leading batsmen throughout his first-class career – even in his last season of 1884 he hit 674 runs, av 28.08. He captained Middlesex from 1873 to 1884 and was a member of the County Committee at the time of his death, having been associated with the running of the Club since its foundation.

Walker, Jack
Amateur. *b:* 2.3.1914, Cobham, Kent. *d:* 29.5.1968, Cobham, Kent. Lower order right-hand batsman, wicket-keeper. *Team* Kent (1949, 1 match).
Career batting
2–4–1–60–26–20.00–0–*ct* 2–*st* 2

His final first-class match was for D. R. Jardine's XI in 1957.

Walker, John
Amateur. *b:* 15.9.1826, Palmers Green, Middlesex. *d:* 14.8.1885, Arnos Grove, Middlesex. Brother of Alfred (Middlesex), A. H. (Middlesex), Frederic (Middlesex), I. D. (Middlesex), R. D. (Middlesex), V. E. (Middlesex). Middle order right-hand batsman, right-hand slow, round-arm or under-arm bowler, wicket-keeper. *Teams* Cambridge U (1846–49, blue 1847–49); Middlesex (1850–66, 9 matches).
Career batting
87–145–20–1355–98–10.84–0–*ct* 51–*st* 20
Bowling 381–16+2–23.81–0–0–4/55

He was joint captain of Middlesex in 1864 and 1865 and assisted in the founding of the County Club. His final first-class match was for Southgate in 1868. He also played for Cambridgeshire and Bedfordshire.

Walker, John
Professional. *b:* 1854, Harrow, Middlesex. Lower order batsman, right-hand fast medium round-arm bowler. *Team* Middlesex (1879, 1 match).
Career batting
1–2–1–6–6–6.00–0–*ct* 0
Bowling 26–0

Walker, John Barnhill
Amateur. *b:* 30.10.1883, Greenock, Renfrewshire, Scotland. *d:* 21.11.1953, Bearsden, Dunbartonshire, Scotland. Brother of W. N. (Scotland). Right-hand batsman. *Team* Scotland (1912).
Career batting
2–4–0–45–34–11.25–0–*ct* 3

Walker, James George
Amateur. *b:* 9.10.1859, Glasgow, Scotland. *d:* 24.3.1923, Nether Auchendrane, Ayrshire, Scotland. Steady middle order right-hand batsman, point field. *Sch* Loretto. *Teams* Oxford U (1880–83, blue 1882 and 1883); Middlesex (1886–90, 44 matches). *Tour* Vernon to Ceylon and India 1889/90 (not first-class).
Career batting
96–167–5–3321–111–20.50–1–*ct* 69
Bowling 52–0

His final first-class match was for MCC in 1892. A noted rugby footballer, he represented Oxford and Scotland.

Walker, Kenneth Gordon Eldridge
Amateur. *b:* 30.11.1922, Wimbledon, Surrey. Middle order left-hand batsman, leg break bowler. *Team* D. R. Jardine's XI (1955).
Career batting
1–1–0–13–13–13.00–0–*ct* 0
Bowling 82–0

Walker, Laurence
Amateur. *b:* 17.7.1901, Belfast. Brother of A. W. (Ireland). Lower order right-hand batsman, right-arm fast medium bowler. *Team* Ireland (1922–26).
Career batting
3–4–2–27–13*–13.50–0–*ct* 0
Bowling 284–9–30.44–1–0–5/125

Walker, Livingstone
Amateur. *b:* 14.6.1879, Urmston, Lancashire. *d:* 10.10.1940, Tonbridge, Kent. Right-hand batsman, right-arm off break bowler. *Sch* The Leys. *Teams* Surrey (1900–03, 56 matches); London County (1900–04).
Career batting
93–147–14–3061–222–23.01–2–*ct* 56–*st* 1
Bowling 911–19–47.94–0–0–4/41

His double century (222) was for London County v MCC at Crystal Palace in 1901. In the same year he hit 1,180 runs, av 31.89.

Walker, Malcolm
Professional. *b:* 14.10.1933, Mexborough, York-

shire. Middle order right-hand batsman, off break bowler. *Team* Somerset (1952–58, 29 matches).
Career batting
29–52–3–574–100–11.71–1–*ct* 8
Bowling 976–28–34.85–2–0–5/45

Walker, Maxwell Henry Norman
Cricketer. *b:* 12.9.1948, West Hobart, Tasmania. Lower order right-hand batsman, right-arm fast medium bowler. *Team* Victoria (1968/9 to 1981/2, 70 matches). *Tours* Australia to England 1975, 1977, to West Indies 1972/3, to New Zealand 1973/4, 1976/7; Robins to South Africa 1975/6; International Wanderers to South Africa 1974/5. *Tests* Australia (1972/3 to 1977, 34 matches).
Career batting
135–170–40–2014–78*–15.49–0–*ct* 49
Bowling 13209–499–26.47–21–0–8/143
Test batting
34–43–13–586–78*–19.53–0–*ct* 12
Bowling 3792–138–27.47–6–0–8/143

In 1975 in England he took 36 wickets in first-class matches, av 29.88, and played in all four Tests. In 1977 he had 53, av 22.33, but was very expensive in the Test matches with 14 wickets, av 39.35

Walker, Niel Alexander McDonald
Amateur. *b:* 22.8.1895, Poona, India. *d:* 10.8.1960. Spink Hill, Derbyshire. Middle order right-hand batsman, right-arm medium pace bowler. *Teams* Europeans (1923/4 to 1926/7); Derbyshire (1931–36, 2 matches).
Career batting
4–6–0–48–18–8.00–0–*ct* 1
Bowling 77–2–38.50–0–0–1/12

Walker, Peter Michael
Professional. *b:* 17.2.1936, Clifton, Bristol. Middle order right-hand batsman, left-arm medium or slow bowler, brilliant short leg field. *Teams* Glamorgan (1956–72, 437 matches); Transvaal (1956/7 to 1957/8); Western Province (1962/3). *Tours* Brown to East Africa 1961/2 (not first-class); Glamorgan to West Indies 1969/70. *Tests* England (1960, 3 matches).
Career batting
469–788–110–17650–152*–26.03–13–*ct* 697
Bowling 23881–834–28.63–25–2–7/58
Test batting
3–4–0–128–52–32.00–0–*ct* 5
Bowling 34–0

He hit 1,000 runs in a season 11 times (best 1,564, av 34.00, in 1959) and took 100 wickets in a season once : 101, av 24.04, in 1961, achieving the 'double' that season. In the same year he held 73 catches. Since retiring from first-class cricket he has become well-known as a cricket commentator and journalist.

Walker, Roger
Amateur. *b:* 18.9.1846, Bury, Lancashire. *d:* 11.11.1919, Reading, Berkshire. Lower order right-hand batsman, wicket-keeper. *Team* Lancashire (1874–75, 2 matches).
Career batting
2–4–1–27–19–9.00–0–*ct* 1–*st* 1

A noted rugby footballer, he appeared five times for England.

Walker, Russell Donnithorne
Amateur. *b:* 13.2.1842, Southgate, Middlesex. *d:* 29.3.1922, Regent's Park, London. Brother of Alfred (Middlesex), A. H. (Middlesex), Frederic (Middlesex), John (Middlesex), I. D. (Middlesex), V. E. (Middlesex). Attacking opening or middle order right-hand batsman, right-hand slow round-arm bowler, good field. *Sch* Harrow. *Teams* Oxford U (1861–65, blue all five years); Middlesex (1862–77, 45 matches).
Career batting
122–202–8–3840–104–19.79–2–*ct* 91
Bowling 5517–313+21–17.62–17–4–8/43

His best season was 1865 with 770 runs, av 24.83. His final first-class match was for MCC in 1878. He was on the Committee of both Middlesex and MCC until he died, being President of the Middlesex Club and a Trustee of MCC. A noted rackets player, he represented Oxford.

Walker, Stanley George
Professional. *b:* 18.5.1908, Pinxton, Derbyshire. Lower order right-hand batsman, left-arm fast medium bowler. *Team* Derbyshire (1932, 1 match).
Career batting
1–2–0–8–7–4.00–0–*ct* 0
Bowling 6–1–6.00–0–0–1/6

He also played for Scotland (not first-class).

Walker, Thomas
Professional. *b:* 16.11.1762, Churt, Surrey. *d:* 1.3.1831, Chiddingfold, Surrey. Brother of Harry (Surrey and Hampshire). Steady opening right-hand batsman, right-hand fast round-arm, later slow under-arm bowler. *Teams* Hampshire (1787–93); Surrey (1788–1810).
Career batting
46–89–4–1111–61–13.07–0–*ct* 25–*st* 2
Bowling 41 wickets, no analyses

The most famous defensive batsman of his day, he was reported to have received 170 balls from David Harris and scored just one run.

He was perhaps the first player to bowl round-arm – it was then banned by the Hambledon Club because of the tremendous pace of Walker's deliveries.

Walker, Thomas
Professional. *b:* 3.4.1854, Leeds, Yorkshire. *d:* 29.8.1925, Roundhay, Leeds, Yorkshire. Hard hitting middle order right-hand batsman. *Team* Yorkshire (1879–80, 14 matches).
Career batting
15–24–2–189–30–8.59–0–*ct* 3
Bowling 7–0
His final first-class match was for T. Emmett's XI in 1883.

Walker, Vyell Edward
Amateur. *b:* 20.4.1837, Southgate, Middlesex. *d:* 3.1.1906, Arnos Grove, Middlesex. Brother of Alfred (Middlesex), A. H. (Middlesex), Frederic (Middlesex), I. D. (Middlesex), John (Middlesex), R. D. (Middlesex). Fine middle order right-hand batsman, right-hand slow under-arm bowler, good field. *Sch* Harrow. *Team* Middlesex (1859–77, 52 matches).
Career batting
145–228–32–3384–108–17.26–1–*ct* 188
Bowling 4797–304+30–15.77–27–9–10/74
His first-class debut was for Gentlemen v Players at Lord's in 1856. He was, around 1860, the best all-round amateur cricketer in England and in 1859 for England v Surrey at the Oval scored 20* and 108 as well as taking 10 for 74 and 4 for 17. He also took 10 for 104 Middlesex v Lancashire at Old Trafford in 1865. He captained Middlesex from 1864 to 1872. He also played for Bedfordshire.

Walker, Willis
Professional. *b:* 24.11.1892, Gosforth, Northumberland. Sound middle order right-hand batsman, right-arm medium pace bowler, good deep field. *Team* Nottinghamshire (1913–37, 405 matches).
Career batting
406–624–60–18259–165*–32.37–31–*ct* 110
Bowling 97–2–48.50–0–0–2/20
He hit 1,000 runs in a season 10 times (best 1,730, av 39.31, in 1933). A good soccer player, he kept goal for South Shields, Sheffield United, Doncaster, Bradford and Leeds.

Walker, William Norman
Amateur. *b:* 23.1.1894, Greenock, Renfrewshire, Scotland. *d:* 14.9.1960, Greenock, Renfrewshire, Scotland. Brother of J. B. (Scotland). Right-hand batsman, right-arm medium pace bowler. *Sch* Glasgow Academy. *Team* Scotland (1922–25).
Career batting
6–11–0–200–58–18.18–0–*ct* 5
Bowling 502–18–27.88–0–0–4/55

Walker, William Percy
Amateur. *b:* 1889, Northampton. *d:* 6.2.1938, Northampton. Middle order right-hand batsman. *Team* Northants (1908–20, 6 matches).
Career batting
7–13–0–113–48–8.69–0–*ct* 1
His final first-class match was for V. W. C. Jupp's XI in 1926.

Walkinshaw, Frank
Amateur. *b:* 28.2.1861. *d:* 14.7.1934, Bramley, Hampshire. Lower order batsman, wicket-keeper. *Sch* Eton. *Team* Hampshire (1885, 3 matches).
Career batting
3–5–0–15–11–3.00–0–*ct* 4–*st* 1

Wall, Henry
Amateur. *b:* 21.4.1852, Wigan, Lancashire. *d:* 13.10.1914, Southport, Lancashire. Brother of Thomas (Lancashire) and William (Lancashire). Middle order right-hand batsman, right-hand fast round-arm bowler. *Team* Lancashire (1877, 3 matches).
Career batting
3–4–0–24–15–6.00–0–*ct* 2

Wall, Thomas
Amateur. *b:* 27.11.1841, Wigan, Lancashire. *d:* 18.4.1875, Wigan, Lancashire. Brother of Henry (Lancashire) and William (Lancashire). Middle order right-hand batsman, right-hand slow round-arm bowler, wicket-keeper. *Team* Lancashire (1868, 2 matches).
Career batting
2–4–0–48–37–12.00–0–*ct* 1
Bowling 17–0

Wall, Thomas Welbourn
Amateur. *b:* 13.5.1904, Semaphore, South Australia. *d:* 26.3.1981, Adelaide, South Australia. Tail end right-hand batsman, right-arm fast bowler, short leg field. *Team* South Australia (1924/5 to 1935/6, 53 matches). *Tours* Australia to England 1930, 1934. *Tests* Australia (1928/9 to 1934, 18 matches).
Career batting
108–135–33–1071–53*–10.50–0–*ct* 54
Bowling 9877–330–29.93–10–2–10/36
Test batting
18–24–5–121–20–6.36–0–*ct* 11
Bowling 2010–56–35.89–3–0–5/14
The fastest bowler in Australian Test cricket, he took 56 wickets, av 29.25, on the 1930 tour to

England and 42, av 30.71, in 1934. He played in all five Tests in 1930 and in four in 1934, but his wickets were very expensive. His best bowling in an innings was 10 for 36 for South Australia v New South Wales at Sydney in 1932/3.

Wall, William
Amateur. *b:* 8.1.1854, Wigan, Lancashire. *d:* 18.4.1922, Southport, Lancashire. Brother of Henry (Lancashire) and Thomas (Lancashire). Lower order right-hand batsman, wicket-keeper. *Team* Lancashire (1877, 1 match).
Career batting
1–2–1–17–17*–17.00–0–*ct* 2–*st* 2

Wallace, Charles William
Amateur. *b:* 24.11.1884, Sunderland. *d:* 5.9.1946, Awbridge, Hampshire. Middle order batsman. *Sch* Winchester. *Team* Worcestershire (1921–22, 4 matches).
Career batting
4–7–1–66–39*–11.00–0–*ct* 1

Wallace, Gary Charles
Cricketer. *b:* 8.2.1958, Salisbury, Rhodesia. Middle order left-hand batsman, left-arm medium pace bowler. *Team* Rhodesia/Zimbabwe (1978/9 to 1982). *Tour* Zimbabwe to England 1982.
Career batting
16–30–2–757–111–27.03–1–*ct* 8
Bowling 238–5–47.60–0–0–3/61

Wallace, George Henry
Amateur. *b:* 18.9.1854, Great Budworth, Cheshire. *d:* 24.11.1927, North Kensington, London. Middle order right-hand batsman. *Sch* Clergy Orphan School, Canterbury. *Team* Cambridge U (1876).
Career batting
1–2–0–13–8–6.50–0–*ct* 1

Wallace, Kenneth William
Cricketer. *b:* 27.8.1936, Romford, Essex. Middle order right-hand batsman, right-arm medium pace bowler. *Team* Essex (1967–72, 10 matches).
Career batting
10–16–0–219–55–13.68–0–*ct* 2

Wallace, Nesbit Willoughby
Amateur. *b:* 20.4.1839, Halifax, Nova Scotia. *d:* 31.7.1931, Guildford, Surrey. Middle order right-hand batsman, right-hand slow under-arm bowler, deep field. *Sch* Rugby. *Teams* Gloucestershire (1871, 2 matches); Hampshire (1884, 2 matches).
Career batting
6–9–1–66–25–8.25–0–*ct* 4
Bowling 6–0
His first-class debut was for Gentlemen of the South in 1863 and his final first-class match for MCC in 1885. He was mainly instrumental in the organising of the English tour of North America in 1872. He also helped to found the Green Jackets CC and was Hon Secretary of that Club until 1894.

Wallace, Walter Mervyn
Amateur. *b:* 19.12.1916, Auckland, New Zealand. Forceful middle order right-hand batsman, good field at mid-off or mid-on. *Team* Auckland (1933/4 to 1956/7). *Tours* New Zealand to England 1937, 1949, to Australia 1937/8. *Tests* New Zealand (1937 to 1952/3, 13 matches).
Career batting
120–190–17–7609–211–43.98–16–*ct* 68
Bowling 18–0
Test batting
13–21–0–439–66–20.90–0–*ct* 5
Bowling 5–0
He hit 1,000 runs on both tours to England (best 1,722, av 49.02, in 1949), but, although he appeared in all Tests on both visits, he made little impact against England. His final first-class match was for the Governor-General's XI in 1960/1. His highest score was 211 for Auckland v Canterbury at Auckland in 1939/40.

Wallach, Benjamin
Amateur. *b:* 18.9.1873, Queenstown, South Africa. *d:* 25.5.1935, Johannesburg, South Africa. Tail end right-hand batsman, wicket-keeper. *Teams* Transvaal (1897/8 to 1904/5); London County (1902–04). *Tour* South Africa to England 1904.
Career batting
15–18–7–100–30–9.09–0–*ct* 16–*st* 11
The reserve wicket-keeper on the 1904 tour, he appeared in only three first-class matches.

Waller, Christopher Edward
Cricketer. *b:* 3.10.1948, Guildford, Surrey. Lower order right-hand batsman, slow left-arm bowler. *Teams* Surrey (1967–73, 40 matches); Sussex (1974–83, 189 matches).
Career batting
229–236–94–1388–51*–9.77–0–*ct* 118
Bowling 16081–557–28.87–20–1–7/64

Waller, Edmund
Amateur. *b:* 7.12.1838, Leamington Spa, Warwickshire. *d:* 6.2.1871, Westminster, London. Opening batsman. *Sch* Marlborough. *Team* Gentlemen of Kent (1865).
Career batting
1–2–0–22–16–11.00–0–*ct* 1

Waller, George
Professional. *b:* 3.12.1864, Pitsmoor, Sheffield, Yorkshire. *d:* 11.12.1937, Ecclesfield, Sheffield, Yorkshire. Lower order right-hand batsman, right-arm medium pace bowler. *Team* Yorkshire (1893–94, 3 matches).
Career batting
3–4–0–17–13–4.25–0–*ct* 1
Bowling 70–4–17.50–0–0–2/10
A noted soccer player, he played for Sheffield Wednesday in the FA Cup Final of 1890. Later he played and then acted as trainer for Sheffield United.

Waller, Guy de Warrene
Cricketer. *b:* 10.2.1950, Ham, Wiltshire. Middle order right-hand batsman, off break bowler. *Sch* Hurstpierpoint. *Team* Oxford U (1973–74, blue 1974).
Career batting
13–25–1–203–29–8.45–0–*ct* 10
Bowling 4–0

Waller, Richmond Campbell Shakespear
Amateur. *b:* 26.7.1879, Barton Regis, Bristol. *d:* 28.6.1950, Colchester, Essex. Lower order batsman, bowler. *Sch* Haileybury. *Team* Navy and Army XI (1910).
Career batting
1–1–0–1–1–1.00–0–*ct* 0
Bowling 22–0

Wallgate, Lamplough
Amateur. *b:* 12.11.1849, Norton, Yorkshire. *d:* 9.5.1887, Harrogate, Yorkshire. Opening right-hand batsman, right-hand round-arm bowler. *Team* Yorkshire (1875–77, 2 matches).
Career batting
2–2–0–3–3–1.50–0–*ct* 2
Bowling 17–1–17.00–0–0–1/17

Wallington, Sir Edward William
Amateur. *b:* 7.12.1854, Oakley Hall, near Basingstoke, Hampshire. *d:* 12.12.1933, Bath, Somerset. Steady middle order right-hand batsman, right-hand slow under-arm bowler. *Sch* Sherborne. *Team* Oxford U (1875–77, blue 1877).
Career batting
6–9–1–100–38–12.50–0–*ct* 3
His final first-class match was for MCC in 1885. He lived for many years in Australia, being at one time Private Secretary to the Governor of New South Wales. He played a little County cricket for Wiltshire and Dorset.

Wallis, Arthur Knight
Amateur. *b: circa* 1868, Donnycarney, Dublin. *d:* 27.11.1905, Dublin. Lower order batsman, useful bowler. *Team* Dublin University (1895).
Career batting
3–5–2–7–5*–2.33–0–*ct* 1
Bowling 319–6–53.16–0–0–3/110
He was a noted rugby footballer, playing for Dublin University and Ireland.

Wallis, William Alfred
Amateur. *b:* 14.12.1878, Long Eaton, Derbyshire. *d:* 12.11.1939, Long Eaton, Derbyshire. Middle order right-hand batsman. *Sch* Trent College. *Team* Derbyshire (1906, 1 match).
Career batting
1–2–0–17–11–8.50–0–*ct* 1

Wallis Mathias
Amateur. *b:* 4.2.1935, Karachi, India. Middle order right-hand batsman, right-arm medium pace bowler, good slip field. *Teams* Sind (1953/4 to 1955/6); Karachi (1956/7 to 1969/70); National Bank (1969/70 to 1976/7). *Tours* Pakistan to West Indies 1957/8, to India 1960/1, to England 1962. *Tests* Pakistan (1955/6 to 1962, 21 matches).
Career batting
146–206–37–7520–278*–44.49–16–*ct* 130
Bowling 555–13–42.69–0–0–2/4
Test batting
21–36–3–783–77–23.72–0–*ct* 22
Bowling 20–0
He achieved little on his tour to England in 1962.

Wallroth, Conrad Adolphus
Amateur. *b:* 17.5.1851, Lee, Kent. *d:* 22.2.1926, Compton, Godalming, Surrey. Steady middle order right-hand batsman, good long stop. *Sch* Harrow. *Teams* Kent (1872, 1 match); Oxford U (1872–74, blue all three years); Derbyshire (1879, 3 matches).
Career batting
21–36–1–596–109–17.02–1–*ct* 8
His first-class debut was for MCC in 1871.

Wallwork, Mark Andrew
Cricketer. *b:* 14.12.1960, Urmston, Lancashire. Lower order right-hand batsman, wicket-keeper. *Team* Lancashire (1982, 1 match).
Career batting
1 match, did not bat –*ct* 3

Walmsley, Walter Thomas
Amateur. *b:* 16.3.1916, Homebush, New South Wales, Australia. *d:* 25.2.1978, Hamilton, New Zealand. Lower order right-hand batsman, leg break and googly bowler. *Teams* New South Wales (1945/6, 1 match); Tasmania (1947/8, 3

matches); Queensland (1954/5 to 1958/9, 28 matches); Northern Districts (1959/60).
Career batting
37–50–11–1064–180*–27.28–2–*ct* 8
Bowling 3861–122–31.64–3–0–6/56
His only match in England was for a Commonwealth XI at Kingston-on-Thames in 1953. His first-class debut in New Zealand was for Combined Northern and Central Districts XI in 1958/9.

Walrond, Sir William Hood
(created 1st Baron Waleren of Uffculme in 1905) Amateur. *b:* 26.2.1849, Exeter, Devon. *d:* 17.5.1925, Westminster, London. Middle order right-hand batsman, deep field. *Sch* Eton. *Team* MCC (1868).
Career batting
1–2–1–26–13*–26.00–0–*ct* 0
He did not appear in any first-class matches whilst at Cambridge. His County cricket was for Devon commencing 1866. From 1880 to 1885 he was Conservative MP for East Devonshire and then until 1905 for Tiverton. He held various Government offices including Chancellor of the Duchy of Lancaster.

Walsh, David Robert
Cricketer. *b:* 17.12.1946, Bombay, India. Middle order right-hand batsman, right-arm medium pace bowler. *Sch* Marlborough. *Team* Oxford U (1966–69, blue 1967–69).
Career batting
39–69–10–1508–207–25.55–2–*ct* 13
Bowling 129–6–21.50–0–0–3/34
He hit 207 for Oxford U v Warwickshire at Oxford in 1969.

Walsh, George
Amateur. *b:* 16.2.1852, Blackburn, Lancashire. *d:* 22.5.1904, Darwen, Lancashire. Middle order batsman. *Sch* Rugby. *Team* Lancashire (1874–77, 2 matches).
Career batting
2–3–0–16–15–5.33–0–*ct* 0
He also played for Cheshire.

Walsh, John Edward
Professional. *b:* 4.12.1912, Sydney, South Wales, Australia. *d:* 20.5.1980, Wallsend, New South Wales, Australia. Attacking lower order left-hand batsman, left-arm slow bowler with chinaman, good close field. *Teams* New South Wales (1939/40, 2 matches); Leicestershire (1937–56, 279 matches). *Tours* Cahn to Ceylon 1936/7, to New Zealand 1938/9.
Career batting
296–460–52–7247–106–17.76–2–*ct* 209
Bowling 29226–1190–24.55–98–26–9/101
His first-class debut was for Sir J. Cahn's XI in 1936. He took 100 wickets in a season seven times (best 174, av 19.56, in 1948). In 1952 he hit 1,106 runs, av 24.04, completing the 'double' in the same season. His best innings analysis was 9 for 101 for Sir J. Cahn's XI v Glamorgan at Newport in 1938.

Walshe, Aubrey Peter
Amateur. *b:* 1.1.1934, Rhodesia. Lower order right-hand batsman, wicket-keeper. *Team* Oxford U (1953–56, blue 1953, 1955 and 1956).
Career batting
46–69–8–900–77–14.75–0–*ct* 49–*st* 12

Walter, Arthur Fraser
Amateur. *b:* 12.9.1846, Wokingham, Berkshire. *d:* 22.2.1910, Bearwood, Berkshire. Son-in-law of T. A. Anson (Cambridge U 1839–42). Middle order right-hand batsman, right-hand medium pace round-arm bowler, good deep field. *Sch* Eton. *Team* Oxford U (1867–69, blue 1869).
Career batting
5–9–0–12–3–1.33–0–*ct* 0
Bowling 200–11–18.18–1–0–5/35
He was Chairman of the Times Publishing Company.

Walters, Charley
Professional. *b:* 1.4.1897, Headington, Oxfordshire. *d:* 13.5.1971, Kidlington, Oxfordshire. Middle order batsman, useful bowler. *Team* Minor Counties (1930–34).
Career batting
4–4–0–47–25–11.75–0–*ct* 2
Bowling 148–3–49.33–0–0–2/72
His County cricket was for Oxfordshire.

Walters, Cyril Frederick
Amateur. *b:* 28.8.1905, Bedlinog, Glamorgan. Stylish opening right-hand batsman. *Teams* Glamorgan (1923–28, 75 matches); Worcestershire (1928–35, 137 matches). *Tours* Tennyson to Jamaica 1931/2; MCC to India and Ceylon 1933/4. *Tests* England (1933–34, 11 matches).
Career batting
244–427–32–12145–226–30.94–21–*ct* 101
Bowling 380–5–76.00–0–0–2/22
Test batting
11–18–3–784–102–52.26–1–*ct* 6
He hit 1,000 runs in a season five times, going on to 2,000 twice (best 2,404, av 50.08, in 1933). His only double century was 226 for Worcestershire v Kent at Gravesend in 1933. He captained Worcestershire 1931 to 1935.

Walters, Francis Henry
Amateur. *b:* 9.2.1860, East Melbourne, Victoria, Australia. *d:* 1.6.1922, at sea off Bombay, India. Sound middle order right-hand batsman, right-arm medium pace bowler. *Teams* Victoria (1880/1 to 1893/4, 22 matches); New South Wales (1895/6, 5 matches). *Tour* Australia to England 1890. *Test* Australia (1884/5, 1 match).
Career batting
56–96–9–1755–150–20.17–4–*ct* 31
Bowling 81–1–81.00–0–0–1/17
Test batting
1–2–0–12–7–6.00–0–*ct* 2
He was very disappointing on his tour to England.

Walters, John
Cricketer. *b:* 7.8.1949, Brampton, Yorkshire. Middle order left-hand batsman, right-arm fast medium bowler. *Team* Derbyshire (1977–80, 58 matches).
Career batting
58–80–15–1296–90–19.93–0–*ct* 26
Bowling 1935–47–41.17–0–0–4/100

Walters, Joseph A.
Professional. *b:* 12.2.1940, Bolsover, Derbyshire. Tail end right-hand batsman, leg break bowler. *Team* Nottinghamshire (1958–59, 5 matches).
Career batting
5–9–8–64–21*–64.00–0–*ct* 4
Bowling 464–10–46.40–1–0–6/139

Walters, Kevin Douglas
Cricketer. *b:* 21.12.1945, Dungog, New South Wales, Australia. Attacking middle order right-hand batsman, right-arm medium pace bowler. *Team* New South Wales (1962/3 to 1980/1, 103 matches). *Tours* Australia to England 1968, 1972, 1975, 1977, to Ceylon, India and South Africa 1969/70, to West Indies 1972/3, to New Zealand 1973/4, 1976/7. *Tests* Australia (1965/6 to 1980/1, 74 matches).
Career batting
258–426–57–16180–253–43.84–45–*ct* 149
Bowling 6782–190–35.69–6–0–7/63
Test batting
74–125–14–5357–250–48.26–15–*ct* 43
Bowling 1425–49–29.08–1–0–5/66
A brilliant batsman in Australia, he rarely succeeded in England – on the tours of 1972 and 1977 his record was very poor in the Tests and altogether his best visit came in 1975 with 784 first-class runs, av 60.30. He played in 18 Tests in England. Of his four double centuries, three were made in Australia and the fourth in New Zealand. His highest score was 253 for New South Wales v South Australia at Adelaide in 1964/5. He hit 1,000 runs in a season twice (best 1,332, av 70.10, in 1965/6).

Walters, Percy Melmoth
Amateur. *b:* 30.9.1863, Ewell, Surrey. *d:* 3.10.1936, Ashtead, Surrey. Lower order right-hand batsman, wicket-keeper. *Sch* Charterhouse. *Team* Oxford U (1885).
Career batting
1–1–0–9–9–9.00–0–*ct* 0
A good soccer player, he appeared as left-back for Old Carthusians in the FA Amateur Cup final of 1895 and was capped for England.

Walton, Arthur Christopher
Amateur. *b:* 26.9.1933, Georgetown, British Guiana. Middle order right-hand batsman. *Sch* Radley. *Teams* Oxford U (1955–57, blue all three years); Middlesex (1957–59, 35 matches).
Career batting
85–155–2–3797–152–24.81–3–*ct* 47
Bowling 8–0
He hit 1,200 runs, av 38.70, in 1956. His first-class debut was for Combined Services in 1953.

Walton, Francis
Amateur. *b:* 1832. *d:* 14.7.1871, Surbiton, Surrey. Attacking middle order right-hand batsman, right-hand fast round-arm bowler. *Team* Hampshire (1864–66, 3 matches).
Career batting
3–6–1–55–16–11.00–0–*ct* 1
Bowling 165–6–27.50–0–0–3/48

Walton, George
Professional. *b:* 3.12.1863, Belgrave, Leicester. *d:* 30.6.1921, Belgrave, Leicester. Lower order right-hand batsman, right-arm fast medium bowler. *Team* Leicestershire (1894–95, 9 matches).
Career batting
9–14–1–88–24–6.76–0–*ct* 9
Bowling 424–17–24.94–0–0–4/64
His career with Leicestershire commenced in 1889.

Walton, Herbert
Amateur. *b:* 21.5.1868. *d:* 1930, Scarborough, Yorkshire. Lower order batsman, fast bowler. *Team* Yorkshire (1893, 1 match).
Career batting
1–1–0–5–5–5.00–0–*ct* 1
Bowling 135–5–27.00–0–0–3/93

Walton, James
Professional. *b:* 1857, Greenwich, Kent. Lower order batsman, useful bowler. *Team* Kent (1875, 1 match).

Career batting
1–2–0–13–13–6.50–0–*ct* 1
Bowling 15–1–15.00–0–0–1/15

Walton, J. C.
Amateur. Right-hand batsman, right-arm medium pace bowler. *Team* Ireland (1925).
Career batting
1–2–0–52–48–26.00–0–*ct* 0
Bowling 26–0
He also played for Suffolk.

Walton, Matthew
Professional. Opening batsman. *Team* Lancashire (1867, 1 match).
Career batting
1–2–0–6–6–3.00–0–*ct* 0

Walton, William
Professional. *b:* 7.8.1862, Glossop, Derbyshire. *d:* 16.2.1925, Glossop, Derbyshire. Opening right-hand batsman. *Team* Derbyshire (1887, 1 match).
Career batting
1–2–0–4–3–2.00–0–*ct* 0

Walusimba, Sam
Cricketer. *b:* 1948, Uganda. Middle order right-hand batsman. *Team* East Africa (1973/4 to 1975). *Tour* East Africa to England 1975.
Career batting
2–4–0–78–54–19.50–0–*ct* 1

Wanklyn, James Leslie
Amateur. *b:* 1860, Christchurch, Hampshire. *d:* 6.7.1919, Northampton. Middle order batsman. *Team* MCC (1885).
Career batting
1–1–0–0–0–0.00–0–*ct* 1

Wanostrocht, N. (*See under* Felix, N.)

Waqar Ahmed
Cricketer. *b:* 19.12.1946, Lahore, India. Son of Dilawar Hussain (India). Middle order right-hand batsman. *Teams* Punjab University (1964/5 to 1968/9); Lahore (1966/7 to 1972/3); Punjab (1972/3). *Tour* Pakistan to England 1967.
Career batting
33–51–6–1705–199–37.88–3–*ct* 18
Bowling 67–1–67.00–0–0–1/19
In seven matches he hit 306 runs, av 38.25, on the 1967 tour to England, but was then forced to return home due to the death of his father.

Waqar Hassan
Amateur. *b:* 12.9.1932, Amritsar, India. Brother of Pervez Sajjad (Pakistan). Stylish middle order right-hand batsman, good outfield. *Teams* Punjab University (1948/9); Karachi (1951/2 to 1965/6). *Tours* Pakistan to India 1952/3, to England 1954, to West Indies 1957/8; Pakistan Services to Ceylon 1953/4. *Tests* Pakistan (1952/3 to 1959/60, 21 matches).
Career batting
97–141–11–4620–201*–35.53–8–*ct* 46
Bowling 172–2–86.00–0–0–1/9
Test batting
21–35–1–1071–189–31.50–1–*ct* 10
Bowling 10–0
He hit 1,263 runs, av 32.38, on the 1954 tour to England and played in all four Tests. His highest score was 201* for Cannon's XI v Hasan Mahmood's XI at Karachi in 1953/4.

Warburton, David
Amateur. *b:* 30.5.1919, Huddersfield, Yorkshire. Lower order right-hand batsman, right-arm fast bowler. *Sch* Leeds GS. *Team* Oxford U (1939).
Career batting
1–2–0–4–4–2.00–0–*ct* 0
Bowling 39–0

Warburton, Leslie
Professional. *b:* 30.4.1910, Haslingden, Lancashire. *d:* 11.2.1984, Gloucester. Middle order right-hand batsman, right-arm fast medium bowler, good slip field. *Team* Lancashire (1929–38, 6 matches).
Career batting
8–8–2–171–74*–28.50–*ct* 1
Bowling 289–7–41.28–0–0–3/47
He was unexpectedly selected for the Test Trial of 1936 on the strength of his performances in League cricket. He achieved little in the Trial.

Ward, Alan
Cricketer. *b:* 10.8.1947, Dronfield, Derbyshire. Lower order right-hand batsman, right-arm fast bowler. *Teams* Derbyshire (1966–76, 115 matches); Border (1971/2); Leicestershire (1977–78, 22 matches). *Tours* Norfolk to West Indies 1969/70; MCC to Australia 1970/1. *Tests* England (1969–76, 5 matches).
Career batting
163–157–47–928–44–8.43–0–*ct* 51
Bowling 10495–460–22.81–15–4–7/42
Test Batting
5–6–1–40–21–8.00–0–*ct* 3
Bowling 453–14–32.35–0–0–4/61
Regarded as the best fast bowling prospect in England in 1969, his career was marred by injury.

Ward, Albert
Professional. *b:* 21.11.1865, Waterloo, Leeds, Yorkshire. *d:* 6.1.1939, Bolton, Lancashire. Steady opening right-hand batsman, slow right-

arm bowler, good field. *Teams* Yorkshire (1886, 4 matches); Lancashire (1889–1904, 330 matches). *Tour* Stoddart to Australia 1894/5. *Tests* England (1893 to 1894/5, 7 matches).
Career batting
385–642–51–17809–219–30.13–29–*ct* 168
Bowling 2473–71–34.83–4–0–6/29
Test batting
7–13–0–487–117–37.46–1–*ct* 1

He hit 1,000 runs in a season nine times (best 1,790, av 42.61, in 1895). His only double century was 219 for Stoddart's XI v South Australia at Adelaide in 1894/5.

Ward, Albert Paine
Professional. *b:* 9.11.1896, Highgate, London. *d:* 5.3.1979, Jersey. Lower order right-hand batsman, right-arm fast bowler. *Team* Hampshire (1921, 1 match).
Career batting
1–2–1–11–6–11.00–0–*ct* 1
Bowling 57–1–57.00–0–0–1/28

Ward, Arnold Sandwith
Amateur. *b:* 8.11.1876, Oxford. *d:* 1.1.1950, Kensington, London. Lower order right-hand batsman, right-arm medium pace bowler. *Sch* Eton and Uppingham. *Team* Oxford U (1899).
Career batting
1–2–0–8–6–4.00–0–*ct* 1
Bowling 52–0

His County cricket was for Hertfordshire and Buckinghamshire. He was MP for West Hertfordshire.

Ward, Brian
Cricketer. *b:* 28.2.1944, Chelmsford, Essex. Middle order right-hand batsman, right-arm medium pace bowler. *Team* Essex (1967–72, 128 matches).
Career batting
128–222–19–4799–164*–23.64–4–*ct* 60
Bowling 68–5–13.60–0–0–2/5

His best season was 1971 with 968 runs, av 27.65

Ward, Basil Jordain
Amateur. *b:* 6.8.1889, Dublin. *d:* 29.3.1972, Clapham, London. Left-hand batsman, left-arm fast bowler. *Team* Ireland (1912–20).
Career batting
4–7–2–56–17–11.20–0–*ct* 3
Bowling 273–13–21.00–0–0–4/66

Ward, Rev Charles Gordon
Amateur. *b:* 23.9.1875, Braughing, Herts. *d:* 27.6.1954, South Ormsby, Lincs. Brother of H. F. (Hampshire). Lower order right-hand batsman, useful bowler. *Sch* Aldenham and Denstone. *Team* Hampshire (1897–1901, 14 matches).
Career batting
14–23–0–186–30–8.08–0–*ct* 3
Bowling 135–2–67.50–0–0–1/17

He also played for Lincolnshire and Hertfordshire.

Ward, Donald J.
Professional. *b:* 30.8.1934, Tonypandy, Glamorgan. Lower order right-hand batsman, off break bowler, fine cover-point. *Team* Glamorgan (1954–62, 135 matches).
Career batting
135–206–33–2496–86–14.42–0–*ct* 65
Bowling 4987–187–26.66–5–0–7/60

Ward, Rev Edward Ewer
(changed name from E. E. Harrison in 1869) Amateur. *b:* 16.7.1847, Timworth Hall, Suffolk. *d:* 25.3.1940, Gorleston, Norfolk. Tail end right-hand batsman, left-hand fast round-arm bowler. *Sch* Bury St Edmund's. *Team* Cambridge U (1868–71, blue 1870 and 1871).
Career batting
11–18–5–30–5–2.30–0–*ct* 5
Bowling 548–37–14.81–1–0–6/29

His County cricket was for Suffolk.

Ward, Frank
Professional. *b:* 9.1.1865, Carlisle, Cumberland. Stylish middle order right-hand batsman, right-arm medium pace bowler. *Team* Lancashire (1884–96, 47 matches).
Career batting
47–74–6–986–145–14.50–1–*ct* 11
Bowling 538–27–19.92–0–0–4/14

Ward, Frank
Professional. *b:* 31.8.1881. *d:* 28.2.1948, Nottingham. Lower order batsman, left-arm bowler. *Team* Yorkshire (1903, 1 match).
Career batting
1–1–0–0–0–0.00–0–*ct* 1
Bowling 16–0

Ward, Frank
Amateur. *b:* 3.6.1888. *d:* 1.3.1952, Worthing, Sussex. Middle order batsman, useful bowler. *Team* Army (1926–27).
Career batting
4–6–0–28–10–4.66–0–*ct* 0
Bowling 84–2–42.00–0–0–1/9

Ward, Francis Anthony
Amateur. *b:* 23.2.1909, Sydney, Australia. *d:* 25.3.1974, Sydney, Australia. Stubborn lower

order right-hand batsman, leg break bowler. *Team* South Australia (1935/6 to 1940/1, 38 matches). *Tour* Australia to England 1938. *Tests* Australia (1936/7 to 1938, 4 matches).
Career batting
66–80–17–871–62–13.82–0–*ct* 42
Bowling 7900–320–24.68–24–5–7/51
Test batting
4–8–2–36–18–6.00–0–*ct* 1
Bowling 574–11–52.18–1–0–6/102

In first-class matches on the 1938 tour he came second in the bowling table with 92 wickets, av 19.27, but was only chosen for one Test.

Ward, Hon Gerald Ernest Francis
Amateur. *b:* 9.11.1877, Himley, Staffordshire. *d:* 30.10.1914, Zandvoorde, Belgium. He was killed in action. Tail end right-hand batsman, right-arm fast bowler, moderate field. *Sch* Eton. *Team* MCC (1903).
Career batting
1–1–0–8–8–8.00–0–*ct* 0

Ward, Geoffrey Hubert
Professional. *b:* 22.11.1926, Rainham, Kent. Lower order right-hand batsman, wicket-keeper. *Sch* Sutton Valence. *Teams* Kent (1949, 2 matches); Essex (1950, 1 match).
Career batting
3–6–2–23–6*–5.75–0–*ct* 3–*st* 1

Ward, Herbert Foster
Amateur. *b:* 24.3.1873, Hammersmith, London. *d:* 6.6.1897, Northwood, Winchester, Hampshire. He died of typhoid fever. Brother of C. G. (Hampshire). Stylish middle order right-hand batsman. *Team* Hampshire (1895–97, 33 matches).
Career batting
34–63–1–1367–113–22.04–2–*ct* 20
Bowling 553–19–29.10–0–0–4/17

He also played for Hertfordshire.

Ward, Humphrey Plowden
Amateur. *b:* 20.1.1899, Amotherby, Malton, Yorkshire. *d:* 16.12.1946, Thornton-le-Dale, Yorkshire. Fine forcing middle order right-hand batsman, wicket-keeper. *Sch* Shrewsbury. *Teams* Oxford U (1919–21, blue 1919 and 1921); Yorkshire (1920, 1 match); Europeans (1921/2 to 1945/6); Madras (1926/7 to 1938/9).
Career batting
66–120–10–3591–173–32.64–4–*ct* 67–*st* 17
Bowling 35–1–35.00–0–0–1/13

He went to India in 1922 and played much cricket in Madras. His final first-class match in England was for Leveson-Gower's XI in 1931. A good soccer player, he was an Amateur International.

Ward, John
Amateur. Lower order batsman, fast round-arm bowler. *Team* Hampshire (1877, 1 match).
Career batting
1–2–0–14–11–7.00–0–*ct* 0
Bowling 77–0

Ward, John Daniel
Amateur. *b:* 21.5.1931, South Africa. Lower order batsman, right-arm medium fast bowler. *Team* Cambridge U (1954).
Career batting
1–1–1–5–5*–no av–0–*ct* 0
Bowling 79–1–79.00–0–0–1/39

Ward, John Michael
Cricketer. *b:* 14.9.1948, Sandon, Staffs. Middle order right-hand batsman. *Teams* Oxford U (1970–73, blue 1971–73); Derbyshire (1973–75, 20 matches).
Career batting
49–87–4–1743–104–21.00–1–*ct* 24

He appeared for Staffordshire 1969 and 1970. A useful rugby footballer, he represented Staffordshire.

Ward, John Thomas
Amateur. *b:* 11.3.1937, Timaru, New Zealand. Steady lower order right-hand batsman, wicket-keeper. *Team* Canterbury (1959/60 to 1970/1). *Tours* New Zealand to England 1958, 1965, to South Africa 1961/2, to India and Pakistan 1964/5. *Tests* New Zealand (1963/4 to 1967/8, 8 matches).
Career batting
95–129–39–1117–54*–12.41–0–*ct* 227–*st* 27
Bowling 7–0
Test batting
8–12–6–75–35*–12.50–0–*ct* 16–*st* 1

The reserve wicket-keeper, he played in only 13 matches on the 1958 tour and in none of the Tests. In 1965 he appeared in just six matches, but in one Test. His first-class debut was for South Island in 1957/8.

Ward, Lancelot Edward Seth
Amateur. *b:* 7.8.1875, Hemel Hempstead, Herts. *d:* 27.8.1929, Lambeth, London. Middle order batsman. *Sch* Felsted. *Team* Somerset (1913–20, 3 matches).
Career batting
3–5–0–18–11–3.60–0–*ct* 0

Ward, Rev Leonard Foster
Amateur. *b:* 24.3.1866, Oldham, Lancashire. *d:*

1.9.1945, St Helier, Jersey. Middle order batsman. *Sch* Denstone. *Team* Derbyshire (1899, 1 match).
Career batting
1–2–0–0–0–0.00–0–*ct* 1

Ward, Leslie Maynard
Amateur. *b:* 2.5.1908, Coventry, Warwickshire. *d:* 13.1.1981, Bideford, Devon. Right-hand batsman, right-arm fast medium off break bowler. *Team* Warwickshire (1930, 1 match).
Career batting
1–1–0–5–5–5.00–0–*ct* 1
Bowling 29–1–29.00–0–0–1/29

Ward, Merrik de Sampajo Cecil
Amateur. *b:* 15.7.1908, London. *d:* 13.2.1981, Bath, Avon. Hard hitting middle order left-hand batsman, left-arm medium or slow bowler. *Sch* Eton. *Team* Hampshire (1927–29, 5 matches).
Career batting
5–10–1–141–48–15.66–0–*ct* 3
Bowling 135–0

Ward, R. (*See under* Wright, R. W.)

Ward, Reginald Valentine
Amateur. *b:* 1902, Biggleswade, Bedfordshire. *d:* 1968, Yeovil, Somerset. Lower order right-hand batsman, useful bowler. *Team* Minor Counties (1931).
Career batting
1–1–0–4–4–4.00–0–*ct* 0
Bowling 77–2–38.50–0–0–2/77
His County cricket was for Bedfordshire.

Ward, Thomas Alfred
Amateur. *b:* 2.8.1887, Rawalpindi, India. *d:* 16.2.1936, at the West Springs Gold Mine, South Africa. He was accidentally electrocuted whilst working. Steady opening or middle order right-hand batsman, wicket-keeper. *Team* Transvaal (1909/10 to 1925/6). *Tours* South Africa to England 1912, 1924. *Tests* South Africa (1912–24, 23 matches).
Career batting
92–137–31–1635–75–15.42–0–*ct* 107–*st* 68
Bowling 11–0
Test batting
23–42–9–459–64–13.90–0–*ct* 19–*st* 13
He played in five out of six Tests on the 1912, but achieved little as a batsman. In 1924 he played in all the Tests and, promoted to open the innings, proved a very stubborn defender. His return of 490 runs, av 14.00, does not convey his worth to the team.

Ward, Thomas Fitzgerald
Amateur. *b:* 14.2.1905, Armagh, Co Armagh. Right-hand batsman, right-arm fast bowler. *Team* Ireland (1936–39).
Career batting
2–4–3–7–3*–7.00–0–*ct* 1
Bowling 139–5–27.80–0–0–2/31

Ward, William
Amateur. *b:* 24.7.1787, Islington, Middlesex. *d:* 30.6.1849, Westminster, London. Attacking middle order right-hand batsman, slow under-arm bowler, point field. *Sch* Winchester. *Teams* Surrey (1815–17); Hampshire (1816–45).
Career batting
130–235–23–4022–278–18.97–3–*ct* 49–*st* 4
Bowling 49 wickets, no analyses
At Lord's in 1820 he hit 278 for MCC v Norfolk, which was the highest innings recorded at that time and the first double century. He was for many years regarded as one of the leading batsmen in England. His first important match was for England in 1810. He was for some years MP for the City of London.

Ward, William
Professional. *b:* 24.5.1874, Birmingham. *d:* 13.12.1961, Birmingham. Lower order batsman, slow left-arm bowler. *Team* Warwickshire (1895–1904, 11 matches).
Career batting
11–16–5–79–26–7.18–0–*ct* 3
Bowling 965–30–32.16–2–0–5/61

Ward, Sir William Erskine
Amateur. *b:* 4.2.1838, Bath, Somerset. *d:* 24.12.1916, Ealing, Middlesex. Middle order batsman. *Team* MCC (1871).
Career batting
1–2–0–6–6–3.00–0–*ct* 0

Wardall, Thomas Arthur
Professional. *b:* 19.4.1862, Eston Junction, Middlesbrough, Yorkshire. *d:* 20.12.1932, Burnley, Lancashire. Steady middle order right-hand batsman, right-arm slow bowler, usually 'donkey-drops'. *Team* Yorkshire (1884–94, 45 matches).
Career batting
47–80–3–1163–112–15.10–3–*ct* 30
Bowling 695–30–23.16–1–0–5/13

Warde, Frederick
Amateur. *b:* 18.3.1852, West Farleigh, Kent. *d:* 14.5.1899, Aldon, Kent. Lower order right-hand batsman, right-hand fast medium round-arm bowler. *Sch* Tonbridge and Maidstone. *Team* Kent (1871–77, 6 matches).

Career batting
6–10–1–65–18–7.22–0–*ct* 1
Bowling 56–3–18.66–0–0–2/5

Warden, Jehangir Sorabji
Amateur. *b:* 13.1.1885, Bombay, India. *d:* 16.1.1928, Bombay, India. Middle order left-hand batsman, slow left-arm bowler. *Team* Parsis (1905/6 to 1924/5). *Tour* India to England 1911.
Career batting
41–71–7–1208–115*–18.87–1–*ct* 38
Bowling 2824–183–15.43–17–4–8/91

He was the leading all-rounder on the 1911 tour with 429 runs, av 15.32, and 44 wickets, av 25.59, in first-class matches. In a minor match in Calcutta in 1920 he took five wickets with the first five balls of the match. He was author of *Knotty Cricket Problems Solved.*

Wardill, Benjamin Johnson
Amateur. *b:* 15.10.1842, Everton, Lancashire. *d:* 15.10.1917, Sandringham, Victoria, Australia. Brother of R. W. (Victoria). Lower order right-hand batsman, wicket-keeper. *Team* Victoria (1866/7, 1 match). *Tours* Manager of Australia to England 1886, 1899 and 1902.
Career batting
2–3–1–21–17–10.50–0–*ct* 2

He played in one first-class match on the 1886 tour to England. He was Secretary to Melbourne Cricket Club from 1878 to 1910.

Wardle, Charles
Professional. *b:* 20.2.1837, Arnold, Notts. *d:* 10.8.1907, Arnold, Notts. Lower order right-hand batsman, right-hand fast round-arm bowler, slip field. *Team* Lancashire (1867–72, 3 matches).
Career batting
3–5–2–25–7*–8.33–0–*ct* 4
Bowling 17–0

Wardle, John Henry
Professional. *b:* 8.1.1923, Ardsley, Yorkshire. Hard hitting lower order left-hand batsman, slow left-arm orthodox and chinaman bowler. *Team* Yorkshire (1946–58, 330 matches). *Tours* MCC to West Indies 1947/8, 1953/4, to Australia and New Zealand 1954/5, to South Africa 1956/7; selected for MCC to Australia 1958/9, but invitation withdrawn following his outspoken newspaper articles. *Tests* England (1947/8 to 1957, 28 matches).
Career batting
412–527–71–7333–79–16.08–0–*ct* 256
Bowling 35027–1846–18.97–134–29–9/25
Test batting
28–41–8–653–66–19.78–0–*ct* 12
Bowling 2080–102–20.39–5–1–7/36

He took 100 wickets in a season 10 times (best 195, av 16.14, in 1955). His best analysis in an innings was 9 for 25 for Yorkshire v Lancashire at Old Trafford in 1954. The newspaper articles referred to above caused his dismissal from Yorkshire at the height of his career and the virtual end of his first-class cricket. He later played for Cambridgeshire. His final first-class appearance was in a National Defence Fund Match in India in 1967/8.

Ware, Rev John Hubert
Amateur. *b:* 1863, Ullingswick, Herefordshire. *d:* 28.11.1907, Minehead, Somerset. Tail end right-hand batsman, slow leg break bowler. *Team* Oxford U (1886).
Career batting
1–2–1–14–10–14.00–0–*ct* 0
Bowling 43–0

His County cricket was for Herefordshire.

Waring, John Shaw
Cricketer. *b:* 1.10.1942, Ripon, Yorkshire. Lower order right-hand batsman, right-arm fast medium bowler. *Teams* Yorkshire (1963–66, 28 matches); Warwickshire (1967, 1 match).
Career batting
29–29–15–152–26–10.85–0–*ct* 17
Bowling 1251–55–22.74–2–1–7/40

He also played for Cumberland.

Waring, Seth
Amateur. *b:* 4.11.1838. *d:* 17.4.1919, Keighley, Yorkshire. Middle order batsman. *Team* Yorkshire (1870, 1 match).
Career batting
1–1–0–9–9–9.00–0–*ct* 0

Warke, Laurence
Amateur. *b:* 6.5.1927, Belfast. Father of S. J. S. (Ireland). Right-hand batsman, right-arm medium pace bowler. *Sch* Royal Belfast Academical Institution. *Team* Ireland (1950–61).
Career batting
17–29–0–405–120–13.96–1–*ct* 20
Bowling 326–7–46.57–0–0–1/0

Warke, Stephen John Simon
Cricketer. *b:* 11.7.1959, Belfast, Ireland. Son of Laurence (Ireland). Middle order right-hand batsman. *Team* Ireland (1981–83).
Career batting
2–3–0–112–63–37.33–0–*ct* 1

Warnapura, Bandula
Cricketer. *b:* 1.3.1953, Rambukkana, Ceylon. Opening right-hand batsman, right-arm medium pace bowler. *Team* Sri Lanka (1970/1 to 1982/3).

Tours Sri Lanka to India 1972/3, 1975/6, 1976/7, 1982/3, to Pakistan 1973/4, 1981/2, to England 1975, 1979, 1981, to South Africa 1982/3. *Tests* Sri Lanka (1981/2 to 1982/3, 4 matches).
Career batting
57–99–8–2280–154–25.05–2–*ct* 23
Bowling 628–13–48.30–0–0–2/33
Test batting
4–8–0–96–38–12.00–0–*ct* 2
Bowling 46–0

Captain of Sri Lanka, he led his country in its first Test, but his decision to tour South Africa ended his brief Test career.

Warne, Frank Belmont
Professional. *b:* 3.10.1906, North Carlton, Victoria, Australia. Son of T. S. (Victoria). Middle order left-hand batsman, off break bowler. *Teams* Victoria (1926/7 to 1928/9, 2 matches); Worcestershire (1934–38, 78 matches); Europeans (1934/5 to 1937/8); Transvaal (1941/2). *Tour* Australia to India 1935/6.
Career batting
95–168–15–3275–115–21.40–3–*ct* 31
Bowling 4801–138–34.78–4–1–6/51

His final first-class match was for Rest of South Africa in 1942/3. He hit 1,000 runs, av 20.40, in 1935.

Warner, Alan Esmond
Cricketer. *b:* 12.5.1957, Birmingham. Right-hand batsman, right-arm fast medium bowler. *Team* Worcestershire (1982–83, 20 matches).
Career batting
20–32–7–418–67–16.72–0–*ct* 5
Bowling 1315–46–28.58–0–0–4/72

Warner, Claude Charles
Amateur. *b:* 31.3.1882, Cardiff. *d:* 29.12.1965, Llanelly. Lower order batsman, useful bowler. *Team* Glamorgan (1923, 1 match).
Career batting
1–2–1–14–7*–14.00–0–*ct* 0
Bowling 47–0

Warner, Christopher John
Cricketer. *b:* 15.1.1945, Bloemfontein, South Africa. Son of E. W. (Orange Free State). Left-hand batsman. *Team* Scotland (1978–83).
Career batting
7–12–1–268–70–24.36–0–*ct* 5

Warner, Charles Simon
Amateur. *b:* 19.11.1938, Liverpool, Lancashire. Opening left-hand batsman. *Sch* Repton. *Team* Oxford U (1962).
Career batting
7–14–0–365–77–26.07–0–*ct* 2

Warner, Graham Sydney
Cricketer. *b:* 27.11.1945, Darlaston, Staffs. Middle order right-hand batsman, right-hand off break bowler. *Team* Warwickshire (1966–71, 30 matches).
Career batting
30–48–7–965–118*–23.53–0–*ct* 13
Bowling 14–0

He also played for Staffordshire.

Warner, Sir Pelham Francis
Amateur. *b:* 2.10.1873, The Hall, Port of Spain, Trinidad. *d:* 30.1.1963, West Lavington, Sussex. Brother of R. S. A. (Trinidad). Stylish opening right-hand batsman, right-arm slow bowler, good field. *Sch* Rugby. *Teams* Oxford U (1894–96, blue 1895 and 1896); Middlesex (1894–1920, 345 matches). *Tours* Hawke to West Indies 1896/7, to South Africa 1898/9, to Australia and New Zealand 1902/3; Warner to North America 1897; 1898; MCC to Australia 1903/4, 1911/12, to South Africa 1905/6, to South America 1926/7; joint manager of MCC to Australia and New Zealand 1932/3. *Tests* England (1898/9 to 1912, 15 matches).
Career batting
519–875–75–29028–244–36.28–60–*ct* 183
Bowling 636–15–42.40–0–0–2/26
Test batting
15–28–2–622–132*–23.92–1–*ct* 3

He hit 1,000 runs in a season 14 times, going on to 2,000 once : 2,123, av 46.15, in 1911. His highest innings was 244 for Rest of England v Warwickshire at the Oval in 1911, and he hit two other double centuries, one in New Zealand and one for MCC v Sussex. He captained England in 10 Test matches and the MCC on three major tours, two to Australia and one to South Africa. He led Middlesex from 1908 to 1920. His final first-class match was for MCC v Navy in 1929. From 1905 to 1938 he was intermittantly a Test selector and in 1937 he was knighted for his services to cricket. In 1950–51 he was President of MCC and from 1946 to 1961 a Trustee of the Club. He wrote many books on the game, besides being Editor of *The Cricketer* and cricket correspondent for the *Morning Post* from 1921 to 1932.

Warner, Rev William Sydney Oke
Amateur. *b:* 29.8.1844, Swansea, Glamorgan. *d:* November 1871, Alderbury, Salisbury, Wiltshire. Attacking middle order right-hand batsman, long stop or long leg. *Team* Cambridge U (1865–68, blue 1867 and 1868).
Career batting
13–22–2–323–50–16.15–0–*ct* 7

His County cricket was for Devon. He represented Cambridge at racquets 1866 to 1868.

Warr, Antony Lawley
Amateur. *b:* 15.5.1913, Birmingham. Lower order right-hand batsman, wicket-keeper. *Sch* Bromsgrove. *Team* Oxford U (1933–34).
Career batting
5–7–1–54–24–9.00–0–*ct* 6–*st* 1
His final first-class match was for MCC in 1950. A noted rugby footballer, he played for Oxford and England.

Warr, John James
Amateur. *b:* 16.7.1927, Ealing, Middlesex. Tail end right-hand batsman, right-arm fast medium bowler. *Teams* Cambridge U (1949–52, blue all four years); Middlesex (1949–60, 260 matches). *Tours* MCC to Australia and New Zealand 1950/1, to Canada 1951, to East Africa 1957/8 (not first-class); Swanton to West Indies 1955/6; Norfolk to Jamaica 1956/7. *Tests* England (1950/1, 2 matches).
Career batting
344–454–119–3838–54*–11.45–0–*ct* 117
Bowling 21796–956–22.79–35–5–9/65
Test batting
2–4–0–4–4–1.00–0–*ct* 0
Bowling 281–1–281.00–0–0–1/76
He took 116 wickets, av 18.17, in 1956 and also exceeded 100 wickets in one other season. His best bowling was 9/65 for Middlesex v Kent at Lord's in 1956. From 1958 to 1960 he captained Middlesex.

Warren, Arnold (R.)
(his second initial was used only to distinguish him from another of the same name in his locality)
Professional. *b:* 2.4.1875, Codnor Park, Derbyshire. *d:* 3.9.1951, Codnor, Derbyshire. Lower order right-hand batsman, right-arm fast bowler. *Team* Derbyshire (1897–1920, 250 matches). *Test* England (1905, 1 match).
Career batting
255–445–44–5507–123–13.73–1–*ct* 195
Bowling 23061–939–24.55–72–15–8/69
Test batting
1–1–0–7–7–7.00–0–*ct* 1
Bowling 113–6–18.83–1–0–5/57
He took 100 wickets in a season three times (best 124, av 20.94, in 1904). He played soccer for Derby County.

Warren, Rev Charles
Amateur. *b:* 20.12.1843, Cambridge. *d:* 29.4.1919, Sidmouth, Devon. Forceful opening right-hand batsman, good deep field. *Sch* Oakham. *Teams* Cambridgeshire (1865–67, 11 matches); Cambridge U (1866, blue).
Career batting
20–35–4–577–73–18.61–0–*ct* 4
He was on the Committee of Cambridgeshire CCC in 1866. His final first-class match was for an England Eleven in 1874, but he rarely appeared in important cricket after being ordained. He also played for Lincolnshire.

Warren, Thomas (Henry)
Professional. *b:* 8.10.1859, Hathern, Leics. *d:* 1936, Billesdon, Leics. Attractive middle order right-hand batsman, right-hand fast medium round-arm bowler, good cover point. *Team* Leicestershire (1894–95, 13 matches).
Career batting
15–27–3–313–33–13.04–0–*ct* 7
Bowling 34–2–17.00–0–0–2/34
His debut for Leicestershire was in 1882 and his first-class debut in 1886 for North v South at Lord's.

Warrington, Anthony George
Cricketer. *b:* 28.3.1947, Ipswich, Suffolk. Opening right-hand batsman. *Team* Minor Counties (1973–74).
Career batting
2–4–0–152–92–38.00–0–*ct* 0
His County cricket has been for Suffolk, commencing 1965.

Warrington, John Michael
Amateur. *b:* 7.3.1924, Northampton. Lower order right-hand batsman, right-arm medium pace bowler. *Team* Northants (1951, 2 matches).
Career batting
2–1–0–18–18–18.00–0–*ct* 1
Bowling 164–1–54.66–0–0–1/30

Warsop, Brian
Professional. *b:* 12.1.1904, Willesden, London. Middle order right-hand batsman, slow left-arm bowler. *Team* Essex (1931–32, 5 matches).
Career batting
5–10–2–128–51–16.00–0–*ct* 1
Bowling 18–0

Warsop, Thomas
Professional. *b:* 1779, Nottingham. *d:* 28.2.1845, Nottingham. He died of gout in the brain. Useful middle order batsman, right-hand slow under-arm bowler. *Team* Nottingham (1791–1823).
Career batting
1–2–0–24–18–12.00–0–*ct* 2
Bowling 2 wickets, no analyses
The most famous of four brothers, all of whom played for Nottingham in the late 18th century, he was a good all-rounder and his under-arm bowling was afterwards imitated with great

success by William Clarke. His only 19th century important match was Notts & Leics v Hampshire in 1803.

Washbrook, Cyril
Professional. *b:* 6.12.1914, Barrow, Blackburn, Lancashire. Sound opening right-hand batsman, brilliant cover field. *Team* Lancashire (1933–59, 500 matches). *Tours* MCC to Australia and New Zealand 1946/7, 1950/1, to South Africa 1948/9. *Tests* England (1937–56, 37 matches).
Career batting
592–906–107–34101–251*–42.67–76–*ct* 211
Bowling 309–7–44.14–0–0–2/8
Test batting
37–66–6–2569–195–42.81–6–*ct* 12
Bowling 33–1–33.00–0–0–1/25

With L. Hutton he formed England's opening pair in the Tests immediately following the Second World War, and together they proved most successful. In 1946/7 in Australia they added over 100 for the first wicket in three consecutive innnings and in 1948/9 against South Africa at Johannesburg added 359 for the first England wicket.

Washbrook hit 1,000 runs 17 times in England and three times in overseas seasons. He went on to 2,000 twice, with his highest aggregate being 2,662, av 68.25, in 1947. All his seven double centuries were for Lancashire, the highest being 251* v Surrey at Old Trafford in 1947.

He was a Test selector in 1956 and 1957 and in the former year was brought back into the England side, having been absent for six years; he hit 98.

His benefit in 1948 produced a record, at the time, of £14,000. From 1954 to 1959 he captained Lancashire, being the first professional officially to hold that post. His last first-class match was for MCC in 1964. In 1971 and 1972 he was again chosen for the Test match panel.

Washington, William Arthur Irving
Professional. *b:* 11.12.1879, Mitchell Main, Yorkshire. *d:* 20.10.1927, Wombwell, Yorkshire. Uncle of Norman and Roy Kilner (Yorkshire). Stylish middle order left-hand batsman. *Teams* Yorkshire (1900–02, 44 matches); Griqualand West (1904/5); Transvaal (1906/7).
Career batting
48–69–6–1384–100*–21.96–1–*ct* 18
Bowling 32–0

He hit 1,029 runs, av 26.38, in 1902, but owing to ill-health could not continue in first-class cricket in England after that season.

Wasim Bari
Cricketer. *b:* 23.3.1948, Karachi, Pakistan. Lower order right-hand batsman, wicket-keeper. *Teams* Karachi (1964/5 to 1980/1); Pakistan International Airlines (1967/8 to 1980/1); Sind (1973/4). *Tours* Pakistan to England 1967, 1971, 1974, 1978, 1982, to Ceylon 1972/3, 1975/6, to Australia and New Zealand 1972/3, 1978/9, to Australia 1976/7, 1981/2, to West Indies 1976/7, to India 1979/80; PIA to England 1969 (not first-class). *Tests* Pakistan (1967 to 1982/3, 73 matches).
Career batting
275–343–89–5530–177–21.77–2–*ct* 634–*st* 144
Bowling 30–1–30.00–0–0–1/11
Test batting
73–102–24–1259–85–16.14–0–*ct* 175–*st* 26
Bowling 2–0

He has been the wicket-keeper on five Test tours to England, playing in all three Tests on each tour and was captain of the 1978 team.

Wasim Hasan Raja
Cricketer. *b:* 3.7.1952, Multan, Pakistan. Brother of Rameez (Lahore) and Zaeem (National Bank). Middle order left-hand batsman, right-arm leg break bowler. *Teams* Lahore (1967/8 to 1969/70); Sargodha (1969/70); Punjab University (1969/70); Combined Universities (1972/3); Pakistan International Airlines (1973/4); Punjab (1973/4); National Bank (1974/5 to 1982/3). *Tours* Pakistan to England 1974, 1978, 1982, to Australia and New Zealand 1978/9, to Australia 1981/2, to West Indies 1976/7, to New Zealand 1972/3, to India 1979/80, to Sri Lanka 1973/4, 1975/6. *Tests* Pakistan (1972/3 to 1982/3, 45 matches).
Career batting
221–337–49–10269–165–35.65–14–*ct* 137
Bowling 14922–520–28.69–31–7–8/65
Test batting
45–74–12–2321–117*–37.43–2–*ct* 12
Bowling 1425–39–36.53–0–0–4/68

On his first tour to England in 1974 he topped the batting averages with 486 runs, av 54.00, but he was nothing like as successful in 1978 or 1982, though playing in the Test matches. He has played County cricket for Durham and Northumberland. In the 1973/4 season he hit 1,010 runs, av 32.58, and took 99 wickets, av 22.41.

Wass, George
Professional. *b:* 6.2.1882, Worksop, Notts. *d:* 15.6.1966, Liverpool. Lower order right-hand batsman, right-arm medium pace leg break bowler, slip field. *Team* Nottinghamshire (1910, 1 match).
Career batting
1–1–0–0–0–0.00–0–*ct* 0
Bowling 34–3–11.33–0–0–3/34

Wass, Horace
Professional. *b:* 26.8.1903, Chesterfield, Derby-

shire. Middle order right-hand batsman, change bowler. *Team* Derbyshire (1929, 1 match).
Career batting
1–1–0–9–9–9.00–0–*ct* 0
He played for Scotland in eight non-first-class matches between 1935 and 1938. A good soccer player, he appeared for Chesterfield and Southport.

Wass, Thomas George
Professional. *b:* 26.12.1873, Sutton-in-Ashfield, Notts. *d:* 27.10.1953, Sutton-in-Ashfield, Notts. Tail end right-hand batsman, right-arm fast medium leg break bowler. *Team* Nottinghamshire (1896–1920, 308 matches).
Career batting
312–395–101–2138–56–7.27–0–*ct* 115
Bowling 34092–1666–20.46–159–43–9/67
He took 100 wickets in a season ten times (best 163, av 14.28, in 1907). His best innings analysis was 9 for 67 for Notts v Derbyshire at Blackwell in 1911.

Wassell, Albert
Professional. *b:* 14.6.1892, Aston, Warwickshire. *d:* September 1975, Birmingham. Lower order batsman, slow left-arm bowler. *Team* Warwickshire (1923, 7 matches).
Career batting
7–11–3–24–10–3.00–0–*ct* 4
Bowling 344–10–34.40–0–0–3/67

Wassell, Alan Robert
Professional. *b:* 15.4.1940, Fareham, Hampshire. Lower order left-hand batsman, slow left-arm bowler. *Team* Hampshire (1957–66, 121 matches).
Career batting
122–160–25–1209–61–8.95–0–*ct* 96
Bowling 8667–320–27.08–11–1–7/87

Waterman, Alfred George
Amateur. *b:* 13.5.1911, Walthamstow, Essex. Lower order right-hand batsman, right-arm fast medium bowler. *Sch* Bancroft's. *Team* Essex (1937–38, 10 matches).
Career batting
10–15–1–380–103–27.14–1–*ct* 7
Bowling 348–11–31.63–0–0–4/79

Waterman, Peter Andrew
Cricketer. *b:* 26.3.1961, Pinner, Middlesex. Lower order right-hand batsman, right-arm medium fast bowler. *Team* Surrey (1983, 2 matches).
Career batting
2–2–1–6–6*–6.00–0–*ct* 0
Bowling 151–1–151.00–0–0–1/64

Waters, Albert Edward
Amateur. *b:* 8.5.1902, Bristol. Middle order right-hand batsman, bowler. *Team* Gloucestershire (1923–25, 16 matches).
Career batting
16–24–3–270–42–12.85–0–*ct* 9
Bowling 377–5–75.40–0–0–2/13
He also played for Wiltshire.

Waters, Robin Hugh Clough
Amateur. *b:* 6.12.1937, Calcutta, India. Lower order right-hand batsman, wicket-keeper. *Sch* Shrewsbury. *Teams* Oxford U (1961–62); Sussex (1961–65, 8 matches); Bengal (1962/3); Ireland (1968–69).
Career batting
38–62–11–929–70–18.21–0–*ct* 52–*st* 3
His first-class debut was for L. C. Steven's XI in 1960. He was injured in a road accident just prior to the 1961 University Match and thus missed his 'blue'.

Waterton, Stuart Nicholas Varney
Cricketer. *b:* 6.12.1960, Dartford, Kent. Lower order right-hand batsman, wicket-keeper. *Team* Kent (1980–83, 14 matches).
Career batting
14–16–2–171–40*–12.21–0–*ct* 25–*st* 4

Wathen, Arthur Cave
Amateur. *b:* 27.3.1841, Streatham, Surrey. *d:* 14.3.1937, Bradfield, Berkshire. Brother of W. H. (Kent). Lower order right-hand batsman, wicket-keeper. *Sch* Blackheath Proprietary. *Team* Kent (1863–64, 9 matches).
Career batting
13–24–1–206–42*–8.95–0–*ct* 3–*st* 3
His first-class debut was for Gentlemen of the South in 1861.

Wathen, William Hulbert
Amateur. *b:* 5.5.1836, Streatham, Surrey. *d:* 29.3.1913, Westerham, Kent. Brother of A. C. (Kent). Middle order right-hand batsman, right-hand slow round-arm bowler, slip field. *Sch* Blackheath Proprietary and Rugby. *Team* Kent (1863, 1 match).
Career batting
6–11–0–139–38–12.63–0–*ct* 0
Bowling 100–7–14.28–0–0–2/16
His first-class debut was for Gentlemen of Kent in 1862, and his last for the same team in 1866.

Watkin, Dennis
Professional. *b:* 28.6.1912, Stapleford, Notts. *d:* 23.3.1983, Bramcote, Nottingham. Tail end right-hand batsman, leg break bowler. *Team* Nottinghamshire (1937–39, 9 matches).

Career batting
9–12–4–47–14–5.87–0–*ct* 4
Bowling 748–15–49.86–1–0–6/48

A good soccer player, he appeared for Aston Villa and Reading as outside-right.

Watkins, Albert John
(known as Allan John Watkins)
Professional. *b:* 21.4.1922, Usk, Monmouthshire. Sound middle order left-hand batsman, left-arm medium fast bowler, good short-leg field. *Team* Glamorgan (1939–62, 408 matches). *Tours* MCC to South Africa 1948/9, to India, Pakistan and Ceylon 1951/2, to Pakistan 1955/6. *Tests* England (1948–52, 15 matches).
Career batting
484–753–87–20361–170*–30.57–32–*ct* 461
Bowling 20393–833–24.48–24–0–7/28
Test batting
15–24–4–810–137*–40.50–2–*ct* 17
Bowling 554–11–50.36–0–0–3/20

He hit 1,000 runs in a season 13 times (best 1,640, av 34.89, in 1954) and took 100 wickets in a season twice (best 114, av 20.49, in 1955). He achieved the 'double' twice. His final first-class match was for MCC in 1963. He played soccer for Plymouth Argyle.

Watkins, Bertram Thomas Lewis
Professional. *b:* 25.6.1902, Gloucester. *d:* 22.12.1982, Badminton, Gloucs. Lower order right-hand batsman, wicket-keeper. *Team* Gloucestershire (1932–38, 30 matches).
Career batting
30–44–9–211–25–6.02–0–*ct* 35–*st* 18

Watkins, David
Amateur. *b:* 18.8.1928, St Albans, Hertfordshire. Lower order right-hand batsman, right-arm medium pace bowler. *Sch* Westcliff HS. *Team* Essex (1949–54, 12 matches).
Career batting
12–17–4–210–32–16.15–0–*ct* 5
Bowling 421–8–52.62–0–0–2/45

He played for Essex in 1949, but not again until 1953.

Watkins, Stephen George
Cricketer. *b:* 23.3.1959, Hereford. Opening right-hand batsman, right-arm medium pace bowler. *Team* Worcestershire (1983, 1 match).
Career batting
1–2–0–105–77–52.50–0–*ct* 0

Watkins, William Martin
Amateur. *b:* 18.1.1923, Swansea, Glamorgan. Middle order right-hand batsman. *Team* Glamorgan (1950, 1 match).
Career batting
1–1–0–3–3–3.00–0–*ct* 0

Watkins, William Richard
Professional. *b:* 22.6.1904, Ealing, Middlesex. Middle order right-hand batsman, slow right-arm bowler. *Team* Middlesex (1930–37, 27 matches). *Tour* MCC to East Africa 1957/8, as baggage master.
Career batting
32–53–7–867–115–18.84–1–*ct* 7
Bowling 376–18–20.88–1–0–5/31

His final first-class match was for MCC in 1947.

Watkinson, Michael
Cricketer. *b:* 1.8.1961, Westhoughton, Lancashire. Lower order right-hand batsman, right-arm medium pace bowler. *Team* Lancashire (1982–83, 16 matches).
Career batting
16–20–4–168–29–10.50–0–*ct* 2
Bowling 974–36–27.05–2–0–6/51

Watson, Alexander
Professional. *b:* 4.11.1844, Coatbridge, Lanarkshire, Scotland. *d:* 26.10.1920, Old Trafford, Manchester. Lower order right-hand batsman, originally right-hand fast, but after about 1877, slow round-arm bowler. *Team* Lancashire (1871–93, 283 matches).
Career batting
303–453–96–4492–74–12.58–0–*ct* 277
Bowling 18425–1383–13.32–106–27–9/118

He took 100 wickets, av 14.82, in 1887, but his two best seasons, in both of which he headed the averages, were 1883 with 96 wickets, av 11.82, and 1886 with 99, av 11.20. By some his bowling action was regarded as unfair and for this reason he was rarely chosen for the representative matches of his day. His best bowling was 9/118 for Lancashire v Derbyshire at Old Trafford in 1874.

Watson, Arthur Campbell
Amateur. *b:* 17.3.1884, Reigate, Surrey. *d:* 16.1.1952, Shermanbury, Horsham, Sussex. Hard hitting middle order right-hand batsman, right-arm fast bowler. *Sch* Uppingham. *Teams* Essex (1913–14, 2 matches); Sussex (1922–28, 104 matches).
Career batting
106–178–15–2724–111–16.71–1–*ct* 37
Bowling 209–5–41.80–0–0–3/42

He also played for Norfolk.

Watson, Alexander Garth MacLaren
Cricketer. *b:* 27.12.1945, Lucknow, India. Lower

order left-hand batsman, right-arm fast medium bowler. *Team* Oxford U (1965–68, blue 1965, 1966 and 1968).
Career batting
42–67–16–666–65*–13.05–0–*ct* 13
Bowling 2708–68–39.82–1–0–5/44
His County cricket was for Dorset, commencing 1973.

Watson, Arthur Kenelm
Amateur. *b:* 23.3.1867, Harrow, Middlesex. *d:* 2.1.1947, Harrow-on-the-Hill, Middlesex. Brother of H. D. (Oxford U). Attacking middle order right-hand batsman, slow right-arm bowler. *Sch* Harrow. *Teams* Oxford U (1886–89, blue 1889); Middlesex (1890–94, 15 matches).
Career batting
34–57–0–847–91–14.85–0–*ct* 13
Bowling 38–1–38.00–0–0–1/38
From 1904 he appeared for Norfolk and later for Suffolk.

Watson, Arthur Lacon
Amateur. *b:* 27.8.1866, West Cowes, Isle of Wight. *d:* 28.6.1955, Wootton, Isle of Wight. Opening right-hand batsman, right-arm fast medium bowler, mid off field. *Sch* Winchester. *Teams* Hampshire (1885, 1 match); Cambridge U (1888).
Career batting
2–4–0–26–22–6.50–0–*ct* 0

Watson, Darsie
Amateur. *b:* 15.7.1889, Broughty Ferry, Scotland. *d:* 19.11.1964, Westminster, London. Attacking middle order right-hand batsman. *Sch* Rugby. *Team* Sussex (1920, 1 match).
Career batting
1–2–0–3–3–1.50–0–*ct* 0

Watson, David James Falshaw
Amateur. *b:* 18.11.1919, St Pancras, London. *d:* 3.10.1943, USA. He was killed in a Fleet Air Arm accident. Middle order right-hand batsman, good field. *Sch* Sedbergh. *Team* Oxford U (1939).
Career batting
2–4–1–83–35–27.66–0–*ct* 0

Watson, Frederic
Amateur. *b:* 3.1.1840, Bitteswell, Leicestershire. *d:* 9.9.1885, Cork, Ireland. Middle order right-hand batsman, wicket-keeper. *Sch* Harrow. *Team* MCC (1869–74).
Career batting
12–20–1–222–47–11.68–0–*ct* 7–*st* 1
His first-class debut was for Gentlemen of the North in 1862. His County cricket was for Devonshire.

Watson, Frank (Bramley)
Professional. *b:* 17.9.1898, Nottingham. *d:* 1.2.1976, Warrington, Lancashire. Steady opening right-hand batsman, right-arm medium pace bowler, good slip field. *Team* Lancashire (1920–37, 456 matches). *Tour* MCC to West Indies 1925/6.
Career batting
470–688–50–23596–300*–36.98–50–*ct* 292
Bowling 13083–407–32.14–5–0–5/31
He hit 1,000 runs in a season twelve times, going on to 2,000 three times (best 2,583, av 61.50, in 1928). His highest innings was 300 not out for Lancashire v Surrey at Old Trafford in 1928 and his three double centuries were also for Lancashire.

Watson, Graeme Donald
Cricketer. *b:* 8.3.1945, Kew, Victoria, Australia. Opening or middle order right-hand batsman, right-arm medium pace bowler. *Teams* Victoria (1964/5 to 1970/1, 40 matches); Western Australia (1971/2 to 1974/5, 25 matches); New South Wales (1976/7, 5 matches). *Tours* Australia to South Africa 1966/7, to New Zealand 1969/70, to England 1972. *Tests* Australia (1966/7 to 1972, 5 matches).
Career batting
107–162–19–4674–176–32.68–7–*ct* 73
Bowling 4709–186–25.31–8–0–6/61
Test batting
5–9–0–97–50–10.77–0–*ct* 1
Bowling 254–6–42.33–0–0–2/67
He hit 915 runs, av 36.60, on the 1972 tour to England, but failed in both the Tests in which he played.

Watson, Gregory George
Cricketer. *b:* 29.1.1955, Mudgee, New South Wales, Australia. Lower order right-hand batsman, right-arm fast medium bowler. *Teams* New South Wales (1977/8 to 1978/9, 14 matches); Worcestershire (1978–79, 30 matches); Western Australia (1979/80, 1 match).
Career batting
45–58–15–552–38–12.83–0–*ct* 12
Bowling 3832–102–37.56–1–0–6/45

Watson, George Sutton
Amateur, turned professional in 1934. *b:* 10.4.1907, Milton Regis, Kent. *d:* 1.4.1974, Guildford, Surrey. Sound middle order right-hand batsman, left-arm medium pace bowler, good outfield. *Sch* Shrewsbury. *Teams* Kent (1928–29, 8 matches); Leicestershire (1934–50, 225 matches).

Career batting
236–393–20–8566–145–22.96–5–*ct* 87
Bowling 51–1–51.00–0–0–1/21

He hit 1,000 runs in a season three times (best 1,314, av 25.76, in 1947). A good soccer player, he appeared for Corinthians and won an Amateur International cap for England, before becoming a professional with Charlton Athletic, Crystal Palace and West Ham.

Watson, Harold
Professional. *b:* 1883. *d:* 14.3.1969, Cambridge. Dashing lower order right-hand batsman, right-arm fast medium bowler. *Teams* MCC (1913–21); Minor Counties (1924).
Career batting
13–21–1–189–42–9.45–0–*ct* 5
Bowling 926–37–25.02–1–0–5/70

His County cricket was for Norfolk commencing 1910.

Watson, Haworth
Professional. *b:* 26.9.1880, Barnoldswick, Yorkshire. *d:* 24.11.1951, Doncaster, Yorkshire. Lower order right-hand batsman, wicket-keeper. *Team* Yorkshire (1908–14, 29 matches).
Career batting
30–37–12–189–41–7.56–0–*ct* 46–*st* 10

Watson, Harold Boyes
Amateur. *b:* 23.10.1893. *d:* 19.3.1972, Thorpe Bay, Essex. Middle order batsman, useful bowler. *Team* Oxford U (1919).
Career batting
1–1–0–2–2–2.00–0–*ct* 0
Bowling 35–2–17.50–0–0–2/35

Watson, Hubert Digby
Amateur. *b:* 31.12.1869, Harrow, Middlesex. *d:* 9.10.1947, Inkpen, Berkshire. Brother of A. K. (Middlesex). Attacking middle order right-hand batsman, right-hand slow under-arm bowler. *Sch* Harrow. *Team* Oxford U (1891–92, blue 1891).
Career batting
10–19–0–248–40–13.05–0–*ct* 6

He joined the Indian Civil Service in 1893 and therefore was lost to English first-class cricket.

Watson, Admiral Sir Hugh Dudley Richards
Amateur. *b:* 20.4.1872, Saltfleetby, Lincolnshire. *d:* 29.5.1954, Windsor, Berkshire. Middle order right-hand batsman. *Team* MCC (1908).
Career batting
1–2–0–12–12–6.00–0–*ct* 0

His County cricket was for Wiltshire.

Watson, Ian Ronald
Cricketer. *b:* 9.6.1947, Teddington, Middlesex. Middle order right-hand batsman. *Teams* Middlesex (1969, 1 match); Northants (1971, 1 match); Hampshire (1973, 1 match).
Career batting
3–5–1–37–16–9.25–0–*ct* 3

He had a unique career, playing one match only for three different Counties.

Watson, James Mackman
Amateur. *b:* 17.6.1936, Rotherham, Yorkshire. Middle order right-hand batsman. *Team* Cambridge U (1957–59).
Career batting
5–9–0–74–31–8.22–0–*ct* 1
Bowling 1–1–1.00–0–0–1/1

Watson, John Russell
Amateur. *b:* 22.8.1910, Sherborne, Dorset. *d:* 7.3.1980, Yeovil, Somerset. Middle order right-hand batsman. *Sch* Stowe. *Team* Somerset (1933–36, 19 matches).
Career batting
19–33–2–375–56–12.09–0–*ct* 4

He also played for Dorset.

Watson, Dr Joseph Riley
Amateur. *b:* 28.3.1859, Streeton-in-Craven, Yorkshire. *d:* 18.10.1915, Harrogate, Yorkshire. Lower order batsman, useful bowler. *Team* Cambridge U (1882).
Career batting
2–3–0–2–1–0.66–0–*ct* 1
Bowling 25–0

His final first-class match was for An England Eleven at Harrogate in 1888.

Watson, John Thomas
Amateur. *b:* 1877. *d:* 2.9.1916, Chesterfield, Derbyshire. Middle order batsman. *Team* MCC (1902–03).
Career batting
2–4–1–66–24–22.00–0–*ct* 0

Watson, Hon Ronald Bannatyne
Amateur. *b:* 28.9.1883, Edinburgh, Scotland. *d:* 22.1.1966, Edinburgh, Scotland. Middle order batsman. *Sch* Marlborough. *Team* Scotland (1913).
Career batting
1–2–0–11–6–5.50–0–*ct* 0

Watson, Roger Graeme
Cricketer. *b:* 14.1.1964, Rawtenstall, Lancashire. Middle order left-hand batsman, off break bowler. *Team* Lancashire (1982, 1 match).
Career batting
1–2–0–15–11–7.50–0–*ct* 0

Watson, Richard Martin
Amateur. *b:* 31.12.1921, Bakewell, Derbyshire. Middle order left-hand batsman, leg break bowler. *Sch* Trent. *Team* Derbyshire (1947, 6 matches).
Career batting
6–11–3–68–25*–8.50–0–*ct* 3

Watson, Thomas
Amateur. *b:* 13.10.1896, Larkhall, Lanarkshire, Scotland. *d:* 17.5.1974, Stonehouse, Lanarkshire, Scotland. Right-hand batsman, right-arm fast medium bowler. *Team* Scotland (1928–31).
Career batting
5–6–2–60–25*–15.00–0–*ct* 3
Bowling 300–13–23.07–0–0–3/54

Watson, Thomas Herman
Amateur. *b:* 14.11.1880, Water Orton, Warwickshire. *d:* 15.2.1944, Singleton, Blackpool, Lancashire. Right-hand batsman, right-arm fast medium bowler. *Sch* St Bees. *Teams* Cambridge U (1903); Warwickshire (1904, 2 matches).
Career batting
3–5–0–18–12–3.60–0–*ct* 0
Bowling 169–0

Watson, Thomas Mead
Amateur. *b:* 22.5.1913, Lewisham, Kent. Forceful middle order left-hand batsman. *Sch* Monkton Combe. *Team* Oxford U (1933–34).
Career batting
3–6–1–92–27–18.40–0–*ct* 1

Watson, Willie
Professional. *b:* 7.3.1920, Bolton-on-Dearne, Yorkshire. Sound and stylish middle order left-hand batsman, fine outfield. *Teams* Yorkshire (1939–57, 283 matches); Leicestershire (1958–64, 117 matches). *Tours* MCC to West Indies 1953/4, to Australia and New Zealand 1958/9, to New Zealand 1960/1, to East Africa 1963/4 (he did not play in first-class match); Howard to India 1956/7; Norfolk to Jamaica 1956/7. *Tests* England (1951 to 1958/9, 23 matches).
Career batting
468–753–109–25670–257–39.86–55–*ct* 295
Bowling 127–0
Test batting
23–37–3–879–116–25.85–2–*ct* 8

He hit 1,000 runs in a season 14 times, going on to 2,000 once : 2,212, av 55.30, in 1959. His highest innings was 257 for MCC v British Guiana at Georgetown in 1953/4 and he hit one other double century for Yorkshire and one for Leicestershire. From 1958 to 1961 he captained Leicestershire and in 1962 was appointed a Test Selector, retiring in 1964. A noted soccer player, he appeared at left half for Huddersfield Town, Sunderland and Halifax Town and gained four caps for England.

Watson, William Kenneth
Cricketer. *b:* 21.5.1955, Port Elizabeth, South Africa. Attacking lower order right-hand batsman, right-arm fast medium bowler. *Teams* Border (1974/5); Northern Transvaal (1975/6); Nottinghamshire (1976–80, 22 matches); Eastern Province (1976/7 to 1982/3).
Career batting
88–112–36–1028–99*–13.52–0–*ct* 25
Bowling 7250–294–24.65–10–0–7/50

Watson-Smith, H. (*See under* Smith, H. W.)

Watt, Alan Edward
Professional. *b:* 19.6.1907, Limpsfield Chart, Westerham, Kent. *d:* 3.2.1974, Pembury, Kent. Swashbuckling lower order right-hand batsman, right-arm fast medium bowler. *Team* Kent (1929–39, 226 matches).
Career batting
230–330–37–4098–96–13.98–0–*ct* 134
Bowling 17586–610–28.82–34–6–8/100

He took 108 wickets, av 27.09, in 1938. He hit 42 all in boundaries – five sixes and three fours – for Kent v Notts at Trent Bridge in 1933. His final first-class match was for M. Leyland's XI in 1947. A useful soccer player, he kept goal for Folkestone.

Watt, Jonathan
Amateur. *b:* 11.9.1937, Eastbourne, Sussex. Opening right-hand batsman. *Sch* Eastbourne. *Team* L. C. Steven's XI (1960–61).
Career batting
2–3–0–69–34–23.00–0–*ct* 1

Watt, Thomas Douglas
Amateur. *b:* 21.12.1891, Edinburgh, Scotland. *d:* 13.6.1949, Edinburgh, Scotland. Right-hand batsman, right-arm medium pace bowler. *Team* Scotland (1912–24).
Career batting
11–20–6–149–23–10.64–0–*ct* 5
Bowling 821–21–39.09–0–0–3/47

Watts, Andrew
Cricketer. *b:* 4.10.1960, Chapeltown, Yorkshire. Lower order left-hand batsman, right-arm medium pace bowler. *Team* Derbyshire (1982–83, 3 matches).
Career batting
3–3–1–39–33*–19.50–0–*ct* 1
Bowling 118–1–118.00–0–0–1/28

Watts, Alfred William
Amateur. *b:* 1859, South Stoneham, Hampshire. Lower order batsman, useful bowler. *Team* Hampshire (1882, 2 matches).
Career batting
2–3–0–26–11–8.66–0–*ct* 0
Bowling 42–2–21.00–0–0–1/9

Watts, Charles George
Amateur. *b:* 4.9.1894, Hinckley, Leics. *d:* 30.1.1979, Hinckley, Leics. Middle order right-hand batsman. *Team* Leicestershire (1924, 1 match).
Career batting
1–1–0–16–16–16.00–0–*ct* 0

Watts, Charles John Manning
Amateur. *b:* 30.9.1905, Northampton. Middle order right-hand batsman, wicket-keeper. *Sch* Repton. *Team* Essex (1928, 8 matches).
Career batting
8–11–0–119–41–10.81–0–*ct* 2–*st* 2
Bowling 4–0
He also played for Suffolk.

Watts, Edward Alfred
Professional. *b:* 1.8.1911, Peckham, Surrey. *d:* 2.5.1982, Cheam, Surrey. Middle order right-hand batsman, right-arm fast medium pace bowler. *Team* Surrey (1933–49, 240 matches). *Tours* Brinckman to South America 1937/8; Cahn to New Zealand 1938/9.
Career batting
244–357–69–6158–123–21.38–2–*ct* 155
Bowling 19004–729–26.06–24–2–10/67
He took 100 wickets in a season twice (best 129, av 18.47, in 1938). His best bowling in an innings was 10 for 67 for Surrey v Warwickshire at Edgbaston in 1939.

Watts, Frederic Arthur
Amateur. *b:* 1884, Westbury-on-Severn, Gloucs. *d:* 20.2.1968, Northampton. Lower order batsman, useful bowler. *Team* Gloucestershire (1905, 1 match).
Career batting
1–2–0–0–0–0.00–0–*ct* 0
Bowling 125–3–41.66–0–0–3/125

Watts, Fred Henry George
Amateur. *b:* 29.7.1904, Northampton. Middle order right-hand batsman. *Team* Northants (1932–37, 4 matches).
Career batting
4–5–0–12–6–2.40–0–*ct* 0

Watts, George Herbert
Professional. *b:* 18.2.1867, Fenners, Cambridge. *d:* 22.4.1949, Cambridge. Son of Walter (Cambridgeshire). Right-hand batsman, right-arm fast bowler, wicket-keeper. *Team* Surrey (1890–92, 8 matches).
Career batting
8–16–2–79–20–5.64–0–*ct* 13–*st* 4
Bowling 21–0
He also played for Cambridgeshire.

Watts, Hugh Edmund
Amateur. *b:* 4.3.1922, Stratton-on-the-Fosse, Somerset. Middle order left-hand batsman, leg break bowler. *Sch* Downside. *Teams* Somerset (1939–52, 61 matches); Cambridge U (1947, blue).
Career batting
72–124–8–2958–110–25.50–1–*ct* 24
Bowling 117–1–117.00–0–0–1/15

Watts, Lawrence Dursley
Amateur. *b:* 2.5.1935, Bristol. Middle order right-hand batsman. *Sch* Bristol GS. *Teams* Oxford U (1957–58); Gloucestershire (1958, 1 match).
Career batting
11–20–0–361–69–18.05–0–*ct* 3
A noted rugby footballer, he appeared for Oxford, Bristol and Gloucs.

Watts, Peter David
Professional. *b:* 31.3.1938, Henlow, Bedfordshire. Brother of P. J. (Northants). Lower order left-hand batsman, leg break and googly bowler. *Sch* Bedford Modern. *Teams* Northants (1958–66, 158 matches); Nottinghamshire (1967, 23 matches).
Career batting
183–277–60–4567–91–21.04–0–*ct* 174
Bowling 10067–307–32.79–12–1–7/77
He also played for Bedfordshire.

Watts, Patrick James
Professional. *b:* 16.6.1940, Henlow, Bedfordshire. Brother of P. D. (Northants and Notts). Middle order left-hand batsman, right-arm medium pace bowler. *Team* Northants (1959–80, 372 matches).
Career batting
375–607–90–14449–145–27.94–10–*ct* 279
Bowling 8710–333–26.15–7–0–6/18
He hit 1,000 runs in a season seven times (best 1,798, av 43.85, in 1962). From 1971 to 1974 he captained Northants, but then retired, playing a few matches in 1975, none in 1976 or 1977; in 1978 he was reappointed captain, retiring a second time in 1980. He played for Bedfordshire in 1976 and Berkshire in 1977.

Watts, Thomas
Professional. *b:* 21.8.1899, Kennington, London. *d:* 19.1.1976, St Helens, Lancashire. Lower order right-hand batsman, useful bowler. *Team* Surrey (1922–26, 6 matches).
Career batting
6–8–5–42–21*–14.00–0–*ct* 3
Bowling 327–8–40.87–0–0–2/32

Watts, Walter
Professional. *b:* 7.3.1827, Wimpole, Cambridgeshire. *d:* 29.7.1910, Cambridge. Father of G. H. (Surrey). Tail end right-hand batsman, right-hand slow round-arm bowler, short leg field. Team Cambridgeshire (1866–69, 11 matches).
Career batting
11–18–5–23–9*–1.76–0–*ct* 4
Bowling 752–43–17.48–4–1–7/46
He was groundsman at Fenner's (later called the University Ground) at Cambridge for fifty years.

Waud, Brian Wilkes
Amateur. *b:* 4.6.1837, Chester Court, Selby, Yorkshire. *d:* 30.5.1889, Toronto, Canada. Stylish middle order right-hand batsman, wicket-keeper. *Sch* Eton. *Teams* Oxford U (1857–60, blue all four years); Yorkshire (1862–64, 8 matches).
Career batting
19–34–7–432–42–16.00–0–*ct* 15–*st* 7
He played for Canada v United States in 1881.

Waugh, Hubert Percy
Amateur. *b:* 24.12.1898, West Ham, Essex. *d:* 13.12.1954, Dollis Hill, Middlesex. Opening right-hand batsman, right-arm medium pace bowler. *Sch* Forest. *Team* Essex (1919–29, 8 matches).
Career batting
9–16–0–251–128–15.68–1–*ct* 9
Bowling 168–4–42.00–0–0–1/6
His final first-class match was for the Minor Counties in 1937 and from 1934 he played for Suffolk, being captain of that County for five years.

Wazir Ali, Syed
Amateur. *b:* 15.9.1903, Jullundur, India. *d:* 17.6.1950, Karachi, Pakistan. Brother of Nazir Ali (India), father of Khalid Wazir (Pakistan). Sound opening right-hand batsman, right-arm medium pace bowler, good field. *Teams* Central India (1934/5 to 1937/8); Muslims (1922/3 to 1940/1); Southern Punjab (1926/7 to 1939/40); Patiala (1932/3). *Tours* India to England 1932, 1936; Indian University Occasionals to Ceylon 1935/6. *Tests* India (1932–36, 7 matches).
Career batting
119–205–22–7042–268*–38.48–21–*ct* 59
Bowling 1032–34–30.35–1–0–5/22
Test batting
7–14–0–237–42–16.92–0–*ct* 1
Bowling 25–0
In 1932 he hit 1,229 runs, av 32.34, in first-class matches, also playing in the Test. In 1936, although he appeared in all three Tests, his record was a poor one. His highest score was 268* for Indian University Occasionals v Viceroy's XI at Calcutta in 1935/6. He hit 1,000 runs in a season once in India.

Wazir Mohammad
Amateur. *b:* 22.12.1929, Junagadh, India. Brother of Hanif, Sadiq, Mushtaq (Pakistan) and Raees (Karachi), uncle of Shahid, Asif and Shoaib (PIA). Determined middle order right-hand batsman, good field. *Teams* Karachi (1949/50 to 1963/4); Bahawalpur (1953/4). *Tours* Pakistan to India 1952/3, to England 1954, to West Indies 1957/8; Pakistan Eaglets to England 1963. *Tests* Pakistan (1952/3 to 1959/60, 20 matches).
Career batting
105–149–26–4952–189–40.26–11–*ct* 34
Bowling 41–0
Test batting
20–33–4–801–189–27.62–2–*ct* 5
Bowling 15–0
He topped the first-class averages on the 1954 tour with 628 runs, av 39.25, but owing to injury played in only two Tests.

Weatherby, Charles Thomas
Amateur. *b:* 7.5.1860, Kensington, London. *d:* 24.6.1913, Lindfield, Sussex. Brother of Francis (Oxford U). Middle order right-hand batsman. *Sch* Winchester. *Team* MCC (1882).
Career batting
1–2–0–16–15–8.00–0–*ct* 0
He did not appear in first-class cricket whilst at Oxford U.

Weatherby, Francis
Amateur. *b:* 15.9.1885, Chertsey, Surrey. *d:* 18.11.1969, Ellington, Warwickshire. Brother of C. T. (MCC). Opening right-hand batsman. *Sch* Winchester. *Team* Oxford U (1904).
Career batting
4–6–0–69–24–11.50–0–*ct* 2
His final first-class match was for Gentlemen of England in 1905.

Weaver, Frederick Charles
Amateur. *b:* 10.3.1878, Gloucester. *d:* 29.12.1949, Limpley Stoke, Wilts. Middle order

batsman, useful bowler. *Team* Gloucestershire (1897–1909, 5 matches).
Career batting
5–10–3–31–18*–4.42–0–*ct* 2
Bowling 177–8–22.12–1–0–5/63
He was a notable figure in West Country Club cricket scoring over 35,000 runs and taking more than 5,000 wickets.

Weaver, Philip Humphrey Peter
Amateur. *b:* 12.3.1912, Kalimpong, India. Middle order right-hand batsman, right-arm medium pace bowler. *Sch* King's, Bruton. *Team* Hampshire (1938, 2 matches).
Career batting
2–3–0–55–37–18.33–0–*ct* 1

Weaver, Samuel
Professional. *b:* 8.2.1909, Pilsley, Derbyshire. Lower order left-hand batsman, left-arm bowler. *Team* Somerset (1939, 2 matches).
Career batting
2–4–2–25–19–12.50–0–*ct* 2
Bowling 63–0
A good soccer player, he appeared for Hull, Newcastle United and Chelsea.

Webb, Arthur Geoffrey Gascoigne
Amateur. *b:* 17.8.1896, Newington, Sittingbourne, Kent. *d:* 6.4.1981, Oakham, Rutland. Middle order left-hand batsman, occasional wicket-keeper. *Sch* Wellington. *Team* Leicestershire (1933–38, 3 matches).
Career batting
5–9–0–123–57–13.66–0–*ct* 5
Bowling 22–0
From 1933 to 1938 he was Secretary of Leicestershire CCC. His first-class debut was for the Royal Navy in 1919.

Webb, Arthur Stuart
Professional but amateur in 1912. *b:* 6.8.1868, Bridge, Kent. *d:* 3.12.1952, Briton-Ferry Glamorgan. Middle order right-hand batsman, right-arm medium pace bowler. *Team* Hampshire (1895–1904, 149 matches).
Career batting
151–272–16–5515–162*–21.54–2–*ct* 83
Bowling 1023–22–46.50–0–0–2/18
His final first-class match was for South Wales v South Africans in 1912. He hit 1,020 runs, av 34.00, in 1901.

Webb, Rev Charles Johnston Bourne
Amateur. *b:* 24.11.1874, Bloemfontein, Orange Free State, South Africa. *d:* 18.11.1963, St John's Wood, London. Lower order right-hand batsman, slow right-arm bowler. *Sch* Radley. *Team* Middlesex (1902, 2 matches).
Career batting
2–3–1–18–14–9.00–0–*ct* 1
Bowling 58–0
He also played for Dorset.

Webb, George
Professional. *b:* 1859, Tonbridge, Kent. Lower order batsman, bowler. *Team* Kent (1892, 1 match).
Career batting
1–2–1–0–0*–0.00–0–*ct* 1
Bowling 45–1–45.00–0–0–1/30

Webb, George William
Professional. *b:* 23.10.1857, Barham, Kent. *d:* 26.12.1931, Stoke-by-Nayland, Suffolk. Lower order right-hand batsman, right-arm fast medium bowler. *Team* Kent (1880, 1 match).
Career batting
1–1–1–5–5*–no av–0–*ct* 3
Bowling 30–0

Webb, Hubert Eustace
Amateur. *b:* 30.5.1927, Tonk, India. Middle order right-hand batsman, leg break bowler. *Sch* Winchester. *Teams* Oxford U (1946–48, blue 1948); Hampshire (1954, 1 match).
Career batting
15–23–1–461–145*–20.95–1–*ct* 7
Bowling 15–1–15.00–0–0–1/10

Webb, Herbert George
Amateur. *b:* 1.7.1913, Headington, Oxfordshire. *d:* 7.8.1947, Hill End, St Albans, Herts. Middle order right-hand batsman, wicket-keeper. *Team* Oxford U (1935).
Career batting
3–6–1–88–38–17.60–0–*ct* 1
His County cricket was for Oxfordshire and his final first-class match for Minor Counties in 1936.

Webb, Dr John Kingdon Guy
Amateur. *b:* 29.10.1918, London. Sound opening right-hand batsman. *Sch* Highgate. *Team* Oxford U (1938).
Career batting
1–2–0–5–5–2.50–0–*ct* 0

Webb, Peter Mitchell
Amateur. *b:* 5.2.1932, Dublin. Right-hand batsman, right-arm medium pace bowler. *Team* Ireland (1953).
Career batting
2–2–1–3–3*–3.00–0–*ct* 3
Bowling 59–4–14.75–0–0–2/11

Webb, Robert
Professional. Lower order right-hand batsman, wicket-keeper. *Team* Kent (1864, 1 match).
Career batting
1–2–0–2–1–1.00–0–*ct* 0

Webb, Rupert Thomas
Professional. *b:* 11.7.1922, Harrow, Middlesex. Lower order right-hand batsman, wicket-keeper. *Team* Sussex (1948–60, 256 matches).
Career batting
257–333–104–2685–49*–11.72–0–*ct* 325–*st* 129
Bowling 43–1–43.00–0–0–1/34

Webb, Sidney
Professional. *b:* 1.2.1875, Brompton, Middlesex. *d:* 4.4.1923, Ilford, Essex. Lower order right-hand batsman, right-arm medium pace bowler. *Teams* Middlesex (1897–98, 9 matches); Lancashire (1899–1903, 73 matches); Griqualand West (1904/5).
Career batting
83–110–31–554–38*–7.01–0–*ct* 59
Bowling 6093–302–20.17–17–4–8/36
He took 112 wickets, av 23.18, in 1901.

Webb, William Louis Taggart
Amateur. *b:* 6.2.1898, Camberwell, London. *d:* 3.4.1969, Southport, Lancashire. Middle order right-hand batsman. *Team* Civil Service (1927).
Career batting
1–2–0–76–59–38.00–0–*ct* 0

Webbe, Alexander Josiah
Amateur. *b:* 16.1.1855, London. *d:* 19.2.1941, Abinger Hammer, Surrey. Brother of H. R. (Middlesex) and G. A. (MCC). Stylish opening right-hand batsman, right-arm fast bowler, good mid wicket. *Sch* Harrow. *Teams* Oxford U (1875–78, blue all four years); Middlesex (1875–1900, 247 matches). *Tour* Harris to Australia 1878/9. *Test* England (1878/9, 1 match).
Career batting
370–641–58–14465–243*–24.81–14–*ct* 227–*st* 10
Bowling 2748–109–25.21–2–0–5/23
Test batting
1–2–0–4–4–2.00–0–*ct* 2
His best season was 1887 with 1,244 runs, av 47.84; in the same year he hit his only double century, 243* for Middlesex v Yorkshire at Huddersfield. He captained Middlesex from 1885 to 1898, being joint leader in the last season. He represented Oxford at rackets and was a useful footballer.

Webbe, George Allan
Amateur. *b:* 15.1.1854, Westminster, London. *d:* 19.2.1925, Ascot, Berkshire. Brother of A. J. (Middlesex) and H. R. (Middlesex). Middle order right-hand batsman, good cover point, occasional wicket-keeper. *Sch* Harrow. *Team* MCC (1874–78).
Career batting
2–3–1–37–19*–18.50–0–*ct* 0
He was not in the Eleven whilst at Oxford. His County cricket was for Dorset, but for several years he was abroad with his Regiment.

Webbe, Herbert Ross
Amateur. *b:* 18.5.1856, London. *d:* 9.5.1886, Paddington, London. He collapsed and died whilst conducting prayers. Brother of A. J. (Middlesex) and G. A. (MCC). Stylish middle order right-hand batsman, good cover point. *Sch* Winchester. *Teams* Oxford U (1877–79, blue all three years); Middlesex (1875–79, 21 matches).
Career batting
43–81–6–1387–63–18.49–0–*ct* 16
He also played for Dorset.

Webster, Andrew John
Cricketer. *b:* 5.3.1959, Burton-on-Trent, Staffs. Left-hand batsman, right-arm medium pace bowler. *Team* Worcestershire (1981–82, 9 matches).
Career batting
9–11–5–81–25–13.50–0–*ct* 3
Bowling 734–15–48.93–1–0–5/87

Webster, Charles
Professional. *b:* 9.6.1838, Eccleshall, Sheffield, Yorkshire. *d:* 7.1.1881, Sheffield, Yorkshire. Middle order right-hand batsman. *Team* Yorkshire (1861–68, 4 matches).
Career batting
4–7–1–36–10–6.00–0–*ct* 2

Webster, David
Cricketer. *b:* 22.5.1946, Sheffield, Yorkshire. Middle order left-hand batsman, right-arm medium pace bowler. *Team* Derbyshire (1975, 1 match).
Career batting
1–1–0–26–26–26.00–0–*ct* 0
Bowling 28–1–28.00–0–0–1/28

Webster, Fred
Professional. b: 7.5.1897, Accrington, Lancashire. *d:* 28.7.1931, Burnley, Lancashire. Tail end left-hand batsman, left-arm fast medium bowler. *Team* Lancashire (1925–27, 2 matches).
Career batting
2–3–1–12–10–6.00–0–*ct* 1
Bowling 122–7–17.42–0–0–3/34

Webster, Frederick
Professional. *b:* 19.1.1885, Ecclesall, Yorkshire. *d:* 23.3.1938. Lower order batsman, useful bowler. *Team* Derbyshire (1906, 1 match).
Career batting
1–2–0–11–10–5.50–0–*ct* 0
Bowling 65–1–65.00–0–0–1/65

Webster, Harry Haywood
Professional. *b:* 8.5.1844, Handsworth, Sheffield, Yorkshire. *d:* 1914, Port Elizabeth, South Africa. Middle order right-hand batsman, right-arm medium pace bowler. *Team* Yorkshire (1868, 2 matches).
Career batting
2–3–0–10–10–3.33–0–*ct* 0
He also played for Staffordshire.

Webster, Harold Wynne
Amateur. *b:* 17.2.1889, Sydney, Australia. *d:* 7.10.1949, Randwick, Sydney, Australia. Lower order right-hand batsman, wicket-keeper. *Team* South Australia (1910/1 to 1911/2, 6 matches). *Tours* Australia to England 1912, to North America 1912.
Career batting
19–29–5–346–54–14.41–0–*ct* 21–*st* 4
He was the reserve wicket-keeper on the 1912 tour and did not play in the Tests.

Webster, Jack
Amateur. *b:* 28.10.1917, Bradford, Yorkshire. Lower order right-hand batsman, right-arm medium fast bowler, good field. *Sch* Bradford GS. *Teams* Cambridge U (1938–39, blue 1939); Northants (1946–55, 60 matches).
Career batting
70–95–15–617–65–7.71–0–*ct* 52
Bowling 4649–145–32.06–6–0–7/78
A master at Harrow School, he played County cricket mainly in August.

Webster, Patrick Greenway
(also known as P. G. Fairfield)
Amateur. *b:* 26.11.1907, South Africa. *d:* 21.6.1937, Le Mans, France. Lower order left-hand batsman, left-arm fast bowler. *Team* Cambridge U (1929).
Career batting
2–3–1–21–12–10.50–0–*ct* 2
Bowling 233–6–38.83–0–0–4/86
He was killed in a motor racing accident at Le Mans.

Webster, Dr Rudi Valentine
Amateur. *b:* 10.6.1939, St Philip, Barbados. Lower order right-hand batsman, right-arm fast medium bowler. *Teams* Scotland (1961–64); Warwickshire (1962–66, 60 matches); Otago (1966/7 to 1967/8).
Career batting
70–82–19–867–47–13.76–0 *ct* 21
Bowling 5290–272–19.44–13–4–8/19

Webster, William
Amateur. *b:* 28.6.1876, Aberdeen, Scotland. Right-hand batsman, right-arm fast medium bowler. *Team* Scotland (1907–12).
Career batting
5–9–1–102–65–12.75–0–*ct* 0
Bowling 209–8–26.12–0–0–3/30

Webster, William
Professional. *b:* 1880. *d:* 10.3.1931, Dinnington, Yorkshire. Middle order batsman. *Team* Derbyshire (1911, 1 match).
Career batting
1–2–0–3–3–1.50–0–*ct* 0

Webster, William Hugh
Amateur. *b:* 22.2.1910, Hackney, London. Opening or middle order right-hand batsman, left-arm medium pace bowler. *Sch* Highgate. *Teams* Cambridge U (1930–32, blue 1932): Middlesex (1930–47, 45 matches).
Career batting
65–103–9–1870–111–19.89–1–*ct* 17
Bowling 478–21–22.76–0–0–3/12

Wedel, George
Amateur. *b:* 18.5.1900, Leigh, Lancashire. *d:* 16.4.1981, Amberley, Gloucs. Lower order left-hand batsman, leg break bowler. *Team* Gloucestershire (1925–29, 45 matches).
Career batting
45–71–10–545–53–8.93–0–*ct* 37
Bowling 1629–51–31.94–0–0–4/4

Weeding, T. W. (*See under* Baggallay, T. W.)

Weedon, Mark John Hayley
Amateur. *b:* 28.10.1940, Singapore. Lower order right-hand batsman, right-arm medium pace bowler. *Sch* Harrow. *Team* Cambridge U (1961–62, blue 1962).
Career batting
17–24–11–164–35–12.61–0–*ct* 8
Bowling 1604–45–35.64–2–0–5/67

Weekes, Donald James
Professional. *b:* 8.5.1930, Horsham, Sussex. Tail end right-hand batsman, right-arm fast bowler. *Team* Sussex (1952, 1 match).
Career batting
1–1–0–0–0–0.00–0–*ct* 0
Bowling 34–0

Weekes, Everton de Courcy
Amateur. *b:* 26.2.1925, Bridgetown, Barbados. Cousin of K. H. (Barbados). Attacking middle order right-hand batsman, bowler, excellent field. *Team* Barbados (1944/5 to 1963/4). *Tours* West Indies to England 1950, 1957, to India, Pakistan and Ceylon 1948/9, to Australia and New Zealand 1951/2, to New Zealand 1955/6; Swanton to West Indies 1960/1; International XI to India, Pakistan, New Zealand and South Africa 1961/2. *Tests* West Indies (1947/8 to 1957/8, 48 matches).
Career batting
152–241–24–12010–304*–55.34–36–*ct* 125–*st* 1
Bowling 731–17–43.00–0–0–4/38
Test batting
48–81–5–4455–207–58.61–15–*ct* 49
Bowling 77–1–77.00–0–0–1/8
In 1950 he headed the tourists batting averages with 2,310 runs, av 79.65, including 304* v Cambridge U at Fenner's. On his second visit in 1957, however, he was not so successful and only just topped 1,000 runs in first-class matches – sinus trouble and a broken finger considerably hampered him on the tour. He hit 1,000 runs on the 1948/9 tour.

Weekes, Kenneth Hunnell
Amateur. *b:* 24.1.1912, USA. Cousin of E. de C. (West Indies). Aggressive middle order left-hand batsman, wicket-keeper. *Team* Jamaica (1938/9 to 1947/8). *Tour* West Indies to England 1939. *Tests* West Indies (1939, 2 matches).
Career batting
30–47–4–1731–146–40.25–4–*ct* 21–*st* 1
Bowling 464–12–38.66–0–0–3/84
Test batting
2–3–0–173–137–57.66–1–*ct* 0
He hit 803 runs, av 29.74, on the 1939 tour.

Weeks, Donald
Professional. *b:* 5.2.1903, Lewisham, Kent. *d:* 1967, Battle, Sussex. Lower order right-hand batsman, useful bowler. *Team* Surrey (1933, 2 matches).
Career batting
2–2–0–2–1–1.00–0–*ct* 0
Bowling 165–2–82.50–0–0–1/25

Weeks, Frederick James
Amateur. *b:* 7.6.1903, Stapleton, Bristol. Middle order left-hand batsman, right-arm fast bowler. *Sch* Clifton. *Team* Gloucestershire (1925–28, 7 matches).
Career batting
7–12–1–122–35*–11.09–0–*ct* 3
Bowling 22–0

Weeks, Raymond Thomas
Professional. *b:* 30.4.1930, Camborne, Cornwall. Lower order left-hand batsman, slow left-arm bowler. *Team* Warwickshire (1950–57, 105 matches).
Career batting
107–141–36–1051–51–10.00–0–*ct* 42
Bowling 6198–236–26.26–8–0–7/70
His best season was 1951 with 94 wickets, av 21.75. He also played for Cornwall.

Weigall, Evelyn Henry Villiers
Amateur. *b:* 29.6.1876, Marylebone, London. *d:* 3.9.1946, Tonbridge, Kent. Brother of G. J. V. (Kent). Middle order right-hand batsman, right-arm medium pace bowler. *Sch* Wellington. *Team* G. J. V. Weigall's XI (1908).
Career batting
1–2–0–14–14–7.00–0–*ct* 0
Bowling 48–0

Weigall, Gerald John Villiers
Amateur. *b:* 19.10.1870, Wimbledon, Surrey. *d:* 17.5.1944, Dublin. He died following an operation. Brother of E. H. V. (Weigall's XI). Stylish middle order right-hand batsman, good point field. *Sch* Wellington. *Teams* Cambridge U (1891–92, blue both years); Kent (1891–1903, 127 matches); Europeans (1917/8 to 1919/20). *Tours* Kent to United States 1903; MCC to South America 1926/7; Tennyson to Jamaica 1927/8.
Career batting
232–398–44–6866–138*–19.39–3–*ct* 92
Bowling 45–1–45.00–0–0–1/4
His final first-class match in England was for MCC in 1920.
Commencing 1923, he was coach to Kent CCC. A noted rackets player he represented Cambridge.

Weighell, Rev William Bartholomew
Amateur. *b:* 21.6.1846, Cheddington, Buckinghamshire. *d:* 29.10.1905, Shilton, Oxfordshire. Effective lower order right-hand batsman, right-hand fast round-arm bowler, good deep field. *Sch* Bedford GS. *Teams* Cambridge U (1866–69, blue 1866, 1868 and 1869); Sussex (1868–78, 13 matches).
Career batting
26–49–7–388–38–9.23–0–*ct* 15
Bowling 588–25–23.52–0–0–4/23
He also played for Bedfordshire and Norfolk. His name is pronounced 'Weel'.

Weightman, Neil Ivan
Cricketer. *b:* 5.10.1960, Normanton-on-Trent, Nottinghamshire. Opening left-hand batsman, off

break bowler. *Team* Nottinghamshire (1981–82, 4 matches).
Career batting
4–6–0–175–105–29.16–1–*ct* 3
Bowling 4–0

Weir, Donald St Clair
Amateur. *b:* 23.1.1900, Trinity, Edinburgh, Scotland. *d:* 1.4.1950, Edinburgh, Scotland. Right-hand batsman, right-arm medium pace bowler. *Sch* Edinburgh Academy. *Team* Scotland (1923–26).
Career batting
4–7–0–64–28–9.14–0–*ct* 3
Bowling 306–5–61.20–0–0–2/63

Weir, Gordon Lindsay
Amateur. *b:* 2.6.1908, Auckland, New Zealand. Sound opening or middle order right-hand batsman, right-arm medium pace bowler, good field. *Team* Auckland (1927/8 to 1946/7). *Tours* New Zealand to England 1931, 1937; to Australia 1937/8. *Tests* New Zealand (1929/30 to 1937, 11 matches).
Career batting
107–172–16–5022–191–32.19–10–*ct* 70
Bowling 3997–107–37.35–2–0–6/56
Test batting
11–16–2–416–74*–29.71–0–*ct* 3
Bowling 209–7–29.85–0–0–3/38

He hit 1,035 runs, av 25.87, in 1931 and played in all three Tests. He was not so successful in 1937 and appeared in only one Test.

Weir, Robert Scott
Cricketer. *b:* 1.5.1953, Glasgow, Scotland. Right-hand batsman, right-arm medium pace bowler. *Team* Scotland (1975–82).
Career batting
4–8–2–187–65–31.16–0–*ct* 1

Welch, Thomas Bacon Gascoigne
Amateur. *b:* 31.7.1906, Reigate, Surrey. *d:* 16.3.1972, London. Son of T. H. G. (Northants captain 1889). Middle order right-hand batsman, right-arm fast medium bowler. *Sch* Malvern. *Teams* Northants (1922–31, 23 matches); Oxford U (1926).
Career batting
33–58–6–767–69–14.75–0–*ct* 9
Bowling 227–5–45.40–0–0–1/4

Welch, William Mark
Amateur. *b:* 12.8.1911. *d:* 25.5.1940, Calais, France. Middle order right-hand batsman, right-arm medium off break bowler, good slip field. *Sch* Harrow. *Team* Free Foresters (1935–39).
Career batting
4–5–0–170–104–34.00–1–*ct* 1
Bowling 221–8–27.62–1–0–5/43

Weldrick, George
Professional. *b:* 1.1.1882, Brighouse, Yorkshire. *d:* 14.4.1953, Brighouse, Yorkshire. Middle order right-hand batsman. *Team* Warwickshire (1906–07, 8 matches).
Career batting
8–11–1–53–12–5.30–0–*ct* 3

Welford, James William
Professional. *b:* 27.3.1869, Barnard Castle, Co Durham. *d:* 17.1.1945, Glasgow, Scotland. Middle order right-hand batsman, right-arm fast bowler. *Team* Warwickshire (1896, 13 matches).
Career batting
13–23–2–459–118–21.85–1–*ct* 2
Bowling 180–2–90.00–0–0–1/13

He also played for Durham. A good soccer player, he appeared for Aston Villa.

Wellard, Arthur William
Professional. *b:* 8.4.1902, Southfleet, Kent. *d:* 31.12.1980, Sutton, Surrey. Hard hitting lower order right-hand batsman, right-arm fast medium or off break bowler, good slip field. *Team* Somerset (1927–50, 391 matches). *Tours* Tennyson to India 1937/8; selected for MCC to India 1939/40 (tour cancelled because of war). *Tests* England (1937–38, 2 matches).
Career batting
417–679–46–12485–112–19.72–2–*ct* 375
Bowling 39302–1614–24.35–108–24–8/52
Test batting
2–4–0–47–38–11.75–0–*ct* 2
Bowling 237–7–33.85–0–0–4/81

He hit 1,000 runs in a season four times (best 1,347, av 31.32, in 1935) and took 100 wickets eight times (best 172, av 20.29, in 1938). He completed the 'double' in 1933, 1935 and 1937. Regarded as the biggest hitter in first-class cricket in the late 1930s, he twice hit five sixes off consecutive balls – v Derbyshire at Wells in 1936 and v Kent at Wells in 1938. In the seasons of 1933, 1935, 1936 and 1938 he hit over 50 sixes.

Welldon, James Turner
Amateur. *b:* 3.8.1847, Felsted, Essex. *d:* 6.2.1927, Ashford, Kent. Middle order right-hand batsman, good deep field. *Sch* Tonbridge. *Teams* Kent (1867–69, 4 matches); Cambridge U (1869).
Career batting
7–11–2–88–37–9.77–0–*ct* 3

Wellham, Dirk MacDonald
Cricketer. *b:* 13.3.1959, Summer Hill, New South

Wales, Australia. Middle order right-hand batsman. *Team* New South Wales (1980/1 to 1982/3, 22 matches). *Tours* Australia to England 1981; Young Australia to Zimbabwe 1982/3. *Tests* Australia (1981 to 1981/2, 4 matches).
Career batting
36–58–12–2287–136*–49.71–6–*ct* 17
Bowling 11–1–11.00–0–0–1/11
Test batting
4–7–0–221–103–31.57–1–*ct* 1

On the 1981 tour to England he topped the first-class averages with 497 runs, av 55.22, but played in only one Test.

Wellings, Evelyn Maitland
Amateur. *b:* 6.4.1909, Alexandria, Egypt. Lower order right-hand batsman, right-arm off break bowler. *Sch* Cheltenham. *Teams* Oxford U (1928–31, blue 1929 and 1931); Surrey (1931, 4 matches).
Career batting
36–47–6–836–125–20.39–1–*ct* 10
Bowling 3256–108–30.14–5–0–6/75

His final first-class match was for MCC in 1946. He was for many years cricket correspondent of the London *Evening News* and has written several books on cricket.

Wellington, Livern
Cricketer. *b:* 5.1.1950, Kingston, Jamaica. Lower order batsman, useful bowler. *Team* Jamaica (1969/70 to 1970/1). *Tour* Jamaica to England 1970.
Career batting
11–14–6–208–49–26.00–0–*ct* 7
Bowling 483–12–40.25–0–0–3/29

Wells, Arthur Luty
Amateur. *b:* 23.11.1909, Headingley, Leeds, Yorkshire. Lower order right-hand batsman, right-arm medium pace bowler. *Team* Northants (1954–55, 5 matches).
Career batting
5–6–1–28–18–5.60–0–*ct* 0
Bowling 333–8–41.62–0–0–4/67

Wells, Alan Peter
Cricketer. *b:* 2.10.1961, Newhaven, Sussex. Brother of C. M. (Sussex). Middle order right-hand batsman, right-arm medium pace bowler. *Teams* Sussex (1981–83, 22 matches); Border (1981/2).
Career batting
23–40–7–976–92–29.57–0–*ct* 14
Bowling 42–0

Wells, Bryan Douglas
Professional. *b:* 27.7.1930, Gloucester. Hard hitting tail end right-hand batsman, off break bowler. *Teams* Gloucestershire (1951–59, 141 matches); Nottinghamshire (1960–65, 151 matches). *Tour* Swanton to West Indies 1960/1.
Career batting
302–423–100–2413–55–7.47–0–*ct* 112
Bowling 24219–998–24.26–46–7–8/31

He took 100 wickets in a season three times (best 123, av 18.60, in 1956).

Wells, Clifford
Amateur. *b:* 17.10.1872, London. *d:* 27.2.1952, Crowthorne, Berkshire. Brother of C. M. (Surrey and Middlesex) and L. S. (Middlesex). Middle order batsman, useful bowler. *Sch* Dulwich. *Team* Cambridge U (1894).
Career batting
1–2–0–24–24–12.00–0–*ct* 1
Bowling 46–0

Wells, Colin Mark
Cricketer. *b:* 3.3.1960, Newhaven, Sussex. Brother of A. P. (Sussex). Middle order right-hand batsman, right-arm medium pace bowler. *Teams* Sussex (1979–83, 85 matches); Border (1980/1).
Career batting
88–141–19–3726–135–30.54–5–*ct* 28
Bowling 2584–67–38.56–0–0–4/23

He hit 1,000 runs in a season twice (best 1,248, av 32.84, in 1982).

Wells, Cyril Mowbray
Amateur. *b:* 21.3.1871, St Pancras, London. *d:* 22.8.1963, St John's Wood, London. Brother of L. S. (Middlesex) and Clifford (Cambridge U). Attractive middle order right-hand batsman, slow off break bowler with occasional leg breaks, good slip field. *Sch* Dulwich. *Teams* Cambridge U (1891–93, blue all three years); Surrey (1892–93, 4 matches); Middlesex (1895–1909, 113 matches).
Career batting
143–219–27–4229–244–22.02–4–*ct* 122
Bowling 9235–465–19.86–27–3–8/35

His only double century was 244 for Middlesex v Notts at Trent Bridge in 1899. A noted rugby footballer, he played for Cambridge, Harlequins, Middlesex and England.

Wells, Frederick (sen)
Professional. *b:* 1796, Dorking, Surrey. *d:* 27.1.1849, Brighton, Sussex. Middle order batsman. *Teams* Surrey (1828, 1 match); Sussex (1832–39, 24 matches).
Career batting
29–56–1–407–67–7.40–0–*ct* 8
Bowling 1 wicket, no analysis

Wells, Frederick (jun)
Professional. *b:* 1.6.1868, St John's, Burgess Hill, Sussex. Son of George (Sussex). Lower order right-hand batsman, right-arm medium pace bowler. *Team* Sussex (1891, 2 matches).
Career batting
2–2–0–7–7–3.50–0–*ct* 0
He also played for Hertfordshire.

Wells, George
Professional. *b:* 2.11.1830, Whitechapel, Middlesex. *d:* 23.1.1891, Shoreham-by-Sea, Sussex. Father of Frederick, jun (Sussex). Lower order right-hand batsman, right-hand medium round-arm, or slow under-arm bowler, good point field. *Teams* Sussex (1854–69, 79 matches); Middlesex (1859–64, 7 matches). *Tour* Stephenson to Australia 1861/2.
Career batting
103–181–15–2772–90–16.69–0–*ct* 102–*st* 13
Bowling 1577–85–18.55–3–0–9/105
His best bowling in an innings was 9 for 105 for Sussex v Surrey at Hove in 1860.

Wells, John
Professional. *b:* 1759, Wrecclesham, Surrey. *d:* 15.2.1835, Wrecclesham, Surrey. Middle order right-hand batsman, fast under-arm bowler, good field. *Team* Surrey (1801–15).
Career batting
46–87–9–618–42–7.92–0–*ct* 34–*st* 2
Bowling 159 wickets, no analyses
For several seasons he was one of the 'crack' players of England.

Wells, Joseph
Professional. *b:* 14.7.1828, Penshurst, Kent. *d:* 14.10.1910, Liss, Hampshire. Lower order right-hand batsman, right-hand fast round-arm bowler, slip field. *Team* Kent (1862–63, 7 matches).
Career batting
8–14–3–48–10–4.36–0–*ct* 6
Bowling 128–14+1–9.14–1–0–6/35
He took four wickets with successive balls for Kent v Sussex in 1862. His son was the well-known novelist H. G. Wells.

Wells, Lionel Seymour
Amateur. *b:* 3.2.1870, London. *d:* 26.4.1928, Kennington, London. Brother of C. M. (Surrey and Middlesex) and Clifford (Cambridge U). Forcing middle order right-hand batsman, slow right-arm bowler. *Sch* Dulwich. *Teams* Middlesex (1898–1905, 6 matches); London County (1900–04).
Career batting
13–21–1–196–42–9.80–0–*ct* 17
Bowling 203–11–18.45–0–0–4/46
His final first-class match was for W. G. Grace's XI in 1906.

Wells, Richard Raymond Collingwood
Cricketer. *b:* 19.1.1956, Salisbury, Rhodesia. Middle order right-hand batsman. *Sch* Cranleigh. *Team* Oxford U (1977–78).
Career batting
11–17–1–212–85–13.25–0–*ct* 4

Wells, Thomas Umfrey
Amateur. *b:* 6.2.1927, Panmure, New Zealand. Middle order left-hand batsman, good outfield. *Teams* Cambridge U (1950–51, blue 1950); Worcestershire (1950, 1 match).
Career batting
21–28–1–446–77*–16.51–0–*ct* 8
Bowling 119–5–23.80–0–0–2/25

Wells, William
Professional. *b:* 14.3.1881, Daventry, Northants. *d:* 18.3.1939, Daventry, Northants. Hard hitting lower order right-hand batsman, right-arm fast medium bowler. *Team* Northants (1905–26, 269 matches).
Career batting
269–441–75–6324–119–17.27–2–*ct* 114
Bowling 16202–751–21.57–51–10–8/35

Welman, Frederic Tristram
Amateur. *b:* 19.2.1849, Taunton, Somerset. *d:* 30.12.1931, South Ascot, Berkshire. Lower order right-hand batsman, wicket-keeper. *Teams* Middlesex (1880–88, 17 matches); Somerset (1882–1901, 19 matches). *Tour* Sanders to North America 1886.
Career batting
65–109–27–737–43–8.98–0–*ct* 83–*st* 24
His first-class debut was for MCC in 1874. He also played for Devon.

Wenlock, David Alan
Cricketer. *b:* 16.4.1959, Leicester. Lower order right-hand batsman, right-arm medium pace bowler. *Team* Leicestershire (1980–82, 10 matches). *Tour* Leicestershire to Zimbabwe 1980/1.
Career batting
10–13–4–148–62–16.44–0–*ct* 3
Bowling 268–7–38.28–0–0–3/50

Wenman, Edward Gower
Professional. *b:* 18.8.1803, Benenden, Kent. *d:* 28.12.1879, Benenden, Kent. Father of William (Kent), cousin of G. and J. G. (Kent). Opening or

middle order right-hand batsman, wicket-keeper, slow under-arm bowler. *Teams* Kent (1825–54, 61 matches); Hampshire (1842, 1 match).
Career batting
146–255–15–3204–73*–13.35–0–*ct* 118–*st* 87
Bowling 42 wickets no analyses

He was regarded as the best wicket-keeper of his day. Although his career with Kent spanned 30 years, he did not play regularly after 1844.

Wenman, William
Professional. *b:* 22.5.1832, Benenden, Kent. *d:* 23.11.1921, Souris, Manitoba, Canada. Son of E. G. (Kent). Middle order right-hand batsman. *Team* Kent (1862–64, 11 matches).
Career batting
11–22–3–179–29–9.42–0–*ct* 6

Wensley, Albert Frederick
Professional. *b:* 24.5.1898, Brighton, Sussex. *d:* 17.6.1970, Ware, Hertfordshire. Hard hitting lower order right-hand batsman, accurate right-arm medium fast bowler, good close field. *Teams* Sussex (1922–36, 373 matches); Auckland (1929/30 to 1930/1); Nawanagar (1936/7 to 1939/40); Europeans (1938/9 to 1947/8).
Career batting
399–594–64–10849–154–20.46–9–*ct* 263–*st* 1
Bowling 30217–1141–26.48–56–10–9/36

He hit 1,000 runs in a season four times (best 1,672, av 30.96, in 1928) and took 100 wickets in a season five times (best 126, av 25.04, in 1933). He achieved the 'double' in 1929. He played for Scotland in non-first class matches. His best bowling was 9/36 for Auckland v Otago at Auckland in 1929/30.

Went, Gwilym John Hubert
Amateur. *b:* 25.3.1914, Barry, Glamorgan. Lower order batsman, useful bowler. *Team* Glamorgan (1934, 1 match).
Career batting
1–2–1–14–14*–14.00–0–*ct* 1
Bowling 14–0

Wentworth, Bruce Canning Vernon
Amateur. *b:* 14.12.1862. *d:* 12.11.1951, Rannoch, Perthshire, Scotland. Middle order batsman. *Sch* Harrow. *Team* MCC (1897–1900).
Career batting
3–5–0–133–36–26.60–0–*ct* 0

He was MP for Brighton.

Wenyon, Herbert John
Amateur. *b:* 18.4.1888, Canton, China. *d:* 19.8.1944, Northwood, Middlesex. Middle order right-hand batsman, slow right-arm bowler. *Team* Middlesex (1921–24, 11 matches).
Career batting
11–14–1–158–51*–12.15–0–*ct* 5
Bowling 71–2–35.50–0–0–2/31

Wesley, Colin
Amateur. *b:* 5.9.1937, Durban, South Africa. Aggressive middle order left-hand batsman, slow left-arm bowler, good field. *Team* Natal (1957/8 to 1965/6). *Tour* South Africa to England 1960. *Tests* South Africa (1960, 3 matches).
Career batting
51–79–9–1892–131–27.02–3–*ct* 20
Bowling 354–15–23.60–0–0–4/51
Test batting
3–5–0–49–35–9.80–0–*ct* 1

He appeared in three Tests on the 1960 tour but made little impact, and in all first-class games hit 595 runs, av 22.03. His first-class debut was for South African Universities in 1956/7. A noted baseball player, he represented Natal.

Wessels, Kepler Christoffel
Cricketer. *b:* 14.9.1957, Bloemfontein, South Africa. Opening left-hand batsman, off break bowler. *Teams* Orange Free State (1973/4 to 1975/6); Northern Transvaal (1977/8); Sussex (1976–80, 53 matches); Western Province (1976/7); Queensland (1979/80 to 1982/3). *Tour* Australia to Sri Lanka 1982/3. *Tests* Australia (1982/3, 5 matches).
Career batting
125–221–20–10142–254–50.45–25–*ct* 92
Bowling 112–4–28.00–0–0–1/0
Test Batting
5–9–0–527–162–58.55–2–*ct* 8

He hit 1,000 runs in a season twice (best 1,800, av 52.94, in 1979). His highest score was 254 for Sussex v Middlesex at Hove in 1980. He also hit 1,000 runs in a season in Australia twice.

West, Albert Richard
Professional. *b:* 7.11.1920, Earl Shilton, Leics. Lower order left-hand batsman, slow left-arm bowler. *Team* Leicestershire (1939, 3 matches).
Career batting
3–5–0–50–22–10.00–0–*ct* 1
Bowling 205–2–102.50–0–0–2/46

West, Gordon Harry Sinclair
Professional. *b:* 7.8.1923, Upton Park, Essex. Sound middle order right-hand batsman, good field. *Team* Essex (1949–53, 2 matches).
Career batting
2–4–0–79–55–19.75–0–*ct* 0

West, John
Professional. *b:* 16.10.1844, Little Sheffield, Yorkshire. *d:* 27.1.1890, Little Sheffield, York-

shire. Lower order left-hand batsman, left-hand fast round-arm bowler. *Team* Yorkshire (1868–76, 38 matches).
Career batting
52–88–17–605–41–8.52–0–*ct* 16
Bowling 1097–75–14.62–5–0–7/42

His final first-class match was for MCC in 1883.

At the time of his death he had been on the staff at Lord's for over 20 years and for many years had been standing as umpire in County matches.

West, John Edward
Professional. *b:* 11.11.1861, Stepney, Middlesex. *d:* 14.3.1920, Bow, London. Lower order right-hand batsman, right-arm medium pace bowler, wicket-keeper. *Team* Middlesex (1885–96, 76 matches).
Career batting
86–143–15–1523–83–11.89–0–*ct* 78–*st* 25
Bowling 2213–89–24.86–4–0–6/31

He was on the Lord's ground staff from 1886 to 1908 and in his later years a well-known first-class umpire. He also played for Durham.

West, Leslie Harold
Professional. *b:* 24.1.1905, Leytonstone, Essex. *d:* 12.11.1982, Essex. Middle order right-hand batsman. *Team* Essex (1928, 3 matches).
Career batting
3–5–0–33–30–6.60–0–*ct* 0

West, Richard
Amateur. *b:* 8.4.1916, Berkhamsted, Hertfordshire. *d:* 18.6.1983, Dry Sandford, Berkshire. Lower order right-hand batsman, right-arm fast medium bowler. *Sch* Rugby. *Team* Oxford U (1936–37).
Career batting
8–11–2–43–18–4.77–0–*ct* 5
Bowling 689–28–24.60–1–0–5/74

West, William Arthur John
Amateur, turned professional 1886. *d:* 17.11.1863, Birmingham. *d:* 22.2.1938, Northampton. Middle order right-hand batsman, right-arm fast bowler, slip. *Team* MCC (1888–91).
Career batting
5–8–1–182–74–26.00–0–*ct* 1
Bowling 100–5–20.00–0–0–3/42

He played for Northants commencing about 1883 until 1890 and for Warwickshire in 1891 (all pre-first-class). For many years a first-class umpire he officiated in some Test matches. A noted boxer, he won the Queensberry Heavyweight Cup in 1884.

Westcott, Albert Harold
Professional. *b:* 6.11.1870, Bridgwater, Somerset. *d:* 6.2.1929, Salisbury, Wilts. Lower order batsman, useful bowler. *Team* Somerset (1894–1902, 6 matches).
Career batting
6–11–6–46–14*–9.20–0–*ct* 3
Bowling 28–0

Westerman, Peter
Amateur. *b:* 12.8.1920, East Sheen, Surrey. Lower order right-hand batsman, right-arm fast bowler. *Team* Surrey (1949–51, 9 matches).
Career batting
9–12–5–25–10–3.57–0–*ct* 1
Bowling 596–21–28.38–2–0–5/49

Western, Edward
Amateur. *b:* 12.5.1845, Taunton, Somerset. *d:* 1919, Williton, Somerset. Middle order right-hand batsman. *Team* Somerset (1882–84, 2 matches).
Career batting
3–4–1–19–13–6.33–0–*ct* 0

He was Hon Secretary of Somerset CCC until 1885.

Westhorp, John White
Amateur. *b:* 1868, London. *d:* 24.3.1935, Purley, Surrey. Lower order right-hand batsman, right-arm medium pace bowler. *Sch* Ipswich. *Team* Middlesex (1893–94, 7 matches).
Career batting
7–11–0–97–39–8.81–0–*ct* 1
Bowling 123–3–41.00–0–0–1/7

Westley, Roger Bancroft
Cricketer. *b:* 21.3.1947, Preston, Lancashire. *d:* 12.5.1982, Haileybury, Herts. Twin brother of S. A. (Lancashire). Lower order right-hand batsman, off break bowler. *Sch* Lancaster GS. *Team* Oxford U (1969).
Career batting
5–7–0–32–14–4.57–0–*ct* 1
Bowling 270–4–67.50–0–0–2/65

Westley, Stuart Alker
Cricketer. *b:* 21.3.1947, Preston, Lancashire. Twin brother of R. B. (Oxford U). Lower order right-hand batsman, wicket-keeper. *Sch* Lancaster GS. *Teams* Oxford U (1968–69, blue both years); Gloucestershire (1969–71, 10 matches).
Career batting
34–55–18–577–93*–15.59–0–*ct* 71–*st* 9

Commencing 1973 he appeared for Suffolk and his final first-class match was for Minor Counties in 1976. A noted rugby footballer, he played for Oxford and Fylde.

Weston, Alan Gibbons
Amateur. *b:* 30.9.1907, Leicester. Middle order right-hand batsman. *Team* Leicestershire (1933–34, 5 matches).
Career batting
5–9–1–72–31*–9.00–0–*ct* 0

Weston, Henry
Amateur. *b:* 2.1.1888, Hurlingham, Putney, London. Middle order left-hand batsman, left-arm slow medium pace bowler. *Team* Middlesex (1910–14, 19 matches).
Career batting
19–27–7–402–79*–20.10–0–*ct* 7
Bowling 736–30–24.53–0–0–4/49

Weston, Martin John
Cricketer. *b:* 8.4.1959, Worcester. Middle order right-hand batsman, right-arm medium pace bowler. *Team* Worcestershire (1979–83, 46 matches).
Career batting
46–79–3–1703–115–22.40–1–*ct* 18
Bowling 445–8–55.62–0–0–3/42

Wettimuny, Sidath
Cricketer. *b:* 12.8.1956, Colombo, Ceylon. Brother of S. R. de S.and M. de S. (Sri Lanka). Middle order right-hand batsman, right-arm medium pace bowler. *Team* Sri Lanka (1975/6 to 1982/3). *Tours* Sri Lanka to India 1976/7, 1980/1, to England 1981, to Pakistan 1981/2, to Australia and New Zealand 1982/3, to Zimbabwe 1982/3, *Tests* Sri Lanka (1981/2 to 1982/3, 4 matches).
Career batting
27–45–3–1303–157–31.02–2–*ct* 9
Bowling 39–1–39.00–0–0–1/7
Test batting
4–8–0–331–157–41.37–1–*ct* 2
Bowling 21–0

Wettimuny, Sunil Ramsay de Silva
Cricketer. *b:* 2.2.1949, Colombo, Ceylon. Brother of Sidath and M. de S. (Sri Lanka). Sound right-hand opening batsman, right-arm medium pace bowler, wicket-keeper or good slip field. *Team* Sri Lanka (1969/70 to 1981/2). *Tours* Sri Lanka to India 1970/1, 1972/3, 1975/6, to Pakistan 1973/4, to England 1975, 1979.
Career batting
39–70–1–1693–121–24.53–2–*ct* 17–*st* 1
Bowling 49–1–49.00–0–0–1/10

Whale, George
Professional. *b:* 27.3.1833, Littleton, Guildford, Surrey. *d:* 1896, Lambeth, London. Lower order left-hand batsman, right-arm fast medium pace bowler. *Team* Surrey (1861–67, 4 matches).
Career batting
5–7–1–46–26–7.66–0–*ct* 2
Bowling 288–5+10–57.60–1–1–6/?

Whalley-Tooker, Edward
Amateur. *b:* 15.1.1863, Wem, Shropshire. *d:* 23.11.1940, Hambledon, Hampshire. Middle order right-hand batsman, slow under-arm bowler. *Sch* Eton. *Team* Hampshire (1883–85, 2 matches).
Career batting
3–5–0–20–7–4.00–0–*ct* 0
His final first-class match was Hambledon v An England XII in 1908.

Wharmby, George Edward
Professional, changed to amateur in 1914. *b:* 7.12.1870, Sutton-in-Ashfield, Notts. *d:* 15.11.1951, Rustington, Sussex. Lower order right-hand batsman, right-arm medium pace bowler. *Teams* Nottinghamshire (1891–93, 4 matches); Lancashire (1894, 6 matches).
Career batting
10–15–2–36–11–2.76–0–*ct* 4
Bowling 298–9–33.11–0–0–3/35
From 1902 to 1923 he played with success for Bedfordshire.

Wharton, Alan
Professional. *b:* 30.4.1923, Heywood, Lancashire. Dashing opening or middle order left-hand batsman, right-arm medium pace bowler. *Teams* Lancashire (1946–60, 392 matches); Leicestershire (1961–63, 79 matches). *Tour* Howard to India 1956/7. *Test* England (1949, 1 match).
Career batting
482–745–69–21796–199–32.24–31–*ct* 288
Bowling 7488–237–31.59–2–0–7/33
Test Batting
1–2–0–20–13–10.00–0–*ct* 0
He hit 1,000 runs in a season eleven times, going on to 2,000 once : 2,157, av 40.69, in 1959. A good rugby league footballer, he played for Salford.

Wharton, Louis Edgar
Amateur. *b:* 18.1.1896, Trinidad. *d:* 31.12.1957, Trinidad. Middle order right-hand batsman. *Sch* Douai. *Teams* Oxford U (1920); Somerset (1921–22, 11 matches).
Career batting
12–24–1–513–86–22.30–0–*ct* 3
Bowling 235–3–78.33–0–0–1/28

Whately, Ellis George
Amateur. *b:* 27.7.1882, London. *d:* 4.9.1969, Chelsea, London. Middle order right-hand batsman, right-arm slow off break bowler. *Sch*

Eton. *Teams* Oxford U (1902–03); Somerset (1904, 1 match).
Career batting
13–21–1–115–20*–5.75–0–*ct* 5
Bowling 1078–43–25.06–1–0–5/66
He also played for Hertfordshire.

Whatford, George Lumley
Amateur. *b:* 20.7.1878, Eastbourne, Sussex. *d:* 22.11.1915, Ctesiphon, Mesopotamia. Middle order batsman. *Sch* Harrow. *Team* Sussex (1904, 2 matches).
Career batting
2–2–0–21–13–10.50–0–*ct* 0

Whatmough, Francis John
(also known as Whatmuff)
Professional. *b:* 4.12.1856, Wilsden, Bingley, Yorkshire. *d:* 3.6.1904, Rastrick, Yorkshire. Tail end right-hand batsman, right-hand fast round-arm bowler. *Team* Yorkshire (1878–82, 7 matches).
Career batting
7–11–1–51–20–5.10–0–*ct* 4
Bowling 111–5–22.20–0–0–3/58

Whatmough, Thomas
Professional. *b:* 26.3.1844, Manchester, Lancashire. *d:* 1911, Prestwich, Lancashire. Lower order right-hand batsman, right-hand fast round-arm bowler, wicket-keeper. *Team* Lancashire (1871, 2 matches).
Career batting
2–4–2–42–28*–21.00–0–*ct* 1
Bowling 79–3–26.33–0–0–2/52
He also played for Cheshire.

Wheat, Arthur Bradley
Professional. *b:* 13.5.1898, Halam, Notts. *d:* 20.5.1973, Kirkby-in-Ashfield, Notts. Tail end left-hand batsman, wicket-keeper. *Team* Nottinghamshire (1927–39, 91 matches).
Career batting
91–115–31–1127–52*–13.41–0–*ct* 152–*st* 21
He was Nottinghamshire CCC scorer from 1947 until his death.

Wheater, Charles Henry
Amateur. *b:* 4.3.1860, Hunmanby, Yorkshire. *d:* 11.5.1885, Scarborough, Yorkshire. Middle order right-hand batsman, right-arm medium pace bowler, point field. *Team* Yorkshire (1880, 2 matches).
Career batting
2–4–1–45–27–15.00–0–*ct* 3
At Cambridge he played in the Freshmen's Match of 1881.

Wheatley, Garth Angus
Amateur. *b:* 28.5.1923, Twickenham, Middlesex. Right-hand batsman, wicket-keeper. *Sch* Uppingham. *Teams* Oxford U (1946, blue); Surrey (1947, 5 matches).
Career batting
18–30–2–478–66–17.07–0–*ct* 20–*st* 8
His final first-class match was for Free Foresters in 1950.

Wheatley, Jack Brian
Amateur. *b:* 12.10.1903, Wandsworth, London. *d:* 29.4.1982, Sellescombe, Sussex. Correct middle order right-hand batsman, left-arm slow medium bowler. *Sch* St Paul's. *Team* Middlesex (1925–28, 8 matches).
Career batting
10–15–1–216–62–15.42–0–*ct* 4
Bowling 169–6–28.16–0–0–3/49
His final first-class match was for Free Foresters in 1930. He appeared in some Trial matches for Oxford U, but no first-class games.

Wheatley, Keith James
Cricketer. *b:* 20.1.1946, Guildford, Surrey. Middle order right-hand batsman, off break bowler, good field. *Team* Hampshire (1965–70, 79 matches).
Career batting
79–110–14–1781–79*–18.55–0–*ct* 32
Bowling 1954–69–18.31–0–0–4/1

Wheatley, Oswald Stephen
Amateur. *b:* 28.5.1935, Durham. Lower order right-hand batsman, right-arm fast medium bowler. *Sch* KES, Birmingham. *Teams* Cambridge U (1957–58, blue both years); Warwickshire (1957–60, 63 matches); Glamorgan (1961 to 1969/70, 206 matches). *Tours* MCC to South America 1958/9 (not first-class); Swanton to West Indies 1960/1; Glamorgan to West Indies 1969/70.
Career batting
316–362–145–1251–34*–5.76–0–*ct* 111
Bowling 22910–1099–20.84–56–5–9/60
His first-class debut was for Free Foresters in 1956. He took 100 wickets in a season five times (best 136, av 19.32, in 1962). His best bowling was 9/60 for Glamorgan v Sussex at Ebbw Vale in 1968. From 1961 to 1966 he captained Glamorgan. After retiring from first-class cricket he continued his connection with Glamorgan cricket in various capacities and in 1983 was Chairman of the County Club.

Wheeler, Alfred
Professional. *b:* 2.10.1845, Croydon, Surrey.

Lower order right-hand batsman, wicket-keeper. *Team* Surrey (1872–73, 2 matches).
Career batting
2–3–0–15–9–5.00–0–*ct* 0

Wheeler, Heneage Gibbes
Amateur. *b:* 24.2.1870, Axbridge, Somerset. *d:* 4.8.1965, Brighton, Sussex. Middle order batsman. *Sch* St Lawrence College. *Team* Somerset (1904, 1 match).
Career batting
1–2–0–8–5–4.00–0–*ct* 0

Wheeler, Henry James William
Amateur. *b:* 27.3.1840, Gibraltar. *d:* 29.10.1908, Westminster, London. Opening batsman. *Sch* Harrow. *Team* Middlesex (1864, 1 match).
Career batting
1–2–0–44–27–22.00–0–*ct* 1

Wheeler, John
Professional. *b:* 9.12.1844, Sutton Bonington, Notts. *d:* 22.9.1908, Sutton Bonington, Notts. Middle order right-hand batsman, right-hand fast round-arm bowler, wicket-keeper. *Team* Nottinghamshire (1873–77, 2 matches).
Career batting
22–38–3–367–66–10.48–0–*ct* 18–*st* 1
Bowling 68–0

His County cricket was mainly for Leicestershire, his career with that County lasting from 1876 to 1892. From 1877 to 1908 he was also on the groundstaff at Lord's and his final first-class match was for MCC in 1887. Between 1893 and 1901 he umpired regularly in first-class matches.

Wheeler, James Anthony
Amateur. *b:* 10.4.1913, Chippenham, Wiltshire. *d:* 1977, Barnstaple, Devon. Stylish middle order right-hand batsman. *Team* Minor Counties (1949).
Career batting
1–2–0–75–54–37.50–0–*ct* 0

His County cricket was for Wiltshire.

Wheeler, Walter Charles
Professional. *b:* 30.12.1841, Newport, Isle of Wight. *d:* 10.10.1907, Kennington, London. Lower order right-hand batsman, right-hand medium pace round-arm bowler, good field. *Teams* Middlesex (1873, 1 match); Surrey (1875, 5 matches); Hampshire (1878–80, 3 matches).
Career batting
10–20–2–80–15–4.44–0–*ct* 2
Bowling 331–14–23.64–1–0–6/133

Wheelhouse, Alan
Amateur. *b:* 4.3.1934, Nottingham. Lower order left-hand batsman, right-arm medium fast bowler. *Sch* Nottingham HS. *Teams* Cambridge U (1958–59, blue 1959); Nottinghamshire (1961, 1 match).
Career batting
17–26–7–133–17–7.00–0–*ct* 10
Bowling 1705–48–35.52–0–0–4/69

Wheldon, George Frederick
Professional. *b:* 1.11.1869, Langley Green, Worcestershire. *d:* 13.1.1924, Worcester. Sound middle order right-hand batsman, occasional wicket-keeper. *Team* Worcestershire (1899–1906, 138 matches).
Career batting
138–244–25–4938–112–22.54–3–*ct* 95–*st* 1
Bowling 77–0

He also played for Carmarthenshire. A brilliant inside-left he played soccer for Aston Villa, Queens Park Rangers, West Bromwich Albion, Portsmouth and Coventry City and was capped for England.

Whetherly, Robin Evelyn
Amateur. *b:* 23.7.1916, Westminster, London. *d:* 27.11.1943, Yugoslavia, He was killed in action. Lower order right-hand batsman, wicket-keeper. *Sch* Harrow. *Team* Oxford U (1937–38). *Tour* Combined Oxford and Cambridge Univ to Jamaica 1938/9.
Career batting
11–16–4–146–63–12.16–0–*ct* 20–*st* 6

Whewell, John William
Professional. *b:* 1887, Church, Lancashire. *d:* 2.7.1948, Blackpool, Lancashire. Lower order right-hand batsman, wicket-keeper. *Team* Lancashire (1921–27, 12 matches).
Career batting
14–17–6–54–25–4.90–0–*ct* 14–*st* 7

Whiley, Richard Kingscote
Amateur. *b:* 10.10.1935, Gloucester. Sound middle order right-hand batsman. *Sch* Malvern. *Teams* Gloucestershire (1954, 1 match); Oxford U (1958).
Career batting
2–4–2–17–7*–8.50–0–*ct* 0

He also played for Dorset.

Whitaker, John James
Cricketer. *b:* 5.5.1962, Skipton, Yorkshire. Middle order right-hand batsman, off break bowler. *Team* Leicestershire (1983, 10 matches).
Career batting
10–16–4–305–56*–25.41–0–*ct* 4
Bowling 88–0

Whitaker, Mark Robin
Cricketer. *b:* 20.9.1946, Walton-on-Thames, Surrey. Tail end right-hand batsman, right-arm fast medium bowler. *Sch* Bryanston. *Team* Cambridge U (1965–67).
Career batting
12–20–7–16–4*–1.23–0–*ct* 2
Bowling 700–20–35.00–1–0–5/62

Whitby, Hugh Owen
Amateur. *b:* 12.4.1864, Ottery St Mary, Devonshire. *d:* 14.10.1934, Tonbridge, Kent. Lower order right-hand batsman, right-hand fast bowler. *Sch* Leamington College. *Team* Oxford U (1884–87, blue all four years). *Tour* Sanders to North America 1885.
Career batting
29–46–12–224–24–6.58–0–*ct* 17
Bowling 2341–119–19.67–10–2–8/82
He played for Warwickshire 1884 to 1889 (pre-first-class).

Whitby, Robert Lionel
Amateur. *b:* 29.10.1928, Calcutta, India. Lower order right-hand batsman, right-arm medium fast bowler. *Sch* Charterhouse. *Team* Cambridge U (1950).
Career batting
2–2–0–23–12–11.50–0–*ct* 0
Bowling 140–0
His final first-class match was for MCC in 1957.

Whitcher, William
Professional. *b:* 1832, Emsworth, Hampshire. *d:* 1910, Southampton, Hants. Middle order batsman, useful bowler. *Team* Hampshire (1864–67, 2 matches).
Career batting
2–4–2–27–17*–13.50–0–*ct* 0
Bowling 30–0

Whitcombe, Henry Maurice
Amateur. *b:* 15.8.1900, Hardwick, Buckinghamshire. *d:* 2.4.84, Ware, Hertfordshire. Brother of P. S. (Essex), uncle of P. A. (Middlesex). Tail end right-hand batsman, left-arm fast medium bowler. *Sch* Haileybury. *Team* Essex (1922, 3 matches).
Career batting
3–4–2–13–7*–6.50–0–*ct* 1
Bowling 199–1–199.00–0–0–1/34

Whitcombe, Philip Arthur
Amateur. *b:* 23.4.1923, Kensington, London. Son of P. S. (Essex), nephew of H. M. (Essex). Hard hitting lower order right-hand batsman, right-arm fast medium bowler. *Sch* Winchester. *Teams* Oxford U (1947–49, blue all three years); Middlesex (1948, 3 matches).
Career batting
37–56–5–956–68–18.74–0–*ct* 23
Bowling 2489–112–22.22–5–0–7/51
His final first-class match was for the Free Foresters in 1960. He also played for Wiltshire.

Whitcombe, Philip John
Amateur. *b:* 11.11.1928, Worcester. Sound opening right-hand batsman, wicket-keeper. *Sch* Worcester RGS. *Teams* Worcestershire (1949–52, 8 matches); Oxford U (1950–52, blue 1951–52).
Career batting
34–53–6–1156–104–24.59–1–*ct* 30–*st* 8
Bowling 10–1–10.00–0–0–1/8

Whitcombe, Major-General Philip Sidney
Amateur. *b:* 3.10.1893, Windsor, Berkshire. Father of P. A. (Middlesex), brother of H. M. (Essex). Middle order right-hand batsman, right-arm fast medium bowler. *Sch* Winchester. *Teams* Essex (1922, 1 match); Europeans (1928/9 to 1930/1).
Career batting
4–7–2–81–32*–16.20–0–*ct* 1
Bowling 37–0
He also played for Berkshire.

White, A. B. (*See under* Blair-White, A.)

White, A. C.
Amateur. Middle order right-hand batsman. *Team* Surrey (1881, 1 match).
Career batting
1–2–1–15–9*–15.00–0–*ct* 0

White, Allan Frederick Tinsdale
Amateur. *b:* 5.9.1915, Coventry, Warwickshire. Opening right-hand batsman. *Sch* Uppingham. *Teams* Cambridge U (1936–37, blue 1936); Warwickshire (1936–37, 9 matches); Worcestershire (1939–49, 110 matches).
Career batting
142–247–17–5035–95–21.89–0–*ct* 46
Bowling 26–0
He hit 1,179 runs, av 26.79, in 1946 and also reached 1,000 runs in one other season. In 1947, 1948, and jointly in 1949 he captained Worcestershire.

White, Alfred Henry Ebsworth
Amateur. *b:* 18.10.1901, Scone, New South Wales, Australia. *d:* 6.3.1964, Darling Point, New South Wales, Australia. Lower order right-hand batsman, right-arm fast medium bowler. *Teams* Cambridge U (1922–24, blue 1924); New South Wales (1925/6, 1 match).

Career batting
20–25–6–279–53*–14.68–0–*ct* 9
Bowling 1299–45–28.86–1–0–5/66

White, Alison Kingsley Gordon
(later Gordon-White)
Amateur. *b:* 2.1.1881. *d:* 20.3.1962, Crowborough, Sussex. Middle order right-hand batsman, right-arm fast medium bowler. *Sch* Cheltenham. *Team* Gloucestershire (1913–19, 11 matches).
Career batting
13–24–1–442–54–19.21–0–*ct* 7
Bowling 3–0
He also played for Northumberland.

White, Albert Winterton
Amateur. *b:* 1889, Wellingborough, Northants. *d:* 9.3.1965, Rushden, Northants. Middle order right-hand batsman. *Sch* Wellingborough. *Team* Northants (1914–23, 8 matches).
Career batting
8–15–0–139–29–9.26–0–*ct* 5
Bowling 24–0

White, Anthony Wilbur
Amateur. *b:* 20.11.1938, Brighton, Bridgetown, Barbados. Attacking lower order right-hand batsman, right-arm medium pace off break bowler. *Team* Barbados (1958/9 to 1965/6). *Tour* West Indies to England 1963. *Tests* West Indies (1964/5, 2 matches).
Career batting
31–46–7–996–75–25.53–0–*ct* 32
Bowling 2665–95–28.05–1–0–6/80
Test batting
2–4–1–71–57*–23.66–0–*ct* 1
Bowling 152–3–50.66–0–0–2/34
He was co-opted into the 1963 touring team to England due to injury, and appeared in nine matches.

White, Sir Archibald Woollaston
Amateur. *b:* 14.10.1877, Tickhill, Yorkshire. *d:* 16.12.1945, Wigtown, Scotland. Middle order right-hand batsman, right-arm medium pace bowler. *Sch* Wellington. *Team* Yorkshire (1908–20, 97 matches).
Career batting
98–130–28–1471–55–14.32–0–*ct* 50
Bowling 7–0
He captained Yorkshire 1912 to 1914.

White, Colin Derek
Amateur. *b:* 4.4.1937, Chiswick, Middlesex. Middle order left-hand batsman. *Sch* Cranleigh. *Team* Cambridge U (1958–60).
Career batting
23–41–2–606–64–15.53–0–*ct* 7
Bowling 24–0
His final first-class match was for Free Foresters in 1961.

White, David William
Professional. *b:* 14.12.1935, Sutton Coldfield. Lower order left-hand batsman, right-arm fast bowler. *Teams* Hampshire (1957–71, 315 matches); Glamorgan (1972, 1 match). *Tours* MCC to India and Pakistan 1961/2; Cavaliers to West Indies 1964/5. *Tests* England (1961/2, 2 matches).
Career batting
337–395–104–3080–58*–10.58–0–*ct* 106
Bowling 26913–1143–23.54–57–5–9/44
Test batting
2–2–0–0–0–0.00–0–*ct* 0
Bowling 119–4–29.75–0–0–3/65
He took 100 wickets in a season four times (best 124, av 19.10, in 1960). His best innings analysis was 9 for 44 for Hampshire v Leicestershire at Portsmouth in 1966.

White, Edmund
Amateur. *b:* 29.1.1928, Lee, London. Middle order right-hand batsman, wicket-keeper. *Sch* Wellingborough. *Team* Northants (1946–48, 3 matches).
Career batting
3–4–0–44–16–11.00–0–*ct* 1

White, Edward Albert
Amateur. *b:* 16.3.1844, Yalding, Kent. *d:* 3.5.1922, Chiswick, Middlesex. Cousin of L. A. (Kent). Stylish opening right-hand batsman. *Sch* Marlborough. *Team* Kent (1867–75, 29 matches).
Career batting
31–60–7–827–81–15.60–0–*ct* 12

White, Edward Clive Stewart
Amateur. *b:* 17.4.1913, Mosman, New South Wales, Australia. Son of A. B. S. (New South Wales). Lower order right-hand batsman, leg break bowler. *Team* New South Wales (1934/5 to 1938/9, 32 matches). *Tour* Australia to England 1938.
Career batting
56–81–22–1316–108*–22.30–1–*ct* 37
Bowling 3072–115–26.71–2–0–8/31
He had few opportunities on the 1938 tour to England.

White, Francis Sims
Amateur. *b:* 26.8.1883, Philadelphia, USA. *d:* 5.4.1962, Germantown, Philadelphia, USA. Middle order right-hand batsman. *Team* Philadel-

phia (1903–08). *Tour* Philadelphia to England 1908.
Career batting
15–27–1–456–62–17.53–0–*ct* 8

He played for USA v Canada in 1904. On the 1908 tour he hit 346 runs, av 19.22, coming second in the batting table.

White, Gordon Charles
Amateur. *b:* 5.2.1882, Port St John's, Pondoland, Cape Province, South Africa. *d:* 17.10.1918, Gaza, Palestine. He died of wounds. Attractive middle order right-hand batsman, leg break bowler. *Team* Transvaal (1902/3 to 1911/12). *Tours* South Africa to England 1904, 1907 and 1912. *Tests* South Africa (1905/6 to 1912, 17 matches).
Career batting
97–152–17–3740–162*–27.70–4–*ct* 46
Bowling 3109–155–20.05–8–2–7/33
Test batting
17–31–2–872–147–30.06–2–*ct* 10
Bowling 301–9–33.44–0–0–4/47

On the 1904 visit he hit 773 runs, av 29.73, and in 1907 862 runs, av 22.10. On the latter tour he took 56 wickets, av 14.73. In 1912, though he played in five out of six Tests, he was not successful.

White, George Holford
Amateur. *b:* 16.10.1904, Dorchester. *d:* 18.1.1965, Uxbridge, Middlesex. Opening right-hand batsman. *Sch* Felsted. *Team* RAF (1932).
Career batting
1–2–0–50–25–25.00–0–*ct* 0

His County cricket was for Dorset.

White, Gilbert William
Amateur. *b:* 6.7.1912, Farnham, Surrey. *d:* 14.10.1977, La Plaine, Dominica. Son of W. N. (Hampshire). Attractive middle order batsman. *Sch* Winchester. *Team* Army (1938).
Career batting
1–1–0–10–10–10.00–0–*ct* 0
Bowling 12–0

White, Rev Harold
Amateur. *b:* 16.6.1876, Kirkstall, Yorkshire. *d:* 11.1.1965, Taunton, Somerset. Lower order right-hand batsman, right-arm fast bowler. *Sch* Denstone. *Team* Oxford U (1900–01, blue 1900).
Career batting
11–14–5–77–26–8.55–0–*ct* 3
Bowling 725–31–23.38–1–0–6/10

His County cricket was for Northumberland.

White, Henry Albert
Professional. *b:* 17.4.1892, Watford. *d:* 27.11.1972, Barrow Gurney, Somerset. Lower order right-hand batsman, right-arm off break bowler. *Team* Warwickshire (1923, 8 matches).
Career batting
8–15–3–107–32–8.91–0–*ct* 2
Bowling 33–0

A good soccer player, he appeared for Arsenal, Blackpool and Walsall.

White, Horace Arthur
Amateur. *b:* 1894, Wellingborough, Northants. *d:* 1969, Wellingborough, Northants. Middle order right-hand batsman, useful bowler. *Teams* Northants (1923, 5 matches); Europeans (1930/1 to 1933/4); Madras (1932/3).
Career batting
10–17–3–173–70*–12.35–0–*ct* 5
Bowling 529–15–35.26–1–0–5/42

White, Jack
Amateur. *b:* 9.7.1893, Putney, London. *d:* 6.11.1968, East Grinstead, Sussex. Lower order right-hand batsman, right-arm fast bowler. *Sch* Wellingborough. *Teams* Cambridge U (1913); Surrey (1926, 1 match).
Career batting
3–3–1–26–15*–13.00–0–*ct* 3
Bowling 289–6–48.16–1–0–5/75

White, John
Professional. *b:* Bulwell, Notts. Lower order batsman, wicket-keeper. *Teams* North of England (1886); Liverpool and District XI (1886–90).
Career batting
3–4–0–73–62–18.25–0–*ct* 4–*st* 2

He appeared for Nottinghamshire in a non-first-class match in 1887.

White, John Cornish
Amateur. *b:* 19.2.1891, Holford, Somerset. *d:* 2.5.1961, Combe-Florey, Somerset. Lower order right-hand batsman, slow left-arm bowler. *Sch* Taunton. *Team* Somerset (1909–37, 409 matches). *Tours* MCC to South America 1926/7, to Australia 1928/9, to South Africa 1930/1. *Tests* England (1921 to 1930/1, 15 matches).
Career batting
472–765–102–12202–192–18.40–6–*ct* 426
Bowling 43759–2356–18.57–193–58–10/76
Test batting
15–22–9–239–29–18.38–0–*ct* 6
Bowling 1581–49–32.26–3–1–8/126

He took 100 wickets in a season 14 times (best 168, av 15.76, in 1929) and hit 1,000 runs twice (best 1,179, av 27.41, in 1929). In 1929 and 1930 he completed the 'double'. His best innings analysis was 10 for 76 for Somerset v Worcestershire at Worcester in 1921; he took nine wickets in an innings on four other occasions. From 1927 to 1931 he captained Somerset and he led England in four Tests, as well as being a Test Selector for some seasons. He was President of Somerset in 1960.

White, John William
Professional. *b:* 1.8.1877, Annesley, Notts. *d:* 2.12.1958, Mansfield, Notts. Lower order right-hand batsman, wicket-keeper. *Teams* Nottinghamshire (1902–04, 3 matches); Scotland (1906).
Career batting
4–8–1–74–31–10.57–0–*ct* 8–*st* 2
A useful soccer player, he appeared for Nottingham Forest at full-back.

White, Lionel Algernon
Amateur. *b:* 9.11.1850, Wateringbury, Kent. *d:* 25.6.1917, Tunbridge Wells, Kent. Cousin of E. A. (Kent). Careful middle order right-hand batsman, good deep field. *Sch* St Paul's. *Team* Kent (1869, 4 matches).
Career batting
4–8–0–84–34–10.50–0–*ct* 1

White, Hon Luke Robert
(succeeded as 5th Baron Annaly in 1970)
Amateur. *b:* 15.3.1927, London. Opening or middle order right-hand batsman. *Sch* Eton. *Team* Middlesex (1946–47, 3 matches).
Career batting
6–10–1–134–46–14.88–0–*ct* 2
His first-class debut was for England in 1945 and his final first-class match for MCC in 1950.

White, Montague Eric
Professional. *b:* 21.1.1908, London. *d:* 21.6.1970, Wirral, Cheshire. Lower order right-hand batsman, right-arm fast medium bowler. *Sch* Worcester RGS. *Team* Worcestershire (1931–34, 34 matches).
Career batting
34–46–12–238–37–7.00–0–*ct* 11
Bowling 2076–66–31.45–1–0–5/34

White, Malcolm Frank
Amateur. *b:* 15.5.1924, Walsall, Staffs. Lower order right-hand batsman, wicket-keeper. *Team* Warwickshire (1946, 1 match).
Career batting
1–2–0–0–0–0.00–0–*ct* 3–*st* 1

White, Oliver Claude
Amateur. *b:* 11.3.1880, Eton, Buckinghamshire. *d:* 12.1.1956, Redhill, Surrey. Lower order right-hand batsman, slow right-arm bowler. *Sch* Merchant Taylors. *Team* Northants (1920, 5 matches).
Career batting
5–9–3–57–15*–9.50–0–*ct* 1
Bowling 279–10–27.90–0–0–3/49

White, Robert Arthur
Professional. *b:* 6.10.1936, Fulham, London. Sound opening, later middle order left-hand batsman, off break bowler. *Teams* Middlesex (1958–65, 114 matches); Nottinghamshire (1966–80, 298 matches).
Career batting
413–642–105–12452–116*–23.18–5–*ct* 190
Bowling 21138–693–30.50–28–4–7/41
He hit 1,355 runs, av 33.87, in 1963; his best bowling season was 1971 with 81 wickets, av 26.21. His career was remarkable in that he did not take a single wicket during his eight seasons with Middlesex. In 1983 he joined the first-class umpires' list.

White, Raymond Christopher
Amateur. *b:* 29.1.1941, Johannesburg, South Africa. Attacking middle order right-hand batsman, right-arm medium pace bowler. *Teams* Cambridge U (1962–65, blue all four years); Gloucestershire (1962–64, 40 matches); Transvaal (1965/6 to 1972/3).
Career batting
141–248–4–6824–205–27.96–10–*ct* 67
Bowling 589–17–34.64–0–0–3/17
His first-class debut was for South African Universities in 1960/1. His highest score was 205 for Transvaal B v Griqualand West at Johannesburg in 1965/6. He hit 1,000 runs in a season twice (best 1,696, av 29.24, in 1962).

White, Roger Frank
Cricketer. *b:* 22.11.1943, Perivale, Middlesex. Lower order right-hand batsman, slow left-arm bowler. *Team* Middlesex (1964–66, 13 matches).
Career batting
13–11–6–18–7*–3.60–0–*ct* 4
Bowling 518–17–30.47–0–0–4/79

White, Reginald Strelley Moresby
Amateur. *b:* 22.2.1893, Grantham, Lincolnshire. *d:* 3.3.1947, Nairobi, Kenya. Lower order batsman, wicket-keeper. *Sch* Malvern. *Teams* Oxford U (1913–14); Europeans (1924/5).
Career batting
7–10–4–90–36–11.25–0–*ct* 4–*st* 2
His final first-class match was for the Army in 1930. His County cricket was for Lincolnshire.

White, Sidney Grayling
Amateur. *b:* 1892, Staines, Middlesex. *d:* 1.5.1949, Chipstead, Surrey. Lower order left-

hand batsman, left-arm bowler. *Team* Middlesex (1921–23, 2 matches).
Career batting
2–3–1–23–20–11.50–0–*ct* 2
Bowling 33–0

White, Thomas
Professional. *b:* 1740, Reigate, Surrey. *d:* 28.7.1831, Reigate, Surrey. Middle order right-hand batsman. *Team* Surrey (1773–78).
Career batting
not applicable, pre-1800

He represented England against Hampshire and in 1771 he used a bat the width of the wicket, and this innnovation caused the Laws of the game to be altered to include a clause stating that the bat should not be more than four and a quarter inches in width.

White, Thomas Reginald
Amateur. *b:* 3.7.1892, Basingstoke. *d:* 7.5.1979, Camden, London. Middle order right-hand batsman, right-arm fast medium bowler. *Sch* Cranleigh. *Team* Sussex (1928, 1 match).
Career batting
1–2–0–13–9–6.50–0–*ct* 0
Bowling 25–0

White, William Michael Eastwood
Amateur. *b:* 22.5.1913, Barnes, Surrey. Lower order right-hand batsman, right-arm medium fast bowler. *Sch* Dover. *Teams* Cambridge U (1937); Northants (1947–49, 5 matches).
Career batting
21–35–6–398–48–13.72–0–*ct* 15
Bowling 1524–42–36.28–0–0–4/67

White, William Neil
Amateur. *b:* 2.5.1920, Troon, Ayrshire, Scotland. Middle order right-hand batsman, slow left-arm bowler. *Sch* The Leys. *Team* Cambridge U (1948).
Career batting
2–3–0–19–19–6.33–0–*ct* 1
Bowling 106–4–26.50–0–0–4/16

His County cricket was for Cambridgeshire.

White, William Nicholas
Amateur. *b:* 10.9.1879, London. *d:* 27.12.1951, Poltimore, Devon. Father of G. W. (Army). Middle order right-hand batsman. *Sch* Malvern. *Teams* Hampshire (1903–14, 61 matches); Barbados (1903/4 to 1905/6).
Career batting
72–128–5–3225–160*–26.21–2–*ct* 42
Bowling 39–0

His final first-class match was for the Combined Services in 1922. A good soccer player, he captained the Army team.

Whitehead, Alan Geoffrey Thomas
Professional. *b:* 28.10.1940, Butleigh, Somerset. Tail end left-hand batsman, slow left-arm bowler. *Team* Somerset (1957–61, 38 matches).
Career batting
38–49–25–137–15–5.70–0–*ct* 20
Bowling 2306–67–34.41–3–0–6/74

He was appointed to the first-class umpires' list in 1970 and was a Test umpire in 1982.

Whitehead, George William Edendale
Amateur. *b:* 27.8.1895, Bromley, Kent. *d:* 17.10.1918, near Halluin, France. He was killed in action. Brother of J. H. E. (MCC). Stylish middle order right-hand batsman, leg break and googly bowler. *Sch* Clifton. *Team* Kent (1914, 2 matches).
Career batting
2–4–0–12–5–3.00–0–*ct* 3

Whitehead, Harry
Professional. *b:* 19.9.1874, Barlestone, Leics. *d:* 14.9.1944, Leicester. Attractive opening right-hand batsman, right-arm medium pace bowler, good field. *Team* Leicestershire (1898–1922, 380 matches).
Career batting
382–680–25–15112–174–23.07–14–*ct* 407
Bowling 3401–106–32.08–1–0–5/80

He hit 1,000 runs in a season four times (best 1,391, av 30.91, in 1911). A good soccer player, he appeared for Leicester Fosse.

Whitehead, James George
Professional. *b:* 1877, Cape Province, South Africa. *d:* 23.1.1940, Mowbray, Cape Town, South Africa. Lower order batsman, left-arm medium fast bowler. *Teams* Warwickshire (1902, 1 match); Western Province (1904/5 to 1920/1); Griqualand West (1912/3 to 1913/4).
Career batting
30–47–16–351–42–11.32–0–*ct* 10
Bowling 2228–118–18.88–7–2–7/58

Whitehead, James Hugh Edendale
Amateur. *b:* 8.7.1890, Bromley, Kent. *d:* 13.3.1919, Marylebone, London. Brother of G. W. E. (Kent). Middle order batsman, leg break bowler. *Sch* Clifton. *Team* MCC (1912).
Career batting
1–2–0–3–2–1.50–0–*ct* 1

Whitehead, John Parkin
Professional. *b:* 3.9.1925, Upper Mill, Yorkshire.

Lower order right-hand batsman, right-arm fast medium bowler. *Teams* Yorkshire (1946–51, 37 matches); Worcestershire (1953–55, 33 matches).
Career batting
74–91–26–1246–71–19.16–0–*ct* 25
Bowling 4297–147–29.23–4–0–5/10

Whitehead, Lees
Professional. *b:* 14.3.1864, Birchen Bank, Friarmere, Yorkshire. *d:* 22.11.1913, West Hartlepool, Co Durham. He died of pneumonia. Lower order right-hand batsman, right-arm fast bowler. *Team* Yorkshire (1889–1904, 119 matches).
Career batting
136–202–43–2433–67*–15.30–0–*ct* 81
Bowling 2799–109–25.67–3–0–6/45

Whitehead, Luther
Professional. *b:* 25.6.1869, Hull, Yorkshire. *d:* 16.1.1931, Buenos Aires, Argentine. Middle order right-hand batsman, deep field. *Team* Yorkshire (1893, 2 matches).
Career batting
2–4–0–21–13–5.25–0–*ct* 0

Whitehead, Philip James
Amateur. *b:* 1881, Woodstock, Oxfordshire. *d:* 1957, Greenwich, Kent. Middle order batsman. *Team* Northants (1908–09, 2 matches).
Career batting
2–4–2–24–10*–12.00–0–*ct* 0
Bowling 11–1–11.00–0–0–1/11

Whitehead, Ralph
Professional. *b:* 16.10.1883, Ashton-under-Lyne, Lancashire. *d:* 23.8.1956, Winwick, Lancashire. Patient middle order right-hand batsman, right-arm medium fast bowler. *Team* Lancashire (1908–14, 107 matches).
Career batting
108–160–36–2578–131*–20.79–4–*ct* 37
Bowling 7260–300–24.20–17–5–8/77

He had a sensational debut – Lancashire v Notts at Old Trafford in 1908 – when he hit 131* and later was no-balled four times in one over for throwing.

Whitehead, Stephen James
Professional. *b:* 2.9.1860, Enfield, Middlesex. *d:* 9.6.1904, Small Heath, Birmingham. Lower order right-hand batsman, right-arm medium off break bowler. *Team* Warwickshire (1894–1900, 55 matches).
Career batting
56–76–28–494–46–10.50–0–*ct* 33
Bowling 4214–178–23.67–11–4–8/47

He died the day following the match between Warwickshire and Essex at Edgbaston, the proceeds of which had been set aside for the benefit of himself and Richards. Whitehead had attended the match and seemed in good health.

Whitehead, Thomas
Amateur. *b:* 1852. *d:* 2.11.1937, Brindle, Preston, Lancashire. Lower order batsman, useful bowler. *Team* Lancashire (1884, 1 match).
Career batting
3–4–2–33–17*–16.50–0–*ct* 1
Bowling 186–5–37.20–0–0–2/40

His final first-class match was for Liverpool and District in 1892.

Whitehill, William K.
Professional. *b:* 13.6.1934, Newport, Monmouthshire. Lower order right-hand batsman, wicket-keeper. *Team* Glamorgan (1960, 7 matches).
Career batting
7–11–3–60–16–7.50–0–*ct* 8

Whitehouse, John
Cricketer. *b:* 8.4.1949, Nuneaton, Warwickshire. Stylish middle order right-hand batsman, right-arm off break bowler. *Team* Warwickshire (1971–80, 179 matches).
Career batting
180–309–38–8693–197–32.07–15–*ct* 120
Bowling 471–6–78.50–0–0–2/55

He hit 1,000 runs in a season three times (best 1,543, av 42.86, in 1977). In 1978 and 1979 he captained Warwickshire.

Whitehouse, Percy Gilbert
Amateur. *b:* 1.8.1893, Edgbaston, Warwickshire. *d:* 24.9.1959, Knowle, Solihull, Warwickshire. Right-hand batsman, right-arm off break bowler. *Team* Warwickshire (1926, 3 matches).
Career batting
3–6–3–41–13–13.66–0–*ct* 6
Bowling 122–8–15.25–0–0–4/23

Whitehouse, Peter Michael William
Amateur. *b:* 27.4.1917, Birchington, Kent. *d:* 19.11.1943, Archi, Italy. He was killed in action. Middle order right-hand batsman, right-arm medium pace bowler. *Sch* Marlborough. *Teams* Oxford U (1936–38, blue 1938); Kent (1937–38, 8 matches).
Career batting
24–39–7–927–91*–28.96–0–*ct* 4
Bowling 1167–43–23.13–1–0–5/33

Whitelaw, William Frederick Martin
Amateur. *b:* 16.6.1906, Edinburgh, Scotland. *d:* May 1982, Polton, Midlothian, Scotland. Right-hand batsman, right-arm medium pace bowler. *Sch* Merchiston. *Team* Scotland (1932)
Career batting
1–2–0–1–1–0.50–0–*ct* 0
Bowling 54–2–27.00–0–0–2/48

Whiteley, John Peter
Cricketer. *b:* 28.2.1955, Otley, Yorkshire. Lower order right-hand batsman, off break bowler. *Team* Yorkshire (1978–82, 45 matches).
Career batting
45–38–17–231–20–11.00–0–*ct* 21
Bowling 2410–70–34.42–0–0–4/14

Whiteley, Peter
Professional. *b:* 12.8.1935, Rochdale, Lancashire. Middle order right-hand batsman, slow left-arm bowler. *Team* Lancashire (1957–58, 5 matches).
Career batting
5–8–2–86–32–14.33–0–*ct* 2
Bowling 266–9–29.55–0–0–3/70

Whiteside, John Parkinson
Professional. *b:* 11.6.1861, Fleetwood, Lancashire. *d:* 8.3.1946, Leicester. Tail end right-hand batsman, wicket-keeper. *Teams* Lancashire (1888–90, 6 matches); Leicestershire (1894–1906, 215 matches).
Career batting
231–362–141–1362–50–6.16–0–*ct* 340–*st* 98
He was on the Lord's ground staff from 1889 to 1920.

Whiteside, Peter George
Amateur. *b:* 21.2.1930, New Malden, Surrey. Lower order right-hand batsman, wicket-keeper. *Sch* Denstone. *Team* Cambridge U (1955).
Career batting
2–2–0–1–1–0.50–0–*ct* 3

Whitfeld, Francis Barry
Amateur. *b:* 23.5.1852, Lewes, Sussex. *d:* 8.1.1924, Lewes, Sussex. Father of G. S., brother of Herbert (Sussex). Middle order batsman, excellent field. *Sch* Uppingham. *Team* Sussex (1878, 1 match).
Career batting
2–4–0–7–5–1.75–0–*ct* 3
His final first-class match was for G. N. Wyatt's XI in 1886.

Whitfeld, George Sulivan
Amateur. *b:* 20.3.1878, Lewes, Sussex. *d:* 29.7.1945, Kensington, London. Son of F. B., nephew of Herbert (Sussex). Hard hitting middle order batsman. *Sch* Eton. *Team* Sussex (1908, 3 matches).
Career batting
3–5–2–191–71*–63.66–0–*ct* 0

Whitfeld, Herbert
Amateur. *b:* 15.11.1858, Lewes, Sussex. *d:* 6.5.1909, Chailey, Sussex. Brother of F. B. (Sussex), uncle of G. S. (Sussex). Opening or middle order right-hand batsman, left-hand medium pace round-arm bowler, good slip field. *Sch* Eton. *Teams* Cambridge U (1878–81, blue all four years); Sussex (1878–85, 39 matches).
Career batting
75–133–14–2400–116–20.16–1–*ct* 65
Bowling 282–6–47.00–0–0–2/35
He captained Sussex in 1883 and 1884. His final first-class match was for I Zingari in 1889. An all-round athlete, he represented Cambridge in the mile and at soccer, also being in the tennis doubles with Hon Ivo Bligh.

Whitfield, Edward Walter
Professional. *b:* 31.5.1911, Clapham, London. Right-hand batsman, right-arm medium pace bowler. *Teams* Surrey (1930–39, 106 matches); Northants (1946, 19 matches).
Career batting
125–189–21–3995–198–23.77–6–*ct* 36
Bowling 1562–35–44.62–0–0–4/63
He hit 1,005 runs, av 38.89, in 1938.

Whiting, Algernon Oswald
Amateur. *b:* 23.4.1861, Kensington, London. *d:* 23.1.1931, Worcester Park, Surrey. Stylish middle order right-hand batsman, wicket-keeper. *Sch* Sherborne and Charterhouse. *Team* Oxford U (1881–82, blue both years).
Career batting
9–17–0–317–80–18.64–0–*ct* 6
He was for many years a tea planter in Ceylon and played much cricket there.

Whiting, Charles Percival
Professional. *b:* 19.4.1888, Bridlington, Yorkshire. *d:* 14.1.1959, Great Driffield, Yorkshire. Lower order right-hand batsman, right-arm fast bowler. *Team* Yorkshire (1914–20, 6 matches).
Career batting
6–10–2–92–26–11.50–0–*ct* 2
Bowling 416–15–27.73–1–0–5/46

Whiting, John George Benjamin
Amateur. *b:* 19.2.1894, Newport Pagnell, Buckinghamshire. *d:* 15.7.1975, Newport Pagnell, Buckinghamshire. Lower order batsman, useful bowler. *Sch* Wellingborough. *Team* Leveson-Gower's XI (1921).
Career batting
2–4–0–34–27–8.50–0–*ct* 0
Bowling 272–6–45.33–0–0–4/76
His County cricket was for Buckinghamshire.

Whiting, Norman Harry
Professional. *b:* 2.10.1920, Wollaston, Worcestershire. Middle order right-hand batsman, off break bowler. *Team* Worcestershire (1947–52, 59 matches).
Career batting
59–96–11–1583–118–18.62–2–*ct* 33
Bowling 657–13–50.53–0–0–2/27

Whiting, Walter Sydney
Amateur. *b:* 23.10.1888, Bath, Somerset. *d:* 15.1.1952, Bath, Somerset. Lower order right-hand batsman, leg break bowler. *Team* Somerset (1921–23, 8 matches).
Career batting
8–12–3–133–28–14.77–0–*ct* 9
Bowling 646–27–23.92–0–0–4/28

Whitington, Richard Smallpeice
Amateur. *b:* 30.6.1912, Unley Park, Adelaide, Australia. *d:* 13.3.1984, Sydney, Australia. Opening right-hand batsman. *Team* South Australia (1932/3 to 1939/40, 36 matches). *Tours* Australian Forces to England 1945, to India 1945/6.
Career batting
54–90–4–2782–155–32.34–4–*ct* 32
Bowling 91–1–91.00–0–0–1/4
His final first-class match was for Australian Services in Australia in 1945/6. He was a noted author and journalist, having written a number of books on cricket, several of them jointly with K. R. Miller.

Whitley, Robert Thomas
Professional. *b:* 1837, Pimlico, Middlesex. *d:* 26.10.1887, Fulham, Middlesex. Middle order batsman. *Team* Surrey (1873, 1 match).
Career batting
1–2–0–8–5–4.00–0–*ct* 2

Whitman, Eric Ioan E.
Amateur. *b:* 1909, Barry, Glamorgan. Lower order batsman, fast bowler. *Team* Glamorgan (1932, 2 matches).
Career batting
2–3–0–27–16–9.00–0–*ct* 0
Bowling 172–3–57.33–0–0–2/113
He also played for Cambridgeshire.

Whitney, Michael Roy
Cricketer. *b:* 24.2.1959, Surry Hills, Sydney, New South Wales, Australia. Lower order right-hand batsman, left-arm fast medium bowler. *Teams* New South Wales (1980/1 to 1982/3, 22 matches); Gloucestershire (1981, 3 matches). *Tours* Australia to England 1981 (co-opted into team due to injuries); Young Australia to Zimbabwe 1982/3. *Tests* Australia (1981, 2 matches).
Career batting
31–28–8–74–28*–3.70–0–*ct* 19
Bowling 3083–103–29.93–4–0–5/29
Test batting
2–4–0–4–4–1.00–0–*ct* 0
Bowling 246–5–49.20–0–0–2/50
He was just about to play for Gloucestershire v Hampshire at Cheltenham on 11 August 1981 when he was summoned to Old Trafford to play for Australia in the fifth Test, a move which created a talking point at the time. His last first-class match in England was for D. B. Close's XI in 1983.

Whittaker, Charles Gustavus
Amateur. *b:* 8.9.1819, Barming, Kent. *d:* 15.11.1886, Barming, Kent. Lower order right-hand batsman, right-hand fast round-arm bowler. *Sch* Westminster. *Team* Kent (1839–47, 36 matches).
Career batting
70–125–20–844–55–8.03–0–*ct* 26
Bowling 12–0+45–no av–1–0–6/?
His final important match was for Gentlemen of Kent in 1848 when he sustained a compound fracture of his right thumb and was unable to continue to appear in great matches.

Whittaker, David
Professional. *b:* 25.10.1857, Church, Lancashire. *d:* 17.12.1901, Rishton, Lancashire. He was found drowned in the canal. Middle order left-hand batsman, left-arm medium pace bowler, good point field. *Team* Lancashire (1884–88, 9 matches).
Career batting
9–14–1–128–26–9.84–0–*ct* 4
Bowling 46–1–46.00–0–0–1/26

Whittaker, Edwin
Amateur. *b:* 4.12.1834, Ashton-under-Lyne, Lancashire. *d:* 25.6.1880, Matlock, Derbyshire. Stylish middle order right-hand batsman, occasional wicket-keeper. *Sch* Wesley College, Sheffield. *Team* Lancashire (1865–68, 11 matches).
Career batting
14–25–2–291–39–12.65–0–*ct* 4
Bowling 125–1–125.00–0–0–1/26
He was a notable player for Gentlemen of Lancashire. His first-class debut was for North of England in 1863.

Whittaker, Geoffrey James
Professional. *b:* 29.5.1916, Peckham, London.

Aggressive middle order right-hand batsman. *Team* Surrey (1937–53, 124 matches).
Career batting
129–191–20–4988–185*–29.16–8–*ct* 48
Bowling 47–1–47.00–0–0–1/31
He hit 1,439 runs, av 39.97, in 1951, and also completed 1,000 runs in 1949.

Whittaker, Robert Christopher Cornwallis
Amateur. *b:* 26.8.1908, Melton, Suffolk. Lower order right-hand batsman, slow left-arm bowler. *Sch* Eton. *Team* Sussex (1927, 2 matches).
Career batting
3–3–1–31–31–15.50–0–*ct* 2
Bowling 84–6–14.00–1–0–5/36
His final first-class match was for the Army in 1929.

Whitting, Edward Jewel
Amateur. *b:* 1.9.1872, Uphill, Somerset. *d:* 8.3.1938, Abergavenny, Monmouthshire. Forceful lower order right-hand batsman, right-arm fast bowler. *Sch* Rugby. *Team* H. T. Hewett's XI (1892).
Career batting
1–2–1–6–5–6.00–0–*ct* 0
He played in the Cambridge Freshmen's Match of 1892.

Whittingham, Norman Barrie
Professional. *b:* 22.10.1940, Silsden, Yorkshire. Middle order left-hand batsman, off break bowler. *Team* Nottinghamshire (1962–66, 77 matches).
Career batting
77–141–7–2964–133–22.11–2–*ct* 41
Bowling 122–1–122.00–0–0–1/9
He played for Cumberland 1967 to 1971

Whittington, Thomas Aubrey Leyson
Amateur. *b:* 29.7.1881, Neath, Glamorgan. *d:* 17.7.1944, St Pancras, London. Opening right-hand batsman. *Sch* Weymouth and Merchiston. *Team* Glamorgan (1921–23, 47 matches). *Tours* MCC to West Indies 1910/11 and 1912/13.
Career batting
70–124–8–2302–154–19.84–2–*ct* 23
Bowling 12–0
His first-class debut was for West in 1910 and he appeared regularly for Glamorgan prior to the First World War. He captained the County in 1922 and 1923.

Whittle, Albert Edward Mark
Professional. *b:* 16.9.1877, Bristol. *d:* 18.3.1917, Charminster, Dorset. Middle order right-hand batsman, right-arm medium pace bowler. *Teams* Warwickshire (1900–06, 60 matches); Somerset (1907–11, 29 matches).
Career batting
89–134–18–2552–104–22.00–1–*ct* 38
Bowling 2421–64–37.82–2–0–5/28

Whittle, Charles James Richardson
Amateur. *b:* 26.9.1921, Birkenhead, Cheshire. Middle order right-hand batsman. *Sch* Sedbergh. *Team* Oxford U (1947).
Career batting
2–4–0–23–10–5.75–0–*ct* 1

Whitty, John Henry Hamlyn
Amateur. *b:* 4.2.1910. *d:* 23.10.1944. He died on active service. Attacking lower order right-hand batsman, right-arm bowler. *Sch* Clifton. *Team* Army (1936).
Career batting
1–2–0–23–22–11.50–0–*ct* 0
Bowling 46–4–11.50–0–0–2/19

Whitty, William James
Amateur. *b:* 15.8.1886, Sydney, New South Wales, Australia. *d:* 30.1.1974, Tantanoola, South Australia. Lower order right-hand batsman, left-arm fast medium bowler. *Teams* New South Wales (1907–08, 1 match); South Australia (1908/09 to 1925/6, 43 matches). *Tours* Australia to England 1909, 1912, to North America 1912, to New Zealand 1909/10. *Tests* Australia (1909–12, 14 matches).
Career batting
119–171–44–1465–81–11.53–0–*ct* 35
Bowling 11489–491–23.39–26–4–8/27
Test batting
14–19–7–161–39*–13.41–0–*ct* 4
Bowling 1373–65–21.12–3–0–6/17
On his 1909 tour to England he had moderate success, but in 1912 was the leading Australian bowler with 109 wickets, av 18.08, in first-class games and 25 wickets, av 19.80, in the Tests.

Whitwell, Joseph Fry
Amateur. *b:* 22.2.1869, Saltburn-by-the-Sea, Yorkshire. *d:* 6.11.1932, Langbaurgh, Great Ayton, Yorkshire. Brother of W. F. (Yorkshire). Middle order right-hand batsman, right-arm medium pace bowler. *Sch* Uppingham. *Team* Yorkshire (1890, 1 match).
Career batting
1–2–0–8–4–4.00–0–*ct* 0
Bowling 11–1–11.00–0–0–1/11
He played for Durham, being captain from 1899 to 1902.

Whitwell, William Fry
Amateur. *b:* 12.12.1867, Saltburn-by-the-Sea,

Yorkshire. *d:* 12.4.1942, Newcastle-on-Tyne. Brother of J. F. (Yorkshire). Lower order right-hand batsman, right-arm fast bowler. *Sch* Uppingham. *Team* Yorkshire (1890, 10 matches). *Tour* Hawke to North America 1894.
Career batting
13–19–3–93–26–5.81–0–*ct* 8
Bowling 682–38–17.94–2–0–5/25
He captained Durham 1893 to 1896. His final first-class match was for Gentlemen in 1900.

Whyatt, Christopher
Cricketer. *b:* 12.6.1954, Old Whittington, Chesterfield, Derbyshire. Lower order right-hand batsman, wicket-keeper. *Team* Derbyshire (1976, 1 match).
Career batting
1–1–0–6–6–6.00–0–*ct* 2

Whysall, William Wilfrid
Professional. *b:* 31.10.1887, Woodborough, Notts. *d:* 11.11.1930, Nottingham. He died of blood poisoning after a fall on a dance floor. Sound opening right-hand batsman, right-arm medium pace bowler, wicket-keeper. *Team* Nottinghamshire (1910–30, 346 matches). *Tours* MCC to Australia 1924/5; Cahn to Jamaica 1928/9. *Tests* England (1924/5 to 1930, 4 matches).
Career batting
371–601–44–21592–248–38.76–51–*ct* 316–*st* 16
Bowling 200–6–33.33–0–0–3/49
Test batting
4–7–0–209–76–29.85–0–*ct* 7
Bowling 9–0
He hit 1,000 runs in a season ten times, going on to 2,000 five times (best 2,716, av 51.24, in 1929). He hit three double centuries, all for Notts, the highest being 248 v Northants at Trent Bridge in 1930.

Wickham, Preb Archdale Palmer
Amateur. *b:* 9.11.1855, South Holmwood, Surrey. *d:* 13.10.1935, East Brent, Highbridge, Somerset. Lower order right-hand batsman, wicket-keeper. *Sch* Marlborough. *Teams* Oxford U (1876–78, blue 1878); Somerset (1891–1907, 82 matches).
Career batting
92–152–66–760–28–8.83–0–*ct* 91–*st* 59
Bowling 3–0
He appeared for Norfolk before representing Somerset.

Wicks, Frank Cowlin
Amateur. *b:* 1891, Bristol. *d:* 26.4.1965, Ham Green, Somerset. Lower order batsman, wicket-keeper. *Team* Gloucestershire (1912, 1 match).
Career batting
1–2–0–2–2–1.00–0–*ct* 2

Wickstead, Archibald
Professional. *b:* 6.11.1884, Meltham Mills, Yorkshire. *d:* 1.2.1966, Rainworth, Notts. Steady middle order left-hand batsman. *Team* Derbyshire (1911–12, 14 matches).
Career batting
14–26–3–385–68–16.73–0–*ct* 3
Bowling 2–0

Widdowson, Albert
Professional. *b:* 31.3.1864, Bingham, Notts. *d:* 28.4.1938, Duffield, Derbyshire. Lower order batsman. *Team* Derbyshire (1894, 1 match).
Career batting
1–1–0–1–1–1.00–0–*ct* 0
He was the groundsman on the County Ground at Derby and was pressed into service in emergency in one match. He also played for Staffordshire.

Widdowson, Sam Weller
Amateur. *b:* 16.4.1851, Hucknall Torkard, Notts. *d:* 9.5.1927, Beeston, Notts. Middle order right-hand batsman, right-hand fast round-arm bowler. *Team* Nottinghamshire (1878, 1 match).
Career batting
1–2–0–15–11–7.50–0–*ct* 0
An excellent soccer player, he appeared as centre-forward for Nottm Forest and England; he was also well-known on the athletic field as a hurdler and sprinter.

Wigan, Denis Grey
Amateur. *b:* 21.6.1893, Walton-on-Thames, Surrey. *d:* 31.12.1958, Pettistree, Suffolk. Stylish middle order right-hand batsman, slow right-arm bowler. *Sch* Eton. *Team* Oxford U (1913–14).
Career batting
6–10–2–119–73*–14.87–0–*ct* 4
Bowling 45–4–11.25–0–0–3/14

Wigginton, Searson Harry
Professional. *b:* 26.3.1909, Leicester. *d:* 15.9.1977, Bulawayo, Rhodesia. Opening or middle order right-hand batsman, right-arm medium pace bowler. *Sch* Wyggeston. *Team* Leicestershire (1930–34, 49 matches).
Career batting
49–85–4–1426–120*–17.60–1–*ct* 20
Bowling 90–3–30.00–0–0–2/14
He emigrated to Rhodesia in 1947, having been appointed coach to the Rhodesian Cricket Association.

Wigglesworth, Cecil George
Amateur. *b:* 17.10.1893, Tadcaster, Yorkshire. *d:* 8.8.1961, Lymington, Hampshire. Middle order right-hand batsman. *Team* RAF (1927).
Career batting
1–1–0–19–19–19.00–0–*ct* 0
Bowling 9–0

Wiggs, Robert James
Cricketer. *b:* 6.9.1950, Essex. Lower order right-hand batsman, slow left-arm bowler. *Team* Cambridge U (1970).
Career batting
1–2–1–6–6–6.00–0–*ct* 0
Bowling 44–1–44.00–0–0–1/44

Wight, Claude Vibart
Amateur. *b:* 28.7.1902, Georgetown, British Guiana. *d:* 1969, Guyana. Brother of O. S. (British Guiana). Middle order right-hand batsman. *Team* British Guiana (1925/6 to 1938/9). *Tour* West Indies to England 1928. *Tests* West Indies (1928 to 1929/30, 2 matches).
Career batting
40–61–11–1547–130–30.94–3–*ct* 20
Bowling 209–3–69.66–0–0–1/18
Test batting
2–4–1–67–23–22.33–0–*ct* 0
Bowling 6–0

He only had a moderately successful visit to England in 1928 and played in one Test.

Wight, Peter Bernard
Professional. *b:* 25.6.1930, Georgetown, British Guiana. Brother of G. L. (West Indies), H. A. and N. (British Guiana). Middle order right-hand batsman, off break bowler. *Teams* British Guiana (1950/1); Somerset (1953–65, 321 matches); Canterbury (1963/4). *Tour* Brown to East Africa 1961/2 (not first-class).
Career batting
333–590–53–17773–222*–33.09–28–*ct* 204
Bowling 2262–68–33.26–1–0–6/29

He hit 1,000 runs in a season ten times going on to 2,000 twice (best 2,375 runs, av 41.66, in 1960). Both his double centuries were for Somerset, the highest being 222* v Kent at Taunton in 1959. He was appointed to the first-class umpires' list in 1966.

Wignall, Eric W. E.
Professional. *b:* 25.12.1932, Edgware, Middlesex. Lower order right-hand batsman, leg break bowler. *Team* Gloucestershire (1952–53, 3 matches).
Career batting
3–4–1–24–14–8.00–0–*ct* 2
Bowling 63–2–31.50–0–0–2/50

Wignall, William Harold
Professional. *b:* 24.12.1908, Hendon, Middlesex. *d:* April 1982, Brent, Middlesex. Lower order right-hand batsman, right-arm bowler. *Team* Middlesex (1934–36, 4 matches).
Career batting
6–11–4–152–72–21.71–0–*ct* 5
Bowling 153–3–51.00–0–0–1/9

His first-class debut was for MCC in 1932 and his final first-class match for MCC in 1938. He also played for Berkshire and Dorset.

Wigram, Sir Clive
(later 1st Baron Wigram)
Amateur. *b:* 5.7.1873, Madras, India. *d:* 3.9.1960, Westminster, London. Brother of Kenneth (Europeans). Lower order right-hand batsman, right-hand medium pace bowler. *Sch* Winchester. *Teams* MCC (1897); Europeans (1906/7).
Career batting
3–5–1–47–22*–11.75–0–*ct* 3
Bowling 165–4–41.25–0–0–1/3

He was stationed in India for some years, being ADC to the Viceroy. In 1910 he was appointed Assistant Private Secretary to the King.

Wigram, Ernest Money
Amateur. *b:* 20.11.1862, Kensington, London. *d:* 10.6.1906, Eastry, Kent. Lower order batsman, useful bowler. *Sch* Winchester. *Team* Orleans Club (1883).
Career batting
1–2–1–9–6–9.00–0–*ct* 1
Bowling 40–0

Wijesuriya, Roger Gerald Christopher Ediriweera
Cricketer. *b:* 18.2.1960, Moratuwa, Ceylon. Lower order right-hand batsman, slow left-arm bowler. *Team* Sri Lanka (1978/9 to 1982/3). *Tours* Sri Lanka to England 1979, 1981, to Pakistan 1981/2, to Australia 1982/3. *Test* Sri Lanka (1981/2, 1 match).
Career batting
14–12–4–69–25–8.62–0–*ct* 11
Bowling 1157–31–37.32–1–0–5/35
Test batting
1–2–0–3–3–1.50–0–*ct* 0
Bowling 105–0

Wilcock, Howard Gordon
Cricketer. *b:* 26.2.1950, New Malden, Surrey. Lower order right-hand batsman, wicket-keeper. *Team* Worcestershire (1971–78, 99 matches).
Career batting
99–137–31–1697–74–16.00–0–*ct* 177–*st* 17
Bowling 3–0

Wilcox, Alfred George Sidney
Amateur. *b:* 10.7.1920, Cheltenham, Gloucs. Enterprising middle order left-hand batsman. *Team* Gloucestershire (1939–49, 39 matches).
Career batting
39–58–5–835–73–15.75–0–*ct* 21

Wilcox, Denys Robert
Amateur. *b:* 4.6.1910, Westcliff-on-Sea, Essex. *d:* 6.2.1953, Westcliff-on-Sea, Essex. Father of J. W. T. (Essex). Stylish middle order right-hand batsman, off break bowler. *Sch* Dulwich. *Teams* Essex (1928–47, 118 matches); Cambridge U (1931–33, blue all three years). *Tours* Martineau to Egypt 1934, 1935, 1936, 1937 and 1938 (not first-class).
Career batting
179–296–11–8399–157–29.47–15–*ct* 130
Bowling 136–3–45.33–0–0–1/0

He hit 1,000 runs in a season four times (best 1,390, av 44.83, in 1937). Owing to his scholastic duties he was unable to play regularly in County cricket, but was joint captain of Essex from 1933 to 1939. His final first-class match was for Free Foresters in 1951.

Wilcox, John Warren Theodore
Amateur. *b:* 16.8.1940, Newton Abbot, Devon. Son of D. R. (Essex). Middle order right-hand batsman, off break bowler, good outfield. *Sch* Malvern. *Teams* Cambridge U (1961–62); Essex (1964–67, 19 matches).
Career batting
31–54–7–903–87–19.21–0–*ct* 15

Wilcox, Sidney Charles
Professional. *b:* 28.2.1893, Bridgend, Glamorgan. *d:* 1973, Glamorgan. Lower order right-hand batsman, wicket-keeper. *Team* Wales (1930).
Career batting
1–2–1–7–6–7.00–0–*ct* 3–*st* 1

His County cricket was for Monmouthshire.

Wild, Duncan James
Cricketer. *b:* 28.11.1962, Northampton. Son of John (Northants). Lower order left-hand batsman, right-arm medium pace bowler. *Team* Northants (1980–83, 19 matches).
Career batting
19–28–5–403–48–17.52–0–*ct* 4
Bowling 616–9–68.44–0–0–2/15

Wild, F. (*See under* Wyld, F.)

Wild, Harold
Professional. *b:* 3.2.1891, Hadfield, Derbyshire. *d:* 8.8.1977, Glossop, Derbyshire. Middle order right-hand batsman, right-arm medium pace bowler. *Team* Derbyshire (1913–20, 32 matches).
Career batting
32–59–7–628–12.07–0–*ct* 29
Bowling 129–2–64.50–0–0–1/3

Wild, John
Professional. *b:* 24.2.1935, Northampton. Father of D. J. (Northants). Middle order right-hand batsman, off break bowler. *Team* Northants (1953–61, 39 matches).
Career batting
41–51–4–664–95–14.12–0–*ct* 26
Bowling 2588–57–45.40–0–0–4/44

Wild, John Vernon
Amateur. *b:* 26.4.1915, Wallasey, Cheshire. Middle order right-hand batsman, right-arm slow bowler. *Sch* Taunton. *Team* Cambridge U (1938, blue).
Career batting
11–17–0–193–34–11.35–0–*ct* 5
Bowling 1047–29–36.10–2–0–6/125

Wild, T.
Professional. Opening batsman. *Team* Hampshire (1880, 2 matches).
Career batting
2–3–0–40–25–13.33–0–*ct* 0

Wild, William
Professional. *b:* 21.2.1846, Thorncombe, Dorset. Lower order right-hand batsman, right-hand fast round-arm bowler. *Team* Hampshire (1877, 1 match).
Career batting
1–2–1–10–8–10.00–0–*ct* 0
Bowling 11–0

Wilde, David
Cricketer. *b:* 3.7.1950, Glossop, Derbyshire. Tail end left-hand batsman, left-arm fast medium bowler. *Team* Derbyshire (1971–72, 13 matches).
Career batting
13–15–5–31–12–3.10–0–*ct* 1
Bowling 860–23–37.39–0–0–3/27

Wilde, Thomas Montague Morrison
(succeeded as 3rd Baron Truro in 1891)
Amateur. *b:* 11.3.1856, Chorlton-cum-Hardy, Lancashire. *d:* 8.3.1899, Mentone, France. Middle order right-hand batsman, right-arm medium pace bowler. *Sch* Harrow. *Team* MCC (1881–83).
Career batting
4–7–2–117–37–23.40–0–*ct* 2
Bowling 23–0

Wilde, Walter Stanley
Professional. *b:* 1908, Long Ashton, Somerset. *d:* 1968, Weston-super-Mare, Somerset. Tail end batsman, wicket-keeper. *Team* Somerset (1929, 7 matches).
Career batting
7–13–5–45–21–5.62–0–*ct* 9–*st* 1

Wilder, George
Amateur. *b:* 9.6.1876, Emsworth, Hampshire. *d:* 10.6.1948, Las Vegas, USA. Middle order batsman, useful bowler. *Sch* Eton. *Teams* Sussex (1905–06, 6 matches); Hampshire (1909, 1 match).
Career batting
8–16–1–203–43–13.53–0–*ct* 2
Bowling 51–4–12.75–0–0–3/14

Wilenkin, Boris Charles Gregory
Amateur. *b:* 20.6.1933, London. Middle order right-hand batsman. *Sch* Harrow and Loretto. *Teams* Free Foresters (1955–59); Cambridge U (1956, blue).
Career batting
16–28–1–661–105–24.48–1–*ct* 4
Bowling 4–0

Wiles, Charles Archibald
Amateur. *b:* 11.8.1892, Bridgetown, Barbados. *d:* 4.11.1957, Diego Martin, Trinidad. Stylish middle order right-hand batsman. *Team* Trinidad (1919/20 to 1935/6). *Test* West Indies (1933, 1 match).
Career batting
38–69–5–1766–192–27.59–2–*ct* 7
Test batting
1–2–0–2–2–1.00–0–*ct* 0

Although playing in one Test, he achieved little on the 1933 tour.

Wiley, John Walter Eddington
Amateur. *b:* 7.2.1927, South Africa. Brother of W. G. A. (Oxford U). Middle order right-hand batsman. *Teams* Western Province (1947/8); Oxford U (1949–51).
Career batting
12–23–1–410–70–18.63–0–*ct* 8

His final first-class match in South Africa was for South African Universities in 1948/9.

Wiley, William Gordon Anthony
Amateur. *b:* 7.11.1931, Cape Town, South Africa. Brother of J. W. E. (Oxford U). Opening right-hand batsman, leg break and googly bowler. *Teams* Oxford U (1952, blue); Western Province (1952/3 to 1953/4).
Career batting
16–29–0–666–100–22.96–1–*ct* 14
Bowling 5–0

Wilkes, Alexander John
Amateur. *b:* 1900, Kidderminster, Worcs. *d:* 12.7.1937, Kidderminster, Worcs. Middle order right-hand batsman. *Team* Worcestershire (1925–27, 11 matches).
Career batting
11–22–2–113–25–5.65–0–*ct* 12

Wilkes, William Harry Walters
Amateur. *b:* 1866, Aston, Birmingham. *d:* 18.2.1940, Birmingham. Middle order right-hand batsman. *Team* Worcestershire (1899–1902, 14 matches).
Career batting
14–25–1–419–109–17.45–1–*ct* 5

Wilkin, Charles Lucien Arthur
Cricketer. *b:* 1.1.1949, St Kitts, West Indies. Lower order right-hand batsman, slow left-arm bowler. *Teams* Cambridge U (1969–70, blue 1970); Leeward Islands (1973/4 to 1976/7).
Career batting
19–30–10–302–26–15.10–0–*ct* 4
Bowling 1440–30–48.00–0–0–3/74

Wilkins, Alan Haydn
Cricketer. *b:* 22.8.1953, Cardiff. Lower order right-hand batsman, left-arm medium pace bowler. *Teams* Glamorgan (1976–83, 65 matches); Gloucestershire (1980–81, 40 matches); Northern Transvaal (1981/2). *Tour* Overseas XI to India 1980/1.
Career batting
107–124–29–902–70–9.49–0–*ct* 34
Bowling 7511–243–30.90–9–0–8/57

Wilkins, Christopher Peter
Cricketer. *b:* 31.7.1944, Kingwilliamstown, South Africa. Middle order right-hand batsman, right-arm medium pace bowler, occasional wicket-keeper. *Teams* Border (1962/3 to 1970/1); Derbyshire (1970–72, 71 matches); Eastern Province (1972/3 to 1977/8); Natal (1978/9 to 1982/3).
Career batting
198–357–21–10966–156–32.63–18–*ct* 211–*st* 6
Bowling 5013–142–35.30–0–0–4/19

He hit over 1,000 runs in each of his three seasons with Derbyshire (best 1,638, av 39.95, in 1970).

Wilkins, Donald Albert
Amateur. *b:* 13.10.1903, Bristol. *d:* 22.1.1972, Saltford, Somerset. Middle order right-hand batsman. *Team* Somerset (1927, 2 matches).
Career batting
2–3–0–6–3–2.00–0–*ct* 1

Wilkinson, Arthur
Professional. *b:* 28.12.1872, Nottingham. Dashing lower order right-hand batsman, right-arm medium pace bowler. *Team* Nottinghamshire (1894–95, 19 matches).
Career batting
19–35–5–293–62–9.76–0–*ct* 9
Bowling 926–33–28.06–1–0–5/56

Wilkinson, Anthony John Anstruther
Amateur. *b:* 28.5.1835, Mount Oswald, Co Durham. *d:* 11.12.1905, Anerley, Kent. Father of C. T. A. (Surrey). Steady opening or middle order right-hand batsman, right-hand slow round-arm bowler, good third man. *Sch* Shrewsbury. *Teams* Middlesex (1864–74, 19 matches); Yorkshire (1865–68, 5 matches).
Career batting
61–103–4–1351–84*–13.64–0–*ct* 43
Bowling 1199–53–22.62–2–0–6/52
His first-class debut was for Gentlemen of the South in 1862. He did not play in any important matches whilst at Cambridge U. In 1874 he took the chair at the meeting during which the Durham County Cricket Club was formed. He also played for Durham and Lincolnshire.

Wilkinson, Burton
Amateur. *b:* 25.4.1900, Nebraska, USA. Tail end left-hand batsman, slow left-arm bowler. *Team* Northants (1932, 1 match).
Career batting
1–1–0–0–0–0.00–0–*ct* 1
Bowling 22–1–22.00–0–0–1/22

Wilkinson, Cyril Theodore Anstruther
Amateur. *b:* 4.10.1884, Durham. *d:* 16.12.1970, Honiton, Devon. Son of A. J. A. (Middlesex and Yorkshire). Middle order right-hand batsman, right-arm fast medium bowler. *Sch* Blundell's. *Team* Surrey (1909–20, 53 matches).
Career batting
54–78–8–1773–135–25.32–3–*ct* 25
Bowling 724–23–31.47–1–0–6/43
He captained Surrey in 1914 and in 1919–20. A great club cricketer, he took all ten wickets for Sidmouth in 1953, when he was 69. A brilliant hockey player, he captained England and appeared for Great Britain in the 1920 Olympics, where he won a gold medal. He was Registrar of the Probate and Divorce Registry from 1936 to 1959.

Wilkinson, Donald John
Cricketer. *b:* 14.2.1955, Irvine, Ayrshire, Scotland. Lower order left-hand batsman, leg break bowler. *Team* Oxford U (1975–76).
Career batting
4–8–2–11–4–1.83–0–*ct* 3
Bowling 350–7–50.00–0–0–4/89

Wilkinson, Edward Obert Hindley
Amateur. *b:* 16.10.1853, Chesfield, Stevenage, Hertfordshire. *d:* 8.2.1881, Scheins Hoogte, South Africa. He drowned crossing a flooded stream after the Battle of Ingogo. Middle order right-hand batsman, wicket-keeper. *Sch* Eton. *Team* Cambridge U (1873).
Career batting
5–8–1–39–22*–5.57–0–*ct* 2–*st* 2
His final match was for MCC in 1875. His County cricket was for Hertfordshire. He was very successful in military matches for his Regiment.

Wilkinson, Frank
Professional. *b:* 23.5.1914, Hull, Yorkshire. Lower order right-hand batsman, right-arm medium fast bowler. *Team* Yorkshire (1937–39, 14 matches).
Career batting
14–14–1–73–18*–5.61–0–*ct* 12
Bowling 590–26–22.74–1–1–7/68

Wilkinson, Francis William
Amateur. *b:* 4.10.1895, Norton-on-Tees, Co Durham. Lower order right-hand batsman, leg break bowler. *Team* Minor Counties (1939).
Career batting
1 match, did not bat–*ct* 0
Bowling 24–1–24.00–0–0–1/24
In his only first-class match – v Oxford U – he was forced to retire injured after bowling 8 overs and took no further part in the match, a substitute batting for him. His County cricket was for Cambridgeshire.

Wilkinson, Henry
Amateur. *b:* 11.12.1877, Huddersfield, Yorkshire. *d:* 15.4.1967, Cape Province, South Africa. Stylish middle order right-hand batsman. *Team* Yorkshire (1903–05, 48 matches).
Career batting
51–80–3–1367–113–17.75–1–*ct* 21
Bowling 121–3–40.33–0–0–2/28
His final first-class match was for C. B. Fry's XI in 1912.

Wilkinson, John
Amateur. *b:* 16.7.1876. *d:* 15.5.1948, Kensington, London. Tail end right-hand batsman, right-arm fast bowler. *Team* Gloucestershire (1899–1920, 10 matches).

Career batting
10–16–7–64–17*–7.11–0–*ct* 9
Bowling 587–17–34.52–0–0–4/39

Wilkinson, John William
Amateur. *b:* 1892, Dudley, Worcestershire. *d:* 3.8.1967, Edgbaston, Birmingham. Lower order batsman, useful bowler. *Team* Worcestershire 1927, 1 match).
Career batting
1–2–2–4–4*–no av–0–*ct* 0
Bowling 45–1–45.00–0–0–1/45
He also played for Devon.

Wilkinson, Kenneth
Amateur. *b:* 11.1.1908, Newbold, Derbyshire. *d:* 15.12.1943, near Naples, Italy. Lower order batsman, right-hand fast medium bowler. *Sch* Uppingham. *Team* Cambridge U (1927).
Career batting
1 match, did not bat –*ct* 0
Bowling 99–0

Wilkinson, Keith William
Cricketer. *b:* 15.1.1950, Fenton, Stoke-on-Trent, Staffs. Middle order left-hand batsman, left-arm medium pace bowler. *Team* Worcestershire (1969–75, 49 matches).
Career batting
49–77–11–1657–141–25.10–2–*ct* 29
Bowling 1651–48–34.39–1–0–5/60

Wilkinson, Leonard Litton
Professional. *b:* 5.11.1916, Northwich, Cheshire. Lower order right-hand batsman, slow leg break bowler, good close field. *Team* Lancashire (1937–47, 63 matches). *Tour* MCC to South Africa 1938/9. *Tests* England (1938/9, 3 matches).
Career batting
77–69–27–321–48–7.64–0–*ct* 53
Bowling 7121–282–25.25–17–3–8/53
Test batting
3–2–1–3–2–3.00–0–*ct* 0
Bowling 271–7–38.71–0–0–2/12
He created a great impression during his first full season of County cricket, taking 151 wickets, av 23.38; selected for the winter tour to South Africa in 1938/9, he topped the averages with 44 wickets, av 18.86. In 1939 however he fell away, and after the Second World War very little of him was seen in first-class cricket.

Wilkinson, Philip Alan
Cricketer. *b:* 23.8.1951, Hucknall, Notts. Lower order right-hand batsman, right-arm medium pace bowler. *Team* Nottinghamshire (1971–77, 92 matches).
Career batting
92–117–38–949–77–12.01–0–*ct* 28
Bowling 6335–175–36.20–2–0–6/81

Wilkinson, Robert William
Professional. *b:* 23.12.1939, Rotherhithe, London. Middle order right-hand batsman, right-arm medium pace bowler. *Team* Kent (1959–63, 23 matches).
Career batting
23–39–7–635–63–19.84–0–*ct* 11
Bowling 626–10–62.60–0–0–2/31

Wilkinson, Stephen George
Cricketer. *b:* 12.1.1949, Hounslow, Middlesex. Middle order right-hand batsman, slow left-arm bowler. *Team* Somerset (1972–74, 18 matches).
Career batting
18–27–5–452–69–20.54–0–*ct* 11
Bowling 9–0

Wilkinson, William
Professional. *b:* 5.7.1859, Kimberley, Notts. *d:* 6.10.1940, Nottingham. Lower order batsman, right-arm fast medium bowler. *Team* Nottinghamshire (1892–93, 5 matches).
Career batting
5–7–2–34–16*–6.80–0–*ct* 4
Bowling 133–5–26.60–0–0–3/41

Wilkinson, William Alexander Camac
Amateur. *b:* 6.12.1892, Sydney, Australia. *d:* 19.9.1983, Storrington, Sussex. Son of W. O'B. C. (Middlesex). Opening or middle order right-hand batsman, slow right-arm bowler. *Sch* Eton. *Team* Oxford U (1913–14, blue 1913). *Tour* MCC to Australia and New Zealand 1922/3.
Career batting
89–162–10–4785–129–31.48–8–*ct* 49
Bowling 385–12–32.08–0–0–4/32
His first-class debut was for H. K. Foster's XI in 1912 and his final match for MCC in 1939. He was a noted batsman in military matches between the wars.

Wilkinson, William Herbert
Professional. *b:* 12.3.1881, Thorpe Hesley, Yorkshire. *d:* 4.6.1961, Birmingham. Sound middle order left-hand batsman, left-arm bowler, moderate field. *Team* Yorkshire (1903-10, 126 matches).
Career batting
127–194–14–3912–103–21.62–1–*ct* 93
Bowling 971–31–31.32–0–0–4/23
He hit 1,382 runs, av 29.40, in 1908. He was also a noted soccer player for Sheffield United.

Wilkinson, Dr William O'Brien Camac
Amateur. *b:* 15.9.1857, Sydney, New South Wales, Australia. *d:* 2.2.1946, Virginia Water, Surrey. Father of W. A. C. (Oxford U). Middle order right-hand batsman, right-arm medium pace bowler. *Team* Middlesex (1881–82, 5 matches).
Career batting
8–14–2–189–52–15.75–0–*ct* 2
Bowling 156–8–19.50–0–0–4/49
His final first-class match was for A. J. Webbe's XI in 1899.

Willard, Michael James Lewis
Amateur. *b:* 24.3.1938, Hawkhurst, Kent. Middle order left-hand batsman, right-arm medium pace bowler. *Team* Cambridge U (1959–61, blue all three years).
Career batting
41–75–1–1866–101*–25.21–1–*ct* 33
Bowling 2326–73–32.30–3–1–7/62

Willatt, Guy Longfield
Amateur. *b:* 7.5.1918, Nottingham. Sound opening left-hand batsman, right-arm bowler. *Sch* Repton. *Teams* Cambridge U (1938–47, blue 1946, 1947); Nottinghamshire (1939–48, 22 matches); Derbyshire (1950–56, 125 matches); Scotland (1948–50).
Career batting
185–303–17–8325–146–29.11–13–*ct* 51
Bowling 135–3–45.00–0–0–2/18
He hit 1,000 runs in a season four times (best 1,624, av 35.30, in 1952). From 1951 to 1954 he captained Derbyshire, but after 1954 he was unable to play regular first-class cricket owing to his profession. His final first-class match was for MCC in 1961. He also played for Cumberland. A good soccer player, he obtained his blue at Cambridge.

Willes, Canon Edmund Henry Lacon
Amateur. *b:* 7.7.1832, Hythe, Southampton. *d:* 9.9.1896, Monk Sherborne, Dorset. Cousin of G. E. (Cambridge U). Middle order right-hand batsman, right-hand fast round-arm bowler, deep field. *Sch* Winchester. *Teams* Hampshire (1850–65, 2 matches); Oxford U (1852–54, blue all three years); Kent (1852–53, 2 matches).
Career batting
22–34–4–416–69–13.86–0–*ct* 12
Bowling 22–3+17–7.33–0–0–4/?
He also played for Oxfordshire, Northants and Warwickshire (pre-first-class).

Willes, Rev George Edward
Amateur. *b:* 16.8.1844, Hamstall Ridware, Rugeley, Staffordshire. *d:* 8.9.1901, Burnham, Bucks. Cousin of E. H. L. (Hampshire and Kent). Middle order right-hand batsman, long stop. *Sch* Rugby. *Team* Cambridge U (1865–66).
Career batting
5–9–1–114–51–14.25–0–*ct* 0
His County cricket was for Warwickshire (pre-first-class) and Buckinghamshire.

Willes, John
Amateur. *b:* 1778, Headcorn, Kent. *d:* 5.8.1852. Staunton, nr Gloucester. Brother of William (Kent 1807). Middle order batsman, fast round-arm bowler. *Team* Kent (1806–22).
Career batting
5–7–0–9–5–1.28–0–*ct* 2
Bowling 6 wickets, no analyses
He tried to introduce round-arm bowling during the early years of the 19th century, but in 1822 when playing for Kent v MCC he was no-balled for throwing and was so annoyed by the umpire's ruling that he left the match, vowing that he would never play again.

Willett, Elquemedo Tonito
Cricketer. *b:* 1.5.1953, Nevis, Leeward Island. Lower order left-hand batsman, slow left-arm bowler. *Team* Leeward Islands (1970/1 to 1982/3). *Tours* West Indies to England 1973, to India, Sri Lanka and Pakistan 1974/5. *Tests* West Indies (1972/3 to 1974/5, 5 matches).
Career batting
80–107–34–914–56–12.52–0–*ct* 53
Bowling 6805–242–28.11–10–3–8/73
Test batting
5–8–3–74–26–14.80–0–*ct* 0
Bowling 482–11–43.81–0–0–3/33
He took 30 wickets, av 23.13, on his tour to England, but did not play in any Tests.

Willett, Dr Frederic Stovin Dealtry
Amateur. *b:* 10.11.1853, Marylebone, London. *d:* 23.4.1884, Ventnor, Isle of Wight. Middle order right-hand batsman, right-hand fast round-arm bowler, cover point field. *Sch* Rugby. *Team* MCC (1882).
Career batting
1–2–0–9–5–4.50–0–*ct* 0
He did not play in any first-class matches whilst at Cambridge.

Willett, Michael David
Professional. *b:* 21.4.1933, Norwood, London. Right-hand batsman, right-arm medium pace bowler. *Team* Surrey (1955–67, 172 matches).
Career batting
172–273–45–6535–126–28.66–8–*ct* 95
Bowling 1105–23–48.04–0–0–3/36

He hit 1,000 runs in a season three times (best 1,789, av 45.87, in 1964). A good soccer player, he was inside-right for Corinthian-Casuals.

Willetts, Frank Terence
Cricketer. *b:* 20.11.1939, Birmingham. Middle order left-hand batsman. *Team* Somerset (1964–67, 16 matches).
Career batting
16–30–0–333–38–11.10–0–*ct* 4
He also played for Shropshire and Cornwall.

Willey, Peter
Cricketer. *b:* 6.12.1949, Sedgefield, Co Durham. Middle order right-hand batsman, off break bowler. *Teams* Northants (1966–83, 319 matches); Eastern Province (1982/3). *Tours* Robins to South Africa 1972/3, to Sri Lanka 1977/8; England to Australia and India 1979/80, to West Indies 1980/1; SAB to South Africa 1981/2. *Tests* England (1976–81, 20 matches).
Career batting
365–601–91–15134–227–29.67–24–*ct* 141
Bowling 15639–530–29.50–20–3–7/37
Test batting
20–38–5–923–102*–27.96–2–*ct* 3
Bowling 441–6–73.50–0–0–2/73
He hit 1,000 runs in a season four times (best 1,783, av 50.94, in 1982). He was banned from Test cricket for three years following his 1981/2 tour to South Africa. His highest score was 227 for Northants v Somerset at Northampton in 1976.

Williams, Ambrose C.
Professional. *b:* 1.3.1887. *d:* 1966, Lancaster. Tail end right-hand batsman, right-arm fast bowler. *Team* Yorkshire (1911–19, 12 matches).
Career batting
12–14–10–95–48*–23.75–0–*ct* 6
Bowling 678–30–22.60–2–1–9/29
He took 9 wickets for 29 in the first innings for Yorkshire v Hampshire at Dewsbury in 1919, but after two further matches was dropped from the County side!

Williams, Alfred Edward Augustus
Professional. *b:* 20.11.1844, Ashford, Kent. *d:* 7.1.1914, Lyminge, Kent. Lower order left-hand batsman, right-hand fast round-arm bowler. *Team* Kent (1865, 3 matches).
Career batting
3–5–2–28–13*–9.33–0–*ct* 1
Bowling 16–3–5.33–0–0–3/9

Williams, Cecil Beaumont
Amateur. *b:* 8.3.1926, Bridgetown, Barbardos. Lower order right-hand batsman, leg break and googly bowler. *Team* Barbados (1947/8 to 1956/7). *Tour* West Indies to England 1950.
Career batting
37–39–5–987–133–29.02–2–*ct* 27
Bowling 2183–75–29.10–4–0–7/55
He took 31 wickets, av 27.61, on the 1950 tour. After the visit he remained in England to go to Durham University.

Williams, Charles Cuthbert Powell
Amateur. *b:* 9.2.1933, Oxford. Middle order right-hand batsman. *Sch* Westminster. *Teams* Oxford U (1952–55, blue 1953–55); Essex (1954–59, 40 matches).
Career batting
87–153–8–4090–139*–38.20–6–*ct* 60
Bowling 61–1–61.00–0–0–1/33
He hit 1,000 runs in a season twice (best 1,219, av 31.25, in 1955). He also played for Oxfordshire.

Williams, Charles Derek
Amateur. *b:* 24.11.1924, Cardiff. Middle order right-hand batsman, right-arm medium pace bowler. *Team* Oxford U (1946).
Career batting
1–2–0–3–3–1.50–0–*ct* 0
Bowling 9–0

Williams, Christopher Mark Bebb
Cricketer. *b:* 11.1.1955, Stamford Hill, Middlesex. Middle order right-hand batsman, right-arm medium pace bowler. *Team* Cambridge U (1976).
Career batting
1–2–0–31–29–15.50–0–*ct* 0

Williams, David
Cricketer. *b:* 25.5.1948, Barnsley, Yorkshire. Lower order right-hand batsman, slow left-arm bowler. *Team* Oxford U (1968–73).
Career batting
29–50–10–497–52–12.42–0–*ct* 15
Bowling 847–24–35.29–1–0–5/19

Williams, Dyson Bransby
(also known as Dyson Brock Williams)
Amateur. *b:* 1877, Sketty, Swansea, Glamorgan. *d:* 18.4.1922, City of London. Middle order right-hand batsman. *Sch* Malvern. *Team* Glamorgan (1921, 1 match).
Career batting
1–2–0–14–9–7.00–0–*ct* 0

Williams, David Lawrence
Cricketer. *b:* 20.11.1946, Tonna, Neath, Glamorgan. Tail end left-hand batsman, right-

arm fast medium bowler. *Team* Glamorgan (1969–76, 150 matches). *Tour* Glamorgan to West Indies 1969/70.
Career batting
151–146–73–403–37*–5.52–0–*ct* 38
Bowling 9883–364–27.15–13–1–7/60
He was also a good rugby footballer.

Williams, D. P.
Amateur. Tail end batsman, useful bowler. *Team* London County (1901).
Career batting
1 match, did not bat – *ct* 0
Bowling 46–0

Williams, Dennis Stanley
Amateur. *b:* 15.11.1936, Surrey. Middle order right-hand batsman. *Team* Combined Services (1959–64).
Career batting
8–15–1–225–82–16.07–0–*ct* 6

Williams, Ernest Albert Vivian
Amateur. *b:* 10.4.1914, Bridgetown, Barbados. Attacking middle order right-hand batsman, right-arm fast medium bowler. *Team* Barbados (1934/5 to 1948/9). *Tour* West Indies to England 1939. *Tests* West Indies (1939 to 1947/8, 4 matches).
Career batting
42–63–8–1479–131*–26.89–2–*ct* 19
Bowling 3387–116–29.19–1–0–5/73
Test batting
4–6–0–113–72–18.83–0–*ct* 2
Bowling 241–9–26.77–0–0–3/51
He hit 370 runs, av 30.83, and took 14 wickets, av 32.92, in first-class matches on the 1939 tour, playing in one Test.

Williams, Edward Lovell
Amateur. *b:* 15.9.1925, Shaftesbury, Dorset. Lower order right-hand batsman, left-arm fast medium bowler. *Sch* Charterhouse. *Team* Leicestershire (1949, 1 match).
Career batting
1–2–0–17–14–8.50–0–*ct* 0
Bowling 33–2–16.50–0–0–2/33

Williams, Edward Stephen Bruce
Amateur. *b:* 2.11.1892, Pinhoe, Devon. *d:* 20.1.1977, Bramdean, Hampshire. Forceful opening right-hand batsman. *Sch* Winchester. *Teams* Services (1922–31); Army (1922–33). *Tour* Martineau to Egypt 1931 (not first-class).
Career batting
29–51–2–2029–228–41.40–4–*ct* 13–*st* 1
Bowling 23–0
Both his double centuries were for the Army, his highest being 228 v Royal Navy at Lord's in 1928. He was for some years captain of the Army team and the leading batsman of that side. His final first-class match was for Free Foresters in 1935. His County cricket was for Devon.

Williams, G. E.
Amateur. Middle order batsman. *Team* Hampshire (1904, 1 match).
Career batting
1–2–0–16–15–8.00–0–*ct* 0

Williams, Gwyfr Lloyd
Amateur. *b:* 30.5.1925, Kidwelly, Carmarthenshire. Middle order right-hand batsman, good close field. *Sch* Christ College, Brecon. *Team* Somerset (1955, 3 matches).
Career batting
3–6–0–30–24–5.00–0–*ct* 4

Williams, H.
Professional. Lower order batsman, slow left-arm bowler. *Team* Worcestershire (1927, 4 matches).
Career batting
4–6–3–7–4–2.33–0–*ct* 0
Bowling 185–2–92.50–0–0–1/13

Williams, Harold
Amateur. *b:* 30.10.1903. Lower order batsman, useful bowler. *Sch* Berkhamsted. *Teams* Northants (1923–24, 6 matches); Europeans in Ceylon (1930/1).
Career batting
7–13–1–104–27–8.66–0–*ct* 2
Bowling 125–5–25.00–0–0–2/29

Williams, Herbert Reginald (Hewett)
Amateur. *b:* 7.6.1900, Hendon, Middlesex. *d:* 17.7.1974, Denmark Hill, London. Lower order right-hand batsman, wicket-keeper. *Sch* Charterhouse. *Team* Essex (1919–20, 10 matches).
Career batting
10–12–2–67–23*–6.70–0–*ct* 18–*st* 7

Williams, Herbert Scott
(later known as Scott-Williams)
Amateur. *b:* 4.9.1860, Woolland, Dorset. *d:* 30.11.1942, Dorchester. Lower order batsman, wicket-keeper. *Sch* Harrow. *Team* Middlesex (1890, 1 match).
Career batting
1–2–0–1–1–0.50–*ct* 1–*st* 1

Williams, I.
Amateur. Middle order batsman. *Team* Glamorgan (1931, 2 matches).
Career batting
2–4–0–10–7–2.50–0–*ct* 0

Williams, Joseph
Professional. *b:* 1892. *d:* 10.7.1916, Thiepval, France. Lower order batsman, useful bowler. *Team* MCC (1914).
Career batting
1–2–1–19–11*–19.00–0–*ct* 0
Bowling 26–0

Williams, John Nathaniel
Amateur. *b:* 24.1.1878, St Austell, Cornwall. *d:* 25.4.1915, Gaba Tepe, Gallipoli Peninsula, Turkey. He was killed in action. Brother of P. F. C. (Gloucs). Hard hitting middle order right-hand batsman. *Sch* Eton. *Teams* Hawke's Bay (1903/4); Gloucestershire (1908, 3 matches). *Tour* Hawke to New Zealand 1902/3 (he appeared in emergency in non-first-class matches only).
Career batting
4–7–0–52–20–7.42–0–*ct* 2
He did not appear in any first-class matches whilst at Oxford and after leaving the University emigrated to New Zealand. He also played for Dorset.

Williams, John Stewart
Amateur. *b:* 4.1.1911, South Croydon, Surrey. *d:* 12.12.1964, Haywards Heath, Sussex. Lower order left-hand batsman, right-arm slow bowler. *Sch* Repton. *Team* Oxford U (1931).
Career batting
4–2–2–16–16*–no av–0–*ct* 0
Bowling 229–6–38.16–0–0–2/49

Williams, Leoline
Amateur. *b:* 15.5.1900, Dursley, Gloucs. *d:* 29.2.1984, Lower Sticker, Cornwall. Brother of P. V. (Sussex) Middle order right-hand batsman, wicket-keeper. *Sch* Winchester. *Teams* Sussex (1919–30, 24 matches); Gloucestershire (1922, 11 matches); Army (in India) (1926/7).
Career batting
43–70–7–1440–107–22.85–3–*ct* 20–*st* 5
Bowling 5–0
His final first-class match was for the Army in 1931.

Williams, Lewis Erskine Wyndham
Amateur. *b:* 28.11.1900, Bonvilston, Cardiff. *d:* 24.4.1974, St Hilary, Glamorgan. Middle order batsman, useful bowler. *Sch* Oratory. *Team* Glamorgan (1928–30, 4 matches).
Career batting
4–8–2–145–53*–24.16–0–*ct* 1
Bowling 42–0

Williams, Neil FitzGerald
Cricketer. *b:* 2.7.1962, Hopewell, St Vincent. Right-hand batsman, right-arm fast medium bowler. *Teams* Middlesex (1982–83, 37 matches); Windward Islands (1982/3).
Career batting
41–43–13–653–63–21.76–0–*ct* 10
Bowling 2845–103–27.62–1–0–5/77

Williams, Norman Roy
Amateur. *b:* 4.1.1931, March, Cambridgeshire. Lower order right-hand batsman, right-arm fast medium bowler, slip field. *Team* Combined Services (1961).
Career batting
1–1–0–5–5–5.00–0–*ct* 1
Bowling 101–5–20.20–0–0–4/67
Not a member of the armed forces, he played in emergency. He appeared for Nottinghamshire 2nd XI.

Williams, Owen Leslie
Cricketer. *b:* 8.4.1938, Cape Town, South Africa. Lower order right-hand batsman, slow left-arm bowler. *Team* Warwickshire (1967, 1 match).
Career batting
1–2–1–6–6*–6.00–0–*ct* 0
Bowling 60–1–60.00–0–0–1/32

Williams, Rev Philip
Amateur. *b:* 7.9.1824, Eton, Bucks. *d:* 18.11.1899, Bath, Somerset. Middle order batsman. *Sch* Winchester. *Teams* Oxford U (1844–47, blue all four years); Nottinghamshire (1845, 2 matches).
Career batting
20–35–2–174–20–5.27–0–*ct* 16
His final first-class match was for MCC in 1849.

Williams, Sir Philip Francis Cunningham
Amateur. *b:* 6.7.1884, Kensington, London. *d:* 6.5.1958, Westminster, London. Brother of J. N. (Gloucs). Attractive middle order right-hand batsman, slow under-arm bowler. *Sch* Eton. *Team* Gloucestershire (1919–25, 112 matches). *Tour* MCC to New Zealand 1906/07 (played in emergency).
Career batting
113–199–10–3084–87–16.31–0–*ct* 45
Bowling 173–2–86.50–0–0–1/10
His first-class debut was for MCC in New Zealand in 1906/07. He appeared in the Oxford Freshmen's match of 1904, but no first-class matches for the University. He played occasionally for Dorset.

Williams, Peter Victor
Amateur. *b:* 10.7.1897, Wolverhampton, Staffs. *d:* 1.4.1971, New Zealand. Brother of Leoline (Gloucs). Sound middle order right-hand

batsman, wicket-keeper. *Sch* Winchester. *Team* Sussex (1919, 10 matches).
Career batting
23–40–0–810–146–20.25–2–*ct* 13–*st* 2
His final first-class match was for the Army in 1927.

Williams, Ralph Augustin
Amateur. *b:* 2.2.1879, Reading, Berkshire. *d:* 1.12.1958, Reading, Berkshire. Sound lower order right-hand batsman, right-arm medium pace bowler. *Sch* Winchester. *Team* Oxford U (1899–1902, blue 1901 and 1902). *Tour* Oxford University Authentics to India 1902/3.
Career batting
15–25–1–584–105–24.33–1–*ct* 14
Bowling 1099–40–27.47–3–0–5/30
His County cricket was for Oxfordshire, Berkshire and Buckinghamshire.

Williams, Richard Grenville
Cricketer. *b:* 10.8.1957, Bangor, Caernarvonshire. Middle order right-hand batsman, off break bowler. *Team* Northants (1974–83, 160 matches). *Tour* Robins to New Zealand 1979/80.
Career batting
162–259–32–6918–175*–30.47–12–*ct* 62
Bowling 6877–214–32.13–6–0–7/73
He hit 1,000 runs in a season five times (best 1,305, av 43.50, in 1983).

Williams, Robert Graham
Amateur. *b:* 4.4.1911, Australia. *d:* 31.8.1978, Adelaide, South Australia. Lower order right-hand batsman, right-arm fast medium bowler. *Team* South Australia (1932/3 to 1947/8, 18 matches). *Tour* Australian Services to England 1945.
Career batting
26–41–8–531–75*–16.09–0–*ct* 12
Bowling 1957–67–29.20–3–0–6/21

Williams, Richard Harry
Amateur. *b:* 23.4.1901, Brockmoor, Staffs. *d:* 19.12.1982, Stourbridge, Worcestershire. Middle order left-hand batsman. *Team* Worcestershire (1923–32, 37 matches).
Career batting
37–68–4–713–81–11.13–0–*ct* 17

Williams, Robert James
Amateur. *b:* 12.4.1912, Viljoen's Drift, South Africa. *d:* 14.5.1984, Durban, South Africa. Lower order right-hand batsman, wicket-keeper. *Team* Natal (1930/1 to 1950/1). *Tour* South Africa to England 1935.
Career batting
53–68–16–1156–117*–22.23–1–*ct* 77–*st* 55
The reserve wicket-keeper on the 1935 tour, he played in only seven first-class matches. At the end of the visit he accepted a business appointment in England.

Williams, Rowland Powell
Amateur. *b:* 8.1.1872, Stratford-on-Avon, Warwickshire. *d:* 16.12.1951, Yelverton, Devon. Middle order right-hand batsman. *Teams* Warwickshire (1897–98, 5 matches); London County (1902).
Career batting
7–12–1–105–38–9.54–0–*ct* 9
Bowling 20–0
His final first-class match was for Gentlemen of England in 1905.

Williams, Stephen
Cricketer. *b:* 11.3.1954, Swindon, Wiltshire. Middle order right-hand batsman, leg break bowler. *Team* Gloucestershire (1978, 1 match).
Career batting
1–0–0–0–0–0.00–0–*ct* 0
He has played for Wiltshire since 1975.

Williams, Thomas Brinsmead
Amateur. *b:* 1884, Newport, Monmouthshire. *d:* 12.1.1954, Llandaff, Glamorgan. Middle order batsman. *Team* Wales (1926).
Career batting
1–1–0–43–43–43.00–0–*ct* 1
His County cricket was for Monmouthshire.

Williams, Thomas Christopher
Amateur. *b:* 13.12.1908, Dublin. *d:* August 1982, Dublin. Left-hand batsman, right-arm medium pace, or leg break, bowler. *Team* Ireland (1939).
Career batting
1–2–0–25–23–12.50–0–*ct* 2
Bowling 50–1–50.00–0–0–1/36

Williams, William
Amateur. *b:* 25.11.1844, Arnold Grove, Nottingham. *d:* 12.3.1885, Wandsworth, London. Middle order right-hand batsman, right-hand fast round-arm bowler. *Sch* Oundle. *Team* Nottinghamshire (1865–75, 9 matches).
Career batting
15–28–2–339–31–13.03–0–*ct* 4
Bowling 92–3–30.66–0–0–2/27
His debut in first-class cricket was for Gentlemen of the North in 1862 and his final first-class match for England XI in 1878.

Williams, William
Amateur. *b:* 12.4.1861. *d:* 14.4.1951, Hampton Wick, Middlesex. Lower order right-hand batsman, leg break bowler, wicket-keeper. *Team* Middlesex (1885–1902, 27 matches). *Tour* Priestley to West Indies 1896/7.

Career batting
38–64–10–465–40–8.61–0–*ct* 32–*st* 4
Bowling 1127–63–17.88–3–1–7/38

A noted figure in club cricket, he is reputed to have taken 100 wickets each season for 55 years and appeared for MCC at the age of 74. He was a noted rugby footballer for Harlequins and later a well-known referee. It was mainly due to him that the Twickenham ground was laid out and it was for some time known as 'Billy Williams' cabbage patch'.

Williamson, Archibald Carmichael
Amateur. *b:* 11.11.1892, Hurlingham, Argentine. *d:* 17.9.1972, South Rubery, Birmingham. Opening batsman. *Sch* Fettes. *Team* Oxford (1913).
Career batting
1–2–0–18–10–9.00–0–*ct* 0

His County cricket was for Cheshire.

Williamson, John Gordon
(later Barkass-Williamson)
Professional. *b:* 4.4.1936, Norton-on-Tees, Co Durham. Tail end right-hand batsman, right-arm fast medium bowler. *Team* Northants (1959–62, 55 matches).
Career batting
56–67–19–820–106*–17.08–1–*ct* 28
Bowling 3921–120–32.67–3–0–6/47

His first-class debut was for Combined Services in 1958. He appeared for Durham 1954 to 1956 and returned in 1963.

Willis, Carl Bleackley
Amateur. *b:* 23.3.1893, Daylesford, Victoria, Australia. *d:* 12.5.1930, Berrigan, New South Wales, Australia. Middle order right-hand batsman, excellent field. *Team* Victoria (1913/4 to 1928/9, 36 matches). *Tours* AIF to England 1919; AIF to South Africa 1919/20; Victoria to New Zealand 1924/5.
Career batting
72–116–12–3707–156*–35.64–8–*ct* 38
Bowling 352–7–50.28–0–0–2/10

He was very successful in England in 1919 coming second in the AIF batting averages with 1,652 runs, av 41.30.

Willis, Rev Charles Francis
Amateur. *b:* 15.4.1827, Hawkhurst, Kent. *d:* 19.11.1895, Bressingham, Norfolk. Lower order batsman, useful bowler. *Sch* Tonbridge. *Teams* Oxford U (1847–49, blue all three years); Kent (1850, 1 match).
Career batting
10–19–2–83–16*–4.88–0–*ct* 4
Bowling 53 wickets, no analyses

He also played for Oxfordshire.

Willis, Henry
Amateur. *b:* 17.3.1841, Sydenham, Kent. *d:* 29.9.1926, Horton, Epsom, Surrey. Middle order batsman. *Team* Surrey (1868, 1 match).
Career batting
1–2–0–7–7–3.50–0–*ct* 0

Willis, John William
Amateur. *b:* 1886, Kettering, Northants. *d:* September 1963, Kettering, Northants. Lower order right-hand batsman, useful bowler. *Team* Northants (1919, 1 match).
Career batting
1–2–0–4–4–2.00–0–*ct* 0
Bowling 35–0

Willis, Robert George (Dylan), MBE
Cricketer. *b:* 30.5.1949, Sunderland, Co Durham. Tail end right-hand batsman, right-arm fast bowler. *Teams* Surrey (1969–71, 34 matches); Warwickshire (1972–83, 131 matches); Northern Transvaal 1972/3. *Tours* MCC to Australia and New Zealand 1970/1, 1974/5, to West Indies 1973/4, to India, Sri Lanka and Australia 1976/7; England to Pakistan and New Zealand 1977/8, to Australia 1978/9, 1979/80, to West Indies 1980/1, to India and Sri Lanka 1981/2, to Australia and New Zealand 1982/3 (New Zealand not first-class); Robins to South Africa 1972/3. *Tests* England (1970/1 to 1983, 83 matches).
Career batting
293–317–137–2606–72–14.47–0–*ct* 126
Bowling 21226–865–24.53–34–2–8/32
Test batting
83–117–51–775–28*–11.74–0–*ct* 37
Bowling 7471–305–24.49–13–0–8/43

Despite an erratic first few years in County and Test cricket, Willis developed into one of the best fast bowlers to play for England. His three outstanding Test series have all been against Australia – in 1977 with 27 wickets, av 19.77, in 1978/9 with 20, av 23.05 and in 1981 with 29, av 22.96. He was vice-captain on three England tours overseas, but only succeeded to the post of captain in his own right when Botham proved unsuitable and Brearley retired. Willis led England in the home series of 1982 and then to Australia and New Zealand in 1982/3 and the following home series of 1983, proving to be better equipped for the task than some had suggested.

Injury and latterly Test calls have restricted his appearances in County cricket, and his best season in England was 1978 with 65 wickets, av 18.41.

He was appointed captain of Warwickshire in 1980 and in 1982 received the MBE for his services to cricket.

Willmer, Arthur Franklin
Amateur. *b:* 10.10.1890. *d:* 20.9.1916, near Loos, France. Lower order batsman, useful bowler. *Sch* Birkenhead. *Team* Oxford U (1912).
Career batting
1–2–2–12–7*–no av–0–*ct* 0
Bowling 36–0
His County cricket was for Cheshire.

Willock, Charles Johnstone
Amateur. *b:* 8.4.1862, Shahjehanpore, India. *d:* 19.3.1919, Ryde, Isle of Wight. Lower order right-hand batsman, right-arm medium pace bowler. *Sch* Wellington. *Teams* Sussex (1883, 1 match); Cambridge U (1883).
Career batting
2–4–1–14–8*–4.66–0–*ct* 2
Bowling 34–3–11.33–0–0–2/18

Willoughby, Frederick George
Professional. *b:* 25.4.1862, Edinburgh, Scotland. *d:* 1952, Winchester, Hampshire. Tail end right-hand batsman, left-arm medium pace bowler. *Team* Hampshire (1885, 8 matches).
Career batting
8–15–3–60–19–5.00–0–*ct* 5
Bowling 564–25–22.56–0–0–4/39
He played for Worcestershire in some non-first-class matches commencing 1890. Later he was on the first-class umpires' list.

Willows, Alan
Cricketer. *b:* 24.4.1961, Portslade, Sussex. Lower order right-hand batsman, slow left-arm bowler. *Team* Sussex (1980–83, 5 matches).
Career batting
5–3–1–5–4–2.50–0–*ct* 0
Bowling 253–8–31.62–0–0–4/33

Wills, Arnold Cass Lycett
Amateur. *b:* 17.7.1906, Kensington, London. *d:* 28.2.1978, Northampton. Steady opening right-hand batsman, right-arm medium pace bowler. *Sch* Harrow. *Teams* Northants (1926–29, 15 matches); Cambridge U (1929).
Career batting
16–27–2–338–68–13.52–0–*ct* 5
Bowling 428–6–71.33–0–0–3/68

Wills, Alec Percy Stanley
Amateur. *b:* 13.3.1911, Trincomalee, Ceylon. *d:* 7.11.1941, He was killed in action. Tail end right-hand batsman, useful bowler. *Sch* Haileybury. *Team* Combined Services (1937).
Career batting
1–2–2–3–3*–no av–0–*ct* 0
Bowling 36–0

Wills, James Robertson
Amateur. *b:* 2.5.1899, Killala, Co Mayo. *d:* 16.4.1949, St Saviour, Jersey. Right-hand batsman, right-arm fast medium bowler. *Teams* Dublin University (1922–26); Ireland (1922).
Career batting
4–8–1–66–28–9.42–0–*ct* 1
Bowling 236–7–33.71–0–0–3/5

Wills, Roy
Cricketer. *b:* 5.12.1944, Northampton. Middle order right-hand batsman, slip field. *Team* Northants (1963–69, 33 matches).
Career batting
33–54–6–824–151*–17.16–1–*ct* 26

Wills, Robert Thomas
Cricketer. *b:* 19.7.1950, Belfast. Right-hand batsman. *Team* Ireland (1981–83).
Career batting
3–5–0–95–48–19.00–0–*ct* 0

Wills, Thomas Wentworth Spencer
Amateur. *b:* 19.8.1835, Molonglo Plains, New South Wales, Australia. *d:* 2.5.1880, Heidelberg, Victoria, Australia. He stabbed himself to death. Cousin of T. W. Antill (Victoria). Lower order right-hand batsman, right-hand fast round-arm, or slow under-arm bowler. *Sch* Rugby. *Teams* Cambridge U (1856, blue); Kent (1855–56, 3 matches); Victoria (1856/7 to 1875/6, 16 matches).
Career batting
32–57–8–602–58–12.28–0–*ct* 20
Bowling 1221–121+9–10.09–15–3–7/44
Although he played for Cambridge against Oxford in 1856, he was not a student at either University. His first-class debut was for Gentlemen of Kent in 1854. He was the first to train the aborigines to play cricket.

Willsher, Edgar
Professional. *b:* 22.11.1828, Little Halden, Rolvenden, Kent. *d:* 7.10.1885, Lewisham, Kent. Brother of William (Kent). Steady middle order left-hand batsman, left-hand fast round-arm bowler. *Team* Kent (1850–75, 145 matches). *Tour* Willsher to North America 1868 (not first-class).
Career batting
267–473–63–5089–89–12.41–0–*ct* 233
Bowling 16393–1282+47–12.78–107–30–8/16
He took 113 wickets, av 9.98, in 1868 and for a period of about ten years was regarded as one of the best bowlers in England.

Willson, Bernard John
Cricketer. *b:* 20.6.1935, Strood, Kent. Lower order right-hand batsman, left-arm medium paced bowler. *Team* Combined Services (1964).
Career batting
2–4–0–87–53–21.75–0–*ct* 2
Bowling 197–7–28.14–0–0–4/87

Willson, Erasmus Albert
Amateur. *b:* 13.10.1878, Sittingbourne, Kent. *d:* 17.4.1948, Sittingbourne, Kent. Lower order right-hand batsman, right-arm fast bowler. *Team* Kent (1898, 1 match).
Career batting
1–2–0–9–8–4.50–0–*ct* 1
Bowling 46–1–46.00–0–0–1/21

Willson, Ronald H.
Professional. *b:* 14.7.1933, Seaford, Sussex. Middle order left-hand batsman, slow left-arm bowler. *Teams* Sussex (1955–57, 19 matches); Rhodesia (1961/2).
Career batting
22–34–5–411–113*–14.17–1–*ct* 10
Bowling 390–4–97.50–0–0–1/27
He also played for Devon.

Wilmot, Rev Arthur Alfred
Amateur. *b:* 14.2.1845, Chaddesden, Derbyshire. *d:* 12.5.1876, Morley, Derbyshire. Opening batsman. *Sch* Repton. *Team* Derbyshire (1871, 1 match).
Career batting
1–2–0–0–0–0.00–0–*ct* 1
He also played for Northants (pre first-class) and Staffordshire.

Wilmot, Kilburn
Professional. *b:* 3.4.1911, Chilvers Coton, Nuneaton. Lower order right-hand batsman, right-arm fast pace bowler. *Team* Warwickshire (1931–39, 75 matches).
Career batting
75–101–25–871–54–11.46–0–*ct* 23
Bowling 5018–154–32.58–2–1–7/34
A good soccer player, he appeared for Coventry and Walsall.

Wilmot, William
Professional. *b:* 25.12.1869, Denby, Derbyshire. *d:* 19.5.1957, Leyland, Lancashire. Lower order right-hand batsman, wicket-keeper. *Team* Derbyshire (1897–1901, 10 matches).
Career batting
10–16–3–155–25*–11.92–0–*ct* 11–*st* 1

Wilson, Alan
Professional. *b:* 24.4.1921, Newton-le-Willows, Lancashire. Tail end right-hand batsman, wicket-keeper. *Team* Lancashire (1948–62, 171 matches).
Career batting
171–186–59–760–37*–5.98–0–*ct* 288–*st* 58
He lost his place in Lancashire side in 1959, but made a fleeting re-appearance in 1962.

Wilson, Arthur Edward
Professional. *b:* 18.5.1910, Paddington, London. Dependable opening or middle order left-hand batsman, wicket-keeper. *Teams* Middlesex (1932–33, 7 matches); Gloucestershire (1936–55, 318 matches).
Career batting
328–502–77–10744–188–25.28–7–*ct* 425–*st* 176
Bowling 1–0
He hit 1,000 runs in a season six times (best 1,327, av 31.59, in 1947). For Gloucestershire v Hampshire at Portsmouth in 1953 he held 10 catches in the match. In 1950 he was appointed Gloucs County coach.

Wilson, Arthur Keith
Amateur. *b:* 26.8.1894, Brighton, Sussex. *d:* 8.11.1977, Brighton, Sussex. Middle order right-hand batsman, slow leg break bowler. *Sch* Brighton. *Team* Sussex (1914–34, 16 matches).
Career batting
17–30–2–546–134–19.50–1–*ct* 4
Bowling 179–3–59.66–0–0–2/39
His final appearance for Sussex in 1934 came after an absence of nine years. He was Chairman of Sussex CCC.

Wilson, Benjamin Ambler
Professional. *b:* 22.9.1921, Knaresborough, Yorkshire. Lower order batsman, slow left-arm bowler. *Team* Warwickshire (1951, 1 match).
Career batting
1–1–0–0–0–0.00–0–*ct* 0
Bowling 75–1–75.00–0–0–1/75

Wilson, Benjamin Birdsall
Professional. *b:* 11.12.1879, Scarborough, Yorkshire. *d:* 14.9.1957, Claro, North Yorkshire. Sound opening right-hand batsman, right-arm fast medium bowler. *Team* Yorkshire (1906–14, 185 matches).
Career batting
185–308–12–8053–208–27.20–15–*ct* 53
Bowling 278–2–139.00–0–0–1/16
He hit 1,000 runs in a season five times (best 1,608, av 32.74, in 1914). His only double century was 208 for Yorkshire v Sussex at Bradford in 1914.

Wilson, Rt Rev Cecil
Amateur. *b:* 9.9.1860, Canonbury, London. *d:*

20.1.1941, Perth, Western Australia. Brother of Leslie (Kent). Attractive middle order right-hand batsman. *Sch* Tonbridge. *Team* Kent (1882–90, 28 matches).
Career batting
33–56–6–1193–127–23.86–1–*ct* 28
Bowling 222–5–44.40–0–0–1/2

He did not appear in any first-clas matches whilst at Cambridge. In 1894 he was appointed Bishop of Melanesia.

Wilson, Rev Clement Eustace Macro
Amateur. *b:* 15.5.1875, Bolsterstone, Yorkshire. *d:* 8.2.1944, Calverhall, Shropshire. Brother of E. R. (Yorkshire) and R. A. (Cambridge U), father of D. C. (Cambridge U). Steady middle order right-hand batsman, right-arm fast medium bowler, also left-arm slow (changing from one to the other in the course of a match). *Sch* Uppingham. *Teams* Cambridge U (1895–98, blue all four years); Yorkshire (1896–99, 8 matches). *Tours* Mitchell to North America 1895; Hawke to South Africa 1898/9. *Tests* England (1898/9, 2 matches).
Career batting
50–78–10–1632–115–24.00–1–*ct* 33
Bowling 2283–121–18.86–6–2–7/24
Test batting
2–4–1–42–18–14.00–0–*ct* 0

On being ordained he retired from first-class cricket, his final first-class match being for MCC in 1900.

Wilson, Charles Plumpton
Amateur. *b:* 12.5.1859, Roydon, Norfolk. *d:* 9.3.1938, East Dereham, Norfolk. Middle order right-hand batsman, right-arm medium pace bowler. *Sch* Uppingham and Marlborough. *Team* Cambridge U (1880–81, blue both years).
Career batting
10–18–7–157–24*–14.27–0–*ct* 6
Bowling 439–22–19.95–1–0–5/34

He played County cricket for Norfolk. A remarkable all-round sportsman, he played rugby football for England in 1881 and soccer for England in 1884. Also a noted cyclist, he raced for Cambridge in the 25 miles in 1878.

Wilson, Claude William
Amateur. *b:* 9.9.1858, Banbury, Oxon. *d:* 7.7.1881, Reigate, Surrey. Middle order right-hand batsman, wicket-keeper. *Sch* Brighton. *Teams* Oxford U (1881); Surrey (1881, 1 match).
Career batting
2–4–0–66–51–16.50–0–*ct* 2

Wilson, Donald
Professional. *b:* 7.8.1937, Settle, Yorkshire. Lower order left-hand batsman, slow left-arm bowler. *Team* Yorkshire (1957–74, 392 matches). *Tours* MCC to New Zealand 1960/1, to India 1963/4, to Ceylon 1969/70, to Australia and New Zealand 1970/1; Yorkshire to North America 1964 (not first-class). *Tests* England (1963/4 to 1970/1, 6 matches).
Career batting
422–533–91–6230–112–14.09–1–*ct* 250
Bowling 24977–1189–21.00–50–8–8/36
Test batting
6–7–1–75–42–12.50–0–*ct* 1
Bowling 466–11–42.36–0–0–2/17

He took 100 wickets in a season five times (best 109, av 13.95, in 1968). From 1975 to 1977 he played for Lincolnshire. He is chief coach at Lord's.

Wilson, David Clement
Amateur. *b:* 1.3.1917, Eccleston, Chester. Son of C. E. M. (Yorkshire), nephew of E. R. (Yorkshire) and R. A. (Cambridge U). Lower order right-hand batsman, right-arm medium pace bowler. *Sch* Winchester. *Team* Cambridge U (1938–39). *Tour* Combined Oxford and Cambridge Univ to Jamaica 1938/9.
Career batting
10–17–8–98–23*–10.88–0–*ct* 8
Bowling 729–15–48.60–1–0–5/81

Wilson, Ernest Frederick
Professional. *b:* 24.6.1907, Godstone, Surrey. *d:* 3.3.1981, Swansea, Glamorgan. Sound middle order right-hand batsman. *Team* Surrey (1928–36, 81 matches).
Career batting
81–120–12–2516–110–23.29–1–*ct* 16
Bowling 43–0

Wilson, Evelyn Rockley
Amateur. *b:* 25.3.1879, Bolsterstone, Yorkshire. *d:* 21.7.1957, Winchester, Hampshire. Brother of C. E. M. (Yorkshire) and R. A. (Cambridge U), uncle of D. C. (Cambridge U). Sound middle or lower order right-hand batsman, right-arm slow bowler turning the ball either way. *Sch* Rugby. *Teams* Cambridge U (1899–1902, blue all four years); Yorkshire (1899–1923, 66 matches). *Tours* Bosanquet to North America 1901; Bennett to West Indies 1901/2; MCC to Argentine 1911/12, to Australia 1920/1. *Test* England (1920/1, 1 match).
Career batting
136–190–28–3565–142–22.00–4–*ct* 106
Bowling 8234–467–17.63–26–4–7/16
Test batting
1–2–0–10–5–5.00–0–*ct* 0
Bowling 36–3–12.00–0–0–2/28

A master at Winchester College, his County

cricket was mainly confined to matches in August, though for eleven years between 1903 and 1913 he did not play for Yorkshire.

Wilson, Edward Wardlaw
Amateur. *b:* 19.8.1907, Burntisland, Fife, Scotland. Left-hand batsman. *Team* Scotland (1936).
Career batting
1–2–0–1–1–0.50–0–*ct* 0

Wilson, Frederic Bonhote
Amateur. *b:* 21.9.1881, Paddington, London. *d:* 19.1.1932, Kensington, London. Middle order right-hand batsman, right-arm slow bowler. *Sch* Harrow. *Team* Cambridge U (1902–04, blue all three years).
Career batting
27–49–7–1130–76–26.90–0–*ct* 15
Bowling 181–4–45.25–0–0–2/64

His final first-class match was for Leveson-Gower's XI in 1906. A well known sporting journalist, he began with the *Daily Mirror*, but was associated with *The Times* after the First World War.

Wilson, Francis Tyrwhitt Drake
Amateur. *b:* 9.4.1876, Guilsborough, Northants. *d:* 19.3.1964, Great Horkesley, Essex. Brother of H. L. (Sussex). Lower order right-hand batsman, leg break bowler. *Teams* MCC (1914); Army (1913–20).
Career batting
5–7–0–103–39–14.71–0–*ct* 2
Bowling 297–18–16.50–2–0–5/57

His County cricket was for Suffolk. His first-class debut was for the Combined Army and Navy XI in 1910.

Wilson, Geoffrey
Amateur. *b:* 21.8.1895, Leeds, Yorkshire. *d:* 29.11.1960, Southsea, Hampshire. Hard hitting opening or middle order right-hand batsman. *Sch* Harrow. *Teams* Cambridge U (1919–20, blue 1919); Yorkshire (1919–24, 92 matches). *Tour* MCC to Australia and New Zealand 1922/3.
Career batting
115–129–18–1801–142*–16.22–1–*ct* 44
Bowling 55–1–55.00–0–0–1/44

He captained Yorkshire from 1922 to 1924.

Wilson, George
Amateur. *b:* 30.6.1916, Belfast. Right-hand batsman, off break bowler. *Team* Ireland (1948–51).
Career batting
3–6–0–116–39–19.33–0–*ct* 0
Bowling 12–2–6.00–0–0–2/12

Wilson, George A.
Amateur. *b:* 2.2.1916, Leeds, Yorkshire. Middle order right-hand batsman, slow left-arm bowler. *Team* Yorkshire (1936–39, 15 matches).
Career batting
15–25–5–352–55*–17.60–0–*ct* 7
Bowling 138–1–138.00–0–0–1/5

Wilson, George Alfred
Professional. *b:* 5.4.1877, Amersham, Buckinghamshire. *d:* 3.3.1962, Abbots Langley, Hertfordshire. Father of G. C. (Worcestershire). Lower order right-hand batsman, right-arm fast bowler. *Team* Worcestershire (1899–1906, 154 matches).
Career batting
160–239–42–2238–78–11.35–0–*ct* 57
Bowling 17615–732–24.06–58–18–9/75

He took 100 wickets in a season three times (best 120, av 22.79, in 1901). His best bowling was 9/75 for Worcestershire v Oxford U at Oxford in 1904.

He also played for Buckinghamshire and Staffordshire.

Wilson, George Clifford
Professional. *b:* 27.7.1902, Kidderminster, Worcs. *d:* 1957, Newcastle-on-Tyne. Son of G. A. (Worcs). Lower order right-hand batsman, right-arm fast bowler. *Team* Worcestershire (1924–26, 70 matches).
Career batting
70–119–34–609–40–7.16–0–*ct* 30
Bowling 4049–150–26.99–8–1–8/81

He also played for Northumberland.

Wilson, Gerald Charles
Professional. *b:* 25.12.1936, Hayes, Middlesex. Tail end right-hand batsman, right-arm medium pace bowler. *Team* MCC (1957).
Career batting
2–2–2–10–7*–no av–0–*ct* 2
Bowling 211–3–70.33–0–0–2/85

Wilson, Guy Denis
Amateur. *b:* 30.11.1882, Melbourne, Derbyshire. *d:* 30.11.1917, Cambrai, France. He was killed in action. Middle order batsman. *Sch* Derby School. *Team* Derbyshire (1902–05, 2 matches).
Career batting
2–4–0–19–9–4.75–0–*ct* 0
Bowling 15–0

Wilson, George Lindsay
Amateur. *b:* 27.4.1868, Fitzroy, Melbourne, Australia. *d:* 9.3.1920, St Kilda, Melbourne, Australia. Sound middle order right-hand batsman, right-arm fast medium bowler, slip

field. *Sch* Brighton and Repton. *Teams* Sussex (1887–95, 49 matches); Oxford U (1888–91, blue 1890 and 1891); Victoria (1898/9, 2 matches).
Career batting
75–136–7–2605–174–20.19–3–*ct* 41
Bowling 2042–34–60.05–0–0–4/47
His first-class debut was for G. N. Wyatt's XI in 1886.

Wilson, G. T. O. (*See under* Wilson, T. G. O.)

Wilson, Harry
Professional. *b:* 1873, Yorkshire. *d:* 13.8.1906, Kidderminster, Worcs. Lower order batsman, slow left-arm bowler. *Team* Worcestershire (1901–06, 6 matches).
Career batting
6–11–3–64–21–8.00–0–*ct* 2
Bowling 373–13–28.69–1–0–6/86

Wilson, Harry
Amateur. *b:* 1897. *d:* 25.4.1960, Peterborough. Tail end right-hand batsman, right-arm medium pace bowler. *Team* Northants (1931, 1 match).
Career batting
1–2–0–0–0–0.00–0–*ct* 0
Bowling 45–1–45.00–0–0–1/19

Wilson, Herbert
Professional. *b:* 22.5.1892, Eastwood, Notts. *d:* 3.6.1972, Macclesfield, Cheshire. Lower order right-hand batsman, right-arm fast medium bowler, slip field. *Team* Nottinghamshire (1911–19, 6 matches).
Career batting
6–7–3–49–19–12.25–0–*ct* 3
Bowling 318–4–79.50–0–0–1/21
From 1922 to 1933 he played with success for Cheshire.

Wilson, Herbert Langford
Amateur. *b:* 27.6.1881, Guilsborough, Northants. *d:* 15.3.1937, Uckfield, Sussex. Brother of F. T. D. (MCC). Stylish middle order right-hand batsman, slow right-arm bowler. *Sch* Framlingham. *Team* Sussex (1913–24, 140 matches).
Career batting
145–264–12–6226–187–24.70–6–*ct* 57
Bowling 1292–26–49.69–0–0–4/19
He hit 1,000 runs in a season four times (best 1,352, av 29.39, in 1913). He captained Sussex 1919 to 1921. Before playing for Sussex, he represented Suffolk. His final first-class match was for H. D. G. Leveson-Gower's XI in 1930.

Wilson, Ian Barclay Justly
Amateur. *b:* 13.10.1932, Clonmel, Co Tipperary. Left-hand batsman, slow left-arm bowler. *Sch* Wrekin. *Team* Ireland (1956–61).
Career batting
3–5–0–49–18–9.80–0–*ct* 1
Bowling 117–7–16.71–0–0–3/7

Wilson, John
Amateur. *b:* 20.6.1858, Pitsmoor, Sheffield, Yorkshire. *d:* 13.11.1931, Sheffield, Yorkshire. Attacking middle order right-hand batsman, right-hand slow under-arm bowler. *Sch* Trent College. *Team* Yorkshire (1887–88, 4 matches).
Career batting
4–5–1–17–13*–4.25–0–*ct* 3
Bowling 165–12–13.75–0–0–3/28

Wilson, John Devakumar
Cricketer. *b:* 4.9.1944, Jaffna, Ceylon. Middle order left-hand batsman, leg break bowler. *Team* Oxford U (1977).
Career batting
1–2–0–19–18–9.50–0–*ct* 0
Bowling 6–0

Wilson, John Philip
Amateur. *b:* 3.4.1889, Gilling, Yorkshire. *d:* 3.10.1959, Tickton, Beverley, Yorkshire. Middle order right-hand batsman, slow right-arm bowler. *Sch* Harrow. *Team* Yorkshire (1911–12, 9 matches).
Career batting
11–18–1–172–36–10.11–0–*ct* 2
Bowling 24–1–24.00–0–0–1/20
He did not play in first-class cricket whilst at Cambridge. His final first-class match was for Leveson-Gower's XI in 1913. A noted steeplechase jockey, he won the Grand National on Double Chance in 1925.

Wilson, John Stuart
Amateur. *b:* 22.1.1932, Middleton, Manchester. Right-hand batsman, right-arm fast medium bowler. *Team* Scotland (1957–64).
Career batting
16–19–6–66–22–5.07–0–*ct* 8
Bowling 1109–44–25.20–1–0–5/51

Wilson, John Victor
Professional. *b:* 17.1.1921, Scampston, Malton, Yorkshire. Middle order left-hand batsman, fine field. *Team* Yorkshire (1946–62, 477 matches). *Tour* MCC to Australia and New Zealand 1954/5.
Career batting
502–770–79–21650–230–31.33–30–*ct* 548
Bowling 435–9–48.33–0–0–2/1
He hit 1,000 runs in a season 14 times, going on to 2,000 once : 2,027, av 48.26, in 1951. Both his double centuries were for Yorkshire the

highest being 230 v Derbyshire at Sheffield in 1952. He captained Yorkshire 1960 to 1962. His final first-class match was for MCC in 1963. He also played for Lincolnshire. A good soccer player, he appeared for Leeds United.

Wilson, John William
Amateur. *b:* 20.8.1922, Albert Park, Victoria, Australia. Tail end right-hand batsman, slow left-arm bowler. *Teams* Victoria (1949/50, 1 match); South Australia (1950/1 to 1957/8, 55 matches). *Tours* Australia to England 1956, to India 1956/7. *Test* Australia (1956/7, 1 match).
Career batting
78–97–47–287–19*–5.74–0–*ct* 17
Bowling 7019–230–30.51–9–1–7/11
Test batting
1 match, did not bat –*ct* 0
Bowling 64–1–64.00–0–0–1/25
He took 43 wickets, av 23.06, on the 1956 tour to England and did not appear in the Tests.

Wilson, Leslie
Amateur. *b:* 16.3.1859, Canonbury, London. *d:* 15.4.1944, Hastings, Sussex. Brother of Cecil (Kent). Stylish middle order right-hand batsman, right-arm medium pace bowler, good deep field. *Sch* Tonbridge. *Team* Kent (1883–97, 105 matches).
Career batting
110–193–10–3554–132–19.42–1–*ct* 78
Bowling 265–6–44.16–0–0–2/17

Wilson, Mark
Amateur. *b:* 25.11.1890, Whitburn, West Lothian, Scotland. Left-hand batsman, left-arm fast medium bowler. *Team* Scotland (1925).
Career batting
1–2–0–4–4–2.00–0–*ct* 0
Bowling 23–0

Wilson, Peter Hugh L'Estrange
Cricketer. *b:* 17.8.1958, Guildford, Surrey. Lower order right-hand batsman, right-arm fast medium bowler. *Sch* Wellington. *Teams* Surrey (1978–82, 37 matches); Somerset (1983, 11 matches); Northern Transvaal (1979/80). *Tours* MCC to East Africa 1981/2, to Bangladesh 1980/1 (neither first-class).
Career batting
57–48–25–261–29–11.34–0–*ct* 10
Bowling 3218–105–30.64–1–0–5/36

Wilson, Peter James
Cricketer. *b:* 9.8.1942, Weston-super-Mare, Somerset. Lower order left-hand batsman, useful bowler. *Team* Oxford U (1964).
Career batting
2–3–0–56–30–18.66–0–*ct* 1

Wilson, Peter Robert Bain
Cricketer. *b:* 31.10.1944, Rhodesia. Middle order right-hand batsman, leg break bowler. *Team* Oxford U (1968–70, blue 1968 and 1970).
Career batting
23–39–1–664–94–17.47–0–*ct* 9
Bowling 233–7–33.28–0–0–4/60

Wilson, Robert
Amateur. *b:* 8.4.1916, Edinburgh, Scotland. Right-hand batsman, right-arm fast medium bowler. *Team* Scotland (1952).
Career batting
3–3–2–5–4–5.00–0–*ct* 1
Bowling 167–8–20.87–0–0–2/16

Wilson, Robert
Amateur. *b:* 12.2.1935, Paisley, Renfrewshire, Scotland. Left-hand batsman, slow left-arm bowler. *Team* Scotland (1955–56).
Career batting
3–5–0–64–29–12.80–0–*ct* 3

Wilson, Rev Rowland Alwyn
Amateur. *b:* 18.7.1868, Bolderstone, Yorkshire. *d:* 1.10.1959, Hartlebury, Worcestershire. Brother of C. E. M. (Yorkshire) and E. R. (Yorkshire), uncle of D. C. (Cambridge U). Hard hitting lower order right-hand batsman, right-arm fast medium bowler. *Sch* Rugby. *Team* Cambridge U (1888–89).
Career batting
3–4–1–18–15–6.00–0–*ct* 3
Bowling 48–1–48.00–0–0–1/13
His County cricket was for Worcestershire (pre first-class).

Wilson, Robert Colin
Professional. *b:* 18.2.1928, Bapchild, Kent. Sound middle order left-hand batsman, right-arm medium pace bowler. *Team* Kent (1952–67, 365 matches).
Career batting
367–647–39–19515–159*–32.09–30–*ct* 201
Bowling 90–4–22.50–0–0–3/38
He hit 1,000 runs in a season 13 times, going on to 2,000 once: 2,038, av 46.31, in 1964.

Wilson, Robert Greenwood
Amateur. *b:* 20.12.1922, Arnside, Westmorland. *d:* 7.3.1980, Swindon, Wiltshire. Aggressive lower order right-hand batsman, right-arm fast medium bowler. *Sch* Bradfield. *Team* Combined Services (1948–52).

Career batting
14–25–2–660–100–28.64–1–*ct* 6
Bowling 655–24–27.29–1–0–5/41
He was Secretary of Nottinghamshire CCC 1972 to 1977.

Wilson, Robin John
Cricketer. *b:* 3.3.1935, London. Lower order right-hand batsman, slow left-arm and chinaman bowler. *Team* Cambridge U (1964).
Career batting
1–1–1–3–3*–no av–0–*ct* 1
Bowling 65–2–32.50–0–0–2/35

Wilson, Robert Warley
Amateur. *b:* 15.7.1934, Warley, Worcestershire. Lower order right-hand batsman, off break bowler. *Sch* Warwick. *Team* Oxford U (1956-57, blue 1957).
Career batting
13–24–6–169–36*–9.38–0–*ct* 10
Bowling 1265–34–37.20–0–0–4/42
He also obtained his rugby blue.

Wilson, Sidney John
Amateur. *b:* 22.9.1858, Maidstone, Kent. *d:* 1.2.1917, Flushing, Cornwall. Son of Alfred (Oxford U 1848). Middle order right-hand batsman, right-arm medium pace bowler. *Sch* Winchester. *Team* MCC (1882).
Career batting
1–2–0–8–6–4.00–0–*ct* 0
Bowling 2–0

Wilson, T.
Professional. Tail end batsman, useful bowler. *Team* Middlesex (1880, 1 match).
Career batting
1–1–0–5–5–5.00–0–*ct* 0
Bowling 31–0

Wilson, Thomas Crichton
Amateur. *b:* 18.11.1936, Eastbourne, Sussex. Lower order batsman, useful bowler. *Sch* Eastbourne. *Team* L. C. Steven's XI (1960).
Career batting
1–1–1–0–0*–no av–0–*ct* 0
Bowling 42–1–42.00–0–0–1/25

Wilson, Thomas Grenville Owen
(known as G. T. O. Wilson)
Professional. *b:* 9.4.1932, Elmley Lovett, Worcestershire. Tail end left-hand batsman, left-arm fast bowler. *Team* Worcestershire (1951–53, 13 matches).
Career batting
13–16–7–10–4*–1.11–0–*ct* 2
Bowling 1000–18–55.55–0–0–3/42

Wilson, Thomas Henry
Amateur. *b:* 10.6.1841. *d:* 31.1.1929, Tucuman, Argentine. Lower order batsman, wicket-keeper. *Sch* Harrow. *Team* Hampshire (1870, 2 matches).
Career batting
3–6–0–23–9–3.83–0–*ct* 0–*st* 1
His first-class debut was for MCC in 1869. He also played for Huntingdonshire.

Wilson, Theophilus Stuart Beatty
Amateur. *b:* 15.8.1870, Orion Downs, Queensland, Australia. *d:* 19.5.1941, Orion Downs, Queensland, Australia. Lower order right-hand batsman, right-arm fast bowler. *Sch* Bath College. *Team* Oxford U (1892–93, blue both years).
Career batting
17–31–2–186–36–6.41–0–*ct* 12
Bowling 1013–46–22.02–0–0–4/23
His County cricket was for Monmouthshire.

Wilson, Thomas Ward
Amateur. *b:* 1.4.1849, Nocton, Lincolnshire. *d:* 4.1.1924, Broadstone, Dorset. Tail end right-hand batsman, right-hand fast or medium pace round-arm bowler. *Sch* Repton. *Team* Cambridge U (1869–71, blue 1869).
Career batting
8–13–2–171–50–15.54–0–*ct* 1
Bowling 304–17–17.88–1–0–5/25
He played County cricket for Lincolnshire in 1869, Norfolk in 1870 and Dorset 1873 to 1877. For 36 years he was a master at Sherborne School.

Wiltshire, Edgar
Amateur. *b:* 25.9.1877, Addiscombe, Surrey. *d:* 25.8.1912, Forest Hill, London. Middle order left-hand batsman, left-arm bowler. *Sch* Dulwich. *Team* Surrey (1902–03, 13 matches).
Career batting
13–22–2–219–33–10.95–0–*ct* 3

Wiltshire, Graham George Morley
Professional. *b:* 16.4.1931, Chipping Sodbury, Gloucs. Lower order right-hand batsman, right-arm medium fast bowler. *Team* Gloucestershire (1953–60, 19 matches). *Tour* Gloucestershire to Zambia 1971/2 (not first-class).
Career batting
19–30–4–218–39–8.38–0–*ct* 3
Bowling 835–25–33.40–1–0–7/52
He is coach to the Gloucestershire County Club.

Wincer, Robert Colin
Cricketer. *b:* 2.4.1952, Portsmouth, Hampshire. Lower order left-hand batsman, right-arm fast medium bowler. *Team* Derbyshire (1978–80, 23 matches).

Career batting
23–21–8–131–26–10.07–0–*ct* 8
Bowling 1653–46–35.93–0–0–4/42

Winchilsea, 9th Earl of, George Finch
Amateur. *b:* 4.11.1752, London. *d:* 2.8.1826, Mayfair, London. Middle order right-hand batsman. *Sch* Eton. *Teams* Surrey (1801); Hampshire (1787); MCC (1804).
Career batting
2–3–1–7–4–3.50–0–*ct* 0

He was President of Hambledon Club in 1787 and 1789 and was a member of the White Conduit Club. He, with others, persuaded Thomas Lord to found his cricket ground and thus was amongst the founding members of the MCC. He also staged matches at his country seat at Burley in Rutland. He is incorrectly given as the 8th Earl in volume XV of *Scores and Biographies*.

Windaybank, Stephen James
Cricketer. *b:* 20.10.1956, Pinner, Middlesex. Opening right-hand batsman. *Team* Gloucestershire (1979–82, 15 matches).
Career batting
15–19–4–385–53–25.66–0–*ct* 3

Winder, George Alexander
Amateur. *b:* 16.7.1850, Bolton, Lancashire. *d:* 1.2.1913, Ottery St Mary, Devon. Middle order right-hand batsman, good deep field. *Sch* Rossall. *Teams* Lancashire (1869, 2 matches); Cambridge U (1871).
Career batting
4–8–1–64–22–9.14–0–*ct* 1

In January 1872, when he was out shooting, his gun exploded and he lost his left hand as a result. This ended his serious cricket, but he continued to take part in minor matches. His final first-class match was for Gentlemen of the North in 1871.

Windows, Anthony Robin
Amateur. *b:* 25.9.1942, Bristol. Middle order right-hand batsman, right-arm medium bowler. *Sch* Clifton. *Teams* Gloucestershire (1960–68, 98 matches); Cambridge U (1962-64, blue all three years). *Tour* MCC to Pakistan 1966/7.
Career batting
149–241–33–3537–82–17.00–0–*ct* 42
Bowling 8308–286–29.04–9–0–8/78

He hit 1,003 runs, av 20.89, in 1962.

Windridge, James Edwin
Professional. *b:* 21.10.1882, Sparkbrook, Birmingham. *d:* 23.9.1939, Birmingham. Lower order right-hand batsman, right-arm medium pace bowler. *Team* Warwickshire (1909–13, 7 matches).
Career batting
7–12–1–161–34*–14.63–0–*ct* 2
Bowling 13–1–13.00–0–0–1/13

He played soccer for Chelsea, Middlesbrough and Birmingham.

Windsor, Raymond Thomas Albert
Cricketer. *b:* 9.2.1943, Wellington, Somerset. Middle order right-hand batsman. *Team* Somerset (1969, 1 match).
Career batting
1–1–0–0–0–0.00–0–*ct* 0

Windsor-Clive, Hon Archer
Amateur. *b:* 6.11.1890, Redditch, Worcs. *d:* 25.8.1914, Landrecies, France. Lower order batsman, left-arm medium pace bowler. *Sch* Eton. *Team* Cambridge U (1910–12).
Career batting
7–14–1–108–22–8.30–0–*ct* 1
Bowling 217–3–72.33–0–0–3/56

His County cricket was for Glamorgan (pre-first-class).

Winfield, Hugh Mervyn
Professional. *b:* 13.6.1933, Gainsborough, Lincolnshire. Sound middle order right-hand batsman. *Team* Nottinghamshire (1954–66, 172 matches).
Career batting
172–311–16–6799–134–23.04–7–*ct* 131
Bowling 5–0

He hit 1,000 runs in a season four times (best 1,552, av 30.43, in 1959). He was a noted table tennis player.

Wing, Derek Charles
Cricketer. *b:* 11.2.1943, Wisbech, Cambridgeshire. Lower order right-hand batsman, right-arm fast medium bowler. *Sch* Kimbolton. *Teams* MCC (1967–68); Minor Counties (1969–76). *Tours* MCC to West Africa 1975/6, to Bangladesh 1976/7, to Far East 1981/2 (none first-class).
Career batting
5–5–1–59–42–14.75–0–*ct* 1
Bowling 375–7–53.57–0–0–3/20

His County cricket was for Cambridgeshire, commencing 1964.

Wingfield, W.
Professional. Middle order batsman. *Team* Surrey (1881, 3 matches).
Career batting
3–6–0–13–5–2.16–0–*ct* 2

Wingfield, Rev William
Amateur. *b:* 30.9.1834, Newtown, Montgomeryshire. *d:* 18.4.1913, Coton Hill, Shrewsbury. Attacking middle order right-hand batsman, wicket-keeper. *Sch* Rossall. *Teams* Cambridge U (1855–57, blue all three years); Cambridgeshire (1857, 2 matches).
Career batting
14–25–1–314–69–13.08–0–*ct* 9–*st* 4
He played for Shropshire from 1853 to 1881. His final first-class match was for Gentlemen of the South in 1862. He was coxswain of the Cambridge boat in 1855 and 1856.

Wingfield-Digby, Rev Andrew Richard
Cricketer. *b:* 25.7.1950, Sherborne, Dorset. Lower order left-hand batsman, right-arm medium pace bowler. *Sch* Sherborne. *Team* Oxford U (1971–77, blue 1971, 1975, 1976 and 1977).
Career batting
39–62–4–720–69–12.41–0–*ct* 20
Bowling 3252–96–33.87–4–0–5/79
His County cricket has been for Dorset commencing 1972. After being at Oxford in 1971 and 1972, he returned in 1974 to study theology.

Winlaw, Ashley William Edgell
Amateur. *b:* 8.2.1914, Sydenham, Kent. Brother of R. de W. K. (Surrey). Middle order right-hand batsman, wicket-keeper. *Sch* Winchester. *Team* Minor Counties (1936).
Career batting
1–2–0–13–13–6.50–0–*ct* 1
He appeared in the Cambridge Freshmen's Match of 1934 and his County cricket was for Bedfordshire.

Winlaw, Roger de Winton Kelsall
Amateur. *b:* 28.3.1912, Morden, Surrey. *d:* 31.10.1942, Caernarvon. Brother of A. W. E. (Minor Counties). Middle order right-hand batsman. *Sch* Winchester. *Teams* Cambridge U (1932–34, blue all three years); Surrey (1932–34, 17 matches).
Career batting
52–89–13–2708–161*–35.63–7–*ct* 17
Bowling 31–0
He hit 1,330 runs, av 42.90, in 1934.
His final first-class match was for an England XI in 1937. He also played for Bedfordshire. He was killed in the same flying incident as C. T. Ashton (Essex).

Winn, Christopher Elliott
Amateur. *b:* 13.11.1926, Beckenham, Kent. Forceful middle order left-hand batsman. *Sch* KCS Wimbledon. *Teams* Oxford U (1948–51, blue all four years); Sussex (1948–52, 15 matches).
Career batting
59–100–2–2449–146*–24.98–2–*ct* 40–*st* 1
Bowling 34–1–34.00–0–0–1/21
His final first-class match was for MCC in 1961. A good rugby footballer, he played for Oxford and for England.

Winning, Samuel Charles
Amateur. *b:* 17.7.1889, New South Wales, Australia. *d:* 20.4.1967, Double Bay, Sydney, Australia. Lower order right-hand batsman, right-arm medium pace bowler. *Team* AIF (1919 to 1919/20). *Tours* AIF to England 1919, to South Africa 1919/20.
Career batting
28–35–17–253–30–14.05–0–*ct* 22
Bowling 1605–67–23.95–3–0–6/30
He took 51 wickets, av 22.82, for the AIF in 1919. His final first-class match was for AIF in Australia in 1919/20.

Winnington, John Francis Sartorius
Amateur. *b:* 17.9.1876, Martley, Worcestershire. *d:* 22.9.1918, Ramle, Palestine. Middle order right-hand batsman. *Team* Worcestershire (1908, 1 match).
Career batting
1–2–0–20–20–10.00–0–*ct* 0

Winrow, Frederick Henry
Professional. *b:* 17.1.1916, Manton, Notts. *d:* 19.8.1973, East London, South Africa. Brother of Robert (Notts). Sound middle order left-hand batsman, slow left-arm bowler. *Team* Nottinghamshire (1938–51, 113 matches).
Career batting
113–180–20–4769–204*–29.80–6–*ct* 34
Bowling 4009–95–42.20–3–0–6/65
He hit 1,000 runs in a season twice (best 1,459, av 37.41, in 1950). His only double century was 204* for Notts v Derbyshire at Trent Bridge in 1947. He emigrated to South Africa in 1952/3.

Winrow, Robert
Professional. *b:* 30.12.1910, Manton, Notts. Brother of F. H. (Notts). Middle order left-hand batsman, slow left-arm bowler. *Teams* Nottinghamshire (1932–35, 5 matches); Scotland (1949).
Career batting
7–10–1–237–137–26.33–1–*ct* 2
Bowling 76–1–76.00–0–0–1/27

Winslow, Lyndhurst
Amateur. *b:* 10.1.1855, Leamington, Warwickshire. *d:* 1910, Kingswilliamstown, South Africa. Cousin of O. E. (Sussex). Attacking middle order

right-hand batsman. *Sch* Somerset College. *Team* Sussex (1875, 5 matches).
Career batting
8–11–0–337–124–30.63–1–*ct* 4
Bowling 13–0

He emigrated to South Africa about 1876 and was a noted cricketer there, appearing in the Champion Bat Tournament and against the English touring team of 1888/9, but not in first-class matches.

Winslow, Dr Lyttelton Stewart Forbes
Amateur. *b:* 31.1.1844, London. *d:* 8.6.1913, Marylebone, London. Middle order batsman. *Sch* Rugby. *Team* MCC (1864).
Career batting
1–2–0–3–3–1.50–0–*ct* 0
Bowling 13–0

Winslow, Octavius Evans
Amateur. *b:* 10.9.1849, Leamington, Warwickshire. *d:* 13.10.1896, Bermondsey, London. Cousin of Lyndhurst (Sussex). Opening right-hand batsman, right-hand medium pace round-arm bowler, point field. *Sch* Somerset College. *Team* Sussex (1869, 5 matches).
Career batting
5–10–0–207–56–20.70–0–*ct* 1

Owing to a knee injury he rarely played after 1869.

Winslow, Paul Lyndhurst
Amateur. *b:* 21.5.1929, Johannesburg, South Africa. Forcing middle order right-hand batsman, right-arm leg break bowler, good field. *Teams* Sussex (1949, 1 match); Transvaal (1949/50 to 1955/6); Rhodesia (1956/7 to 1959/60). *Tour* South Africa to England 1955. *Tests* South Africa (1949/50 to 1955, 5 matches).
Career batting
75–124–6–2755–139–23.34–2–*ct* 85
Bowling 61–1–61.00–0–0–1/12
Test batting
5–9–0–186–108–20.66–1–*ct* 1

He was moderately successful on the 1955 tour to England and appeared in three Tests. His final first-class match was for a Rhodesian Invitation XI in 1961/2.

Winstone, Alec Ethelbert
Professional. *b:* 1879, Keynsham, Somerset. *d:* 29.3.1963, Staple Hill, Bristol. Middle order right-hand batsman, slow right-arm bowler. *Team* Gloucestershire (1906–09, 44 matches).
Career batting
44–80–3–975–58–12.66–0–*ct* 19
Bowling 130–4–32.50–0–0–1/12

Winter, Rev Arthur Henry
Amateur. *b:* 4.12.1844, Clapton, Middlesex. *d:* 31.12.1937, Hemingford Abbots, Huntingdonshire. Brother of William (Middlesex), uncle of G. E. (Middlesex) and C. E. (Cambridge U). Stylish opening right-hand batsman, wicket-keeper. *Sch* Westminster. *Teams*, Cambridge U (1865–67, blue all three years); Middlesex (1866–67, 3 matches).
Career batting
29–55–0–1155–121–21.00–1–*ct* 24–*st* 3

His final first-class match was for MCC in 1870. He also played for Huntingdonshire.

Winter, Charles Arthur
Amateur. *b:* 24.12.1903, London. *d:* 4.3.1982, Farnham Common, Buckinghamshire. Son of C. E. (Somerset). Lower order right-hand batsman, right-arm fast medium bowler. *Sch* Repton. *Team* Somerset (1921–25, 26 matches).
Career batting
26–47–7–437–44*–10.92–0–*ct* 5
Bowling 572–15–38.13–0–0–4/61

Winter, Cecil Esdaile
Amateur. *b:* 1.9.1879, Eastry, Kent. *d:* 20.7.1964, Hove, Sussex. Son of William (Middlesex), brother of G. E. (Middlesex), nephew of A. H. (Middlesex). Lower order right-hand batsman, wicket-keeper. *Sch* Uppingham. *Team* Cambridge U (1901–02, blue 1902).
Career batting
10–13–5–53–18–6.62–0–*ct* 7–*st* 11

Winter, Charles Edgar
Amateur. *b:* 9.10.1866, Bermondsey, London. *d:* 3.4.1954, Northwood, Middlesex. Father of C. A. (Somerset). Lower order batsman, right-arm fast bowler. *Team* Somerset (1882–95, 25 matches).
Career batting
25–45–8–319–62–8.62–0–*ct* 11
Bowling 1107–50–22.14–0–0–4/20

Winter, Charles Henry
Amateur. *b:* 17.2.1890, Philadelphia, USA. *d:* 25.1.1969, Wilmington, Delaware, USA. Tail end right-hand batsman, wicket-keeper. *Team* Philadelphia (1908–13). *Tours* Philadelphia to England 1908, to Jamaica 1908/9.
Career batting
12–21–9–52–14*–4.33–0–*ct* 13–*st* 16

He appeared in four matches for USA v Canada and was regarded as the leading wicket-keeper in America for some years.

Winter, Gerald Esdaile
Amateur. *b:* 29.11.1876, London. *d:* 17.1.1923,

Marylebone, London. Son of William (Middlesex), brother of C. E. (Oxford U), nephew of A. H. (Middlesex). Free scoring middle order right-hand batsman, right-hand slow under-arm bowler. *Sch* Winchester. *Teams* Cambridge U (1898–99, blue both years); Middlesex (1900, 2 matches). *Tour* Warner to North America 1898.
Career batting
22–37–2–738–86–21.08–0–*ct* 19
Bowling 527–22–23.95–1–1–6/59
His final first-class match was for Leveson-Gower's XI in 1902. He also appeared for Cambridgeshire.

Winter, H. E.
Amateur. Lower order batsman. *Team* Somerset (1884, 1 match).
Career batting
1–2–1–24–24*–24.00–0–*ct* 0
Bowling 9–0

Winter, John Arundell
Amateur. *b:* 28.7.1851, Taunton, Somerset. *d:* 15.5.1914, Hampton Wick, Middlesex. Middle order batsman. *Team* Somerset (1884, 1 match).
Career batting
1–2–0–4–4–2.00–0–*ct* 1

Winter, William
Amateur. *b:* 24.4.1843, Clapham Green, Surrey. *d:* 22.8.1905, Rosenlaui, near Meiringen, Berne, Switzerland. He was killed while mountaineering. Father of G. E. (Middlesex) and C. E. (Oxford U), brother of A. H. (Middlesex). Opening right-hand batsman, right-hand slow under-arm bowler, wicket-keeper. *Sch* Westminster. *Team* Middlesex (1873, 1 match).
Career batting
1–2–1–14–14*–14.00–0–*ct* 1–*st* 2
He also played for Huntingdonshire.

Winterbotham, Arthur Strachan
Amateur. *b:* 28.6.1864, Dursley, Gloucs. *d:* 15.6.1936, Stonehouse, Gloucs. Middle order right-hand batsman, right-arm slow bowler. *Sch* Rugby. *Team* Gloucestershire (1885, 3 matches).
Career batting
3–5–1–53–35–13.25–0–*ct* 0
Bowling 28–0

Winterbotham, James Percival
Amateur. *b:* 21.6.1883, Cheltenham, Gloucs. *d:* 2.12.1925, Cheltenham, Gloucs. Lower order left-hand batsman, slow left-arm bowler. *Sch* Cheltenham. *Teams* Gloucestershire (1902, 1 match); Oxford U (1903–04).
Career batting
3–6–3–25–12*–8.33–0–*ct* 3
Bowling 206–4–51.50–0–0–2/68
He represented Gloucestershire at both hockey and golf.

Winterburn, Frederick
Professional. *b:* 10.12.1857, London. *d:* 1926, Hackney, London. Tail end right-hand batsman, wicket-keeper. *Team* Middlesex (1883, 4 matches).
Career batting
4–5–1–19–8–4.75–0–*ct* 6–*st* 5

Winterflood, Thomas
Amateur. *b:* 1832. *d:* 20.2.1900, Brixton Hill, Surrey. Middle order batsman. *Team* Surrey Club (1866).
Career batting
1 match, did not bat–*ct* 0
Bowling 6–0
He was on the Committee of Surrey CCC for many years.

Winwood, Thomas Lawson
Amateur. *b:* 7.2.1910, Dudley, Worcestershire. Middle order right-hand batsman. *Team* Worcestershire (1930–34, 18 matches).
Career batting
18–30–4–404–104–15.53–1–*ct* 6
Bowling 10–0

Wisden, John
Professional. *b:* 5.9.1826, Brighton. *d:* 5.4.1884, Westminster, London. Lower order right-hand batsman, originally right-hand fast round-arm, but after about 1857, medium pace round-arm, or slow under-arm, bowler, good slip field. *Team* Sussex (1845–63, 82 matches); Kent (1854, 1 match); Middlesex (1859–63, 3 matches). *Tour* Parr to North America 1859 (not first-class).
Career batting
186–326–33–4140–148–14.12–2–*ct* 170–*st* 1
Bowling 7070–681+428–10.38–112–39–10/58
He took 100 wickets in a season three times (best 129 in 1849). He twice took 10 wickets in an innings, once against odds, and once for North v South at Lord's in 1850 (all bowled). In 1864 he published for the first time *John Wisden's Cricketers' Almanack.*

Wisdom, Nicholas
Cricketer. *b:* 18.3.1953, West Chiltington, Sussex. Lower order right-hand batsman, right-arm medium pace bowler. *Team* Sussex (1974, 2 matches).

Career batting
2–2–1–35–31*–35.00–0–*ct* 0
Bowling 33–2–16.50–0–0–1/0
He is the son of the comedian, Norman Wisdom.

Wisson, Philip Wesley
Amateur. *b:* 26.4.1935, Everton, Bedfordshire. Middle order right-hand batsman. *Sch* Enfield GS. *Team* Cambridge U (1958).
Career batting
2–4–0–24–14–6.00–0–*ct* 0
He was a useful goalkeeper with Cambridge Falcons.

Witchell, Henry Gough
Amateur. *b:* 8.4.1906, Dursley, Gloucs. *d:* 24.8.1965, Cotham Hill, Bristol. Middle order batsman. *Team* Gloucestershire (1923, 1 match).
Career batting
3–3–0–9–5–3.00–0–*ct* 0
His final first-class match was for Minor Counties in 1935, and after leaving Gloucestershire he played for Wiltshire.

Witherden, Edwin George
Professional. *b:* 1.5.1922, Goudhurst, Kent. Middle order right-hand batsman, off break bowler, slip field. *Team* Kent (1951–55, 40 matches).
Career batting
40–71–9–1380–125*–22.25–2–*ct* 13
Bowling 371–9–41.22–1–0–5/32
From 1956 to 1962 he appeared for Norfolk.

Witherington, Denys March
Amateur. *b:* 25.7.1921. *d:* 16.2.1944, Italy. Middle order right-hand batsman, wicket-keeper. *Sch* The Leys. *Team* Cambridge U (1939).
Career batting
4–7–2–147–52*–29.40–0–*ct* 5–*st* 1

Wolfe-Murray, James Archibald
Amateur. *b:* 25.4.1936, Edinburgh, Scotland. Lower order right-hand batsman, right-arm fast medium bowler. *Sch* Eton. *Team* Oxford U (1957).
Career batting
3–5–2–43–25–14.33–0–*ct* 3
Bowling 155–3–51.66–0–0–1/20

Wolfson, Andrew Cecil
Amateur. *b:* 1.5.1890, Santa Cruz, Canary Islands. *d:* 26.7.1978, Forest Row, Sussex. Lower order batsman, right-arm medium pace bowler. *Sch* Marlborough. *Team* Leveson-Gower's XI (1920).
Career batting
2–3–2–14–8–14.00–0–*ct* 0
Bowling 53–2–26.50–0–0–1/4

Wollocombe, Richard Henry
Amateur. *b:* 12.1.1926, Pachmarhi, India. Middle order right-hand batsman, leg break bowler. *Sch* Wellington. *Team* Oxford U (1951–52).
Career batting
9–16–2–314–119–22.42–1–*ct* 1
Bowling 623–10–62.30–0–0–2/33
His County cricket was for Berkshire.

Wolton, Albert Victor George
Professional. *b:* 12.6.1919, Maidenhead, Berkshire. Middle order right-hand batsman, right-arm off break bowler, good cover field. *Team* Warwickshire (1947–60, 296 matches).
Career batting
297–478–61–12930–165–31.00–12–*ct* 117
Bowling 1226–37–33.13–0–0–4/15
He hit 1,000 runs in a season seven times (best 1,809, av 34.13, in 1955). He also played for Berkshire.

Womersley, Leonard Dale
Amateur. *b:* 10.9.1891, Ingatestone, Essex. *d:* 10.2.1971, Chelmsford, Essex. Middle order batsman. *Sch* Marlborough. *Team* Essex (1910, 1 match.
Career batting
1–2–0–9–9–4.50–0–*ct* 0

Wood, Arthur
Professional. *b:* 25.8.1898, Fagley, Bradford, Yorkshire. *d:* 1.4.1973, Ilkley, Yorkshire. Lower order right-hand batsman, wicket-keeper. *Team* Yorkshire (1927–46, 408 matches). *Tours* Yorkshire to Jamaica 1935/6; Brinckman to South America 1937/8. *Tests* England (1938–39, 4 matches).
Career batting
420–500–83–8842–123*–21.20–1–*ct* 631–*st* 257
Bowling 33–1–33.00–0–0–1/33
Test batting
4–5–1–80–53–20.00–0–*ct* 10–*st* 1
He hit 1,249 runs, av 30.46, in 1935. His final first-class match was for an England XI in 1948.

Wood, Rear-Admiral Arthur Edmund
Amateur. *b:* 23.2.1875, Hartley-Wintney, Hampshire. *d:* 30.1.1961, Ryton, Co Durham. Middle order batsman. *Team* Royal Navy (1912).
Career batting
1–2–1–16–11*–16.00–0–*ct* 1
Bowling 12–0

Wood, Alfred Herbert
Amateur. *b:* 23.4.1866, Portsmouth, Hampshire. *d:* 19.4.1941, Southsea, Hampshire. Middle order batsman. *Sch* Wellington. *Team* Hampshire (1901, 1 match).
Career batting
1–2–0–22–11–11.00–0–*ct* 1

Wood, Arthur Hardy
Amateur. *b:* 25.5.1844, Thaddon, Alton, Hampshire. *d:* 10.7.1933, Steyning, Sussex. Middle order right-hand batsman, wicket-keeper. *Sch* Eton. *Team* Hampshire (1870–85, 28 matches).
Career batting
30–52–3–876–82–17.87–0–*ct* 25–*st* 5
Bowling 17–0
He captained Hampshire 1883 to 1885 and was President of the County Club in 1886. Well-known on the hunting field, he was Secretary of the Hampshire Hunt.

Wood, Arthur John
Amateur. *b:* 7.2.1892, Derby. *d:* 1.3.1951, Croydon, Surrey. Opening right-hand batsman, right-arm fast medium bowler. *Sch* Denstone. *Team* Derbyshire (1911–12, 13 matches).
Career batting
13–19–1–264–52–14.66–0–*ct* 5
Bowling 64–0
He appeared in the Cambridge Freshmen's Match of 1912.

Wood, Arthur Machin
Amateur for Derbyshire, but professional 1880 to 1885, then reverted to amateur. *b:* 21.2.1861, Pye Bridge, Derbyshire. *d:* 25.8.1947, Philadelphia, USA. Sound opening right-hand batsman, right-arm slow bowler, excellent field. *Sch* Nottingham HS. *Teams* Derbyshire (1879, 2 matches); Philadelphia (1893–1908). *Tours* Philadelphia to England 1897, 1903 and 1908.
Career batting
59–105–3–2038–132–19.98–2–*ct* 72
Bowling 43–0
He played for Nottinghamshire v Leicestershire (not first-class) in 1878. He was for many years one of the principal batsmen in Philadelphia and represented USA v Canada seven times commencing 1892. His most successful tour to England was in 1897 when he hit 702 runs, av 28.08.

Wood, Barry
Cricketer. *b:* 26.12.1942, Ossett, Yorkshire. Brother of Ronald (Yorkshire). Sound opening right-hand batsman, right-arm medium pace bowler. *Teams* Yorkshire (1964, 5 matches); Lancashire (1966-79, 260 matches); Derbyshire (1980–83, 63 matches); Eastern Province (1971/2 to 1973/4). *Tours* MCC to India, Pakistan and Sri Lanka 1972/3, to New Zealand 1974/5; English Counties to West Indies 1974/5 (not first-class); International Wanderers to Rhodesia 1975/6. *Tests* England (1972-78, 12 matches).
Career batting
357–591–75–17453–198–33.82–30–*ct* 283
Bowling 9160–298–30.73–8–0–7/52
Test batting
12–21–0–454–90–21.61–0–*ct* 6
Bowling 50–0
He hit 1,000 runs in a season eight times (best 1,492, av 38.25, in 1971). In 1981 he captained Derbyshire. His Testimonial in 1979 raised £62,429.

Wood, Christopher H.
Professional. *b:* 23.7.1934, Bradford, Yorkshire. Lower order right-hand batsman, right-arm fast medium bowler. *Team* Yorkshire (1959, 4 matches).
Career batting
4–4–1–22–10–7.33–0–*ct* 1
Bowling 319–11–29.00–0–0–4/39

Wood, Cecil John Burditt
Amateur to 1895, professional 1896, reverted to amateur 1897. *b:* 21.11.1875, Northampton. *d:* 5.6.1960, Leicester. Stubborn opening right-hand batsman, right-arm slow bowler. *Sch* Wellingborough. *Teams* Leicestershire (1896–1923, 423 matches); London County (1900–04).
Career batting
456–823–54–23879–225–31.05–37–*ct* 180
Bowling 6782–172–39.43–3–0–6/79
He hit 1,000 runs in a season 13 times, going on to 2,000 once: 2,033, av 41.48, in 1901. Both his double centuries were for Leicestershire the higher being 225 v Worcs at Worcester in 1906. He captained the County in 1914, 1919 and 1920. He carried his bat through the completed Leicestershire innings no less than 17 times and in the match v Yorkshire at Bradford in 1911 in both innings. He appeared for Northants in 1895 (not first-class). He was Leicestershire Secretary in 1940 and 1941. A good soccer player, he appeared for Leicester Fosse.

Wood, Douglas James
Professional. *b:* 19.5.1914, Horsted Keynes, Sussex. Tail end right-hand batsman, left-arm fast medium bowler. *Team* Sussex (1936–55, 213 matches).

Career batting
214–251–72–1305–42–7.29–0–*ct* 89
Bowling 18140–589–30.79–21–1–7/24
He took 103 wickets, av 24.56, in 1952.

Wood, Major General Edward Alexander
Amateur. *b:* 8.5.1841, Kensington, London. *d:* 22.5.1898, Shorncliffe, Kent. Middle order batsman. *Sch* Radley and Eton. *Team* MCC (1875).
Career batting
1–2–1–8–8–8.00–0–*ct* 1

Wood, Edwin James
Professional. *b:* 1868, Loughborough, Leicestershire. Lower order batsman, wicket-keeper. *Team* Leicestershire (1907, 1 match).
Career batting
1–2–0–1–1–0.50–0–*ct* 2–*st* 1

Wood, Geoffrey Dayrell
Amateur. *b:* 17.8.1891, Hampstead, London. *d:* 13.10.1915, Loos, France. He was killed in action. Lower order batsman, slow left-arm bowler. *Sch* Cheltenham. *Team* Oxford U (1912).
Career batting
1–1–0–0–0–0.00–0–*ct* 0
Bowling 36–2–18.00–0–0–1/16
His County cricket was for Suffolk.

Wood, George Edward Charles
Amateur. *b:* 22.8.1893, Blackheath, Kent. *d:* 18.3.1971, Christchurch, Hampshire. Opening or middle order right-hand batsman, right-arm medium pace bowler, excellent wicket-keeper. *Sch* Cheltenham. *Teams* Cambridge U (1913–20, blue 1914, 1919 and 1920); Kent (1919–27, 41 matches). *Tour* Martineau to Egypt 1929 (not first-class). *Tests* England (1924, 3 matches).
Career batting
100–157–18–2773–128–19.94–1–*ct* 116–*st* 53
Bowling 9–0
Test batting
3–2–0–7–6–3.50–0–*ct* 5–*st* 1
His final first-class match was for H. D. G. Leveson-Gower's XI in 1936.
Whilst at Cambridge he also gained blues for rugby football and hockey.

Wood, George Henry
Amateur. *b:* 21.5.1846, Liverpool. Lower order batsman, useful bowler. *Team* MCC (1880–82).
Career batting
2–3–1–2–2–1.00–0–*ct* 0
Bowling 22–0

Wood, Graeme Malcolm
Cricketer. *b:* 6.11.1956, East Fremantle, Western Australia. Opening left-hand batsman, right-arm medium pace bowler. *Team* Western Australia (1976/7 to 1982/3, 42 matches). *Tours* Australia to West Indies 1977/8, to India 1979/80, to England 1980, 1981, to New Zealand 1981/2, to Pakistan 1982/3, to Sri Lanka 1980/1, 1982/3. *Tests* Australia (1977/8 to 1982/3, 42 matches).
Career batting
112–196–13–6486–151–35.44–15–*ct* 88
Bowling 127–5–25.40–0–0–3/18
Test batting
42–81–5–2554–126–33.60–7–*ct* 32
On the 1981 tour to England he hit 690 runs, av 31.36, and played in all six Tests, but with only moderate success.

Wood, Rev George Robert
Amateur. *b:* 7.12.1865, Reading, Berkshire. *d:* 3.9.1948, Lyme Regis, Dorset. Middle order right-hand batsman. *Sch* Haileybury. *Team* Somerset (1893–94, 3 matches).
Career batting
3–5–0–84–52–16.80–0–*ct* 1

Wood, George William
Professional. *b:* 18.11.1862, Huddersfield, Yorkshire. *d:* 4.12.1948, Huddersfield, Yorkshire. Lower order batsman, wicket-keeper. *Team* Yorkshire (1895, 2 matches).
Career batting
2–2–0–2–2–1.00–0–*ct* 0–*st* 1

Wood, Henry
Amateur. *b:* 1872, Bath, Somerset. *b:* 1.12.1950, Bath, Somerset. Middle order batsman. *Team* Somerset (1904, 1 match).
Career batting
1–2–2–16–12*–no av–0–*ct* 0

Wood, Henry
Professional. *b:* 14.12.1853, Dartford, Kent. *d:* 30.4.1919, Waddon, Surrey. Middle order right-hand batsman, right-hand fast round-arm bowler, excellent wicket-keeper. *Teams* Kent (1876–82, 9 matches); Surrey (1884–1900, 286 matches). *Tours* Warton to South Africa 1888/9; Read to South Africa 1891/2. *Tests* England (1888 to 1891/2, 4 matches).
Career batting
316–422–96–5523–134*–16.94–1–*ct* 556–*st* 118
Bowling 42–0
Test batting
4–4–1–204–134*–68.00–1–*ct* 2–*st* 1
His only first-class century was scored in the 1891/2 Test Match at Cape Town.

Wood, Rev Hugh
Amateur. *b:* 22.3.1855, Sheffield, Yorkshire. *d:*

31.7.1941, Whitchurch, Buckinghamshire. Lower order right-hand batsman, slow left-arm bowler, close field. *Teams* Cambridge U (1878–79, blue 1879); Yorkshire (1879–80, 10 matches).
Career batting
21–26–3–217–36–9.43–0–*ct* 16
Bowling 759–67–11.32–5–1–7.41

Wood, Rev Henry Thellusson
Amateur. *b:* 1850, Aldbury, Hertfordshire. *d:* 21.7.1928, Aldbury, Hertfordshire. Middle order right-hand batsman. *Team* An All England Eleven (1872).
Career batting
1–2–0–43–43–21.50–0–*ct* 2
His County cricket was for Hertfordshire.

Wood, James
Professional. *b:* 26.6.1933, Royton, Lancashire. *d:* 30.6.1977, Blackpool, Lancashire. Lower order right-hand batsman, bowler. *Team* Lancashire (1956, 1 match).
Career batting
1 match, did not bat–*ct* 1
Bowling 103–4–25.75–0–0–3/56

Wood, Sir John Barry
Amateur. *b:* 27.4.1870, Cheltenham, Gloucestershire. *d:* 10.2.1933, Virginia Water, Surrey. Middle order right-hand batsman, right-hand slow under-arm bowler, good field. *Sch* Marlborough. *Team* Oxford U (1891–93, blue 1892 and 1893).
Career batting
16–30–3–384–50–14.22–0–*ct* 10
Bowling 1399–53–26.39–3–0–6/68
He played for Warwickshire in 1890 (pre-first-class).

Wood, J. H.
Amateur. Middle order batsman, long stop. *Team* Yorkshire (1881, 2 matches).
Career batting
2–1–0–14–14–14.00–0–*ct* 0

Wood, Lindsay Jonathan
Cricketer. *b:* 12.5.1961, Ruislip, Middlesex. Lower order left-hand batsman, slow left-arm bowler. *Team* Kent (1981–82, 2 matches).
Career batting
2–2–0–5–5–2.50–0–*ct* 0
Bowling 182–4–45.50–0–0–4/124

Wood, Sir Matthew
Amateur. *b:* 21.9.1857, Isle of Wight. *d:* 13.7.1908, Westminster, London. Middle order right-hand batsman, slow under-arm bowler. *Sch* Winchester. *Team* Hampshire (1876, 1 match).
Career batting
1–2–0–0–0–0.00–0–*ct* 0
He also played for Essex (pre-first-class).

Wood, Maurice
Professional. *b:* 6.7.1933, Nottingham. *d:* 18.3.1978, Nottingham. Lower order right-hand batsman, right-arm fast medium bowler. *Team* Nottinghamshire (1955, 4 matches).
Career batting
4–5–2–5–4–1.66–0–*ct* 2
Bowling 231–4–57.75–0–0–2/68

Wood, Maxmillian David Francis
Amateur. *b:* 22.2.1873, Kamptee, India. *d:* 22.8.1915, Near Ismail Oglu Tepe, Gallipoli Peninsula, Turkey. Middle order right-hand batsman, right-arm fast medium bowler, good outfield. *Sch* Wellington. *Teams* Europeans (1897/8 to 1902/3); Hampshire (1907, 1 match).
Career batting
10–19–0–196–30–10.31–0–*ct* 8
Bowling 483–34–14.20–1–0–6/51
His final first-class match was for Leveson-Gower's XI in 1909.

Wood, Reginald
Amateur. *b:* 7.3.1860, Woodchurch, Cheshire. *d:* 6.1.1915, Manly, New South Wales, Australia. Middle order left-hand batsman, left-arm medium pace bowler. *Sch* Charterhouse. *Teams* Lancashire (1880–84, 6 matches); Victoria (1886/7, 2 matches). *Tour* Lillywhite, Shaw and Shrewsbury to Australia 1886/7 (co-opted into the team for three matches). *Test* England (1886/7, 1 match).
Career batting
12–20–5–235–52–15.66–0–*ct* 4
Bowling 134–8–16.75–0–0–3/19
Test batting
1–2–0–6–6–3.00–0–*ct* 0

Wood, Ronald
Professional. *b:* 3.6.1929, Ossett, Yorkshire. Brother of Barry (Yorkshire, Lancashire and Derbyshire). Lower order left-hand batsman, slow left-arm bowler. *Team* Yorkshire (1952–56, 22 matches).
Career batting
22–18–4–60–17–4.28–0–*ct* 5
Bowling 1346–51–26.39–3–0–8/45

Wood, Russell Brown
Amateur. *b:* 15.12.1929, Ashley Hill, Bristol. Solid lower order right-hand batsman, wicket-keeper. *Team* Gloucestershire (1950–51, 8 matches).
Career batting
8–12–3–110–48–12.22–0–*ct* 1–*st* 2

Wood, Sir Samuel Hill
(assumed name Hill-Wood in 1910)
Amateur. *b:* 21.3.1872, Glossop, Derbyshire. *d:* 4.1.1949, Westminster, London. Father of B. S. H., C. K. H., D. J. C. H., and W. W. H. (all Derbyshire). Middle order right-arm batsman. *Sch* Eton. *Team* Derbyshire (1894–1902, 34 matches).
Career batting
34–54–11–758–81*–17.62–0–*ct* 12
Bowling 50–0

He captained Derbyshire 1899 to 1901. Later he appeared occasionally for Suffolk. A noted figure in football, he built up his own club at Glossop, which played in the Football League prior to the 1914–18 war. In 1927 he became Chairman of Arsenal and remained in office until his death. From 1910 to 1929 he represented the High Peak Division of Derbyshire in the Conservative interest.

Wood, T.
Amateur. Middle order batsman. *Team* Somerset (1894, 1 match).
Career batting
1–1–0–11–11–11.00–0–*ct* 0

Wood, W.
Professional. Lower order batsman, useful bowler. *Team* Surrey (1883, 2 matches).
Career batting
2–4–0–9–8–2.25–0–*ct* 1
Bowling 44–1–44.00–0–0–1/22

Woodcock, Arthur
Professional. *b:* 23.9.1865, Northampton. *d:* 14.5.1910, Billesdon, Leics. He died from self-administered poison. Tail end right-hand batsman, right-arm fast bowler. *Teams* Leicestershire (1894–1908, 121 matches); London County (1900).
Career batting
137–227–41–1547–62*–8.31–0–*ct* 35
Bowling 12211–548–22.28–38–9–9/28

He took 102 wickets, av 19.29, in 1895. His best innings analysis was 9 for 28 for Leicestershire v MCC in 1899 at Lord's. For a few years he was regarded as the fastest bowler in England (bar Kortright). His debut for Leicestershire was in 1889.

Woodcock, Rev George
Amateur. *b:* 21.4.1894, Warrington, Lancashire. *d:* 22.2.1968, Bruton, Somerset. Lower order right-hand batsman, right-arm medium pace bowler. *Team* Somerset (1921, 1 match).
Career batting
1–2–0–68–63–34.00–0–*ct* 0
Bowling 119–4–29.75–0–0–4/119

Woodcock, Roy Gordon
Amateur. *b:* 26.11.1934, Burnley, Lancashire. Lower order right-hand batsman, slow left-arm bowler. *Sch* Worcester RGS. *Team* Oxford U (1956–58, blue 1957 and 1958).
Career batting
29–52–9–779–57–18.11–0–*ct* 17
Bowling 1793–53–33.83–0–0–4/54

Woodford, John Douglas
Cricketer. *b:* 9.9.1943, Little Horton, Bradford, Yorkshire. Opening right-hand batsman, right-arm medium pace bowler. *Team* Yorkshire (1968–72, 38 matches).
Career batting
38–61–2–1204–101–20.40–1–*ct* 12
Bowling 185–4–46.25–0–0–2/20

He played for Northumberland commencing 1975.

Woodfull, William Maldon
Amateur. *b:* 22.8.1897, Maldon, Victoria, Australia. *d:* 11.8.1965, nr Tweed Heads, New South Wales, Australia. He collapsed and died while playing golf. Defensive opening right-hand batsman. *Team* Victoria (1921/2 to 1933/4, 59 matches). *Tours* Australia to England 1926, 1930, 1934, to New Zealand 1927/8; Victoria to New Zealand 1924/5. *Tests* Australia (1926–34, 35 matches).
Career batting
174–245–39–13388–284–64.99–49–*ct* 78
Bowling 24–1–24.00–0–0–1/12
Test batting
35–54–4–2300–161–46.00–7–*ct* 7

He captained Australia on both the 1930 and 1934 tours, as well as during the controversial 1932/3 Bodyline series in Australia. As a batsman he proved successful on all three visits to England, averaging over 50 and scoring over 1,000 runs on each visit (best 1,672, av 57.65, in 1926). His highest score was 284 for Australians v New Zealand XI at Auckland in 1927/8. He played in all Tests on each tour. Of his seven double centuries three were hit in England, the highest being 228* v Glamorgan at Swansea in 1934. In all he led Australia in 25 Tests. His last first-class match was for W. M. Woodfull's XI in 1934/5.

Woodgate, Thomas William
Amateur. *b:* May 1857, Holborn, London. *d:* 30.1.1929, Hammersmith, London. Middle order

right-hand batsman. *Sch* Uppingham. *Team* Surrey (1877, 1 match).
Career batting
1–2–0–11–11–5.50–0–*ct* 0

Woodhams, Edwin Fehrsen
Amateur. *b:* 1880, Eastbourne, Sussex. *d:* 8.2.1933, Brighton, Sussex. Middle order batsman. *Team* Sussex (1905, 1 match).
Career batting
1–2–1–14–14*–14.00–0–*ct* 1

Woodhead, David Leonard
Cricketer. *b:* 17.3.1940, Birmingham. Middle order right-hand batsman, leg break bowler. *Team* Cambridge U (1968).
Career batting
8–15–1–190–68–13.57–0–*ct* 2
Bowling 190–0

Woodhead, Frank Ellis
Amateur. *b:* 29.5.1868, Woodthorpe, Huddersfield, Yorkshire. *d:* 25.8.1943, Edgerton, Huddersfield, Yorkshire. Sound middle order right-hand batsman, right-arm medium fast bowler. *Sch* Loretto. *Teams* Cambridge U (1889); Yorkshire (1893–94, 4 matches).
Career batting
5–10–0–57–18–5.70–0–*ct* 4
Bowling 4–1–4.00–0–0–1/4

Woodhead, Francis Gerald
Professional. *b:* 30.10.1912, Edwinstowe, Notts. Lower order right-hand batsman, right-arm fast medium bowler. *Team* Nottinghamshire (1934–50, 141 matches).
Career batting
141–174–44–1100–52*–8.46–0–*ct* 80
Bowling 10550–320–32.96–11–1–7/24

His best season was 1938 when he took 69 wickets, av 25.04. From 1970 to 1979 he was coach to Nottinghamshire CCC.

Woodhouse, Arthur James Powys
Amateur. *b:* 20.10.1933, Sidcup, Kent. Middle order right-hand batsman, right-arm medium pace bowler. *Sch* Oundle. *Team* Free Foresters (1957).
Career batting
1–2–0–29–17–14.50–0–*ct* 0
Bowling 20–1–20.00–0–0–1/20

Woodhouse, George Edward Sealy
Amateur. *b:* 15.2.1924, Blandford, Dorset. Stylish middle order right-hand batsman. *Sch* Marlborough. *Team* Somerset (1946–53, 58 matches).
Career batting
65–118–14–2048–109–19.69–1–*ct* 18–*st* 1
Bowling 8–1–8.00–0–0–1/8

He played for Cambridge U in 1943 (not first-class). In 1948 he was joint-captain of Somerset and sole captain in 1949. A good rugby footballer, he gained a war-time blue at Cambridge and also appeared for Dorset and Wiltshire.

Woodhouse, William Henry
Amateur. *b:* 16.4.1856, Bradford, Yorkshire. *d:* 4.3.1938, Bradford, Yorkshire. Middle order batsman. *Team* Yorkshire (1884–85, 9 matches).
Career batting
9–13–0–218–63–16.76–0–*ct* 6

Woodland, Albert William
Professional. *b:* 10.6.1895, Conisbrough, Yorkshire. *d:* 31.1.1955, Mansfield, Notts. Lower order right-hand batsman, right-arm fast medium bowler. *Team* Derbyshire (1920, 2 matches).
Career batting
2–4–1–27–19*–9.00–0–*ct* 1
Bowling 69–0

Woodman, Reginald George
Amateur. *b:* 11.8.1905, Bristol. *d:* 20.5.1980, Bristol. Middle order right-hand batsman. *Team* Gloucestershire (1925, 2 matches).
Career batting
2–3–0–4–2–1.33–0–*ct* 0

Woodroffe, Alfred
Professional. *b:* 1.9.1918, Birmingham. *d:* 23.7.1964, Sutton Coldfield, Warwickshire. Middle order left-hand batsman. *Team* Warwickshire (1947–48, 4 matches).
Career batting
4–7–0–77–41–11.00–0–*ct* 3

Woodroffe, Kenneth Herbert Clayton
Amateur. *b:* 9.12.1892, Lewes, Sussex. *d:* 9.5.1915, near Neuve Chapelle, France. He was killed in action. Lower order right-hand batsman, right-arm fast bowler. *Sch* Marlborough. *Teams* Hampshire (1912–13, 2 matches); Cambridge U (1913–14, blue both years); Sussex (1914, 2 matches).
Career batting
18–29–8–172–22*–8.19–0–*ct* 5
Bowling 1500–55–27.27–2–0–6/43

Woods, Basil Joseph Pontifex
Amateur. *b:* 28.8.1922, South Africa. Lower order right-hand batsman, leg break and googly bowler. *Team* Cambridge U (1951).

Career batting
2–2–0–1–1–0.50–0–*ct* 0
Bowling 108–3–36.00–0–0–2/61

Woods, Charles Pound
Amateur. *b:* 1878, Swinton, Lancashire. *d:* 1.7.1940, Llandudno, Caernarvonshire. Middle order right-hand batsman. *Team* Wales (1930).
Career batting
1–2–0–9–5–4.50–0–*ct* 0
He played for Cheshire before the First World War and afterwards captained Caernarvonshire, being also Secretary of the North Wales Cricket Association.

Woods, Samuel Moses James
Amateur. *b:* 13.4.1867, Ashfield, New South Wales, Australia. *d:* 30.4.1931, Taunton, Somerset. Attacking middle order right-hand batsman, right-arm fast medium bowler. *Sch* Brighton. *Teams* Cambridge U (1888–91, blue all four years); Somerset (1891–1910, 299 matches). *Tours* Australia to England 1888; Hawke to North America 1891, to South Africa 1895/6; Priestley to West Indies 1896/7; Ranjitsinhji to North America 1899; MacLaren to Australia 1901/2 (he did not play in first-class matches).- *Tests* Australia (1888, 3 matches); England (1895/6, 3 matches).
Career batting
401–690–35–15345–215–23.42–19–*ct* 279
Bowling 21653–1040–20.82–77–21–10/69
Test batting
6–10–0–154–53–15.40–0–*ct* 5
Bowling 250–10–25.00–0–0–3/28
He hit 1,000 runs in a season four times (best 1,405, av 34.26, in 1895). He took 100 wickets in a season twice (best 153, av 16.83, in 1892). His only double century was 215 for Somerset v Sussex at Hove in 1895, and his best innings bowling analysis 10 for 69 for Cambridge U v C. I. Thornton's XI at Fenner's in 1890. He captained Somerset from 1894 to 1906. He was Secretary of Somerset until 1923. An excellent rugby footballer, he played for Cambridge, Somerset and England as wing forward. He also played soccer for Sussex.

Wood-Sims, William Wood
(originally Sims)
Amateur, changed to professional in 1884. *b:* 10.2.1858, Ironville, Derbyshire. *d:* 30.11.1926, Lambeth, London. Sound opening right-hand batsman. *Team* Derbyshire (1879–86, 23 matches).
Career batting
25–45–2–518–46–12.04–0–*ct* 13
Bowling 70–5–14.00–0–0–3/22

Woodward, Edwin
Professional. *b:* 17.9.1864, Sutton-in-Ashfield, Notts. *d:* 15.12.1953, Mansfield, Notts. Lower order right-hand batsman, right-arm medium pace bowler. *Team* Liverpool and District XI (1888–90).
Career batting
2–4–0–19–13–4.75–0–*ct* 1
Bowling 50–2–25.00–0–0–2/38
His County cricket was for Cheshire 1886–93.

Woodward, Kenneth Alexander
Amateur. *b:* 23.12.1874, Liverpool, Lancashire. *d:* 24.12.1950, Charlton Kings, Gloucs. Middle order right-hand batsman, right-arm medium pace bowler, excellent deep field. *Sch* Harrow. *Teams* Oxford U (1896); Derbyshire (1909, 2 matches).
Career batting
3–6–1–23–7–4.60–0–*ct* 0
He also appeared for Herefordshire.

Woof, William Albert
Professional. *b:* 9.7.1858, Gloucester. *d:* 4.4.1937, Cheltenham, Gloucs. Tail end right-hand batsman, originally fast, then slow left-arm bowler, slip field. *Team* Gloucestershire (1878–1902, 140 matches).
Career batting
160–258–63–1274–43–6.53–0–*ct* 119
Bowling 13369–754–17.73–69–11–8/70
He took 100 wickets in a season twice (best 116, av 18.21, in 1884). He played very little County cricket after 1894 and for some years was a first-class umpire.

Wookey, Stephen Mark
Cricketer. *b:* 2.9.1954, Upavon, Wiltshire. Lower order right-hand batsman, right-arm medium pace bowler. *Sch* Malvern. *Teams* Cambridge U (1975–76, blue both years); Oxford U (1978–80, blue 1978).
Career batting
19–27–6–260–48–12.38–0–*ct* 5
Bowling 1158–28–41.35–0–0–3/61
He attained the unusual distinction of being awarded his cricket blue at both Universities.
His County cricket was for Wiltshire.

Wooler, Charles Robert Dudley
Professional. *b:* 30.6.1930, Bulawayo, Rhodesia. Lower order right-hand batsman, right-arm fast medium bowler. *Teams* Leicestershire (1949–51, 51 matches); Rhodesia (1951/2 to 1956/7).
Career batting
60–93–16–835–49*–10.84–0–*ct* 16
Bowling 4030–130–31.00–3–0–5/47

Wooley, Gilbert George
Amateur. *b:* 1896. *d:* 8.2.1953, Gloucester. Middle order right-hand batsman. *Team* Gloucestershire (1920, 1 match).
Career batting
1–2–0–0–0–0.00–0–*ct* 0

Woolfries, Simon Andrew
Cricketer. *b:* 10.1.1953, Moreton-in-Marsh, Gloucs. Middle order right-hand batsman, off break bowler. *Team* Cambridge U (1972).
Career batting
1–1–0–3–3–3.00–0–*ct* 0

Woolhouse, William Henry
Professional. *b:* 21.1.1791, Sheffield, Yorkshire. *d:* 14.7.1837, London. Opening left-hand batsman, left-hand round-arm bowler. *Team* Yorkshire (1832–34, 6 matches).
Career batting
17–33–2–440–51–14.19–0–*ct* 18

His debut was for Sheffield and Leicester in 1826. He was the most influential Yorkshire cricketer of his day and was responsible of the laying out of two early Sheffield cricket grounds at Darnall and at Hyde Park. He went to London in 1837 to seek medical advice for an ailment, but died before he could return home.

Woollatt, Randal James
Amateur. *b:* 19.7.1909, Surbiton, Surrey. *d:* 9.4.1984, Cheltenham, Gloucs. Middle order right-hand batsman. *Sch* Cheltenham. *Team* Minor Counties (1930).
Career batting
1–1–0–13–13–13.00–0–*ct* 0

He played for Surrey 2nd XI.

Wooller, Wilfred
Amateur. *b:* 20.11.1912, Rhos-on-Sea, Denbighshire. Militant middle order right-hand batsman, right-arm medium fast bowler, brilliant close field. *Sch* Rydal. *Teams* Cambridge U (1935–36, blue both years); Glamorgan (1938–62, 400 matches).
Career batting
430–679–77–13593–128–22.57–5–*ct* 412
Bowling 25830–958–26.96–43–5–8/45

He hit 1,000 runs in a season five times (best 1,270, av 27.02, in 1947) and took 100 wickets twice (best 120, av 24.55, in 1949). In 1954 he completed the 'double'. He captained Glamorgan from 1947 to 1960 and was Secretary of the County Club until 1978. From 1955 to 1962 he was a Test Selector. He played for Denbighshire in 1933 and 1934. A noted rugby footballer he played for Cambridge and Wales.

Woollett, Anthony Frank
Professional. *b:* 20.9.1927, Lambeth, London. Opening left-hand batsman. *Team* Kent (1950–54, 44 matches).
Career batting
44–81–4–1445–96–18.76–0–*ct* 16

He also played for Berkshire.

Woolley, Albert
Professional. *b:* 26.9.1902, Salford, Lancashire. *d:* 5.1.1978, Doncaster, Yorkshire. Lower order right-hand batsman, right-arm fast medium bowler. *Team* Lancashire (1926, 7 matches).
Career batting
7–9–0–61–24–6.77–0–*ct* 9
Bowling 351–11–31.90–0–0–4/56

Woolley, Claud Neville
Professional. *b:* 5.5.1886, Tonbridge, Kent. *d:* 3.11.1962, Northampton. Brother of F. E. (Kent). Sound opening right-hand batsman, right-arm slow medium bowler. *Teams* Gloucestershire (1909, 1 match); Northants (1911–31, 362 matches).
Career batting
365–658–34–15395–204*–24.67–13–*ct* 137
Bowling 11654–352–33.10–12–1–6/30

He hit 1,000 runs in a season seven times (best 1,602, av 29.66, in 1928). His highest score was 214 for Northants v Worcestershire at Northampton in 1921. He was on the first-class umpires' list and stood in one Test. In 1949 he became groundsman at the County Ground, Northampton, retiring in 1961.

Woolley, Frank Edward
Professional. *b:* 27.5.1887, Tonbridge, Kent. *d:* 18.10.1978, Halifax, Nova Scotia. Brother of C. N. (Gloucs and Northants). Attractive middle order left-hand batsman, left-arm medium, later slow, bowler, brilliant slip field. *Team* Kent (1906–38, 764 matches). *Tours* MCC to South Africa 1909/10, 1913/14, 1922/3, to Australia 1911/12, 1920/1, 1924/5, to Australia and New Zealand 1929/30. *Tests* England (1909–34, 64 matches).
Career batting
978–1530–84–58959–305*–40.77–145–*ct* 1018
Bowling 41058–2066–19.87–132–28–8/22
Test batting
64–98–7–3283–154–36.07–5–*ct* 64
Bowling 2815–83–33.91–4–1–7/76

One of the greatest of the game's all-rounders, he holds the record for the most catches taken by a fielder in a first-class career. As a batsman he was both elegant and fast scoring and his bowling was a feature of the early part of his career – for his final ten seasons he was rarely used.

No less than 28 times he scored over 1,000 runs in a season, going on to 2,000 13 times and thence to 3,000 once: 3,352, av 60.94, in 1928. He hit six double centuries for Kent, one for the MCC in Australia and one for the Rest of England v Yorkshire, but his highest innings was 305 not out for MCC v Tasmania at Hobart in 1911/12.

Eight times he reached 100 wickets in a season, his best year being 1920 with 185 wickets, av 14.23. In each of those eight seasons he also completed the 'double' and in four of them the feat of 2,000 runs and 100 wickets – no other cricketer achieved this feat on four occasions.

Although he first appeared for England in the fifth Test of the 1909 series, his first real opportunity for England in England came in 1912 when he headed the Test bowling averages with 17 wickets, av 8.94, and scored 246 runs, av 30.75. His next home series was not until 1921 when he hit 343 runs, av 42.87. In the 1926 series he scored 237 runs, av 39.50, and that was his last Test series against Australia as a regular member of the England side, though he appeared twice in 1930 and made a final appearance, aged 47, in the Oval Test of 1934.

His most successful tour overseas was in 1911/12 in Australia, when he hit 781 runs, av 55.78.

Woolley, Kenneth McDowell
Amateur. *b:* 9.12.1924. Lower order batsman, useful bowler. *Team* Cambridge U (1947).
Career batting
1–2–0–4–4–2.00–0–*ct* 0
Bowling 56–0

Woolmer, Robert Andrew
Cricketer. *b:* 14.5.1948, Kanpur, India. Son of C. S. (Uttar Pradesh). Stylish middle order, later opening right-hand batsman, right-arm medium pace bowler. *Teams* Kent (1968–83, 271 matches); Natal (1973/4 to 1975/6); Western Province (1980/1). *Tours* Robins to South Africa 1973/4; England to India, Sri Lanka and Australia 1976/7; SAB to South Africa 1981/2. *Tests* England (1975–81, 19 matches).
Career batting
342–531–72–15345–203–33.43–33–*ct* 234–*st* 1
Bowling 10817–415–26.06–12–1–7/47
Test batting
19–34–2–1059–149–33.09–3–*ct* 10
Bowling 299–4–74.75–0–0–1/8

He hit 1,000 runs in a season five times (best 1,749, av 47.27, in 1976). Following his 1981/2 tour to South Africa he was banned from Test cricket for three years, but in fact he lost his place in the England team during the 1981 series v Australia. His highest innings was 203 for Kent v Sussex at Tunbridge Wells in 1982.

Woosnam, Maxwell
Amateur. *b:* 6.9.1892, Liverpool. *d:* 14.7.1965, Marylebone, London. Opening batsman. *Sch* Winchester. *Team* Cambridge U (1912).
Career batting
2–2–0–14–13–7.00–0–*ct* 4

His County cricket was for Cheshire. A brilliant all-round sportsman he played soccer for Manchester City and England at centre-half. In 1921 he won the tennis doubles at Wimbledon, and later captained the English Davis Cup Team and he also won an Olympic Gold Medal in Antwerp in 1920 in the men's doubles.

Wooster, Reginald
Amateur. *b:* 1903, Kettering, Northants. *d:* 12.9.1968, Kettering, Northants. Lower order right-hand batsman, right-arm medium pace bowler. *Team* Northants (1925, 1 match).
Career batting
1–1–0–6–6–6.00–0–*ct* 0
Bowling 77–6–12.83–1–0–5/54

He performed the hat-trick in his only first-class match – Northants v Dublin University at Northampton in 1925.

Wootton, George
Professional. *b:* 16.10.1834, Clifton, Notts. *d:* 15.6.1924, Ruddington, Notts. Lower order left-hand batsman, left-hand fast round-arm bowler. *Team* Nottinghamshire (1861–71, 52 matches).
Career batting
186–301–68–2431–64*–10.43–0–*ct* 143
Bowling 12501–962+22–12.99–87–34–10/54

He took 100 wickets in a season four times (best 142, av 11.58, in 1867). His best innings analysis was 10 for 54 for AEE v Yorkshire at Sheffield in 1865.

Wootton, James
Professional. *b:* 9.3.1860, Sutton-at-Hone, Kent. *d:* 21.2.1941, Leytonstone, Essex. Tail end left-hand batsman, left-arm medium pace bowler, good slip field. *Teams* Kent (1880–90, 115 matches); Hampshire (1895–1900, 24 matches).
Career batting
168–277–73–1628–53–7.98–0–*ct* 92
Bowling 13815–760–18.17–60–17–8/27

He took 100 wickets in a season three times (best 143, av 15.95, in 1886).

Wootton, Simon Howard
Cricketer. *b:* 24.2.1959, Perivale, Middlesex. Middle order left-hand batsman, slow left-arm bowler. *Team* Warwickshire (1981–83, matches).

Career batting
11–16–2–364–104–26.00–1–*ct* 4
Bowling 7–0

Worger, Frederick Joseph
Professional. *b:* 1869. *d:* 18.11.1954, Brighton, Sussex. Middle order batsman. *Team* Sussex (1892, 1 match).
Career batting
1–2–0–1–1–0.50–0–*ct* 2

Workman, James Allen
Amateur. *b:* 17.3.1917, Australia. *d:* 23.12.1970, Westminster, London. Opening right-hand batsman. *Team* Australia Services (1945 to 1945/6). *Tours* Australian Services to England 1945, to India and Ceylon 1945/6.
Career batting
16–29–2–549–76–20.33–0–*ct* 5
Bowling 6–1–6.00–0–0–1/6
His final first-class match was for Australian Services in Australia in 1945/6.

Wormald, Alfred
Professional. *b:* 10.5.1855, Morley, Yorkshire. *d:* 6.2.1940, Gomersal, Yorkshire. Middle order right-hand batsman, wicket-keeper. *Team* Yorkshire (1885–91, 7 matches).
Career batting
7–11–3–161–80–20.12–0–*ct* 10–*st* 2

Wormald, Edward
Amateur. *b:* 4.12.1848, Islington, Middlesex. *d:* 16.10.1928, Brighton, Sussex. Lower order right-hand batsman, right-arm fast bowler. *Sch* Eton. *Team* Kent (1870, 1 match).
Career batting
1–2–0–16–15–8.00–0–*ct* 1
Bowling 11–0
He played in the Cambridge Freshmen's Match of 1868.

Wormald, John
Amateur. *b:* 23.2.1882, Mayfair, London. *d:* 13.11.1957, East Dereham, Norfolk. Sound middle order right-hand batsman. *Sch* Eton. *Team* Middlesex (1910–12, 22 matches).
Career batting
23–35–1–548–61–16.11–0–*ct* 8
He also played for Norfolk.

Worrall, John
Amateur. *b:* 12.5.1863, Maryborough, Victoria, Australia. *d:* 17.11.1937, Fairfield Park, Victoria, Australia. Aggressive middle order, later opening, right-hand batsman, right-hand slow round-arm bowler, good close field. *Team* Victoria (1883/4 to 1901/2, 65 matches). *Tours* Australia to England 1888, 1899. *Tests* Australia (1884/5 to 1899, 11 matches).
Career batting
142–245–23–4660–128–20.99–7–*ct* 101
Bowling 2426–105–23.10–4–0–5/20
Test batting
11–22–3–478–76–25.15–0–*ct* 13
Bowling 127–1–127.00–0–0–1/97
He achieved little on the 1888 tour, but in 1899 hit 1,202 runs, av 35.35, and played in four Tests. For many years he was a noted journalist in Melbourne.

Worrell, Sir Frank Mortimer Maglinne
Amateur. *b:* 1.8.1924, Bank Hall, Bridgetown, Barbados. *d:* 13.3.1967, Mona, Kingston, Jamaica. Cousin of L. R. (Hampshire). Stylish opening or middle order right-hand batsman, left-arm medium, or slow, bowler. *Teams* Barbados (1941/2 to 1946/7); Jamaica (1947/8 to 1963/4). *Tours* West Indies to England 1950, 1957, 1963, to Australia and New Zealand 1951/2, to Australia 1960/1; Commonwealth to India, Pakistan and Ceylon 1949/50, to India and Ceylon 1950/1, 1953/4; West Indian XI to England 1964. *Tests* West Indies (1947/8 to 1963, 51 matches).
Career batting
208–326–49–15025–308*–54.24–39–*ct* 139
Bowling 10115–349–28.98–13–0–7/70
Test batting
51–87–9–3860–261–49.48–9–*ct* 43
Bowling 2672–69–38.72–2–0–7/70
He achieved great success on his first tour to England in 1950, heading the Test batting averages with 539 runs, av 89.83, and in all first-class matches hitting 1,775 runs, av 68.26. He was no less successful in 1957 with 350 Test runs, av 39.60, and 1,470 first-class runs, av 58.80. He led the 1963 touring side which won the rubber 3 to 1, his main contribution being his captaincy. He had already led West Indies on the 1960/1 tour to Australia, and in all captained West Indies in 15 Tests. His highest Test innings was 261 for West Indies v England at Trent Bridge in 1950. He hit 1,000 runs in India, Pakistan and Ceylon twice (best 1,900, av 63.33, in 1950/1). His highest first-class innings was 308* for Barbados v Trinidad at Bridgetown in 1943/4. He was knighted for his services to cricket in 1964 and was a Senator in the Jamaican Parliament.

Worrell, Lawrence Roosevelt
Cricketer. *b:* 28.8.1943, St Thomas, Barbados. Cousin of F. M. M. (West Indies). Lower order right-hand batsman, off break bowler. *Team* Hampshire (1969–72, 32 matches).

Career batting
32–42–17–289–50–11.56–0–*ct* 21
Bowling 2116–65–32.55–1–0–5/67
He also appeared for Dorset.

Worsley, Arthington
Amateur. *b:* 9.12.1861, Marylebone, London. *d:* 13.1.1943, Newport, Isle of Wight. Middle order right-hand batsman. *Team* MCC (1888–90).
Career batting
2–4–0–29–17–7.25–0–*ct* 1

Worsley, Arthur Edward
Amateur. *b:* 10.10.1882, Evenley, Brackley, Northants. *d:* 10.8.1969, Watchet, Somerset. Brother of C. E. A. (Northants). Middle order right-hand batsman. *Sch* Malvern. *Teams* Oxford U (1903–06); Northants (1905, 3 matches).
Career batting
16–31–0–478–86–15.41–0–*ct* 6
Bowling 156–4–39.00–0–0–3/20

Worsley, Charles Edward Austen
Amateur. *b:* 30.5.1902, Evenley, Northants. Brother of A. E. (Northants). Middle order right-hand batsman. *Sch* Radley. *Team* Northants (1921, 2 matches).
Career batting
2–4–0–34–23–8.50–0–*ct* 1

Worsley, Duncan Robert
Amateur. *b:* 18.7.1941, Bolton, Lancashire. Steady left-hand opening batsman, off break bowler. *Sch* Bolton. *Teams* Lancashire (1960–67, 62 matches); Oxford U (1961–64, blue all four years).
Career batting
113–205–11–5062–139–26.09–4–*ct* 68
Bowling 1520–37–41.08–0–0–4/21
He hit 1,498 runs, av 31.87, in 1964.

Worsley, Francis Frederick
Amateur. *b:* 2.6.1902, Kensington, London. *d:* 15.9.1949, Stepney, London. Middle order batsman. *Sch* Brighton. *Team* Glamorgan (1922–23, 2 matches).
Career batting
2–3–0–34–21–11.33–0–*ct* 1
He did not appear in any first-class matches whilst at Oxford. He became well-known as the producer of the radio programme 'Itma'.

Worsley, Thomas Cuthbert
Amateur. *b:* 10.12.1907, Durham. *d:* 23.2.1977, Brighton, Sussex. Lower order right-hand batsman, wicket-keeper. *Sch* Marlborough. *Team* Cambridge U (1928).
Career batting
1–1–0–1–1–1.00–0–*ct* 0
He was a well-known author and journalist.

Worsley, William
Professional. *b:* 11.9.1869, Wandsworth, Surrey. *d:* 13.11.1918, Accrington, Lancashire. Lower order right-hand batsman, wicket-keeper. *Team* Lancashire (1903–13, 136 matches).
Career batting
136–167–63–728–37*–7.00–0–*ct* 239–*st* 45

Worsley, Sir William Arthington
Amateur. *b:* 5.4.1890, Malton, Yorkshire. *d:* 4.12.1973, Hovingham, Yorkshire. Middle order right-hand batsman. *Sch* Eton. *Team* Yorkshire (1928–29, 59 matches).
Career batting
59–50–4–722–60–15.69–0–*ct* 32
He did not play in any first-class matches whilst at Oxford. In 1928 and 1929 he captained Yorkshire. His daughter is the present Duchess of Kent.

Worthington, Charles Robert
Amateur. *b:* 28.2.1877, Surbiton, Surrey. *d:* 7.12.1950, Victoria, British Columbia. Stylish middle order right-hand batsman, right-arm medium pace bowler. *Sch* Tonbridge. *Teams* Cambridge U (1898); Kent (1898, 1 match).
Career batting
8–13–0–156–42–12.00–0–*ct* 4
Bowling 66–2–33.00–0–0–2/11

Worthington, Thomas Stanley
Professional. *b:* 21.8.1905, Bolsover, Derbyshire. *d:* 31.8.1973, Kings Lynn, Norfolk. He died whilst on holiday. Vigorous middle order right-hand batsman, right-arm fast medium bowler. *Team* Derbyshire (1924–47, 406 matches). *Tours* MCC to Australia and New Zealand 1929/30, 1936/7; Tennyson to India 1937/8. *Tests* England (1929/30 to 1936/7, 9 matches).
Career batting
453–720–59–19221–238*–29.07–31–*ct* 340
Bowling 19939–682–29.23–16–2–8/29
Test batting
9–11–0–321–128–29.18–1–*ct* 8
Bowling 316–8–39.50–0–0–2/19
He hit 1,000 runs in a season ten times (best 1,774, av 41.25, in 1937). Both his double centuries were for Derbyshire the highest being 238* v Sussex at Derby in 1937. His best bowling season was 1929 with 89 wickets, av 23.51. After leaving Derbyshire he appeared for Northumberland and later was, for ten years, chief coach to Lancashire CCC.

Wrathall, Harry
Professional. *b:* 1.2.1869, Cheltenham, Gloucs. *d:* 1.6.1944, Salisbury, Wiltshire. Powerful opening right-hand batsman, right-arm medium pace bowler. *Teams* Gloucestershire (1894–1907, 263 matches); London County (1900).
Career batting
288–509–20–11023–176–22.54–9–*ct* 195–*st* 3
Bowling 1358–30–45.26–0–0–4/337
He hit 1,000 runs in a season four times (best 1,508, av 31.44, in 1901). He also played for Northumberland.

Wrathmell, Lewis Franklin
Professional. *b:* 22.1.1855, Huddersfield, Yorkshire. *d:* 16.9.1928, Dewsbury, Yorkshire. Middle order batsman. *Team* Yorkshire (1886, 1 match).
Career batting
1–2–0–18–17–9.00–0–*ct* 0

Wreford-Brown, Anthony John
Amateur. *b:* 26.10.1912, Thames Ditton, Surrey. Son of Charles, nephew of O. E. (Gloucs). Opening right-hand batsman. *Sch* Charterhouse. *Teams* Oxford U (1934); Sussex (1934, 1 match).
Career batting
5–10–1–146–39–16.22–0–*ct* 2
His first-class debut was for Leveson-Gower's XI in 1933.

Wreford-Brown, Charles
Amateur. *b:* 9.10.1866, Clifton, Gloucs. *d:* 26.11.1951, Paddington, London. Father of A. J. (Sussex), brother of O. E. (Gloucs). Lower order right-hand batsman, right-arm slow bowler, good field. *Sch* Charterhouse. *Teams* Gloucestershire (1886–98, 5 matches); Oxford U (1887–88). *Tour* Hawke to North America 1891.
Career batting
19–32–6–252–51–9.69–0–*ct* 10
Bowling 969–39–24.84–1–0–5/62
He was a noted soccer player, appearing at centre-half for Oxford, Old Carthusians, Corinthians and England. Later he became Vice-President of the Football Association and Chairman of the FA Selection Committee. He is said to be the first to use the word 'soccer' for Association football.

Wreford-Brown, Oswald Eric
Amateur. *b:* 21.7.1877, Bristol. *d:* 7.7.1916, near Corbie, France. He died of wounds. Brother of Charles (Gloucs), uncle of A. J. (Sussex). Steady middle order right-hand batsman, good cover-point. *Sch* Charterhouse. *Team* Gloucestershire (1900, 1 match).
Career batting
1–1–0–5–5–5.00–0–*ct* 0

Wreghitt, Peter Hadfield
Amateur. *b:* 11.5.1929, Sheffield, Yorkshire. Middle order right-hand batsman, right-arm medium pace bowler. *Team* Oxford U (1951).
Career batting
1–1–0–1–1–1.00–0–*ct* 3
Bowling 105–3–35.00–0–0–3/64

Wright, Albert
Amateur. *b:* 8.8.1899, Kettering, Northants. Brother of E. V. (Northants), Stephen (Northants), R. L. (Northants). Middle order right-hand batsman, right-arm medium pace bowler. *Sch* Wellingborough. *Team* Northants (1919–20, 3 matches).
Career batting
3–6–0–81–27–13.50–0–*ct* 4
Bowling 106–6–17.66–0–0–3/6

Wright, Albert
Professional. *b:* 25.8.1941, Arley, Warwickshire. Lower order right-hand batsman, right-arm medium pace bowler. *Team* Warwickshire (1960–64, 76 matches).
Career batting
76–76–27–315–27–6.42–0–*ct* 29
Bowling 5953–236–25.22–11–2–6/58

Wright, Albert Charles
Professional. *b:* 4.4.1895, Borstal, Kent. *d:* 26.5.1959, Westminster, London. Hard hitting lower order right-hand batsman, right-arm fast medium bowler. *Team* Kent (1921–31, 225 matches).
Career batting
225–298–49–3280–81–13.09–0–*ct* 127
Bowling 14463–596–24.26–24–1–7/31
He took 100 wickets in a season twice (best 107, av 20.38, in 1927).

Wright, Albert Edward
Amateur. *b:* 11.8.1902, Great Leighs, Essex. Lower order right-hand batsman, right-arm fast bowler. *Team* Essex (1931–34, 3 matches).
Career batting
3–5–1–45–14–11.25–0–*ct* 1
Bowling 86–0

Wright, Arthur Edward Hext
Amateur. *b:* 7.2.1886, Georgetown, British Guiana. *d:* 13.11.1970, Chudleigh, Devon. Son of E. F. (Gloucestershire). Middle order right-hand batsman. *Team* Royal Navy (1914).
Career batting
1–2–0–87–57–43.50–0–*ct* 0
His County cricket was for Devon.

Wright, Anthony John
Cricketer. *b:* 27.6.1962, Stevenage, Hertfordshire, Middle order right-hand batsman, right-arm medium pace bowler. *Team* Gloucestershire (1982–83, 20 matches).
Career batting
20–36–4–779–65–24.34–0–*ct* 8
Bowling 3–0

Wright, Alan Jack Barton
Amateur. *b:* 3.3.1905, Northampton. Brother of R. C. B. (Northants). Middle order right-hand batsman. *Sch* Wellingborough. *Team* Northants (1922–23, 2 matches).
Career batting
2–4–0–4–3–1.00–0–*ct* 0

Wright, Bertie
Amateur. *b:* 7.2.1897, Kettering, Northants. *d:* 2.4.1955, Kettering, Northants. Brother of N. E. (Northants) and P. A. (Northants). Middle order right-hand batsman. *Sch* Wellingborough. *Team* Northants (1919–22, 5 matches).
Career batting
5–8–0–28–12–3.50–0–*ct* 3
Bowling 254–6–42.33–0–0–2/11

Wright, Cyril Carne Glenton
Amateur. *b:* 7.3.1887, Oporto, Portugal. *d:* 15.9.1960, Hampstead, London. Opening right-hand batsman. *Sch* Tonbridge. *Team* Cambridge U (1907–09, blue 1907 and 1908).
Career batting
23–44–2–677–87–16.11–0–*ct* 22
His final first-class match was for G. J. V. Weigall's XI in 1914. A noted rugby footballer, he played for Cambridge and England.

Wright, Charles William
Amateur. *b:* 27.5.1863, Harewood, Yorkshire. *d:* 10.1.1936, Saxelby, Melton Mowbray, Leics. Steady opening right-hand batsman, wicket-keeper. *Sch* Charterhouse. *Teams* Cambridge U (1882–85, blue all four years); Nottinghamshire (1882–99, 117 matches). *Tours* Hawke to North America 1891, 1894, to India 1892/3, to South Africa 1895/6. *Tests* England (1895/6, 3 matches).
Career batting
265–461–21–6989–114–15.88–2–*ct* 195–*st* 41
Bowling 55–0
Test batting
3–4–0–125–71–31.25–0–*ct* 0
His final first-class match was for MCC in 1901. He was for some years on the Committee of Nottinghamshire CCC and a Trustee in 1900. He lost the sight of one eye whilst partridge shooting and this ended his serious cricket.

Wright, Douglas Alexander
Amateur. *b:* 1894. *d:* 1.10.1953, Marylebone, London. Middle order right-hand batsman, wicket-keeper. *Sch* Christ's Hospital. *Teams* Ceylon (1926/7 to 1936/7); MCC (1928).
Career batting
5–6–1–149–82–29.80–0–*ct* 7–*st* 5

Wright, Douglas Vivian Parson
Professional. *b:* 21.8.1914, Sidcup, Kent. Lower order right-hand batsman, right-arm medium leg break and googly bowler. *Team* Kent (1932–57, 397 matches). *Tours* MCC to South Africa 1938/9, 1948/9, to Australia and New Zealand 1946/7, 1950/1; Norfolk to Jamaica 1956/7. *Tests* England (1938 to 1950/1, 34 matches).
Career batting
497–703–225–5903–84*–12.34–0–*ct* 182
Bowling 49307–2056–23.98–150–42–9/47
Test batting
34–39–13–289–45–11.11–0–*ct* 10
Bowling 4224–108–39.11–6–1–7/105
Bowling leg breaks at a much greater speed than the normal practitioner of that art, Wright was the only bowler of his type in first-class cricket. On his day he was virtually unplayable, but often he was very erratic in length and direction. His figures in Test cricket are not at all impressive, but the selectors were always mindful that he could produce the unexpected and therefore he played fairly regularly for England between 1938 and 1950.
In first-class cricket he took 100 wickets in a season 10 times, his best year being 1947 with 177 wickets, av 21.12. Some idea of his occasional effectiveness can be gauged by the fact that he achieved the hat-trick seven times. His best bowling in an innings was 9 for 47 for Kent v Gloucestershire at Bristol in 1939.

Wright, Edward Campbell
Amateur. *b:* 23.4.1874, South Shields, Co Durham. *d:* 28.7.1947, Budleigh Salterton, Devon. Middle order right-hand batsman, right-arm slow bowler. *Sch* Clergy Orphan School, Canterbury. *Teams* Gloucestershire (1894–98, 7 matches); Oxford U (1897–99, blue 1897); Kent (1902, 2 matches).
Career batting
23–35–8–420–83–15.55–0–*ct* 17
Bowling 1149–52–22.09–1–0–5/44

Wright, Edward Fortescue
Amateur. *b:* 11.3.1857, Chudleigh, Devon. *d:* 23.11.1904, Kingston, Jamaica. Father of A. E. H. (Royal Navy). Vigorous lower order right-hand batsman, right-hand fast round-arm bowler. *Sch* Sydney College, Bath. *Teams* Glou-

cestershire (1878, 4 matches); British Guiana (1882/3 to 1886/7); Jamaica (1897/8 to 1901/2).
Career batting
18–32–0–759–123–23.71–1–*ct* 11
Bowling 602–47–12.80–3–2–7/15
He also played for Devon.

Wright, Egerton Lowndes
Amateur. *b:* 15.11.1885, Chorley, Lancashire. *d:* 11.5.1918, Barly, France. He was killed in action. Attractive middle order right-hand batsman, wicket-keeper. *Sch* Winchester. *Teams* Oxford U (1905–08, blue all four years); Lancashire (1905–10, 4 matches).
Career batting
37–68–2–1638–95–24.81–0–*ct* 26–*st* 3
Bowling 40–1–40.00–0–0–1/6
A good soccer player, he was awarded his blue.

Wright, Ernest (Vincent)
Amateur. *b:* 24.10.1894, Kettering, Northants. *d:* 16.12.1977, Kettering, Northants. Brother of Albert (Northants), Stephen (Northants) and R. L. (Northants). Middle order right-hand batsman. *Sch* Wellingborough. *Team* Northants (1919, 2 matches).
Career batting
2–2–0–2–2–1.00–0–*ct* 0

Wright, Frank
(known as Francis Moult Wright)
Professional. *b:* 4.5.1870, Ilkeston, Derbyshire. *d:* 9.12.1943, Cotmanhay, Derbyshire. Middle order right-hand batsman. *Team* Derbyshire (1899, 1 match).
Career batting
1–2–0–4–4–2.00–0–*ct* 0
Bowling 37–0

Wright, Frederick
Amateur. *b:* 1855, Sysonby, Melton Mowbray, Leics. *d:* 20.11.1929, Melton Mowbray, Leics. Attacking middle order right-hand batsman, right-arm fast bowler. *Team* Leicestershire (1895–97, 5 matches).
Career batting
5–10–0–110–31–11.00–0–*ct* 4
Bowling 365–17–21.47–1–0–5/78
Most of his County cricket was played before Leicestershire was raised to first-class status, his County debut being in 1887.

Wright, Rev Frank Wynyard
Amateur. *b:* 6.4.1844, Woodstock, Oxfordshire. *d:* 15.2.1924, Eastbourne, Sussex. Son of F. B. (Oxford U 1829), cousin of E. G. Wynyard (Hants). Stylish middle order right-hand batsman. *Sch* Rossall. *Teams* Oxford U (1863–65, blue all three years); Lancashire (1869–75, 14 matches).
Career batting
37–57–4–917–120*–17.30–1–*ct* 41–*st* 9
Bowling 156–3–52.00–0–0–2/44
His first-class debut was for Gentlemen of the North in 1861. He gave up first-class cricket entirely in 1875 when he took up a scholastic post in Eastbourne. He also played occasionally for Cheshire.

Wright, George Henry
Professional. *b:* 15.11.1822, Highfield, Sheffield, Yorkshire. *d:* 28.11.1893, Ecclesall, Sheffield, Yorkshire. Steady middle order right-hand batsman, good bowler, good point field. *Team* Yorkshire (1849–55, 20 matches).
Career batting
42–74–3–703–68–9.90–0–*ct* 48
Bowling 546–53+35–10.30–4–0–7/?
In 1866 he was appointed groundsman at Bramall Lane, Sheffield, and remained there until his death. His first-class debut was for England in 1847 and his final match for Manchester in 1858.

Wright, Harold
Amateur. *b:* 19.2.1884, Barrow-on-Soar, Leics. *d:* 14.9.1915, Leicester. He died of wounds received in the Dardanelles. Middle order left-hand batsman, slow left-arm bowler, good slip field. *Sch* Mill Hill. *Team* Leicestershire (1912–14, 10 matches).
Career batting
11–21–4–243–44–14.29–0–*ct* 10
Bowling 20–0

Wright, Henry
Professional. *b:* 21.4.1852. Lower order batsman, useful bowler. *Team* An England Eleven (1888).
Career batting
1–2–1–4–4–4.00–0–*ct* 2
Bowling 10–1–10.00–0–0–1/10

Wright, Henry FitzHerbert
Amateur. *b:* 9.10.1870, Swanwick, Derbyshire. *d:* 23.2.1947, Yeldersley, Ashbourne, Derbyshire. Middle order right-hand batsman, right-arm medium pace bowler. *Sch* Eton. *Team* Derbyshire (1904–05, 9 matches). *Tour* Hawke to India 1892/3.
Career batting
13–22–4–349–55–19.38–0–*ct* 6
He played in the Cambridge Freshmen's Match of 1890 and the Seniors' Match of the following year. From 1912 to 1918, he was Unionist MP for Leominster.

Wright, H. W.
Professional. Lower order batsman, useful bowler. *Team* Hampshire (1885, 1 match).
Career batting
1–2–0–12–12–6.00–0–*ct* 1
Bowling 70–1–70.00–0–0–1/70

Wright, J.
Amateur. Middle order batsman. *Team* MCC (1882).
Career batting
1–2–1–2–2–2.00–0–*ct* 0

Wright, James
Professional. *b:* 25.3.1874, Newbold, Leics. *d:* 20.8.1961, Sheffield, Yorkshire. Middle order right-hand batsman. *Team* Derbyshire (1898–1906, 6 matches).
Career batting
6–10–1–93–53*–10.33–0–*ct* 0
Bowling 16–0

Wright, John
Professional. *b:* 23.9.1861, Nantwich, Cheshire. *d:* 5.11.1912, Nantwich, Cheshire. Middle order right-hand batsman, right-arm fast medium bowler. *Team* North of England (1885).
Career batting
1–2–0–3–3–1.50–0–*ct* 2
Bowling 16–0
He played for Cheshire, commencing 1884.

Wright, James Egerton Lowndes
Amateur. *b:* 10.5.1912, London. Middle order right-hand batsman. *Sch* Winchester. *Team* Free Foresters (1937).
Career batting
1–2–0–48–48–24.00–0–*ct* 1

Wright, John Geoffrey
Cricketer. *b:* 5.7.1954, Darfield, New Zealand. Sound opening left-hand batsman, right-arm medium pace bowler. *Teams* Northern Districts (1975/6 to 1982/3); Derbyshire (1977–83, 110 matches). *Tours* New Zealand to England 1978, 1983, to Australia 1980/1; Robins to Sri Lanka 1977/8; International XI to Jamaica 1982/3. *Tests* New Zealand (1977/8 to 1983, 25 matches).
Career batting
201–349–25–12952–190–39.97–31–*ct* 119
Bowling 67–1–67.00–0–0–1/4
Test batting
25–44–1–1233–141–28.67–2–*ct* 12
Bowling 2–0
He hit 1,000 runs in a season five times (best 1,830, av 55.45, in 1982).

Wright, John Vaughan
Cricketer. *b:* 31.12.1935, Colchester, Essex. Middle order right-hand batsman. *Team* Essex (1962–67, 4 matches).
Career batting
4–6–0–60–40–10.00–0–*ct* 2

Wright, Leslie
Professional. *b:* 20.1.1903, Durham. *d:* 6.1.1956, Mitcham, Surrey. Right-hand batsman, right-arm medium pace bowler. *Team* Worcestershire (1925–33, 193 matches).
Career batting
193–348–18–6593–134–19.97–5–*ct* 60
Bowling 3649–76–48.01–0–0–3/6
He hit 1,000 runs in a season twice (best 1,402, av 24.17, in 1928).

Wright, Levi George
Amateur. *b:* 15.1.1862, Oxford. *d:* 11.1.1953, Derby. Attacking opening right-hand batsman, brilliant point field, occasional wicket-keeper. *Team* Derbyshire (1883–1909, 317 matches).
Career batting
325–593–12–15166–195–26.10–20–*ct* 237–*st* 6
Bowling 204–1–204.00–0–0–1/4
He hit 1,000 runs in a season six times (best 1,855, av 42.15, in 1906). In 1906 he was joint-captain of Derbyshire and in 1907 sole captain. He was also a useful soccer player, representing Derby County and Notts County.

Wright, Lynden Norman Gordon
Cricketer. *b:* 18.4.1950, Kingston, Jamaica. Lower order batsman, useful bowler. *Team* Jamaica (1968/9 to 1978/9). *Tour* Jamaica to England 1970.
Career batting
24–30–11–316–33–16.63–0–*ct* 23
Bowling 1073–40–26.82–2–0–5/36

Wright, Malcolm Graeme
Amateur. *b:* 2.6.1926, Kandy, Ceylon. Forcing middle order left-hand batsman. *Team* Oxford U (1950).
Career batting
2–4–0–35–17–8.75–0–*ct* 1

Wright, Matthew William
Professional. *b:* 24.7.1858, Keyworth, Notts. *d:* 13.5.1949, Windsor, Berkshire. Middle order batsman, useful bowler. *Team* Nottinghamshire (1889, 1 match).
Career batting
1–2–0–6–6–3.00–0–*ct* 0
Bowling 7–0

He played for Buckinghamshire as an all-rounder from 1891 to 1913, and was coach at Eton College.

Wright, Nicholas Edward
Amateur. *b:* 28.8.1901, Kettering, Northants. *d:* 20.5.1974, Corby, Northants. Brother of Bertie (Northants) and P. A. (Northants). Lower order right-hand batsman, useful bowler. *Sch* Wellingborough. *Team* Northants (1921–22, 8 matches).
Career batting
8–14–3–30–8–2.72–0–*ct* 0
Bowling 147–2–73.50–0–0–2/59

Wright, Oswald Walter
Amateur. *b:* 20.3.1877, Dover, Kent. *d:* 19.12.1933, Cheltenham, Gloucs. Attacking tail end batsman, originally left-arm fast, later slow, bowler, good field. *Sch* Malvern. *Teams* Cambridge U (1899); Somerset (1902, 1 match).
Career batting
3–5–0–21–14–4.20–0–*ct* 2
Bowling 89–2–44.50–0–0–1/16

Wright, Philip Alan
Amateur. *b:* 16.5.1903, Kettering, Northants. *d:* 21.12.1968, Kettering, Northants. Brother of Bertie (Northants) and N. E. (Northants). Forceful lower order right-hand batsman, right-arm medium pace bowler. *Sch* Wellingborough. *Teams* Northants (1921–29, 59 matches); Cambridge U (1922–24, blue all three years).
Career batting
93–151–27–1459–83–11.76–0–*ct* 45
Bowling 8078–343–23.55–19–2–6/37

In 1925, his only full year of first-class County cricket, he took 108 wickets, av 23.27.

Wright, Robert (Ward)
Professional. *b:* 19.7.1852, Adwalton, Yorkshire. *d:* 1891, Oldham, Lancashire. Lower order right-hand batsman, right-hand slow round-arm bowler. *Team* Yorkshire (1877, 2 matches).
Career batting
3–6–1–37–22–7.40–0–*ct* 0

His first-class debut was for North of England in 1875.

Wright, Ronald Charles Barton
Amateur. *b:* 13.3.1903, Northampton. Brother of A. J. B. (Northants). Middle order left-hand batsman, slow left-arm bowler. *Sch* Wellingborough. *Team* Northants (1923–31, 10 matches).
Career batting
10–17–1–160–56*–10.00–0–*ct* 4
Bowling 1–0

Wright, Richard Leslie
Amateur. *b:* 28.10.1903, Kettering, Northants. Brother of Albert (Northants), E. V. (Northants) and Stephen (Northants). Steady middle order right-hand batsman, right-arm medium pace bowler. *Sch* Wellingborough. *Team* Northants (1923–26, 54 matches).
Career batting
54–101–6–1507–112–15.86–2–*ct* 32
Bowling 194–5–38.80–0–0–1/11

Wright, Stephen
Amateur. *b:* 6.8.1897, Kettering, Northants. *d:* 24.6.1975, Weston-super-Mare, Somerset. Brother of Albert (Northants), E. V. (Northants) and R. L. (Northants). Middle order right-hand batsman. *Sch* Wellingborough. *Team* Northants (1922–23, 9 matches).
Career batting
9–18–0–188–44–10.44–0–*ct* 5

Wright, Stephen
Cricketer. *b:* 4.2.1952, Muswell Hill, London. Middle order right-hand batsman. *Sch* Mill Hill. *Team* Cambridge U (1973, blue).
Career batting
10–19–0–277–41–14.57–0–*ct* 2

Wright, Dr Samuel Reginald
Amateur. *b:* 4.1.1869, Markfield, Leics. *d:* 25.1.1947, Romford, Essex. Lower order left-hand batsman, left-arm fast medium bowler. *Sch* Epsom. *Team* Leicestershire (1896–97, 3 matches).
Career batting
3–4–0–75–65–18.75–0–*ct* 0
Bowling 185–2–92.50–0–0–1/14

His debut for Leicestershire was in 1887.

Wright, Thomas
Amateur. *b:* 29.4.1842, Willington, Derbyshire. Steady middle order right-hand batsman, right-hand slow medium round-arm bowler, good field. *Team* Nottinghamshire (1868–74, 9 matches).
Career batting
9–15–0–138–25–9.20–0–*ct* 4

Wright, Thomas John
Amateur. *b:* 5.3.1900, Middlesbrough, Yorkshire. Middle order batsman. *Sch* St Peter's, York. *Team* Yorkshire (1919, 1 match).
Career batting
1–1–0–12–12–12.00–0–*ct* 0

Wright, Walter
Professional. *b:* 29.2.1856, Hucknall Torkard, Notts. *d:* 22.3.1940, Leigh, Lancashire. Lower order right-hand batsman, left-arm fast medium

bowler, deep field. *Teams* Nottinghamshire (1879–86, 72 matches); Kent (1888–99, 191 matches).
Career batting
289–441–110–4075–127*–12.31–1–*ct* 136
Bowling 19047–976–19.51–60–12–9/72

He took 114 wickets, av 12.86, in 1889. His best bowling was 9/72 for Kent v MCC at Lord's in 1889. He appeared for Berkshire in 1904 and was on the first-class umpires' list for five seasons. A noted athlete, in his younger days, he won the Sheffield Handicap twice.

Wright, William Henry
Amateur. *b:* 10.8.1841. *d:* 28.12.1916, Westminster, London. Middle order batsman. *Sch* Marlborough. *Team* MCC (1866).
Career batting
2–3–0–5–3–1.66–0–*ct* 0

Wright, William John
Professional. *b:* 24.2.1909, Bakewell, Derbyshire. Middle order right-hand batsman. *Team* Derbyshire (1932, 2 matches).
Career batting
2–3–0–58–28–19.33–0–*ct* 0

Wrightson, Roger Wilfrid
Cricketer. *b:* 29.10.1939, Elsecar, Yorkshire. Middle order left-hand batsman, wicket-keeper. *Team* Essex (1965–67, 12 matches).
Career batting
12–20–4–332–84–20.75–0–*ct* 8

He also played for Cumberland.

Wrigley, Michael Harold
Amateur. *b:* 30.7.1924, Knutsford, Cheshire. Lower order right-hand batsman, right-arm fast medium bowler. *Sch* Harrow. *Team* Oxford U (1948–50, blue 1949).
Career batting
16–17–5–71–17–5.91–0–*ct* 6
Bowling 1076–48–22.41–3–0–6/57

His first-class debut was for Combined Services in 1946.

Wyatt, Francis Joseph Caldwell
Amateur. *b:* 10.7.1882, Trichinopoly, India. *d:* 5.5.1971, Chichester, Sussex. Lower order right-hand batsman, right-arm medium pace bowler. *Sch* Dulwich and Glenalmond. *Teams* Hampshire (1905–19, 11 matches); Orange Free State (1906/7).
Career batting
21–35–6–168–26–5.79–0–*ct* 16
Bowling 1843–90–20.47–6–0–6/31

His first-class debut was for Gentlemen of England in 1904 and his final first-class match in 1920 for the Army.

Wyatt, Gerald
Professional. *b:* 4.6.1933, New Mills, Derbyshire. Lower order right-hand batsman, wicket-keeper. *Team* Derbyshire (1954–60, 11 matches).
Career batting
11–20–4–184–59–11.50–0–*ct* 7
Bowling 2–0

Wyatt, George Nevile
Amateur. *b:* 25.8.1850, Champaran, India. *d:* 16.2.1926, Clifton, Gloucs. Dashing middle order right-hand batsman, right-hand medium pace round-arm bowler, good deep field. *Sch* Cheltenham. *Teams* Gloucestershire (1871–76, 10 matches); Surrey (1877–79, 10 matches); Sussex (1883–86, 40 matches).
Career batting
72–129–6–2015–112–16.38–1–*ct* 38
Bowling 127–3–42.33–0–0–1/4

Wyatt, Dr Harold Douglas
Amateur. *b:* 1880, Edmonton, Middlesex. *d:* 24.11.1949, Southwark, London. Middle order batsman. *Sch* The Leys. *Team* Middlesex (1905–09, 4 matches).
Career batting
4–6–1–67–23*–13.40–0–*ct* 2

Wyatt, Julian George
Cricketer. *b:* 19.6.1963, Paulton, Somerset. Opening right-hand batsman, right-arm medium pace bowler. *Team* Somerset (1983, 6 matches).
Career batting
6–12–2–352–82*–35.20–0–*ct* 1

Wyatt, Robert Elliott Storey
Amateur. *b:* 2.5.1901, Milford, Surrey. Sound middle order right-hand batsman, right-arm medium-fast bowler. *Teams* Warwickshire (1923–39, 404 matches); Worcestershire (1946–51, 86 matches). *Tours* MCC to India, Burma and Ceylon 1926/7, to South Africa 1927/8, 1930/1, to West Indies 1929/30, 1934/5, to Australia and New Zealand 1932/3, 1936/7; Brinckman to South America 1937/8; Martineau to Egypt 1936, 1939 (not first-class); selected for MCC to India 1939/40 (cancelled because of the war). *Tests* England (1927/8 to 1936/7, 40 matches).
Career batting
739–1141–157–39405–232–40.04–85–*ct* 413–*st* 1
Bowling 29597–901–32.84–30–2–7/43
Test batting
40–64–6–1839–149–31.70–2–*ct* 16
Bowling 642–18–35.66–0–0–3/4

A very consistent, as well as determined, batsman whose career spanned 35 seasons, he hit over 1,000 runs in a season 17 times, plus once overseas, going on to 2,000 five times, with his best year being 1929 with 2,630 runs, av 53.66. His two double centuries were both for Warwickshire, the highest being 232 v Derbyshire at Edgbaston in 1937.

He captained England in the final Test of 1930 v Australia, in four of the five Tests of the 1934 series, during the 1934/5 tour to West Indies and against South Africa in 1935. From 1930 to 1937 he led Warwickshire and then was joint captain of Worcestershire in 1949 and sole captain in 1950 and 1951. He was a Test Selector from 1949 to 1953, being Chairman in 1950.

His final appearance in first-class cricket was for Free Foresters in 1957.

Wyatt, Rev William
Amateur. *b:* 12.11.1842, Islington, London. *d:* 1.3.1908, Scarborough, Yorkshire. Tail end batsman, useful bowler. *Team* Oxford U (1864).
Career batting
3–4–3–3–2*–3.00–0–*ct* 0
Bowling 72–2+3–36.00–0–0–2/?

Wyers, Alick
Amateur. *b:* 15.12.1907, Droitwich, Worcestershire. *d:* 28.11.1980, Kidderminster, Worcestershire. Middle order right-hand batsman. *Team* Worcestershire (1927, 1 match).
Career batting
1–1–0–3–3–3.00–0–*ct* 0

Wykes, Geoffrey Noel
Amateur. *b:* 22.11.1890, Leicester. *d:* 1.5.1926, Hull, Yorkshire. Middle order batsman. *Sch* Charterhouse. *Team* Leicestershire (1923, 2 matches).
Career batting
2–4–0–2–2–0.50–0–*ct* 0

Wykes, James Cochrane
Amateur. *b:* 19.10.1913, Leigh-on-Sea, Essex. Right-hand batsman, wicket-keeper. *Sch* Oundle. *Team* Scotland (1946).
Career batting
1–2–0–38–23–19.00–0–*ct* 1

Wykes, Norman Gordon
Amateur. *b:* 19.3.1906, West Ham, Essex. Opening or middle order left-hand batsman, good field. *Sch* Oundle. *Teams* Essex (1925–36, 30 matches); Cambridge U (1926–28, blue 1928).
Career batting
42–60–6–1277–162–23.64–2–*ct* 13
Bowling 150–1–150.00–0–0–1/5

Wyld, Frederick
(also known as Wild)
Professional. *b:* 28.8.1847, Eastwood, Notts. *d:* 11.2.1893, Nottingham. Forceful opening or middle order right-hand batsman, right-hand fast round-arm bowler, wicket-keeper. *Team* Nottinghamshire (1868–81, 109 matches).
Career batting
180–297–20–3967–104*–14.32–2–*ct* 186–*st* 53
Bowling 109–8–13.62–0–0–4/33

His final first-class match was for MCC in 1885.

Wyld, Hugh James
Amateur. *b:* 16.4.1880, London. *d:* 9.12.1961, Beverstone, Gloucs. Middle order right-hand batsman, slow left-arm bowler. *Sch* Harrow. *Teams* Oxford U (1900–03, blue 1901, 1902 and 1903); Middlesex (1900–01, 5 matches). *Tour* MCC to North America 1905.
Career batting
36–65–5–1124–85–18.73–0–*ct* 21
Bowling 42–2–21.00–0–0–1/10

His final first-class match in England was for Gentlemen of England in 1904. He also was awarded his soccer blue whilst at Oxford.

Wyld, William George
Amateur. *b:* 3.12.1859, Stirling, Scotland. *d:* 16.7.1900, South Kensington, London. Middle order right-hand batsman, right-arm medium pace, or slow under arm, bowler. *Sch* Dulwich. *Team* Surrey (1879–87, 10 matches).
Career batting
10–16–1–169–34–11.26–0–*ct* 4
Bowling 113–3–37.66–0–0–1/12

Wynch, Charles George
Amateur. *b:* 24.7.1833, Calcutta, India. *d:* 21.5.1876, Westminster, London. Attractive middle order right-hand batsman, good deep field. *Sch* Rugby. *Team* Sussex (1852–59, 24 matches).
Career batting
24–42–6–758–87–21.05–0–*ct* 9
Bowling 4–0+2–no av–0–0–1/?

He resided in India 1855 to 1858; his first-class cricket was therefore very restricted. He occasionally appeared in the Essex team. His final first-class match was for MCC in 1865.

Wynne-Finch, Edward Heneage
(changed name from E. H. Wynne in 1863)
Amateur. *b:* 9.12.1842, Voelas, Denbighshire. *d:* 7.1.1914, Stokesley, Yorkshire. Son of C. G. (Oxford U 1836). Middle order right-hand batsman, off break bowler. *Sch* Eton. *Team* MCC (1864–66).

Career batting
3–6–1–24–20–4.00–0–*ct* 0
Bowling 76–2–38.00–0–0–2/68

He played for Cambridge U in 1864 but not in first-class matches. His County cricket was for Norfolk.

Wynyard, Edward George
Amateur. *b:* 1.4.1861, Mussourie, Bengal, India. *d:* 30.10.1936, Knotty Green, Beaconsfield, Bucks. Cousin of F. W. Wright (Lancashire). Forcing opening or middle order right-hand batsman, slow under-arm bowler, fine cover-point or slip. *Sch* Charterhouse and St Edward's, Oxford. *Team* Hampshire (1878–1908, 71 matches). *Tours* Brackley to West Indies 1904/5; MCC to South Africa 1905/6, 1909/10, to New Zealand 1906/7, to North America 1907, to Egypt 1909 (not first-class). *Tests* England (1896 to 1905/6, 3 matches).
Career batting
154–272–20–8318–268–33.00–13–*ct* 163–*st* 5
Bowling 2130–66–32.27–1–0–6/63
Test batting
3–6–0–72–30–12.00–0–*ct* 0
Bowling 17–0

He hit 1,000 runs in a season twice (best 1,281, av 41.32, in 1899). In 1896 he came second in the first-class batting averages with 1,038, av 49.42. He captained Hampshire 1896 to 1899. His two double centuries were both for Hampshire, the highest being 268 v Yorkshire at Southampton in 1896. His final first-class match was for MCC in 1912. In the 1880s he played many fine innings whilst stationed in India.

A good soccer player, he appeared in the forward line for the winners, Old Carthusians, in the FA Cup Final of 1881. He was also a noted figure skater.

YADAV, NANDLAL SHIVLAL
Cricketer. *b:* 26.1.1957, Hyderabad, India. Tail end right-hand batsman, right-arm off break bowler. *Team* Hyderabad (1977/8 to 1982/3). *Tours* India to Australia and New Zealand 1980/1, to England 1982. *Tests* India (1979/80 to 1981/2, 15 matches).
Career batting
50–50–14–630–49–17.50–0–*ct* 22
Bowling 4330–128–33.82–3–0–6/49
Test batting
15–19–6–207–43–15.92–0–*ct* 4
Bowling 1449–41–35.34–0–0–4/35

He achieved very little on the 1982 tour to England and did not appear in the Tests.

Yajurvindra Singh, Jaswantsingh Wala
Cricketer. *b:* 1.8.1952, Rajkot, India. Lower order right-hand batsman, right-arm medium pace bowler, good close field. *Teams* Maharashtra (1971/2 to 1978/9); Saurashtra (1979/80 to 1981/2). *Tour* India to England 1979. *Tests* India (1976/7 to 1979/80, 4 matches).
Career batting
78–115–26–3765–214–42.30–9–*ct* 82
Bowling 1552–50–31.04–2–1–7/20
Test batting
4–7–1–109–43*–18.16–0–*ct* 11
Bowling 50–0

He appeared in one Test on the 1979 tour of England and in only nine first-class matches. His highest score was 214 for Saurashtra v Maharashtra at Satara in 1979/80.

Yaldren, Charles Henry
Professional. *b:* 1891, Southampton. *d:* 23.10.1916, Thiepval, France. Tail end batsman, useful bowler. *Team* Hampshire (1912, 1 match).
Career batting
1–1–0–8–8–8.00–0–*ct* 0
Bowling 60–1–60.00–0–0–1/52

Yalland, William Stanley
Amateur. *b:* 27.6.1889, Bristol. *d:* 23.10.1914, Ypres, Belgium. He was killed in action. Middle order right-hand batsman. *Sch* Clifton. *Team* Gloucestershire (1910, 1 match).
Career batting
1–1–0–1–1–1.00–0–*ct* 0

Yallop, Graham Neil
Cricketer. *b:* 7.10.1952, Balwyn, Victoria, Australia. Hard hitting middle order left-hand batsman. *Team* Victoria (1972/3 to 1982/3, 78 matches). *Tours* Australia to England 1980, 1981, to West Indies 1977/8, to India 1979/80, to Sri Lanka 1980/1, 1982/3, to Pakistan 1979/80. *Tests* Australia (1975/6 to 1982/3, 33 matches).
Career batting
134–236–25–9187–246–43.54–22–*ct* 102–*st* 1
Bowling 745–11–67.72–0–0–4/63
Test batting
33–62–3–2199–172–37.27–6–*ct* 17
Bowling 116–1–116.00–0–0–1/21

He played in the Centenary Test on the brief 1980 tour to England and in all six Tests on the 1981 tour, but apart from an innings of 114 in the Old Trafford Test in 1981, his form was not impressive. He hit 1,418 runs, av 67.52, in Australia in 1982/3.

Yardley, Norman Walter Dransfield
Amateur. *b:* 19.3.1915, Royston, Barnsley, Yorkshire. Sound middle order right-hand batsman, right-arm medium pace swing bowler. *Sch* St Peter's, York. *Teams* Cambridge U (1935–38, blue all four years); Yorkshire (1936–55, 302 matches). *Tours* Tennyson to India 1937/8, MCC to South Africa 1938/9, to Australia and New Zealand 1946/7. *Tests* England (1938–50, 20 matches).
Career batting
446–658–75–18173–183*–31.17–27–*ct* 328–*st* 1
Bowling 8506–279–30.48–5–0–6/29
Test batting
20–34–2–812–99–25.37–0–*ct* 14
Bowling 707–21–33.66–0–0–3/67

He hit 1,000 runs in a season eight times (best 1,906, av 44.32, in 1947). He captained Yorkshire from 1948 to 1955 and England in 14 Tests. A Test Selector from 1951 to 1954, he was Chairman of the Committee in 1951–52. He was also a member of the Yorkshire Committee. An all-round athlete he gained a hockey blue and was six times North of England squash champion.

Yardley, Thomas James
Cricketer. *b:* 27.10.1946, Chaddesley Corbett, Worcs. Middle order left-hand batsman, right-arm medium pace bowler, wicket-keeper. *Teams* Worcestershire (1967–75, 153 matches); Northamptonshire (1976–82, 107 matches).
Career batting
260–390–69–8287–135–25.81–5–*ct* 232–*st* 2
Bowling 38–0

He hit 1,066 runs, av 30.45, in 1971.

Yardley, William
Amateur. *b:* 10.6.1849, Bombay, India. *d:* 28.10.1900, Kingston-upon-Thames, Surrey. Middle order right-hand batsman, right-hand fast round-arm, or left-hand slow under-arm, bowler, cover point or wicket-keeper. *Sch* Rugby. *Teams* Kent (1868–78, 34 matches); Cambridge U (1869–72, blue all four years).
Career batting
83–151–11–3606–130–25.75–3–*ct* 43–*st* 6
Bowling 227–7–32.42–0–0–2/10

He was the first batsman to hit a century in the inter-University match – in 1870 and in 1872 he scored another century in the same fixture. He was racquets champion whilst at Cambridge. Well-known in theatrical circles, he was the author of several plays and also a dramatic critic. The first Champion County v The Rest match in 1901 was played for the benefit of his widow.

Yarnold, Henry
Professional. *b:* 6.7.1917, Worcester. *d:* 13.8.1974, Leamington Spa, Warwickshire. Lower order right-hand batsman, wicket-keeper. *Team* Worcestershire (1938–55, 283 matches).
Career batting
287–417–69–3741–68–10.75–0–*ct* 463–*st* 231

In 1949 he claimed 110 victims behind the wicket – ct 62, st 48. For Worcestershire v Scotland in 1951 he stumped six batsmen in one innings. He was on the first-class umpires' list after retiring from County cricket.

Yarnold, W. Keith
Amateur. *d:* 8.10.1978, Monaco. Lower order batsman. *Team* Northamptonshire (1928, 1 match).
Career batting
1–2–0–3–2–1.50–0–*ct* 1

Yashpal Sharma
Cricketer. *b:* 11.8.1954, Ludhiana, India. Attractive middle order right-hand batsman, right-arm medium pace bowler, occasional wicket-keeper. *Team* Punjab (1973/4 to 1982/3). *Tours* India to Pakistan 1978/9, 1982/3, to England 1979, 1982, to Australia and New Zealand 1980/1, to West Indies 1982/3. *Tests* India (1979 to 1982/3, 33 matches).
Career batting
110–174–39–6287–201*–46.57–13–*ct* 56–*st* 2
Bowling 725–23–31.52–0–0–3/98
Test batting
33–53–11–1650–140–39.28–2–*ct* 13
Bowling 7–1–7.00–0–0–1/6

Although not very prolific in the Tests, he headed the first-class batting averages on the 1979 tour to England with 884 runs, av 58.93. In 1982 he played in all three Tests, but was not so successful in either the Tests or first-class matches.

Yates, Calvert
Professional. *b:* 1852, Church, Lancashire. *d:* 10.6.1904, Church, Lancashire. Middle order batsman. *Team* Lancashire (1882, 1 match).
Career batting
1–2–0–28–24–14.00–0–*ct* 0

Yates, George
Professional. *b:* 6.6.1856, Haslingden, Lancashire. *d:* 21.8.1925, Marple, Cheshire. Middle order right-hand batsman, right-hand fast round-arm bowler. *Team* Lancashire (1885–94, 92 matches).

Career batting
92–135–15–1632–74–13.60–0–*ct* 41
Bowling 934–30–31.33–0–0–4/112

Yates, George
Professional. *b:* 21.8.1858, Bolsover, Derbyshire. *d:* 21.7.1933, Bolsover, Derbyshire. Lower order batsman, useful bowler. *Team* Derbyshire (1883, 1 match).
Career batting
1–1–0–0–0–0.00–0–*ct* 0
Bowling 9–0

Yates, Humphrey William Maghull
Amateur. *b:* 25.3.1883, Eccles, Lancashire. *d:* 21.8.1956, Johannesburg, South Africa. Son of J. M. (Cambridge U). Dashing middle order right-hand batsman, right-arm medium pace bowler, good field. *Sch* Winchester. *Team* Hampshire (1910–13, 13 matches).
Career batting
20–32–7–646–97–0–25.84–*ct* 10
Bowling 87–1–87.00–0–0–1/25
His final first-class match was for the Army in 1920. From 1945 to 1956 he was scorer to the Transvaal Cricket Union.

Yates, Joseph Maghull
Amateur. *b:* 19.6.1844, Chorlton-cum-Hardy, Lancashire. *d:* 17.4.1916, Dunham Woodhouses, Cheshire. Father of H. W. M. (Hampshire). Neat middle order right-hand batsman, round-arm bowler, good long stop. *Sch* Westminster. *Team* Cambridge U (1866).
Career batting
1–1–0–10–10–10.00–0–*ct* 1
His County cricket was for Cheshire.

Yates, Kenneth Clement
Amateur. *b:* 4.8.1938, Keetmanshoop, South-West Africa. Lower order right-hand batsman, wicket-keeper. *Team* Cambridge U (1961).
Career batting
1–1–1–0–0*–no av–0–*ct* 3

Yates, Walter Gerald
Professional. *b:* 18.6.1919, Warsop, Nottinghamshire. Middle order right-hand batsman, right-arm medium pace bowler. *Team* Nottinghamshire (1937–38, 6 matches).
Career batting
6–8–1–69–19–9.85–0–*ct* 1
Bowling 54–1–54.00–0–0–1/43

Yawar Saeed
Professional. *b:* 22.1.1935, India. Son of Mohammad Saeed (Northern India), brother-in-law of Fazal Mahmood (Pakistan). Lower order right-hand batsman, right-arm medium pace bowler. *Teams* Somerset (1953–55, 50 matches); Punjab (1953/4 to 1956/7).
Career batting
59–106–6–1547–64–15.47–0–*ct* 30
Bowling 3610–106–34.05–5–0–5/32
His final first-class match was for Central Zone in 1958/9. He is a member of the Pakistan Test Selection Committee.

Yeabsley, Douglas Ian
Amateur. *b:* 3.1.1942, Exeter, Devon, Lower order left-hand batsman, left-arm medium fast bowler. *Team* Minor Counties (1974–79). *Tour* Minor Counties to Kenya 1977/8 (not first-class).
Career batting
4–6–3–27–14*–9.00–0–*ct* 1
Bowling 389–13–29.92–0–0–3/45
His County cricket has been for Devon commencing 1959.

Yeadon, James
Professional. *b:* 11.12.1861, Yeadon, Yorkshire. *d:* 30.5.1914, Yeadon, Yorkshire. Lower order right-hand batsman, wicket-keeper. *Team* Yorkshire (1888, 3 matches).
Career batting
3–6–2–41–22–10.25–0–*ct* 5–*st* 3

Yeatman, Rex Herbert
Amateur. *b:* 4.10.1919, Kew, Surrey. Middle order right-hand batsman, right-arm medium pace bowler. *Sch* St Pauls. *Team* Surrey (1946–47, 5 matches).
Career batting
6–9–1–53–21–6.62–0–*ct* 1
Bowling 18–0

Yorke, Gerald Joseph
Amateur. *b:* 10.12.1901, Tewkesbury, Gloucestershire. *d:* 29.4.1983, Forthampton, Gloucestershire. Son of V. W. (Gloucestershire). Middle order batsman. *Sch* Eton. *Team* Gloucestershire (1925, 1 match).
Career batting
1–2–0–6–6–3.00–0–*ct* 0

Yorke, Vincent Wodehouse
Amateur. *b:* 21.5.1869, Pimlico, London. *d:* 27.11.1957, Paddington, London. Father of G. J. (Gloucestershire). Middle order batsman. *Sch* Eton. *Team* Gloucestershire (1898, 1 match).
Career batting
1–1–0–10–10–10.00–0–*ct* 0

Youll, Michael
Professional. *b:* 26.4.1939, Newcastle on Tyne.

Lower order left-hand batsman, slow left-arm bowler, good close field. *Team* Warwickshire (1956–57, 4 matches).
Career batting
4–2–0–15–9–7.50–0–*ct* 2
Bowling 302–14–21.57–1–0–5/99
Commencing 1962, he played for Northumberland. He was also a good soccer player.

Young, Archibald
Professional. *b:* 1890, Bath, Somerset. *d:* 2.4.1936, Odd Down, Bath. Middle order right-hand batsman, slow right-arm bowler, good field. *Team* Somerset (1911–33, 310 matches).
Career batting
312–539–22–13159–198–25.45–11–*ct* 217
Bowling 9928–388–25.58–9–2–8/30
He hit 1,000 runs in a season five times (best 1,219 runs, av 25.93, in 1930).

Young, Sir Alfred Joseph Karney
Amateur. *b:* 1.8.1865, Victoria, British Columbia, Canada. *d:* 5.1.1942, Tamboerskloof, Cape Town, South Africa. Middle order right-hand batsman. *Team* Kent (1890, 1 match).
Career batting
1–2–0–10–6–5.00–0–*ct* 0

Young, Charles Robertson
Amateur and professional at various times. *b:* 2.2.1852, Dharwar, India. Lower order left-hand batsman, left-arm medium pace bowler, slip field. *Team* Hampshire (1867–85, 38 matches).
Career batting
38–67–7–717–48–11.95–0–*ct* 35
Bowling 3258–149–21.86–8–3–7/19
He is believed to be the youngest cricketer to appear for a first-class county, being 15 years and 131 days on his debut for Hampshire.

Young, Douglas Edmund
Amateur. *b:* 7.5.1917, London. Lower order right-hand batsman, slow leg break bowler. *Sch* KCS Wimbledon. *Team* Oxford U (1938–39, blue 1938).
Career batting
20–31–6–442–36–17.68–0–*ct* 16
Bowling 1374–50–27.48–2–0–6/58
His County cricket was for Berkshire.

Young, Douglas Martin
Professional. *b:* 15.4.1924, Coalville, Leicestershire. Sound opening right-hand batsman. *Team* Worcestershire (1946–48, 31 matches); Gloucestershire (1949–64, 435 matches).
Career batting
475–842–42–24555–198–30.69–40–*ct* 177
Bowling 172–4–43.00–0–0–2/35
He hit 1,000 runs in a season 13 times, going on to 2,000 twice (best 2,179, av 41.11, in 1959). His highest score was 198 for Gloucestershire v Oxford U at Oxford in 1962, when he assisted R. B. Nicholls in an opening partnership of 395.

Young, Goodwin
Amateur. *b:* 1850, Carrigshane, Co Cork. *d:* 9.1.1915, Cork. Tail end batsman, slow left-arm bowler. *Sch* Shrewsbury. *Team* Cambridge U (1873).
Career batting
3–6–3–17–12*–5.66–0–*ct* 2
Bowling 254–16–15.87–2–1–5/24

Young, Harding Isaac
Professional. *b:* 5.2.1876, Leyton, Essex. *d:* 12.12.1964, Rochford, Essex. Lower order right-hand batsman, left-arm medium pace bowler. *Team* Essex (1898–1912, 128 matches). *Tour* MCC to West Indies 1910/11. *Tests* England (1899, 2 matches).
Career batting
171–257–65–2299–81–11.97–0–*ct* 80
Bowling 12014–514–23.37–27–4–8/54
Test batting
2–2–0–43–43–21.50–0–*ct* 1
Bowling 262–12–21.83–0–0–4/30
He took 139 wickets, av 21.79, in 1899. Owing to muscular rheumatism he was unable to play regularly in first-class cricket. After retiring he was on the first-class umpires' list for some years.

Young, John Albert
Professional. *b:* 14.10.1912, Paddington, London. Lower order right-hand batsman, slow left-arm bowler, fine gully field. *Team* Middlesex (1933–56, 292 matches). *Tour* MCC to South Africa 1948/9. *Tests* England (1947–49, 8 matches).
Career batting
341–392–114–2485–62–8.93–0–*ct* 148
Bowling 26795–1361–19.68–82–17–9/55
Test batting
8–10–5–28–10*–5.60–0–0–*ct* 5
Bowling 757–17–44.52–0–0–3/65
He took 100 wickets in a season eight times (best 163, av 19.88, in 1952). His best innings analysis was 9 for 55 for an England XI v Commonwealth at Hastings in 1951.

Young, John Henry
Professional. *b:* 2.7.1876, Melbourne, Derbyshire. *d:* 2.8.1913, Melbourne, Derbyshire. Lower order right-hand batsman, right-arm fast medium bowler. *Team* Derbyshire (1899–1901, 28 matches).

Career batting
28–48–9–379–42*–9.71–0–*ct* 3
Bowling 996–28–35.57–1–0–5/65

Young, John Villiers
Amateur. *b:* 16.8.1884, Dharwar, India. *d:* 8.9.1960, Eastbourne, Sussex. Brother of R. A. (Sussex). Middle order batsman. *Sch* Eastbourne. *Team* Sussex (1908, 3 matches).
Career batting
3–5–0–105–84–21.00–0–*ct* 0
Bowling 28–0

Young, John William
Professional. *b:* 24.5.1863, Clay Cross, Derbyshire. *d:* 9.5.1933, Bolsover, Derbyshire. Middle order right-hand batsman. *Team* Derbyshire (1894, 2 matches).
Career batting
2–2–0–0–0–0.00–0–*ct* 0

Young, Richard Alfred
Amateur. *b:* 16.9.1885, Dharwar, India. *d:* 1.7.1968, Hastings, Sussex. Brother of J. V. (Sussex). Consistent middle order right-hand batsman, wicket-keeper. *Sch* Repton. *Teams* Cambridge U (1905–08, blue all four years); Sussex (1905–25, 86 matches). *Tour* MCC to Australia 1907/8. *Tests* England (1907/8, 2 matches).
Career batting
139–242–11–6653–220–28.80–11–*ct* 115–*st* 29
Bowling 114–3–38.00–0–0–2/32
Test batting
2–4–0–27–13–6.75–0–0–*ct* 6

He hit 1,000 runs in a season twice (best 1,430, av 35.07, in 1908). His highest innings was 220 for Sussex v Essex at Leyton in 1905. A noted soccer outside right, he played for Cambridge and Corinthians and gained an amateur international cap v Hungary.

Young, Richard James Caldwell
Amateur. *b:* 2.2.1845, Ireland. *d:* 25.1.1885, Londonderry, Ireland. Middle order batsman. *Team* MCC (1873).
Career batting
1–2–0–11–11–5.50–0–*ct* 0

Young, Robert William
Amateur. *b:* 2.1.1933, Perth, Scotland. Right-hand batsman. *Team* Scotland (1962–64).
Career batting
6–9–0–358–96–39.77–0–*ct* 6

Young, Stuart Harrison
Professional. *b:* 6.7.1938, Blackhall, Co Durham. Lower order left-hand batsman, right-arm fast bowler. *Team* Minor Counties (1959–69).
Career batting
3–4–2–16–14–8.00–0–*ct* 1
Bowling 289–12–24.08–0–0–4/44

His County cricket was for Durham.

Young, William
Professional. *b:* 8.3.1861, Staveley, Derbyshsire. *d:* 6.10.1933, Staveley, Derbyshire. Lower order batsman, wicket-keeper. *Team* Liverpool and District XI (1891).
Career batting
1–2–1–21–21*–21.00–0–*ct* 1

Young, Rev Wilfrid Alec Radford
Amateur. *b:* 5.10.1867, Brighton, Sussex. *d:* 19.3.1947, Kimcote, Leics. Middle order right-hand batsman, right-arm slow bowler. *Sch* Harrow. *Team* Somerset (1891–93, 2 matches).
Career batting
2–3–0–13–13–4.33–0–*ct* 1

He did not play in any first-class matches whilst at Cambridge U.

Young, William Sturrock
Amateur. *b:* 15.11.1896, Dundee, Scotland. *d:* 2.1.1966, Dundee, Scotland. Right-hand batsman. *Team* Scotland (1924).
Career batting
1–1–0–5–5–5.00–0–*ct* 0

Younger, Charles Frearson
Amateur. *b:* 9.9.1885, Tillicoultry, Clackmannanshire. *d:* 21.3.1917, nr Aveluy, France. He died of wounds. Lower order batsman, left-arm medium pace bowler. *Sch* Winchester. *Teams* Oxford U (1907); Scotland (1912).
Career batting
2–3–1–42–27–21.00–0–*ct* 3
Bowling 80–4–20.00–0–0–2/18

Youngson, George William
Amateur. *b:* 12.12.1919, Aberdeen, Scotland. Right-hand batsman, right-arm fast medium bowler. *Team* Scotland (1947–55).
Career batting
19–31–14–64–18–3.76–0–*ct* 7
Bowling 1861–75–24.81–3–1–7/42

Younis Ahmed, Mohammad
Cricketer. *b:* 20.10.1947, Jullunder, India. Brother of Saeed Ahmed (Pakistan). Middle order left-hand batsman, left-arm medium, or slow, bowler. *Teams* Lahore (1963/4 to 1964/5); Surrey (1965–78, 262 matches); Karachi (1967/8); PIA (1969/70); South Australia (1972/3, 6 matches);

Worcestershire (1979–83, 85 matches). *Tours* Cavaliers to Jamaica 1969/70; Commonwealth to Pakistan 1970/1; Robins to South Africa 1973/4, 1974/5; International Wanderers to South Africa 1974/5, 1975/6. *Tests* Pakistan (1969/70, 2 matches).
Career batting
392–658–100–21753–221*–38.98–36–*ct* 219
Bowling 1605–39–41.15–0–0–4/10
Test batting
2–4–0–89–62–22.25–0–*ct* 0

He hit 1,000 runs in a season eleven times (best 1,760, av 47.56, in 1969). His highest innings is 221* for Worcestershire v Notts at Trent Bridge in 1979. His first-class debut was for Pakistan Inter-Board XI in 1961/2.

Yuile, Bryan William
Amateur. *b:* 29.10.1941, Palmerston North, New Zealand. Lower order right-hand batsman, slow left-arm bowler. *Team* Central Districts (1959/60 to 1971/2). *Tours* New Zealand to South Africa and Australia 1961/2, to England 1965, 1969, to Australia 1967/8, to Pakistan and India 1964/5, 1969/70. *Tests* New Zealand (1962/3 to 1969/70, 17 matches).
Career batting
123–187–31–3850–146–24.67–1–*ct* 73
Bowling 8209–375–21.89–17–2–9/100
Test batting
17–33–6–481–64–17.81–0–*ct* 12
Bowling 1213–34–35.66–0–0–4/43

Although completely ineffectual in the Tests, he headed the bowling averages on the 1965 tour to England with 24 wickets, av 22.91. In 1969 he did not play in any of the Tests. His best bowling was 9/100 for Central Districts v Canterbury at New Plymouth in 1965/6.

ZAHEER ABBAS, SYED
Cricketer. *b:* 24.7.1947, Sialkot, Pakistan. Attractive middle order right-hand batsman, off break bowler. *Teams* Karachi (1965/6 to 1975/6); PWD (1968/9); PIA (1969/70 to 1982/3); Gloucestershire (1972–83, 191 matches); Sind (1975/6 to 1976/7); Dawood Club (1975/6). *Tours* Pakistan to England 1971, 1974, 1982, to Ceylon, Australia and New Zealand 1972/3, to Sri Lanka 1975/6, to Australia and West Indies 1976/7, to New Zealand and Australia 1978/9, to India 1979/80, to Australia 1981/2; Rest of World to Australia 1971/2; PIA to England 1969 (not first-class). *Tests* Pakistan (1969/70 to 1982/3, 58 matches).
Career batting
408–682–80–32307–274–53.66–105–*ct* 254
Bowling 939–25–37.56–1–0–5/15
Test batting
58–94–7–4073–274–46.81–11–*ct* 31
Bowling 34–0

He has scored 1,000 runs in a season in England eleven times (best 2,554, av 75.11, in 1976). On his first tour to England in 1971 he was outstandingly successful with 1,508 runs, av 55.85, in first-class matches and 386, av 96.50, in Tests, including 274 in the first Test at Edgbaston; in 1974 he again topped the Test batting averages and hit 240 in the Oval Test. On the 1982 tour he hit 664 runs, av 73.77, in first-class matches but was not so prolific in the Tests. In 1982/3 he became the first Pakistan player to hit 100 centuries in his first-class career. He has also hit 1,000 runs in an overseas season six times.

Zuill, Andrew Morison
Amateur. *b:* 22.4.1937, Falkirk, Stirlingshire, Scotland. Middle order right-hand batsman. *Sch* Merchiston. *Team* Scotland (1962–79).
Career batting
9–17–2–231–62–15.40–0–*ct* 1

Zulfiqar Ahmed
Amateur. *b:* 22.11.1926, Lahore, India. Steady lower order right-hand batsman, right-arm off break, occasional leg break, bowler. *Teams* Bahawalpur (1953/4 to 1959/60); Pakistan International Airlines (1964/5). *Tours* Pakistan to India 1952/3, to England 1954, to West Indies 1957/8. *Tests* Pakistan (1952/3 to 1956/7, 9 matches).
Career batting
60–70–19–969–73–19.00–0–*ct* 21
Bowling 3529–163–21.65–12–3–7/69
Test batting
9–10–4–200–63*–33.33–0–*ct* 5
Bowling 366–20–18.30–2–1–6/42

In England in 1954 he took 64 wickets, av 18.50, in first-class matches and appeared in two Tests, but achieved little. His first-class debut was for Punjab Governor's XI in 1948/9.

Zulfiqar Ali
Cricketer. *b:* 1947, Kenya. Right-hand batsman, right-arm medium pace bowler. *Team* East Africa (1973/4 to 1975). *Tour* East Africa to England 1975.
Career batting
2–4–0–30–20–7.50–0–*ct* 1
Bowling 290–8–36.25–0–0–3/43

Bailey, David (page 53)
Tour Minor Counties to Kenya 1977/8 (not first-class).

Bracewell, Brendon Paul (page 129)
Cricketer. *b.* 14.9.1959, Auckland, New Zealand. Brother of J. G. (New Zealand), D. W. (Canterbury) and M. A. (Otago). Lower order right-hand batsman, right-arm medium pace bowler. *Teams* Central Districts (1977/8 to 1979/80); Otago (1981/2 to 1982/3). *Tours* New Zealand to England 1978, to Australia 1980/1. *Tests* New Zealand (1978 to 1980/1, 5 matches).
Career batting
40–53–13–385–36*–9.62–0–*ct* 14
Bowling 2655–91–29.17–0–0–4/41
Test batting
5–10–2–17–8–2.12–0–*ct* 1
Bowling 456–10–45.60–0–0–3/110
He took 24 wickets, av 28.91, on the 1978 tour to England and played in all three Tests.

Bracewell, John Garry (page 129)
Cricketer. *b.* 15.4.1958, Auckland, New Zealand. Brother of B. P. (New Zealand), D. W. (Canterbury) and M. A. (Otago). Lower order right-hand batsman, off break bowler. *Teams* Otago (1978/9 to 1981/2); Auckland (1982/3). *Tours* New Zealand to Australia 1980/1, to England 1983. *Tests* New Zealand (1980/1 to 1983, 8 matches).
Career batting
51–82–12–1449–62–20.70–0–*ct* 40
Bowling 4641–196–23.67–15–3–7/9
Test batting
8–13–2–85–28–7.72–0–*ct* 6
Bowling 654–21–31.14–1–0–5/75
On the 1983 tour to England he took 41 wickets, av 26.70, and played in all four Tests.

Burton, Clifford (page 167)
d: 20.5.1978, Oldham, Lancashire.

Craig, Hartley Samuel (page 241)
Brother of R. J. (South Australia).

Daniel, Wayne Wendell (page 263)
b: Rices, St Philip, Barbados.

Gaekwad, Anshuman Dattajirao (page 370)
Cricketer. *b*: 23.9.1952, Bombay, India. Son of D. K. (India). Opening right-hand batsman, off break bowler. *Team* Baroda (1969/70 to 1982/3). *Tours* India to New Zealand 1975/6, to West Indies 1975/6, 1982/3, to Australia 1977/8, to Pakistan 1978/9, to England 1979; Wadekar to Sri Lanka 1975/6. *Tests* India (1974/5 to 1982/3, 26 matches).
Career batting
142–231–25–8180–225–39.70–21–*ct* 103
Bowling 3186–94–33.89–2–0–6/49
Test batting
26–43–3–1289–102–29.97–1–*ct* 8
Bowling 83–0
He scored 574 runs, av 31.88, on his tour to England, playing in two Tests. His highest score was 225 for Baroda v Gujerat at Baroda 1982/3.

Hands, Barry Onslow (page 434)
d: 1.7.1984.

Hands, Kenneth Charles Myburgh (page 434)
d: Paris, France.

Hands, Philip Albert Myburgh (434)
d: Parys, Orange Free State, South Africa.

Hartley, Fred (page 448)
d: 24.12.76, Bacup, Lancashire.

Heath, Frederick Rhead (page 465)
Team Derbyshire (1924–25, 4 matches).
Career batting
4–6–1–72–17–14.40–0–*ct* 1

Heath, John Stanley (page 465)
Team Derbyshire (1924–25, 6 matches).
Career batting
11–19–2–214–34–12.58–0–*ct* 8

Kidd, Eric Leslie (page 574)
Son of P. M. (Kent).

Kidd, Dr Percy Marmaduke (page 574)
Father of E. L. (Middlesex).

Kinnersley, Kenneth Charles (page 580)
d: 30.6.1984, Bristol.

Rogers, George Howard (page 873)
d: 24.2.1958.

Smith, Arthur Frederick (page 933)
Brother of C. J. (Middlesex).

Smith, Charles John (page 934)
Brother of A. F. (Middlesex).